ROYAL ANCESTRY:

A STUDY IN COLONIAL AND MEDIEVAL FAMILIES

William the Conqueror, Duke of Normandy, between his half-brothers Eudes, Bishop of Bayeux and Robert, Count of Mortain.

Musée de la Tapisserie, Bayeux, France. ©De Agostini/The British Library Board

Royal Ancestry Series

ROYAL ANCESTRY:

A STUDY IN COLONIAL AND MEDIEVAL FAMILIES

Volume II

Douglas Richardson

Kimball G. Everingham, editor

2013
Salt Lake City, Utah

Copyright © 2013
Douglas Richardson
1681 West 1000 North
Salt Lake City, Utah 84116
E-mail: royalancestry@msn.com

All Rights Reserved

Library of Congress Catalogue Card Number 2013905440
International Standard Book Number 9781731047298
Made in the United States of America

Cover artwork by Brian Kelley.

❧ BRYAN ❧

ALICE OF NORMANDY (sister of King William the Conqueror), married **LAMBERT**, Count of Lens.
JUDITH OF LENS, married **WALTHEOF**, Earl of Northumberland.
MAUD OF NORTHUMBERLAND, married **SIMON DE SENLIS**, Earl of Huntingdon and Northampton.
SIMON DE SENLIS, Earl of Huntingdon and Northampton, married **ISABEL** (or **ELIZABETH**) **OF LEICESTER**.
ISABEL DE SAINT LIZ, married **WILLIAM MAUDUIT**, of Hanslope, Buckinghamshire.
ROBERT MAUDUIT, of Hanslope, Buckinghamshire, married **ISABEL BASSET**.
WILLIAM MAUDUIT, of Hanslope, Buckinghamshire, married **ALICE DE NEWBURGH**.
ISABEL MAUDUIT, married **WILLIAM DE BEAUCHAMP**, Knt., of Elmley, Worcestershire.
SARAH DE BEAUCHAMP, married **RICHARD TALBOT**, of Eccleswall, Herefordshire [see TALBOT 9].

10. JOAN TALBOT, married (as his 2nd wife) **JOHN DE CAREW** (or **CARREU**, **CARRU**), Knt., of Carew, Pembrokeshire, Moulsford, Berkshire, Galmpton (in Churston Ferrers), Mamhead, Monkton, Stoke Fleming, and Weston Peverell, Devon, etc., son and heir of Nicholas Carew, Knt., of Moulsford, Berkshire, by Amice, sister of John Peverel, Knt. They had one son, John, Knt. [Justiciar of Ireland], and one daughter, Joan. In 1313 he confirmed the manor of Weston Peverell, Devon to Robert Lendon his servant. SIR JOHN DE CAREW died about 1324. His widow, Joan, married (2nd) **JOHN DE DARTMOUTH**. His widow, Joan, presented to the church of Mamhead, Devon in 1348 and 1350.

Betham *Baronetage of England* 2 (1802): 283–289 (sub Carew). Risdon *Chorographical Desc. or Survey of the County of Devon* (1811): 37–38. Brydges *Collins' Peerage of England* 3 (1812): 1–49 (sub Talbot, Earl of Shrewsbury). Duncumb et al. *Colls. Towards the Hist. & Antiqs. of Hereford* 2(1) (1812): 376–383. *Debrett's Baronetage of England* 1 (1815): 371–374 (sub Carew). Oliver *Ecclesiastical Antiqs. in Devon* 3 (1842): 66. *Visitation of the County of Cornwall, in the Year 1620* (1874): 28–32 (Carew ped.: "(1) Elinor da. & heir of Wm. Mohun of Ottery. = John Carreu Lord of C. &c. ob. 17 E. 2. = (2) Joan da. of Sir Gilbert Talbot."). *Western Antiq.* 11 (1893): 51. Vivian *Vis. of Devon 1531, 1564 & 1620* (1895): 133–136 (Carew ped.). Owen *Description of Penbrokshire* 2 (1897): 325–338. *D.N.B.* 3 (1908): 962–963 (biog. of Sir John Carew). Reichel *Devon Feet of Fines* 2 (Devon & Cornwall Rec. Soc. 1939) (1939): 192–193. Ellis *Cat. Seals in the P.R.O.* 2 (1981): 22 (seal of John de Carew dated 1314 — Hung in a beaded circle, between two wyverns, a shield of arms: three lions passant. Legend: *SIGILLVM.IOHANNIS.DE.CARRV.). Devon Rec. Office: Mamhead, 6252 Z/Z/1-2 (available at www.a2a.org.uk/search/index.asp). Plymouth & West Devon Rec. Office: Bewes, Dickinson & Scott, Solicitors of Plymouth, 81/R/12/6/17 (available at www.a2a.org.uk/search/index.asp).

Children of Joan Talbot, by John de Carew, Knt:

i. **JOHN DE CAREW**, Knt. [see next].

ii. **JOAN DE CAREW**, married (as his 1st wife) **GUY DE BRYAN**, K.G., of Laugharne, Carmarthenshire, Walwyn's Castle, Pembrokeshire, and Northam, Slapton, and Torbrian, Devon, Seneschal of Pembroke, 1340, son and heir of Guy de Bryan, of Walwyn's Castle, Pembrokeshire, Nympton St. George, Slapton, and Torbrian, Devon, etc. He was born about 1309 (being of age in 1330). They had three daughters, Elizabeth, Margaret, and Philippe (wife of Edward de Bohun and John de Chandos, Knt.). He was first armed at Stannow Park in 1327. In 1330 the king settled a dispute between him and his father, Guy de Bryan, senior, relative to the barony and castle of Walwyn, Pembrokeshire. In 1345 John l'Archdeacon owed him a debt of £500. In 1346 he acquired the manor of Brettgrave (in Epsom), Surrey from the Abbot and convent of Chertsey. In 1347 his wife, Joan, obtained a license for a private oratory in her manor of Brettgrave (in Epsom), Surrey. In 1348 he obtained a license for an oratory for his manor of Brettgrave (in Epsom), Surrey. The same year he conveyed the manor of Brettgrave to various feoffees, probably in trust for Henry, Duke of Lancaster. In 1349 he was granted an annuity of 200 marks for bearing the King's Standard against his enemies at Calais. He married (2nd) before 10 July 1350 **ELIZABETH DE MONTAGU**, widow successively of Giles de Badlesmere, Knt., 2nd Lord Badlesmere (died 7 June 1338) [see BADLESMERE 9.i], and Hugh le Despenser, Knt., 3rd Lord Despenser (died 8 Feb. 1348/9) [see DESPENSER 11.i], and daughter of William de Montagu, Knt., 1st Earl of Salisbury, 3rd Lord Montagu, Marshal of England, by Katherine, daughter of William de Grandison, Knt., 1st Lord Grandison [see MONTAGU 7 for her ancestry]. They had three sons, Guy, Knt., William, Knt. [see ECHINGHAM 10], and Philip. He was summoned to Parliament from 25 Nov. 1350 to 6 Dec. 1389, whereby he is held to have become Lord Bryan. He was constantly entrusted with martial and diplomatic affairs of the highest importance. He presented to the church of Torbrian, Devon in 1353. In 1357 he obtained a license for an oratory at his house at Ashley, Hampshire. His wife, Elizabeth, died at Ashley, Hampshire 31 May 1359, and was buried with her 2nd husband in Tewkesbury Abbey. In 1361 he served as ambassador to the Pope. In 1369 he was appointed Admiral of the Fleet. In 1367 he purchased the manor of Woodsford, Dorset from John Whitfield, Knt. In 1377 he gave an endowment to four chaplains for the chapel of St. Mary at Slapton, Devon, which he augmented in 1386 and again in 1389. SIR GUY DE BRYAN, Lord Bryan, died 17 August 1390, and was buried in Tewkesbury Abbey, Gloucestershire. Pole *Colls. towards a Desc. of Devon* (1791): 274–275, 286–287. *Archaeologia* 14 (1803): 143–153. Banks *Dormant & Extinct Baronage of England* 2 (1808): 63–65 (sub Bryan). Brydges *Collins' Peerage of England* 6 (1812): 496–511 (sub Despenser). *Debrett's Baronetage of England* 1 (1815): 371–374 (sub Carew). Nicolas *Controversy between Scrope & Grosvenor* 2 (1832): 245–255 (biog. of Sir Guy Bryan). *Coll. Top. et Gen.* 1 (1834): 227–228. *Gentleman's Mag.* n.s. 12 (1839): 18–22. Beltz *Mems. of the Order of the Garter* (1841): clii. Hutchins *Hist. & Antiq. of Dorset* 1 (1861): 448 (Bryan ped.); 3 (1868): 291 (Montagu ped.). Worthy *Ashburton & its Neighbourhood* (1875): 149–150, 158. Daniel-Tyssen *Royal Charters & Hist. Docs. Rel. the Town & County of Carmarthen* (1878): 48, footnote 4. Vivian *Vis. of Devon 1531, 1564 & 1620* (1895): 133–136 (Carew ped.). *Papal Regs.: Petitions* 1 (1896): 369 (Hugh de Ferrers styled "kinsman" by Guy de Bryan). Green *Feet of Fines for Somerset* 3 (Somerset Rec. Soc. 17) (1902): 182. Owen *Old Pembroke Fams.* (1902): 81–84. *Wrottesley Peds. from the Plea Rolls* (1905): 99, 178, 228, 236–237. VCH *Dorset* 2 (1908): 73–79. *Rpt. & Trans. Devonshire Assoc.* 3rd Ser. 3 (1911): 132, 137, 191, 210–211. VCH *Hampshire* 4 (1911): 150–151. VCH *Surrey* 3 (1911): 275; 4 (1912): 92–102, 249. *C.P.* 2 (1912): 201, footnote b (sub Bohun), 361–362 (sub Bryan); 4 (1916): 271–274 (sub Despenser), 325; 5 (1926): 463-464 (sub Fitzpayn); 11 (1949): 388, footnote b (sub Salisbury); 14 (1998): 118 (sub Bryan). Reichel *Devon Feet of Fines* 2 (Devon & Cornwall Rec. Soc. 1939) (1939): 392, 400. Hethe *Reg. Hamonis Hethe Diocesis Roffensis* 2 (Canterbury & York Soc. 49) (1948): 810. Paget *Baronage of England* (1957) 102:1. Smith *Itinerary of John Leland* 4 (1964): 150–163. Haines *Cal. Reg. of Wolstan de Bransford Bishop of Worcester* (Worcestershire Hist. Soc. n.s. 4) (1966): 79. *Ancient Deeds — Ser. B* 2 (List & Index Soc. 101) (1974): B.7233. VCH *Somerset* 3 (1974): 111–120, 129–153. MacCulloch *Chorography of Suffolk* (Suffolk Rec. Soc. 19) (1976): 28. Edington *Reg. of William Edington Bishop of Winchester 1346–1366* 1 (Hampshire Rec. Ser. 7) (1986): 46; 2 (Hampshire Rec. Ser. 8) (1987): 7, 23, 44. Emery *Greater Medieval Houses of England & Wales* 3 (2006): 687. National Archives, C 241/119/32 (available at www.catalogue.nationalarchives.gov.uk/search.asp).

Children of Joan de Carew, by Guy de Bryan, K.G.:

a. **ELIZABETH DE BRYAN**, married **ROBERT FITZ PAYN**, Knt., of Stogursey, Somerset [see CODNOR 11.ii].

b. **MARGARET DE BRYAN**, married **HUGH DE COURTENAY**, Knt., 3rd Lord Courtenay [see COURTENAY 7.i.a].

11. JOHN DE CAREW, Baron Carew, of Carew Castle, Pembrokeshire, Ottery Mohun (in Luppit), Galmpton(in Churston Ferrers), Devon, Idrone, co. Carlow, Ireland, etc., Sheriff of Cork, King's Escheator in Ireland, 1349, 1352, 1355–6, Justiciar of Ireland, 1349–50. He married (1st) **MARGARET DE MOHUN**, daughter of John de Mohun, Knt., of Dunster, Somerset, Goring, Oxfordshire, Long Compton and Whichford, Warwickshire, etc., by Christian, daughter of John de Segrave, 2nd Lord Segrave [see MOHUN 12 for her ancestry]. They had five sons, Leonard, Knt. [Baron Carew], John, Nicholas, William, and Edward. He was heir in 1324 to his older helf-brother, Nicholas de Carew. He was summoned to Ireland to defend his estates in 1332. In 1345–6 he was appointed one of the three 'custodes pacis' for the county of Carlow, Ireland. About the same time he was entrusted to negotiate with the Irish rebels. About 1359 he was summoned to attend a great council at Waterford. He married (2nd) **ELIZABETH CORBET**. In 1361 he was called to Westminster to consult on the projected Irish expedition of Lionel, afterwards Duke of Clarence. SIR JOHN DE CAREW died in 1362, or 16 May 1363. His widow, Elizabeth, married (2nd) before 18 April 1368 (date of presentation) **JOHN DE GOURNAY**, Knt. He presented to the church of Mamhead, Devon in 1368, in right of his wife, Elizabeth.

Oliver *Ecclesiastical Antiqs. in Devon* 3 (1842): 66. Dugdale *Monasticon Anglicanum* 5 (1846): 692 (Newenham Abbey, Mohun ped.). *Journal of the Royal Hist. & Arch. Assoc. of Ireland* 4th Ser. 1 (1870–71): 167–168. St. George & Lennard *Vis. of Cornwall 1620* (H.S.P. 9) (1874): 29–32 (Carew ped.: "John [Carew] ob. 36 E. 3. =(1) Marg.t da. of John Mohun Lo. of Dunster, =(2) Elizab. Corbet"), 143–146 (Mohun ped.: "Margareta [Mohun] uxor D'ni Johis Carew"). *Arch.*

Jour. 37 (1880): 57–93. *D.N.B.* 9 (1887): 53–54 (biog. of Sir John Carew). Vivian *Vis. of Devon 1531, 1564 & 1620* (1895): 133–136 (Carew ped.). Little *Franciscan Hist. & Legend in English Mediaeval Art* (1937): 70.

Child of Margaret de Mohun, by John Carew:

i. **LEONARD DE CAREW**, Knt., Baron Carew, married **ELIZABETH ARUNDEL** [see CAREW 13].

ಞ BUCHAN ಞ

ALICE OF NORMANDY (sister of King William the Conqueror), married **LAMBERT**, Count of Lens.
JUDITH OF LENS, married **WALTHEOF**, Earl of Northumberland.
MAUD OF NORTHUMBERLAND, married **SIMON DE SENLIS**, Earl of Huntingdon and Northampton.
MAUD DE SENLIS, married **SAHER DE QUINCY**, of Long Buckby, Northamptonshire.
ROBERT DE QUINCY, of Tranent, Fawside, and Longniddry, East Lothian, Scotland, married **ORABEL FITZ NESS**.
SAHER DE QUINCY, Knt., Earl of Winchester, married **MARGARET OF LEICESTER**.
ROGER DE QUINCY, Knt., 2nd Earl of Winchester, married **ELLEN OF GALLOWAY** [see QUINCY 7].

8. ELIZABETH (or **ISABEL**) **DE QUINCY**, 2nd daughter and co-heiress. She was betrothed by contract dated Feb. 1240/1 to marry **HUGH DE NEVILLE**, of Wakering and Wethersfield, Essex, son and heir of John de Neville, of Wethersfield, Essex, Chief Forester of England, by Hawise, daughter of Robert de Courtenay, Knt., of Okehampton, Devon. It is uncertain if this marriage ever took place. Elizabeth subsequently married **ALEXANDER COMYN**, Knt., 6th Earl of Buchan, Justiciar of Scotland, 1251–5, 1257–9, and, in right of his wife, of Whitwick, Leicestershire, and Weston-under-Wetherley, Warwickshire, son and heir of William Comyn, Earl of Buchan, Justiciar of Scotland, by his 2nd wife, Marjorie, daughter and heiress of Fergus, Earl of Buchan. They had four sons, John, Knt. [7th Earl of Buchan, Constable of Scotland], Alexander, Knt., William [Provost of St. Mary's Church in St. Andrews], and Roger, Knt., and five daughters, Marjory, Agnes (wife of Malise, Earl of Strathearn), Elizabeth, Ellen (wife of William de Brechin, Knt.), and Margaret (wife of Nicholas de Soulis, Knt.). He succeeded his mother between 1236 and 1240. He witnessed many charters for King Alexander III of Scotland, one of whose new counselors he became in 1252. He was removed from that office at the instigation of King Henry III of England in Sept. 1255, but was reappointed in 1257, and held the office until his death. In Nov. 1258 King Henry III of England promised counsel and aid to the various magnates who had assumed the government of Scotland, one of them being Alexander Comyn, Earl of Buchan. In 1259 he was one of the Scottish lords who made a bond of alliance with Llywelyn, Prince of Wales. He founded a hospital for six poor prebendaries in Newburgh in Buchan in 1261. About 1263 he renounced all his right and claim to the patronage of the church of Fithkil to the abbot and convent of Inchcolm in his own name and that of Thomas de Meldrum. In 1264 he took part in the expedition to the Western Isles against the rebels who encouraged the Norwegians. In 1270 his wife's sister, Margaret de Ferrers, Countess of Derby, resigned the hereditary office of Constable of Scotland to him. In 1271 his wife, Elizabeth, and her sisters, Ellen and Margaret, gave license for the election of William de Shaldeston as Prior of the Hospital of St. James and St. John at Brackley, Northamptonshire. In 1273 he founded another hospital at Turreth. In 1274–5 Alexander Comyn, Earl of Buchan, and his wife, Elizabeth, and Ellen la Zouche [Elizabeth's sister] sued Margaret de Ferrers, Countess of Derby, regarding possessions in Eynesbury, Huntingdonshire. In 1274–5 he arraigned an assize of novel disseisin against Walter de Wiltesire and others regarding a tenement in Whitwick and Markfield, Leicestershire. In 1277 he suspended his suit against his wife's sister, Ellen la Zouche, in the Scottish courts at the request of King Edward I of England; Alexander and his wife, Elizabeth, alleged that Ellen received a larger share of the Quincy estates than "of right fell to her lot." He appears as Constable of Scotland 15 April 1277 and in Feb. 1281/2; as Constable and

Justiciar north of the Forth 1 July 1282; and, as Constable and Justiciar of Scotland 30 April 1285. In 1277–8 Adam de Antevill arraigned an assize of novel disseisin against him and Elizabeth his wife touching common of pasture in Charnwood, Leicestershire. About 1281 Earl Alexander and his wife, Elizabeth, together with her two sisters, Margaret de Ferrers, Countess of Derby, and Ellen la Zouche, sued Ranulph son of Robert de Neville and his wife, Euphame, regarding 11-½ virgates in Syston, Leicestershire. His wife, Elizabeth, was living in April 1282. In 1282 he excused his absence in attendance on the King of England in Wales on account of a special journey to the Isles by order of the King of Scotland. In 1284 he engaged to maintain the succession of the Scottish crown to Margaret of Scotland. He was one of the six Guardians appointed on the death of King Alexander III of Scotland in 1285. In 1287 he bound himself to pay to Arbroath Abbey half a mark for finding two tapers to be lighted before the altar of St. Mary in the monastery. At an unknown date, he gave ten marks sterling each year in his holding of Kelly (in Methlick) in Buchan to Lindores Abbey, in exchange for the land of Kyncardinbegg. At an unknown date, he gave a pound of wax or forty shillings to light St. Ethernan's beacon on the Isle of May. SIR ALEXANDER COMYN, 6th Earl of Buchan, Constable and Justiciar of Scotland, died shortly before 6 April 1290. His widow, Elizabeth, Countess of Buchan, died before 4 May 1303, when her son and heir, John Comyn, Earl of Buchan, was granted the lands which Elizabeth held before the commencement of the war in Scotland.

Nichols *Hist. & Antiqs. of Leicester* 3(1) (1800): 121; 3(2) (1804): 1112–1116. Baker *Hist. & Antiqs. of Northampton* 1 (1822–30): 563 (Beaumont-Quincy ped.). Clutterbuck *Hist. & Antiqs. of Hertford* 3 (1827): 287–288 (Beaumont-Quincy ped.). Burke *Dict. of the Peerages… Extinct, Dormant & in Abeyance* (1831): 442–443 (sub Quincy). Palgrave *Docs. & Recs. Ill. the Hist. of Scotland* 1 (1837): 288–291. Innes *Registrum Episcopatus Aberdonensis* 2 (1845): 276–277 (charter of Alexander Comyn, Earl of Buchan dated 1261; names his wife, Isabel). *Sessional Papers in Session 1845: Vol. 38 Rpts. from the Commissioners* (1845): 98–99. Skene *Liber Pluscardensis* 1 (Historians of Scotland 7) (1877): 136–137; 2 (Historians of Scotland 10) (1880): 102–103. Flower *Vis. of Yorkshire 1563–4* (H.S.P. 16) (1881): 13. *Annual Rpt. of the Deputy Keeper* 44 (1883): 100, 291; 45 (1885): 169, 357; 47 (1886): 185; 50 (1889): 61, 202 . *C.C.R. 1272–1279* (1900): 225–226, 552. Dowden *Chartulary of the Abbey of Lindores 1195–1479* (1903): 43–43, 157–158 (charter of Alexander Comyn, Earl of Buchan), 165–167, 248, 272–273, 275. *Scottish Hist. Rev.* 1 (1903): 228–231. Macdonald *Scottish Armorial Seals* (1904): 65 (seal of Alexander Comyn, Earl of Buchan — A knight on horseback with sword and shield bearing arms, which are repeated on the caparisons of his horse, viz: — Three garbs. A fan plume of seven feathers on helmet and head of horse), 65 (counterseal of Alexander Comyn, Earl of Buchan — Within a pointed Gothic quatrefoil a shield bearing arms: — Three garbs). *Scots Peerage* 2 (1905): 254–256 (sub Comyn, Earl of Buchan). Wrottesley *Peds. from the Plea Rolls* (1905): 548. Lindsay et al. *Charters, Bulls & Other Docs. Rel. the Abbey of Inchaffray* (Scottish Hist. Soc. 56) (1908): lxxxvi–lxxxix. *C.P.* 1 (1910): 147–148; 2 (1912): 374–375 (sub Buchan) (Alexander Comyn: "one of the most powerful nobles of the time"); 9 (1936): 482–483 (sub Neville). VCH *Hertford* 3 (1912): 380–397. Turner *Cal. Feet of Fines Rel. Huntingdon* (Cambridge Antiq. Soc. 8° Ser. 37) (1913): 35. *Year Books of Edward II* 13 (Selden Soc. 34) (1918): 59–67; 14(2) (Selden Soc. 43) (1927): 75–77. Davis *Rotuli Ricardi Gravesend Episcopi Lincolniensis* (Lincoln Rec. Soc. 20) (1925): 118. *Rpt. on the MSS of Reginald Rawdon Hastings, Esq.* 1 (Hist. MSS Comm. 78) (1928): 323–342 (partition of estates of Roger de Quincy, Earl of Winchester). VCH *Huntingdon* 2 (1932): 346–354. Easson & Macdonald *Charters of the Abbey of Inchcolm* (Scottish Hist. Soc. 3rd Ser. 32) (1938): 25–26 (charter of Alexander Comyn, Earl of Buchan dated c.1263), 141–142 (biog. note of Alexander Comyn, Earl of Buchan). VCH *Warwick* 6 (1951): 252. Paget *Baronage of England* (1957) 141: 3, 464: 1–8 (sub Quincy). Reid *Wigtownshire Charters* (Scottish Hist. Soc. 51) (1960): xxxix–xlv. Sanders *English Baronies* (1960): 61–62, 142. Painter *Feudalism & Liberty* (1961): 230–239. Simpson & Galbraith *Cal. Docs. Rel. Scotland* 5 (1986): 142. Sutton *Rolls & Reg. of Bishop Oliver Sutton, 1280–1299* 8 (Lincoln Rec. Soc. 76) (1986): 87–88. Schwennicke *Europäische Stammtafeln* n.s. 3(4) (1989): 708 (sub Quency). Grant & Stringer *Medieval Scotland: Crown, Lordship & Community* (1993). Douglas *English Hist. Docs.* 3 (1996): 427. Barrow *Kingdom of the Scots* (2003).

Children of Elizabeth (or Isabel) de Quincy, by Alexander Comyn, Knt.:

i. **JOHN COMYN**, Knt., 7th Earl of Buchan, hereditary Constable of Scotland, Sheriff of Banffshire, 1289, Sheriff of Wigtownshire, 1290, son and heir, born about 1260 (aged 30 in 1290). He married **ISABEL OF FIFE**, daughter of Colban, Earl of Fife, by Anne [see GROBY 8], daughter and co-heiress of Alan Durward, Knt., of Coull and Lumphanan, Aberdeenshire, Lintrathen, Angus, Lundin, Fife, Reedie (in Airlie), Forfarshire, Urquhart, Moray, etc., Usher of the King of Scots, Justiciar of Scotland. They had no issue. Sometime before 1289, his father enfeoffed him of the manor of Whitwick, Leicestershire and all his other lands in the counties of Leicester and Warwick. In 1291 he was one of those appointed to authenticate and take charge of the petitions of the competitors for the sovereignty of Scotland. In 1291 he swore fealty to King Edward I of England. He was granted a weekly market and yearly fair to be held at the manor of Whitwick, Leicestershire in 1292. In 1295 he joined Balliol in resisting King Edward I, and was declared an enemy of the King of England, who confiscated the goods in his manor at Whitwick, Leicestershire. In 1296, with six other earls, he besieged Carlisle, but they had to withdraw. The same year he renounced the Scots league with France, submitted to King Edward I, and swore fealty to him, first at Montrose and again at Berwick. In 1297 he joined in putting down a rebellion in Moray. In 1303 he was one of the Scots ambassadors to France, where he acted in opposition to the interests of the English king. He afterwards had to go to England and make his peace with the king. His lands in Scotland and England were restored to him. Sometime before the War of Independence, he received the thanage of Fermartyn and Darley from Balliol. He had been fully reinstated in favor of the English king before the coronation of King Robert de Brus in 1306. His wife, Isabel, as representative of her nephew, placed the crown on the head of King Robert de Brus at Scone 27 March 1306. She never after rejoined her husband. She was imprisoned by the English in an iron cage in a room at Berwick Castle in 1306. She was strictly guarded, but allowed to have the attendance of her women. He encountered King Robert de Brus 26 Dec. 1307, and, again at Inverury 22 May 1308, where he was totally defeated. Brus subsequently devastated the earldom of Buchan with fire and sword. Comyn was appointed by King Edward I to be joint Warden of the Western Marches —Annandale, Carrick, and Galloway. In August 1308 he had letters nominating attorneys in England for two years, he then going to Scotland on the king's service. SIR JOHN COMYN, 7th Earl of Buchan, died in England shortly before 3 Dec. 1308, when the king granted custody to Ralph de Monthermer of the lands of John Comyn, earl of Buchan, deceased, tenant in chief, together with the marriage of his heirs. In 1309 William Comyn, executor of John Comyn, late Earl of Buchan, was sued by William de Herle and Isabel, wife of Robert de Herle, executrix of Robert de Herle. His widow, Isabel, was released from imprisonment 28 April 1313. Nichols *Hist. & Antiqs. of Leicester* 3(2) (1804): 1112–1116. Palgrave *Docs. & Recs. Ill. the Hist. of Scotland* 1 (1837): 288–291. *Genealogist* n.s. 4 (1887): 194–196. *C.P.R. 1307–1313* (1894): 92, 95, 267, 514. *Scottish Hist. Rev.* 1 (1903): 228–231. Macdonald *Scottish Armorial Seals* (1904): 65 (seal of John Comyn, Earl of Buchan — Three garbs. Shield suspended by guige, a lizard at either side), 65 (seal of John Comyn, Earl of Buchan — Three garbs, with a label of as many points in chief). *Scots Peerage* 2 (1905): 256–258 (sub Comyn, Earl of Buchan). Wrottesley *Peds. from the Plea Rolls* (1905): 548. *Arch. Aeliana* 3rd Ser. 6 (1910): 44. *C.P.* 2 (1912): 375 (sub Buchan). *Cal. Various Chancery Rolls 1277–1326* (1912): 98. Easson & Macdonald *Charters of the Abbey of Inchcolm* (Scottish Hist. Soc. 3rd Ser. 32) (1938): 141–142. Reid *Wigtownshire Charters* (Scottish Hist. Soc. 51) (1960): xxxix–xlv. Sutton *Rolls & Reg. of Bishop Oliver Sutton, 1280–1299* 8 (Lincoln Rec. Soc. 76) (1986): 87–88. Brault *Rolls of Arms Edward I* 2 (1997): 117 (arms of John Comyn: Azure, three garbs argent; Azure, three garbs or). McAndrew *Scotland's Hist. Heraldry* (2006): 42 (Comyn chart), 44 ("John Comyn (d. 1308) played a prominent part in the Wars of Independence, finally losing his earldom in the "Hership of Buchan" in 1308, and dying shortly afterwards. He had no children by his wife Isabella, sister of Duncan (III), Earl of Fife (d. 1289), and title to the earldom passed to his nieces, Alice and Margaret, whose careers will be followed later. But their father, Sir Alexander Comyn of Buchan, who bore Argent, three garbs sable in Collins' Roll (Q255), is found bearing a slightly different version in the Lord Marshal's Roll, for Alisaundre Comyn: Or, three garbs sable, tied argent (LM137)."). King & Penman *England & Scotland in the 14th Cent.: New Perspectives* (2007): 78, footnote 22. Online resource: http://www.briantimms.net/era/lord_marshals/Lord_Marshal03/Lord%20Marshal3.htm (Lord Marshal's Roll — arms of Alexander Comyn: Or three garbs sable).

ii. **ALEXANDER COMYN**, Knt. [see next].

iii. [MASTER] **WILLIAM COMYN**, clerk. He swore fealty to King Edward I of England in 1296, being then Provost of St. Mary's Church in St. Andrews. In 1298 King Edward I gave Master William's valuable provostry to one of his own favored clerks, presumably on grounds that William was a "rebel." In 1302 William was granted protection for one year, he staying in the University of Cambridge for study. In 1306, he was deprived of his income from this source until he should swear fealty to the King of Scotland. The same year he was going to Scotland on the king's affairs. In June 1309 he was pardoned for acquiring without the late king's license from his brother, John Comyn, Earl of Buchan, two parts of the manor of Sheepshead, the towns of Markenfield, Whittington Grange, Botcheston, and Neuton, a moiety of the town of Ratby, the town of Whitwick, with the park of Bredon and all the demesnes of the manor of Whitwick, held in chief. In April 1310 he was granted protection until Michaelmas, he then going to the court of Rome. In June 1310 he surrendered the manor of Whitwick, Leicestershire to the king, which John Comyn his brother, sometime earl of Buchan, had held in chief, he "acknowledging that he has no right to it by an alleged feoffment by his brother, but that it is the inheritance of Alice and Margaret, the nieces and co-heiresses of himself and his late brother." He was living 14 July 1311. Nichols *Hist. & Antiqs. of Leicester* 3(2) (1804): 1112–1116. Palgrave *Docs. & Recs. Ill. the Hist. of Scotland* 1 (1837): 338–339. *Genealogist* n.s. 4 (1887): 194–196. *C.P.R. 1307–1313* (1894): 160, 224, 267. *C.P.R. 1292–1301* (1895):

355, 358. *C.P.R.* 1301–1307 (1898): 70, 461. *Scots Peerage* 2 (1905): 256 (sub Comyn, Earl of Buchan) (seal of William Comyn shows a shield bearing three garbs, 2 and 1 between three lions passant). *Cal. Various Chancery Rolls* 1277–1326 (1912): 98. Barrow *Robert Bruce & Scotland* (2005): 124–125. McAndrew *Scotland's Hist. Heraldry* (2006): 42 (Comyn chart), 44.

iv. **ROGER COMYN**, Knt. He served in Wales for his father in 1282. In 1303 his lands were restored to him by King Edward I of England. He fought at the Battle of Bannockburn in 1314. He was living in England in 1324. Palgrave *Docs. & Recs. Ill. the Hist. of Scotland* 1 (1837): 288–291. *Scots Peerage* 2 (1905): 255 (sub Comyn, Earl of Buchan). Bain *Cal. Docs. Rel. Scotland* 3 (1886): 156–157, 427, 429, 477a. *Genealogist* n.s. 4 (1887): 194–196. Brault *Rolls of Arms Edward I* 2 (1997): 117 (arms of Roger Comyn: Azure semy of estoiles or, three garbs argent). McAndrew *Scotland's Hist. Heraldry* (2006): 42 (Comyn chart).

v. **MARJORY COMYN**, married **PATRICK OF DUNBAR**, Knt., 8th Earl of Dunbar (or March) [see CLAVERING 4.iv.a].

vi. **ELIZABETH COMYN**, married **GILBERT DE UMFREVILLE**, Knt., 2nd Earl of Angus [see MALLORY 9].

9. ALEXANDER COMYN, Knt., of Buchan, Sheriff of Wigtownshire and Aberdeenshire, 1304–5, Keeper of Urquhart and Tarwedale Castles, 2nd son. He married **JOAN LE LATIMER**, daughter of William le Latimer, Knt., of Scampston, Yorkshire, by Alice, elder daughter and co-heiress of Walter Ledet, of Corby, Northamptonshire. They had two daughters, Alice and Margaret (or Margery). He was taken prisoner in Dunbar Castle by King Edward I of England, and committed to Bristol Castle. Later in the year he did homage to King Edward I at Berwick. In 1297 he and his brother, John Comyn, Earl of Buchan, took oath to serve the King of England against the King of France. In 1298/1299 he wrote King Edward I of England stating that he had suffered imprisonment and great loss of goods because of the king; he requested that the king provide aid and remedy. In 1304 King Edward I acceded to his request for delivery of Aboyne Castle to him. On the intervention of John de Strathbogie, Earl of Atholl, however, who represented that Comyn already got Urquhart and Tarwedale Castles and had besides the Castle of Aberdeen at his disposal, the order for the delivery of Aboyne Castle was suspended. About 1305 various petitions were submitted by him to the King of England requesting reimbursement of his expenses while Sheriff of Aberdeenshire and also for letters of protection against those whom he might have displeased in the discharge of his office. In Nov. 1308 Robert de Wauton complained that Alice, widow of William le Latimer, Joan Comyn, and others besieged him at his dwelling at Eaton Beauchamp, Bedfordshire, felled his trees and fences, threw them and the hay into the river Use. SIR ALEXANDER COMYN died shortly before 3 Dec. 1308. Sometime in the period, 1308–13, as "Joan Commin of Buchan, sister of William Latimer," she petitioned the king requesting that he grant her the manor of Faxfleet, Yorkshire for a term of four or five years, the said manor previously being granted to her by her brother in compensation for the loss of her lands in Scotland. In 1313 Joan was duly granted custody of the manor of Faxfleet, Yorkshire late of the Templars. In 1314 she was granted protection for one year without clause. The same year she complained that John Torny with others broke her close at Faxfleet, Yorkshire, assaulted her, and carried away her goods. In 1316 she was granted the manor of Malton, Yorkshire by the king, so she might receive out of its issues 84 marks a year, until she have seisin of her lands in Scotland. In 1319 she complained that Gilbert de Aton and others carried away her goods at Malton, Yorkshire. In October 1320 she was granted safe-conduct, she going to Scotland with one knight, six squires, six men of office, and ten grooms to treat with the Scots for the restitution of her lands in Scotland. In 1323 she was granted protection for one year, she going to Scotland on her own business. In 1327 she was granted £40 yearly to be received yearly from the issues of Yorkshire. She was living 1 October 1340.

Nichols *Hist. & Antiqs. of Leicester* 3(1) (1800): 121 (author states Alexander Comyn "retired to his estate at Charley," Leicestershire, cites Sir T. Cave; ex MS Collectionibus Johannis Brydges, armigeri & MS Chetwynd). Nichols *Hist. & Antiqs. of Leicester* 3(2) (1804): 1112–1116. Hardy *Syllabus (in English) of the Docs. Rel. England & Other Kingdoms* 1 (1869):

209. Flower *Vis. of Yorkshire 1563–4* (H.S.P. 16) (1881): 18. *Genealogist* n.s. 4 (1887): 194–196. *C.P.R. 1327–1330* (1891): 63. *C.P.R. 1307–1313* (1894): 125, 569 (Joan, widow of Alexander Comyn, styled "sister of William le Latymer"). *C.C.R. 1327–1330* (1896): 174, 260, 279, 334, 457, 496. *C.C.R. 1330–1333* (1898): 21, 85, 214, 494. *C.C.R. 1333–1337* (1898): 28, 74, 257, 389–390, 616. *C.P.R. 1313–1317* (1898): 89, 139, 539. *C.C.R. 1337–1339* (1900): 48, 207, 377, 603. *C.C.R. 1339–1341* (1901): 66, 198, 389–390, 541. Pratt *Buchan* (1901): 352–353. *C.P.R. 1317–1321* (1903): 470, 512. *Scottish Hist. Rev.* 1 (1903): 228–231. *C.P.R. 1321–1324* (1904): 290. Littlejohn *Recs. of the Sheriff Court of Aberdeenshire* 1 (1904): 398–399 (biog. of Alexander Comyn). Tait *Mediæval Manchester & the Beginnings of Lancashire* (1904): 141–142 (re. Latimer fam.). *Scots Peerage* 2 (1905): 255–256 (sub Comyn, Earl of Buchan) (seal of Alexander Comyn shows a shield with three garbs). Wrottesley *Peds. from the Plea Rolls* (1905): 548. *C.P.* 2 (1912): 60, 375–376 (sub Buchan). Clay *Extinct & Dormant Peerages* (1913): 121–122 (sub Latimer). *Year Books of Edward II* 13 (Selden Soc. 34) (1918): 59–67. Paget *Baronage of England* (1957) 141: 3. Reid *Wigtownshire Charters* (Scottish Hist. Soc. 51) (1960): xxxix–xlv. Sanders *English Baronies* (1960): 62. Simpson & Galbraith *Cal. Docs. Rel. Scotland* 5 (1986): 160. Walker *Wife & Widow in Medieval England* (1993): 119. Brault *Rolls of Arms Edward I* 2 (1997): 117 (arms of Alexander Comyn: Or, three garbs sable; Argent, three garbs sable). McAndrew *Scotland's Hist. Heraldry* (2006): 42 (Comyn chart), 44 ("This Sir Alexander Comyn was the younger brother of [John Comyn] 3rd Comyn Earl of Buchan and his 1297 seal depicts a shield bearing Three garbs on the breast of an eagle, the inscription reading S' ALEXANDRE CVMYN D'BVC (SAS587). He married an English wife, Joanna le Latimer, and died in 1308, shortly before his elder brother, whereupon his daughters were named heiresses to the earldom despite the claims of a further brother, Master William Comyn, Provost of St. Mary's Church in St. Andrews, self-styled earl in a document to which his seal (SAS578) was attached in 1309."). National Archives, SC 8/97/4835; SC 8/176/8762; SC 8/196/9775; SC 8/342/16116; SC 8/342/16118 (available at www.catalogue.nationalarchives.gov.uk/search.asp).

Children of Alexander Comyn, Knt., by Joan le Latimer:

i. **ALICE COMYN**, married **HENRY DE BEAUMONT**, Knt., 1st Lord Beaumont, Earl of Buchan and Moray [see BEAUMONT 7].

ii. **MARGARET** (or **MARGERY**) **COMYN**, younger daughter and co-heiress. She was co-heiress in 1308 to her uncle, John Comyn, Earl of Buchan, she being then an unmarried minor. On 14 Dec. 1312 custody of her purparty as one of the heirs of John Comyn, Earl of Buchan, was granted by King Edward III to her brother-in-law, Henry de Beaumont, to hold until the king "shall restore her purparty to her." In an English lawsuit dated 1313, it is stated that Margaret was then a minor in the wardship of her brother-in-law, Henry de Beaumont "by the king's commission." About 1315 she was contracted by King Robert I of Scotland to marry **JOHN OF ROSS**, Knt., son of William of Ross, Knt., 3rd Earl of Ross, by Euphame, daughter and heiress of Hugh de Barclay, Knt., Justiciar of Lothian. Her inheritance included half of the Earl of Buchan's whole lands in Scotland. According to Wyntoun, this marriage took place. They had no issue. On 25 June 1316 John of Ross granted his brother, Hugh of Ross, Knt. all his lands in the kingdom of Scotland, if he should not have an heir in the future, male or female, of his body. In letters patent dated 17 May 1321, King Edward II stated that because Margaret "adhered to the Scots, his enemies," he had granted her half of the manor of Whitwick, Leicestershire to Henry de Beaumont and Alice his wife (Margaret's sister) and their heirs, "until such time as she should act as she ought towards him." On the death of Sir John of Ross (husband of Margaret Comyn), his half share of the lands of the earldom of Buchan [which consisted of what became the baronies of Kingedward and Philorth] passed to his brother, Hugh of Ross, Knt., 4th Earl of Ross. Nichols *Hist. & Antiqs. of Leicester* 3(2) (1804): 1112–1116. *Genealogist* n.s. 4 (1887): 194–196. *C.P.R. 1307–1313* (1894): 267, 514. Pratt *Buchan* (1901): 352–353. *Scottish Hist. Rev.* 1 (1903): 228–231. *Scots Peerage* 2 (1905): 258–261 (sub Comyn, Earl of Buchan) (states in error that Margaret Comyn "seems to have married" (2nd) William de Lindsay, Knt., of Symington; she did not); 7 (1910): 235, 238 (sub Ancient Earls of Ross). Linzee *Lindeseie & Limesi Fams.* (1917): 294 (states in error that William de Lindsay "married twice, his second wife was Margaret Comyn, Countess of Buchan"). *Year Books of Edward II* 13 (Selden Soc. 34) (1918): 59–67; 14(2) (Selden Soc. 43) (1927): 75–77. Reid *Wigtownshire Charters* (Scottish Hist. Soc. 51) (1960): xxxix–xlv. Barrow *Robert Bruce & Scotland* (1976): 384. Walker *Wife & Widow in Medieval England* (1993): 119. Young *Robert the Bruce's Rivals: The Comyns 1212–1314* (1997): 206. McAndrew *Scotland's Hist. Heraldry* (2006): 42 (Comyn chart), 44, 54, 158 ("Margaret, the younger niece and coheiress of John Comyn, Earl of Buchan, was the ward of Sir John of Ross, a younger son of William, Earl of Ross (d. 1323), but whether she actually married him is uncertain. Her marriage to her 'other' husband is also erroneous, being based on a misdated charter which refers to [an earlier] Margaret/Marjory, Countess of Buchan who married Sir William Lindsay after the death of her Comyn husband. Sir John of Ross, who added a label azure to the Gules, three lions rampant argent of his house (L195), obtained a moiety of the Buchan earldom with lands at Ellon and Dundarg."), 182. National Archives Doc., SC 8/297/14820 (available at www.catalogue.nationalarchives.gov.uk/search.asp). Special thanks go to Andrew B.W. MacEwen for pointing out the misdated charter cited above by McAndrew based on Mr. MacEwen's research.

~ BULKELEY ~

ALICE OF NORMANDY (sister of King William the Conqueror), married LAMBERT, Count of Lens.
JUDITH OF LENS, married WALTHEOF, Earl of Northumberland.
MAUD OF NORTHUMBERLAND, married SIMON DE SENLIS, Earl of Huntingdon and Northampton.
MAUD DE SENLIS, married SAHER DE QUINCY, of Long Buckby, Northamptonshire.
ROBERT DE QUINCY, of Tranent, Fawside, and Longniddry, East Lothian, Scotland, married ORABEL FITZ NESS.
SAHER DE QUINCY, Knt., Earl of Winchester, married MARGARET OF LEICESTER.
ROGER DE QUINCY, Knt., Earl of Winchester, married ELLEN OF GALLOWAY.
ELLEN DE QUINCY, married ALAN LA ZOUCHE, Knt., of Ashby de la Zouch, Leicestershire.
ROGER LA ZOUCHE, Knt., of Ashby de la Zouch, Leicestershire, married ELA LONGESPÉE (desc. King William the Conqueror).
ALAN LA ZOUCHE, Knt., Lord Zouche, married ELEANOR DE SEGRAVE.
ELLEN LA ZOUCHE, married ALAN DE CHERLETON, Knt., of Apley (in Wellington), Shropshire.
ALAN DE CHERLETON, of Aston Eyre (in Morville), Shropshire, married MARGERY FITZ AER.
THOMAS DE CHERLETON, Esq., of Apley (in Wellington), Shropshire, married _____.
ANNE DE CHERLETON, married WILLIAM DE KNIGHTLEY.
THOMAS CHARLTON, of Apley (in Wellington), Shropshire, married CECILY FRAUNCEYS.
ROBERT CHARLTON, Esq., of Apley (in Wellington), Shropshire, married MARY CORBET (desc. King William the Conqueror).
RICHARD CHARLTON, of Apley (in Wellington), Shropshire, married ELIZABETH MAINWARING [see ZOUCHE 17].

18. **ANNE CHARLTON**, married about 1500 **RANDALL GROSVENOR**, Esq., of Bellaport (in Muckleston), Shropshire, son of Randall Grosvenor, Esq., of Bellaport (in Muckleston), Shropshire, by Margaret, daughter of Randall Mainwaring, of Caringham. He was born about 1482 (aged 40 in 1522). They had five sons, Thomas, Geoffrey, Robert, Randall, and Henry, and three daughters, Katherine (wife of _____ Nash), Elizabeth, and Margery. RANDALL GROSVENOR, Esq., died shortly before 3 March 1559/60 (date of inventory). He left a will dated 23 Feb. 1558/9, proved 3 May 1560, requesting burial in the high chancel of Muckleston, Shropshire.

Herald & Genealogist 4 (1867): 481–495; 5 (1870): 322–324, 499–507 (Grosvenor arms: Azure, a garb or). Lennard & Vincent *Vis. of Warwick 1619* (H.S.P. 12) (1877): 384–388 (Grosvenor ped.: "Randall Grosueneur de Belliport 16 H. 7. = Anna fil. W^{mi} Charlton de Apeley.") (Grosvenor arms: Azure, a garb or between three bezants). St. George *Vis. of Staffordshire 1614, 1663–4* (1885): 163–164 (Grosvenor ped.: "Randolph Grosvenor of Bellaport, Shropshire.") (Grosvenor arms: Azure, a garb or between three bezants, a canton of the second for distinction). Jacobus *Bulkeley Gen.* (1933): 6–11. *TAG* 35 (1959): 29–33, 100–106. Young *Blackmans of Knight's Creek* (1980): 79.

19. **ELIZABETH GROSVENOR**, born about 1515. She married **THOMAS BULKELEY**, Esq., of Woore and Buntingsdale (in Market Drayton), Shropshire, son of William Bulkeley, of Woore, Shropshire, by Beatrice, daughter and co-heiress of William Hill, Esq. He was born about 1515. They had two sons, Rowland and [Dr.] Edward, D.D., and three daughters, Margaret (wife of Thomas Smythe), Anne (wife of William Greene), and Katherine (wife of George Baker). His wife, Elizabeth, was a legatee in the 1559 will of her father, who bequeathed her one bay philly. THOMAS BULKELEY died in 1591, and was buried at Market Drayton, Shropshire.

NEHGR 23 (1869): 299–304. St. George *Vis. of London 1633–5* 1 (H.S.P. 15) (1880): 117 (Bulkeley ped.: "Thomas Bulkeley of Woore in co. Salop = [left blank]"). *Advertiser N&Q* (1882): 137–138. Glover et al. *Vis. of Cheshire 1580, 1566, 1533 & 1591* (H.S.P. 18) (1882): 54–56 (Bulklegh ped.: "Thos Bulkley obijt 1591. = Elizabeth d. to Randoll Grosvenor of Bellaport."). Harvey et al. *Vis. of Bedfordshire 1566, 1582, 1634 & 1669* (H.S.P. 19) (1884): 164 (Add'l. Peds.) (Bulkley ped.: "Thomas Bulkley of Wore. = Elizebeth d. of Randall Grosvenor of Bellapre in com.... Esqr.") (Bulkley arms: Sable, a chevron between three bulls' heads argent, armed or, a crescent for difference). Tresswell & Vincent *Vis. of Shropshire 1623, 1569 & 1584* 1 (H.S.P. 28) (1889): 242–246 (Hill ped.: "Thomas Bulkley of Owre."). Jacobus *Bulkeley Gen.* (1933): 3–11. *Trans. Shropshire Arch. & Nat. Hist. Soc.* 51 (1941–43): 111–116. *TAG* 35 (1959): 29–33, 100–106.

20. [**Dr.**] **EDWARD BULKELEY**, D.D., 2nd son, born about 1540. He matriculated pensioner from St. John's College, Cambridge, Michaelmas, 1555; Scholar, 1555; B.A., 1559/60; B.D., 1569; D.D., 1578; Fellow, 1560. He married about 1566 **OLIVE IRBY**, daughter of John Irby, Gent., of Leighthorpe (in Cawthorpe), Lincolnshire, by Rose, daughter of Guthlac Overton. She was born about 1547. They had three sons, Nathaniel, Paul, and [Rev.] Peter, and twelve daughters, including Mary, Frances, Judith, Martha, Deborah, Dorcas, Elizabeth, and Sarah. He obtained the rectorship of Odell, Bedfordshire, probably in 1571. He was Prebendary of Chester, 1574; Westminster, 1583; and Lichfield, 1594. He was Vicar of St. Mary, Shrewsbury, 1578–82. In 1608 he was appointed by the Bishop of Lincoln for the "Levye of Armour in Bedfordshire among the clergy." He resigned his pastorate at Odell, Bedfordshire in 1609, and was succeeded by his son, Peter. His wife, Olive, was buried at Odell, Bedfordshire 10 March 1614/5. [Dr.] EDWARD BULKELEY was buried there 5 Jan. 1620/1.

NEHGR 23 (1869): 299–304. *Advertiser N&Q* (1882): 137–138. Harvey et al. *Vis. of Bedfordshire 1566, 1582, 1634 & 1669* (H.S.P. 19) (1884): 164 (Add'l. Peds.) (Bulkley ped.: "Edward Bulkley (*Rector*) of Odell in com. Bedfford Docter of Divinity had 3 sonns and 12 daughters."). VCH *Bedford* 3 (1912): 69. Jacobus *Bulkeley Gen.* (1933): 14–36. Young *Blackmans of Knight's Creek* (1980): 63 (Bulkeley arms: Argent, 3 bulls' heads cabossed sable).

Children of [Dr.] Edward Bulkeley, by Olive Irby:

i. **FRANCES BULKELEY**, married **RICHARD WELBY**, Esq., of Whaplode and Moulton, Lincolnshire [see WELBY 21].

ii. **MARTHA BULKELEY**, married about 1595 [**Mr.**] **ABRAHAM MELLOWES**, of Odell, Bedfordshire and Boston, Lincolnshire. They had three sons, Oliver, Abraham, and Edward, and three daughters, Elizabeth, Catherine (wife of William Newland), and Anne (wife of John Smith). They immigrated to New England in 1633, where they settled at Charlestown, Massachusetts. He and his wife, Martha, were admitted to the church at Charlestown, Massachusetts in 1633. He was admitted a freeman in 1634, and served as overseer of highways in 1635. In 1638 the General Court granted him 200 acres of land. [Mr.] ABRAHAM MELLOWES died shortly before 30 Dec. 1638. His will was delivered into court 4 June 1639. Pope *Pioneers of Massachusetts* (1900): 310 (biog. of Abraham Mellows). Jacobus *Bulkeley Gen.* (1933): 24–29. Anderson *Great Migration Begins* 2 (1995): 1248–1250 (biog. of Abraham Mellowes).

iii. **DORCAS BULKELEY**, born about 1577. She married by license dated 10 Dec. 1598 (as his 3rd wife) [**Rev.**] **ANTHONY INGOLDSBY**, Rector of Fishtoft, Lincolnshire, 1586–1627. They had three sons, William, Edward, and John, and two daughters, Olive and Annis (or Ann). He was ordained priest 26 March 1586. His wife, Dorcas, was buried at Fishtoft, Lincolnshire 21 October 1616. [Rev.] ANTHONY INGOLDSBY was buried at Fishtoft, Lincolnshire 26 April 1627. He left a will dated 22 April 1627, proved 17 October 1627. Jacobus *Bulkeley Gen.* (1933): 14–17. *TAG* 11 (1934–35): 26–30, 98–101, 143–145, 208–216.

Child of Dorcas Bulkeley, by [Rev.] Anthony Ingoldsby:

a. **OLIVE INGOLDSBY**, baptized at Fishtoft, Lincolnshire 24 June 1602. She married at Fishtoft, Lincolnshire 20 April 1620 (as his 1st wife) [**Rev.**] **THOMAS JAMES**, minister, son of [Rev.] John James, of Skirbeck, Lincolnshire, by his wife, Alice. He was baptized at Boston, Lincolnshire 5 October 1595. They had two sons, [Rev.] Thomas [of East Hampton, New York], and John. He matriculated at Cambridge University, pensioner from Emmanuel, 1611. He obtained a B.A. degree, 1614–5, and a M.A. degree, 1618. He was ordained deacon 16 March 1616/17, priest 17 March 1616/17. His wife, Olive, apparently died before 22 April 1627 (date of her father's will). He married (2nd) before 1632 **ELIZABETH** _____. They had two sons, John and Nathaniel. [Rev.] Thomas and his family immigrated to New England in 1632, where they resided successively at Charlestown, Massachusetts, Providence, Rhode Island, and New Haven, Connecticut. He served as a missionary to Virginia in 1642–3. He returned permanently to England in 1649. He became a minister at Needham Market, Suffolk in 1650, and was ejected in 1662 following the Restoration. [Rev.] THOMAS JAMES, of Needham Market, Suffolk, left a will dated 5 Feb. 1682/3, proved 13 Feb. 1683/4. Pope *Pioneers of Massachusetts* (1900): 255–256 (biog. of [Rev.] Thomas James). *TAG* 11 (1934–35): 26–30, 98–101, 143–145, 208–216. Anderson *Great Migration Begins* 2 (1995): 1072–1076 (biog. of Thomas James).

iv. **ELIZABETH BULKELEY**, born about 1579. She married (1st) **RICHARD WHITTINGHAM**, Gent., of Sutterton, Lincolnshire, son of Baruch Whittingham. They had one son, John. RICHARD WHITTINGHAM,

Gent., left a will dated 6 March 1615/6, proved 18 April 1618. She married (2nd) at Boston, Lincolnshire 9 Jan. 1617/8 **ATHERTON HOUGH** (or **HAUGH**), Gent., of Boston, Lincolnshire, Mayor and Aldeman of Boston, Lincolnshire. They had one son, [Rev.] Samuel. They immigrated in 1633 to New England, where they settled at successively at Charlestown, Boston, and Cambridge, Massachusetts. He and Elizabeth were admitted to the church as members in Nov. 1633. He was chosen an Assistant in 1635, and served as Deputy to the General Court for Boston in 1637 and 1638. His wife, Elizabeth, died at Boston, Massachusetts 14 October 1643. He married (2nd) before 4 April 1646 **SUSANNA HUTCHINSON**, widow of Augustine Storre. They had no issue. ATHERTON HOUGH, Gent., died at Boston, Massachusetts 11 Sept. 1650. His widow, Susanna, died shortly before 29 May 1651 (date of inventory). Pope *Pioneers of Massachusetts* (1900): 241 (biog. of Atherton Hough: "… a man of great strength of character"). Jacobus *Bulkeley Gen.* (1933): 14–17, 33–36. Anderson *Great Migration Begins* 2 (1995): 1005–1010 (biog. of Atheron Hough).

Child of Elizabeth Bulkeley, by Richard Whittingham, Gent.:

a. **JOHN WHITTINGHAM**, Gent., baptized at Boston, Lincolnshire, 29 Sept. 1616. He married **MARTHA HUBBARD**. They had six children. He died at Ipswich, Massachusetts in 1649. Pope *Pioneers of Massachusetts* (1900): 213 (biog. of John Whittingham).

Child of Elizabeth Bulkeley, by Atherton Hough:

a. [**Rev.**] **SAMUEL HOUGH**, baptized at Boston, Lincolnshire, 23 Dec. 1621. He married before 1650 **SARAH SYMMES**, daughter of [Rev.] Zachariah Symmes. They had seven children. He was a minister at Reading, Massachusetts. He died at Boston, Massachusetts 30 March 1662. His widow, Sarah, married (2nd) at Reading, Massachusetts 13 Nov 1662 **JOHN BROCK**. Anderson *Great Migration Begins* 2 (1995): 1005–1010 (biog. of Atheron Hough).

v. **SARAH BULKELEY**, married **OLIVER SAINT JOHN**, Gent., of Keysoe, Bedfordshire [see SAINT JOHN 20].

vi. [**Rev.**] **PETER BULKELEY**, born at Odell, Bedfordshire 31 Jan. 1582/3, B.A., St. John's College, Cambridge, 1604/5, M.A. 1608, ordained deacon and priest June 1608, Canon of Lichfield 1609, University preacher 1610. He was instituted as Rector of Odell, Bedfordshire 12 Jan. 1609/10. He married (1st) at Goldington, Bedfordshire 12 April 1613 **JANE ALLEN**, daughter of Thomas Allen, Gent., of Goldington, Bedfordshire, and Little Waltham, Essex, by Mary, daughter of Thomas Fairclough, Gent. [see ALLEN 17 for her ancestry]. She was baptized at Goldington, Bedfordshire 13 Jan. 1587/8. They had seven sons, [Rev.] Edward, Thomas, Nathaniel, [Rev.] John, Joseph, Daniel, and Jabez, and two daughters, Mary and Mary (again). His wife, Jane, was buried at Odell, Bedfordshire 8 Dec. 1626. He became increasingly Puritan and non-conformist. In 1634 he was suspended for non-attendance at the visitation of Sir Nathaniel Brent, Vicar-General. He married (2nd) about April 1635 **GRACE CHETWODE**, daughter of Richard Chetwode, Knt., of Warkworth, Northamptonshire, by his 2nd wife, Dorothy, daughter of Robert Needham, Esq. [SEE CHETWODE 16 for her ancestry]. She was born about 1602 (aged 33 in 1635). She was a legatee in the 1616 will of her aunt, Elizabeth Needham. They had three sons, [Rev.] Gershom, Eleazer, and [Dr.] Peter, and one daughter, Dorothy. He and his family immigrated to New England in the *Susan & Ellen* in 1635, where they settled initially at Cambridge, Massachusetts. In 1636 he and John Jones organized the church at Concord, Massachusetts. In 1637 he was selected teacher of the Concord church. His wife, Grace, was a legatee in the 1643 will of her sister, Jane Chetwode. In 1651 he published *The Gospel Covenant Opened*, one of the first books published in America. [Rev.] PETER BULKELEY died at Concord, Massachusetts 9 March 1658/9. He left a will dated 14 April 1658, proved 20 June 1659. His widow, Grace, died at New London, Connecticut 21 April 1669. Baker *Hist. & Antiqs. of Northampton* 1 (1822–30): 739–740. *NEHGR* 10 (1856): 167–170; 76 (1922): 307–311. Harvey et al. *Vis. of Bedfordshire 1566, 1582, 1634 & 1669* (H.S.P. 19) (1884): 164 (Add'l. Peds.) ("Peter Bulkley of Odell"). *Misc. Gen. et Heraldica* 2nd Ser. 1 (1886): 45–51, 69–80. Pope *Pioneers of Massachusetts* (1900): 77–78 (biog. of Peter Bulkley). VCH *Bedford* 3 (1912): 69. Foster *Institutions to Eccl. Benefices in Bedford 1535–1660* (Bedfordshire Hist. Rec. Soc. 8) (1924): 155. Jacobus *Hist. & Gen. of the Fams. of Old Fairfield* 1 (1930): 109–115, 707. Jacobus *Bulkeley Gen.* (1933): 92–111. Emmison *Bedfordshire Parish Regs.* 40 (1950): B2. Anderson *Great Migration* 1 (1999): 459–465 (biog. of Peter Bulkeley).

◈ BURES ◈

WILLIAM THE CONQUEROR, King of England, married **MAUD OF FLANDERS**.
HENRY I, King of England, married **MAUD OF SCOTLAND**.
MAUD OF ENGLAND, married **GEOFFREY PLANTAGENET**, Count of Anjou, Duke of Normandy.
HENRY II, King of England, by a mistress, **IDA DE TONY**.
WILLIAM LONGESPÉE, Knt., Earl of Salisbury, married **ELA OF SALISBURY**.
IDA LONGESPÉE, married **WILLIAM DE BEAUCHAMP**, Knt., of Bedford, Bedfordshire.
BEATRICE DE BEAUCHAMP, married **WILLIAM DE MUNCHENSY**, Knt., of Edwardstone, Suffolk.
WILLIAM DE MUNCHENSY, of Edwardstone, Suffolk, married **ALICE** _____.
THOMAS DE MUNCHENSY, Knt., of Edwardstone, Suffolk, married **JOYCE** _____.
THOMAS MUNCHENSY, of Edwardstone, Suffolk, married (1st) **JOAN VAUNCY**.
JOAN MUNCHENSY, married **RICHARD WALDEGRAVE**, Knt., of Smallbridge (in Bures St. Mary), Suffolk.
RICHARD WALDEGRAVE, Knt., of Edwardstone, Suffolk, married **JOAN DOREWARD**.
THOMAS WALDEGRAVE, Knt., of Smallbridge (in Bures St. Mary), Suffolk, married **ELIZABETH FRAY**.
WILLIAM WALDEGRAVE, Knt., of Smallbridge (in Bures St. Mary), Suffolk, married **MARGERY WENTWORTH** (desc. King William the Conqueror) [see WALDEGRAVE 14].

15. ANTHONY WALDEGRAVE (or **WALGRAVE**), Esq., of Ferrers (in Bures), Essex, and, in right of his wife, of Brent Pelham, Hertfordshire, 2nd son. He married before 1512 **ELIZABETH GRAY**, daughter and co-heiress of Ralph Gray, Esq., of Brent Pelham, Hertfordshire, Baron of the Exchequer, by Anne, daughter of Thomas Barnardiston, Knt. They had three sons, William, Thomas, Esq., and Barnaby, and one daughter, Julian. In 1512 they had livery of her manor of Pepsall (in Flamstead), Hertfordshire. ANTHONY WALDEGRAVE, Esq., left a will proved 5 May 1571 (P.C.C. 20 Holney).

Brydges *Collins' Peerage of England* 4 (1812): 235. Hawley et al. *Vis. of Essex 1552, 1558, 1570, 1612 & 1634* 1 (H.S.P. 13) (1878): 122 (Waldegrave ped.: "Anthoney Walgrave 3d sonne. = Elizabeth, da. & heire to Rauffe Gray of Burnt Pelham in Com. Hartford."), 307–310 (Waldegrave ped.: "Anthony Waldegrave of the Feriers in Bewers in com. Essex Esquier 2d sonne. = Elizabeth daugh. and coheire of Rauffe Graye of Burnt Pelham in com. Hertford Esquier one of Barons of ye Exchequer."). Harvey et al. *Vis. of Bedfordshire 1566, 1582, 1634 & 1669* (H.S.P. 19) (1884): 35 (Grey ped.: "Elizabeth [Grey] only daughter and heire maryed to Anthony Walgrave de com. Suff. ar."). Harvey et al. *Vis. of Norfolk 1563 & 1613* (H.S.P. 32) (1891): 295–300 (Waldegrave ped.: "Anthony Waldegrave of Smallbridge. = Elizabeth da. & heir of Raffe Gray of Brent Pelham in co. Hert., one of the Barons of the Exchequer."). VCH *Hertford* 2 (1908): 197; 4 (1914): 82, 94–95. *List of Early Chancery Procs.* 4 (PRO Lists and Indexes 29) (1908): 440; 5 (PRO Lists and Indexes 38) (1912): 9, 498; 7 (PRO Lists and Indexes 50) (1926): 328; 9 (PRO Lists and Indexes 54) (1933): 308, 368; 10 (PRO Lists and Indexes 55) (1936): 203. *Feet of Fines for Essex* 4 (1964): 167, 197, 283. *NEHGR* 154 (2000): 78–108. National Archives, C 1/563/31 (Chancery Proc. dated 1518–29 — John Russell of the Fryth in Surrey [by Byfleet?], Gent., and Anne, his wife, late the wife of Rauf Grey, Esq., and daughter of Thomas Barnerdeston, Knt. v. Antony Walgrave, son of William Waldegrave, Knt., and Elizabeth, his wife, daughter of the said Rauf and Anne.: Recovery before the justices of assize of the manors of Greys and Chamberleyns in Brent Pelham, Hertfordshire and elsewhere.) (available at www.catalogue.nationalarchives.gov.uk/search.asp). Worcestershire Rec. Office: Berrington Coll., 705:24/808 (available at www.a2a.org.uk/search/index.asp).

16. THOMAS WALDEGRAVE, Esq., of Ferrers (in Bures), Essex, 2nd son. He married (1st) **ELIZABETH GURDON**, daughter of Robert Gurdon, Esq., of Waldingfield and Assington, Suffolk, by Rose, daughter of Robert Sexton, of Lavenham, Suffolk. They had three sons, Thomas, Esq., John, and William, and one daughter, Elizabeth (wife of Isaac Wincole). He was appointed supervisor of the 1597 will of Henry Clarke of Lamarsh, Essex, yeoman. He married (2nd) before 1599 **MARY BADBY**. THOMAS WALDEGRAVE, Esq., left a will dated 1 June 1611, proved 11 May 1612 (P.C.C. 48 Fenner).

Hawley et al. *Vis. of Essex 1552, 1558, 1570, 1612 & 1634* 1 (H.S.P. 13) (1878): 122 (Waldegrave ped.: "Thomas Walgrave of Ferrers, 2d sonne. = Elizabeth, da. to Robert Gordon."), 307–310 (Waldegrave ped.: "Thomas Waldegrave of Bewers in Essex 4th sonne. = Elizabeth daugh. to Robart Gurdon of Assington Esquier."). Harvey et al. *Vis. of Norfolk 1563 & 1613* (H.S.P. 32) (1891): 295–300 (Waldegrave ped.: "Thomas Waldegrave of Ferrers. =

Elizabeth da. of Robert Gordon [Gurdon] of Assington in co. Suff."). *Feet of Fines for Essex* 6 (1993): 168, 185. Emmison *Essex Wills* 12 (Essex Rec. Office 143) (2000): 42. *NEHGR* 154 (2000): 78–108.

17. THOMAS WALDEGRAVE, Esq., of Ferrers (in Bures), Essex, eldest son by 1st wife. He married before 1602 (date of fine) **MARGARET HOLMSTEAD**, daughter and co-heiress of John Holmstead, Gent., of Halstead, Essex, by his wife, Palladia. They had four daughters, Mary (wife of Isaac Wincoll), Jemima, Elizabeth, and Margaret. His wife, Margaret, died about 1639. THOMAS WALDEGRAVE, Esq., left a will dated 4 Sept. 1640, proved 14 Sept. 1642 (P.C.C. 107 Cambell).

Hawley et al. *Vis. of Essex 1552, 1558, 1570, 1612 & 1634* 1 (H.S.P. 13) (1878): 122 (Waldegrave ped.: "Thomas Walgrave of Ferrers. = Margarett da. & heire to John Holinshead of Hempsted in Essex."), 209–210, 307–310 (Waldegrave ped.: "Thomas Waldegrave of the same place Gent. sonne & heire. = Margaret daugh. and heire to John Holmstead of Halsted in Essex."), 515. Harvey et al. *Vis. of Norfolk 1563 & 1613* (H.S.P. 32) (1891): 295–300 (Waldegrave ped.: "Thomas Waldegrave of Ferrers. = Margaret da. & heir of John Hollinshed of Hawsted in Essex."). Muskett *Suffolk Manorial Fams.* 1 (1900): 286, 329. *TAG* 18 (1941–42): 137–146. *Feet of Fines for Essex* 6 (1993): 185, 187. *NEHGR* 154 (2000): 78–108.

Child of Thomas Waldegrave, Esq., by Margaret Holmstead:

i. **JEMIMA WALDEGRAVE**, married **HERBERT PELHAM**, Esq., of Cambridge, Massachusetts and Ferrers (in Bures), Essex [see WEST 15.iii.a].

✤ BURGH ✤

1. WALTER DE BURGH, of Burgh near Aylsham, Norfolk. He married **ALICE** _____. They had four sons, William, Hubert, Knt. [Earl of Kent], Thomas, Knt., and Geoffrey [Bishop of Ely], and one daughter, _____. At her death, his wife, Alice, was buried in the church of Walsingham, Norfolk.

Blomefield *Essay towards a Top. Hist. of Norfolk* 3 (1806): 39–41 & 10 (1809): 263–269 (author misidentifies parents of Hubert de Burgh, Earl of Kent, as Reyner de Burgh, and his wife, Joan, daughter and coheir of John Pouchard, of North Tudenham, Norfolk) [see *Curia Regis Rolls* 6 (1932):199–200, for lawsuit dated 1212, which indicates that John Pouchard and his wife, Ita, had two daughters and co-heiresses, namely Maud, wife of Richard de Belhous, and Alice, wife of Robert de Nerford, and no daughter named Joan, wife of Reyner de Burgh). *East Anglian* n.s. 5 (1893–1894): 104–107. *C.P.* 7 (1929): 133, footnote a (Earl Hubert de Burgh gave the advowson of Oulton, Norfolk to Walsingham Priory, Norfolk for the soul of Alice his mother who was buried in Walsingham church). Bullock *Norfolk Portion of the Chartulary of the Priory of St. Pancras of Lewes* (Norfolk Rec. Soc. 12) (1939): 61, 71 (charter dated 1215/16–1226 of Thomas son of Walter de Burgh; charter witnessed by Geoffrey de Burgh).

Children of Walter de Burgh, by Alice _____:

i. **WILLIAM DE BURGH** [see next].

ii. **HUBERT DE BURGH**, Knt., Earl of Kent, married (1st) **BEATRICE DE WARENNE** [see BARDOLF 8]; (2nd) **ISABEL OF GLOUCESTER**, Countess of Gloucester and Essex [see BARDOLF 8; ESSEX 2.i]; (3rd) **MARGARET** (or **MARGERY**) **OF SCOTLAND** [see BARDOLF 8; SCOTLAND 4.iii].

iii. **THOMAS DE BURGH**, Knt., of Upper Arley, Staffordshire (now Worcestershire), and, in right of his wife, of Cockfield, Groton, Kersey, and Semere, Suffolk, Castellan of Norwich. He married c.1201 **NESTA DE COCKFIELD** (or **COKEFELD**), daughter and heiress of Adam de Cockfield, of Cockfield, Groton, Kersey, and Semere, Suffolk, by his wife, Rohese. They had no issue. Sir Thomas and his wife, Nesta, were chief benefactors to the priory of St. Anthony of Kersey, which priory was founded probably by her ancestors about 1184. Thomas is said to have founded a hospital or free chapel of St. Mary and St. Anthony at Kersey, Suffolk before 1218. By another charter, Thomas and Nesta his wife granted three acres of arable land in Groton, Suffolk. In 1218–19 her mother, Rohese, released her dower in the lands of her late husband in Cockfield, Groton, and Semere to Thomas and Nesta. SIR THOMAS DE BURGH was living in 1225, but died in or before March 1227, when his manor at Upper Arleigh, Staffordshire was granted by the king to his brother, Hubert de Burgh, Knt. His widow, Nesta, made several considerable grants to the canons of Kersey. By the first she granted them the mother church of Kersey, with all its appurtenances, eight acres adjoining the cemetery on the south, the two and a half acres on which the house was founded, a messuage where the hospital (*domus hospitalis*) stood, etc. By the same charter she granted the tithes of her mills at Cockfield, Lindsey, and Kersey, to sustain the lights in the Kersey chapel. The church of Kersey was appropriated to the use of the canons by Thomas de Blun[de]ville, Bishop of Norwich, in 1227. Nesta married (2nd) before 10 October 1233 **JOHN DE BEAUCHAMP**. They had no issue. In 1239–40 John and his wife Nesta conveyed lands in Boxford and Alington, Suffolk to Richard Fitz Robert, and lands in Kersey, Suffolk to Geoffrey de Suffolk. In 1240 they confirmed and increased the grants to the priory of lands and pasture in Lindsey and Kersey, and confirmed to them the church of Kersey. At an unknown date, he and his wife, Nesta, conveyed lands in Euston, Suffolk to William de Oddingseles. Following John de Beauchamp's death, she gave the canons the church of Lindsey in order that they might better relieve the poor who flocked there once every week. She married (3rd) before 1241–2 **MATTHEW DE LEYHAM**, of Leyham, Suffolk. They had no issue. In 1241–2, with consent of her husband, Matthew, Nesta gave certain lands in Lindsey and Kersey, Suffolk, together with her body to be buried in the conventual church of Kersey. At the same date, Matthew and Nesta conveyed lands in Cockfield, Suffolk to Henry, Abbot of St. Edmunds. At some unspecified date, Nesta also gave a pasture for six cows in her park of Kersey, Suffolk to Kersey Priory in frankalmoign. Nesta died about 1248. In 1249–50, Matthew de Leyham conveyed lands in Leyham, Suffolk to Peter de Leyham. In 1250–51 Matthew de Leyham conveyed lands in Leyham, Suffolk, together with the advowson, to Peter de Leyham. Dugdale *Monasticon Anglicanum* 6(1) (1830): 592–592 (charters of Thomas de Burgh and his wife, Nesta de Cockfield, to Kersey Priory). Giles *Roger of Wendover's Flowers of History: The History of England from the Descent of the Saxons to A.D. 1235* 2 (1849): 373. Rye *Cal. of the Feet of Fines for Suffolk* (1900): 18, 40–41, 44, 46, 50, 50. Copinger *Manors of Suffolk* 1 (1905): 83–84; 3 (1909): 183. VCH *Worcester* 3 (1913): 6–7. *Yorkshire Archaeological Journal* 30 (1931): 315, citing R. de Libertate, 3 John, 24. Bullock *Norfolk Portion of the Chartulary of the Priory of St. Pancras of Lewes* (Norfolk Rec. Soc. 12) (1939): 61, 71 (charter dated 1215/16–1226 of Thomas son of Walter de Burgh; charter witnessed by Geoffrey de Burgh). *Ancient Deeds—Series A* 1 (List & Index Soc. 151) (1978): 203. Greenway & Sayers *Jocelin of Brakelond, Chronicle of the Abbey of Bury St. Edmunds* (1989): 109 ("Chronicle of the Abbey of Bury St. Edmunds: "On Adam de Cokefield's death [?1198], the abbot could have taken 300 marks for the wardship of Adam's only daughter, but because her grandfather had secretly taken her away, the abbot was not able to get hold of the girl without the help of Archbishop Hubert of Canterbury, so he granted her wardship to the archbishop for the sum of £100. The archbishop sold her wardship for 500 marks to Thomas de Burgh, brother of [Hubert de Burgh] the king's chamberlain, and the girl, with all her rights, was given to him with the abbot's consent. Thomas therefore at once sought possession of the three manors — Cockfield, Semer, and Groton — which were in our hands after Adam's death … Thomas, therefore seeking to get a writ of recognition on this, had knights summoned to go to Tewkesbury to appear on oath before the king [April 1201]."). Harper-Bill *English Episcopal Acta* 6 (1990): 291 (charter dated 1204 witnessed by Geoffrey [de Burgh], Archdeacon of Norwich, and Thomas his brother). VCH *Cambridge* 4 (2002): 206–219. Birmingham City Archives: Lyttleton of Hagley Hall, MS 3279/351062 (grant dated 1227/43 from Hubert de Burgh, Earl of Kent to Robert son of Robert de Gloverina of land which the latter held from Thomas de Burgh, brother of the said Hubert in Erleigh [Upper Arley], Staffordshire) (abstract of document available online at http://www.a2a.org.uk/search/index asp). National Archives, E 40/2948 (Grant by Thomas son of Walter de Burgo, to Thomas de Yford, for 10 marcs, of land called 'Cnoppecroft, ' containing 16 acres, in Utwellys. Witnesses:- Sir Adam de Hagebeche, Robert de Covenham, and others) (available at www.catalogue.nationalarchives.gov.uk/search.asp).

 iv. **GEOFFREY DE BURGH**, Treasurer of the Exchequer. He was appointed Archdeacon of Norwich 14 August 1200. He was Bishop-elect of Ely in 1215–19. He was elected Bishop of Ely in 1225, and was consecrated in that office 29 June 1225. He died 17 Dec. 1228. Dugdale *Monasticon Anglicanum* 6(1) (1830): 592 (Geoffrey de Burgh as witness for charters of his brother, Sir Thomas de Burgh, to Kersey Priory), 487–488 (Geoffrey [de Burgh], Bishop of Ely, styled "kinsman" [nepotem] of Alice Pouchard, wife of Sir Robert de Nerford, and daughter and coheiress of John Pouchard, of Tuddenham, Norfolk). Halliwell *Chronicle of the Monastery of Abingdon* (1844): 2 (sub A.D. 1228: "Eustachius de Fauconberge Londoniensis et Galfridus de Burgo Eliensis epsicopi obierunt."). Thorpe *Florentii Wigorniensis Monachi Chronicon Ex Chronicis* 2 (1849): 174 (sub 1225: "Johannes, episcopus Eliensis, obiit II. non. Maii [6 Maii]; successit ei Galfridus, frater Huberti de Burgo justitiarius"), 174 (sub 1228: "Galfridus de Burgo, episcopus Eliensis, obiit XVI. kal. Januar. [17 Dec.]"). Bullock *Norfolk Portion of the Chartulary of the Priory of St. Pancras of Lewes* (Norfolk Rec. Soc. 12) (1939): 61, 71 (charter dated 1215/16–1226 of Thomas son of Walter de Burgh; charter witnessed by Geoffrey de Burgh). Bedingfield *Cartulary of Creake Abbey* (Norfolk Rec. Soc. 35) (1966): 1–2. Greenway *Fasti Ecclesiae Anglicanae, 1066–1300* 2 (1971): 46, 64; 4 (1991): 120. Harper-Bill *English Episcopal Acta* 6 (1990): 291 (charter dated 1204 witnessed by Geoffrey [de Burgh], Archdeacon of Norwich, and Thomas his brother).

 v. _____ **DE BURGH**, married **ROBERT DE BLUNDEVILLE** (or **BLUNVILLE**), of Newton Flotman, Suffolk. They had two sons, William [Constable of Corfe Castle] and Thomas [Bishop of Norwich].

Child of _____ de Burgh, by Robert de Blundeville:

a. **THOMAS DE BLUNDEVILLE** (or **BLUNVILLE**), King's clerk, Clerk of the Exchequer. He was elected Bishop of Norwich in 1226, and consecrated in that office 20 Dec. 1226. He had a long standing feud with the Binham and Wymondham Priories. He died 16 August 1236. Luard *Annales Monastici* 4 (Rolls Series 36) (1869): 419 (Annals of Worcester sub A.D. 1226 – "T[homas de Blunville] nepos Huberti de Burgo consecratur in episcopum Norwicensem Dominica proxima ante Natale Domini [20 December]."). He died 16 August 1316. His heir to his lands at Glemham, Suffolk was his cousin, Robert de Booton. Thorpe *Florentii Wigorniensis Monachi Chronicon Ex Chronicis* 2 (1849): 174 (sub 1225: "Pandulfus, episcopus Norwicensis, obiit in Italia, XVII. kal. Septemb. [16 August]; successit ei Thomas de Blunville, consecratus VII. kal. Januar. [26 Dec.]."), 176 (sub 1236: "Thomas de Blunvile, episcopus Norwicensis, obiit XVII. kal. Septemb. [16 August]."). *D.N.B.* 5 (1886): 272 (biog. of Thomas de Blundeville or Blunville). Greenway *Fasti Ecclesiae Anglicanae 1066–1300* 2 (1971): 55–58.

2. WILLIAM DE BURGH, of Askeaton, Carrigogunnell, Castleconnell, Kilfeacle, Kilsheelan, Shanid, and Tibberaghny, Seneschal of Munster, 1201. He was closely associated with John, lord of Ireland [future King John], and probably accompanied him on his expedition to Ireland in 1185. He subsequently became John's principal agent in the conquest and organization of northern Munster. He married before 1193 _____, said to be a daughter of Domnall Mór Ua Briain, King of Limerick. They had three sons, Richard [lord of Connacht], Hubert [Prior of Athassel, Bishop of Limerick], and William, and at least one daughter. He erected the Castle of Kilfeacle in 1193, which Domnall Mac Carthaig destroyed three years later. King John make him a speculative grant of Connacht in 1195. By 1200 he held extensive lands in what are now counties Kilkenny, Tipperary, and Limerick. He built the Priory of St. Edmund in Athassel, co. Tipperary about 1200. He intervened in various conflicts in Connacht in 1200, 1202, and 1203, but incurred the wrath of the justiciar, Meiler Fitz Henry, who forced him to abandon Connacht and submit after besieging him in Limerick. In October 1203 the king commanded Meiler Fitz Henry to restore his castles of Askeaton and Kilfeacle. WILLIAM DE BURGH probably died in Jan. or Feb. 1206. His lands were ordered to be taken into the king's hand 7 April 1206.

Herald & Gen. 4 (1867): 337–340. Begley *Diocese of Limerick Ancient & Medieval* (1906): 131–138 (biog. of Hubert de Burgh, Bishop of Limerick). Orpen *Ireland under the Normans* 4 (1920): 159 (Burgh ped.). Pender *Analecta Hibernica* No. 18, The O'Clery Book of Genealogies (Irish MSS. Comm.) (1951) (Burgh pedigree: "... Sir Uilliam Burc (Una ingen Feidhlimthe mic Cathail croibhdeirg a mhathair), m. Uilliam óig frisi n-abarthaoi Uilliam átha an chip m Riocaird mhoir (ingen righ Saxan a mathair), m. Uilliam concuurer .i. Uilliam Adelmisione m Risdeird m Antoin .i. iárla king ..."). Duffy *Medieval Ireland: An Encyclopedia* (2005): 93–95. C. A. Empey, 'Burgh, William de (d. 1206)', Oxford Dictionary of National Biography (2004).

3. RICHARD DE BURGH, Seneschal of Munster, Keeper of Limerick Castle, lord of Connacht, Justiciar of Ireland, 1228–32, son and heir, born about 1193 (came of age in 1214). In 1215 he obtained confirmation of the grant of Connacht previously made to his father. Between June and September 1215 he served in the household of his uncle, Hubert de Burgh. He was in Ireland in 1220, but appears to have made a pilgrimage to Santiago de Compostela in 1222. He married before 21 April 1225 **GILLE DE LACY**, daughter of Walter de Lacy, Knt., of Weobley, Holme Lacy, Mansell Gamage, and Yarkhill, Herefordshire, Ludlow, Rock [Farm] (in Ludlow), and Stanton Lacy, Shropshire, lord of Meath, Ireland, etc., by Margaret (or Margery), daughter of William de Brewes (or Breuse). Her maritagium included the cantred of Joaganach-Cassel and the castle of Ardmayle in Tipperary. They had three sons, Richard, Walter, Knt. [2nd Earl of Ulster], and William Og, and four daughters, Margery, _____ (wife of Gerard de Prendergast), Alice, and _____ (wife of Hamon de Valoines). In 1234 he fought with Hugh de Lacy, Earl of Ulster on the king's side in the conflict with Richard Marshal, Earl of Pembroke. He effectively conquered Connacht in 1235 and 1236. In 1236 he built a castle in the barony of Loughrea in Galway. In Michaelmas term 1241 his wife, Gille, and her sister, Pernel de Tony, together with Rose de Lacy, widow of their nephew, Walter de Lacy, sued the king requesting the land of Walter de Lacy. RICHARD DE BURGH died in

Gascony shortly before 17 Feb. 1242/3. His widow, Gille, married (2nd) **RICHARD DE ROCHESTER**. She was living 22 Feb. 1247.

    Eyton *Antiqs. of Shropshire* 5 (1857): 240 (Lacy ped.). *Herald & Gen.* 4 (1867): 337–340. *Cal. Docs. Rel. Ireland* 1 (1875): 146, 329 (Hubert de Burgh, Earl of Kent styled "uncle" of Richard de Burgh, of Connacht in Ireland in 1234), 428, 445, 450. Bémont *Rôles Gascons* 1 (1885): 197; Supp. Vol. 1 (1895): 95. Orpen *Ireland under the Normans* 4 (1920): 159 (Burgh ped.). Pender *Analecta Hibernica* No. 18, The O'Clery Book of Genealogies (Irish MSS. Comm.) (1951) (Burgh ped.: "... Sir Uilliam Burc (Una ingen Feidhlimthe mic Cathail croibhdeirg a mhathair), m. Uilliam óig frisi n-abarthaoi Uilliam átha an chip m Riocaird mhoir (ingen righ Saxan a mathair), m. Uilliam concuurer .i. Uilliam Adelmisione m Risdeird m Antoin .i. iárla king ..."). Paget *Baronage of England* (1957) 310:6. *C.P.* 12(2) (1959): 170 (footnote d), 171 (footnote f) (sub Ulster). *Curia Regis Rolls* 16 (1979): 360. *Receipt & Issue Rolls for the Twenty-Sixth Year of the Reign of King Henry III 1241–1242* (Pipe Roll Soc. n.s. 49) (1992): 82 (Issues Michaelmas Term 1241: "Egidie uxori Ricardi de Burgo xx m. de prestito per breve de libertate"). Duffy *Medieval Ireland: An Encyclopedia* (2005): 93–95.

Children of Richard de Burgh, by Gille de Lacy:

    i.   **WALTER DE BURGH**, Knt., 2nd Earl of Ulster [see next].

    ii.   **MARGERY DE BURGH**, married **THEBAUD LE BOTELER**, of Arklow, co. Wicklow, Ireland [see BUTLER 4].

    iii.   _____ **DE BURGH**, married **GERALD** (or **GERARD**) **DE PRENDERGAST**, Knt., of Beauvoir (or Carrigaline), co. Cork, Ireland [see PRENDERGAST 7].

4. WALTER DE BURGH, Knt., 2nd Earl of Ulster, lord of Connacht and Munster in Ireland, 2nd son. He married about 1257 **AVELINE FITZ JOHN**, daughter of John Fitz Geoffrey, Knt., of Shere, Surrey, Justiciar of Ireland, by Isabel, daughter of Hugh le Bigod, Earl of Norfolk [see VERDUN 8 for her ancestry]. He was born about 1229. They had four sons, Richard, Knt. [3rd Earl of Ulster, lord of Connacht], Thebaud, William, and Thomas, and one daughter, Giles. He succeeded his older brother, Richard de Burgh, in 1248. Throughout his life, he was continually involved in disputes with the native Irish in Connacht. In 1255 he made a short-lived treaty with Aedh, the son of Felim O'Conor. The next year he led a host of 20,000 men to ravage Connacht. A second peace followed in 1257. In 1260 he plundered Roscommon, and in 1262 he took part in the English expedition when a site was marked out for the castle at the same place. He was created Earl of Ulster in 1264 by Prince Edward in exchange for the Manor of Kilsheelan and other Munster lands. He was in conflict with the Fitzgeralds in 1264. He founded the Priory of St. Peter in Lorrha, co. Tipperary in 1269. In 1270 a general war broke out between the English and the Irish of Connacht, during which he was severely defeated. His actions against the clergy, whom he tried in lay courts and whose lands he despoiled, caused many complaints. SIR WALTER DE BURGH, 2nd Earl of Ulster, died in Galway Castle 28 July 1271, and was buried in the monastery of Athassel-on-the-Suir, co. Tipperary, Ireland. His widow, Aveline, Countess of Ulster, died about 20 May 1274, and was buried in Dunmow Priory, Essex.

    Clutterbuck *Hist. & Antiq. of Hertford* 1 (1815): 293 (Fitz Peter ped.). Montmorency-Morres *Genealogical Memoir of the Fam. of Montmorency* (1817): xxxii–xxxvi. Hunter *Cat. MSS: Lib. of Lincoln's Inn* (1838): 9 (Eleanor, wife of Odo Onel, Rex Kenelean styled "kinswoman" of Walter de Burgh, Earl of Ulster in charter dated 1269). *Herald & Genealogist* 4 (1867): 337–340 (arms of Walter de Burgh: Escartille d'argent et gules, un crois passant gulez). *Notes & Queries* 4th Ser. 3 (1869): 484–485 (Fitz Peter ped.). *Genealogist* n.s. 13 (1896): 36–37. Wrottesley *Peds. from the Plea Rolls* (1905): 137–138. *D.N.B.* 3 (1908): 328–329 (biog. of Walter de Burgh). Kingsford *Stonor Letters & Papers 1290–1483* 1 (Camden 3rd Ser. 29) (1919): 4. Orpen *Ireland under the Normans* 3 (1920): 266–267; 4 (1920): 159 (Burgh ped.). *Rpt. on the MSS of Lord de L'Isle & Dudley* 1 (Hist. MSS Comm. 77) (1925): 31–32. VCH *Buckingham* 3 (1925): 437. *C.P.* 5 (1926): 437 chart, 440–441 (sub FitzJohn); 12(2) (1959): 171–173 (sub Ulster). *Year Books of Edward II* 10 (Selden Soc. 63) (1947): 196–208. Paget *Baronage of England* (1957) 107: 1, 220: 1. Duffy *Medieval Ireland: An Encyclopedia* (2005): 93–95.

Children of Walter de Burgh, Knt., by Aveline Fitz John:

    i.   **RICHARD DE BURGH**, Knt., 3rd Earl of Ulster, lord of Connacht [see next].

    ii.   **GILES DE BURGH**, married (as his 3rd wife) **JAMES [STEWART]** (or **JAMES FITZ ALEXANDER**), Knt., 5th Steward of Scotland, son and heir of Alexander Stewart, Knt., 4th Steward of Scotland, of Dundonald, by his wife, Joan. He was born about 1243. They had four sons, Andrew, Walter, Knt. [6th Steward of Scotland], John, Knt., and James, Knt. [of Durisdeer], and one daughter, Giles (wife of Alexander de Meyners or Menzies, Knt.). He married previously (2nd) before 1278–9 (date of lawsuit) **MURIEL OF STRATHEARN** (died shortly before 12 November 1291), widow of William, 5th Earl of Mar (living 1270), and daughter of Malise, Earl of Strathearn, by which marriage he had no issue. In 1278–9 he and his 2nd wife, Muriel, sued Thomas de Rok in an assize of morte d'ancestor in Northumberland. In the period, 1285–93, he gave all his land in the ville of Tranent, East Lothian to William de Preston. He was one of the six guardians appointed in 1286 on the death of King Alexander III. About 1290, as "James the Steward of Scotland," he confirmed the grant which his ancestor, Alan Fitz Walter, Steward of Scotland, made to Adam Fitz Gilbert sometime before 1177. In 1292 he was one of the auditors appointed by Robert de Brus to represent the said Robert in his claim for the Crown of Scotland. In 1292 he was one of the leading men who opposed the attempts of King Edward I of England to destroy the independence of Scotland. In 1296 King Edward I of England confirmed a charter from Richard de Burgh, Earl of Ulster, to James Stewart, who had married the Earl's sister. He was one of the Scottish parties named in the covenants made by the English 7 July 1297 as part of the Treaty of Irvine. He was present with Wallace at the Battle of Stirling 11 Sept. 1297. On 3 Nov. 1305 he submitted to King Edward I of England. SIR JAMES [STEWART], Steward of Scotland died in 1309. *Liber Cartarum Sancte Crucis* (1840): 67 (charter of James, Steward of Scotland). Riddell *Comments on the Keir Performance with Drumpellier's Exposition* (1860): 197–198. Stevenson *Docs. Ill. of the Hist. of Scotland* 2 (1870): 167–169 (John brother of James the Steward and many others were invited to accompany King Edward I into Flanders in 1297), 183–184, 192–194, 198–200, 200–203 ([James] Steward of Scotland and "his brother" [son frere] named in letter written by ?Hugh de Cressingham to the English king dated July 1297), 216–218, 225–227, 494–496. *Third Rpt.* (Hist. MSS Comm. 2) (1872): 387. Page *Three Early Assize Rolls for Northumberland* (Surtees Soc. 88) (1891): 301. *Scottish Antiquary* 5 (1891): 1–9. Birch *Cat. Seals in the British Museum* 4 (1895): 265 (seal of James Stewart dated c.1270 — Obverse. To the right. In armour: shield of arms. Horse galloping, armorially caparisoned. Arms: a fess chequy, STEWART. Reverse. A shield of arms: as in the obverse. Within a pointed gothic trefoil, background replenished with foliage.). *Scots Peerage* 1 (1904): 13–14 (sub Kings of Scotland), 322 (sub Campbell, Duke of Argyll); 5 (1908): 574–577 (sub Ancient Earls of Mar). Macdonald *Scottish Armorial Seals* (1904): 321 (seal of James Stewart — A shield within a rounded and pointed trefoil panel bearing arms: A fess chequy). *D.N.B.* 3 (1908): 328–329 (biog. of Walter de Burgh). Orpen *Ireland under the Normans* 4 (1920): 159 (Burgh ped.). Moody et al. *New Hist. of Ireland* 9 (1984): 170 (chart).

Child of Giles de Burgh, by James Stewart, Knt:

a. **WALTER STEWART**, Knt., 6th Steward of Scotland, married **MARJORY DE BRUS** [see BRUS 9].

5. RICHARD DE BURGH, Knt., 3rd Earl of Ulster, lord of Connacht, Lieutenant of Ireland, 1299–1300, Keeper of Athlone, Randown, and Roscommon Castles, son and heir, born about 1259 (obtained his lands 5 Jan. 1279/80). He married before 27 Feb. 1280/1 **MARGARET** _____. They had four sons, Walter, John, Thomas, and Edmund, Knt., and six daughters, Eleanor, Elizabeth, Maud, Aveline (wife of John de Bermingham, Earl of Louth), Katherine, and Joan. He was constantly embroiled with the native Irish kings, especially of Connacht, his own lordship. His wife, Margaret, was present in 1282 at the king and queen's court at Rhuddlan Castle, Flintshire. In 1283 Queen Eleanor granted them her manor of Roteneche in Ireland. In 1286 he invaded Connacht, plundering monasteries and churches, and receiving hostages everywhere, and reduced the septs of Cenet Eogtain and Cenel-Connail. In Sept. 1286 he and Thomas de Clare, Knt., made a pact at Turnberry with the Brus party in Scotland. He surrendered the office of Keeper of the Isle of Man to the king in June 1290. In 1292 he attacked Magnus O'Connor, king of Connacht, and forced him to do submission at this castle of Milic. He was summoned for service in Gascony, 1294, and Flanders, 1297, though later allowed to remain in Ireland. He regularly received summons for the Scotch expeditions during the reigns of Kings Edward I and early years of Edward II. In 1294 John Fitz Thomas detained him as a prisoner in his castle from 12 Dec. to 12 March, when he was released by order of Parliament at Kilkenny. The quarrel was not settled until 1302, when John Fitz Thomas was sentenced to forfeit 120 librates in Connacht. In 1296 King Edward I of England confirmed a charter from Richard de Burgh, Earl of Ulster, to James Stewart, who had married the Earl's sister. Richard was co-heir in 1297 to his uncle, Richard Fitz John, Knt., Lord Fitz John, by which he inherited the manors of Moreton-Hampstead, Devon, Bierton and Hulcott in Bierton, Steeple Claydon, and Whaddon, Buckinghamshire, and 6-3/4 townships in the cantred of the Isles of Thomond in Ireland. He founded St. Mary's Priory in Loughrea, co. Galway about 1300. His wife, Margaret, died in 1304. He was granted rights of free chace in his demesne lands in Ireland in 1304. He was appointed Lieutenant of Ireland in June 1308, but his commission was cancelled the next day in favor of Peter de Gavaston. In 1310 he was present at the great Kilkenny Parliament for the pacification of the Irish barons. He was summoned to attend English Parliaments in 1314 and 1317. In 1315 he raised an army to oppose the invasion of Edward de Brus, and followed his retreat towards the Bann. In 1316 he and the other Irish lords took an oath to defend the country. He was apprehended by the Mayor of Dublin in Feb. 1317 and confined in the castle, but was soon released. During his lifetime, he built three castles, Ballimote in co. Sligo, Greencastle in Galway, and Sligo Castle. He also built churches, granted lands to religious foundations and was a benefactor of the Cistercian house of St. Mary at Dunbrody. SIR RICHARD DE BURGH, 3rd Earl of Ulster, died at the monastery at Athassel-on-the-Suir, co. Tipperary 29 July 1326.

Du Chesne *Hist. Gén. des Maisons de Guines, d'Ardres, de Gand, et de Coucy, et de Quelques Autres Fams. Illustres* (1631). Grace *Annales Hiberniæ* (1842): 46 (sub A.D. 1303: "Obiit Comitissa Ultoniæ."), 103 (sub A.D. 1326: "At Whitsuntide, a parliament was held at Kilkenny; Richard Earl of Ulster went to it, although he was ill, and entertained the lords there at a great feast; he died shortly after at Athassell."). Cole *Docs. illus. of English Hist. in the 13th & 14th Cents.* (1844): 71 (Robert le Poer styled "cousin" [cosyn] by Richard de Burgh, Earl of Ulster in petition dated 1289–90). *Notes & Queries* 4th Ser. 10 (1872): 480. *Cal. Docs. Rel. Ireland* 2 (1877): 487 (Richard de Burgh, Earl of Ulster, styled "cousin" by Queen Eleanor of Castile); 3 (1879): 307–308 (Robert le Poer styled "kinsman" of Richard de Burgh, Earl of Ulster in 1290). *Annual Rpt. of the Deputy Keeper* 49 (1888): 31. *Genealogist* n.s. 13 (1896): 36–37. *Scots Peerage* 1 (1904): 322 (sub Campbell, Duke of Argyll). Wrottesley *Peds. from the Plea Rolls* (1905): 137–138. *C.Ch.R.* 2 (1906): 267. *D.N.B.* 3 (1908): 324–325 (biog. of Richard de Burgh). VCH *Buckingham* 2 (1908): 321. *Jour. Flintshire Hist. Soc.* 5 (1915): 91–94. Mills *Cal. Gormanston Reg.* (1916): 2–3. Orpen *Ireland under the Normans* 3 (1920): 267; 4 (1920): 159 (Burgh ped.). VCH *Buckingham* 3 (1925): 437. *Rpt. on the MSS of Lord de L'Isle & Dudley* 1 (Hist. MSS Comm. 77) (1925): 31–32. *C.P.* 5 (1926): 437 chart, 440–441 (sub FitzJohn); 7 (1929): 222 (sub Kildare), footnote l; 9 (1936): 404; 12(2) (1959): 173–177 (sub Ulster). VCH *Buckingham* 4 (1927): 100. *Cal. Chancery Warrants* (1927): 261 (Richard de Burgh, Earl of Ulster, styled "king's cousin" by King Edward I of England). Johnstone *Letters of Edward Prince of Wales* (1931): 17–18 (Richard de Burgh, Earl of Ulster, styled "cher cosin le Counte de Vluester [Ulster]" by Edward, Prince of Wales [afterwards King Edward II]) [see also Prestwich et al. *Procs. of the Durham Conf. 2001* (13th Cent. England 8) (2003): 64]. *Year Books of Edward II* 10 (Selden Soc. 63) (1947): 196–208. Paget *Baronage of England* (1957) 107: 1, 220: 2. *Ancient Deeds — Ser. B* 2 (List & Index Soc. 101) (1974): B.8431. Ellis *Cat. Seals in the P.R.O.* 1 (1978): 13 (seal of Richard de Burgh, Earl of Ulster dated 1305 — Between two small lions rampant, a shield of arms: a cross [BURGH]). *Genealogists' Mag.* 20 (1982): 335–340 (author identifies Margaret, wife of Richard de Burgh, as a possible daughter of Arnoul III, Count of Guines, by his wife, Alice de Coucy) ("Comte Arnoul III of Guines had … a daughter who was married to a mysterious Irish lord", cites Anselme *Hist. de la Maison Royale de France* 8 (1733): 543 ff; Chesnaye-Desbois *Dict. de la Noblesse* 8 (1866): cols. 40–41, and 4, cols. 129–131). *Ancient Deeds — DD Ser.* (List & Index Soc. 200) (1983): 185. Moody et al. *New Hist. of Ireland* 9 (1984): 170 (chart). Blakely *Brus Fam. in England & Scotland* (2005): 86. Duffy et al. *Medieval Ireland: An Encyclopedia* (2005): 93–95 (author states in error that Richard de Burgh "married a distant relative, Margaret, the great-granddaughter of Hubert de Burgh" [Earl of Kent]). National Archives, SC 8/163/8129; SC 8/175/8730; SC 8/329/E945 (available at www.catalogue.nationalarchives.gov.uk/search.asp).

Children of Richard de Burgh, Knt., by Margaret _____:

i. **JOHN DE BURGH** [see next].

ii. **ELEANOR DE BURGH**, married **THOMAS DE MULTON**, Knt., 1st Lord Multon of Egremont [see HARINGTON 9].

iii. **ELIZABETH DE BURGH**, married **ROBERT DE BRUS**, Knt., Earl of Carrick, afterwards **ROBERT I**, King of Scots [see BRUS 8].

iv. **MAUD DE BURGH**, married **GILBERT DE CLARE**, Knt., Earl of Gloucester and Hertford [see CLARE 8.i].

v. **KATHERINE DE BURGH**, married **MAURICE FITZ THOMAS**, 1st Earl of Desmond [see BERKELEY 5.iv.a].

vi. **JOAN DE BURGH**, married (1st) at Greencastle 16 August 1312 **THOMAS FITZ JOHN**, 2nd Earl of Kildare, Justiciar of Ireland. They had three sons, John, Richard [3rd Earl of Kildare], and Maurice, Knt. [4th Earl of Kildare]. THOMAS FITZ JOHN, 2nd Earl of Kildare, died at Maynooth, co. Kildare 5 April 1328. She married (2nd) at Maynooth, co. Kildare 3 July 1329 (as his 2nd wife) **JOHN DARCY**, Knt., 1st Lord Darcy of Knaith [see DARCY 11], of Knaith, Lincolnshire, Oldcotes, Nottinghamshire, etc., and, in right of his 1st wife, of Notton, Yorkshire, Justiciar of Ireland, Steward of the King's Household, Chamberlain to the King, King's Councillor, Constable of Norham and Nottingham Castles, Constable of the Tower of London, Sheriff of Nottinghamshire and Derbyshire, Sheriff of Lancashire, Sheriff of Yorkshire, 1327–8, Knight of the Shire for Nottinghamshire, son and heir of Roger Darcy, Knt., of Oldcotes and Styrrup, Nottinghamshire, by Isabel, daughter of William de Aton, Knt. [see DARCY 10 for his ancestry]. They had one daughter, Elizabeth. In 1323 he was granted the manors of Edgefield and Walcot, Norfolk for life to support his dignity as Justiciar of Ireland. In 1328 he was granted the manor of Wark in Tynedale for life, and in fee 1329, which he sold to the Queen. He was commissioned to treat with the nobles of Aquitaine in 1330. In 1330, having engaged to stay always with the king with 20 men-at-arms in times of war, he was granted the manors of Brocklesby and Grantham, Lincolnshire for life. In 1331 he was appointed a special envoy to the King of France concerning the marriage of Prince Edward. He was summoned to Parliament from 27 Jan. 1331/2 to 2 Jan. 1333/4, by writs directed *Johanni Darcy le cosyn*, whereby he is held to have become Lord Darcy. In 1332 he was granted the manor of Marston Maysey, Wiltshire, Wick, Gloucestershire, etc. for life. In 1335 he took an army to Scotland, and wasted Arran and Bute. For his good services in Ireland and elsewhere, he and his wife, Joan, and the heirs male of their bodies were granted the manors of Rathwer and Kildalk in Ireland in 1335. In 1337 he was appointed to treat with the King of France, the Emperor, the Count of Flanders, etc., and also with the King of Scots. The same year he was granted the reversion of the manors of Temple Newsham and Temple Hurst, Yorkshire, and Torksey, Lincolnshire. In 1340 he was granted the manors of Louth and Garristown in Ireland in fee, and the reversions of the manors of Eckington, Derbyshire and Kirkby in Ashfield, Nottinghamshire for life. He accompanied the Earl of Northampton in his expedition to Brittany in 1342. In 1345 he was granted a weekly market and yearly fair at Torksey, Lincolnshire. He was present at the Battle of Crécy in 1346. SIR JOHN DARCY, 1st Lord Darcy of Knaith, died 30 May 1347. His widow, Joan, died 23 April 1359, and was buried with her 1st husband in the Church of the Friars Minors at Kildare, or in the Holy Trinity Cathedral in Dublin. By his 1st marriage before 1318 (date of fine) to **EMMELINE HERON**, he was the father of John Darcy, 2nd Lord Darcy of Knaith [see DARCY 12]. Poulson *Hist. & Antiqs. of Holderness* 2 (1841): 200–201 (Darcy ped.). Leinster *Earls of Kildare* (1858): 28–31. *List of Sheriffs for England & Wales* (PRO Lists and Indexes 9) (1898): 161. *C.P.* 4 (1916): 54–58 (sub Darcy) (arms of John Darcy: Azure, crusilly and three cinquefoils argent); 7 (1929): 221–225 (sub Kildare). Mills *Cal. Gormanston Reg.* (1916): 2–3. Paget *Baronage of England* (1957) 169: 1. Clay *Yorkshire Deeds* 7 (Yorkshire Arch. Soc. Recs. 83) (1932): 77–78 (demise dated 1337 from John Darcy *le Cosyn* lord of Notton to John Esaude re. a tenement in the vill of Chevet, Yorkshire). Sanders *English Baronies* (1960): 119. Hedley *Northumberland Fams.* (1968): 96. Ellis *Cat. Seals in the P.R.O.* 2 (1981): 32 (seal of John Darcy, Justiciar of Ireland dated 1343 — A ship fills the lower part of the seal, the stern and prow each ending in an ox's head, with a shield of arms: crusilly, three sexfoils pierced, hung aslant over the side. Above the shield is a helm in profile, with mantling flying to right ande crest: on a cap with two large curved horns, … (defaced). From the top of the shield, below the helm, a mailed forearm curves up to left, the hand holding a lance, bendwise, with a triangular pennon charged with a bird. Legend: S'IEHAN/DARCI). Roper *Feet of Fines for the County of York* 1314–1326 (Yorkshire Arch. Soc. Recs. 158) (2006): 30.

Child of Joan de Burgh, by Thomas Fitz John:

a. **MAURICE FITZ THOMAS**, Knt., 4th Earl of Kildare, Justiciar of Ireland, 1356, 1357, 1360, 1371, 1375, 1377, younger son, born in 1318. He was heir in 1331 to his older brother, Richard Fitz Thomas, 3rd Earl of Kildare. He had writ of livery, tested at Dublin, 9 August 1342. In the summer of 1345 he was treacherously arrested and imprisoned in Dublin Castle, but was liberated in April 1346 on finding sureties. In 1347 he was present with King Edward III of England at the Siege and capture of Calais. He married in 1347 **ELIZABETH DE BURGHERSH**, daughter of Bartholomew de Burghersh, Knt., 3rd Lord Burghersh, by Elizabeth, daughter of Thebaud de Verdun, Knt., 2nd Lord Verdun [see BURGHERSH 7 for her ancestry]. They had four sons, Gerald [5th Earl of Kildare], John, Richard, and Thomas. He does not appear to have been invested with the earldom until after 1 Dec. 1354. In 1356 he was instructed to strengthen and maintain his castles at Kilkea, Rathmore, and Ballymore, under pain of forfeiting the same. In 1372 he issued mandates to the Earl of Desmond and others to meet him with all their men-at-arms, hobelars, and archers, horse and foot, in the county of Limerick, to defend it against O'Brien of Thomond. In 1386 he was a member of the council of Robert de Vere, Marquis of Dublin. SIR MAURICE FITZ THOMAS, 5th Earl of Kildare, died 25 August 1390, and was buried in Holy Trinity (now Christ Church Cathedral), Dublin, Ireland. Leinster *Earls of Kildare & their Ancs., from 1057 to 1773* (1858): 31–35. *D.N.B.* 7 (1908): 140–141 (biog. of Maurice Fitzgerald, 4th Earl of Kildare). *C.P.* 7 (1929): 223–225 (sub Kildare).

Child of Joan de Burgh, by John Darcy, Knt.:

    a. **ELIZABETH DARCY**, married **JAMES LE BOTELER** (or **BUTLER**), Knt., 2nd Earl of Ormond [see BUTLER 8].

6. JOHN DE BURGH, 2nd but 1st surviving son and heir apparent, born about 1290. He married at Waltham Abbey, Essex 30 Sept. 1308 (in the king's presence) **ELIZABETH DE CLARE**, daughter of Gilbert de Clare, Knt., Earl of Gloucester and Hertford, by his 2nd wife, Joan of Acre, daughter of Edward I, King of England [see CLARE 8 for her ancestry]. She was probably born at Caerphilly, Glamorgan in Nov. 1295. They had one son, William, Knt. [4th Earl of Ulster]. JOHN DE BURGH died at Galway in Ireland 18 June 1313. His widow, Elizabeth, was co-heiress in 1314 to her brother, Gilbert de Clare, Knt., Earl of Gloucester and Hertford, by which she inherited the honour of Clare, Suffolk, and the castles and manors of Usk, Tregruk [Llangibby], and Carleon in Wales. She subsequently adopted the style, Elizabeth de Burgh, lady of Clare. Elizabeth married (2nd) near Bristol 4 Feb. 1315/6 (without the king's license) (as his 2nd wife) **THEBAUD** (or **TEBAUD**) **DE VERDUN**, Knt., 2nd Lord Verdun, hereditary Constable of Ireland [see VERDUN 11], of Alton, Staffordshire, Weobley, Herefordshire, Farnham Verdon, Buckinghamshire, Brandon (in Wolston) and Bretford (in Wolston), Warwickshire, Wilsford, Wiltshire, etc., Justiciar of Ireland, 2nd but 1st surviving son and heir of Thebaud de Verdun, Knt., 1st Lord Verdun, hereditary Constable of Ireland, by Margery, daughter of Humphrey de Bohun, Knt. [see VERDUN 10 for his ancestry]. He was born 8 Sept. 1278. They had one daughter, Isabel [see VERDUN 11 for the issue of this marriage]. He was knighted by the king in Northumberland 24 June 1298, and fought in the second line at the Battle of Falkirk 22 July 1298. He was summoned to Parliament from 29 Dec. 1299 by writs directed (till his father's death) *Theobaldo de Verdun junior*. SIR THEBAUD DE VERDUN, 2nd Lord Verdun, died testate at Alton, Staffordshire 27 July 1316, and was buried in Croxden Abbey, Staffordshire. His widow, Elizabeth, married (3rd) shortly before 3 May 1317 **ROGER DAMORY** (or **DAMMORY**, **DAMMARY**), Knt., of Bletchingdon, Oxfordshire, Standon, Hertfordshire, Caythorpe, Lincolnshire, Easton in Gordano, Somerset, and Kennington (in Lambeth), Surrey, Warden of the Forest of Dean and Constable of St. Briavels Castle, 1318–20, Constable of Corfe and Knaresborough Castles, younger son of Robert Damory, Knt., of Bucknell and Woodperry, Oxfordshire, Thornborough, Buckinghamshire, and Ubley, Somerset. They had one daughter, Elizabeth. In 1312 he was granted the manor of Bletchingdon, Oxfordshire for life by his older brother, Richard Damory, Knt. For his good services at the Battle of Bannockburn, he and his wife, Elizabeth, were granted the manors of Vauxhall (in Lambeth), Surrey, Holton, Oxfordshire, and Sandal, Yorkshire in 1317. He was summoned to Parliament from 20 Nov. 1317 to 15 May 1321, by writs directed *Rogero Damory* or *Dammory*, whereby he is held to have become Lord Damory. He presented to the church of Pimperne, Dorset in 1317. In 1320 he and his wife, Elizabeth, granted the Prior and convent of St. Augustine at Clare, Suffolk ten quarters of wheat from the grange at Clare and ten quarters of malt from the issue of the mill adjacent to the priory, in return for the prior and convent finding two friars to celebrate mass daily in the Castle of Clare for the duration of the lifetimes of Roger and Elizabeth. He took an active part in the Despenser war in 1321–2. He was one of the principals in this affair, being engaged in the capture of Gloucester, the burning of Bridgnorth, the Siege of Tickhill, and the conflict at Burton-on-Trent. His lands were subsequently confiscated and orders were issued for his arrest. On the retreat before the King's forces, being sick or wounded, he was left behind at Tutbury, where he was captured 11 March 1321/2. He was tried and condemned to death, and his estates forfeited, but his execution was respited 13 March. SIR ROGER DAMORY, Lord Damory, died testate at Tutbury Castle, Staffordshire 13 (or 14) March 1321/2, and was buried at St. Mary's, Ware, Hertfordshire. Following his death, his widow, Elizabeth, was imprisoned in the Barking Abbey, where under duress and fear of death, she was forced to exchange her castles and manors of Usk, Tregruk [Llangibby], and Caerleon, and 19 other manors in Wales for the castles and manors of Swansea, Oystermouth, etc., held by her brother-in-law, Hugh le Despenser *the younger*. At Christmas 1322 she was placed under arrest at York, until she signed a bond not to marry nor dispose of her lands without the King's license. Her lands were taken into the King's hand 7 Jan. 1322/3, as she had left the King without his license. Her lands were subsequently restored to her 17 Feb. 1326/7, including the manor of Vauxhall (in Lambeth), Surrey which formerly belonged to her husband Roger Damory. In 1326–7 she had license to sell 28 acres of her fee in Haveringland, Norfolk to Haveringland Priory. In 1327 she complained that Walter de Burcy, William son of John de Hanlegh, and others entered her free chace at Cranborne, Dorset, hunted therein, carried away her deer, and assaulted her servant. In 1327 she obtained a license to grant the Prior and Convent of Ely her life interest in fifteen messuages, lands, rent, and a fishery in Windelsea Mere, in Lakenheath, Suffolk, with reversion to her heirs. In 1327 she complained that Nicholas Culpeper, Robert de Wendovre, and others broke her park at Tonbridge, Kent, hunted there, and carried away deer. In 1328 she sued Richard Damory regarding the manor of Eston, Somerset. In 1329–30 she conveyed a 1/4th share of the manor of Kirkby Knowle, Yorkshire to Robert le Constable, Knt. and his wife, Avice. In 1331 she obtained a license to grant £20 rent with appurtenances in Lakenheath, Suffolk to the Prior and Convent of Anglesey. In 1333 she obtained papal indults for plenary remission, a portable altar, and to have masses and divine offices celebrated in chapels and oratories where she may be. The same year she obtained a license to grant £14 rent with the appurtenances in Bottisham, Swaffham Bulbeck, and Horningsey, Cambridegshire, together with the advowson of Dunmow, Essex to the Prior and Convent of Anglesey. In 1337 Elizabeth and her daughter and son-in-law, John and Elizabeth Bardolf, exchanged the Damory manors of Kennington and Vauxhall (both in Lambeth), Surrey with the king, for the manors of Clopton and Ilketshall, Suffolk. In 1338 she refounded University Hall at Cambridge University under the name of Clare Hall, and gave it the rectory of Great Gransden, Huntingdonshire. In 1343 she received a papal indult to transmute a vow she made to visit the Holy Land and Santiago de Compostella to some other works of piety. She presented to the churches of Tarrant Gunville, Dorset, 1344, and Pimperne, Dorset, 1348. In 1346 the king ordered her to provide 10 men-at-arms and 20 archers for the Siege of Calais. In 1348 she had license to found a house of Friars Minor at Walsingham, Norfolk. In 1353 the king granted that the executors of her will should have full and free administration of all her goods from the day of her death and dispose of the same according to her last will and testament and the form of administration committed to them by the ordinary. In 1355 she granted a rent to the Prior and Convent of Anglesey to find two secular chaplains to say mass in their church of Anglesey for the said Elizabeth and her ancestors. Elizabeth de Burgh, lady of Clare, died 4 Nov. 1360. She left a will dated 25 Sept. 1355, proved 3 Dec. 1360, requesting burial in the Convent of the Minoresses without Aldgate, London.

Sandford *Gen. Hist. of the Kings of England* (1677): 141–142. Weever *Antient Funeral Monuments* (1767): 311–312. Nichols *Coll. of All the Wills* (1780): 22–43 (will of Elizabeth de Burgh, lady of Clare). Dugdale *Monasticon Anglicanum* 2 (1819): 59–65; 6(1) (1830): 395–396; 6(3) (1830): 1600–1602 (Elizabeth styled "a ladie bright"). Nicolas *Testamenta Vetusta* 1 (1826): 56–59 (will of Elizabeth de Burgh, lady of Clare). Montagu *Guide to the Study of Heraldry* (1840): 37–38. Banks *Baronies in Fee* 1 (1844): 445 (sub Verdon). Gurney *Rec. of the House of Gournay* 1 (1845): 227. Stapleton *De Antiquis Legibus Liber: Cronica Maiorum et Vicecomitum Londoniarum* (Camden Soc. 34) (1846). *Top. & Gen.* 1 (1846): 216–223. Lipscomb *Hist. & Antiqs. of Buckingham* 1 (1847): 200–201 (Clare ped.). Brewer *Monumenta Franciscana* 1 (Rolls Ser. 4) (1858): 513–514. Eyton *Antiqs. of Shropshire* 8 (1859): 62–64. Grainge *Vale of Mowbray* (1859): 236–237. Hutchins *Hist. & Antiqs. of Dorset* 1 (1861): 296; 3 (1868):461. *Herald & Genealogist* 4 (1867): 414 (seal of Elizabeth de Clare). *Jour. British Arch. Assoc.* 26 (1870): 149–160. Hailstone *Hist. & Antiq. of Bottisham* (1873): 255–262. *Annual Rpt. of the Deputy*

Keeper 35 (1874): 6–7. Turner *Cal. Charters & Rolls: Bodleian Lib.* (1878): 129. Waters *Chester of Chicheley* 1 (1878): 140 (ped. chart). Clark *Land of Morgan* (1883): 93–166. *MSS of the Earl of Westmorland, Captain Stewart,... & others* (Hist. MSS Comm. 10th Rpt., Appendix, Pt. 4) (1885): 358–359 (charter of Thebaud de Verdon, Constable of Ireland dated 1315). *Procs. Soc. of Antiqs. of London* 2nd Ser. 10 (1885): 233–234. *Bedfordshire Notes & Queries* 2 (1889): 301. Dickinson *Kirby's Quest for Somerset* (Somerset Rec. Soc. 3) (1889): 63. Wrottesley *Staffordshire Suits: Plea Rolls* (Colls. Hist. Staffs. 10(1)) (1889): 57–62. *C.P.R.* 1327–1330 (1891): 61, 150, 207. Birch *Cat. Seals in the British Museum* 2 (1892): 33, 580 (seal of Elizabeth de Burgh, lady of Clare dated 1333 — A shield of arms: barry nebuly of six, over all a bend [DAMORY]. Between three lions passant guardant [ENGLAND], in reference to her grandfather Edward I.; and within a square panel ornamented with tracery consisting of two interlaced quatrefoils, cusped and pointed. Outside this square are the lobes of two other quatrefoils; those in cross lancet-shaped, those in saltire segmental. Each of the lancet-shaped lobes contains a roundel charged with the following heraldic bearings: 1. a cross, and label of three points [BURGH]; 2, 3, three chevrons [CLARE]; 4. a fret [VERDUN]. Each of the segmental lobes encloses a countersunk trefoil, which in turn contains a castle [CASTILE], and a lion rampant [LEON]. The spandrels outside all these lobes contain countersunk trefoils), 580–581 (seal of Elizabeth de Burgh, lady of Clare dated 1353 — A shield of arms: per pale, dex., CLARE; sin., BURGH, all within a bordure guttée. Between three lions guardant [ENGLAND]; and within a lozenge-shaped panel ornamented with small ball-flowers along the inner edge. Outside this lozenge are the lancet-shaped lobes of a quatrefoil in saltire: each with tracery and containing a trefoil-shaped compartment in which is a bordered roundel charged with the following heraldic bearings: 1, 4, CASTILE; 2, 3, LEON. The intervening spaces between the lobes are filled in each instance with a roundel between two small circular countersunk compartments, and other intermediate details of tracery. These roundels are charged with the following heraldic bearings: 1, 2, CLARE (at top and bottom); 2, VERDUN (left hand); 3, DAMORY (right hand)). *C.P.R.* 1330–1334 (1893): 159, 476–477, 551 (instances of Elizabeth de Burgh styled "king's kinswoman"). *Papal Regs.: Letters* 2 (1895): 404, 410. *Notes & Queries* 8th Ser. 10 (1896): 136, 285–286, 326, 486. *Papal Regs.: Petitions* 1 (1896): 22–23 (Elizabeth styled "queen's kinswoman"), 229–230. Wrottesley *Crécy & Calais* (1898): 103. Rye *Cal. Feet of Fines for Suffolk* (1900): 211. *C.P.R.* 1321–1324 (1904): 382 (Elizabeth styled "king's niece"). *C.P.R.* 1324–1327 (1904): 347, 351. *List of Inqs. ad Quod Damnum* 1 (PRO Lists and Indexes 17) (1904): 308, 330; 2 (PRO Lists and Indexes 22) (1906): 430, 440, 458, 565. *C.P.R.* 1348–1350 (1905): 7. Wrottesley *Peds. from the Plea Rolls* (1905): 7, 66, 133–134, 273. *C.P.R.* 1350–1354 (1907): 493. *Colls. Hist. Staffs.* n.s. 10(2) (1907): 20, 25. *C.Ch.R.* 3 (1908): 400, 428, 463. *D.N.B.* 4 (1908): 376–377 (biog. of Elizabeth de Clare: "She appears to have maintained a high character for piety and love of learning."). *C.P.* 2 (1912): 426 (sub Burghersh); 3 (1913): 245 (sub Clare); 4 (1916): 42–45 (sub Damory) (Damory arms: Barry undy of six, argent and gules, a bend azure), 46–48 (sub Damory), 671 (Appendix H) (chart); 5 (1926): 344–347 (sub Ferrers), 437 (sub FitzJohn), 708, footnote a (sub Gloucester); 12(2) (1959): 177–178 (sub Ulster), 250–252 (sub Verdun); 14 (1998): 619. VCH *Surrey* 4 (1912): 50–64. *Trans. Royal Hist. Soc.* 3rd Ser. 9 (1915): 21–64. Mills *Cal. Gormanston Reg.* (1916): 2–3. Orpen *Ireland under the Normans* 4 (1920): 159 (Burgh ped.). VCH *Buckingham* 3 (1925): 227–228; 4 (1927): 25, 237–242 (Damory arms: Barry wavy argent and gules). *Cal. Chancery Warrants* (1927): 484 (Sir Roger Damary styled "king's nephew"). *Feet of Fines for Essex* 3 (1929–49): 34. Richardson & Sayles *Rotuli Parl. Anglie Hactenus Inediti 1274–1373* (Camden Soc. 3rd Ser. 51) (1935): 151–153, 177–179. *Speculum* 16 (1941): 57–63; 30 (1955): 207–212. Hatton *Book of Seals* (1950): 53, 175–176, 318. Holmes *Estates of the Higher Nobility in 14th Cent. England* (1957): 35–38. VCH *Oxford* 5 (1957): 170–171; 6 (1959): 56–71. Sanders *English Baronies* (1960): 34–35. Smith *Itinerary of John Leland* 4 (1964): 150–163. Mills *Dorset Lay Subsidy Roll of 1332* (Dorset Rec. Soc. 4) (1971): 75, 77, 85, 89. Pugh *Middle Ages: Marcher Lordships of Glamorgan, Morgannwg, Gower & Kilvey* (Glamorgan County Hist. 3) (1971): 167–173. VCH *Cambridge* 5 (1973): 140–147. *Ancient Deeds — Ser. B* 2 (List & Index Soc. 101) (1974): B.6098; 3 (List & Index Soc. 113) (1975): B.9208, B.11607. Rees *Cal. Ancient Petitions Rel. Wales* (Board of Celtic Studies, Hist. & Law 28) (1975): 139–140, 173. *Ancient Deeds — Ser. A* 1 (List & Index Soc. 151) (1978): 60. Ellis *Cat. Seals in the P.R.O.* 1 (1978): 12 (seal of Elizabeth de Burgh, lady of Clare dated 1327 — In a square traceried panel, a shield of arms: barry wavy, and a baston [DAMORY]. The panel contains three lions passant gardant, above and on either side of the shield; outside these more tracery contains four roundels with arms, viz. (above) a cross, and a label of three points [BURGH]; (below) a fret [VERDUN]; (at either side) three chevrons [CLARE]; and also four trefoils, two containing each a castle [CASTILE] and two a lion rampant [LEON]. No legend); 2 (1981): 32 (seal of Roger Damory dated 1316 — A shield of arms, couché: barry wavy (or vair), overall a bend; helm above with mantling and crest: a crown. The background is diapered. Legend lost or illegible). *Ancient Deeds — Ser. AS & WS* (List & Index Soc. 158) (1979): 6 (Deed A.S.29). Frame *English Lordship in Ireland* (1982). *Genealogists' Mag.* 20 (1982): 335–340. *Ancient Deeds — Ser. DD* (List & Index Soc. 200) (1983): 185. Moody et al. *New Hist. of Ireland* 9 (1984): 170 (chart). Schwennicke *Europäische Stammtafeln* 3(1) (1984): 156 (sub Clare). Harper-Bill *Cartulary of the Augustinian Friars of Clare* (1991): 32–33. Hicks *Who's Who in Late Medieval England* (1991): 87–88 (biog. of Elizabeth Burgh, lady of Clare: "… Elizabeth's widowhood is illuminated by the finest set of household accounts still surviving… she ran her household and estates efficiently, obtained value for her money… from the early 1330s was giving property to Ely cathedral priory, Tremenhall and Anglesey priories, and West Dereham Abbey. Her attention was attracted by 1336 to the notoriously under-financed University Hall at Cambridge, which she was persuaded to take over as Clare Hall, to endow (1346), and for which she devised statutes in 1359"). Barron & Sutton *Medieval London Widows* (1994). Ward *Women of the English Nobility & Gentry 1066–1500* (1995): 116–119. VCH *Gloucester* 5 (1996): 413–415. Underhill *For Her Good Estate* (1999). Morrison *Women Pilgrims* (2000): 72–73. Gee *Women, Art & Patronage from Henry III to Edward III: 1216–1377* (2002): 149–150. Müller & Stöber *Self-Representation of Medieval Religious Communities* (2009). Sandler *Gothic Manuscripts 1285–1385* II: Cat., no. 12. Canterbury Cathedral Archives: Dean & Chapter Archive, CCA-DCc-ChAnt/F/58 (available at www.a2a.org.uk/search/index.asp). National Archives, SC 8/35/1722; SC 8/35/1723; SC 8/35/1724; SC 8/35/1726; SC 8/36/1763; SC 8/81/4007; SC 8/92/4554; SC 8/134/6697; SC 8/194/9664; SC 8/233/11602; SC 8/233/11603; SC 8/233/11604 (available at www.catalogue.nationalarchives.gov.uk/search.asp).

Child of John de Burgh, by Elizabeth de Clare:

i. **WILLIAM DE BURGH**, Knt., 4th Earl of Ulster, lord of Connacht [see next].

Child of Elizabeth de Clare, by Thebaud de Verdun, Knt.:

i. **ISABEL DE VERDUN**, married **HENRY DE FERRERS**, 2nd Lord Ferrers of Groby [see GROBY 10].

Child of Elizabeth de Clare, by Roger Damory, Knt.:

i. **ELIZABETH DAMORY**, married **JOHN BARDOLF**, Knt., 3rd Lord Bardolf [see BARDOLF 13].

7. WILLIAM DE BURGH, Knt., 4th Earl of Ulster, lord of Connacht in Ireland, and of Clare, Suffolk, Justiciar of Ireland, 1331, son and heir, born 17 Sept. 1312. He married before 16 Nov. 1327 (by papal dispensation dated 1 May 1327, he being dispensed to marry a noble lady of England related to him in the 4th degree) **MAUD OF LANCASTER**, daughter of Henry of Lancaster, Knt., Earl of Lancaster and Leicester (grandson of King Henry III of England), by Maud, daughter and heiress of Patrick de Chaworth, Knt. [see LANCASTER 8 for her ancestry]. They had one daughter, Elizabeth. He was summoned to Parliament from 10 Dec. 1327 to 15 June 1328 by writs directed *Willelmo de Burgh*, whereby he is held to have become Lord Burgh. SIR WILLIAM DE BURGH, Earl of Ulster, was murdered at Le Ford (now Belfast) 6 June 1333, by Richard de Mandeville, Knt., John de Logan, and others. His widow, Maud, fled to England, where she married (2nd) before 8 August 1343 **RALPH DE UFFORD**, Knt., Constable of Corfe Castle, 1341–4, Justiciar of Ireland, 1344–6, younger son of Robert de Ufford, Knt., 1st Lord Ufford, by Cecily, younger daughter and co-heiress of Robert de Valoines, of Ixworth and Walsham, Suffolk. They had one daughter, Maud. In 1343 he was granted an annuity of £200 at the exchequer by the king. In 1343 she was present at the papal court, where she was absolved of a vow of visiting Santiago. SIR RALPH DE UFFORD died testate at Kilmainham, Ireland 9 April 1346. His widow, Maud, became an Augustinian canoness at Campsey, Suffolk. She had license in 1364 to transfer to the Order of St. Clare. She was a legatee in the 1368 will of her brother-in-law, Robert de Ufford, K.G., 1st Earl of Suffolk, Lord Ufford. Maud of Lancaster, Countess of Ulster, died 5 May 1377, and was buried with her 2nd husband at Campsey Priory, Suffolk.

Sandford *Gen. Hist. of the Kings of England* (1677): 110. Rymer *Fædera* 6 (1727): 613. Blore *Hist. & Antiqs. of Rutland* 1(2) (1811): 98 (Lancaster ped.). Dugdale *Monasticon Anglicanum* 2 (1819): 59–65; 6(1) (1830): 585 (Maud styled "kinswoman" by King Edward III of England); 6(3) (1830): 1600–1602. Rymer *Fædera* 2(2) (1821): 811 (William styled "kinsman" by King Edward III of England), 1019 (Maud styled "kinswoman" by King Edward III of England). Banks *Baronies in Fees* 1 (1844): 437–440 (sub Ufford). Hawley *Royal Fam. of England* (1851): 20–21. *Top. & Gen.* 2 (1853): 271–277 (Ufford ped.). *Notes & Queries* 4th Ser. 5 (1870): 131–132. *C.P.R. 1327–1330* (1891): 334 (William de Burgh, Earl of Ulster, styled "king's kinsman"). Birch *Cat. Seals in the British Museum* 3 (1894): 390 (seal of Maud of Lancaster, Countess of Ulster dated 1347 — Four shields of arms, arranged in cross: 1, wanting; 2, diapered lozengy, in each interstice a roundle. A cross [ULSTER]; 3, a cross lozengy or engrailed, in the first quarter a fleur-de-lis [UFFORD]; 4, a cross lozengy-shaped, barruly an orle of martlets [CHAWORTH]. In the centre of the seal a rose. Within a richly cusped gothic quatrefoil, ornamented along the inner edge with small quatrefoils. *Papal Regs.: Letters* 2 (1895): 257; 3 (1897): 17, 109, 112, 137, 201, 237 (Queen Philippe of Hainault styled "kinswoman" by Maud of Lancaster, Countess of Ulster); 4 (1902): 37–38. *C.P.R. 1334–1338* (1895): 31 ([Maud], Countess of Ulster, styled "king's kinswoman"), 320–321. *Papal Regs.: Petitions* 1 (1896): 69, 74 (Robert de Walkynton [Walkington], clerk, styled "kinsman" by Maud de Lancaster, Countess of Ulster). *C.P.R. 1340–1343* (1900): 41, 63, 187, 514. *C.P.R. 1345–1348* (1903): 96. Lane *Royal Daughters of England* 1 (1910): 132–135. *C.P.* 2 (1912): 421 (sub Burgh); 3 (1913): 245 (sub

Clare); 12(2) (1959): 150 (sub Ufford), 178–179 (sub Ulster). Mills *Cal. Gormanston Reg.* (1916): 2–3. Holmes *Estates of the Higher Nobility in 14th Cent. England* (1957): 35–38. Smith *Itinerary of John Leland* 4 (1964): 150–163. Maccullough *Chorography of Suffolk* (Suffolk Rec. Soc. 19) (1976): 34. *Ancient Deeds — Ser. AS & WS* (List & Index Soc. 158) (1979): 136 (W.S.339). Ellis *Cat. Seals in the P.R.O.* 2 (1981): 70 (seal of Maud of Lancaster, Countess of Ulster dated 1336 — In a cusped circle, a small shield of arms: a cross [BURGH] impaling three leopards, and a label of three points [LANCASTER]; surrounded by a band of fine tracery enclosing four decorative M's and four roundels containing the arms of England, Old France, Clare and Valence. Legend: SIGILLVM/MAT…/COMITISSE/VLTONI…S). Frame *English Lordship in Ireland* (1982). Moody et al. *New Hist. of Ireland* 9 (1984): 170 (chart). Fryde & Greenway *Handbook of British Chronology* (1996): 162. Underhill *For Her Good Estate* (1999). Rickard *Castle Community* (2002): 181. Duffy *Medieval Ireland: An Encyclopedia* (2005): 93–95. National Archives, SC 8/170/8498; SC 8/180/8954 (available at www.catalogue.nationalarchives.gov.uk/search.asp).

Child of William de Burgh, Knt., by Maud of Lancaster:

i. **ELIZABETH DE BURGH** [see next].

Child of Maud of Lancaster, by Ralph de Ufford, Knt.:

i. **MAUD DE UFFORD**, married **THOMAS DE VERE**, 8th Earl of Oxford, hereditary Chamberlain of England [see VERE 5.ii].

8. ELIZABETH DE BURGH, daughter and heiress, born at Carrickfergus Castle, Ireland 6 July 1332. She married at the Tower of London 15 August 1342 (by agreement dated 5 May 1341) (as his 1st wife) **LIONEL OF ANTWERP**, K.G. [see ENGLAND 9.v], of Brimpsfield, Gloucestershire, Chief Governor of Ireland, and, in right of his wife, 5th Earl of Ulster, lord of Clare and Connacht, 3rd but 2nd surviving son of Edward III, King of England, by Philippe, daughter of Guillaume *le Bon*, Count of Hainault, Holland, and Zeeland, lord of Friesland [see ENGLAND 9 for his ancestry]. He was born at Antwerp in Brabant 29 Nov. 1338.[1] They had one daughter, Philippe. By this marriage, Lionel acquired the vast estates in Ireland of the Burgh family, as well as a large part (including the honour of Clare) of the estates of the Earls of Gloucester and Hertford, in right of his wife's paternal grandmother. He was appointed Regent of England during the king's absence abroad in 1346. In 1355 he went with his father on an expedition to the north of France. He presented to the churches of Tarrant Gunville, Dorset, 1361 and 1363, and Dunmow, Essex, 1361. He was created Duke of Clarence 13 Nov. 1362. His wife, Elizabeth, Duchess of Clarence, died at Dublin, Ireland 10 Dec. 1363, and was buried at Bruisyard Abbey, Suffolk. In Feb. 1368 he presented to the church of Pebmarsh, Essex, by the minority of John son and heir of John Fitz Ralph, Knt. He married (2nd) before the door of Milan Cathedral, Italy 28 May (or 5 June) 1368 (by treaty dated 15 May 1367) **VIOLANTE VISCONTI**, daughter of Galeazzo Visconti, signore of Pavia, Como, Novara, etc., by Bianca, daughter of Aimo, Count of Savoy. They had no issue. LIONEL OF ANTWERP, Duke of Clarence, died testate at Alba (Longuevil) in Piedmont in Italy 17 October 1368. He was buried first at Pavia, but his body was removed to England and buried at convent of the Austin Friars at Clare, Suffolk beside his 1st wife. His widow, Violante, married (2nd) 2 August 1377 **OTHON II PALÆOLOGUS**, Marquis of Monferrato, signore of Ivrea (murdered 16 Dec. 1378), and (3rd) 18 July 1381 **LUDOVICO VISCONTI**, Governor of Lodi, Governor and signore of Parma (died 3 July 1404). She died at Pavia in Nov. 1386.

Weever *Ancient Funerall Monuments* (1631): 740–742. Sandford *Gen. Hist. of the Kings of England* (1677): 219–221. Rymer *Fœdera* 6 (1727): 509–510, 547–548, 564–566. Nichols *Coll. of All the Wills* (1780): 88–91 (will of Lionel, Duke of Clarence). Blore *Hist. & Antiqs. of Rutland* 1(2) (1811): 37 (Kent/Holand ped.). Dugdale *Monasticon Anglicanum* 2 (1819): 59–65; 6(3) (1830): 1600–1602. Nicolas *Testamenta Vetusta* 1 (1826): 70–71 (will of Lionel, Duke of Clarence). Banks *Dormant & Extinct Baronage of England* 4 (1837): 336–337. Beltz *Mems. of the Order of the Garter* (1841): cli. Hawley *Royal Fam. of England* (1851): 23–27. Hutchins *Hist. & Antiqs. of Dorset* 3 (1868):461. Hardy *Syllabus (in English) of the*

---

[1] Note: For contemporary examples of Lionel being styled "Lionel of Antwerp," see Hunter *South Yorkshire* 1 (1828): 110–111; *C.P.R.* 1348–1350 (1905): 130 ("… the king and his son, Lionel de Andewerp [sic]"); *C.P.R.* 1370–1374 (1914): 130.

Docs. Rel. England & Other Kingdoms 1 (1869): 321, 344, 349, 379, 416, 417, 430, 431, 432, 434, 441, 443, 445, 453. *Notes & Queries* 4th Ser. 10 (1872): 258–259 (re. Elizabeth de Burgh's place of burial). Wright *Feudal Manuals of English Hist.* (1872). Turner *Cal. Charters & Rolls: Bodleian Lib.* (1878): 140. Burke *Dormant, Abeyant, Forfeited & Extinct Peerages* (1883): 434 (sub Plantagenet). Doyle *Official Baronage of England* 1 (1886): 396 (sub Clarence). Birch *Cat. Seals in the British Museum* 3 (1894): 388 (seal of Lionel, Duke of Clarence dated 1368 — A shield of arms, couché: quarterly, 1, 4, FRANCE (ancient); 2, 3, ENGLAND, with a label of three points [each charged with a canton], CLARENCE. Crest on a helmet and cap-of-maintenance, the lion crest of ENGLAND. Supporters, dex., a lion; sin., an eagle rising. Inner border ornamented with cusps or engrailings, terminated in trefoils. Legend: ……. ducis · clarencie · comitis …..). *Papal Regs.: Letters* 3 (1897): 626, 630; 4 (1902): 1, 27–28, 38, 49, 84. *Genealogist* n.s. 15 (1898): 30–31. Kirby *Wykeham's Reg.* 2 (1899): 94–95, 564. Wrottesley *Peds. from the Plea Rolls* (1905): 226–227. *D.N.B.* 11 (1909): 1214–1217 (biog. of Lionel of Antwerp: "… a man of strength and beauty of person, and exceedingly tall in stature"). *C.P.R.* 1358–1361 (1911): 456 (Elizabeth, Countess of Ulster, styled "king's kinswoman" by King Edward III of England). *C.P.* 3 (1913): 245 (sub Clare), 257–258 (sub Clarence); 8 (1932): 445–448 (sub March); 12(2) (1959): 180 (sub Ulster); 14 (1998): 184 (sub Clarence). *Somerset & Dorset Notes & Queries* 14 (1915): 45–46. *C.Ch.R.* 5 (1916): 140. Mills *Cal. Gormanston Reg.* (1916): 2–3. Wall *Handbook of the Maude Roll* (1919) unpaginated (ped. dated c.1461–85: "Leonel dux Clarentie = [Anna heredem Ultonie]"). *List of Diplomatic Docs., Scottish Docs. & Papal Bulls* (PRO Lists and Indexes 49) (1923): 25. Fowler *Reg. Simonis de Sudbiria* 1 (Canterbury & York Soc. 34) (1927): 225, 257. Harvey et al. *Vis. of the North* 3 (Surtees Soc. 144) (1930): 2–5 ("Leonellus dux Clarencie = Elizabeth filia et heres comitis Vlstrie in Hibernia"). *Reg. of Edward the Black Prince* 4 (1933): 68 ("Sir Lionel, the prince's brother"). Holmes *Estates of the Higher Nobility in 14th Cent. England* (1957): 35–38. Trautz *Die Könige von England und das Reich 1272–1377* (1961): 396–399. *Coat of Arms* 7 (1962): 80–84 (arms of Lionel: Quarterly France ancient and England, a label of three points argent, each charged with a canton gules). Smith *Itinerary of John Leland* 4 (1964): 150–163. *Urbain V (1362–1370): Lettres Communes* 2 (1964): 238. Maccullough *Chorography of Suffolk* (Suffolk Rec. Soc. 19) (1976): 34. Paget *Lineage & Anc. of Prince Charles* 1 (1977): 20–21. *Ancient Deeds — Ser. AS & WS* (List & Index Soc. 158) (1979): 124 (W.S.233). *TG* 2 (1981): 123–128. Moody et al. *New Hist. of Ireland* 9 (1984): 170 (chart). Schwennicke *Europäische Stammtafeln* 2 (1984): 84 (sub England), 185 (sub Montferrat). *Jour. British Studies* 26 (1987): 398–422. Taylor *English Hist. Lit. in the 14th Cent.* (1987): 293 (Wigmore Chron. sub 1364: "Eodem anno [rectius 1363] obiit domina Elizabeth ducissa Clarencie, Comitissa de Olstre, uxor leonelli filii Regis Edwardi tercii a conquestu, mater Philippe uxoris domini Emundi de Mortimer in hibernia."), 295 (Wigmore Chron. sub 1368: "Eodem anno obiit dominus leonellus dux clarensis et comes de Ullestre secundus filius Regis Edwardi tercii in lumbardia hoc est in Melan."). Williamson *Kings & Queens of Britain* (1991): 79. Leese *Blood Royal* (1996): 80–92, 143–149. Duffy *Medieval Ireland: An Encyclopedia* (2005): 93–95. Taylor *Debating the Hundred Years War* (2006): 46-47, 159.

Child of Elizabeth de Burgh, by Lionel of Antwerp, K.G.:

i. **PHILIPPE OF CLARENCE**, Countess of Ulster, married **EDMUND DE MORTIMER**, Knt., 3rd Earl of March, 6th Earl of Ulster [see MORTIMER 13].

❧ BURGHERSH ❧

ALICE OF NORMANDY (sister of King William the Conqueror), married **LAMBERT**, Count of Lens.
JUDITH OF LENS, married **WALTHEOF**, Earl of Northumberland.
ALICE OF NORTHUMBERLAND, married **RALPH DE TONY**, of Flamstead, Hertfordshire.
ROGER DE TONY, of Flamstead, Hertfordshire, married **IDA OF HAINAULT**.
RALPH DE TONY, of Flamstead, Hertfordshire, married **MARGARET OF LEICESTER**.
IDA DE TONY, married **ROGER LE BIGOD**, Knt., Earl of Norfolk.
HUGH LE BIGOD, Earl of Norfolk, married **MAUD MARSHAL**.
ISABEL LE BIGOD, married **GILBERT DE LACY**, of Ewyas Lacy, Herefordshire.
MARGERY DE LACY, married **JOHN DE VERDUN**, Knt., of Alton, Staffordshire.
THEBAUD DE VERDUN, Knt., 1st Lord Verdun, married **MARGERY DE BOHUN** (desc. King William the Conqueror).
THEBAUD DE VERDUN, Knt., 2nd Lord Verdun, married **MAUD DE MORTIMER** (desc. King William the Conqueror) [see VERDUN 11].

12. **ELIZABETH DE VERDUN**, 2nd daughter and co-heiress, born about 1306. She married before 11 June 1320 **BARTHOLOMEW DE BURGHERSH**, Knt., 3rd Lord Burghersh, of Burghersh, Sussex, Chiddingstone, Kent, Haydor and Culverthorpe, Lincolnshire, Heytesbury, Stert,

and Colerne, Wiltshire, etc., Constable of Dover Castle and Warden of the Cinque Ports, 1326–30, 1343–55, Justice of the Forest south of Trent, 1335–43, Chamberlain of the King's Household, Seneschal of Ponthieu and Montreuil, Admiral of the Fleet west of Thames, 1337–8, Privy Councilor, Constable of the Tower of London, 1355, and, in right of his wife, of Ewyas Lacy Castle, Herefordshire, Bourton-on-Dunsmore, Brandon (in Wolston), Bretford (in Wolston), and Sheldon, Warwickshire, and Bishampton, Worcestershire, etc., 3rd son of Robert de Burghersh, 1st Lord Burghersh, of Burghersh, Sussex, Chiddingstone, Kent, Haydor and Culverthorpe, Lincolnshire, etc., by Maud, daughter of Guncelin de Badlesmere, of Badlesmere, Kent. He was born about 1304 (aged 36 in 1340). They had three sons, Henry, Bartholomew, K.G. [4th Lord Burghersh], and Thomas (clerk), and two daughters, Joan and Elizabeth. He served in the wars of Scotland *temp.* King Edward II. He joined Thomas, Earl of Lancaster in his rebellion, and was defeated with him at the Battle of Boroughbridge 16 March 1321/2, and was taken prisoner, but was restored by Isabel the Queen Consort. He was summoned to Parliament from 25 Jan. 1329/30 to 15 March 1353/4. He and his wife, Elizabeth, received a papal indult for plenary remission in 1330. He was heir in 1340 to his brother, Henry de Burghersh, Bishop of Lincoln, by which he inherited the manors of Studham, Hertfordshire and Heytesbury, Colerne, and Stert, Wiltshire. In 1343 he formed part of an important embassy to the Pope. In 1343–4 Thomas de Canterburi, and other executors of Ralph de Upton, sometime Citizen and draper of London, conveyed to him tenements in Coleman Street ward and in the parish of St. Mary Bow, London, formerly belonging to Ralph de Upton. He fought at the Battle of Crécy 25 August 1346. In 1349 he accompanied Henry, Earl of Lancaster, to Gascony to suppress a rebellion there. The same year he petitioned the king that he with 20 knights, 30 esquires, and their attendants may visit the Holy Land "and there remain fighting at their pleasure." He presented to the church of Carlton Colville, Suffolk in 1349. In 1352 he acquired the manor of Mildenhall, Wiltshire from his son-in-law, John de Mohun, K.G., 2nd Lord Mohun. SIR BARTHOLOMEW DE BURGHERSH, 3rd Lord Burghersh, died intestate at Dover, Kent 3 August 1355, and was buried in the Angel Choir, Lincoln Cathedral. In 1355–6 his administrators gave a receipt for £40 received from Wenlock Priory due him as Warden of Dover Castle. His widow, Elizabeth, died 1 May 1360.

Dugdale *Antiqs. of Warwickshire* (1730): 44 (Verdon ped.). *Gentleman's Mag.* 33 (1763): 192–193. Nichols *Hist. & Antiqs. of Leicester* 3(2) (1804): 640 (Verdon ped.). Blore *Hist. & Antiqs. of Rutland* 1(2) (1811): 204 (Burghersh ped.). Hoare *Hist. of Modern Wiltshire: Hundred of Heytesbury* (1824): 88 (Burghersh ped.). Burke *Dict. of the Peerages… Extinct, Dormant & in Abeyance* (1831): 100–101, 534–535. Westcote *View of Devonshire* (1845): 477. Suckling *Hist. & Antiqs. of Suffolk* 1 (1846): 242. *Sussex Arch. Colls.* 21 (1869): 126 (chart). Chandos Herald *Life & Feats of Arms of Edward the Black Prince* (1883): 303. Burke *Dormant, Abeyant, Forfeited & Extinct Peerages* (1883): 92–93. *Genealogist* n.s. 10 (1893): 212; n.s. 13 (1896): 241. Wrottesley *Staffordshire Suits: Plea Rolls* (Colls. Hist. Staffs. 14) (1893): 81–82. *Papal Regs.: Letters* 2 (1895): 312; 3 (1897): 250, 327–328, 375, 510. *Papal Regs.: Petitions* 1 (1896): 50 (Master John de Bourne styled "kinsman" of Bartholomew de Burghersh), 128, 167 (Bartholomew de Bourn styled "kinsman" of Bartholomew de Burghersh), 207, 253. *English Hist. Rev.* 18 (1903): 112–116. Wrottesley *Peds. from the Plea Rolls* (1905): 59, 71, 160–161, 200. *D.N.B.* 3 (1908): 333–334 (biog. of Bartholomew Burghersh). VCH *Hertford* 2 (1908): 274–275. *C.P.R.* 1396–1399 (1909): 123. *C.Ch.R.* 4 (1912): 454; 5 (1916): 11. *C.P.* 2 (1912): 426 (sub Burghersh); 7 (1929): 223–225 (sub Kildare); 12(2) (1959): 250–252 (sub Verdun). VCH *Surrey* 4 (1912): 183 (Burghersh arms: Gules a lion or with a forked tail). *Cal. IPM* 8 (1913): 210–212. VCH *Worcester* 3 (1913): 261. Kingsford *Grey Friars of London* (1915): 70–133 ("Et in eodem loco jacet dominus Bartholemeus Burwesche, et domina Elizabeth vxor eius."), 134–139. VCH *Buckingham* 3 (1925): 422. *Reg. of Edward the Black Prince* 4 (1933): 105 (Sir Geoffrey de Stowell styled "kinsman" of Bartholomew de Burghersh). Rough *Reg. of Daniel Rough Common Clerk of Romney* (Kent Arch. Soc. Recs. 16) (1945): 55, 90–91 (states Bartholomew de Burghersh was buried in the chantry of St. Catharine at Lincoln). VCH *Warwick* 4 (1947): 201; 6 (1951): 39, 271, 276. Paget *Baronage of England* (1957) 108: 1 (chart only), 557: 7. Sanders *English Baronies* (1960): 95–96. VCH *Cambridge* 5 (1973): 201. Elrington *Abs. of Feet of Fines Rel. Wiltshire* (Wiltshire Rec. Soc. 29) (1974): 70–71. *Ancient Deeds* — Ser. B 3 (List & Index Soc. 113) (1975): B.9751–9756, B.9977. Ellis *Cat. Seals in the P.R.O.* 1 (1978): 13 (seal of Bartholomew de Burghersh dated 1352 — A shield of arms: a lion with a forked tail [BURGHERSH], hanging from a leopard's head and flanked by two mantled helms in profile, each with crest: a lion with a forked tail issuing from an embattled gatehouse. Below, a scroll with legend My Word/My Word); 2 (1981): 19

(seal of Bartholomew de Burghersh, Knt. dated 1316 — Hung from a triple bush or sheaf, between two wyverns, a shield of arms: a lion rampant, queue fourchy [BURGHERSH]). *Ancient Deeds — Ser. AS & WS* (List & Index Soc. 158) (1979): 40 (Deed A.S.238), 120 (Deeds W.S.196, 198), 174 (W.S.722). VCH *Wiltshire* 12 (1983): 128–129. Moody et al. *New Hist. of Ireland* 9 (1984): 173. Brault *Rolls of Arms Edward I* 2 (1997): 85 (arms of Bartholomew de Burghersh: Gules, a lion rampant with a forked tail or). Morganstern *Gothic Tombs of Kinship* (2000): 108–116. Hagger *Fortunes of a Norman Fam.* (2001). Gibson *Recs. of Early English Drama: Kent: Diocese of Canterbury* 3 (2002): 1404 (biog. of Bartholomew Burghersh). National Archives, E 42/238; E 43/196; E 43/198 (available at www.catalogue.nationalarchives.gov.uk/search.asp).

Children of Elizabeth de Verdun, by Bartholomew de Burghersh, Knt.:

i. **HENRY DE BURGHERSH**, married **ISABEL DE SAINT JOHN** [see PAULET 11].

ii. **BARTHOLOMEW DE BURGHERSH**, K.G., 4th Lord Burghersh [see next].

iii. **JOAN DE BURGHERSH**, married **JOHN DE MOHUN**, K.G., 2nd Lord Mohun [see MOHUN 13].

iv. **ELIZABETH DE BURGHERSH**, married **MAURICE FITZ THOMAS**, Knt., 4th Earl of Kildare [see BURGH 5.vi.a].

13. BARTHOLOMEW DE BURGHERSH, K.G., 4th Lord Burghersh, of Ewyas Lacy, Herefordshire, Burwash, Sussex, Ashbocking, Buxhall, Clopton, Carlton Colville, Henley, Swiland, and Tunstall, Suffolk, Bourton-on-Dunsmore and Brandon (in Wolston), Warwickshire, Heytesbury, Mildenhall, Stert, and Colerne, Wiltshire, etc., Steward and Constable of Wallingford and St. Valery, Justiciar of Chester, 2nd but 1st surviving son and heir, born say 1323 (but aged 26 at his father's death). He married (1st) before 10 May 1335 **CECILY DE WEYLAND**, daughter and heiress of Richard de Weyland, Knt., of Blaxhall, Cockfield, Middleton, and Wantisden, Suffolk, by Joan, daughter of Robert de Ufford, Knt., 1st Lord Ufford. They had one daughter, Elizabeth. He was one of the most distinguished warriors of the age. He accompanied King Edward III to Flanders in 1339, and took part in the first invasion of French territories. In 1342 he and William de Bohun were commanded by the king to suppress the rising in Norwich against the visitation of John Stratford, Archbishop of Canterbury. He accompanied the king on his campaign in Brittany in 1342–3. He fought at the Battle of Crécy in 1346, in the retinue of Edward *the Black Prince*. He was a Founder Knight of the Order of the Garter in 1348. He and his wife, Cecily, had grant of free warren in their lands at Witnesham, Henley, Swilland, etc., Suffolk in 1349. In 1354 he fulfilled a religious vow by taking a journey to the Holy Land. His wife, Cecily, was living 2 August 1354. He fought at the Battle of Poitiers in 1356. In 1359 he again accompanied King Edward III on his last and most formidable invasion of France, ending in the decisive Treaty of Bretigny, 8 May 1360. He presented to the church of Carlton Colville, Suffolk in 1361. In 1362 he conveyed the manor of Mildenhall, Wiltshire to Thomas Hungerford, Knt. He married (2nd) before August 1366 **MARGARET GISORS**, widow of Henry Picard, Citizen and vintner of London (living 1363), and daughter and co-heiress of Thomas Gisors, of London. In 1366 he received a license to have mass celebrated in his manor of Henden (in Sundridge), Kent. In 1366–7 he conveyed to Joan, widow of John de Coupland, tenements in Coleman Street, Middlesex which formerly belonged to Ralph de Upton. In 1369 he sold the manors of Bourton-on-Dunsmore and Brandon (in Wolston), Warwickshire to John de Delves, Knt. SIR BARTHOLOMEW DE BURGHERSH, 4th Lord Burghersh, died testate 5 April 1369, and was buried in the lady chapel of Walsingham Abbey, Norfolk. His widow, Margaret, married (3rd) before 16 July 1382 **WILLIAM BURCESTER**, Knt. (died 1407), of Lesnes (in Erith), Kent, Sheriff of Kent, 1389–90, Knight of the Shire for Kent, 1393. In 1382 William and his wife, Margaret, complained that Katherine Engaine, Edward Dallingridge, Knt., and others disseised them of 80 marks rent in the parish of St. Martin in the Vintry, London. In 1385 he and his wife, Margaret, purchased one messuage and lands in Dunsden (in Sonning), Berkshire from Geoffrey Blancmuster and his wife, Joan. In 1385 Thomas Haithorp, George de Bursalle, and Thomas le Walsh sued William and his wife, Margaret, for the manor of

Foxgrove, Kent. His wife, Margaret, died 1 July 1393. He married (2nd) by royal license dated 6 Jan. 1395/6 **MARGARET CHEYNE**, widow of Thomas de Brewes, Knt. (died 2 Sept. 1395) [see TETBURY 9.i.b], of Manningford Bruce, Wiltshire, Tetbury, Gloucestershire, Chesworth, Sedgwick, and Bidlington, Sussex, Little Bookham and Bramley, Surrey, etc., Knight of the Shire for Surrey, 1391, 1393, and daughter of Ralph de Cheyne, Knt. They had one son, John, Knt., and one daughter, Willelma (wife of Walter Urry). In Trinity term 1402 Richard Forster, Dennis Lopham, and others, executors of the will of John Boseham, Citizen and Mercer of London, sued Margaret Burcestre, excutrix of the will of Thomas Brewes, Knt., and her current husband, William Burcestre, Knt., in the Court of Common Pleas regarding the debt of £27 owed them on a bond. In 1403 William and his wife, Margaret, arraigned an assize of novel disseisin against John Brewes, Knt., George Brewes, Richard Brewes, etc. regarding the manors of Chesworth and Sedgwick, Sussex and the tenements in Horsham, Nuthurst, and Broadwater, Sussex. SIR WILLIAM BURCESTER died in 1407. He left a will dated 31 July 1407. His widow, Margaret, married (3rd) before 1409–10 (date of fine) **WILLIAM BRETON**, Esq. Sometime in the period, 1407–27, he and his wife, Margaret, as "residuary legatee and late the wife of William Burcestre, Knt." sued Richard Wakehurst and Richard Aylard, feoffees to uses and executors of the said William Burcestre, in Chancery regarding the manor of Burwash, Sussex and personalty. WILLIAM BRETON, Esq., was living 1409–10. His widow, Margaret, married (4th) after 14 October 1412 and before 8 June 1427 (as his 3rd wife) **JOHN BERKELEY**, Knt. [see FISHER 8], of Beverstone, Compton Greenfield, Over (in Almondsbury), Syde, Tockington, and Woodmancote (in Dursley), Gloucestershire, Lower Ham and Tickenham, Somerset, etc., Knight of the Shire for Gloucestershire, 1388, 1397, Knight of the Shire for Somerset, 1390, 1394, Sheriff of Somerset and Dorset, 1390–1, 1394–5, Sheriff of Gloucestershire, 1392–3, 1397–8, 1414–15, Knight of the Shire for Wiltshire, 1402, 1406, Sheriff of Hampshire, 1402–3, 1406–7, Sheriff of Wiltshire, 1410–11. They had no issue. SIR JOHN BERKELEY died 5 March 1427/8. Margaret died 12 (or 20) August 1444.

Gentleman's Mag. 33 (1763): 192–193. Blore *Hist. & Antiqs. of Rutland* 1(2) (1811): 204 (Burghersh ped.). Hoare *Hist. of Modern Wiltshire: Hundred of Heytesbury* (1824): 88 (Burghersh ped.). Nicolas *Testamenta Vetusta* 1 (1826): 76–77 (will of Bartholomew Burghersh, Knt.). Cartwright *Parochial Topog. of the Rape of Bramber* 2(2) (1830): 369. Burke *Dict. of the Peerages… Extinct, Dormant & in Abeyance* (1831): 100–101. Beltz *Mems. of the Order of the Garter* (1841): cxlix, 45–47. Suckling *Hist. & Antiqs. of Suffolk* 1 (1846): 242. *Sussex Arch. Colls.* 21 (1869): chart betw. 126–127. Chandos Herald *Life & Feats of Arms of Edward the Black Prince* (1883): 303, 336–338. Burke *Dormant, Abeyant, Forfeited & Extinct Peerages* (1883): 92–93. Fisher *Cat. of the Tombs in the Churches of the City of London* (1885): 21. *Desc. Cat. Ancient Deeds* 2 (1894): 25–38; 4 (1902): 218–235. *Genealogist* n.s. 13 (1896): 251. *Papal Regs.: Petitions* 1 (1896): 207, 253. *Papal Regs.: Letters* 3 (1897): 528. Wrottesley *Peds. from the Plea Rolls* (1905): 164. Copinger *Manors of Suffolk* 2 (1908): 123–125, 365–366; 3 (1909): 32–33; 4 (1909): 230. *D.N.B.* 3 (1908): 334–335 (biog. of Bartholomew Burghersh). Hervey *Whelnetham Parish Regs.* (Suffolk Green Books 15) (1910): 365–373. *C.P.* 2 (1912): 426–427 (sub Burghersh); 4 (1916): 274–278 (sub Despenser). VCH *Surrey* 4 (1912): 183. VCH *Worcester* 3 (1913): 261–262. *C.Ch.R.* 5 (1916): 118. Fowler *Reg. Simonis de Sudbiria* 1 (Canterbury & York Soc. 34) (1927): 226, 260. Salzman *Abs. of Feet of Fines Rel. Sussex* 3 (Sussex Rec. Soc. 23) (1916): 223–227. Harvey et al. *Vis. of the North* 4 (Surtees Soc. 146) (1932): 162 (arms of Sir Bartholmew Burghersshe: gules a double-tailed lion rampant gules). *C.C.R. 1422–1429* (1933): 70–71. Watkin *Inventory of Church Goods temp. Edward III* (Norfolk Rec. Soc. 19(2)) (1948): 203 (biog. of Sir Bartholomew de Burghersh). VCH *Warwick* 6 (1951): 39, 276. Langham *Reg. Simonis Langham Cantuariensis Archiepiscopi* (Canterbury & York Soc. 53) (1956): 139. Paget *Baronage of England* (1957) 108: 1 (chart). Chew *London Possessory Assizes* (1965): 46–72 (no. 164). Stow *Survey of London* (1971): 141. VCH *Cambridge* 5 (1973): 201. *Ancient Deeds — Ser. B* 2 (List & Index Soc. 101) (1974): B.6467; 3 (List & Index Soc. 113) (1975): B.9757–9761, B.9764, B.9814, B.9927. VCH *Wiltshire* 12 (1983): 128–129. Kirby *Abs. of Feet of Fines Rel. Wiltshire* (Wiltshire Rec. Soc. 41) (1986): 10, 25–26. Keene & Harding *Hist. Gaz. of London before the Great Fire* (1987): 448–455. *Cal. IPM* 17 (1988): 132. Booth *Account of Master John de Burnham the Younger* (Lanc. & Cheshire Rec. Soc. 125) (1991): 123–124 (biog. of Bartholomew de Burghersh). Roskell *House of Commons 1386–1421* 2 (1992): 197–199 (biog. of Sir John Berkeley), 353–354 (biog. of Sir Thomas Brewes), 410–412 (biog. of Sir William Burcester). Kirby *Hungerford Cartulary* (Wiltshire Rec. Soc. 49) (1994): 160–162. Court of Common Pleas, CP 40/566, rot. 416d (available at www.british-history.ac.uk/source.aspx?pubid=1272). National Archives, C 1/69/154 (available at www.catalogue.nationalarchives.gov.uk/search.asp). National Archives, CP 25/1/191/23, #54 [see abstract of fine at http:// www.medievalgenealogy.org.uk/index.html]. Special thanks go to Doug Thompson for his identification of the maiden name and parentage of Margaret Cheyne, wife successively of Thomas de Brewes, Knt., William Burcester, Knt., William Brereton, Esq., and John Berkeley, Knt.

Child of Bartholomew de Burghersh, K.G., by Cecily de Weyland:

i. **ELIZABETH BURGHERSH**, married **EDWARD LE DESPENSER**, K.G., 4th Lord Despenser [see DESPENSER 13].

❧ BURGUNDY ❧

WILLIAM THE CONQUEROR, King of England, married **MAUD OF FLANDERS**.
ADÈLE OF ENGLAND, married **ÉTIENNE HENRI**, Count of Blois, Chartres, etc.
THIBAUT IV, Count of Blois, Champagne, and Troyes, married **MATHILDE OF CARINTHIA** [see BLOIS 3].

4. MARIE OF BLOIS, married 1145 **EUDES II**, Duke of Burgundy, son and heir of Hugues II Borel, Duke of Burgundy, by Mathilde, daughter of Gautier IV, seigneur of Mayenne. He was born about 1120. They had one son, Hugues [III] [Duke of Burgundy], and three daughters, Alix, Mahaut (wife of Robert IV, Count of Auvergne and Clermont), and _____ (wife of Robert, seigneur of Boisleux). EUDES II, Duke of Burgundy, died 26 (or 27) Sept. 1162, and was buried in the church of the Abbey of Cîteaux (Côte-d'Or). His widow, Marie, served as Regent of Burgundy in 1162–1165. She subsequently became a nun at Fontevrault Abbey, where she was elected Abbess in 1174. She died 11 March, probably in 1190, and was buried before the door of the church of Fontevrault Abbey.

Anselme *Hist. de la Maison Royale de France* 1 (1726): 540 (sub Ducs de Bourgogne). Arbois de Jubainville *Histoire des Ducs et des Comtes de Champagne* 3 (1861): 454 (Marie, Duchess of Burgundy, styled "sister" [sororis] by Henri I, Count Palatine of Troyes, in charter dated 1174). Lalore *Coll. des Principaux Obituaires et Confraternités du Diocèse de Troyes* (Coll. de Docs. Inédits relatif a la Ville de Troyes et a la Champagne Méridionale, vol. 2) (1882): 273 (Foundations: 13 March – "Mémoire de Marie, fille de Thibaut [II], comte de Champagne, et femme d'Eudes (II), duc de Bourgogne. Elle a sa sépulture à Fontevrault, où elle est décédé le 11 de ce mois"), 314. Petit *Hist. des Ducs de Bourgogne de la Race Capétienne* 5 (1894): 393 (Obituaire de Molême: "V kal. [octobr.] [27 September] obiit Odo, dux Burgundie."), 404 (Obituaire de Citeaux: "VI kalendas octobris []27 September], obierunt Hugo et Odo, duces Burgundie."). Brandenburg *Die Nachkommen Karls des Großen* (1935) XIII 63, XIII 245. Schwennicke *Europaische Stanmtafeln* 2 (1984): 20 (sub Burgundy), 47 (sub Champagne, Blois, Navarre). Winter *Descs. of Charlemagne (800–1400)* (1987): XIII.66, XIII.435. Van Kerrebrouck *Les Capétiens 987–1328* (2000): 570–571.

Children of Marie of Blois, by Eudes II of Burgundy:

i. **HUGUES III**, Duke of Burgundy [see next].
ii. **ALIX OF BURGUNDY**, married **ARCHAMBAUD VII DE BOURBON**, seigneur of Bourbon-l'Archambaud [see ARCHAMBAUD 5].

5. HUGUES III, Duke of Burgundy, Count of Viennois, Albon, and Grenoble, Pair de France, son and heir, born about 1148. He married (1st) in 1165 **ALIX OF LORRAINE**, daughter of Mathieu I, Duke of Upper Lorraine, by Bertha (alias Judith), daughter of Friedrich II, Duke of Swabia. They had two sons, Eudes [III] [Duke of Burgundy] and Alexandre, and one daughter, Marie (wife of Simon I, seigneur of Semur-en-Brionnais). Hugues repudiated Alix in 1183 (and she died about 1200). He married (2nd) at Saint-Gilles-en-Languedoc 1 Sept. 1183 **BÉATRIX D'ALBON**, Countess of Viennois, Albon, and Grenoble, widow of Albéric [?or Guillaume??] Taillefer, Count of Toulouse and Saint-Gilles (died 1183), and daughter and heiress of Guigues X, Count of Viennois and Albon, by his wife, Béatrix. They had one son, André (or Guigues VI) [Dauphin of Viennois), and two daughters, Mathilde (or Mahaut) (wife of Jean, Count Palatine of Burgundy) and Marguerite. HUGUES III, Duke of Burgundy died at Tyre 25 August 1192, and was buried in the church of the Abbey of Cîteaux (Côte-d'Or), near Dijon. His widow, Béatrix, died testate at Château de Vizille 15 Dec. 1228, and was buried at Hayes Abbey near Grenoble.

Duchesne *Histoire Généalogique de la Maison Royale de Dreux* (1631): Preuves de l'Histoire, 19–20 (charter dated 1179 issued by Hugues III, Duke of Burgundy, Count of Langres; charter his "uncle" [patruo], Walter; his sons, Eudes and Alexandre; and his "kinsman" [consanguineus], Henri I, Count of Bar, and Thibaut, Renaud, and Hugues, younger brothers of Count Henri). Pérard *Recueil de plusieurs Pièces curieuses servant à l'Histoire de Bourgogne* (1664): 340 (Hugues [III], Duke of Burgundy, styled "kinsman" [consanguineus] by Philippe-Auguste, King of France in charter dated 1183). Anselme *Hist. de la Maison Royale de France* 1 (1726): 540–542 (sub Ducs de Bourgogne). Migne *Nouvelle Encyclopédie Théologique* 18 (1852): 610 (biog. of Hugues III, duc de Bourgogne). Petit *Histoire des Ducs de Bourgogne de la Race Capétienne* 5 (1894): 400 (Obituaire de Cîteaux: "IV nonas martii [4 March], obiit pie memorie domina Alaydis quondam ducissa Burgundie."), 403 (Obituaire de Cîteaux: "VIII idus augusti [6 August], obiit Hugo, dux Burgundie, qui obiit ultra mare."). Warner *Giraldi Cambrensis Opera* (Rolls Ser., vol. 21, no. 8) (1891): 228 ([Hugues III], Duke of Burgundy, styled "cousin" [consanguineo] of Philippe-Auguste, King of France). Delaville le Roulx *Cartulaire Général de l'Ordre des Hospitaliers de S. Jean de Jérusalem* 1 (1894): 287 (charter dated 1170 by Hugues (III), Duke of Burgundy, with assent of Alix [Aalydis] his wife, and his son, Eudes [Odonis]), 348–349 (charter dated 1177 of Hugues (III), Duke of Burgundy), 470 (charter dated 1185 issued by Hugues (III), Duke of Burgundy and Albon; charter confirmed by his son, Eudes), 551 (charter dated 1189 issued by Hugues (III), Duke of Burgundy, Count of Albon, confirms the gift of Mathilde de Magne [Mayenne], formerly Duchess of Burgundy, to the Hospitaliers). Brandenburg *Die Nachkommen Karls des Großen* (1935) XIV 368, XIII 363. Cox *Eagles of Savoy* (1974). Schwennicke *Europaische Stanmtafeln* 2 (1984): 20 (sub Burgundy). Winter *Descs. of Charlemagne (800–1400)* (1987): XIV.120, XIV.601, XIV.881. Van Kerrebrouck *Les Capétians 987–1328* (2000): 571–574. Poull *Maison Ducale de Lorraine* Pt. 1 (Les Ducs de Lorraine du Moyen Age): 38. Online resource: http:// www.binetti.ru/bernardus/217.shtml (charter dated 1179 issued by Hugues III, Duke of Burgundy, Count of Langres, names his uncle [patruo], Walter; his sons, Eudes and Alexandre; and his "kinsman" [consanguineus], Henri I, Count of Bar). Gilbert of Mons *Chronicle of Hainaut* (2005): 76 (sub A.D. 1181: Henry [recte Hugues], Duke of Burgundy, and Henry, Count of Bar, named as "nephews" of Henry, late Count Palatine of Troyes).

Child of Hugues III of Burgundy, by Alix of Lorraine:

i. **EUDES III**, Duke of Burgundy [see next].

Child of Hugues III of Burgundy, by Béatrix d'Albon:

i. **MARGUERITE OF BURGUNDY**, married **AMÉDÉE** (or **AMEDEO**) **IV**, Count of Savoy, Marquis in Italy [see SALUZZO 6].

6. EUDES III, Duke of Burgundy, son and heir, born in 1166. He married (1st) in 1193 **MAHAUT** (or **MAFALDA**) **OF PORTUGAL**, widow of Philippe, Count of Flanders, and daughter of Affonso I, King of Portugal, by Mathilde, daughter of Amédée III, Count of Maurienne and Savoy. They had no issue. Their marriage was dissolved in 1195 on grounds on consanguinity. He married (2nd) in summer 1199 **ALIX** (or **ALAYDIS**) **DE VERGY**, daughter and heiress of Hugues, seigneur of Vergy, Autry, and Châtel-Censoir, by Gisle, daughter of Garnier II, seigneur of Trainel. She was born about 1182. They had one son, Hugues [IV] [Duke of Burgundy], and two daughters, Alix (wife of Béraud II, seigneur of Mercœur, and Robert I, Count of Clermont in Auvergne), and Béatrix (wife of Humbert III, seigneur of Thoire and Villars en Bresse). EUDES III, Duke of Burgundy, died at Lyon (Rhône) 6 July 1218, and was buried in the church of the Abbey of Cîteaux (Côte-d'Or). His widow, Alix, died at Prenois-en-Montagne after 8 March 1251/2, and was buried in the church of the Abbey of Cîteaux (Côte-d'Or).

Pérard *Recueil de plusieurs Pièces curieuses servant à l'Histoire de Bourgogne* (1664): 321 (Eudes [III], Duke of Burgundy, styled "kinsman" [consanguineo] by Étienne, Count of Burgundy, in charter dated 1217), 341 (charters of Eudes, Duke of Burgundy dated 1193 and 1196), 342 (charter of Alix [Aalidis], Duchess of Burgundy dated 1218). Anselme Hist. de la Maison Royale de France 1 (1726): 542–543 (sub Ducs de Bourgogne). Bernard *Recueil des Chartes de l'Abbaye de Cluny* 5 (Coll. de Docs. inédits sur l'histoire de France 1st ser. Histoire Politique) (1876): 724 (charter of Eudes, Duke of Burgundy). *Archives des missions scientifiques et littéraires* 3rd ser. 6 (1880): 341 (Eudes [III], Duke of Burgundy, styled "kinsman" [consanguineo] by King Philippe Auguste of France in 1208). Petit *Hist. des Ducs de Bourgogne de la Race Capétienne* 3 (1889): 87–251 (biog. of Eudes III, Duke of Burgundy), 383, 395, 452–453, 470 [charters dated 1202, 1204, 1215, and 1218 for "La reine Mathilde, comtesse de Flandre (divorcée du duc Eudes III)], 472 (Thibaud, Duke of Lorraine, refers to his uncle "oncle," [Eudes], Duke of Burgundy, in 1218), 473 (Eudes, Duke of Burgundy, refers to Thibaud, Duke of Lorraine, as his "cousin" in 1218); 5 (1894): 389 (Obituaire de Molème: "XVII kal. Julii [15 June], obiit Odo, dux Burgundie."), 399 (Obituaire de Cîteaux: "XV kalendas martii [15 February], obiit Alix ducissa

Burgundie."), 402 (Obituaire de Cîteaux: "II nonas julii [6 July], anno ab incarnatione Domini MoCCoXVIIIo, pridie nonas julii [6 July], obiit Odo, dux Burgundie, et anniversarium ducum et ducissarum."). Delaville le Roulx *Cartulaire Général de l'Ordre des Hospitaliers de S. Jean de Jérusalem* 2 (1897): 254–255 (charter of Alix [Alaydis], duchess of Burgundy, dated 1218). Thatcher & McNeal *Source Book for Mediæval Hist.* (1905): 371 (Thibaud, Count of Troyes, styled "relative" [i.e., kinsman] by Eudes, Duke of Burgundy in 1200. Schwennicke *Europäische Stammtafeln* 2 (1984): 7 (sub Flanders), 20 (sub Burgundy); 3 (1985): 436 (sub Vergy). Winter *Descs. of Charlemagne (800–1400)* (1987): XV.161. Monicat *Recueil des Actes de Philippe Auguste Roi de France* 3 (1996): 98-99 (Eudes, Duke of Burgundy, styled "kinsman" [consanguineo] by King Philippe-Auguste of France). Van Kerrebrouck *Les Capétiens 987–1328* (2000): 575–577. Evergates *Littere Baronum: The Earliest Cartulary of the Counts of Champagne* (2003): 50, 66, 89 (instances of Thibaut III, Count of Troyes, styled "kinsman" [consanguineus] by Eudes III, Duke of Burgundy).

7. HUGUES IV, Duke of Burgundy, Count of Chalon-sur-Saône and Auxonne, [titulary] King of Thessalonica, Pair de France, son and heir, born 9 March 1212/3. He married (1st) by contract dated 1229 **YOLANDE DE DREUX**, Countess of Auxonne, daughter of Robert III, Count of Dreux and Braine, by Annor (or Aénor), daughter and heiress of Thomas de Saint-Valéry [see DREUX 8 for her ancestry]. She was born about 1212. They had three sons, Eudes [Count of Nevers, Auxerre, and Tonnerre], Jean [seigneur of Bourbon], and Robert II [Duke of Burgundy], and two daughters, Alix (or Alaydis) and Marguerite (wife of Guillaume III de Mont-Saint-Jean and Guy VI, Vicomte of Limoges). His wife, Yolande, died 30 October 1248, and was buried in the church of the Abbey of Cîteaux (Côte-d'Or). He married (2nd) by contract dated Nov. 1258 **BÉATRICE OF NAVARRE**, daughter of Teobaldo (or Thibaut) I, King of Navarre, Count Palatine of Champagne and Brie, by his 3rd wife, Marguerite, daughter of Archambaud VIII de Dampierre, seigneur of Bourbon [see BLOIS 6 for her ancestry]. They had one son, Hugues (seigneur of Montréal), and four daughters, Béatrice (wife of Hugues XIII de Lusignan, Count of La Marche and Angoulême), Marguerite (wife of Jean I de Chalon, seigneur of Arlay), Jeanne (nun), and Isabelle (wife of Rudolf I, King of Germany, Duke of Austria). HUGUES IV, Duke of Burgundy died at Château Villaines-en-Duesmois 27 October 1272, and was buried in the church of the Abbey of Cîteaux (Côte-d'Or). His widow, Béatrix, died at Château Villaines-en-Duesmois (Côte-d'Or) in 1295, after July.

Duchesne *Histoire Généalogique de la Maison Royale de Dreux* (1631): 69–82. Pérard *Recueil de plusieurs Pièces curieuses servant à l'Histoire de Bourgogne* (1664): 439–440 (Hugues [IV], Duke of Burgundy, styled "kinsman" [consanguineo] by Jean [I], Count of Burgundy and Chalon, in charter dated 1237). Anselme *Hist. de la Maison Royale de France* 1 (1726): 426–427 (sub Comtes de Dreux), 543–546 (sub Ducs de Bourgogne). *L'Art de Vérifier les Dates* 2 (1784): 670–674. Teulet *Layettes du Trésor des Chartes* 2 (1866): 347 (Hugues [IV], Duke of Burgundy styled "kinsman" by Jean de Châlon, Count of Burgundy and Chalon). Petit *Histoire des Ducs de Bourgogne de la Race Capétienne* 5 (1894): 405 (Obituaire de Cîteaux: "III kalendas novembris [30 October], anno Domini MoCCoLXXoIIo, obiit dominus Hugo, dux Burgundie, quondam filius Odonis."), 406 (Obituaire de Cîteaux: "III kalendas novembris [30 October], Anno Domini MoCCoXLoVIIIo obiit domina Hyolandis, ducissa Burgundie."). Schwennicke *Europaische Stanmtafeln* 2 (1984): 20 (sub Burgundy); 3(1) (1984): 63 (sub Dreux). Kerrebrouck *Les Capétians 987–1328* (2000): 314, 577–583.

Children of Hugues IV of Burgundy, by Yolande de Dreux:

i. **EUDES**, Count of Nevers, Auxerre, and Tonnerre [see next].

ii. **ROBERT II**, Duke of Burgundy, Count of Auxonne and Chalon, married **AGNÈS OF FRANCE** [see FRANCE 9.iii].

iii. **ALIX** (or **ALAYDIS**) **OF BURGUNDY**, married **HENRI III**, Duke of Lorraine and Brabant [see BRABANT 7].

8. EUDES OF BURGUNDY, in right of his wife, Count of Nevers, Auxerre, and Tonnerre, seigneur of Bourbon-l'Archambaud, Baron of Donzy and Perche-Gouët (1254–62), son and heir apparent, born 1230. He married Feb. 1247/8 **MATHILDE** (or **MAHAUT**) **DE BOURBON**, daughter and co-heiress of Archambaud IX de Dampierre-Bourbon, seigneur of Bourbon-l'Archambault, by Yolande, daughter of Guy I de Châtillon, Count of Saint-Pol [see DONZY 8 for her ancestry]. They had four daughters, Yolande, Marguerite, Alix (wife of Jean de Chalon, Chev.,

Count of Auxerre), and Jeanne. His wife, Mahaut, died 1 October 1262. EUDES OF BURGUNDY, Count of Nevers, Auxerre, and Tonnerre was slain in battle at Acre 4 August 1266, and was buried in the cemetery of Saint-Nicholas, Acre.

Anselme *Hist. de la Maison Royale de France* 1 (1726): 543–546 (sub Ducs de Bourgogne). *L'Art de vérifier les Dates* 3 (1818): 97–99 (sub Barons de Donzi); 11 (1818): 205–231 (sub Comtes de Auxerre & Nevers), 287. Lebeuf *Mémoires concernant l'Hist. civile & ecclésiastique d'Auxerre* 3 (1855): 184–191. Hervey *Paper read before the Archaeological Institute of Suffolk ... 1856* (1858): App. I, 117–121 (Donzi ped.). Pertz *Annales et Chronica aevi Salici* (Monumenta Germaniae Historica, Scriptorum 5) (1864): 50 (Annales S. Benigni Divionensis: "1267. Hoc anno Oddo, primogenitus ducis Burgundie, miles bonus prudens atque catholicus, obiit in partibus transmarinis."). Gillois *Chroniques du Nivernois: Les Comtes et les Ducs de Nevers* (1867). *Bull. de la Société Nivernaise des Sciences, Lettres et Arts* 2nd Ser. 5 (1872): 65–106. Petit *Histoire des Ducs de Bourgogne de la Race Capétienne* 5 (1894): 239 (Guillaume de Courtenay styled "cousin" by Eudes of Burgundy, Count of Nevers, in 1264), 393 (Obituaire de Moleme: "Kalendis octobris [1 October] — Obiit Mathildis, comitissa Nivernensis."), 403 (Obituaire de Cîteaux: "Anno Domini M°CC°LX°VI° [1266] — II nonas augusti [4 August] obit Odo, quondam comes Nivernensis."). Molinier *Obituaires de la Province de Sens* 1(2) (Recueil des Historiens de la France — Obituaires) (1902): 995 (sub Chapelle Saint-Blaise, à Provins: "13 March. Ob. Odo, comes Nivernensis [1266]."), 995 (sub Chapelle Saint-Blaise, à Provins: "14 March. Ob. Mathildis, comitissa Nivernensis [1262]."). Schwennicke *Europaische Stammtafeln* 2 (1984): 21 (sub Burgundy); 3(1) (1984): 51 (sub Dampierrre). Van Kerrebrouck *Les Capétians 987–1328* (2000): 599–602.

Child of Eudes of Burgundy, by Mahaut de Dampierre:

i. **YOLANDE OF BURGUNDY**, married (1st) **JEAN TRISTAN OF FRANCE**, Count of Nevers, Valois, and Crécy [see FLANDERS 8]; (2nd) **ROBERT III**, Count of Flanders and Nevers [see FLANDERS 8].

ii. **MARGUERITE OF BURGUNDY**, married **CHARLES OF FRANCE**, King of Jerusalem and Sicily [see SICILY 9].

❧ BURNELL ☙

ROGER D'AUBENEY, married **AMICE** _____.
WILLIAM D'AUBENEY, of Buckenham, Norfolk, married **MAUD LE BIGOD**.
WILLIAM D'AUBENEY, of Buckenham, Norfolk, married **ALICE OF LOUVAIN**, Queen of England.
WILLIAM D'AUBENEY, 2nd Earl of Arundel, married **MAUD DE SAINT HILARY**.
WILLIAM D'AUBENEY, Earl of Arundel, married **MABEL OF CHESTER** (desc. King William the Conqueror).
ISABEL D'AUBENEY, married **JOHN FITZ ALAN**, of Clun, Shropshire.
JOHN FITZ ALAN, Knt., of Oswestry, Shropshire, married **MAUD DE VERDUN**.
JOHN FITZ ALAN, of Arundel, Sussex, married **ISABEL DE MORTIMER** (desc. King William the Conqueror) [see FITZ ALAN 8].

9. **MAUD FITZ ALAN**, married (1st) before 5 June 1283 **PHILIP BURNELL**, Knt., of Holgate, Acton Burnell, Condover, Eudon Burnell (in Chetton), Hope Bowdler, Norton (in Condover), and Rushbury, Shropshire, Wymington, Bedfordshire, East and West Ham (in East Ham) and Great Holland, Essex, Little Rissington, Gloucestershire, Letchworth, Hertfordshire, Upton (in Upton Noble), Somerset, Ham (in Kingston-upon-Thames) and Hatcham, Surrey, Great Cheverell, Wiltshire, Kidderminster Burnell, Worcestershire, etc., King's yeoman, son and heir of Hugh Burnell, Knt., of Wellington and Eudon Burnell, Shropshire, by his wife, Sibyl. He was born 1 August 1264. She had the manors of Cound, Frodesley, and Kenley, Shropshire as her maritagium. They had one son, Edward, Knt. [Lord Burnell], and one daughter, Maud. In 1291 Roesia Trussel acknowledged that she owed him £12, to be levied, in default of payment, of her lands and chattels in Northamptonshire. He was heir in 1292 to his uncle, Robert Burnell, Bishop of Bath and Wells, Chancellor of England. In 1292 a certain individual named "A." brought an assize of novel disseisin for his common of pasture appurtenant to his freehold, etc. against the Abbot of Buildwas; the Abbot said that he could not answer as to the pasture ... for Philip Burnel held that pasture in common with the Abbot, in undivided shares, and he was not named in the writ. In 1293 he

brought an assize of novel disseisin against Gilbert de Clare, Earl of Gloucester, and others regarding unspecified tenements formerly held by Robert Burnel. In 1294 he and John Hastang acknowledged that they owed a debt of £10 to William de Hamelton, clerk. SIR PHILIP BURNELL died 26 June 1294, and was buried in the White Friars church at Oxford, Oxfordshire. His widow, Maud, married (2nd) by license dated 19 Sept. 1295 (as his 2nd wife) **ROBERT DE BRUS**, Knt. (died shortly before 4 April 1304), Earl of Carrick (in Scotland), lord of Annandale (in Scotland), Lord Brus (in England) [see BRUS 7], of Hatfield Broad Oak and Writtle, Essex, Governor of Carlisle Castle, son and heir of Robert de Brus, Knt., lord of Annandale (nicknamed *the Competitor*), by his 1st wife, Isabel, daughter of Gilbert de Clare, Knt., Earl of Gloucester and Hertford, Magna Carta Baron [see BRUS 6 for his ancestry]. He was born in July 1243. They had no issue. In Feb. 1296 Robert de Brus, knight, Earl of Carrick, and Robert de Brus, his son, and three others owed £120 to John de Abingdon, citizen of London. He accompanied Edward I into Scotland, and fought at the Battle of Dunbar 28 April 1296. He again swore fealty to King Edward I at Berwick 28 April 1296. However, on his claims to the throne being thwarted by Edward, he again retired to England, where he resided chiefly at Broomshawbury, Essex. In August 1296 Robert de Brus, knight, Earl of Carrick, his son, Robert, and two others owed a debt of £60 to Nicholas Daleroun, Simon Daleroun, and Henry Daleroun, Citizens and merchants of Winchester. In October 1296 he and his wife, Maud, were involved in a plea of dower regarding her English lands. Robert was summoned to attend the King of England at Salisbury 26 Jan. 1296/7. This marriage ended in divorce sometime before Easter term [6 May–1 June] 1299, when Maud "formerly the wife of Philip Burnel" sued regarding her right of dower in a messuage in Gunton, Norfolk, without any reference to Robert de Brus as her spouse. In the same term, she likewise sued Ralph Springehose for a third of a messuage, lands, and £10 of rent in Wolverhampton, Staffordshire and various other tenants in Wolverhampton for a third of their holdings as her dower. In 1302, as "Maud widow of Philip Burnel," she petitioned the king and council in England regarding socages and burgages held in various counties by her late husband, Philip Burnell. In 1309 Henry son of Henry de Erdington sued Maud widow of Philip Burnell for a third part of the manor of Wellington, Shropshire, and Maud's son, Edward Burnell, for two parts of the same manor. She presented to the church of Sparkford, Somerset in 1310, and to the church of Great Cheverell, Wiltshire in 1314 and in 1315. Maud married (3rd) before 19 June 1316 **SIMON DE CRIKETOT** (or **CRIKETOFT**, **KIRKETOFT**). In 1280–1 Peter de Reding arraigned an assize of novel disseisin against him and others regarding a tenement in Tuddenham, Suffolk. In 1296 Simon de Criketot, while with the king's army in Scotland, was attached to answer Robert de Escores on a plea of trespass, regarding which plea he had license to make an agreement, saving to the marshal his right; they submitted themselves to the arbitration of William Talemasch and Thomas de Hauville. In Feb. 1320 he had letters nominating John le Longe his attorney in Ireland for one year. SIMON DE CRIKETOT was living 7 March 1320. His wife, Maud, was living 19 June 1316, but died shortly before 17 Nov. 1326 (death date of her nephew, Edmund, Earl of Arundel), as indicated by a petition to the king and council dated c.1330 submitted by her daughter and son-in-law, Maud and John de Haudlo).

Hasted *Hist. & Top. Survey of Kent* 2 (1797): 184–203. Surtees *Hist. & Antiqs. of Durham* 3 (1823): 94 (Brus ped.). Tierney *Hist. & Antiqs. of the Castle & Town of Arundel* 1 (1834): chart foll. 192, cites Vincent *A Discoverie of Errours* (1622): 34 (places Maud in wrong generation of Fitz Alan family). Eyton *Antiqs. of Shropshire* 6 (1858): 71–72, 90, 105, 121–136, 294; 9 (1859): 45. *Year Books of Edward I: Years XX & XXI* 1 (Rolls Ser. 31a) (1866): 284–285; *Years XXI & XXII* 2 (Rolls Ser. 31a) (1873): 280–283. *Wiltshire Arch. & Nat. Hist. Mag.* 12 (1869): 17. Burke *Dormant, Abeyant, Forfeited & Extinct Peerages* (1883): 93–94 (sub Burnell). Rye *Some Rough Materials for a Hist. of the Hundred of North Erpingham* 1 (1883): 82–85. *Arch. Cambrensis* 5th Ser. 1 (1884): 219–221 (Fitzalan ped.). Bain *Cal. Docs. Rel. Scotland* 2 (1884): pg. 217, no. 826 (agreement dated 29 Aug. 1296 between Christiana widow of Robert de Brus, lord of Annandale plaintiff and Robert de Brus his son and heir defendant as to dower both in England and Scotland. Robert grants her dower from the freehold of his father in the valley of Annan and Moffet as in John late king of Scotland's time ... She also grants to the said Robert her dower in the rents of the burghs of Annan and Lochmaben), pg. 223, no. 850 ("On 13 Oct. 1296 at Kirkham. The King [Edward I.] to John de Langetone to his chancellor. Empowers him to appoint some fit person to receive the attorneys of Robert de Brus Earl of Carrick and lord of Annandale, and Matill[idis] his wife, in a plea of dower whereof the said earl's clerk, the bearer, will acquaint him. Privy Seals (Tower), 24 Edward I. Bundle 5."). Wrottesley *Staffordshire Suits: Plea Rolls* (Colls. Hist. Staffs. 7(1)) (1886): 51–52; (Colls. Hist. Staffs. 9) (1888): 19; (Colls. Hist. Staffs. 12) (1891): 11–12. *Annual Rpt. of the Deputy Keeper* 50 (1889): 232. Tresswell & Vincent *Vis. of Shropshire 1623, 1569 & 1584* 1 (H.S.P. 28) (1889): 92–93 (1623 Vis.) (Burnell ped.: "Sʳ Philippe Burnell Kᵗ baron of Holgate in com. Salop. nephew & heire to Robert [Burnell]. = Mawde sister to Rich. fitzallen vide Claud 11 E. 3 m. 7.") (Burnell arms: Argent, a lion rampant sable crowned or within a bordure azure). Weaver *Somerset Incumbents* (1889): 185. *Trans. Shropshire Arch. & Nat. Hist. Soc.* 2ⁿᵈ Ser. 6 (1894): 196–202. Birch *Cat. Seals in the British Museum* 4 (1895): 249 (seal of Robert de Brus, Earl of Carrick dated circa A.D. 1285 — Obverse. To the right. In armour: hauberk of mail, short surcoat, grated vizor, sword, and shield of arms. Horse galloping. Arms: a saltire (with curved branches), and on a chief a leopard passant, guardant for "*Le Comte de Karrick.*" Legend: S. ROBERTI (DE BRVS) COMITIS DE CARRIK.). Reverse. A shield of arms: as in the obverse. Legend: SIGILLVM ROBERTI DE [BRUS COMIT]IS DE CARRIK.). *C.P.R. 1292–1301* (1895): 147 (license dated 19 Sept. 1295 for Maud, late the wife of Philip Burnel, tenant in chief, to marry Robert de Brus, lord of Annandale), 404, 581. *C.P.R. 1313–1317* (1898): 479. *Feudal Aids* 2 (1900): 130, 134, 159, 216, 218; 3 (1904): 469; 4 (1906): 229, 306, 319, 321, 349. *Desc. Cat. Ancient Deeds* 4 (1902): 85–86 (A. 6814: "Counterpart indenture of agreement between Sir Hugh le Despenser and Sir John de Haudlo, of the one part, and Simon Criketot, of the other part, viz. that whereas certain covenants between the said Sir Hugh and Sir John of the one part and Dame Maud Burnell, now wife of the said Simon, of the other part, on the marriage between the said Sir John and Dame Maud Lovel, daughter of the said Dame Maud Burnel, in many points have not been carried out, the said Simon agrees to brng the said Dame Maud, his wife, to Temedeburi [Tenbury, Worcestershire] before St. James's day, next, to perform the said covenants ...."). *C.C.R. 1279–1288* (1902): 235 (Maud, wife of Philip Burnell, styled sister of Richard Fitz Alan, Earl of Arundel). *C.P.R. 1317–1321* (1903): 418, 423, 429. *C.C.R. 1288–1296* (1904): 204, 382. *Scots Peerage* 1 (1904): 7–8 (sub Kings of Scotland); 5 (108): 578, footnote 7 (sub Mar). *C.F.R.* 1 (1911): 340. VCH *Surrey* 3 (1911): 505; 4 (1912): 43–43 (Burnell arms: Argent a lion sable crowned or in a border azure), 87. *Cal. IPM* 3 (1912): 116–126, 443–444. *C.P.* 2 (1912): 360–361 (sub Brus), 434 (sub Burnell); 3 (1913): 56 (sub Carrick); 6 (1926): 109–111 (sub Grendon). VCH *Bedford* 3 (1912): 117–122. VCH *Hertford* 3 (1912): 118–124. VCH *Worcester* 3 (1913): 161. *Year Books of Edward II* 13 (Selden Soc. 34) (1918): 234–242. *Cal. Chancery Warrants* (1927): 74. Moor *Knights of Edward I* 1 (H.S.P. 80) (1929): 167. Maxwell-Lyte *Hist. Notes of Some Somerset Manors* (Somerset Rec. Soc. Extra Ser. 1) (1931): 395–398. *Trans. Shropshire Arch. & Nat. Hist. Soc.* 47 (1933–34): 49–53. Gandavo *Reg. Simonis de Gandavo Diocesis Saresbiriensis 1297–1315* 2 (Canterbury & York Soc. 41) (1934): 638, 827, 830, 833. VCH *Warwick* 3 (1945): 52–53 (Burnell arms: Argent a lion sable with a crown or in a bordure azure). Sanders *English Baronies* (1960): 29. Wagner *Hist. Heraldry of Britain* (1972): 44–45. VCH *Essex* 4 (1973): 10–11. VCH *Wiltshire* 10 (1975): 42–43 (errs in stating Maud died in late 1315 or early 1316). Barrow *Robert Bruce & Scotland* (1976): 92–93. VCH *Shropshire* 11 (1985): 215. Neville "A Plea Roll of Edward I's Army in Scotland, 1296" in *Misc. of the Scottish Hist. Soc.* 11 (1990). Brault *Rolls of Arms Edward I* 2 (1997): 42 (arms of Philip Burnel: Argent, a lion rampant sable surmounted by a bend gules). VCH *Somerset* 7 (1999): 59–63. Blakely *Brus Fam. in England & Scotland 1100–1295* (2005): 232 (charter dated 29 May 1298 Robert de Brus senior, Earl of Carrick and lord of Annandale, releases and quitclaims to John Heroloff a half virgate of land in Writtle, Essex, cites Essex Rec. Office, Charter D/DP T1/1770). *Trans. Monumental Brass Soc.* 18 (2010): 119–132. National Archives, C 241/18/59 (Debtor: Robert de Brus, Knt., Earl of Carrick, Robert de Brus, his son, William de Roding, Knt., William de Badew, and John de Writtle, called Serich. Creditor: John de Abingdon, citizen of London. Amount: £120. Before whom: John Breton, Warden of London; John de Bakewell, Clerk. First term: 16/02/1296. Last term: 25/03/1296. Writ to: Sheriff of Essex.); C 241/31/103 (Debtor: Robert de Brus, knight, Earl of Carrick, Robert de Brus, his son, John de Sawbridgeworth, poulterer, and John ....; Creditor: Nicholas Daleroun, Simon Daleroun, and Henry Daleroun, Citizens and merchants of Winchester. Amount: £60. Before whom: John Breton, Warden of London; ...., Clerk. First term: 08/04/1296. Last term: 08/04/1296. Writ to: Sheriff of Middlesex.); SC 8/52/2570 (petition dated c.1330 by John de Haudlo and Maud his wife to the king and council) (see abs. further below); SC 8/80/3993B; SC 8/313/E63 (petition dated 1302 from Maud, widow of Philip Burnel, to king and council, requesting remedy as whereas her late husband held socages and burgages in various counties of which he died seised and although Burnel ought to have and hold these socages and burgages for the upbringing of Edward her son, who is under age, these socages and burgages are retained in the king's hand) (available at www.catalogue.nationalarchives.gov.uk/search.asp).

Children of Maud Fitz Alan, by Philip Burnell, Knt.:

i. **EDWARD BURNELL**, Knt., of Holgate, Acton Burnell, Condover, Eudon Burnell (in Chetton), Hope Bowdler, and Norton (in Condover), Shropshire, East and West Ham (in East Ham) and Great Holland, Essex, Little Rissington, Gloucestershire, Letchworth, Hertfordshire, Upton (in Upton Noble), Somerset, Ham (in Kingston-upon-Thames) and Hatcham, Surrey, Great Cheverell, Wiltshire, Kidderminster Burnell, Worcestershire, etc., son and heir, born about 1286 (proved his age in 1307). He married after 3 May 1302 **ALINE LE DESPENSER**, 1st daughter of Hugh le Despenser, Knt., Earl of Winchester, by Isabel, daughter of William de Beauchamp, Knt., 9th Earl of Warwick [see DESPENSER 10 for her ancestry]. They had no issue. He presented to the church of Wyck Rissington, Gloucestershire in 1309 and 1312. In 1310 Alice, widow of Walter de Beauchamp, was summoned to answer him of a plea wherefore she made waste and sale of the lands, houses, woods, and gardens which she had in the wardship of the inheritance of the said Edward in Broom Court near Bidford, Warwickshire to his disherison. He served in the Scottish wars, 1311–14. He was summoned to Parliament from 19 Dec. 1311 to 24 October 1314, by writs directed *Edwardo Burnell*, whereby he is held to have become Lord Burnell. SIR EDWARD BURNELL, Lord Burnell, died testate shortly before 1 Sept. 1315. In 1316 the Warden of the Schools of Balliol at Oxford appeared by attorney against John de Haudlo and his wife, Maud, "sister and heir of Edward Burnel," in a plea that they should warrant to him the third part of two messuages and ten shops in Oxford which Aline widow of Edward Burnel claimed as dower. His widow, Aline, presented to the church of Chetton, Shropshire in 1318 and again in 1321, and to the prebendal portion of the church of Holdgate, Shropshire in 1322. She was appointed Constable of Conway Castle 30 Jan. 1325/6. In 1326 she sued Robert de Staundon in a plea that he had taken and abducted John son and heir of Peter de Saltmarsh from Morton, Worcestershire, who was under age and whose marriage belonged to her. In Nov. 1329 his widow, Aline, and Hawise de Kaynes were granted protection for one year, they going on pilgrimage to Santiago. In April 1330 she was granted protection until the Feast of the Purification, she going on pilgrimage to Santiago. In Feb. 1331 Aline had simple protection for one year, she going again going on pilgrimage to Santiago. In March 1331 she had letters nominating attorneys in England for one year. In June 1331 she was again granted protection for one year. In 1338 she obtained a license to found a chantry of two chaplains in the chapel of St. Giles, Lulsley, Worcestershire to pray for her soul and that of late husband, Edward Burnell, and for the soul of her late brother, Hugh le Despenser. She received a papal indult for plenary remission at the hour of death in 1347. Aline, Lady Burnell, died shortly before 28 Nov. 1353. Hasted *Hist. & Top. Survey of Kent* 2 (1797): 184–203. Blore *Hist. & Antiqs. of Rutland* 1(2) (1811): 19 (Despener ped.). Brydges *Collins' Peerage of England* 6 (1812): 496–511 (sub Despener). Rye *Some Rough Materials for a Hist. of the Hundred of North Erpingham* 1 (1883): 82–85. Wrottesley *Staffordshire Suits: Plea Rolls* (Colls. Hist. Staffs. 9) (1888): 6, 19, 24, 33, 64, 113, 124; (Colls. Hist. Staffs. 13) (1892): 10. Tresswell & Vincent *Vis. of Shropshire 1623, 1569 & 1584* 1 (H.S.P. 28) (1889): 92–93 (1623 Vis.) (Burnell ped.: "Sr Edw. Burnell Knight baron of Holgatte died Ao 1315, 9 E. 2. s. p'l. = Ela da. to Hughe le Despenser."). *C.P.R. 1327–1330* (1891): 455, 514. *C.P.R. 1330–1334* (1893): 69, 84, 123. *C.P.R. 1292–1301* (1895): 404, 581. *Papal Regs.: Letters* 3 (1897): 249. Amphlett *Lay Subsidy Roll 1332–3* (Worcestershire Hist. Soc. 6(3)) (1899): 1, 3, 5, 8, 9. Maitland *Year Books of Edward II* 3 (Selden Soc. 20) (1905): 90–91; 13 (Selden Soc. 34) (1918): 191–192. *List of Inqs. ad Quod Damnum* 2 (PRO Lists and Indexes 22) (1906): 569. Orleton *Cal. Reg. of Adam de Orleton 1317–1327* (1907): 209–210, 234, 385, 387. *Ancestor* 8 (1904): 167–185. *C.P.* 2 (1912): 434 (sub Burnell). VCH *Bedford* 3 (1912): 117–122. VCH *Surrey* 4 (1912): 42–43 (Burnell arms: Argent a lion sable crowned or in a border azure). VCH *Hertford* 3 (1912): 118–124. VCH *Worcester* 3 (1913): 161; 4 (1924): 354–361. Reynolds *Reg. of Walter Reynolds Bishop of Worcester* (Dugdale Soc. 9) (1928): 148, 154. Martival *Regs. of Roger Martival, Bishop of Salisbury 1315–1330* 3 (Canterbury & York Soc. 59) (1965): 32. VCH *Wiltshire* 8 (1965): 61–74. Ellis *Cat. Seals in the P.R.O.* 1 (1978): 13 (seal of Edward Burnell dated 1315 — Hanging from a triple bush, between two wyverns, a shield of arms: a lion rampant crowned. Legend: SIGILLVM. EDWARDI. BURNEL.). VCH *Shropshire* 10 (1998): 44–52, 135–147. VCH *Somerset* 7 (1999): 59–63. Morrison *Women Pilgrims* (2000): 157–158. *Trans. Monumental Brass Soc.* 18 (2010): 119–132. National Archives, SC 8/70/3464 (petition dated 1327 from Richard de la Rivere to the king and council. Places mentioned: la Wieke (Sewardswick, Wick), [Keynsham hundred, Somerset]; Keynsham, [Somerset]; Compton Dando, [Somerset]. Other people mentioned: Alyne Burnele, daughter of Hugh le Despenser); SC 8/195/9741B (available at www.a2a.org.uk/search/index.asp).

   ii.   **MAUD BURNELL** [see next].

10. MAUD BURNELL, born about 1290–4 (aged 21 or 25 in 1315). She married before 1315 **JOHN LOVEL**, 2nd Lord Lovel [see LOVEL 11], of Titchmarsh, Northamptonshire, Minster Lovell, Oxfordshire, etc., son and heir of John Lovel, Knt., 1st Lord Lovel, of Minster Lovell, Oxfordshire, Docking, Norfolk, Titchmarsh, Northamptonshire, Elcombe (in Wroughton), Wiltshire, etc., Sheriff of Norfolk, by his 2nd wife, Joan, daughter of Robert de Roos, Knt., of Helmsley, Yorkshire [see LOVEL 10 for his ancestry]. He was born about 1288 (aged 22 in 1310). They had one son, John, Knt. [3rd Lord Lovel], and one daughter, Joan. He was summoned to Parliament from 16 June 1311 until his death. JOHN LOVEL, 2nd Lord Lovel, was slain at the Battle of Bannockburn 24 June 1314. She was heiress in 1315 to her brother, Edward Burnell, Knt., Lord Burnell, by which she inherited the barony of Castle Holgate, Shropshire and the manors of Little Rissington, Gloucestershire, Letchworth, Hertfordshire, Billingford, East Riston, and

Thurning, Norfolk, Ham (in Kingston-upon-Thames) and Hatcham, Surrey, etc. She married (2nd) without license before 4 Dec. 1315 (as his 2nd wife) **JOHN DE HAUDLO** (or **HADLOWE**), Knt., of Hadlow, Ashendon, Crundale, Ore, Trentworth (in Crundale), and Vanne (in Crundale), Kent, Warden of the Forest of Dean and Constable of St. Briavels Castle, benefactor of Queen's College, Oxford, and, in right of his 1st wife, of Boarstall, Addingrove (in Oakley), and Oakley, Buckinghamshire, and Muswell (in Piddington), Oxfordshire, Keeper of the Bernewood Forest, and in right of his 2nd wife, of East and West Ham (in East Ham), Essex, Billingford, Norfolk, Upton (in Upton Noble), Somerset, Hatcham, Surrey, Great Cheverell and Fenny Sutton (in Sutton Veny), Wiltshire, Kidderminster Burnell, Worcestershire, etc., son of Richard de Haudlo. They had two sons, Thomas [Burnell] and Nicholas [Burnell], Knt. [1st Lord Burnell], and three daughters, Joan (wife of Amaury de St. Amand, Knt., 3rd Lord Saint Amand), Margaret (wife of Walter de Norwich), and Elizabeth. He married (1st) before 28 Dec. 1299 **JOAN FITZ NIGEL**, daughter and heiress of John Fitz Nigel, Knt., of Boarstall and Oakley, Buckinghamshire, by which marriage he had one son, Richard de Haudlo, Knt. [see SAINT AMAND 12]. In 1299 he served as a valet to Hugh le Despenser. In 1304 he complained that Henry Fitz Nigel, parson of Haseley, broke his chest at Oseney, Oxfordshire, and carried away charters, writings, and muniments. John was summoned to serve against Scotland in 1301, 1316, and 1319. He went overseas with Hugh le Despenser in 1305, 1309, and 1313, and with the Earl of Surrey in 1308. He was knighted 21 May 1306. In 1307 he was owed debts of 64 marks by William de Tracy, of Gloucestershire, and £26 13s. 4d. by John, son of John de Grenville and James, son of Peter de la Rokele. In 1311 he was owed debts of 25 marks by Walter de Cranford, of Buckinghamshire, and £80 by Simon le Bere and Robert de Dene, both of Witney, Oxfordshire. The same year he was owed a debt of £84 by Henry Fetplace, of Denchworth, Berkshire, and Walter de Cranford, of Doddershall, Buckinghamshire. In 1312 he was granted permission to crenellate his house at Boarstall, Buckinghamshire. In 1313 he was owed a debt of 140 marks by Robert de Mohaut. In 1315 he was taken prisoner by Edmund, Earl of Arundel, at Clun, Shropshire and detained until his friends made fine for his delivery by £4000 with the Earl. In 1316 the Warden of the Schools of Balliol at Oxford appeared by attorney against John de Haudlo and his wife, Maud, "sister and heir of Edward Burnel," in a plea that they should warrant to him the third part of two messuages and ten shops in Oxford which Aline widow of Edward Burnel claimed as dower. He was going to Spain with Hugh le Despenser in 1319. In 1319 and 1331 he and his wife, Maud, presented to the church of Haselbech, Northamptonshire. In 1320 Thomas Fillol gave John and his wife, Maud, a release of his right in 140 acres of land and 4s. of rent in Hatfield Peverel and Boreham, Essex, which he impleaded them in the king's court by writ of entry. He was going overseas with the king in 1320 and 1322, and for the king in 1321. In 1321 his estates were greatly damaged by the confederate Barons who took part against his kinsman, Hugh Despenser *the younger*. In 1323 he and his wife, Maud, granted the reversion of a third part of the manor of Great Cheverel, Wiltshire to Robert de Haudlo, clerk. In 1331 he was owed a debt of 10 marks by Thomas le Povere, Robert Vincent, and William de Tackley. In 1332 he was owed a debt of £10 by Thomas Bigenet, of Witney, Oxfordshire, merchant. His wife, Maud, died before 18 July (date of her obit), before 1338. In 1341 he had license to alienate in mortmain to the Dean and Chapter of St. Mary's, Salisbury, a mill and 30 acres of land with £10 rent in Knight's-Enham, Hampshire, and the advowson of the church to provide 4 vicars to celebrate divine service daily for his good estate in life, for his soul after death, for the souls of his wife, Maud, and of Thomas Burnell their son, and for all the souls of their ancestors, of Edward II and of Hugh le Despenser, the elder, and cause vicars to distribute to the poor 20s. 10d. In 1345 he was owed a debt of £22 19d. by Walter de Leeton and Thomas his son. SIR JOHN DE HAUDLO died testate 5 August 1346.

Bridges *Hist. & Antiqs. of Northamptonshire* 2 (1791): 37. Hasted *Hist. & Top. Survey of Kent* 2 (1797): 184–203. Brydges *Collins' Peerage of England* 7 (1812): 319–395 (sub Perceval, Lord Lovel and Holland). Dugdale *Monasticon Anglicanum* 6(3) (1830): 1598–1599. Burke *Gen'l & Heraldic Dict. of the Peerages of England, Ireland & Scotland* (1831): 318–321 (sub Lovel). Banks *Baronies in Fee* 1 (1844): 243 (sub Handlo), 295–297 (sub Lovel). Lipscomb *Hist. & Antiqs. of Buckingham* 1 (1847): 59–61, 66 (Haudlo arms: Sable a lion rampant argent). Eyton *Antiqs. of Shropshire* 6 (1858): 134 (chart). Burke *Gen. Hist. of the Dormant, Abeyant, Forfeited & Extinct Peerages* (1866): 260 (sub Handlo). Harvey et al. *Vis. of Oxford 1566, 1574, 1634 & 1574* (H.S.P. 5) (1871): 202–203. Stubbs *Annales Londonienses* (Chrons. of the Reigns of Edward I and Edward II 1) (Rolls Ser. 76) (1882): 231 ("Nomina interfectorum militum ad bellum de Strivelyn de Anglis [Names of the English knights slain at Bannockburn]: Johannes Lovell le Riche"). Burke *Dormant, Abeyant, Forfeited & Extinct Peerages* (1883): 93–94 (sub Burnell), 332–334 (sub Lovel). *Trans. Shropshire Arch. & Nat. Hist. Soc.* 6 (1883): 328. Grazebrook *Barons of Dudley* 1 (Colls. Hist. Staffs. 9(2)) (1888): 124. Wrottesley *Staffordshire Suits: Plea Rolls* (Colls. Hist. Staffs. 9) (1888): 64, 124; (Colls. Hist. Staffs. 12) (1891): 11–12; (Colls. Hist. Staffs. 14) (1893): 83; (Colls. Hist. Staffs. 17) (1896): 112–113. Tresswell & Vincent *Vis. of Shropshire 1623, 1569 & 1584* 1 (H.S.P. 28) (1889): 92–93 (1623 Vis.) (Burnell ped.: "Mawde sister & heire to Edward Burnell baro. of Holgate died A° 1300, [1] = John Louell baron of Tichmarshe died 10 E. 2., [2] = Sr John Handlowe [*Handlow*] K^t 2 husband died 20 E. 3."). *Trans. Shropshire Arch. & Nat. Hist. Soc.* 2nd Ser. 6 (1894): 196–201. Lewis *Pedes Finium; or, Fines Rel. Surrey* (Surrey Arch. Soc. Extra Vol. 1) (1894): 90, 218, 219. *C.C.R.* 1318–1323 (1895): 221. *Papal Regs.: Letters* 2 (1895): 4 (William de Handlo [recte Haudlo], clerk, probable brother of John, styled "kinsman" of Hugh le Despenser in 1306), 541. *C.P.R.* 1301–1307 (1898): 281. Green *Feet of Fines for Somerset* 2 (Somerset Rec. Soc. 12) (1898): 121–122, 239, 248. *Ancestor* 8 (1904): 167–185. *Index of Placita de Banco 1327–1328* 1 (PRO Lists and Indexes 17) (1904): 31, 136, 144, 156, 168, 417; 2 (PRO Lists and Indexes 22) (1906): 569, 685, 552, 569, 707, 713, 723. Wrottesley *Peds. from the Plea Rolls* (1905): 95. *Cal. IPM* 5 (1908): 390–394; 8 (1913): 488–496. *C.Ch.R.* 3 (1908): 108. Boyd & Wrottesley *Final Concords* (Colls. Hist. Staffs. 3rd Ser. 1911) (1911): 96–97, 110–111. *VCH Surrey* 3 (1911): 505; 4 (1912): 42–43, 87. *C.P.* 2 (1912): 434–435 (sub Burnell); 8 (1926): 217–218 (sub Lovel); 9 (1936): 765 (sub Norwich); 11 (1949): 299–300 (sub Saint Amand) (misidentifies wife of Amaury de St. Amand). *VCH Hertford* 3 (1912): 118–124. Wedgwood *IPM: Staffs.* (Colls. Hist. Staffs. 3rd Ser. 1913) (1913): 113–114. *VCH Worcester* 3 (1913): 161. *Feet of Fines for Essex* 2 (1913–28): 225, 227, 242. Moor *Knights of Edward I* 2 (H.S.P. 81) (1929): 200–201. Salter *Boarstall Cartulary* (Oxford Hist. Soc. 1st Ser. 88) (1930): 65–75, 108. Maxwell-Lyte *Hist. Notes of Some Somerset Manors* (Somerset Rec. Soc. Extra Ser. 1) (1931): 395–398. Veale *Great Red Book of Bristol* 1 (Bristol Rec. Soc. 2) (1931): 80. *Trans. Shropshire Arch. & Nat. Hist. Soc.* 47 (1933–34): 49–53. *Cal. Inqs. Misc.* 3 (1937): 285. Pugh *Abs. of Feet of Fines Rel. Wiltshire* (Wiltshire Arch. & Nat. Hist. Soc. Recs. Branch 1) (1939): 127–128. Stokes et al. *Warwickshire Feet of Fines* 2 (Dudgale Soc. 15) (1939): 120, 140–141, 181–182. *VCH Warwick* 3 (1945): 52–53. Hatton *Book of Seals* (1950): 245. Paget *Baronage of England* (1957) 337: 6. *English Hist. Rev.* 74 (1959): 70–89; 99 (1984): 1–33. Sanders *English Baronies* (1960): 9–10, 29. *Year Books of Edward II* 25 (Selden Soc. 81) (1964): 130–132. *VCH Wiltshire* 8 (1965): 61–74; 10 (1975): 42–43. *VCH Essex* 4 (1973): 10–11. Elrington *Abs. of Feet of Fines Rel. Wiltshire* (Wiltshire Rec. Soc. 29) (1974): 51. Edington *Reg. of William Edington Bishop of Winchester 1346–1366* 1 (Hampshire Recs. 7) (1986): 30. Lefferts *Rules & the Summa* (1990): 8 (re. Robert de Handlo, near kinsman of John de Haudlo). *VCH Gloucester* 5 (1996): 413–415. Montacute *Cal. Reg. of Simon de Montacute Bishop of Worcester 1334–1337* (Worcestershire Hist. Soc. n.s. 15) (1996): 298. Brault *Rolls of Arms Edward I* 2 (1997): 212 (arms of John de Haudlo: Argent, a lion rampant azure goutté or) (author identifies Richard de Haudlo, father of John de Haudlo [died 1346], as a son of Nicholas de Hadlow, of Street, Kent), 266–267. *VCH Somerset* 7 (1999): 59–63. *Trans. Monumental Brass Soc.* 18 (2010): 119–132. National Archives, C 131/174/49; C 241/59/47; C 241/76/89; C 241/76/92; C 241/76/97; C 241/80/45; C 241/98/8; C 241/101/151; C 241/104/121; C 241/104/123; C 241/119/158; SC 8/52/2570 (petition dated c.1330 by John de Haudlo and Maud his wife to the king and council who state that Philip Burnell and Maud his wife were seised of certain tenements which were given in free marriage by Richard Fitz Alan, Earl of Arundel, Maud's brother; which tenements Maud leased to Edmund Earl of Arundel after Philip's death. Because they ought to descend to Maud de Haudlo, daughter of Maud and Philip, John and Maud brought a writ of formedon against Edmund after Maud's death, but Edmund died while it was being pleaded. The tenements came into the king's hand, and he gave them to Roger de Mortemer, formerly Earl of March. They are now again in the king's hand through his forfeiture, and John and Maud ask him to consider their right, and do justice to them. Endorsement: The heir of the Earl of Arundel is restored to his lands, because of which they are to be at common law.) (available at www.catalogue.nationalarchives.gov.uk/search.asp).

Child of Maud Burnell, by John Lovel:

i. **JOHN LOVEL**, Knt., 3rd Lord Lovel, married **ISABEL** _____ [see LOVEL 12].

Children of Maud Burnell, by John de Haudlo, Knt.:

i. **THOMAS BURNELL** (or **DE HAUDLO**), of Great Cheverell, Wiltshire, married **JOAN DE BERKELEY** [see COBHAM 8].

ii. **NICHOLAS BURNELL**, Knt. [see next].

11. NICHOLAS BURNELL (or **DE HAUDLO**), Knt., of Holgate, Acton Burnell, and Condover, Shropshire, East and West Ham (in East Ham) and Great Holland, Essex, Little Rissington, Gloucestershire, Letchworth, Hertfordshire, Billingford, Norfolk, Ham (in Kingston-upon-Thames) and Hatcham, Surrey, Great Cheverell and Fenny Sutton (in Sutton Veny), Wiltshire, Kidderminster Burnell, Worcestershire, etc., younger son by father's 2nd marriage, born about 1323 (aged 23 in 1346). He succeeded to his mother's inheritance and assumed her surname. He married **MARY** _____. They had one son, Hugh, K.G. [2nd Lord Burnell]. His wife, Mary, was living 12 July 1339. He served in the wars in France. In 1346 Nicholas son of John de Haudlo sued William de Gravele in respect of waste in gardens in Acton Burnell, Shropshire, which he held for the life of Thomas Oseberne. He was summoned to Parliament from 25 Nov. 1350 to 7 Jan. 1382/3, by writs directed *Nicholao Burnell*, whereby he is held to have become Lord Burnell. He presented to the churches of Haselbech, Northamptonshire, 1358, 1360, 1363, 1365, 1375, Rollright, Oxfordshire, 1366, Great Holland, Essex, 1367, 1369, 1371, Acton Burnell, Shropshire, 1369, 1375, Pitchford, Shropshire, 1380, and Smethcott, Shropshire, 1381, and to the free chapel of Acton Pigot (in Worthen), Shropshire, 1379. SIR NICHOLAS BURNELL, 1st Lord Burnell, died 19 Jan. 1382/3, and was buried at Acton Burnell, Shropshire.

Hasted *Hist. & Top. Survey of Kent* 2 (1797): 184–203. Bridges *Hist. & Antiqs. of Northamptonshire* 2 (1791): 37. Banks *Baronies in Fee* 1 (1844): 243 (sub Handlo). Lipscomb *Hist. & Antiqs. of Buckingham* 1 (1847): 66. Eyton *Antiqs. of Shropshire* 6 (1858): 134 (chart). Burke *Gen. Hist. of the Dormant, Abeyant, Forfeited & Extinct Peerages* (1866): 260 (sub Handlo). Burke *Dormant, Abeyant, Forfeited & Extinct Peerages* (1883): 93–94 (sub Burnell). Tresswell & Vincent *Vis. of Shropshire 1623, 1569 & 1584* 1 (H.S.P. 28) (1889): 92–93 (1623 Vis.) (Burnell ped.: "Nicholas Burnell baron of Holgate [brass in Acton Burnell Church 1360]."). Wrottesley *Staffordshire Suits: Plea Rolls* (Colls. Hist. Staffs. 14) (1893): 83, 139–140. *Trans. Shropshire Arch. & Nat. Hist. Soc.* 2nd Ser. 6 (1894): 196–201. Amphlett *Lay Subsidy Roll 1332–3* (Worcestershire Hist. Soc. 6(3)) (1899): 4, 5. *Ancestor* 8 (1904): 167–185. Colls. Hist. Staffs. n.s. 10(2) (1907): 198, 201, 206, 210, 211–213. *Year Books of Edward III: Year XX (1st part)* 14 (Rolls Ser. 31b) (1908): 342–346. VCH *Surrey* 3 (1911): 505; 4 (1912): 42–43, 87. *C.P.* 2 (1912): 435 (sub Burnell). VCH *Hertford* 3 (1912): 118–124. *Cal. IPM* 8 (1913): 488–496. VCH *Worcester* 3 (1913): 161. *C.F.R.* 9 (1926): 374. Sudbury *Reg. Simonis de Sudbiria Diocesis Londoniensis 1362–1375* 1 (Canterbury & York Soc. 34) (1927): 255, 268, 277. Veale *Great Red Book of Bristol* 1 (Bristol Rec. Soc. 2) (1931): 80. *Trans. Shropshire Arch. & Nat. Hist. Soc.* 47 (1933–34): 49–53. Stokes et al. *Warwickshire Feet of Fines* 2 (Dugdale Soc. 15) (1939): 181–182. VCH *Warwick* 3 (1945): 52–53. St. George et al. *Wiltshire Vis. Peds. 1623, 1628* (H.S.P. 105-6) (1954): 89–90 (Hungerford ped.: "Nicholas Burnell miles = [left blank]"). VCH *Wiltshire* 8 (1965): 61–74; 10 (1975): 42–43. VCH *Essex* 4 (1973): 10–11. *Trans. Monumental Brass Soc.* 18 (2010): 119–132.

12. HUGH BURNELL, K.G., 2nd Lord Burnell, of Holgate and Acton Burnell, Shropshire, East and West Ham (in East Ham), Essex, Billingford and Thurning, Norfolk, Rollright, Oxfordshire, Compton Dando, Somerset, Ham (in Kingston-upon-Thames), Hatcham, and Rotherhithe, Surrey, Bidford, Warwickshire, Great Cheverell, Wiltshire, Kidderminster Burnell and Upton Snodsbury, Worcestershire, etc., Governor of Bridgnorth, Cefnllys, Dolforwyn, and Montgomery Castles, Trier of Petitions in Parliament, 1407, 1411, 1413, and, in right of his 2nd wife, of Weoley, Worcestershire, Woughton, Buckinghamshire, Cantley and Upton, Norfolk, Great Bradley, Suffolk, etc., son and heir, born about 1347 (aged 36 in 1383). He married (1st) before 1370 **ELIZABETH** _____. They had one son, Edward, Knt. His wife, Elizabeth, was living in 1370. He was summoned to Parliament from 20 August 1383. He served under the Duke of Lancaster in Scotland in 1383. In 1385–6 he conveyed the manor of Kidderminster Burnell, Worcestershire to John Beauchamp, Knt., of Holt, Worcestershire. He married (2nd) before 21 April 1386 **JOYCE BOTETOURT**, *suo jure* Lady Botetourt, daughter of John Botetourt, of Little Linford and Woughton, Buckinghamshire, by Maud, daughter of John de Grey, K.G., 1st Lord Grey of Rotherfield [see BOTETOURT 10.i for her ancestry]. She was born about 1364 (aged 22 in 1386). They had no issue. She was heiress before 1386 to her brother, John Botetourt. In 1386 he made a settlement of Woughton, Buckinghamshire on his wife, Joyce's step-father, Thomas Harcourt, Knt. He was excluded from court in Jan. 1388 by order of the Lords Appellant. On the king's recovering his power, however, he was restored to favor, and granted a sixpence per diem for life in recompense of his losses and services. He presented to the churches of Haselbech, Northamptonshire, 1394, 1397, Sutton Veny, Wiltshire, 1398, West Chiltington, Sussex, 1401, 1406, 1415, Wick Rissington, Gloucestershire, 1403, Bagthorpe, Norfolk, 1404, and Great Bradley, Suffolk, 1404. He was one of lords who received the abdication of King Richard II in the Tower of London in 1399. He subsequently became a zealous and able adherent of King Henry IV. In 1395 his wife, Joyce's cousin, Hugh la Zouche, Knt., 3rd Lord Zouche, and his wife, Joan, settled on Hugh Burnell and Joyce his wife the reversion of the manors of Ashby de la Zouch, Leicestershire, Fulbourn and Swavesey, Cambridgeshire, and Treve (or River) (in Tillington) and Nutbourn (in Pulborough), Sussex, together with the advowsons of the priory and chapel of Swavesey, Cambridgeshire, and the church of West Chiltington, and the chapel of Trever (or River), Sussex; which properties Hugh and Joyce subsequently obtained on the death of Hugh la Zouche, Knt., in 1399. In 1400 he furnished a ship at his own expense for the defense of the realm. His wife, Joyce, died 1 Jan. 1406/7, and was buried at Hales Abbey, Shropshire. He married (3rd) after 1 July 1407 **JOAN DEVEREUX**, widow of Walter Fitz Walter, Knt., 4th Lord Fitz Walter (died at Venice 16 May 1406) [see FITZ WALTER 12], and daughter of John Devereux, K.G., 1st Lord Devereux, of Lyonshall, Dorstone, and Whitechurch Maund (in Bodenham), Herefordshire, and Dinton, Buckinghamshire, Seneschal of Rochelle, Captain of Calais, Steward of the King's Household, Constable of Dover Castle, Warden of the Cinque Ports, by Margaret, daughter of John de Vere, Knt., 7th Earl of Oxford [see LOVAINE 6 for her ancestry]. She was born about 1380 (aged 17 in 1397). They had no issue. He was appointed to treat with French representatives in 1408. In 1408–9 he conveyed the manors of Trever (or River) (in Tillington), Nutbourn (in Pulborough), and West Chiltington, together with the advowson of the church of West Chiltington, Sussex, to trustees. His wife, Joan, died 10 (or 11) May 1409, and was buried at Dunmow Priory, Essex. He received a papal indult to choose a confessor in 1412. SIR HUGH BURNELL, 2nd Lord Burnell, died 27 Nov. 1420. He left a will dated 2 October 1417, requesting burial in the choir of Halesowen Abbey near the body of Joyce his 2nd wife.

Blomefield *Essay towards a Top. Hist. of Norfolk* 4 (1775): 16; 11 (1810): 133. Nash *Colls. for the Hist. of Worcestershire* 1 (1781): 525. Bridges *Hist. & Antiqs. of Northamptonshire* 2 (1791): 37. Hasted *Hist. & Top. Survey of Kent* 2 (1797): 184–203. Nichols *Hist. & Antiqs. of Leicester* 3(2) (1804): 635 (Zouch ped.). *Antiqs. & Top. Cabinet* 1 (1807) (sub Hales Owen Abbey), not paginated. Blore *Hist. & Antiqs. of Rutland* 1(2) (1811): 90, 209 (Botetourt peds.). Nicolas *Controversy between Scrope & Grosvenor* 2 (1832): 456–460 (biog. of Hugh Burnell). Beltz *Mems. of the Order of the Garter* (1841): clvi. Grazebrook *Heraldry of Worcestershire* 1 (1873): 66–67. Elwes *Hist. of the Castles, Mansions & Manors of Western Sussex* (1876): 238. Burke *Dormant, Abeyant, Forfeited & Extinct Peerages* (1883): 63–64 (sub Botetourt), 93–94 (sub Burnell). Mason *Hist. of Norfolk* 5 (1885): 139. Tresswell & Vincent *Vis. of Shropshire 1623, 1569 & 1584* 1 (H.S.P. 28) (1889): 92–93 (1623 Vis.) (Burnell ped.: "Hugh Burnell Baro. of Holgate died Aº 5 H. 5. = [left blank]."). Hill *Hist. of Upton, Norfolk* (1891): following 8 (Botetourt ped.), 9–10. Wrottesley *Staffordshire Suits: Plea Rolls* (Colls. Hist. Staffs. 13) (1892): 197–198; (Colls. Hist. Staffs. 15) (1894): 10, 12; (Colls. Hist. Staffs. 17) (1896): 78–79. *Desc. Cat. Ancient Deeds* 2 (1894): 515–516 (C.2398); 3 (1900): 383–399 (Hugh Burnell, Knt., styled "cousin" by Richard Talbot, lord of Irchenefeld and Blakemere, in grant dated 1394). *Trans. Shropshire Arch. & Nat. Hist. Soc.* 2nd Ser. 6 (1894): 196–201. Wylie *Hist. of England under Henry IV* 2 (1894): 427. *Genealogist* n.s. 14 (1897): 21; n.s. 15 (1898): 97; n.s. 19 (1903): 103–104. Bull *Hist. of Newport Pagnell* (1900): 27–44. *Ancestor* 8 (1904): 167–185. *Papal Regs.: Letters* 6 (1904): 386. Wrottesley *Peds. from the Plea Rolls* (1905): 177, 235, 418. Rede *Reg. of Robert Rede Bishop of Chichester* 2 (Sussex Rec. Soc. 11) (1910): 262, 290. VCH *Surrey* 3 (1911): 505; 4 (1912): 42–43, 87. *C.P.* 2 (1912): 235 (sub Botetourt), 435–436 (sub Burnell) (incorrectly identifies 1st wife as Philippe de la Pole, a ficticious person); 4 (1916): 301–302 (sub Devereux), 744–745 (Appendix H); 5 (1926): 480–482 (sub FitzWalter); 12(2) (1959): 962–963 (sub Zouche). VCH *Hertford* 3 (1912): 118–124. VCH *Worcester* 3 (1913): 161; 4 (1924): 209. Salzman *Feet of Fines Rel. Sussex* 3 (Sussex Rec. Soc. 23) (1916): 205, 222. VCH *Buckingham* 4 (1927): 515–519. *Report on the MSS of Reginald Rawdon Hastings, Esq.* 1 (Hist. MSS Comm. 78) (1928): 280–283. *Feet of Fines for Essex* 3 (1929–49): 268. *Trans. Shropshire Arch. & Nat. Hist. Soc.* 47 (1933–34): 49–53. *Cal. Inqs. Misc.* 3 (1937): 285. Chichele *Reg. of Henry Chichele* 2 (Canterbury & York Soc. 42) (1937): 644 (biog. of Hugh Burnell, kt.); 3 (Canterbury & York Soc. 46) (1945): 452. VCH *Warwick* 3 (1945): 52–53. Watkin *Inv. of Church Goods temp. Edward III* (Norfolk Rec. Soc. 19(2)) (1948): 180. St.

George et al. *Wiltshire Vis. Peds. 1623, 1628* (H.S.P. 105-6) (1954): 89–90 (Hungerford ped.: "Hugh Burnell miles fil: et heres = [left blank]"). VCH *Wiltshire* 8 (1965): 61–74; 10 (1975): 42–43. *Ancient Deeds — Ser. B* 1 (List & Index Soc. 95) (1973): 46 (B.4377). VCH *Essex* 4 (1973): 10–11. *Cal. IPM* 16 (1974): 77–79. Clifford *Reg. of Richard Clifford Bp. of Worcester* (1976): 121. Ellis *Cat. Seals in the P.R.O.* 1 (1978): 13 (seal of Hugh Burnell, knight, lord Burnell dated 1416 — Hung from a twin bush, between lunettes of tracery, a shield of arms: quarterly, 1 and 4, a lion rampant [BURNELL], 2 and 3, a saltire engrailed [BOTETOURT]. Legend: SIGILLUM.HV[GONIS] BVRNELL.). *Ancient Deeds — Ser. E* (List & Index Soc. 181) (1981): 171, 184. Hector *Westminster Chron. 1381–1394* (1982): 230–231. VCH *Cambridge* 9 (1989): 381–386. Somerset *Recs. of Early English Drama: Shropshire* 2 (1994): 698. *Cal. IPM* 20 (1995): 163. National Archives, SC 8/183/9122 (available at www.catalogue.nationalarchives.gov.uk/search.asp).

13. EDWARD BURNELL, Knt., of Billingford, East Riston and Thurning, Norfolk, East and West Ham (in East Ham) and Great Holland, Essex, etc., son and heir apparent by his father's 1st marriage. He married (1st) before 1396 **ALINE LE STRANGE**, presumably daughter of John le Strange, Knt., 6th Lord Strange of Knockin, by Maud, daughter of John de Mohun, K.G., 2nd Lord Mohun [see STRANGE 9 for her ancestry]. They had three daughters, Joyce (wife of Thomas Erdington, Knt., 5th Lord Erdington), Katherine, and Margery (wife of Edmund Hungerford, Knt.). He married (2nd) before 18 June 1415 (date of settlement) **ELIZABETH DE LA POLE** [see DE LA POLE 9.iv], daughter of Michael de la Pole, Knt., 2nd Earl of Suffolk, by Katherine, daughter of Hugh de Stafford, K.G., 2nd Earl of Stafford [see DE LA POLE 9 for her ancestry]. They had no issue. SIR EDWARD BURNELL died 23 Sept. 1415 of the flux in camp before the Siege of Harfleur. His widow, Elizabeth, is named in a roll of the receiver of her late father, Michael de la Pole the elder, and her brother, Michael the younger, dated 1416–7, she then being assigned £13 6s. 8d. yearly for her maintenance. Elizabeth was a legatee in the 1419 will of Elizabeth Elmham. She married (2nd) on or about 30 June 1422 (date of property settlement) (as his 1st wife) **THOMAS KERDESTON**, Knt., of Claxton, Kerdeston, Bircham Newton (in Bircham), East Ruston, and Syderstone, Norfolk, Bulchamp, Henham, and Stratford, Suffolk, etc., son and heir of Leonard Kerdeston, Knt., of Claxton and Kerdeston, Norfolk, by his wife, Margaret, granddaughter of Hugh de Hastings, Knt. [see GANT 8.i.a for his ancestry]. They had one son, William, and one daughter, Margaret (or Marguerite) (wife of Jean de Foix, K.G., Vicomte of Châtillon, Earl of Kendal, Captal de Buch) [see DE LA POLE 9.iv.a]). In 1422 he presented to the church of Reepham, Norfolk. In the period, 1424–6, he and his wife, Elizabeth, made a settlement of the manors of Kerdeston, Claxton, Heloughton, Bircham Newton, Ruston, and Syderstone, Norfolk. In 1427 he and his wife, presented to the church of Reepham, Norfolk. His wife, Elizabeth, died 3 April 1440. In 1442 he quitclaimed his right in the manors of Bulchamp and Henham, Suffolk to William de la Pole, Duke of Suffolk, and Alice his wife. Thomas married (2nd) before 5 May 1443 **PHILIPPE TRUSSELL**, widow of Alexander Bosom (or Bosun, Bozoun), Esq. (living 20 October 1440), of Flore, Northamptonshire, Olney, Buckinghamshire, etc., and daughter and heiress of John Trussell, Knt., of Flore and Gayton, Northamptonshire, Theddingworth, Leicestershire, etc., Knight of the Shire of Northamptonshire [see DESPENSER 12.ii], by his 2nd wife, Margaret (possibly Ardern). They had one daughter, Elizabeth (wife of Terry Robsart, Knt.). Sometime in the period, 1440–3, he and his wife, Philippe, sued John Mauntell, Esq., regarding a place called the Greyhound (Girhound) in Northampton, Northamptonshire. In 1443 he and his wife, Philippe, conveyed the manor of Bosoms (in Stagsden), together with 8 messuages, lands, and 5 marks of rent in Stagsden, Turvey, Bromham, Felmersham, and Radwell (in Felmersham), Bedfordshire to John Harpur and William Lowe. In 1445 he and his wife, Philippe, conveyed the manor of Gayton, Northamptonshire, together with the advowson of the churches of Gayton and Creaton, Northamptonshire to James Swetenham, Esq. for 300 marks of silver. In 1445–6 he and his wife, Philippe, made settlements of the manors of Kerdeston, Claxton, East Ruston, Heloughton, Bircham Newton (in Bircham), Swanton Novers, and Syderstone, Norfolk, and Bulchamp and Henham, Suffolk. SIR THOMAS KERDESTON died 20 July 1446, and was buried at Norwich, Norfolk. He left a will dated 1 July

1446. In the period, 1446–54, Thomas Bernere, kinsman of Thomas Kerdeston, Knt. sued Philippe, late the wife and executrix of the said Thomas Kerdeston, in Chancery regarding a gown and two horses promised by the deceased. In 1452 his widow, Philippe, presented to the church of Reepham, Norfolk. The same year she conveyed 10 messuages, lands, and 52*s.* of rent in Theddingworth and Carlton Curlieu, Leicestershire to John Harpur, of Rushall. Philippe died before Michaelmas term 1454 (date of lawsuit).

> Hasted *Hist. & Top. Survey of Kent* 2 (1797): 184–203. Blomefield *Essay towards a Top. Hist. of Norfolk* 8 (1808): 243, 245; 10 (1809): 111–115. Nicolas *Controversy between Scrope & Grosvenor* 2 (1832): 456–460 (Edward Burnell's 1st wife identified as "Alice, daughter of Lord Strange," cites Dugdale's *Baronage of England* 1 (1675): 222). Nicolas *Treatise on the Law of Adulterine Bastardy* (1836): 552–553. Beltz *Mems. of the Order of the Garter* (1841): clx. Banks *Baronies in Fee* 1 (1844): 269–271 (sub Kerdeston). Page *Supp. to Suffolk Traveller* (1844): 196–197. Suckling *Hist. & Antiqs. of the County of Suffolk* 2 (1847): 190–192. Burke *Gen. Hist. of the Dormant, Abeyant, Forfeited & Extinct Peerages* (1866): 260 (sub Handlo). Candler & Candler *Candler's Suffolk & Essex Peds.* 1 (1868): 120–121 (De la Pole ped. dated c.1660: "Phillip [de la Pole] wife to the Lord Burnell"). Burke *Dormant, Abeyant, Forfeited & Extinct Peerages* (1883): 93–94 (sub Burnell) (Edward's wife identified as "Alice, daughter of Thomas, Lord Strange"). Rye *Short Cal. Feet of Fines for Norfolk* 2 (1886): 408, 423. Bull *Hist. of Newport Pagnell* (1900): 27–44. *Desc. Cat. Ancient Deeds* 3 (1900): 455–456. Rye *Cal. Feet of Fines for Suffolk* (1900): 290, 302. Wrottesley *Staffordshire Suits: Plea Rolls* (Colls. Hist. Staffs. n.s. 4) (1901): 100–101. *List of Early Chancery Procs.* 1 (PRO Lists and Indexes 12) (1901): 87, 94. *Genealogist* n.s. 18 (1902): 187–188; n.s. 19 (1903): 108. *Ancestor* 8 (1904): 167–185. Wrottesley *Peds. from the Plea Rolls* (1905): 413, 422–423. *Norfolk Antiq. Misc.* 2nd Ser. 1 (1906): 89. Copinger *Manors of Suffolk* 2 (1908): 29–31, 80–81. VCH *Surrey* 4 (1912): 42–43. *C.P.* 2 (1912): 435–436 (sub Burnell); 5 (1926): 89–90 (sub Erdington), 484–485 (sub FitzWalter). VCH *Bedford* 3 (1912): 96–100. *Feet of Fines for Essex* 3 (1929–49): 268. *Trans. Shropshire Arch. & Nat. Hist. Soc.* 47 (1933–34): 49–53. *C.C.R. 1435–1441* (1937): 428. *C.C.R. 1441–1447* (1937): 55, 57–58, 119–120, 140, 270–271, 441, 443. St. George et al. *Wiltshire Vis. Peds. 1623, 1628* (H.S.P. 105-6) (1954): 89–90 (Hungerford ped.: "Edw Burnell miles ob: ante Patrem fil et haer Dni Burnell interfectus apud Agincourt = Aliena filia D[omi]ni Strange"). VCH *Leicester* 5 (1964): 312–321. VCH *Shropshire* 8 (1968): 7. VCH *Essex* 4 (1973): 10–11. *Ancient Deeds — Ser. B* 3 (List & Index Soc. 113) (1975): B.12779. *TG* 6 (1985): 160–165. *Genealogists' Mag.* 22 (1988): 373–377. *Cal. IPM* 20 (1995): 163. Ward *Women of the English Nobility & Gentry 1066–1500* (1995): 75–76 (Lady Elizabeth Burnell identified as daughter of Sir Michael de la Pole, late Earl of Suffolk in contemporary record dated 1416–17). Farnham *Leicestershire Medieval Village Notes, Theddingworth–Upton* [FHL 804160]. National Archives, C 1/9/16; C 1/11/87; C 1/11/139; C 1/11/263; C 1/16/248; C 1/29/67; E 210/1020; E 210/10861; E 212/38 (available at www.cataloguenationalarchives.gov.uk/search.asp). National Archives, CP 25/1/6/80, #25; CP 25/1/126/77, #78; CP 25/1/179/95, #116 [see abstract of fines at http://www.medievalgenealogy.org.uk/index.html]. British Library, Kerdeston Hunting Book dated c.1440–6 (includes a miniature featuring portraits of Thomas Kerdeston and his 2nd wife, Philippe, and their respective coats of arms; Thomas' arms: Gules a saltire engrailed argent [KERDESTON]; Philippe's arms: Argent a cross fleury gules [TRUSSELL], quartering Argent on a bend azure three mullets pierced or [COKESEY]; see www.invaluable.com/auction-lot/leaves-from-the-kerdeston-hunting-book,-in-englis-1-c-rc1cssqbmf).

14. KATHERINE BURNELL, 2nd daughter and co-heiress, born about 1405–6 (aged 9 in 1416 and aged 14 in 1420). She was contracted to marry about 22 June 1416 (date of settlement) **JOHN TALBOT**, afterwards 2nd Earl of Shrewsbury [see TALBOT 15]. This marriage contract was voided or annulled. Katherine subsequently married before 8 Dec. 1420 (date of conveyance) (as his 2nd wife) **JOHN RADCLIFFE**, K.G., in right of his 1st wife, of Attleborough, Norfolk, Foxton and Newnham, Cambridgeshire, etc., and, in right of his 2nd wife, of Billingford, East Ruston, and Thurning, Norfolk, and Holgate, Acton Burnell, Onibury, etc., Shropshire, King's knight, Knight of the Shire for Norfolk, 2nd Baron of the Exchequer of Ireland, joint Chief Butler of Ireland, Bailli of Évreux, Constable of Bordeaux, Captain of Fronsac, Seneschal of Aquitaine, Chamberlain of North Wales, Deputy Lieutenant of Calais, younger son of James Radcliffe, of Radcliffe, Lancashire. They had one son, John, Esq. He married (1st) perhaps in 1405 **CECILY MORTIMER**, widow of John Herling, Knt. (died before 1 July 1403), and daughter and co-heiress of Thomas Mortimer, Knt., of Attleborough, Norfolk and Newnham, Cambridgeshire, by Mary, daughter of Nicholas Park. John and his 1st wife, Cecily, had one son, John, who died young. In the period, 1406–7, or 1417–24, John Radcliffe, Knt., then Constable of Bordeaux, was sued in Chancery by Giles de Taville, merchant, of Algarbe regarding wines captured in the barge St. Katerine of Spain, and sold at

Fowey, Cornwall. In 1420 William Lovel, Lord Lovel, Burnel, and Holand conveyed the manor of Lovels (in Southmere and Docking), Norfolk to John and his 2nd wife, Katherine. In 1435 he was sent on an embassy to Arras to treat for peace between England and France. By charters dated 1439 and 1440, William Lovel likewise conveyed the manors of Billingford, Riston, Southmere and Docking, and Thurning, Norfolk to John and his wife, Katherine. SIR JOHN RADCLIFFE died testate 26 Feb. (or 4 March) 1440/1, and was buried at Attleborough, Norfolk. In 1444–5 his executors made part payment of a royal debt to the collectors of Customs at Bridgwater. His widow, Katherine, married (2nd) before 1451 (date of presentment) **JOHN FERRERS**. He was appointed a commissioner of array in Norfolk in 1450. In 1451 he and his wife, Katherine, presented to the church of Billingford, Norfolk. Katherine died 13 October 1452, and was buried at Attleborough, Norfolk.

> Blomefield *Essay towards a Top. Hist. of Norfolk* 1 (1739): 215 (Herling ped.); 5 (1775): 1303. Beltz *Mems. of the Order of the Garter* (1841): clix. Barrett *Mems. of Attleborough* (1848): 189–191 (Ratcliffe ped.). Burke *Gen. Hist. of the Dormant, Abeyant, Forfeited & Extinct Peerages* (1866): 260 (sub Handlo). Bayne *Royal Ill. Hist. of Eastern England* (1873): 47. Burke *Dormant, Abeyant, Forfeited & Extinct Peerages* (1883): 93–94 (sub Burnell). Tresswell & Vincent *Vis. of Shropshire 1623, 1569 & 1584* 1 (H.S.P. 28) (1889): 92–93 (1623 Vis.) (Burnell ped.: "Katherine [Burnell] da. & heir. = Sir John Ratcliffe Kn^t."). *Desc. Cat. Ancient Deeds* 2 (1894): 515–516 (C.2398). Wrottesley *Staffordshire Suits: Plea Rolls* (Colls. Hist. Staffs. 17) (1896): 112–113, 124. Bull *Hist. of Newport Pagnell* (1900): 27–44. *Ancestor* 8 (1904): 167–201. Copinger *Manors of Suffolk* 1 (1905): 193–195 ("Sir John [Radcliffe] was a distinguished soldier. He was Governor of Trounsak [Fronsac] in Aguitaine and had a thousand marks per annum allowed him for his guard thereof. In the reign of Hen. VI. he was retained by that monarch as seneschal of that duchy, having an assignation of four shillings per day for his own salary and twenty marks a piece per annum for two hundred archers. He was killed at Ferrybridge in 1461."). *C.P.R. 1446–1452* (1909): 389–390. VCH *Hertford* 3 (1912): 118–124. *C.P.* 5 (1926): 89–90 (sub Erdington), 484–485 (sub FitzWalter); 9 (1936): 250 (sub Mortimer); 11 (1949): 704, footnote e (sub Shrewsbury). *Trans. Shropshire Arch. & Nat. Hist. Soc.* 47 (1933–34): 49–53. *C.C.R. 1435–1441* (1937): 416–417, 423–424. *C.C.R. 1441–1447* (1937): 10–11. VCH *Shropshire* 8 (1968): 7. Vale *English Gascony 1399–1453* (1970). *Ancient Deeds — Ser. B* 2 (List & Index Soc. 101) (1974): B.5229. Roskell *Parl. & Politics in Late Medieval England* 3 (1983): 96–97. Richmond *Paston Fam. in the 15th Cent.* (1990): 124 (cites biog. of Sir John Radcliff in Trevor John, *Parl. Representation of Norfolk & Suffolk 1377–1422* (unpublished MA thesis, Nottingham, 1959): 487–511). Roskell *House of Commons 1386–1421* 4 (1992): 155–159 (biog. of Sir John Radcliffe: "… one of the most important military captains of his day"). *Cal. IPM* 20 (1995): 163. National Archives, C 1/4/29; E 122/25/31; SC 8/331/15690 (available at www.catalogue.nationalarchives.gov.uk/search.asp).

15. JOHN RADCLIFFE, Esq., of Attleborough, Norfolk, son and heir by his father's 2nd marriage, born about 1430 (aged 23 in 1453). He married before 27 October 1444 **ELIZABETH FITZ WALTER**, daughter and heiress of Walter Fitz Walter, Knt., 5th Lord Fitz Walter, by Elizabeth, daughter of John Chidiock, Knt. [see FITZ WALTER 13 for her ancestry]. She was born at Henham, Essex 28 July 1430, and baptized there (aged 1-½ in 1432). They had one son, John, Knt. [6th Lord Fitz Walter]. He was granted livery of his wife's lands 28 Jan. 1445, he having proved her age. He presented to the church of Diss, Norfolk in 1452. JOHN RADCLIFFE, Esq., was slain in a skirmish at Ferrybridge on the eve of the Battle of Towton 28 March 1461. His widow, Elizabeth, presented to the church of Diss, Norfolk in 1465. She married (2nd) about 15 March 1466/7 (as his 1st wife) **JOHN DINHAM** (or **DYNHAM**), K.G., Lord Dinham, Lord High Treasurer, 1486–1501 (died 28 Jan. 1500/1) [see DINHAM 8.i]. They had no issue. He was summoned to Parliament from 28 Feb. 1466/7 to 16 Jan. 1496/7, by writs directed *Johanni Dynham de Care Dynham*, whereby he is held to have become Lord Dinham. Elizabeth, Lady Fitz Walter, died before 22 August 1485.

> Blomefield *Essay towards a Top. Hist. of Norfolk* 1 (1739): 2–8, 11, 347–352. Dugdale *Monasticon Anglicanum* 6(1) (1830): 148. Beltz *Mems. of the Order of the Garter* (1841): clxvii. Barrett *Mems. of Attleborough* (1848): 189–191 (Ratcliffe ped.). Fenn & Ramsay *Paston Letters* (1859): 79 (letter of Dame Alice Ogard (née Lovel) dated 1456 addressed to her cousin, John Paston, Esq., which letter also mentions another of her cousins, John Radcliff, of Attleborough, Norfolk). Whitaker *Hist. of Original Parish of Whalley* 2(2) (1876): chart foll. 292. Tresswell & Vincent *Vis. of Shropshire 1623, 1569 & 1584* 1 (H.S.P. 28) (1889): 92–93 (1623 Vis.) (Burnell ped.: "Sir John Ratcliffe Kn^t. = Eliz. da. & sole heir of Walter Lord Fitzwalter."). *Genealogist* n.s. 23 (1907): 242. VCH *Hertford* 3 (1912): 25–28, 244–247. *C.P.* 4 (1916): 378–380 (sub Dinham); 5 (1926): 484–486 (sub FitzWalter). *C.C.R. 1441–1447* (1937): 247. Davis *Paston Letters & Papers of the*

15th *Cent.* 2 (1976): 226. Roskell *House of Commons 1386–1421* 4 (1992): 155–159 (biog. of Sir John Radcliffe). Baker *Rpts. of Cases by John Caryll* 1 (Selden Soc. 115) (1999): 57–58. *Cal. IPM* 23 (2004): 373–381. National Archives, E 328/136 (available at www.catalogue.nationalarchives.gov.uk/search.asp).

16. JOHN RADCLIFFE, Knt., 6th Lord Fitz Walter, of Attleborough, Norfolk, Guilford, Surrey, London and Calais, Knight of the Shire for Norfolk, 1478, (?1483, ?1484), Steward of the King's Household, 1485–7, Steward of the lands of the Duchy of Lancaster in Norfolk and Suffolk, 1485, joint High Steward of England, 1487, joint Justice of the Forest south of Trent, 1486–93, Master Porter of Calais, son and heir, born 1 Jan. 1451/2. In 1470 William Hastings, Knt., presented to the church of Attleborough Major Part, Norfolk, during the minority of John, son and heir of John Radcliffe, deceased. John married about 6 July 1475 (date of settlement) **MARGARET WHETHILL**, widow of Thomas Walden, Gent. (will proved 25 June 1474), of London, Walden, Essex, and Deptford, Kent, Citizen of London, Merchant of the Staple of Calais, and daughter of Richard Whethill, Esq., of Earl's Barton and Sywell, Northamptonshire, London, Calais, and Guines, Merchant of the Staple of Calais, Mayor of Calais, Lieutenant of the Castle of Guines, by his wife, Joan. They had one son, Robert, K.G., K.B. [7th Lord Fitz Walter], and five daughters, Mary (wife of Edward Darrell, Knt.), Bridget, Ursula, Jane (nun), and Anne (wife of Walter Hobart, Knt.). He was summoned to Parliament from 15 Sept. 1485 to 12 August 1495 by writs directed *Johanni Radclyff'*, or *Ratclyff'*, *de FitzWauter*. He was admitted a member of Lincoln's Inn in 1489. He presented to the church of Diss, Norfolk in 1490. SIR JOHN RADCLIFFE, 6th Lord Fitz Walter, was attainted of high treason in October 1495 as a confederate of Perkin Warbeck [see note in YORK 13.vi]. His life was spared and he was sent a prisoner to Guines. After an unsuccessful prison break, he was beheaded at Calais about 24 Nov. 1496. His attainder was reversed in 1504, for the benefit of his son and heir, Robert, afterwards Earl of Sussex. In 1505 there were five fines levied by which his lands were conveyed to Richard, Bishop of Winchester, Thomas Lovell, Knt., and other trustees, who settled the whole on his son, Robert, excepting the manors of Southmere, Docking, Billingford, and East Ruston, Norfolk, which were settled on John's widow, Margaret, for life. In 1516 his widow, Margaret, presented her nephew, George Poley, son of her sister, Agnes Whetehill, as rector of Attleborough Major Part, Norfolk. In 1517 she was admitted to the fraternity of St. Nicholas in London. Margaret, Lady Fitz Walter, was living 6 July 1518 (date of indenture).

Norfolk (England) Fams. MS Misc. Peds. (Early 17th Cent. Hobart Ped.) [FHL Microfilm 599678]. Blomefield *Essay towards a Top. Hist. of Norfolk* 1 (1739): 2–8, 11, 343–352. Bentley *Excerpta Historica* (1833): 111. Barrett *Mems. of Attleborough* (1848): 189–191 (Ratcliffe ped.), 226. Gyll *Hist. of Wraysbury, Ankerwycke Priory & Magna Charta Island* (1862): 205 (Whethill ped.). Turner *Cal. Charters & Rolls: Bodleian Lib.* (1878): 196 (indenture of agreement dated 6 July 1518 between Robert Radclyff, lord Fytzwauter, and Margaret Radclyff, lady Fytzwauter, his mother, of the one part, and sir James Hubert kt., of the other, being a marriage settlement on the marriage of Anne Radcliffe, sister of the said lorde, to sir Walter Hubert, eldest son of the said James, before the feast of All Saints next ensuing."). Tresswell & Vincent *Vis. of Shropshire 1623, 1569 & 1584* 1 (H.S.P. 28) (1889): 92–93 (1623 Vis.) (Burnell ped.: "Sir John Ratcliff Kn[t]. Lord Fitzwalter Burnell & Egremont. = Anne da. of Sir Rich[d] Wheathill of Callais Knight."). Baildon *Recs. of Lincoln's Inn: Admissions* 1 (1896): 25. *English Hist. Rev.* 18 (1903): 112–116. *List of Early Chancery Procs.* 2 (PRO Lists and Indexes 16) (1903): 151, 153. Gairdner *Paston Letters, A.D. 1422–1509* 5 (1904): 256–257 (letter of John Paston dated 12 March 1476). Copinger *Manors of Suffolk* 1 (1905): 193–195. *Genealogist* n.s. 23 (1907): 242. *D.N.B.* 16 (1909): 571–572 (biog. of John Radcliffe). *C.P.* 5 (1926): 486–487 (sub FitzWalter) (erroneously identifies wife of John Radcliffe as Anne Whetehill, not Margaret Whetehill, and creates a ficticious 2nd wife, Margaret); 12(1) (1953): 517, footnote c (sub Sussex). Wedgwood *Hist. of Parl.* 1 (1936): 706 (biog. of John Radcliffe) (states in error that John Radcliffe "married (1) by 12 Mar. 1476, Anne Whetehill, sis. of Richard Whetehill of Calais, and (2) Margaret."). *NEHGR* 102 (1948): 5–9, 241–254 (erroneously identifies wife of John Radcliffe as Anne Whetehill "who must have died s.p. within a few years of her marriage."); 103 (1949): 5–19. Davis *Anc. of Mary Isaac* (1955): 263–272 (correctly identifies wife of John Radcliffe as Margaret Whetehill) (Whetehill arms: Per fesse, azure and or, a pale counterchanged, three lions rampant or). Davis *Paston Letters & Papers of the 15th Cent.* 2 (1976): 448, 456–457, 472 (John Paston, Knt., styled "cousin" in letters dated 1486, c.1488, and 1488–94 by John [Radcliffe], Lord Fitz Walter). Harvey *Vis. of Suffolk 1561* 1 (H.S.P. n.s. 2) (1981): 37–38 (Poley ped.). Arthurson *Perkin Warbeck Conspiracy* (1994): 88.

Baker *Rpts. of Cases by John Caryll* 1 (Selden Soc. 115) (1999): 57–58. James *Bede Roll of the Fraternity of St. Nicholas* 1 (London Rec. Soc. Pubs. 39) (2004): 257. National Archives, DL 39/2/4; DL 39/2/9; DL 39/3/31; DL 39/2/11; DL 39/2/7; E 40/4673 (available at www.catalogue.nationalarchives.gov.uk/search.asp).

17. ROBERT RADCLIFFE, K.G., K.B., 7th Lord Fitz Walter, Privy Councillor, 1526, Chamberlain of the Exchequer, 1532–42, Chief Steward of the Honor of Beaulieu, and the manor of Writtle, both in Essex, Chief Steward of the Duchy of Lancaster, Northern Parts, 1539–40, Great Chamberlain of England, 1540, 1st surviving son and heir, born about 1483 (aged 46 in 1529). He married (1st) shortly after 23 July 1505 [**LADY**] **ELIZABETH STAFFORD**, daughter of Henry (or Harry) Stafford, K.G., K.B., 2nd Duke of Buckingham, by Katherine, daughter of Richard Wydeville, K.G., 1st Earl Rivers, Constable of England, Lord High Treasurer [see STAFFORD 12 for her ancestry]. Elizabeth served as gentlewoman to Queen Elizabeth Plantagenet in 1502–3. They had three sons, Henry, K.G., K.B. [2nd Earl of Sussex], Humphrey, Knt., and George, Esq. He obtained a reversal of the attainder of his father by letters patent dated 3 Nov. 1505, and procured an Act of Parliament to the same effect in 1509. He was summoned to Parliament from 28 Nov. 1511 to 15 April 1523, by writs directed *Roberto Radclyff' de FitzWater, Chivaler*. He accompanied King Henry VIII at the Sieges of Tournai and Thérouanne in 1513. He was heir male about 1513 to his cousin, John Radcliffe, by which he inherited the manor of Peasfurlong (in Culcheth), Lancashire. He and his wife attended the king and queen at the Field of the Cloth of Gold in 1520. He served as admiral of the squadron and chief captain of the vanguard in the expedition of 1522. He was created Viscount Fitzwalter 18 June 1525, and further created Earl of Sussex 8 Dec. 1529. He presented to the churches of Hemingby, Lincolnshire, 1525, and Diss, Norfolk, 1529. His wife, Elizabeth, died before 11 May 1532. He married (2nd) between 11 May and 1 Sept. 1532 **MARGARET STANLEY**, daughter of Thomas Stanley, K.B., 2nd Earl of Derby, 3rd Lord Stanley, Lord Strange of Knockin, by Anne, daughter of Edward Hastings, K.B., 2nd Lord Hastings [see STANLEY 17 for her ancestry]. They had two daughters, Jane and Anne (wife of Thomas Wharton, Knt., 2nd Lord Wharton). His wife, Margaret, died shortly after Jan. 1533/4, and was buried at St. Laurence Pountney, London. In 1536 he proposed at the council that Henry, Duke of Richmond, should be placed before Mary in the succession to the throne. He married (3rd) 14 Jan. 1536/7 **MARY ARUNDELL**, daughter of John Arundell, K.B., of Lanherne, Cornwall, Frampton on Severn, Gloucestershire, etc., by Katherine, daughter of Thomas Grenville, Knt. [see CHIDIOCK 16 for her ancestry]. They had two sons, including John, Knt. He presented to the churches of Lexden, Essex, 1538, and Attleborough Major Part, Norfolk, 1540. He accompanied King Henry VIII to receive Anne of Cleves 3 Jan. 1539/40. SIR ROBERT RADCLIFFE, 1st Earl of Sussex, died at Chelsea 27 Nov. 1542, and was buried at St. Laurence Pountney, London, but subsequently removed to Boreham, Essex. He left a will proved 18 Feb. 1546 (P.C.C. 1 Alen). His widow, Mary, married (2nd) 19 Dec. 1545 (as 2nd wife) **HENRY** (**FITZ ALAN**), K.G., Earl of Arundel, Lord Mautravers, Deputy-General of the Town and Marches of Calais, 1540–44, Lord Chamberlain of the Household, 1545– 50, Privy Councillor, 1545, 1547–50, 1553, 1558, Lord Great Master and Steward of the Household, 1553–4, Lord President of the Council, 1553–64, Lord Steward of the Household, 1554–64, High Steward of the University of Oxford, 1555, Lieutenant-General and Captain of the Forces in England, 1557. They had no issue. His wife, Mary, died at Arundel House, Strand 20 October 1557, and was buried at St. Clement Danes, but afterwards removed to Boreham. HENRY (FITZ ALAN), Earl of Arundel, died 24 Feb. 1579/80.

Blomefield *Essay towards a Top. Hist. of Norfolk* 1 (1739): 2–8, 343–352. Brydges *Collins' Peerage of England* 3 (1812): 50–103 (sub Stanley, Earl of Derby). Baker *Hist. & Antiqs. of Northampton* 1 (1822–30): 564–565. Nicolas *Privy Purse Expenses of Elizabeth of York* (1830):41, 80, 99. Baines *Hist. of Lancaster* 4 (1836): chart facing 10 (Stanley ped.). Beltz *Mems. of the Order of the Garter* (1841): clxxii. Barrett *Mems. of Attleborough* (1848): 189–191 (Ratcliffe ped.), 226. Dugdale *Vis. of Lancaster 1664–5* 3 (Chetham Soc. 88) (1873): 280–283 (Stanley ped.: "Margaret [Stanley], = Robert Radclyffe, lord Egremont, Bottereux and Burnell, earl of Sussex."). Whitaker *Hist. of Original Parish of Whalley* 2(2) (1876): chart foll. 292. Turner *Cal. Charters & Rolls: Bodleian Lib.* (1878): 196. Doyle *Official Baronage of England* 1 (1886): 81–83 (sub Arundel); 3 (1886): 480–481 (sub Sussex). Lawson *Gen. Colls. Ill. the Hist. of Roman Catholic Fams. in England* 3 (1887): 151–152, 221–232 (Arundell Peds.). Tresswell & Vincent *Vis. of Shropshire 1623, 1569 & 1584* 1 (H.S.P. 28) (1889): 92–93 (1623 Vis.) (Burnell ped.: "Sir Robt Ratcliffe Kn^t. created Earle of Sussex by Henry VIII. 1530."). Copinger *Manors of Suffolk* 1 (1905): 193–195. *D.N.B.* 16 (1909): 578 (biog. of Robert Radcliffe: "Sussex was long in very confidential relations with Henry [VIII]"). VCH *Lancaster* 4 (1911): 156–166. Pollard *Reign of Henry VII from Contemporary Sources* 2 (1914): 17–19. *C.P.* 5 (1926): 487 (sub FitzWalter); 9 (1936): 97–99 (sub Montagu); 12(1) (1953): 517–520 (sub Sussex); 12(2) (1959): 598–600 (sub Wharton). Adams & Stephens *Select Docs. of English Constitutional Hist.* (1939): 218–220. Davis *Anc. of Mary Isaac* (1955): 271–272. Mayer & Walters *Corr. of Reginald Pole* 4 (2008): 535.

Child of Robert Radcliffe, K.G., K.B., by Margaret Stanley:

i. **JANE RADCLIFFE**, married **ANTHONY BROWNE**, K.G., K.B., 1st Viscount Montague [see TEMPLE 15].

❧ BURROUGH ❧

WILLIAM THE CONQUEROR, King of England, married **MAUD OF FLANDERS**.
HENRY I, King of England, married **MAUD OF SCOTLAND**.
MAUD OF ENGLAND, married **GEOFFREY PLANTAGENET**, Count of Anjou, Duke of Normandy.
HENRY II, King of England, by a mistress, **IDA DE TONY**.
WILLIAM LONGESPÉE, Knt., Earl of Salisbury, married **ELA OF SALISBURY**.
IDA LONGESPÉE, married **WILLIAM DE BEAUCHAMP**, Knt., of Bedford, Bedfordshire.
BEATRICE DE BEAUCHAMP, married **WILLIAM DE MUNCHENSY**, Knt., of Edwardstone, Suffolk.
WILLIAM DE MUNCHENSY, of Edwardstone, Suffolk, married **ALICE** _____.
THOMAS DE MUNCHENSY, Knt., of Edwardstone, Suffolk, married **JOYCE** _____.
THOMAS MUNCHENSY, of Edwardstone, Suffolk, married (1st) **JOAN VAUNCY**.
JOAN MUNCHENSY, married **RICHARD WALDEGRAVE**, Knt., of Smallbridge (in Bures St. Mary), Suffolk.
RICHARD WALDEGRAVE, Knt., of Edwardstone, Suffolk, married **JOAN DOREWARD**.
THOMAS WALDEGRAVE, Knt., of Smallbridge (in Bures St. Mary), Suffolk, married **ELIZABETH FRAY**.
WILLIAM WALDEGRAVE, Knt., of Smallbridge (in Bures St. Mary), Suffolk, married **MARGERY WENTWORTH** (desc. King William the Conqueror).
GEORGE WALDEGRAVE, Esq., of Smallbridge (in Bures St. Mary), Suffolk, married **ANNE DRURY** (desc. King William the Conqueror) [see WALDEGRAVE 15].

16. PHYLLIS WALDEGRAVE, married **THOMAS HIGHAM** (or **HEIGHAM**), Esq., of Higham Green (in Gazeley) and Denham, Suffolk, son of John Higham, of Higham Green (in Gazeley), Suffolk, by Mary, daughter and heiress of _____ Teringham. They had five sons, Thomas, George, Francis, Henry, and John, and two daughters, Anne (wife of Thomas Randall) and Bridget. THOMAS HIGHAM, Esq., was buried at Gazeley, Suffolk 14 Dec. 1554.

Norfolk (England) Fams. MS Misc. Peds. (Early 17th Cent. Waldgrave ped.: "George Waldgrave of Smallbridge Esqr. Eldest son to Sir Will[ia]m Waldgrave of the same placer Kn^t. (whose other sonne was Anthony Waldgrave of the ffennes) had by his wife Anne Eldest daughter to Sir Robt Drury of Hawsted Kn^t. three sonnes, Will[ia]m, George, and Edward, and two daughters, Anne, and Christian. Christian the second daughter of George [Waldgrave] Abouesaid, was Married to Higham of Higham hall in Denham, who bare him two sonnes, the Eldest having onlely two daughters coheires, the one Married to Cleere of Stokesby in Norff. the other to Lewknor.") [see FHL Microfilm 599678]. Muskett *Suffolk Manorial Fams.* 1 (1900): 311–314, 395. *NEHGR* 108 (1954): 172–178. Harvey *Vis. of Suffolk 1561* 1 (H.S.P. n.s. 2) (1981): 93–95; 2 (H.S.P. n.s. 3) (1984): 391–399.

17. BRIDGET HIGHAM, married (1st) (as his 2nd wife) **THOMAS BURROUGH**, Gent., of Wickhambrook, Suffolk, son of William Burrough, Gent. They had three sons, including [Rev.] George, and one daughter. He married (1st) **ELIZABETH BURRELL**, daughter of Thomas Burrell, of Dullingham, Cambridgeshire, by whom he had two children. He was granted arms 20 June 1586 (they being, Argent, two chevronels vert between three chaplets of the second, the roses or). THOMAS BURROUGH, Gent., died 19 June 1597, and was buried at Wickhambrook, Suffolk. He left a will proved 29 June 1597 (P.C.C. 48 Cobham). His widow, Bridget, married (2nd) at Wickhambrook, Suffolk 2 Dec. 1597 **THOMAS FRENCH**, Gent., of Wethersfield, Essex. He left a will proved 31 October 1599 (P.C.C. 73 Kidd).

Muskett *Suffolk Manorial Fams.* 1 (1900): 310–314. *NEHGR* 108 (1954): 172–178. Harvey *Vis. of Suffolk 1561* 2 (H.S.P. n.s. 3) (1984): 391–399.

18. [REV.] GEORGE BURROUGH, son by his father's 2nd marriage, baptized at Wickhambrook, Suffolk 26 October 1579. He entered Corpus Christi College, Cambridge University, in 1594, LL.B., Trinity Hall, 1600; Rector of Pettaugh, Suffolk, 1604, and of Gosbeck, 1621. He married **FRANCES SPARROW**, daughter of Nicholas Sparrow, of Wickhambrook, Suffolk. They had four sons, William, Charles, Thomas, and Nathaniel, and one daughter, Frances. [REV.] GEORGE BURROUGH was buried at Pettaugh, Suffolk 24 Feb. 1653.

Waters *Gen. Gleanings in England* 1 (1885): 737. Muskett *Suffolk Manorial Fams.* 1 (1900): 294–303, 311–314. Noyes et al. *Gen. Dict. of Maine & N.H.* (1928–39): 122. *NEHGR* 108 (1954): 172–178. *TAG* 60 (1984): 140–142. Barnes *British Roots of Maryland Fams.* 1 (1999): 91–92.

19. NATHANIEL BURROUGH, merchant mariner. He married probably in England about 1649 **REBECCA STILES**, sister of John Stiles, Gent., of Stepney, Middlesex. They had one son, [Rev.] George. They settled on the Patuxent River in Calvert County, Maryland before 1651/2. They subsequently resided alternately at Roxbury, Massachusetts and in Maryland. His wife, Rebecca, joined the church at Roxbury, Massachusetts in 1657. He was a legatee in the 1663 will of his brother, Thomas Burrough, of Newchuch, Isle of Wight. In 1675 he conveyed a 200 acre tract called Knott's Neck on the south side of the Patuxent River. In 1674 his wife, Rebecca, obtained a transfer letter from the Roxbury church, she "going for England." He appeared in court in Maryland 22 May 1676. He soon afterwards returned to England, where he resided at Limehouse in Stepney, Middlesex. NATHANIEL BURROUGH left a will dated 13 Dec. 1681, proved 23 March 1682 (P.C.C. 32 Drax). His wife, Rebecca, evidently predeceased him.

NEHGR 106 (1952): 260 (Burrough arms: Silver two chevrons between three chaplets vert the roses gules); 108 (1954): 172–178. Noyes et al. *Gen. Dict. of Maine & N.H.* (1928–39): 122. *Archives of Maryland* 66 (1954): 182–184. Skordas *Early Settlers of Maryland* (1968): 73. *TAG* 56 (1980): 43–45; 60 (1984): 140–142. Barnes *British Roots of Maryland Fams.* 1 (1999): 91–92.

❧ BUTLER ☙

WALTER DE BURGH, of Burgh near Aylsham, Norfolk, married **ALICE** _____.
WILLIAM DE BURGH, of Askeaton, Carrigogunnell, Castleconnell, etc., Ireland, married _____.
RICHARD DE BURGH, lord of Connacht, married **GILLE DE LACY** [see BURGH 3].

4. MARGERY DE BURGH, married in or before 1242 **THEBAUD** (or **TEBAUD**) **LE BOTELER** (or **LE BOTILLER, BUTLER**), of Arklow, co. Wicklow, Ireland, son and heir of Thebaud Walter (or le Boteler), of Arklow, co. Wicklow, Butler of Ireland, by his 1st wife, Joan, daughter of Geoffrey de Marsh (or Mareys), Knt., Justiciar of Ireland. He was born about 1223. They had one son, Thebaud (or Tebaud). He did homage for his lands 11 June 1244. He adhered to King Henry III in the wars with the Barons. THEBAUD LE BOTELER died shorly before 3 August 1248, and was buried at Arklow Abbey, co. Wicklow. His widow, Margery, was living 1 March 1252/3.

Lodge *Peerage of Ireland* 4 (1789): 1–76 (sub Butler, Viscount Mountgarret). Brydges *Collins' Peerage of England* 9 (1812): 58–136 (sub Butler, Lord Butler). *Antiquarian Mag. & Bibliographical Review* 1 (1882): 88–90. *C.P.* 2 (1912):448–449. Orpen *Ireland under the Normans* 4 (1920): 159 (Burgh ped.).

5. THEBAUD (or **TEBAUD**) **LE BOTELER**, of Arklow, co. Wicklow, Ireland, son and heir, born about 1242 (aged 6 in 1248). He married in or before 1268 **JOAN FITZ JOHN**, daughter of John Fitz Geoffrey, Knt., of Shere, Surrey, Justiciar of Ireland, by Isabel, daughter of Hugh le

Bigod, Earl of Norfolk [see VERDUN 8 for her ancestry]. They had eight sons, Theobald, Edmund, Knt. [Earl of Carrick], Thomas, Knt., John, Richard, Gilbert, Nicholas, and James, and two daughters, Maud (wife of John Pipard) and Joan. He took part with King Edward I in the war with Scotland. THEBAUD LE BOTELER died in Arklow, co. Wicklow 26 Sept. 1285, and was buried at Arklow Abbey. His widow, Joan, was co-heiress in 1297 to her brother, Richard Fitz John, Knt., Lord Fitz John, by which she inherited the manors of Aylesbury, Buckinghamshire, Fambridge, Essex, Shere, Surrey, and Atlingworth (in Brighton) and Twineham Benfield (in Twineham), Sussex, and 6-3/4 townships in the cantred of the Isles in Thomond, in Ireland. She died shortly before 26 May 1303.

Lodge *Peerage of Ireland* 4 (1789): 1–76 (sub Butler, Viscount Mountgarret). Brydges *Collins' Peerage of England* 9 (1812): 58–136 (sub Butler, Lord Butler). Clutterbuck *Hist. & Antiqs. of Hertford* 1 (1815): 293 (chart). Montmorency-Morres *Genealogical Memoir of the Fam. of Montmorency* (1817): xxxii–xxxvi. *Notes & Queries* 4th Ser. 3 (1869): 484–485 (Fitz Peter ped.). *Genealogist* n.s. 13 (1896): 36–37. *C.P.* 2 (1912): 449; 5 (1926): 437 chart, 439–441 (sub FitzJohn); 10 (1945): 533 (sub Pipard). Kingsford *Stonor Letters & Papers 1290–1483* 1 (Camden 3rd Ser. 29) (1919): 4. VCH *Buckingham* 3 (1925): 6–7 (arms of Fitz John: Quarterly or and gules a border vair). Cantle *Pleas of Quo Warranto for Lancaster* (Chetham Soc. n.s. 98) (1937): 128 (Butler ped.). VCH *Sussex* 7 (1940): 186–191, 258. *Year Books of Edward II* 10 (Selden Soc. 63) (1947): 196–208. Brooks *Knights' Fees in Counties Wexford Carlow & Kilkenny* (1950): 208–209. Paget *Baronage of England* (1957). VCH *Sussex* 7 (1940): 186–191. Frame *English Lordship in Ireland* (1982): 30, 37, 344 (chart). Moody et al. *New Hist. of Ireland* 9 (1984): 169 (chart). National Archives, SC 8/329/E945 (available at www.catalogue.nationalarchives.gov.uk/search.asp).Online resource: http://www.briantimms.net/era/lord_marshals/Lord_Marshal02/Lord%20Marshal2.htm (Lord Marshal's roll — arms of Tebaud le Botiller: Or a chief indented azure).

6. EDMUND LE BOTELER (or **BUTLER**), Knt., of Knocktopher, co. Kilkenny, Rathkennan, co. Tipperary, Fritwell, Great Linford, and Rotherfield Peppard, Buckinghamshire, Sopley, Hampshire, La Vacherie (in Cranley) and Shere, Surrey, Twineham Benfield (in Twineham), Sussex, etc., Justiciar of Ireland, 2nd son, born about 1273–4 or 1279 (aged variously 24, 29 or 30 in 1303). He was heir in 1299 to his older brother, Theobald le Boteler. He married in 1302 **JOAN FITZ JOHN**, daughter of John Fitz Thomas Fitz Gerald, Knt., of Sligo Castle, 5th Baron of Offaly, co. Kildare, 1st Earl of Kildare, by Blanche, daughter of John Roche, Baron of Fermoy. They had four sons, James, K.B. [1st Earl of Ormond], Lawrence, Thomas, Knt., and John, and two daughters, Joan (wife to Roger de Mortimer) and _____ (wife of Thomas Dillon, Knt.). In 1302 he recovered the manor of Hollywood near Ballymore from Richard, Archbishop of Dublin. He was knighted in London by King Edward II in 1309. In 1310 his brother-in-law, John Pipard, granted the reversion of his English inheritance to him, including manors of Great Linford and Twyford, Buckinghamshire, Smeeton (in Bulmer), Essex, Fritwell, Oxfordshire, Belweton (in Stanton Drew), Somerset, Great Finborough, Suffolk, and Great Compton (in Long Compton), Warwickshire, and £7 rent in Breen juxta Bledon, Somerset. John Pipard afterwards transferred the manor of Great Linford, Buckinghamshire to him for an annual rent; five years later, as Edmund had not paid the rent for two years, John Pipard re-entered the manor and held it until Edmund's death in 1321. In 1315 Edmund was granted the Earldom of Carrick. In 1316 he was granted free warren in his demesne lands at Fritwell, Oxfordshire. In 1316–7 he commanded the English forces in Ireland against the invasion of Edward de Brus of Scotland. His wife, Joan, died before 2 May 1320. SIR EDMUND LE BOTELER died at London 13 Sept. 1321, after returning from a pilgrimage to Santiago of Compostella in Spain, and was buried at Gowran, co. Kilkenny, Ireland.

Lodge *Peerage of Ireland* 4 (1789): 1–76 (sub Butler, Viscount Mountgarret). Brydges *Collins' Peerage of England* 9 (1812): 58–136 (sub Butler, Lord Butler). Clyn & Dowling *Annals of Ireland* (1849): 14 (sub A.D. 1321: "Obiit Edmundus Pincerna Londonii, in vigilia exaltacionis Sancte Crucis, et in vigilia vigilie beati Martini episcopi et confessoris, apud Baligaveran sepelitur."). Leinster *Earls of Kildare* (1858): 22–28. *C.P.R. 1307–1313* (1894): 213. *Genealogist* n.s. 13 (1896): 36–37; n.s. 14 (1897): 98. Green *Feet of Fines for Somerset* 2 (Somerset Rec. Soc. 12) (1898): 112. Wrottesley *Peds. from the Plea Rolls* (1905): 137–138, 226. *C.P.* 2 (1912): 449–450; 3 (1913): 60 (sub Carrick); 5 (1926): 437 chart, 439–441 (sub FitzJohn); 7 (1929): 218–221, esp. 221, footnote d (sub Kildare); 10 (1945): 533 (sub Pipard). Orpen

Ireland under the Normans 3 (1920): 85; 4 (1920): 175, 191–2, 213. VCH *Buckingham* 4 (1927): 387–392. VCH *Sussex* 7 (1940): 186–191. Woodlock *Reg. Henrici Woodlock* 2 (Canterbury & York Soc. 44) (1941): 724, 746. *C.P.* 10 (1945): 116–117. *Year Books of Edward II* 10 (Selden Soc. 63) (1947): 196–208. VCH *Warwick* 5 (1949): 52–58. Paget *Baronage of England* (1957) 220: 2. VCH *Oxford* 6 (1959): 134–146. *Ancient Deeds — Ser. B* 2 (List & Index Soc. 101) (1974): B.8431. Moody et al. *New Hist. of Ireland* 9 (1984): 169 (chart). Frame *English Lordship in Ireland* (1982): 14n, 37, 344.

7. JAMES LE BOTELER (or **BUTLER**), K.B., of Knocktopher, co. Kilkenney, Turvy, co. Dublin, Nenagh and Thurles, co. Tipperary, Aylesbury, Great Linford, and Rotherfield Peppard, Buckinghamshire, Sopley, Hampshire, Great Finborough, Suffolk, La Vacherie (in Cranley) and Shere, Surrey, Weeton, Lancashire, Great Compton (in Long Compton), Warwickshire, etc., hereditary Chief Butler of Ireland, Lieutenant of Ireland, son and heir. He was a legatee in the 1321 will of his father. He was hostage in Dublin Castle for his father in 1317, and was still under age on 3 Dec. 1325. In 1326 he received a protection in England on going over to Ireland. He married in 1327 **ELEANOR DE BOHUN**, 2nd surviving daughter of Humphrey de Bohun, Knt., Earl of Hereford and Essex, by Elizabeth, daughter of Edward I, King of England [see BOHUN 9 for her ancestry]. They had two sons, John and James, Knt. [2nd Earl of Ormond], and one daughter, Pernel (or Perina). She was a legatee in the 1319 will of her father, who bequeathed her £200 for her apparel against her marriage. In 1327 Joan de Plugenet, widow of Henry de Bohun, Knt., had license to enfeoff Eleanor of the Castle and manor of Kilpeck, and the manor of Trivel, together with the office of forester of la Haye, Herefordshire for life. He was created Earl of Ormond 2 Nov. 1328. In 1328 he and his wife, Eleanor, were granted free warren in their demesne lands at Great Linford and Twyford, Buckinghamshire, Smeeton (in Bulmer), Essex, Cold Aston, Gloucestershire, Fritwell and Rotherfield Peppard, Oxfordshire, Great Finborough, Suffolk, Shere, Surrey, and Long Compton, Warwickshire. He presented to the church of Great Linford, Buckinghamshire in 1329, 1332, and 1336, and to Rotherfield Peppard, Buckinghamshire in 1334. SIR JAMES LE BOTELER, 1st Earl of Ormond, died 6 Jan. 1337/8, and was buried at Gowran (the chief seat of the family before the purchase of Kilkenny Castle). His widow, Eleanor, presented to the churches of Rotherfield Peppard, Buckinghamshire in 1338 and Great Linford, Buckinghamshire in 1341. About 1345 Andrew Peverel, Knt., petitioned the king and council stating that he had brought an assize of novel disseisin against Eleanor, Countess of Ormond, and others, concerning a quarter of the manor of Gomshall [Towerhill] (in Shere), Surrey, but she claimed that she held half the manor, containing this quarter, for the term of her life of the king's lease, with reversion to the king, and that she cannot therefore answer without the king. She married (2nd) at La Vacherie (in Cranley), Surrey by license dated 24 Jan. 1343/4 **THOMAS DE DAGWORTH**, Knt., King's Warden and Captain in Brittany, younger son of John de Dagworth, Knt., of Dagworth (in Old Newton), Suffolk, Bradwell juxta Coggeshall, Essex, etc., Usher of the Exchequer, Marshal of the Eyre, by Alice, elder daughter and co-heiress of William Fitz Warin [see DAGWORTH 10 for his ancestry]. They had one daughter, Eleanor. He was one of the most famous captains of his time. He defeated Charles de Blois at the Battle of La Roche-Derien, near Tréguier, 20 June 1347, and took him prisoner. For this exploit he was awarded 25,000 florins *de scuto* in 1348, and granted all the castles, etc., in Brittany forfeited by Hervé VII, Lord of Léon. He was summoned to Parliament 13 Nov. 1347 and 14 Feb. 1347/8, by writs directed *Thome de Dagworth'*, whereby he is held to have become Lord Dagworth. He presented to the chantry of the manor chapel of Cranleigh, Surrey in 1349. SIR THOMAS DE DAGWORTH, Lord Dagworth, died in July or August 1350, being treacherously slain in time of truce in a skirmish near Aurai in Brittany. In 1352 his widow, Eleanor, was granted safe-conduct by the king. In 1357 she was granted a license for an oratory for one year for her house at La Vacherie (in Cranley), Surrey. She was a legatee in the 1361 will of her brother, Humphrey de Bohun, Earl of Hereford. In 1361 Robert Manfeld and Joan his wife quitclaimed to her all their right in the manors of Breen and

Belweton (in Stanton Drew), Somerset, together with other manors in cos. Bucks and Oxford. In 1363 Eleanor, Countess of Ormond, John Raymundi the younger, and other inhabitants of Pensford in the parish of Stanton Drew, Somerset petitioned the Pope that they they be allowed to have mass and other divine offices upon holidays, etc., in the chapel of St. Thomas the Martyr at Pensford which they have founded and endowed. Eleanor, Countess of Ormond, died testate 7 October 1363.

Morice *Mems. pour Servir de Preuves a l'Hist. de Bretagne* 1 (1742): 1460, 1463–1464, 1478 (Eleanor, Countess of Ormond, styled "kinswoman" [consanguineam] by King Edward III). Lodge *Peerage of Ireland* 4 (1789): 1–76 (sub Butler, Viscount Mountgarret). Brydges *Collins' Peerage of England* 9 (1812): 58–136 (sub Butler, Lord Butler). Baker *Hist. & Antiqs. of Northampton* 1 (1822–30): 544–545 (Mandeville-Fitz Peter-Bohun ped.). Nicolas *Testamenta Vetusta* 1 (1826): 66–68 (will of Humphrey de Bohun, Earl of Hereford and Essex). Dugdale *Monasticon Anglicanum* 6(1) (1830): 134–136 (Bohun ped. in Llanthony Abbey records: "Elianora de Bohun supradicta, senior filii prædicti Humfredi octavi [de Bohun], post decessum patris sui, fuit primo desponsata domino Jacobo le Botyler Hyberniæ, quem dominus rex Edwardus tertius supradictus postea fecit comitem de Urmond: de quibus Jacobus le Botiler, et alii filii et filiæ, qui moriebantur juvenes"). Burke *Dict. of the Peerages… Extinct, Dormant & in Abeyance* (1831): 63–65 (sub Bohun), 155–156 (sub Dagworth). Banks *Baronies in Fee* 1 (1844): 175–176 (sub Dagworth). *Arch. Jour.* 2 (1846): 339–349 (will of Humphrey de Bohun). Lipscomb *Hist. & Antiqs. of Buckingham* 2 (1847): 4–7. *Jour. British Arch. Assoc.* 27 (1871): 179–191. Turner *Cal. Charters & Rolls: Bodleian Lib.* (1878): 57. *Genealogist* 5 (1889): 47; n.s. 14 (1897): 98. *C.P.R. 1327–1330* (1891): 182, 340 (instances of Eleanor de Bohun styled "king's kinswoman"), 340 (James le Botiller, earl of Ormond styled "king's kinsman."), 181, 336, 402, 403. *C.P.R. 1330–1334* (1893): 336 (James le Botiller, Earl of Ormond styled "king's kinsman"). Lewis *Pedes Finium; or, Fines Rel. Surrey* (Surrey Arch. Soc. Extra Vol. 1) (1894): 114. *Genealogist* n.s. 13 (1896): 36–37. *Papal Regs.: Petitions* 1 (1896): 419–445. *Papal Regs.: Letters* 3 (1897): 158, 526; 4 (1902): 87–91. Wrottesley *Crécy & Calais* (1898): 54, 108, 113, 254. *Desc. Cat. Ancient Deeds* 3 (1900): 312; 6 (1915): 400 (settlement of estate of Eleanor, Countess of Ormond, mentions payments to Lady Talbot and Lady Fitz Walter, the latter specifically called "her daughter"). Green *Feet of Fines for Somerset* 3 (Somerset Rec. Soc. 17) (1902): 186–187. *C.P.R. 1348–1350* (1905): 207 (Eleanor, wife of Thomas de Dagworth, styled "sister" of William de Bohun, Earl of Northampton). Wrottesley *Peds. from the Plea Rolls* (1905): 69, 137–138, 226. VCH *Lancaster* 1 (1906): 350–357. *C.P.R. 1350–1354* (1907): 54. VCH *Surrey* 3 (1911): 86–92, 111–121. *C.Ch.R.* 4 (1912): 95. *C.P.* 2 (1912): 450 (sub Butler); 4 (1916): 27–29 (sub Dagworth) (Dagworth arms: Ermine, on a fesse gules three roundlets or); 5 (1926): 437 (sub FitzJohn), 479 (footnote b); 10 (1945): 555, footnote j (sub Plugenet), Appendix B, 116–119; 12(1) (1953): 614–616 (sub Talbot). *C.P.R. 1361–1364* (1912): 422 (Eleanor, late Countess of Ormond, styled "king's kinswoman" by King Edward III of England). Duncumb et al. *Colls. towards the Hist. & Antiqs. of Hereford* 6 (1912): 36–37, 39, 49–50. *Cal. IPM* 8 (1913): 117–127. VCH *Buckingham* 3 (1925): 6–7; 4 (1927): 387–392. *Feet of Fines for Essex* 3 (1929–49): 27–28. *Misc. Gen. et Heraldica* 5th Ser. 8 (1932–34): 229–231. *Cal. Inqs. Misc.* 3 (1937): 144. Stokes et al. *Warwickshire Feet of Fines* 2 (Dugdale Soc. 15) (1939): 151–152. VCH *Warwick* 5 (1949): 52–58. Hatton *Book of Seals* (1950): 254–255, 266–267 (seal of Eleanor de Bohun dated 1358 bears arms of Bohun and Dagworth), 268–270. Paget *Baronage of England* (1957) 73: 1–13 (sub Bohun); 165: 1–4 (sub Dagworth). VCH *Oxford* 6 (1959): 134–146. Sanders *English Baronies* (1960): 73–74. Butler *Gen. of the Butlers of Ireland* 1 (1962): 226–262, 270–290, 293–307; 9 (1962): 1, 5–17. *Norfolk Arch.* 34 (1967): 111–118 (author states in error that Sir Nicholas de Dagworth, of Blicking, Norfolk [died 1402] "may well have been the son of Sir Thomas [de Dagworth]"). Frame *English Lordship in Ireland* (1982). Sutherland *Eyre of Northamptonshire* 1 (Selden Soc. 97) (1983): xii. Moody et al. *New Hist. of Ireland* 9 (1984): 169 (chart). Edington *Reg. of William Edington Bishop of Winchester* 1 (Hampshire Recs. 7) (1986): 91; 2 (Hampshire Recs. 8) (1987): 44. Ward *Women of the English Nobility & Gentry 1066–1500* (1995): 50–51. Leese *Blood Royal* (1996): 119–122. Burghersh *Regs. of Bishop Henry Burghersh* 2 (Lincoln Rec. Soc. 90) (2003): 82, 85, 94, 138, 144, 150, 156. National Archives, SC 8/262/13054 (available at www.catalogue.nationalarchives.gov.uk/search.asp).

Children of James le Boteler (or Butler), K.B., by Eleanor de Bohun:

i. **JAMES LE BOTELER** (or **BUTLER**), Knt., 2nd Earl of Ormond [see next].

ii. **PERNEL** (or **PERINA**) **LE BOTELER** (or **BUTLER**), married **GILBERT TALBOT**, Knt., 3rd Lord Talbot [see TALBOT 12].

Child of Eleanor de Bohun, by Thomas de Dagworth, Knt.:

i. **ELEANOR DE DAGWORTH**, married **WALTER FITZ WALTER**, Knt., 3rd Lord Fitz Walter [see FITZ WALTER 11].

8. JAMES LE BOTELER (or **BUTLER**), Knt., 2nd Earl of Ormond, Chief Governor of Ireland, 1359–61, 1377–9, Constable of Dublin Castle, born at Kilkenny, Ireland 4 October 1331 (aged 7 in

1338). He married by papal dispensation dated 15 May 1346 (they being related in the 4th degree of kindred) **ELIZABETH DARCY**, daughter of John Darcy, Knt., of Knaith, Lincolnshire, by his 2nd wife, Joan, 4th daughter of Richard de Burgh, Knt., 3rd Earl of Ulster, lord of Connacht [see DARCY 11 for her ancestry]. They had four sons, Ralph, James [3rd Earl of Ormond], Thomas, and Maurice, and two daughters, Eleanor (wife of Gerald Fitz Maurice, 3rd Earl of Desmond) and Joan (wife of Tiege O'Carrol). He resided chiefly in Ireland, distinguishing himself in the wars there, and receiving many grants of lands for his good services. He presented to La Vacherie chantry in Cranley, Surrey in 1367. SIR JAMES LE BOTELER, 2nd Earl of Ormond, died in his castle of Knocktopher, co. Kilkenny 18 October (or 6 Nov.) 1382, and was buried in Gowran church. He left a will dated 31 August 1379. His widow, Elizabeth, married (2nd) before 22 August 1383 **ROBERT LUKYN** (alias **DE HEREFORD**), Knt. (living 12 April 1395), Seneschal of the Liberty of Tipperary. She died 24 (or 25) March 1389/90.

    Rymer *Fœdera* 6 (1727): 128–129. Lodge *Peerage of Ireland* 4 (1789): 1–76 (sub Butler, Viscount Mountgarret). Brydges *Collins' Peerage of England* 9 (1812): 58–136 (sub Butler, Lord Butler). Thoresby *Ducatus Leodiensis* (1816): 226–228 (Darcy ped.). Nicolas *Testamenta Vetusta* 1 (1826): 107 (will of James Earl of Ormond). Lipscomb *Hist. & Antiqs. of Buckingham* 2 (1847): 4–7. Flower *Vis. of Yorkshire 1563–4* (H.S.P. 16) (1881): 91–92 (Darcy ped.: "Elsabeth [Darcy] wyff to the Lord Ormond."). *Genealogist* n.s. 13 (1896): 36–37; n.s. 14 (1897): 98. Kirby *Wykeham's Reg.* 1 (1896): 15. *C.P.R. 1381–1385* (1897): 403, 408 (James "last earl of Ormonde" styled "king's kinsman"). *Papal Regs.: Letters* 3 (1897): 216 (James, Earl of Ormond, styled "kinsman" of King Edward III of England in 1347). *Desc. Cat. Ancient Deeds* 3 (1900): 456–457 (his will). *C.P.R. 1345–1348* (1903): 263 (styled "king's kinsman"). Wrottesley *Peds. from the Plea Rolls* (1905): 137–138, 226. *D.N.B.* 3 (1908): 502 (biog. of James Butler, 2nd Earl of Ormond). VCH *Surrey* 3 (1911): 111–121. Duncumb et al. *Colls. towards the Hist. & Antiqs. of Hereford* 6 (1912): 36–37, 50–51. *Cal. IPM* 8 (1913): 117–127. *C.P.* 4 (1916): 243–244 (sub Desmond); 10 (1945): 119–121 (sub Ormond). VCH *Buckingham* 3 (1925): 6–7; 4 (1927): 387–392. *C.F.R.* 9 (1926): 375. *Misc. Gen. et Heraldica* 5th Ser. 8 (1932–34): 229–231 ("… A dispensation was required, because the parties were related in the 4th — 4th degrees of consanguinity: being each descended in the 4th degree from John fitz Geoffrey"). Curtis *Cal. Ormond Deeds* 2 (1934): 193–194 (charters of Elizabeth Darcy, countess of Ormond dated 1383). *Irish Genealogist* 2 (1943–45): 332–333. VCH *Oxford* 6 (1959): 134–146. Butler *Gen. of the Butlers of Ireland* 9 (1962): 18–27. *Ancient Deeds — Ser. B* 1 (List & Index Soc. 95) (1973): 24. Ellis *Cat. Seals in the P.R.O.* 2 (1981): 20 (seal of James le Botiller, Earl of Ormond dated 1371 — Upon a breast of a splayed eagle, a shield of arms: a chief dancetty). Moody et al. *New Hist. of Ireland* 9 (1984): 169 (chart). Fryde & Greenway *Handbook of British Chronology* (1996): 162. Leese *Blood Royal* (1996): 119–122. Burghersh *Regs. of Bishop Henry Burghersh* 2 (Lincoln Rec. Soc. 90) (2003): 92. National Archives, E 210/440: will of James le Botiller, Earl of Ormond dated at La Vacherie, Surrey 31 Aug. 1379, names his kinsman, William de Courtenay, Bishop of London, as supervisor of will (available at www.catalogue.nationalarchives.gov.uk/search.asp).

9. JAMES LE BOTELER (or **BUTLER**), 3rd Earl of Ormond, 2nd but eldest surviving son and heir, born about 1360 (aged 22 in 1382). He was in England to do homage 28 October 1385, and was returning in June 1386 to Ireland, where he mostly resided. Like his father, he was several times Chief Governor of Ireland. He married before 17 June 1386 **ANNE WELLES**, daughter of John de Welle (or Welles), Knt., 4th Lord Welles, by Maud, daughter of William de Roos (or Ros), Knt., 2nd Lord Roos of Helmsley [see WELLES 10 for her ancestry]. They had two sons, James [4th Earl of Ormond] and Richard, Knt. [2], and one daughter, Joan (wife of Teige O'Carroll). By his mistress, Katherine, daughter of Gerald Fitz Maurice, 3rd Earl of Desmond, he had four illegitimate sons, James 'Galdie,' Edmund, Gerald, and Theobald. By an unknown mistress, he had illegitimate sons, Thomas, Knt., and Robert. In 1387 he had license to found a house of Friars Minors at Aylesbury, Buckinghamshire. His wife, Anne, was living 26 June 1397 (date of lease), and died 13 Nov. (year unknown), before 3 Dec. 1399. JAMES LE BOTELER, 3rd Earl of Ormond, died at Gowran 3, 4, 6, or 7 Sept. 1405, and was buried there.

---

[2] Ancestor of [**Dr.**] **Charles Carroll** (1691–1755), of Annapolis, Anne Arundel Co., Maryland. For further particulars regarding this line of descent, see Roberts *Royal Descents of 600 Immigrants* (2004): 323–325.

Lodge *Peerage of Ireland* 4 (1789): 1–76 (sub Butler, Viscount Mountgarret). Brydges *Collins' Peerage of England* 9 (1812): 58–136 (sub Butler, Lord Butler). Lipscomb *Hist. & Antiqs. of Buckingham* 2 (1847): 4–7. Graves *Roll of the Procs. of the King's Council in Ireland* (Rolls Ser. 69) (1877): xv (James le Boteler, Earl of Ormond, styled "kinsman" [consanguinei] by King Richard II of England in 1393), 258–260 ([James le Boteler], Earl of Ormond, styled "trescher et foial cousin" by King Richard II of England in letter dated 1393). Kirby *Wykeham's Reg.* 1 (1896): 204–205, 215. *Genealogist* n.s. 14 (1897): 98. *C.P.R.* 1381–1385 (1897): 330 (James Botiller, son and heir of James Botiller, late earl of Ormond, styled "kinsman" by King Richard II in 1383). *C.P.R.* 1385–1389 (1900): 307 (James, Earl of Ormonde, styled "king's kinsman" in 1387). Wrottesley *Peds. from the Plea Rolls* (1905): 226. VCH *Surrey* 3 (1911): 111–121. Duncumb et al. *Colls. towards the Hist. & Antiqs. of Hereford* 6 (1912): 36–37. VCH *Buckingham* 3 (1925): 6–7; 4 (1927): 387–392. *Misc. Gen. et Heraldica* 5th Ser. 8 (1932–34): 229–231. Veale *Great Red Book of Bristol* 2 (Bristol Rec. Soc. 4) (1933): 202 (charter of James le Botiller, Earl of Ormond dated 1386). Curtis *Cal. Ormond Deeds* 2 (1934): 193 (James Botiller son and heir of James Botiller, lately Earl of Ormond, deceased, styled "dear cousin" by King Richard II in 1383). *C.P.* 10 (1945): 121–123 (sub Ormond). VCH *Warwick* 5 (1949): 52–58. VCH *Oxford* 6 (1959): 134–146. Butler *Gen. of the Butlers of Ireland* 6 (1962): 20–24; 9 (1962): 1, 31–46. Moody et al. *New Hist. of Ireland* 9 (1984): 169 (chart). Given-Wilson *Ill. Hist. of Late Medieval England* (1996): chart opp. 61 (temp. King Edward IV). Worcestershire Rec. Office: Hampton (Pakington) of Westwood Park, Droitwich, Worcestershire, 705:349/12946/492083 — Lease dated 26 June 1397 from Anne, Countess of Ormond, re. manor of Aylesbury, Buckinghamshire (available at www.a2a.org.uk/search/index.asp).

10. JAMES LE BOTELER (or **BUTLER**), 4th Earl of Ormond, Lieutenant of Ireland, son and heir, born at Fruglasse 28 May 1393 (aged 12, 13, or 15 in 1405). He married (1st) on or before 28 August 1413 **JOAN BEAUCHAMP**, daughter of William Beauchamp, K.G., 1st Lord Bergavenny, by Joan, daughter of Richard de Arundel, K.G., 11th Earl of Arundel, 10th Earl of Surrey [see BERGAVENNY 12 for her ancestry]. They had three sons, James, K.G. [5th Earl of Ormond, Earl of Wiltshire], John, Knt. [6th Earl of Ormond], and Thomas, K.B. [7th Earl of Ormond], and two daughters, Elizabeth and Anne. In 1412 he accompanied Thomas, Earl of Lancaster, to France. In 1422 Sir John Talbot arraigned him for treason, but the crown and council ordered the annulment of all proceedings connected with this dispute in 1423. His wife, Joan, died 3 (or 5) August 1430, and was buried in the chapel of St. Thomas Acon, now called Mercer's Chapel, Cheapside, London. He married (2nd) by royal license dated 18 July 1432 (papal dispensation dated 29 April 1432, they being related on their fathers' sides in the 3rd degree, and on his father's and her mother's sides on the 3rd & 4th degrees of kindred) **ELIZABETH FITZGERALD**, widow of John Grey, Knt. (died 14 Sept. 1430), 5th Lord Grey of Codnor, and daughter of Gerald Fitz Maurice, 5th Earl of Kildare, by his 2nd wife, Agnes, 1st daughter of Philip Darcy, Knt., 2nd Lord Darcy of Knaith. She was born about 1398. They had no issue. In 1447 John Talbot, Earl of Shrewsbury, accused him of high treason, but the king declared by patent dated 20 Sept. 1448, that "no one should dare, on pain of his indignation, to revive the accusation or reproach of his conduct." His wife, Elizabeth, died 6 August 1452. JAMES LE BOTELER, 4th Earl of Ormond, died at Ardee, co. Louth 22 (or 23) August 1452, and was buried in St. Mary's Abbey, Dublin. Administration was granted on his estate 10 March 1455/6.

Weever *Ancient Funerall Monuments* (1631): 400. Fisher *Cat. of Most of the Memorable Tombs of London* (1668): 18. Rymer *Fœdera* 11 (1727): 46–47 (James [le Boteler], Earl of Ormond styled "kinsman" by King Henry VI of England in 1443). Lodge *Peerage of Ireland* 4 (1789): 1–76 (sub Butler, Viscount Mountgarret). Brydges *Collins' Peerage of England* 9 (1812): 58–136 (sub Butler, Lord Butler). Nicolas *Testamenta Vetusta* 1 (1826): 171–172 (will of William de Beauchamp). *Coll. Top. et Gen.* 1 (1834): 280–281. Lipscomb *Hist. & Antiqs. of Buckingham* 2 (1847): 4–7. Leinster *Earls of Kildare* (1858): 35–37. Graves *Roll of the Procs. King's Council in Ireland* (Rolls Ser. 69) (1877): 304–305 (James styled "trusty and welbeloved cousin" by King Henry VI). *Genealogist* n.s. 7 (1890): 56. Bull *Hist. of Newport Pagnell* (1900): 44–47. *Desc. Cat. Ancient Deeds* 3 (1900): 401. *Procs. Bath Natural Hist. & Antiq. Field Club* 9 (1901): 188–201. *Papal Regs.: Letters* 7 (1906): 341; 8 (1909): 442–443; 10 (1915): 497–498 (Edmund and Robert, brothers of James, Earl of Ormond, named). *D.N.B.* 3 (1908): 502–503 (biog. of James Butler, 4th Earl of Ormond). *C.P.R.* 1441–1446 (1908): 45 (James le Botiller, Earl of Ormond styled "king's kinsman"). *D.N.B.* 3 (1908): 502–503 (biog. of James Butler, 4th Earl of Ormond). Stow *Survey of London* (1908): 258–276. *C.P.R.* 1413–1416 (1910): 93 (James le Botiller, earl Dormond, styled "king's kinsman"). *C.P.R.* 1416–1422 (1911): 256 (James le Boteler, earl of Ormond styled "king's kinsman"). VCH *Surrey* 3 (1911): 111–121. VCH *Buckingham* 3 (1925): 6–7; 4 (1927): 387–392. *Misc. Gen. et Heraldica* 5th Ser. 8 (1932–34): 202–206, 229–231. *C.P.* 10 (1945): 123–130 (sub Ormond) (Carte describes him as, "… a great student, and lover of history and antiquity… proficient in the laws of arms and matters of honour"); 11 (1949): 704–705 (sub Shrewsbury). Paget *Baronage of England* (1957) 41: 1–3 (sub Beauchamp of Bergavenny). VCH *Oxford* 6 (1959): 134–146. Butler *Gen. of the Butlers of Ireland* 9 (1962): 1, 47–50. Moody et al. *New Hist. of Ireland* 9 (1984): 169 (chart). VCH *Cambridge* 9 (1989): 381–386. Given-Wilson *Ill. Hist. of Late Medieval England* (1996): chart opp. 61 (temp. King Edward IV). Catto "Chron. of John Somer," in *Camden Misc.* 34 (Camden Soc. 5th Ser. 10) (1997): 277 (birth date of James le Boteler).

Children of James le Boteler, by Joan Beauchamp:

i. **JAMES BUTLER** (or **ORMOND**), K.G., 5th Earl of Ormond, of Little Linford and Newport Pagnell, Buckinghamshire, Great Compton (in Long Compton), Warwickshire, Upton Snodsbury, Worcestershire, etc., Chief Governor of Ireland, Privy Councillor, member of Prince Edward's Council, Lord High Treasurer, 1455, 1458–60, Sheriff of cos. Carmarthen and Cardigan, Trier of Petitions in Parliament, and, in right of his 1st wife, of Long Wittenham, Berkshire, Middle Chinnock, Somerset, La Hyde (in Coppenhall), Staffordshire, Burmington, Warwickshire, Amblecote (in Old Swinford), Worcestershire, Laugharn (or Tallagharn), Carmarthenshire, etc., son and heir, born about 1422 (aged 30 in 1452). He married (1st) before 4 July 1438 **AVICE STAFFORD**, daughter and heiress of Richard Stafford, Knt., by Maud, daughter and heiress of Robert Lovel, Esq. [see SOUTHWICK 10.i for her ancestry]. She was born about 1431–2 (aged 14 or 15 in 1436). They had no issue. His wife, Avice, was a legatee in the 1436 will of her mother, Maud Lovel, dowager Countess of Arundel. He served in France in 1435, in the retinue of John, Duke of Bedford, and in 1441, in the retinue of Richard, Duke of York. His wife, Avice, was heiress in 1438 to her half-brother, Humphrey Arundel, Earl of Arundel, by which she inherited the manors of Kingsdon, Somerton Erleigh (in Somerton), and Somerton Randolph (in Somerton), Somerset. He presented to the church of Hazelbury Bryan, Dorset in 1443 and also in 1448, in right of his wife, Avice. In 1444, at the request of William Stafford, Esq. (uncle of Avice), the manor of Kingsdon Cary, Somerset was conveyed to Avice. He was made an honorary member of the Guild of Merchant Taylors of London in 1445–6, as "Sir James de Ormond." He was created Earl of Wiltshire 8 July 1449, and summoned to Parliament 23 Sept. following. He presented to the church of Kingsdon, Somerset in 1451. He succeeded his father as Earl of Ormond 23 August 1452. He was present at the 1st Battle of St. Albans in 1455. His wife, Avice, died 3 June (or 3 July) 1457. He married (2nd) in 1457/8 **ELEANOR BEAUFORT**, daughter of Edmund Beaufort, K.G., Duke of Somerset, by Eleanor, daughter of Richard Beauchamp, K.G., K.B., 13th Earl of Warwick, Lord Despenser and Lisle, hereditary Chamberlain of the Exchequer [see SOMERSET 12 for her ancestry]. They had no issue. SIR JAMES BUTLER, Earl of Wiltshire and Ormond, fought at the Battle of Towton 29 March 1461, where he was taken prisoner. He was beheaded at Newcastle 1 May 1461. He and his two brothers, John and Thomas, were attainted in the English Parliament in 1461 and also attainted in Ireland in 1462. His widow, Eleanor, married (2nd) about 1465 **ROBERT SPENCER**, Knt., of Chilton Foliat, Wiltshire [see CAREY 13 for issue of this marriage]. He presented to the church of Hazelbury Bryan, Dorset in 1493, in right of his wife, Eleanor. In 1496 he and his wife, Eleanor, together presented to the church of Hazelbury Bryan, Dorset. Eleanor, Countess of Wiltshire, died 16 August 1501. Sandford *Gen. Hist. of the Kings of England* (1677): 323–324. Rymer *Fœdera* 11 (1727): 375, 385 (instances of James [Butler], Earl of Wiltshire styled "kinsman" by King Henry VI in 1456 and 1457). Nash *Colls. for the Hist. of Worcestershire* 1 (1781): 507, 525. Lodge *Peerage of Ireland* 4 (1789): 1–76 (sub Butler, Viscount Mountgarret). Pole *Colls. towards a Desc. of Devon* (1791): 286–287. Banks *Dormant & Extinct Baronage of England* 2 (1808): 63–65 (sub Bryan). Brydges *Collins' Peerage of England* 1 (1812): 222–243 (sub Somerset, Duke of Beaufort); 9 (1812): 58–136 (sub Butler, Lord Butler). Nicolas *Testamenta Vetusta* 1 (1826): 224–230 (will of Joan Beauchamp). *Coll. Top. et Gen.* 1 (1834): 280–281; 3 (1836): 250–278; 4 (1837): 321–322. Tierney *Hist. & Antiqs. of the Castle & Town of Arundel* 1 (1834): 303. Beltz *Mems. of the Order of the Garter* (1841): clxii. Hutchins *Hist. & Antiqs. of Dorset* 1 (1861): 279–280, 448 (Bryan ped.); 2 (1863): 179 (Stafford ped.). Campbell *Materials for a Hist. of Henry VII* (1873): 380–383. Clode *Mems. of the Guild of Merchant Taylors* (1875): 619. *Notes & Queries* 5th Ser. 3 (1875): 172. Curtis *Antiqs. of Laugharne* (1880): 77–79. *Genealogist* n.s. 1 (1884): 76–78; n.s. 23 (1907): 26–27; n.s. 31 (1915): 173–178. Doyle *Official Baronage of England* 3 (1886): 674–675 (sub Wiltshire). Weaver *Somerset Incumbents* (1889): 90, 118. *Desc. Cat. Ancient Deeds* 1 (1890): 477, 500, 502, 558. Rogers *Strife of the Roses & Days of the Tudors in the West* (1890): 137–154. *Wiltshire Notes & Queries* 1 (1893–5): 557–559; 2 (1896–8): 255–261; 3 (1899–1901): 193–202. *Archæologia* 56 (1899): 323–336. Bull *Hist. of Newport Pagnell* (1900): 44–47. *C.P.R. 1476–1485* (1901): 106 (Eleanor [Beaufort], Countess of Wiltshire, styled "kinswoman" by King Edward IV of England in 1478). Owen *Old Pembroke Fams.* (1902): 81–84. Wrottesley *Peds. from the Plea Rolls* (1905): 397–398, 418, 472. *D.N.B.* 3 (1908): 503 (biog. of James Butler, 5th Earl of Ormond). *C.P.* 1 (1910): 248, footnote h (sub Arundel); 2 (1912): 361, footnote h (sub Bryan); 10 (1945): 126–129 (sub Ormond); 12(2) (1959): 734 (sub Wiltshire). Bradney *Hist. of Monmouthshire* 2(1) (1911): 25–28 (Somerset ped.). VCH *Surrey* 3 (1911): 111–121. VCH *Worcester* 3 (1913): 217–218; 4 (1924): 209. VCH *Berkshire* 4 (1924): 384–390. VCH *Buckingham* 3 (1925): 6–7; 4 (1927): 387–392. VCH *Warwick* 5 (1949): 26–28, 52–58. VCH *Oxford* 6 (1959): 134–146. VCH

Stafford 5 (1959): 138–143. Myers *English Hist. Docs.* 4 (1969): 428–429 (James Ormonde styled "cousin" by King Henry VI of England in 1449). *Ancient Deeds — Ser. B* 1 (List & Index Soc. 95) (1973): 80 (B.4486); 2 (List & Index Soc. 101) (1974): B.5415–5416, B.5882, B.5883; 3 (List & Index Soc. 113) (1975): B.12110(vi). VCH *Somerset* 3 (1974): 111–120, 129–153. *Ancient Deeds — Ser. A* 2 (List & Index Soc. 152) (1978): 40. Moody et al. *New Hist. of Ireland* 9 (1984): 169 (chart). Leese *Blood Royal* (1996): 229–234. Biancalana *Fee Tail & the Common Recovery in Medieval England* (2001): 353–354. Wagner *Encyclopedia of the Wars of the Roses* (2001): 42–43 (biog. of James Butler). Registered will of Maud (Lovel) (Stafford) Arundel, Countess of Arundel, dated and proved 1436, P.C.C. 21 Luffenam [FHL Microfilm 91983].

ii. **JOHN BUTLER** (otherwise known as **JOHN ORMOND**), Knt., 6th Earl of Ormond, of Newport Pagnell, Buckinghamshire, Fulbourn, Cambridgeshire, Great Compton (in Long Compton), Warwickshire, etc., Esquire for the King's Body, 2nd son. He indented to serve in Normandy and France in 1441 for one year. In 1449 he was taken prisoner by the French. He succeeded his older brother, James, in 1461, but was attainted in the English Parliament in 1461 and in Ireland in October 1462. He was living in exile c.1465. During the temporary restoration of King Henry VI in 1471, his attainder was reversed and he was recognized as Earl of Ormond. By his mistress, Reynalda O'Brien, daughter of Turlogh "The Brown" O'Brien, King of Thomond, he had three illegitimate sons, James Ormond, Knt. [Lord Treasurer of Ireland], John Ormond, and Edward Ormond. He left on a pilgrimage in 1476, and was in Rome in Spring 1476. JOHN BUTLER died unmarried in the Holy Land 14 October 1476. Lodge *Peerage of Ireland* 4 (1789): 1–76 (sub Butler, Viscount Mountgarret). Brydges *Collins' Peerage of England* 9 (1812): 58–136 (sub Butler, Lord Butler). Nicolas *Testamenta Vetusta* 1 (1826): 224–230 (will of Joan Beauchamp). *Coll. Top. et Gen.* 1 (1834): 280–281. Fortescue *De Laudibus Legum Angliæ* (1874): xxvi–xxix (letter to [John], Earl of Ormond by Sir John Fortescue dated c.1465). *Genealogist* n.s. 1 (1884): 76–78. Bull *Hist. of Newport Pagnell* (1900): 44–47. *D.N.B.* 3 (1908): 518 (biog. of John Butler, Earl of Ormond); 14 (1909): 1156–1157 (biog. of Sir James Ormonde). *C.P.* 10 (1945): 129–131 (sub Ormond). VCH *Warwick* 5 (1949): 52–58. VCH *Oxford* 6 (1959): 134–146. Allen *English Hospice in Rome* (1962): 6, 188. Moody et al. *New Hist. of Ireland* 9 (1984): 169 (chart). VCH *Cambridge* 10 (2002): 136–143.

iii. **THOMAS BUTLER** (or **ORMOND**), K.B., 7th Earl of Ormond, Lord Rochford [see next].

iv. **ELIZABETH BUTLER**, married **JOHN TALBOT**, K.G., 2nd Earl of Shrewsbury [see TALBOT 15].

v. **ANNE BUTLER**, contracted to marry in 1428–9 **THOMAS FITZ JAMES (FITZ GERALD)**, 7th Earl of Desmond, Steward of Connacht, Constable of Limerick Castle, Lord Deputy of Ireland to George, Duke of Clarence, 1463–7, son and heir of James Fitz Gerald, 6th Earl of Desmond, by Mary, daughter of Ulick mac Rickard Burk. This marriage appears not to have taken place. Anne le Boteler "daughter of the Earl of Ormond" died 4 Jan. 1435, and was buried in Shere, Surrey. Thomas subsequently married by dispensation dated 22 May 1455 **ELLICE BARRY**, daughter of William Barry, 8th Lord Barry or Barrymore. THOMAS FITZ JAMES, 7th Earl of Desmond, was found guilty of extorting "coyne and livery" by a Parliament held at Drogheda, where he was beheaded 15 Feb. 1467/8, and buried in St. Peter's Church, but subsequently removed to Christ Church, Dublin. His widow, Ellice, married (2ned) (as his 2nd wife) **MAURICE MOR FITZGIBBON**, who was living in 1496. Lodge *Peerage of Ireland* 4 (1789): 1–76 (sub Butler, Viscount Mountgarret). Brydges *Collins' Peerage of England* 9 (1812): 58–136 (sub Butler, Lord Butler). *C.P.* 4 (1916): 247–248 (sub Desmond); 14 (1998): 255–256 (sub Desmond). Stephenson *List of Mon. Brasses in Surrey* (1921): 458. National Archives, C 147/118 (bond dated 7 Henry VI [1428–9] between Thomas, son of James FitzGerald, Earl of Desmond, and Anne, daughter of James le Botiller, Earl of Ormond) (available at www.catalogue.nationalarchives.gov.uk/search.asp).

11. THOMAS BUTLER (otherwise known as **THOMAS ORMOND**), K.B., 7th Earl of Ormond, Chief Butler of Ireland, of Fulbourn and Swavesey, Cambridgeshire, later of Rochford, Foulness, Leigh, Paglesham, and Wakering, Essex, Little Linford and Newport Pagnell, Buckinghamshire, Kingsdon and Somerton Erleigh (in Somerton), Somerset, Fritwell, Oxfordshire, Great Compton (in Long Compton), Warwickshire, Hagley and Cradley (in Halesowen), Worcestershire, etc., Lord Chamberlain to the Queen, 1486–1502, Privy Councillor, 1504, 3rd son. He was a legatee in the 1435 will of his grandmother, Joan Beauchamp, Lady Bergavenny. He married (1st) before 11 July 1445 **ANNE HANKFORD** (or **HANKEFORD**), daughter and co-heiress of Richard Hankford, Knt., of Tawstock, Bampton, Combeinteignhead, Cookbury (in Milton Damerel), Harford, Huish, Instow, North Holne, Nymet Tracey (in Bow), Rolastone, Totnes, Uffculme, West Down, and Yarnscombe, Devon, Norton and Nonnington, Somerset, etc., and, in right of his 1st wife, of Wantage, Berkshire, Dilwyn, Herefordshire, Edgmond, Red Castle (in

Hodnet), and Whittington, Shropshire, etc., his 2nd wife, Anne, eldest daughter of John de Montagu, K.G., 3rd Earl of Salisbury [see HANKFORD 10 and FITZ WARIN 15 for her ancestry]. She was born in 1431 (aged variously 12 weeks or 16 weeks in May 1431). They had two daughters, Anne and Margaret. He was attainted in England in 1461, and in Ireland in 1462. He was living in exile with Queen Margaret of Anjou at Saint-Mihiel in the Duchy of Bar c.1465. His wife, Anne, was a legatee in the 1469 will of her son-in-law, Ambrose Cresacre, Esq. He fought at the Battle of Tewkesbury in 1471, and was subsequently granted a general pardon. The following year he petitioned Parliament for the recovery of his estates, which petition was allowed, and certain estates were restored to him. He was heir in 1476 to his older brother, John Ormond, Knt., 6th Earl of Ormond. He presented to the churches of Littleham, Devon, 1477, 1505, and Kingsdon, Somerset, 1509, and to the free chapel of the Hospital of St. John the Baptist (present day Queen Anne's Hospital) in Newport Pagnell, Buckinghamshire in 1501, 1506, and 1510. In 1478 Fulk Bourchier, Lord Fitz Warin and his wife, Elizabeth, remised and quitclaimed the manors of Clifford (in Dunsford), Little Yarnscombe (in Yarnscombe), and West Down, Devon to Thomas and his wife, Anne. His wife, Anne, died 13 Nov. 1485. In 1486 he was granted a weekly market and two annual fairs to be held at the lordship or manor of Stourbridge, Worcestershire. In 1490 he was jointly in charge of the alterations and additions to Westminster Palace. He married (2nd) before Nov. 1496 **LORA BERKELEY**, widow successively of John Blount, Knt., 3rd Lord Mountjoy, of Hampton Lovett, Worcestershire (died 12 October 1485) and Thomas Montgomery, K.G., of Faulkbourne, Essex (died 2 Jan. 1494/5) [see NORBURY 15.ii], and daughter of Edward Berkeley, Knt., of Beverstone, Gloucestershire, Avon (in Sopley) and Ibsley, Hampshire, etc., by his 1st wife, Christian, daughter of Richard Holt, Esq. [see FISHER 10 for her ancestry]. She was born about 1466 (aged 30 in 1496). They had one daughter, Elizabeth. He served as Ambassador to Burgundy in 1497. His wife, Lora, died 31 October [before 1501], and was buried with her 2nd husband in New Abbey, London. In 1505 he was granted a weekly market and annual fair at Swavesey, Cambridgeshire. SIR THOMAS BUTLER (otherwise ORMOND), 7th Earl of Ormond, Lord Rochford, died 3 August 1515, and was buried in the chapel of St. Thomas Acon, now called Mercer's Chapel, Cheapside, London. He left a will dated 31 July 1515, proved 25 August 1515 (P.C.C. 8 Holder).

Weever *Ancient Funerall Monuments* (1631): 400. Morant *Hist. & Antiqs. of Essex* 1 (1768): 269–271. *Archaeologia* 3 (1775): 20–21 (will of Thomas Butler, Knt., Earl of Ormond). Nash *Colls. for the Hist. of Worcestershire* 1 (1781): 489–490, 507, 540. Lodge *Peerage of Ireland* 4 (1789): 1–76 (sub Butler, Viscount Mountgarret). Brydges *Collins' Peerage of England* 9 (1812): 58–136 (sub Butler, Lord Butler). Ellis *Original Letters Ill. of English Hist.* 1st Ser. 1 (1824): 18–19 ([Thomas] Earl of Ormond styled "cousin" by King Henry VII of England). Nicolas *Testamenta Vetusta* 1 (1826): 224–230 (will of Joan Beauchamp); 2 (1826): 396 (will of Sir Thomas Montgomery). *Coll. Top. et Gen.* 1 (1834): 280–281; 3 (1838): 270–275; 4 (1837): 321–322. Banks *Baronies in Fee* 1 (1844): 126–127 (Blount), 359–360 (sub Ormond de Rochford). Westcote *View of Devonshire* (1845): 483. Lipscomb *Hist. & Antiqs. of Buckingham* 2 (1847): 4–7. *Gentleman's Mag.* n.s. 32 (1849): 491–493. Graves *Hist., Architecture & Antiqs. of the Cathedral Church of St. Canice, Kilkenny* (1857): 192 (Thomas, Earl of Ormond, styled "cousin" by Gerald, Earl of Kildare, in letter dated c.1495), 202, 204–205, 208. Gairdner *Letters & Papers Ill. of the Reigns of Richard III & Henry VII* 2 (Rolls Ser. 24) (1863): xli–xlii (letter dated 1494 from Sir Piers Botiller [Butler] to Sir Thomas, Earl of Ormond, in which Pers styled himself "a poor kinsman"), 55–56 (Gerald, Earl of Kildare, and [Maurice], Earl of Desmond both styled "cousin" of [Thomas], Earl of Ormond). *Trans. Essex Arch. Soc.* 3 (1865): 167–175 (will of Thomas Montgomery). *Testamenta Eboracensia* 4 (Surtees Soc. 53) (1869): 227 (will of Ambrose Cresacre). Brewer & Bullen *Cal. Carew MSS* (1873): 439–441. Campbell *Materials for a Hist. of Henry VII* 2 (1873): 380–383. Fortescue *De Laudibus Legum Anglia* (1874): xxvi–xxix (letter to [John], Earl of Ormond by Sir John Fortescue dated c.1465). St. George & Lennard *Vis. of Cornwall 1620* (H.S.P. 9) (1874): 86–87. Blunt *Dursley & Its Neighbourhood* (1877): 97–135. Rogers *Antient Sepulchral Effigies* (1877): 224–226. *Collectanea Genealogica* 1 (1881): 84–93. Doyle *Official Baronage of England* 3 (1886): 157–158 (sub Rochford). *Trans. Bristol & Gloucs. Arch. Soc.* 12 (1888): 24–53. Weaver *Somerset Incumbents* (1889): 118. *Genealogist* n.s. 1 (1884): 76–78; n.s. 7 (1890): 56; n.s. 22 (1906): 180; n.s. 23 (1907): 26–27, 95. *Desc. Cat. Ancient Deeds* 1 (1890): 415 (Sir Piers Butler, knight, styled "cousin" by Thomas, Earl of Ormond); 4 (1902): 208; 6 (1915): 119 (Sir Peris Butiller, knight, styled "cousin" by Thomas, earl of Ormond). *Notes & Gleanings* 4 (1891): 97. Lewis *Pedes Finium; or, Fines Rel. Surrey* (Surrey Arch. Soc. Extra Volume 1) (1894): 203. *Cal. IPM Henry VII* 1 (1898): 1, 46, 106, 447, 563. Bull *Hist. of Newport Pagnell* (1900): 232. Wrottesley

Peds. from the Plea Rolls (1905): 426–427. Stow *Survey of London* (1908): 258–276. Benolte et al. *Peds. from the Vis. of Hampshire 1530, 1575, 1622 & 1634* (H.S.P. 64) (1913): 56–57 (Berkley ped.: "Loraufida [Berkeley] vx. John Mountioy"). *C.P.R. 1485–1494* (1914): 125–126. *C.P.R. 1494–1509* (1916): 402, 419. VCH *Worcester* 3 (1923): 153–158. VCH *Buckingham* 3 (1925): 6–7; 4 (1927): 387–392. *C.P.* 5 (1926): 211, footnote e (sub Exeter), 506, footnote f (sub Fitzwarin); 9 (1936): 337–338 (sub Mountjoy); 10 (1945): 131–133 (sub Ormond). Wedgwood *Hist. of Parl.* 1 (1936): 605–606 (biog. of Sir Thomas Montgomery). Chichele *Reg. of Henry Chichele* 2 (Canterbury & York Soc. 42) (1937): 534–539 (will of Joan Beauchamp). Hemmant *Select Cases in the Exchequer before all the Justices of England* 2 (Selden Soc. 64) (1948): 138–141. VCH *Warwick* 5 (1949): 52–58; 7 (1964): 63. *C.C.R. 1485–1500* (1955): 167–168 (James Ormond styled "kinsman" by Thomas, Earl of Ormond). VCH *Essex* 4 (1956): 31; 8 (1983): 199–200. Paget *Baronage of England* (1957) 56: 1 (sub Berkeley of Beverstone). VCH *Oxford* 6 (1959): 134–146. Butler *Gen. of the Butlers of Ireland* 9 (1962): 1, 3, 69. *Feet of Fines for Essex* 4 (1964): 87, 114–115, 120–121. *Coat of Arms* 8 (1965): 194–204. *Ancient Deeds — Ser. B* 1 (List & Index Soc. 95) (1973): 80 (B.4486); 2 (List & Index Soc. 101) (1974): B.5652, B.6417, B.6445, B.7577; 3 (List & Index Soc. 113) (1975): B.12065, B.12176, B.12188, B.12270. VCH *Somerset* 3 (1974): 111–120, 129–153. *Ancient Deeds — Ser. A* 2 (List & Index Soc. 152) (1978): 41, 43. Horrox & Hammond *British Lib. Harleian Manuscript 433* 1 (1979): 274. Sutton *Coronation of Richard III* (1983): 375 (biog. of Sir Thomas Montgomery), 375–376 (biog. of Lora, Lady Mountjoy). Moody et al. *New Hist. of Ireland* 9 (1984): 169 (chart). Langton *Reg. of Thomas Langton Bishop of Salisbury* (Canterbury & York Soc. 74) (1985): 23 (Thomas Butler styled "Thomas, earl of Ormond and Lord Rochford"). Williams *England in the 15th Cent.* (1987): 187–198. VCH *Cambridge* 9 (1989): 381–386; 10 (2002): 136–143. Baker *Rpts. of Cases by John Caryll* 1 (Selden Soc. 115) (1999): 12–13. *Cal. IPM* 23 (2004): 296–307. National Archives, CP 25/1/46/92, #43 [see abstract of fine at http:// www.medievalgenealogy.org.uk/index.html].

Children of Thomas Butler (or Ormond), K.B., by Anne Hankford:

i. **ANNE BUTLER**, elder daughter and co-heiress. She married (1st) **AMBROSE CRESACRE** (or **GRISACRE**), Esq., lawyer, Justice of the Peace for Yorkshire, West Riding, 1466, son of Percival Cresacre, of Barnborough, Yorkshire, by Alice, daughter of Thomas Mounteney. They had no issue. In 1468–9 he acquired four manors in Kent from Richard Scrope. AMBROSE CRESACRE, Esq., left a will dated 15 Sept. 1469, proved October 1469 (P.C.C. 28 Godyn), requesting burial in the chapel of St. Thomas Acon, now called Mercer's Chapel, Cheapside, London. His widow, Anne, married (2nd) before 1482 **JAMES SAINT LEGER**, Knt., of Annery (in Monkleigh), Devon, son of John Saint Leger, Esq., of Ulcombe, Kent, by Margery, daughter and heiress of James Donet [see RAYNSFORD 11.i.a for his ancestry]. They had two sons, George, Knt., and James. SIR JAMES SAINT LEGER died in 1509. He left a will proved 11 June 1510 (P.C.C. 29 Bennett). His widow, Anne, was a legatee in the 1515 will of her father. She presented to the church of Littleham, Devon in 1531. She died 5 June 1532. *Archaeologia* 3 (1775): 20–21 (will of Thomas Butler, Knt., Earl of Ormond). Lodge *Peerage of Ireland* 4 (1789): 1–76 (sub Butler, Viscount Mountgarret); 6 (1789): 92–124 (sub St. Leger, Viscount Doneraile). Brydges *Collins' Peerage of England* 9 (1812): 58–136 (sub Butler, Lord Butler). Berry *County Gens.: Kent Fams.* (1830): 287 (St. Leger ped.). *Coll. Top. et Gen.* 4 (1837): 321–322. Burke *Hist. of the Commoners* 3 (1838): 452 (sub Cresacre). Scrope *Hist. of the Manor & Ancient Barony of Castle Combe* (1852): 285–286. Collier *Trevelyan Papers* 1 (Camden Soc. 67) (1857): 84–86. Graves *Hist., Architecture & Antiqs. of the Cathedral Church of St. Canice, Kilkenny* (1857): 208. *Testamenta Eboracensia* 4 (Surtees Soc. 53) (1869): 227 (will of Ambrose Cresacre). Brewer & Bullen *Cal. Carew MSS* (1873): 439–441. St. George & Lennard *Vis. of Cornwall 1620* (H.S.P. 9) (1874): 86–87. *Collectanea Genealogica* 1 (1881): 84–93. Colby *Vis. of Devon 1564* (1881): 186 (St. Leger ped.: "James Sayntleger of Annery, co. Devon. = Anne, eldest d. and h. of Thomas Earl of Ormond."). *MSS of the Marquis of Ormonde* (Hist. MSS Comm. 10th Rpt., App., Pt. 5) (1885): 75. *Notes & Gleanings* 4 (1891): 97. Lewis *Pedes Finium; or, Fines Rel. Surrey* (Surrey Arch. Soc. Extra Volume 1) (1894): 203. *C.P.R. 1461–1467* (1897): 577. Ratcliff *Hist. & Antiqs. of the Newport Pagnell Hundreds* (1900): 259. *Rpt. & Trans. of the Devonshire Assoc. for the Advancement of Science, Lit. & Art* 2nd Ser. 2 (1900): 291. *Ancestor* 8 (1904): 167–185 (re. Saint Leger fam.). Stow *Survey of London* (1908): 258–276. VCH *Worcester* 3 (1913): 130–136. Benolte & Cooke *Vis. of Kent 1530–1, 1574 & 1592* 2 (H.S.P. 75) (1924): 68–69 (1574 Vis.) (St. Leger ped.: "James St legier = Anne daughter and one of theyres of therle of Ormond"). VCH *Buckingham* 4 (1927): 311–316, 387–392. *C.P.* 10 (1945): 133, footnote b (sub Ormond). *C.C.R. 1461–1468* (1949): 369–370, 441–442, 456. VCH *Warwick* 5 (1949): 52–58. *C.C.R. 1468–1476* (1953): 14–15, 70–71, 82, 149. *Arch. Cantiana* 78 (1964): 2. *Ancient Deeds — Ser. B* 2 (List & Index Soc. 101) (1974): B.7565. *Ancient Deeds — Ser. BB* (List & Index Soc. 137) (1977): 116. *Ancient Deeds — DD Ser.* (List & Index Soc. 200) (1983): 318. Petre *Richard III: Crown & People* (1985): 194. Harper-Bill & Harvey *Medieval Knighthood IV* (1992): 123. VCH *Gloucester* 9 (2001): 9–20. VCH *Cambridge* 10 (2002): 136–143. Faraday *Worcestershire Taxes in the 1520s* (2003): 4. VCH *Somerset* 8 (2004): 91–112. National Archives, C 146/782; E 211/713; E 326/3538; E 328/413; SP 46/183/fo 245 (available at www.catalogue.nationalarchives.gov.uk/search.asp).

ii. **MARGARET BUTLER** [see next].

12. MARGARET BUTLER, younger daughter and co-heiress by her father's 1st marriage. She was a legatee in the 1469 will of her brother-in-law, Ambrose Cresacre, Esq. She married before 16 Nov. 1469 (date of grant) **WILLIAM BOLEYN**, K.B., of Blicking and Mulbarton, Norfolk, Hever, Kent, and Offley St. Ledgers, Hertfordshire, Baron of the Exchequer, younger son of Geoffrey Boleyn, Knt., Citizen and mercer of London, Lord Mayor of London, by his 2nd wife, Anne, daughter and co-heiress of Thomas Hoo, K.G., Lord Hoo and Hastings [see HOO 14.i for his ancestry]. He was born about 1451 (aged under 22 on 18 Nov. 1469, aged 36 in 1487). They had six sons, Thomas, K.G., K.B. [Earl of Wiltshire and Ormond], William [Archdeacon of Winchester, Prebendary of St. Paul's], James, Knt., Edward, Knt., John, and Anthony, and five daughters, Margaret, Anne (died unmarried 1479), Anne (wife of John Shelton, Knt.), Alice, and Jane (wife of Philip Calthorpe, Knt.). He was heir in 1471 or 1472 to his older brother, Thomas Boleyn. In 1472 he was admitted to the Mercers' Company, London. He was admitted a member of Lincoln's Inn in 1473. In 1483 John Howard appointed William his deputy as admiral for the coasts of Norfolk and Suffolk. Under the terms of a settlement dated 1473, he obtained the manor of Offley St. Ledgers, Hertfordshire on the death of his uncle, Thomas Hoo, in 1486. In the period, 1493–1500, he, John Devenish, Knt. and Elizabeth his wife, and Richard Carew sued Richard Lewknor, of Brambletye, Sussex, in Chancery regarding the detention of deeds relating to the manors of Hoe, Offeley, Cokernehoe, Mulbarton, and Wrattlyng. He presented to the church of Mulbarton, Norfolk in 1494, 1497, and 1500. SIR WILLIAM BOLEYN died 5 October 1505, and was buried in Norwich Cathedral, Norfolk. He left a will dated 7 October 1505, proved 27 Nov. 1505 (P.C.C. 40 Holgrave). His widow, Margaret, was a legatee in the 1515 will of her father. On her father's death in 1515, she inherited the manors of Aylesbury, Buckinghamshire, Fulbourn and Swavesey, Cambridgeshire, and Fritwell, Oxfordshire. Sometime before 1519, she and her son, Thomas Boleyn, alienated the manor of Fritwell, Oxfordshire to Richard Fermor, merchant of the Staple at Calais. In 1538 she and her son, Thomas Boleyn, sold the manor of Aylesbury, Buckinghamshire to John Baldwin, Knt. She died shortly before 20 March 1539/40.

Morant *Hist. & Antiqs. of Essex* 1 (1768): 269–271. *Archaeologia* 3 (1775): 20–21 (will of Thomas Butler, Knt., Earl of Ormond). Lodge *Peerage of Ireland* 4 (1789): 1–76 (sub Butler, Viscount Mountgarret). Hasted *Hist. & Top. Survey of Kent* 3 (1797): 190–202. Blomefield *Essay towards a Top. Hist. of Norfolk* 4 (1806): 33–35; 5 (1806): 75–83; 6 (1807): 381–409. Brydges *Collins' Peerage of England* 9 (1812): 58–136 (sub Butler, Lord Butler). Nicolas *Testamenta Vetusta* 1 (1826): 299–300 (will of Geoffrey Boleyn), 322 (will of Thomas Boleyn); 2 (1826): 465 (will of William Boleyn, Knt.). Clutterbuck *Hist. & Antiqs. of Hertford* 3 (1827): 91–96 (Hoo-Boleyne ped.). *Coll. Top. et Gen.* 4 (1837): 321–322. Banks *Baronies in Fee* 1 (1844): 359–360 (sub Ormond de Rochford). Lipscomb *Hist. & Antiqs. of Buckingham* 2 (1847): 4–7. *Sussex Arch. Colls.* 8 (1856): 96–131. Graves *Hist., Architecture & Antiqs. of the Cathedral Church of St. Canice, Kilkenny* (1857): 208. *Testamenta Eboracensia* 4 (Surtees Soc. 53) (1869): 227 (will of Ambrose Cresacre). Brewer & Bullen *Cal. Carew MSS* (1873): 439–441. St. George & Lennard *Vis. of Cornwall 1620* (H.S.P. 9) (1874): 86–87. *Collectanea Genealogica* 1 (1881): 84–93. Burke *Dormant, Abeyant, Forfeited & Extinct Peerages* (1883): 58–59 (sub Boleyne). *East Anglian* n.s. 1 (1885–86): 233–234. Sinclair *Sinclairs of England* (1887): 322–329. Farrer *Church Heraldry of Norfolk* 2 (1889): 18. *Genealogist* n.s. 7 (1890): 56. Lewis *Pedes Finium; or, Fines Rel. Surrey* (Surrey Arch. Soc. Extra Volume 1) (1894): 203. Baildon *Recs. of Lincoln's Inn: Admissions* 1 (1896): 18. VCH *Bedford* 2 (1908): 348–375. VCH *Hertford* 3 (1912): 40. VCH *Buckingham* 3 (1925): 6–7. *Misc. Gen. et Heraldica* 5th Ser. 8 (1932–34): 109–118 (1679 Saunders ped.: Ormond arms — Or, a chief indented azure). *C.P.* 10 (1945): 133, footnote b, 137 (sub Ormond); 12(2) (1959): 739 (sub Wiltshire). VCH *Warwick* 5 (1949): 52–58. VCH *Oxford* 6 (1959): 134–146. Butler *Gen. of the Butlers of Ireland* 9 (1962): 1, 3. *Ancient Deeds — Ser. BB* (List & Index Soc. 137) (1977): 116. Sutton *Coronation of Richard III* (1983): 313 (biog. of William Boleyn). Moody et al. *New Hist. of Ireland* 9 (1984): 169 (chart). Horrox *Richard III: A Study in Service* (1989): 78. VCH *Cambridge* 9 (1989): 381–386; 10 (2002): 136–143. Orme *Medieval Children* (2001): 43–44. Hoak *Tudor Political Culture* (2002): 35–36. Berkeley Castle Muniments, BCM/H/1/3/1 (grant dated 16 Nov. 1469 from Thomas [Bourgchier], cardinal archbishop of Canterbury, and others to William Boleyn and Margaret his wife, daughter of Sir Thomas Ormonde, the value of 20 marks a year in the manor of Virworthy (in Pancrasweek), Devon for the life of Thomas Ormonde, any surplus to be rendered to the original feoffees); BCM/H/1/3/2 (agreement dated 18 Nov. 1469, whereas Thomas archbishop of Canterbury and others by a deed dated 16 Nov. 1469, have demised the manor of Virworthy, Devon and other lands and holdings there to Thomas Boleyn, clerk, and others [named], to the use of William Boleyn and Margaret his wife, daughter of Sir Thomas Ormond, Knt., for the life of Thomas Ormond, nevertheless, by the assent of William and Margaret Boleyn, it has been agreed that if William, within two months after his 22nd birthday, makes to Margaret for her life a sufficient jointure in lands in Kent to the value of £20 a year, Thomas Boleyn and the others shall retain the manor of Virworthy, and that if the jointure is not made, then the archbishops and the others shall enter the manor) (available at www.a2a.org.uk/search/index.asp). National Archives, C 1/187/80 (available at www.catalogue..nationalarchives.gov.uk/search.asp).

Children of Margaret Butler, by William Boleyn, K.B.:

i. **THOMAS BOLEYN**, K.G., K.B., Earl of Wiltshire and Ormond [see next].

ii. **MARGARET BOLEYN**, married (as his 1st wife) before 1507 **JOHN SACKVILLE** (or **SACKVILE**, **SAKEVYLE**), Esq., of Withyham and Chiddingley, Sussex, and Mount Bures, Essex, Burgess (M.P.) for East Grinstead, Sheriff of Surrey and Sussex, 1540–1, 1546–7, son and heir of Richard Sackville, Esq., of Withyham, Sussex, by Isabel, daughter of John Digges, Esq. He was born before 17 March 1484. They had three sons, Richard, Knt., Christopher, and John, and three daughters, Anne (wife of Nicholas Pelham, Knt.), Isabel (wife of John Ashburnham), and Mary. He married (2nd) **ANNE TORRELL**, daughter of Humphrey Torrell, of Willingale Doe, Essex. They had no issue. JOHN SACKVILLE, Esq., died 27 Sept. 1557, and was buried at Withyham, Sussex 5 October 1557. He left a will dated 1 July 1555, proved 16 October 1559 (P.C.C. 48 Chaynay). Blomefield *Essay towards a Top. Hist. of Norfolk* 6 (1807): 381–409. Clutterbuck *Hist. & Antiqs. of Hertford* 3 (1827): 91–96 (Hoo-Boleyne ped.). *List of Sheriffs for England & Wales* (PRO Lists and Indexes 9) (1898): 137. Brydges *Collins' Peerage of England* 2 (1812): 90–180 (sub Sackville, Duke of Dorset). Clutterbuck *Hist. & Antiqs. of Hertford* 3 (1827): 94–95 (Hoo-Boleyne ped.). Phillips *Hist. of the Sackville Fam.* 1 (1930): 116. *Coll. Top. et Gen.* 4 (1837): 141. Sackville-West *Hist. Notices of Withyham* (1857): 60. *List of Sheriffs for England & Wales* (PRO Lists and Indexes 9) (1898): 137. *Genealogist* n.s. 34 (1918): 81–82 (re. Sackville fam.). *Arch. Cantiana* 38 (1926): 6–7. Bindoff *House of Commons 1509–1558* 3 (1982): 244 (biog. of John Sackville).

Child of Margaret Boleyn, by John Sackville, Esq.:

a. **MARY SACKVILLE**, married **JOHN LUNSFORD**, Esq., of Lunsford (in Etchingham), Sussex [see LUNSFORD 18].

iii. **ALICE BOLEYN**, married **ROBERT CLERE**, Knt., of Ormesby St. Margaret, Norfolk [see ALSOP 13].

13. THOMAS BOLEYN, K.G., K.B., of Hever, Kent, Hoo (in Luton), Bedfordshire, Fulbourn and Swavesey, Cambridgeshire, Offley St. Ledgers, Hertfordshire, New Inn without Temple Bar, London, Blicking and Mulbarton, Norfolk, etc., Knight of the Body to Henry VIII, 1509, Keeper of the Exchange at Calais and of the Foreign Exchange in England, 1509, Sheriff of Kent, 1511–2, 1517–8, joint Constable of Norwich Castle, 1512, Privy Councillor, 1518, Comptroller of the Household, 1520, Treasurer of the Household, 1521–5, Lord Keeper of the Privy Seal, 1530–6, son and heir, born about 1477. He was in arms against the Cornish rebels with his father at Blackheath in 1497. He married about 1500 (jointure dated summer 1501) [**LADY**] **ELIZABETH HOWARD**, daughter of Thomas Howard, K.G., K.B., Duke of Norfolk, by his 1st wife, Elizabeth, daughter and heiress of Frederick Tilney, Esq. [see HOWARD 14 for her ancestry]. They had three sons, Henry, Thomas, and George, Knt. [Lord Rochford], and two daughters, Mary and Anne. He presented to the church of Mulbarton, Norfolk in 1511 and 1526. He was Ambassador to the Emperor Maximilian in the Low Countries in 1513 and served as Ambassador to France in 1519–20. He and his wife, Elizabeth, attended the king and queen at the Field of the Cloth of Gold in 1520. He was Chief Ambassador to Spain in 1522–3. He was created Viscount Rochford 18 June 1525, and Earl of Wiltshire in England and Earl of Ormond in Ireland 8 Dec. 1529. He was present at the baptism of his granddaughter, Princess Elizabeth [future Queen Elizabeth I] in 1533. His wife, Elizabeth, died at the Abbot of Reading's place, beside Baynard's Castle, 3 April 1538, and was buried in the Howard aisle in Lambeth Church, Surrey. SIR THOMAS BOLEYN, Earl of Wiltshire and Ormond, died at Hever, Kent 12 March 1538/9, and was buried there.

Morant *Hist. & Antiqs. of Essex* 1 (1768): 269–271. Lodge *Peerage of Ireland* 4 (1789): 1–76 (sub Butler, Viscount Mountgarret). Hasted *Hist. & Top. Survey of Kent* 3 (1797): 190–202. Blomefield *Essay towards a Top. Hist. of Norfolk* 5 (1806): 75–83, 235–259; 6 (1807): 381–409. Brydges *Collins' Peerage of England* 4 (1812): 264–283; 9 (1812): 58–136 (sub Butler, Lord Butler). Baker *Hist. & Antiqs. of Northampton* 1 (1822–30): 588–590. Clutterbuck *Hist. & Antiqs. of*

Hertford 3 (1827): 91–96 (Hoo-Boleyne ped.). *Coll. Top. et Gen.* 4 (1837): 321–322. Beltz *Mems. of the Order of the Garter* (1841): clxxii. Lipscomb *Hist. & Antiqs. of Buckingham* 2 (1847): 4–7. *Procs. Soc. of Antiqs. of London* 2nd Ser. 4 (1869): 407–408. Cussans *Hist. of Hertfordshire* 1 (1870–73): 42–44. Brewer & Bullen *Cal. Carew MSS* (1873): 439–441. *Collectanea Genealogica* 1 (1881): 84–93. Burke *Dormant, Abeyant, Forfeited & Extinct Peerages* (1883): 58–59 (sub Boleyne). Doyle *Official Baronage of England* 3 (1886): 158–159 (sub Rochford), 679–681 (sub Wiltshire). *Genealogist* n.s. 3 (1886): 90–91; n.s. 7 (1891): 56. Harvey et al. *Vis. of Norfolk 1563 & 1613* (H.S.P. 32) (1891): 162–164 (1563 Vis.) (Howard ped.: "Lady Elizabeth Howard mar. to Thomas Bolleyn, Earl of Wiltsh."). *List of Sheriffs for England & Wales* (PRO Lists and Indexes 9) (1898): 69. *Antiq.* 42 (1906): 64–67. *Misc. Gen. et Heraldica* 4th Ser. 2 (1908): 246–247; 5th Ser. 8 (1932–34): 109–118 (1679 Saunders ped.: Boleyn arms: Argent, a chevron gules between 3 bulls' heads couped sable, langued of the second). VCH *Hertford* 3 (1912): 40. VCH *Buckingham* 3 (1925): 6–7. Harvey et al. *Vis. of the North* 3 (Surtees Soc. 144) (1930): 86–88 (Moubray ped.: "[Elizabeth Howard] vice-comitissa Rocheforde"). *C.P.* 10 (1945): 137–142 (sub Ormond) ("… he championed the Protestant party and commissioned Erasmus to write religious treatises for him… (quoting Brewer) "his besetting vice was avarice"); 11 (1949): 51 (sub Rochford); 12(2) (1959): 739 (sub Wiltshire). VCH *Oxford* 6 (1959): 134–146. Pakenham-Walsh *Tudor Story* (1963): 31–32. *Ancient Deeds — Ser. B* 2 (List & Index Soc. 101) (1974): B.5651, B.7565; 3 (List & Index Soc. 113) (1975): B.11700, B.12250. Moody et al. *New Hist. of Ireland* 9 (1984): 169 (chart). VCH *Cambridge* 9 (1989): 381–386; 10 (2002): 136–143. Ives *Life & Death of Anne Boleyn* (2004). Denny *Anne Boleyn* (2006). National Archives, C 146/782 (grant dated 20 Feb. 1527/8 by Thomas Bulleyn, Knt., Viscount Rocheford, son and heir of Lady Margaret Bulleyn, alias Butler, Lady Anne Seyntleger, alias Butler, and Lady Margert Bulleyn, alias Butler, daughters and co-heiresses of Thomas Butler, late Earl of Ormond, and George Seyntleger, Knt., son and heir of the said Lady Anne Seyntleger, to Bartholomew Dillon, Knt., of the office of steward and keeper of the courts belonging to their manors of Russh Turvy and Balskaddon, in the county of Dublin, Blakcastell and Donaghmour, county Meath, and Oghterard and Castelwarnyng, county Kildare, Ireland) (available at www.catalogue.nationalarchives.gov.uk/search.asp).

Children of Thomas Boleyn, K.G., K.B., by Elizabeth Howard:

i. **GEORGE BOLEYN**, Knt., Gentleman of the Privy Chamber, 1527, Esquire of the Body to the King, 1528, Master of the Buckhounds, 1528, Governor of the Hospital of St. Mary of Bethlehem, London, 1529, Constable of Kenilworth Castle, 1530, Keeper of Hatfield Park, 1531, Constable of Dover Castle and Warden of the Cinque Ports, 1534–6, Keeper of the manor and park of Penshurst, Kent, and the parks of North Leigh and Northlands, Kent, Steward of Tunbridge, Kent, Receiver and Bailiff of Brasted, Kent, only surviving son and heir apparent. He married before the end of 1525 (jointure agreement signed 4 October 1524) **JANE PARKER**, daughter of Henry Parker, Knt., 10th Lord Morley, by Alice, daughter of John Saint John, Knt. They had no issue. He was appointed Joint Ambassador to France in 1529. He was created Lord Rochford before 13 July 1530. He was appointed Ambassador Extraordinary to France in 1533. SIR GEORGE BOLEYN, Lord Rochford, was indicted for high treason, adultery, and incest 10 May 1536, tried and condemned 15 May 1536, and beheaded with all honours forfeited 17 May 1536. His widow, Jane, is listed as a lady of the Privy Chamber in 1540 to Queen Katherine Howard, fifth wife of King Henry VIII of England. Early in 1541 Queen Katherine embarked upon a light-hearted romance with the courtier, Thomas Culpeper; the couple's secret meetings were arranged by Jane Boleyn. In late 1541 Queen Katherine's past was uncovered and an investigation was launched into her private life. Subsequently, a love letter from the Queen Katherine to Culpeper was discovered and it explicitly mentioned Jane Boleyn's role in arranging their meetings. Jane was arrested and taken to the Tower of London, where she was imprisoned for several months. Jane Boleyn, Lady Rochford, was beheaded 13 Feb. 1541/2, and was buried in the Tower of London. Brydges *Collins' Peerage of England* 9 (1812): 58–136 (sub Butler, Lord Butler). Blomefield *Essay towards a Top. Hist. of Norfolk* 6 (1807): 381–409. Clutterbuck *Hist. & Antiqs. of Hertford* 3 (1827): 91–96 (Hoo-Boleyne ped.). Strickland *Lives of the Queens of England* 2 (1868): 352. Doyle *Official Baronage of England* 3 (1886): 160–161 (sub Rochford). Gibson *Recs. of Early English Drama, Diocese of Canterbury/Kent* 3 (2002): 1453–1454. Fox *Jane Boleyn* (2007).

ii. **MARY BOLEYN**, married (1st) **WILLIAM CAREY**, Esq. [see CAREY 15]; (2nd) **WILLIAM STAFFORD**, K.B., of Rochford, Essex [see CAREY 15].

iii. **ANNE BOLEYN**, Queen of England, married **HENRY VIII OF ENGLAND**, King of England [see TUDOR 15].

◈ CALTHORPE ◈

RICHARD FITZ GILBERT, of Clare, Suffolk, married **ROHESE** (or **ROSE**) **GIFFARD**.
GILBERT FITZ RICHARD, of Clare, Suffolk, married **ALICE DE CLERMONT**.
RICHARD FITZ GILBERT, of Clare, Suffolk, married **ALICE OF CHESTER**.
ROGER DE CLARE, Earl of Hertford, married **MAUD DE SAINT HILARY**.
RICHARD DE CLARE, Knt., Earl of Hertford, married **AMICE OF GLOUCESTER** (desc. King William the Conqueror).
MAUD DE CLARE, married **WILLIAM DE BREWES**, of Bramber, Sussex.
JOHN DE BREWES, of Bramber, Sussex, married **MARGARET OF WALES** [see BREWES 7].

8. RICHARD DE BREWES (or **BREWSE**, **BREUSE**), Knt., in right of his wife, of Stinton (in Salle) and Heydon, Norfolk, Ludborough, Lincolnshire, Akenham, Hasketon, Stradbrooke, and Whittingham (in Fressingfield), Suffolk, Bromley, Surrey, etc., younger son, born before 1232. He married before 9 Sept. 1265 **ALICE LE RUS**, widow of Richard Longespée, Knt. (died shortly before 27 Dec. 1261) [see LONGESPÉE 6.ii], and daughter and heiress of William le Rus, of Akenham, Clopton, Hasketon, Stradbroke, and Whittingham (in Fressingfield), Suffolk, and, in right of his wife, of Stinton (in Salle), Norfolk, Ludborough, Lincolnshire, Bromley, Surrey, etc., by Agatha, daughter and heiress of Roger de Clere [see HUNTINGFIELD 6.ii.b for her ancestry]. She was born 25 Dec. 1245, or 1247, or 1 Jan. 1245/6. They had two sons, Giles, Knt., and Richard, and two daughters, Margaret and Sibyl (wife of Constantine de Mortimer). He was granted part of the manor of Thorganby, Yorkshire, by his brother, William de Brewes, Knt. In 1254–c. 1260 he witnessed various charters of his brother, William de Brewes, to Sele Priory. In 1267 he had the grant of a weekly market and yearly fair at his manor of Whittingham (in Fressingfield), Suffolk. He presented to the church of Thorganby, Yorkshire in 1268 and 1271. In 1269 he and his wife, Alice, released to the Dean and Chapter of Lincoln their claims to services from lands in Fotherby, Lincolnshire, in return for a rent of 12 pence from a toft in Ludborough, Lincolnshire and 60 marks of silver. In 1270 Maud Longespée, tenant of part of the lands late of Maud de Faye, sued Richard and his wife, Alice, regarding an acquittance of debt. In 1274–5 he arraigned an assize of novel disseisin against Henry Hay, parson of Acton, touching a tenement in Thirkleby, Yorkshire. He was summoned *cum equus et armis* 12 Dec. 1276 to 14 June 1287, and to attend the King at Shrewsbury, 28 June 1283, by writs directed *Ricardo de Brehuse* or *Breuse*. In 1279–80 Adam de la Sale arraigned an assize of novel disseisin against him and others touching a tenement in Claydon, Suffolk. In 1280 a commission was issued to enquire as to the persons who broke by night the doors and fences of the park of Richard de Brewes, in Stradbroke, Suffolk, and carried away deer. In 1280–1 John de Ferlington arraigned a jury against Richard and his wife, Alice, regarding the manor of Wilton-in-Pickering Lythe, Yorkshire. SIR RICHARD DE BREWES died shortly before 18 June 1292. His widow, Alice, died shortly before 28 Jan. 1300/1. They were buried in Woodbridge Priory, Suffolk.

Blomefield *Essay towards a Top. Hist. of Norfolk* 6 (1807): 242; 8 (1808): 266–269. Bowles & Nichols *Annals & Antiqs. of Lacock Abbey* (1835): App., i–v (Book of Lacock). Lipscomb *Hist. & Antiqs. of Buckingham* 2 (1847): 557–558. *Notes & Queries* 3rd Ser. 1 (1862): 489–490; 6th Ser. 12 (1885): 478. Hutchins *Hist. & Antiqs. of Dorset* 3 (1868): 287 (Salisbury-Longespée ped.). Waters *Chester of Chicheley* 1 (1878): 197. *Genealogist* 5 (1881): 318–323; 6 (1882): 236–247. *Annual Rpt. of the Deputy Keeper* 44 (1883): 263; 46 (1886): 379; 49 (1888): 42, 111, 190; 50 (1889): 253. *Cal. IPM* 1 (1904): 73–74, 128. Giffard *Reg. of Walter Giffard Archbishop of York* (Surtees Soc. 109) (1904): 50, 57. Rigg *Cal. Plea Rolls of the Exchequer of the Jews* 1 (1905): 238. *C.Ch.R.* 2 (1906): 74. Copinger *Manors of Suffolk* 2 (1908): 228, 318; 3 (1909): 50; 4 (1909): 44, 84–85. *C.F.R.* 1 (1911): 436. VCH *Surrey* 3 (1911): 80–86. *C.P.* 2 (1912): 304 (sub Brewes); 9 (1936): 248–249 (sub Mortimer). Salzman *Chartulary of the Priory of St. Peter at Sele* (1923): 5–6, 67, 73–74, 84–85. Foster *Reg. Antiquissimum of the Cathedral Church of Lincoln* 4 (Lincoln Rec. Soc. 32) (1937): 250–254 (charters of Richard de Breuse, Knt., and his wife, Alice dated 1268 and 1269) (his seal attached to the 1269 charter bears a shield with a lion rampant [BREWES]). Paget *Baronage of England* (1957) 93: 1–2 (sub Braose, of Stinton). *TG* 1 (1980): 80–95; 6 (1985): 85–99. Brown *Eye Priory Cartulary & Charters* 1 (Suffolk Charters 12) (1992): 234; 2 (Suffolk Charters 13) (1994): 77–81. Given-Wilson *Illus. Hist. of Late Medieval England* (1996): 78.

Children of Richard de Brewes, Knt., by Alice le Rus:

i. **GILES DE BREWES**, Knt. [see next].

ii. **MARGARET DE BREWES**, married **ROGER DE COLEVILLE**, Knt., of Bytham, Lincolnshire [see RANDOLPH 9].

9. GILES DE BREWES, Knt., of Stinton (in Salle) and Heydon, Norfolk, Ludborough, Lincolnshire, Akenham, Stradbrooke, and Whittingham (in Fressingfield), Suffolk, etc., son and heir, born about 1273 (aged 28 in 1301). He married (1st) **KATHERINE DE HUNTINGFIELD**, daughter of Laurence de Huntingfield, Knt. They had no issue. He married (2nd) in or before 1303 **JOAN DE BEAUMONT**, daughter and heiress of Richard de Beaumont, of Witnesham, Suffolk. They had four sons, Richard, Robert, John, Knt., and Alexander. SIR GILES DE BREWES died shortly before 6 Feb. 1310/11. His widow, Joan, married (2nd) shortly before 15 Nov. 1311 (as his 1st wife) **EDMUND BACON**, Knt. [see MOLEYNS 13], of Oulton, Suffolk, Hatfield Peverel and Gynge Mounteney, Essex, Gresham, Norfolk, Ewelme, Oxfordshire, etc., Knight of the Household, Keeper of Wallingford Castle and Honour, 1311, and, in right of his 1st wife, of Witnesham, Suffolk, allegedly son of Robert Bacon, of Baconsthorpe, by _____, daughter of Robert de Hingham, Knt. They had one daughter, Margaret (wife of William de Kerdeston, Knt., 2nd Lord Kerdeston [see GANT 8]). He performed military service in Gascony in 1297. The same year he was enfeoffed of the manor of Ewelme, Oxfordshire by his brother, John Bacon. In 1303 he served in Scotland with John de Saint John, Knt. He was present at the Siege of Stirling Castle in 1304. In 1308 he was granted the escheated lands of Robert de Stuteville in Gresham, Norfolk. The same year he and his brother, John Bacon, obtained a license to empark their wood at Gynge Mounteney, Essex. In 1309 he was granted the reversion of the manor of Hatfield Peverel, Essex. He was in the service of Peter de Gavaston, Earl of Cornwall in 1310. In 1314 he accompanied Gilbert de Clare, Earl of Gloucester in Queen Isabel's retinue on an embassy concerning Gascony. The same year he also went on a pilgrimage to Santiago. In 1316 he went to Wales on the king's service. His wife, Joan, was living in 1316. Following her death, Edmund married (2nd) **ELIZABETH LA WARRE**, daughter of John la Warre, Knt., 2nd Lord la Warre, by Joan, daughter of Robert de Grelle (or Grelley), Knt. [see LA WARRE 12 for her ancestry]. They had no issue. In 1320 he accompanied Edmund of Woodstock, Earl of Kent on an embassy to France. He was on the king's service in Wales with Earl Edmund in 1322. In August 1322 he accompanied Edmund, Earl of Arundel on the Scottish campaign. His wife, Elizabeth, died testate in 1323. In 1324 he again went on an embassy with Edmund, Earl of Kent. In 1325 he was sent on an embassy to Jaime, King of Aragón, concerning the proposed marriage between the future Edward III and the Infanta Jolant. The same year he fought in Gascony in the War of Saint-Sardos. He married (3rd) before 1326 (date of settlement) **MARGERY DE POYNINGS** (or **PONYNGES**), daughter of Michael de Poynings, Knt., of Poynings, Sussex, by Margery (or Margaret), daughter of Hugh Bardolf, Knt., 1st Lord Bardolf [see POYNINGS 12 for her ancestry]. They had one daughter, Margery (wife of William de Moleyns, Knt.). In 1326, when Queen Isabel's invasion was threatened, he was empowered to arrest shipping in various Norfolk ports and to superintend the sailing of other vessels to Orwell. In 1334 he was appointed Keeper of the Half Hundred of Lothingland in Suffolk for a year. SIR EDMUND BACON died 6 March 1336. His widow, Margery, married (2nd) before 1337 **NICHOLAS DE LA BECHE**, Knt., of Beaumys (in Swallowfield), Beche, Binfield, Burghfield, Basildon, Cookham, East and West Compton, Berkshire, Constable of the Tower. They had no issue. SIR NICHOLAS DE LA BECHE died shortly before 1 March 1345. On 30 March 1347 his widow, Margery, was forcibly carried off and married to **JOHN DE DALTON**, Knt., King's Serjeant-at-arms, of Bispham, Lancashire, son and heir of Robert de Dalton. He fought at the Battle of Crécy in 1346. On 1 May 1347 he was imprisoned in the Tower of London. In

October 1348 his lands were declared forfeited. She died in Calais 20 March 1349. SIR JOHN DE DALTON died in 1369.

> Blomefield *Essay towards a Top. Hist. of Norfolk* 6 (1807): 242, 248; 8 (1808): 266–269. *Coll. Top. et Gen.* 4 (1837): 391 (arms of Sir Edmund Bacon). Napier *Swyncombe & Ewelme* (1858): 21–22, 40–41, chart opp. 42. Hardy *Syllabus (in English) of the Docs. Rel. England & Other Kingdoms* 1 (1869): 355. Rye *Short Cal. Feet of Fines for Norfolk* 2 (1886): 275. Gibbons *Early Lincoln Wills* (1888): 4. *Colls. Hist. Staffs.* 14 (1893): 71–72. *C.P.R. 1307–1313* (1894): 82, 187. Wrottesley *Crécy & Calais* (1898): 39, 101, 110, 279. Russell *Swallowfield & its Owners* (1901): 39–43. *Feudal Aids* 3 (1904): 390, 414, 462, 464, 488, 536; 5 (1908): 37–38, 41. *Cal. IPM* 5 (1908): 146–147 (1908); 9 (1916): 152–153; 10 (1921): 77–78, 262–267; 11 (1935): 11. Copinger *Manors of Suffolk* 3 (1909): 50, 182; 4 (1909): 44. VCH *Lancaster* 4 (1911): 91–97, 97–101; 6 (1911): 100–102. *C.F.R.* 2 (1912): 81, 118, 136; 3 (1912): 353–354, 361, 413; 4 (1913): 391, 479, 481–482, 485–486; 5 (1915): 424. *C.P.* 2 (1912): 305 (sub Brewes) (Breuse arms: Argent, crusilly, a lion rampant, tail forked, gules); 7 (1929): 191–193. *Feet of Fines for Essex* 2 (1913–28): 110, 111, 171, 228. *English Hist. Rev.* 37 (1922): 273–274; 74 (1959): 70–89. Farrer *Honors & Knights' Fees* 3 (1925): 330. Moor *Knights of Edward I* 1 (H.S.P. 80) (1929): 142. *Sussex Notes & Queries* 4 (1932): 97–98. VCH *Sussex* 9 (1937): 139. Paget *Baronage of England* (1957) 93: 1–2 (sub Braose, of Stinton). VCH Cambridge 5 (1973): 4–16. Hockey *Reg. of William Edington Bishop of Winchester 1346–1366* 2 (Hampshire Rec. Ser. 8) (1987): 9. Richmond *Paston Fam. in the 15th Cent.* (1990): 47–49. Brault *Rolls of Arms Edward I* 2 (1997): 23 (arms of Edmund Bacon: Gules, on a chief argent two mullets sable). *Trans. Monumental Brass Soc.* 16 (1997): 2–25. Rickard *Castle Community* (2002): 91. Dunn *Damsels in Distress or Partners in Crime?* (2007): 158–159.

10. JOHN DE BREWES, Knt., of Stinton (in Salle), Corpusty, Heydon, and Olton, Norfolk, Ludborough, Lincolnshire, Akenham, Suffolk, etc., 3rd but 1st surviving son and heir by his father's 2nd marriage, born 10 August 1306. In 1325 he was heir to his older brother, Robert de Brewes. He married **EVE DE UFFORD**, daughter of Robert de Ufford, Knt., 1st Lord Ufford, by Cecily, younger daughter and co-heiress of Robert de Valoines, of Ixworth and Walsham, Suffolk. They had one son, John, Knt., and one daughter, Cecily. He presented to the church of Heydon, Norfolk in 1330, 1331, 1332, 1335, 1338, and 1340. In 1360 the manor of Heydon, Norfolk was settled on trustees including Robert de Ufford, Knt., Earl of Suffolk, for the use of John Brewes, Knt., the elder. His wife, Eve, and their son, John de Brewes, were legatees in the 1368 will of her brother, Robert de Ufford, K.G., 1st Earl of Suffolk, Lord Ufford. His wife, Eve, was living in 1370. SIR JOHN DE BREWES was living in 1374, when he presented to the church of Heydon, Norfolk as "Sir John Brewse, senior, Knt." He and his wife, Eve, were buried in Woodbridge Priory, Suffolk.

> Blomefield *Essay towards a Top. Hist. of Norfolk* 6 (1807): 242, 248; 8 (1808): 266–269. *Top. & Gen.* 2 (1853): 271–277 (Ufford ped.). Copinger *Manors of Suffolk* 2 (1908): 228; 3 (1909): 50, 82; 4 (1909): 44. *Cal. IPM* 6 (1910): 422–423, 440–441, 458; 8 (1913): 341. *C.P.* 2 (1912): 305–306. Paget *Baronage of England* (1957) 93: 1–2 (sub Braose, of Stinton).

Children of John de Brewes, Knt., by Eve de Ufford:

i. **JOHN DE BREWES**, Knt. [see next].

ii. **CECILY DE BREWES**, married **WILLIAM DE KERDESTON**, Knt., of Claxton and Kerdeston, Norfolk [see GANT 8.i].

11. JOHN DE BREWES, Knt., of Stinton (in Salle), Norfolk, Ludborough, Lincolnshire, Akenham, Whittingham, Witnesham, Suffolk, etc., Sheriff of Norfolk and Suffolk, 1376–7, Keeper of Norwich Castle, and, in right of his 2nd wife, of Caxton, Cambridgeshire, son and heir, born about 1332 (aged 54 in 1386). He married (1st) **JOAN DE SHARDELOW**, daughter of John de Shardelow, Knt., of Shardelowe (in Little Barton), Burton Mills, and Cooling, Suffolk, by his wife, Margaret. They had one son, Robert, Knt. He was at the Siege of Calais in 1346–7. In 1368 he was a legatee in the will of his uncle, Robert de Ufford, K.G., 1st Earl of Suffolk, Lord Ufford. He married (2nd) before 1 April 1376 **AGNES _____**, widow of Richard de Freville, son and heir apparent of John Freville, of Little Shelford, Cambridgeshire. SIR JOHN DE BREWES was living in 1394. At his death, he was buried with his 1st wife in Woodbridge Priory, Suffolk. His widow, Agnes, married (3rd) **WILLIAM ROOS** (or **REES**), Esq., of Tharston, Norfolk and Caxton and West Wratting, Cambridgeshire. She was living in 1401. He died testate in 1410.

Blomefield *Essay towards a Top. Hist. of Norfolk* 5 (1806): 303–308; 6 (1807): 248; 8 (1808): 266–269. Hill *Arch. & Hist. Notices of the Churches of Cambridgeshire* (1880): 144. Rye *Short Cal. Feet of Fines for Norfolk* 2 (1886): 377. *List of Sheriffs for England & Wales* (PRO Lists and Indexes 9) (1898): 87. Copinger *Manors of Suffolk* 3 (1909): 50, 182; 4 (1909): 44. *C.P.* 2 (1912): 306 (cites Weever *Ancient Funerall Monuments* (1631): 752). *C.F.R.* 8 (1924): 369; 9 (1926): 3. *Cal. IPM* 14 (1952): 216. Paget *Baronage of England* (1957) 93: 1–2 (sub Braose, of Stinton). VCH *Cambridge* 5 (1973): 26–35; 6 (1978): 191–198.

12. ROBERT BREWES, Knt., of Stinton (in Salle), Norfolk, Akenham, Suffolk, etc., son and heir by his father's 1st marriage. He married **ELA STAPLETON**, daughter of Miles Stapleton, Knt., of Bedale, Yorkshire, and Ingham, Norfolk, by Ela, daughter of Edmund de Ufford, Knt. [see STAPLETON 11 for her ancestry]. They had one son, Thomas, Knt., and two daughters, Margaret and Ela. Robert and his wife, Ela, were both legatees in the 1414 will of her father, Miles Stapleton, Knt. SIR ROBERT BREWES died shortly before 30 Sept. 1424 (grant of his administration). His widow, Ela, presented to the church of Heydon, Norfolk in 1433. She was appointed one of the executors of the 1438 will of her brother, Brian Stapleton, Knt. Ela left a will dated 16 October 1456. Robert and Ela were buried in Woodbridge Priory, Suffolk.

Blomefield *Essay towards a Top. Hist. of Norfolk* 4 (1775): 419; 6 (1807): 249; 8 (1808): 266–269. Banks *Baronies in Fee* 1 (1844): 266–269 (sub Ingham). *Norfolk Arch.* 4 (1855): 321–322, 327–329; 8 (1879): 183–223. Flower *Vis. of Yorkshire 1563–4* (H.S.P. 16) (1881): 293–295 (Stapleton ped.: "Ella [Stapleton] wyff to …. Brews."). *Yorkshire Arch. & Topog. Jour.* 8 (1884): 223–258. Copinger *Manors of Suffolk* 3 (1909): 50, 182. *C.P.* 2 (1912): 306 (asserts mother of Ela was "Ela, da. of Sir Edmund d'Ufford, le cowyn"). Paget *Baronage of England* (1957) 93: 1–2 (sub Braose, of Stinton); 505: 1.

Children of Robert Brewes, Knt., by Ela Stapleton:

i. **ELA BREWES**, married **WILLIAM YELVERTON**, K.B., of Rougham, Norfolk [see YELVERTON 13].

ii. **MARGARET BREWES** [see next].

13. MARGARET BREWES, married **JOHN SHELTON**, Esq., of Shelton, Great Snoring, Thetford, and Hindringham, Norfolk, and Brent Illegh, Suffolk, son and heir of William Shelton, Esq., of Shelton, Norfolk, by Katherine, daughter of Simon Baret, of Hardwicke and Hecham. He was baptized 7 July 1406. They had one son, Ralph, Knt. JOHN SHELTON died 23 April 1431.

Harvey *Vis. of Norfolk 1563* 2 (1895): 342–352 (1563 Vis. Norfolk) (Shelton arms: Azure, a cross or).

14. RALPH SHELTON, Knt., of Shelton, Norfolk, Sheriff of Norfolk and Suffolk, son and heir, born about January 1431 (aged three months at father's death). He married (1st) **JOAN** _____. They had two daughters, Margaret and Elizabeth (said to be wife of Richard Fitz Lewis, Knt.). He married (2nd) **MARGARET CLERE**, daughter of Robert Clere, Esq., of Ormesby, Norfolk, by Elizabeth, daughter of Thomas Uvedale, Esq. They had three sons, John, Knt., Ralph, Esq., and Richard (clerk), and two daughters, Elizabeth and Alice (wife of John Heveningham). SIR RALPH SHELTON died 16 July 1497. He left a will dated 21 March 1497, proved 13 May 1498 (P.C.C. 33 Horne), requesting burial at Shelton, Norfolk. In 1499 his widow Margaret donated a gold chain weighing nearly eight ounces to the Chapel of St. Mary of Pity. She died 16 Jan. 1499/1500. She left a will dated 23 Dec. 1499, proved 3 Dec. 1500 (Cur. Epis. Norwich).

Harvey *Vis. of Norfolk 1563* 2 (1895): 342–352, 375.

15. RALPH SHELTON, Esq., of Broome and Norwich, Norfolk, 2nd son by his father's 2nd marriage. He married **MARY BROME**, widow of John Jenny, Esq., of Hardwicke, and daughter and co-heiress of Gilbert Brome, of Broome, Norfolk. They had one son, Ralph, Esq., and three daughters, Anne, Mary, and Dorothy (wife of Francis Shardlowe, Gent.). RALPH SHELTON, Esq., was buried at Broome, Norfolk 25 October 1538. He left a will dated 21 October 1538, proved 18 June 1539 (Cur. Epis. Norwich). His widow, Mary, died 29 August 1540, and was buried at Broome, Norfolk 3 Sept. 1540. She left a will dated 26 August 1540, proved 12 Feb. 1542 (Cur. Epis. Norwich).

Harvey *Vis. of Norfolk 1563* 2 (1895): 342–352, 370–371, 397–398.

16. RALPH SHELTON, Esq., of Broome, Norfolk. He married (1st) in 1545 **PRUDENCE CALTHORPE**, daughter of Edward Calthorpe, Esq., of Kirby Cane, Norfolk, by Thomasine, daughter and co-heiress of Thomas Gavell, Esq. [see STAPLETON 16 for her ancestry]. They had four sons, Richard, Edward, Gent., Richard (again), and John, Gent., and three daughters, Thomasine (wife of Thomas Uvedale, Gent., and Charles Crofts, Esq.), Grace, and Frances. His wife, Prudence, was buried at Broome, Norfolk 23 October 1562. He married (2nd) **CECILY STEWARD**, widow of John Pickerell of Cringleford, and daughter of Augustine Steward, alderman of Norwich, Norfolk, by Elizabeth, daughter of William Rede, Esq., of Beccles, Suffolk. They had two children. RALPH SHELTON, Esq., left a will dated 31 October 1592, proved 25 Nov. 1592 (Cur. Episc. Norwich). His widow, Cecily, was buried 13 March 1612. She left a will dated 10 April 1610, proved 25 March 1612 (Cur. Episc. Norwich), requesting burial at Broome, Norfolk.
Norfolk Arch. 9 (1884): 1–19. Harvey *Vis. of Norfolk 1563* 2 (1895): 342–352, 400–401. *Virginia Gen.* 40 (1996): 68–70.

17. GRACE SHELTON, daughter by her father's 1st marriage, baptized at Broome, Norfolk 2 August 1554. She married at Broome, Norfolk 29 April 1582 **JOHN THURTON** (or **THURLTON**), Gent., of Broome, Norfolk. His wife, Grace, was buried at Broome, Norfolk 12 Dec. 1606. JOHN THURTON, Gent., was buried at Broome, Norfolk 20 Sept. 1609. He left a will dated 20 Jan. 1606, proved 1 Nov. 1609 (P.C.C. 108 Dorset).
Norfolk Arch. 9 (1884): 153–179. Harvey *Vis. of Norfolk 1563* 2 (1895): 342–352. *Virginia Gen.* 40 (1996): 68–70.

18. MAUD THURTON, baptized at Ditchingham, Norfolk 17 Nov. 1584. She was a legatee in the will of her step-grandmother, Cecily Shelton, who bequeathed her a gilt pepper box. She married at Broome, Norfolk 8 Sept. 1602 **CHRISTOPHER CALTHORPE**, Esq., of Cockthorpe and East Barsham, Norfolk, son of James Calthorpe, Knt., of Cockthorpe and Blakeney, by Barbara, daughter of John Bacon, Esq., of Hessett, Suffolk. He was baptized at Cockthorpe, Norfolk 29 May 1581. They had seven sons, James, Esq., [Col.] Christopher, Edward, Charles, Oliver, Robert, and Francis, and three daughters, Grace (wife of Robert Strutt), Barbara (wife of Henry Mordaunt), and Matilda. His wife, Maud, was buried 27 March 1624. CHRISTOPHER CALTHORPE, Esq., died at London 14 March 1624/5.
Le Neve's Peds. of the Knights (H.S.P. 8) (1873): 9–10 (Calthorpe ped.: "Christopher Calthorp of Cockthorpe blakney Norff. & cockthorp (*sic*) buried at blakney. = Maud dr & coheir of John Thurton of brome Hall Norff. neer bungay."). *Norfolk Arch.* 9 (1884): 153–179 (Calthorpe ancestry) (no mention of son Christopher). Harvey *Vis. of Norfolk 1563* 2 (1895): 401, 440–485. Palgrave-Moore *Norfolk Peds.* 5 (Norfolk Gen. 22) (1990): 31–32 (Calthorpe ped.). *Virginia Gen.* 40 (1996): 68–70. Dorman *Adventurers of Purse & Person* 1 (2004): 456–467.

19. [COL.] CHRISTOPHER CALTHORPE, 2nd son, baptized at Ditchingham, Norfolk 22 April 1605. He immigrated to Virginia in the *Furtherance* in 1622. In 1628 he owned land near Fort Henry in Elizabeth City, Virginia. He married **ANNE** _____. They had one son, James, and three daughters, Elinor (wife of Thomas Wragg), Barbara, and Ann. In 1635 he patented 500 acres at New Poquoson in York County, Virginia, which plantation he called "Thropland" after his family's estate in England. The church building of New Poquoson Parish stood on the Calthorpe tract. He was a member of the House of Burgesses from York County, 1644–6, 1652–3, 1660, and from Elizabeth City County, 1645. He also served as captain, major and colonel of the militia. In 1661 he removed to North Carolina. [COL.] CHRISTOPHER CALTHORPE died shortly before 24 April 1662. His widow, Anne, died in Charles Parish, York County, Virginia 9 Dec. 1667.
Le Neve's Peds. of the Knights (H.S.P. 8) (1873): 9–10 (Calthorpe ped.: "Xtfer C[althorpe]. went into Virginea maried & hath issue."). Harvey *Vis. of Norfolk 1563* 2 (1895): 440–485. Palgrave-Moore *Norfolk Peds.* 5 (Norfolk Gen. 22) (1990): 31–32 (Calthorpe ped.). *Virginia Gen.* 40 (1996): 68–70. Dorman *Adventurers of Purse & Person* 1 (2004): 456–467.

❧ CALVERT ❧

ALICE OF NORMANDY (sister of King William the Conqueror), married **LAMBERT**, Count of Lens.
JUDITH OF LENS, married **WALTHEOF**, Earl of Northumberland.
MAUD OF NORTHUMBERLAND, married **SIMON DE SENLIS**, Earl of Huntingdon and Northampton.
MAUD DE SENLIS, married **SAHER DE QUINCY**, of Long Buckby, Northamptonshire.
ALICE DE SENLIS, married **ROGER DE HUNTINGFIELD**, of Huntingfield, Suffolk.
WILLIAM DE HUNTINGFIELD, Knt., of Huntingfield, Suffolk, married **ISABEL FITZ WILLIAM**.
SARAH DE HUNTINGFIELD, married **RICHARD DE KEYNES**, of Horsted Keynes, Sussex.
RICHARD DE KEYNES, of Horsted Keynes, Sussex, married **ALICE DE MANKESEY**.
JOAN DE KEYNES, married **ROGER DE LEWKNOR**, Knt., of South Mimms, Middlesex.
THOMAS DE LEWKNOR, Knt., of South Mimms, Middlesex, married **SIBYL** _____.
ROGER DE LEWKNOR, Knt., of Broadhurst (in Horsted Keynes), Sussex, married **KATHERINE BARDOLF**.
THOMAS DE LEWKNOR, Knt., of Broadhurst (in Horsted Keynes), Sussex, married **JOAN D'OYLEY**.
ROGER LEWKNOR, Esq., of Horstead Keynes, Sussex, married **ELIZABETH CAREW**.
THOMAS LEWKNOR, Knt., of Horsted Keynes, Sussex, married **PHILIPPE DALLINGRIDGE**.
ROGER LEWKNOR, Knt., of Broadhurst (in Horsted Keynes), Sussex, married **ELEANOR CAMOYS** (desc. King William the Conqueror).
ELIZABETH LEWKNOR, married **JOHN WROTH**, Esq., of Durants (in Enfield), Middlesex.
JOHN WROTH, of Durants (in Enfield), Middlesex, married **JOAN** _____.
ROBERT WROTH, Esq., of Durants (in Enfield), Middlesex, married **JANE HAUTE**.
THOMAS WROTH, Knt., of Durants (in Enfield), Middlesex, married **MARY RICH** [see WROTH 19].

20. ELIZABETH WROTH. She was a legatee in the 1573 will of her father. She married at Hertingfordbury, Hertfordshire 24 June 1574 **GEORGE MYNNE** (or **MYNN**), Esq., of Hertingfordbury, Hertfordshire, St. Botolph Aldersgate, London, and Gaulden, Somerset, son of John Mynne, Gent., of Fransham, Norfolk, St. Botolph, London, and Hertingfordbury, Hertfordshire, King's Auditor, by his wife, Alice Hale. They had three sons, Robert, John, Esq., and George, and three daughters, Mary, Susan, and Anne. He was born 14 Feb. 1536. He was heir in 1551 to his brother, Edward Mynne, Gent. GEORGE MYNNE, Esq., died 20 May 1581, and was buried at Hertingfordbury, Hertfordshire 21 May 1581. He left a will dated 19 May 1581, proved 7 Nov. 1581 (P.C.C. 41 Darcy). His wife, Elizabeth, married (2nd) **NICHOLAS BUTLER**, Esq. His wife, Elizabeth, was a legatee in the 1606 will of her brother, Robert Wroth, Knt. She died 14 August 1614.

Waller *Loughton in Essex* Pt. 2 (1889–1900): 19–21 (will of Sir Thomas Wroth), 21–22 (will of Sir Robert Wroth). Fry *Abs. of IPM for London* 1 (Index Lib.) (1896): 148; 3 (Index Lib. 36) (1908): 48–50. *C.P.* 1 (1910): 393. Mosby *Heritage of Faith: Calvert, Green & Alvey Fam. Hists.* (1976). Palgrave-Moore *Norfolk Peds.* 3 (Norfolk Gen. 13) (1981): 111–115 (Mynne ped.) (Mynne arms: Argent a fess dancetty, paly of four gules and ermine between six cross crosslets sable). Parish Recs. of Hertingfordbury, Hertfordshire [FHL Microfilm 991383].

21. ANNE MYNNE, married at St. Peter's, Cornhill, London 22 Nov. 1604 (as his 1st wife) **GEORGE CALVERT**, Knt., of Danbywiske, Yorkshire, Under Secretary of State, Clerk of the Privy Council, 1605, Burgess (M.P.) for Bossiney, 1609–11, Knight of the Shire for Yorkshire, 1620–2, Secretary of State, 1619–25, Privy Councillor, son and heir of Leonard Calvert, by Alice, daughter of John Crossland. He was born at Kipling (in Bolton), Yorkshire in 1578 or 1579. They had six sons, Cecil [2nd Lord Baltimore], Leonard, George, Francis, Henry, and John, and five daughters, Anne (wife of William Peasley), Dorothy, Elizabeth, Grace (wife of Robert Talbot, Knt.), and Ellen (or Helen) (wife of James Talbot, Esq.). He matriculated aged 14 at Trinity College, Oxford in 1594, and received a B.A. degree in 1597. He resigned his preferments in February 1624/5, having become a Roman Catholic. But as he had received large grants of land in Ireland, he was created Lord Baltimore of Baltimore, co. Longford, Ireland 16 Feb. 1624/5. He obtained a grant of Maryland from King Charles I. LADY ANNE CALVERT died 8 August 1622, and was buried at Hertingfordbury, Hertfordshire. He married (2nd) in or before 1627 **JOAN** _____. They had one son, Philip. SIR GEORGE CALVERT, 1st Lord Baltimore, died 15 April 1632, and was buried at St. Dunstan's-in-the-West, London. He left a will dated 14 April 1632, proved 21 April 1632. His wife, Joan, predeceased him.

> Glover & St. George *Vis. of Yorkshire 1584–5, 1612* (1875): 500 (1612 Vis. Yorkshire) (Calvert ped.: "Sir George Calvert, of Danby Wiske, co. York, knight, one of his Majesty's principal secretaries of State, a[nn]o 1619, 1st Lord Baltimore = Ann, dau. of George Myms, of Hertingfordbury, co. Herts") (Calvert arms: Paly of six or and sable, a bend counterchanged). *C.P.* 1 (1910): 393 (sub Calvert). O'Gorman *Descs. of Virginia Calverts* (1947): 53–58. Mosby *Heritage of Faith: Calvert, Green & Alvey Fam. Hists.* (1976). Palgrave-Moore *Norfolk Peds.* 3 (Norfolk Gen. 13) (1981): 111–115 (Mynne ped.). Dorman *Adventurers of Purse & Person* 1 (2004): 468–485. Parish Recs. of Hertingfordbury, Hertfordshire [FHL Microfilm 991383].

Children of Anne Mynne, by George Calvert, Knt.:

i. **CECIL CALVERT**, 2nd Lord Baltimore [see next].

ii. **LEONARD CALVERT**, planter, Protonotary and Keeper of Writs in Connacht and Thomond, Ireland, born about 1606. He accompanied his father to Newfoundland, and in August 1628 he returned to England where he petitioned the king that his father might have a share in certain prizes taken from the French by the ships *Benediction* and *Victory*. He immigrated to Maryland in 1634, where he settled in St. Mary's County. He served as Governor of Maryland from 1634–47. In 1641/2 and 1643/4 he returned to England to consult with his brother, Cecilius Calvert, 2nd Lord Baltimore. He married an unidentified wife, _____. They had one son, [Col.] William, Esq., and one daughter, Anne (wife of Baker Brooke, Henry Brent, and [Col.] Richard Marsham). LEONARD CALVERT died in St. Mary's Co., Maryland 11 June 1647. O'Gorman *Descs. of Virginia Calverts* (1947): 53–64. Mosby *Heritage of Faith: Calvert, Green & Alvey Fam. Hists.* (1976). Papenfuse *Biog. Dict. of the Maryland Legislature* 1 (1979): 190 (biog. of Leonard Calvert: "… he had a very difficult task in the initial years of settlement of steering a middle ground between the demands of various groups in colony, especially the Jesuits."). Riley *Tidewater Maryland Ancs.* (1999): 148–151. Dorman *Adventurers of Purse & Person* 1 (2004): 468–485.

22. CECIL (or **CECILIUS**) **CALVERT**, 2nd Lord Baltimore, Proprietor of Maryland, Knight of the Shire, colonial investor and legislator, son and heir, born 8 August 1605 and baptized at Boxley, Kent 2 March 1605/6. He married by settlement dated 20 March 1627/8 **ANNE ARUNDELL**, daughter of Thomas Arundell, Knt., 1st Lord Arundell of Wardour, by his 2nd wife, Anne, daughter of Miles Philipson, Esq. [see CHIDIOCK 19 for her ancestry]. They had three sons, George, Charles [3rd Lord Baltimore], and Cecil, and six daughters, Georgiana, Mary, Frances, Anne, Mary (wife of William Blakiston, Knt.), and Elizabeth. He entered Trinity College, Oxford University in 1621, and was admitted to Gray's Inn 8 August 1633. In 1632 he was granted the proprietorship of the province of Maryland by King Charles I, and he took possession of it early in 1634. As heir to the charter promised his father, he promoted, though in England, the settlement of Maryland. He skillfully lobbied in England with the merchant community and Puritan government to save his colony during the years of the English Civil War and Commonwealth government. His wife, Anne, died 23 July 1649, and was buried at Tisbury, Wiltshire. CECIL CALVERT, 2nd Lord Baltimore, died 30 Nov. 1675, and was buried 7 Dec. 1675 at St. Giles-in-the-Fields, Middlesex. He left a will dated 22 and 28 Nov. 1675, proved 3 Feb. 1675/6.

> Brydges *Collins' Peerage of England* 7 (1812): 40–57 (sub Arundel, Lord Arundel of Wardour). Oliver *Colls. Ill. the Hist. of the Catholic Religion* (1857): 75–91. Glover & St. George *Vis. of Yorkshire 1584–5, 1612* (1875): 500 (Calvert arms: Paly of six or and sable, a bend counterchanged). Lawson *Gen. Colls. Ill. the Hist. of Roman Catholic Fams. in England* 3 (1887): 151–152, 233–241. Vivian *Vis. of Cornwall* (1887): 2–5 (Arundell ped.). *Ancestor* 2 (1902): 209. *C.P.* 1 (1910): 393–394 (sub Baltimore). *NEHGR* 86 (1932): 269 (Calvert arms). O'Gorman *Descs. of Virginia Calverts* (1947): 53–58. Mosby *Heritage of Faith: Calvert, Green & Alvey Fam. Hists.* (1976). Papenfuse *Biog. Dict. of the Maryland Legislature 1635–1789* 1 (1979): 186–187 (biog. of Cecilius Calvert: "… an active promoter of religious toleration"). Barnes *British Roots of Maryland Fams.* 1 (1999): 96–98. Dorman *Adventurers of Purse & Person* 1 (2004): 468–485.

23. CHARLES CALVERT, 3rd Lord Baltimore, Governor of Maryland, 2nd Lord Proprietor of Maryland, colonial entrepreneur, born 27 August 1637. He married (1st) about 1660 **MARY DARNALL**, daughter of Ralph Darnall, of Loughton, Herefordshire. She died in childbirth in Maryland. He was commissioned governor of Maryland 14 Sept. 1661, and served in that capacity until the death of his father in 1675, when he succeeded to the proprietorship of the province. He married (2nd) about 1666 **JANE LOWE**, widow of Henry Sewall, and daughter of Vincent Lowe, Esq., of Denby, Derbyshire, by Anne, illegitimate daughter of Henry Cavendish, Esq. [see LOWE 21 for her ancestry]. They had three sons, Cecilius, Benedict Leonard [4th Lord Baltimore], and Charles, and two daughters, Clare (wife of Edward Maria Somerset) and Anne (wife of Edward Maria Somerset and William Paston, Esq.). In 1684 he departed for England to defend his charter and his territorial jurisdiction from the attacks of William Penn. His government was overthrown in 1689 by a Protestant association led by John Coode, and in 1692 a royal government was established. His wife, Jane, died 19 Jan. 1700/1. He married (3rd) 6 Dec. 1701 **MARY BANKES**, widow of _____ Thorpe, who died 13 March 1710/11. He married (4th) in 1712 **MARGARET CHARLETON**, daughter of Thomas Charleton, of Hexham, Northumberland. He was deprived of the Province at the Revolution of 1689; named in the fabricated plot of Titus Oates, but not arrested; Brig. Gen. 1696, Major Gen. 1704. CHARLES CALVERT, 3rd Lord Baltimore, died testate 21 Feb. 1714/5, and was buried at St. Pancras, Middlesex, England. His widow, Margaret, married (2nd) 9 Nov. 1718 **LAWRENCE ELIOT**. She died testate 20 July 1731.

<small>C.P. 1 (1910): 394 (sub Baltimore); 14 (1998): 61 (sub Baltimore). D.A.B. 3 (1929): 427 (biog. of Charles Calvert). Mosby *Heritage of Faith: Calvert, Green & Alvey Fam. Hists.* (1976). Papenfuse *Biog. Dict. of the Maryland Legislature 1635–1789* 1 (1979): 187–188 (biog. of Charles Calvert: "… continued his father's policy of religious toleration"). Raimo *Biog. Dict. of American Col. & Revolutionary Govs.* (1980): 86 (biog. of Charles Calvert). Dorman *Adventurers of Purse & Person* 1 (2004): 468–485.</small>

❧ CAMOYS ❧

REYNOLD DE COURTENAY, of Sutton, Berkshire, married _____.
REYNOLD DE COURTENAY, of Okehampton, Devon, married **HAWISE DE COURCY**.
ROBERT DE COURTENAY, Knt., of Okehampton, Devon, married **MARY DE VERNON** (desc. King William the Conqueror).
HAWISE DE COURTENAY, married **JOHN DE GATESDEN**, Knt., of Broadwater, Sussex [see DE LA MARE 4].

5. MARGARET (or **MARGERY**) **DE GATESDEN**, daughter and heiress, minor in 1269. She married by contract dated before April 1262 **JOHN DE CAMOYS**, Knt., of Flockthorpe (in Hardingham), Norfolk, Hinxton and Orwell, Cambridgeshire, West Tisted, Hampshire, Great Stukeley, Huntingdonshire, Pilton and Tansor, Northamptonshire, Wotton, Surrey, etc., and, in right of his wife, of Eling and Lasham, Hampshire, Broadwater, Elsted, and Trotton, Sussex, etc., son and heir of Ralph de Camoys, Knt., of Flockthorpe (in Hardingham), Norfolk, Hinxton and Orwell, Cambridgeshire, West Tisted, Hampshire, Great Stukeley, Huntingdonshire, Pilton, Tansor, Torpel, and Upton, Northamptonshire, Wotton, Surrey, etc., Constable of Pevensey, by Asceline, daughter of Roger de Torpel. He was born about 1247–52 (aged variously 25, 26, or 30 in 1277). They had one son, Ralph, Knt. [1st Lord Camoys]. Sometime before 1268 he conveyed a moiety of the manor of Lasham, Hampshire to Robert Walerand. In 1275–6 he and his wife, Margaret, arraigned an assize of mort d'ancestor against Nicholas Blundel touching a messuage and land in Elsted, Sussex. In 1276 John and his wife, Margery, sued Robert del Ostre and his wife, Rose, regarding their right to hospitality in a messuage in St. Michael Cornhill, London. In 1276–7 he was granted letters of protection, he then going in the king's suite to the parts of Wales. In 1279 he and his wife, Margaret, successfully claimed free warren in Broadwater, Sussex. The same year he and his wife, Margaret, reached agreement with Richard de Pevensey and his wife, Isabel de Montagu, regarding the holdings of various manors; the said Richard and Isabel granted John and Margaret and her heirs the manors and advowsons of the churches of Norton [Fitzwarren] and Bradford-on-Tone, Somerset, and quitclaimed to them all their right in the manors of Stockholt (in Akeley),

Buckinghamshire, Broadwater and Bovigeton, Sussex, and Eling, Hampshire. Sometime in the period, 1279–84, he conveyed the manor of Orwell, Cambridgeshire to John Kirkby, Bishop of Ely, and John Lovetot. In 1280 he vindicated his right to the advowson of Broadwater, Sussex against William son of Richard Hubard. The same year he granted Richard de Crofton £10 annual rent from the manor of West Tisted, Hampshire. In 1280 he released the manors of Torpel and Upton, Northamptonshire to the king and queen. The same year he and his wife, Margaret, recognized the right of the Prior of Boxgrove to certain land and a mill in Elsted, Sussex which Margaret's father, John de Gatesden, had held for his life by a lease from a former prior, and 17½ acres in Elsted in the vale of Marden; they likewise granted the prior an acre in Tulonde. In 1280 Peter de Montfort and his wife, Maud, and her half-sister, Hawise le Veel, sued John and his wife, Margaret, regarding the manor of Norton [Fitzwarren], Somerset, which John and Margaret they said had no entry except by John de Gatesden (father of Margaret) who unjustly disseised Joan de la Mare, mother of the said Maud and Hawise. In 1280–1 he and his wife, Margaret, arraigned an assize of novel disseisin against William de Brewes and others touching a tenement in Horsham, Sussex. By a very remarkable document, he transferred his wife, Margaret, and her goods and chattels to Sir William Paynel, and by deeds dated 1285 and 1289, he demised to the said William the greater part of her inheritance. William and Margaret were respectively charged with adultery, he in 1287 by the Archbishop of Canterbury, she in 1295 by the Bishop of Chichester. John presented to the church of Pilton, Northamptonshire in 1285. Sometime before 1289 he sold the manor of Hinxton, Cambridgeshire to John Lovetot, Knt. In 1297–8 Margaret brought a successful suit against Robert Walerand for the manor of Eling, Hampshire. SIR JOHN DE CAMOYS died shortly before 4 June 1298. His widow, Margaret, married (2nd) about 1298 (when she made a fine of 100 marks to marry at will) **WILLIAM PAYNEL**, Knt., Lord Paynel, of Littleton Pannell (in West Lavington), Wiltshire, Hamptonett (in Westhampnett), Pinkhurst, Sidlesham, Trotton and Woolbeding, Sussex, etc., younger son of William Paynel, Knt., of Littleton Pannell (in West Lavington), Wiltshire, by Maud, daughter of Henry Husee. They had no issue. In the Parliaments of 1300–2 they made petition for Margaret's dower from the manor of Torpel, Northamptonshire (a Camoys estate). He was summoned to Parliament from 12 Nov. 1304 to 16 October 1315, by writs directed *Willelmo Paynel*, whereby he is held to have become Lord Paynel. In 1304 he and his wife, Margaret, purchased the reversion of the manor of Cokeham (in Sompting), Sussex from her niece, Hawise de la Hyde, widow of Robert le Veel, Knt. In 1304–5 Hawise likewise conveyed the manor of Stow Bedon, Norfolk to William and his wife, Margaret. In 1308 William and his wife, Margaret, gave a release for land in Compton, Surrey to Henry de Guildford. He and his wife were summoned to attend the Coronation of King Edward II in 1308. His wife, Margaret, died shortly before 4 Jan. 1310/11. He married (2nd) before 6 Nov. 1314 **EVE DE HAUTERIVE** (or **DAUTRY**), widow of Roger de Shelvestrode (living 1308), and daughter amd heiress of John de Hauterive (or Dautry), of Barlavington, East Hampnett (in Boxgrove), and North Marden, Sussex, by Elizabeth, daughter and co-heiress of Peter de la Stane. They had no issue. He was heir in 1314 to his elder brother, Thomas Paynel, Knt. In 1316 he gave the manor of Cokeham (in Sompting), Sussex, together with a ferry across the water of New Shoreham, Sussex, to Hardham Priory to provide four secular chaplains. SIR WILLIAM PAYNEL, Lord Paynel, died 1 April 1317. His widow, Eve, married (2nd) shortly before 8 May 1317 **EDWARD DE SAINT JOHN**, Knt. [see PAULET 7.ii], of Litchfield and Sherborne St. John, Hampshire, younger son of John de Saint John, Knt., of Basing, Hampshire, by Alice, daughter of Reynold Fitz Peter, Knt. [see PAULET 7 for his ancestry]. They had four sons, Edward, Knt., John, William, and Richard, and one possible daughter, Agnes. In 1328 she sued Edmund, Earl of Kent and Ralph de Camoys for dower in Broadwater, Petworth, Trotton, Woolavington, etc., Sussex. SIR EDWARD DE SAINT JOHN died 30 Nov. 1347. His widow, Eve, was granted a license for an oratory for her manor of Empshott, Hampshire for one year in 1353. She died 16 August 1354.

    Blomefield *Essay towards a Top. Hist. of Norfolk* 2 (1805): 278. Dallaway *Hist. of the Western Division of the County of Sussex* 1(2) (1832): 217 (Camoys ped.). *Sussex Arch. Colls.* 3 (1850): 94; 37 (1890): 182; 51 (1908): 190. Eyton *Antiqs. of Shropshire* 3 (1856): 6–7, 9. Roberts *Calendarium Genealogicum* 1 (1865): 136. Carthew *Hundred of Launditch & Deanery of Brisley* 1 (1878): 238–241 (Camoys ped.). *Procs. Somersetshire Arch. & Nat. Hist. Soc.* 28(2) (1882): 197–200. *Annual Rpt. of the Deputy Keeper* 45 (1885): 164; 46 (1886): 260; 50 (1889): 121. Rye *Short Cal. Feet of Fines for Norfolk* 1 (1885): 163. *C.C.R.* 1313–1318 (1893): 231, 472. *Regs. of John de Sandale & Rigaud de Asserio, Bishops of Winchester* (Hampshire Rec. Soc. Ser.) (1897): 32. *C.P.R.* 1313–1317 (1898): 558, 646. *C.P.R.* 1317–1321 (1903): 559–560. *C.P.R.* 1348–1350 (1905): 108. *C.C.R.* 1296–1302 (1906): 494, 608. *Index of Placita de Banco 1327–1328* 2 (PRO Lists and Indexes 22) (1906): 574, 672, 673. VCH *Northampton* 2 (1906): 595–596; 3 (1930): 129–131. *C.P.R.* 1350–1354 (1907): 524. Salzman *Feet of Fines Rel. Sussex* 2 (Sussex Rec. Soc. 7) (1908): 73–74, 107, 112–113, 116–117, 142–143, 145, 178, 181–182; 3 (Sussex Rec. Soc. 23) (1916): 26, 35, 45, 49, 53, 87–88, 89, 91, 127. VCH *Hampshire* 3 (1908): 59–60; 4 (1911): 81–82, 547–548. *C.P.R.* 1354–1358 (1909): 117, 256, 263. *Feet of Fines for York[shire]* 1327–1347 (Yorkshire Arch. Soc. Recs. 42) (1910): 144. VCH *Hampshire* 4 (1911): 158–159, 547–548. VCH *Surrey* 3 (1911): 16–24; 155–156. *C.P.* 2 (1912): 506 (sub Camoys); 10 (1945): 327-331 (sub Paynel). *Cal. IPM* 9 (1916): 43; 10 (1921): 164–165. Farrer *Honors & Knights' Fees* 1 (1923): 12. VCH *Buckingham* 4 (1927): 144–147. Moor *Knights of Edward I* 1 (H.S.P. 80) (1929): 175–176. VCH *Huntingdon* 2 (1932): 230–234. Hill *Rolls & Reg. of Bishop Oliver Sutton, 1280–1299* 2 (Lincoln Rec. Soc. 43) (1950): 58. VCH *Sussex* 4 (1953): 8–10, 34–35 (Camoys arms: Or on a chief gules three roundels argent), 56, 85, 108, 110, 144–145, 176, 213–214, 268; 6(1) (1980): 53–64, 69–70, 77; 7 (1940): 80–83. VCH *Wiltshire* 7 (1953): 198–206. Sanders *English Baronies* (1960): 20, 45. Dibben *Cowdray Archives* 2 (1964): 331. VCH *Cambridge* 5 (1973): 241–251; 6 (1978): 220–230. Elrington *Abs. of Feet of Fines Rel. Wiltshire* (Wiltshire Rec. Soc. 29) (1974): 83-84. Weinbaum *London Eyre of 1276* (London Rec. Soc.) (1976): 107. VCH *Oxford* 4 (1979): 304-305. Edington *Reg. of William Edington Bishop of Winchester 1346–1366* 2 (Hampshire Rec. Ser. 8) (1987): 38. Ward *Women of the English Nobility & Gentry 1066–1500* (1995): 61–63. National Archives, SC 8/37/1814; SC 8/339/15986 (available at http://www.a2a.org.uk/search/index.asp).

6. RALPH DE CAMOYS, Knt., of Flockthorpe (in Hardingham) and Bekerton, Norfolk, Eling and Hambledon, Hampshire, Broadwater, Barcombe, and Trotton, Sussex, Pilton and Tansor, Northamptonshire, etc., Constable of Heleigh and Windsor Castles, Keeper of the Forest of Woolmer, son and heir, born about 1282 (adult in 1303). He married (1st) shortly before 25 June 1303 **MARGARET DE BREWES**, daughter of William de Brewes, Knt., 1st Lord Brewes, by his 3rd wife, Mary, daughter of Robert de Roos, Knt. [see BREWES 8 for her ancestry]. They had one son, Thomas, Knt. [2nd Lord Camoys]. He served in the French and Scottish wars, and was taken prisoner in the latter. At an uncertain date, he successfully claimed his mother's former estate at Lasham, Hampshire on the ground that his father in alienating this property, had violated the statute *de donis conditionalibus*, this in spite of the fact that this statute was not passed until 1285. In 1299 he witnessed a release of Robert de Harwedon to John de Haudlo, of Boarstall, Buckinghamshire, and his 1st wife, Joan. In 1300 he first appears in the company of Hugh le Despenser the elder. In 1303 he was granted free warren in his demesne lands at Hampnett, Sussex. In 1303–4 he and his wife, Margaret, conveyed the manor of Little Bookham, Surrey to her mother, Mary de Brewes. In 1305 he was granted letters of protection, he then going beyond seas with Hugh le Despenser on the king's service. In 1306 he acquired the manor of Woolbeding, Sussex from John son of John de Arundel. In 1309 he was granted free warren in his demesne lands at Woolbeding, Sussex. He presented to the churches of Hardingham, Norfolk, 1309, 1319, and Pilton, Northamptonshire, 1312. A commission was appointed in 1310 touching the persons who felled and carried away the trees of Ralph de Camois at Flockthorpe (in Hardingham), Norfolk. The same year he also witnessed a grant by John de la Mare to Sir Hugh le Despenser of the manor of Asshemere, Dorset. In 1312 he was granted a weekly market and a yearly fair at Broadwater, Sussex. He was summoned to Parliament from 26 Nov. 1313 to 1 April 1335, by writs directed *Radulpho de Camoys*, whereby he is held to have become Lord Camoys. In 1313 he was granted letters of protection, he then going beyond seas with Hugh le Despenser the elder on the king's service. In 1314–15 he obtained permission to cut down diverse trees to the value of 100 marks in his wood at Pilton,

Northamptonshire. He married (2nd) before 20 May 1316 (date of settlement) **ELIZABETH LE DESPENSER**, daughter of Hugh le Despenser, Knt., Earl of Winchester, by Isabel, daughter of William de Beauchamp, Knt. [see DESPENSER 10 for her ancestry]. They had four sons, Hugh, Knt., John, Knt., Ralph, and Richard, and two daughters, Margaret and Isabel [Abbess of Romney]. In 1318 he was granted free warren in his demesne lands at Lasham and Hambledon, Hampshire, Stukeley, Huntingdonshire, and Pilton and Tansor, Northamptonshire. In 1319 he and his wife, Elizabeth, and Hugh le Despenser were pardoned for acquiring to them and the heirs of Ralph the bailiwick of the forestership of Alice Holt and Woolmer, Hampshire from Richard de Venuz without license. The same year he was granted free warren in his demesne lands at Eling, Lasham, and Hambledon, Hampshire, Stukeley, Huntingdonshire, and Pilton and Tansor, Northamptonshire. The same year Ralph obtained judgment against Robert, the warden of the house of St. Nicholas, Portsmouth, with respect to the moiety of the manor of Lasham, Hampshire, which had been assigned to the hospital in 1299. In 1320 he witnessed a release from Thomas Fillol to John de Haudlo, Knt., and his 2nd wife, Maud, regarding Fillol's right in 140 acres of land and 4s. of rent in Hatfield Peverel and Borham, Essex. The same year Ralph de Camoys and William de Clif' were nominated attorneys for Hugh le Despenser the younger, the said Hugh going beyond the seas with the king. In 1321 Ralph and his wife, Elizabeth, granted 12 messuages, a mill, and various lands in Rogate, Didling, Trotton, etc., in Sussex to William de Rogate for life. The same year he settled the manor of Lasham, Hampshire on himself and his wife, Elizabeth, in fee tail. In 1321–2 he conveyed a messuage and lands in Didling, Sussex to Thomas de Dydelyngg and his heirs. In 1323 he settled the manor of Eling, Hampshire on himself and his wife, Elizabeth. In 1323–4 he and his wife, Elizabeth, settled the manor of Cokeham (in Sompting), Sussex on themselves for life, together with the advowson of the hospital of Cokeham, with reversion to their son, Ralph. In 1325–6 he and his wife, Elizabeth, settled a messuage and lands in Woolavington, Sussex on themselves for life, with reversion to their son, John. In 1326 the king out of special grace granted Ralph and his wife, Elizabeth, and their son, John, a yearly fair at Rogate, Sussex, together with free warren at Rogate, Harting, Tortewyk, Tadeham, and Alfradesham, Sussex. He was pardoned in Feb. 1326/7 for his adherence to the Despensers in their rebellion against King Edward II. In March 1327 Margery, widow of Robert Lever, arraigned an assize of novel disseisin against Ralph de Camoys, Elizabeth his wife, and their son, Hugh, for a tenement in Westbury. The said Ralph, Elizabeth, and Hugh proferred a charter of the late king whereby they asserted they held the said tenement; however, it was found by the tenor of the assize that the defendants had disseised the said Margery of the manor of Westbury long before the making of the king's charter. In 1327 he sued John de Saint John regarding a debt. In 1328 he and Edmund, Earl of Kent, were sued by Eve Dautry, wife of Edward de Saint John, for dower in Broadwater, Trotton, Woolavington, Petworth, etc., Sussex. The same year John de Ifeld sued Ralph de Camoys and Richard Macy for trespass at Offington [in Broadwater], Sussex. The same year Ralph sued John de Bohun, of Midhurst, Sussex, for the detention of beasts and Geoffrey Hoghles regarding a debt. His wife, Elizabeth, was living 14 March 1327, but presumably died before 17 February 1331, when Ralph alone granted their son, Hugh de Camoys, for the term of his life the manor of Eling, Hampshire, together with lands and tenements called Winsor, and lands which Margery, once wife of Robert Lewyr held by writ of elegit of the king, remainder to the said Ralph and his heirs. In the period, 1327–8, he sued Walter son of Lucy de Meriet regarding the manor of Bradford, Somerset; Walter de Meriet in turn sued him regarding the wardship of land in Bradford, Somerset during the minority of the heir of Roger Baudrip. In 1335 he complained that certain malefactors broke his park at Trotton, Sussex and hunted deer there. SIR RALPH DE CAMOYS, 1st Lord Camoys, died shortly before June 1336.

Blomefield *Essay towards a Top. Hist. of Norfolk* 2 (1805): 277–281; 10 (1809): 221–227. Blore *Hist. & Antiqs. of Rutland* 1(2) (1811): 19 (Despenser ped.). Brydges *Collins' Peerage of England* 6 (1812): 496–511 (sub Despenser) ("[Hugh le Despenser] married Isabel, daughter of William de Beauchamp, Earl of Warwick, and widow of Sir Patrick Chaworth, and by her had … Ada [sic], married to Sir Ralph Camois, Knt."). Dallaway *Hist. of the Western Div. of Sussex* 1(2) (1832): 217 (Camoys ped.). Lennard & Vincent *Vis. of Warwick* 1619 (H.S.P. 12) (1877): 282–285 (Spencer ped.: "Ada [Despenser] ux. Dn'i St. Amon 2d Rad'i Dn'i Camois."). Carthew *Hundred of Launditch & Deanery of Brisley* 1 (1878): 238–241 (Camoys ped.). *Notes & Queries* 6th Ser. 1 (1880): 234–235, 298–299, 341 (W.D. Macray states "The following short descent, which I have put together from two seventeenth century MSS. in the Bodleian (Rawlinson, B. 74 and 314 [shows] Ralph [Camoys] = Da. of Hugh Le Despenser, Earl of Winchester."). *Genealogist* 6 (1882): 236–247. *Year Books of Edward III, Years XIII & XIV* 3 (Rolls Ser. 31b) (1886): 220–223. *Desc. Cat. Ancient Deeds* 1 (1890): 23. *C.P.R.* 1327–1330 (1891): 20. *C.P.R.* 1307–1313 (1894): 257, 582. *C.C.R.* 1318–1323 (1895): 221. *C.C.R.* 1327–1330 (1896): 71–72. *C.P.R.* 1301–1307 (1898): 382. *C.P.R.* 1317–1321 (1903): 325, 449. VCH *Hampshire* 2 (1903): 206–208; 3 (1908): 239, 241; 4 (1911): 81–82, 547–548. *List of Inqs. ad Quod Damnum* 1 (PRO Lists and Indexes 17) (1904): 63, 83; 2 (PRO Lists and Indexes 22) (1906): 562, 573, 659, 660, 666, 672. Benolte et al. *Vis. of Sussex 1530 & 1633–4* (H.S.P. 53) (1905): 29–30 (Camoys ped.: "Rafe Lord Camoys = ... d. of Hugh le Spencer Erle of Winchester."). VCH *Northampton* 2 (1906): 595–596; 3 (1930): 129–131. *C.Ch.R.* 3 (1908): 36, 127, 194, 397, 417, 469, 493. *C.P.* 2 (1912): 506–507 (sub Camoys). Salzman *Abs. of Feet of Fines Rel. Sussex* 3 (Sussex Rec. Soc. 23) (1916): 46, 50, 53, 59. Davies *Baronial Opposition of Edward II: Its Character & Policy* (1918): 93–94. Moor *Knights of Edward I* 1 (H.S.P. 80) (1929): 176–177. *Sussex Arch. Colls.* 70 (1929): 1–7 (The author, Mr. Lambarde, discusses the Lewknor tapestry dating from the 1560's which tapestry features various coats of arms which involve ancestral marriages of the Lewknor family. Among the coats of arms depicted are the arms of Camoys impaling Despenser. The author, writes: "This records the marriage of Ralph, Lord Camoys, to the daughter of Hugh De Spencer, Earl of Winchester. This is according to the Pedigree recorded in the Visitations of Sussex, 1634, Harl. Soc., LIII, 29."). Salter *Boarstall Cartulary* (Oxford Hist. Soc. 1st Ser. 88) (1930): 108. VCH *Huntingdon* 2 (1932): 230–234. VCH *Sussex* 4 (1953): 34–35 (Camoys arms: Or on a chief gules three roundels argent), 84–87; 6(1) (1980): 53–64, 69–70; 7 (1940): 80–83. Paget *Baronage of England* (1957) 90: 1–12 (sub Braose); 114: 1–7 (sub Camoys). Ellis *Cat. Seals in the P.R.O.* 2 (1981): 21 (seal of Ralph de Camoys, knight dated 1335 — hung from a hook, a shield of arms: on a chief three roundels; the field diapered [CAMOYS]). *English Hist. Rev.* 99 (1984): 1–33. Himsworth *Winchester College Muniments* 2 (1984): 269–274. Hanna *Cartularies of Southwick Priory* 1 (Hampshire Recs. 9) (1988): 209. Brault *Rolls of Arms Edward I* 2 (1997): 89 (arms of Ralph de Camoys: Or, on a chief gules three roundels argent). Coss *Soldiers, Nobles and Gentlemen* (2009): 107. National Archives, E 40/215 (grant dated 17 June 1320 by John de la Mare to Sir Hugh le Despenser of his manor of Asshemere, Dorset. Witnesses:- Sirs John de Handlo [Haudlo], Ralph de Camoys, Knts., and others); SC 8/61/3011A; SC 8/127/6319 (petition dated c.1334 from Walter de Meryet, clerk to the king and council, requesting the intervention of the justices of King's Bench in his dispute with Ralph de Camoys, stating that although his case against Camoys was adjudged in his favour and damages awarded, Camoys has alienated his lands to other people before the judgment was made, and is thus avoiding paying the necessary damages); SC 8/169/8415; SC 8/261/13033 (petition dated 1334–5 from Luke de Burgh, king's attorney of Common Pleas, to the king and council, asking that an exigent might be granted against Ralph de Camoys, who has persistently taken steps to resist arrest in a case before the justices of Common Pleas, losing the King a redemption of 1000 marks or more, and that the same might be done in every case where the capias is granted) (available at www.catalogue.nationalarchives.gov.uk/search.asp).

7. JOHN DE CAMOYS, Knt., in right of his 1st wife, of Gressenhall, East Lexham, and Grimston, Norfolk, and Cowesby, Yorkshire, younger son by his father's 2nd marriage, born in or before 1320 (aged 40 in 1360). In 1325–6 his parents settled the reversion of a messuage and lands in Woolavington, Sussex on him. He married (1st) before 1330 **MARGARET FOLIOT**, younger daughter of Richard Foliot, Knt., of Gressenhall and Weasenham, Norfolk, by Joan, daughter and co-heiress of William de Brewes (or Breuse), Knt. [see MIDHURST 6 for her ancestry]. She was born about 1314 (aged 16 in 1330). They had one daughter, Katherine (wife of Hamon le Strange, Knt). In the period, 1343–5, he and his wife, Margaret, made a settlement of the manors of Gressenhall and East Lexham, Norfolk, together with the advowsons of Gressenhall and Stanfield, Norfolk. In 1344 he and his wife, Margaret, settled the manor and advowson of Cowesby, Yorkshire on themselves and the heirs of their bodies, with remainder to Hugh de Hastings, Knt., and Margery his wife, and the heirs of Margery. He fought at the Battle of Crécy 26 August 1346, and was present at the Siege of Calais in 1346–7. In 1347–8 he and his unnamed wife were residing at Hunstanton, Norfolk. He presented to the church of Gressenhall, Norfolk in 1348, 1349, and 1361. He married (2nd) before 1351 **ELIZABETH LE LATIMER**, daughter of William le Latimer, 3rd Lord Latimer, by Elizabeth, daughter of John Botetourt, Knt., 1st Lord Botetourt [see THWENG 10 for her ancestry]. They had two sons, Thomas, K.G. [1st Lord Camoys] and possibly

Hugh, Esq., and one daughter, Maud. He was summoned to a Council in 1359, by writ directed *Johanni de Camoys*. In 1361 John de Trailly, of Yelden, Bedfordshire owed him and three others a debt of £30. SIR JOHN DE CAMOYS was living 5 May 1362 (date of deed). His widow, Elizabeth, married (2nd) before 1365–6 **RALPH DE UFFORD**. In 1382–3 Elizabeth Camoys, possibly his widow, was paid 50*s*. by Sir Edward Courtenay, Earl of Devon out of his manor of Waddesdon, Buckinghamshire.

> Rymer *Fœdera* 6 (1727): 138. Blomefield *Essay towards a Top. Hist. of Norfolk* 9 (1808): 510–513, 519. Dallaway *Hist. of the Western Div. of Sussex* 1(2) (1832): 217 (Camoys ped.). *Index to the Add'l MSS in the British Museum* (1849): 467. *Sussex Arch. Coll.* 3 (1850): 94. Carthew *Hundred of Launditch & Deanery of Brisley* 1 (1878): 238–241 (Camoys ped.). Rye *Short Cal. Feet of Fines for Norfolk* 2 (1886): 313. *Yorkshire Arch. & Topog. Jour.* 11 (1891): 444–446. Wrottesley *Crécy & Calais* (1898): 31, 91, 142 (Queen's Remembrancer, 21 Edward III [1347]: "Sir John de Camoys, formerly of the retinue of Thomas [de Beauchamp], Earl of Warwick, and now of the retinue of Henry, Earl of Lancaster, for lands in cos. Norfolk, Hunts., and Sussex. Dated 1st July."), 173. *Genealogist* n.s. 17 (1901): 115; n.s. 19 (1903): 102; n.s. 20 (1904): 36. Wrottesley *Peds. from the Plea Rolls* (1905): 332. VCH *Northampton* 2 (1906): 595–596. *Cal. IPM* 7 (1909): 203–204; 10 (1921): 502. *Feet of Fines for York[shire]* 1327–1347 (Yorkshire Arch. Soc. Recs. 42) (1910): 172. Salzman *Abs. of Feet of Fines Rel. Sussex* (Sussex Rec. Soc. 23) (1916): 53, 59. *Archaeologia* 69 (1920): 111–120. *Paget* (1957) 114: 1–7 (sub Camoys). *Devon & Cornwall Notes & Queries* 35 (1983): 156. Himsworth *Winchester College Muniments* 2 (1984): 270–271. Archer *Rulers & Ruled in Late Medieval England* (1995): 18. Coss *Foundations of Gentry Life* (2010): 43, 56–57, 71–72. National Archives, C 241/141/139 (available at www.catalogue.nationalarchives.gov.uk/search.asp). Norfolk Rec. Office: Hare Fam., Baronets of Stow Bardolph, Hare 1504 191 x 6 — deed of grant dated 5 May 1362 from John Simond of Ayschelee (Nhts). to Sir Richard de Walkefar', Knt., Sir Richard de Causton, Knt., Sir John Camoys, Knt., and others regarding lands and tenements in Fyncham and Stradesete (available at www.a2a.org.uk/search/index.asp).

Children of John de Camoys, Knt., by Elizabeth le Latimer:

i. **THOMAS CAMOYS**, Knt., 1st Lord Camoys [see next].

i. **MAUD CAMOYS**, married **EDWARD COURTENAY**, Knt., 11th Earl of Devon, 4th Lord Courtenay [see COURTENAY 8.i].

8. THOMAS CAMOYS, K.G., of Trotton, Barcombe, Broadwater, and Elsted, Sussex, Honydon or Camoys (in Eaton Socon), Bedfordshire, Great Stukeley, Huntingdonshire, Bekerton, Norfolk, Tansor, Northamptonshire, etc., son and heir by his father's 2nd marriage, born in or before 1351 (of age in 1372). He married (1st) **ELIZABETH LOUCHES**, daughter and heiress of William Louches, of Great Milton and Chislehampton, Oxfordshire. They had one son, Richard, Knt., and one daughter, Alice. He was heir in 1372 to his uncle, Thomas Camoys, Knt., by which he inherited the manors of Trotton, Barcombe, Broadwater, and Elsted, Sussex, Great Stukeley, Huntingdonshire, Bekerton, Norfolk, Tansor, Northamptonshire, etc. In 1375 he was granted a weekly market at Broadwater, Sussex. The same year his maternal uncle, William Latimer, K.G., 4th Lord Latimer was granted various tenements and houses in Calais by the king formerly held by John Dayre, with remainder in male tail to Thomas Camoys. In 1378 he disputed the advowson of Broadwater, Sussex with Adam de Hartingdon. He was a legatee in the 1381 will of his cousin, William le Latimer, K.G., 4th Lord Latimer, by which he inherited the manor of Wotton, Surrey. He presented to the church of Wotton, Surrey, 1382, 1383, and 1392, and Lasham, Hampshire, 1392. He was one of the liveried personnel of his brother-in-law, Edward Courtenay, Knt., 11th Earl of Devon, in 1384–5. He saw military service in Castile under John of Gaunt. He was summoned to Parliament from 20 August 1383 to 26 Feb. 1420/1, by writs directed *Thome Camoys ch'r*, whereby he is held to have become Lord Camoys. He was excluded from court in Jan. 1388 by order of the Lords Appellant. In 1389 he made a settlement of the manor of Honydon or Camoy's (in Eaton Socon), Bedfordshire. In 1399 he was granted the bailiwick of the forestership of Alice Holt and Wolmer, Hampshire by the king "as Ralph de Camoys his grandfather had in the time of Edward III." The same year he and his son, Richard, were jointly granted custody of the castle and town of Porchester, Hampshire. In 1400 he manned a ship for service against the Scotch and the French. In 1405–6 he unsuccessfully claimed the manor of Eling, Hampshire against the warden of

Winchester College. He married (2nd) after 3 June 1406 **ELIZABETH MORTIMER**, widow of Henry "Hotspur" Percy, Knt., styled *le Fitz*, K.G., K.B., Justice of Chester, North Wales, and Flintshire, Warden of the East Marches, Captain of Berwick on Tweed [see PERCY 12 for issue of that marriage], and daughter of Edmund de Mortimer, Knt., Earl of March and Ulster, by Philippe, daughter and heiress of Lionel of Antwerp, K.G., Duke of Clarence, 5th Earl of Ulster (younger son of King Edward III of England) [see MORTIMER 13 for her ancestry]. She was born at Usk, Monmouthshire 12 (or 13) Feb. 1370/1, and baptized 16 Feb. 1370/1. She was a legatee in the 1380 will of her father. They had one son, Roger, Knt. [Lord Camoys]. In 1406 he signed the deed of King Henry IV regulating the succession to the crown. In 1408 William Mymecan sued Thomas Camoys, Knt., regarding 40*s.* rents with appurtenances in Wheatley, Oxfordshire. Thomas was heavily involved in the military affairs of both Kings Henry IV and Henry V. He commanded the left wing of the English army at the Battle of Agincourt in 1415. He presented to the church of Broadwater, Sussex in 1416. His wife, Elizabeth, died 20 April 1417. SIR THOMAS CAMOYS, 1st Lord Camoys, died 28 March 1421. He and his 2nd wife, Elizabeth, were buried at Trotton, Sussex.

Gurdon *Hist. of the High Court of Parl.* 1 (1731): 189. Nichols *Coll. of All the Wills* (1780): 104–117 (will of Edmund de Mortimer, Earl of March and Ulster). Blomefield *Essay towards a Top. Hist. of Norfolk* 2 (1805): 277–281. Blore *Hist. & Antiqs. of Rutland* 1(2) (1811): 42 (Mortimer ped.). Nicolas *Testamenta Vetusta* 1 (1826): 108 (will of William Latimer, K.G., 4th Lord Latimer, names his "cousin" Thomas Camoys). Dallaway *Hist. of the Western Div. of Sussex* 1(2) (1832): 217 (Camoys ped.). *Sussex Arch. Coll.* 3 (1850): 96. Hawley *Royal Fam. of England* (1851): 23–27. Davenport *Lords Lieutenant & High Sheriffs of Oxfordshire* (1868): 21. Carthew *Hundred of Launditch & Deanery of Brisley* 1 (1878): 238–241 (Camoys ped.). *Notes & Queries* 6th Ser. 1 (1880): 234–235, 298–299, 341, 401; 10th Ser. 7 (1907): 509–510. Kirby *Wykeham's Reg.* 1 (1896): 132, 137, 182, 184. *Genealogist* n.s. 17 (1901): 115. *Revised Rpts. of Cases in the English Courts of Common Law & Equity* 49 (1901): 195–250 (re. Camoys Peerage). *C.P.R.* 1399–1401 (1903): 46. Benolte et al. *Vis. of Sussex 1530, 1633–4* (H.S.P. 53) (1905): 25–30 (Lewknor ped.: "Tho. Lord Camoys = Elizebeth d. & heire of Wmi. Louches."). Wrottesley *Peds. from the Plea Rolls* (1905): 332. *D.N.B.* 3 (1908): 758–759 (biog. of Thomas de Camoys). Lane *Royal Daughters of England* 1 (1910): 275–277. *C.C.R.* 1369–1374 (1911): 406–407. Ruvigny and Raineval *Plantagenet Roll: Mortimer-Percy* 1 (1911): vi–vii, 2 (erroneously identifies Elizabeth Mortimer as mother of Alice Camoys, wife of Leonard Hastings, Knt., Alice was actually Elizabeth's step-daughter). VCH *Hampshire* 4 (1911): 81–82; 547–548. VCH *Surrey* 3 (1911): 155–156, 378–381. *C.P.* 2 (1912): 507–508 (sub Camoys); 9 (1936): 713–714 (sub Northumberland); 14 (1998): 138 (sub Camoys). VCH *Bedfordshire* 3 (1912): 189–202. *C.C.R.* 1381–1385 (1920): 61. *Feudal Aids* 6 (1920): 521. *Cal. IPM* 13 (1954): 150–151. VCH *Sussex* 4 (1953): 34–35; 6(1) (1980): 69–70, 77; 7 (1940): 80–83. Paget *Baronage of England* (1957) 114: 1–7 (sub Camoys). Hector *Westminster Chron. 1381–1394* (1982): 230–231. *Devon & Cornwall Notes & Queries* 35 (1983): 156 (biog. of Thomas Camoys, knight). Taylor *English Hist. Lit. in the 14th Cent.* (1987): 296 (Wigmore Chron. sub 1371: "Eodem anno Elizabeth primogenita filia domini Edmundi de Mortymer comitis marchie nata est ex philippa uxore dicti domini Edmundi et filia leonelli filii Edwardi tercii Anglie idus ffebruaris [13 Feb.] apud Uske et baptisara XVI die ffebruariis et confirmata eodem die."). *Cal. IPM* 20 (1995): 230; 23 (2004): 153, 388–389. Leese *Blood Royal* (1996): 143–149. Coss *Soldiers, Nobles and Gentlemen* (2009):107. Court of Common Pleas, CP 40/590, rot. 127 (available at http://www.british-history.ac.uk/source.aspx?pubid=1272).

Children of Thomas Camoys, K.G., by Elizabeth Louches:

i. **RICHARD CAMOYS**, Knt. [see next].

ii. **ALICE CAMOYS**, married **LEONARD HASTINGS**, Knt., of Kirby Muxloe, Leicestershire [see HUNTINGDON 13].

Child of Thomas Camoys, K.G., by Elizabeth Mortimer:

i. **ROGER CAMOYS**, Knt., styled Lord Camoys, of Wotton, Surrey, Trotton, Sussex, Calais, France, etc., Seneschal of Guienne, son by his father's 2nd marriage, born about 1406 (aged 22 in 1428). He married (1st) before 3 March 1437/8 **ISABEL** _____. They had no issue. In 1429 he quitclaimed to Thomas Morstede, Esq. all his rights in the manor of Wotton, Surrey by way of mortgage for 200 marcs; three years later he released to the said Thomas all his rights therein and levied a fine. In 1429 Roger claimed that in 1428 Robert Falowefeld used force arms to seize and carry off his goods and chattels at London to the value of £40. In 1433 he ceded his rights in the manors of Stukeley (in Great Stukeley), Huntingdonshire and Barcombe, Broadwater, and Trotton, Sussex to Roger Lewknor and his wife, Eleanor, niece of the said Roger. In 1436 he and the Earl of Huntingdon relieved the garrison at Calais. He was taken prisoner in France in 1443–4, and detained there in great misery. During his captivity, his wife, Isabel, was granted an annuity of £40 for life in October 1443. In 1444 he obtained license from the king to settle his property at Calais upon himself and his heirs male. His wife, Isabel, died shortly before 26 Nov. 1444, and was buried in the Grey Friars, London. In 1448 he married (2nd) by papal license dated 1448 **ISABEL DE BEAUNOY**, of the diocese of Rouen, with whom he had already cohabited. They had no issue. In July 1455 the king gave Richard, Earl of Salisbury the armour, etc. "which were of the Lord Camoys, our rebel …. as forfeited by cause of his rebellion." In 1465 SIR ROGER CAMOYS granted an inn called "Nettelbedd" with two tenements in St. Nicholas, Calais to his nephew, William Hastings, 1st Lord Hastings. His date of death is unknown. Monro *Letters of Queen Margaret of Anjou & Bishop Beckington* (Camden Soc. 86) (1863): 109–110. Lewis *Pedes Finium; or, Fines Rel. Surrey* (Surrey Arch. Soc. Extra Volume 1) (1894): 151. VCH *Surrey* 3 (1911): 154–164. Kingsford *Grey Friars of London* (1915): 77–78. *Papal Regs.: Letters* 10 (1915): 192 (Roger Camoys styled "brother of the earl of Northumberland"). *Rpt. on MSS of the late Reginald R. Hastings* 1 (Hist. MSS Comm. 78) (1928): 273, 275–276. VCH *Huntingdon* 2 (1932): 230–234. *C.C.R.* 1422–1429 (1933): 466. *C.C.R.* 1441–1447 (1937): 166, 460. *C.C.R.* 1447–1454 (1941–7): 324. VCH *Sussex* 4 (1953): 32–39; 6(1) (1980): 66–81; 7 (1940): 80–83. *Paget* (1957) 114: 1–7 (sub Camoys). *Cal. IPM* 23 (2004): 153. Court of Common Pleas, CP 40/674, rot. 370 (available at http:// www.british-history.ac.uk/source.aspx?pubid=1272).

9. RICHARD CAMOYS, Knt., of Camoys (in Great Milton) and Chislehampton, Oxfordshire, son and heir apparent by his father's 1st marriage. He married after 10 June 1387 **JOAN POYNINGS**, daughter of Richard de Poynings, 4th Lord Poynings, by Isabel, daughter and heiress of Robert Fitz Pain (formerly de Grey), Knt. [see POYNINGS 15 for her ancestry]. Joan was a legatee in the 1387 will of her father, who bequeathed her 200 marks for her marriage. They had three sons, John, Ralph, and Hugh [2nd Lord Camoys], and two daughters, Margaret and Eleanor. In 1399 he and his father, Sir Thomas Camoys, were jointly granted custody of the castle and town of Porchester, Hampshire. In 1404 William Mymecan sued Richard Camoys, son and heir of Elizabeth Camoys, former wife of Thomas Camoys, Knt., who for default of the said Thomas had been admitted to the defence of his rights to 40*s.* rents with appurtenances in Wheatley, Oxfordshire. Richard was heir in 1408 to his cousin, Gilbert Wace, Knt., by which he inherited the manors of Tythrop (in Kingsey), Buckinghamshire, and Checkenden, Oxfordshire. SIR RICHARD CAMOYS was living 25 May 1416, but died sometime before 24 June 1416. His widow, Joan, was living 24 June 1416.

Nicolas *Testamenta Vetusta* 1 (1826): 122–123 (will of Richard de Poynings, 3rd Lord Poynings). Dallaway *Hist. of the Western Div. of Sussex* 1(2) (1832): 217 (Camoys ped.). *Sussex Arch. Coll.* 3 (1850): 96. Davenport *Lords Lieutenant & High Sheriffs of Oxfordshire* (1868): 21. Carthew *Hundred of Launditch & Deanery of Brisley* 1 (1878): 238–241 (Camoys ped.). *Notes & Queries* 6th Ser. 1 (1880): 234–235, 298–299, 341; 10th Ser. 7 (1907): 509–510. *Genealogist* n.s. 17 (1901): 115. *Revised Rpts. of Cases in the English Courts of Common Law & Equity* 49 (1901): 195–250 (re. Camoys Peerage). *C.P.R.* 1399–1401 (1903): 46. Benolte et al. *Vis. of Sussex 1530 & 1633–4* (H.S.P. 53) (1905): 25–30 (Lewknor ped.: "Sr Richard Camoys. = Joane d. of Tho. Poynings."). Wrottesley *Peds. from the Plea Rolls* (1905): 332. VCH *Buckingham* 4 (1927): 63–68. Salter *Boarstall Cartulary* (Oxford Hist. Soc. 1st Ser. 88) (1930): 9–10 (undated memorandum in Boarstall Cartulary: "Memorandum quod anno domini millesimo CCLXIIII Gilbertus Wace armiger et Elena uxor eius fuerunt seisiti de omnibus terris vocatis Waceslondes in comitatu Oxonie; qui quidem Gilbertus et Elena habuerunt exitum inter se viz. Willelmum Wace militem. Et predictus Willelmus et Agnes uxor eius habuerunt exitum inter se viz. Hugonem, Willelmum, Iohannem, Humfridum, Thomam, Iohannem, Isabellam, Elenam, Radulfum, et Thomam. Et predictus Willelmus filius predicti Willelmi supervixit. Et predicta Elena maritata fuit Ricardo Louches militi de Miltone … Et predictus Willelmus filius Willelmi et Cecilia uxor eius habuerent exitum inter eos viz. Gilbertum Wace militem, Agnetam, Matildam, Sibillam et Margaretam. Et dictus Gilbertus [Wace] … obiit seisitus de terris predictis. Cuius propinquior heres est Ricardus Camoys miles filius Thome Camoys militis et Elizabeth uxoris eius, filie et heredis Willelmi Louches de Milton, filii et heredis Iohannis Louches de Milton, filii et heredis predicti Ricardi Louches militis de Milton et predicte Elene, filie Willelmo Wace militis, uxoris predicti Ricardi Louches."). VCH *Sussex* 4 (1953): 34–35. Paget *Baronage of England* (1957) 114: 1–7 (sub Camoys). Court of Common Pleas, CP 40/572, rot. 205 (available at http:// www.british-history.ac.uk/source.aspx?pubid=1272).

Children of Richard Camoys, Knt., by Joan Poynings:

i **MARGARET CAMOYS**, married **RALPH RADMYLDE**, Esq., of Lancing, Sussex [see CUDWORTH 10].

ii **ELEANOR CAMOYS**, married **ROGER LEWKNOR**, Knt., of Trotton, Sussex [see LEWKNOR 15].

❧ CANTELOWE ❧

1. WILLIAM DE CANTELOWE (or **DE CANTELU**), of Chilton Cantelo, Somerset. He married _____. They had two sons, Walter and Fulk, Knt. In 1155 King Henry II confirmed the gift of William de Cantelowe to Longueville Priory.

Round *Cal. Docs. Preserved in France* 1 (1899): 77–78.

Children of William de Cantelowe, by _____:

i. **WALTER DE CANTELOWE** [see next].

ii. **FULK DE CANTELOWE**, Knt., of Calstone Wellington, Wiltshire, Sheriff of Berkshire, 1200–1. He witnessed six of the 16 charters of John, Earl of Mortain, between June 1195 and 1198. On the accession of John as king, he became a senior household knight. He was employed by King John to bring the monks to heel about the election of an archbishop. He was lord of the hundred of Calne, Wiltshire as early as 1205. About 1209 King John gave Burton, Northamptonshire to Fulk de Cantelowe to hold at will. Thomas Malemains recovered the manor of Burton in 1216, as part of his wife's inheritance. In 1217, it was again granted to Cantelowe, but presumably he obtained other compensation, since on the death of Thomas Malemains, it was granted during pleasure in 1219 to Malemains' widow, Joan. SIR FULK DE CANTELOWE died c.1234. *List of Sheriffs for England & Wales* (PRO Lists and Indexes 9) (1898): 6. Warner & Ellis *Facsimiles of Royal & Other Charters in the British Museum* 1 (1903): #74(charter of John, Count of Mortain dated 1193; charter witnessed by Fulk de Cantelowe). Rosny *C.C.R. 1231–1234* (1905): 405 (Fulk de Cantelowe styled "uncle" of William de Cantelowe in 1234). G.H. Fowler 'Calendar of Inquisitions Post Mortem. No. I' in *Pubs. Bedfordshire Hist. Rec. Soc.* 5 (1920): 210–215. VCH *Northampton* 3 (1930): 180–186. VCH *Wiltshire* 5 (1957): 44–71. Church *Household Knights of King John* (1999): 21.

2. WALTER DE CANTELOWE, of Brimpton, Berkshire, Adber and Leigh, Dorset, Fontley and Oakley, Hampshire, and Barwick, Camel, and Chilton Cantelo, Somerset. He held two knights' fees of William de Roumare in 1166. He also held lands of William de Roumare in Normandy. He married **AMICE** _____. They had three sons, William, Knt., Robert Barat (or Cantelowe), and Roger Orget, and three daughters, Nichole, Sibyl, and probably Isabel. His name occurs on a role of the Norman Exchequer dated 1184. He was a member of the entourage of John, Count of Mortain [afterwards King John]. In 1195 William de Saint Mary accounted £4 for the farm at Barwick, Somerset of Walter de Cantelowe for half a year. In 1201 he sued Robert de Cantelowe for the vill of Chilton Cantelo, Somerset as being his right and inheritance, whereof his father, William de Cantelowe, was seised during the reign of King Henry II [1154–89]. In 1201–2 he conveyed all his right in the vill of Chilton Cantelo, Somerset to Robert de Cantelowe; for this concession Robert gave Walter 28 marks of money, and thereupon Walter did homage to Robert in the Court. In 1204–5 the king issued a writ to the Sheriff of Norfolk to deliver to Walter certain lands in that county which the king had previously committed to the custody of William his son. At an unknown date, he granted in pure and perpetual alms for the salvation of his soul and those of his wife, Amice, his son and heir, William de Cantelowe, his other children, and his ancestors to Christchurch Priory 1/2 mark a year from his rent at Leigh, Dorset, viz. 20*d.* to be paid each quarter by Sampson de Leigh and his heirs. WALTER DE CANTELOWE was living in 1205, when the king gave him a dolium of wine.

Mémoires de la Société des Antiquaires de Normandie 8 (1834): 349–350, 352. Palgrave *Rotuli Curiæ Regis* 1 (1835): 172. Green *Feet of Fines for Somerset* 1 (Somerset Rec. Soc. 6) (1892): 15. Batten *Hist. & Topog. Colls. Rel. to the early Hist. of Parts of South Somerset* (1894): 1–7, 29–32. Hall *Red Book of the Exchequer* 1 (1896): 376–377. *Trans. Shropshire Arch. & Natural Hist. Soc.* 3rd Ser. 1 (1901): 170–177. VCH *Rutland* 2 (1935): 88–91. *Medieval Miscellany for Doris Mary Stenton* (Pubs. Pipe Roll Soc. n.s. 36) (1962): 77–84. Hanna *Christchurch Priory Cartulary* (Hampshire Rec. Ser. 18) (2007): 169 (charter of Walter de Cantelowe; charter witnessed by his son, Robert de Cantelowe).

Children of Walter de Cantelowe, by Amice _____:

i. **WILLIAM DE CANTELOWE**, Knt. [see next].

ii. **ROBERT DE CANTELOWE** (also known as **ROBERT BARAD** or **ROBERT BARAT**). He held the manor of Great Coxwell. Berkshire between 1201 and 1205. He was a member of the royal household before 1209, and was described as William de Cantelowe's brother on a number of occasions. He witnessed his father's charter to Christchurch Priory. In Jan. 1223 William de Cantelowe was given custody of Robert's son and heir, later named as Eustace de Cantelowe. Hardy *Rotuli de Liberate, ac de Misis, et Praestitis, Regnante Johanne* (1844):189 (Robert Barat and Roger Orget styled "brothers" [fratibus] in 1210). *C.Ch.R.* 4 (1912): 247 (Robert Barad styled "son" of Walter de Cantelowe). *English Hist. Rev.* 110 (1995): 277–302. Church *Household Knights of King John* (1999): 26–27. Hanna *Christchurch Priory Cartulary* (Hampshire Rec. Ser. 18) (2007): 169 (charter of Walter de Cantelowe).

Child of Robert de Cantelowe (otherwise Robert Barad), by _____:

a. **EUSTACE DE CANTELOWE** (or **EUSTACE BARET**), of Barby, Northamptonshire, Lubbesthorpe, Leicestershire, Basford, Nottinghamshire, etc., son and heir, minor in 1223. He married **KATHERINE DE LISLE**, daughter and heiress of Hugh de Lisle, of Barby, Northamptonshire, Lubbesthorpe, Leicestershire, and Thorpe in the Glebe, Nottinghamshire. They had no issue. In 1241 he was sued by Walter de Grendale, who claimed 10 carucates in Barby, Northamptonshire and the advowson of the church and the manor of Lubbesthorpe, Leicestershire and 3 virgates there as his right. In 1242 he had a respite of knighthood. In 1246 William de Harcourt, parson of the church of Ayleston, and all his successors were adjudged to do to Eustace de Cantelowe and his heirs the service of 1/40 fee for 1 virgate in Lubbesthorpe, Leicestershire, which service had always been done to Aveline, late wife of Hugh de Lisle, who had held the manor of Lubbesthorpe in dower of the inheritance of the said Eustace, and also to William de Cantelowe in the name of custody of the said Eustace. In 1247 he sued Henry de Lilleburn regarding a plea of land in Leicestershire. The same year he sued John Fitz Joerg regarding an unknown issue in Northamptonshire. In 1252 Eustace de Cantelowe being deceased without issue, the king restored to William de Cantelowe and his heirs, as their inheritance, the lands of the said Eustace in the manors of Barby, Lubbesthorpe, and Basford. *Coll. Top. et Gen.* 1 (1834): 269, 270. *Trans. Shropshire Arch. & Natural Hist. Soc.* 3rd Ser. 1 (1901): 170–177. Farrer *Honors & Knights Fees* (1923): 171–173. *Pubs. Bedfordshire Hist. Rec. Soc.* 21 (1939): 132, 135. Church *Household Knights of King John* (1999): 27.

iii. **ROGER ORGET**, of Great Bowden and Harborough, Leicestershire. In 1203 the king granted William de Cantelowe lands in Great Bowden and Market Harborough, Leicestershire to hold during pleasure; William in turn entrusted the manors to his brother, Roger Orget. Roger was in possession of these manors in 1221. On Roger's death, the lands were seized by the sheriff 30 March 1228. Hardy *Rotuli de Liberate, ac de Misis, et Praestitis, Regnante Johanne* (1844):189 (Robert Barat and Roger Orget styled "brothers" [fratibus] in 1210). *C.C.R.* 1227–1231 (1902): 426 (Roger Orget, deceased, styled "brother" [fratri] of William de Cantelowe in 1230). VCH *Leicester* 5 (1964): 133–153.

iv. **NICHOLE DE CANTELOWE**. She married _____ **DE WANNEVILLE**. She was living in 1229. *C.C.R.* 1227–1231 (1902): 255 (Nichole de Wannevill' styled "sister" [sorori] of William de Cantelowe in 1229).

v. **SIBYL DE CANTELOWE**, married **GEOFFREY PAUNCEFOTE**, of Exhall, Warwickshire. He was holding a ¼ fee at Exhall, Warwickshire under the Earl of Warwick in 1235, but in 1242 ¼ fee was returned as held by Robert de Exhall and Ralph de Binton of Geoffrey Pauncefote, who was the undertenant of William de Cantelowe and he of the heir of Geoffrey Corbizun of Hunningham under the Earl of Warwick. VCH *Warwick* 3 (1945): 49–57, 88–91 ["Early in the 13th century Richard Corbizun (probably son of a Geoffrey who occurs c.1155) granted the manor to William de Cantilupe, who passed it to his sister Sybil and her husband Geoffrey Pauncefote."].

vi. **ISABEL DE CANTELOWE** (probable daughter).[3] She married (as his 2nd wife) **STEPHEN DEVEREUX**, of Lyonshall and Frome Herbert, Herefordshire, Wilby, Norfolk, etc., son and heir of John Devereux, of Lyonshall, Herefordshire. They had one son, William. In 1227 he and his heirs were granted a weekly market and yearly fair at Lyonshall, Herefordshire. STEPHEN DEVEREUX died in 1228. His widow, Isabel, married (2nd)

---

[3] Isabel de Cantelowe's maiden name is attested by her own charter [see *Coll. Top. et Gen.* 2 (1835): 250]. That Isabel was the sister of Sir William de Cantelowe (died 1239) seems virtually certain. Her son, William Devereux, is known to have had a daughter who married Sir John de Pycheford. Sir John de Pycheford's wife was styled "kinswoman" of Sir George de Cantelowe [died 1273] [see *Cal. IPM* 2 (1906): 16–21]. Sir George de Cantelowe was the great-grandson and heir male of Sir William de Cantelowe (died 1239). For further particulars, see Eyton *Antiqs. of Shropshire* 6 (1858): 273.

RALPH DE PEMBRIDGE (or PENEBRUG). In her second widowhood, she gave to the Hospital of St. Ethelbert for the souls of herself and her two husbands "unam ladum bladi" at the Feast of St. Andrew during her life to be received at her house of Frome. She was living in 1245. *Coll. Top. et Gen.* 2 (1835): 250 (charter of Isabel de Cantelowe dated pre-1244). Duncumb *Colls. towards Hist. & Antiqs. of the County of Hereford: Hundred of Huntington* (1897): 21, 49 (Devereux ped.). Holden *Lords of the Central Marches* (2008): 97–102 (re. Devereux fam.).

3. WILLIAM DE CANTELOWE, Knt., of Leigh, Dorset, Ellesborough and Mentmore, Buckinghamshire, Meole Brace, Shropshire, Barcheston and Studley, Warwickshire, Calne, Wiltshire, etc., Steward of the Household of John, Count of Mortain, 1198, Sheriff of Worcestershire, 1200–15, Sheriff of Warwickshire and Leicestershire, 1201–4, 1209–23, itinerant Justice in Staffordshire, 1203, Sheriff of Herefordshire, 1204–5, Steward of the King's Household, 1204–22, a Norman by birth. He married **MASCELINE** (or **MAZRA**) **DE BRACY** (or **BRASCY**, **BRACI**), daughter of Audulf de Bracy, of Meole Brace, Shropshire, Eaton Bray, Bedfordshire, Mentmore, Buckinghamshire, etc. They had four sons, William, Knt., Robert, Walter [Bishop of Worcester], and Matthew [Rector of Ribston, Yorkshire and Alvechurch, Worcestershire], and one daughter, _____ (wife of Thurstan de Montfort). He witnessed two acts of King John while John was still an earl in 1198. The first was dated 12 July 1198 when William was styled 'tunc senescallus;' the second was dated 4 Dec. 1198, just a few months before King Richard's death. William became one of the king's stewards of the household with Peter de Stokes and Robert de Thornham. In 1203 the king granted him lands in Great Bowden and Market Harborough, Leicestershire to hold during pleasure; William in turn entrusted the manors to his brother, Roger Orget. He took part in the ineffectual expedition to Poitou in 1205. The same year he was granted the manor of Eaton Bray, Bedfordshire, in exchange for 300 marks and the manor of Cockeswall; Eaton Bray subsequently became the head of the Cantelowe barony. In 1208 he was granted custody of the see of Worcester, and was a justice in Nottinghamshire. In 1209 he settled a dispute which he had with the Prior of Dunstaple regarding 50 acres in Shortgrave, Bedfordshire; he quitclaimed the said 50 acres to the Prior, as well as 20 acres in Eaton, Bedfordshire, which was part of the land which the Prior claimed by virtue of a grant made by Audulf de Bracy, father of Masceline, wife of William. He and William Briwerre supervised elections to the vacant sees of York and Carlisle in 1214. Wendover's description of him as one of John's "evil counselors" probably owes much to his role as a gaoler of baronial hostages. Wendover also suggests that Cantelowe may have wavered in his loyalty after the rebel seizure of London in 1215, but this is belied by the stream of royal writs sent to him in 1215–16. In 1215 he also witnessed the royal declaration of free election to sees and abbeys. He took the side of the king in his war with the barons. In 1215–16 he was granted a number of manors belonging to rebels, and was commissioned to treat with those who might return into the king's peace. In 1216 he was granted letters of presentation to the advowson of the church of Preston, Warwickshire, the gift belonging to the king because the land of Thurstan de Montfort was in his hand. In 1217 he was at the Siege of Mountsorrel and at the Battle of Lincoln. He presented to the churches of Ridlington, Rutland, 1217, 1218, 1221, and Hinxworth, Hertfordshire, 1218. In 1218 he witnessed the treaty of Worcester with Llywelyn ap Iorwerth, and was an itinerant justice in Bedfordshire. The same year the Sheriff was ordered to inform the king why he had disseised William of seven hides of land in Eaton. In 1219 he was a commissioner investigating encroachments on the royal forests in Oxfordshire, Buckinghamshire, and Herefordshire. His wife, Masceline, seems to have been living in 1220. Sometime before 1223, he appears to have acquired some of William Martel's lands at Totternhoe, Bedfordshire. In 1223 he joined the armed demonstration of Ranulph, Earl of Chester at the Tower against the government of Hubert de Burgh; he submitted at Northampton on 30 December. He joined the royal Siege of Bedford in the summer of 1224. In 1225 he was allowed £1084 at the exchequer for war expenses under King John; this cancelled a list of debts that included increments due on county farms, scutages, and the fine for the custody of the lands and heir of Robert Chandos. As "William de Cantelowe, senior," he presented his son, [Master] Walter de Cantelowe, to the church of Bulwick, Northamptonshire in 1227. He obtained a confirmation of the manor of Aston Cantlow, Warwickshire in 1227 and 1231. In 1227 Richard Fitz William was called to warranty by William de Cantelowe for a third part of the manor of Ellesborough, Buckinghamshire, which Geva Basset, widow of the said Richard's uncle, also named Richard Fitz William, claimed in dower. He served in Wales in 1228, Brittany in 1230, and Wales again in 1231. In 1229, following the death of his brother, Roger Orget, the king re-granted him the manors of Great Bowden and Market Harborough, Leicestershire. In 1230 he received confirmation from the crown of the vill, market, and manor of Bingley, Yorkshire which he had of the gift and feoffment of Ranulph, Earl of Chester and Lincoln. In 1232 he impleaded William son of William Corbicun to acquit him of service which Thomas, Earl of Warwick, demanded for lands in Barcheston and Studley, Warwickshire. He was heir c.1234 to his uncle, Fulk de Cantelowe, by which he inherited lands in Calstone Wellington, Wiltshire. He signed the confirmation of Magna Carta in 1236. On 23 October 1236 the king granted to him that he may render the 32 marks which were exacted from him by summons of the Exchequer, namely 30 marks for the prest of Hereford and 2 marks for the debts of Robert Barat his brother. At an unknown date, he granted the chapel in his court of Eaton Bray, Bedfordshire one messuage and 12 acres of land in Eaton Bray, six measures of wheat yearly, and 22 solidates of annual rent; with a further grant of 50s. yearly, to support a second chaplain, and of a croft to keep a lamp burning in the chapel. SIR WILLIAM DE CANTELOWE died at Reading, Berkshire 7 April 1239, and was buried at Studley Priory, Warwickshire.

Clutterbuck *Hist. & Antiqs.of Hertford* 3 (1827): 528. Lipscomb *Hist. & Antiqs. of Buckingham* 1 (1847): 176 (Cantilupe ped.). Foss *Judges of England* 2 (1848): 291–292 (biog. of William de Cantilupe). Sackville-West *Hist. Notices of the Parish of Withyham* (1857): 40–46 (re. Cantelowe fam.). Eyton *Antiqs. of Shropshire* 6 (1858): 350–357; 11 (1860): 144–147. Luard *Annales Monastici* 1 (Rolls Ser. 36) (1864): 112 (Tewkesbury Annals sub A.D. 1239: "Obiit Willelmus de Cantilupo senior apud Radinges, in Martio, et delatus est apud Stodlegam."); 4 (Rolls Ser. 36) (1869): 430 (Annals of Worcester sub A.D. 1239: "Dominus W[illelmus] de Cantilupo, pater domini episcopi, obiit."). Batten *Hist. & Topog. Colls. Rel. to the early Hist. of Parts of South Somerset* (1894): 1–7. *List of Sheriffs for England & Wales* (PRO Lists and Indexes 9) (1898): 59, 144, 157. *Trans. Shropshire Arch. & Natural Hist. Soc.* 3rd Ser. 1 (1901): 170–177. *C.C.R. 1227–1231* (1902): 121, 426 (Roger Orget styled "brother" [fratri] of William de Cantelowe in 1230). *C.C.R. 1231–1234* (1905): 220, 405 (Fulk de Cantelowe styled "uncle" of William de Cantelowe in 1234). *Rutland Mag. & County Hist. Rec.* 2 (1906): 100. VCH *Buckingham* 2 (1908): 331–338; 3 (1925): 397–401. G.H. Fowler 'Calendar of Inquisitions Post Mortem. No. I' in *Pubs. Bedfordshire Hist. Rec. Soc.* 5 (1920): 210–215. VCH *Bedford* 3 (1912): 369–375 (Cantlowe arms: Gules a fesse vair between three fleurs de lis coming out of leopards' heads or). Phillimore *Rotuli Hugonis de Welles Episcopi Lincolniensis 1209–1235* 2 (Lincoln Rec. Soc. 6) (1913): 134–135. Fowler *Cal. of Feet of Fines for Buckinghamshire* (Pubs Bedfordshire Hist. Soc. 6) (1919): 39 (fine dated 1209 mentions Auduf de Brascy father of Mascelin, wife of William de Cantelowe), 57–58. *Pubs. Bedfordshire Hist. Rec. Soc.* 12 (1928): 79–81. Jenkins *Cal. of the Rolls of the Justices on Eyre 1227* (Buckinghamshire Arch. Soc. 6) (1945): 8, 16–17, 23–24, 29, 31. VCH *Warwick* 3 (1945): 31–42 (Cantelupe arms: Gules three fleurs de lis coming out of leopards' heads or), 167–172, 193–196; 5 (1949): 5–10. Sanders *English Baronies* (1960): 39–40. VCH *Leicester* 5 (1964): 133–153. Carpenter *Minority of Henry III* (1990). Hoskin *English Episcopal Acta* 13 (1997): xxvii–xxxiii (biog. of Walter de Cantelowe). Church *Household Knights of King John* (1999): 21. Hanna *Christchurch Priory Cartulary* (Hampshire Rec. Ser. 18) (2007): 169 (charter of Walter de Cantelowe). Dryburgh *Cal. of the Fine Rolls of the Reign of Henry III* (2008): 130 (Date: 1226-7. William de Cantilupe gives the king 15 marks for having his confirmation of the manor of Aston, which King John gave him and confirmed to him by charter, and for having a market each week on Mondays at the manor of Peter de Montfort of Beaudesert, and for having a fair there each year to last for three days).

Children of William de Cantelowe, by Masceline (or Mazra) de Bracy:

i. **WILLIAM DE CANTELOWE**, Knt. [see next].

ii. **ROBERT DE CANTELOWE**, of Meole Brace, Shropshire and Bingley, Yorkshire. In 1254 the king granted him permission to use the liberties and quittances in his manor of Bingley, Yorkshire as his father, William de Cantelowe, used by the king's charter. The same year he was granted free warren in all his demesne lands in

Bingley, Yorkshire and Meules, Shropshire. Francisque-Michel *Rôles Gascons* 1 (1885): 470, 497. *C.P.R.* 1247–1258 (1908): 305, 323.

iii. **[MASTER] WALTER DE CANTELOWE**, King's clerk, Archdeacon of Stafford, Bishop of Worcester. He was presented to a series of parish livings, i.e, Eyton in 1208, Burton and Worfield in 1215, Long Itchington, Rampisham, Preston, Priors Hardwick, and a moiety of Stokes in 1216, Hinxworth, Hertfordshire in 1219, Penrith, Cumberland in 1222, and Bulwick, Northamptonshire in 1227, and finally, on 22 July 1231, to a canonry and prebend in Lichfield Cathedral. He was evidently a pluralist, and as such was not wholly disinterested when, at the legatine council of 1237, he pleaded the cause of many noble pluralists, "who have until now lived honourably, giving what hospitality they could and dispensing alms with open doors," who were threatened with impoverishment by being reduced to a single benefice each. He served as king's proctor at the Roman court in 1227 and 1229. He acted as justice in eyre for several counties in 1232, and received a number of papal commissions to serve as a judge-delegate or to execute papal mandates. In January 1235 he was one of three envoys sent to France to bear truce proposals to King Louis IX and to swear on King Henry III's behalf to observe the conditions of the truce. He was elected as Bishop of Worcester 30 August 1236; his election received royal assent 9 September. In April 1237 he was ordained priest at Viterbo by Pope Gregory IX, who consecrated him 3 May. In October 1237 he was enthroned at Worcester in the presence of the papal legate, Cardinal Otto, the Archbishop of Canterbury, and the King and Queen of Scots. In 1237, as bishop-elect of Worcester, he again attended the papal court on the king's behalf. He proved himself a zealous diocesan bishop, sharing with Bishop Grosseteste of Lincoln a concern for the reform of abuses and the improvement of pastoral standards. The synodal statutes he promulgated for the Worcester diocese in 1240, frequently revised and updated, provided a model for the legislation of several of his episcopal colleagues. In 1240 he obtained papal sanction for a drive to remove married clergy from parishes and to deprive those who had succeeded their fathers in their benefices. He displayed the same energy in protecting and extending the temporal and spiritual rights of his see. He attended the Council of Lyons with other English prelates in 1245. In 1246 he stood with Robert Grosseteste in supporting the pope's right to receive financial aid from the clergy. In 1252 he supported Simon de Montfort against charges lodged by the king of extortion and mistreatment in Montfort's rule of Gascony. From 1255 onwards he was chief spokesman for the clerical opposition to King Henry's acceptance of the Sicilian crown for his second son, Edmund. In 1257 he was one of those sent to France to negotiate terms of a permanent peace. He played a leading role in the revolutionary events of the years 1258–65. At the Oxford parliament of June 1258 he was the only cleric chosen by the baronial side to serve on the committee of twenty-four which drafted the provisions of Oxford, and he was subsequently elected a member of the standing council imposed upon the king by the new constitution. In 1259 he was appointed one of the councillors to act as regents while the king was absent in France. Following King Henry's recovery of power in 1261, he remained a stalwart supporter of Montfort and an unyielding upholder of the provisions. He put his name to the baronial letters submitting the cause of the reformers to the arbitration of Louis IX, and his nephew, Thomas de Cantelowe, was entrusted with expounding the baronial case to Louis at Amiens. In March 1264, together with the bishops of Winchester, London, and Chichester, he held talks with the king's representatives at Brackley and Oxford, offering baronial acceptance of Louis' verdict on condition that King Henry expelled unacceptable aliens from court and allowed the council to nominate his ministers. In May, he and Henry de Sandwich, Bishop of London, accompanied Montfort's army on the march to Lewes, and on the eve of the battle made a last effort to mediate between Montfort and the king. But after this overture failed, Cantilupe exhorted Montfort's troops to confess their sins, gave them absolution, and blessed them. He was subsequently present at the Battles of Evesham, 1264, and Lewes, 1265. WALTER DE CANTELOWE, Bishop of Worcester, died at his manor of Blockley, Gloucestershire 12 Feb. 1266, and was buried by the monks beside the high altar in Worcester Cathedral. A zealous pastor, a scholar, and an idealist, as the spiritual mentor of one of the most radical political movements of the middle ages, he ranks among the greatest ecclesiastical leaders of his generation. Lipscomb *Hist. & Antiqs. of Buckingham* 1 (1847): 176 (Cantilupe ped.). Sackville-West Hist. *Notices of the Parish of Withyham* (1857): 40–46 (re. Cantelowe fam.). *C.P.R.* 1216–1225 (1901): 350, 377, 382 (Walter de Cantelowe styled "son of our beloved and faithful William de Cantelowe" by King Henry III in 1223), 413. *Trans. Shropshire Arch. & Natural Hist. Soc.* 3rd Ser. 1 (1901): 170–177. *List of Ancient Corr. of the Chancery & Exchequer* (PRO Lists and Indexes 15) (1902): 98 (letter of Peter de Montfort dated ?July 1261 requesting assistance for [Walter de Cantelowe], bishop of Worcester, his kinsman, and himself). *D.N.B.* 3 (1908): 904–906 (biog. of Walter de Cantelupe). Phillimore *Rotuli Hugonis de Welles Episcopi Lincolniensis 1209–1235* 1 (Lincoln Rec. Soc. 3) (1912): 155; 2 (Lincoln Rec. Soc. 6) (1913): 134–135. VCH *Worcester* 3 (1913): 501–510. G.H. Fowler 'Calendar of Inquisitions Post Mortem. No. I' in *Pubs. Bedfordshire Hist. Rec. Soc.* 5 (1920): 210–215 ("He was, except for Robert Grosseteste of Lincoln, the most distinquished cleric of his time."). *C.P.* 9 (1936): 123, footnote a (sub Montfort) ["Peter de Montfort wrote to Walter de Merton, Chancellor 1261-3, about the business of (Walter de Cauntelo) Lord (Bishop) of Worcester, our uncle [avunculi nostri] (Anc. Corresp., PRO, vol. vii, no. 20)]. Powicke & Cheney *Councils & Synods with other Docs. rel. to the English*

Church, 1205–1313 1 (1964). Greenway *Fasti Ecclesiae Anglicanae 1066–1300* 2 (1971): 101. Treharne & Sanders *Docs. of the Baronial Movement of Reform & Rebellion, 1258–1267* (1973). Maddicott *Simon de Montfort* (1994). Carpenter *Reign of Henry III* (1996): 293–307. Hoskin *English Episcopal Acta* 13 (1997): xxvii–xxxiii (biog. of Walter de Cantelowe).

    iv. **MATTHEW DE CANTELOWE**, clerk, Rector of Ribston, Yorkshire, 1231, Rector of Alvechurch, Worcestershire. Sometime in the period, 1216–17, William de Cornhill, Bishop of Coventry, granted license for the appropriation of the church of West Bromwich subject to the rights of Matthew de Cantelowe. In 1239 Pope Gregory IX granted a dispensation to "Matthew de Cantelupe, clerk of the diocese of York, brother to the Bishop of Worcester, allowing him to hold more benefices than one." At an unknown date, he reached agreement with Philip, Abbot of Bordesley, relative to the fishery in the water called 'Arewe' and common of pasture in the woods and fields in 'Osmerleg' and in the wood called 'Sortwode.' MATTHEW DE CANTELOWE was living in July 1253. Gray *Reg., or Rolls, of Walter Gray, Lord Archbishop of York* (Surtees Soc. 56) (1872): 99n., 158, 163–164, 239–240, 282–282, 287–288. *Yorkshire Arch. & Top. Jour.* 7 (1882): 442; 8 (1884): 295; 9 (1886): 77–78. Speight *Nidderdale & the Garden of the Nidd* (1894): 189. *C.C.R. 1254–1256* (1931): 436 (Robert [no surname] styled "kinsman" [consanguineum] of Matthew de Cantelowe in 1256). Darlington *Cartulary of Worcester Cathedral Priory* (Pipe Roll Soc. n.s. 38) (1968): 105. Hoskin *English Episcopal Acta* 13 (1997): 118–119. National Archives, E 326/2687 (available at http://www.catalogue.nationalarchives.gov.uk/search.asp).

    v. _____ **DE CANTELOWE**, married **THURSTAN DE MONTFORT**, of Beaudesert, Warwickshire [see MONTFORT 4].

4. WILLIAM DE CANTELOWE, Knt., of Eaton Bray, Bedfordshire, Ellesborough, Buckinghamshire, Cold Hatton, Eyton, Harley, Hope Bowdler, Marton, Meole Brace, Stanwardine-on-campo, Stapleton, Whittingslow, and Wilderley, Shropshire, Aston Cantlow, Hunningham, Ipsley, and [Upper] Shuckburgh, Warwickshire, Poulton, Wiltshire, etc., Steward of the Royal Household, 1239–51, Sheriff of Nottinghamshire and Derbyshire, 1239–40, Keeper of the Town of Shrewsbury, Constable of Nottingham Castle, Keeper of Lundy Island, son and heir. He married (1st) before July 1215 or 1216 (date of pardon) **MILICENT DE GOURNAY**, Countess of Évreux, widow of Amaury de Montfort, Count of Évreux in Normandy, Earl of Gloucester in England (died before November 1213), and daughter of Hugh (or Hugues) de Gournay (died 1214), seigneur of Gournay-en-Brie, and of Wendover, Buckinghamshire, Houghton, Bedfordshire, Caister and Cantley, Norfolk, Mapledurham, Oxfordshire, etc, by Juliane, daughter of Aubrey II, Count of Dammartin [see GOURNAY 4 for her ancestry]. They had five sons, William, Knt., [Master] Thomas [Bishop of Hereford, Chancellor of England, Chancellor of Oxford University], [Master] Hugh [Archdeacon of Gloucester], John, and Nicholas, and two daughters, Agnes and Juliane. Like his father, he was named by Roger of Wendover as one of King John's "evil counselors." In 1217 Gilbert de Clare, Earl of Gloucester, granted William's wife, Milicent, the manors of Marlow, Buckinghamshire and Burford, Oxfordshire, together with the life grant of the vill of Hambleden, Buckinghamshire in satisfaction of Milicent's claims to dower in the lands of her former husband, Amaury de Evreux. In 1217 William was at the Siege of Mountsorrel and at the Battle of Lincoln. By the mid-1220s he was a follower of Ranulph, Earl of Chester, and witnessed many of his charters. He participated in Earl Ranulph's armed demonstration at the Tower of London in 1223, but then submitted with the earl. He presented to the churches of Bulwick, Northamptonshire, 1226 and 1247, and Barby, Northamptonshire, 1230. He obtained a confirmation of the manor of Aston Cantlow, Warwickshire in 1227 and again in 1231. He joined Chester on the king's expedition to Brittany in 1230. He married (2nd) after Michaelmas 1233 (date of lawsuit) **MAUD FITZ GEOFFREY**, widow of Henry d'Oilly (died 1232), of Hook Norton, Kidlington, and Little Minster (in Minster Lovell), Oxfordshire, and daughter of Geoffrey Fitz Peter, Knt., Earl of Essex, by his 2nd wife, Aveline, daughter of Roger de Clare, Earl of Hertford [see ESSEX 2 for her ancestry]. They had no issue. Sometime in the period, 1227–36, Maud had the manor of Gussage St. Michael, Dorset by gift from her half-sister, Maud de Mandeville, Countess of Essex and Hereford. In 1234 he served as one of the executors of the will of Ranulph, Earl of Chester. In

1236 he went on pilgrimage to Santiago de Compostela. In 1237 the king granted him the manors of Great Bowden and Market Harborough, Leicestershire for life. In 1241 he was one of the English arbitrators with Dafydd of Gwynedd. He was appointed one of the guardians of the realm during the king's expedition to Poitou in 1242. In 1242 William son of William Marmion sued him. In 1242–3 he presented to the church of Coningsby, Lincolnshire, in right of his ward, Philip Marmion. In 1244 Peter de Freney conveyed the manor of Clipsham, Rutland to him. In 1244–5 William de Cantelowe, senior, levied a fine by which William de Haket was bound not to sell, injure, waste, or spoil any part of the manor of Little Merston (in West Camel), Somerset, as it was only his for life, and afterwards should go to the said William de Cantelowe. He was one of the proctors of the English baronage at the Council of Lyons in 1245, delivering a lengthy complaint against Roman exactions. His wife, Maud, had a gift of bucks from Sherwood Forest by the king in 1245 and 1248. SIR WILLIAM DE CANTELOWE died testate 22 Feb. 1250/1. His viscera was buried at Oseney Abbey, Oxfordshire. In 1252 his widow, Maud, went to Scotland with Margaret, the king's daughter, Queen of Scotland, by order of the king. She held the advowson of the Rectory of Berwick St. James, Wiltshire for life. In 1260 Hawise de London, widow of Patrick de Chaworth, Knt., leased to Maud and to Maud's nephew, John son of John Fitz Geoffrey, the manor of East Garston, Berkshire for a term of 11 years. His widow, Maud, died 1 March 1260/1.

Madox *Formulare Anglicanum* (1702): 184 (charter of Amaury, Count of Évreux). Martene & Durand *Veterum Scriptorum et Monumentorum* 1 (1724): 1068 (charter of King Philippe Auguste of France dated 1206 mentions land given by Hugh de Gournay at Sotteville in Normandy in marriage with his daughter, [Milicent], Countess of Evreux). Bridges *Hist. & Antiqs. of Northamptonshire* 1 (1791): 25; 2 (1791): 289. Blomefield *Essay towards a Top. Hist. of Norfolk* 5 (1806): 507 ("Henry d'Oyly who had two wives, Sibil and Maud, who remarried to William de Cantalupe; he had only one daughter, Maud, who died young. He attended King Ric. I. to Jerusalem, and as he returned, died and was buried in Austria, and was succeeded by his only brother, Robert, who was Baron of Hocknorton, and the King's Constable ..."). *Rotuli Hundredorum* (Record Commission) (1812): 97, 102. Montmorency-Morres *Genealogical Memoir of the Fam. of Montmorency* (1817): xxxii–xxxvi. Roberts *Excerpta è Rotulis Finium in Turri Londinensi Asservatis, A.D. 1216–1272* 2 (1836): 357. Lipscomb *Hist. & Antiqs. of Buckingham* 1 (1847): 176 (Cantilupe ped.). Sackville-West *Hist. Notices of the Parish of Withyham* (1857): 40–46 (re. Cantelowe fam.). Eyton *Antiqs. of Shropshire* 6 (1858): 350–357; 11 (1860): 82. Luard *Annales Monastici* 1 (Rolls Ser. 36) (1864): 143 (sub A.D. 1250: "Obiit ... Willelmus de Cantilupo in Cathedra Sancti Petri"); 3 (Rolls Ser. 36) (1866): 181 (Dunstaple Annals sub A.D. 1250: "Eodem tempore mortuus est Willelmus de Cantilupo secundus."); 4 (Rolls Ser. 36) (1869): 100 (Oseney Annals sub 1250: "Eodem anno obiit dominus Willelmus de Cantilupo, et jacent ejus viscera apud Oseneiam coram altari Sancti Michaelis."), 127 (sub Oseney Annals sub A.D. 1260 [i.e., 1260/1]: "Eodem anno primo die Martii obiit bonæ memoriæ domina Matildis de Cantilupo, cujus animæ propicietur Deus."), 440 (Worcester Annals sub A.D. 1251: Willelmus de Cantilupo frater domini episcopi obiit."). Francisque-Michel *Rôles Gascons* 1 (1885): 373, 422. Worthy *Devonshire Parishes, or the Antiquities, Heraldry & Fam. Hist. of Twenty-Eight Parishes in the Archdeaconry of Totnes* 2 (1889): 31–34. *Genealogist* n.s. 5 (1889): 129 (seal of Amaury, Earl of Gloucester—A shield of arms: Barry pily over the whole field. Legend: Sig. Almarici Comitis Gloverniæ. Counterseal of the same. Legend: Secretum A. Comitis Gloverniæ.). *Desc. Cat. Ancient Deeds* 1 (1890): 9–21. Batten *Hist. & Topog. Colls. Rel. to the early Hist. of Parts of South Somerset* (1894): 1–7. Macray *Cal. of Charters & Docs. rel. to Selborne & its Priory* (1894): 63 (charter of Amaury, Earl of Gloucester dated before 1210, followed by fine dated 1210). *Lincolnshire Notes & Queries* 5 (1898): 190. *List of Sheriffs for England & Wales* (PRO Lists and Indexes 9) (1898): 102. Bates *Two Cartularies of the Benedictine Abbeys of Mulchelney & Athelney* (Somerset Rec. Soc. 14) (1899): 71. *Trans. Shropshire Arch. & Natural Hist. Soc.* 3rd Ser. 1 (1901): 170–177. *Rpt. on MSS in Various Colls.* 4 (Hist. MSS Comm. 55) (1907): 97 (charter of Amaury, Earl of Gloucester). *C.P.R. 1247–1258* (1908): 123, 129, 416. VCH *Buckingham* 2 (1908): 331–338; 4 (1927): 260–263. *C.P.R. 1258–1266* (1910): 125, 184–185. VCH *Bedford* 3 (1912): 369–375. Grosseteste *Rotuli Roberti Grosseteste Episcopi Lincolniensis* (Lincoln Rec. Soc. 11) (1914): 67. *C.C.R. 1242–1247* (1916): 337. G.H. Fowler 'Calendar of Inquisitions Post Mortem. No. I' in *Pubs. Bedfordshire Hist. Rec. Soc.* 5 (1920): 210–215. *C.C.R. 1247–1251* (1922): 66. *C.P. 5* (1926): 692–693 (sub Gloucester). *C.C.R. 1251–1253* (1927): 19, 55, 292, 386, 413. *Pubs. Bedfordshire Hist. Rec. Soc.* 12 (1928): 79–81. *C.C.R. 1254–1256* (1931): 94, 181, 193–194, 208, 240, 275, 353, 380. *C.C.R. 1256–1259* (1932): 21, 257, 264. *C.C.R. 1259–1261* (1934): 303. VCH *Rutland* 2 (1935): 41–45. *C.C.R. 1261–1264* (1936): 178–179. Fowler *Tractatus de Dunstaple et de Hocton* (Pubs. Bedfordshire Hist. Rec. Soc. 19) (1937): 40–41, 74–75. Jenkins *Cal. of the Rolls of the Justices on Eyre 1227* (Buckinghamshire Arch. Soc. 6) (1945): 6, 15, 31. VCH *Warwick* 3 (1945): 31–42, 123–126, 167–172, 193–196; 6 (1951): 117–120, 215–219. Sanders *English Baronies* (1960): 39–40, 52. *Duchy of Lancaster, Descriptive List (with Index) of Cartæ Miscellaneæ*, Lists and Indexes, Supplementary Ser., No. V, vol. 3, reprinted 1964): 85 ("Announcement dated 1227–36 by Maud de Oylly that Maud de Mandevill',

Countess of Essex and Hereford, her sister, has granted her by charter the manor of Gussage St. Michael, co. Dorset."). VCH *Leicester* 5 (1964): 133–153. *C.R.R.* 15 (1972): 36, 40–41, 63, 288–290, 438–440, 443. Barraclough *Charters of the Earls of Chester* (Lanc. & Cheshire Rec. Soc. 126) (1988): 416 · Travers *Cal. of the Feet of Fines for Buckinghamshire 1259–1307* (Buckinghamshire Rec. Soc. 25) (1989): 106. VCH *Oxford* 12 (1990): 188–194; 13 (1996): 118–127; 15 (2006): 184–172. VCH *Wiltshire* 15 (1995): 168–177. Hoskin *English Episcopal Acta* 13 (1997): xxvii–xxxiii (biog. of Walter de Cantelowe). Fine Rolls of Henry III, C 60/32 (Date: 1232 — Henry de Oilly deceased styled "kinsman" of Thomas [Earl] of Warwick).

Children of William de Cantelowe, Knt., by Milicent de Gournay:

i. **WILLIAM DE CANTELOWE**, Knt. [see next].

ii. **JOHN DE CANTELOWE**, of Snitterfield, Warwickshire, married **MARGERY** (or **MARGARET**) **COMYN** [see WEST 5].

iii. **NICHOLAS DE CANTELOWE**, of Ellesborough, Buckinghamshire. He married **EUSTACHE FITZ RALPH**, daughter and heiress of Ralph Fitz Hugh, of Greasley and South Muskham, Nottinghamshire, and Ilkeston, Derbyshire, by Joan, daughter of Ralph de la Haye, Knt., of Burwell, Lincolnshire. They had one son, William. NICHOLAS DE CANTELOWE was living 8 May 1262. His widow, Eustache, married (2nd) in 1268 **WILLIAM DE ROOS** (or **ROS**), Knt., of Ingmanthorpe (in Kirk Deighton), Yorkshire, and, in right of his wife, of Greasley, Nottinghamshire, Ilkeston, Derbyshire, etc. Banks *Baronies in Fees* 1 (1844):149–150 (sub Cantilupe). Lipscomb *Hist. & Antiqs. of Buckingham* 1 (1847): 176 (Cantilupe ped.). *Trans. Shropshire Arch. & Natural Hist. Soc.* 3rd Ser. 1 (1901): 170–177. *D.N.B.* 3 (1908): 900–904 (biog. of Thomas de Cantelupe). Alington *St Thomas of Hereford* (2001): 4. West Yorkshire Archive Service, Leeds: Ingilby Recs., WYL230/30 (enfeoffment dated 1 March 1290 from William de Ros, lord of Ingmanthorp and Eustacia his wife to William their son, of the manors of Wythale and Kynthorp in Lincolnshire, Elkeston with the advowson of the church in Derbyshire, Greseby and Seleston with the advowson of the churches in Nottinghamshire, Claydon with the advowson of the church and Esilbergh [Ellesborough] in Buckinghamshire, lately granted to them for life, with remainder to William, by Ralph son of William, lord of Grimthorpe, for term of their lives, rendering annually £100); WYL230/31 (power of attorney dated 1 March 1290 from William de Ros, land of Ingmanthorp and Eustacia his wife to Robert de Sallow and Adam de Cossall to deliver to William de Ros their son full seisin of the manors of Wythhale and Kynthorp in Lincolnshire, Elkeston with the advowson of the church in Derbyshire, Greseley and Selseton with the advowsons of the churches in Nottinghamshire, Claydon with the advowson of the church and Esilbergh [Ellesborough] in Buckinghamshire) (available at www.a2a.org.uk/search/index.asp).

Child of Nicholas de Cantelowe, by Eustache Fitz Ralph:

a. **WILLIAM DE CANTELOWE**, son and heir. Banks *Baronies in Fees* 1 (1844):149–150 (sub Cantilupe). Lipscomb *Hist. & Antiqs. of Buckingham* 1 (1847): 176 (Cantilupe ped.). *Trans. Shropshire Arch. & Natural Hist. Soc.* 3rd Ser. 1 (1901): 170–177.

iv. **[MASTER] THOMAS DE CANTELOWE**, Archdeacon of Stafford, Precentor of York, Chancellor of Oxford University, Chancellor of England, Bishop of Hereford, born about 1220. He and his brother, Hugh de Cantelowe, went to Paris in the early 1240s where they pursued arts degrees. He was appointed Rector of Wintringham, Lincolnshire in 1244. In 1245 Thomas and his brother, Hugh, attended the 1st Council of Lyons in 1245, where Thomas was appointed papal chaplain by Pope Innocent IV, and also received a dispensation allowing him to hold benefices in plurality. After attaining his Master of Arts at Paris, he completed his studies at Oxford in canon law c.1255, incepting as a doctor in that faculty. He was presented to the church of Deighton, Yorkshire by Agatha Trussebut in 1247. He was Rector of Aston Cantlow, Warwickshire in 1253. In 1261 he was elected Chancellor of Oxford University. In December 1263 he went to Amiens to represent baronial interests in their disputes with King Henry III. He drafted the three documents through which the barons' case was submitted to the arbitrament of Louis IX. The French king's rejection of the baronial proposals, in the mise of Amiens of January 1264, was the catalyst that brought Montfortians into open conflict with King Henry III. After Simon de Montfort's victory at the Battle of Lewes in May 1264, the magnate council of nine, and a compliant King Henry III, in February 1265 appointed Thomas as Chancellor of England. Though his execution of duties as chancellor seems to have been of brief duration, the acts he carried out were performed with his usual fastidious attention to detail and consciousness of responsibility. Following the Battle of Evesham in 1265, he remained abroad for several years, studying theology at Paris. In 1268 he was granted a dispensation to be absent for three years to study theology. About 1272 he had returned to Oxford where, in June 1273, he became a doctor of theology. He was again appointed Chancellor of the university in Jan. 1274, where he played an important part in quelling a student riot between the 'northerners' and the 'southerners'. In May 1274 he attended the 2nd Council of Lyons where, as at the first Lyons council, he was made a papal chaplain. He was elected Bishop of Hereford

15 June 1275, and was consecrated by Archbishop Kilwardby 8 September 1275. THOMAS DE CANTELOWE, Bishop of Hereford, died at Castrum Florenti (Ferento, now in ruins) 25 August 1282. He left a will dated 18 August 1282. His flesh and viscera were buried at the monastery of San Severo outside Orvieto. His bones were returned to England and placed under a slab in the east end of Hereford Cathedral, where they remained until moved into a table tomb in the north transept in 1287. His successor Richard Swinfield (died 1317) became a tireless promoter of Cantelowe's canonization. Between 1287 and 1312 nearly 500 miracles were recorded as evidence of his sanctity, a figure surpassed in the surviving records of medieval England only by the 700 attributed to Thomas Becket. Swinfield's attempts to secure the canonization of his predecessor had little immediate success, though after an inquisition authorized by Clement V found that Cantelowe had died in communion with the church, the pope ordered an investigation of his life and miracles, which took place in London and Hereford. Both inquisitorial processes occurred in 1307. Continued support for the bishop's cause, by Kings Edward I and Edward II and by many other secular and ecclesiastical magnates, resulted in his canonization 17 April 1320. A new shrine was constructed in the east end of the cathedral. On 25 October 1349, in the presence of King Edward III and many other lay and clerical notables, his bones were translated from the north transept to this new location. There the remains lay undisturbed until 1538, when, along with much else that represented papal authority in England, the shrine, its ornaments, and its contents were removed. Lipscomb *Hist. & Antiqs. of Buckingham* 1 (1847): 176 (Cantilupe ped.). *Notes & Queries* 2nd Ser. 9 (1860): 171. Gray *Reg., or Rolls, of Walter Gray, Lord Archbishop of York* (Surtees Soc. 56) (1872): 99. Birch *Cat. Seals in the British Museum* 1 (1887): 238 (seal of Thomas de Cantelowe, Bishop of Hereford — Pointed oval: the Bishop, full-length, lifting up the right hand in benediction, in the left hand a pastoral staff. In the field on each side, three fleurs-de-lis in allusion to the armorial charges of CANTELOWE, viz. three leopards' faces reversed jessants-de-lis. The feet of the Bishop rest on a wolf couchant, enraged, in allusion to the name CANTELOWE. Legend: .... OMAS : DEI : GRA : HEREFORDENSIS : EPS.). *Papal Regs.: Letters* 1 (1893): 205, 228 (Thomas and Hugh, clerks, styled "sons of William de Cantalupo"), 417 (Master Thomas de Cantilupe styled "nephew of the bishop of Worcester" in 1264). *Trans. Shropshire Arch. & Natural Hist. Soc.* 3rd Ser. 1 (1901): 170–177. *List of Ancient Corr. of the Chancery & Exchequer* (PRO Lists and Indexes 15) (1902): 338 (letter dated 17 Aug. 1276 written by Thomas de Cantelowe, Bishop of Hereford, requesting that his nephew, John de Cantelowe, have courtesy of England in Aylestone, Leicestershire [it being the inheritance of John's late wife, Margery de Harcourt]); see also *Index to Ancient Correspondence of the Chancery and the Exchequer, Vol. 1: A–K* (Lists and Indexes, Supplementary Series, No. XV): 221, 535. Giffard *Episc. Reg. Diocese of Worcester, Reg. of Bishop Godfrey Giffard* 1 (Worcester Hist. Soc. 15) (1902): 2–3, 26, 40. Cantilupe *Reg. Thome de Cantilupo Episcopi Herefordensis* (Canterbury & York Soc. 1) (1906): 171 (Nicholas de Hodenet styled "kinsman" [consanguineo] by Bishop Thomas de Cantelowe in charter dated c.1270) [see also Robinson *Hist. of the Mansions & Manors of Herefordshire* (1872): 37]. Capes *Charters & Recs. of Hereford Cathedral* (1908) ·*D.N.B.* 3 (1908): 900–904 (biog. of Thomas de Cantelupe). G.H. Fowler 'Calendar of Inquisitions Post Mortem. No. I' in *Pubs. Bedfordshire Hist. Rec. Soc.* 5 (1920): 210–215. Greenway *Fasti Ecclesiae Anglicanae 1066–1300* 1 (1968): 91–96. Jancey *St.Thomas Cantilupe, Bishop of Hereford: Essays in his Honour* (1982). Prestwich *English Politics in the 13th Cent.* (1990). Finucane *Miracles & Pilgrims: Popular Beliefs in Medieval England* (1995): 136–137, 173–190. Carpenter *Reign of Henry III* (1996): 293–307. Hoskin *English Episcopal Acta* 13 (1997): 118–119. Alington *St Thomas of Hereford* (2001). Hicks *Who's Who in Late Medieval England, 1272–1485* (2001): 14–16 (biog. of St. Thomas Cantilupe).

v. **[MASTER] HUGH DE CANTELOWE**, Rector of Skendleby, Lincolnshire, 1244, Archdeacon of Gloucester, Papal chaplain, Treasurer of Salisbury. He is said to have been installed as Archdeacon of Gloucester 16 April 1256, but first occurs 7 July and 16 August 1255, and prob. the unnamed Archdeacon who occurs 18 May 1255. In 1268 he was granted a dispensation to be absent for three years to study theology. He and his brother, Thomas de Cantelowe, served as executors of the will of their uncle, Walter de Cantelowe, Bishop of Worcester, in 1269. [MASTER] HUGH DE CANTELOWE was living 14 May 1270, and died testate before 6 July 1279. Little *Grey Friars in Oxford* Pt. 2 (1892): 218 (John de Clara was executor of Hugh de Cantelowe, Archdeacon of Gloucester, in 1285). *Papal Regs.: Letters* 1 (1893): 205, 223 (Thomas and Hugh, clerks, styled "sons of William de Cantalupo"), 417. Giffard *Episc. Reg. Diocese of Worcester, Reg. of Bishop Godfrey Giffard* 1 (Worcester Hist. Soc. 15) (1902): 3, 26, 40. Reg. Thome de Cantilupo Episcopi Herefordensis (Canterbury & York Soc. 1) (1906): 213. *D.N.B.* 3 (1908): 900–904 (biog. of Thomas de Cantelupe). Greenway *Fasti Ecclesiae Anglicanae 1066–1300* 2 (1971): 107–109. Alington *St Thomas of Hereford* (2001): 4.

vi. **AGNES DE CANTELOWE**, married (1st) **ROBERT DE SAINT JOHN**, of Basing, Hampshire [see PAULET 6]; (2nd) **JOHN DE TURVILLE** [see PAULET 6].

vii. **JULIANE DE CANTELOWE**, married **ROBERT DE TREGOZ**, Knt., of Ewyas Harold, Herefordshire [see TREGOZ 3].

5. WILLIAM DE CANTELOWE, Knt., of Eaton Bray, Bedfordshire, Ellesborough, Buckinghamshire, Barby and Lubbesthrope, Leicestershire, Aston Cantlow and Studley, Warwickshire, Calne, Wiltshire, etc., Constable of Builth Castle, 1254, and, in right of his wife, of Abergavenny, Monmouthshire, Totnes, Devon, etc., son and heir. He married before July 1241 **EVE DE BREWES** (or **BREUSE**), daughter of William de Brewes, Knt., of Totnes, Devon, Kingston, Herefordshire, Abergavenny, Monmouthshire, etc., by Eve, daughter of William Marshal, Knt., Earl of Pembroke, hereditary Master Marshal [see BRIWERRE 5 for her ancestry]. They had one son, George, Knt., and two daughters, Milicent and Joan. Eve was co-heiress in 1230 to her father, by which she inherited a 1/4th share of a 1/3rd share of the barony of Miles of Gloucester. She was also co-heiress in 1233 to her great-uncle, William Briwerre, Knt. He went on the military expedition to Gascony in 1242–3. He was granted an annual fee of £50 at the exchequer in 1243. He received frequent gifts of deer and timber from the royal forests. He came into fierce conflict with John of Monmouth between 1248 and 1253 over Penrhos Castle. On 3 March 1250/1 he did homage for all lands and tenements which his father held from the king in chief. In June 1253 he gave the advowson of the church of Aston Cantlow, Warwickshire to Studley Priory, Warwickshire to maintain hospitality and a hostel for the poor outside the priory gate. In 1253–4 he served again with the king in Gascony, emerging as one of the king's most important courtiers. He was still with the king in mid-July 1254, but must have returned to England soon afterwards. SIR WILLIAM DE CANTELOWE died testate 25 September 1254, and was buried at Studley Priory, Warwickshire. He left a substantial sum of money in his will to redeem his unfulfilled crusading vow. His widow, Eve, died about 20 July 1255.

Dugdale *Antiqs. of Warwickshire* (1730): 58 (Cantelowe-Zouche ped.). *Topographer* 1 (1789): 195–204. Bridges *Hist. & Antiqs. of Northamptonshire* 2 (1791): 315–318. Baker *Hist. & Antiqs. of Northampton* 2 (1836–41): 239–240 (Bruere or Briwere ped.). Lipscomb *Hist. & Antiqs. of Buckingham* 1 (1847): 176 (Cantilupe ped.). Sackville-West *Hist. Notices of the Parish of Withyham* (1857): 40–46. Eyton *Antiqs. of Shropshire* 6 (1858): 350–357. Luard *Annales Monastici* 3 (Rolls Ser. 36) (1866): 192 (Annals of Dunstable sub A.D. 1254: "Eodem anno, die Veneris ante festum Sancti Michaelis [25 September], mortuus est Willelmus de Cantilupo tertius, et die Mercurii proxima sequente, scilicet, in crastino Sancti Michaelis, apud Stodleam sepultus, præsentibus abbatibus, et prioribus multis, et comitibus; videlicet, Simone de Monteforti comite Leycestriæ, et comite de Heforde, qui corpus defuncti in sepulcro posuerunt."), 196 (Dunstaple Annals sub A.D. 1255: "Eodem anno, circa festum Sanctæ Margaretæ [20 July], mortua est domina Eva, uxor Willelmi de Cantilupo tertii."). Clark *Earls, Earldom, & Castle of Pembroke* (1880): 69–75. Batten *Hist. & Topog. Colls. Rel. to the early Hist. of Parts of South Somerset* (1894): 1–7. *Genealogist* n.s. 13 (1896): 242. Chadwyck-Healey *Somersetshire Pleas* (Somerset Rec. Soc. 11) (1897): 380–381. *Trans. Shropshire Arch. & Natural Hist. Soc.* 3rd Ser. 1 (1901): 170–177. VCH *Buckingham* 2 (1908): 331–338. VCH *Bedford* 3 (1912): 369–375. Fowler 'Calendar of Inquisitions Post Mortem. No. I' in *Pubs. Bedfordshire Hist. Rec. Soc.* 5 (1920): 210–215. *C.C.R. 1251–1253* (1927): 221–222. Fowler *Tractatus de Dunstaple et de Hocton* (Pubs. Bedfordshire Hist. Rec. Soc. 19) (1937): 40–41, 74–75. VCH *Warwick* 3 (1945): 31–42, 193–196. Clanchy *Roll & Writ of the Berkshire Eyre of 1248* (Selden Soc. 90) (1973): 199. Clifford *Reg. of Richard Clifford, Bishop of Worcester, 1401–1407* (1976): 113–114. Hoskin *English Episcopal Acta* 13 (1997): 118–119.

Children of William de Cantelowe, Knt., by Eve de Brewes:

i. **GEORGE DE CANTELOWE**, Knt., of Calne, Wiltshire, Eaton Bray, Bedfordshiire, Ellesborough, Buckinghamshire, Cornworthy, Loddiswell, and Totnes, Devon, Bulwick and Harringworth, Northamptonshire, Meole Brace, Shropshire, Aston Cantlow, Warwickshire, Milston and Brigmerston (in Milston), Wiltshire, etc., son and heir, born at Abergavenny 29 March 1252. He married by contract dated 1 September 1254 **MARGARET DE LACY**, daughter of Edmund de Lacy, Knt., Earl of Lincoln, hereditary Constable of Chester, by Alice, daughter of Manfred III, Marquis of Saluzzo [see LACY 4 for her ancestry]. They had one son who died in infancy. He was knighted 13 October 1272. SIR GEORGE DE CANTELOWE died 18 October 1273. His heart was buried in the church of the Black Friars at Pontefract, Yorkshire. His wife, Margaret, was buried with her infant son in the church of the Black Friars at Pontefract, Yorkshire. Dugdale *Antiqs. of Warwickshire* (1730): 58 (Cantelowe-Zouche ped.). *Topographer* 1 (1789): 195–204. Lipscomb *Hist. & Antiqs. of Buckingham* 1 (1847): 176 (Cantilupe ped.). Sackville-West *Hist. Notices of the Parish of Withyham* (1857): 40–46 (re. Cantelowe fam.). Eyton *Antiqs. of Shropshire* 6 (1858): 350–357. Clark *Earls, Earldom, & Castle of Pembroke* (1880): 69–75. Francisque-Michel *Rôles Gascons* 1 (1885): 501. Batten *Hist. & Topog. Colls. Rel. to the early Hist. of Parts of South Somerset* (1894): 1–7. *Trans. Shropshire Arch. & Natural Hist. Soc.* 3rd Ser. 1 (1901): 170–177. *Cal. IPM* 2 (1906): 16–21. VCH

Buckingham 2 (1908): 331–338. *C.P.* 1 (1910): 23 (sub Abergavenny); 12(2) (1959): 937–938 (sub Zouche). G.H. Fowler 'Calendar of Inquisitions Post Mortem. No. I' in *Pubs. Bedfordshire Hist. Rec. Soc.* 5 (1920): 210–215. VCH *Yorkshire* 3 (1925): 271–273. Fowler *Tractatus de Dunstaple et de Hocton* (Pubs. Bedfordshire Hist. Rec. Soc. 19) (1937): 40–41, 74–75. Fowler *Cal. of Inqs. Post Mortem, No. II* (Pubs. Bedfordshire Hist. Rec. Soc. 19) (1937): 116–118 (Inq. of George de Cantelowe). VCH *Warwick* 3 (1945): 31–42.

ii. **MILICENT DE CANTELOWE** [see next].

iii. **JOAN DE CANTELOWE**, married **HENRY DE HASTINGS**, Knt., of Cavendish, Gazeley, Lidgate, Little Udeley, and Rede, Suffolk [see HASTINGS 9].

6. MILICENT DE CANTELOWE, married (1st) **JOHN DE MOHAUT** (or **MONTALT**), son and heir apparent of Roger de Mohaut, Knt., of Mold and Wirral Neston, Cheshire, Castle Rising, Kenninghall, and Snettisham, Norfolk, Kessingland, Suffolk, Middleton, Sussex, etc., Justice of Chester, by Cecily, daughter of William d'Aubeney, Earl of Arundel [see MORLEY 6 for his ancestry]. They had no known issue. JOHN DE MOHAUT died in 1258. His widow, Milicent, married (2nd) before 13 Dec. 1273 **EUDES LA ZOUCHE**, Knt., in right of his wife, of Harringworth, Northamptonshire, Lubbesthorpe, Leicestershire, Bridgwater, Somerset, Calstone, Wilshire, Bingley, Yorkshire, etc., younger son of Roger la Zouche, Knt., of Black Torrington and King's Nympton, Devon, Fulbourn and Swavesey, Cambridgeshire, Tong, Shropshire, etc., Sheriff of Devonshire, by Margaret, doubtless daughter of Henry Biset, of Kidderminster, Worcestershire, Rockbourne, Hampshire, etc. They had one son, William, Knt. [1st Lord Zouche of Harringworth], and three daughters, Elizabeth, Eve, and Eleanor. About 1250 he and his brother, William la Zouche, Knt., witnessed a charter of Richard de Harcourt, Knt., of Stanton Harcourt, Oxfordshire in favor of his son, William de Harcourt. In 1254 he and his brother, William la Zouche, were granted letters of protection, they then going with the queen to the king in Gascony. In 1257 he witnessed a notification by Robert Fitz William le Espicer at Windsor. His wife, Milicent, was co-heiress in 1273 to her brother, George de Cantelowe, Knt., by which she inherited numerous manors, including Eaton Bray, Edworth, Henlow Zouches (in Henlow), Houghton Regis, Totternhoe, and Wymington, Bedfordshire, Crendon, Ellesborough, Ham (in Waddesdon), and Mentmore, Buckinghamshire, Totnes, Devon, Braunstone and Lubbesthorpe, Leicestershire, Harringworth, Bulwick, and Rothwell, Northamptonshire, Basford, Nottinghamshire, Clipsham, Glaston, and North Luffenham, Rutland, Meole Brace, Shropshire, Bridgwater, Somerset, Calstone (in Calstone Wellington), Calne, Milston and Brigmerston (in Milston), and Rockley (in Ogbourne St. Andrew), Wiltshire, Great Inkberrow, Worcestershire, and Bingley, Yorkshire. In 1274 he pulled down the gallows of the Prior of Dunstable at 'Eddesuthe' [?Edworth] and broke open his gaol at Caldecote (in Houghton Regis), Bedfordshire. He presented to the churches of Clipsham, Rutland, 1274; Hope Bowdler, Shropshire, 1275; and Bulwick, Northamptonshire, 1276. In 1274–5 John de Reyny and Juliane his wife arraigned an assize of novel disseisin against Edmund [sic] de la Susche and others touching a tenement in Bridgwater, Somerset. In the same period, Geoffrey de Someresham arraigned an assize of novel disseisin against him and others touching a tenement in Bulwick, Northamptonshire. In the same period, Richard Gruscet arraigned an assize of novel disseisin against him touching a tenement in Eaton and Totternhoe, Bedfordshire. In 1276–7 Roger de Claston' arraigned an assize of novel disseisin against him and others touching common of pasture in Calstone, Wiltshire. In 1277–8 Nicholas Hausex, Sarah his wife, and Joan la Clackere arraigned an assize of novel disseisin against him and others touching a tenement in Calne, Wiltshire. In 1278 he and his wife, Milicent, sued Geoffrey Saint Leger, Bishop of Ossory, for the advowson of the church of Aghaboe in Ireland. SIR EUDES LA ZOUCHE died between 28 April and 25 June 1279. In 1279–80 William del Exchequer arraigned an assize against Milicent de Montalt touching a fosse levied in Bulwick, Northamptonshire. In the same period, Milicent de Montalt and John de Hastings arraigned an assize of mort d'ancestor against Gilbert de Knouyll

[Knoville] touching possessions in Loddiswell, Devon. In the same period, Stephen de la Quarrera arraigned an assize of novel disseisin against Milicent de Montalt and others touching a tenement in Totternhoe, Bedfordshire. In 1280 Gilbert, Abbot of Kirkstall quit Richard de Kygheley of the service which Milicent, widow of Eudes la Zouche, demanded of him in respect of his free tenement in Keighley, Yorkshire. In 1280 Milicent was granted quittance of the common summons of the eyre. In 1280 Milicent sued Ralph de Neville and Euphame his wife in a plea of a third part of 12 messuages, 4 cottages, 11 virgates of land, etc., in Syston, Leicestershire as dower. Milicent presented to the churches of Hope Bowdler, Shropshire, 1280, 1289, Bulwick, Northamptonshire, 1281, 1282, 1290, 1291, Barby, Northamptonshire, 1291, Hinxworth, Hertfordshire, 1293, 1296, and Clipsham, Rutland, 1294. In 1280–1 she arraigned an assize against William del Escheker, senior, touching a fosse levied in Kirk, Northamptonshire. In the same period, she arraigned an assize of novel disseisin against Gilbert de Knovill regarding the church of Loddiswell, Devon. In the same period, William son of William Aumbroys, of Tilsworth, Bedfordshire, arraigned an assize of novel disseisin against Milicent and others regarding a tenement in Tilsworth, Bedfordshire. In the same period, Thomasine widow of Walter le Bon sued Milicent and others regarding a tenement in Totnes, Devon. In 1281 Ralph Springehoes acknowledged that he owed a debt of 60*s*. to Milicent. In 1285 Milicent granted her daughter, Eleanor la Zouche, and her heirs the manor of Bingley, Yorkshire to hold of the said Milicent during her life at a yearly rent of 40 marks of silver; and, after Milicent's death, Eleanor and her heirs to be quit of that rent and to render 1*d*. yearly to Milicent's heirs at Easter, and doing service to the chief lords. About 1286–7 Richard Peres petitioned king and council concerning a legal dispute between himself and Milicent; he was granted permission to have a writ to bring the record and process before the justices. Sometime in the period, 1289–96, she granted the manor of Lubbesthorpe, Leicestershire to Roger la Zouche son of William la Zouche, Knt. In 1293 she was granted a weekly market and yearly fair to be held at the manor of Bulwick, Northamptonshire. In 1294 Hugh de Stretley, of Mentmore, and Agnes his wife conveyed 11 shillings of rent in Mentmore and Leykeburne, Buckinghamshire to Milicent de Mohaut. In Feb. 1295/6 the king granted a license to Master William de Bois to enfeoff Milicent de Mohaut with a moiety of the manors of Thorpe-Arnold, Leicestershire, Ebrington and Farmcote, Gloucestershire, Brafield and Little Houghton, Northamptonshire, Weston-in-Arden (in Bulkington), Warwickshire, etc., and for Milicent to re-grant these manors to Master William de Bois for life, with remainder to Milicent's son, William la Zouche, and his wife, Maud Lovel, niece of Master William de Bois. In 1298 she purchased three messuages and lands in Totternhoe and Eaton, Bedfordshire from Alelme de Whelton. At an unspecified date, Milicent granted one tun of wine to St. Nicholas at Exeter to celebrate mass. Milicent died shortly before 7 Jan. 1298/9.

Dugdale *Antiqs. of Warwickshire* (1730): 58 (Cantelowe-Zouche ped.). Morice *Histoire Ecclesiastique et Civil de Bretagne* 1 (1750): xxi–xxii (Zouche ped.). *Topographer* 1 (1789): 195–204 (list of heraldic quarterings for Zouche family of Harringworth taken from Glover's *Barona e*, No. 1160, Harleian MSS in the British Library erroneously includes the arms of Quincy, Leicester, Grandmesnil, Galloway, Chester, etc., which set of arms respresents the ancestry of Eudes la Zouche's sister-in-law, Ellen de Quincy). Bridges *Hist. & Antiqs. of Northamptonshire* 1 (1791): 25; 2 (1791): 289, 315–318. Nichols *Hist. & Antiq. of the County of Leicester* 4(1) (1807): 37. Kennett *Parochial Antiq. Attempted in the Hist. of Ambrosden, Burcester & other adjacent Parts* 2 (1818): 465–466 (erroneously identifies Eudes la Zouche as son of Alan la Zouche, by his wife, Hellen de Quincy). Baker *Hist. & Antiq. of Northampton* 1 (1822–30): 563 (Beaumont-Quincy-Zouch ped.) (Eudes la Zouch of Harringworth erroneously identified as son of Alan la Zouch and Ellen de Quincy); 2 (1836–41): 239–240 (Bruere or Briwere ped.). Clutterbuck *Hist. & Antiqs.of Hertford* 3 (1827): 528. *Desc. & Hist. Guide to Ashby-de-la-Zouch & the Neighbourhood* (1831): 7–12 (author erroneously identifies Eudo [Eudes] la Zouche, ancestor of the Zouches of Harringworth, as a younger son of Alan la Zouche, lord of Ashby-de-la-Zouch, and his wife, daughter of Roger de Quincy, Earl of Winchester). *Coll. Top. & Gen.* 1 (1834): 62–63 (charter of Milicent de Mohaut to St. Nicholas at Exeter). Roberts *Excerpta è Rotulis Finium in Turri Londinensi Asservatis, Henrico Tertio rege, AD 1216–1272* 2 (1836): 166. Burke *Hist. of the Commoners* 4 (1838): 227 (sub Whatton) (author erroneously identifies Eudes la Zouche, husband of Milicent de Cantelowe, as "the second son of Sir Alan de la Zouch, baron of Ashby de la Zouch, constable of the Tower, and Helen his wife, daughter and co-heiress of Roger de Quincie, Earl of Winchester). Clive

Docs. connected with the Hist. of Ludlow & the Lords Marchers (1841): 305 (list of heraldic quarterings of Edward, Lord Zouche of Harringworth dated temp. Queen Elizabeth includes the arms of Quincy and Leicester). Banks *Baronies in Fee* 1 (1844): 469 (sub Zouche of Ashby), 469–471 (sub Zouche of Haryngworth) (identifies Eudes la Zouche as son of Alan la Zouche and Ellen de Quincy). Lipscomb *Hist. & Antiqs. of Buckingham* 1 (1847): 176 (Cantilupe-Zouche ped.). Eyton *Antiquities of Shropshire* 5 (1857) : 121; 6 (1858): 350–357. Horwood *Year Books of the Reign of King Edward the First* (1863): xxxi, 40–41, 468–476. *Misc. Gen. et Heraldica* 1 (1868): 158–159 (Saunders ped. dated ?1618 which includes the quarterings of Saunders family arms, including Zouche of Harringworth, Quincy, Cantelowe, Brewes, etc.). Foss *Biographical Dictionary of the Judges of England* (1870): 791 (biog. of William la Zouche) (identifies Eudes la Zouche as son of Alan la Zouche). Clark *Earls, Earldom, & Castle of Pembroke* (1880): 69–75. Glover et al. *Vis. of Cheshire 1580, 1566, 1533 & 1591* (H.S.P. 18) (1882): 181–182 (Monhalt ped.: "Johannes de Montealto sine exitu. = 1. Elena Relicta Rob't Stockport, = 2. Millisent Cantelop postea vxor Eudonis de la Zouch."). *Annual Rpt. of the Deputy Keeper* 44 (1883): 42, 50, 92, 309; 46 (1886): 120, 336; 47 (1886): 179; 49 (1888): 30, 109, 174; 50 (1889): 133, 141, 229, 230. Wrottesley *Staffordshire Suits: Plea Rolls* (Colls. Hist. Staffs. 6(1)) (1885): 124. Christie *Annales Cestrienses, or, Chronicle of the Abbey of S. Werburg at Chester* (Lancashire & Cheshire Rec. Soc. 14) (1887): 78–79 (sub A.D. 1258: 747–8 ("Rogerus de Monte Alto tunc Justitiarius Cestriae graviter infestans D[omi]num Thomam Abbatem et Conventum S. Werburgae de Cestria ... Obiitq. dicti Rogeri primogenitus infra quinde'am illam.")). Birch *Catalogue of Seals in the British Museum* 2 (1892): 393 (seal of Milicent de Montalt—Pointed oval. In tightly-fitting dress, fur cloak, in each hand a shield of arms. Standing on a carved corbel. Arms: right hand a lion rampant, MONTALT; left hand three leopards' heads jessants-de-lis, CANTELOWE. In the field on each side a wavy sprig of foliage. Legend: S' MILISENTE · [DE] MONTE ALTO.). *C.P.R. 1292–1301* (1895): 184. *Genealogist* n.s. 13 (1896): 242. Speight *Chronicles & Stories of Old Bingley* (1899): 112. *C.Ch.R.* 2 (1898): 432. *D.N.B.* 63 (1900): 414–415 (biog. of Alan la Zouche) (erroneously identifies Eudes la Zouche [died 1279] as younger son of Alan la Zouche and Ellen de Quincy). Gerard *Particular Description of the County of Somerset* (Somerset Rec. Soc. 15) (1900): 149–151. Rye *Cal. of Feet of Fines for Suffolk* (1900): 79. *Trans. Shropshire Arch. & Natural Hist. Soc.* 3rd Ser. 1 (1901): 170–177. *C.C.R. 1279–1288* (1902): 46–47, 111, 121. *List of Ancient Corr. of the Chancery & Exchequer* (PRO Lists and Indexes 15) (1902): 411. *Cal. IPM* 1 (1904): 92; 2 (1906): 16–21; 3 (1912): 436; 4 (1913): 112. VCH *Bedford* 1 (1904): 371–377; 2 (1908): 223–226 (Zouche arms: Gules bezanty and a quarter ermine), 280–285; 3 (1912): 117–122, 369–375, 389–394, 447–451. Carrigan *Hist. & Antiqs. of the Diocese of Ossory* 2 (1905): 40–41. *MSS of the Duke of Rutland* 4 (Hist. MSS Comm. 24) (1905): 9 (charter of Richard de Harcourt dated c.1250; charter witnessed by Sir William la Zouche and Sir Eudes la Zouche), 10. Wrottesley *Peds. from the Plea Rolls* (1905): 150, 161, 208–209. Cantilupe *Reg. Thome de Cantilupo Episcopi Herefordensis* (Canterbury & York Soc. 1) (1906): xxi, 16, 28, 185, 235. Sympson *Lincoln: Hist. & Topog. Account of the City* (1906): 311. Harcourt *His Grace the Steward & Trial of Peers* (1907): 314. VCH *Buckingham* 2 (1908): 298–303, 331–338; 3 (1925): 65–77, 397–401; 4 (1927): 41, 107–118. Capes *Reg. Ricardi de Swinfield, Episcopi Herefordensis 1283–1317* (Canterbury & York Soc. 6) (1909): 528. *C.P.* 1 (1910): 22–23; 10 (1945): 674; 12(2) (1959): 937–938 (sub Zouche). VCH *Hertford* 3 (1912): 232–240. VCH *Worcester* 3 (1913): 418–430. *C.P.R. 1374–1377* (1916): 270–271, 278–279. Watkin *Hist. of Totnes Priory & Medieval Town, Devonshire* 2 (1917): 713 (Cantelowe ped.), 718–719. *Feudal Aids* 6 (1920): 21, 23. Fowler *Cal. IPM* 1 (Bedfordshire Hist. Rec. Soc. 5) (1920): 210–215; 2 (Bedfordshire Hist. Rec. Soc. 19) (1937): 116–118. *Transactions Leicestershire Arch. Soc.* 13 (1923–24): 200–202. *Pubs. Bedfordshire Hist. Rec. Soc.* 12 (1928): 27, 55–56. Davis *Rotuli Ricardi Gravesend Episcopi Lincolniensis* (Lincoln Rec. Soc. 20) (1925): 124. *Report on the MSS of Reginald Rawdon Hastings, Esq.* 1 (Hist. MSS Comm. 78) (1928): 60, 143. VCH *Rutland* 2 (1935): 41–45, 182–188, 195–203. Fowler *Tractatus de Dunstaple et de Hocton* (Pubs. Bedfordshire Hist. Rec. Soc. 19) (1937): 40–41, 74–75, 92. VCH *Northampton* 4 (1937): 266–270. Pugh *Abs. of Feet of Fines rel. to Wiltshire for the Reigns of Edward I and Edward II* (Wiltshire Arch. & Nat. Hist. Soc. Records Branch 1) (1939): 25 (settlements by Millicent de Mohaut on her daughters, Eve and Elizabeth la Zouche). Reichel *Devon Feet of Fines* 2 (Devon & Cornwall Rec. Soc.) (1939): 57. Stokes et al. *Warwickshire Feet of Fines* 2 (Dugdale Soc. 15) (1939): 15. VCH *Warwick* 3 (1945): 31–42, 175–187; 6 (1951): 48–57. *Rolls & Reg. of Bishop Oliver Sutton 1280–1299* 2 (Lincoln Rec. Soc. 43) (1946): 112. Hatton *Book of Seals* (1950): 96 (charter of Milicent de Mohaut dated 1287; seal on tag: pointed oval, 2 x 1-3/16 in.; red. A lady standing on a carved corbel, a shield of arms in each hand, dexter, a lion rampant [Mohaut], sinister, three fleur-de-lis [Cantelowe], * S' MILISENTE . DE MONTE ALTO.). *Procs. of Somersetshire Arch. & Nat. Hist. Soc.* 94 (1950): 107–109. Sutton *Rolls & Reg. of Bishop Oliver Sutton, 1280–1299* 2 (Lincoln Rec. Soc. 43) (1950): 8, 19, 81, 88, 91, 112. Slingsby *Feet of Fines for the County of York 1272–1300* (Yorkshire Arch. Soc. Rec. Ser. 121) (1956): 49, 69–70, 73–74. Paget (1957) 581:3. VCH *Leicester* 4 (1958): 420–428, 428–433; 5 (1964): 321–330. Sanders *English Baronies* (1960): 8, 90. *Procs. of the Suffolk Institute of Arch.* 29(1) (1962): 34–66 (Naunton ped. dated 18th Cent.) (Eudes la Zouche, husband of Milicent de Cantelowe, is erroneously identified as the son of Alan la Zouche and his wife, Ellen de Quincy). VCH *Shropshire* 8 (1968): 164. Farnham *Leicestershire Medieval Village Notes* (1969): unpaginated (sub Syston) [FHL Microfilm 804160]. *TAG* 49 (1971): 1–12; 70 (1995): 100. Rosenthal *Nobles & the Noble Life 1295-1500* (1976): 59–63. Weinbaum *London Eyre of 1276* (London Rec. Soc.) (1976): 89. DeWindt *Royal Justice & Medieval English Countryside* 2 (1981): 626 (biog. of Milicent de Mold [Mohaut]). VCH *Wiltshire* 12 (1983): 138–151; 17 (2002): 64–79, 123–135. Sutton *Rolls & Reg. of Bishop Oliver Sutton, 1280–1299* 8 (Lincoln Rec. Soc. 76) (1986): 82, 86. Travers *Cal. of the Feet of Fines for Buckinghamshire 1259–1307* (Buckinghamshire

Rec. Soc. 25) (1989): 71. VCH *Somerset* 6 (1992): 208–213. English *Yorkshire Hundred & Quo Warranto Rolls* (Yorkshire Arch. Soc. Rec. Ser. 151) (1996): 33, 277. Mitchell *Portraits of Medieval Women* (2002): 46 (chart). Berkeley Castle Muniments, BCM/A/2/90/1; BCM/A/2/90/2 (available at www.a2a.org.uk/search/index.asp). National Archives, SC 8/107/5338 (available at www.catalogue.nationalarchives.gov.uk/search.asp).

Children of Milicent de Cantelowe, by Eudes la Zouche, Knt.:

i. **WILLIAM LA ZOUCHE**, Knt., 1st Lord Zouche [see next].

ii. **ELIZABETH LA ZOUCHE**, married **NICHOLAS POYNTZ**, Knt., of Curry-Mallet, Somerset [see OWSLEY 5].

iii. **EVE LA ZOUCHE**, married **MAURICE DE BERKELEY**, Knt., 2nd Lord Berkeley [see BERKELEY 6].

iv. **ELEANOR LA ZOUCHE**, married **JOHN DE HARCOURT**, Knt., of Stanton Harcourt, Oxfordshire [see HARCOURT 10].

7. WILLIAM LA ZOUCHE, Knt., of Harringworth, Binfield, and Bulwick, Northamptonshire, Eaton Bray, Henlow Zouches (in Henlow), Houghton Regis, Totternhoe, Whipsnade, and Wymington, Bedfordshire, Ellesborough, Ham (in Waddesdon), Long Crendon, and Mentmore, Buckinghamshire, Loddiswell and Totnes, Devon, Clipsham, Rutland, Bridgwater, Somerset, Lubbesthorpe, Leicestershire, Bridgwater, Haygrove, and Odcombe, Somerset, Calstone (in Calstone Wellington), Wiltshire, etc., Justice of the Peace for Northamptonshire, 1320 and 1329, Justice in Eyre in Derbyshire, 1330, and, in right of his wife, of Thorpe Arnold and Belgrave, Leicestershire, Ebrington, Gloucestershire, Buckworth, Huntingdonshire, Ilston, Leicestershire, Brafield, Little Houghton, and Weston Favell, Northamptonshire, Bulkington, Foleshill, Ryton (in Bulkington), Weston-in-Arden (in Bulkington), and Wolvershill, Warwickshire, etc., son and heir, born at Harringworth, Northamptonshire 18 (or 21) Dec. 1276 (aged 22 in 1299). He married before 15 Feb. 1295/6 (date of license to settle lands) **MAUD LOVEL**, daughter of John Lovel, 1st Lord Lovel, of Titchmarsh, Northamptonshire and Minster Lovell, Oxfordshire, by his 1st wife, Isabel (or Elizabeth), daughter of Arnold du Bois [see LOVEL 10 for her ancestry]. She was born in or before 1279 (aged 30 in 1310). Her maritagium included the manor of Docking, Norfolk. They had seven sons, Eudes, Knt., William, [Master] John [Rector of Loddiswell, Devon], [Master] Roger, Thomas, John (2nd of name), and Edmund [chaplain of Sopford, Sussex, Canon of Lincoln], and three daughters, Milicent, Isabel, and Thomasine. In 1296 the king granted a license to Master William de Bois to enfeoff Milicent de Mohaut with a moiety of the manors of Thorpe-Arnold, Leicestershire, Tubney, Berkshire, Ebrington and Farmcote, Gloucestershire, Brafield and Little Houghton, Northamptonshire, Standlake, Oxfordshire, Weston-in-Arden (in Bulkington), Warwickshire, etc., and for Milicent to re-grant these manors to the said [Master] William de Bois for life, with remainder to [Master] William's niece, Maud Lovel, and her husband, William la Zouche, their issue, and the heirs of Maud. In 1300–1 various Bois family manors were settled on [Master] William de Bois for life, with remainder to William la Zouche and Maud his wife, and the heirs of William la Zouche by the said Maud, including the manors of Thorpe Arnold, Belgrave, Bushby (in Thurnby), Stretton, Leicestershire, Brafield and Little Houghton, Northamptonshire, and Bulkington, Foleshill, Ryton (in Bulkington), Weston-in-Arden (in Bulkington), and Wolvershill, Warwickshire. His wife, Maud, was co-heiress in 1313 to her brother, [Master] William de Bois. He had free warren in his demesne lands in Harringworth and Bulwick, Northamptonshire 23 March 1300/1. He presented to the churches of Hope Bowdler, Shropshire, 1303, 1349, Hinxworth, Hertfordshire, 1303, 1322, Clipsham, Rutland, 1315, Loddiswell, Devon, 1328, 1343, Bulwick, Northamptonshire, 1331, and Barby, Northamptonshire, 1346, 1350, 1351. He was frequently summoned for service against the Scots in the period, 1301–33, in Ireland 1317 (against Edward de Brus) and 1332, and in Gascony in 1324-1325. He was knighted with Prince Edward at Westminster 22 May 1306. He was summoned to Parliament from 16 August 1308 to 14 Feb.

1347/8, by writs directed *Willelmo la Zouche* and from 26 Dec. 1323 *Willelmo la Zouche de Haryngworth*. His wife, Maud, was co-heiress in 1313 to her great uncle, [Master] William du Bois. In 1313 he was pardoned with his son, Eudes, for their part in the death of Peter de Gavaston, Earl of Cornwall. The same year he and his wife, Maud, were granted free warren in their lands of Bramcote, Bulkington, Foleshill, Rycote, Weston, and Wolvershill, Warwickshire. He had a protection going on pilgrimage to Santiago 7 March 1316/7. In 1317 he settled the manor of Clipsham, Rutland for their lives on his younger sons, William, John, and Roger. He was ordered 12 Nov. 1321 not to attend the meeting of the "Good Peers" which had been convened by Thomas, Earl of Lancaster, at Doncaster. In 1322, in association with the sheriff, he was ordered to summon men at arms and to lead them against the Scotch rebels who had entered the realm. Sometime before 1324, he appears to have transferred his one-third share of the manor of Long Crendon, Buckinghamshire to his cousin, John de Hastings, Lord Hastings. His wife, Maud, died before c.1324, when William petitioned the king requesting grace as Edmund, Earl of Leicester [afterwards Earl of Lancaster] formerly granted to Arnold du Bois two stags and two does in certain seasons annually from the chase of Leicester, and the heirs of the said Arnold enfeoffed him with these and he was seised of them until the chase was forfeited to the king with the other lands of Thomas, Earl of Lancaster. In 1324 he was granted liberty to hunt within the forests of Northampton and Rutland provided he did not damage the king's deer. In 1324–5 he settled the manors of Weston-in-Arden (in Bulkington), Foleshill, and Wolvershill, Warwickshire, and a messuage and 40 acres of land in Marston Jabbett (in Bulkington), Warwickshire on his younger son, William la Zouche. In 1324 he settled the manor of Eaton Bray, Bedfordshire on his son, William la Zouche, which manor was subsequently released by his son in 1333. In 1326 he was granted the privilege of riding armed so that he might not suffer the attack of evil doers. In 1334 he had license to enfeoff [Master] John la Zouche and William Danet of the castle of Totnes and manors of Cornworth and Totnes, Devon, together with the manors of Eaton Bray and Houghton Regis, Bedfordshire, Bridgewater, Haygrove, and Odcombe, Somerset, and Calne and Calstone, Wiltshire, and for them to regrant the castle and the manors of Totnes and Cornworth, Devon to his grandson, William son of Eudes la Zouche, and his wife, Elizabeth de Roos, and the remaining manors to the said William la Zouche [the elder] for life, with remainder to his grandson, William son of Eudes la Zouche. In 1338 he quitclaimed to the Prior and canons of Studley lands and rents in Studley, Marton, and Clifford Ruin (in Stratford-upon-Avon), Warwickshire. In 1344 he alienated the advowson of Hinxworth, Hertfordshire to the Abbot and Convent of Pipewell, Northamptonshire. In 1344 Ralph de Cromwell, the younger, and Avice his wife brought an action against him in respect of warranty of the manor of Basford, Nottinghamshire. In 1345 he obtained a license to found a chantry in St. Mary's Chapel within his manor of Weston-in-Arden (in Bulkington), Warwickshire for two chaplains to sing mass daily for his good estate, for his soul when he is dead, for the soul of William Danet, and for the souls of the fathers, mothers, ancestors, and heirs of the said William and William; in 1347 the king granted his petition that that he may assign the premises to one chaplain only who shall find a second chaplain under him for the celebration of the chantry. In 1346 he gave a messuage, four acres of land, and 51*s*. of rent in Studley and Marton, Warwickshire to the Priory and Convent of Studley. In 1351 he settled the manor of Clipsham, Rutland on his grandson, William son of Eudes la Zouche. SIR WILLIAM LA ZOUCHE, 1st Lord Zouche of Harringworth, died 11 (or 12) March 1351/2.

> Dugdale *Antiqs. of Warwickshire* (1730): 9 (Bois ped.), 58 (Cantelowe-Zouche ped.). Morice *Histoire Ecclesiastique et Civil de Bretagne* 1 (1750): xxi–xxii (Zouche ped.). *Topographer* 1 (1789): 195–204. Bridges *Hist. & Antiqs. of Northamptonshire* 1 (1791): 25; 2 (1791): 289, 315–318. Newcome *Hist. of the Ancient & Royal Foundation, called the Abbey of St. Albam* (1793): 242. Nichols *Hist. & Antiq. of the County of Leicester* 4(1) (1807): 37. Blomefield *Essay towards a Top. Hist. of Norfolk* 10 (1809): 365. Kennett *Parochial Antiq. Attempted in the Hist. of Ambrosden, Burcester & other adjacent Parts* 2 (1818): 465–466. Clutterbuck *Hist. & Antiqs.of Hertford* 3 (1827): 528. Palgrave *Docs. & Recs. illus. the Hist. of Scotland* 1 (1837): 211. Banks *Baronies in Fee* 1 (1844): 469–471 (sub Zouche of Haryngworth). Lipscomb *Hist. & Antiqs. of*

Buckingham 1 (1847): 176 (Cantilupe-Zouche ped.). Foss *Judges of England* 3 (1851): 543–544 (biog. of William la Zouche). Eyton *Antiquities of Shropshire* 5 (1857) : 121. Horwood *Year Books of the Reign of King Edward the First* (1863): xxxi, 40–41, 468–476. Riley *Chronica Monasterii S. Albani; Gesta Abbatum Monasterii Sancti Albani, a Thoma Walsingham, regnante Ricardo Secundo, ejusdem ecclesia praecentore, compilata* 2 (1869): 371 (Thomas de la Mare, Abbot of St. Albans, son of John de la Mare, Knt., and his wife, Joan, daughter of John de Herpesfeld, Knt., styled kinsman of William la Zouche, of Harringworth). Foss *Biographical Dictionary of the Judges of England* (1870): 791 (biog. of William la Zouche). *Colls. Hist. Staffs.* 12 (1891): 62. *C.P.R.* 1330–1334 (1893): 566–567. Birch *Cat. of Seals in the British Museum* 3 (1894): 703 (seal of William La Zouche, of Harringworth, 1st Lord dated 1338—A shield of arms: bezanté, a canton ermine, ZOUCHE. Within a carved panel of eight points. Legend: * : SIGILLVM WILLEL….. LA . ZOV…). *Two Cartularies of the Augustinian Priory of Bruton & Cluniac Priory of Montacute* (Somerset Rec. Soc. 8) (1894): 145–146. *C.P.R.* 1292–1301 (1895): 184. *Genealogist* n.s. 13 (1896): 242. Green *Feet of Fines for Somerset* 2 (Somerset Rec. Soc. 12) (1898): 242. Rye *Cal. of Feet of Fines for Suffolk* (1900): 191. *C.P.R.* 1343–1345 (1902): 198, 243, 455. *C.P.R.* 1345–1348 (1903): 76, 258. *C.P.R.* 1324–1327 (1904): 33. *MSS of the Duke of Rutland* 4 (Hist. MSS Comm. 24) (1905): 10. Pike *Year Books of Edward III, Years XVIII & XIX* (Rolls Ser. 31(17)) (1905): 155. Wrottesley *Peds. from the Plea Rolls* (1905): 161, 166. VCH *Bedford* 2 (1908): 280–285; 3 (1912): 369–375, 447–451. VCH *Buckingham* 2 (1908): 331–338; 3 (1925): 397–401; 4 (1927): 41, 107–118. Capes *Reg. Ricardi de Swinfield, Episcopi Herefordensis 1283–1317* (Canterbury & York Soc. 6) (1909): 535. *D.N.B.* 21 (1909): 1335–1338 (biog. of William la Zouche, Archbishop of York). *Cal. IPM* 3 (1912): 436; 4 (1913): 112. VCH *Hertford* 3 (1912): 232–240. Watkin *Hist. of Totnes Priory and Medieval Town* (1914):.200. *Cal. Charter Rolls* 3 (1914): 21; 4 (1898): 272. *C.P.* 4 (1916): 120–122 (sub Deincourt); 12(2) (1959): 97, 938–940. VCH *Berkshire* 4 (1924): 379–380. Farnham *Leicestershire Medieval Peds.* (1925): 23 (Bosco ped.). Dilks *Bridgwater Borough Archives* (Somerset Rec. Soc. 48) (1933): 109–110 (power of attorney of William la Zouche dated 1349). VCH *Rutland* 2 (1935): 41–45. VCH *Huntingdon* 3 (1936): 22–26. VCH *Northampton* 4 (1937): 107–111, 246–248, 266–270. Stokes et al. *Warwickshire Feet of Fines* 2 (Dugdale Soc. 15) (1939): 39–41. Gollancz *Rolls of the Northamptonshire Sessions of the Peace* (Northamptonshire Rec. Soc. 11) (1940): xvii, xxvii–xxviii, xlviii, 80–81, 88. Hatton *Book of Seals* (1950): 190 (charter of William la Zouche of Harringworth dated 1338; seal on tag: round, 1 in., uncoloured. Within an eight-pointed panel a shield of arms, bezanty [ZOUCH], no legend). VCH *Warwick* 6 (1951): 48–57. *Paget* (1957) 337:5, 581:3–4. VCH *Leicester* 4 (1958): 420–428; 5 (1964): 163–166, 321–330. *Procs. of the Suffolk Institute of Arch.* 29(1) (1962): 34–66 (Naunton ped. dated 18th Cent.). *TAG* 49 (1971): 1–12; 70 (1995): 100. Rosenthal *Nobles & the Noble Life 1295–1500* (1976): 59–63. Sutherland *Eyre of Northamptonshire 3–4 Edward III* 1 (Selden Soc. 97) (1983): 109–110. Crowley *Wiltshire Tax List of 1332* (Wiltshire Rec. Soc. 45) (1989): 39. VCH *Somerset* 6 (1992): 208–213. Brand *Earliest English Law Reports* 1 (Selden Soc. 111) (1996): 106–108. VCH *Wiltshire* 17 (2002): 123–135. Smith *Art, Identity & Devotion in 14th-Cent. England* (2003): 24 (Bois ped.), 25–26, 30–31. Scott-Stokes *Women's Books of Hours in Medieval England* (2006): 154. Devon Rec. Office: Hole of Parke, 312M/TY99 (charter dated 15 April 1306 from William la Zousche, Lord of Totnes, Devon to God and Church of B. Mary of Totnes and monks of S. Sergius Andegavis, grant and confirmation in free alms for souls of Eudo la Zousche his father, Miliscenta his mother and Matillidis his wife of the tite of Priory with Totnes Church; manor and advowson of Ayspryngton; lands of Garston, Faggeslonde, Foleton; churches of Cliston and Brixham, with tithes, saving the patronage and advowson of the Priory; releasing to Brother Galfridus, Prior, and Convent, services due from the men of Aysprinton, free tenants and villeins, in the manor of Corneworthy. The Priory agrees not to claim the fisheries in Derte in his liberty and demesne; pendant seal, armorial) (available at http://www.a2a.org.uk/search/index.asp). National Archives, SC 8/153/7636 (available at www.catalogue.nationalarchives.gov.uk/search.asp).

Children of William la Zouche, Knt., by Maud Lovel:

i. **EUDES LA ZOUCHE**, Knt. [see next].

ii. **WILLIAM LA ZOUCHE**,[4] 2nd son. In 1317 his father settled the manor of Clipsham, Rutland on him and his younger brothers, John and Roger la Zouche, for their lives; they were to pay their father £20 a year for his life,

---

[4] Care should be taken to distinguish William la Zouche (living 1333) above, 2nd son of William la Zouche, Knt., 1st Lord Zouche of Harringworth, from his more prominent cousin, William la Zouche, Clerk of the Wardrobe, Keeper of the Privy Seal, Treasurer of England, Archbishop of York (died 1352). Archbishop Zouche is known to have had a brother, Roger la Zouche, Knt., which Roger can be readily identified as Roger la Zouche, Knt. (living 1353), of Lubbesthorpe, Leicestershire. If so, this would place the Archbishop as a younger son of Roger la Zouche (died 1302), of Lubbesthorpe, Leicestershire, by his wife, Juliane. For further particulars on the Zouche family of Lubbesthorpe, see *MSS of the Duke of Rutland* 4 (Hist. MSS Comm. 24) (1905): 10–11. For evidence that the Archbishop was not the son of William la Zouche, 1st Lord Zouche of Harringworth, see Hingeston-Randolph *Reg. of John de Grandisson, Bishop of Exeter (A.D. 1327–1369)* 1 (1894): 579, which records that Archbishop William la Zouche,

then a rose yearly to his heirs. In 1324–5 his father settled the manors of Weston-in-Arden (in Bulkington), Foleshill, and Wolvershill, Warwickshire, and a messuage and 40 acres of land in Marston Jabbett (in Bulkington), Warwickshire on him; which manors William de Arundel then held for life of the inheritance of the grantor. In 1324 his father had license to grant the manors of Eaton Bray, Houghton Regis, and Thornbury (in Houghton Regis), Bedfordshire, to him, and for him to regrant the same to William la Zouche [the elder] for life, with reversion to the said William son of William and his heirs. In 1325 his father acknowledged that he owed him debts of £2000 and £4000. In 1330 William, John, and Roger la Zouche, sons of William la Zouche, of Harringworth, presented Ralph Turville to the church of Clipsham, Rutland. In 1332 he released his claim to the manors of Eaton Bray, Houghton, and Thornbury (in Houghton Regis), Bedfordshire to his father. In 1333 William, John, and Roger la Zouche, sons of William la Zouche, presented William de Osgoodby to the church of Clipsham, Rutland. *C.C.R. 1323–1327* (1898): 524. *C.P.R. 1324–1327* (1904): 33. VCH *Bedford* 3 (1912): 369–375, citing Feet of F. Beds. East. 6 Edw. III [CP 25/1/4/53, number 15]. VCH *Rutland* 2 (1935): 41–45. Gollancz *Rolls of the Northamptonshire Sessions of the Peace* (Northamptonshire Rec. Soc. 11) (1940): xxvii–xxviii. Bennett *Regs. of Bishop Henry Burghersh, 1326–1342* 2 (Lincoln Rec. Soc.90) (2003): 27, 38.

iii. **[MASTER] JOHN LA ZOUCHE**, M.A. (1st of name). In 1317 his father settled the manor of Clipsham, Rutland on him and his brothers, William and Roger la Zouche, for life. In 1325 his father acknowledged that he owed him a debt of £4000. In 1328 his father presented him as Rector of Loddiswell, Devon. In 1330 William, John, and Roger la Zouche, sons of William la Zouche, of Harringworth, presented Ralph Turville to the church of Clipsham, Rutland. In 1333 the same parties presented William de Osgoodby to the church of Clipsham, Rutland. In 1328 he was dispensed for non-residence until Michaelmas 1329 to study at Oxford, or elsewhere in England. In 1330 he was dispensed for non-residence to study for a year at instance of his kinsman, William la Zouche, Archdeacon of Exeter [future Archbishop of York]. In 1331 the Pope ordered that provision be made for John la Zouche, M.A., to have a canonry and prebend of Lichfield, not withstanding that he was already rector of Loddiswell, Devon. In 1331, 1332, and again in 1336–1337, as Master John la Zouche, Rector of Loddiswell, Devon, he was granted a license of non-residency for a year by John de Grandison, Bishop of Exeter, for the purpose of study. As Master John la Zouche, he served as a trustee for a settlement made by his father, William la Zouche, Knt., 1st Lord Zouche of Harringworth, in 1333–4. In 1338 he granted three acres of land and certain houses built thereon to the Carmelite Priory in York. In May 1338 he was granted license to appoint William de Scargehill, Knt., and Thomas de Thorp his attorneys until Michaelmas. In 1339, as Master John la Zouche, he was again granted a license of non-residency from the church of Loddiswell, Devon by John de Grandison, Bishop of Exeter, in 1339, at the instance of William la Zouche, Treasurer of England (afterwards Archbishop of York). In 1339 William de Weaverham, of Asshton, and others granted a recognizance of 8 marks to Master John la Zouche, prebendary of Tervyn. [MASTER] JOHN LA ZOUCHE was living 6 July 1349, when he held the prebend of Tervin in the diocese of Lichfield. He died before 11 October 1350. *Annual Report of the Deputy Keeper* 36 (1875): 511. *C.P.R. 1327–1330* (1891): 202. Hingeston-Randolph *Reg. of John de Grandisson, Bishop of Exeter (A.D. 1327–1369)* 1 (1894): 429, 507, 579 (William la Zouche, Archdeacon of Exeter [future Archbishop of York] styled "kinsman" [nepotis] of John la Zouche, Rector of Loddiswell, Devon); 2 (1897): 617, 657, 838, 918; 3 (1899): 1267. *Papal Regs.: Letters* 2 (1895): 345; 3 (1897): 318. *C.C.R. 1323–1327* (1898): 524. Green *Feet of Fines for Somerset* 2 (Somerset Rec. Soc. 12) (1898): 242. VCH *Rutland* 2 (1935): 41–45. *Treaty Rolls Preserved in the Public Record Office* 2 (1955): 104. Jones *Fasti Ecclesiae Anglicanae 1300–1541* 10 (1964): 59–61. Bennett *Regs. of Bishop Henry Burghersh, 1326–1342* 2 (Lincoln Rec. Soc.90) (2003): 27, 38.

iv. **[MASTER] ROGER LA ZOUCHE**, M.A. In 1317 his father settled the manor of Clipsham, Rutland on him and his older brothers, William and John la Zouche, for life.. In 1330 William, John, and Roger la Zouche, sons of William la Zouche, of Harringworth, presented Ralph Turville to the church of Clipsham, Rutland. In 1333 the same parties presented William de Osgoodby to the church of Clipsham, Rutland. In 1331 the Pope ordered that provision be made for Roger la Zouche, M.A., to have a canonry of Chichester, with reservation of a prebend. He presumably died before 1351. *Papal Regs.: Letters* 2 (1895): 345. VCH *Rutland* 2 (1935): 41–45. Horn *Fasti Ecclesiae Anglicanae 1300–1541* 7 (1864): 54–60. Bennett *Regs. of Bishop Henry Burghersh, 1326–1342* 2 (Lincoln Rec. Soc.90) (2003): 27, 38.

v. **THOMAS LA ZOUCHE**, of North Luffenham, Rutland. He married **CHRISTINE** _____. His father appears to have settled the manor of Ham (in Waddesdon), Buckinghamshire on him. In 1345 he settled land in North Luffenham, Rutland on himself and his wife, Christine, and their issue, with remainder in default to his

---

then Archdeacon of Exeter, was styled "kinsman" [nepotis] of John la Zouche, Rector of Loddiswell, Devon; this John la Zouche was a known son of Lord Zouche.

brother, Edmund la Zouche, and William la Zouche, of Harringworth. VCH *Buckingham* 4 (1927): 107–118. VCH *Rutland* 2 (1935): 195–203.

vi. **JOHN LA ZOUCHE** (2nd of name), living 26 March 1326.

vii. **EDMUND LA ZOUCHE**, clerk, chaplain of Sopford, Sussex, Canon of London. In 1351 he had the king's license to exchange the prebend of Broomesbury with William de Shrewsbury for the prebend of Bulverhythe in the king's Free Chapel of Hastings, Sussex. He was living 12 July 1357. Dugdale *Hist. of Saint Paul's Cathedral* (1818): 234. *Papal Regs.: Petitions* 3 (1897): 155, 397. *C.P.R. 1350–1354* (1907): 297. *C.P.R. 1354–1358* (1909): 35, 609. VCH *Rutland* 2 (1935): 195–203. Horn *Fasti Ecclesiae Anglicanae 1300–1541* 5 (1963): 20–21.

viii. **MILICENT LA ZOUCHE**, married before 26 March 1326 **WILLIAM DEINCOURT** (or **DEYNCOURT**), Knt., 2nd Lord Deincourt, of Blankney and Branston, Lincolnshire, Wooburn, Buckinghamshire, Elmton, Derbyshire, Granby, Nottinghamshire, Kylthorp, Rutland, etc., 2nd but oldest surviving son of John Deincourt. He was born about 1301 (aged 26 in 1327). They had three sons, William, Thomas, and Robert, Knt., and one daughter, Margaret. He was summoned for military service against the Scots from 5 April 1327 to 23 Dec. 1355. He was summoned to Parliament from 20 July 1332 to 1 June 1363. In 1340 he was appointed a justice in cos. Notts and Derby to hear and determine the oppressions commited by the king's ministers and others. He was a commander at the Battle of Neville's Cross 17 October 1346. On 14 May 1347 he was summoned to join the king before Calais. He was the principal warder of the King of France when that monarch was a prisoner in England in 1359–60. They received a papal indult for plenary remission in 1345. SIR WILLIAM DEINCOURT, 2nd Lord Deincourt, died 2 June 1364. His widow, Milicent, died 22 June 1379. *Papal Regs.: Letters* 3 (1897): 161. *List of Inqs. ad Quod Damnum* 1 (PRO Lists and Indexes 17) (1904): 328. *C.P.* 4 (1916): 120–122 (sub Deincourt); 12(2) (1959): 938.

Child of William Deincourt, Knt., by Milicent la Zouche:

a. **MARGARET DEINCOURT**, married (1st) **ROBERT DE TIBETOT**, Knt., 3rd Lord Tibetot [see TIBETOT 10]; (2nd) **JOHN CHEYNE**, Knt., of Beckford, Gloucestershire [see TIBETOT 10].

8. EUDES LA ZOUCHE, Knt., of Harringworth, Northamptonshire, and, in right of his wife, of Lower Gravenhurst, Bedfordshire, Stoke Mandeville, Buckinghamshire, etc., son and heir apparent, born about 1298 (aged about 24 in 1322). He was pardoned with his father in 1313 for their share in the death of Peter de Gavaston, Earl of Cornwall. He married before June 1322 **JOAN INGE**, daughter and heiress of William Inge, Knt., of Inge's Place (in Wheathampstead), Hertfordshire, King's Worthy, Hampshire, Lower Gravenhurst and Westoning, Bedfordshire, Stoke Mandeville, Buckinghamshire, Ingescourt (in Great Milton), Oxfordshire, etc., King's serjeant, Justice of the Common Bench, Chief Justice of the King's Bench, by his 1st wife, Margery, 2nd daughter and coheiress of Henry Grapnel (or Grapenell). She was born about 1299–1300 (aged 22 or 23 in 1322). They had three sons, William, Knt. [2nd Lord Zouche of Harringworth], Henry [Archdeacon of Sudbury], and Richard, Knt. He fought on the king's side at the Battle of Boroughbridge 16 March 1321/2. He was indicted with others for the death of Roger Belers, of Kirby Bellars, who was slain in the field of Brooksby, Leicestershire 19 Jan. 1325/6, after which Eudes fled to France. SIR EUDES LA ZOUCHE died in Paris, France 24 April 1326, and was buried there in the church of the Augustine Friars. His widow, Joan, married (2nd) before 6 Nov. 1327 **WILLIAM MOTON**, Knt., of Peckleton, Leicestershire, and, in right of his wife, of Stoke Mandeville, Buckinghamshire. They had one son, Robert, Knt. [see RANDOLPH 13]. In 1328 he and his wife, Joan, obtained license to grant land at Latchingdon, Essex to William la Zouch, clerk, for his life, retaining land in Oxfordshire. As "Joan la Zouche, wife of William Moton, knight," she was granted a papal indult for plenary remission in 1345. SIR WILLIAM MOTON was living in 1346, and died before 19 July 1367. Joan died before January 1359/60.

Dugdale *Antiqs. of Warwickshire* (1730): 58 (Cantelowe-Zouche ped.). Morice *Histoire Ecclesiastique et Civil de Bretagne* 1 (1750): xxi–xxii (Zouche ped.). *Topographer* 1 (1789): 195–204. Bridges *Hist. & Antiqs. of Northamptonshire* 2 (1791): 315–318. Hasted *Hist. & Top. Survey of Kent* 5 (1798): 35–36. Blomefield *Essay towards a Top. Hist. of Norfolk* 10 (1809): 365. Kennett *Parochial Antiq. Attempted in the Hist. of Ambrosden, Burcester & other adjacent Parts* 2 (1818): 465–466. Banks *Baronies in Fee* 1 (1844): 469–471 (sub Zouche of Haryngworth). Lipscomb *Hist. & Antiqs. of Buckingham* 1 (1847): 176 (Cantilupe-Zouche ped.). Foss *Judges of England* 3 (1851): 268–270 (biog. of William Inge). Frampton *Glance at the*

Hundred of Wrotham (1881): 80–90. *Colls. Hist. Staffs.* 12 (1891): 62. *Genealogist* n.s. 13 (1896): 242. *Papal Regs.: Letters* 3 (1897): 178. *List of Inqs. ad Quod Damnum* 1 (PRO Lists and Indexes 17) (1904): 279. Wrottesley *Peds. from the Plea Rolls* (1905): 14, 109, 161, 166. VCH *Bedford* 2 (1908): 336–338; 3 (1912): 451–455. VCH *Buckingham* 2 (1908): 361. VCH *Hertford* 2 (1908): 307, 367. VCH *Hampshire* 4 (1911): 431. Farnham *Leicestershire Medieval Peds.* (1925): foll. 62 (Moton ped.). Richardson & Sayles *Rotuli Parliamentorum Anglie Hactenus Inediti 1274–1373* (Camden Soc. 3rd Ser. 51) (1935):148. Hatton *Book of Seals* (1950): 190. Paget (1957) 581:3-4. *Procs. of the Suffolk Institute of Arch.* 29(1) (1962): 34–66 (Naunton ped. dated 18th Cent.). VCH *Oxford* 7 (1962): 117–146. *TAG* 49 (1971): 1–12. Rosenthal *Nobles & the Noble Life 1295-1500* (1976): 59–63. Brand *Earliest English Law Reports* 2 (Selden Soc. 112) (1996): lxi–lxv (biog. of William Inge). Musson *Public Order & Law Enforcement* (1996): 267. National Archives, C 143/200/14 (available at www.catalogue.nationalarchives.gov.uk/search.asp).

Children of Eudes la Zouche, Knt., by Joan Inge:

i. **WILLIAM LA ZOUCHE**, Knt., 2nd Lord Zouche of Harringworth [see next].

ii. **HENRY LA ZOUCHE**, clerk, Canon of York, licentiate in arts, skilled in civil law. He was presented to the rectory of Barby, Northamptonshire in 1346–7 by his grandfather, William la Zouche, Knt,. He was Archdeacon of Subury, 1350–61. He died shortly before 11 August 1361. Dixon *Fasti Eboracenses: Lives of the Archbishops of York* 1 (1863): 437, footnote w. *Papal Regs.: Petitions* 1 (1896): 141 (Henry styled "son of Yvo la Zouche, baron and knight"). *Papal Regs.: Petitions* 1 (1896): 374. *Papal Regs.: Petitions* 3 (1897): 457. Jones *Fasti Ecclesiae Anglicanae 1300–1541* 4 (1963): 30–32.

iii. **RICHARD LA ZOUCHE**, Knt., of Docking, Norfolk. He was granted the manor of Docking, Norfolk and lands in the town of Newbury, Berkshire for life by his brother, William la Zouche, Knt. He died shortly before 7 May 1397. Money *Hist. of Newbury* (1887): 157. *Cal. IPM* 17 (1988): 269, 349.

9. WILLIAM LA ZOUCHE, Knt., 2nd Lord Zouche of Harringworth, of Harringworth and Barby, Northamptonshire, Eaton Bray, Henlow Zouches (in Henlow), Houghton Regis, Totternhoe, Westoning, and Wymington, Bedfordshire, Ellesborough, Ham (in Waddesdon), and Mentmore, Buckinghamshire, Cornworth, Loddiswell, and Totnes, Devon, King's Worthy, Hampshire, Buckworth, Huntingdonshire, Belgrave, Leicestershire, Clipsham and North Luffenham, Rutland, Bridgwater, Haygrove, and Odcombe, Somerset, Calne and Calstone (in Calstone Wellington), Wiltshire, etc., son and heir, born at Christmas 1321 or earlier (aged 30 in 1352, aged 60 in 4 Rich. II [1380–1]). He married before 16 July 1334 (date of license for settlement of lands) **ELIZABETH DE ROOS**, daughter of William de Roos, Knt., 2nd Lord Roos of Helmsley, by Margery, daughter of Bartholomew de Badlesmere, Knt., 1st Lord Badlesmere [see ROOS 9 for her ancestry]. They had three sons, William, Knt. [3rd Lord Zouche of Harringworth], Thomas, Knt., and [Master] Eudes [Chancellor of Cambridge University], and two daughters, Elizabeth and Margery. In 1334 his grandfather, William la Zouche, Knt., 1st Lord Zouche of Harringworth, had license to enfeoff John la Zouche and William Danet of the Castle of Totnes and manors of Cornworth and Totnes, Devon, together with the manors of Eaton Bray and Houghton Regis, Bedfordshire, Bridgwater, Haygrove, and Odcombe, Somerset, and Calne and Calstone, Wiltshire, and for them to regrant the Castle and the manors of Totnes and Cornworth, Devon on William son of Eudes la Zouche and Elizabeth de Roos his wife, and the remaining manors to the said William la Zouche [the elder] for life, with remainder to his grandson, William son of Eudes la Zouche. He accompanied Henry of Lancaster, Earl of Derby to Gascony 1344 and 1345, and later served under him, as Earl of Lancaster, at the Siege of Calais in 1347. In 1346 he and his wife, Elizabeth, were granted a papal indult for plenary remission at the hour of death. The same year he and his cousin, Roger Corbet, of Hadley, Shropshire sued Richard de Dynggeleye for two messuages and two virgates of land in South Denchworth, Berkshire. In his grandfather's lifetime he was summoned to Parliament from 20 Nov. 1348 by writs directed *Willelmo la Zouche de Haryngworth juniori*. He presented to the churches of Hope Bowdler, Shropshire, 1355, 1381, and Barby, Northamptonshire, 1361, 1369, and to the chantry of Weston, Warwickshire, 1357, 1359, 1361. In 1359 he had license to settle the reversion of the manor of Westoning, Bedfordshire on himself and his wife, Elizabeth, for life, with successive remainders to their sons, Thomas and Eudes la Zouche; the heirs male of the said Thomas; the heirs male of the said Eudes; Richard la Zouche, Knt., the heirs male of the said Richard, and the right heirs of the said William. He took part in the last campaign of King Edward III in France in 1359–60. He was going on pilgrimage to the Holy Land in 1362. In 1368 William la Zouche of Harringworth, Knt., defendant, essoined himself in London against Richard de Penbrigg, Knt., by William Russe. In 1369 Emma relict of Simon de Pistoye, defendant, essoined herself in London against William la Souche, kt., lord of Harringworth, by William Gill. In 1372 he had license to grant the manor of Westoning, Bedfordshire to various trustees, and for them to re-grant the same to him and his wife, Elizabeth, for life, with remainder to their son, Thomas, for life, and remainder over to the right heirs of the said William. In 1373 he was sent to France to escort the King of Navarre from Normandy to England. He was co-heir in 1376 to his cousin, William de Cantelowe, by which he inherited the manors of Ilkeston, Derbyshire and Greasley, Nottinghamshire. In 1379 he gave the church of Ebington, Gloucestershire to Biddlesden Abbey, Buckinghamshire in memory of his kinsman, William du Bois. He and his wife, Elizabeth, were members of Trinity Guild of Coventry, Warwickshire. His wife, Elizabeth, died 24 May 1380/2. She left a will dated 16 May 1380. SIR WILLIAM LA ZOUCHE, 2nd Lord Zouche of Harringworth, died 23 April 1382, and was buried in Biddlesden Abbey, Buckinghamshire. He left a will dated 14 March 1381, proved 24 April 1382.

Dugdale *Antiqs. of Warwickshire* (1730): 58 (Cantelowe-Zouche ped.), 61. Morice *Histoire Ecclesiastique et Civil de Bretagne* 1 (1750): xxi–xxii (Zouche ped.). *Topographer* 1 (1789): 195–204. Bridges *Hist. & Antiqs. of Northamptonshire* 1 (1791): 25; 2 (1791): 315–318. Blomefield *Essay towards a Top. Hist. of Norfolk* 10 (1809): 365. Kennett *Parochial Antiqs. of Ambrosden, Burcester* 2 (1818): 465–466. Chitty *Practical Treatise on the Criminal Law* 4 (1819): 299 (Roos-Zouche ped.). Banks *Baronies in Fee* 1 (1844): 469–471 (sub Zouche of Haryngworth). Lipscomb *Hist. & Antiqs. of Buckingham* 1 (1847): 176 (Cantilupe-Zouche ped.). *Cat. MSS: Lib. of the Univ. of Cambridge* 1 (1856): 108, 113, 134–135. Eyton *Antiqs. of Shropshire* 5 (1857): 121. Gibbons *Early Lincoln Wills 1280–1547* (1888): 91–92 (will of Elizabeth la Zouche), 92–93 (will of William la Zouche). Atkinson *Cartularium Abbathiæ de Rievalle* (Surtees Soc. 83) (1889): 359–362. *Colls. Hist. Staffs.* 12 (1891): 62. *C.P.R. 1330–1334* (1893): 566–567. Birch *Cat. Seals in the British Museum* 3 (1894): 704 (seal of William la Zouche, 2nd Lord Zouche dated 1362 — A shield of arms, couché: bezanté, or [ten] bezants, a canton ermine [ZOUCHE]. Crest on a helmet and short lambrequin, out of a ducal coronet a nag's head. Background diapered lozengy, with a small quatrefoil in each interstice. Within a carved gothic panel enriched with open tracery at the sides, and ornamented along the inner edge with small quatrefoils. Legend: S' · Will'i : la : Zou]che : [de : haryngw]orth :. Beaded border). *Genealogist* n.s. 13 (1896): 242. *Papal Regs.: Petitions* 1 (1896): 98. *Papal Regs.: Letters* 3 (1897): 193. Green *Feet of Fines for Somerset* 2 (Somerset Rec. Soc. 12) (1898): 242. Trueman *Hist. of Ilkeston* (1899). *MSS of the Duke of Rutland* 4 (Hist. MSS Comm. 24) (1905): 10–11. VCH *Buckingham* 1 (1905): 365–369; 2 (1908): 331–338; 3 (1925): 397–401; 4 (1927): 107–118. Wrottesley *Peds. from the Plea Rolls* (1905): 119, 161, 166. Jeayes *Desc. Cat. Derbyshire Charters* (1906): 116. *Rpt. on MSS in Various Colls.* 4 (Hist. MSS Comm. 55) (1907): 112, 120. VCH *Bedford* 2 (1908): 280–285; 3 (1912): 117–122, 369–375, 389–394, 447–451, 451–455. VCH *Hertford* 2 (1908): 307, 367. *C.P.R. 1358–1361* (1911): 301. *C.P.R. 1370–1374* (1914): 204. Watkin *Hist. of Totnes Priory & Medieval Town, Devonshire* 2 (1917): 722–726. Harris *Reg. of the Guild of the Holy Trinity, St. Mary, St. John the Baptist & St. Katherine of Coventry* 1 (Dugdale Soc. 13) (1935): 89, 110. VCH *Rutland* 2 (1935): 41–45, 182–188, 195–203. VCH *Huntingdon* 3 (1936): 22–26. Paget *Baronage of England* (1957) 473: 6; 581: 1–11 (sub Zouche). VCH *Leicester* 4 (1958): 420–428. *C.P.* 12(2) (1959): 941–942 (sub Zouche). *Procs. Suffolk Institute of Arch.* 29(1) (1962): 34–66 (Naunton ped. dated 18th Cent.). Chew & Kellaway *London Assize of Nuisance 1301–1431* (1973): 136, 139. Payling *Political Soc. in Lancastrian England* (1991): 243 (chart). VCH *Somerset* 6 (1992): 208–213. Sainty *Judges of England* (Selden Soc. Supp. Ser. 10) (1993): 6, 61 (re. William Inge). VCH *Wiltshire* 17 (2002): 123–135. National Archives, Lincolnshire Archives: MSS of the Earl of Ancaster, 5ANC1/1/14 (notification of an enfeoffment dated 25 April 1376 issued by Robert de Willoughby, Knt. witnessed by William la Zouche, lord of Harringworth) (available at www.a2a.org.uk/search/index.asp).

Children of William la Zouche, Knt., by Elizabeth de Roos:

i. **WILLIAM LA ZOUCHE**, Knt., 3rd Lord Zouche of Harringworth [see next].

ii. **THOMAS LA ZOUCHE**, Knt., of Westoning, Bedfordshire, Ellesborough, Middle Claydon, and Ham, Buckinghamshire, King's Worthy, Hampshire, Ing's (in Wheathampstead), Hertfordshire, Ightham and Eynsford, Kent, Barby, Northamptonshire, and Alvenely, Suffolk, and, in right of his wife, of Colne Engaine, Essex, Knight of the Shire for Bedfordshire, 1390, commissioner of array, 1403, younger son. He married **MARY**

D'ENGAINE, widow of William Bernake, Knt. (died 1386), of Blatherwycke, Northamptonshire, Barkeston, Leicestershire, etc., and younger daughter of John d'Engaine, 2nd Lord Engaine, of Colne-Engaine, Essex, by Joan, daughter of Robert Peverel, Knt. [see ENGAINE 10 for her ancestry]. She was born about 1343 (aged 24 in 1367). She was co-heiress in 1367 to her brother, Thomas Engaine, Knt., by which she inherited the manors of Sandy, Bedfordshire, Dillington, Huntingdonshire, Hallaton, Leicestershire, and Pytchley, Northamptonshire. They had no issue. He was a legatee in the 1380 will of his mother and the 1381 will of his father. In 1392 he was forced to find security that neither he nor his servants would harm certain residents of Totternhoe, Bedfordshire. His wife, Mary, died 14 May 1401. SIR THOMAS LA ZOUCHE died 30 October 1404. Newcourt *Repertorium Ecclesiasticum Parochiale Londinense* 2 (1710): 187. Weever *Antient Funeral Monuments* (1767): 405. Clutterbuck *Hist. & Antiqs. of Hertford* 3 (1827): 178 (Engaine ped.). Lipscomb *Hist. & Antiqs. of Buckingham* 1 (1847): 176 (Cantilupe-Zouche ped.). Mundy et al. *Vis. of Nottingham 1569 & 1614* (H.S.P. 4) (1871): 123–128 (Chaworth ped.: "Marye [Engaine] wiffe to Sr William Barnake Kt"). Gibbons *Early Lincoln Wills 1280–1547* (1888): 91–92 (will of Elizabeth la Zouche), 92–93 (will of William la Zouche). *Genealogist* n.s. 23 (1907): 239. VCH *Buckingham* 2 (1908): 332; 4 (1927): 112. VCH *Hertford* 2 (1908): 307, 367. *C.P.R.* 1358–1361 (1911): 301. VCH *Hampshire* 4 (1911): 431. VCH *Bedford* 3 (1912): 451–455. *C.P.R.* 1370–1374 (1914): 204. *Trans. Leicestershire Arch. Soc.* 13 (1923–24): 146 (Engaine ped.). *C.F.R.* 12 (1931): 298. Bassett *Knights of Bedfordshire* (Bedfordshire Hist. Rec. Soc. 29) (1949): 98–99 (biog. of Sir Thomas Zouche). Paget *Baronage of England* (1957) 581: 1–11 (sub Zouche). VCH *Essex* 10 (2001): 107–110. Northamptonshire Rec. Office: Fitzwilliam (Milton) Charters, F(M) Charter/2033 (grant dated 30 June 1359 by William Bernak, Knt. to Lady Joan, formerly wife of John Engayne, Knt., Sir William Bernak, parson of the church of Bulwick, and another).

iii. [MASTER] **EUDES** (or **EON**) **LA ZOUCHE**, Doctor of Canon Law, Rector of Milton, Cambridgeshire, and Grainsby and Hogsthorpe, Lincolnshire, Prebendary of Langford Manor, 1372–89, 1394–1412, Chancellor of Cambridge University, 1380, 1382, and 1396–1400, Prebendary of Empingham, 1389–94, Archdeacon of Huntingdon, 1394–1414, Prebendary of Sexaginta Solidorum, 1394, Archdeacon of Sudbury, 1406–14, Prebendary of Nassington, 1412–14. He was named one of the executors of the 1381 will of his father, and one of the executors of the 1396 will of his brother, William la Zouche, Knt., 3rd Lord Zouche. [MASTER] EUDES LA ZOUCHE died shortly before 13 March 1414. Fuller *Hist. of the University of Cambridge* (1840): 123–124. *Cat. MSS: Lib. of the Univ. of Cambridge* 5 (1867): 336. Clay *Hist. of the Parish of Milton in the County of Cambridge* (1869): 88–89. Gibbons *Early Lincoln Wills 1280–1547* (1888): 92–93 (will of William la Zouche), 93 (will of William la Zouche). Birch *Cat. Seals in the British Museum* 3 (1894): 701 (seal of Eudo la Zouche, of co. Linc., clerk dated 1396 — A shield of arms: ten bezants or roundels, or bezanté, on a canton ermine a mullet for difference [ZOUCHE]. Within a carved gothic panel. Legend: * Sigillum : Eud…la : Zouche *. Beaded border.). *C.P.R.* 1385–1389 (1900): 278 (Eudes la Zouche styled "king's kinsman" by King Richard II of England). *Papal Regs.: Letters* 4 (1902): 363 (Eudo la Zouche, rector of Grainsby, Lincolnshire styled "kinsman" of King Richard II of England in 1390), 364. *C.P.R.* 1358–1361 (1911): 301. Legge *Anglo-Norman Letters & Petitions* (Anglo-Norman Text Soc. 3) (1941): 49 (Alexander [Totington], Bishop of Norwich, and Eon la Zouche both styled "cousin" by Henry, Prince of Wales [future King Henry V] in letter dated 1408; the prince indicated Eon la Zouche was related to both him and the bishop). *Bull. Inst. Hist. Research* 20 (1943): 211. Paget *Baronage of England* (1957) 581: 1–11 (sub Zouche). King *Fasti Ecclesiae Anglicanae 1300–1541* 1 (1962): 9, 64, 76, 95, 107, 116. Jacob *Essays in the Conciliar Epoch* (1963): 236. Jones *Fasti Ecclesiae Anglicanae 1300–1541* 4 (1963): 30–32. Repingdon *Reg. of Philip Repingdon* 2 (Lincoln Rec. Soc. 58) (1963): 332–335, 340–343.

iv. **ELIZABETH LA ZOUCHE**, married **JOHN BASYNGES** (or **BASING**, **BASYNG**), Knt., of Empingham, Hardwick, Horn, and Normanton, Rutland, Kenardington and Yething, Kent, etc., Knight of the Shire for Rutland, Sheriff of Rutland, 1379–80, son and heir of Thomas de Basynges, Knt., by his wife, Joan. He was born about 1341 (aged 8 in 1349). They had two sons, Thomas and John, Knt., and one daughter, Alice. He and his wife, Elizabeth, were legatees in the 1380 will of her mother. SIR JOHN BASYNGES died 26 April 1384. Hasted *Hist. & Top. Survey of Kent* 7 (1798): 244–249. Blore *Hist. & Antiqs. of Rutland* (1811): 127–130 (Basynges-Mackworth ped.). Burke *Hist. Lands of England* (1848): 112. Camden *Vis. of Rutland 1618–19* (H.S.P. 3) (1870): 48–49 (Mackworth ped.: "Sir John Basings Knt. ob. 7 R. 2."). Gibbons *Early Lincoln Wills 1280–1547* (1888): 91–92 (will of Elizabeth la Zouche). Gomme *Top. Hist. of Nottinghamshire, Oxfordshire & Rutlandshire* (1897): 252 (list of coats of arms in church of Empingham, Rutland includes Normanville, Basynges, Zouche, Ros, etc.). *List of Sheriffs for England & Wales* (PRO Lists and Indexes 9) (1898): 112. VCH *Rutland* 2 (1935): 242–250 (Basing arms: Azure a millrind cross or with a baston gules over all). Paget *Baronage of England* (1957) 581: 1–11 (sub Zouche). *English Hist. Rev.* 113 (1998): 1–17. *Virginia Gen.* 50 (2003): 121–130.

Child of Elizabeth la Zouche, by John Basynges:

a. **ALICE BASYNGES**, born about 1385 (aged 60 in 1445). She married **THOMAS MACKWORTH**, Esq., of Mackworth, Derbyshire, Knight of the Shire for Derbyshire, brother of John Mackworth, LL.D., Dean of Lincoln. They had one son, Henry, Esq.[5] THOMAS MACKWORTH, Esq., was living in 1433–4, and died before 1445. His widow, Alice, was heiress in 1445 to her brother, John Basynges, Knt., by which she inherited the manors of Empingham, Hardwick, and Normanton, Rutland. She presented to the church of Normanton, Rutland in 1448, 1452, and 1457. Betham *Baronetage of England* 1 (1801): 167–170 (sub Mackworth). Blore *Hist. & Antiqs. of Rutland* (1811): 127–130 (Basynges-Mackworth ped.). Camden *Vis. of Rutland 1618–19* (H.S.P. 3) (1870): 48–49 (Mackworth ped.: "Thomas Mackworth Esqr who died before Sir John de Basings & his wife = Alice [Basings]."). VCH *Rutland* 2 (1935): 242–250 (Mackworth arms: Party indented sable and ermine a chevron gules fretty or). *English Hist. Rev.* 113 (1998): 1–17. *Virginia Gen.* 50 (2003): 121–130.

v. **MARGERY LA ZOUCHE**, married **ROBERT WILLOUGHBY**, Knt., 4th Lord Willoughby of Eresby [see WILLOUGHBY 10].

10. WILLIAM LA ZOUCHE, Knt., 3rd Lord Zouche of Harringworth, of Totnes, Devon, Harringworth, Northamptonshire, Eaton Bray, Henlow Zouches (in Henlow), Totternhoe, and Wymington, Bedfordshire, Ham (in Waddesdon) and Mentmore, Buckinghamshire, King's Worthy, Hampshire, Buckworth, Huntingdonshire, Belgrave and Ilston, Leicestershire, Clipsham and North Luffenham, Rutland, Bridgwater, Somerset, Calstone (in Calstone Wellington), Wiltshire, etc., son and heir, born about 1342 (aged 40 in 1382). He married (1st) before 27 October 1351 (date of license to grant lands) **AGNES GREENE**, daughter of Henry Greene, Knt., of Boughton, Drayton, and Green's Norton, Northamptonshire, Chief Justice of the King's Bench, by Katherine, daughter of Simon de Drayton, Knt. They had five sons, William, K.G. [4th Lord Zouche of Harringworth], John, Knt., Edmund, Thomas, and Hugh, and one daughter, Eleanor. In 1351 he and his wife, Agnes, were granted the manor of Bridgwater, Somerset in tail by William la Zouche, of Harringworth. He was a legatee in the 1381 will of his father. He presented to the churches of Hope Bowdler, Shropshire, 1385, 1386, and Barby, Northamptonshire, 1389. He accompanied King Richard II on his expedition into Scotland in 1385. In 1386 he and his wife, Agnes, were granted privileges, prayers, masses, etc., by the Abbot and Convent of Dale, with requiems on their anniversaries and on those of their parents. He had license to fortify his manor of Harringworth, Northamptonshire in 1387. He was banished from court in Jan. 1388 by order of the Lords Appellant. In 1388 he released the advowson of the church of Ilkeston, Derbyshire to the Abbey of "La Dale." He and his wife, Agnes, were members of Trinity Guild of Coventry, Warwickshire. His wife, Agnes, died between 2 Dec. 1391 and 28 April 1393. He married (2nd) apparently after 28 April 1393 **ELIZABETH LE DESPENSER**, widow of John de Arundel, Knt., 2nd Lord Arundel (died 14 August 1390) [see ARUNDEL 10], and daughter of Edward le Despenser, K.G., 4th Lord le Despenser, by Elizabeth, daughter and heiress of Bartholomew de Burghersh, K.G., 4th Lord Burghersh [see DESPENSER 13 for her ancestry]. They had no issue. In 1393 he settled the manor of King's Worthy, Hampshire on his brother, Thomas la Zouche, Knt. SIR WILLIAM LA ZOUCHE, 3rd Lord Zouche of Harringworth, died 13 May 1396. He left a will dated 2 May 1396,

---

[5] Henry Mackworth, Esq. (died 1487), of Mackworth, Derbyshire and Empingham, Rutland [see above] is the ancestor of the 17th Century New World immigrant, **Frances Baldwin**, wife successively of [Capt.] Richard Townshend, Esq. (born c.1606, living 1648, died before 7 Feb. 1650/1), of Northumberland County, Virginia, Richard Jones (died before 28 Dec. 1653), of London and York County, Virginia, and [Lt. Col.] Robert Williams (died shortly bef. 6 June 1665), of Stafford County, Virginia. For details regarding the immediate family and extended ancestry of Frances Baldwin, see Blore *Hist. & Antiqs. of Rutland* (1811): 127–130 (Basynges-Mackworth ped.); *VMHB* 2 (1895): 121; *Wm & Mary Quarterly* 1st Ser. 12 (1904): 249; *VMHB* 30 (1922): 323–325; VCH *Rutland* 2 (1935): 244–245; *Virginia Gen.* 48 (2004): 170–184; Dorman *Adventurers of Purse & Person* 3 (2007): 408–427. *Townsend Soc. Gen. Jour.* 6(1) (2008)]. Jeffery A. Duvall outlined Frances Baldwin's line of descent from the Zouche family of Harringworth in *Virginia Gen.* 50 (2006): 121–129.

proved 4 June 1396, requesting burial in the chapel within the manor at Harringworth, Northamptonshire. His widow, Elizabeth, was granted license for the private celebration of divine services in 1404. Elizabeth died 10 (or 11) April 1408. She left a will dated 4 April 1408, requesting burial at Tewkesbury Abbey, Gloucestershire near her brothers.

> Dugdale *Antiqs. of Warwickshire* (1730): 58 (Cantelowe-Zouche ped.). *Topographer* 1 (1789): 195–204. Bridges *Hist. & Antiqs. of Northamptonshire* 1 (1791): 25; 2 (1791): 315–318. Blomefield *Essay towards a Top. Hist. of Norfolk* 10 (1809): 365. Kennett *Parochial Antiqs. of Ambrosden, Burcester* 2 (1818): 465–466. Chitty *Practical Treatise on the Criminal Law* 4 (1819): 299 (Roos-Zouche ped.). Banks *Baronies in Fee* 1 (1844): 469–471 (sub Zouche of Haryngworth). Lipscomb *Hist. & Antiqs. of Buckingham* 1 (1847): 176 (Cantilupe-Zouche ped.). Eyton *Antiqs. of Shropshire* 5 (1857) : 121. Burke *Dormant, Abeyant, Forfeited & Extinct Peerages* (1883): 165–167 (sub Despenser). Money *Hist. of Newbury* (1887): 157–158. Gibbons *Early Lincoln Wills 1280–1547* (1888): 92–93 (will of William la Zouche), 93 (will of William la Zouche). *Desc. Cat. Ancient Deeds* 2 (1894): 410–421; 3 (1900): 477–488. *Genealogist* n.s. 13 (1896): 242. Trueman *Hist. of Ilkeston* (1899). Wrottesley *Peds. from the Plea Rolls* (1905): 161, 166. Jeayes *Desc. Cat. Derbyshire Charters* (1906): 116 (Sir Henry de la Grene, Knt. named as the father of Agnes, wife of William la Zouche, lord of Totnes and Harringworth, in grant dated 1386), 184 (release of William la Zouche, 3rd Baron of Totnes and Harringworth, dated 1388). *C.P.R.* 1350–1354 (1907): 170, 176. VCH *Bedford* 2 (1908): 280–285; 3 (1912): 117–122, 369–375, 447–451. *C.P.R.* 1350–1354 (1907): 170. VCH *Buckingham* 2 (1908): 332, 361; 3 (1925): 397–401; 4 (1927): 107–118. VCH *Hampshire* 4 (1911): 431. *C.Ch.R.* 5 (1916): 307. Watkin *Hist. of Totnes Priory & Medieval Town, Devonshire* 2 (1917): 722–726. Harris *Reg. of the Guild of the Holy Trinity, St. Mary, St. John the Baptist & St. Katherine of Coventry* 1 (Dugdale Soc. 13) (1935): 90, 110. VCH *Rutland* 2 (1935): 41–45, 182–188, 195–203. VCH *Huntingdon* 3 (1936): 22–26. Paget *Baronage of England* (1957) 581: 1–11 (sub Zouche). VCH *Leicester* 4 (1958): 420–428; 5 (1964): 163–166. *C.P.* 12(2) (1959): 942–943 (sub Zouche). *Procs. Suffolk Inst. of Arch.* 29(1) (1962): 34–66 (Naunton ped. dated 18th century). Repingdon *Reg. of Philip Repingdon* 1 (Lincoln Rec. Soc. 57) (1963): 83. Hector *Westminster Chron. 1381–1394* (1982): 230–231. Taylor *English Hist. Lit. in the 14th Cent.* (1987): 233. Payling *Political Soc. in Lancastrian England* (1991): 243 (chart). VCH *Somerset* 6 (1992): 208–213. Sainty *Judges of England* (Selden Soc. Supp. Ser. 10) (1993): 8, 65 (re. Henry Green). *Nottingham Medieval Studies* 41 (1997): 126–156. VCH *Wiltshire* 17 (2002): 123–135. Saul *14th Cent. England* 5 (2008): 91–92.

Children of William la Zouche, Knt., by Agnes Greene:

i. **WILLIAM LA ZOUCHE**, K.G., 4th Lord Zouche of Harringworth [see next].

ii. **ELEANOR LA ZOUCHE**, married **JOHN LOVEL**, Knt., 6th Lord Lovel, Lord Holand [see LOVEL 13.i].

11. WILLIAM LA ZOUCHE, K.G., 4th Lord Zouche of Harringworth, of Totnes, Devon, Harringworth, Northamptonshire, Eaton Bray, Thorn (in Houghton Regis), and Totternhoe, Bedfordshire, Ellesborough and Stoke Mandeville, Buckinghamshire, Thorpe Arnold, Leicestershire, Clipsham, Rutland, Bridgwater, Haygrove, and Odcombe, Somerset, Calstone (in Calstone Wellington), Wiltshire, etc., Lieutenant of Calais, 1413–14, son and heir, born about 1373 (aged 23 in 1396). He married before 1402 **ELIZABETH** _____, said to be a daughter of William Crosse, Knt. They had two sons, William [5th Lord Zouche of Harringworth] and John, Esq., and one daughter, Margaret (wife of Edmund Lenthall, Esq., and Thomas Tresham, Knt.). In 1400 he was granted 100 marks yearly at the Exchequer. In 1402 he attended the Princess Blanche to Heidelberg for her marriage to the Duke of Bavaria. The same year he was a commissioner to treat with Owain Glyn Dŵr for the ransom of Reynold Grey, Lord Grey of Ruthin. In Nov. 1402–Jan. 1402/3 he escorted Joan of Navarre, Duchess of Brittany, to England for her marriage to King Henry IV of England. He presented to the churches of Barby, Northamptonshire, 1403, 1405, and Bulwick, Northamptonshire, 1406, 1407, and to the chantry of Weston, Warwickshire, 1400. He was heir in 1404 to his uncle, Thomas la Zouche, Knt., by which he inherited the manor of Ellesborough, Buckinghamshire; the reversion had already been granted by William la Zouche to Henry, Bishop of Lincoln, in 1402. In 1404–5 William Keresley and Thomas-atte-Chirche of Stoke were appointed arbitrators to determine the "discord and controversy" between William la Zouche, lord of Harringworth, and John Stones, of Eton, of the one part and Rowland Damet, of Coventry, of the other part, regarding right and title to certain lands and tenements in Folkeshull. In 1413 he was appointed a commissioner to treat with the ambassadors of the King of Aragón and later the same year with the Duke of Burgundy. In 1415 he was one of the peers who took part in the trial of the

Earl of Cambridge and Lord Scrope. SIR WILLIAM LA ZOUCHE, 4th Lord Zouche of Harringworth, died 3 Nov. 1415. His widow, Elizabeth, married (2nd) without license before 1 July 1416 **WILLIAM CARNELL**, Esq., who was living 1 April 1430. Elizabeth, Lady Zouche, died shortly before 20 Nov. 1425.

Rymer *Foedera* 9 (1729): 34–36, 56 (William la Zouche, Lord Zouche, Lieutenant of Calais styled "kinsman" by King Henry V of England in 1413). Dugdale *Antiqs. of Warwickshire* (1730): 58 (Cantelowe-Zouche ped.), 61. *Topographer* 1 (1789): 195–204. Bridges *Hist. & Antiqs. of Northamptonshire* 1 (1791): 25; 2 (1791): 289, 315–318. Blomefield *Essay towards a Top. Hist. of Norfolk* 10 (1809): 365. Kennett *Parochial Antiqs. of Ambrosden, Burcester* 2 (1818): 465–466. Chitty *Practical Treatise on the Criminal Law* 4 (1819): 299 (Roos-Zouche ped.). Lipscomb *Hist. & Antiqs. of Buckingham* 1 (1847): 176 (Cantilupe-Zouche ped.). Money *Hist. of Newbury* (1887): 168–169. Gibbons *Early Lincoln Wills 1280–1547* (1888): 93 (will of William la Zouche). *Genealogist* n.s. 13 (1896): 242. *MSS. of Shrewsbury and Coventry Corporations* (Hist. MSS. Comm.) (1899): 142. *Procs. Bath Natural Hist. & Antiq. Field Club* 9 (1901): 188–201. VCH *Buckingham* 2 (1908): 332, 361. Watkin *Hist. of Totnes Priory & Medieval Town, Devonshire* 2 (1917): 722–726. VCH *Rutland* 2 (1935): 195–203. Paget *Baronage of England* (1957) 581: 1–11 (sub Zouche). C.P. 12(2) (1959): 943–944 (sub Zouche). Roskell *Parl. & Politics in Late Medieval England* 2 (1981): 267–277 (biog. of Sir Thomas Tresham). *Cal. IPM* 20 (1995): 126–133. VCH *Wiltshire* 17 (2002): 123–135.

Children of William la Zouche, K.G., by Elizabeth _____:

i. **WILLIAM ZOUCHE**, Knt., 5th Lord Zouche of Harringworth, and, in right of his 1st wife, Lord Saint Maur, son and heir, born 10 (or 12, 20) May 1402 (or 1404) (aged variously 12 in 1415, 13, 14, or 15 in 1416). He married (1st) before 8 March 1423/4 **ALICE SEYMOUR**, daughter and heiress of Richard Seymour, Lord Saint Maur and Lovel, by Mary, daughter of Thomas Peyvre. She was born in the parish of St. Laurence in Cripplegate Ward, London 24 July 1409. They had one son, William [6th Lord Zouche of Harringworth, Lord Saint Maur and Lovel]. In 1429 he and his wife, Alice, conveyed the manor of Wittenham (in Wingfield), Wiltshire to Walter Hungerford, 1st Lord Hungerford. In 1430 John Peyvre quitclaimed to William and his wife, Alice, the manor of Toddington, Bedfordshire and other manors in Buckinghamshire. He presented to the churches of North Barrow, Somerset, 1428, 1430, 1433, 1439; Almsford, Somerset, 1437, 1449, 1453; Barby, Northamptonshire, 1437; Bratton, Somerset, 1442, 1445, 1451, 1454, 1462; and Bulwick, Northamptonshire, 1447, and to the chantry of Weston, Warwickshire, 1432, 1438, 1441, 1451, 1452. He married (2nd) before 2 April 1450 **ELIZABETH SAINT JOHN** [see SAINT JOHN 15.v], daughter of Oliver Saint John, Knt., of Fonmon and Penmark, Glamorgan, Wales, and Paulerspury, Northamptonshire, by Margaret, daughter of John Beauchamp, Knt. [see SAINT JOHN 15 for her ancestry]. They had one daughter, Margaret (wife of William Catesby, Esq.). SIR WILLIAM ZOUCHE, Lord Zouche and Saint Maur, died 25 Dec. 1462. His widow, Elizabeth, was godmother to the future King Edward V in 1470. She married (2nd) before 10 Dec. 1471 (as his 2nd wife) **JOHN SCROPE**, K.G., 5th Lord Scrope of Bolton, son and heir of Henry le Scrope, Knt., 4th Lord Scrope of Bolton, by Elizabeth, daughter of John le Scrope, Knt., 4th Lord Scrope of Masham, Lord High Treasurer [see TIBETOT 13 for his ancestry]. They had one daughter, Mary (wife of William Conyers, Knt., 1st Lord Conyers). His wife, Elizabeth, was living in 1489, and died before 3 July 1494. He married (3rd) before 3 July 1494 **ANNE HARLING**, widow of William Chamberlain, K.G. (died 1462) and Robert Wingfield (died shortly before 13 Nov. 1481), and daughter and heiress of Robert Harling, Knt., of East Harling, Norfolk, by Jane, daughter and heiress of Edmund Gunville. They had no issue. SIR JOHN SCROPE, 5th Lord Scrope of Bolton, died 17 August 1498. He left a will dated 3 July 1494 and 8 August 1498, proved 8 Nov. 1498. His widow, Anne, died 18 Sept. 1498. She left a will dated 28 August 1498, proved 8 Nov. 1498. Dugdale *Antiqs. of Warwickshire* (1730): 58 (Cantelowe-Zouche ped.), 61. *Topographer* 1 (1789): 195–204. Bridges *Hist. & Antiqs. of Northamptonshire* 1 (1791): 25; 2 (1791): 289, 315–318. Nichols *Hist. & Antiqs. of Leicester* 3(2) (1804): 635 (Zouch ped.). Banks *Dormant & Extinct Baronage of England* 2 (1808): 230 (Zouche ped.). Blomefield *Essay towards a Top. Hist. of Norfolk* 10 (1809): 365. Brydges *Collins' Peerage of England* 6 (1812): 42–61 (sub St. John Viscount Bolingbroke and St. John). Kennett *Parochial Antiqs. of Ambrosden, Burcester* 2 (1818): 465–466. Nicolas *Testamenta Vetusta* 2 (1826): 435–436 (will of Ann Lady Scrope). *Coll. Top. et Gen.* 1 (1834): 310–311 (St. John ped.: "Elizabeth [Saint John], wedded first to the Lord Zouche; after to the Lord Scrope of Bolton), 408. Banks *Baronies in Fee* 1 (1844): 404–405 (sub St. Maur). Lipscomb *Hist. & Antiqs. of Buckingham* 1 (1847): 176 (Cantilupe-Zouche ped.). Charles *Vis. of Huntingdon 1613* (Camden Soc. 43) (1849): 2 (St. John ped.: "Elizabetha [St. John], ux. Wm. Do. Zouche de Haringworth."). *Testamenta Eboracensia* 4 (Surtees Soc. 53) (1869): 94–97 (will of John [Scrope] Lord Scrope). Harvey et al. *Vis. of Bedfordshire 1566, 1582, 1634 & 1669* (H.S.P. 19) (1884): 51–54 (Saint John ped.: "Elizabeth [Saint John] first maryed to William Lord Zouche, after to the Lord Scrope."). *Norfolk Arch.* 10 (1888): 382. Weaver *Somerset Incumbents* (1889): 7, 17, 31. *MSS of the Duke of Rutland* 4 (Hist. MSS Comm. 24) (1905): 87 (seal of William lord la Zouche dated 1439 — Zouche, with a canton ermine, quartering : 1 and 4, two chevrons [SEYMOUR]; 2 and 3, a lion rampant [LOVEL]. Crest an ass's head. Supporters: two eagles. Legend: SIGILLUM WILLMI DNI LA ZOUCHE ET D[E SEYMOR] AC DE

TOTTENEIS ET DE HARINGWORTH.). Macklin *Brasses of England* (1907): 267–268. VCH *Buckingham* 2 (1908): 332. Burke *Gen. & Heraldic Hist. of the Peerage & Baronetage* (76th ed., 1914): 262–264 (sub Bolingbroke). Watkin *Hist. of Totnes Priory & Medieval Town, Devonshire* 2 (1917): 722–726. Beckington *Reg. of Thomas Bekynton Bishop of Bath & Wells* 1 (Somerset Rec. Soc. 49) (1934): 271. *C.P.* 11 (1949): 361–362 (sub Saint Maur), 544–546 (sub Scrope); 12(2) (1959): 944–945 (sub Zouche). VCH *Wiltshire* 7 (1953): 69–76. Paget *Baronage of England* (1957) 581: 1–11 (sub Zouche). Ellis *Cat. Seals in the P.R.O.* 1 (1978): 74 (seal of William la Zouche, Knt., Lord Zouche and Seymour dated 1439 — A shield of arms, couché: quarterly, 1 and 4, bezanty and a canton ermine, 2 and 3, two chevrons quartering a lion rampant; helm above in profile with mantling and crest: a horse's head; upon either side an eagle with wings spread and beak open. Legend: SIGILLU WILLMI DNI LA [ZOU]CHE & DE SEYMO' AC DE [TOTTENEIS & DE HARING]WORTH). *Cal. IPM* 20 (1995): 126–133. VCH *Somerset* 7 (1999): 50–59, 164–170; 192–201, 215. Eales & Tyas *Fam. & Dynasty in Late Medieval England* (Harlaxton Medieval Studies n.s. 9) (2003): 193–210. Nottinghamshire Archives: Foljambe of Osberton: Deeds & Estate Papers, DD/FJ/1/30/5; DD/FJ/1/30/6 (available at www.a2a.org.uk/search/index.asp).

  ii. **JOHN ZOUCHE**, Esq., of Bulwick, Northamptonshire, married **ELIZABETH GREY** [see CODNOR 15].

~ CAREW ~

ROGER D'AUBENEY, married **AMICE** _____.
WILLIAM D'AUBENEY, of Buckenham, Norfolk, married **MAUD LE BIGOD**.
WILLIAM D'AUBENEY, of Buckenham, Norfolk, married **ALICE OF LOUVAIN**, Queen of England.
WILLIAM D'AUBENEY, 2nd Earl of Arundel, married **MAUD DE SAINT HILARY**.
WILLIAM D'AUBENEY, Earl of Arundel, married **MABEL OF CHESTER** (desc. King William the Conqueror).
ISABEL D'AUBENEY, married **JOHN FITZ ALAN**, of Clun, Shropshire.
JOHN FITZ ALAN, Knt., of Oswestry, Shropshire, married **MAUD DE VERDUN**.
JOHN FITZ ALAN, of Arundel, Sussex, married **ISABEL DE MORTIMER** (desc. King William the Conqueror).
RICHARD FITZ ALAN, Knt., Earl of Arundel, married **ALICE DI SALUZZO** (desc. King William the Conqueror).
EDMUND DE ARUNDEL, Knt., Earl of Arundel, married **ALICE DE WARENNE**.
RICHARD DE ARUNDEL, Knt., Earl of Arundel and Surrey, married **ISABEL LE DESPENSER** (desc. King William the Conqueror).
EDMUND DE ARUNDEL, Knt., of Chedzoy, Somerset, married **SIBYL DE MONTAGU** (desc. King William the Conqueror) [see APPLETON 12].

13. ELIZABETH ARUNDEL, daughter and co-heiress. She married (1st) **LEONARD DE CAREW** (or **CARREU**, **CARREW**), Knt., Baron Carew, of Carew Castle, Pembrokeshire, Ottery Mohun (in Luppit), Galmpton (in Churston Ferrers), Mamhead, and Stoke Fleming, Devon, Moulsford, Berkshire, Balymaclythan, co. Meath and Idrone, co. Carlow, Ireland, son and heir of John de Carew, Knt., Baron Carew, of Carew Castle, Pembrokeshire, Ottery Mohun (in Luppit) and Galmpton(in Churston Ferrers), Devon, Idrone, co. Carlow, Ireland, etc., King's Escheator in Ireland, Justiciar of Ireland, by his 1st wife, Margaret, daughter of John de Mohun, Knt. [see BRYAN 11 for his ancestry]. He was born at Stoke Fleming, Devon 23 April 1342. They had one son, Thomas, Knt. [Baron Carew]. SIR LEONARD DE CAREW died 9 October 1369. His widow, Elizabeth, married (2nd) about 29 Sept. 1373 (as his 2nd wife) **JOHN DE MERIET**, Knt., of Merriott, Shepton Mallet, and Welweton (in Midsomer Norton), Somerset, Dullingham, Cambridgeshire, etc. They had no issue. He was co-heir in 1361 to his uncle, John de Beauchamp, 4th Lord Beauchamp of Hatch. In 1382 his wife, Elizabeth, and her sister, Philippe, sued their uncle, Richard de Arundel, Earl of Arundel and Surrey, for possession of tenements in Singleton, Sussex. Elizabeth died between 29 Sept. 1385 and March 1386. SIR JOHN DE MERIET died in 1391.

  Pole *Colls. towards a Desc. of Devon* (1791): 133–136 (Carew arms: Or, three lions passant sable). Betham *Baronetage of England* 2 (1802): 283–289 (sub Carew). Prince *Worthies of Devon* (1810): 158–161. *Journal of the Royal Hist. & Arch. Assoc. of Ireland* 4th Ser. 1 (1870–71): 167–168. St. George & Lennard *Vis. of Cornwall 1620* (H.S.P. 9) (1874): 28–32 (Carew ped.). Colby *Vis. of Devon 1564* (1881): 34–35 (Carew ped.: "Leonard, Baron Carew. = Alice, d. of Edw. Arundell."), 37–41 (Carew ped.: "Leonardus de Carew, miles dnus. et Baro de Hidron, heres Inq. 46 E. 3. = Alicia, f.

Edm. Arundell."). *Procs. Somerset Arch. & Nat. Hist. Soc.* 28(2) (1883): 99–215 (article on Meriet fam.). *D.N.B.* 9 (1887): 53–54 (biog. of Sir John Carew). Rogers *Mems. of the West* (1888): 286–327. Vivian *Vis. of Devon 1531, 1564 & 1620* (1895): 133–136 (Carew ped.). *Genealogist* n.s. 18 (1902): 31–32. *Ancestor* 5 (1903): 19–53. Wrottesley *Peds. from the Plea Rolls* (1905): 208–209, 363. VCH *Hampshire* 4 (1911): 338 (Carew arms: Or three lions passant sable). *C.P.R.* 1370–1374 (1914): 380. VCH *Berkshire* 3 (1923): 505–506. *Cal. IPM* 11 (1935): 469–470; 12 (1938): 376–377, 417–418. Rees *Cal. Ancient Petitions Rel. Wales* (Board of Celtic Studies, Hist. & Law 28) (1975): 485. VCH *Somerset* 4 (1978): 90. *Year Books of Richard II* 2 (Ames Found. 3) (1996): 66–69. National Archives, CP 25/1/44/62, #17 [see abstract of fine at http://www.medievalgenealogy.org.uk/index.html].

14. THOMAS CAREW, Knt., Baron Carew, of Carew Castle, Pembrokeshire, Ottery Mohun (in Luppit), Galmpton (in Churston Ferrers), Mamhead, Stoke Fleming, and Weston Peverell, Devon, Charlton (in Wantage) and Moulsford, Berkshire, Amport, Hampshire, and Balymaclythan, co. Meath, Ireland, etc., King's knight, Constable of Narberth Castle in Pembrokeshire, Captain of Harfleur, son and heir, born about 1368 (aged 1 in 1369). He married before 1395 **ELIZABETH BONVILLE**, daughter of William Bonville, Knt., of Shute and Wiscombe (in Southleigh), Devon, Sock Dennis, Somerset, etc. [see BONVILLE 9], by his 1st wife, Margaret, daughter and co-heiress of William Daumarle, Knt. They had two sons, Nicholas, Knt. [Baron Carew], and Hugh, and one daughter, Elizabeth (wife of Thomas Tremayne). In 1394 he was going to Ireland in the king's company. He took a prominent part in the Welsh wars against Owen Glendower. In 1403 they received a papal indult for a portable altar. He was granted the castle and town of St. Clears in 1404. He was at the Siege of Aberystwyth in 1407. His wife, Elizabeth, was a legatee in the 1407 will of her father. He seems to have engaged in trade in Dartmouth in joint ownership of boats and was active in the capture of shipping from Spain, Gascony, and La Rochelle. He presented to the churches of Mamhead, Devon, 1410, 1417, 1426, and Stoke Fleming, Devon, 1419. He was commissioned to guard the Channel at the time of Emperor Sigismund's visit to England in 1415. He served on the sea under Edmund Mortimer, Earl of March with 40 men-at-arms and 80 archers in 1417. In 1422 he was sent as ambassador to negotiate in secret with the King of Portugal. SIR THOMAS CAREW, Baron Carew, died testate 25 Jan. 1430/1. His widow, Elizabeth, presented to the church of Mamhead, Devon in 1434. She was living 11 Dec. 1435, but died before 1 Nov. 1452.

Pole *Colls. towards a Desc. of Devon* (1791): 130. Betham *Baronetage of England* 2 (1802): 283–289 (sub Carew) ("Sir Thomas Carew ... was a brave soldier, and had the charge of the navy, and 3000 English soldiers committed to him, for securing the Emperor, during his abode in England"). Prince *Worthies of Devon* (1810): 158–161. Oliver *Ecclesiastical Antiqs. in Devon* 3 (1842): 66. St. George & Lennard *Vis. of Cornwall 1620* (H.S.P. 9) (1874): 28–32 (Carew ped.). Colby *Vis. of Devon 1564* (1881): 34–35 (Carew ped.: "Thomas, Baron Carew. = Elizab., d. of Will. Bonvill, Knt."), 37–41 (Carew ped.: "Thomas de Carew, miles Baro de Hydron, Inq. 9 H. 6. = Eliz., f. Will Bonville militis et baronis"). Hingeston-Randolph *Reg. of Edmund Stafford (A.D. 1395–1419)* (1886): 186, 210, 391–393 (will of William Bonevylle, Knt.). *D.N.B.* 9 (1887): 53–54 (biog. of Sir John Carew). Rogers *Mems. of the West* (1888): 286–327. Vivian *Vis. of Devon 1531, 1564 & 1620* (1895): 133–136 (Carew ped.). *Genealogist* n.s. 18 (1902): 31–32. *Papal Regs.: Letters* 5 (1904): 568. *C.P.R.* 1391–1396 (1905): 486. Wrottesley *Peds. from the Plea Rolls* (1905): 208–209, 363. *D.N.B.* 3 (1908): 962–963 (biog. of Sir John Carew). VCH *Hampshire* 4 (1911): 338. *C.P.R.* 1370–1374 (1914): 380. Wedgwood *Hist. of Parl.* 1 (1936): 868 (biog. of Thomas Tremayne). *C.C.R.* 1435–1441 (1937): 161–162. Chichele *Reg. of Henry Chichele* 2 (Canterbury & York Soc. 42) (1937): 644 (biog. of Thomas Carew). *C.C.R.* 1447–1454 (1941–7): 377–378. Palmer *Collectanea III: Coll. of Docs. from various Sources* (Somerset Rec. Soc. 57) (1942): 40. Rees *Cal. Ancient Petitions Rel. Wales* (Board of Celtic Studies, Hist. & Law 28) (1975): 482. *Cal. IPM* 23 (2004): 272–273. National Archives, CP 25/1/44/62, #17 [see abstract of fine at http://www.medievalgenealogy.org.uk/index.html]. Plymouth & West Devon Rec. Office: Bewes, Dickinson & Scott, Solicitors of Plymouth, 81/R/12/6/26; 81/R/12/6/27; 81/R/12/6/28 (available at www.a2a.org.uk/search/index.asp).

15. NICHOLAS CAREW, Knt., Baron Carew, of Carew Castle, Pembrokeshire, Ottery Mohun (in Luppit), Galmpton (in Churston Ferrers), and Mamhead, Devon, Moulsford, Berkshire, and Amport, Hampshire, and, in right of his wife, of Haccombe, Clifford (in Dunsford), Leigh Challons, and Nitherton, Devon, son and heir, born about 1409 (aged 22 in 1431). He married **JOAN COURTENAY**, daughter of Hugh Courtenay, Knt., of Haccombe and Bampton, Devon, by his 3rd wife, Philippe, daughter and co-heiress of Warin l'Arcedekne, Knt. [see COURTENAY 9 for her ancestry]. She was born about 1411–4 (aged 4 in 1418, aged 14 in March 1425). She was co-heiress in 1418 to her aunt, Philippe Talbot, wife of John Tiptoft, 1st Lord Tiptoft and Powis, and co-heiress in 1420 to her aunt, Margery l'Arcedekne, wife of Thomas Arundell, Knt. They had five sons, Thomas, Esq. [Baron Carew], Nicholas, Hugh, Alexander, and William, Knt., and three daughters, Jane (wife of _____ Talbot), Elizabeth (wife of John Challons), and Florence (nun). In 1438 he and his wife, Joan, sued Tristan, Abbot of St. Mary, Newenham, and another for the next presentation of the church of Luppitt, Devon. He presented to the church of Haccombe, Devon in 1434 and 1446. SIR NICHOLAS CAREW died intestate shortly before 20 April 1448. In 1449 William Kyrkeby sued his widow, Joan, and John of Ile, administrators of the estate of the said Nicholas, regarding a bond made in 1446 by the said Nicholas in the amount of £12 12s. Joan married (2nd) by license dated 5 October 1450 **ROBERT VERE**, Knt., in right of his wife, of Haccombe, Devon, Captain of Caen, Normandy, Knight of the Shire for Devonshire, Chamberlain to Henry Holand, Duke of Exeter [see HACCOMBE 8 for issue of this marriage]. SIR ROBERT VERE was slain in Cornwall shortly before 18 April 1461. His widow, Joan, died shortly before 3 August 1465.

Pole *Colls. towards a Desc. of Devon* (1791): 130. Betham *Baronetage of England* 2 (1802): 283–289 (sub Carew). Banks *Dormant & Extinct Baronage of England* 1 (1807): 228 (sub Archdekne). Burke *Hist. of the Commoners* 1 (1836): 557. Fuller *Hist. of the Worthies of England* (1840): 427–428. Oliver *Eccl. Antiqs. in Devon* 1 (1840): 160–161. Monro *Letters of Queen Margaret of Anjou & Bishop Beckington* (Camden Soc. 86) (1863): 96–98 (letter of Queen Margaret of Anjou to Joan Courtenay dated 1447–50). *Vis. of Devon 1620* (H.S.P. 6) (1872): 45 (Carew ped.: "Nicho. Baron Carew, eldest son of Thomas = Jone d. of Sir Hugh Courtney, brother to Edw. Erle of Devon") (Carew arms: Or, three lions passant in pale sable). *Antiq.* 3 (1873): 231–233. St. George & Lennard *Vis. of Cornwall 1620* (H.S.P. 9) (1874): 28–32 (Carew ped.). Maclean *Hist. of Trigg Minor* 2 (1876): 240–241 (chart). Colby *Vis. of Devon 1564* (1881): 34–35 (Carew ped.: "Nicholas, Baron Carew. = Joan, d. of Hugh Courtney, Knt., brother of Edw. Earl of Devon & Philippa, d. & coh. of Warren Archdeacon rem.d to Robert Devere, Knt., from whom co. Oxon."), 37–41 (Carew ped.: "Nicholaus de Carrew. = Johanna, f. Hugonis de Courtenay et Philippa f. et coh. Warreni le Archdeacon militis et heres materne hereditatis."). *Notes & Queries* 6th Ser. 7 (1883): 50–52, 369–371. Loftie *Kensington Picturesque & Hist.* (1888): 56–59 (Vere ped.). Rogers *Mems. of the West* (1888): 286–327. Vivian *Vis. of Devon 1531, 1564 & 1620* (1895): 133–136 (Carew ped.), 243–250 (sub Courtenay). *Feudal Aids* 1 (1899): 455, 482, 491, 594. *Genealogist* n.s. 18 (1902): 31–32. Gairdner *Paston Letters, A.D. 1422–1509* (1904): 269. Wrottesley *Peds. from the Plea Rolls* (1905): 363. VCH *Hampshire* 4 (1911): 338. C.F.R. 17 (1937): 272–273, 286–287. Paget *Baronage of England* (1957) 559: 1–3 (sub Vere). Lacy *Reg. of Edmund Lacy* 1 (Devon & Cornwall Rec. Soc. n.s. 7) (1963): 284–285; 3 (Devon & Cornwall Rec. Soc. n.s. 13) (1967): 86–87, 392. *Cal. IPM* 20 (1995): 237–238; 23 (2004): 272–273. Cornwall Rec. Office: Rashleigh of Menabilly, Tywardreth, R/3026 — deed of entail dated 12 Nov. 1461 from Lady Joan wife of Sir Robert Vere to Nicholas Goffe, et al. (available at www.a2a.org.uk/search/index.asp). Devon Rec. Office: Buckland in the Moor, 74/9/2/2 — charter dated 12 Nov. 1461 by Joan late the wife of Robert Veer Knt., to Nicholas Gosse, et al. (available at www.a2a.org.uk/search/index.asp). Plymouth & West Devon Rec. Office: Woollcombe of Hemerdon, 710/53 — power of atty. dated 12 Nov. 1461 from [Joan] wife of Robert Veer, Knt. (available at www.a2a.org.uk/search/index.asp). Court of Common Pleas, CP 40/755, rot. 407 (available at http:// www.british-history.ac.uk/source.aspx?pubid=1272).

16. THOMAS CAREW, Esq., Baron Carew, of Carew Castle, Pembrokeshire, Mamhead, Ottery Mohun (in Luppit), Galmpton (in Churston Ferrers), and Monkton, Devon, and, in right of his wife, of Ashwater, Devon, son and heir, born about 1427 (of age in 1448). He married **JOAN CARMINOW**, daughter and co-heiress of Thomas Carminow, of Boconnoc, Cornwall and Ashwater, Devon, by Joan, daughter of Robert Hill. They had one son, Nicholas, Knt. [Baron Carew], and two daughters, Isabel and Margaret. THOMAS CAREW, Esq., died before 10 Nov. 1461. His widow, Joan, married (2nd) before Trinity term 1477 (date of lawsuit) **HALNATH MAULEVERER**, of Allerton Mauleverer, Yorkshire, usher in King Edward IV's household, Sheriff of Cornwall, 1470, Sheriff of Devon, 1479–80, 1483–4, Constable of Launceston Castle, Esquire of the Body for King Richard III, younger son of John Mauleverer, by Isabel, daughter of Thomas Markenfield, Knt. He was admitted a member of Lincoln's Inn in 1478. His wife, Joan, left a will proved 12 April 1502 (P.C.C. 73 Blamyr).

Pole *Colls. towards a Desc. of Devon* (1791): 130, 352. Betham *Baronetage of England* 2 (1802): 283–289 (sub Carew). Burke *Hist. of the Commoners* 1 (1836): 557. *Vis. of Devon 1620* (H.S.P. 6) (1872): 45 (Carew ped.: "Thomas Carew, 1 s., of Mohun Awtrie"). *Antiq.* 3 (1873): 231–233. St. George & Lennard *Vis. of Cornwall 1620* (H.S.P. 9) (1874): 28–32 (Carew ped.). Maclean *Hist. of Trigg Minor* 2 (1876): 240–241 (chart); 3 (1879): 155, 160. Colby *Vis. of Devon 1564* (1881): 34–35 (Carew ped.: "Thomas Carew."), 37–41 (Carew ped.: "Thomas, Baron de Carew. = Jana, fil. et h. Tho. Carminow."). *Notes & Queries* 6th Ser. 7 (1883): 369–371. Vivian *Vis. of Cornwall* (1887): 296–300 (Carminowe ped.). Rogers *Mems. of the West* (1888): 286–327. Boase *Reg. of Exeter College, Oxford* (1894): liii, 268. Vivian *Vis. of Devon 1531, 1564 & 1620* (1895): 133–136 (Carew ped.). Baildon *Recs. of Lincoln's Inn: Admissions* 1 (1896): 21. *List of Sheriffs for England & Wales* (PRO Lists and Indexes 9) (1898): 22, 36. *List of Early Chancery Procs.* 1 (PRO Lists and Indexes 12) (1901): 323, 344. *C.F.R.* 20 (1949): 3, 38–39, 132. Kirby *Plumpton Letters & Papers* (Camden Soc. 5th Ser. 8) (1996): 321–322 (biog. of Halnath Mauleverer). Biancalana *Fee Tail & the Common Recovery in Medieval England: 1176–1502* (2001): 399–400.

17. NICHOLAS CAREW, Esq., Baron Carew, of Carew Castle, Pembrokeshire, Ottery Mohun (in Luppit), Devon, Sheriff of Devonshire, 1469–70, son and heir, born about 1444 (of age in 1465). He married after 26 October 1461 (grant of his marriage) **MARGARET** (or **MARGERY**) **DINHAM**, daughter of John Dinham, Knt., of Hartland, Kingskerwell, and Nutwell, Devon, by Joan, daughter of Richard Arches, Knt. [see DINHAM 8 for her ancestry]. They had two sons, Edmund, Knt. [Baron Carew], and John, Knt., and one daughter, Jane (wife of Robert Cary). NICHOLAS CAREW, Esq., died shortly before 21 Nov. 1470. His widow, Margaret, died 13 Dec. 1471. Both were buried in Westminster Abbey.

Pole *Colls. towards a Desc. of Devon* (1791): 130. Betham *Baronetage of England* 2 (1802): 285. Prince *Worthies of Devon* (1810): 158–161 ("… was a very eminent person, and great at court"). Burke *Hist. of the Commoners* 1 (1836): 557. Westcote *View of Devonshire in MDCXXX* (1845): 199–200. St. George & Lennard *Vis. of Cornwall 1620* (H.S.P. 9) (1874): 28–32 (Carew ped.). Maclean *Hist. of Trigg Minor* 2 (1876): 240–241 (chart). Colby *Vis. of Devon 1564* (1881): 37–41 (Carew ped.: "Nicholaus Baron de Carew, Inq. 11 E. 4. =- Margarte, soror et coh. Jo. Dom. Dinham."). Rogers *Mems. of the West* (1888): 286–327. Vivian *Vis. of Devon 1531, 1564 & 1620* (1895): 133–136 (Carew ped.). *List of Sheriffs for England & Wales* (PRO Lists and Indexes 9) (1898): 36. *Rpt. & Trans. of the Devonshire Assoc.* 2nd Ser. 4 (1902): 721–723. *C.P.* 4 (1916): 378–382 (sub Dinham). Brookes *Hist. of Steeple Aston & Middle Aston* (1929): 67–73. *Procs. Cambridge Antiq. Soc.* 33 (1933): 61–82. *C.F.R.* 20 (1949): 38–39, 267. Paget *Baronage of England* (1957) 187: 1–9 (sub Dinan). VCH *Oxford* 10 (1972): 42–49; 11 (1983): 295.

18. EDMUND CAREW, Knt., Baron Carew, of Carew Castle, Pembrokeshire, Mamhead and Ottery Mohun, Devon, Amport, Hampshire, etc., son and heir, born about 1461–1464 (aged 6 in 1470, aged 40 in 1501). He was knighted at Bosworth Field in 1485. He married before 16 Jan. 1478/9 (by settlement dated 26 Dec. 1478) **KATHERINE HUDDESFIELD**, daughter and co-heiress of William Huddesfield, Knt., of Shillingford, Farringdon, Widecombe in the Moor, and Witheridge, Devon, Recorder of Exeter, 1479–82, Attorney General to Kings Edward IV and Henry VII [see POYNTZ 11], by his 1st wife, Elizabeth, daughter and co-heiress of John Bosum (or Bosun). They had four sons, William, Knt., Thomas, George [Dean of Bristol and of Exeter, Dean of St. George's Chapel, Windsor, and chapel royal], and Gawen, Knt., and four daughters, Katherine, Dorothy (wife of John Stowell and Hugh Pollard, Knt.), Anne (nun), and Isabel (nun). In 1497 he marched to the relief of Exeter when that city was besieged by the pretender Perkin Warbeck. The same year he sold the manor of Amport, Hampshire to Bartholomew Reed. He was a legatee in the 1497 will of his grandmother, Lady Joan Dinham. He and his wife, Katherine, were also legatees in the 1497 will of her father, William Huddesfield, Knt. He was co-heir in 1501 to his uncle, John Dinham, K.G., Lord Dinham, Treasurer of the Exchequer. He and his fellow Dinham co-heirs presented to the church of Maperton, Somerset in 1505. In 1513 he accompanied King Henry VIII in his expedition to France. To equip himself as Master of the Ordnance for the expedition, he mortgaged Carew Castle and 7 other manors in Wales to Sir Rhys ap Thomas. SIR EDMUND CAREW was slain by a cannon ball as he sat in council at the Siege of Thérouanne in France 24 June 1513. His widow, Katherine, presented to the church of Shillingford, Devon 9 June 1528.

Pole *Colls. towards a Desc. of Devon* (1791): 130. Betham *Baronetage of England* 2 (1802): 283–289 (sub Carew). Prince *Worthies of Devon* (1810): 168 ("[Edmund Carew] was a gallant soldier"). Burke *Hist. of the Commoners* 1 (1836): 557. Oliver *Eccl. Antiqs. in Devon* 2 (1840): 59. *Vis. of Devon 1620* (H.S.P. 6) (1872): 45 (Carew ped.: "Edm. Baron Carew of Mohun Awtrie in com. Devon = d. & h. of Hudsfield"). *Herald & Genealogist* 7 (1873): 19–24. St. George & Lennard *Vis. of Cornwall 1620* (H.S.P. 9) (1874): 28–32 (Carew ped.). Dymond *Things New & Old* (1876): 35. Maclean *Hist. of Trigg Minor* 2 (1876): 240–241 (chart). Colby *Vis. of Devon 1564* (1881): 36 (Carew ped.: "Edward Carew of Otry Mohun, co. Devon, Knt. = Catherine, d. & h. of Will. Huddesfield, of Shillingford, Knt."), 37–41 (Carew ped.: "Edmundus, Baro de Carew. = Cath., f. et h. Will. Hudfield de Shillingford militis."), 139 (Huddesfield ped.: "Catherine [Huddesfield], d. & coh. = Edw. Baron Carew."). Chitting & Phillipot *Vis. of Gloucester 1623, 1569 & 1582–3* (H.S.P. 21) (1885): 130–135 (Poyntz ped.: "Catherina [Huddesfield] altera filiar' et heredum uxor Edmund baronis Carewe."). Rogers *Mems. of the West* (1888): 286–327. Weaver *Somerset Incumbents* (1889): 136. Vivian *Vis. of Devon 1531, 1564 & 1620* (1895): 133–136 (Carew ped.), 162, 418 (with error). *D.N.B.* 3 (1908): 958–959 (biog. of Sir Edmund Carew). VCH *Hampshire* 4 (1911): 338. *C.P.* 4 (1916): 378–382 (sub Dinham). VCH *Berkshire* 3 (1923): 506. Brookes *Hist. of Steeple Aston & Middle Aston* (1929): 67–73. Emden *Biog. Reg. of Univ. of Oxford 1501–1540* (1974): 101–102 (biog. of George Carew). VCH *Oxford* 11 (1983): 295. Cornwall Rec. Office: Arundell of Lanherne & Trerice, AR/37/26 — Pre-nuptial settlement dated 26 Dec. 1478 between Dame Jane Dynham, late wife of John Dynham Knt., and William Huddesfeld, king's attorney, that Edmund Carew, son and heir of Nicholas Carew Baron of Carew, shall marry Katherine, daughter of William Huddesfeld, 'after the lawe of holy churche' before 'the 4th day upon the feast of St Hillary' next [16 January]; and that William Huddesfeld shall before 2nd Feb next have made an estate in law for persons to be named by William Huddesfeld of the [manors] of Mamhede (Devon) and Anneport (Hampshire), to hold for term of Katherine's life to the use of Edmund and Katherine (available at www.a2a.org.uk/search/index.asp).

Children of Edmund Carew, Knt., by Katherine Huddesfield:

i. **WILLIAM CAREW**, Knt., of Ottery Mohun, Devon, son and heir, born about 1483 (aged 30 in 1513). He married **JOAN** (or **JANE**) **COURTENAY**, daughter of William Courtenay, Knt., of East Coker, Somerset, Powderham and Yelton, Devon, etc., by Margaret, daughter of William Bonville, K.G., Lord Bonville [see DAVIE 10.i for her ancestry]. They had three sons, George, Knt., Philip, Knt., and Peter, Knt., and one daughter, Cecily. Betham *Baronetage of England* 2 (1802): 283–289 (sub Carew). *Coll. Top. et Gen.* 7 (1841): 271. St. George et al. *Vis. of Devon 1620* (H.S.P. 6) (1872): 45 (Carew ped.: "William Carew of Mohuns Awtrie = [left blank]"). Trevelyan & Trevelyan eds. *Trevelyan Papers* 3 (Camden Soc. 105) (1872): 14. *Antiq.* 3 (1873): 231–233. St. George & Lennard *Vis. of Cornwall 1620* (H.S.P. 9) (1874): 28–32 (Carew ped.). Colby *Vis. of Devon 1564* (1881): 36 (Carew ped.: "William Carew, Knt., of Mohun Ottery. = Joan, d. of Will. Courtney of Powderham."), 37–41 (Carew ped.: "Gulielmus Carew, miles. = Joh. f. Will. Courteney de Powderham, militis."). Rogers *Mems. of the West* (1888): 286–327. *Western Antiq.* 8 (1889): 240–241. Vivian *Vis. of Devon 1531, 1564 & 1620* (1895): 133–136 (Carew ped.).

Child of William Carew, Knt., by Joan (or Jane) Courtenay:

a. **CECILY CAREW**, married (as his 2nd wife) **THOMAS KIRKHAM** (or **KYRKEHAM**), Esq., of Blackdown, Devon, son of John Kirkham, Knt., Sheriff of Devonshire, by his 3rd wife, Lucy, daughter of Thomas Tremayle. He was born about 1504 (aged 25 in 1529). They had five sons, Henry, William, Richard, Edward, and George, and one daughter, Thomasine. In the period, 1542–3, Joan Dible, of Paignton, Devon, widow of John Dible, sued Thomas Kyrkeham of "Blakedon," Devon, and others: in the Court of Requests regarding a tenement in the borough of Paignton, Devon, held of the Bishop of Exeter. THOMAS KIRKHAM, Esq., died 31 Jan. 1551/2. His widow, Cecily, was heiress in 1575 to her brother, Peter Carew, Knt., by which she inherited the manor of Ottery Mohun, Devon. *Coll. Top. et Gen.* 4 (1837): 361 ("Sir William Carew's only child that left issue, was Cecily, who was the second wife of Sir Thomas Kirkham of Blackdown, in Devon, Knt., by whom she had a daughter Thomasin, wife of Thomas Southcote of Bovey Tracey, whose grandson Thomas recorded his pedigree at the Heralds' Visitation in 1620"); 7 (1841): 271. St. George et al. *Vis. of Devon 1620* (H.S.P. 6) (1872): 161–162 (Kirkham ped.: "Tho. Kirkham 24 H. 8 = Mary d. & h. of Rich. Ferrers & of Jane d. & h. of Sir John Malehearte"). Trevelyan & Trevelyan eds. *Trevelyan Papers* 3 (Camden Soc. 105) (1872): 14. *Antiq.* 3 (1873): 231–233. St. George & Lennard *Vis. of Cornwall 1620* (H.S.P. 9) (1874): 28–32 (Carew ped.). Colby *Vis. of Devon 1564* (1881): 36 (Carew ped.: "Cicily [Carew] = Tho. Kirkham of Blakdon, co. Devon."). Rogers *Mems. of the West* (1888): 286–327 ("At the death of Sir Peter [Carew] the house and estate [of Mohuns-Ottery] passed to his only sister, Cecily, who had married, as his second wife, Thomas Kirkham, the eldest son of Sir John Kirkham, of Blagdon, South Devon. By him she had four sons and a daughter, Thomazine, and singularly, the distaff again was left to carry on the possession of Mohuns-Ottery. She married Thomas Southcott, of Bovey Tracey; and one of her sons, "Thomas Southcott, Esquier," says the antiquary Sir W. Pole, 'nowe dwelling at Mouns-Ottery, maried Kateryn, my second daughter.' About the middle of the seventeenth century, Thomas Southcott, sold the old ancestral place to Sir Walter Yonge, of Great House, Colyton, as we have previously noted."). *Western Antiq.* 8 (1889): 240–241. Vivian *Vis. of Devon 1531, 1564 & 1620* (1895): 133–136 (Carew ped.), 516–517 (Kirkham ped.). National Archives, REQ 2/7/49 (available at www.catalogue.nationalarchives.gov.uk/search.asp).

Child of Cecily Carew, by Thomas Kirkham, Esq.:

1) **THOMASINE KIRKHAM**, married (as his 2nd wife) **THOMAS SOUTHCOTT**, Esq., of Bovey Tracey, Devon, son of John Southcott, of Indiho (in Bovey Tracey), Devon, by Joanna, daughter of _____ Hankford. They had three sons, Thomas, George, and Peter, and six daughters, Frances (wife of Otho Petre), Cecily (wife of William Petre), Ursula (wife of Robert Tracey), Susanna (wife of Thomas Molford), Margaret (wife of Arthur Hill), and Mary. He presented to the church of Shillingford, Devon in 1557 and 1573. THOMAS SOUTHCOTT, Esq., died 10 August 1600. *Coll. Top. et Gen.* 4 (1837): 361 ("Sir William Carew's only child that left issue, was Cecily, who was the second wife of Sir Thomas Kirkham of Blackdown, in Devon, Knt., by whom she had a daughter Thomasin, wife of Thomas Southcote of Bovey Tracey, whose grandson Thomas recorded his pedigree at the Heralds' Visitation in 1620 …"). Oliver *Eccl. Antiqs. in Devon* 2 (1840): 59. *Vis. of Devon 1620* (H.S.P. 6) (1872): 266–267 (Southcote ped.: "Tho. Southcot of Bowey [1] = Grace d. & h. of Barnham, 1 wife, = 2, Suzan d. of Sir Tho. Kirkham, [3] mar. to his 3d wife Eliz., d. of Fitz Will'm"), 268–269 (Southcott ped.: "Tho. Southcott, 1 s., who had 3 wives"), 269 (Southcot ped.: "Thomas Southcott of Bovye = Suzan d. of Sir Thomas Kirkham"). Colby *Vis. of Devon 1564* (1881): 36 (Carew ped.: "Thomazina [Kirkham] = Thomas Southcott of Bovy Tracy, Esq."). Rogers *Mems. of the West* (1888): 286–327. *Western Antiq.* 8 (1889): 240–241. Vivian *Vis. of Devon* (1895): 516–517 (Kirkham ped.), 697–701 (Southcott ped.).

Child of Thomasine Kirkham, by Thomas Southcott, Esq.:

a) **MARY SOUTHCOTT**, married **WILLIAM STRODE**, Knt., of Newnham (in Plympton St. Mary), Devon [see DAVIE 15].

ii. **KATHERINE CAREW**, married **PHILIP CHAMPERNOUN**, Knt., of Modbury, Devon [see DENNY 17].

❧ CAREY ❧

WILLIAM THE CONQUEROR, King of England, married **MAUD OF FLANDERS**.
HENRY I, King of England, married **MAUD OF SCOTLAND**.
MAUD OF ENGLAND, married **GEOFFREY PLANTAGENET**, Count of Anjou, Duke of Normandy.
HENRY II, King of England, married **ELEANOR OF AQUITAINE**.
JOHN, King of England, married **ISABEL OF ANGOULEME**.
HENRY III, King of England, married **ELEANOR OF PROVENCE**.
EDWARD I, King of England, married **ELEANOR OF CASTILE** (desc. King William the Conqueror).
EDWARD II, King of England, married **ISABEL OF FRANCE** (desc. King William the Conqueror).
EDWARD III, King of England, married **PHILIPPE OF HAINAULT** (desc. King William the Conqueror).
JOHN OF GAUNT, K.G., Duke of Aquitaine and Lancaster, married **KATHERINE DE ROET**.
JOHN BEAUFORT, K.G., 1st Earl of Somerset, married **MARGARET HOLAND** (desc. King William the Conqueror).
EDMUND BEAUFORT, K.G., Duke of Somerset, married **ELEANOR BEAUCHAMP** [see SOMERSET 12].

13. ELEANOR BEAUFORT, married (1st) in 1457/8 (as his 2nd wife) **JAMES BUTLER** (or **ORMOND**), K.G., 5th Earl of Ormond [see BUTLER 10.i], of Upton Snodsbury, Worcestershire, Sheriff of Cardigan and Carmarthen, Chief Governor of Ireland, Privy Councillor, Treasurer of England, 1st son and heir apparent of James Boteler, 4th Earl of Ormond, by his 1st wife, Joan, daughter of William Beauchamp, K.G., Lord Bergavenny [see BUTLER 10 for his ancestry]. He was born about 1422 (aged 30 and more in 1452). They had no issue. He was made an honorary member of the Guild of Merchant Taylors of London in 1445–6, as "Sir James de Ormond." He was created Earl of Wiltshire 8 July 1449, and summoned to Parliament 23 Sept. following. He succeeded his father as Earl of Ormond 23 August 1452. He was present at the 1st Battle of St. Albans in 1455. SIR JAMES BUTLER, Earl of Wiltshire and Ormond, fought at the Battle of

Towton 29 March 1461, where he was taken prisoner. He was beheaded at Newcastle 1 May 1461. She married (2nd) about 1465 **ROBERT SPENCER** (or **SPENSER**), Knt., of Ashbury, Devon, Brompton Ralph, Somerset, and, in right of his wife, of Chilton Foliat, Wiltshire, son and heir of John Spencer, Esq., of Frampton, Dorset, Ashbury, Devon, and Brompton Ralph, Somerset, Knight of the Shire for Dorset, by his 1st wife, Joan. They had two daughters, Margaret and Katherine. His wife, Eleanor, was co-heiress in 1471 to her brother, Edmund Beaufort, styled Duke of Somerset. In the period, 1486–3, or 1504–15, as "Robert Spenser, knight, son and heir of John Spenser, esquire," he sued Robert Cotes, feoffee to uses, in Chancery regarding a moiety of the manor and the advowson of the church of Brompton Ralph, Somerset. He presented to the church of Hazelbury Bryan, Dorset in 1493, in right of his wife, Eleanor. In 1496 he and his wife, Eleanor, presented to the church of Hazelbury Bryan, Dorset. His wife, Eleanor, Countess of Wiltshire, died 16 August 1501. SIR ROBERT SPENCER left a will proved 12 April 1510 (P.C.C. 27 Bennett).

>Sandford *Gen. Hist. of the Kings of England* (1677): 323–324. Strachey *Rotuli Parl.* 6 (1777): 452–454. Brydges *Collins' Peerage of England* 1 (1812): 222–243 (sub Somerset, Duke of Beaufort). Fosbroke *Berkeley Manuscripts: Abs. & Extracts of Smyth's Lives of the Berkeleys* (1821): 150–151 (Berkeley ped.). Baker *Hist. & Antiqs. of Northampton* 1 (1822–30): 54–56. *Coll. Top. et Gen.* 1 (1834): 308–309 (Beaufort ped.: "Alianor Countess of Wiltshire, afterwards wedded to Sir Robert Spencer."). Banks *Dormant & Extinct Baronage of England* 4 (1837): 338–348. Lipscomb *Hist. & Antiqs. of Buckingham* 2 (1847): 4–7. Hutchins *Hist. & Antiqs. of Dorset* 1 (1861): 280. *Vis. of Devon 1620* (H.S.P. 6) (1872): 47–50 (Cary ped.: "Elinor [Beaufort], 4 d. = Sir Robt Spencer Kt."). Flower *Vis. of Yorkshire 1563–4* (H.S.P. 16) (1881): 244–246 (Percy ped.: "Elenor Beaufort on of the doughters & heyres [of] Edmond Duke of Somerset = Sir Robert Spencer.") (Spencer arms: Sable, two bars undée Ermine). Smyth *Berkeley MSS* 2 (1883): 28–34. Cooke & St. George *Vis. of Hertfordshire 1572, 1634 & 1546* (H.S.P. 22) (1886): 134–137 (Cary ped.) (Spencer arms: Sable two bars nebulé ermine). Doyle *Official Baronage of England* 3 (1886): 674–675 (sub Wiltshire). Weaver *Somerset Incumbents* (1889): 90. *Desc. Cat. Ancient Deeds* 1 (1890): 477, 500, 502, 558; 5 (1906): 548–565; 6 (1915): 105–119. *C.P.R. 1476–1485* (1901): 106 (Eleanor [Beaufort], Countess of Wiltshire, styled "kinswoman" by King Edward IV of England in 1478). *D.N.B.* 3 (1908): 503 (biog. of James Butler, 5th Earl of Ormond). Bradney *Hist. of Monmouthshire* 2(1) (1911): 25–28 (Somerset ped.). *List of Early Chancery Procs.* 5 (PRO Lists and Indexes 38) (1912): 264 (identification of parents of Robert Spencer). VCH *Worcester* 4 (1924): 209. *C.P.* 9 (1936): 719–720 (sub Northumberland); 10 (1945): 126–129 (sub Ormond); 12(2) (1959): 734 (sub Wiltshire). Wedgwood *Hist. of Parl.* 1 (1936): 786–787 (biog. of John Spencer), 435 (biog. of Richard Hatfield). *Berkshire Arch. Jour.* 44 (1940): 114–115. *TAG* 19 (1942–43): 197–202. Lamborn *Armorial Glass of the Oxford Diocese* (1949): 14–15. *Ancient Deeds — Ser. B* 1 (List & Index Soc. 95) (1973): 80 (B.4486); 2 (List & Index Soc. 101) (1974): B.5415–5416. VCH *Somerset* 3 (1974): 111–120. VCH *Somerset* 5 (1985): 21. Leese *Blood Royal* (1996): 229–234. Baker *Rpts. of Cases by John Caryll* 2 (Selden Soc. 116) (2000): 650–653. Beadle & Richmond *Paston Letters & Papers of the 15th Cent.* 3 (2005): 26–28 ([Robert] Spencer styled "brother" by William Paston in letter dated 1495). National Archives, C 1/40/112; C 1/160/2; C 1/480/13; C 47/10/28/27; C 146/913; C 146/1145; C 146/1170; SP 46/45/fo 79; SP 46/183/fo 83; SP 46/183/fo 87; SP 46/183/fo 101; SP 46/183/fo 122 (available at www.catalogue.nationalarchives.gov.uk/search.asp).

>Children of Eleanor Beaufort, by Robert Spencer, Knt.

>i. **MARGARET SPENCER** [see next].

>ii. **KATHERINE SPENCER**, married **HENRY** (or **HARRY**) **ALGERNON PERCY**, K.G., K.B., Earl of Northumberland [see PERCY 15.i].

14. MARGARET SPENCER, daughter and co-heiress, born about 1472 (aged 30 in 1502). She married about 1490 **THOMAS CAREY** (or **CARY**), of Chilton Foliat, Wiltshire, Burgess (M.P.) for Wallingford, Berkshire, 1491–2, son of William Carey, Knt., of Cockington, Devon, by his 2nd wife, Alice, daughter of Baldwin Fulford, Knt. They had two sons, John, Knt., and William, Esq., and four daughters, Mary (wife of John Delaval, Knt.), Margaret, Anne, and Eleanor (nun). In the period, 1502–3, Robert Brynklowe sued him in Chancery regarding the detention of deeds relating to a messuage in Chilton, Wiltshire. In 1515 he and Edward Darrell, Knt., entered into a bond with condition in the amount of £20. In the period, 1518–29, he sued John Fulford, Esq., in Chancery in right of his wife, Margaret, "daughter and heir of Robert Spencer, knight, [Robert in turn] son and heir of John Spencer and of Joan, his wife" regarding the detention of deeds relating to the manor of Ashbury, Devon, and half the manor of Brompton Ralph, Somerset. In the period, 1529–32, as "Thomas Cary of Chilton," he sued Robert Byngham, Gent., in Chancery regarding the detention of deeds relating to messuages and land in Blandford Forum and Melcombe Bingham, Dorset. THOMAS CAREY died before 21 June 1536.

> Clutterbuck *Hist. & Antiqs. of Hertford* 1 (1815): 129–130 (Cary ped.); 3 (1827): 181 (Cary ped.). Fosbroke *Berkeley Manuscripts: Abs. & Extracts of Smyth's Lives of the Berkeleys* (1821): 150–151 (Berkeley ped.). Lysons & Lysons *Magna Brittania* 6 (1822): 132–160 ("Sir William Carey had by his second wife, (Alice Fulford), a son, Thomas, who by a co-heiress of Sir Robert Spencer, of Spencer's Combe in Devon (who had married a co-heiress of Beaufort, Duke of Somerset,) had two sons, Sir John and William … William [Carey] … married the only sister of Queen Anne Boleyn, [he] was ancestor of the Barons Hunsdon and the Earls of Monmouth."). *Coll. Top. et Gen.* 1 (1834): 308–309 (Beaufort ped.). Westcote *View of Devonshire* (1845): 509–510. *Herald & Genealogist* 3 (1866): 33–54. St. George et al. *Vis. of Devon 1620* (H.S.P. 6) (1872): 47–50 (Cary ped.: "Elianor d. & h. of Sir Rob. Spencer = Thomas Carye, 2"). Colby *Vis. of Devon 1564* (1881): 43–44 (Cary ped.: "Thomas Cary. = Margaret, d. of Robt. Spencer."). Flower *Vis. of Yorkshire 1563-4* (H.S.P. 16) (1881): 244–246 (Percy ped.: "Margaret Spencer on of the doughters & heyres wyf to = Sir Thomas Cary"). Cooke & St. George *Vis. of Hertfordshire 1572, 1634 & 1546* (H.S.P. 22) (1886): 134–137 (Cary ped.: "Thomas Cary of Chilton, Devon, Esq., 2 son of Sir William = Margaret, da. and co-heir of Sir Robert Spencer by… his wife, da. and heir of… Duke of Somersett") (Cary arms: Argent on a bend sable three roses of the field). *Arch. Aeliana* 12 (1887): 219. *Desc. Cat. Ancient Deeds* 1 (1890): 476–485, 495–505, 546–558; 5 (1906): 548–565; 6 (1915): 119. Vivian *Vis. of Devon 1531, 1564 & 1620* (1895): 150–156. Saintsbury *Minor Poets of the Caroline Period* (1906): 452–453 (Cary ped.). Craster *Hist. of Northumberland* 9 (1909): 169 (Delaval ped.). *List of Early Chancery Procs.* 5 (PRO Lists and Indexes 38) (1912): 264. Wedgwood *Hist. of Parl.* 1 (1936): 156 (biog. of Thomas Cary). *Berkshire Arch. Jour.* 44 (1940): 114–115. *TAG* 19 (1942–43): 197–202. Lamborn *Armorial Glass of the Oxford Diocese* (1949): 14–15 (Cary arms: Silver a bend sable with three roses of the field, a crescent gold for difference). *Hist. Research* 31 (1958): 92–96. Leese *Blood Royal* (1996): 229–234. Baker *Rpts. of Cases by John Caryll* 2 (Selden Soc. 116) (2000): 650–653. Beadle & Richmond *Paston Letters & Papers of the 15th Cent.* 3 (2005): 26–28 (letter to Thomas Carey by William Paston dated 1495). National Archives, C 1/258/67; C 1/480/13; C 1/624/5; C 47/10/28/27; C 146/913; C 146/1145; C 146/1170; SP 46/183/fo 83 (available at www.catalogue.nationalarchives.gov.uk/search.asp).

15. WILLIAM CAREY, Esq., Gentleman of the Privy Chamber, Esquire of the Body to King Henry VIII, 2nd son, born about 1496 (aged 30 in 1526). He married at Greenwich, Kent 4 Feb. 1519/20 **MARY BOLEYN** (also known as **MARY ROCHFORD**), elder daughter and co-heiress of Thomas Boleyn, K.G., K.B., Earl of Wiltshire, Earl of Ormond, Viscount Rochford, by Elizabeth, daughter of Thomas Howard, K.G., K.B., Duke of Norfolk [see BUTLER 13 for her ancestry]. She was born c.1500. She was the sister of Queen Anne Boleyn, second wife of King Henry VIII of England. They had one son, Henry (or Harry), K.G. [1st Lord Hunsdon], and one daughter, Katherine.[6] Mary appears to have been the "Mistress Boleyn" who attended Princess

---

[6] In 1997 Anthony Hoskins published an interesting and well written article in *Genealogists' Mag.* 25 (1997): 345–352, in which he advanced the notion that King Henry VIII *may have been* the father of Mary Boleyn's two Carey children. The chief piece of evidence cited by Hoskins to support this theory consists of a salacious piece of second hand gossip uttered by John Hale, vicar of Isleworth, to the Council in April 1535, who alleged that a certain Mr. Skydmore believed that "yonnge master Care" [i.e., Henry Carey, son of Mary Boleyn] was the king's son [see *Letters & Papers… Henry VIII* 8 (1932): 215]. Hale was summarily executed two weeks later at Tyburn for denying the king's supremacy, not for his accusation of bastardy against the king. While Hoskins termed his argument "a powerful case," he failed to present sufficient evidence that supports his "ineluctable conclusion" that the Careys "must have been the king's children." While it is true that the king by his own admission had an affair at some point with Mary Boleyn, there appears to be no indication in surviving records to indicate exactly when their liaison occurred or that the king and Mary had any children together. Jasper Ridley *Henry VIII* (1985): 152, for example, plainly states "Here again there is no record of when the affair with Mary Boleyn began; " see also Alison Weir *The Six Wives of Henry VIII* (2000): 133 ("… the affair was conducted discreetely, and for this reason it is impossible to pinpoint when it began or ended."). For contemporary evidence of King Henry VIII's affair with Mary Boleyn, see Bridgett *Life of Blessed John Fisher* (1902): 148 (undated letter of Cardinal Reginald Pole to King Henry VIII) and Friedmann *Anne Boleyn: A Chapter of English Hist. 1527–1536* 2 (1884): 325 (letter of Dr. Pedro Ortiz dated 1533). One recent historian, Eric Ives, has dated the affair as taking place either in the 1510s or early 1520s [see Eric Ives *The Life & Death of Anne Boleyn* (2004): 15]; however, another historian, Agnes Strickland, dated the affair as being prior to 1520, in which year Queen Katherine

Mary Tudor in France in 1514. During her stay in France, she is alleged to have had an affair with King François I of France. At some unknown date, Mary was a "long time" mistress to King Henry VIII of England, who eventually discarded her. Following their marriage, William and his wife, Mary, attended the king and queen at the Field of the Cloth of Gold in 1520. In 1526 the King granted him the borough of Buckingham, Buckinghamshire and the manor of Easington (in) Chilton, Buckinghamshire. In 1528 Thomas Gardiner, the king's chaplain, was appointed Prior of Tynemouth, Northumberland through the influence of Lady Mary Carey, to whom he granted an annuity of 100 marks out of the conventual revenues. WILLIAM CAREY, Esq., died of sweating sickness 22 June 1528. His widow, Mary, married (2nd) in 1534 (as his 1st wife) **WILLIAM STAFFORD**, K.B., of Chebsey, Staffordshire, and, in right of his wife, of Rochford, Essex, Colvilles, Manners, Shardelowes, and Zouches (all four in Fulbourn), Cambridgeshire, etc., Esquire of the Body to King Henry VIII before 1541, Gentleman Pensioner, 1540, Burgess (M.P.) for Hastings, Sussex, 1547, Standard Bearer, Gentleman Pensioner, before 20 May 1550–53, 2nd son of Humphrey Stafford, Knt., of Blatherwycke, Northamptonshire, by his 1st wife, Margaret, daughter of John Fogge, Knt. [see HASTANG 16 for his ancestry]. They had one son (died young). Their marriage displeased the king and queen (Mary's sister), as well as Cromwell. He attended the Coronation of Queen Anne Boleyn in 1533 as a servitor. He accompanied King Henry VIII to receive Anne of Cleves at Dover 3 Jan. 1539/40. In 1540 he and his wife, Mary, was allowed to take possession of the manors of Southam and Henden, Kent, together with certain detached lands in Brasted, Hever, Chiddingstone, and Sundridge, Kent, which properties formerly belonged to her late father, Thomas Boleyn, Earl of Wiltshire. In 1541 they exchanged the manor of Henden, Kent with the king for more valuable property in London and Yorkshire. In 1542 William and his wife, Mary, made a settlement of her four manors in Fulbourn, Cambridgeshire on William and his heirs. In 1543 William was committed to the Fleet together with Sir John Clere and others for eating meat on Good Friday. After his release, he served in the military campaign later that year in the Netherlands. His wife, Mary, died 19 July 1543. In 1544 he fought in France, and in 1545 in Scotland, where he was knighted by Edward Seymour, Earl of Hertford. He married (2nd) in 1545 **DOROTHY STAFFORD**, daughter of [Lord] Henry Stafford, Lord Stafford, by Ursula, daughter of Richard Pole, K.G., of Isleworth, Middlesex, London, and Ellesborough and Medmenham, Buckinghamshire [see STAFFORD 13.i for her ancestry]. They had three sons, Edward, Knt. [see CODNOR 19], William, and John, Knt., and three daughters, including Ursula (wife of Richard Drake, Esq.) and Elizabeth (wife of William Drury, K.G., and John Scott, Knt.). In Michaelmas term 1545 he ceded his rights to the manors of Colvilles, Manners, Shardelowes, and Zouches (all four in Fulbourn), Cambridgeshire, together with the advowson of the church of Fulbourn,

---

allegedly brought Mary Boleyn to "confession that she had been at fault" [see Strickland *Lives of the Queens of England* 4 (1864): 93]. Regardless of when king's affair with Mary Boleyn took place, there is no known contemporary record which suggests that either the king or his successors at any time acknowledged Mary Boleyn's two Carey children as the king's issue. For example, when Queen Elizabeth I (the daughter of King Henry VIII) mentioned Mary Boleyn's son, Henry Carey, in a letter dated 1579, she referred to him as "our cousin of Hunsdon," not as her brother [see Boyd *Cal. State Papers Rel. Scotland & Mary, Queen of Scots* 5 (1907): 358–360]. Mary Boleyn's other child, Katherine Carey, Lady Knollys, was similarly styled "kinswoman and good servant" [not sister] of Queen Elizabeth I in a letter written in 1569 by Nicholas White [see Strickland *Letters of Mary, Queen of Scots* 2 (1848): 385–390]. Moreover, it may be noted that Mary Boleyn's son, Henry Carey, in his lifetime was duly acknowledged as the lawful issue of the marriage of Mary Boleyn and her husband, William Carey, and, as their heir, he succeeded to both of his parents' land holdings [see Benton *Hist. of Rochford Hundred* 2 (1888): 810–812; VCH *Buckingham* 3 (1925): 1–11, 471–489; 4 (1927): 25; VCH *Cambridge* 9 (1989): 292–295, 381–386]. Simply put, the argument that King Henry VIII fathered one or both of the Carey children remains an unproven theory which may find a surer footing upon the discovery of additional relevant evidence.

Cambridgeshire to the king to pay certain debts. In 1550 the Earl of Warwick granted him an annuity of £100 for his services to King Henry VIII, and entrusted him with three French hostages from Dover to London. In 1551 he and his wife, Dorothy, and his nephew, Humphrey Stafford, Knt., and his wife, Elizabeth, sold the manor of Abinger, Surrey to Thomas and Edward Elrington. The same year he accompanied 9th Lord Clinton to Paris for the christening of one of the sons of King Henri II of France, and on his return, he took part in the New Year's tournament at court. In 1552 mounting debts induced him to exchange his annuity for £900 in cash. In Nov. 1552 he had a brawl with Adrian Poynings, which reduced his standing in the Council's esteem and led to his recommital to the Fleet. In 1553 he wrote the Privy Council concerning injudicious remarks of a certain Mrs. Huggones, a former servant of the Duchess of Somerset, spoken at supper in his home at Rochford, Essex. Following Queen Mary's accession in 1553, he went into exile on the Continent with his wife and family, where he settled in Geneva by March 1554. He soon became embroiled in its disputes, and, on returning to Geneva after the uprising of 1535, he was almost killed in an affray. SIR WILLIAM STAFFORD died at Geneva, Switzerland 5 May 1556. Following Sir William's death, John Calvin claimed the guardianship of his minor son, John, he being the baptismal godfather, and the Council of Geneva decided in favor of the claim. However, his brother, Robert Stafford, Knt., threatened that if his sister-in-law, Dorothy, and the children of Sir William were not allowed to leave Geneva, he would apply to the English government to take steps against Genevese merchants in England. His widow, Dorothy, subsequently removed to Basel, remaining there until Jan. 1559, when she returned to England. Upon the accession of Queen Elizabeth I, she was appointed Mistress of the Robes (senior lady in the royal household), in which capacity she served the queen from 1559/62 to 1603. In 1575 she was granted the manor and park of Wetheringsett, Suffolk by the queen. In 1589 Dorothy Stafford, widow, purchased the manors of Church Eaton and Wood Eaton (in Church Eaton), Staffordshire, together with 40 messuages, 40 tofts, 2 water mills, etc., and the advowson of the church of Church Eaton, Staffordshire from her brother, Edward Stafford, Lord Stafford, for £500. She presented to the church of Wetheringsett, Suffolk in 1590. In 1593–4 she obtained a license to alienate the manor of Church Eaton, Staffordshire, with the advowson of the church there, to her son-in-law, Richard Drake, Esq. She was named sole executrix of the 1596 will of her son, John Stafford, Esq. (afterwards Knt.), which will was not probated until after her death. Lady Dorothy Stafford died 22 Sept. 1604, and was buried in St. Margaret's, Westminster.

Morant *Hist. & Antiqs. of Essex* 1 (1768): 269–271. Lodge *Peerage of Ireland* 4 (1789): 1–76 (sub Butler, Viscount Mountgarret). Hasted *Hist. & Top. Survey of Kent* 3 (1797): 190–202. Blomefield *Essay towards a Top. Hist. of Norfolk* 6 (1807): 381–409. Brydges *Collins' Peerage of England* 9 (1812): 58–136 (sub Butler, Lord Butler). Clutterbuck *Hist. & Antiqs. of Hertford* 1 (1815): 129–130 (Cary ped.); 3 (1827): 91–96 (Hoo-Boleyne ped.), 181 (Cary ped.). Nichols *Progresses & Public Processions of Queen Elizabeth* 2 (1823): 127. Nicolas *Privy Purse Expences of King Henry the Eighth* (1827): xxxvi, 88. *Retrospective Rev.* 2nd Ser. 1 (1827): 8–10 (letter dated c.1534–1536 to Secretary Cromwell written by Mary Boleyn signed "Mary Stafford."). *Gentleman's Mag.* 101 (1831): 594; n.s. 26 (1846): 31–33. *Coll. Top. et Gen.* 4 (1837): 321–322. Beltz *Mems. of the Order of the Garter* (1841): clxxix. Jerdan *Rutland Papers: Original Docs. Ill. of the Courts & Times of Henry VII & Henry VIII* (Camden Soc. 21) (1842): 28–49, 101. Banks *Baronies in Fees* 1 (1844): 408–413 (sub Stafford). Westcote *View of Devonshire* (1845): 509–510. Nichols *Chron. of Calais* (Camden Soc. 35) (1846): 173. *Topographer & Gen.* 1 (1846): 142–144 (will of John Stafford). Lipscomb *Hist. & Antiqs. of Buckingham* 2 (1847): 4–7; 3 (1847): 154 (Drake ped.). Strickland *Mems. of the Queens* (1853): 88, 93–95, 125, 130–132, 134 ("There was a striking resemblance between Anne Boleyn and her sister [Mary], the previous object of Henry's attention; but Mary was the fairest, the most delicately featured, and the most feminine of the two"), 139, 146–147, 180, 214. Napier *Swyncombe & Ewelme* (1858): 369. Burn *Registrum Ecclesiæ Parochialis: Hist. of Parish Regs. in England* (1862): 275–276, 284, 286 (death of Sir William Stafford). *Herald & Genealogist* 3 (1866): 33–54; 4 (1867): 33–48, 129–144. *Notes & Queries* 3rd Ser. 9 (1866): 375–376. *Misc. Gen. et Heraldica* 1 (1868): 244. Cussans *Hist. of Hertfordshire* 1 (1870–73): 42–44. *Vis. of Devon 1620* (H.S.P. 6) (1872): 47–50 (Cary ped.: "William [Carey], 2 = Marie d. & coh, of Sir Tho. Bullen Kt. Erle of Wiltes"). Brewer & Bullen *Cal. Carew MSS* (1873): 439–441. St. George & Lennard *Vis. of Cornwall 1620* (H.S.P. 9) (1874): 86–87. *Surrey Arch. Colls.* 7 (1880): 203–213 (re. Drake fam.). Flower *Vis. of Yorkshire 1563–4* (H.S.P. 16) (1881): 244–246 (Percy ped.: "William Cary father to Sir Henry Cary, Baron of Hunsdon."). *Western Antiq.* 2 (1882):

121. Bridgeman *Hist. of Church Eaton* (Colls. Hist. Staffs. 4(2)) (1883): 17–18, 35–36. Brewer *Reign of Henry VIII from His Accession to the Death of Wolsey* 2 (1884): 164–165, 169–170, 240, 273, 276. Friedmann *Anne Boleyn: A Chapter of English Hist. 1527–1536* 2 (1884): 13, 324 ("Mary Boleyn was married in February, 1521 (not, as [Mr.] Brewer says, in 1520), to [Mr.] William Carey ... Mr. Froude asserts that "the liaison [with King Henry VIII], if real, must have taken place previous to 1521""). *Collectanea* 1st Ser. (1885): 238–242. Cooke & St. George *Vis. of Hertfordshire 1572, 1634 & 1546* (H.S.P. 22) (1886): 134–137 (Cary ped.: "William Cary, Esq. for the body of H. 8, ob. 1528 = Mary, da. and co-heir of Thomas Bullen, Erle of Wiltshire"). Round *Early Life of Anne Boleyn* (1886). Benton *Hist. of Rochford Hundred* 2 (1888): 810–812 ('William Carey, who married Mary Boleyn, in 1521, in the presence of the Court, was a younger brother of Sir John Carey of Plashey. This marriage was distasteful to the Boleyns, as they considered she had lowered and thrown herself away. He died in 1528. She afterwards married William Stafford, subsequently knighted. This Sir William shared in the Church spoils under Edward VI., and was conspicuous for despoiling the Churches of their bells. He appropriated three of those of Rochford, and others were sold to repair the sea walls. He resided with his wife in a retired manner at Rochford Hall, occasionally corresponding with Sir William Cecil. She died here 19th July, 1543, possessed of many estates in this Hundred, together with the advowsons of the Churches of Pakelsham, Foulness, Hakewell, Ashendon and Lighe. These properties descended to her heir at law ..."). Blaikie *Alliance of the Reformed Churches: Minutes & Procs. of the 4th Gen'l Council London 1888* (1889): 307 ("Sir William Stafford appears, from the [Geneva] City Registers, to have been there as early as 29th March [1555]. He was probably the richest and most influential man among the exiles, and was allowed, as a singular privilege, to wear his sword. He is spoken of in the Registers as Sieur de Rochefort."). *Exhibition of the Royal House of Tudor* (1890): 42. *Letters & Papers of Henry VIII* 12(1) (1890): 363. *English Hist. Rev.* 8 (1893): 53–60, 299–300; 10 (1895): 104. Boyd & Wrottesley *Final Concords* (Colls. Hist. Staffs. 15) (1894): 195. MacNamara *Mems. of the Danvers Fam.* (1895): 546. Vivian *Vis. of Devon 1531, 1564 & 1620* (1895): 150–156. *Antiq.* 42 (1906): 64–67. Hazlitt *Some Prose Writings* (1906): 42–43 ("If any such intimacy as has been alleged took place between Mary Boleyn and her Sovereign, it is probably attributable to a period anterior to her first nuptials, when she was a mere child."). Saintsbury *Minor Poets of the Caroline Period* (1906): 452–453 (Carey ped.). *Remarks & Colls. of Thomas Hearne* 8 (Oxford Hist. Soc. 50) (1907): 77. *D.N.B.* 18 (1909): 870–871 (biog. of William Stafford). Davey *Nine Days' Queen, Lady Jane Gray & Her Times* (1909): 225–226. VCH *Surrey* 3 (1911): 129–134. VCH *Hertford* 3 (1912): 323–332. *Genealogist* n.s. 31 (1915): 173–178 (re. Stafford fam.). *C.P.* 4 (1916): 160; 6 (1926): 627–629 (sub Hunsdon). Bridgett *The Life of St John Fisher* (1922): 148 (letter of Cardinal Pole to King Henry VIII dated 1536). VCH *Buckingham* 3 (1925): 471–489; 4 (1927): 25. Baskerville *English Monks & the Suppression of the Monasteries* (1937): 67. Garrett *Marian Exiles* (1938). *Berkshire Arch. Jour.* 44 (1940): 114–115, 125. *TAG* 19 (1942–43): 197–202. Lamborn *Armorial Glass of the Oxford Diocese* (1949): 14–15. *Hist. Research* 31 (1958): 92–96. *Feet of Fines for Essex* 4 (1964): 234–235, 253. *Ancient Deeds — Ser. B* 3 (List & Index Soc. 113) (1975): B.12685, B.12743. *Burlington Mag.* 123 (1981): 304–305. Bindoff *House of Commons 1509–1558* 3 (1982): 364–366 (biog. of Sir William Stafford). *Camden Misc.* 28 (Camden 4th Ser. 29) (1984): 291, 300. *Hist. Jour.* 28 (1985): 939–952. VCH *Cambridge* 9 (1989): 381–386; 10 (2002): 136–143 (erroneously styles William Stafford the "unacknowledged husband" of Mary Boleyn). Warnicke *Rise & Fall of Anne Boleyn: Fam. Politics at the Court of Henry VIII* (1989): 34–37, 46, 63, 81–82, 135, 147–148, 177, 237. *Genealogists' Mag.* 25 (1997): 345–352. Knighton *Acts of the Dean & Chapter of Westminster* 2 (Westminster Abbey Rec. Ser. 2) (1997): 113. Gibson *Recs. of Early English Drama, Diocese of Canterbury/Kent* 3 (2002): 1283 ("Sir William [Stafford] may have been styling himself 'Lord Rochford,' however, for when he and his family went into exile and settled in Geneva in 1554, he was known there as Lord Rochford."). Ives *The Life & Death of Anne Boleyn* (2004): 15 ("... [Mary Boleyn's] one claim to fame is that, for a time in the 1510s or early 1520s, she was Henry VIII's mistress. Mary is said to have had the reputation of 'a great wanton and notoriously infamous' when she was in France in 1514."). Starkey *Six Wives: The Queens of Henry VIII* (2004): 274. Denny *Anne Boleyn* (2007). Fox *Jane Boleyn* (2007). *Hist. Research* 80 (2007): 315–323. Wilkinson *Mary Boleyn* (2009). Staffordshire & Stoke-on-Trent Archive Service, Staffordshire Rec. Office: Recs. of the Bagot Fam. of Blithfield, Barons Bagot, D5121/3/2/3 (letter dated 1578 from Dorothy, Lady Stafford, to Richard Bagot, Sheriff of Staffordshire, concerning a dispute with Robert Harcourt over the manor of Chebsey, Staffordshire) (available at www.a2a.org.uk/search/index.asp).

Children of William Carey, Esq., by Mary Boleyn:

i. **KATHERINE CAREY** [see below].

ii. **HENRY** (or **HARRY**) **CAREY**, K.G., of Rochford, Essex, Buckingham, Bourton (in Buckingham), and Easington (in Chilton), Buckinghamshire, Fen Drayton and Swavesey, Cambridgeshire, etc., Governor of Berwick, Keeper of Hyde Park, Privy Councillor, 1577, Chamberlain of the Household, 1585–96, Justice of the Forest south of Trent, 1589–96, son and heir, born 4 March 1525/6. He married by license dated 21 May 1545 **ANNE** (or **ANNES**) **MORGAN**, daughter of Thomas Morgan, Esq., of Arkeston (in Kingston), Herefordshire, by Elizabeth, daughter of James Whitney, Esq. They had nine sons, including George [2nd Lord Hunsdon], John [3rd Lord Hunsdon], Henry, Thomas (1st of name), Thomas (2nd of name), William, Edmund, Knt., and Robert [1st Earl of Monmouth], and three daughters, Katherine (wife of Charles Howard, K.G., 1st Earl of Nottingham),

Philadelphia (wife of Thomas Scrope, 10th Lord Scrope), and Margaret (wife of Edward Hoby, Knt.). In the period, 1544–51, Thomas Segrey, of Wooburn, yeoman sued him in Chancery regarding a lease made by the defendant during his minority of his lands and manors in Buckingham, Burton, and Easington, Buckinghamshire, with the office of bailiff thereof. In 1548 he sold the manor of Fen Drayton, Cambridgeshire, together with 200 acres of arable land, to John Batisford. In 1549 he sold the manor of Swavesey, Cambridgeshire to John Cutts, Knt. In 1552 he sold the borough of Buckingham, Buckinghamshire to Robert Brocas. The same year he sold the manor of Rochford, Essex to Richard Rich, Lord Rich. In 1553 he sold the manor of Easington (in Chilton), Buckinghamshire to John Croke and his wife Prudence. In March 1558/9 the queen granted him and his heirs male the manor of Hunsdon, Hertfordshire, together with house and lands. She likewise granted him the manors of Stratfield Mortimer, Berkshire, and Bidborough, Hadlow, Kemsing, Seale, Sevenoke, and Wye, Kent. He presented to the church of Cookley, Suffolk in 1559, 1563, and 1573. In 1564 he obtained leave to alienate the manor of Stratfield Mortimer, Berkshire to William Paulet, Marquess of Winchester. In 1570 he obtained a lease of the manor of Eckington, Derbyshire, formerly belonging to Leonard Dacre. His feoffees presented to the church of Huntingfield, Suffolk in 1571. He presented to the church of Michinhampton, Gloucestershire in 1576. SIR HENRY CAREY, 1st Lord Hunsdon, died at Somerset House, London 23 July 1596, and was buried in St. John the Baptist's Chapel, Westminster Abbey 12 August 1596. His widow, Anne, died 19 Jan. 1606/7, and was buried in St. John the Baptist's Chapel, Westminster Abbey. She left a will dated 10 Jan. 1606/7, proved 22 Jan. 1606/7 (P.C.C. Huddleston). Hasted *Hist. & Top. Survey of Kent* 3 (1797): 32–50, 51–59, 60–105; 5 (1798): 177–193, 272–276; 7 (1798): 340–368. Lysons & Lysons *Magna Britannia* 5 (1817): 142–164. Clutterbuck *Hist. & Antiqs. of Hertford* 3 (1827): 181 (Cary ped.). Wainright *Hist. & Top. Intro. ... of the Wapentake of Stafford & Tickhill* (1829): 187–188. Suckling *Hist. & Antiqs. of Suffolk* 2 (1848): 207, 420. *Herald & Genealogist* 3 (1866): 33–54. *Cal. State Papers, Domestic Ser., Edward VI, Mary, Elizabeth, James I* 7 (1871): xi, 53 ([Henry Carey], Lord Hunsdon styled "our cousin" by Queen Elizabeth I of England in letter dated 1568), 246 (Queen Elizabeth I of England styles herself "your loving kinswoman" in letter to [Henry Carey], Lord Hunsdon dated 1570). Robinson *Hist. of the Mansions & Manors of Herefordshire* (1872): 161. Brewer & Bullen *Cal. Carew MSS* (1873): 439–441. St. George & Lennard *Vis. of Cornwall 1620* (H.S.P. 9) (1874): 86–87. Chester *Regs. of St. Peter, Westminster* (H.S.P. 10) (1876): 108. Chitting & Phillipot *Vis. of Gloucester 1623, 1569 & 1582-3* (H.S.P. 21) (1885): 267 (Whitney ped.: "Anne vx. Henry Cary L. Hunsdon Kt of the Garter"). *Collectanea* 1st Ser. (1885): 194–196 (letter of Henry Carey, Lord Hunsdon, dated 1587). Cooke *Vis. of Herefordshire 1569* (1886): 75–76 (Whitney ped.). Foster *London Marr. Lics. 1521–1869* (1887): 251. Benton *Hist. of Rochford Hundred* 2 (1888): 810–812 ("Henry [Carey], who was seventeen at his mother's death, was cousin german to Queen Elizabeth, and made Knight of the Garter and created Lord Hunsdon in the 1st year of her accession to the throne. He was called an honest courtier. He was made Captain of the Pensioners, and governor of Berwick, in which position he was instrumental in suppressing the rebellion of Thomas, Earl of Northumberland, and Charles Neville, Earl of Westmoreland, and having secured the former, sent him to York, where he was beheaded. He likewise defeated Leonard Dacre, on the river Galt, who was a partizan of the Duke of Norfolk, and Mary, Queen of Scots. He was afterwards, jointly with the Earl of Sussex, one of the commanders against the Scotch, and is said to have given in Tiviotdale three hundred villages to the flames and battered fifty castles. He was now made Lord Chamberlain, and at the time of the expected landing of Spanish troops from the Armada, had charge of the Queen's person, with 2,000 horse and 34,000 foot. He had expected Elizabeth to have created him Earl of Ormond, but it was not until he was on his death-bed, in 1596, that the letters patent for the Earldom were offered him, when he exclaimed 'If I was unworthy of these honours when living, I am unworthy of them now I am dying'."). Fishwick *Hist. of St. Michaels-on-Wyre* (Chetham Soc. n.s. 25) (1891): 47 (Henry [Carey], Lord of Hunsdon styled "most dear kinsman" by Queen Elizabeth I in 1575). Jeayes *Desc. Cat. of the Charters & Muniments in the Possession of the Rt. Hon. Lord Fitzhardinge* (1892): 324–325 ([Henry Carey], Lord Hunsdon styled "cousin" by King James VI of Scotland in letter dated 1584). *Notes & Queries* 9th Ser. 9 (1902): 9, 158–159, 314. *English Hist. Rev.* 18 (1903): 112–116. Saintsbury *Minor Poets of the Caroline Period* (1906): 452–453 (Carey ped.). Boyd *Cal. State Papers Rel. Scotland & Mary, Queen of Scots* 5 (1907): 358–360 (Henry Carey, Lord Hunsdon styled "our cousin of Hunsdon" by Queen Elizabeth I of England in 1579). VCH *Middlesex* 2 (1911): 223–251. VCH *Hertford* 3 (1912): 323–332 (Carey arms: Argent a bend sable with three roses argent thereon). VCH *Berkshire* 3 (1923): 422–428. VCH *Buckingham* 3 (1925): 1–11, 471–489; 4 (1927): 25. Lamborn *Armorial Glass of the Oxford Diocese 1250–1850* (1949): 14–16. VCH *Warwick* 7 (1964): 58. *Ancient Deeds — Ser. B* 2 (List & Index Soc. 101) (1974): B.7567; 3 (List & Index Soc. 113) (1975): B.12126. VCH *Gloucester* 11 (1976): 201–204. VCH *Cambridge* 9 (1989): 292–295, 381–386. Somerset *Recs. of Early English Drama: Shropshire* 2 (1994): 704. Siddons *Vis. by the Heralds in Wales* (H.S.P. n.s. 14) (1996): 91 (Morgan ped.: "Annes [Morgan]"). *Genealogists' Mag.* 25 (1997): 345–352. VCH *Northampton* 5 (2002): 345–374. National Archives, C 1/1265/12; E 134/30&31Eliz/Mich11 (available at www.catalogue.nationalarchives.gov.uk/search.asp).

16. KATHERINE CAREY, born about 1524 (aged 38 in 1562). She was appointed maid of honor for the coming of Anne of Cleves in Nov. 1539. She married 26 April 1540 **FRANCIS**

KNOLLES (or **KNOLLYS**, **KNOWLES**), K.G., of Rotherfield Greys, Oxfordshire, member of Parliament, constituency unknown, 1529, ?1539, Burgess (M.P.) for Horsham, 1545, Burgess (M.P.) for Camelford, 1547, Burgess (M.P.) for Arundel, 1559, Knight of the Shire for Oxfordshire, 1563, 1571–2, 1584, 1586, 1589, 1593, Master of the Horse to Prince Edward by 1547; Constable of Wallingford Castle by 1552; Vice-Chamberlain and Privy Councillor, 1559, Governor of Portsmouth, 1562, High Steward of Oxford, 1564–92; Captain of the Guard, 1565, Treasurer of the Chamber, 1567–70, Treasurer of the Household, 1570–96, Lord Lieutenant of Oxfordshire by 1569, Joint Lord Lieutenant of Oxfordshire and Berkshire, c. 1585, son and heir of Robert Knolles, of Rotherfield Greys, Oxfordshire, Usher of the Privy Chamber, by Lettice, daughter of Thomas Peniston, Knt. He was born before 1512. They had eight sons, Henry ("Harry"), Esq., William, K.G. [Viscount Wallingford, 1st Earl of Banbury], Edward, Robert, K.B., Richard, Francis, Knt., Thomas, Knt., and Dudley, and six daughters, Mary, Lettice (wife of Walter Devereux, K.G., Viscount of Hereford, Earl of Essex, Robert Dudley, K.G., Earl of Leicester, and Christopher Blount, Knt.), Maud, Elizabeth (wife of Thomas Leighton, Knt.), Anne, and Katherine (wife of Gerald FitzGerald, Lord Gerald, and Philip Boteler, Knt.). In 1541 Katherine's mother and stepfather granted Francis and his wife, Katherine, the demesne farmland and pasture rights in her mother's four manors in Fulbourn, Cambridgeshire. At the beginning of King Edward VI's reign, he accompanied the English army to Scotland and was knighted by the Commander-in-Chief, the Duke of Somerset, at the camp at Roxburgh 28 September 1547. His strong Protestant convictions recommended him to the young king and to his sister, the Princess Elizabeth; and he spent much time at court, taking a prominent part, not only in tournaments there, but also in religious discussion. He was present at Sir William Cecil's house in 1551, at a conference between Catholics and Protestants respecting the corporeal presence in the Sacrament. In 1552 he visited Ireland on public business. He and his wife, Katherine, alienated all of their estate in Fulbourn, Cambridgeshire in 1554 to Thomas Docwra. Upon the accession of Queen Mary, he deemed it prudent to cross to Germany. He first took up residence in Frankfort, where he was admitted as a church-member 21 December 1557, but, afterwards, he removed himself to Strasburg. Before Mary's death, he returned to England. He was admitted to the new Queen Elizabeth's privy council in December 1558, while his wife became a woman of the Queen's Privy Chambers. In 1560 his wife, Katherine, and their son, Robert, were granted the manor of Taunton, Somerset for life by Queen Elizabeth I. In 1564 Francis and his wife, Katherine, were granted the manors of Wendover Borough and Wendover Forrens, Buckinghamshire by the queen, which properties passed before 1575 probably by sale to William Hawtrey, of Chequers. Throughout his parliamentary career, he was a frequent spokesman for the government on questions of general politics but, as a zealous puritan, in ecclesiastical matters, he preserved an independent attitude. He was guardian of Mary, Queen of Scots, in 1568–9. His wife, Katherine, died at Hampton Court 15 Jan. 1568/9, while in attendance on the Queen, and was buried in St. Edmund's Chapel, Westminster Abbey. In 1581 he sued Elizabeth Fettiplace and others regarding the manor of Blewbury, Berkshire. He was a legatee in the 1582 will of his brother, Henry Knolles, by which he inherited the manor and hundred of Milverton, Somerset for life, with successive remainders to his sons, William, Robert, Richard, Francis, and Thomas. In 1589 he was placed in command of the land forces of Hertfordshire and Cambridgeshire which had been called together to resist the Spanish Armada. SIR FRANCIS KNOLLES died 19 July 1596, and was buried at Rotherfield Greys, Oxfordshire. He left a will proved 15 Sept. 1596 (P.C.C. 67 Drake).

Clutterbuck *Hist. & Antiqs. of Hertford* 3 (1827): 181 (Cary ped.). Beltz *Mems. of the Order of the Garter* (1841): clxxxiii. Strickland *Letters of Mary, Queen of Scots* 2 (1848): 385–390 ([Katherine Carey], Lady Knollys, styled "kinswoman and good servant" of Queen Elizabeth I in letter dated 1569 written by Nicholas White). Napier *Swyncombe & Ewelme* (1858): 360–388. Leinster *Earls of Kildare* (1858): 217–224. *Annual Rpt. of the Deputy Keeper* 25 (1864): 3. *Herald & Genealogist* 3 (1866): 33–54; 4 (1867): 33–48. *Annual Rpt. of the Deputy Keeper* 38 (1870): 190, 207 (Sir Francis Knowles, plaintiff). *Le Neve's Peds. of the Knights* (H.S.P. 8) (1873): 25–26 (Botiler ped.). Burke *Dormant, Abeyant, Forfeited & Extinct Peerages* (1883): 307–308 (sub Knollys). Lee *Hist., Desc. & Antiqs. of ...Thame* (1883): 591–600 (Knollys ped.). *Genealogist* n.s. 1 (1884): 139–144. Cooke & St. George *Vis. of Hertfordshire 1572, 1634 & 1546* (H.S.P. 22) (1886): 134–137 (Cary ped.: "Catherine [Cary], ux. Sir Francis Knolles, Kt. of the Garter"). Benton *Hist. of Rochford Hundred* 2 (1888): 810–812. Vivian *Vis. of Devon 1531, 1564 & 1620* (1895): 150–156. Saintsbury *Minor Poets of the Caroline Period* (1906): 452–453 (Carey ped.). Benolte et al. *Four Vis. of Berkshire 1532, 1566, 1623 & 1665–6* 1 (H.S.P. 56) (1907): 103 (Knollys ped.: "Franciscus Knowles Ordinis Garterij miles in Aula Regia Elizabethæ Reginæ Thesaurari et e Sacris Consilijs ob: 1596. = Catherina filia Willi. Cary Ar: Soror Henrici Cary Dni. Hunsdon obijt Aº 1568"). *C.P.* 1 (1910): 400–401 (sub Banbury); 4 (1916): 159–160 (sub De la Warr); 5 (1926): 140–141 (sub Essex); 7 (1929): 239 (sub Kildare), 549–552 (sub Leicester). VCH *Buckingham* 3 (1925): 20–31. Garrett *Marian Exiles* (1938): 210–213 (biog. of Sir Francis Knollys). *TAG* 18 (1941–42): 211–218; 19 (1942–43): 197–202. *Camden Misc. XXVII* (Camden 4th Ser. 22) (1979): 123–124. Hasler *House of Commons 1558–1603* 2 (1981): 409–414 (biog. of Sir Francis Knollys: "... Knollys' parliamentary career was unrivalled during Elizabeth's reign. He was a Privy Councillor throughout the 11 parliamentary sessions he attended, and active committeeman and speaker, and from his appointment as Treasurer of the Household the most senior Member in the House."). Bindoff *House of Commons 1509–1558* 2 (1982): 479–481 (biog. of Francis Knollys: "... He sat in every one of Elizabeth's Parliaments until 1593 and at his death... he was the last surviving Member of the Parliament of 1529"). *Genealogists' Mag.* 25 (1997): 345–352. *Cal. Patent Rolls 27 Elizabeth I (1584–1585)* (List and Index Soc. 293) (2002): 96. VCH *Cambridge* 10 (2002): 136–143. *Hist. Research* 80 (2007): 315–323.

Child of Katherine Carey, by Francis Knolles, K.G.:

i. **ANNE KNOLLES**, married **THOMAS WEST**, Knt., 2nd Lord La Warr [see WEST 15].

❧ CARLETON ❧

MALCOLM III (CEANNMORE), King of Scots, married [Saint] **MARGARET**.
DAVID I, King of Scots, married **MAUD OF NORTHUMBERLAND**.
HENRY OF SCOTLAND, Earl of Northumberland, married **ADA DE WARENNE**.
WILLIAM THE LION, King of Scots, by a mistress, _____ **AVENEL**.
ISABEL OF SCOTLAND, married **ROBERT DE ROOS**, of Helmsley, Yorkshire.
ROBERT DE ROOS, Knt., of Wark, Northumberland, married _____.
ROBERT DE ROOS, Knt., of Wark, Northumberland, married **MARGARET DE BRUS**.
WILLIAM DE ROOS, Knt., of Kirkby-Kendal, Westmorland, married **ELIZABETH** _____.
THOMAS DE ROOS, Knt., of Kirkby-Kendal, Westmorland, married _____ **DE PRESTON**.
JOHN DE ROOS, Knt., of Kirkby-Kendal, Westmorland, married **KATHERINE LE LATIMER**.
ELIZABETH DE ROOS, married **WILLIAM PARR**, Knt., of Parr (in Prescot), Lancashire.
JOHN PARR, Knt., of Kirkby-Kendal, Westmorland, married **AGNES CROPHILL**.
THOMAS PARR, Knt., of Kirkby-Kendal, Westmorland, married **ALICE TUNSTALL** [see PARR 13].

14. AGNES PARR, married before 1464–5 (date of settlement) (as his 1st wife) **THOMAS STRICKLAND**, Knt., of Sizergh (in Kendal), Westmorland, son and heir of Walter Strickland, Esq., of Sizergh (in Kendal), Westmorland, by Douce, daughter of Nicholas de Croft, of Dalton and Leighton. He was born about 1443 (aged 24 in 1467). They had three sons, Walter, K.B., Thomas (clerk), and Gervase, and one daughter, Joan (wife of Thomas Middleton). He married (2nd) **MARGARET FOULESHURST**, widow of John Byron, Knt., and daughter of Robert Fouleshurst. SIR THOMAS STRICKLAND died in 1497.

Nicolson & Burn *Hist. & Antiqs. of Westmorland & Cumberland* 1 (1777): 87–103. Burke *Hist. of the Commoners* 1 (1836): 55–59 (sub Strickland). *Top. & Gen.* 3 (1858): 352–360. Clay *Extinct & Dormant Peerages* (1913): 156–158 (sub Parr). Wedgwood *Hist. of Parl.* 1 (1936): 823–824 (biog. of Walter Strickland).

15. WALTER STRICKLAND, K.B., of Sizergh (in Kendal), Westmorland. He married about 14 July 1491 (by dispensation dated 27 and 30 March 1491, they being related in the 3rd and 4th degrees of kindred) **ELIZABETH PENNINGTON**, widow of _____ Salkeld, and daughter of John Pennington, Knt., of Muncaster, Cumberland, by Isabel, daughter of John Broughton. They had two sons, Walter, Knt., and Thomas, and three daughters, Agnes, Mary, and Douce. SIR WALTER

STRICKLAND died 15 Sept. 1506. His widow, Elizabeth, married (3rd) by contract dated 9 August 1508 **RICHARD CHOLMELEY**, Knt., of Thornton-on-the-Hill, Yorkshire, and St. Mary Barking, London, Lieutenant of the Tower of London, Lieutenant-Governor of Berwick, Governor of Hull, Knight of the Body to King Henry VII, son of John Cholmeley, of Golston, by Joan, daughter of Thomas Eyton. SIR RICHARD CHOLMELEY died 27 or (28 or 29) December 1521. He left a will proved 24 March 1521/2 (P.C.C.). She married (4th) before 1527 (as his 2nd wife) **WILLIAM GASCOIGNE**, Knt., of Cardington, Bedfordshire, Justice of the Peace for cos. Bedford, Huntingdon, Northampton, Middlesex, Buckingham, and other counties, Knight of the Shire for Bedfordshire, 1529, 1536, Treasurer of the Household of Cardinal Wolsey, 1523–9, Steward to John Neville, 3rd Lord Latimer, c.1535, son of George Gascoigne, of Cardington, Bedfordshire, by Elizabeth, daughter of Thomas Rufford. SIR WILLIAM GASCOIGNE died shortly after 17 March 1539/40. His widow, Elizabeth, left a will dated 18 April 1546, proved 12 October 1546.

> Nicolson & Burn *Hist. & Antiqs. of Westmorland & Cumberland* 1 (1777): 87–103. Burke *Hist. of the Commoners* 1 (1836): 55–59 (sub Strickland). Foster *Peds. of Fams. of Yorkshire* 2(2) (1874) (Cholmeley ped.). Glover & St. George *Vis. of Yorkshire 1584–5, 1612* (1875): 219–221 (Cholmeley ped.). Foster *Ped. of Sir Josslyn Pennington* (1878): 47. Flower *Vis. of Yorkshire 1563–4* (H.S.P. 16) (1881): 52–54 (Cholmley ped.: "Sir Rychard Cholmondley Lieutenante of the Tower whiche died without issu."), 237 (Pennyngton ped.: "Elsabeth [Pennington] wyff to Water Stryckland."). *Testamenta Eboracensia* 5 (Surtees Soc. 79) (1884): 76–77 (will of Thomas Strickland). Dugdale *Dugdale's Vis. of Yorkshire* 2 (1907): 248–252 (Cholmeley ped.). Harvey et al. *Vis. of the North* 2 (Surtees Soc. 133) (1921): 132 (Cholmondely ped.: "Sir Rychard [Cholmondley], lieutenant of the tower, dyed *sans* issu."). Hornyold *Genealogical Memoirs of the Fam. of Strickland of Sizergh* (1928). Barker *Reg. of Thomas Rotherham Archbishop of York* 1 (Canterbury & York Soc. 69) (1976): 234–235. Bindoff *House of Commons 1509–1558* 2 (1982): 194–195 (biog. of Sir William Gascoigne).

Children of Walter Strickland, K.B., by Elizabeth Pennington:

i. **WALTER STRICKLAND**, Knt. [see next].

ii. **AGNES STRICKLAND**, married (1st) **HENRY FROWICK**, Esq., son of Henry Frowick, Knt., by his 2nd wife, Margaret Leigh. He left a will dated 4 Dec. 1518, proved 5 Feb. 1520/1 (P.C.C.). She married (2nd) (as his 1st wife) **THOMAS CURWEN**, Knt., of Workington, Cumberland, Sheriff of Cumberland, 1536–7, son and heir of Christopher Curwen, Knt., of Workington, Cumberland, Sheriff of Cumberland, by Margaret, daughter of Roger Bellingham, Knt. They had seven children, including one son, Henry (or Harry), Knt., and two daughters, Joan and Lucy (wife of John Lowther, Knt.). In the period, 1532–8, Thomas and Agnes his wife, late the wife of Henry Frowick, Esq., sued John Lane, late of the King's guard in Chancery regarding the forcible ouster from the millhouse and lands in Acton, Middlesex and seizure of deeds. He married (2nd) **FLORENCE WHARTON**, widow of Thomas Forster, of Edderston, and daughter of Thomas Wharton, Knt., by Margaret, daughter of Reginald Warcopp. They had one son, Thomas. SIR THOMAS CURWEN left a will dated 1 Nov. 1543, proved 8 Nov. 1544. Burke *Hist. of the Commoners* 1 (1836): 577–580 (sub Curwen). Jefferson *Hist. & Antiqs. of Allerdale Ward* (1842): 251–257. Tonge *Vis. of Northern Counties 1530* (Surtees Soc. 41) (1863): 100 (Curwyn ped.: "Thomas [Curwen], son of Christofer, maried Agnes, doughter of Walter Strekland"). St. George *Vis. of Cumberland 1615* (H.S.P. 7) (1872): 30 (Curwen ped.: "Sr Thomas Curwen of [left blank] = Agnes dau. of Walter Strickland of [left blank]"). Flower *Vis. of Yorkshire 1563–4* (H.S.P. 16) (1881): 82 (Curwen ped.: "Thomas Curwyn son and heyr to Crystofer. = Agnes doghter to Sir Water Strygland.") (Curwen arms: Argent, fretty Gules, on a chief Azure three escallops Or). Jackson *Papers & Peds. Mainly Rel. Cumberland & Westmorland* 1 (1892): 288–370. *List of Sheriffs for England & Wales* (PRO Lists and Indexes 9) (1898): 28. Hornyold *Genealogical Memoirs of the Fam. of Strickland of Sizergh* (1928). Davis *Ancestry of Mary Isaac* (1955): 253–254. National Archives, C 1/757/12 (available at www.catalogue.nationalarchives.gov.uk/search.asp).

Child of Agnes Strickland, by Thomas Curwen, Knt.:

a. **HENRY** (or **HARRY**) **CURWEN**, Knt., of Workington, Cumberland, married (1st) **MARY FAIRFAX** [see FAIRFAX 18]; (2nd) **JANE CROSBY** [see FAIRFAX 18].

16. WALTER STRICKLAND, Knt., of Sizergh (in Kendal), Westmorland, son and heir, born before 1498. He was a legatee in the 1516 will of his uncle, Thomas Strickland, clerk. He married (1st) **AGNES REDMAN**, daughter of Richard Redman. They had no issue. He married (2nd)

KATHERINE NEVILLE, daughter and co-heiress of Ralph Neville, Esq., of Thornton Bridge [in Brafferton], Yorkshire, by Anne, daughter and co-heiress of Christopher Warde, Knt. [see THORNTON BRIDGE 17 for her ancestry]. She was born about 1501. They had two sons, Walter, Esq., and Thomas, and three daughters, Elizabeth (wife of William Strickland), Anne (wife of Ralph Constable and Edward Holme), and Mary (wife of Lewis Dyve, Knt.). SIR WALTER STRICKLAND died 9 Jan. 1528. His widow, Katherine, married (2nd) in 1529 **HENRY BURGH** (or **BOROUGH**), Esq., of Black Friars, London, gentleman of the household of Cardinal Thomas Wolsey, bastardized son of Edward Burgh, Knt. HENRY BURGH, Esq., died testate before Michaelmas 1531. In Michaelmas 1531 William Gryslyng, Citizen and mercer of London, sued his widow and executrix, Katherine, for a debt of £180. She married (3rd) _____ **DARCY**. They had one daughter, Frances (wife of Peter Gobard). She married (4th) before Michaelmas 1533 (date of fine) (as his 2nd wife) **WILLIAM KNYVET**, Esq., of London and Westminster, Sergeant Porter to Kings Henry VIII and Edward VI, and, in right of his wife, of Thornton Bridge (in Brafferton), Yorkshire, younger son of Edmund Knyvet, Knt., of Buckenham, Norfolk, by Eleanor, daughter of William Tyrrell, Knt. In the period, 1533–8, Elizabeth, late the wife of Jervis Strickland, sued William and Katherine his wife, late the wife of Walter Strickland, Knt., nephew of complainant, and Walter, son and heir of the said Sir Walter, in Chancery regarding an annuity charged on Hackthorpe Hall by Walter Strickland, Esq., father of the said Sir Walter. In the period, 1538–44, Robert Hogan sued Edward Musgrave, Knt., Jane his wife (since deceased), William Knyvet, Katherine his wife, late the wife of Walter Strickland, Knt., and John Constable, Knt., and Jane his wife in Chancery regarding a debt of John Ward, whose brother Christopher Ward, Knt., was his heir, and father of the first-named Jane and grandfather of the said Katherine and Jane Constable. He married (3rd) **ALICE** _____. By his various marriages, he had two sons, William and Harry, and five daughters, Mary, Sibyl, Joan, Dorothy, and Margery. Sometime in the period, 1547–53, William Knyvet sued Walter Robynson and others in the Court of the Star Chamber regarding damage to fences, poaching, etc. in the park of Thornton Bridge, Yorkshire. WILLIAM KNYVET, Esq., left a will dated 13 August 1557, inventory dated 6 Dec. 1557.

> Nicolson & Burn *Hist. & Antiqs. of Westmorland & Cumberland* 1 (1777): 87–103 (Strickland arms: Sable, three escalops within a bordure ingrailed Argent). Burke *Hist. of the Commoners* 1 (1836): 55–59 (sub Strickland). Surtees *Hist. & Antiqs. of Durham* 4 (1840): 158–163 (Nevill peds.). Raine *Wills & Invs. from the Reg. Archdeaconry of Richmond* (Surtees Soc. 26) (1853): 97–102 (will and inv. of William Knyvet). Lennard & Vincent *Vis. of Warwick 1619* (H.S.P. 12) (1877): 292–293 (Gobard ped.: "Filia et hæres Neuill de Thornton bridg. [1] = Strickland primus maritus, [2] = … Darcy of the house of Menell in Com. Eborum 2 maritus."). Flower *Vis. of Yorkshire 1563–4* (H.S.P. 16) (1881): 230 (Nevill ped.: "Kateren [Neville] wyff to William Stryckland."), 262. *Testamenta Eboracensia* 5 (Surtees Soc. 79) (1884): 76–77 (will of Thomas Strickland). Collins *Feet of Fines of the Tudor Period* 1 (Yorkshire Arch. Rec. Ser. 2) (1887): 65, 73. *List of Procs. in the Star Chamber* 1 (PRO Lists and Indexes 13) (1901): 268. *C.P.* 2 (1912): 423, footnote e (sub Burgh). *List of Early Chancery Procs.* 5 (PRO Lists and Indexes 38) (1912): 271; 6 (PRO Lists and Indexes 48) (1922): 21, 350; 7 (PRO Lists and Indexes 50) (1926): 270; 8 (PRO Lists and Indexes 51) (1929): 106. VCH *Yorkshire N.R.* 2 (1923): 100–101. Hornyold *Genealogical Memoirs of the Fam. of Strickland of Sizergh* (1928). *TAG* 17 (1940–41): 105–109. Walker *Yorkshire Peds.* 3 (H.S.P. 96) (1944): 432–434 (Warde ped.). Hasler *House of Commons 1558–1603* 3 (1981): 457–458 (biog. of William Strickland). *Norfolk Arch.* 41 (1993): 260, 266. Baker *Rpts. of Cases from the Time of Henry VIII* 2 (Selden Soc. 121) (2004): 249–250. National Archives, C 1/894/73; C 1/999/17–24 (available at www.catalogue.nationalarchives.gov.uk/search.asp).

17. WALTER STRICKLAND, Esq., of Sizergh (in Kendal), Westmorland, and Thornton Bridge (in Brafferton), Yorkshire, Knight of the Shire for Westmorland, hereditary Deputy Steward of the Kendal barony, son and heir by his father's 2nd marriage, born 5 April 1516 (aged 14 in 1530). He married (1st) by contract dated 1535 **MARGARET HAMERTON**, daughter of Stephen Hamerton. Knt., by his wife, Elizabeth. They had no issue. He was implicated in the uprising called the Pilgrimage of Grace in October 1536, but was subsequently pardoned. Following his pardon, Walter appears to have conformed, and served on juries trying the northern rebels, his late companions. In 1538 he was named a supervisor of the will of his mother-in-law, Elizabeth

Hamerton. He married (2nd) by contract dated 20 Jan. 1560/1 **ALICE TEMPEST**, widow of Christopher Place, Esq., of Halnaby, Yorkshire, and daughter of Nicholas Tempest, Esq., of Stanley and Holmside, co. Durham. They had one son, Thomas, K.B., and one daughter, Alice. By an unknown mistress, he had an illegitimate daughter, Ellen (or Eleanor). In later years he made many additions and improvements to Sizergh Hall and began the decoration which his widow and son completed. WALTER STRICKLAND, Esq., died at Sizergh (in Kendal), Westmorland 8 April 1569. He left a will dated 23 Jan. 1568[/69], proved 15 April 1569. His widow, Alice, married (3rd) before 31 March 1574 (as his 4th wife) **THOMAS BOYNTON**, Knt., of Barmston and Acklam, Yorkshire, Burgess (M.P.) for Boroughbridge, Knight of the Shire for Cumberland, son and heir of Matthew Boynton, of Barmston, Yorkshire, by Ann, daughter of John Bulmer, Knt. He was born about 1537 (aged 3 in 1540). They had no issue. SIR THOMAS BOYNTON was buried at Barmston, Yorkshire 5 Jan. 1582. His widow, Alice, left a will dated 18 Jan. 1586, proved 24 March 1595.

Nicolson & Burn *Hist. & Antiqs. of Westmorland & Cumberland* 1 (1777): 87–103. Burke *Hist. of the Commoners* 1 (1836): 55–59 (sub Strickland). Raine *Wills & Invs. from the Reg. Archdeaconry of Richmond* (Surtees Soc. 26) (1853): 215–224 (will and inv. of Walter Strickland). Dugdale *Dugdale's Vis. of Yorkshire* 2 (1907): 145–152 (sub Boynton). VCH *Yorkshire N.R.* 2 (1923): 100–101. *List of Early Chancery Procs.* 7 (PRO Lists and Indexes 50) (1926): 270. *NEHGR* 93 (1939): 3–46; 114 (1960): 51–58; 115 (1961): 316. *TAG* 17 (1940–41): 105–109. Hasler *House of Commons 1558–1603* 1 (1981): 476 (biog. of Thomas Boynton); 3 (1981): 456 (biog. of Thomas Strickland), 456–457 (biog. of Walter Strickland). National Archives, C 1/894/73 (available at www.catalogue.nationalarchives.gov.uk/search.asp).

18. ELLEN (or **ELEANOR**) **STRICKLAND**, illegitimate daughter. She was a legatee in the 1568 will of her father, who bequeathed her £200, provided she marry with consent of his wife, Alice. Ellen married (1st) after 23 Jan. 1568 _____ **NORTON**. They had one son, Thomas. Ellen married (2nd) before 1582 **JOHN CARLETON**, Gent., of Beeford, Yorkshire, Steward of the Manor Court of Beeford, Yorkshire, 1586–1614, son and heir of Thomas Carleton, of Beeford, Yorkshire, by Jennet, probable daughter of William Wilson. They had five sons, Thomas, George, Walter, Gent., Robert, and John, and one daughter, Anne (or Agnes) (wife of Alan Chamber, Gent., and _____ Strickland). His wife, Ellen, was a legatee in the 1586 will of her step-mother, Lady Alice Boynton (formerly Strickland), who bequeathed her £10. JOHN CARLETON, Gent., was buried 27 Jan. 1622/3, and was survived by his wife, Ellen. He left a will.

Nicolson & Burn *Hist. & Antiqs. of Westmorland & Cumberland* 1 (1777): 84 (Chamber ped.: "… This Alan [Chamber] married Anne daughter of John Carlton of Beeforth near Bridlington in Yorkshire; whose mother was daughter of Walter Strickland of Sizergh esquire.") (According to the authors, this information came from the "family writings" of Alan Chamber, Esq. (living c.1700), great-grandson of Alan Chamber and his wife, Anne Carlton). Raine *Wills & Invs. from the Reg. Archdeaconry of Richmond* (Surtees Soc. 26) (1853): 215–224. *Yorkshire Arch. Jour.* 11 (1891): 226, footnote 11. *NEHGR* 93 (1939): 3–46. *TAG* 17 (1940–41): 105–109.

19. WALTER CARLETON, Gent., of Hornsea Burton, Yorkshire, baptized at Beeford, Yorkshire 29 Dec. 1582. He married at Hornsea, Yorkshire by license dated 1607 **JANE GIBBON**, daughter of Peter Gibbon, of Great Hatfield and Hornsea, Yorkshire, by his wife, Margery. She was born about April 1595 (aged 12 years and 7 months on 23 Nov. 1607). They had three sons, Edward, Gent., Thomas, and William, and one daughter, Anne. WALTER CARLETON, Gent., died testate at Hornsea Burton, Yorkshire 4 October 1623. His widow, Jane, married (2nd) in 1626 **WILLIAM BIRKELL**, Jr. She was living in 1639.

Yorkshire Arch. Jour. 11 (1891): 230. *NEHGR* 93 (1939): 3–46. *TAG* 17 (1940–41): 105–109.

20. EDWARD CARLETON, Gent., of Barmston and Hornsea, Yorkshire, son and heir, baptized at Beeford, Yorkshire, 20 October 1610. He married at St. Martin-Micklegate, City of York, Yorkshire 3 Nov. 1636 **ELLEN NEWTON**, daughter and co-heiress of Launcelot Newton, of Hedon, Yorkshire, Bailiff, Mayor and Alderman of Hedon, Yorkshire, by his wife, Mary Lee [see NEWTON 19 for her ancestry]. She was baptized at Hedon, Yorkshire 24 Feb. 1614. They had two sons, [Lieut.] John and Edward, and two daughters, Mary and Elizabeth. His wife, Ellen, was a legatee in the 1635 will of her aunt, Ellen Bracks, who bequeathed her £10. In 1638 Edward and Ellen sold her inheritance at Ryhill and Camerton, Yorkshire. The same year they immigrated to New England, where they settled at Rowley, Massachusetts. He was made a freeman of Massachusetts Bay Colony in 1642. He served as Deputy to the General Court for Rowley, 1644–7. EDWARD CARLETON, Gent., returned to England shortly before 24 Jan. 1648/9, and was living there 22 May 1651. He died sometime before 27 Nov. 1678, presumably in England.

 Pope *Pioneers of Massachusetts* (1900): 88 (biog. of [Mr.] Edward Carleton). *NEHGR* 93 (1939): 3–46; 94 (1940): 3–18; 96 (1942): chart following 106; 106 (1952): 89; 114 (1960): 51–58; 115 (1961): 316. *TAG* 17 (1940–41): 105–109. Sheppard *Anc. of Edward Carleton* (1978). Craven *Hedon Parish Regs.* 1 (1993): 17.

ಈ CASTILE ಈ

WILLIAM THE CONQUEROR, King of England, married **MAUD OF FLANDERS**.
HENRY I, King of England, married **MAUD OF SCOTLAND**.
MAUD OF ENGLAND, married **GEOFFREY PLANTAGENET**, Count of Anjou, Duke of Normandy.
HENRY II, King of England, married **ELEANOR OF AQUITAINE** [see ENGLAND 4].

5. ELEANOR (or **LEONOR**) **OF ENGLAND**, born at Domfront in Normandy 13 October 1162. She married at Burgos in Sept. 1170 **ALFONSO VIII** *el Noble* or *el de las Navas*, King of Castile, Toledo, and Extremadura, lord of Gascony, son and heir of Sancho III *el Deseado*, King of Castile, by Blanca, daughter of García VI Ramírez, King of Navarre. He was born at Soría 11 Nov. 1155. They had seven sons, Sancho, Fernando, Sancho (again), Enrique, Fernando (again), Fernando (again), and Enrique (I) [King of Castile], and seven daughters, Berenguela, Sancha, Urraca, Blanche (or Blanca), Mafalda, Leonor (wife of Jaime I, King of Aragón), and Constanza [Abbess of Las Huelgas]. The regency which followed Alfonso's father's death in 1158, gave rise to a violent struggle for power, as rival factions within the Castilian nobility, the Laras and the Castros, and the boy's uncle, Fernando II of León, sought to secure custody of the boy-king. In 1159 King Sancho VI of Navarre and Fernando II of León seized a number of Castilian frontier towns, and in 1162, the Leonese monarch took Toledo under his control. By 1166 Toledo was back in Castilian hands, and, in 1169, Alfonso VIII began to rule in his own right. In 1174 he ceded Uclés to the Order of Santiago, and afterwards this became the order's principal seat. From Uclés he began a campaign which culminated in the reconquest of Cuenca in 1177. About 1180 he founded the royal monastery of Las Huelgas de Burgos at the instance of his wife, Doña Eleanor (or Leonor). By the last decade of the century, he had firmly established himself as the pre-eminent ruler among the Christian realms of Iberia. In 1191 the caliph Ya'qūb captured the castle of Alcácer do Sal and a number of other fortresses from the Portuguese. In 1195 he returned to launch a major offensive against Castilian positions in La Mancha. When Alfonso moved to block the Almohad advance, his army was annihilated at Alarcos near Calatrava 19 July 1195, and the king barely escaped with his life. In 1212, through the mediation of Pope Innocent III, a crusade was called against the Almohads. ALFONSO VIII OF CASTILE, King of Castile, Toledo, and Extremadura, died at Gutiérre Muñoz near Arévalo 5 October 1214. His widow, Eleanor (or Leonor), died at Burgos 25 October 1214. They were both buried in Santa María la Real monastery (called de las Huelgas) near Burgos.

 Sandford *Gen. Hist. of the Kings of England* (1677): 70. Llorente *Noticias históricas de las tres provincias Vascongadas Alava, Guipuzcoa y Vizcaya* 4(3) (1808): 221–224 (Sancho VI, King of Navarre, styled "uncle" [avunculo] by Alfonso VIII, King of Castile and Toledo, in petition dated 1177), 297–300 & 303–309 (various charters of Alfonso VIII, King of Castile & Toledo, with his wife, Eleanor, dated 1187), 326–327, 333–338 & 356–357 (various charters of Alfonso VIII, King of Castile & Toledo, with his wife, Eleanor, and their son, Fernando, dated 1192, 1195, 1199). Rymer *Fœdera* 1(1) (1816): 32–34, 94 (Eleanor styled "sister" [soror] by King John of England). Banks *Genealogical Hist. of*

Divers Fams of the Ancient Peerage of England (1826): 308–313. George *Annals of the Queens of Spain* (1850): 205–209 (biog. of Elinor of England, Queen of Castile). Hawley *Royal Fam. of England* (1851): 18–19. Green *Lives of the Princesses of England* 1 (1857): 263–307 (biog. of Eleanora of England). Lalore *Cartulaire de l'Abbaye de Boulancourt* (1869): 93 (Obituaire: 6 Oct. — "Anniversaire de Ildefonse, roi de Castille, de glorieuse mémoire"). Wright *Feudal Manuals of English Hist.* (1872). *Genealogist* n.s. 11 (1894): 31, 34–35. Delaville le Roulx *Cartulaire Général de l'Ordre des Hospitaliers de S. Jean de Jérusalem* 1 (1894): 231, 260, 288–289, 316, 342, 442, 526, 567, 572, 599, 688; 2 (1897): 57–58, 87; 4 (1906): 73–74, 258–260, 268–269. Brandenburg *Die Nachkommen Karls des Großen* (1935) XIV 330, do XIV/114–121. Aguado Bleye *Manual de Hist. de España* 1 (1954): 638–649. Gonzalez *El Reino de Castilla en la Epoca de Alfonso VIII* (1960). Valdeavellano *Hist. de España: de los origines a la baja Edad Media* (1968). *Coat of Arms* n.s. 5 (1983): 153–156 [Eleanor's tomb has a 13th cent. shield depicting her arms as three crowned leopards (lions passant guardant) gold on red]. Schwennicke *Europäische Stammtafeln* 2 (1984): 62 (sub Castile & León), 83. Moriarty *Plantagenet Anc. of Edward III & Philippa* (1985): 108. Winter *Descs. of Charlemagne (800–1400)* (1987): XIV.612 & XIV.172. Williamson *Debrett's Kings & Queens of Europe* (1988): 42. *Studies in Gen. & Fam. Hist. in Tribute to Charles Evans* (1989): 366–417 (Alfonso VIII: "… first to bear the arms of Castilla, Gules a castle or). Williamson *Kings & Queens of England* (1991): 53. van Caenegem *English Lawsuits from William I to Richard I* 2 (Selden Soc. 107(2)) (1991): 538–549 ("Aldefonsum qui filiam regis Henrici Angliæ in uxorem duxit") (Alfonso refers to Sancho, King of Navarre, as his "uncle" [avunculo]). Vann *Queens, Regents & Potentates* (Women of Power 1) (1995). Leese *Blood Royal* (1996): 47–53. Barton *Aristocracy in 12th Cent. León & Castile* (1997). Wheeler *Eleanor of Aquitaine: Lord & Lady* (2003).

Children of Eleanor (or Leonor) of England, by Alfonso VIII of Castile:

i. **BERENGUELA OF CASTILE** [see next].

ii. **URRACA OF CASTILE**, married **AFFONSO II** *el Gordo*, King of Portugal & the Algarve [see PORTUGAL 6].

iii. **BLANCHE** (or **BLANCA**) **OF CASTILE**, married **LOUIS VIII** *le Lion*, King of France [see FRANCE 8].

6. BERENGUELA I OF CASTILE *la Grande*, Queen of Castile and Toledo, eldest daughter, born about 1179–80. She married (1st) at Seligenstadt by contract dated 23 April 1188 **KONRAD II**, Duke of Swabia and Rothenburg, son of Friedrich I Barbarossa, Holy Roman Emperor, Duke of Swabia, King of Burgundy, by his 2nd wife, Béatrice, daughter of Rainald III, Count of Burgundy. He was born in 1177. They had no issue and were subsequently divorced. He was assassinated at Durlach 15 August 1196. She married (2nd) (as his 2nd wife) at Valladolid in Dec. 1197 **ALFONSO IX OF LEÓN**, King of León, Galicia, and Badajoz, son and heir of Fernando II, King of León, by by his 1st wife, Urraca, daughter of Affonso I Enríques, King of Portugal. He was born at Zamora 15 August 1171. They had two sons, [Saint] Fernando (III) [King of Castile and León] and Alfonso [señor of Soria, Molina, Mesa, Cigales], and three daughters, Leonor, Bérengère (or Berenguela), and Constanza (nun at Las Huelgas). A papal dispensation for this marriage was refused, and León was placed under an interdict, 1202–4. The couple separated owing to consanguinity in 1204, after which she returned to her father's dominions, where she became regent for her younger brother, Enrique I, following her parents' deaths in 1214. She was heiress in 1217 to her brother, Enrique I, King of Castile. She abdicated the throne of Castile 31 August 1217, in favor of her son, Fernando. Alfonso IX married (1st) at Guimarães 15 Feb. 1191 **TERESA OF PORTUGAL**, daughter of Sancho I, King of Portugal & the Algarve, by Dulce, daughter of Raymond Bérengar IV, Count of Barcelona. She was born about 1176. They had three children, Fernando, Sancha, and Dulce. The marriage was annulled in 1194 for reason of consanguinity by Pope Celestine III at the 2nd Council of Salamanca. Alfonso and Teresa separated in 1197, and she afterwards became a nun at Lorvão in 1200. By various mistresses, he also had eleven illegitimate children, Pedro Alfonso, Rodrigo Alfonso, Fernando Alfonso, Fernando Alfonso (2nd of name), Martín Alfonso, Urraca Alfonso (wife of Lope Díaz de Haro), Aldonza Alfonso (wife of Diego Ramírez Froilaz and Pedro Ponce de Cabrera), Sancha Alfonso (nun), María Alfonso (wife of Alvar Fernández de Lara and Suero Arias de Valladares), Urraca Alfonso (wife of García Romero and Pedro Nuñez de Guzmán), and Teresa Alfonso (wife of Nuno González, Count of Lara). ALFONSO IX OF LEÓN, King of León, Galicia, and Badajoz, died at Villaneuva de Sarria 24 Sept. 1230, and was buried in the chapel of San Lorenzo in Santiago el Mayor Cathedral at Santiago de Compostela. In 1230 Queen Berenguela [his

2nd wife] was appointed to negotiate with Teresa [his 1st wife] for the renunciation of the rights to the crown of León of Teresa's two daughters in favor of Berenguela's son, Fernando. Berenguela died at Las Huelgas near Burgos 8 Nov. 1246, and was buried there in the Cistercian monastery Santa María la Real (called de la Huelgas). Teresa died at Lorvão 17 (or 18) June 1250.

George *Annals of the Queens of Spain* (1850): 212–220 (biog. of Doña Berengaria, Queen of León, 1196, Regent of Castile, 1214, Queen in her own right of Castile, 1217). *Genealogist* n.s. 11 (1894): 31, 34–35. Delaville le Roulx *Cartulaire Général de l'Ordre des Hospitaliers de S. Jean de Jérusalem* 1 (1894): 299, 371, 567; 2 (1897): 3, 21, 57–58, 169–171, 201, 259, 328, 383–384, 396, 408–409, 586–587; 4 (1906): 259–260. Brandenburg *Die Nachkommen Karls des Großen* (1935) XIV 332. Aguado Bleye *Manual de Hist. de España* 1 (1954): 649–658. Chaplais *Diplomatic Docs.* 1 (1964): 154–155 (King Henry III of England styled "kinsman" [affini/consanguineo] by Berenguela, Queen of Castile and Toledo, in letters dated c.1217–1230). *Jour. Medieval Hist.* 5 (1979): 185–201. Moriarty *Plantagenet Anc. of Edward III & Philippa* (1985): 108. Schwennicke *Europäische Stammtafeln* 1(1) (1998): 15 (sub Staufer) (no mention of Berenguela's 1st marriage); 2 (1984): 38 (sub Portugal), 62 (sub Castile and Leon), 70 (sub Aragón); 3(3) (1985): 530a (sub León). Winter *Descs. of Charlemagne (800–1400)* (1987): XIV.613 & XV.238. Williamson *Debrett's Kings & Queens of Europe* (1988): 42. *Studies in Gen. & Fam. Hist. in Tribute to Charles Evans* (1989): 366–417 ["… He used the emblem of the Lion in perfect heraldic form and left the first contemporary colored representation of the arms of the Kingdom of León (dated 1208, in the Cartulary *Tumbo* A of Santiago), evidence also that the royal lion was purple (morado) and not gules."]. Leese *Blood Royal* (1996): 47–53. Barton *Aristocracy in 12th Cent. León & Castile* (1997). Wheeler *Eleanor of Aquitaine: Lord & Lady* (2003).

Children of Berenguela of Castile, by Alfonso IX of León:

i. [SAINT] **FERNANDO III OF CASTILE-LEÓN** [see next].

ii. **ALFONSO OF CASTILE-LEÓN**, señor of Soria, Molina, Mesa, Cigales, Knight of the Order of Calatrava, younger son, born in Fall 1202. He married (1st) in 1240 **MAFALDA GONZÁLEZ DE LARA**, daughter of Gonzalo Pérez de Lara, señor of Molina and Mesa, by Sancha Gómez de Trastamara. They had one son, Fernando Alfonso, and one daughter, Blanca Alfonso (wife of Alfonso Fernández el Niño). He participated in the conquest of Córdoba in 1236, Murcia in 1242, and Sevilla in 1248. He was sent to England in 1241 to speak with the king. His wife, Mafalda, was dead before Sept. 1244. He married (2nd) after Sept. 1244 **TERESA GONZÁLEZ DE LARA**, daughter of Gonzalo Nuñez de Lara, señor of Belorado, Governor in Monterroso, Toroño and Trastamara, by María Díaz de Haro. They had one daughter, Juana Alfonso (wife of Lope Díaz de Haro). He married (3rd) after 22 July 1260 **MAYOR ALFONSO DE MENESES**, widow of Gonzalo Gil de Villalobos (living 22 July 1260), daughter of Alfonso Téllez de Meneses, señor of Meneses, Montealegre, San Román, Córdoba, etc., by María Annez de Lima, daughter of Juan Fernández de Lima. They had one son, Alfonso Téllez de Meneses, and one daughter, María Alfonso. Mayor was heiress of her brother, Alfonso Téllez de Meneses, by which she inherited Meneses, Montealegre, San Román, etc. By various mistresses, he also had several illegitimate children including Juan Alfonso [Bishop of Palencia], Teresa Alfonso (wife of Nuño González de Lara), Urraca Alfonso (wife of García Gómez Carrillo), Berenguela Alfonso (wife of Gonzalo Ramírez Froílaz), Leonor Alfonso (wife of Álvaro García de Villamayor), and Juana Alfonso. ALFONSO OF CASTILE-LEÓN died at Salamanca 6 Jan. 1272, and was buried at Ciudad Real, castle of Calatrava-la-Nueva. Champeval *Cartulaire des Abbayes de Tulle et de Roc-Amadour* (1903): 346–348 (charter of King Fernando [III] of Castile and Toledo and his brother [fratre] Alfonso dated 1217 granted with the consent of his mother [genetricis], Queen Berenguela). *C.P.R. 1232–1247* (1906): 260. Garcia Carraffa & Garcia Carraffa *Diccionario Heráldico y Genealógico de Apellidos Españoles y Americanos* 54 (1952): 154–158 (sub Meneses). Aguado Bleye *Manual de Hist. de España* 1 (1954): 658. Schwennicke *Europäische Stammtafeln* 3(1) (1984): 127 (sub Molina and Mesa). *Studies in Gen. & Fam. Hist. in Tribute to Charles Evans* (1989): 366–417 ("… his arms display a perfect heraldic brisure; on the obverse of his seal a lion is framed by 17 castles, and on the reverse a castle is framed by 12 lions"). Leese *Blood Royal* (1996): 51.

Child of Alfonso of Castile-León, by Mayor Alfonso de Meneses:

a. **MARÍA ALFONSO DE MOLINA**, married **SANCHO IV** *el Bravo*, King of Castile and León [see CASTILE 9 below].

iii. **BÉRENGÈRE** (or **BERENGUELA**) **OF CASTILE-LEÓN**, married **JEAN DE BRIENNE**, King-Consort of Jerusalem, Emperor-Regent of Constantinople [see BRIENNE 7].

7. FERNANDO III OF CASTILE-LEÓN *el Santo* ["the Saint"], King of Castile, León, Galicia, Toledo, Córdoba, Jaén, and Seville, born en route between Salamanca & Zamora 5/19 August 1201. He was proclaimed King of Castile on the abdication of his mother in 1217. He married (1st) at

Burgos 30 Nov. 1220 **BEATRIZ** (or **ISABEL**) **OF SWABIA**, daughter and co-heiress of Philip, Duke of Swabia and Tuscany, King of the Romans, by Eirene, daughter of Isaac II Angelos, King of Byzantium. She was born in Nürnberg March/May 1205. They had seven sons, Alfonso (X) [King of Castile and León], Fadrique (or Federico), Fernando, Enrique [señor of Ecija, Medellin, Dueñas, etc., Senator of Rome], Felipe [Archbishop of Seville, later señor of Valdeporchena, Piedrahita, etc.], Sancho [Archbishop of Toledo], and Manuel [señor of Elche, Villena, etc.], and three daughters, Leonor, Berenguela (nun at Las Huelgas), and María. His wife, Beatriz, died at Toro 5 Nov. 1235, and was buried in Santa María la Real monastery called de las Huelgas near Burgos. He married (2nd) at Burgos before 31 October 1237 (by papal dispensation dated 31 August 1237, they being related in the 3rd and 4th degree of kindred) **JEANNE** (or **JUANA**) **DE DAMMARTIN**, Countess of Ponthieu, Montreuil, and Aumale, daughter and co-heiress of Simon de Dammartin, Count of Ponthieu and Montreuil (in right of his wife), by Marie, daughter and heiress of Guillaume II Talvas, Count of Ponthieu and Montreuil [see DAMMARTIN 4 for her ancestry]. She was born about 1220, and succeeded to Ponthieu in 1251 on her mother's death. They had four sons, Fernando [Count of Aumale, Baron of Montgomery and Noyelles-sur-Mer], Luis [señor of Marchena and Zuheros], Simón, and Juan, and one daughter, Eleanor (or Leonor). [SAINT] FERNANDO III, King of Castile, León, etc., died at Seville 30 May 1252, and was buried in the Santa María Cathedral at Seville. He was canonized by Pope Clement X in 1671. His widow, Queen Jeanne, returned to France in October 1254, where she took up residence at Abbeville in Ponthieu. Jeanne was co-heiress in 1259 to her cousin, Mahaut de Dammartin, Countess of Boulogne and Dammartin, by which she inherited the county of Aumale. She married (2nd) between May 1260 and 9 Feb. 1261 (as his 2nd wife) **JEAN DE NESLE** (or **NÉELE**) (also styled **DE FALVY**), Chev., seigneur of Falvy-sur-Somme and la Hérelle, and in right of his wife, Count of Ponthieu, Montreuil, and Aumale, son of Raoul de Nesle, seigneur of Falvy-sur-Somme and la Hérelle, by Alix, daughter of Barthelemy de Roye, Chamberlain of France. Jeanne, Queen of Castile & León, Countess of Ponthieu, Montreuil, and Aumale died testate at Abbeville 15 March 1278/9, and was buried at Valoires Abbey. JEAN DE NESLE died 2 Feb. 1292.

Anselme *Hist. de la Maison Royale de France* 2 (1726): 507. *L'Art de vérifier les Dates* 2 (1784): 750–759 (sub Comtes de Ponthieu). George *Annals of the Queens of Spain* (1850): 221–222 (biog. of Doña Beatrix de Suabia, Queen of Castile), 223–224 (biog. of Doña Juana, Queen of Castile & León). Huillard-Bréholles *Hist. Diplomatica Friderica Secundi* 5(1): (1857): 370–371 ([Fernando III], King of Castile styled "kinsman" [affinis] by Emperor Friedrich II in 1239). Pertz *Annales ævi Suevici* (Monumenta Germaniæ Historica, Scriptores 17) (1861): 170 (Annales Marbacenses sub A.D. 1201: "… preclarissimus princeps Phylippus … Habuit enim Phylippus filiam regis Constantinopolitani in coniugio, quam filius Tancradi in Sycilia ducere debebat, sed preventus immatura morte una cum patre in palacio Panormitano remansit, quam Heinricus imperator ibidem inveniens, postea fratri suo tradidit. Qui postea eam cum magno conventu principum in Suevia sollempniter duxit, et ex ea quatuor filias, progenuit, que postea nupserunt, videlicet Ottoni postea imperatori, et regi Hyspanie, et regi Boemie, atque duci Brabantie …"). Boutaric *Actes du Parlement de Paris* 1st Ser. 1 (1863): 28, 36, 219. Teulet *Layettes du Trésor des Chartes* 2 (1866): 372–373 (Louis IX, King of France, styled "kinsman" by King Fernando III), 373 (Louis IX, King of France, styled "kinsman" by Jeanne de Dammartin, Queen of Castile). Luard *Annales Monastici* 4 (Rolls Ser. 36) (1869): 477 (Annals of Worcester sub A.D. 1279 — "… circa Ascensionem Domini [11 May] mare transit rex Edwardus una cum regina; cujus mater, comitissa Pontivi, quondam regina Hyspaniæ, transierat ex hoc mundo."). Thierry *Recueil des Monuments Inédits de l'Hist. du Tiers État* 4 (1870). Gorgue-Rosny *Recherches Géns. sur les Comtés de Ponthieu, de Boulogne, de Guines et Pays Circonvoisins* 4 (1877): 2, 8–9, 12, 25 (letters of Jean de Nesles), 52–53 (charters of Jean de Nesle), 88 (charter of Jean de Néele and his wife, Jeanne). Noulens *Maison d'Amiens, Histoire généalogique* (1888): 133, 263, 387 (charter of Jean de Néelle, Count of Ponthieu, Montreuil, and Aumale, and his wife, Jeanne, Queen of Castile and León dated c.1275). *Genealogist* n.s. 7 (1891): 39 (seal of Jean de Néelle dated 1272 — A shield of arms: barry and a bendlet.); n.s. 11 (1894): 31, 34–35. Piton *Histoire de Paris: le Quartier des Halles* (1891): 279–280 (letter of Jean de Nesle, seigneur of Falvi, to King Edward I of England dated before 1282?). Delaville le Roulx *Cartulaire Général de l'Ordre des Hospitaliers de S. Jean de Jérusalem* 2 (1897): 259, 302, 478, 586–587, 641; 3 (1899): 148. Prarond *Cartulaire du comté de Ponthieu* (1897): 172–173 (Fernando III, King of Castile, styled "kinsman" [consanguinei] by King Louis IX of France), 172–173 (Louis IX, King of France, styled "kinsman" [consanguineo] and [Simon], Count of Ponthieu, styled "father-in-law" [socero] by Fernando III, King of Castile, in letter dated 1237), 234 (Eudes de Ranqueroles, knight styled "kinsman" [consanguineo/consanguineus] by

Jeanne de Dammartin, Queen of Castile in 1257). Champeval *Cartulaire des Abbayes de Tulle et de Roc-Amadour* (1903): 346–348 (charter of King Fernando [III] of Castile and Toledo and his brother [fratre] Alfonso dated 1217 granted with the consent of his mother [genetricis], Queen Berenguela; names his grandfather [avus], Lord Alfonso). Auvray *Regs. de Grégoire IX* 2 (1907): 747 (dispensation for marriage of King Fernando III of Castile and Jeanne de Dammartin). *C.C.R. 1234–1237* (1908): 346 (King Fernando III styled "kinsman" by King Henry III of England). Brunel *Recueil des Actes des Comtes de Ponthieu 1026–1279* (1930): 551–554 (instances of Eudes de Roncherolles (or Ronquereles), Knt. styled "kinsman" [consanguineum] by Jeanne de Dammartin, Countess of Ponthieu), also doc. no. 304. Aguado Bleye *Manual de Hist. de España* 1 (1954): 676–681. *Genealogists' Mag.* 15 (1965): 53–63. Tremlett et al. *Rolls of Arms Henry III* (H.S.P. 113–4) (1967): 193 (arms of Simon de Dammartin: Argent, three bars azure in a border gules). Petit *Le Ponthieu et la Dynastie Anglaise au XIIIᵉ Siècle* (1969). Newman *Les Seigneurs de Nesle en Picardie* 1 (1971): 72–73, chart foll. 287. Fossier *Chartes de Coutume en Picardie (XIᵉ–XIIIᵉ Siècle)* (Coll. de Docs. Inédits sur l'Hist. de France 10) (1974): 286–290, 415–416. Parsons *Court & Household of Eleanor of Castile in 1290* (1977): 41. *Jour. Medieval Hist.* 5 (1979): 185–201. González *Reinado y Diplomas de Fernando III* 1 (1980): 110–113, 117. *Mediæval Studies* 46 (1984): 245–265. Winter *Descs. of Charlemagne (800–1400)* (1987): XV.834 & XV.1017a. Williamson *Debrett's Kings & Queens of Europe* (1988): 43. *Studies in Gen. & Fam. Hist. in Tribute to Charles Evans* (1989): 366–417. Leese *Blood Royal* (1996): 47–53. Brault *Rolls of Arms Edward I* 2 (1997): 92 (he sealed in 1237 with quartered arms of Castile and León), 350 (arms of Jeanne de Dammartin: Quarterly 1 and 4 argent, a lion rampant purpure. 2 and 3 gules, a castle or, impaling argent, three bars azure, a bordure gules [Dammartin], both dimidiated). O'Callaghan *Alfonso X & the Cantigas De Santa Maria* (1998): 43 ("A handsome man with a truly regal presence, Fernando III had high intelligence, was well spoken and courteous, and knew precisely the moment to take action. Alfonso X [his son] also praised his father's personal habits, his skill in the military arts and in playing chess and other 'good games,' and his appreciation of singers, troubadours, and *juglares* who played musical instruments."). Schwennicke *Europäische Stammtafeln* 1(1) (1998): 15 (sub Staufer), 2 (1984): 63 (sub Castile and Leon); 3 (1989): 649; 7 (1979): 16 (sub Châtelains de Brugge). Sayer *Original Papal Docs. in England & Wales (1198–1304)* (1999): 97–99, 159–160, 184–185, 203.

Child of [Saint] Fernando III of Castile-León, by Beatriz of Swabia:

i. **ALFONSO X OF CASTILE-LEÓN** [see next].

Child of [Saint] Fernando III of Castile-León, by Jeanne (or Juana) de Dammartin:

i. **ELEANOR** (or **LEONOR**) **OF CASTILE-LEÓN**, married **EDWARD I OF ENGLAND**, King of England [see ENGLAND 7].

8. ALFONSO X OF CASTILE-LEÓN *el Sabio*, King of Castile, León, Toledo, Galicia, Seville, Córdoba, Murcia, Jaén, and the Algarve, Knt., son and heir by his father's 1st marriage, born at Toledo 23 Nov. 1221. He married at Valladolid 26 Nov. 1248 (by dispensation dated 25 Jan. 1249) **VIOLANTE** (or **YOLANDA**) **OF ARAGÓN**, daughter of Jaime I *el Conquistador*, King of Aragón, Majorca, and Valencia, Count of Barcelona and Urgel, seigneur of Montpellier, by his 2nd wife, Jolanta (or Yolande), daughter of Andras II, King of Hungary, Dalmatia, Croatia, etc. [see HUNGARY 9.i for her ancestry]. She was born about 1236. They had five sons, Fernando de la Cerda, Knt., Sancho (IV) [King of Castile and León], Pedro [señor de Ledesma], Juan [señor of Palencia de Campos], and Jaime [señor de Los Cameros], and six daughters, Berenguela (nun), Beatriz (wife of Guglielmo, Marchese of Monferrato), Leonor, Constanza (nun at Las Huelgas), Isabel, and Violante (wife of Diego López de Haro, señor of Vizcaya). By his mistress, **MAYOR GUILLÉN DE GUZMÁN** (died testate at Alcocer before 1267), daughter of Guillén Pérez de Guzmán, señor of Becilla, he had one illegitimate daughter, Beatris (or Beatriz) Alfonso. By various other mistresses, he also had three illegitimate sons, Alfonso Fernández el Niño, Martin Alfonso [Abbot of Valladolid], and James, king's clerk [Chamberlain of the Exchequer of Receipt for King Edward II of England, canon of York, Exeter, St. Patrick's, Dublin, Wells, St. Paul's, London, Lichfield; Lincoln, Chester-le-Street, and Sarum], and two illegitimate daughters, Berenguela Alfonso (wife of Pedro Nuñez de Guzmán) and Urraca Alfonso. Alfonso was elected King of the Romans in 1257–72. ALFONSO X, King of Castile, León, etc., died at Seville 4 (or 21) April 1284, and was buried at Santa María Cathedral in Seville. He left two wills, one dated 8 Nov. 1282, the other dated 10 Jan. 1284. His widow, Violante, died at Roncesvalles in 1300 after a visit to Rome, and was buried there at Real Casa.

Butkens *Trophées tant sacres que prohanes de la duché de Brabant* 1 (1637): Preuves, 95 (Henry III, Duke of Lorraine & Brabant, styled "kinsman" [consanguinei] by Alfonso X, King of Castile and León in a letter dated 1258). Llorente *Noticias Históricas de las Tres Provincias Vascongadas Alava, Guipuzcoa y Vizcaya* 4(3) (1808): 297–305 (confirmation charters of Alfonso X, King of Castile, Toledo, León, etc., with his wife, Queen Yolant/Violante, and his daughters, Berenguela and Beatriz, dated 1254). Rymer *Fœdera* 1 (1816): 290, 357, 397, 408 (instances of Alfonso X styled "kinsman" by Henry III, King of England). George *Annals of the Queens of Spain* (1850): 225–231 (biog. of Doña Violante, Queen of Castile & León). Shirley *Royal & Other Hist. Letters Ill. of King Henry III* 2 (Rolls Ser. 27) (1866): 107–108 (Alfonso X styled "kinsman" [affinis et consanguineus] by Henry III, King of England). Delaville le Roulx *Cartulaire Général de l'Ordre des Hospitaliers de S. Jean de Jérusalem* 1 (1894): 104; 2 (1897): 302, 586–587, 641, 645–646, 768, 798; 3 (1899): 148–149, 256–257, 260, 373–375, 397–398, 406–409, 434. *C.P.R. 1272–1281* (1901): 176 (Alfonso styled "king's brother" [i.e., brother-in-law] by King Edward I of England). *C.C.R. 1279–1288* (1902): 79, 159 (Jacob [James] de Ispannia styled "queen's kinsman"; James de Ispannia styled "nephew of the queen the king's consort" [Eleanor of Castile, wife of King Edward I of England]. Daumet "Les testaments d'Alphonse X le Savant roi de Castille" in *Bibliothèque de l'École des Chartes* 67 (1906): 70–99 (King Edward I of England styled "kinsman" and "brother-in-law" [consanguineus/levir] by King Alfonso X). *C.P.R. 1247–1258* (1908): 500, 640 (instances of Alfonso X, King of Castile, styled "kinsman" by King Henry III of England). *Cal. Chancery Warrants* (1927): 417 (sons Pedro and Juan styled "king's cousins" by King Edward II of England). *C.C.R. 1261–1264* (1936): 172–173 (Alfonso X styled "kinsman" by King Henry III of England). Aguado Bleye *Manual de Hist. de España* 1 (1954): 681–689. Garcia Carraffa & Garcia Carraffa *Diccionario Heráldico y Genealógico de Apellidos Españoles y Americanos* 40 (1954): 174–175 (sub Guzmán). Emden *Biog. Reg. of the Univ. of Oxford* 3 (1959): 136–138 (biog. of James of Spain — James identified as an illegitimate son of Alfonso X, King of Castile). Ballesteros *Alfonso X* (1963). Chaplais *Diplomatic Docs.* 1 (1964): 181–182 (King Henry III of England styled "kinsman" [consanguineo] by Alfonso X, King of Castile in letter dated 1254), 184–186 (Edward of England [future King Edward I of England] styled "kinsman and brother-in-law" [affinem et sororium] by Alfonso X, King of Castile in letter dated 1254). Keller *Alfonso X, el Sabio* (1967). Cuttino *Gascon Reg. A* 2 (1975): 511–516 (Alfonso X styled "kinsman" by King Henry III of France). *Jour. Medieval Hist.* 5 (1979): 185–201. Schwennicke *Europäische Stammtafeln* 2 (1984): 63 (sub Castile and Leon), 70 (sub Aragón), 200 (sub Montferrat); 3(1) (1984): 123 (sub de la Cerda); 3(3) (1985): 530b (sub Castile and Leon). Williamson *Debrett's Kings & Queens of Europe* (1988): 43. *Studies in Gen. & Fam. Hist. in Tribute to Charles Evans* (1989): 366–417. Burns *Emperor of Culture: Alfonso X the Learned of Castile & His 13th Cent. Renaissance* (1990). Jiménez *Alfonso X 1252–1284* (1993). O'Callaghan *Learned King: Reign of Alphonso X of Castile* (1993). *Atalaya* (Revue Française d'Études Médiévales Hispaniques 5) (1994): 151–179. Leese *Blood Royal* (1996): 47–53. Brault *Rolls of Arms Edward I* 2 (1997): 92 (arms of Alphonso of Castile: Gules, three castles or; he sealed in 1255 with quartered arms of Castile and Leon). O'Callaghan *Alfonso X & the Cantigas De Santa Maria* (1998): 23 ("Alphonso X, King of Castile–León (1252–1284) stands out as a scholar and patron of scholars unrivaled by any of his fellow monarchs… [He] gathered to his court students of law, history, astronomy, and astrology, as well as poets and artists of varying origins and backgrounds. Together with them he collaborated in the production of an enormous number of legal, historical, scientific, literary, and poetic works. Though he failed to win the crown of the Holy Roman Empire, his contribution to European civilization prompted Robert Burns to dub him the 'Emperor of Culture' and to describe his reign as a thirteenth-century renaissance."). Valladolid *Chron. of Alfonso X* (2002).

Child of Alfonso X of Castile-León, by Violante of Aragón:

i. **SANCHO IV OF CASTILE-LEÓN** [see next].

Illegitimate child of Alfonso X of Castile-León, by Mayor Guillén de Guzmán:

i. **BEATRIS** (or **BEATRIZ**) **ALFONSO OF CASTILE-LEÓN**, married **AFFONSO III OF PORTUGAL**, King of Portugal & the Algarve [see PORTUGAL 7].

9. SANCHO IV OF CASTILE-LEÓN *el Bravo*, King of Castile, León, Toledo, Galicia, Seville, Córdoba, Murcia, Jaén, and the Algarve, 2nd son, born at Valladolid 12 May 1258. He married at Toledo in June 1282 **MARÍA ALFONSO DE MOLINA**, daughter of Alfonso Infante of Castile, señor of Molina and Mesa, by his 3rd wife, Mayor Alfonso, daughter of Alfonso Téllez de Meneses Girón, señor of Meneses, Montealegre, San Román, Córdoba, etc. [see CASTILE 6.ii above for her ancestry]. She was born about 1259 (aged 60 in 1319). They had five sons, Fernando (IV) [King of Castile and León], Alfonso, Enrique, Pedro [señor of Los Cameros], and Felipe [señor of Cabrera and Ribera], and two daughters, Isabel (wife of Jaime II, King of Aragón, and Jean III *le Bon*, Duke of Brittany, Earl of Richmond, Vicomte of Limoges) and Beatriz. By various mistresses, he also had three illegitimate children, Alfonso Sánchez, Violante Sánchez (wife of Fernán Rodriguez de

Castro), and Teresa Sánchez (wife of Juan Alfonso de Meneses, Count of Barcelos). SANCHO IV, King of Castile, León, etc., died at Toledo 25 April 1295, and was buried in Santa Cruz chapel in Santa María Cathedral in Toledo. His widow, María, was regent for her son, King Fernando IV, 1295–1314, and for her grandson, King Alfonso XI, 1314–21. She died at Valladolid 1 July 1321, and was buried at Santa María la Real monastery called Las Huelgas de Valladolid.

George *Annals of the Queens of Spain* (1850): 231–264 (biog. of Doña Maria la Grande, Queen Consort, Dowager Queen Regent). Delaville le Roulx *Cartulaire Général de l'Ordre des Hospitaliers de S. Jean de Jérusalem* 3 (1899): 407–409, 434, 436, 469, 491, 559, 578, 618–619, 641–642; 4 (1906): 73–74, 99–100. Birch *Cat. Seals in the British Museum* 6 (1900): 620 (seal of Sancho IV, King of Castile, Toledo, León, etc. dated 1293 — Obverse. The King, full-face, seated on a carved throne, with sceptre and orb or mound. Legend wanting. Reverse. The King, in armour, with surcoat, helmet, [sword], scabbard, and shield of arms, riding on a caparisoned horse turned to the left. The armorial bearings of the shield and caparisons are: quarterly; 1, 4. a tripled-tower castle, CASTILE, 2, 3. a lion rampant, LEÓN. Legend wanting.). C.P. 10 (1945): 818–819 (sub Richmond). Aguado Bleye *Manual de Hist. de España* 1 (1954): 693–705. *Jour. Medieval Hist.* 5 (1979): 185–201 (Maria de Molina: "a strong willed and greatly revered figure"). Schwennicke *Europäische Stammtafeln* 2 (1984): 63 (sub Castile and Leon); 3(1) (1984): 127 (sub Molina and Mesa); 3(3) (1985): 532a (sub Castile & León). Williamson *Debrett's Kings & Queens of Europe* (1988): 43. *Studies in Gen. & Fam. Hist. in Tribute to Charles Evans* (1989): 366–417. Leese *Blood Royal* (1996): 51.

Children of Sancho IV of Castile-León, by María Alfonso de Molina:

i. **FERNANDO IV OF CASTILE-LEÓN**, King of Castile, León, etc. [see next].

ii. **BEATRIS** (or **BEATRIZ**) **OF CASTILE-LEÓN**, married **AFFONSO IV OF PORTUGAL**, King of Portugal & the Algarve [see PORTUGAL 9].

10. FERNANDO IV OF CASTILE-LEÓN *el Aljurno*, King of Castile, León, Toledo, Galicia, Seville, Córdoba, Murcia, Jaén, and the Algarve, señor of Molina, son and heir, born at Seville 6 Dec. 1285. He married at Valladolid Jan. 1302 **CONSTANZA** (or **COSTANÇA**) **OF PORTUGAL**, daughter of Diniz *el Justo*, King of Portugal & the Algarve, King of Portugal, by [Saint] Elizabeth (or Isabel), daughter of Pedro III *el Grande*, King of Aragón, King of Sicily, Count of Barcelona [see PORTUGAL 8 for her ancestry]. She was born 3 Jan. 1290. They had one son, Alfonso (XI) [King of Castile and León], and two daughters, Leonor (wife of Jaime of Aragón and Alfonso IV, King of Aragón) and Constanza. FERNANDO IV, King of Castile, León, etc., died at Jaén 7 Sept. 1312. His widow, Constanza, died at Sahagún 23 Nov. 1313.

Rymer *Fœdera* 2(1) (1818): 65, 92 (instances of Fernando IV styled "kinsman" by King Edward II of England). George *Annals of the Queens of Spain* (1850): 264–265 (biog. of Constanza of Portugal). Delaville le Roulx *Cartulaire Général de l'Ordre des Hospitaliers de S. Jean de Jérusalem* 3 (1899): 711–712; 4 (1906): 72–74, 76–77, 99–100. Birch *Cat. Seals in the British Museum* 6 (1900): 620–621 (seal of Fernando IV, King of Castile, Toledo, León, etc. dated 1298 — Obverse. The King, in armour, with crown, surcoat, and shield of arms; riding to the left on a caparisoned horse. The armorial bearings of the shield and caparisons are: quarterly ; 1, 4. a tripled-tower castle, CASTILE; 2, 3. a lion rampant, LEÓN. Reverse. A *rueda* or circular panel quarterly of the armorial charges of CASTILE and LEÓN as on the shield of arms on the obverse.), 621 (leaden bulla of Fernando IV, King of Castile, Toledo, León, etc. dated 1307 — Obverse. The King, in armour, with hauberk of mail, surcoat, crowned helmet, sword and shield of arms; riding on a caparisoned horse springing to the left. The armorial bearings of the shield and caparisons are: quarterly; 1, 4. a tripled-tower castle, CASTILE, 2, 3. a lion rampant, LEÓN. Legend: * S' FERNANDI ILVSTRIS REGIS CASTELLE LEGIONIS. Reverse. Quarterly; 1, 4. CASTILE; 2, 3. LEÓN as before. Beaded borders, and quartering lines on the reverse.). Champeval *Cartulaire des Abbayes de Tulle et de Roc-Amadour* (1903): 349–351 (charter of King Fernando IV of Castile dated 1304 names his wife [muger] Costança; charter witnessed by his brothers, Pedro and Felipe). C.P. 3 (1913): 434–435 (sub Cornwall). Johnstone *Letters of Edward Prince of Wales 1304–1305* (1931): 23 ([Fernando IV], King of Spain styled "cousin" by Edward, Prince of Wales [afterwards King Edward II of England]). Caetano de Sousa *Provas da História Genealógica de Casa Real Portuguesa* 1(1) (1946): 94–94. Aguado Bleye *Manual de Hist. de España* 1 (1954): 705–710. Minguez *Fernando IV de Castilla (1295–1312)* (1976). *Jour. Medieval Hist.* 5 (1979): 185–201. Schwennicke *Europäische Stammtafeln* 2 (1984): 38–39 (sub Portugal), 63 (sub Castile and Leon), 70 (sub Aragón). Williamson *Debrett's Kings & Queens of Europe* (1988): 43. Minguez *Fernando IV de Castilla 1295–1312* (1995). Brault *Rolls of Arms Edward I* 2 (1997): 92 (arms of Fernando of Castile: Gules, three castles or). *TG* 26 (2012): 77.

11. ALFONSO XI OF CASTILE-LEÓN *el Justo*, Knt., King of Castile, León, Toledo, Galicia, Seville, Córdoba, Murcia, Jaén, the Algarve, and Algesiras, señor of Viscaya and Molina, son and heir, born at Salamanca 13 August 1311. He married (1st) **CONSTANZA MANUEL**, daughter of Juan Manuel of Castile, señor of Villena and Escalona, by his 2nd wife, Constanza, daughter of Jaime II, King of Aragón. This marriage was annulled without issue in 1327 (she died at Santaren 13 Nov. 1345). He married (2nd) at Alfayate in Sept. 1328 **MARÍA OF PORTUGAL**, daughter of Affonso IV, King of Portugal & the Algarve, by Beatriz, daughter of Sancho IV, King of Castile, León, etc. [see PORTUGAL 9 for her ancestry]. They had two sons, Fernando and Pedro (I) [King of Castile and León]. By his mistress, Leonor Nuñes de Guzmán, he had nine sons, Pedro Alfonso, Sancho Alfonso, Enrique (II) [King of Castile and León, Count of Trastamara], Fadrique Alfonso, Fernando Alfonso, Tello Alfonso, Juan Alfonso, Pedro Alfonso, and Sancho Alfonso, and one daughter, Juana Alfonso (wife of Fernando de Castro and Felipe de Castro). ALFONSO XI, King of Castile and León, died at Gibraltar 26 March 1350. His widow, María, died at Evora 13 Jan. 1357.

Rymer *Fœdera* 2(1) (1818): 611 (King Alfonso XI styled "kinsman" by King Edward II of England); 2(2) (1821): 736, 771 (instances of King Alfonso XI styled "kinsman" by King Edward III of England). George *Annals of the Queens of Spain* (1850): 265–270 (biog. of Constanza Manuel), 270–283 (biog. of Doña Maria de Portugal). *C.P.R. 1334–1338* (1895): 571. Lehugeur *Hist. de Philippe le Long, Roi de France (1316–1322)* (1897): 267–268 (Alphonso XI, King of Castile, styled "cousin" by King Philippe V of France in letter dated 1320). Birch *Cat. Seals in the British Museum* 6 (1900): 621–622 (leaden bulla of Alfonso XI, King of Castile, Toledo, León, etc. dated 1329). Déprez *Les Préliminaires de la Guerre de Cent Ans: La Papauté, la France et l'Angleterre* (1902): 427–428 (Alfonso XI, King of Castile and León, styled "kinsman" [consanguineus] in letter by King Philippe VI of France dated 1341). *C.P.R. 1345–1348* (1903): 135. Champeval *Cartulaire des Abbayes de Tulle et de Roc-Amadour* (1903): 351–355 (charter of King Alfonso XI of Castile dated 1318 granted with the consent of his grandmother [avuela], Queen María, and his uncles [tios], Juan and Pedro; charter witnessed by his uncle, Felipe, señor of Cabrera and Ribera). *C.P.R. 1348–1350* (1905): 247. *C.P.R. 1374–1377* (1916): 507 (instances of Alfonso XI styled "kinsman" by King Edward III of England). Aguado Bleye *Manual de Hist. de España* 1 (1954): 710–718. *Urbain V (1362–1370): Lettres Communes* 2 (1964): 130. *Jour. Medieval Hist.* 5 (1979): 185–201. Schwennicke *Europäische Stammtafeln* 2 (1984): 64 (sub Castile and Leon); 3(1) (1984): 126 (sub Escalona). Williamson *Debrett's Kings & Queens of Europe* (1988): 43.

12. PEDRO I OF CASTILE-LEÓN *el Cruel*, King of Castile, León, Toledo, Galicia, Seville, Córdoba, Murcia, the Algarve, and Algesiras, 2nd but eldest surviving son and heir, born at Burgos 30 August 1334. About 17 March 1346 he was contracted to marry **JOAN OF ENGLAND** (otherwise known as **JOAN OF THE TOWER**), 2nd daughter of Edward III, King of England, by Philippe, daughter of William III *le Bon*, Count of Hainault, Holland, and Zeeland, lord of Friesland [see ENGLAND 9 for her ancestry]. JOAN OF ENGLAND died of the plague at Bordeaux, France 2 Sept. 1348 en route to be married, and was buried at Bayonne Cathedral. He married (1st) at Valladolid 3 June 1353 **BLANCHE** (or **BLANCA**) **OF BOURBON**, daughter of Pierre I, Duke of Bourbon, Count of Clermont and la Marche, Chamberlain of France, by Isabelle, daughter of Charles of France, Knt., Count of Valois, Chartres, Alençon, and Anjou [see BOURBON 12 for her ancestry]. She was born about 1335 (aged 18 in 1353). Immediately following their wedding, he deserted Blanche for his mistress, **MARÍA DÍAZ DE PADILLA**, daughter of Juan García de Padilla, señor of Villagera, by María González, daughter of Fernán Gutiérrez de Henestrosa. He and María had one son, Alfonso, and three daughters, Beatriz, Constance (or Constanza), and Isabel. In 1354 he asked the Bishops of Avila and Salamanca to annul his marriage to Blanche of Bourbon. He subsequently married (2nd) at Cuéllar probably in March 1354 **JUANA DE CASTRO**, widow of Diego de Haro, and daughter of Pedro Fernández de Castro, señor of Lemos, Monforte, and Sarria, by Isabel, daughter of Pedro Ponce de León. He soon abandoned Juana, granting her the villa of Dueñas, where she lived until her death with the title of queen. In 1361 he allegedly had his former wife, Blanche of Bourbon, poisoned at Medina Sidonia. His long term mistress, María Díaz de Padilla, died at Seville in July 1361, and was buried at the monastery of Santa Clara de Astudillo. In 1362 the Cortes accepted Pedro's claim that he had married his deceased mistress, María de Padilla, in a clandestine ceremony prior to his 1st marriage to Blanche of Bourbon, by which act María's children were formally acknowledged as Pedro's legitimate heirs. María's remains were reinterred with honors of sovereignty in Seville. The following year, his son by María, namely Alfonso, having died, the Cortes of Bubierca acknowledged María's three surviving daughters as Pedro's heirs. By an unknown mistress (or mistresses), Pedro also had three illegitimate sons, Sancho, Diego, and Juan. PEDRO I, King of Castile and León, was slain at Montiel 23 March 1367/8 by his illegitimate brother, Enrique, Count of Trastamara. His former wife, Juana, died at Galicien 21 August 1374.

> Rymer *Fœdera* 6 (1727): 126–127, 401–403, 480–481 (instances of Pedro, King of Castile & León, styled "kinsman" [consanguinei] by King Edward III of England), 514–520 (Charles, King of Navarre, and Edward, Prince of Aquitaine and Wales, styled "cousins"), 521–533 (instances of John of Gaunt, Duke of Lancaster, styled "kinsman"). George *Annals of the Queens of Spain* (1850): 283–309 (biog. of Blanche of Bourbon). Rosell *Crónicas de los Reyes de Castilla* 1 (Biblioteca de Autores Españoles 66) (1875): 514 (re. Padilla fam.). *Annual Rpt. of the Deputy Keeper* 48 (1887): 587. *Genealogist* n.s. 12 (1895): 181, 185. Birch *Cat. Seals in the British Museum* 6 (1900): 623 (seal of Pedro I, King of Castile, Toledo, León, etc. dated 1351). *C.C.R. 1341–1343* (1902): 554. *C.P.R. 1345–1348* (1903): 430. *C.C.R. 1346–1349* (1905): 55–56, 426, 570, 590. *C.P.R. 1348–1350* (1905): 24, 26, 40, 343. Storer *Peter the Cruel* (1911). *List of Diplomatic Docs., Scottish Docs. & Papal Bulls* (PRO Lists and Indexes 49) (1923): 13. Aguado Bleye *Manual de Hist. de España* 1 (1954): 755–763. Garcia Carraffa & Garcia Carraffa *Diccionario Heráldico y Genealógico de Apellidos Españoles y Americanos* 23 (1955): 136–138 (sub Castro); 65 (1950): 73 (sub Padilla). Russell *English Intervention in Spain & Portugal in the Time of Edward III & Richard II* (1955). *Yorkshire Arch. Jour.* 40 (1962): 265–297. Fernández *Hist. de España* 14 (1966): 1ff. Schwennicke *Europäische Stammtafeln* 2 (1984): 64 (sub Castile and Leon). *Jour. Medieval Hist.* 11 (1985): 61–69. Van Kerrebrouck *La Maison de Bourbon 1256–1987* (1987): 60–61. Williamson *Debrett's Kings & Queens of Europe* (1988): 43. Estow *Pedro the Cruel of Castile* (1995). Gerli *Medieval Iberia* (2003): 629 (biog. of María de Padilla). Online resource: Angel Vaca Lorenzo *Documentación Medieval de la Villa de Astudillo* (PDF file).

Children of Pedro I of Castile-León, by María Díaz de Padilla:

i. **CONSTANCE** (or **CONSTANZA**) **OF CASTILE-LEÓN**, married **JOHN OF GAUNT**, K.G., Duke of Aquitaine and Lancaster, Earl of Derby, Lincoln, and Leicester [see LANCASTER 10].

ii. **ISABEL OF CASTILE-LEÓN**, married **EDMUND OF LANGLEY**, K.G., Duke of York [see YORK 10].

❧ CHAMBERLAIN ❦

ROBERT DE VERE, Knt., Earl of Oxford, married **ISABEL DE BOLEBEC**.
HUGH DE VERE, Knt., Earl of Oxford, married **HAWISE DE QUINCY**.
ROBERT DE VERE, Knt., Earl of Oxford, married **ALICE DE SANFORD**.
ALPHONSE DE VERE, Knt., of Aston Sanford, Buckinghamshire, married **JOAN FOLIOT**.
JOHN DE VERE, Knt., Earl of Oxford, married **MAUD DE BADLESMERE** (desc. King William the Conqueror).
MARGARET DE VERE, married **NICHOLAS DE LOVAINE**, Knt., of Penshurst, Kent.
MARGARET LOVAINE, married **RICHARD CHAMBERLAIN**, Knt., of Coates (in Titchmarsh), Northamptonshire [see LOVAINE 7].

8. RICHARD CHAMBERLAIN, Esq., of Coates (in Titchmarsh), Northamptonshire, Tilsworth, Bedfordshire, Petsoe (in Emberton), Buckinghamshire, etc., son and heir, born about 1391–2 (aged 16 in 1408, 22 in 1413). He married (1st) **ELIZABETH** _____. They had one son, Richard. In 1425 he and his half-brother, Thomas Saint Clair, were sued by Thomas de Pulteney regarding the manors of Penshurst and Yevesfeld, Kent. By 1431 he claimed and perhaps controlled the manor of Cheveley, Cambridgeshire, formerly held by his grandfather, Nicholas de Lovaine, Knt. He married (2nd) before 1436 **MARGARET KNYVET**, daughter of John Knyvet, Knt., of Southwick, Northamptonshire, Hamerton, Huntingdonshire, etc., by Elizabeth, daughter of Constantine de Clifton, Esq. or Gent., 2nd Lord Clifton [see GURDON 14 for her ancestry]. They had two sons, William, Esq., and Richard, Esq. RICHARD CHAMBERLAIN, Esq., died in 1439. His widow,

Margaret, married (2nd) **WILLIAM GEDNEY**, Esq., of Cardington, Bedfordshire, King's esquire, Clerk of the Signet Office, King's serjeant, Secretary for Queen Katherine of France (widow of King Henry V of England), 1433, and for Queen Margaret of Anjou (wife of King Henry VI of England), 1445, Steward of Berkhamstead Honour, Knight of the Shire for Bedfordshire, 1447, Sheriff of Bedfordshire, 1449–50. He acted as one of the king's messengers from time to time, taking letters to the Duke of Gloucester at Tenby in 1440. In 1443 he went on a mission to Normandy. In the period, 1452–4, he and his wife, Margaret, "late the wife of Richard Chamberleyn, Esq., of Cotys [Coates]" sued William Aldewyncle, Esq., feoffee of the said Richard in Chancery regarding the third part of the manors of Denford, Coates (in Titchmarsh), Ringstead, and Raunds, Northamptonshire, and Petsoe (in Emberton) and Okeney, Buckinghamshire. Margaret died shortly before 12 May 1458.

Coll. Top. et Gen. 3 (1836): 95–98. *Misc. Gen. et Heraldica* 1st Ser. 1 (1868): 24–27 (Chamberlain ped.). Harvey et al. *Vis. of Oxford 1566, 1574, 1634 & 1574* (H.S.P. 5) (1871): 235–237 (Chamberlaine ped.: "Richardus Chamberlaine fil. 1. & hæres. = Margareta fil. Willi. (?John) Knevett, militis, per filiam Ducis Buck."). Rye *Pedes Finium or Fines Rel. Cambridge* (1891): 151–152. Birch *Cat. Seals in the British Museum* 2 (1892): 623 (seal of Richard Chaumberlayn, Esq. dated 1428 — A shield of arms: on a chevron, between three escallops, as many roses slipped, or other uncertain charges). *List of Sheriffs for England & Wales* (PRO Lists and Indexes 9) (1898): 2. *Genealogist* n.s. 17 (1901): 25; n.s. 19 (1903): 244 (pleadings state that William Chamberlain, husband of Joan, was uncle, not brother, of Richard Chamberlain, the plaintiff, but charted in error). Wrottesley *Peds. from the Plea Rolls* (1905): 434. *Norfolk Antiq. Misc.* 2nd Ser. 1 (1906): 81–87 (Knyvet ped. dated 1651). *C.P.R. 1441–1446* (1908): 95. VCH *Bedford* 3 (1912): 433. *Rpt. on the MSS of Lord de L'Isle & Dudley Preserved at Penshurst Place* 1 (Hist. MSS Comm. 77) (1925): 13–14 (letters of atty. by Richard Chamburleyn, Esq. dated 1420; a seal with a shield of arms — a chevron between three escallops). VCH *Buckingham* 4 (1927): 340. Colket *English Anc. of Hutchinson & Scott* (1936): 41, 54. Bassett *Knights of Bedfordshire* (Bedfordshire Hist. Rec. Soc. 29) (1949): 43–44 (biog. of William Gedney). *NEHGR* 138 (1984): 317–320. Bodine *Anc. of Dorothea Poyntz* (1995): 27. *Cal. IPM* 20 (1995): 2–3, 15–16. *TG* 13 (1999): 188–198. VCH *Cambridge* 10 (2002): 46–49. National Archives, C 1/18/18 (available at www.catalogue.nationalarchives.gov.uk/search.asp).

9. RICHARD CHAMBERLAIN, Esq., of Coates (in Titchmarsh), Northamptonshire, Stanbridge (in Leighton Buzzard) and Tilsworth, Bedfordshire, Ekeney (in Emberton) and Petsoe (in Emberton), Buckinghamshire, North Reston, Lincolnshire, Barton St. John, Oxfordshire, and Swaffham Prior, Cambridgeshire, younger son by his father's 2nd marriage, born 1436–9. He was heir in 1470 to his older brother, William Chamberlain, Esq. In 1473 he sued Joan, widow of his brother, William Chamberlain, Esq., for the manor of Great Barton, Oxfordshire. He married before 30 Nov. 1476 **SIBYL FOWLER**, daughter of Richard Fowler, of Rycote and Holton, Oxfordshire, Chancellor of the Exchequer to King Edward IV and of the Duchy of Lancaster, by Joan, daughter of John Danvers. They had four sons, Edward, William (a friar in Greenwich), Thomas, and John, and one daughter, Anne. RICHARD CHAMBERLAIN, Esq., died 28 August 1496. He left a will proved 19 October 1496 (P.C.C. 7 Horne). His widow, Sibyl, died in 1525. They were buried at Shirburn, Oxfordshire.

Coll. Top. et Gen. 1 (1834): 329 (Ped. of Danvers &c.: "Sibill, sister to Sir Richard Fowler, was maryed to Richard Chamberlain, and they had issue iii sonnes and one daughter. Edward, the eldest sone, now Knight, maryed one of the daughters of Sir John Verney, and they have issue. William, brother to Sir Edward, was a fryer in Grenewiche. His brother John is not maryed; theire sister Anne was fyrst maryed to Edward Rawley, Knight, and they have a sone maryed to Anne, daughter to Sir Humfry Conysby, Knight, and now Justice: and after, the saide Anne Rawley was maryed to Fulchurch, and they have issue."). Harvey et al. *Vis. of Oxford 1566, 1574, 1634 & 1574* (H.S.P. 5) (1871): 187 (Danvers ped.), 235–237 (Chamberlaine ped.: "Richardus Chamberlaine fil. & hæres. = Sibilla filia Rici. Fowler de Ricott, Cancellarii Ducatus."). Lee *Hist., Desc. & Antiqs. of Thame* (1883): 292–296 (Quartermain ped.). *Genealogist* n.s. 19 (1903): 244. Wrottesley *Peds. from the Plea Rolls* (1905): 434. *D.N.B.* 4 (1908): 7–8 (biog. of Sir Edward Chamberlayne). VCH *Bedford* 3 (1912): 399–417, 433 (errs in stating Richard Chamberlain, died 1496, was "probably" the son of William Chamberlain; Richard and William were actually brothers) (Fowler arms: Azure a cheveron argent between three leopards or with three crosses moline sable in the cheveron). Stephenson *List of Mon. Brasses in the British Isles* (1926): 420. VCH *Buckingham* 4 (1927): 340. VCH *Northampton* 3 (1930): 193. Colket *English Anc. of Hutchinson & Scott* (1936): 42. VCH *Oxford* 5 (1957): 170–171, 285. *NEHGR* 138 (1984): 317–320. Bodine *Anc. of*

Dorothea Poyntz (1995): 20. *TG* 13 (1999): 188–198. Biancalana *Fee Tail & the Common Recovery in Medieval England* (2001): 427–428. *Trans. Monumental Brass Soc.* 17 (2007): 453–466.

Child of Richard Chamberlain, Esq., by Sibyl Fowler:

i. **ANNE CHAMBERLAIN**, married **EDWARD RALEIGH**, Esq., of Farnborough, Warwickshire [see CHESELDINE 18].

❧ CHAMPERNOUN ❦

WILLIAM THE CONQUEROR, King of England, married **MAUD OF FLANDERS**.
HENRY I, King of England, by an unknown mistress, _____.
ROBERT FITZ ROY, Earl of Gloucester, married **MABEL FITZ ROBERT** [see GLOUCESTER 3].

4. ROBERT FITZ ROBERT, of Conarton (in Gwithian), Cornwell, Castellan of Gloucester, younger son. He married **HAWISE DE REDVERS**, daughter of Baldwin de Redvers, 1st Earl of Devon. They had one daughter, Mabel. Sometime in the period, 1141–61, he and his wife, Hawise, made a gift to Quarr Abbey. Sometime in the period, 1147–71, he witnessed a charter of his brother, Earl William, at Bristol to Gilbert Fitz John. Sometime in the period, 1147–50, probably before March 1148/9, he witnessed a treaty between his brother, Earl William, and Roger, Earl of Hereford. Sometime in the period, c. 1147–8, he witnessed a charter of his mother, Countess Mabel, and his brother, Earl William, announcing restorations made to Jocelin, Bishop of Salisbury. In 1154, as Robert son of the Earl of Gloucester, he conveyed to Richard the butler the manor of Conarton (in Gwithian), Cornwall for a payment 400 marks of silver and a silk cloth, and to his wife, "Harvisa" a palfrey. ROBERT FITZ ROBERT (or FITZ COUNT) died in 1170. In the period, c. 1193–1211, his widow, Hawise de Redvers, gave the manors of Fleet and Ibberton, Dorset to her grandson, Jordan de Champernoun.

Madox *Formulare Anglicanum* (1702): 3–4 (charter of Hawise de Rivers daughter of Earl Baldwin). Pole *Colls. towards a Desc. of Devon* (1791): 422–423. Dugdale *Monasticon Anglicanum* 6(2) (1830): 1097–1098. Pertz *Chronica et Annales ævi Salici* (Monumenta Germaniæ Historica, Scriptores 6) (1844): 519 (Roberti de Monte Cronica [Robert de Torigni]) sub 1170 —"Mortuo Roberto filio Roberti comitis Gloecestrie"). *C.P.* 5 (1926): 686, footnote b (sub Gloucester). *Collectanea Archæologica* 1 (1862): 263–284. Patterson *Earldom of Gloucester Charters* (1973): 63, 97–98, 155–156 (Robert and his brother, William styled "my sons" [filii mei] by their mother, Countess Mabel). Bearman *Charters of the Redvers family and the Earldom of Devon, 1090–1217* (Devon & Cornwall Soc. n.s. 37) (1994). Fizzard *Plympton Priory* (2008): 93n. (Hawise de Redvers was "benefactor of Quarr, Christchurch, Hartland Abbey in Devon, and the Knights Hospitallers."). Cornwall Rec. Office: Messrs Harvey and Co, Hay, H/236 (available at available at www.a2a.org.uk/search/index.asp).

5. MABEL FITZ ROBERT, married (1st) **JORDAN DE CHAMPERNOUN** (or **CHAMBERNOUN**), seigneur of Cambernon (Manche, arr. and cant. Coutances) and Maisoncelles[-la-Jourdain] (dept. Calvados, arr. and cant. Vire) in Normandy, and Umberleigh (in Atherington) and High Bickington, Devon, presumably son of Jordan de Champernoun, living 1146. They had two sons, Richard and Jordan. JORDAN DE CHAMPERNOUN was living in 1172, in which year he owed the service of one knight in Normandy, having himself the service of two knights. His widow, Mabel, married (2nd) **GUILLAUME** (or **WILLIAM**) **DE SOLERS** (or **SOLIERS**), of Ellingham, Hampshire, Constable of Moulins-la-Marche, 1180. They had two sons, Guillaume (or William), chev., and Richard, and two daughters, Philippe (wife of _____ Punchardon) and Joan (wife of William Cosyn). In 1163 he gave the church of All Souls, with the chapel of St. Mary, in Ellingham, Hampshire to the Abbey of St. Sauveur-le-Vicomte, Coutances, for the soul of his uncle, Earl Richard. He witnessed a charter of Richard, Bishop of Winchester in 1176. He was present at an assize at Caen in Normandy in 1176–7. He also witnessed a charter for King Henry II for Hôtel-Dieu du Mans. In Jan. 1177 he assisted in the Siege of Baieux. The king gave him lands recovered by inquest at Guillerville and Criquetot. At an unknown date, Mabel, lady of Maisoncelles, [grand]daughter of earl Robert and mother of Jordan de Campo Ernulfi, confirmed to the canons regular of Plessis the gift by her son, Jordan, of the church of St. Amand of Maisoncelles[-la-Jourdain] (dept. Calvados, arr. and cant. Vire) in alms for ever. In the period, c. 1193–1211, his widow, Mabel, confirmed the gift of the manors of Fleet and Ibberton, Dorset made by her mother, Hawise de Redvers, to her son, Jordan de Champernoun. In 1198 she was sued in a plea in Cornwall by Hugh de Beauchamp. In 1200 she appointed her son, Richard [de Champernoun], to represent her in a plea of land against William de Botreaux in Ludgvan, Cornwall. About the year 1200 as "Mabel, daughter of Robert, son of the Earl of Gloucester," she confirmed to John son of Richard the Butler the manor of Conarton (in Gwithian), Cornwall, excepting Penburn and Lugan, for 30 silver marks and one caparisoned horse of value of two marks, together with the service of Philip de Caul, Alfred de Trevitho, and Enoch. In 1201 William de Botreaux sued her in a plea of land at Ludgvan, Cornwall. In 1201, as "Mabil' de Soliis," she held 16 knights' fees of the Honour of Gloucester. Following the loss of Normandy in 1204, her lands at Umberleigh Devon were confiscated and granted in 1205 by King John to Master Serlo. About the same time her lands at Hanford, Dorset were likewise confiscated by the king (they being considered land of the Normans) and were granted to Alan de Roterbiaus.

Pole *Colls. towards a Desc. of Devon* (1791): 422–423. Dugdale *Monasticon Anglicanum* 5 (1825): 198 (charter of Henry de Tracy dated 1146). *Mémoires de la Société des Antiquaires de Normandie* 8(2) (1834): 105, 448. Hardy *Rotuli de Oblatis et Finibus in Turri Londinensi Asservati* (1835): 135, 152, 333. Palgrave *Rotuli Curiæ Regis* 1 (1835): 336. Stapleton *Magni Rotuli Scaccarii Normanniæ* 1 (1840): ci, cxxviii, cxxix, cxxxiv. *Collectanea Archæologica* 1 (1862): 263–284. Hutchins *Hist. & Antiqs. of Dorset* 4 (1870): 61. Vivian *Vis. of Devon 1531, 1564 & 1620* (1895): 160–165 (sub Champernowne). *Feet of Fines of the 7th & 8th Years of the Reign of Richard I A.D. 1196 to A.D. 1197* (Pubs. Pipe Roll Soc. 20) (1896): 55–56. Round *Cal. Doc. Preserved in France* 1 (1899): 192. *C.Ch.R.* 1 (1903): 249. VCH Hampshire 4 (1911): 563–567. Mitchell *Studies in Taxation under John and Henry III* (1914): 43. *C.R.R.* 1 (1922): 264, 438; 15 (1972): 307–308. *Book of Fees* 2 (1923): 1268. Stenton *Great Roll of the Pipe for the 5th Year of the Reign of King John Michaelmas 1203* (Pubs. Pipe Roll Soc. n.s. 16) (1938): 41, 43. Stenton *Great Roll of the Pipe for the 6th Year of the Reign of King John Michaelmas 1201* (Pubs. Pipe Roll Soc. n.s. 18) (1940): 231–232. Smith *Great Roll of the Pipe for the 7th Year of the Reign of King John Michaelmas 1205* (Pubs. Pipe Roll Soc. n.s. 19) (1941): 104–105. Stenton *Great Roll of the Pipe for the 8th Year of the Reign of King John Michaelmas 1206* (Pubs. Pipe Roll Soc. n.s. 20) (1942): 18–19, 143 (sub Michaelmas 1206 sub Devon: "Magister Serlo debet j palefridum (set non debet summoneri quia noin habuit pro quo promisit) pro habendo manerio de Vmbel' quod fuit Mabil' de Solariis tenendum per eandem firmam per quam Ricardus de Greinuill' illud tenuit . per bailliam Willelmi de Faleisia."). Kirkus *Great Roll of the Pipe for the 9th Year of the Reign of King John Michaelmas 1207* (Pubs. Pipe Roll Soc. n.s. 22) (1946): 220. Brown *Memorandum Roll for the 10th Year of the Reign of King John (1207–8) together with the Curia Regis Rolls of Hilary 7 Richard I (1196) and Easter 9 Richard I (1198)* (Pubs. Pipe Roll Soc. n.s. 31) (1957): 104. Powicke *Loss of Normandy* (1961): 72. Loyd *Origins of Some Anglo-Norman Fams.* (1975): 26 (sub Champernowne, de Campo Arnulfi). Franklin *English Episcopal Acta* 8 (1993): 107–108, 111. Bearman *Charters of the Redvers family and the Earldom of Devon, 1090–1217* (Devon & Cornwall Soc. n.s. 37) (1994): 11, 146. Power *Norman Frontier in the 12th & Early 13th Cents.* (2004): 42, 75–76, 78. Cornwall Rec. Office: Arundell of Lanherne and Trerice, AR/1/101, AR/15/130 (available at available at www.a2a.org.uk/search/index.asp). Cornwall Rec. Office: Messrs Harvey and Co, Hay, H/236 (available at available at www.a2a.org.uk/search/index.asp).

6. JORDAN DE CHAMPERNOUN, 2nd son. He married **EMMA DE SOLIGNY**, daughter of Hasculf de Soligny, by Iseult, daughter and heiress of Jean de Dol, seigneur of Dol in Brittany. They had one son, William. At an unknown date, he confirmed to the canons regular of Plessis and Ivrandes the earlier gift of his brother, Richard. In the period, c.1193–1211, his grandmother, Hawise de Redvers, granted him the manors of Fleet and Ibberton, Dorset. In 1206 King John assigned him Umberleigh, Devon and £15 of his mother's lands.

Pole *Colls. towards a Desc. of Devon* (1791): 422–423. *Mémoires de la Société des Antiquaires de Normandie* 8(2) (1834): 105. Hardy *Rotuli Normanniæ in Turri Londinensi Asservati* 1 (1835): 93. Douet d'Arcq *Coll. de Sceaux des Archives de l'Empire* 1(1) (1863): 522 (seal of Jourdain de Champ-Arnoul dated early 13th Cent. — Armorial. Un sautoir de vair. Legend: + SIGILL : IORDANI : DE CHAME ERNVL. Appended to a undated charter of Jordanus de Campo Arnulfi in favor of Savigny Abbey.). Vivian *Vis. of Devon 1531, 1564 & 1620* (1895): 160–165 (sub Champernowne). Round *Cal. Doc. Preserved in France* 1 (1899): 195. *Cal. IPM* 4 (1913): no. 82. Loyd *Origins of Some Anglo-Norman Fams.* (1975): 26 (sub

Champernowne, de Campo Arnulfi). Power *Norman Frontier in the 12th & Early 13th Cents.* (2004): 518–519 (Subligny ped.).

7. WILLIAM DE CHAMPERNOUN, of Umberleigh (in Atherington) and High Bickington, Devon, Hampton Gay and Lower Heyford, Oxfordshire, etc., son and heir. He married **EVE DE BLANCHMINSTER** (or **WHITCHURCH**), daughter and heiress of Reynold de Blanchminster (or Whitchurch), of Shrivenham and Winterbourne (in Chieveley), Berkshire, and Bolney, Oxfordshire, by his 1st wife, Alice, daughter and co-heiress of Nicholas de Bolney. They had one daughter, Joan. In 1228–9 he brought an assize of darrein presentment against the Abbot of Ford regarding the churches of Bickington and Umberleigh, Devon. In 1229 he was involved in a dispute with the Abbot of Tewkesbury. WILLIAM DE CHAMPERNOUN was living in 1235. She married (2nd) before 1236 **HENRY FITZ ROY**, Knt., of Waltham, Ashby, Brigsley, Gonerby (in Hatcliffe), Hawerby, and North Coates, Lincolnshire, and Chilham, Kent, illegitimate son of John, King of England, by an unknown mistress [see ENGLAND 5 for his ancestry]. They had no issue. He was sent as a student to the Prior of Kenilworth in 1207. In 1215 he was granted the lands of Robert Fitz Walter in Cornwall. In 1217 he and Ralph de Raleigh were granted the manor of Waltham, Lincolnshire formerly held by Alan Fitz Count to sustain them in royal service. In 1231 he was granted all of the land of Henri de Avaugor, a Norman, in Waltham, Lincolnshire. On 21 Aug1249, Geoffrey de Grandi Monte was granted all land in Beseby, in the soke of Wautham, and with the dower of Eva de Chambernun there if she should die in this time. SIR HENRY FITZ ROY died shortly before 8 April 1245. His widow, Eve, married (3rd) before 30 June 1252 **GILES DE CLIFFORD** (living 1276–7), of Columbjohn, Everleigh, Combe-in-Teignhead, and Godford (in Awliscombe), Devonshire, younger son of Walter de Clifford, of Clifford, Herefordshire, by Agnes, daughter and heiress of Roger de Condet. They had one son, Reynold. He witnessed a charter of his brother, Walter de Clifford, dated c.1225. In 1257 Giles and his wife, Eve, quitclaimed land in Shrivenham Hundred in Berkshire to William de Valence and his wife, Joan, in exchange for a quitclaim to the plot of land where the manor of Stauelpeth was built. In 1258 he and his wife, Eve, gave 1 mark to have a plea in Wiltshire. Giles presented to the church of Stoke-in-Teignhead, Devon in 1259. In 1266 he was pardoned by the king due to his non-observance of the Provisions of Oxford. In 1274 he and the heirs of Thomas de Hauterive [or Dautry] were recorded as the owners of Shrivenham Hundred in Berkshire. In 1274 the king appointed a commission of oyer and terminer on complaint by Henry son of Adam de Cotes who stated that he had previously impleaded Richard Bernard and another in the court of William de Valence, Giles de Clifford, and Isabel de Hauteryve (or Dautry) of Shrivenham, Berkshire by writ of King Henry III touching a two virgates of land in Kyngescotes and on his complaint of a false judgment. In 1274–5 Joan de Champernoun [his step-daughter] arraigned an assize of mort d'ancestor against him and Reginald de Clifford touching three messuages and land in Godford (in Awliscombe), Combe[-in-Teignhead], and Rocombe, Devon. In 1275–6 Joan de Champernoun arraigned an assize of mort d'ancestor against him touching rent in Figheldean, Wiltshire. In the same period, Reynold son of Giles de Clifford arraigned an assize of novel disseisin against him and others touching a tenement in Over Rocombe and Stoke, Devon. In 1276–7 Alice de Ralegh arraigned an assize of novel disseisin against Giles de Clifford and others touching a tenement in Combe-in-Teignhead, Devon. In 1276–7 Reginald son of Giles de Clifford arraigned an assize of novel disseisin against Alice widow of Giles de Clifford and Wymund de Raleye touching a tenement in Over Rocombe and Stoke, Devon.

Pole *Colls. towards a Desc. of Devon* (1791): 422–423. Kennett *Parochial Antiqs. of Ambrosden, Burcester* 1 (1818): 213 (charter of William de Champernoun). Roberts *Excerpta è Rotulis Finium in Turri Londinensi asservatis, Henrico Tertio rege, AD 1216–1272* 2 (1836): 274. Vivian *Vis. of Devon 1531, 1564 & 1620* (1895): 160–165 (sub Champernowne). *Notes & Queries* 9th Ser. 4 (1899): 212. Gerard *Particular Desc. of the County of Somerset* (Somerset Rec. Soc. 15) (1900): 6. C.P.R. 1247–1258 (1908): 46. VCH *Oxford* 6 (1959): 152–159, 182–195.

8. JOAN DE CHAMPERNOUN, daughter and heiress. She married before 17 July 1238 (date of fine) **RALPH DE WILINGTON**, Knt., of Poulton, Gloucestershire, Cherington, Warwickshire, Calstone Wellington, Wiltshire, etc., and, in right of his wife, of Beaford, Colhays, Manleigh, Stoke Rivers, and Umberleigh (in Atherington), Devon, Constable of Exeter Castle and Sheriff of Devon, 1254–5, son and heir of Ralph de Wilington, of Calstone Wellington, Wiltshire, Constable of Bristol Castle, Keeper of the Town and Castle of Devizes, by Olimpia, daughter and heiress of William Franc Chevaler. They had one son, Ralph, Knt. In 1238 the Abbot of Tewkesbury quitclaimed to Ralph and his wife, Joan, all his right and claim in the advowson of High Bickington, Devon. He was appointed to tallage the royal domain in Gloucestershire in 1252. SIR RALPH DE WILINGTON was living April 1255, and presumably died before 18 Nov. 1256 (date of fine). His widow, Joan, presented to the churches of St. Gwinear, Cornwall, 1261, Huntshaw, Devon, 1277, Beaford, Devon, 1278, and High Bickington, Devon, 1278 and 1283. In 1274–5 she arraigned an assize of mort d'ancestor against Giles de Clifford [her step-father] and Reginald de Clifford touching three messuages and land in Godford (in Awliscombe), Combe[-in-Teignhead], and Rocombe, Devon. In 1275–6 she arraigned an assize of mort d'ancestor against Giles de Clifford touching rent in Figheldean, Wiltshire. She was the mesne tenant of Lower Heyford, Oxfordshire in 1275 and 1284. Sometime during the reign of King Henry III, she founded a chantry at Umberleigh, Devon. Joan died before 1309, when her grandson, John de Wilington, presented to the church of High Bickington, Devon.

> Pole *Colls. towards a Desc. of Devon* (1791): 422–423. Kennett *Parochial Antiqs. Attempted in the Hist. of Ambrosden, Burcester & other adjacent Parts* 1 (1818): 213 (charter of Joan de Champernoun, widow of Ralph de Wylynton). Burke *Genealogical & Heraldic Hist. of the Land Gentry* 4 (1838): 526–529 (sub Willington). *Annual Rpt. of the Deputy Keeper* 44 (1883): 115; 45 (1885): 172. Burke *Dormant, Abeyant, Forfeited, and Extinct Peerages* (1883): 585–586 (sub Willington) (Willington arms: Gules, a saltier, vairée, argent and azure). Hingeston-Randolph *Regs. of Walter Bronescombe & Peter Quivil* (1889): 113, 144, 145, 173, 346. *List of Sheriffs for England & Wales* (PRO Lists and Indexes 9) (1898): 34. *Notes & Queries* 9th Ser. 4 (1899): 212. Gerard *Particular Desc. of the County of Somerset* (Somerset Rec. Soc. 15) (1900): 6. Reichel *Devon Feet of Fines* 1 (1912): 135–136, 290–291. VCH *Berkshire* 4 (1924): 531–543. VCH *Warwick* 5 (1949): 38–41. C.P. 12(2) (1959): 643–645 (sub Wilington). VCH *Oxford* 6 (1959): 152–159, 182–195. *Cal. IPM* 4 (1913): no. 82. VCH *Wiltshire* 17 (2002): 123–135.

9. RALPH DE WILINGTON, Knt., of Umberleigh (in Atherington), Devon, Ablington (in Bibury), Lidney, and Yate, Gloucestershire, Cherington, Warwickshire, Calstone Wellington, Wiltshire, etc., Keeper of Lundy Island, son and heir, born about 1239 (of full age in July 1260). He married **JULIANE** _____.[7] They had five sons, John, Knt. [1st Lord Wilington], Reynold (clerk), Henry, Thomas, and presumably Edmund. He supported the Barons in the Civil War, 1264-5, serving under Geoffrey de Lucy. He forfeited his lands in 1265. He recognized a debt in October 1270. In 1275–6 Reynold son of Giles de Clifford arraigned an assize of mort d'ancestor against Ralph and Juliane his wife touching a messuage and land in Shrivenham, Berkshire, and a similar assize touching a messuage and land in Pattishall, Northamptonshire. In 1277–8 he arraigned a jury against Thomas Vincent touching a messuage and land in La Bruerne, Gloucestershire. He was named as a creditor 12 Feb. 1284/5. In 1286 he owed Alexander de Marwell, and Richard de Wherwell, citizens and merchants of Winchester, a debt of £39 2s. 6d. for cloth sold to him and provided on credit. SIR RALPH DE WILINGTON died before 15 October 1294. His widow, Juliane, was living June 1299, but died before 16 Nov. 1323.

---

[7] Juliane, wife of Sir Ralph de Wilington, was not as sometimes alleged the daughter and co-heiress of Richard de Lomene, Knt., of Uplowman, Gittisham, and Riddlecombe (in Ashreigney), Devon) [see *Year Books of Edward III* 6 (Rolls Ser. 31b) (1891): 254–257 re. a lawsuit dated 1341, in which James Cokyngton sued for the manors of Gittisham and Lomene Richard, Devon, as heir of Christine Lomene, widow of Edmund de Wilington, which Christine was evidently the daughter and sole heiress of Sir Richard de Lomene).]

Pole *Colls. towards a Desc. of Devon* (1791): 422–423. Burke *Genealogical & Heraldic Hist. of the Land Gentry* 4 (1838): 526–529 (sub Willington). Maclean *Hist. of the Deanery of Trigg Minor* 1 (1876): 384 (Wylyngton ped.) (Wylyngton arms: Barry bendy indented or and sable a chief argent). Burke *Dormant, Abeyant, Forfeited, and Extinct Peerages* (1883): 585–586 (sub Willington). *Annual Rpt. of the Deputy Keeper* 45 (1885): 307; 47 (1886): 175. *Trans. Bristol & Gloucs. Arch. Soc.* 11 (1886–87): 139, 144, 147. *Cal. IPM* 4 (1913): no. 82; 6 (1910): 350–351. Reichel *Devon Feet of Fines* 2 (Devon & Cornwall Rec. Soc. 1939) (1939): 69–70, 105. VCH *Warwick* 5 (1949): 38–41. *C.P.* 12(2) (1959): 645–646 (sub Willington). Brault *Rolls of Arms Edward I (1272–1307)* 2 (1997): 456 (arms of Ralph de Willington: Gules, a saltire vair). VCH *Wiltshire* 17 (2002): 123–135. National Archives, C 241/7/36 (available at www.catalogue.nationalarchives.gov.uk/search.asp).

10. HENRY DE WILINGTON, of Gittisham and Uplowman, Devon, Culverdene (in Sandhurst), Gloucestershire, Sheriff of Cornwall, 1316, Under-Sheriff of Cornwall, 1317, 3rd son. He married **MARGARET** (or **MARGERY**) **DE FREVILLE**, daughter of Alexander de Freville, Knt., of Tamworth, Warwickshire, by Joan, daughter and heiress of Ralph de Cromwell, Knt. They had one son, Henry, Knt. In 1313–14 Henry and his wife, Margaret, were granted the manor of Yatesbury, Wiltshire by her parents. Sometime before 1322, he and Christine de Lomene, widow of Edmund de Wilington, were enfeoffed by his brother, John de Wilington, with the manor of Lanteglos [by Fowey], Cornwall, and lands in Fawton, Cornwall for the term of their lives. He and his brother, John, were taken prisoners at the Battle of Boroughbridge in 1322. Henry was subsequently hung, drawn, and quartered for his homicides, and his estates forfeited. In 1323 miracles were said to be worked by his body, then hanging in chains at Bristol.

Pole *Colls. towards a Desc. of Devon* (1791): 422–423. Burke *Genealogical & Heraldic Hist. of the Land Gentry* 4 (1838): 526–529 (sub Willington). Maclean *Hist. of the Deanery of Trigg Minor* 1 (1876): 384 (Wylyngton ped.). Burke *Dormant, Abeyant, Forfeited, and Extinct Peerages* (1883): 585–586 (sub Willington). *Trans. Bristol & Gloucs. Arch. Soc.* 10 (1885–86): 79–80. *List of Sheriffs for England & Wales* (PRO Lists and Indexes 9) (1898): 21. *Feudal Aids* 1 (1899): 381. *Cal. IPM* 7 (1909): 9. *C.P.* 12(2) (1959): 649, footnote d (sub Willington). Martival *Regs. of Roger Martival, Bishop of Salisbury 1315–1330* 3 (Canterbury & York Soc. 59) (1965): 87–88. VCH *Wiltshire* 17 (2002): 172–181. National Archives, C 143/96/16; SC 8/201/10046 (available at www.catalogue.nationalarchives.gov.uk/search.asp). Carthew.

11. HENRY DE WILINGTON, Knt., of Gittisham, Beaford, Manleigh, Riddlecombe (in Ashreigney), Stoke Rivers, and Uplowman, Devon, Steward of the Duchy of Cornwall, born c. 1313–4 (aged 13 or 14 in 1327). He married **ISABEL DE WHALESBOROUGH**, daughter of John de Whalesborough, Knt. They had two sons, John, Knt., and Thomas, and one daughter, Eleanor. In 1348 he owed a debt of £210 to William Bishop, serjeant. In 1341 he was sued by James de Cokyngton, heir of Christine de Lomene, regarding the manors of Gittisham and Lomene Richard, Devon. He witnessed a charter of Henry Fitz Roger, Knt., in 1349. SIR HENRY DE WILINGTON died 23 May 1349. His wife, Isabel, died 20 March 1363.

Pole *Colls. towards a Desc. of Devon* (1791): 422–423. Burke *Genealogical & Heraldic Hist. of the Land Gentry* 4 (1838): 526–529 (sub Willington). Burke *Dormant, Abeyant, Forfeited, and Extinct Peerages* (1883): 585–586 (sub Willington). Maclean *Hist. of the Deanery of Trigg Minor* 1 (1876): 384 (Wylyngton ped.). *Year Books of Edward III* 6 (Rolls Ser. 31b) (1891): 254–257. Wrottesley *Crécy & Calais* (1898): 137. *Feudal Aids* 1 (1899): 412, 417, 423, 426, 432, 433. *List of Foreign Accounts* (Lists & Indexes XI) (1900): 144. VCH *Berkshire* 4 (1924): 531–543. *C.P.* 12(2) (1959): 649, footnote d (sub Willington). VCH *Gloucester* 7 (1981): 29; 11 (1976): 285–286. VCH *Wiltshire* 17 (2002): 123–135. National Archives, C 131/194/40 (available at www.catalogue.nationalarchives.gov.uk/search.asp).

Children of Henry de Wilington, Knt., by Isabel de Whalesborough:

i. **JOHN DE WILINGTON**, Knt. [see next].

ii. **ELEANOR DE WILINGTON**, married **GILES DAUBENEY**, of South Ingleby, Lincolnshire [see MARKHAM 8].

12. JOHN DE WILINGTON, Knt., of Stalpits (in Shrivenham), Berkshire, Ablington (in Bibury) and Westonbirt, Gloucestershire, Calstone Wellington, Wiltshire, etc., born c. 1340–42 (aged 7 in 1349, aged 15 in 1355). He married **MAUD CARMINOW**, daughter of Walter Carminow, Knt., by Alice, daughter of Stephen Tynten, Knt. They had two sons, Ralph and John, and two daughters, Isabel and Margaret (wife of John Wroth, Knt.). He was heir in 1355 to his great-uncle,

Reynold de Wilington, clerk. He presented to the church of Atherington, Devon in 1375. SIR JOHN DE WILINGTON died 19 August 1378. His widow, Maud, died 22 August 1382.

> Pole *Colls. towards a Desc. of Devon* (1791): 422–423. Burke *Genealogical & Heraldic Hist. of the Land Gentry* 4 (1838): 526–529 (sub Willington). Banks *Baronies in Fee* 1 (1844): 461–462 (sub Wilinton). Maclean *Hist. of the Deanery of Trigg Minor* 1 (1876): 384 (Wylyngton ped.). Burke *Dormant, Abeyant, Forfeited, and Extinct Peerages* (1883): 585–586 (sub Willington). Vivian *Vis. of Cornwall* (H.S.P. 9) (1874): 296–300 (Carminowe ped.). Vivian *Vis. of Cornwall* (1887): 72–75 (Carmynowe ped.). VCH *Berkshire* 4 (1924): 531–543. *C.P.* 12(2) (1959): 649, footnote d (sub Wilington). VCH *Gloucester* 7 (1981): 29; 11 (1976): 285-286. VCH *Wiltshire* 17 (2002): 123–135.

13. ISABEL WILINGTON, born about 1370 (aged 26 in 1396). She married **WILLIAM BEAUMONT**, of Heanton Punchardon, Parkham, and Sherwell, Devon, and, in right of his wife, of Stalpits (in Shrivenham), Berkshire, Knighton (in Winfrith), Dorset, Ablington (in Bibury), Culverdene (in Sandhurst), Frampton Coterell, Poulton, Sandhurst, Westonbirt, and Yate, Gloucestershire, Plaish (in Elworthy), Somerset, Steeple Ashton and Calstone Wellington, Wiltshire, etc., son and heir of John de Beaumont, Knt., of Saunton (in Braunton) and Sherwell, Devon, by Joan, daughter and co-heiress of Robert de Stockheye, Esq. They had one son, Thomas, Knt., and one daughter, Maud She was co-heiress in 1396 to her brother, John de Wilington. William presented to the churches of Heanton Punchardon, Devon, 1397, Stoke Rivers, Devon, 1403, Beaford, Devon, 1404, Shirwell, Devon, 1404, and Loxhore, Devon in 1406. WILLIAM BEAUMONT died before 14 Nov. 1406. His widow, Isabel, presented to the churches of Heanton Punchardon, Devon, 1408, and Parkham, Devon, 1420. She died 26 April 1424.

> Pole *Colls. towards a Desc. of Devon* (1791): 395, 407–409, 422–423. Rudge *Hist. of the County of Gloucester* 2 (1803): 154. Risdon *Chorographical Desc. or Survey of Devon* (1811): 339. Burke *Genealogical & Heraldic Hist. of the Land Gentry* 4 (1838): 526–529 (sub Willington). Banks *Baronies in Fee* 1 (1844): 461–462 (sub Wilinton). Maclean *Hist. of the Deanery of Trigg Minor* 1 (1876): 384 (Wylyngton ped.), 554-555 (Bodrigan ped.). Burke *Dormant, Abeyant, Forfeited, and Extinct Peerages* (1883): 585–586 (sub Willington). Stafford *Reg. of Edmund Stafford* (1886): 125, 145, 153, 185, 208, 211. *Notes & Gleanings* 1 (1888): 12. Vivian *Vis. of Devon* (1895): 65 (sub Beaumont). *Rpt. & Trans. of the Devonshire Assoc. for the Advancement of Science, Lit. & Art* 2nd Ser. 8 (1906): 154–160. *C.P.R. 1405–1408* (1907): 268. *C.P.R. 1396–1399* (1909): 263, 434. *C.P.R. 1408–1413* (1909): 166, 182, 183, 472. VCH *Berkshire* 4 (1924): 531–543. *C.F.R.* 13 (1933): 79. *Cornwall Feet of Fines* 2 (1950): 120–121. *C.P.* 12(2) (1959): 649, footnote d (sub Wilington). VCH *Gloucester* 7 (1981): 29. VCH *Wiltshire* 17 (2002): 123–135.

Child of Isabel Wilington, by William Beaumont:

i. **MAUD BEAUMONT**, married **HUGH COURTENAY**, Knt., of Haccombe, Devon [see COURTENAY 9].

❧ CHAUNCY ❧

ALICE OF NORMANDY (sister of King William the Conqueror), married **LAMBERT**, Count of Lens.
JUDITH OF LENS, married **WALTHEOF**, Earl of Northumberland.
ALICE OF NORTHUMBERLAND, married **RALPH DE TONY**, of Flamstead, Hertfordshire.
ROGER DE TONY, of Flamstead, Hertfordshire, married **IDA OF HAINAULT**.
RALPH DE TONY, of Flamstead, Hertfordshire, married **MARGARET OF LEICESTER**.
IDA DE TONY, married **ROGER LE BIGOD**, Knt., Earl of Norfolk.
HUGH LE BIGOD, Earl of Norfolk, married **MAUD MARSHAL**.
RALPH LE BIGOD, Knt., of Settrington, Yorkshire, married **BERTHA DE FERRERS** (desc. King William the Conqueror).
JOHN LE BIGOD, Knt., of Settrington, Yorkshire, married **ISABEL** _____.
ROGER LE BIGOD, Knt., of Settrington, Yorkshire, married **JOAN** _____ [see ASKE 10].

11. JOAN BIGOD, born in March 1339. She married in 1357–8 (date of settlement) **WILLIAM CHAUNCY**, Knt., of Skirpenbeck, Bugthorpe, Kilham, Thoralby, etc., Yorkshire, son and heir of Thomas de Chauncy, Knt., of Skirpenbeck and Thoralby, Yorkshire. He was born about 1342 (aged 44 in 1386). They had one son, John, Esq. He commenced his career in arms in his 15th year and subsequently served in military campaigns in France, Brittany, and Normandy. In 1361 he owed £10 to William de Burton, of York, draper. He owed £10 in 1362 to John de Bourne, Citizen and merchant of York. In 1369 he gave recognizance for 24 marks to Jordan de Barton to be levied, in default of payment, of his lands and chattels in Yorkshire. In 1374 he owed £50 to Maud de Beverley and her son, John de Beverley. In 1377 as "William Chauncy of Skirpenbeck," he owed £10 Robert de Farington, clerk. In 1382 he gave recognizance to John de Hothom, Knt. for £10 to be levied, in default of payment, of his lands and chattels in Yorkshire. He testitified in 1386 in the Scrope and Grosvenor trial. In 1387 he gave recognizance to Robert de Faryngton, clerk for £10 to be levied, in default of payment, of his lands and chattels in Yorkshire. His wife, Joan, was a legatee in the 1388 will of her brother, John le Bigod, of Settrington, Yorkshire. In 1389 as "William Chauncy, knight, of Yorkshire," he owed £8 to Robert de Eure, son and heir of Hugh de Eure, Knt., of Yorkshire. In 1390 he and John de Feriby served as mainpernors for Roger Fauconberge, Knt. and Thomas Fauconberge the cousin that they bring Thomas Fauconberge, brother of Roger, before the Council. In 1392 he and Robert de Eure reached agreement regarding lands in Bugthorpe, Yorkshire held of him by the said Robert by fealty and the rent of 1*d*. yearly. His wife, Joan, was living 9 Sept. 1398. In 1398–9, as "William Chauncy, knight," he conveyed the manor of Skirpenbeck, Yorkshire to Ralph Neville, Earl of Westmorland. In 1399–1400 John Osborne, Citizen and goldsmith of London, granted him a release of all actions, he then being styled "William Chauncy, knight, baron of Skirpenbeck, co. York." SIR WILLIAM CHAUNCY allegedly purchased considerable estates in Stepney, Middlesex, where he died and was buried.

Weever *Ancient Funerall Monuments* (1767): 316–317. Clutterbuck *Hist. & Antiqs. of Hertford* 2 (1821): 400–403 (Chauncy ped.). Chauncy *Hist. Antiqs. of Hertfordshire* 1 (1826): 115 ("Elizabeth Daughter to Sir John Bigott, Kt."). Nicolas *Controversy between Scrope & Grosvenor* 2 (1832): 304–305 (biog. of Sir William Chauncy) (Chauncy arms: Gules, a cross patée Argent, on a chief Or, a lion passant Azure). *Testamenta Eboracensia* 1 (Surtees Soc. 4) (1836): 128–129 (will of John Bigod). *NEHGR* 10 (1856): 256, 259. Fowler *Mems. of the Chaunceys* (1858): 41–42. *Heraldic Jour.* 1 (1865): 187–190. Cooke & St. George *Vis. of Hertfordshire 1572, 1634 & 1546* (H.S.P. 22) (1886): 4 (1572 Vis.) (Chauncy arms: Gules, a cross patonce Argent, on a chief Azure a lion passant Or), 39 (1634 Vis.) (Chauncy ped.: "D'n's Gulielmus Chancy, miles, Baro de Skirpenbeck, temp. R. 2. = [left blank]."). *Misc. Gen. et Heraldica* 2nd Ser. 1 (1886): 21–30. *C.C.R. 1369–1374* (1911): 109. *C.C.R. 1381–1385* (1920): 111, 216. *C.C.R. 1385–1389* (1921): 421, 680. *C.C.R. 1389–1392* (1922): 233. *C.C.R. 1392–1396* (1925): 92. Surtees *Recs. of the Fam. of Surtees* (1925): 240–243. *Yorkshire Arch. Jour.* 32 (1936): 180–190, 201. Paget *Baronage of England* (1957) 65: 1. National Archives, C 143/324/5 (Thomas Chauncy to grant a messuage, land, and rent in Thoralby and Skirpenbeck, Yorkshire to William his eldest son, Joan daughter of Roger Bigot, Knt., and the heirs of their bodies, with remainder to the said Thomas and his heirs, retaining the manor of Skirpenbeck. Date: 31 Edward III [1357–8]); C 143/429/10 (William Chauncy, Knt., to grant his manor of Skirpenbeck and all his lands and tenements in Bugthorpe, Thoralby, Kilham, Swaythorpe, Fridaythorpe, Youlthorpe, Gowthorpe, and Fangfoss, Yorkshire to Ralph Neville, Earl of Westmorland, John Alwent, clerk, Robert de Coverham, John Conyers, and the heirs of the said earl. Date: 22 Richard II [1398–9].

12. JOHN CHAUNCY, Esq., of Pishobury (in Sawbridgeworth), Hertfordshire, son and heir. He married **MARGARET GIFFARD**, daughter of William Giffard, of Gifford's and Netherhall (in Gilston), Hertfordshire, and Giffards (in Great Sampford), Essex. They had one son, John, Esq. His wife, Margaret, was heiress in 1414 to her brother, John Giffard. JOHN CHAUNCY, Esq., died 22 Feb. 1444/5. His widow, Margaret, died at Pishobury (in Sawbridgeworth), Hertfordshire 17 October 1448. They were buried at Sawbridgeworth, Hertfordshire.

Weever *Ancient Funerall Monuments* (1767): 316–317. Clutterbuck *Hist. & Antiqs. of Hertford* 2 (1821): 400–403 (Chauncy ped.). Chauncy *Hist. Antiqs. of Hertfordshire* 1 (1826): 115. *NEHGR* 10 (1856): 256, 259; 148 (1994): 161–166. Fowler *Mems. of the Chaunceys* (1858): 41. *Heraldic Jour.* 1 (1865): 187–190. Cooke & St. George *Vis. of Hertfordshire 1572, 1634 & 1546* (H.S.P. 22) (1886): 39 (1634 Vis.) (Chauncy ped.: "Joh'es Chancy, miles, vixit apud Stebenheath juxta London, temp. H. 4. = [left blank]."). *Misc. Gen. et Heraldica* 2nd Ser. 1 (1886): 21–30 (Chauncy family quartered the Giffard arms followed by Roos and "Aubigny"). Wrottesley *Peds. from the Plea Rolls* (1905): 453–454. VCH *Hertford* 3 (1912): 319–322. Surtees *Recs. of the Fam. of Surtees* (1925): 240–243.

13. JOHN CHAUNCY, Esq., of Pishobury (in Sawbridgeworth) and Gilston, Hertfordshire, son and heir, born about 1408 (aged 40 in 1448). He married **ANNE LEVENTHORPE**, daughter of John Leventhorpe, Esq., of Shinglehall (in Sawbridgeworth), Hertfordshire, Receiver-General of the Duchy of Lancaster, executor of the wills of Kings Henry IV and Henry V, by Katherine, daughter and heiress of William de Riley. They had two sons, including John, Gent., and six daughters. His wife, Anne, died 2 Dec. 1477. JOHN CHAUNCY, Esq., died testate 27 April 1479. He and his wife, Anne, were buried at Sawbridgeworth, Hertfordshire.

> Weever *Ancient Funerall Monuments* (1767): 316–317 (monumental inscription in church of Sawbridgeworth, Hertfordshire: "Hic iacent Johannes Chancy, arm. filius et heres Johannes Chancy, arm. filii et heredis Willelmi Chancy, militis, quondam baronis de Shorpenbek, in com. Ebor. & Anna, vxor eius, vna filiarum Johannis Leuenthorp, arm. qui quidem Johannes obiit vii Maii, M.cccc.lxxix & Anna ii Decembris, M.cccc.lxxvii, quorum animabus, &c."). Clutterbuck *Hist. & Antiqs. of Hertford* 2 (1821): 400–403 (Chauncy ped.). Chauncy *Hist. Antiqs. of Hertfordshire* 1 (1826): 115–116. *NEHGR* 10 (1856): 256, 259; 148 (1994): 161–166. Fowler *Mems. of the Chaunceys* (1858): 41. *Heraldic Jour.* 1 (1865): 187–190. Cooke & St. George *Vis. of Hertfordshire 1572, 1634 & 1546* (H.S.P. 22) (1886): 39 (1634 Vis.) (Chauncy ped.: "Joh'es Chauncy de Gedeleston [Geldsden] in com. Hertford, temp. H. 5. = [left blank]."). *Misc. Gen. et Heraldica* 2nd Ser. 1 (1886): 21–30. Wrottesley *Peds. from the Plea Rolls* (1905): 453–454. Surtees *Recs. of the Fam. of Surtees* (1925): 240–243. *East Hertfordshire Arch. Soc. Trans.* 9 (1934-36): 129–151 (re Leventhorpe). Roskell *House of Commons 1386–1421* 3 (1992): 591–595 (biog. of John Leventhorpe). *TG* 16 (2002): 183–188.

14. JOHN CHAUNCY, Gent., of Gifford's and Netherhall (in Gilston) and Sawbridgeworth, Hertfordshire, son and heir, born about 1452 (aged 27 in 1479). He was a defendant in a dispute over land inherited from his paternal grandmother, Margaret Giffard. He married **ALICE BOYSE**, daughter of Thomas Boyse. They had three sons, John, Esq., George, and William. In 1480 Walter Patsyll and Rose, his wife, sued him for an illegal entry by force into a tenement at Sawbridgeworth, Hertfordshire. JOHN CHAUNCY, Gent., died 8 June 1510, and was buried at Sawbridgeworth, Hertfordshire. His widow, Alice, was living 4 Nov. 1519.

> Clutterbuck *Hist. & Antiqs. of Hertford* 2 (1821): 400–403 (Chauncy ped.). Chauncy *Hist. Antiqs. of Hertfordshire* 1 (1826): 116. *NEHGR* 10 (1856): 256, 260; 120 (1966): 243–247; 148 (1994): 161–166. Fowler *Mems. of the Chaunceys* (1858): 41. *Heraldic Jour.* 1 (1865): 187–190. Cooke & St. George *Vis. of Hertfordshire 1572, 1634 & 1546* (H.S.P. 22) (1886): 39 (1634 Vis.) (Chauncy ped.: "Joh'es Chauncy de Gedeleston, co. Hertf., temp. H. 6. = [left blank]."). *Misc. Gen. et Heraldica* 2nd Ser. 1 (1886): 21–30. *Hertfordshire Gen. & Antiq.* 1 (1895): 4. Wrottesley *Peds. from the Plea Rolls* (1905): 453–454. VCH *Hertford* 3 (1912): 319–322. Surtees *Recs. of the Fam. of Surtees* (1925): 240–243.

Children of John Chauncy, Gent., by Alice Boyse:

  i. **JOHN CHAUNCY**, Esq. [see next].

  ii. **WILLIAM CHAUNCY**, married _____ **GARLAND** [see HARLAKENDEN 15].

15. JOHN CHAUNCY, Esq., of Netherhall (in Gilston) and Pishobury (in Sawbridgeworth), Hertfordshire, and, in right of his 1st wife, of Crayford and East Lenham, Kent, son and heir. He married (1st) before 4 Nov. 1509 **ELIZABETH PROFFIT**, widow of Richard Manfield, Gent., of Middlesex, and daughter and co-heiress of John Proffit, Gent., of Barcombe, Sussex, by Alice, daughter and heiress of John Horne, Gent., of East Lenham, Kent. They had three sons, Maurice [Prior of the English Carthusians at Bruges], Henry, Esq., and Robert, and one daughter, Alice. His wife, Elizabeth, died 10 Nov. 1531. He married (2nd) **KATHERINE** _____. They had no issue. His wife, Katherine, died 30 April 1535. JOHN CHAUNCY, Esq., died testate 8 June 1546. He and his two wives were buried at Sawbridgeworth, Hertfordshire.

> Hasted *Hist. & Top. Survey of Kent* 5 (1798): 415–445. Clutterbuck *Hist. & Antiqs. of Hertford* 2 (1821): 400–403 (Chauncy ped.). Chauncy *Hist. Antiqs. of Hertfordshire* 1 (1826): 116. *NEHGR* 10 (1856): 256, 260. Fowler *Mems. of the Chaunceys* (1858): 41. *Heraldic Jour.* 1 (1865): 187–190. Cooke & St. George *Vis. of Hertfordshire 1572, 1634 & 1546* (H.S.P. 22) (1886): 39 (1634 Vis.) (Chauncy ped.: "John Chauncy of Crafford [Crayford] in Kent. = [left blank]."). *Misc. Gen. et Heraldica* 2nd Ser. 1 (1886): 21–30. *Hertfordshire Gen. & Antiq.* 1 (1895): 138, 140, 142, 143. *NEHGR* 55 (1901): 432–439. VCH *Hertford* 3 (1912): 319–322. Surtees *Recs. of the Fam. of Surtees* (1925): 240–243.

Children of John Chauncy, Esq., by Elizabeth Proffit:

i. **MAURICE CHAUNCY**, first Prior of the English Carthusians at Bruges, later Confessor to Queen Mary, eldest son. He studied common law at Gray's Inn and became a Carthusian monk. He authored *Historia Aliquot Nostril Sæculi Matyrum cum Pia* (1550). He died at Bruges 2 July 1581. Hasted *Hist. & Top. Survey of Kent* 5 (1798): 415–445. Fowler *Mems. of the Chaunceys* (1858): 41–42. Morris *Troubles of Our Catholic Forefathers Related by Themselves* (1872): 25–26.

ii. **HENRY CHAUNCY**, Esq. [see next].

16. HENRY CHAUNCY, Esq., of New Place, Netherhall, and Gifford's (all in Gilston), Hertfordshire, Great Sampford, Hemstead, Little Sampford, and Passebury, Essex, Crayford and East Lenham, Kent, Barcombe, Sussex, etc., 2nd son by his father's 1st marriage. He married (1st) **LUCY** _____. They had four sons, John, George, Esq., Robert, and Edward. He built the capital messuage at New Place (in Gilston), Hertfordshire. In 1544–51 he sued Alice Pylston, of [Bishop's] Stortford, Hertfordshire in Chancery regarding the manor of Netherhall (in Gilston), Hertfordshire. He was a legatee in the 1549 will of his half-brother, John Manfield, Gent., of Standon, Hertfordshire. In 1549 Richard Pylson and others conveyed the manor of Netherhall (in Gilston), together with lands and rents in Gilston, Sawbridgeworth, East Wyke, and Hunsdon, Hertfordshire to him. His wife, Lucy, died 25 April 1566, and was buried at Gilston, Hertfordshire. He married (2nd) at Gilston, Hertfordshire 1 June 1570 **ROSE** _____, widow of John Cockes, of Stanstead Abbots, Hertfordshire. She was living Trinity Term 1571. He married (3rd) by license dated 27 April 1574 **JANE BARRETT**, widow of John Salisbury (will proved 1573), Dean of Norwich, Bishop of Sodor and Man. His wife, Jane, died 12 Dec. 1579, and was buried at Gilston, Hertfordshire. In 1581 Henry Chauncy and his sons, George and Edward, were accused of "seditious practices in favouring popery." HENRY CHAUNCY, Esq., died at Gilston, Hertfordshire 14 April 1587, and was buried there.

Hasted *Hist. & Top. Survey of Kent* 5 (1798): 415–445. Clutterbuck *Hist. & Antiqs. of Hertford* 2 (1821): 400–403 (Chauncy ped.). Chauncy *Hist. Antiqs. of Hertfordshire* 1 (1826): 117. Dod *Manual of Dignities, Privilege & Precedence* (1844): 603. *NEHGR* 10 (1856): 256, 260. Fowler *Mems. of the Chaunceys* (1858): 42. *Heraldic Jour.* 1 (1865): 187–190. Cooke & St. George *Vis. of Hertfordshire 1572, 1634 & 1546* (H.S.P. 22) (1886): 39 (1634 Vis.) (Chauncy ped.: "Henry Chancy of Gedleston, 10 H. 7. = [left blank]."). *Misc. Gen. et Heraldica* 2nd Ser. 1 (1886): 21–30. *Hertfordshire Gen. & Antiq.* 1 (1895): 138, 202, 207, 238, 314; 2 (1897): 35, 80, 177, 178, 220, 253, 341. *Index of Chancery Procs. (Ser. II)* 1 (PRO Lists and Indexes 7) (1896): 288; citation courtesy of John Brandon. *NEHGR* 55 (1901): 432–439. *VCH Hertford* 3 (1912): 319–322. Surtees *Recs. of the Fam. of Surtees* (1925): 240–243. Wyndham *Cal. of Chancery Decree Rolls C 78/46–85* (List & Index Soc. 253) (1994): C 78/51/14; C 78/59/8.

17. GEORGE CHAUNCY, Esq., of New Place and Netherhall (in Gilston), Hertfordshire, and Fairstead, Essex, and, in right of his wife, of Yardley-Bury, Hertfordshire, 2nd son by his father's 1st marriage. He married (1st) at Gilston, Hertfordshire 26 Sept. 1569 **JANE CORNWELL**, daughter and heiress of John Cornwell, Esq., of Yardley, Hertfordshire, and Stebbing, Essex, by his 2nd wife, Jane Stubbs. They had two sons, Henry and Charles, and four daughters, Jane (wife of Edward Coe), Frances (wife of Ambrose Porter), Barbara (wife of Henry Wright), and Mary. The marriage brought him enough money to purchase the manors of Gifford's and Netherhall from his nephew William, son of his older brother John. His wife, Jane, was buried at Gilston, Hertfordshire 12 Dec. 1579. He married (2nd) **AGNES WELSH**, widow of Edward Humberston (died 1583), of Walkern, Hertfordshire, yeoman, and said to be daughter of Edward Welsh, Gent., of Great Wymondley, Hertfordshire. They had three sons, George, Edward, and [Rev.] Charles, and four daughters, Elizabeth (wife of Robert Lane), Lucy, Judith, and Anne. In 1615 he sold the manor of Netherhall (in Gilston), Hertfordshire to Alexander Williams. GEORGE CHAUNCY, Esq., died 1625–7, and was buried at Barking, Essex.

Clutterbuck *Hist. & Antiqs. of Hertford* 2 (1821): 400–403 (Chauncy ped.). Chauncy *Hist. Antiqs. of Hertfordshire* 1 (1826): 118 (son "Charles who married _____ the Daughter of _____ Ayres of Wilts, Esq."). *NEHGR* 10 (1856): 105–120, 251–262, 323–336; 11 (1857): 148–153. Fowler *Mems. of the Chaunceys* (1858): 43, 312. *Heraldic Jour.* 1 (1865): 187–190. Waters *Gen. Gleanings in England* 1 (1885): 107–109. *Misc. Gen. et Heraldica* 2nd Ser. 1 (1886): 21–30. Foster

London Marr. Lics. 1521–1869 (1887): 269. Cooke & St. George *Vis. of Hertfordshire 1572, 1634 & 1546* (H.S.P. 22) (1886): 39 (1634 Vis.) (Chauncy ped.: "George Chauncy of Gedleston, co. Hertf. [1] = Jane, da. and coheir of John Cornwall of Yardley, co. Hertf., 1 wife, [2] = Anne Welch."), 66 (1634 Vis.) (Humberston ped.: "Edward Humberston of Walkarne, co. Hertf. = Annis, da. of William Winch."). *Hertfordshire Gen. & Antiq.* 2 (1897): 50 (will dated 1654 of William Hummerstone, of Brantfeild, Hertfordshire, P.C.C. 451 Alchin, "to bro. Master Charles Chauncie now in New England 40s. if he come over or anie of his sonnes"), 96, 340–341; 3 (1899): 9, 222. VCH *Hertford* 3 (1912): 319–322. Surtees *Recs. of the Fam. of Surtees* (1925): 240–243. Special thanks go to John Brandon for his assistance with this family.

18. [REV.] **CHARLES CHAUNCY**, younger son by his father's 2nd marriage, baptized at Yardley, Hertfordshire 5 Nov. 1592. He was educated at Westminster School. He obtained several degrees: B.A. 1613, M.A. 1617, Fellow, B.D. 1624, Trinity College, Cambridge, Professor of Greek. He married at Ware, Hertfordshire 17 March 1630/1 **CATHERINE EYRE**, baptized 2 Nov. 1604, died 23 Jan. 1667, daughter of Robert Eyre, Esq., of Chilhampton and Salisbury, Wiltshire, Barrister at Law, by Anne, daughter of [Rev.] John Still, Bishop of Bath and Wells. They had six sons, Isaac, Ichabod, Barnabus, Nathaniel, Elnathan, and Israel, and two daughter, Sarah (wife of Gershom Bulkeley) and Hannah. He was Vicar of Ware, Hertfordshire, and imprisoned for nonconformity. He immigrated to New England in 1637, where he served as minister at Scituate and Plymouth, Massachusetts. He was later second President of Harvard College. He was a legatee in the 1657 will of his sister, Judith Chauncey, of Yardley, Hertfordshire. [REV.] CHARLES CHAUNCEY died at Cambridge, Mass. 19 Feb. 1671/2.

Chauncy *Hist. Antiqs. of Hertfordshire* (1700): 57–60. Clutterbuck *Hist. & Antiqs. of Hertford* 2 (1821): 400–403 (Chauncy ped.). *NEHGR* 10 (1856): 251–262 ; 11 (1857): 149–153. *Heraldic Jour.* 1 (1865): 187–190. Cussans *Hist. of Hertfordshire* 1(1) Braughing Hundred (1870): 152–153. Waters *Gen. Gleanings in England* 1 (1885): 107–109. Cooke & St. George *Vis. of Hertfordshire 1572, 1634 & 1546* (H.S.P. 22) (1886): 39 (1634 Vis.) (Chauncy ped.: "3. Charles [Chauncy]."). Gerish *Sir Henry Chauncy* (1907): 4–8. Surtees *Recs. of the Fam. of Surtees* (1925): 240–243. Weis *Col. Clergy of New England* (1934): 53.

✎ CHAWORTH ✎

1. PATRICK (or **PATRICE**) **DE CHAOURCES** (or **DE SOURCHES**), seigneur of Sourches (in Saint-Symphorien) in Maine, and, in right of his wife, of Toddington, Bedfordshire. He married **MAUD DE HESDIN** (or **HESDING**), daughter of Ernulf (or Arnulph) de Hesdin, of Keevil, Wiltshire, Kempsford, Gloucestershire, etc., by his wife, Emmeline. They had two sons, Hugues and Patrick (or Patrice), and two daughters, Sibyl and Cecily (wife of Henry d'Aubeney). He made grants in certain parts of the manor of Toddington, Bedfordshire which eventually devolved on Dunstable Priory. About 1081–90 he gave various rights at Bernay to Geoffrey de Brûlon. He went on Crusade in 1095. Sometime after 1100 he was granted the manor of Great Wishford, Wiltshire by King Henry I. Sometime in the period, 1100–22, he and his wife, Maud, gave the Abbey of St. Pierre de la Couture, Le Mans the church of Toddington, Bedfordshire, for the soul of Ernulf de Hodine [Ernulf de Hesdin]. Sometime before 1127 he granted the manor of Great Wishford, and possibly part of the manor of Berwick St. James, Wiltshire to his son-in-law, Henry Daubeney. At an unknown date, he and his wife, Maud, granted the same Abbey an exchange for the land which its monks previously held in the time of three kings, together with a virgate of Eduine's land to be free and quit. At an unknown date he granted la Couture his rights in the forest of Charnie. Patrick and his wife, Maud, were living in 1133.

Pesche *Dictionnaire topographique, historique et statistique de la Sarthe* 6 (1842): 224–226. Guétanger *Essai historique sur l'Abbaye de Solesmes* (1846): 23 ("On remarque le don fait a l'Abbaye, par Patrice de Sourches et Mathilda sa femme, d'une eglise de Dodington, en Angleterre"). *Herald & Genealogist* 6 (1871): 241–253 (re. Hesding fam.). *Cartulaire des Abbayes de Saint-Pierre de la Couture et de Saint-Pierre de Solesmes* (1881): 30–31, 31 (charter of Patricus de Cadurcis dated

1081–90), 31 (ratification made by Patrice de Sourches and his son, Hugues dated 1095), 48–49 (charter of Patrice de Cardurcis and his wife, Maud, dated c.1120; grant made for the soul of Ernulf de Hodine), 49 (charter of Patrice de Cadurcis and his wife, Maud, dated 1120), 50. Money *Hist. of Newbury* (1887): 72–79 (Chaworth ped.). *Genealogist* n.s. 5 (1889): 209–212 ("According to the pedigree thus admitted in court, it is clear that Sibilla was daughter to the original Patrick de Chaworth, who had acquired, through marrying Matilda, one of Arnulph de Hesding's daiughters, a share of Arnulph's Domesday manors, some of which were afterwards again given as a marriage portion with Sibilla to Walter of Salisbury ... The difficulties as to the dates of the birth of Sibilla's children, supposed to be involved, have no real existence. All that is known as to her son, Earl Patrick, is that he was of age in 1142, and born, therefore, at least as early as 1121, whilst his sister, Hawise, is said to have become the second wife of Rotrou (III), Count of Perche, in 1126, when she may have been, perhaps, sixteen. It seems to follow, from a passage in the *Liber Niger* (p. 171), that Patrick and Matilda de Chaworth had another daughter who married into the family of De Albini, and had a son named Nigel, stated to hold, in 1165, a manor, worth £20 a year, of their fief 'de matrimonio matris suæ.' The hypothesis that Sibilla herself was Nigel's mother, by a second husband, is inadmissible, since Walter of Salisbury lived until 1147 ... Patrick de Cadurcis (I) had a son of the same name, who had apparently succeeded him prior to 1130, when he appears, from the Cartulary of St. Peter's, Gloucester, to have added the mill of Horcote, near Kempsford, to the donations which his grandfather, Arnulph de Hesding, had made to that Abbey."). Round *Cal. Docs. Preserved in France* 1 (1899): 364. *Pubs. of Bedfordshire Hist. Rec. Soc.* 7 (1923): 165–167; 10 (1926): 304–306 ("The family of which the name was anglicized as Chaworth, but latinised as de Cadurcis Cadulcis Chaurciis Chaurces Chaorciis etc., appearing also as Chauarz Chauard Cahurt etc., drew its style from Chaorches, the modern Sourches, near le Mans in the old province of Maine. Something of the early history of this very difficult family has already been sketched, but the line can be extended further backwards. Its founder appears to be Hugh, younger son of Ernauld lord of Marigné in southern Maine, who built a castle at Sourches; he occurs in the Cartulary of Marmoutier about 1046/50 as Hugues de Sourches le Marigné. He gave St. Mars de Ballon (vicum sancti Medardi juxta castrum Baledoni) to the Abbey of la Couture. His son Patric became a monk of la Couture, and under the style Patricus de Cadurcis filius Hugonis de Matrinniaco [Marigné] gave Lavaré to the Abbey about 1050, his sons Hugh and Geoffrey consenting. His successor, probably his grandson and the son of Hugh (who attests 1050 and 1085), is the Patric I de Chaworth who heads the family in the accounts already published by this Society. Having accidentally killed a lad, he made atonement to the father by giving the church of Bernay, and land at Bernay and Sourches to la Couture about 1080/90; when making ready for the First Crusade in 1095, he entrusted his son Hugh to the same Abbey. His wife Matilda was probably a daughter of Ernulf de Hesdin, the Domesday tenant of Toddington; she and her husband granted the church there (Dedingtona Dodingetona) to la Couture, and the grant was confirmed by King Henry I, in a charter of the probable date 1105/7. To St. Peter Gloucester he gave a hide at Ampney before 1104, confirmed by Henry I probably in 1105; in 1115/30 he further gave to the monastery the church of Kempsford with lands and mills there and elsewhere in co. Gloucs.; their last gift is dated 1133. He appears in the Pipe Roll of 1130 as pardoned Danegeld in Oxon. Wilts. Glos. Beds. and Berks.; and it is implied that he was alive in 1135."). Boussard *Le Comte d'Anjou sous Henri Plantegenet & ses Fils (1151–1204)* (1938): 55–57. *C.P.* 11 (1949): 375. Sanders *English Baronies* (1960): 124–125 (the name Chaworth derives from Sourches, Sarthe, arr. Le Mans). VCH *Wiltshire* 15 (1995): 168–177, 284–294. Green *Aristocracy of Norman England* (1997): 375–376. Keats-Rohan *Domesday Descendants* (2002): 391–392, 515.

Children of Patrick de Chaources, by Maud de Hesdin:

i. **PATRICK DE CHAOURCES** (or **DE SOURCHES**) [see next].

ii. **SIBYL DE CHAOURCES**, married **WALTER OF SALISBURY** (also known as **WALTER FITZ EDWARD**), of Chitterne, Wiltshire [see LONGESPÉE 2].

2. **PATRICK** (or **PATRICE**) **DE CHAOURCES** (or **DE SOURCHES**), of Kempsford, Gloucestershire, son and heir. He married **WIBURGE** (or **GUIBURGE**, **GUIBOURGE**) _____. They had two sons, Pain (or Payen) [de Mondoubleau] and Hugh (or Hugues). In 1130 he granted to St. Peter's, Gloucester the mill of Horcote, near Kempsford, Gloucestershire. At an unknown date he and his son, Pain, granted the monks of la Couture their right to the patronage of the churches of Brûlon, Bernay, and Saint-Mars-sous-Ballon. PATRICK DE CHAOURCES was deceased before 1149. About 1149 Wilburge, and her son, Pain, founded Tironneau Abbey (commune de Saint-Aignan, canton de Marolles-les-Braux).

Pesche *Dictionnaire topographique, historique et statistique de la Sarthe* 6 (1842): 224–226. Guéranger *Essai historique sur l'Abbaye de Solesmes* (1846): 23 ("En 1147, Patrice de Sourches et Guiburge sa mère [fonda l'abbaye] de Tironneau."). *Herald & Genealogist* 6 (1871): 241–253. *Cartulaire des Abbayes de Saint-Pierre de la Couture et de Saint-Pierre de Solesmes* (1881): 42 (charter of Patrick de Sourches and his son, Pain). *Inventaire-Sommaire des Archives Départementales antérieures à 1790: Sarthe* 3 (1881): 414 ("Abbaye de Tironneau. XIIe siècle. Chartes ... que les religieux avaient payé a Guiburge de

Cadurcis (Chaourses) 25 sols, et à Massile, son fils aîné, 5 sols, pour que l'un et l'autre ratifiassent cette donation comme seigneurs suzerains ..."). Duc des Cars *Le Chateau de Sourches au Maine & ses Seigneurs* (1887). Money *Hist. of Newbury* (1887): 72–79 (Chaworth ped.). *Genealogist* n.s. 5 (1889): 209–212 ("Patrick de Cadurcis (I) had a son of the same name, who had apparently succeeded him prior to 1130, when he appears, from the Cartulary of St. Peter's, Gloucester, to have added the mill of Horcote, near Kempsford, to the donations which his grandfather, Arnulph de Hesding, had made to that Abbey. This Patrick (II), however, seems, from the Pipe Roll of 31 Hen. I, to have had his lands seized by the King, and there is some reason to suppose that they were never restored to him. Not improbably he succeeded to the headship of the family in France, and, dying there, left sons too young to assert a claim to their English heritage, which, during the confusion of the Civil war, came into the hands of the other descendants of Arnulph de Hesding of Domesday."). *Province du Maine* 5 (1897): 179–180. *Bull. de la Société Archéologique, Scientifique & Littéraire du Vendomois* 43 (1904): 100–104 ("Geoffroy de Brulon ... ce personnage tenait ce lieu de sa mère N... de Mondoubleau, fille probablement de Payen de Mondoubleau et mariée avant 1167 à Payen de Sourches qui devint seigneur de Brulon par le fait même de son mariage."). *Pubs. of Bedfordshire Hist. Rec. Soc.* 7 (1923): 165–167; 10 (1926): 304–306 ("Patric II de Chaworth hardly appears in records, and probably died young and in his father's lifetime. With his son Payn he confirmed to la Couture three churches in Maine; there is also a notification possibly granted by him. His wife Wiburga seems to have long survivived him."). Boussard *Le Comte d'Anjou sous Henri Plantegenet & ses Fils (1151–1204)* (1938): 55–57. Sanders *English Baronies* (1960): 125. Keats-Rohan *Domesday Descendants* (2002): 391–392.

3. PAIN DE CHAOURCES (or **DE SOURCHES**) (also known as **PAIN DE MONDOUBLEAU**), of Kempsford, Gloucestershire, seigneur of Brûlon, son and heir. He married _____. They had three sons, Patrick, Hugh (or Hugues), and Geoffroi de Brûlon [seigneur of Chaurellières]. About 1149 he and his mother, Wilburga (or Guiburge), founded Tironneau Abbey (commune de Saint-Aignan, canton de Marolles-les-Braux). Sometime before 1151 he and his mother, Wiburga, confirmed the family grants to la Couture. In 1155 King Henry II restored to him all the lands which his *grandfather*, Patrick de Sourches, previously held in England. He went on crusade in 1158 with Geoffrey de Mayenne. He appears to have lost control of his lands some time between March 1166 and Michaelmas 1167, but to have regained possession of them by 1168. In 1167 he confirmed to Abbey of St. Pierre de la Couture all their lands at Brûlon, Saint-Mars-sous-Ballon, Bernay, and Toddington in England which had been granted to them by his predecessors. PAIN DE CHAOURCES (or DE MONDOUBLEAU) was living in 1170.

Cauvin *Essai sur la statistique de l'Arrondissement de la Flèche* (1831): 59–61. Pesche *Dictionnaire topographique, historique et statistique de la Sarthe* 6 (1842): 224–226. Guéranger *Essai historique sur l'Abbaye de Solesmes* (1846): 23 ("En 1147, Patrice de Sourches et Guiburge sa mere, [fonda l'abbaye] de Tironneau."). *Herald & Genealogist* 6 (1871): 241–253. *Cartulaire des Abbayes de Saint-Pierre de la Couture et de Saint-Pierre de Solesmes* (1881): 42 (charter of Patrick de Sourches and his son, Pain), 82–83. Duc des Cars *Le Chateau de Sourches au Maine & ses Seigneurs* (1887). Money *Hist. of Newbury* (1887): 72–79 (Chaworth ped.). Comte de Charencey *Cartulaire de l'Abbaye de Notre-Dame de la Trappe* (1889): 319, footnote 3 (Tyronneau, commune de Saint-Aignan, canton de Marolles-les-Braux, Abbaye de l'Ordre de Citeaux, fondée, en 1151, par Payen de Sourches et Guiburge, sa mère (Cauvin, *Geographie ancienne du diocese du Mans*, p. 202 et 529). *Genealogist* n.s. 5 (1889): 209–212 ("On the accession of Henry II, however, Patrick's eldest son, Pagan de Mundublel, appeared on the scene, and on 1 January, 1155, obtained a charter from the youthful King restoring to him all the lands which his *grandfather*, Patrick de Cadurcis, had held throughout England. As the city of Cadurcæ (Cahors) was the capital of the dominions of the new Queen, Eleanor of Guyenne, it seems not improbable that Pagan may have come over in her suite, or at any rate obtained this charter throiugh her influence. Its tenor must have been unwelcome to some of Henry's chief supporters ... It is, to say the least, remarkable that Pagan got a grant of the lands of his *grandfather*, Patrick (I), had held in England, not a word being said of his *father*. And again, in the Cartulary of St. Peter's, Gloucester, which furnishes the only actual proof of the existence of a Patrick (II), son of Patrick (I) (vol. i, p. 91), is it not stranger still that Pagan de Mundublel is found confirming to the Abbey, Kempsford and everything which his *grandfather*, Patrick, had given it (No. cccxxvi), not a word being said about his father's gift, whilst Pagan's son and heir, Patrick (III), confines himself to confirming, with even greater distinctness, what had been given by his *great grandfather (proavus)*, Patrick, *and his wife Matilda* (No. cccxxviii).")."). Auvry *Histoire de la Congrégation de Savigny* 3 (1898): 24–25 (En l'année 1149, l'abbaye de S. André en Goffern, dont on a parlé ailleurs, en fonda une untre, dans la province du Maine, à six lieues de la ville du Mans, et à deux lieues de Bonnétable. La seigneur de Clinchamp, nommé Payen de Sourche, ou comme portent les titres, de Chaourches, s'adresse à Raoul, abbé de S. André, pour avoir une communauté de religieux, afin de l'établir dans une de ses terres apeléee Tironnel, laquelle on donna depuis ce nom, car il n'est pas certain que cet endroit se nommait ainsi alors). On voit dans le sanctuaire de l'église de ce monastère, sous une arcade du côté de l'Evangile, le tombeau de deux seigneurs de Saint-Agnan, qui est une paroisse voisine de l'abbaye de Tironneau, car il est constant que Payen de Sourches est le légitime fondateur de ce monastère. On trouve dans la première charte de la fondation de l'abbaye de Perseigne, aussi de l'Ordre de Citeaux, au même diocèse, les souscriptions de Richard, abbé de Savigny, de Raoul, abbé de Saint-André et celle de Payen de Sourches,. seigneur de Clinchamp, mais cette charte étant sans date, on n'n peut rien conclure pour le temps de la fondation de Tironneau."). Round *Cal. Docs. Preserved in France* 1 (1899): 364–365. *Annales fléchoises et la Vallée du Loir* 3 (1904): 230 ("En premier lieu, le manoir des *Chaurellières*, possédé a la fin du XIIIᵉ siècle (et non XVIᵉ) par Geoffroy de Brûlon, fils de Payen de Sourches et de N. de Mondoubleau, dame de Brulon."). *Pubs. of Bedfordshire Hist. Rec. Soc.* 7 (1923): 165–167; 10 (1926): 304–306 ("Payn I, the son of Patric II and Wiburga, is generally recorded as Payn de Montdubleil (de monte Dublelli), clearly an instance of the then not uncommon practice of taking name from the mother, especially is she were an heiress; he seems to have derived his font-name from her father, the Payn de Montdubleil who occurs in the Ecclesiastical History of Orderic and other contemporary records about 1080/96. At the some date before 1151 Payn with his mother Wiburga confirmed the family grants to la Couture; the date is interesting, because he did not receive his English lands till 1155, when a royal charter granted to him all the lands which his grandfather Patric [I] had held in England; the phrasing in consonant with the suggestion of the early death of Patric II. Payn's carta of knights is duly recorded in 1166, but about that date the 12-½ fees which were his share of Ernulf de Hesdin's Honour are returned as held either by Earl Patric of Salisbury his first cousin, or by Geoffrey de Vere then warden of another share of Ernulf's fief; possibly he preferred to live in Maine, and they administered the English lands for him. Payn is apparently last mentioned in 1170. He appears in confirmations to la Couture with his sons Hugh and Patric in 1167, and to St. Peter Gloucester and to Dunstable as Payn de Cadurcis."). Sanders *English Baronies* (1960): 123, 125. Lemesle *Société aristocratique dans le Haut-Maine, XIᵉ-XIIᵉ Siècles* (1999): 246. Keats-Rohan *Domesday Descendants* (2002): 606.

4. PATRICK (or **PATRICE**) **DE CHAOURCES** (or **DE SOURCES**), seigneur of Sourches, Malicorne, and Brûlon, and Kempsford, Gloucestershire, son and heir. He married **AGNÈS** _____. They had four sons, Pain, Hugh (or Hugues), Patrick (or Patrice), and Geoffrey (or Geoffroi), and two daughters, ____ (wife of _____ de Adverton) and Cécile (nun at La Fontaine-Saint-Martin). He confirmed to St. Peter Gloucester the gifts of his father, Pain, and his [great] grandfather, Patrick. Sometime in the period, 1170–99, he gave and confirmed to his uncle, H[ugh] de Chaworth, one hide of land in Milton appendent to Kempsford, Gloucestershire, to give in alms with his body for burial wherever he may wish. In the period, 1190–c.1201, he gave to the Priory of La Fontaine-Saint-Martin, 100 sous mançais of rent on his lands at Malicorne, Sourches, and Brûlon, in exchange for the tithe of his bread at the same places. At an unknown date he and his wife, Agnes, gave to the nuns of Champagne two cart loads of wood to be taken from the Forest of Sourches. At an unknown date, he and his son, Pain, abandoned their rights to the church of Beaufay to the Abbey of Saint-Vincent du Mans. PATRICK DE CHAOURCES was living in 1201. In 1212 their son, Patrick, granted the Priory of La Fontaine-Saint-Martin 10 sous mançais of rent on his mill at Gravier for the celebration of the anniversary of Agnès his mother.

Herald & Genealogist 6 (1871): 241–253. *Inventaire-Sommaire des Archives Départementales antérieures à 1790: Sarthe* 3 (1881): 41 ("Charte de Patrice de Sourches (de Chaurciis) et de Payen, son fils, par laquelle, du consentement des autre fils dudit Patrice et de sa femme Agnès, ils cèdent à l'abbaye de Saint-Vincent tous leurs droits sur l'église de Beaufay (de Belligafio). Cette donation est faire en présence de Hamelin, évêque du Mans ...(Sans date. Fin du XIIᵉ siècle."), 147 ("Deux sentences, l'une rendue a l'officialité de Tours, et l'autre arbitrale, par lesquelles il paraît que Patry de Chaources or Souches a donné une rente de 3 lives 10 sols aux religieuses, sur ses moulins de Bernay et du Gravier, en Bernay, en faveur d'une de ses filles qui avait pris le voile au prieuré, laquelle rent Jeanne Le Cornu, comme dame de Bernay, est condamnée à servir et continuer (Date: 1438), 147 ("Une copie de donation faite par Patrice, seigneur de Sourches, Malicorne et Brulon, aux religieuses, de 100 sols mançais de rente, sur sesdites seigneuries, en échange de la dime du pain de sa maison qu'il leur avait d'abord accordée (sans date)."), Prieure de La Fontaine-Saint-Martin. - Rentes. - Paroisses de Brûlon, Malicorne et Saint-Symphorien. - Vidimus, par l'official du Mans: 1° d'une charte, sans date, mais de la fin du XIIᵉ siècles ou du commencement du XIIIᵉ, par laquelle Patrice de Chaources ou Sourches (de Caduclis), pour le bien de son âme et des âmes de son père, de sa mère, de sa femme, de ses fils et de ses filles, donne aux religieuses de La Fontaine-Saint-Martin, au lieu de la dime de son pain de Malicorne, de Sourches et de Brulon qu'il leur avait précédemment aumônée, 100 sols mançais de rente sur ses domaines de Malicorne, de Brûlon et de Sourches ... sur la fraction de ladite rente payable sur le domaine de Malicorne reserve est faite de 10 sols qui devront être attribués chaque année à Cécile, sans doute une des filles de Patrice, qu'il avait fait entrer comme religieuse a La Fontaine-Saint-Martin; la donation, scellée des sceaux de Hamelin, évêque du Mans (1190–1214), et de Payen, fils ainé de Patrice, est faite en présence des personnages suivants: Goffredus de Bruslone, frater meus, Agnes, uxor mea,

Paganus, Hugo, Patricius, Goffredus, filii mei, qui hoc donum laudaverunt et consenserunt ...; 2º d'une charte de 1212, par laquelle Patrice de Chourcis, donne aux religieuses, pour la célébration de l'anniversaire d'Agnès, sa mère, 10 sols mançais de rente, sur son moulin de Gravier, et leur confirme 15 autres sols mançais de rente, que ladite Agnes leur avait déjà assignés sur ledit moulin."), 357 ("Titre latin, sur parchemin, contenant une donation pure et simple aux religieux de Champagne par Patrice de Sourches et Agnès, sa femme, d'une charretée à deux chevaux de bois mort tombé par terre, à prendre tous les jours dans la forêt de Sourches."), 414 ("Abbaye de Tironneau. XIIe siècle. Chartes ... que les religieux avaient payé a Guiburge de Cadurcis (Chaourses) 25 sols, et à Massile, son fils aîné, 5 sols, pour que l'un et l'autre ratifiassent cette donation comme seigneurs suzerains ..."). Duc des Cars *Le Chateau de Sourches au Maine & ses Seigneurs* (1887). Money *Hist. of Newbury* (1887): 72–79 (Chaworth ped.). Comte de Charencey *Cartulaire de l'Abbaye de Notre-Dame de la Trappe* (1889): 286 (undated charter of Patrick de Sourches to La Trappe Abbey). *Revue historique et archéologique du Maine* 58 (1905): 33. *Pubs. of Bedfordshire Hist. Rec. Soc.* 7 (1923): 165–167; 10 (1926): 304–306 ("Patric III de Chaworth appears in the Liber Rubeus from 1172 to 1200, and in the Pipe Rolls from 1172 to 1201, for the 12-½ fees of the family. He confirmed to St. Peter Gloucester the gifts of his father Payn and [gt.] grandfather Patric. During his tenure of the fief occurred the obscure partition of Toddington to which the present writer has called attention, when a part fell temporararily into the King's hand as an Escheat. If, as is surmised, this manor was the marriage portion of Sibil de Chaworth, the Counts of Perche would receive it through her daughter Haweise; they undoubtedly held the manor when it was escheated in 1189 and again in 1205, when the Chaworths certainly retained the Gloucestershire lands."). Sanders *English Baronies* (1960): 125. London *Cartulary of Bradenstoke Priory* (Wiltshire Rec. Soc. 35) (1979): 191.

5. PAIN DE CHAWORTH (or **CHAOURCES**, **DE SOURCHES**), of Kempsford, Gloucestershire, and, in right of his wife, of Alphington, Devon, son and heir. He married **GUNDRED DE LA FERTÉ**, daughter and heiress of William de la Ferté, Knt., of Lavington (in Market Lavington), Wiltshire, and Alphington, Devon, by Margery (or Margaret), daughter of William Briwerre, Knt. [see BRIWERRE 3.vii for her ancestry]. They had three sons, Patrick, Adam (clerk), and Hervey. In 1212 he granted the Priory of La Fontaine-Saint-Martin 10 sous mançais of rent on his mill at Gravier for the celebration of the anniversary of Agnès his mother. In 1218 William Longespée Earl of Salisbury and his wife, Ela, sued him regarding an unnamed manor in Gloucestershire which Patrick de Chaources, ancestor of the said Pain, gave in marriage to his daughter, Sibyl, from whom it descended to Patrick her son and thence to his daughter, Ela, wife of the said William. At at unknown date, he granted property to Mottisfont Priory, Hampshire for the souls of William Briwerre, Knt., their founder and for William de la Ferté, Knt., his wife's father. He is possibly the Payen de Chaources who witnessed a charter in 1220 for his cousin and friend, Jean, seigneur of Amboise. In 1226 Richard de Argentan was granted full seisin of the land that Pain de Chaworth had in Linley and Willey, Herefordshire. His wife, Gundred, was living 9 March 1233. In 1236, with the assent of Patrick his eldest son, he granted a rent of £7 from the manor of Kempsford, Gloucestershire to Tronell St. Mary, which grant was made for the souls of the said Pain and Gundred his wife. He was granted seisin of all lands formerly of Margaret de la Ferté in Hampshire 4 Feb. 1237; on 1 April following, he made fine with the king by 200 marks for having custody of the land and heir of Margery de la Ferté. PAIN DE CHAWORTH died shortly before 2 June 1237.

Dugdale *Monasticon Anglicanum* 1 (1817):482. *Inventaire-Sommaire des Archives Départementales antérieures à 1790: Sarthe* 3 (1881): 153. Merlet *Cartulaire de l'Abbaye de la Sainte-Trinité de Trion* 1 (1883): 61, footnote 1 ("En 1220, Payen de Chaources est témoin d'une charte donnée par son parent et ami, Jean, seigneur d'Amboise."). Duc des Cars *Le Chateau de Sourches au Maine & ses Seigneurs* (1887): 43–44 (Au XIIIe siècle vivait un Payen de Sourches, chevalier, sire de Clinchamp, fils de Patrice de Sourches et de Odeline de Clinchamp. En 1265, un arret du Parlement confirmait à ce Payen la justice du larron dans l'étendue de la vavassorerie de Clinchamp. En 1323, Amete de Beaumont, dame de Clinchamp, veuve de Payen de Sourches, chevalier, en son nom et en celui de ses enfants, soutient un procès contre Guiart de Manchecourt. Boutaric, *Actes du Parlement de Paris*, nos 989, 7175 et 7972. — Ménage cites dans son *Histoire de Sablé*, p. 104: Payen de Sourches, mari de Anne, fille de Jean de Brienne-Beaumont, Ier du nom, et de Jeanne de la Guerche."). Maitland *Bracton's Note Book* 2 (1887): 3–4. Comte de Charencey *Cartulaire de l'Abbaye de Notre-Dame de la Trappe* (1889): 314–315 (charter dated 1255 of Payen de Sourches, chevalier, seigneur of Clinchamp; charter granted with consent of his wife, Odeline, lady of Clinchamp). Birch *Cat. Seals in the British Museum* 2 (1892): 263 (seal of Pain de Chaorciis dated early 13th Cent.— Obverse. To the right. In armour: hauberk of mail, surcoat, flat helmet, sword, shield of arms. Arms appear to be: barry of eight. The arms of Chaworth are: barry an orle of martlets. Legend: *SIGILL' PA[G]ANI DE CHAORCIIS. Reverse. A smaller counterseal. A shield of arms much defaced, but apparently: barry unnumbered. Legend: * SECRETVM PAGANI DE CHAORCIIS.). *C.Ch.R.* 1 (1903): 221–222. Tait *Mediæval Manchester & the Beginnings of Lancashire* (1904): 108–109. *Revue historique et archéologique du Maine* 58 (1905): 33. *Rpt. & Trans. of the Devonshire Assoc.* 2nd Ser. 7 (1905): 450. *C.P.R.* 1232–1247 (1906): 26 (Fulk de Adverton styled "nephew" of Payn de Chaorcis). VCH *Hampshire* 4 (1911): 469–480. *Pubs. of Bedfordshire Hist. Rec. Soc.* 10 (1926): 304–306 ("Payn II de Chaworth seems to make his first appearance on the records in 1202/3; nothing has been noticed to show that he had any interest in Toddington. At the separation of Normandy from England Payn evidently remained loyal, and was rewarded by the gift of several forfeited manors. His brothers Hugh IV and Patric IV were captured by the French during the war, but were freed on an exchange of prisoners in 1203. Payn married Gundreda, daughter of William de la Ferté (de Feritate), and received her lands in Devon in 1216. He is also said to have married Odeline daughter of Emeric de Clinchamp. In 1236 Payn, with his wife Gundreda, gave 7 li. yearly from their manor of Kempsford co. Glouc. to St. Mary 'Tronell,' apparently a foreign monastery. He died in 1237. The last mention of a Chaworth at Toddington seems to be in 1228 at the death of Hugh IV, when Payn II disclaimed heirship to his brother, there or elsewhere, in the lands which Hugh had pledged to a Jew. The family appears to have no further relation to Beds., and need not to be traced further for our purposes; it ended in an heiress Matilda who, by her marriage in 1291 to Henry of Lancaster, became an ancestress of the royal house."). Sanders *English Baronies* (1960): 123, 125. VCH *Wiltshire* 10 (1975): 82–106. Henry III Fine Rolls Project (available at www.finerollshenry3.org.uk/home.html).

6. PATRICK DE CHAWORTH, Knt., of Kempsford, Gloucestershire, North Standen (in Hungerford), Berkshire, Holsworthy, Devon, King's Somborne and Stockbridge, Hampshire, Anderton and Stoke Bruerne, Northamptonshire, Berwick and Oakhill (in Froxfield), Wiltshire, etc., son and heir, born in or before 1216. In 1237 he was granted livery of his inheritance and the right to marry himself to whom he would wish. In Hilary 1237/8 the king granted that he pay the prest of Ireland and Poitou at the terms granted by writ to his father. He married before 19 Dec. 1243 **HAWISE DE LONDON**, widow successively of Walter de Brewes (died before 14 Jan. 1234) [see BREWES 6.iv], and Henry de Turberville, Knt., of Bradninch, Devon, Cottesey, Norfolk, etc., Seneschal of Gascony, Warden and Lord of Isle of Guernsey (died shortly before 23 Jan. 1240), and daughter and heiress of Thomas de London, of Kidwelly, Carmarthenshire, Ogmore, Glamorgan, East Garston, Berkshire, and Hannington, Wiltshire, by Eve, daughter of Fulk Fitz Warin, of Alveston, Gloucestershire, Tadlow, Cambridgeshire, Alberbury, Shropshire, etc. She was the half-sister of Henry de Tracy, Knt., of Barnstaple, Devon [see MARTIN 7]. They had three sons, Pain, Knt., Patrick, Knt., and Hervey, Knt., and three daughters, Emma, Eve (wife of Robert de Tibetot, Knt.), and Agnes. In 1237 he gave 500 marks to the king to have livery of lands formerly belonging to his father and his maternal grandmother, Margery Briwerre (or Brewer), both of whom were dead. In Hilary 1237/8 the king granted that he pay the prest of Ireland and Poitou at the terms granted by writ to his father. In 1243 he owed a debt of 120 marks to Peter Arnaldi de Alto Villarii. Sometime before 1249 he demised the manor of North Standen (in Hungerford), Berkshire to Peter Chaceporc, Keeper of the King's Wardrobe. In 1252 he obtained a license from the king to enclose How Wood located within the bounds of Bere Forest and convert it into a park. Sometime before 1258 he granted a market and fair at the manor of Holsworthy, Devon to his brother-in-law, Henry de Tracy. SIR PATRICK DE CHAWORTH died shortly before 23 Sept. 1258. Sometime in the period, 1258–74, John de Chilmerford gave bond in favor of Lady Hawise de London and Payne her son and heir to pay them 100 marks if the grantees should be impleaded in respect of a charter granted to them by the said John of all his right in the manor of Standon and Ochulle, Wiltshire. In 1259 William Fowell, a burgess of Stockbridge, Hampshire, released a claim to damage to his heirs, due to the erection of a mill at Stockbridge by the said Patrick. In 1260 his widow, Hawise, leased the manor of East Garston, Berkshire, except the advowson of the church, to Maud Fitz Geoffrey, widow of William de Cantelowe, Knt., and John Fitz John Fitz Geoffrey for a term of 11 years. Hawise was heiress in 1267 to Mabel de Cantelowe, by which she inherited an itinerant forge in Dean Forest. Hawise died before 23 Sept. 1274.

Flower *Ped. of the Chaworth Fam.* (1581). *Placita de Quo Warranto, Edward I–Edward III in Curia Receptae Scaccarii Westm. Asservati* (1818): 76. Dugdale *Monasticon Anglicanum* 5 (1825): 591. Baker *Hist. & Antiqs. of Northampton* 2 (1836–41): 239–240 (Chaworth ped.). *Coll. Top. et Gen.* 6 (1840): 152–153. *Arch. Cambrensis* n.s. 3 (1852): 13–20. Hardy *Syllabus (in English) of the Docs. Rel. England & Other Kingdoms* 1 (1869): 29–31, 35. Mundy et al. *Vis. of Nottingham 1569 & 1614* (H.S.P. 4) (1871): 123–128 (Chaworth ped.: "Patric de Carducis = Helwise d. & heire of Thomas de Lounders"). *Annual Rpt. of the Deputy Keeper* 35 (1874): 17. Hazlitt *Tenures of Land & Customs of Manors* (1874): 110. Sweetman *Cal. Docs. Rel. Ireland 1171–1251* (1875): 364. *Arch. Jour.* 36 (1879): 119. Dallas & Porter *Note-book of Tristram Risdon* (1897): 65, 74–75. C.P.R. 1216–1225 (1901): 134. Turbervill *Ewenny Priory* (1901): 36–38. C.Ch.R. 1 (1903): 221–222. Madge *Abs. of IPM for Gloucestershire* 4 (Index Lib. 30) (1903): 20–23. Cal. IPM 1 (1904): 113–115. Tait *Medieval Manchester & the Beginnings of Lancashire* (1904): 109–110 (Hawise de London identified as the niece of Fulk Fitz Warin). Clark *English Reg. of Godstow Nunnery, near Oxford* 1 (1905): 122–125. *Rpt. & Trans. of the Devonshire Assoc.* 2nd Ser. 7 (1905): 439. C.P.R. 1232–1247 (1906): 17, 33, 369. Jones *Hist. of Kidwelly* (1908): 23 (London-Chaworth ped.). C.P.R. 1258–1266 (1910): 125. C.C.R. 1237–1242 (1911): 169. VCH *Hampshire* 4 (1911): 469–480, 483–486. Lloyd *Hist. of Wales* 2 (1912): 658, footnote 16. Marsh *English Rule in Gascony* (1912): 56–69. C.P.R. 1266–1272 (1913): 94. Cannon *Great Roll of the Pipe A.D. 1241–1242* (1918): 250, 265. VCH *Berkshire* 4 (1924): 183–200, 247–248, 531–543. Fowler *Digest of Charters of the Priory of Dunstable* (Bedfordshire Hist. Rec. Soc. 10) (1926): ped. 12 at end. Moor *Knights of Edward I* 1 (H.S.P. 80) (1929): 199–200. *Bull. of Celtic Studies* 9(2) (1938): 149–154. Paget *Baronage of England* (1957) 90: 1–12 (sub Braose); 533: 1–5 (sub Tracy). Sanders *English Baronies* (1960): 123, 125. Painter *Feudalism & Liberty* (1961): 240–243. *Duchy of Lancaster* 3 (PRO Lists and Indexes, Supp. Ser. 5) (1964): 66. Colvin *Building Accounts of King Henry III* (1971): 417, 421. *Curia Regis Rolls* 15 (1972): 46; 16 (1979): 374 (Hawise de London identified as daughter of Eve de Tracy). VCH *Wiltshire* 10 (1975): 82–106; 16 (1999): 149–165. *Inventory of the Ancient Monuments in Glamorgan* 3(1b) (1976): 125. Summerson *Crown Pleas of the Devon Eyre of 1238* (Devon & Cornwall Rec. Soc. n.s. 28) (1985): 28. Stacey *Politics, Policy & Finance* (1987): 174–178. Carpenter *Minority of Henry III* (1990): 83, 314. *Great Roll of the Pipe* Michaelmas 1221 (Pipe Roll Soc. n.s. 48) (1990): 92. Church *Household Knights of King John* (1999): 44, 126. *Great Roll of the Pipe* Michaelmas 1222 (Pipe Roll Soc. n.s. 51) (1999): 220. Huffman *Social Politics of Medieval Diplomacy* (2000): 260. VCH *Northampton* 5 (2002): 374–413. *Great Roll of the Pipe* Michaelmas 1224 (Pipe Roll Soc. n.s. 54) (2005): 257. *Great Roll of the Pipe* Michaelmas 1223 (Pipe Roll Soc. n.s. 56) (2008): 24. National Archives, DL 25/2299 (agreement (chirograph) between Patrick de Chaworth (Chauz) and Hawise de London, his wife, and Henry de Tracy, concerning the manor of East Garston, Berkshire and the advowson of the church. If the said Patrick have no heirs by the said Hawise, the manor and advowson to revert to the heris of Hawise. If Hawise die before she have heirs by the said Patrick, the manor and advowson, which they have granted to Eve de Tracy for life, shall revert at the death of the said Eve to Patrick, for life, and at his death to the heirs of Hawise) (available online at www.catalogue.nationalarchives.gov.uk/search.asp). Henry III Fine Rolls Project (fine of Eve de Tracy dated 23 June 1222 for having married her daughter, Hawise, without license) (available at www.finerollshenry3.org.uk/home.html).

Children of Patrick de Chaworth, by Hawise de London:

i. **PAIN DE CHAWORTH**, Knt., son and heir, minor at father's death. In 1274–5 the king (by reason of the lands and heirs of Walter de Merton) arraigned an assize of darrein presentment against Payn de Chaworth and William Herigaud touching the church of Broadhembury, Devon. In the same period, he arraigned an assize of darrein presentment against William Herigaud touching the church of Broadhembury, Devon. In the same period, Payn de Cahors [sic] arraigned an assize of darreign presentment against John Wyger and William Heringaud touching the church of Broadhembury, Devon. Sometime in the period, 1274–84, John de Basynges conveyed to him in fee and inheritance a rent from the garden in Aldermansbury, London, formerly belonging to Robert de Basynges, father of the said John. SIR PAIN DE CHAWORTH died shortly before 20 Sept. 1279. Dugdale *Monasticon Anglicanum* 5 (1825): 591 (charter of Pain de Chaworth, son and heir of Hawise de London dated 1270; charter witnessed by Patrick and Hervey his brothers both knights). *Annual Rpt. of the Deputy Keeper* 35 (1874): 17–18; 44 (1883): 45; 45 (1885): 121. Birch *Cat. Seals in the British Museum* 2 (1892): 263 (seal of Pain de Chaurciis dated 1270 — To the right. In armour: hauberk of mail, surcoat, sword, [shield of arms]. Horse caparisoned. Arms: barry, an orle of martlets, CHAWORTH. Legend: .... [CH]AVRC[IIS].). Moor *Knights of Edward I* 1 (H.S.P. 80) (1929): 200. *Littere Wallie preserved in Liber A in the Public Rec. Office* (1940): 48, 197, 199. Sanders *English Baronies* (1960): 125.

ii. **PATRICK DE CHAWORTH**, Knt. [see next].

iii. **EVE DE CHAWORTH**, married **ROBERT DE TIBETOT**, Knt., of Nettlestead, Suffolk [see TIBETOT 7].

7. PATRICK DE CHAWORTH, Knt., of Kidwelly, Carmarthenshire, Wales, East Garston and North Standen (in Hungerford), Berkshire, Kempsford, Gloucestershire, King's Somborne, Hampshire, Stoke Bruerne, Northamptonshire, Berwick St. James, Lavington (in Market Lavington), and Standon Chaworth, Wiltshire, etc., younger son, born about 1254 (aged 24 in 1278). He married **ISABEL DE BEAUCHAMP**, daughter of William de Beauchamp, Knt., 9th Earl of Warwick, by Maud, daughter of John Fitz Geoffrey, Knt. [see BEAUCHAMP 9 for her ancestry]. She had the manor of Chedworth, Gloucestershire in free marriage. They had one daughter, Maud. In 1275–6 he arraigned an assize of novel disseisin against Nicholas Attewode and others touching a tenement in Weston Chaurz, Hampshire. In 1276 he witnessed a deed of his older brother, Pain de Chaworth, to Aaron son of Vives, a Jew. He was Captain of the king's munition in Wales in 1277. Sometime during the period, c.1278–82, Patrick witnessed a charter of Guy de Bryan to the burgesses of Laugharne, Carmarthenshire, Wales. He was heir in 1279 to his older brother, Pain de Chaworth, Knt. In 1279–80 Walter atte Berewe arraigned an assize of novel disseisin against Patrick de Chaworth and others touching a tenement in Etloe, Gloucestershire. In 1280–1 the king granted murage to the bailiffs and men of Kidwelly, Carmarthenshire for a term of five years at the instance of Patrick de Chaworth their lord. Patrick fought in Wales in 1282. On 6 June 1283, he confirmed the gift of his brother, Pain de Chaworth, to Godstow Abbey, which provided for the anniversaries of the obits of their mother, Hawise, and grandmother, Eve. SIR PATRICK DE CHAWORTH died testate shortly before 7 July 1283. His widow, Isabel, married (2nd) between 10 Sept. 1285 (record of Highworth Hundred Rolls) and 27 Jan. 1287 (date of fine for marrying without royal license) **HUGH LE DESPENSER**, Knt., Earl of Winchester, 1st Lord le Despenser, Justice of the Forest south of Trent (hanged 27 October 1326) [see DESPENSER 10 for the issue of this marriage and subsequent history of this couple]. Isabel died shortly before 30 May 1306.

Dugdale *Monasticon Anglicanum* 5 (1825): 591 (charter of Pain de Chaworth, son and heir of Hawise de London dated 1270; charter witnessed by Patrick and Hervey his brothers both knights). Baker *Hist. & Antiqs. of Northampton* 2 (1836–41): 218–219 (Beauchamp ped.), 239–240 (Bruere or Briwere ped.). *Arch. Cambrensis* 3rd Ser. 8 (1862): 281 (13th Cent. Chronicle: "Anno mcclxxxiiio. [A.D. 1283] — Obiit Patricius Chavard."); 4th Ser. 9 (1878): 99–100. Doyle *Official Baronage of England* 3 (1886): 695–697 (sub Winchester). *Annual Rpt. of the Deputy Keeper* 45 (1885): 354; 46 (1886): 119; 49 (1888): 62; 50 (1889): 127. Birch *Cat. Seals in the British Museum* 2 (1892): 631 (seal of Patrick de Chaworth dated 1280 — A shield of arms lozenge-shaped: nine barrules, or barruly, four martlets in cross or orle, for CHAWORTH. Between four small quatrefoil panels. * S' PATRICI DE CHAW..ORZ *.). Dallas & Porter *Notebook of Tristram Risdon* (1897): 74–75. *C.C.R. 1272–1279* (1900): 345. Clark *English Reg. of Godstow Nunnery, Near Oxford* 1 (1905): 122–125. Wrottesley *Peds. from the Plea Rolls* (1905): 544. *Cal. IPM* 2 (1906): 182, 288–290. Fry *Abs. of Wiltshire IPM* 2 (Index Lib. 37) (1908): 124–125. Jones *Hist. of Kidwelly* (1908): 23 (London-Chaworth ped.). VCH *Hampshire* 4 (1911): 470–471. VCH *Surrey* 3 (1911): 381–390. C.P. 4 (1916): 262–266 (sub Despenser); 7 (1929): 400 (sub Lancaster); 12 (2) (1959): 754 (sub Winchester). *Cal. Inqs. Misc.* 2 (1916): 245 (In 1327 William Fitz Matthew, former keeper of Odiham park, claimed he was removed as keeper by Hugh le Despenser the younger because he "levied hue and cry" upon Isabel the said Hugh's mother who was taking 5 bucks in the park without warrant). VCH *Berkshire* 4 (1924): 194, 247–248 (Chaworth arms: Burelly argent and gules an orle of martlets sable). *Year Books of Edward II* 20 (Selden Soc. 52) (1934): 110–113. Richardson & Sayles *Rotuli Parl. Anglie Hactenus Inediti 1274–1373* (Camden Soc. 3rd Ser. 51) (1935): 12. Paget *Baronage of England* (1957) 125: 3. Sanders *English Baronies* (1960): 125. Farr *Rolls of Highworth Hundred 1275–1287* (Wiltshire Arch. & Nat. Hist. Soc. Recs. Branch 21) 1 (1966): 142, 144–147, 149–150, 152, 154, 156–157; 2 (Wiltshire Arch. & Nat. Hist. Soc. Recs. Branch 22) (1968): 201, 203, 206, 208, 211–212, 215–216, 219, 221, 223, 251–252, 294–297. VCH *Wiltshire* 10 (1975): 82–106. VCH *Gloucester* 7 (1981): 98(99, 168. Ellis *Cat. Seals in the P.R.O.* 2 (1981): 24 (seal of Patrick de Chaworth dated 1281 — A lozenge of arms: barruly, four martlets in orle; between four small cinquefoils. Legend: +S PATARICI.DE.CHAUWORZ). *Rolls & Reg. of Bishop Oliver Sutton 1280–1299* 8 (Lincoln Rec. Soc. 76) (1986): 42. Parsons *Eleanor of Castile: Queen & Soc.* (1997): 44, 163, 171. VCH *Northampton* 5 (2002): 374–413. National Archives, SC 8/2/83; SC 8/56/2769; SC 8/58/2860; SC 8/123/6149; SC 8/240/11977 (available at www.catalogue.nationalarchives.gov.uk/search.asp).

Child of Patrick de Chaworth, Knt., by Isabel de Beauchamp:

i   **MAUD DE CHAWORTH**, married **HENRY OF LANCASTER**, Knt., Earl of Lancaster and Leicester, Lord of Monmouth [see LANCASTER 8].

✥ CHERLETON ✥

WILLIAM THE CONQUEROR, King of England, married **MAUD OF FLANDERS**.
HENRY I, King of England, married **MAUD OF SCOTLAND**.
MAUD OF ENGLAND, married **GEOFFREY PLANTAGENET**, Count of Anjou, Duke of Normandy.
HENRY II, King of England, married **ELEANOR OF AQUITAINE**.
JOHN, King of England, by a mistress, **CLEMENCE** _____.
JOAN OF ENGLAND, married **LLYWELYN AP IORWERTH**, Prince of North Wales.
GWLADUS DDU OF WALES, married **RALPH DE MORTIMER**, of Wigmore, Herefordshire.
ROGER DE MORTIMER, Knt., of Wigmore, Herefordshire, married **MAUD DE BREWES**.
EDMUND DE MORTIMER, Knt., 1st Lord Mortimer, married **MARGARET DE FIENNES** (desc. King Henry II).
ROGER DE MORTIMER, Knt., 1st Earl of March, married **JOAN DE GENEVILLE** [see MORTIMER 10].

11. MAUD DE MORTIMER, married before 13 April 1319 **JOHN DE CHERLETON** (or **CHARLETON**), Knt., 2nd Lord Cherleton of Powis, North Wales, of Pole (Welshpool), Montgomeryshire, Pontesbury, Shropshire, etc., Chamberlain of the Household to King Edward III, son and heir of John de Cherleton, Knt., 1st Lord Cherleton of Powis, Chamberlain to King Edward II, Justiciar of Ireland, by Hawise (nicknamed *Gadarn*, i.e., *the Hardy*), *suo jure* Lady of Powis, daughter of Owain ap Gruffudd ap Wenwynwyn (otherwise known as Owen de la Pole). He was born about 1316 (aged 37 in 1353). They had two sons, John, Knt. [3rd Lord Cherleton] and Roger, Knt., and one daughter, Joan. He was summoned to Parliament from 15 March 1353/4 to 20 Nov. 1360, by writs directed *Johanni de Cherleton*. He served in the wars of Gascony. His wife, Maud, was living August 1345. He married (2nd) before 1346/7 **AVICE** _____. SIR JOHN DE CHERLETON, 2nd Lord Cherleton of Powis, died shortly before 30 August 1360.

Blore *Hist. & Antiqs. of Rutland* 1(2) (1811): 42 (Mortimer ped.). Eyton *Antiqs. of Shropshire* 9 (1855): 319 (John's father, John de Cherleton, senior, was the brother of Alan de Cherleton, Knt. [see ZOUCHE 11]). *Herald & Genealogist* 6 (1871): 97–124. *Colls. Hist. & Arch. Rel. Montgomeryshire* 15 (1882): 361–404. Burke *Dormant, Abeyant, Forfeited & Extinct Peerages* (1883): 113–116 (sub Cherlton — Barons Cherlton of Powys). *Papal Regs.: Letters* 3 (1897): 192. *List of Inqs. ad Quod Damnum* 2 (PRO Lists and Indexes 22) (1906): 420. *C.P.* 3 (1913): 161 (sub Cherleton); 4 (1916): 757–760 (Appendix H); 10 (1945): 641–642 (sub Powis). Griffith *Peds. of Anglesey & Carnarvonshire Fams.* (1914): 26 (Powys ped.). Harrison *Royal Ancestry of George Leib Harrison* 2 (1914): 28–42. Stokes et al. *Warwickshire Feet of Fines* 3 (Dugdale Soc. 18) (1943): 20. *Trans. Shropshire Arch. & Nat. Hist. Soc.* 53 (1949–50): 258–292. Paget *Baronage of England* (1957) 128: 1. *Dict. Welsh Biog.* (1959): 74, 316–317. VCH *Shropshire* 8 (1968): 264–265; 11 (1985): 313. *Welsh Hist. Rev.* 10 (1980–81): 1–42. Fryde *Handbook of British Chron.* (1986): 55. Mortimer *Greatest Traitor* (2003). National Archives, C 143/280/13 (available at www.catalogue.nationalarchives.gov.uk/search.asp).

Children of Maud de Mortimer, by John de Cherleton, Knt.

i. **JOHN DE CHERLETON**, Knt., 3rd Lord Cherleton, feudal Lord of Powis [see next].

ii. **JOAN DE CHERLETON**, married **JOHN DE BEAUCHAMP**, Knt., of Powick, Worcestershire [see POWICK 11].

12. JOHN DE CHERLETON, Knt., 3rd Lord Cherleton, feudal Lord of Powis, Montgomeryshire, son and heir, born about 1334 (aged 26 in 1360). He married in or before 1344 **JOAN DE STAFFORD**, daughter of Ralph de Stafford, K.G., 1st Earl of Stafford, 2nd Lord Stafford, by his 2nd wife, Margaret, daughter and heiress of Hugh de Audley, Knt., Earl of Gloucester [see STAFFORD 7 for her ancestry]. They had two sons, John [4th Lord Cherleton] and Edward, K.G. [5th Lord Cherleton]. By an unknown mistress, he had an illegitimate daughter. He was summoned to Parliament from 14 August 1362 to 4 October 1373, by writs directed *Johanni de Cherleton de Powys*. In 1371 he obtained a plat of land from John Perle, of Shrewsbury, Shropshire, for the purpose of making a *staindelf* for the behalf of the friars of the order of Minors of Shropshire. He was appointed a Trier of Petitions in Parliament in 1372. SIR JOHN DE CHERLETON, 3rd Lord Cherleton, died 13 July 1374, and was buried at Strata Florida Abbey,

Cardiganshire 20 August 1374. His widow, Joan, married (2nd) shortly before 7 Feb. 1377 (as his 2nd wife) **GILBERT TALBOT**, 3rd Lord Talbot, of Archenfield, Eccleswall (in Linton), and Goodrich Castle, Herefordshire, Ley (in Westbury upon Severn), Lydney Shrewsbury, Moreton Valence, and Painswick, Gloucestershire [see TALBOT 12], son and heir of Richard Talbot, Knt., 2nd Lord Talbot, of Goodrich Castle, Herefordshire, Blaenllyfni and Bwlch-y-dinas, Breconshire, Wales, etc., by Elizabeth, daughter of John Comyn, Knt., of Badenoch in Scotland [see TALBOT 11 for his ancestry]. He was born about 1332. He was summoned to Parliament from 14 August 1362 to 8 August 1386. In 1370 he owed a debt of 900 marks to Reynold de Grey, Knt., of Wilton, Herefordshire. In 1373 he was granted license for the alienation in mortmain to the Prior and convent of Wormesley of the advowson of the church of Credenhill, Herefordshire. He presented to the church of Great Melton, Norfolk in 1377, as "Sir Gilbert Talbot, Knt., lord of Irchinfield, Blakmere [Blackmere], and Godric's castle [Goodrich Castle]," and again to the same church in 1382. In 1380 he owed a debt of £800 to John de Kingsfold, which debt was unpaid in 1389. He accompanied Edmund of Langley, Earl of Cambridge, on his expedition to Portugal, 1381–2, and was with John of Gaunt's unsuccessful expedition to Spain and Portugal from July 1386. His wife, Joan, was a legatee in the 1385 will of her brother, Hugh de Stafford, K.G., 2nd Earl of Stafford. SIR GILBERT TALBOT, 3rd Lord Talbot, died of the pestilence at Roales, Spain 24 April 1387. His widow, Joan, died shortly before 2 August 1397.

Nicolas *Testamenta Vetusta* 1 (1826): 118–120 (will of Hugh de Stafford, Earl of Stafford). Dugdale *Monasticon Anglicanum* 6(1) (1830): 403. *Colls. Hist. & Arch. Rel. Montgomeryshire* 15 (1882): 361–404. Burke *Dormant, Abeyant, Forfeited & Extinct Peerages* (1883): 113–116 (sub Cherlton — Barons Cherlton of Powys), 526–528 (sub Talbot). Birch *Cat. Seals in the British Museum* 3 (1894): 570–571 (seal of Gilbert Talbot dated 1376 — A shield of arms: a lion rampant, within a bordure engrailed [TALBOT]; over all a label of three points. Crest on a helmet, cappiline and chapeau, a lion sejant, differenced as in the shield. Within a carved gothic panel with open tracery at the sides, and small quatrefoils along the inner edge). *C.P.R.* 1385–1389 (1900): 415 (son John, lord of Cherleton and Powys, styled "king's kinsman"). Wrottesley *Peds. from the Plea Rolls* (1905): 84. *C.P.* 3 (1913): 161 (sub Cherleton); 4 (1916): 757–760 (Appendix H). Harrison *Royal Ancestry of George Leib Harrison* 2 (1914): 28–42. *Trans. Shropshire Arch. & Nat. Hist. Soc.* 53 (1949–50): 258–292. Hatton *Book of Seals* (1950): 60 (seal of John de Cherleton, lord of Powis dated 1368 — On a reticulated background a shield of arms, a lion rampant; [Legend:] * Sigillu . Johis : de : Cherleton : dni : Powisie). *Cal. IPM* 14 (1952): 19–23. *National Lib. of Wales Jour.* 23 (1984): 292–318. Taylor *English Hist. Lit. in the 14th Cent.* (1987): 284, 287, 298 (Extract from a newly discovered Wigmore chronicle written during the 1360s and 1370s: "Eodem anno [1374] obiit Johannes de Cheorlton / dominus de Powys et XIII kalendas septembris [20 Aug.] honorifice apud monasterium de Strathmathhull sepultus."). National Archives, C 131/205/66; C 241/163/2; C 241/175/17; SC 8/103/5104 (available at www.catalogue.nationalarchives.gov.uk/search.asp).

Children of John de Cherleton, Knt., by Joan de Stafford:

i. **JOHN CHERLETON**, 4th Lord Cherleton, married **ALICE ARUNDEL** [see FITZ ALAN 13.v; STRADLING 11].

ii. **EDWARD CHERLETON**, K.G., 5th Lord Cherleton [see next].

13. EDWARD CHERLETON (or **CHARLETON**), K.G., 5th Lord Cherleton, feudal lord of Powis, younger son, born about 1371 (aged 30 in 1401). He married (1st) shortly after 19 June 1399 (date of license) **ELEANOR HOLAND**, widow of Roger Mortimer, Knt., Earl of March and Ulster, Lord Mortimer (died 1398) [see MORTIMER 14 for issue of this marriage], and daughter of Thomas de Holand, K.G., 2nd Earl of Kent, by Alice, daughter of Richard de Arundel, Knt., Earl of Arundel and Surrey [see KENT 10 for her ancestry]. She was born 13 October 1370. They had two daughters, Joan and Joyce. He was heir in 1401 to his older brother, John de Cherleton, Knt., 4th Lord Cherleton [see FITZ ALAN 13.v]. He was summoned to Parliament from 2 Dec. 1401 to 26 Feb. 1421, by writs directed *Edwardo de Cherleton* (or *Charleton de Powys*). He presented to the church of Headbourne Worthy, Hampshire in 1403, in right of his wife, Eleanor. His wife, Eleanor, died in childbirth 23 October 1405. He married (2nd) before 1408 **ELIZABETH BERKELEY**, daughter of John Berkeley, Knt., of Beverstone, Gloucestershire, by Elizabeth, daughter and heiress of John Betteshorne (or Bistorne), Knt. [see FISHER 8 for her ancestry]. They had no issue. In 1402 Owen Glendower overthrew his castles of Usk and Caerleon, but, in the following year, Edward appears to have regained possession of them. In 1404 the council allowed him to make a private truce with the Welsh. In 1410 he sustained great loss by the rebellion of Owain Glyn Dŵr. In 1417 he received the thanks of Parliament for apprehending John Oldcastle, Knt., Lord Oldcastle, a Lollard, within his territory of Powis. SIR EDWARD CHERLETON (or CHARLETON), 5th Lord Cherleton, died testate 14 March 1420/1. His widow, Elizabeth, married (2nd) before 28 June 1421 **JOHN SUTTON** (or **DUDLEY**), K.G., 1st Lord Dudley (died 30 Sept. 1487) [see SUTTON 7 for issue of this marriage]. She died shortly before 8 Dec. 1478.

Nash *Colls. for the Hist. of Worcestershire* 2 (1782): 201. Blore *Hist. & Antiqs. of Rutland* 1(2) (1811): 37 (Kent/Holand ped.). Clutterbuck *Hist. & Antiqs. of Hertford* 3 (1827): 287–288 (Beaumont-Quincy ped.). *Coll. Top. et Gen.* 1 (1834): 296 (Holand ped.). Beltz *Mems. of the Order of the Garter* (1841): clvii. *Colls. Hist. & Arch. Rel. Montgomeryshire* 2 (1869): i–xxvii. *Vis. of Devon 1620* (H.S.P. 6) (1872): 345–347 (Holland ped.: "Elinor [Holand] Countess of March, aft. mar. to Carleton Lord Powis"). Blunt *Dursley & Its Neighbourhood* (1877): 121, footnote 1. *Colls. Hist. & Arch. Rel. Montgomeryshire* 15 (1882): 361–404. Burke *Dormant, Abeyant, Forfeited & Extinct Peerages* (1883): 113–116 (sub Cherlton — Barons Cherlton of Powys). Tresswell & Vincent *Vis. of Shropshire 1623, 1569 & 1584* 1 (H.S.P. 28) (1889): 105 (1623 Vis.) (Charleton ped.: "Edward Charleton Do. Powisiæ frater & heres Joh'is Dom. Powisiæ ob. a[nn]o 1420, 7 H. 5. [1] = Elianora soror et una heredum Edmundi Holland Comitis Kancij, [2] = Elizab. filia Joh'is Berckley militis renupta Baroni Dudley"). Kirby *Wykeham's Reg.* 1 (1896): 243. *Genealogist* n.s. 15 (1898): 30–31; n.s. 18 (1902): 182. Usk *Chronicon Adæ de Usk 1377–1421* (1904): 238 (Edward Cherleton: "a most graceful youth"). *C.P.R. 1391–1396* (1905): 313 (Edward Charleton, Knt. styled "king's kinsman"). *C.P.R. 1401–1405* (1905): 139 (Edward Cherlton of Powys styled "king's kinsman"), 318 (Eleanor [Holand] "late the wife of the earl of March" styled "king's kinswoman"). Wrottesley *Peds. from the Plea Rolls* (1905): 226–227, 380–381. *D.N.B.* 6 (1908): 123–124 (biog. of Edward Charlton). *C.P.* 3 (1913): 161–162 (sub Cherleton); 4 (1916): 480, 757–760 (Appendix H); 6 (1926): 136–138 (sub Grey); 8 (1932): 448–450 (sub March); 12(2) (1959): 305 (sub Wake). Griffith *Peds. of Anglesey & Carnarvonshire Fams.* (1914): 26 (Powys ped.). Harrison *Royal Ancestry of George Leib Harrison* 2 (1914): 28–42. *Yorkshire Inqs.* 5 (Yorkshire Arch. Soc. Recs. 59) (1918): 92–93. *C.F.R.* 13 (1933): 1, 7, 16, 17, 21, 116, 135; 15 (1935): 81; 16 (1936): 77, 81 (Edward Cherleton styled "late lord de Powys"). *Trans. Shropshire Arch. & Nat. Hist. Soc.* 53 (1949–50): 258–292. *Trans. Bristol & Gloucestershire Arch. Soc.* 70 (1951): 94–95. Paget *Baronage of England* (1957) 56: 1 (sub Berkeley of Beverstone). VCH *Shropshire* 8 (1968): 164. Ellis *Cat. Seals in the P.R.O.* 1 (1978): 16 (seal of Elizabeth, widow of Edward Cherleton, Knt., lord of Powys, dated 1421 — In a traceried circle, a shield of arms: a lion rampant [CHERLETON] impaling a chevron between ten crosses paty [BERKELEY]). *Ancient Deeds — Ser. AS & WS* (List & Index Soc. 158) (1979): 46 (Deed A.S.260). Leese *Blood Royal* (1996): 128–134. Wilson *Uncrowned Kings of England* (2005): xiv–xv (Dudley ped.). Psalter. K.26, St. John's College, Cambridge ("Oct. 13. a. d. 1370. Nata est domina alianora co[mit]issa Marchie.") (transcript of doc. available at www.joh.cam.ac.uk/library/special_collections/manuscripts/medieval_manuscripts/mmk26/).

Children of Edward Cherleton, K.G., by Eleanor Holand:

i. **JOAN CHERLETON**, married **JOHN GRAY**, K.G., 1st Count of Tancarville [see LLOYD 8].

ii. **JOYCE CHERLETON**, married **JOHN TIPTOFT**, K.B., 1st Lord Tiptoft and Powis [see INGALDESTHORPE 11].

∽ CHESELDINE ∽

ALICE OF NORMANDY (sister of King William the Conqueror), married **LAMBERT**, Count of Lens.
JUDITH OF LENS, married **WALTHEOF**, Earl of Northumberland.
MAUD OF NORTHUMBERLAND, married **SIMON DE SENLIS**, Earl of Huntingdon and Northampton.
SIMON DE SENLIS, Earl of Huntingdon and Northampton, married **ISABEL** (or **ELIZABETH**) **OF LEICESTER**.
ISABEL DE SAINT LIZ, married **WILLIAM MAUDUIT**, of Hanslope, Buckinghamshire.
ROBERT MAUDUIT, of Hanslope, Buckinghamshire, married **ISABEL BASSET**.
WILLIAM MAUDUIT, of Hanslope, Buckinghamshire, married **ALICE DE NEWBURGH**.
ISABEL MAUDUIT, married **WILLIAM DE BEAUCHAMP**, Knt., of Elmley, Worcestershire.
SARAH DE BEAUCHAMP, married **RICHARD TALBOT**, of Eccleswall (in Linton), Herefordshire.
GILBERT TALBOT, Knt., 1st Lord Talbot, married **ANNE LE BOTELER** (desc. King William the Conqueror).
RICHARD TALBOT, Knt., 2nd Lord Talbot, married **ELIZABETH COMYN**.
GILBERT TALBOT, Knt., 3rd Lord Talbot, married **PERNEL BUTLER** (desc. King William the Conqueror).
RICHARD TALBOT, Knt., 4th Lord Talbot, married **ANKARET LE STRANGE** (desc. King William the Conqueror).
MARY TALBOT, married **THOMAS GREENE**, Knt., of Green's Norton, Northamptonshire.
THOMAS GREENE, Knt., of Green's Norton, Northamptonshire, married **PHILIPPE FERRERS** (desc. King Edward I) [see GREENE 15].

16. ELIZABETH GREENE, married **WILLIAM RALEIGH** (or **RALEGH**), Esq., of Farnborough, Warwickshire, Claydon, Oxfordshire, and Charles, West Hagington, West Buckland, and Assh Raff, Devon, etc., son and heir of John Raleigh, of Mollington, Oxfordshire, by Idoine, daughter and heiress of Thomas Cotesford (or Cottesford), Knt. They had four sons, Edward, Knt., Thomas, Giles, and William, and one daughter, Margaret. WILLIAM RALEIGH, Esq., died 15 October 1460.

Dugdale *Antiqs. of Warwickshire* (1760): 382. Lennard & Vincent *Vis. of Warwick 1619* (H.S.P. 12) (1877): 76–78 (Raleigh ped.: "William Raleigh Kt. = Elizb. Da. of Sr Tho. Greene Kt."). Royce *Hist. Notices of the Parish of Cropredy, Oxon* (Trans. North Oxfordshire Arch. Soc.) (1880): 6–7. *Genealogist* n.s. 13 (1896): 136. *Greene Fam. in England & America* (1901): Greene Ped. II following 147: "Elizabeth [Greene] wife of Sir William Rowley of Com. Warwick."). Colket *English Anc. of Hutchinson & Scott* (1936): 37, 53 (cites Greene ped., British Lib., P 13573 Harl. 1412). *NEHGR* 123 (1969): 180–181; 145 (1991): 3–21.

17. EDWARD RALEIGH, Knt., of Farnborough, Warwickshire, and Charles, West Hagington, and West Buckland, Devon, Sheriff of Warwickshire and Leicestershire, 1467–8, 1495–6, 1506–7, son and heir, born 20 Jan. 1441. He married in 1467 **MARGARET VERNEY**, daughter of Ralph Verney, Knt., Lord Mayor of London, by his wife, Emma. They had two sons, Edward, Esq., and Anthony, and five daughters, Anne, Alice, Joan, Elizabeth (wife of Austin Gainsford), and Emma. His wife, Margaret, was living in 1509. SIR EDWARD RALEIGH left a will dated 20 June 1509, proved 4 May 1513 (P.C.C. 14 Fetiplace), requesting burial in the Chapel of Our Lady at Farnborough, Warwickshire.

Lennard & Vincent *Vis. of Warwick 1619* (H.S.P. 12) (1877): 76–78 (Raleigh ped.: "Sr Edward Raleigh Kt. = Margt. Da. of Sr Raph Verney Kt."). Royce *Hist. Notices of the Parish of Cropredy, Oxon* (Trans. North Oxfordshire Arch. Soc.) (1880): 6–7. *List of Sheriffs for England & Wales* (PRO Lists and Indexes 9) (1898): 146. Colket *English Anc. of Hutchinson & Scott* (1936): 37. *NEHGR* 145 (1991): 3–21. Warwickshire County Rec. Office: Holbech of Farnborough, L1/96 — enfeoffment dated 16 Nov. 1476 by Ralph Verney Alderman of London and John Reigny Gent. to Edward Ralegh Knt. and Margaret his wife (available at www.a2a.org.uk/search/index.asp).

18. EDWARD RALEIGH, Esq., of Farnborough, Warwickshire, born about 1470. He married between 1496 and 1505 **ANNE CHAMBERLAIN**, daughter of Richard Chamberlain, of Coates (in Titchmarsh), Northamptonshire, by Sibyl, daughter of Richard Fowler, of Sherburne, Oxfordshire, Chancellor of the Exchequer to King Edward IV [see CHAMBERLAIN 9 for her ancestry]. They had five sons, George, Edward, Leonard, Anthony, and Thomas, and three daughters, Bridget, Margaret (wife of Richard Musket), and Mary. EDWARD RALEIGH, Esq., left a will dated 25 August 1508, proved 20 Sept. 1508 (P.C.C. 5 Bennett). His widow, Anne, married (2nd) **RALPH FOULSHURST**. They had issue. He left a will proved 2 Sept. 1530 (P.C.C. 20 Jankyn).

> *Coll. Top. et Gen.* 1 (1834): 329 (Ped. of Danvers &c.: "Sibill, sister to Sir Richard Fowler, was maryed to Richard Chamberlain, and they had issue iii sonnes and one doughter. Edward, the eldest sone, now Knight, maryed one of the doughters of Sir John Verney, and they have issue. William, brother to Sir Edward, was a fryer in Grenewiche. His brother John is not maryed; theire sister Anne was fyrst maryed to Edward Rawley, Knight, and they have a sone maryed to Anne, doughter to Sir Humfry Conysby, Knight, and now Justice: and after, the saide Anne Rawley was maryed to Fulchurch, and they have issue."). Harvey et al. *Vis. of Oxford 1566, 1574, 1634 & 1574* (H.S.P. 5) (1871): 235–237 (Chamberlaine ped.: "Anna [Chamberlaine] uxor Edwardi Raleigh."). Lennard & Vincent *Vis. of Warwick 1619* (H.S.P. 12) (1877): 76–78 (Raleigh ped.: "Edward Raleigh. = Anne d. of Sʳ Wm. Chamberleyn Kt. al's Tankeruill."). Metcalfe *Vis. of Northamptonshire 1564 & 1618–9* (1887): 15 (1564 Vis.) (Cope ped.), 56 (1564 Vis.) (Woodhull ped.). MacNamara *Mems. of the Danvers Fam.* (1895): 173–174. Colket *English Anc. of Hutchinson & Scott* (1936): 37. *NEHGR* 138 (1984): 317–320; 145 (1991): 3–21. *TG* 13 (1999): 188–198.

Children of Edward Raleigh, Esq., by Anne Chamberlain:

i. **BRIDGET RALEIGH** [see next].

ii. **MARY RALEIGH**, married **NICHOLAS WODHULL**, Esq., of Warkworth, Northamptonshire [see CHETWODE 13].

19. BRIDGET RALEIGH, married (as his 1st wife) **JOHN COPE** (or **COOPE**), Knt., of Canons Ashby, Northamptonshire, Sheriff of Northamptonshire, 1545–6, Knight of the Shire for Northamptonshire, 2nd son of William Cope, Esq., of Banbury, Oxfordshire, Cofferer to King Henry VIII, by his 2nd wife, Jane, daughter of John Spencer, Esq., of Hodnell, Warwickshire. He was born before 1513. They had three sons, Erasmus, Esq., George, Esq., and Anthony, Esq., and two daughters, Elizabeth and Joan (wife of Stephen Boyle and Ferdinand Freckleton). He married (2nd) **MARY MALLORY**, widow of _____ Cave, and daughter of Nicholas Mallory. They had no issue. He married (3rd) before June 1542 **MARGARET TAME**, widow of Humphrey Stafford [see HASTANG 17], and daughter and co-heiress of Edmund Tame, Knt., of Fairford, Gloucestershire, by his 1st wife, Agnes, daughter of John Greville, of Drayton, Oxfordshire. They had no issue. She was co-heiress in 1544 to her brother, Edmund Tame, Knt. SIR JOHN COPE died 22 Jan. 1557/8. He left a will proved 21 May 1558 (P.C.C. 25 Noodes). His wife, Margaret, survived him.

> Wotton *English Baronetage* 1 (1741): 113–114 (Cope arms: Argent, on a chevron azure, between three roses gules, flipt proper, as many fleur de lis, or). Kimber & Johnson *Baronetage of England* 1 (1771): 50–55 (sub Cope). Bigland *Account of Fairford* (1791): 12. Bridges *Hist. & Antiqs. of Northamptonshire* 1 (1791): 224–225; 2 (1791): 275–280. Betham *Baronetage of England* 1 (1801): 87. Rudge *Hist. of Gloucester* 1 (1803): 255, 309. Baker *Hist. & Antiqs. of Northampton* 2 (1836–41): 13. Beesley *Hist. of Banbury* (1841): 193. Lee *Hist. of the Town & Parish of Tetbury* (1857): 79. *Warwickshire Antiqs. Mag.* Pt. 8 (1859): 148 (Verney ped.: "… [Thame] ux. Sʳ. Hump: Stafford of Blatherwick Kᵗ."). Holt *Tames of Fairfield* (1870). *Notes & Queries* 4ᵗʰ Ser. 6 (1870): 250–251. Lennard & Vincent *Vis. of Warwick 1619* (H.S.P. 12) (1877): 76–78 (Raleigh ped.: "Bridgett [Raleigh] ux. John Cope miles."). Chitting & Phillipot *Vis. of Gloucester 1623, 1569 & 1582–3* (H.S.P. 21) (1885): 260 (1623 Vis.) (Tame ped.: "Margerett [Tame] ux. Humfrey Stafford Knight sonn and heire of Sʳ Humfrey of Blatherwick in com. Northampton."). Metcalfe *Vis. of Northamptonshire 1564 & 1618–9* (1887): 15 (1564 Vis.) (Cope ped.: "Sir John Cope of Copes Ashby, co. North'ton, Kt., second son to William by Jone his second wife, mar., to his first wife, Bridgett, da. to Edward Rawleigh of Farnborough, co. Warwick, Esq., son and heir to Sir Edward Rawleigh, Kt., … after, the said Sir John mar., to his second wife, Mary, dau. of …. Mallory."). *Trans. Bristol & Gloucs. Arch. Soc.* 14 (1889–90): 224–226. *List of Sheriffs for England & Wales* (PRO Lists and Indexes 9) (1898): 94. *Misc. Gen. et Heraldica* 3ʳᵈ Ser. 4 (1902): 208–223 (Cope peds.) (Raleigh arms: Chequy or and gules; a chief vair). Gun *Studies in Hereditary Ability* (1928): 122–127. Colket *English Anc. of Hutchinson & Scott* (1936): 37 (cites Barron *Northamptonshire Fams.* (1906): 370). VCH *Warwick* 6 (1951): 115f. VCH *Wiltshire* 9 (1970): 119–124. Bindoff *House of Commons 1509–1558* 1 (1982): 693–694 (biog. of John Cope: "… [He] became a grazier and wool-producer, occasionally visiting Calais to transact business with the staple, and cut a figure in local administration"). *NEHGR* 145 (1991): 3–21. VCH *Gloucester* 8 (2001): 42–69; 11 (1976): 264–269.

20. ELIZABETH COPE, married **JOHN DRYDEN**, Gent., of Canons Ashby, Northamptonshire, son of David Dryden, Esq., of Staffle Hill, Cumberland, by Isabel, daughter and heiress of William Nicholson, of Staffle Hill. They had eight sons, Anthony, Erasmus, Knt., Edward, George, Gent., John, Thomas, Gent., [Rev.] Stephen, Gent., and Nicholas, Gent., and four daughters, Mary, Elizabeth, Bridget, and Emma (wife of William Bury, Gent.). JOHN DRYDEN, Gent., died 3 Sept. 1584, and was buried at Canons Ashby, Northamptonshire. He left a will dated 15 August 1584, proved 10 Sept. 1584 (P.C.C. 24 Watson).

>Wotton *English Baronetage* 1 (1741): 114, 349–350. Bridges *Hist. & Antiqs. of Northamptonshire* 1 (1791): 224–226. Baker *Hist. & Antiqs. of Northampton* 2 (1836–41): 6–7. Metcalfe *Vis. of Northamptonshire 1564 & 1618–9* (1887): 15 (1564 Vis.) (Cope ped.: "Elizabeth [Cope], mar. to John Dryden of Copes Ashby, Gent."), 178 (Appendix) (Dryden ped.: "John Dryden of Copes Ashbie, co. North'ton = Elizabeth, da. of Sir John Cope of Copes Ashbie"). *Notes & Queries* 8th Ser. 4 (1893): 461–462 (re. Bury family). *Misc. Gen. et Heraldica* 3rd Ser. 3 (1900): 257 (will of John Dryden); 4 (1902): 208–223 (Cope peds.). *Desc. Cat. Ancient Deeds* 5 (1906): 478, 527–528. Bysshe *Vis. of Lincoln 1666* (Lincoln Rec. Soc. 8) (1917): 11 (Bury ped.). Glencross *Administrations in the P.C.C.* 2 (1917): 9. Longden *Vis. of Northampton 1681* (H.S.P. 87) (1935): 66–67 (Dryden ped.: "John Driden of Cannons Ashby in com. Northt. = *Elizabeth*, daur. of *Sir John Cope* of Cannons Ashby aforesaid"). Colket *English Anc. of Hutchinson & Scott* (1936): 37. *NEHGR* 98 (1944): 18–19 (Dryden arms: Azure, a lion rampant and in chief a sphere between two estoiles, or); 145 (1991): 3–21. Ward *Life of John Dryden* (1961).

Children of Elizabeth Cope, by John Dryden, Gent.:

i. [REV.] STEPHEN DRYDEN, Gent. [see next].

ii. MARY DRYDEN, married FRANCIS FOXLEY, Esq., of Foxley, Northamptonshire [see FOXLEY 18].

iii. BRIDGET DRYDEN. She was a legatee in the 1584 will of her father. She married (1st) about 1587 (as his 2nd wife) [REV.] FRANCIS MARBURY (or MERBURY), Gent., minister, playwright, 3rd son of William Marbury, Gent., of Girsby (in Burgh on Bain), Lincolnshire, by Agnes, daughter of John Lenton, Esq. He was baptized at St. Pancras, Soper Lane, London 27 October 1555 (aged 49 in 1605). They had seven sons, John, Francis, Erasmus, Anthony, Jeremuth, Daniel, and Anthony, and eight daughters, Mary (wife of William Layton), Anne, Bridget, Emma (wife of William Bury, Esq.), Bridget (again), Elizabeth, Elizabeth (again), and Katherine. He was matriculated pensioner from Christ's College, Cambridge in May 1571. He was ordained deacon in 1578. His preaching at Northampton brought about his imprisonment for a time. On his release he returned to that place, notwithstandiung he had been forbidden to go there. He was brought before the High Commission in 1578. He was subsequently imprisoned in the Marshalsea, where he wrote an allegorical play entitled *The Contract of Marriage between Wit & Wisdom* in 1579. He married (1st) at Stoke, Warwickshire 24 May 1580 ELIZABETH MOORE, by whom he had two daughters, Susan (wife of _____ Twyford) and Mary. By 1585 he was curate and Master of the Grammar School in Alford, Lincolnshire. He was inhibited for causes unknown to him, and, in a letter to Lord Burghley dated 1590, he laid before him a statement of his teachings and beliefs in religious and civil matters. He was ordained priest in 1605, and successively became Rector of St. Martin's Vintry, London, 1605–11, Rector of St. Pancras, Soper Lane; London, 1608–10, Vicar of St. Pancras, London, 1608–10, and Rector of St. Margaret's, New Fish Street, London, 1610–1611. [REV.] FRANCIS MARBURY died 12 Feb. 1610/11. He left a will dated 25 Jan. 1610/11, proved 14 Feb. 1610/11 [Consistory Court, London, 56 Hamer]. His widow, Bridget, married (2nd) about Dec. 1620 (date of indenture before marriage) (as his 2nd wife) [REV.] THOMAS NEWMAN, B.D., Rector of Berkhamstead St. Peter, Hertfordshire, chief Burgess and Mayor of Berkhamstead, 1631. He admitted sizar from Peterhouse, Cambridge University, 1584. He obtained a B.A. degree, 1588, M.A. degree, 1591, and B.D. degree, 1607. He was ordained deacon and priest in 1591. He served as Vicar of Stanstead Abbots, Hertfordshire, 1593–7, and as Rector of Great Berkhamstead from 1598. The rectory at Great Berkhamstead was sequestered from him by Parliament in 1645 by reason of his delinquency, he being a staunch Anglican. His wife, Bridget, left a will dated 12 Feb. 1644[/45]; administration granted 2 April 1645 [Hitchin Div., Archdeaconry Ct. of Huntingdon, 32HW98 (will); H22/795 (adm. bond)]. [REV.] THOMAS NEWMAN was living at Berkhamstead, Hertford 5 Dec. 1647. Wotton *English Baronetage* 1 (1741): 351. Baker *Hist. & Antiqs. of Northampton* 2 (1836–41): 6–7. *NEHGR* 20 (1866): 355–367; 86 (1932): 262 (Marbury arms); 98 (1944): 11–25 (Marbury arms: Argent, on a fess engrailed gules, three sheaves or); 145 (1991): 3–21. Cobb *Two Lectures on the Hist. & Antiqs. of Berkhamsted* (1883): 38, 134–140. Urwick *Nonconformity in Herts* (1884): 373–376. *Middlesex & Hertfordshire N&Q* 4 (1898): 197–199. *Misc. Gen. et Heraldica* 3rd Ser. 3 (1900): 257 (will of John Dryden). Maddison *Lincolnshire Peds.* 2 (H.S.P. 51) (1903): 637–640 (Marbury ped.). Peile *Biog. Reg. of Christ's College, 1505–1905* 1 (1910): 118. *NYGBR* 45 (1914): 17–26, 164–169. *Procs. Massachusetts Hist. Soc.* 48 (1915): 280–291. Venn & Venn *Alumni Cantabrigiensis to 1751* 1(3) (1924): 139, 250. *Notes & Queries* 156 (1929): 195, 287 (will of Bridget Dryden). Colket *English Anc. of Hutchinson* & Scott (1936): 25–34. Longden *Northamptonshire & Rutland Clergy from 1500* 9 (1940): 121–122 (biog. of Francis Merbury). Matthews *Walker Revised* (1948): 202 (biog. of Thomas

Newman). Powell *Puritan Village* (1970): 28–29, 34. Crawley *Wills at Hertford 1415–1858* (2007): 395. Hertfordshire Archives & Local Studies: Title Deeds & Papers of the Duncombe Fam., 1534-1895, DE/B664/29479 (available at www.a2a.org.uk/search/index.asp). Northamptonshire Rec. Office: Dryden (Canons Ashby) Coll., D (CA)/518 (available at www.a2a.org.uk/search/index.asp). Bishop's Transcripts for Stoke, Warwickshire [FHL Microfilm 501449].

Children of Bridget Dryden, by [Rev.] Francis Marbury:

a. **ANNE MARBURY**, baptized at Alford, Lincolnshire 20 July 1591. She married at St. Mary Woolnoth, London 9 August 1612 **WILLIAM HUTCHINSON**, Gent., of Alford, Lincolnshire, son and heir of Edward Hutchinson, of Alford, Lincolnshire, by his wife, Susanna. He was baptized at Alford, Lincolnshire 14 August 1586. They had seven sons, [Capt.] Edward, Richard, Francis, William, Samuel, William (again), and Zuriel, and eight daughters, Susanna, Faith (wife of Thomas Savage), Bridget (wife of [Gov.] John Sanford and William Phillips), Elizabeth, Anne (wife of William Collins), Mary, Katherine, and Susanna (again) (wife of John Cole). They immigrated in 1634 on the ship *Griffin* to New England, where they settled successively in Boston, Massachusetts, and Portsmouth and Providence, Rhode Island. He served as Deputy for Boston to the Massachusetts Bay General Court, 1635–6; Magistrate for Particular Court for Boston, Roxbury, etc., 1636, Boston selectman, 1636–7, and Portsmouth treasurer, 1638. WILLIAM HUTCHINSON, Gent., died soon after June 1641. His widow, Anne, was killed by the Indians with several of her children in late summer 1643 in an area which is present day Westchester County, New York. *NEHGR* 19 (1865): 13–20; 20 (1866): 355–367. Pope *Pioneers of Massachusetts* (1900): 250 (biog. of William Hutchinson). Maddison *Lincolnshire Peds.* 2 (H.S.P. 51) (1903): 637–640 (Marbury ped.). *NYGBR* 45 (1914): 17–26, 164–169. Raimo *Biog. Dict. of American Col. & Revolutionary Govs.* (1980): 370–371 (biog. of William Hutchinson). Anderson *Great Migration* 3 (2003): 477–484 (biog. of William Hutchinson). LaPlante *American Jezebel* (2005).

Child of Anne Marbury, by William Hutchinson:

1) [Capt.] **EDWARD HUTCHINSON**, of Boston, Massachusetts, married (1st) **KATHERINE HAMBY** [see HAMBY 22]; (2nd) **ABIGAIL FIRMAGE** [see HAMBY 22].

b. **KATHERINE MARBURY**, married at Berkhampstead, Hertfordshire 7 June 1632 **RICHARD SCOTT**. They had two sons, John and Richard, and four daughters, Mary (wife of Christopher Holder), Hannah (wife of [Gov.] Walter Clarke), Patience (wife of Henry Beere), and Deliverance (wife of William Richardson). They immigrated to New England, where they resided successively at Boston and Ipswich, Massachusetts and at Providence, Rhode Island. RICHARD SCOTT died at Providence, Rhode Island in 1679/80. His widow, Katherine, died at Newport, Rhode Island 2 May 1687. *NEHGR* 20 (1866): 355–367; 60 (1906): 168–175; 96 (1942): 3–27, 192–194. Pope *Pioneers of Massachusetts* (1900): 404 (biog. of Richard Scott). *NYGBR* 45 (1914): 17–26, 164–169. *TAG* 16 (1939–40): 81–88.

21. [Rev.] **STEPHEN DRYDEN**, Gent., of Bulwick, Northamptonshire, 7th son. He was a legatee in the 1584 will of his father. He was admitted to Middle Temple 20 Feb. 1589/90. He married **ELLEN NEALE**, daughter of John Neale, of Yelden, Bedfordshire, and Wollaston, Northamptonshire, by his 2nd wife, Grace, daughter of John Butler, Esq. They had one son, Stephen, and three daughters, _____ (wife of _____ Warren), Grace, and Mary (wife of Thomas Harper). His wife, Ellen, was a legatee in the 1607 will of her father. He was installed as Rector of Bulwick, Northamptonshire 14 August 1615. His wife, Ellen, was buried at Bulwick, Northamptonshire 21 Nov. 1632. [Rev.] STEPHEN DRYDEN, Gent., was buried at Bulwick, Northamptonshire Feb. 1636/7. He left a nuncupative will dated 12 Dec. 1636, proved 19 Jan. 1636/7 (P.C.C. 2 Goare).

Baker *Hist. & Antiqs. of Northampton* 2 (1836–41): 6–7. Camden *Vis. of Rutland 1618–19* (H.S.P. 3) (1870): 21. Metcalfe *Vis. of Northamptonshire 1564 & 1618–9* (1887): 118 (Neale ped.: "Ellen [Neale], ux. Stephen Dryden of Bulwick, co. North'ton, brother of Erasmus Dryden."). *Misc. Gen. et Heraldica* 3rd Ser. 3 (1900): 257 (will of John Dryden). Hopwood *Middle Temple Recs.* (1904): 378. *Maryland Hist. Mag.* 7 (1912): 201–218. Burghill et al. *Vis. of Rutland 1681–2* (H.S.P. 73) (1922): 28. VCH *Rutland* 2 (1935): 34, 96, 98. Longden *Northamptonshire & Rutland Clergy from 1500* 4 (1939): 153 (biog. of Stephen Dryden). Barnes *British Roots of Maryland Fams.* 1 (1999): 171–172.

22. GRACE DRYDEN, married at Bulwick, Northamptonshire 5 June 1624 (by petition dated 3 June 1624) [Rev.] **KENELM CHESELDINE** (or **CHESELDYNE**), Gent., clerk, of Braunston,

Rutland, son of Edward Cheseldyne, of Uppingham, Rutland, by Bridget, daughter of Anthony Faulkner. He was born about 1603 (aged 15 in 1618). They had five sons, including Thomas, Kenelm, Esq., and Stephen, and two daughters. He was admitted to Sidney Sussex College, Cambridge University 28 June 1617. He matriculated in 1617, and obtained a B.A. degree in 1621. He was ordained deacon 20 May 1627, and priest 9 June 1639. He was a legatee and named one of the executors in the 1636 will of her father. He was presented as an intruder to the rectory of Deene, Northamptonshire in 1647. He was appointed Vicar of Bloxham, Lincolnshire in 1655. In 1655 he and his son, Thomas, sold the manor of Braunston, Rutland. [REV.] KENELM CHESELDINE died about 1667.

> Camden *Vis. of Rutland 1618–19* (H.S.P. 3) (1870): 21–22 (Cheseldine ped.: "Kenelme Cheselden æt. 15 ao 1618 Clarke 1624. = Grace d. of Stephen Dryden 3 brother to Sir Erasmus Dryden Kt & Baronett. Stephen was of Bulwik in Com' Northampton."). *Genealogist* n.s. 10 (1893): 255–256. Burghill et al. *Vis. of Rutland 1681–2* (H.S.P. 73) (1922): 27–28. Venn & Venn *Alumni Cantabrigiensis to 1751* 1(1) (1922): 329. Longden *Northamptonshire & Rutland Clergy from 1500* 3 (1939): 103 (biog. of Kenelm Chessledine); 4 (1939): 153 (biog. of Stephen Dryden). Beitzell *Cheseldine Fam.* (1949): 20–24. Barnes *British Roots of Maryland Fams.* 1 (1999): 111–113.

23. KENELM CHESELDINE, Esq., practicing attorney, 2nd son, born about 1640, immigrated to Maryland about 1669, where he settled in St. Mary's County. He married (1st) 9 October 1669 **BRIDGET FAULKNER**. They had no surviving issue. She died in 1677. He married (2nd) before 1677 **MARY GERARD**, daughter of Thomas Gerard, Gent., surgeon and planter, of St. Mary's County, Maryland, and Westmoreland County, Virginia, by his 1st wife, Susanna, daughter of John Snow [see GERARD 19 for her ancestry]. They had one son, Kenelm, and three daughters, Mary (wife of James Hay and George Fobes), Susanna (wife of Thomas Trueman Greenfield), and Dryden (wife of Henry Peregrine Jowles and John Fobes). He served as a member of the Provincial Assembly (Speaker of the Lower House), member of the Provincial Council, Burgess of St. Mary's County, Attorney of the Provincial Court, Attorney General of Maryland, commissary general. He represented the Protestant Associators' government before the colonial authorities in England, 1690–1. He was a founder of King William College in Annapolis. KENELM CHESELDINE, Esq., died testate in Dec. 1708, and was buried in St. Ann's churchyard in Annapolis, Maryland.

> Papenfuse *Biog. Dict. of the Maryland Legislature 1635–1789* 1 (1979): 216–217 (biog. of Kenelm Cheseldyne). Christou & Wright *Col. Fams. of the Eastern Shore of Maryland* 4 (1998): 49–52. Riley *Tidewater Maryland Ancs. 1634 to 1999* (1999): 152–154. Barnes *British Roots of Maryland Fams.* 1 (1999): 111–113.

∽ CHESTER ∾

WILLIAM THE CONQUEROR, King of England, married **MAUD OF FLANDERS**.
HENRY I, King of England, by an unknown mistress, _____.
ROBERT FITZ ROY, Earl of Gloucester, married **MABEL FITZ ROBERT** [see GLOUCESTER 3].

4. MAUD OF GLOUCESTER, married before 1135 **RANULPH DE GERNONS**, Knt., 5th Earl of Chester, lord of Eastham and Macclesfield, Cheshire, Coventry, Warwickshire, Barrow upon Soar, Leicestershire, and Greetham, Lincolnshire, etc., hereditary Vicomte of Avranches in Normandy, son and heir of Ranulph (nicknamed *le Meschin*), 4th Earl of Chester, hereditary Vicomte of Bayeux, by Lucy, widow of Ives de Taillebois and Roger Fitz Gerold, and heiress (and possibly daughter) of Thorold, Sheriff of Lincoln. He was probably born about 1105. She had the manor of Chipping Campden, Gloucestershire by the gift of her father. They had two sons, Hugh [6th Earl of Chester] and Richard. By an unknown mistress, he apparently had an illegitimate son, Robert Fitz Count. He was present at royal councils in Northampton, 1131, Westminster, 1132, and Windsor, 1132. He accepted King Stephen's accession in 1135, and attended the royal council at Westminster in 1136. In 1136 he witnessed the Oxford charter of liberties. In 1136 or 1137 he led a disastrous expedition into Wales from which he was one of the few to escape alive. In 1140 he attempted to capture Henry of Scotland and his wife on their return from King Stephen's court. The same year he surprised the city of Lincoln and manned it for the empress. The king's response was to visit Lincolnshire, where he peaceably renewed a pact with Ranulph. King Stephen left for London before Christmas, but made a surprise return during the festival to lay siege to Lincoln Castle. Ranulph managed to escape, obtained the armed assistance of his father-in-law, Robert, Earl of Gloucester, and other Angevin adherents, raised soldiers from Cheshire and Wales, and marched back to Lincoln, where his wife and half-brother were continuing to resist the siege. At the subsequent Battle of Lincoln 2 February 1141 the king was captured, and Ranulph followed up his victory with sack and slaughter in the city itself. At the Siege of Winchester in September 1141 he initially joined the queen's army, only to encounter such suspicion and hostility that he switched to the empress's camp. In 1144 he was besieged in Lincoln by the king. He met King Stephen at Stamford probably early in 1146, where he apparently renewed his fealty to the king. The king granted him royal manors in Warwickshire, Leicestershire, Nottinghamshire, and Lincolnshire, the towns of Newcastle under Lyme, and Derby, land in Grimsby, and the soke of Grantham, plus the honors of William d'Aubeny Brito (Belvoir), Roger de Bully (Tickhill), and Roger de Poitou (Lancaster, although that which lay north of the Ribble was under Scottish control). He was also confirmed in his tenure of Lincoln Castle. He duly helped Stephen to capture Bedford town and besiege Wallingford Castle in 1146, but the king and the royalist magnates remained deeply suspicious of his failure to restore revenues from royal lands and castles he had seized. He was again with the king at Northampton 29 August 1146, but his refusal to give hostages or restore royal property led to his sudden arrest and imprisonment. He was released after agreeing to Stephen's terms and taking an oath not to resist the king in future, whereupon he set about trying to recover by force what he had been obliged to surrender. Subsequent campaigns led to armed confrontations with Stephen's son Eustache, and on at least two occasions, near Coventry (probably early in 1147) and Lincoln (1149), with the king himself. He did homage to David I, King of Scots at Carlisle in 1149, who granted him the honour of Lancaster (including lands north of the Ribble) in exchange for a renunciation of claims to Carlisle. In 1150, in alliance with Madog ap Maredudd, king of Powys, he prepared an attack on Owain Gwynedd, but the enterprise collapsed after defeat at Coleshill. Some time between 1149 and 1153, he made a formal agreement with Robert, Earl of Leicester, whereby each pledged to bring only twenty knights if obliged by his liege lord to fight against the other. Both earls joined the Angevin campaign in 1153. At Devizes in 1153, Henry, Duke of Normandy gave him lavish grants in the north midlands, including the estates of several royalist barons which the earl was effectively being invited to seize; Ranulph was also restored in his 'Norman inheritance,' which has been interpreted to include Breuil, the castle of Vire, and other holdings once associated with his family, together with comital status and extensive lordship in the Avranchin. During his lifetime, Ranulph founded four religious houses, including an abbey for Savignac monks at Basingwerk, Flintshire, in 1131, priories for Benedictine monks and nuns at Minting, Lincolnshire, and Chester respectively (both at uncertain dates), and, on his deathbed, a priory for Augustinian canons at Trentham, Staffordshire. RANULPH DE GERNONS, Earl of Chester, died at Gresley, Derbyshire 17 Dec. 1153, and was buried at St. Werburg's, Chester. Sometime in the period, 1153–59, his widow, Maud, with consent of her son, Hugh, gave the canons of Calke, then part of Ticknall, the church of St. Wiestan-in-Repton, Derbyshire. Probably in 1158 Queen Eleanor, wife of Henry II, gave confirmation to his widow, Maud, of her wapentake and hundred of Repton, Derbyshire. In 1172 she founded Repton Priory, Derbyshire. Maud, Countess of Chester, died 29 July 1189.

Banks *Dormant & Extinct Baronage of England* 1 (1807): 215–216. Hanshall *Hist. of the County Palatine of Chester* (1823): 19–21, 28 (ped.), 284. *Coll. Top. et Gen.* 2 (1835): 247–249. Dugdale *Monasticon Anglicanum* 3 (1846): 217–218 (sub

Spalding Monastery — Hugonis, primi Comitis Cestriæ et Lincolniæ.... prosapia: "... post quem successit Ranulfus de Gernons filius ejus, qui moriens decimo sexto kalendas Januarii [17 December], jacet juxta patrem suum. Post hunc successit Hugo filius ejus, qui moriens secundo kalendas Julii [30 June], jacet juxta patrem suum."); 4 (1823): 313–314 (charter of Ranulph, Earl of Chester); 6(1) (1830): 410–411 (Ranulph, Earl of Chester, styled "uncle" [avunculi] by Richard Bacun), 430 (""Ranulphus dictus Gernons, comes Cestriæ, obiit xvii. kal. Januarii [16 Dec.], anno MCLIII. et regis Stephani xviii. Qui Ranulphus cepit Mathildem filiam Roberti comitis Gloverniæ; quæ quidem Mathildis fundavit prioratum de Repindon S. Trinitatis anno MCLXXII. decimo octavo Henrici secundi, quæ Matildis obiit quarto kal. Augusti [29 July] anno MCLXXXIX."). Hibbert-Ware *Ancient Parish Church of Manchester* (1848): 16–18 (charter of Ranulph, Earl of Chester). *Arch. Jour.* 15 (1855): 242–246 (charter of Ranulph, Earl of Chester). Bigsby *Hist. & Topog. Desc. of Repton* (1854): 56-57 (charter of Maud, Countess of Chester), 57–58 (charter of Maud, Countess of Chester naming her parents, Robert, Earl of Gloucester, and Countess Mabel, and her grandfather, King Henry I), 58. *Arch. Jour.* 15 (1858): 242 (charter of Ranulph, Earl of Chester). Luard *Annales Monastici* 2 (Rolls Ser. 36) (1865): 235 (Annals of Waverley sub A.D. 1153: "Rannulfus comes Cestrensis hoc anno obiit, cui successit Hugo filius ejus."). *Annual Rpt. of the Deputy Keeper* 35 (1874): 7 (charter and letter of Ranulph, Earl of Chester). Ormerod *Hist. of the County Palatine & City of Chester* 1 (1882): 20–26 (Robert Malet styled "uncle" [avunculus] of Earl Ranulph's mother [Lucy] in charter of Henry, Duke of Normandy [afterwards King Henry II] dated c.1152). *Cat. of a Selection from the Stowe MSS* (1883): 10–11 (charter of Maud, Countess of Chester). Christie *Annales Cestrienses, or, Chronicle of the Abbey of S. Werburg at Chester* (Lancashire & Cheshire Rec. Soc. 14) (1887): 22–23 (sub A.D. 1153: "Obiit Ranulphus II. comes Cestrie."). Birch *Cat. of Seals in the British Museum* 2 (1892): 380 (seal of Maud, Countess of Chester dated mid-12th Cent.—Pointed oval. In tight-fitting dress and a long maunch, standing. Legend wanting.). Round *Feudal England* (1895). Prou & Vidier *Recueil des Chartes de l'Abbaye de Saint-Benoit-sur-Loire* (1900–1907): 356–364 (charter of Ranulph, Earl of Chester dated 1147–53). *C.P.R. 1399–1401* (1903): 296–297. Warner & Ellis *Facsimiles of Royal & Other Charters in the British Museum* 1 (1903): #51 (charter of Hugh, Earl of Chester to his mother, Countess Maud, dated c.1162–7; charter names his father, Earl Ranulph), #52 (charter of Maud, Countess of Chester, dated c.1162–7, granted with consent of her son, Earl Hugh; charter names her aunt [amita], Empress Maud, her parents, Robert, Earl of Gloucester, and Countess Mabel, and her husband, Earl Ranulph). Jeayes *Desc. Cat. of Derbyshire Charters* (1906): 242–243 (charter of Maud, Countess of Chester, dated 1153–60 names her grandfather, King Henry I of England, and her parents, Robert, Earl of Gloucester, and Countess Mabel), 244 (charter of Maud, Countess of Chester, dated c.1162-1167 names her parents, Robert, Earl of Gloucester, and Countess Mabel), 244 (Maud, Countess of Chester, styled "kinswoman" [cognata] by King Henry II of England in charter dated ?1175). Marx ed. *Gesta Normannorum Ducum* (1914): 331 (Guillaume de Jumièges: "Predictus autem Rannulfus comes accepit uxorem Mathildem, filiam Roberti comitis de Gloecestria, ex qua genuit duos filios, Hugonem et Ricardum."). Farrer *Early Yorkshire Charters* 2 (1915): 195 (chart). Stenton *Docs. illus. of the Social & Economic Hist. of the Danelaw* (1920): 360–361. Farrer *Honors & Knights' Fees* 2 (1924): 34. *Colls. Hist. Staffs. 1924* (1926): 30–31 (charter of Countess Maud and her son, Earl Hugh). *Trans. Royal Hist. Soc.* 4th Ser. 20 (1937): 103–134 (biog. of Ranulf de Gernons, Earl of Chester: "The man was haughty and proud; touchy upon the point of honour, but faithless and utterly untrammelled by any scruple in the pursuit of his ends; determined as a spoilt child to gratify his desires and ambitions."). Hatton *Book of Seals* (1950): 356–357 (charter of Robert Fitz Count, Constable of Chester). *C.P.* 3 (1913): 166–167; 4 (1916): 670 (chart), 5 (1926): 686, footnote b (sub Gloucester); 7 (1929): 677; 12(1) (1953): 274 (re. Robert Fitz Count). Barraclough *Earldom & County Palatinate of Chester* (1953): 57–58 (Benedict styled "brother of the Earl" in charter issued by Ranulph, 5th Earl of Chester). *English Hist. Rev.* 75 (1960), 654–660; 91 (1976): 555–565. Sanders *English Baronies* (1960): 32–33. Stenton *First Cent. of English Feudalism, 1066–1166* (1961). Davis *King Stephen* (1967): 132–134. Patterson *Earldom of Gloucester Charters* (1973): 5, 171 (Appendix, No. 227: Donor: Earl William [of Gloucester]; Date: Before 1135; Beneficiary: Matilda the earl's daughter; Description: Chipping Campden (Glos.); Source: *Misc. D.M. Stenton*, 26). Schwennicke *Europaische Stanmtafeln* 3(2) (1983): 354. Barraclough *Charters of the Anglo-Norman Earls of Chester, c.1071–1237* (Lancashire & Cheshire Rec. Soc. 126) (1988) 81 (Richard Bacun styled "kinsman and retainer" [cognatus meus et familiaris] by Ranulph de Gernons, Earl of Chester, in charter dated 1143–44). *Anglo-Norman Studies* 14 (1991): 39–59. Brown *Eye Priory Cartulary & Charters* 2 (Suffolk Rec. Soc.) (1994): 28 (Robert Malet called "uncle" of Earl Ranulph's mother in 1153 by King Henry II). Katherine Keats-Rohan 'Parentage of Countess Lucy made Plain,' in *Prosopon Newsletter* (1995): 1–3 (identifes Lucy, wife of Ranulph, 4th Earl of Chester, as daughter of Turold, Sheriff of Lincoln). Johns *Noblewomen, Aristocracy & Power in the 12th Cent. Anglo-Norman Realm* (2003): 88. Graeme White, 'Ranulf (II), fourth earl of Chester (d. 1153)', in *Oxford Dictionary of National Biography* (2004). National Archives, DL 25/36 (charter dated 1129–53 by Ranulph, Earl of Chester, addressed to his Bishop of Bangor, etc., notifying that Robert, Earl of Gloucester, gave to Maud his daughter, Countess of Chester, [Chipping] Campden [Campadene], and that he has confirmed it to her) (available at www.catalogue.nationalarchives.gov.uk/search.asp).

5. HUGH, 6th Earl of Chester, hereditary Vicomte of Avranches in Normandy, seigneur of Saint Sever and Briquessart, son and heir, born about 1141 (of age in 1162). He is sometimes called Hugh of Cyfeiliog, because, according to a late writer, he was born in that district of Wales. According to the chronicler, John of Hexham, it was agreed at Carlisle in 1150 that a son of Ranulph, Earl of Chester, should marry one of the daughters of Henry, son of the king of Scotland. The son of Earl Ranulph was presumably his eldest son, Hugh. The projected marriage never took place. In the period, 1154–7, Earl Hugh and his mother, Countess Maud, gave Styvechale (south of Coventry) to Walter, Bishop of Chester, and his successors for the absolution of Hugh's father, Lord Earl Ranulph, and the redemption of his soul and that of his ancestors. Sometime in the period, 1155–63, the king ordered Earl Hugh and his mother, Countess Maud, to give to the Abbot and monks of Gloucesterr the rents which Hugh's father, Earl Ranulph, gave them in the mills of Oldney and Tadwell. He was present in 1163 at Dover for King Henry II's renewal of the Flemish money fief, and also attended the Council of Clarendon in January 1164. Sometime in the period, 1166–87, he confirmed the former grant made to Saint-Étienne Abbey, Caen by Ranulph, Vicomte of Bayeux, his ancestor, of all the land the said Ranulph possessed at Bretteville-l'Orgueilleuse. He married in 1169 **BERTRADE DE MONTFORT**, daughter of Simon de Montfort, Count of Évreux, seigneur of Montfort-l'Amaury, by his wife, Maud. She was born about 1156 (aged 29 in 1185). They had one son, Ranulph, Knt. [Earl of Chester and Lincoln], and five daughters, Maud, Mabel, Agnes, Hawise, and _____ (wife of Llywelyn ap Iorwerth, Prince of North Wales). By an unknown mistress (or mistresses), he also had two illegitimate sons, William (or Pain) (of Milton), and Roger, and one illegitimate daughter, Amice. Hugh joined the rebellion of King Henry II's sons in 1173. He was captured by King Henry II at Dol in August 1173. In 1174 he was deprived of his lands for rebellion. He was subsequently regranted his honours and lands at the Council of Northampton in 1177. In March 1178 he witnessed King Henry II's award in the dispute between Alfonso IX, King of Castile, and Sancho V, King of Navarre. During his lifetime, he granted some lands in the Wirral to the Abbey of St. Werburgh, Chester, and made other special gifts to Stanlow Priory, St Mary's, Coventry, and the nuns of Bullington and Greenfield priories. He also confirmed his mother's grants to her foundation of Augustinian canons at Calke, Derbyshire, and those of his father to his convent of the Benedictine nuns of St Mary's, Chester. In 1171 he confirmed the grants of his father to the Abbey of St. Stephen in the diocese of Bayeux. He likewise granted the church of Belchford, Lincolnshire to Trentham Priory, and the church of Combe, Gloucestershire to the Abbey of Bordesley, Warwickshire. HUGH, Earl of Chester, died at Leek, Staffordshire 30 June 1181, and was buried next to his father in the chapter house of St Werburgh's, Chester. Sometime in the period, 1188–99, his widow, Bertrade, witnessed a charter of her son, Ranulph, Earl of Chester. In the period, 1190–1200, she reached agreement with the abbot and convent of Troarn in Normandy regarding the construction of a mill and fishpond on the boundary between her wood and theirs. Sometime before 1194–1203, she exchanged lands with the canons of Repton. Sometime in the period, 1200–10, she granted to Ralph Carbonel, of Halton, Lincolnshire, for his homage and service a half a knight's fee which he held of the said countess in Halton. In 1223 Richard Duket and Simon de Sees brought a plea of novel disseisin against her touching a tenement in Harmston, Lincolnshire. In 1226 she presented to the church of Waddington, Lincolnshire. In 1227 she arraigned an assize of last presentation to the church of Waddington, Lincolnshire against the abbot of St. Sever. Bertrade, Countess of Chester, died in 1227, after 31 March.

Banks *Dormant & Extinct Baronage of England* 1 (1807): 217–218. Hanshall *Hist. of the County Palatine of Chester* (1823): 21, 28 (ped.). D'Anisy *Extrait des Chartes, et autres Actes Normands ou Anglo-Normands* 1 (1834): 276 (charter of Hugh, Earl of Chester). *Coll. Top. et Gen.* 2 (1835): 247–249. Dugdale *Monasticon Anglicanum* 3 (1846): 217–218 (sub Spalding Monastery — Hugonis, primi Comitis Cestriæ et Lincolniæ.... prosapia: "... post quem successit Ranulfus de Gernons filius ejus, qui moriens decimo sexto kalendas Januarii [17 December], jacet juxta patrem suum. Post hunc successit Hugo filius ejus, qui moriens secundo kalendas Julii [30 June], jacet juxta patrem suum."); 4 (1823): 314 (charter of Hugh, Earl of Chester). Bigsby *Hist. & Topog. Desc. of Repton* (1854): 58 (charter of Hugh, Earl of Chester, naming his father, Ranulf, Earl of Chester, and his grandfather, Robert, Earl of Gloucester), 59–61 (charter of Hugh, Earl of Chester). Stevenson *Church Historians of England* 4(1) (1856): 27 (Chronicle of John of Hexham). Luard *Annales Monastici* 1 (Rolls Ser. 36) (1864): 244 (Burton Annals sub A.D. 1227: "Obiit Bertrudis comitissa Cestriae."). Leycester

& Mainwaring *Tracts written in the Controversy respecting the Legitimacy of Amicia, daughter of Hugh Cyveliok, Earl of Chester* 1–3 (Chetham Soc. 78–80) (1869). *Reliquary* 11 (1870–71): 196 (Harleian MS. 1486 [Derbyshire Visitation] alleges Hugh, Earl of Chester, had [illegitimate] son, William de Mylton). Ormerod *Hist. of the County Palatine & City of Chester* 1 (1882): 26–33. *Cat. of a Selection from the Stowe MSS* (1883): 10 (charter of Hugh, Earl of Chester). Christie *Annales Cestrienses, or, Chronicle of the abbey of S. Werburg at Chester* (Lancashire & Cheshire Rec. Soc. 14) (1887): 20–21 (sub A.D. 1147: "Natus comes Hugo II."), 24–25 (sub A.D. 1169: "In hoc anno factus Hugo comes Cestrie miles, eodem vero anno duxit Hugo comes Cestre uxorem filiam Simonis comitis Ebroensis nomine Bertrad quam Rex Henricus II. Angliæ ei tradidit quia ipsius cognata fuit."), 28–29 (sub A.D. 1181: "Obiit Hugo II. ij kal. Julii comes Cestre apud Lech."), 54–55 (sub A.D. 1227: "Item obiit Bertrudis comitissa Cestre."). Birch *Cat. of Seals in the British Museum* 2 (1892): 381 (seal of Bertrade, Countess of Chester dated at end of 12th Cent.—Pointed oval. Full face, tightly-fitting dress with long maunches at the wrists, standing. Legend: * SIGILL' BERTREE COMITISSE CESTRIE.). *C.P.R.* 1225–1232 (1903): 156. *C.P.R.* 1399–1401 (1903): 296–297. Warner & Ellis *Facsimiles of Royal & Other Charters in the British Museum* 1 (1903): #51 (charter of Hugh, Earl of Chester to his mother, Countess Maud, dated c.1162–7; charter names his father, Earl Ranulph), #52 (charter of Maud, Countess of Chester, dated c.1162–7, granted with consent of her son, Earl Hugh; charter names her parents, Robert, Earl of Gloucester, and Countess Mabel, and her husband, Earl Ranulph). Wrottesley *Peds. from the Plea Rolls* (1905): 531–532. Jeayes *Descriptive Catalogue of Derbyshire Charters* (1906): 69, 242–245. Delisle *Recueil des Actes de Henri II, Roi d'Angleterre et Duc de Normandie* (1909): 387 (biog. of Hugh, Earl of Chester). Round *Rotuli de Dominabus et Pueris et Puellis de XII Comitatibus [1185]* (Pipe Roll Soc. 35) (1913): 15 (Date 1185: "Bertreia comitissa filia comitis de Everews, uxor Hugonis comitis Cestrie, est de donatione Domini Regis, et est .xxix. annorum."). Davis *Rotuli Hugonis de Welles Episcopi Lincolniensis 1209–1235* 3 (Lincoln Rec. Soc. 9) (1914): 154. Farrer *Early Yorkshire Charters* 2 (1915): 195 (chart). Tait *Chartulary or Reg. of the Abbey of St. Werburgh, Chester* (Chetham Soc. 82) (1923). Farrer *Honors & Knights' Fees* 2 (1924): 103, 200. *Colls. Hist. Staffs. 1924* (1926): 30–31 (charter of Earl Hugh and his mother, Countess Maud). *Rpt. on the MSS of Reginald Rawdon Hastings, Esq.* 1 (Hist. MSS Comm. 78) (1928): 83. Hatton *Book of Seals* (1950): 238 (writ of King Henry II to Hugh, Earl of Chester, and Bertrade his wife dated 1177–81). Barraclough *Earldom & County Palatinate of Chester* (1953). Sanders *English Baronies* (1960): 18, 32. Barraclough *Charters of the Anglo-Norman earls of Chester, c.1071–1237* (Lancashire & Cheshire Rec. Soc. 126) (1988): 140–196. Johns *Noblewomen, Aristocracy & Power in the 12th Cent. Anglo-Norman Realm* (2003): 65–66. T. F. Tout, 'Hugh, fifth earl of Chester (1147–1181)', rev. Thomas K. Keefe, in *Oxford Dictionary of National Biography* (2004).

Children of Hugh, Earl of Chester, by Bertrade de Montfort:

i   **RANULPH**, Knt., Earl of Chester, Vicomte of Avranches in Normandy, Judge in the King's Court, 1193, Constable of Sermilly Castle, 1201–4, Constable of the Tower of Avranches, 1203, Governor of the Peak Castle and Forest, 1215, Sheriff of Lancashire, 1216–22, Sheriff of Shropshire and Staffordshire, 1216, 1217–23, Steward of the Town and Honour of Lancaster, 1216–23, Constable of Fotheringay Castle, 1221–2, Steward of the Honour of Leicester, 1222, and, in right of his 1st wife, Duke of Brittany, Earl of Richmond, son and heir, born at Oswestry in Powys c.1172. He was knighted by the king at Caen 1 Jan. 1187/8. He married (1st) 3 Feb. 1187/8 (or 1189) **CONSTANCE OF BRITTANY** [see BRITTANY 6], widow of Geoffrey of England, Duke of Brittany, Earl of Richmond (killed in a tournament at Paris 19 August 1186) [see ENGLAND 4.v], and daughter and heiress of Conan IV *le Petit*, Duke of Brittany, Earl of Richmond, by Margaret, daughter of Henry of Scotland, Earl of Northumberland [see BRITTANY 5 for her ancestry]. She was born about 1162. They had no issue. In 1194 he was commander of the forces for King Richard I. He took part in the second Coronation of King Richard I, which was solemnised in Winchester Cathedral 17 April 1194. In 1196 Ranulph captured his wife, Constance, en route to her finalizing negotiations with King Richard I and confined her at Benvron for at least a year. Soon after her release, she sought the annulment of their marriage, which was granted in 1199, presumably on grounds on consanguinity; she subsequently married (3rd) before October 1199 (as his 1st wife) **GUY DE THOUARS**, in right of his 1st wife, Count (or Duke) of Brittany, Earl of Richmond [see BRITTANY 6]. Constance died testate at Nantes 4 (or 5) Sept. 1201. Ranulph married (2nd) before 7 October 1200 **CLEMENCE DE FOUGÈRES**, widow of Alain de Vitré (or Dinan) (died 1198), seigneur of Dinan, and daughter of Guillaume de Fougères, seigneur of Fougères, by Agatha, daughter of Guillaume du Hommet, Constable of Normandy [see FOUGÈRES 5 for her ancestry]. Her maritagium included land in the valley of Mortain. They had no issue. He was engaged in warfare with the Welsh from 1209 to 1214. He was faithful to King John against the rebellious Barons. He was one of the executors of King John who died 19 October 1216; and one of most zealous supporters of the young king, Henry III. In 1217, as Joint Commander of the royal army, he contributed to the defeat of the rebels under the Count of Perche. He was created Earl of Lincoln 23 May 1217. He went on crusade to the Holy Land in May 1218, and distinguished himself at the Siege of Damietta. He returned to England in August 1220. In 1223 he was required to surrender his castles. In 1229 he opposed in Parliament the grant of a tenth to the Pope, and forbade its collection in his own domain. In 1229 Earl Ranulph granted tithes in Wilsford, Wiltshire, formerly held of the Earl of Lincoln, to Roger, Succentor of Salisbury. He served as Chief Commander of the royal troops in Brittany, 1230–1, and in June 1231 was a Joint Commissioner to treat with France. Sometime between April 1231 and his death, he resigned the earldom of Lincoln to his sister, Hawise de Quincy. RANULPH, Earl of Chester, died at Wallingford 28 October 1232, and was buried at St. Werburg's, Chester, his heart being interred at Dieulacres Abbey. His widow, Clemence, died in 1252. Sandford *Gen. Hist. of the Kings of England* (1677): 67–68. Madox *Formulare Anglicanum* (1702): 187 (charter of Ranulph, Earl of Chester). *Gallia Christiana* 2 (1720): 1333 (abstract of charter of Guy de Thouars dated 1208 naming his mother, Aumuz, and his wife, [Constance] Countess of Brittany). Anselme *Hist. de la Maison Royale de France* 1 (1725): 445–461 (sub Bretagne). Morice *Méms. pour Servir de Preuves a l'Hist. de Bretagne* 1 (1742): 37–38, 912–913, 917. Morice *Histoire Ecclesiastique et Civil de Bretagne* 1 (1750): xvii–xviii (Counts of Penthievre ped.). Banks *Dormant & Extinct Baronage of England* 1 (1807): 218–220. Hanshall *Hist. of the County Palatine of Chester* (1823): 21–23, 28 (ped.). Dugdale *Monasticon Anglicanum* 5 (1825): 325 (charter of Ranulph, Earl of Chester dated 1230), 574–575 (Jerveaux Abbey — Genealogy of the Counts of Richmond). *Coll. Top. et Gen.* 2 (1835): 247–249. *Extracta e Variis Cronicis Scocie* (1842): 70 ("Henricus, regis Dauid filius, comes Huntyntoune et Northumbrie vxorem duxit Adam filiam Willelmi senioris, sororis Willelmi junioris comitis de Warenna, et sororem comitis Roberti Legecestrensis, et Walranni comitis de Melent, cuius mater fuit soror Rodulphi comitis de Perona, regis Francorum Ludouici consanguinea, ex qua suscepit tres inclitos filios ... Genuit eciam idem princeps Henricus totidem filias ex uxore sua predicta Ada, scilicet, Adam, que lege conjugii tradita est comiti Holandie Florentino : secundam, Margaretam Conano duci Britannie comiti de Richmonth nuptam, ex qua genuit filiam nomine Constanciam Gaufrido, comiti Andigauie, fratri regis Anglie Richardi Primi, disponsatam, de qua Gaufridus genuit filium nomine Arthurum, postea in mare mersum, vnam eciam filiam, Aleciam nomine, que a Petro Mauclerk concepit et peperit filium, nomina Johannem, postea ducem Britannie, et aliam filiam nomine Alienoram, que cum Arthuro fratre in mare periit."). *Top. & Gen.* 1 (1846): 301–320. Hawley *Royal Fam. of England* (1851): 18–19. *Jour. British Arch. Assoc.* 7 (1852): 123–132 (letter of Clemence, Countess of Chester, names her aunt [amite], Aline, Prioress of Mortain, and Raoul de Fougères her grandfather [avus]). *Mémoires de la Société des Antiquaries de l'Ouest* 29 (1865): 365–369 (re. Thouars fam.). Stubbs *Gesta Regis Henrici Secundi Benedicti Abbatis* 1 (Rolls Ser. 49) (1867): 207. Marchegay & Mabille *Chroniques des Églises d'Anjou* (1869): 45 (Chronicæ Sancti Albini Andegavensis: death of Geoffrey). Wright *Feudal Manuals of English Hist.* (1872). *Annual Rpt. of the Deputy Keeper* 35 (1874): 8–9 (charter of Ranulph, Earl of Chester). Demay *Inv. des Sceaux de la Normandie* (1881): 5–6 (undated seal of Constance, Duchess of Brittany, Countess of Richmond — Dame debout, coiffée en tresses, revêtue d'un sur___ ajusté du corsage, des hanches et des bras, et recouvert d'une chape, un faucon sur le poing, en fleuron dans la main droite. [Légende:] * CONSTANCIA DVCISS .... [COM]ITISSA RICH[EMUN]DIE). Ormerod *Hist. of the County Palatine & City of Chester* 1 (1882): 33–41. Robertson *Materials for the Hist. of Thomas Becket* 6 (Rolls Ser. 67) (1882): 170–174. Doyle *Official Baronage of England* 1 (1886): 365–366 (sub Chester); 3 (1886): 107–109 (sub Richmond). *Annales Cestrienses* (Lanc. & Cheshire Rec. Soc. 14) (1887): 40–41 (Chron. of St. Werburg sub 1188: "Rannulphus comes cestrie ... Cui etiam dedit Henricus rex anglie in uxorem relictam v Kl. [recte Galfridi filii sui] Cui comitissam britannie filia Alani [recte Conani] Comitis britannie nominee Constancia et toto comittatu de Richemund quam ipse comes Cestrie Rannulphus desponsavit in die Sancte Werburge virginis, id est, tertia nonas Februarii [3 Feb.] apud ..."), 46 (Chron. of St. Werburg sub 1200: "Rannulphus comes Cestrie desponsavit uxorem filiam Radulphi de Feugis, nomine Clementiam, relicta comitissa Britannie, nomine Constancia."). La Borderie *Recueil d'Actes inédits des Ducs et Princes de Bretagne (XIe, XIIe, XIIIe Siècles)* (1888). Birch *Cat. Seals in the British Museum* 2 (1892): 378 (seal of Constance, Duchess of Brittany, Countess of Richmond dated 1190–1198 — Pointed oval. To the right. Standing, with tightly-fitting dress, long fur-lined cloak fastened at the throat, in the right hand a lily-flower, on the left hand a hawk with long jesses.). *Inventaire Sommaire des Archives Départementales antérieures à 1790, Loire-Inférieure* 2(2) Ser. C &D (1898): 147. *List of Sheriffs for England & Wales* (PRO Lists and Indexes 9) (1898): 72, 117. Wrottesley *Peds. from the Plea Rolls* (1905): 531–532. *C.P.R. 1232–1247* (1906): 355. Dunbar *Scottish Kings* (1906): 58-70. Delisle *Recueil des Actes de Henri II, Roi d'Angleterre et Duc de Normandie* Introduction (1909): 103–106, 371–372 (biog. of Geoffrey Fitz Roy, Count of Brittany). VCH *Hertford* 3 (1912): 441–458. Farrer *Early Yorkshire Charters* 2 (1915): 195 (chart). *Le Moyen Age* 35 (1924-5): 63–70. Farnham *Leicestershire Medieval Peds.* (1925): 11 (ped. of Earls of Chester). Brunel et al. *Recueil des Actes de Philippe Auguste Roi de France* 2 (1943): 542. *C.P.* 3 (1913): 167–169 (sub Chester); 10 (1945): 780 (chart), 794–805 (sub Richmond). *Annales de Bretagne* 53 (1946), 1–27. VCH *Wiltshire* 6 (1962): 213–221. Painter *Scourge of the Clergy: Peter of Dreux, Duke of Brittany* (1969). *BIHR* 50 (1977): 112–115. Ellis *Cat. Seals in the P.R.O.* 2 (1981): 13 (seal of Ranulph, Earl of Chester dated c.1200 — A shield of arms: a lion passant. Legend: + SIGILLVM [R]A[NVF]I COMITIS CESTRIE). Schwennicke *Europäische Stammtafeln* 2 (1984): 75 (sub Brittany), 83 (sub England); 3 (1989): 810 (sub Thouars). *Hist. Research* 63 (1990): 1–16. Everard *Charters of Duchess Constance of Brittany & her Fam.* (1999). Everard *Brittany & the Angevins* (2000). Van Kerrebrouck *Les Capétiens 987–1328* (2000): 347–360. Jones *Between France & England* (2003): 38–40. Wheeler & Parsons *Eleanor of Aquitaine: Lord & Lady* (2003): 101. Richard Eales, 'Ranulf (III), sixth earl of Chester and first earl of Lincoln (1170-1232)', in *Oxford Dict. of National Biog.* (2004). Bull & Léglu *World of Eleanor of Aquitaine* (2005).

ii **MAUD OF CHESTER**, married **DAVID OF SCOTLAND**, Earl of Huntingdon [see BALLIOL 4].

iii. **MABEL OF CHESTER**, married **WILLIAM D'AUBENEY**, 3rd Earl of Arundel [see CLIFTON 5].

iv. **AGNES OF CHESTER**, married **WILLIAM DE FERRERS**, Knt., 4th Earl of Derby [see FERRERS 6].

v. **HAWISE OF CHESTER**, Countess of Lincoln, married **ROBERT DE QUINCY** [see QUINCY 6.i].

Child of Hugh, Earl of Chester, by an unknown mistress, _____:

vi. **AMICE OF CHESTER**, married **RALPH DE MAINWARING**, Seneschal of Chester [see AUDLEY 6].

❧ CHETWODE ❧

WILLIAM MALET, of Curry-Mallet, Somerset, married _____.
MABEL MALET, married **HUGH DE VIVONNE**, Knt., of Chewton, Somerset [see MALET 2].

3. HAWISE DE VIVONNE, married before 1256 **WALTER DE WAHULL** (or **WODHULL**), Knt., of Odell and Langford, Bedfordshire, son and heir of Saher de Wahull, of Odell and Langford, Bedfordshire, by his wife, Alice. He was born about 1227 (aged 23 in 1250). They had one son, John, Knt., and one daughter, Beatrice (wife of Henry Fitz Morgald). In 1255 Hugh Chaceporc, Knt., with the assent of Walter de Wahull, son and heir of Saher de Wahull, surrendered the land of Peter Chaceporc in Ravenstone, Buckinghamshire to the king, who gave it, in memory of the said Peter, and in recognition of his services and for the soul of Hugh de Vivonne, Peter's uncle, to Austin canons then established at Ravenstone, Buckinghamshire. In 1257 Walter received protection to make a pilgrimage to the shrine at Santiago de Compostela in Spain. In 1260 and 1263 he was summoned for military service in Wales. He appears to have joined the Barons against King Henry III and was pardoned 9 May 1266. SIR WALTER DE WAHULL died shortly before 15 July 1269. His widow, Hawise, had license to remarry granted to her 23 July 1269.

Dugdale *Monasticon Anglicanum* 6(1) (1830): 498. Roberts *Excerpta è rotulis finium in Turri Londinensi asservatis, Henrico Tertio rege, AD 1216–1272* 2 (1836): 221–222. *Coll. Top. et Gen.* 7 (1841): 136–138. Harvey et al. *Vis. of Bedfordshire 1566, 1582, 1634 & 1669* (H.S.P. 19) (1884): 67–69 (Wahull ped.: "Walt'us de Wahull Baro' de Wahull ob. 52 H. 3. = Havisia d'na de Longford vidua 1225 filia Hugonis de Viuonia Senescalli Gasconiæ & Pictaviæ."). *Misc. Gen. et Heraldica* 2nd Ser. 1 (1886): 45–51, 69–80. *Journals of the House of Lords* 124 (1892): 194–201. Wrottesley *Peds. from the Plea Rolls* (1905): 87. VCH *Bedford* 2 (1908): 234–237; 3 (1912): 71–72 ("He was summoned by special writ, one of the privileges attached to the rank of majores barones in the Great Charter of 1215, for military purposes in 1260, 1261, and 1263"). Farrer *Honors & Knights' Fees* 1 (1923): 61–68. Fowler *Digest of Charters of the Priory of Dunstable* (Bedfordshire Hist. Rec. Soc. 10) (1926): ped. 6 at end. VCH *Buckingham* 4 (1927): 439–445 (Wahull arms: Or three crescents gules). Paget *Baronage of England* (1957) 564: 3–4. Sanders *English Baronies* (1960): 69. *TG* 7-8 (1986): 4–127.

4. JOHN DE WAHULL, Knt., of Odell, Flitton and Silsoe, Langford, Podington, and Wymington, Bedfordshire, Pattishall, Lamport, Orlingbury, and Wootton, Northamptonshire, etc., son and heir, born about 1248 (of full age 5 Nov. 1269). He married **AGNES DE PINKNEY**, daughter of Henry de Pinkney, Knt., of Weedon Pinkney, Northamptonshire, Enborne, Berkshire, Fulmer and Datchet, Buckinghamshire, Elmdon, Essex, Pirton, Hertfordshire, etc. [see PINKNEY 7 for her ancestry]. They had one son, Thomas, Knt. He fought in Wales in 1277, 1282 and 1283. He was summoned to the military council in 1283 at Shrewsbury which passed sentence of death on David, brother of Llewellyn, Prince of Wales. He presented to the church of Odell, Bedfordshire in 1284 and 1298. In 1287 he held a market at Odell, Bedfordshire, by right of a previous charter for the same granted in 1245 to his grandfather, Saher de Wahull. In 1290 Ralph de Beauchamp acknowledged that he owed him a debt of 45 marks. He fought in Gascony in 1294. SIR JOHN DE WAHULL died shortly before 5 April 1296. His widow, Agnes, was assigned dower 13 June 1296.

Baker *Hist. & Antiqs. of Northampton* 2 (1836–41): 107. Harvey et al. *Vis. of Bedfordshire 1566, 1582, 1634 & 1669* (H.S.P. 19) (1884): 67–69 (Wahull ped.: "Joh'es de Wahull Baro' de Wahull d'n's de Longford sum[s] int. Barones ad pugnand. contra Wallos A° 1 E. 1 ob. 24 E. 1. = [left blank]."). *Misc. Gen. et Heraldica* 2nd Ser. 1 (1886): 45–51, 69–80. *Journals of the House of Lords* 124 (1892): 194–201. *C.C.R. 1288–1296* (1904): 120, 484. *Scots Peerage* 3 (1906): 6–7 (sub Lindsay, Earl of Crawford). VCH *Bedford* 2 (1908): 325–333; 3 (1912): 71–72 ("John de Wahull received nine writs as a baron between the years 1276 and 1295. These were not summons to Parliament, but undoubtedly military writs"), 80–87, 117–122. Farrer *Honors & Knights' Fees* 1 (1923): 61–68. VCH *Buckingham* 4 (1927): 489–496. VCH *Northampton* 4 (1937): 195–200, 204–207, 292–296. Hatton *Book of Seals* (1950): 36–37. Paget *Baronage of England* (1957) 564: 4. *C.P.* 12(2) (1959): 294. Sanders *English Baronies* (1960): 69. Sutton *Rolls & Reg. of Bishop Oliver Sutton, 1280–1299* 8 (Lincoln Rec. Soc. 76) (1986): 98, 110. *TG* 7-8 (1986): 4–127.

5. THOMAS DE WAHULL, Knt., of Odell, Bedfordshire, Pattishall, Lamport, Orlingbury, and Wootton, Northamptonshire, Wymington, Bedfordshire, etc., son and heir, born about 1273 (aged 23 in 1296). He married **HAWISE DE PRAYERS**, daughter of Henry de Prayers, Knt., of Durnford and Liddiard, Wiltshire. They had one son, John. He was summoned to the so-called Parliament at Salisbury on 26 Jan. 1297, and fought in Scotland in 1298. SIR THOMAS DE WAHULL died shortly before 30 Jan. 1304. His widow, Hawise, married (2nd) in 1305–6 **ROBERT DE ETON**.

Harvey et al. *Vis. of Bedfordshire 1566, 1582, 1634 & 1669* (H.S.P. 19) (1884): 67–69 (Wahull ped.: "Thomas de Woodhall miles Baro' de Woodhall ob. 32 E. 1. = Havisia filia Henr. Praiers renupta Rob'to de Grey de Eyton."). *Misc. Gen. et Heraldica* 2nd Ser. 1 (1886): 45–51, 69–80. *Journals of the House of Lords* 124 (1892): 194–201. Wrottesley *Peds. from the Plea Rolls* (1905): 87. VCH *Bedford* 3 (1912): 71–72 ("Thomas de Wahull received three writs of summons, two in 1297 of a military character, and one in 1296–7 endorsed 'De Parliamento tenendo apud Sarum' … this meeting is not technically recognized as a Parliament"). *Cal. IPM* 4 (1913): 139–141. Farrer *Honors & Knights' Fees* 1 (1923): 61–68. Paget *Baronage of England* (1957) 564: 4. *C.P.* 12(2) (1959): 294. Sanders *English Baronies* (1960): 69. *TG* 7-8 (1986): 4–127.

6. JOHN DE WAHULL, of Odell and Langford, Bedfordshire, Pattishall, Northamptonshire, etc., son and heir, born 1 Nov. 1302. He married **ISABEL** _____. They had two sons, John, Knt., and Thomas. He acquired the manor of Little Durnford, Wiltshire from Henry de Préaux, Knt., in 1322. He did homage for his father's lands in 1323. In 1332 he reached agreement with the Prior of the Hospital of St. John of Jerusalem regarding the tithes of the water mill at Langford, Bedfordshire. JOHN DE WAHULL died shortly before 30 April 1336. His widow, Isabel, was living 4 August 1336.

Harvey et al. *Vis. of Bedfordshire 1566, 1582, 1634 & 1669* (H.S.P. 19) (1884): 67–69 (Wahull ped.: "Joh'es de Wahull Baro' de Woodhall Inq. A° 10 E. 3. = Isabella filia …. vidia 10 E. 3."). *Misc. Gen. et Heraldica* 2nd Ser. 1 (1886): 45–51, 69–80. *Journals of the House of Lords* 124 (1892): 194–201. Wrottesley *Peds. from the Plea Rolls* (1905): 87. VCH *Bedford* 3 (1912): 71–72. *Cal. IPM* 4 (1913): 139–141. Paget *Baronage of England* (1957) 564: 4–5. *C.P.* 12(2) (1959): 294. Sanders *English Baronies* (1960): 69. *TG* 7-8 (1986): 4–127. VCH *Wiltshire* 15 (1995): 79–93.

7. THOMAS DE WODHULL, of Little Durnford, Wiltshire, younger son, born about 1322. He married an unidentified wife, _____. They had three sons, including Nicholas. THOMAS DE WODHULL died before February 1375/6.

Harvey et al. *Vis. of Bedfordshire 1566, 1582, 1634 & 1669* (H.S.P. 19) (1884): 67–69 (Wahull ped.) [this generation omitted in ped.]. *Misc. Gen. et Heraldica* 2nd Ser. 1 (1886): 45–51, 69–80. VCH *Bedford* 3 (1912): 71–72 (omits this generation). Jacobus *Bulkeley Gen.* (1933): 61. Paget *Baronage of England* (1957) 564: 5 (names only his father's son and heir, John, husband of Eleanor, daughter of John de Moleyns, with issue John, son and heir, and Nicholas "who succeeded to the property on the deaths of his nieces, 1376; his descendants flourished till the middle of the 16th Century"). *TG* 7-8 (1986): 4–127.

8. NICHOLAS DE WODHULL (or **WODEHYLL**), of Odell and Langford, Bedfordshire, and Pattishall, Northamptonshire, Sheriff of Wiltshire, 1381–2. He married before 1366–7 (date of grant) **MARGARET FOXCOTE**, daughter of John Foxcote, of Wiltshire, by his wife, Christian. They had two sons, Thomas, Knt., and Richard, and two daughters, Edith (wife of _____ Knesworth) and Margaret (wife of Simon Browne). He was heir in 1376 to Elizabeth and Eleanor de Wodhull, minor daughters of his first cousin, John de Wodhull, Knt. The same year Gerard de

Braybrooke, Knt., and Isabel his wife remised and quitclaimed to him all their right in the manors of Tyderle, Great Durnford, and Little Durnford, Wiltshire for £100. In 1405 he and his wife, Margaret, and their children were granted a license for the private celebration of divine services presumably at his manor of Odell, Bedfordshire. His wife, Margaret, was living 29 August 1405. NICHOLAS DE WODHULL died 24 October 1410.

>Harvey et al. *Vis. of Bedfordshire 1566, 1582, 1634 & 1669* (H.S.P. 19) (1884): 67–69 (Wahull ped.: "Nich'us de Woodhall consangineus & heres pronep'tu' Elizabethæ & Elianoræ Inq. 50 E. 3 ob. 12 H. 4. = Margareta filia & heres Joh'es Foxcott de com. Wiltes."). *Misc. Gen. et Heraldica* 2nd Ser. 1 (1886): 45–51, 69–80. *Journals of the House of Lords* 124 (1892): 194–201. *List of Sheriffs for England & Wales* (PRO Lists and Indexes 9) (1898): 153. VCH *Bedford* 3 (1912): 71–72. Paget *Baronage of England* (1957) 564: 5, 7 (but as son of John and Eleanor). Repingdon *Reg. of Philip Repingdon* 1 (Lincoln Rec. Soc. 57) (1963): 44. Elrington *Abs. of Feet of Fines Rel. Wiltshire* (Wiltshire Rec. Soc. 29) (1974): 147. *TG* 7-8 (1986): 4–127. VCH *Wiltshire* 15 (1995): 79–93.

9. THOMAS WODHULL, Knt., of Odell, Bedfordshire, born about 1387 (aged 23 in 1410). He married **ELIZABETH CHETWODE**, daughter of John Chetwode, Knt., of Warkworth, Northamptonshire, Hockliffe, Bedfordshire, and Chetwode, Buckinghamshire, by his 2nd wife, Amabil, daughter of Thomas Greene, Knt., of Green's Norton, Northamptonshire. They had two sons, Thomas, Esq., and William. In 1413 he and his wife, Elizabeth, were granted a license for the private celebration of divine services at his manor of Odell, Bedfordshire. SIR THOMAS WODHULL was slain in the retinue of the Duke of Clarence at the Battle of Beaugé in Anjou 22 March 1420/1. His widow, Elizabeth, married (2nd) **WILLIAM LOUDESOP** (died 27 October 1454). She was heiress c.1456 to her brother, Thomas Chetwode, Knt., of Warkworth, Northamptonshire. Elizabeth died 24 August 1475, and was buried at Warkworth, Northamptonshire.

>Willis *Hist. & Antiqs. of the Town, Hundred, & Deanry of Buckingham* (1755): 172–174. Harvey et al. *Vis. of Bedfordshire 1566, 1582, 1634 & 1669* (H.S.P. 19) (1884): 67–69 ("Thomas Woodhall miles Baro' Woodhall ob. 23 Junij 9 H.5 = Elizabeth filia Jo. Chetwood mil. soror et heres Thomæ & heres Joh'es de Lyons renupt' Will'o Ludsup ob. 1475."). *Journals of the House of Lords* 124 (1892): 194–201. VCH *Surrey* 3 (1911): 252–262. VCH *Bedford* 3 (1912): 71–72, 383–386. VCH *Buckingham* 4 (1927): 163–168. Jacobus *Bulkeley Gen.* (1933): 61 (Elizabeth "was heiress of the elder Chetwood Line"). Paget *Baronage of England* (1957) 564: 7. Repingdon *Reg. of Philip Repingdon* 2 (Lincoln Rec. Soc. 58) (1963): 317. VCH *Oxford* 11 (1983): 209–222. *TG* 7-8 (1986): 4–127. VCH *Wiltshire* 15 (1995): 79–93. *Cal. IPM* 23 (2004): 11–12.

10. THOMAS WODHULL, Esq., of Odell and Langford, Bedfordshire, Pattishall, Northamptonshire, son and heir, born about 1410–12 (aged 11 in 1421, 16 in 1428). In 1422 William Darell and Elizabeth his wife sued Richard Wodhull regarding £5 of rent in Little Durnford, Wiltshire; Richard vouched to warranty Thomas, son and heir of Thomas Wodhull, Knt., who was then of minor age. He married **ISABEL TRUSSELL**, daughter of William Trussell, Knt., of Elmesthorpe, Leicestershire, and of Marston-Trussel, Northamptonshire, by Margery, daughter of John Ludlow, Knt. [see SAINT PHILIBERT 12 for her ancestry]. They had two sons, John, Esq., and Thomas, Esq., and one daughter, Isabel (wife of _____ Bowden). THOMAS WODHULL, Esq., died 8 August 1441. His widow, Isabel, married (2nd) by license dated 8 Feb. 1448/9 **JOHN HOTON**, Gent.

>Baker *Hist. & Antiqs. of Northampton* 1 (1822–30): 711–712, 739–740. Glover et al. *Vis. of Cheshire 1580, 1566, 1533 & 1591* (H.S.P. 18) (1882): 225–226 (Trussell ped.: "… [Trussell] uxor…. Wodhull de Com. Bedford"). Harvey et al. *Vis. of Bedfordshire 1566, 1582, 1634 & 1669* (H.S.P. 19) (1884): 67–69 (Wahull ped.: "Thomas Baro' de Woodhall ob. 19 H. 6. = Isabella filia Will'i seu Thomæ Trussell de Elmthorp mil."). *Misc. Gen. et Heraldica* 2nd Ser. 1 (1886): 45–51, 69–80. *Journals of the House of Lords* 124 (1892): 194–201. VCH *Bedford* 3 (1912): 71–72. VCH *Buckingham* 4 (1927): 163–168. Jacobus *Bulkeley Gen.* (1933): 59–62. *Year Books of Henry VI: 1 Henry VI 1422* (Selden Soc. 50) (1933): 58–60. Lamborn *Armorial Glass of the Oxford Diocese* (1949): 115–117 (Woodhull arms: Gold three crescents gules). Paget *Baronage of England* (1957) 564: 7. *TG* 7-8 (1986): 4–127. *Cal. IPM* 23 (2004): 11–12.

11. JOHN WODHULL, Esq., of Warkworth, Northamptonshire, Odell, Hockliffe, and Langford, Bedfordshire, Chetwode, Buckinghamshire, etc., son and heir, born about 1436 (aged 5 in 1441).

He married before Feb. 1456 **JOAN ETWELL**, daughter of Henry Etwell, of Puttenhoe (in Goldington), Bedfordshire, Governor of Lincoln's Inn, by his wife, Mary. They had four sons, Fulk, Esq., Thomas, William, and John, and three daughters, Elizabeth, Anne, and Mary. In 1474 he joined in a sale of the manor of Little Durnford, Wiltshire to Thomas Tropenell. His wife, Joan, was living 16 June 1475, but predeceased her husband. JOHN WODHULL, Esq., died 12 Sept. 1490.

Baker *Hist. & Antiqs. of Northampton* 1 (1822–30): 711–712, 739–740. Harvey et al. *Vis. of Bedfordshire 1566, 1582, 1634 & 1669* (H.S.P. 19) (1884): 67–69 (Wahull ped.: "Joh'es Baro' de Woodhall filius & heres Tho. Woo. & Isabella Trussell ætatis vnius anni ad mortem p'ris ob. 6 H. 7. = Johanna filia Henrici Etwall in legibus doctoris in London."). *Misc. Gen. et Heraldica* 2nd Ser. 1 (1886): 45–51, 69–80. *Journals of the House of Lords* 124 (1892): 194–201. VCH *Bedford* 3 (1912): 71–72. VCH *Buckingham* 4 (1927): 163–168. Jacobus *Bulkeley Gen.* (1933): 59–62. *TG* 7-8 (1986): 4–127. VCH *Wiltshire* 15 (1995): 79–93.

12. FULK WODHULL, Esq., of Warkworth, Northamptonshire, Odell, Hockliffe, and Langford, Bedfordshire, Chetwode, Buckinghamshire, etc., and, in right of his wife, of Thenford, Northamptonshire, Sheriff of Northamptonshire, 1500–1, born about 1458. He married (1st) about June 1475 **ANNE NEWENHAM**, daughter and co-heiress of William Newenham, of Thenford, Northamptonshire, by Margaret, daughter and co-heiress of Thomas Lamporte, Esq. They had three sons, Nicholas, Esq., Lawrence, Esq., and Thomas, and three daughters, Mary, Jane (wife of William Bellingham), and Isabel (wife of Richard Tresham). He married (2nd) **ELIZABETH WEBB**, daughter of John Webb, Esq. FULK WODHULL, Esq., died in 1508/9. His widow, Elizabeth, married (2nd) **ROBERT CHEYNE**, of Chesham Bois, Buckinghamshire (died 9 Dec. 1552). She died before 17 May 1511.

Baker *Hist. & Antiqs. of Northampton* 1 (1822–30): 711–712, 739–740. Harvey et al. *Vis. of Bedfordshire 1566, 1582, 1634 & 1669* (H.S.P. 19) (1884): 67–69 (Wahull ped.: "Fulco Woodhall Baro' de Woodhall ob. 24 H. 7. = Anna filia & coh. Will'i Newnham de Themford & Margeriæ vnis coh. Tho. Longports."). *Misc. Gen. et Heraldica* 2nd Ser. 1 (1886): 45–51, 69–80. Metcalfe *Vis. of Northamptonshire 1564 & 1618–9* (1887): 56 (1564 Vis.) (Woodhull ped.: "Fulke, Lord Woodhull, co. Bedford, mar. Anne, da. and one of the heirs of William Newenham.") (Wodhull arms: Or, three crescents Gules). *Journals of the House of Lords* 124 (1892): 194–201. *List of Sheriffs for England & Wales* (PRO Lists and Indexes 9) (1898): 93. VCH *Bedford* 3 (1912): 69–76. VCH *Buckingham* 4 (1927): 163–168. Jacobus *Bulkeley Gen.* (1933): 59–62. Lamborn *Armorial Glass of the Oxford Diocese* (1949): 115–117 (Newenham arms: Silver a cross gules a bendlet azure over all). *TG* 7-8 (1986): 4–127. VCH *Wiltshire* 15 (1995): 79–93.

Children of Fulk Wodhull, Esq., by Anne Newenham:

  i. **NICHOLAS WODHULL**, Esq. [see next].

  ii. **LAWRENCE WODHULL**, Esq., of Thenford, Northamptonshire, married **ELIZABETH HALL** [see ELKINGTON 13].

  iii. **MARY WODHULL**, married **EDWARD COPE**, Esq., of Helmdon, Northamptonshire [see BRENT 13].

13. NICHOLAS WODHULL, Esq., of Warkworth, Middleton, Pattishall, and Thenford, Northamptonshire, Odell, Hockliffe, and Langford, Bedfordshire, Chetwode, Buckinghamshire, etc., Sheriff of Northamptonshire, 1527–8, son and heir by his father's 1st marriage, born about 1482. He married (1st) about 1508 **MARY RALEIGH**, daughter of Edward Raleigh, Esq., of Farnborough, Warwickshire, by Anne, daughter of Richard Chamberlain, Esq. [see CHESELDINE 18 for her ancestry]. They had one son, Anthony, Esq., and one daughter, Joyce (wife of Edmund Midwinter, Esq.). His wife, Mary, died before 1522/3. He married (2nd) about 1523 **ELIZABETH PARR** [see PARR 16], daughter and co-heiress of William Parr, Knt., of Black Friars, London, and Horton, Northamptonshire, by Mary, daughter and co-heiress of William Salisbury, Knt. [see PARR 15 for her ancestry]. They had one son, Fulk, Esq., and two daughters, Mary (wife of David Seymour, Gent.) and Anne. NICHOLAS WODHULL, Esq., died 6 May 1531. He left a will dated 29 March 1531, requesting burial in the chapel of Warkworth church, Northamptonshire. His wife, Elizabeth, predeceased him.

Bridges *Hist. & Antiqs. of Northamptonshire* 1 (1791): 367. Baker *Hist. & Antiqs. of Northampton* 1 (1822–30): 711–712, 739–740. *Coll. Top. et Gen.* 5 (1838): 309–311 (will of Nicholas Wodhull, Esq.). Beesley *Hist. of Banbury* (1841): 161. *Top. & Gen.* 3 (1858): 352–360. Harvey et al. *Vis. of Bedfordshire 1566, 1582, 1634 & 1669* (H.S.P. 19) (1884): 67–69 (Wahull ped.: "Nich'us Woodhall Baro' de Woodhall cui Rex H. 8 27 Maij Ao 3 p'donavit intrasionem & Anna. [1] = Maria filia Ed'r'i Raleigh de Farnborow in com.... mil. vxor 1a., [2] = Elizabeth filia & coheres Will'i Parre militis & Mariæ ux'is eis vxor 2a fuit Baro' de Horton in co. Northt."). *Misc. Gen. et Heraldica* 2nd Ser. 1 (1886): 45–51, 69–80. Metcalfe *Vis. of Northamptonshire 1564 & 1618–9* (1887): 56 (1564 Vis.) (Woodhull ped.: "Nicholas, Lord Woodhull, co. Bedford, mar., to his first wife, the da. to ..... Rawley of Thornbury, co. Oxon, Esq. ..... after, the said Nicholas mar., to his second wife, *Alice* (Elizabeth), da. to *William, Lord Parr* of Horton, co. North'ton ...") (Woodhull arms: Or, three crescents Gules), 159 (1618–19 Vis.) (Woodhull of Thenford ped.: "Nicholas, Lord Wodhull of Wodhull, co. Bedf.; ob. 23 H. 8, [1] = ... da. of Edward Raleigh of Farnburgh, co. Warwick, 1 ux., [2] = Elizabeth, da. and heir of William, Lord Parr of Horton, co. North'ton, 2 ux."). *Journals of the House of Lords* 124 (1892): 194–201. *List of Sheriffs for England & Wales* (PRO Lists and Indexes 9) (1898): 93. VCH *Bedford* 3 (1912): 69–76. Clay *Extinct & Dormant Peerages* (1913): 156–158 (sub Parr). VCH *Buckingham* 4 (1927): 163–168. Jacobus *Bulkeley Gen.* (1933): 59–62. Bull *Fam. of Stephen Bull* (1961): 93. *TG* 7-8 (1986): 4–127; 13 (1999): 188–198. *NEHGR* 145 (1991): 3–21. VCH *Wiltshire* 15 (1995): 79–93.

Child of Nicholas Wodhull, Esq., by Mary Raleigh:

i. **ANTHONY WODHULL**, Esq. [see next].

Child of Nicholas Wodhull, Esq., by Elizabeth Parr:

i. **ANNE WODHULL**, married **RICHARD BURNABY**, Esq., of Watford, Northamptonshire [see PARR 17].

14. **ANTHONY WODHULL**, Esq., of Warkworth, Middleton, Overthorp, and Pattishall, Northamptonshire, Hockliffe and Langford, Bedfordshire, Chetwode, Buckinghamshire, Durnford, Wiltshire, etc., son and heir by his father's 1st marriage, born about 1517 (aged 14 in 1531). He married **ANNE SMITH**, daughter of John Smith, Esq., of Cressing, Essex, Baron of the Exchequer, by Agnes, daughter of John Harewell, Esq., of Wootton Wawen, Warwickshire. They had one daughter, Agnes. ANTHONY WODHULL, Esq., died 4 Feb. 1541/2. He left a will dated 4 Feb. 1538/9, proved 11 October 1542 (P.C.C. 9 Spert). His widow, Anne, married (2nd) **JOHN LEVESON**, Esq., of Halling, Kent, and Wolverhampton, Staffordshire (died 1549), and (3rd) **EDWARD GRIFFIN**, Knt. (died 16 Dec. 1569), of Dingley, Attorney-General under King Edward VI. She predeceased her 3rd husband.

Baker *Hist. & Antiqs. of Northampton* 1 (1822–30): 711–712, 739–740. *Coll. Top. et Gen.* 7 (1841): 42–44 (will of Anthony Wodhull, Esq.), 267. *Misc. Gen. et Heraldica* 2nd Ser. 1 (1886): 45–51, 69–80. Metcalfe *Vis. of Northamptonshire 1564 & 1618–9* (1887): 56 (1564 Vis.) (Woodhull ped.: "Anthony, Lord Woodhull of Woodhull, co. Bedford, eldest son and heir to Nicholas, mar. *Anne*, da. of *Sir John Smith*, Baron of the Exchequer, of Bradfield, co. Essex, Kt."), 159 (1618–19 Vis.) (Woodhull of Thenford ped.: "Anthony, Lord Wodhull of Wodhull; ob. 34 H. 8. = Anne, da. of Sir John Smyth, Kt., Baron of the Exchequer."). *Journals of the House of Lords* 124 (1892): 194–201. VCH *Bedford* 3 (1912): 69–76. VCH *Buckingham* 4 (1927): 163–168. Jacobus *Bulkeley Gen.* (1933): 59–62. *TG* 7-8 (1986): 4–127. *NEHGR* 145 (1991): 3–21. VCH *Wiltshire* 15 (1995): 79–93.

15. **AGNES WODHULL**, daughter and heiress, born 18 Jan. 1541/2 (aged 17 days at the death of her father). She married (1st) before Jan. 1555/6 **RICHARD CHETWODE** (or **CHETWOOD**, **CHYTWOOD**), Esq., Gentleman of the Privy Chamber, and, in right of his wife, of Chetwode, Buckinghamshire, Pattishall, and Warkworth, Northamptonshire, etc., 3rd son of Roger Chetwode, of Oakley, Staffordshire, by Ellen, daughter of Thomas Masterson. They had one son, Richard, Knt. In 1555 he was committed to the Tower of London for "his lewde and presumptuouse woordes to my Lorde Stewarde [Mr. Walgrave]" and for his "evill behaviour" before the Council. About 1556 Charles Tyrrell, Gent., brought suit to have Richard and Agnes' marriage annulled, after which Cardinal Pole declared their marriage invalid. In 1559 the Court of Audience rescinded the annulment. RICHARD CHETWODE, Esq., was buried at St. Dunstan's-in-the-West, London 12 Jan. 1559/60. He left a will dated 6 Jan. 1559/60, proved 26 October 1560 (P.C.C. 51 Mellershe). His widow, Agnes, married (2nd) in 1561 **GEORGE CALVERLEY**, Knt. (died 5 August 1585), of

Lea, Cheshire, and, in right of his wife, of Hockliffe, Bedfordshire. They had two sons, George and Hugh. She died at Hockliffe, Bedfordshire 20 March 1575/6.

>Willis *Hist. & Antiqs. of the Town, Hundred, & Deanry of Buckingham* (1755): 172–174. *Coll. Top. et Gen.* 7 (1841): 267. Law *Ecclesiastical Statutes at Large* 1 (1847): 152–153. Sheahan *Hist. & Topog. of Buckinghamshire* (1862): 267–269. Nichols *Wills from Doctors' Commons* (Camden Soc. 83) (1863): 28–41 (will of Charles Brandon). *Recs. of Buckinghamshire* 2 (1863): 151–156. Glover et al. *Vis. of Cheshire 1580, 1566, 1533 & 1591* (H.S.P. 18) (1882): 62 (Chitwood ped.: "Richard [Chetwood] 3ᵈ son. = Agnes d. & heire to Antᵒ Baron Woodhull after mar. to Sʳ George Calveley of the Lea."). (Chitwood arms: Quarterly Argent and Gules, four crosses patée counterchanged). *Misc. Gen. et Heraldica* 2ⁿᵈ Ser. 1 (1886): 45–51, 69–80. Metcalfe *Vis. of Northamptonshire 1564 & 1618-9* (1887): 56 (1564 Vis.) (Woodhull ped.: "Agnes [Woodhull], his only dau. and heir, mar. Richard Chetwood, co. Chester, Esq."), 159 (1618–19 Vis.) (Woodhull ped.: "Agnes [Wodhull], da. and sole heir, ux. Richard Chetwood of Warkworth, co. Northampton, [2] = Sir George Calverley, Kt., 2 vir."). *Journals of the House of Lords* 124 (1892): 194–201. Stapleton *Three Oxfordshire Parishes* (1893): 330–331. Philipot et al. *Vis. of Buckingham 1634 & 1566* (H.S.P. 58) (1909): 151–152 (Chetwood ped.: "Richard Chetwood 3 son of yᵉ privy chamber to K. E. 6 and Capt. of a tr. of hors at yᵉ sieg of Hanington. = Agnes da. and h. of Anthony Baron Woodhull [in Co.] Bedf."). VCH *Bedford* 3 (1912): 69–76, 383–386. *NEHGR* 76 (1922): 307–311; 145 (1991): 20. VCH *Buckingham* 4 (1927): 163–168. Jacobus *Bulkeley Gen.* (1933): 55–62. Smith *Chetwode Fam.* (1945): 37–41. Lamborn *Armorial Glass of the Oxford Diocese* (1949): 115–117 (Chetwode arms: Quarterly silver and gules four crosses formy counter-coloured). VCH *Oxford* 11 (1983): 209–222. *TG* 7-8 (1986): 4–127. VCH *Wiltshire* 15 (1995): 79–93.

16. RICHARD CHETWODE, Knt., of Warkworth, Middleton, Overthorp, and Pattishall, Northamptonshire, Hockliffe and Langford, Bedfordshire, Chetwode, Buckinghamshire, Begbroke and Duns Tew, Oxfordshire, Durnford, Wiltshire, etc., Sheriff of Northamptonshire, 1597–8, son and heir, born about 1560 (aged 16 in 1576). He married (1ˢᵗ) **JANE DRURY**, daughter and co-heiress of William Drury, sometime Deputy Lieutenant of Ireland, by Margery, daughter of Thomas Wentworth, Knt., 1ˢᵗ Lord Wentworth, Lord Chamberlain of the Household to King Edward VI. They had two sons, William and Richard, and three daughters, Katherine (wife of William Skeffington, Knt., and Michael Bray), Elizabeth, and Anne (wife of Giles Bray, Knt.). He was admitted a member of Inner Temple in 1579. In the period, 1579–87, Henry Hill; and Agnes his wife sued Richard Chetwode and John Manning in Chancery regarding a messuage and land in Begbroke, Oxfordshire, formerly granted to the plaintiff Agnes by the said Richard's deceased parents, Richard and Agnes Chetwode. In 1583 Richard and the inhabitants of Chetwode, Buckinghamshire sued William Rysley, Esq., regarding the partial destruction and misuse of the parish church of Chetwode. He married (2ⁿᵈ) **DOROTHY NEEDHAM**, daughter of Robert Needham, Esq., of Shavington (in Adderley), Shropshire, by Frances, daughter of Edward Aston, Knt. [see NEEDHAM 17 for her ancestry]. She was born in 1570. They had four sons, Robert, Thomas, John, D.D., and Tobias (or Toby), and seven daughters, Frances (wife of George Reinsham, Esq.), Mary, Dorothy, Jane, Grace, Abigail, and Beatrice. He sold the manor of Duns Tew, Oxfordshire to Thomas Read in 1598. In 1599 he sold the manor of Begbroke, Oxfordshire to William Spencer, Knt. In 1602 he conveyed the manors of Great and Little Durnford, Wiltshire to Richard Griffith, Gent., of Gray's Inn, Middlesex, and two others. He sold the manor of Southend (in Durnford), Wiltshire to Arthur Matravers in 1612. In 1613 he petitioned the king to establish his right to the ancient Barony of Woodhull, but his claim was not accepted. He and his wife, Dorothy, were named in the 1616 will of her sister, Elizabeth Needham. In 1632 he and his wife, Dorothy, conveyed the manors of Great and Little Odell, Bedfordshire by fine to Roger Nicholls and Thomas Tirrell, preliminary to a sale the following year to William Alston. SIR RICHARD CHETWODE was buried in the high chancel of Temple Church, London 21 May 1635.

>Willis *Hist. & Antiqs. of the Town, Hundred, & Deanry of Buckingham* (1755): 172–174, 180. Clifford & Clifford *Top. & Hist. Desc. of Tixall* (1817): 149. Baker *Hist. & Antiqs. of Northampton* 1 (1822–30): 711–712, 739–740. *3ʳᵈ Gen. Rpt. on Dignity of a Peer* (House of Lords Sessional Papers 135) (1822): 219–222. Glover et al. *Vis. of Cheshire 1580, 1566, 1533 & 1591* (H.S.P. 18) (1882): 62 (Chitwood ped.: "Richard Chitwood."). *Misc. Gen. et Heraldica* 2ⁿᵈ Ser. 1 (1886): 45–51,

69–80. Metcalfe *Vis. of Northamptonshire 1564 & 1618–9* (1887): 159 (1618–19 Vis.) (Woodhull ped.: "Richard Chetwood of Wodhull, co. Bedf.; now living, 1618."). Earwaker *Hist. of Sandbach* (1890): 198–199 (Needham ped.). Harrod *Hist. of Shavington* (1891): 123–126. Stapleton *Three Oxfordshire Parishes* (1893): 330–331. Inderwick *Cal. of the Inner Temple Recs.* 1 (1896): 296. *List of Sheriffs for England & Wales* (PRO Lists and Indexes 9) (1898): 94. Reade *Rec. of the Redes of Barton Court, Berks* (1899): 13. Muskett *Suffolk Manorial Fams.* 1 (1900): 358 (Drury ped.). *Reg. of Burials at the Temple Church, 1628–1853* (1905): 3. Philipot et al. *Vis. of Buckingham 1634 & 1566* (H.S.P. 58) (1909): 151–152 (Chetwood ped.: "Richard Chetwood."). VCH *Bedford* 3 (1912): 69–76. *NEHGR* 76 (1922): 307–311; 107 (1953): 44 (Chetwood arms: Quarterly silver and gules four crosses patty counter-changed). VCH *Buckingham* 4 (1927): 163–168. *D.A.B.* 3 (1929): 249–250. Jacobus *Bulkeley Gen.* (1933): 55–59, 62–66. Smith *Chetwode Fam.* (1945): 42–46. VCH *Oxford* 11 (1983): 209–222; 12 (1990): 5–10. *TG* 7-8 (1986): 4–127. Wyndham *Cal. of Chancery Decree Rolls C 78/46–85* (List & Index Soc. 253) (1994): C 78/71/9. VCH *Wiltshire* 15 (1995): 79–93. Northamptonshire Rec. Office: Cartwright (Aynhoe), C(A)Box 103/1/4 (available at www.a2a.org.uk/search/index.asp).

Child of Richard Chetwode, Knt., by Dorothy Needham:

i. **GRACE CHETWODE**, married [**REV.**] **PETER BULKELEY**, of Concord, Massachusetts and Odell, Bedfordshire [see BULKELEY 20.vi].

CHEYNE

MALCOLM III (**CEANNMORE**), King of Scots, married [**SAINT**] **MARGARET**.
DAVID I, King of Scots, married **MAUD OF NORTHUMBERLAND**.
HENRY OF SCOTLAND, Earl of Northumberland, married **ADA DE WARENNE**.
MARGARET OF SCOTLAND, married **HUMPHREY DE BOHUN**, hereditary Constable of England.
HENRY DE BOHUN, Earl of Hereford, married **MAUD DE MANDEVILLE**, Countess of Essex.
HUMPHREY DE BOHUN, Knt., Earl of Hereford and Essex, married **MAUD OF EU** (desc. King William the Conqueror).
ELEANOR DE BOHUN, married **JOHN DE VERDUN**, Knt., of Alton, Staffordshire.
MAUD DE VERDUN, married **JOHN DE GREY**, Knt., 2nd Lord Grey of Wilton.
ROGER DE GREY, Knt., 1st Lord Grey of Ruthin, married **ELIZABETH DE HASTINGS** (desc. King William the Conqueror).
REYNOLD DE GREY, Knt., 2nd Lord Grey of Ruthin, married **ELEANOR LE STRANGE** (desc. King William the Conqueror) [see GREY 10].

11. IDA GREY, married before 1394 **JOHN COKAYNE**, of Berwardecote, Brunaldeston, and Hatton, Derbyshire, Recorder of London, 1394, Chief Baron of the Exchequer, 1401, Justice of the Common Pleas, 1405–29, Chief Steward of the Duchy of Lancaster (Northern parts), 2nd son of John Cokayne, Knt., of Ashbourne, Derbyshire, by Cecily, daughter of William de Vernon, Knt. They had five sons, including Reginald, Henry, John, and Thomas (clerk), and five daughters, including Cecily (wife of Edward Fitz Simon), Elizabeth, and Margaret (wife of Edmund Odingsells, Knt.). He was named one of the executors of the 1397 will of John of Gaunt, Duke of Aquitaine and Lancaster. They received a papal indult to choose a confessor in 1405. In 1409 he had license to hunt in Sutton and Potton, Bedfordshire. In 1417 he purchased the manor of Cockayne Hatley, Bedfordshire from Edward Boteler, Knt. His wife, Ida, died 1 June 1426. **JOHN COKAYNE** died 22 May 1429, and was buried with his wife at Cockayne Hatley, Bedfordshire. He left a will dated 10 Feb. 1427/8, proved August 1429 (P.C.C. 12 Luffenam).

Nichols *Coll. of All the Wills* (1780): 145–176 (will of John of Gaunt). Nicolas *Testamenta Vetusta* 1 (1826): 140–145 (will of John, Duke of Lancaster). Glover *Hist. of Derby* 2(1) (1829): 41–42 (Cokayne ped.). Cockayne *Cockayne Memoranda* (1869): 7; (1873): 81–83, 147–148, chart. Cox *Notes on the Churches of Derbyshire* 2 (1877): 382–383. Waters *Chester of Chicheley* 1 (1878): 156–157. Harvey et al. *Vis. of Bedfordshire 1566, 1582, 1634 & 1669* (H.S.P. 19) (1884): 17–18 (1566 Vis.) ("Cokayne ped.: Sir John Cokayne of Cokayne Hatley in com. Bedf. K. [ob. 5 H. 6, 1427] = Ede (alibi Edith) daughter of [Reignold] Lord Grey of Ruthyn") (Cokayne arms: Argent, three cocks gules, membered and beaked azure). *Misc. Gen. et Heraldica* 3rd Ser. 3 (1900): 221–230. *Papal Regs.: Letters* 6 (1904): 21. *MSS of the Duke of Rutland* 4 (Hist. MSS Comm. 24) (1905): 53. VCH *Bedford* 2 (1908): 215–216 (Cokayne arms: Argent three cocks gules having their beaks, combs and wattles sable). VCH *Hertford* 3 (1912): 25–28, 244–247. Somerville *Hist. of the Duchy of Lancaster* 1 (1953): 367–368. McGregor *Bedfordshire Wills proved in the P.C.C. 1383–1548* (Bedfordshire Hist. Rec. Soc.

58) (1979): 8–11 (will of John Cokayn). Ellis *Cat. Seals in the P.R.O.* 2 (1981): 26 (seal of John Cockayne (Cokayn) the uncle dated 1418 — A cock, standing, facing to the left; on either side of his head, lettering CO'H/… No legend.). Garratt *Derbyshire Feet of Fines 1323–1546* (Derbyshire Rec. Soc. 11) (1985): 63–65, 70. Roskell *House of Commons 1386–1421* 2 (1992): 609–610 (biog. of Henry Cockayne). National Archives, E 210/4184 (Date: 13 Henry IV [1411–12] — Walter Taylard of Wrestlingworth the elder to John Cokayn and William Hesunhull, Esq.: Bond for the payment of £10 endorsed with condition that the said Walter shall not trespass against the said John and Ida his wife or their tenants of the manor of Hatley Cockayne, Bedfordshire, or do anything to their disherison) (available at www.catalogue.nationalarchives.gov.uk/search.asp).

12. ELIZABETH COKAYNE, married (1st) before 1412 **PHILIP LE BOTELER** (or **BUTLER**), Knt., of Watton Woodhall (in Watton at Stone) and Sele (in St. Andrew Hertford), Hertfordshire, Bromham, Bedfordshire, Pulverbatch, Shropshire, etc., son and heir of Philip le Boteler, Knt., of Watton Woodhall (in Watton at Stone), Hertfordshire, by his wife, Elizabeth. He was born in 1388. They had two sons, Edward and Philip, Gent. He was heir in 1412 to his cousin, Edward le Boteler, Knt., by which he inherited the manors of Pulverbatch, Shropshire, Norbury, Staffordshire, Higham-Gobion, Bedfordshire, etc. He presented to the church of Pulverbatch, Shropshire in 1413. SIR PHILIP LE BOTELER died 5 (or 6) Nov. 1420, and was buried at Watton at Stone, Hertfordshire. His widow, Elizabeth, married (2nd) by license dated 13 Dec. 1421 **LAURENCE CHEYNE** (or **CHENEY**), Esq., of Fen Ditton, Fen Drayton, and Long Stanton, Cambridgeshire, Eaton (in Eaton Socon) and Pavenham, Bedfordshire, Irchester, Northamptonshire, etc., Sheriff of Cambridgeshire and Huntingdonshire, 1429–30, 1435–6, Knight of the Shire for Cambridgeshire, 1431, 1432, 1435, 1442, Escheator of Bedfordshire and Buckinghamshire, 2nd son of William Cheyne, Knt., of Long Stanton and Fen Ditton, Cambridgeshire, by Katherine, daughter of Laurence Pabenham, Knt. [see ENGAINE 12 for his ancestry]. He was born about 1396 (aged 40 in 1436). They had one son, John, Knt., and two daughters, Elizabeth and Mary (wife of John Allington). Sometime in the period, 1428–36, he was heir to his older brother, John Cheyne. In 1422 he and his wife, Elizabeth, released the manor of Eaton (in Eaton Socon), Bedfordshire to Katherine, widow of Thomas Aylesbury, Thomas Brake, and others. He and his wife, Elizabeth, were legatees in the 1428 will of her father, John Cokayne. In 1439 he and his wife, conveyed 8 acres of wood and 100s. of rent in Horton, Northamptonshire to Thomas Reynes, Esq. LAURENCE CHEYNE, Esq., died testate 31 Dec. 1461, and was buried at Barnwell Priory, Cambridgeshire.

Coll. Top. et Gen. 4 (1837): 43–45. Fuller *Hist. of the Worthies of England* (1840): 244–247. Banks *Baronies in Fees* 1 (1844): 199–200 (sub Engaine). Cockayne *Cockayne Memoranda* (1873): 81–83. Hailstone *Hist. & Antiqs. of Bottisham* (1873): 113–114, chart following 116. Waters *Chester of Chicheley* 1 (1878): 138–139, 156–157. *Genealogist* n.s. 7 (1890): 57; n.s. 22 (1906): 90; n.s. 23 (1907): 239. Rye *Pedes Finium or Fines Rel. Cambridge* (1891): 149, 151. Cooke & St. George *Vis. of Cambridge 1575 & 1619* (H.S.P. 41) (1897): 14–17 (Allington ped.), 118–119 (Cheney ped.: "Sr Lawrance Cheney Knt. = Elizebeth d. of … Cockayne of Bury Hatley") (Cheney arms: Argent, a bend lozengy gules). *List of Sheriffs for England & Wales* (PRO Lists and Indexes 9) (1898): 13. Wrottesley *Peds. from the Plea Rolls* (1905): 284–285, 358. Tregelles *Hist. of Hoddesdon* (1908): 31–32, 68. VCH *Bedford* 2 (1908): 345; 3 (1912): 76–80, 189–202. C.P.R. 1416–1422 (1911): 437. VCH *Hertford* 3 (1912): 162. *Yorkshire Inqs.* 5 (Yorkshire Arch. Soc. Recs. 59) (1918): 160–161. C.P. 5 (1926): 80 (chart) (sub Engaine); 9 (1936): 612–615 (sub Norfolk). Bassett *Knights of Bedfordshire* (Bedfordshire Hist. Rec. Soc. 29) (1949): 25–26 (biog. of Sir Edward Butler). C.C.R. 1422–1429 (1933): 31. Wedgwood *Hist. of Parl.* 1 (1936): 145 (biog. of Philip Butler), 183 (biog. of Laurence Cheyne). VCH *Northampton* 4 (1937): 21–22. Paget *Baronage of England* (1957) 82: 4. VCH *Shropshire* 8 (1968): 134. McGregor *Bedfordshire Wills proved in the P.C.C. 1383–1548* (Bedfordshire Hist. Rec. Soc. 58) (1979): 8–11 (will of John Cokayn). VCH *Cambridge* 9 (1989): 223, 294; 10 (2002): 123–124. Payling *Political Soc. in Lancastrian England* (1991): 83, 85, 242 (chart). *Cal. IPM* 23 (2004): 98–99. National Archives, CP 25/1/179/94, #92 [see abstract of fine at http://www.medievalgenealogy.org.uk/index.html].

Child of Elizabeth Cokayne, by Philip le Boteler, Knt.:

i. **PHILIP BOTELER**, Gent., of Watton Woodhall, Hertfordshire, married **ISABEL WILLOUGHBY** [see LOVETT 13].

Children of Elizabeth Cokayne, by Laurence Cheyne, Esq.:

i. **JOHN CHEYNE**, Knt. [see next].

ii. **ELIZABETH CHEYNE**, married (1st) **FREDERICK TILNEY**, Esq., of Ashwellthorpe, Norfolk [see STRATTON 13]; (2nd) **JOHN SAY**, Knt., of Baas (in Broxbourne), Hertfordshire [see STRATTON 13].

13. JOHN CHEYNE, Knt., of Fen Ditton, Fen Drayton, and Long Stanton, Cambridgeshire, Eaton (in Eaton Socon), Bedfordshire, Irchester, Northamptonshire, etc., King's Serjeant, Knight of the Shire for Cambridgeshire, 1449–50, Sheriff of Cambridgeshire and Huntingdonshire, 1463–4, 1474–5, lawyer, son and heir, born about 1424 (aged 38 in 1462). He was admitted a member of Lincoln's Inn in 1445–6. He married before 1449 **ELIZABETH REMPSTON**, 1st daughter and co-heiress of Thomas Rempston, Knt., of Beckering (in Holton) and Tuxford, Nottinghamshire, by Alice, daughter and heiress of Thomas Beckering. She was born about 1418 (aged 40 in 1458). They had two sons, Thomas, Knt., and William, and three daughters, Elizabeth, Katherine (wife of Henry Barlee, Esq.), and Anne (wife of John Appleyard). SIR JOHN CHEYNE died 13 (or 14) July 1489. He left a will dated 31 July 1488, proved 21 July 1489, requesting burial at Barnwell Priory, Cambridgeshire.

Banks *Baronies in Fees* 1 (1844): 199–200 (sub Engaine). *East Anglian* 1 (1864): 226–227 (Barlee ped.). Birch *Catalogue of Seals in the British Museum* 2 (1892): 397 (seal of John Cheyne dated 1475 — A goat's head erased, ducally gorged. In the field an uncertain motto. Cabled border.). Cooke & St. George *Vis. of Cambridge 1575 & 1619* (H.S.P. 41) (1897): 118–119 (Cheney ped.: "Sr John Cheney Knt. = Elizebeth d. & heire of Sr Thom. Rempston Knt."). Baildon *Recs. of Lincoln's Inn: Admissions* 1 (1896): 10. *List of Sheriffs for England & Wales* (PRO Lists and Indexes 9) (1898): 13. *Desc. Cat. Ancient Deeds* 3 (1900): 144. *Genealogist* n.s. 22 (1906): 90; n.s. 23 (1907): 239. VCH *Bedford* 3 (1912): 189–202. C.P. 5 (1926): 80 (sub Engaine). Wedgwood *Hist. of Parl.* 1 (1936): 181–182 (biog. of Sir John Cheyne). VCH *Northampton* 4 (1937): 21–22. *Ancient Deeds — Ser. B* 2 (List & Index Soc. 101) (1974): B.6006, B.6065. VCH *Cambridge* 9 (1989): 223, 294; 10 (2002): 123–124. Payling *Political Soc. in Lancastrian England* (1991): 43, 60, 239. Roskell *House of Commons 1386–1421* 4 (1992): 192–194 (biog. of Sir Thomas Rempston).

Child of John Cheyne, Knt., by Elizabeth Rempston:

i. **ELIZABETH CHEYNE**, married **JOHN HASILDEN**, Esq., of Meldreth, Cambridgeshire [see HASILDEN 13].

❧ CHIDIOCK ☙

ALICE OF NORMANDY (sister of King William the Conqueror), married **LAMBERT**, Count of Lens.
JUDITH OF LENS, married **WALTHEOF**, Earl of Northumberland.
ALICE OF NORTHUMBERLAND, married **RALPH DE TONY**, of Flamstead, Hertfordshire.
ROGER DE TONY, of Flamstead, Hertfordshire, married **IDA OF HAINAULT**.
RALPH DE TONY, of Flamstead, Hertfordshire, married **MARGARET OF LEICESTER**.
ROGER DE TONY, Knt., of Flamstead, Hertfordshire, married **CONSTANCE DE BEAUMONT** (desc. King William the Conqueror).
RALPH DE TONY, Knt., of Flamstead, Hertfordshire, married **PERNEL DE LACY**.
CONSTANCE DE TONY, married **FULK FITZ WARIN**, Knt., of Whittington, Shropshire.
FULK FITZ WARIN, Knt., of Whittington, Shropshire, married **MARGARET DE LA POLE** [see FITZ WARIN 9].

10. WILLIAM FITZ WARIN, K.G., styled *the brother*, of Whittington, Shropshire, Brians (in Wantage), Berkshire, Winterbourne Houghton, Dorset, and Blunsdon St. Andrew, Wiltshire, Governor of Montgomery Castle, and, in right of his wife, of Caundle Haddon, Lidlinch, and Up Cerne, Dorset, and Isle-Brewers and Pitney and Wearne, Somerset, younger son. He married before 1337 **AMICE DE HADDON**, daughter and heiress of Henry de Haddon, Knt., of Caundle Haddon, Lidlinch, Up Cerne, Dorset, etc., by Eleanor, daughter of Matthew de Furneaux, Knt., of Ashington and Kilve, Somerset. She was born about 1323 (aged 25 in 1348). They had one son, Ives, Knt., and two daughters, Margaret and Philippe (nun at Wilton). In 1317 he was going to Ireland on the king's service in the company of his elder brother, Fulk Fitz Warin. In 1336 he was granted the borough of Wilton, Wiltshire in tail male for services previously rendered to Queen Philippe. He presented to the church of Winterbourne Houghton, Dorset in 1340, 1345, 1348, 1349, 1350, 1351, and 1353. He was summoned to a Council 25 Feb. 1341/2, by writ directed *Willelmo filio Warini*. In 1345–6 John de Mere, Knt., quitclaimed to William and his wife, Amice, lands, etc., he had from Adam de Grymstede, son and heir of Sir John de Grymstede, in Wantage, Berkshire. His wife, Amice, was living 5 March 1348. In 1351 he had license to found a chantry at Wantage, Berkshire. In 1351 Nicholas Poyntz owed him a debt of 1000 marks. SIR WILLIAM FITZ WARIN died of the pestilence 28 October (or 3 Nov.) 1361. He and his wife were buried at Wantage, Berkshire.

Banks *Dormant & Extinct Baronage of England* 1 (1807): 304–305 (sub Fitz-Warine). *Coll. Top. et Gen.* 1 (1834): 243–248 ("Be it remembred that Matthew de Furneaux had issew three sonnes, Symond, Henry, and Thomas, and 4 doughters, Elianor, Havise, Jane, and Margarete… the first doughter Elianor was married to Henry Haddon, knt. and had issew a doughter calld Mary [recte Amice], which was married to Wm. Fitzwaren, knt. and had issew Iwon Fitzwarren, knt. and Iwon had issue Jone [recte Eleanor] that was maried to John Chidok, knt. and had for her part 50*li*. of land, that is to saie Kelve, and oder lands, that Henry Rogers now hath."); 6 (1840): 397–398. Beltz *Mems. of the Order of the Garter* (1841): 96–98 (In 1339 he attended the King into Flanders and in the same year was in the war against Scotland. He was again in Flanders in 1340, and in 1342, In France, with the rank of banneret, having in his retinue one knight, eight esquires, and ten mounted archers. Froissart numbers him among the commanders in the expedition to France in 1346. He was Knight of the Body to Queen Philippe in 1349). Hutchins *Hist. & Antiqs. of Dorset* 1 (1861): 330; 3 (1868): 664–667. *Notes & Queries* 4th Ser. 8 (1871): 211–212; 5th Ser. 9 (1878): 194–195. Lettenhove *Oeuvres de Froissart* 21 (1875): 204. *C.P.R. 1313–1317* (1898): 618. *Misc. Gen. et Heraldica* 3rd Ser. 3 (1900): 272–276 (Fourneaux ped.); 5th Ser. 10 (1938): 110–113 (ancestry of Amice de Haddon). *C.C.R. 1364–1368* (1910): 5–6. Fry & Fry *Abs. of Feet of Fines Rel. Dorset* 2 (Dorset Rec. Soc. 10) (1910): 11–12, 26–27, 30, 33–36, 54, 91. *Cal. IPM* 9 (1916): 94–95. VCH *Berkshire* 4 (1924): 323, 328, 329. *C.P.* 5 (1926): 512–513 (sub FitzWarin) ("He was, no doubt, a yr. br. of that Fulk Fitz Warin of Whittington who died in 1349, but there is no actual proof. His arms were: Quarterly, per pale and per fesse indented, Ermine and Gules, i.e., those of FitzWarin of Whittington, with a difference"). Harvey et al. *Vis. of the North* 4 (Surtees Soc. 146) (1932): 159 (arms of Sir Willm. Fitzwaren: quarterly per fess indented ermine and gules). Paget *Baronage of England* (1957) 232: 2. VCH *Wiltshire* 6 (1962): 8–9. Elrington *Abs. of Feet of Fines Rel. Wiltshire* (Wiltshire Rec. Soc. 29) (1974): 112, 120 (he was styled "of Whittington, co. Salop," to distinguish him from his contemporary kinsman, William Fitz Warin "of Penleigh" in Westbury, Wiltshire, for whom see VCH *Wiltshire* 8 (1965): 148–163). *Ancient Deeds — Ser. B 2* (List & Index Soc. 101) (1974): B.8232. Rees *Cal. Ancient Petitions Rel. Wales* (Board of Celtic Studies, Hist. & Law 28) (1975): 399. Ellis *Cat. Seals in the P.R.O.* 2 (1981): 43 (seal of William Fitz Warin, Knt. dated 1352 — On a diapered background, a shield of arms, couché: quarterly, per fesse indented (or dancetty); helm above with mantling and crest: a swan, to left of helm a bird, to right a lion rampant. Legend lost.). VCH *Somerset* 5 (1985): 98. *Antiquaries Jour.* 69 (1989): 257–259. Fein *Studies in the Harley MS.* (2000): 89. Cornwall Rec. Office: Arundell of Lanherne & Trerice, AR/1/782/1, 2, gift in fee tail dated 10 April 1342 between John de Haddon and Sir Henry de Haddon, Knt., and Eleanor his wife the manor of Pitney and Wearne, Somerset… after the death of the said Henry and Eleanor, the manors shall remain to Sir William fitz Waryn and Amice his wife and their heirs of body; AR/1/786 (Date: 1342, 7th Jun. at Ilebruere. Instructions to tenants to transfer their rent. Henry de Haddone and Eleanor his wife = (1)-(2). Sir William fitz Waryn = (3). (1)-(2) to their tenants, free and others, of their manors of Puttenye & Werne: they have granted and assigned to (3), their son (a nostre trescher filtz et bien amez mons' Williame le filtz Waryn) £20 of yearly rent from those manors, to be paid at Michaelmas and Easter from year to year, until full payment is made of a debt of £99 which they owe to (3), together with power to (3) to take distraint from the tenants if the rent is in arrears. Therefore (1)-(2) instruct the tenants to pay their rent directly to (3), until such time as full payment has been made.); AR/1/1023, gift in fee tail dated 5 March 1348 between Henry de Haddon and Eleanor his wife, and William Fitz Warin and Amice his wife to Roger de Staunton 1 acre of wood in North Braddon, Devon (available at www.a2a.org.uk/search/index.asp). National Archives, C 143/271/3; C 148/71; C 148/89; C 241/133/103; E 326/8232; 8/181/9020 (petition dated 1331 from William Fitz Waryn *the brother* to the king, requesting that the king order the establishment of an assize of novel disseisin for his cousin Peter Fitz Waryn against Robert de Wyleby regarding land in Wilby, Northamptonshire) (available at www.catalogue.nationalarchives.gov.uk/search.asp).

11. IVES FITZ WARIN, Knt., of Caundle Haddon, Lidlinch, Lydlinch Baret, Up Cerne, Winterbourne Houghton, Dorset, Brians (in Wantage), Berkshire, Pitney and Wearne, and Isle-Brewers, Somerset, Blunsdon St. Andrew and Wilton, Wiltshire, etc., Knight of the Shire for Dorset, Devon and Somerset, Keeper of Mere Castle, Governor of Southampton, and, in right of his wife, of Clopton Bury (in Clopton), Cambridgeshire, Gernons (in Steeple Bumpstead), Essex, Pachesham (in Leatherhead), Surrey, etc., son and heir, born 30 Nov. 1347. He married about 20 Jan. 1372 (date of license) **MAUD ARGENTINE**, widow of Richard de Merton, Knt., of Merton and Sutcombe, Devonshire (died 25 Sept. 1370), and daughter and co-heiress of John Argentine, Knt., of Melbourne, Cambridgeshire, Great and Little Wymondley, Hertfordshire, Ketteringham, Norfolk, Halesworth, Suffolk, etc., by Margaret, daughter and heiress of Robert Darcy [see ARGENTINE 5 for her ancestry]. They had two daughters, Eleanor and Alice (wife of Richard Whittington, Knt.). He presented to the churches of Winterbourne Houghton, Dorset, 1378, 1381, 1390, 1397, 1404, 1411, and Sutcombe, Devon, 1405, 1408, and to the rectory or chapel of St. James in the Castle of Great Torrington, Devon in 1401. He was present at the Siege of Nantes in 1380. He served as guardian in 1394–1404 for minor cousin, Fulk Fitz Warin, of Whittington, Shropshire. He owed a debt of 1000 marks to William Beauchamp, Knt. in 1400. In 1401 his wife, Maud, was co-heiress to her cousin, Baldwin Bereford, Knt., by which she inherited a one sixth share of the manor of Clopton Bury (in Clopton), Cambridgeshire, and a half share in the manors of Bryghtwell Huscarlon and Newenham, Oxfordshire, and Biscote (in Luton), Bedfordshire. In 1410 he witnessed charters for his cousin, Elizabeth Mautravers, widow of Roger Foliot and William le Latimer. SIR IVES FITZ WARIN died 6 Sept. 1414, and was buried at Wantage, Berkshire. He left a will dated 6 Nov. 1412, proved 5 Feb. 1414/5.

Blomefield *Essay towards a Top. Hist. of Norfolk* 5 (1806): 7–12. Banks *Dormant & Extinct Baronage of England* 1 (1807): 304–305 (sub Fitz-Warine). Brydges *Collins' Peerage of England* 7 (1812): 42. Clarke *Parochial Top. of the Hundred of Wanting* (1824): 196. Dugdale *Monasticon Anglicanum* 6(2) (1830): 738–747. *Coll. Top. et Gen.* 1 (1834): 243–248; 6 (1840): 355–356, 397–398. Beltz *Mems. of the Order of the Garter* (1841): 96–98 (In 1380 he was at the Siege of Nantes and, in 1381, he went on Buckingham's expedition to Brittany. In 1385 he attended John of Gaunt, Duke of Lancaster in his expedition for the recovery of the inheritance of Constance of Castile). Suckling *Hist. & Antiqs. of Suffolk* 2 (1847): 326–329 (re. Argentine fam.). *Wiltshire Arch. & Nat. Hist. Mag.* 2 (1855): 282. *Arch. Jour.* 13 (1856): 278–279 ("On a label is the seal of Sir Ivo Fitz Waryn [dated 1399]… device a shield, with his arms, viz., quarterly, per fess indented ermine and [gules], hanging on a tree between two storks (?); a legend, S' : IUONIS : FYWARYN : in black letter."), 279–280. Hutchins *Hist. & Antiqs. of Dorset* 1 (1861): 330; 3 (1868): 664–667. Burke *Gen. Hist. of the Dormant, Abeyant, Forfeited & Extinct Peerages* (1866): 10–11 (sub Argentine). Lettenhove *Oeuvres de Froissart* 21 (1875): 204–205. Rogers *Antient Sepulchral Effigies* (1877): 143–144 ("The brass effigy of Sir Ivo Fitzwarren represents him in early plate armour with roundels at the shoulders and elbows, hip-belt and long sword."), 374 (ped. chart). *Notes & Queries* 5th Ser. 9 (1878): 194–195. *Arch. Jour.* 38 (1881): 76. Hore *Hist. of Newmarket* 1 (1885): 41–48 (re. Argentine fam.). Hingeston-Randolph *Reg. of Edmund Stafford (A.D. 1395–1419)* (1886): 187, 212, 214. Birch *Cat. Seals in the British Museum* 2 (1892): 807 (seal of Ivo Fywaryn, als. Fitzwaryn dated late 14th Cent. — A shield of arms: quarterly, per fess indented ermine, and ____, FITZ-WARREN. Suspended by a strap from a tree on a mount. Supporters two swans. Legend: * : s' : iuonis : * * fywaryn : *. Inner border carved with ball-flowers, outer border cabled.). *Genealogist* n.s. 13 (1896): 242. *C.P.R. 1381–1385* (1897): 260. Giffard & Bowett *Regs. of Walter Giffard & Henry Bowett Bishops of Bath & Wells* (Somerset Rec. Soc. 13) (1899): 76. Gibbons *Wantage Past & Present* (1901): 43–46. *Procs. Bath Natural Hist. & Antiq. Field Club* 9 (1901): 188–201. Wrottesley *Peds. from the Plea Rolls* (1905): 162, 241. VCH *Bedford* 2 (1908): 362. Fry & Fry *Abs. of Feet of Fines Rel. Dorset* 2 (Dorset Rec. Soc. 10) (1910): 124–125. *C.P.* 1 (1910): 196–197 (sub Argentine). Stawell *Quantock Fam.* (1910): 325. *C.P.R. 1370–1374* (1914): 166. VCH *Berkshire* 4 (1924): 323, 328, 329. *Procs. Somerset Arch. & Nat. Hist. Soc.* 80 (App. II) (1935): 73–74. Chichele *Reg. of Henry Chichele* 2 (Canterbury & York Soc. 42) (1937): xlii, 18–21 (will of Sir Ives Fitz Warin), 32, 653 (biog. of Sir Ivo Fitzwaryn). *Devon & Cornwall Notes & Queries* 20 (1939): 256. Stokes et al. *Warwickshire Feet of Fines* 3 (Dugdale Soc. 18) (1943): 105–106. Paget *Baronage of England* (1957) 7: 1–2 (sub Argentine); 232: 2. VCH *Wiltshire* 6 (1962): 8–9. Dunning *Hylle Cartulary* (Somerset Rec. Soc. 68) (1968): 127–128. VCH *Somerset* 3 (1974): 51–52. Rees *Cal. Ancient Petitions Rel. Wales* (Board of Celtic Studies, Hist. & Law 28) (1975): 316–317. Ellis *Cat. Seals in the P.R.O.* 1 (1978): 25 (seal of Ives Fitz Warin (Wareyn), Knt. dated 1404: Hanging from a twin bush, which grows from a mount, a shield of arms: quarterly, per fesse indented, ermine and (plain) [FITZ WARIN]; supported on the backs of two swans which turn their beaks to the shield's upper points). VCH *Cambridge* 8 (1982): 34. *Year Books of Richard II* 4 (Ames Found. 7) (1987): 80–81. *Antiquaries Jour.* 69 (1989): 257–258. Roskell *House of Commons 1386–1421* 2 (1992): 50–52 (biog. of Sir William Argentine). *Camden Misc.* 32 (Camden Soc. 5th Ser. 3) (1994): 1–190. *Cal. IPM* 20 (1995): 67–69. Middleton-Stewart *Inward Purity & Outward Splendour* (2001): 96, 101–102. National Archives, C 131/215/14; E 329/30 (available at www.catalogue.nationalarchives.gov.uk/search.asp). Cornwall Rec. Office: Arundell of Lanherne and Trerice, AR/39/2 (ped. of Fitz Warin-Chidiock fams.) (available at www.a2a.org.uk/search/index.asp).

12. ELEANOR FITZ WARIN, daughter and co-heiress, born about 1384/90 (aged variously 24, 27, or 30 in 1314). She married (1st) before 26 August 1390 **JOHN CHIDIOCK** (or **CHEDIOK**), Knt., of Chideock, Dorset, Frampton on Severn, Gloucestershire, Allowenshay, Somerset, etc., Knight of the Shire for Dorset, son and heir of John Chidiock, Knt., of Chideock and More Crichel, Dorset, Frampton on Severn, Gloucestershire, by Joan, daughter and co-heiress of John de Saint Loe (or Seintlo), Knt. He was born about 1375–8 (aged 12 or 15 in 1390). They had one son, John, Knt., and one daughter, Elizabeth. His wife, Eleanor, was co-heiress in 1414 to her father, by which she inherited the manors of Caundle Haddon, Lidlinch, Up Cerne, Winterbourne Houghton, Dorset, Brians (in Wantage), Berkshire, Iles-Brewers, Pitney, and Wearne, Somerset, etc. His wife, Eleanor, was likewise co-heiress in 1414 to her cousin, Alice Blount (wife successively of Richard Stafford and Richard Stury, Knt. [see ARDERNE 8.i]), by which she inherited the manor of Kilve and lands in Kilton and Holford, Somerset. In 1415 he and his wife, Eleanor, conveyed 200 acres of wood in Purton, Purton Stoke, Great Chelworth, etc., Wiltshire to Robert Andrewe for 100 marks. SIR JOHN CHIDIOCK died 25 (or 28) Sept. 1415, probably at the Siege of Harfleur. Administration on his estate was granted in 1415 (P.C.C. 30 Marche). His widow, Eleanor, married (2nd) between October 1415 and 11 February 1415/6 (as his 2nd wife) **RALPH BUSH** (or **BUSSH**, **BUSCHE**), Esq., in right of his wife, of Biscote (in Luton), Bedfordshire, Caundle Haddon, Dorset, etc., Clerk of the Household to Elizabeth, Lady Harington, Knight of the Shire for Dorset, 1419, 1429, son of Ralph Bush, of Corfe, Dorset, by Edith, daughter of William Canon. They had two sons, William and John, and one daughter, Margery. He was admitted to the fraternity of St. Albans Abbey in 1408. In 1419 he and his wife, Eleanor, conveyed the manor of Biscote (in Luton), Bedfordshire to William Acworth. His wife, Eleanor, died 1 (or 7) Dec. 1433. RALPH BUSH, Esq., died 11 July 1441.

Banks *Dormant & Extinct Baronage of England* 1 (1807): 304–305 (sub Fitz-Warine). Brydges *Collins' Peerage of England* 7 (1812): 42. *Coll. Top. et Gen.* 1 (1834): 243–248. Fuller *Hist. of the Worthies of England* (1840): 462. *Arch. Jour.* 13 (1856): 279–280 (seal of John Chidioke [dated 1397] ... device, within a curvilinear triangle, an escutcheon charged with an inescutcheon in a bordure of eight martlets; legend, SIGILLV IOHANNIS CHIDYOK, in black letter."). Hutchins *Hist. & Antiqs. of Dorset* 3 (1868): 664–667. Rogers *Ancient Sepulchral Effigies* (1877): 374 (ped. chart). *Notes & Queries* 5th Ser. 9 (1878): 194–195. *Misc. Gen. et Heraldica* 2nd Ser. 2 (1888): 314–317. Wood *Colls. for a Parochial Hist. of Chew Magna* (1903): 111–139. Wrottesley *Peds. from the Plea Rolls* (1905): 322. VCH *Bedford* 2 (1908): 362. Fry & Fry *Abs. of Feet of Fines Rel. Dorset* 2 (Dorset Rec. Soc. 10) (1910): 279–280, 308–309, 318–320, 357–358. Bubwith *Reg. of Nicholas Bubwith Bishop of Bath & Wells* 1 (Somerset Rec. Soc. 29) (1914): 94–95. Maxwell-Lyte *Docs. & Extracts illus. History of the Honour of Dunster* (1921): 173. VCH *Berkshire* 4 (1924): 323. *C.P.* 5 (1926): 457–459 (sub Fitzpayn), 482–484 (sub Fitzwalter). *Feet of Fines for Essex* 3 (1929–49): 272. VCH *Gloucester* 10 (1972): 143–148. *Ancient Deeds — Ser. B* 2 (List & Index Soc. 101) (1974): B.6350, B.7043. VCH *Somerset* 3 (1974): 51–52, 205; 5 (1985): 98. Kirby *Abs. of Feet of Fines Rel. Wiltshire* (Wiltshire Rec. Soc. 41) (1986): 73. VCH *Cambridge* 8 (1989): 34. Roskell *House of Commons 1386–1421* 2 (1992): 447–448 (biog. of Ralph Bush), 564–565 (biog. of John Chideock). *Cal. IPM* 20 (1995): 150–151. National Archives, CP 25/1/179/94, #93 [see abstract of fine at http:// www.medievalgenealogy.org.uk/index.html]. Cornwall Rec. Office: Arundell of Lanherne and Trerice, AR/39/2 (ped. of Fitz Warin-Chidiock fams.) (available at www.a2a.org.uk/search/index.asp).

Children of Eleanor Fitz Warin, by John Chidiock, Knt.:

i. **JOHN CHIDIOCK**, Knt. [see next].

ii. **ELIZABETH CHIDIOCK**, married (1st) **WILLIAM MASSEY** [see FITZ WALTER 13]; (2nd) **WALTER FITZ WALTER**, Knt., 5th Lord Fitz Walter [see FITZ WALTER 13].

13. JOHN CHIDIOCK, Knt., of Chideock, Buckham (in Beaminster), Caundle Haddon, East Chelborough, Kingston (in Yeovil), Lydlinch, and More Crichel, Dorset, Frampton on Severn, Gloucestershire, Allowenshay, Isle-Brewers, Pitney, and Wearne, Somerset, etc., Knight of the Shire for Dorset, Sheriff of Somerset and Dorset, 1447–8, son and heir, born at Chideock, Dorset 1 Nov. 1401. He married between 24 April 1418 and 25 March 1425 **KATHERINE LUMLEY**, daughter of Ralph Lumley, Knt., 1st Lord Lumley, by Eleanor, daughter of John Neville, K.G., 3rd Lord

Neville of Raby [see LUMLEY 14 for her ancestry]. They had two daughters, Katherine (or Catherine) and Margaret (wife of William Stourton, [2nd Lord Stourton], and John Cheyne, K.G. [Lord Cheyne]). Katherine was a legatee in the 1418 will of her brother, John Lumley, Knt. In 1433 he and his wife, Katherine, sued Katherine of France, Queen of England, regarding an annuity of 40 marks for good service performed and to be performed. He was made an honorary member of the Guild of Merchant Taylors of London in 1436–7. SIR JOHN CHIDIOCK died testate 6 March 1449/50. His widow, Katherine, died 2 June 1461.

> Lodge *Peerage of Ireland* 4 (1789): 254 (sub Lumley). Banks *Dormant & Extinct Baronage of England* 1 (1807): 304–305 (sub Fitz-Warine). Brydges *Collins' Peerage of England* 7 (1812): 42. *Wills & Invs.* 1 (Surtees Soc. 2) (1835): 60–63. Nicolas *Controversy between Scrope & Grosvenor* 2 (1832): 255–257. Fuller *Hist. of the Worthies of England* (1840): 462. Beltz *Mems. of the Order of the Garter* (1841): clxvii. Clode *Mems. of the Guild of Merchant Taylors* (1875): 619. Rogers *Ancient Sepulchral Effigies* (1877): 374 (ped. chart). Lawson *Gen. Colls. Ill. the Hist. of Roman Catholic Fams. in England* 3 (1887): 221–232. Birch *Cat. Seals in the British Museum* 2 (1892): 640 (seal of John Chidiock dated 1425 — A shield of arms, couché: an escutcheon between eight martlets in orle, CHIDIOCK. Crest on a helmet, ornamental mantling and wreath, a garb. Legend: Sigill'u * : * iohis * : * chidiok : *. Cabled borders.). *List of Sheriffs for England & Wales* (PRO Lists and Indexes 9) (1898): 123. Wordsworth *Ceremonies & Processions of the Cathedral Church of Salisbury* (1901): 24–30 ("We shalle pray ... for Dame Kateryn chydiok' soule."). Fry & Fry *Abs. of Feet of Fines Rel. Dorset* 2 (Dorset Rec. Soc. 10) (1910): 318–320, 357–358, 398. Clay *Extinct & Dormant Peerages* (1913): 128–131 (sub Lumley). *C.P.* 3 (1913): 191–192 (sub Cheyne); 5 (1926): 459–461 (sub FitzPayn); 12(1) (1953): 302–303 (sub Stourton). *Cal. MSS Dean & Chapter of Wells* 2 (Hist. MSS Comm. 12B) (1914): 668, 669. *C.C.R.* 1429–1435 (1933): 328–329. *C.C.R.* 1447–1454 (1941–7): 153–155. VCH *Gloucester* 10 (1972): 143–148. VCH *Somerset* 3 (1974): 205. VCH *Cambridge* 8 (1989): 34. Roskell *House of Commons 1386–1421* 2 (1992): 564–565 (biog. of John Chideock). *Cal. IPM* 20 (1995): 150–151. National Archives, CP 25/1/179/94, #93 [see abstract of fine at http:// www.medievalgenealogy.org.uk/index.html]. Cornwall Rec. Office: Arundell of Lanherne and Trerice, AR/39/2 (ped. of Fitz Warin-Chidiock fams.) (available at www.a2a.org.uk/search/index.asp). Year Books Search, Boston Univ. School of Law (online database found at www.bu.edu/law/seipp/index.html: Seipp Case # 1433.042: Plaintiffs: Sir John Chideoke and Katherine his wife vs. Katherine, Queen of England). Warwickshire County Rec. Office, Deed 1886/282.

14. KATHERINE (or **CATHERINE**) **CHIDIOCK**, daughter and co-heiress, born about 1428 (aged 22 in 1450). She married (1st) by contract dated 11 March 1436/7 **WILLIAM STAFFORD**, Esq. [see SOUTHWICK 10.iii], of Stinsford, Bomston, and Puriton, Dorset, etc., and, in right of his wife, of Frampton on Severn, Gloucestershire, Sheriff of Somerset and Dorset, 1437–8, 1441–2, Sheriff of Gloucestershire, 1438–9, Knight of the Shire for Dorset, 1439–40, Sheriff of Wiltshire, 1446–7, 3rd son of Humphrey Stafford, Knt., of Hooke, Dorset, Perton, Staffordshire, and Southwick (in North Bradley), Wiltshire, by Elizabeth, daughter and co-heiress of John Mautravers, Knt. [see SOUTHWICK 10 for his ancestry]. They had one son, Humphrey Stafford, Knt. [Earl of Devon]. WILLIAM STAFFORD, Esq., was slain 18 June 1450. She married (2nd) by settlement dated 5 March 1450/1 (as his 2nd wife) **JOHN ARUNDELL**, Knt., of Lanherne, Penpoll (in Phillack), Trenoweth (in Crowan), etc., Tregear (in Crowan), etc., Cornwall, Ravensbury, Surrey, etc., Vice Admiral of Cornwall, Under-Sheriff of Cornwall, 1457, Sheriff of Cornwall, 1469–70, son of John Arundell, Esq., of Lanherne, Cornwall and Bideford, Devon, by Margaret, daughter and co-heiress of John de Burghersh, Knt. [see GANT 11 for his ancestry]. He was born at Bideford, Devon 9 June 1421. They had one son, Thomas, K.B., and six daughters, Elizabeth (wife of Giles Daubeney, K.G., Lord Daubeney), Katherine (wife of Walter Courtenay, Knt., and John Moyle, Esq.), Ellen (wife of Ralph Coppleston), Margaret, Thomasine (wife of Henry Marney, K.G., K.B., 1st Lord Marney), and Dorothy (wife of Henry Strangeways, Knt.). John Arundell married (1st) **ELIZABETH MORLEY**, daughter of Thomas Morley, Knt., 5th Lord Morley, *de jure* Lord Marshal [see MORLEY 14 for issue of this marriage]. He served in France, and was knighted by King Edward IV in 1463. He fought at the Battle of Tewkesbury in 1471. In 1472–3 he and his wife, Katherine, conveyed the manor of Ravensbury, Surrey to Thomas Stonor, Esq., Humphrey Forster, Thomas Hampden, Esq., etc. SIR JOHN ARUNDELL died 12 Nov. 1473. His widow, Katherine, married (3rd) (as his 3rd wife) **ROGER LEWKNOR**, Knt. [see LEWKNOR 15], of

Trotton, Broadhurst (in Horsted Keynes), Dedisham (in Slinfold), Iteford, and Selmeston, Sussex, etc., Knight of the Shire for Sussex, Sheriff of Surrey and Sussex, 1439–40, 1467–8, Keeper of the Temporalities of the Archbishopric of Canterbury. SIR ROGER LEWKNOR died 4 August 1478. He left a will dated 23 July 1478, proved 28 Nov. 1478 (P.C.C. 1 Logge), requesting burial in St. George's, Trotton, Sussex. In the period, 1478–9, his widow, Katherine, sued Giles Daubeney and others, feoffees to uses, in Chancery regarding several manors, including Dedisham (in Slinfold), Bolebrook (in Hartfield), Broadhurst (in Horsted Keynes), Iteford, and Selmeston, Sussex, South Mimms, Middlesex, etc. Katherine died 9 April 1479.

Strachey *Rotuli Parl.* 6 (1777): 325–326. Banks *Dormant & Extinct Baronage of England* 1 (1807): 304–305 (sub Fitz-Warine). Bridges *Hist. & Antiqs. of Northamptonshire* 1 (1791): 125. Brydges *Collins' Peerage of England* 7 (1812): 40–57 (sub Arundel, Lord Arundel of Wardour) ("Sir John Arundel, Knt. … one of those valiant commanders who served King Henry VI. in France"). Burke *Gen'l & Heraldic Dict. of the Peerages of England, Ireland & Scotland* (1831): 492–493 (sub Stafford). *Coll. Top. et Gen.* 1 (1834): 306–307 (Arundell ped.: "Sir John Arundell [1] = Dau. of the Lord Morley, [2] = Dame Katherine, dau. of Sir John Chideoke, and widow of William Stafford"). Hutchins *Hist. & Antiqs. of Dorset* 2 (1863): 178–182 (Stafford ped.); 3 (1868): 431. Rogers *Ancient Sepulchral Effigies* (1877): 374 (ped. chart). Flower *Vis. of Yorkshire 1563-4* (H.S.P. 16) (1881): 154–156 (Hastings ped.: "Elsabeth [Morley] wyff to Sir John Arundell who had a doughter wyff to James Tyrrell of Gyppynge."). Cooke & St. George *Vis. of Hertfordshire 1572, 1634 & 1546* (H.S.P. 22) (1886): 113–114 (Capell ped.: "Sir John Arundell, Kt. = Katherin, da. to Sir John Chidioke, Kt."). Lawson *Gen. Colls. Ill. the Hist. of Roman Catholic Fams. in England* 3 (1887): 151–152, 221–232. *Misc. Gen. et Heraldica* n.s. 2 (1887): 73–76. Vivian *Vis. of Cornwall* (1887): 2–5 (Arundell ped.). Rogers *Strife of the Roses & Days of the Tudors in the West* (1890): 137–154. *Wiltshire Notes & Queries* 1 (1893–5): 556–560; 2 (1896–8): 255–261; 3 (1899–1901): 193–202. Lewis *Pedes Finium; or, Fines Rel. Surrey* (Surrey Arch. Soc. Extra Vol. 1) (1894): 195. *List of Sheriffs for England & Wales* (PRO Lists and Indexes 9) (1898): 22, 50, 123, 136, 153. Wrottesley *Peds. from the Plea Rolls* (1905): 472. VCH *Worcester* 3 (1913): 217–218. *Genealogist* n.s. 31 (1915): 173–178 (re. Stafford fam.). *C.P.* 4 (1916): 102–105 (sub Daubeney), 327–328 (sub Devon); 5 (1926): 459–462 (sub FitzPayn); 8 (1932): 523 (sub Marney); 14 (1998): 348–349 (sub Grane). Kingsford *Stonor Letters & Papers 1290–1483* 1 (Camden Soc. 3rd Ser. 29) (1919): 128–129 (letter of Lady Katherine Arundell (née Chidiock) dated ?1473 names her cousins, Thomas Stonor, Esq. [see DE LA POLE 10], and Richard Harcourt, Knt. [see WITHAM 9]). Harvey et al. *Vis. of the North* 3 (Surtees Soc. 144) (1930): 106–109 (Strangwais ped.). Comber *Sussex Gens.* 3 (1933): 148–158 (sub Lewknor). Beckington *Reg. of Thomas Bekynton Bishop of Bath & Wells* 1 (Somerset Rec. Soc. 49) (1934): 119, 237, 259. Wedgwood *Hist. of Parl.* 1 (1936): 795 (biog. of William Stafford). Chichele *Reg. of Henry Chichele, Archbishop of Canterbury* 2 (Canterbury & York Soc. 42) (1937): 620–624 (will of Humphrey Stafford, Knt.). *Bridgwater Borough Archives* 4 (Somerset Rec. Soc. 60) (1948): 50–55. VCH *Warwick* 5 (1949): 26–28. Paget *Baronage of England* (1957) 224: 2. VCH *Wiltshire* 8 (1965): 218–234. VCH *Gloucester* 10 (1972): 143–148. VCH *Somerset* 3 (1974): 111–120. VCH *Cambridge* 8 (1982): 34. Cornwall Rec. Office: Arundell of Lanherne & Trerice, AR/19/10 — lease dated 5 Mar. 1451; AR/39/2 (ped. of Fitz Warin-Chidiock fams.) (available at www.a2a.org.uk/search/index.asp).

Children of Katherine Chidiock, by John Arundell, Knt.:

i. **THOMAS ARUNDELL**, K.B. [see next].

ii. **MARGARET ARUNDELL**, married before 1485 **WILLIAM CAPELL** (or **CAPEL**), Knt., of London, Essex, Master of the Drapers Company, Alderman of London, 1485–1515, Sheriff of London, 1489–90, M.P. for London, 1491–2, 1512–4, 1515, Lord Mayor of London, 1503–4, 1509–10, 2nd son of John Capell, of Stoke Nayland, Suffolk, by his wife, Joan (or Jane). They had one son, Giles, Knt., and three daughters, Dorothy (wife of John Zouche [Lord Zouche of Harringworth]), Cecily, and Elizabeth. In 1478 he was in custody for vilifying alderman Robert Drope, and the Chancellor remitted him to be punished at the discretion of the Mayor and aldermen of London. In 1484 he was elected one of the auditors of the accounts of the Chamber. In 1486 he purchased the manor of Little Raynes, Essex. The same year he was shipping wool to the Mediterranean. He was committed to the Tower by Dudley and Empson in 1509. SIR WILLIAM CAPELL died 7 Sept. 1515, and was buried in the south chapel of St. Bartholomew-by-the-Exchange which he had rebuilt. He left a will dated 1 Sept. 1515, proved 17 March 1516 (P.C.C. 13 Holder), requesting that four clerks be present at his funeral and 4*d.* paid to each clerk present at his trental of diriges and masses after burial. His widow, Margaret, was living in 1517. Brydges *Collins' Peerage of England* 7 (1812): 40–57 (sub Arundel, Lord Arundel of Wardour). Clutterbuck *Hist. & Antiqs. of Hertford* 1 (1815): 243 (Capel ped.). Nicolas *Testamenta Vetusta* 2 (1826): 532–533 (will of Sir William Capel). *Coll. Top. et Gen.* 1 (1834): 306–307 (Arundell ped.: "Margaret [Arundell], wedd. to Sir Will. Capel of London."). Dingley *Hist. from Marble* 2 (Camden Soc. 97) (1868): 137. Hawley et al. *Vis. of Essex 1552, 1558, 1570, 1612 & 1634* 1 (H.S.P. 13) (1878): 171–172 (Capell ped.: "Sr William Capell of London Shrive ao 1489 and twice Lord Mayor ao 1503 and 1509 = Margarett daugh. to Sr Thomas Arundell Knight.") (Capel arms: Gules, a lion rampant between three cross crosslets fitchée or). Cooke & St. George *Vis. of Hertfordshire 1572, 1634 & 1546* (H.S.P. 22) (1886): 113–114 (Capell ped.: "Sir William Capell, Kt., Lord Maior of London and Draper 1503, knighted by H. 7. = Margaret, da. to Sir Thomas Arundell, Kt."). Lawson *Gen. Colls. Ill. the Hist. of Roman Catholic Fams. in England* 3 (1887): 151–152, 221–232. Vivian *Vis. of Cornwall* (1887): 2–5 (Arundell ped.). Harvey *Vis. of Wiltshire 1565* (1897): 43–44 (Sowche ped.). Sharpe *Cal. Letter-Books of London: L* (1912): 210–227. Wedgwood *Hist. of Parl.* 1 (1936): 153–154 (biog. of William Capel). *C.P.* 12(2) (1959): 948 (sub Zouche). *Ancient Deeds — Ser. B* 2 (List & Index Soc. 101) (1974): B.7140, B.8726. James *Bede Roll of the Fraternity of St. Nicholas* 1 (London Rec. Soc. Pubs. 39) (2004): 254, 256, 257, 259.

Child of Margaret Arundell, by William Capell, Knt.:

a. **ELIZABETH CAPELL**, married **WILLIAM PAULET**, K.G., 1st Marquess of Winchester [see PAULET 16].

15. THOMAS ARUNDELL, K.B., of Lanherne, Cornwall, Frampton on Severn, Gloucestershire, etc., son and heir by his father's 2nd marriage, born about 1458–60 (aged 14 in 1474, 21 in 1479). He married before 26 Jan. 1474 (by marriage settlement dated 14 Dec. 1473) **KATHERINE DINHAM** (or **DYNHAM**), 4th daughter of John Dinham, Knt., of Hartland, Kingserwell, and Nutwell, Devon, by Joan, daughter of Richard Arches, Knt. [see DINHAM 8 for her ancestry]. They had five sons, John, K.B., Thomas, Humphrey, Roger, and Edward, and three daughters, Eleanor (wife of Nicholas St. Low and Thomas Sydenham), Elizabeth, and Alice (wife of John Speke). There was a long dispute over lands with James Tyrrell, Knt., husband of his half-sister, Anne Arundell, which was settled in Tyrrell's favor. Giles Daubeney, husband of his full sister, Elizabeth Arundell, was also involved in this dispute. Thomas was summoned for knighthood at King Edward V's Coronation and knighted at the Coronation of King Richard III. He joined Buckingham's rebellion in 1483 and was subsequently attainted by King Richard III. His wife, Katherine, was granted £100 per annum from his forfeited estates in Feb. 1484. He fought at the Battle of Bosworth in 1485 for Henry Tudor, Earl of Richmond (afterwards King Henry VII), who restored his estates. SIR THOMAS ARUNDELL died 5 (or 11) October 1485. He left a will dated 3 October 1485, proved 12 Dec. 1488 (P.C.C. 29 Milles). His wife, Katherine, was living 3 October 1485.

Brydges *Collins' Peerage of England* 7 (1812): 40–57 (sub Arundel, Lord Arundel of Wardour). *Coll. Top. et Gen.* 1 (1834): 306–307 (Arundell ped.: "Sir Thos. Arundell, wedded Katherine, sister of the Lord Dynham."). Westcote *View of Devonshire in MDCXXX* (1845): 199–200. Flaherty *The Annals of England* (1876): 265. Rogers *Ancient Sepulchral Effigies* (1877): 374 (ped. chart). Lawson *Gen. Colls. Ill. the Hist. of Roman Catholic Fams. in England* 3 (1887): 151–152, 221–232. *Misc. Gen. et Heraldica* n.s. 2 (1887): 73–76. Vivian *Vis. of Cornwall* (1887): 2–5 (Arundell ped.). Weaver *Somerset Medieval Wills* 1 1383–1500 (Somerset Rec. Soc. 16) (1901): 256–257. *Rpt. & Trans. of the Devonshire Assoc.* 2nd Ser. 4 (1902): 721–723. *C.P.* 4 (1916): 381–382 (sub Dinham); 5 (1926): 461–462 (sub FitzPayn). Brookes *Hist. of Steeple Aston & Middle Aston* (1929): 67–73. Paget *Baronage of England* (1957) 187: 1–9 (sub Dinan). VCH *Gloucester* 10 (1972): 143–148. VCH *Oxford* 10 (1972): 42–49; 11 (1983): 295. Sutton *Coronation of Richard III* (1983): 304 (biog. of Thomas Arundell). Cornwall Rec. Office: Arundell of Lanherne & Trerice, AR/19/18 (marriage settlement dated 14 Dec. 1473); AR/19/22 (appointment of attorneys dated 26 Jan. 1474) (available at www.a2a.org.uk/search/index.asp).

Children of Thomas Arundell, K.B., by Katherine Dinham:

i. **JOHN ARUNDELL**, K.B. [see next].

ii. **ELIZABETH ARUNDELL**, married **EDWARD STRADLING**, Knt., of St. Donat's Castle, Glamorgan [see STRADLING 15].

16. JOHN ARUNDELL, K.B., of Lanherne, Cornwall, Frampton on Severn, Gloucestershire, etc., son and heir, born about 1473–5 (aged 10 or 11 in 1485, aged 28 in 1501). He married (1st) in 1496 [**LADY**] **ELIZABETH GREY**, daughter of Thomas Grey, K.G., K.B., 1st Marquess of Dorset, Lord Ferrers of Groby, Harington, Bonville, and Astley, by his 2nd wife, Cecily, *suo jure* Lady Harington and Bonville, daughter of William Bonville, Knt., 6th Lord Harington [see GROBY 17 for her ancestry]. They had two sons, John, Knt., and Thomas, K.B., and one daughter, Elizabeth (wife of Richard Edgecombe, Knt.). He was co-heir in 1501 to his uncle, John Dinham, K.G., Lord Dinham, Treasurer of the Exchequer. His wife, Elizabeth, was living 24 Feb. 1501/2. He married (2nd) before 7 Dec. 1503 (date of dispensation, they being related in the 3rd & 4th degrees of both kindred and affinity) **KATHERINE GRENVILLE**, daughter of Thomas Grenville, Knt., of Kilkhampton (in Stowe), Cornwall, by his 1st wife, Isabel, daughter of Otes Gilbert, Esq. They had three daughters, Jane, Mary (wife of Robert Radcliffe, K.G., K.B., 1st Earl of Sussex, Viscount Fitzwalter], and Henry [Fitz Alan], Earl of Arundel [see BURNELL 17]), and Eleanor. He and his fellow Dinham co-heirs presented to the church of Maperton, Somerset in 1505. He was attended King Henry VIII at the Sieges of Thérouanne and Tournai in 1513, for which service he was made a Knight Banneret in 1514. His wife, Katherine, was living 21 October 1536. SIR JOHN ARUNDELL died 8 Feb. 1544/5, and was buried at St. Mary Woolnoth, London.

Weever *Ancient Funerall Monuments* (1631): 411. Nichols *Hist. & Antiqs. of Leicester* 3(2) (1804): 682–684 (Grey ped.). Brydges *Collins' Peerage of England* 3 (1812): 340–370 (sub Grey, Earl of Stamford); 7 (1812): 40–57 (sub Arundel, Lord Arundel of Wardour). *Coll. Top. et Gen.* 1 (1834): 306–307 (Arundell ped.: "John Arundell."). Wood *Letters of Royal & Ill. Ladies* 1 (1846): 312–314 ([John] Arundel of Lanherne styled "cousin" by Mary Zouch [daughter of John Zouche, 9th Lord Zouche and his 1st wife, Dorothy Capel] in letter dated pre-1529). Oliver *Colls. Ill. the Hist. of the Catholic Religion* (1857): 75–91. Burke *Gen. Hist. of the Dormant, Abeyant, Forfeited & Extinct Peerages* (1866): 249–250 (sub Grey). Morris *Troubles of our Catholic Forefathers* (1872): 138. Rogers *Ancient Sepulchral Effigies* (1877): 374 (ped. chart). *Notes & Queries* 5th Ser. 9 (1878): 377. Boase *Bibliotheca Cornubiensis* 3 (1882): 1039 (biog. of Sir John Arundell). Burke *Dormant, Abeyant, Forfeited & Extinct Peerages* (1883): 249–250 (sub Grey). Lawson *Gen. Colls. Ill. the Hist. of Roman Catholic Fams. in England* 3 (1887): 151–152, 221–232. *Misc. Gen. et Heraldica* n.s. 2 (1887): 73–76. Vivian *Vis. of Cornwall* (1887): 2–5 (Arundell ped.), 190–197 (Grenville ped.). Weaver *Somerset Incumbents* (1889): 136. Rogers *Strife of the Roses & Days of the Tudors in the West* (1890): 67–69. *Rpt. & Trans. of the Devonshire Assoc.* 2nd Ser. 4 (1902): 721–723. *C.P.* 1 (1910): 250–252 (sub Arundel); 4 (1916): 381–382 (sub Dinham); 12(1) (1953): 517–520 (sub Sussex). Brookes *Hist. of Steeple Aston & Middle Aston* (1929): 67–73. VCH *Gloucester* 10 (1972): 143–148. *Ancient Deeds — Ser. B* 2 (List & Index Soc. 101) (1974): B.5695. VCH *Oxford* 11 (1983): 295. Cornwall Rec. Office: Arundell of Lanherne & Trerice, AR/19/30, AR/19/32, AR/19/33, AR/19/34, AR/19/42, 43, AR/19/44, AR/19/45 (available at www.a2a.org.uk/search/index.asp).

17. THOMAS ARUNDELL, K.B., of Wardour, Wiltshire and Shaftesbury, Dorset, Sheriff of Somerset and Dorset, 1530–1, 1540–1, Knight of the Shire for Dorset, Receiver-General of Duchy of Cornwall, Surveyor and Receiver for Court of Augmentations, Steward of Shaftesbury Abbey, Chancellor of the Household to Queen Katherine Parr, 2nd son by his father's 1st marriage, born about 1502. He married by settlement dated 20 Nov. 1530 **MARGARET HOWARD**, daughter and co-heiress of [Lord] Edmund Howard, Knt., by his 1st wife, Joyce, daughter of Richard Culpeper, Esq. [see HOWARD 15 for her ancestry]. They had two sons, Matthew, Knt., and Charles, Knt., and two daughters, Dorothy (wife of Henry Weston, K.B.) and Jane (wife of William Bevyle, Knt.). He was educated at Lincoln's Inn. He served both Wolsey and Cromwell. He was knighted at the Coronation of Queen Anne Boleyn in 1533. He was one of the royal commissioners for the suppression of religious houses in the west of England. His wife, Margaret, was one of the "ladies attendant" of the queen's household in 1540 to her sister, Queen Katherine Howard, fifth wife of King Henry VIII of England. He served in the French campaign in 1544. He presented to the church of Sutton Mandeville, Wiltshire in 1549. In 1552 he was arrested and charged with conspiring to murder John Dudley, Duke of Northumberland. SIR THOMAS ARUNDELL was beheaded on Tower Hill 26 Feb. 1552. His estates were forfeited to the crown. His widow, Margaret, presented to the church of Kingsdon, Somerset in 1558 and 1561. She died 10 October 1571, and was buried at Tisbury, Wiltshire.

Blomefield *Essay towards a Top. Hist. of Norfolk* 5 (1806): 235–259. Brydges *Collins' Peerage of England* 1 (1812): 50–143; 7 (1812): 40–57 (sub Arundel, Lord Arundel of Wardour). Allen *Hist. & Antiqs. of the Parish of Lambeth* (1826): ped. chart foll. 276. Burgon *Sir Thomas Gresham* 1 (1839): 466–471. Ellis *Original Letters Ill. of English Hist.* 3rd Ser. 3 (1846): 230–231. Oliver *Colls. Ill. the Hist. of the Catholic Religion* (1857): 75–91. Strickland *Lives of the Queens of England* 2 (1868): 352. Lawson *Gen. Colls. Ill. the Hist. of Roman Catholic Fams. in England* 3 (1887): 151–152, 233–241. Vivian *Vis. of Cornwall* (1887): 2–5 (Arundell ped.). Weaver *Somerset Incumbents* (1889): 118. *List of Sheriffs for England & Wales* (PRO Lists and

Indexes 9) (1898): 124. Brenan & Statham *House of Howard* 1 (1907): 268, footnote 1. *C.P.* 1 (1910): 263–264 (sub Arundell). Glenross *Admins. in the P.C.C.* 1 (1912): 124; 2 (1917): 2. *C.P.R. 1547–1553* (1926): 31–32. Davis *Anc. of Mary Isaac* (1955): 354. *Ancient Deeds — Ser. B 2* (List & Index Soc. 101) (1974): B.5695, B.7126 (Thomas Arrendell styled "cousin" by Harry Daubney, Knt.), B.7128; 3 (List & Index Soc. 113) (1975): B.12181 (Thomas Arundell, Esq., styled "kinsman" by John Dudley, Knt.), B.12143 (Thomas Arundell, Knt. styled "kinsman" by Henry [Grey], Marquess of Dorset). Bindoff *House of Commons 1509–1558* 1 (1982): 336–337 (biog. of Sir Thomas Arundell); 3 (1982): 588 (biog. of Henry Weston).

18. MATTHEW ARUNDELL, Knt., of Wardour, Wiltshire, Burgess (M.P.) for Shaftesbury, Dorset, son and heir, born about 1532–4. He was restored in blood in the 1st Parliament of Queen Mary I, and in July 1554 recovered the greater part of his inheritance by grant of the queen. He repurchased the lordship and castle of Wardour, Wiltshire from William, Earl of Pembroke. He married by settlement dated 20 Dec. 1559 **MARGARET WILLOUGHBY**, daughter of Henry Willoughby, Knt., of Wollaton, Nottinghamshire, by Anne, daughter of Thomas Grey, K.G., K.B., 2nd Marquess of Dorset [see FREVILLE 16 for her ancestry]. They had two sons, Thomas, Knt. [1st Lord Arundell of Wardour], and William, Esq. SIR MATTHEW ARUNDELL died 24 Dec. 1598, and was buried at Tisbury, Wiltshire. He left a will proved 6 Feb. 1599 (P.C.C. 12 Kidd).

Brydges *Collins' Peerage of England* 7 (1812): 40–57 (sub Arundel, Lord Arundel of Wardour). Oliver *Colls. Ill. the Hist. of the Catholic Religion* (1857): 75–91. Mundy et al. *Vis. of Nottingham 1569 & 1614* (H.S.P. 4) (1871): 145–149 (Willoughby ped.: "Margerett [Willoughby] ux. Sir Mathew Arundell Knt."). Lawson *Gen. Colls. Ill. the Hist. of Roman Catholic Fams. in England* 3 (1887): 151–152, 233–241. Vivian *Vis. of Cornwall* (1887): 2–5 (Arundell ped.). Weaver *Somerset Incumbents* (1889): 118. *C.P.* 1 (1910): 263 (sub Arundell); 14 (1998): 40 (sub Arundell). *Ancient Deeds — DD Ser.* (List & Index Soc. 200) (1983): 272.

19. THOMAS ARUNDELL, Knt., son and heir, born about 1560. He was imprisoned in the summer of 1580 for his zeal in the Catholic cause. He married (1st) by settlement dated 19 June 1585 **MARY WRIOTHESLEY**, daughter of Henry Wriothesley, Earl of Southampton, by Mary, daughter of Anthony Browne, K.G., K.B., 1st Viscount Montague. They had two sons, Thomas [2nd Lord Arundell] and William, Esq., and one daughter, Elizabeth Mary (wife of John Philpot, Knt.). He served in 1588 as a volunteer with the Imperial army in Hungary against the Turks, and, having taken a standard from the enemy at Gran, in Hungary, he was created by the Emperor Rudolph II, 14 Dec. 1595, a Count of the Holy Roman Empire. He was subsequently created Lord Arundell of Wardour, Wiltshire 4 May 1605. His wife, Mary, was buried at Tisbury, Wiltshire 27 June 1607. He married (2nd) at St. Andrew's Holborn, London 1 July 1608 **ANNE PHILIPSON**, daughter of Miles Philipson, Esq., of Crook, Westmorland, by Barbara, daughter of William Sandys, of Conishead, Lancashire. They had three sons, Matthew, Thomas, and Frederick, and six daughters, Katherine (wife of Ralph Eure), Mary, Anne, Frances (wife of John Talbot, Earl of Shrewsbury), Margaret (wife of John Fortescue, Bart.), and Clare (wife of Humphrey Weld, Esq.). His wife, Anne, died at Lennox House, Drury Lane 28 June 1637. SIR THOMAS ARUNDELL, 1st Lord Arundell of Wardour, died at Wardour Castle, Wiltshire 7 Nov. 1639. He left a will dated 5 Nov. 1639, proved 3 Dec. 1639 (P.C.C. 199 Harvey). They were buried at Tisbury, Wiltshire.

Nicolson & Burn *Hist. & Antiqs. of the Counties of Westmorland & Cumberland* 1 (1777): 142 (re. Philipson fam.). West *Antiqs. of Furness* (1805): 325–327 (re. Sandys fam.). Brydges *Collins' Peerage of England* 7 (1812): 40–57 (sub Arundel, Lord Arundel of Wardour). Wright *Queen Elizabeth & Her Times: A Ser. of Original Letters* 2 (1838): 494 (Thomas Arundell styled "the Counte Arundell of Warder" in letter dated 1603 from William Camden to Sir Robert Cotton). St. George *Heraldic Vis. of Westmoreland* (1853): 47–50 (Philipson ped.) (Philipson arms: Gules, a chevron between three boars heads couped ermine). Oliver *Colls. Ill. the Hist. of the Catholic Religion* (1857): 75–91. Hitchman *Richard Burton, K.C.M.G.* 2 (1887): 445 (Thomas, Lord Arundell styled "kinsman" [consanguineus] by Queen Elizabeth I). Lawson *Gen. Colls. Ill. the Hist. of Roman Catholic Fams. in England* 3 (1887): 151–152, 233–241. Vivian *Vis. of Cornwall* (1887): 2–5 (Arundell ped.). *Ancestor* 2 (1902): 209, 210. *C.P.* 1 (1910): 263–264 (sub Arundell); 11 (1949): 718 (sub Shrewsbury). Sterry *Eton College Reg.* (1943): 11.

Children of Thomas Arundell, Knt., by Anne Philipson:

i. **ANNE ARUNDELL**, married **CECIL** (or **CECILIUS**) **CALVERT**, 2nd Lord Baltimore [see CALVERT 22].

ii. **MARY ARUNDELL**, married [LORD] **JOHN SOMERSET**, Knt., of Pauntley, Gloucestershire [see SOMERSET 19].

❧ CLARE ❧

1. RICHARD FITZ GILBERT, of Bienfaite and Orbec, Normandy, lord of Clare, Suffolk, Tonbridge, Kent, Standon, Hertfordshire, Blechingley, Surrey, etc., son of Gilbert Fitz Godfrey, Count of Brionne, born about 1030–35. He married **ROHESE** (or **ROHAIS**, **ROHAÏDI**, **ROAXDIS**) **GIFFARD**, daughter of Walter Giffard, of Longueville-sur-Scie (Seine-Maritime), Normandy, Long Crendon, Buckinghamshire, etc., by Agnes, daughter of Gerard Flaitel (or Fleitel). They had six sons, Roger, Gilbert, Walter, Richard [Abbot of Ely], Robert, and Godfrey, and four daughters, Rohese, Alice (wife of Walter Tirel), and Avice. He was among those consulted about the proposed invasion of England in the assembly at Bonneville-sur-Touques in 1066, but there is no direct evidence of his personal participation at Hastings or in the campaign. Nevertheless, he was a significant figure soon afterwards and occurs as a witness of royal charters throughout the reign of King William the Conqueror. He was rewarded with no fewer than 176 lordships, which consisted of two concentrations of lands, one in Kent and Surrey, and the other in Suffolk and Essex. His holdings at Tonbridge, Kent and Clare, Suffolk were both given motte and bailey castles. During the king's absence, he served as Joint Chief Justiciar. He played a leading role in suppressing the rebellion of Roger de Breteuil, Earl of Hereford and Ralph de Gael in 1075 or 1076. In 1078 or 1079 he and his wife, Rohese, sent to Bec Abbey for a colony of monks to replenish the vacant convent at Neotsbury, Huntingdonshire. Sometime before 1086 he granted the monks of Bec his manors of Tooting and Streatham, and land in Horsham (in Walton-on-Thames), all in Surrey. Sometime before 1090 he confirmed to the monks of Bec two thirds of his demesne tithes and one villain in Standon, Hertfordshire; and two thirds of his demesne tithes in Blechingley, Chivington, Woodmansterne, Tolworth, Chipstead, Betchworth, and Walton Leigh, Surrey and houses in Southwark, Surrey and Tonbridge, Kent. RICHARD FITZ GILBERT died about 1090, and was buried at St. Neots, Huntingdonshire. His widow, Rohese, was still living in 1113, when she granted the whole of her manor of Eynesbury, Huntingdonshire to St. Neot's Priory, Huntingdonshire.

Gorham *Hist. & Antiqs. of Eynesbury & St. Neot's* (1820): 61–63, 68–69, 184. Clutterbuck *Hist. & Antiqs. of Hertford* 3 (1827): 225–226 (Clare ped.). Dugdale *Monasticon Anglicanum* 3 (1846): 462–463; 5 (1846): 269 (sub Tintern Abbey — Genealogia Fundatoris: "Walterum de Giffard primogenitum, qui alium Walterum procreavit, et dictus fuit Walterius Giffard secundus. Rohesia una sororum Walteri (duas plures enim habuit) conjuncta in matrimonio Ricardo filio comitis Gisleberti, qui in re militari, tempore Conquestoris omnes sui temporis magnates præcessit. Prædicta Rohesia supervixit et renupta Eudoni, dapifer Regis Normanniæ, qui construxit castrum Colecestriæ, cum coenobio, in honore sancti Johannis, ubi sepultus fuit, cum conjuge sua, tempore Henrici primi. Margareta filia eorum nupta fuit Willielmo de Mandevill, et fuit mater Gaufridi filii comitis Essexiæ et jure matris, Normanniæ dapifer. Prædictus Ricardus apud sanctum Neotum jacet sepultus. Huic rex Willielmus concessit baroniam de Clare, villam verò cum castello de Tunbridge, de archiepiscopo Cantuariensi, pro aliis terris in Normannia, perquisivit in escambium."). Lipscomb *Hist. & Antiqs. of Buckingham* 1 (1847): 200–201 (Clare ped.). *Recueil des Historiens des Gaules et de la France* 8 (1871): 269 (Ex Historia Willelmi Gemetic [William de Jumièges]: "His Gislebertus genuit Richardum strenuissimum militem; qui tam ipse, quàm filii ejus, Gislebertus, Rogerius, Walterius, Rodbertus."). *Recueil des Historiens des Gaules et de la France* 11 (1876): 58 (Ex Willelmi Calculi, Gemeticensis Monachi, Historia Normannorum [William de Jumièges]: "Genuit autem idem Galterius secundum Galterium Giffardum et plures filias, quarum una nomine Rohais nupsit Richardo filio Comitis Gisleberti."). Round *Feudal England* (1895): 468–479. *Arch. Jour.* 2nd Ser. 6 (1899): 221–231. Porée *Hist. de l'Abbaye du Bec* 1 (1901): 454. Copinger *Manors of Suffolk* 1 (1905): 45–46. Marx ed. *Gesta Normannorum Ducum* (1914): 325–326 (Guillaume de Jumièges: "Ricardus autem frater Balduini, genuit ex Rohais quatuor filios, Gislebertum, Rogerium, Walterium, Robertum, et duas filias; altera quarum matrimonio copulata est Rodulfo de Felgeriis, natique sunt ex ea Fransvalo, Henricus, Robertus Giffardus. Gislebertus autem, qui illam terram, quam pater eorum habuerat in Anglia, post ipsum adeptus est; Rogerius enim, frater ejus, terram de Normannia optinuit."). *C.P.* 3 (1915): 242 (sub

Clare). Douglas *Feudal Docs. from Bury St. Edmunds* (1932): 152–153. Douglas *Domesday Monachorum of Christ Church, Canterbury* (1944). Chibnall *Select Docs. of the English Lands of the Abbey of Bec* (Camden 3rd Ser. 73) (1951): 21–22 (charters of Richard Fitz Gilbert lord of Clare dated *ante* 1090 and *ante* 1086). Paget (1957) 130:2. Sanders *English Baronies* (1960): 34–35. Fauroux *Recueil des Actes des Ducs de Normandie de 911 à 1066* (1961). Blake *Liber Eliensis* (Camden Soc. 3rd Ser. 92) (1962). *Anglo-Norman Studies* 3 (1980): 119–141. *Arch. Cantiana* 96 (1980): 119–131. *Jour. Ecclesiastical Hist.* 32 (1981): 427–437. Barlow *William Rufus* (1983). Hollister *Monarchy, Magnates, & Institutions in the Anglo-Norman World* (1986). Brown *Anglo-Norman Studies* 11 (1989): 261–278. Blair *Early Medieval Surrey* (1991). Duby *Rural Economy & Country Life in the Medieval West* (1998): 429–430. Van Houts *Memory & Gender in Medieval Europe: 900–1200* (1999): 156–157. Keats-Rohan *Domesday People* 1 (1999): 413, 456–457. Tanner *Fams., Friends, & Allies* (2004): 316 (Clare ped.).

Children of Richard Fitz Gilbert, by Rohese Giffard:

i. **GILBERT FITZ RICHARD** [see next].

ii. **ROBERT FITZ RICHARD**, of Little Dunmow, Essex, married **MAUD DE SENLIS** [see FITZ WALTER 4].

iii. **ROHESE** (or **ROSE**) **FITZ RICHARD**, married **EUDES THE STEWARD** (or **EUDES FITZ HUBERT**), of Colchester, Essex [see SAY 2].

iv. **AVICE FITZ RICHARD**, married **RAOUL [I] DE FOUGÈRES**, seigneur of Fougères [see FOUGÈRES 2].

2. GILBERT FITZ RICHARD (also styled **DE CLARE** and **DE TONBRIDGE**), of Clare, Suffolk, Tonbridge, Kent, etc., born before 1066. He succeeded to the English possessions of his father. He married **ALICE** (or **ADELICIA, ADELIZ, ADALICIA, ADELIDÆ, HADALAIDIS**) **DE CLERMONT**, daughter of Hugues, seigneur of Clermont, Breuil-le-Vert, Creil, Luzarches, and Mouchy-Saint-Elou, by Marguerite, daughter of Hildouin de Rameru, Count of Montdidier and Roucy [see CLERMONT 1 for her ancestry]. They had four sons, Richard, Gilbert, Walter, and Baldwin, and four daughters, Rohese (or Rose), Avice, Margaret, and Alice. In 1088 he joined the revolt of Eudes, Bishop of Bayeux, and others against King William Rufus in favor of Robert Curthose. He was besieged at Tonbridge, Kent by the king, but wounded and forced to surrender. He was evidently pardoned, as he afterwards witnessed a number of royal charters. He founded the Priory of Clare in 1090. He served in the king's army in 1091. He was involved in a conspiracy with Robert de Mowbray and others to dethrone King William Rufus in 1095 but, joining the king's army, he informed on his fellow conspirators as the army moved to suppress Mowbray. He was once again pardoned, but does not reappear in the king's company. He was granted the lordship of Cardigan, 1107–11, by King Henry I. He raised an army and subdued the region, building castles at Castles of Aberystwyth and Llanbadarn. He was a patron of Bec, granting the collegiate church at Clare to be colonized by Benedictines from the Norman house, and confirmed his mother's endowment of St. Neots. He also made grants to Lewes Priory from his Surrey lands and granted the church of Llanbadarn to Gloucester Abbey. At an unknown date, his wife, Alice, founded an anniversary at the Priory of Saint-Leu d'Esserent for herself and for her parents, Hugues de Clermont and his wife, Marguerite. **GILBERT FITZ RICHARD** last appears at Westminster 16 September 1115. The Welsh annals note his death in 1117. His widow, Alice, married (2nd) before 1123 **BOUCHARD DE MONTMORENCY**. They had one son, Hervé de Montmorency [Constable of Ireland]. In the period, 1136–38, she confirmed in alms to Thorney Abbey, Cambridgeshire the gift of a half a yardland and ten acres in Lowick and four yardlands in Rounds made by a certain Tovi.

Dugdale *Monasticon Anglicanum* 2 (1819): 601 (charter dated 1136–38 of Adeliz, uxor Gilberti filii Ricardi to Thorney Abbey), 602 (charter of Robert, Bishop of Lincoln, confirming previous gift of Alice de Montmorency [Adelidæ de Montemoraci] to Thorney Abbey), 603 (charter of Alice, mother of Earl Gilbert [Adeliz, mater comitis Gilberti] to Thorney Abbey; charter names Earl Gilbert and Walter his brother); 6(2) (1830): 834–835. Clutterbuck *Hist. & Antiqs. of Hertford* 3 (1827): 225–226 (Clare ped.). Lipscomb *Hist. & Antiqs. of Buckingham* 1 (1847): 200–201 (Clare ped.). Williams ab Ithel *Annales Cambriæ* (Rolls Ser.) (1860): 36 (sub A.D. 1117: "Gilebertus filius Ricardi obiit."). Hart *Historia et Cartularium Monasterii Sancti Petri Gloucestriae* 2 (Rolls Ser. 33) (1865): 73–74. *Jour. of the British Arch. Assoc.* 26 (1870): 149–160 ("The first of the Clares who wrote himself Earl of Hertford is said to have been Richard, eldest son of Gilbert de Tonbridge, by his wife Adeliza, who is stated by Guillaume de Jumièges to have been the daughter of a Comte de Clermont .... It would be desirable to affiliate this wife of Gilbert more distinctly, by showing which of the Counts of Clermont was her father. According to Père Anselme (*Hist. Généalogique*) she was the daughter of Hugh, first Comte de Clermont en Beauvaisis, by his wife Marguerite de Rouey, daughter of Hildouin, fourth Comte de Rouey, and Alex. de Chastillon; but though he states this in the genealogy of Clare, he gives no such daughter to Count Hugh in that of Clermont, naming only three daughters, — 1, Ermentrude, wife of Hugh, Earl of Chester; 2, Richilde, wife of Dreux, second Seigneur de Mello; and 3, Emma, wife of Matthieu, first Comte de Beaumont sur l'Oise. The fact of her parentage depends, therefore, at present on the statement of Guillaume de Jumièges, and the authenticity of a note appended to her charter in the Register of Thorney Abbey, and thus printed by Dugdale: 'Adelicia de Claramonte dicta (folio 11, cap. 9, parte 4).' The charter itself commences thus: 'Adeliz mater Comitis Gilberti omnibus amicis et hominibus suis Francie et Anglie salutem,' etc.; and ends with 'Sciendum est anterior hæc esse facta coram Comite Gilberti et Waltero frater ejus.'"). Delisle *Recueil des Historiens des Gaules et de la France* 14 (1877): 7 (Genealogia Regum Francorum Tertiae Stirpis: "Secundam filiam præfati Comitis Helduini de Rameruth, dictam Margaretam, duxit Hugo Comes de Claromonte, de qua nati sunt Guido dictus Qui-non-dormit, et Hugo Paper, et Comes Rainaldus, et sorores eorum. Rainaldus duxit Adelidem Comitissam Viromandensium, defuncto priore viro suo, scilicet Hugone Magno, quæ peperit ei filiam Margaretam, quam duxit Comes Karolus Flandriæ; quo mortuo, tradita est Comiti Sancti-Pauli Hugoni, qui dictus est Campus-avenæ. Prædictus Rainaldus, defuncta Adelide, duxit Comitissam de Dammartin, filiam Comitis de Rainaldi de Monzuns, de qua genuit Guidonem, et Rainaldum, et Hugonem archidiaconum Metensem, et Galterum, cum aliis utriusque sexus. Unda sororum Comitis Rainaldi nupsit in Anglia Comiti Hugoni de Cestre; alteram duxit Gislebertus filius Richardi Anglici; tertiam copulavit sibi Matthæus Comes de Bellomonte, de qua genuit alterum Matthæum Comitem, et fratrem ejus, et filias."). Round *Feudal England* (1895): 468–479, 519–527. *Arch. Jour.* 2nd Ser. 6 (1899): 221–231. Muller *Prieuré de Saint-Leu d'Esserent: Cartulaire* 1 (Pubs. Soc. Hist. du Vexin) (1900): 44 (charter of Adelaide de Clermont, wife of Gilbert de Anglia [Hadalaidis, filia Hugonis de Claromonte, scilicet uxor Gisleberti de Anglia]). Depoin *Cartulaire de l'Abbaye de Saint-Martin de Pontoise* 3 (1904): 302–305. Copinger *Manors of Suffolk* 1 (1905): 45–46. Delisle *Rouleau Mortuaire du B. Vital abbé de Savigni* (1909), titre no. 182 (Gilbert Fitz Richard styled "uncle" [avunculi] of Fransualo [de Fougères]). *C.P.* 3 (1913): 242–243 (sub Clare), 10 (1945):441 (Round in *Feudal England*, ped. at p. 472 suggests that Alice, wife of William de Percy, was the daughter of Gilbert Fitz Richard [died 1117], but see next generation). Marx ed. *Gesta Normannorum Ducum* (1914): 325–326 (Guillaume de Jumièges: "Gislebertus autem, qui illam terram, quam pater eorum habuerat in Anglia, post ipsum adeptus est; Rogerius enim, frater ejus, terram de Normannia optinuit. Hic, inquam, Gislebertus ex filia comitis de Claro Monte habuit tres filios, Ricardum, qui ei successit, et Gislebertum, et Walterium, et unam filiam, nomine Rohais."). Stenton *Facsimiles of Early Charters from Northamptonshire Colls.* (Northamptonshire Rec. Soc. 4) (1930): 52–54 (charter dated c.1136–38 of Alice wife of Gilbert Fitz Richard, and Gilbert, Walter, Baldwin, and Rohese, Gilbert's children). Douglas *Feudal Docs. from Bury St. Edmunds* (1932): 152–153. Chibnall *Select Docs. of the English Lands of the Abbey of Bec* (Camden 3rd Ser. 73) (1951): 21–22. *Paget* (1957) 130: 3–4. Sanders *English Baronies* (1960): 34–35, 62–63. *Sussex Arch. Colls.* 72 (1980): 97–126. Schwennicke *Europäische Stammtafeln* 3(4) (1989): 653 (sub Clermont). Brown *Anglo-Norman Studies* 11 (1989): 261–278. Jackson *Words, Names, & Hist.: Selected Papers Cecily Clark* (1995): 335 (Margareta de ierborai [Gerberoy] entered in LV as sister of Alice de Clermont), 336 (Burchardus de muntmorenci entered in LV as 2nd husband of Alice de Clermont) [Note: LV =.Liber Vitae of Thorney Abbey (BL., Add. MS. 40,000, entry record before c.1135–1140; for Alice de Clermont's sister, Marguerite de Clermont, wife of Gérard de Gerberoy, see *Prieuré de Saint-Leu d'Esserent: Cartulaire* 1 (Pubs. Soc. Hist. du Vexin) (1900): 34–36). Ward *Women of the English Nobility & Gentry 1066–1500* (1995): 126–127 (confirmation charter of Alice mother of Earl Gilbert dated c.1138–48), 127 (letter of Earl Roger de Clare to Alice de Claremont dated c.1152). Cownie *Religious Patronage in Anglo-Norman England, 1066–1135* (1998): 123. Keats-Rohan *Domesday People* 1 (1999): 52, 332–333. Tanner *Fams., Friends, & Allies* (2004): 316 (Clare ped.).

Children of Gilbert Fitz Richard, by Alice de Clermont:

i. **RICHARD FITZ GILBERT** [see next].

ii. **GILBERT FITZ GILBERT**, 1st Earl of Pembroke, married **ISABEL OF MEULAN** [see PEMBROKE 3].

iii. **BALDWIN FITZ GILBERT**, of Bourne, Lincolnshire, married **ALINE** (or **ADELINE**) **DE ROLLOS** [see WAKE 3].

iv. **ROHESE** (or **ROSE**) **FITZ GILBERT**. She consented to a gift of her mother, Alice, to Thorney Abbey dated c.1136–38. She married **BADERON DE MONMOUTH**, of Monmouth, Monmouthshire. They had two sons, Gilbert and James, and one probable daughter, Rohese (or Rose) (wife of Hugh de Lacy). He and his wife, Rohese, witnessed a charter of Roger, Earl of Hereford to St. Mary, Monmouth dated 1148–55. In the period, c.1150–60, he granted the monks of Monmouth three forges in his borough of Monmouth on the bank of the Wye in exchange for Hadnock, Monmouthshire. He and his wife, Rohese, granted property to St. Florent Abbey.

His wife, Rohese, evidently died before 1166, when Baderon gave a knight's fee to the Hospitallers of Quenington for the soul of his wife, Rohese. BADERON DE MONMOUTH was living in 1169–70. Dugdale *Monasticon Anglicanum* 2 (1819): 601 (charter dated 1136–38 of Adeliz, uxor Gilberti filii Ricardi to Thorney Abbey). Clutterbuck *Hist. & Antiqs. of Hertford* 3 (1827): 225–226 (Clare ped.). Lee *Hist. of the Town & Parish of Tetbury* (1857): 209. Warner & Ellis *Facsimiles of Royal & Other Charters in the British Museum* 1 (1903): #41 (charter of Baderon de Monmouth dated c.1150–60; charter granted with consent of his sons, Gilbert and James). *Cat. of the MSS rel. to Wales in the British Museum* 3 (Cymmrodorion Rec. Ser. 4) (1908): 710. Copinger *Manors of Suffolk* 1 (1905): 45–46. Stenton *Facsimiles of Early Charters from Northamptonshire Colls.* (Northamptonshire Rec. Soc. 4) (1930): 52–54. Meale *Women & Literature in Britain, 1150–1500* (1996): 17–18. Johns *Noblewomen, Aristocracy & Power in the 12th-Cent. Anglo-Norman Realm* (2003): 90. Tanner *Fams., Friends, & Allies* (2004): 316 (Clare ped.).

v. **MARGARET FITZ GILBERT**, married **WILLIAM DE MONTFICHET**, of Stansted Montfichet, Essex [see PLAIZ 3].

vi. **ALICE DE TONBRIDGE**, married **WILLIAM DE PERCY**, of Topcliffe, Yorkshire [see PERCY 3].

3. RICHARD FITZ GILBERT (also known as **RICHARD DE CLARE**), of Clare, Suffolk, Tonbridge, Kent, and Cardigan, son and heir. He married **ALICE** (or **ALICIA**) **OF CHESTER**, daughter of Ranulph *le Meschin*, Earl of Chester, by his wife, Lucy. They had three sons, Gilbert [Earl of Hertford], Roger [Earl of Hertford (or Clare)], and Richard, and two daughters, Alice and Rohese. In 1124 he removed the Priory of Clare, Suffolk from its original site to Stoke by Clare, a few miles away, and rebuilt the church and monastic buildings for the monks. In 1130 he had pardons from exactions in four counties; the king also assisted him in the matter of a large debt to the Jewish moneylenders of London. He rebuilt the clas church of Llanbadarn Fawr, which his father had given to Gloucester Abbey, as a priory of the house. He founded a priory at Tonbridge, Kent. He was also active as a patron of Cardigan Priory. RICHARD FITZ GILBERT, lord of Clare, was surprised and slain by the Welsh, near Abergavenny 15 April 1136, and was buried at the Chapter House at Gloucester. Sometime before 1143 his widow, Alice, was rescued from the Welsh by Miles of Gloucester. About 1148 she gave the mill of Taddewell to the monks of St. Peter, Gloucester for the soul of her late husband, Richard Fitz Gilbert; this gift was confirmed by King Henry II in 1153–4.

Clutterbuck *Hist. & Antiqs. of Hertford* 3 (1827): 225–226 (Clare ped.). *Coll. Top. et Gen.* 1 (1834): 388. Lipscomb *Hist. & Antiqs. of Buckingham* 1 (1847): 200–201 (Clare ped.). Hart *Historia et Cartularium Monasterii Sancti Petri Gloucestriæ* 1 (1863): 104 (undated record that Alice, sister of Ranulph, Earl of Chester, gave the mill of Taddewell for the soul of Richard Fitz Gilbert her husband in the time of Abbot Hamelin [i.e., c. 1148]). *Jour. British Arch. Assoc.* 26 (1870): 149–160. *Arch. Jour.* 2nd Ser. 6 (1899): 221–231. Copinger *Manors of Suffolk* 1 (1905): 45–46 ("Gilbert Lord of Tonbridge died about 1091 and the manor passed with most of the estates to Richard who was taken prisoner by Robert de Beleswe at the siege of Couci in 1091 and is erroneously stated to have died from the effects of his incarceration which was the result. He was the first of the family who bore the title of Earl of Hertford. He acquired vast possessions in Wales as the result of a long continued warfare which he waged somewhat on his own account there. He was in 1136 killed in a combat with the Welsh chieftains Joworth and his brother Morgan-ap-Owen in a woody tract called 'the ill-way of Coed Grano,' near the Abbey of Llanthony."). *C.P.* 3 (1913):243 (sub Clare), 6:498–499, 10 (1945): 441 (author identifies Alice de Tonbridge, wife of William de Percy, on chronological grounds as more likely to be the daughter of Richard Fitz Gilbert; instead of the suggestion made by Round [see preceding generation] that her father was Richard's father Gilbert, who, moreover, had a da. Alice who m. Aubrey de Vere). Marx ed. *Gesta Normannorum Ducum* (1914): 325–326 (Guillaume de Jumièges: "Ricardus autem duxit sororem comitis Rannulfi junioris, comitis Cestriae, et habuit ex ea tres filios: Gislebertum, qui ei successit et fratres ejus."), 331 (Guillaume de Jumièges: "Hujus autem Rannulfi sororem duxit Ricardus, filius Gisleberti; ex qua suscepit tres filios."). Delisle *Recueil des Actes de Henri II* 1 (1916): 67–68 (confirmation charter of King Henry II dated 1153–4). Paget (1957) 130:4–5 (Founder of Stoke-Clare Priory; slain near Brecknock, being ambushed and surprised by Jorwerth, brother of Morgan of Caerleon). Harper-Bill *Stoke by Clare Cartulary* 1 (Suffolk Charters 4) (1982): 30–31 (confirmation charter of Richard Fitz Gilbert, lord of Clare dated 1124–36). Rohan *Domesday Descendants* (2002): 399. Tanner *Fams., Friends, & Allies* (2004): 316 (Clare ped.).

Children of Richard Fitz Gilbert, by Alice of Chester:

i. **GILBERT DE CLARE**, Lord of Clare, etc., son and heir, born before 1115; hostage for his uncle Ranulph, Earl of Chester; succeeded his father in the great family estates (which, besides the honour of Clare, included

Tonbridge Castle), 15 April 1136. He married **LUCY** _____. They had no issue. He was created Earl of Hertford probably by King Stephen in (?1138). He and his uncle, Baldwin Fitz Gilbert, witnessed a charter for King Stephen in 1142. He witnessed a charter of his uncle, Gilbert, Earl of Pembroke, c.1147–8. GILBERT DE CLARE, 1st Earl of Hertford, died between 1151 and 1153, and was buried at Clare Priory. His widow, Lucy, married (2nd) between 1151/1155 (as his 2nd wife) **BALDWIN DE REDVERS**, 1st Earl of Devon (died 4 June 1155). Clutterbuck *Hist. & Antiqs. of Hertford* 3 (1827): 225–226 (Clare ped.). Lipscomb *Hist. & Antiqs. of Buckingham* 1 (1847): 200–201 (Clare ped.). *Jour. of the British Arch. Assoc.* 26 (1870): 149–160. Copinger *Manors of Suffolk* 1 (1905): 45–46. *C.P.* 3 (1913): 244 (sub Clare); 4 (1916): 311–312 (sub Devon); 6 (1926): 498–499 (sub Hertford) ("The Earl of Hertford's wife is unknown: he is generally supposed not to have married"). Leys *Sandford Cartulary* 1 (Oxfordshire Rec. Soc. 19) (1938): 35; 2 (Oxfordshire Rec. Soc. 22) (1941): 229 (charter of Gilbert, Earl of Pembroke dated c.1147–8; charter witnessed by [his nephew] Earl Gilbert de Clare). Ellis *Cat. Seals in the P.R.O.* 2 (1981): 25 (seal of Gilbert, Earl of Clare dated 1139–49 — On horseback, riding to the right. He wears chain mail and conical helmet with nasal, and holds a drawn sword and a shield charged with chevrons of which half only are visible.). Harper-Bill *Stoke by Clare Cartulary* 1 (Suffolk Charters. 4) (1982): 49–50. Beaman *Charters of the Redvers Family & the Earldom of Devon, 1090–1217* (Devon & Cornwall Rec. Soc. n.s. 37) (1994): 5–11, 44, 80–82, 84–85.

ii. **ROGER DE CLARE** (otherwise **ROGER FITZ RICHARD**), 2nd Earl of Hertford [see next].

iii. **ALICE DE CLARE**, married before 1151 **CADWALADR AP GRUFFUDD AP CYNAN,** Prince of North Wales, of Cynfael, Meirion, younger son of Gruffudd ap Cynan, by Angharad, daughter of Owain ab Edwin. They had four sons, Cunedda (or Conan), Randwlff, Gruffudd, and Richard. During his father's lifetime he accompanied his elder brother, Owain, on many predatory excursions against rival princes. In 1121 they ravaged Meirionydd, and apparently conquered it. In 1135 and 1136 they led three successful expeditions to Ceredigion, and managed to get possession of at least the northern portion of that district. In 1137 Owain succeeded, on Gruffudd ap Cynan's death, to the sovereignty of Gwynedd or North Wales. Cadwaladr appears to have found his portion in his former conquests of Meirionydd and northern Ceredigion. The intruder from Gwynedd soon became involved in feuds both with his south Welsh neighbours and with his family. In 1143 his men slew Anarawd, son of Gruffudd of South Wales, to whom Owain Gwynedd had promised his daughter in marriage. Repudiated by his brother, who sent his son Howel to ravage his share of Ceredigion and to attack his castle of Aberystwith, Cadwaladr fled to Ireland, whence he returned next year with a fleet of Irish Danes, to wreak vengeance on Owain. The fleet had already landed at the mouth of the Menai Straits when the intervention of the 'goodmen' of Gwynedd reconciled the brothers. Disgusted at what they probably regarded as treachery, the Irish pirates seized and blinded Cadwaladr, and only released him on the payment of a heavy ransom of 2,000 bondmen (some of the chroniclers say cattle). Their attempt to plunder the country was successfully resisted by Owain. In 1146, however, fresh hostilities broke out between Cadwaladr and his brother's sons Howel and Cynan. They invaded Meirionydd and captured his castle of Cynvael, despite the valiant resistance of his steward, Morvran, abbot of Whitland. This disaster lost Cadwaladr Meirionydd, and so hard was he pressed that, despite his building a castle at Llanrhystyd in Ceredigion (1148), he was compelled to surrender his possessions in that district to his son, apparently in hope of a compromise; but Howel next year captured his cousin and conquered his territory, while the brothers of the murdered Anarawd profited by the dissensions of the princes of Gwynedd to conquer Ceredigion as far north as the Aeron, and soon extended their conquests into Howel's recent acquisitions. Meanwhile Cadwaladr was expelled by Owain from his last refuge in Mona. Cadwaladr now seems to have taken refuge with the English, with whom, if we may believe a late authority, his marriage with a lady of the house of Clare had already connected him (Powel, History of Cambria, p. 232, ed. 1584). The death of Stephen put an end to the long period of Welsh freedom under which Cadwaladr had grown up. In 1156 he was temporarily granted an estate at Ness, Shropshire worth £7 a year. In 1157 Henry II's first expedition to Wales, though by no means a brilliant success, was able to effect Cadwaladr's restoration to his old dominions. Despite his blindness, Cadwaladr had not lost his energy. In 1158 he joined the marcher lords and his nephews in an expedition against Rhys ap Gruffudd of South Wales. In 1165 Cadwaladr took part in the general resistance to Henry II's third expedition to Wales. In 1169 the death of Owain Gwynedd probably weakened his position. In March 1172 Cadwaladr himself died, and was buried in the same tomb as Owain, before the high altar of Bangor Cathedral (Gir. Cambr. It. Camb. in Op. (Rolls ed.), iii. 133).

In 1156 he was temporarily granted an estate at Ness, Shropshire worth £7 a year.

He died in 1172, and was buried before the high altar of Bangor Cathedral. Wynn *Hist. of the Gwydir Fam.* (1827): 20. Price *Hanes Cymru* (1942): 549 (charter of Cadwalader brother of Owain to Haughmond Abbey). Dwnn *Heraldic Vis. of Wales* 2 (1846): 17 ("Kynneda a Rickart a Randiolff, meibion oeddynt hwy y Gydwaladr ab Gr^h ab Kynan o Adles v^h Iarll Kaer y mam hwyntey."). Lipscomb *Hist. & Antiqs. of Buckingham* 1 (1847): 200–201 (Clare ped.).

Burke *Gen. & heraldic Dictionary of the landed Gentry of Great Britain* 1 (1852): 743. *Arch. Cambrensis* 3rd Ser. 6 (1860): 332 (charter of Cadwaladr brother of Owain; charter witnessed by Aliz de Clare his wife); 4th Ser. 6 (1875): 117. Eyton *Antiqs. of Shropshire* 10 (1860): 256–257 ("In 1151, says the Welsh Chronicle, 'Cadwalader, the brother of Prince Owen, escaped out of his Nephew Howel's prison and subdued part of the Ile of Môn, or Anglesey, to himselfe; but his brother Owen sent an armie against him, and chased him thence, who fled to England for succour to his wife's friends, for she was the *daughter* of Gilbert Earl of Clare.' Between 1151 and 1152 Ranulf, Earl of Chester ... confirmed the Monks of Shrewsbury in the possession of all their lands between the Ribble and the Mersey. The Earl's Charter is dated at Chester, and attested as follows. - Testibus, Comite de Clara, et Cadwaladro ... The Earl of Clare here alluded to, was Gilbert. He was Nephew of Earl Ranulph himself, and, in the year 1146, had been given up to Stephen as a hostage for his Uncle's good faith and allegiance. His flight from Stephen's Court is recorded by the Chroniclers. It is evident that he took refuge with his Uncle. He died, in 1152, without issue, and was succeeded by his brother Roger. This fact, as well as a comparison of dates and ages, will show that Cadwalader's wife, Alice, was a *Sister* of Earl Gilbert and a *daughter* of Earl Richard de Clare, and, finally, a niece of Ranulph, Earl of Chester. For a time he [Cadwallader] remained in alliance with the English, as when, in 1159, he assisted the Earls of Clare and of Bristol to relieve Carmarthen, then besieged by Prince Rese of South Wales. He was also a munificent Benefactor to Haughmond Abbey. In 1165 he is found leagued with Owen Gwyneth against the English, and probably retained that adverse position till his death in 1172."). Nicholas *Annals & Antiqs. of the Counties & County Fams. of Wales* 1 (1872): 43; foll. 442. Lloyd *Hist. of the Princes, the Lords Marcher & the Ancient Nobility of Powys Fadog* 1 (1881): 96, 107, 151; 4 (1884): 323, 341; 5 (1885): 367. *D.N.B.* 3 (1908): 642–643 (biog. of Cadwaladr). Lloyd *Hist. of Wales* 2 (1911): 76, 93–101, 315, 317. Fryde *Handbook of British Chron.* (1996): 50. Maund *Gruffudd ap Cynan* (1996). *Jour. Medieval Military Hist.* 2 (2004): 58. Pryce *Acts of Welsh rulers, 1120–1283* (2005): 330–331. Hosler *Henry II* (2007): 54.

Child of Alice de Clare, by Cadwaladr:

a. CONAN AP CADWALADR. Ward *Women of the English Nobility & Gentry 1066–1500* (1995): 42; 93–94 (charter of Maud, wife of Roger earl of Clare dated 1152–73; charter witnessed by Richard brother of the earl and Conan nephew of the earl).

iv. **ROHESE DE CLARE**, married (1st) **GILBERT DE GANT**, Earl of Lincoln [see GANT 2.i], (2nd) **ROBERT FITZ ROBERT**, of Ilkley, Yorkshire [see GANT 2.i].

4. ROGER DE CLARE (otherwise **ROGER FITZ RICHARD**), 2nd Earl of Hertford (also styled Earl of Clare), younger son. He married **MAUD DE SAINT HILARY**, daughter and heiress of James de Saint Hilary, of Field Dalling, Norfolk, by his wife, Aveline. They had four sons, Richard [3rd Earl of Hertford (or Clare)], John, Richard [2nd of name], and James, and one daughter, Aveline. He was heir in 1153 to his older brother, Gilbert de Clare, 1st Earl of Hertford. In the period, 1153–73, he confirmed the grant which Walter Fountains and subsequently Tebaud Sorrel made of four acres in Norton in Finchingfield, Essex to the Hospitallers. He accompanied King Henry II to France on at least two occasions, once probably in 1156, when he is found at the Siege of Chinon, and once in the winter of 1160–61. In 1157, and in the following years, he was engaged against Rhys ap Gryffydd in Wales. In 1163 he disputed with Thomas Becket, Archbishop of Canterbury regarding the latter's claim for fealty in respect of Tonbridge Castle. In 1164 he took part in the Constitutions of Clarendon. Sometime before 1164 he and his brother, Richard, witnessed a charter of Walter Giffard, Earl of Buckingham, to Newington Longueville Priory. In 1166 he certified his barony as consisting of 149 knights fees. In 1170 he was a commissioner to enquire into the proceedings of the sheriffs in Kent, Surrey, Middlesex, Berkshire, Oxfordshire, and Bedfordshire. Sometime before his death, he gave the church of Barton Bendish, Norfolk to the monks of Bec dwelling at St. Neot's. His wife, Maud, gave a mark of silver to the nuns of Godstow for the health of the soul of the Earl her husband. ROGER DE CLARE, 2nd Earl of Hertford (or Clare), died in 1173, and was buried at Stoke by Clare Priory, Suffolk. In the period, 1173–76, his widow, Maud, granted the monks of St. Andrew, Northampton her mill of Shipton under Wychwood, Oxfordshire. She married (2nd) before Michaelmas 1176 **WILLIAM D'AUBENEY**, 2nd Earl of Arundel (or Sussex) [see CLIFTON 4], Chief Butler of England, Privy Councillor, Constable of Windsor Castle, 1191–3, son and heir of William d'Aubeney, 1st Earl of Arundel (or Sussex), Chief

Butler of England, by Alice, Queen Dowager of England, daughter of Gottfried (or Godefroy) I, Duke of Lower Lorraine, Count of Louvain [see CLIFTON 3 for his ancestry]. They had three sons, William [3rd Earl of Arundel], Alan, and Godfrey (or Geoffrey). In 1176/7 he was confirmed as Earl of Sussex, but the Castle and Honour of Arundel were, in accordance with the policy of King Henry II, retained by the Crown. He served as assessor in the royal court in 1177 to arbitrate between the Kings of Castile and Navarre. He was granted restoration of the Castle and Honour of Arundel by King Richard I 27 June 1190, when he became Earl of Arundel. In 1194 he was one of the Receivers of the money raised for the king's ransom. At an unknown date, he granted various lands in Quiddenham, Norfolk to Reading Abbey, Berkshire. WILLIAM D'AUBENEY, Earl of Arundel, died 24 Dec. 1196, and was buried at Wymondham Priory, Norfolk.

Dugdale *Monasticon Anglicanum* 3 (1821): 24 (charter of Maud de Clare), 474 (charters of Roger de Clare, Earl of Hertford to Priory of St. Neot); 6(2) (1830): 834 (reference to a charter to Templars by Maud, Countess of Clare, wife of William [sic] Earl of Clare, and mother of Richard, Earl of Clare). Clutterbuck *Hist. & Antiqs. of Hertford* 3 (1827): 225–226 (Clare ped.). Tierney *Hist. & Antiqs. of the Castle & Town of Arundel* 1 (1834): 179–180. Lipscomb *Hist. & Antiqs. of Buckingham* 1 (1847): 200–201 (Clare ped.). Barrett *Memorials of the parochial Church ... in the Parish of Attleborough* (1848): 12–41. *Arch. Journal* 22 (1865): 154 (undated charter of William d'Aubeney, Earl of Sussex to Reading Abbey; charter names Queen Alice his mother [Regine Adelize matris mee], Jocelin the castellan his uncle [avunculi], charter is witnessed by Reiner his brother [fratre]), 155 (undated charter of William d'Aubeney, Earl of Sussex to Reading Abbey; charter names Jocelin his uncle [avunculi]; charter is witnessed by Reiner his brother [fratre]). *Jour. British Arch. Assoc.* (1867): 21–33; 26 (1870): 149–160. Delisle *Chronique de Robert de Torigni* 2 (1873): 41 (sub A.D. 1173 — "Obiit etiam Rogerius, comes de Clara, cui successit Ricardus, filius ejus, qui duxit filiam Guillermi comitis Gloecestriæ."), 63–64 (sub A.D. 1176 — "Qui Guillermus [de Albineio] duxit relictam Rogerii comitis de Clara, filiam Jacobi de Sancto Hilario, cum omni terra quam idem Jacobus habuerat in Anglia."). Doyle *Official Baronage of England* 1 (1886): 66–67 (sub Arundel). *C.P.* 1 (1910): 235–236, 237 (chart) (sub Arundel); 3 (1913): 244 (1913); 5 (1926): 124; 6 (1926): 499–501 (sub Clare). *Genealogist* n.s. 34 (1918): 181–189. Harvey et al. *Vis. of the North* 3 (Surtees Soc. 144) (1930): 152–156 (Daubeny ped.: "Willelmus (nomen cepit in parliamento consulatus [sic MS.] Sussex et Arundell construxit capellam beate Thome in Wimondham et sepelitur in abbathia predicta) *Daubeney comes Arundel ob. 22 H. 2.* = [empty roundel] *Matilda filia et heres Iacobi de Sancto Hillario relicta Rogeri comitis Clara.*"). Stenton *Facsimiles of Early Charters from Northamptonshire Colls.* (Northamptonshire Rec. Soc. 4) (1930): 130–131 (charter of Maud, Countess of Clare, daughter of James de Saint Hilaire dated 1173–76; charter witnessed by her son, James). *Paget* (1957) 130:5. Sanders *English Baronies* (1960): 34–35, 44. Ross *Cartulary of Cirencester Abbey* 2 (1964): 526–568. Holdsworth *Rufford Charters* (Thoroton Soc. Rec. Ser. 30) (1974): 392. Harper-Bill *Stoke by Clare Cartulary* 1 (Suffolk Charters 4) (1982): 20 (confirmation charter of Roger, Earl of Hertford dated 1152–73; charter witnessed by his son, Richard, and his brother, Richard), 20 (writ of Roger de Clare, Earl of Hertford, dated 1152–73), 21 (confirmation charter of Roger, Earl of Hertford dated shortly after 1152 granted for the soul of Gilbert his brother deceased; charter names his grandfather, Gilbert Fitz Richard), 21–22 (charter of Roger de Clare, Earl of Hertford dated 1166–73; charter witnessed by his brother, Richard de Clare), 22 (writ of Roger, Earl of Hertford possibly dated 1157), 22–23 (writ of Roger, Earl of Clare dated shortly after 1152 to his grandmother, Aelicie de Clermunt, Peter his seneschal, and her men of Norfolk; charter names his father, Richard, and his grandfather, Gilbert) 23 (confirmation charter of Roger de Clare, Earl of Hertford dated 1152–73), 23–24 (confirmation charter of Roger de Clare, Earl of Hertford dated 1152–66; charter names Earl Gilbert his brother; charter witnessed by his brother, Richard de Clare), 24 (notification by Roger, Earl of Clare dated 1152–73), 24–25 (confirmation charter of Roger de Clare, Earl of Hertford dated 1152–73; charter names his brother, Earl Gilbert, his father, Richard, and his grandfather, Gilbert), 25–30 (general confirmation charter of Roger, Earl of Clare dated 1152–73). Cheney *English Episcopal Acta III: Canterbury 1193–1205* (1986): 254–255. Barraclough *Charters of the Anglo-Norman Earls of Chester, c. 1071–1237* (Roger Fitz Richard styled "nephew" [nepos] of Ranulph II, Earl of Chester). Gervers *Cartulary of the Knights of St. John of Jerusalem in England: Secunda Camera/ Essex* 1 (Recs. of Social & Econ. Hist. n.s. 6) (1982): 216 (charter of Earl Roger de Clare dated c.1152–c.1173). Ward *Women of the English Nobility & Gentry 1066–1500* (1995): 42; 93–94 (charter of Maud, wife of Roger earl of Clare dated 1152–73; charter witnessed by Richard brother of the earl and Conan nephew of the earl).

Children of Roger de Clare, by Maud de St. Hilary:

i. **RICHARD DE CLARE**, 3rd Earl of Hertford [see next].

ii. **AVELINE DE CLARE**, married (1st) before 1186 **WILLIAM DE MUNCHENSY**, Knt., of Swanscombe, Kent, Winfarthing and Gooderstone, Norfolk, etc., younger son of Warin de Munchensy, by Agnes, daughter and co-heiress of Pain Fitz John. They had two sons, William and Warin, Knt. He was heir before Michaelmas 1190 to his older brother, Ralph de Munchensy, Knt. In 1198 he was serving in Normandy. He was one of the guarantors of the treaty between King John and the Count of Flanders at Roche d'Andelys in 1199. He was fined for not serving overseas in 1201. He was a benefactor of the religious houses of West Dereham and Missenden. SIR WILLIAM DE MUNCHENSY died before 7 May 1204. His widow, Aveline, married (2nd) before 29 May 1205 (date of grant) (as his 2nd wife) **GEOFFREY FITZ PETER**, Knt., Earl of Essex [see ESSEX 2], of Wellsworth (in Chalton), Hampshire, Cherhill and Costow, Wiltshire, Chief Forester, Sheriff of Northamptonshire, 1184–89, 1191–94, Sheriff of Essex and Hertfordshire, 1190–93, Constable of Hertford Castle, Justiciar of England, 1198–1213, Sheriff of Staffordshire, 1198, Sheriff of Yorkshire, 1198–1200, 1202–4, Sheriff of Bedfordshire and Buckinghamshire, 1199–1204, Sheriff of Westmorland, 1199–1200, Sheriff of Hampshire, 1201–4, Sheriff of Shropshire, 1201–4, and, in right of his 1st wife, of Streatley, Berkshire, Amersham and Quarrendon, Buckinghamshire, Pleshey, Essex, Digswell, Hertfordshire, Kimbolton, Huntingdonshire, etc., younger son of Peter de Ludgershall, of Cherhill and Linley (in Tisbury), Wiltshire, and Gussage Saint Andrew (in Sixpenny Handley), Dorset, by his wife, Maud. He was born before 1145. They had one son, John, Knt., and four daughters, Hawise, Cecily, _____, and Maud. Sometime in the period, 1157–66, he witnessed an exchange of land between Roger de Tichborne and the Bishop of Winchester. He held a fee in Cherhill, Wiltshire of new enfeoffment in 1166. Sometime in the period, c.1166–90, Elias de Studley conveyed to him his land held of the fee of William Malbanc in Heytesbury and Cherhill, Wiltshire at an annual rent of 20s. In 1184 he accounted for the farm of Kinver before the itinerant justices in Oxfordshire. He married (1st) before 25 Jan. 1184/5 **BEATRICE DE SAY** (died before 19 April 1197), daughter and co-heiress of William de Say, of Kimbolton, Huntingdonshire, and Saham, Norfolk [see SAY 4.i for her ancestry]. They had three sons, Geoffrey de Mandeville [5th Earl of Essex], William de Mandeville, Knt. [6th Earl of Essex], and Henry [Dean of Wolverhampton], and two daughters, Maud and Alice. In 1186–7 King Henry II granted him the manor of Cherhill, Wiltshire, to hold in fee and inheritance by the service of one knight, as his father Peter or his brother Robert held it. In the period, 1186–89, he and his two half-brothers, William and Hugh de Buckland, witnessed a charter of William, Earl of Ferrers, to Ralph Fitz Stephen. In the period, c.1189–99, he founded Shouldham Abbey, Norfolk, to which he gave the manor and the advowson of the church of Shouldham, Norfolk, together with the churches of Shouldham Thorpe, Stoke Ferry, and Wereham, Norfolk. In 1190 he obtained the lands to which his 1st wife's grandmother, Beatrice, had become heir on the death of her nephew, William de Mandeville, Earl of Essex. From Easter 1190 he received the third penny of the county of Essex. Sometime in the period, 1190–1213, Sibyl de Fiennes, daughter of Pharamus of Boulogne, conveyed to him 300 acres on Hyngeshill [?in Quarrendon, Buckinghamshire] at an annual rent of an unmewed sparrowhawk, or 12d. Sometime in the period, 1190–1213, he granted the manor of Cherhill, Wiltshire to his younger son, William de Mandeville. He was one of those excommunicated for his part in removing Longchamp in 1191. About 1195 he and his two half-brothers, William and Geoffrey de Buckland, witnessed a charter of Geoffrey Fitz Nigel de Gardino to William de Ultra la Haia. In 1195 he owed £4 4s. in the vill of Lydford, Devon for making the market of the king there. In 1198 Eustace de Balliol and his wife, Pernel (widow of Geoffrey's brother Robert), quitclaimed all their right to lands in Salthrop (in Wroughton), Wiltshire to Geoffrey, in return for 30 marks silver. In the period, 1199–1216, Geoffrey further gave Shouldham Priory, Norfolk twelve shops, with the rooms over them, in the parish of St. Mary's Colechurch, London, for the purpose of sustaining the lights of the church and of providing the sacramental wine. Sometime in or before 1199, he made a grant to William de Wrotham, Archdeacon of Taunton, of all his land of Sutton at Hone, Kent to make a hospital for the maintenance of thirteen poor men and three chaplains in honour of the Holy Trinity, St. Mary, and All Saints. In the period, 1200–13, he made notification that Abbot Ralph and the convent of Westminster had at his petition confirmed to the nuns of Shouldham all tithes pertaining to them in Clakelose Hundred, Norfolk, in return for £1 10s. due annually to the almoner of Westminster. In the same period, Abbot Ralph and the convent of Westminster granted him the vill of Claygate, Surrey to hold of them for his lifetime. In 1204 King John granted him the manor of Winterslow, Wiltshire, and, in 1205, the honour of Berkhampstead, Hertfordshire with the castle at a fee farm of £100 per annum. He campaigned against the Welsh in 1206 and 1210. He was granted a significant part of the lands forfeited by Normans, including the manors of Depden and Hatfield Peverel, Essex, and other lands in Norfolk and Suffolk, all worth over £100 per annum. In 1207 the king confirmed his possession of the manor of Notgrove, Gloucestershire, which Geoffrey had by the gift of John Eskelling. Sometime before 1212, he was granted the manor of Gussage Dynaunt (or Gussage St. Michael), Dorset, which manor was forfeited by Roland de Dinan. At some unspecified date, when already earl, he granted all his right in St. Peter's chapel in Drayton to the canons of St. Peter's Cathedral, York. He was the founder of the first church of Wintney Priory, Hampshire. SIR GEOFFREY FITZ PETER, Earl of Essex, died 14 October 1213, and was buried in Shouldham Priory, Norfolk. In 1213–4 the king commanded Geoffrey de Buckland to let the king have, at the price any others would give for them, the corn, pigs, and other chattels at Berkhampstead, Hertfordshire which belonged his brother, Geoffrey Fitz Peter, lately deceased. About 1214 his widow, Aveline, granted the canons of Holy Trinity, London, in frank almoin, a half mark quit rent out of her manor of Towcester, Northamptonshire, part of whose body is buried there. In 1221 the Prior of the Hospital of Jerusalem in England sued her regarding two virgates and five acres of land in Towcester, Northamptonshire.

Aveline, Countess of Essex, died before 4 June 1225. Blomefield *Essay towards a Top. Hist. of Norfolk* 7 (1807): 414–427. Clutterbuck *Hist. & Antiq. of the County of Hertford* 1 (1815): 293 (Fitz Peter ped.). Montmorency-Morres *Genealogical Memoir of the Fam. of Montmorency* (1817): xxxii–xxxvi. Baker *Hist. & Antiqs. of Northampton* 1 (1822–1830): 544–545 (Mandeville-Fitz Peter-Bohun ped.). Dugdale *Monasticon Anglicanum* 5 (1825): 721–722; 6(1) (1830): 339–340; 6(3) (1830): 1191 (charter of Geoffrey Fitz Peter). Clutterbuck *Hist. & Antiqs. of Hertford* 3 (1827): 190–194 (Mandeville-Say ped.). Luard *Annales Monastici* 2 (Rolls Ser. 36) (1865): 273 (Annals of Waverley sub A.D. 1213: "Obiit Gaufridus filius Petri comes de Essexe, et justitiarius totius Angliæ, tunc temporis cunctis in Anglia præstantior."). *Notes & Queries* 4th Ser. 3 (1869): 484–485 (Fitz Peter ped.). Clark *Earls, Earldom, & Castle of Pembroke* (1880): 76–114. Lee *Hist., Desc. & Antiqs. of ...Thame* (1883): 332 (Mandeville ped.). Maitland *Bracton's Note Book* 2 (1887): 193–194; 3 (1887): 452–453. Round *Ancient Charters Royal & Private Prior to A.D. 1200* (Pipe Roll Soc. 10) (1888): 97–99 (confirmation by King Richard I dated 1191 to Geoffrey Fitz Peter and Beatrice his wife, as rightful and next heirs, of all the land of Earl William de Mandeville, which was hers by hereditary right), 108–110 (confirmation by King Richard I dated 1198 of the division of their inheritance made by Beatrice and Maud, daughters and co-heirs of William de Say, in the time of his father, King Henry II). *Desc. Cat. Ancient Deeds* 2 (1894): 91, 93. Moore *Cartularium Monasterii Sancti Johannis Baptiste de Colecestria* 2 (1897): 349–350, 354, 371–372. *Feet of Fines of King Richard I A.D. 1197 to A.D. 1198* (Pubs. Pipe Roll Soc. 23) (1898): 36–37, 58–59, 85, 130–131. *List of Sheriffs for England & Wales* (PRO Lists and Indexes 9) (1898): 1, 43, 54, 92, 117, 127, 150, 161. *Feet of Fines of King Richard I A.D. 1198 to A.D. 1199* (Pubs. Pipe Roll Soc. 24) (1900): 15. VCH *Norfolk* 2 (1906): 412–414. VCH *Essex* 2 (1907): 110–115; 4 (1956): 158–162. Salter *Eynsham Cartulary* 2 (Oxford Hist. Soc. 51) (1908): 224–225. VCH *Hertford* 3 (1912): 81–85, 501–511. *Genealogist* n.s. 34 (1918): 181–189 (two charters of Geoffrey Fitz Peter, Earl of Essex, and two charters of his widow, Aveline, Countess of Essex). *Book of Fees* 1 (1920): 91–92. Fowler & Hughes *Cal. of the Pipe Rolls of the Reign of Richard I for Buckinghamshire & Bedfordshire, 1189–1199* (Pubs. Bedfordshire Hist. Rec. Soc. 7) (1923): 215, 218–219. VCH *Berkshire* 3 (1923): 511–516. VCH *Buckingham* 3 (1925): 141–155; 4 (1927): 100–102. *C.P.* 5 (1926): 122–125 (sub Essex), 437 (chart) (sub Fitz John); 9 (1936):420 (sub Munchensy). VCH *Kent* 2 (1926): 175–176. Foster *Registrum Antiquissimum of the Cathedral Church of Lincoln* 3 (Lincoln Rec. Soc. 29) (1935): 216–218. Gibbs *Early Charters of the Cathedral Church of St. Paul* (Camden Soc. 3rd Ser. 58) (1939): 34–37, 41, 92–93, 255–256. *C.R.R.* 10 (1949): 24, 103, 228. Hassall *Cartulary of St. Mary Clerkenwell* (Camden 3rd ser. 71) (1949): 100–101. *Paget* (1957) 130:5 (see *Genealogist* n.s. 14:181). West *Justiciarship in England, 1066–1232* (1966). Elvey *Luffield Priory Charters* 1 (Buckingham Rec. Soc. 22) (1968): 174–176. Chew & Weimbaum *London Eyre of 1244* (London Rec. Soc. 6) (1970): 118. VCH *Hampshire* 2 (1973) 149–151; 3 (1908): 107; 4 (1911): 79–81. Burton *Cartulary of the Treasurer of York Minster* (Borthwick Texts & Cals.: Recs. of the Northern Province 5) (1978): 52–53 (charter of Geoffrey Fitz Peter, Earl of Essex dated 1199–1212). London *Cartulary of Bradenstoke Priory* (Wiltshire Rec. Soc. 35) (1979): 85, 165–168. Mason *Beauchamp Cartulary Charters* (Pipe Roll Soc. n.s. 43) (1980): 186–187, 189–190, 191 (charter dated 1190–1213 of Geoffrey Fitz Peter, Earl of Essex, to his son, William de Mandeville), 194–197. Holt *Acta of Henry II and Richard I* (List & Index Soc. Special Ser. 21) (1986): 193, 202–203. Mason *Westminster Abbey Charters, 1066–c.1214* (London Rec. Soc. 25) (1988): 308–309 (charter of Geoffrey Fitz Peter, Earl of Essex; charter witnessed by Geoffrey de Bocland. Seal on tag — obverse: earl of horseback, brandishing a sword. Legend: SI[GILLUM GAUFRIDI COMITI]S EXIE +; Counterseal: six-petalled flower (worn); Legend: ...IL...ETRI...), 309, 314–315 (charter of Geoffrey Fitz Peter, Earl of Essex). Brand *Earliest English Law Reports* 1 (Selden Soc., vol. 111) (1996): 16–17, 84–91. Turner *Men Raised from the Dust* (1988): 35–70 (biog. of Geoffrey Fitz Peter), App. Chart A (Fitz Peter ped.). *Haskins Soc. Jour.* 1 (1989): 147–172. Franklin *English Episcopal Acta* 8 (1993): 78–79. Ward *Women of the English Nobility & Gentry 1066–1500* (1995): 100–101. Thorley *Docs. in Medieval Latin* (1998): 53–55. Breay *Cartulary of Chatteris Abbey* (1999): 151. Greenway *Book of the Foundation of Walden Monastery* (1999): xxviii–xxx. Norfolk Rec. Office: Hare Family, Baronets of Stow Bardolph, Hare 2706 198 x 4 (available at www.a2a.org.uk/search/index.asp).

Child of Aveline de Clare, by William de Munchensy:

a. **WARIN DE MUNCHENSY**, Knt., of Swanscombe, Kent, married (1st) **JOAN MARSHAL** [see MARSHAL 4]; (2nd) **DENISE DE ANESTY** [see MARSHAL 4].

Children of Aveline de Clare, by Geoffrey Fitz Peter, Knt.:

a. **JOHN FITZ GEOFFREY**, Knt., of Shere, Surrey, Fambridge, Essex, etc., married **ISABEL LE BIGOD** [see VERDUN 8].

b. **HAWISE FITZ GEOFFREY**, married **REYNOLD DE MOHUN**, Knt., of Dunster, Somerset [see MOHUN ??].

c. **CECILY FITZ GEOFFREY**, married **SAVARY DE BOHUN**, of Midhurst, Sussex [see MIDHURST 3].

d. _____ **FITZ GEOFFREY**. She married **WILLIAM DE LA ROCHELLE**, of South Ockendon, Essex, Market Lavington, Wiltshire, etc. [see HARLESTON 3].

e. **MAUD FITZ GEOFFREY**, married (1st) **HENRY D'OILLY**, of Hook Norton, Oxfordshire, King's Constable [see CANTELOWE 4]; (2nd) **WILLIAM DE CANTELOWE**, Knt., of Eaton Bray, Bedfordshire, Steward of the Royal Household [see CANTELOWE 4].

5. RICHARD DE CLARE, Knt., 3rd Earl of Hertford (also styled Earl of Clare), of Clare, Suffolk, son and heir. He married **AMICE OF GLOUCESTER**, daughter and co-heiress of William Fitz Robert, 2nd Earl of Gloucester, lord of Glamorgan and Caerleon, seigneur of Torigny in Manche, Normandy, etc., by Hawise, daughter of Robert of Meulan, Knt., 1st Earl of Leicester [see GLOUCESTER 4 for her ancestry]. Her maritagium included the town of Sudbury, Suffolk and 6-½ knights fees in Kent. They had four sons, Gilbert, Knt. [Earl of Gloucester and Hertford], Richard, Roger, and Henry, and three daughters, Maud, Hawise, and [?Joan] (wife of Rhys Gryg, lord of Dynevor or Ystradtywi, Prince of South Wales). Sometime in or before 1172 he gave assent to the grant of his father, Earl Roger de Clare to the Hospital of St. John of Jerusalem of the advowson of Tonbridge, Kent. He and his father-in-law, William, Earl of Gloucester, were both suspected of complicity, if not direct involvement, in the rebellion of Earl Hugh le Bigod in 1173–4. Clare subsequently supported the king, when the king's son, Henry, rebelled against his father. In the period, 1185–1214, he gave the advowson of the church of Yalding with the chapel of Brenchley, Kent to the church of St. Mary Magdalene, Tonbridge, Kent. In 1188 he and Roger le Bigod, Earl of Norfolk, disputed for the honor of carrying the banner of St. Edmund in battle. He was present at the Coronation of King Richard I at Westminster in 1189. In 1191 he was one of the eleven appointed by the Chancellor to determined the questions between himself and Prince John. In 1193 he was enjoined by the Chancellor to accompany him on his return to King Richard, then a prisoner in Germany. In 1194/5 he had acquittance as being with the King in the army in Normandy. At the start of the reign of King Richard I the barony of Long Crendon, Buckinghamshire (which had escheated to the crown in 1164) was divided between him and William Marshal, Knt., later Earl of Pembroke. He had a grant from King John of a moiety of the Giffard estates in Normandy and England. In 1198 he excused himself from personal attendance on the king at Hertford. Sometime before Michaelmas 1198, Earl Richard and his wife, Amice, were separated by order of the Pope on grounds of consanguinity, at which date she claimed the town of Sudbury, Suffolk, which had been her marriage portion. They were evidently divorced by 1200, when Amice was styled "formerly the Countess of Clare." In 1202–3 she repeated her claim to the town of Sudbury, Suffolk, and, in 1205–7, she claimed the advowson of St. Gregories, Sudbury, Suffolk, which the Prioress of Eton said had been granted to Eton by Earl William, Amice's father. The issue of the validity of their marriage was presumably resolved, as Amice styled herself in later charters the "Countess of Clare." Regardless, they appeared to have been estranged at the time of Earl Richard's death, as her charters make no mention of her husband, but only their son and heir, Gilbert. In 1201 he paid £100 in order to obtain possession of the manor of Saham, Norfolk by writ of mort d'ancestor against Roger de Tony, but Tony subsequently recovered the manor. Sometime prior to 1206, he granted the church of Yalding, Kent with the chapelry of Brenchley to Tonbridge Priory. In 1211 Amice, Countess of Clare, offered 40 marks for the recovery of certain fees of which she had been disseised by Guy de Chanceaux. In 1214 the canons of Nutley Abbey secured the church of Bottesham, Cambridgeshire against Richard de Clare. He joined the confederacy of the barons against the king in 1215. He was one of the twenty-five barons elected to guarantee the observance of Magna Carta, which King John signed 15 June 1215. In consequence he was among the barons excommunicated by Pope Innocent III 16 Dec. 1215. On 9 Nov. 1215 he was one of the commissioners on the part of the Barons to treat of peace with the king. On returning to fealty 5 October 1217, he had restitution of his lands. On the death of her sister,

Isabel, Countess of Gloucester (former wife of King John) in 1217, Amice became sole heir to their father, William, Earl of Gloucester. SIR RICHARD DE CLARE, Earl of Hertford, died between 30 October and 28 Nov. 1217. Following his death, Tonbridge Priory petitioned the bishop to grant indulgence "to all who pray for the soul of Sir Richard de Clare, formerly Earl of Hertford, whose body lies in the church of St. Mary Magdalen of Tonbridge, and the souls of all faithful departed deceased and those who have assisted in the building or upkeep of the lights, etc." of the church of St. Mary Magdalen in Tonbridge. His widow, Amice, caused the earl's body to be carried to Tewkesbury Abbey, Gloucestershire, where it was buried in the choir of the Abbey. In the period, 1217–23, in her widowhood ["viduetate mea"], she gave to Stoke by Clare Priory a messuage and possessions of the hospital of St. Sepulchre in Sudbury, Suffolk. In the period, 1217–36, Amice, Countess of Clare, in her widowhood ["viduitate mea'] confirmed grants made to Margam Abbey by her grandfather, Robert, Earl of Gloucester, and William, Earl of Gloucester. At an unknown date, Countess Amice founded the hospital of St. Sepulchre in Sudbury, Suffolk, as well as one dedicated to Jesus Christ and the Blessed Virgin Mary. At an unknown date, Amice granted Abraham Fitz Ralph of Thaxted three acres at Holgate in her fee at Sudbury, Suffolk at a yearly rent of 12*d*. Amice, Countess of Clare, allegedly died 1 January 1224/5.[8]

Placitorum in Domo Capitulari Westmonasteriensi Asservatorum Abbrevatio (1811): 36. Dugdale *Monasticon Anglicanum* 2 (1819): 59–65; 6(2) (1830): 806–807 (charter of Richard de Clare, Earl of Hertford), 913 (charter of Richard [de Clare], Earl of Hertford); 6(3) (1830): 1658–1659 (charters of Amice, Countess of Clare, daughter of William Earl of Gloucester). Clutterbuck *Hist. & Antiqs. of Hertford* 3 (1827): 225–226 (Clare ped.). Thomson *Hist. Essay on the Magna Charta of King John* (1829): 270–272 (biog. of Richard de Clare). Palgrave *Rotuli Curiæ Regis* 2 (1835): 180. Lipscomb *Hist. & Antiqs. of Buckingham* 1 (1847): 200–201 (Clare ped.). *Jour. British Arch. Assoc.* 26 (1870): 149–160. Delisle *Chronique de Robert de Torigni* 2 (1873): 41 (sub A.D. 1173 — "Obiit etiam Rogerius, comes de Clara, cui successit Ricardus, filius ejus, qui duxit filiam Guillermi comitis Gloecestriæ."). Matthew of Paris *Chronica Majora* 2 (Rolls Ser. 57) (1874): 604–605, 642–644. Turner *Cal. Charters & Rolls: Bodleian Lib.* (1878): 127. Clark *Land of Morgan* (1883): 64–92 ("Earl Richard's seal is extant, and bears the three chevrons."). Doyle *Official Baronage of England* 2 (1886): 176 (sub Hertford). Birch *Cat. Seals in the British Museum* 2 (1892): 268–269 (seal of Richard de Clare, Earl of Hertford — To the right. In hauberk, surcoat, conical helmet, sword, kite-shaped shield. Legend wanting.). Delaville le Roulx *Cartulaire Général de l'Ordre des Hospitaliers de S. Jean de Jérusalem* 1 (1894): 298–299 (charter dated 1172-99 by Richard de Clare, Earl of Hertford); charter names his father, Earl Roger; and his mother, Countess Maud; charter witnessed by

---

[8] *C.P.* 6 (1926): 503 (sub Hertford) says Amice de Clare, Countess of Hertford "is stated to have died 1 January 1224/5, before which date she appears to have been recognized as Countess of Gloucester." This statement regarding her being acknowledged Countess of Gloucester appears to be without foundation. In Amice's own charters which have survived and in contemporary records, she is styled solely as Countess of Clare (i.e., Hertford), and never as Countess of Gloucester [see, for instance, Dugdale *Monasticon Anglicanum* 6(3) (1830): 1658–1659 (charters of Amice, Countess of Clare, daughter of William Earl of Gloucester); Fry & Fry *Abs. of Feet of Fines Rel. Dorset* 1 (Dorset Rec. Soc. 5) (1896): 26; Clark *Cartæ et Alia Munimenta de Glamorgancia* 2 (1910): 358 (charter of Amice, Countess of Clare, widow); Harper-Bill *Stoke by Clare Cartulary* 1 (Suffolk Charters 4) (1982): 41-48 (charters of Amice, Countess of Clare); Mortimer *Charters of St. Bartholomew's Priory* (Suffolk Charters 15) (1996): 25–26 (charter of Amice, Countess of Clare)]. Rather, Dugdale *Monasticon Anglicanum* 1 (1817): 33 states that Amice's son and heir, Gilbert de Clare, took up the twin earldoms of Gloucester and Hertford in 1217, which occurred during his mother's lifetime. In Nov. 1217, shortly after the death of his aunt, Isabel, Countess of Gloucester, Gilbert confirmed several benefactions as Earl of Gloucester and Hertford [see Stevenson *Durford Cartulary* (Sussex Rec. Soc. 90) (2006): 81]. In the same month there was a plea between Gilbert de Clare, Earl of Gloucester, and William de Cauntelo and his wife, Milicent, widow of Amaury, Count of Evreux. Livery of various lands was also ordered [see *C.P.* 5 (1926): 694 (sub Gloucester)]. Gilbert certainly had possession of the Gloucester inheritance before 1220/1, when the Pipe Rolls sub Norfolk and Suffolk state that "Isti habunt quietancias per brevia … Comes de Clara de 131 f etc." [see *Great Roll of the Pipe* Michaelmas 1221, cited in *C.P.* 6 (1926): 503, footnote c]. Presumably Amice was excluded from the Gloucester inheritance by the terms of her father's agreement with King Henry II in 1176, by which King Henry's son, John (later King John) was acknowledged as heir to William Earl of Gloucester (as future husband of his youngest daughter, Isabel); in return for this grant, the king agreed to give £100 yearly rental to Earl William's older daughters, Mabel and Amice [see Lambert *Bletchingley: A Parish Hist.* 1 (1921): 53–54, 59, footnote 2].

his "brothers" [fratribus], Richard de Clare and James de Clare. Fry & Fry *Abs. of Feet of Fines Rel. Dorset* 1 (Dorset Rec. Soc. 5) (1896): 26. *Genealogist* n.s. 13 (1896): 98; n.s. 34 (1918): 181–189 (charter of Richard de Clare, Earl of Hertford; charter names his parents, Earl Roger and Countess Maud). Rye *Cal. Feet of Fines for Suffolk* (1900): 13. Ramsay *Angevin Empire* (1903): 195. VCH *Buckingham* 1 (1905): 377. Wrottesley *Peds. from the Plea Rolls* (1905): 146. VCH *Hampshire* 3 (1908): 85–93. Clark *Cartæ et Alia Munimenta de Glamorgancia* 2 (1910): 343, 358 (charter of Amice, Countess of Clare, widow to Margam Abbey). Lambert *Bletchingley* 1 (1921): 52–59. *Curia Regis Rolls* 1 (1922): 186, 249; 4 (1929): 13, 15, 139–140, 172; 6 (1932): 3, 30, 89, 108, 358; 14 (1961): 92; 15 (1972): 343. *C.P.* 5 (1926): 694–696 (sub Gloucester); 6 (1926): 501–503 (sub Hertford) ("Whatever the nature of the separation of the Earl and Countess, it did not affect the position of their son, Gilbert."). *English Hist. Rev.* 61 (1946): 292, footnote 2. Hethe *Reg. Hamonis Hethe Diocesis Roffensis* 1 (Canterbury & York Soc. 48) (1948): 15, 17 (charter of Richard de Clare dated 1185–1214), 18–19, 45. Paget *Baronage of England* (1957) 130: 6. Sanders *English Baronies* (1960): 6, 34–35, 63. Ross *Cartulary of Cirencester Abbey* 2 (1964): 436–437, 563–564. Cheney *Letters of Pope Innocent III 1198–1216* (1967): 172. Gervers *Hospitaller Cartulary in the British Museum* (1981): 304 (charter of Richard de Clare). Gervers *Cartulary of the Knights of St. John of Jerusalem in England, Secunda Camera, Essex* (Recs. of Social and Econ. Hist. n.s. 6) (1982): 548 (charter of Richard de Clare, Earl of Hertford). Harper-Bill *Stoke by Clare Cartulary* 1 (Suffolk Charters 4) (1982): 3, 12, 23, 30 (notification of Richard, Earl of Clare dated 1173–80; charter witnessed by his brother, Richard de Clare), 31–32 (charter of Richard de Clare, Earl of Hertford dated 1185–88; charter witnessed by his uncle [avunculus], Richard de Clare), 32 (charter of Richard de Clare dated 1173–89), 33 (confirmation charter of Richard de Clare, Earl of Hertford dated 1173–85), 33–34 (charter of Richard de Clare, Earl of Hertford dated c.1192–1217; charter witnessed by Sir Richard de Clare), 37, 41–48 (charters of Amice, Countess of Clare); 2 (Suffolk Charters 5) (1983): 321, 323, 325. Merrick *Morganiae Archaiographia* (South Wales Rec. Soc. 1) (1983): 41–52. Schwennicke *Europäische Stammtafeln* 3(1) (1984): 156 (sub Clare); 3(2) (1983): 354. Smith *English Episc. Acta* 6 (1990): 109–110, 216–217, 333–334, 365. Ward *Women of the English Nobility & Gentry 1066–1500* (1995): 24–25 (charter of Richard de Clare, Earl of Hertford dated 1173–90; charter witnessed by Richard de Clare and John de Clare). Mortimer *Charters of St. Bartholomew's Priory* (Suffolk Charters 15) (1996): 25–26 (charter of Amice, Countess of Clare).

Children of Richard de Clare, Knt., by Amice of Gloucester:

i. **GILBERT DE CLARE**, Knt., Earl of Gloucester and Hertford [see next].

ii. **RICHARD DE CLARE**, younger son. He was murdered at London 4 May 1228. Lipscomb *Hist. & Antiqs. of Buckingham* 1 (1847): 200–201 (Clare ped.). Luard *Annales Monastici* 1 (Rolls Ser. 36) (1864): 70. Clark *Land of Morgan* (1883): 64–92. *C.P.* 6 (1926): 503, footnote d (sub Hertford). Schwennicke *Europäische Stammtafeln* 3(1) (1984): 156 (sub Clare).

iii. **ROGER DE CLARE**, of Middleton, Norfolk, and, in right of his wife, of Norton, Suffolk, Chipstead, Surrey, and Southwick and Wickham, Sussex, younger son. Probably about 1223 he witnessed a confirmation charter of his brother, Earl Gilbert de Clare, to the priory of St. Gregory, Clerkenwell. In Feb. 1225 Roger had the grant of land in Ashingdon, Essex formerly belonging to John de Beauchamp, which land he restored in March 1225. In 1226 he received the grant of an annual fee of £25 from the Exchequer, on going to Gascony with Richard, Earl of Cornwall. In 1230 he was granted £15 in lands, and his annual wage accordingly reduced to £10. He married before Feb. 1231 **ALICE DE DAMMARTIN**, widow of John de Wauton (died shortly before Sept. 1230), of Walton-on-the Hill, Surrey, and daughter of Eudes Dammartin, of Strumpshaw, Norfolk, and Chipstead, Effingham, Mickleham, and Tandridge, Surrey, presumably by _____, sister of Richard de Lucy. They had no issue. His wife, Alice, was heiress in 1225 to her brother, Eudes de Dammartin. In 1232 he was one of those sent to accompany Margaret, Countess of Kent, to London. In March 1233 he had a gift of the king of two stags and ten hinds to be taken from his late brother, Earl Gilbert's park at Bletchingley, Surrey. He served in the Welsh campaign of 1233–4. In 1236 he had the gift of two stags from the king to be taken from his nephew, Earl Richard's park at Hundon, Suffolk. Before Jan. 1241 he left for the Holy Land, presumably in the English expedition led by Richard, Earl of Cornwall. In May 1241 his essoin in an action was adjourned for five weeks, he then returning from the Holy Land. ROGER DE CLARE presumably died on the way home shortly before August 1241, when an order was issued to take his lands into the king's hands. In Jan. 1241/2 his widow, Alice, agreed to pay 200 marks to the king at the rate of £25 a year to have seisin of Roger's lands in Middleton, Norfolk, until his unnamed heirs were of age or married. She evidently died about 1255. Clark *Land of Morgan* (1883): 64–92 ("Roger de Clare, Earl Gilbert's brother, was allowed £12 on the 11th February 1226, for his expenses in the King's service with the Earl of Cornwall in Poitou."). *Cal. Liberate Rolls* 1 (1916): 1, 77, 105, 125, 177. Lambert *Bletchingley* 1 (1921): 66–69. *Surrey Arch. Colls.* 54 (1955): 58–65. Woodcock *Cartulary of the Priory of St. Gregory, Canterbury* (Camden 3rd Ser. 88) (1956): 68–69. *Curia Regis Rolls* 14 (1961): 327, 332–333; 16 (1979): 112; 17 (1991): 84, 277, 394, 465. Meekings *1235 Surrey Eyre* 1 (Surrey Rec. Soc. 31) (1979): 180–182 (biog. of Roger de Clare). Schwennicke *Europäische Stammtafeln* 3(1) (1984): 156 (sub Clare).

iv. **HENRY DE CLARE**, younger son. In 1228 he was granted a yearly wage of £20, being then in the king's service. His subsequent history is unknown. *Cal. Liberate Rolls* 1 (1916): 77 (Henry styled "brother" of Roger de Clare). Lambert *Bletchingley* 1 (1921): 67.

v. **MAUD DE CLARE**, married **WILLIAM DE BREWES**, of Bramber, Sussex [see BREWES 6].

vi. **HAWISE DE CLARE**, married **GEOFFREY DE SAY**, Knt., of Edmonton, Middlesex [see SAY 6].

vii. **[?JOAN] DE CLARE**, married in 1219 (as his 2nd wife) **RHYS GRYG**, lord of Dynevor or Ystradtywi, Prince of South Wales, younger son of Lord Rhys ap Griffith, Prince of South Wales. They had two sons, Maredudd and Howel. RHYS GRYG died in 1233, and was buried in St. David's Cathedral. Vincent *A Discoverie of Errours* (1622): 122. Thomson *Hist. Essay on the Magna Charta of King John* (1829): 270–272 (biog. of Richard de Clare). *Jour. British Arch. Assoc.* 26 (1870): 149–160. Bridgeman *Hist. of the Princes of South Wales* (1876): 73–110, 185–202. Clark *Land of Morgan* (1883): 64–92 ("The Chronicles state that the daughter of the Earl of Clare in 1217 married Rhys Bahan (Vachan). She may have been a natural daughter."). *Arch. Cambrensis* 5th Ser. 15 (1898): 226–227. Caradog of Llancarvan *Brut y Tywysogion* 1 (2001): 304–305 (sub A.D. 1219: "The ensuing year, Rhys the Hoarse [Rhys Gryg] married the daughter of the earl of Clare.").

Children of [?Joan] de Clare, by Rhys Gryg:

a. **MAREDUDD AP RHYS GRYG**, of Dryslwyn and Llandovery, Carmarthenshire, younger son by his father's 2nd marriage, born in or before 1222. He married 1234/41 _____, niece of Gilbert Marshal, 7th Earl of Pembroke, hereditary Master Marshal of England, and granddaughter of William Marshal, Knt., 4th Earl of Pembroke, by Isabel, daughter of Richard de Clare. They had one son, Rhys, Knt. Sometime before 1241, he was granted the commotes of Ystlwyf and Newcastle Emlyn, Carmarthenshire by Gilbert Marshal, Earl of Pembroke. He was at variance with his nephew, Rhys Fychan ap Rhys Mechyll, during the greater part of their lives. He accompanied Llywelyn ap Gruffudd on his victorious expeditions of 1256, and was rewarded with grants of lands around Llanbadarn and Cantref Buellt. He took a leading part in the Welsh victory of Cymerau in 1257. In 1258 he went over to the English king, who conceded to him all the lands he then held, as well as lands belonging to his nephew, Rhys, in Mabuderith, Mabelneu, etc. In 1258 he concluded an alliance with Llywelyn ap Gruffudd. In 1259 he defected from Llywelyn, who had him imprisoned. Llywelyn demanded that he surrender Newcastle Emlyn and Dinefwr to him that year. Maredudd sided with the Welsh in 1261. In 1265–6 he was again taken into the English king's pay. MAREDUDD AP RHYS died at his castle at Dryslwyn, Carmarthenshire 22 July 1271, and was buried at Whitland Abbey. Bridgeman *Hist. of the Princes of South Wales* (1876): 111–150, 174–179, 185–202. Davies *Age of Conquest* (2000): 226, 319.

Child of Maredudd ap Rhys Gryg, by _____, niece of Gilbert Marshal:

1) **RHYS AP MAREDUDD**, Knt., of Dryslwyn and Ystlwyf, Carmarthenshire, son and heir. He married by papal dispensation dated 10 Dec. 1283 (they being related in the 3rd and 4th degrees of kindred) **ADA DE HASTINGS**, daughter of Henry de Hastings, Knt., of Lidgate, Cavendish, Gazeley, Little Udeley, Rede, etc., Suffolk, Nailstone and Wistow, Leicestershire, Yardley Hastings, Northamptonshire, Aston (in Munslow), Shropshire, Fillongley, Warwickshire, etc., hereditary Steward of the liberty of Bury St. Edmunds Abbey, by Joan, daughter of William de Cantelowe, Knt. [see HASTINGS 9 for her ancestry]. Her maritagium included Emlyn Is Cuch (in the hundred of Cilgerran), Pembrokeshire, and St. Clear's, Carmarthenshire. They had no issue. In the crisis of 1276–7, he confirmed his loyalty to King Edward I of England. The king granted him Dinefwr Castle, together with the commotes of Maenordeilo, Mallaen, Caeo, and Mabelfyw, all in Cantref Mawr; he was also granted the commotes of Gwynionydd and Mabwynion, Cardiganshire on a limited basis. In 1277, with the defeat of Prince Llywelyn, King Edward I retook possession of Dinefwr Castle and later reclaimed Maenordeilo. In 1282 Rhys was granted a yearly fair to be held at the manor of Dryslwyn. In 1282 Rhys was required to required to give up any formal claims to Dinefwr Castle; however, he was granted the lands of Rhys Wyndod in Caeo and Mallaen and given formal seisin of the commotes of Gwynionydd and Mabwynion, Cardiganshire. In 1285 he was granted a weekly market and yearly fair to be held at the manor of Lampeter, Cardiganshire. In June 1287 he rebelled against King Edward I of England and captured Dinefwr, Carreg Cennen, and Llandovery Castles. The king mustered a force of 22,000 men to meet the danger; by Sept. 1287 his castle of Dryslwyn had been captured. In Nov. 1287, however, Rhys renewed the struggle, moving to Carmarthenshire where he captured Newcastle Emlyn. He held out there against royalist forces until Jan. 1288, when the castle was taken. In 1290 his forfeited lands in Wales were granted to Robert de Tibetot, to hold until Easter next, and for the four years after. In 1290, having raised a new insurrection, Rhys was opposed by Robert de Tibetot, the king's justiciar. Four thousand Welshmen were slain and Rhys was taken prisoner. SIR RHYS AP MAREDUDD was tried at York soon after Michaelmas [29 Sept.] 1291

and there cruelly executed. On 14 June 1293 his widow, Ada, was allowed to retain all the lands which she held in her own right. Ada married (2nd) before 1306 (date of settlement) (as his 2nd wife) **ROBERT DE CHAMPAINE** (or **CHAMPAYNE, CHAMPAGNE, CHAUMPAYNE**), of Thurlaston and Wigston, Leicestershire, and Great Doddington, Northamptonshire, son and heir of Nicholas de Champaigne, of Great Doddington, Northamptonshire, by Joan, daughter and heir of Adam son of Philip, of Northampton. He was a minor in 1274, he already being married. By his previous marriage, he was the father of one son, Robert. In 1279–80 Robert de Skeftinton and Joan his wife arraigned an assize of novel disseisin against him and others touching a tenement in Great Doddington, Northamptonshire. In the same period, Isabel widow of Robert le Freman arraigned an assize of novel disseisin against him and others touching a tenement in Great Doddington, Northamptonshire. In 1280–1 Michael Fitz Durand and Mabel his wife arraigned an assize of novel disseisin against Robert de Champaigne and Stephen de Ouensby regarding a tenement in Doddington, Northamptonshire. In 1280–1 Robert de Skefinton and Joan his wife arraigned an assize of novel disseisin against him regarding a tenement in Thurleston and Castre, Leicestershire. In 1281–2 he quitclaimed a croft of land in Collingtree, Northamptonshire to John de Wotton. In 1282 he remitted and quitclaimed to Devorguille of Gallloway, wife of John de Balliol, his right in the manor of Borgue in Galloway. He presented to the church of Thurlaston, Leicestershire in 1288. In 1296 an assize came to recognize whether Robert de Champaine, John de Champaine, and others disseised Robert Skeffington [step-father of Robert de Champaine] of his free tenements in Wigston, Leicestershire; the jury found in favor of Robert de Champaine. In 1301 he sued Thomas Skeffington regarding 11 messuages, 5 virgates of land, and 2s. of rent in Collingtree, Northamptonshire. His wife, Ada, died sometime before 1308–9. In 1313 Robert settled the manors of Thurleston, Leicestershire and Great Doddington, Northamptonshire on himself for life, with reversion to his son and heir, Robert de Champaine the younger, and his wife, Margaret. He married (3rd) **MAUD** _____. ROBERT DE CHAMPAINE died shortly before 27 May 1315, when his widow, Maud, acknowledged that she owed a debt of £20 to Richer de Refham, to be levied, in default of payment, of her lands and chattels in Essex. His widow, Maud, married (2nd) before Hilary term 1320 (date of lawsuit) **RICHARD TABOURER**, of Albrighton. In 1320 Robert son of Robert de Champaine sued Richard and his wife, Maud, and Margaret daughter of the said Maud in a plea of a messuage, five acres of land, one acre of meadow, and 57s. rent in Wigston, Leicestershire, which he claimed as his right. In Hilary term 1322 Richard and his wife, Maud, sued Robert de Champaine and his wife, Margaret, in a plea of a third part of the manor of Thurleston, together with the advowson of the church of the said manor, and £10 rent in Wigston, Leicestershire, which they demanded as dower of the said Maud. Dugdale *Baronage of England* 1 (1675): 574–579 (sub Hastings). Bridges *Hist. & Antiqs. of Northamptonshire* 2 (1791): 140. Nichols *Hist. & Antiqs. of Leicester* 3(2) (1804): 607–608 (Hastings ped.). Brydges *Collins' Peerage of England* 6 (1812): 643–645 (sub Lord Hastings). Williams ab Ithel *Annales Cambriæ* (Rolls Ser.) (1860): 109–110. *Cambrian Jour.* 6 (1863): 185. *Arch. Jour.* 26 (1869): 236–256. Bridgeman *Hist. of the Princes of South Wales* (1876): 185–202. Flower *Vis. of Yorkshire 1563–4* (H.S.P. 16) (1881): 154–156 (Hastings ped.: "Alda [de Hastings] wyff fyrst to John ap Meredyth & after to Robert de Champayne, Knight."). Bain *Cal. of Docs. Rel. to Scotland* 2 (1884): 67. *Annual Rpt. of the Deputy Keeper* 49 (1888): 56; 50 (1889): 71, 227. *Papal Regs.: Letters* 1 (1893): 470. Morris *Welsh Wars of Edward I* (1901): 205, 214. *C.C.R. 1279–1288* (1902): 189. Hulme *Hist. of Thurlaston* (1904): 25–26, 103 (Champayne ped.). *C.Ch.R.* 2 (1906): 253, 303. Farnham *Leicestershire Medieval Peds.* (1925): foll. 126 (Champaine ped.), 127–128. VCH *Northampton* 4 (1937): 113–116 (Champayne arms: Argent three bars wavy gules). Powicke *13th Cent., 1216–1307* (1953): 410, 438–440. *Welsh Hist. Rev.* 3 (1966): 121–143. Rees *Cal. Ancient Petitions Rel. Wales* (Board of Celtic Studies, Hist. & Law 28) (1975): 71–72, 512, 524. Hill *Rolls & Reg. of Bishop Oliver Sutton 1280–1299* 8 (Lincoln Rec. Soc. 76) (1986): 40. Walker *Medieval Wales* (1990): 152–154 (Rhys ap Maredudd: "He was, beyond question, the leading figure in the dynasty of Deheubarth; his gains were small and local, but he was building up a compact lordship."). National Archives, E 42/207 (available at www.catalogue.nationalarchives.gov.uk/search.asp).

b. **HOWEL AP RHYS GRYG**, of Landarak, Carmarthenshire, younger son by his father's 2nd marriage. In 1277 he was one of those who remained faithful to Prince Llywelyn ap Griffith. He made peace with the English king at the commencement of the following year. He took part in the wars of 1282–3, and was taken after the capture of Prince David in 1283 and imprisoned in London. His land was forfeited in 1283. His subsequent history is unknown. Bridgeman *Hist. of the Princes of South Wales* (1876): 202–203. Brault *Rolls of Arms Edward I* 2 (1997): 11 (arms of Howel ap Rhys: Gules, a chevron between three mullets argent).

6. GILBERT DE CLARE, Knt., 4th Earl of Hertford, Lord of Harfleur and Mostrevilliers in Normandy, 1202, son and heir, born about 1180. In 1211 he held 6-½ knights fees in Kent of his mother's maritagium. He and his father joined the confederacy of the barons against the king in 1215. He was as one of the twenty-five barons elected to guarantee the observance of Magna Carta, which King John signed 15 June 1215. In consequence he and his father were excommunicated by Pope Innocent III 16 Dec. 1215, but at this time, he was a party to the negotiations for peace. He had a safe-conduct from the king 9 Nov. 1215, which was repeated 27 March 1216, after the fall of Colchester. He fought on the side of Louis of France at the Battle of Lincoln 19 May 1217, and was taken prisoner by William Marshal, Earl of Pembroke. He was afterwards released, and his lands restored. He married 9 October 1217 **ISABEL MARSHAL**, 2nd daughter of William Marshal, Knt., 4th Earl of Pembroke (or Strigoil), hereditary Master Marshal, by Isabel, daughter of Richard Fitz Gilbert (nicknamed *Strongbow*), 2nd Earl of Pembroke (or Strigoil) [see MARSHAL 3 for her ancestry]. She was born at Pembroke Castle 9 October 1200. They had three sons, Richard, Knt. [Earl of Gloucester and Hertford], William, Knt., and Gilbert, and three daughters, Amice, Agnes, and Isabel. He was recognized as Earl of Gloucester (in his mother's lifetime) in November 1217. In 1217 he gave the manor of Hambleden, Buckinghamshire to Milicent de Cantelowe for life in settlement of her other claims in dower on the estates of her former husband, Amaury, Count of Evreux (Gilbert's 1st cousin). In 1218 Hugh de Vivonne was ordered to give up the Forest of Keynsham to him. In July 1222 he was forbidden to attack the castle of Dinas Powys in Glamorgan. From this time forward he frequently attests royal grants. In 1223 he joined his brother-in-law, the Earl Marshal, in an expedition into Wales. Probably about 1223 he confirmed the grant of Hamo de Blean (alias Crevequer) to the Priory of St. Gregory, Clerkenwell. In 1224 the king ordered his bailiffs of Bristol to cause Earl Gilbert to have five tuns of the 40 tuns of wine that he lately took to the king's use in the vill of Bristol at the same market price. He was present in 1225 at the confirmation of Magna Carta by King Henry III. In 1227 he sued William de Similly for the manor of Princes Risborough, Buckinghamshire, which he claimed as his right. In 1227 he served as witness to the king's charter permitting the removal of the cathedral from Old to New Salisbury and confirming the same rights to the new city as Winchester enjoyed. The same year he supported Richard, Earl of Cornwall, against the king, with regard to the forest laws and the misgovernment of Hubert de Burgh. The king soon gave way to the barons' threats, and meeting them at Northampton in August, promised them satisfaction of their demands. In Sept. 1227 he was one of the nobles accredited to meet the princes of the Empire at Antwerp. He led an army against the Welsh in 1228 and captured Morgan Gam, who was released the following year. In Feb. 1228 he had a gift of 40 rafters in the wood of Auvour to house himself at Cranborne, Dorset. In 1228 he again led an army against the Welsh and discovered iron, lead, and silver mines in Wales. In Feb. 1230 he and William Earl Marshal were ordered to yield up to the Archdeacon of Llandaff all the possessions of the bishopric which they had taken on the bishop's death. Early in 1230 he crossed over into Brittany with the king, where he served as a commander in the royal army. SIR GILBERT DE CLARE, Earl of Gloucester and Hertford, died at Penros in that duchy 25 October 1230, and was buried 11 November 1230 before the high altar at Tewkesbury Abbey, Gloucestershire. His funeral was conducted with great state. He left two wills, one dated 30 April 1230, the other 23 October 1230, proved before Michaelmas, 1233. By the terms of his will, he left a gilt silver cross to Tewkesbury Abbey, as well as the wood of Mythe by Severn side during the minority of his son. His widow, Isabel, married (2nd) 30 March 1231 (as his 1st wife) **RICHARD OF ENGLAND**, Earl of Cornwall, Count of Poitou [see CORNWALL 6], Lieutenant of Guienne, 1226–7, Keeper of Castle and Honour of Wallingford, 1230–1, Lord of the Manor, Castle, and Honour of Knaresborough, 1235, Lord of the Manor and Castle of Lideford, 1239, Commander-in-Chief of the Crusaders, 1240–1, Privy Councillor, 1253, Joint Guardian of England, 1253–4, younger son of John, King of England, by his 2nd wife, Isabel, daughter of Adémar, Count of Angoulême [see ENGLAND 5 for his ancestry]. They had three sons, John, Henry, Knt., and

Nicholas, and one daughter, Isabel. He was granted the borough of Wilton, Wiltshire by his brother, King Henry III, on the occasion of his marriage. In 1232–3 he fought in Wales against Llywelyn ap Iorwerth. In 1237 he openly rebuked his brother the king for his greed and maladmininistration. He was on an embassy to Emperor Frederick in 1237. By March 1233 he had driven Llywelyn back and strongly fortified Radnor Castle. His wife, Isabel, died testate at Berkhampstead, Hertfordshire in childbed of jaundice 17 Jan. 1239/40. Her body was buried at Beaulieu Abbey, Hampshire, her bowels went to Missenden, and her heart was sent to Tewkesbury Abbey for burial in her 1st husband's grave. In 1240 he left for the Holy Land on crusade, in the company of a large number of English knights and nobles. In 1241 negotiated a treaty with the sultan of Krak, by which many French captives were restored to liberty. He fought in Poitou in 1242–3. Richard married (2nd) at Westminster Abbey 23 Nov. 1243 **SANCHE** (or **SANCHIA**) **OF PROVENCE**, daughter and co-heiress of Raymond Bérenger V, Count and Marquis of Provence, Count of Forcalquier, by Béatrice, daughter of Thomas (or Tommaso) I, Count of Savoy, Marquis in Italy. She was the sister of Eleanor of Provence, wife of his brother, King Henry III of England. She was born about 1225 at Aix-en-Provence. They had two sons, one unnamed and Edmund, Knt. [Earl of Cornwall]. In December 1243 the king demanded a written renunciation of any rights that Richard might possess in Ireland or Gascony, together with an explicit disclaimer of the award that had been made at Saintes. In return, Richard was confirmed in possession of Cornwall and of the honours of Wallingford and Eye. He was granted the honour of Bradninch, Devon in 1244. In 1246, together with King Henry III, he sought unsuccessfully to oppose the efforts of Charles of Anjou, husband of Sanche's younger sister, Béatrice, to claim the entire dominion of Count Raymond Bérengar V of Provence. He served as principal governor of the mint between 1247 and 1258, an office from which he derived considerable profit. He was Joint Plenipotentiary to France and Ambassador to Pope Innocent IV in 1250. He was elected King of the Romans (also styled King of Almain) 13 Jan. 1256/7, and was crowned at Aachen 17 May 1257. He failed to establish his authority in Germany, however, was soon dispossessed, and returned to England in Jan. 1259. In April 1261 he was elected senator of Rome for life, a purely honorary title which he made no attempt to exercise in person, and in which he was subsequently supplanted by Charles of Anjou. His wife, Sanche, died at Berkhampstead, Hertfordshire 9 Nov. 1261. In 1263 he secured a temporary truce after war had broken out between his brother the king and the English barons. In 1264, when conflict became inevitable, he supported his brother. He was taken prisoner with his brother at the Battle of Lewes 14 May 1264. After the Battle of Evesham 4 August 1265, he was released and his lands restored. He married (3rd) at Kaiserslautern, Germany 16 June 1269 **BEATRICE DE FALKENBURG** (or **FAUQUEMONT**), daughter of Dietrich II de Falkenburg, seigneur of Montjoye, by Berta, daughter of Walram of Limburg, seigneur of Montjoye. They had no issue. By an unknown mistress (or mistresses), he had several illegitimate children, including Philip (clerk), Richard, Knt., and Walter, Knt. He purchased the honour of Trematon, Cornwall in 1270. RICHARD, King of the Romans, Earl of Cornwall, died testate at Berkhampstead, Hertfordshire 2 (or 3) April 1272, and was buried with his 2nd wife, Sanche, at Hailes Abbey, Gloucestershire, his heart being interred in the choir of the Franciscan church at Oxford. His widow, Beatrice, died testate 17 October 1277, and was buried before the high altar at the Friars Minors, Oxford.

Sandford *Gen. Hist. of the Kings of England* (1677): 95–100. Rymer *Fœdera* 1 (1816): 484 ("Richard de Romeyns" [i.e., Richard, King of the Romans] styled "uncle" by King Edward I of England). Dugdale *Monasticon Anglicanum* 2 (1819): 59–65; 6(3) (1830): 1658–1659 (charter of Amice, Countess of Clare, daughter of William Earl of Gloucester). Banks *Genealogical Hist. of Divers Fams of the Ancient Peerage of England* (1826): 315–321. Clutterbuck *Hist. & Antiqs. of Hertford* 3 (1827): 225–226 (Clare ped.). Thomson *Hist. Essay on the Magna Charta of King John* (1829): 270–272 (biog. of Richard de Clare). *Coll. Top. et Gen.* 8 (1843): 120–122 (two charters of Richard, King of the Romans). Lipscomb *Hist. & Antiqs. of Buckingham* 1 (1847): 200–201 (Clare ped.). Shirley *Royal & Other Hist. Letters Ill. of King Henry III* 2 (Rolls Ser. 27) (1866): 101–102 & 106–107 (letters of Richard, Earl of Cornwall), 132–133 (Richard, King of the Romans, styled "brother" [fratri] by King Henry III of England), 174–175, 193–194 & 197–198 (letters of Richard, King of the Romans). Luard *Annales Monastici* 4 (Rolls Ser. 36) (1869): 72 (Annals of Oseney sub A.D. 1231 — "Eodem anno venit Willelmus Marescallus de Britannia, et dedit sororem suam comitissam Gloucestriæ Ricardo comiti Cornubiæ, fratri regis, in conjugium"), 223–224 (Annals of Oseney sub A.D. 1269 — "Eodem anno et eodem tempore idem Ricardus rex Alemanniæ, quinto idus Junii [9 June], duxit in uxorem quandam nobilem puellam et decoram valde, nomine Beatricem de Falkestan, quæ propter ejus pulchritudinem vocabatur gemma mulierum"), 248 (Annals of Oseney sub A.D. 1272 — "Eodem anno quarto nonas Aprilis [2 April] apud castrum de Berkamestede obiit Ricardus rex Alemanniæ, et sepultus est in abbatia de Hailes, quam a fundamentis sumptibus suis construxerat."). *Jour. British Arch. Assoc.* 26 (1870): 149–160. Matthew of Paris *Chronica Majora* 2 (Rolls Ser. 57) (1874): 604–605, 642–644. Maclean *Hist. of Trigg Minor* 1 (1876): 189–190 (obit at Grey Friars, Bodmin, Cornwall: "Richardus Rex Almaniæ obiit 3 die Aprilis"). *Arch. Jour.* 34 (1877): 180–186 (charter of Richard, Earl of Poitou and Cornwall dated 1256) ("He [Richard] was for a time heir to the throne, and always exercised great influence in the affairs of the kingdom … He was a far wiser man than his brother, who seems to have consulted him on many occasions, although they were often at variance. Wallingford … was his chief seat, where he lived with great splendour … The seal [on the charter] is imperfect, but what remains is well cut and clear … On the upper side … is a knight on horseback galloping to the proper left. He wears a loose plaited surcoat, girdled at the waist, and with the skirt freely flowing backwards, shewing the right leg from the knee in armour, apparently mail, with a prick-spur. The right arm, in mail, is extended backwards, and holds upright a long straight sword. Above the upper edge of the surcoat is seen the throat, closely fitted with mail, and on the head a flat-topped helmet. The left arm is covered with a heater shield, with conceals the breast and bears a lion rampant, with probably a border. The saddle is raised below and behind, and the two girths cross saltire fashion under the horse's belly. Over the knight's right shoulder is a narrow embossed belt, for sword or dagger. The horse is cut with great freedom, and does not appear to be in armour. The legend is: 'SIGIL[LUM RICARDI COMITIS CORNU]BIE.' Upon the obverse is large, bold heater shield, about two inches high, bearing a lion rampant within a plain border, charged with fourteen roundels. Round and behind the shield is scroll work of an early English character. The legend, in place of the usual cross, commences with a crescent 'SIG[ILLVM] RICARDI COMITIS [CORN]UBIE.' It is remarkable that Richard did not bear the arms of England, but those of Poictou. 'Argent, a lion rampant gules, crowned or,' which he placed within 'a border sable, bezantée,' derived from the old Earls of Cornwall, and thus, as was not unsual, represented both his earldoms on his shield."). *Table chronologique des Chartes et Diplômes imprimés concernant Belgique* 5 (1877): 385–386 (Baudouin d'Avesnes [seigneur de Beaumont] styled "cher cousin et vassal" by Richard, King of the Romans in 1267). *Genealogist* 3 (1879): 225–230; n.s. 13 (1896): 98. *Antiq.* 2 (1880): 273; 21 (1890): 232. Clark *Earls, Earldom, & Castle of Pembroke* (1880): 69–75. Stubbs *Historical Works of Gervase of Canterbury* 2 (Rolls Ser. 73) (1880): 110–111. Clark *Land of Morgan* (1883): 64–92. Doyle *Official Baronage of England* 1 (1886): 436–437 (sub Cornwall); 2 (1886): 13 (sub Gloucester), 177 (sub Hertford). Hart & Lyons *Cartularium Monasterii de Rameseia* 2 (Rolls Ser. 79) (1886): 330–331 (charter of Richard, Earl of Cornwall, to Ramsey Abbey). Clark *Survey of the Antiqs. of Oxford* 1 (1889): 366; 2 (1890): 295–297, 299, 303, 383–384, 407–408, 415, 417, 434. Hingeston-Randolph *Regs. of Walter Bronescombe & Peter Quivil* (1889): 178, 200 (charters of Richard, Earl of Cornwall and Poitou). Birch *Cat. Seals in the British Museum* 2 (1892): 268 (seal of Gilbert de Clare, Earl of Gloucester and Hertford, dated 1218 — Obverse: To the right. In armour: hauberk of mail, surcoat, shield of arms. Horse caparisoned. Arms: three chevrons [CLARE]. Legend wanting. Reverse — a smaller counterseal. A shield of arms as above. Legend: * SIGILL' GILEBERTI DE CLARA), 338 (seal of Richard, Earl of Cornwall, Count of Poitou dated before 1257 — To the right. In armour: hauberk of mail, coif, flat-topped helmet with vizor down, sword, shield of arms slung by the strap round the neck. Horse galloping with ornamental breast-band, crossed girths, and embroidered saddle. For the arms see the reverse. Legend: SIG[ILLVM :] RICARDI : COMITIS : PICTAVIE :; Reverse. On a background of foliage forming a tree of three branches elegantly designed with fruit in clusters, a shield of arms: a lion rampant crowned, POITOU, within a bordure bezantée, ANCIENT DUCHY OF CORNWALL. Legend: SIGILLVM : RICARDI : COMITIS : CORNVBIE.), 338 (another seal of Earl Richard dated 1227 — Obverse. To the right. In armour: hauberk of mail, surcoat of arms, flat-topped helmet, sword, convex shield of arms. Horse galloping, caparisoned. Arms as in reverse. Legend: SIGILL'M RICARDI FI……; Reverse. A shield of arms: a lion rampant, crowned, within a bordure charged with nine roundels. The art of this seal is apparently French, and it is of poor workmanship. Legend: ………TAVIENSIS.). *Recueil des Historiens des Gaules et de la France* 23 (1894): 474 (Ex Obituariis Lirensis Monasterii: "25 October. [Obiit] Gilebertus de Clare, comes."). Fry & Fry *Abs. of Feet of Fines Rel. Dorset* 1 (Dorset Rec. Soc. 5) (1896): 26. Browne *Corporation Chrons.* (1904): 95 (charter of Richard, Earl of Cornwall). Clark *English Reg. of Godstow Nunnery* 1 (1905): 264–265 (charters of Richard, King of the Romans), 281 (charter of Richard, Earl of Cornwall). Wrottesley *Peds. from the Plea Rolls* (1905): 133–134, 146. Auvray *Registres de Grégoire IX* 2 (1907): 977 (Roger, clerk, styled "nephew" [nepoti] of [Henry III] King of England and R[ichard], Earl of Cornwall in 1238); 3 (1908): 132 (papal dispensation dated 1239: "Rogero, clerico, nepoti regis Angliae et Riccardi, comitis Cornubiae, - cum quo olim ipse papa, intuitu devotionis quam praedictus comes Cornubiae, ejus patruus, …"). *D.N.B.* 4 (1908): 378 (biog. of Gilbert de Clare); 16 (1909): 1051–1061 (biog. of Richard, Earl of Cornwall and King of the Romans) ("… Richard was the only Englishman who attempted to rule the holy Roman empire… He was at all times bountiful to the church.")John, Bishop of Lübeck, a contemporary of Richard's, described him as "orthodox, prudent, strenuous, wealthy, well connected, energetic, and moderate."). *C.Ch.R.* 3 (1908): 489–491 (various charters of Richard, Earl of Cornwall). VCH *Buckingham* 2 (1908): 260–267, 348; 3 (1925): 47, 70–71; 4 (1927): 396. Clark *Cartæ et Alia Munimenta de Glamorgancia* 2 (1910): 359 (charter of Gilbert de Clare, Earl of Gloucester & Hertford dated c.1218), 359–360 (charter of Gilbert de Clare, Earl of Gloucester & Hertford dated 1218–29. Seal, dark wax, 2 7/8in. diam. The Earl, with a hauberk of mail, surcoat, flat-topped helmet, vizor closed, right arm extended, sword uplifted, shield covering his breast, slung with strap round his neck; on a horse galloping to the proper left; caparisons charged with the chevrons of Clare. Counterseal, 1-1/8in. diam. Heater-shaped shield, with three chevrons as above), 360 (letter of Gilbert de Clare, Earl of Gloucester and Hertford dated 1218–30. Seal, dark green, fine but imperfect, 3 in. diam. Device, the earl in armour, riding to the proper left; on his shield three chevrons. Reverse, a heater-shaped shield of arms: three chevrons). VCH *Hertford* 3 (1912): 232–240. *C.P.* 3 (1913): 244, 430–432 (sub Cornwall); 5 (1926): 694–696 (sub Gloucester); 6 (1926): 503 (sub Hertford); 10 (1945): 364, footnote a. Davis *Rotuli Hugonis de Welles Episcopi Lincolniensis 1209–1235* 3 (Lincoln Rec. Soc. 9) (1914): 10, 11, 14, 54. Lambert *Bletchingley* 1 (1921): 59–63. Moor *Knights of Edward I* 2 (H.S.P. 81) (1929): 238 (Richard, Earl of Cornwall: "…'a man of much more enterprise than his brother,' and accounted in his time the peace-maker of Europe…. One of the most interesting personages noted in the pages of English history."). *Antiqs. Jour.* 18 (1938): 142–145 ("A Portrait of Beatrix of Falkenburg"). Leys *Sandford Cartulary* 1 (Oxfordshire Rec. Soc. 19) (1938): 156 (confirmation charter of Richard, Count of Poitou and Cornwall dated c.1233–4). Jenkins *Cal. of the Rolls of the Justices on Eyre 1227* (Buckinghamshire Arch. Soc. 6) (1945): 1, 32. Denholm-Young *Richard of Cornwall* (1947). Hatton *Book of Seals* (1950): 306–307 (charter of Richard, King of the Romans dated 1262). Woodcock *Cartulary of the Priory of St. Gregory, Canterbury* (Camden 3rd Ser. 88) (1956): 68–69 (charter of Gilbert de Clare, Earl of Gloucester & Hertford). Paget *Baronage of England* (1957) 130: 6–7. Sanders *English Baronies* (1960): 9–10, 14, 20–21, 34–35, 60, 62–64, 90–91, 93. *Curia Regis Rolls* 14 (1961): 61, 124, 433–435, 506–507, 520; 15 (1972): 50, 102–103, 343. Hull *Cartulary of St. Michael's Mount* (Devon & Cornwall Rec. Soc. n.s. 5) (1962): 32 (charter of Richard, King of the Romans dated 1265). Ross *Cartulary of Cirencester Abbey* 2 (1964): 563–564. Tremlett *Rolls of Arms Henry III* (H.S.P. 113-4) (1967): 64 (arms of Gilbert de Clare: Or, three chevrons gules). Cheney *Letters of Pope Innocent III 1198–1216* (1967): 172. *Ancient Deeds — Ser. B* 2 (List & Index Soc. 101) (1974): B.8659. Hockey *Beaulieu Cartulary* (Southampton Recs. Ser. 17) (1974): 202 (charter of Richard, Count of Poitou, Earl of Cornwall dated 1240–2; charter granted for the soul of his late wife, Isabel, Countess of Gloucester), 217–218. London *Cartulary of Bradenstoke Priory* (Wiltshire Rec. Soc. 35) (1979): 195 (charter of Gilbert de Clare, Earl of Gloucester & Hertford dated 1217–30). Gervers *Hospitaller Cartulary in the British Museum* (1981): 303 (charter of Gilbert de Clare). Gervers *Cartulary of the Knights of St. John of Jerusalem in England, Secunda Camera, Essex* (Recs. of Social and Econ. Hist. n.s. 6) (1982): 547–548 (charter of Gilbert de Clare, Earl of Hertford & Gloucester). Merrick *Morganiae Archaiographia* (South Wales Rec. Soc. 1) (1983): 41–52. Schwennicke *Europäische Stammtafeln* 3(1) (1984): 156 (sub Clare). Leese *Blood Royal* (1996): 61–65. Gee *Women, Art & Patronage from Henry III to Edward III: 1216–1377* (2002): 156. Stevenson *Durford Cartulary* (Sussex Rec. Soc. 90) (2006): 81 (charter of Gilbert de Clare, Earl of Gloucester & Hertford dated c.Nov. 1217 names his "kinsman" [i.e., 1st cousin], Amaury [de Montfort], Earl of Gloucester), 91–92 (charter of Gilbert de Clare, Earl of Gloucester & Hertford dated c.Nov. 1217).

Children of Gilbert de Clare, Knt., by Isabel Marshal:

i. **AMICE DE CLARE**, eldest daughter, born 27 May 1220. She married (1st) after 29 October 1226 (date of grant of his marriage) **BALDWIN DE RIVERS** (or **REVIERS**), Knt., 6th Earl of Devon, Lord of the Isle of Wight, son and heir of Baldwin de Rivers, by Margaret, daughter and heiress of Warin Fitz Gerold, King's Chamberlain. They had one son, Baldwin, Knt. [7th Earl of Devon], and two daughters, Isabel [Countess of Aumale and Devon] and Margaret (nun at Lacock). He was knighted by the king, and invested with the Earldom of Devon 25 Dec. 1239 at Winchester. He accompanied Richard, Earl of Cornwall, to the Holy Land in June 1240. He was with the King in Gascony in 1242. SIR BALDWIN DE RIVERS, 6th Earl of Devon, died 15 Feb. 1244/5, and was buried at Breamore Priory, Hampshire. Sometime in the period, 1245–58, his widow, Amice, gave to Breamore Priory, Hampshire all her land of Hordle, Hampshire and her rights therein, which she bought of Ralph Bardulf. She had permission 10 Jan. 1247/8 to marry (2nd) **ROBERT DE GUINES**, younger son of Arnold II, Count of Guines, if she consented. There is no evidence this marriage ever took place. In 1253 she took two beasts in New Forest, Hampshire, when returning from the court of the queen. In 1255 she went on a pilgrimage to St. Edmund's at Pontigny [Yonne]. In 1257 she was charged with enclosing a six acre tract at Langel' with a hedge without warrant, which hedge was ordered to be thrown down. In 1258 she was again going beyond seas. In 1276–7 John le Boteler arraigned an assize of novel disseisin against her and others touching a tenement in Stanton-Drew, Somerset. In 1278 she founded Buckland Abbey, Devon. Amice, Countess of Devon, Lady of the Isle (otherwise styled Countess of Wight), died shortly before 21 Jan. 1283/4, and was buried at Buckland, Devon. Baker *Hist. & Antiqs. of Northampton* 1 (1822–30): 619–620 (Rivers ped.). Dugdale *Monasticon Anglicanum* 5 (1825): 712–713 (charter of Amice, Countess of Devon, Lady of the Isle), 714 (charter of Amice, Countess of Devon, Lady of the Isle). *Jour. British Arch. Assoc.* 11 (1855): 213–227; 26 (1870): 149–160. *Trans. Royal Hist. Soc.* 6 (1877): 293–294.

Rowe *Contributions to a Hist. of the Cistercian Houses of Devon* (1878): 25–33 (charters of Amice, Countess of Devon, Lady of the Isle). Clark *Land of Morgan* (1883): 64–92. *Annual Rpt. of the Deputy Keeper* 46 (1886): 286. Doyle *Official Baronage of England* 1 (1886): 573 (sub Devon). *Desc. Cat. Ancient Deeds* 1 (1890): 270; 2 (1894): 432. Benolte et al. *Vis. of Surrey 1530, 1572 & 1623* (H.S.P. 43) (1899): 66–68 (Lisle ped.: "Baldwin 3 Erle of Devon = Amicia Clare."). *MSS of the Duke of Rutland* 4 (Hist. MSS Comm. 24) (1905): 57–58 (charter of Amice de Rivers, Countess of Devon, Lady of the Isle). *Rpt. & Trans. Devonshire Assoc.* 37 (1905): 426; 39 (1907): 219. Wrottesley *Peds. from the Plea Rolls* (1905): 535. *C.P.R. 1247–1258* (1908): 408, 630. *C.P.* 4 (1916): 318–319 (sub Devon); 5 (1926): 695, footnote m (sub Gloucester). Cam *Hundred & Hundred Rolls* (1930): 263–264. Jenkinson & Fermoy *Select Cases in the Exchequer of Pleas* (Selden Soc. 48) (1932): 58–60. Paget *Baronage of England* (1957) 466: 1–7 (sub Redvers). VCH *Oxford* 6 (1959): 196–205; 11 (1983): 21–44, 143–159, 259–295. *Ancient Deeds — Ser. B* 2 (List & Index Soc. 101) (1974): B.5540. Ellis *Cat. Seals in the P.R.O.* 1 (1978): 54 (seal of Amice de Rivers, Countess of Devon dated 1274 — Hung from a three-branched tree, a shield of arms: a lion rampant with forked tail [RIVERS]. Legend: [S']AMICIE COMITISSE DEVON.). Rogers *Lacock Abbey Charters* (Wiltshire Rec. Soc. 34) (1979): 109–111 (charter of Amice, Countess of Devon dated 1245–65). Stagg *Cal. New Forest Docs. 1244–1334* (Hampshire Rec. Ser. 3) (1979); 71, 74–75. VCH *Wiltshire* 12 (1983): 86–105, 105–119; 16 (1999): 50–69, 149–165, 164–181. Schwennicke *Europäische Stammtafeln* 3(1) (1984): 156 (sub Clare). Hicks *Who's Who in Late Medieval England* (1991): 11–13 (biog. of Isabella Forz). Hobbs *Cartulary of Forde Abbey* (Somerset Rec. Soc. 85) (1998): 99 (charter of Amice). Gee *Women, Art & Patronage from Henry III to Edward III: 1216–1377* (2002): 13, 15–16, 20, 27, 31, 35, 36, 78, 128, 130, 140–141. Hanna *Christchurch Priory Cartulary* (Hampshire Rec. Ser. 18) (2007): 21–22. Dryburgh *Cal. of Fine Rolls of the Reign of Henry III* 2 (2008): 113.

Children of Amice de Clare, by Baldwin de Rivers, Knt.:

a. **BALDWIN DE RIVERS** (otherwise known as **BALDWIN DE LISLE**), Knt., 7th Earl of Devon, son and heir, born 1 Jan. 1235/6. He married in 1257 **MARGARET OF SAVOY**, daughter of Thomas of Savoy, sometime Count of Flanders and Hainault, by his 2nd wife, Béatrice, daughter of Tedisio di Fiesco. She was a 1st cousin to Queen Eleanor of Provence, wife of King Henry III of England. They had one son, John (died young). The king took his homage and he had livery of his father's lands and the rest of his inheritance 29 Jan. 1256/7. He accompanied the king to France in July 1262. SIR BALDWIN DE RIVERS, 7th Earl of Devon, died in France shortly before 13 Sept. 1262, and was buried at Breamore Priory, Hampshire. His widow, Margaret, married (2nd) in 1269 (as his 2nd wife) **ROBERT D'AGUILLON**, Knt., of Addington, Surrey, Stapleford and Watton at Stone, Hertfordshire, Bures, Suffolk, Fulking and Perching (in Fulking), Sussex, etc., Custodian of Arundel Castle, son and heir of William d'Aguillon, of Perching, Sussex, by Joan, daughter of Peter son of Henry Fitz Ailwin. They had no issue. In 1270 he was granted license to fortify his house at Addington, Surrey. In 1278 he claimed view of frankpledge in his manor of Stapleford, Hertfordshire. SIR ROBERT D'AGUILLON died 15 Feb. 1285/6. His widow, Margaret, Countess of Devon, died shortly before 14 May 1292. Baker *Hist. & Antiqs. of Northampton* 1 (1822–30): 619–620 (Rivers ped.). Dugdale *Monasticon Anglicanum* 5 (1825): 714. *Jour. British Arch. Assoc.* 11 (1855): 213–227. *Notes & Queries* 5th Ser. 10 (1878): 390–391. Rowe *Contributions to a Hist. of the Cistercian Houses of Devon* (1878): 25–33. Doyle *Official Baronage of England* 1 (1886): 573 (sub Devon). *Annual Rpt. of the Deputy Keeper* 50 (1889): 181. Benolte et al. *Vis. of Surrey 1530, 1572 & 1623* (H.S.P. 43) (1899): 66–68 (Lisle ped.: "Baldwin the last Erle of Devon."). *Rpt. & Trans. Devonshire Assoc.* 37 (1905): 426. Wrottesley *Peds. from the Plea Rolls* (1905): 535. *C.P.* 4 (1916): 319–322 (sub Devon). VCH *Essex* 4 (1956): 262–269. Paget *Baronage of England* (1957) 466: 1–7 (sub Redvers). VCH *Oxford* 5 (1957): 234–249; 6 (1959): 196–205; 11 (1983): 143–159. Ellis *Cat. Seals in the P.R.O.* 1 (1978): 54 (seal of Baldwin de Rivers, earl of Devon dated 1262 — A shield of arms: a lion rampant [RIVERS]. Legend: +S'BAL[D]EWINI:DE:IN[S]VLA.). *Ancient Deeds — Ser. AS & WS* (List & Index Soc. 158) (1979): 13 (Deed A.S.67). VCH *Wiltshire* 12 (1983): 86–105, 105–119; 16 (1999): 50–69, 149–165, 164–181. Gee *Women, Art & Patronage from Henry III to Edward III: 1216–1377* (2002): 8, 15, 20, 35. Hanna *Christchurch Priory Cartulary* (Hampshire Rec. Ser. 18) (2007): 22–23, 322–323, 339–342. Online resource: http://www.briantimms.net/rolls_of_arms/rolls/gloversB1.htm (Glover's Roll dated c.1252 — arms of Baldwin de Reviers, Earl of Devon: Or a lion rampant azure).

b. **ISABEL DE RIVERS**, elder daughter, born in July 1237 (aged 54 in 1292). She married (as his 2nd wife) in 1248–9 (date of fine) **WILLIAM DE FORZ**, Knt., titular Count of Aumale, Lord of Holderness, Sheriff of Cumberland, 1255–60, Keeper of Carlisle Castle, Privy Councillor, son and heir of William de Forz, Knt., titular Count of Aumale, Lord of Holderness, Magna Carta baron, 1215, by Aveline, daughter of Richard Montfitchet, of Stanstead, Essex. They had three sons, John, Thomas [titular Count of Aumale], and William, and five daughters, Avice, Joan, Sibyl, Mabel, and Aveline. He married (1st) before 1241 **CHRISTIAN OF GALLOWAY**, daughter of Alan Fitz Roland, Lord of Galloway, by his 2nd wife, Margaret, daughter of David of Scotland, Earl of Huntingdon [SEE BALLIOL 5 for her ancestry]. In 1255 he was appointed joint ambassador to Scotland. In 1259 he was appointed joint special deputy to ratify the peace with France. SIR WILLIAM DE FORZ, Count of Aumale, died at Amiens 23 May 1260, and was buried in Thornton Abbey. His widow, Isabel, was heiress in 1262 to her brother, Baldwin de Rivers, 7th Earl of Devon. She had livery of her brother's lands 17 August 1263, after which she styled herself Countess of Aumale and Devon, Lady of the Isle. She presented to the church of Naseby, Northamptonshire in 1262 and 1286. In 1281 Philip son of Simon le Chaumpyon arraigned an assize of mort d'ancestor against her regarding two parts of a messuage and land in Multon, Northamptonshire. In Nov. 1293 she sold the king the Isle of Wight for 6,000 marks. ISABEL, Countess of Aumale and Devon, Lady of the Isle, died testate at Stockwell, Surrey 10 Nov. 1293, and was buried in Breamore Priory, Hampshire. Mastin *Hist. & Antiqs. of Naseby* (1792): 64–65, 94. Baker *Hist. & Antiqs. of Northampton* 1 (1822–30): 619–620 (Rivers ped.), 672–673 (Aumale ped.). Dugdale *Monasticon Anglicanum* 5 (1825): 712–713, 713–714 (charter of Isabel de Forz, Countess of Aumale & Devon, Lady of the Isle), 714. Cooper *Account of the Most Important Public Recs. of Great Britain* 2 (1832): 476–480. Palgrave *Antient Kalendars & Inventories of the Treasury of His Majesty's Exchequer* 1 (1836): 42, 45, 55, 63. *Coll. Top. et Gen.* 6 (1840): 261–265. *Extracta e Variis Cronicis Scocie* (1842): 94–95. *Arch. Aeliana* 2 (1852): 384–386 (Forz ped.). *Jour. British Arch. Assoc.* 11 (1855): 213–227. Jones *Hist.& Antiq. of Harewood* (1859). *Trans. Royal Hist. Soc.* 6 (1877): 293–294. Rowe *Contributions to a Hist. of the Cistercian Houses of Devon* (1878): 25–33 (confirmation charter of Isabel de Forz, Countess of Aumale & Devon dated 1291). *Annual Rpt. of the Deputy Keeper* 44 (1883): 56; 45 (1885): 77, 148, 205–206, 325; 46 (1886): 130, 216, 279; 47 (1886): 140, 144, 163, 179; 48 (1887): 153; 49 (1888): 15, 93; 50 (1889): 30, 160, 181. Doyle *Official Baronage of England* 1 (1886): 27 (sub Albemarle), 574 (sub Devon). Birch *Cat. Seals in the British Museum* 2 (1892): 296 (seal of William de Forz, Count of Aumale dated 1251 — Obverse. To the right. In armour: hauberk and coif of mail, flat-topped helmet with vizor closed, [sword], shield of arms suspended by an embroidered strap round his neck. Horse galloping with ornamental breast-band. Arms as in reverse. Legend: * SIGILLVM WILLELMI DE FORTIBVS CO[MI]TIS ALBEMARLIE. Reverse: a shield of arms: a cross formée vairée [FORZ]; suspended by a strap on an ornamental tree of conventional and elegant design, between two wavy branches of foliage. Legend: * SIGILLVM WILLELMI DE FORTIBVS COMITIS ALBEMARLIE. Beaded borders.), 822 (seal of Isabel de Forz, Countess of Aumale and Devon dated 1276 — A shield of arms: a cross patonce, vair, AUMALE. Between three lions rampant, in allusion to the armorial charge of REDVERS. Legend: [S]ECRET' : ISABELLE : DE FORTIB' : COMIT[ISSE : D]EVONIE : ET : INSU……. Beaded borders. The art of this seal is very fine.), (another seal of Isabel de Forz dated 1259–62 — Pointed oval: a shield of arms: illegible. Suspended from a tree and between two wavy scrolls of foliage. Legend: ………. FORTIB ; COMITISSE ALB……….). *Genealogist* n.s. 8 (1892): 153. *List of Sheriffs for England & Wales* (PRO Lists and Indexes 9) (1898): 26. Benolte et al. *Vis. of Surrey 1530, 1572 & 1623* (H.S.P. 43) (1899): 66–68 (Lisle ped.: "Willm. de fortibus Comes Albemarle. = Issabella Comitissa Devon."). *Rpt. & Trans. Devonshire Assoc.* 37 (1905): 426; 39 (1907): 219. Wrottesley *Peds. from the Plea Rolls* (1905): 535. *C.P.* 1 (1910): 353–356 (sub Aumale); 4 (1916): 322–323 (sub Devon). VCH *Yorkshire N.R.* 2 (1923): 492–497. VCH *Berkshire* 4 (1924): 168–174. VCH *Northampton* 3 (1930): 196–203 (Forz arms: Gules a cross paty vair); 4 (1937): 69–73. *Early Yorkshire Charters* 7 (Yorkshire Arch. Soc. Extra Ser. 5) (1947): 1–30. Tremlett *Stogursey Charters* (Somerset Rec. Soc. 61) (1949): xxiv (Curci ped.). VCH *Essex* 4 (1956): 262–269. Paget *Baronage of England* (1957) 466: 1–7 (sub Redvers). VCH *Oxford* 5 (1957): 234–249; 6 (1959): 134–146, 196–205; 8 (1964): 80–91; 11 (1983): 21–44, 143–159, 194–208, 259–295. VCH *Somerset* 3 (1973): 235–249. *Ancient Deeds — Ser. B* 3 (List & Index Soc. 113) (1975): B.11728. *Ancient Deeds — Ser. BB* (List & Index Soc. 137) (1977): 21–22, 76, 95–96. Rogers *Lacock Abbey Charters* (Wiltshire Rec. Soc. 34) (1979): 111–112 (charter of Isabel de Forx, Countess of Aumale and Devon dated c.1265). VCH *Wiltshire* 12 (1983): 86–105, 105–119; 16 (1999): 50–69, 149–165, 164–181. Hockey *Charters of Quarr Abbey* (1991). Mitchell *Portraits of Medieval Women* (2003). Gee *Women, Art & Patronage from Henry III to Edward III: 1216–1377* (2002): 15, 16, 20, 35, 61, 78, 156–157. VCH *Yorkshire E.R.* 7 (2002): 213–223, 273–295, 340–349. Hanna *Christchurch Priory Cartulary* (Hampshire Rec. Ser. 18) (2007): 24–29, 56, 73, 92–93, 519–520. Legg *Lost Cartulary of Bolton Priory* (Yorkshire Arch. Soc. Rec. Ser. 160) (2009): 82–84, 86, 88, 236–239.

Children of Isabel de Rivers, by William de Forz:

1) **THOMAS DE FORZ**, titular Count of Aumale, son and heir by his father's 2nd marriage, born 9 Sept. 1253. He died without issue before 6 April 1269, and was buried in the Church of the Black Friars, Stamford, Lincolnshire. *Coll. Top. et Gen.* 6 (1840): 261–265. *Arch. Aeliana* 2 (1852): 384–386 (Forz ped.). Doyle *Official Baronage of England* 1 (1886): 27 (sub Albemarle). Benolte et al. *Vis. of Surrey 1530, 1572 & 1623* (H.S.P. 43) (1899): 66–68 (Lisle ped.: "Thomas ob. a child."). *C.P.* 1 (1910): 356 (sub Aumale); 4 (1916): 322–323 (sub Devon). VCH *Yorkshire N.R.* 2 (1923): 492–497. *Early Yorkshire Charters* 7 (Yorkshire Arch. Soc. Extra Ser. 5) (1947): 1–30. Paget *Baronage of England* (1957) 466: 1–7 (sub Redvers). Legg *Lost Cartulary of Bolton Priory* (Yorkshire Arch. Soc. Rec. Ser. 160) (2009): 82–84, 86.

2) **AVELINE DE FORZ**, occasionally styled Countess of Aumale, married **EDMUND OF ENGLAND**, Earl of Lancaster, Leicester, and Derby [see LANCASTER 7].

c. **MARGARET DE RIVERS**, nun at Lacock Abbey, younger daughter. Dugdale *Monasticon Anglicanum* 5 (1825): 712–714. Rowe *Contributions to a Hist. of the Cistercian Houses of Devon* (1878): 25–33. *Rpt. & Trans. Devonshire Assoc.* 37 (1905): 426. *C.P.* 4 (1916): 319, footnote f (sub Devon). Gee *Women, Art & Patronage from Henry III to Edward III: 1216–1377* (2002): 78.

ii. **RICHARD DE CLARE**, Knt., Earl of Gloucester and Hertford [see next].

iii. **AGNES DE CLARE**. Dugdale *Monasticon Anglicanum* 2 (1819): 59–65. *Jour. British Arch. Assoc.* 26 (1870): 149–160. Clark *Land of Morgan* (1883): 64–92.

iv. **ISABEL DE CLARE**, married **ROBERT DE BRUS**, Knt., of Annandale in Scotland [see BRUS 6].

v. **WILLIAM DE CLARE**, Knt., of Petersfield and Mapledurham (in Buriton), Hampshire, and Walsingham, Wells, and Warham, Norfolk, Constable of Winchester Castle, 2nd son, born 18 May 1228. Sometime in the period, 1245–58, he witnessed a charter of his sister, Amice de Rivers, Countess of Devon, to Breamore Priory, Hampshire. In Nov. 1247 his brother, Richard, had a great tournament at Northampton in honor of William's knighthood. In 1248 William went beyond seas on a pilgrimage with his brother, Earl Richard, to St. Edmund's at Pontigny [Yonne]. The same year he was granted free warren in his demesne lands at Petersfield and Mapledurham (in Buriton), Hampshire. In 1252 he was granted a weekly market and a yearly fair at his manor of Little Walsingham, Norfolk. In 1255 he was granted two yearly fairs at his manor of Petersfield, Hampshire. In 1256 he was granted an annuity of 100 marks at the Exchquer until the king provide for him in an equivalent in wards or escheats. The same year William Finamour and Joan his wife conveyed the manor of Sunworth (in Buriton), Hampshire to him, in exchange for 53 acres of arable land, 15 acres of wood, and 2 acres of meadow in Mapledurham (in Buriton), Hampshire. In 1257 he was granted free warren in his demesne lands in Great and Little Walsingham, Wells, and Warham, Norfolk, and Sunworth (in Buriton), Hampshire, and a weekly market at his manor of Little Walsingham, Norfolk. Sometime before 1258, he gave 30 acres of wood to Durford Priory, Sussex outside their close next to their land on the north side of the manor of Sunworth (in Buriton), Hampshire, one virgate within the canons' close at Holte, and 6s. yearly rent, together with pasture for 200 sheep and 16 animals in the demesne pasture of Sunworth. He was poisoned in May 1258, with his brother, Richard, while at breakfast with Prince Edward at Winchester, Hampshire. SIR WILLIAM DE CLARE died from the effects at Retherford. He was initially buried at Durford Abbey, Sussex 23 July 1258, but was later reinterred beside his father at Tewkesbury Abbey, Gloucestershire. He left no issue. In 1259 Walter de Scotenay, seneschal of Earl Richard de Clare, was condemned for having administered poison to William de Clare, was dragged into the city of Winchester by a horse of the said William, and afterwards hanged. Dugdale *Monasticon Anglicanum* 2 (1819): 59–65. Dugdale *Monasticon Anglicanum* 6(2) (1830): 932–935. Halliwell *Chron. of the Monastry of Abingdon* (1844): 13, 50–51. Luard *Annales Monastici* 1 (Rolls Ser. 36) (1864): 165. *Jour. British Arch. Assoc.* 26 (1870): 149–160. Clark *Land of Morgan* (1883): 64–92. *C.Ch.R.* 1 (1903): 333, 334, 377, 449, 475. *C.P.R. 1232–1247* (1906): 497. *MSS of the Duke of Rutland* 4 (Hist. MSS Comm. 24) (1905): 57–58 (Sir William de Clare styled "my brother" [fratre meo] in charter of Amice de Rivers, Countess of Devon). *Rpt. on MSS in Various Colls.* 4 (Hist. MSS Comm. 55) (1907): 101 ("Will. de Clare, brother of Richard Earl of Gloucester" witness to deed), 256. *C.P.R. 1247–1258* (1908): 9, 12, 66, 456, 505, 638, 644. *D.N.B.* 4 (1908): 393–396 (biog. of Richard de Clare). VCH *Hampshire* 3 (1908): 85–93. *Desc. Cat. Ancient Deeds* 6 (1915): 228. Lambert *Bletchingley* 1 (1921): 82–83. *C.P.* 5 (1926): 695, footnote m (sub Gloucester). Schwennicke *Europäische Stammtafeln* 3(1) (1984): 156 (sub Clare). Stevenson *Durford Cartulary* (Sussex Rec. Soc. 90) (2006): 67 (charter of William de Clare), 71–72. Online resource: http://www.briantimms.net/rolls_of_arms/rolls/gloversB1.htm (Glover's Roll dated c.1252 — arms of William de Clare: Gules three chevrons or a label azure).

vi. **GILBERT DE CLARE**, 3rd son, born 12 Sept. 1229. In 1241 the abbot of Tewkesbury was permitted to present William de Staneway to the church of Great Marlow, Buckinghamshire, allowing Gilbert de Clare, a minor ["*pupilli*"], a pension of 16 marks in compensation for the benefice until other provisions could be made for him. In 1244, being then a resident of the diocese of Worcester, he was granted a papal dispensation at the request of his step-father, Richard, Earl of Cornwall, to hold beneficies to the yearly value of 300 silver marks. His subsequent history is unknown. Dugdale *Monasticon Anglicanum* 2 (1819): 59–65. *Jour. British Arch. Assoc.* 26 (1870): 149–160. Clark *Land of Morgan* (1883): 64–92. *Papal Regs.: Letters* 1 (1893): 207. Grosseteste *Rotuli Roberti Grosseteste Episcopi Lincolniensis* (Lincoln Rec. Soc. 11) (1914): 362–363. Lambert *Bletchingley* 1 (1921): 72–73. VCH *Buckingham* 3 (1925): 76. *C.P.* 5 (1926): 695, footnote m (sub Gloucester). Schwennicke *Europäische Stammtafeln* 3(1) (1984): 156 (sub Clare).

7. RICHARD DE CLARE, Knt., 6th Earl of Gloucester, 5th Earl of Hertford, High Marshal and Chief Butler to the Archbishop of Canterbury, Privy Councillor, 1255, 1258, Warden of the Isle of Portland, Weymouth, and Wyke, 1257, son and heir, born 4 August 1222. His wardship was granted to Hubert de Burgh. He married (1st) at St. Edmund's Bury before Michaelmas 1236 **MARGARET DE BURGH**, daughter of Hubert de Burgh, Knt., Earl of Kent, by his 3rd wife, Margaret, daughter of William *the Lion*, King of Scotland [see BARDOLF 8 and SCOTLAND 4.iii for her ancestry]. They had no issue. When the marriage was discovered, the couple was at once parted, he being interned in his own castle at Bletchingley, Surrey. Margaret died in November 1237. He married (2nd) about 25 Jan. 1237/8 **MAUD DE LACY**, daughter of John de Lacy, Knt., Earl of Lincoln, Magna Carta Baron, by Margaret (or Margery), daughter and heiress of Robert de Quincy [see LACY 3 for her ancestry]. Her maritagium included the manor of Naseby, Northamptonshire. They had three sons, Gilbert, Thomas, Knt., and Boges (or Beges) (clerk) [Treasurer of York], and four daughters, Isabel, Margaret, Rose, and Eglantine. By an unknown mistress, he also had an illegitimate son, Guy (or Gaudin), Knt. He served as a captain in the king's army in Guienne in 1241. In 1243–51 he reached agreement with Walter de Cantelowe, Bishop of Worcester, regarding the charging of tolls for the bishop's men coming to the market at Fairford and the presence of the earl's pigs in the bishop's glade in the forest of Malvern. He engaged in an expedition against the Welsh in 1244–5, and was knighted by the king in London 4 June 1245. He was co-heir in 1245 to his uncle, Anselm Marshal, 9th Earl of Pembroke, by which he inherited a fifth part of the Marshal estates, including Kilkenny and other lordships in Ireland. Sometime after June 1247 he confirmed the grants of Hamo de Blean, John son of Terric, and William Box to the Priory of St. Gregory, Clerkenwell. He went on pilgrimages to St. Edmund at Pontigny in Champagne in 1248 and to Santiago in 1250. In 1248 Isabel, wife of William de Forz, Count of Aumale, sued Earl Richard and his wife, Maud, on a plea of warranty of charter. In 1250 he settled a dispute with the Abbot of Tewkesbury about the right of infangthef or punishment of thieves taken on the Abbey's lands, allowing the jurisdiction and gallows-right of the abbey. The same year he was appointed joint Ambassador to Pope Innocent IV. In 1254 he was appointed joint Ambassador to Castile. He was sent to Edinburgh in 1255 for the purpose of freeing the young king and queen of Scotland from the hands of Robert de Roos. In 1256 he and Richard, Earl of Cornwall, were employed by the king in settling differences between Archbishop Boniface and the Bishop of Rochester. In March 1258 he was appointed joint Ambassador to France. In July 1258 he fell ill, being poisoned with his brother, as it was supposed, by his steward, Walter de Scotenay. He recovered, with the loss of his hair and nails, but his brother died. In 1259 he was appointed chief Ambassador to treat with the Duke of Brittany. At the commencement of hostilities between the king and the nobles, occasioned by Henry's predilection for his Poitevin relatives, he favored the Baronial cause. SIR RICHARD DE CLARE, Earl of Gloucester and Hertford, died testate at Ashenfield (in Waltham), Kent 15, 16, or 22 July 1262 (rumored that he had been poisoned at the table of Peter of Savoy, the Queen's uncle). On the Monday following, his body was taken to the Cathedral Church of Christ at Canterbury, where his entrails were buried before the altar of St. Edward the Confessor; the body was forthwith taken to the Collegiate Church of Tonbridge, Kent, where the heart was buried; and thence the body was finally borne to Tewkesbury, Gloucestershire, and buried there in the choir at Tewkesbury Abbey at his father's right hand 28 July 1262. In 1276–7 John de Aulton, chaplain, arraigned an assize of novel disseisin against his widow, Countess Maud, and others touching common of pasture in Dauntsey, Wiltshire. In 1284 she founded an Augustinian nunnery for forty nuns at the church of St. John the Evangelist and St. Etheldreda at Legh, Devon. Maud, Countess of Gloucester and Hertford, died 29 December, sometime before 10 March 1288/9.

Mastin *Hist. & Antiqs. of Naseby* (1792): 63–65. Dugdale *Monasticon Anglicanum* 2 (1819): 59–65,603 (charter of Richard de Clare, Earl of Gloucester & Hertford dated 1254); 5 (1825): 89, 266 (Obit. of Tintern Abbey: "Matilda de Clare comitissa Gloucestriæ et Herefordiæ [sic] obiit die xix. Decembris."). *Coll. Top. et Gen.* 8 (1843): 72 (sub Kent). Lipscomb *Hist. & Antiqs. of Buckingham* 1 (1847): 200–201 (Clare ped.). Luard *Annales Monastici* 1 (Rolls Ser. 36) (1864): 169 (Tewkesbury Annals sub 1262: "Obiit vir nobilis et omni laude dignus, Ricardus de Clara comes Gloverniæ et Hertfordiæ, idus Julii [15 July]. Et sepultus est apud Theokesberiam quinto kal. augusti [28 July], ad cujus sepulturam interfuerunt episcopus Wygorniæ Walterus de Cantilupo, et Willelmus episcopus Landavensis, et viii. abbates"); 2 (Rolls Ser. 36) (1865): 353 (Annals of Waverley sub A.D. 1262: "Obiit Ricardus comes Glocestriæ."); 4 (Rolls Ser. 36) (1869): 131 (Annals of Oseney sub A.D. 1262: "Die Sabbati proxima ante festum dicti Sancti Kenelmi [16 July] obiit vir nobilis Ricardus comes Gloverniæ in partibus Cantuariæ, et cum magno honore sepultus est ad patres suos apud Teokesbury."). Shirley *Royal & Other Hist. Letters Ill. of King Henry III* 2 (Rolls Ser. 27) (1866): 377–378 (Appendix I). *Jour. British Arch. Assoc.* 26 (1870): 149–160. *Arch. Cambrensis* 4th Ser. 3 (1872): lxxiv–lxxv (grant of lease dated 1275 by Maud de Clare, Countess of Gloucester & Hertford, to Aline Despenser, Countess of Norfolk). *Fifth Rpt.* (Hist. MSS Comm. 4) (1876): 448 (composition dated 1258 between Boniface, Archbishop of Canterbury and Richard de Clare, Earl of Gloucester). Turner *Cal. Charters & Rolls: Bodleian Lib.* (1878): 49 (charter of Maud de Clare, Countess of Gloucester & Hertford dated c.1280). Clark *Land of Morgan* (1883): 93–166. *Annual Rpt. of the Deputy Keeper* 46 (1886): 143. Doyle *Official Baronage of England* 2 (1886): 14 (sub Gloucester), 177 (sub Hertford). Birch *Cat. Seals in the British Museum* 2 (1892): 269 (seal of Richard de Clare, Earl of Gloucester and Hertford dated c.1250 — Obverse. To the right. In armour: hauberk of mail, surcoat, [flat helmet], sword, shield of arms. Horse caparisoned. Arms: three chevrons [CLARE]. Legend wanting. Reverse. A shield of arms of CLARE, as in obverse, suspended by a strap, and supported by two lions rampant addorsed. Legend wanting.). *Papal Regs.: Letters* 1 (1893): 282 (Elmer [recte Oliver] de Traci, clerk, of the diocese of Exeter, styled "earl's kinsman"). *Recueil des Historiens des Gaules et de la France* 23 (1894): 473 (Ex Obituariis Lirensis Monasterii: "22 Jul. Obiit Ricardus, comes de Clare."). *Genealogist* n.s. 13 (1896): 98. Rigg et al. *Cal. Plea Rolls of the Exchequer of the Jews* 1 (1905): 60–61. Wrottesley *Peds. from the Plea Rolls* (1905): 133–134, 146, 470–471. *Rpt. on MSS in Various Colls.* 4 (Hist. MSS Comm. 55) (1907): 256. *C.P.R. 1247–1258* (1908): 12. *D.N.B.* 4 (1908): 393–396 (biog. of Richard de Clare: "[He] was the most powerful English noble of his time …. Avarice … was the leading characteristic of his mind … [he] appeared as one pre-eminently skilled in the laws of his country … He was a great lover of tournaments."). VCH *Hampshire* 3 (1908): 85–93. *C.P.R. 1258–1266* (1910): 266. Clay *Extinct & Dormant Peerages* (1913): 115–116 (sub Lacy). *C.P.* 3 (1913): 244; 5 (1926): 696–702 (sub Gloucester); 6 (1926): 503 (sub Hertford). Turner *Cal. Feet of Fines Rel. Huntingdon* (Cambridge Antiq. Soc. 8° Ser. 37) (1913): 30. *Desc. Cat. Ancient Deeds* 6 (1915): 5–6, 276. Foster *Final Concords of Lincoln from the Feet of Fines A.D. 1244–1272* 2 (Lincoln Rec. Soc. 17) (1920): 280–294. Lambert *Bletchingley* 1 (1921): 64–66, 69–87. VCH *Buckingham* 3 (1925): 70–71, 104; 4 (1927): 300, 510. Cam *Hundred & Hundred Rolls* (1930): 266. Richardson & Sayles *Rotuli Parl. Anglie Hactenus Inediti 1274–1373* (Camden Soc. 3rd Ser. 51) (1935): 192–193. *C.C.R. 1261–1264* (1936): 83. Powicke *Henry III & Lord Edward* (1947). Woodcock *Cartulary of the Priory of St. Gregory, Canterbury* (Camden 3rd Ser. 88) (1956): 160–161 (charter of Richard de Clare, Earl of Gloucester & Hertford). Paget *Baronage of England* (1957) 130: 7–8. Clay *York Minster Fasti* 2 (Yorkshire Arch. Soc. Recs. 124) (1959): 54. Sanders *English Baronies* (1960): 34–35. Ross *Cartulary of Cirencester Abbey* 2 (1964): 41–44, 400–402, 436–437, 563–564; 3 (1977): 1117. London *Cartulary of Canonsleigh Abbey* (Devon & Cornwall Rec. Soc. n.s. 8) (1965): 1–2, 77 (charter of Maud), 77–80, 92–93, 95–97, 97 (acknowledgement of Maud), 98, 99 (charter of Maud), 99–102, 104. Clanchy *Civil Pleas of the Wiltshire Eyre 1249* (Wiltshire Rec. Soc. 26) (1971): 120. Clanchy *Roll & Writ of the Berkshire Eyre of 1248* (Selden Soc. 90) (1973): 199, 288. Adams *Select Cases from Eccl. Courts of Canterbury 1200–1301* (Selden Soc. 95) (1981): 138–144 (suit dated c.1271–2, in which Earl Richard's widow, Maud, claimed one third of his moveables valued at £12,000). Harper-Bill *Stoke by Clare Cartulary* 1 (Suffolk Charters 4) (1982): 33 (acquittance of Richard de Clare, Earl of Gloucester and Hertford, dated 1247). Schwennicke *Europäische Stammtafeln* 3(1) (1984): 156 (sub Clare). Powicke *Henry III & Lord Edward* (1947). Merrick *Morganiae Archaiographia* (South Wales Rec. Soc. 1) (1983): 41–52. Sutton *Rolls & Reg. of Bishop Oliver Sutton, 1280–1299* 8 (Lincoln Rec. Soc. 76) (1986): 125. Kemp *Reading Abbey Cartularies* 2 (Camden 4th Ser. 33) (1987): 230 (charter of Richard de Clare, Earl of Gloucester & Hertford dated c.1247), 230 (Richard de Clare, Earl of Gloucester & Hertford styled "son" [i.e., son-in-law] in charter of Margaret de Lacy, Countess of Lincoln & Pembroke, dated 1247). Harper-Bill *Cartulary of the Augustinian Friars of Clare* (1991). Hoskin *English Episcopal Acta* 13 (1997): 93, 100–102, 107–109, 148, 151, 163. Mitchell *Portraits of Medieval Women* (2003). Legg *Lost Cartulary of Bolton Priory* (Yorkshire Arch. Soc. Rec. Ser. 160) (2009): 50 (memorandum names Richard de Brus as son of Isabel, sister of Richard de Clare, Earl of Gloucester and Hertford). Online resource: http://www.briantimms.net/rolls_of_arms/rolls/gloversB1.htm (Glover's Roll dated c.1252 — arms of Richard de Clare, Earl of Gloucester: Or three chevrons gules.

Children of Richard de Clare, Knt., by Maud de Lacy:

i. **GILBERT DE CLARE**, Knt., Earl of Gloucester and Hertford [see next].

ii. **THOMAS DE CLARE**, Knt., of Thomond in Connacht, Ireland, married **JULIANE FITZ MAURICE** [see BADLESMERE 8].

iii. **BOGES** (or **BOEGHES, BEGES**) **DE CLARE**, clerk, papal chaplain, king's clerk, born 21 July 1248. In 1258 his father, Earl Richard, presented him to the church of Rotherfield, Sussex, but the appointment was disallowed. Boges occurs as Canon of York from 5 Nov. 1265, Canon of Exeter, 1267, parson of St. Peter in the East, Oxford, Papal chaplain by 1282, Canon of Wells, 1284, King's Clerk by 1285, Treasurer of York, 1285–93, Chancellor of Llandaff, 1287–90, Canon of Chichester, 28 Sept. 1294, Dean of Stafford. In the period, 1275–85, he surrendered to Queen Eleanor of Castile his tenement in Sideyard Street, Oxford called "la Oriole." In 1277–8 John de Kent and Isabel his wife arraigned an assize of novel disseisin against Boges de Clare, parson of the church of Dorking, and others regarding a tenement in Dorking, Surrey. In 1280, acting as parson of Fordingbridge, Hampshire, he disputed the right of William le Brune to the assize of bread and ale in Fordingbridge, Hampshire; the case was tried before the justices in eyre, and was decided in favor of William le Brune. In 1290 Boges was fined £1,000 for summoning the Earl of Cornwall to appear before the Archbishop of Canterbury during Parliament. In 1291 he and his successors were granted a market and a fair at his manor of Tollerton, Yorkshire. His extensive pluralism is shown in part in a letter from the Archbishop of York to the Archbishop of Canterbury dated 16 Feb. 1290/1 which gives a list of his benefices in the diocese and province of York. In 1293 Boges de Clare, Dean of Stafford, and the Chapter, were sued by William Wyger in a writ of darrein presentement; Boges answered that he had the church to his own use by gift from the king. In 1294 he held the churches of Dunmow, Essex, Polstead and Soham, Suffolk, Leverington, Cambridgeshire, and a moiety of the church of Walpole, Norfolk. BOGES DE CLARE died at London 26 October 1294. Dugdale *Monasticon Anglicanum* 2 (1819): 59–65. *Year Books of Edward I: Years XX & XXI* 1 (Rolls Ser. 31a) (1866): 408–409. *Jour. British Arch. Assoc.* 22 (1866): 214; 26 (1870): 149–160. Simpson *Docs. Ill. the Hist. of St. Paul's Cathedral* (Camden Soc. n.s. 26) (1880): 42 (sub 1294: "Obiit Dominus Bogo de Clare multarum Rector Ecclesiarum vel potius incubator."). Clark *Land of Morgan* (1883): 93–166. *Annual Rpt. of the Deputy Keeper* 47 (1886): 207; 50 (1889): 39. Burton *Hist. & Antiqs. of the Parish of Hemingsbrough* (1888): 48–50 (biog. of Bogo de Clare: "One consequence of this mass of preferment was that De Clare was always in litigation. He was never out of the king's and the bishop's courts, and he seems to have defied them all alike. He had a little army of bailiffs and receivers, whom he often did not pay. The bishops were continually attacking him for non-residence and plurality, but he had his papal dispensations to flourish in their face …. In 1290 a poor wretched officer of the law went into De Clare's house in London to serve a writ. The servants, after making the poor wretch eat the document, seals and all, beat and imprisoned him. In this case De Clare was obliged to answer in person, but he threw the blame upon his servants, who took care to be out of the way when searched for. … Here we have a man, receiving an income from his ecclesiastical preferments of not less than 50,000*l*. a year in our money, neglecting every duty, and yet strong enough in his influence with the Court and at Rome to defy everyone who strove to call him to account. … De Clare died in London on 1st November, 1294, leaving an evil name behind."). Rogers *Oxford City Docs., Financial & Judicial 1258–1665* 3 (Oxford Hist. Soc. 18) (1890): 96–97. *Papal Regs.: Letters* 1 (1893): 466, 486, 509–510, 519, 570. *C.P.R. 1292–1301* (1895): 63–65 (Boeghes de Clare styled "brother" [frere] by Margaret [de Clare], Countess of Cornwall), 118. *Sussex Arch. Colls.* 41 (1898): 52–53. *VCH Hampshire* 4 (1911): 567–577. *Assoc. Architectural Socs.' Rpts. & Papers* 33 (1915–16): 35–73. *Archæologia* 70 (1920): 1–56. Dew *Hist. of the Parish & Church of Kilhampton* (1928): 26, 30, 33. Jenkinson & Fermoy *Select Cases in the Exchequer of Pleas* (Selden Soc. 48) (1932): 113–116. *Jour. Hist. Soc. of the Church in Wales* 1 (1947): 15–25. Emden *Biog. Reg. of the Univ. of Oxford* 1 (1957): 423–424. Clay *York Minster Fasti* 1 (Yorkshire Arch. Soc. Recs. 123) (1957): 26–27; 2 (Yorkshire Arch. Soc. Recs. 124) (1959): 54. Labarge *Mistress, Maids & Men: Baronial Life in the 13th Cent.* (1965). Prestwich *Three Edwards: War & State in England* (1980): 109. Schwennicke *Europäische Stammtafeln* 3(1) (1984): 156 (sub Clare). *Rolls & Reg. of Bishop Oliver Sutton 1280–1299* 8 (Lincoln Rec. Soc. 76) (1986): 173. Hicks *Who's Who in Late Medieval England* (1991): 19–20 (biog. of Bogo Clare: "… the most notorious pluralist in medieval England."). Neve *Fasti Ecclesiæ Anglicanæ 1066–1300* 5 (1996): 14, 38; 9 (2003): 21. Hoskin *English Episcopal Acta* 13 (1997): 41–43. Parsons *Eleanor of Castile* (1997): 186, 202. Mitchell *Portraits of Medieval Women* (2003). Schofield *Peasant & Community in Medieval England 1200–1500* (2003): 194 ("Bogo de Clare … at his death in 1291 held, amongst other offices, 24 parishes and the income they generated (more than £2000), was atypical in his assiduity.").

iv. **ISABEL DE CLARE**, married at Lyons 28 March 1257 (as his 1st wife) **GUGLIELMO** (or **WILLIAM**) **VII**, Marquis [Marchese] of Monferrato, son and heir of Bonifacio II, Marquis of Monferrato, by Margherita, daughter of Amadeo IV, Count of Savoy. He was near kinsman of King Edward I of England. They had one daughter, Margarita (or Margherita). He married (2nd) in 1271 **BEATRICE** (or **BEATRIZ**) **OF CASTILE**, daughter of Alfonso X, *el Sabio*, King of Castile, León, Toledo, Galicia, Seville, Córdoba, Murcia, Jaén & the Algarve, by Violante (or Yolanda), daughter of Jaime I *el Conquistador*, King of Aragón, Majorca & Valencia, Count of Barcelona and Urgel, seigneur of Montpellier. They had one son, Giovanni (I) [Marquis of Monferrato] and two daughters, Yolanda (wife of Andronikas II Palæologus) and Alasina (wife of Poncello Orsini, signore of

Montefiascone, senator of Rome). His wife, Beatrice, was living in 1280. GUGLIELMO VII, Marquis of Monferrato, died in captivity at Alexandria 6 Feb. 1292. Dugdale *Monasticon Anglicanum* 2 (1819): 59–65. *Jour. British Arch. Assoc.* 26 (1870): 149–160. Clark *Land of Morgan* (1883): 93–166. *C.P.R. 1247–1258* (1908): 662. Lambert *Bletchingley* 1 (1921): 82. *Hidalguía* Nos. 172–173 (1982): 324 (chart). Schwennicke *Europäische Stammtafeln* 2 (1984): 63 (sub Castile), 200 (sub Montferrat); 3(1) (1984): 156 (sub Clare). Sayer *Original Papal Docs. in England & Wales (1198–1304)* (1999): 426 (William, marquis of Monferrato, styled "cousin" of King Edward I of England).

Child of Isabel de Clare, by Guglielmo VII of Monferrato:

a. **MARGARITA** (or **MARGHERITA**) **OF MONFERRATO**, married at Burgos in 1281 (as his 1st wife) **JUAN OF CASTILE**, señor of Valencia de Campos, Oropesa, Baena, Ponferrada, etc., younger son of Alfonso X, *el Sabio*, King of Castile, León, Toledo, Galicia, Seville, Córdoba, Murcia, Jaén & the Algarve, by Violante (or Yolanda), daughter of Jaime I *el Conquistador*, King of Aragón, Majorca & Valencia, Count of Barcelona and Urgel, seigneur of Montpellier. They had one son, Alfonso [señor of Valencia de Campos and Mansilla]. His wife, Margherita, was living in 1286. He married (2nd) before 11 May 1287 **MARÍA DÍAZ DE HARO**, señora of Vizcaya, daughter of Lope Díaz de Haro, señor of Vizcaya. They had two sons, Lope and Juan (señor of Vizcaya) and one daughter, María Díaz (wife of Juan Nuño de Lara, señor of Lara). **JUAN OF CASTILE** died at Vega de Granada 25 June 1319. Vilena *El Limeño Don Juan de Valencia el del Infante* (1952). *Hidalguía* Nos. 172–173 (1982): 324 (chart). Schwennicke *Europäische Stammtafeln* 2 (1984): 63 (sub Castile), 200 (sub Montferrat); 3(1) (1984): 124A (Valencia de Campos). Martinez *Alfonso X, el Sabio* (2003).

v. **MARGARET DE CLARE**, married **EDMUND OF CORNWALL** (usually styled **EDMUND OF ALMAIN**), Knt., Earl of Cornwall [see CORNWALL 6.ii].

vi. **ROSE DE CLARE**, married **ROGER DE MOWBRAY**, Knt., 1st Lord Mowbray [see MOWBRAY 3].

vii. **EGLANTINE DE CLARE**. Dugdale *Monasticon Anglicanum* 2 (1819): 59–65. *Jour. British Arch. Assoc.* 26 (1870): 149–160. Clark *Land of Morgan* (1883): 93–166. Schwennicke *Europäische Stammtafeln* 3(1) (1984): 156 (sub Clare).

Illegitimate child of Richard de Clare, Knt., by an unknown mistress, _____:

i. **GUY** (or **GAUDIN**) **DE CLARE**, Knt. In 1280–1 Thomas del Park' arraigned an assize of novel disseisin against him and others touching a tenement in East Brightwell, Oxfordshire. In 1301 he witnessed a grant of land by Sir Robert Wandak (or Wandard), of Shotteswell, Oxfordshire, to his brothers, Robert, Rector of Shotteswell, and Thomas. Sometime prior to 1307, his brother Earl Gilbert de Clare's widow, Joan, granted him the manor of Easington (in Chilton), Buckinghamshire for life, of which he died seised. Royce *Hist. Notices of the Parish of Cropredy, Oxon* (Trans. North Oxfordshire Arch. Soc.) (1880): 6. *Annual Rpt. of the Deputy Keeper* 50 (1889): 36. VCH *Buckingham* 4 (1927): 25. Brault *Rolls of Arms Edward I* 2 (1997): 105 (arms of Gaudin de Clare: Argent, three chevrons gules, in chief two lions rampant sable). Online resource: http://www.briantimms.net/era/lord_marshals/Lord_Marshal05/Lord%20Marshal5.htm.

8. GILBERT DE CLARE, Knt., 7th Earl of Gloucester, 6th Earl of Hertford, Steward of St. Edmund's Abbey, son and heir, born at Christchurch, Hampshire 2 Sept. 1243. He married (1st) in the spring of 1253 **ALICE** (or **ALIX**) **DE LUSIGNAN** (or **DE LA MARCHE**), daughter of Hugues [XI] *le Brun* (or de Lusignan), Count of La Marche and Angoulême, seigneur of Lusignan in Poitou (uterine brother of Henry III, King of England), by Yolande, daughter of Pierre de Braine *styled* Mauclerc, Knt., Duke of Brittany, Earl of Richmond [see LUSIGNAN 6 for her ancestry]. They had two daughters, Isabel and Joan. Earl Gilbert played an important role in the constitutional crisis and the Barons' War, 1258–67. Initially he supported the Baronial cause. He and Simon de Montfort, Earl of Leicester captured Rochester, Kent 18 April 1264, but shortly afterwards Tonbridge and Rochester fell to the royalists, who soon gained control over southeast England. On 6 May the royalist forces were camped at Lewes, Sussex. Attempts at arbitration failed, and on 14 May the Battle of Lewes was fought. Earl Gilbert commanded the 2nd line at the battle, where the king and his brother, Richard, Earl of Cornwall, were captured. Prince Edward and his cousin, Henry of Almain, became hostages, being initially sent to Dover Castle. The king and Richard of Cornwall were taken to London with Montfort. Montfort made every effort to secure peace, as unrest within the realm continued. Earl Gilbert, then the most powerful lord in the kingdom, was annoyed because Bristol had passed into Montfort's hands. Furthermore, the earl was jealous of Montfort's monopoly of power. Consequently early in 1265 Earl Gilbert withdrew to the Welsh March, the home of Montfort's intractable enemies. In Feb. 1265 Montfort banned a tournament at Dunstable for fear of conflict between his men and the followers of Earl Gilbert. All efforts to arrange a meeting between Montfort and Earl Gilbert failed. On 28 May 1265 Prince Edward escaped from captivity to join Mortimer and Earl Gilbert at Wigmore. The following month, Prince Edward and Earl Gilbert were denounced as rebels by Montfort. Earl Gilbert shared Prince Edward's victory at Kenilworth 31 July–August 1265, and, at the Battle of Evesham, 4 August 1265, he commanded the 2nd division and contributed largely to the victory. At the end of 1266, Earl Gilbert quarreled with Mortimer, who favored a more violent policy of repression. Sometime before 1267, Earl Gilbert conveyed the manor of Sunworth (in Buriton), Hampshire to Roger de Loveday, to hold to him and his heirs by the annual payment of a pair of gilt spurs at Easter. Earl Gilbert and his wife, Alice, were legally separated at Norwich, Norfolk 18 July 1271. In 1271 he had license to enditch his new castle of Caerphilly in Wales. At the death of King Henry III 16 Nov. 1272, Earl Gilbert took the lead in swearing fealty to King Edward I, who was then in Sicily returning from the Crusade. He was Joint Guardian of England during the king's absence. In 1274–5 William de Valence and Joan his wife arraigned an assize of novel disseisin against Gilbert [de Clare], Earl of Gloucester, and Robert de Boyton touching a tenement in Woolstone, Buckinghamshire. In 1275 Gilbert went to France to negotiate for peace. He was summoned to serve against the Welsh in 1277 and 1282. In 1278 he was among those selected to escort King Alexander III of Scotland to the king. He failed to recover his ancestors' lands in Normandy in the Paris Parlement in 1279. In May 1283 he was contracted to marry the king's daughter, Joan, provided he be formally divorced from his wife, Alice, and be free to marry where he will, and also that he obtain a dispensation from the Pope to marry to Joan, a 1st cousin once removed of Alice. In 1285 Gilbert was absolved from the contract of marriage between him and his former wife, Alice. He granted Alice various properties for her support, including the park and manor of Thaxted, Essex, and the manors of Warham, Wells, and Wiveton, Norfolk, Burford, Oxfordshire, and Speenhamland, Berkshire; she subsequently married Gilbert de Lindsey.9 In 1286 and 1287 he was beyond seas with the king, and, in June 1287, he was again in Wales on the king's service. In 1287 he sued Cecily de Vivonne, widow of John de Beauchamp, and others regarding the wardship of Thomas de Hawy. He married (2nd) at Westminster Abbey 23 April 1290 (by dispensation dated 16 Nov. 1289, they being related in the 2nd & 3rd degrees of affinity) **JOAN OF ENGLAND** [sometimes styled **JOAN OF ACRE**], daughter of Edward I, King of England, by his 1st wife, Eleanor, daughter of [Saint] Fernando III, King of Castile, León, Galicia, Toledo, Córdoba, Jaén, and Seville [see ENGLAND 7 for her ancestry]. She was born at Acre in Palestine in Spring 1272. They had one son, Gilbert, Knt. [Earl of Gloucester and Hertford], and three daughters, Eleanor, Margaret, and Elizabeth. In 1291 his quarrels with the Earl of Hereford about Brecknock culminated in a private war between them. Both earls were imprisoned by the king, Earl Gilbert being fined 10,000 marks as the aggressor. In 1291 his wife, Joan, received a papal indult to enter Cistercian monasteries accompanied by eight honest matrons. In 1293 he was appointed Captain of the forces in Ireland, and resided there until some time in 1294. He presented to the churches of Marlow, Buckinghamshire, 1295, and Thurning, Northamptonshire, 1295. SIR GILBERT DE

---

9 For evidence of Alice's 2nd marriage, see *Cal. IPM* 3 (1912): 234–251; *Genealogist* n.s. 38 (1922): 169–172. Alice's 2nd husband, Gilbert de Lindsey, is presumably Gilbert de Lindsey, Knt., of Molesworth, Huntingdonshire, who occurs in the period, 1279–1305/6 [see VCH *Huntingdon* 3 (1936): 92–96; DeWindt *Royal Justice & the Medieval English Countryside* 2 (1981): 617; McAndrew *Scotland's Hist. Heraldry* (2006): 93–94]. Presumably she is the Alice de la Marche, tenant in chief, who died shortly before 24 March 1290 [see *C.F.R.* 1 (1911): 277].

CLARE, Earl of Gloucester and Hertford, died at Monmouth Castle 7 Dec. 1295, and was buried at Tewkesbury Abbey, Gloucestershire. His widow, Joan, married (2nd) early in 1297 **RALPH DE MONTHERMER**, Knt., Privy Councillor, Keeper of Caerlyon, Cardiff, Caerfilly, Lantrissan, Newburgh, and Usk Castles, 1307, Steward of the lands of Earl of Buchan, 1308, Guardian and Lieutenant in Scotland, 1311, Steward of the lands of John ap Adam, 1311, Justice of the Forest south of Trent, 1315–20. Ralph was a native of Wales. Ralph was a native of Wales, and was near related to John Bluet, Knt., who served as his bachelor in Scotland in 1303. Ralph and Joan had two sons, Thomas, Knt. [2nd Lord Monthermer], and Edward, Knt. [Lord Monthermer], and one daughter, Mary (wife of Duncan of Fife, Knt., 10th Earl of Fife [see CLARE 8.ii.a below]). Their marriage enraged her father, the king, and he committed Ralph to prison in Bristol Castle 10–22 July 1297, and all of Joan's lands were seised into the king's hand. By the mediation of Anthony Bek, Bishop of Durham, peace was made between the king and his daughter, and her lands were restored to her 31 July 1297, save Tonbridge and the Isle of Portland. The king afterwards became much attached to his new son-in-law, who was summoned to Parliament as Earl of Gloucester and Hertford during the minority of his step-son, Gilbert de Clare. By Sept. 1297 Ralph and his wife were allowed to stay in the outer bailey of Windsor Castle, which the king had lent them. In 1297 he was summoned to serve with the king's overseas expedition. In 1298 he was appointed Captain of the 4th Division of the king's army in Scotland. He was summoned to serve against the Scots in 1299, 1300, and frequently thereafter. He fought at the Battle of Falkirk 22 July 1298, and was present at the Siege of Caerlaverock Castle in 1300. He presented to the churches of Pimperne, Dorset, 1299, and Naseby, Northamptonshire, 1305. He signed the Barons' letter to Pope Boniface VIII in 1301 as *Rad'us de Monte H'meri Com' Glouc' & Herf*. In 1303 he and his wife, Joan, arraigned an assize of novel disseisin against Gilbert son of Thomas de Clare concerning a tenement in Plashes (in Standon), Hertfordshire. He was briefly Earl of Atholl in Scotland, 1306–7, he being defeated by King Robert de Brus in 1307. JOAN OF ENGLAND died 7 April 1307, and was buried in the Austin Friars at Clare, Suffolk. In August 1307 he surrendered to King Edward II custody of the lands of his step-son, Gilbert de Clare, a minor, and had a grant of 5,000 marks in lieu thereof. In 1308 John de Huntley, of cos. Somerset and Gloucester, owed him a debt of £15. The same year he had license to hunt in the king's forests or chases when passing through them. He was granted a charter for a weekly market and two yearly fairs at his manor of Llanfair Discoed, Monmouthshire in Nov. 1308. He was summoned to Parliament from 4 March 1308/9 to 13 Sept. 1324, by writs directed *Radulpho de Monte Hermerii*, whereby he is held to have become Lord Monthermer. In 1309 he was granted the barony of Erlestoke, Wiltshire, including the manors of Stokenham, Oakford, Pyworthy, and Sterte, Devon and Hunton, Hampshire. A similar grant of Warblington, Hampshire was made to him in Dec. 1310. He was going beyond seas in the king's service in May 1313. In 1313 Henry Fitz Alan brought a writ of replevin against him and complained that he had wrongfully seised his beasts, namely two bullocks, one calf, and two mares in Dodbrooke Burgh, Devon, whereby Henry claimed he suffered damages to the amount of £20. Ralph fought at the Battle of Bannockburn 24 June 1314, where he was taken prisoner. In 1315 he had permission to go on pilgrimage to Santiago of Compostella in Spain. The same year he presented to the church of Stokenham, Devon. He likewise presented to the church of Shorncote, Wiltshire in 1316 and 1317, by reason of the land and heir of John ap Adam being in his hand. He married (2nd) before 20 Nov. 1318 (without the king's permission) **ISABEL LE DESPENSER**, widow successively of Gilbert de Clare, Knt. (died shortly before 16 Nov. 1307) [see BADLESMERE 8.i] and John de Hastings, Knt., 1st Lord Hastings (died 10 Feb. 1312/3) [see HASTINGS 10], and daughter of Hugh le Despenser, Knt., Earl of Winchester, 1st Lord Despenser, by Isabel, daughter of William de Beauchamp, Knt., 9th Earl of Warwick [see DESPENSER 10 for her ancestry]. In Dec. 1318 perambulation was made by the mayor, sheriffs, and aldermen of

London of the land of the Dean and Chapter of St. Paul's in the parish of St. Dunstan [? in the East], London on complaint of Thomas de Neusom, clerk of Sir Ralph de Monthermer, who stated that because the tenement of the Dean and Chapter adjoining that of Ralph was not built up along the street, vagabonds crossing the tenement by night broke down Ralph's party-walls and entered and done damage there. Ralph and his wife, Isabel, were pardoned by the king 12 August 1319 for marrying without the king's permission. In 1324 he was summoned for military service in Gascony in person. After the reduction of the Queen's household in 1324, the king's daughters, Eleanor and Joan, were put in charge of Ralph and his wife in the king's castle of Marlborough. SIR RALPH DE MONTHERMER, 1st Lord Monthermer, died 10 May (or 5 April) 1325, and was buried at Grey Friars, Salisbury, Wiltshire. He left a will enrolled 15 July 1325. On 19 Feb. 1325/6 his widow, Isabel, was appointed custodian of the *corpus* of Marlborough Castle and of the houses within the walls for the safe dwelling of herself and of the king's daughters living with her. Isabel died testate 4 (or 5) Dec. 1334, and was buried at Grey Friars, Salisbury, Wiltshire.

Weever *Ancient Funerall Monuments* (1631): 734–740. Sandford *Gen. Hist. of the Kings of England* (1677): 139–143. Pole *Colls. towards a Desc. of Devon* (1791): 287. Mastin *Hist. & Antiqs. of Naseby* (1792): 94. Brydges *Collins' Peerage of England* 6 (1812): 496–511 (sub Despenser). Dugdale *Monasticon Anglicanum* 2 (1819): 59–65; 6(1) (1830): 148 ("1307. Obiit Johanna de Acres comitissa de Clare"); 6(3) (1830): 1600–1602 ("Dame Johan of Acris"). Nicolas *Siege of Carlaverock* (1828): 275–279 (biog. of Ralph de Monthermer). Palgrave *Docs. & Recs. Ill. the Hist. of Scotland* 1 (1837): 301. Banks *Baronies in Fee* 1 (1844): 328–329 (sub Monthermer). Lipscomb *Hist. & Antiqs. of Buckingham* 1 (1847): 200–201 (Clare ped.). Hawley *Royal Fam. of England* (1851): 22–23. Green *Lives of the Princesses of England* 2 (1857): 318–362. *Monthermer Peerage. In the House of Lords. Case on Behalf of William Lowndes* (1860). Hutchins *Hist. & Antiqs. of Dorset* 1 (1861): 296. *Archives Hist. de Département de la Gironde* 6 (1864): 345–346. *Year Books of Edward I: Years XXXII–XXXIII* 4 (Rolls Ser. 31a) (1864): 176–179. Haddan *Councils & Eccl. Docs. Rel. Great Britain & Ireland* 1 (1869): 612–613. Hardy *Syllabus (in English) of the Docs. Rel. England & Other Kingdoms* 1 (1869): 145, 153, 158, 163, 183, 184, 204. Luard *Annales Monastici* 4 (Rolls Ser. 36) (1869): 502 (Annals of Worcester sub A.D. 1290 — "Pridie kal. Maii [30 April] G[ilbertus] comes Gloucestriæ Johannam filiam regis duxit uxorem."). *Jour. British Arch. Assoc.* 26 (1870): 149–160. Wright *Feudal Manuals of English Hist.* (1872). *Fifth Rpt.* (Hist. MSS Comm. 4) (1876): 302 (charters of Gilbert de Clare, Earl of Gloucester & Hertford, and his wife, Joan, dated 1290–91; "the third [seal] is a large one of the Earl on a horse in chain armour, with sword and shield charged with three chevrons; the horse's trappings are charged with the same (well cut); the heads of the horse and man and the feet of the horse are gone; on the obverse is a large shield of arms; the fourth [seal] is that of the Countess, a small seal, three lions."). Lennard & Vincent *Vis. of Warwick 1619* (H.S.P. 12) (1877): 282–285 (Spencer ped.: "Isabella [Despenser] ux. Joh'is Hastinges Dn'i Abergauennie, 2 Rad'i Monthermer"). *Arch. Cambrensis* 4th Ser. 9 (1878): 51–59. Turner *Cal. Charters & Rolls: Bodleian Lib.* (1878): 687. *Annual Rpt. of the Deputy Keeper* 44 (1883): 65, 74, 96, 102, 135, 202, 215, 232, 259, 266, 279, 302, 303. Clark *Land of Morgan* (1883): 93–166. Doyle *Official Baronage of England* 1 (1886): 93 (sub Athol); 2 (1886): 15–17 (sub Gloucester). Stafford *Reg. of Edmund Stafford* (1886): 339–340. Bain *Cal. Docs. Rel. Scotland* 4 (1888): 370 (Sir John Bluet styled "bacheler and cousin" of Ralph de Monthermer, Earl of Gloucester in 1303). *Trans. Hist. Soc. of Lanc. & Cheshire* n.s 5 (1889): 39 ("The first observed instance of a mantling or lambrequin, as it was then called, — a term still applied to it by the modern French heralds, — occurs in the large seal of Ralph de Monthermer, Earl of Gloucester and Hertford, 1299. This is engraved in Nicholas Upton, *De Usu Militari* [Bisse edition, 1654, p. 63]. In Planché's *Poursuivant* the helmet and mantling alone are engraved from this seal. It is represented as a square handkerchief or shawl fastened at one end under the crest, and flying out loose behind. There is no hacking. Ralph de Monthermer was a 'plain esquire,' but attracted the attention and secured the love of Joan of Acres, daughter of Edward I. and relict of Gilbert de Clare, Earl of Gloucester. May we be allowed to fancy we see here the kerchief of the fair lady whose favour led to his advancement, and whose marriage eventually brought him his title?"). *Desc. Cat. Ancient Deeds* 1 (1890): 108. Stevenson *Rental of all the Houses in Gloucester, A.D. 1455* (1890): 122 (ped. in Hist. of the Kings of England dated c.1470). Birch *Cat. Seals in the British Museum* 2 (1892): 268 (undated seal of Gilbert de Clare, Earl of Gloucester and Hertford — Obverse. To the left. In armour: hauberk of mail, surcoat, flat helmet with vizor down, sword, shield of arms. Horse galloping. Arms: three chevrons [CLARE]. Legend: SIGILL' GILBERTI · DE · CLARE : COMITIS : …..VERNIE. Reverse. To the right. In armour: hauberk of mail, surcoat, flat helmet with vizor down, sword, shield of arms. Horse caparisoned, galloping. Arms: CLARE. Legend: SIGILL' GIL[EBE]RTI : DE : CLARE : COMITIS : HERTFORDIE. Beaded borders), 324 (seal of Ralph de Monthermer, Earl of Gloucester & Hertford dated 1301 — Obverse. A shield of arms, as in reverse, suspended by a loop from a forked tree, and between two wyverns with tails floriated. Legend: [….CO]M' : G[L]OV'NIE : HERTF[OR]D' …. Reverse. To the left. In armour: hauberk of mail, surcoat, helmet with vizor down and furnished with a lambrequin (the crest, an eagle displayed, see Doyle *Official Baronage of England* 2 (1886): 16, is wanting), sword, shield of arms. Horse galloping, caparisoned and plumed, with the crest of an eagle displayed. Arms: an eagle displayed [MONTHERMER]. Legend: …. RTFORD : KILKENI ET DNI GLA…. Beaded borders.). *Papal Regs.: Letters* 1 (1893): 525. Fry & Fry *Abs. of Feet of Fines Rel. Dorset* 1 (Dorset Rec. Soc. 5) (1896): 245–246, 248. *Genealogist* n.s. 13 (1896): 98; n.s. 20 (1904): 71, 162–163; n.s. 21 (1905): 78–82; n.s. 38 (1922): 169–172. *C.Ch.R.* 1 (1903): 438–439 (Alice, contracted wife of Gilbert de Clare, styled "niece" by Aymer de Valence, Bishop elect of Winchester, and Sir William de Valence in 1255); 3 (1908): 72, 131–132. *English Hist. Rev.* 18 (1903): 112–116. Howard de Walden *Some Feudal Lords & Their Seals* (1903): 9–10 (biog. of Ralph de Monthermer). *C.P.R. 1321–1324* (1904): 203. *List of Inqs. ad Quod Damnum* 1 (PRO Lists and Indexes 17) (1904): 238. Wrottesley *Peds. from the Plea Rolls* (1905): 7, 133–134, 146, 341, 470–471. Hervey *Suffolk in 1327* (Suffolk Green Books No. IX Vol. II) (1906): 131, 209, 211. *Rpt. on MSS in Various Colls.* 4 (Hist. MSS Com. 55) (1907): 75. *D.N.B.* 4 (1908): 378–382 (biog. of Gilbert de Clare: "[He] was the most powerful English noble of his day."); 13 (1909): 773–774 (biog. of Ralph de Monthermer). VCH *Buckingham* 2 (1908): 298–299, 348; 3 (1925): 6, 70; 4 (1927): 23, 25, 300, 395–401, 510. VCH *Hampshire* 3 (1908): 85–93, 134–136, 408–413. *C.P.* 1 (1910): 346 (sub Audley); 3 (1913): 244 (sub Clare); 4 (1916): 267–271 (sub Despenser), Appendix H, 671 (chart); 5 (1926): 346–349 (sub Hastings), 373, 702–712 (sub Gloucester), 753; 6 (1926): 503 (sub Hertford); 9 (1936): 140–142 (sub Monthermer). Lane *Royal Daughters of England* 1 (1910): 182–192. *C.F.R.* 3 (1912): 357. *Cal. Various Chancery Rolls 1277–1326* (1912): 69, 348 (Joan styled "king's daughter"). VCH *Surrey* 4 (1912): 87. *C.P.R. 1266–1272* (1913): 684 (Alice, 1st wife of Gilbert de Clare, styled "king's niece"). Turner *Cal. Feet of Fines Rel. Huntingdon* (Cambridge Antiq. Soc. 8° Ser. 37) (1913): 39. *Feet of Fines for Essex* 2 (1913–28): 128, 219, 237. *Year Books of Edward II* 15 (Selden Soc. 36) (1918): 218–225; 25 (Selden Soc. 81) (1964): 78–82. Wall *Handbook of the Maude Roll* (1919) unpaginated (ped. dated c.1461–85: "Johanna comitissa de Gloucester"). Lambert *Bletchingley* 1 (1921): 88–105. Cam *Hundred & Hundred Rolls* (1930): 263–265, 267, 271–272, 276. Moor *Knights of Edward I* 3 (H.S.P. 82) (1930): 190–192 (sub Sr Ralph de Monthermer). *C.C.R. 1405–1419* (1931): 444–445 (will of Ralph de Monthermer). Johnstone *Letters of Edward Prince of Wales 1304–1305* (1931): 70 [Joan styled "very dear sister" [treschere soer] by Edward, Prince of Wales (afterwards King Edward II)]. Thomas *Cal. Plea & Memoranda Rolls of London 1381–1412* (1932): 291. Gandavo *Reg. Simonis de Gandavo Diocesis Saresbriensis 1297–1315* 2 (Canterbury & York Soc. 41) (1934): 569–570. *English Hist. Rev.* 58 (1943): 51–78 (St. Edmundsbury Chronicle, 1296–1301: "Mortuo comite Glovernie Gilberto adhesit quidem iuvenis nomine Radulphus de marchia oriundus cognomine Mowhermer a secretis comitisse; quo militaribus a rege peticione dicte comitisse accincto sollempnitate tepide vel publice non promulgata dictam comitassam desponsavit."). Hethe *Reg. Hamonis Hethe Diocesis Roffensis* 1 (Canterbury & York Soc. 48) (1948): 137–138. Hatton *Book of Seals* (1950): 67–68. Watkin *Great Chartulary of Glastonbury* 3 (Somerset Rec. Soc. 64) (1956): 631–632 (charter of Gilbert de Clare dated 1281). Paget *Baronage of England* (1957) 130: 13. Martival *Regs. of Roger Martival, Bishop of Salisbury 1315–1330* 1 (Canterbury & York Soc. 55) (1959): 55, 95. Sanders *English Baronies* (1960): 6, 34–35, 42. Smith *Itinerary of John Leland* 4 (1964): 150–163. Ross *Cartulary of Cirencester Abbey Gloucestershire* 2 (1964): 436–437, 603–604. Altschul *The Clares* (1965). London *Cartulary of Canonsleigh Abbey* (Devon & Cornwall Rec. Soc. n.s. 8) (1965): xiii, 11–12, 96 (charter of Gilbert de Clare). Darlington *Cartulary of Worcester Cathedral Priory* (Pipe Roll Soc. n.s. 38) (1968): 288–289. Mills *Dorset Lay Subsidy Roll of 1332* (Dorset Rec. Soc. 4) (1971): 75. Chew & Kellaway *London Assize of Nuisance 1301–1431* (1973): 41–54 (no. 250). Treharne & Sanders *Docs. of the Baronial Movement of Reform & Rebellion 1258–1267* (1973). Rosenthal *Nobles & Noble Life* (1976): 174–175. Ellis *Cat. Seals in the P.R.O.* 1 (1978): 46 (seal of Ralph de Monthermer, earl of Gloucester and Hertford dated 1305 — In a cusped circle, hung from a hook, between two small leopards, a shield of arms: an eagle displayed [MONTHERMER]). DeWindt *Royal Justice & Medieval English Countryside* 2 (1981): 574. *Ancient Deeds — Ser. DD* (List & Index Soc. 200) (1983): 125. Merrick *Morganiae Archaiographia* (South Wales Rec. Soc. 1) (1983): 41–52. *Mediæval Studies* 46 (1984): 245–265. Schwennicke *Europäische Stammtafeln* 3(1) (1984): 156 (sub Clare); n.s. 3(4) (1989): 816 (sub Lusignan). *Rolls & Reg. of Bishop Oliver Sutton 1280–1299* 8 (Lincoln Rec. Soc. 76) (1986): 86, 126, 161, 162. Williams *England in the 15th Cent.* (1987): 187–198. Harper-Bill *Cartulary of the Augustinian Friars of Clare* (1991). *TAG* 69 (1994): 129–139 (birth dates of daughters Eleanor and Margaret). Gervers *Cartulary of the Knights of St. John of Jerusalem in England* 2 (Recs. of Soc. & Econ. Hist. n.s. 23) (1996): 46–47. Leese *Blood Royal* (1996): 264–271. Brault *Rolls of Arms Edward I* 2 (1997): 106 (arms of Gilbert de Clare: Or, three chevrons gules), 300–301 (arms of Ralph de Monthermer: Or, an eagle displayed vert; at Caerlaverock, he displayed the arms of the earldom of Gloucester on his banner, they being Or, three chevrons gules). Sayer *Original Papal Docs. in England & Wales (1198–1304)* (1999): 419. Underhill *For Her Good Estate* (1999). VCH *Wiltshire* 16 (1999): 8–49. Biancalana *Fee Tail & the Common Recovery in Medieval England* (2001): 154. Gee *Women, Art & Patronage from Henry III to Edward III: 1216–1377* (2002): 157–158. Brand *Earliest English Law Rpts.* 3 (Selden Soc. 122) (2005): 245–249. Legg *Lost Cartulary of Bolton Priory* (Yorkshire Arch. Soc. Rec. Ser. 160) (2009): 50. Burton et al. *Thirteenth Century England XIII* (2011): 154. National Archives, C 241/66/3; SC 7/31/14; SC 8/61/3004; SC 8/86/4286; SC 8/182/9085; SC 8/327/E825 (available at www.catalogue.nationalarchives.gov.uk/search.asp).

Children of Gilbert de Clare, Knt., by Alice de Lusignan:

i. **ISABEL DE CLARE**, married (1st) **GUY DE BEAUCHAMP**, Knt., 10th Earl of Warwick [see BEAUCHAMP 10]; (2nd) **MAURICE DE BERKELEY**, Knt., 2nd Lord Berkeley [see BERKELEY 6].

ii. **JOAN DE CLARE**, married (1st) **DUNCAN OF FIFE**, 9th Earl of Fife (in Scotland), son and heir of Colban of Fife, Knt., 8th Earl of Fife, by Anne [see GROBY 8], daughter and co-heiress of Alan Durward, Knt., of Coull and Lumphanan, Aberdeenshire, Lintrathen, Angus, Lundin, Fife, Reedie (in Airlie), Forfarshire, Urquhart, Moray, etc., Usher of the King of Scots, Justiciar of Scotland. He was born about 1262 (aged 8 in 1270). They had one son, Duncan, Knt. [10th Earl of Fife]. He was admitted to the possession of his Earldom in 1284. He was chosen one of the six Regents of the Kingdom [Scotland] in 1286. DUNCAN OF FIFE, 9th Earl of Fife, was murdered by Sir Patrick de Abernethy and others on the king's highway at Pitpollok 10 Sept. 1289, and was buried at Coupar Angus Abbey, Perthshire. In 1292 his widow, Countess Joan, paid a fine of 1,000 marks of silver to King Edward I to have her marriage and for leave to marry whomever she pleased. In 1299, while on her way between Stirling Castle and Edinburgh, she was abducted by Herbert de Morham, Knt., of Scotland, who imprisoned her in the house of Thomas his brother in an aborted attempt to get her to marry him. In April 1299 she complained to King Edward I that Morham had also taken her jewels, horses, robes, and other goods to the value of £2,000, and "committed other enormities to the scandal of the countess and the king's contempt." On 1 Nov. 1299 she granted John de Hastings, lord of Abergavenny, the manors of Clapthorne, Northamptonshire, and Carlton [le Moorland], Lincolnshire, together with her lands in Scotland, namely Strazhurd, Kimile, and Loygiastre, Perthshire and Coull and Lumphanan, Aberdeenshire, to hold the said lands for the term of his life, paying to the said Joan £80 per year. Joan married (2nd) after 1 Nov. 1299 (date of grant) **GERVASE AVENEL**, Knt., of Scotland. In 1305 the Earl of Atholl petitioned King Edward I to deliver Coull, Aberdeenshire to Joan, Countess of Fife. In 1316 King Edward II ordered Gervase and Joan to hand over various tenements in Carlton le Moorland, Lincolnshire to the Abbot of Thornton. In 1317 the king granted Hugh le Despenser the younger the manor of Glapthorn, Northamptonshire, "which Gervase Avenel and Joan, his wife, and Douegal de Fyf, son of the said Joan, held of the inheritance of the said Joan, … which was forfeited to the king because they lately adhered to his Scotch enemies." The same year her estate in Hampshire also escheated to the Crown. In 1322 the king granted Hugh le Despenser the younger the manor of Carlton le Moorland, Lincolnshire, "late of Gervase Avenel and Joan his wife, who adhered to the Scots, and whose lands therefore escheated to the king." Stevenson *Ill. of Scottish Hist.* (1834): 43. Palgrave *Antient Kalendars & Inventories of the Treasury of His Majesty's Exchequer* 1 (1836): 76. *Book of Bon-Accord* (1839): 348. Stevenson *Docs. Ill. of the Hist. of Scotland* 1 (1870): 220–221 (Joan, Countess of Fife, styled sister ["soer"] of Isabel de Clare in letter of King Edward I of England dated 4 March 1291), 295, 317; 2 (1870): 399–400. Cockburn-Hood *House of Cockburn of that Ilk & the Cadets Thereof* (1888): 343–344. *Desc. Cat. Ancient Deeds* 1 (1890): 162. *C.C.R.* 1313–1318 (1893): 492. *C.P.R.* 1292–1301 (1895): 466. *C.C.R.* 1327–1330 (1896): 13–14. Sharpe *Cal. Letter-Books of London: A* (1899): 162 (Isabel [de Clare] and her sister, Joan, styled "kinswomen" by King Edward I in 1285). *C.P.R.* 1317–1321 (1903): 10. *Scottish Hist. Rev.* 2 (1905): 14–29. *C.Ch.R.* 3 (1908): 451. Lambert *Bletchingley* 1 (1921): 102. *Genealogist* n.s. 38 (1922): 169–172. *C.P.* 5 (1926): 373–374 (sub Fife), 707, footnote j (sub Gloucester). Richardson & Sayles *Rotuli Parl. Anglie Hactensis Inediti 1274–1373* (Camden Soc. 3rd Ser. 51) (1935): 147, 283–284. Altschul *The Clares* (1965): 38–39, 45, 47, 51, 165–166. Fryde *Tyranny & Fall of Edward II* (1979): 34. Schwennicke *Europäische Stammtafeln* 3(1) (1984): 156 (sub Clare). Jones & Vale *England & Her Neighbours 1066–1453* (1989): 191. Ward *English Noblewomen in the Later Middle Ages* (1992): 41. Grant & Stringer *Medieval Scotland: Crown, Lordship & Community* (1993): 33 (ped. of Fife). Boardman & Ross *Exercise of Power in Medieval Scotland* (2003): 136. National Archives, SC 8/175/8743 (available at www.catalogue. nationalarchives.gov.uk/search.asp). Online resource: http:// www.briantimms.net/era/lord_marshals/ Lord_Marshal02/Lord%20Marshal2.htm (Lord Marshal's Roll — arms of [Duncan] Earl of Fife: Argent three pallets gules).

Child of Joan de Clare, by Duncan of Fife:

a. **DUNCAN OF FIFE**, Knt., 10th Earl of Fife (in Scotland), and, of Glapthorn and Cotterstock, Northamptonshire, son and heir, born posthumously in late 1289 or early 1290. In 1292, being then under age, King Edward I of England appointed John de Saint John to officiate for him at the Coronation of John de Balliol, King of Scotland. Duncan married by papal dispensation dated 3 Nov. 1307 (they being related in the 4th degree of kindred) **MARY DE MONTHERMER**, daughter of Ralph de Monthermer, by Joan, daughter of King Edward I of England [see CLARE 8 above for her ancestry]. She was born about 1298 (aged 9 in 1307). They had one daughter, Isabel (or Elizabeth) [Countess of Fife]. In 1314 he and his family were granted safe-conduct by the king of England, they going abroad. In 1316 he did homage to the Abbot of Dunfermline for the lands of Cluny in Fife held by the earl of the abbot. At some unknown date, he made an entail of his earldom in favor of Alan II de Menteith, 7th Earl of Menteith. Like many of his contemporaries, he changed sides, sometimes holding with the English faction, at other times with the patriot Scots. He was the first of the Earls who signed the famous letter to the Pope, asserting the independence of Scotland in the Parliament at Arbroath 6 April 1320. About 1320 he granted lands in Luthile, Balbreky (in Kennoway), and Ballenkerc (in Kennoway), Fife to Adam de Ramsay. On attaching himself to King Robert I de Brus, he received a charter of the earldom of Fife. He was also granted the baronies of O'Neil,

Aberdeenshire, Kinnoul, Perthshire, and Calder, Midlothian, and, in default of legitimate issue, reversion of the property was to go to the king's nephew, Thomas Randolph, Earl of Moray. In 1320 his wife, Mary, had safe-conduct granted to her by King Edward II of England, she then going into Scotland for the deliverance of Ellen, widow of Robert de Neville. In 1321 Robert de Compton was granted protection by the king of England, he going to Berwick on the affairs of the countess of Fife. The same year protection was granted by the king of England to the servants of Mary, Countess of Fife, they coming from Scotland to London. In 1330 he consented to the erection of the parish church of Kincardine Oneill, Aberdeenshire into a prebend of Aberdeen Cathedral, reserving to him and his heirs every third presentation of the prebend and the patronage. He was taken prisoner at the Battle of Dupplin Moor 12 August 1332. He submitted to Edward de Balliol, and assisted at his Coronation at Scone 24 September following. He fought at the Battle of Halidon Hill in 1333. In 1335 he was granted license by King Edward III of England to grant the manor of Calder in Midlothian to his first cousin, Thomas de Ferrers. Sometime in the period, 1335–8, Earl Duncan granted the barony of West Calder, Midlothian to Beatrice de Douglas in liferent and to her son and heir, John de Douglas, in fee. In 1336 he took part in resisting King Edward III's forces in Fife. In March 1336 King Edward III granted Mary Countess of Fife 40*s.* a week while she remained in England. In Sept. 1336 a warrant was issued for the payment of the arrears of the pension of 40*s.* a week granted to Mary, Countess of Fife. In 1337 he and the Earl of March defeated Lord Montfort near Panmure near Angus. In 1339 he granted the right of patronage of the church of Kincardine Oneill, Aberdeenshire, together with the annexed chapels, to Alexander, Bishop of Aberdeen, saving the right of the present rector until he resigned or died. In May 1340 Mary, Countess of Fife, was granted 40*s.* a week at the Exchequer, two robes a year by the hands of the clerk of the Great Wardrobe, and the manor of Kempton (in Sunbury), Middlesex "for her to stay in" during pleasure. In May 1341 Thomas de Crosse, Keeper of the Great Wardrobe, was ordered to deliver the robes granted to Mary, Countess of Fife. On the return of King David II of Scotland from France in 1341, Earl Duncan joined that party. In May 1345 the king of England granted safe-conduct to Mary de Monthermer, Countess of Fife, "who has long been in England in the king's peace and fealty," she returning to Scotland. Earl Duncan was taken prisoner with King David II of Scotland and many other Scottish magnates at the Battle of Neville's Cross in 1346. In Dec. 1346 the king of England ordered Robert de Ogle to send his prisoners to the Tower of London, including Duncan, Earl of Fife. Earl Duncan was subsequently tried for treason by King Edward III of England, and sentenced to a traitor's death 22 Feb. 1347, but he was reprieved owing to his relationship to the king. In April 1350 safe-conduct was granted until Christmas for Duncan, Earl of Fife, a prisoner in the Tower of London, he going to Scotland to obtain his ransom set at £1,000. SIR DUNCAN OF FIFE, 10th Earl of Fife, died in Scotland in 1353. His widow, Countess Mary, was living 30 March 1371. Rymer *Fœdera* 1(2) (1816): 1002; 2(1) (1818): 5–6. Buchanan *Tracts Ill. of the Traditionary & Hist. Antiqs. of Scotland* (1836): 155–156. Innes *Registrum Episcopatus Aberdonensis* 1 (1845): 51 (charter of Duncan, Earl of Fife dated 1330), 64–66 (two charters of Duncan, Earl of Fife, one dated 1338/9). Laing *Desc. Cat. Impressions from Ancient Scottish Seals* (1850): 61 (seal of Duncan, Earl of Fife dated ?1360 — An armed knight on horseback at full speed, a sword in his right hand, and on his left arm a shield charged with a lion rampant, which is repeated on the caparisons of the horse). Green *Lives of the Princesses of England* 2 (1857): 359. Hardy *Syllabus (in English) of the Docs. Rel. England & other Kingdoms in Rymer's Fœdera* 1 (1869): 142, 184, 206 (Mary, Countess of Fife, styled "king's niece" by King Edward II of England), 210, 211, 213, 280, 282, 285, 321, 342, 353, 366. *Sixth Rpt.* (Hist. MSS Comm. 5) (1877): 690 (Sir Robert de Menzies, Knt. styled "kinsman" by Duncan, Earl of Fife, is charter dated c.1342). *Papal Regs.: Letters* 2 (1895): 30 (dispensation dated 3 Non. Nov. [3 Nov.] 1307 granted to Duncan, earl of Fife, and Mary de Monte Hermeri [Monthermer], the king's niece to intermarry). *C.P.R. 1338–1340* (1898): 480. Hutchinson *Lake of Menteith* (1899): 233 (cites Fraser *Red Book of Menteith*, vol. ii, pg. 257). Burnett *Fam. of Burnett of Leys* (Aberdeen Univ. Studies 4) (1901): 152–153 (Duncan, Earl of Fife styled "kinsman" [consanguineo] by King Robert I of Scotland). *C.P.R. 1343–1345* (1902): 471. *C.P.R. 1317–1321* (1903): 10. Macdonald *Scottish Armorial Seals* (1904): 114 (seal of Duncan, Earl of Fife: An armed knight on horseback to sinister with sword in right hand, and on left arm shield bearing arms: — A lion rampant. These arms are repeated on the caparisons of his horse). *C.P.R. 1348–1350* (1905): 558. *Scottish Hist. Rev.* 2 (1905): 14–29. *Scots Peerage* 4 (1907): 11–12 (sub Fife) (Mary styled "niece" by King Edward II of England). Ramsay *Bamff Charters, A. D. 1232–1703* (1915): 13–15. *Genealogist* n.s. 38 (1922): 169–172. *C.P.* 5 (1926): 374 (sub Fife). *Cal. Chancery Warrants* (1927): 256. *Misc.* 5 (Scottish Hist. Soc. Ser. 3 21) (1933): 7–8 (charter of Duncan, Earl of Fife dated c.1320), 24–26 (undated charter of Duncan, Earl of Fife). VCH *Middlesex* 3 (1962): 53–57. Chew & Kellaway *London Assize of Nuisance 1301–1431* (1973): 41–54 (no. 250). *Ancient Deeds — Ser. AS & WS* (List & Index Soc. 158) (1979): 128 (W.S. 271), 164 (W.S.621). Ellis *Cat. Seals in the P.R.O.* 2 (1981): 68 (seal of Mary, Countess of Fife, dated 1336 — In a cusped and traceried circle, the field diapered with fleur-de-lys, the countess standing, wearing a hood and a long gown with three leopards on the front [ENGLAND], holding in either hand by its strap a shield of arms: (L) a lion rampant, (R) a splayed eagle [MONTHERMER]; under her feet a crouching leopard). Grant & Stringer *Medieval Scotland: Crown, Lordship & Community* (1993): 33 (ped. of Fife). Martin *Knighton's Chron. 1337–1396* (Oxford Medieval Texts) (1995): 77 ("The earl of Fife was later reprieved, as [King] Edward [III]'s kinsman," cites *Fædera*, 1344–61, pg. 108). Brault *Rolls of Arms Edward I* 2 (1997): 164–165 (arms of Duncan of Fife: Argent, three pales gules; Or, three piles gules surmounted by a bend sable). National Archives of Scotland, GD124/1/408 (Duncan, Earl of Fife styled "king's kinsman" by King David II of Scotland in charter dated 1351–2) (available at www.nas.gov.uk).

Child of Duncan of Fife, Knt., by Mary de Monthermer:

1) **ISABEL** (or **ELIZABETH**) **OF FIFE**, *suo jure* Countess (or Lady) of Fife, daughter and heiress. She was made a prisoner at Perth in 1332 by Edward de Balliol. She married (1st) before 1341 (as his 2nd wife) **WILLIAM DE FELTON**, Knt., of Edlingham, Nafferton, and West Matfen, Northumberland, Medomsley and Hamsterley, co. Durham, Boddington, Northamptonshire, etc., Constable of Roxburgh Castle, 1337, Knight of the Shire for Northumberland, Sheriff of Northumberland, 1341–4, Keeper of Newcastle-upon-Tyne, 1342, son and heir of William de Felton, Knt., of Edlingham, Northumberland, by his wife, Eustancia. He was born about 1299 (aged 30 in 1329). They had two sons, John, Knt., and Duncan (clerk), and one daughter, Constance. He took part in the Battle of Halidon Hill in 1333. In 1335 he was granted £20 out of the farm and rents of Matfen and Nafferton, Northumberland for a term of five years. In 1338 he acknowledged he owed a debt of 250 marks to Nicholas de la Beche, Knt., to be levied, in default of payment, of his goods and chattels in Northumberland. In 1338 Queen Philippe of Hainault granted him the manor of Wark in Tindale, Northumberland, and two parts of the lands within the lordship of the manor late of David de Strathbogie, Earl of Atholl, together with two parts of the manor of Henshaw and of the forest of Lowes, Northumberland excepted for a term of seven years. In 1338, in consideration of his good service in Scotland, the king granted him a release of a rent of £25 in the towns of West Matfen and Nafferton, Northumberland. In 1340, for his faithful counsel and aid, the Canons of Dryburgh granted him the advowson of Abbotsley, Huntingdonshire and associated pension, which he subsequently granted to Balliol College, Oxford. He was summoned to a council 25 Feb. 1341/2, by a writ directed *Willelmo de Felton'*. In 1345 he owed a debt of 22s. 4d. to William de Ravendale, clerk. In 1347 he was constituted Justiciary of those parts of Scotland in the possession of England. SIR WILLIAM DE FELTON died testate 21 Sept. 1358, and was buried in Edlingham, Northumberland. His widow, Isabel, married (2nd) **WALTER STEWART**, in right of his wife, lord of Fife [see BRUS 10.ii], 2nd son of Robert II, King of Scots, by his 1st wife, Elizabeth, daughter of Adam Mure, Knt. [see BRUS 10 for his ancestry]. They had no issue. He was living 14 August 1362. His widow, Isabel, married (3rd) shortly after 10 Jan. 1362/3 (date of endowment) and before 8 June 1363 (as his 2nd wife) **THOMAS BISET** (or **BISSET**, **BYSETH**), Knt., of Upsetlington, Berwickshire. They had no issue. He witnessed charters of King David II of Scotland in 1358 and 1363. In 1359 a papal petition on his behalf for leave to visit the Holy Sepulchre in recorded. On 10 Jan. 1362/3 he endowed Isabel of Fife, Lady of Fife, before their marriage, with the life rent of his barony of Glasclune, in the region of Lethendy, Perthshire, together with other lands. In 1363–4, as "Thomas Bisset of Glasclune," he granted Maurice Drummond and his wife, Marion Erskine, the lands of Carnbady in the barony of Megginch. Thomas was granted the earldom of Fife by King David II of Scotland 8 June 1363. SIR THOMAS BISET, Earl of Fife, died before 17 April 1365. His widow, Isabel, married (4th) **JOHN DE DUNBAR**. In 1371 she resigned the reversion of the earldom of Fife following her death to Robert Stewart, Earl of Menteith, afterwards Duke of Albany. In 1373 King Robert II of Scotland confirmed a donation which Isabel, late Countess of Fife, made of an annual rent out of lands at Over and Nether Sydserf. She was living 12 August 1389. Rymer *Fædera* 6 (1727): 123, 128–129. Hutchinson *Hist. & Antiqs. of Durham* 2 (1787): 372. Surtees *Hist. & Antiqs. of Durham* 2 (1820): 285 (Felton ped.). *Wills & Invs.* 1 (Surtees Soc. 2) (1835): 29. *Top., Statistical & Hist. Gaz. of Scotland* 1 (1842): 545. Laing *Desc. Cat. Impressions from Ancient Scottish Seals* (1850): 61 (seal of Isabel, Countess of Fife dated 1369 — A prettily designed seal. A tree in the centre, from the branches of which two shields are suspended; the dexter bearing a lion rampant, for the Earldom of Fife; and the sinister, a fess chequé, for Stuart). Burke *Gen. Hist. of the Dormant, Abeyant, Forfeited & Extinct Peerages* (1866): 196 (sub Felton). *Procs. Soc. Antiqs. Scotland* 8 (1871): 435–436. Glover & St. George *Vis. of Yorkshire 1584–5, 1612* (1875): 372–373 (Hastings ped.: "William de Felton, of Northumberland, ob. 32 Edward III. He had two wives. = Isabella."). *Annual Rpt. of the Deputy Keeper* 45 (1885): 194–195. *Athenaeum* July-Dec. 1886 (1886): 16. *D.N.B.* 18 (1889): 311 (biog. of Sir William Felton). *Arch. Aeliana* 14 (1890): 290 (arms of William de Felton: Gules, two lions passant within a double tressure argent); 3rd Ser. 20 (1923): 69–178 (seal of William de Felton: "Red, round, 26 mm., armorial, two lions passant within a tressure. Shield is in a traceried panel."). *C.P.R. 1334–1338* (1895): 173. *C.P.R. 1338–1340* (1898): 109, 119–120, 445–446, 461, 517. *List of Sheriffs for England & Wales* (PRO Lists and Indexes 9) (1898): 97. *C.P.R. 1343–1345* (1902): 234. Martin *Regs. of Edlingham* (Durham &

Northumberland Parish Reg. Soc. 8) (1903): 19. Hodgson *Hist. of Northumberland* 7 (1904): 114–122, 127–129. Macdonald *Scottish Armorial Seals* (1904): 115 (seal of Isabel, Countess of Fife: From a tree in the centre of the seal are suspended two shields bearing arms, viz.: — On dexter shield: A lion rampant [FIFE]. On sinister shield: A fess chequy [STEWART]. Legend: S' ISABELLE COMITISSE DE FYFF.), 324 (seal of Walter Stewart: — A fess chequy.). *Scots Peerage* 1 (1904): 15–17 (sub Kings of Scotland); 4 (1907): 13–14 (sub Fife) (confuses Isabel's marriages); 7 (1910): 32 (sub Drummond, Earl of Perth). *Scottish Hist. Rev.* 2 (1905): 14–29. *Wrottesley Peds. from the Plea Rolls* (1905): 100–101. Dunbar *Scottish Kings* (1906): 166. Maxwell *Scalacronica ... as recorded by Sir Thomas Gray* (1907): 126 ("Which earldom [Fife] the King declared was in his right to bestow owing to the forfeiture, as he said, of Duncan Earl of Fife in the time of Robert de Brus, his father, for the slaying of an esquire named Michael Beton, whom he had caused to be slain in anger at a hawking party, wherefore the said [King David II] alleged that the said earl, in order to obtain from the king remission of the forfeiture, had by indenture devised the reversion of the earldom to the said king his [David's] father, in the event of his [Duncan's] dying without heir-male, which he did. But the said earl had a daughter by his wife, the King of England's daughter, the Countess of Gloucester. This daughter was in England, and it was intended that she should be sold to Robert the Steward of Scotland, but she married for love William de Felton, a knight of Northumberland, who was her guardian at the time, and she laid claim to the earldom which had been renounced by contract."). *Trans. Dumfriesshire & Galloway Nat. Hist. & Antiq. Soc.* n.s. 22 (1911): 81 (transcript of *Scalacronica* [Ladder of Time]). *Arch. Aeliana* 3rd Ser. 20 (1923): 76–78. *C.P.* 5 (1926): 294 (sub Felton), 374–375 (sub Fife) (confuses Isabel's marriages). Dodds *Hist. of Northumberland* 12 (1926): 273–275. VCH *Huntingdon* 2 (1932): 257–260. Easson *Charters of the Abbey of Coupar-Angus* 1 (Scottish Hist. Soc. 3rd Ser. 40) (1947): 246–249 (re. Thomas Biset). Stringer *Essays on the Nobility of Medieval Scotland* (1985): 57, 61. Saul *14th Cent. England* 1 (2000): 29. *Burke's Landed Gentry of Great Britain* (2001): lxiii-lxv (sub Scottish Royal Lineage). National Archives, C 131/7/4 (available at www.catalogue.nationalarchives.gov.uk/search.asp).

Children of Isabel of Fife, by William de Felton, Knt.:

a) **JOHN FELTON**, Knt., of Edlingham, Northumberland, Hamsterley and Medomsley, co. Durham, Boddington, Northamptonshire, etc., son by his father's 2nd marriage, born about 1339–41 (aged 28 in 1367, 30 in 1371). He married (1st) _____. They had two daughters, Elizabeth (born c.1379–81, wife of Edmund Hastings, Knt., of Roxby (in Pickering Lythe), Yorkshire) and Joan (born c.1383, living 1396, died before 1402). He married (2nd) **ELIZABETH** _____. They had one son, John (born c.1386, died 1402). He was heir in 1367 to his older half-brother, William de Felton, Knt., Seneschal of Poitou. SIR JOHN FELTON died shortly before 24 July 1396. His widow, Elizabeth, married (2nd) **HENRY BOYNTON**, Knt. She died shortly before 8 May 1422. Collins *English Baronetage* 1 (1741): (sub Boynton). Hutchinson *Hist. & Antiqs. of Durham* 2 (1787): 372 ("This John [de Felton] appears in bishop Hatfield's Survey ... Several subsequent inquisitions shew that John [de Felton] was half brother to William by a second venter, and succeeded to the estates by virtue of an intail, created by a general ancestor, under a fine levied of the premises. John, son of John de Felton, dying without issue, the manor descended to his sister, Elizabeth; she married Edmund Hastings, esq.; and by him had John her son and heir; Henry Boynton was her second husband."). Betham *Baronetage of England* 1 (1801): 156 (sub Boynton). Burke *Gen. Hist. of the Dormant, Abeyant, Forfeited & Extinct Peerages* (1866): 196 (sub Felton). *Annual Rpt. of the Deputy Keeper* 33 (1872): 184, 188; 45 (1885): 170, 194–196, 198. Whellan *Hist., Top. & Dir. of Northamptonshire* (1874): 445. Flower *Vis. of Yorkshire 1563–4* (H.S.P. 16) (1881): 153 (Hastynges ped.: "Sir Edward Hastynges of Rowesby in Yorkshyre. = ... doughter of Sir John Felton of Northumberland."). *Arch. Aeliana* 14 (1890): 14, 290. Martin *Regs. of Edlingham* (Durham & Northumberland Parish Reg. Soc. 8) (1903): 19. *Wrottesley Peds. from the Plea Rolls* (1905): 100–101. VCH *Yorkshire N.R.* 2 (1923): 492–497. Dodds *Hist. of Northumberland* 12 (1926): 372–373. Roskell *House of Commons 1386–1421* 3 (1992): 317–319 (biog. of Sir Edmund Hastings).

b) **CONSTANCE FELTON**, married **THOMAS DE FAUCONBERGE**, Knt., 5th Lord Fauconberge [see FAUCONBERGE 11].

Children of Gilbert de Clare, Knt., by Joan of England:

i. **GILBERT DE CLARE**, Knt., 9th Earl of Gloucester, 7th Earl of Hertford, Chief Guardian and Lieutenant of Scotland, 1308–9, Chief Captain in Scotland and the North, 1309, Guardian and Lieutenant of England, 1311, son and heir, born at Winchcombe, Gloucestershire 10 (or 11) May 1291. He was knighted by the king 22 May 1306. In October 1306 his lands were ordered to be seized at the King's hands and his body to be arrested in consequence of his having absented himself from the King's army in Scotland without license. After the death of his mother in April 1307, he was styled Earl of Gloucester and Hertford. On 18 August 1307 all his lands in Wales were granted to him, and, on 28 Nov. following, he had livery of his father's lands, though still under age, and also had livery of his lands in London and others held in socage. Sometime in the period, 1307–11, Gilbert de Clare, Earl of Gloucester and Hertford, Henry de Lacy, Earl of Lincoln, and other earls and barons, while assembled in the Parliament in London, wrote to the Pope praying for the canonization of Thomas de Cantelowe, late Bishop of Hereford. He married at Waltham Abbey 29 Sept. 1308 **MAUD DE BURGH**, daughter of Richard de Burgh, Knt., 3rd Earl of Ulster, lord of Connacht, by his wife, Margaret [see BURGH 5 for her ancestry]. They had one son, John. He took no part in the disputes occasioned by the favors showered by his uncle, the King, on the king's favorite, Peter de Gavaston. In 1308 he was made chief Captain of the expedition into Scotland to relieve Rutherglen Castle in Scotland. He presented to the church of Rendcombe, Gloucestershire in 1308. He was forbidden to tourney in June 1309 and again in Jan. 1313. He was appointed one of the Lords Ordainer of Reform in 1310. In August 1310 he accompanied the King to Berwick. In 1310–11 he granted land at Deineck [?Deviock], Cornwall for the use of poor students in the University of Oxford. In 1311 he was appointed Keeper of the Realm during the king's absence in Scotland. He was with the king in Scotland in April 1311, and in June was with him at Berwick. In 1312, after the murder of Peter de Gavaston, he and the Earl of Richmond tried to make peace between the king and Thomas, Earl of Lancaster. In May 1313 he was again appointed regent during the king's absence in France. In 1314 he was going overseas on the king's service in the train of Queen Isabel on an embassy concerning Gascony. SIR GILBERT DE CLARE, Earl of Gloucester and Hertford, fought at the Battle of Bannockburn 24 June 1314, where he was slain while leading a fierce attack on the Scots. His body was buried at Tewkesbury Abbey, Gloucestershire at his father's right hand. His widow, Maud, presented to the church of Bletchingley, Surrey 4 July 1320. She died testate shortly before 11 August 1320, and was buried at Tewkesbury Abbey at her husband's left side. Sandford *Gen. Hist. of the Kings of England* (1677): 140. Dugdale *Monasticon Anglicanum* 2 (1819): 59–65. *Archæologia* 26 (1836): 341. Lipscomb *Hist. & Antiqs. of Buckingham* 1 (1847): 200–201 (Clare ped.). Brewer *Monumenta Franciscana* 1 (Rolls Ser. 4) (1858): 513–514. Luard *Annales Monastici* 4 (Rolls Ser. 36) (1869): 505 (Annals of Worcester sub A.D. 1291 — "Quinto idus Maii [11 May] Johanna comitissa Gloucestriæ peperit filium, a Bathoniense baptizatum; cui nomen imponitur Gilebertus."). *Jour. British Arch. Assoc.* 26 (1870): 149–160. White *Hist. of the Battle of Bannockburn* (1871): 172–173 (biog. of Gilbert de Clare). *Fifth Rpt.* (Hist. MSS Comm. 4) (1876): 302 (charter of Gilbert de Clare, Earl of Gloucester & Hertford dated 1314; seal, three chevronels). Kellawe *Reg. of Richard de Kellawe, Lord Palatine & Bishop of Durham 1314–1316* 4 (1878): xxxi. Stubbs *Annales Londonienses* (Chrons. of the Reigns of Edward I and Edward II 1) (Rolls Ser. 76) (1882): 231 ("Nomina interfectorum militum ad bellum de Strivelyn de Anglis [Names of the English knights slain at Bannockburn]: Primo Gilbertus de Clare comes Gloucestriæ, ætate circa xxiii. annos"). Clark *Land of Morgan* (1883): 93–166. Doyle *Official Baronage of England* 2 (1886): 17–18 (sub Gloucester). *Papal Regs.: Letters* 2 (1895): 209. Fry & Fry *Abs. of Feet of Fines Rel. Dorset* 1 (Dorset Rec. Soc. 5) (1896): 265. *Regs. of John de Sandale & Rigaud de Asserio, Bishops of Winchester* (Hampshire Rec. Soc. 12) (1897): 17, 114, 434–435. Wrottesley *Peds. from the Plea Rolls* (1905): 7, 133–134, 273, 470–471. *Rpt. on MSS in Various Colls.* 4 (Hist. MSS Comm. 55) (1907): 75. *D.N.B.* 4 (1908): 382–383 (biog. of Gilbert de Clare). *C.F.R.* 1 (1911): 543. Mills *Cal. Gormanston Reg.* (1916): 2–3. VCH *Buckingham* 3 (1925): 47–48, 70, 422; 4 (1927): 23, 25. *C.P.* 5 (1926): 712–715 (sub Gloucester); 6 (1926): 503 (sub Hertford). *Cal. Chancery Warrants* (1927): 387, 392 (Gilbert styled "king's nephew"). Reynolds *Reg. of Walter Reynolds* (Dugdale Soc. 9) (1928): 148. Gandavo *Reg. Simonis de Gandavo Diocesis Saresbriensis* 2 (Canterbury & York Soc. 41) (1934): 760. Ross *Cartulary of Cirencester Abbey* 2 (1964): 603–604. London *Cartulary of Canonsleigh Abbey* (Devon & Cornwall Rec. Soc. n.s. 8) (1965): xiii–xiv, 100 (charter of Gilbert), 100–102, 104. VCH *Cambridge* 5 (1973): 140–147. Merrick *Morganiae Archaiographia* (South Wales Rec. Soc. 1) (1983): 41–52. Schwennicke *Europäische Stammtafeln* 3(1) (1984): 156 (sub Clare). Brault *Rolls of Arms Edward I* 2 (1997): 106 (arms of Gilbert de Clare: Or, three chevrons gules). Catto "Chron. of John Somer," in *Camden Misc.* 34 (Camden Soc. 5th Ser. 10) (1997): 270 (birth date of Gilbert de Clare). VCH *Wiltshire* 16 (1999): 8–49. National Archives, SC 8/327/E825 (available at www.catalogue.nationalarchives.gov.uk/search.asp).

Child of Gilbert de Clare, Knt., by Maud de Burgh:

- a. **JOHN DE CLARE**, son and heir apparent, born at Cardiff, Wales 3 April 1312, died the same year, and was buried at St. Mary's Chapel, Tewkesbury, Gloucestershire. Dugdale *Monasticon Anglicanum* 2 (1819): 59–65. *Jour. British Arch. Assoc.* 26 (1870): 149–160. Clark *Land of Morgan* (1883): 93–166. *C.P.* 5 (1926): 715 (sub Gloucester).

- ii. **ELEANOR DE CLARE**, married (1st) **HUGH LE DESPENSER**, Knt., 2nd Lord Despenser [see DESPENSER 11]; (2nd) **WILLIAM LA ZOUCHE MORTIMER**, Knt., 1st Lord Zouche of Richard's Castle [see BEAUCHAMP 10].

iii. **MARGARET DE CLARE**, married (1st) **PETER DE GAVASTON**, Knt., Earl of Cornwall [see STRATTON AUDLEY 10]; (2nd) **HUGH DE AUDLEY**, Knt., Lord Audley, Earl of Gloucester [see STRATTON AUDLEY 10].

iv. **ELIZABETH DE CLARE**, married (1st) **JOHN DE BURGH** [see BURGH 6]; (2nd) **THEBAUD DE VERDUN**, Knt., 2nd Lord Verdun [see VERDUN 11 and BURGH 6]; (3rd) **ROGER DAMORY**, Knt., Lord Damory [see BURGH 6; VERDUN 11].

Children of Joan of England, by Ralph de Monthermer, Knt.:

i. **MARY DE MONTHERMER**, married **DUNCAN OF FIFE**, Knt., 10th Earl of Fife [see CLARE 8.ii.a above].

ii. **THOMAS DE MONTHERMER**, Knt., 2nd Lord Monthermer, of Stokenham, Oakford, Sterte, and Pyworthy, Devon, Warblington, Hampshire, Erlestoke, Wiltshire, son and heir, born 4 October 1301, and was baptized by the Bishop of Llandaff 8 October 1301. He married after 23 July 1326 **MARGARET DE BREWES**, widow of Henry le Tyeys, Knt., 2nd Lord Tyeys, of Chilton Foliat, Draycot Foliat, and Lydiard Tregoze, Wiltshire, Noke, Oxfordshire, etc. (executed 3 April 1322) [see MONTAGU 5.ii.a], and daughter of Peter de Brewes, Knt., of Tetbury, Gloucestershire, Bidlington, Chesworth, Findon, Grinstead, Sedgwick, and Washington, Sussex, etc., by his wife, Agnes de Clifford [see TETBURY 9 for her ancestry].[10] They had one daughter, Margaret. He was not summoned to Parliament. He was knighted in 1327. He presented to the church of Stokenham, Devon in 1328. In 1329 he acknowledged that he owed the king 1,000 marks, to be levied, in default of payment, of his lands and chattels in Norfolk. He was pardoned in 1330 for adhering to Henry, Earl of Lancaster, and other rebels. He was one of the guardians of the coast against the Scots in July 1333. He was on commissions of array, etc., in Cornwall in 1336, and in Devon in 1338. He was heir in 1340 to his younger brother, Edward de Monthermer, Knt., Lord Monthermer, by which he inherited the manors of Lantyan, Cornwall, Hunton (in Crawley), Hampshire, and Erlestoke, Wiltshire. SIR THOMAS DE MONTHERMER, 2nd Lord Monthermer, died 24 June 1340, being slain at the Battle of Sluys. In March 1341 the king requested that his widow, Margaret, pay 100 marks a year to the Earl of Salisbury for the support of her daughter, Margaret de Monthermer, whose wardship the king has granted to him. His widow, Margaret, received a papal indult for plenary remission in 1346. She died 15, 22, or 26 May 1349. Pole *Colls. towards a Desc. of Devon* (1791): 287. Rymer *Fœdera* 2(2) (1821): 694 (Thomas de Monthermer styled "kinsman" by King Edward III of England), 1146, 1153. Banks *Baronies in Fee* 1 (1844): 328–329 (sub Monthermer). Green *Lives of the Princesses of England* 2 (1857): 359. *Monthermer Peerage. In the House of Lords. Case on Behalf of William Lowndes* (1860). Hardy *Syllabus (in English) of the Docs. Rel. England & other Kingdoms in Rymer's Fœdera* 1 (1869): 319, 320. Luard *Annales Monastici* 4 (Rolls Ser. 36) (1869): 550 (Annals of Worcester sub A.D. 1301 — "Quarto non. Octobris [4 Oct.] Johanna comitissa Gloucestriæ peperit filium, quem octavo idus ejusdem [8 Oct.] Johannes episcopus Landavensis Thomam in baptismate nominavit."). Stafford *Reg. of Edmund Stafford* (1886): 339–340. Thompson *Chronicon Galfridi le Baker de Swynebroke* (1889): 69 (sub A.D. 1340: Thomas de Monthermer styled "king's kinsman" [consanguineus regis]). *C.P.R. 1327–1330* (1891): 547 (Thomas de Monthermer styled "king's kinsman"). *C.C.R. 1327–1330* (1896): 530. *Papal Regs.: Letters* 3 (1897): 193. Déprez *Les Préliminaires de la Guerre de Cent Ans: La Papauté, la France et l'Angleterre* (1902): 319–321. *Wiltshire Notes & Queries* 4 (1902–4): 481–493 ("Thomas de Monthermer born 1300–1; Lord Monthermer killed in naval battle, 1340 = Margaret, dau. of … Tiptoft"). *C.P.R. 1324–1327* (1904): 302. Wrottesley *Peds. from the Plea Rolls* (1905): 341. *Index of Placita de Banco 1327–1328* 2 (PRO Lists and Indexes 22) (1906): 708, 716, 831. *Rpt. & Trans. of the Devonshire Assoc.* 2nd Ser. 8 (1906): 346. *C.Ch.R.* 3 (1908): 131 (Thomas styled "king's nephew"). VCH *Hampshire* 3 (1908): 134–136, 408–413. *Cal. IPM* 9 (1916): 286. *C.P.* 9 (1936): 86–88 (sub Montagu), 143 (sub Monthermer);

---

[10] Contemporary records indicate that Margaret de Brewes, wife of Thomas de Monthermer, was earlier the wife of Henry le Tyeys, whom she married in or before 1316 [see Pugh *Abs. of Feet of Fines Rel. Wiltshire* (Wiltshire Arch. & Nat. Hist. Soc. Recs. 1) (1939): 25]. In 1320 Henry le Tyeys and his wife, Margaret, were granted lands in Bockhampton (in Lambourn), Berkshire, for life; Bockhampton was held after Henry's death by Margaret de Monthermer [see VCH *Berkshire* 4 (1924): 258; *Feudal Aids* 1 (1899): 62]. Thomas and Margaret de Monthermer also possessed part of the manor of Lydiard Tregoze, Wiltshire, which was previously held by Henry le Tyeys [see VCH *Wiltshire* 9 (1970): 83]. *Cal. Inqs. Misc.* 2 (1916): 457 shows that Margaret de Monthermer held this property in dower, evidently in right of her first marriage. Elsewhere, the *IPM* of Alice, sister of Henry le Tyeys, taken in 1350 indicates that Margeret "who was the wife of Henry Tieys" previously held a one-third share in the manor of Bracken, Yorkshire, in dower, and that the said Margaret died 20 May 1349. This is virtually the same death date given for Thomas de Monthermer's wife Margaret recorded in her own IPM taken in the previous year [see *Cal. IPM* 9 (1916): nos. 344, 571; *C.F.R.* 6 (1921): 277; Abs. of IPM — Alice "Tyies," wife of Warin de Insula (see FHL Microfilm 917256)].

12(2) (1959): 103–105 (sub Tyeys). VCH *Oxford* 6 (1959): 268–276. Myers *English Hist. Docs. 1327–1485* (1969): 67–68 (account of Battle of Sluys in 1340). VCH *Wiltshire* 9 (1970): 75–90; 16 (1999): 88–109. Ellis *Cat. Seals in the P.R.O.* 2 (1981): 108 (seal of Margaret widow of Henry le Tyeys dated 1323 — in a cusped quatrefoil, hung from a triple bush, two shields of arms: (L) a chevron, the field hatched [TYEYS], and (R) crusily (?) a lion rampant, queue fourchy [BREWES]). Williams *England in the 15th Cent.* (1987): 187–198. Crowley *Wiltshire Tax List of 1332* (Wiltshire Rec. Soc. 45) (1989): 125. Hanna *Christchurch Priory Cartulary* (Hampshire Rec. Ser. 18) (2007): 157. National Archives, SC 8/86/4286 (available at www.catalogue.nationalarchives.gov.uk/search.asp).

Child of Thomas de Monthermer, by Margaret de Brewes:

a **MARGARET DE MONTHERMER**, married **JOHN DE MONTAGU**, Knt., Lord Montagu [see MONTAGU 8].

iii. **EDWARD DE MONTHERMER**, Knt., of Lantyan, Cornwall, Hunton (in Crawley) and Warblington, Hampshire, and Erlestoke, Wiltshire, younger son. He served as a surety for his step-mother, Isabel, in 1325, for repayment of a loan of £200. He was knighted in 1327. In 1330 he was suspected of being implicated in the so-called plot of Edmund of Woodstock, Earl of Kent. His lands were confiscated and he was confined to Winchester Castle for "certain seditions." The king ordered that his lands be restored 3 Dec. 1330. In 1334 and 1335 he was summoned for military service against the Scots. He was summoned to Parliament on 23 April and 21 June 1337, by writs directed *Edwardo de Monte Hermerii*, whereby he is held to have become Lord Monthermer. In 1337 he mortgaged the manor of Hunton (in Crawley), Hampshire to Peter de la Mare. He took part in Edward III's expedition to Antwerp in 1338. SIR EDWARD DE MONTHERMER, Lord Monthermer, was mortally wounded at Vironfosse 23 October 1339. He died testate in early Dec. 1339, apparently unmarried, and was buried near his mother in the church of the Austin Friars at Clare, Suffolk. Banks *Baronies in Fee* 1 (1844): 328–329 (sub Monthermer). Green *Lives of the Princesses of England* 2 (1857): 359. *Monthermer Peerage. In the House of Lords. Case on Behalf of William Lowndes* (1860). Wrottesley *Peds. from the Plea Rolls* (1905): 341. *Rpt. & Trans. of the Devonshire Assoc.* 2nd Ser. 8 (1906): 346. VCH *Hampshire* 3 (1908): 134–136, 408–413. *Feet of Fines for Essex* 2 (1913–28): 219. *C.P.* 9 (1936): 144–145 (sub Monthermer). Crowley *Wiltshire Tax List of 1332* (Wiltshire Rec. Soc. 45) (1989): 48. Ward *English Noblewomen in the Later Middle Ages* (1992): 102. Ward *Women of the English Nobility & Gentry 1066–1500* (1995): 81. McCash *Cultural Patronage of Medieval Women* (1996): 270. National Archives, SC 8/86/4286; SC 8/177/8809 (petition dated ?c.1340 from John de Holdich, executor of the testament of Edward de Mounthermer, to the king, requesting that the king command writs for him to the treasurer, barons and chamberlains to pay to him the sum owed to Mounthermer, whose executor he is, or make an assignment of the farm of Waltham until the sum be paid) (available at www.catalogue.nationalarchives.gov.uk/search.asp).

✤ CLARELL ✤

MALCOLM III (CEANNMORE), King of Scots, married [SAINT] **MARGARET**.
DAVID I, King of Scots, married **MAUD OF NORTHUMBERLAND**.
HENRY OF SCOTLAND, Earl of Northumberland, married **ADA DE WARENNE**.
WILLIAM THE LION, King of Scots, by a mistress, _____ **AVENEL**.
ISABEL OF SCOTLAND, married **ROBERT DE ROOS**, of Helmsley, Yorkshire.
WILLIAM DE ROOS, Knt., of Helmsley, Yorkshire, married **LUCY FITZ PETER** [see ROOS 6].

7. ALICE DE ROOS (or ROS), married (1st) about 1260 (as his 2nd wife) **JOHN COMYN**, Knt., of Badenoch in Scotland, Justiciar of Galloway, son and heir of Richard Comyn, of Badenoch. Her maritagium included the manor of Ulceby, Lincolnshire. They had two sons, John, Knt., and Robert, Knt., and one daughter, Alice. He was previously married (1st) about 1240 to **EVE** _____ , possibly daughter of Walter Stewart, Steward of Scotland, by whom he had three sons, John, Knt., William, and Alexander, and four daughters, Mary (wife of Richard Siward, Knt.), _____ (wife of Geoffrey Mowbray, Knt.), _____ (wife of Alexander of Argyll, Knt.), and _____ (wife of Andrew Moray, Knt.). In 1262 he had a confirmation of the grant by King David I of Scotland to his great-grandfather, Richard Comyn, and his wife, Hextilde, of the inheritance of Uchtred Fitz Waltheof, father of Hextilde, in Tindale, viz., Walwick, Thornton, Staincroft, and Hethingishalt, Northumberland. In 1268 he was granted a license to crenellate a camera (a long narrow building) which he proposed to build within his manor of Tarset, Northumberland. He adhered to King

Henry III against the Barons. In 1266 he had a grant of £300 per annum from the lands of the king's enemies beyond the Trent. In 1269 he and his wife, Alice, had a grant of free warren in Ulceby, Lincolnshire. In June 1276 the king appointed justices to determine the trespasses committed by Thomas de Whitewell and other evil doers in taking forcibly, carrying away, and still detaining corn, wine, and other victuals and goods of John Comyn at Tindale, as well as in a certain ship within the port of the vill of Newcastle-upon-Tyne. SIR JOHN COMYN died shortly before 18 July 1278. His widow, Alice, married (2nd) before 18 Nov. 1279 **JAMES DE BYRON**, Knt., of Cadney, Lincolnshire, son of Richard de Byron, Knt. In 1277 he was going to Wales on the king's service. In 1282 he witnessed a deed of Henry de Lacy, Earl of Lincoln. Lady Alice de Roos, noblewoman, died testate on or shortly before 29 April 1286, and was buried in the church of the Friars Minor, Lincoln. In 1285–6 [sic] Sir James de Byron paid to his wife's executors £98 for the third part of her moveable goods, and also gave for the health of his soul and that of Alice his wife to the men of Husum a selion [or ridge] of land. In 1287 he had letters of protection, he going to the Holy Land. In 1296 Oliver de Sutton, Bishop of Lincoln, committed to the subdean and to Masters John le Fleming and William of Langworth to grant probate of Alice's will. SIR JAMES DE BYRON died about 1300.

 Brydges *Collins' Peerage of England* 6 (1812): 91–92. Douglas *Peerage of Scotland* 1 (1813): 160–163. Bain *Cal. Docs. Rel. Scotland* 2 (1884): 51. *Annual Rpt. of the Deputy Keeper* 45 (1885): 286. *Genealogist* n.s. 9 (1892): 13. *C.P.R. 1281–1292* (1893): 78, 268. *C.P.R. 1272–1281* (1901): 189, 222. *Scots Peerage* 1 (1904): 506–507 (sub Comyn). Wrottesley *Peds. from the Plea Rolls* (1905): 27, 555. *Lincolnshire Notes & Queries* 9 (1907): 249–250. Lindsay et al. *Charters, Bulls & other Docs. Rel. the Abbey of Inchaffray* (Scottish Hist. Soc. 56) (1908): 99–100. Romeyn *Reg. of John le Romeyn Archbishop of York* 1 (Surtees Soc. 123) (1913): 13. Easson *Charters of the Abbey of Coupar Angus* 1 (Scottish Hist. Soc. 3rd Ser. 40) (1947): 134–135 (charter dated 1289 by Alice de Roos' step-son, John Comyn, which names his father J[ohn] Comyn and lady Eve his mother, proving Alice was not the mother of her husband's older Comyn children). Sutton *Rolls & Reg. of Bishop Oliver Sutton* 3 (Lincoln Rec. Soc. 48) (1954): 21; 5 (Lincoln Rec. Soc. 60) (1965): 186. Paget *Baronage of England* (1957) 142: 12. Hedley *Northumberland Fams.* (1968): 224–231 (Ros ped.). Brault *Rolls of Arms Edward I* 2 (1997): 88 (arms of James de Byron: bendy argent and gules, a label azure), 117. Special thanks go to Andrew B.W. MacEwen for his assistance with this account.

8. JOHN COMYN, Knt., of Ulceby, Lincolnshire, younger son by his father's 2nd marriage. He was a minor in 1279, when his eldest brother, John Comyn, of Badenoch, settled on him £20 land in Thornton-juxta-Symondburn, Northumberland. He married **MAUD** _____. They had one son, Robert, and one daughter, Isabel. In the period, 1300–10, he granted a moiety of the mill in Ulceby, Lincolnshire called Skythe to Newhouse. In 1302 he leased the common of pasture in Ulceby, Lincolnshire to the Abbot and Convent of Thornton for use every other year for the maintenance of the poor in their hospital. He had a safe-conduct from King Edward I in 1302, and again in 1308. SIR JOHN COMYN died sometime before 1321. In 1331 his widow, Maud, had two brass pots stolen at Ulceby, Lincolnshire by Henry Stavyn, a common thief.

 Bain *Cal. Docs. Rel. Scotland* 2 (1884): 51, 168, 963. *Scots Peerage* 1 (1904): 507 (sub Comyn). Wrottesley *Peds. from the Plea Rolls* (1905): 27, 555. *Lincolnshire Notes & Queries* 9 (1907): 249–250. McLane *1341 Royal Inquest in Lincolnshire* (Lincoln Rec. Soc. 78) (1988): 127, 131. *Cal. IPM* 8 (1913): 340; 17 (1988): 213. Paget *Baronage of England* (1957): 142:12. Nottinghamshire Archives: Foljambe of Osberton: Deeds & Estate Papers, DD/FJ/1/165/2 — lease dated 7 April 1302 from John Comyn of Ulseby, Lincolnshire to the Abbot and Convent of Thorenton, for maintenance of the poor in their hospital, the common of pasture in Ulseby to use every other year for 20 years (available at www.a2a.org.uk/search/index.asp).

Children of John Comyn, Knt., by Maud _____:

i.   **ROBERT COMYN**, of Ulceby, Lincolnshire, adult by 1321. The name of his wife is unknown. He had one son, Thomas, Knt. In 1321 he sued Richard Byron and other tenants for land in Ulceby, Lincolnshire, which William de Roos gave to Alice his daughter (Robert Comyn's paternal grandmother). In 1331 he claimed land at Thurton, Newbrugh, Whesley, and Thesyde, Northumberland. In 1335 he demanded against Roger Comyn and Agnes his wife and others land in Ulceby, Lincolnshire. The same year, as "Robert son of John Comyn of Ulseby," he sued Robert de Sutheby, of Ulceby. ROBERT COMYN was living 19 April 1340, when Robert

Belhone, of Scawby, was charged with stealing four sheep from him at Ulceby, Lincolnshire. Wrottesley *Peds. from the Plea Rolls* (1905): 27, 555. *Lincolnshire Notes & Queries* 9 (1907): 249–250. *Arch. Aeliana* 3rd Ser. 6 (1910): 46, 47. McLane *1341 Royal Inquest in Lincolnshire* (Lincoln Rec. Soc. 78) (1988): 127, 131.

Child of Robert Comyn, by _____:

a. **THOMAS COMYN**, Knt., of Ulceby, Lincolnshire, son and heir. He was knighted before 1349. He married before 1349 **MARGARET DANYEL**, widow of Hervey Bek, of Normanby, Lincolnshire, and sister of Robert Danyel. They had no issue. SIR THOMAS COMYN died testate before 1359. His widow, Margaret, was living 11 Feb. 1375/6. *Lincolnshire Notes & Queries* 6 (1901): 125–127; 9 (1907): 249–250. Foster *Lincoln Wills* (Lincoln Rec. Soc. 5) (1914): 7–11.

ii. **ISABEL COMYN** [see next].

9. ISABEL COMYN, married before 21 June 1335 (date of deed) **THOMAS CLARELL**, Knt., of Aldwark, Adwick, etc., Yorkshire, son and heir of William Clarell, Knt., of Aldwark, Adwick, etc., Yorkshire, by Agnes, daughter and heiress of William Walleis. They had one son, William. Thomas was of age before 1 Dec. 1331, when his father settled on him certain rent of tenants in Thorp, Barley, and Scoles. In 1335 John Hyghe of Roderham conveyed lands in Thorpe, Aldwark, and Thrybergh to him and his wife, Isabel. In 1338 he leased all of his lands in Adwick, Yorkshire except woods, certain rents, and ½ mill to his brother, Robert, for 12 years at £6 per year. In 1341 he and Brian de Thornhill, Knt. reached an agreement regarding lands in Thurlstone, Yorkshire. SIR THOMAS CLARELL was living 2 Feb. 1354/5.

Hunter *South Yorkshire* 2 (1831): 51–56 (misidentifies Isabel, wife of Thomas Clarell, as "daughter and heir of Sir John Philibert"). Foster *Peds. of Fams. of Yorkshire* 1(1) (1874): Clarell ped. Madan *Gresleys of Drakelowe* (Colls. Hist. Staffs. n.s. 1) (1898): 245 (Clarell ped.). Dodsworth *Yorkshire Church Notes 1619–1631* (Yorkshire Arch. Soc. Recs. 34) (1904): 107–111 (Clarell arms: Gules six martlets argent). *Misc. Gen. et Heraldica* 4th Ser. 4 (1912): 70 (Clarell ped.: "Sir Thomas Clarell son and heyre. = Izabell Dor. & heyre of Redcomyn."). *Inscriptions & Memorial Bearings from the Parish Church of Leeds, Yorkshire* (19??): 305 (Clarell ped.). Nottinghamshire Archives: Foljambe of Osberton: Deeds and Estate Papers, DD/FJ/4/32/3 — grant dated 1 Dec. 1331 from William Clarell, Knt., to Thomas his son re. rent of tenants in Thorp, Barley and Scoles, with suit of court in Thorp, rent in Kynehirst and Great and Little Dalton, and watermill and suit of same in Aldewerk, £10 per annum; DD/FJ/4/32/8 — grant dated 21 June 1335 from John Hyghe of Roderham, chaplain to Thomas Clarell and his wife Isabel in tail lands in Thorpe, 1 water mill and 1 fulling mill in Aldewerk, Osterneheeng meadow in Thrybergh, and lands in Kilnehirst and Great and Little Dalton, of which Thomas had previously enfeoffed the grantor (available at www.a2a.org.uk/search/index.asp).

10. WILLIAM CLARELL, of Aldwark, Adwick, Newton upon Derwent, Peniston, etc., Yorkshire, son and heir, born about 1340 (adult by 1371). He married **ELIZABETH DE REYGATE**, daughter of William de Reygate, of Stiveton (in Sherburn), Yorkshire. They had two sons, Thomas, Esq., and William, and one daughter, Agnes. He was heir sometime before 1359 to his cousin, Sir Thomas Comyn, by which he inherited the manor of Ulceby, Lincolnshire. His wife, Elizabeth, was co-heiress c.1375 to her brother, James de Reygate, by which she inherited the manors of Stiveton (in Sherburn) and Woodhall near Milford, Yorkshire. He had a license for an oratory at Aldwark, Yorkshire in 1379. WILLIAM CLARELL died before 15 Jan. 1379/80. His widow, Elizabeth, married (2nd) before 14 Jan. 1382/3 **THOMAS DE LEEDS**, Knt., of Steeton, Yorkshire (died before 3 May 1388). They had one son, John, and three daughters, Maud, Katherine, and Margaret.

Hunter *South Yorkshire* 2 (1831): 51–56. Foster *Peds. of Fams. of Yorkshire* 1(1) (1874): Clarell ped. Madan *Gresleys of Drakelowe* (Colls. Hist. Staffs. n.s. 1) (1898): 245 (Clarell ped.). *Misc. Gen. et Heraldica* 4th Ser. 4 (1912): 70 (Clarell ped.) ("William Clarell son and heyre" placed in the wrong generation of the ped.). *Inscriptions & Memorial Bearings from the Parish Church of Leeds, Yorkshire* (19??): 305 (Clarell ped.). Nottinghamshire Archives: Foljambe of Osberton: Deeds and Estate Papers, DD/FJ/1/165/3 — grant dated 11 Feb. 1375/6 from William Clarell, Lord of Ulceby to Sir Gilbert, rector of Rawmarsh, Yorkshire et al. of the manor of Ulceby, Lincolnshire, subject to the reversion of dower of dame Margaret, widow of Sir Thomas Comyn (available at www.a2a.org.uk/search/index.asp).

11. THOMAS CLARELL, Esq., of Aldwark, Newton upon Derwent, Penistone, and Stiveton (in Sherburn), Yorkshire, son and heir, adult by 1389. He married **MAUD MONTGOMERY**, daughter of Nicholas Montgomery, Knt. (died 1424), of Cubley and Marston Montgomery, Derbyshire. They had three sons, Thomas, Esq., John, Esq., and Robert, and two daughters, Elizabeth and Margaret. In 1400 he took a release of a croft in Tickhill, Yorkshire from Thomas Johnson, of Wadworth. THOMAS CLARELL, Esq., left a will dated 20 Nov. 1441, proved 20 June 1442, requesting burial in the Austin Friars at Tickhill, Yorkshire. His widow, Maud, died shortly before 17 March 1456/7, when administration on her estate was granted to her son John Clarell, Esq., of Marshburgh Hall.

> Hunter *South Yorkshire* 2 (1831): 51–56 (Fitzwilliam Fam. Kalendar: "Maii. Kal. Obitus Thomæ Clarell et Matildis uxoris suæ"). *Coll. Top. et Gen.* 1 (1834): 338–339. *Testamenta Eboracensia* 3 (Surtees Soc. 45) (1865): 247n., 271n.; 4 (Surtees Soc. 53) (1869): 209–212 (will of Elizabeth Fitzwilliam (née Clarell) dated 1502 names her grandfather, Thomas Clarell, senior). Foster *Peds. of Fams. of Yorkshire* 1(1) (1874): Clarell ped. Madan *Gresleys of Drakelowe* (Colls. Hist. Staffs. n.s. 1) (1898): 245 (Clarell ped.). *Misc. Gen. et Heraldica* 4th Ser. 4 (1912): 66–70 (Clarell ped.: "Thomas Clarell of Aldwarke Esquyer, [1] = Maude Daughter of Nicolas Mongomery Knight, [2] = Elenor Dr of Roger of Aisford."). *Desc. Cat. Ancient Deeds* 6 (1915): 235. Harvey et al. *Vis. of the North* 3 (Surtees Soc. 144) (1930): 65–67 (Scrope ped.: "Thomas Clarell armiger = Matildis filia domini Nicholai de Mongomebry"). *Yorkshire Deeds* 6 (Yorkshire Arch. Soc. Recs. 76) (1930): 15–18, 27, 154; 8 (Yorkshire Arch. Soc. Recs. 102) (1940): 20; 10 (Yorkshire Arch. Soc. Recs. 120) (1955): 62–63. *Inscriptions & Memorial Bearings from the Parish Church of Leeds, Yorkshire* (19??): 305 (Clarell ped.). Foljambe of Osberton: Deeds and Estate Papers, DD/FJ/13/3/4 — exchange dated 29 Sept. 1437 between Thomas Clarell, snr., Esq. Thomas Clarell, jr., and Thomas Momforthe of Kilnhirste re. lands in Kilnhirst and Swinton (available at www.a2a.org.uk/search/index.asp).

Children of Thomas Clarell, Esq., by Maud Montgomery:

i. **THOMAS CLARELL**, Esq. [see next].

ii. **ELIZABETH CLARELL**, married **JOHN GRESLEY**, Knt., of Drakelow, Derbyshire [see GRESLEY 12].

iii. **MARGARET CLARELL**, married (1st) by contract dated 19 Jan. 1410 **JOHN FITZWILLIAM**, Knt., of Sprotborough, Yorkshire and Plumtree, Nottinghamshire [see SALTONSTALL 16], son and heir of John Fitzwilliam, of Sprotborough, Yorkshire, by Eleanor, daughter of Henry Greene, Knt. [see FITZWILLIAM 15 for his ancestry]. He was born at Sprotborough, Yorkshire 27 May 1397 (aged 20 in 1417). They had two sons, William, Knt., and John, and one daughter, Eleanor. In 1421 he presented to the church of Sprotborough, Yorkshire. SIR JOHN FITZWILLIAM died at Rouen 17 Sept. 1421, and was buried at Sprotborough, Yorkshire. His widow, Margaret, married (2nd) in 1422 (as his 3rd wife) **ROBERT WATERTON**, Esq., of Methley, Yorkshire, Master of the Horse, Master of the Hounds, Chief Forester of Knaresborough, Keeper of Pontefract Castle, Steward, Master Forester, and Bailiff of Hatfield. He and his wife, Margaret, presented to the church of Sprotborough, Yorkshire 3 Dec. 1424. ROBERT WATERTON, Esq., died 17 Jan. 1424/5. His widow, Margaret, married (3rd) clandestinely 7 Feb. 1425/6 **WILLIAM GASCOIGNE**, Knt., of Gawthorpe, Thorp Arch, etc., Yorkshire, Knight of the Shire of Yorkshire, 1431, 1435, 1452, Sheriff of Yorkshire, 1441–2, son and heir of William Gascoigne, of Gawthorpe, Thorp Arch, Shipley, etc., Yorkshire, Knight of the Shire for Yorkshire, by Joan (or Jane), said to be a daughter and heiress of Henry Wyman. He was born about 1405 (aged 18 in 1423). They had four sons, William, Knt., Robert, John, and Ralph, and five daughters, Joan (wife of Henry Vavasour, Knt.), Anne, Margaret (wife of William Scargill, Esq.), _____ (wife of Robert Dransfeld), and _____ (wife of Hamon Sutton). In Feb. 1425/6 he and his wife, Elizabeth, presented to the church of Sprotborough, Yorkshire. In 1434 he was one of those required to take the oath not to maintain peacebreakers. In 1444 he was pardoned for any flight or withdrawal wherewith he was charged in the indictment against him and others for the killing of Thomas Dawson, collier. SIR WILLIAM GASCOIGNE was living in Feb. 1448/9, but died before March 1453/4, when his widow, Margaret, petitioned in Chancery that his feoffees of the manor of Thorp Arch would not perform his wishes with regard to the estate. She was living in 1465/7, when she sued her late husband's feoffees for the manor of Thorp Arch, Yorkshire. Lodge *Peerage of Ireland* 2 (1789): 158–181 (sub Fitz-William). Brydges *Collins' Peerage of England* 4 (1812): 374–400 (sub Fitz-William). Hunter *South Yorkshire* 2 (1831): 51–56, 484. *Testamenta Eboracensia* 3 (Surtees Soc. 45) (1865): 247n., 271n. Banks *Walks in Yorkshire: Wakefield & its Neighbourhood* (1871): 186–191. Foster *Peds. of Fams. of Yorkshire* 1(1) (1874): Clarell and Fitzwilliam peds. Glover & St. George *Vis. of Yorkshire 1584–5, 1612* (1875): 7 (Fitzwilliam ped.: "Sir John Fitzwilliam, of Sprotborough, lord of Emley, died at Rouen. = Margaret, dau. of Thos. Clarell, ye elder, wid. to Sir William Gascoigne, and Sir Robert Waterton."). Hawley et al. *Vis. of Essex 1552, 1558, 1570, 1612 & 1634* 1 (H.S.P. 13) (1878): 197–199

(1612 Vis.) (Fitzwilliam ped.: "Sr John Fitz Williams Lo. of Ellmyn sonne and he."). Flower *Vis. of Yorkshire 1563–4* (H.S.P. 16) (1881): 124–127 (Fitzwilliam ped.: "Sir John Fytz William, Knight, of Sprotborough, son & heyr. = Margaret doughter to Thomas Clarell, after to Robert Waterton, and last to William Gaskon, Knight."), 133–136 (Gaskon ped.: "Sir William Gaskon son & heyr = Margaret doughter to Thomas Clarell, to her 2 husband, Robert Waterton, & after to John Fytz William of Sprotboroo."). *Yorkshire Arch. & Topog. Jour.* 7 (1882): 421 (re. Waterton fam.). *List of Sheriffs for England & Wales* (PRO Lists and Indexes 9) (1898): 162. Madan *Gresleys of Drakelowe* (Colls. Hist. Staffs. n.s. 1) (1898): 245 (Clarell ped.). *List of Early Chancery Procs.* 1 (PRO Lists and Indexes 12) (1901): 347. Dodsworth *Yorkshire Church Notes 1619–1631* (Yorkshire Arch. Soc. Recs. 34) (1904): 135–137. Clay *Yorkshire Church Notes* (Yorkshire Arch. Soc. Rec. Ser. 34) (1904): 154. Phillimore *Abs. of IPMs Rel. Nottinghamshire* 1 (Thoroton Soc. Rec. Ser. 3) (1905): vii, 18–20. Colman *Hist. of Parish of Barwick-in-Elmet* (Thoresby Soc. 17) (1908): 244–245 (re. Waterton fam.). *Misc. Gen. et Heraldica* 4th Ser. 4 (1912): 66–70 (Clarell ped.: "Margaret [Clarell] (1) = Sir John Fitzwilliam of Spratboro, (2) to Robt Waterton, = (3) Wm Gaskon."). Clay *Extinct & Dormant Peerages* (1913): 76–78 (sub Fitzwilliam). *Yorkshire Inqs.* 5 (Yorkshire Arch. Soc. Recs. 59) (1918): 144–147. *C.P.* 5 (1926): 191 (sub Everingham). Harvey et al. *Vis. of the North* 3 (Surtees Soc. 144) (1930): 65–67 (Scrope ped.: "*Domina* Margareta [Clarell] nupta Iohanni Fitzwilliam de Sprotborough et postea domino Willelmo Gascoigne militi"), 74–76 (Fitzwilliam ped.: "Iohannes Fitzwilliam obijt apud Rothomagum *1 fil.* = Margareta nupta (*sic Ms.*) *filia* (Iohanni filio) Thome Clarel postea nupta Roberto Waterton et postea Willelmo Gascoyn militi"). *Yorkshire Arch. Jour.* 30 (1931): 383–384. Gooder *Parl. Representation of York* 1 (Yorkshire Arch. Soc. Recs. 91) (1935): 180 (biog. of William Gascoigne), 186–188 (biog. of William Gascoigne). Train *Abs. of IPMs Rel. Nottinghamshire* 2 (Thoroton Soc. Recs. 12) (1952): 176, 191–192. Reese *Royal Office of Master of the Horse* (1976): 341 (biog. of Robert Waterton). Gillespie *Age of Richard II* (1997): 192. *Inscriptions & Memorial Bearings from the Parish Church of Leeds, Yorkshire* (19??): 305 (Clarell ped.). Ormrod *Lord Lieutenants & High Sheriffs of Yorkshire, 1066–2000* (2000): 86 (biog. of Sir William Gascoigne). Sheffield Archives: Estate papers of the Copley Fam., Baronets, of Sprotborough, CD/2 — Pre-nuptial settlement dated 19 Jan. 1410, between John Fitzwilliam and Thomas Clarell, in consideration of a marriage to be had between John, son and heir of John Fitzwilliam, and Margaret, daughter of Thomas Clarell; CD/3 (available at www.a2a.org.uk/search/index.asp). Sheffield Archives: Wentworth Woodhouse Muniments, WWM/D/77; WWM/D/83 (available at www.a2a.org.uk/search/index.asp).

Children of Margaret Clarell, by John Fitzwilliam, Knt.:

a. **WILLIAM FITZWILLIAM**, Knt., of Sprotborough, Yorkshire, married **ELIZABETH CHAWORTH** [see SALTONSTALL 17].

b. **ELEANOR FITZWILLIAM**, married **WILLIAM RYTHER**, Knt., of Ryther, Yorkshire [see RYTHER 14].

Children of Margaret Clarell, by William Gascoigne, Knt:

a. **WILLIAM GASCOIGNE**, Knt., of Gawthorpe, Yorkshire, married **JOAN** (or **JANE**) **NEVILLE** [see GASCOIGNE 16].

b. **ANNE GASCOIGNE**, married **HUGH HASTINGS**, Knt., of Fenwick, Yorkshire [see ELSING 16].

12. THOMAS CLARELL, Esq., of Aldwark, Yorkshire, hereditary patron of Austin Friars, Tickhill, Yorkshire, and, in right of his wife, of Birkby, Haldenby, and Sedbury (in Gilling), Yorkshire, son and heir, born about 1402 (aged 40 in 1442). He married about 8 May 1408 (date of bond) **ELIZABETH SCROPE**, daughter and co-heiress of John le Scrope, Knt., of Hollinhall and Haldenby, Yorkshire, and Hay (in Therfield), Hertfordshire, by Elizabeth, daughter and co-heiress of David de Strathbogie, 12th Earl of Atholl [see ATHOLL 16 for her ancestry]. They had three daughters, Elizabeth, Maud (wife of _____ Ughtred), and Alice [Prioress of Hampole]. His wife, Elizabeth, was a legatee in the 1405 will of her father, John le Scrope, Knt. She was heiress after 1415 to her sister, Joan, wife of Richard Hastings, Knt. In 1423 John Anabyll granted Thomas Clarell, Junior, esquire, and John Marsburgh his lands and tenements in Yorkshire. THOMAS CLARELL, Esq., died shortly before 15 July 1450, when administration of his estate was granted to his mother, Maud Clarell. He was buried at Austin Friars, Tickhill, Yorkshire. His widow, Elizabeth, married (2nd) before 18 July 1455 (date of demise) **JOHN PILKINGTON**, Knt., of Pilkington Hall, Yorkshire, Whitingham, Lancashire, etc., King's esquire, Chief Forester of Sowerby

Chase, 1461, Constable of Chester Castle, 1461, Steward and Bailiff of the lordship and liberty of Howden, Yorkshire, 1462, Escheator of Lancashire, Seneschal of the barony of Sherburn, 1475, Chamberlain of the Exchequer, 1477, son and heir of Robert Pilkington. His wife, Elizabeth, was living 18 July 1455. In 1461 he was granted the manors of Aylesthorp, Edenham, Grimesthorpe, Hoall, and Senthorp, Lincolnshire, and Hoton, Linton-super-Ouse, Malteby, Thornton in Craven, and Turnham Hall, Yorkshire by the king. In 1463 he conveyed the manors of Therfeld, Hertfordshire, Thorpe Constantine, Staffordshire, and Birkby and Hollinhall, Yorkshire to George, Duke of Clarence, and other feoffees. Following his wife, Elizabeth's death, he married (2nd) in 1464 **JOAN** (or **JANE**) **BALDERSTON**, daughter and co-heiress of William Balderston, of Balderston, Lancashire, by his 2nd wife, Margaret, daughter of William Stanley. They had two sons, including Edward. By an unknown mistress, he also had an illegitimate son, Robert. In the period, 1460–5, he and Robert Harington, Esq., sued William Sengleton, Esq., in Chancery regarding the manor of Singleton, Lancashire belonging to petitioners in right of their wives and seizure of tenants' goods. In 1475 he built and endowed a chantry chapel in the parish church of All Saints, Wakefield, Yorkshire. SIR JOHN PILKINGTON died 29 Dec. 1478. He left a will dated 28 June 1478, proved 30 June 1479. His widow, Joan, married (2nd) **THOMAS WORTLEY**, Knt., from whom she was divorced. William, Bishop of Dromore, was directed to veil her 10 Sept. 1488. She left a will dated 2 Jan. 1497, requesting burial in the nun's quire in the Priory of Nun Monkton, Yorkshire.

Hunter *South Yorkshire* 2 (1831): 51–56 (Fitzwilliam Fam. Kalendar: "Februarii VI°.id. Obitus Thomæ Clarell et Elisabethæ uxoris ejus"). Nicolas *Controversy between Scrope & Grosvenor* 2 (1832): 127–129, 134–135 (Scrope ped.). *Testamenta Eboracensia* 1 (Surtees Soc. 4) (1836): 338–339 (will of John le Scrope, Knt.); 3 (Surtees Soc. 45) (1865): 247n. *Coll. Top. et Gen.* 4 (1837): 73. Fisher *Hist. & Antiqs. of Masham & Mashamshire* (1865): 221–243. Burke *Gen. Hist. of the Dormant, Abeyant, Forfeited & Extinct Peerages* (1866): 482–483 (sub Scrope of Masham). Foster *Peds. of Fams. of Yorkshire* 1(1) (1874): Clarell ped. Glover & St. George *Vis. of Yorkshire 1584–5, 1612* (1875): 415 (Burgh ped.: "filia [Scrope] nupta Thomæ Clarell"). Whitaker *Hist. & Antiqs. of the Deanery of Craven* (1878): 118, 120. *Yorkshire Arch. Jour.* 11 (1891): 46–47; 12 (1893): 258–259. Pilkington *Hist. of the Lancashire Fam. of Pilkington* (1894): 28–33. James *Desc. Cat. MSS in the Fitzwilliam Museum* (1895): 87–88, 429. Madan *Gresleys of Drakelowe* (Colls. Hist. Staffs. n.s. 1) (1898): 245 (Clarell ped.). Benolte et al. *Vis. of Surrey 1530, 1572 & 1623* (H.S.P. 43) (1899): 5–6 (Clarell arms: Gules, six martlets argent). Reade *House of Cornwall* (1908): 61–62. VCH *Lancashire* 6 (1911): 313–319. *Misc. Gen. et Heraldica* 4th Ser. 4 (1912): 66–70 (Clarell ped.: "Thomas Clarell son & heyre. = Elizabeth Dot. & on heyres of Sir John Scrope."). VCH *Hertford* 3 (1912): 276–284. VCH *Yorkshire* 1 (1913): 280–281. VCH *Yorkshire N.R.* 1 (1914): 79, 399. Harvey et al. *Vis. of the North* 3 (Surtees Soc. 144) (1930): 65–67 (Scrope ped.: "Elizabeth filia et heres domini Iohannis le Scrope militis = Thomas Clarell armiger de Aldwarke 2 vir."). *Yorkshire Deeds* 6 (Yorkshire Arch. Soc. Recs. 76) (1930): 16–18; 9 (Yorkshire Arch. Soc. Recs. 111) (1948): 146. Gooder *Parl. Representation of York* 1 (Yorkshire Arch. Soc. Recs. 91) (1935): 157–158 (biog. of John le Scrope), 183–185 (biog. of Richard Hastings). Paget *Baronage of England* (1957) 492: 1–2 (sub Scrope of Masham). National Archives, SC 8/117/5838 (petition dated 1450 from the Prioress and convent of Hampole which mentions Elizabeth, widow of Thomas Clarell; Thomas Clarell; John Pilkyngton (Pilkington) of Pilkington Hall, Gent., etc.) (available at www.catalogue.nationalarchives.gov.uk/search.asp). Nottinghamshire Archives: Foljambe of Osberton: Deeds and Estate Papers, DD/FJ/4/38/2 — defeasance of demise dated 18 July 1455, from Edmund Fitzwilliam, Esq., and feoffees to Robert Nevyll, Esq., William Skargill, jun., and others; demise of grantors and father Edmund Fitzwilliam of premises in Waddeworth and Bilham to be void if Richard Fitzwilliam and wife make estate to grantees of either manor of Steton and lands there and in Milford worth £13 6s. 8d. per annum 6 months after death of Maud late wife of Thomas Clarell; or of manor of Haldenby worth £13 6s. 8d. per annum 6 months after death of Elizabeth wife of John Pillyngton [Pilkington] and late wife of Thomas Clarell; on condition that grantees within 6 months after 7 years settle same on Thomas Fitzwilliam and Joan daughter of William Mirfeld if they marry, or to Joan for life with remainder to Elizabeth wife of Richard Fitzwilliam (available at www.a2a.org.uk/search/index.asp).

Child of Thomas Clarell, Esq., by Elizabeth Scrope:

i. **ELIZABETH CLARELL**, married **RICHARD FITZWILLIAM**, Knt., of Wadworth, Yorkshire [see HOTHAM 14].

❧ CLARKE ❧

WILLIAM THE CONQUEROR, King of England, married **MAUD OF FLANDERS**.
HENRY I, King of England, by an unknown mistress, _____.
ROBERT FITZ ROY, Earl of Gloucester, married **MABEL FITZ ROBERT**.
MAUD OF GLOUCESTER, married **RANULPH DE GERNONS**, Earl of Chester.
HUGH, Earl of Chester, married **BERTRADE DE MONTFORT**.
AGNES OF CHESTER, married **WILLIAM DE FERRERS**, Knt., Earl of Derby.
WILLIAM DE FERRERS, Knt., Earl of Derby, married **MARGARET DE QUINCY**.
WILLIAM DE FERRERS, Knt., of Groby (in Ratby), Leicestershire, married **ANNE DURWARD** (desc. King William the Conqueror).
WILLIAM DE FERRERS, Knt., 1st Lord Ferrers of Groby, married [?**MARGARET**] **DE SEGRAVE**.
HENRY DE FERRERS, 2nd Lord Ferrers of Groby, married **ISABEL DE VERDUN** (desc. King William the Conqueror).
WILLIAM DE FERRERS, Knt., 3rd Lord Ferrers of Groby, married **MARGARET DE UFFORD**.
HENRY DE FERRERS, Knt., 4th Lord Ferrers of Groby, married **JOAN DE POYNINGS** (desc. King William the Conqueror).
WILLIAM FERRERS, Knt., 5th Lord Ferrers of Groby, married **PHILIPPE CLIFFORD** (desc. King William the Conqueror) [see GROBY 13].

14. THOMAS FERRERS, Esq., of Hethe and Flecknoe, Warwickshire, Walton-on-Trent, Derbyshire, Champeyns (in Woodham Ferrers), Essex, Tettenhall, Staffordshire, etc., 2nd son by his father's 1st marriage and heir male, born 1392/1402 (aged 40 and more in 1445, 50 and more in 1452). He married before 1418 **ELIZABETH FREVILLE**, daughter of Baldwin Freville, Knt., of Tamworth, Warwickshire, by Maud, daughter of Stephen le Scrope, Knt., 2nd Lord Scrope of Masham [see FREVILLE 11 for her ancestry]. She was born about 1394 (aged 24 in 1418 and 26 in 1420). They had two sons, Thomas, Knt., and Henry, Knt. His wife, Elizabeth, was co-heiress in 1418 to her brother, Baldwin de Freville, by which she inherited the castle and lordship of Tamworth, Warwickshire, the manors of Marston and Lea (both in Lea Marston), Stivichall, and Stratford juxta Tamworth, Warwickshire, and a one-third share of the manor of Yatesbury, Wiltshire. She was a legatee in the 1418 will of her uncle, Stephen le Scrope, Archdeacon of Richmond, who bequeathed her £10 for her marriage. He and his wife Elizabeth's fellow Freville co-heirs presented to the church of Great Harborough, Warwickshire in 1421 and 1450. In 1422 he and his wife, Elizabeth, leased one acre of pasture in Stebbing, Essex to John Clerk, of Stebbing, and Maud his wife. In 1440 Roger Aston, Knt., Thomas Ferrers, Esq., and Hugh Willoughby, Knt., sued John Prynce, yeoman, of Warwick for waste and destruction in houses, woods, and gardens which had been demised to him for a term of years. He presented to the church of Great Harborough, Warwickshire alone in 1458. THOMAS FERRERS, Esq., died 6 Jan. 1458/9.

Dugdale *Antiqs. of Warwickshire* (1730): 94. Manning *Hist. & Antiqs. of Surrey* 2 (1809): 626–628. Blore *Hist. & Antiqs. of Rutland* 1(2) (1811): 90 (Botetourt ped.). Clutterbuck *Hist. & Antiqs. of Hertford* 1 (1815): 360 (Ferrers ped.). Baker *Hist. & Antiqs. of Northampton* 1 (1822–30): 103–104. Nicolas *Controversy between Scrope & Grosvenor* 2 (1832): 134–137, 142–148. Carthew *Hundred of Launditch & Deanery of Brisley* 1 (1877): 343–344. Lennard & Vincent *Vis. of Warwick 1619* (H.S.P. 12) (1877): 4–5 (Ferrers ped.: "Sr Tho. Firrers of Tamworth Kt. 2 sonne to Will'm Lord Firrers of Grobie. = Elizb. eldist da. & cohey. of Baldwine Freuille Kt. Lo. of Tamworth.") (Ferrers arms: Gules, seven mascles conjoined or, a canton ermine), 6–7 (Ferrers ped.: Sr Tho. Ferrers Kt. of Tamworth 2 sone to Will'm Lo. Ferrers of Groby. = Elizb. eldest Da. & Cohey. to Sr Baldwyne Freuile Kt Lo. of Tamworth."). Burke *Dormant, Abeyant, Forfeiarted & Extinct Peerages* (1883): 63–64 (sub Botetourt). Birch *Cat. Seals in the British Museum* 2 (1892): 792 (seal of Thomas Ferrers dated 1435 — A shield of arms, couché: seven mascles, three, three and one [FERRERS]. Crest on a helmet, ornamental mantling, and chapeau, a horse statant. Beaded borders. Legend: ** s' thome * ferrers * de * groby **.). Norris *Baddesley Clinton* (1897): 112–117. Wrottesley *Staffordshire Suits: Plea Rolls* (Colls. Hist. Staffs. n.s. 3) (1900): 153. *Genealogist* n.s. 19 (1903): 34–35, 103–104, 163. Wrottesley *Peds. from the Plea Rolls* (1905): 413–414, 418. *Surrey Arch. Colls.* 19 (1906): 27–32. May *Vis. of Warwick 1683* (H.S.P. 62) (1911): 165–167 (Ferrers ped.: "Sir Tho: Ferrers of Tamworth Kt 2 son of William Lo: Ferrers of Grooby. = Elizabeth da. & heire of Sr Baldwin Freville Lord of Tamworth."). *C.P.* 5 (1926): 333 (chart), 356, footnote a, 357, footnote a, 358, footnote c (sub Ferrers). *C.C.R.*

1422–1429 (1933): 81–82. Paget *Baronage of England* (1957) 207: 6–7 (sub Ferrers). *Genealogists' Mag.* 21 (1984): 185–190. Carpenter *Locality & Polity* (1992): 160. VCH *Wiltshire* 17 (2002): 172–181. Hertfordshire Archives & Local Studies: Personal & Fam. Papers of the Capells, Earls of Essex, DE/M/134 (lease by Thomas Ferrers, son and heir of William de Ferrers of Groby, and his wife, Elizabeth, dated 15 June 1422) (available at http://www.a2a.org.uk/search/index.asp).

15. HENRY FERRERS, Knt., of Peckham, Kent, and Hambleton, Rutland, Knight of the King's Bodyguard, Sheriff of Kent, 1487–8, Knight of the Shire for Kent, Keeper of the Chaylesmore Park, 2nd son. He married before 30 Sept. 1481 (date of grant) **MARGARET HEXSTALL**, widow of William Whetenhall (or Whetnall), Gent., of East Peckham, Kent, and daughter and co-heiress of William Hexstall, Esq., of Heckstall, Staffordshire, and East Peckham, Kent, by his wife, Joan. They had four sons, including Edward, Knt., and Richard, and five daughters, including Margaret and Elizabeth. SIR HENRY FERRERS died 28 Dec. 1499. He left a will dated 22 Dec. 1499, proved 20 August 1500 (P.C.C. 4 Moore), requesting burial besides his wife in the parish church at Peckham, Kent.

Hasted *Hist. & Top. Survey of Kent* 5 (1798): 280–294. Lennard & Vincent *Vis. of Warwick 1619* (H.S.P. 12) (1877): 4–5 (Ferrers ped.: "Sr Hen. Firrers of Chilmore Kt. 2 sonne. = Margt da. & Coheire of Will'm Hortall relicta William Wittenhall."). Tresswell & Vincent *Vis. of Shropshire 1623, 1569 & 1584* 1 (H.S.P. 28) (1889): 71–78 (Bromley ped.: "Margareta [Hextall] vxor Henrici Ferrers de Est Peckham in Kent militis"). *Desc. Cat. Ancient Deeds* 1 (1890): 420, 427–428, 458. Norris *Baddesley Clinton* (1897): 112–117. *List of Sheriffs for England & Wales* (PRO Lists and Indexes 9) (1898): 68. May *Vis. of Warwick 1683* (H.S.P. 62) (1911): 165–167 (Ferrers ped.: "Henricus Ferrers de Chillesmore miles fil. 2. = Margareta filia et cohæres Wm Hexstall de Hexstall in com. Staff et de Peckham in com. Kanc."). Benolte & Cooke *Vis. of Kent 1530–1, 1574 & 1592* 2 (H.S.P. 75) (1924): 115–116 (1592 Vis.) (Whetnhall ped.: "William Whetenhall of Est Peckham in the Countie of Kent gent. Sonne and heire to Whetnhall aforesaide maried Margaret Daughter and sole heire to William Hexstall of Est Peckham aforesaide Esquire and of …. his wife Daughter and heir to Hewet gent., and had issue William."). *C.P.* 5 (1926): 333 (chart), 357 footnote a (sub Ferrers). McSheffrey *Marriage, Sex & Civil Culture in late Medieval London* (2006): 104. National Archives, C 146/431 (grant dated 30 Sept. 1481 by Henry Ferrers, knight of the King's body-guard, and Margaret his wife, daughter and heiress of William Hexstall, Esq., deceased, to Robert Weston, and two others, Citizens of London, of lands &c., in the parishs of Halstow and St. Mary's in the hundred of Hoo in Kent) (available at www.catalogue.nationalarchives.gov.uk/search.asp). Surrey History Centre: Loseley MSS, Recs. of the More & More Molyneux Fam. of Loseley Park, LM/341/73; LM/342/18 (available at http://www.a2a.org.uk/search/index.asp).

16. ELIZABETH FERRERS, married about 1508 **JAMES CLERKE**, Esq., of Forde Hall (in Wrotham), Kent, son and heir of John Clerke, Esq., of Forde Hall (in Wrotham), Kent, Kent, by Lucy, daughter of Walter Moyle, Knt. They had four sons, Henry, Walter, George, Gent., and John. JAMES CLERKE, Esq., died at Wrotham, Kent 20 Sept. 1553.

Arch. Cantiana 4 (1861): 247 (1619 Vis. Kent) (Elizabetha, filia Ed'ri Ferrers, de Badesley et Peckham, in co. Cantii, militis). Lennard & Vincent *Vis. of Warwick 1619* (H.S.P. 12) (1877): 4–5 (Ferrers ped.: "Elizb. [Ferrers] ux. Jams Clarke of Fordhall in Kent."). Norris *Baddesley Clinton* (1897): 112–117. May *Vis. of Warwick 1683* (H.S.P. 62) (1911): 165–167 (Ferrers ped.: Elizabeth [Ferrers] wife of Ja: Clarke of Fordhall in com. Canc."). *NEHGR* 74 (1920): 68–76, 130–140 (Forde Hall lay about a mile and a half eastward from Wrotham church, near Addington Common, said to be still standing in 1920). Benolte & Cooke *Vis. of Kent 1530–1, 1574 & 1592* 1 (H.S.P. 74) (1923): 38 (1574 Vis.) (Clerke ped.: "James Clerke of Wrotam = Elizabeth daughter of Sir Edward Ferrys of Badfly, knight") (Clerke arms: Or, on a bend engrailed azure a cinquefoil of the field).

17. GEORGE CLERKE (or **CLARKE**), Gent., of Wrotham, Kent, son and heir, born in 1510. He married about 1533 **ELIZABETH WILSFORD**, daughter of Thomas Wilsford, Esq., of Hartridge (in Cranbrook), Kent [see BARNE 18], by his 1st wife, Elizabeth, daughter of Walter Culpeper, Esq. They had seven sons, William, Esq., James, Gent., George, Gent., Thomas, Gent., Reginald, Robert, and Richard, and seven daughters, Elizabeth (wife of Thomas Goulden or Godden), Anne, Constance, Margaret, Katherine, Lucy, and Mary. He was a legatee in the 1535 will of his uncle, Edward Ferrers, Knt. He participated in the suppression of Wyatt's Rebellion with a defeat of rebels near Wrotham, Kent 10 Feb. 1553/4. GEORGE CLERKE, Gent., died at Wrotham, Kent 6 March 1558/9, and was buried there the 8th March following.

Arch. Cantiana 4 (1861): 247. *NEHGR* 74 (1920): 68–76, 130–140. Benolte & Cooke *Vis. of Kent 1530–1, 1574 & 1592* 1 (H.S.P. 74) (1923): 38 (1574 Vis.) (Clerke ped.: "George Clerke of Worton [Wrotham] mar. Elizabeth dau. of Tho. Willford of Tanbroke [Cranbroke]"). Shakespeare Centre Library & Archive: Ferrers of Baddesley Clinton, DR 3/307 (will of Edward Ferrers, Knt.) (available at www.a2a.org.uk/search/index.asp).

18. JAMES CLERKE (or **CLARKE**), Gent., of East Farleigh, Kent, 2nd son. He married **MARY SAXBY**, daughter and heiress of Edward Saxby (or Saxilby), Knt., Clerk in the Remembrancer's Office, Baron of the Exchequer, by his 2nd wife, Elizabeth, daughter of _____ Fisher, Esq., of Longworth, Oxfordshire. They had four sons, Walter, William, Gent., Peter, and Edward, and four daughters, Elizabeth, Anne (wife of Humphrey Browne), Grace, and Barbara (wife of Nicholas Crump). JAMES CLERKE, Gent., left a will dated 13 July 1614, proved 1 Nov. 1614 (P.C.C. 118 Lawe).

Chalmers *Gen'l Biog. Dict.* 29 (1816): 447. *Gentleman's Mag.* n.s. 12 (1839): 488. Foss *Judges of England* 5 (1857): 539 (biog. of Edward Saxby, or Saxilby). *Arch. Cantiana* 4 (1861): 247. Cooke & St. George *Vis. of Hertfordshire 1572, 1634 & 1546* (H.S.P. 22) (1886): 161 (Appendix II) (Purvey ped.). Benolte et al. *Vis. of Sussex 1530, 1633–4* (H.S.P. 53) (1905): 210–211 (Crump ped.: "James Clerke of Farley in Kent uncle to Sr John Clerke of Ford in Kent knt. = Marid on of ye dau. & heires of Edw. Saxbie Baron of the Exchequer.") (Clerke arms: Or, a bend engrailed azure; impaling, Gules, a bend vaire between six escallops argent). *NEHGR* 74 (1920): 68–76, 130–140. Benolte & Cooke *Vis. of Kent 1530–1, 1574 & 1592* 1 (H.S.P. 74) (1923): 38 (1574 Vis.) (Clerke ped.: "Jeames Clerke = Mary daughter & heire of Edward Saxby Boron of ye Exchequere").

19. WILLAM CLERKE, Gent., of East Farleigh, Kent, and St. Botolph, Aldgate, London, younger son. He married at St. Andrew's, Holborn, London, by license dated 10 Feb. 1598/9 **MARY WESTON**, daughter of Jerome Weston, Knt., of Skreens (in Roxwell), Essex, by Mary, daughter of Anthony Cave, Gent. [see LOVETT 18 for her ancestry]. She was baptized at Roxwell, Essex 26 April 1579. They had eight sons, Weston, William, James, [Rev.] Essex, George, Jeremy (or Jeremiah), Richard, and John, and one daughter, Mary. WILLIAM CLERKE, Gent., was buried at East Farleigh, Kent 12 June 1610. His widow, Mary, probably died before 13 July 1614.

Waters *Chester of Chicheley* 1 (1878): 96–97. *NEHGR* 74 (1920): 68–76, 130–140; 82 (1928): 154 (arms of Jeremy Clarke: Or, on a bend engrailed azure a cinqfoil of the field). Benolte & Cooke *Vis. of Kent 1530–1, 1574 & 1592* 1 (H.S.P. 74) (1923): 38 (1574 Vis.) (Clerke ped.).

20. [Mr.] JEREMY (or **JEREMIAH**) **CLARKE**, younger son, baptized at East Farleigh, Kent 1 Dec. 1605. He married in England about 1637 **FRANCES LATHAM**, widow of William Dungan, of St. Martin in the Fields, Middlesex, and daughter of Lewis Latham, Gent., of Elstow, Bedfordshire, Sergeant Falconer to King Charles I, by his 1st wife, Elizabeth. She was baptized at Kempston, Bedfordshire 15 Feb. 1609/10. They had five sons, [Mr.] Walter, Esq. [Governor of Rhode Island], Jeremiah, Latham, Weston, and [Rev.] James, and two daughters, Mary (wife of [Gov.] John Cranston and John Stanton) and Sarah (wife of John Pinner and [Gov.] Caleb Carr). He and his family immigrated to New England before 1638, in which year he was admitted an inhabitant of the island of Aquidneck, later Newport, Rhode Island. He and eight others signed a compact at Portsmouth, Rhode Island 28 April 1639, prepatory to the settlement of Newport. The same year he was present at a meeting of the inhabitants, and was made treasurer. In 1640 he and two others were chosen to lay out the remainder of the lands at Newport, Rhode Island. He was made freeman 16 March 1640/1. He held various important positions in Newport and the colony of Rhode Island, namely town constable, 1639–40; Lieutenant, 1642; Captain, 1644; Treasurer for Newport, 1644–7; and Treasurer for the four towns of the colony, 1647–9. In 1648 he was chosen one of the governor's assistants. During that year, pending the clearing of certain accusations against [Gov.] William Coddington, Clarke was elected interim governor under the title of president regent. [Mr.] JEREMY CLARKE was buried at Newport, Rhode Island Jan. 1651/2. His widow, Frances, married (3rd) before 18 Jan. 1656 [**Rev.**] **WILLIAM VAUGHAN**, pastor of the First Baptist church of Newport, Rhode Island. In 1656 he, with others, separated from the First church and organized a new society known as the Second Baptist church. [REV.] WILLIAM VAUGHAN died on or about 2 Sept. 1677 (date of letter). His wife, Frances, is thought to have died about the same time or soon afterwards, and was buried at Newport, Rhode Island.

>   Bartlett *Recs. of Rhode Island* 1 (1856): 87, 93, 98, 102, 110, 121, 127, 148, 209, 210, 211, 213, 219. *Newport Hist. Mag.* 1 (1881): 75–96, 129–155. Austin *Gen. Dict. of Rhode Island* (1887): 44. Harting *Bibliotheca Accipitraria* (1891): 250–251. Leach *Gen. & Biog. Mems.* (1898): 217–222. Cutter *New England Fams.* 1 (1913): 34–35. NEHGR 74 (1920): 68–76, 130–140; 82 (1928): 154 (arms of Jeremy Clarke: Or, on a bend engrailed azure a cinqfoil of the field). Justice *Ancestry of Jeremy Clarke of Rhode Island & Dungan Gen.* (1922). Raimo *Biog. Dict. of American Col. & Revolutionary Govs.* (1980): 374 [biog. of Jeremiah (or Jeremy) Clarke]. TG 4 (1983): 187–202; 10 (1982): 167–194. Dungan *Quest for Origins* (1997).

ꝏ CLARKSON ꝏ

MALCOLM III (CEANNMORE), King of Scots, married [SAINT] **MARGARET**.
DAVID I, King of Scots, married **MAUD OF NORTHUMBERLAND**.
HENRY OF SCOTLAND, Earl of Northumberland, married **ADA DE WARENNE**.
MARGARET OF SCOTLAND, married **HUMPHREY DE BOHUN**, hereditary Constable of England.
HENRY DE BOHUN, Earl of Hereford, married **MAUD DE MANDEVILLE**, Countess of Essex.
HUMPHREY DE BOHUN, Knt., Earl of Hereford and Essex, married **MAUD OF EU** (desc. King William the Conqueror).
ELEANOR DE BOHUN, married **JOHN DE VERDUN**, Knt., of Alton, Staffordshire.
MAUD DE VERDUN, married **JOHN DE GREY**, Knt., 2nd Lord Grey of Wilton.
ROGER DE GREY, Knt., 1st Lord Grey of Ruthin, married **ELIZABETH DE HASTINGS** (desc. King William the Conqueror).
REYNOLD DE GREY, Knt., 2nd Lord Grey of Ruthin, married **ELEANOR LE STRANGE** (desc. King William the Conqueror)
REYNOLD GREY, Knt., Lord of Hastings, Wexford, and Ruthin, married **JOAN ASTLEY** (desc. King William the Conqueror) [see GREY 11].

12. ROBERT GREY, Esq., of Enville and Whittington (in Kinver), Staffordshire, and, by gift of his father, of Nailstone, Leicestershire, Wootton, Northamptonshire, and Barford, Bedfordshire, 4th son, but 3rd son by his father's 2nd marriage. He married before 1447 **ELEANOR LOWE**, daughter and heiress of Humphrey Lowe, Esq., of Enville, Staffordshire, by Alice, daughter of William Botoner, of Withybrook, Warwickshire. They had two sons, Humphrey, Esq., and Henry, and two daughters, Anne and Rebecca. ROBERT GREY, Esq., died before 20 June 1460.

>   Shaw *Hist. & Antiqs. of Staffordshire* 2(1) (1801): 268. Nichols *Hist. & Antiqs. of Leicester* 3(2) (1804): 684; 4(2) (1811): 811. Blore *Hist. & Antiqs. of Rutland* 1(2) (1811): 165–166 (Grey Peds.). Erdeswicke *Survey of Staffordshire* (1844): 378–385 (Grey ped.). Lennard & Vincent *Vis. of Leicester 1619* (H.S.P. 2) (1870): 17, 74–75 (Grey ped.: "Rob'tus Gray de Whittington et Envill in Comitat. Staff. cuius posteritas in eo loco adhuc continuatur"). Lennard & Vincent *Vis. of Warwick 1619* (H.S.P. 12) (1877): 42–43 (Grey ped.: "Robt. Graye of Whitington in Com. Staff. = Elianor Da. & hey. of Hump. Loue of Enuille.") [Grey arms: Three bars and in chief as many roundles (untinctured)]. *List of Early Chancery Procs.* 8 (PRO Lists and Indexes 51) (1929): 96. VCH *Northampton* 4 (1937): 293. VCH *Warwick* 8 (1969): 209, 353. Paget *Baronage of England* (1957) 261: 1. VCH *Stafford* 20 (1984): 106, 135. NYGBR 127 (1996): 193–201. TG 17 (2003): 86–95.

13. HUMPHREY GREY, Esq., of Enville and Whittington (in Kinver), Staffordshire, Nailstone, Leicestershire, Saxthorp, Norfolk, Withybrook, Warwickshire, etc., son and heir, born about 1448 (aged 12 in 1460). He married **ANNE FIELDING**, daughter of William Fielding, Knt., by his wife, Agnes. They had two sons, Edward, Knt., and Robert, and three daughters, Elizabeth (wife of Sampson Erdeswicke, Esq.), Margery, and Mary (wife of John Dixwell). HUMPHREY GREY, Esq., died 11 Dec. 1499.

>   Shaw *Hist. & Antiqs. of Staffordshire* 2(1) (1801): 268. Nichols *Hist. & Antiqs. of Leicester* 3(2) (1804): 684. Blore *Hist. & Antiqs. of Rutland* 1(2) (1811): 166 (Grey ped.). Erdeswicke *Survey of Staffordshire* (1844): 378–385 (Grey ped.). Lennard & Vincent *Vis. of Warwick 1619* (H.S.P. 12) (1877): 42–43 (Grey ped.: "Humphry Gray of Enuill & Whitingto'. = Anna Da. of Will'm Felding of Warw."). *List of Early Chancery Procs.* 8 (PRO Lists and Indexes 51) (1929): 96. VCH

Northampton 4 (1937): 293. VCH *Warwick* 6 (1951): 266. Davis *Anc. of Abel Lunt* (1963): 194. *NYGBR* 127 (1996): 193–201. *C.C.R. 1468–1476* (1953): 374. *TG* 17 (2003): 86–95.

Children of Humphrey Grey, Esq., by Anne Fielding:

i. **EDWARD GREY**, Knt. [see next].

ii. **MARGERY GREY**, married **RICHARD SAINT BARBE**, Gent., of Homington, Wiltshire [see BATT 16].

14. EDWARD GREY, Knt., of Enville, Staffordshire, Sheriff of Staffordshire, 1519–20, 1524–6, son and heir, born about 1472 (aged 28 in 1500). He married (1st) **JOYCE HORDE**, daughter of John Horde, Esq., of Bridgnorth, Shropshire, by Alice, daughter of William Bulkeley. They had seven sons, including Thomas, Esq., Richard, Francis, and Robert, and ten daughters, including Agnes. He married (2nd) **ANNE MIDDLETON**, widow of John Harewell (died 10 April 1505), of Wootton, Worcestershire, and daughter and co-heiress of Richard Middleton, of Great Lyneford, Buckinghamshire and London, by Maud, daughter of John Throckmorton, Knt. SIR EDWARD GREY died 14 Feb. 1528/9, and was buried at Kinver, Staffordshire. He left a will proved 4 May 1529 (P.C.C. 6 Jankyn).

Nichols *Hist. & Antiqs. of Leicester* 3(2) (1804): 684. Blore *Hist. & Antiqs. of Rutland* 1(2) (1811): 166 (Grey ped.). Erdeswicke *Survey of Staffordshire* (1844): 378–385 (Grey ped.). *Top. & Gen.* 1 (1846): 33–42. Lennard & Vincent *Vis. of Warwick 1619* (H.S.P. 12) (1877): 42–43 (Grey ped.: "Edw. Graye of Enuill. = Joyce Da. of John Hoord of Bredgnorth in Com. Salop."). Tresswell & Vincent *Vis. of Shropshire 1623, 1569 & 1584* 1 (H.S.P. 28) (1889): 251–253 (Hoorde ped.: "Jocosa [Hoorde] vxor Edw. Greye de Envile in co. Staff. mil.") (Hoorde arms: Argent, on a chief or a bird sable). *List of Sheriffs for England & Wales* (PRO Lists and Indexes 9) (1898): 128. Dodds *Hist. of Northumberland* 13 (1930): chart facing 327. *NYGBR* 127 (1996): 193–201.

15. AGNES GREY, daughter by her father's 1st marriage. She married (as his 1st wife) **RICHARD MITTON**, Esq., of Halston near Oswestry, Shropshire, Burgess (M.P.) for Shrewsbury, Shropshire, son of William Mitton, of Shrewsbury, Shropshire, by Cecily, daughter of Henry Delves, Knt., of Doddington, Cheshire. He was born about 1501. They had ten sons, Edward, Thomas, Francis, William, Gent., Richard, Roland, Robert, John, George, and Hankin, and five daughters, Cecily (wife of Richard Acton, Esq.), Ursula (wife of John Lewis), Elizabeth, Anne, and Katherine. He married (2nd) **ELEANOR HARBURNE**, daughter and heiress of George Harburne, Recorder of Shrewsbury. They had one son, Adam, and two daughters, Jane (wife of Edward Ireland, Gent., and Thomas Higgon, D.D.) and Isabel (wife of Thomas Oteley, Esq.). RICHARD MITTON, Esq., died 28 Nov. 1591, and was buried at St. Chad's, Shrewsbury, Shropshire. His widow, Eleanor, died 30 Jan. 1602, aged 90.

Tresswell & Vincent *Vis. of Shropshire 1623, 1569 & 1584* 2 (H.S.P. 29) (1889): 361–363 (Mitton ped.: "Richardus Mitton de Salop [1] = Agnes fil. Ed'r'i Grey de Enuile in co. Staff. mil., [2] = Elianora filia Geo. Harburne Recordatoris Salop vxor 2.") (Mitton arms: Per pale azure and gules, an eagle displayed with two heads or within a bordure engrailed of the last). *Colls. Hist. & Arch. Rel. Montgomeryshire* 27 (1893): 366–369. Howard & Crisp *Vis. of England & Wales* 13 (1919): 1–5 (Mitton ped.). Bindoff *House of Commons 1509–1558* 2 (1982): 654–656 (biog. of Richard Mytton). *NYGBR* 127 (1996): 193–201; 128 (1997): 227.

16. ELIZABETH MITTON, daughter by her father's 1st marriage. She married (1st) **NICHOLAS GROSVENOR**, of Whitmore (in Bobbington), Staffordshire. NICHOLAS GROSVENOR died before 14 Feb. 1558/9. She married (2nd) **RICHARD DEWE** (or **DEYE**, **DIER**) (died 1587), of Hallon, Shropshire.

Herald & Genealogist 5 (1870): 46–47. Tresswell & Vincent *Vis. of Shropshire 1623, 1569 & 1584* 2 (H.S.P. 29) (1889): 361–363 (Mitton ped.: "Elizabetha [Mitton] vx. Nich'i Grosvernor renupta Ric'o Deun *Dewe*"). *Colls. Hist. & Arch. Rel. Montgomeryshire* 27 (1893): 366–369 (Nicholas Grosvenor, husband of Elizabeth Mitton, identified as being "of Showlde"). Howard & Crisp *Vis. of England & Wales* 13 (1919): 1–5 (Mitton ped.). *NYGBR* 127 (1996): 193–201.

17. ELEANOR GROSVENOR, married **JASPER LODGE**, of Woore, Shropshire, son and heir apparent of Edward Lodge, Gent., of Woore, Shropshire, by Margery, daughter of Robert

Mainwaring, of Woore, Shropshire. They had one daughter, Elizabeth. JASPER LODGE died before 1576.

> Herald & Genealogist 5 (1870): 46–47. Tresswell & Vincent Vis. of Shropshire 1623, 1569 & 1584 2 (H.S.P. 29) (1889): 284–285 (Kenrick ped.: "Jasperus Lodge de Ower in com. Salop = Elianora fil. Nich'i Grosuenor of Whitint' et Elizab. fil. Ric'i Mitton et Agnetis fil. Edwardi Grey militis"). Trans. Shropshire Arch. & Nat. Hist. Soc. 51 (1941–43): 111–116. Craine & Hazard Matthew Clarkson (1971): 9. NYGBR 127 (1996): 193–201.

18. ELIZABETH LODGE, daughter and heiress, baptized at Ashley, Staffordshire 14 Dec. 1574. She married about 1594 **JOHN KENRICK**, Gent., of Mucklestone and Ashley, Staffordshire, and, in right of his wife, of Woore, Shropshire, son of Richard Kenrick, of Acton Burnell, Shropshire, by Agnes, daughter of Edward Norton. He was born about 1570. They had ten sons, Humphrey, Richard, William, Edward, Andrew, Esq., Matthew, George, Edward (again), John, Thomas, and three daughters, Jane, Dorothy, and Bridget. JOHN KENRICK, Gent., was buried at Ashley, Staffordshire 9 May 1628. His widow, Elizabeth, was buried at Ashley, Staffordshire 1 May 1646. She left a will proved 6 July 1646 (P.C.C. 111 Twisse).

> Herald & Genealogist 5 (1870): 46–47. Tresswell & Vincent Vis. of Shropshire 1623, 1569 & 1584 2 (H.S.P. 29) (1889): 284–285 (Kenrick ped.: "Joh'es Kenwrick de… in com. Salop ao 1623. = Elizabethæ fil. et hæres Jasperi Lodge de Ower in com. Salop.") (Kenrick arms: Ermine, a lion rampant sable). Trans. Shropshire Arch. & Nat. Hist. Soc. 51 (1941–43): 111–116. Howells Cal. Letters Rel. North Wales (Board of Celtic Studies, Hist. & Law 23) (1967): 23–24, 184–185. Craine & Hazard Matthew Clarkson (1971): 9. NYGBR 127 (1996): 193–201.

19. MATTHEW KENRICK, Citizen and fishmonger of London, of St. Catherine Cree, London, 6th son, baptized at Mucklestone, Staffordshire 27 Sept. 1599. He married **REBECCA PERCIVAL**, 6th daughter of [Dr.] Thomas Percival, Gent., Professor of Physick, of London, by Katherine, daughter of Anthony Ludford, of Rowington, Warwickshire and London. He owned the manors of Heydon and Withibridge, Gloucestershire, and was a mortgagor of Farthinglow manor, etc., in Kent. He was an executor of 1653 will of his brother, Andrew Kenrick, Esq., of London. He was mentioned in the 1654 will of his brother, Edward Kenrick, Merchant, of Rotterdam, Holland. MATTHEW KENRICK left a will dated 7 July 1656, proved 25 Feb. 1656/7 (P.C.C. 59 Ruthen).

> Nichols Hist. & Antiqs. of Leicester 4(2) (1811): 1025 (Ludford ped.). Munk Roll of the Royal College of Physicians of London 1 (1878): 122. Misc. Gen. et Heraldica 2nd Ser. 1 (1886): 149 (Funeral certificates for Mr. Thomas Percival, Professor of Physick [died 1630], and his wife, Katherine Ludford [died 1633]). Tresswell & Vincent Vis. of Shropshire 1623, 1569 & 1584 2 (H.S.P. 29) (1889): 284–285 (Kenrick ped.: "Mathew [Kenrick] 6 [son]"). VCH Surrey 2 (1905): 299–300. Howard & Crisp Vis. of England & Wales: Notes 6 (1906): 37 (Kenrick ped.) (citation courtesy of John Brandon). Price English Patents of Monopoly (1913): 217. Craine & Hazard Matthew Clarkson (1971): 8–9. Godfrey Development of English Glassmaking, 1560–1640 (1975): 60, 65, and 90. NYGBR 127 (1996): 193–201.

20. ELIZABETH KENRICK, married (1st) **WALRAVE** (or **WALDRAVE**) **LODWICK** (died July 1662), of Hackney St. John, London, and Tooting (in Stretham), Surrey, citizen and fishmonger of London, son of Walgrave Lodwick. He was baptized at the Dutch Reformed Church, Austin Friars, London 17 Jan. 1628/9. They had four children. WALRAVE LODWICK left a will dated 1 July 1662, proved 28 July 1662 (P.C.C. 98 Laud). His widow, Elizabeth, married (2nd) at St. Lawrence, Jewry, London 15 Feb. 1663/4 (as his 2nd wife) [**REV.**] **DAVID CLARKSON**, of St. Faith's, London, son of Robert Clarkson, of Bradford, Yorkshire, by his wife, Agnes Lilly. He was baptized at Bradford, Yorkshire 3 March 1621/2. They had three sons, David, Matthew, and Robert, and four daughters, Rebecca (wife of _____ Combe), Mary, Gertrude, and Katherine. He was graduated from Cambridge University, B.D., in 1644. He was among the chief champions of nonconformity and was ejected from his charge at Mortlake, near Battersea, Surrey under the Act of Uniformity (1662). He published many religious works. [REV.] DAVID CLARKSON died at St. Dunstan's, Stepney, Middlesex 14 June 1686, and was buried in Bunhill Fields Cemetery, Islington,

Middlesex. He left a will proved 23 Sept. 1686 (P.C.C. 115 Lloyd). His widow, Elizabeth, was living 10 May 1706.

NEHGR 112 (1958): 248 (Clarkson arms: Silver a bend engrailed sable on the bend three annulets gold). Craine & Hazard *Matthew Clarkson* (1971): 1, 5, 7–8, 12–14. *NYGBR* 127 (1996): 193–201.

21. MATTHEW CLARKSON, younger son by his father's 2nd marriage, born about 1664. He immigrated to New York, appointed 28 Dec. 1689, 1st Secretary of the New York Colony; vestryman, Trinity Church, New York City, New York, 1698–1700, 1702. He married 19 Jan. 1692 **CATHARINE VAN SCHAICK**, daughter of [Capt.] Goosen Gerritsz Van Schaick, of Albany, New York, brewer, by his wife, Anna/Annetje Lievens. They had three sons, David, Levinus, and Matthew, and one daughter, Anne. His wife, Catherine, was a legatee in the 1702 will of her mother, Anna van Schaick. His wife, Catherine, died 1 July 1702. MATTHEW CLARKSON died testate in a yellow fever epidemic at Jamaica, Long Island, 20 July 1702. He left a will dated 18 July 1702, proved 19 Nov. 1702.

Berrian *Hist. Sketch of Trinity Church, New-York* (1847): 353. *Abs. of Wills Surrogate's Office, City of New York* 1 (Colls. New-York Hist. Soc. 25) (1893): 348–349 (will of Anna van Schayk), 349 (will of Matthew Clarkson). Reynolds *Hudson-Mohawk Gen. & Fam. Mems.* 3 (1911): 992–994 (re. Van Schaick). Craine & Hazard *Matthew Clarkson* (1971). *NYGBR* 127 (1996): 193–201.

✣ CLAVERING ✣

1. RICHARD, of unknown parentage, had a brother Thomas de "Candelent" (or Cantelowe). He married _____ **LE BIGOD**, daughter of Roger le Bigod, Domesday tenant. They had one son, Roger, Knt. RICHARD was living after 1135.

Keats-Rohan *Domesday Descendants* (2002): 948.

2. ROGER FITZ RICHARD, Knt., of Warkworth, Northumberland. He married in or after ?1145 (date of her charter) **ALICE DE VERE**, widow of Robert de Essex, of Rayleigh and Clavering, Essex (died 1132–1140), and former wife of William de Sackville, of Great Braxsted, Essex (divorced 1141 or 1143), and daughter of Aubrey de Vere, of Hedingham, Essex, Great Addington and Drayton, Northamptonshire, etc., by his wife, Alice. She was born about 1125 (aged 60 in 1185). In ?1145 Alice granted assarted land called Stanheye in Ugley, Essex to the Hospitallers for the health of her soul, and those of her late husband, Robert de Essex, her father, [Aubrey] de Vere, and her brother, Robert de Vere. He was granted Warkworth, Northumberland, by the king in 1157. Following the disgrace of Alice's step-son, Henry de Essex in 1163, his lordship of Clavering, Essex was given to Alice's husband, Roger Fitz Richard. ROGER FITZ RICHARD died by the end of 1177. His widow, Alice, was living in 1185.

Fowler *Chartularium Abbathiæ de Novo Monasterio* (Surtees Soc. 66) (1878): 301. *Trans. Essex Arch. Soc.* n.s. 3 (1889): 243–251. Hall *Court Life under the Plantagenets* (1890): 211. *Archaeological Journal* n.s. 14 (1907): 217–226. *Paget* (1957) 132:1 (Roger Fitz Richard styled "nepos" of Hugh Bigod, Earl of Norfolk (Hist. of S. Osyth's by William de Vere). The statement in Dugdale and elsewhere, that he was the son of Richard Fitz Eustace, Constable of Chester, will not bear inspection. In 1166 he certified that he held Warkworth. He likewise held two fees, de novo, of Earl Hugh Bigod, and one fee and three parts of William Earl of Essex) (wife Alice was "aged 60 or 80 in 1185; for her, see Essex Arch. Trans, n.s. 3:243-251"). Sanders *English Baronies* (1960): 150. *Nomina: Jour. of the Soc. for Name Studies in Britain & Ireland* 17–19 (1994): 104. Keats-Rohan *Domesday Descendants* (2002): 948. Gervers *Cartulary of the Knights of St. John of Jerusalem in England* 1 (Recs. of Soc. & Econ. Hist. n.s. 6) (1982): 225 (charter of Alice de Vere dated ?1145).

Children of Roger Fitz Richard, Knt., by Alice de Vere:

i. **ROBERT FITZ ROGER** [see next].

ii. **ALICE FITZ ROGER**, married **JOHN**, Constable of Chester [see LACY 1].

3. ROBERT FITZ ROGER, of Warkworth, Northumberland, Clavering, Essex, etc., Sheriff of Norfolk and Suffolk, 1193–94, 1197–1200, Sheriff of Northumberland, 1200–12, son and heir. He married **MARGARET DE CHESNEY**, widow of Hugh de Cressy (died before Michaelmas 1189), and daughter and heiress of William Fitz Walter (also known as William de Chesney or de Norwich), of Horsford, Norfolk, Blythborough, Suffolk, etc., Sheriff of Norfolk and Suffolk. They had one son, John, and one daughter, Alice. He was granted the manor of Iver, Buckinghamshire in 1197. In 1199 he received a confirmation of the grant of Warkworth, Northumberland and Clavering, Essex. In 1200 he was sent with other nobles to escort William *the Lion*, King of Scots to do homage to King John at Lincoln. He was granted the manors of Corbridge, Newburn, Rothbury, and Whalton, Northumberland in 1205. In 1212 he held Clavering, Essex of the fee of Henry de Essex. At an unknown date, he granted Brinkburn Priory a saltpan in Warkworth, Northumberland. He founded Langley Abbey, Norfolk. ROBERT FITZ ROGER died shortly before 22 Dec. 1214. His widow, Margaret, died in 1230.

>Gardner *Hist. Account of Dunwich, Blithburgh, Southwold* (1754): 135–136. Blomefield *Essay towards a Top. Hist. of Norfolk* 5 (1775): 1356. Stubbs *Chronica Magistri Rogeri de Houedene* 4 (Rolls Ser. 51) (1871): 140 (sub A.D. 1200). Fowler *Chartularium Abbathiæ de Novo Monasterio* (Surtees Soc. 66) (1878): 301. Page *Chartulary of Brinkburn Priory* (Surtees Soc. 90) (1893): 142 (undated charter of Robert Fitz Roger). *List of Sheriffs for England & Wales* (PRO Lists and Indexes 9) (1898): 86, 97. *Paget* (1957) 132:1. Sanders *English Baronies* (1960): 16, 150.

Children of Robert Fitz Roger, by Margaret de Chesney:

i. **JOHN FITZ ROBERT** [see next].

ii. **ALICE FITZ ROBERT**, married **PETER FITZ HERBERT**, of Blaen Llyfni (in Cathedine), Breconshire [see FITZ HERBERT 4].

4. JOHN FITZ ROBERT, of Warkworth, Corbridge, Newburn, Rothbury, and Whalton, Northumberland, Iver, Buckinghamshire, Clavering, Essex, Aynho, Northamptonshire, etc., Sheriff of Norfolk and Suffolk, 1213–15, Sheriff of Northumberland, 1224–8, son and heir of Robert Fitz Roger, of Warkworth, Corbridge, Newburn, and Rothbury, Northumberland, Iver, Buckinghamshire, Blythburgh, Suffolk, etc., Sheriff of Norfolk and Suffolk, Sheriff of Northumberland, by Margaret (or Margery), daughter and heiress of William Fitz Walter (also known as William de Chesney), of Blythburgh, Suffolk. He was born before 1191 (of age at his father's death in 1212). He married **ADA DE BALLIOL**, daughter of Hugh de Balliol, of Barnard Castle, Durham, Bywell, Northumberland, etc., by Cecily, daughter of Aléaume de Fontaines, Chevalier, seigneur de Fontaines. Her maritagium included the barony of Stokesley, Yorkshire. She was aunt of John de Balliol, King of Scots. They had five sons, Roger, Robert [Fitz John or de Eure], Knt., Hugh [de Eure], Knt., [Master] Stephen [de Balliol or Eure] [Rector of Mitford], and Ingram, and four daughters, Cecily, Alice, Annor, and Margery. He joined the confederacy of the barons against the king in 1215. He was one of the twenty-five barons elected to guarantee the observance of Magna Carta, signed by King John 15 June 1215. In 1219 he sued the Abbot of Langley for the presentation to the church of Iver, Buckinghamshire. He fought at the Siege of Bytham Castle, Lincolnshire in 1221. In 1224 he obtained a charter for a fair to be held yearly at Stokesley, Yorkshire. In 1225–6 he was appointed an itinerant justice in Yorkshire. In 1232 he was sued in the king's court by Simon de Divelston for a fishery in the Tyne and estovers in the wood and turbary of Corbridge, Northumberland. At an uncertain date, he reached agreement with the Abbot of Newminster regarding pasture at West Ritton, Northumberland. JOHN FITZ ROBERT died shortly before 20 Feb. 1241. Sometime in the period, 1241–51, his widow, Ada, granted a toft and 12 acres of land in Lintune to Hosbert de Stredlam. She presented to the Hospital of Aynho, Northamptonshire in 1243. In the summer of 1250 she settled the manor of Stokesley, Yorkshire, with half of that barony, and the advowson of fifteen churches, and half of the forest of Bedale, Yorkshire on her two younger son, Robert and Hugh de Eure. Some months later they granted the manor of Stokesley back to her. In 1250 she sued William de Kyme regarding an agreement between herself and Simon de Kyme (brother of Willam) regarding the manors of Newton, Thorpe, and Thornton in Craven, Yorkshire. Ada de Balliol died 29 July 1251.

Blomefield *Essay towards a Top. Hist. of Norfolk* 5 (1775): 1356–1357. Bridges *Hist. & Antiqs. of Northamptonshire* 1 (1791): 142. Hodgson *Hist. of Northumberland* Pt. 2 Vol. 1 (1827): 372 (ped.) (assigns John Fitz Robert two wives: Joan and Ada de Balliol; no documentation or dates are provided for Joan). Ord *Hist. & Antiqs. of Cleveland* (1846): 392–397. Suckling *Hist. & Antiqs. of Suffolk* 2 (1847): 131–135. Hartshorne *Feudal & Military Antiqs. of Northumberland* (1858): 186–194. Belleval *Jean de Bailleul: Roi d'Écosse et Sire de Bailleul-en-Vimeu* (1886): 53–56. *Fourth Rpt.* (Hist. MSS Comm. 3) (1874): 442–451. Matthew of Paris *Chronica Majora* 2 (Rolls Ser. 57) (1874): 604–605. Glover & St. George *Vis. of Yorkshire 1584–5, 1612* (1875): 607–617 (Eure ped.). Fowler *Chartularium Abbathiæ de Novo Monasterio* (Surtees Soc. 66) (1878): 10–11. Atkinson *Cartularium Abbathiae de Rievalle* (Surtees Soc. 83) (1889): 221–222 (charter of Hugh de Balliol). Blackburne *Reg. Booke of Inglebye iuxta Grenhow* (1889): xli–xlv. *Arch. Aeliana* 14 (1891): 81–166 ("On the seal of the charter [of John Fitz Robert] by which he conveyed his meadow of Braineslawe to the monks of Durham, we see him careering in a cynlindrical helm, which viewed in profile presents a concave line behind, the front part rounded below and pierced with holes to enable him to breathe, his surcoat considerably shorter than his father's, but the other equipments similar, and the sword equally ponderous. For the charter see Raine's *North Durham*, App. p. 242. The seal (1. 1. Spec. 51 in the Treasury, Durham) is engraved on steel in Surtees, *Durham*, I. Seals, plate 7, No. 4; and also has been reproduced on the annexed plate, with greater fidelity, by 'Lichtdruck.' The secretum is the same as that of Robert fitz Roger's seal."). *Lincolnshire Notes & Queries* 5 (1898): 155. *List of Sheriffs for England & Wales* (PRO Lists and Indexes 9) (1898): 86, 97. *Hist. of Northumberland* 5 (1899): 18–32; 6 (1902): 72–73 (Balliol ped.); 10 (1914): 59–87; 13 (1930): 142–144. St. George & Dugdale *Peds. Rec. at the Heralds' Vis. of Northumberland* (1903): 30–31 (Clavering ped.: "Iohannes filius Rob[ti] Baro de Werkworth et Clavering. = Ada filia et hæres… de Balliolo."). *Norfolk Arch.* 15 (1904): 267–292. Wrottesley *Peds. from the Plea Rolls* (1905): 527. Huyshe *Royal Manor of Hitchin* (1906): 100–117. Salter *Eynsham Cartulary* 1 (Oxford Hist. Soc. 49) (1907): 415 (re. Chesney fam.). Clay *Extinct & Dormant Peerages* (1913): 4–6 (sub Baliol), 20–21 (sub Clavering). Scott *Norman Balliols in England* (1914). Cannon *Great Roll of the Pipe for 26th Year of the Reign of King Henry the Third A.D. 1241–1242* (1918): 45. *Arch. Aeliana* 3rd Ser. 20 (1923): 83, 96 (undated seal of Ada da Baliol — Oval, a robed figure of Ada, standing holding in her right hand a shield of arms quarterly a bend and in her left a shield bearing an orle [BALLIOL]. Legend: + SIGILLVM. ADAE. DE. BALIOLO. VXORIS. JOHANNIS. FILII. ROBERT.) . VCH *Yorkshire N.R.* 2 (1923): 302–303. Oliver *Northumberland & Durham Deeds* (Newcastle-upon-Tyne Recs. Comm. 7) (1929): 226. *Pubs Bedfordshire Hist. Soc.* 13 (1930): Ped. 8 (Engaine ped.). Paget *Baronage of England* (1957) 22: 1–10 (sub Baliol); 132: 2. Sanders *English Baronies* (1960): 16, 150. Hedley *Northumberland Fams.* (1968): 160–183. Tremlett *Rolls of Arms Henry III* (H.S.P. 113-4) (1967): 66 (Matthew Paris Shields: "Hoc etiam anno obiit Johannes filius Roberti, vir nobilis et unus de præcipiis baronibus in plaga Anglie borealis; Arms: Quarterly or and gules a bend sable). Hedley *Northumberland Fams.* 1 (1968): 160–163 (Clavering ped.), 203–208 (Balliol ped.). *Coat of Arms* n.s. 3 (1979): 161–163. *TG* 9 (1988): 229–241. English *Yorkshire Hundred & Quo Warranto Rolls* (Yorkshire Arch. Soc. Recs. 151) (1996): 148–149 (Date: 1279/81: "Hugh de Euere comes; and says that one Hugh de Balliol and his ancestors held the manor [Stokesley, Yorkshire] from the conquest of England with infangthief, market and with gallows, which Hugh gave that manor to John son of Robert in marriage with Ada his daughter, who held the manor with the said liberties until the death of John. Afterwards Ada gave that manor to one Robert her son, after whose death Hugh entered the manor as brother and heir, and still holds that with the liberties…"). Rollason *Durham Liber Vitæ: Prosopographical Commentary* (2007): 566.

Children of John Fitz Robert, by Ada de Balliol:

i. **ROGER FITZ JOHN** (or **DE BALLIOL**) [see next].

ii. **ROBERT DE EURE** (or **FITZ JOHN**), Knt., of Stokesley, Yorkshire, married **ISABEL DE MERLAY** [see SOMERVILLE 8].

iii. **HUGH DE EURE**, Knt., of Stokesley, Yorkshire, married **ELLEN** _____ [see EURE 5].

iv. **CECILY FITZ JOHN**, married before 1242 **PATRICK OF DUNBAR**, 7th Earl of Dunbar, son and heir of Patrick, 6th Earl of Dunbar, by Euphame, daughter of William de Brus. He was born about 1213 (aged 35 in 1248). They had three sons, Patrick, Knt. [8th Earl of Dunbar, also called Earl of March], John, Knt., and Alexander, Knt. He was a steadfast adherent of the English party. In 1255 he and others procured the dismissal of the Comyns and their faction from power. The same year he was nominated Regent and Guardian of the King and Queen. In 1258, the Comyns prevailed, and Earl Patrick was excluded from the government. He commanded a division of the Scottish army at the Battle of Largs in 1263. He was present at the signing of the treaty between King Alexander III and the King of Norway in 1266, which provided for the cession of the Hebrides and the Isle of Man to Scotland. He was one of the witnesses to the marriage contract of Princess

Margaret of Scotland and King Eric of Norway in 1281. In 1284 he attended the Parliament at Scone which declared the Princess Margaret of Norway to be heir to the Scottish Crown. PATRICK, Earl of Dunbar, died at Whittingham, East Lothian 24 August 1289, and was buried at Dunbar. *Scots Peerage* 3 (1906): 257–262 (sub Dunbar). *C.P.* 4 (1916): 506 (sub Dunbar). Hedley *Northumberland Fams.* 1 (1968): 238–241 (Dunbar ped.). *TG* 9 (1988): 229–241.

Child of Cecily Fitz John, by Patrick of Dunbar:

    a. **PATRICK OF DUNBAR**, Knt., 8th Earl of Dunbar (or March), son and heir. He married c.1270 **MARJORY COMYN**, daughter of Alexander Comyn, Knt., 6th Earl of Buchan, Constable of Scotland, by Elizabeth (or Isabel), daughter and co-heiress of Roger de Quincy, Knt., 2nd Earl of Winchester, Constable of Scotland [see BUCHAN 8 for her ancestry]. They had one son, Patrick [9th Earl of Dunbar]. He had livery of his father's lands 14 May 1290. He was one of the competitors for the Crown of Scotland in 1291, in right of his great-grandmother, Ada, Countess of Dunbar, illegitimate daughter of William *the Lion*, King of Scots [see DUNBAR 5]. He soon withdrew his claim, swearing fealty to King Edward I of England 25 March 1296. In 1298 he was King's Lieutenant for Scotland, and in 1300 was present at the Siege of Caerlaverock Castle with his son, Patrick. Patrick, 8th Earl of Dunbar, died 10 October 1308. *Scottish Hist. Rev.* 1 (1903): 228–231. *Scots Peerage* 2 (1905): 256 (sub Comyn, Earl of Buchan). *C.P.* 4 (1916): 506–507 (sub Dunbar). Reid *Wigtownshire Charters* (Scottish Hist. Soc. 51) (1960): xxxix–xlv. Hedley *Northumberland Fams.* 1 (1968): 238–241 (Dunbar ped.). Ellis *Cat. Seals in the P.R.O.* 2 (1981): 35 (seal of Patrick de Dunbar, Earl of March dated 1300 — Hung by its strap, between two twining plants (ivy?), a shield of arms: a lion rampant, within a bordure charged with eight roundels. Legend: *S'[DNI:PATRICII:DE.DVNBAR COM MARC']).

    v. **ALICE FITZ JOHN**. In 1251 Alice and her two sisters, Annor and Margery, sued William de Kyme, regarding an earlier agreement reached between their mother, Ada de Balliol, and Simon de Kyme regarding the manors of Newton, Thorpe, and Thornton in Craven, Yorkshire. *Arch. Aeliana* 14 (1891): chart facing 90 (Clavering ped.). Hodgson *Hist. of Northumberland* 5 (1899): 25–26 (Clavering ped.). *Lincolnshire Notes & Queries* 5 (1898): 155. Rollason *Durham Liber Vitæ: Prosopographical Commentary* (2007): 566.

    vi. **ANNOR FITZ JOHN**. In 1251 Annor and her two sisters, Alice and Margery, sued William de Kyme, regarding an earlier agreement reached between their mother, Ada de Balliol, and Simon de Kyme regarding the manors of Newton, Thorpe, and Thornton in Craven, Yorkshire. *Arch. Aeliana* 14 (1891): chart facing 90 (Clavering ped.). *Lincolnshire Notes & Queries* 5 (1898): 155. Hodgson *Hist. of Northumberland* 5 (1899): 25–26 (Clavering ped.). Rollason *Durham Liber Vitæ: Prosopographical Commentary* (2007): 566.

    vii. **MARGERY FITZ JOHN**. In 1251 Margery and her two sisters, Alice and Annor, sued William de Kyme, regarding an earlier agreement reached between their mother, Ada de Balliol, and Simon de Kyme regarding the manors of Newton, Thorpe, and Thornton in Craven, Yorkshire. *Arch. Aeliana* 14 (1891): chart facing 90 (Clavering ped.). *Lincolnshire Notes & Queries* 5 (1898): 155. Hodgson *Hist. of Northumberland* 5 (1899): 25–26 (Clavering ped.). Rollason *Durham Liber Vitæ: Prosopographical Commentary* (2007): 566.

5. ROGER FITZ JOHN (or **DE BALLIOL**), of Warkworth, Corbridge, and Whalton, Northumberland, Clavering, Essex, Iver, Buckinghamshire, Horsford, Norfolk, etc., son and heir, born after 1219 (a minor at his father's death). He married **ISABEL OF DUNBAR**, daughter of Patrick, 6th Earl of Dunbar, by Euphame, daughter of William de Brus [see DUNBAR 6 for her ancestry].[11] They had one son, Robert, Knt. [Lord Fitz Roger], and one daughter, Euphame (wife of William Comyn, Knt., of Kilbride, and Andrew de Moray, Knt.). ROGER FITZ JOHN died at a tournament in Normandy shortly before 22 June 1249. In 1259 his widow, Isabel, gave £300 to

---

[11] Evidence relating to Isabel of Dunbar's parentage and her 2nd marriage to Simon Baard is discussed at length by Andrew B.W. MacEwen in his brilliant article, "A Clarification of the Dunbar Pedigree," published in *TG* 9 (1988): 229–241. Since publication of this article, Mr. MacEwen has located further evidence which conclusively proves Isabel's parentage. This evidence is found in *Fourth Rpt.* (Hist. MSS Comm. 3) (1874): 460, which source cites a charter dated c.1270–80, in which Isabel's son and heir, Robert Fitz Roger, specifically names his grandmother, "E[upheme], Countess of Dunbar." As for Isabel's 2nd marriage, recent research by Mr. Richardson has located additional evidence which shows that Isabel and her 2nd husband, Simon Baard, presented to the Hospital of Aynho, Northamptonshire in 1268. The patronage of the hospital belonged to the Clavering family. Isabel presumably held the patronage of the hospital in dower as a Clavering widow

have the farm of Corbridge, Northumberland. She married (2nd) before 13 October 1261 (date of lawsuit) **SIMON BAARD** (or **BAYARD**), of Northumberland. In 1262 he and his wife, Isabel, were summoned to answer William Comyn and Euphame his wife (Isabel's daughter) in a plea that they should deliver to them 540 marks which which owed and unjustly detained. He and his wife, Isabel, presented to the Hospital of Aynho, Northamptonshire 19 Sept. 1268. In 1268–9 an assize was arraigned to determine if Isabel, widow of Roger Fitz John, Simon Baard, and others had unjustly disseised Simon Fitz Waltheof of his free tenement in Corbridge, Northumberland. In the same period, Richard de Gosebek and his wife, Margery, sued Simon and his wife, Isabel, regarding an agreement made between them regarding the maner of Eydene, Northumberland.

Bridges *Hist. & Antiqs. of Northamptonshire* 1 (1791): 142. Dugdale *Monasticon Anglicanum* 3 (1821): 636–637 (Priory of St. Faith at Horsham, Norfolk — Genealogia Fundatoris: "Idem Rogerus genuit filium nomine Robertum, filium Rogeri, nunc patronum, qui post obitum Stephani de Crescy successit in hæreditate baroniæ de Horsford, quasi hæres dominæ Margeriæ de Cheny, quæ duobus nupsit viris, ut prædictum est."); 5 (1825): 559–560 (Sibton Abbey — Linea Consanguinitatis, de Stirpe Fundatorum Abbaciæ de Sybeton: "… Idem Rogerus genuit filium nomine Robertum fiilum Rogeri nunc patronum, qui post obitum Stephani de Cressi successit in hæreditatem baroniæ de Horsford quasi hæres dominæ Margaretæ de Cheney, quæ duobus nupsit viris, ut prædictum est."). Hodgson *Hist. of Northumberland* Pt. 2 Vol. 1 (1827): 372 (ped.). Ord *Hist. & Antiqs. of Cleveland* (1846): 392–397. Hartshorne *Feudal & Military Antiqs. of Northumberland* (1858): 186–194. *Fourth Rpt.* (Hist. MSS Comm. 3) (1874): 460. Glover & St. George *Vis. of Yorkshire 1584–5, 1612* (1875): 607–617 (Eure ped.). *Arch. Aeliana* 14 (1891): 81–166 ("Roger fitz John de Baliol …. must have been a youth of great promise. Matthew of Paris says he was the most noble knight and baron in the North of England, and had already displayed remarkable activity in the arts of war. His career was cut short by his being ridden over in a tournament at Argences in Normandy in 1249."). Page *Three Early Assize Rolls for Northumberland* (Surtees Soc. 88) (1891): 165–166, 174–175, 200, 222. *Hist. of Northumberland* 5 (1899): 18–32; 10 (1914): 59–87; 13 (1930): 142–144. *Norfolk Arch.* 15 (1904): 267–292. St. George & Dugdale *Peds. Rec. at the Heralds' Vis. of Northumberland* (1903): 30–31 (Clavering ped.: "Rogerus filius Johis. Baro de Warkmouth et Clavering. = [left blank]."). *Scots Peerage* 3 (1906): 255–257 (sub Dunbar). C.P. 3 (1913): 274 (sub Clavering). Clay *Extinct & Dormant 1241–1242* (1918): 45. VCH *Yorkshire* N.R. 2 (1923): 302–303. Pubs *Bedfordshire Hist. Soc.* 13 (1930): Ped. 8 (Engaine ped.). Paget *Baronage of England* (1957) 132: 2. Sanders *English Baronies* (1960): 150. Hedley *Northumberland Fams.* 1 (1968): 160–163 (Clavering ped.). *Coat of Arms* n.s. 3 (1979): 161–163 (author states Roger Fitz John bore a quarterly coat of arms). Barrow *Anglo-Norman Era in Scottish Hist.* (1980): 10. *TG* 9 (1988): 229–241; 22 (2008): 28–29. Hedley *Northumberland Fams.* 1 (1968): 160–183, 238–241. Cassidy *1259 Pipe Roll*: 198 (available at www.cmjk.com/1259/1259_pipe_roll.html).

6. ROBERT FITZ ROGER, Knt., of Warkworth, Corbridge, Newton on the Moor, Rothbury, and Whalton, Northumberland, Clavering, Essex, Horsford, Norfolk, etc., King's Lieutenant in Northumberland, son and heir, born about 1247 (aged 1½ in 1249, and came of age at Martinmas 1268). He was heir in 1263 to his cousin, Stephen de Cressy, by which he inherited the barony of Blythburgh, Suffolk. He married in 1265 **MARGERY LA ZOUCHE**, daughter of Alan la Zouche, Knt., of Ashby de la Zouch, Leicestershire, by Ellen, daughter and co-heiress of Roger de Quincy, Knt., 2nd Earl of Winchester, hereditary Constable of Scotland [see ZOUCHE 8 for her ancestry]. They had seven sons, John, Knt. [Lord Clavering], Alexander, Knt., Roger, Alan, Knt. (of Callaley), Robert, [Master] Henry [Rector of Carleton Rode and Reepham, Norfolk], and Edmund [Vicar of Ardeley, Hertfordshire], and two daughters, Euphame and Ellen. Her maritagium included lands at Syston, Leicestershire and Boxworth, Cambridgeshire. Sometime between 1260 and 1266, Robert acquired the drengage holding of Callaly and the vill of Yetlington, Northumberland from Gilbert de Callaly. In 1269 he was party to an agreement with Thomas de Divelston touching the woods and pastures of Corbridge, Northumberland, which agreement was later modified in 1274–8. About 1270–80 he provided maintenance for a chaplain at the Hospital of St. Mary and St. James at Aynho, Northamptonshire to celebrate for the soul of his grandmother, Euphame, Countess of Dunbar. In 1275–6 William de Stuteville and Ermentrude his wife arraigned an assize of novel disseisin against him touching a tenement in Horsford and Horsham, Norfolk. In 1276–7 Emma daughter of Henry de Brumfeld arraigned an assize of novel disseisein against him touching a tenement in Warkworth, Northumberland. He was summoned to serve against the Welsh in 1277,

1282 and 1283, against the Scots in 1291 and frequently to 1309, and in Gascony 1294. In 1278 he confirmed the grants of all his predecessors to Blythburgh Priory, Suffolk of his fee in Bulcamp and Blythburgh. The following year he remitted the annual Christmas feast provided by the Blythburgh canons to his men at Walberswick, Suffolk, on condition they maintain a resident chaplain. He was summoned to attend the King at Shrewsbury 28 June 1283, by writ directed *Roberto filio Rogeri*. He granted £20 yearly secured on his lands in Buckingham, Northumberland, etc. to Balliol College, Oxford. In 1291 he was granted weekly markets and annual fairs to be held at his manors of Newton on the Moor and Rothbury, Northumberland. He presented to the Hospital of Aynho, Northamptonshire, 1293, 1299, and to the church of Iver, Buckinghamshire, 1295. In the assizes at Newcastle in 1294, he claimed free warren in Whalton, Northumberland. He distinguished himself in the war with Scotland, 1294–8, and was taken prisoner at the Battle of Stirling 11 Sept. 1297. He was summoned to Parliament from 2 Nov. 1295 to 26 October 1309, by writs directed *Roberto filio Rogeri*, whereby he is held to have become Lord Fitz Roger. He was joint Captain of the Scotch Marches 4 Nov. 1297. He was present at the Siege of Caerlaverock Castle with his son John in 1300. In 1300–1 he was attached to answer John de Chiggewell, varlet of Walter, Bishop of Coventry and Lichfield, regarding a debt of 120 marks as payment for two horses which the said Chiggewell previously sold to the said Robert and his son, John, at London. He signed the Barons' letter to Pope Boniface VIII in 1301 as *Robertus filius Rogeri, dominus de Claveryng*. He accompanied John de Segrave in a foray from Berwick in 1302. In 1304 he made an agreement with Lucy widow of Thomas de Dyvelston respecting boats crossing the water of Tyne at Corbridge, Northumberland. He was ordered to serve under Aymer de Valence in 1306, who defeated the Scots at Methven near Perth 19 June. In 1307 he was granted free warren in his demesne lands in Corbridge, Northumberland by the king. In 1309 he brought an assize of novel disseisin against Bishop Walter Langton and others regarding an one third part of the manor of Ling, Norfolk. He was one of the fifteen barons appointed Lords Ordainers 25 March 1310. At an uncertain date, he granted pasture at Hesilhurst, Northumberland to Newminster Abbey, Northumberland. SIR ROBERT FITZ ROGER, Lord Fitz Roger, died shortly before 29 April 1310. At the time of his death, he owed the Crown the sum of £149 in arrears of the farm of Corbridge town.

Gardner *Hist. Account of Dunwich, Blithburgh, Southwold* (1754): 135–136. Blomefield *Essay towards a Top. Hist. of Norfolk* 5 (1775): 1356–1357. Bridges *Hist. & Antiqs. of Northamptonshire* 1 (1791): 142. Dugdale *Monasticon Anglicanum* 3 (1821): 636–637 (Priory of St. Faith at Horsham, Norfolk — Genealogia Fundatoris: "Prædictus veró Robertus duxit uxorem nomine Margeriam de la Souche, de qua genuit multos filios et filias, videlicet, Johannem, Alexandrum, Rogerum, Robertum, Alanum, Henricum, et Edmundum."); 5 (1825): 559–560 (Sibton Abbey — Linea Consanguinitatis, de Stirpe Fundatorum Abbaciæ de Sybeton: "… Idem Rogerus genuit filium nomine Robertum fiilum Rogeri nunc patronum, qui post obitum Stephani de Cressi successit in hæreditatem baroniæ de Horsford quasi hæres dominæ Margaretæ de Cheney, quæ duobus nupsit viris, ut prædictum est. Prædictus vero Robertus duxit uxorem nominee Margeriam de la Suche, de qua genuit multos filios et filias, videlicet Johannem, cujus cognomen rex Edwardus filius regis Henrici fecit vocari Clavering, à principali manerio suo; Alexandrum, Rogerum, Robertum, Alanum, Henricum, et Edmundum."). Hodgson *Hist. of Northumberland* Pt. 2 Vol. 1 (1827): 371, 372 (ped.). Nicolas *Siege of Carlaverock* (1828): 115–116 (biog. of Robert Fitz Roger). Montagu *Guide to the Study of Heraldry* (1840): 39. Suckling *Hist. & Antiqs. of Suffolk* 2 (1847): 133–135. Hartshorne *Feudal & Military Antiqs. of Northumberland* (1858): 186–194 (identifies wife as "Margaret, daughter of Lord de la Zouche."). *Fourth Rpt.* (Hist. MSS Comm. 3) (1874): 442, 460. Fowler *Chartularium Abbathiæ de Novo Monasterio* (Surtees Soc. 66) (1878): 11 (charter of Robert Fitz Roger; charter names his ancestor, John Fitz Robert), 11–12, 13 (charter of Robert Fitz Roger). Glover et al. *Vis. of Cheshire 1580, 1566, 1533 & 1591* (H.S.P. 18) (1882): 90–91 (Clavering ped.: "Rob't fiz Roger, lord of Claveringe."). *Annual Rpt. of the Deputy Keeper* 45 (1885): 207; 46 (1886): 313. *Arch. Aeliana* 14 (1891): 81–166 ("A beautiful seal attached to a document dated 1276 and preserved at Paris shows us Robert fitz Roger with a fan-crested helmet mounted on a horse with plain housings but also adorned with a fan-crest."). Birch *Cat. Seals in the British Museum* 2 (1892): 290–291 (seal of Robert Fitz Roger dated late 13th century — To the right. In armour: hauberk of mail, surcoat, plumed helmet, sword, shield of arms. Horse galloping, caparisoned and plumed. Arms: quarterly, a bend [FITZ ROGER]. Fine style of workmanship. Legend: : SIGILLVM : ROBERTI : FILII : ROGERI.). Hodgson *Hist. of Northumberland* 5 (1899): 18–32; 10 (1914): 59–87; 13 (1930): 142–144. Howard de Walden *Some Feudal Lords & Their Seals* (1903): 185–186 (biog.

of Robert Fitz Roger). St. George & Dugdale *Peds. Rec. at the Heralds' Vis. of Northumberland* (1903): 30–31 (Clavering ped.: "Robertus filius Rogeri Baro de Warkworth et Clavering, sumon. ad parl, 23 Ed. I. and 4 E. II. = Margeria de la Zouche."). *Feudal Aids* 3 (1904): 419. *Norfolk Arch.* 15 (1904): 267–292. Wrottesley *Peds. from the Plea Rolls* (1905): 10. *C.Ch.R.* 2 (1906): 404. Rye *Norfolk Fams.* (1911): 219. *C.P.* 3 (1913): 274–275 (sub Clavering); 14 (1998): 186 (sub Clavering). Clay *Extinct & Dormant Peerages* (1913): 20–21 (sub Clavering). Moor *Knights of Edward I* 2 (H.S.P. 81) (1929): 59 (biog. of Sir Robert Fitz Roger) (his arms at Caerlaverock: Quarterly or and gules a bend sable). Oliver *Northumberland & Durham Deeds* (Newcastle-upon-Tyne Recs. Comm. 7) (1929): 77–79, 227, 283 (Hugh de Balliol, seigneur of Helicourt, styled "dear Uncle" by Robert Fitz Roger). Cam *Hundred & Hundred Rolls* (1930): 266. *Pubs Bedfordshire Hist. Soc.* 13 (1930): Ped. 8 (Engaine ped.). Jenkinson & Fermoy *Select Cases in the Exchequer of Pleas* (Selden Soc. 48) (1932): 211–212. Hatton *Book of Seals* (1950): 463. Paget *Baronage of England* (1957) 132: 3 (eventual heir to the Barony of Horsford, Norfolk, on the failure of the family of Cressy) (identifies wife and younger sons citing Dugdale *Monasticon Anglicanum* 1 (1817): 415b n 10 [wife only as "Marjery de la Zouche, with no indication of parentage]). Craster *Hist. of Northumberland* 10 (1914): 59. *Year Books of Edward II* 14(2) (Selden Soc. 43) (1927): 157–158. Dodds *Hist. of Northumberland* 13 (1930): 142. Sanders *English Baronies* (1960): 150. Beardwood *Trial of Walter Langton, Bishop of Lichfield 1307–1312* (Trans. American Philosophical Soc. n.s. 54 (3)) (1964): 21. Hedley *Northumberland Fams.* 1 (1968): 160–163 (Clavering ped.). *Coat of Arms* n.s. 3 (1979): 161–163 (Robert Fitz Roger "was one of a handful of knights during the late thirteenth and early fourteenth centuries to bear two distinct coats; lists seals dated 1279, 1280, 1296, and 1303/4 [all quarterly and a bend] and 1284 [a lion rampant]). Harper-Bill *Blythburgh Priory Cartulary* 1 (Suffolk Charters 2) (1980): 7, 46, 50–51; 2 (Suffolk Charters 3) (1981): 155, 238–239 (notification of Robert Fitz Roger to prior and canons of Blythburgh dated 1279 mentions his wife, Margery). Sutton *Rolls & Reg. of Bishop Oliver Sutton, 1280–1299* 8 (Lincoln Rec. Soc. 76) (1986): 161. *TG* 9 (1988): 229–241; 22 (2008): 28–29. VCH *Cambridge* 9 (1989): 271–274. Brault *Rolls of Arms Edward I* 2 (1997): 173 (arms of Robert Fitz Roger: Argent, a lion rampant sable; Quarterly or and gules, a bend sable).

Children of Robert Fitz Roger, Knt., by Margery la Zouche:

i. **JOHN FITZ ROBERT** (or **DE CLAVERING**), Knt., Lord Clavering [see next].

ii. **ALEXANDER DE CLAVERING**, Knt., of Burgh St. Margaret and Ling, Norfolk, 2nd son, adult before 1295. He married before 1293–4 (date of fine) **JOAN DE BURGH**, daughter and heiress of Walter de Burgh, Knt., of Runham, Norfolk, by Euphame, daughter and co-heiress of Walter de Evermere (or Evermue). They had no issue. In 1295 he was granted an annual fair to be held at the manor of Lyng, Norfolk. In 1296–7 he and his wife, Joan, conveyed a moiety share of the manor of Aylmerton, Norfolk to Richard de Refham, of London. He presented to the churches of Reepham, Norfolk in 1303, and Ling, Norfolk in 1304 and 1305. In 1304–5 he and his wife, Joan, conveyed a moiety share of the advowson of the church of Reepham, Norfolk to Robert Bourgilion. In 1304–5 he and his wife, Joan, conveyed lands in Oby, Clippesby, Burgh St. Margaret, and Flegg, Norfolk to Walter de Filby. In 1309–10 he and his wife, Joan, conveyed a third part of the manor of Runham, Norfolk to Ralph de Holbeck and Beatrice his wife. He was appointed to a commission of oyer and terminer in 1314 on complaint by Humphrey de Littlebury that John Maignard and others carried away his goods at Upwelle, Norfolk and assaulted his men and servants. SIR ALEXANDER DE CLAVERING was living in 1318–9, but died in or before 1319. His widow, Joan, presented to the churches of Ling, Norfolk in 1317, and Burgh St. Margaret, Norfolk in 1319 and again in 1321. Blomefield *Essay towards a Top. Hist. of Norfolk* 4 (1775): 407–408; 8 (1808): 245; 11 (1810): 153, 155, 170–171, 242. Montagu *Guide to the Study of Heraldry* (1840): 39. *Coll. Top. et Gen.* 7 (1841): 197–202. Rye *Some Rough Materials for a Hist. of the Hundred of North Erpingham* 1 (1883): 85–86. Rye *Short Cal. Feet of Fines for Norfolk* 1 (1885): 145, 149, 162, 165; 2 (1886): 265. Birch *Cat. Seals in the British Museum* 2 (1892): 645 (seal of Alexander de Clavering, of Essex, dated 1318–9 — A shield of arms: quarterly, on a bend three mullets [CLAVERING]. Hodgson *Hist. of Northumberland* 5 (1899): 18–32. *Feudal Aids* 3 (1904): 398, 470. *C.Ch.R.* 2 (1906): 457. Clay *Extinct & Dormant Peerages* (1913): 20–21 (sub Clavering). *Cal. MSS in Various Colls.* 7 (Hist. MSS Comm. 55) (1914): 227. *Genealogist's Mag.* 6 (1932–34): 607. Hedley *Northumberland Fams.* 1 (1968): 160–163 (Clavering ped.).

iii. **ROGER DE CLAVERING**, younger son. He married **BEATRICE** _____. They had one daughter, Margery, who died underage in 1307. In 1298 his father settled the manor of Callaly on him and his brother, Alan, jointly. ROGER DE CLAVERING died shortly before 27 April 1306. His widow, Beatrice, was pardoned 19 October 1306 for the death of Hervey de Bylton at the instance of Robert Fitz Roger. No living descendants. *C.P.R. 1301–1307* (1898): 430, 461, 469, 473, 515. Hodgson *Hist. of Northumberland* 5 (1899): 18–32. Clay *Extinct & Dormant Peerages* (1913): 20–21 (sub Clavering). Hedley *Northumberland Fams.* 1 (1968): 160–163 (Clavering ped.).

iv. **ALAN DE CLAVERING**, Knt., of Callaly (in Whittingham), Northumberland, younger son, born about 1279 (aged 28 in 1307). He married before 1304 **ISABEL RYDDELL**, daughter and co-heiress of William Ruddell, Knt., of Tillmouth in Norhamshire. She was born about 1288–98 (aged 30 in 1328). They had three sons,

William, Alan, Knt., and John, Knt. In 1306 he was pardoned for the death of his brother, Roger de Clavering, at the request of Patrick, Earl of March, Ingram de Umfreville, John de Mowbray, and Alexander de Abernathy. In 1326 he had license to grant land in Yetlington and two parts of the manor of Callaly to his son William and Maud his wife. SIR ALAN DE CLAVERING died before 18 Jan. 1327/8. His widow, Isabel, married **WALTER DE CRAKES**, Knt., Sheriff of Berwick. She was living 9 April 1349. Hodgson *Hist. of Northumberland* Pt. 2 Vol. 1 (1827): 372 (ped.). *C.P.R. 1301–1307* (1898): 430. Hodgson *Hist. of Northumberland* 5 (1899): 18–32. St. George & Dugdale *Peds. Rec. at the Heralds' Vis. of Northumberland* (1903): 30–31 (Clavering ped.: "Alanus de Clavering, miles ob. 2 E. 3. = Isabella filia primogenita et una hæredum Willmi Riddill militis de cujus hæreditate Duddo et aliæ possessiones in co. Northumbr. fuerent, quæ usque in hunc diem ejus posteri tenent."). *C.P.R. 1324–1327* (1904): 241. Clay *Extinct & Dormant Peerages* (1913): 20–21 (sub Clavering). Oliver *Northumberland & Durham Deeds* (Newcastle-upon-Tyne Recs. Comm. 7) (1929): 195–196. Hedley *Northumberland Fams.* 1 (1968): 160–163 (Clavering ped.). Given-Wilson *Fourteenth Century England* 2 (2002): 21.

v. [MASTER] **HENRY DE CLAVERING**, clerk. He was appointed Rector of Reepham Norfolk in 1303 and Rector of Carleton Rode, Norfolk in 1307. He was living in 1313–14. He died about 1317. Blomefield *Essay towards a Top. Hist. of Norfolk* 3 (1769): 83; 8 (1808): 245. *Papal Regs.: Letters* 2 (1895): 36, 79–93. Hodgson *Hist. of Northumberland* 5 (1899): 18–32. Rye *Cal. Feet of Fines for Suffolk* (1900): 131. Clay *Extinct & Dormant Peerages* (1913): 20–21 (sub Clavering). Hedley *Northumberland Fams.* 1 (1968): 160–163 (Clavering ped.). Given-Wilson *Fourteenth Century England* 2 (2002): 19.

vi. **EDMUND DE CLAVERING**, chaplain. He was presented to the church of Ardeley, Hertfordshire in 1291. In 1331 he and his brother, John de Clavering, and the mayor, bailiffs and others of Dunwich, were ordered to appear in Chancery to inform the king and his council concerning disputes and disturbances between them. Gardner *Hist. Account of Dunwich, Blithburgh, Southwold* (1754): 135–136. Chauncy *Hist. Antiqs. of Hertfordshire* 1 (1826): 126. Cussans *Hist. of Hertfordshire* 1(1) Braughing Hundred (1870): 95. Hall *Hist. of the Custom-Revenue in England* 2 (1885): 19. Hodgson *Hist. of Northumberland* 5 (1899): 18–32. Sutton *Rolls & Reg. of Bishop Oliver Sutton, 1280–1299* 8 (Lincoln Rec. Soc. 76) (1986): 75–76. Waugh *England in the Reign of Edward III* (1991): 42–43. National Archives, C 47/14/3/14; C 47/14/3/15; C 143/86/15; SC 8/107/5342; SC 8/258/12864; SC 8/277/13812 (available at www.catalogue.nationalarchives.gov.uk/search.asp).

vii. **EUPHAME DE CLAVERING**, married **RANULPH DE NEVILLE**, of Ashby, Lincolnshire [see NEVILLE 10].

viii. **ELLEN DE CLAVERING**, married before 30 Dec. 1296 **JOHN D'ENGAINE**, Knt., of Laxton, Blatherwycke, and Pytchley, Northamptonshire, Dillington, Gidding, and Graffham, Huntingdonshire, etc., son and heir of John d'Engaine, Knt., of Colne Engaine, Essex, Laxton and Pytchley, Northamptonshire, etc., by Joan, daughter and heiress of Gilbert de Greinville, Knt. They had no issue. He was born about 1263–73 (aged variously 24 and more, 26, 30, 30 and more, and 34 in 1297). He accompanied the King to France in 1286. He was summoned to Parliament from 6 Feb. 1298/9 to 15 May 1321, by writs directed *Johanni Engayne, Engaigne, Dengayne,* or *Dengaigne,* whereby he is held to have become Lord Engaine. He was present at the Battle of Falkirk 22 July 1298, and at the Siege of Caerlaverock in July 1300. He signed the Barons' letter to Pope Boniface VIII in 1301 as *Johannes Engayn' dominus de Colum.* SIR JOHN ENGAINE, 1st Lord Engaine, died 28 Sept. 1322. His widow, Ellen, died shortly before 2 June 1339. Clutterbuck *Hist. & Antiqs. of Hertford* 3 (1827): 178 (Engaine ped.). *C.C.R. 1339–1341* (1901): 183. *MSS of the Duke of Rutland* 4 (Hist. MSS Comm. 24) (1905): 8. *Trans. Leicestershire Arch. & Hist. Soc.* 13 (1923–4): 146 (Engaine chart). *C.P.* 5 (1926): 73–74 (sub Engaine).

7. JOHN FITZ ROBERT (or **DE CLAVERING**), Knt., of Clavering, Essex, Cotessey and Horsford, Norfolk, Whalton, Northumberland, Blythburgh, Suffolk, etc., son and heir, born about 1266 (aged 44 in 1310). He married by contract dated about 11 Sept. 1277 **HAWISE DE TIBETOT**, daughter of Robert de Tibetot, of Nettlestead, Suffolk, by Eve, daughter of Patrick de Chaworth, Knt. [see TIBETOT 7 for her ancestry]. They had one daughter, Eve. He was summoned to Parliament from 16 July 1299 to 20 Nov. 1331, by writs directed *Johanni de Clavering*, whereby he is held to have become Lord Clavering. He was summoned to serve against the Scots in 1299. He and the Abbas and Convent of St. Osyth presented to the church of Blythburgh, Suffolk in 1310. In the period, 1310–32, he granted his fishing rights in his river at Blythburgh to the canons of Blythburgh, Suffolk. He fought with distinction in the Scotch wars and was taken prisoner at the Battle of Bannockburn 24 June 1314. In 1311 he obtained the king's license to settle upon the king his castle of Warkworth and manor of Rothbury, Northumberland in reversion upon his own death, the manor of Eure, Buckinghamshire in reversion upon his own death and that of Hawise his wife, and the reversion of the manors of Newburn and Corbridge, Northumberland in default of male issue. In return for the grant, which comprised lands of the yearly value of £700, the king granted him a life interest in various manors and hundreds in the counties of Norfolk, Suffolk and Northamptonshire to the yearly vaue of £400. The same year he received license to alienate the manor of Whalton, Northumberland to Geoffrey le Scrope, Knt. He also granted land in fee-farm in Horsford, Norfolk to William son of Robert Joynt. About 1312 he petitioned King and Council requesting remedy in his suit against Aymer de Valence, Earl of Pembroke, regarding the manors of Postwick, Norfolk, and Reydon, Suffolk, and a messuage and lands in Filby, Norfolk. In 1312 he and his wife, Hawise, settled the manors of Clavering, Essex and Blythburgh, Suffolk, in default of male issue, on his brother Edmund for life, and then to Ralph de Neville and his heirs. He also conveyed the reversion of the manors of Aynho, Northamptonshire and Horsford, Norfolk and his life interest in Newburn, Northumberland to Ranulph de Neville in default of his own male issue. In 1319 he gave to the Hospital of Aynho, Northamptonshire a half a virgate of land, a messuage, and a mill called Goldsbolte with the adjacent meadow and water-course, and the custom of his tenants at the said mill; the master and brethren acquired further lands in Aynho from the same lord in 1331 to the value of 5 marks yearly. In 1320 he sold the reversion of the manor of Ling, Norfolk to Walter de Norwich, Knt. In 1320–1 he was ordered to furnish his castle of Wark, Northumberland with men-at-arms, victuals, and all other necessaries for its defense against the Scots. He presented to the Hospital of Aynho, Northamptonshire in 1323. In 1324 he was granted a market and fair to be held at the manor of Aynho, Northamptonshire and the same at the manor of Blythburgh, Suffolk. In 1327 he petitioned the king, requesting to be released from the arrears of the £40 farm of Corbridge, Northumberland owing to the great impoverishment of Corbridge produced by frequent Scottish attacks. In Feb. 1327 he was granted the town of Corbridge for life, free from any payment of rent. In 1328 Richard Touchet sued him regarding service exacted by Robert de Vere, Earl of Oxford, from a tenement in Uggle, Essex. In 1331 he and his brother, Edmund de Clavering, and the mayor, bailiffs and others of Dunwich, were ordered to appear in Chancery to inform the king and his council concerning disputes and disturbances between them. SIR JOHN DE CLAVERING, Lord Clavering, died at Aynho, Northamptonshire 18 Jan. 1331/2, and was buried in the choir at Langley Abbey, Norfolk. His widow, Hawise, died 18 Feb. 1345.

Gardner *Hist. Account of Dunwich, Blithburgh, Southwold* (1754): 135–136. Blomefield *Essay towards a Top. Hist. of Norfolk* 4 (1775): 407; 5 (1775): 1356–1357; 11 (1810): 144, 189. Bridges *Hist. & Antiqs. of Northamptonshire* 1 (1791): 142. Blore *Hist. & Antiqs. of Rutland* 1(2) (1811): 44 (Tybetot ped.). Dugdale *Monasticon Anglicanum* 3 (1821): 636–637 (Priory of St. Faith at Horsham, Norfolk — Genealogia Fundatoris: "Johannes duxit uxorem nomine Hawisiam, de qua genuit nomine Evam, cujus cognomen rex Edwardus filius Henrici fecit vocari Clavering, à principali manerio suo, de qua genuit filiam Evam, quæ nunc se clamat advocatricem domus de Sibeton, de Langley, sanctæ Fidis, et de Bliburg; et hoc jure hæreditario."). Dugdale *Monasticon Anglicanum* 5 (1825): 559–560 (Sibton Abbey — Linea Consanguinitatis, de Stirpe Fundatorum Abbaciæ de Sybeton: "… Johannes [de Clavering] duxit uxorem nomine Hawisiam, de qua genuit filiam nomine Evam, quæ nunc se clamat advocatam domus de Sybeton, de Langele, sanctæ Fidis, et de Bliburg, et hoc jure hæreditario, …"). Hodgson *Hist. of Northumberland* Pt. 2 Vol. 1 (1827): 372 (ped.). Nicolas *Siege of Carlaverock* (1828): 117–119 (biog. of John de Clavering). Palgrave *Antient Kalendars & Inventories of the Treasury of His Majesty's Exchequer* 1 (1836): 65. Montagu *Guide to the Study of Heraldry* (1840): 39. *Coll. Top. et Gen.* 7 (1841): 49–52, 197–202; 8 (1843): 159. Cole *Docs. Ill. of English Hist. in the 13th & 14th Cents.* (1844): 19–20, 24–25 (instances of Stephen de Cressy styled "kinsman" of John de Clavering). Suckling *Hist. & Antiqs. of Suffolk* 2 (1847): 131–135, 161. Hartshorne *Feudal & Military Antiqs. of Northumberland* (1858): 186–194. Fowler *Chartularium Abbathia de Novo Monasterio* (Surtees Soc. 66) (1878): 12 (charter of John de Clavering). Glover et al. *Vis. of Cheshire 1580, 1566, 1533 & 1591* (H.S.P. 18) (1882): 90–91 (Clavering ped.: "John de Claveringe. = Elizab. d. to Sr Paine Tiptoft."). Rye *Short Cal. Feet of Fines for Norfolk* 2 (1886): 259, 265. *Arch. Aeliana* 14 (1891): 81–166. *Genealogist* n.s. 8 (1892): 154. *Norfolk Arch.* 15 (1904): 267–292. *MSS of the Duke of Rutland* 4 (Hist. MSS Comm. 24) (1905): 57. Hodgson *Hist. of Northumberland* 5 (1899): 18–32; 10 (1914): 59–87; 13 (1930): 142–144. St. George & Dugdale *Peds. Rec. at the Heralds' Vis. of Northumberland* (1903): 30–31 (Clavering ped.: "Johannes, dictus de Clavering, miles, Baro de Warkworth et Clavering, ob. s. hær. max. = Haursia, filia Roberti de Tybetot."). *Feudal Aids* 3 (1904): 473, 547. *Index of Placita de Banco 1327–1328* 1 (PRO Lists and

Indexes 17) (1904): 158. Wrottesley *Peds. from the Plea Rolls* (1905): 10. VCH *Northampton* 2 (1906): 150–151. *C.Ch.R.* 3 (1908): 463. Rye *Norfolk Fams.* (1911): 219. *C.P.* 3 (1913): 275–276; 12(2) (1959): 93, footnote c. Clay *Extinct & Dormant Peerages* (1913): 20–21 (sub Clavering). *Feet of Fines for Essex* 2 (1913–28): 140. *Cal. MSS in Various Colls.* 7 (Hist. MSS Comm. 55) (1914): 36, 184 (grant by Sir John de Clavering dated 1311). *Year Books of Edward II* 14(2) (Selden Soc. 43) (1927): 157–158. Jenkinson & Fermoy *Select Cases in the Exchequer of Pleas* (Selden Soc. 48) (1932): 211–212. Richardson & Sayles *Rotuli Parl. Anglie Hactenus Inediti 1274–1373* (Camden Soc. 3rd Ser. 51) (1935): 81–82. *Norfolk Arch.* 30 (1952): 263–286. Dalton *MSS of St. George's Chapel* (1957): 405. Paget *Baronage of England* (1957) 132: 4–5. Holmes *Estates of the Higher Nobility in 14th Cent. England* (1957): 134–142. Sanders *English Baronies* (1960): 150. Hedley *Northumberland Fams.* 1 (1968): 160–163 (Clavering ped.). Harper-Bill *Blythburgh Priory Cartulary* 1 (Suffolk Charters 2) (1980): 7, 45. VCH *Cambridge* 9 (1989): 271–274. Waugh *England in the Reign of Edward III* (1991): 42–43. Britnell & Pollard *McFarlane Legacy* (1995): 39. Brault *Rolls of Arms Edward I* 2 (1997): 107 (arms of John de Clavering: Argent, a lion rampant purpure, a label vert; Quarterly or and gules, a bend sable, a label azure). Biancalana *Fee Tail & the Common Recovery in Medieval England* (2001): 154. Given-Wilson *Fourteenth Century England* 2 (2002): 15, 18. National Archives, C 47/14/3/14; C 47/14/3/15; C 143/86/15; SC 8/39/1928; SC 8/99/4937; SC 8/258/12864; SC 8/277/13812 (available at www.catalogue.nationalarchives.gov.uk/search.asp).

8. EVE DE CLAVERING, *suo jure* Lady Clavering, born about 1295–1305 (aged 40 and more in 1345). She married (1st) **THOMAS DE AUDLEY**, of Heleigh, Audley, Endon, etc., Staffordshire, Marchamley, Shropshire, etc., son and heir of Nicholas de Audley, Knt., of Heleigh (in Audley), Audley, Talk, Tunstall, etc., Staffordshire, by Katherine, daughter of John Giffard, Knt., 1st Lord Giffard [see AUDLEY 9 for his ancestry]. He was born in or before 1289 (aged over 10 in 1299). They had no issue. He died a minor shortly before 21 Nov. 1307. His widow, Eve, married (2nd) before 2 December 1308 **THOMAS DE UFFORD**, Knt., 2nd son of Robert de Ufford, Knt., of Ufford, Suffolk, Justiciar of Ireland, 1268–9, 1276–81, Justice of Chester before October 1276, by his 2nd wife, Joan. He was born before 1286–7 (date of fine). He was younger brother of the half-blood to Robert de Ufford, Knt., 1st Lord Ufford, and uncle of Robert de Ufford, K.G., 1st Earl of Suffolk, Lord Ufford. They had three sons, John, Knt. [Lord Ufford], Robert, Knt., and Edmund, Knt. In 1313 Nicholas de Audley appeared by attorney against Thomas de Ufford and Eve his wife for causing waste and destruction in the woods, lands, and iron mines which they held as dower of the said Eve in Audley, Endon, and Chesterton (in Wolstanton), Staffordshire. SIR THOMAS DE UFFORD was slain at the Battle of Bannockburn 24 June 1314 (when his father-in-law was taken prisoner), and was buried in Langley Abbey, Norfolk. His widow, Eve, married (3rd) before 1 Nov. 1319 (date of lease) **JAMES DE AUDLEY**, Knt. [see STRATTON AUDLEY 9.i], of Stratton (in Stratton Audley), Oxfordshire, Chesterton (in Wolstanton), Cold Norton (in Chebsey), and Mere, Staffordshire, and, in right of his wife, of Audley, Staffordshire, son and heir of Hugh de Audley, Knt., Lord Audley, of Stratton (in Stratton Audley), Oxfordshire, Raunds, Northamptonshire, and Bradwell and Chesterton (both in Wolstanton), Gratton, and Mere, Staffordshire, Justice of North Wales, Steward of the King's Household, by his wife, Iseult [see STRATTON AUDLEY 9 for his ancestry]. They had two sons, James, K.G. (the hero of the Battle of Poitiers), and Peter, Knt., and three daughters, Katherine, Anne, and Hawise. In 1316 he was granted the manor of Brucebury (in Kempston), Bedfordshire for life by the king. In 1323 he sued Philip de Wenlok for 46 marks. He served in Gascony in 1324, and in Scotland in 1327. In 1327 he was taxed for his wife, Eve's dower lands at Audley, Chesterton, and Cold Norton (in Chebsey), Staffordshire. In 1330 he and his wife, Eve, made settlements of the manor of Stratton (in Stratton Audley), Oxfordshire and a fourth part of the manor of Mere, Staffordshire. On 21 April 1331, he had letters nominating attorneys in England for two years, he then going on pilgrimage to Santiago in Spain. In 1332, as "Eve de Audley," she and the Convent presented to the church of Blythburgh, Suffolk. In 1332, as "Eva de Offord [Ufford]," she was taxed for her dower property in Chesterton, Staffordshire, while James was taxed for his lands at Mere, Staffordshire and his wife, Eve's dower lands at Audley, Staffordshire. SIR JAMES DE AUDLEY died shortly before 1 March 1333/4, when the king granted his manor of Brucebury (in Kempston), Bedfordshire held for his life to another party.

Following his death, the legality of his marriage to Eve de Clavering and the legitimacy of their issue appears to have been challenged; his brother, Hugh de Audley, Knt., Earl of Gloucester, was styled his heir in a legal proceeding dated 1342. In 1334 she presented to a mediety of the church of Newton, Norfolk, as "Eve daughter of Sir John Clavering guardian to William son and heir of William Blumville." His widow, Eve, married (4th) in 1335, after 29 Sept. (date of notification record) **ROBERT DE BENHALE**, Knt., in right of his wife, of Audley, Balterley, and Mere, Staffordshire. They had no issue. In 1331 he remitted to Robert de Rokewood, of Acton, Suffolk, an annual rent of £20 issuing from his lands in Acton, Suffolk. He attended the 2nd Dunstable Tournament in 1334. In 1337 he quitclaimed to the Prior and convent of Holy Trinity, Norwich, John Curteys, and Thomas de Brisele one piece of land in Riston, and one half of the advowson of the church of Fordham, Norfolk. In 1337–8 Robert and his wife, Eve, conveyed lands in Ilketshall and Spexhall, Suffolk to Elizabeth de Burgh, lady of Clare. He presented to the church of Burgh St. Margaret, Norfolk in right of his wife in 1338, 1346, 1348, 1349, and 1356. He served in the king's retinue in the Crécy and Calais campaigns of 1346 and 1347. In 1342 Eve and Robert released their right to the manors of Clavering, Essex, Aynho, Northamptonshire, Eure, Buckinghamshire, and Blythburgh, Suffolk to Ralph de Neville and her mother, Hawise de Clavering. In 1347 he conveyed to Alexander, parson of Horsham, Robert de Marcham, and others lands and tenements in Benhale, Sternfield, Farnham, and Snape, Suffolk, which property the grantees lately had by his gift. In 1351 Robert and his wife, Eve, sought the manor of Benhall, Suffolk against Robert de Ufford, Earl of Suffolk. In 1352–3 Robert and his wife, Eve, sued Richard, son of Peter de Thiknes for 20 acres of land in Balterley, Staffordshire, which they claimed as the right of Eve. In 1354 Richard le Cooper, parson of Audley, Staffordshire, was attached at the suit of Robert de Benhale for forcibly breaking into his park at Audley, Staffordshire in 1351, chasing his game, cutting down his trees, and taking his goods and chattels to the value of £10, and likewise three hares, six rabbits, forty partridges, and ten pheasants worth 100s., and for which he claimed £100 as damages. In 1354 Lady Eve de Audley and her two daughters were admitted to the Fraternity of the Abbey of St. Benet of Holm, Norfolk. In 1357 Robert and his wife, Eve, sued John de Beauchamp, of Holt, and Henry Puse for unjustly disseising them of the fourth part of the manor of Mere, Staffordshire; Robert atte Gate answered for the defendants and denied the disseisin. He was summoned to a Council in 1359, by writ directed *Roberto de Benhale*. He was summoned to Parliament 3 April 1360, by writ directed *Roberto de Benhale*, whereby he may be held to have become Lord Benhale. He was not subsequently summoned. In 1361 he and his wife, Eve, and the Convent presented to the church of Blythburgh, Suffolk. In 1362 she and her son, James de Audley, Knt., were admitted to the Fraternity of the Abbey of St. Benet of Holm, Norfolk. He presented to the church of Great Bromley, Essex in 1363. **SIR ROBERT DE BENHALE**, Lord Benhale, died shortly before 28 Feb. 1365. In 1368 John de Catfield, rector of Stratton, held Isaac's Hall (now called the Music House) in Norwich, Norfolk as trustee for Lady Eve de Audley and her son, James de Audley, Knt. In 1369 the king pardoned William de Upgate for the death of Walter Halleman, at the request of Eve de Audley, late the wife of Robert de Benhale. Eve died 20 Sept. 1369, and was buried at Langley Abbey, Norfolk, with her four husbands.

<small>Rymer *Fœdera* 6 (1727): 138. Blomefield *Essay towards a Top. Hist. of Norfolk* 3 (1769): 43; 5 (1775): 1140, 1356–1357; 11 (1810): 52–53, 155. Dugdale *Monasticon Anglicanum* 3 (1821): 636–637 (Priory of St. Faith at Horsham, Norfolk — Genealogia Fundatoris: "Quæ quidem Eva nupsit cuidam nomine Thomæ de Audele, qui mortuus est sine prole de se. Item nupsit cuidam militi Radulfo de Ufford, qui genuit ex ea tres filios, videlicet, dominos Johannem, Robertum, et Edmundum, milites. Prædicto Radulfo mortuo, nupsit Jacobo de Audele, qui genuit duos filios et duas filias, videlicet, Jacobum et Petrum, Annam et Hawisiam. Mortuo prædicto domino Jacobo viri, prædicta Eva nupta fuit Roberto Benhalle militi, qui obiit sine hærede. Defuncta prædicta Eva et sepulta in monasterio de Langley …"); 5 (1825): 559–560 (Sibton Abbey — Linea Consanguinitatis, de Stirpe Fundatorum Abbaciæ de Sybeton: "…quæ quidem Eva [de Clavering] nupsit cuidam nomine …. qui mortuus est sine prole de se. Item nupsit cuidam militi nomine Radulfus de Ufford, qui genuit ex ea tres filios, videlicet, dominos Johannem, Robertum, et Edmundum milites. Prædicto Radulfo</small>

mortuo nupsit ... de Audle, qui genuit ex ea duos filios et duas filias, videlicet Jacobum et Petrum, Aviciam, et Hawisiam."). Hodgson *Hist. of Northumberland* Pt. 2 Vol. 1 (1827): 372–373 (ped.). *Coll. Top. et Gen.* 2 (1835): 126; 7 (1841): 49–52. Banks *Dormant & Extinct Baronage of England* 4 (1837): 11–12 (sub Benhale). Beltz *Mems. of the Order of the Garter* (1841): 83 ("In a roll of arms between 2 and 7 Edw. II, 1308–1314, 'sir James de Audele of Gloucestershire' is stated to have borne on his banner the arms of Audeley [Gules fretty or], differenced by 'a label Azure charged with three lioncels rampant Or,' evidently in commemoration of his descent from *Longspee*."). Banks *Baronies in Fees* 1 (1844): 437–440 (sub Ufford). Suckling *Hist. & Antiqs. of Suffolk* 2 (1847): 161. *Top. & Gen.* 2 (1853): 271–277 (Ufford ped.); 8 (1843): 159. Hartshorne *Feudal & Military Antiqs. of Northumberland* (1858): 186–194. *Annual Rpt. of the Deputy Keeper* 28 (1867): 22. *Notes & Queries* 4th Ser. 4 (1869): 44. *Herald & Genealogist* 5 (1870): 63–68. Waters *Chester of Chicheley* 1 (1878): 337–338. Turner *Cal. Charters & Rolls: Bodleian Lib.* (1878): 210–211 (charter of Robert de Benhale, Knt.). Duncumb et al. *Colls. towards the Hist. & Antiq. of Hereford* 3 (1882): 4–10 (Audley ped.). Glover et al. *Vis. of Cheshire 1580, 1566, 1533 & 1591* (H.S.P. 18) (1882): 90–91 (Clavering ped.: "Eua [de Clavering] had 4 husbands, 1. Thos Audley, 2. Sr Thos Ufford, 3. Sr James Audley 3 husband, 4. Rob't Benhalle sine prole."). Wrottesley *Staffordshire Suits: Plea Rolls* (Colls. Hist. Staffs. 7(1)) (1886): 108, 114; (Colls. Hist. Staffs. 9(1)) (1888): 43–44, 52, 78, 90, 101, 106; (Colls. Hist. Staffs. 11) (1890): 131; (Colls. Hist. Staffs. 12) (1891): 9, 110, 159–160; (Colls. Hist. Staffs. 14) (1893): 82. *Colls. Hist. Staffs.* 7(1) (1886): 202, 205, 206; 10 (1889): 94, 100–101. *C.P.R. 1327–1330* (1891): 466. Birch *Cat. Seals in the British Museum* 2 (1892): 645 (seal of Eve de Clavering dated 1334 — A shield of arms: per pale, dex., a cross lezengy, dimidiated, over all a bend [UFFORD]; sin., fretty of six pieces [AUDLEY]. Within a carved gothic panel of three points and five semicircular cusps, ornamented with ball-flowers along the inner edge. Outside this the carving and tracery, which is very elaborate, contains three cusped countersunk panels in triangle, in each of which is a lozenge-shaped shield of arms: quarterly a bendlet [CLAVERING]). *C.P.R. 1330–1334* (1893): 102, 512, 522. *C.P.R. 1334–1338* (1895): 181. *Year Books of Edward III: Year XVI* 7 (Rolls Ser. 31b) (1896): 81–82. *C.P.R. 1313–1317* (1898): 510. Wrottesley *Crécy & Calais* (1898): 143, 185. Hodgson *Hist. of Northumberland* 5 (1899): 18–32. Rye *Cal. Feet of Fines for Suffolk* (1900): 90, 94, 95, 184, 205. Foster *Some Feudal Coats of Arms* (1902): 21 (arms of Robert de Benhale: Argent, a bend between three fizures (cotises) wavy sable). St. George & Dugdale *Peds. Rec. at the Heralds' Vis. of Northumberland* (1903): 30–31 (Clavering ped.: "Eva [de Clavering], unica filia et hæres, per quam tota hæres itas in com. Essexia Suffolciæ et Northamptoniæ familiæ de Nevill, accesit. = Thomas de Gifford, miles"). *Norfolk Arch.* 15 (1904): 267–292; 28 (1945): 36. Wedgwood *Parentage of Sir James Audley* (Colls. Hist. Staffs. n.s. 9) (1906): 245–268. Chetwynd *Hist. of Pirehill Hundred* 1 (Colls. Hist. Staffs. n.s. 12) (1909): 228–229 (Audley ped.). *C.P.* 1 (1910): 339 (sub Audley), 348 (sub Audley); 3 (1913): 275–276 (sub Clavering); 12(2) (1959): 154–155; 14 (1998): 186 (sub Clavering). *Colls. Hist. Staffs.* 1911 (1911): 466–467. Martin *Percy Chartulary* (Surtees Soc. 117) (1911): 264. Rye *Norfolk Fams.* (1911): 219. *C.P.R. 1364–1367* (1912): 141. VCH *Bedford* 3 (1912): 299. *C.P.R. 1367–1370* (1913): 223. Clay *Extinct & Dormant Peerages* (1913): 20–21 (sub Clavering). *C.F.R.* 8 (1924): 58. Fowler *Reg. Simonis de Sudbiria* 1 (Canterbury & York Soc. 34) (1927): 235. VCH *Northampton* 4 (1937): 30–31. *Cal. IPM* 13 (1954): 72. Paget *Baronage of England* (1957) 17: 1–4 (sub Audley); 132: 4. VCH *Oxford* 6 (1959): 325–326. Hedley *Northumberland Fams.* 1 (1968): 160–163 (Clavering ped.) (seal of Eve daughter of John de Clavering dated 1346 — A shield of arms: cross lozengy, over all a bendlet [UFFORD] impaling by dimidiation fretty [AUDLEY], on a shield set in a richly cusped circular panel, between three lozenges with the arms of CLAVERING, quarterly a bendlet, in smaller panels). Maccullough *Chorography of Suffolk* (Suffolk Rec. Soc. 19) (1976): 34, 51. VCH *Stafford* 7 (1976): 70. Bothwell *Edward III & the English Peerage* (2004): 119. Suffolk Rec. Office, Ipswich Branch: Iveagh (Phillipps) Suffolk MSS, HD 1538/12 Vol.12/fol.23/2 — quitclaim dated 20 April 1347 from Robert de Benhale, Knt. to Sir Alexander, parson of Horham church, and three others, all lands and tenements which grantees lately had by grantors's gift in Benhale, Sternefeld [Sternfield], Farnham, and Snape, Suffolk (available at www.a2a.org.uk/search/index.asp). Shropshire Archives: Phillipps Coll., 52/32 — notification dated 29 Sept. 1335 that Richard de Venables, steward of Eva who was the wife of James de Audeley has received from Richard, Prior of St Thomas a coffin to keep on behalf of his said lady (available at www.a2a.org.uk/search/index.asp).

9. EDMUND DE UFFORD, Knt., of Great Belstead, Suffolk, and Burgh St. Margaret and Horsford, Norfolk, 3rd son. He married **SIBYL DE PIERREPOINT** (or **PIERPOINT**), daughter and heiress of John de Pierrepoint, Knt., of Wrentham, Benacre, and Henstead, Suffolk, and Hurstpierpoint, Sussex, by Ela, daughter of William de Calthorpe, Knt. They had one son, Robert, Knt., and one daughter, Ela. In 1346 Edmund was granted an annual rent of 40 marks by his kinsman, Henry, Earl of Lancaster, from the manor of Higham Ferrers, Northamptonshire. He was heir in 1361 to his brother, John de Ufford, Lord Ufford. On his mother's death in 1369, he succeeded *de jure* to his mother's barony of Clavering. He presented to the church of Blythburgh, Suffolk in 1371. SIR EDMUND DE UFFORD left a will dated 1 Sept. 1374, proved 3 October 1375. He was buried at Langley Abbey, Norfolk.

Blomefield *Essay towards a Top. Hist. of Norfolk* 5 (1775): 1356–1357. Dugdale *Monasticon Anglicanum* 3 (1821): 636–637 (Priory of St. Faith at Horsham, Norfolk — Genealogia Fundatoris: "… successit Edmundus Ufford miles, ut filius et hæres dictæ Evæ, qui quidem Edmundus maritatus erat Sibillæ filiæ Simonis Perpoint militis, qui genuit ex ea Robertum Ufford militem et alios filios et filias, qui obierunt in pueritia."). *Coll. Top. et Gen.* 7 (1841): 197–202. Suckling *Hist. & Antiqs. of Suffolk* 2 (1847): 161. *Top. & Gen.* 2 (1853): 271–277 (Ufford ped.). *Sussex Arch. Colls.* 11 (1859): 50–88. Waters *Chester of Chicheley* 1 (1878): 338–339. Glover et al. *Vis. of Cheshire 1580, 1566, 1533 & 1591* (H.S.P. 18) (1882): 90–91 (Clavering ped.: "Sr Edm. Ufford. = Sibill d. to Sr Simon Perpoint."). *Genealogist* n.s. 16 (1899): 41 (plea roll ped. correctly identifies Sibyl as daughter of John Perpount, by Ela, daughter of William de Calthorp, which John was the son of Simon Perpount, Knt., of Wrentham, Benacre, and Henstede, Suffolk, living 4 Edward III [1330–1]). *Norfolk Arch.* 15 (1904): 267–292. Wrottesley *Peds. from the Plea Rolls* (1905): 270. Copinger *Manors of Suffolk* 2 (1908): 5–7, 42–43, 86–87. *C.P.* 10 (1945): 518–519 (sub Pierrepoint); 12(2) (1959): 154 footnote f, 156 footnote f. *Coat of Arms* 6 (1961): 350–355. Fowler *King's Lieutenant* (1969): 234 (Edmund de Ufford styled "cousin" by Henry, Earl of Lancaster, in 1347). National Archives, DL 27/155: Indenture between Henry Earl of Lancaster and Esmond, son of Thomas de Ufford, witnessing that the said Earl has granted to the said Esmond, an annual rent of forty marks issuing from the manor of Higham Terrers, for term of his life. Witnessed by M. Reygnaud de Mohan, M. John de Sayton, M. Richard de Roucliff, knights, Symon Symeon, Payen de Mohun, at London, March 1. 21 Edward III [1347] (available at www.catalogue.nationalarchives.gov.uk/search.asp).

Children of Edmund de Ufford, Knt., by Sibyl de Pierrepoint:

    i.   **ROBERT DE UFFORD**, Knt. [see next].

    ii.   **ELA UFFORD**, married **MILES STAPLETON**, Knt., *de jure* Lord Ingham, of Ingham, Norfolk [see STAPLETON 11].

10. ROBERT DE UFFORD, Knt., *de jure* Lord Clavering, of Burgh St. Margaret and Horsford, etc., Norfolk, Wrentham, Suffolk, etc., son and heir. He married **ELEANOR FELTON**, daughter and co-heiress of Thomas de Felton, K.G., of Litcham, Banham, Dersingham, Great Ryburgh, Ingaldesthorp, Little Ryburgh, and Wilby, Norfolk, Barrow, Suffolk, etc., Seneschal of Aquitaine, Seneschal of Gascony, by Joan, daughter and co-heiress of Richard de Walkfare, Knt. [see FELTON 7 for her ancestry] She was born about 1361 (aged 20 in 1381). They had three daughters, Ela (wife of Richard Bowet, Esq.), Joan, and Sibyl (nun at Barking). On the death of his cousin, William de Ufford, K.G., 2nd Earl of Suffolk, Lord Ufford [see BLACKMERE 12.i; NORFOLK 8.iii.e] in 1382, he became the heir male of the Ufford family. He presented to the church of Blythburgh, Suffolk in 1382. SIR ROBERT DE UFFORD was living 7 Jan. 1389/90, and died before 1393. His widow, Eleanor, married (2nd) in or before Feb. 1394/5 (date of demise) (as his 1st wife) **THOMAS HOO**, Knt. [see HOO 13], of Luton Hoo (in Luton), Bedfordshire, Brundale and Mulbarton, Norfolk, Ockley, Surrey, Wartling, Sussex, etc., son and heir of William de Hoo, Knt., of Maulden, Bedfordshire, Knebworth and Wheathampstead, Hertfordshire, Brundale, Ketteringham, and Mulbarton, Norfolk, Bucksteep, Dallington, and Wartling, by his 1st wife, Alice, daughter and co-heiress of Thomas de Saint Omer, Knt. [see HOO 12 for his ancestry] They had one son, Thomas, K.G. [Lord Hoo and Hastings] [see HOO 14]. In 1394 he quitclaimed to his uncle, John de Hoo, and John Glemham all his right in the manor of Stameleshoo by Portsmouth, Hampshire. In 1395 and 1396 he and his wife, Eleanor, and the Convent presented to the church of Blythburgh, Suffolk. His wife, Eleanor, died 8 August 1400. He married (2nd) after 15 Jan. 1414/15 (date of inquisition) **ELIZABETH ECHINGHAM**, daughter of William Echingham, Knt. [see ECHINGHAM 10], of Etchingham and Udimore, Sussex, by his 1st wife, Alice, daughter and co-heiress of William Batisford. They had one son, Thomas, Esq. (of Horsham and Roughey, Sussex, and Southwark, Surrey). He fought at the Battle of Agincourt in 1415. In 1417 he levied a fine to settle the manor and advowson of the church of Mulbarton, Norfolk on himself and heirs. The same year he conveyed to Thomas Huchon, of Ukkefeld, lands and tenements called Sturgislondes together in 7 crofts at Cowbeech (in Wartling), Sussex. He was present at the Siege of Rouen in 1418. In 1420 Richard Osbarn and others, executors of the will of Stephen Speleman, Citizen and mercer of London, sued Thomas Hoo, Knt., of Bedfordshire, alias of Wartling, Sussex, in the Court of Common Pleas claiming that the said Thomas owed them £31 2s. 8d. which the late Stephen Speleman had loaned to the said Thomas. In 1422 John Harris, Citizen and skinner of London, sued him in the Court of Common Pleas regarding a debt of £8 4d. as per a bond dated 1419. SIR THOMAS HOO died 23 August 1420. His widow, Elizabeth, married (2nd) (as his 2nd wife) **THOMAS LEWKNOR**, Knt. [see LEWKNOR 14], of Horsted Keynes, Sussex, South Mimms, Middlesex, Stoke Doyle, Northamptonshire, etc., Sheriff of Surrey and Sussex, 1426, 1431–2, son and heir of Roger Lewknor, Esq., of Horstead Keynes, Iteford, and Selmeston, Sussex, by Elizabeth, evidently daughter of Nicholas Carew [see LEWKNOR 13 for his ancestry]. He was born about 1392 (aged 12 in 1404, aged 19 in 1411). They had five sons, John, Knt., Thomas, Richard, Esq., Walter, and Nicholas [see CUDWORTH 11], and three daughters, Alice (wife of John Pelham, Knt.), Jane (wife of Thomas Goode), and Joan (wife of Henry Frowick). In 1432 he was a supervisor of the will of his grandfather, Nicholas Carew. In 1435 he presented to the church of Stoke Doyle, Northamptonshire. He served as a witness to a charter of Thomas Hoo, Knt., in 1445. SIR THOMAS LEWKNOR died in 1452. In 1454 his widow, Elizabeth, and Joan Rykhill, daughters of Alice Batisford, disputed with their cousin, Sir Richard Fiennes, grandson of Alice's sister, Elizabeth, for possession of the manor of Buckholt (in Bexhill), Sussex. Elizabeth was named in the 1455 will of her step-son, Thomas Hoo, Knt., Lord Hoo. Sometime before 1464, she sued John Cheyne, son and heir of Sir William Cheyne, Knt., feoffee to uses regarding a tenement called 'the Christopher,' in St. Peter's, Cornhill, London, demised for the maintenance of the chantry of Goring, Sussex. In the same period, she sued her step-son, Roger Lewknor, in Chancery regarding the manors of Goring and Preston, Sussex. Elizabeth left a will dated 21 March 1450, proved 23 Feb. 1464 (P.C.C. 8 and 59 Godyn).

Blomefield *Essay towards a Top. Hist. of Norfolk* 5 (1775): 1356–1357; 5 (1806): 75–83; 7 (1807): 162–167, 219–221; 10 (1809): 335–336. Bridges *Hist. & Antiqs. of Northamptonshire* 1 (1791): 125. Dugdale *Monasticon Anglicanum* 3 (1821): 636–637 (Priory of St. Faith at Horsham, Norfolk — Genealogia Fundatoris: "…Et dictus Robertus Ufford maritatus fuit Elionoræ filiæ Thomæ Felton militis, qui genuit Elam, Sibillam, et Joannam filias, quæ dicta Ela desponsata fuit Ricardo Bowes armigero, quæ obiit sine hærede, et Sibilla monialis de Berkinge, et prædicta Johanna nupta Willielmo Bowes armigero, fratri Ricardi Bowes prædicti, qui genuit ex ea filiam, nuptam domino Dacres, et genuit ex ea filiam nomine Johannam quæ nupta fuit Ricardo Fines militi, camerario domini regis Edwardi quarti"). Dallaway *Hist. of the Western Division of the County of Sussex* 2(2) (1832): 339–340 (Hoo-Copley ped.). Beltz *Mems. of the Order of the Garter* (1841): 274–279 (biog. of Sir Thomas Felton). *Coll. Top. et Gen.* 7 (1841): 197–202. Suckling *Hist. & Antiqs. of Suffolk* 2 (1847): 161. *Top. & Gen.* 2 (1853): 271–277 (Ufford ped.). *Sussex Arch. Colls.* 8 (1856): 104–131; 11 (1859): 50–88; 30 (1880): 142–143. *Procs. Suffolk Inst. of Arch. & Nat. Hist.* 4 (1864): 49–56 (Felton ped.). Waters *Chester of Chicheley* 1 (1878): 339–340. Carthew *Hundred of Launditch & Deanery of Brisley* 3 (1879): 310–311 (Hoo ped.). Glover et al. *Vis. of Cheshire 1580, 1566, 1533 & 1591* (H.S.P. 18) (1882): 90–91 (Clavering ped.: "Sr Robt. Ufford. = Elenor d. to Sr Thoms ffelton."). Sinclair *Sinclairs of England* (1887): 322–329. Harvey et al. *Vis. of Norfolk 1563 & 1613* (H.S.P. 32) (1891): 158–160 (Hoo ped.: "Sir Thomas Hoo [1] = Elenor da. of Thomas Felton, [2] = Elizabeth da. of William Eckington."). *MSS of Rye & Hereford Corporations* (Hist. MSS Comm. 13th Rep., App., Part IV) (1892): 422–425 (docs. re. Felton and Walkfare fams.). Birch *Cat. Seals in the British Museum* 3 (1894): 606 (seal of Eleanor, widow of Sir Robert de Ufford dated 1393 — A shield of arms: per pale, dex., a cross lozengy, or engrailed, over all a bendlet [UFFORD], with a bendlet for difference; sin., two lions passant in pale, crowned [FELTON]. Suspended by a strap from a forked tree. Within a carved panel, with open tracery at the sides, and ball-flowers or small quatrefoils along the inner edge. Cabled borders). *Desc. Cat. Ancient Deeds* 2 (1894): 509; 6 (1915): 256–267. *Genealogist* n.s. 16 (1899): 41. *Papal Regs.: Letters* 4 (1902): 55. *Feudal Aids* 3 (1904): 599, 644. *Norfolk Arch.* 15 (1904): 267–292. Wrottesley *Peds. from the Plea Rolls* (1905): 270. Benolte et al. *Four Vis. of Berkshire 1532, 1566, 1623 & 1665–6* 2 (H.S.P. 57) (1908): 203–205 (Reade ped.: "Eliz: da: and heire to Wm Wichingham *William de Echingham. 2d wife.* = Tho: Lo: Hoo ob. 23 Aug : 1420. = Ellenor da: to Thomas Felton. *First wife.*"). Copinger *Manors of Suffolk* 2 (1908): 5–7. VCH *Bedford* 2 (1908): 348–375. VCH *Surrey* 3 (1911): 150–153. VCH *Hertford* 3 (1912): 39–44. *C.P.* 5 (1926): 292–294 (sub Felton); 6 (1926): 561–567 (sub Hoo); 12(2) (1959): 154 footnote f, 156 footnote f. Watkin *Inventory of Church Goods temp. Edward III* (Norfolk Rec. Soc. 19(2)) (1948): 172 (biog. of Sir Thomas de Saint Omer), 199 (biogs. of Lady Margaret de Walkfare and Lady Joan de Felton). *Coat of Arms* 6 (1961): 350–355. *Cal. Inqs. Misc.* 7 (1968): 280; 8 (2003): 250–251. VCH *Cambridge* 10 (2002): 426–437. Rose *Misericords of Norwich Cathedral* (2003): 12, 16, 44. Court of Common Pleas, CP 40/638, rot. 423 (available at http:// www.british-history.ac.uk/source.aspx?pubid=1272). East Sussex Rec. Office: Addl. MSS, Cat. J, AMS5647/5, AMS5647/6, AMS5647/7 (available at www.a2a.org.uk/search/index.asp).

(available at www.a2a.org.uk/search/index.asp). Court of Common Pleas, CP 40/659, rot. 425 (available at www.british-history.ac.uk/source.aspx?pubid=1272).

11. JOAN UFFORD, daughter and co-heiress, minor in 1402. She married after 29 Sept. 1402 (as his 1st wife) **WILLIAM BOWET**, Knt., of Blackhall, Botcherby, and Stainton, Cumberland, and, in right of his wife, of Wrentham, Benacre, and Henstead, Suffolk, Burgh St. Margaret, Great Hautbois, and Horsford, Norfolk, and Hurstpierpoint, Sussex, son and heir of Thomas Bowet, of Blackhall, Botcherby, and Stainton, Cumberland, by his wife, Margaret. They had one daughter, Elizabeth. His wife, Joan, was co-heiress c.1401 to her great-grandmother, Lady Ela de Pierrepont, and sole heiress after 29 Sept. 1402 to her older sister, Ela, wife of Richard Bowet, Esq. Joan presented to the rectory of Benacre, Suffolk jointly with her husband in 1409. In 1409–10 William and his wife, Joan, settled the manor of Horsford, Norfolk on trustees. In 1411 he and his wife, Joan, sued Thomas Aleyn and his brothers., William and Richard, regarding unjust disseisin in Henstead, Suffolk. He presented alone to the rectory of Hurstpierpont, Sussex in 1413. He and his wife, Joan, presented to the church of Benacre, Suffolk in 1409, and he alone in 1418. He was a witness of the will of Robert Ty, Knt., of Barsham, Suffolk in 1414. At some unknown date, he and two others were sued in Chancery by John Frelond and William Scardeburgh, vintners, of London regarding goods, etc., of the ship Leonard of Newcastle-on-Tyne wrecked near Fissherdepe. He married (2nd) before 1 Feb. 1417/8 **AMY** (or **AMICE**) **WYTHE**, widow of John Calthorpe, Knt. (died 1415), and daughter and heiress of John Wythe, Knt., of Smallborough, Norfolk, by Sibyl, daughter and heiress of Edmund Saint Omer, Knt. They had one daughter, Sibyl (wife of Robert Osbern). He presented to the church of Blythburgh, Suffolk in 1418. He was wounded and taken prisoner at the Battle of Beaugé 22 March 1420/1. His wife, Amy, and the Convent presented to the church of Blythburgh, Suffolk in 1420 [1420/1 intended?]. SIR WILLIAM BOWET was living in May 1421, when he and his wife, Amy, obtained the wardship and marriage of Amy's son, William Calthorpe. SIR WILLIAM BOWET died soon afterwards, and was buried at Langley Abbey, Norfolk with his 1st wife, Joan. On 20 June 1422 his widow, Amy, leased the manor of Horsford, Norfolk for seven years to the Prior of St. Faith. On 14 Jan. 1422/3 she granted a cottage and land in Dilham, Norfolk to Geoffrey and John Haldeyn. Amy married (2nd) before 1427 **HENRY INGLOSE**, Knt., of Dilham, Norfolk, Knight of the Shire for Suffolk and Norfolk, son and heir of Henry Inglose, Knt., of Dilham, Norfolk, by Anne, daughter and heiress of Roger Gyney. They had no issue. He served in the retinue of King Henry V at the Battle of Agincourt in 1415. Henry was Lieutenant to John, Duke of Bedford, Admiral of England in 1428. In 1429 John, Bishop of Bath and Wells, appealed a judgment of his as Lieutenant of the Dukes of Norfolk and Suffolk given against the Almayne merchants. He was one of the knights present at the Council 24 Feb. 1439. His wife, Amy, was living in 1439–40. SIR HENRY INGLOSE died 1 July 1451. He left a will dated 20 June 1451, proved 4 July 1451, requesting burial at Horsham Priory, Norfolk.

Blomefield *Essay towards a Top. Hist. of Norfolk* 5 (1775): 1356–1357; 11 (1810): 153. Dugdale *Monasticon Anglicanum* 3 (1821): 636–637 (Priory of St. Faith at Horsham, Norfolk — Genealogia Fundatoris: "…Et dictus Robertus Ufford maritatus fuit Elionoræ filiæ Thomæ Felton militis, qui genuit Elam, Sibillam, et Joannam filias, quæ dicta Ela desponsata fuit Ricardo Bowes armigero, quæ obiit sine hærede, et Sibilla monialis de Berkinge, et prædicta Johanna nupta Willielmo Bowes armigero, fratri Ricardi Bowes prædicti, qui genuit ex ea filiam, nuptam domino Dacres, et genuit ex ea filiam nomine Johannam quæ nupta fuit Ricardo Fines militi, camerario domini regis Edwardi quarti"). *Coll. Top. et Gen.* 7 (1841): 197–202. Suckling *Hist. & Antiqs. of Suffolk* 2 (1847): 130, 161–162. *Top. & Gen.* 1 (1846): 299–300; 2 (1853): 271–277 (Ufford ped.). *Sussex Arch. Colls.* 11 (1859): 50–88. Waters *Chester of Chicheley* 1 (1878): 339–340. Glover et al. *Vis. of Cheshire 1580, 1566, 1533 & 1591* (H.S.P. 18) (1882): 90–91 (Clavering ped.: "Jone [Ufford] vxor Sr Wm Bowett."). *Norfolk Arch.* 9 (1884): 1, et seq. (re. Calthope fam.); 15 (1904): 267–292. Rye *Short Cal. Feet of Fines for Norfolk* 2 (1886): 400, 417, 418. Harvey et al. *Vis. of Norfolk 1563 & 1613* (H.S.P. 32) (1891): 65–66 (Calthrop ped.: "Sir John Calthrop, knight. = Ann da. & heir of John Withe."). *Genealogist* n.s. 16 (1899): 41. *Feudal Aids* 3 (1904): 569, 599. Wrottesley *Peds. from the Plea Rolls* (1905): 270. Parker "Cal. of Feet of Fines for Cumberland" in *Trans. Cumberland & Westmorland Antiq. Soc.* n.s. 7 (1907): 246. Copinger *Manors of Suffolk* 2 (1908): 5–7, 42–43, 86–87. Rede *Reg. of Robert Rede Bishop of Chichester* (Sussex Rec. Soc. 11) (1910): 322–323. Thompson *Vis. of Religious Houses in the Diocese of Lincoln* (Lincoln Rec. Soc. 14) (1914): 219. Wedgwood *Hist. of Parl.* 1 (1936): 492–493 (biog. of Sir Henry Ingles). VCH *Sussex* 7 (1940): 116–119, 172–178. Watkin *Inventory of Church Goods temp. Edward III* (Norfolk Rec. Soc. 19(2)) (1948): 189 (biog. of Sir William Bowet) (Bowet arms: Argent, three stags heads caboshed sable). *Coat of Arms* 6 (1961): 350–355.Richmond *Paston Fam. in the 15th Cent.: First Phase* (1990): 216-218. National Archives, C 146/230 (grant dated 20 Jan. 1422/3 by Amy, late the wife of William Bowet, Knt., to Geoffrey Haldeyn, vicar of Dilham, and John Haldeyn, of Becklys, of land with a cottage thereon in Dilham, Norfolk); C 1/6/311 (Chancery Proc. dated 1404–7, 1413–17, or 1424–6 — John Frelond and William Scardeburgh, vintners, of London. v. George Felbrig, Knt. William Bowet, Knt. and Henry Inglose, Esq. re. goods &c., of the ship Leonard of Newcastle-on-Tyne, wrecked near Fissherdepe, the crew being saved); C 1/19/40 (Chancery Proc. dated 1452-4 — Robert Osbern and Sibil, his wife, daughter of Sir William Bowet, Knt., deceased v. Edmund Wichingham, Robert Inglose, and Sir John Parram, priest, executors of Sir Henry Inglose, Knt., husband of Dame Amy Bowet, deceased, mother of the said Sibyl re. money arising from the sale of said Sibil's wardship and marriage and the half of the manors of Blackhall, Botcherby (Botchardby) and Stainton, Cumberland by the said Sir William to lord Dacres); C 1/21/44 & C 1/22/157 (Chancery Proc. dated 1452-4 — Robert Osbern, Esq., of Barking. v. Dame Elizabeth Daker [Dacre], and Henry Inglose, and John Colvyle, Knts., and other feoffees re. profits of the manor of Great Hautbois, Norfolk, being the dower of petitioner's wife Sibyl, sister of the said Dame Elizabeth) (available at www.catalogue.nationalarchives. gov.uk/search.asp).

Child of Joan Ufford, by William Bowet, Knt.:

i. **ELIZABETH BOWET**, married **THOMAS DACRE**, Knt. [see DACRE 14.i].

❧ CLERMONT ✥

1. HUGUES, seigneur of Clermont, Breuil-le-Vert, Creil, Gournay, Luzarches, and Mouchy-Saint-Elou, son and heir of Renaud, seigneur of Clermont, Chamberlain of France for King Henri I, by his wife, Ermentrude. He married about 1080 **MARGUERITE DE MONTDIDIER**, daughter of Hildouin (or (or Hellouin) II, Count of Montdidier, by Alix, daughter of Eblès I, Count of Reims and Roucy. They had four sons, Renaud (II) [seigneur of Clermont, later Count of Clermont-en-Beauvaisis), Guy, Hugues le Pauvre, and Raoul [Canon of Beauvais], and five daughters, Ermentrude (wife of Hugues d'Avranches, Earl of Chester), Alice, Marguerite (wife of Gérard de Gerberoy), Richilde (wife of Dreux II, seigneur of Mello), and Béatrice (wife of Mathieu, Count of Beaumont-sur-Oise). He witnessed a grant of his father, Renaud, to Fécamp Abbey. At an unknown date, as "Hugues, son of Renaud the Chamberlain," he granted the monks of Fécamp free passage of their ships through Creil. Sometime after 1067 he approved the gift to Engelard, abbot of St. Martin des Champs, by his cousin Waleran the Chamberlain, of half of the land of Rungis. In the period, 1096–99, he gave the Abbey of Saint-Germer-de-Flay the church of Breuil-le-Vert and the tithes of Villiers-St.-Leu. HUGUES, seigneur of Clermont, died between 1101 and 1103. Following his death, his daughter, Alice, wife of Gilbert de Clare, styled "daughter of Hugues de Clermont," founded an anniversary at the Priory of Saint-Leu d'Esserent for herself and for her parents, Hugues and Marguerite.

Revue Historique Nobiliaire et Biographique 3rd Ser. 1 (1876): 273–275. Delisle *Recueil des Historiens des Gaules et de la France* 14 (1877): 7 (Genealogia Regum Francorum Tertiae Stirpis: "Secundam filiam præfati Comitis Helduini de Rameruth, dictam Margaretam, duxit Hugo Comes de Claromonte, de qua nati sunt Guido dictus Qui-non-dormit, et Hugo Paper, et Comes Rainaldus, et sorores eorum. Rainaldus duxit Adelidem Comitissam Viromandensium, defuncto priore viro suo, scilicet Hugone Magno, quæ peperit ei filiam Margaretam, quam duxit Comes Karolus Flandriæ; quo mortuo, tradita est Comiti Sancti-Pauli Hugoni, qui dictus est Campus-avenæ. Prædictus Rainaldus, defuncta Adelide, duxit Comitissam de Dammartin, filiam Comitis de Rainaldi de Monzuns, de qua genuit Guidonem, et Rainaldum, et Hugonem archidiaconum Metensem, et Galterum, cum aliis utriusque sexus. Unda sororum Comitis Rainaldi nupsit in Anglia Comiti Hugoni de Cestre; alteram duxit Gislebertus filius Richardi Anglici; tertiam copulavit sibi Matthæus Comes de Bellomonte, de qua genuit alterum Matthæum Comitem, et fratrem ejus, et filias."). Lépinois *Recherches historiques et critiques sur l'ancient Comté et les Comtes de Clermont en Beauvoisis* (1877). Luçay *Le Comté de Clermont en Beauvaisis* (1878): 9–11 ("Ni Suger, ni les chartes que nous avons eues sous les yeux, ne donnent à Hugues le titre de comte; elles le qualifient seulement seigneur de Clermont."). *Monumenta Germaniæ Historica* SS XIII (1881): 251–256: (Genealogiæ Scriptoris Fusniacensis: "Secundam filiam prefati comitis Helduini de Rameruth dictam Margaretam duxit Hugo comes de Claro-monte; de qua nati sunt Guido dictus Qui-non-dormit et Hugo Pauper et comes Rainaldus et sorores eorum."); SS XXIII (1925): 793–794 (Chronica Alberici Monachi Trium Fontium:"Tertia soror Margareta comiti Hugoni de Claromonte Baluacensis peperit comitem Renaldeum et sorores eius, et quarum una fuerent comites Bellimontis."). Muller *Prieuré de Saint-Leu d'Esserent: Cartulaire* 1 (Pubs. Soc. Hist. du Vexin) (1900): 34–36 (testament of Marguerite de Gerberoy "daughter of Hugues de Clermont" [filia Hugonis de Claromonte], who having arranged for her burial at the Priory of Saint-Leu d'Esserent, gave the Priory the sixth part of the tithe of Courlaye for the foundation of her anniversary; this document mentions her husband, Gerard; Pierre son of the said Gerard; and Count Renaud brother of the said Marguerite), 44 (charter of Adelaide de Clermont, wife of Gilbert de Anglia [Hadalaidis, filia Hugonis de Claromonte, scilicet uxor Gisleberti de Anglia]), 195. Depoin *Cartulaire de l'Abbaye de Saint-Martin de Pontoise* 3 (1904): 302–305. Brandenburg *Die Nachkommen Karls des Großen* (1935) Teil II XI 220. Winter *Descs. of Charlemagne (800–1400)* (1987): XI.199. Schwennicke *Europäische Stammtafeln* 3(4) (1989): 653 (sub Clermont).

Children of Hugues de Clermont, by Marguerite de Montdidier:

i. **RENAUD II**, seigneur of Clermont, afterwards Count of Clermont-en-Beauvaisis [see next].

ii. **ALICE DE CLERMONT**, married (1st) **GILBERT FITZ RICHARD** (also styled **DE CLARE**, **DE TONBRIDGE**), of Clare, Suffolk, Tonbridge, Kent, etc. [see CLARE 2]; (2nd) **BOUCHARD DE MONTMORENCY**, seigneur of Montmorency [see CLARE 2].

2. RENAUD II, seigneur of Clermont, afterwards Count of Clermont-en-Beauvaisis, Châtelain of Creil, and, in right of his 1st wife, Count of Vermandois, son and heir. He went on Crusade in 1099. He married (1st) before 1104 **ADÈLE DE VERMANDOIS**, Countess of Vermandois, widow of Hugues *le Grand*, Count of Crépy (died 1101) [see VERMANDOIS 4], and daughter of Heribert IV, Count of Vermandois, by Adèle, daughter of Raoul III, Count of Valois. She was born about 1065. They had one daughter, Marguerite (wife of Charles *le Bon*, Count of Flanders, Hugues II Candevène, Count of Saint-Pol, and Baudouin d'Encre). In 1115 he granted a fair of three days at Saint-Jean to the collégiale of Clermont. His wife, Adèle, died 28 September, between 1120 and 1124. He married (2nd) **CLÉMENCE OF BAR**, daughter of Renaud I, Count of Bar-le-Duc, by Gisèle, daughter of Gérard, Count of Vaudémont. They had seven sons, Raoul (I) *le Roux* [Count of Clermont, Constable of France], Simon, Chev., Étienne, Guy, Renaud, Hugues [Dean of Metz, Abbot of Saint-Germer, Saint-Lucien, and Cluny], and Gautier, and three daughters, Marguerite (wife of Guy III de Senlis, seigneur of Chantilly, Boutillier of France), Mahaut (or Mathilde), and Comtesse (wife of Rogues de la Tournelle). In 1152 he confirmed the gifts of his parents, Hugues and Marguerite, and Hugh and Richard, Earls of Chester, to St.-Leu d'Esserent. RENAUD II, Count of Clermont-en-Beauvaisis, died before 1162. His widow, Clémence, married (3rd) **THIBAUT III DE NANTEUIL**, seigneur of Nanteuil-le-Haudouin and Crépy, son and heir of Thibaut II, seigneur of Nanteuil-le-Haudouin and Crépy, by his 1st wife, Mathilde. They had three sons, Philippe [seigneur of Nanteuil-le-Haudouin], Guy [seigneur of Bouillancy], and Gautier (or Gaucher). THIBAUT III DE NANTEUIL died 20 Jan. 1183. His widow, Clémence, was living in 1185.

Carlier *Histoire du Duché de Valois* 1 (1764): 346–352, 394–398. Teulet *Layettes du Trésor des Chartes* 2 (1866): 282 (Mahaut de Dammartin, Countess of Boulogne, styled "kinswoman" [consanguinea] by Philippe de Nanteuil, Knt. in 1235 [editor states it is Nanteuil-le-Haudoin, Oise, arr. de Senlis in Valois]). *Revue Historique Nobiliaire et Biographique* 3rd Ser. 1 (1876): 275–281. Delisle *Recueil des Historiens des Gaules et de la France* 14 (1877): 7 (Genealogia Regum Francorum Tertiae Stirpis: "Secundam filiam præfati Comitis Helduini de Rameruth, dictam Margaretam, duxit Hugo Comes de Claromonte, de qua nati sunt Guido dictus Qui-non-dormit, et Hugo Paper, et Comes Rainaldus, et sorores eorum. Rainaldus duxit Adelidem Comitissam Viromandensium, defuncto priore viro suo, scilicet Hugone Magno, quæ peperit ei filiam Margaretam, quam duxit Comes Karolus Flandriæ; quo mortuo, tradita est Comiti Sancti-Pauli Hugoni, qui dictus est Campus-avenæ. Prædictus Rainaldus, defuncta Adelide, duxit Comitissam de Dammartin, filiam Comitis de Rainaldi de Monzuns, de qua genuit Guidonem, et Rainaldum, et Hugonem archidiaconum Metensem, et Galterum, cum aliis utriusque sexus. Unda sororum Comitis Rainaldi nupsit in Anglia Comiti Hugoni de Cestre; alteram duxit Gislebertus filius Richardi Anglici; tertiam copulavit sibi Matthæus Comes de Bellomonte, de qua genuit alterum Matthæum Comitem, et fratrem ejus, et filias."). Lépinois *Recherches historiques et critiques sur l'ancient*

Comté et les Comtes de Clermont en Beauvoisis (Mémoires de la Société Académique d'Archéologie, Sciences & Arts du Département de l'Oise 10) (1877): 21, footnote 1 ["D. Brial, s'étayant sur ces mots de la Généalogie des rois de la troisième race: Rainaldus defuncta Adelide, duxit comitissam da Dammartin (Hist. de France, XIV, 7), pense que Clémence était veuve du comte de Dammatin lors de son mariage avec Renaud de Clermont. L'Art de vérifier les dates, le P. Anselme (Hist. généal., II, 268), A. Duchesne (Hist. de la maison de Bar), disent au contraire que Clémence ne devint comtesse de Dammatin qu'après la mort de Renaud. L'opinion de D. Brial est confirmée par une charte sans date, mais parfaitement authentique, par laquelle Clémence, comtesse de Dammartin, et Guy, son fils, approuvaient la donation d'un bois faite à l'abbaye de Chaalis par Gautier de Alneto, leur sénéchal, en présence de Renaud, seigneur de Clermont (arch. de l'Oise: Fonds de Chaalis, charmant petite charte avec sceau de la comtesse, assez frustre, mais sur lequel on lit distinctement Artini com. Guy de Dammattin, fils de Clémence et de Lancelin, comte de Dammartin, n'est pas mentionné dans l'Art de vérifier les dates. Il est probable qu'il mourut jeune, car on ne connaît aucun acte de lui comme comte de Dammartin."]. Luçay *Comté de Clermont en Beauvaisis* (1878): 11–17. Muller *Prieuré de Saint-Leu d'Esserent: Cartulaire* 1 (Pubs. Soc. Hist. du Vexin) (1900): 45 (charter of Renaud, Count of Clermont [R(enaldus) Claromontensis comes]), 45–47, 195, 197 (Dammartin ped.). Depoin *Cartulaire de l'Abbaye de Saint-Martin de Pontoise* 3 (1904): 302–305. Brandenburg *Die Nachkommen Karls des Großen* (1935) XII/346-353, XIII/98-104 (do). Winter *Descs. of Charlemagne (800–1400)* (1987): XI.17, XII.29, XII.317, XIII.224, XIII.510-XIII.516, XIV.328-XIV.330. Schwennicke *Europäische Stammtafeln* 3(4) (1989): 653 (sub Clermont); 6 (1978): 147 (ancestry of Clementia of Bar). Power *Norman Frontier in the 12th & Early 13th Cents.* (2004): 256–259.

Child of Renaud II de Clermont, by Clémence of Bar:

i. **RAOUL (I)** le Roux, Count of Clermont, Constable of France, Châtelain de Creil, and, in right of his wife, of seigneur of Breteuil-en-Beauvaisis. He married before 1162 (date of charter) **ALIX** (or **AELIS**) **DE BRETEUIL**, daughter and co-heiress of Waleran (or Valéran) III, seigneur of Breteuil-en-Beauvaisis, by his 1st wife Holdeburge (or Hildeburge), lady of Ailly sur Noie and Tartigny, and daughter of _____, by his wife, Béatrice. They had one son, Raoul, and three daughters, Catherine (or Katherine), Mathilde (or Mahaut) (wife of Guillaume I, seigneur of Vierzon), and Alice. In 1175 he joined Count Baudouin V in his expedition against Jacques d'Avesnes. RAOUL, Count of Clermont, was killed in battle at Acre 15 October 1191. His widow, Alice, Countess of Clermont, lady of Breteuil, was living in 1195. At her death, she was buried in the church of the Priory of Variville. Peigné-Delacourt *Cartulaire de l'Abbaye de Notre-Dame d'Ourscamp* (1865): 157 (charter of Raoul, Count of Clermont dated 1178; charter granted with consent of his wife, Alix [Adelidis], and his daughters, Katherine and Alix [Adelidis]; charter witnessed by his brother, Simon, and his nephew/kinsman [nepotis], Pierre of Amiens), 158 (charter of Raoul, Count of Clermont dated 1162; charter mentions his wife, Alix [Adelidis], and his sister, Mathilde; his brothers, Simon and Étienne, give their consent), 161–162 (charter of Raoul, Count of Clermont dated 1177). *Revue Historique Nobiliaire et Biographique* 3rd Ser. 1 (1876): 282–294. Lépinois *Recherches historiques et critiques sur l'ancient Comté et les Comtes de Clermont en Beauvoisis* (Mémoires de la Société Académique d'Archéologie, Sciences & Arts du Département de l'Oise 10) (1877). Luçay *Comté de Clermont en Beauvaisis* (1878): 18–30. *Mémoires de la Société Académique d'Archéologie, Sciences et Arts du département de l'Oise* 10(3) (1879): 677 (agreement dated 1174 between Lannoy Abbey and Raoul, Count of Clermont), 678. *Mémoires de la Société de l'Histoire de Paris et de l'Île de France* 10 (1884): 191–242. Toulgoët-Tréanna *Histoire de Vierzon* (1884): 105–109. *Recueil des Historiens des Gaules et de la France* 23 (1894): 421 (Ex Obituario Gemmeticensi: "4 Oct. [Obiit] Radulfus, comes Clari Montis."). Muller *Prieuré de Saint-Leu d'Esserent: Cartulaire* 1st Pt. (1900): 82 (Renaud de Haute-Pierre, Prior of Saint-Leu, styled "kinsman" [consanguineum] by Raoul, Count of Clermont in charter dated 1176). Vernier *Chartes de l'Abbaye de Jumièges* 2 (1916): 3–5 (charter of Raoul, Count of Clermont, dated 1170; charter witnessed by his brother, Simon). Schwennicke *Europäische Stammtafeln* 3(4) (1989): 653 (sub Clermont). Power *Norman Frontier in the 12th & Early 13th Cents.* (2004): 490 (Breteuil ped.).

Child of Raoul I de Clermont, by Alix de Breteuil:

   a. **CATHERINE** (or **KATHERINE**) **DE CLERMONT**, married **LOUIS**, Count of Blois and Clermont, seigneur of Breteuil [see WYDEVILLE 4.i].

ii. **SIMON I DE CLERMONT** (or **D'AILLY**), Chev. [see next].

iii. **MAHAUT** (or **MATHILDE**) **OF CLERMONT**, married **AUBREY II DE DAMMARTIN**, Count of Dammartin [see DAMMARTIN 3].

3. SIMON DE CLERMONT (or **D'AILLY**), Chev., in right of his wife, seigneur of Ailly sur Noie and Tartigny, 2nd son. He married **MAHAUT** (or **MATHILDE**) **DE BRETEUIL**, daughter and co-heiress of Waleran III, seigneur of Breteuil-en-Beauvaisis, by his 1st wife, Hildeburge (or Holdeburge), lady of Ailly sur Noie and Tartigny. They had two sons, Raoul [seigneur of Ailly-sur-Noye] and Guy, and two daughters, Jeanne (or Beatrice) (wife of Baldwin de Darges) and Clémence (wife of Simon de Beausault). In 1162 he consented to a grant of his brother, Raoul, Count of Clermont, to the Abbey of Notre-Dame d'Ourscamp. He witnessed a charter of his brother, Raoul, Count of Clermont, to Jumièges dated 1170. In 1174 Raoul, Count of Clermont, seigneur of Breteuil reached agreement with Lannoy Abbey concerning his fiefs in Monceaux-l'Abbaye; this agreement was made with the consent of his wife, Countess Alix, his daughter, Katherine, and his brother, Simon, with his wife, Mathilde. In 1176 he consented to a grant of his brother, Raoul, Count of Clermont, to the Priory of Saint-Leu d'Esserent. In 1178 he witnessed a charter of his brother, Raoul, Count of Clermont, to the Abbey of Notre-Dame d'Ourscamp. SIMON DE CLERMONT was living in 1187. In 1193 Thibaut, Bishop of Amiens stated that he had received a charter granted by Simon d'Ailly, his wife Mathilde, and their sons, Raoul and Guy, concerning a gift of grain from the tithes of Ailly to the Priory of Saint-Leu d'Esserent. His widow, Mahaut, died 14 March 1208.

Peigné-Delacourt *Cartulaire de l'Abbaye de Notre-Dame d'Ourscamp* (1865): 157 (charter of Raoul, Count of Clermont dated 1178; charter granted with consent of his wife, Alix [Adelidis], and his daughters, Katherine and Alix [Adelidis]; charter witnessed by his brother, Simon, and his nephew/kinsman [nepotis], Pierre of Amiens), 158 (charter of Raoul, Count of Clermont dated 1162; charter mentions his wife, Alix [Adelidis], and his sister, Mathilde; his brothers, Simon and Étienne, give their consent). *Revue Historique Nobiliaire et Biographique* 3rd Ser. 1 (1876): 283–284 ("Simon, lequel épousa la belle-sœur de son frère, Mahaud ou Mathilde, fille puînée de Valeran IV de Breteuil. Il devint par son mariage seigneur d'Ailly-sur-Noye et de Tartigny en Picardie et fut la tige des Clermont d'Ailly et Clermont Nesle, seigneurs d'Offémont et de Mello, qui ne s'éteignirent que dans le courant du seizième siècle."). Luçay *Comté de Clermont en Beauvaisis* (1878): 14–15, 41. *Mémoires de la Société Académique d'Archéologie, Sciences et Arts du département de l'Oise* 10(3) (1879): 677 (agreement dated 1174 between Lannoy Abbey and Raoul, Count of Clermont), 678. *Mémoires de la Société de l'Histoire de Paris et de l'Île de France* 10 (1884): 191–242. *Prieuré de Saint-Leu d'Esserent: Cartulaire* 1 (Pubs. Soc. Hist. du Vexin) (1900): 81–82 (charter of Raoul, Count of Clermont dated 1176; charter granted with consent of his brothers, Hugues, Dean of Metz, and Simon, Chev.), 86, 90. Vernier *Chartes de l'Abbaye de Jumièges* 2 (1916): 3–5 (charter of Raoul, Count of Clermont, dated 1170; charter witnessed by his brother, Simon). Winter *Descs. of Charlemagne (800–1400)* (1987): XIII.514, XIV.727-XIV.730, XIV.821. Schwennicke *Europäische Stammtafeln* 3(4) (1989): 654 (sub Clermont). Power *Norman Frontier in the 12th & Early 13th Cents.* (2004): 256–259, 490 (Breteuil ped.).

4. RAOUL DE CLERMONT, seigneur of Ailly-sur-Noye. He married before 1203 **GERTRUDE DE NESLE**, widow of Renaud de Mello, of Mello (died 1201), and daughter of Jean I, seigneur of Nesle-en-Picardie, Falvy-sur-Somme, and La Hérelle, Châtelain of Bruges, by Elisabeth, daughter of Johann de Peteghem, lord of Peteghem. They had eight children, including five sons, Jean, Simon, Chev., Thibaut [canon of Beauvais], Renaud [Bishop of Beauvais], and Raoul [seigneur of Ailly], and one daughter, Mahaut. In 1223 he renounced his rights to the county of Clermont to Philippe *dit* Hurepel, Count of Boulogne and Clermont, and King Louis of France. RAOUL DE CLERMONT, seigneur of Ailly-sur-Noye, died 30 March 1225/26. His widow, Gertrude, was heiress in 1239 to her brother, Jean, seigneur of Nesle. She died after June 1239.

Du Chesne *Prevves de l'Histoire de la Maison de Montmorency* (1624): 338–339 (Raoul de Clermont, seigneur of Ailly, occurs in charter dated March 1224). *La Picardie, Revue Littéraire et Scientifique* 4 (1858): 137–142 (Clermont-Nesle arms: Gueles à deux bars adossés d'or, semé de trèfles de même). Lépinois *Recherches Historiques et Critiques sur l'Ancien Comté et les Comtes de Clermont en Beauvoisis* (1877): 490–491 (charter of Raoul de Clermont). Piton *Histoire de Paris: le Quartier des Halles* (1891): 278 (Clermont ped.). Birch *Cat. Seals in the British Museum* 5 (1898): 528 (seal of Raoul de Clermont dated 1203 — To the right. In armour, with hauberk of mail, short surcoat or tunic, cap-shaped helmet, sword, and shield of arms: five garbs in cross. Horse springing. Legend: SIGILL' RADVLPHI DE : CLAROMONTE.). Winter *Descs. of Charlemagne (800–1400)* (1987): XIV.456, XIV.727; (1991): XV.644-XV.651. Schwennicke *Europäische Stammtafeln* 3(4) (1989): 654 (sub Clermont); 7 (1979): 16 (ancestry of Gertrude de Nesle). Power *Norman Frontier in the 12th & Early 13th Cents.* (2004): 490 (Breteuil ped.).

5. SIMON DE CLERMONT, Chev., seigneur of Nesle, Beaulieu-les-Fontaines, and Ailly-sur-Noye, Constable of France. He married before February 1242 **ALIX DE MONTFORT**, daughter of Amaury VI, Duke of Narbonne, Count of Toulouse, Vicomte of Béziers and Carcasonne, Count of Montfort-l'Amaury, Constable of France, by Béatrix, daughter of André of Burgundy, Dauphin of Viennois, Count of Albon, Grenoble, etc. They had five sons, Raoul [Vicomte of Châteaudun, Constable of France], Guy [seigneur of Breteuil and Offemont, Marshal of France), Amaury [Prevost of St. Pierre de Lille, Canon of Beauvais], and Simon [Bishop of Noyon and Beauvais], and Jean, and one daughter, Béatrix (wife of Jean IV, Châtelain of Lille). His wife, Alix, was given the manor of Houdan in partage in 1248. He was appointed Regent of the kingdom with the Abbot of Saint-Denis in 1270, on the departure of the king for Tunis. His wife, Alix, died testate 28 May 1279, and was buried at Beaupré. SIMON DE CLERMONT, seigneur of Nesle, died 1 Feb. 1286.

La Picardie, Revue Littéraire et Scientifique 4 (1858): 137–142 (charter of Simon de Clermont seigneur of Nesle dated 1241; charter names his uncle [oncle], Jean, seigneur of Nesle). *Musée des Archives Nationales: Docs. originaux de l'Histoire de France* (1872): 155–156. Piton *Histoire de Paris: le Quartier des Halles* (1891): 278 (Clermont ped.). *Revue de Bretagne de Vendée & d'Anjou* 16 (1896): 37 ("Nous avons vu Houdan donné en partage à Alix en 1248, quand elle épousa Simon de Clermont, seigneur de Nesle"). Schwennicke *Europäische Stammtafeln* 3(4) (1989): 642 (sub Montfort-l'Amaury), 654 (sub Clermont). *Winter Descs. of Charlemagne (800–1400)* (1991) XV.645 & XV.2035.

6. RAOUL DE CLERMONT, seigneur of Nesle, Ailly, Beaulieu-les-Fontaines, Bray-sur-Somme, and Briost, Constable of France, and, in right of his 1st wife, Vicomte of Châteaudun. He married (1st) before 1268 **ALIX DE DREUX**, daughter of Robert de Dreux, Vicomte of Châteaudun, seigneur of Bû, Nesle-en-Tardenois, etc., by his 1st wife, Clémence, daughter and co-heiress of Geoffroi VI de Châteaudun, Vicomte of Châteaudun [see DREUX 9 for her ancestry]. She was born about 1255. They had three daughters, Alix (or Aelis), Isabeau (wife of Hugh Larchévêque, seigneur of Montfort-le-Rotrou) and Beatrice (or Béatrix). In 1270 he participated in the crusade against Tunis launched by King Louis IX of France. In 1283 he was put in command of troops sent against the King of Aragón. His wife, Alix, died before January 1292/3. In 1294 he defended Bordeaux against the attacks of the king of England. The following year he was sent by the king with his army to the aid of the Count of Valois during the Siege of Riole. He married (2nd) before 9 June 1297 **ISABELLE OF HAINAULT**, daughter of Jean (or Jan) II d'Avesnes, Count of Hainault, Holland, and Zeeland, lord of Friesland, by Philippe (or Philippine), daughter of Henri V, Count of Luxembourg and La Roche, Marquis of Arlon [see HAINAULT 8 for her ancestry]. They had no issue. He fought in Guyenne in 1296. RAOUL DE CLERMONT, seigneur of Nesle, was slain at the Battle of Courtrai 11 July 1302, and was buried in the Abbey of Beaupré. In 1303 his widow, Isabelle, did homage for the land of Briost and its appurtenances, which had been given to her by grant of her late husband. His widow, Isabelle, died testate in December 1305.

Duchesne *Histoire Généalogique de la Maison Royale de Dreux* (1631): 129–145. Bernier *Histoire de Blois* (1682): 223–228. Rymer *Foedera* 1 (1816): 512 (Raoul de Clermont styled "cousin" by King Edward I of England). Cartier *Recherches sur les Monnaies au type Chartrain* (1846): 112–117. *Compte rendu des Séances de la Commission Royale d'Histoire* 2nd Ser. 4 (1852): 13–14, 30, 32–33, 40, 41–42 (Isabelle, widow of R[aoul] de Clermont, seigneur of Nesle, Constable of France, styled "daughter of the Count of Hainault" in record dated 1303), 49–50 (late Isabelle, lady of Nesle, styled "sister" [sœur] of Jean of Hainault in record dated 6 March 1306), 76–77, 102–103, 111. *La Picardie, Revue Littéraire et Scientifique* 4 (1858): 137–142. Magen & Tholin *Archives municipales d'Agen: Chartes 1st Ser. (1189–1328)* (1876): 140 (lettres of Philippe, King of France to Raoul de Clermont, seigneur of Nesle, Constable of France dated 1293), 173 (letter of the Consuls of Agen to Raoul de Clermont, Constable of France, seigneur of Nesle, dated 1293). *Bulletins de la Société Dunoise* 8 (1896): 112–113. Birch *Cat. Seals in the British Museum* 5 (1898): 528 (seal of Raoul de Clermont dated 1292 — Obverse. To the right. In armour, with hauberk of mail, surcoat, helmet crested with a fan-plume on which is a lion rampant contourné, queue fourchée, sword, and a shield of arms. Horse springing, armorially caparisoned. The armorial bearings of the shield and caparisons are: two bars addorsed, on a field semé of trefoils slipped, NESLE, or NEELLE. Legend: S' RADVLPHI : DE : CL........ DE : NIGELLA. Beaded borders. Reverse. A smaller round counterseal. A shield of arms, as described in the obverse. Legend: * CONT · S · RADVLPHI · DNI · DE · NIGELLA.). Schwennicke *Europäische Stammtafeln* 3(1) (1984): 64 (sub Dreux); 3(4) (1989): 654 (sub Clermont). Winter *Descs. of Charlemagne (800–1400)* (1991) XVI.937 & XVI.3093. Van Kerrebrouck *Les Capétians 987–1328* (2000): 327.

Children of Raoul de Clermont, by Alix de Dreux:

i. **ALIX DE CLERMONT**, married (1st) **GUILLAUME OF FLANDERS**, Chev., seigneur of Termonde, Arleux, Crèvecœur, and Richebourg [see TERMONDE 8]; (2nd) **JEAN DE CHÂLON**, Chev., seigneur of Arlay and Nesle [see TERMONDE 8].

  ii. **BEATRICE** (or **BÉATRIX**) **DE CLERMONT**, married **AYMER DE VALENCE**, Knt., Earl of Pembroke, Lord of Wexford and Montignac [see MARSHALL 5.iii].

❧ CLIFFORD ☙

RICHARD FITZ GILBERT, of Clare, Suffolk, married **ROHESE GIFFARD**.
GILBERT FITZ RICHARD, of Clare, Suffolk, married **ALICE DE CLERMONT**.
BALDWIN FITZ GILBERT, of Bourne, Lincolnshire, married **ALINE** (or **ADELINE**) **DE ROLLOS** [see WAKE 3].

4. ROHESE (or **ROSE**) **FITZ BALDWIN**, daughter and co-heiress, born about 1135 (aged 50 in 1185). She married **WILLIAM DE BUSSEY** (or **BUSSEI**), of Essendine, Rutland, son and heir of William de Bussey, by Hawise, sister of Walter Espec. They had two sons, Bartholomew and Walter, and two daughters, Cecily and Maud (wife of Hugh Wake). He was co-heir in 1158 to his uncle, Walter Espec. In 1162 he accounted for five marks of scutage in Buckinghamshire and Bedfordshire. WILLIAM DE BUSSEY died about 1165. His widow, Rose, married (2nd) before 1165 **BALDWIN BUELOT**. He was one of the king's ambassadors to Sicily in 1176, from which journey he never returned. His widow, Rose, was living in 1185. At an unknown date, she gave to the monks of St. Andrew, Northampton 12 acres of the demesne in Essendine, Rutland, together with 18 acres of her demesne and the tithes of the assarts in Essendine, Rutland.

Lipscomb *Hist. & Antiqs. of Buckingham* 2 (1847): 123–126. *Pubs. Bedfordshire Hist. Rec. Soc.* 11 (1927): 5–17, 20–23. Fowler *Cartulary of the Abbey of Old Wardon* (Pubs. Bedfordshire Hist. Rec. Soc. 13) (1930): 66, 294–295, 318, 326. VCH *Rutland* 2 (1935): 250–254. *C.P.* 12(2) (1959): 296, footnote d (sub Wake).

5. CECILY DE BUSSEY, married **JOHN DE BUILLI** (or **BUILLY**), of Kimberworth (in Rotherham), Yorkshire, Constable of Scarborough Castle, 1204, son of Richard de Builli, founder of Roche Abbey. They had two daughters, Joan (wife of Thomas Gravenel) and Idoine (wife of Robert de Vipont). His wife, Cecily, was co-heiress about 1182, to her brother, Walter de Bussey. In 1182 he and Hugh Wake accounted for a debt of Walter de Bussey for a fine of land. In 1195 he owed ten marks for acquittance of scutage and for not serving in the second army of Normandy. In 1198 he and his wife, Cecily, and Hugh Wake and his wife, Maud (Cecily's sister) sued the Abbot of Wardon for the church of Wardon, Bedfordshire; in 1200 the Abbot demanded against John and his wife, Cecily, a moiety of the church of St. Leonard in Wardon, Bedfordshire, which William de Bussey (father of Cecily) gave in alms. In 1200 Robert, Dean of Lincoln sued John and his wife, Cecily, and Hugh Wake and his wife, Maud (Cecily's sister) regarding the advowson of the church of Buckland, Buckinghamshire. In 1201 John held three fees of the Honour of Wardon. In 1205 his wife, Cecily, obtained custody of the land of Guy de Aselakesby in Aislaby, Yorkshire. At an unknown date, he gave the monks of St. John of Pontefract a half an acre of land with its toft in Kimberworth for a light in the chapel of St. Victor the Martyr. JOHN DE BUILLI died in 1213.

Lipscomb *Hist. & Antiqs. of Buckingham* 2 (1847): 123–126. *Third Rpt. of Royal Comm. on Hist. MSS* (1872): Appendix, 223 (charter of John de Builli). *Yorkshire Arch. & Topog. Jour.* 9 (1885):286–292. Holmes *Chartulary of St. John of Pontefract* 2 (Yorkshire Arch. Soc. Recs. 30) (1902): 528 (undated charter of John de Builli), 607–609 (Builli ped.), 654. *Curia Regis Rolls* 1 (1922): 76, 238, 278, 283, 346, 356, 471. *Pubs. Bedfordshire Hist. Rec. Soc.* 11 (1927): 5–16. VCH *Rutland* 2 (1935): 250–254.

6. IDOINE DE BUILLI, daughter and co-heiress. She married **ROBERT DE VIPONT**, of Appleby and Brough under Stainmoor, Westmorland, Temple Wycombe (in High Wycombe), Buckinghamshire, Prescote, Oxfordshire, etc., and, in right of his wife, of Eyworth, Bedfordshire,

Buckland, Buckinghamshire, and Essendine, Rutland, son of William de Vipont, by Maud, sister of Hugh de Morville. They had one son, John. In 1204 King John confirmed to him the inheritance of his mother. In 1220 he and his wife, Idoine, sued Alice, Countess of Eu, for the castle and town of Tickhill, Yorkshire; in 1222 Robert and Idoine consented to a final concord by which they acknowledged the right of the Countess to the Castle and Honour of Tickhill, saving and excepting the right to 6-½ knights' fees in Maltby Sandbeck and Kimberworth, Yorkshire and divers manors in Nottinghamshire. ROBERT DE VIPONT died in 1228. His widow, Idoine, died in 1241.

> Lipscomb *Hist. & Antiqs. of Buckingham* 2 (1847): 123–126. Shirley *Royal & Other Historical Letters Illustrative of the Reign of King Henry III* 1 (Rolls Ser. 27) (1862): 38 (Roger Bertram, Knt., styled "kinsman" [nepotis] by Robert de Vipont in 1219). Clark *Mediæval Military Architecture in England* 1 (1884): 292–293. *Yorkshire Arch. & Topog. Jour.* 9 (1885):286–292. Taylor *Old manorial Halls of Westmorland & Cumberland* (1892): 17–24. *Pubs. Bedfordshire Hist. Rec. Soc.* 11 (1927): 5–16. *Curia Regis Rolls* 10 (1949): 128; 17 (1991): 62–63. *Trans. Dumfriesshire & Galloway Nat. Hist. & Antiq. Soc.* 3rd Ser. 33 (1956): 91–106 (Vipont family). McAndrew *Scotland's Hist. Heraldry* (2006): 168.

7. JOHN DE VIPONT (or **VIEUXPONT**), of Appleby and Brough under Stainmoor, Westmorland, Eyworth, Bedfordshire, Buckland, Buckinghamshire, Prescote, Oxfordshire, Essendine, Rutland, Kimberworth (in Rotherham), Yorkshire, etc., son and heir. He married _____ **DE FERRERS**, daughter of William de Ferrers, Knt., 4th Earl of Derby, by Agnes, daughter of Hugh, Earl of Chester [see FERRERS 6 for her ancestry]. They had one son, Robert. JOHN DE VIPONT died shortly before 25 July 1241.

> *Coll. Top. et Gen.* 1 (1834): 256. Lipscomb *Hist. & Antiqs. of Buckingham* 2 (1847): 123–126. Clark *Mediæval Military Architecture in England* 1 (1884): 292–293. Taylor *Old manorial Halls of Westmorland & Cumberland* (1892): 17–24. *Cal. IPM* 2 (1906): 315–316 (Inq. post mortem of Roger de Leyburn). *C.P.R. 1232–1247* (1906): 255. VCH *Bedford* 2 (1908): 230–233. VCH *Buckingham* 2 (1908): 328; 3 (1925): 112–134. *C.P.R. 1258–1266* (1910): 327, 371, 551. Farrer *Honors & Knights' Fees* 1 (1923): 242. VCH *Rutland* 2 (1935): 250–254. VCH *Oxford* 10 (1972): 206–210. Power *Norman Frontier in the 12th & Early 13th Cents.* (2004): 528–529 (Vieuxpont ped.). National Archives, SC 8/172/8596 (available at www.catalogue.nationalarchives.gov.uk/search.asp).

8. ROBERT DE VIPONT, of Appleby, Westmorland, Eyworth, Bedfordshire, Buckland, Buckinghamshire, Staveley, Derbyshire, Perlethorpe, Nottinghamshire, Essendine, Rutland, Winderton (in Brailes), Warwickshire, Kimberworth (in Rotherham), Yorkshire, etc., son and heir, born about 1234 (a minor at his father's death in 1241, and came of age c.1254/6). He married after 19 Nov. 1242 **ISABEL FITZ JOHN**, daughter of John Fitz Geoffrey, Knt., of Shere, Surrey, Justiciar of Ireland, by Isabel, daughter of Hugh le Bigod, Earl of Norfolk [see VERDUN 8 for her ancestry]. They had two daughters, Isabel and Idoine (wife of Roger de Leybourne and John Cromwell, Knt., Lord Cromwell). In 1256 he made fine with the king by five marks of gold for having respite from his knighthood, and for having a charter for a market, fair, and warren. In 1258 he sued Walter, parson of Newbiggin, Northumberland for poaching in his deer park. The same year he fought in Wales. In 1258 John de Gravenel granted him by fine the manor of Eyworth, Bedfordshire, for which Robert granted him a moiety of the manor of Buckland, Buckinghamshire for life, except the hall, with 12 librates of land in Newbottle, Northamptonshire. He was one of the most violent of the barons in arms against King Henry III, he being an adherent of Simon de Montfort. His name occurs among the list of barons whose seal was required to ratify the peace between King Henry III and the barons in 1261. In 1263 he excused his absense as plaintiff in a plea in Westmorland on the ground of infirmity. ROBERT DE VIPONT died testate shortly before 5 July 1264.

> Nicolson & Burn *Hist. & Antiqs. of the Counties of Westmorland & Cumberland* 1 (1777): 265–292. Clutterbuck *Hist. & Antiqs. of Hertford* 1 (1815): 293 (chart). Montmorency-Morres *Genealogical Memoir of the Fam. of Montmorency* (1817): xxxii–xxxvi. *Coll. Top. et Gen.* 1 (1834): 256. Lipscomb *Hist. & Antiqs. of Buckingham* 2 (1847): 123–126. Eddison *Hist. of Worksop* (1854): 170–171. *Notes & Queries* 4th Ser. 3 (1869): 484–485 (Fitz Peter ped.). Aveling *Hist. of Roche Abbey* (1870): xxi–xxii. Taylor *Old manorial Halls of Westmorland & Cumberland* (1892): 17–24. *Genealogist* n.s. 13 (1896): 36–37. Prescott *Reg. of the Priory of Wetherhal* (Cumb. & West. Antiq. & Arch. Soc. Recs. 1) (1897): 328–330, 363–364. Wrottesley *Peds. from the Plea Rolls* (1905): 137–138. VCH *Bedford* 2 (1908): 230–233. VCH *Buckingham* 2 (1908): 328

(Vipont arms: Or six rings gules). Fowler *Cal. of Feet of Fines for Bedfordshire* (Pubs Bedfordshire Hist. Soc. 6 (1919): 168. Kingsford *Stonor Letters & Papers 1290–1483* 1 (Camden 3rd Ser. 29) (1919): 4. Foster *Final Concords of Lincoln from the Feet of Fines A.D. 1244–1272* 2 (Lincoln Rec. Soc. 17) (1921): 179–180. *C.P.* 5 (1926): 437 chart, 439–441 (sub FitzJohn). *Pubs. Bedfordshire Hist. Rec. Soc.* 11 (1927): 5–16. VCH *Rutland* 2 (1935): 250–254 (Vipont arms: Or six rings gules). Fowler *Cal. of IPM* 2 (Bedfordshire Hist. Rec. Soc. 19) (1937): facing 170 (Vipont chart 6). *Year Books of Edward II* 10 (Selden Soc. 63) (1947): 196–208. VCH *Warwick* 5 (1949): 17–26. *Trans. Dumfriesshire & Galloway Nat. Hist. & Antiq. Soc.* 3rd Ser. 33 (1956): 91–106. Paget *Baronage of England* (1957) 220: 1, 562: 4. Sanders *English Baronies* (1960): 103–104. VCH *Oxford* 10 (1972): 206–210. National Archives, SC 8/172/8596 (available at www.catalogue.nationalarchives.gov.uk/search.asp).

Children of Robert de Vipont, by Isabel Fitz John:

i. **ISABEL DE VIPONT** [see next].

ii. **IDOINE DE VIPONT**, younger daughter and co-heiress, born about 1259 (aged 25 in 1284). She married (1st) before 1276 **ROGER DE LEYBOURNE** (or **LEYBURNE**), in right of his wife, of Brough under Stainmoor, Westmorland, Buckland, Buckinghamshire, Perlethorpe, Nottinghamshire, Kimberworth (in Rotherham), Yorkshire, etc., younger son of Roger de Leybourne, Knt., of Elham, Kent, Steward of the King's Household, Warden of the Cinque Ports, Warden of the Forests beyond Trent. They had one son, John. In 1276–7 Emma wife of Alan de Galwithia arraigned an assize of mort d'ancestor against Roger and his wife, Idoine, touching a tenement in Kimberworth (in Rotherham), Yorkshire. In 1280–1 Thomas de Hellebek' arraigned an assize against Roger and his wife, Idoine, touching common of pasture in Brough-under-Stainmore, Westmorland. ROGER DE LEYBOURNE died shortly before 21 Feb. 1283/4. In 1293–4 his widow, Idoine, was summoned to answer the king by what warrant she claimed to have free warren in Bawtry, Kimberworth, and Austerfield, gallows, infangthief, and outgangthief in Bawtry, and a market and fair in Kimberworth, all in Yorkshire. She was co-heir in 1297 to her uncle, Richard Fitz John, Knt., Lord Fitz John. Idoine married (2nd) before 25 June 1302 (later dispensation dated 15 March 1317, they being related in the 4th degree of kindred) (as his 2nd wife) **JOHN DE CROMWELL**, Knt., of Carlton on Trent, Nottinghamshire, Beeston, Cheshire, Englefield, Flintshire, Hope, Shropshire, Austerfield, Yorkshire, etc., Constable of Chepstow Castle, 1307–8, Constable of the Tower of London, 1307/8, 1310–23, 1326/7–35, Justice of the Forest south of Trent, 1317, Admiral of the Fleet, 1324, and, in right of his 2nd wife, of Eyworth, Bedfordshire, Amersham, Buckland, and Singleborough (in Great Horwood), Buckinghamshire, Staveley, Derbyshire, Moulton, Cromwells (in Potterspury), and Yardley, Northamptonshire, Perlethorpe, Nottinghamshire, Essendine, Rutland, Winderton (in Brailes), Warwickshire, West Winterslow, Wiltshire, Kimberworth (in Rotherham) and Maltby, Yorkshire, etc., younger son of Ralph de Cromwell, Knt., of Cromwell, Nottinghamshire, by his 2nd wife, Margaret, daughter of Roger de Somery [see STAFFORD 4 for his ancestry]. They had no issue. He was engaged in the French and Scottish wars. In 1305 he accused Nicholas de Segrave, Knt. of treason and was defied by him to battle. He was summoned to Parliament 10 March 1307/8 to 1 April 1335, by writs directed *Johanni de Crumwell'* or *Crumbewell'*, whereby he is held to have become Lord Cromwell. In 1308 he and his wife, Idoine, obtained a grant of free warren in several manors including Kimberworth (in Rotherham), Yorkshire, Eyworth, Bedfordshire, Buckland, Buckinghamshire, and Essendine, Rutland. In 1313 he obtained a papal indult for a portable altar. In 1317 he and his wife, Idoine, obtained a papal indult to choose their confessors. In 1318 he complained that his park in Essendine, Rutland was broken into. In 1319 he and Robert de Umfreville, Knt. were appointed wardens of Northumberland, and the parts adjacent. In 1320–1 John and his wife, Idoine, settled various manors, including Amersham, Buckland, and Singleborough (in Great Horwood), Buckinghamshire, Moulton, Potterspury, and Yardley, Northamptonshire, Perlethorpe, Nottinghamshire, Essendine, Rutland, Winderton (in Brailes), Warwickshire, West Winterslow, Wiltshire, etc. on themselves for the life of Idoine, with successive remainders to Hugh le Despenser, Knt., the younger and Hugh le Despenser, Knt. the elder for life, and thence to Edward son of Hugh le Despenser, Knt. the younger and his heirs. He fought on the part of the king at the Battle of Boroughbridge 16 March 1321/2. In 1325 Robert de Wombwell and Robert Tree were fined £300 for damages done by wilful entry of the manors of Moulton and Yardley, Northamptonshire, where they devastated the goods and furniture of John de Cromwell and expelled him by force and arms. He was a supporter of Queen Isabel and fled abroad with her in 1326. That year King Edward II seized all of John's lands, including those held in right of his wife, because he stayed out of England without license. In August 1326 his wife, Idoine, was allowed to receive the issues and profits of the manors of Buckland, Buckinghamshire, Moulton, Northamptonshire, and Essendine, Rutland during pleasure, and to retain her own robes, beds, and jewels, and other things pertaining to her chamber. John probably returned to England early in the reign of King Edward III, as he was suing his bailiff touching his accounts for the manor of Essendine, Rutland in 1327. He was granted a weekly market and a yearly fair at his manor of Carlton on Trent, Nottinghamshire in 1328. In 1330 John and his wife, Idoine, claimed view of frankpledge in the manor of Moulton, Northamptonshire. In 1331 he and his wife, Idoine, and his son, Richard, obtained papal indults for

plenary remission at the hour of death. In 1331 John and his wife, Idoine, took advantage of the statute annulling all fines levied by force and duress after the exile of the Despensers, and tried to obtain an annulment of the fine of 1320–1, which they said had been so levied. They were evidently unsuccessful. His widow, Idoine, died shortly before 18 Nov. 1333. SIR JOHN DE CROMWELL, Lord Cromwell, died shortly before 8 October 1335.
    Whatley *England's Gaz.* 2 (1751) (sub Perlethorp). Throsby *Thoroton's Hist. of Nottinghamshire* 3 (1790): 169–171. Banks *Dormant & Extinct Baronage of England* 2 (1808): 120–124 (sub Cromwell). *Coll. Top. et Gen.* 1 (1834): 256. Palgrave *Docs. & Recs. Ill. the Hist. of Scotland* 1 (1837): 217 ("Idonea de Leyburne filia et una heredum Rob'ti de Wespunt" included on list of people owing military service in 1300). Lipscomb *Hist. & Antiqs. of Buckingham* 2 (1847): 123–126. Eddison *Hist. of Worksop* (1854): 170–171. *Wiltshire Arch. & Nat. Hist. Mag.* 12 (1869): 24. Aveling *Hist. of Roche Abbey* (1870): xxi–xxii. Cox *Notes on the Churches of Derbyshire* 4 (1879): 478. *Annual Rpt. of the Deputy Keeper* 44 (1883): 10; 45 (1885): 128–129; 46 (1886): 203; 47 (1886): 147; 50 (1889): 39, 162. *D.N.B.* 33 (1893): 209–212 (biog. of Roger de Leybourne). *Papal Regs.: Letters* 2 (1895): 111 (Richard de Cromwell, rector of Olney, Buckinghamshire, styled "kinsman and clerk" of King Edward II in 1313 [but see, however, *English Hist. Rev.* 11 (1896): 564 which corrects entry to read that Richard de Cromwell was actually kinsman of John de Cromwell, not King Edward II), 115, 137 (dispensation dated Id. March [15 March] 1317 granted to John de Cromuel, knight and Ydona, his wife, to remain in marriage which they contracted), 143–144, 353, 430, 443. *Genealogist* n.s. 13 (1896): 36–37. Prescott *Reg. of the Priory of Wetherhal* (Cumb. & West. Antiq. & Arch. Soc. Recs. 1) (1897): 328–330, 363–364. Wrottesley *Peds. from the Plea Rolls* (1905): 137–138. *Cal. IPM* 2 (1906): 315–316. *C.Ch.R.* 3 (1908): 121; 4 (1912): 85, 285, 300. VCH *Bedford* 2 (1908): 230–233. VCH *Buckingham* 2 (1908): 328; 3 (1925): 372–376. *C.P.* 3 (1913): 553 (sub Cromwell); 5 (1926): 437 chart, 439–441 (sub FitzJohn); 14 (1998): 224 (sub Cromwell). Carter *Lay Subsidy Roll for Warwickshire of 6 Edward III* (1332) (Dugdale Soc. 6) (1926): 16. *Pubs. Bedfordshire Hist. Rec. Soc.* 11 (1927): 5–16. VCH *Rutland* 2 (1935): 250–254. VCH *Northampton* 4 (1937): 88–94; 5 (2002): 289–345. Pugh *Abs. of Feet of Fines Rel. Wiltshire* (Wiltshire Arch. & Nat. Hist. Soc. Recs. Branch 1) (1939): 129. Stokes et al. *Warwickshire Feet of Fines* 2 (Dugdale Soc. 15) (1939): 111–112. *Year Books of Edward II* 10 (Selden Soc. 63) (1947): 196–208. VCH *Warwick* 5 (1949): 17–26. Ellis *Cat. Seals in the P.R.O.* 2 (1981): 30 (seal of John de Cromwell dated 1316 — A shield of arms: six annulets; between two wyverns.). English *Yorkshire Hundred & Quo Warranto Rolls* (Yorkshire Arch. Soc. Recs. 151) (1996): 239–241. Vale *Princely Court* (2001): 313. National Archives, SC 8/11/525; SC 8/172/8596 (available at www.catalogue.nationalarchives.gov.uk/search.asp).

9. ISABEL DE VIPONT, daughter and co-heiress, born say 1251 (of age on 15 June 1269). She married shortly after 28 June 1265 **ROGER DE CLIFFORD**, Justice of the Forest south of Trent, 1270–81, and, in right of his wife, of Appleby, Brougham, King's Meaburn, etc., Westmorland, Eyworth, Bedfordshire, Buckland, Buckinghamshire, Perlethorpe, Nottinghamshire, Essendine, Rutland, etc., son and heir apparent of Roger de Clifford, Knt., of Tenbury and Severn Stoke, Worcestershire, Bridge Sollers and Eardisley, Herefordshire, etc., Justiciar of Wales, Justice of the Forest south of Trent, by his 1st wife, Maud, widow of Hugh de Gournay [see TREGOZ 2.i for his ancestry]. He was born about 1242. They had two sons, Robert, Knt. [1st Lord Clifford] and Roger. In 1277–8 he and his wife, Isabel, and Roger de Leyburn and Idoine his wife arraigned an assize of mort d'ancestor against Richard de la Vache touching a messuage and land in Aston Clinton, Buckinghamshire. He fought in Wales in 1277. ROGER DE CLIFFORD was drowned while crossing a bridge of boats near the Menai Straits in Wales 6 Nov. 1282. His widow, Isabel, died testate shortly before 14 May 1292.
    Collins *Supp. to the Four Volumes of the Peerage of England* 2 (1750): 402–469 (sub Clifford, Baroness Clifford). .Nicolson & Burn *Hist. & Antiqs. of the Counties of Westmorland & Cumberland* 1 (1777): 265–292. Clutterbuck *Hist. & Antiqs. of Hertford* 1 (1815): 293 (chart). *Coll. Top. et Gen.* 1 (1834): 256. Lipscomb *Hist. & Antiqs. of Buckingham* 2 (1847): 123–126. Eddison *Hist. of Worksop* (1854): 170–171. Aveling *Hist. of Roche Abbey* (1870): xxi–xxii. *Annual Rpt. of the Deputy Keeper* 44 (1883): 10; 45 (1885): 128–129; 47 (1886): 147; 50 (1889): 162. *Genealogist* n.s. 13 (1896): 36–37. Prescott *Reg. of the Priory of Wetherhal* (Cumb. & West. Antiq. & Arch. Soc. Recs. 1) (1897): 328–330, 363–364. *English Hist. Rev.* 18 (1903): 112–116. Wrottesley *Peds. from the Plea Rolls* (1905): 137–138. VCH *Bedford* 2 (1908): 230–233. VCH *Buckingham* 2 (1908): 328. *C.P.* 3 (1913): 290 (sub Clifford); 5 (1926): 437 chart, 439–441 (sub FitzJohn). *Pubs. Bedfordshire Hist. Rec. Soc.* 11 (1927): 5–16. VCH *Rutland* 2 (1935): 250–254. Fowler *Cal. of IPM* 2 (Bedfordshire Hist. Rec. Soc. 19) (1937): facing 170 (Vipont chart 6). *Year Books of Edward II* 10 (Selden Soc. 63) (1947): 196–208. VCH *Warwick* 5 (1949): 17–26. Paget *Baronage of England* (1957) 134: 2–3 (sub Clifford); 220: 1; 562: 4. Sanders *English Baronies* (1960): 103–104. *Curia Regis Rolls* 18 (1999): 79, 217. *Genealogists' Mag.* 23 (1990): 260–263. Cumbria Rec. Office, Carlisle Headquarters: Wybergh Fam., D/WYB/2/46 — lease dated 1293 mentions John de St. John and Thomas Paynel, executors of the will of lady Isabel de Clifford (available at www.a2a.org.uk/search/index.asp).

10. **ROBERT DE CLIFFORD**, Knt., of Appleby, Brougham, Stainmore, etc., Westmorland, Singleborough (in Great Horwood), Buckinghamshire, Hart, Durham, Essendine, Rutland, Winderton (in Brailes), Warwickshire, Stoke Severn and Tenbury, Worcestershire, etc., hereditary Sheriff of Westmorland, Governor of Carlisle and Nottingham Castles, Warden of the Marches of Scotland, Guardian of Norham Castle, son and heir, born about 5 April 1276 (8 years old in 1282). He married 13 Nov. 1295 **MAUD DE CLARE**, daughter of Thomas de Clare, Knt., of Thomond in Connacht, Ireland, by Juliane, daughter of Maurice Fitz Maurice, Knt., Justiciar of Ireland [see BADLESMERE 8 for her ancestry]. They had two sons, Roger [2nd Lord Clifford] and Robert [3rd Lord Clifford], and two daughters, Idoine and Margaret. In 1297 he was co-heir to his great-uncle, Richard Fitz John, Knt., Lord Fitz John. He served in the wars of King Edward I with Scotland. He was summoned to Parliament from 29 Dec. 1299 to 26 Nov. 1313, by writs directed *Roberto de Clifford*. He was present at the Siege of Caerlaverock in 1300. He signed the Barons' letter to Pope Boniface VIII in 1301 as *Robertus de Clifford Castellanus de Appelby*. In 1306 he was granted the manor of Hart, the borough of Hartlepool, and other property in the bishopric of Durham forfeited by Robert de Brus for the murder of John Comyn. In 1308 his aunt, Idoine de Vipont (wife of John de Cromwell, Knt.) granted him her share of the honour of Appleby, Westmorland, in return for his share of the barony of Staveley, Derbyshire. In 1310 he was granted the manor of Skipton in Craven, Yorkshire by the king. The same year he was granted a weekly market and yearly fair to be held at his manor of Severn Stoke, Worcesstershire. He received a pardon 16 October 1313 for participation in the death of Peter de Gavaston, Knt., Earl of Cornwall. SIR ROBERT DE CLIFFORD, 1st Lord Clifford, was slain at the Battle of Bannockburn 24 June 1314, and was buried with his mother at Shap Abbey, Westmorland. He left a will. His widow, Maud, was abducted by John le Irish, Keeper of Barnard Castle, in Nov. 1315, while travelling near Bowes Castle, Durham. A force of some 40 men-at-arms headed by William de Montagu, Knt., was immediately dispatched to her rescue. She married (2nd) without license before 16 Dec. 1315 **ROBERT DE WELLE** (or **DE WELLES**), Knt., of Worcestershire, Warden of the Marches of Cumberland and Westmorland, Constable of Pendragon Castle, Warden of Malrestang Forest, probable son of Robert de Welle, by Isabel, daughter and co-heiress of Adam de Periton. They had no issue. In 1316 the king entrusted Brough Castle, Westmorland to him, ordering that he maintain 15 men-at-arms fully mailed and mounted and 20 hobelars or light lancers. His wife, Maud, was co-heiress in 1321 to her nephew, Thomas de Clare, by which she inherited Thomond, Inkisty, Knockany, etc. in Ireland, as well as a moiety share of the manor of Tarrant Rushton, Dorset and the Stewardship of Essex. In 1322 he was granted the houses late of Roger de Clifford, a rebel, in the parish of St. Dunstan in the West, London. In 1323 he and Richard de Ayremynne were appointed keepers of the bishopric of Winchester. He was granted protection in August 1325, he then going beyond seas on the king's business. SIR ROBERT DE WELLE was living 29 August 1326, when he was empowered to name a day and place to treat for peace with the Scots. Maud, Lady Clifford, died shortly before 24 May 1327.

Collins *Supp. to the Four Volumes of the Peerage of England* 2 (1750): 402–469 (sub Clifford, Baroness Clifford). .Nicolson & Burn *Hist. & Antiqs. of the Counties of Westmorland & Cumberland* 1 (1777): 265–292 ("This Robert de Clifford is said to have been the greatest man of all this family, being of a most martial and heroic spirit"). *Topographer* 3 (1791): 20 (Clare ped.). *Topographer* 3 (1791): 20 (Clare ped.). Clifford *Collectanea Cliffordiana* 3rd Pt. (1817): 103–104. Nicolas *Siege of Carlaverock* (1828): 185–189 (biog. of Robert de Clifford). Gray *Scalacronica* (1836): 147. Banks *Baronies in Fee* 1 (1844): 155. Lipscomb *Hist. & Antiqs. of Buckingham* 2 (1847): 123–126. Fordyce *Hist. & Antiqs. of the County Palatine of Durham* 2 (1857): 238–239. Hutchins *Hist. & Antiqs. of Dorset* 3 (1868): 462–463. Luard *Annales Monastici* 4 (Rolls Ser. 36) (1869): 523 (Annals of Worcester sub A.D. 1295 — "Decimo tertio die Novembris [13 November] Robertus de Clifford duxit uxorem filiam Thomæ de Clare neptem comitis Geleberti"). Aveling *Hist. of Roche Abbey* (1870): xxi–xxii. White *Hist. of the Battle of Bannockburn* (1871): 176–178 (biog. of Robert de Clifford). Stubbs *Annales Londonienses* (Chrons. of the Reigns of Edward I and Edward II 1) (Rolls Ser. 76) (1882): 231 ("Nomina interfectorum militum ad bellum de Strivelyn de Anglis [Names of the English knights slain at Bannockburn]: Robertus de Clifford baro").

D.N.B. 11 (1887): 70–72 (biog. of Robert de Clifford). *Genealogist* n.s. 13 (1896): 36–37. *Regs. of John de Sandale & Rigaud de Asserio, Bishops of Winchester* (Hampshire Rec. Soc. 12) (1897): xxix–xxx, 376, 581, 587. *C.P.R. 1321–1324* (1904): 210. *C.P.R. 1324–1327* (1904): 161, 315. Wrottesley *Peds. from the Plea Rolls* (1905): 137–138. VCH *Buckingham* 2 (1908): 328; 3 (1925): 372–376. *C.F.R.* 4 (1913): 43. *C.P.* 3 (1913): 247, footnote c (sub Clare), 290–291 (sub Clifford); 10 (1945): 461–462; 12(2) (1959): 440, footnote h. St. John Hope *Heraldry for Craftsmen & Designers* (1913): 171 (seal of Robert de Clifford, with arms surrounded by rings in allusion to his mother Isabel [de] Vipont). VCH *Berkshire* 4 (1924): 168–174. VCH *Worcester* 4 (1924): 68–76, 193. Reynolds *Reg. of Walter Reynolds Bishop of Worcester* (Dugdale Soc. 9) (1928): 155. VCH *Durham* 3 (1928): 254–263. Harvey et al. *Vis. of the North* 4 (Surtees Soc. 146) (1932): 17–24 (Lassels ped.: "Robt Lord Clifford = ... d. of Humphrey Bohum"). Gandavo *Reg. Simonis de Gandavo Diocesis Saresbiriensis* 2 (Canterbury & York Soc. 41) (1934): 633. VCH *Northampton* 4 (1937): 88–94. *Year Books of Edward II* 10 (Selden Soc. 63) (1947): 196–208. VCH *Warwick* 5 (1949): 17–26. Paget *Baronage of England* (1957) 134: 3–4, 220: 1. Sanders *English Baronies* (1960): 103–104. Schwennicke *Europäische Stammtafeln* 3(1) (1984): 156 (sub Clare). Brault *Rolls of Arms Edward I* 2 (1997): 109 (arms of Robert de Clifford: Checky or and azure, a fess gules). *Northern Hist.* 38 (2001): 187–195.

Children of Robert de Clifford, Knt., by Maud de Clare:

i. **ROBERT DE CLIFFORD**, 3rd Lord Clifford [see next].

ii. **IDOINE DE CLIFFORD**, married **HENRY DE PERCY**, Knt., 2nd Lord Percy [see PERCY 9].

iii. **MARGARET DE CLIFFORD**, married **PETER DE MAULEY**, Knt., 3rd Lord Mauley [see MAULEY 8].

11. ROBERT DE CLIFFORD, 3rd Lord Clifford, of Appleby, Westmorland, Tarrant Rushton, Dorset, Hart, Durham, Bridge Sollers, Herefordshire, Shalford, Surrey, Winderton (in Brailes), Warwickshire, Severn Stoke and Tenbury Wells, Worcestershire, Skipton in Craven, Yorkshire, etc., hereditary Sheriff of Westmorland, younger son, born 5 Nov. 1305. He was heir to his older brother, Roger de Clifford, Knt., 2nd Lord Clifford, who was taken prisoner at the Battle of Boroughbridge and executed at York in 1322. He married at Berkeley Castle June 1328 **ISABEL DE BERKELEY**, daughter of Maurice de Berkeley, Knt., 2nd Lord Berkeley, by Eve, daughter of Eudes la Zouche, Knt. [see BERKELEY 6 for her ancestry]. They had three sons, Robert [4th Lord Clifford], Roger, Knt. [5th Lord Clifford], and Thomas, Knt. He was restored in blood by King Edward III. He was summoned to Parliament from 1327 to 1344. He was heir in 1333 to his great-aunt, Idoine de Vipont (wife of Roger de Leybourne, Knt., and John de Cromwell, Knt., Lord Cromwell), by which he inherited her share of the Vipont estates. He served in the Scottish wars. SIR ROBERT DE CLIFFORD, 3rd Lord Clifford, died 20 May 1344, and was buried in Shap Abbey, Westmorland. His widow, Isabel, married (2nd) shortly before 9 June 1345 (date of pardon for marrying without the king's license) (as his 2nd wife) **THOMAS DE MUSGRAVE**, Knt., Knight of the Shire for Westmorland, 1340–44, son and heir of Thomas de Musgrave, by Sarah, sister of Andrew de Harcla, Knt., Earl of Carlisle. He was of age before 1328. He was summoned to Parliament from 25 Nov. 1350 to 4 October 1373, by writs directed *Thome Musgrave*, whereby he is held to have become Lord Musgrave. In 1352 Thomas and his wife, Isabel, sued Reynold de Lucy and his wife, Euphame de Neville (widow of Isabel's deceased son, Robert de Clifford), for one-third of one-third of the manor of Caveley, Derbyshire. Isabel was a legatee in the 1358 will of John de Morland, Rector of Long Marton, Westmorland, who bequeathed her a mazer. She died 25 July 1362. SIR THOMAS DE MUSGRAVE, Lord Musgrave, died about 1385.

Collins *Supp. to the Four Volumes of the Peerage of England* 2 (1750): 402–469 (sub Clifford, Baroness Clifford). .Nicolson & Burn *Hist. & Antiqs. of the Counties of Westmorland & Cumberland* 1 (1777): 265–292. Nash *Colls. for the Hist. of Worcestershire* 2 (1782): 346–347. Blore *Hist. & Antiqs. of Rutland* 1(2) (1811): 15 (Clifford ped.). Brydges *Collins' Peerage of England* 6 (1812): 512–541 (sub Southwell, Lord de Clifford). Burke *Dormant, Abeyant, Forfeited & Extinct Peerages* (1883): 122–124 (sub Clifford). Jeayes *Desc. Cat. of the Charters & Muniments in the Possession of the Rt. Hon. Lord Fitzhardinge* (1892): xxii–xxiii (chart). *Genealogist* n.s. 10 (1893): 213; n.s. 13 (1896): 36–37. Wrottesley *Peds. from the Plea Rolls* (1905): 72, 137–138. *Yorkshire Arch. Jour.* 18 (1905): 354–411. *C.P.* 3 (1913): 291 (sub Clifford); 7 (1929): 642–643 (sub Leyburn); 9 (1936): 434–436 (sub Musgrave). Clay *Extinct & Dormant Peerages* (1913): 21–27 (sub Clifford); 143–144 (sub Musgrave). VCH *Worcester* 4 (1924): 193 (Clifford arms: Checky or and azure a fesse gules). VCH *Durham* 3 (1928): 254–263. Pugh *Abs. of Feet of Fines Rel. Wiltshire* (Wiltshire Arch. & Nat. Hist. Soc. Recs. 1) (1939):

129. VCH *Warwick* 5 (1949): 17–26. Paget *Baronage of England* (1957) 55: 1–2 (sub Berkeley); 134: 4–5, 404: 9. Sanders *English Baronies* (1960): 83–84, 103–104. Ellis *Cat. Seals in the P.R.O.* 2 (1981): 26 (seal of Robert de Clifford dated 1331 — In a cusped circle, a shield of arms: checky, and a fesse [CLIFFORD]; between six rings [VIPONT]). Montacute *Cal. Reg. of Simon de Montacute Bishop of Worcester* (Worcestershire Hist. Soc. n.s. 15) (1996). Whelton *Reg. of Gilbert Whelton Bishop of Carlisle* (Canterbury & York Soc. 88) (1999): 39–40. Berkeley Castle Muniments, BCM/A/3/3/1 — charter dated 14 Aug. 1344 issued by Sir Maurice de Berkeley styled "brother of the lady de Clifford" and William de Corbrig' (available at www.a2a.org.uk/search/index.asp).

12. ROGER DE CLIFFORD, Knt., 5th Lord Clifford, of Appleby, Brough, Brougham, and King's Meaburn, Westmorland, Hart and Hartlepool, Durham, Bridge Sollers, Herefordshire, Eckington and Tenbury, Worcestershire, etc., hereditary Sheriff of Westmorland, Warden of the East and West Marches of Scotland, hereditary Sheriff of Cumberland, Governor of Carlisle Castle, younger son, born 10 July 1333. He was heir in 1345 to his older brother, Robert de Clifford, 4th Lord Clifford. In 1350 he was present in the sea fight with the Spaniards near Winchelsea. In 1355 he served in the expedition to Gascony and in 1356 was employed in the defense of the Marches of Scotland. He married before 20 March 1357 **MAUD DE BEAUCHAMP**, daughter of Thomas de Beauchamp, K.G., 11th Earl of Warwick, by Katherine, daughter of Roger de Mortimer, Knt., 1st Earl of March [see BEAUCHAMP 11 for her ancestry]. They had three sons, Thomas, Knt. [6th Lord Clifford], Roger, and William, Knt., and three daughters, Philippe, Katherine, and Margaret. He was summoned to Parliament from 15 Dec. 1356 to 28 July 1388. In 1357 he had license to settle the manors of Hart and Hartlepool, Durham on himself and his wife, Maud. He served in the wars with Scotland and France. He assisted Lionel, Duke of Clarence, in his Irish expedition in 1361. In 1361 he successfully claimed the manor of Eckington, Worcestershire, which he stated was held by his grandfather, Robert de Clifford, who granted it for a term of years to Alma Poer. He served as a Trier of Petitions in Parliament in 1363, 1373, and 1376–7. As "Roger de Clifford, lord of Westmorland," he presented to the church of Cranleigh, Surrey in 1363. His wife, Maud, was a legatee in the 1369 wills of both of her parents. In 1373 he served in the French expedition of John, Duke of Lancaster. He testified in the famous Scrope-Grosvenor case in 1386. He accompanied Richard de Arundel, Earl of Arundel into Brittany in 1388. SIR ROGER DE CLIFFORD, 5th Lord Clifford, died testate 13 July 1389. In 1396 Walter Skirlaw, Bishop of Durham granted license to the Mayor and Commonalty of Hartlepool, Durham to found a chantry of one chaplain at the altar of St. Helen, to pray for the good estate of Bishop Skirlaw, of Maud wife of Roger Clifford, and of the said Mayor and Commonalty, and for the rest of their souls after death. Maud received papal indults for plenary remission and a portable altar in 1398. She was a legatee in the 1400 will of her brother, Thomas Beauchamp, Earl of Warwick. Maud, Lady Clifford, died Jan. or Feb. 1402/3.

Collins *Supp. to the Four Volumes of the Peerage of England* 2 (1750): 402–469 (sub Clifford, Baroness Clifford). Nicolson & Burn *Hist. & Antiqs. of the Counties of Westmorland & Cumberland* 1 (1777): 265–292 ("Roger de Clifford … was accounted one of the wisest men of his time. He was a man of much gallantry and valour, being often in the wars both in France and Scotland."). Nash *Colls. for the Hist. of Worcestershire* 2 (1782): 346–347. Blore *Hist. & Antiqs. of Rutland* 1(2) (1811): 15 (Clifford ped.). Brydges *Collins' Peerage of England* 6 (1812): 512–541 (sub Southwell, Lord de Clifford). Clutterbuck *Hist. & Antiqs. of Hertford* 1 (1815): 358 (Beauchamp ped.). Surtees *Hist. & Antiqs. of Durham* 3 (1823): 117. Nicolas *Testamenta Vetusta* 1 (1826): 78 (will of Katherine Beauchamp, Countess of Warwick), 79–80 (will of Thomas Beauchamp, Earl of Warwick), 153–155 (will of Thomas Beauchamp, Earl of Warwick). Nicolas *Controversy between Scrope & Grosvenor* 2 (1832): 469–472 (biog. of Roger Clifford). Baker *Hist. & Antiqs. of Northampton* 2 (1836–41): 218–219 (Beauchamp ped.). Surtees *Hist. & Antiqs. of Durham* 4 (1840): 65 (Beauchamp ped.). Fordyce *Hist. & Antiqs. of the County Palatine of Durham* 2 (1857): 255. Flower *Vis. of Yorkshire 1563–4* (H.S.P. 16) (1881): 60 (Clifford ped.: "Robert Clyfford Lord Clyfford second son, brother & heyre to Roger maryed = Mawde doughter to… Becham Erl of Warwyke"). Burke *Dormant, Abeyant, Forfeited & Extinct Peerages* (1883): 122–124 (sub Clifford). D.N.B. 11 (1887): 74–75 (biog. of Roger de Clifford). *Genealogist* n.s. 13 (1896): 36–37. *C.P.R. 1381–1385* (1897): 307 ([Roger], Lord of Clifford, styled "king's kinsman"). *List of Sheriffs for England & Wales* (PRO Lists and Indexes 9) (1898): 26. *C.P.R. 1385–1389* (1900): 239 ([Roger], lord of Clifford, styled "king's kinsman"). *Papal Regs.: Letters* 5 (1904): 134, 143. Wrottesley *Peds. from the Plea Rolls* (1905): 137–138. *Yorkshire Arch. Jour.* 18 (1905): 354–411. *List of Inqs. ad Quod Damnum* 2 (PRO Lists and Indexes 22) (1906): 516, 544, 586–587, 612, 637. *C.P.* 3 (1913): 292 (sub

Clifford); 5 (1926): 354–357 (sub Ferrers); 6 (1926): 195–196 (sub Greystoke). Clay *Extinct & Dormant Peerages* (1913): 21–27 (sub Clifford). *Yorkshire Inqs.* 5 (Yorkshire Arch. Soc. Recs. 59) (1918): 28, 89. VCH *Worcester* 4 (1924): 68–76; 193. VCH *Durham* 3 (1928): 254–263. Paget *Baronage of England* (1957) 39: 1–13 (sub Beauchamp of Elmley); 134: 7. *Ancient Deeds — Ser. B* 1 (List & Index Soc. 95) (1973): 24. Ellis *Cat. Seals in the P.R.O.* 1 (1978): 16 (seal of Roger de Clifford dated 1357 — In a traceried circle, a shield of arms: checky, a fesse. Legend broken away.). *Ancient Deeds — Ser. AS & WS* (List & Index Soc. 158) (1979): 29 (Deed A.S.157: "Roger de Clifford, lord of Westmorland"). Edington *Reg. of William Edington Bishop of Winchester 1346–1366* 1 (Hampshire Recs. 7) (1986): 224. National Archives, CP 25/1/288/49, #743 [see abstract of fine at http:// www.medievalgenealogy.org.uk/index.html].

Children of Roger de Clifford, Knt., by Maud de Beauchamp:

i. **THOMAS DE CLIFFORD**, Knt., 6th Lord Clifford [see next].

ii. **PHILIPPE CLIFFORD**, married **WILLIAM FERRERS**, Knt., 5th Lord Ferrers of Groby [see GROBY 13].

iii. **KATHERINE CLIFFORD**, married **RALPH GREYSTOKE**, Knt., 3rd Lord Greystoke [see GREYSTOKE 12].

iv. **MARGARET CLIFFORD**, married **JOHN MELTON**, Knt., of Aston and Kilham, Yorkshire [see MELTON 11].

13. THOMAS DE CLIFFORD, Knt., 6th Lord Clifford, Knight of the chamber, hereditary Sheriff of Westmorland, Governor of Carlisle Castle, Warden of the East Marches, son and heir, born about 1363 (aged 26 in 1389). He married before 1378/9 (date of settlement) **ELIZABETH DE ROOS** (or **ROS**), daughter of Thomas de Roos, Knt., 4th Lord Roos of Helmsley, by Beatrice, daughter of Ralph de Stafford, K.G., 1st Earl of Stafford [see ROOS 10 for her ancestry]. They had one son, John, K.G. [7th Lord Clifford], and one daughter, Maud. He was excluded from court in Jan. 1388 by order of the Lords Appellant. He was summoned to Parliament from 6 Dec. 1389. He presented to the church of Cranleigh, Surrey in 1390. In 1390 he procured a safe-conduct for William de Douglas, who was coming to the English court with forty knights to a wager of battle with Clifford regarding certain disputed lands. He accompanied Thomas, Duke of Gloucester, on his expedition to Prussia against the infidels in 1391. SIR THOMAS DE CLIFFORD, 6th Lord Clifford, died abroad 18 August 1391. His widow, Elizabeth, was a legatee in the 1392 will of her brother, John de Roos, Knt., 5th Lord Roos of Helmsley. She received a papal indult for a portable altar in 1423. Elizabeth, Lady Clifford, died in March 1424.

Rymer *Fœdera* 7 (1728): 526, 552 (Thomas de Clifford styled "kinsman" by King Richard II of England). Collins *Supp. to the Four Volumes of the Peerage of England* 2 (1750): 402–469 (sub Clifford, Baroness Clifford). .Nicolson & Burn *Hist. & Antiqs. of the Counties of Westmorland & Cumberland* 1 (1777): 265–292. Blore *Hist. & Antiqs. of Rutland* 1(2) (1811): 15 (Clifford ped.). Brydges *Collins' Peerage of England* 6 (1812): 483–495 (sub De Roos, Baroness de Roos), 512–541 (sub Southwell, Lord de Clifford). Clutterbuck *Hist. & Antiqs. of Hertford* 3 (1827): 393 (Roos ped.). Burke *Dormant, Abeyant, Forfeited & Extinct Peerages* (1883): 122–124 (sub Clifford). D.N.B. 11 (1887): 77 (biog. of Thomas de Clifford). Gibbons *Early Lincoln Wills 1280–1547* (1888): 70–71 (will of John de Roos, Knt.). Atkinson *Cartularium Abbathiæ de Rievalle* (Surtees Soc. 83) (1889): 359–362. Kirby *Wykeham's Reg.* 1 (1896): 173. C.P.R. 1381–1385 (1897): 176, 192, 212 (instances of Thomas de Clifford styled "king's kinsman"). C.P.R. 1385–1389 (1900): 65 (Thomas de Clifford styled "king's kinsman"). *List of Early Chancery Procs.* 1 (PRO Lists and Indexes 12) (1901): 14, 138. *Yorkshire Arch. Jour.* 18 (1905): 354–411. *List of Inqs. ad Quod Damnum* 2 (PRO Lists and Indexes 22) (1906): 612. *Papal Regs.: Letters* 7 (1906): 314. Clay *Extinct & Dormant Peerages* (1913): 21–27 (sub Clifford), 181–185 (sub Ros). C.P. 3 (1913): 292 (sub Clifford). VCH *Worcester* 4 (1924): 193. C.F.R. 9 (1926): 257. VCH *Durham* 3 (1928): 254–263. Harvey et al. *Vis. of the North* 3 (Surtees Soc. 144) (1930): 161–164 (Espec [Roos] ped.: "Elizabeth [Roos]"). Train *Abs. of IPMs Rel. Nottinghamshire* 2 (Thoroton Soc. Recs. 12) (1952): 118–119. *Coat of Arms* 9 (1967): 177–182. Hedley *Northumberland Fams.* (1968): 224–230. Hector *Westminster Chron. 1381–1394* (1982): 230–231. Cal. IPM 17 (1988): 13–20.

Children of Thomas de Clifford, Knt., by Elizabeth de Roos:

i. **JOHN CLIFFORD**, K.G., 7th Lord Clifford [see next].

ii. **MAUD CLIFFORD**, married (1st) **JOHN DE NEVILLE**, Knt., 6th Lord Latimer [NEVILLE 12.i]; (2nd) **RICHARD OF YORK**, Knt., Earl of Cambridge [see YORK 11].

14. JOHN CLIFFORD, K.G., 7th Lord Clifford, hereditary Sheriff of Westmorland, son and heir, born about 1389 (aged 3 in 1392, 13 in 1403, 21 in 1411, 26 in 1419). He married between August 1403 and 5 Nov. 1412, probably in 1404, **ELIZABETH PERCY**, daughter of Henry 'Hotspur' Percy, K.G., K.B., by Elizabeth, daughter of Edmund de Mortimer, Knt., 3rd Earl of March [see PERCY 12 for her ancestry]. They had two sons, Thomas [8th Lord Clifford] and Henry, and two daughters, Mary and Blanche (wife of Robert Waterton, Knt.). He was summoned to Parliament from 21 Sept. 1412. They received a papal indult for a portable altar in 1412. He took part in a great tournament at Carlisle between six English and six Scottish Knights, as also in the French war. He was heir in 1418 to his uncle, William Clifford, Knt. He was a legatee in the 1421 will of his cousin, King Henry V of England. SIR JOHN CLIFFORD, 7th Lord Clifford, was slain at the Siege of Meaux in France 13 March 1421/2, and is said to have been buried at Bolton Priory, Yorkshire. His widow, Elizabeth, married (2nd) by contract dated 7 May 1426, license dated 20 July 1426 (dispensation *ex post facto* dated 28 Nov. 1426, they being related in the 3rd and 4th degrees of kindred) (as his 1st wife) **RALPH NEVILLE**, Knt., 2nd Earl of Westmorland (died 3 Nov. 1484) [see NEVILLE 14.i], son and heir of John de Neville, Knt., of Sutton (in Galtres), Yorkshire, by Elizabeth, 5th daughter of Thomas de Holand, K.G., 2nd Earl of Kent [see NEVILLE 14 for his ancestry]. They had one son, John, Knt. She died 26 October 1436, and was buried at Staindrop, Durham.

Collins *Supp. to the Four Volumes of the Peerage of England* 2 (1750): 402–469 (sub Clifford, Baroness Clifford). Nicolson & Burn *Hist. & Antiqs. of the Counties of Westmorland & Cumberland* 1 (1777): 265–292. Nash *Colls. for the Hist. of Worcestershire* 2 (1782): 346–347. Blore *Hist. & Antiqs. of Rutland* 1(2) (1811): 15 (Clifford ped.). Brydges *Collins' Peerage of England* 2 (1812): 217–366 (sub Duke of Northumberland); 6 (1812): 512–541 (sub Southwell, Lord de Clifford). Rowland *Noble Fam. of Nevill* (1830). Beltz *Mems. of the Order of the Garter* (1841): clviii. *Testamenta Eboracensia* 3 (Surtees Soc. 45) (1865): 325 (abs. of dispensation). Atkinson *Cartularium Abbathiæ de Whitby* 2 (Surtees Soc. 72) (1881): 690–696 (Percy ped.: "Elizabeth Percy, the Daughter of the foresayd Syr Henry, Knight, first was maried to John Lord Clyfford .... hyr second Husband was Raffe Erle of Westmorland"). Flower *Vis. of Yorkshire 1563-4* (H.S.P. 16) (1881): 241–244 (Percy ped.: "Elsabeth [Percy] fyrst wyf to… Clyfford & after to Raff Erl to Westmerland"). Burke *Dormant, Abeyant, Forfeited & Extinct Peerages* (1883): 122–124 (sub Clifford). Birch *Cat. Seals in the British Museum* 2 (1892): 651 (seal of John Clifford dated 1417 — A shield of arms, couché: quarterly, 1, 4, chequy a fess [CLIFFORD]; 2, 3, quarterly, i., iv., six annulets [VIPONT], ii., iii., indistinct, perhaps three water bougets [?ROOS of Hemsley]. Crest on a helmet and lambrequins, a wyvern rising with wings expanded. Supporters two wyverns.). *Papal Regs.: Letters* 6 (1904): 383. *Yorkshire Arch. Jour.* 18 (1905): 354–411; 30 (1931): 385–386. Ruvigny and Raineval *Plantagenet Roll: Mortimer-Percy* 1 (1911): 2. Clay *Extinct & Dormant Peerages* (1913): 21–27 (sub Clifford). *C.P.* 3 (1913): 293 (sub Clifford); 9 (1936): 741, footnote f; 12(2) (1959): 549–550 (sub Westmorland). *Yorkshire Inqs.* 5 (Yorkshire Arch. Soc. Recs. 59) (1918): 28, 89, 182–184. VCH *Worcester* 4 (1924): 193. VCH *Durham* 3 (1928): 254–263. *Coat of Arms* 9 (1967): 177–182 (his seal). *English Hist. Rev.* 96 (1981): 79–102 (John [Clifford], lord of Clifford, styled "kinsman" [consanguineo] by King Henry V of England). Pollard *Richard III & Princes in the Tower* (1991): 30 (chart). Leese *Blood Royal* (1996): 143–149. *Cal. IPM* 21 (2002): 11.

Children of John Clifford, K.G., by Elizabeth Percy:

i. **THOMAS CLIFFORD**, 8th Lord Clifford [see next].

ii. **MARY CLIFFORD**, married **PHILIP WENTWORTH**, Knt., of Nettlestead, Suffolk [see NETTLESTEAD 16].

15. THOMAS CLIFFORD, 8th Lord Clifford, hereditary Sheriff of Westmorland, son and heir, born 25 March 1414. He married after March 1424 **JOAN** (or **JANE**) **DACRE**, daughter of Thomas Dacre, Knt., 6th Lord Dacre of Gilsland, by Philippe, daughter of Ralph de Neville, 1st Earl of Westmorland, 4th Lord Neville of Raby [see DACRE 14 for her ancestry]. They had four sons, John, Knt. [9th Lord Clifford], Roger, Knt., Robert, Knt., and Thomas, Knt., and five daughters, Elizabeth, Maud, Anne (wife of Richard Tempest, Knt., and William Conyers, Esq.), Joan (or Jane) (wife of Simon Musgrave, Knt.), and Margaret (wife of Robert Carr). He was summoned to Parliament from 19 Dec. 1436 to 1453. In 1435 he was a member of the Duke of Bedford's retinue in France. He defended Pontoise against the French king about 1439. In May 1453 he contracted to marry Isabel _____, widow of John Dacre, Knt., a lady in waiting to Queen Margaret of Anjou. This marriage never took place, she marrying instead in 1454 John Boteler (or Butler), Knt., of Bewsey (in Warrington), Lancashire [see TROUTBECK 11]. THOMAS CLIFFORD, 8th Lord Clifford, a Lancastrian, was slain fighting for King Henry VI at the 1st Battle of St. Albans 22 May 1455, and was buried in the Lady Chapel within St. Albans Abbey.

Collins *Supp. to the Four Volumes of the Peerage of England* 2 (1750): 402–469 (sub Clifford, Baroness Clifford). Weever *Antient Funeral Monuments* (1767): 337. Nicolson & Burn *Hist. & Antiqs. of the Counties of Westmorland & Cumberland* 1 (1777): 265–292. Blore *Hist. & Antiqs. of Rutland* 1(2) (1811): 15 (Clifford ped.). Brydges *Collins' Peerage of England* 6 (1812): 512–541 (sub Southwell, Lord de Clifford). Dugdale *Monasticon Anglicanum* 2 (1819): 203. Burke *Dict. of the Peerages… Extinct, Dormant & in Abeyance* (1831): 153–155. *Coll. Top. et Gen.* 1 (1834): 302–303. *Testamenta Eboracensia* 3 (Surtees Soc. 45) (1865): 338 (abs. of license to marry). French *Shakspeareana Genealogica* 1 (1869): 160–161. Riley *Chronica Monasterii S. Albani* 1: *Registrum Abbatiæ Johannis Whethamstede* (Rolls Ser. 28) (1872): 175–178. Flower *Vis. of Yorkshire 1563–4* (H.S.P. 16) (1881): 83–85 (Dacre ped.: "Jane [Dacre] = Thomas Lord Clyfford"). Burke *Dormant, Abeyant, Forfeited & Extinct Peerages* (1883): 122–124 (sub Clifford). *D.N.B.* 11 (1887): 77–78 (biog. of Thomas Clifford). *Yorkshire Arch. Jour.* 18 (1905): 354–411. VCH *Lancaster* 1 (1906): 347 (cites Lichfield Episc. Reg. Bothe as source for Thomas Dacre's 2nd marriage); 6 (1911): 162; 8 (1914): 120–121. Clay *Extinct & Dormant Peerages* (1913): 21–27 (sub Clifford), 36–39 (sub Dacre). *C.P.* 3 (1913): 293 (sub Clifford). *Yorkshire Inqs.* 5 (Yorkshire Arch. Soc. Recs. 59) (1918): 182–184. VCH *Worcester* 4 (1924): 193. VCH *Durham* 3 (1928): 254–263. *Genealogists' Mag.* 5 (1929): 353–354. Harvey et al. *Vis. of the North* 3 (Surtees Soc. 144) (1930): 23–32 (Neville ped.: "Iohanna [Dacre] nupta Thome domino de Clifford"). Paget *Baronage of England* (1957) 164: 1–2 (sub Dacre). *Bull. John Rylands Lib.* 40 (1957–8): 79–113, 391–431; 42 (1959–60): 113–131. *Trans. Monumental Brass Soc.* 18 (2010): 33–44.

Children of Thomas Clifford, by Joan Dacre:

i. **JOHN CLIFFORD**, Knt., 9th Lord Clifford [see next].

ii. **ROGER CLIFFORD**, Knt., married **JOAN** (or **JANE**) **COURTENAY** [see SOMERSET 11.vi.d].

iii. **ELIZABETH CLIFFORD**, married (1st) **WILLIAM PLUMPTON**, Knt., of Knaresborough, Yorkshire [see PLUMPTON 10]; (2nd) **JOHN HAMERTON** [see PLUMPTON 14].

iv. **MAUD CLIFFORD**, married (1st) **JOHN HARINGTON**, Knt., of Hornby, Lancashire [see SUTTON 8]; (2nd) **EDMUND SUTTON** (or **DUDLEY**), Knt., of Dudley, Staffordshire [see SUTTON 8].

16. **JOHN CLIFFORD**, Knt., 9th Lord Clifford, of Appleby, Westmorland, son and heir, born at Conisbrough Castle, Yorkshire 8 April 1435. He was a legatee in the 1446 will of his great aunt and godmother, Maud Clifford, widow of Richard of York, Knt., Earl of Cambridge [see YORK 11]. He married **MARGARET BROMFLETE** [see BROMFLETE 16], daughter and heiress of Henry (or Harry) Bromflete, Knt., Lord Vescy, of Londesborough, Yorkshire, by his 2nd wife, Eleanor, daughter of Henry Fitz Hugh, K.G., 3rd Lord Fitz Hugh, Lord High Treasurer [see BROMFLETE 15 for her ancestry]. She was born about 1443 (aged 26 in 1469). They had two sons, Henry, K.B. [10th Lord Clifford] and Richard, Esq., and one daughter, Elizabeth. He was summoned to Parliament 30 July 1460, by writ directed *Johanni Clifford domino de Clyfford chivaler*. He was one of the Lancastrian leaders at the Battle of Wakefield, where he was knighted 31 Dec. 1460, and where "for slaughter of men he was called the Butcher." SIR JOHN CLIFFORD, 9th Lord Clifford, Lancastrian, was slain at Ferrybridge by a chance arrow 28 March 1461, on the eve of the Battle of Towton, and was said to have been buried in a pit with others slain there. He was attainted 4 Nov. 1461, whereby his peerage was forfeited and his estates confiscated. His widow, Margaret, married (2nd) before 14 May 1467 **LANCELOT THRELKELD**, Knt., of Threlkeld, Cumberland [see BROMFLETE 16 for issue of this marriage]. Margaret, Lady Clifford, died testate 12 April 1493, and was buried at Londesborough, Yorkshire.

Collins *Supp. to the Four Volumes of the Peerage of England* 2 (1750): 402–469 (sub Clifford, Baroness Clifford). .Nicolson & Burn *Hist. & Antiqs. of the Counties of Westmorland & Cumberland* 1 (1777): 265–292. Strachey *Rotuli Parl.* 6 (1777): 95. Nash *Colls. for the Hist. of Worcestershire* 2 (1782): 346–347. Blore *Hist. & Antiqs. of Rutland* 1(2) (1811): 15 (Clifford ped.). Brydges *Collins' Peerage of England* 6 (1812): 512–541 (sub Southwell, Lord de Clifford). *Testamenta Eboracensia* 2 (Surtees Soc. 30) (1855): 118–124 (will of Maud of York, Countess of Cambridge). Burke *Gen. Hist. of the Dormant,*

Abeyant, Forfeited & Extinct Peerages (1866): 75 (sub Bromflete). Glover & St. George *Vis. of Yorkshire 1584–5, 1612* (1875): 120–121 (Vaughan ped.: "Margaret, daughter and heir of Henry Bromflett, Lord Vescy, [1] = John, Lord Clifford (*1st husband*), [2] = Sir Lancelot Thirkeld, Knt. (2nd husband)"). Flower *Vis. of Yorkshire 1563–4* (H.S.P. 16) (1881): 62–63 (Clifford ped.: "John Lord Clyfford = Margaret Bromflete"). Burke *Dormant, Abeyant, Forfeited & Extinct Peerages* (1883): 122–124 (sub Clifford). *Trans. Cumberland & Westmorland Antiq. & Arch. Soc.* 9 (1888): 307–308. Jackson *Papers & Peds. Mainly Rel. Cumberland & Westmorland* 2 (1892): 120–136, foldout ped. *Yorkshire Arch. Jour.* 18 (1905): 354–411. *North Country Wills* 1 (Surtees Soc. 116) (1908): 53–54 (will of Henry Brounflete, Knt., Lord Vessey). Clay *Extinct & Dormant Peerages* (1913): 21–27 (sub Clifford). *C.P.* 3 (1913): 293–294 (sub Clifford). VCH *Worcester* 4 (1924): 193. VCH *Durham* 3 (1928): 254–263. *Yorkshire Deeds* 9 (Yorkshire Arch. Soc. Recs. 111) (1948): 116–117.

Children of John Clifford, Knt., by Margaret Bromflete:

i. **HENRY CLIFFORD**, K.B., 10th Lord Clifford [see next].

ii. **ELIZABETH CLIFFORD**, married **ROBERT ASKE**, Knt., of Aughton, Yorkshire [see ASKE 15].

17. HENRY (or **HARRY**) **CLIFFORD**, K.B., 10th Lord Clifford, Lord Vescy, son and heir, born in 1454. He was said to have been concealed by his mother from the Yorkists and brought up without education as a shepherd (hence called "The Shepherd Lord"). He received a general pardon 16 March 1471/2, and attainder reversed with restoration of the estates on the accession of King Henry VII in 1485. He was summoned to Parliament from 15 Sept. 1485, by writs directed *Henrico Clifford de Clifford ch'r*. He married (1st) **ANNE SAINT JOHN**, daughter of John Saint John, K.B., of Bletsoe, Bedfordshire, by his 1st wife, Alice, daughter of Thomas Bradshagh, Knt., of Haigh, Lancashire [see SAINT JOHN 16 for her ancestry]. They had four sons, Henry, Henry, K.G. [11th Lord Clifford, 1st Earl of Cumberland], Thomas, Knt., and Edward, and six daughters, Elizabeth, Jane (or Joan) (wife of John Huddleston, Knt.), Mabel (wife of William Fitzwilliam, Knt., Earl of Southampton), Anne, Eleanor, and Margaret (wife of Cuthbert Ratcliffe). In the period, 1486–93, as "Henry, lord Clifford, son of Margaret, daughter of Henry, son of Margaret, daughter of Edward Seynt John," he sued Richard Clifford, executor of his mother, Margaret, in Chancery regarding the detention of deeds relating to the manors of Weighton, Weaverthorpe, Londesborough, Aton, Hotton, Langton, Wellom, Winteringham, and Brompton, Yorkshire. On 5 April 1495, as "lord Clyfford, Westmorland, and Vescy, knight," he cancelled a grant of 600 marks made to him by Sir Thomas Darcy, Knt., contained in a deed dated 4 April same year. His wife, Anne, was living 12 May 1506, and was buried in the church of Skipton-in-Craven, Yorkshire. He married (2nd) before 11 July 1511 **FLORENCE PUDSEY**, widow of Thomas Talbot, Knt., of Bashall in Craven, Yorkshire, and daughter of Henry Pudsey, of Bolton-by-Bolland and Barforth, Yorkshire, by Margaret, daughter of Christopher Conyers [see PUDSEY 12 for her ancestry]. They had two sons and one daughter, Dorothy (wife of Hugh Lowther, Knt.). By an unknown mistress, he also had an illegitimate son, Anthony, Esq. He was appointed to a principal command over the army which fought against the Scots at Flodden Field 9 Sept. 1513. In 1521 his wife, Florence, brought a suit against him in the ecclesiastical court at York for restitution of her conjugal rights, he refusing to let her live and sleep with him at Barden. SIR HENRY CLIFFORD, 10th Lord Clifford, died 23 April 1523. His widow, Florence, married (3rd) [**LORD**] **RICHARD GREY**, Knt., son of Thomas Grey, K.G., K.B., 1st Marquess of Dorset, Lord Ferrers of Groby, Harington, Bonville, and Astley, by his 2nd wife, Cecily, *suo jure* Lady Harington and Bonville, daughter of William Bonville, Knt., 6th Lord Harington [see GROBY 17 for his ancestry]. They had no issue. He left a will dated 28 March 1541, proved 9 May 1542 (P.C.C. 5 Spert). His widow, Florence, died in 1558.

Collins *Supp. to the Four Volumes of the Peerage of England* 2 (1750): 402–469 (sub Clifford, Baroness Clifford). Nicolson & Burn *Hist. & Antiqs. of the Counties of Westmorland & Cumberland* 1 (1777): 265–292. Nash *Colls. for the Hist. of Worcestershire* 2 (1782): 346–347. Nichols *Hist. & Antiqs. of Leicester* 3(2) (1804): 661–680, 682–684 (Grey ped.). Blore *Hist. & Antiqs. of Rutland* 1(2) (1811): 15 (Clifford ped.). Brydges *Collins' Peerage of England* 6 (1812): 512–541 (sub Southwell, Lord de Clifford) (quoting Whitaker's *Hist. & Antiqs of Craven* (1878): 224 [based on "Lady Pembroke's MS Memoirs"]: On the accession of Henry the Seventh emerged from the Fells of Cumberland, where he had been principally concealed for twenty-five years, Henry Lord Clifford, with the manners and education of a shepherd. He was almost altogether illiterate; but far from deficient in natural understanding… depressed by a consciousness of his own deficiencies. On this account he retired to the solitude of *Bardin*… The narrow limits of his residence shew that he had learned to despise the pomp of greatness… [at Flodden he] shewed that the military genius of the family had neither been chilled in him by age, nor extinguished by habits of peace"), 741–751 (sub St. John, Lord St. John of Bletshoe). Nicolas *Testamenta Vetusta* 2 (1826): 692 (will of Richard Grey, Knt.). *Coll. Top. et Gen.* 1 (1834): 310–311 (Saint John ped.), 408. Beltz *Mems. of the Order of the Garter* (1841): clxxiv. Charles *Vis. of Huntingdon 1613* (Camden Soc. 43) (1849): 2 (St. John ped.: "Anna [St. John], ux. Hen. Domini Clifford."). *Testamenta Eboracensia* 3 (Surtees Soc. 45) (1865): 368 (abs. of license to marry). St. George *Vis. of Cumberland 1615* (H.S.P. 7) (1872): 22–24 (Hudleston ped.). Flower *Vis. of Yorkshire 1563–4* (H.S.P. 16) (1881): 62–63 (Clifford ped.: "Henry Lord Clyfford = Ann St. John daughter of Sir John St. John"). Burke *Dormant, Abeyant, Forfeited & Extinct Peerages* (1883): 122–124 (sub Clifford). Taylor *Anecdotæ Eboracenses: Yorkshire Anecdotes* (1883): 95–96 (biog. of Henry Clifford). Harvey et al. *Vis. of Bedfordshire 1566, 1582, 1634 & 1669* (H.S.P. 19) (1884): 51–54 (Saint John ped.: "Anne [Saint John] maryed to Henry Lord Clifforde."). *Desc. Cat. Ancient Deeds* 3 (1900): 518 (Henry Clifford styled himself "lord Clyfford, Westmorland and Vescy" in instrument dated 5 April 10 Henry VII [1495]). *Yorkshire Arch. Jour.* 18 (1905): 354–411. *List of Early Chancery Procs.* 3 (PRO Lists and Indexes 20) (1906): 47, 163. *C.P.* 3 (1913): 294–295 (sub Clifford). Clay *Extinct & Dormant Peerages* (1913): 21–27 (sub Clifford). Littledale *Pudsay Deeds* (Yorkshire Arch. Soc. Recs. 56) (1916). VCH *Worcester* 4 (1924): 193. VCH *Durham* 3 (1928): 254–263. Dickens *Clifford Letters of the 16th Cent.* (Surtees Soc. 172) (1962): 128–132 ("Anne St. John: "… a woman of great goodness, piety & devotion… By the half blood she was cosin germain to King Henry the 7th, for her father was half brother to the Kings mother, Margaret Countess of Richmond & Derby"). Bartrum *Welsh Gens. 1400–1500* 9 (1983): 1567 [St. John 1: "Ann [St. John] = Henry Clifford Baron Clifford d. 1523"]. Owen *Lowther Fam.* (1990): 58–59. Spence *Shepherd Lord of Skipton Castle* (1994). National Archives, C 1/89/2 (available at www.catalogue.nationalarchives.gov.uk/search.asp).

Children of Henry Clifford, K.B., by Anne Saint John:

i. **ELIZABETH CLIFFORD**, married **RALPH BOWES**, Knt., of Streatlam, Durham [see BOWES 16].

ii. **ANNE CLIFFORD**, married (1st) **ROBERT CLIFTON**, Esq., of Clifton, Nottinghamshire [see NEED 18]; (2nd) **RALPH MELFORD**, Esq., of Arnold, Nottinghamshire [see NEED 18].

iii. **ELEANOR CLIFFORD**, married (1st) **NINIAN MARKENFIELD**, Knt. [see MAULEVERER 15]; (2nd) **JOHN CONSTABLE**, Knt., of Halsham, Yorkshire [see MAULEVERER 15].

❧ CLIFTON ❧

1. ROGER D'AUBENEY. He married **AMICE** _____. They had two sons, William and Nigel.
Barrett *Memorials of the parochial church … in the Parish of Attleborough* (1848): 12–41. Ellis *Antiqs. of Heraldry* (1869): 206–207 (Aubigny ped.). Green *Henry I: King of England & Duke of Normandy* (2006): 50.

2. WILLIAM D'AUBENEY, of Buckenham, Norfolk, Chief Butler of England. He married **MAUD LE BIGOD**, daughter of Roger le Bigod, Earl of Norfolk, probably by his 2nd wife, Alice, daughter of Robert de Tosny, of Belvoir. They had three sons, William [1st Earl of Arundel], Nigel, and Oliver, and one daughter, Olive (wife of Ralph de la Haye). He attested the treaty with the Count of Flanders in 1101. Sometime in the period, 1101–7, he founded Wymondham Priory, Norfolk. He distinguished himself at the Battle of Tinchebrai in 1106. He and his brother, Nigel, witnessed a charter of King Henry I dated 1111–16. Following the death of his wife, Maud, he gave the monks of Wymondham the manor of Happisburgh, Norfolk in pure alms. He was also a benefactor of Thetford Priory, Rochester Priory, and the Abbey of St. Stephen, Caen, Normandy. WILLIAM D'AUBENEY died in 1139. He and his wife, Maud, were buried before the high altar in the church of Wymondham Priory, Norfolk.
Barrett *Memorials of the parochial Church … in the Parish of Attleborough* (1848): 12–41. Ellis *Chronica Johannis de Oxenedes* (Rolls Ser.) (1859): 51 (sub A.D. 1139: "Willelmus, pincerna regis, fundator cœnobii de Wymundeham, obiit, a qua fundatione anno l. primo, die Omnium Sanctorum."). Ellis *Antiqs. of Heraldry* (1869): 206–207 (Aubigny ped.). *C.P.* 1 (1910): 233–235 (sub Arundel); 14 (1998): 37 (sub Arundel). Round *King's Serjeants & Officers of State* (1911): 140–165. Harvey et al. *Vis. of the North* 3 (Surtees Soc. 144) (1930): 152–156 (Daubeny ped.: "Willelmus Daubeney venit in Angliam cum Willelmo Conquestore et fundauit abbathiam de Wymondeham et ibidem sepelitur = (Matildis filia

Rogeri Bigot comitis Norffolcij).""). Hollister *Anglo-Norman Political Culture & the 12th-Cent. Renaissance* (1997): 70–71. Holt *Colonial England, 1066–1215* (1997): 176–178. Cownie *Religious Patronage in Anglo-Norman England, 1066–1135* (1998): 90. Keats-Rohan *Domesday Descendants* (2002): 273. Green *Henry I: King of England & Duke of Normandy* (2006): 50.

3. WILLIAM D'AUBENEY, of Buckenham, Kenninghall, and Wymondham, Norfolk, hereditary Chief Butler of England, Privy Councillor to King Henry I, and, in right of his wife, of Arundel, Sussex and Waltham, Essex, son and heir. He married after Dec. 1136 but not later than summer 1139 **ALICE** (or **AELIZ, ALEIDE, ALEYDA, AELIDIS, ADELIDE, ADELIDIS, ADELAIDIS, ADELIZA, ADELIZE, ATHELICE**) **OF LOUVAIN**, widow of Henry I, King of England (died 1 Dec. 1135) [see ENGLAND 2], and daughter of Gottfried (or Godefroy) I, Duke of Lower Lorraine, Count of Louvain, by his 1st wife, Ida, daughter of Otto II, Count of Chiny. She was born about 1103. They had four sons, William [2nd Earl of Arundel or Sussex], Reiner, Henry, and Godfrey, and two daughters, Alice and Olive. In the period, c.1132/38, he granted the ville of Ham to Chartres Saint-Père. He was a witness to King Stephen's 2nd Charter of Liberties in 1136. He was created Earl of Lincoln c.1138. He gave shelter to Empress Maud at Arundel Castle in 1139, but afterwards adhered to King Stephen. His earldom was transferred from Lincoln to Sussex before Christmas 1141. In his own later charters he is styled Earl of Chichester. About 1145 he witnessed a charter of Henry Hussey as "Consul Willelmo de Cicestrr." His wife, Alice, presented to the prebend of West Dean in 1150. About 1150, as "William Earl of Chichester," he granted 120 acres of land at Wymondham, Norfolk to the church of St. Lazarus of Jerusalem. Alice, dowager Queen of England, died as a nun at Affligem Abbey in Brabant 25 (or 26) March 1151, and was buried at Reading Abbey, Berkshire. He was influential in arranging the treaty of 1153, whereby the Crown continued with King Stephen for life, though the inheritance thereof was secured to Henry II. He subscribed his name to this instrument as "Comes Cicestrie." By grant dated c.1155, King Henry II confirmed to him as "William, Earl of Arundel" the Castle of Arundel, with the whole honour of Arundel and all its appurtenances. He served as Joint Ambassador to France and to the Pope in 1163/4. He served as Chief Ambassador with Princess Maud to Germany in 1168. He was appointed joint Commander of the royal army in Normandy in 1173. In Sept. 1173 he assisted in the defeat near Bury St. Edmunds of the Earl of Leicester. He founded Buckenham Abbey, Norfolk and Pynham Priory, Sussex. WILLIAM D'AUBENEY, 1st Earl of Arundel (or Sussex or Chichester), died at Waverley Abbey, Surrey 4 (or 12) October 1176, and was buried at Wymondham Priory, Norfolk.

D'Achery *Spicilegium* 10 (1671): 612–613 (Continuatio Chronici Afflegemiensis: "Filia præfati Ducis Aleidis juncta matrimonio Regi Angliæ, post obitum secundi conjugis Afflegemiensis Claustri solitudinem ad reliquum vitæ ad humandum corpus elegit in domo turri Ecclesiæ contigua, cum una aut altera ancilla in Fratrum Afflegemiensium quieta taciturna multitudine solitaria habitavit, & beato fine quievit, de qua epitaphium: Aleidis Regina Angliæ, filia Ducis Godefridi cum barba, Regnum suscepit in Anglia an MCXXI. obiit 9 Kal. Maii [23 April], sepulta è regione horologii nostri."). Brequigny & Mouchet *Table Chronologique des Diplômes, Chartes, Titres ... concernant l'Histoire de France* 3 (1783): 236 (charter dated c.1155 of Alice Queen of the English [Adelaidis reginæ Anglorum]). Banks *Genealogical Hist. of Divers Fams of the Ancient Peerage of England* (1826): 301–305. Tierney *Hist. & Antiqs. of the Castle & Town of Arundel* 1 (1834): 169–179. Guérard *Cartulaire de l'Abbaye de Saint-Père de Chartres* 2 (1840): 611–612 (charter of William d'Aubeney). Strickland *Lives of the Queens of England* 1 (1840): 212–256 (biog. of Adelicia of Louvaine). Barrett *Memorials of the parochial Church ... in the Parish of Attleborough* (1848): 12–41. *Arch. Journal* 20 (1863): 283 ("Adeliza appears to have used the identical matrux of the seal which had belonged to the first queen of Henry I., the name—Aalidis—having been substituted for Mat[i]ldis), 287–288 (charter of Queen Alice [Aelidis regina] ... There is appended ... a pointed oval seal of white wax .... device, a female figure standing ... The legend is + SIGILLVM · AALIDIS · SECVND[AE · DE]I · GRACIA · REGINAE · ANGLIE.), 288–289 (charter of Queen Alice [A. Dei gracia Reginæ]); 22 (1865): 152–153 (charter of William [d'Aubeney], Earl of Lincoln; charter names Queen Alice his wife [regina Adelidis]). Luard *Annales Monastici* 1 (Rolls Ser. 36) (1864): 14 (Margam Annals sub 1151: "Obiit Adelidis, regina secunda Henrici regis."); 3 (Rolls Ser. 36) (1866): 433 (Bermondsey Annals sub A.D. 1121: "Hoc anno rex Henricus primus duxit Adelizam, filiam ducis Lovaniae, in uxorem, tertio nonas Februarii [3 February]."). Burke *Gen. Hist. of the Dormant, Abeyant, Forfeited & Extinct Peerages* (1866): 2–3 (sub Albini, Earls of Arundel). *Jour. British Arch. Assoc.* (1867):

21–33 ("In the Register of the Priory of Bromhale, we find the record of his death under the date of the 4th day of October, 22nd of Henry II (A.D. 1176), in the following words, 'obiit Willielmus Comes Arundel' (no mention of Sussex or Chichester), et 'sepultus est in prioratus de Wymondham.'"). Ellis *Antiqs. of Heraldry* (1869): 206–207 (Aubigny ped.). *Recueil des Historiens des Gaules et de la France* 13 (1869): 314 (Ex Roberti de Monte [Robert de Torigni]: "Johannes Comes Aucensis moritur, ei successit ei filius ejus Henricus, quem genuerat ex filia Willermi de Albineio, quem vocant Comitem de Arundel. Hic duxit Aelizam Reginam, relictam Henrici senioris Regis Anglorum, ex qua genuit Guillermum primogenitum suum, et Godefridum, et istam comitissam uxorem Johannis Aucensis, de quo sermo est."). Delisle *Chronique de Robert de Torigni* 1 (1872): 215 (sub A.D. 1139: "Invitarerat enim eos Willermus de Albinneio, qui duxerat Aeliz quondam reginam, quæ habebat castellum et comitatum Hardundel, quod rex Henricus dederat ei in dote."); 2 (1873): 63–64 ("Cessit etiam in fata Willermus de Albineio, quem vocabant comitem d'Arundel, relinquens filios quatuor, scilicet Guillermum de Albineio primogenitum, et alios tres natos ex Aeliza regina, uxore primi Henrici regis Anglorum."). Matthew of Paris *Chronica Majora* 2 (Rolls Ser. 57) (1874): 298 (sub 1176: "comes etiam Willemus de Arundel obiit quarto idus Octobris [12 October] apud Waverle, et sepultus est apud Wimundham, cellam scilicet ecclesiæ Sancti Albani, cujus cellæ patronus fuisse dinoscitur."). *D.N.B.* 1 (1885): 137–138 (biog. of Adeliza of Louvain). Doyle *Official Baronage of England* 1 (1886): 66 (sub Arundel). Luard *Flores Historiarum* 2 ((Rolls Ser.) 1890): 69 ("Anno gratiæ MCLIº [1151]. Obiit Adelicia regina, uxor regis Stephani;" the editor notes that the name "Stephani" is erased in Ch. and altered to "Henrici I."). *Recueil des Historiens des Gaules et de la France* 23 (1894): 471 (Ex Obituariis Lirensis Monasterii: "25 Mart. Obiit Adelicia regina."), 476 (Ex Necrologio Monasterii Crucis Sancti Leufredi: "25 Mart. [Obiit] Adeliza, regina Anglorum."), 580 (Notæ Monasterii Montis Sancti Michaelis: "12 Oct. [Obiit] Guillermus, comes de Arundel."). Napier & Stevenson *Crawford Coll. of early Charters & Docs. now in the Bodleian Library* (1895): 31 (William [d'Aubeney], Earl of Chichester dated c.1150; charter names his wife, Queen Alice [regina Adelide]). *Trans. East Herts Arch. Soc.* 1(1) (1901): 129–135 (charter of Queen Alice wife of King Henry I dated 1136 [Adelidis regina uxor nobilissimi regis Henrici & filia Godefridi ducis lotharingie]. Warner & Ellis *Facsimiles of Royal & Other Charters in the British Museum* 1 (1903): #14 (charter of William [de Albini], Earl of Lincoln dated c.1139–40; charter names his wife, Queen Adeleidis), #27 (charter of William [de Albini], Earl of Chichester dated 1151-2; charter names his wife, Queen Athelice). *C.P.* 1 (1910): 233–235, 237 (chart) (sub Arundel). Round *King's Serjeants & Officers of State* (1911): 140–165. Harvey et al. *Vis. of the North* 3 (Surtees Soc. 144) (1930): 152–156 (Daubeny ped.: "Willelmus Daubeney creatus Comes Darundell fundauit prioratum de Boukenham et sepultus est in domo capitulari de Wymondham *ob. 3 H. 2.* = Adeliza relicta Henrici primi regis."). Leys *Sandford Cartulary* 2 (Oxfordshire Rec. Soc. 22) (1941): 216. Davis *King Stephen* (1967): 137 ("[King] Stephen recognized three successive earls of Lincoln ... The first was William d'Aubigny *pincerna* who married Queen Adeliza, widow of King Henry I, and in her right became lord of the honour and castle of Arundel. He styles himself William Earl of Lincoln in three charters in which his identity is proved by references to his wife. They are in favour of Lewes Priory and the abbeys of Reading and Affligem—and in the case of Affligem there is also a charter of Adeliza referring to her husband as earl of Lincoln (Round, *Geoffrey de Mandeville* 324–325; Warner and Ellis, *Facsimiles*, no. 14; E. de Marneffe, *Cartulaire de l'Abbaye de Affligem* in *Analectes pour servir à l'Histoire ecclésiastique de la Belgique*, 2º section, pp. 104, 106). In royal charters it is usually impossible to distinguish him from his successor, William de Roumare, since the normal style of both was *Willelmus comes de Lincolnia*, or (before he was an earl) from his father, William d'Aubigny *pincerna*, who died before June 1139 (Reg. iii. 973). If Robert de Torigny is right (*Chronicles* iv. 137) William had married Adeliza by September 1139, and it is tempting to assume that it was on his marriage that he was made earl of Lincoln, his connection with that county being that his mother, Maud Bigod, was a grand-daughter, and possible co-heiress, of Robert de Tosny of Belvoir. We do not know precisely when he was transferred from Lincoln to Sussex, but it was certainly by Christmas 1141 when he attested a charter as *Comite Willelmo de Sudsexa* (Reg. iii. 276)."). Kemp *Reading Abbey Cartularies* 1 (Camden Soc. 4th Ser. 31) (1986): 301, 369, 476. Schwennicke *Europaische Stanmtafeln* 1 (1980): 95 (sub Hainault, Brabant). Meyer *Culture of Christendom* (1993): 136 (Canterbury Obituary Lists: "7 Kal. [Apr.] [26 March]. Obiit Atheliza regis."). Vincent *Acta of Henry II and Richard I* Pt. 2 (List and Index Soc. Special Ser. 27) (1996): 143 (confirmation c. 1172/81 of grant made by Queen Adela) (original published in *Jour. of British Architetural Assoc.* 17: 312). Holt *Colonial England, 1066–1215* (1997): 176–178. Weller *Die Heiratspolitik des deutschen Hochadels im 12. Jahrhundert* (2004): 464–476 (biog. of Königin Adelheid von England) ("On page 476, Weller states: "Seine Gattin Adelheid von Löwen, die ehemalige Königin von England, war schon 1151 während des Bürgerkrieges verschieden und wurde in Reading beigesetzt ... Der Begräbnisort Kgn. Adelheids geht aus einem Schreiben Jocelins v. Löwen an Bf. Hilarius v. Chichester eindeutig hervor; vgl. *Reading Abbey Cartularies* 1, No. 551, 416f.; s.a. Bartlett, *England* 596. Nicht stichhaltig ist demgegenüber die van Sanderus, Chorographia 1, 45, verbreitete Nachricht, wonach Adelheid vor ihrem Tod in ihre Heimat übergesiedelt und im Kloster Affligem gestoren und begraben sei; heirnach auch John Horace Round in dem Art.: Adeliza of Louvain, in *DNB* 1 (1885): 137f.; *Complete Peerage* 1, 235. Allerdings ist Kgn. Adelheid als Wohltäterin von Affligem aufgetreten unde hat dem Kloster einigen Besitz in England gestiftet; vgl. Cart. Affligem, No. 79, 121-124 (hier 122)."). Verbeke *Medieval Narrative Sources* (2005): 21–36.

Children of William d'Aubeney, by Alice of Louvain:

i. **WILLIAM D'AUBENEY**, 2nd Earl of Arundel (or Sussex) [see next].

ii. **ALICE D'AUBENEY**, married (1st) **JEAN** (or **JOHN**) **I**, 5th Count of Eu [see EU 5]; (2nd) **ALVRED DE SAINT MARTIN** [see EU 5].

4. WILLIAM D'AUBENEY, 2nd Earl of Arundel (or Sussex), Chief Butler of England, Privy Councillor, Constable of Windsor Castle, 1191–3, son and heir. He married before Michaelmas 1176 **MAUD DE SAINT HILARY**, widow of Roger de Clare (otherwise Roger Fitz Richard), 2nd Earl of Hertford (died 1173) [see CLARE 4], and daughter and heiress of James de Saint Hilary, of Field Dalling, Norfolk, by his wife, Aveline. They had three sons, William [3rd Earl of Arundel], Alan, and Godfrey (or Geoffrey), and one daughter, Maud. In 1176/7 he was confirmed as Earl of Sussex, but the Castle and Honour of Arundel were, in accordance with the policy of King Henry II, retained by the Crown. He served as Assessor in the royal court in 1177 to arbitrate between the Kings of Castile and Navarre. He was granted restoration of the Castle and Honour of Arundel by King Richard I 27 June 1190, when he became Earl of Arundel. At an unknown date, he granted various lands in Quiddenham, Norfolk to Reading Abbey, Berkshire. WILLIAM D'AUBENEY, Earl of Arundel, died 24 Dec. 1193, and was buried at Wymondham Priory, Norfolk.

Tierney *Hist. & Antiqs. of the Castle & Town of Arundel* 1 (1834): 179–180. Barrett *Memorials of the parochial Church ... in the Parish of Attleborough* (1848): 12–41. *Arch. Journal* 22 (1865): 154 (undated charter of William d'Aubeney, Earl of Sussex to Reading Abbey; charter names Queen Alice his mother [Regine Adelize matris mee], Jocelin the castellan his uncle [avunculi], charter is witnessed by Reiner his brother [fratre]), 155 (undated charter of William d'Aubeney, Earl of Sussex to Reading Abbey; charter names Jocelin his uncle [avunculi]; charter is witnessed by Reiner his brother [fratre])). Luard *Annales Monastici* 2 (Rolls Ser. 36) (1865): 249 (Annals of Waverley sub A.D. 1193: "Obiit Willelmus comes junior de Arundel in vigilia Natalis Domini."). *Jour. British Arch. Assoc.* (1867): 21–33. Delisle *Chronique de Robert de Torigni* 2 (1873): 63–64 (sub A.D. 1176 — "Qui Guillermus [de Albineio] duxit relictam Rogerii comitis de Clara, filiam Jacobi de Sancto Hilario, cum omni terra quam idem Jacobus habuerat in Anglia."). Doyle *Official Baronage of England* 1 (1886): 66–67 (sub Arundel). *C.P.* 1 (1910): 235–236, 237 (chart) (sub Arundel). Harvey et al. *Vis. of the North* 3 (Surtees Soc. 144) (1930): 152–156 (Daubeny ped.: "Willelmus (nomen cepit in parliamento consulatus [*sic* MS.] Sussex et Arundell construxit capellam beate Thome in Wimondham et sepelitur in abbathia predicta) *Daubeney comes Arundel ob. 22 H. 2.* = [empty roundel] *Matilda filia et heres Iacobi de Sancto Hillario relicta Rogeri comitis Clara.*"). Ward *Women of the English Nobility & Gentry 1066–1500* (1995): 42; 93–94 (charter of Maud, wife of Roger earl of Clare dated 1152–73; charter witnessed by Richard brother of the earl and Conan nephew of the earl).

Children of William d'Aubeney, by Maud de Saint Hilary:

i. **WILLIAM D'AUBENEY**, 3rd Earl of Arundel [see next].

ii. **MAUD D'AUBENEY**, married **WILLIAM DE WARENNE**, Knt., 6th Earl of Surrey [see WARENNE 8].

5. WILLIAM D'AUBENEY, 3rd Earl of Arundel, Chief Butler of England, Privy Councillor, Judge in the King's Court, 1198, 1200, 1218, son and heir. He married **MABEL OF CHESTER**, daughter of Hugh, Earl of Chester, by Bertrade, daughter of Simon de Montfort, Count of Évreux, seigneur of Montfort-l'Amaury [see CHESTER 5 for her ancestry]. They had two sons, William [4th Earl of Arundel] and Hugh [5th Earl of Arundel], and four daughters, Maud, Nichole (or Colette), Cecily, and Isabel. In 1194 he was one of the Receivers of the money raised for the king's ransom. He assisted at the Coronation of King John in 1199. In 1213 he witnessed the instrument by which King John resigned the crown of England into the hands of the Pope. He served a joint envoy to treat with the Barons in 1215. He went on Crusade in 1218 and was present at the Siege of Damietta later that year. WILLIAM D'AUBENEY, 3rd Earl of Arundel, died at Cainell near Rome 1 Feb. 1220/1. His remains were conveyed to England and buried in Wymondham Priory, Norfolk.

Placitorum in Domo Capitulari Westmonasteriensi Asservatorum Abbreviatio (1811): 30, 44. Dugdale *Monasticon Anglicanum* 3 (1821): 330 (sub Wymondham Monastery: "Memorandum, quod Willielmus de Albaneio, pincerna regis Henrici, fundavit ecclesiam monachorum de Wymundham. Qui quidem Willielmus habuit unum filium Willielmum, comitem Arundeliae; qui Willielmus comes habuit unum filium Willelmum, comitem Sussexiae; qui Willielmus comes habuit unum filium Willielmum, comitem Sussexiæ; qui Willielmus habuit unum fratrem Hugonem, comitem Sussexiæ; qui Hugo moriebatur sine hærede de corpore suo, et quatuor sorores fuerunt propinquiores hæredes ejus, et diviserunt totum comitatum Sussexiæ inter eas: quarum unam desponsavit dominus le Fitz Allen, et aliam dominus de Montealto, et aliam domus Robertus de Tathesale, et aliam dominus de Somerie, et advocatio ecclesiæ de Wymundeham allocata fuit domino Roberto de Tateshale, et uxori ejus, tenenda de se et hæredibus suis in puram et perpetuam elemosinam; qui quidem Robertus de Tathesale, habuit filium et hæredem Robertum de Tathesale, cujus erant tres filiae, quarum unam desponsavit dominus Johannes Orby, aliam dominus de Dryby, et tertiam dominus Thomas Caily qui habuit unum filium et hæredem, scilicet Thomam Caily, qui obiit sine hærede de corpore suo, cujus sororem duxit Rogerus de Clyfton armiger prædicti Thomæ. Iste Rogerus habuit unum filium et hæredem, scilicet, dominum Adam de Clyfton, qui habuit filium et hæredem Constantinum de Clyfton, qui gabuit filium et haeredem dominum Johannem de Clyfton, qui habuit filium et hæredem Constantinum de Clyfton, qui quidem Constantinus habuit unum filium et hæredem dominum Johannem de Clyfton, qui nunc est dominus de Wymundham."). Tierney *Hist. & Antiqs. of the Castle & Town of Arundel* 1 (1834): 181–185. *Coll. Top. et Gen.* 2 (1835): 247–249. Burke *Gen. Hist. of the Dormant, Abeyant, Forfeited & Extinct Peerages* (1866): 2–3 (sub Albini, Earls of Arundel). *Jour. British Arch. Assoc.* (1867): 21–33. Flower *Vis. of Yorkshire 1563–4* (H.S.P. 16) (1881): 176–177 (Knevet ped.: "Willielmus Dawbeny Comes Arundell nupcit Mabillam filiam et unam heredum Radulphi Comitis Cestrie et Lincolnie."). Ormerod *Hist. of the County Palatine & City of Chester* 1 (1882): 26–33. Doyle *Official Baronage of England* 1 (1886): 67 (sub Arundel). *C.P.* 1 (1910): 236–238, 237 (chart) (sub Arundel). Farrer *Early Yorkshire Charters* 2 (1915): 195 (chart). *Genealogist* n.s. 34 (1918): 181–189 (William d'Aubeney, Earl of Arundel, styled "uncle" [avunculus] of Warin de Munchensy in 1213, he being half-brother of Warin's mother, Aveline de Clare). Farrer *Honors & Knights' Fees* 2 (1924): 10–11. Harvey et al. *Vis. of the North* 3 (Surtees Soc. 144) (1930): 152–156 (Daubeny pedigree: "Willelmus Daubeney comes de Arundell sepultus in Abbathia predicta *ob. 1 Io.* = [empty roundel] *Mabilia filia et coh. Ranulfi co. Cestrie.*"). Meyer *Culture of Christendom* (1993): 132 (Canterbury Obituary Lists: "Kal. [Feb.] [1 Feb.]. Obiit Willelmus Comes de Arundel.").

Children of Mabel of Chester, by William d'Aubeney:

i. **HUGH D'AUBENEY**, Knt., 5th Earl of Arundel, Chief Butler of England, 2nd son of William d'Aubeney, 3rd Earl of Arundel, by Mabel, 2nd daughter of Hugh, Earl of Chester. He was born about 1214 (of age in 1235). He was heir in 1224 to his older brother, William d'Aubeney, 4th Earl of Arundel. He was co-heir in 1232 to his uncle, Ranulph, Earl of Chester and Lincoln. In 1233 he made fine with the king by 2500 marks to have the lands of his late brother, William d'Aubeney, Earl of Arundel, until his legal age, as well as the lands which fell to Hugh by hereditary right of the lands formerly of his uncle, Ranulph, Earl of Chester and Lincoln. He married in 1234 **ISABEL DE WARENNE**, daughter of William de Warenne, Knt., 6th Earl of Surrey, Warden of the Cinque Ports, by Maud, daughter of William Marshal, Knt., 4th Earl of Pembroke (or Striguil), hereditary Master Marshal [see WARENNE 8 for her ancestry]. They had no issue. In 1240 he was summoned to restore the manor of Whaddon, Buckinghamshire to the king as an escheat of the Normans. Hugh stated that he, his brother, and his father had all been given livery of the lands, but, though he quoted the terms of the original grant made to his father in 1207, Whaddon was surrendered to the king. In 1242 he accompanied the King in his expedition to Guienne. SIR HUGH D'AUBENEY, Earl of Arundel, died 7 May 1243, and was buried at Wymondham Priory, Norfolk. In 1244 his widow, Countess Isabel, sued Robert de Sheney for the third part of one carucate of land in Smisby, Derbyshire, and Ralph de Kenninghall for the third part of nine acres of land and one acre of pasture in Kenninghall, Norfolk, and the one third part of 14 acres of land in Riddlesworth, Norfolk. The same year she also sued Thomas le Ireys for the third part of one carucate of land in Attleborough, Norfolk, William de Oddingseles for the third part of one-half carucate of land in Leeds, Yorkshire, Roger de Somery and Nichole his wife for the third part of two carucates of land in Chipping Campden, Gloucestershire, and one third part of one carucate of land in Great Tew, Oxfordshire, and Hugh le Bigod for the one third part of one carucate of land in Stoughton, Sussex. In 1249 Countess Isabel founded the Abbey of Marham, Norfolk. She presented to the church of Shenley, Buckinghamshire in 1272. In 1271 Roger de Somery was engaged in a lengthy lawsuit with her regarding the advowson of the church of Olney, Buckinghamshire; in 1273 it was noted that the patronage of the church was to remain with Roger by a concord between him and Countess Isabel. In 1277–8 Master John de Croft arraigned an assize of novel disseisin against her and others touching a tenement in Bilsham, Sussex. In 1278–9 Nigel le Got arraigned an assize of novel disseisin against her and others touching a tenement in Wymondham, Norfolk. Isabel, Countess of Arundel, died shortly before 23 Nov. 1282, and was buried at Marham, Norfolk. Blomefield *Essay towards a Top. Hist. of Norfolk* 1 (1805): 216–218; 4 (1775): 125–128; 9 (1808): 42–59. Dugdale *Monasticon Anglicanum* 5 (1825): 743, 744 (charter of Isabel d'Aubeney, Countess of Arundel; charter witnessed by her brothers, Sir Roger Bigod, Earl of Norfolk, Sir Hugh Bigod, and John de Warenne). *Dignity of a Peer of the Realm* (1826): 389–434. Hunter *South Yorkshire* 1 (1828): 105 (Warenne ped.). Wainright *Hist. & Top. Intro. of the Wapentake of Stafford & Tickhill* (1829): 168–169, 195–196 (Warenne ped.). Dallaway *Hist. of the Western Div. of Sussex* 2(1) (1832): 128 (Warenne ped.). Tierney *Hist. & Antiqs. of the Castle & Town of Arundel* 1 (1834): 186–192. Brewer *Monumenta Franciscana* 1 (Rolls Ser. 4) (1858): 331, 639–640. Burke *Gen. Hist. of the Dormant, Abeyant, Forfeited & Extinct Peerages* (1866): 2–3 (sub Albini, Earls of Arundel). Matthew of Paris *Matthæi Parisiensis* 2 (Rolls Ser. 44) (1866): 477 (sub A.D. 1243: "Anno sub eodem, nonis Maii [7 May], obiit comes

Harundeliæ Hugo de Albineto, in ætate juvenili, cum jam vix metas adolescentiæ pertransisset. Et apud Wimundham, in ecclesia Sanctæ Mariæ, videlicet prioratum Sancto Albano pertinentem, est sepultus, cum patribus suis dictæ ecclesiæ patronis et fundatoribus."). *Jour. British Arch. Assoc.* (1867): 21–33. Matthew of Paris *Chronica Majora* 5 (Rolls Ser. 57) (1880): 336-337 (Countess Isabel de Warenne, widow of Hugh d'Aubeney, Earl of Arundel, styled "king's kinswoman" [regis cognate]). Flower *Vis. of Yorkshire 1563–4* (H.S.P. 16) (1881): 176–177 (Knevet ped.: "Hugo Comes Arundell post mortem Willielmi fratris sui non habuit exitum et sepelitur in Abathia predicta."). *Annual Rpt. of the Deputy Keeper* 47 (1886): 163; 48 (1887): 214. Doyle *Official Baronage of England* 1 (1886): 68 (sub Arundel). Maitland *Bracton's Note Book* 3 (1887): 280–283. Grazebrook *Barons of Dudley* 1 (Colls. Hist. Staffs. 9(2)) (1888): 20. Ratcliff *Hist. & Antiqs. of the Newport Pagnell Hundreds* (1900): 415–416. C.P.R. 1272–1281 (1901): 30. Wrottesley *Peds. from the Plea Rolls* (1905): 85, 550. *Year Books of Edward II* 3 (Selden Soc. 20) (1905): 60–63. Martin *Hist. of the Manor of Westhope* (1909): 15–33. C.P. 1 (1910): 237 (chart), 238–239 (sub Arundel). Round *King's Serjeants & Officers of State* (1911): 140–165. Clay *Extinct & Dormant Peerages* (1913): 236–238 (sub Warenne). Farnham *Leicestershire Medieval Peds.* (1925): 11 (ped. of Earls of Chester). VCH *Buckingham* 3 (1925): 435–442. *Romania* 55 (1929): 332–381. Harvey et al. *Vis. of the North* 3 (Surtees Soc. 144) (1930): 152–156 (Daubeny ped.: "Hugo comes Arundell post mortem Willelmi fratris sui non habuit exitum et sepelitur in abbathia predicta ob. 28 H. 3. = filia domini [left blank]."). C.C.R. 1268–1272 (1938): 391–392. Paget *Baronage of England* (1957) 12: 1–6 (sub Aubigny). C.R.R. 16 (1979): 499; 18 (1999): 151–152, 216, 222, 241, 247, 261, 310. VCH *Oxford* 11 (1983): 194–208. Gee *Women, Art & Patronage from Henry III to Edward III: 1216–1377* (2002): 157. Morris *Bigod Earls of Norfolk in the 13th Cent.* (2005): opp. 1 (chart). Henry III Fine Rolls Project (R[anulph] Earl of Chester and Lincoln styled "uncle" of Hugh d'Aubeney, brother and heir of William d'Aubeney, Earl of Arundel in a fine roll item dated 1233) (abs. of record available at www.finerollshenry3.org.uk/content/calendar/roll_033.html).

ii. **MAUD D'AUBENEY** [see next].

iii. **NICHOLE** (or **COLETTE**) **D'AUBENEY**, married **ROGER DE SOMERY**, Knt., of Dudley (in Sedgley), Staffordshire [see SOMERY 3].

iv. **CECILY D'AUBENEY**, married **ROGER DE MOHAUT**, Knt., of Mold, Cheshire, Castle Rising, Norfolk, etc. [see MORLEY 6].

v. **ISABEL D'AUBENEY**, married **JOHN FITZ ALAN**, of Clun and Oswestry, Shropshire [see FITZ ALAN 6].

6. MAUD D'AUBENEY, married before 1222 **ROBERT DE TATESHALE**, Knt., of Tattershall, Candlesby, Kirkby, Maltby, and Toft, Lincolnshire, Fleckney and Slawston, Leicestershire, Denton, Babingley, Tibenham, and Topcroft, Norfolk, etc., son and heir of Walter de Tateshale, by Iseult, daughter and co-heiress of William Pantolf, of Breedon, Leicestershire. He was born about 1200 (minor in 1214). They had one son, Robert. He was heir in 1212 to his uncle, Robert de Tateshale, of Tattershall, Lincolnshire. He served at the Siege of Bytham Castle in 1221 and in the Welsh campaign of 1228. In 1223, being then in the king's service with horses and arms, he obtained livery of the lands of his mother, Iseult, which had been taken into the king's hand by reason of her debt to the Crown. In 1224 he joined the pursuit of Fawkes de Breauté across England. In 1226 and 1227 he was granted custody of the castles and towns of Bolsover, Derbyshire and Lincoln. In 1229 he was going overseas in the king's service. He served in Brittany in 1230. His wife, Maud, was living in 1238, but died before 1243. In 1242 orders were issued for him to be supplied with one or two ships to accompany the king abroad. In 1244 he and his son, Robert, were going on service in Scotland and Wales. He was summoned before the King's Court at Chester in 1245 for having tourneyed in defiance of the royal commands. He presented to the churches of Candlesby, Lincolnshire, 1242, Gunby, Lincolnshire, 1245, Knossington, Leicestershire, 1249, and Tattershall, Lincolnshire, 1249. SIR ROBERT DE TATESHALE died 18 July 1249.

Dugdale *Antiqs. of Warwickshire* (1730): 95 (Stuteville-Pantolf ped.). *Topographer* 1 (1789): 327–336. Blomefield *Essay towards a Top. Hist. of Norfolk* 9 (1808): 42–59. Dugdale *Monasticon Anglicanum* 3 (1821): 330 (sub Wymondham Monastery). Burke *Gen. Hist. of the Dormant, Abeyant, Forfeited & Extinct Peerages* (1866): 2–3 (sub Albini, Earls of Arundel). Flower *Vis. of Yorkshire 1563–4* (H.S.P. 16) (1881): 176–177 (Knevet ped.: "Anabilia Dawbeny, filia prima, Roberto Tateshall."). Grazebrook *Barons of Dudley* 1 (Colls. Hist. Staffs. 9(2)) (1888): 17–29. *Lincolnshire Notes & Queries* 6 (1901): 33–41. Wrottesley *Peds. from the Plea Rolls* (1905): 244–245, 531–532, 550. C.P. 1 (1910): 237; 12(1) (1953): 648–649 (sub Tateshal). Grosseteste *Rotuli Roberti Grosseteste Episcopi Lincolniensis* (Lincoln Rec. Soc. 11) (1914):

68, 84, 115, 424–425. Farrer *Honors & Knights' Fees* 2 (1924): 10–11. Farnham *Leicestershire Medieval Village Notes* 1 (1929): 1–6; 5 (1931): 65–74, 219–222. Harvey et al. *Vis. of the North* 3 (Surtees Soc. 144) (1930): 152–156 (Daubeny ped.: "Robertus Tateshall miles = Anabilia *Amabilia* Daubeney prima filia *et coh.*"). Paget *Baronage of England* (1957) 524:2-3 (Amabel). Sanders *English Baronies* (1960): 2, 88. VCH *Leicester* 5 (1964): 84–90, 297–303.

7. ROBERT DE TATESHALE, of Tattershall and Candlesby, Lincolnshire, Ab-Kettleby, Breedon, Holwell, and Somerby, Leicestershire, Denton, Babingley, Buckenham, Tibenham, and Topcroft, Norfolk, etc., son and heir, born about 1223 (aged 26 in 1249). He married before 1249 **NICHOLE DE GREY**, daughter of John de Grey, Knt., of Shirland, Derbyshire, by his 1st wife, Emma, daughter and heiress of Roger de Cauz. Her maritagium included the manor of Shalbourne, Berkshire (now Wiltshire). They had two sons, Robert, Knt. [1st Lord Tateshale] and Hugh, and three daughters, Emma, Joan, and Isabel (wife of John de Orreby, Knt., Lord Orreby). In 1243 he was co-heir to his uncle, Hugh d'Aubeney, Earl of Arundel, by which he inherited the Castle and manor of Buckenham, Norfolk, the manor of Tortington, Sussex, and an one-fourth share in the manor of Walderton (in Stoughton), Sussex. In 1243 he and Roger de Mohaut gave the king three palfreys for making a partition between them of the lands formerly of Hugh, Earl of Arundel, which fell to them as inheritance. He served with his father in 1244. He went to Gascony with the king in 1253. He was going on the king's service to Wales in 1257. He was summoned to muster at Chester for service against Llywelyn in 1258. In 1260 he promised to deliver 70 sacks of wool to Arnold Griffun and partners at the fair at Boston, Lincolnshire. He was summoned for service against the Welsh in 1260, 1263, and 1264. In 1263 he was a commissioner to complete the eyre in Lincolnshire. During the Barons' War, he supported the king. He was taken prisoner at the Battle of Lewes 14 May 1264. After the royal victory at Evesham, he aided the Crown in restoring peace. In 1267 he served as one of the royal commanders in East Anglia. In 1267 his grandmother, Iseult widow of Walter de Tateshale, sued him for one third part of a messuage, two watermills, and lands in Breedon, Leicestershire, with lands in Holwell, Somerby, and Dalby, Leicestershire, as her dower. The same year as "Robert de Tateshale the elder," he sued Ralph Chamberleng, Adam Hubert, and others, claiming that in the time of the disturbance of the realm, they plundered and scattered his goods and chattels in the manors of Breedon, Somerby, and Holwell, Leicestershire to his grave damage. In 1268 he was called in to aid in the enforcement of order in the realm. ROBERT DE TATESHALE died 22 July 1273, probably at Tattershall, Lincolnshire. His widow, Nichole, had the manors of Topcroft, Norfolk, Bredon, Leicestershire, and Candlesby and Maltby, Lincolnshire assigned for her dower. In 1274–5 she arraigned an assize of novel disseisin against Peter Bacon touching common of pasture in Fortesbyr' [?Fosbury], Berkshire. In the same period, William son of Peter le Clere arraigned an assize of mort d'ancestor against her touching a messuage and land in Swakeston, Derbyshire. On 30 May 1277 a royal inquisition reported that Hugh de Estgate and others by order of Nicholas de Stuteville came by night to the gallows of Nichole de Tateshale at Topcroft, Norfolk, overthrew them, and carried them away. In 1277–8 and 1279–80 Ralph Basset, of Drayton, arraigned an assize of mort d'ancestor against her touching the manor of Bredon, Leicestershire.

Topographer 1 (1789): 327–336. Dugdale *Monasticon Anglicanum* 3 (1821): 330 (sub Wymondham Monastery). *Coll. Top. et Gen.* 7 (1841): 142–144 (sub Tateshale). *Annual Rpt. of the Deputy Keeper* 44 (1883): 108, 257; 47 (1886): 171; 49 (1888): 27. *Staffordshire Suits: Plea Rolls* (Colls. Hist. Staffs. 4) (1883): 121–133. Wrottesley *Peds. from the Plea Rolls* (1905): 244–245, 531–532, 550. Round *King's Serjeants & Officers of State* (1911): 140–165. *Cal. Inqs. Misc.* 1 (1916): 331. Foster *Final Concords of Lincoln from the Feet of Fines A.D. 1244–1272* 2 (Lincoln Rec. Soc. 17) (1920): 127–144. Farnham *Leicestershire Medieval Village Notes* 1 (1929): 1–6; 5 (1931): 65–74, 219–222. C.P. 12(1) (1953): 649–650 (sub Tateshal). VCH *Sussex* 4 (1953): 121–126; 5(1) (1997): 190–204, 214–224. Paget *Baronage of England* (1957) 524:3-4 (coheir of the Earldom of Arundel). Sanders *English Baronies* (1960): 88. Moore *Fairs of Medieval England* (1995): 47–48. Oggins *Kings & Their Hawks: Falconry in Medieval England* (2004): 80. C.R.R. 18 (1999): 151–152.

Children of Robert de Tateshale, by Nichole de Grey:

    i. **EMMA DE TATESHALE** [see next].

    ii. **JOAN DE TATESHALE**, married **ROBERT DE DRIBY**, of Tumby, Lincolnshire [see BERNAKE 8].

8. EMMA DE TATESHALE, married before 1284 (as his 1st wife) **ADAM DE CAILLY**, of Cranwich, Norfolk. They had one son, Thomas, Knt., and one daughter, Margaret.

Topographer 1 (1789): 327–336. Dugdale *Monasticon Anglicanum* 3 (1821): 330 (sub Wymondham Monastery). *Coll. Top. et Gen.* 7 (1841): 142–144 (sub Tateshale). *Norfolk Archaeology* 3 (1852): 126–127 (Cailly-Clifton ped.). Flower *Vis. of Yorkshire 1563–4* (H.S.P. 16) (1881): 176–177 (Knevet ped.: "Emma prima filia Roberti Tateshall. = Osbertus Caylye Knight."). *Notes & Queries* 6th Ser. 6 (1882): 353. Burke *Gen. & Heraldic Hist. of the Colonial Gentry* 2 (1895): 750–753 (sub Cayley). *Lincolnshire Notes & Queries* 6 (1901): 33–41. Wrottesley *Peds. from the Plea Rolls* (1905): 244–245. Farrer *Honors & Knights' Fees* 3 (1925): 384. Farnham *Leicestershire Medieval Village Notes* 1 (1929): 1–6; 5 (1931): 65–74, 219–222. Harvey et al. *Vis. of the North* 3 (Surtees Soc. 144) (1930): 152–156 (Daubeny ped.: "Emma prima filia Robert Tateshall et coh. = Osbertus Cayly (miles)."). VCH *Sussex* 4 (1953): 121–126.

9. MARGARET DE CAILLY, married **ROGER DE CLIFTON**. They had one son, Adam, Knt. ROGER DE CLIFTON died shortly before 24 June 1330.

Dugdale *Monasticon Anglicanum* 3 (1821): 330 (sub Wymondham Monastery). *Coll. Top. et Gen.* 7 (1841): 142–144 (sub Tateshale). Barrett *Mems. of Attleborough* (1848): 183 (Caily-Clifton ped.). *Norfolk Archaeology* 3 (1852): 126–127 (Cailly-Clifton ped.). Flower *Vis. of Yorkshire 1563–4* (H.S.P. 16) (1881): 176–177 (Knevet ped.: "Emma filia et heres Thome Caly nupta = Rogero Clyfton Militi."). Burke *Gen. Hist. of the Dormant, Abeyant, Forfeited & Extinct Peerages* (1883): 124 (sub Clifton). Burke *Gen. & Heraldic Hist. of the Colonial Gentry* 2 (1895): 750–753 (sub Cayley). Wrottesley *Peds. from the Plea Rolls* (1905): 244–245. *C.F.R.* 4 (1913): 182. *C.P.* 3 (1913): 307, footnote a. Leadam *Select Cases before the King's Council 1243–1482* (Selden Soc. 35) (1918): 35–37. Harvey et al. *Vis. of the North* 3 (Surtees Soc. 144) (1930): 152–156 (Daubeny ped.: "Margeria filia et heres domini Thome Cayly = Rogerus Cliffton (miles)."). VCH *Sussex* 4 (1953): 121–126. Sanders *English Baronies* (1960): 88. Round: *King's Serjeants*, pp. 149 seq.

10. ADAM DE CLIFTON, Knt., of Buckenham, Cranwich, Denver, Hilborough, and Topcroft, Norfolk, Little Waltham, Essex, Shelley, Suffolk, Hunmanby, Yorkshire, etc., son and heir, born about 1307 (aged 9 in 1316, minor in 1323 and 1327). He was heir in 1316 to his uncle, Thomas de Cailly, Knt., by which he inherited the manors of Hilborough and West Bradenham, Norfolk and a one-fourth share of the manor of Walderton (in Stoughton), Sussex. He married **ELEANOR DE MORTIMER**, daughter of Robert de Mortimer, Knt., of Attleborough, Norfolk. They had two sons, Constantine and Adam, Knt., and one daughter, Eleanor (wife of John Mauteby). In 1327 he petitioned the king and council requesting that his minority not be turned to his disadvantage as he held the castle of Buckenham, Norfolk from the king in chief by homage and by the service of being chief butler for a fee and to do service at the coronation. In 1331 he impleaded several persons for fishing in his waters at Hilborough, Norfolk. In 1335 he had letters of protection, he then going to Scotland. He presented to the free chapel of St. Margaret, Hilborough, Norfolk in 1335, 1338, 1345, 1347, and 1349. In 1340 he complained that while he was beyond seas with the king, John, parson of Forncett, Richard le Smyth, and others came armed to his manor of Buckenham Castle, Norfolk, and took away 15 horses and 20 cows worth £40 and assaulted his men and servants. In 1342 the manor of Hilborough, Norfolk was settled on him and his wife, Eleanor. In 1347 he was granted a weekly market and two yearly fairs at his manor of Hilborough, Norfolk. In 1353 he had license to alienate in mortmain to the Prior and convent of Buckenham one messuage and lands in West Bradenham, Norfolk, together with the advowson of the same church. In 1356 he complained that Geoffrey Maloysel, Simon de Dunmowe, and others came armed to his manor of Hilborough, Norfolk, broke his gates, close and houses of the manor, drove away 200 sheep, carried away his goods, and assaulted his men and servants. In 1356–7 he claimed the manor of Blo Norton, Norfolk. In 1362–3 he granted land and rent in Buckenham, Norfolk and Cratfield, Suffolk to the Prior and convent of Buckenham, Norfolk. SIR ADAM DE CLIFTON died shortly before 11 May 1367.

Blomefield *Essay towards a Top. Hist. of Norfolk* 6 (1807): 112–118. Dugdale *Monasticon Anglicanum* 3 (1821): 330 (sub Wymondham Monastery). *Coll. Top. et Gen.* 7 (1841): 142–144 (sub Tateshale). Barrett *Mems. of Attleborough* (1848):

183 (Caily-Clifton ped.). *Norfolk Archaeology* 3 (1852): 126–127 (Cailly-Clifton ped.), 153 (Mauteby ped.); 4 (1855): 23 (Mawtby ped.). Flower *Vis. of Yorkshire 1563–4* (H.S.P. 16) (1881): 176–177 (Knevet ped.: "Dominus Adam Clyfton Militis = Alienora filia Domini Roberti Mortymer de Atylboroo Militis."). Burke *Gen. Hist. of the Dormant, Abeyant, Forfeited & Extinct Peerages* (1883): 124 (sub Clifton). *C.C.R.* 1323–1327 (1898): 1–11. *C.P.R.* 1338–1340 (1898): 118–119, 518. *C.P.R.* 1340–1343 (1900): 88. *C.C.R.* 1339–1341 (1901): 150–151. *C.P.R.* 1343–1345 (1902): 226. *C.P.R.* 1345–1348 (1903): 545. Wrottesley *Peds. from the Plea Rolls* (1905): 244–245. *C.P.R.* 1350–1354 (1907): 440. *C.C.R.* 1354–1360 (1908): 266–267. *C.P.R.* 1354–1358 (1909): 452. *C.P.R.* 1361–1364 (1912): 498. *C.P.R.* 1364–1367 (1912): 401, 405, 424. *C.P.* 3 (1913):307, footnote a. Leadam *Select Cases before the King's Council 1243–1482* (Selden Soc. 35) (1918): 35–37. *C.F.R.* 7 (1923): 349, 388. Harvey et al. *Vis. of the North* 3 (Surtees Soc. 144) (1930): 152–156 (Daubeny ped.: "Dominus Adam Clifton miles = Aleonora filia domini (Roberti) Mortimer de Atilborough militis."). VCH *Sussex* 4 (1953): 121–126. Sanders *English Baronies* (1960): 88. National Archives, C 143/345/5; SC 8/211/10505; SC 8/266/13284; SC 8/340/16045 (available at www.catalogue.nationalarchives.gov.uk/search.asp).

11. CONSTANTINE DE CLIFTON, of Little Waltham, Essex, Shelley, Suffolk, and Hunmanby, Yorkshire, son and heir apparent. He married before 20 May 1340 (date of license to grant lands) **KATHERINE DE LA POLE**, daughter of William de la Pole, Knt., of Kingston upon Hull, Yorkshire, Baron of the Exchequer, by Katherine, daughter of Walter de Norwich, Knt. They had two sons, John, Knt. [1st Lord Clifton] and Adam, Knt. CONSTANTINE DE CLIFTON died shortly before 20 Jan. 1363. His widow, Katherine, died shortly before 17 Feb. 1363.

Blomefield *Essay towards a Top. Hist. of Norfolk* 6 (1807): 112–118. Dugdale *Monasticon Anglicanum* 3 (1821): 330 (sub Wymondham Monastery). *Coll. Top. et Gen.* 7 (1841): 142–144 (sub Tateshale). Barrett *Mems. of Attleborough* (1848): 183 (Caily-Clifton ped.). *Norfolk Arch.* 3 (1852): 126–127 (Cailly-Clifton ped.). Flower *Vis. of Yorkshire 1563–4* (H.S.P. 16) (1881): 176–177 (Knevet ped.: "Dominus Constantinus Clyfton. = Katerina filia Domini Willielmi Dela pole Militis."). Burke *Dormant, Abeyant, Forfeited & Extinct Peerages* (1883): 124 (sub Clifton). *C.P.R.* 1338–1340 (1898): 518. Wrottesley *Peds. from the Plea Rolls* (1905): 244–245. *C.P.* 3 (1913): 307. *C.F.R.* 7 (1923): 249, 251. *Report on the MSS of Lord de L'isle & Dudley* 1 (Hist. MSS Comm. 77) (1925): 28. Harvey et al. *Vis. of the North* 3 (Surtees Soc. 144) (1930): 152–156 (Daubeny ped.: "Dominus Constantinus Clifton miles = Catherina filia domini Willielmi de la Powlle militis."). Paget *Baronage of England* (1957) 134a:1 (chart only).

12. JOHN DE CLIFTON, Knt., 1st Lord Clifton, of Buckenham, Babingley, Denton, Hilborough, West Bradenham, etc., Norfolk, son and heir, born about 1353 (aged 15 in 1368). He married **ELIZABETH DE CROMWELL**, daughter of Ralph de Cromwell, Knt., 1st Lord Cromwell, by Maud, daughter of John de Bernake, Knt. [see CROMWELL 8 for her ancestry]. They had one son, Constantine, Esq. or Gent. [2nd Lord Clifton], and one daughter, Katherine (wife of Ralph Greene, Esq., and Simon Felbrygg, K.G. [see FELBRIGG 9]). He was summoned to Parliament from 1 Dec. 1376 to 28 July 1388, by writs directed *Johanni de Clyfton*, whereby he is held to have become Lord Clifton. SIR JOHN DE CLIFTON, 1st Lord Clifton, died at Rhodes 10 August 1388. His widow, Elizabeth, married (2nd) **EDWARD BENSTEAD** (or **BENSTEDE**), Knt., of Hertingfordbury, Hertfordshire, Sheriff of Essex and Hertfordshire, 1379–80, 1399–1400, Knight of the Shire for Hertfordshire, 1384, 1397. Elizabeth, Lady Clifton, died 24 Sept. 1391.

Topographer 1 (1789): 327–336. Throsby *Thoroton's Hist. of Nottinghamshire* 3 (1790): 169–171. Blomefield *Essay towards a Top. Hist. of Norfolk* 5 (1806): 23–33. Banks *Dormant & Extinct Baronage of England* 1 (1807): 268–269 (Clifton ped.); 2 (1808): 120–124 (sub Cromwell). Dugdale *Monasticon Anglicanum* 3 (1821): 330 (sub Wymondham Monastery). *Coll. Top. et Gen.* 7 (1841): 142–144 (sub Tateshale). Barrett *Mems. of Attleborough* (1848): 183 (Caily-Clifton ped.). *Norfolk Arch.* 3 (1852): 126–127 (Cailly-Clifton ped.). Napier *Swyncombe & Ewelme* (1858): 296–299. Mundy et al. *Vis. of Nottingham 1569 & 1614* (H.S.P. 4) (1871): 5–8 (Stanhop ped.) ("John Clifton of Burnam Castell in Norfolk = Elizabeth [Cromwell] d. & coheire = Edmond Bensted"). Flower *Vis. of Yorkshire 1563–4* (H.S.P. 16) (1881): 176–177 (Knevet ped.: "Dominus Johannes Clyfton Miles. = Elsabeth Cromwell."). Burke *Dormant, Abeyant, Forfeited & Extinct Peerages* (1883): 124 (sub Clifton) (Clifton arms: Chequy, or and gules, a bend ermine). Phillimore *Abs. of IPMs Rel. Nottinghamshire* 1 (Thoroton Soc. Rec. Ser. 6) (1905): vii, 18–20. Wrottesley *Peds. from the Plea Rolls* (1905): 244–245, 383–384. *List of Inqs. ad Quod Damnum* 2 (PRO Lists and Indexes 22) (1906): 600. VCH *Hertford* 3 (1912): 462–468. *C.P.* 3 (1913): 307–308 (sub Clifton). *C.F.R.* 7 (1923): 251, 349, 388. Farnham *Leicestershire Medieval Peds.* (1925): opp. 18 (Pantulf-Tatshall ped.). Harvey et al. *Vis. of the North* 3 (Surtees Soc. 144) (1930): 152–156 (Daubeny ped.: "Elizabeth Cromwell soror et coheres = Dominus Iohannes Clifton miles"). VCH *Sussex* 4 (1953): 121–126. Paget *Baronage of England* (1957) 134a: 1. *Cal. IPM* 17 (1988): 140–141.

13. **CONSTANTINE DE CLIFTON**, Esq. or Gent., 2nd Lord Clifton, of Buckenham, Attleborough, Babingley, and Hilborough, Norfolk, Little Waltham, Essex, etc., son and heir, born about 1372 (aged 16 in 1388, aged 19½ in 1391). He married after Feb. 1389/90 **MARGARET HOWARD**, daughter of Robert Howard, Knt., of East Winch, Fersfield, and Wiggenhall, Norfolk, by Margaret (or Margery), daughter of Robert de Scales, 3rd Lord Scales [see HOWARD 10 for her ancestry]. They had one son, John, Knt. [3rd Lord Clifton], and one daughter, Elizabeth. He was summoned to Parliament from 13 Nov. 1393 to 20 Nov. 1394. In 1395 he quitclaimed his rights to various lands in Hunmanby, Yorkshire to Henry de Percy, 1st Earl of Northumberland. CONSTANTINE DE CLIFTON, Esq. or Gent., 2nd Lord Clifton, died 19 Feb. 1395/6. His widow, Margaret, married (2nd) before 1397 (as his 3rd wife) **GILBERT TALBOT**, Knt. [see RICHARD'S CASTLE 6.ii], of Wadley, Hanney, Letcombe Regis, and Wicklesham, Berkshire, Knight of the Shire for Berkshire, 1386, Justice of the Peace for Berkshire, 1383–97, Justice of the Peace for Wiltshire, 1391–4, 2nd son of John Talbot, Knt., of Richard's Castle, Herefordshire, by Juliane, daughter of Roger de Grey, Knt., 1st Lord Grey of Ruthin [see RICHARD'S CASTLE 6 for his ancestry]. He was born about 1346. They had one son, Richard. SIR GILBERT TALBOT died 6 Feb. 1398/9. His wife (later widow), Margaret, presented to the church of Sandringham, Norfolk in 1396, 1405, 1408, 1410, and, together with the prior of Westacre, in 1422 and 1427. She also presented to the churches of Attleborough, Norfolk, 1404, and Babingley, Norfolk, 1425. In 1415 she sold the manor and advowson of Hatford, Berkshire to John Philip, Knt., and his wife, Alice. Margaret, Lady Clifton, died 25 March 1434, and was buried at Black Friars, Norwich, Norfolk.

Throsby *Thoroton's Hist. of Nottinghamshire* 3 (1790): 169–171. Blomefield *Essay towards a Top. Hist. of Norfolk* 5 (1806): 242; 9 (1808): 71–72. Banks *Dormant & Extinct Baronage of England* 1 (1807): 268–269 (Clifton ped.). Brydges *Collins' Peerage of England* 1 (1812): 50–143. Dugdale *Monasticon Anglicanum* 3 (1821): 330 (sub Wymondham Monastery). Burke *Dict. of the Peerages… Extinct, Dormant & in Abeyance* 2 (1832): 231–235 (sub Howard) (assigns wrong parentage to Margaret Howard). Nicolas *Controversy between Scrope & Grosvenor* 2 (1832): 397–398 (biog. of Sir Gilbert Talbot). Causton *Rights of Heirship* (1842): 118–119. Barrett *Mems. of Attleborough* (1848): xiv, 9, 183 (Caily-Clifton ped.), 224. Flower *Vis. of Yorkshire 1563–4* (H.S.P. 16) (1881): 176–177 (Knevet ped.: "Constantinus Clyfton. = Margeria filia Domini Roberti Howard de Est wynch Militis."). Burke *Dormant, Abeyant, Forfeited & Extinct Peerages* (1883): 124 (sub Clifton). Phillimore *Abs. of IPMs Rel. Nottinghamshire* 1 (Thoroton Soc. Rec. Ser. 3) (1905): vii, 18–20. Wrottesley *Peds. from the Plea Rolls* (1905): 244–245, 383–384. C.P.R. 1413–1416 (1910): 281. C.P. 3 (1913): 308 (sub Clifton) (Margaret Howard's parentage and death date incorrectly stated). VCH *Berkshire* 4 (1924): 461–463, 489–499. VCH *Buckingham* 4 (1927): 425–429. Harvey et al. *Vis. of the North* 3 (Surtees Soc. 144) (1930): 152–156 [Daubeny ped.: "Constantinus Clifton = (Margareta filia domini Roberti Howard de Estwynche militis)"]. C.F.R. 16 (1936): 166–167. Legge *Anglo-Norman Letters & Petitions* (Anglo-Norman Text Soc. 3) (1941): 13–16. Chichele *Reg. of Henry Chichele* 3 (Canterbury & York Soc. 46) (1945): 470. VCH *Sussex* 4 (1953): 121–126. Paget *Baronage of England* (1957) 134a: 1, 488: 4. Salvin *Salvin Papers* (1965): 61 (quitclaim of Constantine de Clifton dated 11 Feb. 1395). *Cal. IPM* 17 (1988): 239–240, 495–499; 20 (1995): 45; 23 (2004): 45–47. Roskell *House of Commons 1386–1421* 3 (1992): 431–433 (biog. of Sir John Howard) (correctly states Margaret Howard's parentage); 4 (1992): 560–563 (biog. of Sir Gilbert Talbot) (correctly states Margaret Howard's death date). Norfolk Rec. Office: Wodehouse Fam. of Kimberley, KIM 2P/3 (agreement dated 2 Sept. 1415 between William Wyngefeld and Katherine, his wife, and Lady Margaret, widow of Constantine de Clifton, Gent., re. the manor of Butordes in Kimberley, Norfolk) (available at www.a2a.org.uk/search/index.asp). Durham County Rec. Office, Salvin fam. of Croxdale, D/Sa/D 1627 (quitclaim of Constant de Clifton to Henry de Percy, Earl of Northumberland, et al. dated 11 Feb. 1395) (available at www.durham.gov.uk/recordoffice/ register.nsf/7da41db46fbaf08880256ff80053d88c/cadba69fede04160802568ff004d5449?OpenDocument).

Child of Constantine de Clifton, Esq. or Gent., by Margaret Howard:

i. **ELIZABETH CLIFTON**, married **JOHN KNYVET**, Knt., of Southwick, Northamptonshire [see GURDON 14].

҈ CLINTON ҈

ALICE OF NORMANDY (sister of King William the Conqueror), married **LAMBERT**, Count of Lens.
JUDITH OF LENS, married **WALTHEOF**, Earl of Northumberland.
MAUD OF NORTHUMBERLAND, married **SIMON DE SENLIS**, Earl of Huntingdon and Northampton.
MAUD DE SENLIS, married **ROBERT FITZ RICHARD**, of Little Dunmow, Essex.
WALTER FITZ ROBERT, Knt., of Little Dunmow, Essex, married **MAUD DE LUCY**.
ROBERT FITZ WALTER, of Little Dunmow, Essex, married (2nd) **ROHESE** (or **ROSE**) _____.
WALTER FITZ ROBERT, of Woodham Walter, Essex, married **IDA LONGESPÉE** (desc. King William the Conqueror).
ELA FITZ WALTER, married **WILLIAM DE ODDINGSELES**, Knt., of Solihull, Warwickshire [see ODDINGSELES 8].

9. IDA DE ODDINGSELES, eldest daughter and co-heiress, born about 1265. She married (1st) **ROGER DE HERDEBURGH**, Knt., of Prilleston, Norfolk, son and heir of Hugh de Herdeburgh, Knt., of Great Harborough, Pailton (in Monks Kirkby), and Willey, Warwickshire, Weston Turville, Buckinghamshire, Messing, Essex, and Carshalton, Surrey, by Isabel, daughter and co-heiress of William de Turville. They had two daughters, Ela and Isabel. SIR ROGER DE HERDEBURGH died before 9 Feb. 1284. She married (2nd) after 29 Sept. 1286 **JOHN DE CLINTON** (or **CLYNTON**), Knt., of Amington (in Tamworth) and Coleshill, Warwickshire, Dunton Bassett, Leicestershire, Lydiard Millicent, Wiltshire, etc., and, in right of his wife, of Oxborough, Norfolk, and Cavendish and Newton, Suffolk, Knight of the Shire for Warwickshire, Constable of Wallingford Castle, Seneschal of Ponthieu, 2nd but 1st surviving son and heir of Thomas de Clinton, of Amington (in Tamworth), Warwickshire, by Maud, daughter of Ralph de Bracebridge, Knt. He was born probably in 1258. They had three sons, John, Knt. [2nd Lord Clinton], William, Knt. [Earl of Huntingdon, Lord Clinton], and Thomas, and two daughters, Joan (wife of Edmund Deincourt) and probably Elizabeth. He was heir before 1276 to his brother, Osbert de Clinton. He was going to Scotland with Ralph Basset of Drayton in 1291 and 1292. His wife, Ida, was co-heiress in 1295 to her brother, Edmund de Oddingseles, by which she inherited the manors of Maxstoke and Budbrooke, Warwickshire and a moiety share of the manor of Pirton, Hertfordshire. He served in the Scottish and French wars. He was summoned to Parliament 6 Feb. 1298/9, by writ directed *Johanni de Clinton*, whereby he is held to have become Lord Clinton. In 1300 he had a grant of free warren in his demesne lands in Amington, Warwickshire. In 1302 a lawsuit filed against John and his wife, Ida, and her sister, Margaret, wife of John de Grey, by their sisters, Ela de Bermingham and Alice de Caunton, regarding tenements in Weeford, Staffordshire was dismissed, owing to Ela and Alice's failure to prosecute their writ of novel disseisin. In 1304–5 two of his valets were given robes as "hawkers." He was going to Ponthieu for Edward, Prince of Wales, in 1306. In 1309 king ordered that the Castle and honour of Wallingford, the honour of St. Valery, and the town of Chichester be delivered to him. SIR JOHN DE CLINTON, 1st Lord Clinton, died shortly before 7 Jan. 1310/11, on which date his executors and heirs were granted remission of a payment of £31 10s. 4-½d. in which he was indebted to the king for the time in which he was seneschal of Ponthieu, also £61 2s. 2d. as Steward of Wallingford. In 1311 his widow, Ida, was jointly bound with John de Bracebridge, Knt., for the proper debt of 450 marks of the said Ida to Edmund Deincourt, Knt., to be levied in default upon her land, etc., in Warwickshire and Wiltshire. Lady Ida de Clinton was one of the ladies of the Queen's Chamber in 1311–12. On 3 May 1313 and 20 Feb. 1313/4 there are protections recorded for Ida, she going beyond seas with Queen Isabel. In Sept. 1313 Adam de Kyngesford and Richard Folky were pardoned by the king at the request of Ida de Clinton for a disseisin made by them upon Maud daughter of William de Olton of a tenement in Solihull, Warwickshire. In 1319 she was summoned to answer William la Zouche [Mortimer] concerning a plea that she surrender to him [her son] John son and heir of John de Clinton of Maxstoke, whose wardship belonged to the said William, for reason that John de Clinton held his land of him by knight's service. The said Ida came by William de Coleshill her attorney and said that she held the aforesaid wardship by the lease of William la Zouche [Mortimer], lord of Ashby, Alice the widow of Sir Guy de Beauchamp, Simon de Sutton, and William de Wellesbourne, executors of the will of Guy de Beauchamp, late earl of Warwick; she vouched to warranty the said William, Alice, etc. On 1 March 1321/2 the king ordered John de Walewayn, escheator this side Trent, to permit her to have the easement of houses in the manor of La Grove until further order. In Feb. 1322 she was granted protection for one year. Ida subsequently became Prioress of Wroxall, and died testate in office in 1325. In 1328 her executors sued John Pecche the elder.

Dugdale *Antiqs. of Warwickshire* (1730): 73 (Herdeburgh ped.), 92 (Herdeburgh ped.). *British Mag.* 3 (1762): 625–634. Morant *Hist. & Antiqs. of Essex* 2 (1768): 176. Brydges *Collins' Peerage of England* 2 (1812): 181–216 (sub Duke of Newcastle). Clutterbuck *Hist. & Antiqs. of Hertford* 3 (1827): 119–120 (Odingsells-Clinton ped.). Bowles & Nichols *Annals & Antiqs. of Lacock Abbey* (1835): 162–163. King *Some Observations Rel. Four Deeds from the Muniment Room at Maxstoke Castle* (1861). *Wiltshire Arch. & Nat. Hist. Mag.* 12 (1869): 19. *Procs. Soc. Antiqs.* 2nd Ser. 5 (1870): 304–305. *Rpt. from Commissioners* 33 (1872): 262. *Genealogist* 4 (1880): 50–58. Wrottesley *Staffordshire Suits: Plea Rolls* (Colls. Hist. Staffs. 7(1)) (1886): 64, 107. *Trans. Hist. Soc. of Lanc. & Cheshire* n.s 5 (1889): 24 ("Now, also, two, three, or more shields appear, conjointed or standing side by side. The earliest instance I have noticed in Sigillum Ide de Clinton, 1298–1300, with three heater shields, points to the centre [Nicholas Upton, pg. 82].") [Note: At this author's request, the description of Ida de Clinton's seal reported by Upton was examined at the British Library. Upton's notes indicates that Ida de Oddingseles' seal bore the arms of three families: Clinton, Oddingseles, and Fitz Walter]. *C.C.R.* 1313–1318 (1893): 11–12. *Desc. Cat. Ancient Deeds* 3 (1900): 511–523. *C.C.R.* 1279–1288 (1902): 424–425. *Ancestor* 10 (1904): 32–51. *C.P.R. 1321–1324* (1904): 70. *Feudal Aids* 3 (1904): 448, 478, 496; 5 (1908): 27, 43, 206. Wrottesley *Peds. from the Plea Rolls* (1905): 31, 95, 544–545. *Index of Placita de Banco 1327–1328* 2 (PRO Lists and Indexes 22) (1906): 681, 685. VCH *Buckingham* 2 (1908): 367–369. VCH *Hertford* 2 (1908): 261–264; 3 (1912): 48. VCH *Warwick* 2 (1908): 71, 431; 3 (1945): 65; 4 (1947): 138, 247. *C.P.* 3 (1913): 312–313 (sub Clinton); 4 (1916): 119, footnote f; 10 (1945): 343, footnote l (sub Pecche). *Year Books of Edward II* 6 (Selden Soc. 26) (1914): 13–14; 25 (Selden Soc. 81) (1964): 13–14. *Cal. Chancery Warrants* (1927): 533. Moor *Knights of Edward I* 1 (H.S.P. 80) (1929): 215. Stokes et al. *Warwickshire Feet of Fines* 2 (Dugdale Soc. 15) (1939): 104. *NEHGR* 102 (1948): 45. VCH *Warwick* 6 (1951): 100, 176, 259. *Norfolk Arch.* 30 (1952): 19–25. *Genealogists' Mag.* 12 (1958): 535–539. Skipp *Medieval Yardley* (1970): 35. Blackley & Hermansen *Household Book of Queen Isabella of England* (1971): xiv, 156–157, 176–177. Brault *Rolls of Arms Edward I* 2 (1997): 110 (arms of John de Clinton: Argent, on a chief azure two mullets or). Oggins *Kings & Their Hawks* (2004): 179.

Children of Ida de Oddingseles, by Roger de Herdeburgh, Knt.:

i. **ELA DE HERDEBURGH**, married (1st) **WALTER DE HOPTON**, Knt., of Hopton, Shropshire [see BLACKMERE 10]; (2nd) **WILLIAM LE BOTELER**, 1st Lord Boteler of Wem [see BLACKMERE 10].

ii. **ISABEL DE HERDEBURGH**, married before 1304 **JOHN DE HULLES**, in right of his wife, of Harborough Magna and Pailton (in Monks Kirby), Warwickshire, Puttenham, Hertfordshire, Prilleston and Overstrand, Norfolk, and Messing, Essex. They had two daughters, Denise and Alice. JOHN DE HULLES died before 6 Nov. 1311. His widow, Isabel, was living 6 Nov. 1311, but was presumably dead in or before 1316, when Alice le Bigod, Countess of Norfolk, presented to the church of Prilleston, Norfolk as "guardian," evidently of her two minor daughters. Dugdale *Antiqs. of Warwickshire* (1730): 73 (Herdeburgh ped.), 92 (Herdeburgh ped.). Wrottesley *Peds. from the Plea Rolls* (1905): 31. VCH *Hertford* 2 (1908): 261–264. VCH *Warwick* 6 (1951): 100, 176, 259. *Norfolk Arch.* 30 (1952): 19–25. *Genealogists' Mag.* 12 (1958): 535–539. Leicestershire, Leicester & Rutland Rec. Office: Recs. of the Shirley Fam., Earls Ferrers, of Staunton Harold, Leicestershire, 26D53/100 — quitclaim dated 6 Nov. 1311 from John Torald of Norwich and Agnes his wife to William le Butiller [Boteler] de Wemme, Elen his wife, and Isabella who was wife of John de Hulles, of life interest of Agnes in manors of Asphall and Debenham, Suffolk (available at www.a2a.org.uk/search/index.asp).

Children of Isabel de Herdeburgh, by John de Hulles:

a. **DENISE DE HULLES**, born about 1299. She married before 1323 **JOHN DE WATEVILLE**, in right of his wife, of Prilleston, Norfolk and Harborough Magna, Warwickshire. They had no issue. She died before 1326. In 1326 he conveyed a moiety of the manor and the advowson of the church of Prilleston, Norfolk to Alice and John de Peyto, reserving for himself an annuity of 21 silver marks. The same year it was recorded that he held a life estate in a moiety of the manor of Harborough Magna, Warwickshire for life. Dugdale

Antiqs. of Warwickshire (1730): 73 (Herdeburgh ped.), 92 (Herdeburgh ped.). Rye *Short Cal. Feet of Fines for Norfolk* 2 (1886): 274. Wrottesley *Peds. from the Plea Rolls* (1905): 31. VCH *Warwick* 6 (1951): 100, 176. *Norfolk Arch.* 30 (1952): 19–25.

b. **ALICE DE HULLES**, born about 1305. She married (1st) before 1323 **JOHN DE LANGLEY**. He died in 1324. She married (2nd) before 8 Nov. 1324 (as his 1st wife) **JOHN DE PEYTO**, Knt., styled the younger, of Loxley, Sheldon, Shottery, etc., Warwickshire, and, in right of his 1st wife, of Overstrand and Prilleston, Norfolk, and Harborough Magna, Pailton (in Monks Kirby), Willey, and Wodecote (in Leek Wootton), Warwickshire, son of John Peyto. They had no issue. In 1330 John and his wife, Alice, sold six marks of rent in Overstrand, Norfolk, together with the advowson of the church, to Alan son of Geoffrey, of Shypedene for 100 silver marks. In 1337 he presented to the church of Prilleston, Norfolk, in right of his wife. Alice was living in February 1339, but evidently died in or before October 1339, when a previous family settlement was remade in favor of her nephew, Walter de Hopton, Knt. In 1339 Wolstan de Bransford, Bishop of Worcester, farmed the manor of Stratford (in Stratford-upon-Avon), Warwickshire to John de Peyto, junior, for life at £60 a year, which amount was afterwards reduced to £30 annually, in lieu of a pension of that amount which the bishop had previously granted him. He married (2nd) before 28 June 1344 **BEATRICE** _____, widow of John Bishopsdon, Knt. (living 1339), of Waresley (in Hartlebury), Warwickshire. In 1345 he and his wife, Beatrice, were assigned lands in Bysspewode, Lapworth, and Rouhinton, and rents and services in Lyndon (in Solihull), Warwickshire by Beatrice's son (or step-son), Roger de Bishopsdon. In 1347 he and his wife, Beatrice, leased the manor of Sheldon, Warwickshire for life at an annual rent of £10. In 1351 he granted 14 messuages and various lands in Loxley, Warwickshire to Kenilworth Priory. In 1370 he was involved in a lawsuit with the Abbot of Combe over waste committed in the manor of Harborough Magna, Warwickshire. The same year he was summoned into Chancery and ordered to account for £30, the equivalent of the pension, for every year since 1339, except for those years when the see of Worcester was vacant. In 1372 the bishop was ordered to ordered to account for the £30 rent in the manor of Stratford (in Stratford-upon-Avon), Warwickshire received from John de Peyto since the beginning of the lease, and with this proviso, the manor was restored to Peyto the following year. SIR JOHN DE PEYTO died in June 1373. His wife, Beatrice, was living in 1374. Dugdale *Antiqs. of Warwickshire* (1730): 73 (Herdeburgh ped.), 92 (Herdeburgh ped.). Blomefield *Essay towards a Top. Hist. of Norfolk* 5 (1806): 322. Rye *Short Cal. Feet of Fines for Norfolk* 2 (1886): 274. *Misc. Gen. et Heraldica* 2nd Ser. 2 (1888): 273–283 (Langley ped.). Wrottesley *Peds. from the Plea Rolls* (1905): 31. VCH *Worcester* 3 (1913): 380–387. VCH *Warwick* 3 (1945): 129–134, 258–266; 4 (1947): 100–205, 214–229; 6 (1951): 100, 167–170, 176, 259. *Norfolk Arch.* 30 (1952): 19–25.

Children of Ida de Oddingseles, by John de Clinton, Knt.:

i. **JOHN DE CLINTON**, Knt., 2nd Lord Clinton [see next].

ii. **WILLIAM DE CLINTON**, Knt., of Maxstoke, Warwickshire, and, in right of his wife, of Eltham and Ashford, Kent, and Fulbrook, Warwickshire, Constable of Halton Castle, 1326, Chief Justice of Chester, 1330, Constable of Dover Castle and Warden of the Cinque Ports, 1330, Privy Councillor, 1333, Captain and Admiral of the Cinque Ports and the West, 1333–5, Captain and Admiral from the Thames to Portsmouth, 1340, Captain and Admiral of the West, 1341–2, joint Warden of the Marches towards Scotland, 1342, Justice of the Forest south of Trent, 1343–5, joint Warden in Kent, 1352, younger son. He and his brother, John, were squires of the household of Queen Isabel of France, wife of King Edward II, in 1311–12. He was summoned to serve in Gascony in 1325. He married before 17 October 1328 **JULIANE DE LEYBOURNE** (or **LEYBURNE**), widow successively of John de Hastings, 2nd Lord Hastings (died 20 Jan. 1324/5) [see HASTINGS 11] and Thomas le Blount, Knt., of Tibberton, Gloucestershire, Steward of the King's Household (died 17 August 1328) [see HASTINGS 11], and daughter and heiress of Thomas de Leybourne, Knt., of Leybourne, Kent, by Alice, daughter of Ralph de Tony, Knt. [see TONY 9.ii and BEAUCHAMP 10 for her ancestry]. They had no surviving issue. He was summoned to Parliament from 6 Sept. 1330 to 14 Jan. 1336/7, by writs directed *Willelmo de Clynton*, whereby he is held to have become Lord Clinton. He presented to the churches of Birdingbury, Warwickshire, 1334, 1342, 1353, 1353, 1359, Allesley, Warwickshire, 1337, 1341, Fulbrook, Warwickshire, 1337, and Ripley, Kent, 1349. On 10 March 1336/7, he was created Earl of Huntingdon. In 1337 he founded a priory of Austin Canons at Maxstoke, Warwickshire. He fought in the Scottish wars and in Edward III's wars with France. In 1341 he purchased the manor of Cherry Hinton, Cambridgeshire from John de Kyriel, which he transferred by exchange to John Mowbray, Lord Mowbray. In 1342 he and Richard de Arundel, Earl of Arundel, secured a one year truce with Scotland. In 1342 William de Clinton, Earl of Huntingdon complained that Warin Trussell, Knt., Henry son of John Trap, of Shelfhull, and others broke his park at Shelfhull and entered his free warren at Aston Cantlow, Warwickshire, hunted in these, carried away his goods there with deer from the park and hares, rabbits, and partridges from the warren, and beat his men and servants so that he lost their service for a long time. In 1345 he granted to the

Abbot and Convent of Maxstoke land in Aston Cantlow, Warwickshire, with the advowsons of the churches of Aston Cantlow and Fillongley, Warwickshire. In 1350 he gave to John de Bertulmeu, of Maxstoke, Warwickshire, a piece of land called Sotecroft, in exchange for a piece of land in the Ruddynge. SIR WILLIAM DE CLINTON, Earl of Huntingdon, died testate 24 (or 25) August 1354, and was buried at Maxstoke, Warwickshire. In 1356–7 his widow, Countess Juliane, granted the manor of Harrietsham, Kent to Richard de Alleslee, rector of Harrietsham, with rent of the weald, for the term of his life. She presented to the churches of Allesley, Warwickshire, 1357, Winchfield, Hampshire, 1361, and Birdingbury, Warwickshire, 1361, 1366. In 1357–8 Stephen de Valoines quitclaimed to her and two others lands in Ashford, Eaststour (in Ashford), Great Chart, Hothfield, Mersham, and Willesborough, Kent, which he lately acquired from William de Suddynton, burgess of Berkeley. Juliane, Countess of Huntingdon, died testate 31 October, 1 or 2 Nov. 1367, and was buried in St. Anne's Chapel in St. Augustine's, Canterbury, Kent. Dugdale *Antiqs. of Warwickshire* (1730): 130, 324–325. *British Mag.* 3 (1762): 625–634. Brydges *Collins' Peerage of England* 2 (1812): 181–216 (sub Duke of Newcastle) ("William [de Clinton], a younger son, whose great actions, and great employments, do so sufficiently manifest his great abilities, that he may well be reputed one of the chiefest worthies of the kingdom."). Nicolas *Testamenta Vetusta* 1 (1826): 55 (will of William, Lord Clinton), 69 (will of Julian de Clinton). Clutterbuck *Hist. & Antiqs. of Hertford* 3 (1827): 119–120 (Odingsells-Clinton ped.). *Gentleman's Mag.* 99 (1829): 124–125. Burke *Gen'l & Heraldic Dict. of the Peerages of England, Ireland & Scotland* (1831): 252–255 (sub Hastings). Baker *Hist. & Antiqs. of Northampton* 2 (1836–41): 315. Lipscomb *Hist. & Antiqs. of Buckingham* 1 (1847): 202 (Hastings ped.). King *Some Observations Rel. Four Deeds from the Muniment Room at Maxstoke Castle* (1861) ("William de Clinton …. the grantor in the second Deed …. On the seal appended to this Deed are six crosses crosslet fitchy, and on a chief two mullets of six points, Clinton: the shield is inclosed in a foliated circle of nine-foils, and accompanied by six lions rampant of Leybourne in the area of the seal, two over the shield, and two on each side, the Earl having married Juliana, daughter and heir of Sir Thomas Leybourne."). *Procs. Soc. Antiq.* 2nd Ser. 5 (1870): 104–105. *Arch. Cantiana* 14 (1882): 267–268. Doyle *Official Baronage of England* 2 (1886): 225–227 (sub Huntingdon). *Desc. Cat. Ancient Deeds* 1 (1890): 276; 3 (1900): 511–523; 5 (1906): 195 (Katherine de Lucy styled "cousin" [cognate] of Julian de Hastynges, countess of Huntyngdon). Rye *Pedes Finium or Fines Rel. Cambridge* (1891): 105. *Genealogist* n.s. 8 (1892): 36. Birch *Cat. Seals in the British Museum* 3 (1894): 194 (seal of Juliane de Leybourne, wife of William de Clinton dated 14th century — A shield of arms: six lioncels rampant, three, two, and one [LEYBOURNE]. Within a finely carved gothic six-foil panel). *Desc. Cat. Ancient Deeds* 2 (1894): 173 (charter of Juliane de Hastings, Countess of Huntingdon dated 1356). *Papal Regs.: Petitions* 1 (1896): 50–51, 76, 92–93, 150, 175, 192–193, 207, 217, 237, 246–247, 258, 404 (Juliane de Leybourne, Countess of Huntingdon, styled "king's kinswoman" in papal petition dated 1363). *Papal Regs.: Letters* 2 (1895): 557; 3 (1897): 512. *C.P.R. 1340–1343* (1900): 588. *List of Ancient Corr. of the Chancery & Exchequer* (PRO Lists and Indexes 15) (1902): 649 (letter of William de Clinton and Julia his wife to Desiderata de Lucy dated 1329). *English Hist. Rev.* 18 (1903): 112–116. *Ancestor* 10 (1904): 32–51. *C.C.R. 1346–1349* (1905): 84. Wrottesley *Peds. from the Plea Rolls* (1905): 7. Jeayes *Desc. Cat. Derbyshire Charters* (1906): 116. *List of Inqs. ad Quod Damnum* 2 (PRO Lists and Indexes 22) (1906): 430. *Colls. Hist. Staffs.* n.s. 10(2) (1907): 19, 25. Tuker *Cambridge* (1907): 299 (Valence ped.). *C.P.* 2 (1912): 195 (sub Blount); 3 (1913): 324 (sub Clinton); 6 (1926): 349–350 (sub Hastings), 648–650 (sub Huntingdon); 7 (1929): 638–639 (sub Leyburn). *Cal. IPM* 10 (1921): 171ff. Moor *Knights of Edward I* 1 (H.S.P. 80) (1929): 216. VCH *Warwick* 3 (1945): 91–94; 4 (1947): 69–75, 138 (arms of Clinton, Earl of Huntingdon: Argent six crosslets fitchy sable with a chief azure charged with two molets or), 205–210. Hethe *Reg. Hamonis Hethe Diocesis Roffensis* 1 (Canterbury & York Soc. 48) (1948): 481, 496, 535, 572, 578; 2 (Canterbury & York Soc. 49) (1948): 641–642, 729, 747, 756, 778, 789. Blackley & Hermansen *Household Book of Queen Isabella of England* (1971): 74–75, 160–161, 182–183. *Ancient Deeds — Ser. B* 2 (List & Index Soc. 101) (1974): B.8931, B.8932. Ellis *Cat. Seals in the P.R.O.* 1 (1978): 17 (seal of Juliane de Clinton, countess of Huntingdon dated 1340 — In a cusped and traceried circle, a shield of arms: a maunch (HASTINGS) impaling six lions rampant (LEYBOURNE). The circle is surrounded by an outer ring of elaborate tracery containing six roundels, each of which contains a lozenge of arms (charges not clear), 17 (seal of William de Clinton, Earl of Huntingdon dated 1342 — In a cusped and traceried circle, surrounded by six small lions rampant, a shield of arms: six crosses crosslet fitchy, 3, 2, and 1, on a chief two rowels. Legend: *SIGILLVM. WILLELMI.DE.CLINTVN.). *Ancient Deeds — Ser. AS & WS* (List & Index Soc. 158) (1979): 14 (Deeds A.S.71, 73), 15 (Deed A.S.81), 20 (Deed A.S.106), 26 (Deed A.S.139), 99 (Deed A.S. 533). Sutherland *Eyre of Northamptonshire 3–4 Edward III* 1 (Selden Soc. 97) (1983): 104–106. *English Hist. Rev.* 99 (1984): 1–33. Edington *Reg. of William Edington Bishop of Winchester 1346–1366* 1 (Hampshire Recs. 7) (1986): 207. Taylor *English Hist. Lit. in the 14th Cent.* (1987): 294 (Wigmore Chron. sub 1368: "Eodem anno [rectius 1367] obiit domina Juliana comitissa de hontyndone."). Montacute *Cal. Reg. of Simon de Montacute Bishop of Worcester* (Worcestershire Hist. Soc. n.s. 15) (1996): 60, 304. Gee *Women, Art & Patronage from Henry III to Edward III: 1216–1377* (2002): 161 (re. Juliana de Leybourne). VCH *Cambridge* 10 (2002): 106–109. *Coat of Arms* 3rd Ser. 3(2) (2007): 93–101. Birmingham City Archives: Wingfield Digby Fam. of Sherborne Castle, Dorset & Coleshill, Warwickshire: Warwickshire Estate Papers, MS 3888/A252 (available at www.a2a.org.uk/

search/index.asp). Warwickshire County Rec. Office: Fetherston-Dilke of Maxstoke, CR 2981/Dining Room/Cabinet/Drawer 4/7 (available at www.a2a.org.uk/search/index.asp).

Child of William de Clinton, Knt., by an unidentified wife or mistress, _____, not Juliane de Leybourne:

a. **ELIZABETH DE CLINTON**, married **JOHN FITZWILLIAM**, Knt., of Sprotborough, Yorkshire [see FITZWILLIAM 13].

iii. **ELIZABETH DE CLINTON**, probable daughter, married **EBLE DE MOUNTS** (or **MONTZ**), Knt., of Heydor, Lincolnshire, King's esquire, Constable of Stirling Castle, Sheriff and Constable of Edinburgh Castle, Steward to Queen Isabel of France (wife of King Edward II of England). They had one son, Edward. Sometime prior to 1290, Queen Eleanor of Castile (wife of King Edward I of England) granted him the manor of Shirling, Kent. In 1312 he was granted the Templars' manors of Askeby, Kirkby, Rowston, and Temple Bruer, Lincolnshire "on account of his good service to the late king [Edward I]" and in order that he may better serve Queen Isabel, "in whose train he is by the king's command." He retired from his position as Steward to the Queen Isabel in Feb. 1314. In 1316 he brought news to the king of the birth of his second son, John of Eltham. William Tolymer conveyed a moiety of the manor of Oxhey Richard (in Watford), Hertfordshire to him and his wife, Elizabeth in 1316. In 1317 he served as king's envoy to Edward, Count of Bar. The same year the king sent John Pecok junior from Nottingham to Maxstoke to defray Elizabeth's expenses and those of her suite. SIR EBLE DE MOUNTS died shortly before 15 Feb. 1317/8. His widow, Elizabeth, was going overseas with Queen Isabel in 1320. Sometime before 23 October 1321 the Queen delivered the Great Seal to Elizabeth de Mounts to be enclosed in a chest in Rochester, Kent, and afterwards it came to the king. *Archæologia* 26 (1836): 318-345. Palgrave *Docs. & Recs. Ill. the Hist. of Scotland* 1 (1837): 272. *Rpt. from Commissioners* 33 (1872): 262. *C.P.R. 1317–1321* (1903): 449. VCH *Hertford* 2 (1908): 371–386, 451–464. Moor *Knights of Edward I* 3 (H.S.P. 82) (1930): 195. Blackley & Hermansen *Household Book of Queen Isabella of England* (1971): xii–xiii, xv, 6, 7, 22, 23, 26, 27, 114, 115, 156–157, 176–177, 206–209. Ellis *Cat. Seals in the P.R.O.* 2 (1981): 75 (seal of Ebule de Monts, knight dated 1317 — Within a circle of knotted rope, a shield of arms: a bend cotised, and a label of three points. Legend: *SIGILL':ELIL…MOVNS.).

10. JOHN DE CLINTON, Knt., 2nd Lord Clinton, of Maxstoke, Coleshill, etc., Warwickshire, and Pirton, Hertfordshire, Justice of the Peace for Warwickshire, 1329, 1332, patron of Wroxall Priory, son and heir. He and his brother, William, were squires of the household of Queen Isabel of France, wife of King Edward II, in 1311–12. He fought on the king's side at the Battle of Boroughbridge in 1322. He married before 7 April 1325 **MARGERY CORBET**, daughter of William Corbet, Knt., of Chaddesley-Corbet and Impney, Worcestershire. They had one son, John, Knt. [3rd Lord Clinton], and four daughters, Ida, and allegedly Margery, Isabel, and Margaret. He was summoned to Parliament from 27 Jan. 1331/2 to 1 April 1335, the words "*Mortuus est*" added to the last writ. In 1325 he was granted permission to give the church of Snitterfield, Warwickshire to the Prior and Convent of St. Sepulchres, Warwick. In 1329 he and his wife, Margery, and the heirs of their bodies, were granted £200 of yearly rent from the manor of Chaddlesley-Corbet, Worcestershire by William Corbet, Knt., of Chaddesley (father of the said Margery). SIR JOHN DE CLINTON, 2nd Lord Clinton, died shortly before 1 April 1335. On 14 May 1343, a commission of oyer and terminer was ordered on complaint of his widow, Margery, that Richard de Herthull, Knt., and others broke her close at Amington, Warwickshire, felled her trees, and burned and plundered her goods.

British Mag. 3 (1762): 625–634. Brydges *Collins' Peerage of England* 2 (1812): 181–216 (sub Duke of Newcastle). Clutterbuck *Hist. & Antiqs. of Hertford* 3 (1827): 119–120 (Odingsells-Clinton ped.). Ellis *Plea for the Antiq. of Heraldry* (1853): 12 ("Thus the mullets on the arms of Sir John de Clinton were taken from the coat of Odingsell, his mother."). *C.C.R. 1327–1330* (1896): 518. *Ancestor* 10 (1904): 32–51. Wrottesley *Peds. from the Plea Rolls* (1905): 95. VCH *Warwick* 2 (1908): 71; 4 (1947): 50, 138, 205–210. VCH *Hertford* 3 (1912): 48. *C.P.* 3 (1913): 313–314 (sub Clinton). Moor *Knights of Edward I* 1 (H.S.P. 80) (1929): 215. Jeayes *Desc. Cat. Charters & Muniments Belonging to the Marquis of Anglesey* (Colls. Hist. Staffs. 1937) (1937): 128–129 (charter of John Clinton, of Maxstoke, knt. dated 1333 names his great-grandfather, Osbert fil. Dom. Thome de Clinton). Stokes et al. *Warwickshire Feet of Fines* 2 (Dugdale Soc. 15) (1939): 121. *Year Books of Edward II* 25 (Selden Soc. 81) (1964): 13–14. Blackley & Hermansen *Household Book of Queen Isabella of England* (1971): 74–75, 160–161, 182–183. *Ancient Deeds — Ser. BB* (List & Index Soc. 137) (1977): 10.

Children of John de Clinton, Knt., by Margery Corbet:

i. **JOHN DE CLINTON**, Knt., 3rd Lord Clinton [see next].

ii. **IDA DE CLINTON**, married (1st) **JOHN LE STRANGE**, Knt., of Middle, Shropshire [see FREVILLE 9]; **BALDWIN DE FREVILLE**, Knt., of Tamworth, Warwickshire [see FREVILLE 9].

11. JOHN DE CLINTON, Knt., 3rd Lord Clinton, of Maxstoke, Budbrooke, and Shustoke, Warwickshire, Pirton, Hertfordshire, and Folkestone, Kent, Constable of Warwick Castle, son and heir, born about 13 April 1328. In 1345 his uncle, William de Clinton, Earl of Huntingdon, had license to build a castle for him at Maxstoke, Warwickshire. He presented to the church of Arley, Warwickshire in 1349, 1358, and 1361. He married (1st) probably in 1350 **IDOINE DE SAY**, daughter of Geoffrey de Say, Knt., 2nd Lord Say, Admiral of the Fleet from the mouth of the Thames westward, by Maud, daughter of Guy de Beauchamp, Knt., 10th Earl of Warwick [see SAY 10 for her ancestry]. They had three sons, William, Knt., Thomas, Knt., and Edward, and two daughters, Margaret and Katherine (wife of Thomas Berkeley, Knt., 5th Lord Berkeley). He was heir in 1354 to his uncle, William de Clinton, Knt., Earl of Huntingdon. In 1354–5 he quitclaimed the manor of Kingshurst (in Coleshill), with appurtenances in Coleshill, Bromwich, and Sheldon, Warwickshire to Peter de Montfort, Knt., 3rd Lord Montfort. He served in 1355 in the French wars, and was at the Battle of Poitiers in 1356. In 1356 he reached an agreement with John de Montfort, Knt., of Coleshill, regarding fishing rights in the river Blythe. He was summoned to Parliament from 15 Dec. 1357 to 5 Nov. 1397. In 1360 he was lord of Prilleston, Norfolk for life, jointly with his cousin, Walter de Hopton, Knt. In 1368 he sued Hugh le Cook for land in Austrey, Warwickshire. In 1369–70 he conveyed property in Cavendish, Suffolk, together with the advowson of the church, to John de Cavendyssh and his wife, Alice. In 1371 and again in 1372, he was ordered to go to his manor of Folkestone, Kent to resist an apprehended invasion by the French. He married (2nd) before 19 Sept. 1379 **JOAN** _____, widow of Philip Limbury, Knt., of Limbury, Bedfordshire (died at Constantinople 6 July 1367). They had no issue. In 1380 he was again in the wars with France. His wife, Joan, died 21 Feb. 1387/8. He married (3rd) before 24 Oct 1388 (date of pardon for marrying without license) **ELIZABETH DE LA PLAUNCHE**, widow successively of John de Bermingham, Knt., of Birmingham, Warwickshire, and Robert de Grey, Knt., 4th Lord Grey of Rotherfield (died 12 or 14 Jan. 1387/8) [see ODDINGSELES 11.v], and daughter and eventually sole heiress of William de la Plaunche, of Haversham, Buckinghamshire, by Elizabeth, daughter of Roger Hillary, Knt., Chief Justice of the Common Pleas. She was born about 1347 (aged 9 in 1356). They had no issue. In 1390 the king confirmed to him a weekly market at Folkestone, Kent. The same year he was appointed keeper of the lands of the attainted Earl of Warwick. SIR JOHN DE CLINTON, 3rd Lord Clinton, died 6 Sept. 1398, and was buried at Haversham, Buckinghamshire. His widow, Elizabeth, married (4th) (as his 3rd wife) **JOHN RUSSELL**, Knt. [see WINGFIELD 13], of Strensham, Worcestershire, Knight of the Shire for Worcestershire, Master of the King's Horse, Member of the King's Council. She was co-heiress in 1400 to her uncle, Roger Hillary, Knt., by which she inherited the manor of Fisherwick, Staffordshire. SIR JOHN RUSSELL died testate in 1405. His widow, Elizabeth, presented to the church of Arley, Warwickshire in 1407 and 1409. She was made an honorary member of the Guild of Merchant Taylors of London in 1420. Elizabeth, Lady Clinton, died testate 6/17 Sept. 1423, and was buried at Haversham, Buckinghamshire. She left a will dated 29 August 1422, proved 9 Nov. 1423.

Dugdale *Antiqs. of Warwickshire* 1 (1730): 104–105. *British Mag.* 3 (1762): 625–634. Blomefield *Essay towards a Top. Hist. of Norfolk* 5 (1806): 319. Hughson *London* 6 (1809): 395. Brydges *Collins' Peerage of England* 2 (1812): 181–216 (sub Duke of Newcastle); 7 (1812): 16–39 (sub Twisleton, Lord Say and Sele). Bridgman *Hist. & Top. Sketch of Knole, in Kent* (1821): 3. Clutterbuck *Hist. & Antiqs. of Hertford* 3 (1827): 119–120 (Odingsells-Clinton ped.), 190–194 (Mandeville-Say ped.). *Coll. Top. et Gen.* 7 (1841): 57–66. *Sussex Arch. Colls.* 8 (1856): 96–131. Hardy *Syllabus (in English) of the Docs. Rel. England & Other Kingdoms* 1 (1869): 457, 460. Cloe *Mems. of the Guild of Merchant Taylors* (1875): 618. Bridgeman *Hist. of the Parish of Blymhill* 1 (Colls. Hist. Staffs. 1) (1880): 365–366. *Procs. of Somersetshire Arch. & Nat. Hist. Soc.* n.s. 8

(1883): 214. Willmore *Hist. of Walsall & its Neighbourhood* (1887): 142–143, 243–245, 246 (Hillary ped.). *Desc. Cat. Ancient Deeds* 1 (1890): 276. Wrottesley *Staffordshire Suits: Plea Rolls* (Colls. Hist. Staffs. 17) (1896): 78, 132–135. *Genealogist* n.s. 16 (1899): 90–91. Kirby *Wykeham's Reg.* 2 (1899): 1–3. *C.P.R. 1385–1389* (1900): 518. Ratcliff *Hist. & Antiqs. of the Newport Pagnell Hundreds* (1900): 272. Rye *Cal. Feet of Fines for Suffolk* (1900): 238. *C.P.R. 1388–1392* (1902): 184. *Ancestor* 10 (1904): 32–51. *C.C.R. 1346–1349* (1905): 84. Stretton *Regs. of Bishops of Coventry & Lichfield* (Colls. Hist. Staffs. n.s. 8) (1905): 78. Wrottesley *Peds. from the Plea Rolls* (1905): 95, 283–284, 437. Jeayes *Desc. Cat. Derbyshire Charters* (1906): 184, 221. *List of Inqs. ad Quod Damnum* 2 (PRO Lists and Indexes 22) (1906): 430. *Colls. Hist. Staffs.* n.s. 10(2) (1907): 19–20. VCH *Bedford* 2 (1908): 348–375. *D.N.B.* 17 (1909): 875–876 (biog. of Geoffrey de Say). VCH *Hertford* 3 (1912): 48. *C.P.* 2 (1912): 152 (sub Bermingham); 3 (1913): 314–315 (sub Clinton); 4 (1916): 53 (sub Darcy); 6 (1926): 149–150 (sub Grey); 11 (1949): 478, footnote g (sub Say). *Cal. MSS in Various Colls.* 7 (Hist. MSS Comm. 55) (1914): 37–38. Farnham *Leicestershire Medieval Peds.* (1925): 22 (Haversham ped.). *Rpt. on the MSS of Reginald Rawdon Hastings, Esq.* 1 (Hist. MSS Comm. 78) (1928): 79–80. Harris *Reg. of the Guild of the Holy Trinity, St. Mary, St. John the Baptist & St. Katherine of Coventry* 1 (Dugdale Soc. 13) (1935): 28–29. VCH *Buckingham* 4 (1927): 368. *Misc. Gen. et Heraldica* 5th Ser. 9 (1935–37): 232–245. Chichele *Reg. of Henry Chichele* 2 (Canterbury & York Soc. 42) (1937): 647 (biog. of Lady Elizabeth Clinton). Stokes et al. *Warwickshire Feet of Fines* 3 (Dugdale Soc. 18) (1943): 75. VCH *Warwick* 3 (1945): 65; 4 (1947): 10, 138, 207; 5 (1949): 154; 7 (1964): 58–59. *TAG* 26 (1950): 12–25. Paget *Baronage of England* (1957) 485: 6. VCH *Oxford* 6 (1959): 127, 291–292. *Ancient Deeds — Ser. B* 3 (List & Index Soc. 113) (1975): B.10472. Ellis *Cat. Seals in the P.R.O.* 1 (1978): 17 (seal of John de Clinton dated 1354 — A shield of arms: on a chief, two rowels, the field diapered; surrounded by eight circles each containing a cross crosslet fitchy. Legend: *SIGILLVM. IOHANNIS.DE.CLYNTONE.). VCH *Cambridge* 6 (1978): 230–246. *Ancient Deeds — Ser. AS & WS* (List & Index Soc. 158) (1979): 91 (Deed A.S.492). Coss *Langley Cartulary* (Dugdale Soc. 32) (1980): 65. VCH *Stafford* 14 (1990): 237–252. Sainty *Judges of England* (Selden Soc. Supp. Ser. 10) (1993): 63 (re. Roger Hillary). Birmingham City Archives: Wingfield Digby Fam. of Sherborne Castle, Dorset and Coleshill, Warwickshire, Warwickshire Estate Papers, MS 3888/A286 (available at www.a2a.org.uk/search/index.asp).

Child of John de Clinton, Knt., by Idoine de Say:

i. **MARGARET DE CLINTON**, married **BALDWIN DE MONTFORT**, Knt., of Coleshill, Warwickshire [see MONTFORT 10].

ii. **KATHERINE CLINTON**, married **THOMAS BERKELEY**, Knt., 5th Lord Berkeley [see BERKELEY 8.i].

❧ CLOPTON ❧

ALICE OF NORMANDY (sister of King William the Conqueror), married **LAMBERT**, Count of Lens.
JUDITH OF LENS, married **WALTHEOF**, Earl of Northumberland.
MAUD OF NORTHUMBERLAND, married **SIMON DE SENLIS**, Earl of Huntingdon and Northampton.
MAUD DE SENLIS, married **SAHER DE QUINCY**, of Long Buckby, Northamptonshire.
ALICE DE SENLIS, married **ROGER DE HUNTINGFIELD**, of Huntingfield, Suffolk.
WILLIAM DE HUNTINGFIELD, Knt., of Huntingfield, Suffolk, married **ISABEL FITZ WILLIAM**.
ROGER DE HUNTINGFIELD, Knt., of Huntingfield, Suffolk, married **JOAN DE HOWBRIDGE**.
WILLIAM DE HUNTINGFIELD, Knt., of Huntingfield, Suffolk, married **EMMA DE GREY**.
ROGER DE HUNTINGFIELD, Knt., of Huntingfield, Suffolk, married **JOYCE D'ENGAINE**.
JOAN DE HUNTINGFIELD, married **RICHARD BASSET**, Knt., 1st Lord Basset of Weldon.
RALPH BASSET, Knt., 2nd Lord Basset of Weldon, married **JOAN** _____.
ELEANOR BASSET, married **JOHN KNYVET**, Knt., of Southwick, Northamptonshire.
ROBERT KNYVET, Knt., of Stanway, Essex, married **MARGARET CASTELAYN**.
THOMAS KNYVET, Esq. of Stanway, Essex, married **ELEANOR DOREWARD**.
JOHN KNYVET, Esq., of Stanway, Essex, married **JOAN BAYNARD**.
THOMAS KNYVET, Esq., of Stanway, Essex, married **ELIZABETH LUNSFORD** [see KNYVET 16].

17. THOMASINE KNYVET (or **KNYVETT**), born about 1475 (aged 60 and more in 1535). She married (as his 3rd wife) **WILLIAM CLOPTON**, Knt., of Kentwell (in Long Melford), Suffolk, and London, son and heir of John Clopton, Esq., of Kentwell, by Alice, daughter of Robert Darcy, Knt., of Malden, Essex, Keeper of the Writs for the Common Pleas, Knight of the Shire for Essex, Burgess (M.P.) for Maldon. He was born about 1458 (aged 40 in 1498). They had three sons, Francis, Gent., Richard, and John. His wife, Thomasine, was co-heiress in 1508 to her niece,

Elizabeth (or Isabel) Knyvet, wife of John Raynsford, Esq. In the period, 1507–14, William and his wife, Thomasine, with John Clopton and Elizabeth his wife, and Thomas Barney and Katherine his wife, heiresses of Elizabeth, late the wife of John Raynsford sued Thomas Bonham and Katherine his wife in Chancery regarding the detention of deeds relating to the reversions of the two manors of Castlins in Waldingfield and Groton, and to the manors of Sampfords in Waldingfield, Newton Bellhouse, and Down Hall in cos. Suffolk, Kent, and Essex. In the same period, the same plaintiffs sued the same defendants and Robert Drury, Philip Calthorp, Knts., John Akerman and Thomas Croxston, feoffees to uses in Chancery regarding the manors of Bellhouse Olivers and Ramsden Bellhouse, lands in Howes, Kirton, and Shrubbe, in Stanway and Colchester, and Wheteley in cos. Essex and Suffolk. In the period, 1515–18, William and his wife, Thomasine, together with John Clopton, Esq., and Elizabeth his wife, and John Hastings, Gent., and Katherine his wife sued Thomas Bonham, Esq., in Chancery regarding the detention of deeds relating to the manors of Newton Bellhouse, Ramsden Bellhouse, Whetley, Stanway, Downhall, Shenfield, Castlyns in Groton, and Sampford and Castlyns in Waldingfield, in cos. Kent, Essex, and Suffolk, late of Edward Knyvet, brother of the said Thomasine, and uncle of the said Elizabeth and Katherine. In the same period, William and his wife, Thomasine, sued John Raynesford, Knt. in Chancery regarding the detention of deeds relating to the manors of Newton Bellhouse, Wheteley, and Ramsden Bellhouse, tenements called 'Stewards,' and messuages and lands in Thunderley, Waldingfield, and Groton, Essex, late of Edward Knyvet, whose daughter Elizabeth was married to defendant's son, John. SIR WILLIAM CLOPTON died 20 Feb. 1530/1. He left a will dated 14 October 1530, requesting burial at Long Melford, Suffolk "nyhte unto the places wheras Jane & Dame Katherine late my wyffes lieth buried." His widow, Thomasine, died in 1538.

> Morant *Hist. & Antiqs. of Essex* 1 (1768): 202–3; 2 (1768): 190–191. Hasted *Hist. & Top. Survey of Kent* 8 (1799): 199–202; 9 (1800): 347. *Coll. Top. et Gen.* 7 (1841): 273–278. D'Ewes *Autobiography & Correspondence of Sir Simonds D'Ewes* 1 (1845): 326–346. Harvey *Vis. of Suffolk 1561* 1 (1866): 20–136. Hawley et al. *Vis. of Essex 1552, 1558, 1570, 1612 & 1634* 1 (H.S.P. 13) (1878): 179 (1612 Vis.). Muskett *Suffolk Manorial Fams.* 1 (1900): 144 (Clopton ped.). Copinger *Manors of Suffolk* 1 (1905): 113–115. *Letters & Papers… Henry VIII* 1(1) (1920): 210, 240. Erwin *Anc. of William Clopton* (1939). Ward *Fam. of Twysden & Twisden* (1939): 75–76. *List of Early Chancery Procs.* Maccullough *Chorography of Suffolk* (Suffolk Rec. Soc. 19) (1976): 34. Barnes *British Roots of Maryland Fams.* 2 (2002): 156–160. National Archives, C 1/298/48; C 1/298/49; C 1/298/51; C 1/298/52; C 1/392/35; C 1/392/36; C 1/392/38; C 1/400/56 (available at www.catalogue.nationalarchives.gov.uk/search.asp).

18. RICHARD CLOPTON, of Ford Hall (in Long Melford), Suffolk, 2nd son of his father's 3rd marriage. He married (1st) **MARGARET BOZUN**, daughter of Richard Bozun, Knt., of Baraby, Lincolnshire, by Thomasine, daughter and heiress of James Dene. They had one daughter, Mary (1st of name) (wife of William Cordell, Knt., Master of the Rolls). He married (2nd) **MARGERY PLAYTERS**, daughter of William Playters, Esq., of Sotterley, Suffolk, by Jane, daughter of Edmund Jenney, Knt. They had three sons, William, Esq., Richard, and Edward, and six daughters, Thomasine (wife of Thomas Aldham, Gent., and Thomas Kighley, Esq.), Frances (wife of Martin Bowes and Henry Hutton, Archbishop of York), Elizabeth (wife of Nicholas Hobart, Gent.), Emma (wife of George Smith, Esq.), Julian (wife of Thomas Wye and John Throckmorton), and Mary (2nd of name) (wife of Edward King). He was appointed one of the executors of the 1530 will of his father.

> D'Ewes *Autobiography & Correspondence of Sir Simonds D'Ewes* 1 (1845): 326–346. Suckling *Hist. & Antiqs. of Suffolk* 1 (1846): 86 (Playters ped.). Harvey *Vis. of Suffolk 1561* 1 (1866): 20–136. Muskett *Suffolk Manorial Fams.* 1 (1900): 144 (Clopton ped.).

19. WILLIAM CLOPTON, Esq., of Castelyns (in Groton), Suffolk, and Ramsden and Belhouse, Essex, son and heir. He married **MARGERY WALDEGRAVE**, daughter of Edward Waldegrave, Esq., of Rivers Hall (in Boxted), later of Lawford Hall, Essex, by Joan, daughter of George Acworth, Esq. [see WALDEGRAVE 15.ii for her ancestry]. They had four sons, William, Esq.,

Walter, Gent., Waldegrave, and Thomas, and six daughters, Anne (wife of John Maidstone), Bridget (wife of John Sampson, Esq.), Thomasine, Mary (wife of George Jenney, Gent.), Margery (wife of Thomas Doggett, Gent.), and Elizabeth (wife of George Cocke). His wife, Margery, was a legatee in the 1584 will of her father, Edward Waldegrave, Esq. WILLIAM CLOPTON, Esq., died 9 August 1616, and was buried at Groton, Suffolk. He left a will dated 5 Sept. 1615, proved 28 Nov. 1616 (P.C.C. 83 Cope).

Norfolk (England) Fams. MS Misc. Peds. (Early 17th Cent. Waldegrave ped.: "Margaret [Waldgrave] his youngest daughter Married to Will[ia]m Clopton of Grotton Esqr.") [FHL Microfilm 599678]. Hawley et al. *Vis. of Essex 1552, 1558, 1570, 1612 & 1634* 1 (H.S.P. 13) (1878): 119–122 (Waldegrave ped.: "Margery [Walgrave] ux. William Clopton of Bretton in Essex."), 307–310 (Waldegrave ped.: "Margery [Waldegrave] mar. to William Clopton of Castlyns in Grotton in com. Suffolk Esquier."). Harvey et al. *Vis. of Norfolk 1563 & 1613* (H.S.P. 32) (1891): 295–300 (Waldegrave ped.: "Margery [Waldgrave] ux. William Clopton of Groton in co. Suff."). Muskett *Suffolk Manorial Fams.* 1 (1900): 26 (Winthrop ped.), 144 (Clopton ped.). *Wm & Mary Quarterly* 11 (1903): 67–73. Erwin *Anc. of William Clopton* (1939): 10–13, 29–30. *TAG* 46 (1970): 117–118. Harvey *Vis. of Suffolk 1561* 1 (H.S.P. n.s. 2) (1981): 20–28; 2 (H.S.P. n.s. 3) (1984): 341–346.

Children of William Clopton, Esq., by Margery Waldegrave:

i. **WALTER CLOPTON**, Gent. [see next].

ii. **THOMASINE CLOPTON**, married [Gov.] **JOHN WINTHROP**, of Groton, Suffolk and Boston, Massachusetts [see TYNDALL 16].

20. WALTER CLOPTON, Gent., of Boxted, Essex, 2nd son, baptized at Groton, Suffolk 30 June 1585. He married at Boxted, Essex 21 April 1612 **MARGARET MAIDSTONE**, daughter of Robert Maidstone, Gent., of Great Horkesley, Essex. They had two sons, [Rev.] William and Walter, and one daughter, Margaret. WALTER CLOPTON, Gent., died at Boxted, Essex in 1622. He left a will dated 24 Dec. 1622. His widow, Margaret, married (2nd) by settlement dated 16 August 1631 **ROBERT CRANE**, Gent., of Coggeshall, Essex, grocer. He was living in May 1645. His wife, Margaret, died in 1666.

Muskett *Suffolk Manorial Fams.* 1 (1900): 144 (Clopton ped.). Erwin *Anc. of William Clopton* (1939): 13–14. *TAG* 46 (1970): 117–118.

21. [Rev.] WILLIAM CLOPTON, baptized at Boxted, Essex 19 April 1613. He attended Emmanuel College, Cambridge University, receiving B.A. in 1634 and M.A. in 1637. He was Rector of Great Horkesley, Essex, then in 1654 Rector at All Saints, Rettendon, Essex. He married before 1653 **ELIZABETH SUTCLIFFE**, daughter of [Rev.] Isaiah Sutcliffe, of Rettendon, Essex, by Elizabeth, daughter of [Rev.] Thomas Jolye. They had one son, William, Gent. They were devised part of the manor of Eastwoodbury after her mother's death. He was ejected "for conscience sake" in 1662, and thereafter resided at or near Eastwood, Essex. [REV.] WILLIAM CLOPTON, of Eastwood, Essex, left a will dated 24 October 1670, proved 14 June 1671. His widow, Elizabeth, died at Paglesham, Essex in 1683.

Calamy *Nonconformist's Memorial* 2 (1802): 212–213. Davids *Annals of Evangelical Nonconformity in the County of Essex* (1863): 447–448. Muskett *Suffolk Manorial Fams.* 1 (1900): 144 (Clopton ped.). Erwin *Anc. of William Clopton* (1939): 14–18. *NEHGR* 107 (1953): 190 (Clopton arms: Sable a bend silver cotised dancetty gold).

22. WILLIAM CLOPTON, Gent., of Paglesham, Essex, born about 1655 (aged 30 in 1685). He was apprenticed in London to Joshua White. He subsequently immigrated to Virginia in 1673. He married **ANNE BOOTH**, widow of Thomas Dennett, and daughter of Robert Booth. They had three sons, Robert, William, and Walter, and two daughters, Anne (wife of Nicholas Mills) and Elizabeth (wife of William Walker and Alexander Moss). He was living in York County, Virginia in 1683, where he served as Constable of Hampton Parish in York County. He later removed to New Kent County, Virginia, where he served as clerk of St. Peter's church, New Kent. His wife, Anne, died in 1716, and was buried in St. Peter's churchyard, New Kent. He was a legatee in the 1732 will of his nephew, William Hammond, Gent., of Ratcliffe (in Stepney), Middlesex, who bequeathed him lands in Eastwood and Thundersley, Essex in England for life, with remainder to his children. WILLIAM CLOPTON died at New Kent County, Virginia before 1733.

Wm & Mary Quarterly 11 (1903): 67–73. *NEHGR* 59 (1905): 219. Crozier *Virginia Heraldica* (1908): 21. *VMHB* 28 (1920): 238–239; 30 (1922): 41–42. Erwin *Anc. of William Clopton* (1939). MacDonald & Slatten *Surry County [Virginia] Tithables, 1668–1703* (2007): xxi.

↣ COBHAM ↢

JOHN DE SOMERY, married **HAWISE PAYNELL**.
RALPH DE SOMERY, of Dudley (in Sedgley), Staffordshire, married **MARGARET LE GRAS**.
JOAN DE SOMERY, married **THOMAS DE BERKELEY**.
MAURICE DE BERKELEY, Knt., of Berkeley, Gloucestershire, married **ISABEL DE DOVER** (desc. King William the Conqueror).
THOMAS DE BERKELEY, Knt., 1st Lord Berkeley, married **JOAN DE FERRERS** (desc. King William the Conqueror).
MAURICE DE BERKELEY, Knt., 2nd Lord Berkeley, married **EVE LA ZOUCHE**.
THOMAS DE BERKELEY, Knt., 3rd Lord Berkeley, married **MARGARET DE MORTIMER** (desc. King William the Conqueror) [see BERKELEY 7].

8. JOAN DE BERKELEY, married (1st) by dispensation dated 17 Jan. 1337 (they being related in the 4th degree of kindred) **THOMAS BURNELL** (or **DE HAUDLO**), of Great Cheverell, Wiltshire, son of John de Haudlo, Knt., of Boarstall and Oakley, Buckinghamshire, and Hadlow, Ashendon, Crundale, Ore, Trentworth (in Crundale), and Vanne (in Crundale), Kent, by his 2nd wife, Maud, daughter of Philip Burnell, Knt. [see BURNELL 10 for his ancestry]. They had no issue. THOMAS DE HAUDLO died in or before 1339. His widow, Joan, presented to the church of Haselbech, Northamptonshire 15 Jan. 1340/1. She married (2nd) before 1342–3 (date of fine) **REYNOLD DE COBHAM**, K.G., of Sterborough (in Lingfield), Surrey, Admiral of the Fleet for the West, son and heir of Reynold de Cobham, Knt., of Orkesden (in Eynesford), Kent, by Joan, daughter and heiress of William de Hever. He was born in 1300. They had one son, Reynold, Knt. [2nd Lord Cobham], and one daughter, Joan. He was distinguished in nearly all the battles in France and Flanders from 1327 to 1360. In 1341 he was granted the manor of Cippenham, Buckinghamshire by the king. He formed one of an important embassy to the Pope in 1343. He received an annuity of £500 in 1347. He was summoned to Parliament from 13 Nov. 1347 to 20 Nov. 1360, by writs directed *Reginaldo de Cobham*, whereby he is held to have become Lord Cobham. In 1353 John Mohaut and Joan his wife remised and quitclaimed their right in the manor of la Leygh, Wiltshire held for the term of the life of the said Joan to Reynold de Cobham and his wife, Joan, for 100 marks. Reynold was Marshal of the Prince's army at the Battle of Poitiers in 1356, where he conducted the French king, Jean, to the English quarters. In 1358 they were granted a license for mass to be celebrated in any suitable place in the diocese of Hampshire at the bishop's discretion. SIR REYNOLD DE COBHAM, 1st Lord Cobham of Sterborough, died testate of pestilence 5 October 1361, and was buried in Lingfield, Surrey. His widow, Joan, died 2 October 1369. She left a will dated 13 August 1369, proved 23 May 1370, directing burial at Southwark, Surrey.

Bridges *Hist. & Antiqs. of Northamptonshire* 2 (1791): 37. Nicolas *Testamenta Vetusta* 1 (1826): 81–82 (will of Joan de Cobham). Clutterbuck *Hist. & Antiqs. of Hertford* 3 (1827): 131 (Cobham ped.). Beltz *Mems. of the Order of the Garter* (1841): cl, 103–105 (biog. of Reynold de Cobham: "… His judgement and valour were… so conspicuous that he shared in almost every martial expedition of that reign, and was engaged in its most important diplomatic transactions until the conclusion of the treaty of Bretigny, in May 1360… Vincent has preserved (No. 40, fo. 51, in Coll. Arm.) sketches of the arms on eight shields which adorn [his] tomb, viz.: 1. Cobham; 2. Cobham, impaling Stafford; 3. Badlesmere; 4. Berkeley; 5. Valenges; 6. Cosyngton; 7. Paveley; 8. Roos."). *Surrey Arch Colls.* 2 (1864): 115–194. Burke

Dormant, Abeyant, Forfeited & Extinct Peerages (1883): 125–126 (sub Cobham). Smyth *Berkeley MSS* 1 (1883): 348. *Genealogist* n.s. 5 (1889): 129 (seal of Joan, Lady Cobham dated 1368–9 — An eagle displayed, on its breast the arms of Lady Cobham, viz., BERKELEY, on its wings, the arms of her two husbands, on a chevron three mullets [COBHAM], and a lion rampant [HAUDLO]. Legend: S' Johanne de Cobham.). Jeayes *Desc. Cat. of the Charters & Muniments in the Possession of the Rt. Hon. Lord Fitzhardinge* (1892): xxii–xxiii (chart). Lewis *Pedes Finium; or, Fines Rel. Surrey* (Surrey Arch. Soc. Extra Volume 1) (1894): 221. *Papal Regs.: Letters* 2 (1895): 541. Kirby *Wykeham's Reg.* 2 (1899): 179. *C.C.R. 1341–1343* (1902): 75, 620. *C.C.R. 1343–1346* (1904): 380. VCH *Surrey* 4 (1912): 312–321. *C.P.* 3 (1913): 353 (sub Cobham); 6 (1926): 127 (sub Grey). *Misc. Gen. et Heraldica* 5th Ser. 8 (1932–34): 205. Paget *Baronage of England* (1957) 55: 1–2 (sub Berkeley). VCH *Wiltshire* 8 (1965): 61–74; 10 (1975): 42–43. Haines *Cal. Reg. of Wolstan de Bransford Bishop of Worcester* (Worcestershire Hist. Soc. n.s. 4) (1966): 110–111, 480–485. Elrington *Abs. of Feet of Fines Rel. Wiltshire* (Wiltshire Rec. Soc. 29) (1974): 101. Ellis *Cat. Seals in the P.R.O.* 2 (1981): 26 (seal of Reynold de Cobham, Knt. dated 1335 — In a cusped circle, a shield of arms: on a chevron, three stars (the field diapered). Legend: SIGILL'/ROGINAL…EHAM.). Edington *Reg. of William Edington Bishop of Winchester* 2 (Hampshire Recs. 8) (1987): 45, 52. Saul *Death, Art & Memory in Medieval England* (2001). Coss & Keen *Heraldry, Pageantry & Social Display in Medieval England* (2002): 169–194 ("The tomb of Reginald, Lord Cobham (d. 1361) at Lingfield (Surrey) is … a fairly standard London-made job with a relief effigy, bears all the hallmarks of the taste of his wife's Berkeley kin; it is almost identical to the tomb of Reginald's in-laws at Berkeley (Gloucestershire) and the two were probably ordered at the same time. However, the rich display of heraldry on the sides is very much a reflection of Reginald's own career and achievements: virtually all the arms are those of his comrades-in-arms and associates.").

Children of Joan de Berkeley, by Reynold de Cobham, K.G.:

i. **REYNOLD COBHAM**, Knt., 2nd Lord Cobham [see next].

ii. **JOAN DE COBHAM**, married **HENRY DE GREY**, Knt. [see CODNOR 13].

9. REYNOLD COBHAM, Knt., 2nd Lord Cobham of Sterborough, of Sterborough (in Lingfield) and Oxted, Surrey, son and heir, born about 1348 (aged 13 in 1361). He married (1st) after Easter term 1370 (date of lawsuits) **ELIZABETH DE STAFFORD**, widow successively of Fulk le Strange, Lord Strange of Blackmere (died 6 Sept. or 22 or 30 August 1349) [see BLACKMERE 11.i], and John de Ferrers, Knt., *de jure* 4th Lord Ferrers of Chartley (died 2 April 1367) [see FERRERS 11], and daughter of Ralph de Stafford, K.G., 1st Earl of Stafford, by Margaret, daughter of Hugh de Audley, Knt., Earl of Gloucester, Lord Audley [see STAFFORD 7 for her ancestry]. They had no issue. He distinguished himself in the wars of Gascony and France. He presented to the church of Oxted, Surrey in 1370, 1373, 1383, 1385, 1390, and 1398. He was summoned to Parliament from 8 Jan. 1370/1 to 6 October 1372. His wife, Elizabeth, died 7 August 1375. He married (2nd) 9 August 1380 (they being related in the 2nd and 3rd degrees of kindred) **ELEANOR MAUTRAVERS**, widow of John Arundel, Knt., 1st Lord Arundel, Marshal of England (died 15 Dec. 1379) [see ARUNDEL 9 for issue of this marriage], and daughter of John Mautravers, Knt., of Woolcombe and Witchampton, Dorset, by his wife, Gwenthlian [see ARUNDEL 8 for her ancestry]. She was born about 1345 (aged 5 in 1350 and 19 in 1364). They had three sons, John, Reynold, Knt. [3rd Lord Cobham], and Thomas, and two daughters, Elizabeth and Margaret (wife of Reginald Courteys, Esq.). She was sole heiress in or after 1376 to her sister, Joan Mautravers, wife of Robert Rous, Knt., by which she became *de jure* Lady Mautravers. He presented to the church of Langton Matravers, Dorset in 1383, 1395, and 1400, in right of his wife. In 1384 they were divorced on account of their consanguinity and afterwards allowed to remarry at Trottiscliffe, Kent 29 Sept. 1384. He presented to the Hospital of Aynho, Northamptonshire in 1401. SIR REYNOLD COBHAM, 2nd Lord Cobham of Sterborough, died testate 3 (or 6) July 1403, and was buried in the church at Lingfield, Surrey. His widow, Eleanor, Lady Mautravers, died testate 12 Jan. 1404/5, and was buried with her 1st husband at Lewes Priory, Sussex.

Bridges *Hist. & Antiqs. of Northamptonshire* 1 (1791): 142. Clutterbuck *Hist. & Antiqs. of Hertford* 3 (1827): 131 (Cobham ped.). Dallaway *Hist. of the Western Div. of Sussex* 2(1) (1832): 143 (Mautravers ped.). Tierney *Hist. & Antiqs. of the Castle & Town of Arundel* 1 (1834): chart following 192. *Coll. Top. et Gen.* 6 (1840): 1–20, 334–361. Beltz *Mems. of the Order of the Garter* (1841): cliv. *Top. & Gen.* 2 (1853): 317–325, 336. *Surrey Arch Colls.* 2 (1864): 115–194. Hutchins *Hist. & Antiqs. of Dorset* 3 (1868): 314–325. Flower *Vis. of Yorkshire 1563–4* (H.S.P. 16) (1881): 337–338 (Warren ped.: "John

Fytzallen Knight 2 son maryed = Ellyn doughter & heyre to John, Lord Maltravers"). Burke *Dormant, Abeyant, Forfeited & Extinct Peerages* (1883): 125–126 (sub Cobham). Birch *Cat. Seals in the British Museum* 2 (1892): 395–396 (seal of Eleanor Mautravers, widow of John de Arundel dated 1404 — A shield of arms: per pale, dex., a lion rampant [ARUNDEL]; sin., A FRET [MAUTRAVERS]. Suspended by a strap from a forked tree. Within a finely-carved gothic panel.). Wrottesley *Staffordshire Suits: Plea Rolls* (Colls. Hist. Staffs. 13) (1892): 68, 77, 79, 80, 123. Kirby *Wykeham's Reg.* 1 (1896): 36, 49, 143–144, 154, 175, 176, 216; 2 (1899): 548. *Genealogist* n.s. 15 (1898): 216; n.s. 16 (1899): 46, 163–164. *C.P.R.* 1401–1405 (1905): 321. Wrottesley *Peds. from the Plea Rolls* (1905): 125–126, 275, 294. *C.P.* 1 (1910): 253, 259–260 (sub Arundel); 3 (1913): 353–354 (sub Cobham); 8 (1932): 585–586 (sub Mautravers); 11 (1949): 102–103 (sub Ros). VCH *Surrey* 3 (1911): 173–174, 316; 4 (1912): 312–321. Hemmant *Select Cases in the Exchequer Chamber* 1 1377–1461 (1933): 23–27. *Cal. Inqs. Misc.* 3 (1937): 377–378; 7 (1968): 384–385. Legge *Anglo-Norman Letters & Petitions* (Anglo-Norman Text Soc. 3) (1941): 376–377 (letter of Eleanor de Cobham dated 1399), 409 ([Eleanor?], Lady Cobham, styled "cousin" by an unidentified king of England). VCH *Warwick* 6 (1951): 276–277. Paget *Baronage of England* (1957) 304: 6 (sub Keynes). *Cal. IPM* 15 (1970): 77–80. *Year Books of Richard II* 2 (Ames Found. 3) (1996): 191–205. *Nottingham Medieval Studies* 41 (1997): 154–155 (chart). Deed #310, English Deeds Coll., Harvard Law School Lib. — available at http://hollis.harvard.edu//?itemid=%7clibrary%2fm%2faleph%7c003306988.

10. REYNOLD COBHAM, Knt., 3rd Lord Cobham of Sterborough, of Sterborough (in Lingfield) and Oxted, Surrey, 1st surviving son and heir by his father's 2nd marriage, born in 1381. He married (1st) **ELEANOR CULPEPER**, daughter of Thomas Culpeper, Knt., by his 1st wife, Eleanor, daughter and heiress of Nicholas Greene, of Exton, Rutland, Steward of Higham Ferrers and Glatton [see EXTON 11 for her ancestry]. They had two sons, Reynold, Knt., and Thomas, Knt., and three daughters, Elizabeth, Eleanor, and Anne (nun at Barking). In 1408–9 he granted the manor of Oxted, Surrey to Thomas Culpeper and others, evidently in trust for his wife, Eleanor. His wife, Eleanor, died in 1422, and was buried at Lingfield, Surrey. He married (2nd) shortly before 9 July 1422 **ANNE BARDOLF**, widow of William Clifford, Knt. (died 25 March 1418), and daughter and co-heiress of Thomas Bardolf, Knt., 5th Lord Bardolf, by Anice (or Amice), daughter of Ralph de Cromwell, Knt., 1st Lord Cromwell [see BARDOLF 14.i for her ancestry]. She was born 24 June 1389. They had no issue. He presented to the churches of Garveston, Norfolk, 1425, and Gedling, Nottinghamshire, 1428. In 1431 he and his wife, Anne, founded the College of Lingfield, Surrey. He was granted custody of Louis, Duke of Orléans (afterwards King Louis XII) in 1436. He presented to the church of Plumpton, Sussex in 1441. SIR REYNOLD COBHAM, 3rd Lord Cobham of Sterborough, left a will dated 12 August 1446, requesting burial at Lingfield, Surrey. His widow, Anne, died 6 Nov. 1453, and was buried at Lingfield, Surrey.

Blomefield *Essay towards a Top. Hist. of Norfolk* 11 (1810): 202–203. Nicolas *Testamenta Vetusta* 1 (1826): 246–247 (will of Reginald Cobham). Clutterbuck *Hist. & Antiqs. of Hertford* 3 (1827): 131 (Cobham ped.). Stapleton *De Antiquis Legibus Liber: Cronica Maiorum et Vicecomitum Londoniarum* (Camden Soc. 34) (1846). Suckling *Hist. & Antiqs. of Suffolk* 1 (1846): 113–114. Eller *Mems.: Arch. & Eccl. of the West Winch Manors* (1861): 68–75. *Surrey Arch Colls.* 2 (1864): 115–194. Burke *Dormant, Abeyant, Forfeited & Extinct Peerages* (1883): 125–126 (sub Cobham). *Genealogist* n.s. 17 (1901): 246–247. Deedes *Extracts from the Episcopal Regs. of Richard Paty, S.T.P., Lord Bishop of Chichester* (Sussex Rec. Soc. 4) (1905): 122–123. Wrottesley *Peds. from the Plea Rolls* (1905): 311, 352. Gerring *Hist. of Gedling* (1908): 175–179. VCH *Surrey* 4 (1912): 312–321. *C.P.* 3 (1913): 354 (sub Cobham). Dudding *Hist. of the Manor & Parish of Saleby with Thoresthorpe* (1922): 44–53 (re. Culpeper fam.). Hemmant *Select Cases in the Exchequer Chamber* 1 1377–1461 (1933): 23–27. *C.F.R.* 14 (1934): 441; 15 (1934): 66. VCH *Sussex* 7 (1940): 109–113. Chichele *Reg. of Henry Chichele* 3 (Canterbury & York Soc. 46) (1945): 471. Somerville *Hist. of the Duchy of Lancaster* 1 (1953): 371, 385. Train *Lists of Clergy of Central Nottinghamshire* (Thoroton Soc. Rec. Ser. 15(1)) (1953): 53–54. Paget *Baronage of England* (1957) 24: 1–2 (sub Bardolf). VCH *Oxford* 5 (1957): 170–171. VCH *Leicester* 5 (1964): 123.

Children of Reynold Cobham, Knt., by Eleanor Culpeper:

i. **ELIZABETH COBHAM**, married (1st) **RICHARD LE STRANGE**, Lord Strange of Knockin [see STRANGE 10]; (2nd) **ROGER KYNASTON**, Knt., of Middle, Shropshire [see LLOYD 10].

ii. **ELEANOR COBHAM**, married **HUMPHREY OF LANCASTER**, K.G., Duke of Gloucester [see LANCASTER 11.v].

❧ CODNOR ❧

ALICE OF NORMANDY (sister of King William the Conqueror), married **LAMBERT**, Count of Lens.
JUDITH OF LENS, married **WALTHEOF**, Earl of Northumberland.
ALICE OF NORTHUMBERLAND, married **RALPH DE TONY**, of Flamstead, Hertfordshire.
ROGER DE TONY, of Flamstead, Hertfordshire, married **IDA OF HAINAULT**.
GODEHILDE DE TONY, married **WILLIAM DE MOHUN**, of Dunster, Somerset.
WILLIAM DE MOHUN, of Dunster, Somerset, married **LUCY** _____.
REYNOLD DE MOHUN, Knt., of Dunster, Somerset, married **ALICE BRIWERRE**.
REYNOLD DE MOHUN, Knt., of Dunster, Somerset, married **HAWISE FITZ GEOFFREY** [see MOHUN 8].

9. LUCY DE MOHUN, married **JOHN DE GREY**, Knt., of Codnor, Beeley, Hazelbache, Heanor, Normanton, and Shirland, Derbyshire, Thurrock, Essex, Hoo and Aylesford, Kent, Evington, Leicestershire, Sherringham, Norfolk, etc., son and heir of Richard de Grey, Knt., of Codnor, Derbyshire, Thurrock, Essex, Aylesford and Hoo, Kent, Governor of the Channel Isles, Seneschal of Gascony and Poitou, Constable of Devises, Dover, and Kenilworth Castles, Warden of the Cinque Ports, by Lucy, daughter and heiress of John du Hommet (or de Humez), of Humberstone, Leicestershire, Sherringham, Norfolk, and Newbottle Northamptonshire. Her maritagium included the manor of Tunworth, Hampshire. They had one son, Henry, Knt. [1st Lord Grey of Codnor] and two daughters, Joan and Lucy (wife of Brian le Waleys). He was knighted in 1244, and joined with his father against King Henry III. He is said to have brought Carmelites (White Friars) from the Holy Land about 1240 and settled them at Aylesford, Kent. He acquired the manor of Upton Grey, Wiltshire from William de Arundel. SIR JOHN DE GREY died shortly before 5 Jan. 1271/2. In 1272-3 John de Evington arraigned an assize of novel disseisin against his widow, Lucy, touching common of pasture in Evington, Leicestershire. Lucy married (2nd) before 4 July 1281 (date of pardon for marrying without a license) **ARNOLD MURDAC**, Knt. In 1284 he acknowledged that he owed Philip de Montgomery 4 marks; to be levied, in default of payment, of his lands and chattels in Leicestershire. In 1285, as Arnold Murdak, Knt., of Northamptonshire, he owed a debt of £17 to Baroncinus Galteri, and others their partners and merchants of Lucca. On 19 May 1290 he and his wife, Lucy, were acquitted of 100*l.* of the 200*l.* by which they made fine with the king for their trespass in marrying without the king's license. SIR ARNOLD MURDAC was living in June 1290.

Banks *Baronies in Fee* 1 (1844): 227–230 (sub Grey of Codnor). Vivian *Vis. of Cornwall* (H.S.P. 9) (1874): 143–146 (Mohun ped.: "Lucia [de Mohun] uxor Johis Grey de Codner."). Cox *Notes on the Churches of Derbyshire* 4 (1879): 233-234. *Arch. Jour.* 37 (1880): 57–93. *Annual Rpt. of the Deputy Keeper* 42 (1881): 551; 49 (1888): 161. *C.C.R.* 1279–1288 (1902): 100, 346. *C.C.R.* 1288–1296 (1904): 29, 34, 80, 134. *Cal. IPM* 1 (1904): 276-277. *Reg. of William Wickwane, Lord Archbishop of York 1279-1285* (Surtees Soc. 114) (1907): 75. VCH *Hampshire* 3 (1908): 383 (Grey arms: Barry argent and azure, with three roundels gules in the chief); 4 (1911): 174-175. Maxwell-Lyte: *Hist. of Dunster* 1 (1909): 18–34. *C.P.* 6 (1926): 123, 126 footnote n, 135. *C.F.R.* 11 (1929): 151. *Paget* (1957) 259: 3 (sub Grey of Codnor). *TG* 8 (1988): 3–38. National Archives, C 241/6/198; C 241/8/418; C 241/14/19 (available at www.catalogue.nationalarchives.gov.uk/search.asp).

10. HENRY DE GREY, Knt., of Codnor, Derbyshire, Grays Thurrocks, Essex, Tunworth and Upton Grey, Hampshire, Aylesford and Hoo, Kent, Evington, Leicestershire, Sherringham, Norfolk, Eastwood and Toton, Nottinghamshire, etc., son and heir, born about 1255/8 (aged 14, 15, or 17 in 1272). He married (1st) **ELEANOR** _____. They had four sons, Richard, Knt. [2nd Lord Grey of Codnor], Nicholas, Thomas and Henry, and two daughters, Lucy and Joan (nun). He fought in Wales in 1282. In 1294 he was going to Gascony in the retinue of Edmund, the king's brother. He was again on service in Gascony in 1295 and 1297. He presented to the church of Heanor, Derbyshire in 1298 and 1304. He was constantly employed in the Scottish wars of King Edward I. He was summoned to Parliament from 6 Feb. 1298/9 to 16 August 1308, by writs directed *Henrico de Grey*, whereby he is held to have become Lord Grey. He was present at the Siege of Caerlaverock in 1300. He signed the Barons' letter to Pope Boniface VIII in 1301 as *Dominus de Codnore*. In 1306, in consideration of his services in Scotland and elsewhere, he had a pardon for all debts due from him or his ancestors to the Exchequer. He married (2nd) shortly before 6 June 1301 **JOAN DE SOMERVILLE**, widow of Ralph de Cromwell, Knt., of Cromwell and Lambley, Nottinghamshire (died before 2 March 1298/9) [see CROMWELL 5], and daughter of Robert de Somerville, Knt., of Wichnor (in Tatenhill), Staffordshire, by Isabel, daughter and co-heiress of Roger de Merlay, Knt. [see SOMERVILLE 8 for her ancestry]. In 1305 he conveyed the manor of Barton le Street, Yorkshire to his son, Nicholas de Grey. SIR HENRY DE GREY, 1st Lord Grey of Codnor, died shortly before 18 Sept. 1308. He left a will dated 9 Sept. 1308, proved 16 and 19 Sept. and 15 and 22 October 1309, requesting burial in the Carmelite Friars at Aylesford, Kent.

Banks *Baronies in Fee* 1 (1844): 227–230 (sub Grey of Codnor). Cox *Notes on the Churches of Derbyshire* 4 (1879): 233-234. Wrottesley *Staffordshire Suits: Plea Rolls* (Colls. Hist. Staffs. 7) (1886): 47–48, 97, 108, 113. Birch *Cat. Seals in the British Museum* 3 (1894): 36–37 (seal of Henry de Grey, lord of Codnor dated 1301 — A shield of arms: barry of six, GREY. Suspended by a strap from a tree of three branches, with two smaller branches at the side. Legend: * DE LEIAVTE SE....VNTE(?). Beaded borders.). *Cal. IPM* 1 (1904): 276-277; 5 (1908): 50-51. Brown *Yorkshire Inquisitions* 4 (Yorkshire Arch. Soc. Rec. Ser. 37): (1906): 116. VCH *Hampshire* 3 (1908): 383; 4 (1911): 174-175. *Register of John le Romeyn Lord Archbishop of York* 1 (Surtees Soc. 123) (1913): 320. *C.P.* 6 (1926): 123-124 ("said to have m., 1stly, Eleanor, da. of Sir Hugh de Courtenay"). Paget (1957) 259: 3-4 (sub Grey of Codnor) (no identification of parents of wife). *List of Ancient Correspondence of the Chancery & the Exchequer* (PRO, Lists and Indexes 15): 393 (letter re. marriage of daughter Lucy to John de Somery). *Index to Ancient Correspondence of the Chancery & the Exchequer* 1 (PRO, Lists and Indexes, Supp. Ser., No. 15): 509.

Children of Henry de Grey, Knt., by Eleanor _____:

i. **RICHARD DE GREY**, Knt., 2nd Lord Grey of Codnor [see next].

ii. **LUCY DE GREY**, married **JOHN DE SOMERY**, Knt., Lord Somery [see SOMERY 4.ii].

11. RICHARD DE GREY, Knt., 2nd Lord Grey of Codnor, of Codnor and Denby, Derbyshire, Thurrock, Essex, Tunworth and Upton Grey, Hampshire, Aylesford and Hoo, Kent, Evington and Newbold, Leicestershire, Sherringham, Norfolk, Eastwood and Barton, Nottinghamshire, etc., Seneschal of Gascony, Steward of Aquitaine, Constable of Nottingham Castle, son and heir by his father's 1st marriage, born about 1281 or 1282 (aged 26, 26-1/2, or 27 in 1308). He married **JOAN FITZ PAYN**, daughter of Robert Fitz Payn, Knt., Lord Fitz Payn, by Isabel, daughter of John Clifford, Knt., of Frampton-on-Severn, Gloucestershire. They had four sons, John, Knt. [3rd Lord Grey of Codnor], Robert [Fitz Payn], Knt., Gilbert, and Henry, and two daughters, Joan and Maud. He was continually employed in the Scottish wars. He was summoned to Parliament from 4 March 1308/9 by writs directed *Ricardo de Grey*. He presented to the church of Heanor, Derbyshire in 1320. In 1323 he was granted 20 does by the king for burying the body of his kinsman, John de Grey, Knt., 2nd Lord Grey of Ruthin. SIR RICHARD DE GREY, 2nd Lord Grey of Codnor, died testate shortly before 10 March 1334/5.

Banks *Baronies in Fee* 1 (1844): 227–230 (sub Grey of Codnor). Cox *Notes on the Churches of Derbyshire* 4 (1879): 233-234. *Year Books of Edward III* 3 (Rolls Ser. 31) (1886): 122–131. *C.P.R. 1330–1334* (1893): 598. Rye *Cal. Feet of Fines for Suffolk* (1900): 182, 297. VCH *Hampshire* 3 (1908): 383. *Cal. IPM* 5 (1908): 50-51; 7 (1909): 468-469. *Report on the MSS of Lord Middleton* (Hist. Mss. Comm. 69) (1911): 91. VCH *Hampshire* 4 (1911): 174-175. Chaplais *War of Saint-Sardos (1323-1325)* (Camden 3rd Ser. 87) (1954): 78 (Richard styled "trescher cousin" in 1324 by Hugh le Despenser). Paget (1957) 224:1, 259:4-5 (identifies other children Henry, Gilbert and Joan, but no daughter Agnes). *List of Inquisitions ad Quod Damnum* 1 (PRO, Lists and Indexes, No. 17) (repr. 1963): 232, 238. Goodall "Heraldry in the Decoration of English Medieval Manuscripts," in *Antiquaries Journal* 77 (1997): 179-220. Gee *Women, Art & Patronage from Henry III to Edward III: 1216–1377* (2002): 159.

Children of Richard de Grey, Knt., by Joan Fitz Payn:

i. **JOHN DE GREY**, Knt., 3rd Lord Grey of Codnor [see next].

ii. **ROBERT FITZ PAYN**, Knt., 2nd son, of Stogursey, Bridghampton, Cary Fitzpaine, Charlton Mackrell, Cheddon Fitzpaine, Rodway, Speckington, and Staple Fitzpaine, Somerset, Okeford Fitzpaine and Wraxall,

Dorset, Stourton, Wiltshire, Wisley, Surrey, etc., younger son, born about 1321. He married before 16 October 1354 **ELIZABETH DE BRYAN**, daughter of Guy de Bryan, K.G., Lord Bryan, of Laugharne, Carmarthenshire, Walwyn's Castle, Pembrokeshire, and Torbrian, Devon, by his 1st wife, Joan, daughter of John de Carew, Knt. [see BRYAN 10.ii for her ancestry]. They had two daughters, Isabel and Elizabeth. In 1354 he was in the king's service with Guy de Bryan in parts beyond sea. In 1359 he and his wife, Elizabeth, conveyed the manors of Wraxall, Dorset and Stourton, Wiltshire to John de Vere, Earl of Oxford, and Maud his wife, for the life of Maud, at an annual rent of 200s., with reversion to himself and Elizabeth, and his heirs. He was with the king in the invasion of France, October 1359 to 1360, serving in the retinue of Sir Guy de Bryan. He presented to the church of Wisley, Surrey in 1387 and 1388. SIR ROBERT FITZ PAYN died 21 May 1393. His wife, Elizabeth, predeceased him. Pole *Colls. towards a Desc. of Devon* (1791): 286–287. Banks *Dormant & Extinct Baronage of England* 2 (1808): 63–65 (sub Bryan). Willement *Heraldic Notices of Canterbury Cathedral* (1827): 121 (Gules, three lions passant, in pale, argent, a bendlet, azure [Fitz Pain], impaling Or, three piles, in chief, azure [Brian].). Banks *Baronies in Fee* 1 (1844): 227–230 (sub Grey of Codnor). Kirby *Wykeham's Reg.* 1 (1896): 165, 169. Green *Feet of Fines for Somerset* 2 (Somerset Rec. Soc. 12) (1898): 93, 120–121; 3 (Somerset Rec. Soc. 17) (1902): 182–183. VCH *Surrey* 3 (1911): 378–381. *C.P.* 2 (1912): 361, footnote h; 5 (1926): 452, 463-464 (sub Fitzpayn); 6 (1926): 125, footnote j; 10 (1945): 663. *Paget* (1957) 259: 4-5. *List of Inquisitons ad Quod Damnum* 1 (PRO, Lists and Indexes, No. 17) (repr. 1963): 232-233.

Children of Robert Fitz Payn, Knt., by Elizabeth de Bryan:

- a. **ISABEL FITZ PAYN**, married **RICHARD DE POYNINGS**, Knt., 3rd Lord Poynings [see POYNINGS 15].
- b. **ELIZABETH FITZ PAYN**, married (1st) **THOMAS DE AUDLEY**, Knt., of Kingston, Devon and Stogursey, Somerset [see AUDLEY 11.iii]; (2nd) **HUGH DE COURTENAY**, Knt., of Goodrington (in Paignton), Devon [see COURTENAY 9].

iii. **JOAN DE GREY**, married (1st) **WILLIAM DE HARCOURT**, Knt., of Stanton Harcourt, Oxfordshire [see HARCOURT 11];(2nd) **RALPH DE FERRERS**, Knt., of Bilton, Warwickshire [see HARCOURT 11].

iv. **MAUD DE GREY**, married (1st) **JOHN DE GRAVESENDE**, of Gravesend, Kent. He died before 25 July 1332, when her father granted her 40l. of rent in his manor of Sheringham, Norfolk, in exchange for the manor of Gravesend, Kent, which she granted him for the term of her life. His widow, Maud, married (2nd) before 1336-7 (date of fine) **ROGER DE LOUDHAM**, Knt., of Herringfleet and Lound, Suffolk. They had three sons, Roger, John, and Nicholas. In 1332 he acknowledged that he owed £400 to Richard de Grey, of Codnor; to be levied, in default of payment, of his lands and chattels in Suffolk. In 1336-7 Geoffrey de Corton conveyed the manor of Gunton, Suffolk to him and his wife, Maud. He presented to the church of Gunton, Suffolk in 1346. SIR ROGER DE LOUDHAM died 15 March 1347. Suckling *Hist. & Antiqs. of Suffolk* 2 (1847): 1, 9, 12. Rye *Some Rough Materials for a Hist. of the Hundred of North Erpingham* 1 (1883): 98. *C.C.R.* 1330–1333 (1898): 598. Rye *Cal. Feet of Fines for Suffolk* (1900): 182, 297. Copinger *Manors of Suffolk* 5 (1910): 40. *Rpt. on the MSS of Lord Middleton* (Hist. Mss. Comm. 69) (1911): 91. *Cal. IPM* 9 (1916): 2.

12. JOHN DE GREY, Knt., 3rd Lord Grey of Codnor, of Codnor, Derbyshire, Tunworth and Upton Grey, Hampshire, Aylesford and Hoo, Kent, Barton-on-Trent, Nottinghamshire, etc., son and heir, born about 1305/11 (aged variously 24, 27, 28, or 30 in 1335). He married (1st) before 4 Sept. 1325 **ELEANOR DE COURTENAY**, daughter of Hugh de Courtenay, Knt., 9th Earl of Devon, 1st Lord Courtenay, by Agnes, daughter of John de Saint John, Knt. [see COURTENAY 6 for her ancestry]. He and his wife, Eleanor, presented to the church of High Halstow, Kent 12 July 1326. He married (2nd) before 20 October 1330 **ALICE DE LISLE**, daughter of Warin de Lisle, Knt., of Kingston Lisle (in Sparsholt) and Beedon, Berkshire, Mundford, Norfolk, etc., by Alice, daughter of Henry le Tyeys, Knt., 1st Lord Tyeys [see KINGSTON LISLE 8 for her ancestry]. They had three sons, Henry, Knt., John, and Richard, and two daughters, Alice (wife of William Everingham) and Margaret (wife of Roger Beler, Knt.). By an unknown mistress, he also had an illegitimate son, Nicholas. He had livery of his father's lands 26 March 1335. He was summoned to Parliament from 1 April 1335 to 23 Nov. 1392, by writs directed *Johanni de Grey de Codenore* or *Johanni filio Ricardi de Grey de Codenore* or *Johanni Grey de Codenore*. He served in Scotland at great expense in 1335, when he had a respite of debts due to the Exchequer. In 1344 he and his wife, Alice, were granted a papal indult for plenary remission. In 1345 he crossed over with the Earls of Derby and

Pembroke to Gascony. He was in the Crécy expedition in 1346, and afterwards joined the king during the Siege of Calais in 1346–7. In 1347 he had a grant of free warren in his demesne lands at Barton-on-Trent, Nottinghamshire. He presented to the churches of High Halstow, Kent, 1347, 1349, Heanor, Derbyshire, 1348, 1349, 1370, 1385, and Tunworth, Hampshire, 1348, 1349, 1351, 1367, 1373, 1377, 1388. He obtained a papal indult for a portable altar in 1355. In 1359 he was granted at farm the city of Rochester and the keepership of the castle there for life. The same year he was granted a protection, he then going abroad in the retinue of John, Earl of Richmond. He was going on a pilgrimage in 1365. SIR JOHN DE GREY, 3rd Lord Grey of Codnor, died 14 Dec. 1392, and was buried in the Carmelite church at Aylesford, Kent.

> Blomefield *Essay towards a Top. Hist. of Norfolk* 8 (1808): 161-164. Banks *Baronies in Fee* 1 (1844): 227–230 (sub Grey of Codnor). Cox *Notes on the Churches of Derbyshire* 4 (1879): 233-234. *Year Books of Edward III* 3 (Rolls Ser. 31) (1886): 122–131. Kirby *Wykeham's Reg.* 1 (1896): 7, 50, 92, 169. *Papal Regs.: Letters* 3 (1897): 110, 560. *List of Inqs. ad Quod Damnum* 1 (PRO Lists and Indexes 17) (1904): 247. VCH *Hampshire* 3 (1908): 383; 4 (1911): 174–175. *C.P.* 6 (1926): 125–126 (sub Grey). Hethe *Reg. Hamonis Hethe Diocesis Roffensis* 2 (Canterbury & York Soc. 49) (1948): 887. Dalton *Manuscripts of St. George's Chapel, Windsor Castle* (1957): 405. *Paget* (1957) 259:5-7. Edington *Reg. of William Edington Bishop of Winchester 1346–1366* 1 (Hampshire Recs. 7) (1986): 47, 65, 106, 124. National Archives, C 143/249/21 (Date: 1339-40 — John de Grey of Codnor, Knt., to grant the reversion of land in Toton and of the advowson of the church of Attenborough, now held for life by Thomas de Vaus, to the Prior and convent of Felley, retaining the manors of Codnor (Derby) and Toton (Notts)); C 143/271/12; C 143/277/7 (Date: 1345-46 — Nicholas de Poyntz, Knt., to grant the manor of Hoo (Kent), except the advowsons of the churches there, to John de Grey of Codnor, Knt., in exchange for the manors of Broadway and East Elworth (Dorset). Kent. Dorset); C 143/292/2 (Date: 1349-50 — Nicholas de Poyntz, Knt., to grant the right of alternate presentation to the churches of St. Mary at Hoo and St. Margaret at [High] Halstow, with land in Hoo, Kent to John de Grey of Codnor.) (available at www.catalogue.nationalarchives.gov.uk/search.asp). National Archives, CP 25/1/177/81, #467 [see abstract of fine at http:// www.medievalgenealogy.org.uk/index.html].

13. HENRY DE GREY, Knt., son and heir apparent. He obtained a papal indult for plenary remission at the hour of death in 1355. He married at Sterborough (in Lingfield), Surrey by license dated 13 April 1358 **JOAN DE COBHAM**, daughter of Reynold de Cobham, K.G., 1st Lord Cobham of Sterborough, by Joan, daughter of Thomas de Berkeley, Knt., 3rd Lord Berkeley [see COBHAM 8 for her ancestry]. They had one son, Richard, K.G. [4th Lord Grey of Codnor], and one daughter, Joan. He was abroad with John of Gaunt, Duke of Lancaster, in 1369. Joan was a legatee in the 1369 will of her mother. SIR HENRY DE GREY died sometime prior to 14 Dec. 1392. His widow, Joan, received a papal indult for plenary remission in 1396.

> Baker *Hist. & Antiqs. of Northampton* 1 (1822–30): 658–659 (Grey ped.). Glover *Hist. of Derby* 2 (1829): 308–312 (Grey ped.). Banks *Baronies in Fee* 1 (1844): 227–230 (sub Grey of Codnor). Burke *Gen. Hist. of the Dormant, Abeyant, Forfeited & Extinct Peerages* (1866): 247–249 (sub Grey). *Misc. Gen. et Heraldica* 2nd Ser. 5 (1894): 76–78. *Papal Regs.: Letters* 3 (1897): 553; 5 (1904): 31. *C.P.* 6 (1926): 127 (sub Grey). Edington *Reg. of William Edington Bishop of Winchester 1346–1366* 2 (Hampshire Recs. 8) (1987): 45.

14. RICHARD GREY, K.G., 4th Lord Grey of Codnor, Admiral of the Fleet north of the Thames, Keeper of Brecknock and Horston Castles, King's Chamberlain, deputy Constable and Marshal of England, Constable of Nottingham Castle, Justice of South Wales, joint Warden of the East and West Marches, Captain of Argentan in Normandy, son and heir, born about 1371 (aged 21 in 1392). He married **ELIZABETH BASSET**, daughter and co-heiress of Ralph Basset, Knt., Lord Basset of Sapcote, by his 2nd wife, Alice, daughter and heiress of John de Driby [see RANDOLPH 12 for her ancestry]. They had two sons, John, Knt. [5th Lord Grey of Codnor] and Henry (or Harry), Knt. [6th Lord Grey of Codnor], and three daughters, Elizabeth, Eleanor (wife of Thomas Newport, Knt.), and Lucy. He was summoned to Parliament from 13 Nov. 1393 to 3 Sept. 1416, by writs directed *Ricardo Grey de Codenore*. SIR RICHARD GREY, 4th Lord Grey of Codnor, died in Normandy 1 August 1418, and was buried in the Church of the White Friars at Aylesford, Kent. His widow, Elizabeth, died 6 August 1451. She left a will dated 7 April 1445, testament dated 4 Jan.

1448/9, requesting in the latter document to be buried by her mother in the Chapel of Holy Trinity in the Church of the Black Friars at Stamford, Lincolnshire.

Rymer *Fœdera* 9 (1729): 141, 151, 183–188 (instances of Richard, Lord of Grey styled "kinsman" [consanguineo] by King Henry V of England). Bridges *Hist. & Antiqs. of Northamptonshire* 2 (1791): 398. Baker *Hist. & Antiqs. of Northampton* 1 (1822–30): 658–659 (Grey ped.). Glover *Hist. of Derby* 2 (1829): 308–312 (Grey ped.). Dugdale *Monasticon Anglicanum* 6(1) (1830): 423. Beltz *Mems. of the Order of the Garter* (1841): clvi. Banks *Baronies in Fee* 1 (1844): 227–230 (sub Grey of Codnor). Burke *Gen. Hist. of the Dormant, Abeyant, Forfeited & Extinct Peerages* (1866): 27–28 (sub Basset), 247–249 (sub Grey). Wild *Hist. of Castle Bytham* (1871): 46–68. *Trans. Leicestershire Arch. & Arch. Soc.* 4 (1878): foll. 30 (Basset ped.). Birch *Cat. Seals in the British Museum* 3 (1894): 40–41 (seal of Richard Grey, Lord Grey of Codnor dated 1412 — A shield of arms: barry of six [GREY]. Within a plaited wreath or garland. Below, in a park, a badger passant, between two ears of barley. Legend: "Sigillum domini ricardi domini de grey." Cabled borders.). *Misc. Gen. et Heraldica* 2nd Ser. 5 (1894): 76–78; 5th Ser. 8 (1932–34): 202–206. *List of Early Chancery Procs.* 1 (PRO Lists and Indexes 12) (1901): 31; 2 (PRO Lists and Indexes 16) (1903): 504; 3 (PRO Lists and Indexes 20) (1906): 452. *C.P.R. 1401–1405* (1905): 122, 285, 483 (instances of Richard, Lord of Grey/Richard de Grey of Codnor styled "king's kinsman"). *C.P.R. 1405–1408* (1907): 20, 84, 145 (instances of Richard, Lord of Grey, styled "king's kinsman"). *C.P.* 6 (1926): 127–129, 132–133 (sub Grey). *C.C.R. 1441–1447* (1937): 313–316, 466–471. Legge *Anglo-Norman Letters & Petitions* (Anglo-Norman Text Soc. 3) (1941): 432–433 ([Richard], Sire de G[rey], styled "cousin" by King Henry IV of England). Paget *Baronage of England* (1957) 30: 1 (sub Basset). Ellis *Cat. Seals in the P.R.O.* 2 (1981): 49 (seal of Richard Grey, Lord Grey dated 1414 — In an eight-sided panel a sheaf of wheat ears, with the ends passing downwards through a crown and ending in tassels, enclosing a lily plant. No legend.).

Children of Richard Grey, K.G., by Elizabeth Basset:

i. **HENRY** (or **HARRY**) **GREY**, Knt., 6th Lord Grey of Codnor, son and heir, born about 1404–6 (aged variously 24, 25, or 26 in 1430). He was heir in 1430 to his older brother, John Grey, Knt., 5th Lord Grey of Codnor. He married before 5 May 1434 **MARGARET PERCY**, daughter and co-heiress of Henry Percy of Atholl, Knt., by Elizabeth, daughter of William Bardolf, Knt., 4th Lord Bardolf [see BARDOLF 14.iii for her ancestry]. They had one son, Henry (or Harry), Knt. [7th Lord Grey of Codnor], and one daughter, Elizabeth (wife of Thomas Bodulgate, Knt., and John Welles, Esq.). He was summoned to Parliament from 27 Nov. 1430 to 3 Dec. 1441, by writs directed *Henrico Grey de Codenore*. He presented to the church of Heanor, Derbyshire in 1434 and 1440. He had a general pardon to March 1440/1 for offences prior to Whitsuntide 1439, and another pardon 14 Nov. 1442. SIR HENRY GREY, 6th Lord Grey of Codnor, died 17 July 1444. His widow, Margaret, married (2nd) about 3 Dec 1445 (date of enfeoffment) **RICHARD VERE** (or **VEER**), Knt., of Ashlyns (in High Ongar), Essex, son of Richard Vere, K.G., 11th Earl of Oxford, by Alice, 3rd daughter of Richard Sergeaux, Knt. [see VERE 7 for his ancestry]. In 1445 Richard Vere, Knt., brother of John Vere, Earl of Oxford, owed 1,000 marks to Thomas, Lord Scales, and Elizabeth Grey, daughter of Henry, Lord Grey. He obtained letters of protection in 1454, he then serving in France in the retinue of his brother, John Vere, Earl of Oxford. In the period, 1460–5, he sued Robert Foulman, Esq., regarding the detention of a deed of feoffment of his manor of Ashlyns (in High Ongar), Essex made on his marriage with his wife, Margaret. In 1462 he sold the reversion of the manor of Ashlyns (in High Ongar), Essex to Thomas Winslow. His wife, Margaret, Lady Grey, died 22 Sept. 1464. SIR RICHARD VERE was living 21 Dec. 1466. Brydges *Collins' Peerage of England* 2 (1812): 217–366 (sub Duke of Northumberland). Glover *Hist. of Derby* 2 (1829): 308–312 (Grey ped.). Dugdale *Monasticon Anglicanum* 6(1) (1830): 423. Hodgson *Hist. of Northumberland* Pt. 2 Vol. 2 (1832): 41–44 (ped.); Pt. 2 Vol. 3 (1840): 364–366 (Tindale ped.). Banks *Baronies in Fee* 1 (1844): 110–111 (sub Athol), 227–230 (sub Grey of Codnor). *Coll. Top. et Gen.* 5 (1838): 156. *Memoirs illus. of the Hist. & Antiqs. of Northumberland* 2 (1858): 259 (Percy ped.). Burke *Gen. Hist. of the Dormant, Abeyant, Forfeited & Extinct Peerages* (1866): 247–249 (sub Grey). Wild *Hist. of Castle Bytham* (1871): 46–68. Glover & St. George *Vis. of Yorkshire 1584–5, 1612* (1875): 415 (Burgh ped.: "Margareta [Percy] [1] = Henricus Dominus Grey de Codnor, [2] Ricardus Vere, miles, secundus maritus."). Cox *Notes on the Churches of Derbyshire* 4 (1879): 233-234. *Rpt. of the Deputy Keeper* 48 (1887): 400. Loftie *Kensington Picturesque & Hist.* (1888): 56–59 (Vere ped.). Wrottesley *Final Concords* (Colls. Hist. Staffs. 11) (1890): 233. Bridgeman *Hist. of Weston-under-Lizard* (Colls. Hist. Staffs. n.s. 2) (1899): 159–167. Gairdner *Paston Letters* 2 (1904): 144 (Sir Richard de Vere, Knt., styled "welbeloved brothir" in letter of [John Vere], Earl of Oxford dated ?1450). *C.P.* 6 (1926): 130 (sub Grey). Wedgwood *Hist. of Parl.* 1 (1936): 87–88 (biog. of Sir Thomas Bodulgate). *Ancient Deeds — Ser. B* 2 (List & Index Soc. 101) (1974): B.6293. Payling *Political Soc. in Lancastrian England* (1991): 92. Horrox *Fifteenth-Century Attitudes* (1994): 65. *Cal. IPM* 23 (2004): 235–237. National Archives, C 1/27/144; C 1/38/113; C 1/66/399; C 131/241/21; SC 8/29/1448 (available at www.catalogue.nationalarchives.gov.uk/search.asp). Royal College of Physicians of London: College Legal Status, RCP-LEGAC/ASHLYNS BOX, TITLE DEEDS 1, 2, 3, 4, 5, 6, 7, 8, 9, 10, 11, 14, 15, 18, 19; RCP-LEGAC/ASHLYNS, BDL. 3 (available at www.a2a.org.uk/search/index.asp).

Child of Henry Grey, Knt., by Margaret Percy:

a. **HENRY** (or **HARRY**) **GREY**, Knt., 7th Lord Grey of Codnor, son and heir, born about 1435 (aged 9 in 1444, 28 in 1464). He married (1st) **KATHERINE STRANGEWAYS** (or **STRANGWAYS**) [see MOWBRAY 8.ii], daughter and co-heiress of Thomas Strangeways, Esq., by Katherine, daughter of Ralph Neville, K.G., 1st Earl of Westmorland, 4th Lord Neville of Raby [see MOWBRAY 8 for her ancestry]. They had no issue. He married (2nd) 2 October 1465 **MARGARET STANLEY**, widow of William Troutbeck, Knt. [see TROUTBECK 15], of Dunham-on-the-Hill, Cheshire (slain 23 Sept. 1459) and John Boteler (or Butler), Knt. [see BOTELER 13], of Bewsey (in Warrington), Lancashire (died 26 Feb. 1462/3), and daughter of Thomas Stanley, K.G., 1st Lord Stanley, by Joan, daughter and co-heiress of Robert Goushill, Knt. [see STANLEY 14 for her ancestry]. They had one daughter, Anne. In 1467 he sold the manors of Tunworth and Upton, Hampshire to Richard Illingworth, Knt. In 1474 he and his wife, Margaret, sold all the wood, trees, underwood, etc. between Butterley and Codnor Parks to William Roodes for a term of four years. His wife, Margaret, died about 1481. He married (3rd) before 1489 **KATHERINE STOURTON**, widow of William Berkeley, Knt. (died 1485), of Beverstone, Gloucestershire, Bisterne (in Ringwood), Exbury, and Minstead, Hampshire, etc. [see FISHER 9.i.a], and daughter of William Stourton, 2nd Lord Stourton, by Margaret, 1st daughter and co-heiress of John Chidiock, Knt. [see CHIDIOCK 13]. They had no issue. By an unknown mistress (or mistresses), he had three illegitimate sons, Richard, Harry, and Harry. SIR HENRY GREY, 7th Lord Grey of Codnor, died 8 April 1496. He left a will dated 10 Sept. 1492, proved 28 October 1496. His widow, Katherine, married (3rd) married before 26 April 1497 (date of presentment) **WILLIAM [DE LA] POLE**, Knt. [see DE LA POLE 10.i.e], of Wingfield, Suffolk, younger son of John [de la] Pole, Duke of Suffolk, by Elizabeth, daughter of Richard Plantagenet, K.G., 3rd Duke of York, 6th Earl of March, 9th Earl of Ulster, lord of Mortimer, Herefordshire and Clare, Suffolk [see DE LA POLE 10.i for his ancestry]. They had no issue. Sometime in or after 1496 Werburgh Brereton, daughter of Katherine, sister of William Berkeley, Knt., sued William Pole, Knt., son of John, Duke of Suffolk, and Katherine, lady Grey, his wife in Chancery regarding the detention of deeds relating to the castles and manors of Beverstone, Hatherley, Leckhampton, and Syde, Gloucestershire, etc. In 1503 William Stourton presented to the church of Great Kington, Dorset by grant of Katherine Grey, lady of the manor. William [de la] Pole was attainted in Parliament with his two brothers in Jan. 1503/4. He was still a prisoner in the Tower of London after the execution of his older brother, Edmund, Earl of Suffolk, in 1513. A bill was introduced in the House of Lords 10 Dec. 1515 for Katherine, wife of "William de la Poole." His wife, Katherine, Lady Grey died in London 25 Nov. 1521. William was listed first among the prisoners in the Tower in 1535 and again in 1538. SIR WILLIAM [DE LA] POLE was apparently living in October 1539, it is said in the Tower, but died before 20 Nov. 1539, when his name no longer appears in the list of the prisoners there. Nichols *Hist. & Antiqs. of Leicester* 3(2) (1804): 863 (Grey ped.). Ormerod *Hist. of Chester* 2 (1819): 28 (Troutbeck ped.), 42. *Testamenta Vetusta* 2 (1826): 411–414 (will of Henry Lord Grey). Glover *Hist. of Derby* 2 (1829): 308–312 (Grey ped.). Banks *Baronies in Fee* 1 (1844): 227–230 (sub Grey of Codnor). *Jour. Architectural, Arch., & Hist. Soc. of Chester* 1 (1857): 217–233. Burke *Gen. Hist. of the Dormant, Abeyant, Forfeited & Extinct Peerages* (1866): 247–249 (sub Grey). Wild *Hist. of Castle Bytham* (1871): 46–68. Beamont *Annals of the Lords Warrington* 2 (Chetham Soc. 87) (1872): 263–302. Foster *Royal Lineage of Our Noble & Gentle Fams.* (1883): 3–10. Child *English & Scottish Popular Ballads* 6 (1889): 327–330. *Desc. Cat. Ancient Deeds* 1 (1890): 59–70. Bridgeman *Hist. of Weston-under-Lizard* (Colls. Hist. Staffs. n.s. 2) (1899): 159–167. Jeayes *Desc. Cat. Derbyshire Charters* (1906): 110, 111. *C.P.* 6 (1926): 130–133 (sub Grey). *Rpt. on the MSS of Reginald Rawdon Hastings, Esq.* 1 (Hist. MSS Comm. 78) (1928): 94 (seal of Henry Grey, Lord de Grey dated 1468 — A shield of arms, barry of six; the shield couchée from helm surmounted by crest — a peacock's head and neck between two wings erect. Legend: SIGILLUM MEUM DOMINI DE GREY.). Harvey et al. *Vis. of the North* 3 (Surtees Soc. 144) (1930): 106–109 (Strangwais ped.: "Catherina nupta Gray"). Garratt *Derbyshire Feet of Fines 1323–1546* (Derbyshire Rec. Soc. 11) (1985): 92. Biancalana *Fee Tail & the Common Recovery in Medieval England* (2001): 355. Nottinghamshire Archives: Charlton of Chilwell, DD/CH/32/20 (will of Henry Grey, Lord Grey) (available at www.a2a.org.uk/search/index.asp). National Archives, C 1/84/73 (available at www.catalogue.nationalarchives.gov.uk/search.asp).

ii. **ELIZABETH GREY** [see next].

iii. **LUCY GREY**, married **ROLAND LENTHALL**, Knt., of Lenthall and Hampton Court, Herefordshire [see FITZ ALAN 12.viii].

15. ELIZABETH GREY, married (2nd) before 11 June 1444 (date of conveyance) **JOHN ZOUCHE**, Esq., of Bulwick, Northamptonshire, younger son of William la Zouche, K.G., 4th Lord Zouche of Harringworth, by Elizabeth, said to be daughter of William Crosse, Knt. [see

CANTELOWE 11 for his ancestry]. They had one son, John, Esq. In 1444 her mother, Elizabeth, Lady Grey, conveyed the manor and the advowson of the church of Benefield, Northamptonshire to John and his wife, Elizabeth. His wife, Elizabeth, was living 10 May 1445. He presented to the church of Benefield, Northamptonshire in 1449, 1460, 1463, and 1475.

> Bridges *Hist. & Antiqs. of Northamptonshire* 2 (1791): 398. Glover *Hist. of Derby* 2 (1829): 308–312 (Grey ped.). Banks *Baronies in Fee* 1 (1844): 227–230 (sub Grey of Codnor). Burke *Gen. Hist. of the Dormant, Abeyant, Forfeited & Extinct Peerages* (1866): 27–28 (sub Basset), 247–249 (sub Grey). Wild *Hist. of Castle Bytham* (1871): 46–68. Bridgeman *Hist. of Weston-under-Lizard* (Colls. Hist. Staffs. n.s. 2) (1899): 159–167. VCH *Northampton* 3 (1930): 76–80. *C.C.R. 1441–1447* (1937): 287, 313–316, 466–471. *C.C.R. 1447–1454* (1941–7): 316. Paget *Baronage of England* (1957) 581: 1–11 (sub Zouche). *C.P.* 12(2) (1959): 944, footnote o (sub Zouche). Eales & Tyas *Fam. & Dynasty in Late Medieval England* (Harlaxton Medieval Studies n.s. 9) (2003): 193–210 (author erroneously identifies John Zouche, husband of Elizabeth Grey, as the son of William la Zouche, Knt., 5th Lord Zouche, by his wife, Elizabeth Saint John). Nottinghamshire Archives: Foljambe of Osberton: Deeds & Estate Papers, DD/FJ/1/30/5; DD/FJ/1/30/6 (available at www.a2a.org.uk/search/index.asp).

16. JOHN ZOUCHE (or **SOUCHE**), Esq., of Benefield, Northamptonshire, Westoning, Bedfordshire, etc. He married before 1489 **ELEANOR SAINT JOHN**, daughter of John Saint John, K.B., of Bletsoe, Bedfordshire, Paulerspury, Northamptonshire, Fonmon and Penmark, Glamorgan, Wales, etc., by Alice, daughter of Thomas Bradshagh, Knt. [see SAINT JOHN 16 for her ancestry]. They had three sons, John, Knt., David, and Lionel, and four daughters, Elizabeth (wife of Gerald Fitz Gerald, 9th Earl of Kildare), Cecily, Margaret, and Agnes (nun at Sempringham). He presented to the church of Benefield, Northamptonshire in 1488. In 1489 Henry Grey, 7th Lord Grey of Codnor, agreed to sell his cousin, John Zouche, the reversion of the Castle and manor of Codnor (in Heanor), Derbyshire, and the manors of Heanor, Losco, and Langley (in Heanor), Derbyshire, and Eastwood, Nottinghamshire, which the said Zouche was to have immediately on the decease of Lord Grey; together with the reversion of lands in Bytham and Castle Bytham, Lincolnshire, and lands in Essex and Kent worth £100 yearly. In spite of these arrangements, King Henry VII intervened and persuaded Lord Grey to sell Codnor to the crown for the use of the king's son, Henry, Duke of York [afterwards King Henry VIII] on more favorable terms to Lord Grey. Through the invervention of the king's mother, Margaret Beaufort, Countess of Richmond, the king eventually agreed to return Codnor to Zouche. In the period, 1496–1500, John Newport and John Lenthall, Esqs., cousins and heirs of Harry, Lord Grey sued John Zouche, another cousin and heir of Lord Grey, in Chancery regarding his entry into the lordship of Codnor (in Heanor), Derbyshire and other lands of the said Lord Grey and Katherine, his wife, to the prejudice of complainants' suit against Thomas Leeke and Roger Johnson. In 1500, on the payment of £300, Thomas Leeke and Roger Johnson, representatives of the late Henry Lord Grey, duly conveyed a lawful estate of the premises to Zouche's feoffees. JOHN ZOUCHE, Esq., died testate 20 October 1501. His widow, Eleanor, married (as his 2nd wife) **JOHN MELTON**, Knt., *de jure* 7th Lord Lucy, of Aston, Yorkshire, Bentworth, Hampshire, Radston, Northamptonshire, etc., son and heir of John Melton, Knt., of Aston and Kilham, Yorkshire, Bentworth, Hampshire, etc., by Margaret, daughter of Roger de Clifford, Knt., 5th Lord Clifford [see MELTON 11 for his ancestry]. They had no issue. SIR JOHN MELTON died 11 June 1510. His widow, Eleanor, died testate 12 Feb. 1518/9. Administration on her estate was granted 19 March 1518/9 to her son, David Zouche and daughter, Cecily Zouche. In the period, 1518–29, David, son of John Zouche, Esq., of Codnor, sued John Saint John, Knt., and Richard Burton, Esq., feoffees to uses in Chancery regarding refusal to convey parcel of the manors of Westoning, Bedfordshire, Benefield, Northamptonshire, and Codnor (in Heanor), Heanor, and Loscoe, Derbyshire as devised by complainant's said father, whose executors are the said Richard and Eleanor, late wife of the testator.

> Bridges *Hist. & Antiqs. of Northamptonshire* 2 (1791): 398. Banks *Dormant & Extinct Baronage of England* 2 (1808): 229 (Grey ped.), 230 (Zouche ped.). Brydges *Collins' Peerage of England* 6 (1812): 741–751 (sub St. John, Lord St. John of Bletshoe). Chitty *Practical Treatise on the Criminal Law* 4 (1819): 299 (Roos-Zouche ped.). Baker *Hist. & Antiqs. of*

Northampton 1 (1822–30): 672–673 (Melton ped.). Glover *Hist. of the County of Derby* 2 (1829): 308–309 (Grey-Zouch ped.). Hunter *South Yorkshire* 2 (1831): 162 (Melton ped.). Banks *Baronies in Fee* 1 (1844): 227–230 (sub Grey of Codnor), 298–299 (sub Lucy) (Lucy-Melton ped.). Charles *Vis. of Huntingdon 1613* (Camden Soc. 43) (1849): 2 (St. John ped.: "Eleonora [St. John], uxor Joh'is Zouche de Codnor"). Wild *Hist. of Castle Bytham* (1871): 46–68. Whellan *Hist., Top. & Dir. of Northamptonshire* (1874): 708. Flower *Vis. of Yorkshire 1563–4* (H.S.P. 16) (1881): 202–203 (Melton ped.: "Sir John Melton [1] = Ales daughter of Sir John Stanley of the Pype, [2] = Elenor daughter of …. St. John that maryed …. daughter of ….. Bradshaw, [and widow of] …. Sowche."). *Desc. Cat. Ancient Deeds* 1 (1890): 59–70; 5 (1906): 42, 522. Gairdner & Brodie *Letters & Papers, Foreign & Domestic, Henry VIII* 14(1) (1894): 598. Bridgeman *Hist. of Weston-under-Lizard* (Colls. Hist. Staffs. n.s. 2) (1899): 159–167. Cox *Royal Forests of England* (1905): 252–253. Hampshire Field Club & Arch. Soc. 4 (1905): 12–13. Jeayes *Desc. Cat. Derbyshire Charters* (1906): 111. C.P.R. 1494–1509 (1916): 583. VCH *Northampton* 3 (1930): 76–80. VCH *Rutland* 2 (1935): 155–157. Bowker *Episcopal Court Book for the Diocese of Lincoln, 1514–1520* (Lincoln Rec. Soc. 61) (1967): 84, 86. Colvin *Hist. of the King's Works* 3(1)(1982): 228. Jones *King's Mother* (1992): 113–114. Harris *English Aristocratic Women 1450–1550* (2002): 96. Nottinghamshire Archives: Charlton of Chilwell, DD/CH/32/20 (will of Henry Grey, Lord Grey) (available at www.a2a.org.uk/search/index.asp). National Archives, C 1/216/20; C 1/599/55; C 142/34/81; E 150/683/4 (available at www.catalogue.nationalarchives.gov.uk/search.asp).

Children of John Zouche, Esq., by Eleanor Saint John:

i. **DAVID ZOUCHE**, married **MARGARET BOURGCHIER**, Lady Bryan [see BOURCHIER 13.ii].

ii. **MARGARET ZOUCHE** [see next].

17. MARGARET ZOUCHE, married (as his 2nd wife) **ROBERT SHEFFIELD**, Knt., of Butterwick, Lincolnshire, son of Robert Sheffield, Knt., of Butterwick, Lincolnshire, Recorder of London, Speaker of the House of Commons, by his 1st wife, Ellen (or Helen), daughter and co-heiress of John Delves, Knt., of Doddington, Cheshire. They had three sons, Thomas, Edmund, Knt. [1st Lord Sheffield], and David, and one daughter, Eleanor (wife of Thomas Watton, Esq.). His wife, Margaret, was a legatee in the 1530 will of her sister-in-law, Margaret Willoughby, widow of John Zouche, Knt., who bequeathed her a brooch of gold. Robert married (1st) before c.1515 **JOAN** (or **JANE**) **STANLEY**, daughter of George Stanley, K.G., K.B., Lord Strange of Knockin, by Joan Strange [see STANLEY 16 for her ancestry]. They had no issue. Joan was a legatee in the 1504 will of her grandfather, Thomas Stanley, 1st Earl of Derby. She was also a legatee in the 1514/19 will of her brother, Thomas Stanley, 2nd Earl of Derby. SIR ROBERT SHEFFIELD died 15 Nov. 1531. His widow, Margaret, married (2nd) before 1538 **JOHN CANDISHE** (or **CAUNDISH**, **CAVENDISH**), Knt., of Melwood (in Owston) and Burnham (in Haxey), Lincolnshire. They had no issue. Sometime in the period, 1509–47, Alexander Banaster sued Sir John Candyshe, Richard Browne, John Shawe, and others in the Court of the Star Chamber regarding a right of way through Melwood Park (in Epworth), Lincolnshire. In the same period, James Fox sued Sir John Cavendish, John Shawe, and others in the Court of the Star Chamber regarding seizure of corn at Haxey and Butterwick, Lincolnshire. In the period, 1551–3, Robert [Holgate], Archbishop of York, sued John Candishe, Knt., and John Sutton, Esq., regarding corn-rent of the parsonages of Owston and Haxey, Lincolnshire. SIR JOHN CANDISHE left a will dated 19 October 1553, proved 8 Nov. 1554 (P.C.C. 11 More), naming his wife, Margaret, and his sister-in-law, Cecily Zouche, among others. In the period, 1553–4, Richard Thorne sued Margaret, late the wife of John Cavendysshe, Knt., kinsman of the complainant, and formerly the wife of Robert Sheffelde, Knt., in Chancery regarding an annuity granted by the said Sir John for past service out of the manors of Woode [Melwood] and Burnham and messuages and land in Woodeburnham and Axholme, Lincolnshire. Margaret was a legatee in the 1554/7 will of her sister, Cecily Zouche, who bequeathed her 20 marks of money, a silver piece, and a ring of gold.

Kent *Banner Display'd* (1726): 266–268 (sub Sheffield). Banks *Dormant & Extinct Baronage of England* 2 (1808): 230 (Grey ped.). *Gentleman's Mag.* n.s. 3 (1810): 34–36. Brydges *Collins' Peerage of England* 3 (1812): 50–103; 7 (1812): 410–415 (sub Morton, Lord Ducie). Baker *Hist. & Antiqs. of Northampton* 1 (1822–30): 564–565. Grace *Memoirs of the Family of Grace* (1823): 57–61. Nicolas *Testamenta Vetusta* 2 (1826): 589–590 (will of Thomas Stanley, Earl of Derby).

Glover *Hist. of the County of Derby* 2 (1829): 308–309 (Grey-Zouch ped.). Burke *Gen'l & Heraldic Dict. of the Peerages of England, Ireland & Scotland* (1831): 483–485 (sub Sheffield). Baines *Hist. of Lancaster* 4 (1836): chart facing 10 (Stanley ped.). Stonehouse *Hist. & Topog. of the Isle of Axholme* (1839): 256, 268–271. *Top. & Gen.* 1 (1846): 263–265. Nichols *Narrative of the Days of the Reformation* (Camden Soc. 77) (1859): 57. Flower *Vis. of Lancaster 1567* (Chetham Soc. 81) (1870): 78–79 (Erle of Derby/Stanley peds.: "Jane [Stanley], maryed to … Sheffeild of the Isle of Axham."). *Testamenta Eboracensia* 5 (Surtees Soc. 79) (1884): 297–298 (will of Dame Margaret Zouche, widow). Gairdner *Letters & Papers, Foreign & Domestic, Henry VIII* 13(1) (1892): 522 ("Master Candish" styled "worshipful father-in-law" [stepfather] by Edmund Sheffield in letter dated 1538. Fielding *Memories of Malling & its Valley* (1893): 49–50 (re. Watton fam.). *List of Procs. in the Court of Star Chamber* 1 (Lists & Indexes 13) (1901): 61. *D.N.B.* 18 (1909): 16 (biogs. of Sir Robert Sheffield and Edmund Sheffield, first Baron Sheffield). Clay *Extinct & Dormant Peerages* (1913): 205–208 (sub Sheffield). *C.P.* 11 (1949): 661 (sub Sheffield). *Chancery Decree Rolls (C.78)* (List & Index Soc. 160) (1979): 59. *Chancery Decree Rolls: Elizabeth I (C78/15–45)* (List & Index Soc. 198) (1983): 81. Registered will of Cecily Zouche proved 24 Sept. 1557, Cons. Court of Lincoln, Will Register 1557, vol. 2, pg. 112 [FHL Microfilm 198815]. Lincolnshire Archives: MSS of the Earl of Ancaster, 1ANC11/A/2 (available at www.a2a.org.uk/search/index.asp). National Archives, C 1/1303/47-49; C 1/1386/23-25; STAC 2/3; STAC 2/15 (available at www.catalogue.nationalarchives.gov.uk/search.asp).

18. EDMUND SHEFFIELD, Knt., of Butterwick, Lincolnshire, son and heir by his father's 2nd marriage, born 22 Nov. 1521. He married before 31 Jan. 1537/8 **ANNE VERE**, 2nd daughter of John Vere, K.G., 15th Earl of Oxford, by his 2nd wife, Elizabeth, daughter of Edward Trussell, Gent. [see HACCOMBE 10 for her ancestry]. They had one son, John, K.B. [2nd Lord Sheffield], and three daughters, Eleanor (wife of Denzil Holles), Frances (wife of William Metham, Esq.), and Elizabeth. He was in the vanguard of the army in France, with 50 horsemen and 500 foot from Lincolnshire. He was created Lord Sheffield 16 Feb. 1546/7. In 1547 John Sleford sued him in Chancery regarding lands called Wadnyng's lands in Isle of Axholme, Lincolnshire. SIR EDMUND SHEFFIELD, 1st Lord Sheffield, was slain at Norwich, Norfolk 31 July 1549, in an unsuccessful attempt to suppress Kett's rebellion in Norfolk, and was buried at St. Martin's at the Palace, Norwich, Norfolk. He left a will dated 20 May 1544, proved 10 March 1549/50 (P.C.C. 6 Coode). His widow, Anne, married (2nd) (as his 1st wife) **JOHN BROCK**, Esq., of Colchester, Essex, son and heir of John Brock, of Little Leighs, Essex, by Agnes, daughter of _____ Wiseman. They had no issue. Anne, Lady Sheffield, was buried at Stepney, Middlesex 14 Feb. 1571/2. John married (2nd) at Langford, Essex in 1581 **MARY PASCALL**.

Kent *Banner Display'd* (1726): 266–268 (sub Sheffield). Buckler *Stemmata Chicheleana* (1765): 19, 55. *Gentleman's Mag.* n.s. 3 (1810): 34–36. Grace *Memoirs of the Family of Grace* (1823): 57–61. Burke *Gen'l & Heraldic Dict. of the Peerages of England, Ireland & Scotland* (1831): 483–485 (sub Sheffield). Stonehouse *Hist. & Topog. of the Isle of Axholme* (1839): 268–271. *Top. & Gen.* 1 (1846): 263–265 (Sheffield arms: Argent a chevron between three garbs gules). Hawley et al. *Vis. of Essex 1552, 1558, 1570, 1612 & 1634* 1 (H.S.P. 13) (1878): 47–48 (Vere ped.: "Anne [Vere], uxor Edward L…. Sheffe…"); 2 (H.S.P. 14) (1879): 554 (Misc. Peds.) (Brock ped.: "John Brock of Colchester, [1]= Anne d. of John Vere Earl of Oxford & widow of Edmond Lord Sheffield, [2] = Mary d. of …. Pascall of Springfield 2 wife."). John de Veere Earle of Oxford obiit 31 H. 8, 1539. = Elizabeth, da. and heire to Sr Edward Trussell, Knight."). Loftie *Kensington Picturesque & Hist.* (1888): 56–59 (Vere ped.). *D.N.B.* 18 (1909): 16 (biogs. of Sir Robert Sheffield and Edmund Sheffield, first Baron Sheffield). Clay *Extinct & Dormant Peerages* (1913): 205–208 (sub Sheffield). Monson *Lincolnshire Church Notes* (Lincoln Rec. Soc. 31) (1936): 297–298 (re. Metham fam.). *C.P.* 11 (1949): 661–662 (sub Sheffield). Smith *Itinerary of John Leland* 1 (1964): 145–150 (Vere ped.: "Anne [Vere] maried to Edmund Shefefeld."). *Chancery Decree Rolls (C.78)* (List & Index Soc. 160) (1979): 36. Nelson *Monstrous Adversary* (2003): 16.

19. JOHN SHEFFIELD, K.B., 2nd Lord Sheffield, of Butterwick, Lincolnshire, son and heir, born about 1538. He was admitted to Gray's Inn in 1561. He married about 1562 **DOUGLAS HOWARD**, daughter of William Howard, K.G., 1st Lord Howard of Effingham, by his 2nd wife, Margaret, daughter of Thomas Gamage, Knt. [see HOWARD 14.i for her ancestry]. She was born about 1535. They had one son, Edmund, K.G., K.B. [1st Earl of Mulgrave, 3rd Lord Sheffield], and one daughter, Elizabeth (wife of Thomas Butler, K.G. [Earl of Ormond]). SIR JOHN SHEFFIELD, 2nd Lord Sheffield, died 10 Dec. 1568. He left a will proved 31 Jan. 1568/9 (P.C.C. 1 Sheffell). His widow, Douglas, had a notorious affair with Robert Dudley, K.G. (died 4 Sept.

1588), Earl of Leicester, Chancellor of Oxford University, Lord Steward of the Household, 5th son of John Dudley, Duke of Northumberland, by Jane, daughter of Edward Guilford, Knt. They had one illegitimate son, Robert Dudley, Knt. Around 1579 the earl ended his affair with her, agreeing to pay her £700 pounds a year in support. Douglas subsequently married (2nd) 29 Nov. 1579 (as his 2nd wife) **EDWARD STAFFORD**, Knt., of Grafton, Staffordshire, Ambassador to France, 1583–90, son and heir of William Stafford, K.B., of Chebsey, Staffordshire, Rochford, Essex, etc., by his 2nd wife, Dorothy, daughter of Henry (or Harry) Stafford, Lord Stafford [see CAREY 15 for his ancestry]. They had no surviving issue. In 1603 her son, Robert Dudley, tried to establish his claim to the title of Earl of Leicester. The case ended up in the Star Chamber and aroused great public interest. Lady Sheffield declared in writing that her former paramour, Leicester, had solemnly contracted to marry her in Cannon Row, Westminster in 1571, and that they were married at Esher, Surrey, in 1573. The court rejected the evidence, however, and fined several of the witnesses. SIR EDWARD STAFFORD died 5 Feb. 1604/5. Douglas, Lady Sheffield was buried at St. Margaret's, Westminster, Middlesex 11 Dec. 1608. She left a will proved 16 Feb. 1608/9 (P.C.C. 29 Dorset).

Kent *Banner Display'd* (1726): 266–268 (sub Sheffield). *Cat. of the Harleian Coll. of MSS* 2 (1759): Num. 6993 ("A Folio, Vol. v. containing Letters of considerable Persons from 1581 to 1585: 68. Sir Edw. Stafford to the L.L. of the Council, under Imprisonment for marrying the Queen's Kinswoman. No Date, nor Place."). Buckler *Stemmata Chicheleana* (1765): 55. *Gentleman's Mag.* n.s. 3 (1810): 34–36. Brydges *Collins' Peerage of England* 4 (1812): 264–283. Grace *Memoirs of the Family of Grace* (1823): 57–61. Burke *Gen'l & Heraldic Dict. of the Peerages of England, Ireland & Scotland* (1831): 483–485 (sub Sheffield). *Top. & Gen.* 1 (1846): 263–265. Cooper & Cooper *Athena Cantabrigienses* 1 (1858): 263 (biog. of John Sheffield). Boyd & Wrottesley *Final Concords* (Colls. Hist. Staffs. 16) (1895): 97–98. Warner *Voyage of Robert Dudley to the West Indies, 1594–1595* (1899). Clay *Extinct & Dormant Peerages* (1913): 205–208 (sub Sheffield). *C.P.* 7 (1929): 549–552 (sub Leicester); 11 (1949): 662–663 (sub Sheffield). *English Hist. Rev.* 44 (1929): 203–219. Read "Letter from Robert, Earl of Leicester, to a Lady" in *Huntington Library Bull.* 9 (1936). Wilson *Sweet Robin* (1981). Bindoff *House of Commons 1509–1558* 2 (1982): 66–67 (biog. of Sir Robert Dudley). Adams *Leicester & the Court* (2002). Rickman *Love, Lust, & License in Early Modern England* (2008). Lincolnshire Archives: Sheffield, Sheff/B/1; Sheff/B/1a (available at www.a2a.org.uk/search/index.asp).

20. EDMUND SHEFFIELD, K.G., K.B., 3rd Lord Sheffield, of West Butterwick, Conesby, Flixborough, and Normanby, Lincolnshire, Governor of the Fort and Island of Brill (Holland), 1598, Lord Lieutenant, co. York, 1603–19, Lord President of the North, 1603–19, Councillor for the Colony of Virginia, 1609, Vice-Admiral, co, York, 1616, Councillor of the North, 1625, son and heir, born 7 Dec. 1565. He married (1st) before 13 Nov. 1581 **URSULA TYRWHIT** (or **TYRWHITT**), daughter of Robert Tyrwhit, Knt., of Kettleby, Lincolnshire, by Elizabeth, daughter of Thomas Oxenbridge, Knt. [see TYRWHIT 20 for her ancestry]. They had six sons, Charles, John, K.B., Edmund, K.B., William, Philip, and George, and eleven daughters, Mary (wife of Ferdinando Fairfax [2nd Lord Fairfax]), Magdalen (wife of Walter Walsh), Elizabeth (wife of Edward Swift, Knt., and John Bourchier, Knt.), Tryphena (wife of George Verney), Dorothy, Douglas, Margaret, Ursula, Sarah, Anne, and Frances. In 1582 he was one of the lords ordered to accompany the Duke of Anjou to Antwerp. In 1585 he served as a volunteer under Leicester in the Netherlands. In 1588 he commanded the *White Bear*, one of the queen's ships, in the defeat of the Spanish Armada. In 1589–90 he and his wife, Ursula, together with his step-father and mother, Edward Stafford, Knt. and Douglas his wife, sold the manor of Cold Norton (in Chebsey), Staffordshire, and two messuages, two cottages, ten tofts, etc. in Cold Norton, Chebsey, and Somerton, Staffordshire to Stephen Slaney, Esq. for £1,050. He was admitted to Gray's Inn in 1595. He was a member of the councils of the Virginia Company in 1609 and of the New England Company in 1620. His wife, Ursula, was living May 1617, but died before 4 August 1618. He married (2nd) 4 March 1618/9 **MARIANA IRWIN**, daughter of William Irwin, Knt., Gentleman of the Privy Chamber to Prince Henry, later Gentleman Usher to King Charles I. They had three sons, James, Thomas, and Robert, and two daughters, Margaret (wife of Simon Thelwall) and Sarah. He was one of the signers of the first Plymouth patent in 1621. He was created Earl of Mulgrave 5 Feb.

1625/6. He took the side of the Parliament during the civil war. SIR EDMUND SHEFFIELD, 1st Earl of Mulgrave, 3rd Lord Sheffield, died 6 October 1646, and was buried at Hammersmith.

    Kent *Banner Display'd* (1726): 266–268 (sub Sheffield). Buckler *Stemmata Chicheleana* (1765): 55. Graves *Hist. of Cleveland* (1808): 301 (ped.). *Gentleman's Mag.* n.s. 3 (1810): 34–36. Baker *Hist. & Antiqs. of Northampton* 1 (1822–30): 114. Grace *Memoirs of the Family of Grace* (1823): 57–61. Stonehouse *Hist. & Topog. of the Isle of Axholme* (1839): 268–271. Beltz *Mems. of the Order of the Garter* (1841): clxxxiii. *Top. & Gen.* 1 (1846): 263–265. *Genealogist* 5 (1881): 45–46 (Vis. Lincolnshire) (Tirwitt ped.: "Ursula [Tirwitt], wife to Edm. Lo. Sheffeild"). Doyle *Official Baronage of England* 2 (1886): 541–542 (sub Mulgrave). Foster *Reg. of Admissions to Gray's Inn 1521–1889* (1889): 87. Boyd & Wrottesley *Final Concords* (Colls. Hist. Staffs. 16) (1895): 97–99. Maddison *Lincolnshire Peds.* 3 (H.S.P. 52) (1904): 1018–1021 (Tyrwhit ped.). *D.N.B.* 18 (1909): 11–12 (biog. of Edmund Sheffield). Murray *English Dramatic Companies, 1558–1642* 2 (1910): 65. Clay *Extinct & Dormant Peerages* (1913): 205–208 (sub Sheffield). *C.P.* 9 (1936): 388–390 (sub Mulgrave); 11 (1949): 663 (sub Sheffield). Lincolnshire Archives: Sheffield, Sheff/A/53/4; Sheff/B/1; Sheff/B/1a; Sheff/B/2; Sheff/B/3 (available at www.a2a.org.uk/search/index.asp).

Child of Edmund Sheffield, K.G., K.B., by Ursula Tyrwhit:

i. **FRANCES SHEFFIELD**, married **PHILIP FAIRFAX**, Knt., of Steeton, Yorkshire [see BLADEN 15].

❧ CONINGTON ❧

MALCOLM III (**CEANNMORE**), King of Scots, married [SAINT] **MARGARET**.
DAVID I, King of Scots, married **MAUD OF NORTHUMBERLAND**.
HENRY OF SCOTLAND, Earl of Northumberland, married **ADA DE WARENNE**.
DAVID OF SCOTLAND, Earl of Huntingdon, married **MAUD OF CHESTER** (desc. King William the Conqueror).
ISABEL OF HUNTINGDON, married **ROBERT DE BRUS**, Knt., of Annandale in Scotland [see BRUS 5].

6. BERNARD DE BRUS, of Conington, Huntingdonshire, Exton, Rutland, Buecesford, Donington, and Golksby, Lincolnshire, etc., younger son. He married (1st) **ALICE DE BEAUCHAMP**, daughter of William de Beauchamp, of Elmley and Salwarpe, Worcestershire, hereditary Sheriff of Worcestershire, by Isabel, daughter of William Mauduit, hereditary Chamberlain of the Exchequer [see BEAUCHAMP 8 for her ancestry]. They had two sons, Bernard, Knt., and John. He received robes, gifts, and expenses from King Henry III between 1247 and 1257. Sometime before 1268 he and his wife, Alice, were granted lands and rents in Cottesmore and Greetham, Rutland by her uncle, William Mauduit, Earl of Warwick. He forfeited his lands by taking part against the king in the Barons' War. He married (2nd) **CONSTANCE DE MERSTON**, widow of John de Morteyn (living 1254, died about 1265), of Marston (in Marston Moretaine), Bedfordshire, and daughter of Ralph de Merston, of Marston, Bedfordshire. BERNARD DE BRUS died shortly before August 1266. In 1274–5 his widow, Constance, arraigned an assize of novel disseisin against Radulph son of Richard de Marston touching common of pasture in Marston, Bedfordshire. In 1276 she disputed with the Abbot of St. Albans regarding the presentation of the church of Turville, Buckinghamshire. In 1278–9 she sued William Fitz Henry in a novel disseisin plea regarding meadow in Conington, Huntingdonshire. She married (3rd) before 8 May 1281 (date of presentation) **ROBERT DE WOTTON** (or **DE WYTTON**), in right of his wife, of Marston (in Marston Moretaine), Bedfordshire. In 1280–1 Robert de Brus, senior, arraigned an assize of darrein presentment against Robert and his wife, Constance, and Bernard de Brus touching the church of Conington, Huntingdonshire. He and his wife, Constance, presented Master Walter de Wotton as rector of the church of Marston Moretaine, Bedfordshire in 1281. Later a dispute ensued in the king's court between Robert and his wife, Constance, and Richard d'Argentine concerning the right of presentation to the dependant chapel of Roxhill, Bedfordshire; the court subsequently ruled in favor of Robert and Constance. In 1282 and the said Walter was re-instituted to the church of Marston Moretaine, this time with the addition of the chapel of Roxhill.

In 1281 Adam del Cokedaek [or Crokedaek] had a plea against Constance, wife of Robert Wotton. In 1283 she granted the manor of Turville, Buckinghamshire to her son, Eustace de Morteyn, in tail-male. Constance died about 1293.

> Wright *Hist. & Antiqs. of Rutland* (1684): 51 (Brus ped.). Burke *Gen. Hist. of the Dormant, Abeyant, Forfeited & Extinct Peerages* (1866): 80–81 (sub Bruce). Riley *Chronica Monasterii S. Albani; Gesta Abbatum Monasterii Sancti Albani, a Thoma Walsingham, Regnante Ricardo Secundo* 1 (1867): 431. *Herald & Genealogist* 8 (1874): 325–348. *Misc. Gen. et Heraldica* n.s. 1 (1874): 337–340. *Annual Rpt. of the Deputy Keeper* 44 (1883): 180; 50 (1889): 61. *Scots Peerage* 2 (1905): 430–432 (sub Bruce, Earl of Carrick). Wrottesley *Peds. from the Plea Rolls* (1905): 330. *Rutland Mag. & County Hist. Rec.* 3 (1908): 97–106, 130–137. VCH *Bedford* 3 (1912): 309. *Cal. Inq. Misc.* 1 (1916): 239, 262. *NEHGR* 79 (1925): 135. VCH *Buckingham* 3 (1925): 102. VCH *Rutland* 2 (1935): 128 (Brus arms: Azure a saltire and a chief or). VCH *Huntingdon* 3 (1936): 144–151. Mason *Beauchamp Cartulary Charters* (Pipe Roll Soc. n.s. 43) (1980): 140. DeWindt *Royal Justice & Medieval English Countryside* 2 (1981): 580, 627. Sutton *Rolls & Reg. of Bishop Oliver Sutton, 1280–1299* 8 (Lincoln Rec. Soc. 76) (1986): 94. *Burke's Landed Gentry of Great Britain* (2001): lxiii-lxv (sub Scottish Royal Lineage). Blakely "Scottish Bruses and the English Crown" (13th Cent. England 9) (2003): 101–113.

7. BERNARD DE BRUS, Knt., of Conington, Huntingdonshire, Exton, Rutland, Tutland, Staffordshire, etc., son and heir by his father's 1st marriage. He married (1st) **ISABEL FALKNEY** (or **FALKNER**), daughter of Ralph Falkney. They had one son, John. He married (2nd) **AGATHA** _____. They had one son, Bernard, Knt. In 1274–5 he arraigned two assizes of mort d'ancestor against Robert de Brus touching land, rent, and possessions in Exton, Rutland. In 1280 his uncle, Robert de Brus, lord of Annandale, quitclaimed all his right to the manor of Exton, Rutland to him. In 1283 Bernard gave the monks of St. Andrew of Northampton the church of Exton, Rutland and its liberties and also confirmed the gift of pasture for eight animals given earlier to the monks by his grandmother, Isabel de Brus. In 1286 he defended his claim to view of frankpledge and waif against the Crown. He was summoned to serve against the Scots and overseas in 1295–7. SIR BERNARD DE BRUS died 21 Nov. 1301. His widow, Agatha, was living in 1303.

> *Herald & Genealogist* 8 (1874): 325–348. *Misc. Gen. et Heraldica* n.s. 1 (1874): 337–340. *Procs. Soc. Antiquaries of Scotland* 14 (1880): 345–346. *Annual Rpt. of the Deputy Keeper* 44 (1883): 99; 50 (1889): 61. *Rutland Mag. & County Hist. Rec.* 3 (1908): 97–106, 130–137. VCH *Rutland* 2 (1935): 128. VCH *Huntingdon* 3 (1936): 144–151. DeWindt *Royal Justice & Medieval English Countryside* 2 (1981): 565.

8. BERNARD DE BRUS, Knt., of Conington, Huntingdonshire and Exton, Rutland, son by his father's 2nd marriage, born about 1275 (aged 26 in 1301). He married **AGNES DE HARDRESHULL**, daughter of John de Hardeshull, of Hardreshull, Warwickshire. They had two sons, Bernard and John. In 1320 he made a settlement with his cousin, Bernard de Brus, of Thrapston, Northamptonshire, son of his father's younger brother, John, as to the manor of Exton, Rutland. In 1325 he settled two thirds of the manor of Exton, Rutland on himself, with remainder to his son and heir, Bernard, and his wife, Maud, at the same time granting the remaining third to them and their issue in fee tail.

> *Herald & Genealogist* 8 (1874): 325–348. *Misc. Gen. et Heraldica* n.s. 1 (1874): 337–340. *Rutland Mag. & County Hist. Rec.* 3 (1908): 97–106, 130–137. Turner *Cal. Feet of Fines Rel. Huntingdon* (Cambridge Antiq. Soc. 8° Ser. 37) (1913): 62. VCH *Rutland* 2 (1935): 128. VCH *Huntingdon* 3 (1936): 144–151.

9. JOHN DE BRUS, of Conington, Huntingdonshire and Exton, Rutland, 2nd son, born 13 June 1317. He was heir in 1336 to his older brother, Bernard de Brus. He married **MARGARET DE BEAUCHAMP**. They had one son, Bernard, and four daughters, Agnes, Joan, Elizabeth (nun at Bullington Priory), and Ellen (nun at Bullington Priory). In 1342 he settled the manor of Conington, Huntingdonshire on himself and his wife, Margaret, and his heirs. In the same year he was called upon to answer the Abbot of Ramsey for disseising the abbey of lands in Walton. JOHN DE BRUS died in 1346.

> *Herald & Genealogist* 8 (1874): 325–348. *Misc. Gen. et Heraldica* n.s. 1 (1874): 337–340. *Rutland Mag. & County Hist. Rec.* 3 (1908): 97–106, 130–137. VCH *Rutland* 2 (1935): 128. VCH *Huntingdon* 3 (1936): 144–151.

Children of John de Brus, by Margaret de Beauchamp:

i. **AGNES DE BRUS** [see next].

ii. **JOAN DE BRUS**, married **NICHOLAS GREENE**, of Exton, Rutland [see EXTON 10].

10. AGNES DE BRUS, born 4 August 1336 (aged 19 in 1358). She was co-heiress in 1348 to her brother, Bernard de Brus. She married (1st) about 1353 **HUGH DE WESENHAM**, Knt., son and heir of John de Wesenham, merchant. They had one son, Robert. SIR HUGH DE WESENHAM was living 14 May 1358. His widow, Agnes, married (2nd) before 1364 (date of partition) **ROBERT LOVETOT** (or **LOVETOFT**), of Conington, Huntingdonshire, Knight of the Shire for Huntingdonshire, 1378, 1383–4, 1386, 1391, Justice of the Peace for Huntingdonshire, 1384–93. In 1367 she and her sister, Joan, and their husbands received quitclaims as to their holdings in Conington, Huntingdonshire and Cottesmore, Exton, and Greetham, Rutland from Athelina (or Alana), daughter of Bernard de Brus, of Thrapston, Northamptonshire. ROBERT LOVETOT died 20 Sept. 1393. His wife, Agnes, predeceased him.

Herald & Genealogist 8 (1874): 325–348. *Misc. Gen. et Heraldica* n.s. 1 (1874): 337–340. *C.C.R. 1364–1368* (1910): 366, 464. VCH *Rutland* 2 (1935): 128. VCH *Huntingdon* 3 (1936): 144–151 (Wesenham arms: Sable a fesse dancetty between three molets argent.). Roskell *House of Commons 1386–1421* 3 (1992): (biog. of Robert Lovetot).

11. ROBERT WESENHAM, of Conington, Huntingdonshire, son and heir, born about 1363 (aged 30 in 1393). He married **ELFRED** _____. They had two sons, Thomas, Esq., and Robert, and one daughter, Joan. ROBERT WESENHAM died 9 August 1400.

Herald & Genealogist 8 (1874): 325–348. *Misc. Gen. et Heraldica* n.s. 1 (1874): 337–340. VCH *Rutland* 2 (1935): 128. VCH *Huntingdon* 3 (1936): 144–151.

12. JOAN WESENHAM, married **JOHN FOLVILLE**, Esq., of Sileby, Rotherby, Queniborough, etc., Leicestershire. They had three daughters, Mary, Anne (wife of Walter Kebell, Esq.), and Cecily (wife of _____Rydyll). She died before Sept. 1477.

Herald & Genealogist 8 (1874): 325–348. *Misc. Gen. et Heraldica* n.s. 1 (1874): 337–340. VCH *Rutland* 2 (1935): 128. VCH *Huntingdon* 3 (1936): 144–151. Ives *Common Lawyers of Pre-Reformation England: Thomas Kebell, a Case Study* (1983): 26, 27 (chart), 28–29, 33.

Child of Joan Wesenham, by John Folville, Esq.:

i. **MARY FOLVILLE**, married (1st) **WILLIAM COTTON** [see LACY 10]; (2nd) **THOMAS LACY**, of Grantchester, Cambridgeshire [see LACY 10]; (3rd) **THOMAS BILLINGE**, Chief Justice of the King's Bench [see LACY 10].

❧ CONSTABLE ❧

ALICE OF NORMANDY (sister of King William the Conqueror), married **LAMBERT**, Count of Lens.
JUDITH OF LENS, married **WALTHEOF**, Earl of Northumberland.
MAUD OF NORTHUMBERLAND, married **SIMON DE SENLIS**, Earl of Huntingdon and Northampton.
SIMON DE SENLIS, Earl of Huntingdon and Northampton, married **ISABEL** (or **ELIZABETH**) **OF LEICESTER**.
ISABEL DE SAINT LIZ, married **WILLIAM MAUDUIT**, of Hanslope, Buckinghamshire.
ROBERT MAUDUIT, of Hanslope, Buckinghamshire, married **ISABEL BASSET**.
WILLIAM MAUDUIT, of Hanslope, Buckinghamshire, married **ALICE DE NEWBURGH**.
ISABEL MAUDUIT, married **WILLIAM DE BEAUCHAMP**, Knt., of Elmley, Worcestershire.
WILLIAM DE BEAUCHAMP, Knt., Earl of Warwick, married **MAUD FITZ JOHN**.
ISABEL DE BEAUCHAMP, married **HUGH LE DESPENSER**, Knt., Earl of Winchester.
PHILIP LE DESPENSER, Knt., of Goxhill, Lincolnshire, married **MARGARET DE GOUSHILL** (desc. King William the Conqueror).
PHILIP LE DESPENSER, Knt., of Goxhill, Lincolnshire, married **JOAN DE COBHAM** (desc. King William the Conqueror).
PHILIP LE DESPENSER, Knt., 1st Lord Despenser, married **ELIZABETH** _____.
PHILIP LE DESPENSER, Knt., 2nd Lord Despenser, married **ELIZABETH TIBETOT** (desc. King William the Conqueror).
MARGERY DESPENSER, married **ROGER WENTWORTH**, Esq., of Nettlestead, Suffolk [see NETTLESTEAD 15].

16. AGNES WENTWORTH, married **ROBERT CONSTABLE**, Knt., of Flamborough, Yorkshire, and Somerby, Lincolnshire, Sheriff of Yorkshire, 1461–3, 1478–9, Sheriff of Lincolnshire, 1466–7, Knight of the Shire for Yorkshire, Knight of the Shire for Lincolnshire, Mayor of York, Justice of the Peace for East Riding, Yorkshire, 1453–88, son and heir of Robert Constable, Knt., of Flamborough, Yorkshire, and Somerby, Lincolnshire, by Agnes, daughter of William Gascoigne, of Gawthorpe, Yorkshire, Chief Justice of the King's Bench. He was born at Holme on Spalding Moor, Yorkshire 4 April 1423. They had six sons, Marmaduke, Knt., Robert, Esq., Philip, John [Dean of Lincoln], William, Knt., and Roger, and seven daughters, Elizabeth (wife of Thomas Metham, Knt.), Margaret, Agnes (wife of Walter Griffith, Knt., and Gervase Clifton, Knt.), Margery (wife of Ralph Bigod, Knt.), Anne, Agnes (wife of William Scargill, Knt.), and Katherine. He was appointed keeper of Fastolf's lands in Suffolk, 1448–53. He was summoned to a Great Council for Yorkshire in 1455 as a Lancastrian. He was pardoned by the Yorkists later the same year. In 1461 he was appointed steward of all the lands in Yorkshire and Lincolnshire forfeited by the Earl of Northumberland and Lord Roos. He was pardoned in 1462. He was sent on an embassy to Scotland in 1464. He was negotiating a truce with the Scots at Newcastle in 1466. He presented to the church of Scremby, Lincolnshire in 1466. He was part owner of a pirate ship in 1473. He was one of the appointed to keep the border in 1484. He remained on the Bench throughout every revolution. He was pardoned by King Henry VII in 1486. SIR ROBERT CONSTABLE died testate 23 May 1488. His widow, Agnes, died 20 April 1496.

Mundy et al. *Vis. of Nottingham 1569 & 1614* (H.S.P. 4) (1871): 40 (Constable ped.: "Sr Robert Constable of Flamborough Knt. = Anne d. of Phillip (Roger) Wentworth of Gowshill in com. York"). Glover & St. George *Vis. of Yorkshire 1584–5, 1612* (1875): 524 (Griffith ped.). Flower *Vis. of Yorkshire 1563–4* (H.S.P. 16) (1881): 63–67 (Constable ped.: "Sir Robert Constable Knyght son & heyre. = Agnes daughter of Sir Robert Wentworth or of Sir Phelyp Wentworth of Suffolk."). *C.P.R. 1461-1467* (1897): 86. *Northern Gen.* 3 (1897): 42. *List of Sheriffs for England & Wales* (PRO Lists and Indexes 9) (1898): 79, 162. *Lincolnshire Notes & Queries* 6 (1901): 184. *Genealogist* n.s. 20 (1904): 128; n.s. 25 (1909): 89. *MSS of the Duke of Rutland* 4 (Hist. MSS Comm. 24) (1905): 11. Dugdale *Dugdale's Vis. of Yorkshire* 2 (1907): 287–294 (sub Constable). Harvey et al. *Vis. of the North* 1 (Surtees Soc. 122) (1912): 46–47 (Constable ped.: "Syr Robert Constable, son and heyre of Sir Marmaduke, maryed Agnes, dowghter to Phylip Wentworth, off Suffolk"); 2 (Surtees Soc. 133) (1921): 160–161 (Constable ped.: "Sir Robert [Constable], son and heyre = Agnes, doter to Sir Phelyp Wentworth of Suffolk."); 3 (Surtees Soc. 144) (1930): 159–160 (Constable ped.: "Dominus Robertus Constable miles = Agnes filia Rogeri Wentworth"). Wedgwood *Hist. of Parl.* 1 (1936): 213 (biog.

of Sir Robert Constable). Harvey *Vis. of Suffolk 1561* 1 (H.S.P. n.s. 2) (1981): 162–168. Sainty *Judges of England* (Selden Soc. Supp. Ser. 10) (1993): 8 (re. William Gascoigne). *TAG* 70 (1995): 96–103. Kirby *Plumpton Letters & Papers* (Camden Soc. 5th Ser. 8) (1996): 305–309 ("A political trimmer, he remained on the East Riding bench throughout every political revolution from 1453 until his death").

Children of Agnes Wentworth, by Robert Constable, Knt.:

i. **MARMADUKE CONSTABLE**, Knt. [see next].

ii. **ROBERT CONSTABLE**, Esq., of North Cliffe (in Sancton), Yorkshire, married **BEATRICE HAWCLIFF** [see GREYSTOKE 14].

iii. **ANNE CONSTABLE**, married **WILLIAM TYRWHIT**, Knt., of Kettleby, Lincolnshire [see TYRWHIT 17].

iv. **MARGARET CONSTABLE**, married **WILLIAM EURE** Knt., Malton and Stokesley, Yorkshire [see EURE 11].

v. **KATHERINE CONSTABLE**, married **RALPH RYTHER**, Esq., of Ryther, Yorkshire [see RYTHER 15].

17. MARMADUKE CONSTABLE, Knt., of Flamborough, Yorkshire, Knight of the Body to Kings Richard III and Henry VII, Steward of Tutbury, Donington, and High Peak, Sheriff of Staffordshire, 1484–5, Sheriff of Yorkshire, 1488–9, 1493–4, Knight of the Shire for cos. York, Stafford, and Lincoln, Ambassador to Scotland, son and heir, born about 1443 (aged 31 in 1488, aged 40 and more in 1496, aged 70 in 1513). He married (1st) **MARGERY FITZ HUGH**, daughter of Henry Fitz Hugh, 5th Lord Fitz Hugh, of Ravensworth, Yorkshire, by Alice, daughter of Richard Neville, K.G., 5th Earl of Salisbury [see FITZ HUGH 16 for her ancestry]. They had no issue. He married (2nd) **JOYCE STAFFORD**, daughter of Humphrey Stafford, Knt., of Grafton, Worcestershire, by Eleanor, daughter of Thomas Aylesbury, Knt. [see HASTANG 14 for her ancestry]. They had four sons, Robert, Knt., Marmaduke, Knt., William, Knt., and John, Knt., and two daughters, Agnes (wife of Henry Ughtred, Knt. and William Percy, Knt.) and Eleanor. He served in France with King Edward IV in 1475. He was knighted by the Earl of Northumberland during the Scottish campaign of 1480–3. He accompanied King Henry VII to France in 1492. He was Captain of the Left Wing at Flodden 9 Sept. 1513. SIR MARMADUKE CONSTABLE died 20 Nov. 1518, and was buried at Flamborough, Yorkshire. He left a will dated 1 May 1518, proved 27 April 1520.

Nash *Colls. for the Hist. of Worcestershire* 1 (1781): 157. Plumpton *Plumpton Corr.* (1839): 207–208 (Sir William Gascoigne styled "cousin" by Marmaduke Constable in letter dated 1514; Constable also refers to his cousins Plumpton and Roclife). *Arch. Aeliana* n.s. 2 (1858): 190–192 (letter of King Henry VIII to Marmaduke Constable dated 1514). Cooper & Cooper *Athenæ Cantabrigienses* 1 (1858): 22–23 (biog. of Marmaduke Constable). Mundy et al. *Vis. of Nottingham 1569 & 1614* (H.S.P. 4) (1871): 40 (Constable ped.: "Sr Marmaduke Constable of Flamborough = Joyce d. of Humfrey Stafford of Blatherwick"). *Genealogist* n.s. 20 (1904): 128–129. Glover & St. George *Vis. of Yorkshire 1584–5, 1612* (1875): 178–179 (Constable ped.: "Sir Marmaduke Constable, *called little Sir Marmaduke*, [1] = … dau. of the Lord Fitz-Hugh, *d.s.p.*, [2] = Joyce, dau. of Sir Humphrey Stafford, *of Grafton (2nd wife)*."). Flower *Vis. of Yorkshire 1563–4* (H.S.P. 16) (1881): 63–67 (Constable ped.: "Sir Marmaduke Constable, Knight, son & heyre [1] = … filia D'ni Fytzhugh 1st wyff, by her no issu, [2] = Joyce doughter to Sir Humfrey Stafford of Graufton, 2 wyff.") (Constable arms: Barry of six, or and azure). *Testamenta Eboracensia* 5 (Surtees Soc. 79) (1884): 88–93 (will of Marmaduke Constable, Knt.). *List of Sheriffs for England & Wales* (PRO Lists and Indexes 9) (1898): 128, 162. Wrottesley *Staffordshire Suits: Plea Rolls* (Colls. Hist. Staffs. n.s. 4) (1901): 176. Dugdale *Dugdale's Vis. of Yorkshire* 2 (1907): 287–294 (sub Constable). *D.N.B.* 4 (1908): 967–969 (biog. of Sir Marmaduke Constable). Harvey et al. *Vis. of the North* 1 (Surtees Soc. 122) (1912): 46–47 (Constable ped.: "Syr Marmaduk [Constable], sone and heyre to Syr Robert, maryed to his first wyff Marye, dowghter to FytzHue, and by her had no yssu. After maryed to his second wyff Joyes, dowghter to Vmfrey Stafford, of Goranston"); 2 (Surtees Soc. 133) (1921): 160–161 (Constable ped.: "Marmaduke [Constable], 2 son, maryed Barbara, doter and heyre of John Sotell."); 3 (Surtees Soc. 144) (1930): 159–160 (Constable ped.: "(Dominus) Marmeducus Constable (miles) [1] = Margeria filia Domini Fitzhugh, [2] = Ioysa filia domini Humfredi Stafford (of Grafton) *militis*"); 4 (Surtees Soc. 146) (1932): 5–6 (Constable ped.: "Mary, d. to…. Fitzhugh, sans issu = Sr Marmaduke Costable of Flamborowgh = Joice d. to Sr Humfrey Stafford"). Wedgwood *Hist. of Parl.* 1 (1936): 212 (biog. of Sir Marmaduke Constable). Walker *Yorkshire Peds.* 3 (H.S.P. 96) (1944): 400–402 (Ughtred ped.). Petre *Richard III: Crown & People* (1985): 218–223. *TAG* 70 (1995): 96–103. Kirby *Plumpton Letters & Papers* (Camden

Soc. 5th Ser. 8) (1996): 310–311 (biog. of Sir Marmaduke Constable: "… Like his father a consummate trimmer"). Biancalana *Fee Tail & the Common Recovery in Medieval England* (2001): 393.

Children of Marmaduke Constable, Knt., by Joyce Stafford:

- i. **MARMADUKE CONSTABLE**, Knt. [see next].
- ii. **ELEANOR CONSTABLE**, married (1st) **JOHN INGLEBY**, of Ripley, Yorkshire [see BERKELEY 12]; (2nd) **THOMAS BERKELEY**, Knt., of Thornbury, Gloucestershire [see BERKELEY 12].

18. MARMADUKE CONSTABLE, Knt., in right of his wife, of Everingham, Yorkshire, member of the Council in the North, Sheriff of Yorkshire, 1509–10, Sheriff of Lincolnshire, 1513–4, Knight of the Shire for Yorkshire, 2nd son, born about 1480. He married **BARBARA SOTHILL**, daughter of John Sothill, Esq., of Everingham, Yorkshire, by his 1st wife, Agnes, daughter of William Ingleby, Knt. She was born about 1474 (aged 28 in 1502). They had two sons, Robert, Knt., and William (clerk), and one daughter, Everild. His wife, Barbara, was co-heiress in 1502 to her brother, George Sothill, an embecile. He fought at Flodden with his father and three brothers, and was knighted after the battle 9 Sept. 1513. He attended the queen at the Field of the Cloth of Gold in 1520. He took an active part in the Scotch wars of 1522 and 1523. He distinguished himself at the capture of Jedburgh and Fernieherst, both in Sept. 1523. His wife, Barbara, died 4 October 1540. He had a grant of Drax Priory founded by his wife's ancestors. He served in the Scottish campaign of 1544. SIR MARMADUKE CONSTABLE died testate 12 Sept. 1545, and was buried with his wife at Everingham, Yorkshire.

Kimber & Johnson *Baronetage of England* 1 (1771): 441 (sub Ingleby). *Testamenta Eboracensia* 4 (Surtees Soc. 53) (1869): 185–186. Mundy et al. *Vis. of Nottingham 1569 & 1614* (H.S.P. 4) (1871): 40 (Constable ped.: "Sr Marmaduke Constable of Everingham = Barbara d. & heire of John Suthill of Everingham"). Skaife *Reg. of the Guild of Corpus Christi in the City of York* (Surtees Soc. 57) (1872): 82–83 (re. John Sothill). Glover & St. George *Vis. of Yorkshire 1584–5, 1612* (1875): 178–179 (Constable ped.: "Sir Marmaduke Constable, *of Everingham, knt., ob. 7 Sept. 1545, 37 H. VIII.* = Elizabeth, dau. and heir to John Sothill, *of Everingham. She died 4Oct. 1540.*"). Flower *Vis. of Yorkshire 1563–4* (H.S.P. 16) (1881): 63–67 (Constable ped.: "D'n's Marmaducus Counstable 2 son.= Barbara doughter & heyre of John Sowtell de Everingham."). *List of Sheriffs for England & Wales* (PRO Lists and Indexes 9) (1898): 80, 163. *Testamenta Eboracensia* 6 (Surtees Soc. 106) (1902): 200. Dodsworth *Yorkshire Church Notes* (Yorkshire Arch. Soc. Recs. 34) (1904): 203–205. *Genealogist* n.s. 20 (1904): 130. Dugdale *Dugdale's Vis. of Yorkshire* 2 (1907): 287–294 (sub Constable). *D.N.B.* 4 (1908): 967–969 (biog. of Sir Marmaduke Constable). Harvey et al. *Vis. of the North* 1 (Surtees Soc. 122) (1912): 46–47 (Constable ped.: "Syr Marmaduke [Constable], second sone to Sir Marmaduk, maryed Barbara, dowghter and heyre to John Sottell"); 3 (Surtees Soc. 144) (1930): 159–160 (Constable ped.: "Marmeducus Constable"); 4 (Surtees Soc. 146) (1932): 5–6 (Constable ped.: "Sr Marmaduke Constable of Everingham = Barbara d. to Sr Jno Suthill of Everingham"). Bindoff *House of Commons 1509–1558* 1 (1982): 685–686 (biog. of Sir Marmaduke Constable I). Kirby *Plumpton Letters & Papers* (Camden Soc. 5th Ser. 8) (1996): 311 (biog. of Sir Marmaduke Constable).

19. ROBERT CONSTABLE, Knt., of Everingham, Yorkshire, Justice of the Peace for Yorkshire (East and North Ridings), 1545–58, Knight of the Shire for Yorkshire, 1553, ?1555, Sheriff of Yorkshire, 1557–8, born before 1495. He married before 1530 **KATHERINE MANNERS**, daughter of George Manners, Knt., 11th Lord Roos of Helmsley, by Anne, daughter and heiress of Thomas Saint Leger, Knt. [see MANNERS 11 for her ancestry]. They had six sons, Marmaduke, Knt., Robert, Knt., John, Michael, George, and Thomas, and five daughters, Barbara (wife of William Babthorp), Margaret (wife of Thomas Saltmarsh), Everild (wife of Thomas Crawthorne), Elizabeth (wife of Edward Ellerker), and Eleanor. He was knighted by the Earl of Hertford 19 May 1544 during the campaign against the Scots. SIR ROBERT CONSTABLE died testate 29 October 1558.

Wotton *English Baronetage* 2 (1741): 328 (Constable arms: Quarterly, gules and vaire, a bend, or). Brydges *Collins' Peerage of England* 1 (1812): 465. Mundy et al. *Vis. of Nottingham 1569 & 1614* (H.S.P. 4) (1871): 40 (Constable ped.: "Sr Robert Constable of Everingham = Catherin d. of George Mannors Lord Roos, sister of the Earle of Rutland"). Glover & St. George *Vis. of Yorkshire 1584–5, 1612* (1875): 178–179 (Constable ped.: "Sir Robert Constable, *of Everingham, knt., d. 5 & 6, P. & M., 1558.* = Katherine, dau. to *George Manners*, Lord Roos, *of Hamlake, by Anne St. Leger.*"). Flower *Vis. of Yorkshire 1563–4* (H.S.P. 16) (1881): 63–67 (Constable ped.: "Sir Robert Counstable son & heyre to Sir Marmaduke. =

Kateren doughter to George Maners Lord Rosse and syster to Thomas Erl of Rutland."). Fletcher *Leicestershire Peds. & Royal Descents* (1887): 1–8. Dugdale *Dugdale's Vis. of Yorkshire* 2 (1907): 287–294 (sub Constable). Ruvigny and Raineval *Plantagenet Roll: Anne of Exeter* (1907): 2, 52. Harvey et al. *Vis. of the North* 1 (Surtees Soc. 122) (1912): 46–47 (Constable ped.: "Sir Robert [Constable], son and heyre of Sir Marmaduke, maryed Katheryn, dowghter to George Manners, Lord Roose, and suster to Thomas, erle of Rutland"); 4 (Surtees Soc. 146) (1932): 5–6 (Constable ped.: "Sʳ Robart Constable of Everingham mar: Katherin d. to George Maners Lord Ross sister to yᵉ erle of Rutland"). Vickers *Hist. of Northumberland* 11 (1922): 444–445 (Manners chart). Bindoff *House of Commons 1509–1558* 1 (1982): 687–688 (biog. of Sir Robert Constable).

20. **MARMADUKE CONSTABLE**, Knt., of Everingham, Yorkshire, son and heir. He married **JANE CONYERS**, daughter of Christopher Conyers, Knt., 2nd Lord Conyers, of Hornby, Yorkshire, by Anne, daughter of Thomas Dacre, Lord Dacre of Gilsland [see CONYERS 19 for her ancestry]. They had four sons, Philip, Knt., Roger, Robert, and William, and two daughters, Everild (wife of William Constable) and Katherine. His wife, Jane, died 4 Dec. 1558, and was buried at Everingham, Yorkshire. SIR MARMADUKE CONSTABLE died 1 Feb. 1574.

Wotton *English Baronetage* 2 (1741): 328. Betham *Baronetage of England* 1 (1801): 335. Whitaker *Hist. of Richmondshire* 2 (2) (1823): unpaginated Conyers ped. Mundy et al. *Vis. of Nottingham 1569 & 1614* (H.S.P. 4) (1871): 40 (Constable ped.: "Sʳ Marmaduke Constable of Everingham = Jane d. of Wm. Lord Conyers"). Glover & St. George *Vis. of Yorkshire 1584–5, 1612* (1875): 71–72 (Conyers ped.: "Jane [Conyers], *wife of Sir Marmaduke Constable, of Everingham.*"), 178–179 (Constable ped.: "Sir Marmaduke Constable, *of Everingham, knt.,*1ˢᵗ son, *ob. 1 Feb., 17 Q. Eliz.,* 1574. = Jane, daughter of *William or Christopher* Lo. Conyers, *of Hornby.*"). Flower *Vis. of Yorkshire 1563–4* (H.S.P. 16) (1881): 63–67 (Constable ped.: "Sir Marmaduke Counstable son & heyre to Sir Robert. = Jane doughter to Crystofer Lord Conyers."), 72–73 (Conyers ped.: "Jane Conyers. = Sir Marmaduke Counstable of Everyngham Knight."). Dodsworth *Yorkshire Church Notes* (Yorkshire Arch. Soc. Recs. 34) (1904): 203–205. Ruvigny and Raineval *Plantagenet Roll: Anne of Exeter* (1907): 52. Dugdale *Dugdale's Vis. of Yorkshire* 2 (1907): 287–294 (sub Constable). Clay *Extinct & Dormant Peerages* (1913): 35 (sub Conyers). Harvey et al. *Vis. of the North* 1 (Surtees Soc. 122) (1912): 46–47 (Constable ped.: "Sir Marmaduke Constable, son and heyre to Syr Robert, maryed Jane, dowghter to Christopher Lord Conyers"); 4 (Surtees Soc. 146) (1932): 5–6 (Constable ped.: "Sʳ Marmaduke Constable of Everingham = Jane d. to Wᵐ Lord Coniers").

Child of Marmaduke Constable, Knt., by Jane Conyers:

i. **KATHERINE CONSTABLE**, married **ROBERT STAPLETON**, Knt., of Wighill, Yorkshire [see NELSON 17].

❧ CONYERS ❧

EUSTACHE I, Count of Boulogne, married **MATHILDE** (or **MAHAUT**) **OF LOUVAIN**.
EUSTACHE II, Count of Boulogne, by an unknown mistress, _____.
GEOFFREY OF BOULOGNE, of Carshalton, Surrey, married **BEATRICE DE MANDEVILLE**.
WILLIAM OF BOULOGNE, of Carshalton, Surrey, married _____.
ROHESE OF BOULOGNE, married **RICHARD DE LUCY**, Knt., of Chipping Ongar, Essex, Justicar of England.
ALICE DE LUCY, married **ODINEL DE UMFREVILLE**, Knt., of Prudhoe, Northumberland.
ALICE DE UMFREVILLE, married **WILLIAM BERTRAM**, of Mitford, Northumberland.
ROGER BERTRAM, Knt., of Mitford, Northumberland, married **AGNES** _____.
ISABEL BERTRAM, married **PHILIP DARCY**, Knt., of Cawkwell, Lincolnshire.
ROGER DARCY, of Blyth, Nottinghamshire, married **ISABEL DE ATON**.

JOHN DARCY, Knt., of Knaith, Lincolnshire, married **EMMELINE HERON**.
JOHN DARCY, Knt., 2nd Lord Darcy of Knaith, married **ELIZABETH DE MEINILL**.
PHILIP DARCY, 4th Lord Darcy of Knaith, married **ELIZABETH GRAY**.
JOHN DARCY, Knt., 5th Lord Darcy of Knaith, 4th Lord Meinell, married **MARGARET GREY** (desc. King William the Conqueror).
PHILIP DARCY, Knt., 6th Lord Darcy of Knaith, married **ELEANOR FITZ HUGH** (desc. King William the Conqueror) [see DARCY 15].

16. MARGERY DARCY, daughter and co-heiress, born posthumously at Ravensworth, Yorkshire 1 Sept. 1418 (aged 1 in 1419, 13 in 1431). She was a legatee in the 1427 will of her grandmother, Elizabeth Fitz Hugh. She married before 20 Nov. 1431 **JOHN CONYERS**, K.G., of Hornby, Yorkshire, Sheriff of Yorkshire, 1467–8, 1474–5, Steward of the lordship of Middleham, Bailiff and Steward of Richmond Liberty, Constable of Middleham, son of Christopher Conyers, by his 1st wife, Eleanor, daughter of Thomas Rolleston, of Mablethorpe, Lincolnshire. They had seven sons, John, Knt., Richard, Christopher, Henry, Philip, Robert and William, Esq., and five daughters, Eleanor, Elizabeth (wife of William Fitzwilliam, Knt.), Margaret (wife of Richard Ascue), Margery and Joan. He and his wife, Margery, presented to the church of Kirkby-in-Ashfield, Nottinghamshire in 1465, and he alone in 1482, 1483, 1489, and 1490. His wife, Margery, died between 20 March 1468/9 and 20 April 1469. In 1473 he conveyed the manor of Pinchingthorpe (in Guisborough), Yorkshire to his half-brother, Brian Conyers, of York, merchant. He was present at the Coronation of King Richard III in 1483. He received an annuity of £200 and the manors of Aldebrough and Catterick by grant of King Richard III. SIR JOHN CONYERS died 14 March 1489/90, and was buried at Hornby, Yorkshire.

Betham *Baronetage of England* 1 (1801): 335. Thoresby *Ducatus Leodiensis* (1816): 226–228 (Darcy ped.). Whitaker *Hist. of Richmondshire* 2 (2) (1823): unpaginated Conyers ped. Beltz *Mems. of the Order of the Garter* (1841): clxvii. Poulson *Hist. & Antiqs. of Holderness* 2 (1841): 200–201 (Darcy ped.). Banks *Baronies in Fee* 1 (1844): 178–179 (sub Darcy). Ord *Hist. & Antiqs. of Cleveland* (1846): 445–446 (Meinell-Darcy ped.). Tonge *Vis. of Northern Counties 1530* (Surtees Soc. 41) (1863): 48–49 (Conyers ped.: "Syr John Coniers, of Horneby, maried Margery, doughter and quo heyre of the Lord Darcy") (Conyers arms: Azure, a maunch or charged in chief with an annulet [sable], for difference). Glover & St. George *Vis. of Yorkshire 1584–5, 1612* (1875): 71–72 (Conyers ped.: "Sir John Conyers, of Hornby, Knt. = Margery, 1st dau. and one of ye heires of Philip Lord Darcy, and Meignill."). Flower *Vis. of Yorkshire 1563–4* (H.S.P. 16) (1881): 72–73 (Conyers ped.: "Sir John Conyers of Hornby. = Margery doughter & quoheyre of the Lord Darcy."), 91–92 (Darcy ped.: "Dame Margery [Darcy] wyf to Sir John Conyers Knyght of the Garter"). *Cal. IPM Henry VII* 1 (1898): 259–261, 278. *List of Sheriffs for England & Wales* (PRO Lists and Indexes 9) (1898): 162. Hodgson *Hist. of Northumberland* 5 (1899): 411. *Genealogical Mag.* 5 (1902): 189–198. Wrottesley *Peds. from the Plea Rolls* (1905): 377–378. *Yorkshire Deeds* 1 (Yorkshire Arch. Soc. Recs. 39) (1909): 137–138, 207; 10 (Yorkshire Arch. Soc. Recs. 120) (1955): 126–129. Harvey et al. *Vis. of the North* 1 (Surtees Soc. 122) (1912): 51 (Conyers ped.); 2 (Surtees Soc. 133) (1921): 144 (Conyers ped.); 3 (Surtees Soc. 144) (1930): 92–94 (Conyers ped.: "Dominus Iohannes Cogniers miles de Hornby = Margeria filia et (vna heredem) heres Philippi domini Darcy"). VCH *Hertford* 3 (1912): 451. Clay *Extinct & Dormant Peerages* (1913): 32–35 (sub Conyers), 41–42 (sub Darcy). *C.P.* 4 (1916): 66–67, 71 (sub Darcy). *Yorkshire Inqs.* 5 (Yorkshire Arch. Soc. Recs. 59) (1918): 156–157. VCH *Yorkshire N.R.* 2 (1923): 309–319. Train *Abs. of IPMs Rel. Nottinghamshire* 2 (Thoroton Soc. Recs. 12) (1952): 168–169. Train *Lists of Clergy of Central Nottinghamshire* (Thoroton Soc. Rec. Ser. 15(1)) (1953): 76–77. Langley *Reg. of Thomas Langley* 3 (Surtees Soc. 169) (1959): 62–64. VCH *Yorkshire N.R.* 2 (1973): 360. Roskell *Parl. & Politics in Late Medieval England* 2 (1981): 279–306 (biog. of Sir James Strangeways). Sutton *Coronation of Richard III* (1983): 325. *Cal. IPM* 23 (2004): 358–360.

Children of Margery Darcy, by John Conyers, K.G.:

i. **JOHN CONYERS**, Knt. [see next].

ii. **ELEANOR CONYERS**, married **THOMAS MARKENFIELD**, Knt., of Markenfield, Yorkshire [see MAULEVERER 14].

iii. **MARGERY CONYERS**, married (1st) **ROWLAND PLACE**, Esq., of Halnaby, Yorkshire [see BLAKISTON 12].

17. JOHN CONYERS, Knt., of Hornby, Yorkshire, son and heir apparent. He married **ALICE NEVILLE**, 3rd daughter and co-heiress of William Neville, K.G., Earl of Kent, 6th Lord

Fauconberge, by Joan, daughter and heiress of Thomas Fauconberge, Knt., 5th Lord Fauconberge [see FAUCONBERGE 12 for her ancestry]. She was born about 1437 (aged 26 in 1463). They had two sons, John and William, Knt. [1st Lord Conyers], and two daughters, Margery (wife of William Bulmer, Knt.) and Anne (wife of Richard Lumley, 4th Lord Lumley). SIR JOHN CONYERS was slain at Edgcote Field near Banbury 26 July 1469. His widow, Alice, died before 21 April 1491 (date of inquisition post mortem for her mother).

> Betham *Baronetage of England* 1 (1801): 335. Whitaker *Hist. of Richmondshire* 2 (2) (1823): unpaginated Conyers ped. Rowland *Noble Fam. of Nevill* (1830). *Coll. Top. et Gen.* 1 (1834): 300–301 (Neville ped.). Baker *Hist. & Antiqs. of Northampton* 2 (1836–41): 295–297. Surtees *Hist. & Antiqs. of Durham* 4 (1840): 158–163 (Nevill peds.). Poulson *Hist. & Antiqs. of Holderness* 2 (1841): 200–201 (Darcy ped.). Banks *Baronies in Fee* 1 (1844): 178–179 (sub Darcy). *Gentleman's Mag.* n.s. 23 (1845): 593–599. Ord *Hist. & Antiqs. of Cleveland* (1846): 445–446 (Meinell-Darcy ped.). Tonge *Vis. of Northern Counties 1530* (Surtees Soc. 41) (1863): 48–49 (Conyers ped.: "Syr John Conyers, son of John, maried the doughter and quo heyre of Willyam Lord Fauconberge"). Glover & St. George *Vis. of Yorkshire 1584–5, 1612* (1875): 71–72 (Conyers ped.: "Sir John Conyers, K.G., of Hornby, = Alice, daughter and one of the heirs of Sir Wm. Nevill, Lord Fauconbridge, and Earl of Kent."). Flower *Vis. of Yorkshire 1563–4* (H.S.P. 16) (1881): 72–73 (Conyers ped.: "Sir John Conyers, Knight, son & heyr. = Alicia doughter quo heyr of William Lord Faconbrydge sive Nevell."). *Genealogical Mag.* 5 (1902): 189–198. *C.P.* 2 (1912): 418 (sub Bulmer); 3 (1913): 404 (sub Conyers); 4 (1916): 67, 71 (sub Darcy); 5 (1926): 281–287 (sub Fauconberge); 8 (1932): 274–275 (sub Lumley). Harvey et al. *Vis. of the North* 1 (Surtees Soc. 122) (1912): 51; 2 (Surtees Soc. 133) (1921): 144; 3 (Surtees Soc. 144) (1930): 92–94 (Conyers ped.: "Iohannes Cogniers miles = Alicia filia et vna heredum domini Willelmi de Neuille comitis Kancij"), 99–101 (Brus ped.: "Alicia [Neville] = Iohannes Cognyers"). Clay *Extinct & Dormant Peerages* (1913): 32–35 (sub Conyers), 71 (sub Nevile).

18. WILLIAM CONYERS, Knt., of Hornby, Yorkshire, Bailiff of the Liberty of Richmond, Constable of Richmond and Middleton Castles, 2nd but 1st surviving son and heir, born 21 Dec. 1468 (aged 22 in 1491). He married (1st) by license dated 24 Sept. 1479 (they being related in the 4th degree) **MARY SCROPE**, widow of his brother, John Conyers (living 1472), and daughter of John Scrope, K.G., 5th Lord Scrope of Bolton, by his 2nd wife, Elizabeth, daughter of Oliver Saint John, Knt. [see SAINT JOHN 15.v for her ancestry]. They had one daughter. He succeeded his grandfather 14 March 1489/90, and built Hornby Castle. He married (2nd) before 6 Feb. 1498/9 **ANNE NEVILLE**, daughter of Ralph Neville, K.B., 3rd Earl of Westmorland, Lord Neville, by Isabel, daughter of Roger Booth, Esq. [see NEVILLE 16 for her ancestry]. They had one son, Christopher, Knt. [2nd Lord Conyers], and two daughters, Katherine (wife of Francis Bigod, Knt.) and Margaret (wife of Richard Cholmeley, Knt.). He was summoned to Parliament from 17 October 1509 by writs directed *Willelmo Conyers de Conyers chivaler*. He fought at the Battle of Flodden Field in 1513 and served under George Talbot, Earl of Shrewsbury in Scotland in 1522. SIR WILLIAM CONYERS, 1st Lord Conyers, died shortly before 14 April 1524. His widow, Anne, married (2nd) at Aldwark, Yorkshire 12 Nov. 1525 (as his 2nd wife) **ANTHONY SALTMARSHE**, Gent., of Strubby (in Langton-by-Wragby), Lincolnshire, son of John Saltmarshe. He left a will dated 28 July 1550, proved 9 October 1550.

> Betham *Baronetage of England* 1 (1801): 335. Whitaker *Hist. of Richmondshire* 2 (2) (1823): unpaginated Conyers ped. Rowland *Noble Fam. of Nevill* (1830). Surtees *Hist. & Antiqs. of Durham* 4 (1840): 158–163 (Nevill peds.). Poulson *Hist. & Antiqs. of Holderness* 2 (1841): 200–201 (Darcy ped.). Banks *Baronies in Fee* 1 (1844): 164–165 (sub Coniers or Conyers), 178–179 (sub Darcy). Ord *Hist. & Antiqs. of Cleveland* (1846): 445–446 (Meinell-Darcy ped.). Tonge *Vis. of Northern Counties 1530* (Surtees Soc. 41) (1863): 28–29 (Neville ped.: "Rauff Erle of Westmerland, son of John, maried the doughter of Bouth, and by her he had yssue, Rauff Lord Nevill, whiche died before his father; and Anne Lady Conyers."), 48–49 (Conyers ped.: "Willyam, furst Lord Coniers, son of Syr John, maried Anne, doughter of Rauff Erle of Westmerland"). *Testamenta Eboracensia* 3 (Surtees Soc. 45) (1865): 341 (abs. of license to marry), 373 (abs. of license to marry). Glover & St. George *Vis. of Yorkshire 1584–5, 1612* (1875): 71–72 (Conyers ped.: "Sir William Conyers, the first Lord Conyers of Hornby, mar. Ann, daughter to Ralph Nevill, Earl of Westmoreland."). Flower *Vis. of Yorkshire 1563–4* (H.S.P. 16) (1881): 72–73 (Conyers ped.: "William fyrst Lord Conyers. = Anne doughter of Raff Erl of Westmerland."), 224–226 (Nevill ped.: "Anne [Neville] Lady Conyers."), 278–281 (Scrope ped.: "Mary [Scrope] wyff to William Lord Conyers."). Foster *Royal Lineage of our Noble & Gentle Fams.* 1 (1883): 11–13 (sub Nevill, Earl of Westmorland, etc.). *Cal. IPM Henry VII* 1 (1898): 259–261. *Genealogist* n.s. 15 (1898): 165. *Genealogical Mag.* 5 (1902):

189–198. Maddison *Lincolnshire Peds.* 3 (H.S.P. 52) (1904): 846–848. Harvey et al. *Vis. of the North* 1 (Surtees Soc. 122) (1912): 51 (Conyers ped.: "Wylliam, fyrst Lorde Conyers, sone and heyre of Sir John, maryed Anne, dowghter of Raff, erle of Westmorlond"); 2 (Surtees Soc. 133) (1921): 144 (Conyers ped.); 3 (Surtees Soc. 144) (1930): 92–94 (Conyers ped.). Clay *Extinct & Dormant Peerages* (1913): 32–35 (sub Conyers). *C.P.* 3 (1913): 404 (sub Conyers); 4 (1916): 67, 71 (sub Darcy); 5 (1926): 286–287 (sub Fauconberge); 12(2) (1959): 551–552 (sub Westmorland).

19. CHRISTOPHER CONYERS, Knt., 2nd Lord Conyers, of Hornby, Yorkshire, son and heir by his father's 2nd marriage. He married at Kirkoswald, Cumberland 28 Sept. 1515 **ANNE DACRE**, daughter of Thomas Dacre, K.G., K.B., 3rd Lord Dacre of the North, by Elizabeth, daughter and heiress of Robert Greystoke, Knt. [see DACRE 16 for her ancestry]. They had two sons, John [3rd Lord Conyers] and Leonard, and two daughters, Elizabeth (wife of George Place) and Jane. He was summoned to Parliament from 9 August 1529 by writs directed *Christofero domino Conyers chivaler*. He presented to the church of Kirkby-in-Ashfield, Nottinghamshire in 1534. SIR CHRISTOPHER CONYERS, 2nd Lord Conyers, died testate 14 June 1538. His widow, Anne, left a will dated 16 Dec. 1547, proved 21 April 1548. They were buried at Skelton, Yorkshire.

Betham *Baronetage of England* 1 (1801): 335. Whitaker *Hist. of Richmondshire* 2 (2) (1823): unpaginated Conyers ped. Poulson *Hist. & Antiqs. of Holderness* 2 (1841): 200–201 (Darcy ped.). Banks *Baronies in Fee* 1 (1844): 164–165 (sub Coniers or Conyers), 178–179 (sub Darcy). Ord *Hist. & Antiqs. of Cleveland* (1846): 445–446 (Meinell-Darcy ped.). Tonge *Vis. of Northern Counties 1530* (Surtees Soc. 41) (1863): 48–49 (Conyers ped.: "Christofer, 2nd Lord Coniers, son of William, maried Anne, doughter to Thomas Lord Dacres"). Glover & St. George *Vis. of Yorkshire 1584–5, 1612* (1875): 71–72 (Conyers ped.: "Christopher Lord Conyers, of Hornby, mar. Ann, daughter of Thomas, Lord Dacre, of Gilsland."). *Desc. Cat. Ancient Deeds* 1 (1890): 81. Flower *Vis. of Yorkshire 1563–4* (H.S.P. 16) (1881): 72–73 (Conyers ped.: "Crystofer Lord Conyers son & heyr. = Anne doughter to Thomas Lord Dacres of Gyllesland."), 83–85 (Dacre ped.: "Anne [Dacre] Lady Conyers."). *Genealogical Mag.* 5 (1902): 189–198. Harvey et al. *Vis. of the North* 1 (Surtees Soc. 122) (1912): 51; 2 (Surtees Soc. 133) (1921): 144. Clay *Extinct & Dormant Peerages* (1913): 32–35 (sub Conyers), 36–39 (sub Dacre). *C.P.* 3 (1913): 404–405 (sub Conyers); 4 (1916): 71 (sub Darcy). Train *Lists of Clergy of Central Nottinghamshire* (Thoroton Soc. Rec. Ser. 15(1)) (1953): 76–77. Dickens *Clifford Letters of the 16th Cent.* (Surtees Soc. 172) (1962): 95 (transcript of letter from Lady Anne Conyers, widow, dated 1538 to Henry Clifford, 1st Earl of Cumberland).

Child of Christopher Conyers, Knt., by Anne Dacre:

i. **JANE CONYERS**, married **MARMADUKE CONSTABLE**, Knt., of Everingham, Yorkshire [see CONSTABLE 20].

❦ CORBET ❦

JOHN DE SOMERY, married **HAWISE PAYNELL**.
RALPH DE SOMERY, of Dudley (in Sedgley), Staffordshire, married **MARGARET LE GRAS**.
ROGER DE SOMERY, Knt., of Dudley (in Sedgley), Staffordshire, married **NICHOLE D'AUBENEY** (desc. King William the Conqueror) [see SOMERY 3].

4. MAUD DE SOMERY, 4th daughter. She married **HENRY DE ERDINGTON** (or **ERDINTON**, **HERDINGTON**), Knt., of Erdington (in Aston), Warwickshire, Little Withyford, Shawbury, and Wellington, Shropshire, etc., and, in right of his wife, of Chipping Campden, Gloucestershire, and Barrow on Soar, Leicestershire, son of Giles de Erdington, of Besford, Shawbury, Wellington, and Withyford, Shropshire. They had two sons, Giles and Henry, Knt. In 1274–5 Thomas le Frounceys arraigned an assize of novel dissseisin against him and others touching a tenement in Rowton, Shropshire. In 1274 Ralph de Limesi sued him for the advowson of Yardley, Worcestershire; Ralph acknowledged the advowson to be the right of the said Henry. Just before this, Henry had given the advowson to the Abbot and convent of Halesowen, but they had afterwards restored it to him with the charter. In 1279 he gave the same advowson to Catesby Priory on condition that the nuns should appoint a canon of their house, as soon as the appropriation had been made, to say mass for him and his family, and that he should be buried before the altar in the chapel dedicated to St. Edmund of Canterbury. At an unknown date, he gave to the church of St. Mary, Shawbury, Shropshire a messuage, curtilage, and lands for the sustenance of the chaplain in the said church. At an unknown date, as "Henry de Erdington, heir of Giles de Erdington," he granted Sir John de Kirkeby, Dean of Wymburn, Dorset the homage and service of Jordan Loky and an annual rent of 12*d*. he paid for a tenement in Wymburn, Dorset. At an unknown date, he quitclaimed to the Canons of Lilleshall all right of common which he had in their grange at Cherleton. SIR HENRY DE ERDINGTON died shortly before 26 March 1282. In Easter Term 1282 his widow, Maud, sued Walter de Eylesburi for a third of the manors of Roulton and Elwerthyn, Shropshire as her dower; Walter called to warranty Giles, son and heir of Henry de Erdington, who was within age, and in ward to the king. In Michaelmas term 1282 she sued Roger Pride for a third of the manor of Besford; Shropshire, Roger Sprencheheuse for a third of the manor of Wellington, Shropshire (excepting eight messuages and twenty acres of land), and Hugh Burnel for a third of the manor of Wellington (sic), and other tenants in Shropshire for a third of their holdings as her dower; the defendants called to warranty Giles the son and heir of Henry, who was in ward to the king; it was adjudged that the tenants should be quit of the dower claimed, and that Maud should be endowed out of lands of the heir in the custody of the king in Dorset. His widow, Maud, married (2nd) before Spring 1285–6 **WILLIAM DE BIFELD** (or **BYFIELD**), Knt., in right of his wife, of Olney, Buckinghamshire, Barrow on Soar, Leicestershire, and Great Tew, Oxfordshire. They had issue. SIR WILLIAM DE BIFIELD died shortly before 9 July 1302. His wife predeceased him.

Eyton *Antiqs. of Shropshire* 8 (1859): 137–145. Burke *Gen. Hist. of the Dormant, Abeyant, Forfeited & Extinct Peerages* (1866): 2–3 (sub Albini, Earls of Arundel). *Annual Rpt. of the Deputy Keeper* 44 (1883): 228. *Colls. Hist. Staffs.* 6(1) (1885): 121–126; 8 (1887): 7–9, 137–145. Grazebrook *Barons of Dudley* 1 (Colls. Hist. Staffs. 9(2)) (1888): 17–29. *Desc. Cat. Ancient Deeds* 1 (1890): 21–33. Rushen *Hist. & Antiqs. of Chipping Campden* (1899): 1–15. Wrottesley *Peds. from the Plea Rolls* (1905): 529, 531–532. *Cal. IPM* 2 (1906): 11–23. VCH *Northampton* 2 (1906): 121–125. *C.F.R.* 1 (1911): 176. VCH *Worcester* 3 (1913): 238–245. Le Strange *Le Strange Recs.* (1916): 159 (Somery ped.). *C.P.* 5 (1926): 85–86 (sub Erdington). VCH *Buckingham* 4 (1927): 429–439.

5. HENRY DE ERDINGTON, Knt., of Erdington (in Aston), Warwickshire, Olney, Buckinghamshire, Corfe Mullen, Dorset, Barrow-on-Soar, Leicestershire, Shawbury, Shropshire, etc., Knight of the Shire for Leicestershire, 1309, 2nd son, born about 1274 (of age in 1295, aged 24 in 1302). He was heir c.1292 to his older brother, Giles de Erdington. He married before June 1315 **JOAN DE WOLVEY**, daughter of Thomas de Wolvey, Knt., of Wolvey, Warwickshire, by Alice, daughter of James de Clinton. They had one son, Giles, Knt., and one daughter, _____ (wife of John de Grafton). He had livery of his father's lands 21 July 1295. He was summoned for military service from May 1297 to 28 July 1317. He had livery of his mother's lands 9 July 1302, on the death of his step-father, William de Bifield, Knt. In 1303 he disputed the right of the nuns of Catesby to the advowson of Yardley, Worcestershire. He was knighted by Edward, Prince of Wales [future King Edward II] at Westminster 22 May 1306. Sometime in the period, 1307–27, he conveyed 3 messuages, 2 mills, and land in Shawbury and Withyford, Shropshire to Robert de Staunton. He was summoned to Parliament 22 Jan. 1335/6, by writ directed *Henrico de Erdyngton'*, whereby he is held to have become Lord Erdington. HENRY DE ERDINGTON was living in 1341/2.

Eyton *Antiqs. of Shropshire* 8 (1859): 137–145. Wrottesley *Peds. from the Plea Rolls* (1905): 531–532. VCH *Worcester* 3 (1913): 238–245. *C.P.* 5 (1926): 85–86 (sub Erdington). VCH *Buckingham* 4 (1927): 429–439.

6. GILES DE ERDINGTON, Knt., of Erdington (in Aston), Warwickshire, Corfe Mullen, Dorset, Barrow-on-Soar, Branston, Houghton, and Knossington, Leicestershire, Shawbury, Shropshire, Withybrook, Warwickshire, etc., son and heir. He married **ELIZABETH DE TOLETHORPE**, daughter and co-heiress of William de Tolethorpe, of Tolethorpe (in Little Casterton), Rutland, by Alice, daughter of Ralph de Normanville, of Empingham, Rutland. They had three sons, Henry, John, and Thomas, Knt., and one daughter, Margaret. In 1343 he received a pardon for having acquired without license the manor of Shawbury, Shropshire from his father. In 1345 he was pardoned for not having taken up knighthood by the previous Feast of St. Lawrence, pursuant to the proclamation. He quitclaimed his right to the advowson of Yardley, Worcestershire in 1346. He was on the king's service in Flanders in 1346 in the retinue of John de Montgomery, Knt., but returned to England before 20 Jan. 1346/7, owing to severe illness. SIR GILES DE ERDINGTON was living 10 June 1359. His widow, Elizabeth, died 26 May 1375.

VCH *Worcester* 3 (1913): 238–245. *C.P.* 5 (1926): 86–87 (sub Erdington). VCH *Rutland* 2 (1935): 236–242.

7. MARGARET DE ERDINGTON, married **ROGER CORBET**, Knt., of Moreton Corbet, Habberley, Rowton, and Shawbury, Shropshire, Justice of the Peace for Shropshire, 1383–9, 1390–95, Knight of the Shire for Shropshire, 1383, 1391, 3rd son of Robert Corbet, Knt., of Moreton Corbet, Shropshire, by Elizabeth, daughter of Fulk le Strange, 1st Lord Strange of Blackmere, Seneschal of Aquitaine. They had two sons, Robert, Esq., and Roger, and two daughters, Joan and Eleanor. ROBERT CORBET, Esq., died shortly before 22 Sept. 1395. His widow, Margaret, died 14 Nov. 1395.

Burke *Gen. & Heraldic Hist. of the Extinct & Dormant Baronetcies* (1841): 131–132 (sub Corbet). Vincent *Vis. of Warwick 1619* (H.S.P. 12) (1877): 63 (Corbett ped.: "Geo. Corbett de Morton Corbett in Com. Salop miles. = Margt. Da. of Tho. Erdington"). *Trans. Shropshire Arch. & Natural Hist. Soc.* 4 (1881): 81–86 (Corbet ped.). Tresswell & Vincent *Vis. of Shropshire 1623, 1569 & 1584* 1 (H.S.P. 28) (1889): 132–144 (Corbet ped.: "Rogerus Corbet de Morton in com. Salopiæ miles ob. 18 Ric. 2. = Margareta fil. et hær. Erdington D'n's de Shawbery ob. 19 R. 2."). Corbet *Fam. of Corbet* 2 (1920): 209–261. *C.P.* 5 (1926): 88, footnote a (sub Erdington). *TG* 10 (1989): 35–72.

8. ROBERT CORBET, Esq., of Moreton Corbet, Shropshire, Justice of the Peace for Shropshire, 1410–1416, Knight of the Shire for Shropshire, 1413, 1419, Sheriff of Shropshire, 1419–20, son and heir, born at Moreton Corbet, Shropshire 8 Dec. 1383 (aged 12 in 1395/6). He married before 1410 **MARGARET** _____. They had two sons, Thomas and Roger, Knt., and three daughters, Juliane (or Anne) (wife of John Sandford, Knt., and Hugh Peshale, Knt.), Dorothy (wife of Philip Kynaston), and Mary. ROBERT CORBET, Esq., died 12 August 1420. His widow, Margaret, married (2nd) **WILLIAM MALLORY**, of Papworth, Cambridgeshire. She died 26 Jan. 1439.

Burke *Gen. & Heraldic Hist. of the Extinct & Dormant Baronetcies* (1841): 131–132 (sub Corbet). Vincent *Vis. of Warwick 1619* (H.S.P. 12) (1877): 63 (Corbett ped.: "Robt. Corbett de Morton Corbett. = Margt. Da. of Wm. Malorye miles."). *Trans. Shropshire Arch. & Natural Hist. Soc.* 4 (1881): 81–86 (Corbet ped.). Tresswell & Vincent *Vis. of Shropshire 1623, 1569 & 1584* 1 (H.S.P. 28) (1889): 132–144 (Corbet ped.: "Rob'tus Corbet obijt a⁰ 17 H. 6. = Margareta filia Will'i Mallory militis."). *C.P.R. 1396–1399* (1909): 219. Corbet *Fam. of Corbet* 2 (1920): 209–261.

Children of Robert Corbet, by Margaret Mallory:

i. **ROGER CORBET**, Knt.

ii. **MARY CORBET**, married **ROBERT CHARLTON** (or **CHARLETON**), Esq., of Apley (in Wellington), Shropshire [see ZOUCHE 16].

9. ROGER CORBET, Knt., of Moreton Corbet and Shawbury, Shropshire, Sheriff of Shropshire, 1453–4, 1459–60, 2nd but eldest surviving son and heir of Robert Corbet, Esq., of Moreton Corbet and Shawbury, Shropshire, by his wife, Margaret. He was born about 1415. He was heir in 1436 to his older brother, Thomas Corbet, Knt. He married before 1448 **ELIZABETH HOPTON**, daughter of Thomas Hopton, Knt., Knt., of Staunton-on-Arrow, Herefordshire, and Hopton, Burwarton, Eaton Constantine, Fitz, and Sandford, Shropshire, by Eleanor, daughter of Walter Lucy, Knt. [see LUCY 15 for her ancestry]. She was born about 1427 (aged 34 in 1461). They had two sons, Richard, Knt., and Robert, and four daughters, Anne (wife of John Sturry, Esq.), Mary, Jane (or Joan), and Elizabeth (wife of Richard Cholmondeley, Knt.). His wife, Elizabeth, was heiress in 1461 to her brother, Walter Hopton, Esq., by which she inherited the manors of Gaddesden (in Little Gaddesden), Hertfordshire, Hopton, Shropshire, Great Harborough,

Warwickshire, and a moiety share of Richard's Castle, Shropshire, Newington, Kent, Elerky, Cornwall, Cublington, Fowlers (in Stewkley), and Linslade, Buckinghamshire, and Woodham Mortimer, Essex, together with lands in Pailton (in Monks Kirby), Warwickshire. In 1462 he was pardoned for the forfeiture of £120 for which he was bound to the king. He was knighted in 1465 on the eve of the Coronation of Queen Elizabeth Wydeville. The same year he presented to the church of Prilleston, Norfolk, in right of his wife. SIR ROGER CORBET died 8 June 1467. His widow, Elizabeth, married (2nd) at Ludlow, Shropshire about Sept. 1467 (pardon for marrying without license dated 9 May 1468) (as his 3rd wife) **JOHN TIPTOFT**, K.G., 1st Earl of Worcester, 2nd Lord Tiptoft [see INGALDESTHORPE 11.i], Lord High Treasurer, 1452–5, 1462–3, 1470, Privy Councillor, 1453, Deputy of Ireland, 1456–7, Chief Justice of North Wales, 1461, Constable of the Tower of London, 1461, Constable of England, 1462–7, 1470, Lord Steward of the Household, 1463, Chancellor of Ireland, 1464, Lord Deputy of Ireland, 1467, Lieutenant of Ireland, 1470, Chamberlain of the Exchequer, 1470, son and heir of John Tiptoft, K.B., 1st Lord Tiptoft and Powis, by his 2nd wife, Joyce, daughter and co-heiress of Edward Cherleton, K.G., 5th Lord Cherleton, feudal lord of Powis [see see INGALDESTHORPE 11 for his ancestry]. They had one son, Edward [2nd Earl of Worcester, 3rd Lord Tiptoft]. He was beheaded on Tower Hill 18 October 1470, and was buried in the Church of the Black Friars by Ludgate. She married (3rd) before 7 Dec. 1471 (as his 2nd wife) **WILLIAM STANLEY**, K.G., of Holt, Bromfield, and Yale, Denbighshire, Ridley, Cheshire, etc., Chamberlain of the Household to King Henry VII, Chamberlain of Chester, Sheriff of Flintshire, Constable of Beaumaris, Caernafon, Flint and Rhuddlan Castles, Steward of Denbigh, younger son of Thomas Stanley, K.G., 1st Lord Stanley, by Joan, daughter and co-heiress of Robert Goushill, Knt. [see STANLEY 14 for his ancestry]. By an uncertain wife, he had one son, William, Knt., and two daughters, Joan (or Jane) (wife of John Warburton, Knt.) and Katherine (wife of Thomas Cocat). By an unidentified mistress, he also had an illegitimate son, Thomas (living in 1517). In 1471 he presented to the church of Prilleston, Norfolk, in right of his wife, Elizabeth. In 1489 Joan Ingaldesthorpe settled the manors of Wickham and Brewers, Kent on various feoffees, including John Fyneux, John Morton, Archbishop of Canterbury, and others; Fyneux was to hold the manors to the use of indenture between himself and the said Joan, according to which he was to pay £50 yearly to Joan for her life, less £16 13s. 4d. to Elizabeth, wife of William Stanley, as her dower; then to hold to the use of Joan's last will. SIR WILLIAM STANLEY was found guilty of treason for his support of Perkin Warbeck [see YORK 13.vi] and beheaded on Tower Hill 16 Feb. 1494/5, and was buried at Sion. His widow, Elizabeth, died 22 June 1498.

Morant *Hist. & Antiqs. of Essex* 1 (1768): 340–341. Bridges *Hist. & Antiqs. of Northamptonshire* 1 (1791): 493. Blomefield *Essay towards a Top. Hist. of Norfolk* 5 (1806): 322. Blore *Hist. & Antiqs. of Rutland* 1(2) (1811): 44 (Tybetot ped.). Brydges *Collins' Peerage of England* 3 (1812): 50–103 (sub Stanley, Earl of Derby). Clutterbuck *Hist. & Antiqs. of Hertford* 1 (1815): 393–395. Baker *Hist. & Antiqs. of Northampton* 1 (1822–30): 129–131. Ireland *New & Complete Hist. of Kent* 4 (1830): 27–29. Burke *Gen'l & Heraldic Dict. of the Peerages of England, Ireland & Scotland* (1831): 519–520 (sub Tibetot). Bentley *Excerpta Historica* (1833): 101–102. Baines *Hist. of Lancaster* 4 (1836): chart facing 10 (Stanley ped.). Beltz *Mems. of the Order of the Garter* (1841): clxiii, clxvii. Lipscomb *Hist. & Antiqs. of Buckingham* 1 (1847): 270–271; 3 (1847): 328–329, 464–466. *Letters & Papers… Henry VIII* 2(2) (1864): 1163–1164. Lennard & Vincent *Vis. of Warwick 1619* (H.S.P. 12) (1877): 63 (Corbett ped.: "Roger Corbett de Morton ob. 7 Ed. 4. = Elizab. Da. & hey. of Tho. Hopton."). Earwaker *East Cheshire* 2 (1880): 602–605 (Stanley ped.). *Trans. Shropshire Arch. & Natural Hist. Soc.* 4 (1881): 81–86 (Corbet ped.); 6 (1883): 255–256, 454–455 (discussion of Hopton and Corbet quarterings). Glover et al. *Vis. of Cheshire 1580, 1566, 1533 & 1591* (H.S.P. 18) (1882): 44 (Brereton ped.: "Sr Wm Stanley of the Holt brother to Tho. 1 Earle of Derby Decollats an'o 1494. = Elizabeth d. to…. Hopton widow to Jno Tiptoft Earle of Worcester."), 216 (Stanley ped.: "Sr Wm Stanley of Holt Chamberlaine to K. H. 7 decollats 1494. = Elizab. d. to Tho. Hopton sister & heire to Sr Walter Hopton widow to John Tiptoft Earle of Worcr."), 239–240 (Warburton ped.). *Arch. Cambrensis* 4th Ser. 14 (1883): 57–77; 6th Ser. 7(1) (1907): 1–34. Doyle *Official Baronage of England* 3 (1886): 718–720 (sub Worcester). Tresswell & Vincent *Vis. of Shropshire 1623, 1569 & 1584* 1 (H.S.P. 28) (1889): 132–144 (1623 Vis.) (Corbet ped.: "Rogerus Corbet miles ob. = Elizabetha filia et hæres Thomæ Hopton renupta Tiptoft Comiti Wigorniæ et 3o Wo Stanley"), 253–256 (Hopton ped.: "Elizabeth [Hopton] da. & sole heire [1] Sir Roger Corbett Knt. 1 husband, [2] ux….. Tiptofte Earle of Worcester 2d husband, [3] = Sir Wm Stanley Knt. Chamberlayne to Henry VII, 3 husband"); 2 (H.S.P. 29) (1889): 448–449 (Stury ped.). *List of Sheriffs for England & Wales* (PRO Lists and Indexes 9) (1898): 118. *Trans. Essex Arch. Soc.* n.s. 6 (1898): 28–59. *English Hist. Rev.* 14 (1899): 529–534. *Arch. Cambrensis* 6th Ser. 7 (1907): 18–19, 20–23. VCH *Hertford* 2 (1908): 211. *Misc. Gen. et Heraldica* 4th Ser. 3 (1910): 140. *C.P.* 4 (1916): 206 (sub Derby); 8 (1932): 262–263 (sub Lucy); 12(2) (1959): 842–846 (sub Worcester). Corbet *Fam. of Corbet* 2 (1920): 238–261. VCH *Buckingham* 3 (1925): 339 (Corbet arms: Or, a raven sable), 388, 422. Mitchell *John Tiptoft 1427–70* (1938). VCH *Warwick* 6 (1951): 100, 176. Paget *Baronage of England* (1957) 146: 4; 342: 5; 343: 5. Weiss *Humanism in England during the 15th Cent.* (1957). Myers *Household of Edward IV* (1959): 286. *TAG* 40 (1964): 95–99 [asserts Robert Corbet's wife, Margaret, was a daughter of William Malory]. *NEHGR* 124 (1970): 85–87. VCH *Cambridge* 8 (1982): 180. *National Lib. of Wales Jour.* 25 (1988): 387–398. *Welsh Hist. Rev.* 14 (1988–89): 1–22. Hicks *Who's Who in Late Medieval England* (1991): 320–321 (biog. of John Tiptoft: "… was 'the English nobleman of his age who came closest to the Italian prince of the renaissance.' A conventional chivalric unbringing enabled him to draft ordinances for jousts and umpire tournaments. Worcester was highly complex. [He possessed] a marked sense of humour and a talent for friendship. He cared little for English public opinion, yet wanted respect from humanists not for his rank but as a scholar. When Edward [IV] was deposed in 1470, Worcester was captured, and he alone was executed to great public rejoicing."). *Ricardian* 9 (1992): 206–210, 315–318; 10 (1994): 21–22. Roskell *House of Commons 1386–1421* 2 (1992): 653–654 (sub Robert Corbet); 3 (1992): 674, footnote 1 (sub William Mallory). Biancalana *Fee Tail & the Common Recovery in Medieval England* (2001): 420. Berkeley Castle Muniments: BCM/D/4/3/1 (William Stanley, Knt., King's Chamberlain styled "cousin" by William Berkeley, Earl Marshal and of Nottingham, in grant dated 1486).

Children of Roger Corbet, Knt., by Elizabeth Hopton:

i. **RICHARD CORBET**, Knt. [see next].

ii. **JANE** (or **JOAN**) **CORBET**, married (1st) **JOHN TWYNYHO**, of Cayford, Somerset [see MORE 10]; (2nd) **THOMAS CRESSETT**, Esq., of Upton Cressett, Shropshire [see MORE 10].

iii. **MARY CORBET**, married **THOMAS THORNES**, Esq., of Shelvock (in Ruyton-of-the-Eleven-Towns), Shropshire [see LITTLETON 10].

10. RICHARD CORBET, Knt., of Moreton Corbet and Shawbury, Shropshire, son and heir, born in 1451. He was knighted at the Battle of Tewkesbury in May 1471. He married before 1478 **ELIZABETH DEVEREUX**, daughter of Walter Devereux, K.G., Lord Ferrers of Chartley, by his 1st wife, Anne, daughter and heiress of William Ferrers, Knt., of Chartley, Staffordshire [see FERRERS 15 for her ancestry]. They had two sons, Robert, Knt., and George, and five daughters, Katherine (wife of Thomas Onslow), Margaret (wife of Richard Clyve), Mary (wife of Thomas Lacon, Knt.), Anne (wife of Thomas Cornwall, Knt.), and Elizabeth. In 1475 he went on an expedition to France with the king. In 1477 he received a general pardon for all offences. In 1485 he joined Henry Tudor at Shrewsbury and fought at the Battle of Bosworth. In 1488 he went to Brittany under Sir Robert Willoughby. In 1492 he served on a French expedition. SIR RICHARD CORBET died 6 Dec. 1493. His widow, Elizabeth, married (2nd) **THOMAS LEIGHTON**, Knt., of Wattlesborough, Shropshire, Sheriff of Shropshire, 1494–5. She died in 1516, and was buried in the church of Burford, Shropshire.

Clutterbuck *Hist. & Antiqs. of Hertford* 1 (1815): 393–395. Baker *Hist. & Antiqs. of Northampton* 1 (1822–30): 129–131. Lipscomb *Hist. & Antiqs. of Buckingham* 3 (1847): 464–466. Botfield *Stemmata Botevilliana* (1858): 169. Lennard & Vincent *Vis. of Warwick 1619* (H.S.P. 12) (1877): 63 (Corbett ped.: "Rich. Corbett de Morton miles. = Elizb. da. of Walt. Devereux Dom' de Ferrers de Chartley."), 278–280 (Devereux ped.: "Elizab. [Devereux] ux. Rici Corbet militis postea Thomæ Leighton militis."). *Trans. Shropshire Arch. & Natural Hist. Soc.* 4 (1881): 81–86 (Corbet ped.). Tresswell & Vincent *Vis. of Shropshire 1623, 1569 & 1584* 1 (H.S.P. 28) (1889): 132–144 (1623 Vis. Shropshire) (Corbet ped.: "Richardus Corbet de Morton Corbet in com. Salop miles ob. 8. H. 7. = Elizabetha filia Walteri D'ni Ferrers de Chartley renupta Tho. Leighton de Watlesburgh militi."). *Cal. IPM Henry VII* 1 (1898): 476. *List of Sheriffs for England & Wales* (PRO Lists and Indexes 9) (1898): 119. *Misc. Gen. et Heraldica* 4th Ser. 3 (1910): 140. Burke *Gen. & Heraldic Hist. of the Peerage & Baronetage* (1914): 1000–1002 (sub Hereford). Corbet *Fam. of Corbet* 2 (1920): 238–261. VCH *Buckingham* 3 (1925): 338–339. *Ricardian* 9 (1992): 206–210, 315–318.

Children of Richard Corbet, Knt., by Elizabeth Devereux:

i. **ROBERT CORBET**, Knt. [see next].

ii. **ELIZABETH CORBET**, married **THOMAS TRENTHAM**, Esq., of Shewsbury, Shropshire [see TRENTHAM 11].

11. ROBERT CORBET, Knt., of Moreton Corbet, Shropshire, Chelmscott (in Soulbury) and Cublington, Buckinghamshire, etc., Sheriff of Shropshire, 1506–7, son and heir, born about 1478 (aged 16 in 1494). He married **ELIZABETH VERNON**, daughter of Henry (or Harry) Vernon, Knt., of Haddon, Derbyshire, by Anne, daughter of John Talbot, K.G., 2nd Earl of Shrewsbury [see VERNON 17 for her ancestry]. They had three sons, Roger, Esq., Richard, and Reginald, and four daughters, Jane (wife of Thomas Lee), Joan (wife of Thomas Newport), Mary (wife of Thomas Powell), and Dorothy. He had order for livery of his inheritance 10 Dec. 1498. In 1500 an action was brought by his cousin, Sir Nicholas Vaux, against him for refusing to divide the manor of Cublington, Buckinghamshire. In the period, 1504–15, Richard Charleton sued Henry Vernon, Knt., in Chancery regarding a bond given on behalf of Richard Corbett, Knt., concerning the marriage of Robert, his son, with Elizabeth, defendant's daughter. SIR ROBERT CORBET died 11 April 1513. He left a will proved 16 Nov. 1513 (P.C.C. 27 Fetiplace). His widow, Elizabeth, died 29 March 1563. He and his wife were buried at Moreton Corbet, Shropshire.

Baker *Hist. & Antiqs. of Northampton* 1 (1822–30): 129–131. Burke *Hist. of the Commoners* 3 (1836): 190 ("she survived her husband fifty years, and was called "the old Lady Corbet, of Shawbury"). Lipscomb *Hist. & Antiqs. of Buckingham* 3 (1847): 464–466. Lennard & Vincent *Vis. of Warwick 1619* (H.S.P. 12) (1877): 63 (Corbett ped.: "Roge Corbett de Morton miles. = Elizb. da. of Hen. Vernon. de Hadon Miles."). *Trans. Shropshire Arch. & Natural Hist. Soc.* 4 (1881): 81–86 (Corbet ped.). Tresswell & Vincent *Vis. of Shropshire 1623, 1569 & 1584* 1 (H.S.P. 28) (1889): 132–144 (1623 Vis.) (Corbet ped.: "Robertus Corbet de Morton miles obijt ao 5 H. 8 [Sheriff 1501] = Elizabetha filia Henrici Vernon de Haddon in co. Derby militis ob. ao 1563"); 2 (H.S.P. 29) (1889): 469–474 (Vernon ped.: "Elizabetha [Vernon] vxor Roberti Corbet de Moreton in com. Salop."). *Jour. Derbyshire Arch. & Nat. Hist. Soc.* 18 (1896): 81–93. *Cal. IPM Henry VII* 1 (1898): 476. *List of Sheriffs for England & Wales* (PRO Lists and Indexes 9) (1898): 119. *Trans. Shropshire Arch. & Nat. Hist. Soc.* 3rd Ser. 8 (1908): 159–160. *Misc. Gen. et Heraldica* 4th Ser. 3 (1910): 140. *C.P.R. 1494–1509* (1916): 175. Corbet *Fam. of Corbet* 2 (1920): 238–261. VCH *Buckingham* 3 (1925): 338–339. *TG* 5 (1984): 164. Edwards *Derbyshire Wills Proved in the P.C.C. 1393–1574* (Derbyshire Rec. Soc. 26) (1998): 44–50. National Archives, C 1/294/74 (available at www.catalogue.nationalarchives.gov.uk/search.asp).

Child of Robert Corbet, Knt., by Elizabeth Vernon:

i. **DOROTHY CORBET**, married **RICHARD MAINWARING**, Knt., of Ightfield, Shropshire [see MAINWARING 10].

✢ CORBIN ✢

EUSTACHE I, Count of Boulogne, married **MATHILDE** (or **MAHAUT**) **OF LOUVAIN**.
EUSTACHE II, Count of Boulogne, by an unknown mistress, _____.
GEOFFREY OF BOULOGNE, of Carshalton, Surrey, married **BEATRICE DE MANDEVILLE**.
WILLIAM OF BOULOGNE, of Carshalton, Surrey, married _____.
ROHESE OF BOULOGNE, married **RICHARD DE LUCY**, Knt., of Chipping Ongar, Essex, Justiciar of England.
ALICE DE LUCY, married **ODINEL DE UMFREVILLE**, Knt., of Prudhoe, Northumberland.
ALICE DE UMFREVILLE, married **WILLIAM BERTRAM**, of Mitford, Northumberland.
ROGER BERTRAM, Knt., of Mitford, Northumberland, married **AGNES** _____.
ADA BERTRAM, married **SIMON DE VERE**, Knt., of Goxhill, Lincolnshire.
ISABEL DE VERE, married **WILLIAM DE ATON**, of West Ayton, Yorkshire.
GILBERT DE ATON, Knt., of West Ayton, Yorkshire, married _____.
WILLIAM DE ATON, Knt., married **ISABEL DE PERCY** (desc. King William the Conqueror).
ELIZABETH DE ATON, married **JOHN DE CONYERS**, Knt., of Sockburn, Durham.
ROBERT CONYERS, Esq., of Sockburn, Durham, married **ISABEL PERT** [see SURTEES 14].

15. ISABEL CONYERS, married **THOMAS CLERVAUX**, younger son of John Clervaux, of Croft, Yorkshire, by Isabel, daughter of Richard de Richmond. They had one son, Robert, and one daughter, Alice. Thomas and Isabel were legatees in the 1431 will of her father, Robert Conyers, Esq.

>Nichols *Hist. & Antiqs. of Leicester* 4(1) (1807): 174–175 (Clervaux and Faunt peds.). Surtees *Hist. & Antiqs. of Durham* 3 (1823): 247–248 (Conyers ped.). *Wills & Invs.* 1 (Surtees Soc. 2) (1835): 80–82 (will of Robert Conyers). Longstaffe *Hist & Antiq. Parish Darlington* (1854), tabular ped.; Div. VI, lix–lxxx. Glover & St. George *Vis. of Yorkshire 1584–5, 1612* (1875): 412–414 (Clervaux ped.: "Thomas [Clervaux], mar. Isabel, da. of *Thomas* Thoresby, but, as saith Glover, the dau. of Thos. Conyers, of Sockborne, o.s.p."). Flower *Vis. of Yorkshire 1563–4* (H.S.P. 16) (1881): 58–59 (Clervaux ped.: "Thomas Clervaux dyd mary Izabell doughter to Robert Conyers.").

16. ALICE CLERVAUX, daughter and heiress. She married **JOHN FAUNT** (or **FAUNTE**), Esq., of Wistow and Ramsey, Huntingdonshire, and of London, attorney, King's Serjeant, son of William Faunt, of Wistow, Huntingdonshire, by Joan, daughter of John Moulton, Knt. They had three sons, John, William, and Thomas. JOHN FAUNT, Esq., died at Wistow after 1499.

>Nichols *Hist. & Antiqs. of Leicester* 4(1) (1807): 174–175 (Clervaux and Faunt peds.). Longstaffe *Hist & Antiq. Parish Darlington* (1854), tabular ped.; Div. VI, lix–lxxx. Lennard & Vincent *Vis. of Leicester 1619* (H.S.P. 2) (1870): 28 (Faunt ped.: "John Faunt a Counceller of the Lawe ob. at Wistowe. = _____ Da. & hey of Tho. Claruaux.") (Faunt arms: Argent, a lion rampant between five cross crosslets fitchée gules). Glover & St. George *Vis. of Yorkshire 1584–5, 1612* (1875): 413. *C.P.R.* 1494–1509 (1916): 9, 643.

17. WILLIAM FAUNT, of Wistow, Huntingdonshire. He married **ISABEL SAYER**, daughter of John Sayer. They had three sons, John, William, and Anthony. He was a servant to Lord Poynings. WILLIAM FAUNT was buried at Wistow, Huntingdonshire.

>Nichols *Hist. & Antiqs. of Leicester* 4(1) (1807): 175 (Faunt ped.). Lennard & Vincent *Vis. of Leicester 1619* (H.S.P. 2) (1870): 28 (Faunt ped.: "William Faunt seruant to the Lo. Poyninges buried at Winstow. = _____ Da. of Scot.").

18. WILLIAM FAUNT, Esq., of Foston and Newton Burdett, Leicestershire, Justice of the Peace for Rutland, 1542–59, Justice of the Peace for Leicestershire, 1543–59, Burgess (M.P.) for Leicester, 1553, Knight of the Shire for Leicestershire, 1555, 2nd son, born about 1496. He married (1st) **ANNE FIELDING**, widow of Richard Cave, of Pickwell, Leicestershire, and daughter of William Fielding, of Newnham, Warwickshire. They had no issue. His name appears as attorney in land transactions in the late 1520s and early 1530s. He married (2nd) in 1546 **JANE VINCENT**, widow of Nicholas Purefoy, Esq., of Drayton, and daughter of George Vincent, Esq., of Peckleton, Leicestershire, by his 1st wife, Anne, daughter of William Slorey [see RANDOLPH 19 for her ancestry]. They had four sons, William, Anthony, Arthur (Jesuit priest), and Vincent, and four daughters, Dorothy (wife of Ralph Burton, Esq.), Frideswide (wife of John Hales and Roger Cotton), Alice (wife of Humphrey Purefoy and John Plumbe, Esq.), and Mary. He was appointed one of the executors of the 1556 will of George Giffard, Knt., of Middle Claydon, Buckinghamshire. WILLIAM FAUNT, Esq., was buried at Foston, Leicestershire 4 Sept. 1559. He left a will proved 10 Nov. 1559 (P.C.C. 53 Chaynay). His widow, Jane, died in 1585.

>Nichols *Hist. & Antiqs. of Leicestershire* 4(1) (1807): 169 (William Faunt: "a very respectable lawyer, of the Inner Temple"), 175 (Faunt ped.), 176 ("The whole manor of Foston about the latter end of the reign of king Henry VIII. came (by purchase) to William Faunt, of Wistow, esq.; an apprentice of the law, and fellow of the Inner Temple in London; a man of great learning, wisdom, and judgement, of great esteem and grace in his country, having been chosen twice knight of the shire for the parliament by voice of the shire; and in those busy, various, and uncertain times of the latter end of king Henry VIII. king Edward VI. and queen Mary, ever carried himself just and upright …"); 4(2) (1811): 870 (Moton and Vincent ped.). Oliver *Colls. towards Ill. the Biog. of the Scottish, English & Irish Members of the Soc. of Jesus* (1845): 89 (re. Laurence Arthur Faunt, a Jesuit priest). Lennard & Vincent *Vis. of Leicester 1619* (H.S.P. 2) (1870): 28 (Faunt ped.: "Will'm Faunt a man of Law of fosson in Com. Leic. ob. 1 Elizab. 1559 ætat. 63., [1] = Anne Da. of Sr Wm Feilding of Newn' in Com. Warw. sine p'le., [2] = Jane [Da.] of Geo. Vincent of Pecleton ob. 7. Elizab."), 50–51 (Vincent ped.: "Jane [Vincent] first mar. to Nicholas Purifoy after to Faunt of Foston."), 80–81 (Vincent ped.: "Jana [Vincent] nupta Nicho' Purifoy de Draiton et postea Will'mo Faunt de Foston in Com' Leic."). Mundy et al. *Vis. of Nottingham 1569 & 1614* (H.S.P. 4) (1871): 138–139 (Vincent ped.: "Jane [Vincent] 1 m. to Nicholas Pureffoy of Drayton 2 to Wm. Faunt of Foston"). *D.N.B.* 18 (1889): 247 (biog. of Arthur Faunt, in religion Laurence Arthur). *Acts of the Privy Council of England* n.s. 4 (1892): 371. Farnham *Quorndon Recs.* (1912): 189, 200. *NEHGR* 74 (1920): 271–272 (will of Sir George Giffard). *C.P.R. Elizabeth I* 1 (1939): 215. Bindoff *House of Commons*

1509–1558 2 (1982): 121–122 (biog. of William Faunt). Leicestershire, Leicester & Rutland Rec. Office: Docs. rel. to the Manor & Soke of Rothley, 44'28/315 (available at www.a2a.org.uk/search/index.asp).

19. MARY FAUNT, daughter by her father's 2nd marriage. She married **GEORGE CORBIN**, of Hallend and Polesworth, Warwickshire, son of Thomas Corbin, by his wife, Anne, daughter of William Repington. He was born at Hallend, Warwickshire about 1543 (of age in 1564). They had two sons, Henry and Thomas, Esq., and two daughters, Anne (wife of John Dawkins) and Jane (wife of James Prescott). In 1564 George's father, Thomas Corbin, made a settlement of a cottage and land at Polesworth, Warwickshire in favor of George. In 1568 he signed a deed relating to his cottage at Polesworth, Warwickshire. His wife, Mary, died in 1614. GEORGE CORBIN died 26 Sept. 1636, and was buried at King's Swinford, Staffordshire.

Nichols *Hist. & Antiqs. of Leicester* 4(1) (1807): 175 (Faunt ped.). Lennard & Vincent *Vis. of Leicester 1619* (H.S.P. 2) (1870): 28 (Faunt ped.: "Mary [Faunt] ux. Geo. Kerkin of Hallend in Warw.sh."). *VMHB* 28 (1920): 281–283, 370–373. Ligon *Madresfield Muniments* (1929): 50–59.

20. THOMAS CORBIN, Esq., of Hallend, Warwickshire, 2nd son, born 24 May 1594. He married about 25 August 1620 (date of settlement) **WINIFRED GROSVENOR**, daughter of Gawen Grosvenor, Esq., of Sutton Coldfield, Warwickshire, by Dorothy, daughter of George Pudsey, Esq., of Elsfield, Oxfordshire [see PUDSEY 17 for her ancestry]. She was born 29 April 1605. They had five sons, Thomas, George, Henry, Gawin, and Charles, and one daughter, Lettice (wife of Thomas Okeover). THOMAS CORBIN, Esq., died 1 July 1637. He left a will dated 5 June 1637, proved 1 June 1638 (P.C.C. 74 Lee). He was buried at King's Swinford, Staffordshire. His widow, Winifred, married (2nd) _____ **HOVELL** (or **HOWELL**), by whom she had a son, Richard. She married (3rd) before 13 Nov. 1653 **HENRY HURDMAN**. She was living 12 June 1688.

Herald & Genealogist 5 (1870): 427 (Winifred's birth date). King & Dugdale *Staffordshire Peds. Based on the Vis. of that County 1663–4 & 1680–1700* (H.S.P. 63) (1912): 58 (Corbin ped.: "Thomas Corbin of Corbins hall in p[arish] de K[ing]s. Swinford [*co. Stafford*] and Hall end born 24. Maij 1594 ob. Jun. 1637 sep. apd Swinford. = Winifrid d. of Gawen Grosvenor of Sutton Colefield [*co: Warwick*] gent married ao 1620."). *VMHB* 28 (1920): 281–283, 370–373; 29 (1921): 124–125, 243–251, 374–382, 520–526. Ligon *Madresfield Muniments* (1929): 50–59.

21. HENRY CORBIN, of London, draper, 3rd son, born about 1629 (aged 25 in 1654). He immigrated to Virginia in the ship *Charity* in 1654, where he settled at Middlesex County, Virginia. He married before 5 April 1658 **ALICE ELTONHEAD**, widow of Rowland Burnham (will proved 14 Jan. 1656/7), of York and Lancaster Counties, Virginia [see ELTONHEAD 21.v for issue of this marriage], and daughter of Richard Eltonhead, Gent., of Eltonhead (in Prescot), Lancashire, by Anne, daughter of Edward Sutton, Gent. [see ELTONHEAD 21 for her ancestry]. They had three sons, Henry, Thomas, and Gawin, and five daughters, Letitia (wife of Richard Lee, Esq.), Alice (wife of [Mr.] Philip Lightfoot [see ASKE 20.ii]), Winifred (wife of [Col.] Leroy Griffin), Ann (wife of [Col.] William Tayloe), and Frances (wife of [Col.] Edmund Jennings, Esq.) [see JENNINGS 23.i]. HENRY CORBIN died testate 8 Jan. 1675. His widow, Alice, married (3rd) before 22 April 1677 [**CAPT.**] **HENRY CREYKE** (or **CREEKE**) (will proved 6 October 1684), of Middlesex County, Virginia. They had no issue. She left a will dated 23 March 1684/5, proved in King and Queen County, Virginia.

Dugdale *Vis. of Lancaster 1664–5* 1 (Chetham Soc. 84) (1872): 103 (Eltonhead ped.: "Alice [Eltonhead], wife of… Durnham."). Hayden *Virginia Gens.* (1891): 221–290. King & Dugdale *Staffordshire Peds. Based on the Vis. of that County 1663–4 & 1680–1700* (H.S.P. 63) (1912): 58 (Corbin ped.: "Henry [Corbin]."). *VMHB* 28 (1920): 281–283, 370–373; 29 (1921): 374–382, 520–526. Ligon *Madresfield Muniments* (1929): 50–59. Lee *Abs. of Lancaster County, Virginia Wills 1653–1800* (1959): 30. Hopkins *Middlesex County, Virginia Wills & Invs. 1673–1812* (1989): 282. Sparacio & Sparacio *Virginia County Court Recs.: Deed & Will Abs. of Lancaster County, Virginia 1654–1661* (1991): 22–24, 78. Sparacio & Sparacio *Virginia County Court Recs.: Order Book Abs. of Middlesex County, Virginia 1680–1686* (1994): 76–77.

❧ CORNWALL ❧

WILLIAM THE CONQUEROR, King of England, married **MAUD OF FLANDERS**.
HENRY I, King of England, married **MAUD OF SCOTLAND**.
MAUD OF ENGLAND, married **GEOFFREY PLANTAGENET**, Count of Anjou, Duke of Normandy.
HENRY II, King of England, married **ELEANOR OF AQUITAINE**.
JOHN, King of England, married **ISABEL OF ANGOULEME** [see ENGLAND 5].

6. RICHARD OF ENGLAND, Knt., Earl of Cornwall, Count of Poitou, Lieutenant of Guienne, 1226–7, Keeper of Castle and Honour of Wallingford, 1230–1, Lord of the Manor, Castle, and Honour of Knaresborough, 1235, Lord of the Manor and Castle of Lideford, 1239, Commander-in-Chief of the Crusaders, 1240–1, Privy Councillor, 1253, Joint Guardian of England, 1253–4, 2nd son, born at Winchester Castle 5 Jan. 1209. He was knighted by his brother, King Henry III, 2 Feb. 1224/5. He was granted the honour of Launceston, Cornwall in 1225 and the honour of Berkhampstead, Hertfordshire in 1229. He fought for his brother in Brittany in 1230. He married (1st) at Fawley, Buckinghamshire 30 March 1231 **ISABEL MARSHAL**, widow of Gilbert de Clare, 4th Earl of Gloucester, 5th Earl of Hertford [see CLARE 6], and 2nd daughter of William Marshal, Knt., 4th Earl of Pembroke (or Striguil), hereditary Master Marshal, by Isabel, daughter of Richard Fitz Gilbert (nicknamed *Strongbow*), 2nd Earl of Pembroke (or Striguil) [see MARSHAL 3 for her ancestry]. She was born at Pembroke Castle 9 October 1200. They had four children (see below). He was granted the borough of Wilton, Wiltshire by his brother, King Henry III, on the occasion of his marriage. In 1232–3 he fought in Wales against Llywelyn ap Iorwerth. In 1237 he openly rebuked his brother the king for his greed and maladmininistration. He was on an embassy to Emperor Frederick in 1237. By March 1233 he had driven Llywelyn back and strongly fortified Radnor Castle. His wife, Isabel, died testate at Berkhampstead, Hertfordshire in childbed of jaundice 17 Jan. 1239/40. Her body was buried at Beaulieu Abbey, Hampshire, her bowels went to Missenden, and her heart was sent to Tewkesbury Abbey for burial in her 1st husband's grave. In 1240 he left for the Holy Land on crusade, in the company of a large number of English knights and nobles. In 1241 he negotiated a treaty with the sultan of Krak, by which many French captives were restored to liberty. He fought in Poitou in 1242–3. He married (2nd) at Westminster Abbey 23 Nov. 1243 (by contract dated 17 July 1242) **SANCHE (or SANCHIA, SENCHIA) OF PROVENCE**, 3rd daughter and co-heiress of Raymond Bérenger V, Count and Marquis of Provence, Count of Forcalquier, by Béatrice, daughter of Thomas (or Tommaso) I, Count of Savoy, Marquis in Italy. She was the sister of Eleanor of Provence, wife of his brother, King Henry III of England [see ENGLAND 6]. She was born about 1225 at Aix-en-Provence. They had two sons (see below). In Dec. 1243 the king demanded a written renunciation of any rights that Richard might possess in Ireland or Gascony, together with an explicit disclaimer of the award that had been made at Saintes. In return, Richard was confirmed in possession of Cornwall and of the honours of Wallingford and Eye. In 1244 he negotiated a treaty with Scotland and sat on the committee to investigate baronial grievances against the crown. The same year he was granted the honour of Bradninch, Devon. In 1245 he allowed his nephew the Welsh rebel, Dafydd ap Llywelyn, to take shelter at Tintagel Castle in Cornwall. In 1246, together with King Henry III, he sought unsuccessfully to oppose the efforts of Charles of Anjou, husband of Sanche's younger sister, Béatrice, to claim the entire dominion of Count Raymond Bérengar V of Provence. He served as principal governor of the royal mint between 1247 and 1258, during which period he organized the first complete recoinage since 1180. In 1247 he presented to the churches of Ambrosden, Horspath, and Brightwell. He was Joint Plenipotentiary to France and Ambassador to Pope Innocent IV in 1250. In 1252 he determined the amount of Simon de Montfort's expenses while lieutenant in Gascony. He served as Regent of England in 1253–4, 1264, and *de facto* 1270–2. He was elected King of the Romans (also styled King of Almain) 13 Jan. 1256/7, and was crowned at Aachen 17 May 1257. He failed to establish his authority in Germany, however, was soon dispossessed, and returned to England in Jan. 1259. In 1260 he mediated between the Earl of Gloucester and the Lord Edward and the king. In April 1261 he was elected senator of Rome for life, a purely honorary title which he made no attempt to exercise in person, and in which he was subsequently supplanted by Charles of Anjou. His wife, Sanche (or Sanchia), died at Berkhampstead, Hertfordshire 9 Nov. 1261. In 1263 he secured a temporary truce after war had broken out between his brother the king and the English barons. In 1264, when conflict became inevitable, he supported his brother. He was taken prisoner with his brother at the Battle of Lewes 14 May 1264. After the Battle of Evesham 4 August 1265, he was released and his lands restored. He married (3rd) at Kaiserslautern, Germany 16 June 1269 **BEATRICE DE FALKENBURG** (or **FAUQUEMONT**), daughter of Dietrich II de Falkenburg, seigneur of Montjoye, by Berta, daughter of Walram of Limburg, seigneur of Montjoye. They had no issue. By an unknown mistress (or mistresses), he had several illegitimate children, including three sons, Philip (clerk), Richard, Knt., and Walter, Knt., and one daughter, Joan. He presented to the church of St. Stithian's, Cornwall in 1268. In 1270 he purchased from Roger de Vautort the honour of Trematon, Cornwall, consisting of 60-½ knights' fees, including the Castle and manor of Trematon, Cornwall and the manor and advowson of Calstock, Cornwall. RICHARD, King of the Romans, Earl of Cornwall, died testate at Berkhampstead, Hertfordshire 2 (or 3) April 1272, and was buried with his 2nd wife, Sanche, at Hailes Abbey, Gloucestershire, his heart being interred in the choir of the Church of the Grey Friars, Oxford. His widow, Beatrice, died testate 17 October 1277, and was buried before the high altar at the Church of the Grey Friars, Oxford.

Sandford *Gen. Hist. of the Kings of England* (1677): 95–100. Morice *Mems. pour Servir de Preuves a l'Hist. de Bretagne* 1 (1742): 876 (letter of Richard, Count of Poitou & [Earl of] Cornwall). Rymer *Fœdera* 1 (1816): 484 ("Richard de Romeyns" styled "uncle" by King Edward I of England). Kennett *Parochial Antiqs. of Ambrosden, Burcester* 1 (1818): 297–299 (charters of Richard, Earl of Cornwall), 300, 327, 332–333, 353–354, 358, 409. Lysons & Lysons *Magna Britannia* 6 (1822): 306–326. Banks *Genealogical Hist. of Divers Fams of the Ancient Peerage of England* (1826): 315–321. Burke *Dict. of the Peerages… Extinct, Dormant & in Abeyance* (1831): 421–422. Gilbert *Parochial Hist. of Cornwall* 3 (1838): 448–449. *Coll. Top. et Gen.* 8 (1843): 120–122 (two charters of Richard, King of the Romans). Hawley *Royal Fam. of England* (1851): 19–20. Brewer *Monumenta Franciscana* 1 (Rolls Ser. 4) (1858): 292 (letter to S[anche], Countess of Cornwall). Wurstemberger *Peter der Zweite, Graf von Savoyen, Markgraf in Italien* 4 (1858): 86–87, 90. Oliver *Hist. of Exeter* (1861): 280–281 (charters of Richard, King of the Romans). Riley *Chrons. of the Mayors & Sheriffs of London* (1863): 140–141 (Richard, King of the Romans and Almain, Earl of Cornwall styled "dear cousin and friend" [karissimo consanguineo suo et amico] by Philippe III, King of France in 1271). Shirley *Royal & Other Hist. Letters Ill. of King Henry III* 2 (Rolls Ser. 27) (1866): 101–102 & 106–107 (letters of Richard, Earl of Cornwall), 132–133 (Richard, King of the Romans, styled "brother" [fratri] by King Henry III of England), 174–175, 193–194 & 197–198 (letters of Richard, King of the Romans). Teulet *Layettes du Trésor des Chartes* 2 (1866): 122–123. Luard *Annales Monastici* 4 (Rolls Ser. 36) (1869): 72 (Annals of Oseney sub A.D. 1231 — "Eodem anno venit Willelmus Marescallus de Britannia, et dedit sororem suam comitissam Gloucestriæ Ricardo comiti Cornubiæ, fratri regis, in conjugium"), 223–224 (Annals of Oseney sub A.D. 1269 — "Eodem anno et eodem tempore idem Ricardus rex Alemanniæ, quinto idus Junii [9 June], duxit in uxorem quandam nobilem puellam et decoram valde, nomine Beatricem de Falkestan, quæ propter ejus pulchritudinem vocabatur gemma mulierum"), 248 (Annals of Oseney sub A.D. 1272 — "Eodem anno quarto nonas Aprilis [2 April] apud castrum de Berkamestede obiit Ricardus rex Alemanniæ, et sepultus est in abbatia de Hailes, quam a fundamentis sumptibus suis construxerat."). Matthew of Paris *Matthæi Parisiensis, Monachi Sancti Albani, Historia Anglorum* 3 (Rolls Ser. 44) (1869): 280 (sub A.D. 1239: "Obiit Ysabella, Cornubiae comitissa, in partus discrimine."). Wright *Feudal Manuals of English Hist.* (1872). *Notes & Queries* 5th Ser. 2 (1874): 431; 5th Ser. 3 (1875): 209–211. Maclean *Hist. of Trigg Minor* 1 (1876): 189–190 (obit at Grey Friars, Bodmin, Cornwall: "Richardus Rex Almaniæ obiit 3 die Aprilis"). Stow *Survey of London* (1876): 134. *Arch. Jour.* 34 (1877): 180–186 (charter of Richard, Earl of Poitou and Cornwall dated 1256) ("He [Richard] was for a time heir to the throne, and always exercised great influence in the affairs of the kingdom … He was a far wiser man than his brother, who seems to have consulted him on many occasions, although they were often at variance. Wallingford … was his chief seat, where he lived with great splendour … The seal [on the charter] is imperfect, but what remains is well cut and clear … On the upper side … is a knight on horseback galloping to the proper left. He wears a loose plaited surcoat, girdled at the waist, and with the skirt freely flowing backwards, shewing the right leg from the knee in armour, apparently mail, with a prick-spur. The right arm, in mail, is extended backwards, and holds upright a long straight sword. Above the upper edge of the surcoat is seen the throat, closely fitted with mail, and on the head a flat-topped helmet. The left arm is covered with a heater shield, with conceals the breast and bears a lion rampant, with probably a border. The saddle is raised below and behind, and the two girths cross saltire fashion under the horse's belly. Over the knight's right shoulder is a narrow embossed belt, for sword or dagger. The horse is cut with great freedom, and does not appear to be in armour. The legend is: 'SIGIL[LUM RICARDI COMITIS CORNU]BIE.' Upon the obverse is large, bold heater shield, about two inches high, bearing a lion rampant within a plain border, charged with fourteen roundels. Round and behind the shield is scroll work of an early English character. The legend, in place of the usual cross, commences with a crescent 'SIG[ILLVM] RICARDI COMITIS [CORN]UBIE.' It is remarkable that Richard did not bear the arms of England, but those of Poictou. 'Argent, a lion rampant gules, crowned or,' which he placed within 'a border sable, bezantée,' derived from the old Earls of Cornwall, and thus, as was not unusual, represented both his earldoms on his shield."). *Table chronologique des Chartes et Diplômes imprimés concernant Belgique* 5 (1877): 385–386 (Baudouin d'Avesnes [seigneur of Beaumont] styled "cher cousin et vassal" by Richard, King of the Romans in 1267). *Genealogist* 3 (1879): 225–230. *Antiq.* 2 (1880): 273; 21 (1890): 232. *Recueil des Historiens des Gaules et de la France* 19 (1880): 231 (Ex Brevi Historia Comitum Provinciæ : "Idelfonsus autem Comes Provinciæ factus Gersendem neptem Comitis Folcalquerii in uxorem duxit, ex qua Berengarium-Raimundus ultimum Comitem Catalonum habuit, qui in uxorem habuit filiam ducis Sabaudi, in cujus Berengarii minibus Nicentini juramentum fidelitatum præstiterunt sub anno MCCXXIX, die nona mensis novembris. Et hic Berengarius fuit famosus pulchritudine quatuor filiarum suarem, videlicit ... Sanciæ tertio genitæ, quam Richardo, Cornubiæ Duci, et demum, deposito Federico, creato Imperatori, in matrimonium dedit ..."). Clark *Earls, Earldom, & Castle of Pembroke* (1880): 69–75. Clark *Land of Morgan* (1883): 64–92. Francisque-Michel *Rôles Gascons* 1 (1885): 158. Doyle *Official Baronage of England* 1 (1886): 436–437 (sub Cornwall). Hart & Lyons *Cartularium Monasterii de Rameseia 2* (Rolls Ser. 79) (1886): 330–331 (charter of Richard, Earl of Cornwall, to Ramsey Abbey). Clark *Survey of the Antiqs. of Oxford* 1 (1889): 366; 2 (1890): 295–297, 299, 303, 383–384, 407–408, 415, 417, 434. Hingeston-Randolph *Regs. of Walter Bronescombe & Peter Quivil* (1889): 178, 200 (charters of Richard, Earl of Cornwall and Poitou). Birch *Cat. Seals in the British Museum* 2 (1892): 338 (seal of Richard, Earl of Cornwall, Count of Poitou before 1257 — To the right. In armour: hauberk of mail, coif, flat-topped helmet with vizor down, sword, shield of arms slung by the strap round the neck. Horse galloping with ornamental breast-band, crossed girths, and embroidered saddle. For the arms see the reverse. Legend: SIG[ILLVM :] RICARDI : COMITIS : PICTAVIE :. Reverse. On a background of foliage forming a tree of three branches elegantly designed with fruit in clusters, a shield of arms: a lion rampant crowned, POITOU, within a bordure bezantée, ANCIENT DUCHY OF CORNWALL. Legend: SIGILLVM : RICARDI : COMITIS : CORNVBIE.), 338 (another seal of Earl Richard dated 1227 — Obverse. To the right. In armour: hauberk of mail, surcoat of arms, flat-topped helmet, sword, convex shield of arms. Horse galloping, caparisoned. Arms as in reverse. Legend: SIGILL'M RICARDI FI...... Reverse. A shield of arms: a lion rampant, crowned, within a bordure charged with nine roundels. The art of this seal is apparently French, and it is of poor workmanship. Legend: ....TAVIENSIS.). *Misc. Gen. et Heraldica* 2nd Ser. 5 (1894): 76–78. Petit *Hist. des Ducs de Bourgogne de la Race Capétienne* 5 (1894): 278 (Baudouin d'Avesnes styled "cher cousin" [dear cousin] by Richard, King of the Romans, in 1267). Giffard *Episc. Reg. Diocese of Worcester, Reg. of Bishop Godfrey Giffard* 2(2) (Worcester Hist. Soc. 15) (1899): 91. Wordsworth *Ceremonies & Processions of the Cathedral Church of Salisbury* (1901): 234 (Obit Kalendar: "1 April — Obitus comitis Cornubie."). *Procs. Suffolk Inst. of Arch. & Nat. Hist.* 11 (1903): 304–305. Browne *Corporation Chrons.* (1904): 95 (charter of Richard, Earl of Cornwall). Clark *English Reg. of Godstow Nunnery* 1 (1905): 264–265 (charters of Richard, King of the Romans), 281 (charter of Richard, Earl of Cornwall). *C.P.R.* 1232–1247 (1906): 408. *Desc. Cat. Ancient Deeds* 5 (1906): 49–61 (Deeds A. 10842, A. 10843). Auvray *Registres de Gregoire IX* 2 (1907): 977 (Roger, clerk, styled "nephew" [nepoti] of [Henry III] King of England and R[ichard], Earl of Cornwall in 1238); 3 (1908): 132 (papal dispensation dated 1239: "Rogero, clerico, nepoti regis Angliae et Riccardi, comitis Cornubiae, - cum quo olim ipse papa, intuitu devotionis quam praedictus comes Cornubiae, ejus patruus, ..."). *Rpt. on MSS in Various Colls.* 4 (Hist. MSS Com. 55) (1907): 68. Baddeley *Cotteswold Shrine* (1908): 66–67. *C.Ch.R.* 3 (1908): 489–491 (various charters of Richard, Earl of Cornwall). Reade *House of Cornewall* (1908). VCH *Buckingham* 2 (1908): 261–262. *D.N.B.* 16 (1909): 1051–1061 (biog. of Richard, Earl of Cornwall and King of the Romans) ("... Richard was the only Englishman who attempted to rule the holy Roman empire... He was at all times bountiful to the church." John, Bishop of Lübeck, a contemporary of Richard's, described him as "orthodox, prudent, strenuous, wealthy, well connected, energetic, and moderate."). *C.P.R.* 1258–1266 (1910): 495 (Richard, king of Almain, styled "king's brother"). VCH *Hertford* 3 (1912): 232–240. *C.P.R.* 1266–1272 (1913): 369 (Richard, king of the Romans, styled "king's brother" [germanus]). *C.P.* 3 (1913): 244, 430–432 (sub Cornwall); 5 (1926): 694–696 (sub Gloucester); 6 (1926): 503 (sub Hertford); 10 (1945): 364, footnote a. Wall *Handbook of the Maude Roll* (1919) unpaginated (ped. dated c.1461–85: "Ricardus rex Almanie"). Lambert *Bletchingley* 1 (1921): 59–63. VCH *Berkshire* 3 (1923): 484–492. VCH *Buckingham* 3 (1925): 45–54. *Rpt. on the MSS of Reginald Rawdon Hastings* 1 (Hist. MSS Comm. 78) (1928): 276–279. Moor *Knights of Edward I* 2 (H.S.P. 81) (1929): 238 (Richard, Earl of Cornwall: "...'a man of much more enterprise than his brother,' and accounted in his time the peace-maker of Europe.... One of the most interesting personages noted in the pages of English history."). *English Hist. Rev.* 52 (1937): 279–282; 115 (2000): 21–38. *Antiqs. Jour.* 18

(1938): 142–145 ("A Portrait of Beatrix of Falkenburg"). Leys *Sandford Cartulary* 1 (Oxfordshire Rec. Soc. 19) (1938): 156 (confirmation charter of Richard, Count of Poitou and Cornwall dated c.1233–4). Gibbs *Early Charters of the Cathedral Church of St. Paul* (Camden Soc. 3rd Ser. 58) (1939): 140–142. Lawrance *Heraldry from Military Monuments before 1350* (H.S.P. 98) (1946): 11. Denholm-Young *Richard of Cornwall* (1947). *Speculum* 23 (1948): 81–101. Hatton *Book of Seals* (1950): 306–307 (charter of Richard, King of the Romans dated 1262). Dunham *Casus Placitorum & Rpts. of Cases in the King's Courts 1272–1278* (Selden Soc. 69) (1952): 59–64 ("Henry, Count of Luxembourg [?]," styled uncle of Beatrice de Falkenburg). Williams *Collectanea* (Wiltshire Arch. & Natural Hist. Soc. Recs. Branch 12) (1956): 87, 113–114. Sanders *English Baronies* (1960): 9–10, 14, 20–21, 60, 62–64, 90–91, 93. Powicke *Handbook of British Chron.* (1961): 33. *Coat of Arms* 7 (1962): 18–24 (arms of Richard as Earl of Cornwall: Argent, a lion rampant gules crowned or within a bordure sable bezanty; arms of Richard as King of the Romans: The same, the shield suspended from the beak of a single-headed eagle), 93. Hull *Cartulary of St. Michael's Mount* (Devon & Cornwall Rec. Soc. n.s. 5) (1962): 32 (charter of Richard, King of the Romans dated 1265). VCH *Wiltshire* 6 (1962): 8–9. *NEHGR* 119 (1965): 94–102. Tremlett et al. *Rolls of Arms Henry III* (H.S.P. 113-4) (1967): 192–193 (Cornwall arms: Argent a lion rampant gules crowned or a bordure sable besanty or). *Chancery Miscellanea Vol. III* (List & Index Soc. 26) (1967): 167. *Ancient Deeds — Ser. B* 2 (List & Index Soc. 101) (1974): B.8659. Hockey *Beaulieu Cartulary* (Southampton Recs. Ser. 17) (1974): 202 (charter of Richard, Count of Poitou, Earl of Cornwall dated 1240-2; charter granted for the soul of his late wife, Isabel, Countess of Gloucester), 217–218. Paget *Lineage & Anc. of Prince Charles* 1 (1977): 15–16. Schwennicke *Europäische Stammtafeln* 6 (1978): 22 (sub Valkenburg). *Ancient Deeds — Ser. AS & WS* (List & Index Soc. 158) (1979): 5 (Deed A.S.22), 99 (Deed A.S.530). *Ancient Deeds — DD Ser.* (List & Index Soc. 200) (1983): 312. Hull *Cartulary of Launceston Priory* (Devon & Cornwall Rec. Soc. n.s. 30) (1987) 12. Rosser *Medieval Westminster 1200–1540* (1989): 25. Williamson *Kings & Queens of England* (1991): 66. Brand *Earliest English Law Rpts.* 1 (Selden Soc. 111) (1996): 21–27 (Henry, Count of Lutenburg', styled "uncle" [avunculi] by Beatrice de Falkenburg). Leese *Blood Royal* (1996): 61–65. Duggan *Queens & Queenship in Medieval Europe* (1997): 76–77. Tyerman *Who's Who in Early Medieval England 1066–1272* (2001): 324–329 (biog. of Richard, Earl of Cornwall: "His career exemplifies the ambition and reality of Angevin rule in the mid-thirteenth century. Politically, his contacts with the higher nobility and his proximity and influence over the king made him a ubiquitous arbiter of potentially damaging disputes between nobles and the crown. Richard was almost a sort of a vice-king … Richard had little consistent political philosophy … Some saw Richard as a trickster, a man who would do anything for the right price. Nonetheless, Richard's influence lent an element of cohesion to English politics. For a few years it seemed possible that it would be possible to persuade the pope to crown him emperor … although crowned king of the Romans (i.e., emperor designate) at Aachen in May 1257, he was never more than king of the Rhineland and even that was largely honorific, his four brief visits (1257–9, 1260, 1262–3, 1268–9) having more ceremonial than political significance."). Gee *Women, Art & Patronage from Henry III to Edward III: 1216–1377* (2002): 168–169.

Children of Richard of England, by Isabel Marshal:

i. **JOHN OF CORNWALL**, born at Great Marlow, Buckinghamshire 31 Jan. 1231/2, died there 22 Sept. 1232, buried at Reading Abbey, Berkshire. Sandford *Gen. Hist. of the Kings of England* (1677): 98. Banks *Genealogical Hist. of Divers Fams of the Ancient Peerage of England* (1826): 315–321. Hawley *Royal Fam. of England* (1851): 19–20. *Antiq.* 21 (1890): 232. *Misc. Gen. et Heraldica* 2nd Ser. 5 (1894): 76–78. Reade *House of Cornewall* (1908). *C.P.* 3 (1913): 432 (sub Cornwall). Leese *Blood Royal* (1996): 61–65.

ii. **ISABEL OF CORNWALL**, born at Great Marlow, Buckinghamshire about 9 Sept. 1233, died 6 October 1234, buried by the side of her brother, John, at Reading Abbey, Berkshire. Sandford *Gen. Hist. of the Kings of England* (1677): 99. Hawley *Royal Fam. of England* (1851): 19–20. *Antiq.* 21 (1890): 232. *Misc. Gen. et Heraldica* 2nd Ser. 5 (1894): 76–78. Reade *House of Cornewall* (1908). Leese *Blood Royal* (1996): 61–65.

iii. **HENRY OF CORNWALL**, Knt. (usually styled **HENRY OF ALMAIN**), Constable of Corfe Castle, 2nd but 1st surviving son, born at Haughley Castle, Suffolk 2 Nov. 1235. In 1247 and also in 1250 he accompanied his father on trips to France. He was knighted by his father at Aachen 18 May 1257. In 1260 he became a regular partisan of Simon de Montfort. In June 1263 he was arrested at Boulogne and imprisoned by Enguerrand de Fiennes. On 23 August 1263, he was again in England, and was sent to treat with Llywelyn of Wales. In Sept. 1263 he was again sent to France. On his return, he joined Prince Edward, under whose strong influence he remained the rest of the baronial war. He was taken prisoner with his father at the Battle of Lewes 14 May 1264. He was released 4 Sept. 1264, and was allowed under stringent conditions to go to France to treat with King Louis. He and his brother, Edmund, witnessed two charters of their father to Burnham Abbey, one dated 1266. He married at Windsor, Berkshire 15 May 1269 **CONSTANCE DE BÉARN**, Countess of Bigorre, Vicomtesse of Marsan, widow of Alfonso, Infante of Aragón (died before 25 March 1260), and 1st daughter and co-heiress of Gaston VII, Vicomte of Béarn, lord of Montcada and Castelvielh, by his 1st wife, Mathe (or Mata), Vicomtesse of Marsan, daughter of Bozon de Matha, Count of Bigorre, seigneur of Cognac. They had no issue. Between May and August 1269 he was engaged at Paris in the negotiation of terms with Louis IX for the Lord Edward's participation in the forthcoming crusade, and in August 1270 he sailed with Edward's crusading army. He went first to Gascony, where he left his wife, and thence proceeded to Aigues Mortes, where he joined his cousin, Prince Edward. They arrived at Tunis to find King Louis of France dead, and a peace made with the infidels. Early in 1271 he was sent north by Edward to accompany the funeral cortège of King Louis. Edward commissioned Henry to return to the west to settle the disorderly affairs of Gascony. Henry accompanied the kings of France and Spain in their journey through southern and central Italy. They arrived at Viterbo on 9 March. SIR HENRY OF ALMAIN was cruelly murdered while attending mass in the church of San Silvestro (now the Chiesa di Gesù) at Viterbo, Italy 13 March 1270/1, by his cousins, Simon and Guy de Montfort. His cold blooded murder excited universal horror. Henry's viscera were buried in the cathedral church of Viterbo 'between two popes.' His bones and heart were conveyed to England. His heart encased in a costly vase was deposited in Westminster Abbey, where it became an object of popular veneration. His bones were buried before the high altar at Hailes Abbey, Gloucestershire. In 1278–9 Robert de Wyston arraigned an assize of mort d'ancestor against his widow, Constance, touching a messuage and land in Wiston, Nottinghamshire. Constance married (3rd) Sept. 1279 (by contract dated at Paris 5 July 1279) (as his 2nd wife) **AIMON II**, Count of Geneva, and, in right of his 2nd wife, Vicomte de Marsan, son of Rodolph, Count of Geneva, by Marie, daughter of Albert III, seigneur of la Tour-du-Pin and Coligny. They had no issue. He died 18 Nov. 1280. He left a will dated 18 Nov. 1280. In 1280–1 Edmund, Earl of Cornwall, arraigned two assizes of mort d'ancestor against her touching land and rents in Stockwith, Misterton, and Walkeringham, Nottinghamshire. In October 1309 King Edward II of England granted her respite for two years for her debts due to him. Constance de Béarn, Viscountess of Marsan, died 25 April 1310. She left a will dated 6 April 1310. Marca *Hist. de Bearn* (1640). Sandford *Gen. Hist. of the Kings of England* (1677): 98. Rymer *Fœdera* 1(1) (1816): 481 (Gaston VII, vicomte de Béarn, styled "cousin"); 1(1) (1816): 478 & 2(2) (1816): 569, 656 (instances of Constance styled "cousin" by King Edward I of England); 2(1) (1818): 214. d'Avezac-Macaya *Essais Hist. sur la Bigorre* 1 (1823): 253–282. Banks *Genealogical Hist. of Divers Fams of the Ancient Peerage of England* (1826): 315–321. *Coll. Top. et Gen.* 8 (1843): 120–122. *Annual Rpt. of the Deputy Keeper* 7 (1846): 269; 45 (1885): 180; 46 (1886): 220 (Henry of Almain deceased styled "king's cousin" by King Edward I in 1276–7); 48 (1887): 209; 49 (1888): 6; 50 (1889): 215. Green *Letters of Royal & Ill. Ladies* (1846): 46–47 (Lady Constance [evidently Constance de Béarn, widow of Henry of Almain] styled "cousin" by Queen Eleanor of Castile in latter dated 1274/79), 47–50 (letter of Constance of Béarn dated c.1279). Hawley *Royal Fam. of England* (1851): 19–20. Capgrave *Liber de Illustribus Henricis* (1858): 151–155 (biog. of Henry, son of Richard, King of the Romans). Riley *Chrons. of the Mayors & Sheriffs of London* (1863): 140–141 (Sir Henry [of Almain] styled "cousin" by Philippe III, King of France, in 1271). *Régeste Genevois* (1866): 282 (Aimon II, Count of Geneva, styled "cousin" [cosyn] by King Edward I of England in 1279), 284–285 (will of Aimon II, Count of Geneva). Hardy *Syllabus (in English) of the Docs. Rel. England & Other Kingdoms* 1 (1869): 159. Luard *Annales Monastici* 4 (Rolls Ser. 36) (1869): 222–223 (Annals of Oseney sub A.D. 1269: "Eodem anno dominus Henricus, filius domini Ricardi regis Alemanniæ, desponsavit filiam Gasti de Bierne apud Windesowre in die Sancti Dunstani, patre suo in Alemannia moram faciente."). Wright *Feudal Manuals of English Hist.* (1872). *Notes & Queries* 5th Ser. 2 (1874): 431. Stubbs *Hist. Works of Gervase of Canterbury* 2 (Rolls Ser. 73) (1880): 206, 215–216, 219, 222, 224, 226, 229, 232, 238, 249. *Annual Rpt. of the Deputy Keeper* 44 (1883): 277 (Henry de Almain styled "nephew" [nepos] of William de Valence, Earl of Pembroke in acquittance dated 1275); 45 (1885): 179. Cristofori *Il conclave del MCCLXX in Viterbo: l'assassinio di Enrico di Cornovaglia da Gvido di Monforte* (1888): 53 (Henry of Almain styled "kinsman" [consanguineo] by Charles I, King of Sicily). *Antiq.* 21 (1890): 232. *Misc. Gen. et Heraldica* 2nd Ser. 5 (1894): 76–78. Delaville le Roulx *Cartulaire Général de l'Ordre des Hospitaliers de S. Jean de Jérusalem* 3 (1899): 392–394. *Desc. Cat. Ancient Deeds* 4 (1902): 34 (Sir Henry of Almain styled "kinsman" of Edward, son of King Henry III (afterwards King Edward I in letter patent dated 1265). Giffard *Reg. of Walter Giffard Archbishop of York* (Surtees Soc. 109) (1904): 79 (Sir Henry of Almain styled "kinsman" [consanguineo] by Prince Edward [afterwards King Edward I] in letter dated 1268). Bémont *Rôles Gascons* 3 (1906): 313, 427 & 476(Constance [de Béarn], Vicomtess of Marsan, styled "kinswoman of the king" [consanguinee regis] in 1295, 1304, and 1305). *C.Ch.R.* 2 (1906): 146 (Henry styled "king's nephew"). *C.C.R. 1234–1237* (1908): 340 (B[oson] de Mastak' [Matha], count of Bigorre, styled "kinsman" by King Henry III of England). *C.P.R. 1247–1258* (1908): 388 (Henry son of R[ichard] earl of Cornwall styled "king's nephew" in 1254). *D.N.B.* 9 (1908): 547–551 (biog. of Henry of Cornwall: "… Henry was a good soldier and a man of ability, though somewhat fickle and inconstant"). Reade *House of Cornewall* (1908). *C.P.R. 1258–1266* (1910): 460, 549, 638–639 (instances of Henry "son of the king of Almain" styled "king's nephew"). *C.P.R. 1266–1272* (1913): 323. *C.P.* 3 (1913): 432 (sub Cornwall). *Cal. Inqs. Misc.* 2 (1916): 385. Wall *Handbook of the Maude Roll* (1919) unpaginated (ped. dated c.1461–85: "Henricus de Almania"). *List of Diplomatic Docs., Scottish Docs. & Papal Bulls* (PRO Lists and Indexes 49) (1923): 8. Denholm-Young *Richard of Cornwall* (1947). Powicke *King Henry III & the Lord Edward* (1947). Ellis *Gaston de Béarn* (Univ. of Oxford D.Phil. thesis, 1952). Sanders *English Baronies* (1960): 147–148. *Coat of Arms* 7 (1962): 18–24 (arms of Henry: A lion rampant and a bordure bezanty; an eagle above the shield and another at each side). Chaplais *Diplomatic Docs.* 1 (1964): 304–305

(Constance [of Béarn], widow of Henry of Almain, styled "kinswoman" [consanguinee] by Queen Eleanor of Castile in letter dated 1272). Treharne & Sanders *Docs. of the Baronial Movement of Reform & Rebellion 1258–1267* (Oxford Medieval Texts) (1973): 194–195. Cuttino *Gascon Reg. A* 1 (1975): 173–182, 186–187; 2 (1975): 454–455, 553, 597–598, 604–605, 608–611 (Henry of Almain and Gaston VII, Vicomte of Béarn, both styled "kinsman" by King Edward I of England), 611–612 (Esquivat II [de Chabanais], Count of Bigorre, styled "kinsman" by Constance), 624–625 (Gaston VII, Vicomte of Béarn, styled "kinsman" by King Edward I of England), 716–717. Ellis *Cat. Seals in the P.R.O.* 1 (1978): 54 (seal of Richard, Earl of Cornwall dated 1260 — A shield of arms: a lion rampant wthin a bordure bezanty. Legend: +:S':SECRETI:COMITIS:RICARDI). Hunnisett & Post *Medieval Legal Recs. edited in Memory of C. A. F. Meekings* (1978). Schwennicke *Europäische Stammtafeln* 2 (1984): 70 (sub Aragon); 3(4) (1989): 642 (sub Montfort). Jodar-Galindo *Tableaux Géns. des Grands Feudataires* 1 (1985). Maddicott "Edward I and the Lessons of Baronial Reform: Local Government, 1258–60" (13th Cent. England 1) (1985): 3 ("The murder of Henry of Almain in church at Viterbo in March 1271 by Guy de Montfort and the young Simon, in revenge for their father's death at Evesham, had shown the depth and savagery of the conflicts engendered by the barons' war."). Rosser *Medieval Westminster 1200–1540* (1989): 25. Studd "The Marr. of Henry of Almain and Constance of Béarn" (13th Cent. England 3) (1990). Maddicott *Simon de Montfort* (1994). Foulds *Thurgarton Cartulary* (1994): cxxxiii. Leese *Blood Royal* (1996): 61–65. Howell *Eleanor of Provence* (1998): 229, 245–246. Crawford *'Templar of Tyre': Pt. III of the 'Deeds of the Cypriots'* (Crusade Texts in Translation 6) (2003): 46–47. *Oxford Dict. of National Biog.* (2004–2008) (biog. of Henry of Almain (1235–1271): doi:10.1093/ref:odnb/12958).

iv. **NICHOLAS OF CORNWALL**, born and died at Berkhampstead Jan. 1240, and was buried at Beaulieu Abbey, Hampshire. Sandford *Gen. Hist. of the Kings of England* (1677): 98. Banks *Genealogical Hist. of Divers Fams of the Ancient Peerage of England* (1826): 315–321. Hawley *Royal Fam. of England* (1851): 19–20. *Misc. Gen. et Heraldica* 2nd Ser. 5 (1894): 76–78. *Antiq.* 21 (1890): 232. Reade *House of Cornewall* (1908). Leese *Blood Royal* (1996): 61–65.

Children of Richard of England, by Sanche (or Sanchia) of Provence:

i. _____ **OF CORNWALL** (son), born July 1246, died 15 August 1246. Leese *Blood Royal* (1996): 61–65.

ii. **EDMUND OF CORNWALL** (usually styled **EDMUND OF ALMAIN**), Knt., Earl of Cornwall, of Wallingford, Berkshire, Launceston and Trematon, Cornwall, Bradninch, Devon, Berkhampstead, Hertfordshire, Clopton, Suffolk, etc., Joint and Sole Guardian of the Realm, Sheriff of Cornwall, 1288–1300, Sheriff of Rutland, 1288, Councillor to the Prince of Wales, born about 1 Jan. 1250. He and his brother, Henry, witnessed two charters of their father to Burnham Abbey, one dated 1266. He married at Ruislip, Middlesex 7 October 1272 **MARGARET DE CLARE**, daughter of Richard de Clare, Knt., Earl of Gloucester and Hertford, by his 2nd wife, Maud, daughter of John de Lacy, Knt., Earl of Lincoln [see CLARE 7 for her ancestry]. She was born in 1250. Her maritagium included the manor of Hambledon, Buckinghamshire. They had no issue. He presented to the churches of Lydford, Devon, 1272, 1285, Sancreed, Cornwall, 1275, Lanteglos by Camelford, Cornwall, 1276, St. Stephen's by Saltash, Cornwall, 1276, Ladock, Cornwall, 1279, 1281, Michaelstow, Cornwall, 1279, 1282, Manton, Rutland, 1280, 1296, Yardley Hastings, Northamptonshire, 1280, St. Stithian's, Cornwall, 1283, North Stoke, Oxfordshire, 1291, Beckley, Oxfordshire, 1291, 1299, and Hambledon, Buckinghamshire, 1295. In 1273 John le Bret and Sara his wife sold one messuage and four virgates of land in Chesterton, Oxfordshire to Earl Edmund for 44 marks. In 1274 William de Lisle sold the advowson of Great Chesterton, Oxfordshire to Earl Edmund for 80 marks. In 1275 William le Frankeleyn and Emma his wife sold one messuage in the suburb of Oxford to Earl Edmund for 100*s*. The same year John le Cupere and Alice his wife sold one messuage in the suburb of Oxford to Earl Edmund for 40*s*. In 1276 John Tumbur and Amice his wife sold one messuage in the suburb of Oxford to Earl Edmund for 16 marks. In 1278 commission was granted to Peter de Tregluthenou, coroner of Cornwall, and John de Treisgeu to take inquisition on which John Morsel put himself, who was lately indicted of receiving persons who broke the park of Edmund, Earl of Cornwall, at Lanteglos, Cornwall, hunted therein, and carried away deer. The same year commission was likewise granted to Oliver de Dinham and Walter de Wynburn touching the persons who entered the free chace of Edmund, Earl of Cornwall, of Dartmoor, Devon and his parks of Clymeslond, Liskaret, Restormel, and Lanteglos, Cornwall, hunted therein and carried away deer. In 1280-1 he arraigned three assizes of mort d'ancestor against his former sister-in-law, Constance de Béarn, touching land and rent in Stockwith, Misterton, and Walkeringham, Nottinghamshire. About 1282 he granted Rewley Abbey 60*s*. of rent paid to him by Thame Abbey on two knights' fees in Stoke Talmage, Oxfordshire. In 1283 he founded the first college for the order of Bonhommes at Ashridge, Buckinghamshire. In 1285 Robert d'Oilly and John le Mouner and Eve his wife sold a mill in Watlington, Oxfordshire to Earl Edmund for 8 marks. In 1285 Roger de Lisle quitclaimed various lands and rent in Little Chesterton, Oxfordshire to Earl Edmund for 40 marks. The marriage of Earl Edmund and his wife, Margaret, was dissolved in Feb. 1293/4; he granted her £800 a year in lands. In 1296 the Bishop of Lincoln suspended a chantry in Hambledon, Buckinghamshire which was newly built without license by Earl Edmund, because superstitious things were venerated, miracles said to be performed, and pilgrimages made there under color of devotion. The chapel doubtless contained the relics of St. Thomas de Cantelowe, who had bequeathed his heart to his friend, Earl Edmund. Later in the same year, however, the bishop withdrew the suspending order. In 1297 the earl obtained a license to alienate in mortmain to the rector and brethren of Ashridge a fee farm rent of £8 in Aldbury, Hertfordshire for the maintenance of a chaplain celebrating divine service daily in the chapel of Hambledon, Buckinghamshire. SIR EDMUND OF ALMAIN, Earl of Cornwall, died testate at Ashridge Abbey, Buckinghamshire on or before 25 Sept. 1300, on which date his cousin and heir, King Edward I, commanded celebration of exequies for the late earl. Earl Edmund was buried at Hailes Abbey, Gloucestershire. In 1302 his former wife, Margaret, successfully sued the Abbot of Thame in a plea of dower regarding the third part of 60s. of annual rent in Stoke Talmage, Oxfordshire. In 1303 she claimed the one third part of the manors of Ambrosden, Asthall, Chesterton, Holton, and Yarnton, Oxfordshire in dower. In 1311 she presented to the church of Bradninch, Devon. Margaret de Clare, Countess of Cornwall, died shortly before Nov. 1312. She left a will probated before 3 July 1315. One of executors of her will included her nephew, Master Richard de Clare, Rector of Dunmow, Essex. Sandford *Gen. Hist. of the Kings of England* (1677): 101. Kennett *Parochial Antiqs. of Ambrosden, Burcester* 1 (1818): 124, 392, 409–410, 423–424 (charter of Edmund, Earl of Cornwall, dated 1283), 427, 435–436, 438–440, 445, 448, 456, 462–465, 469, 472–473 (charter of Edmund, Earl of Cornwall dated 1298), 480, 485–487, 509. Dugdale *Monasticon Anglicanum* 2 (1819): 59–65; 6(2) (1830): 832 (reference of charter to Templars by Edmund, Earl of Cornwall). Banks *Genealogical Hist. of Divers Fams of the Ancient Peerage of England* (1826): 315–321. *Coll. Top. et Gen.* 8 (1843): 120–122, 122–124 (three charters of Edmund, Earl of Cornwall dated variously 1294, 1297, one undated). *Arch. Jour.* 5 (1848): 224; 18 (1861): 184. Hawley *Royal Fam. of England* (1851): 19–20. Forester *Chron. of Florence of Worcester* (1854): 350 (sub A.D. 1272: "Edmund of Almaine, earl of Cornwall, was married to Margaret, sister of Gilbert, earl of Gloucester, on the morrow of St. Faith [7th Oct.], and was knighted … on the feast of the Translation of St. Edward [13th Oct.]."). Green *Lives of the Princesses of England* 2 (1857): 298 (Edmund [of Almain], Earl of Cornwall, styled "cousin" by Eleanor of England, daughter of King Edward I, in letter dated 1286/1289). *Cat. MSS: Lib. of the Univ. of Cambridge* 4 (1861): 150 (charter of Edmund, Earl of Cornwall dated 1295). Oliver *Hist. of Exeter* (1861): 281–282. *Jour. British Arch. Assoc.* 26 (1870): 149–160. Wright *Feudal Manuals of English Hist.* (1872). *Notes & Queries* 5th Ser. 2 (1874): 431. *Annual Rpt. of the Deputy Keeper* 44 (1883): 63, 88, 94, 167, 192, 217, 272; 45 (1885): 131, 280, 341, 342; 46 (1886): 104, 127, 159, 192, 201, 207, 212, 230–231; 47 (1886): 186, 216; 49 (1888): 60; 50 (1889): 32, 76, 127, 215. Clark *Land of Morgan* (1883): 93–166. Doyle *Official Baronage of England* 1 (1886): 437 (sub Cornwall). *Procs. Suffolk Inst. of Arch.* 6 (1888): 131–135. Clark *Survey of the Antiqs. of Oxford* 1 (1889): 103 ("Edmund, Earl of Cornwall, a great lover of religious orders"), 366; 2 (1890): 168, 295–300, 303, 478, 484–485. Hingeston-Randolph *Regs. of Walter Bronescombe & Peter Quivil* (1889): 149, 151–152, 155–156, 170, 173, 178, 348, 349, 354, 355, 361–362 (charter of Edmund, Earl of Cornwall dated 1284), 394–395. *Antiq.* 21 (1890): 232. Brewer & Martin *Registrum Malmesburiense* 2 (Rolls Ser. 72) (1890): 387 (charter of Edmund, Earl of Cornwall, dated 1292). Luard *Flores Historiarum* 2 (Rolls Ser. 95) (1890): 363 (birth of Edmund of Cornwall). Birch *Cat. Seals in the British Museum* 2 (1892): 334 (seal of Edmund, Earl of Cornwall dated 1275 — Obverse. To the right. In armour: hauberk of mail, surcoat, sword, shield of arms slung by the strap over the shoulder. Horse galloping. Arms as on reverse. Legend wanting. Reverse. A shield of arms: a lion rampant crowned, within a bordure, charged with fourteen roundels. Fine Italian workmanship. Legend wanting.). *Notes & Gleanings* 5 (1892): 83 (charter of Edmund; seal of Edmund bears shield with a lion rampant). Stapeldon *Reg. of Walter de Stapeldon, Bishop of Exeter (A.D. 1307–1326)* (1892): 193, 278. Baddeley *Queen Joanna I. of Naples, Sicily & Jerusalem, Countess of Provence, Forcalquier & Piedmont* (1893): 299–325. *Misc. Gen. et Heraldica* 2nd Ser. 5 (1894): 76–78. C.P.R. 1292–1301 (1895): 63–65 (Boeghes de Clare styled "my brother" [mon frere] by Margaret, Countess of Cornwall), 311. Wigram *Cartulary of the Monastery of St. Frideswide at Oxford* (Oxford Hist. Soc. 31) (1896): 312 (charter of Edmund, Earl of Cornwall dated 1298). C.P.R. 1301–1307 (1898): 30, 50, 51, 60, 98, 130, 197, 224, 339. C.P.R. 1313–1317 (1898): 304, 459. *List of Sheriffs for England & Wales* (PRO Lists and Indexes 9) (1898): 21, 112. C.P.R. 1272–1281 (1901): 284, 292. Giffard *Episc. Reg. Diocese of Worcester, Reg. of Bishop Godfrey Giffard* 1 (Worcester Hist. Soc. 15) (1902): 51 (Edmund, Earl of Leicester, styled "kinsman" of Edmund of Almain, Earl of Cornwall, in letter dated 1272). *Papal Regs.: Letters* 4 (1902): 89. *Procs. Suffolk Inst. of Arch. & Nat. Hist.* 11 (1903): 304–305. *Year Books of Edward II* 2 (Selden Soc. 19) (1904): 75–76. C.Ch.R. 2 (1906): 183 (Edmund of Almain styled "king's nephew" in 1272), 383–386 (various charters of Edmund, Earl of Cornwall), 463 (Edmund, Earl of Cornwall, styled "king's kinsman" in 1293); 3 (1908): 489–491 (various charters of Edmund, Earl of Cornwall). *Rpt. on MSS in Various Colls.* 4 (Hist. MSS Com. 55) (1907): 72–73. Baddeley *Cotteswold Shrine* (1908): 66–67. Reade *House of Cornewall* (1908). VCH *Buckingham* 2 (1908): 261–262; 3 (1925): 47–48. Fox-Davies *Complete Guide to Heraldry* (1909): 524. C.P.R. 1266–1272 (1913): 668 (Edmund son of Richard, king of Almain, styled "nephew" to Queen Eleanor of Provence), 669 (Edmund de Allemania styled "king's nephew"). C.P. 3 (1913): 433 (sub Cornwall). Wall *Handbook of the Maude Roll* (1919) unpaginated (ped. dated c.1461–85: "Edmundus dux Cornubie"). Ehrlich *Procs. Against the Crown (1216–1377)* (Oxford Studies in Social & Legal Hist. 6) (1921): 261. VCH *Berkshire* 3 (1923): 484–492. VCH *Buckingham* 3 (1925): 45–54. *Cal. Chancery Warrants* (1927): 9, 25, 29 (instances of Edmund styled "king's cousin"). *Rpt. on the MSS of Reginald Rawdon Hastings* 1 (Hist. MSS Comm. 78) (1928): 276–277. Cam *Hundred & Hundred Rolls* (1930): 264, 276–277, 283. Salter *Boarstall Cartulary* (Oxford Hist. Soc. 1st Ser. 88) (1930): 253–254 (charter of Edmund, Earl of Cornwall dated 1280), 255 (charter of Edmund, Earl of Cornwall dated 1300). Salter *Feet of Fines for Oxfordshire 1195–1291* (Oxfordshire Rec. Soc. 12) (1930): 204, 206–207, 218, 220. Johnstone *Letters of Edward Prince of Wales 1304–1305* (1931): 17 [(Edmund), Earl of Cornwall, styled "cousin" by Edward, Prince of Wales (afterwards King Edward II)]. Jenkinson & Fermoy *Select Cases in the Exchequer of Pleas* (Selden Soc. 48) (1932): 113–118, 119–121. Midgley *Ministers' Accounts of the Earldom of Cornwall 1296–1297* 1 (Camden Soc. 3rd Ser. 66) (1942): vii–xxxiv. *English Hist. Rev.* 58 (1943): 51–78 (St. Edmundsbury Chronicle, 1296–1301: "Memorandum quod die sancti Remigii [1 Oct.] obiit pie memorie dominus Edmundus comes Cornubie."). Lawrance *Heraldry from Military Monuments before 1350* (H.S.P. 98) (1946): 11. Salter *Thame Cartulary* 1 (Oxfordshire Rec. Soc. 25) (1947): 33–38, 97–98 (charter of Edmund, Earl of Cornwall dated c.1282), 164–165 (charter of Margaret widow of Edmund, Earl of Cornwall dated 1302); 2 (Oxfordshire Rec. Soc. 26) (1948): 164–165. Sutton *Rolls & Reg. of Bishop Oliver Sutton, 1280–1299* 2 (Lincoln Rec. Soc. 43) (1950): 4, 137; 8 (Lincoln Rec. Soc. 76) (1986): 162, 173, 201. Williams *Collectanea* (Wiltshire Arch. & Natural Hist. Soc. Recs. Branch 12) (1956): 87, 113–114. VCH *Oxford* 5 (1957): 170. Sanders *English Baronies* (1960): 14, 20–21, 60, 90–91, 93. Bigwood *Les Livres des Comptes des Gallerani* 2 (1961): 216. *Coat of Arms* 7 (1962): 18–24 (arms of Edmund: Argent, a lion rampant gules crowned or within a bordure sable bezanty). VCH *Wiltshire* 6 (1962): 8–9. Stone *Oxfordshire Hundred Rolls of 1279* (Oxford Rec. Soc. 46) (1968): 29, 33–35, 37–38, 40. Phillips *Household Book of Queen Isabella of England, for the 5th Regnal Year* (1971): 139. Treharne & Sanders *Docs. of the Baronial Movement of Reform & Rebellion 1258–1267* (Oxford Medieval Texts) (1973): 194–195. Weinbaum *London Eyre of 1276* (London Rec. Soc.) (1976): 89–98, 101 (Edmund of Almain, Earl of Cornwall, styled "brother" [i.e., brother-in-law] by Thomas de Clare, Knt.). Ellis *Cat. Seals in the P.R.O.* 1 (1978): 22–23 (seal of Edmund of Almain, earl of Cornwall dated 1275 — Obverse. On horseback, riding to right. He wears chain mail, helmet and surcoat, and holds a drawn sword and a shield of his arms. Reverse. A shield of arms: a lion rampant within a bordure bezanty: held by its strap in the beak of an eagle behind. Legend lost.). Schwennicke *Europäische Stammtafeln* 3(1) (1984): 156 (sub Clare). *Rolls & Reg. of Bishop Oliver Sutton 1280–1299* 8 (Lincoln Rec. Soc. 76) (1986): 176, 201. Sayles *Functions of the Medieval Parl. of England* (1988): 135 (letter of Edmund of Almain dated 1272/74). Travers *Cal. Feet of Fines for Buckinghamshire 1259–1307* (Bucks. Rec. Soc. 25) (1989): 49. English *Yorkshire Hundred & Quo Warranto Rolls* (Yorkshire Arch. Soc. Recs. 151) (1996): 167–168, 210–211. Leese *Blood Royal* (1996): 61–65. Gee *Women, Art & Patronage from Henry III to Edward III: 1216–1377* (2002): 66 ("The earliest surviving example of such a vestment owned by a lay patron in England appears to be the Clare Chausable in the Victoria and Albert Museum. This has been cut but part of the missing embroidery was described in 1786 as being decorated with the shields of Clare, Cornwall, Lacy and England. This indicates that the chausable was made for Margaret de Clare, daughter of Richard, Earl of Gloucester and Hertford, and Maud de Lacy, who married Edmund, Earl of Cornwall, Edward I's 1st cousin, in 1272. The Clare Chausable is decorated with blue foliate scrolls framing griffins and lions in gold on a blue background."). Mitchell *Portraits of Medieval Women* (2003). Wild *If Stones Could Speak: Stories from the Stone Heads of St. Andrew's, Kirton-in-Lindsey* (2005): 104. Legg *Lost Cartulary of Bolton Priory* (Yorkshire Arch. Soc. Rec. Ser. 160) (2009): 222–223.

Illegitimate children of Richard of England, by an unknown mistress (or mistresses), _____:

i. **PHILIP DE CORNWALL**, clerk. On 20 March 1248 Pope Innocent IV granted an indult at the request of Philip of Savoy, Archbishop elect of Lyons, for Philip, son of the Earl of Cornwall, clerk, to hold an additional benefice with cure of souls. It is remotely possible that he is the Master Philip de Cornwall, late Archdeacon of Llandaff, canon of Glasney, Cornwall, who died shortly before 23 Jan. 1319/20, of whom little is known. Berger *Les Registres d'Innocent IV* 1 (1884): 570 ("Philippo clerico dilecti filii nobilis viri comitis Cornubie."). Hingeston-Randolph *Regs. of Walter Bronescombe & Peter Quivil* (1889): 418, 427. Stapledon *Reg. of Walter de Stapeldon, Bishop of Exeter, (A.D. 1307–1326)* (London, 1892): 124, 219. Peter *Hist. of Glasney Collegiate Church, Cornwall* (1903): 120. Reade *House of Cornewall* (1908): 31. NEHGR 119 (1965): 94–102.[12]

---

[12] NEHGR 119 (1965): 98 (author alleges in error that Philip, son of the Earl of Cornwall, is the same person as a much later individual, Master Philip de Saint Austell (otherwise le Cornwaleys), Archbishop's clerk, Archdeacon of Winchester. Master Philip first occurs in April 1285, when King Edward I gave him safe conduct, he then going to Rome. In 1292 the king granted him protection for two years, he then going beyond seas with John de Pontissara, Bishop of Winchester. In 1294 the king licensed him to assign one acre of land in "monte de Tremur" near St. Clether, Cornwall, together with the advowson and patronage of St. Clether, Cornwall, to maintain certain chaplains celebrating divine service. In May 1299 the king granted him protection until Easter, he then going beyond seas with John de Pontissara, Bishop of Winchester. In 1301 the king granted him authority to convey one messuage and 30

ii. **RICHARD DE CORNWALL**, Knt. [see next].

iii. **WALTER DE CORNWALL**, Knt., of Brannel, Cornwall, married _____ [see HUNGERFORD 7].

iv. **JOAN DE CORNWALL**. She married (1st) **RICHARD DE CHAMPERNOUN**, of Inswork, Cornwall, younger son of Henry de Champernoun, Knt., of Ilfracombe, Devon and Jacobstowe, Trevelowen, and Tywardraith, Cornwall, by Denise, daughter of Gilbert English. They had one son, Richard, Knt. In 1280–1 Andrew Trellok arraigned an assize of novel disseisin against Richard and his wife, Joan, regarding a tenement in Meyswerk, Cornwall. In 1281–2 her half-brother, Edmund, Earl of Cornwall allegedly referred to Joan, wife of Richard de Champernoun, as his "sister." In 1286 he terminated a plea brought by him in City Court against Master Henry de Bollegh, Archdeacon of Cornwall. His widow, Joan, married (2nd) before 1300 **PETER DE FISSACRE** (or **FISHACRE**), Knt., of Morleigh and Woodleigh, Devon, Seneschal of Dartmouth, and, in right of his wife, of Inswork, Cornwall, son of Peter de Fissacre, by his wife, Beatrice. They had no issue. He presented to the churches of Moreleigh, Devon, 1280, and Stoke Rivers, Devon, 1282, 1285. He served as attorney for Oliver de Dinham in 1297, and for Josce de Dinham in 1301. He was summoned to serve overseas in 1297. SIR PETER DE FISSACRE living in 1303. In 1316 his wife, Joan, put in a claim regarding a fine relating to Modbury, Devon. Pole *Colls. towards a Desc. of Devon* (1791): 309 ([Joan, wife of Richard Champernoun] … whom Edmond Erle of Cornwall calleth by the name of his sister, in a grant made by hym unto the said Richard and Jone, of theassise of breade & ale, dated anno 12 of Kinge Edw. I."). Lysons *Magna Britannia* 6 (1822): 342. Burke *Hist. of the Commoners* 2 (1836): 271–273 (sub Champernowne). Gilbert *Parochial Hist. of Cornwall* 3 (1838): 448–449. *Notes & Queries* 5th Ser. 2 (1874): 431 ("But a pedigree given in Harl. MS. 3288, fol. 50, states that 'Joan, daughter of Edmund, Earl of Cornwall' — query if not Richard rather ? — married Ralph Valletorte, and her daughter Joan married Richard Champernoun."); 5th Ser. 3 (1875): 209–211. *Annual Rpt. of the Deputy Keeper* 50 (1889): 155. Hingeston-Randolph *Regs. of Walter Bronescombe & Peter Quivil* (1889): 157, 356. Jackson *Wadham College Oxford* (1893): 25 (Tregarthen ped.). *MSS of the Duke of Somerset, the Marquis of Ailesbury & the Rev. Sir T.H.G. Puleston, Bart.* (Hist. MSS Comm. 43) (1898): 136. *Jour. of the Royal Institution of Cornwall* 17 (1907): 409–424. *C.Ch.R.* 3 (1908): 36. Woodbine *Bracton De legibus et consuetudinibus Angliæ* 1 (1915): 86, footnote 1. Chope *Early Tours in Devon & Cornwall* (Devon & Cornwall Notes & Queries 9) (1918): 58. *Genealogists' Mag.* 7 (1937): 536–537 (re. Fissacre family). *NEHGR* 119 (1965): 94–102.

7. RICHARD DE CORNWALL (or **CORNWAILLE**, **CORNEWEYLE**), Knt., of Asthall and Asthall Leigh, Oxfordshire, Thonock, Lincolnshire, and Cornwalls (in Iver), Buckinghamshire, Steward of Knaresborough, illegitimate son. He married before 1280 **JOAN** _____, allegedly daughter of John Fitz Alan, Knt. (died 1267), of Oswestry, Clun, and Acton Round, Shropshire, Boarhunt, Hampshire, Keevil, Wiltshire, etc., by Maud, daughter of Thebaud le Boteler, 2nd Lord Boteler [see FITZ ALAN 7 for her possible ancestry]. They had three sons, Edmund, Knt., Geoffrey, Knt., and Richard (king's clerk), and one daughter, Joan. Sometime in the period, 1270–90, William son of William Gayland, of Asthall, Oxfordshire, granted Richard and his wife, Joan, a tenement in Asthall and Asthall Leigh, Oxfordshire. In 1276–7 William le Heyr arraigned an assize of novel disseisin against him and others touching a tenement in Asthall and Aston, Oxfordshire. He performed military service for his brother, Edmund, Earl of Cornwall, in 1277. The same year he and his brother, Edmund, witnessed a charter of John de Saint John to Nutus Fulberti of Florence. In 1277–8 Thomas de Asthall arraigned an assize of novel disseisin against him and John

---

acres of land in Menkudel for the maintenance of three chaplains to celebrate divince services daily for the good of his soul in the chapel of St. Michael in the town of Saint Austell, Cornwall. In 1303 he was granted protection by the king for one year, he then going beyond seas with John de Pontissara, Bishop of Winchester. He died shortly before 10 June 1304. In Feb. 1305 the king pardoned Reynold son of Richard de Penres for acquiring in fee simple 3s. 7-3/4d. rent in Landewynnek and the advowson of the church of St. Cross, Kerrier, Cornwall from Master Philip de Saint Austell, sometime Archdeacon of Winchester, who held them in chief. *C.P.R. 1281–1292* (1893): 157. *C.P.R. 1292–1301* (1895): 92, 179, 415, 600. Hammond *A Cornish Parish: Being an Account of St. Austell, Town, Church, District & People* (1897): 15–17, 110. *C.P.R. 1301–1307* (1898): 127, 314. VCH *Hampshire* 4 (1911): 337–344. Pontissara *Reg. Johannis de Pontissara* 1 (Surrey Rec. Soc. 1) (1913): 29 (J. de Saint Austell, clerk, styled nephew/kinsman [nepos] of Philip de Saint Austell, Archdeacon of Winchester, in 1287). Jones *Fasti Ecclesiae Anglicanae 1300–1541* 4 (1963): 50–51. Horn *Fasti Ecclesiae Anglicanae 1300–1541* 12 (1967): 58–61. Greenway *Fasti Ecclesiae Anglicanae 1066-1300* 2 (1971): 92–93).

de Asthall touching a tenement in Asthall, Oxfordshire. In 1277–8 he arraigned an assize of novel disseisin against Walter de Esthall touching a tenement in Asthall, Oxfordshire. He witnessed various charters for his brother, Edmund, Earl of Cornwall, in the period, 1278–95, including one to Rewley Abbey, Oxfordshire dated c.1282 and one to the Master and brothers of the Holy Trinity dated 1293. In 1280 he was granted the manor of Thonock, Lincolnshire by his brother, Edmund, Earl of Cornwall. The same year he was granted letters of protections, he then going beyond seas. In 1286 he came into Chancery and stated that he had lost his seal through the cutting of his purse. In 1290 John de Sapy and Pernel his wife conveyed a messuage and a moiety of a carucate of land in Asthall, Asthall Leigh, and Aston, Oxfordshire to Richard and his wife, Joan. He witnessed an undated charter of his brother, Edmund, Earl of Cornwall, to Burnham Abbey, Buckinghamshire. SIR RICHARD DE CORNWALL was killed by an arrow at the siege of Berwick in 1296. He left a will proved 17 April 1297. In 1303 his widow, Joan, arraigned an assize of novel disseisin against her son, Edmund, and others concerning a tenement in Thonock, Lincolnshire. She was living 10 October 1321, when she gave five messuages, four crofts of land, two virgates of arable land, and 10s. rent in Asthall and Asthall Leigh, Oxfordshire to John, master, and brethren of the Hospital of St. John Evangelist to find one priest to celebrate daily in the church of Asthall for souls of Richard de Cornwall, herself, and their children. At her death, she was buried in a chantry chapel in the church of Asthall, Oxfordshire.

Sandford *Gen. Hist. of the Kings of England* (1677): 99. Kennett *Parochial Antiqs. of Ambrosden, Burcester* 1 (1818): 456 (Sir Richard de Cornwall styled "brother" [fratre] by Edmund, Earl of Cornwall, in charter dated 1293), 486–487 (erroneously identifies Sir Richard de Cornwall as illegitimate son of Edmund, Earl of Cornwall). Banks *Genealogical Hist. of Divers Fams of the Ancient Peerage of England* (1826): 315–321. Gilbert *Parochial Hist. of Cornwall* 3 (1838): 448–449. *Coll. Top. et Gen.* 8 (1843): 124–125. Cole *Docs. illus. of English Hist. in the 13th & 14th Cents.* (1844): 198–199. Hawley *Royal Fam. of England* (1851): 19–20 (erroneously identifies Richard of Cornwall, died 1297, as a legitimate son of Richard, Earl of Cornwall). Luard *Annales Monastici* 3 (Rolls Ser. 36) (1866): 403 (Annals of Dunstable sub A.D. 1296: "De gente vero domini regis nullus nobilis, nullus magni valoris, ibi, ut dicitur, fuerat interfectus, nisi solum dominus Ricardus, germanus Edmundi comitis Cornubyæ, qui cum quarello perculsus, cerebro violato."); 4 (Rolls Ser. 36) (1869): 526 (Annals of Worcester sub A.D. 1296: "Penultimo die Martii rex civitatem Berewyk vi et armis superatam ante vesperam expugnavit; et iratus exercitus pro morte Ricardi fratris comitis de Cornubia et pro quibusdam nautis interfectis, multos de civibus trucidavit."). *Notes & Queries* 5th Ser. 2 (1874): 431; 5th Ser. 3 (1875): 29–30, 209–211. *Genealogist* 3 (1879): 225–230. *Annual Rpt. of the Deputy Keeper* 46 (1886): 86; 47 (1886): 146–147. Tresswell & Vincent *Vis. of Shropshire 1623, 1569 & 1584* 1 (H.S.P. 28) (1889): 145–148 (1623 Vis.) (Cornwall ped.: "Rich. de Cornewall 2 sonne to Rich. E. of Cornewall = Joane da. to Jo. Fitz Allen [Fitz Alan] Lo. of Clunn."). *Antiq.* 21 (1890): 232 (erroneously identifies Richard de Cornwall as a legitimate son of Richard, Earl of Cornwall, King of the Romans). Jackson *Wadham College Oxford* (1893): 25 (Tregarthen ped.). *Misc. Gen. et Heraldica* 2nd Ser. 5 (1894): 76–78 (chart identifies Joan, wife of Richard de Cornwall, as "Joan, da. of Lord St. Owen"). *C.P.R. 1301–1307* (1898): 197. *C.P.R. 1313–1317* (1898): 475. *Desc. Cat. Ancient Deeds* 3 (1900): 540. *C.P.R. 1272–1281* (1901): 211. *C.C.R. 1279–1288* (1902): 178. *C.P.R. 1317–1321* (1903): 495. *Genealogical Mag.* 6 (1903): 525–532. *C.C.R. 1296–1302* (1906): 491, 542. *C.Ch.R.* 2 (1906): 331–332, 443 (Sir Richard of Cornwall styled "brother of the earl"), 443 (Richard de Cornwall styled "the earl's brother"); 3 (1908): 208, 489–491 (Sir Richard de Cornubia [Richard of Cornwall] styled "the donor's brother" [that is, brother of Edmund, Earl of Cornwall]). VCH *Oxford* 2 (1907): 154. Reade *House of Cornwall* (1908): 25–53. *Cal. Various Chancery Rolls 1277–1326* (1912): 72. *Cal. IPM* 3 (1912): 482–483, 487–488; 7 (1909): 505. *C.P.* 3 (1913): 431, footnote g (sub Cornwall). Gretton *Burford Recs.* (1920): 587–588. VCH *Buckingham* 3 (1925): 288–289. Salter *Feet of Fines for Oxfordshire 1195–1291* (Oxfordshire Rec. Soc. 12) (1930): 226–227. Price *Two Effigies in the Churches of Asthall & Cogges in Oxfordshire* (1938): 103–110. Reichel *Devon Feet of Fines* 2 (Devon & Cornwall Rec. Soc.) (1939): 231–232. Midgley *Ministers' Accounts of the Earldom of Cornwall 1296–1297* 1 (Camden Soc. 3rd Ser. 66) (1942): xx, xxxiii; 2 (Camden Soc. 3rd Ser. 68) (1945): 201. Denholm-Young *Richard of Cornwall* (1947): 165, 168. Salter *Thame Cartulary* 1 (Oxfordshire Rec. Soc. 25) (1947): 97–98. Lamborn *Armorial Glass of the Oxford Diocese* (1949): 104. *NEHGR* 119 (1965): 94–102. *Rolls & Reg. of Bishop Oliver Sutton 1280–1299* 5 (Lincoln Rec. Soc. 60) (1965): 215. Stone *Oxfordshire Hundred Rolls of 1279* (Oxfordshire Rec. Soc. 46) (1968): 38–40. *Oxoniensia* 62 (1997): 241–242. Leese *Blood Royal* (1996): 61–65. Brault *Rolls of Arms Edward I* 2 (1997): 121 (arms of Richard de Cornwall — HE 315, A 184, E 534, F 254, Q 266: Argent, on a fess sable three roundels or; LM 376: Argent, on a fess sable three roundels argent). Gee *Women, Art & Patronage from Henry III to Edward III: 1216–1377* (2002): 158–159 (identifies Joan, wife of Richard de Cornwall, as the daughter of John Fitz Alan, of Clun and Oswestry, by Isabel, daughter of Roger de Mortimer,

Knt.). Burghersh *Regs. of Bishop Henry Burghersh* 2 (Lincoln Rec. Soc. 90) (2003): 78. Weiler *Thirteenth Cent. England XI* (2007): 186.

Children of Richard de Cornwall, Knt., by Joan _____:

i. **EDMUND DE CORNWALL**, Knt., King's yeoman, of Asthall, Oxfordshire, Thonock, Lincolnshire, etc., and, in right of his wife, of Kinlet, Shropshire, Over Hall (in Hampton Lovett), Worcestershire, etc., King's yeoman. He married before 7 Dec. 1309 **ELIZABETH DE BROMPTON**, daughter and co-heiress of Brian de Brompton, of Kinlet, Shropshire. She was born 16 Dec. 1294. They had three sons, Edmund, Knt., Brian, Knt., and Peter. In 1300 he was empowered to levy scutage on the tenants of the lands of Brian de Brompton deceased for several armies of Scotland. In 1301 he sought to replevy his land in Asthall, Oxfordshire, which was taken into the king's hands for his default before the justices of the Bench against Margaret, late the wife of Edmund, Earl of Cornwall; he also sought to replevy to his mother, Joan, her land in Asthall, which was also taken into the king's hands for the same reason. The same year he was granted free warren in Asthall, Oxfordshire and Thonock, Lincolnshire. In 1303 his mother, Joan, arraigned an assize of novel disseisin against him concerning a tenement in Thonock, Lincolnshire. The same year the Abbot of Hailes arraigned an assize of novel disseisin against him concering a tenement in Asthall, Oxfordshire. In 1305 he was granted view of frankpledge in his manor of Thonock, Lincolnshire. In 1308 he and his brother, Geoffrey, owed a debt of £270 to John Knockin. In 1309 his wife, Elizabeth. did homage to the king for her purparty of her father's lands. He owed money to Cambinus Fulberti of Florence in 1316. SIR EDMUND OF CORNWALL died 28 Feb. (or 22 March) 1354. His widow, Elizabeth, quitclaimed her rights to the manor of Hampton Lovet, Worcestershire to her son, Peter, on 7 Dec. 1354. She was living 18 May 1355. Eyton *Antiqs. of Shropshire* 4 (1857) : 244 (Brompton ped.), 254–255. *Year Books Edward I* 3 (Rolls ser. 31a) (1863): 320–321. *C.P.R. 1301–1307* (1898): 308 & 332 (instances of Edmund of Cornwall styled "king's kinsman" by King Edward I of England in 1305). *C.C.R. 1313–1318* (1893): 331. *Misc. Gen. et Heraldica* 2nd Ser. 5 (1894): 76–78. *C.P.R. 1301–1307* (1898): 197. *C.C.R. 1296–1302* (1906):491. *C.Ch.R.* 3 (1908): 42 (Edmund of Cornwall styled "king's kinsman" by King Edward I of England in 1304). Reade *House of Cornewall* (1908): 25–53. *Trans. Shropshire Arch. & Nat. Hist. Soc.* 3rd Ser. 8 (1908): 112–117. *Cal. Various Chancery Rolls* 1277–1326 (1912): 67, 69, 72, 75, 138, 141. VCH *Worcester* 3 (1913): 153–158. Price *Two Effigies in the Churches of Asthall & Cogges in Oxfordshire* (1938): 103–110. Brault *Rolls of Arms Edward I* 2 (1997): 121 (arms of Edmund de Cornwall — L 211, O 188: Argent, a lion rampant gules crowned or surmounted by a bend semy of roundels or); N 343: Argent, a lion rampant gules crowned or surmounted by a bend sable). National Archives, C 241/65/161 (available at www.catalogue.nationalarchives.gov.uk/search.asp). Worcestershire Rec. Office: Hampton (Pakington) of Westwood Park, Droitwich, Worcestershire, 705:349/12946/475234 (available at www.a2a.org.uk/search/index.asp).

ii. **GEOFFREY DE CORNWALL**, Knt., of Burford, Shropshire [see next].

iii. **RICHARD DE CORNWALL**, King's clerk, King's Clerk of the Markets, Rector of Pytchley, Hampshire and Fotheringhay, Northamptonshire, Prebendary of North Newbald, Yorkshire, 1310–1325, Rector of Walsoken, Norfolk, 1312–32, Prebendary of Fridaythorpe, Yorkshire, 1325–29. He was instituted Rector of Radclive, Buckinghamshire in 1296. In 1311 the king ordered that his kinsman, Richard of Cornwall, not be molested by papal citations in respect to his possession of the prebend of North Newbald in the church of York. In 1313 he was granted a papal dispensation at the request of King Edward II of England to retain the churches of Pytchley, Hampshire and Fotheringhay, Northamptonshire, and to hold other benefices to the number of four, value £200. In 1320 he was charged with having received fines and amercements of those who had been convicted of using false measures at St. Giles' Fair near Winchester, Hampshire; for this trespass, he asked redress. In 1330 the Pope ordered that he be provided a canonry of Lincoln (or Lichfield) with reservation of a prebend, on condition of resigning the prebend of Fridaythorpe, Yorkshire. *Cat. of the Harleian Coll. of MSS* 2 (1759): Num. 5804 ("A thick Book in folio with a large variety of Matters containing: 16. A Grant from Richardus de Cornubia to John Howard & Johanna his wife, Sister of the said Richard for inhabiting his Manors in Norf. f. 26."). Blomefield *Essay towards a Top. Hist. of Norfolk* 9 (1808): 121–131. Hardy *Syllabus (in English) of the Docs. Rel. England & Other Kingdoms* 1 (1869): 167. *C.P.R. 1307–1313* (1894): 386–387 (Richard of Cornwall styled "king's kinsman" by King Edward I of England in 1305). *Papal Regs.: Letters* 2 (1895): 109 (Richard de Cornwall styled "kinsman" of King Edward II of England in 1313), 174, 175, 201, 322, 324. *Regs. of John de Sandale & Rigaud de Asserio, Bishops of Winchester* (Hampshire Rec. Soc. Ser.) (1897): xix. Reade *House of Cornewall* (1908): 25–53. *Cal. Chancery Warrants* (1927): 379, 386 (instances of Richard of Cornwall styled "king's cousin"). Jones *Fasti Ecclesiae Anglicanae 1300–1541* 6 (1963): 50–52, 68–70. *Rolls & Reg. of Bishop Oliver Sutton 1280–1299* 8 (Lincoln Rec. Soc. 76) (1986): 163.

iv. **JOAN DE CORNWALL**, married **JOHN HOWARD**, Knt., of Wiggenhall, East Winch, etc., Norfolk [see HOWARD 8.

8. GEOFFREY DE CORNWALL, Knt., King's Bachelor, and, in right of his wife, of Burford, Shropshire, King's Nympton, Devon, Hamperden (in Depden), Essex, Rochford, Herefordshire, Norton and Thrupp (in Norton), Northamptonshire, Stapleton (in Presteigne), Herefordshire, Carkedon (in Clifton upon Teme), Clifton (in Clifton upon Teme), Ham Castle (in Clifton upon Teme), and Kyre Wyard, Worcestershire, etc. In 1297–8 he was granted lands and tenements in Iver, Bukinghamshire by his uncle, Edmund, Earl of Cornwall. He married before 1308 **MARGARET DE MORTIMER**, daughter and co-heiress of Hugh de Mortimer, Knt., of Richard's Castle, Herefordshire, King's Nympton, Devon, Farleigh Wallop, Hampshire, Norton, Northamptonshire, Burford, Shropshire, Farnborough, Warwickshire, Cotheridge, Worcestershire, etc., by his wife, Maud [see RICHARD'S CASTLE 4 for her ancestry]. She was born on or about 14 Sept. 1295 (aged 8 on 14 Sept. 1313, 10 in 1304, 14-½ in Nov. 1308). They had three sons, Richard, Knt., Geoffrey, and John, Knt., and two daughters, Joan (wife of James Neville, Knt.) and Maud (wife of William Boure). His wife, Margaret, was co-heiress in 1308 to her great-uncle, William de Mortimer, Knt., of Ham (in Clifton upon Teme), Worcestershire. In 1308 he and his brother, Edmund, owed a debt of £270 to John Knockin. He presented to the second portion of the prebendal church of Burford, Shropshire, 1316, 1320, 1321, 1325, and to the third portion of the prebendal church of Burford, Shropshire, 1316, 1333. In 1316 he was granted free warren in his demesne lands in Stapleton (in Presteigne), Herefordshire, Burford, Shropshire, Norton, Northamptonshire, Hamperden (in Depden), Essex, and King's Nympton, Devon. In 1317 he was granted a moiety of the hundred of Cures, Shropshire by the king. In 1328 he settled the manor of Cornwallis (in Iver), Buckinghamshire on his son, Richard, and his wife, Sibyl, in tail male. SIR GEOFFREY DE CORNWALL died shortly before 1 June 1335. His widow, Margaret, married (2nd) **WILLIAM DEVEREUX**, of Holme Lacy and Stoke Lacy, Herefordshire. WILLIAM DEVEREUX died shortly before 6 March 1336/7. His widow, Margaret, married (3rd) before 9 Feb. 1338/9 **THOMAS DE HULHAMPTON**. Margaret died shortly before 25 Dec. 1345.

Baker *Hist. & Antiqs. of the County of Northampton* 1 (1822-1830): 414–415. Banks *Baronies in Fee* 1 (1844): 337–338 (sub Mortimer). Whellan *Hist., Gazetteer, & Directory of Northamptonshire* (1849): 462. Eyton *Antiqs. of Shropshire* 4 (1857): 302–321, 323–326. Tresswell & Vincent *Vis. of Shropshire 1623, 1569 & 1584* 1 (H.S.P. 28) (1889): 145–148 (Cornwall ped.: "Sr Geoffrey Cornwall Kt. = Margrett da. & coheire to Sr Hugh de Mortimer Baron of Burford."). *C.P.R. 1327–1330* (1891): 36 & 530 (instances of Geoffrey de Cornubia/Cornewaill [Cornwall] styled "king's kinsman"). Bund *Inqs. Post Mortem for the County of Worcester* 1 (1894): xxvii, 34. *C.P.R. 1307–1313* (1894): 457. *Misc. Gen. et Heraldica* 2nd Ser. 5 (1894): 76–78 (Cornwall ped.). *Feudal Aids* 1 (1899): 373; 2 (1900): 178, 393; 4 (1906): 30, 234; 5 (1908): 305. Amphlett *Lay Subsidy Roll, A.D. 1603 for the County of Worcester* (1901): xxv–xxvii. *Genealogical Mag.* 6 (1903): 525–532. *C.C.R. 1343–1346* (1904): 274. *Year Books of Edward II* 3 (Selden Soc. 20) (1905): 157–158. *Trans. Shropshire Arch. & Natural Hist. Soc.* 3rd Ser. 7 (1907): 358–359. *C.Ch.R.* 3 (1908): 330. Reade *House of Cornewall* (1908): 25–53. *Trans. Worcestershire Naturalists' Club* 4 (1911): 342. *Cal. Various Chancery Rolls 1277–1326* (1912): 114, 119, 139, 143. Farrer *Honors & Knights' Fees* 1 (1923): 35. VCH *Worcester* 4 (1924): 246–255, 279–285, 362–371. VCH *Buckingham* 3 (1925): 286–294. Price *Two Effigies in the Churches of Asthall & Cogges in Oxfordshire* (1938): 103–108. Rennell *Valley on the March* (1958): 130. Beardwood *Trial of Walter Langton, Bishop of Lichfield 1307–1312* (Trans. American Philosophical Soc. n.s. 54) (1964): 182. Orleton *Cal. Reg. of Adam de Orleton* (Worcestershire Hist. Soc. n.s. 10) (1979): 354–355. Sutherland *Eyre of Northamptonshire* 1 (Selden Soc. 97) (1983): 311. Brault *Rolls of Arms Edward I* 2 (1997): 121 (arms of Geoffrey de Cornwall — O 187: Argent, a lion rampant gules crowned or surmounted by a bend sable charged with three mullets or). Rickard *Castle Community* (2002): 249. National Archives, C 241/65/161; SC 8/11/548 (available at www.catalogue.nationalarchives.gov.uk/search.asp). National Archives, CP 25/1/205/21, #15 [see abstract of fine at http://www.medievalgenealogy.org.uk/index.html].

9. RICHARD DE CORNWALL, Knt., of Burford, Shropshire, Cornwallis (in Iver), Buckinghamshire, Norton and Thrupp (in Norton), Northamptonshire, etc. He married before 1328 (date of settlement) **SIBYL DE BODRUGAN** (or **BOTRINGHAM**), sister of John de Botringham. They had two sons, Geoffrey, Knt., and John. In 1341 he was granted letters of protection while serving in Scotland. SIR RICHARD DE CORNWALL died 6 October 1343. His widow, Sibyl, died 23 May 1349.

Whellan *Hist., Gazetteer, & Directory of Northamptonshire* (1849): 462. Tresswell & Vincent *Vis. of Shropshire 1623, 1569 & 1584* 1 (H.S.P. 28) (1889): 145–148 (Cornwall ped.: "Sr Rich. de Cornwall Baron of Burford ob. 13 E. 3. = Sibell sister to John de Botringham ."). *Genealogical Mag.* 6 (1903): 525–532. *Misc. Gen. et Heraldica* 2nd Ser. 5 (1894): 76–78 (Cornwall ped.). Wrottesley *Crécy & Calais* (1898): 34, 85, 149. *C.C.R.* 1343–1346 (1904): 274. *C.F.R.* 4 (1913): 463. VCH *Buckingham* 3(1925): 286–294. Simpson & Galbraith *Cal. Docs. rel. Scotland* 5 (1986): 514.

10. GEOFFREY DE CORNWALL, Knt., of Burford, Shropshire, Cornwallis (in Iver), Buckinghamshire, King's Nympton, Devon, Hamperden (in Depden), Essex, Rochford and Stapleton (in Presteigne), Herefordshire, Norton and Thrupp (in Norton), Northamptonshire, etc., son and heir, born about 1335–6 (13 or 14 in 1349, age 22 in 1357). In 1346 his wardship was granted to Thomas de Beauchamp, Earl of Warwick. He married before 1355 **CECILY** _____. They had three sons, Brian, Knt., Richard, Esq., and Geoffrey, Knt., and one daughter, Ellen. In 1358 Reynold de la Mare, Knt., complained that Geoffrey son of Richard de Cornwall, Geoffrey son of Geoffrey de Cornwall, Knt., and many others of their confederacy, "arrayed as for war," assaulted him in the church of Greet, Shropshire. Geoffrey presented to the church of Burford, Shropshire in 1362 and 1364. SIR GEOFFREY DE CORNWALL died 18 May 1365. His widow, Cecily, married before 5 April 1368 (date of pardon for marrying without the king's license) **RICHARD DE BITERLE**. She died 26 July 1369.

Eyton *Antiqs. of Shropshire* 4 (1857): 326. Tresswell & Vincent *Vis. of Shropshire 1623, 1569 & 1584* 1 (H.S.P. 28) (1889): 145–148 (Cornwall ped.: "Sr Geoffrey [Cornwall]. = … ."). *Misc. Gen. et Heraldica* 2nd Ser. 5 (1894): 76–78 (Cornwall ped.). *C.P.R.* 1358–1361 (1895): 160. *Genealogical Mag.* 6 (1903): 525–532. *C.F.R.* 5 (1915): 496. VCH *Buckingham* 3(1925): 286–294.

11. RICHARD CORNWALL, Esq., of Burford, Shropshire, Cornwallis (in Iver), Buckinghamshire, Stapleton (in Presteigne), Herefordshire, etc., 2nd son. He married (1st) before 1402 **CECILY SEYMOUR**, possibly daughter of Ralph Seymour, Knt., living 1375, Sheriff of Glamorgan and Morganou, 1373. They had three sons, Richard, Brian, and Edmund, Knt. He was heir in 1400 to his older brother, Brian Cornwall, Knt. In 1402 he made a settlement on himself and his wife, Cecily, and their heirs of the manor of Burford, Shropshire and a moiety of the manors of Ham (in Clifton upon Teme) and Carkedon (in Clifton upon Teme), Worcestershire. In 1407 he obtained license to grant his castle of Stapleton (in Presteigne), Herefordshire to himself and his wife, Cecily, and to their heirs. He married (2nd) before 1418 **ALICE** _____. In 1418 he and his wife, Alice, granted power of attorney to John Penne and Simon Byrchore to deliver seisin of the patronage and advowson of the church of Churchill, Worcestershire to Walter Kebbyll, Esq., and others. RICHARD CORNWALL, Esq., died in 1443.

Eyton Antiqs. of Shropshire 4 (1857): 326. Tresswell & Vincent Vis. of Shropshire 1623, 1569 & 1584 1 (H.S.P. 28) (1889): 145–148 (Cornwall ped.: "Sr Richard Cornwall K^t 2 sonne Baron of Burford. = Cicely da. to S^r Jo. Seymer."). *Misc. Gen. et Heraldica* 2nd Ser. 5 (1894): 76–78 (Cornwall ped.). *Genealogical Mag.* 6 (1903): 525–532. *C.P.R.* 1401–1405 (1905): 104. *C.P.R.* 1405–1408 (1907): 382. VCH Buckingham 3(1925): 286–294. Jeayes *Desc. Cat. of the Charters & Muniments of the Lyttelton Fam.* (1893): 73–74. *Foundations* 2(6) (2008): 390–422 (author identifies Cecily Seymour, wife of Richard Cornwall, as daughter of Roger de Seymour, Knt., of Undy, Monmouthshire, by Cecily, daughter of John de Beauchamp, Knt., 2nd Lord Beauchamp of Somerset). Birmingham City Archives, Lyttleton of Hagley Hall Muniments, MS 3279/351335) (available at www.catalogue.nationalarchives.gov.uk/search.asp). National Archives, CP 25/1/191/26, #41 & CP 25/1/191/26, #44 [two fines dated 1421 both of which include reversions to several parties including Gilbert and Ralph, sons of William Gamage, Knt., and Richard and Brian, sons of Richard Cornwall, Baron of Burford, with the eventual reversion to the "right heirs of Ralph Seymour, Knt."] [see abstract of fines at http:// www.medievalgenealogy.org.uk/index.html].

12. EDMUND CORNWALL, Knt., of Burford, Shropshire, Cornwalls (in Iver), Buckinghamshire, Over Hall (in Hampton Lovett), Worcestershire, etc., son and heir. He married (1st) before 1415 **ALICE** _____. He married (2nd) **ELIZABETH BARRE**, daughter of Thomas Barre, Knt., of Rotherwas (in Dinedor), Herefordshire, by Alice, daughter of Richard Talbot, Knt., 4th Lord Talbot [see TALBOT 13.v for her ancestry]. They had three sons, Thomas, Richard, and allegedly Otis, and one daughter, Eleanor. In 1432 he and his wife, Elizabeth, enfeoffed Thomas Mokhale, John Saunders, and others the manor of Cornwalls (in Iver), Buckinghamshire. SIR EDMUND CORNWALL died in his father's lifetime at Cologne in 1436, following which his heart was taken and interred at Burford, Shropshire. His widow, Elizabeth, was living in 1455.

> Waters *Chester of Chicheley* 2 (1878): 596 (ped. chart). *Procs. Soc. of Antiqs. of London* 2nd Ser. 11 (1886): 216–219 (seal of Edmund Cornwall dated 1432 — Field filled with foliage; on a shield penché, a lion rampant, perhaps crowned, surmounted by a label, all within a bordure engrailed, charged with roundels. Ensigned with a helm. Supporters, two birds, with long open beaks. Legend: le * seel * emunt * Cornewayll * escuier.). Tresswell & Vincent *Vis. of Shropshire 1623, 1569 & 1584* 1 (H.S.P. 28) (1889): 145–148 (Cornwall ped.: "Sr Edm. Cornwall Knight Baron of Burford. = Eliza. da. & coheir to Sr James Barre Kt 2 wife."). *Misc. Gen. et Heraldica* 2nd Ser. 5 (1894): 76–78 (Cornwall ped.). *C.P.R.* 1467–1477 (1900): 425. *Genealogical Mag.* 6 (1903): 525–532. Williams *Llyfr Baglan* (1910): 63 (Barrye ped.: "The said Sr Tho. de Barrie ye 3 had 3 daughters and coheires, the 1 ma. [blank] delaber, the 2 ma. [blank] Cornwall of Byrford, the 3 mar. [blank] a gent. of northwales."). VCH *Worcester* 3 (1913): 153–158 (Cornwall arms: Ermine a lion gules crowned or and a border engrailed sable bezanty). VCH *Buckingham* 3 (1925): 286–294. Bartrum *Welsh Gens. 1400–1500* 1 (1983): 53 (Barry 1: "Elizabeth [Barry] = Edmund ap Richard Cornwall of Burford.").

13. ELEANOR CORNWALL, married (1st) before 1455 **HUGH MORTIMER**, Knt., of Martley and Kyre Wyard, Worcestershire, Tedstone Wafer and Sapey, Herefordshire, younger son of John Mortimer, Knt., of Martley and Kyre Wyard, Worcestershire, etc. He was born about 1434 (came of age in 1455). They had one son, John, and one daughter, Elizabeth. SIR HUGH MORTIMER died in 1460. His widow, Eleanor, married (2nd) before 1465 **RICHARD CROFT**, Knt., of Croft Castle, Herefordshire, Sheriff of Herefordshire, 1471, 1475–6, 1484–5, Knight of the Shire for Herefordshire, Treasurer and Keeper of the Wardrobe, Steward of the Household for Prince Arthur, 1488, son and heir of William Croft, of Croft Castle, by Margaret, daughter of Thomas Walwyn. They had three sons, Edward, Knt., John, and Robert, and five daughters, Anne (wife of Thomas Blount, Knt.), Elizabeth (wife of John Whittington, Esq.), Joyce (wife of Thomas Mill, Esq.), Jane (or Alice) (wife of Edward Darrell), Sibyl (wife of George Herbert, Knt.). By an unknown mistress, he also had one illegitimate son, Thomas. He and his wife, Eleanor, were governor and governess to Edward Mortimer, Earl of March and his brother in 1456. He was appointed general receiver for the Earldom of March in Herefordshire, Shropshire, Wigmore, Radnor and Melleneth. In 1467 he was one of the commissioners appointed to arrest John Morgan, of Worcester, and others and bring them before the king in Chancery. He fought at the Battle of Tewkesbury 4 May 1471, where he captured Edward, Prince of Wales, who was subsequently executed. In 1472 he served with George, Duke of Clarence, Richard, Duke of Gloucester, Thomas Cornwall, Knt., and others on a commission of array in Herefordshire. He fought at the Battle of Stoke 16 June 1487, and was afterward made a Knight Banneret by King Henry VII. SIR RICHARD CROFT died 29 July 1509, and was interred in the church of St. Michael, Croft Castle, Herefordshire. He left a will dated 11 July 1509, proved 11 November 1509 (P.C.C. 22 Bennett).

> Waters *Chester of Chicheley* 2 (1878): 596 (ped. chart). *C.P.R.* 1467-1477 (1900): 29, 350. *Retrospective Review* 2nd Ser. 1 (1827): 472–474. Cooke *Vis. of Herefordshire 1569* (1886): 20–22 (Croft ped.: "Sir Richard Crofte, sonne of William (d. 1509.) = Elynor, daughter to Sir John Bare. = Sir Hugh Mertymer, Knight (Mortimer, Ash. 831.).") (Croft arms: Quarterly, indented per fess Az. and Arg. in the first quarter a lion passant guardant Or.). *List of Sheriffs for England & Wales* (PRO Lists and Indexes 9) (1898): 60. Williams *Llyfr Baglan* (1910): 190 (Croft ped.: "Sr Richerd croft, knight, lord of crofte, ma. Elnor, da. to Sr Edmond Cornwall, knight."). VCH *Worcester* 4 (1924): 279–285. Williams *Parliamentary Hist. of the County of Hereford* (1896): 35. VCH *Worcester* 4 (1924): 279–285. Wedgwood *Hist. of Parliament 1439-1509* 1 (1836): 237–238. Gairdner *Paston Letters 1422–1509* (3): 9, 304. Croft *House of Croft of Croft Castle* (1949): 40–46. Bartrum *Welsh Gens. 1400–1500* 2 (1983): 343 [Croft ped.: "Sir Richard [Croft] d. 1509 (a) = Eleanor f. Sir Edmund Cornwall, (b) = NN Blunt"). Herefordshire Rec. Office: Recs. of the Garnstone Estate, F 78/II/19 (available at www.a2a.org.uk/search/index.asp).

Child of Eleanor Cornwall, by Hugh Mortimer, Knt.:

i. **ELIZABETH MORTIMER**, married **THOMAS WEST**, Knt., 8th Lord la Warre, 5th Lord West [see WEST 12].

Child of Eleanor Cornwall, by Richard Croft, Knt.:

i. **EDWARD CROFT**, Knt. [see next].

14. EDWARD CROFT, Knt., of Croft Castle, Herefordshire, Sheriff of Herefordshire, 1504–5, 1509–10, 1513–14, 1517–18, 1522, 1526, 1529–30, 1533–34, Receiver General of the Earldom of March, 1509–46, son and heir, born about 1465. He married **JOYCE SKULLE**, daughter and heiress of Walter Skulle, Knt., of Hereford and London, and, in right of his 1st wife, of Holt, Worcestershire, Keeper of the King's Wardrobe, Treasurer of the Household [see HAVILAND 16], by his 2nd wife, Frances, daughter and heiress of Edmond Winchcombe, of Woodrising, Norfolk. They had three sons, Richard, Thomas, and George, and five daughters, Eleanor (wife of Thomas Scryven, Esq.), Elizabeth, Margaret (wife of John Aprice alias Gwynne, Esq..), Anne (wife of John Harley, Esq.), and Joyce. In 1525 he was appointed one of the learned counsel to Princess Mary Tudor [afterwards Queen Mary I]. In 1535 John Scudamore of Holme Lacy sued him in Chancery; he was also sued in Chancery by the executors of the testament of his kinsman, Sir Richard Cornwall. SIR EDWARD CROFT died 23 March 1547. He left a will dated 23 Feb. 1545/6, proved 24 March 1546/7 (P.C.C. 30 Alen).

Retrospective Review 2nd Ser. 1 (1827): 472–474. Cooke *Vis. of Herefordshire 1569* (1886): 20–22 (Croft ped.: "Sir Edwarde Croft, maried (*d. 1546.*) = Joys, doughter and soule heire to Sir Walter Scoule of the Holte in Wostershir (*Skull, Ash. 831.*)"), 65 (Skull ped.: . "(Joyce [Skull], d. and sole h., ux. Sr. Edw. Crofte, Kt.)"). House of Commons Papers (1841) (1): 275. *List of Sheriffs for England & Wales* (PRO Lists and Indexes 9) (1898): 61. Croft *House of Croft of Croft Castle* (1949): 47–51. Bindoff *House of Commons 1509-1558* 1 (1982): 284. Bartrum *Welsh Gens. 1400–1500* 2 (1983): 343 [Croft ped.: "Edward [Croft] d. 1541 = Joyce f. Walter Skull"). Somerset *Recs. of Early English Drama: Shropshire* 2 (1994): 699–700. Siddons *Vis. by the Heralds in Wales* (H.S.P. n.s. 14) (1996): 89 (Croft ped.: "Sir Edwarde Croft knight, of the house of Croft, maryed Joyce, doughter and sole heyre to Sir Walter Stowle of the Holte in Worcestrshire.").

Children of Edward Croft, Knt., by Joyce Skulle:

i. **JOYCE CROFT**, married **HENRY** (or **HARRY**) **OWEN**, Knt., of Pulborough and Newtimber, Sussex, and London [see LANCASTER 12.i.a].

ii. **ELIZABETH CROFT** [see next].

15. ELIZABETH CROFT, married **JAMES VAUGHAN**, Esq., of Hergest, Herefordshire, Sheriff of Radnorshire, 1541–2, son of Watkin Vaughan, Esq., of Hergest, Herefordshire, by Elizabeth, daughter of James Baskerville, Knt. They had one son, Charles, and one daughter, Isabel.

Retrospective Review 2nd Ser. 1 (1827): 472–474. Cooke *Vis. of Herefordshire 1569* (1886): 20–22 (Croft ped.: "Elizabeth [Croft], married to James Vaughan (*of Hergest.*)."), 97 (Vaughan ped.: "James Vaughan of Hergest."). Watkins *Coll. Hist. & Antiqs. of the County of Hereford, Hundred of Huntington* (1897): 73–74. *List of Sheriffs for England & Wales* (PRO Lists and Indexes 9) (1898): 269. Croft *House of Croft of Croft Castle* (1949): 51. Bindoff *House of Commons 1509–1558* 1 (1982): 514. Bartrum *Welsh Gens. 1400–1500* 2 (1983): 343 [Croft ped.: "Elizabeth [Croft] = James ap Watkin Vaughan"); 3 (1983): 457 (Drymbenog 2(B₁) ped.: "James Vaughan = Elizabeth d. Edward Croft"). Siddons *Vis. of Herefordshire 1634* (H.S.P. n.s. 15) (2002): 164–166 (Vaughan ped.: "James Vaughan of Hargest Esqr = daughter of Sr Edward Croft knight."). Siddons *Vis. by the Heralds in Wales* (H.S.P. n.s. 14) (1996): 89 (Croft ped.: "Elsabeth [Croft] maryed James Vaghan of Hargeste in Kyntons lande in the lordship of Huntyngdon.").

16. ISABEL VAUGHAN, married **GEORGE PARRY** (or **AP HARRY**), Esq., of Poston, Herefordshire, Sheriff of Herefordshire, 1563–4, son of Richard ap Harry (or Parry), by Elizabeth, daughter of Christopher Mathew, Knt., of Llandaff. They had six sons, James, Esq., Thomas, John, Esq., Hugh, Roger, and Richard, and five daughters, Elizabeth, Katherine, Eleanor, Jane, and Sybil. George was a legatee in the 1522 will of his grandfather, Thomas ap Harry, of Poston. In 1547 he purchased the rectory and church of Peterchurch, Herefordshire from Richard Taverner, Esq., of London and Roger Taverner, Gent., for £74. In 1567 his uncle, Hugh ap Harry, of Aconbury, Herefordshire granted him a moiety of Snodhill Castle and other lands in Peterchurch, Herefordshire. On 28 June 1578 he granted land with a barn in Peterchurch, Herefordshire, together with various tithes of corn and grain, to his daughter Jane Parry for "advancing" her marriage. **GEORGE PARRY**, Esq., died before 16 April 1580. Administration of the will of George Parry, of Poston, Herefordshire, Esq., was granted 2 May 1584 to his next of kin, John Parry.

> Jones *Hist. of the County of Brecknock* 2(2) (1809): 558 (Parry ped.: "George Parry m. Eliz. d. James Vaughan of Hergest."). Cooke *Vis. of Herefordshire 1569* (1886): 3–5 (Apharry or Parry ped.: "George Aphenry of Paston (*Poston*). = Isabell, daughter to James Vauhan of Hergest (*in Kington*)."). *List of Sheriffs for England & Wales* (PRO Lists and Indexes 9) (1898): 61. Parry *Genealogical Abstracts of Parry Wills* (1911): 26, no. 149; 27, no. 156. Bartrum *Welsh Gens. 1400–1500* 3 (1983): 457 (Drymbenog 2(B₁) ped.: "Isabel [Vaughan] = George Parry"), 484 (Drymbenog 12(A) ped.: "George Parry = Isabel f. James Vaughan of Hergest"); 6 (1983): 972 (Gwaithford 5(A) [Matthew ped.]. Siddons *Vis. by the Heralds in Wales* (H.S.P. n.s. 14) (1996): 46–47 (Mathew ped.: "Elysabeth [Mathew] maryed Rychard ap Harry and had yssue George and Katherine."). Siddons *Vis. of Herefordshire 1634* (H.S.P. n.s. 15) (2002): 57–58 (Parry ped.: "George ap Harry of Poston in Com. Hereford = Isabell daughter of James Vaughan of Hargest.") (Parry arms: Argent a fess between three lozenges a bordure Azure), 178–179 (Parry ped.: "George Parry of Poston Esq. = Isabell da: of James Vaughan of Hergest Esq."). Herefordshire Rec. Office: Guy's Hospital, London, AW28/25/2; AW28/25/4 (available at www.a2a.org.uk/search/index.asp). Herefordshire Rec. Office: Snodhill Papers, F94/II/2 (available at www.a2a.org.uk/search/index.asp).

17. [**REV.**] **ROGER PARRY**, clerk, 5th son, of Hinton-Ampner, Hampshire, born about 1548. He attended Hart Hall, Oxford before 1568, where he received a B.A. degree 26 February 1572/3 and a M.A. degree 5 July 1575. He married (1st) **MARY CROSLEY**, daughter of Henry Crosley, of Woodstock, Oxfordshire. They had three sons, George, Alexander, and William, and seven daughters, Blanche (wife of James Williams and Thomas Lawrence), Elizabeth, Jane (wife of Samuel West), Mary (wife of Rev. Daniel Evans), Katherine (wife of John Lamphere), Frances (wife of Thomas Good), and Rebecca. He was instituted to the church of Hinton-Ampner, Hampshire in 1576. His wife, Mary, was buried at Hinton-Ampner, Hampshire 14 November 1605. He married (2nd) by license dated 14 Sept. 1611 **ELEANOR** _____, widow of _____ Ewyns, of Tarring, Sussex. [REV.] ROGER PARRY was buried at Winchester Cathedral 18 May 1634.

> Cooke *Vis. of Herefordshire 1569* (1886): 3–5 (Apharry or Parry ped.: "Roger [Parry], 5 sonne."). Foster *Alumni Oxonienses* 3 (1891): 1121. Hampshire Parish Regs. 4 (Phillimore Par. Reg. Ser. XXXIV) (1902): 16. *Hampshire Marriage Licenses 1607–1640* (1960): 16. *Virginia Gen.* 42 (1998): 217–233. Siddons *Vis. of Herefordshire 1634* (H.S.P. n.s. 15) (2002): 57–58 (Parry ped: "Roger Apparey, Rector of Hinton Com. Southampton = Mary da: of Henry Crosley of Woodstock Co: Oxon."). Parish Regs. for Hinton-Ampner, Hampshire, 1561–1877 [available on FHL Microfilm 1041252].

18. ELIZABETH PARRY, baptized at Hinton Ampner, Hampshire 15 July 1582. She married at Hinton Ampner, Hampshire 7 Feb. 1603/4 (as his 2nd wife) [**REV.**] **ROBERT BATTE**, clerk, Rector of Newton Tony, Wiltshire, son of John Batte, by his wife, Margaret. He was baptized at Birstall, Yorkshire 6 June 1560. They had four sons, [Capt.] John, Henry, William, and Robert, and five daughters, Mary, Elizabeth (wife of Dr. Richard Marsh), Mary (wife of Reresby Eyre and Henry Hirst), Katherine (wife of [Rev.] Philip Mallory [see MALLORY 19.ii]), and Rebecca. He matriculated at Brasenose College, Oxford 9 Nov. 1579, aged 19. He received a B.A. degree, 1583, M.A. degree from University College, 29 April 1586, and a B.D. degree 27 June 1594. He was licensed to preach 27 October 1595. [REV.] ROBERT BATTE was buried at Newton Tony, Wiltshire 18 Jan. 1617/8. He left a will dated 1 Dec. 1617, proved 6 Feb. 1617/8 (P.C.C. 10 Meade). His widow, Elizabeth, married (2nd) at Birstall, Yorkshire 4 June 1629 [**MR.**] **ANTHONY RAWLINSON**. She was buried at Birstall, Yorkshire 1 August 1633.

> Dugdale *Vis. of York 1665-6* (Surtees Soc. 36) (1859): 233 (Batte ped. "Robert Batte, brothr and heire of John, died circa an. 1617. = Eliz. daughter of … Parrey of .. in com. Heref. "). *NEHGR* 39 (1885): 163–165; 51 (1897): 356 (will of Robert Batte). Foster *Alumni Oxoniensis* 1 (1891): 87 (sub Robert Batt). Dugdale *Dugdale's Visitation of Yorkshire* Pt. 4 (1899): 352–355 (sub Batte). *Yorkshire Fines for the Stuart Period* 1 (Yorkshire Arch. Soc. Rec. Ser. 53) (1915): 62. *Virginia Gen.* 42 (1998): 217–233. Siddons *Vis. of Herefordshire 1634* (H.S.P. n.s. 15) (2002): 57–58 (Parry ped.: "Elizabeth Parry wife to Robert Batt of Okewell Co. Yorke").

19. [CAPT.] JOHN BATTE, of Oakwell Hall (in Birstall), Yorkshire, son and heir, baptized at Newton Tony, Wiltshire 24 June 1606. He married **MARTHA MALLORY**, daughter of Thomas Mallory, D.D., Dean of Chester, by Elizabeth, daughter of Richard Vaughan, D.D., successively Bishop of Bangor, Chester, and London [see MALLORY 19 for her ancestry]. They had six sons, Henry, John, William, Esq., Robert, Thomas, Gent., and [Capt.] Henry, and three daughters, Martha, Elizabeth, and Mary. He was a Royalist and is said to have been a Captain and present at the Battle of Adwalton Moor. His wife, Martha, was buried at Birstal, Yorkshire 9 Feb. 1644/5. He immigrated with his children to Charles City County, Virginia in 1649. [CAPT.] JOHN BATTE died "beyond the seas" in 1652. His estate was administered in England Sept. 1653.

> Dugdale *Vis. of York 1665–6* (Surtees Soc. 36) (1859): 233 (Batte ped.: "John Batte of Okewell in co. Ebor. died in aº 1652. = Martha, dau. of Tho. Mallory, Dʳ in Divinity and Deane of Chestʳ."). *NEHGR* 39 (1885): 163–165. *Genealogist* n.s. 15 (1898): 88. Dugdale *Dugdale's Visitation of Yorkshire* Pt. 4 (1899): 352–355 (sub Batte). Boddie *Virginia Hist. Gens.* (1954): 103–121. *Virginia Gen.* 42 (1998): 217–233.

Children of [Capt.] John Batte, by Martha Mallory:

i. **WILLIAM BATTE**, Esq., baptized at Newton-Tony, Wiltshire 15 July 1632. He immigrated to Virginia, where he resided at Spring Gardens in Charles City County, Virginia. He married (1st) before 5 Sept. 1655 **SUSAN** (or **SUSANNAH**) **ASTON**, widow of [Lieut. Col.] Edward Major, and daughter of [Lieut. Col.] Walter Aston, Gent., of Charles City County, Virginia [see ASTON 19 for her ancestry]. He removed to Isle of Wight County, Virginia before 28 Feb. 1657, but soon returned to England. They had no known issue. He married (2nd) **ELIZABETH HORTON**, daughter of William Horton, of Barkisland, Yorkshire, by Elizabeth, daughter of Thomas Gledhill. She was baptized at Elland, Yorkshire 29 March 1637. They had three sons, William, John, and Gledhill, and three daughters, Elizabeth, Judith, and Martha (wife of John Murgatroyd). WILLIAM BATTE, Esq. was buried at Birstal, Yorkshire 7 Sept. 1673. His widow, Elizabeth, was buried at Birstal, Yorkshire 10 August 1685. Dugdale *Vis. of York 1665–6* (Surtees Soc. 36) (1859): 233 (Batte ped.: "William Batte of Okewell in com. Ebor. Esqʳ, now one of his Majesties justices of yᵉ Peace in the West-Riding, ætatius 33 annor. 2º Apr. 1666. = Elizabeth, daughter unto William Horton of Barkislond in com. Eborum."). *NEHGR* 39 (1885): 163–165. Dugdale *Dugdale's Visitation of Yorkshire* Pt. 4 (1899): 352–355 (sub Batte). Cabell *Majors & Their Marrs.* (1915): 27–28. Boddie *Virginia Hist. Gens.* (1954): 103–121. Boddie *Southside Virginia Fams.* 1 (1955): 25–28. *Virginia Gen.* 42 (1998): 217–233.

ii. **THOMAS BATTE**, Gent., of Henrico and Charles City Counties, Virginia, born about 1642. He married **MARY** _____. They had five children. He headed an expedition which crossed the Allegheny Mountains in 1671. He was living in Jan. 1693/4. Dugdale *Vis. of York 1665–6* (Surtees Soc. 36) (1859): 233 (Batte ped.: "Thomas [Batte], now in Virginia."). *NEHGR* 39 (1885): 163–165. Dugdale *Dugdale's Visitation of Yorkshire* Pt. 4 (1899): 352–355 (sub Batte). Boddie *Virginia Hist. Gens.* (1954): 103–121. Boddie *Southside Virginia Fams.* 1 (1955): 25–28. *Virginia Gen.* 42 (1998): 217–233.

iii. **[CAPT.] HENRY BATTE**, of Charles City County, Virginia, born about 1643. He married **MARY LOUND**, daughter of Henry Lound, of Henrico County, Virginia, by his wife, Ann. They had two sons, William and Henry, and five daughters, Mary (wife of John Poythress), Elizabeth (wife of William Ligon), Anne (wife of Edward Stratton), Rachel (wife of James Parham), and Sarah (wife of Abraham Jones).. He was a member of the House of Burgesses, 1685–86, 1691–92, 1695. He died testate in Charles City County, Virginia before 1 June 1700. His widow, Mary, was living in Prince George County, Virginia in Dec. 1717. She died before 10 Sept 1720. Dugdale *Vis. of York 1665–6* (Surtees Soc. 36) (1859): 233 (Batte ped.: "Henry [Batte], now in Virginia."). *NEHGR* 39 (1885): 163–165. Dugdale *Dugdale's Visitation of Yorkshire* Pt. 4 (1899): 352–355 (sub Batte). *VMHB* 29 (1921): 102. Boddie *Virginia Hist. Gens.* (1954): 103–121. Boddie *Southside Virginia Fams.* 1 (1955): 25–28. *Virginia Gen.* 42 (1998): 217–233.

⁂ COURTENAY ⁂

1. REYNOLD DE COURTENAY (or **CURTENAY**, **CORTENAY**), of Sutton, Berkshire, and Waddesdon, Buckinghamshire, and, in right of his 2nd wife, of Okehampton and Musbury, Devon, Hemington, Somerset, etc., of uncertain parentage. He married (1st) an unidentified wife, _____, kinswoman of Queen Eleanor of Aquitaine (wife of King Henry II of England). They had three sons, William, Robert, and Reynold, and one daughter, Egeline. He was a witness in 1150 at Rouen in Normandy of a charter of Henry, Duke of Normandy (afterwards King Henry II of England). He held lands in Sutton, Berkshire in 1160–1, and received a grant of the manor from King Henry II sometime in the period, 1175–84. He witnessed numerous charters of King Henry II issued in the period, 1164–88. He was frequently in the king's train on his itineraries in England and France. In 1171 he accompanied the king in his campaign in Ireland. He married (2nd) after 1173 **MAUD FITZ ROBERT**, daughter of Robert Fitz Roy (illegitimate son of King Henry I of England), by Maud, daughter of Robert d'Avranches [see ENGLAND 2.i for her ancestry]. In 1174 he witnessed an agreement between King Henry II and William *the Lion*, King of Scots. He wa first recorded as holding lands in Devon in 1175–6. Sometime prior to his death, he granted two islands in the Thames between Witteneiam [?Wittenham] and Wadeiam [?Waddeson] to Abingdon Abbey. REYNOLD DE COURTENAY was living Michaelmas 1190, and died before Michaelmas 1191. In 1204–5 the king presented to the chapel of Musbury, Devon, which should have been in his widow, Maud's gift. In 1213 Maud obtained letters of safe conduct permitting her to return to England and petition for the king's favor. In 1215 the king directed the Constable of Wallingford to deliver to her seisin of the vill of Waddesdon, Buckinghamshire, which formed part of her dower. She presented to the church of Waddesdon, Buckinghamshire about 1215. In 1220 she sued Robert de Courtenay and Reynold de Courtenay (her nephews and step-grandsons) for the manors of Oakhampton, Chawleigh, Chulmleigh, Kenn, and Musbury, and Sampford, Devon and Hemington, Somerset, which she claimed as her right; Robert answered that no claims under French titles were valid; Maud rebutted that the properties were in England and she was English. Maud died shortly before 3 August 1224. In 1227 a mandate was sent to the sheriff of Gloucestershire ordering him to make enquiry of Peter Fitz Herbert concerning scutage for the manor of Okehampton, Devon which belonged to Maud de Courtenay.

Pole *Colls. towards a Desc. of Devon* (1791): 2–5 (charter of Maud de Courtenay, lady of Oakhampton; another charter of Reynold de Courtenay granted with consent of Maud his wife). Kennett *Parochial Antiqs. of Ambrosden, Burcester* 1 (1818): 277. *Coll. Top. et Gen.* 1 (1834): 189 (undated charter of Reynold de Courtenay and his wife, Maud; charter witnessed by William and Robert de Courtenay). Dugdale *Monasticon Anglicanum* 5 (1846): 377–382 (Ford Abbey, Fundationis et Fundatorum Historia: "Fuit autem iste dictus Reginaldus de Courtney filius domini Flori, filii regis Franciae Ludovici, cognomento Grossi; ac etiam ista Hawisia vicecomitissa uxor ejus secunda, de sanguine regio Anglicano, ex parte dominae Albredae neptis etiam regis Willielmi Bastardi matris aviae suae dominae Adeliciae vicecomitissae primitus memoratae generosae exorta."). *Collectanea Archæologica* 1 (1862): 263–284. Bain *Cal. of Docs. rel. to Scotland* 2 (1884): 15 (Robert de Courtenay [son of Reynold] styled "kinsman" [cognatus] of Queem Eleanor of Aquitaine). Maitland *Bracton's Note Book* 2 (1887): 133–134, 137–138; 3 (1887): 355–356, 450–452. *Notes & Queries* 6th Ser. 3 (1881): 1–3; 7th Ser. 4 (1887): 430; 8th Ser. 7 (1895): 441–443. *Note-book of Tristram Risdon* (1897): 53–56. Round *Cal. Docs. Preserved in France* 1 (1899): 316–317. Phillimore *Rotuli Hugonis de Welles Episcopi Lincolniensis 1209–1235* 2 (Canterbury & York Soc. 3) (1907): 49. *C.P.* 4 (1916): 465, footnote b (Courtenay in Gâtinais. The arms of the Courtenays, both English and French, were, Or, three roundlets Gules (with various brisures). These were borne (seals, 1205, 1212) by Pierre, Sire de Courtenay, Count of Nevers, Auxerre, and Tonnerre, s. and h. of Pierre de France, citing Du Bouchet, *Maison de Courtenay* (1661): 89–99, preuves, 13–15). *C.P.* 4 (1916): 317 (sub Devon) (ped.) (author alleges without evidence that Renaud de Courtenay, seigneur of Courtenay, living 1149, is the same person as Reynold de Courtenay, died 1190–1, of Sutton, Berkshire). Stenton *Great Roll of the Pipe Michaelmas 1190* (Pubs. Pipe Roll Soc. n.s. 1) (1925): 31. Stenton *Great Rolls of the Pipe Michaelmas 1191 & Michaelmas 1192* (Pubs. Pipe Roll Soc. n.s. 2) (1926): 162, 276. *C.R.R.* 8 (1938): 32, 213; 9 (1952): 36–37, 71–72, 293–294;10 (1949): 22, 53. Seversmith *Colonial Fams. of Long Island, New York & Connecticut* 5 (1958): 2419–2424. Darlington *Cartulary of Worcester Cathedral Priory* (Pipe Roll Soc. n.s. 38) (1968): 132–133. *Traditio* 41 (1985): 145–179 (author suggests that Reynold de Courtenay above is possibly the "Renaud" or "Renaud Pauper" who witnessed charters dated 1152 and 1155 as "cognatus" [kinsman] for Robert, Count of Dreux, younger son of King Louis VI of France). Kemp *Reading Abbey Cartularies* 1 (Camden 4th Ser. 31) (1986): 232; 2 (Camden 4th Ser. 33) (1987): 232–233. Schwennicke *Europaische Stanmtafeln* 3(2) (1983): 354 (illegitimate children of King Henry I of England); 3(4) (1989): 629. Slade & Lambrick *Two Cartularies of Abingdon Abbey* 1 (Oxford Hist. Soc. n.s. 32) (1990): 170–171 (charter of Reynold de Courtenay dated pre-1194). Hanna *Christchurch Priory Cartulary* (2007): 281. Cornwall Rec. Office: Arundell of Lanherne and Trerice, AR/1/557 (no date [12th century?]; in his court at Cuwyk [Cowick]. Confirmation by Reginald de Courtenay, for the souls of himself and Maud his wife, and of his children and parents, of the gift by Osbert [sic, for Osbern] de Hyduna and Geoffrey his brother, and later by Richard de Hydona and John his son, to the church and canons of Tanton, of the land of Middelduna, as freely as attested by charters of Robert son of King Henry and of John de Hydona; also of a ferling of Madecombe which John de Hydona gave, and of the land of Sinderhull which Agnes daughter of the said Osbert gave; Witnesses: Robert de Courtenay and William his brother, William Dapifer, Henry the chaplain, William de Punchard[un], Guy de Bryan, Anthony de la Bruer', Henry his brother, Richard Ottele [?], 'Hatelinus' de Hydona, William de Hemiok, Henry Hostiar', Simon Delpyt, Roger his brother, Walter Pipinus, Richard son of Brian, Brian his brother, William Talebot, Richard his son, Richard de Hydona, Arnold de Burdeuyle, Robert Anechorus Cophinus (available at http://www.a2a.org.uk/search/index.asp). National Archives, DL 34/1/34 (Writ of H[ubert] de Burgh, justiciar, to Hugh de Neville requesting him to restrain the bailiffs of Brill forest from exacting unjust services from Maud de Courtenay and from her manor of Waddesdon, Bucks. Date: 1215–1224) (available at http:// www.catalogue.nationalarchives.gov.uk/search.asp). Devon Rec. Office: Petre, 123M/TB281 (grant dated late 12th c. in fee farm with warranty Matilda de Curtenai lady of Oke [Okehampton] to Ailmar de Siete. Mill of Misbire [Musbury], which was at farm for 18*s*. annually, to hold at fee farm by hereditary right to Ailmar from Matilda. Rent 20*s*. Consideration Ailmar's homage and service --- a certain gold ring and 100s. which Ailmar gave to Matilda in her court of Cuwic [Cowick, St. Thomas's Exeter] in aid of her --- her relief and fine made to the king. Matilda should warrant the mill for 20s. with all mulcture, land, meadow, pasture, common.) (available at http://www.a2a.org.uk/search/index.asp).

Children of Reynold de Courtenay, by _____:

i. **REYNOLD DE COURTENAY**, of Okehampton, Devon [see next].

ii. **EGELINE DE COURTENAY**, married **GILBERT BASSET**, of Bicester, Headington, Stratton (in Stratton Audley), and Wretchwick, Oxfordshire, Holmer (in Little Missenden) and Stony Stratford, Buckinghamshire, Uxbridge, Middlesex, etc., son and heir of Thomas Basset, by Alice, daughter of Walter de Dunstanville. Her maritagium included the manor of Westcott (in Waddesdon), Buckinghamshire. They had one son, Thomas, and one daughter, Eustache. In 1182 he founded Bicester Priory, Oxfordshire. Sometime before 1188 he was granted a market in his town of Uxbridge, Middlesex. In 1194 he and his wife, Egeline, were granted a weekly market in their manor of Stony Stratford, Buckinghamshire. GILBERT BASSET died in 1205. In 1209 his widow, Egeline, sued for a larger dowry out of the lands of her late husband. She was living in 1219. Kennett *Parochial Antiqs. of Ambrosden, Burcester* 1 (1818): 185–189 (three undated charters of Gilbert Basset, two of which name his wife, Egeline), 210–211 (charter of Gilbert Basset and his wife, Egeline; charter witnessed by Reynold son of William de Courtenay, 237, 240–242 (charter of Egeline de Courtenay; charter names her late husband, Gilbert Basset, her late son, Thomas Basset, her late grandson, Thomas de Camville, son of her daughter, Eustache), 248–250, 272–273, 391–392. *Notes & Queries* 6th Ser. 3 (1881): 1–3. Clarke *Parochial Topog. of the Hundred of Wanting* (1824): 54–55. VCH *Buckingham* 2 (1908): 354–360; 4 (1927): 107–118. Hatton *Book of Seals* (1950): 203. VCH *Oxford* 6 (1959): 324–333. VCH *Middlesex* 4 (1971): 69–75. Reedy *Basset Charters c. 1120 to 1250* (Pub. Pipe Roll Soc. n.s. 50) (1995): xiv, 128–129 (charter of Egeline de Courtenay dated 1205–6; charter names her late father, Reynold de Courtenay; her late husband, Gilbert Basset; and her late son, Thomas Basset; charter witnessed by Robert de Courtenay).

Child of Egeline de Courtenay, by Gilbert Basset:

a. **EUSTACHE BASSET**, daughter and heiress. She married (1st) **THOMAS DE VERDUN**, of Farnham Royal, Buckinghamshire, Hethe, Oxfordshire, etc., son and heir of Bertram de Verdun, of Farnham Royal, Buckinghamshire, Hethe, Oxfordshire, etc.. They had no issue. THOMAS DE VERDUN died in 1199. She married (2nd) in 1200 **RICHARD DE CAMVILLE**, of Avington, Berkshire, Godington and Middleton (in Middleton Stoney), Oxfordshire, and, in right of his wife, of Bicester, Stratton (in Stratton Audley), and Wretchwick, Oxfordshire, son and heir of Gerard de Camville, of Brattleby, Lincolnshire, Godington and Middleton (in Middleton Stoney), Oxfordshire, King's Sutton, Northamptonshire, Charlton and Henstridge, Somerset, etc., Constable of Lincoln Castle, by Nichole, and co-heiress of Richard de la Haye, of Brattleby, Lincolnshire. They had one son, Richard, and one daughter, Idoine. His wife, Eustache, was living in 1209, and died before 1215. In December 1215 his castle of Middleton, Oxfordshire was committed to the keeping of Engelard de Cigogné, one of the king's most hated servants, and in the following May a royal order was issued for its destruction. RICHARD DE CAMVILLE died in early March 1217. Blore *Hist. & Antiqs. of Rutland* 1(2) (1811): 150–151 (De La Hay/Deincourt ped.). *Placitorum in Domo Capitulari Westmonasteriensi Asservatorum Abbreviatio* (1811): 47. Kennett *Parochial Antiqs. of Ambrosden, Burcester* 1 (1818):

240 (charter of Richard de Camville and Eustache his wife), 240–242, 248–250 (charter of Richard de Camville and Eustache Basset his wife), 250–251 (charter of Richard de Camville, charter granted with consent of his wife, Eustache Basset), 391–392. VCH *Berkshire* 4 (1924): 158–162. VCH *Buckingham* 3 (1925): 225–231. VCH *Oxford* 6 (1959): 14–56, 146–152, 174–181, 243–251, 324–333. Sanders *English Baronies* (1960): 109. Jobson *English Government in the 13th Cent.* (2004): 110–119.

Child of Eustache Basset, by Richard de Camville:

1) **IDOINE DE CAMVILLE,** married **WILLIAM LONGESPÉE,** Knt., of Amesbury, Wiltshire [see LONGESPÉE 6].

2. REYNOLD DE COURTENAY, in right of his wife, of Okehampton, Alphington, Kenn, Musbury, Wimple, and Winkleigh, Devon, younger son by his father's 1st marriage, born about 1150. He married after 1173 and before 1178 **HAWISE DE COURCY,** daughter and heiress of William de Courcy (or ?Geoffrey de Crimes?), by Maud, daughter of Robert d'Avranches. She was born before 1162, and was the older half-sister of his father's 2nd wife, Maud Fitz Robert. They had three sons, Robert, Knt., Reynold, Knt., and Henry. In 1178 he and his wife, Hawise, were granted license to have a free chapel at Oakhampton, Devon. At an unknown date, he witnessed a charter of his brother, Robert de Courtenay. REYNOLD DE COURTENAY died 27 Sept. 1194, and was buried at Ford Abbey, Dorset. In 1199 she fined for 300 marks for the lands of her mother, which included 40 librates in England and just as many in Normandy. In 1201 she owed 40 marks and one palfrey for 18 knights' fees. The same year she paid 40 marks for permission to cross the seas. In 1205 she owed 500 pounds and five palfreys to have livery of the honour of Oakhampton, Devon. An at unknown date, she confirmed to Christchurch Priory the land of Wicha in the manor of Chulmleigh, Devon, which land her predecessor, Richard Fitz Baldwin, previously gave to William Martel. Sometime during her widowhood, she granted the advowson of the church of Alphington, Devon to Henry de Courtenay. At an unknown date, she gave Ford Abbey the whole land of Haregrave, Devon in frankalmoin for maintaining three poor persons in the infirmary of the said house. Hawise died 31 July 1219, and was buried at Ford Abbey, Dorset. On 14 August 1219 the king ordered the Sheriff of Devon to take into the king's hand all lands and tenements in his bailiwick formerly of Hawise de Courtenay, and keep them safely until the king orders otherwise. The same year her sister, Maud de Courtenay, brought a lawsuit against her, but the action was stayed due to Hawise's death.

Pole *Colls. towards a Desc. of Devon* (1791): 2–5 (undated charter of Hawise de Courtenay; charter names her sister, Maud; charter witnessed by her sons, Robert de Courtenay and Reynold his brother). *Coll. Top. et Gen.* 1 (1834): 62. Dugdale *Monasticon Anglicanum* 5 (1846): 377–382 (Ford Abbey, Fundationis et Fundatorum Historia: "[Reynold de Courtenay] … Dilectus igitur a Deo et hominibus, cujus memoria in benedictione, quinto calendas Octobris [27 Sept.] anno Domini M.CXCIV. et regni regis Ricardi quarto fæliciter obiit in Christo, et apud Fordam in aquilonari parte presbyterii sepultus quiescit … [Hawise, widow of Reginaldi de Courtenay] obiit tandem plenam dierum in senectute bona pridie calendas Augusti [31 July] anno Dom. MCCIX [recte 1219]. et anno regni Johannis decimo, quæ in ecclesia Fordensi in australi parte presbyterii sepelitur."). Lipscomb *Hist. & Antiqs. of Buckingham* 1 (1847): 471–472 (Courtenay ped.). *Collectanea Archæologica* 1 (1862): 263–284. *Reliquary* 17 (1876–7): 97–104. *Notes & Queries* 6th Ser. 3 (1881): 1–3; 8th Ser. 7 (1895): 441–443. Maitland *Bracton's Note Book* 2 (1887): 404–405; 3 (1887): 450–452. *MSS of the Marquess of Abergavenny* (Hist. MSS Comm.) (1887): 72–73 (undated charter of Robert de Courtenay; charter names his wife, Maud, and is witnessed by Reynold and William de Courtenay). *Note-book of Tristram Risdon* (1897): 53–56. *C.P.* 4 (1916): 317 (sub Devon) (ped.), 465, footnote c. *C.R.R.* 1 (1922): 127; 8 (1938): 32. Stenton *Great Roll of the Pipe Michaelmas 1201* (Pubs. Pipe Roll Soc. n.s. 14) (1936): 223. Seversmith *Colonial Fams. of Long Island, New York & Connecticut* 5 (1958): 2419, 2425–2426. Schwennicke *Europaische Stammtafeln* 3(4) (1989): 629 (sub Courtenay). Slade & Lambrick *Two Cartularies of Abingdon Abbey* 1 (Oxford Hist. Soc. n.s. 32) (1990): 171 (charter of Reynold de Courtenay dated pre-1194). Hanna *Christchurch Priory Cartulary* (2007): 281.

3. ROBERT DE COURTENAY, Knt., of Okehampton, Kenn, Musbury, and Sampford Courtenay, Devon, Sutton Courtenay, Berkshire, Waddesdon, Buckinghamshire, Iwerne, Dorset, etc., Sheriff of Devonshire, 1215, 1218, Justice for Berkshire and Wiltshire, 1235, son and heir. He was heir in 1209 to his uncle, Robert de Courtenay. He married in 1210–11 (grant of her marriage)

MARY DE VERNON, widow of Peter de Preaux, Knt.,[13] of Alton, Hampshire, Sudbury (in West Ham), Essex, etc., lord of the Channel Islands, Constable of Rouen (living 1209), and daughter of William de Vernon, Knt., 5th Earl of Devon, by Mabel, daughter of Robert II, Count of Meulan [see VERMANDOIS 8 for her ancestry]. Her maritagium included lands in Crewkerne, Somerset, with the foreign hundred and the chace there. They had three sons, John, Knt., William, Knt., and Robert [Dean of Auckland], and two daughters, Egeline and Hawise. In 1209 he paid a fine to the king of 400 marks and two great horses to have seisin of the manor of Sutton, Berkshire. In 1211 he owed 1,200 marks to have the honour of Oakhampton, Devon, which had been in the king's hands. In 1217 he was ordered by the king to release Exeter Castle and the stannaries and coinage of Devon to the queen mother. In 1214 he sued Roger Chike and two others regarding lands in Sutton, Berkshire. In April 1218 he offered 5 marks to have a jury concerning the hundred of Redlane which he said was his and pertains to his manor of Iwerne, which hundred, and the hundred of Gillingham, were withdrawn from him and his ancestors. In July 1218 the king committed custody of the manor of Sutton, Berkshire to John of Wiggonholt for as long as it pleases the king, so that he answer for the issues of the same manor to Stephen de Croy, merchant of Amiens, for the debt which Robert de Courtenay owed him. In 1219 the king ordered the Sheriff of Devon that he cause Robert de Courtenay to have full seisin of all lands and appurtenances in Devonshire formerly of Hawise de Courtenay, his mother, which fell to the said Robert by inheritance. In 1220 he was granted a two day fair at his manor of Okehampton, Devon. In 1220 John de Saint Helen sued him regarding half a hide of land in Sutton, Berkshire. The same year Maud de Courtenay (his aunt and step-grandmother) sued him regarding the manors of Oakhampton, Chulmleigh, Kenn, and Musbury, and Sampford, Devon and Hemington, Somerset, which she claimed as her right. In 1224 he made fine with the king to render £30 to him annually at the Exchequer of the £190 8s. 7d. due from him to the king; he was allowed such costs he incurred, by order of the king and the same justiciar, to fill a breach in the wall of Exeter castle. In 1227 the king committed the manor of Sedborough (in Parkham), Devon with its appurtenances to his wife, Mary. In 1230 he was overseas in the service of the king. In the period, 1230–2, he settled a long standing dispute with Abingdon Abbey regarding digging turves from the manor of Culham for the repair of Sutton mill, Berkshire. SIR ROBERT DE COURTENAY died at Iwerne, Dorset about 27 July 1242, and was buried at Ford Abbey, Dorset. His widow, Mary, was living 15 July 1250.

Brooke *Discoverie of Certaine Errours* (1724): 75–76. Risdon *Chorographical Desc. or Survey of the County of Devon* (1811): 356–357. Burke *Gen'l & Heraldic Dict. of the Peerages of England, Ireland & Scotland* (1831): 142–146 (sub Courtenay). *Coll. Top. et Gen.* 1 (1834): 62; 2 (1835): 390. Stapleton *Magni Rotuli Scaccarii Normanniæ* 1 (1840): clxix–clxx, clxxii–clxxiii; 2 (1844): cxliv–cxlvi, cc, ccxxix–ccxxxii (Peter de Préaux styled "brother" [fratris] by Alice, Countess of Eu). Dugdale *Monasticon Anglicanum* 5 (1846): 377–382 (Ford Abbey, Fundationis et Fundatorum Historia: "Qui Robertus [de Courtenay] cum tandem vitæ suæ laudabilem cursum fœliciter consummasset in stadio, septimo calend. Augusti [26 July] apud Ywren, manerium suum, diem clausit extremum anno Domini M.CCXLII. [1242] et regni regis Henrici III. 26...."). Lipscomb *Hist. & Antiqs. of Buckingham* 1 (1847): 464–472. (Courtenay ped.) Adams *Hist., Topog., & Antiqs. of the Isle of Wight* (1856): 132–133. Le Quesne *Constitutional Hist. of Jersey* (1856): 109–110. *Collectanea Archæologica* 1 (1862): 263–284. Shirley *Royal & Other Historical Letters illus. of the Reign of King Henry III* 1 (1862) (Rolls ser. 27): 40–41, 160, 232–233 (letters of Robert de Courtenay). Teulet *Layettes du Trésor des Chartes* 1 (1863): 250–252. *Notes & Queries*

---

[13] Mary de Vernon married (1st) in 1201 (date of charter) (betrothal dated early 1200) Peter de Préaux, Knt., of Alton, Hampshire, Sudbury (in West Ham), Essex, etc., lord of the Channel Islands, Constable of Rouen, younger son of Osbert de Préaux, of Normandy. They had no issue. He accompanied King Richard I on crusade in 1190. He distinguished himself at the Siege of Acre in 1192. In the period, 1194–9, he served King Richard I throughout his wars against Philip II of France. In 1203 he was in charge of the escheats of Normandy and the Jews, except for the Jews of Rouen and Caen. The same year he was granted all the land which Peter de Meulan (his wife's uncle) held at Sens, Normandy. In 1204, in agreement with the leading men of the city, he surrendered Rouen to King Philippe Auguste of France. He was living in 1209.

4th Ser. 6 (1870): 388; 6th Ser. 3 (1881): 1–3; 8th Ser. 7 (1895): 441–443. *Bibliothèque de l'École des Chartes* 32 (1871): 403–404. *Reliquary* 17 (1876–7): 97–104. *MSS of the Marquess of Abergavenny* (Hist. MSS Comm.) (1887): 72–73. Ouless *Ecréhous, Illustrated* (1884): 8–10. Worthy *Hist. of the Suburbs of Exeter* (1885): 61–62, 81–82, 149. Maitland *Bracton's Note Book* 2 (1887): 133–134, 137–138 (Robert de Courtenay testified in lawsuit dated 1222 that he was the son of Hawise, the first born daughter of Maud d'Avranches; Hawise's sister, Maud de Courtenay, who was the plaintiff in the lawsuit, in turn testified that the said Hawise was the daughter of Geoffrey de Crimes (or Crunes, Cruues), the 1st husband of Maud d'Avranches), 404–405; 3 (1887): 320, 450–452 (Robert de Courtenay testified in lawsuit dated 1222 that his mother, Hawise, was the daughter of William de Curcy, husband of Maud d'Avranches). Archer *Crusade of Richard I, 1189–92* (1889): 326. *Notes & Gleanings* 2 (1889): 65–68; 5 (1892): 21 (charter of Robert de Courtenay). Curtis *Short Hist. & Desc. of the Town of Alton* (1896): 21–22. *Note-book of Tristram Risdon* (1897): 53–56. *List of Sheriffs for England & Wales* (PRO Lists and Indexes 9) (1898): 34. *C.P.R. 1216–1225* (1901): 53 (Robert de Courtenay styled "king's kinsman" by King Henry III of England). *Desc. Cat. Ancient Deeds* 4 (1902): 69. Wrottesley *Peds. from the Plea Rolls* (1905): 535. *C.Ch.R.* 2 (1906): 60. *Devon Notes & Queries* 4 (1907): 148–149, 229–232 (re. Preaux fam.). Phillimore *Rotuli Hugonis de Welles Episcopi Lincolniensis 1209–1235* 2 (Canterbury & York Soc. 3) (1907): 79. *C.P.* 4 (1916): 317 (sub Devon) (ped.), 323 (sub Devon), 465. *C.R.R.* 7 (1935): 51, 97, 134, 146, 192–193, 244, 259, 333; 9 (1952): 26, 36–37, 104, 237, 294, 305–306, 322, 330, 362; 10 (1949): 22, 115–116, 119–120; 17 (1991): 166. Hatton *Book of Seals* (1950): 136. *Great Roll of the Pipe Michaelmas 1211* (Pubs. Pipe Roll Soc. n.s. 28) (1953): 61. Seversmith *Col. Fams. of Long Island* 5 (1958): 2413–2419, 2439–2440. Sanders *English Baronies* (1960): 70. VCH Essex 6 (1973): 68–74. VCH Somerset 4 (1978): 4–38. Schwennicke *Europaische Stanmtafeln* 3(4) (1989): 629 (sub Courtenay). Bearman *Charters of the Redvers family and the Earldom of Devon, 1090–1217* (Devon & Cornwall Soc. n.s. 37) (1994): 172. Reedy *Basset Charters c. 1120 to 1250* (Pub. Pipe Roll Soc. n.s. 50) (1995): 128–129 (charter of Egeline de Courtenay, widow of Gilbert Basset dated 1205–6; charter names her late father, Reynold de Courtenay; charter witnessed by Robert de Courtenay). Barlow *English Episcopal Acta* XII (1996): 215. Golb *Jews in Medieval Normandy* (1998): 372. Hobbs *Cartulary of Forde Abbey* (Somerset Rec. Soc. 85) (1998): 90 (charter of Robert de Courtenay dated 1225–42; charter witnessed by his sons, John and William, and Reynold de Courtenay [presumably his brother]); 109 (charter of Robert de Courtenay dated 1225–42; charter witnessed by his brother, Reynold de Courtenay), 152–153 (charter of John son of Ellis, parson of Crewkerne dated 1228–36; charter witnessed by Sir Robert de Courtenay and Reynold his brother). Church *King John: New Interpretations* (1999): 135 footnote 114, 202 ("The Courtenays to whom Henry II awarded landed in England, although related to the original Courtenay line, appear to have been only distant cousins. Nonetheless, cousins they were, so that in 1217, when Robert de Courtenay was asked to surrender Exeter to Isabella, he is described in King Henry III's letter as 'our kinsman.' Perhaps because of his kinship to one of the leading families of France, Robert de Courtenay of Okehampton appears to have been singled out for particularly harsh treatment by Louis and the French during the civil war of 1216–17, being deprived of his lands in one of Louis' few surviving English charters. The fact that the original of this charter survived amongst the Courtenay family archives in France provides further proof, if such were needed, of the kinship between the English and French Courtenays. Robert appears as witness to Isabella's charter in favour of the monks of St. Nicholas Exeter, issued at Exeter in May 1217."). Knight *Great Roll of the Pipe Michaelmas 1222* (Pubs. Pipe Roll Soc. n.s. 51) (1999): 51. Sayer *Original Docs. in Eng. & Wales (1198–1304)* (1999): 165–166 ("Lyons, 1250 Jul. 15. 369. Innocentius IV <<dilecte in Christo filie nobili mulieri Marie de Cortenay Bathonien. dioc.>> Protection for the noble lady, Mary de Cortenay of the diocese of Bath, Hawise de Neville and her other sons and daughters, with all their goods."). Barratt *Receipt Rolls, Easter 1223, Michaelmas 1224* (Pubs. Pipe Roll Soc. n.s. 55) (2007): 85.

Children of Robert de Courtenay, Knt., by Mary de Vernon:

i. **JOHN DE COURTENAY**, Knt. [see next].

ii. **ROBERT DE COURTENAY**, Dean of Auckland, dead 1 Jan. 1258. C.P.R. 1232–1247 (1906): 190 (Robert le Clerc, son of Robert de Curtenay, styled "king's kinsman").

iii. **EGELINE DE COURTENAY**, married **PHILIP DE COLUMBERS**, of Nether Stowey, Honibere (in Lilstock), Huntworth, Puriton, Woolavington, and Woolstone (in Stogursey), Somerset and Battisford, Suffolk, son and heir of Philip de Columbers, of Nether Stowey and Honibere (in Lilstock), Somerset. They had two sons, Philip and John. At an unknown date, he confirmed William de Rokelle in his land in Akot and Beningham, which property the said Philip's grandfather, Philip de Columbers, gave in free marriage to Richard de Rokelle and Maud de Columbers his daughter, parents of the said William and Philip de Rokelle. PHILIP DE COLUMBERS died in 1262. In 1272 his widow, Egeline, settled 100 librates of land in South Kelsey, Lincolnshire and Blacktoft, Yorkshire, together with the advowson of the church of Torrington, Lincolnshire, on Gilbert Hansard and Joan his wife. Egeline was living in 1297. Roberts *Excerpta è Rotulis Finium in Turri Londinensi asservatis* 2 (1836): 256, 378, 384. Gairdner *Letters & Papers, Foreign & Domestic, Henry VIII* 7 (1883): 326–357. Moore *Cartularium Monasterii Sancti Johannis Baptiste de Colecestria* 2 (1897): 389–390 (confirmation charters of Philip de Columbers *tertius*). *Cal. IPM* 1 (1904): 145–146; 2 (1906): 126–133. Foster *Final Concords of Lincoln from the Feet of Fines A.D. 1244–1272* 2 (Lincoln Rec. Soc. 17) (1920): 292. Farrer *Honors & Knights' Fees* (1923): 137–140. Tremlett *Stogursey Charters* (Somerset Rec. Soc. 61) (1949): xxv (Columbers ped.). VCH Somerset 5 (1985): 103–107; 6 (1992): 137–145; 8 (2004): 210–223. Schwennicke *Europaische Stanmtafeln* 3(4) (1989): 629 (sub Courtenay).

    iv. **HAWISE DE COURTENAY**, married (1st) **JOHN DE NEVILLE**, Knt., of Essex [see DE LA MARE 10]; (2nd) **JOHN DE GATESDEN**, Knt., of Broadwater, Sussex [see DE LA MARE 10].

4. JOHN DE COURTENAY, Knt., of Okehampton, Chulmeleigh, Kenn, Musbury, and Sampford Courtenay, Devon, Sutton Courtenay, Berkshire, Hillesden and Waddesdon, Buckinghamshire, Iwerne Courtney, Dorset, Hemington, Somerset, etc., son and heir. He married (1st) **EMMA _____**. In 1235 he gave all his lands at East Hirst [Hirst Courtney] and his right of common in the woods at West Hirst [Temple Hirst], Yorkshire to the Knights Templar for the health of his soul and the soul of Emma his wife. He married (2nd) before 2 Jan. 1233/4 **MAUD DE CANEVILLE** (she died testate shortly before 6 October 1240), widow of Nele de Mowbray (died 1230), of Thirsk, Yorkshire, and niece of Hugh de Pateshull, Bishop of Coventry and Lichfield. He and his 2nd wife, Maud, were defendants in a lawsuit in Yorkshire in 1237. He married (3rd) after 6 October 1240 **ISABEL DE VERE**, daughter of Hugh de Vere, Knt., Earl of Oxford, by Hawise, daughter of Saher de Quincy, 1st Earl of Winchester [see VERE 2 for her ancestry]. Her maritagium included the manors of Hillesden and Wavendon, Buckinghamshire. They had one son, Hugh, Knt. He served in Poitou, 1242, Wales, 1244, 1257, and 1258, and Gascony, 1248 and 1253. In 1254 he was granted a market and fair at Chawleigh and Newton Poppleford, Devon, and free warren in all his demesne lands in cos. Berks, Bucks, Devon, Dorset, and Somerset. He was granted a weekly market and a yearly fair at Iwerne Courtney, Dorset in 1261. In 1263 he was granted a a weekly market and yearly fair at Faukland, Somerset. The same year he was pardoned 10 marks by the king for his good services. In 1264 he was commanded to come to the king with all speed. SIR JOHN DE COURTENAY died testate 3 May 1274, and was buried at Ford Abbey, Dorset. His widow, Isabel, married (2nd) before 24 Jan. 1276/7 (royal license 18 or 19 May 1280 for a fine of £100) **OLIVER DE DINHAM** (or **DYNHAM**), Knt., of Hartland, Ilsington, etc., Devon, Corton Dinham and Sandford Orcas, Somerset, Constable of Exeter and Taunton Castles, Keeper of Lundy Isle, son and heir of Geoffrey de Dinham, Knt., of Hartland, Devon. He was born about 1234 (aged 24 in 1258). They had two sons, Josce, Knt., and Geoffrey. Oliver was pardoned for non-observance of the Provisions of Oxford 28 March 1264. In 1265 he supported the king's cause in the West against the adherents of Simon de Montfort. The same year he presented to the church of Corton Dinham, Somerset. He took possession of Hartland Abbey during a voidance about 1272, when the Bishop of Exeter was absent abroad, and extorted large sums of money from the canons. He bought the manors of Nutwell and Harpwell, Devon from Marmoutier Abbey in 1272/3. In 1274–5 Simon de Torm arraigned an assize of mort d'ancestor against him and others touching common of pasture in Buckland, Somerset. In 1276–7 he arraigned an assize of novel disseisin against the abbot of Hartland touching a tenement in Hartland, Devon. He was in the army of Wales in 1277 and 1282. He presented to the church of Waddesdon, Buckinghamshire 13 March 1277. He was summoned to attend the king at Shrewsbury 28 June 1283. In 1286 he was granted a fair at Hartland, Devon. His wife, Isabel, died testate 11 August, year uncertain, sometime before 7 Jan. 1290/1. He was summoned to Parliament from 24 June 1295 to 26 August 1296, by writs directed *Olivero de Dynham* or *Dynaunt*, whereby he is held to have become Lord Dinham. SIR OLIVER DE DINHAM, Lord Dinham, died 26 Feb. 1298/9. He and his wife, Isabel, were buried in the church of the Black Friars, Exeter, Devon.

    Dugdale *Baronage of England* 2 (1676): 635 (chart), 636–637 (sub Courtenay). Brydges *Collins' Peerage of England* 6 (1812): 214–271 (sub Courtenay, Viscount Courtenay). Kennett *Parochial Antiqs. of Ambrosden, Burcester* 2 (1818): 447–456. Baker *Hist. & Antiqs. of Northampton* 1 (1822–30): 619–620 (Rivers ped.). Clutterbuck *Hist. & Antiqs. of Hertford* 3 (1827): 104–105 (Vere ped.). Westcote *View of Devonshire in MDCXXX* (1845): 570–573 (sub Courtenay). Lipscomb

Hist. & Antiqs. of Buckingham 1 (1847): 471–472 (Courtenay ped.). *Reliquary* 17 (1876–7): 97–104. *Annual Rpt. of the Deputy Keeper* 44 (1883): 49, 189; 46 (1886): 183. Maitland *Bracton's Note Book* 2 (1887): 404–405. *Notes & Queries* 7th Ser. 4 (1887): 430. Loftie *Kensington Picturesque & Hist.* (1888): 56–59 (Vere ped.). *Notes & Gleanings* 2 (1889): 50–56, 65–68, 89–93, 97. Dickinson *Kirkby's Quest for Somerset* (Somerset Rec. Soc. 3) (1889): 26. *Genealogist* n.s. 12 (1895): 228. Vivian *Vis. of Devon 1531, 1564 & 1620* (1895): 243–250 (sub Courtenay). *Note-book of Tristram Risdon* (1897): 53–56. Giffard & Bowett *Regs. of Walter Giffard & Henry Bowett Bishops of Bath & Wells* (Somerset Rec. Soc. 13) (1899): 5. *Rpt. & Trans. of the Devonshire Assoc.* 2nd Ser. 4 (1902): 721–723 (author identifies Oliver de Dinham, husband of Isabel de Vere, as son of Oliver de Dinham, by Mary, daughter of Hugh Courtney of Hanington, cites Plac. Quo. Warr. 8 Edw. I., Somerset Rot. 62). Wrottesley *Peds. from the Plea Rolls* (1905): 68–69, 129, 225–226, 535. *C.Ch.R.* 2 (1906): 329. *Cal. IPM* 2 (1906): 50–53. *C.C.R. 1234–1237* (1908): 520. *C.P.R. 1258–1266* (1910): 323 (John de Eyvile styled "nephew" [i.e., kinsman] of John de Courtenay in 1264). *C.P.* 3 (1913): 465 (sub Courtenay); 4 (1916): 317 (sub Devon) (ped.), 323 (sub Devon), 369–371 (sub Dinham); 9 (1936): 375 (sub Mowbray); 10 (1945): 215, footnote h (sub Vere). *Cornwall Feet of Fines* 1 (Devon & Cornwall Rec. Soc. 1914a) (1914): 119, 49, 54–55. Ehrlich *Procs. against the Crown (1216–1377)* (Oxford Studies in Social & Legal Hist. 6) (1921): 217. VCH *Berkshire* 4 (1924): 372–373. Davis *Rotuli Ricardi Gravesend Episcopi Lincolniensis* (Lincoln Rec. Soc. 20) (1925): 255. *Somersetshire Pleas* 3 (Somerset Rec. Soc. 41) (1926): 36–37. VCH *Buckingham* 4 (1927): 109–110, 174–175. *Somersetshire Pleas* 4(1) (Somerset Rec. Soc. 44) (1929): 59–60. Moor *Knights of Edward I* 1 (H.S.P. 80) (1929): 296 (biog. of Sir Oliver de Dynaunt) (his arms: Gules a fesse fusilly ermine). Cam *Hundred & Hundred Rolls* (1930): 263. *Genealogist's Mag.* 6 (1932–34): 606–626. Paget *Baronage of England* (1957) 151: 1–3 (sub Courtenay); 187: 1–9 (sub Dinan). Seversmith *Col. Fams. of Long Island* 5 (1958): 2407–2413 ("John de Courtenay is said to have been a particularly upright and just man, and he was a strong friend and benefactor to the monks of Ford abbey"). Sanders *English Baronies* (1960): 70. London *Cartulary of Canonsleigh Abbey* (Devon & Cornwall Rec. Soc. n.s. 8) (1965): 99, 102–103. Hedley *Northumberland Fams.* 1 (1968): 24–26. VCH *Somerset* 4 (1978): 4–38. Hull *Cartulary of Launceston Priory* (Devon & Cornwall Rec. Soc. n.s. 30) (1987): 100–101. Schwennicke *Europaische Stammtafeln* 3(4) (1989): 629 (sub Courtenay). Hobbs *Cartulary of Forde Abbey* (Somerset Rec. Soc. 85) (1998): 97. Special thanks go to John P. Ravilious for his correction of the death date of Isabel de Vere.

Child of John de Courtenay, Knt., by Isabel de Vere:

i. **HUGH DE COURTENAY**, Knt. [see next].

Child of Isabel de Vere, by Oliver de Dinham, Knt.:

i. **JOSCE DE DINHAM**, Knt., of Hartland, Devon, married **MARGARET DE HYDON** [see DINHAM 4].

5. HUGH DE COURTENAY, Knt., of Okehampton, Aylesbeare, Belstone, Dolton, Kenn, Newton, and Sampford Courtney, Devon, Sutton Courtenay, Berkshire (now Oxfordshire), Hillesdon and Waddesdon, Buckinghamshire, Iwerne Courtney, Dorset, Crewkerne, Somerset, etc., son and heir, born 25 March 1251. He married **ELEANOR LE DESPENSER**, daughter of Hugh le Despenser, of Loughborough, Leicestershire, Ryhall, Rutland, Parlington, Yorkshire, etc., Justiciar of England, by Aline (or Aveline), daughter and heiress of Philip Basset, Knt., of Wycombe, Buckinghamshire, and Wootton Basset, Wiltshire. Her maritagium included a messuage and three carucates of land, excepting 110 acres, in Wootton Courtney, Somerset by the gift of Philip Basset, Eleanor's grandfather. They had three sons, Hugh, Knt. [Earl of Devon, 1st Lord Courtenay], John, and Philip, and four daughters, Isabel, Aveline, Egeline, and Margaret (or Margery). In 1274–5 Hugh de Pruz and Maud his wife arraigned an assize of novel disseisin against him and others touching common of pasture in Colyton, Devon. In 1275–6 Robert Malet arraigned an assize of novel disseisin against him and others regarding a tenement in Waddesdon, Buckinghamshire. In the same period, Matthew, parson of the church of Wootton, arraigned an assize of novel disseisin against him and others touching common of pasture in Wootton, Somerset. In 1277 he was granted protection, he then going to Wales on the king's service. In 1280 Ela, widow of Philip Basset, sued Hugh and his wife, Eleanor (Ela's step-granddaughter) for a messuage and lands in Wootton Courtney, Somerset which Ela claimed to be her right by the gift of Hugh de Neville; the jury found in favor of Hugh and Eleanor. He was in the army of West Wales in 1282. He was summoned to attend the King at Shrewsbury 28 June 1283. He presented to the church of Waddesdon, Buckinghamshire in 1290. SIR HUGH DE COURTENAY died at Colecombe (or Cullicomb), Devon 28 Feb. 1291/2. His widow, Eleanor, presented to the churches of Waddesdon,

Buckinghamshire, 1295, 1323, Hemington, Somerset, 1316, Parkham, Devon, 1322, and Wrington, Somerset, 1327. She died testate at London when returning from Canterbury 30 Sept. 1328. Hugh and Eleanor were buried at Cowick Priory near Exeter, Devon.

Brydges *Collins' Peerage of England* 6 (1812): 214–271 (sub Courtenay, Viscount Courtenay). Baker *Hist. & Antiqs. of Northampton* 1 (1822–30): 619–620 (Rivers ped.). Dugdale *Monasticon Anglicanum* 5 (1825): 377–382 (Ford Abbey: "… Erexit se ergo Hugo de Courtney primus dominus, in progenitorum suorem hæreditatem et dominium; sed quantum in ipsis viguit et floruit devotio et affectio in Deo et Forden. cœnobium, tantum in isto tepuit et hebuit mentis sinceritas, pietas, puritas, præcordia suorem. Duxerat autem in uxorem Elianorum filiam proceris incliti domini Hugonis le Despenser primi."). Westcote *View of Devonshire in MDCXXX* (1845): 570–573 (sub Courtenay). Lipscomb *Hist. & Antiqs. of Buckingham* 1 (1847): 471–472 (Courtenay ped.). *Reliquary* 17 (1876–7): 97–104. *Annual Rpt. of the Deputy Keeper* 44 (1883): 71; 45 (1885): 313, 346, 367. *Notes & Gleanings* 1 (1888): 11; 2 (1889): 50–56, 65–68, 89–93, 97. Weaver *Somerset Incumbents* (1889): 99, 304. Grandisson *Reg. of John de Grandisson Bishop of Exeter* 1 (1894): 601 (re. probate of will of Eleanor de Courtenay). Vivian *Vis. of Devon 1531, 1564 & 1620* (1895): 243–250 (sub Courtenay). *Note-book of Tristram Risdon* (1897): 53–56. Bates *Two Cartularies of the Benedictine Abbeys of Muchelney & Athelney* (Somerset Rec. Soc. 14) (1899): 27. *List of Foreign Accounts* (Lists & Indexes XI) (1900): 206. Wrottesley *Peds. from the Plea Rolls* (1905): 225–226, 535. *Cal. IPM* 2 (1906): 50–53. Guilloreau *Cartulaire de Loders* (1908): 61, 116. *C.P.* 3 (1913): 465–466 (sub Courtenay); 4 (1916): 323 (sub Devon); 5 (1926): 644–647 (sub Giffard); 6 (1926): 123–124 (sub Grey) (Henry de Grey "is said to have m., 1stly, Eleanor, da. of Sir Hugh de Courtenay … If this is correct, she was presumably da. of Sir Hugh de Courtenay, of Okehampton, by Eleanor, da. of Hugh le Despenser, Lord Le Despenser… Dugdale mentions a grant by Henry de Grey of a cottage in Sheringham, Norfolk, for the health of his soul and the soul of his wife, Eleanor, to the monks of Notley."). VCH *Berkshire* 4 (1924): 372–373. Davis *Rotuli Ricardi Gravesend Episcopi Lincolniensis* (Lincoln Rec. Soc. 20) (1925): 257. VCH *Buckingham* 4 (1927): 109–110, 174–175. Schofield *Mulchelney Memoranda* (Somerset Rec. Soc. 42) (1927): 79–80. *Somersetshire Pleas* 4(1) (Somerset Rec. Soc. 44) (1929): 59–60, 80–82, 135, 137, 219–220, 254–255, 324–325. Cam *Hundred & Hundred Rolls* (1930): 263–264, 278. *Genealogist's Mag.* 6 (1932–34): 606–626. *Somerset & Dorset Notes & Queries* 25 (1950): 32. Paget *Baronage of England* (1957) 151: 1–3 (sub Courtenay). Seversmith *Col. Fams. of Long Island* 5 (1958): 2402–2407. Sanders *English Baronies* (1960): 70. *TAG* 38 (1962): 180. London *Cartulary of Canonsleigh Abbey* (Devon & Cornwall Rec. Soc. n.s. 8) (1965): 96, 99–100, 100 (charter of Hugh de Courtenay). VCH *Somerset* 4 (1978): 4–38. Sutton *Rolls & Reg. of Bishop Oliver Sutton, 1280–1299* 8 (Lincoln Rec. Soc. 76) (1986): 126, 160. Schwennicke *Europaische Stamtafeln* 3(4) (1989): 629 (sub Courtenay). Brault *Rolls of Arms Edward I* 2 (1997): 123–124 (arms of Hugh de Courtenay: Or, three roundels gules, a label azure; Argent, three roundels gules, a label azure; Or, three roundels gules surmounted by a bend azure). Burghersh *Regs. of Bishop Henry Burghersh* 2 (Lincoln Rec. Soc. 90) (2003): 129.

Children of Hugh de Courtenay, Knt., by Eleanor le Despenser:

i. **HUGH DE COURTENAY**, Knt., Earl of Devon, 1st Lord Courtenay [see next].

ii. **JOHN DE COURTENAY**, of Little Hillegh, Somerset, died in or before 1306. No issue. Vivian *Vis. of Devon 1531, 1564 & 1620* (1895): 243–250 (sub Courtenay). Schofield *Mulchelney Memoranda* (Somerset Rec. Soc. 42) (1927): 79–80.

iii. **PHILIP DE COURTENAY**, of Moreton and Little Hillegh, Somerset. He was slain at the Battle of Bannockburn 24 June 1314. No known issue. Brydges *Collins' Peerage of England* 6 (1812): 214–271 (sub Courtenay, Viscount Courtenay). Westcote *View of Devonshire in MDCXXX* (1845): 570–573 (sub Courtenay). Vivian *Vis. of Devon 1531, 1564 & 1620* (1895): 243–250 (sub Courtenay). Schofield *Mulchelney Memoranda* (Somerset Rec. Soc. 42) (1927): 79–80. Paget *Baronage of England* (1957) 151: 1–3 (sub Courtenay).

iv. **ISABEL DE COURTENAY**, married **JOHN DE SAINT JOHN**, Knt., 1st Lord Saint John of Basing [see PAULET 8].

v. **AVELINE DE COURTENAY**, married before 6 Nov. 1311 **JOHN GIFFARD**, Knt., 2nd Lord Giffard, of Brimpsfield, Badgeworth, Rockhampton, etc., Gloucestershire, Keeper of the Castle and town of Dryslwyn, Carmarthenshire, son and heir of John Giffard, Knt., 1st Lord Giffard, by his 2nd wife, Margaret. He was probably born 24 June 1287. They had no issue. He was summoned to Parliament from 8 October 1311 to 15 May 1321, by writs directed *Johanni Giffard de Brymmesfeld'*. In 1313 he was ordered under pain of forfeiture to abstain from attending a tournament at Newmarket. The same year he was enjoined to abstain from tourneying, bourding, jousting, seeking adventures, or performing any other feat of arms without the king's license. He was taken prisoner at the Battle of Bannockburn 24 June 1314. In 1316 he was sent to Wales to check the depredations of Llywelyn ab Rhys in Morgannwg. In 1316 he granted the privilege of free-pasturage in Buckholt to Gloucester Abbey. On 30 Dec. 1316 he was granted 200 marks a year, being a banneret of the King's Household, having agreed to remain with the king for life and serve him in peace and war with 30 men-at-arms. This grant was revoked 9 June 1318, by reason of the Ordinances drawn up by the barons which King Edward II was forced to accept. In 1321 he joined the disaffected barons in the west who were preparing for hostilities in South Wales. The king summoned a number of barons, including Giffard, to a Council of Magnates to be held in Gloucester 5 April 1321, but they ignored the command. He was one of those who ravaged the lands of the Despensers in May and June, for which he received a pardon 20 August 1321. At the outbreak of hostilities the following Dec., he successfully held Gloucester against the king. Soon afterwards he joined Thomas, Earl of Lancaster, at the Siege of Tickhill Castle, and was present at the conflict at Burton-on-Trent 11 March. SIR JOHN GIFFARD was taken prisoner at the Battle of Boroughbridge 16 March 1321/2. He was subsequently hanged at Gloucester at the end of April or beginning of May 1323, and his body cut in quarters. His widow, Aveline, died 27 April 1327. Brydges *Collins' Peerage of England* 6 (1812): 214–271 (sub Courtenay, Viscount Courtenay). Westcote *View of Devonshire in MDCXXX* (1845): 570–573 (sub Courtenay). Lipscomb *Hist. & Antiqs. of Buckingham* 1 (1847): 471–472 (Courtenay ped.). Vivian *Vis. of Devon 1531, 1564 & 1620* (1895): 243–250 (sub Courtenay). *C.P.* 5 (1926): 644–649 (sub Giffard). Richardson & Sayles *Rotuli Parl. Anglie* (Camden Soc. 3rd Ser. 51) (1935): 154–155. *Trans. Bristol & Gloucs. Arch. Soc.* 65 (1944): 105–128. Paget *Baronage of England* (1957) 151: 1–3 (sub Courtenay). Schwennicke *Europaische Stamntafeln* 3(4) (1989): 629 (sub Courtenay).

vi. **EGELINE DE COURTENAY**, married **ROBERT DE SCALES**, Knt., 2nd Lord Scales [see SCALES 6].

vii. **MARGARET** (or **MARGERY**) **DE COURTENAY**, married **NICHOLAS DE MOELS**, 2nd Lord Moels [see MOELS 9.i].

6. HUGH DE COURTENAY, Knt., of Okehampton, Cadeleigh, Honiton, and Plympton, Devon, Sutton Courtenay, Berkshire (now Oxfordshire), Waddesdon, Buckinghamshire, Ibberton and Iwerne Courtney, Dorset, Crowell and Nuneham (in Nuneham Courtenay), Oxfordshire, etc., Chief Warden of the Ports and Coasts for cos. Cornwall and Devon, 1324, Chief Justiciar of the Woods and Parks in cos. Gloucester, Somerset, Dorset, Wilts, and Hants, 1328, Warden of Buddeleigh Hundred, 1330, son and heir, born 14 Sept. 1276 (came of age in 1297). He married in 1292 **AGNES DE SAINT JOHN**, daughter of John de Saint John, Knt., of Basing, Hampshire, by Alice, daughter of Reynold Fitz Peter, Knt. [see PAULET 7 for her ancestry]. They had four sons, John [Abbot of Tavistock], Hugh, Knt. [10th Earl of Devon, 2nd Lord Courtenay], Robert, and Thomas, Knt., and two daughters, Eleanor and Elizabeth (wife of Bartholomew de Lisle). About 1285 he granted an acre of arable land in the manor of Iwerne Courtney, Dorset, together with the advowson of the church, to Christchurch Priory. He was heir in 1293 to his cousin, Isabel de Forz, Countess of Aumale and Devon [see CLARE 6.i.b], by which he inherited the various manors, including Breamore and Lymington, Hampshire and Nuneham (in Nuneham Courtenay), Oxfordshire. He served in the Scottish wars, 1298–1303. He was summoned to Parliament from 6 Feb. 1298/9 by writs directed *Hugoni de Curtenay*, whereby he is held to have become Lord Courtenay. He was in the Scottish wars, and was present at the Siege of Caerlaverock Castle in 1300. He was knighted by Edward, Prince of Wales 22 May 1306. He presented to the chantry of Brightleigh (in Chittlehampton), Devon in 1309. In 1311–12 Robert de Mandeville brought an action against him and others for disseising him of a tenement in East Coker and West Coker, Somerset; in 1315 Mandeville acknowledged that he owed Hugh and another 2000 marks, and he granted them all his lands in East Coker and South Coker, Somerset; he likewise released all his right in the manor of Coker with East Coker, West Coker, and South Coker, and in the hundred of Coker. Hugh was chosen one of the Lords Ordainers in 1313, and was a member of the King's Council 9 August 1318. He presented to the churches of Honiton, Devon, 1325, Waddesdon, Buckinghamshire, 1326, 1329, Kenn, Devon, 1328, Chawleigh, Devon, 1328. He presented to the prebendal church of Chulmleigh, Devon, 1328, and the chantry of the chapel of Sticklepath, Devon, 1329. In the period, 1327–8, William de Fauconberge and his wife, Maud, sued him regarding the manors of East Coker and West Coker, Somerset. On 22 Feb. 1334/5 he was declared Earl of Devon. In 1338 he presented to the church of Crewkerne, Somerset, First Portion. SIR HUGH DE COURTENAY, 9th Earl of Devon, 1st Lord Courtenay, died testate at Tiverton, Devon 23 Dec.

1340, and was buried 5 Feb. 1340/1. His widow, Agnes, died 11 June 1345. They were buried in the conventual church of Cowick Priory near Exeter, Devon.

Brydges *Collins' Peerage of England* 6 (1812): 214–271 (sub Courtenay, Viscount Courtenay). Baker *Hist. & Antiqs. of Northampton* 1 (1822–30): 619–620 (Rivers ped.). Nicolas *Rpt. of Procs. on the Claim of the Earldom of Devon in the House of Lords* (1832): 5–16. Palgrave *Docs. & Recs. Ill. the Hist. of Scotland* 1 (1837): 225 ("Hugo de Curtenay Miles" included on list of people owing military service in 1300). Westcote *View of Devonshire in MDCXXX* (1845): 570–573 (sub Courtenay). Lipscomb *Hist. & Antiqs. of Buckingham* 1 (1847): 471–472 (Courtenay ped.). *Reliquary* 17 (1876–7): 97–104. Doyle *Official Baronage of England* 1 (1886): 574–575 (sub Devonshire). *Notes & Gleanings* 2 (1889): 50–56, 65–68, 89–93, 97. Birch *Cat. Seals in the British Museum* 2 (1892): 695 (seal of Hugh de Courtenay dated 1298 — A rose of five leaves, or cinquefoil, between three small shields of arms, conjoined in triangle at the angular points of their chiefs: (1) COURTENAY; (2) Three bars wavy [BASSET]; (3) DESPENSER. With a small rose or cinquefoil in each space between two shields.). Stapeldon *Reg. of Walter de Stapeldon, Bishop of Exeter (A.D. 1307–1326)* (1892): 197, 213. Grandisson *Reg. of John de Grandisson Bishop of Exeter* 1 (1894): 204 ([Agnes de Saint John], lady de Courtenay, styled "very dear cousin" [treschere Chosine] by John de Grandison, Bishop of Exeter in letter dated 1328–9); 3 (1899): lii. Vivian *Vis. of Devon 1531, 1564 & 1620* (1895): 243–250 (sub Courtenay). *Note-book of Tristram Risdon* (1897): 53–56. Grandisson *Reg. of John de Grandisson Bishop of Exeter* 3 (1899): 1264, 1267, 1272. *List of Ancient Corr. of the Chancery & Exchequer* (Lists and Indexes 15) (1902): 552; see also *Index to Ancient Corr. of the Chancery & Exchequer* 1 (Lists and Indexes, Supp. Ser. 15) (1969): 308, 351 (John de Dynham styled "kinsman" by Hugh de Courtenay in 1316). Wrottesley *Peds. from the Plea Rolls* (1905): 225–226, 535. *List of Inqs. ad Quod Damnum* 2 (PRO Lists and Indexes 22) (1906): 566. Parker "Cal. of Feet of Fines for Cumberland" in *Trans. Cumberland & Westmorland Antiq. Soc.* n.s. 7 (1907): 237. *C.P.* 3 (1913): 466 (sub Courtenay); 4 (1916): 323–324 (sub Devon). VCH *Berkshire* 4 (1924): 372–373. VCH *Buckingham* 4 (1927): 109–110. *Genealogist's Mag.* 6 (1932–34): 606–626. Gandavo *Reg. Simonis de Gandavo Diocesis Saresbiriensis* 2 (Canterbury & York Soc. 41) (1934): 648, 775. Richardson & Sayles *Rotuli Parl. Anglie Hactenus Inediti 1274–1373* (Camden Soc. 3rd Ser. 51) (1935): 66–68. Paget *Baronage of England* (1957) 151: 1–3 (sub Courtenay). Holmes *Estates of the Higher Nobility in 14th Cent. England* (1957): 33 (ped.). VCH *Oxford* 5 (1957): 234–249. Seversmith *Colonial Fams. of Long Island, New York & Connecticut* 5 (1958): 2392–2402. Sanders *English Baronies* (1960): 70. Mills *Dorset Lay Subsidy Roll of 1332* (Dorset Rec. Soc. 4) (1971): 19, 61. VCH *Somerset* 4 (1978): 4–38. Ellis *Cat. Seals in the P.R.O.* 2 (1981): 29 (seal of Hugh de Courtenay dated 1326 — Hung from a hook, a shield of arms: three roundels, and a label of five points [COURTENAY]; on either side a small stylized leopard). *Rolls & Reg. of Bishop Oliver Sutton 1280–1299* 8 (Lincoln Rec. Soc. 76) (1986): 137. Schwennicke *Europaische Stanmtafeln* 3(4) (1989): 629 (sub Courtenay). Brault *Rolls of Arms Edward I* 2 (1997): 124 (arms of Hugh de Courtenay: Or, three roundels gules, a label azure). Burghersh *Regs. of Bishop Henry Burghersh* 2 (Lincoln Rec. Soc. 90) (2003): 135, 140. Hanna *Christchurch Priory Cartulary* (Hampshire Rec. Ser. 18) (2007): 71, 195–196. Nathan *Annals of West Coker* (2011). SC 8/3/101 (petition dated ?1315 from Hugh de Courtenay to king and council, requesting that his grievances be remedied and the king should wish to give him £18 6s. 8d. which sum was from a fee of the county of Devon which Isabel de Forz his ancestor held. As her heir, upon her death he was seised of the same as appears by a writ of Edward I of his 26th year, but subsequently the king ousted Courtenay, and moreover demanded by resummons of his Exchequer the money that he had received in the time of Edward I. It seems to Courtenay that he is being oppressed by the king, and that the money was given to him by Edward I as his right and heritage with other lands which descended to him on the death of the countess); SC 8/41/2017 (petition dated c.1327 by Hugh de Courtenay to king and council. Courtenay shows that he has sued for a long time for his right in the Isle of Wight and Christchurch. At the last parliament at Lincoln during the time of the king's father he was adjourned before the king's council at Westminster at the quinzene of Easter next following when a writing of Isabel de Forz granting and quitclaiming the same to which Courtenay requested an advisement to the next parliament. He requests that the writing be enquired of, and if she died seised, then the lands be rendered to him as his right); SC 8/82/4087; SC 8/99/4923 (available at www.catalogue.nationalarchives.gov.uk/search.asp).

Children of Hugh de Courtenay, Knt., by Agnes de Saint John:

i. **JOHN DE COURTENAY**, clerk, eldest son, born c. 1296. He received first tonsure at Bradninch, Devon 4 April 1310, he being then a monk at Tavistock Abbey. He became an acolyte at Totnes, Devon 6 March 1310/11. He was admitted into holy orders at Totnes, Devon 22 Dec. 1313. In 1325 Robert Bosse was elected Abbot of Tavistock in a disputed election. John de Courtenay, the disappointed candidate, together with two other monks contested the election and submitted 31 accusations against Bosse ranging from bastardy to incontinence and assault. Despite the charges, Busse's election was upheld. Bosse and Courtenay refused to accept the decision of the Bishop of Exeter, and appealed the Roman Curia. Bosse subsequently resigned his election and Courtenay was removed to Lewes Priory. In 1329 the pope endeavored to introduce John de Courtenay, a monk of Tavistock, as prior of Lewes, to which the king opposed a firm resistance. The prior of Christ Church, Canterbury, was suspected of supporting John de Courtenay, but replied that he had never so much as heard of him. In 1334 John de Courtenay elected Abbot of Tavistock. In 1337, as Abbot of Tavistock, John de Courtenay acknowledged that he and his convent owed a debt to Boniface Busket and Andrew Bertone, merchants of Chieri. He was suspended as Abbot of Tavistock in 1338 and again in 1348. On the last occasion, the bishop ultimately forgave him for alienating monastic property, but prohibited him from keeping hounds. JOHN DE COURTENAY, Abbot of Tavistock, died shortly before 11 July 1349. Brydges *Collins' Peerage of England* 6 (1812): 214–271 (sub Courtenay, Viscount Courtenay). Westcote *View of Devonshire in MDCXXX* (1845): 570–573 (sub Courtenay). *Sussex Arch. Colls.* 3 (1850): 200. Stapeldon *Reg. of Walter de Stapeldon, Bishop of Exeter (A.D. 1307–1326)* (1892): 469–470, 478, 490–492. Worthy *Hist. of the Suburbs of Exeter* (1892): 93 ("John Courtenay ... He had become Abbot of Tavistock in 1334, but he is described as having been throughout his career, 'very vain and much addicted to dress,' and to some other more reprehensible 'pomps and vanities of this wicked world.' He permitted 'feasting and revelry' in the private chambers of the Abbey, ... he was more than once censured by the Bishop of Exeter, for riotous living, and he involved the community over which he presided, to the extent of over £1,300, an enormous amount in those days."). Grandisson *Reg. of John de Grandisson Bishop of Exeter* 1 (1894): 230–231 (John de Courtenay, Prior of Lewes styled "kinsman" [consanguineo] by John de Grandison, Bishop of Exeter in letter dated 1329), 304; 2 (1897): 725–726, 740–741, 745, 817–819, 887–890, 996–998, 1050–1051, 1071–1073. Vivian *Vis. of Devon 1531, 1564 & 1620* (1895): 243–250 (sub Courtenay). Hoskins & Finberg *Devonshire Studies* (1952): 198–211. Finberg *West-Country Hist. Studies* (1969). VCH *Sussex* 2 (1973): 64–71. Wasson *Recs. of Early English Drama: Devon* (1986): lii, 451–452. Smith & London *Heads of Religious Houses, England & Wales* 2 (2001): 72–73, 234–235. SC 8/310/15470 (petition dated 1325–1327 by the Chaplains of Tavistock Abbey to the king, requesting that the king appoint another monk to lead their house, stating that the convent of Tavistock have elected two abbots, John de Courtenay and Robert Bosse, who are pleading their case at Rome. The Prior of Tavistock has been given custody of the house, but has cut down woods, reduced alms from 5*s*. to 12*d*. per day and done other things, to the destruction of the house) (available at www.catalogue.nationalarchives.gov.uk/search.asp).

ii. **HUGH DE COURTENAY**, Knt., 10th Earl of Devon [see next].

iii. **THOMAS DE COURTENAY**, Knt., of Woodhuish and Dunterton, Devon, and Cricket Malherbie and Wootton Courtenay, Somerset, and, in right of his wife, of King's Carswell, Devon, Maperton, South Cadbury, Somerset, Over Wallop, Hampshire, Over Worton, Oxfordshire, etc., 4th son, born in or before 1315. He married before 27 August 1337 (pardon for marrying without a license) **MURIEL DE MOELS**, elder daughter and co-heiresss of John de Moels, Knt., 4th Lord Moels, by Joan, daughter of Richard Lovel, Knt., Lord Lovel of Castle Cary [see MOELS 10 for her ancestry]. She was born in Dorset about 1322 (aged 15 in 1337). They had one son, Hugh, and two daughters, Muriel and Margaret. They received their share of her father's lands 6 October 1337, and their share of her father's knights' fees 3 March 1337/8. He presented to the churches of Cricket Malherbie, Somerset in 1340, 1349; Maperton, Somerset, 1343, 1351, and South Cadbury, Somerset, 1351. In 1346 he and his wife, Muriel, petitioned the Pope for an indult for plenary remission at the hour of death. SIR THOMAS DE COURTENAY died 9 June 1362. His widow, Muriel, died 12 August 1369. Brydges *Collins' Peerage of England* 6 (1812): 214–271 (sub Courtenay, Viscount Courtenay). Clutterbuck *Hist. & Antiqs. of Hertford* 2 (1821): 30–32 (Moels-Botreaux ped.). Dugdale *Monasticon Anglicanum* 5 (1825): 380 (Ford Abbey: "… Thomam [de Courtenay] postea conjugem Murielæ senioris filiæ et hæredis domini Johannis de Mules, militem strenuum"). Westcote *View of Devonshire in MDCXXX* (1845): 570–573 (sub Courtenay). Benolte *Vis. of Somerset 1531, 1573 & 1591* (1885): 50–51 (Moeles ped.: "Muriel [de Moeles]. = Sir Thos. Courtenay."). Weaver *Somerset Incumbents* (1889): 41, 136, 345. *C.P.R. 1334–1338* (1895): 501, 507. Vivian *Vis. of Devon 1531, 1564 & 1620* (1895): 243–250 (sub Courtenay). *Papal Regs.: Petitions* 1 (1896): 114 (Thomas de Courtenay styled "legitimate brother of the Earl of Devon"). Ralph of Shrewsbury *Reg. of Ralph of Shrewsbury Bishop of Bath & Wells* 2 (Somerset Rec. Soc. 10) (1896): 490, 592, 687–689. *Somerset & Dorset Notes & Queries* 6 (1899): 289–295. *C.C.R. 1349–1354* (1906): 18. VCH *Hampshire* 4 (1911): 531. *C.F.R.* 6 (1921): 114; 7 (1923): 245; 9 (1926): 136. VCH *Buckingham* 3 (1925): 363–367. *Genealogist's Mag.* 6 (1932–34): 606–626. *Cal. IPM* 11 (1935): 242–243. *C.P.* 9 (1936): 8 (sub Moels). Reichel *Devon Feet of Fines* 2 (Devon & Cornwall Rec. Soc. 1939) (1939): 150, 229–230, 314, 321–322. St. George et al. *Wiltshire Vis. Peds. 1623, 1628* (H.S.P. 105-6) (1954): 89–91 (Hungerford ped.: "Thomas Courtney miles = Muriell Da: et hey of John Moiles = …. Dns Botreux"). Paget *Baronage of England* (1957) 151: 2 (sub Courtenay); 368: 1–7 (sub Moels). Seversmith *Col. Fams. of Long Island* 5(1) (1958): 2396. VCH *Oxford* 11 (1983): 295. Deed #174, English Deeds Coll., Harvard Law School Lib. — available at http://hollis.harvard.edu//?itemid=%7clibrary%2fm%2faleph%7c002832257.

Children of Thomas de Courtenay, Knt., by Muriel de Moels:

a. **MURIEL DE COURTENAY**, married **JOHN DE DINHAM** (or **DYNHAM**), Knt., of Hartland, Devon [see DINHAM 6].

    b. **MARGARET COURTENAY**, married **THOMAS PEVERELL**, Esq., of Hamatethy (in St. Breward), Cornwall [see HUNGERFORD 10].

 iv. **ELEANOR DE COURTENAY**, married **JOHN DE GREY**, Knt., 3rd Lord Grey of Codnor [see CODNOR 12].

7. HUGH DE COURTENAY, Knt., 10th Earl of Devon, 2nd Lord Courtenay, of Okehampton, Cadeleigh, Colcombe, Honiton, Huntebeare, Plympton, Tiverton, and Whitwell (in Colyton), Devon, Hillesdon and Wavendon, Buckinghamshire, Ibberton, Dorset, Crowell and Nuneham (in Nuneham Courtenay), Oxfordshire, East Coker and Hemington, Somerset, etc., Joint Warden of Devon and Cornwall, Chief Warden of Devon, 2nd surviving son and heir, born 12 July 1303. He married 11 August 1325 (by marriage agreement dated 27 Sept. 1314) **MARGARET DE BOHUN**, daughter of Humphrey de Bohun, Knt., Earl of Hereford and Essex, by Elizabeth, daughter of Edward I, King of England [see BOHUN 9 for her ancestry]. She was born 3 April 1311. She was a legatee in the 1319 will of her father, who bequeathed her 200 marks for her apparel against her marriage. They had eight sons, Hugh, K.G., Thomas [Canon of Crediton and Exeter], Edward, Knt., Robert, [Master] William [Bishop of Hereford and London, Archbishop of Canterbury, Chancellor of England], Philip, Knt., Peter, K.G., and Humphrey, and five daughters, Margaret, Elizabeth, Katherine, Anne, and Joan. He served in the Scottish and French wars, and was Knight Banneret 20 Jan. 1327. He was summoned to Parliament 23 April 1337, by writ directed *Hugoni de Courteney juniori*, whereby he is held to have become Lord Courtenay. He succeeded to the Earldom of Devon on his father's death in 1340. He repulsed the French descent on Cornwall in 1339. In 1339–40 he granted the reversion of one burgage tenement and a half in Culliford, Devon to John Wylemot and his wife, Julian. In 1343 he was given a protection and safe conduct, he then going on a pilgrimage beyond seas. He presented to the churches of East Coker, Somerset, 1344, 1349, 1352, Sampford Courtenay, Devon, 1347, Misterton, Somerset, 1349, Hemington, Somerset, 1352, Luffincott, Devon, 1360, 2nd portion of Crewkerne, Somerset, 1362, Sutton Courtenay, Berkshire, 1372, and West Coker, Somerset, 1372, and to the prebendal churches of Chulmleigh, Devon, 1360, and Cutton, Exeter Castle, Devon, 1360. He attended the tournament held at Lichfield 9 April 1347, as one of the Knights of the King's Chamber. In 1350 he took out a license to pass to foreign parts, and to absent himself from the realm for one year. He and his wife, Margaret, were legatees in the 1361 will of her brother, Humphrey de Bohun, Earl of Hereford and Essex. SIR HUGH DE COURTENAY, 10th Earl of Devon, 2nd Lord Courtenay, died 2 May 1377. In 1382 the king granted his widow, Margaret, her household, tenants, servants, and possessions free ingress and egress from the city of Exeter, Devon. Margaret, Countess of Devon, died 16 Dec. 1391. She left a will proved Dec. 1391 (P.C.C. 2 Rous). Hugh and Margaret were buried at Cathedral Church of St. Peter, Exeter, Devon.

    Rymer *Fœdera* 6 (1727): 138. Brydges *Collins' Peerage of England* 6 (1812): 214–271 (sub Courtenay, Viscount Courtenay). Baker *Hist. & Antiqs. of Northampton* 1 (1822–30): 544–545 (Mandeville-Fitz Peter-Bohun ped.). Dugdale *Monasticon Anglicanum* 5 (1825): 381 (Ford Abbey: "… dominus Hugo [de Courtenay] tertius patre adhuc vivente anno Domini MCCCXXV. iij. die idus Augusti, generosæ dominæ Margaretæ filiæ comitis Herefordiæ domini Humphredi de Bohun, tironis strenuissimi… Hæc Margareta matrem habuit ingenuam, dominam Elizabetham illustrissimi principis et regis incliti Edwardi post conquestum Angliæ primi filiam, anno Domini MCCCxj. iij. nonas Aprilis nata"); 6(1) (1830): 134–136 (Bohun ped. in Llanthony Abbey records: "Margareta de Bohun supradicta, secunda filia prædicti Humfredi ocatavi [de Bohun], post decessum dicti patris sui, desponsata fuit domino Hugoni de Cortney, quem supradictus rex Edwardus postea fecit domitem de Devonschire"). Nicolas *Testamenta Vetusta* 1 (1826): 66–68 (will of Humphrey de Bohun, Earl of Hereford and Essex), 127–128 (will of Margaret de Courtenay, Countess of Devon). Nicolas *Siege of Carlaverock* (1828): 193–196 (biog. of Hugh de Courtenay). Burke *Dict. of the Peerages… Extinct, Dormant & in Abeyance* (1831): 63–65 (sub Bohun). Nicolas *Rpt. of Procs. on the Claim to the Earldom of Devon* (1832): 5–16. Beltz *Mems. of the Order of the Garter* (1841): cxxxxix, 51–54. Westcote *View of Devonshire in MDCXXX* (1845): 570–573 (sub Courtenay). *Arch. Jour.* 2 (1846): 339–349 (will of Humphrey de Bohun). Lipscomb *Hist. & Antiqs. of Buckingham* 1 (1847): 471–472 (Courtenay ped.: adds son Humphrey). *Procs. Soc. Antiqs.* 2nd Ser. 5 (1870): 36–37 (deed of Hugh de Courtenay dated at Colcombe 13 Edward III [1339–40]: "The finely engraved seal attached to this deed … bears on an escucheon placed between mullets, and surrounded by a border of tracery, the arms of Courtenay, three roundels (torteaux) and a label."). *Jour. British Arch. Assoc.* 27 (1871): 179–191. *Annual Rpt. of the Deputy Keeper* 35 (1874): 5–6 (marriage contract of Humphrey & Margaret dated 27 Sept. 1314). Maclean *Hist. of Trigg Minor* 2 (1876): 240–241 (chart). *Reliquary* 17 (1876–7): 97–104. Burke *Dormant, Abeyant, Forfeited & Extinct Peerages* (1883): 139–142 (sub Courtenay). Doyle *Official Baronage of England* 1 (1886): 575 (sub Devonshire). Vivian *Vis. of Cornwall* (1887): 105–118 (Courtenay ped.). *Notes & Gleanings* 2 (1889): 50–56, 65–68, 89–93, 97. Birch *Cat. Seals in the British Museum* 2 (1892): 695–696 (seal of Hugh de Courtenay, Earl of Devon, dated 1341 — A shield of arms: COURTENAY, with a label of three points, enclosed in a design of elaborate gothic tracery; the center is a six-foil, ornamented with ball-flowers along the inner edge. A second seal dated 1349; a copy of, but slightly larger than, the first seal of arms). *Papal Regs.: Letters* 2 (1895): 367; 3 (1897): 158, 195. Vivian *Vis. of Devon 1531, 1564 & 1620* (1895): 243–250 (sub Courtenay). *Genealogist* n.s. 13 (1896): 242. Kirby *Wykeham's Reg.* 1 (1896): 43. Ralph of Shrewsbury *Reg. of Ralph of Shrewsbury Bishop of Bath & Wells* (Somerset Rec. Soc. 10) (1896): 464, 467, 503, 516, 518, 531–534 (license and charter of Hugh de Courtenay), 562, 587, 601–602, 623, 695, 760, 766. *C.P.R. 1381–1385* (1897): 183 (Margaret, Countess of Devon, styled "king's kinswoman" by King Richard II of England). *Note-book of Tristram Risdon* (1897): 53–56. *C.P.R. 1313–1317* (1898): 267. Grandisson *Reg. of John de Grandisson Bishop of Exeter* 3 (1899): 1359, 1399, 1458. *C.P.R. 1340–1343* (1900): 282. Wrottesley *Peds. from the Plea Rolls* (1905): 164, 225–226, 425. *List of Inqs. ad Quod Damnum* 2 (PRO Lists and Indexes 22) (1906): 415, 454, 585, 589–590. *Cal. MSS Dean & Chapter of Wells* 1 (Hist. MSS Comm. 12B) (1907): 294–295. *Colls. Hist. Staffs.* n.s. 10(2) (1907): 136–137. *Rpt. on MSS in Various Colls.* 4 (Hist. MSS Comm. 55) (1907): 81. *Devon Notes & Queries* 5 (1909): 209–212 (Margaret styled "king's kinswoman" by King Richard II of England). *C.P.* 3 (1913): 344–345 (sub Cobham), 466 (sub Courtenay); 4 (1916): 324 (sub Devon); 5 (1926): 77–78 (sub Engaine); 14 (1998): 259 (sub Devon). *Genealogist* n.s. 34 (1918): 29–30. Kingsford *Stonor Letters & Papers 1290–1483* 1 (Camden Soc. 3rd Ser. 29) (1919): 27–28 (letter of Margaret, Countess of Devon dated c.1380). VCH *Berkshire* 4 (1924): 372–373 (Courtenay arms: Or three roundels gules with a label azure). VCH *Buckingham* 4 (1927): 109–110. *Reg. of Edward the Black Prince* 2 (1931): 194. *Genealogist's Mag.* 6 (1932–34): 606–626. Reichel *Devon Feet of Fines* 2 (Devon & Cornwall Rec. Soc. 1939) (1939): 324, 357–358, 374–375, 382–383, 395–396, 420–421. Holmes *Estates of the Higher Nobility in 14th Cent. England* (1957): 32–35, 47–48. Paget *Baronage of England* (1957) 73: 1–13 (sub Bohun). VCH *Oxford* 5 (1957): 240. Seversmith *Colonial Fams. of Long Island, New York & Connecticut* 5 (1958): 2380–2392. *Yorkshire Arch. Jour.* 40 (1962): 265–297. Dunning *Hylle Cartulary* (Somerset Rec. Soc. 68) (1968): 73. VCH *Somerset* 4 (1978): 4–38. Ellis *Cat. Seals in the P.R.O.* 2 (1981): 29 (seal of Hugh de Courtenay, Earl of Devon, dated 1365 — In a circle, surrounded by fine tracery, a shield of arms: three roundels and a label of three pieces. The tracery is based on an inner circle contained in a triangle and contains quatrefoils and roses). Schwennicke *Europaische Stanmtafeln* 3(4) (1989): 630 (sub Courtenay). Ward *Women of the English Nobility & Gentry 1066–1500* (1995): 29–30 (marriage agreement dated 28 Feb. 1315), 50–51. Leese *Blood Royal* (1996): 116–119. McKardy *Royal Writs addressed to John Buckingham Bishop of Lincoln 1363–1398* (Lincoln Rec. Soc. 86) (1997): 166–167. Given-Wilson *English Nobility in the Late Middle Ages* (2003): xvi. Hanna *Christchurch Priory Cartulary* (Hampshire Rec. Ser. 18) (2007): 288–289. Nathan *Annals of West Coker* (2011). Deed #23, English Deeds Coll., Harvard Law School Lib. — available at http://hollis.harvard.edu// ?itemid=%7clibrary%2fm%2faleph%7c005528652. National Archives, DL 27/13 (indenture and articles of agreement dated 8 Edward II [1314–15] for marriage of Hugh de Courtenay and Margaret de Bohun); SC 8/13/606 (available at www.catalogue.nationalarchives.gov.uk/search.asp). National Archives, CP 25/1/44/61, #406 [see abstract of fine at http:// www.medievalgenealogy.org.uk/index.html].

Children of Hugh de Courtenay, Knt., by Margaret de Bohun:

i. **HUGH DE COURTENAY**, K.G., of Wavendon, Buckinghamshire, Honiton, Devon, Ibberton, Dorset, Crowell and Nuneham (in Nuneham Courtenay), Oxfordshire, East Coker, Somerset, etc., son and heir apparent, born 22 March 1326/7. He married before 3 Sept. 1341 (date of license to grant property to him and his wife) **ELIZABETH DE VERE**, daughter of John de Vere, Knt., 7th Earl of Oxford, by Maud, daughter of Bartholomew de Badlesmere, Knt., 1st Lord Badlesmere [see VERE 5 for her ancestry]. They had one son, Hugh, Knt. [3rd Lord Courtenay]. In 1348 he was a Founder Knight of the Order of the Garter. SIR HUGH DE COURTENAY died shortly after Easter term 1348, and was buried at Ford Abbey, Somerset. On 2 Sept. 1349 Queen Philippe of Hainault, while on a progress through Dorsetshire, placed a piece of cloth of gold as an oblation upon his tomb. His widow, Elizabeth, married (2nd) before papal dispensation dated 4 May 1351 (they being related in the 3rd and 4th degrees of kindred) (as his 3rd wife) **JOHN DE MOWBRAY**, Knt., 3rd Lord Mowbray [see MOWBRAY 5]. They had no known issue. SIR JOHN DE MOWBRAY, 3rd Lord Mowbray, died of pestilence at York 4 October 1361, and was buried at the church of Friars Minor, Bedford, Bedfordshire. His widow, Elizabeth, married (3rd) before 18 Jan. 1368/9 **WILLIAM DE COSSINGTON**, Knt. (living 6 July 1380), son and heir of Stephen de Cossington, of Cosynton (in Aylesford) and Acrise, Kent. She died 16 August 1375. Brydges *Collins' Peerage of England* 6 (1812): 214–271 (sub Courtenay, Viscount Courtenay). Nicolas *Rpt. of Procs. on the Claim to the Earldom of Devon* (1832): 5–16. Beltz *Mems. of the Order of the Garter* (1841): 51–54. Westcote *View of Devonshire in MDCXXX* (1845): 570–573 (sub Courtenay). *Reliquary* 17 (1876–7): 97–104. Vivian *Vis. of Devon*

1531, 1564 & 1620 (1895): 243–250 (sub Courtenay). *C.P.R. 1340–1343* (1900): 282. *C.P.* 3 (1913): 466–467 (sub Courtenay); 4 (1916): 325 (sub Devon); 10 (1945): 223, footnote n (sub Oxford). VCH *Buckingham* 3 (1925): 444–445. *Genealogist's Mag.* 6 (1932–34): 606–626. Holmes *Estates of the Higher Nobility in 14th Cent. England* (1957): 33 (ped.). VCH *Oxford* 5 (1957): 240. Schwennicke *Europaische Stanmtafeln* 3(4) (1989): 630 (sub Courtenay). Leese *Blood Royal* (1996): 116–119. VCH *Cambridge* 10 (2002): 86–90.

Child of Hugh de Courtenay, K.G., by Elizabeth de Vere:

a. **HUGH DE COURTENAY**, Knt., 3rd Lord Courtenay, of Sutton Courtenay, Berkshire and Waddesdon, Buckinghamshire, son and heir. He married (1st) **MARGARET DE BRYAN**, daughter of Guy de Bryan, K.G., Lord Bryan, of Laugharne, Carmarthenshire, Walwyn's Castle, Pembrokeshire, Clifton Dartmouth and Hardness and Slapton, Devon, Woodsford, Dorset, etc., by his 1st wife, Joan, daughter of John de Carew, Knt., of Carew, Pembrokeshire, Moulsford, Berkshire, Galmpton (in Churston Ferrers), Ottery Mohun (in Luppit), Monkton, and Stoke Fleming, Devon, etc. [see BRYAN 11.ii for her ancestry]. They had no issue. His wife, Margaret, was living in 1361. He married (2nd) by marriage settlement dated 3 October 1362 (dispensation dated 29 August 1363, they being related in the 3rd and 4th degree of kindred) **MAUD DE HOLAND** (also known as **MAHAUT DE REUS**) [see KENT 9.v], daughter of Thomas de Holand, K.G., 1st Earl of Kent, by Joan, daughter of Edmund of Woodstock, Earl of Kent (son of King Edward I) [see KENT 9 for her ancestry]. They had no issue. In 1366 they received an indult for a portable altar, to have mass celebrated before daybreak, etc. He was knighted by Edward the *Black Prince* before Vittoria in 1367, and was at the Battle of Nájera the same year. He was summoned to Parliament 8 Jan. 1370/1, by writ directed *Hugoni de Courteney le fitz*, whereby he is held to have become Lord Courtenay. In 1373 King Edward III of England granted a pardon at the request of Maud de Courtenay his kinswoman to William del Langhous for the death of William del Kechin. In 1374 the king likewise granted a pardon at the request of Lady de Courtenay his kinswoman to Walter Hydon for the death of Walter Robyn. SIR HUGH DE COURTENAY, 3rd Lord Courtenay, died 20 Feb. 1373/4. His widow, Maud, married (2nd) at Windsor, Berkshire in Easter week, 1380 (as his 1st wife) **WALERAN DE LUXEMBOURG**, Knt., Count of Ligny (in Namur) and Saint-Pol (in Artois), seigneur of Fiennes and Bohain, Châtelain of Lille and Bourbourg, Constable of France [see KENT 9.v], son and heir of Guy de Luxembourg, Count of Ligny (in Namur), seigneur of Roussy, Beauvoir (in Arrouaise), and Richebourg, Châtelain of Lille, Governor of Arras and Picardy, and, in right of his wife, Count of Saint-Pol, by Mahaut, daughter of Jean de Châtillon, Count of Saint-Pol [see WYDEVILLE 10 for his ancestry]. They had one daughter, Jeanne (wife of Antoine de Bourgogne, Duke of Lorraine, Brabant, and Luxembourg, Count of Rethel, Marquis of the Holy Empire). In 1390 King Richard II of England granted a pardon at the supplication of his sister, Maud, Countess of Saint-Pol, to John Wallere, of Horstead, Sussex, who was indicted for murdering Peter Gracyan, a Lombard. His wife, Maud, was buried at Westminster Abbey 23 April 1392. WALERAN DE LUXEMBOURG, Count of Ligny and Saint-Pol, died at Ivois Castle in Chiny 19 April 1415, and was buried in the church of Notre Dame in that town. Anselme *Hist. de la Maison Royale de France* 3 (1728): 724 (sub Ligny) (identifies Maud, 1st wife of Waleran de Luxembourg, as "Mahaud de Roeux"). Rymer *Fœdera* 7 (1728): 675 (Maud, Countess of Ligny and Saint-Pol, styled "sister" by King Richard II of England in 1390). Brydges *Collins' Peerage of England* 6 (1812): 214–271 (sub Courtenay, Viscount Courtenay). Clutterbuck *Hist. & Antiqs. of Hertford* 1 (1815): 371 (Longespée-Zouch ped.). Nicolas *Controversy between Scrope & Grosvenor* 2 (1832): 245–255 (biog. of Sir Guy Bryan). Nicolas *Rpt. of Procs. on the Claim to the Earldom of Devon* (1832): 5–16. Westcote *View of Devonshire in MDCXXX* (1845): 570–573 (sub Courtenay). Lipscomb *Hist. & Antiqs. of Buckingham* 1 (1847): 471–472 (Courtenay ped.). Hulton *Coucher Book, or Chartulary, of Whalley Abbey* 4 (Chetham Soc. 20) (1849): 977–979 (Holand ped.). Goethals *Dictionnaire Gén. & Héraldique des Fams. Nobles du Royaume de Belgique* 4 (1852). Neÿen *Biographie Luxembourgeoise* 2 (1861): 52 (biog. of Walram de Luxembourg-Ligny). Johnes *Chronicles of Enguerrand de Monstrelet* 1 (1869): 327. De Robaulx de Soumoy *Considérations sur le Gouvernement des Pays-Bas* 1 (Coll. de Méms. Relatifs à l'Hist. de Belgique) (1872): 9. *Méms. de la Soc. des Lettres, Sciences et Arts de Bar-le-Duc* 2 (1872): 140–142; 2nd Ser. 3 (1884): 362–363. *Méms. de la Société des Sciences, de l'Agriculture et des Arts de Lille* 1873 3rd Ser. 12 (1874): 167–187. Le Fevre *Chronique de Jean Le Févre, Seigneur de Saint-Remy* 1 (1876): 212 ("Le XIXᵉ jour d'avril, mil IIIIᶜ et XV, morut et la ville d'Ivix, en la duchie de Luxembourg, le conte Walleran, conte de Ligny et de Saint-Pol, soy-disant encores connestable de France, et fut enterré en l'église Nostre-Dame en ladicte ville d'Ivix, devant le grant autel"). Duchet & Giry *Cartulaires de l'Église de Térouane* (1881): 285–286 (letter dated 1406 of Waleran de Luxembourg, Count of Ligny and Saint-Pol, seigneur of Fiennes). Haigneré "Cartulaire de l'Église abbatiale Notre-Dame de Boulogne-sur-Mer, Ordre de Saint-Augustin, 1067–1567" in *Mémoires de la Société académique de l'Arrondissement de Boulogne-sur-Mer* 13 (1882–6): 216 (charter of Waleran de Luxembourg, Count of Ligny and Saint-Pol, seigneur of Fiennes dated 13 April 1392, naming his deceased wife, Mahaut de Reus [i.e., Maud de Holand]). *Notes & Gleanings* 2 (1889): 50–56, 65–68, 89–93, 97; 5 (1892): 78–80. Vivian *Vis. of Devon 1531, 1564 & 1620* (1895): 243–250 (sub Courtenay). *Papal Regs.: Petitions* 1

(1896): 453. *C.P.R. 1388–1392* (1902): 256, 364, 420 (instances of [Waleran], Count of St. Paul/St. Pol, styled "king's brother"), 313 ([Maud], Countess of St. Paul [sic] styled "king's sister"). *C.P.R. 1391–1396* (1905): 212. Wrottesley *Peds. from the Plea Rolls* (1905): 225–226. *C.C.R. 1360–1364* (1909): 262. *C.P.* 3 (1913): 466–467 (sub Courtenay); 4 (1916): 325 (sub Devon). VCH *Berkshire* 4 (1924): 372–373. VCH *Buckingham* 4 (1927): 109–110. *Genealogist's Mag.* 6 (1932–34): 606–626. Barroux *Les Fêtes royales de Saint-Denis en Mai 1389* (1936): 17–18, 62. *John of Gaunt's Reg.* 1 (Camden Soc. 3rd Ser. 56) (1937): 151–153. Legge *Anglo-Norman Letters & Petitions* (Anglo-Norman Text Soc. 3) (1941): 368. Harvey *Westminster Abbey & its Estates in the Middle Ages* (1977): 378. Schwennicke *Europaische Stanmtafeln* 3(4) (1989): 630 (sub Courtenay); 6 (1978): 28 (sub Luxemburg). Leese *Blood Royal* (1996): 116–119. Maillard-Luypaert *Papauté, Clercs et Laïcs* (2001): 307. Preest *Chronica maiora of Thomas Walsingham, 1376–1422* (2005): 104.

ii. **THOMAS DE COURTENAY**, clerk, born about 1329–31 (aged 15 in 1344, 18 in 1349). He was Canon of Crediton and Exeter. Brydges *Collins' Peerage of England* 6 (1812): 214–271 (sub Courtenay, Viscount Courtenay). *Papal Regs.: Petitions* 1 (1896): 80 (Thomas son of Hugh [de Courtenay], Earl of Devon styled "king's kinsman" in 1344). *Papal Regs.: Letters* 3 (1897): 165, 304 (Thomas de Courtenay, son of Hugh [de Courtenay], Earl of Devon, styled "kinsman" of King Edward III of England in 1349). Emden *Biog. Reg. of the Univ. of Oxford* 1 (1957): 502 (biog. of Thomas Courtenay). Schwennicke *Europaische Stanmtafeln* 3(4) (1989): 630 (sub Courtenay).

iii. **EDWARD DE COURTENAY**, Knt. [see next].

iv. [MASTER] **WILLIAM COURTENAY**, 4th son, born at St. Martin's, Exeter, Devon about 1342. He was granted a license for mass to be celebrated in his lodgings at Oxford, 1363. He was a Licentiate of Civil Law before 1366; Doctor of Civil Law, 1366 or 1367. He was elected Chancellor of Oxford University, 1367. He was appointed a Rector of a portion of Crewkerne, Somerset before 1361; Canon of York, 1361; Canon of St. Crantock, Cornwall, 1362; Canon of Wells before 1366; Bishop of Hereford by papal provision, 1369; Bishop of London, 1375. He was reprimanded publishing at St. Paul's Cross a bull of Gregory XI against the Florentines, which resulted in the pillage of those resident in London by a mob in 1376. He was threatened by John of Gaunt, Duke of Lancaster, for his repeated publication of sentence of excommunication against those guilty of sacrilege at Westminster Abbey when Robert Hawley was killed by members of the duke's following in 1378. He was made Archbishop of Canterbury in 1381. He served as Chancellor of England, 1381. He crowned Anne of Bohemia queen in Westminster Abbey 22 Jan. 1382. In 1382 he summoned a council in London 17 May 1382, for the silencing of Wyclif and his followers. He was appointed one of the executors of the 1385 will of his cousin, Hugh de Stafford, K.G., 2nd Earl of Stafford. In 1385 he was threatened in council by King Richard II for his intervention on behalf of John of Gaunt, and his temporalities were ordered to be seised. He took a prominent part in the negotiations between the king and the Lords appellant in Nov. 1387. [MASTER] WILLIAM COURTENAY, Archbishop of Canterbury, died at Maidstone, Kent 31 July 1396, and was buried at Canterbury, Kent 4 August 1396, eastward of the tomb of Edward *the Black Prince*. He left a will dated 1396, codicil dated 28 July 1396, proved 15 Sept. 1396. Weever *Ancient Funerall Monuments* (1631): 285–286. Brydges *Collins' Peerage of England* 6 (1812): 214–271 (sub Courtenay, Viscount Courtenay). Nicolas *Testamenta Vetusta* 1 (1826): 118–120 (will of Hugh de Stafford, Earl of Stafford). Dugdale *Monasticon Anglicanum* 6(3) (1830): 1394–1395 (William late Archbishop of Canterbury styled "kinsman" by King Richard II). Nicolas *Rpt. of Procs. on the Claim of the Earldom of Devon in the House of Lords* (1832): 5–16; Appendix, xxxv–xxxvi. Westcote *View of Devonshire in MDCXXX* (1845): 570–573 (sub Courtenay). Lipscomb *Hist. & Antiqs. of Buckingham* 1 (1847): 471–472 (Courtenay ped.). Foss *Judges of England* 4 (1851): 48–51 (biog. of William de Courtenay: "… He is represented as having a noble presence and courtly manners; with the learning fit for his position, a clear and acute understanding; and, what speaks more in his praise, he was a favourite with the monks of his cathedral"). *Collectanea Arch.* 1 (1862): 232–262. *Notes & Gleanings* 2 (1889): 50–56, 65–68, 89–93, 97. Vivian *Vis. of Devon 1531, 1564 & 1620* (1895): 243–250 (sub Courtenay). *Papal Regs.: Petitions* 1 (1896): 284 (William Courtenay styled "kinsman" by William de Bohun, Earl of Northampton), 291, 374 (instances of William de Courtenay styled "kinsman" by Edward, Prince of Wales). *Arch. Cantiana* 23 (1898): 31–54 (burial place of William Courtenay, Archbishop of Canterbury), 55–67 (will of William Courtenay, Archbishop of Canterbury) (will names William's "kinswoman" [consanguinee], Lady Elizabeth nun of Canonle [Canonsleigh]). *C.Ch.R.* 5 (1916): 287 (William de Courtenay, Archbishop of Canterbury, styled "king's cousin" in 1383). *Genealogist's Mag.* 6 (1932–34): 606–626. Emden *Biog. Reg. of the Univ. of Oxford* 1 (1957): 502–504 (biog. of William Courtenay). Holmes *Estates of the Higher Nobility in 14th Cent. England* (1957): 33–34. Dahmus *William Courtenay, Archbishop of Canterbury* (1966). Schwennicke *Europaische Stanmtafeln* 3(4) (1989): 630 (sub Courtenay). Hicks *Who's Who in Late Medieval England* (1991): 158–160 (biog. of William Courtenay) ("… .one of the ablest English primates in the later middle ages … he was conscientious in performance of such Episcopal duties as visitation and ordination … He was a sympathetic pastor, who allowed offenders like John Ball time for reflection, forgave those who repented their errors … He 'aspired to be a churchman, not an agent of the crown'."). National Archives, E 210/440 — will of James le Botiller, 2nd Earl of Ormond dated at La Vacherie, Surrey 31

v. **PHILIP COURTENAY**, Knt., of Powderham, Devon, married **ANNE WAKE** [see DAVIE 8].

vi. **PETER COURTENAY**, K.G., of Hardington-Mandeville and Stewley (in Ashill), Somerset, Honiton, Milton Damarel, and Moreton, Devon, and, in right of his wife, of Aller and Newton St. Loe, Somerset, King's Chamberlain, Keeper of the Mews, Master of the King's Falcons, Constable of Windsor Castle, Keeper of Clarendon Park, Captain of Calais, Privy Councillor, Knight of the Shire for Somerset, 1382. He married before Trinity term 1390 (date of lawsuit) **MARGARET CLYVEDON**, widow of John de Saint Loe (or Seintlo), Knt. (died 8 Nov. 1375), and daughter and heiress of John de Clyvedon, of Aller, Cricket, and Yeovilton, Somerset, by his wife, Elizabeth. They had no issue. He received knighthood in 1367 from Edward *the Black Prince* at Vittoria before the Battle of Nájera. In 1377 in company with his brother, Philip, they encountered the Spanish fleet near the coast of Brittany and, after a desperate naval conflict, they were compelled to surrender; and Peter was taken prisoner. Upon his release, he returned to England and was granted a military appointment at Calais. In 1388 he was authorized to proceed to Calais for the purpose of enquiring with the French regarding certain intended feats of arms. In 1389 he claimed the advowson of Landbeach, Cambridgeshire as remainderman under an earlier settlement dated 1303; in 1392 he and his wife, Margaret, released his right to the advowson to Corpus Christi College, Cambridge for 100 marks. In 1390 he jousted three challengers at St. Inghelbert with various success. He was a legatee in the 1396 will of his brother, William Courtenay, Archbishop of Canterbury. He presented to the churches of Newton St. Loe, Somerset in 1402, Alphington, Devon in 1403, Aller, Somerset in 1403 and 1404, and Hardington Mandeville, Somerset in 1403 and 1404. SIR PETER COURTENAY died 2 Feb. 1404/5, and was buried by the side of his parents in the Cathedral church of St. Peter's, Exeter, Devon. His widow, Margaret, presented to the church of Newton St. Loe, Somerset in 1409 and 1410. Margaret died 5 Jan. 1411/2. She left a will dated 14 Nov. 1412 [recte 1411], proved 26 Jan. 1411/2 (P.C.C. 24 Marche), requesting burial in the Cathedral church of Bath by her 1st husband, John de Saint Lo, Knt. Rymer *Fœdera* 7 (1728): 415, 580, 666 (instances of Peter de Courtenay styled "kinsman" by King Richard II of England); 8 (1727): 120 (Peter de Courtenay styled "kinsman" by King Henry IV of England). Brydges *Collins' Peerage of England* 6 (1812): 214–271 (sub Courtenay, Viscount Courtenay). Nicolas *Rpt. of Procs. on the Claim of the Earldom of Devon in the House of Lords* (1832): 5–16; Appendix, xxxvii. Oliver *Eccl. Antiqs. in Devon* 1 (1840): 75. Beltz *Mems. of the Order of the Garter* (1841): cliv, 328–332 (Peter de Courtenay: "… the lustre of his birth, his ardent and romantic devotion to chivalrous exercises, and his martial skill and undaunted valour in the field, may claim for this knight a conspicuous station among the heroes of his time"). Westcote *View of Devonshire in MDCXXX* (1845): 570–573 (sub Courtenay). Lipscomb *Hist. & Antiqs. of Buckingham* 1 (1847): 471–472 (Courtenay ped.). Hingeston *Royal & Hist. Letters during the Reign of Henry IV* (Rolls Ser. 18) (1860): 7–8 (Peter de Courtenay styled "kinsman" by King Henry IV of England). *Misc. Gen. et Heraldica* 2nd Ser. 2 (1888): 314–317. *Notes & Gleanings* 2 (1889): 50–56, 65–68, 89–93, 97. Weaver *Somerset Incumbents* (1889): 5, 95, 278. Rye *Pedes Finium or Fines Rel. Cambridge* (1891): 137. Vivian *Vis. of Devon 1531, 1564 & 1620* (1895): 243–250 (sub Courtenay). *Genealogist* n.s. 14 (1897): 24–25. *Arch. Cantiana* 23 (1898): 55–67 (will of William Courtenay, Archbishop of Canterbury). *Somerset & Dorset Notes & Queries* 6 (1899): 241–245. Weaver *Somerset Medieval Wills* 1 (Somerset Rec. Soc. 16) (1901): 50–52 (will of Margaret de Courtenay). C.P.R. 1399–1401 (1903): 75 (Peter de Courtenay styled "king's kinsman"). Wood *Colls. for a Parochial Hist. of Chew Magna* (1903): 111–139. Wrottesley *Peds. from the Plea Rolls* (1905): 180–181, 241. *Rpt. on the MSS of Reginald Rawdon Hastings, Esq.* 1 (Hist. MSS Comm. 78) (1928): 252. *Genealogist's Mag.* 6 (1932–34): 606–626. Holmes *Estates of the Higher Nobility in 14th Cent. England* (1957): 33–34. VCH *Oxford* 5 (1957): 240. Dunning *Hylle Cartulary* (Somerset Rec. Soc. 68) (1968): 73. VCH *Cambridge* 5 (1973): 68–87. VCH *Wiltshire* 12 (1973): 143. VCH *Somerset* 3 (1974): 63, 169; 4 (1978): 134–135. *Devon & Cornwall Notes & Queries* 35 (1984): 219–220 (biog. of Peter Courtenay). Schwennicke *Europaische Stanmtafeln* 3(4) (1989): 630 (sub Courtenay). VCH *Cambridge* 9 (1989): 151–155. Leese *Blood Royal* (1996): 116–119. Devon Rec. Office: Petre, 123M/TB227 (available at www.a2a.org.uk/search/index.asp).

vii. **HUMPHREY DE COURTENAY**, died young without issue. Brydges *Collins' Peerage of England* 6 (1812): 214–271 (sub Courtenay, Viscount Courtenay). Nicolas *Rpt. of Procs. on the Claim of the Earldom of Devon in the House of Lords* (1832): Appendix, xxxvi–xxxvii. Westcote *View of Devonshire in MDCXXX* (1845): 570–573 (sub Courtenay). Vivian *Vis. of Devon 1531, 1564 & 1620* (1895): 243–250 (sub Courtenay). Schwennicke *Europaische Stanmtafeln* 3(4) (1989): 630 (sub Courtenay).

viii. **MARGARET DE COURTENAY**, married **JOHN COBHAM**, Knt., 3rd Lord Cobham [see WYATT 13].

ix. **ELIZABETH DE COURTENAY**, married (1st) **JOHN DE VERE**, Knt., of Whitchurch, Buckinghamshire [see VERE 5.i]; (2nd) **ANDREW LUTTRELL**, Knt., of Chilton (in Thorverton), Devon [see LOWELL 8].

x. **KATHERINE COURTENAY**, married **THOMAS D'ENGAINE**, Knt., 3rd Lord Engaine [see ENGAINE 10.i].

xi. **JOAN DE COURTENAY**, married before 1367 **JOHN DE CHEVERSTON** (or **CHIVERSTON**), Knt., of Cheverston, Marlborough, Portlemouth, Salcombe, South Huish, and Thurlestone, Devon, Stoneaston, Somerset, etc., Knight of the Shire for Devon, 1334, Captain of Calais, 1347, Seneschal of Gascony, 1351–62, Seneschal of Aquitaine, 1362, son of William de Cheverston, Knt., of Ilton (in Marlborough), Devon. He was born about 1300. They had no issue. In 1367 his wife, Joan, obtained a papal indult to have a portable altar. In 1371 he and his wife, Joan, conveyed the manor of Stoneaston, Somerset to William Cheddre for 100 marks of silver. SIR JOHN DE CHEVERSTON died c.1375. Risdon *Surevey of the County of Devon* (1811): 121–122. Brydges *Collins' Peerage of England* 6 (1812): 214–271 (sub Courtenay, Viscount Courtenay). Vivian *Vis. of Devon 1531, 1564 & 1620* (1895): 243–250 (sub Courtenay). Green *Feet of Fines for Somerset* 3 (Somerset Rec. Soc. 17) (1902): 80. *Papal Regs.: Letters* 4 (1902): 1, 3, 60. *Rpt. & Trans. of the Devonshire Assoc. for the Advancement of Science, Lit. & Art* 3rd Ser. 5 (1913): 257 (biog. of John de Cheverston). *C.C.R. 1389–1392* (1922): 442–443. Ellis *Cat. Seals in the P.R.O.* 2 (1981): 25 (seal of John de Cheverston dated 1374(?) — In a traceried circle, a shield of arms: on a bend, three goat's heads (?). Legend: [S'...DE CHEVERE]STON [MILITIS]).

8. EDWARD DE COURTENAY, Knt., in right of his wife, of Goodrington (in Paignton), South Allington, and Stancombe (in Sherford), Devon, Mudford Terry and Hinton, Somerset, Prince's Bachelor to Edward *the Black Prince*, 3rd son, born about 1331/2. He married **EMELINE** (or **EMME**) **DAUNEY**, daughter and heiress of John Dauney, Knt., of Mudford Terry and Hinton, Somerset, Sheviock, Anthoney, Landulph, and Portlove, Cornwall, Goodrington (in Paignton), Stancombe, and South Allington (in Chivelstone), Devon, by Sibyl, daughter of Walter de Treverbyn, of Treverbyn, Cornwall. She was born about 1329 (aged 18 in 1347). They had two sons, Edward, Knt. [11th Earl of Devon, 4th Lord Courtenay] and Hugh, Knt. SIR EDWARD COURTENAY died between 2 Feb. 1368 and 1 April 1371. His widow, Emeline, died 28 Feb. 1370/1.

Brydges *Collins' Peerage of England* 6 (1812): 214–271 (sub Courtenay, Viscount Courtenay). Nicolas *Rpt. of Procs. on the Claim of the Earldom of Devon in the House of Lords* (1832): 5–16. *Coll. Top. et Gen.* 4 (1837): 264. Westcote *View of Devonshire in MDCXXX* (1845): 570–573 (sub Courtenay). Lipscomb *Hist. & Antiqs. of Buckingham* 1 (1847): 471–472 (Courtenay ped.). Maclean *Hist. of Trigg Minor* 2 (1876): 240–241 (chart). *Reliquary* 17 (1876–7): 97–104. Burke *Dormant, Abeyant, Forfeited & Extinct Peerages* (1883): 139–142 (sub Courtenay). Vivian *Vis. of Cornwall* (1887): 105–118 (Courtenay ped.). *Notes & Gleanings* 2 (1889): 50–56, 65–68, 89–93, 97. *Genealogist* n.s. 9 (1892): 205; n.s. 15 (1898): 24. Vivian *Vis. of Devon 1531, 1564 & 1620* (1895): 243–250 (sub Courtenay). *Papal Regs.: Petitions* 1 (1896): 498. Bates *Particular Desc. of Somerset* (Somerset Rec. Soc. 15) (1900): 179–180. *List of Foreign Accounts* (Lists & Indexes XI) (1900): 221–222. Wrottesley *Peds. from the Plea Rolls* (1905): 208, 220–221, 225–226. *C.C.R. 1369–1374* (1911): 407. *C.P.* 4 (1916): 325 (sub Devon). VCH *Buckingham* 4 (1927): 109–110. *Reg. of Edward the Black Prince* 1 (1930): 15, 16, 119; 2 (1931): 155, 183; 4 (1933): 101, 246, 271, 388, 404, 410 (Sir Edward de Courtenay styled "prince's kinsman" by Edward *the Black Prince*), 479. *Genealogist's Mag.* 6 (1932–34): 606–626. Holmes *Estates of the Higher Nobility in 14th Cent. England* (1957): 32–35, 47–48. Paget *Baronage of England* (1957) 151: 3. Dunning *Hylle Cartulary* (Somerset Rec. Soc. 68) (1968): 74–75, 85.

Children of Edward de Courtenay, Knt., by Emeline Dauney:

i. **EDWARD COURTENAY**, Knt., 11th Earl of Devon, 4th Lord Courtenay, Marshal of England, Lieutenant of the Duchy of Lancaster in Devon, 1386, Admiral of the West, 1383–5, Privy Councillor, son and heir, born about 1357 (of age in 1378, aged 40 and more in 1405). He proved his age and had livery of the lands of his mother and his grandfather the earl in 1378. He married before 31 May 1383 (date of fine) **MAUD CAMOYS**, daughter of John de Camoys, Knt., of Gressenhall, Norfolk, by his 2nd wife, Elizabeth, daughter of William le Latimer, 3rd Lord Latimer [see CAMOYS 7 for her ancestry]. They had three sons, Edward, Knt. [Lord Courtenay], Hugh, Knt. [12th Earl of Devon, 5th Lord Courtenay], and James, and one daughter, Elizabeth. He served as Captain of the English army in Picardy in 1380. He was one of the suite that conducted Anne of Bohemia from Gravelines to London in 1381 for her marriage to King Richard II. He was commander of 60 men-at-arms and 60 arches in Scotland in 1385. He presented to a portion of the church of Waddesdon, Buckinghamshire, 1394, and to the church of Misterton, Somerset, 1410 and 1413. He went on the French campaign in 1415. He was appointed to treat with the French ambassador in October and Nov. 1417. SIR EDWARD COURTENAY, 11th Earl of Devon, 4th Lord Courtenay, died 5 Dec. 1419, and was buried in Ford Abbey. He left a will dated 29 June 1419, proved 5 Dec. 1419. Rymer *Fædera* 7 (1728): 193–194 (Edward styled "cousin" by King Richard II of England).

Brydges *Collins' Peerage of England* 6 (1812): 214–271 (sub Courtenay, Viscount Courtenay). Nicolas *Rpt. of Procs. on the Claim to the Earldom of Devon* (1832): 5–16. Westcote *View of Devonshire in MDCXXX* (1845): 570–573 (sub Courtenay). Lipscomb *Hist. & Antiqs. of Buckingham* 1 (1847): 471–472 (Courtenay ped.). *Sussex Arch. Coll.* 3 (1850): 94 (identifies Elizabeth [recte Maud], wife of Edward Courtenay, Earl of Devon as daughter of Sir John de Camoys). *Reliquary* 17 (1876–7): 97–104. *Notes & Queries* 6th Ser. 1 (1880): 234–235, 298–299, 341. Doyle *Official Baronage of England* 1 (1886): 575–576 (sub Devonshire). Weaver *Somerset Incumbents* (1889): 401. Vivian *Vis. of Devon 1531, 1564 & 1620* (1895): 243–250 (sub Courtenay). Kirby *Wykeham's Reg.* 1 (1896): 193–194. Giffard & Bowett *Regs. of Walter Giffard & Henry Bowett Bishops of Bath & Wells* (Somerset Rec. Soc. 13) (1899): 15–16, 57. *Procs. Bath Natural Hist. & Antiq. Field Club* 9 (1901): 188–201. Benolte et al. *Vis. of Sussex 1530 & 1633–4* (H.S.P. 53) (1905): 29–30 (Camoys ped.: "Elizabeth [Camoys] ux. Edw. Courtney Erle of Devon."). Wrottesley *Peds. from the Plea Rolls* (1905): 208, 220–221, 225–226, 425. *Yorkshire Arch. Jour.* 18 (1905): 369. *C.C.R. 1369–1374* (1911): 407. *C.P.* 3 (1913): 467 (sub Courtenay); 4 (1916): 325–326 (sub Devon). Bubwith *Reg. of Nicholas Bubwith Bishop of Bath & Wells* 1 (Somerset Rec. Soc. 29) (1914): 94, 168, 242, 295. *C.C.R. 1377–1381* (1914): 149. VCH *Buckingham* 4 (1927): 107–118. *Genealogist's Mag.* 6 (1932–34): 606–626. Chichele *Reg. of Henry Chichele* 2 (Canterbury & York Soc. 42) (1937): 178 (will of Edward Courtenay), 649 (biog. of Edward Courtenay). *Cornwall Feet of Fines* 2 (1950): 67–68. Paget (1957) 114: 1–7 (sub Camoys). *Ancient Deeds — Ser. BB* (List & Index Soc. 137) (1977): 41, 76. VCH *Somerset* 4 (1978): 4–38. *Devon & Cornwall Notes & Queries* 35 (1984): 151–158 (incorrectly identifies Earl Edward's wife, Maud, as daughter of Sir Thomas Camoys), 189–193, 219–224. Leese *Blood Royal* (1996): 116–119. National Archives, SC 8/183/9116 (available at www.catalogue.nationalarchives.gov.uk/search.asp).

Children of Edward Courtenay, Knt., by Maud Camoys:

a. **EDWARD COURTENAY**, Knt., styled Lord Courtenay, Warden of the King's Forests in Devon and Cornwall, Keeper of the New Forest, 1415, Admiral of the Fleet, 1418, son and heir apparent, born say 1385 (adult by 1406). He married before 20 Nov. 1409 **ELEANOR MORTIMER**, daughter of Roger Mortimer, Knt., 4th Earl of March, 7th Earl of Ulster, by Eleanor, daughter of Thomas de Holand, K.G., 2nd Earl of Kent [see MORTIMER 14 for her ancestry]. They had no issue. His wife, Eleanor, was living Jan. 1413/4. He fought at the Battle of Agincourt in 1415. SIR EDWARD COURTENAY died in or shortly after August 1418. Sandford *Gen. Hist. of the Kings of England* (1677): 224–226. Rymer *Fœdera* 9 (1729): 8. Nicolas *Controversy between Scrope & Grosvenor* 2 (1832): 235–240. Hardy *Rotuli Normanniæ in Turri Londinensi Asservati* 1 (1835): 167, 170 (instances of Edward Courtenay styled "kinsman" by King Henry V of England in 1417). Hawley *Royal Fam. of England* (1851): 23–27. *Annual Rpt. of the Deputy Keeper* 44 (1883): 545. Vivian *Vis. of Devon 1531, 1564 & 1620* (1895): 243–250 (sub Courtenay). Giffard & Bowett *Regs. of Walter Giffard & Henry Bowett Bishops of Bath & Wells* (Somerset Rec. Soc. 13) (1899): 63. *Papal Regs.: Letters* 6 (1904): 383. Wrottesley *Peds. from the Plea Rolls* (1905): 208. *C.P.R. 1408–1413* (1909): 144. *C.P.R. 1413–1416* (1910): 128 (Edward Courtenay styled "king's kinsman"). Lane *Royal Daughters of England* 1 (1910): 281. *C.P.R. 1416–1422* (1911): 10 (Edward Courtenay styled "king's kinsman"). *C.P.* 4 (1916): 326 (sub Devon). Leese *Blood Royal* (1996): 143–149.

b. **HUGH COURTENAY**, K.B., 12th Earl of Devon, 5th Lord Courtenay, 2nd but 1st surviving son and heir, born in 1389. He married **ANNE TALBOT**, daughter of Richard Talbot, Knt., 4th Lord Talbot, by Ankaret, daughter of John le Strange, Knt., 4th Lord Strange of Blackmere [see TALBOT 13 for her ancestry]. They had one son, Thomas, Knt. [13th Earl of Devon, 6th Lord Courtenay]. He was appointed captain of the fleet to guard the sea in 1418. He served as lieutenant of the king at sea in 1419. SIR HUGH DE COURTENAY, 12th Earl of Devon, 5th Lord Courtenay, died 16 June 1422. Administration on his estate was granted 4 July 1423. His widow, Anne, presented to the churches of Hemington, Somerset in 1423, and Misterton, Somerset in 1428. She married (2nd) by license dated 1432-3 **JOHN BOTREAUX**. Anne, Countess of Devon, died 16 Jan. 1440/1. Rymer *Fœdera* 10 (1727): 97 (Hugh Courtenay, Earl of Devon, styled "kinsman" by King Henry V in 1421). Rogers *Antient Sepulchral Effigies* (1877): 197–200 (Hugh Luttrell styled "dear and beloved cousin" by Sir Hugh Courtenay [12th Earl of Devon] in 1419). Doyle *Official Baronage of England* 1 (1886): 576 (sub Devonshire). Weaver *Somerset Incumbents* (1889): 99, 341, 344, 401. Vivian *Vis. of Devon 1531, 1564 & 1620* (1895): 243–250 (sub Courtenay). *Rpt. on MSS in Various Colls.* 4 (Hist. MSS Comm. 55) (1907): 82. *C.P.* 3 (1913): 467 (sub Courtenay); 4 (1916): 326 (sub Devon). Chichele *Reg. of Henry Chichele* 2 (Canterbury & York Soc. 42) (1937): 649 (biog. of Hugh Courtenay). VCH *Somerset* 4 (1978): 4–38. Wasson *Recs. of Early English Drama: Devon* (1986): 476.

Child of Hugh Courtenay, by Anne Talbot:

1) **THOMAS COURTENAY**, Knt., 13th Earl of Devon, 6th Lord Courtenay, married **MARGARET BEAUFORT** [see SOMERSET 11.vi].

c. **ELIZABETH COURTENAY**, married (1st) **JOHN HARINGTON**, Knt., 4th Lord Harington [see HARINGTON 12.i]; (2nd) **WILLIAM BONVILLE**, K.G., 1st Lord Bonville [see BONVILLE 11].

ii. **HUGH COURTENAY**, Knt. [see next].

9. HUGH COURTENAY, Knt., of Goodrington (in Paignton), South Allington, and Stancombe (in Sherford), Devon, Corton, Dorset, and Hinton (in Mudford) and Mudford Terry, Somerset, and, in right of his 3rd wife, Combehill, Combenetherton, Haccombe, Milton (or Middleton), Ringmore, and Shobrooke, Devon, Knight of the Shire for Devonshire, 1395, 1397, 1421, Sheriff of Devonshire, 1418–19, younger son, born after 1358. He accompanied his uncles, Peter and Philip Courtenay, in the naval expedition of 1378, which was all but destroyed by the Spaniards. He was taken prisoner in the struggle, but was quickly ransomed. He married (1st) shortly after 14 March 1386/7 (date of marriage arrangements) **ELIZABETH FITZ PAYN**, widow of Thomas de Audley, Knt. (died before 1 April 1386) [see AUDLEY 11.iii], of Kingston, Devon, and Stogursey, Somerset, and daughter of Robert Fitz Payn (formerly de Grey), Knt., of Stogursey, Bridghampton, Cheddon Fitzpaine, Rodway, etc., Somerset, by Elizabeth, daughter of Guy de Bryan, K.G., Lord Bryan [see CODNOR 11.ii for her ancestry]. They had no issue. He served at sea as a member of his brother's retinue from March 1387, under the admiral, Richard de Arundel, Earl of Arundel and Surrey. In 1388 he and his wife, Elizabeth, sued Fulk Fitz Warin, Knt., for dower in the manor of Kingston, Devon. She was living at Michaelmas Term 1389. She reportedly died 1 June 139[2?]. He married (2nd) after 1 July 1392 and before 11 Feb. 1392/3 (date of pardon for marrying without a license) **ELIZABETH COGAN**, widow of Fulk Fitz Warin, Knt. (died 8 August 1391), 5th Lord Fitz Warin [see FITZ WARIN 13], of Whittington, Shropshire, Wantage, Berkshire, etc., and daughter of William Cogan, Knt., of Bampton, Devon, and Huntspill, Somerset, by Isabel, daughter and co-heiress of Nigel (or Neel) Loring, Knt., of Chalgrave, Bedfordshire. She was born about 1374 (aged 8 in 1382). She was heiress in 1382 to her minor brother, John Cogan. They had no surviving issue. She died 29 October 1397. In 1399 he went to Ireland with King Richard II. He married (3rd) before 1407 **PHILIPPE L'ARCEDEKNE** (or **L'ARCEDEAKEN**), daughter and co-heiress of Warin l'Arcedekne, Knt., of Elerky (in Veryan), Lanihorne (in Ruan Lanihorne), and Roseworthy (in Gwinear), Cornwall, Haccombe, Devon, etc., by Elizabeth, daughter of John Talbot, Knt. [see RICHARD'S CASTLE 8 for her ancestry]. She was born about 1386 (age 21 in 1407). They had two daughters, Elizabeth and Joan. He presented to the church of Haccombe, Devon in 1409 and 1413. He married (4th) by license dated 16 October 1417 **MAUD BEAUMONT**, daughter of William Beaumont, Knt., of Heanton Punchardon, Devon, by Isabel, daughter of Henry Wilington, Knt. [see CHAMPERNOUN 13 for her ancestry]. Her maritagium appears to have included the manor of Stalpits (in Shrivenham), Berkshire. They had two sons, Edward, Knt., and Hugh, Knt. SIR HUGH COURTENAY died 5 (or 6) March 1425, and was buried at Haccombe, Devon with his 3rd wife, Philippe. His widow, Maud, died 3 July 1467. She left a will dated 10 Jan. 1466/7 (P.C.C. 20 Godyn).

Banks *Dormant & Extinct Baronage of England* 1 (1807): 176–179 (sub Talbot), 228 (sub Archdekne). Brydges *Collins' Peerage of England* 6 (1812): 214–271 (sub Courtenay, Viscount Courtenay). Nicolas *Rpt. of Procs. on the Claim of the Earldom of Devon* (1832): 5–16. *Coll. Top. et Gen.* 3 (1836): 250–278 (re. Bryan fam.); 6 (1840): 79–80 (re. Cogan fam.). Oliver *Eccl. Antiqs. in Devon* 1 (1840): 160. Westcote *View of Devonshire in MDCXXX* (1845): 570–573 (sub Courtenay). Lipscomb *Hist. & Antiqs. of Buckingham* 1 (1847): 471–472 (Courtenay ped.). *Antiq.* 3 (1873): 231–233. Maclean *Hist. of Trigg Minor* 1 (1876): 384 (Wylyngton ped.); 2 (1876): 240–241 (chart); 3 (1879): 259 (Lercedekne ped.). Colby *Vis. of Devon 1564* (1881): 15 (Beamond ped.). Burke *Dormant, Abeyant, Forfeited & Extinct Peerages* (1883): 139–142 (sub Courtenay). *Notes & Queries* 6th Ser. 7 (1883): 50–52, 369–371. Stafford *Reg. of Edmund Stafford* (1886): 71–72. *Jour. Royal Institution of Cornwall* 9 (1886–9): 425–448 (re. Lerchedekne fam.). Vivian *Vis. of Cornwall* (1887): 105–118 (Courtenay ped.). Lawson *Gen. Colls. Ill. the Hist. of Roman Catholic Fams. in England* 3 (1887): 221–232. Birch *Cat. Seals in the British Museum* 2 (1892): 696 (seal of Hugh de Courtenay dated 1391-2 — A shield of arms: COURTENAY, with a label of three points. Suspended by a strap from a tree, and within a carved gothic panel ornamented with ball-flowers along the inner edge). Jackson *Wadham College Oxford* (1893): 25 (Tregarthen ped.). *Desc. Cat. Ancient Deeds* 2

(1894): 438–439; 3 (1900): 464–465. Wrottesley *Staffordshire Suits: Plea Rolls* (Colls. Hist. Staffs. 15) (1894): 6–7. Vivian *Vis. of Devon 1531, 1564 & 1620* (1895): 65–66 (sub Beaumont), 243–250 (sub Courtenay). *Genealogist* n.s. 15 (1898): 215; n.s. 17 (1901): 114. *List of Sheriffs for England & Wales* (PRO Lists and Indexes 9) (1898): 35. *C.P.R. 1391–1396* (1905): 225. Wrottesley *Peds. from the Plea Rolls* (1905): 208, 259, 331. *Rpt. on MSS in Various Colls.* 4 (Hist. MSS Comm. 55) (1907): 82. *C.P.* 1 (1910): 187–188; 5 (1926): 463–464 (sub Fitzpayn), 502–503 (sub Fitzwarin). Strange *Le Strange Recs.* (1916): 333. VCH *Berkshire* 4 (1924): 534. *Genealogist's Mag.* 6 (1932–34): 606–626. *Year Books of Richard II* 5 (Ames Found. 8) (1937): 158–163. Paget *Baronage of England* (1957) 6 (sub Archdekne); 151: 3. *Cal. Inqs. Misc.* 6 (1963): 22–23. *Ancient Deeds — Ser. B* 3 (List & Index Soc. 113) (1975): B.11770. *Ancient Deeds — Ser. BB* (List & Index Soc. 137) (1977): 41 (Hugh Courtenay, Knt. styled "brother" of Edward Courtenay, Earl of Devon). *Devon & Cornwall Notes & Queries* 35 (1984): 192–193 (biog. of Hugh Courtenay). *Cal. IPM* 17 (1988): 519–520; 20 (1995): 237–238; 23 (2004): 307–308. Roskell *House of Commons 1386–1421* 2 (1992): 668–670 (biog. of Sir Hugh Courtenay). VCH *Somerset* 6 (1992): 136–137; 8 (2004): 91–112. Ward *Women of the English Nobility & Gentry 1066–1500* (1995): 30–31 (arrangements Sir Hugh's for 2nd marriage). Leese *Blood Royal* (1996): 116–119. National Archives, E 210/494 — grant dated 14 March 1386/7 by Edward Courtenay, Earl of Devon, and Hugh Courtenay, his brother, to Hamo de Breirton, clerk, and others, of their manors of Gothelyngton [Goodrington], Stancombe, and Alyngton, Devon, and further grant by the said earl, to the same, of his manors of Hynton and Modeford, Somerset, on condition that after the said Hugh shall have married Elizabeth de Audeleye (available at www.catalogue.nationalarchives.gov.uk/search.asp).

Children of Hugh Courtenay, Knt., by Philippe l'Arcedekne:

i. **ELIZABETH COURTENAY**, born about 1413 (aged 5 in 1418). She was co-heiress in 1418 to her aunt, Philippe Talbot, wife of John Tiptoft, 1st Lord Tiptoft and Powis. Banks *Dormant & Extinct Baronage of England* 1 (1807): 228 (sub Archdekne). *Cal. IPM* 20 (1995): 237–238.

ii. **JOAN COURTENAY**, married (1st) **NICHOLAS CAREW**, Knt., Baron Carew [see CAREW 15]; (2nd) **ROBERT VERE**, Knt., of Haccombe, Devon [see HACCOMBE 8].

Child of Hugh Courtenay, Knt., by Maud Beaumont:

i. **HUGH COURTENAY**, Knt. [see next].

10. HUGH COURTENAY, Knt., of Boconnoc, Cornwall, Hinton (in Mudford), Somerset, etc., Knight of the Shire for Cornwall, 1447, 1449–50, son and heir by his father's 4th marriage, born about 1427 (aged 40 & more in 1467). He married **MARGARET CARMINOW**, daughter and co-heiress of Thomas Carminow, of Boconnoc, Cornwall and Ashwater, Devon, by Joan, daughter of Robert Hill. They had two sons, Edward, K.G. [17th Earl of Devon] and Walter, Knt., and four daughters, Isabel (wife of William Mohun), Maud (wife of John Arundell), Elizabeth, and Florence (wife of John Trelawney). She was born about 1422 (aged 20 in 1442). He took part with the Earl of Devon in his private warfare against William Bonville, Lord Bonville, in 1457. In April 1471 he joined Queen Margaret of Anjou at Exeter and went with her to Tewkesbury. He was proclaimed a rebel by King Edward IV 27 April 1471. SIR HUGH COURTENAY fought at the Battle of Tewkesbury, where he was taken and beheaded 6 May 1471. His widow, Margaret, left a will dated or proved 14 Nov. 1512.

Wotton *English Baronetage* 2 (1741): 87–98 (sub Trelawney). Brydges *Collins' Peerage of England* 6 (1812): 214–271 (sub Courtenay, Viscount Courtenay). Nicolas *Rpt. of Procs. on the Claim of the Earldom of Devon in the House of Lords* (1832): 5–16. Westcote *View of Devonshire in MDCXXX* (1845): 570–573 (sub Courtenay). Maclean *Hist. of Trigg Minor* 1 (1876): 317 (chart). Burke *Dormant, Abeyant, Forfeited & Extinct Peerages* (1883): 139–142 (sub Courtenay). *Notes & Queries* 6th Ser. 7 (1883): 50–52, 369–371. Vivian *Vis. of Cornwall 1530, 1573, & 1620* (1887): 105–118 (Courtenay ped.), 296–300 (Carminowe ped.). Jackson *Wadham College Oxford* (1893): 25 (Tregarthen ped.). Vivian *Vis. of Devon 1531, 1564 & 1620* (1895): 243–250 (sub Courtenay). *Genealogist's Mag.* 6 (1932–34): 606–626. Wedgwood *Hist. of Parl.* 1 (1936): 229 (biog. of Sir Hugh Courtenay). *Ancient Deeds — Ser. B* 3 (List & Index Soc. 113) (1975): B. 10,333–10,334, B. 10,358. Biancalana *Fee Tail & the Common Recovery in Medieval England: 1176–1502* (2001): 399–400.

Children of Hugh Courtenay, Knt., by Margaret Carminow:

i. **EDWARD COURTENAY**, K.G., 17th Earl of Devon, Constable of Restormell Castle, 1486, son and heir. He married **ELIZABETH COURTENAY**, daughter of Philip Courtenay, Knt., of Molland, Kingston, and Exeter, Devon, by his wife, Elizabeth [see DAVIE 11 for her ancestry]. They had one son, William, K.B. [18th Earl of

Devon]. He attended the Coronation of King Henry VII in 1485, where he was the bearer of the Second Sword. In 1490 the king restored the manor of Lymington, Hampshire to him. He served as a Captain in the king's army in France in 1492, and as a Captain in the royal army in the West in 1497. EDWARD COURTENAY, 17th Earl of Devon, died 28 May 1509. He left a will dated 27 May 1509, proved 11 July 1509, requesting burial in the chapel of Tiverton, Devon near the grave of his late wife. Brydges *Collins' Peerage of England* 6 (1812): 214–271 (sub Courtenay, Viscount Courtenay). Nicolas *Testamenta Vetusta* 2 (1826): 494–495 (will of Edward Courtenay, Knt., Earl of Devon). Westcote *View of Devonshire in MDCXXX* (1845): 570–573 (sub Courtenay). Colby *Vis. of Devon 1564* (1881): 72–73 (Courtney ped.: "Elizab. [Courtney] = Edw. Courtney, co. Devon."). Doyle *Official Baronage of England* 1 (1886): 579–580 (sub Devonshire). Boase *Reg. of Exeter College, Oxford* (1894): liii, 268. Vivian *Vis. of Devon 1531, 1564 & 1620* (1895): 243–252 (sub Courtenay). VCH *Hampshire* 4 (1911): 639–649. VCH *Buckingham* 4 (1927): 107–118. *Ancient Deeds — Ser. B* 2 (List & Index Soc. 101) (1974): B.6972. VCH *Somerset* 4 (1978): 4–38. *Ancient Deeds — DD Ser.* (List & Index Soc. 200) (1983): 206. James *Bede Roll of the Fraternity of St. Nicholas* 1 (London Rec. Soc. Pubs. 39) (2004): 222, 225.

Child of Edward Courtenay, K.G., by Elizabeth Courtenay:

a. **WILLIAM COURTENAY**, K.B., 18th Earl of Devon, son and heir, born about 1475. He attended the Coronation of Queen Elizabeth Plantagenet 25 Nov. 1487. He married in or before October 1495 [**LADY**] **KATHERINE PLANTAGENET** [see YORK 13.ix], daughter of Edward IV, King of England, by Elizabeth, daughter of Richard Wydeville, K.G., 1st Earl Rivers, Constable of England, Lord High Treasurer [see YORK 13 for her ancestry]. She was born at Eltham, Kent about 14 August 1479. They had two sons, Henry, K.G. [19th Earl of Devon, Marquess of Exeter], and Edward, and one daughter, Margaret. He became the object of jealousy to King Henry VII, by whom he was imprisoned in 1503–9, for alleged (but not proven) complicity in the Earl of Suffolk's rebellion. He was attainted by Parliament Feb. 1504. He was received into favor by King Henry VIII, at whose Coronation in 1509 he bore the Third Sword. The same year his wife, Katherine, was granted an annuity of 200 marks by the king. His attainder was reversed 9 May 1511 on his petition and that of his wife, Katherine. He was created Earl of Devon 10 May 1511. In 1511 the king granted the reversion of the manor of Lymington, Hampshire to William and his wife, Katherine. WILLIAM COURTENAY, 18th Earl of Devon, died testate at Greenwich, Kent 9 June 1511, and was buried at Black Friars, London. His widow, Katherine, took a vow of perpetual chastity in 1511. In 1512 the king granted Katherine and her heirs the reversion of the manors of Sutton Courtenay, Berkshire and Breamore, Hampshire. In 1519–20, as Katherine, Countess of Devonshire, "daughter, suster and awnte to kynges," she leased a close in Waddesdon, Berkshire, to Nicholas Latham, Joan his wife, and John his son. Katherine, Countess of Devon, died testate at Tiverton, Devon 15 Nov. 1527. Sandford *Gen. Hist. of the Kings of England* (1677): 397–399. Brydges *Collins' Peerage of England* 6 (1812): 214–271 (sub Courtenay, Viscount Courtenay). Hardyng *Chronicle of John Hardyng* (1812): 472 ("Katheryne, yᵉ yōgest doughter was maryed to lorde Willyā Courtney, sonne to yᵉ earle of Deuōshire, which lōgtyme tossed in ether fortune, somtyme in welth after in aduersitiee, tyl yᵉ benignitee of her nephewe kyng Hērye yᵉ viii. brought her into a sure estate, accordyng to her degre & progeny."). Nicolas *Privy Purse Expenses of Elizabeth of York* (1830). *Coll. Top. et Gen.* 1 (1834): 297 (York ped.: "The Lady Katherine, wedded to the Earl of Devonshire's son and heir."). Westcote *View of Devonshire in MDCXXX* (1845): 570–573 (sub Courtenay). Green *Lives of the Princesses of England* 4 (1857): 15–43 (biog. of Katherine Plantagenet). *Archæologia* 48 (1884): 157–166. Doyle *Official Baronage of England* 1 (1886): 580–581 (sub Devonshire). Vivian *Vis. of Devon 1531, 1564 & 1620* (1895): 243–250 (sub Courtenay). *Devon N&Q* 5 (1909): 33–37. Lane *Royal Daughters of England* 1 (1910): 316–317. VCH *Hampshire* 4 (1911): 426–427, 596–602, 639–649. Clay *Extinct & Dormant Peerages* (1913): 169–171 (sub Plantagenet). C.P. 4 (1916): 330–331 (sub Devon); 5 (1926): 216 (sub Exeter); 12(2) (1959): 851–852 (sub Worcester). *Letters & Papers… Henry VIII* 1(1) (1920): 77 (Katherine styled "king's aunt" by King Henry VIII of England), 404–405. VCH *Berkshire* 4 (1924): 372–373. VCH *Buckingham* 4 (1927): 107–118. Chrimes *Henry VII* (1972): 35–36. *Ancient Deeds — Ser. B* 2 (List & Index Soc. 101) (1974): B.6072, B.7208, B.8477. VCH *Somerset* 4 (1978): 4–38. *Ancient Deeds — DD Ser.* (List & Index Soc. 200) (1983): 118, 206. Fryde *Handbook of British Chron.* (1986): 41–42. Gray et al. *Tudor & Stuart Devon* (1992): 13–38. National Archives, E 312/12/10 (available at www.catalogue.nationalarchives.gov.uk/search.asp).

Children of William Courtenay, K.B., by Katherine Plantagenet:

1) **HENRY COURTENAY**, K.G., 19th Earl of Devon, Privy Councillor, 1520, Gentleman of the Privy Chamber, 1520, Keeper of Birling Park, Kent, 1522, High Steward of the Duchy of Cornwall and Warden of the Stanneries, 1523, Constable of Windsor Castle, 1525, Seneschal of the Duchy of Cornwall, 1528, son and heir, born about 1498. In 1512 he obtained a reversal of his father's attainder, by which he succeeded to the earldom of Devon. He married (1st) after June 1515 **ELIZABETH GREY**, *suo jure*

Lady Lisle, daughter and heiress of John Grey, 4th Viscount Lisle, by Muriel, daughter of Thomas Howard, Duke of Norfolk. They had no issue. She was born on or about 25 March 1505. They had no issue. His wife, Elizabeth, died shortly before 12 May 1519. His wife, Elizabeth, died soon after their marriage. He married (2nd) 25 October 1519 **GERTRUDE BLOUNT**, daughter of William Blount, K.G., K.B., 4th Lord Mountjoy, by his 1st wife, Elizabeth, daughter and co-heiress of William Say, Knt. They had two sons, Henry and Edward, K.B. [20th Earl of Devon]. He and his wife, Gertrude, attended the king and queen at the Field of the Cloth of Gold in 1520. He was created Marquess of Exeter 18 June 1525. He supported King Henry VIII in his attempt to obtain a divorce, and was rewarded with the Stewardship of numerous Abbies and Priories in the west of England. He assisted in suppressing the rebellion called the Pilgrimage of Grace in 1536. He conspired with the Pole family, endeavoring to raise the men of Devon and Cornwall. HENRY COURTENAY, Marquess of Exeter, was taken prisoner and was tried by his Peers 3 Dec. 1538. He was found guilty of high treason and beheaded on Tower Hill 9 Jan. 1538/9, and was subsequently attainted. He left a will dated 25 Sept. 1538. His widow, Gertrude, was arrested 5 Nov. 1558, and was attainted as his widow July 1539. She was granted a special pardon by the king 21 Dec. 1539. She became a lady in waiting to Queen Mary I. Gertrude, Marchioness of Exeter, died 25 Sept. 1558, and was buried in Wimborne Minster, Dorset. Brydges *Collins' Peerage of England* 6 (1812): 214–271 (sub Courtenay, Viscount Courtenay). Tytler *England under Edward VI & Mary* 2 (1839): 473–474 (letter of Gertrude, Marchioness of Exeter dated 1555). Beltz *Mems. of the Order of the Garter* (1841): clxxii, clxxiv. Westcote *View of Devonshire in MDCXXX* (1845): 570–573 (sub Courtenay). Hutchins *Hist. & Antiqs. of Dorset* 3 (1868): 294. Hardy *Syllabus (in English) of the Docs. Rel. England & Other Kingdoms* 2 (1873): 778. Rogers *Antient Sepulchral Effigies* (1877): 101. Doyle *Official Baronage of England* 1 (1886): 581 (sub Devonshire), 714–715 (sub Exeter). Vivian *Vis. of Devon 1531, 1564 & 1620* (1895): 243–250 (sub Courtenay). *Notes & Queries for Somerset & Dorset* 6 (1899): 15. *Desc. Cat. Ancient Deeds* 3 (1900): 549–561 (D.1202). VCH *Hampshire* 4 (1911): 596–602, 639–649. *C.P.* 4 (1916): 330–332 (sub Devon). VCH *Berkshire* 4 (1924): 372–373. VCH *Buckingham* 4 (1927): 107–118. *Ancient Deeds — Ser. B* 2 (List & Index Soc. 101) (1974): B.6066, B.6072, B.6076; 3 (List & Index Soc. 113) (1975): B.11649, B.12150, B.12241, B.12690. *Ancient Deeds — Ser. BB* (List & Index Soc. 137) (1977): 75–76, 85. VCH *Somerset* 4 (1978): 4–38. *Ancient Deeds — DD Ser.* (List & Index Soc. 200) (1983): 116, 200, 317. Cooper *Propaganda & the Tudor State* (2003): 148 (Henry Courtenay styled "king's near kinsman"). Routledge *Hist. Dict. of British Women* (2003): 119 (biog. of Gertrude Blount).

    2) **[LADY] MARGARET COURTENAY**, married **HENRY SOMERSET**, Knt., 2nd Earl of Worcester [see SOMERSET 15].

  ii. **ELIZABETH COURTENAY** [see next].

11. ELIZABETH COURTENAY, married before 1477 **JOHN TRETHERFF**, Esq., of Tretherff (in Ladock), Argallas (in St. Enoder), Burngullow (in St. Mewan), Pettigrew (in Gerrans), Skewys [in Cury], Tresamble (in Gwennap), Trevelwyth, etc., Cornwall, son and heir of Reynold (or Reginald) Tretherff, Esq., of Tretherff (in Ladock), Cornwall, by Margaret (or Margery), daughter and co-heiress of John Saint Aubyn, Esq. [see RYME 16.ii for his ancestry] They had three sons, including Thomas, Esq., and Reynold, Esq. In 1480 he sued Thomas Glasen for breaking into his closes at Saint Elven, Trewoen in the parish of Saint Breock, and other places in Cornwall. In the period, 1502–3, as "John, son and heir of Reynold Tretherff," he sued John Tregasowe, executor of Stephen Tregasowe in Chancery regarding the detention of deeds relating to the manor of Pettigrew (in Gerrans), and messuages and land in Sorne and Trevelwyth, Cornwall. His wife, Elizabeth, was a legatee in the 1509 will of her brother, Edward Courtenay, K.G., Earl of Devon. JOHN TRETHERFF, Esq., died testate 17 (or 20) June 1510.

Brydges *Collins' Peerage of England* 6 (1812): 214–271 (sub Courtenay, Viscount Courtenay). Gilbert *Hist. Survey of Cornwall* 2 (1820): 303. Nicolas *Rpt. of Procs. on the Claim of the Earldom of Devon in the House of Lords* (1832): 5–16. Gilbert *Parochial Hist. of Cornwall* 2 (1838): 353–354. Westcote *View of Devonshire in MDCXXX* (1845): 570–573 (sub Courtenay). Maclean *Hist. of Trigg Minor* 1 (1876): 317 (chart). Burke *Dormant, Abeyant, Forfeited & Extinct Peerages* (1883): 139–142 (sub Courtenay). Vivian *Vis. of Cornwall 1530, 1573, & 1620* (1887): 437 (St. Aubyn ped.), 497 (Trethurff ped.). Jackson *Wadham College Oxford* (1893): 25 (Tregarthen ped.). Vivian *Vis. of Devon 1531, 1564 & 1620* (1895): 243–250 (sub Courtenay). Wrottesley *Peds. from the Plea Rolls* (1905): 452. *Desc. Cat. Ancient Deeds* 5 (1906): 59, 74, 142, 149–150, 403. *List of Early Chancery Procs.* 5 (PRO Lists and Indexes 38) (1912): 551, 554; 6 (PRO Lists and

Indexes 48) (1922): 1. Abs. of *IPM* — John Tretherff, Esq., dated 1511 and 1513 [FHL Microfilm 917256]. *Cal. IPM* 23 (2004): 221–222. National Archives, C 1/272/48 (available at www.catalogue.nationalarchives.gov.uk/search.asp).

12. **THOMAS TRETHERFF**, Esq., of Tretherff (in Ladock), Cornwall, Street (in Whimple), Devon, etc., son and heir, born about 1478 (aged 33 in 1511). He married **MAUD TREVISA**, daughter of _____ Trevisa, of Trevisa, Cornwall. They had two daughters, Elizabeth (wife of John Vivian) and Margaret. In the period, 1515–18, Elizabeth, daughter of Christopher Crekhay sued him in Chancery regarding his refusal to make conveyance of a cottage and land in defendant's manor of Street [in Rockbere], Devon, for which part of the fine had been paid by her said father, in contemplation of her marriage with John Leche. In the period, 1518–29, as "Thomas Tretherff, esquire, son and heir of John Tretherff, esquire," he sued Reynold Tretherff, his younger brother regarding a petition to examine witnesses as to complainant's title to the manors of Argallas (in St. Enoder), Trewynyan, Treverbyn [in St. Austell], Trelosek, Trevelwith, Tyndele, Penlane; Chalons Leigh and Strete Ralegh; and messuages and lands in Millynowith, Nansawsyn, Nanskilly, Brothoga, Merther, Myler, Brongullowe, Trewyns, Goenrownsyn, Street (in Whimple), Stretewoode, and Chalons Leigh (in Plympton St. Mary), which defendant claims to the disinheriting of complainant's heirs female, with the will annexed of the said John Tretherff. THOMAS TRETHERFF, Esq., died testate 10 Sept. 1529. In the period, 1529–32, John Arundell of Tolvern the elder and the younger, and John Skewys sued John Vyvyan, Alice, wife of William Cristoferys, executors of Thomas Tretherf, and the said William in Chancery regarding the failure of the said Thomas to pay the annuity for the finding of a priest charged on the manors of Tretherff (in Landrake) and Argallas (in St. Enoder), Cornwall, and Stretewode, Devon, by his father, John Tretherf, to the uses of whose will complainants are feoffees.

    Maclean *Hist. of Trigg Minor* 1 (1876): 317 (chart). Vivian *Vis. of Cornwall 1530, 1573, & 1620* (1887): 497 (Trethurff ped.). Jackson *Wadham College Oxford* (1893): 25 (Tregarthen ped.). *List of Early Chancery Procs.* 5 (PRO Lists and Indexes 38) (1912): 554; 6 (PRO Lists and Indexes 48) (1922): 1, 171. Stoate *Cornwall Subsidies in 1524, 1543 & 1545* (1985): 73, 152–153. Abs. of *IPM* — Thomas Tretherff, Esq., dated 1532 [FHL Microfilm 917256]. National Archives, C 1/396/17; C 1/583/50a; C 1/601/1 (available at www.catalogue.nationalarchives.gov.uk/search.asp).

13. **MARGARET TRETHERFF**, younger daughter and co-heiress, born about 1506 (aged 26 in 1532). She married (1st) **JOHN BOSCAWEN**, of Tregothnan, Cornwall, son and heir of John Boscawen, by Elizabeth, daughter of Nicholas Lower. He was born about 1494 (aged 21 in 1515). They had one son, Thomas. JOHN BOSCAWEN died 29 Feb. 1523/4. His widow, Margaret, married (2nd) before 1532 **EDWARD COURTENAY**, of Landrake, Cornwall, son of Edward Courtenay, Esq., by Alice, daughter and heiress of John Wotton. They had three sons, Peter, Esq., William, and Edward, and one daughter, Katherine (wife of George Kekewich, Esq.). In the period, 1529–32 Reynold, son of John Tretherff, Esq. sued John Vyvyan and Elizabeth his wife, Edward Courtenay and Margaret, his wife, daughters of Thomas Tretherf, and Robert Vyvian in Chancery regarding the manors of Tretherff [in Ladock], Pettigrew [in Gerrans], Trevelwyth, Burngullow, Argallas [in St. Enoder], Penlen, Skewys [in Cury], Treverbyn [in St. Austell], Trelesike, Tyndelle and Trewynyan, and messuages, land and rent there and in Melennowith, Nansawfyn, Nanskilly, etc., Cornwall, late of the said John Tretherffe. His widow, Margaret, married (3rd) before 1544 (date of subsidy) **RICHARD BULLER**, Esq., of Shillingham (in St. Stephen-juxta-Saltash) and Tregarrick (in Pelynt), Cornwall, younger son of Alexander Buller, of Lillesdon, Somerset, by his 2nd wife, Elizabeth, daughter of John Horsey, Knt. They had one son, Francis, Esq., and one daughter, Mary. In the period, 1544–7, he and his wife, Margaret, styled "late Margaret Courteney," sued Reynold Mohone and others in Chancery regarding the detention of deeds relating to the manors of Leigh Challons (in Plympton St. Mary) and Street (in Rockbere), Devon, and Argallas (in St. Enoder), and Trevewyth, Cornwall, and lands, rents, services, a mill, and woods in Blakesdon (in Tamerton Folliott ?), Devon. In the period, 1547–51, he and his wife, Margaret, and his step-son, William

Courtenay, were sued in Chancery by Gilbert Flamake and Joan his wife regarding the detention of deeds relating to messuages, lands, rents, and services in Millbrook (in Maker), St. Germans, Rudelond, and Castle Trematon, and a rent in Landrake, St. Neot, and St. Pinnock, Cornwall. His wife, Margaret, was co-heiress in 1556 to her cousin, Edward Courtenay, Earl of Devon, by which she inherited a 1/8th interest in the castles, manors, etc. of Okehampton, Plympton, Tiverton, Colyton, etc., Devon. RICHARD BULLER, Esq., died 9 Dec. 1555. He left a will dated Nov. 1555, proved 12 May 1556 (P.C.C. 6 Ketchyn). His widow, Margaret, died 28 June 1576.

> Gilbert *Hist. Survey of Cornwall* 2 (1820): 38–39, 303. St. George & Lennard *Vis. of Cornwall 1620* (H.S.P. 9) (1874): 20–21 (Boscawen ped.: "John Boscawen son of John = Margaret Da. of Tho. Trethurf & Coh. of Edw. Courtney Erle of Devon"), 24–25 (Buller ped.), 51 (Courtenay ped.: "Edw. Courtney of Lanrake in Com. Cornwall = Margaret 2 Da. and Coh. of Thomas Tredurff"), 108–109 (Kekewich ped.). Rogers *Ancient Sepulchral Effigies & Monumental & Memorial Sculpture of Devon* (1877): 314–315. Burke *Hist. of the Landed Gentry* 1 (1879): 220–221. Colby *Vis. of Devon 1564* (1881): 73 (Courteney ped.: "Edward Courtenay. = Margaret, d. & coh. of Tho. Tretherff, of Tretherff, co. Cornw."). Benolte *Vis. of Somerset 1531, 1573 & 1591* (1885): 12–13 (Buller ped.: "Richard Buller of Wood 1573. = Margt., wid. of Courtney of Cornwall and coh. Jo. Tretherf."). Vivian *Vis. of Cornwall 1530, 1573, & 1620* (1887): 56–57 (Buller ped.), 105–107 (Courtenay ped.), 497 (Tretthurff ped.). *List of Early Chancery Procs.* 6 (PRO Lists and Indexes 48) (1922): 171; 9 (PRO Lists and Indexes 54) (1933): 211. Glenross *Cornish Wills in P.C.C.* 1 (1940): 51. Stoate *Cornwall Subsidies in 1524, 1543 & 1545* (1985): 118, 163. Neal *Cal. of Patent Rolls 28 Elizabeth I (1585–86)* (List & Index Soc. 294) (2002). Abs. of *IPM* — John Boscawen dated 1524 [FHL Microfilm 917525]. Abs. of *IPM* — Margaret Buller ("kinswoman & heir of Edward, late earl of Devon") dated 1576 [FHL Microfilm 917525]. Abs. of *IPM* — Richard Buller, Esq., dated 1556 [FHL Microfilm 917525]. National Archives, C 1/681/30; C 1/1108/52-53; C 1/1219/9-10; C 1/1294/71-72; C 1/1328/19; C 1/1394/64 (available at www.catalogue.nationalarchives.gov.uk/search.asp).

14. FRANCIS BULLER, Esq., of Shillingham (in St. Stephen-juxta-Saltash) and Tregarrick (in Pelynt), Cornwall, Sheriff of Cornwall, 1600–1, son and heir, born about 1546 (aged 10 in 1556). He married **THOMASINE WILLIAMS**, daughter of Thomas Williams, Esq., of Stowford (in Harford), Devon, Burgess (M.P.) for Bodwin, 1555, Burgess (M.P.) for Saltash, Cornwall, 1558, Burgess (M.P.) for Exeter, Devon, 1563, Speaker of the House of Commons, 1563, by Emlyn, daughter and co-heiress of William Crewse, Esq. They had three sons, Richard, Knt., Matthew, and Francis, and six daughters, Margaret (wife of Richard Kendall and Thomas Honywood, Knt.), Thomasine (wife of Robert Dodson), Mary (wife of Arthur Burell), Margery (wife of Pierce Mannington), Frances (wife of John Vivian), and Emlyn (wife of Henry Chiverton). In the period, 1603–16, he and his wife, Thomasine, sued Alexander Maunder, George Maundley, and others in Chancery regarding messuages and lands in Trewyn, Athill, Whitehowse, Ugborough, Innaton, and Cruse Morchard, Devon, settled on Francis and Thomasine by her late mother, Emlyn Williams. FRANCIS BULLER, Esq., died 28 Sept. 1615, and was buried at Pelynt, Cornwall. He left a will 10 May 1615, proved 27 October 1616 (P.C.C. 94 Rudd). His widow, Thomasine, was buried at St. Stephen-juxta-Saltash 29 October 1627.

> Gilbert *Hist. Survey of Cornwall* 2 (1820): 38–39. Gilbert *Parochial Hist. of Cornwall* 3 (1838): 463. *Le Neve's Peds. of the Knights* (H.S.P. 8) (1873): 176–177 (Chiverton ped.). St. George & Lennard *Vis. of Cornwall 1620* (H.S.P. 9) (1874): 24–25 (Buller ped.: "Francis Buller of Shillingham 2 sonne = Thomasine da. of Tho. Williams Esq."). Burke *Hist. of the Landed Gentry* 1 (1879): 220–221. Benolte *Vis. of Somerset 1531, 1573 & 1591* (1885): 12–13 (Buller ped.: "Francis Buller of Shillingham, Cornwall. = Thomasin, d. Williams."). Vivian *Vis. of Cornwall 1530, 1573, & 1620* (1887): 56–57 (Buller ped.). *List of Sheriffs for England & Wales* (PRO Lists and Indexes 9) (1898): 23. *D.N.B.* 21 (1909): 454 (biog. of Thomas Williams). Index of Chancery Procs. (Ser. I) (PRO Lists and Indexes 47) (1922): 98. Abs. of *IPM* — Francis Buller, Esq. dated 1616 [FHL Microfilm 917525].

15. RICHARD BULLER, Knt., of Shillingham (in St. Stephen-juxta-Saltash), Cornwall, Knight of the Shire for Cornwall, Sheriff of Cornwall, 1611–12, 1636–37, son and heir, born about 1579 (aged 37 in 1616). He married before 1603 **ALICE HAYWARD**, daughter of Rowland Hayward, Knt., of Elsinge Spital, London, Hackney, Middlesex, and Cound, Shropshire, Lord Mayor of London, by his 2nd wife, Katherine, daughter of Thomas Smythe, Knt. They had six sons, Francis, Esq., George, Richard, John, Anthony, and Samuel, and six daughters, Katherine, Julian (wife of Bernard

Tanner), Alice (wife of George Kekewich), Mary, Maria, and Thomasine (wife of Josias Calmady). SIR RICHARD BULLER was buried at St. Andrew's, Plymouth, Devon 1 Dec. 1642. He left a will dated 30 March 1640, proved 1 March 1646/7 (P.C.C. 48 Fines). His widow, Alice, was living in 1647 (date of the probate of his will).

> Buckler *Stemmata Chicheleana* (1765): 1, 3 (Katherine Smythe was "Founder's Kin"); Supp. (1) (1775): i, Supp. (2): 20. Gilbert *Hist. Survey of Cornwall* 2 (1820): 38–39. Gilbert *Parochial Hist. of Cornwall* 3 (1838): 463. St. George & Lennard *Vis. of Cornwall 1620* (H.S.P. 9) (1874): 24–25 (Buller ped.: "Sr Richard Buller of Shillingham Kt now living 1620 = Alice da. of Sr Rowland Haward of London Kt"). Burke *Hist. of the Landed Gentry* 1 (1879): 220–221. Benolte *Vis. of Somerset 1531, 1573 & 1591* (1885): 12–13 (Buller ped.: "Richard [Buller] of Swell. = Alice, d. Rowland Howard of London."). Vivian *Vis. of Cornwall 1530, 1573, & 1620* (1887): 56–57 (Buller ped.). *List of Sheriffs for England & Wales* (PRO Lists and Indexes 9) (1898): 23. *Ancestor* 2 (1902): 224.

16. KATHERINE BULLER, married at St. Stephen-juxta-Saltash, Cornwall 31 Dec. 1616 **JAMES PARKER**, Esq., of St. Stephen-juxta-Saltash, Trengoff (in Warleggon), and Blisland, Cornwall, son and heir of [Rev.] William Parker, of Blisland, Cornwall, Archdeacon of Cornwall, by Joan, daughter of _____ Panchard, of Wiltshire. He was born about 1590 (aged 30 in 1620). They had eight sons, William, Esq., Robert, Richard, John, M.A., Francis, Anthony, George, and Rowland, and eleven daughters, Katherine, Alice (wife of George Smith), Jane, Katherine (again), Elizabeth, Cordelia (wife of [Rev.] John Fathers), Katherine (again), Mary (wife of Thomas Lower), Jane (again), Joan (wife of _____ Nicholls), and Katherine (again) (wife of _____ Bray). In 1625 he and his wife, Katherine, acquired lands in Trengoff, Downland, Helligan, Trevorder, and West Wood from John Reade, of Truro, and his wife, Anne. In 1630 he acquired lands in Higher Trevorder parks and other fields from Nathan Lobb, of Warleggon, Cornwall, yeoman, and his father, George Lobb. The same year John, Lord Mohun of Okehampton, Devon assigned him a lease of lands in Trevorder, Cornwall for a term of 99 years. In 1633 he leased part of Trevorder, Cornwall to George Lobb, of Warleggon, Cornwall, yeoman and his wife, Martha, for a term of 99 years. In 1635 he granted a lease of Blisland Green for a term of 200 years of Obadiah Reynolds. In 1639 he sold lands in Trevorder, Cornwall to Samuel Hill, of Warleggon, Cornwall, clerk. In 1649 he and his wife, Katherine, conveyed lands in Blisland, Simonsward, Trevorder, and Warleggon, Cornwall to William Orchard and Francis Reynolds, Gents. In 1657 he and his wife, Katherine, their son, James Parker, junior, and Samuel Hill, clerk, and his wife, Judith, conveyed lands in Trenay and Trevorder, Cornwall to John Gregor, Gent. In 1658 he and his wife, Katherine, sold lands in Trengoff, Downland, Helligan, and Westwood (in Warleggon), Crabbs Hill, Penquite, and Trenay (in St. Neot) to John Colchester, of London, linen-draper, and John Wintle, of London, Gent. In 1663 he conveyed lands in West Mood to Thomas Hambly, of St. Neot, Cornwall, yeoman. JAMES PARKER, Esq., was buried at Warleggon, Cornwall 22 Feb. 1672/3. His widow, Katherine, was buried at Warleggon, Cornwall 25 April 1686. She left a will dated 23 April 1686, proved 25 June 1686 [Archdeaconry Court of Cornwall].

> Buckler *Stemmata Chicheleana* (1765): 3, 88. Maclean *Parochial & Fam. Hist. of Blisland* (1868): 34, 67. St. George & Lennard *Vis. of Cornwall 1620* (H.S.P. 9) (1874): 24–25 (Buller ped.: "Catheryne [Buller] wife to James Parker of Blisland"), 161 (Parker ped.: "Jacobus Parker filius et hæres ætatis 30 annoru' = Katherin filia Rici Buller de Com. Cornub. Militis"). Boase & Courtney *Bibliotheca Cornubiensis* 2 (1878): 424 (sub [Rev.] William Parker, D.D.). Vivian *Vis. of Cornwall 1530, 1573, & 1620* (1887): 56–57 (Buller ped.), 352 (Parker ped.). Jewers *Heraldic Church Notes from Cornwall* (1889): 103, 127, 136, 146. Foster *Alumni Oxonienses* 3 (1891): 1115 (sub John Parker). *Western Antiq.* 11 (1893): 82–83. *VMHB* 5 (1898): 442–444. Crozier *Virginia Heraldica* (1908): 93. Stoate *Cornwall Hearth & Poll Taxes 1660–1664* (1981): 107. Matthews & Calamy *Calamy Revised* (1988): 192 (biog. of John Fathers). Powell *Three Richard Parkers of Virginia* (1990). Cornwall Rec. Office, Gregor Fam. of Trewarthenick, Cornelly, Cornwall, G/690/1,2; G/691; G/719; G/720/1,2; G/721; G/723/1,2½; G/735; G/804; G/806 (available at www.a2a.org.uk/search/index.asp). Royal Institution of Cornwall, Marriage Settlements & Various Parishes, BRA/551/2/35 (available at www.a2a.org.uk/search/index.asp). Parish regs. of Warleggon, Cornwall [FHL Microfilm 1596316]. Online resource: www.kinnexions.com/smlawson/parkere.htm#JParker.

Children of Katherine Buller, by James Parker, Esq.:

i. **[Mr.] RICHARD PARKER**, chirurgeon, baptized at Warleggon, Cornwall 29 Nov. 1630 (aged 31 in 1660). He immigrated to Virginia before 1654, where he settled in Charles City County. He married about 5 Sept. 1656 **MARY** _____, widow of Nicholas Perkins. They had six children, including one son, Richard. He and his family removed to Henrico County, Virginia in 1664. In 1669 he patented a 350 acre tract in Henrico County at the head of Four Mile Creek on the north side of the James River. RICHARD PARKER was last mentioned in the records of Henrico County, Virginia in Feb. 1679/80. Vivian *Vis. of Cornwall 1530, 1573, & 1620* (1887): 352 (Parker ped.). *VMHB* 5 (1898): 442–444. Crozier *Virginia Heraldica* (1908): 93. Nugent *Cavaliers & Pioneers* 2 (1977): 71. Foley *Early Virginia Fams. Along the James River* 1 (1974): 20–21. McSwain *Some Ancs. & Descs. of Richard Parker* (1980). *Gens. of Virginia Fams. from VMHB* 4 (1981): 584–586. Powell *Three Richard Parkers of Virginia* (1990). Special thanks go to Fred Olen Ray and Waunita Powell for their contribution of original research for this account.

ii. **GEORGE PARKER**, baptized at Warleggon, Cornwall 1 May 1640. He was apprenticed to a woolen draper in England. He immigrated before 1673 to Virginia. His subsequent history is unknown. Vivian *Vis. of Cornwall 1530, 1573, & 1620* (1887): 352 (Parker ped.). Crozier *Virginia Heraldica* (1908): 93. McSwain *Some Ancs. & Descs. of Richard Parker* (1980). Powell *Three Richard Parkers of Virginia* (1990).

✤ COVERT ✤

RICHARD SUTTON, Knt., of Sutton-on-Trent, Nottinghamshire, married **ISABEL PATRICK**.
JOHN DE SUTTON, Knt., of Aston le Walls, Northamptonshire, married **MARGARET DE SOMERY**.
JOHN DE SUTTON, Knt., of Dudley (in Sedgley), Staffordshire, married **ISABEL DE CHERLETON**.
JOHN DE SUTTON, Knt., of Dudley (in Sedgley), Staffordshire, married **JOAN DE CLINTON**.
JOHN DE SUTTON, Knt., of Greathampstead Someries (in Luton), Bedfordshire, married **ALICE LE DESPENSER** (desc. King William the Conqueror).
JOHN SUTTON, Knt., of Dudley (in Sedgley), Staffordshire, married **CONSTANCE BLOUNT**.
JOHN SUTTON, K.G., 1st Lord Dudley, married **ELIZABETH BERKELEY** (desc. King William the Conqueror) [see SUTTON 7].

8. JOHN DUDLEY, Esq., of Atherington (in Climping), Sussex, Justice of the Peace for Hampshire, 1470, Justice of the Peace for Sussex, 1471–5, 1481–3, 1484–1501, Knight of the Shire for Sussex, 1478, Sheriff of Surrey and Sussex, 1483–4, Esquire of the Body to King Henry VII, 1490–1500, Burgess (M.P.) for Arundel, 1491–2, Sheriff of Hampshire, 1493–4, and, in right of his wife, of Gatcombe, Hampshire, and Compton, Sussex, 2nd son. He married before 1462 **ELIZABETH BRAMSHOTT**, daughter and co-heiress of John Bramshott, of Bramshott and Gatcombe, Hampshire, Compton, Lordington (in Racton), and Terwick, Sussex, etc., by Katherine, daughter of John Pelham, Knt., of Laughton, Bivelham, Burwash, Crowhurst, etc., Sussex, Chamberlain to Queen Katherine of France (wife of King Henry V of England) [see BRAMSHOTT 11 for her ancestry]. They had three sons, Edmund, Esq., John, and Peter, and two daughters, Elizabeth and Anne (wife of Robert Hall). His wife, Elizabeth, died in 1498. JOHN DUDLEY, Esq., died 6 Feb. 1500/1501. He left a will dated 1 October 1500, proved 26 June 1501 (P.C.C. Moone 19 & 23), requesting burial in the College Church of Arundel, "in my tombe of marbill there, where Elizabeth, late my wife, lyeth buried."

Grazebrook *Barons of Dudley* 1 (Colls. Hist. Staffs. 9(2)) (1888): 1–152. *List of Sheriffs for England & Wales* (PRO Lists and Indexes 9) (1898): 55, 137. Benolte et al. *Vis. of Sussex 1530 & 1633–4* (H.S.P. 53) (1905): 44–45 (Bramshott ped.: "Elizebeth [Bramshott]. = John Dudley Esqr ob. 14 H. 7."). *D.N.B.* 6 (1908): 100–102 (biog. of Edmund Dudley). VCH *Hampshire* 3 (1908): 165–170; 5 (1912): 246–249. Wedgwood *Hist. of Parl.* 1 (1936): 286 (biog. of John Dudley). VCH *Sussex* 4 (1953): 28–30, 91–94. Loades *John Dudley, Duke of Northumberland 1504–1553* (1996): 1. Adams *Leicester & the Court: Essays on Elizabethan Politics* (2002): 314–315. Wilson *Uncrowned Kings of England* (2005): xiv–xv (Dudley ped.).

Children of John Dudley, Esq., by Elizabeth Bramshott:

i. **EDMUND DUDLEY**, Esq., of Atherington and Findon, Sussex, Balderston, Lancashire, and London, lawyer, Knight of the Shire (or Burgess) (M.P.) for Lewes, some Sussex boro. or Sussex, 1483–7, 1489–90, Burgess (M.P.) for Lewes, 1491–2, Knight of the Shire for Sussex, 1495, (?1497), 1504, Speaker of the House of Commons, 1504,

President of the Council, 1506–9, son and heir. He was a student at Oxford, and afterwards studied law at Gray's Inn. He married (1st) **ANNE WINDSOR**, daughter of Thomas Windsor, Esq., of Stanwell, Middlesex, Usher of the Chamber, by Elizabeth, daughter of John Andrew (or Andrews), Esq. [see LUDLOW 12 for her ancestry]. They had one daughter, Elizabeth (wife of William Stourton, 7th Lord Stourton). He was present at the Coronation of King Richard III in 1483. He helped negotiate peace at Boulogne in 1492. His wife, Anne, was living 1 October 1500. He married (2nd) **ELIZABETH GREY**, *suo jure* Lady Lisle of Kingston Lisle, daughter of Edward Grey, Knt., 3rd Viscount Lisle, by his 1st wife, Elizabeth, daughter of John Talbot, Knt., 1st Viscount Lisle [see GROBY 15.ii for her ancestry]. She was born about 1482–5 (aged 20 or 23 in 1505). They had three sons, John, K.G. [1st Duke of Northumberland], Jerome, and Andrew, Knt. He was granted letters of fraternity by the Prior and Convent of Durham in 1508. EDMUND DUDLEY, Esq., was beheaded on Tower Hill 18 August 1510, and was buried in the church of the Blackfriars. His widow, Elizabeth, married (2nd) 12 Nov. 1511 (as his 1st wife) **ARTHUR PLANTAGENET**, K.G. [see YORK 13.ii], King's Spear, Esquire of the Body, Sheriff of Hampshire, 1513–14, Vice-Admiral of England, 1525, Trier of Petitions in Parliament, Governor of Calais, 1533–40, Warden of the Cinque Ports, 1536–42, Privy Councillor, 1540, illegitimate son of King Edward IV of England [see YORK 13 for his ancestry]. He was probably born about 1470 (presumed to be "my Lord the Bastard" mentioned in an Exchequer account dated mid-1471). They had three daughters, Frances (wife of John Basset and Thomas Monke), Elizabeth (wife of Francis Jobson, Knt.), and Bridget (wife of William Carden, Knt.). He was admitted a member of Lincoln's Inn 4 Feb. 1510/11. His wife, Elizabeth, was co-heiress in 1519 to her niece, Elizabeth Grey, Countess of Devon, Viscountess Lisle, and sole heiress before 1523 to her sister, Anne Grey, wife of John Willoughby, Knt. He presented to the church of Bedworth, Warwickshire in 1521, in right of his wife, Elizabeth. He and his wife, Elizabeth, presented to the church of Uphill, Somerset in 1522; he presented alone in 1528. In consequence of his marriage, he was created Viscount Lisle 25 April 1523. In 1526 he was acting as Lieutenant of Henry Fitz Roy, Duke of Richmond. In 1528 he purchased the manors of Segenworth, Chark, Lee, Sutton, West Stratton, etc., Hampshire from his cousin, John Wayte, Esq., of Titchfield, Hampshire. His wife, Elizabeth, was living 10 August 1530. He married (2nd) before 20 Feb. 1530/1 **HONOR GRENVILLE**, widow of John Basset, Knt. (died 31 Jan. 1522/9), and daughter of Thomas Grenville, Knt., of Kilkhampton (in Stowe), Cornwall, by his 1st wife, Isabel, daughter of Otes Gilbert, Esq. They had no issue. He was imprisoned in the Tower of London on suspicion of treason 19 May 1540. SIR ARTHUR PLANTAGENET, Viscount Lisle, died there 3 March 1541/2. On 9 March 1541/2 the king's council commanded the Deputy of Calais to set at liberty Lady Lisle and her daughters, and to restore to them their apparel and jewels, and that Lady Lisle have £900 for the payment of her debts, transportation, and other necessaries. Honor, Lady Lisle, was buried at Logan, Cornwall 30 April 1566. Sandford *Gen. Hist. of the Kings of England* (1677): 399, 421–424. Dugdale *Antiqs. of Warwickshire* (1730): 107 (Astley-Grey ped.), 121. Nichols *Hist. & Antiqs. of Leicester* 3(2) (1804): 682–684 (Grey ped.). Clarke *Parochial Topog. of the Hundred of Wanting* (1824): 167–168. Ellis *Original Letters Ill. of English Hist.* 2nd Ser. 2 (1827): 104–106. *Rpt. on the Procs. on the Claim to the Barony of L'Isle* (1829). Burke *Dict. of the Peerages… Extinct, Dormant & in Abeyance* (1831): 433, 513–514. Banks *Dormant & Extinct Baronage of England* 4 (1837): 386–389. Nicolas *Procs. & Ordinances of the Privy Council* 7 (1837): 89, 113, 144, 146, 268, 271, 321. Montagu *Guide to the Study of Heraldry* (1840): 42. Beltz *Mems. of the Order of the Garter* (1841): clxxii. Jerdan *Rutland Papers: Original Docs. Ill. of the Courts & Times of Henry VII & Henry VIII* (Camden Soc. 21) (1842): 28–49. Ellis *Three Books of Polydore Vergil's English Hist.* (Camden Soc. 29) (1844): 172 (Arthur Plantagenet: "base gotten … of very verteuous and lovely disposytion"). Ebchester & Burnby *Obit. Roll* (Surtees Soc. 31) (1856): 115. Lennard & Vincent *Vis. of Leicester 1619* (H.S.P. 2) (1870): 74–75 (Gray ped.: "Elizab. [Gray] Nupta Edm. Dudley postea Arthur Plantagenet"). Abram *Hist. of Blackburn* (1877): 416. Holton *Farwell Ancestral Mem.: Henry Farwell, of Concord & Chelmsford* (1879): viii (Monk ped.). Flower *Vis. of Yorkshire 1563–4* (H.S.P. 16) (1881): 308–310 (Talbot ped.: "Anne daughter of the Lord Wyndsore = Edmond Dudley on of the Prevy Consell to Kyng Henry 7th. = Elsabeth [Grey] daughter & sole heyre = Arthur Plantagenet bastard son to Edward IV. 2 husband"). Chitting & Phillipot *Vis. of Gloucester 1623, 1569 & 1582–3* (H.S.P. 21) (1885): 113–116 (Newton ped.: "Elizabetha [Grey] ux. Edwardi Dudley relicta Arthuri Plantageneti."). Doyle *Official Baronage of England* 2 (1886): 400–401 (sub Lisle). Vivian *Vis. of Cornwall* (1887): 190–197 (Grenville ped.). Weaver *Somerset Incumbents* (1889): 202. Woodward & Burnett *Treatise on Heraldry, British & Foreign* 2 (1892): 557. Vivian *Vis. of Devon 1531, 1564 & 1620* (1895): 45–48 (sub Basset), 568–570 (sub Monk). Baildon *Recs. of Lincoln's Inn: Admissions* 1 (1896): 34. *List of Sheriffs for England & Wales* (PRO Lists and Indexes 9) (1898): 55. *Desc. Cat. Ancient Deeds* 4 (1902): 47; 5 (1906): 309, 338, 386, 424, 459. Benolte et al. *Vis. of Sussex 1530 & 1633–4* (H.S.P. 53) (1905): 44–45 (Bramshott ped.: "Edmund Sutton of Dudley. = 1st …. d. & heire of John Grey Viscount Lisle."). *Rpt. on MSS in Various Colls.* 4 (Hist. MSS Comm. 55) (1907): 88. *D.N.B.* 6 (1908): 100–102 (biog. of Edmund Dudley); 15 (1909): 1285–1287 (biog. of Arthur Plantagenet). VCH *Lancaster* 6 (1911): 313–319. *List of Early Chancery Procs.* 5 (PRO Lists and Indexes 38) (1912): 288, 358, 465, 472, 473; 6 (PRO Lists and Indexes 48) (1922): 109, 134. Maxwell-Lyte *Docs. & Extracts illus. Hist. of the Honour of Dunster* (1921): 283. Scofield *Life & Reign of Edward IV* 2 (1923): 56, 161. VCH *Worcester* 4 (1924): 297–317. *C.P.* 5 (1926): App. A, 755; 8 (1932): 63–68 (sub Lisle); 12(1) (1953): 305–306 (sub Stourton); 14 (1998):

443 (sub Lisle). Fox *Letters of Richard Fox 1486–1527* (1929): 130–131 (letter to Sir Arthur Plantagenet dated ?1522). Wedgwood *Hist. of Parl.* 1 (1936): 285–286 (biog. of Edmund Dudley). *Regs. of Thomas Wolsey, Bishop of Bath and Wells, 1518–1523, John Clerke, Bishop of Bath and Wells, 1523–1541, etc.* (Somerset Rec. Soc. 55) (1940): 51. *Ancient Deeds — Ser. B* 2 (List & Index Soc. 101) (1974): B.8898; 3 (List & Index Soc. 113) (1975): B.10780, B.12180. Himsworth *Winchester College Muniments* 1 (1976): 242; 2 (1984): 53. VCH *Gloucester* 11 (1976): 65–70. *Ancient Deeds — Ser. BB* (List & Index Soc. 137) (1977): 80–81, 83, 90. *Chancery Decree Rolls (C.78)* (List & Index Soc. 160) (1979): 69. VCH *Sussex* 6 (1) (1980): 20–34. Byrne *Lisle Letters* 1 (1981): 481; 2 (1981): 63 (Arthur Plantagenet styled "cousin" by Margaret Pole, Countess of Salisbury); 4 (1981): 140 (instances of Henry Pole, Lord Montagu, styled "cousin" to Arthur Plantagenet). *Ancient Deeds — DD Ser.* (List & Index Soc. 200) (1983): 193, 207. *Chancery Decree Rolls: Elizabeth I (C78/15–45)* (List & Index Soc. 198) (1983): 9. Given-Wilson *Royal Bastards of Medieval England* (1984): 158, 161–174. Fryde *Handbook of British Chron.* (1986): 41–42. Wasson *Recs. of Early English Drama: Devon* (1986): 500. Hockey *Charters of Quarr Abbey* (1991): 5. Loades *John Dudley, Duke of Northumberland, 1504–1553* (1996). *Ricardian* 13 (2003): 229–233. Online resource: www.a2a.org.uk/search/doclist.asp?nb=0&nbKey=1&com=1&keyword="Arthur%20Plantagenet"&properties=0601

Child of Edmund Dudley, Esq., by Elizabeth Grey:

a. **JOHN DUDLEY**, K.G., of Dudley Castle, Staffordshire, Halden, Kent, Durham Place, London, Chelsea and Syon, Middlesex, Kingston Lisle, Berkshire, etc., joint Constable of Warwick Castle, 1532–50, Knight of the Body to King Henry VIII by 1533, Master of the Armoury in the Tower, 1534–44, Knight of the Shire for Kent, 1529, Knight of the Shire for Staffordshire, 1542, Sheriff of Staffordshire, 1536–7, Vice-Admiral, 1537–43, Ambassador Extraordinary to Spain, 1537, Warden of the Scottish Marches, 1542–3, 1551–53, Lord High Admiral, 1543–7, 1549–50, Privy Councillor, 1543–53, Governor of Boulogne, 1544–5, Lieutenant General of the Army and Armada upon the sea in outward parts, 1546, Lord Great Chamberlain, 1547–50, Lieutenant of all the Northern counties, 1547, Lord President of the Council of Wales, 1549–50, Great Master (High Steward) of the Household, 1550–3, Lord President of the Council, 1550–3, Governor of Northumberland and Warden-Gen. for life of the Marches towards Scotland and in the king's lordship of Scotland, 1550–3, Earl Marshal of England, 1551, Chancellor of Cambridge University, 1552–3, Trier of Petitions in Parliament, 1553, son and heir by his father's 2nd marriage, born in 1504–6 (aged under 8 in 1512). He was restored in blood in 1512. He married before 1526 **JANE GUILDFORD**, daughter and heiress of Edward Guildford, Knt., of Halden and Hempsted (in Benenden), Kent, Marshal of Calais, Constable of Dover Castle and Warden of the Cinque Ports, by his 1st wife, Eleanor, daughter of Thomas West, K.G., 8th Lord la Warre [see WEST 12.ii for her ancestry]. She was born about 1504 (aged 50 in 1554). They had eight sons, Henry, Thomas, John, Knt. [Earl of Warwick], Ambrose, Henry, Robert [Earl of Leicester], Guildford, Esq., and Charles, and five daughters, including xMary (wife of Henry Sidney, Knt.) and Katherine (wife of Henry Hastings, K.G., 3rd Earl of Huntingdon). On the death of his mother c.1530, he is held to have succeeded her as Lord Lisle. In 1538 he sold the manor of Kingston Lisle, Berkshire to William Hyde, Esq. In 1537 he purchased Dudley Castle from Lord Dudley. On the death of his mother's 2nd husband, Arthur Plantagenet, Viscount Lisle, in 1542, he became entitled to the Viscountcy of Lisle under the terms of the patent creating that dignity in 1523; nevertheless, he was created Viscount Lisle 12 March 1541/2. He took part in the expedition against Scotland in 1544, when Edinburgh was sacked. He was present at the capture of Boulogne in 1544. He was appointed a commissioner to conclude peace with France in 1546. He was created Earl of Warwick 16 Feb. 1546/7. He was in command of the army against the Scots in 1547, and won the Battle of Pinkie. In 1549 he suppressed the agrarian rebellion raised by Robert Kett. He was created Duke of Northumberland 20 October 1551. He was the first of 26 peers who signed the document settling the crown on Lady Jane Grey 16 June 1553, to the exclusion of the king's sisters. On the death of King Edward VI 6 July 1553, he proclaimed his daughter-in-law, Lady Jane Grey, as Queen. On 23rd July, however, he was arrested at Cambridge and lodged in the Tower, 25 July. JOHN DUDLEY, Duke of Northumberland, was found guilty of high treason 18 August 1553, and executed at Tower Hill 22 August 1553. He was subsequently attainted and his honours forfeited. His wife, Jane, was taken to the Tower 23 July 1553 with her son, Guildford, and his wife, Lady Jane Grey. She was co-heiress in 1554 to her uncle, Thomas West, K.G., K.B., 9th Lord la Warre, 6th Lord West. She died at Chelsea, Middlesex 22 Jan. 1554/5, and was buried there 1 Feb. 1554/5. Edmondson *Hist. & Genealogical Acount of the Noble Fam. of Greville* (1766): 61–62. Brydges *Collins' Peerage of England* 5 (1812): 1–28 (sub West, Earl Delawarr). *British Plutarch* 1 (1816): 239–255 (biog. of John Dudley). Clarke *Parochial Topog. of the Hundred of Wanting* (1824): 167–168. *Rpt. on the Procs. on the Claim to the Barony of L'Isle* (1829). Beltz *Mems. of the Order of the Garter* (1841): clxxv, clxxvii. Nichols *Diary of Henry Machyn* (Camden Soc. 42) (1848): 81. Hutchins *Hist. & Antiqs. of Dorset* 3 (1868): 141 (West ped.). Lennard & Vincent *Vis. of Leicester 1619* (H.S.P. 2) (1870): 74–75 (Gray ped.: "Joh'es Dudley Dux Northumb'."). Flower *Vis. of Yorkshire 1563–4* (H.S.P. 16) (1881): 308–310 (Talbot ped.: "John Dudley Vyscount Lysley Erl of Warwyke & after created Duc of Northumberland."). Doyle *Official Baronage of England*

2 (1886): 401–402 (sub Lisle), 656–659 (sub Northumberland); 3 (1886): 591–592 (sub Warwick). Boyd & Wrottesley *Final Concords* (Colls. Hist. Staffs. 11) (1890): 280. *List of Sheriffs for England & Wales* (PRO Lists and Indexes 9) (1898): 128. Benolte et al. *Vis. of Sussex 1530 & 1633–4* (H.S.P. 53) (1905): 44–45 (Bramshott ped.: "John Duke of Northumberland. = Jane d. & heire of Sr Edward Guilford Warden of the 5 Ports."). *D.N.B.* 6 (1908): 109–111 (biog. of John Dudley, Duke of Northumberland). *C.P.* 4 (1916): 157, footnote a (sub De la Warr); 6 (1926): 656–657 (sub Huntingdon); 8 (1932): 68 (sub Lisle); 9 (1936): 722–726 (sub Northumberland); 12(2) (1959): 397 (sub Warwick). *Ancient Deeds — Ser. B* 2 (List & Index Soc. 101) (1974): B.5266, B.5582, B.6013, B.6443, B.6470, B.6473, B.6485, B.6768, B.6940, B.8688; 3 (List & Index Soc. 113) (1975): B.12008 (Geoffrey Dudley styled "kinsman" by John Dudley, Earl of Warwick), B.12106, B.12181 (Thomas Arundell, Esq., styled "kinsman" by John Dudley, Knt.), B.12832. *Ancient Deeds — Ser. BB* (List & Index Soc. 137) (1977): 25–26, 80–81, 83, 90. Ellis *Cat. Seals in the P.R.O.* 1 (1978): 22 (seal of John Dudley, Duke of Northumberland dated 1553 — A shaped and curled shield of arms: quarterly of eight, (1) two lions passant [SOMERY]; (2) barry of six, a label of three pieces [GREY]; (3) a lion rampant, queue fourché [DUDLEY]; (4) checky a chevron ermine [NEWBURGH]; (5) a fesse between six crosses crosslet [BEAUCHAMP]; (6) a chevron between ten crosses paty (6 and 4); (7) a fesse between two chevrons [LISLE]; (8) a lion passant gardant crowned [GERARD]. The shield is encircled by the Garter and the duke's coronet is above. No legend.). *Chancery Decree Rolls (C.78)* (List & Index Soc. 160) (1979): 3, 32. Bindoff *House of Commons 1509–1558* 2 (1982): 63–66 (biog. of Sir John Dudley). VCH *Somerset* 6 (1992): 283–300. Loades *John Dudley, Duke of Northumberland, 1504–1553* (1996). *Trans. Monumental Brass Soc.* 17 (2004): 132–135.

Child of John Dudley, K.G., by Jane Guildford:

1) [**Lord**] **GUILDFORD DUDLEY**, Esq., married [**Lady**] **JANE GREY**, Queen of England [see GROBY 18.i.a].

ii. **ELIZABETH DUDLEY** [see next].

9. ELIZABETH DUDLEY, married before 1483 **THOMAS ASHBURNHAM**, Esq., of Guestling and Winchelsea, Sussex, and London, Sheriff of Surrey and Sussex, 1499–1500, Mayor of Winchelsea, Sussex, 1509–10, 1521–2, Burgess (M.P.) for Winchelsea, Sussex, 1510, 1523, younger son of Thomas Ashburnham, of Ashburnham, Sussex, by Elizabeth, daughter of Henry Wanses. They had two sons, including Thomas, Esq., and two daughters, Ellen and Ann (wife of Roger Horne and John Goldwell). THOMAS ASHBURNHAM, Esq., died in 1523. He left a will dated 13 April 1523, requesting burial in the church of Guestling, Sussex.

List of Sheriffs for England & Wales (PRO Lists and Indexes 9) (1898): 137. Berry *County Gens.: Sussex Fams.* (1830): 28 (sub Ashburnham). Bindoff *House of Commons 1509–1558* 1 (1982): 340 (biog. of Thomas Ashburnham). Wilson *Uncrowned Kings of England* (2005): xiv–xv (Dudley ped.).

10. ELLEN ASHBURNHAM, married before 1520 (as his 1st wife) **WALTER HENDLEY**, Knt., of Coursehorne (in Cranbrook), Kent, and Gray's Inn, London, Counsel for the Cinque Ports, Counsel for Rye, Solicitor for the Court of Augmentations, 1537–40, Attorney-General for the Court of Augmentations, 1540–7, Burgess (M.P.) for Canterbury, Kent, 1542, son and heir of Gervase Hendley, of Canterbury, Kent, by Elizabeth, daughter of Walter Roberts. They had three daughters, Elizabeth (wife of William Waller, Esq., and George Fane, Esq.), Ellen (wife of Thomas Culpeper), and Anne. His wife, Ellen, died before 1523. In 1526 the Brotherhood of the Cinque Ports granted him an annual fee of 13*s*.4*d*., which was increased the following year to 40*s*. About this same time he acted for Sandwich in its suit against Edward Ryngeley, Knt. He married (2nd) by license dated 1 July 1527 **MARGERY PIGOTT**, widow of Thomas Cotton, of Landwade, Cambridgeshire, and daughter of Thomas Pigott, Esq., of Whaddon, Buckinghamshire, Serjeant-at-law. He served as a commissioner for the suppression of the monasteries in 1539. He acquired 11 manors in Kent, most of them ex-monastic but including Matham which he obtained from Thomas Wyatt, Knt., and Cockride and Crowthorne purchased from John Cheyne. In 1540 he had a lease of Holborn manor in the suburbs of London for a term of 89 years from the Bishop of Bangor. In 1546 he was considered for the chancellorship of Ireland, but being ill and almost blind, he did not wish for the promotion. SIR WALTER HENDLEY died 1 March 1550. He left a will proved 26 April 1550 (P.C.C. 10 & 30 Coode), requesting burial before his pew in the church of Cranbrook, Kent. His widow, Margery, married (3rd) **THOMAS ROBERTS**, Esq.

>Ireland *New & Complete Hist. of Kent* 2 (1829): 299. Berry *County Gens.: Sussex Fams.* (1830): 28 (sub Ashburnham). Poste *Hist. of the College of All Saints, Maidstone* (1847): 51. *Arch. Cantiana* 13 (1880): 132–135. *C.P.R. 1547–1553* (1926): 327. *Chancery Decree Rolls (C.78)* (List & Index Soc. 160) (1979): 56. Bindoff *House of Commons 1509–1558* 1 (1982): 340 (biog. of Thomas Ashburnham); 2 (1982): 332–333 (biog. of Walter Hendley).

11. ANNE HENDLEY, daughter by her father's 1st marriage. She married (as his 1st wife) **RICHARD COVERT**, Esq., of Slaugham, Bradbridge, Hangleton, Peathorne, Rustington, and Twineham, Sussex, Sheriff of Surrey and Sussex, 1564–5, son and heir of John Covert, Esq., of Slaugham, Sussex, Burgess (M.P.) for Shoreham, 1529, Knight of the Shire for Sussex, 1555, by Joan, daughter and co-heiress of Thomas Cooke, Esq., of Rustington, Sussex. They had seven sons, Walter, Walter, Knt. (again), John, Thomas, Minors, Alexander, and Francis, and seven daughters, Mary (wife of Richard Bartelott), Ellen/Eleanor (wife of Bessels Fettiplace), Ann, Joan (wife of Henry Smith), Elizabeth (wife of Richard Sheppard), Dulcibella (wife of William Vyne), and Margery (perhaps wife of Ninian Chaloner). He was admitted to Gray's Inn in 1536. He and his wife, Anne, were legatees in the 1550 will of her father. He married (2nd) **CECILY BOWES**, widow of Henry Harte, and daughter of Martin Bowes, Knt. He married (3rd) **MARY HERON**, daughter of Nicholas Heron, Knt. RICHARD COVERT, Esq., died 10 Sept. 1579. He left a will proved 26 April 1580 (P.C.C. 14 Arundell).

>Ireland *New & Complete Hist. of Kent* 2 (1829): 299. Berry *County Gens.: Sussex Fams.* (1830): 18–19 (Covert ped.). *List of Sheriffs for England & Wales* (PRO Lists and Indexes 9) (1898): 137. *Sussex Arch. Colls.* 46 (1903): 170–180; 47 (1904): 116–147; 48 (1905): 1–15. Comber *Sussex Gens.* 2 (1932): 179–186 (sub Covert). Bindoff *House of Commons 1509–1558* 2 (1982): 332–333 (biog. of Walter Hendley).

12. JOHN COVERT, of Ewhurst, Sussex, Burgess (M.P.) for East Grinstead, Sussex, 1586, 3rd son. He married **CHARITY BOWES**, daughter of Martin Bowes, Knt. She was the niece of his father's 2nd wife. They had one daughter, Anne. He was a legatee in the 1580 will of his father. His wife, Charity, was buried at Ifield, Sussex 2 August 1583. JOHN COVERT died 22 October 1589. He left a will proved 5 Dec. 1589 (P.C.C. 98 Leicester).

>*Sussex Arch. Colls.* 46 (1903): 170–180; 47 (1904): 116–147; 48 (1905): 1–15. *Survey of London: St. Leonard, Shoreditch* (1922): 89–90. Comber *Sussex Gens.* 2 (1932): 179–186 (sub Covert).

13. ANNE COVERT, daughter and heiress. She married **WALTER COVERT**, Knt., of Maidstone, Kent, son and heir of William Covert, of Leeds and Vinters, by Elizabeth, daughter of William Steed, Knt., of Harrietsham, Kent. They had three sons, Walter, Thomas, and John, Knt., and two daughters, Elizabeth and Anne. He was admitted to Gray's Inn in 1608. His wife, Anne, was a legatee in the 1604 will of her uncle, Thomas Covert. He presented to the Rectory of Slaugham, Sussex in 1615 and 1626. His wife, Anne, was heiress in 1632 to her uncle, Walter Covert, Knt. SIR WALTER COVERT died 22 Sept. 1632. He left a will dated 20 Sept. 1632, proved 13 Nov. 1632 (P.C.C. 111 Audley).

>*Sussex Arch. Colls.* 46 (1903): 170–180; 47 (1904): 116–147; 48 (1905): 1–15. Comber *Sussex Gens.* 2 (1932): 179–186 (sub Covert).

Child of Anne Covert, by Walter Covert, Knt.:

i. **ELIZABETH COVERT**, married **JOHN FENWICK**, Esq., of Brockham, Surrey, Binfield, Berkshire, and Salem, New Jersey [see FENWICK 16.ii].

COYTEMORE

    WILLIAM THE CONQUEROR, King of England, married **MAUD OF FLANDERS**.
    HENRY I, King of England, by an unknown mistress, _____.
    ROBERT FITZ ROY, Earl of Gloucester, married **MABEL FITZ ROBERT**.
    MAUD OF GLOUCESTER, married **RANULPH DE GERNONS**, Earl of Chester.
    HUGH, Earl of Chester, married **BERTRADE DE MONTFORT**.
    AGNES OF CHESTER, married **WILLIAM DE FERRERS**, Knt., Earl of Derby.
    WILLIAM DE FERRERS, Knt., Earl of Derby, married **MARGARET DE QUINCY**.
    ROBERT DE FERRERS, Knt., Earl of Derby, married **ELEANOR DE BOHUN**.
    JOHN DE FERRERS, Knt., 1st Lord Ferrers of Chartley, married **HAWISE DE MUSCEGROS**.
    ELEANOR DE FERRERS, married **THOMAS DE LATHOM**, Knt., of Lathom, Lancashire.
    THOMAS DE LATHOM, Knt., of Lathom, Lancashire, married **JOAN VENABLES**.
    ISABEL LATHOM, married **JOHN STANLEY**, K.G., of Lathom, Lancashire.
    JOHN STANLEY, Knt., of Lathom, Lancashire, married **ELIZABETH HARINGTON**.
    THOMAS STANLEY, K.G., 1st Lord Stanley, married **JOAN GOUSHILL**.
    MARGARET STANLEY, married **WILLIAM TROUTBECK** Knt., of Dunham-on-the-Hill, Cheshire [see TROUTBECK 15].

16. JOAN TROUTBECK, born in 1459. She married (1st) **WILLIAM BOTELER** (or **BUTLER**), Knt., 2nd but 1st surviving son and heir of John Boteler, Knt., of Bewsey (in Warrington), Burtonwood, Great Sankey, etc., Lancashire, by his 1st wife, Margaret, daughter of Peter Gerard. He was born 25 Nov. 1450. They had no issue. SIR WILLIAM BOTELER died 8 June 1471. His widow, Joan, married (2nd) (as his 1st wife) **WILLIAM GRIFFITH**, K.B., of Penrhyn, Caernarvonshire, Marshal of the King's Hall, Chamberlain of North Wales, son of Gwilym Fychan ap Gwilym (otherwise known as William Griffith), Marshal of the King's Hall, deputy to various Chamberlains of North Wales, by his 1st wife, Alice, daughter of Richard Dalton, Knt. He was born about 1447. They had one son, William, Knt., and three daughters, Jane (wife of William Herbert, Knt.), Margaret (wife of Nicholas Dutton, Knt., and Simon Thelwall), and Ann (wife of _____ Winnington). He married (2nd) **ELIZABETH GREY**, daughter of Robert Grey, Esq., Constable of Ruthin Castle. They had one son, William Grey, and one daughter, Alice (wife of Pierce Vychan, of Coetmor). SIR WILLIAM GRIFFITH died in 1505 or 1506.

    Williams *Observations on the Snowdon Mountains* (1802): 163–177. Ormerod *Hist. of Chester* 2 (1819): 28 (Troutbeck ped.). *Jour. Architectural, Arch., & Hist. Soc. of Chester* 1 (1857): 217–233. *Notes & Queries* 4th Ser. 4 (1869): 369–370. Beamont *Annals of the Lords Warrington* 2 (Chetham Soc. 87) (1872): 263–302, 324–332. Glover et al. *Vis. of Cheshire 1580, 1566, 1533 & 1591* (H.S.P. 18) (1882): 223 (Troutbeck ped.: "Jone [Troutbeck] vxr Sr Wm Boteler and after to Wm Griffith."). *Literary Era* 5 (1898): 26–28. Griffith *Peds. of Anglesey & Carnarvonshire Fams.* (1914): 26 (Carreglwyd ped.), 184–185 (Griffith ped.). *Chester & North Wales Arch. Soc.* n.s. 28 (1929): 167. Glenn *Fam. of Griffith* (1934): chart opp. 208. *Genealogists' Mag.* 8 (1938): 204. *NEHGR* 108 (1954): 172–178. *TAG* 32 (1956): 9–23. Bartrum *Welsh Gens. 1400–1500* 8 (1983): 1265 [Marchudd 6 (B1)], 1267 [Marchudd 6 (B3): "Sir William Griffith Hen, b. c.1445, d. c.1505, (1) = Jane d. William Troutbeck, (2) = Elsbeth d. Robt. Grey, Constable of Rhuthun"]. *National Lib. of Wales Jour.* 25 (1988): 387–398. *Welsh Hist. Rev.* 14 (1988–89): 1–22.

17. WILLIAM GRIFFITH, Knt., of Penrhyn, Caernarvonshire, Esquire of the Body to King Henry VIII, Chamberlain of North Wales, Deputy Justice of North Wales, son and heir by his father's 1st marriage, born about 1480. He married (1st) **JANE STRADLING**, daughter of Thomas Stradling, of St. Donat's, Glamorgan, by Janet, daughter of Thomas Mathew, Esq. [see STRADLING 14 for her ancestry]. They had five sons, William, Edward, Esq., Rhys, Knt., John, and Hugh, and eight daughters, Grace (wife of William Stanley, Knt.), Jane (wife of Thomas Mostyn), Elin/Elinor (wife of Hugh Conway, Esq.), Catherine (wife of Richard Bulkeley, Knt.), Anne (wife of Hugh Lewis, Esq.), Elizabeth (wife of John Philipps, Esq.), Dorothy, and Margaret (wife successively of Peter Mytton, Thomas Griffith, and Hugh Thelwall). He served in the French campaign in 1513, being present at the Siege of Thérouanne, the Battle of the Spurs, and the Siege of Tournai. His wife, Jane, died before 1520. He married (2nd) by marriage settlement dated 2 August 1522 **JANE PULESTON**, widow of Robert ap Maredudd, of Glynllifon, Caernarvonshire, and daughter of John Puleston, of Hafod-y-Wern, Wrexham, and Bersham, Denbighshire, Constable of Caernarvon, Chamberlain of North Wales, by Eleanor, daughter of Robert Whitney, Esq., of Whitney, Herefordshire. They had three sons, William, Esq., Rowland, and George [Archdeacon of Anglesey], and two daughters, Mary (wife of Randall Brereton, Knt., and Hugh Cholmondeley, Knt.) and Sibyl (or Isabel). SIR WILLIAM GRIFFITH died in 1531.

> Williams *Observations on the Snowdon Mountains* (1802): 163–177. Traherne *Stradling Corr.* (1840): xvii–xx (Stradling ped.). Heard *Glamorganshire Peds.* (1845): 26 (Stradling ped.: "Thomas Stradling, Esqr. married Jonet, daughter to Thomas Mathew, of Radyr, Esqr. and issued Edward, and Hary Stradling … [and] Jane Stradling, that married Sir William Griffith, Knt. Chamberlain of North Wales."). Dwnn *Heraldic Vis. of Wales* 2 (1846): 89, 167–168 (Griffith ped.: "Sr Wm Grifd marchg Chamberlin Gwynedd, [1] = Sian v: Sr. Thos Stradling, [2] = Sian v: Sr. Joh Pulston kt chwaer Sr. John"). *Literary Era* 5 (1898): 26–28. Griffith *Peds. of Anglesey & Caernarvonshire Fams.* (1914): 184–185 (Griffith ped.). *West Wales Hist. Recs.* 7 (1918): 161–164. Glenn *Fam. of Griffith* (1934): 221, chart opp. 208. *Genealogists' Mag.* 8 (1938): 204. *NEHGR* 108 (1954): 172–178. *TAG* 32 (1956): 9–23. Bartrum *Welsh Gens. 1400–1500* 8 (1983): 1268 [Marchudd 6 (B4): "Sir William Griffith Ail, b. c. 1480, d. 1531, (1) = Jane d. Thomas Stradling; (2) = Jane d. John Puleston"]; 9 (1983): 1454 [Puleston A1]; 10 (1983): 1621–1623 (Stradling ped.: "Jane [Stradling] = Sir William Griffith."). *National Lib. of Wales Jour.* 25 (1988): 387–398. Online resource: Welsh Biography Online (biog. of William Griffith) (William Griffith styled "blood relation" by Charles Brandon, Duke of Suffolk in 1516, cites Penrhyn MSS 48) (available at http:// wbo.llgc.org.uk/en/s1-GRIF-PEN-1300.html).

Child of William Griffith, Knt., by Jane Stradling:

i. **DOROTHY GRIFFITH** [see next].

Child of William Griffith, Knt., by Jane Puleston:

i. **SIBYL** (or **ISABEL**) **GRIFFITH**, married **OWEN AP HUGH AB OWEN**, Esq., of Bodeon, Anglesey, Wales [see OWEN 18].

18. DOROTHY GRIFFITH, 4th daughter by her father's 1st marriage. She married (1st) **WILLIAM WILLIAMS**, Esq., of Cochwillan (in Llechwedd Uchav), Caernarvonshire, Sheriff of Caernarvonshire, 1591–2, son and heir of William Williams, Esq., of Cochwillan (in Llechwedd Uchav), Caernarvonshire, by Lowry, daughter of Henry Salusbury, Esq., of Llanrhaidadr. They had eight sons, William, Rowland, John, Rhys, Edmund, Richard, Arthur, and Thomas, and three daughters, Jane, Catherine (wife of John ap Humphrey Meredydd), and Margaret (wife of John Lloyd). His widow, Dorothy, married (2nd) (as his 1st wife) **ROBERT WYNNE**, Esq., of Plas Mawr (in Conway), Caernarvonshire, Sheriff of Caernarvonshire, 1590–1. They had no issue. ROBERT WYNNE, Esq., was buried at Conway, Caernarvonshire 30 Nov. 1598.

> Betham *Baronetage of England* 2 (1802): 276–282 (sub Williams: "Sometimes called William Wynn Williams, by way of distinction"). Williams *Observations on the Snowdon Mountains* (1802): 163–185. Dwnn *Heraldic Vis. of Wales* 2 (1846): 167–168 (Griffith ped.: "Dorety [Griffith] = Wm. ab Wm. o Gwchwillan"). Jones *Cymru* 2 (1875): 152. Lloyd *Hist. of the Princes: Lords Marcher, Powys Fadog, Arwystli, Cedewen & Meirionwdd* 6 (1887): 200, 428 (arms: Gules, a chevron ermine, inter three English men's heads couped in profile ppr). *List of Sheriffs for England & Wales* (PRO Lists and Indexes 9) (1898): 248. *Literary Era* 5 (1898): 26–28. Griffith *Peds. of Anglesey & Caernarvonshire Fams.* (1914): 184–185 (Griffith ped.), 186 (Cochwillan, and Penrhyn ped.), 360. Glenn *Fam. of Griffith* (1934): chart opp. 208. *Genealogists' Mag.* 8 (1938): 204. *NEHGR* 108 (1954): 172–178. *TAG* 32 (1956): 9–23. Bartrum *Welsh Gens. 1400–1500* 8 (1983): 1268, 1271 (Marchudd 6 D2).

19. JANE WILLIAMS, married **WILLIAM COYTEMORE** (or **COETMORE**), Esq., of Coetmor (in Llechwedd Uchav), Caernarvonshire, son of William Coetmor, of Coetmor (in Llechwedd Uchav), Caernarvonshire, by Elin, daughter of John Puleston, of Tir Môn, Anglesey. They had six sons, including Robert and Rowland, and seven daughters, including Alice. He married (2nd) **MARY LEWIS**, daughter of William Lewis, of Presaddfed. They had four children.

> Betham *Baronetage of England* 2 (1802): 276–282 (sub Williams). Dwnn *Heraldic Vis. of Wales* 2 (1846): 166. Jones *Cymru* 2 (1875): 152. Lloyd *Hist. of the Princes: Lords Marcher, Powys Fadog, Arwystli, Cedewen & Meirionwdd* 6 (1887): 200–201 (Coetmor ped.) (Ancient Coetmor arms: Gules, a chevron inter three stag's heads caboshed argent, attired or).

Griffith *Peds. of Anglesey & Carnarvonshire Fams.* (1914): 186 (Cochwillan, and Penrhyn ped.), 277. Glenn *Fam. of Griffith* (1934): 277. *Genealogists' Mag.* 8 (1938): 204. *NEHGR* 108 (1954): 172–178. *TAG* 32 (1956): 9–23.

Children of Jane Williams, by William Coytemore, Esq.:

  i. **ROWLAND COYTEMORE** [see next].

 ii. **ALICE COYTEMORE**, 7th daughter. She married about 1610 **HUGH WYNNE**, of Evenechtyd (in Llandysilio-in-Yale), Denbighshire, son of John and Goleubryd (Gethin) Wynne, of Ruthin, Denbighshire. Descendants include Sarah Kenrick (1755–1815), wife of Ralph Eddowes, of "Stapeley," Foxchase, Philadelphia County, Pennsylvania — see *TAG* 32 (1956): 9–23; Roberts *Royal Descents of 600 Immigrants* (2004): 199–200.

20. ROWLAND COYTEMORE, 2nd son, of Wapping (in Stepney), Middlesex, born say 1565. He moved to London, became a mariner, and made several voyages to India and the East Indies as captain of ships belonging to the East India Company. He married (1st) at Stepney, Middlesex 13 Jan. 1590/1 **CHRISTIAN HAYNES**. He married (2nd) at St. Mary's, Whitechapel, Middlesex 28 March 1594/5 **DOROTHY [?LANE]**, widow of William Harris, mariner of Wapping, and daughter of Dorothy (?Burton) Lane, widow, of St. Dunstan's-in-the-East, London. They had two daughters. He married (3rd) at Harwich, Essex 27 Dec. 1610 **KATHERINE MYLES**, widow of Thomas Gray, of Harwich, Essex (buried 7 May 1607), and daughter of Robert Myles, of Sutton, Suffolk, by his wife, Parnel Reve. She was baptized at Sutton, Suffolk 17 March 1576. He was a grantee of the second Charter of Virginia 23 May 1607. He was master of the *Royal James* at Swally Roads north of Bombay in 1617. In 1618 he and other mariners made a contribution of £180 towards the building of new chapel at Wapping (in Stepney), Middlesex. In 1619 he was appointed chief commander of the *Lesser James*. ROWLAND COYTEMORE left a will dated 5 June 1626, proved 24 Nov. 1626 (P.C.C. 125 Hele). His widow, Katherine, immigrated to New England about 1636, accompanied by her son, Thomas, and followed by her daughter, Elizabeth. She was admitted an inhabitant at Charlestown, Massachusetts in 1637. She died there 29 Nov. 1659.

Wyman *Gens. & Estates of Charlestown* 1 (1879): 227–228. *NEHGR* 34 (1880): 253–259; 40 (1886): 158; 106 (1952): 15–16; 108 (1954): 172–178; 138 (1984): 39–41. Waters *Gen. Gleanings in England* 1 (1885): 158–159, 160–161 (his will). *Genealogists' Mag.* 8 (1938): 204. *TAG* 32 (1956): 9–23. Roberts *English Origins of New England Fams.* 2nd Ser. 2 (1985): 107–113.

Children of Rowland Coytemore, by Katherine Myles:

  i. **THOMAS COYTEMORE**, sea captain, born at Prittlewell, Essex about 1611–12, educated at Charlwood School, matriculated Christ's College, Cambridge 1628. He married at Wapping (in Stepney), Middlesex 14 June 1635 **MARTHA RAINSBOROUGH**, daughter of [Capt.] William Rainsborough, by his wife, Judith Hoxton. They had two sons, Thomas and William, and one daughter, Katherine, all of whom died in infancy. They immigrated to New England in 1636 and settled at Charlestown, Massachusetts. THOMAS COYTMORE was lost at sea in shipwreck off the coast of Spain 27 Dec. 1644. Pope *Pioneers of Massachusetts* (1900): 121 (biog. of [Mr.] Thomas Coytmore). *NEHGR* 108 (1954): 32 (Coytemore arms: Gules a chevron between three stag's heads cabossed argent, on the chevron a crescent for difference).

 ii. **ELIZABETH COYTEMORE**, born about 1617. She married about 1636/7 (as his 2nd wife) [**Capt.**] **WILLIAM TYNG** (or **TING**). They had four daughters, Elizabeth (wife of Thomas Brattle), Anna (wife of [Rev.] Thomas Shepard, Gent.), Bethia (wife of Richard Wharton, Esq.), and Mercy (wife of Samuel Bradstreet). William and Elizabeth immigrated to New England in 1638, where they settled at Boston, Massachusetts. He subsequently served as Treasurer of Massachusetts Bay Colony. His wife, Elizabeth, died at Boston, Massachusetts before Jan. 1648/9. [Capt.] WILLIAM TYNG died at Braintree, Massachusetts 18 Jan. 1652/3. Pope *Pioneers of Massachusetts* (1900): 467 (biog. of William Tyng). *NEHGR* 108 (1954): 172–178.

❧ CROMER ❧

EUSTACHE I, Count of Boulogne, married **MATHILDE** (or **MAHAUT**) **OF LOUVAIN**.
EUSTACHE II, Count of Boulogne, by an unknown mistress, _____.
GEOFFREY OF BOULOGNE, of Carshalton, Surrey, married **BEATRICE DE MANDEVILLE**.
WILLIAM OF BOULOGNE, of Carshalton, Surrey, married _____.
FARAMUS OF BOULOGNE, married **MAUD** _____.
SIBYL OF BOULOGNE, married **ENGUERRAND DE FIENNES**, Knt., seigneur of Fiennes.
WILLIAM (or **GUILLAUME**) **DE FIENNES**, seigneur of Fiennes, married **AGNÈS DE DAMMARTIN**.
ENGUERRAND DE FIENNES, Knt., seigneur of Fiennes, married [?**ISABEAU**] **DE CONDÉ**.
GILES DE FIENNES, of Old Court (in Wartling), Sussex, married **SIBYL FILLIOL**.
JOHN DE FIENNES, of White Waltham, Berkshire, married **JOAN LE FORESTER**.
JOHN DE FIENNES, Knt., of White Waltham, Berkshire, married **MAUD DE MONCEUX**.
WILLIAM DE FIENNES, Knt., of Herstmonceux, Sussex, married **JOAN DE SAY** (desc. King William the Conqueror).
WILLIAM DE FIENNES, Knt., of Herstmonceux, Sussex, married **ELIZABETH BATISFORD** [see FIENNES 13].

14. JAMES FIENNES (or **FENYS**), Knt., of Hever and Knole (in Sevenoke), Kent, Ascot (in Great Milton), Oxfordshire, seigneur of Court-le-Comte and Carentan in Normandy, etc., Bailiff of Caux, Captain of Arques, 1419, Lieutenant of Caudebec, 1421, Captain of Evreux, 1430, Sheriff of Kent, 1436–7, Esquire of the Body to King Henry VI, Sheriff of Surrey and Sussex, 1438–9, Sheriff of Worcestershire, 1446–9, Knight of the Shire for Kent, 1441–2, 1446, High Steward of the Archbishopric of Canterbury, 1443, Constable of Rochester Castle, Constable of Dover Castle and Warden of the Cinque Ports, 1447, King's Serjeant, Lord Chamberlain of the Household, 1447, Privy Councillor, 1447, Constable of the Tower of London, 1447, Lord High Treasurer, 1449–51, 2nd son, born about 1395. He married (1st) **JOAN** _____. They had one son, William, Knt. [2nd Lord Saye and Sele], and one daughter, Elizabeth. He served in the war in France of King Henry V and, for his services, obtained the lordship of Court-le-Comte and the bailivy of Caux. He attended King Henry VI at his Coronation in Paris in 1431. In 1440 he was granted an annuity of £100, he being an esquire of the body to the king. At her death, his wife, Joan, was buried in the church of the Grey Friars, London, by her sister, Isabel. He married (2nd) before 5 August 1441 **EMELINE** (or **EMELYN**) **CROMER** (or **CROWMER**), daughter of _____ Cromer, of Willingham, by _____, daughter and co-heiress of _____ Trillow. They had two daughters, Emeline (wife of Robert Radmylde, Esq.) and Jane. In 1445 he received a grant of £20 per year from the Earl of Warwick. James was created Lord Saye and Sele 3 March 1447. The following November he obtained a confirmation and quitclaim of his title, together with the arms of Say, from his cousin, John Clinton, Lord Clinton. In 1448 William Wykeham, Esq. owed him a debt of £4000. As an adherent of William de la Pole, Duke of Suffolk, James became very unpopular. He was generally accused of complicity in the supposed murder of Humphrey, Duke of Gloucester. He was indicted by the Commons as responsible for the loss of Anjou and Maine. SIR JAMES FIENNES, 1st Lord Saye and Sele, was beheaded by a mob during the rising of Jack Cade at the Standard in Cheapside 4 July 1450. His body was drawn naked at a horse's tail into Southwark to St. Thomas of Waterings, and there hanged and quartered. He left a will dated 12 April 1449. In 1450 Thomas Clemens Gent. and another settled a dispute between his widow, Emeline, Lady Saye, and John Barton and Thomas Barton, yeomen, regarding ownership of land called Panteres in Sevenoaks, Kent. In the period, 1450–2, she sued Gervase Clifton, Roger Cliderowe, and John Fineux, feoffees, in Chancery regarding the manors, lands, advowsons, etc. in Kent and Sussex late of William Septvans, Knt. Emeline, Lady Saye and Sele, died intestate 5 Jan. 1451/2. James and his wife, Emeline, were buried in the church of the Grey Friars, London.

Fisher *Cat. of Most of the Memorable Tombs of London* (1668): 76. Brydges *Collins' Peerage of England* 6 (1812): 555–590 (sub Brand, Baroness Dacre); 7 (1812): 16–39 (sub Twisleton, Lord Say and Sele) (wife Emmeline identified as "daughter of ____ Cromer, of Willingham, and by her mother, one of the coheirs of Trillow."). Clutterbuck *Hist. & Antiqs. of Hertford* 2 (1821): 9–11 (Fiennes ped.). Nicolas *Testamenta Vetusta* 1 (1826): 264 (will of James Fienes, Lord Say). Vautier *Extrait du Registre des Dons, Confiscations, Maintenues, et autres Actes* (1828): 53. Beltz *Mems. of the Order of the Garter* (1841): ccxxiv. *Coll. Top. et Gen.* 7 (1841): 57–66; 8 (1843): 167–168. Lipscomb *Hist. & Antiq. of the County of Buckingham* 2 (1847): 469–472 (Fiennes ped.). *Docs. rel. to the University & Colleges of Cambridge* 1 (1852): 46. Monro *Letters of Queen Margaret of Anjou & Bishop Beckington* (Camden Soc. 86) (1863): 73, 79–80. French *Shakspeareana Genealogica* 1 (1869): 163–164. Harvey et al. *Vis. of Oxford 1566, 1574, 1634 & 1574* (H.S.P. 5) (1871): 213 (Fynes ped.: "Sir James Fynes of Knowle in co. Canc. 2 son. = Emelyn d. of [left blank]"). Doyle *Official Baronage of England* 3 (1886): 268–269 (sub Saye and Sele). *Desc. Cat. Ancient Deeds* 1 (1890): 530. *List of Sheriffs for England & Wales* (PRO Lists and Indexes 9) (1898): 68, 136, 158. Benolte et al. *Vis. of Sussex 1530 & 1633–4* (H.S.P. 53) (1905): 11–12 (Fynes ped.: "James Fynes Lord Say and Seale."). *D.N.B.* 6 (1908): 1292–1293 (biog. of James Fiennes). *Cal. IPM Henry VII* 2 (1915): 161–166. Kingsford *Grey Friars of London* (1915): 73 ("Et ad eorum dexteram in plano jacet domina Johanna de Fenys, et domina Isabella, soror, eius, sub pavimento."), 76 ("In primis ad sinistram aultaris versus boriam jacet Jacobus Fenys, dominus de Say: qui obiit 4° die mensis Julii, A° dni. 1450°. Et domina Elonina vxor eius: que obiit 5° die mensis Januarii A° dni. 1452°;" Editor's note: Emeline de Say "is called Enomie, daughter of — Cromer in the English List."), 134–139. *C.P.R. 1494–1509* (1916): 644. *C.P.* 4 (1916): Appendix H, 729; 11 (1949): 479–481 (sub Saye and Sele). *C.F.R.* 15 (1935): 269. Paget *Baronage of England* (1957) 485: 1–10 (sub Say). VCH *Oxford* 7 (1962): 126–127. Du Boulay *Docs. Ill. of Medieval Kentish Soc.* (Kent Arch. Soc. 18) (1964): 225–226, 233–234. Owen *Catalogue of Lambeth MSS 889 to 901* (1968): 35, 50, 75–76. Harriss & Harriss "John Benet's Chron. for the Years 1400 to 1462," in *Camden Misc.* 24 (Camden Soc. 4th Ser. 9) (1972): 164–165, 197, 199–201. Harvey *Jack Cade's Rebellion of 1450* (1991). National Archives, C 1/19/46; C 4/2/79; C 241/240/6 (available at www.catalogue.nationalarchives.gov.uk/search.asp).

Children of James Fiennes, Knt., by ____:

i. **WILLIAM FIENNES** (or **FENYS**), Knt., 2nd Lord Saye and Sele, Knight of the Body, Privy Councillor, 1454, Constable of Porchester Castle, 1461, Keeper of the New Forest, 1461–7, Constable of Pevensey Castle, 1461, son and heir, born about 1428. He married **MARGARET WYKEHAM**, daughter and heiress of William Wykeham, Esq., of Broughton and North Newington (in Broughton), Oxfordshire, and Otterbourne, Hampshire, by his wife, Joan. They had two sons, Richard and Henry [3rd Lord Saye and Sele]. He was summoned to Parliament 13 April 1451. He accompanied Richard Wydeville, Lord Rivers to France to defend Calais and Guisnes in 1451. He was present in Parliament 30 March 1454. In 1457 he owed a debt of £125 18s. 11d. to Thomas Wenslowe, Citizen and draper of London. In 1458 he sold the manor of Otterbourne, Hampshire to William Waynflete, Bishop of Winchester. He fought at the Battle of Northampton 10 July 1460 on the side of the Yorkists. In Feb. 1461 he conveyed messuages, lands, etc., in Hever and Chydryngton, Kent to Geoffrey Boleyn, Citizen and mercer of London. In Feb. 1462 he released the manors of Hever Cobham and Hever Brokays, Kent, together with lands, tenements, etc. in the parishes of Hever and Chydryngton, Kent to Geoffrey Boleyn, Citizen and mercer of London. He served as Vice-Admiral to Richard Neville, Earl of Warwick in 1462. He attended King Edward IV on his flight from Lynn to the Low Countries in October 1470. He returned with King Edward IV the next year from Flushing. SIR WILLIAM FIENNES, 2nd Lord Saye and Sele, was slain at the Battle of Barnet 14 April 1471, and was buried in the Church of St. Thomas's Hospital, Southwark, Surrey. His widow, Margaret, married (2nd) **JOHN HERVEY**. She died shortly before 30 May 1477. Lipscomb *Hist. & Antiq. of the County of Buckingham* 2 (1847): 469–472 (Fiennes ped.). Burke *Royal Descents & Peds. of Founders' Kin* (1864): 57 (ped.). Doyle *Official Baronage of England* 3 (1886): 269 (sub Saye and Sele). *Desc. Cat. Ancient Deeds* 1 (1890): 268, 399, 471. VCH *Hampshire* 3 (1908): 440–444. *C.P.* 11 (1949): 482–483 (sub Saye and Sele). VCH *Oxford* 9 (1969): 85–102. National Archives, C 131/236/22 (available at www.catalogue.nationalarchives.gov.uk/search.asp).

ii. **ELIZABETH FIENNES** [see next].

15. ELIZABETH FIENNES, daughter by her father's 1st marriage. She married (1st) **WILLIAM CROMER** (or **CROWMER**), Esq., of Tunstall (in Sittingbourne), Kent, King's Esquire, Sheriff of Kent, 1449–50, son of William Cromer, Knt., draper, of St. Martin's Orgar, London, and Tunstall, Kent, Mayor of London, Alderman of London, 1403–34, by his 2nd wife, Margaret, elder daughter of Thomas Squery, of Westerham, Kent. He was born about 1422 (of age in 1443). They had three sons, James, Knt., William, and Nicholas. He was a principal target of Jack Cade's rising, and was confined in the Fleet Prison by King Henry VI in an attempt to appease the rebels. WILLIAM

CROMER, Esq., was dragged from the Fleet and beheaded at Mile End in Cade's presence in 1450. His widow, Elizabeth, married (2nd) **ALEXANDER IDEN** (or **EDEN**), Esq., of Milton, Kent and London, Sheriff of Kent, 1450, 1456–7, Governor of Rochester Castle. They allegedly had one son, William. He left a will proved 19 Nov. 1457 (P.C.C. 11 Stokton). She married (3rd) (as his 1st wife) **LAURENCE RAYNSFORD**, Knt., of London, Colchester and Bradfield, Essex, Alpheton and Great Whelnetham, Suffolk, Sheriff of Essex and Hertfordshire, 1465–6, Sheriff of Wiltshire, 1469–70, son of William Raynsford, Esq., of Bradfield, Essex, Rockland Tofts, Norfolk, and Alpheton, Suffolk, by Eleanor, daughter and heiress of Edmund Brokesbourne, of Bradfield, Essex and Rockland Tofts, Norfolk. He was born about 1419 (aged 15 in 1434). They had one son, John, Knt. Laurence was heir in 1433 to his aunt, Elizabeth Bourgchier, *suo jure* Lady Bourgchier. In 1450–1 he was granted safe-conduct, he then trading between Normandy and England to defray his ransom when taken prisoner in Normandy. He married (2nd) before 24 June 1470 (date of conveyance) **ANNE PERCY**, widow of Thomas Hungerford, Knt. [see HUNGERFORD 14], of Rowden (in Chippenham), Wiltshire (executed 1469), and daughter of Henry Percy, K.G., 2nd Earl of Northumberland, 5th Lord Percy, by Eleanor, daughter of Ralph Neville, K.G., 1st Earl of Westmorland, 4th Lord Neville of Raby [see PERCY 13 for her ancestry]. They had issue. SIR LAURENCE RAYNSFORD died 18 Sept. 1490, and was buried at St. John's Abbey, Colchester, Essex. He left a will proved 6 Nov. 1490 (P.C.C. 26 Milles). His widow, Anne, married (3rd) before Dec. 1493 (probably as his 2nd wife) **HUGH VAUGHAN**, Knt., of St. Peter, Westminster, and Littleton, Middlesex, Gentleman usher and Esquire of the Body to King Henry VII, Lieutenant of the Tower, Captain of the King's Guard, Bailiff of Westminster, Privy Councillor, Captain of Jersey, 1507–32 [see HUNGERFORD 14 for details of this marriage and possible issue]. Anne died 5 July 1522, and was buried in St. Michael's Chapel in Westminster Abbey with her 3rd husband, Sir Hugh Vaughan.

Dart *Westmonasterium* 2 (1723): 60. Blomefield *Essay towards a Top. Hist. of Norfolk* 1 (1739): 322, 325. Morant *Hist. & Antiqs. of Essex* 1 (1768): 463–464. Hasted *Hist. & Top. Survey of Kent* 6 (1798): 86–88. Brydges *Collins' Peerage of England* 2 (1812): 217–366 (sub Duke of Northumberland); 5 (1812): 391 (sub Percy, Earl of Northumberland); 7 (1812): 16–39 (sub Twisleton, Lord Say and Sele). Clutterbuck *Hist. & Antiqs. of Hertford* 2 (1821): 9–11 (Fiennes ped.). Berry *County Gens.: Kent Fams.* (1830): 318. *England's Topographer* 4 (1830): 47–48. Bentley *Excerpta Historica* (1833): 89. *Coll. Top. et Gen.* 1 (1834): 298. French *Shakspeareana Genealogica* 1 (1869): 168–169. Parker *Hist. of Long Melford* (1873): 55–56, 69. Hawley et al. *Vis. of Essex 1552, 1558, 1570, 1612 & 1634* 1 (H.S.P. 13) (1878): 96 (1558 Vis.) (Raynsford ped.): "Sr Laurance Reynesford of Bradfild in Essex Knt.") (Raynsford arms: Gules, a chevron engrailed between three fleurs de lis argent). *Jour. British Arch. Assoc.* 40 (1884): 400–408. *Annual Rpt. of the Deputy Keeper* 48 (1887): 385. *Desc. Cat. Ancient Deeds* 1 (1890): 413. Kriehn *English Rising in 1450* (1892): 99. *Cal. IPM Henry VII* 1 (1898): 257–258, 310. *List of Sheriffs for England & Wales* (PRO Lists and Indexes 9) (1898): 45, 68, 153. Copinger *Manors of Suffolk* 1 (1905): 14. *C.P.R. 1441–1446* (1908): 89. Hervey *Whelnetham Parish Regs.* (Suffolk Green Books 15) (1910): 351–356. *C.P.* 2 (1912): 247–248 (sub Bourchier). Mundy *Middlesex Peds.* (H.S.P. 65) (1914): 65 (Vaughan ped.: "Sr Hugh Vaughan of Litleton in com. Midlesex knight m. to his 1 wife Anne d. of Hen. Erle of Northumberland widow of Thom. Hungerford, [2] = Blanch d. of… Castell by… d. of Melford. ob. 1553. 2 wife."). Benolte & Cooke *Vis. of Kent 1530–1, 1574 & 1592* 1 (H.S.P. 74) (1923): 43–44 (1574 Vis.) (Crowmer ped.: "William Crowmer of Tunstall in Kent. Beheaded by Cades rebells = daughter of the Lord Say = Laurence Raynsford 2 husband") (Crowmer arms: Argent, a chevron engrailed sable between three crows). *C.P.* 6 (1926): 621 (sub Hungerford); 10 (1945): 663–664 (sub Poynings). *C.C.R. 1422–1429* 1 (1933): 265. Wedgwood *Hist. of Parl.* 1 (1936) (biog. of Alexander Iden). Thrupp *Merchant Classs of Medieval London* (1948): 336. *C.C.R. 1485–1500* (1953): nos. 731, 733. *Bull. Inst. Hist. Research* 34 (1961): 148–164. Du Boulay *Docs. Ill. of Medieval Kentish Soc.* (Kent Arch. Soc. 18) (1964): 236. Reaney & Fitch *Feet of Fines for Essex* 4 (1964): 97. *Ancient Deeds — Ser. A* 1 (List & Index Soc. 151) (1978): 178. Harvey *Jack Cade's Rebellion of 1450* (1991). *English Hist. Rev.* 108 (1993): 22–49. Baker *Rpts. of Cases by John Caryll* 2 (Selden Soc. 116(2)) (2000): 653–654.

Child of Elizabeth Fiennes, by William Cromer, Esq.:

i. **JAMES CROMER**, Knt. [see next].

Child of Elizabeth Fiennes, by Laurence Raynsford, Knt.:

i. **JOHN RAYNSFORD**, Knt., of Colchester and Bradfield, Essex, Alpheton and Great Whelnetham, Suffolk, etc., Esquire and Knight of the Body to King Henry VII, born about 1461. He married (1st) **ANNE STARKEY**, widow of John Writtle, Esq., and daughter and co-heiress of Humphrey Starkey, Knt., of Littlehall (in Woldham), Kent, Chief Baron of the Exchequer. They had one son, John, Knt. His wife, Anne, died 26 Dec. 1488. He married (2nd) shortly after 3 March 1503/4 (date of marriage arrangements) **MARGARET ILAM**, widow of John Shaa, Knt. (died 26 Dec. 1503), of London, goldsmith, Mayor of London, 1501–2, and daughter of Thomas Ilam, of London, mercer, Alderman of London. She was born about 1467 (aged 12 in 1479). They had one daughter, Julian. He was knighted June 1497 at the foot of London bridge, when Henry VII entered London after defeating the Cornish rebels at the Battle of Blackheath. He served as a captain in the French wars under Kings Henry VII and Henry VIII. He attended the king at the Field of the Cloth of Gold in 1520. SIR JOHN RAYNSFORD left a will dated 17 Sept. 1521, proved Feb. 1521/2 (P.C.C. 21 Maynwaring). Morant *Hist. & Antiqs. of Essex* 1 (1768): 463–464 (confuses father and son). Hawley et al. *Vis. of Essex 1552, 1558, 1570, 1612 & 1634* 1 (H.S.P. 13) (1878): 96 (1558 Vis.) (Raynsford ped.: "Sr John Reynesford Kt. [1] = Anne da. & coheire to Sr Humphrey Starkey Kt., [2] = Margarett Lady Shaw 2 wiffe widow to Sr Edw. Shaw of Lon."). *Cal. IPM Henry VII* 1 (1898): 194, 422. Hervey *Whelnetham Parish Regs.* (Suffolk Green Books 15) (1910): 351–356. Thrupp *Merchant Classs of Medieval London* (1948): 350, 366. Reaney & Fitch *Feet of Fines for Essex* 4 (1964): 97. Sainty *Judges of England* (Selden Soc. Supp. Ser. 10) (1993): 94 (re. Humphrey Starkey). VCH *Essex* 9 (1994): 64 (confuses father and son).

Child of John Raynsford, Knt., by Margaret Ilam:

a. **JULIAN RAYNSFORD**, married **WILLIAM WALDEGRAVE**, Knt., of Smallbridge (in Bures St. Mary), Suffolk [see WALDEGRAVE 16].

16. JAMES CROMER (or CROWMER), Knt., of Tunstall, Kent, Knight of the Shire for Kent, Justice of the Peace for Kent, born about 1448. He married **KATHERINE CANTELOWE**, daughter of William Cantelowe, Knt., of Milk Street, St. Mary Magdalen, London, Mercer and Merchant of the Staple, Alderman of London, 1446–61, Sheriff of London, 1448, Member of Parliament for London, 1453, 1455, by Margaret, daughter of Richard Barry, of London. They had four sons, William, Knt., John, [Dr.] George [Archbishop of Armagh, Lord Chancellor of Ireland, Master of Cobham College], and Lewis, and three daughters, Elizabeth, Anne, and Margaret (wife of John Rickhill). He fought on the Yorkist side at the Battle of Tewkesbury in 1471. His wife, Katherine, was a legatee in the 1490 will of her brother, Henry Cantelowe, mercer. SIR JAMES CROMER was living in 1502, but evidently dead before 1503.

Berry *County Gens.: Kent Fams.* (1830): 318. *Arch. Cantiana* 11 (1877): 394 (Cromer arms: Argent, a chevron engrailed three crows sable); 18 (1889): 449–450. Baddeley *Aldermen of Cripplegate Ward* (1900): 34–35 (biog. of William Cantelowe). *List of Early Chancery Procs.* 4 (PRO Lists and Indexes 29) (1908): 65. Benolte & Cooke *Vis. of Kent 1530–1, 1574 & 1592* 1 (H.S.P. 74) (1923): 43–44 (1574 Vis.) (Crowmer ped.: "Sir James Crowmer, Knight = Katheryn daughter of Sir William Cantelupe"). Thrupp *Merchant Classs of Medieval London* (1948): 328. O'Flanagan *Lives of the Lord Chancellors & Keepers of the Great Seal of Ireland* 1 (1971): 181–186 (biog. of George Cromer, Lord Chancellor of Ireland). Ball *Judges in Ireland 1221–1921* (2005): 198 (biog. of George Cromer, Archbishop of Armagh).

Children of James Cromer, Knt., by Katherine Cantelowe:

i. **WILLIAM CROMER**, Knt., of Tunstall, Kent, married **ALICE HAUTE** [see BRODNAX 17].

ii. **ELIZABETH CROMER**, married (1st) **RICHARD LOVELACE**, Knt. [see FINCH 18]; (2nd) **WILLIAM FINCH**, Knt., of the Moat by Canterbury, Kent [see FINCH 18].

iii. **ANNE CROMER** [see next].

17. ANNE CROMER (or CROWMER), married by settlement dated 1489 **WILLIAM WHETENHALL** (or **WHETNALL**), Esq., of Hextall's Court (in East Peckham), Kent, Wallbury (in Great Hallingbury), Hassingbroke (in Stanford le Hope), and Fanges, Essex, etc., Sheriff of Kent, 1526–7, Justice of the Peace for Kent, son and heir of William Whetenhall, of Hextall's Court (in East Peckham), Kent, by Margaret, daughter and co-heiress of William Hexstall, Esq. He was born at East Peckham, Kent 8 Nov. 1467, and baptized there. They had two sons, George, Esq., and Lewis, and six daughters, Margaret, Alice, Jane (wife of John Culpeper, Esq.), Rose, Ursula (wife of James Blechenden, Gent.), and Juliane (nun). His wife, Anne, was living in 1520. WILLIAM

WHETENHALL, Esq., left a will proved 27 Nov. 1539 (P.C.C. 34 Dyngeley), requesting burial in Our Lady chapel in the church of East Peckham, Kent.

> Hasted *Hist. & Top. Survey of Kent* 5 (1798): 101–102. Berry *County Gens.: Kent Fams.* (1830): 134. Ayre *Early Works of Thomas Becon* (1843): 307. *Letters & Papers… Henry VIII* 3(1) (1867): 381; 3(2) (1867): 1143–1144. *Trans. of the St. Paul's Ecclesiological Soc.* 3 (1895): 281. *Cal. IPM Henry VII* 1 (1898): 190. *List of Sheriffs for England & Wales* (PRO Lists and Indexes 9) (1898): 69. *C.P.R. 1485–1494* (1914): 271. Benolte & Cooke *Vis. of Kent 1530–1, 1574 & 1592* 1 (H.S.P. 74) (1923): 43–44 (1574 Vis.) (Crowmer ped.: "Anne [Crowmer] maried vnto Will'm Whetnall"); 2 (H.S.P. 75) (1924): 115–116 (1592 Vis.) (Whetenhall ped.: "William Whetnall of Est Peckham aforsaide gent. Sonne and heire to William maried Anne Daughter to Sr James Cromer of Tunstall in the Countie of Kent Knight") (Whetnall arms: Vert, a bend ermine).

Children of Anne Cromer, by William Whetenhall, Esq.:

i. **MARGARET WHETENHALL** [see next].

ii. **ALICE WHETENHALL**, married (1st) **THOMAS HODDE** [see GRESLEY 16]; (2nd) **THOMAS DARRELL**, Esq., of Scotney (in Lamberhurst), Kent [see GRESLEY 16].

iii. **ROSE WHETENHALL**, married **THOMAS WILSFORD**, Esq., of Hartridge (in Cranbrook), Kent [see BARNE 18].

18. MARGARET WHETENHALL, married about 6 August 1511 (date of conveyance) **THOMAS ROYDON**, Esq., of Roydon Hall (or Fortune) (in East Peckham) and Ringes (in Woldham), Kent, Justice of the Peace of Kent, 2nd son of Thomas Roydon, of Ramsay. He was born about 1484. They had three sons, George, William, and John, and six daughters, Margaret (wife of Hugh Catlin, Esq., and Everard Digby), Anne (wife of Henry Delahay), Elizabeth, Mary, Alice (wife of William Heron and Oliver St. John), and Katherine. In 1515 he was in the retinue of George Neville, Lord Bergavenny. He served as a feoffee for his father-in-law, William Whetenhall in 1520. In 1521 he and his wife, Margaret, were given the manor or tenement called Gore (in Tunstall), Kent by her father. He was a surety in 1522 for the payment of Lord Bergavenny's fine of 10,000 marks. In 1532 he was one of the feoffees for the fulfillment of the same lord's will. He was mentioned in the 1535 will of his cousin, Edward Ferrers, Knt., of Baddesley Clinton, Warwickshire. In 1536, on the occasion of the Northern Rebellion, he was one of the Kentish gentlemen appointed to attend on the king's own person and was to bring 20 men. In 1552 he purchased the manor of the Rectory of Hadlow, Kent from Elizabeth Lady Fane. **THOMAS ROYDON**, Esq., died 10 August 1557. He left a will dated 10 August 1557, proved 9 March 1559 (P.C.C. 19 Mellershe). His widow, Margaret, was buried at East Peckham, Kent 23 June 1576. She left a will dated 19 Jan. 1575/6, proved 2 August 1576.

> Hasted *Hist. & Top. Survey of Kent* 5 (1798): 95–96 (Roydon arms: Chequy, argent and gules, a cross azure). Ayre *Early Works of Thomas Becon* (1843): 307. *Letters & Papers… Henry VIII* 2(2) (1864): 134; 3(1) (1867): 381; 3(2) (1867): 1143; 5 (1880): 129, 430, 703. *Arch. Cantiana* 11 (1877): 401 (in 1542 he contributed twenty marks towards a loan to the king). *Misc. Gen. et Heraldica* 3rd Ser. 1 (1896): 68 (will of Thomas Roydon, Esq.). Benolte & Cooke *Vis. of Kent 1530–1, 1574 & 1592* 2 (H.S.P. 75) (1924): 115–116 (1592 Vis.) (Whetenhall ped.: "Margaret [Whetenhall] maried to Thomas Roydon gent."). Royden *Three Roydon Fams.* (1924): 83–115. *List of Early Chancery Procs.* 10 (PRO Lists and Indexes 55) (1936): 31. Cook *Manor through Four Cents.* (1938). Ward *Fam. of Twysden & Twisden* (1939). National Archives, 30/75/69, Jenkinson Papers.

Children of Margaret Whetenhall, by Thomas Roydon, Esq.:

i. **ELIZABETH ROYDON** [see next].

ii. **MARY ROYDON**, married **THOMAS DARRELL**, Esq., of Scotney (in Lamberhurst), Kent [see GRESLEY 17].

19. ELIZABETH ROYDON, born about 1523 (aged 42 in 1565). She married (1st) **WILLIAM TWYSDEN**, Esq., of Wye and Chelmington (in Great Chart), Kent, son and heir of Roger Twysden, Esq., of Wye and Chelmington (in Great Chart), Kent, by Jane, daughter of Christopher

Cooper, of Stone, Kent. They had one son, Roger, and three daughters, Margaret, Katherine, and Bennet. WILLIAM TWYSDEN, Esq., died 19 Nov. 1549. He left a will dated 9 Nov. 1549, proved 14 May 1550 (P.C.C. 13 Coode). His widow, Elizabeth, married (2nd) at Wye, Kent 30 Sept. 1550 **CUTHBERT VAUGHAN**, Esq., of Hargest, Herefordshire, and Great Chart, Kent, Queen's servant, Keeper of the King's bulls, bears, and dogs. They had no issue. In 1554 he joined in Wyatt's Rebellion, leading an attack on Whitehall. He was arrested and taken to the Tower of London 9 Feb. 1553/4. He pleaded guilty at his trial, but claimed his life as having been promised by a herald on the field. He was condemned to death and on 28 Feb. 1553/4 was sent with others to be executed in Kent. On 12 March 1553/4 he was brought back to the Tower of London from Kent by the suit of his wife, Elizabeth. Next month he turned queen's evidence at the trial of Nicholas Throckmorton, whom the jury refused to convict. He was afterwards in the service of Queen Elizabeth. His wife, Elizabeth, was mentioned in the 1557 will of her father. CUTHBERT VAUGHAN, Esq., left a will dated 21 July 1563, proved 21 October 1563 (P.C.C. Chayre). His widow, Elizabeth, married (3rd) at Great Chart, Kent 25 May 1564 **THOMAS GOLDINGE**, Knt., of St. Paul's Belchamp, Essex, Sheriff of Essex and Hertfordshire, 1561–2, Sheriff of Essex, 1569–70, 2nd son of John Goldinge, of Halstead, Essex. They had no issue. His wife, Elizabeth, was co-heiress in 1565 to her nephew, Thomas Roydon, by which she inherited the manor of Roydon Hall (or Fortune) (in East Peckham), Kent. In 1565 she settled the reversion of the manor of Eastbridge, Kent on her daughter and son-in-law, Richard and Margaret Dering. In 1571 she settled the reversion of manor of Honichild (in Hope All Saints), Kent on her son, Roger Twysden. SIR THOMAS GOLDINGE died in 1571. Elizabeth was the residuary legatee in the 1576 will of her mother. Elizabeth died 19 August 1595, and was buried at East Peckham, Kent. She left a will dated 4 October 1591, proved 5 May 1596 (P.C.C.).

> Hasted *Hist. & Top. Survey of Kent* 5 (1798): 95–96 (Twysden arms: Girony of four, argent and gules, a saltire between four cross-croslets, all countercharged). *Arch. Cantiana* 11 (1877): 400. *List of Sheriffs for England & Wales* (PRO Lists and Indexes 9) (1898): 45. Philipot *Vis. of Kent 1619–1621* (H.S.P. 42) (1898): 134–136 (1619 Vis.). Benolte & Cooke *Vis. of Kent 1530–1, 1574 & 1592* 2 (H.S.P. 75) (1924): 41 (1574 Vis.) (Twysden ped.: "William Twsyden of Wye = Elizabeth daughter and heire of Thomas Raydan [Roydon] of great Pecham [Esquire]"). Royden *Three Roydon Fams.* (1924): 83–115. *List of Early Chancery Procs.* 10 (PRO Lists and Indexes 55) (1936): 108. *C.P.R. 1558–1560* (1939): 236, 437. Ward *Fam. of Twysden & Twisden* (1939). *C.P.R. 1560–1563* (1948): 2, 78, 254–255, 389, 400, 528. *C.P.R. 1563–1566* (1960): 299. *C.P.R. 1569–1572* (1966): 297, 322. *Chancery Decree Rolls: Elizabeth I (C78/15–45)* (List & Index Soc. 198) (1983): 30. Neal *Cal. of Patent Rolls 26 Elizabeth I (1583–1584)* (List & Index Soc. 287) (2001): 44. *Cal. Patent Rolls 43 Elizabeth I (1600–1601)* (List and Index Soc. 339) (2011): 184. Deeds #630, 634, 760, English Deeds Coll., Harvard Law School Lib. — available at http://hollis.harvard.edu//?itemid=%7clibrary%2fm%2faleph%7c005978339, http://hollis.harvard.edu//?itemid=%7clibrary%2fm%2faleph%7c005999669 and http://hollis.harvard.edu//?itemid=%7clibrary%2fm%2faleph%7c006859855.

Child of Elizabeth Roydon, by William Twysden, Esq.:

i. **MARGARET TWYSDEN**, married **RICHARD DERING**, Esq., of Surrenden, Kent [see FISHER 14].

CROMWELL

JOHN DE SOMERY, married **HAWISE PAYNELL**.
RALPH DE SOMERY, of Dudley (in Sedgley), Staffordshire, married **MARGARET LE GRAS**.
ROGER DE SOMERY, Knt., of Dudley (in Sedgley), Staffordshire, married **NICHOLE D'AUBENEY** (desc. King William the Conqueror).
MARGARET DE SOMERY, married **RALPH DE CROMWELL**, Knt., of Cromwell, Nottinghamshire [see STAFFORD 4].

5. RALPH DE CROMWELL (or **CRUMWELL, CRUMBEWELL**), Knt., of Cromwell and Lambley, Nottinghamshire, son and heir. He married in 1292–3 (date of marriage settlement)

JOAN DE SOMERVILLE, daughter of Robert de Somerville, Knt., of Wichnor (in Tatenhill), Staffordshire, by Isabel, daughter of Roger de Merlay, Knt. [see SOMERVILLE 8 for her ancestry]. Her maritagium included an estate in Little Curborough (in Streethay), Staffordshire. They had two sons, Ralph, Knt., and John (clerk), and two daughters, Margaret and Joan. In 1292 he and William de Kendal owed a debt of £9 to William de Chadworth, Sheriff of Nottinghamshire. In 1295–6 he had license to clear a way around his wood of Lambley, Nottinghamshire, and to sell all the trees in the clearing. In 1298 he sued Isabel, widow of Robert de Somerville, and two others, executors of the will of the said Robert, for a debt of 20 marks. The same year Isabel widow of Robert de Somerville sued him and his wife, Joan, for a third part of 26 messuages, lands, and rent in Shirescote and Curborough, Staffordshire as her dower; Robert and Joan called to warranty Edmund son of Robert de Somerville. SIR RALPH DE CROMWELL died shortly before 2 March 1298/9. His widow, Joan, married (2nd) before 6 June 1301 (as his 2nd wife) **HENRY DE GREY**, Knt., 1st Lord Grey of Codnor [see CODNOR 10], of Codnor, Derbyshire, Grays Thurrock, Essex, Aylesford and Hoo, Kent, etc., son and heir of John de Grey, Knt., of Codnor, Derbyshire, Thurrock, Essex, Hoo and Aylesford, Kent, Evington, Leicestershire, Sherringham, Norfolk, etc., by Lucy, daughter of Reynold de Mohun, Knt. [see CODNOR 9 for his ancestry]. He was born about 1255/8 (aged 14, 15, or 17 in 1272). In 1294 he was going to Gascony in the retinue of Edmund, the king's brother. He was again on service in Gascony in 1295 and 1297. He presented to the church of Heanor, Derbyshire in 1298 and 1304. He was constantly employed in the Scottish wars of King Edward I. He was summoned to Parliament from 6 Feb. 1298/9 to 16 August 1308, by writs directed *Henrico de Grey*, whereby he is held to have become Lord Grey. He was present at the Siege of Caerlaverock in 1300. He signed the Barons' letter to Pope Boniface VIII in 1301 as *Dominus de Codnore*. In 1306, in consideration of his services in Scotland and elsewhere, he had a pardon for all debts due from him or his ancestors to the Exchequer. SIR HENRY DE GREY, 1st Lord Grey of Codnor, died shortly before 18 Sept. 1308. He left a will dated 9 Sept. 1308, proved 16 and 19 Sept. and 15 and 22 October 1309, requesting burial in the Carmelite Friars at Aylesford, Kent.

_{Throsby *Thoroton's Hist. of Nottinghamshire* 3 (1790): 15–18, 169–171. Shaw *Hist. & Antiqs. of Staffordshire* 1 (1798): 119. Banks *Baronies in Fee* 1 (1844): 227–230 (sub Grey of Codnor). Wrottesley *Staffordshire Suits: Plea Rolls* (Colls. Hist. Staffs. 7) (1886): 47–48, 97, 108, 113. Cox *Notes of the Churches of Derbyshire* 4 (1879): 234. Birch *Cat. Seals in the British Museum* 3 (1894): 36–37 (seal of Henry de Grey, lord of Codnor dated 1301 — A shield of arms: barry of six, GREY. Suspended by a strap from a tree of three branches, with two smaller branches at the side. Legend: * DE LEIAVTE SE....VNTE(?). Beaded borders.). *Papal Regs.: Letters* 2 (1895): 354. *C.C.R. 1296–1302* (1906): 241. *Cal. IPM* 2 (1906): 488; 3 (1912): 395. *C.P.* 3 (1913): 551 (sub Cromwell); 6 (1926): 123–124 (sub Grey). *Paget* (1957) 162:1. VCH *Stafford* 14 (1990): 278. National Archives, C 143/25/15; C 241/16/27 (available at www.catalogue.nationalarchives.gov.uk/search.asp).}

6. **RALPH DE CROMWELL**, Knt., of Cromwell, Hucknall Torkard, and Lambley, Nottinghamshire, West Hallam, Derbyshire, etc., son and heir, born about 1292 (aged 7 in 1299). He married **JOAN DE LA MARE**. They had one son, Ralph, Knt. He presented to the churches of West Hallam, Derbyshire, 1322 and 1331; and Lambley, Nottinghamshire, 1323, 1327, and 1348. In 1331–2 he had license to grant a messuage, land, and rent in Lambley, Nottinghamshire to a chaplain in the church of the Holy Trinity there to sing forever for his ancestors and successors; the said Ralph retaining the manors of Cromwell, Nottinghamshire and Hallam, Derbyshire; he was likewise granted license to assart waste land of his own soil in Lambley, Nottinghamshire in Sherwood Forest without arrenting it. In 1340–1, as "Ralph de Crumbewell, the elder," he had license to grant a messuage and rent in Lambley, Nottinghamshire to a chaplain in the church of the Holy Trinity there, retaining land and rent in Lambley and Cromwell, Nottinghamshire. In 1354 Richard de Goldsborough, Knt. owed him a debt of 1000 marks. SIR RALPH DE CROMWELL died testate shortly before 15 October 1356.

Throsby *Thoroton's Hist. of Nottinghamshire* 3 (1790): 15–18, 169–171. Banks *Baronies in Fee* 1 (1844): 167–169 (sub Cromwell). Cox *Notes on the Churches of Derbyshire* 4 (1879): 219–222. *C.C.R.* 1354–1360 (1908): 77, 280. *Cal. IPM* 3 (1912): 395. *C.P.* 3 (1913): 551. *C.F.R.* 5 (1915): 513. *Cal. Inqs. Misc.* 2 (1916): 446. Blagg *Abs. of IPMs & other Inqs. Rel. to Nottinghamshire* 3 (Thoroton Soc. Rec. Ser. 6) (1939): 120–121. Train *Second Miscellany of Nottinghamshire* (Thoroton Soc. Rec. Ser. 14) (1951): 41–45. Train *Lists of Clergy of Central Nottinghamshire* (Thoroton Soc. Rec. Ser. 15(1)) (1953): 82–83. *Paget* (1957) 162:1. VCH *Stafford* 14 (1990): 278. National Archives, C 131/10/2; C 143/214/2; C 143/214/12; C 143/254/1; SC 8/243/12110; SC 8/241/12011; SC 8/243/12114 (available at www.catalogue.nationalarchives.gov.uk/search.asp).

7. RALPH DE CROMWELL, Knt., of Cromwell, Basford, and Lambley, Nottinghamshire, West Hallam, Derbyshire, etc., son and heir. He married **AMICE** (or **AVICE**, **ANICE**) **BELERS**, daughter of Roger Belers, Knt., of Kirby Bellars, Leicestershire. They had two sons, Ralph, Knt. [1st Lord Cromwell] and Richard, Knt., and two daughters, Margaret (wife of Nicholas Monboucher, Knt.) and Joan. He presented to the church of Bulwick, Northamptonshire in 1338 and 1344. In 1344 Ralph de Cromwell the younger and Avice his wife brought an action against William la Zouche of Harringworth in respect of warranty of the manor of Basford, Nottinghamshire. He and his wife, Amice, obtained a papal indult for plenary remission at the hour of death in 1355. SIR RALPH DE CROMWELL died shortly before 28 October 1364. His widow, Amice, presented to the churches of Bulwick, Northamptonshire, 1365, and Lambley, Nottinghamshire 21 April 1367.

Throsby *Thoroton's Hist. of Nottinghamshire* 3 (1790): 15–18, 169–171. Bridges *Hist. & Antiqs. of Northamptonshire* 2 (1791): 289. Banks *Baronies in Fee* 1 (1844): 167–169 (sub Cromwell). Mundy et al. *Vis. of Nottingham 1569 & 1614* (H.S.P. 4) (1871): 5–8 (Stanhope ped.: "Robertus Cromwell Miles = Alice fil. et hæres Rogeri Bellers de Kirkby Bellers militis"). Cox *Notes on the Churches of Derbyshire* 4 (1879): 219–222. *Papal Regs.: Letters* 3 (1897): 556. Phillimore *Abs. of IPMs Rel. to Nottinghamshire* 1 (Thoroton Soc. Rec. Ser. 3) (1905): vii, 18–20. Pike *Year Books of Edward III, Years XVIII & XIX* (Rolls Ser. 31(17)) (1905): 155. *Lincolnshire N & Q* 10 (1909): 66-73. *C.P.* 3 (1913): 551 (sub Cromwell). *C.F.R.* 9 (1926): 295. Train *Abs. of IPMs Rel. to Nottinghamshire 1350–1436* 1 (Thoroton Soc. Rec. Ser. 12(1)) (1949): 86; 2 (Thoroton Soc. Rec. Ser. 12(2)) (1952): 170. Train *Lists of Clergy of Central Nottinghamshire* (Thoroton Soc. Rec. Ser. 15(1)) (1953): 82–83. *Paget* (1957) 162:1. Payling *Political Soc. in Lancastrian England* (1991): 95–96. Foulds *Thurgarton Cartulary* (1994): 646.

8. RALPH DE CROMWELL, Knt., of Cromwell, Basford, Bleasby, Hucknall Torkard, Lambley, Little Markham, and Tuxford, Nottinghamshire, and West Hallam, Derbyshire, and, in right of his wife, of Tattershall, Candlesby, and Woodthorpe, Lincolnshire, and Lutton, Northamptonshire, son and heir. He married before 20 Jan. 1351/2 (date of fine) **MAUD DE BERNAKE**, daughter of John de Bernake, Knt., of Buckenham, Besthorpe, Denton, Hethersett, and Wymondham, Norfolk, and Woodthorpe, Lincolnshire, by Joan, daughter of John Marmion, Knt., 2nd Lord Marmion [see BERNAKE 10 for her ancestry]. She was born about 1335–8 (aged 23 in 1360, and 24 or 26 in 1361, aged 36 in 1382). They had five sons, Ralph, Knt. [2nd Lord Cromwell], Robert, William, Knt., Thomas, and John, and three daughters, Elizabeth, Amice (or Avice), and Maud. His wife, Maud, was heiress in 1360 to her brother, William de Bernake. He presented to the churches of Lambley, Nottinghamshire, 1370, and West Hallam, Derbyshire, 1374, 1387, 1393, and 1396. He was summoned to Parliament from 28 Dec. 1375 by writs directed *Radulfo de Crombwell'*, whereby he is held to have become Lord Cromwell. In 1375–6 he and two others had license to grant the advowson of the church of Garthorpe, Leicestershire to the Prior and convent of Kirby Bellars, retaining the manor of Burgh-on-the-Hill, Leicestershire. He was heir in 1382 to his 1st cousin, Thomasine Belers, daughter of Roger Belers, Knt., by which he inherited lands in Bunny, Nottinghamshire. His wife, Maud, was heiress in 1386 to her uncle, Robert de Bernake, of Driby and Baston, Lincolnshire, whose will dated 1386 bequeathed her a missal and two doublets, one of red cloth and another of white linen. In 1386–7 Ralph was a Banneret, and retained to serve the King in the event of invasion. In 1392–3 he and Richard de Outhorp, chaplain, had license to grant messuages, land, and rent in Nottingham, Rampton, Costock, and Bunny, Nottinghamshire to the Prior and convent of Kirkby-on-Wreak, Nottinghamshire. They also had license to grant messuages, land, and rent in Kirby Bellars, Leicester, Stapleford, Wymondham, Leesthorpe, Buckminster, Sewstern, Market Harborough, and Ab-Kettleby, Leicestershire to the Prior and convent of Kirby Bellars, the said Ralph retaining land in Buckminster and Sewstern, Leicestershire. His wife, Maud, was co-heiress in 1394 to her cousin, Mary Percy, wife of John Roos, 5th Lord Roos of Helmsley, by which she inherited the manor and advowson of Candlesby, Lincolnshire. In 1394 he and his wife, Maud, obtained a papal indult to celebrate mass before daybreak. SIR RALPH DE CROMWELL, 1st Lord Cromwell, died 27 August 1398. His widow, Maud, presented to the church of Candlesby, Lincolnshire in 1409. Maud, Lady Cromwell, died 10 April 1419. She left a will dated 14 Sept. 1416, codicil dated 1 Jan. 1417.

Topographer 1 (1789): 327–336. Throsby *Thoroton's Hist. of Nottinghamshire* 3 (1790): 15–18, 169–171. Bridges *Hist. & Antiqs. of Northamptonshire* 2 (1791): 462–464. Blomefield *Essay towards a Top. Hist. of Norfolk* 5 (1806): 23–33. Banks *Dormant & Extinct Baronage of England* 2 (1808): 120–124 (sub Cromwell). Dugdale *Monasticon Anglicanum* 6(3) (1830): 1432–1433. *Coll. Top. et Gen.* 7 (1841): 142–144 (sub Tateshale). Banks *Baronies in Fee* 1 (1844): 167–169 (sub Cromwell). *Procs. Soc. Antiq.* 2nd Ser. 2 (1861-4): 63–65. Mundy et al. *Vis. of Nottingham 1569 & 1614* (H.S.P. 4) (1871): 5–8 (Stanhop ped.: "Rad'us Cromwell Miles d'nus de Tatishall iure vxoris = Matild. fillia heridator' Joh'is Bernake militis."). Cox *Notes on the Churches of Derbyshire* 4 (1879): 219–222. *Genealogist* 4 (1880): 254 (1562–4 Vis. Lincolnshire) (Massingbeard ped.: "Maude [Barnak], da. and heir = Sir Ralph Cromwell, Kt."); n.s. 15 (1898): 25. Flower *Vis. of Yorkshire 1563–4* (H.S.P. 16) (1881): 176–177 (Knevet ped.: "Dominus Radulphus Cromwell Miles = Matilda filia et heres domini Johannis Bernake."), 336–338 (Warren ped.: "Mawd doughter & heyr of Sir John Barnake wyf to = Sir Raff Cromwell, Knight, Lord of Tattersall Castell by his wyff."). Burke *Dormant, Abeyant, Forfeited & Extinct Peerages* (1883): 147–148 (sub Cromwell). Birch *Cat. Seals in the British Museum* 2 (1892): 707 (seal of Maud de Bernake, wife of Sir Ralph de Cromwell dated 1370 — A shield of arms: per pale, dex., ermine, a fess [BERNAKE], sin., a chief (diapré) and baton [CROMWELL]. Within a carved and pointed gothic quatrefoil with three shields of arms thereon: viz., 1, chequy, a chief ermine, with a label of four points [TATTERSHALL]; 2, three cinquefoils and a canton [DRIBY]; vairé, a fess [MARMION]. Legend between the small shields: — Sigill'_ matildi de cro_mwelle. Beaded border.), 708 (seal of Ralph de Cromwell, Knt. dated 1370 — A shield of arms: a chief (diapered) and bendlet [CROMWELL]. Within a carved and traced gothic cinquefoil, ornamented along the inner edge with small ball-flowers. Legend: Si': Radulphi de Coūwelle: Milit'. Beaded border.). *Desc. Cat. Ancient Deeds* 2 (1894): 233. *C.P.R.* 1381–1385 (1897): 487 (George, son and heir of Nicholas Monbocher, styled "nephew"[nepos] of Ralph de Crumwell) (for the Monboucher family, see *Lincolnshire Notes & Queries* 10 (1909): 66–73). *Genealogist* n.s. 15 (1898): 149. *Lincolnshire Notes & Queries* 6 (1901): 33–41, 71–77. *Papal Regs.: Letters* 4 (1902): 498. Phillimore *Abs. of IPMs Rel. Nottinghamshire* 1 (Thoroton Soc. Rec. Ser. 3) (1905): vii, 18–20. Wrottesley *Peds. from the Plea Rolls* (1905): 221, 244–245, 339–340, 353. Jeayes *Desc. Cat. Derbyshire Charters* (1906): 164. *List of Inqs. ad Quod Damnum* 2 (PRO Lists and Indexes 22) (1906): 626. VCH *Northampton* 2 (1906): 584–585. *C.C.R.* 1360–1364 (1909): 225. *C.P.* 1 (1910): 419–420 (sub Bardolf), 3 (1913): 551–552 (sub Cromwell), 5 (1926): 519 (sub FitzWilliam). *Cal. IPM* 10 (1921): 497–498, 11 (1935): 54; 12 (1938): 4–7, 127–128; 23 (2004): 37–43. Dudding *Hist. of the Manor & Parish of Saleby with Thoresthorpe* (1922): 98–104 (re. Woodthorpe-Bernake fams.). *C.F.R.* 7 (1923): 151, 317–318, 388; 9 (1926): 295; 10 (1929): 130–131, 136, 212, 279; 11 (1929): 41, 145, 272. Farnham *Leicestershire Medieval Peds.* (1925): opp. 18 (Pantulf-Tatshall ped.), 42 (Beler of Kirby ped.). *Rpt. on the MSS of Lord de L'Isle & Dudley* 1 (Hist. MSS Comm. 77) (1925): 16 & 171–172 (charters of Ralph & Maud de Cromwell) (seal of Maud de Bernake attached to charter dated 1396: in good condition showing the four shields: Barnack impaling Cromwell; Tateshale; Dryby; and Barnack [not Marmyon as described in Birch *Cat. Seals in the British Museum* 2 (1892): 707; see seal in *Archæologia* 65 (1914): Plate xxx, 9]), 204–206 (will of Maud de Cromwell, lady of Tateshale). Harvey et al. *Vis. of the North* 3 (Surtees Soc. 144) (1930): 152–156 (Daubeny ped.: "Dominus Radulphus Cromwell miles = Matildis filia et heres domini Iohannis Barnake"). VCH *Rutland* 2 (1935): 53–54. Train *Abs. of IPMs Rel. Nottinghamshire* 1 (Thoroton Soc. Recs. 12(1)) (1949): 86; 2 (Thoroton Soc. Recs. 12(2)) (1952): 134, 165, 170. Train *Lists of Clergy of Central Nottinghamshire* (Thoroton Soc. Rec. Ser. 15(1)) (1953): 82–83. Paget *Baronage of England* (1957) 162: 1. Garratt *Derbyshire Feet of Fines 1323–1546* (Derbyshire Rec. Soc. 11) (1985): 64. Payling *Political Soc. in Lancastrian England* (1991): 95–96. Owen *Medieval Lindsey Marsh* (Lincoln Rec. Soc. 85) (1996): 92, 113–116. National Archives, C 143/387/11; C 143/400/29; C 143/421/10; C 143/421/29; SC 8/83/4144; SC 8/185/9248 (available at www.catalogue.nationalarchives.gov.uk/search.asp). National Archives, CP 25/1/141/127, #8; CP 25/1/141/127, #9; CP 25/1/141/127, #10; CP 25/1/141/130, # 5; CP 25/1/142/135, #2; CP 25/1/185/34, #448 [see abstract of fines at http:// www.medievalgenealogy.org.uk/index.html].

Children of Maud de Bernake, by Ralph de Cromwell, Knt., by Maud de Bernake:

i. **RALPH CROMWELL**, Knt., 2nd Lord Cromwell, of Cromwell, Basford, Bleasby, Hucknall Torkard, and Lambley, Nottinghamshire, and West Hallam, Derbyshire, Constable of Castle Rising, Norfolk, 1404–17, son and heir, born about 1358/68 (aged 30 and more in 1398). He married (1st) before 30 May 1372 (date of fine)

ELIZABETH _____. They had no issue. He married (2nd) about 29 Sept. 1387 (by contract dated 3 July 1387) **JOAN GRAY**, widow of John Heron, Knt., and daughter of Thomas Gray, Knt., of Heaton (in Norham), Doddington, etc., Northumberland, by Margaret, daughter and heiress of William de Presfen (or Pressen). They had one son, Ralph, Knt. [3rd Lord Cromwell], and two daughters, Maud and Juliane (wife of John Culpeper, Knt., John Braunspath, Knt., and Robert Fenne, Esq.). He was summoned to Parliament from 19 August 1399 to 3 Sept. 1417, by writs directed *Radulfo de Comwell'*. In 1399–1400 he had license to grant land in Skirbeck. Lincolnshire to the Prior and Carmelite friars of Boston, he retaining land in Boston and Skirbeck, Lincolnshire. In 1400 he sued William Newport, Knt., for the manor of Curborough, Staffordshire. In 1407 he presented to the perpetual chantry of Lambley, Nottinghamshire. SIR RALPH CROMWELL, 2nd Lord Cromwell, shortly died before 2 May 1417. His widow, Joan, left a will dated 26 July 1434, proved 10 August 1434. He and his wife were buried in the church at Lambley, Nottinghamshire. *Topographer* 1 (1789): 327–336. Bartlett *Hist. & Antiqs. of Manceter* (1791): 60–66. Banks *Dormant & Extinct Baronage of England* 2 (1808): 120–124 (sub Cromwell). Mundy et al. *Vis. of Nottingham 1569 & 1614* (H.S.P. 4) (1871): 5–8 (Stanhop ped.: "Rad'us Cromwell d'nus de Tatshall = [left blank]"). Flower *Vis. of Yorkshire 1563-4* (H.S.P. 16) (1881): 176–177 (Knevet ped.: "Radulphus Cromwell Miles. = [left blank]."). Wrottesley *Staffordshire Suits: Plea Rolls* (Colls. Hist. Staffs. 15) (1894): 93. Phillimore *Abs. of IPMs Rel. to Nottinghamshire* 1 (Thoroton Soc. Rec. Ser. 3) (1905): 18–20. Wrottesley *Peds. from the Plea Rolls* (1905): 339–340, 353, 439. Jeayes *Desc. Cat. Derbyshire Charters* (1906): 164. *Rutland Mag. & County Hist. Rec.* 3 (1907–8): 129–132. *C. P.* 3 (1913): 552 (sub Cromwell). Dudding *Hist. of the Manor & Parish of Saleby with Thoresthorpe* (1922): 98–104 (re. Woodthorpe-Bernake fams.). Farnham *Leicestershire Medieval Peds.* (1925): 42 (Beler of Kirby ped.). Harvey et al. *Vis. of the North* 3 (Surtees Soc. 144) (1930): 152–156 (Daubeny ped.: "Radulphus Cromwell miles"). Train *Abs. of IPMs Rel. Nottinghamshire* 2 (Thoroton Soc. Recs. 12(2)) (1952): 170. Payling *Political Soc. in Lancastrian England* (1991): 95–96. Kirby *York Sede Vacante Reg. 1405–1408* (2002): 46. *Cal. IPM* 23 (2004): 37–43. Sheffield Archives: Estate Papers of the Copley Fam., Baronets of Sprotborough, CD/385 — marriage settlement dated 3 July 1387 for Ralph de Cromwell, Knt., and Lady Joan Heron, sister of Thomas Gray (available at www.a2a.org.uk/search/index.asp). National Archives, C 1/1489/90; C 143/430/18 (available at www.catalogue.nationalarchives.gov.uk/search.asp). National Archives, CP 25/1/142/135, #2; CP 25/1/185/34, #448 [see abstract of fines at http:// www.medievalgenealogy.org.uk/index.html].

Children of Ralph Cromwell, Knt., by Joan Gray:

a. **RALPH CROMWELL**, Knt., 3rd Lord Cromwell, Privy Councillor, Captain of Harfleur, Constable of Rising Castle, 1431, King's Chamberlain, Lord High Treasurer, 1433–43, Master of the King's Mews and Falcons, 1436, Constable of Nottingham Castle and Warden of Sherwood Forest, 1445, son and heir, born Jan. 1393. As a young man, he fought at the Battle of Agincourt in 1415. He became a trusted captain in 1417, and was present at the successful assault that year on Caen and on other major towns in Normandy. He acted as lieutenant for Thomas of Lancaster, Duke of Clarence, in 1418, and, then as a member of the king's general staff, he helped to negotiate the Treaty of Troyes which marked the zenith of English power in France. He was summoned to Parliament from 29 Sept. 1422 to 26 May 1455. In 1422 he was one of four knights appointed to help the thirteen great lords of the Council to rule England during Henry VI's minority. He married before 3 Nov. 1423 **MARGARET DEINCOURT**, daughter of John Deincourt, Knt., 5th Lord Deincourt, by Joan, daughter of Robert Grey, Knt., 4th Lord Grey of Rotherfield [see ODDINGSELES 11.v.a for her ancestry]. She was born 21 Sept. 1405. They had no issue. His wife, Margaret, was co-heiress in 1422 to her brother, William Deincourt, 6th Lord Deincourt. He presented to the churches of Whitwell, Derbyshire, 1429, and Lambley, Nottinghamshire, 1446. In 1430 John Gra, Knt. owed him a debt of £1000. In 1432 he was dismissed from the Council and the office of king's chamberlain, but was restored to power upon Bedford's return to England in 1433. In 1440 he founded a college of chantry priests and almshouse at Tattershall, Lincolnshire. In 1453 he was suspected of complicity in a Yorkist Rising; he was examined by the Star Chamber and cleared himself. His wife, Margaret, died 15 Sept. 1454. In 1454–5 he had license to grant the manors of Woodthorpe, Maltby, and Cherry Willingham, and a messuage, land, and rent in Waddington, Washingborough, Haydor, and Birton, Lincolnshire to the Master and chaplains of the almshouse of Tattershall, retaining the manor of Burwell, Lincolnshire. SIR RALPH CROMWELL, 3rd Lord Cromwell, died at Wingfield, Derbyshire 4 Jan. 1455/6. He left a will dated 18 Dec. 1451, proved 19 Feb. 1455/6. He and his wife were buried in Tattershall Collegiate Church, Lincolnshire. At his death, all of his chattels and moveables were sold to provide for the endowment of Tattershall College and the rebuilding of the church of Lambley, Nottinghamshire. *Topographer* 1 (1789): 327–336. Banks *Dormant & Extinct Baronage of England* 2 (1808): 120–124 (sub Cromwell). Mundy et al. *Vis. of Nottingham 1569 & 1614* (H.S.P. 4) (1871): 5–8 (Stanhop ped.: "Rad'us Cromwell d'nus Thesauri' Angliæ ob. s. p. 13 H. 6 mar. Margerett heire of Will'm Lord Deincourt of Thurgaston."). Cox *Notes on the Churches of Derbyshire* 4 (1879): 482. Flower *Vis. of Yorkshire 1563-4* (H.S.P. 16) (1881): 176–177 (Knevet ped.: "Dominus Radulphus Dominus de Cromwell, obiit sans issu."). Phillimore *Abs. of IPMs Rel. to Nottinghamshire* 1 (Thoroton Soc. Rec. Ser. 3) (1905): 18–20.

Wrottesley *Peds. from the Plea Rolls* (1905): 339–340, 353, 394. Jeayes *Desc. Cat. Derbyshire Charters* (1906): 293, 323. McCall *Early Hist. of Bedale* (1907): 56–73. *C.P.* 3 (1913): 552–553 (sub Cromwell); 4 (1916): 127–128 (sub Deincourt). Hawes *Edmond Hawes of Yarmouth* (1914): 77–78. Dudding *Hist. of the Manor & Parish of Saleby with Thoresthorpe* (1922): 98–104 (re. Woodthorpe-Bernake fams.). Farnham *Leicestershire Medieval Peds.* (1925): 42 (Beler of Kirby ped.). *C.Ch.R.* 6 (1927): 50. Harvey et al. *Vis. of the North* 3 (Surtees Soc. 144) (1930): 152–156 (Daubeny ped.: "Dominus Radulphus dominus de Cromwell obijt sine liberis"). Train *Abs. of IPMs Rel. Nottinghamshire* 2 (Thoroton Soc. Recs. 12(2)) (1952): 170. *Bull. John Rylands Lib.* 55 (1973): 459–482. *Nottingham Medieval Studies* 30 (1986): 67–96; 32 (1988): 227; 34 (1990): 93–112. VCH *Stafford* 14 (1990): 278. Payling *Political Soc. in Lancastrian England* (1991): 95–96. Archer *Rulers & Ruled in Late Medieval England* (1995): 117–136. Siddons *Vis. by the Heralds in Wales* (H.S.P. n.s. 14) (1996): 5 (arms of Ralph Cromwell, Lord Cromwell). Emery *Greater Medieval Houses of England & Wales* 2 (2000): 205–206, 312–315 (biog. of Ralph, Lord Cromwell: "… able, hardworking, and authoritative … He was one of the most capable, energetic, and efficient of medieval treasurers … one of the richest men in England"). Biancalana *Fee Tail & the Common Recovery in Medieval England* (2001): 391. *Cal. IPM* 23 (2004): 37–43. National Archives, C 1/1489/90; C 1/13/129; C 1/26/75; C 1/26/84; C 1/26/236; C 131/63/1; C 143/451/28; C 143/451/38; C 241/224/22; C 241/225/25; C 241/226/4; C 241/231/21; E 40/4248; E 40/4478; E 40/4488; SC 8/40/1993 (available at www.catalogue.nationalarchives.gov.uk/search.asp).

   b. **MAUD CROMWELL**, married (as his 2nd wife) **RICHARD STANHOPE**, Knt., of Rampton, Nottinghamshire. They had one son, Henry, and two daughters, Maud and Joan. SIR RICHARD STANHOPE died in 1436. Banks *Dormant & Extinct Baronage of England* 2 (1808): 120–124 (sub Cromwell). Brydges *Collins' Peerage of England* 3 (1812): 407–434 (sub Stanhope, Earl of Chesterfield). Glover *Hist. of Derby* 2(1) (1829): 190–193 (Stanhope ped.). Mundy et al. *Vis. of Nottingham 1569 & 1614* (H.S.P. 4) (1871): 5–8 (Stanhop ped.: "Ricardus Stanhop miles tenet maner de Rampton ob. 14 H. 6. [1] = Johanna fil. Rob'ti Staley soror Rad'i Staley militis, [2] = Matilda soror et heres Rad'i Cromwell et renup' Sr Will'm Fitzwilliams of Emley."). Flower *Vis. of Yorkshire 1563–4* (H.S.P. 16) (1881): 176–177 (Knevet ped.: "Matilda [Cromwell] = Dominus Willielmus Stanhope Miles."). Phillimore *Abs. of IPMs Rel. to Nottinghamshire* 1 (Thoroton Soc. Rec. Ser. 3) (1905): 18–20. *C.P.* 3 (1913): 552–554 (sub Cromwell). Dudding *Hist. of the Manor & Parish of Saleby with Thoresthorpe* (1922): 98–104 (re. Woodthorpe-Bernake fams.). Harvey et al. *Vis. of the North* 3 (Surtees Soc. 144) (1930): 152–156 (Daubeny ped.: "Matildis [Cromwell] soror et heres = Dominus Ricardus Stannope miles").

Children of Maud Cromwell, by Richard Stanhope, Knt.:

1) **MAUD STANHOPE**, married (1st) **ROBERT WILLOUGHBY**, K.G., 6th Lord Willoughby of Eresby [see WILLOUGHBY 11.i]; (2nd) **THOMAS NEVILLE**, Knt. [see WILLOUGHBY 11.i]; (3rd) **GERVASE CLIFTON**, Knt. [see HODSOCK 14].

2) **JOAN STANHOPE**, married (1st) **HUMPHREY BOURGCHIER**, Knt., Lord Cromwell [see YORK 11.i.b]; (2nd) **ROBERT RADCLIFFE**, Knt. [see YORK 11.i.b].

ii. **ELIZABETH DE CROMWELL**, married (1st) **JOHN DE CLIFTON**, Knt., of Buckenham, Norfolk [see CLIFTON 12]; (2nd) **EDWARD BENSTEAD**, Knt., of Hertingfordbury, Hertfordshire [see CLIFTON 12].

iii. **AMICE** (or **AVICE**) **CROMWELL**, married **THOMAS BARDOLF**, Knt., 5th Lord Bardolf [see BARDOLF 14.i].

iv. **MAUD CROMWELL**, married **WILLIAM FITZWILLIAM**, Knt., of Sprotborough, Yorkshire [see FITZWILLIAM 14].

CRYMES

WILLIAM MALET, of Curry-Mallet, Somerset, married _____.
MABEL MALET, married **HUGH DE VIVONNE**, Knt., of Chewton, Somerset.
WILLIAM DE FORZ (or **DE VIVONNE**), Knt., of Chewton, Somerset, married **MAUD DE FERRERS** (desc. King William the Conqueror).
JOAN DE VIVONNE, married **REYNOLD FITZ PETER**, Knt., of Blaen Llyfni (in Cathedine), Breconshire.
REYNOLD FITZ REYNOLD, of Hinton Martell, Dorset, married **JOAN MARTEL**.
HERBERT FITZ REYNOLD, of Hinton Martell, Dorset, married **LUCY PEVEREL**.
REYNOLD FITZ HERBERT, Knt., of Midsomer Norton, Somerset, married **JOAN HAKELUYT**.
ALICE FITZ HERBERT, married **THOMAS WEST**, Knt., of Roughcombe, Wiltshire.
THOMAS WEST, Knt., 1st Lord West, married **JOAN LA WARRE** (desc. King William the Conqueror).
REYNOLD WEST, Knt., 6th Lord la Warre, 3rd Lord West, married **MARGARET THORLEY**.
RICHARD WEST, Knt., 7th Lord la Warre, 4th Lord West, married **KATHERINE HUNGERFORD** (desc. King William the Conqueror).
THOMAS WEST, K.G., 8th Lord la Warre, 5th Lord West, married **ELEANOR COPLEY** (desc. King William the Conqueror) [see WEST 12].

13. OWEN WEST, Knt., of Wherwell, Hampshire, son by his father's 3rd marriage. He married **MARY GUILDFORD**, daughter of George Guildford, Esq., of Rolvenden and Benenden, Kent, Esquire of the Body to King Henry VIII, by Elizabeth, daughter and heiress of Robert Mortimer, Esq. [see GUILDFORD 15 for her ancestry]. They had two daughters, Mary and Anne. He was a legatee in the 1525 will of his father. He was plaintiff in a fine for Lurgashall in 1527 and Buckingham in 1550/1. He was defendant in fines for Compton and Blatchingdon, 1542, Folkington, 1543, and Torryng Peverell, 1547. In 1545 Thomas Jurden, of Wilmington, Sussex sued him in Chancery regarding an enforced obligation. SIR OWEN WEST died 18 July 1551, and was buried at Wherwell, Hampshire. He left a will dated 17 July 1551, proved 30 October 1551 (P.C.C. 30 Bucke). His widow, Mary, was a legatee in the 1554 will of her brother-in-law, Thomas West, K.G., 9th Lord la Warre. She was living Hilary term 1559 (date of fine).

Morant *Hist. & Antiqs. of Essex* 1 (1768): 441. Brydges *Collins' Peerage of England* 5 (1812): 1–28 (sub West, Earl Delawarr). Nicolas *Testamenta Vetusta* 2 (1826): 605–606 (will of Thomas West, Lord La Warre), 728 (will of Sir Owen West). *Retrospective Rev.* 2nd Ser. 2 (1828): 300. *Coll. Top. et Gen.* 2 (1835): 8–9; 8 (1843): 223–224. Hutchins *Hist. & Antiqs. of Dorset* 3 (1868): 141 (West ped.). *Antiq.* 3 (1873): 213. Watson *Tendring Hundred in the Olden Time* (1877): 161–164. Gairdner & Brodie *Letters & Papers, Foreign & Domestic, Henry VIII* 15 (1896): 219, 408. Clutterbuck *Notes on the Parishes of Fyfield, Kimpton, Penton Mewsey, Weyhill & Wherwell* (1898): 167–170, 178–185. *Notes & Queries for Somerset & Dorset* 6 (1899): 22, 23, 118. Round *Peerage & Ped.* 1 (1910): 56–58. Benolte et al. *Peds. from the Vis. of Hampshire 1530, 1575, 1622 & 1634* (H.S.P. 64) (1913): 58–59 (West ped.: "Owen West ob. s.p. masculo."). Dunkin *Sussex Manors, Advowsons, etc., recorded in the Feet of Fines, Henry VIII to William IV (1509–1833)* 1 (Sussex Rec. Soc. 19) (1914): 45–46. *C.P.* 4 (1916): 157 footnote d (sub De la Warr), 158 footnote b (sub De la Warr); 12(2) (1959): 522 (sub West). Comber *Sussex Gens.* 3 (1933): 304–308 (sub Lords West). Welch *Willoughby Letters of the 1st Half of the 16th Cent.* (Thoroton Soc. Rec. Ser. 24) (1967): 33 (letter of Sir Owen West dated c.1527). *Chancery Decree Rolls (C.78)* (List & Index Soc. 160) (1979): 9. Bernard *King's Reformation* (2005): 424–425.

14. MARY WEST, daughter and co-heiress. She was a legatee in the 1551 will of her father. Sometime after 1551, she was sole heiress of her sister, Anne West. She married (1st) before Hilary term 1559 (date of fine) **ADRIAN POYNINGS**, Knt., of Wherwell, Hampshire, Burnegate, Dorset, Lieutenant of Boulogne citadel, 1546, Lieutenant of Boulogne base town, 1546, Captain of Boulogne, 1546–7, Lieutenant of Calais, 1552, Captain of Portsmouth, 1559–71, Burgess (M.P.) for Tregony, 1559, Justice of the Peace for Hampshire from c. 1559, Justice of the Peace for Dorset, 1561, Marshal of Boulogne, 1562, Steward of the Duchy of Lancaster for Dorset, 1566, Vice Admiral of Hampshire by 1570, illegitimate son of Edward Poynings, K.G., of Westenhanger, Kent, Treasurer of the Household to King Henry VIII, Warden of the Cinque Ports, by his mistress, Rose, daughter of Adrian Whethill. He was born in Ghent when his father was ambassador to the Emperor. They had three daughters, Elizabeth (wife of Andrew Rogers), Mary (wife of Edward

More), and Anne. He was a member of the household of Thomas Cromwell by 1538. He became a soldier, succeeding Thomas Wyatt to commands at Boulogne. He gained large sums from the ransoms of prisoners. He was present at the Battle of St. Quintin in 1557, with 48 foot soldiers. In June 1558 he was appointed lieutenant to Lord Talbot in the army which was being sent northwards, but the commission was cancelled a month later because he was unwilling to serve. He was second in command under Ambrose Dudley in the expedition to France in 1562. The same year he received a patent of denization, and his title to his Dorset manors was confirmed. In 1567 he unsuccessfully claimed the barony of la Warre in right of his wife. His last years were spent at Portsmouth, quarrelling with the mayor and burgesses, who accused him of high-handedness and violence as captain of the town. SIR ADRIAN POYNINGS died at St. Benet Paul's Wharf, London 15 Feb. 1570/1, and was buried in the parish church there. Administration was granted on his estate to his widow, Mary, 22 Feb. 1570/1. Lady Mary West married (2nd) (as his 2nd wife) **RICHARD ROGERS**, Knt., of Bryanston, Dorset, Knight of the Shire for Dorset, 1572, Sheriff of Dorset, 1573–4, 1587–8, Lieutenant of the Isle of Purbeck, 1588, son and heir of John Rogers, Knt., of Bryanston, Dorset, by Katherine, daughter of Richard Weston, Knt. He was born about 1527. They had one son. In the period, 1556–8, he and John Chettell, Gent. were sued by Richard's parents regarding an annuity which was promised in return for a mortgage of the manor of Langton and Littleton (in Blandford St. Mary), Dorset, and lands there to raise money for the said Richard's relief. He was deeply involved in the piracy scandal of 1577, being fined £100 and bound over to return his loot. He commanded one of the five Dorset defence divisions from 1587 to 1600. SIR RICHARD ROGERS left a will proved 11 May 1605 (P.C.C. Hayes).

    Brydges *Collins' Peerage of England* 5 (1812): 1–28 (sub West, Earl Delawarr); 9 (1812): 475–476 (sub Poynings, Lord Poynings). *Gentleman's Mag.* n.s. 16(2) (1823): 492–493. Nicolas *Testamenta Vetusta* 2 (1826): 728 (will of Sir Owen West). *Retrospective Rev.* 2nd Ser. 2 (1828): 300. *Coll. Top. et Gen.* 8 (1843): 223–224 ("The right of Mary Poynings to the barony of La Warre is set forth in Harl. MSS 1323, f. 280"). Gyll *Hist. of Wraysbury, Ankerwycke Priory & Magna Charta Island* (1862): 205 (Whethill ped.). Burke *Gen. Hist. of the Dormant, Abeyant, Forfeited & Extinct Peerages* (1866): 444–445 (sub Poynings). Hutchins *Hist. & Antiqs. of Dorset* 3 (1868): 141 (West ped.). *Antiq.* 4 (1873): 213. Clutterbuck & Webb *Notes on the Parishes of Fyfield…* (1898): 178–185. *List of Sheriffs for England & Wales* (PRO Lists and Indexes 9) (1898): 39. *Notes & Queries for Somerset & Dorset* 6 (1899): 117, 118. Round *Peerage & Ped.* 1 (1910): 56–58. VCH *Hampshire* 4 (1911): 87–98. *C.P.* 4 (1916): 157 footnote d (sub De la Warr) ("Adrian Poynings considered that his issue had, in right of their mother, a right to the [la Warre] Barony, and in the 9 Eliz. 1567 a case was prepared in which that claim was urged; but the heralds of that day, upon what principle it is impossible now to say, were of a different opinion"), 158, footnote b (sub De la Warr). Comber *Sussex Gens.* 3 (1933): 304–308 (sub Lords West). Hasler *House of Commons 1558–1603* 3 (1981): 241–242 (biog. of Adrian Poynings), 302–303 (biog. of Richard Rogers). National Archives, C 1/1465/51-55 (Chancery Proc. dated 1556–8 — John Rogers, Knt., and Katherine his wife v. Richard Rogers, Esq., his son and heir apparent, and John Chettell, Gent.) (available at www.catalogue.nationalarchives.gov.uk/search.asp).

15. ANNE POYNINGS, daughter and co-heiress. She married (as his 1st wife) **GEORGE MORE**, Knt., of Loseley, Godalming, Compton Westbury, Polsted, and Piccards, Surrey, Provost Marshal for Surrey, 1589, Sheriff of Surrey and Sussex, 1597–8, Chamberlain of the Receipt in the Exchequer, 1601, Treasurer and Receiver General to Henry, Prince of Wales, Chancellor of the Order of the Garter, 1611–30, Lieutenant of the Tower of London, 1615–17, Justice of the Peace for Surrey and Sussex, Deputy Lieutenant for Surrey, Verderer of Windsor Forest, Constable of Farnham Castle, Burgess (M.P.) for Guildford, 1584, 1586, 1589, 1593, 1604, 1624, Knight of the Shire for Surrey, 1597, 1601, 1614, 1621, 1625, 1626, son and heir of William More, Knt., of Loseley, Surrey, Chamberlain of the Exchequer, Provost Marshal for Surrey, 1552, Sheriff of Surrey and Sussex, 1558–9, by his 2nd wife, Margaret, daughter of Ralph Daniell, of Swaffham, Norfolk. He was born 28 Nov. 1553. They had four sons, Robert, Knt., George, William, and John, and five daughters, Mary (wife of Nicholas Carew, Knt.), Margaret, Anne (wife of John Donne, D.D.), Elizabeth (wife of John Mills, Knt., Bart.), and Frances. His wife, Anne, died at Loseley, Surrey 19 Nov. 1590, and was buried in the chapel there. In 1601 he was granted the lordship and hundred of

Godalming, Surrey by the queen. He married (2nd) before 6 July 1622 (date of deed) **CONSTANCE MICHELL**, widow of Richard Knight, Esq., of Highclere, Hampshire, and daughter and co-heir of John Michell, of Stamerham (in Horsham), Sussex. They had no issue. SIR GEORGE MORE died 16 October 1632, and was buried in the chapel at Loseley, Surrey.

> *Coll. Top. et Gen.* 8 (1843): 223–224. *Antiq.* 3 (1873): 213. *List of Sheriffs for England & Wales* (PRO Lists and Indexes 9) (1898): 137. Benolte et al. *Vis. of Surrey 1530, 1572 & 1623* (H.S.P. 43) (1899): 2–3 (Moore ped.: "Sr George Moore of Loseley Knt. Justice of the peace Chancellor of the order of the garter 1623. = Anne d. & heire of Sr Ardian Poynings of Burnegate in com. Dorssett Knt.") (Moore arms: Azure, on a cross argent five martlets sable). Hasler *House of Commons 1558–1603* 3 (1981): 80–83 (biog. of George More). Bindoff *House of Commons 1509–1558* 2 (1982): 624–625 (biog. of William More II). *Cal. Patent Rolls 43 Elizabeth I (1600–1601)* (List and Index Soc. 339) (2011): 94, 208, 245.

16. MARGARET MORE, daughter by her father's 1st marriage. She married before 1603 **THOMAS CRYMES** (or **GRYMES**), Knt., of Peckham (in Camberwell) and Bredinghurst (in Camberwell), Surrey, Burgess (M.P.) for Stockbridge, 1601, Justice of the Peace for Surrey, 1608, Burgess (M.P.) for Haslemere, 1614, 1621, Knight of the Shire for Surrey, 1624, Deputy Lieutenant for Surrey, 1627, Governor of Camberwell Free Grammar School, Trustee of Dulwich College, son and heir of Thomas Crymes, Esq., of St. Lawrence Jewry, London, Peckham (in Camberwell), Ashtead, Headley, and Leatherhead, Surrey, and Stoke-by-Nayland and Polstead, Suffolk, Fountains Fell (in Kirkby Malhamdale), Yorkshire, haberdasher, by Jane, daughter and co-heiress of Thomas Muschamp, of London and Bredinghurst (in Camberwell), Surrey, goldsmith, born about 1574 (aged 12 in 1586). They had four sons, George, Knt. [1st Baronet], Arthur, Thomas, and Richard, and twelve daughters, including Frances, Mary, Margaret, and Jane. He was a legatee in the 1586 will of his father. He was trained as a lawyer, and was admitted to Gray's Inn in 1594. He was knighted at Hanworth 25 June 1603. He sat regularly on the bench at the Surrey Assizes. In 1625 Nicholas Canon and William Butler, laborers, of Peckham, Surrey, were indicted of grand larceny on a charge of stealing six sheep worth £3 from Sir Thomas Crymes. In Feb. 1631 he acquired the manor of Tadworth, Surrey, together with three messuages and 640 acres of land. In 1631 he and his wife, Margaret, sold the rectory of Lubbenham, Leicestershire to Francis Nevill, Thomas Stringer, and Thomas Beckwith for £2950. In 1637 he and his wife, Margaret, obtained a license to alienate the rectory and advowson of the vicarage of Sileby, Leicestershire. SIR THOMAS CRYMES died 28 April 1644, and was buried at Camberwell, Surrey.

> Manning & Bray *Hist. & Antiqs. of Surrey* 1 (1804): 96, 659; 3 (1814): 670–671. Cooke *Vis. of London 1568* (H.S.P. 1) (1869): 41. Foster *Reg. of Admissions to Gray's Inn 1521–1889* (1889): 83. Benolte et al. *Vis. of Surrey 1530, 1572 & 1623* (H.S.P. 43) (1899): 2–3 (Moore ped.: "Margerett [Moore] vx. Sr Thomas Grymes of Pech… [?Peckham] Knt."), 144 (Grymes ped.: "Sr Thomas Grymes of Peckham Knt. Justice of the peace 1623. = Margerett d. of Sr George Moore of Losley in com. Surrey Knt.") (Grymes arms: Or, three bars gules and as many martlets, two and one, argent, a chief barry nebulée argent and azure). VCH *Surrey* 3 (1911): 258; 4 (1912): 31, 229–234. Somerville Hist. of the Duchy of Lancaster 1 (1953): 338–340. Cooke *Vis. of London 1568, 1569–90* (H.S.P. 109-10) (1963): 55. Hasler *House of Commons 1558–1603* 2 (1981): 231 (biog. of Thomas Grymes). Crimes *C(h)rymes or C(h)rimes* (1985): 149–163 (Sir Thomas Grimes styled "brother" [i.e., brother-in-law] in letter of [Dr.] John Donne dated 1615).

17. GEORGE CRYMES, Knt., of Peckham (in Camberwell) and South Tadworth, Surrey, Burgess (M.P.) for Haslemere, 1628–9, son and heir, baptized at Camberwell, Surrey 10 Feb. 1604/5. He married at St. Margaret's, Lothbury, London 25 May 1637 **ALICE LOVELL**, daughter and co-heiress of Charles Lovell, Esq., of Spridlington, Lincolnshire and East Harling, Norfolk, by his 2nd wife, Elizabeth, daughter of Thomas Le Gros, Knt. [see EAST HARLING 21 for her ancestry]. They had seven sons, Thomas, Knt. [2nd Baronet], Charles Lovell, Esq., George, Richard, [Dr.] William, Gent., Henry, and Benjamin, and four daughters, Margaret, Mary (wife of Lodowick Jackson), Elizabeth, and Sarah. He matriculated at Brasenose College, Oxford 6 Dec. 1622, aged 14. He was knighted by King Charles I at Theobalds, Essex 19 Dec. 1628. He was accused by Parliament of having taken part in the Battle of Edgehill in 1642, and his estates were sequestered. Sometime in the period, 1642–57, he sued Richard Farrer and others in Chancery regarding money matters in Surrey. In 1644 he twice petitioned the Parliamentary Committee for Compounding, seeking to take the oath of allegiance to the government; the Committee for Compounding proposed a fine of £500, which he paid in October 1644. By the mid-1640s, he was in a desperate financial position, he owing a total of £5220 in outstanding debts. He tried to ease his difficulties in 1645 or 1646 by writing to the Parliamentary Committee for Compounding. In 1647 he was sued by James Paycocke and others in Chancery regarding property in Kirkby Malham, Yorkshire. In 1652 he and Thomas Aberly sued Harbottle Grimston, Knt., baronet, Chaloner Chute, and others in Chancery regarding property in Putney, Surrey. He was created a Baronet in 1654 by the future King Charles II of England. In 1657 Dame Arabella Bryers, widow, sued him in Chancery regarding property in Peckham, Surrey. SIR GEORGE CRYMES, 1st Baronet, was buried at Camberwell, Surrey 15 October 1657. Administration on his estate was granted to his widow, Alice, 16 March 1657/8. Alice married (2nd) **ANDREW KNIVETON**, Knt., 3rd Baronet, of Mercaston, Derbyshire, son and heir of Gilbert Kniveton, Knt., 2nd Baronet, of Mercaston and Bradley, Derbyshire, by his 1st wife, Mary, daughter and co-heiress of Andrew Grey. They had no issue. He was admitted to Gray's Inn 10 October 1634. In 1661 Dame Mary Pratt, widow sued Andrew Kniveton and Alice his wife and Thomas Brograve regarding money matters in Middlesex. SIR ANDREW KNIVETON was buried 24 Dec. 1669, at St. Giles in the Fields, Middlesex. Administration on his estate was granted to his widow, Alice, 5 Jan. 1669/70.

Coll. Top. et Gen. 3 (1836): 155–157. Benolte et al. *Vis. of Surrey 1530, 1572 & 1623* (H.S.P. 43) (1899): 144 (Grymes ped.: "George Grymes 18 yere old 1623."). Cokayne *Complete Baronetage* 1 (1900): 51 (sub Kniveton); 3 (1903): 15–16 (sub Crymes). Armytage *Vis. of Surrey 1662–1668* (1910): 33 (Crymes ped.: Sr George Crymes of Peckham, Knt & Bart. = Alice da. & Coh. of Charles Lovell of East-harling in Com. Norf. Ar.") (Crymes arms: Or, three bars gules charged with as many martlets of the first, on a chief argent, two bars nebulée azure). VCH *Surrey* 3 (1911): 258; 4 (1912): 31. Crimes *C(h)rymes or C(h)rimes* (1985). *Surrey Heraldic Vis.*: 53 (Crimes ped.: "Sr. George Crimes of Peckham Sur Kted Decr. 19. 1628 aged 18. 1623."). National Archives, C 3/445/80; C 5/416/116; C 6/135/30; C 6/155/111; C 10/15/23 (available at www.catalogue.nationalarchives.gov.uk/search.asp).

18. [DR.] **WILLIAM CRYMES**, Gent., surgeon or doctor, younger son, born about 1646. He was a legatee in the 1659 will of his brother, Charles Lovell Crymes, Esq., of Peckham, Surrey. He immigrated to Virginia as early as 1676, when a bond was recorded in Middlesex County, Virginia from William Crimes and Robert Littlefield, both of Gloucester County, and John Purvis, of London, for 53 pounds sterling to secure payment to merchant Robert Harwood. In 1678 he patented 450 acres on Poropotank adjoining the land of Capt. Richard Dudley and other. He was a member of the vestry of Petsworth Parish, Gloucester County, Virginia, 1682–90, at which time he became Warden. In 1686, as "William Crimes of Petsoe Parish in Gloucester County Gent.," he purchased 500 acres of land in Rappahannock County, Virginia from Edward Adcock, which property he in turn sold in 1688 to John Scott. He married (1st) before 1694 _____. They had one daughter. In 1698 he served as an overseer of highways for the upper part of the parish. From 1704 through 1705, he was listed on the parish rent roll as owner of 400 acres, and in 1707, the owner of lot 18 in the town of Gloucester. He married (2nd) **CHRISTIANA** _____. They had one son, [Dr.] George. [DR.] WILLIAM CRYMES, Gent., died in Gloucester, Virginia 24 Nov. 1712, aged 66. In 1720 there was a chancery suit recorded in Essex County, Virginia by George Crymes, "infant son of William Crymes, late of Gloucester County deceased." His widow, Christiana, died 6 October 1758.

Coll. Top. et Gen. 3 (1836): 155–157. Cokayne *Complete Baronetage* 3 (1903): 15–16 (sub Crymes). *VMHB* 20 (1912): 200. Tyler *Encyclopedia of Virginia Biography* 1 (1915): 249. Blanton *Medicine in Virginia in the 17th Cent.* (1930): 265. Chamberlayne *Vestry Book of Petsworth Parish, Gloucester County, Virginia, 1677–1793* (1933): 29, 50, 86, 89, 130, 132, 150, 173. Mason *Recs. of Colonial Gloucester County, Virginia* 1 (1946): 22, 86; 2 (1946): 54, 96–97, 126. Crimes *C(h)rymes or C(h)rimes* (1985). Essex County Orders, No. 5, 1716–1723, part 2, pp. 555, 613, 724. Essex County Recs., Old Rappahannock County Deed Book 7, 1682–1688, pp. 337–344. Clark-Crymes Fam. Bible rec., 1692–1949, available electronically through the Library of Virginia at http:// image.lva.virginia.gov/Bible/29401/index.html. Registered

❧ CUDWORTH ❧

REYNOLD DE COURTENAY, of Sutton, Berkshire, married _____.
REYNOLD DE COURTENAY, of Okehampton, Devon, married **HAWISE DE COURCY**.
ROBERT DE COURTENAY, Knt., of Okehampton, Devon, married **MARY DE VERNON** (desc. King William the Conqueror).
HAWISE DE COURTENAY, married **JOHN DE GATESDEN**, Knt., of Broadwater, Sussex.
MARGARET (or **MARGERY**) **DE GATESDEN**, married **JOHN DE CAMOYS**, Knt., of Flockthorpe (in Hardingham), Norfolk.
RALPH DE CAMOYS, Knt., of Flockthorpe (in Hardingham), Norfolk, married **ELIZABETH LE DESPENSER**.
JOHN DE CAMOYS, Knt., of Gressenhall, Norfolk, married **ELIZABETH LE LATIMER** (desc. King William the Conqueror).
THOMAS CAMOYS, K.G., 1st Lord Camoys, married **ELIZABETH LOUCHES**.
RICHARD CAMOYS, Knt., of Camoys (in Great Milton), Oxfordshire, married **JOAN POYNINGS** [see CAMOYS 9].

10. MARGARET CAMOYS, born about 1402 (aged 24 in 1426). Margaret married (as his 1st wife) **RALPH RADMYLDE** (or **RADMYLD**, **RADMYLL**, **RADEMELDE**), Esq., of Lancing, Sussex, Knight of Shire for Sussex, 1420. They had one son, Robert, Esq., and two daughters, Margaret (wife of John Goring, Esq.) and Elizabeth (or Isabel). He was heir in 1400 to his brother, Richard Radmyld. His wife, Margaret, was co-heiress in 1426 to her brother, Hugh Camoys, 2nd Lord Camoys, by which she inherited the manors of Great Milton, Oxfordshire and Albourne, Sussex, and a moiety of the manors of Camoys (in Great Stukeley), Huntingdonshire, Baldon St. Lawrence (in Toot Balden), Chislehampton, and Wheatley (in Cuddesdon), Oxfordshire, and Barcombe, Bevendean (in Falmer), and Trotton, Sussex. In 1428 Margaret, together with Roger Lewknor and his wife, Eleanor (Margaret's sister), were plaintiffs in a suit for the manors of Didling, Elsted, and Trotton, Sussex. In 1432 he and Roger Lewknor disputed the right of presentation to the church of Broadwater, Sussex. He and Roger Lewknor presented to the churches of Trotton, Sussex, 1439, 1442, and Itchingfield, Sussex, 1440, and to the chantry of St. Mary in Broadwater, Sussex, 1439. He married (2nd) before 1440 **AGNES** _____. In 1442 his feoffees presented to the church of East Hoathly, Sussex. RALPH RADMYLDE, Esq., died 3 August 1443. He left a will dated 1442. His wife, Agnes, was living in 1457.

Sussex Arch. Colls. 3 (1850): 94–95, 101–102 (Lewknor-Camoys-Radmylde ped.). Hervey *Vis. of Suffolke* 2 (1871): 230–232 (Radmylde arms: Argent, 3 bars Sable, on a canton Sable a leopard's face Or). Elwes *Hist. of the Castles, Mansions & Manors of Western Sussex* (1876): viii, 51, 127. Ellis *Parks & Forests of Sussex* (1885): 172. *Sussex Arch. Colls.* 41 (1898): 123–124, 136. *English Rpts.: House of Lords* 7 (1901): 895–924 (Camoys Peerage). Benolte et al. *Vis. of Sussex 1530 & 1633–4* (H.S.P. 53) (1905): 25–30 (Lewknor ped.: "Ralph Radnelle = Margarett d. & heire of Ric. Camoys."). Edward Lewknor of Kingston Bewsey. = Margarett d. of …. Copley."). Deedes *Extracts from the Episcopal Regs. of Richard Paty, S.T.P., Lord Bishop of Chichester* (Sussex Rec. Soc. 4) (1905): 112–113, 114–115, 124–125, 126–127. *C.P.* 2 (1912): 508, 510 (sub Camoys). VCH *Buckingham* 4 (1927): 63–68. VCH *Huntingdon* 2 (1932): 230–234. Comber *Sussex Gens.* 3 (1933): 148–162. *C.F.R.* 15 (1935): 234, 269. *Sussex Notes & Queries* 6 (1937): 73. VCH *Sussex* 7 (1940): 80–83, 223–227. VCH *Oxford* 5 (1957): 47–56, 96–116; 7 (1962): 5–16, 117–146. Kerridge *Hist. of Lancing* (1979): 15.

11. ELIZABETH (or **ISABEL**) **RADMYLDE**, was a legatee in the 1442 will of her father. She married **NICHOLAS LEWKNOR**, of Kingston Bowsey (in Kingston by Sea), Sussex, younger son of Thomas Lewknor, Knt., of Horsted Keynes, Sussex, South Mimms, Middlesex, Stoke Doyle, Northamptonshire, etc., by his 2nd wife, Elizabeth, daughter of William Echingham, Knt. [see LEWKNOR 14 for his ancestry]. They had three sons, Edward, Thomas, and John (clerk) [Parson of Broadwater, Sussex], and one daughter, Joan (or Jane) (wife successively of Thomas Moore, John

Massingberd, and Thomas Thatcher). Elizabeth was co-heir in 1499 to her nephew, William Radmylde, Knt. She died before 1503.

> Gurney *Rec. of the House of Gournay* 2 (1848): 469–470 (Lewknor ped.). *Sussex Arch. Colls.* 3 (1850): 89–102. Hervey *Vis. of Suffolke* 2 (1871): 230–232. Elwes *Hist. of the Castles, Mansions & Manors of Western Sussex* (1876): 51. Ellis *Parks & Forests of Sussex* (1885): 172. *English Rpts.: House of Lords* 7 (1901): 895–924 (Camoys Peerage). Benolte et al. *Vis. of Sussex 1530 & 1633-4* (H.S.P. 53) (1905): 25–30 (Lewknor ped.: "Elizebeth d. & coheire of Raffe Radnelle. = Nicholas Lewknor, 6 sonn of Thomas 14 E. 4, 1473."). *C.P.* 2 (1912): 510 (sub Camoys). Comber *Sussex Gens.* 3 (1933): 148–162. VCH *Oxford* 7 (1962): 5–16.

12. EDWARD LEWKNOR, Esq., of Kingston Bowsey (in Kingston by Sea), Sussex, Gentleman Usher to Kings Henry VII and Henry VIII, Escheator for Surrey and Sussex, 1485–6, Commissioner of Array for Sussex, 1490, Burgess (M.P.) for Lewis, 1491–2, Sheriff of Surrey and Sussex, 1510–11, son and heir. He married (1st) **MARGARET** _____. They had one son, Edward, Esq. He married (2nd) **SIBYL** _____. In 1503 he and his wife, Sibyl, and his cousin, John Goring, and his wife, Constance, released all their right in the manor of Great Milton, Oxfordshire to Reginald Bray, Knt., and others. Edward married (3rd) **ANNE EVERARD**, daughter of John Everard, of Cratfield, Suffolk, by Margaret Bedingfield. They had one son, Richard, and three daughters, Eleanor, Elizabeth, and Dorothy. EDWARD LEWKNOR, Esq., left a will dated 22 Dec. 1522 [sic], proved 31 October 1522 (P.C.C. 28 Maynwaryng). His widow, Anne, married (2nd) (as his 2nd wife) **EDWARD ECHINGHAM**, Knt., of Barsham, Suffolk, son of John Echingham, of Barsham, Suffolk, by Anne, daughter of John Wingfield, K.B. He served in the naval expedition against the French before Brest in 1513. SIR EDWARD ECHINGHAM died at Barsham, Suffolk 8 July 1527. He left a will dated 18 June 1527, proved 7 Feb. 1527/8 (P.C.C. 28 Porch). His widow, Anne, died at Barsham, Suffolk 14 Nov. 1538. She left a will dated 14 Nov. 1538, proved 3 July 1539 (P.C.C. 15 Crumwell).

> Gurney *Rec. of the House of Gournay* 2 (1848): 469–470 (Lewknor ped.). *Sussex Arch. Colls.* 3 (1850): 89–102. *List of Sheriffs for England & Wales* (PRO Lists and Indexes 9) (1898): 137. *English Rpts.: House of Lords* 7 (1901): 895–924 (Camoys Peerage). Benolte et al. *Vis. of Sussex 1530 & 1633-4* (H.S.P. 53) (1905): 25–30 (Lewknor ped.: "Edward Lewknor ob. 14 H. 7. [1] = Margarett d. of …. 1 wyffe, [2] = Ann d. of …. 2 wiffe, [which Ann] = Sr Edmond Edlingham 2 husband."). *Genealogist* n.s. 22 (1906): 52–61. Comber *Sussex Gens.* 3 (1933): 148–162. Wedgwood *Hist. of Parliament* 1 (1936): 540 (biog. of Edward Lewkenor). VCH *Oxford* 7 (1962): 117–146.

13. EDWARD LEWKNOR, Esq., of Kingston Bowsey (in Kingston by Sea), Ham, Hamsey, and Parham, Sussex, son and heir by his father's 1st marriage. He married **MARGARET COPLEY**, daughter of Roger Copley, Esq., of London and Roughey (in Horsham), Sussex, by Anne, 2nd daughter and co-heiress of Thomas Hoo, Knt., Lord Hoo and Hastings [see HOO 15 for her ancestry]. They had two sons, Edward, Esq., and Anthony, and three daughters, Eleanor (wife of Giles Saint Barbe), Mary (wife of John Michell), and Barbara (wife of John Dawtrey, Knt.). He was a legatee in the 1522 will of his father. In 1524 he was assessed for tax with his nine servants at half the total for Kingston and Southwick together. EDWARD LEWKNOR, Esq., died 7 July 1528. He left a will dated 1 October 1527, proved 7 Nov. 1528 (P.C.C. 39 Porch). In the period, 1533–38, Margaret "executrix and late the wife of Edward son and executor of Edward Lewkenour" sued Thomas Thatcher in Chancery regarding the marriage settlement of the said Thomas with Jane, sister of the said Edward Lewknor the elder. In 1537 the manor of Kingston Bowsey (in Kingston by Sea), Sussex was settled on Edward's widow, Margaret, for life and an additional 20 years, with remainder in tail male on her younger son, Anthony Lewknor. In 1548 Margaret was the demesne lessee of the manor of King's Barns (in Upper Beeding), Sussex. In 1550 Margaret Lewknor, of Kingston Bowsey, widow, and her son, Edward Lewknor, Esq., of same, sold Thomas Woulder, and William Woulder, both of West Angmering, husbandmen, four tenements, three barns, and lands, being part of the customary land of the manor of Ham, Sussex.

> Dallaway *Hist. of the Western Division of the County of Sussex* 2(2) (1832): 339–340 (Hoo-Copley ped.). Gurney *Rec. of the House of Gournay* 2 (1848): 469–470 (Lewknor ped.). *Sussex Arch. Colls.* 3 (1850): 89–102. *English Rpts.: House of Lords* 7

(1901): 895–924 (Camoys Peerage). Benolte et al. *Vis. of Sussex 1530 & 1633–4* (H.S.P. 53) (1905): 25–30 (Lewknor ped.: "Edward Lewknor of Kingston Bewsey. = Margarett d. of …. Copley."), 111 (Copley ped.: "Margarett [Copley] ux. Edward Lewknor of Kingston Bowsey."). *Genealogist* n.s. 33 (1917): 74, 79. Comber *Sussex Gens.* 1 (1931): 70–73 (sub Copley); 3 (1933): 148–162. Copley *Letters of Sir Thomas Copley* (1970): xvi. VCH *Sussex* 6(1) (1980): 132–138; 6(3) (1987): 34–37; 7 (1940): 83–87. National Archives, C 1/843/23 (available at www.catalogue.nationalarchives.gov.uk/search.asp). West Sussex Rec. Office: Holmes, Campbell & Co MSS, Holmes, Campbell & Co/983 (available at www.a2a.org.uk/search/index.asp).

14. EDWARD LEWKNOR, Esq., of Kingston Bowsey (in Kingston by Sea) and Hamsey, Sussex, Groom Porter to King Edward VI and Queen Mary I, Burgess (M.P.) for Horsham, Sussex, 1553, son and heir, born about 1518 (aged 11 in 1529). He was a legatee in the 1527 will of his father. He married before 1542 **DOROTHY WROTH**, daughter of Robert Wroth, Esq., of Durants (in Enfield), Middlesex, by Jane, daughter of Thomas Haute, Knt. [see WROTH 18 for her ancestry]. They had four sons, Edward, Knt., Thomas, Gent., Stephen, and William, and five daughters, Leverest [or Lucrece?] (wife of William Jackson), Anne, Mary, Dorothy (wife of Benjamin Pellatt, Esq.), and Elizabeth. In 1550 he sold the manor of Ham, Sussex to Thomas Wolder for £80. In 1551 the king and Council recommended him for the packership of London, but the City refused on the ground that the yield of the office had been allocated to the poor. In 1553 he was granted the manor of King's Barns (in Upper Beeding) and an estate called New Park (in Lower Beeding), Sussex by the king. In Feb. 1556 he and his cousin, William West, the disabled heir of the 9th Lord la Warre, were informed by Henry Peckham of the conspiracy being hatched by Henry Dudley, Knt., against Queen Mary I, and asked to procure a copy of the will of King Henry VIII as proof of the queen's ineligibility to wear the crown. Lewknor sent the document to West's house in St. Dunstan's, Farringdon Without, where it was handed over to Peckham. Lewknor was also said to have had meetings with sympathizers both at his house in Sussex and in London, and more vaguely to have been privy to a plot to kill the Queen during a card game. On 6 June 1556 he was taken to the Tower of London and on 15 June following he was tried at Guildhall and sentenced to death for treason. EDWARD LEWKNOR, Esq., died a prisoner in the Tower of London 6 Sept. 1556. Following his attainder in 1556, the Crown granted the manors of Kingston Bowsey (in Kingston by Sea) and Hamsey, Sussex to his widow, Dorothy. In 1558 a private act was passed in Parliament for the restitution in blood of the children of Edward Lewknor, Esq. Dorothy and his brother, Anthony Lewknor, appear to have broken the entail on the manor of Kingston Bowsey, Sussex in 1559. She was a legatee in the 1573 will of her brother, Thomas Wroth, Knt. Dorothy left a will dated 1587, proved 26 August 1589 (P.C.C. 68 Leicester).

Strype *Eccl. Mems.* 3(1) (1822): 494. Gurney *Rec. of the House of Gournay* 2 (1848): 469–470 (Lewknor ped.). Nichols *Diary of Henry Machyn* (Camden Soc. 42) (1848): 108, 114. *Sussex Arch. Colls.* 3 (1850): 89–102. Elwes *Hist. of the Castles, Mansions & Manors of Western Sussex* (1876): 130–131. Benolte *Vis. of Somerset 1531, 1573 & 1591* (1885): 91–93 (Wrothe ped.: "Dorothy [Wrothe] = Sir Edw. Lewknor."). Waller *Loughton in Essex* Pt. 2 (1889–1900): 19–21 (will of Sir Thomas Wroth). *English Rpts.: House of Lords* 7 (1901): 895–924 (Camoys Peerage). *Denham Parish Regs.: 1539–1850* (1904): 86–93, 198–219. Benolte et al. *Vis. of Sussex 1530 & 1633–4* (H.S.P. 53) (1905): 25–30 (Lewknor ped.: "Edward Lewknor of Kingston Bewsey. = Dorathey d. of Sr Rob. Wroth of Enffeild knight."). Comber *Sussex Gens.* 3 (1933): 148–162. Davis *Anc. of Mary Isaac* (1955): 177–178. VCH *Sussex* 6(1) (1980): 132–138; 6(3) (1987): 34–37; 7 (1940): 83–87. Bindoff *House of Commons 1509–1558* 2 (1982): 528–529 (biog. of Edward Lewknor). East Sussex Rec. Office: Archive of Drake & Lee of Lewes, solicitor, SAS-D/105 (available at www.a2a.org.uk/search/index.asp). Parliamentary Archives: House of Lords, HL/PO/PB/1/1558/E1n32 (available at www.a2a.org.uk/search/index.asp). West Sussex Rec. Office: Holmes, Campbell & Co MSS, Holmes, Campbell & Co/983, 984, 985, and 1087 (available at www.a2a.org.uk/search/index.asp).

15. MARY LEWKNOR, married by license dated 1 July 1568 **MATTHEW MACHELL**, Gent., of London and Shacklewell (in Hackney), Middlesex, Citizen and haberdasher of London, younger son of John Machell, Citizen and haberdasher of London, Sheriff of London, 1555–6, Alderman of London, 1556–8, by Jane (or Joan), daughter of Henry Luddington, Gent. He was born after 1545. They had one son, John, Gent., and five daughters, Dorothy, Jane (wife of Henry Walsh), Elizabeth (wife of John Cave), Ann (wife of _____ Gibbs), and Mary. In 1570 Queen Elizabeth I sued Matthew Machell regarding money lent by the said Matthew to Thomas Lord Wentworth for the supposed sale of sugar to Lord Wentworth agreed upon by the defendant and Robert Savadge to escape the penalties of the statute of usury. In the period, 1587–91, John Machell sued Matthew Machell regarding the manors of Guilden Sutton, Cheshire, and Burneside [Burnside], Westmorland; and property in London; Tottenham, Middlesex; Hatfield, Hertfordshire; Hinton Admiral, Hampshire; Sandbach, Holmes Chapel and Goostrey, Cheshire; and Dorset. MATTHEW MACHELL, Gent., died 23 August 1593.

Sussex Arch. Colls. 3 (1850): 89–102. Burke *Gen. & Heraldic Hist. of the Landed Gentry of Great Britain & Ireland* 2 (1871): 851 (sub Machell). Hawley et al. *Vis. of Essex 1552, 1558, 1570, 1612 & 1634* 1 (H.S.P. 13) (1878): 441–442 (1634 Vis. Essex) (Machell ped.: "Mathew Machell. = Mary d. of Edward Lewknor of Sussex.") (Machell arms: Sable, three greyhounds courant in pale argent, collared or, a bordure of the second). Bellasis *Machells of Crackenthorpe* (1886): Machell of Kendal ped. at end. Chester *Allegations for Marr. Lics.: London* 1 (H.S.P. 25) (1887): 39. Sharpe *Cal. Wills proved & enrolled in the Court of Husting, London* 2 (1890): 655–668 (will of Sir William Laxton, step-father of Joan Luddington). Fry *Abs. of IPMs Rel. London* 1 (Index Lib. 15) (1896): 173–174 (inquisition of John Machell). Benolte et al. *Vis. of Sussex 1530 & 1633–4* (H.S.P. 53) (1905): 25–30 (Lewknor ped.: "Mary [Lewknor] ux. Mathew Machell of Hackney."). Beaven *Alderman of London* (1908): 205–215. *Index of Chancery Procs. (Ser. II)* 2 (PRO Lists and Indexes 24) (1908): 68. Philipot et al. *Vis. of Buckingham 1634 & 1566* (H.S.P. 58) (1909): 88 (Matchell ped.: "Mathew Matchell of Hatfield in Hartfordshire 2d son. = Mary da: of Edward Lewknor of Okeington Bewsey Com. Sussex."). Mundy *Middlesex Peds.* (H.S.P. 65) (1914): 7 (Machell ped.: "Mathew Machell hath yssue as in Buckinghamshire."). Walker *Yorkshire Peds.* 2 (H.S.P. 95) (1943): 279–280 (Luddington ped.: "Matthew [Machell] = … dau. of …. Cotton"). *Sussex Notes & Queries* 16 (1964): 114–121. VCH *Middlesex* 10 (1995): 51–59. Boyd *Peds. with index of London Citizens* (1954): #9845 [John Machell] & #9846 [Matthew Machell] [found on FHL Microfilm 94550]. National Archives, C 3/227/10; E 133/1/94; E 133/10/1588 (available at www.catalogue.nationalarchives.gov.uk/search.asp).

16. MARY MACHELL, nurse to Prince Henry, eldest son of King James I of England. She married (1st) at St. Mary, Newington, Surrey 18 June 1611 [**REV.**] **RALPH CUDWORTH**, D.D., Fellow of Emmanuel College, Cambridge. They had three sons, [Major] James, Gent., Ralph, D.D. [Fellow of Emmanuel College, Master of Clare College, Master of Christ's College], and John, and three daughters, Elizabeth (wife of [Rev.] Josias Beacham/Beachamp), Mary, and Jane. He was born in 1572. He matriculated at Emmanuel College, Cambridge, Lent, 1588–9, where he obtained the following degrees: B.A., 1592–3, M.A., 1596, B.D., 1603, and D. D., 1619. He served as Curate of Westley Waterless, Cambridgeshire c.1600, and was also a minister of St. Andrew's, Cambridge. He was instituted Vicar of Coggeshall, Essex in 1604. He was appointed Rector of Aller, Somerset in 1609. He was appointed Rector of Aller, Somerset in 1609. [REV.] RALPH CUDWORTH, D.D. was buried at Aller, Somerset 30 August 1624. He left a will dated 17 August 1624, proved 29 October 1624 (P.C.C. 116 Byrde). His widow, Mary, married (2nd) [**REV.**] **JOHN STOUGHTON**, D.D., Fellow of Emmanuel College, younger son of [Rev.] Thomas Stoughton, of Naughton, Suffolk and Coggeshall, Essex, by his 1st wife, Katherine. He was baptized at Naughton, Suffolk 23 Jan. 1592/3. He was admitted sizar of Emmanuel College, Cambridge in 1607, where he obtained the following degrees: B.A., 1610–11, M.A., 1614, B.D., 1621, and D.D., 1626. He was appointed Rector of Aller, Somerset 24 August 1624. In 1632 he was appointed curate of St. Mary, Aldermanbury, London. His wife, Mary, was living in December 1634. He married (2nd) at Frampton, Dorset in 1637 **JANE BROWNE**, widow of [Rev.] Walter Newburgh (will proved 7 Nov. 1632), of Symondsbury, Dorset, and daughter of John Browne, Esq., of Frampton, Dorset. They had two daughters, Jane and Mary. He was prosecuted in the high commission at the instigation of Archbishop Laud. [REV. DR.] JOHN STOUGHTON died 4 May 1639, and was buried 9 May 1639. He left a will dated 4 May 1639, proved 20 May 1639 (P.C.C. 69 Harvey).

Brook *Lives of the Puritans* 3 (1813): 527 ("Dr. John Stoughton, D.D. was fellow of Emmanuel college, Cambridge … He is classed among the learned writers and fellows of that college, and is denominated a pious and learned divine."). Chalmers *Gen'l Biog. Dict.* 11 (1813): 104–111 (biog. of Ralph Cudworth [the younger]: "[He] was son of Dr. Ralph Cudworth, and born 1617, at Aller, Somerset, of which place his father was rector. His mother was of the family of

Machell, and had been nurse to prince Henry, eldest son of James I. His father dying when he was only seven years of age, and his mother marrying again, his education was superintended by his father-in-law, Dr Stoughton"). Hutchins *Hist. & Antiqs. of Dorset* (1815). Chauncy *Hist. Antiqs. of Hertfordshire* 1 (1826): 77–78. *Coll. Top. et Gen.* 1 (1834): 172–173 (re. Beacham fam.). Green *Diary of John Rous* (Camden Soc. 66) (1856): 79–80 (sub 1635: "In Oct., Doctor Stoughton, of Aldermanbury, in London, who married Cudworth's widow, of Emm[anuel] and had the same living given by the colledge in the West country, from when a carrier bringing some monyes for his wives children's portions, he was traduced (as it seemeth) to be a favourer of New England, and a collector of contributions for those ministers there, &c."). *Notes & Queries* 2nd Ser. 7 (1859): 230. *NEHGR* 14 (1860): 101–104 (letter of James Cudworth dated 1634 addressed to his "very Louinge & Kinde ffather Dr. Stoughton at his howse in Aldermanbury"); 21 (1867): 249–250; 30 (1876): 464; 40 (1886): 306–307 (will of John Stoughton, D.D.); 53 (1899): 433 (will of John Cudworth, Esq.); 64 (1910): 85–86. Bellasis *Machells of Crackenthorpe* (1886): Machell of Kendal ped. at end. Weaver *Somerset Incumbents* (1889): 4. *Notes & Queries for Somerset & Dorset* 7 (1901): 143–144. *D.N.B.* 5 (1908): 271–272 (biog. of Ralph Cudworth). Bartlett *Newberry Genealogy* (1914): 24–26. Holman *Scott Gen.* (1919): 259–262. Burghill et al. *Vis. of Rutland 1681–2* (H.S.P. 73) (1922): 19 (Beacham ped.). Venn & Venn *Alumni Cantabrigiensis to 1751* 1 (1922): 431 (sub Ralph Cudworth); 4(1) (1927): 171 (sub John Stoughton). Calder & Cudworth *Recs. of the Cudworth Fam.* (1974). Emerson *Letters from New England* (1976): 138–139, 142–143. Spear *Search for the Passengers of the Mary & John 1630* 18 (1992): 39–43; 26 (1997): 101–104 (sub Stoughton). Parish Regs. of Aller, Somerset [FHL Microfilm 1517680]. Registered will of John Machell, Gent., of Wonersh, Surrey dated 17 Oct. 1646, codicil dated 14 Jan. 1646/7, proved 16 July 1647, P.C.C. 163 Fines [FHL Microfilm 92165] — brother of Mary Machell, wife of Ralph Cudworth; testator bequeaths his cousin/kinswoman [i.e., niece], Jane Cudworth, £125 at her marriage.

17. [MAJOR] **JAMES CUDWORTH**, Gent., salter, Deputy Governor Plymouth Colony, 1640, 1642; Assistant, 1656–7, 1674–80, Plymouth commissioner to New England Confederation, 1655, 1657, 1678, 1681, Deputy to Plymouth General Court for Barnstable, 1640, 1642, and for Scituate, 1649–56, 1652, son and heir, baptized at Aller, Somerset 2 August 1612. He married at Northam, Devon 1 Feb. 1633/4 **MARY PARKER**. They had five sons, James, Jonathan [1st of name], Israel, unnamed, and Jonathan [2nd of name], and two daughters, Mary (wife of Robert Whitcomb) and Joanna (wife of _____ Jones). He and his wife, Mary, immigrated to New England in 1634, where they initially settled at Scituate, Massachusetts. He was admitted freeman of Plymouth Colony 1 Jan. 1634/5. He and his wife, Mary, joined the Scituate, Massachusetts church 18 Jan. 1634/5. In 1639 he and his family removed to Barnstable, Massachusetts, but in 1646, they returned to Scituate, Massachusetts. He was sent by Scituate as a Deputy to the Plymouth General Court in 1659, but was not approved by the Court. In 1660 he was disenfranchised of his freedom of the Plymouth Colony, being found a "manifest opposer of the laws of the government" owing to his support of the Quakers. He was readmitted to freemanship 4 July 1673, and on the same day was made magistrate for Scituate. In 1673 he was authorized to solemnize marriages, grant subpoenas for witnesses, and to administer oaths to witnesses. In Dec. 1673 he was chosen to lead a military expedition against the Dutch. In 1675 he was chosen to take charge of the Plymouth Colony military forces. His wife, Mary, was living 17 Dec. 1673. [MAJOR] JAMES CUDWORTH left a will dated 15 Sept. 1681, proved 7 July 1682.

Deane *Hist. of Scituate, Massachusetts* (1831): 245–249. *NEHGR* 14 (1860): 101–104 (letter of James Cudworth dated 1634 names his cousin, [Zachariah] Symmes, of Charlestown, Massachusetts). Pope *Pioneers of Massachusetts* (1900): 125 (biog. of James Cudworth). Holman *Scott Gen.* (1919): 259–262. Pratt *Early Planters of Scituate* (1929): 210–235. Calder & Cudworth *Recs. of the Cudworth Fam.* (1974). Spear *Search for the Passengers of the Mary & John 1630* 18 (1992): 39–43. Anderson *Great Migration* 2 (2001): 249–258 (biog. of James Cudworth). Parish Regs. of Aller, Somerset [FHL Microfilm 1517680].

❧ CULPEPER ❧

WILLIAM MALET, of Curry-Mallet, Somerset, married _____.
HAWISE MALET, married **HUGH POYNTZ**, Knt., of Tockington, Glloucestershire.
NICHOLAS POYNTZ, Knt., of Tockington, Gloucestershire, married **ISABEL DYALL**.
HUGH POYNTZ, 1st Lord Poyntz, married _____.
NICHOLAS POYNTZ, 2nd Lord Poyntz, married **ELIZABETH LA ZOUCHE**.
NICHOLAS POYNTZ, Esq., of North Ockendon, Essex, married _____ [see WYCHE 6].

7. EDWARD POYNTZ, Esq., of Essex, younger son. He married an unidentified wife, _____. They had one son, Robert, and one daughter, Maud.

Hawley et al. *Vis. of Essex 1552, 1558, 1570, 1612 & 1634* 1 (H.S.P. 13) (1878): 267–271 (1612 Vis. Essex) (Poyntz ped.: "Edwarde Poyntz Esquier, 2d sonne. = …. Daugh. to …."). *Hist. & Gen. Mem. of the Fam. of Poyntz* (1886): 47.

8. MAUD POYNTZ, married **THOMAS BARRETT**, Esq., of Belhouse (in Aveley), Essex, son and heir of John Barrett, Esq., of Hawkhurst, Kent and Belhouse (in Aveley), Essex, by Alice, daughter and co-heiress of Thomas Belhouse, of Belhouse (in Aveley), Essex. They had one son, Robert, Esq. His widow, Maud, was living in 1440–41.

Brydges *Collins' Peerage of England* 6 (1812): 558–590 (sub Brand, Baroness Dacre). Hawley et al. *Vis. of Essex 1552, 1558, 1570, 1612 & 1634* 1 (H.S.P. 13) (1878): 145–146 (1612 Vis.) (Barrett ped.: "Thomas Barrett of Belhowse in Alvethley in com. Essex, esquire, sonne and heire. = Mawde daugh. to Edward Poyntz of Essex, Esquier"), 267–271 (1612 Vis. Essex) (Poyntz ped.: "Mawde [Poyntz], mar. to Thomas Barrett of Belhowse Esquier."). Maclean *Hist. & Gen. Mem. of the Fam. of Poyntz* (1886): 47. Barrett-Lennard *Account of the Fams. of Lennard & Barrett* (1908): 340–391. *Misc. Gen. et Heraldica* 5th Ser. 6 (1926–28): 81–87 (Barrett arms: Barry of four, argent and gules, per pale counterchanged).

9. ROBERT BARRETT, Esq., of Belhouse (in Aveley), Essex, son and heir. He married (1st) **MARGARET CHICHELEY**. They had no issue. He married (2nd) **MARGERY KNOLLES**, daughter of Robert Knolles, Esq., of North Mimms, Hertfordshire, by Elizabeth, daughter of Bartholomew Seman, goldsmith. They had one son, John, Esq. In 1453 he made a grant of lands called Gossards in South Ockendon, Essex. ROBERT BARRETT, Esq., was living in 1458–9, when Walter Sergeant released to him his moiety of the manor of Belhouse in Aveley) alias Nortons, Essex. His widow, Margery, married (2nd) **JOHN EDWARDS**, Citizen and salter of London.

Brydges *Collins' Peerage of England* 6 (1812): 558–590 (sub Brand, Baroness Dacre) (Margery Knolles identified as "daughter of Thomas Knolles, son of Sir Thomas Knolles, Knight, Lord Mayor of London, in 1st and 11th of Hen. IV."). Hawley et al. *Vis. of Essex 1552, 1558, 1570, 1612 & 1634* 1 (H.S.P. 13) (1878): 145–146 (1612 Vis.) (Barrett ped.: "Robart Barrett of Belhowse in Alvethley in com. Essex, esquire, sonne and heire. = Margery daugh. to Chichley, ar."). Barrett-Lennard *Account of the Fams. of Lennard & Barrett* (1908): 340–391. *Misc. Gen. et Heraldica* 5th Ser. 6 (1926–28): 81–87 (married "Margaret, dau. of . . . . Knolles. Gules, on a chevron argent three roses gules"). Thrupp *Merchant Classs of Medieval London* (1948): 351 (re. Knolles fam.).

10. JOHN BARRETT, Esq., of Belhouse (in Aveley), Essex, and London, son and heir by his father's 2nd marriage. He married (1st) **ELIZABETH BRAYTOFT**, daughter and heiress of Richard Braytoft, by Elizabeth, daughter of Edward Odingsells. They had six sons, George, Gent., and Thomas (clerk), and four sons who died young, and one daughter, Elizabeth (wife of Thomas Cumberford). In the period, 1500–1, he sued John Fowlar and Robert Howghton regarding the detention of deeds relating to a messuage and land in Havering-atte-Bower, Essex. He married (2nd) before 1509 (date of deeds) **PHILIPPE HARPESFIELD** (or **HARPESFELD**), widow of Thomas Dyneley, Esq. (died 29 May 1502) [see FITZ HERBERT 15], of Stanford Dingley and Wokefield (in Stratfield Mortimer), Berkshire, Southam (in Bishop's Cleeve), Gloucestershire, Foxcott (in Andover) and Wolverton, Hampshire, etc., and daughter of Nicholas Harpesfield, Esq., of Harpesfield (in St. Peters, St. Albans), Hertfordshire, by Agnes, daughter of John Norton, Esq., of Nutley and East Tisted, Hampshire. They had six daughters, Cecily, Muriel (wife of John Champneys, Mayor of London), Anne (wife of Martin Bowes, Esq.), Joyce (wife of James Wilford,

Knt.), Margaret (wife of Walter Crompton, Esq.), and Bridget. She was a legatee in the 1500 will of her aunt, Jane Norton, Viscountess Lisle, widow successively of Robert Drope, and Edward Grey, Viscount Lisle. His wife, Philippe, died before 1517. He married (3rd) **MARGARET NORRIS**, daughter of Edward Norris, of Ricot, Berkshire. They had no issue. He married (4th) before July 1526 **MARY BROOKE**, widow of Robert Blagge (died 13 Sept. 1522), of Broke Montacute, Somerset, Baron of the Exchequer, and daughter of John Brooke, Knt., 7th Lord Cobham, by Margaret, daughter of Edward Neville, Knt., Lord Bergavenny [see WYATT 18 for her ancestry]. They had no issue. JOHN BARRETT, Esq., died in 1526. His widow, Mary, married (3rd) (as his 2nd wife) **RICHARD WALDEN**, Knt., of Erith, Kent. In the period, 1529–32, Edward Cobham, Knt., younger son of John Brooke, Lord Cobham sued Richard and his wife, Mary, his wife, regarding an annuity charged by the will of complainant's father on Lufton manor, Somerset. SIR RICHARD WALDEN died 25 March 1536, and was buried in Erith, Kent. In the period, 1533–8, Ralph Folvyle sued Mary, late the wife of Richard Walden, Knt., George Blagge, her son, and others in Chancery regarding the occupation of messuages and lands in Dartford and Wilmington, Kent in contempt of divers judgments. Mary died in 1543–4.

> Hasted *Hist. & Top. Survey of Kent* 2 (1797): 375–376. Brydges *Collins' Peerage of England* 6 (1812): 558–590 (sub Brand, Baroness Dacre). Evelyn *Life of Mrs. Godolphin* (1848): 278–279 (Blagge ped.). Foss *Judges of England* 5 (1857): 136 (biog. of Robert Blagge). *Herald & Genealogist* 5 (1870): 127–130 (re. Harpesfeld fam.). Hawley et al. *Vis. of Essex 1552, 1558, 1570, 1612 & 1634* 1 (H.S.P. 13) (1878): 145–146 (1612 Vis.) (Barrett ped.: "John Barrett of Belhowse in Alvethley in Essex, ar. sonne and he. [1] = Phillip daugh. to Thomas Bardfelde, ar. first wyfe, [2] = Elizabeth daughter to Harpsfild 2nd wyfe, [3] = and he mar. 3dly Elizabeth daugh. to Sr Edward Odingsells, Knight."). *Arch. Cantiana* 16 (1886):1 214. Barrett-Lennard *Account of the Fams. of Lennard & Barrett* (1908): 340–391. VCH *Hampshire* 4 (1911): 270–272, 345–358. Woodruff & Churchill *Sede Vacante Wills* (Kent Arch. Soc. Recs. 3) (1914): 127–145 (will of Jane Viscountess Lisle). VCH *Berkshire* 3 (1923): 422–428; 4 (1924): 110–114. *Misc. Gen. et Heraldica* 5th Ser. 6 (1926–28): 81–87. VCH *Gloucester* 8 (1968): 2–25. National Archives, C 1/237/22; C 1/621/1; C 1/793/9-10 (available at www.catalogue.nationalarchives.gov.uk/search.asp).

11. CECILY BARRETT, daughter by her father's 2nd marriage. She married by settlement dated 4 Jan. 1529/30 **WILLIAM CULPEPER**, Esq., of Hunton, Losenham (in Newenden), and Heryngdon (in Tenterden), Kent, Wigsell (in Salehurst), Sussex, etc., Justice of the Peace for Kent, 3rd but eldest surviving son of Walter Culpeper, Esq., of Losenham (in Newenden) and Woods (in Newenden), Kent, Wigsell (in Salehurst), Sussex, Calais, France, etc., Under Marshal of Calais, by Anne, daughter and heiress of Henry (or Harry) Aucher, Esq., born about 1509 (came of age about 1530). Her maritagium consisted of lands called Scotts in Sandhurst and Newenden, Kent. They had seven sons, John, Esq., Francis, Martin, Walter, Thomas, Richard, and Edmund, and two daughters, Elizabeth (wife of John Wildgose), and Anne (wife of Simon Edolphe). He was admitted to Gray's Inn in 1530, and was subsequently servant to Thomas Cromwell, then Lord Privy Seal. In 1539 he had seisin of the lands of the dissolved Priory of Losenham, Kent. WILLIAM CULPEPER, Esq., left a will dated 16 Nov. 1559, proved 6 Dec. 1559 (P.C.C. 61 Chaynay), requesting burial in the chapel of the parish church of Salehurst, Sussex besides his late wife, Cecily.

> Hawley et al. *Vis. of Essex 1552, 1558, 1570, 1612 & 1634* 1 (H.S.P. 13) (1878): 145–146 (1612 Vis.) (Barrett ped.: "Cecylie [Barrett] mar. to William Culpeper, ar. sonne and he. to Walter."). Philipot *Vis. of Kent 1619–21* (H.S.P. 42) (1898): 61–63 (Colepeper ped.: "Willielmus Colepeper = Cicilia [Cecilia] filia [Joh'is] Barrett."). Benolte & Cooke *Vis. of Kent 1530–1, 1574 & 1592* 1 (H.S.P. 74) (1923): 69–71 (1574 Vis.) (Coulpeper ped.: "William Coulpeper = Cysseley dau: of [John] Barrett"). *Sussex Arch. Colls.* 47 (1904): 47–81. *Gens. of Virginia Fams. from VMHB* 2 (1981): 396–439.

12. JOHN CULPEPER, Esq., of Wigsell (in Salehurst), Sussex, Losenham (in Newenden), Kent, etc., Justice of the Peace, son and heir. He married **ELIZABETH SEDLEY** (or **SIDLEY**), daughter of William Sedley, Esq., of Southfleet, Kent, Sheriff of Kent, by his 1st wife, Anne, daughter and heiress of Roger Grove, of Bishopsgate Ward, London, Grocer. They had four sons, Thomas, William, John, Esq., and Alexander, and one daughter, Cecily (wife of William Stede, Knt.). His wife, Elizabeth, was a legatee in the 1574 will of her brother, Nicholas Sidley, and in the 1581 will of her brother, John Sidley. JOHN CULPEPER, Esq., died 20 October 1612, and was buried at Salehurst, Sussex. His widow, Elizabeth, was buried at Salehurst, Kent 17 May 1618.

Burke *Gen. & Heraldic Hist. of the Extinct & Dormant Baronetcies* (1844): 27–29 (sub Aucher), 482–483. Harvey *Vis. of Norfolk 1563* 1 (1878): 111 (Sedley ped.). Philipot *Vis. of Kent 1619–21* (H.S.P. 42) (1898): 60 ("Eliza Sidley ux. Joh'is Colpeper de Wigsell") (Sidley arms: Azure, a fesse wavy argent between three goats' heads erased [of the second]), 61–63 (Colepeper ped.: "Johannes Colepeper = [left blank]."). Benolte & Cooke *Vis. of Kent 1530–1, 1574 & 1592* 1 (H.S.P. 74) (1923): 70. Beaven *Aldermen of London* 2 (1913): 21 (re Roger Grove). *Sussex Arch. Colls.* 47 (1904): 47–81. Benolte & Cooke *Vis. of Kent 1530–1, 1574 & 1592* 1 (H.S.P. 74) (1923): 69–71 (1574 Vis.) (Coulpeper ped.: "John Coulpeper"); 2 (H.S.P. 75) (1924): 30–31 (1574 Vis.) (Sedley ped.: "Elizabeth Sedley maried vnto John Colpeper of Wigshill"). *Gens. of Virginia Fams. from VMHB* 2 (1981): 396–439.

13. JOHN CULPEPER, Esq., of Greenway Court (in Harrietsham and Hollingbourne), Kent, Salehurst, Sussex, and Astwood (in Feckenham), Worcestershire, Sheriff of Worcestershire, 1623–4, 3rd son. He entered Middle Temple in 1587. He married (1st) in 1600 **URSULA WOODCOCK**, widow of Solomon Pordage, of Rodmersham, Kent (died 1599), and daughter of Ralph Woodcock, of Portsoken & Coleman Street Wards, London, Grocer. She was baptized at St. Lawrence Jewry, London 27 Jan. 1565/6. They had two sons, Thomas and John, and two daughters, Cecily and Frances (wife of James Medlicote). He was a member of the Virginia Company, 1609–25. His wife, Ursula, was buried at Feckenham, Worcestershire 2 June 1612. He married (2nd) **ELEANOR NORWOOD**, widow of George Blount, Knt., of Sodington, Worcestershire, and daughter of William Norwood, Esq., of Leckhampton, Gloucestershire, by his 1st wife, Elizabeth, daughter of William Ligon, Esq., of Madresfield, Redgrove, and Lower Mitton, Worcestershire [see LIGON 17.v for her ancestry]. His wife, Eleanor, died in February 1623/4, and was buried at Mamble, Worcestershire. He married (3rd) **ANN** _____, widow of Hugh Goddard, Citizen and draper of London. In 1628 he sold the manors of Losenham (in Newenden) and Woods (in Newenden), Kent to Adrian Moore, Esq. JOHN CULPEPER, Esq., was buried at Hollingbourne, Kent 18 Dec. 1635. He left a will dated 14 Dec. 1635, proved 23 Jan. 1635/6 (P.C.C. 4 Pile). His widow, Ann, died at St. Giles, Cripplegate, London, in 1645.

Hasted *Hist. & Top. Survey of Kent* 7 (1798): 167–168. Burke *Gen. & Heraldic Hist. of the Extinct & Dormant Baronetcies* (1844): 27–29 (sub Aucher). Chitting & Phillipot *Vis. of Gloucester 1623, 1569 & 1582–3* (H.S.P. 21) (1885): 117–118 (Northwood ped.: "Ellenor Northwod."). *List of Sheriffs for England & Wales* (PRO Lists and Indexes 9) (1898): 159. Philipot *Vis. of Kent 1619–21* (H.S.P. 42) (1898): 61–63 (Colepeper ped.: "John Colepeper of Wigsale in com. Sussex = [left blank]."). Philipot *Vis. of Kent 1619–21* (H.S.P. 42) (1898): 62. Beaven *Aldermen of London* 2 (1913): 41 (re. Ralph Woodcock). *Sussex Arch. Colls.* 47 (1904): 47–81. VCH *Worcester* 4 (1924): 285–289. *Gens. of Virginia Fams. from VMHB* 2 (1981): 488–516.

Children of John Culpeper, Esq., by Ursula Woodcock:

i. **THOMAS CULPEPER**, of Hollingbourne, Kent, son and heir by his father's 1st marriage, born about 1602 (of age by 1623). He was admitted Middle Temple 7 May 1621, and was a member of Virginia Company, 1623. He married at Ulcombe, Kent 10 July 1628 **KATHERINE SAINT LEGER**, daughter of Warham Saint Leger, Knt., of Ulcombe, Kent, by Mary, daughter of Rowland Hayward, Knt. [see SAINT LEGER 21 for her ancestry]. They had three sons, John, [Capt.] Alexander, Esq., and John, Gent., and three daughters, Mary, Anne (wife of Christopher Danby), and Frances. He was an original patentee of the Northern Neck of Virginia in 1649. He was co-owner of the ship *Thomas & John* which carried many immigrants to Virginia. He reportedly lost all his estate, life, and liberty in the king's service (as per a letter written by his son-in-law, [Gov.] William Berkeley of Virginia). THOMAS CULPEPER probably died in Virginia before 1652. His widow, Katherine, removed to Maidstone, Kent, where she died shortly before 28 Aug. 1658 (date of the administration of her estate). *Le Neve's Peds. of the Knights* (H.S.P. 8) (1873): 436 (Danby ped.). *Cal. State Papers, Col. Ser., America & West Indies 1669–1674* (1889): 234. *VMHB* 20 (1912): 93–94. *Sussex Arch. Colls.* 47 (1904): 47–81. Powell *Dict. of North Carolina Biog.* 1 (1979): 470–472 (biog. of John Culpeper). *Gens. of Virginia Fams. from VMHB* 2 (1981): 488–516. Dorman *Adventurers of Purse & Person* 3 (2007): 103–113.

Children of Thomas Culpeper, by Katherine Saint Leger:

a. **FRANCES CULPEPER**, baptized at Hollingbourne, Kent 27 May 1634. She married (1st) soon after 1 Jan. 1652/3 [**Capt.**] **SAMUEL STEPHENS**, Gent., of Bolthorpe, Warwick County, Virginia, Commander of

Albemarle [Southern Plantation], son and heir of [Capt.] Richard Stephens, of Warwick County, Virginia, by Elizabeth, daughter of Abraham Peirsey. He was born about 1629, and died intestate before 7 March 1669/70. They had no issue. She married (2nd) about 21 June 1670 (as his 2nd wife) [Gov.] **WILLIAM BERKELEY**, Knt. [see LIGON 17.ii.a.1], of Green Spring, near Jamestown, Virginia, Governor of Virginia, son of Maurice Berkeley, Knt., of Bruton, Somerset, by Elizabeth, daughter of William Killigrew, Knt. [see LIGON 17.ii.a for his ancestry]. He was baptized at Hanworth, Middlesex 16 July 1608. They had no issue. He died testate 9 July 1677, and was buried at Twickenham, Middlesex. She married (3rd) about 1680 (as his 2nd wife) [Gov.] **PHILIP LUDWELL**, of James City County, Virginia, member of the Council, deputy Secretary of State of Virginia, Governor of North Carolina, and of both North and South Carolina. He was born in 1638. They had no issue. His wife, Frances, was living in July 1690. He returned to England about 1700, and was buried at Stratford le Bow, Middlesex in 1717. *North Carolina Hist. & Gen. Reg.* 2 (1901): 101–103. *VMHB* 20 (1912): 93–94; 68 (1960): 408–428 (letters of Frances Culpeper dated 1670–1671 mentions her cousins, Robert Filmer, cousin Hormansden, cousin Anthony St. Leger, cousin Warham, and an unnamed brother). *Wm & Mary Quarterly* 2nd Ser. 16 (1936): 289–315. Powell *Dict. of North Carolina Biog.* 1 (1979): 470 (biog. of Frances Culpeper). Raimo *Biog. Dict. of American Col. & Revolutionary Govs.* (1980): 284 (biog. of Samuel Stephens), 289 (biog. of Philip Ludwell), 419–420 (biog. of Philip Ludwell), 472–473 (biog. of Sir William Berkeley). *Gens. of Virginia Fams. from VMHB* 2 (1981): 488–516. Kneebone *Dict. of Virginia Biog.* 1 (1998): 450–451 (biog. of Frances Culpeper Stephens Berkeley), 454–458 (biog. of Sir William Berkeley). Dorman *Adventurers of Purse & Person* 3 (2007): 103–113, 246–248. Grizzard & Smith *Jamestown Colony: a Political, Social, & Cultural Hist.* (2007): 25–26 (biog. of Lady Frances Berkeley), 27–30 (biog. of Sir William Berkeley).

b. [**Capt.**] **ALEXANDER CULPEPER**, Esq., of Leeds Castle and Hollingbourne, Kent, son and heir. He was a legatee in the 1645 will of his great-uncle, Alexander Culpeper. In 1658 he was appointed administrator of the estate of his mother. He served as secretary to his cousin, Thomas Culpeper, 2nd Lord Culpeper. He was commander of Cowes Castle and Vice-Admiral's Deputy in the Isle of Wight, 1664–66. In 1666 he and his cousin, Cheyney Culpeper, purchased the manor of Newport, Hampshire from Levinus Bennett, Knt. He went to Virginia before June 1671. On his return to England, he was granted the office of Surveyor General of Virginia 25 October 1671. He subsequently remained in England. He served as administrator of the estate of his brother-in-law, Gov. William Berkeley, in 1677. He was removed from office as Sureveyor-General in 1694. [Capt.] ALEXANDER CULPEPER was buried at Broomfield, Kent 26 Dec. 1694. He left a will dated 29 Nov. 1691, proved 5 Jan. 1694/5 (P.C.C. 3 Irby). VCH *Hampshire* 5 (1912): 253–265. *Gens. of Virginia Fams. from VMHB* 2 (1981): 488–516. Dorman *Adventurers of Purse & Person* 3 (2007): 103–113.

c. [**Mr.**] **JOHN CULPEPER**, Gent., born about 1644 (aged 31 in 1675), merchant-planter, Surveyor General of South Carolina, member of Parliament in South Carolina, younger son. He was appointed administrator of the estate of his brother-in-law, Samuel Stephens', in North Carolina in 1670. He later resided in Albemarle County, North Carolina, where he participated in Culpeper's Rebellion. He was tried for treason in England in 1679, of which charges he was subsequently acquitted. He married (1st) **JUDITH** _____, who was living Dec. 1671. He married (2nd) before March 1680 **MARGARET** _____, widow of [Capt.] Valentine Byrd (died c.1679), of Albemarle County, North Carolina. In 1681 she sued Phillip Langdon in Suffolk County, Massachusetts regarding the transportation of a female from South Carolina. He married (3rd) 23 May 1688 **SARAH MAYO**, daughter of Edward Mayo, Esq., of Barbadoes, Charlestown, South Carolina, and Perquimans County, North Carolina, by his 1st wife, Sarah, daughter of George Magges. Sarah was a legatee in the 1677 will of her grandfather, George Magges, of Barbadoes. They had one daughter, Sarah Culpeper (wife of Benjamin Pritchard). JOHN CULPEPER, Gent., was living 11 June 1691, and died testate in Albemarle County, North Carolina before Feb. 1693/4. His widow, Sarah, married (2nd) before 6 June 1694 (as his 2nd wife) [**Mr.**] **PATRICK HENLEY**, of Albemarle County, North Carolina and Philadelphia, Pennsylvania. They had one son, John, and two daughters, Elizabeth (wife of William Evergin) and Anne (wife of William Newby). PATRICK HENLEY died 28 April 1698, and was buried in the Friends' Burying Ground, Philadelphia, Pennsylvania. He left a will dated 24 July 1696, proved in Philadelphia County, Pennsylvania 20 May 1698. His widow, Sarah, married (3rd) at Philadelphia MM (Quaker), Pennsylvania 9 May 1699 **MATTHEW PRITCHARD** (or **PRICHARD**), son of Thomas Pritchard, of Philadelphia, Pennsylvania, cordwainer, by his wife, Barbara. They had one son, Thomas. He was styled "relative" by John Roberts, of Denbigh, Denbighshire, Wales in a letter dated 1710. MATTHEW PRICHARD died at Pasquotank County, North Carolina 26 Dec. 1726, aged about 50 years. Saunders *Colonial Recs. of North Carolina* 1 (1886). Sainsbury *Cal. of State Papers, Colonial Ser., America & West Indies, 1669–1674* (1889). *Colls. South Carolina Hist. Soc.* 5 (1897). *Suffolk Deeds* Liber 10 (1899): ff. 179, 180;180, 181; Liber 11 (1900): ff. 51, 52; 180, 181. *North Carolina Hist. & Gen. Reg.* 2 (1901): 101–103. *National Cyclopædia of Amer. Biog.* 12 (1904):

223 (biog. of John Culpepper). Lloyd *Lloyd M.S.S.* (1912): 355 (letter of John Roberts). Trueblood *Hist. of Trueblood Fam.* (1931): App., III–VI. Hinshaw *Encyclopedia of American Quaker Gen.* 1 (1936): 115, 162; 2 (1938): 444, 547, 628. *Abs. & Index of the Recs. of the Inferior Court of Pleas (Suffolk County Court) 1680–1698* (1940): 114. Hineman *Some of the Anc. & Desc. of Joseph and Naomi (Dicks) Newby* (1962): 91 (will of Patrick Henley). Sirmans *Colonial South Carolina* (1966): 31–32. *North Carolina Hist. Rev.* 45 (1968): 111–127. Parker *North Carolina Higher-Court Recs. 1670–1696* (1968). *North Carolina Gen.* 17 (1971): 2617–2622. Parker *North Carolina Higher-Court Recs. 1697–1701* (1971). Powell *Dict. of North Carolina Biog.* 1 (1979): 470–472 (biog. of John Culpeper). *Gens. of Virginia Fams. from VMHB* 2 (1981): 488–516. *Gens. of Barbadoes Fams.* (1983): 567–569. *Dict. of North Carolina Biog.* 1 (1986): 161–162 (biog. of Valentine Bird), 470–472 (biog. of John Culpeper). Dorman *Adventurers of Purse & Person* 3 (2007): 103–113.

ii. **JOHN CULPEPER**, merchant, baptized at Harrietsham, Kent, 26 October 1606. He was admitted to the Middle Temple in 1621. He married **MARY** _____. He was part owner with his brother, Thomas, of the ship, Thomas and John, in the Virginia trade. In 1651, being then "beyond seas," he claimed a rent charge in England upon the forfeited estate of his 1st cousin, John Culpeper, Lord Culpeper, of Thoresway, then in exile. He is believed to be identical with the John Culpeper who was Sheriff and Clerk of Northumberland County, Virginia, 1671–1674. His widow, Mary, petitioned the Council for an allowance from his estate about 1675. Philipot *Vis. of Kent 1619–21* (H.S.P. 42) (1898): 61–63 (Colepeper ped.: "John [Colepeper]."). *Gens. of Virginia Fams. from VMHB* 2 (1981): 488–516.

ꙮ DACRE ꙮ

ALICE OF NORMANDY (sister of King William the Conqueror), married **LAMBERT**, Count of Lens.
JUDITH OF LENS, married **WALTHEOF**, Earl of Northumberland.
ALICE OF NORTHUMBERLAND, married **RALPH DE TONY**, of Flamstead, Hertfordshire.
ROGER DE TONY, of Flamstead, Hertfordshire, married **IDA OF HAINAULT**.
RALPH DE TONY, of Flamstead, Hertfordshire, married **MARGARET OF LEICESTER**.
IDA DE TONY, married **ROGER LE BIGOD**, Knt., Earl of Norfolk.
MARY LE BIGOD, married **RANULPH FITZ ROBERT**, of Middleham, Yorkshire.
RALPH FITZ RANULPH, Knt., of Middleham, Yorkshire, married **ANASTASIA DE PERCY**.
MARY FITZ RANULPH, married **ROBERT DE NEVILLE**, of Middleham, Yorkshire.
RANULPH DE NEVILLE, Knt., 1st Lord Neville of Raby, married **EUPHAME DE CLAVERING**.
RALPH DE NEVILLE, Knt., 2nd Lord Neville of Raby, married **ALICE DE AUDLEY** (desc. King William the Conqueror).
JOHN DE NEVILLE, K.G., 3rd Lord Neville of Raby, married **MAUD DE PERCY** (desc. King William the Conqueror).
RALPH NEVILLE, K.G., 1st Earl of Westmorland, married **MARGARET STAFFORD** (desc. King William the Conqueror) [see NEVILLE 13].

14. PHILIPPE NEVILLE, 3rd daughter, married before 20 July 1399 **THOMAS DACRE**, Knt., 6th Lord Dacre of Gilsland (or Gillesland), of Dacre, Blackhall, Brackenthwaite, Castle Carrock, Farlam, and Kirkoswald, Cumberland, Holbeach, Lincolnshire, Barton, Westmorland, etc., Chief Forester of Inglewood Forest, son and heir of William Dacre, Knt., 5th Lord Dacre of Gilsland, by Joan, illegitimate daughter of William de Douglas, Knt., 1st Earl of Douglas [see GROBY 8.ii.b]. He was born at Naworth Castle, Cumberland 27 October 1387. They had eight sons, John, Knt. (living 1439, dead by c.1454), Thomas, Knt., Randolf, Knt. [1st Lord Dacre of the North], Humphrey, Knt. [2nd Lord Dacre of the North], Ralph, Richard, George, and John, and two daughters, Joan (or Jane) and Margaret (wife of John le Scrope). In 1411 they received a papal indult for a portable altar. He was summoned to Parliament from 1 Dec. 1412 to 26 May 1455, by writs directed *Thome de Dacre de Gillesland*. His wife, Philippe, was a legatee in the 1440 will of her father. In 1447 he and his wife, Philippe, acquired the manor of Ainstable, Cumberland from John Denton. Philippe was living 8 July 1453, but predeceased her husband. SIR THOMAS DACRE, 6th Lord Dacre of Gilsland, died 5 Jan. 1457/8, and was buried in Lanercost Priory, Cumberland.

Brydges *Collins' Peerage of England* 6 (1812): 555–590 (sub Brand, Baroness Dacre). Riddell *Reply* (1828): Appendix III, pp. 6, 8, 10 (Thomas Dacre, 6th Lord Dacre, is styled "kin" to Gavin Douglas, Bishop of Dunkeld [died 1522]).

Rowland *Noble Fam. of Nevill* (1830). Burke *Dict. of the Peerages… Extinct, Dormant & in Abeyance* (1831): 153–155. *Coll. Top. et Gen.* 1 (1834): 302–303, 407; 5 (1838): 317–328. *Wills & Invs.* 1 (Surtees Soc. 2) (1835): 68–74. Surtees *Hist. & Antiqs. of Durham* 4 (1840): 158–163 (Nevill peds.). Tonge *Vis. of Northern Counties 1530* (Surtees Soc. 41) (1863): 28–29 (Neville ped.: "Philip [Neville], maried to the Lord Dacres"). Towneley *Abs. of IPM* 2 (Chetham Soc. 99) (1876): 65–66. Howard *Selections from Household Books of the Lord William Howard* (Surtees Soc. 68) (1878): 365–395, 514–516. Flower *Vis. of Yorkshire 1563–4* (H.S.P. 16) (1881): 83–85 (Dacre ped.: "Thomas Lord Dacres of Gylsland = Phelyppa doughter of Raff Nevell Earl of Westmerland"). *Genealogist* n.s. 3 (1886): 31–35, 107–111 (Neville ped.: "Philippam, dominam de Dacre"). *Papal Regs.: Letters* 6 (1904): 338. Parker "Cal. of Feet of Fines for Cumberland" in *Trans. Cumberland & Westmorland Antiq. Soc.* n.s. 7 (1907): 247–249. Clay *Extinct & Dormant Peerages* (1913): 36–39 (sub Dacre). VCH *Lancaster* 8 (1914): 120–121, 142. *C.P.* 4 (1916): 7–8, 18 (sub Dacre); 11 (1949): 568–569 (sub Scrope). Harvey et al. *Vis. of the North* 3 (Surtees Soc. 144) (1930): 23–32 (Neville ped.: "Philippa [Neville] nupta domino Dacre Thomas nomine"). *Bull. John Rylands Lib.* 40 (1957–8): 79–113, 391–431. Paget *Baronage of England* (1957) 164: 1–2 (sub Dacre). *Bull. Inst. Hist. Research* 41 (1968): 95–99. *Ancient Deeds — Ser. B* 2 (List & Index Soc. 101) (1974): B.6435. *Cal. IPM* 17 (1988): 515–517. Winchester *John Denton's Hist. of Cumberland* (Surtees Soc. 213) (2010): 86–87, 114.

Children of Philippe Neville, by Thomas Dacre, Knt.:

i. **THOMAS DACRE**, Knt., in right of his wife, of Horsford, Burgh St. Margaret's, and Great Hautbois, Norfolk, Benacre, South Cove, and Wrentham, Suffolk, Hurstpierpoint and Westmeston, Sussex, etc., son and heir apparent. He married before 1427 (date of presentment) **ELIZABETH BOWET**, daughter and co-heiress of William Bowet, Knt., of Wrentham, Benacre, and Henstead, Suffolk, Horsford, Burgh St. Margaret's and Great Hautbois, Norfolk, Hurstpierpoint and Westmeston, Sussex, etc., by his 1st wife, Joan, daughter and co-heiress of Robert de Ufford, Knt. [see CLAVERING 11 for her ancestry]. They had two daughters, Joan and Philippe (wife of Robert Fiennes, Knt.). He and the Convent presented to the church of Blythburgh, Suffolk in 1427 and 1431. He presented to the churches of Benacre, Suffolk, 1434, 1453; Westmeston, Sussex, 1439, 1444; and Hurstpierpoint, Sussex, 1440, 1441. In 1435 he contracted to give military service for life to Richard Neville, Earl of Salisbury. His wife, Elizabeth, was living in 1447–8. SIR THOMAS DACRE was living in 1453 (date of presentment), but died before 5 Jan. 1457/8. Blomefield *Essay towards a Top. Hist. of Norfolk* 5 (1775): 1356–1357; 11 (1810): 153. Brydges *Collins' Peerage of England* 6 (1812): 555–590 (sub Brand, Baroness Dacre). Dugdale *Monasticon Anglicanum* 3 (1826): 636–637 (Horsham Priory Founders Gen.: "… Et dictus Robertus Ufford maritatus fuit Elionoræ filæ Thomæ Felton militis, qui genuit Elam, Sibillam, et Joannam filias,… et prædicta Johanna nupta Willielmo Bowes armigero,… qui genuit ex ea filiam, nuptam domino Dacres, et genuit ex filiam nomine Johannam quæ nupta fuit Ricardo Fines militi, camerario domini regis Edwardi quarti"). Burke *Dict. of the Peerages… Extinct, Dormant & in Abeyance* (1831): 153–155. *Coll. Top. et Gen.* 1 (1834): 302–303 ("Thomas, Lord Dacre, wedded Elizabeth, the daughter of Sir William Bowett"), 407; 5 (1838): 317–328; 7 (1841): 197–202. Suckling *Hist. & Antiqs. of Suffolk* 2 (1848): 130, 162. Howard *Selections from Household Books of the Lord William Howard* (Surtees Soc. 68) (1878): 365–395, 514–516. Waters *Chester of Chicheley* 1 (1878): 339–340. Flower *Vis. of Yorkshire 1563–4* (H.S.P. 16) (1881): 83–85 (Dacre ped.: "Sir Thomas Dacres Knyght fyrst son dyed in his father's lyef tyme = Elsabeth doughter to Sir William Bowes"). Glover et al. *Vis. of Cheshire 1580, 1566, 1533 & 1591* (H.S.P. 18) (1882): 85–86 (Clavering ped.: "Elizabeth Bowett vxor Tho. L: Dacres."). Rye *Short Cal. Feet of Fines for Norfolk* 2 (1886): 400, 417, 418. *Norfolk Arch.* 15 (1904): 275–277, 291 (chart). Benolte et al. *Vis. of Sussex 1530 & 1633–4* (H.S.P. 53) (1905): 11–12 (Fynes ped.: "Thomas Dacres. = Ellizebeth d. & heire of Wi'm Blewett."). Deedes *Extracts from the Episcopal Regs. of Richard Paty, S.T.P., Lord Bishop of Chichester* (Sussex Rec. Soc. 4) (1905): 112–113, 118–119, 120–121, 130–131. Copinger *Manors of Suffolk* 2 (1908): 5–7, 42–43. Clay *Extinct & Dormant Peerages* (1913): 36–39 (sub Dacre). VCH *Lancaster* 8 (1914): 120–121, 142. *C.P.* 4 (1916): 7–8 (sub Dacre). Salzman *Feet of Fines Rel. Sussex* 3 (Sussex Rec. Soc. 23) (1916): 262. *Genealogist* n.s. 34 (1918): 166–167. Harvey et al. *Vis. of the North* 3 (Surtees Soc. 144) (1930): 23–32 (Neville ped.: "Dominus Thomas dominus Dacre nupsit Elizabetham filiam domini Willelmi Bowet"). VCH *Sussex* 7 (1940): 172–178. Paget *Baronage of England* (1957) 164: 1–2 (sub Dacre). *Coat of Arms* 6 (1961): 350–355. National Archives, C 1/21/44 & C 1/22/157 (Chancery Proc. dated 1452-4 — Robert Osbern, Esq., of Barking. v. Dame Elizabeth Daker [Dacre], and Henry Inglose, and John Colvyle, Knts., and other feoffees re. profits of the manor of Great Hautbois, Norfolk the dower of petitioner's wife Sibyl, sister of the said Dame Elizabeth (available at www.catalogue.nationalarchives.gov.uk/search.asp). Northamptonshire Rec. Office: Fitzwilliam (Milton) Charters, F(M) Charter/2049 (available at www.a2a.org.uk/search/index.asp).

Child of Thomas Dacre, Knt., by Elizabeth Bowet:

a. **JOAN DACRE**, married **RICHARD FIENNES**, Knt., 7th Lord Dacre of the South [see FIENNES 15].

ii. **HUMPHREY DACRE**, Knt., 2nd Lord Dacre of the North [see next].

iii. **JOAN** (or **JANE**) **DACRE**, married **THOMAS CLIFFORD**, 8th Lord Clifford [see CLIFFORD 15].

15. HUMPHREY DACRE, Knt., Chief Forester of Inglewood Forest, Governor of Carlisle Castle, Warden of the West Marches, younger son. He married **MABEL PARR**, daughter of Thomas Parr, Knt., of Kirkby-Kendal, Westmorland, by Alice, daughter of Thomas Tunstall, Knt. [see PARR 13 for her ancestry]. They had six sons, Thomas, K.G., K.B. [3rd Lord Dacre of the North], Hugh (clerk), Christopher, Philip, Ralph, and Humphrey, and three daughters, Anne (wife of Thomas Strangeways, Knt.), Elizabeth (wife of Richard Huddleston), and Katherine (wife of George Fitz Hugh, K.B., 7th Lord Fitz Hugh, and Thomas Neville, Knt.). He was a legatee in the 1457 will of his uncle, Robert Neville, Bishop of Durham. He and his older brother, Randolf Dacre, Knt. [1st Lord Dacre of the North], fought on the Lancastrian side at the Battle of Towton in 1461, at which battle his brother was killed and the estates and honors of both forfeited. He received a general pardon for all offenses committed by him before 21 June 1468. His brother's attainder was reversed on petition in the Parliament 12–13 Edward IV, whereby he became heir to most of the Dacre estates including Gilsland, although possession was disputed by his niece, Lady Joan Fiennes, the heir general. He was summoned to Parliament from 15 Nov. 1482 to 9 Dec. 1483, by writs directed *Humfrido Dacre de Gillesland'*. He was present at the Coronation of King Richard III in 1483. SIR HUMPHREY DACRE, 2nd Lord Dacre of the North, died 30 May 1485. His widow, Mabel, died testate 14 Nov. 1508. They were buried at Lanercost Priory, Cumberland.

Brydges *Collins' Peerage of England* 6 (1812): 555–590 (sub Brand, Baroness Dacre). Burke *Dict. of the Peerages… Extinct, Dormant & in Abeyance* (1831): 153–155. *Coll. Top. et Gen.* 1 (1834): 302–303, 407–408; 5 (1838): 317–328. *Historiæ Dunelmensis Scriptores Tres* (Surtees Soc. 9) (1839): Appendix, cccxli–cccxliii (will of Robert Neville, Bishop of Durham). *Top. & Gen.* 3 (1858): 352–360. Howard *Selections from Household Books of the Lord William Howard* (Surtees Soc. 68) (1878): 365–395, 514–516. Flower *Vis. of Yorkshire 1563–4* (H.S.P. 16) (1881): 83–85 (Dacre ped.: "Humfrey Dacres 3 son = Izabell doughter of Sir Thomas Parre"). Cooke & St. George *Vis. of Cambridge 1575 & 1619* (H.S.P. 41) (1897): 26–28 (Hudleston ped.). *C.P.R. 1467–1477* (1900): 183 (Humphrey styled "king's kinsman"). *C.P.R. 1476–1485* (1901): 388 (Humphrey Dacre, Knt. styled "king's kinsman" in 1484). VCH *Lancaster* 6 (1911): 162; 8 (1914): 120–121. Clay *Extinct & Dormant Peerages* (1913): 36–39 (sub Dacre), 156–158 (sub Parr). *C.P.* 4 (1916): 18–20 (sub Dacre); 5 (1926): 430–431 (sub FitzHugh), 764–767. Harvey et al. *Vis. of the North* 3 (Surtees Soc. 144) (1930): 23–32 (Neville ped.: "Humfredus dominus Dacre desponsauit filiam Thome a Par militis"), 106–109 (Strangwais ped.). Paget *Baronage of England* (1957) 164: 1–2 (sub Dacre). Winchester *John Denton's Hist. of Cumberland* (Surtees Soc. 213) (2010): 86–87 (MS Cumberland hist. dated early 17th Cent. usually attributed to John Denton states: "Afterwards the Lord Humphrid Dacre, by marrying of Dame Mabell Parr, the daughter of the king's favorite, recovered the Dacres' lands < and right > and kept still Ainstiplighe [Ainstable] by his father's pretended right, & so to his posteritye …").

16. THOMAS DACRE, K.G., K.B., 3rd Lord Dacre of the North, of Gilsland and Greystoke, Cumberland, Lieutenant of the West Marches, son and heir, born 25 Nov. 1467. He married about 1488 **ELIZABETH GREYSTOKE**, *suo jure* Lady Greystoke, daughter and heiress of Robert Greystoke, Knt., by his 1st wife, Elizabeth, daughter of Edmund Grey, Knt., 1st Earl of Kent, 4th Lord Grey of Ruthin [see GREYSTOKE 15 for her ancestry]. She was born and baptized at Morpeth, Northumberland 10 July 1471. They had two sons, William [4th Lord Dacre] and Humphrey, and six daughters, Mary (wife of Francis Talbot, K.G., 5th Earl of Shrewsbury), Anne, Jane (wife of Lord Tailboys), Mabel (wife of Henry Scrope, 7th Lord Scrope of Bolton), Philippe, and Jane (2nd of name). He also had one illegitimate son, Thomas, Knt. He fought at the Siege of Norham Castle in 1494. He was summoned to Parliament from 17 October 1509 to 23 Nov. 1514, by writs directed *Thome Dacres de Dacres*. He was a legatee in the 1509 will of his brother, Hugh Dacre, clerk. He distinguished himself at the head of a troop of horse at Flodden Field in 1513. His wife, Elizabeth, died 13 (or 14) August 1516. SIR THOMAS DACRE, 3rd Lord Dacre of the North, died intestate on the Borders 24 October 1525, by a fall from his horse. They were buried at Lanercost Priory, Cumberland.

Cat. MSS: in the Cottonian Lib. Deposited in the British Museum (1802). Garbet *Hist. of Wem* (1818): 46–50. Dugdale *Monasticon Anglicanum* 5 (1825): 401. Riddell *Reply to the Misstatements of Dr. Hamilton of Bardowie* (1828): Appendix III, pp. 6, 8, 10 (Thomas Dacre, 3rd Lord Dacre of the North, styled "kin" [kyne] to "my Lord of Angus" [Archibald

Douglas, 6th Earl of Angus], cites letter dated 1515 in Cottonian MSS Caligula B. VI. in British Lib.). Burke *Dict. of the Peerages… Extinct, Dormant & in Abeyance* (1831): 153–155. Hodgson *Hist. of Northumberland* 2(2) (1832): 374–379. *Coll. Top. et Gen.* 1 (1834): 302–303; 2 (1835): 160–161 (Greystock ped.: "Elizabeth [Greystock], mar. to [Thomas] Lord Dacre"); 5 (1838): 313–317 (sub Greystoke), 317–328 (sub Dacre of Gillesland). Beltz *Mems. of the Order of the Garter* (1841): clxxi. Ellis *Original Letters Ill. of English Hist.* 3rd Ser. 1 (1846): 287–288 (Thomas [Dacre], Lord Dacre styled "cousin" by John [Stewart], 2nd Duke of Albany in letter dated 1521), 291–292 (letter of Thomas Dacre, Lord Dacre). Green *Lives of the Princesses of England* 4 (1857): 198 (Thomas Dacre, Lord Dacre styled "cousin" by Margaret Tudor, dowager Queen of Scotland in letter dated 1515). *Testamenta Eboracensia* 4 (Surtees Soc. 53) (1869): 20–21 (will of Sir Ralph Greystock). *Yorkshire Arch. & Top. Jour.* 2 (1873): 195–214. Howard *Selections from Household Books of the Lord William Howard* (Surtees Soc. 68) (1878): 365–395, 514–516. Flower *Vis. of Yorkshire 1563–4* (H.S.P. 16) (1881): 83–85 (Dacre ped.: "Thomas Lord Dacre son of Humfrey = Elsabeth Greystock daughter & heyre to Robert Grestock"). *Arch. Aeliana* 24 (1903): 120. *North Country Wills* 1 (Surtees Soc. 116) (1908): 83. *List of Early Chancery Procs.* 4 (PRO Lists and Indexes 29) (1908): 214. VCH *Bedford* 3 (1912): 191–192 (Dacre arms: Gules three scallops argent). Clay *Extinct & Dormant Peerages* (1913): 36–39 (sub Dacre), 95–98 (sub Greystock). VCH *Lancaster* 8 (1914): 120–121. *C.P.* 4 (1916): 20–21 (sub Dacre); 6 (1926): 99–100 (sub Greystoke); 14 (1998): 232. *Letters & Papers… Henry VIII* 1(1) (1920): 170–171. Harvey et al. *Vis. of the North* 3 (Surtees Soc. 144) (1930): 23–32 (Neville ped.: "Thomas lo. Dacre = Elizabeth filia et heres Roberti Domini Greistoke"). Paget *Baronage of England* (1957) 164: 1–2 (sub Dacre). VCH *Yorkshire E.R.* 3 (1976): 164–170.

Child of Thomas Dacre, K.G., K.B., by Elizabeth Greystoke:

i. **ANNE DACRE**, married **CHRISTOPHER CONYERS**, Knt., 2nd Lord Conyers [see CONYERS 19].

✃ DADE ✃

ROGER D'AUBENEY, married **AMICE** _____.
WILLIAM D'AUBENEY, of Buckenham, Norfolk, married **MAUD LE BIGOD**.
WILLIAM D'AUBENEY, of Buckenham, Norfolk, married **ALICE OF LOUVAIN**, Queen of England.
WILLIAM D'AUBENEY, 2nd Earl of Arundel, married **MAUD DE SAINT HILARY**.
WILLIAM D'AUBENEY, Earl of Arundel, married **MABEL OF CHESTER** (desc. King William the Conqueror).
ISABEL D'AUBENEY, married **JOHN FITZ ALAN**, of Clun, Shropshire.
JOHN FITZ ALAN, Knt., of Oswestry, Shropshire, married **MAUD DE VERDUN**.
JOHN FITZ ALAN, of Arundel, Sussex, married **ISABEL DE MORTIMER** (desc. King William the Conqueror).
RICHARD FITZ ALAN, Knt., Earl of Arundel, married **ALICE DI SALUZZO** (desc. King William the Conqueror).
EDMUND DE ARUNDEL, Knt., Earl of Arundel, married **ALICE DE WARENNE**.
RICHARD DE ARUNDEL, Knt., Earl of Arundel and Surrey, married **ISABEL LE DESPENSER** (desc. King William the Conqueror).
EDMUND DE ARUNDEL, Knt., of Chedzoy, Martock, Sutton Montagu, and Thurlbear, Somerset, married **SIBYL DE MONTAGU** (desc. King William the Conqueror).
PHILIPPE ARUNDEL, married **RICHARD SERGEAUX**, Knt., of Colquite, Cornwall.
PHILIPPE SERGEAUX, married **ROBERT PASHLEY**, Knt., of Pashley (in Ticehurst), Sussex [see PASHLEY 14].

15. ANNE PASHLEY, married (1st) **JOHN BASSINGBOURNE**, of Manuden Hall, Essex. They had one son, John. She married (2nd) **EDWARD TYRRELL**, Esq., of Downham, Lancaster (in Hatfield Broad Oak), and Mountnessing, Essex, Harrow on the Hill, Middlesex, etc., Escheator of Essex and Hertfordshire, 1426–7, Sheriff of Essex and Hertfordshire, 1436–7, Knight of the Shire for Essex, 1427, 1432, 1435, younger son of Walter Tyrrell, of Avon, Hampshire, by Eleanor, daughter and heiress of Edmund Flambard, of Shepreth, Cambridgeshire. They had one son, Edward, and two daughters, Philippe and Margaret. EDWARD TYRRELL, Esq., died 17 Dec. 1442, and was buried in the Church of the Franciscans at Chelmsford, Essex. He left a will dated 1 October 1442, codicil dated 9 Dec. 1442.

Brydges *Collins' Peerage of England* 2 (1812): 538. Burke *Royal Descents & Peds. of Founders' Kin* (1864): 105 (ped.). Mundy et al. *Vis. of Nottingham 1569 & 1614* (H.S.P. 4) (1871): 161 (1614 Vis.). *Trans. Shropshire Arch. & Nat. Hist. Soc.* 5 (1882): 139. *List of Sheriffs for England & Wales* (PRO Lists and Indexes 9) (1898): 44. Muskett *Suffolk Manorial Fams.* 2

(1908): 268. Copinger *Manors of Suffolk* 3 (1909): 239. Chichele *Reg. of Henry Chichele* 2 (Canterbury & York Soc. 42) (1937): 628–636, 679 (biog. of Edward Tyrell). *Genealogists' Mag.* 11 (1954): 541–543. *NEHGR* 109 (1955): 31. McFarlane *England in the Fifteenth Cent.* (1981): 164, footnote 51. Roskell *House of Commons 1386–1421* 3 (1992): 323–324 (biog. of Sir Nicholas Haute); 4 (1992): 683–686 (biog. of John Tyrell).

16. PHILIPPE TYRRELL. She was a legatee in the 1442 will of her father. She was co-heiress after 1442 to her brother, Edward Tyrrell. She married before 1446–7 (date of fine) **THOMAS CORNWALLIS**, Esq., of Brome, Suffolk, Basildon, Essex, and London, Knight of the Shire for Suffolk, son and heir of John Cornwallis, of Brome and Oakley, Suffolk, by Philippe, daughter and co-heiress of Robert Bucton, Esq. He was born about 1421 (did homage for lands in 1441/2). They had four sons, John, Esq., Edward, Esq., Robert, and William, Esq., and one daughter, Katherine (wife of Francis or Thomas Froxmere). In 1479 he was suing a bargeman of London for the "Crane Wharf Dock" in the Vintry. THOMAS CORNWALLIS, Esq., died 26 May 1484.

Brydges *Collins' Peerage of England* 2 (1812): 538. Mundy et al. *Vis. of Nottingham 1569 & 1614* (H.S.P. 4) (1871): 161–162 (Cornwallis ped.: "Thomas Cornwallis of Brome in Com. Suff. = Phillip d. & coheire of Edward Tirrell of Downham in Com. Essex"). Harvey et al. *Vis. of Suffolk 1561, 1577 & 1612* (1882): 21 (Cornwallys ped.: "Thomas Cornwallys of Brome, co. Suff., Esq., son and heir to John Cornwallys, mar. Philippe, da. and one of the heirs of Edward Tyrrell of Downham, co. Essex, Esq."). *Trans. Shropshire Arch. & Nat. Hist. Soc.* 5 (1882): 139. *Gen. Memoranda Rel. Fam. of Dade* (1888): [n.p.]. Rye *Pedes Finium or Fines Rel. Cambridge* (1891): 153. Muskett *Suffolk Manorial Fams.* 2 (1908): 268. Copinger *Manors of Suffolk* 3 (1909): 239. *VMHB* 28 (1920): 375–392. Wedgwood *Hist. of Parl.* 1 (1936): 225 (biog. of Thomas Cornwallis). Harvey *Vis. of Suffolk 1561* 1 (H.S.P. n.s. 2) (1981): 147–153 (Cornwallis ped.).

17. WILLIAM CORNWALLIS, Esq., of Brome and Oakley, Suffolk, London, Bedfordshire, and Norfolk, Justice of the Peace for Suffolk, 4th son, born about 1470 (aged 40 in 1510). He married **ELIZABETH STANFORD** (or **STAMFORD**), daughter and co-heiress of John Stanford, Esq., of Stagsden, Bedfordshire and Banks (in Wimpole), Cambridgeshire, by Joan, daughter and heiress of John Butler (or Boteler), of Meppershall, Bedfordshire. They had five sons, John, Knt., Thomas (clerk), Edward, William, and Francis, and six daughters, Elizabeth (wife of William Singleton), Affra, Dorothy (wife of John Head), Katherine (nun at Elstow Abbey), Prudence (wife of _____ Roydon), and Edith (wife of William Barwike). He was heir in 1510 to his older brother, Edward Cornwallys, Esq. WILLIAM CORNWALLIS, Esq., died 20 Nov. 1519, and was buried in the chancel in St. Nicholas's, Oakley, Suffolk. He left a will proved 29 Nov. 1519 (P.C.C. 24 Ayloffe). His widow, Elizabeth, died testate 1 April 1537, and was buried in the chancel at Thrandeston, Suffolk.

Brydges *Collins' Peerage of England* 2 (1812): 540–542. *East Anglian* 1 (1864): 396–398, 417. Mundy et al. *Vis. of Nottingham 1569 & 1614* (H.S.P. 4) (1871): 161–162 (Cornwallis ped.: "William Cornwallis of Brome = Elizebeth d. & coheire of John Staunford"). Harvey et al. *Vis. of Suffolk 1561, 1577 & 1612* (1882): 21 (Cornwallys ped.: "William Cornwallys of Brome, co. Suff., Esq., fourth son and heir to Thomas Cornwallys, mar. Eliza, da. and one of the heirs of John Stamford, Esq."). Muskett *Suffolk Manorial Fams.* 2 (1908): 268. VCH *Bedford* 2 (1908): 289. Copinger *Manors of Suffolk* 3 (1909): 241. *VMHB* 28 (1920): 375–392. VCH *Cambridge* 5 (1973): 267. Harvey *Vis. of Suffolk 1561* 1 (H.S.P. n.s. 2) (1981): 147–153 (Cornwallis ped.).

Children of William Cornwallis, Esq., by Elizabeth Stanford:

i. **JOHN CORNWALLIS**, Knt. [see next].

ii. **AFFRA CORNWALLIS**, married **ANTHONY AUCHER**, Knt., of Bishopsbourne, Kent [see LOVELACE 18].

18. JOHN CORNWALLIS, Knt., of Brome, Suffolk, son and heir, Steward of the Household to Edward Tudor, Prince of Wales (later King Edward VI). He married **MARY SULLIARD**, daughter of Edward Sulliard (or Sulyard), Esq., of London and Otes (in High Laver), Essex, by his 2nd wife, Anne, daughter of John Norris, of Bray, Lancashire. They had four sons, Thomas, Knt., Henry, Esq., Richard, Esq., and William, and three daughters, Elizabeth, Anne (wife of Thomas

Kent), and Mary (wife of William Halse and Roger Warren). SIR JOHN CORNWALLIS died at Ashridge, Buckinghamshire 23 April 1544, and was buried at Berkhamstead, Hertfordshire, with a monument in the chancel at Brome, Suffolk. He left a will proved 9 July 1544 (P.C.C. 11 Pynnyng).

> Brydges *Collins' Peerage of England* 2 (1812): 542–544. *East Anglian* 1 (1864): 396–398, 417. Mundy et al. *Vis. of Nottingham 1569 & 1614* (H.S.P. 4) (1871): 161–162 (Cornwallis ped.: "Sʳ John Cornwallis of Brome Knt. = Mary d. of Edward Sulliard of Ottes in Com. Essex"). *Genealogist* 4 (1880): 226–234 (Sulyard ped.). Harvey et al. *Vis. of Suffolk 1561, 1577 & 1612* (1882): 21 (Cornwallys ped.: "Sir John Cornwallys, of Brome, co. Suff., Kt., son and heir of William, mar. Mary, da. of Edward Sulyard of Otes, co. Essex, Esq."). *Gen. Memoranda Rel. Fam. of Dade* (1888): [n.p.]. Muskett *Suffolk Manorial Fams.* 2 (1908): 268. Copinger *Manors of Suffolk* 3 (1909): 242–243. Throckmorton *Gen. & Hist. Account of the Throckmorton Fam.* (1930): 202. *NEHGR* 98 (1944): 271–278. Harvey *Vis. of Suffolk 1561* 1 (H.S.P. n.s. 2) (1981): 147–153 (Cornwallis ped.).

Children of John Cornwallis, Knt., by Mary Sulliard:

i. **RICHARD CORNWALLIS**, Esq. [see next].

ii. **ELIZABETH CORNWALLIS**, married **JOHN BLENNERHASSET**, Esq., of Barsham by Beccles, Suffolk [see THROCKMORTON 19].

19. RICHARD CORNWALLIS, Esq., of Shotley and Okenhill Hall (in Badingham), Suffolk, 3rd son. He married **MARGARET LOUTHE**, daughter and heiress of Lionel Louthe, of Sawtrey Beaumes, Huntingdonshire, and Cretingham, Suffolk, by Elizabeth, daughter of Thomas Blennerhasset, Knt., of Frenze, Suffolk. She was born about 1529 (aged 4 in 1533). They had two sons, Thomas and John, and five daughters, including Anne. RICHARD CORNWALLIS, Esq., is said to have died before 1581. His widow, Margaret, then of Tannington, Suffolk, left a will proved in 1603, and was buried at Cretingham, Suffolk.

> Brydges *Collins' Peerage of England* 2 (1812): 543. Charles *Vis. of Huntingdon 1613* (Camden Soc. 43) (1849): 11 (Louthe ped.: "Margareta Louthe, consanguinea et hæres de Thomæ Louthe armigeri, in forma præd'c'a, æt. 4 annor' et amplius 26 H. 8."). Nichols ed. *Narrative of the Days of the Reformation* (Camden Soc. 77) (1859): 1–59. *East Anglian* 1 (1864): 396–398, 417. Mundy et al. *Vis. of Nottingham 1569 & 1614* (H.S.P. 4) (1871): 161–162 (Cornwallis ped.: "Richard Cornwallis of Arowton in Com. Suff. = Margerett d. & sole heire of Lionell Lowth of Sawtrey in Com. Lincon"). *Gen. Memoranda Rel. Fam. of Dade* (1888): [n.p.]. Wedgwood *Hist. of Parl.* 1 (1936): 557 (biog. of Thomas Lowth). *VCH Huntingdon* 3 (1936): 206–207 (Louthe arms: Sable, a leaping wolf argent with a crescent argent in the quarter for a difference). Harvey *Vis. of Suffolk 1561* 1 (H.S.P. n.s. 2) (1981): 147–153 (Cornwallis ped.); 2 (H.S.P. n.s. 3) (1981): 354–361 (Blennerhasset ped.).

20. ANNE CORNWALLIS, married about 1575 (as his 1st wife) **THOMAS DADE**, Gent., of Tannington, Suffolk, son and heir of William Dade, Gent., of Witton, Norfolk, by Margery, daughter and heiress of Nicholas Godbold, Gent., of Badingham, Suffolk. He was born about 1556. They had four sons, William, Esq., Thomas, Henry, Esq., and John, and six daughters, Audrey (wife of Nicholas Garneys, Gent.), Anne, Frances, Margaret (wife of John Fox), Elizabeth (wife of Thomas Fletcher, Gent.), and Ellen. His wife, Anne, died 2 May 1612, and was buried at Tannington, Suffolk. He married (2nd) **ANNE HASELOP**, daughter of Thomas Haselop, of Trumpington, Cambridgeshire. They had one son, Thomas, and three daughters, Anne, Frances, and Margery (wife of George Harrison, Gent.). THOMAS DADE, Gent., died at Tannington, Suffolk 13 April 1619, and was buried there in the chancel. He left a will proved in 1619 (P.C.C. 80 Parker).

> Mundy et al. *Vis. of Nottingham 1569 & 1614* (H.S.P. 4) (1871): 161–162 (Cornwallis ped.: "Anne [Cornwallis] ux. Thomas Dade of Tanington in Suff."). *Gen. Memoranda Rel. Fam. of Dade* (1888): [n.p.] (Dade arms: Gules, a chevron between three garbs or, in chief a crescent sable for difference). Byshhe *Vis. of Suffolk 1664–1668* (H.S.P. 61) (1910): 96 (1664 Vis.). *Heraldry of Suffolk Churches* 31 (n.d.): 12–15 (shield on effigy in chancel of Tannington, Suffolk displays Dade arms impaling quarterly of six: (1) Cornwallis [Sable gutty Argent on a fess Argent three Cornish cloughs proper], (2) Buckton, (3) Braham, (4) Tye, (5) Tyrell [Argent two chevrons Azure a bordure engrailed Gules], and (6) Stanford [Azure a chevron between three seapies Argent]).

21. WILLIAM DADE, Esq., of Tannington and Ipswich, Suffolk, son and heir, born about 1580. He married (1st) in 1612 **MARY WINGFIELD**, daughter of Henry Wingfield, of Crowfield, Suffolk, by Elizabeth, daughter of Thomas Risby [see HANKFORD 15 for her ancestry]. They had seven sons, Thomas, Esq., William, Henry, Robert, Gent., Anthony, [Maj.] Francis, and Charles, and six daughters, Elizabeth, Mary (wife of John Soanes), Anne (wife of John Vere, Gent., and George Gosnell), Frances (wife of Samuel Aldus), Martha (wife of John Glanville, Gent.), and Audrey (wife of Robert Neale). His wife, Mary, died at Tannington, Suffolk 3 Feb. 1624/5. He married (2nd) **ELIZABETH REVETT**, widow of Robert Armiger, of Freston, and daughter of John Revett, Esq., of Brandeston, Suffolk. They had one daughter, Joan. His wife, Elizabeth, died at Tannington, Suffolk 24 Feb. 1656/7. WILLIAM DADE, Esq., died 22 Feb. 1659/60, and was buried at Tannington, Suffolk with both of his wives. He left a will proved 26 April 1660 (P.C.C. 35 Nabbs).

> Charles *Vis. of Huntingdon 1613* (Camden Soc. 43) (1849): 125–128 (Wingfield ped.: "Mary [Wingfield], wiffe of Wm. Dade, sonne and heire of Tho. Dade of Tannington in Suff. Esq."). *Gen. Memoranda Rel. Fam. of Dade* (1888): [n.p.] (identification of children). Harvey et al. *Vis. of Norfolk 1563 & 1613* (H.S.P. 32) (1891): 312–318 (Wingfield ped.: "Mary [Wingfield] ux. William Dade of Tanington in co. Suffolk; she died 3 Feb. 1624."). *Procs. Suffolk Institute of Arch. & Natural Hist.* 7 (1891): 57–68 (Wingfield peds.). Byssshe *Vis. of Suffolk 1664–1668* (H.S.P. 61) (1910): 96 (1664 Vis.). NEHGR 107 (1953): 269 (Dade arms). Dorman *Adventurers of Purse & Person* 1 (2004): 217–225. *Heraldry of Suffolk Churches* 31 (n.d.): 12–15.

22. [Major] FRANCIS DADE, born about 1622. He immigrated to Virginia, where he settled at Patomak in Westmoreland County. He married in 1652 **BEHEATHLAND BERNARD**, daughter of [Capt.] Thomas Bernard, by Mary, daughter of Robert Beheathland. They had one son, Francis, and one daughter, Mary (wife of [Capt.] Robert Massey and [Col.] Rice Hooe). He served as a member of House of Burgesses from Warwick County and as Speaker of the House of Burgesses, 1658 (under alias as John Smith). [Major] FRANCIS DADE died on a return voyage from England in 1662/3. He left a nuncupative will proved 1 May 1663. His widow, Beheathland, married (2nd) [Major] **ANDREW GILSON**, of Lancaster, Rappahannock, and Stafford Counties, Virginia. They had issue. She left a will dated 20 August 1716, proved 3 March 1720/1.

> Hayden *Virginia Gens.* (1891): 731–733 (cites Provincial Court of Maryland, Lib. B.B., fol. 44). *VMHB* 11 (1903): 363. Withington *Virginia Gleanings in England* (1980): 56. Dorman *Adventurers of Purse & Person* 1 (2004): 217–225.

✢ DAGWORTH ✢

ALICE OF NORMANDY (sister of King William the Conqueror), married **LAMBERT**, Count of Lens.
JUDITH OF LENS, married **WALTHEOF**, Earl of Northumberland.
MAUD OF NORTHUMBERLAND, married **SIMON DE SENLIS**, Earl of Huntingdon and Northampton.
MAUD DE SENLIS, married **SAHER DE QUINCY**, of Long Buckby, Northamptonshire.
ALICE DE SENLIS, married **ROGER DE HUNTINGFIELD**, of Huntingfield, Suffolk.
WILLIAM DE HUNTINGFIELD, Knt., of Huntingfield, Suffolk, married **ISABEL FITZ WILLIAM** [see HUNTINGFIELD 6].

7. ISABEL DE HUNTINGFIELD, married before 1221 **RICHARD DE DAGWORTH**, of Dagworth, Suffolk, Doddinghurst, Essex, etc., son and heir of Osbert Fitz Hervey, of Dagworth and Leyland, Suffolk, by Margaret (or Margery), daughter of William Fitz Roscelin, of Linstead, Suffolk. He was a minor at his father's death in 1205. They had two sons, Osbert and William (clerk) [Parson of Bradwell]. Sometime in the 1220s, as "Ricardus de Dagwrthe filius Margerie de Rye," he confirmed the grant of a mill in Walpole, Suffolk made to Sibton Abbey made by his uncle, William son of William Fitz Roscelin. In 1227–8 he was a party to a fine concerning Dagworth (in Old Newton), Suffolk. RICHARD DE DAGWORTH was dead before 16 October 1234. His widow, Isabel, died 15 Sept. 1262.

Rye *Cal. Feet of Fines for Suffolk* (1900): 27. *C.P.* 4 (1916): 27, footnote e. Paget *Baronage of England* (1957) 165: 1–4 (sub Dagworth), 299: 1–5 (sub Huntingfield). Brown *Sibton Abbey Cartularies* 1 (Suffolk Charters 7) (1985): 90–92; 2 (Suffolk Charters 8) (1986): 123–124 (charter of Richard de Dagworth dated 1220s); 3 (Suffolk Charters 9) (1987): 190. National Archives, E210/153 (available at www.catalogue.nationalarchives.gov.uk/search.asp).

8. OSBERT DE DAGWORTH, of Dagworth (in Old Newton) and Thrandeston, Suffolk, and Bradwell juxta Coggeshall, Essex, son and heir. He married **HAWISE** _____. They had one son, John. He fought in Gascony in 1253 and in Wales in 1257. In 1254 he was granted the right to hold a weekly market and yearly fair at Bradwell juxta Coggeshall, Essex, as well as free warren in all his demesne lands in Dagworth and Thrandeston, Suffolk. He and his brother, William, witnessed an undated conveyance from John de Frampton to Roger de Huntingfield, rector of Frampton, of a messuage and land in Frampton, Lincolnshire. At an unknown date, he granted to the monks of St. Mary of Mendham, Suffolk a certain Roger Cokerel, of Thrandeston, Suffolk, with all his family, together with the tenement which the said Roger held of him in Thrandeston. OSBERT DE DAGWORTH died shortly before 15 July 1260. His widow, Hawise, was living 17 Nov. 1260.

Morant *Hist. & Antiqs. of Essex* 2 (1768): 155. Blomefield *Essay towards a Top. Hist. of Norfolk* 6 (1807): 383–385. Francisque-Michel *Rôles Gascons* 1 (1885): 322, 337. *C.P.R. 1247–1258* (1908): 278, 289. Copinger *Manors of Suffolk* 6 (1910): 162–164. *C.P.* 4 (1916): 27, footnote e. Paget *Baronage of England* (1957) 165: 1–4 (sub Dagworth). Brown *Sibton Abbey Cartularies* 1 (Suffolk Charters 7) (1985): 90–92. Lincolnshire Archives: MSS of the Earl of Ancaster, Huntingfield Cartulary, 3ANC2/1 (available at www.a2a.org.uk/search/index.asp). Suffolk Rec. Office, Ipswich Branch: Iveagh (Phillipps) Suffolk MSS, HD 1538/301/15 — charter of Osbert de Dagworth to the monks of St. Mary of Mendham, Suffolk (available at www.a2a.org.uk/search/index.asp).

9. JOHN DE DAGWORTH, of Dagworth (in Old Newton), Suffolk, son and heir, born about 1251 (aged 9 in 1260). He married about 1275 **MAUD DE L'ESCHEKER**, eldest daughter of Laurence de l'Escheker (or de Scaccario), of Twinsted, Essex, Exchequers (in Stokenchurch), Buckinghamshire, and Abbefeld (in Aston Rowant), Oxfordshire, Usher of the Exchequer, Marshal of the Eyre, Sheriff of Essex and Hertfordshire, 1275–8, by his wife, Gunnor. She was born about 1251, and was sister and co-heiress to Simon de l'Escheker, by which she inherited the office of Usher of the Exchequer, and one third interest in the Marshalsy of the Eyre and the manors of Exchequers and Dagworth in Pebmarsh. They had one son, John, Knt., and one daughter, Hawise (wife of Reginald de Herlison, of Essex). In 1275–6 he arraigned an assize of novel disseisin against Walter de Fanacourt and others touching a tenement in Walton, Trimley, Croxton, and Alteston, Suffolk. JOHN DE DAGWORTH died 17 October 1290. In 1304–5 his widow, Maud, was given license to grant the one third part of the bailiwick of the Usher of the Exchequer to her son and heir, John de Dagworth. Maud died shortly before 8 May 1308.

Morant *Hist. & Antiqs. of Essex* 2 (1768): 155, 261–262, 270–271. Blomefield *Essay towards a Top. Hist. of Norfolk* 6 (1807): 383–385. Palgrave *Antient Kalendars & Inventories of the Treasury of His Majesty's Exchequer* 1 (1836): 79. Banks *Baronies in Fee* 1 (1844): 175–176 (sub Dagworth). *Annual Rpt. of the Deputy Keeper* 45 (1885): 348. Hardy & Page *Cal. to Feet of Fines for London & Middlesex* 1 (1892): 74. *C.P.R. 1301–1307* (1898): 219. *List of Sheriffs for England & Wales* (PRO Lists and Indexes 9) (1898): 43. Rye *Cal. Feet of Fines for Suffolk* (1900): 60. *C.P.R. 1317–1321* (1903): 63. *Feudal Aids* 3 (1904): 50. Copinger *Manors of Suffolk* 6 (1910): 162–164. *C.P.* 4 (1916): 27, footnote e. *Cambridge Hist. Jour.* 1 (1924): 126–137. VCH *Buckingham* 3 (1925): 43, 98. Moor *Knights of Edward I* 1 (H.S.P. 80) (1929): 215. Salter *Boarstall Cartulary* (Oxford Hist. Soc. 1st Ser. 88) (1930): 304. Jenkinson & Fermoy *Select Cases in the Exchequer of Pleas* (Selden Soc. 48) (1932): 132. Paget *Baronage of England* (1957) 165: 1–4 (sub Dagworth). Cam *Liberties & Communities in Medieval England* (1963). VCH *Oxford* 8 (1964): 105. Davies *Baronial Opposition to Edward II* (1967): 51–52. Keene & Harding *Hist. Gazetteer of London before the Great Fire* (1987): 805-810 (will of Reginald de Herlison).

10. JOHN DE DAGWORTH, Knt., of Dagworth (in Old Newton) and Thrandeston, Suffolk, and Bradwell juxta Coggeshall and Elmdon, Essex, Usher of the Exchequer, Marshal of the Eyre, son and heir, born 25 April 1276. He married after 4 July 1292 **ALICE FITZ WARIN**, daughter and co-heiress of William Fitz Warin, of Elmdon and Whatley (in Rayleigh), Essex, Gentleman of the Bedchamber to King Edward I, by Alice, daughter and co-heiress of John Hardel, Knt. She was born about 1285 (aged 30 in 1315). They had two sons, Nicholas, Esq., and Thomas, Knt. [Lord Dagworth]. In 1309 he owed a debt of 9 marks to William Trente. In 1312–13 Alan son of Robert de Heythe granted him 22*d*. rent in Dagworth and Old Newton, Suffolk. In 1313 he confirmed a grant made by his uncle, Simon de l'Escheker, to John Dymmok of a moiety of the serjeantry of the ushership of the Exchequer. In 1313 he owed a debt of £25 to Anthony Usumaris, merchant of Genoa. In August 1320 he was pardoned for acquiring in fee without license a third part of the ushership of the Exchequer from his 1st cousin, Hamo Peverel. About 1320 he and his aunt, Lora Peyforer, petitioned King and council stating that they held the office of Usher of the Exchequer, together with that of crier of Common Bench and marshal of all the eyres of England; they claimed this office before the justices in the last eyre at the Tower of London, but the mayor and aldermen of London had the office without profits, while the justices' marshals took the fees. About 1321/5 he acquired the interests of the other de l'Escheker co-heirs to the office of Marshal of the Eyre. In 1325 he owed a debt of £20 to Walter de Beauchamp. SIR JOHN DE DAGWORTH died 27 July 1332. His widow, Alice, died 15 May 1333.

> Morant *Hist. & Antiqs. of Essex* 1 (1768): 276–277; 2 (1768): 155, 190, 261–262, 598. Blomefield *Essay towards a Top. Hist. of Norfolk* 6 (1807): 383–385. Palgrave *Antient Kalendars & Inventories of the Treasury of His Majesty's Exchequer* 1 (1836): 79. Palgrave *Docs. & Recs. Ill. the Hist. of Scotland* 1 (1837): 266, 272. Banks *Baronies in Fee* 1 (1844): 175–176 (sub Dagworth). D'Ewes *Autobiography & Correspondence of Sir Simonds D'Ewes* 1 (1845): 326–346. Hardy & Page *Cal. to Feet of Fines for London & Middlesex* 1 (1892): 74. *C.P.R. 1317–1321* (1903): 63, 495. *Feudal Aids* 5 (1908): 34. Copinger *Manors of Suffolk* 6 (1910): 162–164. *Feet of Fines for Essex* 2 (1913–28): 33, 122, 231. *C.P.* 4 (1916): 27. *Cambridge Hist. Jour.* 1 (1924): 126–137. *Year Books of Edward II* 23 (Selden Soc. 65) (1950): 92–93. *Norfolk Arch.* 30 (1952): 263–286. Paget *Baronage of England* (1957) 165: 1–4 (sub Dagworth). Cam *Liberties & Communities in Medieval England* (1963). Davies *Baronial Opposition to Edward II* (1967): 51–52. *Norfolk Arch.* 34 (1967): 111–118. Sutherland *Eyre of Northamptonshire* 1 (Selden Soc. 97) (1983): xii, xlviii–xlix, 24–27 (John de Dagworth, Knt. styled "kinsman and heir" of Lora, widow of William de Pyferer). National Archives, C 131/1/57; C 131/2/23; C 131/171/3E; C 143/325/17; C 241/70/133; C 241/96/43; E 210/8696; SC 8/8/381 (available at www.catalogue.nationalarchives.gov.uk/search.asp).

Children of John de Dagworth, Knt., by Alice Fitz Warin:

i. **NICHOLAS DE DAGWORTH**, Esq., of Dagworth (in Old Newton), Suffolk, Bradwell juxta Coggeshall and Elmdon, Essex, etc., son and heir, born about 1306 (aged 26 in 1332). He married before 20 Sept. 1334 **MARGARET** _____. They had two sons, John, Knt., and Nicholas, Knt., and one daughter, Alice (wife of Henry Shardelowe). In 1333 he owed a debt of £40 to Robert de Holverston, Citizen of Norwich. In 1335 he had license to settle the manor of Dagworth (in Old Newton), Suffolk on himself and his wife, Margaret, and the heirs of their bodies. In 1346 he was discharged from finding a man-at-arms, because his brother, Thomas, was on the king's service in Brittany, and his son [John] was with Thomas, and he himself was too infirm to labour. NICHOLAS DE DAGWORTH, Esq., died 12 October 1351. Blomefield *Essay towards a Top. Hist. of Norfolk* 6 (1807): 383–385. *C.P.R. 1334–1338* (1895): 74. Copinger *Manors of Suffolk* 6 (1910): 162–164. *C.P.* 4 (1916): 27, footnote c (sub Dagworth). *Feet of Fines for Essex* 3 (1929–49): 267. Cam *Liberties & Communities in Medieval England* (1963). *Norfolk Arch.* 34 (1967): 111–118. National Archives, C 143/229/12; C 241/104/19 (available at www.catalogue.nationalarchives.gov.uk/search.asp).

ii. **THOMAS DE DAGWORTH**, Knt., Lord Dagworth, married **ELEANOR DE BOHUN** [see BUTLER 7].

❧ DAMMARTIN ❧

1. AUBREY, Chamberlain to King Louis VI of France, 1122–29. He married an unknown wife, _____. They had two sons, Aubrey [Count of Dammartin] and William. The date of his death is uncertain. In 1162 Amauri, Bishop of Senlis, attested in the presence of King Louis that Aubrey the Chamberlain and his son, Aubrey, Count of Dammartin, had confirmed to the Abbey of Chaalis all that the Abbey possessed in the county of Dammartin.

> *L'Art de Vérifier les Dates* 2 (1784): 661–663 (sub Comtes de Dammartin). Tardif *Monuments Historiques* (Inv. & Docs. publiées par Ordre de l'Empereur) (1866): 214–215 (charter of King Louis VI dated 1122; charter witnessed by

"Aubrey the chamberlain" [Alberici camerarii]), 215–216 (charter of King Louis VI dated 1123; charter witnessed by "Aubrey the chamberlain" [Alberici chamerarii]), 216 (charter of King Louis VI dated 1123; charter witnessed by "Aubrey the cham0berlain" [Alberici camerarii]), 218 (charters of King Louis VI dated 1124; charter witnessed by "Aubrey the chamberlain" [Alberici camerarii]), 219–220 (charter of King Louis VI dated 1122; charter witnessed by "Aubrey the chamberlain" [Alberici camerarii]), 223 (charter of King Louis VI dated 1127; charter witnessed by "Aubrey the chamberlain" [Alberici camerarii]). *Annales de la Faculté des Lettres de Bordeaux* 3 (1881): 369–370, 372–373. Luchaire *Remarques sur la Succession des Grands Officiers de la Couronne* (1881): 23, 25–26 ("M. de Wailly, reproduisant textuellement une indication de du Cange, place entre Mathieu I et Matheiu II un Aubri qui souscrivait en 1152 (du Cange dit 1162) et vivait encore en 1181. Cet Aubri n'apparaît, à notre connaissance, sur aucune charte de Louis VII. L'erreur de Du Cange provient sans doute de l'interprétation erronée d'un texte publié en partie et dans lequel on voit Aubri II, comte de Dammartin, fils du chambrier de Louis VI, "Alberico patre meo camerario," faire une donation à l'abbaye de Chaalis, donation expédiée à Senlis en 1162."). *Genealogists' Mag.* 15 (1965): 53–63.

2. AUBREY DE DAMMARTIN, Count of Dammartin-en-Goële, of Little Haugh (in Norton), Suffolk, and, in right of his 2nd wife, of Piddington, Oxfordshireson and heir, born say 1100 . He married (1st) **MAUD** _____, possibly daughter of William de Saint Clair, of Hamerton, Huntingdonshire. They had one son, Aubrey II [Count of Dammartin]. In 1130-35 King Henry I of England confirmed to him all the land of his father in the manor of Norton, Suffolk. In the period, 1148-53?, he and Eudes de Dammartin were granted lands in Wrestlingworth, Bedfordshire and Beachampstead (in Great Staughton), Huntingdonshire. He was granted the manor of Hamerton, Huntingdonshire about 1152-3, to hold by the service of one knight. In the period, 1147-65, he and his wife, Maud, confirmed the earlier grant of the church of Hamerton, Huntingdonshire made by William de Saint Clair to the monks of Colchester Monastery. About 1150–60 he witnessed a charter of Manasser de Dammartin to Missenden Abbey. In 1162 Amauri, Bishop of Senlis, attested in the presence of King Louis that Aubrey, Count of Dammartin, and his father, Aubrey the Chamberlain, confirmed to the Abbey of Chaalis all that the Abbey possessed in the county of Dammartin. Sometime after c.1162 and before 1166, as Aubrey, Count of Dammartin, he granted the manor of Norton, Suffolk to his brother, William de Dammartin (living 1166, died ante 1170). He married (2nd) before 1164 **JOAN BASSET**, widow successively of Guy de Ryhall (otherwise Fitz Pain, de Cahaines) (died c. 1151–52), of Ryhall, Rutlandshire and Piddington, Oxfordshire, and Simon de Gerardmoulin (living 1152–53), of Merton and Piddington, Oxfordshire, and daughter of Gilbert Basset, of Bicester and Wallingford, by his wife, Edith d'Oilly. In 1174 either he or his son, Aubrey, as "Aubrey Count of Dammartin," witnessed a charter of Ralph Fitz Ralph Fitz Reinger and his brother, Hugh, to Rufford Abbey. AUBREY I, Count of Dammartin-en-Goële, died before c.1175.

L'Art de Vérifier Les Dates 2 (1784): 661–663 (sub Comtes de Dammartin). Kennett *Parochial Antiqs. of Ambrosden, Burcester* 1 (1818): 147–148. Dunkin *Oxfordshire: Hist. & Antiqs. of the Hundreds of Bullington & Ploughley* 2 (1823): 129–130. Dugdale *Monasticon Anglicanum* 6(1) (1849): 549 (charter of Joan de Piddington, widow of Guy de Ryhall), 549 (charter of Simon de Gerardmulin). Revue *Historique Nobiliaire et Biographique* 3rd Ser. 1 (1876): 281, footnote 1 ("*L'Art de Vérifier les Dates*, le P. Anselme et Bosquillon se bornent à énoncer l'identité sans apporter de preuves à l'appui. André Duchesne, qui a avancé le fait le premier, Histoire de la maison de Bar, fo 23, est plus explicite et en meme temps moins affirmatif. 'Il est vrai, dit-il, que l'historien Albéric ne parle point du second mariage de Clémence de Bar avec le comte de Dammartin, mais je l'ai recueilli de plusieurs conjectures et raisons fort vraisemblables. Car en premier lieu quelques titres de l'abbaye de Saint-Denis en France font mention d'une Clémence, comtesse de Dammartin, veuve en l'année 1153. Secondement par une charte de l'abbaye d'Andres, Hugues de Clairemont, abbé de Cluny, fils de Clemence, est dit oncle de Renaut, comte de Boulogne et de Dammartin, fils d'Albéric II, ce qui ne pourroit convenir, sinon en accordant qu'Albéric et Hugues étoient frères utérins. On bien il faudroit que Mahaut, mère de comte Renaud, eut été sœur du mesme Hugues. En quoi il n'y a point d'apparence, vu qu'après la mort de Catherine, comtesse de Clermont, fille du comte Raoul et d'Alix de Breteuil, les enfants de cette Mahaut ne participèrent point à la succession d'icelle, comme firent ceux de Marguerite de Clermont, sœur de Hugues et de Raoul. En troisième lieu, Rigordus, auteur du siècle, dit sous l'année 1212 que la comtesse de Clermont lors vivante, savoir est Catherine, fille de Raoul, étoit cousine de Renaut de Dammartin. Bref Albéric écrit qu'en la même année Renaut sortant du royaume se retira par devers le comte de Bar, Thibaut Ier, lequel il qualifie aussi son cousin. D'où il s'ensuit que Clémence, comtesse de Dammartin, son aïeule, doit avoir eté de la maison de Bar et la même que

Clémence de Bar, conjointe avec Renaut, comte de Clairmont en Beauvaisis.). *Annales de la Faculté des Lettres de Bordeaux* 3 (1881): 372–373. Wigram *Cartulary of the Monastery of St. Frideswide at Oxford* 2 (Oxford Hist. Soc. 31) (1896): 96–97. Moore *Cartularium Monasterii Sancti Johannis Baptiste de Colecestria* 1 (1897): 162 (charter dated 1147–65 of Aubrey de Dammartin and his wife, Maud; charter witnessed by Hubert de Saint Clair, brother of William de Saint Clair). Ellis & Bickley *Index to the Charters & Rolls in the Department of MSS British Museum* 1 (1900): 64, 330, 930. Muller *Prieuré de Saint-Leu d'Esserent: Cartulaire* 1 (Pubs. Soc. Hist. du Vexin) (1900): 197 (Dammartin ped.). Copinger *Manors of Suffolk* 1 (1905): 352. Salter *Boarstall Cartulary* (Oxford Hist. Soc.1st Ser. 88) (1930): 68–69, 102–103. VCH *Huntingdon* 2 (1932): 354–369; 3 (1936): 66–69. Jenkins *Cartulary of Missenden Abbey* 1 (1938): 17–18, 70–72 (charter of Manasser de Dammartin). Leys *Sandford Cartulary* 1 (Oxfordshire Rec. Soc. 19) (1938): 35; 2 (Oxfordshire Rec. Soc. 22) (1941): 279–280 (charter of Simon, Earl of Northampton dated 1152–3). VCH *Oxford* 5 (1957): 249–258. *Genealogists' Mag.* 15 (1965): 53–63 (Charles F.H. Evans foolishly argues that Aubrey I de Dammartin, Count of Dammartin, is "more likely" a son of Eudes de Dammartin, of England). *Sussex Arch. Colls.* 116 (1978): 399. Smith *English Episcopal Acta* 1 (1980): 102. *Surrey Arch. Colls.* 54 (1955): 58–65 ("... an undated deed in the Minet Library [G. 127] by which Alberic 'Comes Dommartini' grants Norton to William de Donomart' [his brother]. Among the ten witnesses, all Dammartins, is Walter, a name with occurs also among the witnesses to the grant by William de Dammartin to Lewes Priory."); 72 (1980): 123 ("A Tandridge charter of Aubrey, earl Dammartin of c.1130–50 (Minet Library Surrey Deed 3603) is witnessed by many members of the family."). Holdsworth *Rufford Charters* 2 (Thoroton Soc. Rec. Ser. 30) (1974): no. 746 (charter of Ralph Fitz Ralph Fitz Reinger and his brother, Hugh, dated 1174). Châtelain *Châteaux Forts et Féodalité en Ile de France* (1983): 23 ("Les seigneurs de Dammartin en Goele, qui tenaient leurs terres en franc-alleu, n'attendirent pas de se rebeller contre Philippe Auguste pour donner du souci aux rois …Les successeurs Albéric Ier et II seront, â leur tour, fidèles; le premier sera chambrier de Louis VII en 1155 et le second soutiendra d'abord Philippe Auguste contre le comte de Flandre, ce qui lui coûtera son château, ravagé en 1183 par celui-ci."). Schwennicke *Europaische Stanmtafeln* 3 (1984): 649 (Alberic (Aubri) I Comte de Dammartin-en-Goele, married _____ (perhaps Clémence) de Dammartin), 650 (identification of parentage of Aubri I de Dammartin) (Aubri's mother married, second, Lancelin II de Beauvais, Verweser d Gfschft Dammartin-en-Goéle). Mathieu *Recherches sur les premiers Comtes de Dammartin* (1996). Yorkshire Arch. Soc.: H. L. Bradfer-Lawrence Coll., MD335/7/17 (deed of Ralph son of Ralph, son of Reinger, and Hugh his brother to the Monks of Rufford) (available at available at www.a2a.org.uk/search/index.asp).

3. AUBREY DE DAMMARTIN, Count of Dammartin-en-Goële, seigneur of Lillebonne-en-Normandie, and Rouville, lord of Beachampton (in Great Staughton) and Southoe, Huntingdonshire, Piddington, Oxfordshire, South Norton and Thurston, Suffolk, etc., son and heir, born say 1130. He married **MAHAUT** (or **MATHILDE**) **OF CLERMONT**, daughter of Renaud II, Count of Clermont-en-Beauvaisis, by Clémence, Countess of Dammartin, daughter of Renaud I, Count of Bar-le-Duc [see CLERMONT 2 for her ancestry]. They had three sons, Renaud [Count of Boulogne, Dammartin, and Mortain], Simon [Count of Aumâle, Ponthieu, and Monstreuil], and Raoul, and four daughters, Alix (or Aleide, Adelicia) (wife of Jean II, seigneur of Trie), Agnès, Clémence (wife of Jacques de Prische, 4th son of Guillaume, Châtelain of Saint Omer), and Juliane. In 1174 either he or his father, Aubrey, as "Aubrey Count of Dammartin," witnessed a charter of Ralph Fitz Ralph Fitz Reinger and his brother, Hugh, to Rufford Abbey. About 1175, as Aubrey, Count of Dammartin, he granted Missenden Abbey the hermitage and chapel of Muswell, together with the tithe of the demesne of Piddington, Oxfordshire; this grant was made with the consent of his son and heir, Renaud. In 1177, as "Aubrey Count of Dammartin," he witnessed a charter of his brother-in-law, Raoul, Count of Clermont. Some time before 1184 he successfully claimed to have an hereditary right to Merton, Oxfordshire; he subsequently obtained a charter from King Henry II confirming the manor of Merton to himself and his son Renaud with all the rights that their ancestors had enjoyed under King Henry I. In 1183–4, as "Aubrey, Count of Dammartin," he issued a charter confirming the previous grant of Merton, Oxfordshire to the Templars, excepting the fee and tenement of Guy of Merton and his heirs, the overlordship of which Aubrey reserved to himself. Sometime before 1184 Earl Simon de Senlis confirmed to Aubrey and his son, Renaud, lands in Beachampton (in Great Staughton) and Southoe, Huntingdonshire. In 1185 he and his wife, Countess Mathilde, and his son, Renaud, Count of Boulogne, issued a charter to the canons and prior of Dammartin. In 1193 he and his wife, Mathilde, witnessed a charter of their son-in-law, Jean de Trie, to the Abbey of St.-Paul. In 1194 the manor of Piddington, Oxfordshire, was described as lately belonging to the Count of Dammartin, it then being in royal hands as an escheat. In 1200 he granted the Priory of Saint-Leu d'Esserent 40 shillings Parisien of rent. In 1202 [sic] he and his wife, Mathilde, gave the chapel of their manor of Rouville to the church of Alisay. AUBREY II, Count of Dammartin-en-Goële, died at London 19 Sept. 1200, and was buried in the Abbey of Jumièges. He left a testament dated 20 [sic] Sept. 1200. His widow, Mahaut, was co-heiress in 1218 to her great-nephew, Thibaut, Count of Blois and Clermont. In 1218 she quitclaimed her rights in the comté of Clermont to King Philippe Auguste.

Du Plessis *Histoire de l'Église de Meaux* 2 (1731): 73–74 (charter dated 1185 of Aubrey, Count of Dammartin, and Renaud his son, Count of Boulogne, and Countess Mathilde his wife), 93–94. *L'Art de Vérifier les Dates* 2 (1784): 661–663 (sub Comtes de Dammartin). Dugdale *Monasticon Anglicanum* 6(1) (1830): 421 (charter issued by Renaud, Count of Boulogne, naming [his parents], Aubrey, Count of Dammartin, and Maud his wife), 549 (charter of Aubrey Count of Dammartin, granted with consent of his son, Renaud). Herckenrode *Coll. de Tombes, Épitaphes et Blasons, recueillis dans les Églises et Couvents de la Hesbaye* (1845): 671–673. Peigné-Delacourt *Cartulaire de l'Abbaye de Notre-Dame d'Ourscamp* (1865): 158 (charter of Raoul, Count of Clermont dated 1162; charter mentions his wife, Alix [Adelidis], and his sister, Mathilde; his brothers, Simon and Étienne, give their consent). Ellis *Notices of the Ellises* (1866): 34–35 ("M. D'Anisy speaks of Alisay as a place where councils were held in the ninth century. Alberic Comte de Dammartin, about the year 1200, made a donation to the abbey of Fontaine-Guérard, which was dated 'at Alisi, in the monastery of St. Germain.'"), 34 footnote 3 ("In 1202, Alberic Comte de Dammartin, Mathilda his wife, and Renaud their son, united to the living a chapel, which they had built and endowed, in the manor of Rouville, and to which they gave the tithes of all newly assarted or cleared land in the manor of Alisay. In November, 1258, Mathilda Countess of Bologne gave the patronage to the Archbishop of Rouen."). Pinio et al. *Acta Sanctorum Augusti* 5 (1868): 484–485 (document indicates that Aubrey II, Count of Dammartin [Albericus II comes Domni-Martini] had two children, Renaud [Raynaldum], Count of Dammartin and Boulogne, and Aleide, wife of Jean, seigneur of Trie). *Annuaire administratif, statistique et historique du Département de l'Eure* 2nd Ser. 8th Year (1869): 266. Lépinois *Recherches Historiques et Critiques sur l'Ancien Comté et les Comtes de Clermont en Beauvoisis* (1877): 434–435. Luçay *Comté de Clermont en Beauvaisis* (1878): 16–17 ("Et en effet une charte de Raoul, comte de Clermont, sans date déterminée, mais que la collection Moreau place entre 1177 et 1203, inscrit au nombre des témoins Albéric comte de Dammartin et Mahaut comtesse de Dammartin, sœur dudit Raoul, mais cette charte même est une preuve de plus a l'appui de l'existence d'une troisième fille de Renaud II et de Clémence. Cette Mathilda, comtesse de Dammartin, nous la retrouverons d'ailleurs en 1218 cédant a Philippe Auguste ses droits sur le comté de Clermont moyennant une rent annuelle de cent livres sur la prévoté de Crépy … par une charte de l'abbaye d'Andres, Hugues de Clairemont, abbé de Cluny, fils de Clémence, est dit oncle de Renaut, comte de Boulogne et de Dammartin, fils d'Albéric II … Ou bien il faudroit que Mahaut, mère de comte Renaud, eût été sœur du mesme Hugues … Rigordus, auteur du siècle, dit sous l'année 1212 que la comtesse de Clermont lors vivante, savoir est Catherine, fille Raoul, étoit cousine de Renaut de Dammartin. Bref Albéric écrit qu'en la même année Renaut sortant du royaume se retira par devers le comte de Bar, Thibaut Ier, lequel il qualifie aussi son cousin."), 41. *Mémoires de la Société de l'Histoire de Paris et de l'Île de France* 10 (1884): 191–242. Malo *Un Grand Feudataire, Renaud de Dammartin et la Coalition de Bouvines* (1898): 263–264 (charters of Aubrey, Count of Dammartin, dated 1200; charters witnessed by M[ahaut], his wife, Countess of Dammartin, and Renaud, Count of Boulogne, his son). Muller *Prieuré de Saint-Leu d'Esserent: Cartulaire* 1 (Pubs. Soc. Hist. du Vexin) (1900): 94 (charter of Aubri, Count of Dammartin, dated 1200; charter granted with consent of his wife, Mathilde, and their son, Renaud, Count of Boulogne), 195 (Clermont ped.), 197 (Dammartin ped.). Chavanon *Études & Docs. sur Calais avant la Domination Anglaise (1180–1346)* (1901): 15 (charter dated 1196 of Renaud, Count of Boulogne, and Ida, his wife, Countess of Boulogne; charter witnessed by [his father] A[ubrey] Count of Dammartin). Depoin *Cartulaire de l'Abbaye de Saint-Martin de Pontoise* 3 (1904): 302–305. VCH *Huntingdon* 2 (1932): 354–369. Leys *Sandford Cartulary* (Oxfordshire Rec. Soc. 22) (1941): 281–282 (charter of Aubrey, Count of Dammartin dated 1183-4). Davis *Kalendar of Abbot Samson of Bury St. Edmunds and Related Docs.* (Camden Soc. 3rd Ser. 84) (1954): 4, 12, 41. VCH *Oxford* 5 (1957): 221–234, 249–258. *Genealogists' Mag.* 15 (1965): 53–63. Holdsworth *Rufford Charters* 2 (Thoroton Soc. Rec. Ser. 30) (1974): no. 746 (charter of Ralph Fitz Ralph Fitz Reinger and his brother, Hugh, dated 1174). Pinoteau *Origines des Armoiries* (1983): 26 ("Avant cette date, ils n'usent pas systématiquement du sceau armorié: Aubri de Dammartin, en 1189, selle d'un equestre simple, alors qu'en 1185, son sceau portait un bouclier quatre fasces."). Schwennicke *Europaische Stanmtafeln* 3 (1989): 649, 653 (ancestry of Mahaut de Clermont). Manchester University, John Rylands Library: Beaumont Charters, BMC/78 (charter dated c.1200 issued to the Abbey of La Trinité at Fécamp: --For the weal of their souls, for that of Mathieu, Count of Boulogne and Marie, his wife, that of Aubry, Count of Dammartin, and Mathilde, his wife, the grantor's father and mother, [the grantor] Renaud, Count of Boulogne, Ida his wife, and Mathilde, their daughter, grant to the Abbey the free passage at Harfleur [Seine Inférieure Con Montivilliers in the viscounty of Caux]) (available at available at www.a2a.org.uk/search/index.asp). Yorkshire Arch. Soc.: H. L. Bradfer-Lawrence

Coll., MD335/7/17 (deed of Ralph son of Ralph, son of Reinger, and Hugh his brother to the Monks of Rufford) (available at available at www.a2a.org.uk/search/index.asp).

Children of Aubri de Dammartin, by Mahaut de Clermont:

i. **RENAUD DE DAMMARTIN**, of Beachampton (in Great Staughton) and Southoe, Huntingdonshire, Piddington, Oxfordshire, Ryhall, Rutlandshire, Norton, Suffolk, and, in right of his 2nd wife, Count of Boulogne, and of Kirton-in-Lindsay, Dunham, Nottinghamshire, Bampton and Cold Norton, Oxfordshire, etc., son and heir, born 1165. He married (1st) **MARIE DE CHÂTILLON**, daughter of Guy de Châtillon, whom he subsequently repudiated. They had no issue. He married (2nd) c.1191 **IDA OF BOULOGNE**, Countess of Boulogne, widow of Gérard III, Count of Guelders and Zutphen, contracted wife of Berthold V, Duke of Zeringhen, and daughter and co-heiress of Mathieu of Flanders, Count of Boulogne, lord of Kirton-in-Lindsey, Lincolnshire, Dunham, Nottinghamshire, Bampton and Cold Norton, Oxfordshire, Exning, Suffolk, etc., by his 1st wife, Mary (or Marie), daughter of Stephen, King of England [see BRABANT 4 for her ancestry]. They had one daughter, Mahaut (or Mathilde, Mafalda) [Countess of Boulogne and Dammartin] (wife successively of Philippe *dit* Hurepel, Count of Clermont-en-Beauvaisis and Mortain, and Affonso III, King of Portugal and the Algarve [see PORTUGAL 7]). Sometime before 1184 Simon Earl of Huntingdon and Northampton granted him the manor of Wrestlingworth, Bedfordshire. In 1189 he was granted the castle and forest of Lillebonne, Normandy by King Henry II. In 1198 King Richard I confirmed to him the forest of Lillebonne and the inheritance in England and in Normandy of his wife, Ida, as count Mathieu held it, and all the inheritance of his father count Aubrey de Dammartin. The same year the king granted him the manor of Bampton, Oxfordshire. In 1202 King Philippe granted him the fortress and county of Aumale. Following Renaud's defection from the England king in 1203, the manor of Bampton passed in custody to Geoffrey Fitz Peter, Earl of Essex. In 1204–6 King Philippe Auguste granted Mortain and Saint-James in Normandy to Count Renaud and his brother, Simon, only to confiscate them once more in 1211. In 1212 King John restored to him the manors of Wrestlingworth, Bedfordshire, Kirton-in-Lindsay, Lincolnshire, Bampton, Cold Norton, and Piddington, Oxfordshire, Ryhall, Rutland, and Little Haugh (in Norton), Suffolk. He was defeated by King Philippe *Auguste* at the Battle of Bouvines in 1214, and forfeited his title of count. Although still regarded as part of Renaud's honour of Boulogne after his capture at the Battle of Bouvines, the manor of Bampton, Oxfordshire was granted at pleasure in 1217 to Fawkes de Breauté. Du Plessis *Histoire de l'Église de Meaux* 2 (1731): 73–74 (charter dated 1185 of Aubrey, Count of Dammartin, and Renaud his son, Count of Boulogne, and Countess Mathilde his wife), 93–94. *L'Art de Vérifier les Dates* 2 (1784): 661–663 (sub Comtes de Dammartin). Blore *Hist. & Antiqs. of Rutland* 1(2) (1811): 30–31. Dugdale *Monasticon Anglicanum* 6(2) (1830): 1006 (undated charter of Ida, Countess of Boulogne, to Westwood Priory, Worcestershire, which names her "father" [pater], Mathieu, Count of Boulogne, and her "uncle" [avunculus]," Philippe, Count of Flanders), 1007 (undated charter of Ida, Countess of Boulogne, to Westwood Priory, which names her father [patris], Mathieu, Count of Boulogne, and her "aunt" [materteræ], M[athilde of Flanders], Abbess of Fontrevault). Herckenrode *Coll. de Tombes, Épitaphes et Blasons, recueillis dans les Églises et Couvents de la Hesbaye* (1845): 671–673. Pinio *Acta Sanctorum Augusti* 5 (1868): 484–485. La Gorgue-Rosny *Recherches Généalogiques sur les Comtés de Ponthieu, de Boulogne, de Guines et Pays Circonvoisins: Documents Inédits* (1877): 42–43 (charter of Renaud, Count of Boulogne, and his wife dated 1201). *Desc. Cat. Ancient Deeds* 2 (1894): 154–165. Malo *Un Grand Feudataire, Renaud de Dammartin et la Coalition de Bouvines* (1898): 250–251 (charter dated 1192 by Renaud, Count of Boulogne; charter names his wife, Ida, Countess of Boulogne, and her uncle [patruus], Philippe, Count of Flanders). Ellis & Bickley *Index to the Charters & Rolls in the Department of MSS British Museum* 1 (1900): 553, 588, 633, 845. Muller *Prieuré de Saint-Leu d'Esserent: Cartulaire* 1 (Pubs. Soc. Hist. du Vexin) (1900): 197 (Dammartin ped.). Chavanon *Études & Docs. sur Calais avant la Domination Anglaise (1180–1346)* (1901): 15 (charter dated 1196 of Renaud, Count of Boulogne, and Ida, his wife, Countess of Boulogne; charter witnessed by A[ubrey] Count of Dammartin), 15–16 (charter dated 1210 of Renaud, Count of Boulogne, and Ida his wife, Countess of Boulogne). Copinger *Manors of Suffolk* 1 (1905): 352. VCH *Bedford* 2 (1908): 255–259. VCH *Huntingdon* 2 (1932): 354–369. Landon *Itinerary of King Richard I* (Pipe Roll Soc. n.s. 13) (1935): 137. VCH *Rutland* 2 (1935): 268–275. VCH *Oxford* 5 (1957): 249–258; 13 (1996): 22–30. *Genealogists' Mag.* 15 (1965): 53–63. Evergates *Littere Baronum: The earliest Cartulary of the Counts of Champagne* (2003): 74 (charter of Renaud of Dammartin, count of Boulogne, announces that Gaucher III of Châtillon-sur-Marne, count of Saint-Pol, and Guillaume III des Barres will conduct an inquest in order to resolve his dispute with Countess Blanche over the residence and village of Brégy. The village has been held by Count Henri I, Countess Marie, Count Henri II, and Renaud's father, Alberic. The inquest will also determine who may collect the head tax at Brégy.). Power *Norman Frontier in the 12th & Early 13th Cents.* (2004): 39, 454. Online resources: http://www.briantimms.com/rolls/chiffletprinetCP01.htm (Chifflet-Prinet Roll, Part 1, No. 33: Arms of Renaut de Dammartin - Barry of six argent and azure a bordure gules and a martlet sable); http://www.mittelalter-genealogie.de/dammartin_grafen_von/rainald_1_von_dammertin_graf_von_boulogne_1227.html.

ii. **AGNÈS DE DAMMARTIN**, married **GUILLAUME** (or **WILLIAM**) **DE FIENNES**, seigneur of Fiennes (Pas de Calais) [see BOULOGNE 7].

iii. **JULIANE DE DAMMARTIN**, married **HUGH DE GOURNAY**, seigneur of Gournay-en-Brie, Normandy [see GOURNAY 4].

4. SIMON DE DAMMARTIN Count of Aumale, and, in right of his wife, Count of Ponthieu and Montreuil, 2nd son. He married at Compiègne by settlement dated September 1208 **MARIE OF PONTHIEU**, Countess of Ponthieu and Montreuil (1225), daughter and heiress of Guillaume Talvas II, Count of Ponthieu, by Alix, daughter of Louis VII, King of France [see FRANCE 6.ii for her ancestry]. She was born before 17 Sept. 1199. They had four daughters, Jeanne, Mathilde (wife of Jean de Châtellerault), Philippe (wife successively of Raoul de Lusignan, Count of Eu, Raoul de Coucy, seigneur of Coucy, and Otton II, Count of Guelders), and Marie (wife of Jean II, Count of Roucy). In 1204–6 King Philippe *Auguste* granted Mortain and Saint-James in Normandy to Count Renaud and his brother, Simon, only to confiscate them once more in 1211. In 1208 his brother, Renaud, Count of Boulogne, gave him 500 livrées of land in Normandy. He fought against King Philippe *Auguste* at the Battle of Bouvines, after which he was banished from the kingdom and his goods confiscated. In 1221, on the death of his father-in-law, Guillaume, Count of Ponthieu, his lands held in right of his wife were taken. In 1225 Marie obtained a pardon, and resumed the administration of Ponthieu. Simon obtained permission to return to France in 1231. In 1233 Marie was coming to England on pilgrimage. SIMON DE DAMMARTIN, Count of Aumale, Ponthieu, and Montreuil, died 21 Sept. 1239, and was buried at Valoires Abbey. His widow, Marie, married (2nd) between September 1240 and 15 Dec. 1241 **MATHIEU DE MONTMORENCY**, seigneur of Attichy, and, in right of his wife, Count of Ponthieu and Montreuil (slain at Mansurah February 1250), son of Mathieu II, seigneur of Montmorency, Constable of France, by his 1st wife, Gertrude, daughter of Raoul II, Count of Soissons. In 1244 Mathieu and his wife, Marie, issued a charter regarding a difference between Corbie Abbey and Jean de Maisnières, Chev. His widow, Marie, died at Abbeville in September 1250.

Martene & Durand *Veterum scriptorum et monumentorum* 1 (1724): 1202 (Marie, Countess of Ponthieu, styled "kinswoman" [consanguinea] by King Louis VIII of France), 1305–1306. *L'Art de Vérifier les Dates* 2 (1784): 661–663 (sub Comtes de Dammartin), 750–759 (sub Comtes de Ponthieu). *Mémoires de la Société des Antiquaires de Normandie* 2nd Ser. 6 (1852): 314 (Marie, wife of Simon, Count of Ponthieu, styled "kinswoman" [consanguineam] by King Louis IX of France in charter dated 1233). Guigniaut *Recueil des Historiens des Gaules et de la France* 21 (1855): 626–627 (Chronicle of Alberic of Trois Fontaines (sub anno 1239): "… Obiit comes de Pontivi, Simon cujus uxor filia Guillelmi comitis de Pontivo, quatuor relinquens filias, quarum unam duxit rex Castellae de Hispania Fernandus, et filius ejus Alfunsus duxit filiam regis Arragonensis (ex qua genuit Sancium, regem Castellae qui nunc est); alteram, natu majorem, filius vicecomitis de Castro Araudi; tertiam filius vicecomitis de Augo (dein, illo mortuo, nupsit Radulfo de Couci; tertio vero, Ottoni comiti Gelriae, cui peperit Raynaldum comitem qui nunc est); quartem comes de Roceio (comiti autem de Roceio peperit Johannem comitem de Roceio qui nunc est)"). Teulet *Layettes du Trésor des Chartes* 2 (1866): 56–57, 62, 185, 195, 199–200 ("Simone de Bolonia comite Pontivi"), 257, 281–282 (Maud [de Dammartin], Countess of Boulogne, styled "niece" [nepte] by Simon de Dammartin), 311–312, 550–552. Thierry *Recueil des Monuments Inédits de l'Histoire du Tiers État* 4 (1870): 22–23, 26–28. La Gorgue-Rosny *Recherches Généalogiques sur les Comtés de Ponthieu, de Boulogne, de Guines & Pays Circonvoisins: Documents Inédits* (1877): 12, 40–41, 44. Delisle *Cartulaire Normand* (1882): 28. Müller *Le Prieuré de Saint-Leu d'Esserent: Cartulaire (1080-1538)* (1901): 113–114, 121–122. *C.P.R. 1232-1247* (1906): 25. *Recherches généalogiques sur la Famille des Seigneurs de Nemours* 2 (1908): 139. *Genealogists' Mag.* 15 (1965–68): 53–63; 23 (1989): 141–144. Parsons (1977): 42 (The Dammartin descent in *L'Art de verifier les dates* is badly out of date and must be corrected by use of H. Morainvillé, "Origine de la maison de Ramerupt-Roucy," *BEC* 86 (1925) 169–184; Newman *Seigneurs de Nesle en Picardie* I:82-83). Winter *Descs. of Charlemagne (800–1400)* (1987): XIV.744c & XV.198. Schwennicke *Europaische Stanmtafeln* 3 (1989): 638 (ancestry of Marie de Ponthieu). Power *Norman Frontier in the 12th & Early 13th Cents.* (2004): 39.

Child of Simon de Dammartin, by Marie of Ponthieu:

i. **JEANNE** (or **JUANA**) **DE DAMMARTIN**, Countess of Ponthieu, Montreuil, and Aumale, married [**SAINT**] **FERNANDO III**, King of Castile and León [see CASTILE 7].

❧ DARCY ✣

EUSTACHE I, Count of Boulogne, married **MATHILDE** (or **MAHAUT**) **OF LOUVAIN**.
EUSTACHE II, Count of Boulogne, by an unknown mistress, _____.
GEOFFREY OF BOULOGNE, of Carshalton, Surrey, married **BEATRICE DE MANDEVILLE**.
WILLIAM OF BOULOGNE, of Carshalton, Surrey, married _____.
ROHESE OF BOULOGNE, married **RICHARD DE LUCY**, Knt., of Chipping Ongar, Essex, Justiciar of England.
ALICE DE LUCY, married **ODINEL DE UMFREVILLE**, Knt., of Prudhoe, Northumberland.
ALICE DE UMFREVILLE, married **WILLIAM BERTRAM**, of Mitford, Northumberland.
ROGER BERTRAM, Knt., of Mitford, Northumberland, married **AGNES** _____.
ISABEL BERTRAM, married **PHILIP DARCY**, Knt., of Cawkwell, Lincolnshire [see BERTRAM 9].

10. ROGER DARCY (or **DE ARCY**), of Blyth, Oldcotes, and Styrrup, Nottinghamshire, younger son. He married **ISABEL DE ATON**, daughter of William de Aton, Knt. They had one son, John, Knt. [1st Lord Darcy of Knaith]. He purchased the manor of Sproatley, Yorkshire from Simon de Veer. In 1272 he agreed to make Ingram de Oldcotes a knight, and to provide food and clothing for him, as well as an esquire and two grooms, and three horses for life, in return for the use of all of Ingram's lands for life in Blyth, Oldcotes, and Styrrup, Nottinghamshire; this agreement subsequently led to nearly four decades of litigation between the Darcy and Oldcotes families. In 1272–3 he arraigned an assize of novel disseisin against Ingram de Oldcotes touching a tenement in Oldcotes, Buggethorp, and Styrrup, Nottinghamshire. In 1275–6 William de Hochem and Maud his wife and Radulph le Rendu and Sibyl his wife arraigned an assize of novel disseisin against him and others touching a tenement in Kelby, Lincolnshire. In 1277 he was granted letters of protection, he then going with Edmund the king's brother to Wales. SIR ROGER DARCY died before 12 May 1284.

Annual Rpt. of the Deputy Keeper 42 (1881): 626; 46 (1885): 199, 259. Prestwich *Three Edwards* (2003): 122. Janin *Medieval Justice* (2004): 112–113.

11. JOHN DARCY, Knt., of Knaith, Kexby, Sturton by Stow St. Mary, and Upton, Lincolnshire, Blyth, Kirkby in Ashfield, Oldcotes, Sturton-in-the-Clay, and Styrrup, Nottinghamshire, etc., Constable of Norham Castle, 1317, Sheriff of Nottinghamshire and Derbyshire, 1319–22, Knight of the Shire for Nottinghamshire, 1320, Sheriff of Lancashire, 1323, Justiciar of Ireland, 1323–7, 1328–31, 1332–37, 1340–44, Sheriff of Yorkshire, 1327–8, Steward of the King's Household, 1337–40, Chamberlain to the King, 1341–6 or later, Constable of Nottingham Castle, 1344–7, Constable of the Tower of London, 1346–7, and, in right of his 1st wife, of Notton, Yorkshire, son and heir, minor on 15 June 1292. He was outlawed for felony in or before 1306, and lost his lands in Oldcotes, etc. He was pardoned 19 May 1307 at the request of Aymer de Valence, Earl of Pembroke, in whose retinue he was in 1313, 1320, and 1321. He married (1st) before 1317 **EMMELINE HERON**, daughter and heiress of Walter Heron, of Silkestone, Yorkshire, by Alice, daughter of Nicholas de Hastings. She was aged 7-½ years in May 1297. They had three sons, John, Knt. [2nd Lord Darcy of Knaith], Aymer, and Roger. He served in the expedition to Scotland in 1322. In 1323 he was granted the manors of Edgefield and Walcot, Norfolk for life to support his dignity as Justiciar of Ireland. In 1328 he was granted the manor of Wark in Tynedale for life, and in fee 1329, which he sold to the Queen. He married (2nd) at Maynooth, co. Kildare 3 July 1329 **JOAN DE BURGH**, widow of Thomas Fitz John, 2nd Earl of Kildare, Justiciar of Ireland (died 5 April 1328) [see BURGH 5.vi], and daughter of Richard de Burgh, Knt., 3rd Earl of Ulster, lord of Connacht, Lieutenant of Ireland, 1299–1300, by his wife, Margaret [see BURGH 5 for her ancestry]. They had one son, William, and one daughter, Elizabeth. He was commissioned to treat with the nobles of Aquitaine in 1330. In 1330, having engaged to stay always with the king with 20 men-at-arms in times of war, he was granted the manors of Brocklesby and Grantham, Lincolnshire for life.

In 1331 he was appointed a special envoy to the King of France concerning the marriage of Prince Edward. He was summoned to Parliament from 27 Jan. 1331/2 to 2 Jan. 1333/4, by writs directed *Johanni Darcy le cosyn*, whereby he is held to have become Lord Darcy. In 1332 he was granted the manor of Marston Maysey, Wiltshire, Wick, Gloucestershire, etc. for life. In 1335 he took an army to Scotland, and wasted Arran and Bute. For his good services in Ireland and elsewhere, he and his wife, Joan, and the heirs male of their bodies were granted the manors of Rathwer and Kildalk in Ireland in 1335. In 1337 he was appointed to treat with the King of France, the Emperor, the Count of Flanders, etc., and also with the King of Scots. The same year he was granted the reversion of the manors of Temple Newsham and Temple Hurst, Yorkshire, and Torksey, Lincolnshire. In 1340 he was granted the manors of Louth and Garristown in Ireland in fee, and the reversions of the manors of Eckington, Derbyshire and Kirkby in Ashfield, Nottinghamshire for life. He accompanied the Earl of Northampton in his expedition to Brittany in 1342. In 1342–3 as "John Darcy le Cosyn," he obtained a license to grant a messuage, land, and rent in Tewin, Hertingfordbury, and Panshanger, Hertfordshire to the Prior and convent of St. Bartholomew's, Smithfield. In 1345 he was granted a weekly market and yearly fair at Torksey, Lincolnshire. He was present at the Battle of Crécy in 1346, and was one of those sent from before Calais, 8 Sept. 1346, to announce the victory in Parliament. SIR JOHN DARCY, 1st Lord Darcy of Knaith, died 30 May 1347. His widow, Joan, died 23 April 1359, and was buried with her 1st husband in the Church of the Friars Minors at Kildare, or in the Holy Trinity Cathedral in Dublin.

Throsby *Thoroton's Hist. of Nottinghamshire* 3 (1790): 298. *Gentleman's Mag.* 76 (1806): 115–117. Poulson *Hist. & Antiqs. of Holderness* 2 (1841): 200–201 (Darcy ped.). Banks *Baronies in Fee* 1 (1844): 178–179 (sub Darcy). Leinster *Earls of Kildare* (1858): 28–31. *List of Sheriffs for England & Wales* (PRO Lists and Indexes 9) (1898): 72, 102, 161. *List of Inqs. ad Quod Damnum* 1 (PRO Lists and Indexes 17) (1904): 389. *C.P.* 4 (1916): 54–58 (sub Darcy) (arms of John Darcy: Azure, crusilly and three cinquefoils argent); 7 (1929): 221–225 (sub Kildare). Mills *Cal. Gormanston Reg.* (1916): 2–3. Paget *Baronage of England* (1957) 169: 1. Clay *Yorkshire Deeds* 7 (Yorkshire Arch. Soc. Recs. 83) (1932): 77–78 (demise dated 1337 from John Darcy *le Cosyn* lord of Notton to John Esaude re. a tenement in the vill of Chevet, Yorkshire). D'Arcy *Life of John, First Baron Darcy of Knayth* (1933). Riess *Hist. of the English Electoral Law in the Middle Ages* (1940): 66. Sanders *English Baronies* (1960): 119. Hedley *Northumberland Fams.* (1968): 96. Ellis *Cat. Seals in the P.R.O.* 2 (1981): 32 (seal of John Darcy, Justiciar of Ireland dated 1343 — A ship fills the lower part of the seal, the stern and prow each ending in an ox's head, with a shield of arms: crusilly, three sexfoils pierced, hung aslant over the side. Above the shield is a helm in profile, with mantling flying to right ande crest: on a cap with two large curved horns, … (defaced). From the top of the shield, below the helm, a mailed forearm curves up to left, the hand holding a lance, bendwise, with a triangular pennon charged with a bird. Legend: S'IEHAN/DARCI). Fryde & Greenway *Handbook of British Chronology* (1996): 162. Roper *Feet of Fines for the County of York* 1314–1326 (Yorkshire Arch. Soc. Recs. 158) (2006): 30.

Child of John Darcy, Knt., by Emmeline Heron:

i. **JOHN DARCY**, Knt., 2nd Lord Darcy of Knaith [see next].

Child of John Darcy, Knt., by Joan de Burgh:

i. **ELIZABETH DARCY**, married (1st) **JAMES LE BOTELER** (or **BUTLER**), Knt., 2nd Earl of Ormond [see BUTLER 8]; (2nd) **ROBERT LUKYN** (alias **DE HEREFORD**), Knt. [see BUTLER 8].

12. JOHN DARCY, Knt., 2nd Lord Darcy of Knaith, of Knaith, Lincolnshire, Hedstone, Northumberland, Notton (in Royston), Yorkshire, etc., King's Councillor, Constable of the Tower of London, 1347–52, son and heir by his father's 1st marriage, born about 1317 (aged 30 and more in 1347). He married (1st) before 8 July 1332 **ELEANOR DE HOLAND**, daughter of Robert de Holand, Knt., 1st Lord Holand, by Maud, 2nd daughter and co-heiress of Alan la Zouche, Knt., Lord Zouche [see HOLAND 11 for her ancestry]. They had no male issue. He had a grant in 1341 of £40 a year to him and his heirs for his long and gratuitous services. His wife, Eleanor, died before 21 Nov. 1341. In 1344 he was appointed Keeper of the manor of Burstwick, Yorkshire, with its members, and Escheator in Holderness for life. He married (2nd) by dispensation dated 7 Jan. 1344/5 (she being related to his 1st wife in the 3rd and 4th degrees of kindred) **ELIZABETH DE**

MEINILL, *de jure* Lady Meinill of Whorlton, daughter and heiress of Nicholas de Meinill, Knt., Lord Meinell of Whorlton, by Alice, daughter of William de Roos, Knt., 1st Lord Roos of Helmsley [see THWENG 9.i for her ancestry]. She was born at Whorlton, Yorkshire 15 October 1331. They had three sons, John [3rd Lord Darcy of Knaith], Philip, Knt. [4th Lord Darcy of Knaith], and Thomas, and one daughter, Alice (wife of John Colville, Knt.). He was granted an annuity of £200 for life in 1346 at La Hogue to maintain himself as a banneret. He fought at the Battle of Crécy in 1346, and was present at the Siege of Calais in 1347, he being in the king's retinue. In 1347 he was appointed a commissioner to treat with the Cardinals concerning peace with France. John and Elizabeth were granted seisin of her father's lands held in chief in Yorkshire and Northumberland 10 October 1348, as she had proved her age. He was summoned to Parliament from 20 Nov. 1348 to 15 March 1353/4, by writs directed *Johanni Darcy de Knayth'*. In 1350 he complainted that Thomas, Prior of St. Oswald's, Nostell, Geoffrey de Ledes, and others broke his park at Notton (in Royston), Yorkshire, hunted therein, carried away his goods, with deer from the park, and assaulted his men and servants. He and his wife, Elizabeth, obtained a papal indult for plenary remission at the hour of death in 1355. SIR JOHN DARCY, 2nd Lord Darcy of Knaith, died at Notton, Yorkshire 5 March 1355/6, and was buried at Guisborough Priory, Yorkshire. His widow, Elizabeth, married (2nd) before 18 Nov. 1356 (pardon for marrying without license dated 30 October 1357) (as his 1st wife) **PETER DE MAULEY**, Knt., 4th Lord Mauley [see MAULEY 9], of Mulgrave, Bainton, Doncaster, Kilnwick, and Lockington, Yorkshire, Warden of the East March, son and heir of Peter de Mauley, Knt., 3rd Lord Mauley, of Mulgrave, Bainton, Bramham, Doncaster, Etton, Kilnwick, Lockington, and Rossington, Yorkshire, by Margaret, daughter of Robert de Clifford, Knt., 1st Lord Clifford, by Maud, daughter of Thomas de Clare, Knt. [see MAULEY 8 for his ancestry]. They had one son, Peter. In 1360 he and his wife, Elizabeth, conveyed the third part of the manor of Mears Ashby, Northamptonshire (which she held in right of dower) to Henry Greene, Knt. In 1361 he and others were pardoned for their part in the death of two persons for which they had been indicted. In 1362 he complained of violence done in his park of Bainton, Yorkshire, and again in 1366 at other places in Yorkshire. In 1367 custody of the town of Berwick was granted to him. The same year he was appointed conservator of the truce in the Scottish Marches. In 1368 he was made one of the wardens of the East March. His wife, Elizabeth, died 9 July 1368. He married (2nd) before 9 October 1371 (date of license to settle lands) **CONSTANCE SUTTON**, daughter and co-heiress of Thomas de Sutton, Knt., of Bransholme, Southcoates (in Drypool), Sutton, and Atwick, Yorkshire, by Agnes, daughter of John Hothom, Knt. They had female issue, including one daughter, Margaret. In 1372 he was indicted for sheltering felons, but was not to be arrested. In 1378 he complained that John Snell and others had broken into his parks at Kilnwick and Lockington, Yorkshire, and taken away his deer and other game. SIR PETER DE MAULEY, 4th Lord Mauley, died 19 (or 20) March 1382/3. He left a will dated 8 March 1381/2, requesting burial in the church of the Friars Minor, Doncaster, Yorkshire. His widow, Constance, married (2nd) before December 1384 (date of pardon for marrying without license) **JOHN GODDARD**, Knt., in right of his wife, of Bransholme, Yorkshire, King's knight, Knight of the Shire for Yorkshire, 1386, 1391, Escheator of Yorkshire, 1387–8, Sheriff of Yorkshire, 1388–9. He was born about 1346. They had two sons, John, Knt., and Henry, and three daughters, Agnes (wife of Brian Stapleton, Knt.), Maud (wife of Robert Waddesle, Esq.), and Margaret (wife of _____ Ughtred). He served his first campaign under John of Gaunt in Spain in 1367. In 1385 he took part in the expedition of King Richard II against the Scots. He was examined as a witness in the Scrope-Grosvenor controversy in 1386. SIR JOHN GODDARD was living March 1392. His widow, Constance, married (3rd) before 28 August 1395 **ROBERT DE HILTON**, Esq., of Swine in Holderness. She died 9 June 1401.

Frost *Notices rel. to the early Hist. of the Town and Port of Hull* (1827): facing 99 (Sutton ped.). Mackenzie *Desc. & Hist. Account of the Town & County of Newcastle upon Tyne* 1 (1827): 265. Poulson *Hist. & Antiqs. of Holderness* 2 (1841): 198 (Hilton ped.), 200–201 (Darcy ped.), 326 (Sutton ped.), 330. Banks *Baronies in Fee* 1 (1844): 178–179 (sub Darcy), 311–312 (sub Mauley), 313–314 (sub Meinell); 2 (1843): 139–141 (sub Sutton). Ord *Hist. & Antiqs. of Cleveland* (1846): 445–446 (Meinell-Darcy ped.). Flower *Vis. of Yorkshire 1563–4* (H.S.P. 16) (1881): 91–92 (Darcy ped.: "Elenor [rectius Elizabetha] doughter & heyr of the Lord Mennell = John Darcy"). *Papal Regs.: Petitions* 1 (1896): 1, 78. *Papal Regs.: Letters* 3 (1897): 580. *Genealogical Mag.* 5 (1902): 189–198. Wrottesley *Peds. from the Plea Rolls* (1905): 377–378. *C.P.R. 1350–1354* (1907): 27. VCH *Hertford* 3 (1912): 441–458. Clay *Extinct & Dormant Peerages* (1913): 41–42 (sub Darcy), 135–136 (sub Meynell). *C.P.* 4 (1916): 58–61 (sub Darcy); 7 (1929): 225–227 (sub Kildare); 8 (1932): 567–568, 634–635. *Cal. Inqs. Misc.* 3 (1937): 212, 243. VCH *Yorkshire N.R.* 2 (1923): 309–319. Paget *Baronage of England* (1957) 169: 1. Ellis *Cat. Seals in the P.R.O.* 2 (1981): 32 (seal of John Darcy dated 1349 — In a circle, on a background of feathers, a shield of arms: crusilly, three cinquefoils pierced [DARCY]). Edington *Reg. of William Edington Bishop of Winchester* 1 (Hampshire Recs. 7) (1986): 46.

Child of John Darcy, Knt., by Elizabeth de Meinell:

i. **PHILIP DARCY**, Knt., 4th Lord Darcy of Knaith [see next].

Child of Peter de Mauley, Knt., by Elizabeth de Meinill:

i. **PETER DE MAULEY**, of Mulgrave, Yorkshire, married **MARGERY DE SUTTON** [see MAULEY 10].

13. PHILIP DARCY, Knt., 4th Lord Darcy of Knaith, of Knaith, Lincolnshire, Darcies (in Cheshunt), Hertfordshire, Notton (in Royston), Yorkshire, etc., Admiral from the Thames Northwards, 1386, younger son by his father's 2nd marriage, born in the House of the Friars Preachers at York 21 May 1352. He was heir in 1362 to his older brother, John Darcy [3rd Lord Darcy]. He had livery of his inheritance 31 Jan. 1373/4. He married **ELIZABETH GRAY**, daughter of Thomas Gray, Knt., of Heton (in Norham), Northumberland, by Margaret, daughter of William de Presfen (or Pressen). They had four sons, John, Knt. [5th Lord Darcy of Knaith, 4th Lord Meinell], Philip, Thomas, and William, and four daughters, Agnes, Elizabeth, Joan, and Eleanor. He served under the Duke of Lancaster in his raid into Picardy and Caux, July to Nov. 1369, and under the Earl of Buckingham in his raid into Brittany, July 1380 to April 1381. He did homage to King Richard II at his Coronation 16 July 1377. He was summoned to Parliament from 4 August 1377 to 5 Nov. 1397, by writs directed *Philippo Darcy* or *de Darcy*. He was in the expeditions to Scotland under the Duke of Lancaster in April 1384, and under the king in August 1385. In 1392 he was sent to Ireland to recover the king's lordships and his own inheritance, and defend the same against the Irish rebels. SIR PHILIP DARCY, 4th Lord Darcy of Knaith, died 24 April 1399, and was buried at Henes Priory, Lincolnshire. He left a will dated 16 April 1399, proved 3 May 1399. His widow, Elizabeth, Lady Darcy, died 11 August 1412. She left wills dated 20 Dec. 1411 and 7 August 1412, proved 16 August 1412.

Poulson *Hist. & Antiqs. of Holderness* 2 (1841): 200–201 (Darcy ped.). Banks *Baronies in Fee* 1 (1844): 313–314 (sub Meinell). Ord *Hist. & Antiqs. of Cleveland* (1846): 445–446 (Meinell-Darcy ped.). Flower *Vis. of Yorkshire 1563–4* (H.S.P. 16) (1881): 91–92 (Darcy ped.: "Phelyp Lord Darcy of Mennell = Elsabeth doughter of Thomas Grey of Heydon"). *Genealogical Mag.* 5 (1902): 189–198. Wrottesley *Peds. from the Plea Rolls* (1905): 377–378. VCH *Hertford* 3 (1912): 441–458. Clay *Extinct & Dormant Peerages* (1913): 41–42 (sub Darcy). *C.P.* 4 (1916): 61–63 (sub Darcy). VCH *Yorkshire N.R.* 2 (1923): 309–319. Train *Abs. of IPMs Rel. Nottinghamshire* 1 (Thoroton Soc. Recs. 12) (1949): 29–30. Paget *Baronage of England* (1957) 169. Repingdon *Reg. of Philip Repingdon* 2 (Lincoln Rec. Soc. 58) (1963): 264–267 (will of Elizabeth Darcy). *Ancient Deeds — Ser. B* 2 (List & Index Soc. 101) (1974): B.8621. Ellis *Cat. Seals in the P.R.O.* 2 (1981): 32 (seal of Philip Darcy, Lord Darcy dated 1386 — Hung from a twin bush, between lunettes of tracery, a shield of arms: quarterly, 1 and 4, crusilly, three cinquefoils pierced [DARCY], 2 and 3, barry, a chief [MEINELL]. Legend: …LIPPI DARCY…MENYLL..).

14. JOHN DARCY, Knt., 5th Lord Darcy of Knaith, 4th Lord Meinell, of Knaith, Lincolnshire, Darcies (in Cheshunt), Hertfordshire, Notton (in Royston), Yorkshire, etc., son and heir, born about 1376–7 (aged 22 or 23 in 1399). He married shortly after 9 July 1397 (date of recognizances) **MARGARET GREY**, daughter of Henry de Grey, Knt., 5th Lord Grey of Wilton, by Elizabeth, daughter of Gilbert Talbot, Knt., 3rd Lord Talbot [see WILTON 11 for her ancestry]. They had two sons, Philip, Knt. [6th Lord Darcy of Knaith] and John, and four daughters, Elizabeth, Maud, Margery, and Joan. He was summoned to Parliament from 19 August 1399 to 21 Sept. 1411, by writs directed *Johanni Darcy*. He and his wife, Margaret, received a papal indult for a portable altar in 1403. SIR JOHN DARCY, Lord Darcy and Meinell, died 9 Dec. 1411, and was buried at Selby Abbey, Yorkshire. He left a will dated at his manor of Temple Hurst 2 August 1411, proved 18 Feb. 1411/2. His widow, Margaret, married (2nd) (as his 2nd wife) before 12 July 1421 **THOMAS SWYNFORD** (or **SWINFORD**), Knt., of Kettlethorpe, Lincolnshire, Sheriff of Lincoln, 1401–2, Governor of Calais, 1405, son and heir of Hugh de Swynford, Knt., of Kettlethorpe and Coleby, Lincolnshire, by Katherine, daughter and co-heiress of Gilles dit Paonet de Roet (or Ruet, etc.), Knt., Marshal of the Household for Queen Philippe of Hainault [wife of King Edward III of England], Master knight of the Household for Marguerite, Countess of Hainault, Guienne King of Arms in England. He was born about 1368 (aged 4 in 1372). He was the step-son of John of Gaunt, K.G., Duke of Aquitaine and Lancaster (younger son of King Edward III) [see LANCASTER 10]. They had one son, William. He married (1st) before 14 October 1399 **JOAN CROPHILL**, by whom he had one son, Thomas, Knt. [see POWICK 12.ii], and one daughter, Katherine (wife of William Drury, Knt., and Thomas Curzon, Esq.). He was in the retinue of Henry, Earl of Derby [afterwards King Henry IV] as early as 1382. In 1386 he was admitted a member of the fraternity of Lincoln Cathedral. He accompanied Earl Henry on his expedition to Prussia in 1390–1. He was a legatee in the 1398 will of his step-father, John of Gaunt, Duke of Lancaster, who bequeathed him 100 marks. He supported King Henry IV on his accession to the throne. He is thought to have been Henry's instrument in procuring the death of King Richard II at Pontefract Castle, where he was at the time. In 1399 he was granted custody of the king's castle of Somerton, Lincolnshire. In 1404 he was lieutenant for his half-brother, John Beaufort, Duke of Exeter, then Captain of Calais. He was sent on several important missions of treaty to France and Flanders in the period, 1405–10. In 1411 he obtained letters patent for the purpose of inheriting property in Hainault left to him by his mother, Katherine de Roet, Duchess of Lancaster. SIR THOMAS SWYNFORD died 2 April 1432. Margaret, Lady Darcy, died 1 June 1454. Administration on her estate was granted 29 August 1454 to her son, William Swynford, Esq. (Lincoln Cons. Court, 18 Chedworth).

Rymer *Fœdera* 8 (1727): 694–712. Blore *Hist. & Antiqs. of Rutland* 1(2) (1811): 164 (Grey ped.). Thoresby *Ducatus Leodiensis* (1816): 226–228 (Darcy ped.). Nicolas *Testamenta Vetusta* 1 (1826): 254, footnote 2. *Retrospective Rev.* 2nd Ser. 1 (1827): 341. Poulson *Hist. & Antiqs. of Holderness* 2 (1841): 200–201 (Darcy ped.). Banks *Baronies in Fee* 1 (1844): 178–179 (sub John Darcy). Ord *Hist. & Antiqs. of Cleveland* (1846): 445–446 (Meinell-Darcy ped.). Williams *Chron. de la Traïson et Mort de Richart Deux* (1846): lviii, lxxi–lxxii. *Mems. Ill. of the Hist. & Antiqs. of York* (1848): Holy Trinity Priory, York, 222–223. *Archæologia* 40 (1866): 451–482. Burke *Gen. Hist. of the Dormant, Abeyant, Forfeited & Extinct Peerages* (1866): 245–247 (sub Grey, Barons Grey of Wilton). Hardy *Syllabus (in English) of the Docs. Rel. England & Other Kingdoms* 2 (1873): 551, 552, 569. Turner *Cal. Charters & Rolls: Bodleian Lib.* (1878): 679–680 (charter of John, lord Darcy of Menell). Flower *Vis. of Yorkshire 1563–4* (H.S.P. 16) (1881): 90–92 (Danyell ped.: "John Darcy Lord Darcy. = Margaret daughter of the Lord Grey of Wylton."). Gibbons *Early Lincoln Wills 1280–1547* (1888): 183 (admin. of Margaret, Lady Darcy). *Somerset & Dorset Notes & Queries* 1 (1890): 241–246. Fowler *Coucher Book of Selby* 2 (Yorkshire Arch. & Top. Assoc. Rec. Ser. 13) (1893): l–liv. *Yorkshire Arch. Jour.* 12 (1893): 288 (Darcy arms: Semée of crosses crosslet, three cinquefoils). Smith *Expeditions to Prussia & the Holy Land made by Henry Earl of Derby in the Years 1390–1 & 1392–3* (Camden Soc. n.s. 52) (1894). *D.N.B.* 55 (1898): 243–244 (biog. of Catherine Swynford). *List of Sheriffs for England & Wales* (PRO Lists and Indexes 9) (1898): 79. Hodgson *Hist. of Northumberland* 5 (1899): 411 (Darcy ped.). *Life-Recs. of Chaucer* (1900): xxxiii. Foster *Cals. of Lincoln Wills* 1 (Index Lib. 28) (1902): 5. *Genealogical Mag.* 5 (1902): 189–198. *C.P.R. 1399–1401* (1903): 42, 295. *Papal Regs.: Letters* 5 (1904): 569. Wrottesley *Peds. from the Plea Rolls* (1905): 377–378. *C.P.R. 1408–1413* (1909): 323–324. *C.P.R. 1446–1452* (1909): 229. VCH *Hertford* 3 (1912): 451 (Darcy arms: Azure crusilly and three cinqfoils argent). Clay *Extinct & Dormant Peerages* (1913): 41–42 (sub Darcy). *C.P.* 4 (1916): 63–65, 71 (sub Darcy). *Yorkshire Inqs.* 5 (Yorkshire Arch. Soc. Recs. 59) (1918): 93–95. VCH *Yorkshire N.R.* 2 (1923): 309–319. *C.C.R. 1396–1399* (1927): 198–201 (bond, recognizance, and indenture evidently involving marriage arrangements of John Darcy and Margaret Grey). Clay *Yorkshire Deeds* 7 (Yorkshire Arch. Soc. Recs. 83)

(1932): 151. Campling *Hist. of the Fam. of Drury* (1937): 17–19, 96–97 (ped.). *TAG* 21 (1944–45): 169–177. Chichele *Reg. of Henry Chichele* 4 (Canterbury & York Soc. 47) (1947): 222–223. Train *Abs. of IPMs Rel. Nottinghamshire* 2 (Thoroton Soc. Recs. 12) (1952): 153. Worcester *Itineraries [of] William Worcestre* (1969): 355, 359. *Ancient Deeds — Ser. B* 2 (List & Index Soc. 101) (1974): B.8793. Harvey *Vis. of Suffolk 1561* 2 (H.S.P. n.s. 3) (1984): 404–407 (Grimston ped.). *Cal. IPM* 23 (2004): 358–359. *Foundations* 1(3) (2004): 164–174.

Children of John Darcy, Knt., by Margaret Grey:

i. **PHILIP DARCY**, Knt., 6th Lord Darcy of Knaith [see next].

ii. **JOHN DARCY**, of Temple Hurst, Yorkshire, married **JOAN GREYSTOKE** [see LAUNCE 15].

iii. **JOAN DARCY**, married (1st) **JOHN BEAUCHAMP**, Esq. [see MARKHAM 10]; (2nd) **GILES DAUBENEY**, Knt., of Barrington and South Petherton, Somerset, South Ingleby, Lincolnshire, etc. [see MARKHAM 10].

15. PHILIP DARCY, Knt., 6th Lord Darcy of Knaith, of Knaith, Lincolnshire, Darcies (in Cheshunt), Hertfordshire, Notton (in Royston), Yorkshire, etc., son and heir, born about 1398 (aged 14 in 1412). He married before 28 October 1412 (by settlement dated 11 October 1411) **ELEANOR FITZ HUGH**, daughter of Henry Fitz Hugh, K.G., 3rd Lord Fitz Hugh, Lord High Treasurer, by Elizabeth, daughter and heiress of Robert de Grey, Knt. [see FITZ HUGH 14 for her ancestry]. They had two daughters, Elizabeth (wife of James Strangeways, Knt. [see STRANGEWAYS 8]) and Margery. SIR PHILIP DARCY, 6th Lord Darcy of Knaith, died 2 August 1418. His widow, Eleanor, received a papal indult for a portable altar in 1423. Eleanor married (2nd) before 18 Feb. 1426/7 (date of pardon for marrying without license) **THOMAS TUNSTALL**, Knt., of Thurland (in Tunstall), Lancashire [see TUNSTALL 15 for the issue of that marriage]. She was a legatee in the 1427 will of her mother. SIR THOMAS TUNSTALL was about to proceed to France 4 May 1431. Eleanor married (3rd) (as his 2nd wife) **HENRY** (or **HARRY**) **BROMFLETE**, Knt., of Londesborough, Yorkshire (afterwards Lord Vescy) (died testate 16 Jan. 1468/9) [see BROMFLETE 15 for the issue of that marriage]. She died 30 Sept. 1457.

Thoresby *Ducatus Leodiensis* (1816): 226–228 (Darcy ped.). Whitaker *Hist. of Richmondshire* 2 (2) (1823): unpaginated Tunstall ped. *Wills & Invs.* 1 (Surtees Soc. 2) (1835): 74–76 (will of Elizabeth Lady Fitzhugh). Poulson *Hist. & Antiqs. of Holderness* 2 (1841): 200–201 (Darcy ped.). Banks *Baronies in Fee* 1 (1844): 178–179 (sub John Darcy). Ord *Hist. & Antiqs. of Cleveland* (1846): 445–446 (Meinell-Darcy ped.). Flower *Vis. of Yorkshire 1563–4* (H.S.P. 16) (1881): 90–92 (Danyell ped.: "Phelyp Lord Darcy of Mennell. = Elenor doughter to Sir Henry Fytzhugh & syster to the Lord William Fytzhvgh."). Hodgson *Hist. of Northumberland* 5 (1899): 411 (Darcy ped.). *Genealogical Mag.* 5 (1902): 189–198. Wrottesley *Peds. from the Plea Rolls* (1905): 377–378. *Papal Regs.: Letters* 7 (1906): 317. VCH *Hertford* 3 (1912): 451. Clay *Extinct & Dormant Peerages* (1913): 18 (sub Bromflete), 41–42 (sub Darcy), 72–75 (sub Fitz Henry). C.P. 4 (1916): 65–67, 71 (sub Darcy). *Yorkshire Inqs.* 5 (Yorkshire Arch. Soc. Recs. 59) (1918): 93–95, 156–157. VCH *Yorkshire N.R.* 2 (1923): 309–319. Harvey et al. *Vis. of the North* 3 (Surtees Soc. 144) (1930): 132–133 (Fitzhugh ped.: "Aleonora [Fitz Hugh] nupta domino Darcy postea domino Thome Tunstall et postea domino Vescy"). Clay *Yorkshire Deeds* 7 (1932): 141–142. Chippindall *Hist. of Tunstall* (Chetham Soc. n.s. 104) (1940). Walker *Yorkshire Peds.* 3 (H.S.P. 96) (1944): 395–396 (Tunstall ped.). Train *Abs. of IPMs Rel. Nottinghamshire* 2 (Thoroton Soc. Recs. 12) (1952): 168–169. Langley *Reg. of Thomas Langley Bishop of Durham* 3 (Surtees Soc. 169) (1959): 62–64. Roskell *Parl. & Politics in Late Medieval England* 2 (1981): 279–306 (biog. of Sir James Strangeways). *Cal. IPM* 23 (2004): 358–360.

Child of Philip Darcy, Knt., by Eleanor Fitz Hugh:

i. **MARGERY DARCY**, married **JOHN CONYERS**, K.G., of Hornby, Yorkshire [see CONYERS 16].

❧ DAUBENEY ❧

ALICE OF NORMANDY (sister of King William the Conqueror), married **LAMBERT**, Count of Lens.
JUDITH OF LENS, married **WALTHEOF**, Earl of Northumberland.
MAUD OF NORTHUMBERLAND, married **SIMON DE SENLIS**, Earl of Huntingdon and Northampton.
MAUD DE SENLIS, married **ROBERT FITZ RICHARD**, of Little Dunmow, Essex.

5. MAUD DE SENLIS, born about 1125 (aged 60 in 1185). She married (1st) **WILLIAM D'AUBENEY** (or **D'AUBENY**, **DE ALBENEY**), of Belvoir, Leicestershire, son and heir of William d'Aubeney, of Belvoir, Leicestershire, by Cecily, daughter of Roger Bigod. She had the manor of Cratfield, Suffolk in free marriage. They had one son, William, and one daughter, Maud. At an unknown date, he granted Belvoir Priory, Leicestershire and its monks "omnimodas sectas et adventus curiarum" of all their men and tenants. He and his wife, Maud, gave the same Priory the advowson of the church of Cratfield, Suffolk. She gave one-third of the manor of Cratfield, Suffolk to the Priory of St. Neot, Cambridgeshire. WILLIAM D'AUBENEY died in 1167. His widow, Maud, married (2nd) in or after 1180 (as his 2nd wife) **RICHARD DE LUVETOT**, Knt., of Sheffield, Aston, Aughton (in Aston), Brampton-en-le-Morthen, Handsworth, Todwick, and Treeton, Yorkshire, Worksop, Nottinghamshire, etc., son and heir of William de Luvetot, of Sheffield, Yorkshire, Worksop, Nottinghamshire, etc., by his wife, Emma. About 1160 he confirmed the gifts of his parents to Worksop Priory, Nottinghamshire, and added valuable grants of his own, including half the church of Clarborough; two bovates of land in Hardwick Grange, near Clumber, the whole site of the town of Worksop near the church, enclosed by a great ditch as far as Bracebridge meadow; a mill, mansion, and Buselin's meadow; a mill at Manton; and all Sloswick. He further granted to the canons the privileges of feeding as many pigs as they possessed in Rumwood, and of having two wagons for the collecting of all the dry wood they required in the park of Worksop. In 1161 he had a dispute with Ecclesfield Priory, Yorkshire, as to the extent of their respective rights and territories. He held 5 knights' fees of William Paynel in 1166. He accounted for the issues of the honour of Belvoir from midsummer 1168 to 1171. With the consent of his son, William, he gave the hermitage of St. John in the parish of Ecclesfield, Yorkshire to Kirkstead Abbey, Lincolnshire. SIR RICHARD DE LUVETOT died in 1171, and was buried in the church of Worksop, Nottinghamshire. His widow, Maud, was living in 1185.

<small>Thoroton & Throsby *Thoroton's Hist. of Nottinghamshire* 1 (1790): 62–65, 232–236. Dugdale *Monasticon Anglicanum* 3 (1821): 472 (charter of Maud de Senlis, daughter of Robert Fitz Richard to the Priory of St. Neot), 475 (charter of Walter Fitz Robert to Priory of St. Neot; charter names his father, Robert Fitz Richard; his wife, Maud, and his sister, Maud); 5 (1825): 416, 419 (charter of Richard de Luvetot); 6(1) (1830): 118–119 (charter of Richard de Luvetot), 122–124. Holland *Hist., Antiqs., & Desc. of the Town & Parish of Worksop* (1826): 18 (Luvetot-Furnival ped.). Eastwood *Hist. of the Parish of Ecclesfield* (1862): 56–59 (charter of Richard de Luvetot), 81–86. *Notes & Queries* 4th Ser. 11 (1873): 305–308. Round *Feudal England* (1895): 468–479, 575 (ped.). Porée *Hist. de l'Abbaye du Bec* 1 (1901): 454–456. *MSS of the Duke of Rutland* 4 (Hist. MSS Comm. 24) (1905): 99 (charter of Simon de Senlis, Earl of Northampton, to Belvoir Priory; charter witnessed by Richard de Luvetot and his wife, Maud de Senlis), 106, 108 (charter of William d'Aubeney to Belvoir Priory), 127, 165–166, 177. VCH *Nottingham* 2 (1910): 125–129. *Early Yorkshire Charters* 6 (1939): 209–211. Tanner *Fams., Friends, & Allies* (2004): 313 (Scotland ped.), 316 (Clare ped.).</small>

Children of Maud de Senlis, by William d'Aubeney:

i. **WILLIAM D'AUBENEY** [see next].

ii. **MAUD D'AUBENEY**, married (as his 1st wife) **GILBERT**, 3rd Earl of Strathearn, son of Ferteth (or Ferquhard), 2nd Earl of Strathearn, by his wife, Ethen (or Ethne). They had seven sons, Gilchrist, William, Ferteth, Robert [Earl of Strathearn], Fergus, Knt., Malise (parson of Gask), and Gilbert, Knt., and three daughters, Maud (wife of Malcolm, Earl of Fife), Cecily (wife of Walter Ruthven), and probably Ethna (or Helen) (wife of David Hay, of Erroll). He first appears on record as a witness to a charter by King Malcolm in 1164. Sometime in the period, 1178–85, he was granted lands in Kinveachy. In 1185 he had a charter of Maderty. In 1200 he founded an abbey on his own lands at Inchaffray. He was a benefactor to the cathedral of Dunblane. His wife,

Maud, was living in 1210. He married (2nd) **YSENDA DE GASK**, sister of Richard and Geoffrey de Gask. Sometime in the period, 1211–14, he was granted the lands of Ure and Lethindie, which formerly belonged to his brother, Malise. Gilbert, Earl of Strathearn, died in 1223. Innes *Liber Insule Missarum* (1847): 3, 6, 7, 8, 9, 10, 11, 12, 15, 16, 17, 18, 21, 25, 26, 27, 28, 29, 33, 67, 68, 70, 71, 76. Dowden *Chartulary of the Abbey of Lindores* (Scottish Hist. Soc. 42) (1903): xxxiv–xxxviii. Cowan *Royal House of Stuart* 1 (1908): 54–60 (charter of Gilbert, Earl of Strathearn, and his wife, Maud d'Aubeney). *Scots Peerage* 1 (1904): 450–451, & 452, footnote 4 (sub Murray, Duke of Atholl); 8 (1911): 240–244 (sub Ancient Earls of Strathearn). Prestwich et al. *Procs. of the Gregynog Conf. 2005* (13th Cent. England 11) (2007): 88–89.

Child of Maud d'Aubeney, by Gilbert, Earl of Strathearn:

a. **ROBERT**, 4th Earl of Strathearn, 4th but eldest surviving son and heir by his father's 1st marriage. He married ____ **OF MORAY**, daughter of Hugh de Moray, by Annabelle, daughter of Duncan, Earl of Fife. They had three sons, Malise [5th Earl of Strathearn], Hugh [Prior of Inchaffray], and Gilbert, Knt., and four daughters, Annabelle (wife of John de Restalrig and Patrick Graham, Knt.), Mary (wife of John Johnstone, Knt.), Maud, and Amice. He first appears as a witness to his father's charters in 1199. In 1219, as heir-apparent to his father, he confirmed all his father's grants to Inchaffray Abbey. He witnessed a charter of his brother, Fergus, in 1234. In 1237 he was with King Alexander II at York, where he witnessed the treaty with King Henry III regarding Northumberland. ROBERT, Earl of Strathearn, died in or before 1244. His widow was living in 1246. Dowden *Chartulary of the Abbey of Lindores* (Scottish Hist. Soc. 42) (1903): xxxiv–xxxviii. *Scots Peerage* 8 (1911): 244–245 (sub Ancient Earls of Strathearn).

6. WILLIAM D'AUBENEY (or **D'AUBENY**, **DE ALBENEY**), Knt., of Belvoir and Bottesford, Leicestershire, Uffington, Woolsthorpe, and Wyville, Lincolnshire, Stoke Albany and Wilbarston, Northamptonshire, Orston, Nottinghamshire, etc., Sheriff of Rutland, 1195, Sheriff of Bedfordshire and Buckinghamshire, 1197, Sheriff of Warwickshire and Leicestershire, 1197, Governor of Rochester Castle, son and heir, minor in 1168. He married (1st) **MARGARET** (or **MARGERY**) **DE UMFREVILLE**, daughter of Odinel de Umfreville, of Prudhoe, Northumberland, by Alice, daughter of Richard de Lucy, Knt., Justiciar of England [see MALLORY 6 for her ancestry]. They had four sons, William, Knt., Odinel, Knt., Robert, and Nicholas [Rector of Bottesford, Lincolnshire]. He fought in Normandy 1192 and 1194. His wife, Margaret (or Margery), died 20 September, year unknown, and was buried in Belvoir Priory, Leicestershire. He married (2nd) about 29 Sept. 1198 **AGATHA TRUSSEBUT**, widow of Hamo Fitz Hamo (died 1196/7), of Wolverton, Buckinghamshire, and daughter of William Trussebut, of Warter and Hunsingore, Yorkshire, by his wife, Aubrey de Harcourt. They had no issue. In 1193 she was co-heiress to her brother, Robert Trussebut, by which she inherited a one-third share of the barony of Hunsingore, Yorkshire. On 15 Jan. 1200 King John confirmed to him the grant of the manor of Orston, Nottinghamshire, which he had received earlier from King Richard I. In 1200/1 he had license from the king to enclose his park at Stoke Albany, Northamptonshire, and to hunt fox and hare in the royal forests. He fought in Ireland in 1210. He joined the confederacy of the barons against the king in 1215. He was one of the twenty-five barons elected to guarantee the observance of Magna Carta, which King John signed 15 June 1215. He was appointed by the Barons Governor of Rochester Castle, but was compelled to surrender it to the King on 30 Nov. 1215, and was imprisoned in Corfe Castle. He and his son, William, were among the barons excommunicated by Pope Innocent III 16 Dec. 1215. In December and the ensuing months, his wife, Agatha, and on some occasions, his son William, had letters of safe-conduct for coming to the king to speak for his deliverance. On 6 August 1216 seisin of all his lands was given to his wife for the payment of 6,000 marks, for which he made a fine with the king. In the period July to October 1216, she made several payments amounting to upwards of 1,000 marks for his redemption and his knights and tenants had orders to make an aid for the purpose. On 23 March 1216/7, and again on 29 May 1217, orders were issued for the delivery of Agatha to her husband, satisfactory arrangements being made for hostages in her place. He was subsequently restored by King Henry III. In 1220 he, William de Roos, and Hilary Trussebut presented to the church in Braunston,

Northamptonshire. He presented to the churches of Bottesford, Leicestershire, c.1220, 1223, 1224, and 1233, and Wilbarston, Northamptonshire, 1223. In 1231–2 he presented to the church of Grayingham, Lincolnshire, in right of his wife, Agatha. At an unknown date, he gave the church of Cratfield, Suffolk to the Priory of St. Neot. He founded the hospital of Newstead by Stamford, Lincolnshire. SIR WILLIAM D'AUBENEY died 7 May 1236, and was buried at Newstead, Lincolnshire, his heart at Belvoir Priory, Leicestershire. Following his death, his widow, Agatha, was again in royal favour, receiving gifts in 1236 and 1240. In 1237 she and her sister, Hilary Trussebut, and their great-nephew, William de Roos, presented to the church of Braunston, Northamptonshire. In 1238 she had license to go overseas on the king's business and in 1241 she had license to visit Normandy. In 1241 she was co-heiress to her sister, Hilary Trussebut, by which her share in the barony of Hunsingore, Yorkshire increased from one-third to one-half. She presented to the church of Deighton, Yorkshire in 1247, as "Dame Agatha Trussebut." She died at Chalfont St. Giles, Buckinghamshire shortly before 28 Feb. 1247.

Throsby *Thoroton's Hist. of Nottinghamshire* 1 (1790): 218–221. Bridges *Hist. & Antiqs. of Northamptonshire* 1 (1791): 30. Nichols *Hist. & Antiqs. of Leicester* 2(1) (1795): 96; Appendix, 8–10 (charters of William d'Aubeney III), 23, 29 (anniversary of William d'Aubeney III kept at Belvoir Priory 7 May), 35 (anniversary of Margery, wife of William d'Aubeney III, kept at Belvoir Priory 20 September). Dugdale *Monasticon Anglicanum* 3 (1821): 474 (charter of William d'Aubeney, son of Maud de Senlis to the Priory of St. Neot). Lipscomb *Hist. & Antiqs. of Buckingham* 4 (1847): 99–102. Foss *Judges of England* 2 (1848): 204–207 (biog. of William de Albini). *Reliquary* 7 (1866–7): 72–77. Hardy *Syllabus (in English) of the Docs. Rel. England & Other Kingdoms* 1 (1869): 21, 22. Gray *Reg., or Rolls, of Walter Gray, Lord Archbishop of York* (Surtees Soc. 56) (1872): 99. Matthew of Paris *Chronica Majora* 2 (Rolls Ser. 57) (1874): 604–605, 642–644. Birch *Cat. Seals in the British Museum* 3 (1894): 598 (seal of Agatha Trussebut, widow of William de Aubeny — Dark-green: fine. 1⅝ in. A water bouget, in allusion to the arms of the Trussebut family, viz. three water-bougets, etc.). Round *Feudal England* (1895): 575 (ped.). *List of Sheriffs for England & Wales* (PRO Lists and Indexes 9) (1898): 1, 112, 144. *Jour. British Arch. Assoc.* n.s. 7 (1901): 300–326. Porée *Hist. de l'Abbaye du Bec* 1 (1901): 454–456. *C.Ch.R.* 1 (1903): 387. *MSS of the Duke of Rutland* 4 (Hist. MSS Comm. 24) (1905): 13, 17, 103, 115, 119–121, 126, 129–131, 136, 144, 147–149, 164, 167 (various charters of William d'Aubeney), 121 (charter of Agatha Trussebut). *Notes & Queries for Somerset & Dorset* 9 (1905): 308–310. Phillimore *Rotuli Hugonis de Welles Episcopi Lincolniensis 1209–1235* 2 (Lincoln Rec. Soc. 6) (1913): 48–50, 100, 114. *Early Yorkshire Charters* 1 (1914): 460–461; 10 (1955): 5–19, 63, also 43, 49–51, 61, 126 (charters of William d'Aubeney and Agatha Trussebut). Grosseteste *Rotuli Roberti Grosseteste Episcopi Lincolniensis* (Lincoln Rec. Soc. 11) (1914): 168, 212, 388. Dodds *Hist. of Northumberland* 12 (1926): 79–112. Foster & Major *Reg. Antiquissimum Lincoln* 3 (Lincoln Rec. Soc. 29) (1932): 313–314; 10 (Lincoln Rec. Soc. 67) (1973): 283. Paget *Baronage of England* (1957) 14: 1–4 (sub Aubigny); 546: 2. Sanders *English Baronies* (1960): 12, 56, 100. Leys *Sandford Cartulary* 2 (Oxfordshire Rec. Soc. 22) (1941): 253–254. Cheney *Letters of Pope Innocent III 1198–1216* (1967): 172. Tremlett et al. *Rolls of Arms Henry III* (H.S.P. 113-4) (1967): 23 (arms of William d'Aubeney: Or, two chevrons and a bordure gules), 40. Major *Registrum Antiquissimum of the Cathedral Church of Lincoln* 10 (Lincoln Rec. Soc. 67) (1973): 282–283. Elvey *Luffield Priory Charters* 2 (Northamptonshire Rec. Soc. 26) (1975): xlii, lxxii (chart). Smith *English Episc. Acta* 9 Winchester 1205–1238 (1994): 82–86, 87–88. Raban *White Book of Peterborough* (Northamptonshire Rec. Soc.) (2001): 52. Weiler *Thirteenth Cent. England XI* (2007).

Children of William d'Aubeney, Knt., by Margaret (or Margery) de Umfreville:

i. **WILLIAM D'AUBENEY**, Knt. [see next].

ii. **ODINEL D'AUBENEY**, Knt., of Barkestone and Plungar, Leicestershire, and Naburn and North Dalton, Yorkshire, 2nd son. He married **HAWISE** _____. They had two sons, William and John, Knt., and four daughters. He was taken prisoner with his father at Rochester Castle in 1215, and imprisoned in Corfe Castle. He died 26 November, in or after 1235–6, and was buried at Belvoir Priory, Leicestershire. In 1238 Richard de Waterville recovered custody of the lands of Odinel d'Aubeney at Dalton, Yorkshire against Roger de Coleville, until the heir of Odinel should come of age. Sometime before his brother William d'Aubeney's death in 1242, William gave custody of Barkestone and Plungar, Leicestershire to the four daughters of Odinel in payment of money owed to Odinel by their father's will. His widow, Hawise, married (2nd) **ROGER DE BIRMINGHAM**. They were both living in Hilary term 1253 (date of fine). Nichols *Hist. & Antiqs. of Leicester* 2(1) (1795): Appendix, 23, 38 (anniversary of Odinel d'Aubeney kept at Belvoir Priory 26 November). *Reliquary* 7 (1866–7): 72–77. *Jour. British Arch. Assoc.* n.s. 7 (1901): 300–326. *Lincolnshire N & Q* 7 (1904): 141–142. *MSS of the Duke of Rutland* 4 (Hist. MSS Comm. 24) (1905): 71, 103, 121, 124, 131, 136, 164, 167, 169. *C.C.R. 1237–1242* (1911): 119, 472–473. *Early Yorkshire Charters* 1 (1914): 462. *Yorkshire Deeds* 2 (Yorkshire Arch. Soc. Recs. 50) (1914): 78. *Lincolnshire N*

& *Q* 15 (1919): 25. Foster *Final Concords of Lincoln from the Feet of Fines A.D. 1244–1272* 2 (Lincoln Rec. Soc. 17) (1920): 282–283. *C.C.R. 1251–1253* (1927): 264. Leys *Sandford Cartulary* 2 (Oxfordshire Rec. Soc. 22) (1941): 253–254. Paget *Baronage of England* (1957) 14: 1–4 (sub Aubigny). Farnham *Leicestershire Medieval Village Notes* (sub Barkstone) [FHL 804152].

Children of Odinel d'Aubeney, by an unknown wife, _____:

a. **WILLIAM D'AUBENEY**, of Barkestone and Plungar, Leicestershire, son and heir, living in 1253. He married _____. They had two daughters, Isabel (presumably wife of _____ de Bringhurst) and Sarah. He died before Michaelmas 1261. *Lincolnshire N & Q* 7 (1904): 141–142. Foster *Final Concords of Lincoln from the Feet of Fines A.D. 1244–1272* 2 (Lincoln Rec. Soc. 17) (1920): 282–283. *C.C.R. 1251–1253* (1927): 264. Farnham *Leicestershire Village Notes* 5 (1931): 131. Farnham *Leicestershire Medieval Village Notes* (sub Barkstone) [FHL 804152].

   Child of William d'Aubeney, by _____:

   1) **SARAH D'AUBENEY**, daughter and co-heiress, minor in 1261. She married **RICHARD DE BERNAKE**, Knt., in right of his wife, of Barkestone, Leicestershire. They had one son, William, Knt. In 1274–5 he and his wife, Sarra, arraigned an assize of novel disseisin against Robert de Ros and others touching a tenement in Barkestone and Plungar, Leicestershire. In the same period, Richard and his wife, Sarra, arraigned an assize of novel disseisin against Robert de Ros and others touching a tenement in North Dalton, Yorkshire. In 1275–6 Sampson son of William de Burleigh arraigned an assize of novel disseisin against him touching common of pasture in Barnack and Burghley, Northamptonshire. RICHARD DE BERNAKE died testate shortly before 15 Nov. 1293. Descendants include William de Bernake, Knt. (died 1386), of Blatherwycke, Northamptonshire, Barkestone, Leicestershire, etc. [see CANTELOWE 9.ii]. *Annual Rpt. of the Deputy Keeper* 44 (1883): 18, 80; 45 (1884): 86. Harvey et al. *Vis. of Bedfordshire 1566, 1582, 1634 & 1669* (H.S.P. 19) (1884): 12–15 (1566 Vis.) (Cheyney ped.: "Ricardus Barnacke miles. = Sara filia et hær. Will'm Dawbney de Barkeston.") (Barnacke arms: Argent, a horse barnacle sable). VCH *Bedford* 2 (1908): 242–246 (Barnacke arms: Argent a horse-barnacle sable). Farnham *Leicestershire Village Notes* 5 (1931): 131. *Rolls & Reg. of Bishop Oliver Sutton 1280–1299* 4 (Lincoln Rec. Soc. 52) (1958): 134. Farnham *Leicestershire Medieval Village Notes* (sub Barkstone) [FHL 804152].

b. **JOHN D'AUBENEY**, Knt., of Croxton, Leicestershire, Kirmington, Lincolnshire, North Dalton, Yorkshire, etc., 2nd son, adult by 1253. He was living in 1270. He presumably died without issue before 1314, as by that date his land holdings at Croxton and Kirmington were held jointly by William de Bernake and William de Bringhurst, who were presumably the lineal representatives of John Daubeney's two nieces, Sarah and Isabel Daubeney. *Cal. IPM* 1 (1904): 254–255. *Lincolnshire N & Q* 7 (1904): 141–142. *Cal. IPM* 5 (1908): 257–258. Foster *Final Concords of Lincoln from the Feet of Fines A.D. 1244–1272* 2 (Lincoln Rec. Soc. 17) (1920): 282–283. Moor *Knights of Edward I* 1 (H.S.P. 80) (1929): 8 (biog. of Sr John de Albini). Farnham *Leicestershire Village Notes* 5 (1931): 131. Farnham *Leicestershire Medieval Village Notes* (sub Barkstone) [FHL 804152].

iii. **ROBERT D'AUBENEY**, of Wyville and Hungerton, Lincolnshire, and Normanton, Rutland, 3rd son. He married **EUSTACHE** _____. They had one son, William. Robert presented to the chuch of Normanton, Rutland in 1227 and again in 1234. Sometime before 1236, he granted a sheaf yearly from every acre of his demesne at Wyville and Hungerton, Lincolnshire to Belvoir Priory, for the refreshment of the sick monks. ROBERT D'AUBENEY died in or before 1237, when his widow, Eustache, claimed dower in 20 virgates and 5 acres of land in Normanton, Rutland against Gilbert de Umfreville. *Reliquary* 7 (1866–7): 72–77. *MSS of the Duke of Rutland* 4 (Hist. MSS Comm. 24) (1905): 164 (charters of Robert d'Aubeney and his son, William d'Aubeney). Phillimore *Rotuli Hugonis de Welles, Episcopi Lincolniensis 1209–1235* 2 (Lincoln Rec. Soc. 6) (1913): 180. VCH *Rutland* 2 (1935): 86–88. Paget *Baronage of England* (1957) 14: 1–4 (sub Aubigny). Lincolnshire Archives: 1 Pearson-Gregory, 1 PG/1/1 (undated gift and confirmation from William de Aubeny III to Robert de Aubeny his son, for his homage and service, of the whole vill of Wivelle and of Hungerton with all its appurtenances within the vill to be held by the service of half a knight's fee) (available at www.a2a.org.uk/search/index.asp).

   Child of Robert d'Aubeney, by an unknown wife, _____:

   a. **WILLIAM D'AUBENEY**, son and heir. He married _____. They had one daughter, Eustache. He was living c.1249, when he confirmed his father's gift to Belvoir Priory. *MSS of the Duke of Rutland* 4 (Hist. MSS Comm. 24) (1905): 164.

      Presumed child of William d'Aubeney, by an unknown wife, _____:

1) **EUSTACHE D'AUBENEY**, daughter and heiress. She married **GERARD DE FANCOURT**, Knt., of Hickling and Kinoulton, Nottinghamshire, and, in right of his wife, of Wyville and Hungerton, Lincolnshire and Normanton, Rutland, son and heir of Gerard de Fancourt, of Hickling and Kinoulton, Nottinghamshire, Harby, Leicestershire, etc. They had no issue. In 1261 he had letters of protection, he then going on pilgrimage to Santiago. In 1265, following the Battle of Evesham, he seized lands of the abbot of Peterborough in Nottinghamshire and the bishop of Lincoln in Lincolnshire. In 1266 he was granted Harston Castle, Leicestershire by the king for life at an annual rent of £15 per annum, provided he fortify it at his own cost. In 1270 he went on crusade with Prince Edward, and to pay his expenses, he mortgaged his lands to Master Elias, a Jewish moneylender. In 1271 he and Eustache his wife granted a messuage and 8 virgates of land in Normanton, Rutland, together with the advowson of the church, to Thomas de Normanville to be held of them and the heirs of Eustache. In 1274–5 he granted 16 bovates and the free service of 12 bovates in Hickling and Cropwell Bishop, Nottinghamshire to Thurgarton Priory. In the period, 1285–95, she quitclaimed her right in one messuage and 2s. rent per annum in Hickling, Nottinghamshire to Thurgarton Priory. In 1286 she confirmed all the endowments given to the monks of Belvoir Priory by her predecessors in her fee of Wyvillle and Hungerton, Lincolnshire. In 1287 she conveyed to her cousin, Robert son of Robert de Roos [see GEDNEY 8], one messuage and various lands in Wyville, Hungerton, Denton, Bottesford, North Stoke, and South Stoke, Lincolnshire. She withdrew her candidate for the church of Wyville, Lincolnshire in 1291. In 1292 Roger, prior of Belvoir, accepted Eustache into fraternity, and granted that for life she should have a mass celebrated for her every July 20th. She presented to the church of Normanton, Rutland in 1295, acting as guardian for Edmund heir of Sir Thomas de Normanville. She died 3 November, year unknown. Throsby *Thoroton's Hist. of Nottinghamshire* 1 (1790): 142. *Annual Rpt. of the Deputy Keeper* 45 (1885): 117. *MSS of the Duke of Rutland* 4 (Hist. MSS Comm. 24) (1905): 164. *Lincolnshire N & Q* 11 (1910): 2. VCH *Rutland* 2 (1935): 86–88. Foulds *Thurgarton Cartulary* (1994): cxxviii–cxxxiv, 330–335. Prestwich *Plantagenet England 1225–1360* (2005): 417.

iv. **NICHOLAS D'AUBENEY**, clerk, 4th son. He was Rector of Bottesford, Leicestershire. He held Belvoir Castle for his father in 1216, but was compelled to surrender it to King John. He was delivered into the custody of Philip Marc 22 Mar. 1217. The king ordered that he be released from custody 4 Nov. 1217. He died 26 April 1222. Nichols *Hist. & Antiqs. of Leicester* 2(1) (1795): 96; Appendix: 28 (anniversary of Nicholaus [d'Aubeney], parson of Bottesford, kept at Belvoir Priory 26 April). *Reliquary* 7 (1866–7): 72–77. *C.P.R.* 1216–1225 (1901): 45, 47, 66, 120. *MSS of the Duke of Rutland* 4 (Hist. MSS Comm. 24) (1905): 121, 124, 144. Paget *Baronage of England* (1957) 14: 1–4 (sub Aubigny).

7. WILLIAM D'AUBENEY (also known as **WILLIAM DE BEAUVOIR**), Knt., of Belvoir and Bottesford, Leicestershire, Turvey and Oakley, Bedfordshire, Deeping, Tallington, Uffington, and Woolsthorpe, Lincolnshire, Stoke Albany, Northamptonshire, Orston and Thoroton, Nottinghamshire, Naburn, Yorkshire, etc., son and heir by his father's 1st marriage. He married (1st) before 1212 **AUBREY BISET**, probable daughter and co-heiress of Henry Biset (son of William the Carpenter), of West Allington, Lincolnshire, by Aubrey de Lisours, daughter of Richard Fitz Eustace, hereditary Constable of Chester. Her maritagium or inheritance included the manor of West Allington, Lincolnshire. They had no issue. He fought in Ireland in 1210. He and his father, William, were among the barons excommunicated by Pope Innocent III 16 Dec. 1215. He presented to the church of Bottesford, Leicestershire in 1223–4 and again in 1233–4. His wife, Aubrey, was living 28 Sept. 1226. She died 23 November, year unknown. He married (2nd) before 1239 **ISABEL** _____. They had one daughter, Isabel. He was summoned for military service in Gascony in 1242, but gave twenty marks to be excused. SIR WILLIAM D'AUBENEY died 4 Sept. 1242. His body was buried before the high altar at Beauvoir Priory, Leicestershire, and his heart at Croxton Abbey, Leicestershire. In 1261 his widow, Isabel, demanded against John d'Aubeney a fourth part of nine marks rent in Croxton, Leicestershire as dower. She was living in 1285.

Thoroton & Throsby *Thoroton's Hist. of Nottinghamshire* 1 (1790): 218–221. Nichols *Hist. & Antiqs. of Leicester* 2(1) (1795): Appendix, 10 (charter of William d'Aubeney IV), 23, 35 (anniversary of William d'Aubeney IV kept at Belvoir Priory 4 September), 38 (anniversary of Aubrey Biset, wife of William d'Aubeney IV kept at Belvoir Priory 23 November). Lipscomb *Hist. & Antiqs. of Buckingham* 4 (1847): 99–102. *Reliquary* 7 (1866–7): 72–77. Matthew of Paris *Chronica Majora* 2 (Rolls Ser. 57) (1874): 642–644. *Jour. British Arch. Assoc.* n.s. 7 (1901): 300–326. *Cal. IPM* 1 (1904): 4. *MSS of the Duke of Rutland* 4 (Hist. MSS Comm. 24) (1905): 18 (quit-claim and deed of feoffment of William d'Aubeney), 121 (charter of William d'Aubeney). Phillimore *Rotuli Hugonis de Welles, Episcopi Lincolniensis 1209–1235* 2 (Lincoln Rec. Soc. 6) (1913): 291, 292, 310–311, 324. Farnham *Leicestershire Village Notes* 5 (1931): 131. *C.P.* 11 (1949): 96, footnote c. Hatton *Book of Seals* (1950): 8–9 (charter of William d'Aubeney IV dated 1239–48; seal on cord. Shield of arms curved at top and sides, two chevrons and a bordure charged with roundels). Paget *Baronage of England* (1957) 14: 1–4 (sub Aubigny). Sanders *English Baronies* (1960): 12. Cheney *Letters of Pope Innocent III 1198–1216* (1967): 172. VCH *Yorkshire E.R.* 3 (1976): 74–82.

Child of William d'Aubeney, Knt., by Isabel _____:

i. **ISABEL D'AUBENEY**, married **ROBERT DE ROOS**, Knt., of Helmsley, Yorkshire [see ROOS 7].

↬ DAUNTSEY ↫

RICHARD DE MONTAGU, of Shepton Montague, Somerset, married **ALICE** _____.
WILLIAM DE MONTAGU, of Shepton Montague, Somerset, married **ISABEL** _____.
DREW DE MONTAGU, married **ALINE BASSET**.
WILLIAM DE MONTAGU, Knt., of Shepton Montague, Somerset, married **BERTHA** _____.
SIMON DE MONTAGU, Knt., 1st Lord Montagu, married **HAWISE DE SAINT AMAND**.
WILLIAM DE MONTAGU, Knt., 2nd Lord Montagu, married **ELIZABETH DE MONTFORT** (desc. King William the Conqueror) [see MONTAGU 6].

7. **HAWISE DE MONTAGU**, married before 1337 (date of fine) **ROGER DE BAVENT**, Knt., of Cocking, Sussex, Brandeston (in Waldingfield), Suffolk, Fifield-Scudamore (now Fifield-Bavant) and Norton Bavent, Trow (in Alvediston), Wiltshire, son and heir of Roger de Bavent, Lord Bavent, of Cocking, Sussex, Norton-Scudamore and Fifield-Scudamore (now Fifield-Bavant), Wiltshire, etc., by his wife, Joan. They had one son, John (Franciscan friar), and one daughter, Joan. He was never summoned to Parliament. In 1344 he granted all his lands except the manors of Chiltington and Sloughterford, Sussex to the king, who regranted them to him for life. SIR ROGER BAVENT died 23 April 1355. His widow, Hawise, was living in 1362.

Wigram *Cartulary of the Monastery of St. Frideswide at Oxford* (Oxford Hist. Soc. 31) (1896): 8–13 (charter dated 1348 names Lady Elizabeth de Montagu, her late husband, Sir W[illiam] de Montagu, and their ten children; including Lady Hawise Bavent). Copinger *Manors of Suffolk: Hundred of Babergh & Blackbourn* (1905): 241. *C.C.R.* 1360–1364 (1909): 383. *C.P.* 2 (1912): 33–34 (sub Bavent). VHC *Wiltshire* 8 (1965): 47–48; 13 (1987): 9–10, 62–63.

8. **JOAN DE BAVENT**, married before Nov. 1373 **JOHN DAUNTSEY**, Knt., of Dauntsey, Bremilham, Marden, Smithcot (in Dauntsey), Wilsford Dauntsey, and Winterbourne-Dauntsey, Wiltshire, Sheriff of Wiltshire, 1373–4, Knight of the Shire for Wiltshire, 1378, 1379, 1381, 1382, 1388, son of Richard Dauntsey, of Wilsford Dauntsey, Wiltshire, by Katherine, daughter of John Gernon, of Steeple Lavington, Wiltshire. They had three sons, John, Knt., Edmund, and Edward. His wife, Joan, was heiress before 1373 to her brother, John de Bavent. In 1372 he was serving in the retinue of Edward le Despenser, Lord Despenser. In 1373 he and his wife, Joan, gave up their claim to the manors of Fifield Bavant and Norton Bavent, Wiltshire, in exchange for a royal grant of the manor of Marden, Wiltshire. He presented to the church of Dauntsey, Wiltshire in 1376 and 1379, Smithcot Chapel in Dauntsey, Wiltshire, 1387, and the church of Bremilham, Wiltshire in 1390. In 1386 he acquired the manors of Oakhanger and Newton Valence, Hampshire, by the terms of a settlement. In 1386 he was granted an annuity of £20 annually for life by Richard, Earl of Arundel. In 1387 he enlisted in the force which put to sea under the earl as admiral. SIR JOHN DAUNTSEY died testate 31 October 1391, requesting burial at Dauntsey, Wiltshire.

Wiltshire Arch. & Nat. Hist. Mag. 2 (1855): 281–282. MacNamara *Mems. of the Danvers Fam.* (1895): 227–305. *C.C.R.* 1381–1385 (1920): 420, 427. *C.C.R.* 1385–1389 (1921): 144. VHC *Wiltshire* 8 (1965): 47–48; 10 (1975): 120, 204–214; 13 (1987): 9–10, 62–63; 14 (1991): 10, 68. Roskell *House of Commons 1386–1421* 2 (1992): 758–759 (biog. of Sir John Dauntsey).

9. JOHN DAUNTSEY, Knt., of Dauntsey, Bremilham, Marden, Smithcot (in Dauntsey), Wilsford Dauntsey, and Winterbourne-Dauntsey, Wiltshire, and, in right of his wife, of Minsdenbury (in Hitchin), Hertfordshire, son and heir, born about 1357 (aged 34 in 1391). He married before 1383 **ELIZABETH BEVERLEY**, daughter and co-heiress of John Beverley, Knt., of London, Bucknell, Oxfordshire, Minsdenbury (in Hitchin), Hertfordshire, and Penkridge, Staffordshire, King's yeoman, by Amice, daughter and co-heiress of Alan Buxhall. They had one son, Walter, Knt., and one daughter, Joan (or Jane). He presented to the church of Dauntsey, Wiltshire in 1393. His wife, Elizabeth, died in 1395. SIR JOHN DAUNTSEY died in Feb. 1404/5.

Clutterbuck *Hist. & Antiqs. of Hertford* 3 (1827): 33 (Beverley ped.). *Wiltshire Arch. & Nat. Hist. Mag.* 2 (1855): 281–282. Boyd & Wrottesley *Final Concords* (Colls. Hist. Staffs. 11) (1890): 225. MacNamara *Mems. of the Danvers Fam.* (1895): 227–305. VCH *Hertford* 3 (1912): 3–12. *C.C.R.* 1385–1389 (1921): 144, 363. VCH *Stafford* 5 (1959): 103–126. VHC *Wiltshire* 10 (1975): 120; 14 (1991): 10, 68. Timmins *Reg. of John Chandler Dean of Salisbury 1404–17* (Wiltshire Rec. Soc. 39) (1984): 26–27.

10. JOAN (or **JANE**) **DAUNTSEY**, born about 1396 (aged 25 in 1421). She married (1st) before 1412 (as his 2nd wife) **MAURICE RUSSELL**, of Kingston Russell, Dorset, Dyrham, Gloucestershire, etc., Sheriff of Gloucestershire, 1390–1, 1395–6, 1400–1, 1406–7, Coroner for Gloucestershire, 1392–4, Knight of the Shire for Gloucestershire, 1402, 1404, 3rd son but eventual heir of Ralph Russell, Knt., of Kingston Russell, Dorset, by his wife, Alice. He was born 2 Feb. 1356. They had one son, Thomas. SIR MAURICE RUSSELL died 27 June 1416, and was buried at Dyrham, Gloucestershire. His widow, Joan, married (2nd) before 8 July 1418 (date of pardon for marrying without license) **JOHN STRADLING**, Knt., in right of his wife, of Dauntsey, Bremilham, Marden, Pertenall, Smithcot (in Dauntsey), Trow(in Alvediston), Wilsford, and Winterbourne-Dauntsey, Wiltshire, Penkridge, Staffordshire, etc., 2nd son of William Stradling, Knt., of St. Donat's, Glamorgan, by Isabel, daughter and heiress of John Saint Barbe, of South Brent, Somerset. They had two sons, Richard and Edmund. His wife, Joan, was heiress in 1420 to her brother, Walter Dauntsey, Knt. He presented to the church of Bremilham, Wiltshire in 1430 and 1433, and Dauntsey, Wiltshire in 1433. SIR JOHN STRADLING died in 1435. His widow, Joan, married (3rd) after 17 July 1437 (date of bond) and before 1439 **JOHN DEWALL** (or **DEWALE**), Esq., of Dauntsey, Bremilham, Pertenall, Smithcot (in Dauntsey), Trow (in Alvediston), Wilsford, and Winterbourne-Dauntsey, Wiltshire, and London, lawyer, Escheator for Wiltshire, 1438–9, Knight of the Shire for Wiltshire, 1449–50. He presented to the church of Bremilham, Wiltshire in 1439, 1444, and 1445. He and his wife, Joan, presented to the church of Dauntsey, Wiltshire in 1439. JOHN DEWALL, Esq., died shortly before 16 March 1453. His widow, Joan, died in 1457. She and her 3rd husband were buried in the church of Dauntsey, Wiltshire.

Traherne *Stradling Corr.* (1840): xvii–xx (Stradling ped.). Scrope *Hist. of the Manor & Ancient Barony of Castle Combe* (1852): 219. *Wiltshire Arch. & Nat. Hist. Mag.* 2 (1855): 281–282. Boyd & Wrottesley *Final Concords* (Colls. Hist. Staffs. 11) (1890): 229. MacNamara *Mems. of the Danvers Fam.* (1895): 227–305. *Wiltshire Notes & Queries* 3 (1902): 47–48. Wedgwood *Hist. of Parl.* 1 (1936): 273 (biog. of John Dewall). Williams *Collectanea* (Wiltshire Arch. & Natural Hist. Soc. Recs. Branch 12) (1956): 169–170 (bond dated 1437), 171–173. VHC *Wiltshire* 10 (1975): 120; 14 (1991): 10, 12, 68. Kirby *Abs. of Feet of Fines Rel. Wiltshire* (Wiltshire Rec. Soc. 41) (1986): 88, 121, 123. Roskell *House of Commons 1386–1421* 4 (1992): 251–253 (biog. of Sir Maurice Russell).

11. EDMUND STRADLING, Esq., of Dauntsey, Castle Combe, Marden, Pertenall, Trow (in Alvediston), and Winterbourne-Dauntsey, Wiltshire, Sheriff of Wiltshire, 1452–3, 2nd but eldest surviving son and heir, born about 1429 (aged 28 in 1457). He married before 1446 (date of fine) **ELIZABETH ARUNDELL**, daughter of Renfrey Arundell, Knt., of Treloy and Trefink, Cornwall, by Joan, daughter and heiress of John Coleshull, Knt. They had three sons, John, Edmund, and Renfrey, and one daughter, Margaret (wife of John Hethe). In 1460 he owed a debt of £2,000 to Edward Langford, Esq. EDMUND STRADLING, Esq., died in 1460. His widow, Elizabeth, married (2nd) before 1465 **WILLIAM LYGON**, of Madresfield, Worcestershire. He and his wife, Elizabeth, presented to the churches of Dauntsey, Wiltshire and Bremilham, Wiltshire in 1465. WILLIAM LYGON died about 1484.

> Brydges *Collins' Peerage of England* 9 (1812): 507–508 (sub Add. & Corr.). *Coll. Top. et Gen.* 1 (1834): 306–307 (Arundell ped.: "Eliz. [Arundell] first wedded Edward Stradling, after to Will. Lygon."). Traherne *Stradling Corr.* (1840): xvii–xx (Stradling ped.). Vivian *Vis. of Cornwall* (1887): 2–5 (Arundell ped.). MacNamara *Mems. of the Danvers Fam.* (1895): 227–305. Putnam *Procs. before the Justices of the Peace* (1938): 434. VHC *Wiltshire* 10 (1975): 120; 13 (1987): 9–10; 14 (1991): 10, 12, 68. Kirby *Abs. of Feet of Fines Rel. Wiltshire* (Wiltshire Rec. Soc. 41) (1986): 123. National Archives, C 131/77/14; C 131/243/21; C 241/254/53 (available at www.catalogue.nationalarchives.gov.uk/search.asp).

12. JOHN STRADLING, of Dauntsey, Bremilham, Trow (in Alvediston), and Marden, Wiltshire, son and heir, born about 1449 (aged 11 in 1460). He married by dispensation dated 1468 **ALICE LANGFORD**, daughter of Edward Langford, Esq., of Bradfield, Berkshire and Langley and Minsdenbury (both in Hitchin), Hertfordshire, by Sanche, daughter of Sir Thomas Blount. They had one son, Edward, Esq., and one daughter, Anne. JOHN STRADLING died in 1471. His widow, Alice, married (2nd) before 28 June 1483 (as his 1st wife) **RICHARD POLE** (or **POOLE**), K.G. [see POLE 17], of Isleworth, Middlesex, London, and Ellesborough and Medmenham, Buckinghamshire, Esquire of the Body to Kings Richard III and Henry VII, Knight of the Body to King Henry VII, Constable of Rising, Harlech, and Montgomery Castles, Sheriff of Norfolk and Suffolk, 1484–5, Chamberlain of Arthur, Prince of Wales, Chamberlain of Chester, son and heir of Geoffrey Pole, Esq., of Pebidiog, Pembrokeshire, and Ellesborough and Medmenham, Buckinghamshire, Esquire of the Body to King Henry VI, Constable of Haverfordwest, Pembrokeshire, Serjeant and Keeper of the king's tents and pavilions, by Edith, daughter of Oliver Saint John, Knt. [see POLE 16 for his ancestry]. They had no known issue. He married (2nd) in or about Nov. 1487 **MARGARET PLANTAGENET**, Governess of Princess Mary Tudor, daughter of George Plantagenet, K.G., K.B., Duke of Clarence, Lord of Richmond, by Isabel, elder daughter and co-heiress of Richard Neville, K.G., Earl of Warwick and Salisbury [see MONTAGU 13 for her ancestry]. SIR RICHARD POLE died shortly before 15 Nov. 1504. In 1513 his widow, Margaret, was restored to the dignity of Countess of Salisbury upon the removal of the attainder of her late brother Edward. His widow, Margaret, Countess of Salisbury, was transferred to the Tower of London, attainted by Act of Parliament without trial 12 May 1539, and beheaded in the Tower 28 May 1541. She left a will dated Sept. 1538.

> Clutterbuck *Hist. & Antiqs. of Hertford* 3 (1827): 33 (Langford ped.). *Coll. Top. et Gen.* 1 (1834): 306–307 (Arundell ped.: "John Stradling, wedd. Alice, dau. of Langford."). Baker *Hist. & Antiqs. of Northampton* 2 (1836–41): 218–219 (Beauchamp ped.). Traherne *Stradling Corr.* (1840): xvii–xx (Stradling ped.). MacNamara *Mems. of the Danvers Fam.* (1895): 227–305. C.P.R. 1476–1485 (1901): 475–476. VCH *Hertford* 3 (1912): 3–12. C.P.R. 1485–1494 (1914): 5, 66, 75, 78, 192, 299, 481–482. *Misc. Gen. et Her.* 5th Ser. 3 (1918–19): 206. *Papal Regs.: Letters* 12 (1933): 608. VHC *Wiltshire* 10 (1975): 120; 13 (1987): 9–10; 14 (1991): 10, 68. Pierce *Margaret Pole, Countess of Salisbury, 1473–1541* (2003). National Archives, C1/67/36 (available at www.catalogue.nationalarchives.gov.uk/search.asp).

13. ANNE STRADLING, born about 1469 (aged 2 in 1471, 19 in 1488). She married 13 Dec. 1487 **JOHN DANVERS**, Knt., of Culworth and Sulgrave, Northamptonshire, Prescott, Oxfordshire, etc., Sheriff of Northamptonshire, 1494, Sheriff of Wiltshire, 1503, 1513, and, in right of his wife, of Dauntsey, Marden, and Smithcot (in Dauntsey), Wiltshire, 2nd son of Richard Danvers, Esq., of Prescott, Oxfordshire. They had four sons, Thomas, Richard, William, and John, and six daughters, Dorothy (wife of John Fettiplace and Anthony Hungerford, Knt.), Anne, Margaret (wife of Edward Fiennes [*de jure* 5th Lord Say and Sele] and Thomas Neville, Knt.), Elizabeth, Susan (wife of Walter Hungerford, Knt. [Lord Hungerford]), and Constance (wife of John Staveley). His wife, Anne, was sole heiress in 1487 to her brother, Edward Stradling, Esq., and co-heiress in 1507 to her cousin, Anne Arundell, wife of John Crocker. He presented to the church of Dauntsey, Wiltshire in 1503 and 1508. He was heir in 1505 to his older brother, Richard Danvers. SIR JOHN DANVERS died 3 Jan. 1514/5. He left a will dated 2 Jan. 1514/5, proved 24

Jan. 1514/5 (P.C.C. 4 Holder). His widow, Anne, presented to the church of Dauntsey, Wiltshire in 1517. She died 29 Dec 1539. She left a will proved 21 Jan. 1539/40 (P.C.C. Alenger). He and Anne were buried in the chancel of Dauntsey, Wiltshire.

Coll. Top. et Gen. 1 (1834): 306–307 (Arundell ped.: "Anne [Stradling], wedded to John Danvers."). Traherne *Stradling Corr.* (1840): xvii–xx (Stradling ped.). *Wiltshire Arch. & Nat. Hist. Mag.* 2 (1855): 281–282. MacNamara *Mems. of the Danvers Fam.* (1895): 227–305. VHC *Wiltshire* 10 (1975): 120; 14 (1991): 10, 68, 69, 72. National Archives, C 1/467/62, C 1/773/6-7 (available at www.catalogue.nationalarchives.gov.uk/search.asp).

Child of Anne Stradling, by John Danvers, Knt.:

i. **ANNE DANVERS**, married **THOMAS LOVETT**, Esq., of Astwell (in Wappenham), Northamptonshire [see LOVETT 16].

✒ DAVIE ✑

REYNOLD DE COURTENAY, of Sutton, Berkshire, married _____.
REYNOLD DE COURTENAY, of Oakhampton, Devon, married **HAWISE DE COURCY**.
ROBERT DE COURTENAY, Knt., of Okehampton, Devon, married **MARY DE VERNON** (desc. King William the Conqueror).
JOHN DE COURTENAY, Knt., of Okehampton, Devon, married **ISABEL DE VERE**.
HUGH DE COURTENAY, Knt., of Okehampton, Devon, married **ELEANOR LE DESPENSER**.
HUGH DE COURTENAY, Knt., Earl of Devon, married **AGNES DE SAINT JOHN**.
HUGH DE COURTENAY, Knt., Earl of Devon, married **MARGARET DE BOHUN** (desc. King William the Conqueror) [see COURTENAY 7].

8. PHILIP COURTENAY, Knt., of Powderham, Devon, King's knight, Knight of the Shire for Devonshire, 1383, 1386, 1388, 1390, 1393, 1395, 1399, 1401, Admiral of the Western Fleet, 1372–80, Lieutenant of Ireland, 1383–6, Steward of the Duchy of Cornwall (in Cornwall), 1388–92, member of the King's Council, 1405, born about 1355 (aged 50 in 1405). He married about 1378 **ANNE WAKE**, daughter of Thomas Wake, Knt., of Blisworth, Northamptonshire, by Alice, daughter of John de Pateshulle, Knt. [see PATESHULLE 12 for her ancestry] They had three sons, [Master] Richard [Bishop of Norwich, Chancellor of Oxford University], John, Knt., and William, Knt., and two daughters, Agnes (wife of Otes Champernoun, Knt.) and Margaret (wife of Robert Carew, Knt.). He served in the Spanish War *temp.* Edward III. In 1394 he was granted an annuity of £200 by King Richard II, which annuity was reconfirmed by Richard's successor, King Henry IV. He was a legatee in the 1396 will of his brother, William Courtenay, Archbishop of Canterbury. He was heir by reversion in 1405 to his brother, Peter Courtenay, Knt., by which he inherited the manor of Stewley (in Ashill), Somerset. He was appointed an executor of the 1391 will of his mother. His wife, Anne, was living about 30 March 1404. He presented to the churches of Hardington Mandeville, Somerset, 1403 and 1404, and East Coker, Somerset, 1405. SIR PHILIP COURTENAY died 29 July 1406.

Rymer *Fœdera* 7 (1728): 504–505. Brydges *Collins' Peerage of England* 6 (1812): 214–271 (sub Courtenay, Viscount Courtenay). Burke *Dict. of the Peerages… Extinct, Dormant & in Abeyance* (1831): 142–147. Brydges *Collins' Peerage of England* 6 (1812): 214–271 (sub Courtenay, Viscount Courtenay). Nicolas *Rpt. of Procs. on the Claim of the Earldom of Devon in the House of Lords* (1832): 5–16; Appendix, xxxviii. Westcote *View of Devonshire in MDCXXX* (1845): 570–574 (sub Courtenay). Maclean *Hist. of Trigg Minor* 2 (1876): 240–241 (chart). Vivian *Vis. of Cornwall* (1887): 105–118 (Courtenay ped.). *Notes & Gleanings* 2 (1889): 50–56, 65–68, 89–93, 97. Weaver *Somerset Incumbents* (1889): 68, 95. *Misc. Gen. et Heraldica* 2nd Ser. 3 (1890): 349 (Audley-Touchet ped.). Vivian *Vis. of Devon 1531, 1564 & 1620* (1895): 243–252 (Courtenay ped.). *C.P.R. 1381–1385* (1897): 293 (Philip Courtenay styled "king's kinsman"). *Arch. Cantiana* 23 (1898): 55–67 (will of William Courtenay, Archbishop of Canterbury). Green *Feet of Fines for Somerset* 3 (Somerset Rec. Soc. 17) (1902): 146; 3 (Somerset Rec. Soc. 22) (1906): 16. Wrottesley *Peds. from the Plea Rolls* (1905): 298, 425. *C.P.* 4 (1916): 335 (sub Devon). *C.P.R. 1374–1377* (1916): 308, 386 (Philip Courtenay styled "king's kinsman"). *Genealogist's Mag.* 6 (1932–34): 606–626. Curtis *Cal. Ormond Deeds* 2 (1934): 193. Holmes *Estates of the Higher Nobility in 14th Cent. England* (1957): 33–34. Paget *Baronage of England* (1957) 151: 1–3 (sub Courtenay); 566: 1–5 (sub Wake).

VCH *Oxford* 5 (1957): 240. Dunning *Hylle Cartulary* (Somerset Rec. Soc. 68) (1968): 73. *Devon & Cornwall Notes & Queries* 35 (1984): 220 (biog. of Richard Courtenay). Schwennicke *Europaische Stanmtafeln* 3(4) (1989): 630 (sub Courtenay). Roskell *House of Commons 1386–1421* 2 (1992): 670–673 (biog. of Sir Philip Courtenay: "… remembered for acts of gratuitous savagery and vindictiveness, occasionally tempered with some real skill in military and naval affairs… a man of energy and ability in national and local affairs whose predilection for violence and thuggery was extreme even by medieval standards"). Leese *Blood Royal* (1996): 116–119.

Children of Philip Courtenay, Knt., by Anne Wake:

i. [MASTER] **RICHARD COURTENAY**, King's councilor, Treasurer of the Household, Keeper of the King's Jewels, son and heir, born about 1381. He was a legatee in the 1396 will of his uncle, William Courtenay, Archbishop of Canterbury. He rented rooms at Exeter College at Oxford University in 1402–3. He was appointed Canon of Wingham, Kent, 1392; Canon of the King's free chapel of Bosham, Sussex, 1393; Canon of St. Paul's, London, 1394; Canon of Lincoln, 1394; Canon of Wells before 1395; Canon of Chichester before 1395; Dean of South Malling, Sussex, 1395; Canon of Exeter, 1399; Archdeacon of Northampton, 1402; Dean of St. Asaph, 1402; Rector of Alphington, Devon, 1403; Canon of York, 1403; Canon of York and Lincoln, 1404. He was chosen Chancellor of Oxford University, 1406. He accompanied the lady Philippe, daughter of King Henry IV, to Copenhagen in 1406 for her marriage to Eric, King of Denmark. He was appointed Rector of Yelvertoft, Northamptonshire, 1407; Dean of Wells, 1410; and Rector of Holcot, Northamptonshire, 1410. He presented to the church of Sampford Bret, Somerset in 1408, 1409, 1412, 1413, and 1415. He was made an honorary member of the Guild of Merchant Taylors of London in 1411–2. He was chosen Bishop of Norwich by papal provision in 1413. He accompanied King Henry V to Normandy on his invasion of Normany in 1415. RICHARD COURTENAY, Bishop of Norwich, contracted dysentery at the Siege of Harfleur, where he died 15 Sept. 1415. He was buried in the chapel of St. Edward the Confessor in Westminster Abbey. Rymer *Fœdera* 8 (1727): 419 (Master Richard Courtenay styled "kinsman" by King Henry IV of England); 9 (1729): 141, 150–151, 183–188 (instances of Richard Courtenay, Bishop of Norwich, styled "kinsman" by King Henry V of England). Brydges *Collins' Peerage of England* 6 (1812): 214–271 (sub Courtenay, Viscount Courtenay). Nicolas *Rpt. of Procs. on the Claim of the Earldom of Devon in the House of Lords* (1832): Appendix, xxxviii–xxxix. Hardy *Rotuli Normanniæ in Turri Londinensi Asservati* 1 (1835): 373–374. Oliver *Eccl. Antiqs. in Devon* 1 (1840): 75. *Collectanea Arch.* 1 (1862): 232–262. Clode *Mems. of the Guild of Merchant Taylors* (1875): 618. Weaver *Somerset Incumbents* (1889): 429. Vivian *Vis. of Devon 1531, 1564 & 1620* (1895): 243–250 (Courtenay ped.). *Arch. Cantiana* 23 (1898): 55–67 (will of William Courtenay, Archbishop of Canterbury). *Procs. Bath Natural Hist. & Antiq. Field Club* 9 (1901): 188–201. Wrottesley *Peds. from the Plea Rolls* (1905): 298. Wylie *Reign of Henry V* 2 (1919): 42–43. Curtis *Cal. Ormond Deeds* 2 (1934): 193. Emden *Biog. Reg. of the Univ. of Oxford* 1 (1957): 500–502 (biog. of Richard Courtenay). Paget *Baronage of England* (1957) 151: 1–2 (sub Courtenay of Powderham). Dunning *Hylle Cartulary* (Somerset Rec. Soc. 68) (1968): 73–74. Turner *Recollections of a Westminster Antiq.* (1969): 179–181. *Ancient Deeds — Ser. B* 2 (List & Index Soc. 101) (1974): B.6900. Taylor & Roskell *Gesta Henrici Quinti: Deeds of Henry V* (1975): 45. Harvey *Westminster Abbey & its Estates in the Middle Ages* (1977): 381. *Devon & Cornwall Notes & Queries* 35 (1984): 220 (biog. of Richard Courtenay). *Cal. IPM* 20 (1995): 140–142. Leese *Blood Royal* (1996): 116–119.

ii. **JOHN COURTENAY**, Knt. [see next].

9. **JOHN COURTENAY**, Knt., 2nd son. He married **JOAN CHAMPERNOUN**, widow of James Chudleigh, Knt., of Ashton and Shirwell, Devon (living June 1401), and daughter of Richard Champernoun, Knt., of Modbury, Devon, by his 1st wife, Alice, daughter of Thomas de Astley, 3rd Lord Astley [see MODBURY 12 for her ancestry]. They had two sons, Philip, Knt., and Humphrey, Knt. SIR JOHN COURTENAY died before 1415. His widow, Joan, died in 1419.

Nichols *Hist. & Antiqs. of Leicester* 2(1) (1795): 132. Brydges *Collins' Peerage of England* 6 (1812): 214–271 (sub Courtenay, Viscount Courtenay). Nicolas *Rpt. of Procs. on the Claim of the Earldom of Devon in the House of Lords* (1832): Appendix, xxxviii–xxxix. Westcote *View of Devonshire in MDCXXX* (1845): 573–574 (sub Courtenay). Maclean *Hist. of Trigg Minor* 2 (1876): 240–241 (chart). Vivian *Vis. of Cornwall* (1887): 105–118 (Courtenay ped.). *Misc. Gen. et Heraldica* 2nd Ser. 3 (1890): 349 (Audley-Touchet ped.). Vivian *Vis. of Devon 1531, 1564 & 1620* (1895): 243–252 (Courtenay ped.). Wrottesley *Peds. from the Plea Rolls* (1905): 298, 425. *C.P.* 4 (1916): 335 (sub Devon). Paget *Baronage of England* (1957) 151: 1–2 (sub Courtenay of Powderham). Roskell *House of Commons 1386–1421* 2 (1992): 573–574 (biog. of Sir James Chudleigh), 670–673 (biog. of Sir Philip Courtenay). Leese *Blood Royal* (1996): 116–119. Inq. re. Proof of Age of Philip de Courtenay taken 12 Feb. 1424/5, Ref. Inq., 3 Henry V, file 20 (50) [FHL Microfilm 915526] ([Joan] wife of John Courtenay, Knt. [mother of Philip] stated to be daughter of Richard Champernoun, Knt.).

10. PHILIP COURTENAY, Knt., of Powderham and Honiton, Devon, King's knight, Forester of Dartmoor, 1446–56, Knight of the Shire for Devonshire, 1455–6, son and heir, born at Ashton, Devon 18 Jan. 1403/4 (aged 11 in 1415). He was heir in 1415 to his uncle, Richard Courtenay, Bishop of Norwich. He was likewise heir in 1419 to his uncle, William Courtenay, Knt. In 1419 the king presented to the church of Hardington Mandeville, Somerset by reason of his minor age. He married about 1426 **ELIZABETH HUNGERFORD**, daughter of Walter Hungerford, K.G., K.B., 1st Lord Hungerford, Speaker of the House of Commons, Steward of the Household to Kings Henry V and Henry VI, Lord High Treasurer, by his 1st wife, Katherine, daughter and co-heiress of Thomas Peverell, Esq. [see HUNGERFORD 11 for her ancestry]. Her maritagium included the manor of Molland Botreaux, Devon. They had seven sons, William, Knt., Philip, Knt., [Master] Peter [Bishop of Exeter and Winchester], Walter, Knt., Edmund, Humphrey, and John, Knt., and four daughters, Anne (wife of William Palton, Knt., and Richard Densell, Esq.), Elizabeth, Philippe (wife of Thomas Fulford, Knt.), and Katherine. He presented to the churches of East Coker, Somerset, 1427, 1435, 1438, 1443, 1448, 1449, and Sampford Bret, Somerset, 1449, 1456. He was made an honorary member of the Guild of Merchant Taylors of London in 1433–4. In 1440 he was joint commander of a fleet to repress pirates. In 1445 he obtained license for his ship *Trinity Cou[r]tenay* to take pilgrims to St. James in Galicia. In 1448 he and his wife obtained a papal indult for a portable altar. SIR PHILIP COURTENAY died 16 Dec. 1463. His widow, Elizabeth, died 14 Dec. 1476.

Brydges *Collins' Peerage of England* 6 (1812): 214–271 (sub Courtenay, Viscount Courtenay). Nicolas *Rpt. of Procs. on the Claim of the Earldom of Devon* (1832): Appendix, xxxix–xl. Hardy *Rotuli Normanniæ in Turri Londinensi Asservati* 1 (1835): 373–374. Fuller *Hist. of the Worthies of England* (1840): 427–428. Westcote *View of Devonshire in MDCXXX* (1845): 573–574 (sub Courtenay). Clode *Mems. of the Guild of Merchant Taylors* (1875): 619. Maclean *Hist. of Trigg Minor* 2 (1876): 240–241 (chart). Rogers *Antient Sepulchral Effigies* (1877): 183–185. Colby *Vis. of Devon 1564* (1881): 72–73 (Courtney ped.: "Philip Courtney of Powderham, Knt., s & h., of Phil. Courtney of Powderham, Knt., who was living in the time of E. 3 and R. 2. = Elizabeth, d. of Walter, Lord Hungerford."). Chitting & Phillipot *Vis. of Gloucester 1623, 1569 & 1582-3* (H.S.P. 21) (1885): 87–90 (1623 Vis.) (Hungerford ped.: "Elizebeth [Hungerford] vx. Sir William Courtney Knt. [of Powderham — Harleian 1041]"). Vivian *Vis. of Cornwall* (1887): 105–118 (Courtenay ped.). Weaver *Somerset Incumbents* (1889): 68, 95, 429. *Misc. Gen. et Heraldica* 2nd Ser. 3 (1890): 349 (Audley-Touchet ped.). *Notes & Gleanings* 4 (1891): 188; 5 (1892): 18–19. Vivian *Vis. of Devon 1531, 1564 & 1620* (1895): 243–252 (Courtenay ped.). Wrottesley *Peds. from the Plea Rolls* (1905): 298, 425. Green *Feet of Fines for Somerset* 4 (Somerset Rec. Soc. 22) (1906): 97–98. *Papal Regs.: Letters* 10 (1915): 387. *C.P.* 4 (1916): 335 (sub Devon). Beckington *Reg. of Thomas Bekynton Bishop of Bath & Wells* 1 (Somerset Rec. Soc. 49) (1934): 111, 270. Wedgwood *Hist. of Parl.* 1 (1936): 229–230 (biog. of Sir Philip Courtenay). St. George et al. *Wiltshire Vis. Peds. 1623, 1628* (H.S.P. 105-6) (1954): 89–91 (Hungerford ped.: "Elizab. [Hungerford] ux: Phill: Courtney de Powderham militis"). Paget *Baronage of England* (1957) 151: 1–2 (sub Courtenay of Powderham). Lacy *Reg. of Edmund Lacy* 3 (Devon & Cornwall Rec. Soc. n.s. 13) (1968): 71. *Bull. Inst. Hist. Research* 45 (1972): 230–246. Roskell *House of Commons 1386–1421* 3 (1992): 446–453 (biog. of Sir Walter Hungerford). *Cal. IPM* 20 (1995): 140–142. *Devon & Cornwall Notes & Queries* 37 (1996): 328–334; 38 (1997): 10–15. Wasson *Recs. of Early English Drama: Devon* (1986): 476–477. Inq. re. Proof of Age of Philip de Courtenay taken 12 Feb. 1424/5, Ref. Inq., 3 Henry V, file 20 (50) [FHL Microfilm 915526].

Children of Philip Courtenay, Knt., by Elizabeth Hungerford:

i. **WILLIAM COURTENAY**, Knt., of East Coker, Somerset, Powderham and Yelton, Devon, etc., Knight of the Shire for Somerset, 1455–6, Sheriff of Devonshire, 1482–3, son and heir, born about 1428 (aged 35 in 1463). He married **MARGARET BONVILLE**, daughter of William Bonville, K.G., Lord Bonville, by his 1st wife, Margaret, daughter of Reynold Grey, Knt., 3rd Lord Grey of Ruthin [see BONVILLE 11 for her ancestry]. They had four sons, William, Knt., Edward, Philip, and James, and one daughter, Joan (or Jane). He presented to the churches of East Coker, Somerset in 1453, and Hardington Mandeville, Somerset in 1472. He was ordered to be arrested and brought before the Council in March 1470. He was denounced as a rebel with Clarence and Warwick. He served the Readeption goverment, crossed or double-crossed with Clarence, and evaded the Battle of Tewkesbury in 1471. He was one of ten knights who swore allegiance to the infant Prince of Wales 18 July 1471. He was king's servant to King Richard III who granted him an annuity of £20. SIR WILLIAM COURTENAY died shortly before 20 Sept. 1485, and was buried at Powderham, Devon. His widow, Margaret, left a will dated July 1487, proved 22 Sept. 1487. Brydges *Collins' Peerage of England* 6 (1812): 214–271 (sub

Courtenay, Viscount Courtenay). *Trans. Exeter Diocesan Arch. Soc.* 2nd Ser. 1 (1867): 177. Colby *Vis. of Devon 1564* (1881): 72–73 (Courtney ped.: "William Courtney of Powderham, Knt., 1. = Margaret, d. of Lord de Boneville."), 73 (Courteney ped.: "Sir William Courtenay of Powderham. = Margaret, d. of the lord Bonville."). Vivian *Vis. of Cornwall* (1887): 105–118 (Courtenay ped.). Weaver *Somerset Incumbents* (1889): 68, 95. Rogers *Strife of the Roses & Days of the Tudors in the West* (1890): 65. *Notes & Gleanings* 4 (1891): 192–196. Vivian *Vis. of Devon 1531, 1564 & 1620* (1895): 243–252 (Courtenay ped.). *List of Sheriffs for England & Wales* (PRO Lists and Indexes 9) (1898): 36. Wrottesley *Peds. from the Plea Rolls* (1905): 425. Wedgwood *Hist. of Parl.* 1 (1936): 231–232 (biog. of Sir William Courtenay). Wasson *Recs. of Early English Drama: Devon* (1986): 477.

Child of William Courtenay, Knt., by Margaret Bonville:

- a. **JOAN** (or **JANE**) **COURTENAY**, married **WILLIAM CAREW**, Knt., of Ottery Mohun, Devon [see CAREW 18.i].

- ii. **PHILIP COURTENAY**, Knt. [see next].

- iii. [**MASTER**] **PETER COURTENAY**, Doctor of Canon Law. He was educated at Oxford and at the University of Padua. He was Archdeacon of Exeter, 1453; Archdeacon of Wiltshire, 1464; Dean of Windsor, 1476; and Dean of Exeter, 1477. He was elected Bishop of Exeter 14 June 1478, and consecrated as Bishop 8 Nov. following. In 1483 he joined the rebellion of Henry Stafford, Duke of Buckingham against King Richard III, and fled to Brittany when this enterprise failed. He was restored to his dignities and estates in 1485 by King Henry VII, whom he had accompanied to England. He was translated to the see of Winchester 29 Jan. 1487. He served as Keeper of the Privy Seal, 1485–87. PETER COURTENAY, Bishop of Winchester, died 22 Sept. 1492. Brydges *Collins' Peerage of England* 6 (1812): 214–271 (sub Courtenay, Viscount Courtenay). *Collectanea Arch.* 1 (1862): 232–262. *Papal Regs.: Letters* 11 (1921): 685 (Peter Courtenai, archdeacon of Exeter, doctor of degrees, styled "of the lineage" of King Edward IV in 1463). Emden *Biog. Reg. of the Univ. of Oxford* 1 (1957): 499–500 (biog. of Peter Courtenay). Horn *Fasti Ecclesiae Anglicanae 1300–1541* 9 (1964): 1–3, 3–6, 12–15, 53–60. Wagner *Encyclopedia of the Wars of the Roses* (2001): 88 (biog. of Peter Courtenay).

- iv. **WALTER COURTENAY**, Knt., of Bouryslegh, Sourton, and Spreyton, Devon, married **ALICE COLBROKE** [see HACCOMBE 9].

- v. **KATHERINE COURTENAY**, married (1st) **SEINTCLERE POMEROY**, Knt., of Sinclere Pomeroy, Devon [see POYNTZ 11]; (2nd) **THOMAS ROGERS**, of Bradford, Wiltshire [see POYNTZ 11]; (3rd) **WILLIAM HUDDESFIELD**, Knt., of Shillingford, Devon [see POYNTZ 11].

- vi. **ELIZABETH COURTENAY**, married (1st) **JAMES LUTTRELL**, Knt., of Dunster, Somerset [see LOWELL 11]; (2nd) **HUMPHREY AUDLEY**, Knt., of Carlton, Suffolk [see TUCHET 15.i]; (3rd) **THOMAS MALET**, Esq., of Enmore, Somerset [see LOWELL 11].

11. PHILIP COURTENAY, Knt., of Molland, Kingston, and Exeter, Devon, Knight of the Shire for Devonshire, [?1470–1], 1472–5, 1484, [?1485–6 or 1487], Sheriff of Devonshire, 1470–1, Knight of the Body to King Richard III, 1484–5, 2nd son. He married (1st) about 1459 **ELIZABETH** _____, widow of William Hyndeston (or Henston, Hingston) (died c. 1455), of Wonwell (in Kingston), Devon. They had three sons, John, Esq., Philip, and William, and two daughters, Elizabeth and Margaret. He and Clarence were ordered to be arrested as rebels in April 1470. He presumably fought at the Battle of Barnet 14 April 1471. His wife, Elizabeth, died in 1482. He married (2nd) before 1485 **ELIZABETH ASHFORD**, widow and executrix of William Marwood, Esq., of Westacot (in Marwood), Devon, and daughter of William Ashford, of Ashford (in Burlescombe), Devon. In the period, 1475–80, or 1483–85, John Broughton and Alice, his wife, daughter and heiress of Elizabeth Squire, and Lewis Pollard, son and heir of Jane Pollard, sister to the said Alice, sued Sir Philip Courteney, Knt., and Elizabeth, his wife, executrix and previously the [2nd] wife of William Marwood (whose 1st wife was the said Elizabeth Squire) regarding the detention of deeds relating to messuages and land in Exeter, Barnstaple, etc.., Devon. He fell with Clarence in 1478 and was restored by King Richard III who made him a knight of the body and granted him a pension of £40 a year. SIR PHILIP COURTENAY died 7 Dec. 1489.

Brydges *Collins' Peerage of England* 6 (1812): 214–271 (sub Courtenay, Viscount Courtenay). Burke *Hist. of the Commoners* 2 (1836): 162 ("m. a daughter of Robert Hingeston, of Wonewell") (children: John, William [father of Philip of

Loughtorr], Elizabeth, wife of Edward, Earl of Devonshire, and Margaret, wife of John Champernoun, of Modbury). Westcote *View of Devonshire in MDCXXX* (1845): 573–575 (sub Courtenay). *Notes & Queries* 3rd ser. 4 (1863): 143–144 (re. Marwood fam.). Maclean *Hist. of Trigg Minor* 2 (1876): 240–241 (chart). Colby *Vis. of Devon 1564* (1881): 72–73 (Courtney ped.: "Philip [Courtney], 2, of Molland. = Eliz., d. & h., of Hingeston."), 190–191 (Squire ped.). Vivian *Vis. of Cornwall* (1887): 105–118 (Courtenay ped.). *Genealogist* n.s. 7 (1891): 126–127. Vivian *Vis. of Devon 1531, 1564 & 1620* (1895): 243–252 (Courtenay ped.). *List of Sheriffs for England & Wales* (PRO Lists and Indexes 9) (1898): 36. *List of Early Chancery Procs.* 2 (PRO Lists and Indexes 16) (1903): 254. *Rpt. & Trans. of the Devonshire Assoc. for the Advancement of Science, Lit. & Art* 3rd Ser. 6 (1914): 491 (biog. of William Hingston). Wedgwood *Hist. of Parl.* 1 (1936): 230–231 (biog. of Sir Philip Courtenay). Paget *Baronage of England* (1957) 151: 1–2 (sub Courtenay of Powderham). *Bull. Inst. Hist. Research* 45 (1972): 230–246. National Archives, C 1/58/142 (available at www.catalogue.nationalarchives.gov.uk/search.asp).

Children of Philip Courtenay, Knt., by Elizabeth _____:

i. **PHILIP COURTENAY** [see next].

ii. **ELIZABETH COURTENAY**, married **EDWARD COURTENAY**, K.G., 17th Earl of Devon [see COURTENAY 10.i]

iii. **MARGARET COURTENAY**, married **JOHN CHAMPERNOUN**, Knt., of Modbury, Devon [see DENNY 16].

12. **PHILIP COURTENAY**, of Loughtor (in Plympton St. Mary), Devon, 2nd son. He married **JANE FOWELL**, daughter of Richard Fowell, of Fowelscomb (in Ugborough), Devon. They had one daughter, Elizabeth. PHILIP COURTENAY died 26 March 1514. His widow, Jane, married (2nd) **HUMPHREY PRIDEAUX**, Esq., of Thuborough (in Sutcombe), Devon.

Brydges *Collins' Peerage of England* 6 (1812): 214–271 (sub Courtenay, Viscount Courtenay). Burke *Hist. of the Commoners* 1 (1833): 203–206 (sub Prideaux); 2 (1838): 162. Westcote *View of Devonshire in MDCXXX* (1845): 574–575 (sub Courtenay). Colby *Vis. of Devon 1564* (1881): 72–73 (Courtney ped.: "Philip Courtney de Loughter. = [left blank]."). Vivian *Vis. of Cornwall* (1887): 105–118 (Courtenay ped.). Vivian *Vis. of Devon 1531, 1564 & 1620* (1895): 243–252 (Courtenay ped.). Howard & Crisp *Vis. of England & Wales: Notes* 12 (1917): 121.

13. **ELIZABETH COURTENAY**, daughter and heiress, born about 1513 (aged 6 months at her father's death in 1514). She married **WILLIAM STRODE** (or **STROWDE**), Esq., of Newnham (in Plympton St. Mary), Devon, son and heir of Richard Strode (or Stroud), of Newnham (in Plympton St. Mary), Devon, by Agnes, daughter of John Milliton. He was born at Newnham (in Plympton St. Mary), Devon 16 June 1504. They had seven sons, Richard, Esq., John, William, Philip, Arthur, Sampson, and Thomas, and five daughters, Agnes (wife of Edward Yarde), Katherine (wife of George Whyte), Maria (wife of Thomas Prestwood and Nicholas Martyn), Joan (wife of Stephen Vaughan), and Elizabeth (wife of Walter Hele). He was imprisoned at Exeter in the 1530s on suspicion of heresy. WILLIAM STRODE, Esq., died at Newnham (in Plympton St. Mary), Devon 5 May 1579. His widow, Elizabeth, was living 4 October 1581.

Brydges *Collins' Peerage of England* 6 (1812): 214–271 (sub Courtenay, Viscount Courtenay). Burke *Hist. of the Commoners* 3 (1836): 568–569. Westcote *View of Devonshire in MDCXXX* (1845): 542–543 (sub Strode), 574–575 (sub Courtenay). *Vis. of Devon 1620* (H.S.P. 6) (1872): 278 (Strode ped.: "Wm. Strowde of Newnham = Elizb. d. of Wm. Courtney of Molland") (Strode arms: Argent, a chevron between three conies couchant sable). Colby *Vis. of Devon 1564* (1881): 72–73 (Courtney ped.: "Elizab. [Courtney], d. & h. = Will. Strode of Yewnam [Newnham.]"), 195–196 (Strode ped.: "William Stowde. = Eliz., d. & h. of Phil. Courtney of Molland."). Vivian *Vis. of Cornwall* (1887): 105–118 (Courtenay ped.). Vivian *Vis. of Devon 1531, 1564 & 1620* (1895): 243–252 (Courtenay ped.), 718–720 (Stode ped.). Howard & Crisp *Vis. of England & Wales: Notes* 12 (1917): 121. Bindoff *House of Commons 1509–1558* 3 (1982): 401 (biog. of Richard Strode).

14. **RICHARD STRODE**, Esq., of Newnham (in Plympton St. Mary), Devon, Burgess (M.P.) of Plympton Erle, Devon, Escheator of Devon and Cornwall, son and heir, born in 1528. He married at Compton, Hampshire 11 Nov. 1560 **FRANCES CROMWELL**, daughter of Gregory Cromwell, K.B., 2nd Lord Cromwell, by Elizabeth, daughter of John Seymour, Knt. [see SEYMOUR 19.v for her ancestry]. She was born about 1544. They had one son, William, Knt. His wife, Frances, died 7

Feb. 1561/2, and was buried at Plympton St. Mary, Devon. RICHARD STRODE, Esq., died testate 5 August 1581.

> Banks *Dormant & Extinct Baronage of England* 2 (1808): 124–129 (sub Cromwell). Burke *Dict. of the Peerages… Extinct, Dormant & in Abeyance* (1831): 152–153 (sub Cromwell). Westcote *View of Devonshire in MDCXXX* (1845): 542–543 (sub Strode). *Vis. of Devon 1620* (H.S.P. 6) (1872): 278 (Strode ped.). Carthew *Hundred of Launditch & Deanery of Brisley* 2 (1878): 522–523 (Cromwell ped.). Colby *Vis. of Devon 1564* (1881): 195–196 (Strode ped.: "Richard Strowde of Newnam. = Frances, d. of Gregory Lord Cromwell by Eliz. Semer."). Vivian *Vis. of Devon 1531, 1564 & 1620* (1895): 718–720 (Strode ped.). Howard & Crisp *Vis. of England & Wales: Notes* 12 (1917): 121–122. Hasler *House of Commons 1558–1603* 3 (1981): 458–459 (biog. of Richard Strode). Bindoff *House of Commons 1509–1558* 3 (1982): 401 (biog. of Richard Strode).

15. WILLIAM STRODE, Knt., of Newnham (in Plympton St. Mary), Devon, Sheriff of Devonshire, 1593–4, Knight of the Shire for Devon, 1597, 1624, Burgess (M.P.) for Plympton Erle, 1601, 1604, 1621, 1625, Burgess (M.P.) for Plymouth, 1614, Recorder of Plymouth, son and heir, born 1 Feb. 1561/2. He was admitted to the Inner Temple in 1580. He married (1st) at Bovey Tracey, Devon 15 July 1581 **MARY SOUTHCOTT**, 2nd daughter of Thomas Southcott, of Bovey Tracey, Devon, by his 2nd wife, Susan, daughter of Thomas Kirkham, Knt. [see CAREW 18.i.a.1 for her ancestry]. They had three sons, Richard, Knt., William, and John, and seven daughters, Mary (wife of George Chudleigh, 1st Bart.), Joanna (wife of Francis Drake, Knt., and John Trefusis), Ursula (wife of John Chichester, Knt.), Frances (wife of Samuel Somaster, Knt.), Julian, Margaret (wife of John Yonge/Younge, Knt.), and Elizabeth (wife of Edmond Speccot, Esq.). His wife, Mary, was buried at Plympton St. Mary, Devon 24 Feb. 1617/18. He married (2nd) at Tavistock, Devon 31 March 1624 **DEWNES** (or **DUNES**) **GLANVILLE**, widow of Stephen Vosper, of Liskeard, Cornwall, and daughter of Nicholas Glanville, of Tavistock, Devon, by Elizabeth, daughter of William Ridley, Esq. They had no issue. His wife, Dewnes, was buried at Plympton St. Mary, Devon 16 Sept. 1635. SIR WILLIAM STRODE died 27 June 1637, and was buried at Plympton St. Mary, Devon. He left a will proved 21 Feb. 1638 (P.C.C. 18 Lee).

> Wotton *English Baronetage* 2 (1741): 267. Westcote *View of Devonshire in MDCXXX* (1845): 542–543 (sub Strode). St. George & Lennard *Vis. of Cornwall 1620* (H.S.P. 9) (1874): 77 (Glanville ped.: "Dewnes [Glanvile]."). Colby *Vis. of Devon 1564* (1881): 195–196 (Strode ped.: "Sir Wm. Strowde, Knt."). Glanville-Richards *Recs. of the Anglo-Norman House of Glanville* (1882): 75–76. Vivian *Vis. of Devon 1531, 1564 & 1620* (1895): 697–701 (Southcott ped.), 718–720 (Strode ped.). *List of Sheriffs for England & Wales* (PRO Lists and Indexes 9) (1898): 36. *TAG* 23 (1946–47): 207, 210. Hasler *House of Commons 1558–1603* 3 (1981): 459–460 (biog. of William Strode).

16. JULIAN STRODE, 5th daughter. She married (as his 1st wife) **JOHN DAVIE**, Knt., of Creedy (in Sandford), Devon, Member of Parliament (M.P.) for Tiverton, Sheriff of Devonshire, 1629–30, son and heir of John Davie, of Sandford and Kirton, Devon, Mayor of Exeter, Devon, by Margaret, daughter of George Southcote, Esq. They had five sons, John, Knt. [2nd Baronet], William, Robert, Robert (again), and Humphrey, Esq., and four daughters, Mary (wife of John Willoughby, Esq.), Elizabeth (wife of Arthur Copleston, Esq.), Julian (wife of Thomas Beare, Esq.), and Margaret (wife of Richard Beavis, Esq.). He was matriculated aged 16 at Exeter College, Oxford 22 Feb. 1604/5. His wife, Julian, died 14 May 1627, and was buried 25 May following at Sandford, Devon. He married (2nd) about 1630 **ISABEL HELE**, daughter of Walter Hele, of Gnaton (in Newton Ferrers), Devon. They had one daughter, Isabel (wife of Walter Yonge, Bt.). He was created a Baronet by King Charles I 2 Sept. 1641. SIR JOHN DAVIE, 1st Baronet, was buried at Sandford, Devon 13 October 1654. He left a will dated 20 June 1639, proved 7 August 1655 (P.C.C. 101 Aylett). His widow, Isabel, was buried at Sandford, Devon 28 October 1656. She left a will dated 20 July 1656, proved 18 Nov. 1657 (P.C.C. 433 Ruthen).

> Wotton *English Baronetage* 2 (1741): 267–268. Kimber & Johnson *English Baronetage* 1 (1771): 416–419 (sub Davie). Betham *Baronetage of England* 1 (1801): 453–457 (sub Davie). Westcote *View of Devonshire in MDCXXX* (1845): 542–543 (sub Strode). *Hist. Mag.* 1 (1857): 282. St. George et al. *Vis. of Devon 1620* (H.S.P. 6) (1872): 85 (Davye ped.: "John Davy of Sandford s. & h., living 1620 = Julian d. of Sir William Strowd of Newnam"). *NEHGR* 48 (1894):

139–140 (wills of John Davie, 1st Bt. and his 2nd wife, Isabel); 86 (1932): 269. Vivian *Vis. of Devon 1531, 1564 & 1620* (1895): 269–270 (sub Davie) (Davie arms: Azure three cinquefoils 2 and 1 or, on a chief of the last a lion passant gules), 698, 719. *List of Sheriffs for England & Wales* (PRO Lists and Indexes 9) (1898): 37. *Rpt. & Trans. Devonshire Assoc.* 2nd Ser. 6 (1904): 116–122. Howard & Crisp *Vis. of England & Wales: Notes* 12 (1917): 127. *TAG* 23 (1946–47): 206.

17. HUMPHREY DAVIE, Esq., baptized at Sandford, Devon 24 August 1625. He was a legatee in the 1639 will of his father, who bequeathed him £500. He was a wealthy merchant in London and a zealous Puritan. He married (1st) **MARY WHITE**, daughter of Edmund White, Citizen and haberdasher of London, by Elizabeth, daughter of Rowland Wilson. They had five sons, Edmund, Humphrey, John, Knt. [5th Baronet], Rowland, and Humphrey (again), and five daughters, Elizabeth (wife of Daniel Taylor), Anne, Anne (again), Margaret (wife of Henry Franklin), and Mary. He and his family immigrated in 1662 to Boston, Massachusetts, where he became a prominent man. He was admitted a member of the Artillery Company in 1665. His wife, Mary, was a legatee in the 1674 will of her father, Edmund White. He married (2nd) by settlement dated 14 Dec. 1683 **SARAH GIBBONS**, widow of James Richards (died 16 July 1680), of Hartford, Connecticut, and daughter of William Gibbons, of Hartford, Connecticut, by his wife, Ursula. She was born at Hartford, Connecticut 17 August 1645. They had two sons, Humphrey and William, Gent. Following his second marriage, he removed to Hartford, Connecticut. HUMPHREY DAVIE, Esq., died at Hartford, Connecticut 18 Feb. 1688/9. His widow, Sarah, married (3rd) at Boston, Massachusetts 30 May 1706 (as his 2nd wife) [**COL.**] **JONATHAN TYNG**, Esq., of Boston, Dunstable, and Woburn, Massachusetts. She died at Woburn, Massachusetts 8 Feb. 1713/4.

Wotton *English Baronetage* 2 (1741): 263–269 (sub Davie). Kimber & Johnson *English Baronetage* 1 (1771): 416–419 (sub Davie). Betham *Baronetage of England* 1 (1801): 453–457 (sub Davie). *Hist. Mag.* 1 (1857): 282. Hoadly *Public Recs. of the Colony of Connecticut* 5 (1870): 455. Sibley *Biog. Sketches of Graduates of Harvard University* 3 (1885): 231–236 (biog. of John Davie). Winsor *Memorial Hist. of Boston* 1 (1885): 578. *NEHGR* 48 (1894): 136–137 (will of Edmund White), 139–140 (wills of John Davie, 1st Bt. and his 2nd wife, Isabel). Caulkins *Hist. of New London, Connecticut* (1895): 415–417. Roberts *Hist. of the Military Company of the Massachusetts* 1 (1895): 216 (biog. of Jonathan Tyng). Vivian *Vis. of Devon 1531, 1564 & 1620* (1895): 269–270 (sub Davie). *Papers of the New Haven Colony Hist. Soc.* 6 (1900): 369–371 (letters and receipts of Humphrey Davie, one letter dated 1685 naming his son-in-law, Mr. Daniel Taylor). Manwaring *Digest of Early Connecticut Probate Recs.* 1 (1902): 437. *Rpt. & Trans. Devonshire Assoc.* 2nd Ser. 6 (1904): 116–122. Barbour *Fams. of Early Hartford, Connecticut* (1977): 208, 476. Parish regs. of St. Christopher-le-Stocks, London, England [FHL Microfilm 396896].

☙ DEIGHTON ❧

JOHN DE SOMERY, married **HAWISE PAYNELL**.
RALPH DE SOMERY, of Dudley (in Sedgley), Staffordshire, married **MARGARET LE GRAS**.
JOAN DE SOMERY, married **THOMAS DE BERKELEY**.
MAURICE DE BERKELEY, Knt., of Berkeley, Gloucestershire, married **ISABEL DE DOVER** (desc. King William the Conqueror).
THOMAS DE BERKELEY, Knt., 1st Lord Berkeley, married **JOAN DE FERRERS** (desc. King William the Conqueror).
MAURICE DE BERKELEY, Knt., 2nd Lord Berkeley, married **EVE LA ZOUCHE** [see BERKELEY 6].

7. MAURICE DE BERKELEY, Knt., of Uley, Rockhampton, and Stoke Gifford, Gloucestershire, Kingston Seymour, Somerset, Milston, Wiltshire, etc., Custodian of Prudhoe Castle, Constable of Gloucester and Bristol Castles, Steward of the Duchy of Aquitaine, younger son. He married by papal dispensation dated 29 Dec. 1331 (they being related in the 4th degree of kindred) **MARGERY DE VERE**, perhaps daughter of Alphonse de Vere, Knt., of Aston Sandford, Buckinghamshire and Great Hormead, Hertfordshire, by Joan, daughter of Jordan Foliot [see VERE 4 for her possible ancestry]. They had three sons, Thomas, Knt., Maurice, and Edward,

Knt., and one daughter, Isabel. His lands were seized by King Edward II when his father rebelled against the king and the Despensers. With his elder brother, Thomas, he pillaged Despenser property. He had restitution of his lands after the fall of the Despensers. In 1330 King Edward III retained him for life "to attend him always." The same year Maurice purchased the manors of Aylburton (in Lydney) and King's Weston (near Bristol), Gloucestershire from Sir Thomas ap Adam. In 1337 the king granted Maurice the manor of Sherrington, Wiltshire, and, in 1339, the manor of Brimpsfield, Gloucestershire, both of which formerly belonged to his brother-in-law, John Mautravers. He served King Edward III in France, and was created a knight banneret in 1341–2. He fought at the Battle of Crécy in 1346. SIR MAURICE DE BERKELEY died testate 12 Feb. 1346/7. His memory is commemorated in the great east window of Gloucester Cathedral in the display of shields of the knights who fought in the Crécy and Calais campaigns of 1346 and 1347. His widow, Margery, died 21 May 1351.

Dugdale *Baronage of England* 2 (1676): 355–356 (sub Berkeley). Blore *Hist. & Antiqs. of Rutland* 1(2) (1811): 210 (Berkeley ped.). Brydges *Collins' Peerage of England* 3 (1812): 591–627 (sub Earl of Berkeley). Burke *Dormant, Abeyant, Forfeited & Extinct Peerages* (1883): 45–46 (sub Berkeley). Smyth *Berkeley MSS* 1 (1883): 245–254. Benolte *Vis. of Somerset 1531, 1573 & 1591* (1885): 5–6 (Berkley ped.: "Sr. Morris [Berkeley] of Ewley [Uley, Glos.], d. 21 E. III.= Margaret."). C.P.R. 1327–1330 (1891): 507. Jeayes *Desc. Cat. of the Charters & Muniments in the Possession of the Rt. Hon. Lord Fitzhardinge* (1892): xxii–xxiii (chart). C.P.R. 1334–1338 (1895): 3, 428, 519. *Papal Regs.: Letters* 2 (1895): 368. Ralph of Shrewsbury *Reg. of Ralph of Shrewsbury Bishop of Bath & Wells* 2 (Somerset Rec. Soc. 10) (1896): 543. Wrottesley *Crécy & Calais* (1898): 196. C.P.R. 1345–1348 (1903): 368. C.C.R. 1346–1349 (1905): 198, 201, 225. *List of Inqs. ad Quod Damnum* 2 (PRO Lists and Indexes 22) (1906): 474. C.P. 2 (1912): 129, footnote c (sub Berkeley). *Cal. IPM* 9 (1916): 28–29. *Trans. Bristol & Gloucs. Arch. Soc.* 71 (1952): 100–121. Paget *Baronage of England* (1957) 55: 1–2 (sub Berkeley). Ross *Cartulary of St. Mark's Hospital Bristol* (Bristol Rec. Soc. 21) (1959): 23–28. Sabin *Some Manorial Accounts of Saint Augustine's Abbey* (Bristol Rec. Soc. 22) (1960): 56. Orleton *Cal. Reg. of Adam de Orleton 1327–1333* (Worcestershire Hist. Soc. n.s. 10) (1979): 107. Saul *Knights & Esquires* (1981): 58, 276, 281. VCH *Gloucester* 7 (1981): 143, 203; 4 (1988): 279, footnote 71. VCH *Wiltshire* 15 (1995): 138–139, 237, 257. Brault *Rolls of Arms Edward I* 2 (1997): 456 (arms of Sir Alphonse ("Aumphons") de Vere: Quarterly gules and or, in the first quarter a mullet ermine).

8. **THOMAS DE BERKELEY**, Knt., of Uley, Aylburton (in Lydney), Bradley, and Kings Weston, Gloucestershire, Kingston Seymour, Somerset, Milston, Wiltshire, etc., son and heir, born about 1334 (aged 13 in 1347). He attended his father at the siege of Calais, and, in respect to his father's service, was granted by the King the profits of his father's lands during his minority, together with his own marriage. He married before 1350 **KATHERINE BOTETOURT**, daughter of John Botetourt, Knt., 2nd Lord Botetourt, by Joyce, daughter of William la Zouche Mortimer, Knt., Lord Zouche [see BOTETOURT 10 for her ancestry]. They had one son, Maurice, Knt., and one daughter (living 1400 unmarried). He fought at the Battle of Poitiers in 1356. SIR THOMAS DE BERKELEY died shortly before 29 Sept. 1361. His widow, Katherine, married (2nd) **JOHN DE THORPE**, Knt. (died 10 Dec. 1386), of East Boscome (in Boscome), Wiltshire, Knight of the Shire for Gloucestershire, Knight of the Shire for Wiltshire. They had two sons, Edward and Henry. In 1382 Thomas Berkeley, Knt., 5th Lord Berkeley sued John and his wife, Katherine, for the manors of Brigmerston (in Milston) and Milston, Wiltshire. Katherine died 22 Jan. 1387/8.

Nichols *Hist. & Antiqs. of Leicester* 3(2) (1804): 635 (Zouch ped.). Blore *Hist. & Antiqs. of Rutland* 1(2) (1811): 90, 209 (Botetourt peds.), 210 (Berkeley ped.). Grazebrook *Heraldry of Worcestershire* 1 (1873): 66–67. Smyth *Berkeley MSS* 1 (1883): 254–257. Burke *Dormant, Abeyant, Forfeited & Extinct Peerages* (1883): 45–46 (sub Berkeley), 63–64 (sub Botetourt). Benolte *Vis. of Somerset 1531, 1573 & 1591* (1885): 5–6 (Berkley ped.: Sr. Thos. [Berkeley] of Ewley, d. 35 E. III. = Kath. d. Sr. Joh. Bitton.") (ped. inserts additional generation: "Sir Morris [Berkeley] of Ewley, d. 4 H. IV. = Kath., s. and coh., Joh. De la Botetourt, L. of Weley."). *Genealogist* n.s. 13 (1896): 172–173. Wrottesley *Staffordshire Suits: Plea Rolls* (Colls. Hist. Staffs. 17) (1896): 78–79. Bull *Hist. of Newport Pagnell* (1900): 27–44. *Trans. Bristol & Gloucs. Arch. Soc.* 26 (1903): 257–262. *Genealogist* n.s. 19 (1903): 103–104. Wrottesley *Peds. from the Plea Rolls* (1905): 150, 418. *List of Inqs. ad Quod Damnum* 2 (PRO Lists and Indexes 22) (1906): 474, 485. VCH *Hampshire* 4 (1911): 99. C.P. 2 (1912): 234 (chart) (in error calls him "Maurice"). VCH *Worcester* 3 (1913): 194–201. *Cal. IPM* 11 (1935): 6–7, 452–455. Paget *Baronage of England* (1957) 55: 1–2 (sub Berkeley). VCH *Warwick* 7 (1964): 58. Saul *Knights & Esquires* (1981): 285. VCH *Gloucester* 7 (1981): 143. Roskell *House of Commons 1386–1421* 2 (1992): 201–202 (biog. of Sir Maurice Berkeley), 4 (1992): 600–601 (biog. Henry Thorpe). VCH *Wiltshire* 15 (1995): 9, 57, 138–139, 220. National

Archives, SC 8/226/11297 (petition dated c.1361–4 from Robert de Danhurst, clerk and avener of the queen, to the king, requesting that it be granted to his kinsman, John de Thorpe, who recently returned from Rome, a charter of exemption and liberty that he not be put on assizes, juries or any other manner of recognisance, nor be a collector of fifteenth or serve in other offices) (available at www.catalogue.nationalarchives.gov.uk/search.asp).

9. MAURICE BERKELEY, Knt., of Uley, Aylburton (in Lydney), Kings Weston, and Rockhampton, Gloucestershire, Rotherwick, Hampshire, Milston, Wiltshire, etc., Knight of the Shire for Gloucestershire, Justice of the Peace for Gloucestershire, 1389–90, son and heir, born at Uley, Gloucestershire 1 June 1358. He was heir in 1364 by prior settlement to his cousin, John Mautravers, Lord Mautravers, by which he inherited the manors of Stoke Gifford, Rockhampton, and Wallscourt, Gloucestershire. He served in the French war as a minor, and was knighted in 1379 on the voyage to France. He accompanied John of Gaunt, Duke of Lancaster, to Aquitaine. He married before May 1400 **JOAN DINHAM** (or **DYNHAM**), daughter of John de Dinham, Knt., of Hartland, Devon, by Muriel, daughter of Thomas de Courtenay, Knt. [see DINHAM 6 for her ancestry]. They had one son, Maurice, Knt. SIR MAURICE BERKELEY died 2 October 1400. His widow, Joan, died 22 August 1412.

Blore *Hist. & Antiqs. of Rutland* 1(2) (1811): 90, 209 (Botetourt peds.), 210 (Berkeley ped.). Grazebrook *Heraldry of Worcestershire* 1 (1873): 66–67. Smyth *Berkeley MSS* 1 (1883): 257–259. Burke *Dormant, Abeyant, Forfeited & Extinct Peerages* (1883): 45–46 (sub Berkeley), 63–64 (sub Botetourt). Benolte *Vis. of Somerset 1531, 1573 & 1591* (1885): 5–6 (Berkley ped.: "Sr. Morris of Ewley and Stoke Gifford, Glos., d. 10 H. V. = Joan, d. Sr. John Denham."). Bull *Hist. of Newport Pagnell* (1900): 27–44. *C.P.R. 1399–1401* (1903): 288. *Genealogist* n.s. 19 (1903): 103–104. Wrottesley *Peds. from the Plea Rolls* (1905): 418. *C.P.* 2 (1912): 234 (chart); 8 (1932): 584, footnote k. Stawell *Quantock Fam.* (1910): 324. VCH *Hampshire* 4 (1911): 99. *C.C.R. 1399–1402* (1927): 237–238, 242. Ross *Cartulary of St. Mark's Hospital Bristol* (Bristol Rec. Soc. 21) (1959): 23–28. VCH *Warwick* 7 (1964): 58. Saul *Knights & Esquires* (1981): 289. Roskell *House of Commons 1386–1421* 2 (1992): 201–202 (biog. of Sir Maurice Berkeley). VCH *Wiltshire* 15 (1995): 138–139.

10. MAURICE BERKELEY, Knt., of Stoke Gifford and Uley, Gloucestershire, Milston, Wiltshire, etc., Knight of the Shire for Gloucestershire, Sheriff of Gloucestershire, 1430–1, 1436–7, son and heir, born posthumously 2 Feb. 1400/1. He was co-heir in 1407 to his cousin, Joyce Botetourt, wife of Hugh Burnell, K.G., 2nd Lord Burnell, by which he inherited a one-third share of the barony of Botetourt. He married before 1427/8 (date of receipt) **ELLEN** (or **ELEANOR**) **MONTFORT**, daughter of William Montfort, Knt., of Coleshill, Warwickshire, by his 1st wife, Margaret, daughter and co-heiress of John Pecche, Knt. [see MONTFORT 11 for her ancestry]. They had three sons, William, K.B., Thomas, and Maurice. In 1431 he and Joan Beauchamp, Lady Bergavenny, held the manor of Northfield, Worcestershire jointly, but by subsequent arbitration, it was decided that the Castle of Weoley (in Northfield) (thereafter his chief residence) and the manors of Northfield and Cradley (in Halesowen) should pass to Maurice, as well as 40s. out of the manor of Old Swinford, Worcestershire. He served in France in the army of John of Lancaster, Duke of Bedford. In 1446 Thomas, Bishop of Worcester, and William Wynde, Master of the house of St. Mark, Bristol were summoned in the king's court to answer Maurice de Berkeley on a plea that they should permit him to present a suitable person to the church of the house of St. Mark of Bristol. This suit was decided against Maurice. He presented to the church of Kingston Seymour, Somerset in 1463. SIR MAURICE BERKELEY died 26 Nov. 1464. His widow, Ellen, was living in 1475. They were buried in the Lord Mayor's Chapel in St. Mark's, Bristol.

Blore *Hist. & Antiqs. of Rutland* 1(2) (1811): 90, 209 (Botetourt peds.), 210 (Berkeley ped.). Fuller *Hist. of the Worthies of England* (1840): 567–568. Foss *Judges of England* 5 (1857): 144–145. Grazebrook *Heraldry of Worcestershire* 1 (1873): 66–67. Smyth *Berkeley MSS* 1 (1883): 260–261. Burke *Dormant, Abeyant, Forfeited & Extinct Peerages* (1883): 45–46 (sub Berkeley). Benolte *Vis. of Somerset 1531, 1573 & 1591* (1885): 5–6 (Berkley ped.: "Sr. Morris [Berkeley] of Stoke, d. 4 Ed. IV. = Ellen, d. Sir Wm. Mountford."). Weaver *Somerset Incumbents* (1889): 274. *List of Sheriffs for England & Wales* (PRO Lists and Indexes 9) (1898): 50. Bull *Hist. of Newport Pagnell* (1900): 27–44. *Trans. Bristol & Gloucs. Arch. Soc.* 26 (1903): 257–262. *Genealogist* n.s. 19 (1903): 103–104. Wrottesley *Peds. from the Plea Rolls* (1905): 418. Green *Feet of Fines for Somerset* 4 (Somerset Rec. Soc. 22) (1906): 192. *Feudal Aids* 5 (1908): 240. *List of Early Chancery Procs.* 4 (PRO Lists and Indexes 29) (1908): 4. VCH *Hampshire* 4 (1911): 99. *C.P.* 2 (1912): 234 (chart). VCH *Worcester* 3 (1913): 143, 194–

195. Beckington *Reg. of Thomas Bekynton Bishop of Bath & Wells* 1 (Somerset Rec. Soc. 49) (1934): 384. Ross *Cartulary of St. Mark's Hospital Bristol* (Bristol Rec. Soc. 21) (1959): 23–28. VCH *Oxford* 10 (1972): 201. Hallum *Reg. of Robert Hallum Bishop of Salisbury 1407–17* (Canterbury & York Soc. 72) (1982): 33. Roskell *House of Commons 1386–1421* 2 (1992): 201–202 (biog. of Sir Maurice Berkeley). VCH *Wiltshire* 15 (1995): 138–139. Gloucestershire Rec. Office: Badminton Muniments Vol. II, Estate and Household, D2700/MJ1/6 — receipt dated: 1427/8 by Dame Ellen Berkeley for money (available at www.a2a.org.uk/search/index.asp).

11. WILLIAM BERKELEY, K.B., of Weoley (in Northfield), Worcestershire, Stoke Gifford and Uley, Gloucestershire, Milston, Wiltshire, Bristol, etc., Sheriff of Gloucestershire, 1484–5, Knight of the Shire for Worcestershire, son and heir, born about 1436 (aged 28 in 1464). He married **ANNE STAFFORD**, widow of Thomas Skulle, of Wigginton, Oxfordshire (died before 1459), and daughter of Humphrey Stafford, Knt., of Grafton, Worcestershire, by Eleanor, daughter of Thomas Aylesbury, Knt. [see HASTANG 14 for her ancestry]. They had one son, Richard, Esq., and two daughters, Anne and Katherine (wife of Maurice Berkeley). In 1467 William Berkeley and his cousins, Margaret Freville, Thomas Ferrers, and John Aston, jointly claimed the manor of Ashby de la Zouch, Leicestershire, as lineal descendants and heirs of William la Zouche Mortimer, 1st Lord Zouche of Richard's Castle (died 1337) [see BEAUCHAMP 10], by virtue of a fine dated 1304. In 1485, following the forfeiture of his cousin, William Berkeley, Knt., of Bettesthorne, he was granted the castle or lordship of Beverstone, Gloucestershire. He fought for King Richard III at the Battle of Bosworth in 1485. He was subsequently attainted 7 Nov. 1485, and all of his estates were declared forfeited. In the period, 1486–93, he was sued in Chancery by John Brereton, Esq., and Katherine, his wife, sister and heir to William Berkeley, of Bettesthorne (in Sopley), Hampshire regarding detention of deeds relating to the manor of Bettesthorne and other lands late of the said William Berkeley, of Bettesthorne. In 1486 the king granted the manor of Northfield, Worcestershire to the king's uncle, Jasper Tudor, Duke of Bedford, and his heirs male, who sold it ten days later to John Lord Dudley. In 1489 William was restored in blood, and was granted the reversion of the manor of Northfield, Worcestershire after the death of Duke Jasper Tudor. In spite of this, on the death of Duke Jasper Tudor in 1495, the king took possession of the manor of Northfield. In Dec. 1495 William Berkeley, Knt., formerly of Weoley (in Northfield), Worcestershire, and his son, Richard Berkeley, owed a debt of 1,000 marks to John Walsh, Esq., formerly of Olveston, Gloucestershire. In 1496 he and his wife, Anne, made a settlement of the manors of Zouches, Manners, Shardelowes, and Fulbourn [all in Fulbourn], and Swavesey, Cambridgeshire, together with lands in Fen Drayton, Fulbourn, and Swavesey, Cambridgeshire. SIR WILLIAM BERKELEY died in 1501. His widow, Anne, was living in 1503.

Nash *Colls. for the Hist. of Worcestershire* 1 (1781): 157. Fosbrooke *Abs.of Recs.& MSS respecting the County of Gloucester* 2 (1807): 86–87. Blore *Hist. & Antiqs. of Rutland* 1(2) (1811): 210 (Berkeley ped.). Burke *Dormant, Abeyant, Forfeited & Extinct Peerages* (1883): 45–46 (sub Berkeley). Smyth *Berkeley MSS* 1 (1883): 261–262. Benolte *Vis. of Somerset 1531, 1573 & 1591* (1885): 5–6 (Berkley ped.: "Sr. William [Berkeley] of Stoke, d. 1501. = Anne, d. Hum. Stafford."). C.P.R. 1461–1467 (1897): 549–550. *List of Sheriffs for England & Wales* (PRO Lists and Indexes 9) (1898): 50. C.P.R. 1476–1485 (1901): 530–531. *List of Early Chancery Procs.* 1 (PRO Lists and Indexes 12) (1901): 226; 4 (PRO Lists and Indexes 29) (1908): 42, 44. *Genealogist* n.s. 19 (1903): 103–104. Wrottesley *Peds. from the Plea Rolls* (1905): 418. VCH *Hampshire* 4 (1911): 99. C.P. 2 (1912): 135–136 (sub Berkeley), 234 (chart) ; 6 (1936): 131, footnote j (sub Grey). VCH *Worcester* 3 (1913): 194–201. Wedgwood *Hist. of Parl.* 1 (1936): 69 (biog. of Sir William Berkeley). VCH *Oxford* 9 (1969): 166. *Ancient Deeds — Ser. B* 3 (List & Index Soc. 113) (1975): B.12684. Horrox *British Lib. Harleian MS 433* 1 (1979): 269. Sutton *Coronation of Richard III* (1983): 312 (biog. of William Berkeley). Langton *Reg. of Thomas Langton Bishop of Salisbury 1485–93* (Canterbury & York Soc. 74) (1985): 14. VCH *Wiltshire* 15 (1995): 138–139. Biancalana *Fee Tail & the Common Recovery in Medieval England* (2001): 392–393. VCH *Cambridge* 10 (2002): 136–143. National Archives, C 1/85/48; C 131/90/3; C 131/90/8; C 131/253/6 (available at www.catalogue.nationalarchives.gov.uk/search.asp). Shakespeare Centre Library & Archive, Archer of Tanworth, DR 37/2/Box 88/6 (John Archer styled "worshipful cousin" by William Berkeley, Knt., of Wigginton in letter dated c.1489) (available at www.a2a.org.uk/search/index.asp).

Children of William Berkeley, K.B., by Anne Stafford:

i. **RICHARD BERKELEY**, Esq. [see next].

ii. **ANNE BERKELEY**, married (1st) **JOHN GYSE**, Knt., of Elmore, Gloucestershire [see HAVILAND 18]; (2nd) **WILLIAM KINGSTON**, K.G., of the Blackfriars, London, and Painswick, Gloucestershire [see HAVILAND 18].

12. RICHARD BERKELEY, Esq., of Stoke Gifford, Bradley, Kings Weston, and Uley, Gloucestershire, son and heir. He married **ELIZABETH CONINGSBY**, daughter of Humphrey Coningsby, Knt., of Aldenham, Hertfordshire, and Rock, Worcestershire, Justice of the King's Bench, Serjeant at law, counsel to Queen Elizabeth, by Alice, daughter and heiress of _____ Fereby, of Lincolnshire. They had two sons, John, Knt., and Maurice, Knt., and three daughters, Dorothy (wife of Nicholas Wadham and William Gibbes, Esq.), Anne (wife of Thomas Speke, Knt.), and Mary (wife of William Francis). In 1500–1 Richard son and heir of Sir William Berkeley, Knt. sued Humfrey Pepwall, Henry Shelton, and Richard Colmore, feoffees to uses in Chancery regarding a messuage and land in Aston, Warwickshire. In 1501 he petitioned the king for license to purchase the manor of Northfield, Worcestershire, (formerly held by his father) from Lord Dudley; permission to acquire the manor was granted to him, but he never seems to have done so. In 1508 he and his wife, Elizabeth, sold the manor and advowson of Kingston Seymour, Somerset to Thomas Trye, Gent. for £200. RICHARD BERKELEY, Esq., died in 1513, and was buried in the College of Westbury, Gloucestershire. His widow, Elizabeth, married (2nd) **JOHN FITZ JAMES**, Knt., Chief Justice of the King's Bench. She left a will dated 30 Nov. 1545, proved 8 May 1546 (P.C.C. 9 Alen).

<small>Fosbrooke *Abs.of Recs.& MSS respecting the County of Gloucester* 2 (1807): 86–87. Blore *Hist. & Antiqs. of Rutland* 1(2) (1811): 210–211 (Berkeley ped.). Foss *Judges of England* 5 (1857): 144–145 (biog. of Humphrey Coningsby). Smyth *Berkeley MSS* 1 (1883): 263. Burke *Dormant, Abeyant, Forfeited & Extinct Peerages* (1883): 45–46 (sub Berkeley). Benolte *Vis. of Somerset 1531, 1573 & 1591* (1885): 5–6 (Berkley ped.: "Richard [Berkeley] of Stoke, d. 1514. = Eliz., d. Sr. Hum. Coningsby, she d. 1546."). Chitting & Phillipot *Vis. of Gloucester 1623, 1569 & 1582-3* (H.S.P. 21) (1885): 8–9 (Barkley ped.: "Richard Barkley of Stoke in com. Gloster Esq're ob. 3 or 4 H. 8. = Elizabeth d. of Sir Humffrey Conningsby of… in com.… Knt."). Cooke & Mundy *Vis. of Worcester 1569* (H.S.P. 27) (1888): 43–44 (Coningsby ped.: "… Coningsby ux… Barkley of Glostershire.") ("Coningsby arms: Gules, three coneys couchant argent within a bordure engrailed sable"). Worthy *Devonshire Wills* (1896): 486–487 (re. Gibbes fam.). Weaver *Somerset Medieval Wills* 3 1531–1558 (Somerset Rec. Soc. 21) (1905): 86–88 (will of Elizabeth Fitz-James). C.P. 2 (1912): 234 (chart). VCH *Worcester* 3 (1913): 194–201. *Trans. Shropshire Arch. & Nat. Hist. Soc.* 47 (1933–34): 142. Wedgwood *Hist. of Parl.* 1 (1936): 69 (biog. of Sir William Berkeley). *Notes & Queries* 208 (1963): 5–9. Bindoff *House of Commons 1509–1558* 3 (1982): 359–360 (biog. of Sir Thomas Speke). Thorne *Readings & Moots at the Inns of Court in the 15th Cent.* 2 (Selden Soc. 105) (1990): cxxiv (biog. of Humphrey Conyngesby). National Archives, C 1/237/58; C 131/90/3; C 131/90/8; C 131/253/6; C 131/253/9 (available at www.catalogue.nationalarchives.gov.uk/search.asp). National Archives, CP 25/1/202/42, #61 [see abstract of fine at http:// www.medievalgenealogy.org.uk/index.html].</small>

13. JOHN BERKELEY, Knt., of Stoke Gifford, Gloucestershire, son and heir, born about 1510 (aged 3 in 1513). He married **ISABEL DENNIS**, daughter of William Dennis, Knt., of Dyrham, Gloucestershire, by his 1st wife, Anne, daughter of Maurice Berkeley, Knt. [see DENNIS 15 for her ancestry]. They had one son, Richard, Knt., and two daughters, Mary (wife of Nicholas Walshe and William Herbert, Knt.) and Elizabeth. SIR JOHN BERKELEY died in 1545. His widow, Isabel, married (2nd) (as his 2nd wife) **ARTHUR PORTER**, Esq. (died 31 May 1559), of Newent and Alvington, Gloucestershire, Sheriff of Gloucestershire, 1548–9, Knight of the Shire for Gloucestershire, son and heir of Thomas Porter, by Katherine, daughter and heiress of John Hayward. They had no issue.

<small>Fosbrooke *Abs.of Recs.& MSS respecting the County of Gloucester* 2 (1807): 86–87. Blore *Hist. & Antiqs. of Rutland* 1(2) (1811): 210 (Berkeley ped.). Smyth *Berkeley MSS* 2 (1883): 178–187. Burke *Dormant, Abeyant, Forfeited & Extinct Peerages* (1883): 45–46 (sub Berkeley). Benolte *Vis. of Somerset 1531, 1573 & 1591* (1885): 5–6 (Berkley ped.: "Sir John [Berkeley] of Stoke, d. 1546. = Isabel, d. Sr. W. Dennis of Dyrham, Glos."). Chitting & Phillipot *Vis. of Gloucester 1623, 1569 & 1582-3* (H.S.P. 21) (1885): 8–9 (Barkley ped.: "Sir John Barkley of Stoke Knt. ob. 1545. = Issabell d. of Sir William Dennis Knt."), 49–52 (Dennis ped.: "Isabel [Dennis] wife of John Barkley 2d Arther Porter"), 126–127 (Porter ped.: "Arthur Porter sonn and heire [1] = Allice d. of John Arnold sister of Sir Nicholas Arnold Knight, [2] =</small>

Issabell Laydy Barkley d. of Sir Wm. Dennys Knight"). *List of Sheriffs for England & Wales* (PRO Lists and Indexes 9) (1898): 51. *C.P.* 2 (1912): 234 (chart). *Trans. Bristol & Gloucestershire Arch. Soc.* 64 (1943): 120–125 (Arthur Porter, Esq. styled "nephew" in will of Cecily [Arnold], Lady Berkeley). *Notes & Queries* 208 (1963): 5–9. Bindoff *House of Commons 1509–1558* 3 (1982): 136–137 (biog. of Arthur Porter).

14. ELIZABETH BERKELEY, married **HENRY LIGON** (or **LYGON**), of Upton St. Leonard's, Gloucester, Gloucestershire, 4th son of Richard Lygon, Knt., of Madresfield, Worcestershire, and Kemerton, Gloucestershire, by Margery, daughter of William Greville, Knt., of Cheltenham, Gloucestershire, Justice of the Common Pleas [see LIGON 16 for his ancestry]. They had two sons, Arnold, Knt., and Henry, and two daughters, Mary (wife of Samuel Clinton, Esq.) and Isabel (or Elizabeth). He had a lease of a wood at Cromhall in 1554 from his older brother, William Ligon. In 1560 and 1568 he was in the service of Henry, Lord Berkeley. HENRY LIGON died 31 July 1577. He left a will dated 30 July 1577, proved 15 August 1577.

Fosbrooke *Abs. of Recs. & MSS respecting the County of Gloucester* 2 (1807): 86–87. Blore *Hist. & Antiqs. of Rutland* 1(2) (1811): 210 (Berkeley ped.). Brydges *Collins' Peerage of England* 9 (1812): 507–516 (sub Add. & Corr.). Smyth *Berkeley MSS* 2 (1883): 180. Chitting & Phillipot *Vis. of Gloucester 1623, 1569 & 1582-3* (H.S.P. 21) (1885): 8–9 (Barkley ped.: "Elizabeth [Berkeley] ux. Hen. Lison [sic] of Upton St Leonards"). Cooke & Mundy *Vis. of Worcester 1569* (H.S.P. 27) (1888): 90–91 (Lygon ped.: "Henry [Lygon] m. Eliz. da. to Sr John Berckly K."). Ligon *Madresfield Muniments* (1929): 18–47. *TAG* 9 (1932-33): 212–222. *Wm & Mary Quarterly* 2nd Ser. 16 (1936): 289–315. Ligon *Ligon Fam.* 1 (1947): 42–43.

15. ISABEL (or **ELIZABETH**) **LIGON**, was a legatee in her father's 1577 will. She married **EDWARD BASSET**, Gent., of Uley, Gloucestershire, son and heir of William Basset, of Uley and Highfield, Gloucestershire, by Jane (or Joan), daughter of John Ashe (or Asshe), Esq. [see ASHE 17 for his ancestry]. They had four sons, William, Esq., Barnaby, Edward, and Giles, and four daughters, Elizabeth (wife of William Clayfield, Gent., and Thomas Poyntz, Gent.), Margery (or Margaret) (wife of Samuel Shellom), Susanna (wife of Michael Dorney), and Jane. EDWARD BASSET, Gent., left a will dated 3 June 1601, proved 5 Nov. 1602 (P.C.C. 77 Montague), requesting burial in the chapel of Uley, Gloucestershire. His widow, Isabel, married (2nd) (as his 2nd wife) **RICE** (or **REES**) **DAVIS** (or **DAVIES**), Esq., of Tickenham, Somerset. They had no issue. At some unknown date, Rice and his wife, Isabel, conveyed a 1/9th share of the manor of Furnax (in Warminster), Wiltshire to Simon Sloper, of Warminster. Following her death, he married (3rd) **MARY PITT**, widow of Robert Owen, of Bristol, merchant, by whom he had a daughter, Eleanor (wife of Nicholas Poyntz). RICE DAVIS, Esq., left a will dated 28 August 1638, proved 23 April 1639 (P.C.C. 41 Fairfax), requesting burial at the chapel of Backwell, Somerset between his 1st wife, Dorothy Rodney and his 2nd wife, Isabel Ligon.

Brydges *Collins' Peerage of England* 9 (1812): 507–516 (sub Add. & Corr.). *Le Neve's Peds. of the Knights* (H.S.P. 8) (1873): 89 (Basset ped.: "Edward Basset of Uley in Glouc. see Atkyn's Glouc. pag. 791. = …. dr of …. Ligon."). Ellacombe *Hist. of Bitton* (1881): 119 (Basset ped.). Smyth *Berkeley MSS* 1 (1883): 121, 2: 182–183. Chitting & Phillipot *Vis. of Gloucester 1623, 1569 & 1582-3* (H.S.P. 21) (1885): 204–207 (Bassett ped.: "Edward Bassett of Yewley = Elizabeth d. of Henry Lygon") (Bassett arms: Ermine, on a canton gules a mullet or). Brown *Abs. of Somersetshire Wills* 2 (1888): 30 (will of Rice Davis). Byrchmore *Colls. for a Parochial Hist. of Tickenham* (1895): 9–11. *TAG* 9 (1932-33): 212–222; 10 (1933-34): 20–24. *Wm & Mary Quarterly* 2nd Ser. 16 (1936): 289–315. VCH *Wiltshire* 8 (1965): 96–103. Gloucestershire Archives, Deeds of the Dorney Fam. of Uley, D3365/2 (available at www.a2a.org.uk/search/index.asp). Gloucestershire Archives, Gloucestershire Parish Deeds, D2957/65/116 (available at www.a2a.org.uk/search/index.asp).

16. JANE BASSET. She was a legatee in her father's 1601 will. She married at St. Nicholas, Gloucester, Gloucestershire 12 April 1605 **JOHN DEIGHTON**, Gent., of St. Nicholas, Gloucester, Gloucestershire, surgeon, Sheriff of the City of Gloucester, son of Thomas Deighton, of Cirencester, Gloucestershire, by his wife, Anne (or Agnes). He was baptized at Cirencester, Gloucestershire 18 Nov. 1568. They had three sons, John, John (again), and Thomas, and five daughters, Jane, Frances, Katherine, Damaris, and Mary. His wife, Jane, died 23 April 1631. JOHN

DEIGHTON, Gent., died 16 May 1640. He left a will dated 30 Jan. 1639, proved 21 May 1640. He and his wife, Jane, were buried in the south aisle of the church of St. Nicholas, Gloucester, Gloucestershire.

Smyth *Berkeley MSS* 2 (1883): 183. *TAG* 9 (1932–33): 212–222 (Deighton arms: Argent a lion passant between three crosses patty fitchee gules); 10 (1933–34): 20–29. Waters *Gen. Gleanings in England* 1 (1885): 551–552. *NEHGR* 45 (1891): 303. Bassette *One Basset Fam. in America* (1926): 522–523. Ligon *Ligon Fam.* 1 (1947): 43–44. Harleian MSS 5814: 49 (unpublished manuscript Deighton ped., original held at the British Lib., London). *TG* 6 (1985): 195–231. Special thanks go to Ellen Shaw for her assistance with this account.

Children of Jane Bassett, by John Deighton, Gent.:

i. **JANE DEIGHTON**, baptized at St. Nicholas, Gloucester, England 5 April 1609. She married (1st) St. Nicholas, Gloucester 3 Jan. 1627/8 **JOHN LUGG**. They had one son, John, and two daughters, Elizabeth and Mary (wife of Nathaniel Barnard). They immigrated to New England in 1637–8, where JOHN LUGG died after 1644. His widow, Jane, married (2nd) at Boston, Massachusetts 27 October 1647 **JONATHAN NEGUS**, of Boston, Massachusetts, Clerk of the Writs. He was born about 1601. They had one son, Isaac, and one daughter, Maria. His wife, Jane, was living at Boston, Massachusetts in 1671. JONATHAN NEGUS died there shortly before 11 April 1682. Pope *Pioneers of Massachusetts* (1900): 295 (biog. of John Lugg), 326 (biog. of Jonathan Negoose). *TAG* 9 (1932–33): 212–222. *TG* 6 (1985): 195–231.

ii. **FRANCES DEIGHTON**, baptized at St. Nicholas, Gloucester, England 1 March 1611/2. She married at Great Witcombe, Gloucestershire 11 Feb. 1632/3 **RICHARD WILLIAMS**, baptized at Wotton under Edge, Gloucestershire 28 Jan. 1607/8, son of William Williams, of Synwell (in Wotton under Edge), Gloucestershire, yeoman, by his 2nd wife, Jane Woodward. They had six sons, John, Samuel, Nathaniel, Joseph, Thomas, and Benjamin, and three daughters, Elizabeth, Elizabeth (again) (wife of John Bird), and Hannah (wife of John Parmenter). He was a legatee in the 1618 will of his father. He and his family immigrated to New England about 1636 or 1637, where they settled at Taunton, Massachusetts. RICHARD WILLIAMS died at Taunton, Massachusetts in August 1693. His widow, Frances, died there in Feb. 1705/6. Pope *Pioneers of Massachusetts* (1900): 500 (biog. of Richard Williams). *TAG* 9 (1932–33): 136–144, 212–222; 10 (1933–34): 24–29.

iii. **KATHERINE DEIGHTON**, baptized at St. Nicholas, Gloucester, Gloucestershire 16 Jan. 1614/5. She married (1st) at St. Nicholas, Gloucester, Gloucestershire 25 Dec. 1633 **SAMUEL HACKBURNE** (or **HAGBORNE**). They had two sons, Samuel and John, and two daughters, Elizabeth (wife of John Chickering) and Hannah (wife of Samuel Hunting). They immigrated to New England, where they settled at Roxbury, Massachusetts. SAMUEL HACKBORNE was buried 27 Dec. 1642. She married (2nd) at Roxbury, Massachusetts 4 April 1644 (as his 2nd wife) [**Gov.**] **THOMAS DUDLEY** [see DUDLEY 21]. They had two sons, Joseph and Paul, and one daughter, Deborah (wife of Jonathan Wade). [**Gov.**] THOMAS DUDLEY died at Roxbury, Massachusetts 31 July 1653. She married (3rd) at Dedham, Massachusetts 8 Nov. 1653 (as his 2nd wife) [**Rev.**] **JOHN ALLIN**, of Dedham, Massachusetts. They had three sons, Benjamin, Daniel, and Eliezer. She died 20 August 1671. Pope *Pioneers of Massachusetts* (1900): 14 (biog. of [Rev.] John Allen), 145–146 (biog. of [Mr.] Thomas Dudley), 206 (biog. of Samuel Hagborne). *TAG* 9 (1932–33): 212–222. Anderson *Great Migration Begins* 1 (1995): 581–588.

❧ DE LA MARE ❧

HUGUES CAPET, King of France, married **ALIX OF POITOU**.
ROBERT II *le Pieux*, King of France, married **CONSTANCE OF PROVENCE**.
HENRI I, King of France, married **ANNE OF KIEV**.
HUGUES LE GRAND, Count of Crépy, married **ADÈLE DE VERMANDOIS**.
ISABEL DE VERMANDOIS, married **WILLIAM DE WARENNE**, 2nd Earl of Surrey.
REYNOLD DE WARRENE, of Wormegay, Norfolk, married **ALICE DE WORMEGAY** [see BARDOLF 6].

7. GUNDRED DE WARENNE. She married (1st) **PETER DE VALOINES**, of Dersingham, Norfolk. They had no issue. He was dead at Michaelmas 1160. His widow, Gundred, married (2nd) **WILLIAM DE COURCY** (or **CURCY**), of Stogursey, Somerset, Nuneham (in Nuneham Courtenay), Oxfordshire, etc., King's Steward, son and heir of William de Courcy, of Stogursey, Somerset, Nuneham (in Nuneham Courtenay), Oxfordshire, etc., by Avice de Rumilly, daughter of

William Meschin. They had one son, William, and one daughter, Alice. In the period, 1162–71, he granted St. Andrew of Stokes a mill called Mervines Milne at Northamp'. **WILLIAM DE COURCY** died in 1171. His widow, Gundred, married (3rd) **GEOFFREY HOSE**, Sheriff of Oxfordshire, 1179–82. They had one son, Henry. He died between Michaelmas 1192 and Michaelmas 1193. In 1194 she sued the Abbot of Abingdon regarding the advowson of the church of Nuneham Courtenay, Oxfordshire. At an unknown date, she gave the Priory of St. Denis near Southampton the advowson of the church of Little Fakenham, Suffolk, which was of her maritagium. Gundred died shortly before 9 May 1225.

> *Memoirs illustrative of the Hist. & Antiqs. of the County & City of York* (1848): 34–48 (undated confirmation charter of William de Courcy, Steward of the King of England; charter names his mother, Avice de Rumilly). *List of Sheriffs for England & Wales* (PRO Lists and Indexes 9) (1898): 107. Farrer *Honors & Knights' Fees* 2 (1924): 103–110. *Early Yorkshire Charters* 7 (Yorkshire Arch. Soc. Extra Ser. 5) (1947): 4–9. Clay *Early Yorkshire Charters* 8 (1949): 26–35. Tremlett & Blakiston *Stogursey Charters* (Somerset Rec. Soc. 61) (1949): xxiv (chart), 5–6 (charter of William son of William de Coucy dated 1162–71). VCH *Oxford* 5 (1957): 234–249. VCH *Somerset* 6 (1992): 136–137.

8. ALICE DE COURCY. She married (1st) **HENRY DE CORNHILL** (also known as **HENRY FITZ GERVASE**, of London, Wakering, Essex, and Oxted, Surrey, Sheriff of London, Sheriff of Kent, 1189–92, Sheriff of Surrey, 1183–91, joint Sheriff of London, 1187–9, son and heir of Gervase Fitz Roger (also known as Gervase de Cornhill), joint Sheriff of London, 1155–6, Sheriff of Surrey, 1163–82, Sheriff of Kent, 1168–74, by Agnes, daughter of Edward de Cornhill. They had one daughter, Joan. **HENRY DE CORNHILL** died in 1193. His widow, Alice, married (2nd) before 1194 **WARIN FITZ GEROLD**, King's Chamberlain, of Heyford Warren (in Upper Heyford), Oxfordshire, and, in right of his wife, of Stogursey and Wootton, Somerset, Nuneham (in Nuneham Courtenay), Oxfordshire, Harewood, Yorkshire, etc., son and heir of Henry Fitz Gerold, by Maud de Chesney. He was born about 1167 (aged 18 in 1185). They had one daughter, Margaret (wife of Baldwin de Rivers [or Reviers] and Fawkes de Breauté). He came of age in 1189. His wife, Alice, was heiress in 1194 to her brother, William de Courcy. In 1200 he claimed the right of presentation to the church of Harewood, Yorkshire in right of his wife, Alice. He joined the party of the barons towards the end of 1215. Sometime before 1216, Warin forfeited the honour of Stogursey, Somerset to the king. **WARIN FITZ GEROLD** died in 1216. His wife, Alice, died about 1218.

> Round *Geoffrey de Mandeville* (1892): 304–312. *List of Sheriffs for England & Wales* (PRO Lists and Indexes 9) (1898): 67, 135, 200. Round *Commune of London* (1899): 107. Farrer *Honors & Knights' Fees* 2 (1924): 103–110. Maxwell-Lyte *Hist. Notes of Some Somerset Manors* (Somerset Rec. Soc. Extra Ser. 1) (1931): 308. Clay *Early Yorkshire Charters* 8 (1949): 26–35. Tremlett & Blakiston *Stogursey Charters* (Somerset Rec. Soc. 61) (1949): xxiv (chart), 29–30. VCH *Oxford* 5 (1957): 234–249; 6 (1959):196–205. VCH *Somerset* 6 (1992): 136–137. Young *Making of the Neville Family in England: 1166–1400* (1996): 46–49.

9. JOAN DE CORNHILL, daughter and heiress. She married before 30 April 1200 (as his 1st wife) **HUGH DE NEVILLE**, of Great Hallingbury, Essex, Chief Forester and Justice of the King's Forest, Sheriff of Essex and Hertfordshire, 1197–1200, 1202–4, Keeper of the Seaports from Cornwall to Hampshire, 1213, and, in right of his wife, of Nuneham (in Nuneham Courtenay), Oxfordshire and Stogursey, Somerset, son of Ralph de Neville. They had two sons, John, Knt., and Herbert, and one daughter, Agnes. He accompanied King Richard I on the Third Crusade in 1190, and took part in the Siege of Jaffa in 1192. In 1194 he became farmer and Keeper of Marlborough. In 1203 he had a charter for life of the office of Forester. He was made Treasurer before 27 Jan. 1208/9, and became one of the king's chief advisors. He remained faithful to King John during the trouble with the Barons, being one of 27 who appeared on the king's side at Runnymeade in June 1215. However, when the Dauphin overran Kent, he did homage to the invader and surrendered the royal castle of Marlborough, thus forfeiting his lands and offices. He returned to his fealty, and his lands and the Forestship were restored to him in October 1217. In 1220 he claimed half of the honor of Stogursey, Somerset, in right of his wife's inheritance; but he was not successful until after the fall of Fawkes de Breauté in 1224. His wife, Joan, was living 9 May 1225. In the period, 1225–34, he granted the monks of Stogursey the church of St. Andrew in Stogursey, various tithes, and the chaplaincy of his house when he was in town. He was granted free warren in his lands at Stogursey, Somerset in 1228. He married (2nd) before April 1230 **BEATRICE DE TURNHAM**, widow of Ralph de Fay, of Bromley, Surrey (died about 1223), and daughter and co-heiress of Stephen de Turnham. In 1233 the king ordered him to fortify and remain permanently in the castle of Stogursey, Somerset, in order to prevent the landing of an enemy. HUGH DE NEVILLE died shortly before 21 July 1234, and was buried at Waltham Abbey, Essex. His widow, Beatrice, married (3rd) (as his 2nd wife) **HUGH DE PLAIZ**, Knt. [see PLAIZ 6], of Feltwell and Weeting, Norfolk, Barford, Oxfordshire, Chailey, Iford, Kingston, Newick, Wapsbourne, and Worth, Sussex, etc., son and heir of Ralph de Plaiz. She attempted to have this marriage dissolved and was falsely accused of having been excommunicated. She appears to have died in or before Dec. 1245. SIR HUGH DE PLAIZ died before 18 August 1244.

<small>List of Sheriffs for England & Wales (PRO Lists and Indexes 9) (1898): 43. Archaeologia 2nd Ser. 6 (1899): 351–370. D.N.B. 14 (1909): 260–262 (biog. of Hugh de Neville). Farrer Honors & Knights' Fees 2 (1924): 103–110. Maxwell-Lyte Hist. Notes of Some Somerset Manors (Somerset Rec. Soc. Extra Ser. 1) (1931): 308. C.P. 9 (1936): 479–480 (sub Neville); 10 (1945): 537–538 (sub Plaiz). Clay Early Yorkshire Charters 8 (1949): 26–35. Tremlett & Blakiston Stogursey Charters (Somerset Rec. Soc. 61) (1949): xxiv (chart), 29–30 (charter of Hugh de Neville dated 1225–34; charter granted with consent of his son and heir, John). VCH Oxford 5 (1957): 234–249. VCH Somerset 6 (1992): 136–137. Young Making of the Neville Family in England: 1166–1400 (1996): 46–49.</small>

10. JOHN DE NEVILLE, Knt., of Little Hallingbury, Essex, Stogursey, Somerset, South Stoke, Sussex, West Harnham, Wiltshire, etc., Chief Forester and Justice of the King's Forest throughout England, son and heir. He married in 1230 **HAWISE DE COURTENAY**, daughter of Robert de Courtenay, Knt., Okehampton, Kenn, Musbury, and Sampford Courtenay, Devon, Sutton Courtenay, Berkshire, Waddesdon, Buckinghamshire, Iwerne, Dorset, etc., by Mary, daughter of William de Vernon, Knt., 5th Earl of Devon [see COURTENAY 3 for her ancestry]. Her maritagium included eleven librates of land in Waddesdon, Buckinghamshire and 24 librates of land and the advowson of the church in Alphington, Devon. They had two sons, Hugh, Knt., and John, and one daughter, Joan. In 1231 he sued William, Prior of Cowick, regarding the advowson of the church of Alphington, Devon. In 1234, before his father's death, he fined to have the bailiwick of the King's Forest in Oxfordshire, Northamptonshire, Buckinghamshire, and Huntingdonshire for life; after his father's death, he did homage 21 July 1234. He was appointed Chief Forester and Justice of the whole of the King's Forest through England 21 October 1235. Sometime in the period, 1234–46, he confirmed the grants of his father and ancestors to the monks of Stogursey. In 1240 he sailed with Richard, Earl of Cornwall, for Palestine. After his return to England, he was so rapacious and oppressive in the execution of his office as Forester that he escaped prison only by payment of a very heavy fine. He retired in disgrace to Wethersfield, Essex. SIR JOHN DE NEVILLE died at Wethersfield, Essex shortly before 8 June 1246, and was buried at Waltham Abbey, Essex. His widow, Hawise, married (2nd) before Easter 1254 (date of fine) **JOHN DE GATESDEN**, Knt., of Broadwater, Barcombe, Didling, Dumpford, Elsted, and Trotton, Sussex, Stockholt (in Akeley), Buckinghamshire, Eling and Lasham, Hampshire, Compton, Surrey, etc. They had one daughter, Margaret (or Margery). Sometime before 1262 he granted the Dean and Chapter of Chichester one acre of land in Didling, Sussex. SIR JOHN DE GATESDEN died shortly before 17 October 1262. In 1264 his widow, Hawise, was given two deer as a gift of the king. Sometime in the period, 1265–9, she and her daughter, Joan, witnessed an alleged miracle in Sussex, which was accredited to the late Simon de Montfort, Earl of Leicester. Hawise was a benefactress of Beeleigh (Maldon) Abbey, and founded a chantry at the Priory of Mottenden in Headcorn, Kent. She died shortly before 8 April 1269.

Burke *Gen'l & Heraldic Dict. of the Peerages of England, Ireland & Scotland* (1831): 142–146 (sub Courtenay). Dallaway *Hist. of the Western Division of the County of Sussex* 1 (1815): 202. Halliwell-Phillipps *Chron. of William de Rishanger* (Camden Soc. 15) (1840): 90, 101–102 (Hawise de Courtenay and Joan de la Mare both styled "noblewomen"). Wood *Letters of Royal & Ill. Ladies* (1846): 42–46 (letter dated c.1258 from Lady Hawise de Neville (née Courtenay) to her son, Hugh de Neville, dated c.1258, in which she says: "Sir Walter de la Hide, Joan your sister, and all our household salute you."; see also Blauuw *Barons' War* (1871): 184, footnote 1). Lipscomb *Hist. & Antiqs. of Buckingham* 1 (1847): 471–472 (Courtenay ped.). Matthew of Paris *Chronica Majora* 4 (Rolls Ser. 57) (1877): 563–564 (death of John de Neville). Maitland *Bracton's Note Book* 2 (1887): 404–405. *Archaeologia* 2nd Ser. 6 (1899): 351–370. *C.C.R.* 1272–1279 (1900): 378. *Desc. Cat. Ancient Deeds* 3 (1900): 19–30 (A. 4008 — Demise of John de Gatesden, 2nd husband of Hawise de Courtenay, witnessed by Walter de la Hide, Knt.), 19–30 (A. 4010 — Release by Hawise de Neville, widow of Sir John de Gatesden, witnessed by Walter de la Hyde, Knt.). Salzman *Feet of Fines Rel. Sussex* 2 (Sussex Rec. Soc. 7) (1908): 8, 25, 62–63, 73–74, 116–117. *Sussex Arch. Colls.* 51 (1908): 190. *VCH Surrey* 3 (1911): 16–24. Farrer *Honors & Knights' Fees* 2 (1924): 103–110. *Sussex Notes & Queries* 1 (1927): 215–216. *VCH Buckingham* 4 (1927): 107–118, 144–147. *C.P.* 9 (1936): 481–482 (sub Neville). *C.C.R.* 1264–1268 (1937): 8. Peckham *Chartulary of the High Church of Chichester* (Sussex Rec. Soc. 46) (1942/3): 102. Tremlett *Stogursey Charters* (Somerset Rec. Soc. 61) (1949): xxiv (Curci ped.), 43 (charter of John de Neville son of Hugh de Neville dated 1234–46). *VCH Sussex* 4 (1953): 8–10; 7 (1940): 80–83. Weinbaum *London Eyre of 1276* (London Rec. Soc.) (1976): 107, 109–110 (charter of John de Gatesdene; mentions his wife, Hawise). Meekings *1235 Surrey Eyre* (Surrey Rec. Soc. 31) (1979): 196–199. Schwennicke *Europaische Stamtafeln* 3(4) (1989): 629 (sub Courtenay). *VCH Somerset* 6 (1992): 136–137. Barlow *English Episcopal Acta* XII (1996): 215. Young *Making of the Neville Family in England: 1166–1400* (1996): 46–49. Meel & Simms *Fragility of her Sex?* (2006): 130. Stewart *1263 Surrey Eyre* (Surrey Rec. Soc. 40) (2006): lxxxvi, cii, cxviii, cxxi. Ward *Women in England in the Middle Ages* (2006): 75. National Archives, E 40/4008, E 40/4010, DL 25/168; DL 25/193; DL 25/1293; DL 25/3469; DL 27/70; DL 34/1/2; SC 7/64/2 (available at www.catalogue.nationalarchives.gov.uk/search.asp).

Child of Hawise de Courtenay, by John de Neville, Knt.:

i. **JOAN DE NEVILLE** [see next].

Child of Hawise de Courtenay, by John de Gatesden, Knt.:

i. **MARGARET** (or **MARGERY**) **DE GATESDEN**, married (1st) **JOHN DE CAMOYS**, Knt., of Flockthorpe (in Hardingham), Norfolk [see CAMOYS 5]; (2nd) **WILLIAM PAYNEL**, Knt., Lord Paynel [see CAMOYS 5].

11. **JOAN DE NEVILLE**, married (1st) **HENRY DE LA MARE**, Knt., of Ashtead, Surrey, and Diddenham (in Shinfield), Farley Hill (in Swallowfield), Hinton (in Hurst), and Sheepbridge (in Swallowfield), Berkshire, royal justice, Seneschal of William Longespée, Earl of Salisbury, Constable of Stogursey Castle, son and heir of William de la Mare, Knt., of Ashtead and Mitcham, Surrey, and Harlaxton and Londonthorpe, Lincolnshire, deputy Sheriff of Surrey and Sussex, 1217–26, by his wife, Basile. They had one daughter, Maud. In 1243 he was exempted from being put on juries, assizes, or recognitions, as long as he was with William Longespée. In 1245 he was granted letters of protection, he then going as a royal messenger to the court of Rome. In 1246 he delivered Stogursey Castle to the king, he then acting as constable for John de Neville. SIR HENRY DE LA MARE died testate in 1257. His widow, Joan, married (2nd) before 1260 **WALTER DE LA HYDE**, Knt., of Cokeham (in Sompting), Stammerham (in Horsham), and Waldron, Sussex, Stow Bedon, Norfolk, etc. They had one daughter, Hawise (wife of Robert le Veel, Knt.). In 1275 he had the assize of bread and ale at Stow Bedon, Norfolk by warrant of Baldwin Wake. His wife, Joan, died before 1280 (date of lawsuit). SIR WALTER DE LA HYDE was living in 1281, and died before 1285.

Blomefield *Essay towards a Top. Hist. of Norfolk* 2 (1805): 278. *Placitorum Abbreviatio* (Rec. Commission) (1811): 152. Roberts *Excerpta e Rotuilis Finium* 2 (1836): 228. Halliwell-Phillipps *Chron. of William de Rishanger* (Camden Soc. 15) (1840): 90, 101–102. Wood *Letters of Royal & Ill. Ladies* (1846): 42–46. Foss *Judges of England* 2 (1848): 397. *Sussex Arch. Colls.* 13 (1861): 85–96, 99. Roberts *Calendarium Genealogicum* 1 (1865): 136. Matthew of Paris *Chronica Majora* 4 (Rolls Ser. 57) (1877): 551, 560; 5 (Rolls Ser. 57) (1880): 56–57, 443, 560, 618, 628, 629. *Procs. Somersetshire Arch. & Nat. Hist. Soc.* 28(2) (1882): 197–200. Rye *Short Cal. Feet of Fines for Norfolk* 1 (1885): 96, 118, 129. Maitland *Bracton's Note Book* 3 (1887): 286–287. *List of Sheriffs for England & Wales* (PRO Lists and Indexes 9) (1898): 135. *Archaeologia* 2nd Ser. 6 (1899): 351–370. *C.C.R.* 1272–1279 (1900): 378. *C.P.R.* 1232–1247 (1906): 357, 453, 468, 483. *Surrey Arch. Colls.* 19 (1906): 27–32. *C.P.R.* 1247–1258 (1908): 463, 478. Salzman *Feet of Fines Rel. Sussex* 2 (Sussex Rec. Soc. 7)

(1908): 54. VCH *Surrey* 3 (1911): 248. Foster *Final Concords of the County of Lincoln, A.D. 1244–1272* (Lincoln Rec. Soc. 17) (1921): 62. Farrer *Honors & Knights' Fees* 1 (1923): 12. VCH *Berkshire* 3 (1923): 253. *Sussex N&Q* 1 (1927): 215–216. *Somersetshire Pleas* 4(1) (Somerset Rec. Soc. 44) (1929): 60–62. C.C.R. 1254–1256 (1931): 277. C.C.R. 1256–1259 (1932): 159. C.C.R. 1259–1261 (1934): 11, 473. C.C.R. 1264–1265 (1937): 55. Hatton *Book of Seals* (1950): 136–138. Watkin *Great Chartulary of Glastonbury* 3 (Somerset Rec. Soc. 64) (1956): 631–632. Meekings *1235 Surrey Eyre* (Surrey Rec. Soc. 31) (1979): 218–220. VCH *Sussex* 6(1) (1980): 53–64; 6(2) (1986): 156–166. Meekings *Studies in 13th Cent. Justice & Administration* (1981): I 218, VII 141, VIII 1, IX lxx–IX lxxi, XV 168, XV 172. Kemp *Reading Abbey Cartularies* 2 (Camden 4th Ser. 33) (1987): 100–101, 101 (acknowledgement by Henry de la Mare to Reading Abbey dated c.1238–50). Stewart *1263 Surrey Eyre* (Surrey Rec. Soc. 40) (2006): 5–6. National Archives, C 49/66/5; C 143/1/5; E 40/536; E 210/141; JUST 1/870 (available at www.catalogue.nationalarchives.gov.uk/search.asp). Cassidy *1259 Pipe Roll*: 282 (available at http:// www.cmjk.com/1259/1259_pipe_roll.html).

Child of Joan de Neville, by Henry de la Mare, Knt.:

i. **MAUD DE LA MARE**, married **PETER DE MONTFORT**, Knt., of Beaudesert, Warwickshire [see MONTFORT 6].

❧ DE LA POLE ❧

JOHN DE SOMERY, married **HAWISE PAYNELL**.
RALPH DE SOMERY, of Dudley (in Sedgley), Staffordshire, married **MARGARET LE GRAS**.
ROGER DE SOMERY, Knt., of Dudley (in Sedgley), Staffordshire, married **NICHOLE D'AUBENEY** (desc. King William the Conqueror).
MARGARET DE SOMERY, married (1st) **RALPH BASSET**, of Drayton Basset, Staffordshire.
RALPH BASSET, 1st Lord Basset of Drayton, married **HAWISE** _____.
MARGARET BASSET, married **EDMUND DE STAFFORD**, 1st Lord Stafford.
RALPH DE STAFFORD, K.G., 1st Earl of Stafford, married **MARGARET DE AUDLEY** (desc. King William the Conqueor).
HUGH DE STAFFORD, K.G., 2nd Earl of Stafford, married **PHILIPPE DE BEAUCHAMP** (desc. King William the Conqueror) [see STAFFORD 8].

9. KATHERINE STAFFORD, married about 13 April 1383 **MICHAEL DE LA POLE**, Knt., 2nd Earl of Suffolk, 2nd Lord de la Pole, lord of the Honour of Eye, Guardian and Justice of the Peace for Suffolk, 1403, Privy Councillor, 1411, Justice of the Peace for Norfolk, 1414, son and heir of Michael de la Pole, 1st Earl of Suffolk, Lord de la Pole, Admiral of the Northern Fleet, Joint Governor to King Richard II, Lord Chancellor of England, Keeper of the Great Seal, by Katherine, daughter and heiress of John Wingfield, Knt. He was born in or before 1367 (presumably of age in 1388). They had five sons, Michael, Knt. [3rd Earl of Suffolk], William, K.G. [1st Duke of Suffolk, 1st Marquess of Suffolk, 4th Earl of Suffolk], Alexander, Knt., John, Knt., and Thomas (clerk), and five daughters, Isabel, Elizabeth, Joan, Philippe, and Katherine [Abbess of Barking]. He served as Captain of Men at Arms and Archers for Calais in 1386. In 1388 he and his wife, Katherine, were granted livery of the manors of Harpswell and Blyborough, Lincolnshire, and Grassthorpe, Nottinghamshire. In 1389 he and his wife, Katherine, petitioned the king and council, requesting the grant of the king to them of lands and tenements be executed giving them lands, tenements, rents or farms from Michael de la Pole, the father or from others, as it was agreed on the marriage of the petitioners that Pole would settle on the petitioners £100 of land. He accompanied Thomas of Woodstock, Duke of Gloucester to Prussia in 1391. In 1392 he and his wife, Katherine, were granted an annuity of £50 out of the fee-farm rent of Kingston-upon-Hull, Yorkshire. He was restored to his father's dignities by Parliament 28 Jan. 1397/8. The following year, however, Parliament annulled its previous proceedings and he fell again under his father's attainder. On 15 Nov. 1399, "in consideration of his services after the king's advent," he was again restored as Earl of Suffolk. He was made an honorary Brother of Christ Church Priory, Canterbury, Kent in 1405. He represented England at the Council of Pisa in April 1409. He was one of the peers to decide the guilt of Cambridge and Scrope in 1415. The same year he was appointed Joint Justiciar to enquire into treasons and felonies in Hampshire. SIR MICHAEL DE LA POLE, 2nd Earl of Suffolk, died of dysentery at the Siege of Harfleur 18 Sept. 1415. He left a will dated 1 July 1415, proved 5 Nov. 1415. His widow, Katherine, presented to the church of Cookley, Suffolk in 1418. Katherine, Countess of Suffolk, died 8 April 1419. They were buried at Wingfield, Suffolk.

    Hutchinson *Hist. & Antiqs. of the County Palatine of Durham* 3 (1794): 69–70. Blomefield *Essay towards a Top. Hist. of Norfolk* 2 (1805): 406–419. Nicolas *Testamenta Vetusta* 1 (1826): 189–190 (will of Michael de la Pole, Earl of Suffolk). Burke *Dict. of the Peerages… Extinct, Dormant & in Abeyance* (1831): 435–438. Suckling *Hist. & Antiqs. of Suffolk* 2 (1847): 206. Napier *Swyncombe & Ewelme* (1858): 313–318, chart facing 322. Candler & Candler *Candler's Suffolk & Essex Peds.* 1 (1868): 120–121 (De la Pole ped. dated c.1660). *Annual Rpt. of the Deputy Keeper* 45 (1885): 250–251. Doyle *Official Baronage of England* 3 (1886): 434–435 (sub Suffolk). Travis-Cook *Notes Rel. the Manor of Myton* (1890). Birch *Cat. Seals in the British Museum* 3 (1894): 399 (seal of Michael de la Pole, Earl of Suffolk dated 1408 — A shield of arms: quarterly, 1, 4, a fess between three leopards' heads [DE LA POLE]; 2, 3, on a bend three pairs of wings [WINGFIELD]. Above the shield a monogram or numeral *ii*, wth a label or sprig of foliage behind it. Probably to represent the owner's being the second of that name. Within a finely traced gothic panel, ornamented along the inner edge with a quatrefoil and slipped trefoils. Legend: * : Sigillū : michaelis : de : la : pole ….. [: s]uffolchie.). Kirby *Wykeham's Reg.* 1 (1896): 220. Wrottesley *Peds. from the Plea Rolls* (1905): 268. *North Country Wills* 1(Surtees Soc. 116) (1908): 8–9 (will of Michael de la Pole, Earl of Suffolk). Copinger *Manors of Suffolk* 4 (1909): 108–111. Clay *Extinct & Dormant Peerages* (1913): 51–52. *Yorkshire Inqs.* 5 (Yorkshire Arch. Soc. Recs. 59) (1918): 150–151. Wylie *Reign of Henry V* 2 (1919): 44–45. *Rpt. on the MSS of Lord de L'Isle & Dudley* 1 (Hist. MSS Comm. 77) (1925): 28. VCH *Buckingham* 4 (1927): 206–207. *C.P.* 9 (1936): 218–219 (sub Morley); 10 (1945): 566–567 (sub Pole); 12(1) (1953): 441–442 (sub Suffolk) ("… a knight of the most excellent and gracious reputation"); 14 (1998): 602. Chichele *Reg. of Henry Chichele* 2 (Canterbury & York Soc. 42) (1937): 49, 57–60, 671 (biog. of Michael de la Pole). Lamborn *Armorial Glass of the Oxford Diocese* (1949): 125–127 (De la Pole arms: Azure a fesse between three leopards' faces gold). Paget *Baronage of England* (1957) 176: 1. *Cal. Inqs. Misc.* 5 (1962): 40–42, 66, 134–136, 143–147, 199–200. McFarlane *Nobility of Later Medieval England* (1973): 244–245. Horrox *De La Poles of Hull* (East Yorkshire Local Hist. Soc. 38) (1983): 22–23 (chart). *TAG* 69 (1994): 129–139. *Cal. IPM* 20 (1995): 134–138. Ward *Women of the English Nobility & Gentry 1066–1500* (1995): 75–77, 120 (cites *Rotuli Parl.* 3: 245). Atherton *Norwich Cathedral: Church, City, & Diocese, 1096–1996* (1996): 458–460. National Archives, C 143/437/17 (Michael de la Pole, earl of Suffolk, cousin and heir of John de Wyngefeld, knight, deceased, to grant the manor of Benhall, etc. to the master and chaplains of a chantry in the church of Wingfield founded by Eleanor late the wife of the said John, retaining land in Wingfield, Eye, Lowestoft, and elsewhere. Date: 7 Henry IV.); SC 8/21/1026; SC 8/173/8637 (available at www.catalogue.nationalarchives.gov.uk/search.asp).

Children of Katherine Stafford, by Michael de la Pole, Knt.:

i. **MICHAEL DE LA POLE**, Knt., 3rd Earl of Suffolk, son and heir, born about 1392–4 (aged 21 or 23 in 1415). He married before 24 Nov. 1403 **ELIZABETH MOWBRAY**, daughter of Thomas Mowbray, K.G., 1st Duke of Norfolk, Earl of Nottingham, Earl Marshal, by Elizabeth, daughter of Richard de Arundel, K.G., Earl of Arundel and Surrey [see MOWBRAY 7 for her ancestry]. They had three daughters, Katherine [Abbess of Bruisyard], Elizabeth, and Isabel. He was made an honorary Brother of Christ Church Priory, Canterbury, Kent in 1409. He served in France in the campaign of 1415, being present with his father at the Siege of Harfleur in Sept. 1415. He served as commander of the Rear Guard of the King's Army in France Sept.–October 1415. SIR MICHAEL DE LA POLE, 3rd Earl of Suffolk, was slain at the Battle of Agincourt 25 October 1415. His widow, Elizabeth, took the veil at Bruisyard, Suffolk before 17 Jan. 1419/20. She was living 1 Dec. 1423. Blore *Hist. & Antiqs. of Rutland* 1(2) (1811): 114 (Mowbray ped.). Clutterbuck *Hist. & Antiqs. of Hertford* 2 (1821): 516–517 (Mowbray-Berkeley ped.). Candler & Candler *Candler's Suffolk & Essex Peds.* 1 (1868): 120–121 (De la Pole ped. dated c.1660). *Annual Rpt. of the Deputy Keeper* 45 (1885): 250–251. Doyle *Official Baronage of England* 3 (1886): 435 (sub Suffolk). Travis-Cook *Notes Rel. the Manor of Myton* (1890). *Rpt. on MSS in Various Colls.* 4 (Hist. MSS Com. 55) (1907): 195–197. Copinger *Manors of Suffolk* 4 (1909): 108–111. *C.C.R. 1419–1422* (1932): 247 ([Elizabeth Mowbray, widow of Michael de la Pole] styled "king's cousin it is said" in 1422; her daughter, Katherine de la Pole, styled "near akin to the king."). *C.P.* 12(1) (1953): 442–443 (sub Suffolk). *Cal. IPM* 20 (1995): 134–140. *Ricardian* 13 (2003): 12–26 (discusses evidence that Michael de la Pole had a 4th daughter, Jane "with the Blemysh").

ii. **WILLIAM [DE LA] POLE**, K.G., Duke, Marquess and Earl of Suffolk [see next].

iii. **ISABEL DE LA POLE**, married **THOMAS MORLEY**, Knt., 5th Lord Morley [see MORLEY 13].

iv. **ELIZABETH DE LA POLE**. She married (1st) before 18 June 1415 (as his 2nd wife) **EDWARD BURNELL**, Knt., of Billingford, Thurning, and East Ruston, Norfolk [see BURNELL 13], son and heir apparent of Hugh Burnell, K.G., 2nd Lord Burnell, of Holdgate, Shropshire, by his 1st wife, Elizabeth. They had no issue. He died of the flux at the Siege of Harfleur 23 Sept. 1415. His widow, Elizabeth, is named in a roll of the receiver of her late father, Michael de la Pole the elder, and her brother, Michael the younger, dated 1416–7, she then being assigned £13 6s. 8d. yearly for her maintenance. Elizabeth was a legatee in the 1419 will of Elizabeth Elmham. She married (2nd) on or about 30 June 1422 (date of property settlement) (as his 1st wife) **THOMAS KERDESTON**, Knt., of Claxton, Kerdeston, Bircham Newton (in Bircham), East Ruston, and Syderstone, Norfolk, Bulchamp, Henham, and Stratford, Suffolk, etc., son and heir of Leonard Kerdeston, Knt., of Claxton and Kerdeston, Norfolk, Bulchamp, Henham, and Stratford, Suffolk, etc., by his wife, Margaret, granddaughter of Hugh de Hastings, Knt. [see GANT 8.i.a for his ancestry]. They had one son, William, and one daughter, Margaret (or Marguerite). In 1422 he presented to the church of Reepham, Norfolk. In the period, 1424–6, he and his wife, Elizabeth, made a settlement of the manors of Kerdeston, Claxton, Heloughton, Bircham Newton (in Bircham), Ruston, and Syderstone, Norfolk. In 1427 he and his wife, presented to the church of Reepham, Norfolk. His wife, Elizabeth, died 3 April 1440. In 1442 he quitclaimed his right in the manors of Bulchamp and Henham, Suffolk to William de la Pole, Duke of Suffolk, and Alice his wife. Thomas married (2nd) before 5 May 1443 **PHILIPPE TRUSSELL**, widow of Alexander Bosom (or Bosun, Bozoun), Esq. (living 20 October 1440), of Flore, Northamptonshire, Olney, Buckinghamshire, etc., and daughter and heiress of John Trussell, Knt., of Flore and Gayton, Northamptonshire, Theddingworth, Leicestershire, etc., Knight of the Shire of Northamptonshire [see DESPENSER 12.ii], by his 2nd wife, Margaret (possibly Ardern). They had one daughter, Elizabeth (wife of Terry Robsart, Knt.). Sometime in the period, 1440–3, he and his wife, Philippe, sued John Mauntell, Esq., regarding a place called the Greyhound (Girhound) in Northampton, Northamptonshire. In 1443 he and his wife, Philippe, conveyed the manor of Bosoms (in Stagsden), together with 8 messuages, lands, and 5 marks of rent in Stagsden, Turvey, Bromham, Felmersham, and Radwell (in Felmersham), Bedfordshire to John Harpur and William Lowe. In 1445 he and his wife, Philippe, conveyed the manor of Gayton, Northamptonshire, together with the advowson of the churches of Gayton and Creaton, Northamptonshire to James Swetenham, Esq. for 300 marks of silver. In 1445–6 he and his wife, Philippe, made settlements of the manors of Kerdeston, Claxton, East Ruston, Heloughton, Bircham Newton, Swanton Novers, and Syderstone, Norfolk, and Bulchamp and Henham, Suffolk. SIR THOMAS KERDESTON died 20 July 1446, and was buried at Norwich, Norfolk. He left a will dated 1 July 1446. In the period, 1446–54, Thomas Bernere, kinsman of Thomas Kerdeston, Knt. sued Philippe, late the wife and executrix of the said Thomas Kerdeston, in Chancery regarding a gown and two horses promised by the deceased. In 1452 his widow, Philippe, presented to the church of Reepham, Norfolk. The same year she conveyed 10 messuages, lands, and 52s. of rent in Theddingworth and Carlton Curlieu, Leicestershire to John Harpur, of Rushall. Philippe died before Michaelmas term 1454 (date of lawsuit).

Blomefield *Essay towards a Top. Hist. of Norfolk* 4 (1775): 402–406; 8 (1808): 243, 245; 10 (1809): 111–115. Nicolas *Treatise on the Law of Adulterine Bastardy* (1836): 552–553. Banks *Baronies in Fee* 1 (1844): 269–271 (sub Kerdeston). Page *Supp. to Suffolk Traveller* (1844): 196–197. Suckling *Hist. & Antiqs. of the County of Suffolk* 2 (1847): 190–192, 349–350. Napier *Swyncombe & Ewelme* (1858): 316–318, charts facing 42, 322. Candler & Candler *Candler's Suffolk & Essex Peds.* 1 (1868): 120–121 (De la Pole ped. dated c.1660: "Phillip [de la Pole] wife to the Lord Burnell"). Rye *Short Cal. Feet of Fines for Norfolk* 2 (1886): 408, 423. *Desc. Cat. Ancient Deeds* 3 (1900): 455–456. Rye *Cal. Feet of Fines for Suffolk* (1900): 290, 302. Wrottesley *Staffordshire Suits: Plea Rolls* (Colls. Hist. Staffs. n.s. 4) (1901): 100–101. *List of Early Chancery Procs.* 1 (PRO Lists and Indexes 12) (1901): 87, 94. *Genealogist* n.s. 18 (1902): 187–188; n.s. 19 (1903): 108. Wrottesley *Peds. from the Plea Rolls* (1905): 413, 422–423. *Norfolk Antiq. Misc.* 2nd Ser. 1 (1906): 89. *Ancestor* 8 (1904): 167–185. Copinger *Manors of Suffolk* 2 (1908): 29–31 (Kerdeston arms: Gules, a saltier engrailed, Argent), 80–81. *C.P.* 2 (1912): 435 (sub Burnell); 5 (1926): 89–90 (sub Erdington); 7 (1929): 196–199 (sub Kerdeston). VCH *Bedford* 3 (1912): 96–100. Harvey et al. *Vis. of the North* 4 (Surtees Soc. 146) (1932): 157 (arms of Sir T[homas] Kerdeston: gules a saltire engrailed silver a label of three points checky gold and azure). *C.C.R.* 1435–1441 (1937): 428. *C.C.R.* 1441–1447 (1937): 55, 57–58, 119–120, 140, 270–271, 441, 443. VCH *Leicester* 5 (1964): 312–321. *Fam. Hist.* 2 (1969): 143–149 (1st correct identification of daughter Margaret in print). *Ancient Deeds — Ser. B* 3 (List & Index Soc. 113) (1975): B.12779. *TG* 3 (1982): 171–174; 6 (1985): 160–165. *Genealogists' Mag.* 22 (1988): 373–377. Ward *Women of the English Nobility & Gentry 1066–1500* (1995): 75–77 (Lady Elizabeth Burnell identified as daughter of Sir Michael de la Pole, late Earl of Suffolk, in contemporary record dated 1416–17). *Foundations* 1(3) (2004): 178–192. *Revue de Pau et du Béarn* 33 (2006): 32–34. Registered will of Elizabeth Elmham (née Hastings) dated 1 Dec. 1419, proved 18 Feb. 1419/20, 56–57 Hyrning, Cons. Court of Norwich [FHL Microfilm 94857]. Farnham *Leicestershire Medieval Village Notes, Theddingworth–Upton* [FHL 804160]. National Archives, C 1/9/16; C 1/11/87; C 1/11/139; C 1/11/263; C 1/16/248; C 1/29/67; E 210/1020; E 210/10861; E 212/38 (available at www.catalogue.nationalarchives.gov.uk/search.asp). National Archives, CP 25/1/6/80, #25; CP 25/1/126/77, #78; CP 25/1/179/95, #116 [see abstract of fines at http://www.medievalgenealogy.org.uk/index.html]. British Library, Kerdeston Hunting Book dated c.1440–6 (includes a miniature featuring portraits of Thomas Kerdeston and his 2nd wife, Philippe, and their respective coats of arms; Thomas' arms: Gules a saltire engrailed argent [KERDESTON]; Philippe's arms: Argent a cross fleury gules [TRUSSELL], quartering Argent on a bend azure three mullets pierced or [COKESEY]; see www.invaluable.com/

auction-lot/leaves-from-the-kerdeston-hunting-book,-in-englis-1-c-rc1cssqbmf). Online resource: www.tuddenham.org/History/Calendar_of_the_rolls.htm.

Child of Elizabeth de la Pole, by Thomas Kerdeston, Knt.:

a. **MARGARET KERDESTON**, daughter and co-heiress. She married before 12 May 1446 **JEAN DE FOIX**, K.G., Vicomte of Châtillon, Earl of Kendal [otherwise Count of Candale], Captal de Buch, Count of Bénauges, Vicomte of Meilles in Aragón, Castellan of Mauleon and Soule & Baili of La Bort, 1446, son and heir of Gaston de Foix, Captal de Buch, Vicomte of Bénauges and Longueville, by Marguerite, daughter of Arnaud-Amanieu d'Albret, Knt., Count of Dreux, Vicomte of Tartas, High Chamberlain of France. They had two sons, Gaston [Count of Candale and Bénauges, Captal de Buch, Seneschal of Guyenne] and Jean [Count of Gurson and Fleix, Vicomte of Meilles], and two daughters, Cathérine (wife of Charles d'Armagnac, Count of Armagnac, Vicomte of Fezensaguet) and Marguerite/Margherita (wife of Ludovico II, Marquis/Marchese of Saluzzo). He was created Earl of Kendal in England 12 May 1446. The same year he was granted the seigneuries of Castillon, Lamarque, Mouton, Saussac, Castelnau, Milhou, Budos, Listrac, and Montignac by King Henry VI of England. He presumably resigned his earldom in England in 1462, when he became a subject of the French king. JEAN DE FOIX, Count of Candale, left a will made at Saint-Laurent dated 5 Dec. 1485, in which he bequeathed his wife, Marguerite, a life estate in the baronies of Gurson and Fleix. Following his death sometime before 31 Dec. 1493, he was buried in the church of Castelnau by Médoc. Descendants include Queen Henriette Marie of France (otherwise known as Queen Mary), wife of Charles I, King of England. Plantin *Abbregé de l'Hist. Generale de Suisse* (1666): 509–510. Rymer *Fœdera* 11 (1727): 71 ([Gaston de Foix], Count of Longueville and Bénauges, Captal de Buch, and his son, Jean [de Foix], Vicomte of Châtillon, both styled "kinsman" by King Henry VI of England in 1444), 147–148 (instances of Jean de Foix, Earl of Kendale styled "kinsman" by King Henry VI of England in 1446). Anselme *Hist. de la Maison Royale de France* 3 (1728): 382–383 (sub Foix) (identifies Marguerite, wife of Jean de Foix, as daughter of Richard [de la Pole], Duke of Suffolk, and Marie dite de Sicile "suivant une preuve d'un chanoine de S. Jean de Lyon," confusing her with her younger cousin, Marguerite de la Pole, wife of Sibeud de Thivoley [see DE LA POLE 9.i.f.1 below]). La Chesnaye Des Bois *Dict. de la Noblesse* 6 (1773): 456–457 (sub Foix). Strachey *Rotuli Parl.* 5 (1777): 177–180 (Articles presented in Parliament against William de la Pole, Duke of Suffolk dated 1450: "[Article] 31. Item, the seid Duke, for the singuler enrichyng of his Neece, and hir husbond, sonne to the Capidawe, caused you to make the seid sonn Erle of Kendale, to yeve him hym grete possessions and enherituancez in Englond; and over that, to graunte him dyvers Castelles, Lordshippes and grete possessions, in youre Duchie of Guyan, to the yerely value of M li. and more...."). Muletti *Memorie Storico-diplomatiche appartenenti alla cittla ed ai Marchesi di Saluzzo* 5 (1831): 328. Beltz *Mems. of the Order of the Garter* (1841): clx. Ribadieu *Châteaux de la Gironde* (1856): 79. Napier *Swyncombe & Ewelme* (1858): 316–318 (Margaret styled "niece" of William, Duke of Suffolk, in 1450). Vallet de Viriville *Hist. de Charles VII* 3 (1865): 229 ("Jean de Foix, comte de Candale, marié à Marguerite, nièce de W., duc de Suffolk"). Burke *Dormant, Abeyant, Forfeited & Extinct Peerages* (1866): 603 (sub Foix, Earl of Kendal) (erroneously identifies wife Margaret as "dau. of Michael de la Pole, Earl of Suffolk."). *Third Rpt.* (Hist. MSS. Comm. 2) (1872): Appendix, 279–280 (Paper roll of charges against [William de la Pole], Duke of Suffolk temp. Henry VI [1450]: "... First, for asmoche as he [Duke William] gat to [Jean de Foix] the Erle of Kendale the honour, name, title, and astate [estate] of the erle, &c. ... and maried to him his nece. Therefore he hath by slypper [dishonest] eschaunge the lordship and castell of Glaxton [Claxton], Resham [Reepham], and other landes and tenements in Norfolk and Suffo[lk] wich were of the enheritaunce of his seid nece, to the yerely value, with fees and offices and services, cc li."). Legeay *Hist. de Louis XI* 1 (1874): 117 ("Jean de Foix, neveu par alliance de Suffolk"). Doyle *Official Baronage of England* 2 (1886): 268 (sub Kendal). *Notes & Queries* 8th Ser. 3 (1893): 101–102, 197, 272, 370–371 (identifies Margaret, wife of Jean de Foix, as the niece of William de la Pole, Duke of Suffolk, she being the daughter of one of his siblings). *Archives Hist. de Département de la Gironde* 30 (1895): 24 (biog. of Gaston de Foix). *Századok* 29 (1895): 689–695. Prudhomme *Inventaire-sommaire des Archives Départementales antérieures à 1790, Isère* 3 (1899): 345–348. Calmette *Louis XI, Jean II et la Révolution Catalane* (Bibliothèque Méridionale 2nd Ser. 8) (1903): 168–169. *English Hist. Rev.* 22 (1907): 93–95 (Jean de Foix styled "cousin" by King Henry VI of England in 1446). Dubois *Inv. des Titres de la Maison d'Albret* (Receuil des Travaux de la Soc. d'Agriculture, Sciences et Arts d'Agen 2nd Ser. 16) (1913): 19. Haggard *Louis XI & Charles the Bold* (1913): 57 ("At the same time the Earl of Suffolk, who had married his niece to a member of the House of Foix"). Kingsford *English Hist. Lit. in the 15th Cent.* (Burt Franklin Bibliog. & Ref. 37) (1913): 360 (Colls. of a Yorkist Partisan dated c.May 1452: "Article 5. The Duke of Suffolk hath marryed his nese, His Suster Dowghter to ye Capdawe [i.e., Captal de Buch] &c:"). *Rpt. on the MSS of Lord de L'Isle & Dudley* 3 (Hist. MSS Comm. 77) (1925): 309–310 (erroneously identifies Margaret, wife of Jean de Foix, as "Margaret Pole, daughter of the Duke of Suffolk."). *C.P.* 7 (1929): 108–110 (sub Kendal) (Jean de Foix styled "king's cousin" in 1446). Fryde *Handbook of British*

Chron. (1961): 433. Desgranges *Nobiliaire du Berry* 1 (1965): 62–63. Fam. Hist. 2 (1969): 143–149 (1st correct identification of parentage of Margaret Kerdeston, wife of Jean de Foix in print). Vale *English Gascony* (1970): 133–135, 142–144, 207, 221. *Intermédiaire des Chercheurs et Curieux* 22 (1972): 553. TG 3 (1982): 171–173; 6 (1985): 160–165. Schwennicke *Europäische Stammtafeln* 3(1) (1984): 149 (sub Foix). Boureau *Lord's First Night* (1998): 96 (erroneously identifies Marguerite, wife of Jean de Foix, as "Marguerite de la Pole, who brought him the county of Candale."). Collins *Order of the Garter, 1348–1461* (2000): 142. *Foundations* 1(3) (2004): 178–192. *Revue de Pau et du Béarn* 33 (2006): 32–34.

v. **KATHERINE DE LA POLE**, nun, Abbess of St.Mary the Virgin of Barking. She died shortly before 10 April 1473. Monro *Letters of Queen Margaret of Anjou & Bishop Beckington* (Camden Soc. 86) (1863): 103 (Katherine, Abbess of Barking, styled "cousin" by Margaret of Anjou, Queen of England). Candler & Candler *Candler's Suffolk & Essex Peds.* 1 (1868): 120–121 (De la Pole ped. dated c.1660: "Katherine [de la Pole] Abbess of Barking"). C.P.R. 1467–1477 (1900): 388. Erler *Women, Reading & Piety in Late Medieval England* (2006): 17. National Archives, E 210/5183 (Alice late the wife of William de la Pole, Duke of Suffolk to Thomas Tyrell, knight, and others: Grant indented, of an annuity of £10 for the life of Katharine de la Poole, the duke's sister, Abbess of Barking, charged on the manor of Langham. Essex. Date: 29 Henry VI [1450–1]); C 1/33/135 (Chancery Proc. dated 1386–1473 — Catherine de la Pole, Abbess of St. Mary the Virgin of Barking, and Eleanor and Alice Chamberleyn, nuns there, daughters of Ralph Chamberleyn. v. Sir John Doreward, Knt., and William Doreward, feoffees to uses.: £20 issuing out of manors of Lawshall (Losehall) and Naughton (Naunton), alias Baxsters, in Naunton.) (available at www.catalogue.nationalarchives.gov.uk/search.asp).

10. WILLIAM [DE LA] POLE, K.G., 4th Earl of Suffolk, Admiral of Normandy, Captain of Avranches, Coutances, Pontorson, and St. Lô, Governor of the marches of Normandy, Guardian of the Cotentin, Governor of Chartres, Lieutenant-General of Caen, Lieutenant of Caen and the Cotentin, Privy Councillor, Lord Steward of the Household, Steward and Constable of the Honour and Castle of Wallingford Castle, High Steward of the Duchy of Lancaster north of Trent, Chief Justice of South Wales, Lord Great Chamberlain of England, Constable of Dover Castle and Warden of the Cinque Ports, Admiral of England, Governor and Protector of the Staple of Calais, younger son, born at Cotton, Suffolk 16 October 1396 (aged 20 in 1417, 22 in 1419, 26 in 1423, 30 and more in 1430). He was with his father at the Siege of Harfleur in Sept. 1415. He was heir male in October 1415 to his brother, Michael de la Pole, Knt., 3rd Earl of Suffolk. He served in the French wars continuously for 17 years from July 1417, taking part in the Sieges of Cherbourg and Rouen, 1418–9, the Siege of Melun, 1420, the Battle of Verneuil, 1424, and the Siege of Montargis, 1427. He was granted the lordships of Hambye and Briquebec in Normandy in March 1418, which lands consolidated his authority as a military commander and landowner in western Normandy. He was Cupbearer at the Coronation of Queen Katherine in 1421. He was active with Thomas Montagu, Earl of Salisbury, in extending English authority in Champagne in 1423. In 1424 he besieged Ivry and took part in the Battle of Verneuil. In reward for his services, he was created Count of Dreux in Normandy 27 July 1424. In 1425 he besieged the Mont-Saint-Michel by sea, and led a raid into Brittany in 1425–26. In 1429 he was tightening his grip around the walls of Orléans, when he was totally outmaneuvered in a few, simple breathtaking moves by Joan of Arc. He retreated to Jargeau, a little way up the Loire, where he was forced to surrender 12 June 1429. He and his brother, John, were taken prisoner. He was released in March 1429/30 in exchange for a ransom of £20,000, the payment of which compelled him to sell his lordship of Bricquebec by special permission to Bertram Entwistle, a Lancashire esquire. By an unknown mistress (allegedly Malyne de Cay, a nun he seduced the night before he surrendered at Jargeau), he had an illegitimate daughter, Joan (or Jane).[14] He took Aumale in July 1430, after which the captaincies which he held

---

[14] In 1450 it was directly stated in a charge made in Parliament against William de la Pole, Duke of Suffolk, that he had fathered an illegitimate daughter who was then the wife of "Stonard of Oxonfordshire": "Copy of a Paper Roll, temp. Henry 6, containing Charges against the Duke of Suffolk," which says that, "… The nighte before he was yolden [prisoner at Jargeau, 12 June 1429] he laye in bede with a Nonne whom he toke oute of holy profession and defouled,

were placed in the hands of lieutenants. He married by license dated 11 Nov. 1430 **ALICE CHAUCER**, widow successively of John Philip (or Phelip), Knt., of Castle Donnington and Hatford, Berkshire, King's knight (died at Harfleur 2 October 1415) [see HARCOURT 12.ii], and Thomas Montagu, 4th Earl of Salisbury (died 3 Nov. 1428) [see MONTAGU 10], and daughter and heiress of Thomas Chaucer, Esq., of Ewelme, Hook Norton, and Kidlington, Oxfordshire, Hatfield Peverel, Essex, etc., Chief Butler to Kings Richard II and Henry IV, Speaker of the House of Commons, Constable of Taunton and Wallingford Castles, by Maud, daughter and co-heiress of John de Burghersh, Knt. [see GANT 10.ii for her ancestry]. She was born about 1404–5 (aged 11 in 1415, aged 30 in 1434 and 1435, aged 32 in 1437). They had one son, John, K.G. [2nd Duke of Suffolk, 2nd Marquess of Suffolk, 5th Earl of Suffolk]. By an uncertain wife or mistress, he had one daughter, Anne. He was heir male in 1430 to his 1st cousin, Thomas de la Pole, by which he inherited the manor of Grafton Regis, Northamptonshire. About 1430 he extended the chancel and its chapels at Wingfield church in Suffolk. In 1431 his wife, Alice, settled the manor of Hatford, Berkshire on her parents, Thomas Chaucer, Esq., and his wife, Maud, for the term of their lives. He attended the congress of Arras in 1435. In 1437 he and his wife, Alice, were granted a license to establish an almshouse at Ewelme, Oxfordshire. The same year Bishop Thomas Hatfield granted him free warren in his demesne lands of the Isle, Bradbury, Chilton, Preston upon Skerne Foxden, Fishburn, and Bolam, Durham. In 1440 he and his wife, Alice, obtained a grant in tail of the manors of Nedding and Kettlebaston, Suffolk, which had formerly been granted to Alice and her 1st husband, Sir John Philip, shortly before the latter's death in 1415. He presented to the churches of Grafton, Northamptonshire, 1438, Frostenden, Suffolk, 1446, Bugbrooke, Northamptonshire, 1447, and Huntingfield, Suffolk, 1447. He was Chief Ambassador to France in 1444. In 1444 he was created Marquess of Suffolk. In 1445 he was granted two annual fairs to be held at the town of Lowestoft, Suffolk. Under Suffolk's influence negotiations for peace with France continued through 1446, with little tangible result. The government, nonetheless, passed wholesale into Suffolk's hands. The king was completely alienated from his uncle, Humphrey, Duke of Gloucester, who made Suffolk the object of repeated open attacks. To Suffolk and the queen, the complete

---

whos name was Malyne de Cay, by whom he gate a daughter, nowe married to Stonard of Oxonfordshire." [see *Third Report* (Hist. MSS. Comm. 2) (1872): Appendix, 279–280]. The statement made in 1450 is supported by a later Stonor family pedigree in the 1574 visitation of Oxfordshire, which indicates that Thomas Stoner, Esq., of this generation, married Joan, the "natural daughter" of "Delapole, Duke of Suffolk" [see Harvey et al. *Vis. of Oxford 1566, 1574, 1634 & 1574* (H.S.P. 5) (1871): 143–144]. Joan Stonor's existence is well attested in the contemporary records, including letters of denization granted to her in 1453, she being "born in Normandy" [see *C.P.R. 1452–1461* (1910): 70]. Further evidence of Joan Stonor's parentage is afforded by Joan Stonor's son, William Stonor, being styled "cousin" by Sir Edmund Rede, which Sir Edmund was a descendant of the de la Pole family) [see Kingsford *Stonor Letters & Papers 1290–1483* 2 (Camden Soc. 3rd Ser. 30) (1919): 80–81]. Elsewhere the 16th Century antiquarian Leland claimed that Duke William de la Pole secretly married Jacob (or Jacque) of Bavaria, Countess of Hainault [see LANCASTER 9.v], by whom he had a unnamed daughter, afterwards the wife of a certain man named Barentine (grandfather of Sir William Barentine then living), which daughter was later proved to be a bastard by Duke William's wife, Alice Chaucer [see Smith *Itinerary of John Leland* 2 (1964): 19; 5 (1964): 233]. No evidence was advanced by Leland to support this claim. In 1924 Eric St. John Brooks suggested that this child was possibly Beatrix, 2nd wife of Drew Barantyne, of Chalgrove, Oxfordshire [see *Notes & Queries* 146 (1924): 299], but like Leland, he gave no evidence that Duke William de la Pole was ever married to Jacob (or Jacque) of Bavaria, or that they had a child together. Brooks seems not to have realized that Sir William Barentine's grandfather mentioned by Leland who married Duke William's illegitimate daughter was not his paternal grandfather at all, but rather his maternal grandfather, Thomas Stonor, Esquire. Even so, the usually careful historian, Wedgwood, accepted that Beatrix, wife of Drew Barantyne, as the Duke's daughter without any qualification [see Wedgwood *Hist. of Parliament* 1 (1936): 40 (biog. of Drewe Barentyne)]. Stranger still, in 1952 Robert Julian Stonor collapsed the various accounts of the illegitimate daughters of William de la Pole into one [see Robert Julian Stonor *Stonor: A Catholic Sanctuary in thwe Chilterns from the 5th Century till To-day* (1952): 124–131].

overthrow of Humphrey's power seemed of paramount importance. When Duke Humphrey arrived to attend Parliament held 10 Feb. 1446/7 at Bury St. Edmunds, he was not allowed to see the king, but instead was conducted to St. Saviour's Hospital outside the town and arrested; he died two weeks later at Bury St. Edmunds, Suffolk 23 Feb. 1446/7. William and his wife, Alice, were made Earl and Countess of Pembroke in 1447. In 1448 the manors of Eaton, Fyfield, Garford, and Philiberts (in East Hanney), Berkshire were settled on him and his wife, Alice, for life. The same year he was further created Duke of Suffolk. On the loss of Normandy and cessation of Maine, he became extremely unpopular. SIR WILLIAM [DE LA] POLE, Duke, Marquess and Earl of Suffolk, was committed to the Tower and impeached in 1450. He was charged with mismanagement, waste of the public treasure, the loss of divers provinces in France, with many other high crimes and misdemeanors. On the intervention of Queen Margaret, he was ordered banished by the king for five years 17 March 1449/50. Embarking at Ipswich for France, his vessel was boarded by the captain of a ship of war belonging to the Duke of Exeter, then Constable of the Tower of London. Being brought into Dover Road, he was murdered in open boat 2 May 1450. His head was struck off on the gunwhale of a boat, and his body thrown into the sea. He was buried under a purfled arch in the Collegiate Church at Wingfield, Suffolk. He left a will dated 17 Jan. 1448/9, proved 3 June 1450. In June 1451 two men, Thomas Smyth, late of Calais, yeoman, alias late of Dover, shipman, and Richard Lenard, late of Bosham, Sussex were indicted for the duke's murder. In 1455, his widow, Alice, Duchess of Suffolk, was Constable of Wallingford Castle. Alice was a legatee in the 1458 will of John Hampden, Esq., of Great Hampden, Buckinghamshire, who bequeathed her one standing gilt silver cup. She presented to the churches of Cookley, Suffolk, 1461, 1467, Huntingfield, Suffolk, 1462, and Bugbrooke, Northamptonshire, 1470. In 1475, "being broken with age," she was granted a papal indult to choose a priest secular or religious as her confessor. Alice, Duchess of Suffolk, died 20 May (or 9 June) 1475, and was buried in a magnificent tomb at Ewelme, Oxfordshire.

Rymer *Fœdera* 10 (1727): 91–92, 153 (instances of William de la Pole styled "kinsman" by King Henry V of England); 11 (1727): 53, 60, 63, 74, 80 (instances of William de la Pole styled "kinsman" by King Henry VI of England), 122–123 (William de la Pole styled "kinsman" by Charles VII, King of France). Bridges *Hist. & Antiqs. of Northamptonshire* 1 (1791): 301, 487. Hutchinson *Hist. & Antiqs. of the County Palatine of Durham* 3 (1794): 69–70. Blomefield *Essay towards a Top. Hist. of Norfolk* 1 (1805): 360–368; 2 (1805): 406–419; 8 (1808): 241–244; 9 (1808): 336–340; 10 (1809): 111–115. Nicolas *Testamenta Vetusta* 1 (1826): 256–257 (will of William de la Pole, Marquess of Suffolk). Vautier *Extrait du Registre des Dons, Confiscations, Maintenues, et autres Actes* (1828): 36, 102. Burke *Dict. of the Peerages… Extinct, Dormant & in Abeyance* (1831): 435–438. Nicolas *Controversy between Scrope & Grosvenor* 2 (1832): 404–412 (biog. of Geoffrey Chaucer). Bentley *Excerpta Historica* (1833): 3–4 ([Wiliam de la Pole], Earl of Suffolk, styled "cousin" by King Henry VI of England). Nicolas *Procs. & Ordinances of the Privy Council of England* 6 (1837): 245–246. Fenn & Ramsay *Paston Letters* 1 (1840): 17–18 (transcript of letter of William de la Pole, Duke of Suffolk, to his son, John, dated 1450). Beltz *Mems. of the Order of the Garter* (1841): clviii, clxiv. *Coll. Top. et Gen.* 8 (1843): 73–75 (sub Kerdeston). Suckling *Hist. & Antiqs. of the County of Suffolk* 2 (1847): 190–192, 207, 324, 349–350, 420. Gurney *Supp. to the Rec. of the House of Gournay* (1858): 932–935 (Alice Whalesborough, wife of John Fitz Ralph, styled "cosyn vnto myn lady of Suff[olk]" [that is, Alice Chaucer]"); see also Richmond *Paston Fam. in the 15th Cent.* (1990): 235–236. Napier *Swyncombe & Ewelme* (1858): 30–38, 46–89, charts 21, 67, 68, facing 42, 322. Stevenson *Letters & Papers Ill. of the Wars of the English in France* 1 (Rolls Ser. 22) (1861): 79–82 ([William] Marquess and Earl of Suffolk, styled "cousin" by Richard, Duke of York), 474–475, 496–499 (instances of [William] Marquess and Earl of Suffolk styled "cousin" by King Henry VI of England). Candler & Candler *Candler's Suffolk & Essex Peds.* 1 (1868): 120–121 (De la Pole ped. dated c.1660). French *Shakspeareana Genealogica* 1 (1869): 157–159. *Third Rpt.* (Hist. MSS Comm. 2) (1872): Appendix, 279–280: ("Copy of a Paper Roll, temp. Henry 6, containing Charges against the Duke of Suffolk," which says that, "… The nighte before he was yolden [prisoner at Jargeau, 12 June 1429] he laye in bede with a Nonne whom he toke oute of holy profession and defouled, whos name was Malyne de Cay, by whom he gate a daughter, nowe married to Stonard of Oxonfordshire."). Riley *Chronica Monasterii S. Albani* 1: *Registrum Abbatiæ Johannis Whethamstede* (Rolls Ser. 28) (1872): 266–268. Marshall *Early Hist. of Woodstock Manor & its Environs* (1873): 107–121. Turner *Cal. Charters & Rolls: Bodleian Lib.* (1878): 521. Luce *Chronique du Mont-Saint-Michel (1343–1468)* 2 (1883): 44–45 ([William de la Pole], Earl of Suffolk, styled "cousin" by John [of Lancaster], Duke of Bedford in 1434), 180–181 ([William de la Pole], Earl and Marquis of Suffolk, styled "cousin" by Richard, Duke of York, in 1445). Money *First & 2nd Battles of Newbury & the*

Siege of Donnington Castle (1884): 263–265. Benolte *Vis. of Somerset 1531, 1573 & 1591* (1885): 52 (Montacute ped.: "Thomas [Montacute], E. of Sarum, [1] = Elinor, d. Thos. [Edm.] Holland E. of Kent, =2. Alice, d. Thos. Chaucer, ob. 1475."), 68 (Raleigh ped.: "Alice [Chaucer], only child, b. 1404. = Wm. de la Pole D. of Suffolk, ob. 1450, æt. 54."). *Annual Rpt. of the Deputy Keeper* 45 (1885): 251–252. Doyle *Official Baronage of England* 3 (1886): 13–14 (sub Pembroke), 436–438 (sub Suffolk). Rye *Short Cal. Feet of Fines for Norfolk* 2 (1886): 423. Birch *Cat. Seals in the British Museum* 1 (1887): 137–138; 2 (1892): 158 (seal of William de la Pole — Obverse. The Earl, armed cap-à-pie, with hauberk, surcoat with open sleeves, helmet, [sword], and shield of arms slung over the right shoulder, riding on the right on a caparisoned horse with plume on head. The armorial bearings of the shield and caparisons are as described below for the reverse. Background replenished with sprigs of foliage and flowers. Reverse. On an ornamental tree of conventional foliage, and with a central flower, a shield of arms: quarterly, 1, 4, a fess between three leopards' heads [DE LA POLE], 2, 3, a chief, and over all a lion rampant queue fourchée [CHAUCER]. Supporters, two wild boars collared), 168; 3 (1894): 397 (seal of Alice, widow of William de la Pole, Duke of Suffolk dated 1459 — A shield of arms: per pale., dex., a fess between three lions' faces [DE LA POLE]; sin., a lion rampant, queue fourchée [CHAUCER]. Within an engrailed panel. Cabled border), 400 (seal of William de la Pole, Earl of Suffolk, Count of Dreux dated 1430 — A shield of arms, couché : quarterly, 1, 4, a fess between three lions' faces or leopards' heads [DE LA POLE]; 2, 3, on a bend three pairs of wings conjoined in lure [WINGFIELD]. Crest on a helmet, and wreath, an old man's head bearded, wearing a tufted cap. Supporters, two heraldic antelopes; field replenished with sprigs of foliage and flowers. Legend: S' willermi · de · la · pole · comit' · suffolchie · et · de · dreux : *. Cabled border.). Travis-Cook *Notes Rel. the Manor of Myton* (1890). Owen *Desc. of Penbrokshire* (Cymmrodorion Rec. Ser. 1) (1892): 26–27. Morris *Poetical Works of Geoffrey Chaucer* 1 (1893): 114. Skeat *Complete Works of Geoffrey Chaucer* (1894): xlviii–xlix. *C.P.R. 1461–1467* (1897): 446 (Alice styled "king's kinswoman"). Williams *Parl. Hist. of Worcester* (1897): 25 (biog. of Sir John Phelipp). *Gentleman's Mag. Library: English Topog., Part XI* (1899): 222–223. *C.P.R. 1467–1477* (1900): 417 (Alice, Duchess of Suffolk, and her son, John, Duke of Suffolk, styled "king's kinsfolk"). Rye *Cal. Feet of Fines for Suffolk* (1900): 302. *Genealogist* n.s. 18 (1902): 187–188. Searle *Christ Church, Canterbury* (Cambridge Antiq. Soc., Octavo Pubs. 34) (1902): 49 (Chronicle of John Stone: "Item hoc anno [1450] in vigilia apostolorum Philippi et Iacobi [30 Apr.], viz. vj[a] feria, captus erat in mare dominus Willelmus Pole dux de Suffolk. Et die sequente [1 May] in aurora decapitatus erat in mare, et iactauerunt corpus eius cum capite super litus maris ante villam Douorie. Et die sequente [2 May] maior ville Douorie et alii acceperunt corpus eius et portauerunt ad ecclesiam sancti Martini, et ibidem habuit exequias et tres misses cum nota, et terciam missam celebrauit prior Douorie in ecclesia pariochiali. Item xj[o] kal' Junii [22 May], videlicet feria vj[a] ante Pentecosten, delatum erat corpus predicti domini ad ecclesiam Cant', et ibidem habuit exequias cum tribus lectionibus; deinde delatum erat corpus eius ad ecclesiam Rofens' deinde."). Copinger *Manors of Suffolk* 1 (1905): 391–392 ("It is said that he espoused the Countess of Hainault, and by her had a daughter, but that afterwards marrying Alice daughter and heir of Thomas Chancer, granddaughter of Geoffrey Chaucer the poet, that daughter was proved a bastard"); 2 (1908): 29–31, 80–82; 3 (1909): 327; 4 (1909): 108–111. Wrottesley *Peds. from the Plea Rolls* (1905): 386. *List of Inqs. ad Quod Damnum* 2 (PRO Lists and Indexes 22) (1906): 745, 747–749. *C.P.R. 1436–1441* (1907): 41, 61 (instances of William de la Pole styled "king's kinsman"). *Rpt. on MSS in Various Colls.* 4 (Hist. MSS Comm. 55) (1907): 27 (ref. to correspondence of [Alice Chaucer], Duchess of Suffolk). Le Cacheux *Actes de la Chancellerie d'Henri VI concernant la Normandie sous la Domination Anglaise* 2 (1908): 127–129 ([William de la Pole], Earl of Suffolk and Dreux styled "amé et feal cousin" by King Henry VI of England in 1428). *North Country Wills* 1 (Surtees Soc. 116) (1908): 50–51 (will of William de la Pole, Duke, Marquess, and Earl of Suffolk). *C.P.R. 1441–1446* (1908): 49 (William de la Pole styled "king's kinsman"). Philipot et al. *Vis. of Buckingham 1634 & 1566* (H.S.P. 58) (1909): 68–69 (Hampden ped.: "…There was a Knight in Cornwall called Sir John Rayle which had 2 sons and a daugh. … when Sir John Rayle was dead his wife mar. a Knight whose name was Sir John Boroughwash (Burrowash) and by him had 2 daughters, the one mar. to M[r]. Chawser and by him had one daughter [Alice] that was married to Sir John Phillip(s) and after to y[e] Earle of Salesbury, and after to y[e] Duke of Suffolke"). *C.P.R. 1413–1416* (1910): 281. VCH *Bedford* 3 (1912): 399–417. VCH *Surrey* 4 (1912): 229–234. *Cal. MSS in Various Colls.* 7 (Hist. MSS Comm. 55) (1914): 38. *Yorkshire Inqs.* 5 (Yorkshire Arch. Soc. Recs. 59) (1918): 150–151. Kingsford *The Stonor Letters & Papers 1290–1483* 1 (Camden 3rd Ser. 29) (1919): 154 (letter of Alice [Chaucer], Duchess of Suffolk dated ?1475). Lyle *Original Identity of the York & Towneley Cycles* (1919). Wood & Rawlinson *Parochial Colls.* 2 (Oxfordshire Rec. Soc. 4) (1922): 133–135, 138–139. VCH *Berkshire* 4 (1924): 91–92, 287–288, 461. Kingsford *Prejudice & Promise in 15th Cent. England* (1925). VCH *Buckingham* 3 (1925): 88–92; 4 (1927): 206–207. *C.Ch.R.* 6 (1927): 1, 2 (William de la Pole styled "king's kinsman"), 59. Stillington & Fox *Regs. of Robert Stillington & Richard Fox* (Somerset Rec. Soc. 52) (1937): 16, 31. *C.P.* 10 (1945): 397 (sub Pembroke); 11 (1949): 393–395 (sub Salisbury); 12(1) (1953): 443–448 (sub Suffolk). Lamborn *Armorial Glass of the Oxford Diocese* (1949): 65–70, 86, 125–127. Somerville *Hist. of the Duchy of Lancaster* 1 (1953): 420, 428. *Coat of Arms* 3 (1955): 241–242. *Papal Regs.: Letters* 13(2) (1955): 550. VCH *Oxford* 5 (1957): 240. *Bull. John Rylands Lib.* 47 (1964–65): 489–502. Du Boulay *Docs. Ill. of Medieval Kentish Soc.* (Kent Recs. 18) (1964): 248. Smith *Itinerary of John Leland* 2 (1964): 19 ("William Pole Duke of Southfolk maried the Countes of Henaude secretely; and gotte a doughtter by her that was maried to Syr William Barentine's graundfather now being but Chaucher doughter and heir was after solemnly maried to William Duke of Southfolk by whom he had very fair landes, and she provid Barentines wife doughter to the Countes of Henault to be but a bastarde. Barentine for making a riot on Duke William's wife lost a 100 *li*. by the yere."); 5 (1964): 233 ("Barentine's graundfather now lyvynge maried the Countes of Henaults dowghtar, begotten on hir by Gullim Duke of Suffolke that first maried hir, and aftar *facto divortio* to Chaucer's heire"). Harriss & Harriss "John Benet's Chron. for the Years 1400 to 1462," in *Camden Misc.* 24 (Camden Soc. 4th Ser. 9) (1972): 162, 168–169, 172, 179, 182, 190, 194–198 (death of William de la Pole), 202. VCH *Cambridge* 5 (1973): 4–16. *Ancient Deeds — Ser. B* 2 (List & Index Soc. 101) (1974): B.5981, B.6901. MacCulloch *Chorography of Suffolk* (Suffolk Rec. Soc. 19) (1976): 48. Rosenthal *Nobles & Noble Life* (1976): 109–110, 115–116. *Speculum* 54 (1979): 528–542. Griffiths *Reign of Henry VI* (1981). McFarlane *England in the 15th Cent.* (1981): 79–113. Allmand & Armstrong *English Suits before the Parlement of Paris* (Camden Soc. 4th Ser. 26) (1982): 306–307 (biog. of [William de la Pole], Earl of Suffolk). Horrox *De La Poles of Hull* (East Yorkshire Local Hist. Soc. 38) (1983): 22–23 (chart). Scarfe *Suffolk in the Middle Ages* (1986): 156–162. *Jour. Hist. Sociology* 1 (1988): 233–252. VCH *Oxford* 12 (1990): 8, 41, 189, 351. Hicks *Who's Who in Late Medieval England* (1991): 272–274 (biog. of William de la Pole: "… A poet, reputedly 'the embodiment of chivalry', and genuinely pious, his life was spent in service to the crown… He held no ministerial office after 1446, yet dominated through his personal influence on the king. Decisions were made outside council, which became thinly attended and was purged of critics and rivals. Patronage was confined to Suffolk's adherents, who were placed about the king and on key positions in the localities… the king became dangerously identified with a narrow clique that proved to be incompetent… Suffolk and his adherents also enjoyed profits of extortion, coercion and manipulation of justice."). Roskell *House of Commons 1386–1421* 2 (1992): 524–532 (biog. of Thomas Chaucer); 3 (1992): 16 (biog. of Sir William Elmham); 4 (1992): 68–69 (biog. of Sir John Phelip). *Cal. IPM* 20 (1995): 111–113, 138–140, 268–269; 23 (2004): 136–152, 206–209, 269–272. Catto "Chron. of John Somer," in *Camden Misc. 34* (Camden Soc. 5th Ser. 10) (1997): 277 (birth date of William de la Pole). Pernoud & Clin *Joan of Arc: Her Story* (1999): 203–205 (biog. of William de la Pole). Castor *King, the Crown & the Duchy of Lancaster* (2000): 71–72, 75–76, 84–125. VCH *Essex* 10 (2001): 165–169. VCH *Northampton* 5 (2002): 142–176. *Foundations* 1(3) (2004): 178–192. Wright *Music & Ceremony at Notre Dame of Paris, 500–1550* (2008): 207. National Archives, CP 25/1/179/94, #99 [see abstract of fine at http://www.medievalgenealogy.org.uk/index.html]. National Archives, E 41/204 (William de la Pole, earl of Suffolk, holder of the lands late of Michael de la Pole formerly earl of Suffolk, father of William, and of Michael de la Pole son of the said earl Michael: Quittance to the king of certain sums of money, parcel of a surplus owed to Pole, on account of a certain expedition to France in the service of Henry V; in consideration of Pole's quittance at the Exchequer in respect of certain jewels (described) granted by Henry V to the said Michael earl of Suffolk and Michael his son in return for their service and provision of men in France, and of a certain other sum owed by William Pole in respect of an embassy undertaken by him to Arras. Date: 28 March 1436, enrolled on the K.R. Memoranda Roll, Easter 14 Hen VI, r.l) (available at www.catalogue.nationalarchives.gov.uk/search.asp).

Child of William [de la] Pole, K.G., by Alice Chaucer:

i. **JOHN [DE LA] POLE**, K.G., 2nd Duke of Suffolk, 2nd Marquess of Suffolk, 5th Earl of Suffolk, Constable of Wallingford Castle, High Steward of Oxford University, son and heir, born 27 Sept. 1442. He married (1st) 28 Jan./7 Feb. 1450 (by dispensation dated 18 August 1450, they being related in the 4th and 4th degrees of kindred) **MARGARET BEAUFORT** [see TUDOR 13], daughter and heiress of John Beaufort, K.G., Duke of Somerset, Earl of Kendal, by Margaret, daughter of John Beauchamp, Knt. [see TUDOR 12 for her ancestry]. She was born 31 May 1443, allegedly at Bletsoe, Bedfordshire. The king allowed a divorce between the couple shortly before 6 March 1452/3. He married (2nd) before 1 Feb. 1458 **ELIZABETH PLANTAGENET**, 2nd daughter of Richard Plantagenet, K.G., 3rd Duke of York, 6th Earl of March, 9th Earl of Ulster, lord of Mortimer, Herefordshire and Clare, Suffolk, by Cecily, daughter of Ralph Neville, K.G., 1st Earl of Westmorland, 4th Lord Neville of Raby [see YORK 12 for her ancestry]. She was born at Rouen, Normandy 22 April 1444, and baptized there 22 Sept. 1444. They had six sons, John, K.B. [Earl of Lincoln], Edmund, K.G., K.B. [3rd Duke of Suffolk (degraded to Earl of Suffolk), 3rd Marquess of Suffolk], Edward [Archdeacon of the East Riding, Archdeacon of Richmond, Precentor of Salisbury], Humphrey, Doctor of Canon Law [Prebendary of Wenlocksbarn], William, Knt., and Richard, and four daughters, Elizabeth, Anne (nun), Katherine (wife of William Stourton, K.B., 5th Lord Stourton), and Dorothy. He fought as a Yorkist at the Battles of St. Albans (2nd), Ferrybridge, and presumably Towton, all in 1461. He served as Lord High Steward for the Coronation of his brother-in-law, King Edward IV, in 1461. His wife, Elizabeth, was admitted to the Fraternity of St. Nicholas in London in 1461. He presented to the churches of Cookley, Suffolk, 1464, 1474, and 1479, Huntingfield, Suffolk, 1487, and Frostenden, Suffolk, 1488. He bore St. Edward's sceptre at the Coronation of Queen Elizabeth Wydeville in 1465. In 1465 the attainder of 1387/8 was reversed, whereby the Barony of de la Pole was revived and he probably (then or later) became Lord de la Pole. He took part in King Edward IV's expedition to France in 1475. In the Parliament of 1477, he gave the manors of Eastworldham and Westworldham, Suffolk to the king, in exchange for the manors of Deddington and Ascot, Oxfordshire. He was appointed Lieutenant of Ireland in 1478, but he never assumed the office. In Dec. 1479 and June 1480 he and his wife, Elizabeth, received mortmain licenses for gifts to St. George's Chapel, Westminster. He presented to the church of Reepham, Norfolk in 1481 and 1490. He was present at the

Coronation of King Richard III in 1483, where he bore the sceptre with the dove. Following the Battle of Bosworth in 1485, he quickly submitted to King Henry VII, receiving as reward the constableship of Wallingford Castle. In 1489 he was sued in the Court of the Star Chamber by William Parker, Knt., 9th Lord Morley regarding the possession of the manors of Hingham and Buxton, Norfolk. He bore the Queen's sceptre at the Coronation of his wife's niece, Queen Elizabeth Plantagenet, in 1487. SIR JOHN [DE LA] POLE, 2nd Duke of Suffolk, 2nd Marquess of Suffolk, died shortly before 24 July 1492. His widow, Elizabeth, Duchess of Suffolk, died between 7 Jan. 1502/3 and 3 May 1504. They were buried at Wingfield, Suffolk. Sandford *Gen. Hist. of the Kings of England* (1677): 378–380. Rymer *Fœdera* 11 (1727): 401 (John [de la Pole], Duke of Suffolk, styled "kinsman" by King Henry VI of England). Strachey *Rotuli Parl.* 6 (1777): 477–478. Blomefield *Essay towards a Top. Hist. of Norfolk* 2 (1805): 406–419; 5 (1806): 358–372; 8 (1808): 243, 245; 9 (1808): 336–340. Dugdale *Monasticon Anglicanum* 6(3) (1830): 1361–1362. Dallaway *Hist. of the Western Div. of Sussex* 2(1) (1832): 150–151. *Coll. Top. et Gen.* 1 (1834): 297 (York ped.: "Elizabeth Duchess of Suffolk."). Beltz *Mems. of the Order of the Garter* (1841): clviii, clxiv, clxix, ccxxiv. Suckling *Hist. & Antiqs. of the County of Suffolk* 2 (1847): 190–192, 207, 324, 420. Napier *Swyncombe & Ewelme* (1858): 108–197, chart facing 322. Collier *Trevelyan Papers* 2 (Camden Soc. 84) (1863): 53–54 (charter of John [de la Pole], Duke of Suffolk dated 1488 as "kinsman and heir of Thomas Chaucers [Chaucer], Esq."). Candler & Candler *Candler's Suffolk & Essex Peds.* 1 (1868): 120–121 (De la Pole ped. dated c.1660). Beaurepaire *Fondations Pieuses du Duc de Bedford à Rouen* (Bibliothèque de l'École des Chartes 34) (1873): 6, footnote 4. Burke *Dormant, Abeyant, Forfeited & Extinct Peerages* (1883): 440–442 (sub Pole). Doyle *Official Baronage of England* 3 (1886): 438–439. Travis-Cook *Notes Rel. the Manor of Myton* (1890). Birch *Cat. Seals in the British Museum* 3 (1894): 398 (seal of John de la Pole, Duke of Suffolk dated 1488 — A lion rampant, queue fourchée). *Archæologia* 56 (1899): 323–336. *C.P.R.* 1467–1477 (1900): 261, 312 (instances of Elizabeth, wife of John, Duke of Suffolk, styled "king's sister"), 417 (John, Duke of Suffolk, and his mother, Alice, Duchess of Suffolk, styled "king's kinsfolk"). Leadam *Select Cases Before the King's Council in the Star Chamber* (Selden Soc. 16) (1903): 15–18. Copinger *Manors of Suffolk* 1 (1905): 391–392; 3 (1909): 327; 4 (1909): 108–111. Wrottesley *Peds. from the Plea Rolls* (1905): 388. *Genealogist* n.s. 23 (1907): 25–26, 88, 90–91. Lane *Royal Daughters of England* 1 (1910): 300. Clay *Extinct & Dormant Peerages* (1913): 169–171 (sub Plantagenet). *Papal Regs.: Letters* 10 (1915): 472–473 [John de la Pole and his 1st wife, Margaret Beaufort, were related in the 4th degree of kindred (i.e., 3rd cousins) through their respective great-grandmothers, Katherine de Roet (wife of John of Gaunt) and Philippe de Roet (wife of Geoffrey Chaucer), who were sisters]; 13(1) (1955): 272 (son Edward called "nephew" by Richard III, King of England); 13(2) (1955): 714 (son Edward called "nephew of Edward IV, King of England"). *C.P.* 4 (1916): 19, footnote f; 7 (1929): 688–690 (sub Lincoln); 9 (1936): 220 (sub Morley); 10 (1945): 567 (sub Pole); 12(1) (1953): 304 (sub Stourton), 448–454 (sub Suffolk), Appendix I: 21–25 (list of sons, includes possible son Geoffrey). Wall *Handbook of the Maude Roll* (1919) unpaginated (ped. dated c.1461–85: "Elizabeth ducissa Suthfolcie"). VCH *Berkshire* 4 (1924): 91–92, 461. Venn & Venn *Alumni Cantabrigiensis to 1751* 3 (1924): 378 ("Some doubt exists as to the identity" of son, Geoffrey … Possibly a mistake for Humphrey, as also the *Grace* 1494, to admit to congregations 'William de la Pole, son of the Duke of Suffolk,' as neither of these names occurs in the pedigrees"). Harvey et al. *Vis. of the North* 3 (Surtees Soc. 144) (1930): 2–5 ("Elizabeth nupta Iohanni duci Suffolcij"). Lamborn *Armorial Glass of the Oxford Diocese* (1949): 134–135. VCH *Oxford* 5 (1957): 240; 12 (1990): 40–44. Harriss & Harriss "John Benet's Chron. for the Years 1400 to 1462," in *Camden Misc.* 24 (Camden Soc. 4th Ser. 9) (1972): 209, 224–225. MacCulloch *Chorography of Suffolk* (Suffolk Rec. Soc. 19) (1976): 48, 72–73. *Speculum* 54 (1979): 528–542. Griffiths *Reign of Henry VI* (1981): 679, 707, 841. *Ricardian* 7 (1985–87): 18–25; 13 (2003): 341–358. Scarfe *Suffolk in the Middle Ages* (1986): 156–162. Bates & Curry *England & Normandy in the Middle Ages* (1994): 307. Ward *Women of the English Nobility & Gentry 1066–1500* (1995): 58. Leese *Blood Royal* (1996): 159–163. Michalove & Reeves *Estrangement, Enterprise & Education in 15th-Cent. England* (1998): 113–116. VCH *Essex* 10 (2001): 165–169. Wagner *Encyclopedia of the Wars of the Roses* (2001): 210–211 (biog. of John de la Pole). James *Bede Roll of the Fraternity of St. Nicholas* 1 (London Rec. Soc. Pubs. 39) (2004): 56–59.

Children of John [de la] Pole, K.G., by Elizabeth Plantagenet:

a. **JOHN [DE LA] POLE**, K.B., son and heir apparent, born about 1462. He was created Earl of Lincoln 13 March 1466/7. He was ceremonially knighted, K.B., 14 May 1475, in company with the king's sons. He married **MARGARET ARUNDEL**, daughter of Thomas Arundel, K.G., K.B., 17th Earl of Arundel, by Margaret, daughter of Richard Wydeville, K.G., 1st Earl Rivers, Constable of England, Lord High Treasurer [see ARUNDEL 13 for her ancestry]. They had no issue. He attended the funeral of King Edward IV 16/17 April 1483. He was bearer of the Orb at the Coronation of King Richard III 6 July 1483. Although never publicly declared heir to the throne by his uncle, King Richard III, the king signaled his acceptance of Lincoln as his heir in 1484 by granting him lands worth over £300 and a pension of £176 per year drawn from the duchy of Cornwall, which grant was usually made to the heir to the throne. He was appointed President of the Council of the North in July 1484. He was appointed Chief Governor of Ireland, as the King's Lieutenant

21 August 1484. He is said to have fought for King Richard III at the Battle of Bosworth 22 August 1485, but, like his father, he quickly submitted to King Henry VII. He was in King Henry VII's service up to the middle of 1486, when he fled to Flanders. He took an active part there in promoting the cause of the imposter Lambert Simnel. He proclaimed Simnel in Dublin, 24 May 1487, and, crossing to England, landed at Furness 4 June. JOHN [DE LA] POLE, Earl of Lincoln, was slain at the Battle of Stoke 16 June 1487. His lands were subsequently declared forfeit from 9 March 1486/7. In the period, 1493–9, his widow, Margaret, Countess of Lincoln, sued the prior of Bromholme regarding a rent of £20 payable out of the manor of Bacton, Norfolk given by John de la Pole, Duke of Suffolk, on complainant's marriage with the Earl of Lincoln. In the same period, she sued Richard Drylond regarding the detention of deeds relating to lands and tenements called 'Wyghtes' in West Cheam and Cuddington, Surrey. Margaret, Countess of Lincoln, presented to the church of Drayton, Norfolk in 1501, 1503, and 1531, and to the church of Felthorpe, Norfolk in 1525. Her date of death is unknown. Strachey *Rotuli Parl.* 6 (1777): 474–478. Hasted *Hist. & Top. Survey of Kent* 1 (1797): 340–371. Blomefield *Essay towards a Top. Hist. of Norfolk* 1 (1805): 360–368; 8 (1808): 241–244; 10 (1809): 412, 415. Hutchins *Hist. & Antiqs. of Dorset* 3 (1868): 322–323 (Arundel ped.). Doyle *Official Baronage of England* 2 (1886): 379 (sub Lincoln). Birch *Cat. Seals in the British Museum* 3 (1894): 398 (seal of John de la Pole, Earl of Lincoln dated 1484–1485 — A shield of arms, couché: quarterly, 1, 4, DE LA POLE; 2, 3, a lion rampant, queue fourchée, CHAUCER, in chief over all a label of three points. Crest on a helmet, ornamental foliated mantling and wreath, an old man's head, couped at the neck, wreathed with a chaplet of quatrefoiled flowers about the head. Supporters, two heraldic antelopes, spotted with roundles, collared, chained and ringed. Legend on a scroll: : S' : ioh'is : comit' : lincoln : nepot' : rici : t'cij : reg' : angl' : etc' : locutenet : tre : sue : hib'nie. Outer border carved and ornamented with small quatrefoils.). *Trans. Royal Hist. Soc.* n.s. 18 (1904): 157–194. VCH *Surrey* 4 (1912): 229–234. *C.P.* 7 (1929): 689–690 (sub Lincoln); 12(1) (1953): Appendix I, 21–25. *Norfolk Arch.* 36 (1977): 305–326. Leese *Blood Royal* (1996): 159–163. Michalove & Reeves *Estrangement, Enterprise & Education in 15th-Cent. England* (1998): 113–116. Wagner *Encyclopedia of the Wars of the Roses* (2001): 211–212 (biog. of John de la Pole). National Archives, C 1/212/18; C 1/212/19 (available at www.catalogue.nationalarchives.gov.uk/search.asp).

b. **EDMUND DE LA POLE**, K.G., K.B., 3rd Duke of Suffolk, Keeper of Wolmer Forest, Constable of Eye Castle, 2nd son but eldest surviving son and heir. On 26 Feb. 1492/3 he was allowed to have certain lands of his brother, as if there had been no attainder. He presented to the church of Reepham, Norfolk in 1493. He married before 10 October 1496 **MARGARET SCROPE**, daughter and co-heiress of Richard Scrope, Esq., of Bentley, Arksey, Hamthwayte, and Wighton under the Wold, Yorkshire, by Eleanor, daughter of Norman Washbourne, Esq. [see TIBETOT 14 for her ancestry]. They had one daughter, Elizabeth (nun in the Convent of the Minoresses without Aldgate). He was a captain in the king's army in France in 1492. He presented to the church of Reepham, Norfolk in 1493. In 1494 he took a leading part in the tournament at the creation of prince Henry as duke of York, and gained one of the prizes for the second day's achievements. After his father's death, as the family estate had been considerably reduced by his brother's attainder, in 1495 he agreed to surrender the title of duke and accept that of earl. He was a captain in the king's army at the Battle of Blackheath in 1497. His family fell under suspicion of conspiracy and treason in 1499, which caused Edmund and his brother, Richard, to flee abroad to the Emperor Maximilian. They were allowed to travel about the Low Countries. Edmund was officially attainted in England Jan. 1504. In 1506 the Archduke Philip and his wife, Joanna, were shipwrecked on the coast of Dorset and forced to attend King Henry VII at Windsor. On 4 April 1506 Philip signed an authorization to adjust the treaty of 1496 and agreed to the surrender of Edmund de la Pole to King Henry VII. SIR EDMUND DE LA POLE, late Earl of Suffolk, was executed 4 May 1513. His widow, Margaret, Countess of Suffolk, died Feb. 1514/5. She left an undated will, proved 15 May 1515 (P.C.C. 6 Holder). Strachey *Rotuli Parl.* 6 (1777): 474–477. Blomefield *Essay towards a Top. Hist. of Norfolk* 1 (1805): 360–368; 2 (1805): 406–419; 8 (1808): 243, 245; 9 (1808): 336–340; 10 (1809): 111–115. *Coll. Top. et Gen.* 1 (1834): 408. Ellis *Original Letters Ill. of English Hist.* 3rd Ser. 1 (1846): 117–142 (letters of Edmund [de la] Pole, Earl of Suffolk). Suckling *Hist. & Antiqs. of Suffolk* 2 (1847): 349–350, 420. Gairdner *Letters & Papers Ill. of the Reigns of Richard III & Henry VII* 1 (Rolls Ser. 24) (1861): xxxv–lvii (Edmund de la Pole: "He is described as a man of violent temper, rash, and headstrong. His letters certainly give us the impression of a rude and careless writer."), 143–149 (instances of [Edmund de la Pole], Earl of Suffolk, styled "cousin" by Maximilian, King of the Romans and Hungary, in letters dated 1501–1503). Brewer *Letters & Papers, Foreign & Domestic, Henry VIII* 1 (1862): 65. Flower *Vis. of Yorkshire 1563–4* (H.S.P. 16) (1881): 278–281 (Scrope ped.: "Margaret [Scrope] wyff to Edmond Delapole Duke of Suffolk."). Doyle *Official Baronage of England* 3 (1886): 440–441. *Trans. Royal Hist. Soc.* n.s. 18 (1904): 157–194. *List of Early Chancery Procs.* 3 (PRO Lists and Indexes 20) (1906): 439. Copinger *Manors of Suffolk* 3 (1909): 327. VCH *Berkshire* 4 (1924): 287–288. *C.P.* 7 (1929): 690, footnote b (sub Lincoln); 12(1) (1953): 451–453 (sub Suffolk), Appendix I, 21–25. VCH *Oxford* 5 (1957): 240; 12 (1990): 40–44. VCH *Cambridge* 5 (1973): 4–16. MacCulloch *Chorography of Suffolk*

(Suffolk Rec. Soc. 19) (1976): 48, 72–73. *Renaissance Studies* 2(2) (1988): 240–250. Leese *Blood Royal* (1996): 159–163. Michalove & Reeves *Estrangement, Enterprise & Education in 15th-Cent. England* (1998): 113–116. *Trans. Monumental Brass Soc.* 17 (2003): 2–13. Sutton *Mercery of London* (2005): 331–333. National Archives, C 43/2/43; C 43/2/45 (available at www.catalogue.nationalarchives.gov.uk/search.asp).

c. **EDWARD POLE**, clerk, Canon of Salisbury, 3rd son, born c.1468 (aged 12 in 1480). He was instituted as Prebendary of Netheravon in the diocese of Salisbury 21 Nov. 1478. He was collated as Prebendary of Hurstborne and Burbage in the diocese of Salisbury 27 Feb. 1479, which position he resigned by Jan. 1485. He was collated as Precentor of Salisbury 17 April 1480, which position he resigned by 20 March 1485. He was admitted Archdeacon of the East Riding 15 October 1480. In October 1480 the Univ. of Oxford requested that King Edward IV send his nephew, "Lord Edward Pole," to study at Oxford. In March 1482 the University wrote to the king praising his nephew's gifts of intellect and heart. Edward was collated Archdeacon of Richmond 2 Jan. 1484/5, and admitted 6 Jan. 1484/5. EDWARD POLE died shortly before 28 Sept. 1485. Venn *Biog. Hist. of Gonville & Caius College* 3 (1901): 279. *English Hist. Rev.* 36 (1921): 419. *C.P.* 12(1) (1953): Appendix I, 21–25. *Papal Regs.: Letters* 13(1) (1955): 272 ("Edward Poole" called "nephew" by Richard III, King of England in 1484); 13(2) (1955): 714 ("Edward Poole" called "nephew of Edward IV, King of England" in 1480). Horn *Fasti Ecclesiæ Anglicanæ 1300–1541* 3 (1962): 15–16, 64; 12 (1967): 54–57. Jones *Fasti Ecclesiae Anglicanae 1300–1541* 6 (1963): 22–23, 25–27. Myers *English Hist. Docs. 1327–1485* (1969): 698–699. Carpenter *Kingsford's Stonor Letters & Papers 1290–1483* (1996): 393–394. Leese *Blood Royal* (1996): 159–163. Michalove & Reeves *Estrangement, Enterprise & Education in 15th-Cent. England* (1998): 113–116.

d. **HUMPHREY [DE LA] POLE**, clerk, 4th son. He was Rector of Barrowby, Lincolnshire in 1490. He was a pensioner at Gonville Hall, Cambridge University, 1490–1505. He was ordained an acolyte by the Bishop of Ely at Downham 25 Sept. 1491. He was appointed Prebendary of Wenlocksbarn in St. Paul's, London 25 Jan. 1493/4, which position he resigned by 2 July 1509. He obtained the following degrees: Bach. Civil Law, 1496–7, Bach. Canon Law, 1500–1, Doctorate Canon Law, 1501. He was Rector of Leverington, Cambridgeshire 8 Nov. 1500, and Rector of Hingham, Norfolk to 1513. HUMPHREY POLE died shortly before 15 Feb. 1513. He was allegedly buried at Babraham, Cambridgeshire. Blomefield *Essay towards a Top. Hist. of Norfolk* 2 (1805): 424. Venn *Biog. Hist. of Gonville & Caius College* 1 (1897): 14, 15; 3 (1901): 279, 282. Hennesey *Novum Repertorium Ecclesiasticum Parochiale Londinense* (1898): 53. Caius *Annals of Gonville & Caius College* (1904): 13, 29. *C.P.* 12(1) (1953): Appendix I, 21–25. Horn *Fasti Ecclesiae Anglicanae 1300–1541* 5 (1963): 68; 12 (1967): 62–65. Zutshi *Medieval Cambridge: Essays on the Pre-Reformation Univ.* (1993): 56. Leese *Blood Royal* (1996): 159–163. Michalove & Reeves *Estrangement, Enterprise & Education in 15th-Cent. England* (1998): 113–116.

e. **WILLIAM [DE LA] POLE**, Knt., of Wingfield, Suffolk, 5th son, born about 1478 (aged about 18 in 1496–7). He was educated at Cambridge about 1494. He married before 26 April 1497 (date of presentment) **KATHERINE STOURTON**, widow successively of William Berkeley, Knt. (died 1485), of Beverstone, Gloucestershire, Bisterne (in Ringwood), Exbury, and Minstead, Hampshire, etc. [see FISHER 9.i.a], and Henry (or Harry) Grey, Knt., 7th Lord Grey of Codnor (died 8 April 1496) [see CODNOR 14.i.a], and daughter of William Stourton, 2nd Lord Stourton, by Margaret, 1st daughter and co-heiress of John Chidiock, Knt. [see CHIDIOCK 13]. They had no issue. Sometime in or after 1496 Werburgh Brereton, daughter of Katherine, sister of William Berkeley, Knt., sued William Pole, Knt., son of John, Duke of Suffolk, and Katherine, lady Grey, his wife in Chancery regarding the detention of deeds relating to the castles and manors of Beverstone, Hatherley, Leckhampton, and Syde, Gloucestershire, etc. He was knighted at the Battle of Blackheath 17 June 1497. He attended the king at his meeting of Archduke Philip of Austria at Calais in 1500. He was appointed to meet Katherine of Aragón at St. George's Fields in Nov. 1501. He was present at the ceremony of betrothal of Princess Margaret Tudor to King James IV of Scotland 25 Jan. 1501/2. A few weeks later, in 1502, he was arrested and sent to the Tower for alleged complicity in the projected rebellion of his brother, Edmund [de la] Pole, Earl of Suffolk. In 1503 William Stourton presented to the church of Great Kington, Dorset by grant of Katherine Grey, lady of the manor. William [de la] Pole was attainted in Parliament with his two brothers in Jan. 1503/4. He was still a prisoner in the Tower of London after the execution of his older brother, Edmund, Earl of Suffolk, in 1513. A bill was introduced in the House of Lords 10 Dec. 1515 for Katherine, wife of "William de la Poole." His wife, Katherine, Lady Grey died in London 25 Nov. 1521. William was listed first among the prisoners in the Tower in 1535 and again in 1538. SIR WILLIAM [DE LA] POLE was apparently living in October 1539, it is said in the Tower, but died before 20 Nov. 1539, when his name no longer appears in the list of the prisoners there. *Jour. of the House of Lords* 1 (1802): 52. Nichols *Hist. & Antiqs. of Leicester* 3(2) (1804): 863 (Grey ped.). Glover *Hist. of Derby* 2 (1829): 308–312 (Grey ped.). Burke *Gen. Hist. of the Dormant, Abeyant, Forfeited & Extinct Peerages* (1866): 247–249 (sub Grey). Hutchins *Hist. & Antiqs. of Dorset* 4 (1870): 72. Wild *Hist. of Castle Bytham* (1871): 46–68. Weaver

Somerset Incumbents (1889): 368. *Desc. Cat. Ancient Deeds* 1 (1890): 59–70. Bridgeman *Hist. of Weston-under-Lizard* (Colls. Hist. Staffs. n.s. 2) (1899): 159–167. *C.P.* 6 (1936): 130–132 (sub Grey); 12(1) (1953): 302–303 (sub Stourton), Appendix I, 21–25. Leese *Blood Royal* (1996): 159–163. Michalove & Reeves *Estrangement, Enterprise & Education in 15th-Cent. England* (1998): 113–116. Emery *Greater Medieval Houses of England & Wales 1300–1500* 3 (2006): 646. National Archives, C 1/84/73 (available at www.catalogue.nationalarchives.gov.uk/search.asp).

f. **RICHARD [DE LA] POLE** (nicknamed the *White Rose*), titular Duke of Suffolk and Earl of Lincoln, of Wingfield, Suffolk, 6th son. He attended the king at his meeting of Archduke Philip of Austria at Calais in 1500. Supporting the (alleged) projected rebellion of his older brother, Edmund, Earl of Suffolk, he fled fled abroad with him in August 1501, never to return to England. At Calais they encountered James Tyrrell, Knt. (husband of their kinswoman, Anne Arundell [see MORLEY 15]); Tyrrell was subsequently arrested in 1502 and executed as their accomplice. From Calais they went to court of their aunt, Margaret, Duchess of Burgundy. By the treaty of Augsberg in 1502, Emperor Maximilian agreed to give them no more support. However, he allowed them to settled in the city of Aix-la-Chapelle. He was attainted in Parliament with his two brothers in Jan. 1503/4. In 1506 Erard de la March, Bishop of Liège, intervened to enable Richard to leave Aix-la-Chapelle. He went to the court of Ladislaus VI, King of Hungary, who gave him a pension. In 1510 Richard had returned to Imperial territory, he being at Freiburg in that year. In or before 1510, in the lifetime of his brother, Edmund, he styled himself Duke of Suffolk. As such he claimed the crown of England, and was supported in this by France from 1512. Sometime between 1510/12, he entered the service of King Louis XII of France, who granted him a pension of 6,000 crowns. He commanded a band of German mercenaries in an unsuccessful invasion of Navarre in October-Nov. 1512. In 1512, as "Richard, Duke of Suffolk," he issued letters to his cousin, Marguerite/Margherita de Foix, Marquise of Saluzzo, promising to grant her the earldom of Kendale in England, if he could restablish himself in the kingdom "qu'il dit lui appartient." In 1513 he commanded 6,000 troops against the English at the Siege of Thérouanne. In 1514 he was in command of 12,000 men in Normandy in preparation for an invasion of England. England and France concluded peace, however, which agreement was sealed by the marriage of King Louis XII to Mary Tudor, sister of King Henry VIII of England. Louis gave Richard letters to the civic authorities of Metz, requesting they give him a good reception. On 2 Sept. 1514 Richard entered the city of Metz with an escort of 60 cavalry and a guard of honour provided by the Duke of Lorraine. In 1516 he visited King François I of France at Lyons, and at Christmas secretly came to the king at Paris. In 1517 he went to Venice and Milan. In 1519 he was sent by King François as his emissary to King Louis of Bohemia. Until Feb. 1519 he had the use of a house in Metz called Passe-Temps, after which date he rented a mansion there from the Cathedral Chapter. He lived in great magnificence on the pensions he received from France and Hungary, and introduced horse-racing to Metz. After seducing the wife of a local goldsmith, Sebille, wife of Nicholas Robert, which caused a public scandal, he went to Toul where he resided between 1519 and 1522. When war resumed between France and England in 1522, he joined King François I in Paris. In 1523 he and the Duke of Albany went to Brittany, where they prepared a joint invasion of England and Scotland. On 21 Sept. 1523 they parted company at sea. Richard went to Switzerland to recruit mercenaries for King François I. They joined up again at the Siege of Marseilles in 1524. In 1525 he accompanied King François I on his Italian campaign. RICHARD [DE LA] POLE, titular Duke of Suffolk, was slain at the Battle of Pavia 24 Feb. 1524/5, and was buried in the Augustinian Priory at Pavia. Following his death, a "messe anniversaire" was founded by the metropolitan chapter of Metz Cathedral for the repose of his soul. By a mistress or wife, allegedly Marie of Sicily, he had one daughter, Marguerite. Ellis *Original Letters Ill. of English Hist.* 3rd Ser. 1 (1846): 117–142 (letters of Richard [de la] Pole), 202–212. *L'Union des Arts* (Soc. de l'Union des Arts) (1851): 366–383. *Méms. de la Soc. d'Arch. Lorraine* 3rd Ser. 6 (1859): 239–268 (biog. of Richard de la Pole). Gairdner *Letters & Papers Ill. of the Reigns of Richard III & Henry VII* 1 (Rolls Ser. 24) (1861): xxxv–lvii, 309 (Richard de la Pole styled "your kinsman" [vestrum consanguineum] in his letter to Erard de la Marck, Bishop of Liège dated 1507). Candler & Candler *Candler's Suffolk & Essex Peds.* 1 (1868): 120–121 (De la Pole ped. dated c.1660: "Richard [de la Pole] slaine in Italy"). *Notes & Queries* 8th Ser. 3 (1893): 101–102, 197, 272, 370–371. Prudhomme *Inventaire-sommaire des Archives Départementales antérieures à 1790, Isère* 3 (1899): 348 (Marguerite/Margherita de Foix, Marquise of Saluzzo styled "cousine" by Richard [de la Pole], Duke of Suffolk in letters dated 1512). *C.P.* 12(1) (1953): Appendix I, 21–25. Giono *Battle of Pavia* (1965). *Norfolk Arch.* 36 (1977): 305–326 (author confuses Richard [de la] Pole with another individual, Richard Pole). *Ricardian* 7 (1985–87): 18–25 (Richard de la Pole: "… his outstanding quality seems to have been his gallantry as a soldier."). Demarolle *Chron. de Philippe de Vigneules et la Mém. de Metz* (1993): 90–91. Leese *Blood Royal* (1996): 159–163. Michalove & Reeves *Estrangement, Enterprise & Education in 15th-Cent. England* (1998): 113–116. Baker *Rpts. of Cases by John Caryll* 2 (Selden Soc. 116) (2000): 693–695 (lawsuit refers to Richard de la Pole as "a traitor to the said lord king … being in parts beyond the seas, in subversion of this realm of England.").

Soc. of Antiquaries of London: MSS in the Soc. of Antiquaries of London, SAL/MS/654 (receipt signed by Richard de la Pole, styling himself Duke of Suffolk dated 1516).

Child of Richard de la Pole, allegedly by Marie of Sicily:

1) **MARGUERITE DE LA POLE** (otherwise **SUFFOLK**), lady of honour of the Queen of Navarre. She married at Fontainebleau by contract dated 21 May 1539 (signed in the presence of the Queen and her kinsman, Gabriel, Marquis of Saluzzo[15]) **SIBEUD** (or **CYBAUD**) **DE THIVOLEY** (or **TIVOLEY**), seigneur of Brenieu in Vivarais and La Motte-Galaure in Dauphiné, Esquire ordinaire of Queen Éléonore of Austria, judge of la terre d'Ay. They had three sons, Jean (seigneur of Brénieu in Vivarais), Pierre (priest) [canon of Saint-Denis], and Claude (priest) [canon of Evry], and five daughters, Catherine (wife of Gilbert de Colomb), Eléonore (wife of Jean de Secondat de Montesquieu, seigneur of Roques), Marguerite (wife of Claude d'Orgeoise, seigneur of Montferrier), Louise (wife of Jean de Montchenu), and Sébastienne (wife of André Berenger du Gua). Sibeud de Thivoley was living in 1547, and died before 1568. His widow, Marguerite, left a will dated 1599. Anselme *Hist. de la Maison Royale de France* 3 (1728): 383 (sub Foix) (refers to a certain Marguerite, daughter of Richard [de la Pole], Duke of Suffolk and Marie dite de Sicile "suivant une preuve d'un chanoine de S. Jean de Lyon," but confuses her with her cousin, Margaret/Marguerite Kerdeston, wife of Jean de Foix [see DE LA POLE 8.iv.a above]). Rivoire de La Bâtie *L'Armorial de Dauphiné* (1867): 106–107. *Notes & Queries* 8th Ser. 3 (1893): 101–102, 197, 272, 370–371. *Procs. of the Huguenot Soc. of London* 16 (1937–41): 53 (erroneously identifies Margaret de la Pole, wife of Cybaud de Brénieu, as a descendant of George, Duke of Clarence). *Le Pays Lorrain* 73 (1992): 84–85. Loriol Chandieu *Anc. List Francois-Louis de Buade* (1999): Ref.: 78. Marriage contract dated 21 May 1539 of Sibeud de Tivoley, seigneur of Brénieu, and Marguerite de la Pole Suffolk, daughter of Richard de la Pole, document discovered at Fonds Montravel: Bibliothèque municipal de Lyon by Pierre Henri Chaix, citation kindly supplied by Peter de Loriol. Online resources: http://jeromereynaud.free.fr/download/Mise_au_point_Genealogies_COLOMB_COPPIER_ROCHETTE.pdf.

g. **ELIZABETH [DE LA] POLE**, married at Wingfield, Suffolk **HENRY LOVEL**, Knt., 8th Lord Morley and *de jure* Lord Marshal, son and heir of William Lovel, Knt., 7th Lord Morley, by Eleanor, daughter and heiress of Robert Morley, 6th Lord Morley. He was born about 1466 (aged 10 in 1476). They had no issue. He was made a knight 18 Jan. 1477/8, at the marriage of Richard, Duke of York. In 1481 John de la Pole, Duke of Suffolk, presented to the church of Foulsham, Norfolk, by reason of the minority of Henry Lovel, Lord Morley. He took part in the funeral of King Edward IV in 1483, and attended the Coronation of King Richard III 6 July 1483. On 5 Feb. 1488/9 livery of his estates was granted to him. He was not summoned to Parliament. SIR HENRY LOVEL, 8th Lord Morley, was slain at Dixmude in Flanders 13 June 1489, and was buried at Calais. Dower was assigned to his widow, Elizabeth, 31 Dec. 1489. At her death at aged 51, she was buried in the church at Hallingbury, Essex. Blomefield *Essay towards a Top. Hist. of Norfolk* 8 (1808): 208. Brydges *Collins' Peerage of England* 7 (1812): 319–395 (sub Perceval, Lord Lovel and Holland). *C.P.* 9 (1936): 219–220 (sub Morley).

Child of William [de la] Pole, K.G., by uncertain wife or mistress:

i. **ANNE [DE LA] POLE**, married **GAILLARD DE DURFORT**, K.G., seigneur of Duras (Lot-et-Garonne, arrond. de Marmande), Blanquefort, and Villandraut, Governor of Calais, Chamberlain of Charles, Duke of Burgundy, son and heir of Gaillard de Durfort, seigneur of Duras and Blanquefort, Provost of Bayonne, Seneschal of Landes, by Indie, daughter of Jean de Lalande, seigneur of La Brède. They had three sons, Amaury (or Aimery), Jean [seigneur of Duras, Blanquefort, and Villandraut], and Georges [seigneur of Tilh, Tirou, Bussac, and Bussaguet], and one daughter, Marguerite (wife of Jean de Saint-Gelais, seigneur of Montlieu). He negotiated the surrender of Bordeaux in 1451 to the French. In 1452 he renounced his homage to King Charles VII of France and joined in the pro-English revolt in the province of Aquitaine. After the defeat of the English at Castillon in 1453, his French lands were forfeited and he fled to England. He was nominated Knight of the Garter sometime before 22 April 1463. He was granted the lordship of Lesparre in Aquitaine by King Edward IV of England in 1473. He was pardoned by King Louis XI of France in 1476, afterwhich he recovered his French lands. He was degraded from the honour of the Garter before 4 Nov. 1476. GAILLARD DE DURFORT left a will dated 4 Feb. 1480, requesting burial in the Friars Minors of Bordeaux. Anselme *Hist. de la Maison Royale de France* 5 (1730):

---

[15] Gabriel, Marquis of Saluces, was a third cousin to Marguerite de la Pole, wife of Sibeud de Brénieu. His mother, Marguerite de Foix, wife of Louis II, Marquis of Saluces, was a granddaughter of Elizabeth de la Pole, wife of Thomas Kerdeston, Knt. [see DE LA POLE 8.iv above].

734 (Anne, wife of Gaillard de Durfort, identified as "Anne de Sufolc fille du duc de Sufolc en Angleterre"). Beltz *Mems. of the Order of the Garter* (1841): clxiii, clxv (footnote 3). *Archives Hist. de Département de la Gironde* 7 (1865): 444–446; 16 (1878): 258–259. Vallet de Viriville *Hist. de Charles VII* 3 (1865): 229. *Revue de l'Agenais* 8 (1881): 509–510 (Anne, wife of Gaillard de Durfort, identified as "Anne de La Pole Suffolck .... fille de N. .... de La Pole, duc de Suffolck, et d'Elizabeth d'Angleterrre dite d'Yorck."). *L'intermédiaire des chercheurs et curieux* 19 (1886): 215–216. Durand *La Maison de Durfort à l'Époque Moderne* (1975): 28–30 (Anne, wife of Gaillard de Durfort, identified as "fille du duc de Suffolk"). Peña *Docs. sur la Maison de Durfort (XIe-XVe Siècle)* (1977): xxxi (Anne, wife of Gaillard de Durfort, identified as "fille du duc de Suffolk"). *TG* 4 (1983): 131–136. Schwennicke *Europäische Stammtafeln* 10 (1986): 113 (sub Durfort).

Illegitimate child of William [de la] Pole, K.G., allegedly by Malyne de Cay, a nun:

i. **JOAN** (or **JANE**) **DE LA POLE** [see next].

11. JOAN (or **JANE**) **[DE LA] POLE**, illegitimate child of William [de la] Pole, K.G., allegedly by Malyne de Cay, born in Normandy evidently early in 1430. She married before 1450 **THOMAS STONOR** (or **STONER**, **STONOUR**, **STONAR**), Esq., of Stonor (in Pyrton), Oxfordshire, Bierton-Stonors (in Bierton), Buckinghamshire, Ermington, Devon, Penton Mewsy, Hampshire, etc., Knight of the Shire for Oxfordshire, Sheriff of Oxfordshire and Berkshire, 1453–4, 1465–6, Justice of the Peace for Oxfordshire, 1466, 1468–71, 1473–4, son and heir of Thomas Stonor, Esq., of Stonor (in Pyrton), Oxfordshire, Ermington, Devon, Penton Mewsey, Hampshire, etc., Knight of the Shire for Oxfordshire, by Alice, daughter and heiress of Thomas Kirby, of Horton Kirby, Kent. He was born 23 March 1424 (aged 7 in 1431). They had three sons, William, K.B., Thomas, and Edmund, and four daughters, Alice, Joan (wife of John Cottesmore), Mary, and Elizabeth (or Isabel). His wife, Joan, had letters of denization granted to her 11 May 1453, she being born in Normandy and dwelling in England from the time of her marriage. In 1458 he was pardoned as one of the trustees of the lands of his wife's late father, William de la Pole, Duke of Suffolk. In 1465 the king granted him 100 marks from the issues of the counties and Oxford and Berkshire. In 1469 he and his wife, Joan, sold the manor of Bierton-Stonors (in Bierton), Buckinghamshire to Ralph Verney, Knt. In 1471 he witnessed a conveyance of the manor of Swerford, Oxfordshire in favor of Alice de la Pole, Duchess of Suffolk. He was pardoned in 1472, after his lapse with the Lancastrians in 1470. In 1472 John Arundell, Knt. conveyed all his title and rights to a moiety share of the manors of Stratford, Suffolk, Ewelme, Oxfordshire, Hatfield Peverel, Essex, and East Worldham, Hampshire to Alice de la Pole, Duchess of Suffolk, Thomas Stonor, and Humphrey Forster, Esq. THOMAS STONOR, Esq., died testate 23 April 1474, and was buried at Pyrton, Oxfordshire. In 1480 the king granted an annuity of 80 pounds to his secretary, John Kendale, "during the life of Jane mother of Sir William Stonor, rebel." Joan (or Jane) died 28 Feb. 1494. She left a will dated 13 April 1493, proved 16 Nov. 1494 (P.C.C. 16 Vox), requesting burial in the church of Henley-on-Thames, Oxfordshire.

Burke *Dict. of the Peerages... Extinct, Dormant & in Abeyance* (1831): 435–438. Burke *Hist. of the Commoners* 2 (1836): 440–441. Harvey et al. *Vis. of Oxford 1566, 1574, 1634 & 1574* (H.S.P. 5) (1871): 143–144 (Stonor ped.: "Thomas Stoner, armiger. = Johanni filia naturalis ... Delapole, ducis Suffolciæ."). *C.P.R.* 1461–1467 (1897): 363–364, 479, 538, 570. *Cal. IPM Henry VII* 1 (1898): 436. *List of Sheriffs for England & Wales* (PRO Lists and Indexes 9) (1898): 108. *C.P.R.* 1467–1477 (1900): 248–249, 285, 350, 406, 625. VCH *Buckingham* 2 (1908): 321–322 (Stonor arms: Azure two bars dancetty or and a chief argent). *C.P.R.* 1452–1461 (1910): 70, 467–468. VCH *Hampshire* 4 (1911): 381–384. Kingsford *Stonor Letters & Papers 1290–1483* 1 (Camden Soc. 3rd Ser. 29) (1919): chart opp. vii, vii–xlvii, 62–63 (letter of J[oan] Stonor dated 1463 mentions her cousin Langforth [presumably Edward Langford intended], 69–70 (Thomas Stonor styled "cousin" by Thomas Hampden, of Hampden, and his wife, Margery Popham, in letter dated c.1465), 70–71 (Thomas Stonor styled "cousin" by Thomas Hampton, of Kimble in letter dated c.1465), 97–98 (Thomas Stonor styled "cousin" by John Crocker in letter dated 1468), 99–100, 119–120 (instances of Thomas Stonor styled "cousin" by Richard Quatermayns in letters dated 1467 or 1468 and ?1471), 107 (Thomas Stonor styled "cousin" by R[ichard] Restwold in letter dated 1470 or earlier), 112–114 (Thomas Stonor styled "father" [fadyr] by Sir Richard Harcourt [see WITHAM 9] in letter dated ?1470), 128–129 (Thomas Stonor styled "cousin" by Lady Katherine Arundell (née Chidiock) in letter dated ?1473 [see ARUNDELL 10]). Wedgwood *Hist. of Parl.* 1 (1936): 814–815 (biog. of Thomas Stonor). Lamborn *Armorial Glass of the Oxford Diocese* (1949): 65–70, 86, 125–127. Stonor *Stonor* (1952): 131 ([Edward] Langford styled "cousin" by Joan Stonor in 1463). *C.C.R.* 1468–1476 (1953): 176, 217, 321–322, 331, 383. Weaver & Beardwood *Some Oxfordshire Wills* (Oxfordshire Rec. Soc. 39) (1958): 50 (will of Dame Jane Stonar, the elder). Briers *Henley Borough Recs.* (Oxfordshire Rec. Soc. 41) (1960): 89, 93, 96, 98, 144. VCH *Oxford* 8 (1964): 154. Hassall *Index of Persons in Oxfordshire Deeds* (Oxfordshire Rec. Soc. 45) (1966): 196. *Chancery Misc.* 3 (List & Index Soc. 26) (1967): 43–59. Jones *Gentry & Lesser Nobility in Late Medieval Europe* (1986): 68–70. Roskell *House of Commons 1386–1421* 4 (1992): 483485 (biog. of Thomas Stonor [died 1431]). Archer & Walker *Rulers & Ruled in Late Medieval England* (1995): 175–200. *Cal. IPM* 23 (2004): 240–241.

Children of Joan [de la] Pole, by Thomas Stonor, Esq.:

i. **WILLIAM STONOR**, K.B. [see next].

ii. **ALICE STONOR**, married **RICHARD HARCOURT**, Knt., of Witham, Berkshire [see WITHAM 14].

iii. **MARY STONOR**, married **JOHN BARANTYNE**, Esq., of Little Haseley, Oxfordshire [see POPHAM 16].

12. WILLIAM STONOR, K.B., of Stonor (in Pyrton), Oxfordshire, Ermington, Devon, Penton Mewsey, Hampshire, and London, and, in right of his 2nd wife, of Clist Barneville and Hode (in Dertington), Devon, and Wolston, Cornwall, Steward of Thame and Dorchester, Oxfordshire, Knight of the Body to King Henry VII, Knight of the Shire for Oxfordshire, Sheriff of Oxfordshire and Berkshire, 1485, Sheriff of Devonshire, 1490–1, High Steward of Oxford University, joint Constable of Wallingford Castle, son and heir, born about 1450 (aged 24 in 1474). He married (1st) in 1475 **ELIZABETH CROKE** (died 1479), widow of Thomas Rich and John Fenne (died 3 Sept. 1474), and daughter of John Croke, Alderman of London. He married (2nd) before Jan. 1480/1 **AGNES WINNARD** (or **WENARD**) (died 4 May 1481), widow of John Wideslade, and daughter and heiress of John Winnard, of Hatherleigh, Devonshire. He married (3rd) in Autumn 1481 **ANNE NEVILLE**, daughter of John Neville, K.G., Earl of Northumberland, afterwards Marquess of Montagu, by Isabel, daughter and heiress of Edmund Ingaldesthorpe, Knt. [see INGALDESTHORPE 13 for her ancestry]. They had one son, John, and one daughter, Anne. He was present at the Coronation of King Richard III in 1483. His wife, Anne, was co-heiress in 1483 to her brother, George Neville, formerly Duke of Bedford. He joined in the rebellion of Henry Stafford, Duke of Buckingham, and was attainted October or Nov. 1485. He probably accompanied Thomas Grey, Marquess of Dorset, in his flight to Brittany. His estates were restored on the accession of King Henry VII, who made him a banneret at the Battle of Stoke 16 June 1487. His wife, Anne, died shortly before 5 Nov. 1486. In 1491 he sued Thomas Dormer and others in the Court of Star Chamber regarding a riotous assembly at Nursling, Hampshire. He was a legatee and appointed an executor in the 1493 will of his mother, Jane Stonor. SIR WILLIAM STONOR died 21 May 1494. He left a will dated 11 April 1489, proved in 1494 (P.C.C. 20 Vox).

Rowland *Noble Fam. of Nevill* (1830). Burke *Dict. of the Peerages… Extinct, Dormant & in Abeyance* (1831): 389–390. Dallaway *Hist. of the Western Division of the County of Sussex* 2(2) (1832): 250 (Montacute-Neville-Pole ped.). *Coll. Top. et Gen.* 1 (1834): 300–301 (Neville ped.: "… [Neville], wedded to William Stonor."); 8 (1843): 75–77 (sub Barony of Bradstone). Surtees *Hist. & Antiqs. of Durham* 4 (1840): 158–163 (Nevill peds.). *Annual Rpt. of the Deputy Keeper* 38 (1870): 219. Harvey et al. *Vis. of Oxford 1566, 1574, 1634 & 1574* (H.S.P. 5) (1871): 143–144 (Stonor ped.: "Willmus. Stoner, miles. = Anna filia primogenita & coheires Johannis Nevill, Marchionis de Monteacuto."). *Desc. Cat. Ancient Deeds* 1 (1890): 495–505 (C.1112). Gurney *Ref. Handbook for Readers, Students & Teachers of English Hist.* (1890): 42–44. *Cal. IPM Henry VII* 1 (1898): 106, 410, 416, 418–419, 440–441, 483, 520–521. *List of Sheriffs for England & Wales* (PRO Lists and Indexes 9) (1898): 36, 108. Benolte et al. *Vis. of Surrey 1530, 1572 & 1623* (H.S.P. 43) (1899): 19 (Browne ped.: "Ann [Nevell] vx. Sir Will'm Stoner"). VCH *Hertford* 2 (1908): 266–267. *C.C.R.* 1485–1494 (1914): 399–400, 439–441. Kingsford *Stonor Letters & Papers 1290–1483* 1 (Camden Soc. 3rd Ser. 29) (1919): chart opp. vii, vii–xlvii, 125–127 (William Stonor styled "cousin" by Thomas Mull), 148 (William Stonor styled "cousin" by W[alter Elmes]), 150–151 (William Stonor styled "cousin" by Richard Harcourt); 2 (Camden Soc. 3rd Ser. 30) (1919): 29, 75–76 (instances of William Stonor styled "cousin" by Thomas Hampden), 57–58 (William Stonor styled "cousin" by Edmund Hampden), 80–81 (William Stonor styled "cousin" by Sir Edmund Rede), 116 (William Stonor styled "cousin" by James Tyrrell [see MORLEY 11]), 132–133 (William Stonor styled "cousin" by William Sandys, Knt.), 150, 162–163 (instances of William Stonor styled "cousin" by Francis Lovell, Lord Lovell), 154–157 (instances of

William Stonor styled "cousin" by Philip Fitzlewis). *English Hist. Rev.* 35 (1920): 421–432. Stopes *Life of Henry, 3rd Earl of Southampton* (1922): 487–488. VCH *Berkshire* 3 (1923): 333, 509. Wedgwood *Hist. of Parl.* 1 (1936): 815–816 (biog. of Sir William Stonor). Lamborn *Armorial Glass of the Oxford Diocese* (1949): 65–70, 125–127. Stonor *Stonor* (1952). Emden *Biog. Reg. of the Univ. of Oxford* 3 (1959): 1790–1791 (biog. of Sir William Stonor). Briers *Henley Borough Recs.* (Oxfordshire Rec. Soc. 41) (1960): 88, 105. VCH *Oxford* 7 (1962): 178; 8 (1964): 154, 197. *Chancery Misc.* 3 (List & Index Soc. 26) (1967): 43–59, 303. Jones *Gentry & Lesser Nobility in Late Medieval Europe* (1986): 68–70. *TG* 9 (1988): 163–225. Hicks *Who's Who in Late Medieval England* (1991): 355–356 (biog. of Sir William Stonor: "… the central figure of the Stonor Letters, represents the normal lifestyle and aspirations of a country gentleman"). Abstract of *IPM* — Agnes Stonore dated 1481 and William Stoner, Knt. dated 1494 [FHL Microfilm 917256]. National Archives, STAC 1/1/45 (available at www.catalogue.nationalarchives.gov.uk/search.asp).

13. ANNE STONOR, daughter by her father's 3rd marriage. She was heiress in 1498 to her brother, John Stonor. She married before 17 October 1499 (as his 1st wife) **ADRIAN FORTESCUE**, K.B., of Stonor (in Pyrton) and Shirburn, Oxfordshire, and St. Clement Danes, London, Gentleman of the Privy Chamber, Knight of Saint John, younger son of John Fortescue, Knt., of Ponsbourne (in Hatfield), Brookmans (in North Mimms), Darkes (in South Mimms), and Windridge (in St. Michael's par., St. Albans), Hertfordshire, Eyworth, Bedfordshire, Arnolds (in Trumpington) and Steeple Morden, Cambridgeshire, etc., Chief Butler of England, Esquire and Knight of the Body, Porter of Calais, by his 1st wife, Alice, daughter of Geoffrey Boleyn, Knt. [see HOO 14.i.c for his ancestry]. He was born about 1481. They had two daughters, Margaret and Frances (wife of Thomas Fitz Gerald, 10th Earl of Kildare). In 1507 he and his wife, Anne, sold the manor of Hood (in Dartington), Devon to Thomas Hobson for 200 marks of silver. In 1509 he and his wife, Anne, sold the manor of Knowle, Somerset to William Carant, Esq., for £200. He served as a captain in the expedition to France in 1513. His wife, Anne, died at Stonor (in Pyrton), Oxfordshire 14 June 1518, and was buried at Pyrton, Oxfordshire. He attended the queen at the Field of the Cloth of Gold in 1520. He served in the short and uneventful French war of 1522. He married (2nd) in 1530 **ANNE READE**, widow of Giles Greville, Knt. (died 1 April 1528), and daughter of William Reade, Knt., of Boarstall, Buckinghamshire, by his 2nd wife, Anne, daughter of Nicholas Warham. She was born about 1510. They had three sons, John, Knt., Thomas, Knt., and Anthony, Knt., and two daughters, Mary (wife of William Norris) and Elizabeth (wife of Thomas Bromley, Knt.). In 1532 he was admitted a knight of St. John of Jerusalem. In 1533 he was admitted into the confraternity of the Black Friars of St. Dominic at Oxford. In 1534 he was committed to the Marshalsea, and released in 1535. In Feb. 1539 he was again arrested and sent to the Tower. SIR ADRIAN FORTESCUE was beheaded on Tower Hill 8, 9, or 10 July 1539, owing to his refusal to take the oath of supremacy. His widow, Anne, married (3rd) **THOMAS PARRY** (or **AP HARRY**), Knt., of Hampstead Marshall and Welford, Berkshire, Comptroller of the Household, Privy Councillor, Master of the Court of Wards and Liveries, Burgess (M.P.) for Wallingford, 1547, 1552, 1555, Knight of the Shire for Hertfordshire, 1559, Lord Lieutenant of Berkshire, 1559, son and heir of Henry Vaughan, Esq., of Tretower, Breconshire. They had two sons, Thomas, Knt., and Edward, and three daughters, Muriel (wife of Thomas Knyvet, Knt.), Anne (wife of Griffin Hampden), and Frances (wife of John Abrahall). In 1557 his wife, Anne, was granted the manors of Gotherington (in Bishop's Cleeve) and Washbourne (in Great Washbourne), Gloucestershire. SIR THOMAS PARRY died 15 Dec. 1560, and was buried in Westminster Abbey. In the period, 1560–79, Richard Woodward sued his widow, Anne, and others regarding a parcel of the manor of Welford, Berkshire. Anne died 5 Jan. 1585, and was buried at Welford, Berkshire.

Fortescue *De Laudibus Legum Angliæ* (1775): liv–lx. Clutterbuck *Hist. & Antiqs. of Hertford* 2 (1821): 348–349 (Fortescue ped.). Napier *Swyncombe & Ewelme* (1858): Fortescue chart opp. 390. Leinster *Earls of Kildare* (1858): 128–170. *Herald & Gen.* 1 (1863): 337 (ped.). Harvey et al. *Vis. of Oxford 1566, 1574, 1634 & 1574* (H.S.P. 5) (1871): 143–144 (Stonor ped.: "Adrianus fortescue, miles, filius ætate minimus. = Anna filia et hæres Willmi. Stoner, militis."). *Le Neve's Peds. of the Knights* (H.S.P. 8) (1873): 21–23 (Knyvet ped.). Fortescue *Hist. of the Fam. of Fortescue* (1880): 234–279. Morris *Venerable Sir Adrian Fortescue* (1887). *Index of Chancery Procs. (Ser. II)* 1 (PRO Lists and Indexes 7) (1896): 420. *Pubs. Catholic Truth Soc.* 29 (1896): 1–9. *Notes & Queries* 9th Ser. 7 (1901): 327, 435–436; 9th Ser. 8 (1901): 73, 449–451.

Downside Rev. n.s. 3 (1903): 163–176. Benolte et al. *Vis. of Sussex 1530 & 1633–4* (H.S.P. 53) (1905): 32–36 (Fortescue ped.: "Sr Adrian Fortescue knight, [1] = Anne d. & heire of S^r W^m. Stoner & of Ann his wiffe d. & heire of John Marques Mountague, [2] = Ann d. of S^r W^m. Read of Borestall knight and widdow of Sr Georg Grevell."). Benolte et al. *Four Vis. of Berkshire 1532, 1566, 1623 & 1665–6* 2 (H.S.P. 57) (1908): 191 (Parry ped.: "Sr Tho: ap harry (alias) Parry Kn^t Treasurer of the Qu: house house [sic] ob: 1560: sepult: apud Westminst. = Anne da: to Sr Wm Reade of Borestall widow to Sr Gyles Grevell, and Sr Adrian Fortescue quæ ob: 1585.). *D.N.B.* 7 (1908): 476–477 (biog. of Sir Adrian Fortescue). Mundy *Middlesex Peds.* (H.S.P. 65) (1914): 48–50 (Fortescue ped.: "Sr Adrian Fortescue Knight. [1] = [left blank], [2] = Anne d. of Sr Wm Reade of Borstall in Com. Buckingham."). *C.P.R.* 1494–1509 (1916): 191, 553, 596 (1916). *C.P.* 4 (1916): 293, footnote d (sub Despenser); 12(2) (1959): 497–499 (sub Wentworth). VCH *Berkshire* 3 (1923): 333, 509; 4 (1924): 116–125, 178–183. Wedgwood *Hist. of Parl.* 1 (1936): 349 (biog. of Sir John Fortescue, father of Adrian Fortescu). Lamborn *Armorial Glass of the Oxford Diocese* (1949): 65–70, 125–127. Stonor *Stonor* (1952). VCH *Oxford* 7 (1962): 178; 8 (1964): 154, 197. VCH *Gloucester* 6 (1965): 232–237; 8 (1968): 2–25; 11 (1976): 1–3. *Ancient Deeds — Ser.* B 3 (List & Index Soc. 113) (1975): B.12287. *Ancient Deeds — Ser. A* 2 (List & Index Soc. 152) (1978): 37. Harvey *Vis. of Suffolk 1561* 1 (H.S.P. n.s. 2) (1981): 162–168 (Wentworth ped.). *Ancient Deeds — Ser. DD* (List & Index Soc. 200) (1983): 155. *TG* 9 (1988): 163–225. *Analecta Bollandiana* 115 (1997): 307–353. Biancalana *Fee Tail & the Common Recovery in Medieval England* (2001): 417–418. Mayer & Walters *Corr. of Reginald Pole* 4 (2008): 205 (biog. of Sir Adrian Fortescue). National Archives, C 1/134/67 (Chancery Proc. dated 1506–15 — Adrian Fortescu, Knt., and Anne, his wife, daughter and heir of Sir William Stonour, Knt., and Anne, his wife, Elizabeth, lady Scrope, Margaret, late the wife of Sir John Mortymer, Knt., and Lucy Browne, late the wife of Sir Anthony Browne, Knt. v. The abbot of St. Augustine's, Canterbury re. detention of deeds rel. lands not specified, late of John Nevyll, marquis of Montagu, and Isabel (Elizabeth), his wife, parents of the said Anne lady Stonour, Elizabeth, Margaret, and Lucy.: York, Kent, Camb. Essex, Wilts, Glouc. and other counties.) (available at www.catalogue.nationalarchives.gov.uk/ search.asp). National Archives, CP 25/1/46/93, #44; CP 25/1/202/42, #60 [see abstract of fines at http://www.medievalgenealogy.org.uk/index.html].

Child of Anne Stonor, by Adrian Fortescue, K.B.:

i. **MARGARET FORTESCUE**, married **THOMAS WENTWORTH**, Knt., Lord Wentworth [see NETTLESTEAD 19].

⊷ DENNIS ⊶

WILLIAM THE CONQUEROR, King of England, married **MAUD OF FLANDERS**.
HENRY I, King of England, married **MAUD OF SCOTLAND**.
MAUD OF ENGLAND, married **GEOFFREY PLANTAGENET**, Count of Anjou, Duke of Normandy.
HENRY II, King of England, married **ELEANOR OF AQUITAINE**.
JOHN, King of England, married **ISABEL OF ANGOULEME**.
HENRY III, King of England, married **ELEANOR OF PROVENCE**.
EDWARD I, King of England, married **ELEANOR OF CASTILE** (desc. King William the Conqueror).
EDWARD II, King of England, married **ISABEL OF FRANCE** (desc. King William the Conqueror).
EDWARD III, King of England, married **PHILIPPE OF HAINAULT** (desc. King William the Conqueror).
JOHN OF GAUNT, K.G., Duke of Aquitaine and Lancaster, married **KATHERINE DE ROET** (or RUET).
HENRY BEAUFORT, Cardinal of England, allegedly by his mistress, **ALICE ARUNDEL** (desc. King William the Conqueror).
JOAN BEAUFORT, married **EDWARD STRADLING**, Knt., of St. Donat's, Glamorgan [see STRADLING 12].

13. JOAN (or **KATHERINE**) **STRADLING**, married (as his 1st wife) **MAURICE DENNIS** (or **DENYS**), Esq., of Olveston and Earthcott, Gloucestershire, Sheriff of Gloucestershire, 1461–3, son and heir of Gilbert Dennis, Knt., of Siston, Gloucestershire, Knight of the Shire for Gloucestershire, Sheriff of Gloucestershire, by his 2nd wife, Margaret, elder daughter of Maurice Russell, Knt. He was born about 1410 (aged 12 in 1422). They had two sons, Walter, Knt., and John. On his father's death in 1422, Maurice's wardship was granted to Edward Stradling, Knt. (his future father-in-law). He was granted seisin of his father's lands 20 Nov. 1431. In the period, 1433–43, he sued John Dalden, clerk, and other feoffees to uses in Chancery regarding the manors of Siston and Alston [?Olveston], Gloucestershire, and the manor and lordship of Lawrenny, Pembrokeshire. He married (2nd) before 1 Nov. 1437 (date of settlement) **ALICE POYNTZ**, daughter of Nicholas Poyntz, Esq., of Iron Acton, Gloucestershire, by his 2nd wife, Elizabeth, daughter of Henry Hussey, Knt. [see OWSLEY 8 for her ancestry]. They had three sons, Hugh, Maurice, and Francis, and four daughters, Isabel (wife of Reyborne Mathew), Jane, Emma, and Alice. MAURICE DENNIS, Esq., was living in 1466. He was buried at Olveston, Gloucestershire. His wife, Alice, was living in 1473.

> Chitting & Phillipot *Vis. of Gloucester 1623, 1569 & 1582–3* (H.S.P. 21) (1885): 49–52 (Dennis ped.: "Morrys Dennys [1] = Katherine d. of [Sr] Edward Stradling [K. 1 wiffe], [2] = Alice d. of Nicholas Poyntz [2 wiffe]."). (Dennis arms: Gules, a bend engrailed azure between two leopards' faces jessant de lis or), 128–129 (Poyntz ped.: "Alice [Poyntz] ux. Morris Dennis."). Clark *Limbus Patrum Morganiæ et Glamorganiæ* (1886): 381–382 (sub Dennis), 433–439 (sub Stradling). *Trans. Bristol & Gloucs. Arch. Soc.* 12 (1888): 326–327; 23 (1900): 64–65. *C.P.R. 1461–1467* (1897): 531. *List of Sheriffs for England & Wales* (PRO Lists and Indexes 9) (1898): 50. *Procs. Bath Natural Hist. & Antiq. Field Club* 9 (1901): 58–70 (Katherine, daughter of Sir Edward Stradling identified as 1st wife of Maurice Dennis). *Desc. Cat. Ancient Deeds* 4 (1902): 291. *List of Early Chancery Procs.* 2 (PRO Lists and Indexes 16) (1903): 1. *C.P.R. 1436–1441* (1907): 120. *C.C.R. 1429–1435* (1933): 137–138. *C.F.R.* 14 (1934): 100, 441–442. Lewis *Inv. of Early Chancery Procs. Concerning Wales* (Board of Celtic Studies, Hist. & Law 3) (1937): 61. *C.C.R. 1454–1461* (1947): 134. *C.C.R. 1468–1476* (1953): 305. Ross *Cartulary of St. Mark's Hospital Bristol* (Bristol Rec. Soc. 21) (1959): 234–235. Colwell *Fam. Hist. Book* (1980): 15 (Dennis ped. dated c.1530 College of Arms, Muniment Room, MS 3/54). Roskell *House of Commons 1386–1421* 2 (1992): 771–772 (biog. of Sir Gilbert Denys); 4 (1992): 251–253 (biog. of Sir Maurice Russell). Roberts *Royal Descents of 600 Immigrants* (2004): 259–262.

14. WALTER DENNIS, Knt., of Olveston, Aust, Dyrham, and Siston, Gloucestershire, and Kingston Russell and Lutton, Dorset, Escheator of Gloucestershire, 1457, Sheriff of Gloucestershire, 1479–80, 1493–4, son and heir by his father's 1st marriage. He married (1st) _____ **FIENNES**, daughter of _____ Fiennes, Lord Dacre of the South. They had no issue. He married (2nd) before 1467 **AGNES DANVERS**, daughter and co-heiress of Robert Danvers, Knt., of Ipwell, Oxfordshire, Chief Justice of the Common Pleas, by his 1st wife, Agnes, daughter of Richard Delabar, Knt. She was born about 1445 (aged 22 in 1467). They had three sons, William, Knt., Richard, and John, and three daughters, Anne, Jane, and Katherine. In 1469 Walter released any right he had by his wife, Agnes, to Thomas Unton regarding a tenement and garden in More Street, St. Giles Cripplegate, London. He married (3rd) **AGNES MYNNE**, a widow. They had no issue. He married (4th) before 10 Nov. 1503 **ALICE WALWYN**, widow of Thomas Baynham, Esq. (died 16 Feb. 1499/1500), and daughter and heiress of William Walwyn, of Bickerton, Herefordshire. They had no issue. SIR WALTER DENNIS died 1 Sept. 1505, and was buried at Olveston, Gloucestershire. His widow, Alice, died 22 October 1518.

> Foss *Judges of England* 4 (1851): 428–429 (biog. of Robert Danvers). Harvey et al. *Vis. of Oxford 1566, 1574, 1634 & 1574* (H.S.P. 5) (1871): 187–188 (Danvers ped.). *Trans. Bristol & Gloucs. Arch. Soc.* 6 (1882): 139–160, 181–187; 23 (1900): 64–65. Duncumb et al. *Colls. towards the Hist. & Antiqs. of Hereford* 3 (1882): 38–41. Chitting & Phillipot *Vis. of Gloucester 1623, 1569 & 1582–3* (H.S.P. 21) (1885): 49–52 (Dennis ped.: "Sr Walter Dennys [K.] [1] = …. da. to… ffines L. Dacres of the South 1 wiffe — Harleian 1041], [2] = Agnes d. and co-heire of Sr Robert Davers [K. Judge of the Comon place — Harleian 1041], [3] = Agnes Mynns 3 wiffe — Harleian 1041, [4] = Alice d. of… Baynham [4 wiffe]."). (Danvers arms: Argent, on a bend gules three martlets or). Clark *Limbus Patrum Morganiæ et Glamorganiæ* (1886): 381–382 (sub Dennis). MacNamara *Mems. of the Danvers Fam.* (1895): 102–116, 122. *List of Sheriffs for England & Wales* (PRO Lists and Indexes 9) (1898): 50. *Procs. Bath Natural Hist. & Antiq. Field Club* 9 (1901): 58–70. *List of Early Chancery Procs.* 3 (PRO Lists and Indexes 20) (1906): 180. Matthews *Colls. towards the Hist. & Antiqs. of Hereford* 6 (Hundred of Wormelow) (1912): 54–56. *Cal. IPM Henry VII* 2 (1915): 442–443; 3 (1955): 96–97. *Misc. Gen. et Heraldica* 5th Ser. 6 (1926–28): 288–294. *List of Escheators for England & Wales* (List & Index Soc. 72) (1971): 55. Colwell *Fam. Hist. Book* (1980): 15 (Dennis ped. dated c.1530, College of Arms, Muniment Room, MS 3/54). Roberts *Royal Descents of 600 Immigrants* (2004): 259–262. Deeds & related papers of the Salters' Company, H1/23/4 (conveyance dated 1469 between Walter Denys, Esq., and Thomas Unton) (available at www.a2a.org.uk/search/index.asp).

15. WILLIAM DENNIS, Knt., of Dyrham, Olveston and Iscote, Gloucestershire, Sheriff of Gloucestershire, 1519–20, son and heir by his father's 2nd marriage, born about 1470 (aged 35 in 1505). He married (1st) **ANNE BERKELEY**, daughter of Maurice Berkeley, Knt., by Isabel, daughter of Philip Meade (or Mede), Esq. [see BERKELEY 11 for her ancestry]. They had six sons, Walter, Knt., Maurice, Knt., William, Thomas, Francis, and John, and seven daughters, Anne, Isabel, Katherine (wife of Edmund Tame, Knt., Walter Buckler, Knt., and Roger Lygon, Esq.), Eleanor, Bridget, Mary (nun at Lacock Abbey), and Margaret (wife of Nicholas Arnold, Knt.). His wife, Anne, was living Easter term 1523 (date of fine). He married (2nd) **EDITH TWINIHOE**. They had one daughter, Anne. SIR WILLIAM DENNIS died 22 June 1533.

>Dugdale *Baronage of England* 2 (1676): 367 (sub Berkeley). Bigland *Account of Fairford* (1791): 27–28. Nicolas *Testamenta Vetusta* 2 (1826): 655–656 (will of Thomas Berkeley, Knt., Lord Berkeley). Bruce *Corr. of Robert Dudley, Earl of Leycester* (Camden Soc. 27) (1844): 180–183 (letter dated 1586 mentions "one Mr. Mawryce Dennys" a kinsman of Anne Russell, wife of Ambrose Dudley, Earl of Warwick). Smyth *Berkeley MSS* 2 (1883): 178–187. Chitting & Phillipot *Vis. of Gloucester 1623, 1569 & 1582–3* (H.S.P. 21) (1885): 49–52 (Dennis ped.: "Sir Wm. Dennys K. [1] = Lady Anne d. of Morris Lord Barkley brother to Wm. Marquis Barkley, [2] = Edith d. of… Twinihoe") (Dennis arms: Gules, a bend engrailed azure between two leopards' faces jessant de lis or). Clark *Limbus Patrum Morganiæ et Glamorganiæ* (1886): 381–382 (sub Dennis). Tresswell & Vincent *Vis. of Shropshire 1623, 1569 & 1584* 1 (H.S.P. 28) (1889): 31 (1623 Vis.) (Barkley ped.: "Anne [Berkeley] wife to Sir Wm. Dennis of Dirham Kt."). Jeayes *Desc. Cat. of the Charters & Muniments in the Possession of the Rt. Hon. Lord Fitzhardinge* (1892): xxii–xxiii (chart). *List of Sheriffs for England & Wales* (PRO Lists and Indexes 9) (1898): 51. *Notes & Queries for Somerset & Dorset* 6 (1899): 27. *Trans. Bristol & Gloucs. Arch. Soc.* 23 (1900): 64–65. *Procs. Bath Natural Hist. & Antiq. Field Club* 9 (1901): 58–70. *Cal. IPM Henry VII* 3 (1955): 96–97. Colwell *Fam. Hist. Book* (1980): 15 (Dennis ped. dated c.1530, College of Arms, Muniment Room, MS 3/54). Bindoff *House of Commons 1509–1558* 2 (1982): 31–33 (biog. of Sir Maurice Denys), 36–37 (biog. of Sir Walter Denys). *Virginia Gen.* 38 (1994): 48–51. Roberts *Royal Descents of 600 Immigrants* (2004): 259–262.

Children of William Dennis, Knt., by Anne Berkeley:

i. **ANNE DENNIS**, married (1st) **JOHN RAGLAN**, Knt., of Carn-Lwyd (in Llancarfan), Glamorgan [see AUBREY 16]; (2nd) **EDWARD CARNE**, Knt., Doctor of Canon Law, of Ewenny, Glamorgan [see AUBREY 16].

ii. **ISABEL DENNIS**, married (1st) **JOHN BERKELEY**, Knt., of Stoke Gifford, Gloucestershire [see DEIGHTON 13]; (2nd) **ARTHUR PORTER**, Esq., of Newent, Gloucestershire [see DEIGHTON 13].

iii. **ELEANOR DENNIS**, married **WILLIAM LIGON**, Esq., of Madresfield, Worcestershire [see LIGON 17].

❧ DENNY ❧

RICHARD DE MONTAGU, of Shepton Montague, Somerset, married **ALICE** _____.
WILLIAM DE MONTAGU, of Shepton Montague, Somerset, married **ISABEL** _____.
DREW DE MONTAGU, married **ALINE BASSET**.
WILLIAM DE MONTAGU, Knt., of Shepton Montague, Somerset, married **BERTHA** _____.
SIMON DE MONTAGU, Knt., 1st Lord Montagu, married **HAWISE DE SAINT AMAND**.
WILLIAM DE MONTAGU, Knt., 2nd Lord Montagu, married **ELIZABETH DE MONTFORT** (desc. King William the Conqueror).
ALICE DE MONTAGU, married **RALPH DAUBENEY**, Knt., of South Ingleby, Lincolnshire.
GILES DAUBENEY, Knt., of South Ingleby, Lincolnshire, married **ELEANOR DE WILINGTON** (desc. King William the Conqueror).
KATHERINE DAUBENEY, married **RICHARD CHAMPERNOUN**, Knt., of Modbury, Devon [see MODBURY 12].

13. RICHARD CHAMPERNOUN (or **CHAMBERNON**), Knt., of Modbury, Bridford, Buckland Dinham, and Dodbrook, Devon, son by his father's 2nd marriage. He married **ISABEL BONVILLE**, daughter of John Bonville, Knt., of Chewton, Somerset, by Elizabeth, daughter of John Fitz Roger [see BONVILLE 10 for her ancestry]. They had one son, Hugh, Esq. In 1419 Isabel, wife of Richard Champernoun, junior, esquire, was granted an oratory within the residence of Richard Champernoun, Knt. He was a legatee in the 1419 will of his father. SIR RICHARD CHAMPERNOUN died 20 Jan. 1419/20. His widow, Isabel, was living 5 Feb. 1421.

Nichols *Hist. & Antiqs. of Leicestershire* 2(1) (1795): 132. *Reliquary* 7 (1866–7): 167–172. Vivian *Vis. of Devon 1531, 1564 & 1620* (1895): 162. *Devon & Cornwall Notes & Queries* 14 (1927): 218–221. Champernowne *Champernowne Fam.* (1954): 47, ped. II. Paget *Baronage of England* (1957) 80: 2.

14. HUGH CHAMPERNOUN, Esq., of Modbury, Devon, Burgess (M.P.) for Barnstaple, Devon, son and heir, born 24 Nov. 1417 (aged 2 in 1420). He married **ALICE BOIS**, daughter and heiress of John Bois, of Wood. They had two sons, William, Esq., and Thomas. HUGH CHAMPERNOUN, Esq., left a will dated 8 October 1443, proved 10 Jan. 1443/4 (Cons. Court of London).

Nichols *Hist. & Antiqs. of Leicestershire* 2(1) (1795): 132. Vivian *Vis. of Devon 1531, 1564 & 1620* (1895): 162. Hingeston-Randolph *Reg. of Edmund Lacy Bishop of Exeter (A.D. 1420–1455)* 1 (1909): 123–125. *Devon & Cornwall Notes & Queries* 14 (1927): 218–221. Champernowne *Champernowne Fam.* (1954): 47, ped. II.

15. WILLIAM CHAMPERNOUN, Esq., of Modbury, Bridford, and Dodbrook, Devon, born c.1438 (minor in 1449). He married before 1458 **ELIZABETH CHUDERLEGH**, daughter and heiress of John Chuderlegh, of Chedderlegh, Devon, by his wife, Alice Moore. He was admitted a member of Lincoln's Inn in 1453. In the period, 1460–64, he sued Thomas Danvers, feoffee, regarding the manor of Aston-Rowant, Oxfordshire mortgaged for a loan; usury, etc. In the period, 1460–64, he sued Hugh Rowe alias Chamburn, Esq., in Chancery regarding assaults on himself and his men, hindering them from protecting Plymouth, Modbury, etc, Devon, against the French; and protecting the king's enemies. In the period, 1460–64, he sued Thomas Danvers, feoffee, regarding the manor of Aston-Rowant, Oxfordshire mortgaged for a loan; usury, etc. In 1461–4 he likewise sued the said Hugh in Chancery regarding an assault on his servant, Nicholas Jay, obstruction of a royal commission, riot. WILLIAM CHAMPERNOUN, Esq., died 7 October 1464. He left a will proved 20 Nov. 1464 (P.C.C. 7 Godyn).

Nichols *Hist. & Antiqs. of Leicestershire* 2(1) (1795): 132. *Reliquary* 7 (1866–7): 167–172. Vivian *Vis. of Devon 1531, 1564 & 1620* (1895): 162. Baildon *Recs. of Lincoln's Inn: Admissions* 1 (1896): 12. *Devon & Cornwall Notes & Queries* 14 (1927): 218–221. National Archives, C 1/1/97; C 1/29/193; C 1/29/327 (available at www.catalogue.nationalarchives.gov.uk/search.asp).

16. JOHN CHAMPERNOUN, Knt., of Modbury, Bridford, and Dodbrook, Devon, son and heir, born about 1458 (aged 6 in 1464). He married **MARGARET COURTENAY**, daughter of Philip Courtenay, Knt., of Molland, Devon, by his wife, Elizabeth [see DAVIE 11 for her ancestry]. They had one son, Philip, Knt. He presented to the church of Bridford, Devon in 1473 and 1498. SIR JOHN CHAMPERNOUN died at Aston-Rowant, Oxfordshire 30 April 1503. His widow, Margaret, married (2nd) **JOHN WEST**. In the period, 1504–15, he and his wife, Margaret, and Philip Courtenay were sued in Chancery by her son, Philip Champernoun, regarding the detention of deeds relating to the manors of Modbury, Dodbrooke, and Bridford, and messuages and lands in South Ludbrook, Shipham, Buckland Dinham, and Woodleigh, Devon. Margaret married (3rd) _____ **FORTESCUE**. She died in 1536.

Brydges *Collins' Peerage of England* 6 (1812): 214–271 (sub Courtenay, Viscount Courtenay). Burke *Hist. of the Commoners* 2 (1835): 271–273 (sub Champernowne). Oliver *Eccl. Antiqs. in Devon* 2 (1840): 130. *Reliquary* 7 (1866–7): 167–172. Maclean *Hist. of Trigg Minor* 2 (1876): 240–241 (chart). Colby *Vis. of Devon 1564* (1881): 72–73 (Courtney ped.: "Margaret [Courtney] = John Champernon of Modbury."). Vivian *Vis. of Cornwall* (1887): 105–118 (Courtenay ped.). Vivian *Vis. of Devon 1531, 1564 & 1620* (1895): 162. Champernowne *Champernowne Fam.* (1954). National Archives, C 1/296/18 (available at www.catalogue.nationalarchives.gov.uk/search.asp).

17. PHILIP CHAMPERNOUN, Knt., of Modbury, Devon, Sheriff of Devonshire, 1526–7, son and heir, born about 1479 (aged 24 in 1503). He married **KATHERINE CAREW**, daughter of Edmund Carew, Knt., Baron Carew, of Carew Castle, Pembrokeshire, Mamhead and Ottery Mohun, Devon, Amport, Hampshire, etc., by Katherine, daughter and co-heiress of William Huddesfield, Knt. [see CAREW 18 for her ancestry]. They had two sons, John, Esq., and Arthur, Knt., and six daughters, including Jane (or Joan) (wife of Robert Gamage, Esq.), Joan (wife of

Anthony Denny, Knt.), and Katherine (wife of Walter Raleigh, Knt.). His wife, Katherine, was first Governess to Princess Elizabeth Tudor (afterwards Queen Elizabeth I). He presented to the church of Bridford, Devon in 1508. SIR PHILIP CHAMPERNOUN died at Modbury, Devon 2 August 1545. He left a will dated 1 August 1545, proved 5 Feb. 1545/6 (P.C.C. 3 Alen), naming his wife, Katherine.

> Burke *Hist. of the Commoners* 2 (1836): 272. Oliver *Eccl. Antiqs. in Devon* 2 (1840): 130. *Reliquary* 7 (1866–7): 167–172. St. George & Lennard *Vis. of Cornwall 1620* (H.S.P. 9) (1874): 28–32 (Carew ped.). Maclean *Hist. of Trigg Minor* 2 (1876): 240–241 (chart). *Macmillan's Mag.* 65 (1881): 385–386 ("During all this time of her residence at Hatfield, varied by visits to Hunsdon or Ashridge, [Princess] Elizabeth [Tudor] was making great progress in her education. Her first governess, or 'tutoress,' was Lady Champernoun, the wife of Sir Philip Champernoun. Ascham mentions 'the counsels of this accomplished lady,' as having contributed to Elizabeth's advancement in education, and Bohun describes her 'as a person of great worth, who formed this great wit (Elizabeth) from her infancy, and improved her native modesty with wise counsels, and a liberal and sage advice'."). Vivian *Vis. of Devon* (1895): 133–136 (Carew ped.), 162. *List of Sheriffs for England & Wales* (PRO Lists and Indexes 9) (1898): 36. Champernowne *Champernowne Fam.* (1954). Dickens *English Reformation* (1991): 218. Starkey *Elizabeth: Struggle for the Throne* (2001): 25–27, 79. National Archives, C 1/296/18 (available at www.catalogue.nationalarchives.gov.uk/search.asp).

Children of Philip Champernoun, Knt., by Katherine Carew:

i. **JANE** (or **JOAN**) **CHAMPERNOUN**, married **ROBERT GAMAGE**, Esq., of Coity, Glamorgan, Wales [see GAMAGE 19].

ii. **JOAN CHAMPERNOUN** [see next].

18. JOAN CHAMPERNOUN, married by license dated 4 Feb. 1538 **ANTHONY DENNY**, Knt., of Cheshunt, Hertfordshire, Burgess (M.P.) for Ipswich, Suffolk, King's Remembrancer, Gentleman of the Bed Chamber, Yeoman of the Royal Wardrobe, Chief Gentleman of the Privy Chamber, Groom of the Stole to King Henry VIII, Privy Councillor, Knight of the Shire for Hertfordshire, 1547, 4th but 2nd surviving son of Edmund Denny, Knt., of Cheshunt, Hertfordshire, King's Remembrancer to King Henry VII, Chief Baron of the Exchequer, by his 2nd wife, Mary, daughter and heiress of John Coke, Gent., of Newbury, Berkshire. He was born at Cheshunt, Hertfordshire 16 Jan. 1500/1. They had five sons, Henry, Anthony, Charles, Edward, Knt., and Edmund, and four daughters, Anne, Mary, Douglas (wife of John Dive, Knt.), and Honora (wife of Thomas Wingfield, Esq.). As a youth, he was educated at St. Paul's School, London. His education was completed at St. John's College, Cambridge. At the dissolution of the monasteries, and at various subsequent periods, he received from the king immense gifts of lands. In 1538 he and his wife, Joan, received a grant of the Priory of Hertford, Hertfordshire, together with divers other lands and manors. In 1539 he obtained the manor of Butterwick (in St. Peter's parish, St. Albans), the manors of the rectory and the nunnery in Cheshunt, and Great Amwell, all in Hertfordshire. The same year he and his wife, Joan, were among those appointed to receive Anne of Cleves. In 1541 he was granted several lands which had belonged to the Abbey of St. Albans, Hertfordshire. The same year he also acquired a 31-year lease of Waltham Abbey in Essex; the mansion of the Abbots of Waltham subsequently became the chief seat of the family. He accompanied the king on his expedition to France in 1544. He fought at the Siege of Boulogne-sur-Mer, where he was knighted by the king in Sept. 1544. In 1547 he was granted further properties and rights on Cheshunt manor, Hertfordshire, together with a reversion of Waltham Grange and Claverhambury, all formerly belonging to Waltham Abbey. He was legatee in the will of King Henry VIII, who bequeathed him the sum of £300 and named him one of his executors. In 1549 he was one of those sent to quell Kett's rebellion in Norfolk. SIR ANTHONY DENNY died at Cheshunt, Hertfordshire 10 Sept. 1549, and was buried in the parish church there. He left a will dated 7 Sept. 1549, proved 19 Sept. 1549 (P.C.C. 37 Populwell). His widow, Joan, died 15 May 1553, probably at Dallance, Essex. She left a will proved 27 May 1553 (P.C.C. 11 Tashe).

Blomefield *Essay towards a Top. Hist. of Norfolk* 4 (1775): 407. Britton *Architectural Antiqs. of Great Britain* 3 (1812): 21 (biog. of Sir Anthony Denny). Dugdale *Monasticon Anglicanum* 3 (1821): 301 (transcript of royal charter dated 1538 granting Hertford Priory, Hertfordshire to Anthony Denny ["Anthonio Denny"] and Joan Champernoun ["Johannæ Champernon"]). Clutterbuck *Hist. & Antiqs. of Hertford* 2 (1821): 105–108 (Denny ped.). Chauncy *Hist. Antiqs. of Hertfordshire* 1 (1826): 584 ("Pedigree of the Fam. of the Denny's, taken by Sir Matthew Cary, one of the Masters of the Chancery, partly out of a Book, which a Benedictine Fryar of that Name, shewed him in France"); 2 (1826): 390–391. Burke *Dict. of the Peerages… Extinct, Dormant & in Abeyance* (1831): 170–171. Madden *Privy Purse Expenses of the Princess Mary, Daughter of King Henry the Eighth, Afterwards Queen Mary* (1831): 227 (biog. of Anthony Denny: "His Lady was Joan, daughter of Sir Philip Champernoun, Knt., by whom he had two sons and one daughter. Among the Lansdowne Charters, No. 15 is the 'Audit of Dame Johan, widow of Sir Anth. Denny'."). Lodge *Portraits of Ill. Personages* 1 (1835): (biog. of Sir Anthony Denny "He carried with him an eminent reputation for universal learning."). Foss *Judges of England* 5 (1857): 157–158 ("was a zealous promoter of the Reformation"). *Top. & Gen.* 3 (1858): 207–210 (re. Denny fam.). Nichols *Narrative of the Days of the Reformation* (Camden Soc. 77) (1859): 311–312. *Notes & Queries* 4th Ser. 4 (1869): 276, 369–370 (author states in error that Robert Troutbeck [maternal grandfather of Anthony Denny] was younger son of William Troutbeck, Knt., by Margaret Stanley). Burke *Dormant, Abeyant, Forfeited & Extinct Peerages* (1883): 164–165 (sub Denny). Harvey et al. *Vis. of Norfolk 1563 & 1613* (H.S.P. 32) (1891): 101–103 (Denny ped.: "Sir Anthony Denny, knt., born 18 Jan., 16 Hen. 7, 1500. = Joane da. of Sir Philip Champnoone of Modbury, co. Devon, knt."). *East Herts Arch. Soc. Trans.* 3(2) (1906): 197–216 (biog. of Sir Anthony Denny). *List of Early Chancery Procs.* 3 (PRO Lists and Indexes 20) (1906): 393. *D.N.B.* 5 (1908): 823–824 (biog. of Sir Anthony Denny). VCH *Hertford* 3 (1912): 447. *Notes & Queries* 12th Ser. 10 (1922): 111–112. Chambers *Faculty Office Regs. 1534–1549* (1966): 121 (citation courtesy of John Brandon). *Ancient Deeds — Ser. B* 3 (List & Index Soc. 113) (1975): B.11693, B.12130. *Ancient Deeds — Ser. BB* (List & Index Soc. 137) (1977): 71. Bindoff *House of Commons 1509–1558* 2 (1982): 27–29 (biog. of Anthony Denny). *Ancient Deeds — DD Ser.* (List & Index Soc. 200) (1983): 156. Sil *Tudor Placemen & Statesmen: Select Case Hists.* (2001). Starkey *Elizabeth: Struggle for the Throne* (2001): 25–27. National Archives, C 1/198/40 (available at www.catalogue.nationalarchives.gov.uk/search.asp).

19. MARY DENNY, married (1st) in 1557 (as his 2nd wife) **THOMAS CRAWLEY**, Esq., of Chrishall, Essex, son of Robert Crawley. They had two daughters, Anne (wife of Edward Penruddock, Knt.) and Jane. THOMAS CRAWLEY, Esq., left a will dated 5 Feb. 1559, proved 18 May 1559. His widow, Mary, married (2nd) before 1562-3 **THOMAS ASTLEY** (or **ASTELEY**), Esq., of Writtle, Essex, Groom of the Privy Chamber to Queen Elizabeth I, son of Thomas Astley, of Hillmorton, Warwickshire, and Melton Constable, Norfolk, by his 3rd wife, Anne Cruse. They had two sons, Andrew, Knt., and Thomas, and two daughters, Elizabeth and Frances (wife of William Harris, Knt.). In 1588 he purchased from Nicholas Collins, Gent., and Judith his wife and George Glascock, Gent. and Susan his wife one messuage, one garden, and 120 acres of land in Writtle and Margaretting, Essex for £200. THOMAS ASTLEY died in 1595.

Clutterbuck *Hist. & Antiqs. of Hertford* 2 (1821): 105–108 (Denny ped.). Nichols *Progresses & Public Processions of Queen Elizabeth* 1 (1823): 127. Chauncy *Hist. Antiqs. of Hertfordshire* 1 (1826): 584; 2 (1826): 390–391. Hawley et al. *Vis. of Essex 1552, 1558, 1570, 1612 & 1634* 1 (H.S.P. 13) (1878): 336–337 (Astley ped.: "Thomas Astley of Writtle in com. Essex esqre Grome of the chamber to Q. Elizabeth buried in Writtle Church. = Mary d. of Sr Anthony Denny of … in com Hertford one of the privy counsell to H. 8."). Burke *Dormant, Abeyant, Forfeited & Extinct Peerages* (1883): 164–165 (sub Denny). Farrer *Church Heraldry of Norfolk* 2 (1889): 392–402. Harvey et al. *Vis. of Norfolk 1563 & 1613* (H.S.P. 32) (1891): 101–103 (Denny ped.: "Mary [Denny], 1 ux. .... Crawley. 2, to Thomas Ashley of Writtell in Essex, Groom of the Privy Chamber."). *East Herts Arch. Soc. Trans.* 3(2) (1906): 197–216. St. George & Lennard *Wiltshire Vis. Peds. 1623, 1628* (H.S.P. 105-6) (1954): 149 (Penruddock ped.). Emmison *Elizabethan Life: Wills of Essex Gentry & Merchants* (Essex Rec. Office Pubs. 71) (1978): 72–73 (will of Thomas Crawley). Emmison *Feet of Fines for Essex* 6 (1993): 58. Mears *Queenship & Political Discourse in the Elizabethan Realms* (2005): 68. National Archives, C 43/6/69 (Parties: Thomas Asteley and Mary his wife, late wife of Thomas Crawley junior, and one of the daughters of Sir Anthony Denny, Knt. Subject: Traverse of inquisition taken on death of the said Thomas, Anna sole daughter and heir. Judgment Places: Chrishall Bury manor; Chrishall Magna, manor, etc., called Barnes; Chrishall Parva, manor, etc., called Fryers alias Chrishall Grange; Wenden Lofts, Strathall manor, lands etc.; Chishill Magna, Chishill Parva, Elmdon, Lithbury, Chesterford Magna and Parva, Langley, Clavering and Askisden messuages, lands, etc. County: Essex. Date: 1562-3.) (available at www.catalogue.nationalarchives.gov.uk/search.asp).

Child of Mary Denny, by Thomas Astley, Esq.:

i. **ELIZABETH ASTLEY**, married **EDWARD DARCY**, Knt., of Dartford, Kent [see LAUNCE 20].

❧ DEREHAUGH ❦

WILLIAM THE CONQUEROR, King of England, married **MAUD OF FLANDERS**.
HENRY I, King of England, married **MAUD OF SCOTLAND**.
MAUD OF ENGLAND, married **GEOFFREY PLANTAGENET**, Count of Anjou, Duke of Normandy.
HENRY II, King of England, by a mistress, **IDA DE TONY**.
WILLIAM LONGESPÉE, Knt., Earl of Salisbury, married **ELA OF SALISBURY**.
IDA LONGESPÉE, married **WILLIAM DE BEAUCHAMP**, Knt., of Bedford, Bedfordshire.
BEATRICE DE BEAUCHAMP, married **WILLIAM DE MUNCHENSY**, Knt., of Edwardstone, Suffolk.
WILLIAM DE MUNCHENSY, of Edwardstone, Suffolk, married **ALICE** _____.
THOMAS DE MUNCHENSY, Knt., of Edwardstone, Suffolk, married **JOYCE** _____.
THOMAS MUNCHENSY, of Edwardstone, Suffolk, married (1st) **JOAN VAUNCY**.
JOAN MUNCHENSY, married **RICHARD WALDEGRAVE**, Knt., of Smallbridge (in Bures St. Mary), Suffolk.
RICHARD WALDEGRAVE, Knt., of Edwardstone, Suffolk, married **JOAN DOREWARD**.
THOMAS WALDEGRAVE, Knt., of Smallbridge (in Bures St. Mary), Suffolk, married **ELIZABETH FRAY**.
WILLIAM WALDEGRAVE, Knt., of Smallbridge (in Bures St. Mary), Suffolk, married **MARGERY WENTWORTH** (desc. King William the Conqueror) [see WALDEGRAVE 14].

15. DOROTHY WALDEGRAVE, married **JOHN SPRING**, Knt., of Hitcham and Cockfield, Suffolk, son and heir of Thomas Spring, Gent. or Esq., of Lavenham, Suffolk, and London, merchant, clothmaker, and clothier, by his 1st wife, Anne, daughter of _____ King, Esq., of Boxford, Suffolk. They had one son, William, Knt., and two daughters, Frances and Bridget (wife of Thomas Fleetwood, Esq., and Robert Wingfield, Knt.). He was a legatee in the 1523 will of his father. SIR JOHN SPRING died 12 August 1547, and was buried at Hitcham, Suffolk. He left a will dated 8 June 1544, proved 21 May 1549 (P.C.C. 31 Populwell). They had son, William, Knt., and two daughters, Bridget (wife of Thomas Fleetwood and Robert Wingfield, Knt.) and Frances. His widow, Dorothy, was buried at Cockfield, Suffolk 10 April 1564. She left a will dated 15 April [sic] 1564, proved 10 Nov. 1564 (P.C.C. 30 Stevenson).

> Blomefield *Essay towards a Top. Hist. of Norfolk* 2 (1805): 372. McKeon *Inquiry into the Rights of the Poor, of the Parish of Lavenham* (1829): 85–89. Burke *Gen. & Heraldic Hist. of the Extinct & Dormant Baronetcies* (1844): 500–502 (sub Spring). Hawley et al. *Vis. of Essex 1552, 1558, 1570, 1612 & 1634* 1 (H.S.P. 13) (1878): 119–122 (Waldegrave ped.: "Dorothey [Waldegrave] ux. Sr John Springe of Lanham."), 307–310 (Waldegrave ped.: "Dorathe [Waldegrave] mar. to Sr John Springe Knight."). *Procs. Suffolk Institute of Arch. & Natural Hist.* 5 (1886): 238. Harvey et al. *Vis. of Norfolk 1563 & 1613* (H.S.P. 32) (1891): 295–300 (Waldegrave ped.: "Dorothy [Waldegrave] ux. Willm Spring of Lanham in co. Suff."). Reyce *Suffolk in the XVIIth Cent.: Breviary of Suffolk* (1902): 170–171 (Spring ped.: "Sr John Spring Kt lyeth buried at Hitcham 2: Ed: 6. 1547. = Dorothy da: of Sr Will: Waldegrave kt lyeth buried at Cockfield"). *Rpt. on the MSS of the Earl of Ancaster* (Hist. MSS Comm.) (1907): 488, 489, 490, 491, 493, 494. Brewer *Letters & Papers, Foreign & Domestic, Henry VIII* 1 (1920): 234–256. Harvey *Vis. of Suffolk 1561* 1 (H.S.P. n.s. 2) (1981): 32–35. *NEHGR* 155 (2001): 367–390; 156 (2002): 39–61, 390. Registered will of Thomas Spryng, of Lavenham, Suffolk proved 3 July 1523 (P.C.C. Bodfelde).

16. FRANCES SPRING, married before 8 June 1544 (as his 2nd wife) **EDMUND WRIGHT**, Esq., of Sutton Hall and Burnt Bradfield, Suffolk, and Little Buckenham, Norfolk, Burgess (M.P.) for Steyning, Suffolk, 1559, Escheator for Norfolk and Suffolk, 1553–4, 1560–1, son and heir of Robert Wright, of Burnt Bradfield, Suffolk, by Anne, daughter and co-heiress of Thomas Russell. They had two sons, William and Edmund, and five daughters, Anne (wife of Sir John Heigham), Frances (wife of Thomas Bell), Bridget (wife of Robert Rolfe), Millicent (wife of John Thurston, Esq.), and Mary. In 1554 he and his wife, Frances, were granted the reversion of the manor of Bardsall, Yorkshire. EDMUND WRIGHT, Esq., left a will dated 20 July 1582, proved 4 Feb. 1583/4.

> *Concise Desc. of Bury St. Edmund's* (1827): 261–262. McKeon *Inquiry into the Rights of the Poor, of the parish of Lavenham* (1829): 85–89. Burke *Hist. of the Commoners* 2 (1836): 614–616 (sub Wright). Burke *Gen. & Heraldic Hist. of the Extinct & Dormant Baronetcies* (1844): 500–502 (sub Spring). Hervey *Vis. of Suffolke* 2 (1868): 288–289 (Russell-Wright-Heigham ped.). Harvey et al. *Vis. of Norfolk 1563 & 1613* (H.S.P. 32) (1891): 323 (Wright ped.: "Edmund Wright of

Sutton in Suffolk, after of Little Bucknam in Norfolk. = Frances da. of Sir John Spring.") (Wright arms: Sable, a chevron engrailed between three fleurs-de-lis or, on a chief of the second three spears' heads azure). Reyce *Suffolk in the XVII*[th] *Cent.: Breviary of Suffolk* (1902): 170–171 (Spring ped.: "Frances [Spring] 2: da: = Edmond Wright Esq."). *C.P.R. 1550–1553* (1926): 109. *C.P.R. 1554–1555* (1936): 133. Harvey *Vis. of Suffolk 1561* 2 (H.S.P. n.s. 3) (1984): 270–271. Hasler *House of Commons 1558–1603* 3 (1981): 656–657 (biog. of Edmund Wright). *NEHGR* 155 (2001): 367–390; 156 (2002): 39–61, 390.

17. MARY WRIGHT, daughter and co-heiress. She married about 1578 **WILLIAM DEREHAUGH**, of Badingham, Suffolk, son of John Derehaugh, of Badingham, Suffolk, by Agnes, daughter of Nicholas Thurston. He was born on or about 10 Feb. 1559 (aged 30 in 1590). They had four sons, Edmund, John, Thomas, and Samuel, and six daughters, Mary (wife of John Blome, Gent.), Alice (wife of Reginald Bokenham), Anne, Susan, Dorothy (wife of Francis Noone), and Bridget. He was heir in 1577 to his uncle, George Derehaugh. WILLIAM DEREHAUGH was buried at Badingham, Suffolk 4 Sept. 1610. His widow, Mary, was buried at Badingham, Suffolk 4 March 1621/2. She left a will dated 3 July 1619, proved 14 March 1621/2.

Harvey et al. *Vis. of Suffolk 1561, 1577 & 1612* (1882): 189 (Derhaugh ped.: "William Derhaugh of Colston Hall, co. Suff. = Margaret, youngest da. and co-heir of Edmund Wright of Sutton Hall, co. Suff., and of Little Buckenham, co. Norf.") (Derhaugh arms: Sable three martlets in bend between two bendlets). Harvey et al. *Vis. of Norfolk 1563 & 1613* (H.S.P. 32) (1891): 323 (Wright ped.: "Mary [Wright] ux.... Drew."). *NEHGR* 155 (2001): 367–390; 156 (2002): 39–61, 390.

Child of Mary Wright, by William Derehaugh:

i. **ANNE DEREHAUGH**, married **JOHN STRATTON**, Gent., of Kirkton Hall (in Shotley), Suffolk [see STRATTON 19].

✥ DESPENSER ✥

ALICE OF NORMANDY (sister of King William the Conqueror), married **LAMBERT**, Count of Lens.
JUDITH OF LENS, married **WALTHEOF**, Earl of Northumberland.
MAUD OF NORTHUMBERLAND, married **SIMON DE SENLIS**, Earl of Huntingdon and Northampton.
SIMON DE SENLIS, Earl of Huntingdon and Northampton, married **ISABEL** (or **ELIZABETH**) **OF LEICESTER**.
ISABEL DE SAINT LIZ, married **WILLIAM MAUDUIT**, of Hanslope, Buckinghamshire.
ROBERT MAUDUIT, of Hanslope, Buckinghamshire, married **ISABEL BASSET**.
WILLIAM MAUDUIT, of Hanslope, Buckinghamshire, married **ALICE DE NEWBURGH**.
ISABEL MAUDUIT, married **WILLIAM DE BEAUCHAMP**, Knt., of Elmley, Worcestershire.
WILLIAM DE BEAUCHAMP, Knt., Earl of Warwick, married **MAUD FITZ JOHN** [see BEAUCHAMP 9].

10. ISABEL DE BEAUCHAMP, married (1st) **PATRICK DE CHAWORTH**, Knt. [see CHAWORTH 7], of Kidwelly, Carmarthenshire, Wales, East Garston and North Standen (in Hungerford), Berkshire, Kempsford, Gloucestershire, King's Somborne, Hampshire, Stoke Bruerne, Northamptonshire, Berwick St. James and Standon Chaworth, Wiltshire, etc., younger son of Patrick de Chaworth, Knt., of Kempsford, Gloucestershire, North Standen (in Hungerford), Berkshire, King's Somborne, Hampshire, Stoke Bruerne, Northamptonshire, etc., by Hawise, daughter and heiress of Thomas de London, of Kidwelly, Carmarthenshire, Ogmore, Glamorgan, East Garston, Berkshire, and Hannington, Wiltshire [see CHAWORTH 6 for his ancestry]. He was born about 1254 (aged 24 in 1278). Isabel had the manor of Chedworth, Gloucestershire in free marriage. They had one daughter, Maud. In 1275–6 he arraigned an assize of novel disseisin against Nicholas Attewode and others touching a tenement in Weston Chaurz, Hampshire. In 1276 he witnessed a deed of his older brother, Pain de Chaworth, to Aaron son of Vives, a Jew. He was Captain of the king's munition in Wales in 1277. Sometime during the period, c.1278–82, Patrick witnessed a charter of Guy de Bryan to the burgesses of Laugharne, Carmarthenshire, Wales. He was heir in 1279 to his older brother, Pain de Chaworth, Knt. In 1279–80 Walter atte Berewe arraigned an assize of novel disseisin against Patrick de Chaworth and others touching a tenement in Etloe, Gloucestershire. In 1280–1 the king granted murage to the bailiffs and men of Kidwelly, Carmarthenshire for a term of five years at the instance of Patrick de Chaworth their lord. Patrick fought in Wales in 1282. On 6 June 1283, he confirmed the gift of his brother, Pain de Chaworth, to Godstow Abbey, which provided for the anniversaries of the obits of their mother, Hawise, and grandmother, Eve. SIR PATRICK DE CHAWORTH died testate shortly before 7 July 1283. His widow, Isabel, married (2nd) between 10 Sept. 1285 (record of Highworth Hundred Rolls) and 27 Jan. 1287 (date of fine for marrying without license) **HUGH LE DESPENSER**, Knt., of Loughborough, Arnesby, Barrow, Beaumanor, and Hugglescote (in Ibstock), Leicestershire, Ryhall, Rutlandshire, Wycombe, Buckinghamshire, Maplederwell, Hampshire, Woking, Surrey, Broad Town (then in Cliff-Pippard), Fastern (in Wootton Basset), Wootton Basset, Wiltshire, Barrowby, Hillam, Parlington, and Shippen [Ho], Yorkshire, etc., Justice of the Forest south of Trent, 1297–1307, 1308–11, 1312–15, 1324–6, Privy Councillor, 1297, Warden of the Coasts south of Trent, 1303, Constable of Devizes, Marlborough, Odiham, St. Briavel's, and Striguil Castles, son and heir of Hugh le Despenser, Knt., of Loughborough, Leicestershire, Justiciar of England, by Aline (or Aveline), daughter and heiress of Philip Basset, Knt., Justiciar of England. He was born 1 March 1260/1 (aged 14 in 1275). They had two sons, Hugh, Knt. [2nd Lord Despenser], and Philip, Knt., and four daughters, Aline (wife of Edward Burnell, Knt., Lord Burnell), Isabel, Margaret, and Elizabeth. He was heir in 1275 to his cousin, John le Despenser, by which he inherited the manor of Arnesby, Leicestershire. A letter of William de Valence to John de Kirkby indicates that the Queen exacted 1,000 marks from Hugh because of his marriage. In Jan. 1285 the king took the manor of Bollington, Cheshire because Hugh took emends of ale without warrant. In 1286 and again in 1287, he appointed attorneys, he then going beyond seas. He released all right to his lands and tenements in Soham, Cambridgeshire and Bollington in Macclesfield, Cheshire to the king in 1286–7. He was with the king in Gascony in 1287. In 1289 he was going beyond seas with Roger le Bigod, Earl of Norfolk. He presented to the churches of Cossington, Leicestershire, 1289, Stoke Bruerne, Northamptonshire, 1292, 1304, and Winterbourne Houghton, Dorset, 1316, 1317. In 1292 he was granted a weekly market and year fair at Arnesby, Leicestershire. In 1293 he had license to enclosed 30 acres of wood adjoining his park at Fastern (in Wootton Basset), Wiltshire. In 1293–4 he claimed to have view of frankpledge in his manor of Barrowby, Hillam, Parlington, and Shippen [Ho], Yorkshire, and that he and his men were free from suits of counties, hundreds/wapentakes/ridings, and from sheriff's aid and murdrum and view of frankpledge. He was appointed an envoy to treat with the King of the Romans in 1294. He was summoned to Parliament from 24 June 1295 to 14 March 1321/2, by writs directed *Hugoni le Despenser*, whereby he is held to have become Lord Despenser. In 1295 he was going beyond seas on the king's service. The following year he was going beyond seas on an embassy for the king. In 1297 he was granted 20 oaks fit for timber by the king. The same year he took part in the expedition to Flanders. In 1297 he demised the manor of Arnesby, Leicestershire to two tenants for a term of seven years. In 1298 Maud le Barber of Garscherch testified in London court that Saer le Barber said that Sir Hugh le Despenser "kept more robbers with him than any man in England." In 1299 he was granted the manors of Chelworth and Somerford, Wiltshire, together with the bailiwick of the Forest of Braydon, by his kinsman, Robert de Kaynes (or Kaignes). He was present at the Siege of Caerlaverock in 1300. In 1300 he was going to the court of Rome on the king's special affairs. In 1301 Ralph Pipard granted him the manor of Great Haseley, Oxfordshire. In 1302 Robert de Kaynes, Knt. conveyed to him the manors of Tarrant Keyneston, Dorset and two parts of the manor of Newentone, Wales, together with the reversion of the manors of Dodford, Northamptonshire, Oxhill, Warwickshire, Coombe Keynes, Wiltshire, and a third part of Newentone, Wales. He took part in the negotiations with France which preceded the peace of

1303. In 1305 he was sent as Joint Ambassador to Pope Clement V at Lyons, where he obtained a bull absolving the king from the oaths which he had taken to his people. In Feb. 1306 Hugh received a papal indult to have a portable altar. His wife, Isabel, died shortly before 30 May 1306. At the Coronation of King Edward II in 1308, he carried part of the royal insignia. In the quarrel about Peter de Gavaston in 1308, Hugh alone sided with the king against the barons. He was regarded as a deserter from the common cause, and the parliament which met at Northampton procured his dismissal from the king's council. His disgrace was not of long duration; he received the castles of Devizes and Marlborough, and became the chief adviser of the king. On the death of Gavaston in 1312, he became the chief man of the court party, and encouraged the king to form plans of revenge against the barons. He was present at the Battle of Bannockburn 24 June 1314, and accompanied the king in his flight to Dunbar, and thence by sea to Berwick. About this time his son, Sir Hugh le Despenser, joined the king's side. He was appointed Ambassador to Pope John XXII in 1319, and Joint Ambassador to the Pope in 1320. In May and June 1321 the barons of the Welsh Marches and their adherents ravaged the lands of the younger Despenser in Wales and those of the elder throughout the country. In August of that year both Despensers were accused in Parliament, chiefly on account of the son's misconduct, of many misdeeds, including appropriating royal power to themselves, counselling the King evilly, and replacing good ministers by bad ones. They were then disinherited and exiled from the realm. The elder Hugh accordingly retired to the Continent. The sentence on the Despensers was pronounced unlawful at a provincial council of the clergy about 1 Jan. 1321/2. In March following, the elder Hugh accompanied the King against the contrariants, and was present at the judgment on Thomas, Earl of Lancaster. The proceedings against the Despensers were annulled and cancelled, and his lands restored 7 May 1322. He was created Earl of Winchester 10 May 1322, and granted £20 yearly from the issues of Hampshire, together with the Castle and manor of Brimpsfield, Gloucestershire, and the manors of Badgeworth and Syde, Gloucestershire, Ashton Giffard, Codford St. Peter, Sherrington, and Stapleford, Wiltshire (formerly belonging to John Giffard), as well as other lands formerly belonging to Thomas Mauduit, Henry le Tyeys, Warin de Lisle, and John de Kyngeston. The queen hated the Despensers, and when some difficulty arose in France, she gladly left the kingdom on an embassy to her brother, King Charles IV of France. When the queen landed in England with an armed force in Sept. 1326, she put out a proclamation against the Despensers. On the king's flight to Wales in October 1326, Earl Hugh was dispatched to defend Bristol, which, however, he at once surrendered on the arrival of the Queen. The next day, 27 October 1326, SIR HUGH LE DESPENSER, Earl of Winchester, was tried — without being allowed to speak in his own defence — condemned to death as a traitor, and hanged on the common gallows, all his honours forfeited. His head was sent to Winchester.

Bridges *Hist. & Antiqs. of Northamptonshire* 1 (1791): 325. Nichols *Hist. & Antiqs. of Leicester* 3(1) (1800): 136–137. Cobbett's *Complete Coll. of State Trials* 1 (1809): 23–38 (Proceedings against Hugh and Hugh le Despenser). Blore *Hist. & Antiqs. of Rutland* 1(2) (1811): 19 (Despenser ped.), 32–35. Brydges *Collins' Peerage of England* 6 (1812): 496–511 (sub Despenser). Dugdale *Monasticon Anglicanum* 5 (1825): 591. Nicolas *Siege of Carlaverock* (1828): 190–192 (biog. of Hugh le Despenser). Baker *Hist. & Antiqs. of Northampton* 2 (1836–41): 218–219 (Beauchamp ped.), 239–240 (Bruere or Briwere ped.). Palgrave *Antient Kalendars & Inventories of the Treasury of His Majesty's Exchequer* 1 (1836): 62. Palgrave *Docs. & Recs. Ill. the Hist. of Scotland* 1 (1837): 226 ("Hug' le Despenc[er] Mil[es]" included on list of people owing military service in 1300). Hutchins *Hist. & Antiqs. of Dorset* 1 (1861): 296. *Arch. Cambrensis* 3rd Ser. 8 (1862): 281 (13th Cent. Chronicle: "Anno mcclxxxiii°. [A.D. 1283] — Obiit Patricius Chavard."); 4th Ser. 9 (1878): 99–100. Lennard & Vincent *Vis. of Warwick 1619* (H.S.P. 12) (1877): 282–285 (Spencer ped.: "Hugo le Despensor Comes Wintoniæ 18 E. 2 decollatus 19 E. 2. = Isabella fil. Willi Beauchamp Com. Warw."). Burke *Dormant, Abeyant, Forfeited & Extinct Peerages* (1883): 165–167 (sub Despenser). *Annual Rpt. of the Deputy Keeper* 45 (1885): 354; 46 (1886): 119; 49 (1888): 62; 50 (1889): 127. Doyle *Official Baronage of England* 3 (1886): 695–697 (sub Winchester). C.P.R. 1281–1292 (1893): 248, 267–268, 325. *Cal. Entries Papal Regs.: Letters* 2 (1895): 4 (William de Handlo [Haudlo], clerk, styled "kinsman" of Hugh le Despenser), 9, 541. C.P.R. 1292–1301 (1895): 42, 72–73, 170, 206–207, 211, 224, 226, 293, 306, 535, 561, 600. Fry & Fry *Abs. of Feet of Fines Rel. Dorset* 1 (Dorset Rec. Soc. 5) (1896): 264–265. Dallas & Porter *Note-book of Tristram Risdon* (1897): 74–75. C.C.R. 1272–1279 (1900): 345. *Desc. Cat. Ancient Deeds* 3 (1900): 97–107, 107–118 (Sir

Hugh le Despenser styled "kinsman" by Robert de Kaynes in 1299), 226–238; 4 (1902): 48 (Sir Alan de Elsefeld [Ellesfield] styled "kinsman" by Hugh le Despenser in undated grant), 89. *C.P.R. 1272–1281* (1901): 439. *English Hist. Rev.* 18 (1903): 112–116; 99 (1984): 1–33. Wrottesley *Peds. from the Plea Rolls* (1905): 544. *D.N.B.* 5 (1908): 863–865 (biog. of Hugh le Despenser, the elder: "Both the Despensers received many large grants from the crown; they were generally hated, and were accused of many acts of oppression and wrong dealing … Greedy and ambitious, they used the influence they gained over the king for their own aggrandisement."). VCH *Hampshire* 4 (1911): 150–151. VCH *Surrey* 3 (1911): 381–390. Wedgwood *Staffordshire Coats of Arms* (Colls. Hist. Staffs. 3rd Ser. 1913) (1913): 298 (his seal bearing a shield displaying quarterly, in the 2nd and 3rd quarters, a fret, over all a bend). *C.P.* 4 (1916): 262–266 (sub Despenser); 9 (1936): 142; 11 (1949): 298–299 (sub Saint Amand); 12 (2) (1959): 754 (sub Winchester). *Cal. Inqs. Misc.* 2 (1916): 245 (In 1327 William Fitz Matthew, former keeper of Odiham park, claimed he was removed as keeper by Hugh le Despenser the younger because he "levied hue and cry" upon Isabel the said Hugh's mother who was taking 5 bucks in the park without warrant). Farrer *Honors & Knights' Fees* 1 (1923): 233–234. Thomas *Cal. Early Mayor's Court Rolls 1298–1307* (1924): 23. VCH *Berkshire* 4 (1924): 158–162. Salter *Boarstall Cartulary* (Oxford Hist. Soc. 1st Ser. 88) (1930): 107–108, 300, 312, 318. Richardson & Sayles *Rotuli Parl. Anglie Hactenus Inediti 1274–1373* (Camden Soc. 3rd Ser. 51) (1935): 12. Stokes et al. *Warwickshire Feet of Fines* 2 (Dugdale Soc. 15) (1939): 111–112. Hethe *Reg. Hamonis Hethe Diocesis Roffensis* 1 (Canterbury & York Soc. 48) (1948): 334–335. Paget *Baronage of England* (1957) 28: 1–5 (sub Basset). Farr *Rolls of Highworth Hundred 1275–1287* (Wiltshire Arch. & Nat. Hist. Soc. Recs. Branch 21) 1 (1966): 142, 144–147, 149–150, 152, 154, 156–157; 2 (Wiltshire Arch. & Nat. Hist. Soc. Recs. Branch 22) (1968): 201, 203, 206, 208, 211–212, 215–216, 219, 221, 223, 251–252, 294–297. VCH *Gloucester* 11 (1976): 285–288. *Ancient Deeds — Ser. A* 1 (List & Index Soc. 151) (1978): 166 (Hugh styled "kinsman" by Robert de Kaines [Kaynes] son of Sir Robert de Kaines [Kaynes]). *Ancient Deeds — Ser. AS & WS* (List & Index Soc. 158) (1979): 5 (Deed A.S.20), 8 (Deed A.S.41), 12 (Deed A.S.63). Rogers *Lacock Abbey Charters* (Wiltshire Rec. Soc. 34) (1979): 80 (charter of Hugh le Despenser dated 1299). Hill *Rolls & Reg. of Bishop Oliver Sutton 1280–1299* 8 (Lincoln Rec. Soc. 76) (1986): 42. *NEHGR* 145 (1991): 258–268. Kirby *Hungerford Cartulary* (Wiltshire Rec. Soc. 49) (1994): 154. English *Yorkshire Hundred & Quo Warranto Rolls* (Yorkshire Arch. Soc. Recs. 151) (1996): 274. Parsons *Eleanor of Castile: Queen & Soc.* (1997): 44, 163, 171. VCH *Cambridge* 10 (2002): 500. Online resource: http:// www.briantimms.net/era/ lord_marshals/Lord_Marshal02/Lord%20Marshal2.htm (Lord Marshal's Roll — arms of Hugh le Despenser: Quarterly argent and gules fretty or overall a bendlet sable).

Child of Isabel de Beauchamp, by Patrick de Chaworth, Knt.:

i. **MAUD DE CHAWORTH**, married **HENRY OF LANCASTER**, Knt., Earl of Lancaster and Leicester, Lord of Monmouth [see LANCASTER 8].

Children of Isabel de Beauchamp, by Hugh le Despenser, Knt.:

i. **HUGH LE DESPENSER**, Knt., 2nd Lord Despenser [see next].

ii. **PHILIP LE DESPENSER**, Knt., of Goxhill, Lincolnshire, married **MARGARET DE GOUSHILL** [see NETTLESTEAD 11].

iii. **ALINE LE DESPENSER**, married **EDWARD BURNELL**, Knt., Lord Burnell [see BURNELL 9.i].

iv. **ISABEL LE DESPENSER**, married (1st) **GILBERT DE CLARE** [see BADLESMERE 8.i]; (2nd) **JOHN DE HASTINGS**, Knt., 1st Lord Hastings [see HASTINGS 10]; (3rd) **RALPH DE MONTHERMER**, Knt., 1st Lord Monthermer [see CLARE 8].

v. **MARGARET LE DESPENSER**, married **JOHN DE SAINT AMAND**, Knt., 2nd Lord Saint Amand [see SAINT AMAND 11].

vi. **ELIZABETH LE DESPENSER**, married **RALPH DE CAMOYS**, Knt., 1st Lord Camoys [see CAMOYS 6].

11. HUGH LE DESPENSER, Knt., styled "the younger," of Hanley Castle, Worcestershire, King's Chamberlain, Constable of Odiham Castle, Keeper of the castle and town of Dryslwyn, and Cantref Mawr, Carmarthenshire, Keeper of the Castle and town of Portchester, Keeper of the Castle, town and barton of Bristol, Keeper of the Castles, manor, and lands of Brecknock, Hay, Cantref Selyf, etc., Breconshire, and Huntington, Herefordshire, son and heir. He married at Westminster shortly after 14 June 1306 **ELEANOR DE CLARE**, daughter of Gilbert de Clare, Knt., Earl of Gloucester and Hertford, by his 2nd wife, Joan of Acre, daughter of Edward I, King of England [see CLARE 8 for her ancestry]. She was born at Caerphilly, Glamorgan shortly before 23 Nov. 1292 (date of her mother's churching). They had five sons, Hugh, Knt. [3rd Lord le

Despenser], Edward, Knt., Gilbert, Knt., John, and Philip, and five daughters, Isabel, Joan (nun at Shaftesbury Abbey), Eleanor (nun at Sempringham Priory), Margaret (nun at Whatton Priory), and Elizabeth. In 1310 he purchased the manor of Winstone, Gloucestershire from Geoffrey de Pulham. He presented to the church of Winstone, Gloucestershire in 1311. He accompanied the King to Pontoise in 1313. His wife, Eleanor, was co-heiress in 1314 to her brother, Gilbert de Clare, Knt., Earl of Gloucester and Hertford, by which she inherited the lordship of Glamorgan in Wales, including the castles of Llanblethian, Kenfeg, Neath, Llantrisant, Caerphilly, and Whitchurch, and the manor of Stanford in the Vale, Berkshire. He was summoned to Parliament from 29 July 1314 to 10 October 1325, by writs directed *Hugoni le Despenser juniori*. From Nov. 1317 his influence at court rapidly increased, and, by the end of the following year, he won a lasting ascendancy over the king's mind. In 1320–1 John de Cromwell, Knt., Lord Cromwell, and his wife, Idoine, settled the manors of Amersham, Buckland, and Singleborough (in Great Horwood), Buckinghamshire, Moulton, Potterspury, and Yardley, Northamptonshire, Perlethorpe, Nottinghamshire, Winderton (in Brailes), Warwickshire, West Winterslow, Wiltshire, etc. on themselves for the life of Idoine, with successive remainders to Hugh le Despenser, Knt., the younger and Hugh le Despenser, Knt. the elder for life, and to Edward son of Hugh le Despenser, Knt. the younger and his heirs. In 1320 the king seized the lordship of Gower in Wales, as a means of conferring it on him. The dispute over this seizure united a powerful group of Welsh marcher lords in a coalition against Hugh; moreover, his rule in Glamorgan was intensely unpopular with the Welsh. Civil war broke out May 4, 1321, and the lordship of Glamorgan was quickly overrun and devastated. Hugh and his father were subsequently banished by Parliament 14 August 1321. The royalist counter-offensive against the baronial opposition began in October 1321. Following the royalist victory at the Battle of Boroughbridge 16 March 1321/2, Parliament in May 1322 reversed the sentences on the Despensers, who were allowed to return from exile. Hugh recovered the lordships of Glamorgan and Gower. From 1322 to 1326 he directed England's internal and foreign policy. By fraud and violence, he accumulated enormous possessions in both England and Wales. The revolution of 1326 was the inevitable result of the misgovernment of the Despensers. In Sept. 1326 Queen Isabel (wife of King Edward II) and Roger de Mortimer landed at Orwell, Suffolk, with a force of 700 mercenaries hired from the Count of Hainault. In a matter of weeks, the government of the Despensers collapsed. On October 2, King Edward II left London and fled to south Wales, accompanied by Hugh the younger. They were captured near Llantrisant, Glamorgan 16 Nov. 1326. SIR HUGH LE DESPENSER, 2nd Lord le Despenser, was taken to Hereford, and executed there 24 Nov. 1326. In 1330 his bones were collected and buried at Tewkesbury Abbey, Gloucestershire. His widow, Eleanor, was treated with remarkable leniency and her inheritance was restored to her 22 April 1328. Shortly before 26 Jan. 1328/9, she was abducted from Hanley Castle, Worcestershire and married without royal license **WILLIAM LA ZOUCHE MORTIMER**,[16] Knt., 1st Lord Zouche of Richard's Castle, of Ashby de la Zouch, Leicestershire, Fulbourn and Swavesey, Cambridgeshire, and Nutbourn (in Pulborough) and Treve (or River) (in Tillington), Sussex, Justice

---

[16] For instances of the style "William la Zouche Mortimer" in contemporary records, see Horwood *Year Books of Edward III: Years XI & XII* (Roll Ser. 31(6)) (1883): 346–349; *Year Books of Edward III, Years XIV & XV* (Rolls Ser. 31(10)) (1889): 122–125; *Genealogist* n.s. 8 (1892): 36; *C.P.R. 1334–1338* (1895): 164; *Papal Regs.: Letters* 2 (1895): 394; Ralph of Shrewsbury *Reg. of Ralph of Shrewsbury Bishop of Bath & Wells* 1 (Somerset Rec. Soc. 9) (1896): 275, 338; Wrottesley *Crécy & Calais* (1898): 100; *Year Books of Edward III, Years XVIII & XIX* (Rolls Ser. 31(17)) (1905): 302–313; *Year Books of Edward III, Year XIX* (Rolls Ser. 31(18)) (1906): 92–95. For an instance of the style "William la Zouche de Mortimer," see National Archives, SC 8/179/8915 (available at www.catalogue.nationalarchives.gov.uk/search.asp). For instance of the styles "William la Souche" and "William de la Zouche," see Crowley *Wiltshire Tax List of 1332* (Wiltshire Rec. Soc. 45) (1989): 17, 112.

in Eyre for forest pleas in Essex, Joint Keeper of Caerphilly Castle, Keeper of Glamorgan and Morganno, Chamberlain of Cardiff, Keeper of the Tower of London, Justice of the Forest south of Trent, 1328, and, in right of his 1st wife, of Walthamstow, Essex, Flamstead, Hertfordshire, Wyke or Rumboldswyke (in Rumboldswyke), Sussex, Cherhill, Newton Tony, and Stratford Tony, Wiltshire, Elmley Lovett, Worcestershire, etc., younger son of Robert de Mortimer, of Richard's Castle and Puddlestone, Herefordshire, Burford, Milson, and Tilsop (in Burford), Shropshire, by Joyce, daughter of William la Zouche [see RICHARD'S CASTLE 3 for his ancestry] [see BEAUCHAMP 10 for the details of the remaining portion of their lives]. They had two sons, Hugh, Knt., and William (clerk). Sir William la Zouche Mortimer, 1st Lord Zouche of Richard's Castle, died 28 Feb. 1336/7, and was buried at Tewkesbury Abbey, Gloucestershire. His widow, Eleanor, died testate 30 June 1337.

Sandford *Gen. Hist. of the Kings of England* (1677): 140–141. Nichols *Hist. & Antiqs. of Leicester* 3(2) (1804): 635 (Zouch ped.). *Cobbett's Complete Coll. of State Trials* 1 (1809): 23–38 (Procs. against Hugh and Hugh le Despenser). Blore *Hist. & Antiqs. of Rutland* 1(2) (1811): 19 (Despenser ped.), 35–36. Brydges *Collins' Peerage of England* 6 (1812): 496–511 (sub Despenser). Clutterbuck *Hist. & Antiqs. of Hertford* 1 (1815): 354 (Tony ped.), 358 (Beauchamp ped.). Dugdale *Monasticon Anglicanum* 2 (1819): 59–65; 6(1) (1830): 110 (charter of William la Zouche). Burke *Dict. of the Peerages… Extinct, Dormant & in Abeyance* (1831): 171–174 (sub Despenser), 587 (sub Zouche). Banks *Baronies in Fee* 1 (1844): 337–338 (sub Mortimer), 472 (sub Zouche of Mortimer). Lipscomb *Hist. & Antiqs. of Buckingham* 1 (1847): 200–201 (Clare ped.). Brewer *Monumenta Franciscana* 1 (Rolls Ser. 4) (1858): 513–514. Luard *Annales Monastici* 4 (Rolls Ser. 36) (1869): 511 (Annals of Worcester sub A.D. 1292 — "Die Sancti Clementis [23 November] … et Johanna comitissa Gloucestriæ in castro de Kaerfili post partum filiæ purificata"). *Jour. British Arch. Assoc.* 26 (1870): 149–160. Lennard & Vincent *Vis. of Warwick 1619* (H.S.P. 12) (1877): 282–285 (Spencer ped.: "Hugo le Despensor Com. Gloucest. creat's 20 E. 2 iure uxoris, decollatus 1326. = Elianor fil. et heres Gilb'ti de Clare Comitis. Glou' et Hertford."). Turner *Cal. Charters & Rolls: Bodleian Lib.* (1878): 674. Burke *Dormant, Abeyant, Forfeited & Extinct Peerages* (1883): 165–167 (sub Despenser). Clark *Land of Morgan* (1883): 93–166. *Trans. Shropshire Arch. & Nat. Hist. Soc.* 6 (1883): 327–328. *Desc. Cat. Ancient Deeds* 1 (1890): 21 (Hugh le Despenser the younger styled "kinsman" by Alice de Lacy, wife of Thomas, Earl of Lancaster). *Genealogist* n.s. 8 (1892): 36; n.s. 18 (1902): 110. *Papal Regs.: Letters* 2 (1895): 394. Fry & Fry *Abs. of Feet of Fines Rel. Dorset* 1 (Dorset Rec. Soc. 5) (1896): 328–329. *English Hist. Rev.* 12 (1897): 755–761; 70 (1955): 261–267; 99 (1984): 1–33. Wrottesley *Peds. from the Plea Rolls* (1905): 7, 133–134, 273. *Year Books of Edward III, Years XVIII & XIX* 12 (Rolls Ser. 31b) (1905): 302–313; *Year XIX* 13 (Rolls Ser. 31b) (1906): 92–95. *C.Ch.R.* 3 (1908): 448 (wife Eleanor styled "king's niece"). *D.N.B.* 5 (1908): 865–867 (biog. of Hugh le Despenser, the younger). VCH *Buckingham* 2 (1908): 328; 3 (1925): 70–71; 4 (1927): 25. *C.P.* 1 (1910): 242–244 (sub Arundel); 2 (1912): 130 (sub Berkeley); 4 (1916): 267–271 (sub Despenser), Appendix H, 671 (chart); 5 (1926): 708, footnote a (sub Gloucester); 7 (1929): 222, footnote m (sub Kildare). Clark *Cartæ et Alia Munimenta de Glamorgancia* 4 (1910): 1213–1227. VCH *Hampshire* 4 (1911): 560–563. VCH *Surrey* 4 (1912): 92–102. *Trans. Leicestershire Arch. Soc.* 11 (1913–20): 377–378. *Cal. MSS in Various Colls.* 7 (Hist. MSS Comm. 55) (1914): 36 (grant by Hugh le Despenser the younger). *Trans. Royal Hist. Soc.* 3rd Ser. 9 (1915): 21–64. Kingsford *Stonor Letters & Papers 1290–1483* 1 (Camden Soc. 3rd Ser. 29) (1919): 3 (letter of Eleanor le Despenser dated c.1326). Gretton *Burford Recs.* (1920). VCH *Berkshire* 4 (1924): 100, 479–480 (Despenser arms: Argent quartered with gules fretty or on a bend sable over all). *Cal. Chancery Warrants* (1927): 519 & 529 (Hugh styled "king's nephew"), 526 (Eleanor styled "king's niece"). Reynolds *Reg. of Walter Reynolds Bishop of Worcester* (Dugdale Soc. 9) (1928): 153. Reichel *Devon Feet of Fines* 2 (Devon & Cornwall Rec. Soc. 1939) (1939): 234–236. Stokes et al. *Warwickshire Feet of Fines* 2 (Dugdale Soc. 15) (1939): 111–112. Hatton *Book of Seals* (1950): 125. Chaplais *War of Saint-Sardos 1323–1325* (Camden Soc. 3rd Ser. 87) (1954): vi, 75 & 80 (Ralph Basset of Drayton styled "cousin" by Hugh le Despenser), 78 (Richard de Grey of Codnor styled "cousin" by Hugh le Despenser), 88 (Hugh le Despenser styled "cousin" by John de Segrave), 217 (Hugh le Despenser styled "cousin" by John de Warenne, Earl of Surrey). *Speculum* 30 (1955): 207–212. Paget *Baronage of England* (1957) 182: 1–2 (sub Despenser). Sanders *English Baronies* (1960): 6, 9–10. Smith *Itinerary of John Leland* 4 (1964): 150–163. *Year Books of Edward II* 25 (Selden Soc. 81) (1964): 13–14. Pugh *Middle Ages: Marcher Lordships of Glamorgan, Morgannwg, Gower & Kilvey* (Glamorgan County Hist. 3) (1971): 167–204 ("… Chroniclers of Edward II's reign depict [Hugh le Despenser] as a man of reckless and unbounded ambition… Throughout his tenure of power, Despenser's acts were the consequence of necessity or self-interest"). VCH *Middlesex* 4 (1971): 71, 156. VCH *Cambridge* 5 (1973): 201. *Ancient Deeds — Ser. B* 2 (List & Index Soc. 101) (1974): B.8538. VCH *Gloucester* 11 (1976): 147–148. *Ancient Deeds — Ser. AS & WS* (List & Index Soc. 158) (1979): 9 (Deed A.S.49). Fryde *Tyranny & Fall of Edward II* (1979). London *Cartulary of Bradenstoke Priory* (Wiltshire Rec. Soc. 35) (1979): 133 (charter of William de la Zouche, lord of Glamorgan and Margam, and Eleanor his wife), 134. Ellis *Cat. Seals in the P.R.O.* 2 (1981): 33 (seal of Hugh le Despenser the younger dated 1319 — Hung from a leopard's face between two branches, a shield of arms: quarterly, in the second and third quarters a fret, overall a bend and a label of three points. The first and fourth quarters are stippled. On either side, a wyvern. Legend: S'HVGONIS LE DEPE[NS]ER.). Merrick *Morganiae Archaiographia* (South Wales Rec. Soc. 1) (1983): 41–52. Schwennicke *Europäische Stammtafeln* 3(1) (1984): 156 (sub Clare). *Bull. Inst. Hist. Research* 58 (1985): 95–100. Hicks *Who's Who in Late Medieval England* (1991): 63–65 (biog. of Hugh Despenser the younger: "… the evil genius of the Despenser dictatorship of 1322–26… He was greedy, arrogant and supremely self-confidant."). *TAG* 69 (1994): 129–139. Given-Wilson *Ill. Hist. of Late Medieval England* (1996): chart opp. 61 (temp. King Edward IV). Brault *Rolls of Arms Edward I* 2 (1997): 140–141 (arms of Hugh le Despenser the younger: Quarterly argent, and gules fretty or, a bend sable, a label azure). *Nottingham Medieval Studies* 41 (1997): 153 (chart). Underhill *For Her Good Estate* (1999). Vale *Princely Court* (2001): 313. Roper *Feet of Fines for the County of York* 1314–1326 (Yorkshire Arch. Soc. Recs. 158) (2006): 107. National Archives, E 40/198 (Hugh le Despenser the younger styled "kinsman" in 1322 by Alice de Lacy, widow of Thomas, Earl of Lancaster); SC 8/120/5962 (available at www.catalogue.nationalarchives.gov.uk/search.asp). National Archives, CP 25/1/205/21, #15 [see abstract of fine at http://www.medievalgenealogy.org.uk/index.html].

Children of Hugh le Despenser, Knt., by Eleanor de Clare:

i. **HUGH LE DESPENSER**, Knt., lord of Glamorgan and Morgannwg, Wales, and of Tewkesbury, Gloucestershire, Maplederwell, Hampshire, Tooting Bec (in Streatham), Surrey, Broad Town (then in Cliff-Pippard), Wiltshire, Hanley, Worcestershire, etc., and, in right of his wife, of Barrow, Suffolk, son and heir, born about 1308 (aged 18 in 1326). He successfully defended Caerphilly Castle against Queen Isabel's forces in 1327, until he obtained pardon of his life. He was imprisoned at Bristol Castle 15 Dec. 1328, and not released until 5 July 1331. In 1332 he was about to go on a pilgrimage to Santiago. In 1332 he was granted manors of Thorley, Hampshire and Frithby, Leicestershire. In 1334 the king granted him the manor of Ashley, together with lands in Little Somborne, Hampshire. In 1336 Hugh le Despenser, Knt., his step-father, William la Zouche Mortimer, and four others acknowledged that they owed debts of £266 to Asselmo Symonete, and £1600 to Gwido de La Chouche, merchants of Lucca, which debts they had not paid. He had livery of his mother's lands 21 July 1337. He was summoned to Parliament from 15 Nov. 1338 to 1 Jan. 1348/9 by writs directed *Hugoni le Despenser*, whereby he is held to have become Lord Despenser. He was in the Scottish wars, Nov. 1337–1338, and present at the Battle of Sluys 24 June 1340. He married after 31 May 1341 (by dispensation dated 27 April 1341, he and her former husband being related in the 3rd degree of kindred) **ELIZABETH DE MONTAGU**, widow of Giles de Badlesmere, Knt., 2nd Lord Badlesmere (died 7 June 1338) [see BADLESMERE 9.i], and daughter of William de Montagu, Knt., 1st Earl of Salisbury, 3rd Lord Montagu, Marshal of England, by Katherine, daughter of William de Grandison (or Graunson), Knt., 1st Lord Grandison [see MONTAGU 7 for her ancestry]. They had no issue. During the Breton civil war, he served as a captain in the English army which defeated the French at Morlaix in 1342. In 1343 he gave a yearly rent of 10 marks from his manor of Broad Town, Wiltshire to Shaftesbury Abbey, Dorset, for the life of his sister, Joan, a nun in the Abbey. In 1344 he sued Anthony Citroun regarding waste in the manor of Great Marlow, Buckinghamshire. The same year he and his wife, Elizabeth, were granted an indult for a portable altar. He accompanied the King to France in July 1346, and was in the King's retinue at the Battle of Crécy. He was present at the Siege of Calais, which surrendered 4 August 1347. SIR HUGH LE DESPENSER, 3rd Lord le Despenser, died 8 Feb. 1348/9, and was buried in Tewkesbury Abbey, Gloucestershire. He left a will proved in 1349. His widow, Elizabeth, married (3rd) before 10 July 1350 (as his 2nd wife) **GUY DE BRYAN** (or **BRIAN**), K.G., Lord Bryan [see CAREW 10.ii], of Laugharne, Carmarthenshire, Clifton Dartmouth and Hardness and Slapton, Devon, etc., Governor of St. Briavel's Castle, Warden of the Forest of Dean, son and heir of Guy de Bryan, Knt., of Walwyns Castle, Pembrokeshire, Battleford (in Ipplepen), Clifton Dartmouth and Hardness, Tor Bryan, Devon, etc., by Gwenllian, daughter of Gruffudd ap Lloyd. He was born about 1309 (being of age in 1330). They had three sons, Guy, Knt., William, Knt. [see ECHINGHAM 10], and Philip. He was first armed at Stannow Park in 1327. In 1330 the king settled a dispute between him and his father, Guy de Bryan, senior, relative to the barony and castle of Walwayn, Pembrokeshire. In 1349 he was granted an annuity of 200 marks for bearing the King's Standard against his enemies at Calais. He was summoned to Parliament from 25 Nov. 1350 to 6 Dec. 1389, whereby he is held to have become Lord Bryan. He was constantly entrusted with martial and diplomatic affairs of the highest importance. His wife, Elizabeth, died at Ashley, Hampshire 30 (or 31) July 1359, and was buried with her 2nd husband in Tewkesbury Abbey, Gloucestershire. In 1361 he was Ambassador to the Pope. In 1369 he was appointed Admiral of the Fleet. In 1367 he purchased the manor of Woodsford, Dorset from John Whitfield, Knt. In 1377 he gave an endowment to four chaplains for the chapel of St. Mary at Slapton, Devon, which he augmented in 1386 and again in 1389. SIR GUY DE BRYAN, Lord Bryan, died 17 August 1390, and was buried in Tewkesbury Abbey, Gloucestershire. Pole *Colls. towards a Desc. of Devon* (1791): 274–275, 286–287. *Archaeologia* 14 (1803): 143–153. Banks *Dormant & Extinct Baronage of England* 2 (1808): 63–65 (sub Bryan). Blore *Hist. & Antiqs. of Rutland* 1(2) (1811): 19 (Despenser ped.), 36–37. Brydges *Collins' Peerage of England* 6 (1812): 496–511 (sub Despenser). Dugdale *Monasticon Anglicanum* 2 (1819): 59–65. Nicolas *Controversy between Scrope & Grosvenor* 2 (1832): 245–255 (biog. of Sir Guy Bryan). *Coll. Top. et Gen.* 3 (1836): 250–

278 (re. Bryan fam.). *Gentleman's Mag.* n.s. 12 (1839): 18–22. Beltz *Mems. of the Order of the Garter* (1841): clii. Hutchins *Hist. & Antiqs. of Dorset* 1 (1861): 448 (Bryan ped.); 3 (1868): 291 (Montagu ped.). *Fifth Rpt.* (Hist. MSS Comm. 4) (1876): 603 (charter of Guy de Bryan). Daniel-Tyssen *Royal Charters & Hist. Docs. Rel. the Town & County of Carmarthen* (1878): 48, footnote 4. Burke *Dormant, Abeyant, Forfeited & Extinct Peerages* (1883): 165–167 (sub Despenser). *Year Books of Edward III: Years XIV & XV* 5 (Rolls Ser. 31b) (1889): 122–125; *Year Books of Edward III: Years XVIII & XIX* 12 (Rolls Ser. 31b) (1905): 302–313; *Year XIX* 13 (Rolls Ser. 31b) (1906): 92–95. *Genealogist* n.s. 8 (1892): 36. *Cal. Entries Papal Regs.: Letters* 2 (1895): 553. *Papal Regs.: Petitions* 1 (1896): 103 (Hugh styled "king's kinsman"). Ralph of Shrewsbury *Reg. of Ralph of Shrewsbury Bishop of Bath & Wells* 1 (Somerset Rec. Soc. 9) (1896): 275, 338. *Papal Regs.: Letters* 3 (1897): 146. *C.P.R. 1338–1340* (1898): 4, 201, 447, 518 (instances of Hugh styled "king's kinsman"), 328. Wrottesley *Peds. from the Plea Rolls* (1905): 228, 236–237. VCH *Dorset* 2 (1908): 73–79. *Rpt. & Trans. Devonshire Assoc.* 3rd Ser. 3 (1911): 132, 137, 191, 210–211. VCH *Hampshire* 4 (1911): 150–151, 481; 5 (1912): 284–285. *C.P.* 2 (1912): 201, footnote b (sub Bohun), 361–362 (sub Bryan); 4 (1916): 271–274 (sub Despenser); 14 (1998): 118 (sub Bryan). VCH *Surrey* 4 (1912): 92–102, 249. Woodruff & Churchill *Sede Vacante Wills* (Kent Arch. Soc. Recs. 3) (1914): 38. *C.C.R. 1381–1385* (1920): 167–168. VCH *Buckingham* 3 (1925): 70–71. *C.F.R.* 10 (1929): 359. Reichel *Devon Feet of Fines* 2 (Devon & Cornwall Rec. Soc. 1939) (1939): 392, 400. Hethe *Reg. Hamonis Hethe Diocesis Roffensis* 2 (Canterbury & York Soc. 49) (1948): 810. Paget *Baronage of England* (1957) 20: 1 (sub Badlesmere). Smith *Itinerary of John Leland* 4 (1964): 150–163. Haines *Cal. Reg. of Wolstan de Bransford Bishop of Worcester* (Worcestershire Hist. Soc. n.s. 4) (1966): 79. VCH *Wiltshire* 9 (1970): 23–43. Pugh *Middle Ages: Marcher Lordships of Glamorgan, Morgannwg, Gower & Kilvey* (Glamorgan County Hist. 3) (1971): 176–177. *Ancient Deeds — Ser. B* 2 (List & Index Soc. 101) (1974): B.7233, B.8656. VCH *Somerset* 3 (1974): 111–120, 129–153. MacCulloch *Chorography of Suffolk* (Suffolk Rec. Soc. 19) (1976): 28. Ellis *Cat. Seals in the P.R.O.* 2 (1981): 18 (seal of Guy de Bryan dated 1383 — Hanging from a twin oak tree, growing from a mount below, a shield of arms: three piles in point (hatched). Upon either side, holding the strap in its beak, a gryphon. Legend: SIGILLUM: GUYDO/NIS: DE: BRYENE). Merrick *Morganiae Archaiographia* (South Wales Rec. Soc. 1) (1983): 41–52. Higginbotham *Traitor's Wife* (2005): 471–472. Emery *Greater Medieval Houses of England & Wales* 3 (2006): 687.

ii. **EDWARD LE DESPENSER**, Knt. [see next].

iii. **GILBERT LE DESPENSER**, Knt., younger son. He was granted the manor of Melton Mowbray, Leicestershire by his uncle, King Edward II, in 1322, subject to a life estate reserved to his mother, Eleanor. As an adult, he was granted the manors of Thorley, Hampshire and Broad Town (in Cliffe Pypard), Wiltshire by his brother, Hugh le Despenser. He served as a knight in King Edward III's household. In 1368 he received a grant of 40 marks per annum at the Exchequer for life. SIR GILBERT LE DESPENSER died without issue 23 April 1381. Nichols *Hist. & Antiqs. of Leicester* 2(1) (1795): Appendix: 126–127. Blore *Hist. & Antiqs. of Rutland* 1(2) (1811): 19 (Despenser ped.). Brydges *Collins' Peerage of England* 6 (1812): 496–511 (sub Despenser). Dugdale *Monasticon Anglicanum* 2 (1819): 59–65. Burke *Dormant, Abeyant, Forfeited & Extinct Peerages* (1883): 165–167 (sub Despenser). VCH *Hampshire* 5 (1912): 284–285. *C.C.R. 1381–1385* (1920): 167–168. VCH *Wiltshire* 9 (1970): 23–43. Allington-Smith *Henry Despenser* (2003): 4. Higginbotham *Traitor's Wife* (2005): 471–472. National Archives, SC 8/120/5962 (available at www.catalogue.nationalarchives.gov.uk/search.asp).

iv. **JOHN LE DESPENSER**, younger son. In 1351 he received lands in Carleton le Moorland, Lincolnshire, by reversion settled on him by his brother, Hugh le Despenser. He may be the John le Despenser who died shortly before 10 June 1366. *C.C.R. 1349–1354* (1906): 322. *C.F.R.* 7 (1923): 344. Higginbotham *Traitor's Wife* (2005): 471–472.

v. **PHILIP LE DESPENSER**, buried in the Chapter House of the Austin Friars, London. *Gentleman's Mag.* n.s. 8 (1860): 372–376.

vi. **ISABEL LE DESPENSER**, married **RICHARD DE ARUNDEL**, Knt., 10th Earl of Arundel, 9th Earl of Surrey [see FITZ ALAN 11].

vii. **JOAN LE DESPENSER**. A dispensation was granted 1 June 1323 for her to marry John son of Thomas, Earl of Kildare, they being related in the 4th degree of kindred. This marriage did not take place. Joan subsequently became a nun at Shaftesbury Abbey, where she died in 1384. *Papal Regs.: Letters* 2 (1895): 231. *C.C.R. 1381–1385* (1920): 167–168. Allington-Smith *Henry Despenser* (2003): 4. Higginbotham *Traitor's Wife* (2005): 471–472.

viii. **ELIZABETH LE DESPENSER**, married (1st) **MAURICE DE BERKELEY**, Knt., 4th Lord Berkeley [see BERKELEY 8]; (2nd) **MAURICE WYTHE**, Knt., of Portbury, Somerset [see BERKELEY 8].

Children of William la Zouche Mortimer, Knt., by Eleanor de Clare:

i. **HUGH LA ZOUCHE** (otherwise **HUGH MORTIMER LA ZOUCHE**), Knt. In 1362 he was granted an indult for a portable altar and plenary remission at the hour of death. He was a man-at-arms in Italy, where he became Captain-General of the White Company, a calvary company of 5,000 men. In July 1365, while fighting in Italy at San Mariano, he was taken prisoner and placed in jail in Perugia. In Sept. 1368 Pope Urban V wrote the governors and commune of the city of Perugia exhorting them to grant the request of Lionel, Duke of Clarence, for the liberation of Hugh la Zouche, Knt., of England, detained by them in prison. He was released from imprisonment in Sept. 1369. Dugdale *Monasticon Anglicanum* 2 (1819): 59–65 (Tewkesbury Abbey: "Elianoræ de Clare .... Post mortem ejus maritata fuit domino Willielmo le Sowch, de quo genuit Hugonem Souch."). Burke *Dict. of the Peerages... Extinct, Dormant & in Abeyance* (1831): 587 (sub Zouche). *Papal Regs.: Petitions* 1 (1896): 388, 397 (instances of Hugh la Zouche, 3rd Lord Zouche, styled "king's kinsman"). *Papal Regs.: Letters* 4 (1902): 28. *C.P.R. 1364–1367* (1912): 236. Pugh *Middle Ages: Marcher Lordships of Glamorgan, Morgannwg, Gower & Kilvey* (Glamorgan County Hist. 3) (1971): 605 footnote 60. Sumption *Hundred Years War II: Trial by Fire* (2002): 470 (erroneously identifies Hugh la Zouche Mortimer as grandson of Roger de Mortimer, 1st Earl of March). Villalon & Kagay *Hundred Years War: A Wider Focus* (Hist. of Warfare 25) (2005): 203–204. Caferro *John Hawkwood* (2006): 120.

ii. **WILLIAM LA ZOUCHE**, monk at Glastonbury Abbey. In 1355–6 he leased an estate at Bletchingdon, Oxfordshire from his aunt, Elizabeth de Burgh, lady of Clare. In 1367 Edward le Despenser, lord of Glamorgan and Morgannwg, granted in mortmain to the Abbot of Glastonbury a rent of 100*s*. out of his manor of Sherston, Wiltshire for the life of his uncle, William la Zouche, fellow-monk of the abbot. He was living 6 March 1377. *C.P.R. 1377–1381* (1895): 597. *C.P.R. 1374–1377* (1916): 438. *Procs. Dorset Nat. Hist. & Arch. Soc.* 85 (1964): 137 ("Brother William Zouche" mentioned in a letter of Walter de Monynton, Abbot of Glastonbury). Pugh *Middle Ages: Marcher Lordships of Glamorgan, Morgannwg, Gower & Kilvey* (Glamorgan County Hist. 3) (1971): 176, 605 footnote 60. Underhill *For Her Good Estate* (1999): 87.

12. EDWARD LE DESPENSER, Knt., of Buckland, Buckinghamshire, Eyworth, Bedfordshire, Potterspury, Yardley, and Yelvertoft, Northamptonshire, Perlethorpe, Nottinghamshire, Essendine, Rutland, West Winterslow, Wiltshire, etc., 2nd son. He married at Groby (in Ratby), Leicestershire 20 April 1335 **ANNE DE FERRERS**, daughter of William de Ferrers, Knt., 1st Lord Ferrers of Groby, by his 1st wife, [?Margaret], daughter of John de Segrave, Knt., 2nd Lord Segrave [see GROBY 9 for her ancestry]. They had five sons, Edward, K.G. [4th Lord le Despenser], Hugh, Knt., Thomas, Knt., Henry [Bishop of Norwich], and Gilbert. In 1341 he and his wife, Anne, bought two messuages, 118 acres of land, and 10*s*. of rent in Eyworth, Bedfordshire from John de Purley and Joan his wife for 100 marks. SIR EDWARD LE DESPENSER was slain at Morlaix 30 Sept. 1342, while serving on an expedition. Administration on his estate was granted 18 Feb. 1342/3 to his widow, Anne, and Ralph de Donyngton, vicar of Ryhall, Rutland. In 1352 John de Hotham granted his widow, Anne, and her brother, Thomas de Ferrers, Knt., the castle of Kilkenny and other estates in Ireland for life, with remainder to her son, Hugh. In 1363 the king granted her the manor of Burley, Rutland, in exchange for the Castle of Moor End (in Potterspury) and the manors of Plumpton Pury (in Paulerspury) and Yardley Gobion, Northamptonshire. In 1364 Anne endowed a chaplain with certain rents from Burley, Rutland to pray daily in the church of Burley for the souls of the king, Queen Philippe, and Anne herself, and for John de Lisle and Henry de Lisle. In the following year she settled half the manor of Burley, Rutland on herself for life, with remainder to her son, Sir Thomas le Despenser. She died 8 August 1367.

Bridges *Hist. & Antiqs. of Northamptonshire* 1 (1791): 607–608. Blore *Hist. & Antiqs. of Rutland* 1(2) (1811): 19 (Despenser ped.). Brydges *Collins' Peerage of England* 6 (1812): 496–511 (sub Despenser). Dugdale *Monasticon Anglicanum* 2 (1819): 59–65 (Tewkesbury Cartulary: "Edwardus [le Despenser] igitur primus, frater Hugonis tertii, ex Anna filia domini de Ferrers, genuit Edwardum secundum, Thomas, Henricum, et Gilbertum secundum, et fortunio belli ante fratrem suum decessit."). Hunter *South Yorkshire* 1 (1828): 71 (Despenser ped.). Burke *Dict. of the Peerages... Extinct, Dormant & in Abeyance* (1831): 171–174. Eddison *Hist. of Worksop* (1854): 170–171. Lennard & Vincent *Vis. of Warwick 1619* (H.S.P. 12) (1877): 282–285 (Spencer ped.: "Edw. Dn's Spencer 2 fil. Hugonis le Despensor = Anna fil. Hen. Dn'i Ferrers."). Burke *Dormant, Abeyant, Forfeited & Extinct Peerages* (1883): 165–167 (sub Despenser). Gibbons *Early Lincoln Wills 1280–1547* (1888): 16 (administration of estate of Edward le Despenser). Thompson *Adæ Murimuth Continuatio Chronicarum* (Rolls Ser. 93) (1889): 127, 227. *Notes & Queries* 8th Ser. 10 (1896): 136, 285–286, 326, 486. *Papal Regs.: Petitions* 1 (1896): 261 (Edward le Despenser styled "king's kinsman"). Norris *Baddesley Clinton, its Manor,*

Church & Hall (1897): 112–117. *Desc. Cat. Ancient Deeds* 3 (1900): 105–106, 137; 5 (1906): 557–558 (Anne, widow of Edward le Despenser, styled "cousin" by King Edward III of England). Wrottesley *Peds. from the Plea Rolls* (1905): 205. VCH *Bedford* 2 (1908): 230–232. VCH *Buckingham* 2 (1908): 328. Clark *Cartæ et Alia Munimenta de Glamorgancia* 4 (1910): 1292. *C.P.R. 1361–1364* (1912): 417. Saltmarshe *Hist. & Chartulary of the Hothams of Scorborough* (1914): 209, 214–215. Stokes *Abs. of Wiltshire IPM* 3 (Index Lib. 48) (1914): 341–342. *C.P.* 4 (1916): 272 footnote j, 274–275 (sub Despenser), Appendix H, 671 (chart). VCH *Rutland* 2 (1935): 114–115, 119, 252 (Despenser arms: Quarterly argent gules fretty or with a bend sable over all). VCH *Northampton* 4 (1937): 89. Pugh *Abs. of Feet of Fines Rel. Wiltshire* (Wiltshire Arch. & Nat. Hist. Soc. Recs. 1) (1939): 129. Stokes et al. *Warwickshire Feet of Fines* 2 (Dugdale Soc. 15) (1939): 111–112. Brooks *Knights' Fees in Counties Wexford Carlow & Kilkenny* (1950): 200. Paget *Baronage of England* (1957) 182: 1–2 (sub Despenser). *Cal. Inqs. Misc.* 4 (1957): 6–8. Smith *Itinerary of John Leland* 4 (1964): 150–163. Ellis *Cat. Seals in the P.R.O.* 1 (1978): 21 (seal of Anne, widow of Edward le Despenser, knight, dated 1363 — A shield of arms: quarterly, in the second and third quarters a fret, over all a bend [DESPENSER] impaling four mascles [FERRERS]. Within a cusped circle, surrounded by a band of pointed tracery broken by four roundels of arms containing (above) a sleeping lion (below) a pierced cinquefoil [BEAUMONT], (left) three chevrons [CLARE], (right) a lion rampant crowned [SEGRAVE]). *Ancient Deeds — Ser. AS & WS* (List & Index Soc. 158) (1979): 5 (Deed A.S.21). O'Connor *Cal. Cartularies of John Pyel & Adam Fraunceys* (Camden Soc. 5th Ser. 2) (1993): 83–84, 432. Ayton *Knights & Warhorses* (1994): 148. *TAG* 69 (1994): 129–139. *Nottingham Medieval Studies* 41 (1997): 153 (chart). Underhill *For Her Good Estate* (1999). Allington-Smith *Henry Despenser* (2003): 2 (wife Anne identified as the "daughter of William, Lord Ferrers of Groby"), 53. Higginbotham *Traitor's Wife* (2005): 471–472. National Archives, SC 8/122/6062 (available at www.catalogue.nationalarchives.gov.uk/search.asp).

Children of Edward le Despenser, Knt., by Anne de Ferrers:

i. **EDWARD LE DESPENSER**, K.G., 4th Lord le Despenser, lord of Glamorgan and Morgannwg [see next].

ii. **HUGH LE DESPENSER**, Knt., in right of his wife, of Colyweston, Northamptonshire, Bonby, Lincolnshire, Cranswick, Hotham, and Kennythorpe, Yorkshire, etc., 2nd son. He married **ALICE DE HOTHAM**, daughter and heiress of John de Hotham, Knt., of Bonby, Lincolnshire, Fishhide, Essex, Solihull, Warwickshire, Hotham, Yorkshire, etc. She was born about 1335 (aged 16 in 1351). They had one son, Hugh, Knt., and one daughter, Anne. In 1352 the Chancellor of Ireland was instructed to deliver Kilkenny Castle in Ireland to them. SIR HUGH LE DESPENSER died at Padua in Lombardy 2 March 1374. In Sept. 1374 his widow, Alice, staying in England, had letters appointing William Ilger and another her attorneys in Ireland. Alice married (2nd) before 7 Nov. 1374 (as his 1st wife) **JOHN TRUSSELL**, Knt., of Flore and Gayton, Northamptonshire, Theddingworth, Leicestershire, etc., Knight of the Shire of Northamptonshire, son and heir of Theobald Trussell, of Flore and Gayton, Northamptonshire, Theddingworth, Leicestershire, etc., by his wife, Katherine. He was born about 1349. They had one son, John. He presented to the church of Solihull, Warwickshire in 1375 and again in 1379, in right of his wife. His wife, Alice, died 6 October 1379. He married (2nd) before 1396 **MARGARET** _____ (possibly **ARDERN**). They had one daughter, Philippe (wife of Alexander Bosom, Esq., and Thomas Kerdeston, Knt. [see DE LA POLE 9.iv; BURNELL 13]). By an uncertain wife, he also had one son, Geoffrey. In 1403 he had license to impark 300 acres in Gayton, Northamptonshire. In 1406 he and his son, John, conveyed their right in the manor and advowson of Colyweston, Northamptonshire to Richard Norton. In 1417 he sued Laurence Estwyk, Esq., John Boorn, Esq., Peter Brereton, and others in a plea of maheem and breach of the peace; the said Trussell appeared in court and stated that the defendants, together with Richard le Strange, of Knockin, and Joan his wife, laid in wait for him in the parish of St. Dunstan in the East, London and that said Boorn and Brereton violently attacked and maimed him; the jury assessed 1,000 marks in damages, costs, and expenses to the said Trussell. SIR JOHN TRUSSELL died intestate 21 March 1424. His widow, Margaret, died in Nov. 1442. She left a will dated 1441. Bridges *Hist. & Antiqs. of Northamptonshire* 2 (1791): 434–435 (Hothum ped.). Brydges *Collins' Peerage of England* 6 (1812): 496–511 (sub Despenser). Whellan *Hist., Gaz. & Dir. of Northamptonshire* (1849): 458. Gibbons *Early Lincoln Wills 1280–1547* (1888): 172–173 (will of Margaret Trussell). Wrottesley *Staffordshire Suits: Plea Rolls* (Colls. Hist. Staffs. 17) (1896): 34–35; (Colls. Hist. Staffs. n.s. 4) (1901): 100–101. *List of Early Chancery Procs.* 1 (PRO Lists and Indexes 12) (1901): 87. Wrottesley *Peds. from the Plea Rolls* (1905): 95, 129. *C.P.R. 1436–1441* (1907): 477. *C.P.R. 1441–1446* (1908): 359–360. Saltmarshe *Hist. & Chartulary of the Hothams of Scarborough* (1914): 207–210, 214–216. *C.P.R. 1374–1377* (1916): 15. VCH *Warwick* 4 (1947): 214–229. Brooks *Knights' Fees in Counties Wexford Carlow & Kilkenny* (1950): 199–200. Hatton *Book of Seals* (1950): 182 (indenture of Margaret, widow of John Trussell, Knt. dated 1426; attached seal has shield bearing coat of arms: Ermine a fess checky [presumably ARDERN]. VCH *Leicester* 5 (1964): 312–321. Ellis *Cat. Seals in the P.R.O.* 2 (1981): 33 (seal of Hugh le Despenser dated 1359 — A shield of arms: quarterly, in the second and third quarters a fret, over all a bendlet [DESPENSER]. Legend: [+SIGI]LLVM [HUGONIS.LE.D]ESPE[NSER].). *Year Books of Richard II* 4 (Ames Found. 7) (1987). Roskell *House of Commons 1386–1421* 4 (1992): 666–669 (biog. of Sir John Trussell). Allington-Smith *Henry Despenser* (2003): 3–4. Farnham *Leicestershire Medieval Village Notes, Theddingworth–Upton* [FHL 804160].

National Archives, CP 25/1/179/91, #53 [see abstract of fine at http://www.medievalgenealogy.org.uk/index.html]. Court of Common Pleas, CP 40/662, rot. 119d (available at http://www.british-history.ac.uk/source.aspx?pubid=1272).

Children of Hugh le Despenser, Knt., by Alice de Hotham:

- a. **HUGH LE DESPENSER**, Knt., of Colyweston, Northamptonshire, Bonby, Lincolnshire, Sheldon and Solihill, Warwickshire, Hotham, Yorkshire, etc., Governor of Henry, Prince of Wales [afterwards King Henry V], Justiciar of South Wales, 1401, Knight of the Passion of Jesus Christ, son and heir, born about 1359 (aged 16 in 1375). He married before Sept. 1388 **SIBYL** _____. They had one daughter, Elizabeth, living 1400. In 1383 he was beyond the seas in the king's service. In 1383 and again in 1386 he had a dispute with John Hotham, Knt., of Scorborough regarding the manor of Hotham, Yorkshire. In 1401 he was appointed Steward of Macclesfield and Surveyor, Keeper and Master of the Forests of Macclesfield and Mara for life. SIR HUGH LE DESPENSER died 14 October 1401. He left a will dated 1 July 1400, requesting burial in the chapel of the Friars Preachers at Stamford, Lincolnshire. His widow, Sibyl, died 16 August 1415. Bridges *Hist. & Antiqs. of Northamptonshire* 2 (1791): 434–435 (Hothum ped.). Brydges *Collins' Peerage of England* 6 (1812): 496–511 (sub Despenser). *Annual Rpt. of the Deputy Keeper* 36 (1875): 145. *Archives de l'Orient Latin* 1 (1881): 362–364. Gibbons *Early Lincoln Wills 1280–1547* (1888): 98–99 (will of Hugh le Despenser, Knt. dated 1 July 1400, mentions his land in Caldeford, Sulihull, Fencot, and Morecot, which he had by the gift of his uncle, Sir Ralph de Ferrers). Birch *Cat. Seals in the British Museum* 2 (1892): 733 (seal of Hugh le Despenser dated 1385 — A shield of arms couché: quarterly, in the 2nd and 3rd quarters a fret, over all a bend, in the 1st quarter a martlet for difference, DESPENSER. Crest on a helmet and lambrequin, on a wreath a griffin's head (?) and wings erect. Background enriched with sprigs of foliage. Within a carved gothic panel. Legend: Sigillū : hug[onis] ..e : Spencer.). *Wrottesley Peds. from the Plea Rolls* (1905): 179. Saltmarshe *Hist. & Chartulary of the Hothams of Scarborough* (1914): 64, 214–216. Legge *Anglo-Norman Letters & Petitions* (Anglo-Norman Text Soc. 3) (1941): 284–286, 302–304 (Hugh le Despenser styled "cousin" by King Henry IV of England). VCH *Warwick* 4 (1947): 214–229. Brooks *Knights' Fees in Counties Wexford Carlow & Kilkenny* (1950): 199–200. *Cal. Inqs. Misc.* 7 (1968): 293. *Year Books of Richard II* 4 (Ames Found. 7) (1987). *Cal. IPM* 20 (1995): 120 (alleges that Hugh le Despenser died 12 Dec. 1399). Allington-Smith *Henry Despenser* (2003): 3–4. National Archives, SC 8/182/9094 (available at www.catalogue.nationalarchives.gov.uk/search.asp).

- b. **ANNE LE DESPENSER**, born about 1371 (aged 30 in 1401). She married **EDWARD LE BOTELER**, Knt., of Pulverbatch, Shropshire, Higham-Gobion, Bedfordshire, and Norbury, Staffordshire, and, in right of his wife, of Colyweston, Northamptonshire and Bonby, Lincolnshire, 2nd son of John le Boteler, Knt., of Pulverbatch, Shropshire, by Joan, daughter of John d'Argentine, Knt. He was born 20 July 1337. They had no surviving issue. He was heir in 1348 to his older brother, Ralph le Boteler. In 1406 he and his wife, Anne, conveyed all their right in the manor and advowson of Colyweston, Northamptonshire to Richard Norton. His wife, Anne, died in 1409. SIR EDWARD LE BOTELER died 10 Nov. 1412. Bridges *Hist. & Antiqs. of Northamptonshire* 2 (1791): 434–435 (Hothum ped.). Brydges *Collins' Peerage of England* 6 (1812): 496–511 (sub Despenser). Waters *Chester of Chicheley* 1 (1878): 138–139 (Boteler ped.). VCH *Bedford* 2 (1908): 344–347. Saltmarshe *Hist. & Chartulary of the Hothams of Scarborough* (1914): 214–216. Legge *Anglo-Norman Letters & Petitions* (Anglo-Norman Text Soc. 3) (1941). VCH *Warwick* 4 (1947): 214–229. Paget *Baronage of England* (1957) 82: 1–11 (sub Boteler). *Cal. IPM* 20 (1995): 85, 120. Allington-Smith *Henry Despenser* (2003): 3–4. National Archives, CP 25/1/179/91, #52 [see abstract of fine at http://www.medievalgenealogy.org.uk/index.html].

iii. **THOMAS LE DESPENSER**, Knt., of Buckland, Buckinghamshire, and Maplederwell, Hampshire. In 1363 he and his mother, Anne, granted the king the Castle of Moor End (in Potterspury) and the manors of Plumpton Pury (in Paulerspury) and Yardley Gobion, Northamptonshire. In 1365 his mother, Anne, settled half the manor of Burley, Rutland on herself for life, with remainder to her son, Sir Thomas. In 1369 he was in possession of the whole manor. In 1373 he was taken prisoner in France at a skirmish at Ouchy-les-Soissons. In 1375 he had a grant of a court leet and view of frankpledge and a fair at Burley, Rutland, and quittance of suit of counties and hundreds for his men of the manor. The reason for this grant was that the vill of Burley having been destroyed by fire, and the inhabitants being so impoverished by excessive amercements for suits of hundreds and other demands by the sheriff, they threatened to abandon their holdings unless some assistance was given them. In 1380 he granted the manor of Burley, Rutland to various trustees, among whom were his brother, Henry le Despenser, Bishop of Norwich, his nephew, Hugh le Despenser, and his cousin, Philip le Despenser, Knt. SIR THOMAS LE DESPENSER died without issue in Feb. 1381. Blore *Hist. & Antiqs. of Rutland* 1(2) (1811): 19 (Despenser ped.). Brydges *Collins' Peerage of England* 6 (1812): 496–511 (sub Despenser). *C.P.R. 1377–1381* (1895): 452–453. *Desc. Cat. Ancient Deeds* 3 (1900): 106, 133. VCH *Buckingham* 2 (1908): 328. VCH *Hampshire* 4 (1911): 150–151. *C.P.R. 1367–1370* (1913): 219 (Thomas le Despenser styled "king's kinsman" in 1369). VCH *Rutland* 2

(1935): 114–115. Allington-Smith *Henry Despenser* (2003): 4. National Archives, SC 8/122/6062 (available at www.catalogue.nationalarchives.gov.uk/search.asp).

iv. **HENRY LE DESPENSER**, 4th son, born about 1343. He was appointed Canon of Salisbury, 1354; Rector of Bosworth, Leicestershire, 1361; Canon of Lincoln, 1364; Rector of Elsworth, Cambridgeshire, 1364; Archdeacon of Llandaff, 1364; and Canon of Llandaff, 1366. He was chosen Bishop of Norwich by papal provision, 1370. He was constantly placed on committees of parliament. He quarreled with King's Lynn in 1377, when he sought to have a mace carried before him in the town and was attacked and wounded by the townsmen. During the Peasants' Revolt in Norfolk in 1381, he personally led an assault at North Walsham and overpowered the rebels in a hand-to-hand fight. The rigor with with he put down the rebellion made him highly unpopular among Norfolk men. In 1382 he was chosen by Pope Urban VI to lead a campaign against the followers of Clement VII in Flanders. In May 1383 the expedition crossed to Calais and quickly took Gravelines and Dunkirk. The Siege of Ypres was long and disastrous. The mediation of the Duke of Brittany put an end to the war. When Parliament met in Nov. 1383, his temporalities were seized into the king's hands, they being restored in 1385. In 1385 he accompanied King Richard II in his march northward to repel the French invasion of Scotland. He took part in the naval expedition of Richard, Earl of Arundel, against the Flemish coast, 1386–7. In 1389 he took active steps to suppress lollardy. On the accession of King Henry IV in 1399, he remained loyal to King Richard II, was arrested, and suffered imprisonment. He was reconciled to the new king in 1401. HENRY LE DESPENSER, Bishop of Norwich, died 23 August 1406, and was buried in his cathedral church. Weever *Ancient Funerall Monuments* (1631): 793–794. Rymer *Fœdera* 7 (1728): 392, 395–396, 399 (instances of Henry styled "kinsman" by King Richard II of England). Blore *Hist. & Antiqs. of Rutland* 1(2) (1811): 19 (Despenser ped.). Brydges *Collins' Peerage of England* 6 (1812): 496–511 (sub Despenser). Capgrave *Liber de Illustribus Henricis* (1858): 170–174 (biog. of Henry le Despenser, Bishop of Norwich). Boutell *English Heraldry* (1867): 189–190 (The secretum or private seal of Bishop Despenser "displays his Shield of Despencer, differenced with his bordure of mitres, couché from a large mantled helm, surmounted by a mitre, in place of a crest-coronet, with supports the Despencer crest, a silver griffin's head of ample size; on either side are the Shields of the see of Norwich, and of Ferrers (the Bishop's mother was Anne, daughter of William Lord Ferrers of Groby) — Or, seven mascles, three three and one, gules; the legend is, S . HENRICI . DESPENCER . NOWWICENSIS . EPISCOPI."). *Procs. Soc. of Antiqs. of London* 2nd Ser. 10 (1884): 103–104 (seal of Henry le Despenser dated 1385). *Papal Regs.: Petitions* 1 (1896): 261, 364 (Henry le Despenser styled "kinsman" by King Edward III of England). Usk *Chronicon Adæ de Usk 1377–1421* (1904): 16–17. *D.N.B.* 5 (1908): 860–862 (biog. of Henry Despenser: "… He had all the faults of an arrogant and headstrong noble … his energy and practical ability were early appreciated at court."). *Hist. Research* 10 (1932): 40–44. *VCH Rutland* 2 (1935): 114–115. Legge *Anglo-Norman Letters & Petitions* (Anglo-Norman Text Soc. 3) (1941): 46–47, 112 (Henry le Despenser styled "cousin" by King Henry IV of England in letters dated 1403), 50, 52 (instances of Henry le Despenser styled "cousin" by Henry, Prince of Wales [later King Henry V] in letters dated 1399–1406), 78–79 (Henry le Despenser, Bishop of Norwich styled "cousin" by Thomas la Warre, 5th Lord la Warre, in letter dated c.1399), 90, 98, 100–101, 106–108 (instances of Henry le Despenser styled "cousin" by Margaret Ferrers, Countess of Warwick in letters dated 1401-6), 92–93 (Henry le Despenser styled "uncle" by Anne le Despenser, Lady Botiller), 97 (Henry le Despenser styled "cousin" by Isabel Beauchamp, Countess of Suffolk), 101–102 (Henry le Despenser styled "cousin" by John Beaufort, Earl of Somerset in letter dated 1397–1406), 125–127 (Henry le Despenser styled "uncle" by Thomas Morley, Lord Morley in letter dated 1405–6), 366 (an unidentified niece of Henry le Despenser mentions Ralph Greene, husband of her cousin [presumably Katherine Clifton]), 372–373 (Henry le Despenser styled "cousin" by Philippe of Lancaster, Queen of Portugal), 383–384 ([Elizabeth de Beaumont], Lady Audley styled "cousin" by Henry le Despenser). Langham *Reg. Simonis Langham Cantuariensis Archiepiscopi* (Canterbury & York Soc. 53) (1956): 61 (Henry styled "king's kinsman"). Emden *Biog. Reg. of the Univ. of Oxford* 3 (1959): 2169–2170 (biog. of Henry Despenser). Hicks *Who's Who in Late Medieval England* (1991): 172–173 (biog. of Henry Despenser) ("… [He] achieved rapid promotion at an early age. This was due rather to his birth than his conventional qualifications, for he was not particularly learned, discreet, or spiritual. He remained an impulsive nobleman, sensitive about his honour and rights, and with a marked taste for warfare"). Allington-Smith *Henry Despenser* (2003). Higginbotham *Traitor's Wife* (2005): 471–472.

13. EDWARD LE DESPENSER, K.G., 4th Lord le Despenser, lord of Glamorgan and Morgannwg, Wales, and, in right of his wife, of Ewyas Lacy, Herefordshire, son and heir, born at Essendine, Rutland about 24 March 1335/6. He was heir in 1349 to his uncle, Hugh le Despenser, Knt., 3rd Lord le Despenser. He married before 2 August 1354 **ELIZABETH BURGHERSH**, daughter and heiress of Bartholomew de Burghersh, K.G., 4th Lord Burghersh, by his 1st wife, Cecily, daughter of Richard de Weyland, Knt. [see BURGHERSH 13 for her ancestry]. She was born in 1342 (aged 27 in 1369). They had three sons, Edward, Hugh, and Thomas, K.G. [5th Lord le Despenser], and four daughters, Cecily, Elizabeth, Anne, and Margaret. He accompanied the Prince of Wales to Gascony in Sept. 1355, and fought at the Battle of Poitiers 19 Sept. 1356. He was summoned to Parliament from 15 Dec. 1357 to 6 October 1372, by writs directed *Edwardo le Despenser*. He was with the king in the invasion of France in 1359–60. In 1362 he obtained license to grant to Little Marlow Priory two quarters of corn and three quarters of barley from his manor of Barlow, Buckinghamshire. He and his wife received a papal indult for a portable altar in 1365. In 1367 Edward le Despenser, lord of Glamorgan and Morgannwg, granted in mortmain to the Abbot of Glastonbury a rent of 100*s*. out of his manor of Sherston, Wiltshire for the life of his uncle, William la Zouche, fellow-monk of the abbot. In 1368 he went with Lionel, Duke of Clarence, to Milan. He subsequently took service with Pope Urban in his war against the Visconti of Milan, winning a great reputation in battles in Lombardy. At the request of John of Gaunt, Duke of Lancaster, he returned to England in 1372. He was Constable of the Army in the Duke's unsuccessful expedition in France in 1373–4. He assisted the Duke of Brittany in his campaign in that province in 1375. SIR EDWARD LE DESPENSER, 4th Lord le Despenser, died at Llanblethian, Glamorgan 11 Nov. 1375. He left a will dated 6 Nov. 1375 (Linc. Episc. Reg., 163 Bokingham). In 1382/7 his widow, Elizabeth, sold the manors of Heytesbury, Colerne, and Stert, Wiltshire to Thomas Hungerford. She presented to the church of Fordley, Suffolk in 1387. She was mentioned in the 1396 will of her son-in-law, William la Zouche, Knt., 3rd Lord Zouche of Harringworth. She presented to the church of Carlton Colville, Suffolk in 1399. Elizabeth, Lady Despenser died testate about 26 July 1409. They were buried at Tewkesbury Abbey, Gloucestershire.

Rymer *Fœdera* 6 (1727): 136. *Gentleman's Mag.* 33 (1763): 192–193. Bridges *Hist. & Antiqs. of Northamptonshire* 1 (1791): 607–608. Blore *Hist. & Antiqs. of Rutland* 1(2) (1811): 19 (Despenser ped.). Brydges *Collins' Peerage of England* 6 (1812): 496–511 (sub Despenser). Dugdale *Monasticon Anglicanum* 2 (1819): 59–65 (Tewkesbury Cartulary: "Edwardus [le Despenser] vero secundus, filius istius Edwardi, successit Hugoni tertio, et copulavit sibi in matrimonium dominam Elizabetham, filiam domini Bartholomei de Borowashe, de qua genuit Edwardum tertium, qui obiit duodenus apud Kardif, sed apud Theokes. sepelitur in capella sanctæ Mariæ, et Hugonem quartum, qui obiit cito postquam natus erat et sepelitur cum fratre suo. Deinde genuit quator filias, quarum nomina sunt ista, scilicet Ceciliam, quæ obiit iuvenis, et sepulta est cum fratribus suis: deinde Elizabetham dominam de la Sowch, et relictam domini Johannis de Arundell, et dominam Annam quæ fuit desponsata Hugoni Hastings, et post Thomæ Morley et Margaretam quæ fuit nupta domino Roberto de Ferrers; et prædictus Edwardus in ultima ætate sua genuit Thomam le Despenser et comitem Gloucestriæ."). Hoare *Hist. of Modern Wiltshire: Hundred of Heytesbury* (1824): 88 (Burghersh ped.). Nicolas *Testamenta Vetusta* 1 (1826): 99–100 (will of Edward, Lord Despenser), 174–175 (will of Elizabeth de Burghersh, Lady Despenser). Hunter *South Yorkshire* 1 (1828): 71 (Despenser ped.). Burke *Dict. of the Peerages… Extinct, Dormant & in Abeyance* (1831): 100–101, 171–174. Beltz *Mems. of the Order of the Garter* (1841): cli. Suckling *Hist. & Antiqs. of Suffolk* 1 (1846): 242; 2 (1848): 316. *Sussex Arch. Colls.* 21 (1869): chart betw. 126–127. Lennard & Vincent *Vis. of Warwick 1619* (H.S.P. 12) (1877): 282–285 (Spencer ped.: "Edwardus Dn's Despensor eques Garterij hæres avunculi Sui Hugonis. = Elizab. fil. et hær. Bartholmei Burwash militis."). Burke *Dormant, Abeyant, Forfeited & Extinct Peerages* (1883): 165–167 (sub Despenser). Gibbons *Early Lincoln Wills 1280–1547* (1888): 45 (will of Edward le Despenser), 93 (will of William la Zouche). Birch *Cat. Seals in the British Museum* 2 (1892): 732–733 (seal of Elizabeth, Lady Despenser dated 1401 — A shield of arms: per pale, dex., DESPENSER; sin., a lion rampant, queue fourchée, BURGHERSH. Above the shield a griffin couchant. At the sides the initial letters [E.] S. Within a finely carved gothic panel ornamented with small ball-flowers along the inner edge. Legend: · le : Seal : elizabet : dame : la : despensere.). *Papal Regs.: Petitions* 1 (1896): 261 (Edward le Despenser styled "king's kinsman"). *Papal Regs.: Letters* 3 (1897): 528; 4 (1902): 47. Kirby *Wykeham's Reg.* 2 (1899): 256. *C.P.R. 1385–1389* (1900): 416 (Elizabeth, lady Despenser styled "king's kinswoman"). Copinger *County of Suffolk* 1 (1904): 206. Wrottesley *Peds. from the Plea Rolls* (1905): 200, 205. *Archæologia* 60 (1906): 25–42. VCH *Buckingham* 2 (1908): 328; 3 (1925): 70–71. Copinger *Manors of Suffolk* 2 (1908): 123–125, 365–366; 3 (1909): 32–33; 4 (1909): 230. Hervey *Whelnetham Parish Regs.* (Suffolk Green Books 15) (1910): 291, 365–373. *C.P.* 1 (1910): 247, 260 (sub Arundel); 2 (1912): 427 (sub Burghersh); 4 (1916): 274–278 (sub Despenser), Appendix H, 671 (chart); 5 (1926): 315–317 (sub Ferrers); 6 (1926): 355–357 (sub Hastings); 9 (1936): 216–217 (sub Morley). Clark *Cartæ et Alia Munimenta de Glamorgancia* 4 (1910): 1298–1301, 1333–1334, 1443–1445. VCH *Hampshire* 4 (1911): 150–151. *C.P.R. 1374–1377* (1916): 30–31, 45, 68, 95, 442–443 (instances of Edward le Despenser styled "king's kinsman"), 438. Gretton *Burford Recs.* (1920). VCH *Berkshire* 4 (1924): 480. *Speculum* 4 (1929): 270–281. Fowler *Reg. Simonis de Sudbiria* 1 (Canterbury & York Soc. 34) (1927): 230. VCH *Rutland* 2 (1935): 114–115, 252. Hatton *Book of Seals* (1950): 334

(charter of Edward le Despenser). *Cal. IPM* 14 (1952): 214–227. Paget *Baronage of England* (1957) 182: 1–2 (sub Despenser). *Cal. Inqs. Misc.* 4 (1957): 53–54, 132. *Yorkshire Arch. Jour.* 40 (1962): 265–297. Smith *Itinerary of John Leland* 4 (1964): 150–163. Pugh *Middle Ages: Marcher Lordships of Glamorgan, Morgannwg, Gower & Kilvey* (Glamorgan County Hist. 3) (1971): 167–204 ("Froissart eulogizes him [Edward] as the most handsome, most courteous and most honourable knight of his time in England"). Merrick *Morganiae Archaiographia* (South Wales Rec. Soc. 1) (1983): 41–52. Kirby *Abs. of Feet of Fines Rel. Wiltshire* (Wiltshire Rec. Soc. 41) (1986): 10, 25–26. Kirby *Hungerford Cartulary* (Wiltshire Rec. Soc. 49) (1994): 160–162, 195. *TAG* 69 (1994): 129–139. McKardy *Royal Writs addressed to John Buckingham Bishop of Lincoln 1363–1398* (Lincoln Rec. Soc. 86) (1997): 146. *Nottingham Medieval Studies* 41 (1997): 126–156. Higginbotham *Traitor's Wife* (2005): 471–472. Hanna *Christchurch Priory Cartulary* (Hampshire Rec. Ser. 18) (2007): 188. Saul *14th Cent. England* 5 (2008): 91–92. National Archives, SC 8/85/4205; SC 8/106/5275; SC 8/106/5288; SC 8/106/5293; SC 8/106/5295; SC 8/107/5316; SC 8/158/7884; SC 8/226/11298 (available at www.catalogue.nationalarchives.gov.uk/search.asp).

Children of Edward le Despenser, K.G., by Elizabeth Burghersh:

i. **THOMAS LE DESPENSER**, K.G., Earl of Gloucester, 5th Lord le Despenser [see next].

ii. **ANNE LE DESPENSER**, married (1st) **HUGH DE HASTINGS**, Knt., of Elsing, Norfolk [see ELSING 13]; (2nd) **THOMAS MORLEY**, K.G., 4th Lord Morley, Marshal of Ireland [see MORLEY 11].

iii. **ELIZABETH LE DESPENSER**, married (1st) **JOHN DE ARUNDEL**, Knt., 2nd Lord Arundel [see ARUNDEL 10]; (2nd) **WILLIAM LA ZOUCHE**, Knt., 3rd Lord Zouche of Harringworth [see CANTELOWE 10].

iv. **MARGARET LE DESPENSER**, married **ROBERT FERRERS**, Knt., of Chartley, Staffordshire [see FERRERS 12].

14. THOMAS LE DESPENSER, K.G., 5th Lord le Despenser, Constable of Gloucester Castle, Constable of St. Briavel's Castle and Warden of the Forest of Dean, 1397, Knight of the Passion of Jesus Christ, 3rd but 1st surviving son and heir, born 22 Sept. 1373 (aged 2 in 1376). He married shortly before 7 Nov. 1379 (recorded date of gift for their marriage) **CONSTANCE OF YORK**, daughter of Edmund of Langley, K.G., Duke of York (5th son of King Edward III of England), by Isabel, younger daughter and co-heiress of Pedro *the Cruel*, King of Castile and León [see YORK 10 for her ancestry]. She was born about 1374. They had one son, Richard, and two daughters, Elizabeth and Isabel. He was licensed to go to Prussia 20 May 1391. He served as a captain in the king's army in Ireland in 1394. He was summoned to Parliament from 30 Nov. 1396 to 30 Sept. 1399, by writs directed *Thome le Despenser*, with the addition of *Comiti Gloucestrie* on or after 5 Nov. 1397. He was created Earl of Gloucester 29 Sept. 1397. On petition in the same Parliament, he obtained the reversal of the sentence of disheritance and exile on his ancestors, Hugh the elder and Hugh the younger. He was one of King Richard II's chief lieutenants on his 2nd expedition to Ireland in 1399. He had an interview with Art McMurrough, whom the Leinster Irish had accepted as their king, but failed to bring him to terms. The campaign was interrupted by the news of the landing of Henry of Lancaster [future King Henry IV]. On Henry IV's ascension to the throne in 1399, he was degraded from his earldom and lost various lands granted to him in 1397. In Jan. 1400, he joined the Earls of Kent, Huntingdon, and Salisbury in a bid to restore the deposed Richard II to the throne, and was with their army at Cirencester 6 Jan. 1400. The conspiracy was betrayed by Rutland. The rebel lords were attacked by the townsmen, who burnt the house in which Despenser lodged. He jumped from a window, and then fled and escaped to his castle at Cardiff. Hearing that the king had sent to take him, he went on board a ship in the Severn. The captain refused to take him anywhere except Bristol; he resisted, was overpowered, and taken before the mayor of the town. The Bristol people, who hated his family, demanded that he should be brought forth; the mayor yielded to their clamor. SIR THOMAS LE DESPENSER, Earl of Gloucester, 5th Lord le Despenser, was beheaded at Bristol 16 Jan. 1399/1400, and was buried in Tewkesbury Abbey. Because of her kinship with the king, his widow, Constance, was treated with great generosity. She was granted the greater part of her husband's lands for life and given custody of their son and heir, Richard. About this time she was allegedly betrothed to marry Edmund Holand, K.G., 4th Earl of Kent [see KENT 11], by whom she had a daughter, Eleanor Holand. It is doubtful that this betrothal, if valid, ever resulted in marriage. In Feb. 1405 Constance appeared before the Council on a charge of being concerned in the abduction of the young Mortimer brothers from Windsor Castle. During the interrogation, she incriminated her brother, Edward, Duke of York. She was sent to Kenilworth Castle, and her property was seized, later restored in 1406. She died 28 Nov. 1416, and was buried in Reading Abbey, Berkshire.

Sandford *Gen. Hist. of the Kings of England* (1677): 360–361. Bridges *Hist. & Antiqs. of Northamptonshire* 1 (1791): 607–608. Blore *Hist. & Antiqs. of Rutland* 1(2) (1811): 19 (Despenser ped.). Brydges *Collins' Peerage of England* 6 (1812): 496–511 (sub Despenser). Dugdale *Monasticon Anglicanum* 2 (1819): 59–65 (Tewkesbury Cartulary: "Thomam le Despenser … Iste successit patri suo in hæreditatem et copulavit sibi in matrimonium dominam Constantiam filiam domini Edmundi de Langley, filii regis Edwardi tertii et ducis Eboracensis, de qua Constantia præfatus Thomas genuit Ricardum, Elizabetham, et Isabellam."). Hunter *South Yorkshire* 1 (1828): 71 (Despenser ped.). Burke *Dict. of the Peerages… Extinct, Dormant & in Abeyance* (1831): 171–174. Beltz *Mems. of the Order of the Garter* (1841): cliv. Hawley *Royal Fam. of England* (1851): 23–27. Lennard & Vincent *Vis. of Warwick 1619* (H.S.P. 12) (1877): 282–285 (Spencer ped.: "Tho. Despensor Comes Gloucest. p. R. 2, 1388, decollatus 1 H. 4. = Constancia fil. Edm. Plantagenet Ducis Eboracensis illa ob. 1417, et sepultus in Abbatia de Readinge"). *Archives de l'Orient Latin* 1 (1881): 362–364. Burke *Dormant, Abeyant, Forfeited & Extinct Peerages* (1883): 165–167 (sub Despenser). Doyle *Official Baronage of England* 2 (1886): 21 (sub Gloucester). Birch *Cat. Seals in the British Museum* 2 (1892): 734 (seal of Thomas le Despenser, Earl of Gloucester dated 1397 — A shield of arms, couché: quarterly, in the 2nd and 3rd quarters, a fret, over all a bendlet, DESPENSER. Crest on a helmet and mantling, out of a ducal coronet a griffin's head and wings erect. Between two trees eradicated, on each, suspended by a strap, a lozenge-shaped shield of arms: dex., three chevrons, CLARE; sin., a lion rampant, queue fourchée, BURGHERSH. All within a carved gothic quadrilobe ornamented with ball-flowers along the edge. Legend: * Sigillum : thome : * * : dni : le despenser : *). *C.P.R. 1381–1385* (1897): 364 (Constance styled "king's kinswoman"). *C.P.R. 1399–1401* (1903): 204, 223, 226 (instances of Constance styled "king's kinswoman"). *C.P.R. 1391–1396* (1905): 271, 314, 327, 376 (instances of Thomas le Despenser styled "king's kinsman"). Wrottesley *Peds. from the Plea Rolls* (1905): 205. *D.N.B.* 5 (1908): 867 (biog. of Thomas le Despenser); 15 (1909): 1289 ("… Lady le Despenser was not a woman of the highest character"). VCH *Buckingham* 2 (1908): 328; 3 (1925): 70–71. Copinger *Manors of Suffolk* 2 (1908): 123–125; 3 (1909): 32–33; 4 (1909): 230. *C.P.* 1 (1910): 26–27 (sub Abergavenny); 2 (1912): 427 (sub Burghersh); 4 (1916): 278–282 (sub Despenser), Appendix H, 671 (chart). Clark *Cartæ et Alia Munimenta de Glamorgancia* 4 (1910): 1409–1426, 1450, 1456–1457. Hervey *Whelnetham Parish Regs.* (Suffolk Green Books 15) (1910): 291, 365–373. Lane *Royal Daughters of England* 1 (1910): 265–274. VCH *Hampshire* 4 (1911): 150–151. Clay *Extinct & Dormant Peerages* (1913): 169–171 (sub Plantagenet). *Yorkshire Inqs.* 5 (Yorkshire Arch. Soc. Recs. 59) (1918): 128–129. Gretton *Burford Recs.* (1920): 578–579. VCH *Berkshire* 4 (1924): 100, 480. Haythornthwaite *Parish of King's Langley* (1924): 29–32. VCH *Buckingham* 3 (1925): 70–71. Harvey et al. *Vis. of the North* 3 (Surtees Soc. 144) (1930): 2–5 ("Constancia [of York] nupta Thome domino le despenser"). VCH *Rutland* 2 (1935): 252. *John of Gaunt's Reg.* 1 (Camden Soc. 3rd Ser. 56) (1937): 50 (gift recorded 7 Nov. 1379 by John of Gaunt, Duke of Lancaster, made to his niece, Constance of York, on "the day of her marriage"). Legge *Anglo-Norman Letters & Petitions* (Anglo-Norman Text Soc. 3) (1941): 110–112 ([Constance], Lady Despenser styled "niece" by Henry le Despenser, Bishop of Norwich). Train *Abs. of IPMs Rel. Nottinghamshire* 2 (Thoroton Soc. Recs. 12) (1952): 159–160. Paget *Baronage of England* (1957) 182: 1–2 (sub Despenser). Smith *Itinerary of John Leland* 4 (1964): 150–163. *Coat of Arms* 8 (1965): 251–255 (arms of Thomas le Despenser: Quarterly, 1 and 4, Or, three chevrons gules (Clare); 2 and 3, Quarterly argent and gules, a fret or and over all a baston sable (Despenser). Pugh *Middle Ages: Marcher Lordships of Glamorgan, Morgannwg, Gower & Kilvey* (Glamorgan County Hist. 3) (1971): 167–204. Rees *Cal. Ancient Petitions Rel. Wales* (Board of Celtic Studies, Hist. & Law 28) (1975): 382. Ellis *Cat. Seals in the P.R.O.* 2 (1981): 33 (seal of Thomas le Despenser, Earl of Gloucester dated 1398 — In a cusped quatrefoil, a shield of arms, couché: quarterly, in the second and third quarters a fret, overall a bend; helm above with mantling and crest: a griffin's head and wings within a crown; all flanked by two trees with lozenges of arms hung therefrom, (left) three chevrons [CLARE], (right) a lion rampant, queue fourchy [BURGHERSH]. Legend: :SIGILLUM:THOME:/ DNI:LE:DESPENSER.). Hector *Westminster Chron. 1381–1394* (1982): 474–475. Merrick *Morganiae Archaiographia* (South Wales Rec. Soc. 1) (1983): 41–52. Pugh *Henry V & Southampton Plot of 1415* (1988): 78–79 ("To call her [Constance] 'a thoroughly bad lot' (as McFarlane did) seems exaggerated condemnation, but she was a woman of doubtful fame."). *Cal. IPM* 20 (1995): 91–92, 193–198. Leese *Blood Royal* (1996): 149–168. VCH *Gloucester* 5 (1996): 413–415. *Nottingham Medieval Studies* 41 (1997): 126–156. Hamilton *14th Cent. England* 4 (2006): 146–158. National Archives, SC 8/182/9051 (available at www.catalogue.nationalarchives.gov.uk/search.asp).

Children of Thomas le Despenser, K.G., by Constance of York:

i. **RICHARD LE DESPENSER**, son and heir, born 30 Nov. 1396. He married **ELEANOR NEVILLE**, daughter of Ralph Neville, K.G., 1st Earl of Westmorland, 4th Lord Neville of Raby, by his 2nd wife, Joan Beaufort, legitimated daughter of John of Gaunt, K.G., Duke of Aquitaine and Lancaster, Earl of Derby, Lincoln, and Leicester (son of King Edward III) [see NEVILLE 13 for her ancestry]. He was heir in 1409 to his cousin, Anne le Despenser, wife of Edward le Boteler, Knt. RICHARD LE DESPENSER died before 16 April 1414. His widow, Eleanor, married (2nd) at Berwick shortly after October 1414 **HENRY PERCY**, Knt., 2nd Earl of Northumberland, 5th Lord Percy [see PERCY 13]. Eleanor, Countess of Northumberland, died about 1472/3. Blore *Hist. & Antiqs. of Rutland* 1(2) (1811): 19 (Despenser ped.). Brydges *Collins' Peerage of England* 6 (1812): 496–511 (sub Despenser). Dugdale *Monasticon Anglicanum* 2 (1819): 59–65. Burke *Dormant, Abeyant, Forfeited & Extinct Peerages* (1883): 165–167 (sub Despenser). *C.P.R.* 1413–1416 (1910): 192–193. VCH *Hampshire* 4 (1911): 150–151. *C.P.* 4 (1916): 282 (sub Despenser). VCH *Buckingham* 3 (1925): 70–71. VCH *Warwick* 4 (1947): 214–229. Merrick *Morganiae Archaiographia* (South Wales Rec. Soc. 1) (1983): 41–52. Leese *Blood Royal* (1996): 149–168.

ii. **ISABEL LE DESPENSER**, married (1st) **RICHARD BEAUCHAMP**, K.B., Earl of Worcester [see BERGAVENNY 13]; (2nd) **RICHARD BEAUCHAMP**, K.G., K.B., Earl of Warwick, Lord Despenser and Lisle, hereditary Chamberlain of the Exchequer [see BEAUCHAMP 13].

❧ DINHAM ☙

ROBERT DE VERE, Knt., Earl of Oxford, married **ISABEL DE BOLEBEC**.
HUGH DE VERE, Knt., Earl of Oxford, married **HAWISE DE QUINCY**.
ISABEL DE VERE, married **OLIVER DE DINHAM** (or **DYNHAM**), Knt., Lord Dinham [see COURTENAY 4].

4. JOSCE DE DINHAM (or **DYNHAM**), Knt., of Hartland, Harpford, and Nutwell, Devon, Buckland Dinham and Corton Dinham, Somerset, Cardinham, Cornwall, etc., and, in right of his wife, of Clayhidon, Devon, son and heir, born about 1273–5 (aged 24–26 in 1299). The King took his homage, and he had livery of his father's lands 2 April 1299. He married after 12 April 1288 (grant of her marriage) and before 23 April 1292 **MARGARET DE HYDON**, daughter of Richard de Hydon, Knt. (died about October 1285), of Clayhidon and Hemyock, Devon, by Isabel, daughter of Peter de Fissacre. They had two sons, John, Knt., and Oliver, Knt. He was summoned for military service in 1300 and 12 March 1300/1, by writs directed *Joceo de Dynham* or *Dyneham*. SIR JOSCE DE DINHAM died 30 March 1301. His widow, Margaret, married (2nd) before 24 Jan. 1308/9 (as his 2nd wife) **GILBERT DE KNOVILLE**, Knt., of Battishorne, Ideford, and Loddiswell, Devon, Puckington, Somerset, etc., Justice in eyre, commissioner of forests. They had no issue. SIR GILBERT DE KNOVILLE died 20 Jan. 1313/4. She married (3rd) after 30 August 1316 and before 24 Sept. 1324 **PETER DE UVEDALE**, Knt., of Titsey, Surrey, Tacolneston, Norfolk, etc., and, in right of his wife, of Clayhidon and Hemyock, Devon, son and heir of John d'Uvedale, Knt., by his 1st wife, Mary, daughter and co-heiress of Peter de Champaine. He was born 9 August 1290 at Saxilby, Lincolnshire. He was serving in the Welsh marches in Jan. 1321/2. In 1322 his wife, Margaret, nominated attorneys, she going on pilgrimage to St. Edmund's, Potigny. He was granted royal protection 12 June 1324, before service in Gascony, where he was in October 1325. In 1326 he was one of those appointed to array the men of Devon and Cornwall for service against the rebels. In 1330 he and his wife, Margaret, founded a chantry in St. Katherine's chapel in Hemyock, Devon. He was summoned to Parliament from 27 Jan. 1331/2 to 22 Jan. 1335/6, by writs directed *Petro de Uvedale*, whereby he may be held to have become Lord Uvedale. He was summoned against the Scots in 1336. Sir Peter de Uvedale, Lord Uvedale, died shortly before 2 May 1336. In 1348 his widow, Margaret, settled the manor of Camlerton, Somerset on her grandson, Oliver de Dinham, Knt., and his wife, Joan. She died 15 May 1357, and was buried in St. Katherine's chapel in Hemyock, Devon.

Palgrave *Docs. & Recs. Ill. the Hist. of Scotland* 1 (1837): 219 ("Joceus de Dynaunt" included on list of people owing military service in 1300). *Arch. Jour.* 13 (1856): 70–72. Weaver *Somerset Incumbents* (1889): 74. Rye *Pedes Finium or Fines*

Rel. Cambridge (1891): 107. *Genealogist* n.s. 12 (1895): 228. Green *Feet of Fines for Somerset* 3 (Somerset Rec. Soc. 17) (1902): 12–13. *Rpt. & Trans. of the Devonshire Assoc.* 2nd Ser. 4 (1902): 721–723. *Year Books of Edward II* 1 (Selden Soc. 17) (1903): 58–61. Wrottesley *Peds. from the Plea Rolls* (1905): 68–69, 129. C.P. 4 (1916): 371–372 (sub Dinham); 12(2) (1959): 199–200 (sub Uvedale). *Rpt. & Trans. of the Devonshire Assoc.* 4th Ser. 1 (1919): 181–210. Moor *Knights of Edward I* 1 (H.S.P. 80) (1929): 296–297 (biog. of Joyce de Dynaunt); 2 (H.S.P. 81) (1929): 294 (biog. of Sir Gilbert de Knoville). *Genealogist's Mag.* 6 (1932–34): 606–626. Paget *Baronage of England* (1957) 187: 1–9 (sub Dinan). Erskine *Devonshire Lay Subsidy of 1332* (Devon & Cornwall Rec. Soc. n.s. 14) (1969): 8, 37–38, 41–42, 59, 71, 89, 120. Cornwall Rec. Office: Arundell of Lanherne & Trerice, AR/1/874; AR/1/1038 — gift dated 6 Mar. 1339 from Margaret de Douuedale who was wife of Joce de Dynham in her pure and independent (ligia) widowhood gives to Walter de Sutton 2 knight's fees in Devon, one in Kynwardeslegh (hundred of Criditon), the other in Uleburgh, Clyst and Wodeham (hundred of Clyston) (available at www.a2a.org.uk/search/index.asp).

5. JOHN DE DINHAM (or **DYNHAM**), Knt., of Hartland, Devon, Bodardel and Cardinham, Cornwall, Buckland Dinham and Corton Dinham, Somerset, etc., son and heir, born at Nutwell, Devon 14 Sept. 1295 (minor in 1310). He married in or before 1310 **MARGARET DE BOTREAUX**, probable daughter of William de Botreaux, Knt., of Boscastle, Cornwall. They had one son, John, Knt., and one daughter, Joan. He presented to the church of Corton Dinham, Somerset in 1316. About Sept. 1316 his cousin, Hugh de Courtenay, wrote a letter to William de Airmyn dated c. September 1316, in which he requested assistance for him in obtaining seisin of his lands. The king took his homage, and he had livery of his lands 18 October 1316. He was summoned for military service from 20 May 1317 to 20 Feb. 1324/5, and to a Council May 1323, by writs directed *Johanni de Dynham*. In 1328 he obtained license to grant his manor of Buckland Denham, Somerset to Maud de Multon for life. In 1329 he was summoned to appear before the Bishop of Exeter on a charge of adultery and incest commited with his cousin, Alice (or Maud) de Multon, but he did not attend and was excommunicated. He subsequently obtained an inhibition from the Court of the Metropolitan. The Archbishop informed the Bishop of Exeter that Dinham was to appear before him 12 Sept. 1331. In October 1331, Dinham was about go beyond seas on pilgrimage, probably as penance. SIR JOHN DE DINHAM died on or just before 14 April 1332. His widow, Margaret, died 28 Nov. 1361.

Weaver *Somerset Incumbents* (1889): 74. *Genealogist* n.s. 12 (1895): 228. *List of Ancient Corr. of the Chancery & Exchequer* (Lists and Indexes 15) (1902): 552; see also *Index to Ancient Corr. of the Chancery & Exchequer* 1 (Lists and Indexes, Supp. Ser. 15) (1969): 308, 351 (John de Dynham styled "kinsman" by Hugh de Courtenay in 1316). *Rpt. & Trans. of the Devonshire Assoc.* 2nd Ser. 4 (1902): 721–723. Wrottesley *Peds. from the Plea Rolls* (1905): 68–69, 129. C.P. 4 (1916): 372–373 (sub Dinham). *Genealogist's Mag.* 6 (1932–34): 606–626 (mistakenly identifies wife as Emma, daughter of Sir William de Widworthy, Knt.: see *Somersetshire Pleas* 3 (Somerset Rec. Soc. 41) (1926): 27 for suit dated 1275 which shows that Emma de Widworthy was wife of *Robert* de Dynham, and daughter of *Hugh* de Widworthy). Paget *Baronage of England* (1957) 187: 1–9 (sub Dinan). Erskine *Devonshire Lay Subsidy of 1332* (Devon & Cornwall Rec. Soc. n.s. 14) (1969): 105. Kleineke "The Dinham Fam. in the Later Middle Ages" (1998): 27, note 99 (seal used by Margaret Botreaux, wife of John de Dinham, attached to Cornwall Rec. Office Doc., AR1/397: "a tree surmounted by two shields of arms, the first one being DINHAM, the other chequy, a bend [BOTREAUX]). Cornwall Rec. Office: Arundell of Lanherne & Trerice, AR/1/397 — agreement for adjustment of dower dated 29 March 1343 between Lady Margaret widow of Sir John de Dyneham, Knt., and Sir John [de Dyneham], son and heir of Sir John de Dyneham (available at www.a2a.org.uk/search/index.asp).

6. JOHN DE DINHAM (or **DYNHAM**), Knt., of Hartland and Harpford, Devon, Cardinham, Cornwall, Buckland Dinham and Corton Dinham, Somerset, etc., son and heir, born about 1318 (aged 14 in 1332). He had livery of his father's lands 12 May 1340. He presented to the church of Corton Dinham, Somerset in 1344. In 1346 he quitclaimed lands in Whyteleigh (in Hartford) to his cousin, Oliver de Dinham. He married before 27 March 1357 (date of charter) **MURIEL DE COURTENAY**, daughter of Thomas de Courtenay, Knt., of Woodhuish and Dunterton, Devon, and Wootton Courtenay and Cricket Malherbie, Somerset, by Muriel, daughter of John de Moels, Knt., 4th Lord Moels [see COURTENAY 6.iii for her ancestry]. They had one son, John, Knt., and one daughter, Joan. His wife, Muriel, died before 12 August 1369, and was buried at Hartland Abbey, Devon. SIR JOHN DE DINHAM died 7 Jan. 1382/3, being murdered by robbers.

Weaver *Somerset Incumbents* (1889): 74. *Genealogist* n.s. 12 (1895): 228. Vivian *Vis. of Devon 1531, 1564 & 1620* (1895): 243–250 (sub Courtenay). Ralph of Shrewsbury *Reg. of Ralph of Shrewsbury Bishop of Bath & Wells* 2 (Somerset Rec. Soc. 10) (1896): 511, 566. *Somerset & Dorset Notes & Queries* 6 (1899): 289–295. Green *Feet of Fines for Somerset* 3 (Somerset Rec. Soc. 17) (1902): 111. *Rpt. & Trans. of the Devonshire Assoc.* 2nd Ser. 4 (1902): 721–723. Wrottesley *Peds. from the Plea Rolls* (1905): 68–69, 129. VCH *Hampshire* 4 (1911): 531. *C.P.* 4 (1916): 373–374 (sub Dinham). *C.F.R.* 9 (1926): 136. *Genealogist's Mag.* 6 (1932–34): 606–626. Paget *Baronage of England* (1957) 187: 1–9 (sub Dinan); 368: 1–7 (sub Moels). VCH *Oxford* 11 (1983): 295. Cornwall Rec. Office: Arundell of Lanherne & Trerice, AR/1/912 (available at www.a2a.org.uk/search/index.asp).

Children of John de Dinham, Knt., by Muriel de Courtenay:

i. **JOHN DINHAM**, Knt. [see next].

ii. **JOAN DINHAM**, married **MAURICE BERKELEY**, Knt., of Uley, Gloucestershire [see DEIGHTON 9].

7. JOHN DINHAM, Knt., of Hartland, Harpford, Kingskerwell, and Nutwell, Devon, Buckland Dinham, Somerset, Cardinham, Cornwall, Over Worton, Oxfordshire, etc., son and heir, born about 1358–9 (aged 10 or 11 in 1369). He was co-heir in 1369 to his uncle, Hugh de Courtenay, by which he inherited the manors of Kingskerwell, Woodhuish, and Dunterton, Devon, Cricket Malherbie and Northome, Somerset, Over Wallop, Hampshire, etc. He married (1st) before 3 Feb. 1379/80 **ELEANOR** (or **ELLEN**) **MONTAGU**, daughter of John de Montagu, Knt., Lord Montagu, by Margaret, daughter and heiress of Thomas de Monthermer, Knt., 2nd Lord Monthermer [see MONTAGU 8 for her ancestry].[17] They had one daughter, Muriel. In 1383 he did homage to the Abbot of Mulchelney for his lands in Hillegh, Somerset (a Courtenay property). The same year he was pardoned for killing Robert Tuwyng and imprisoning John Broun, notorious thieves, after their conviction for murdering his father. His wife, Eleanor, was a legatee in the 1389 will of her father, who bequeathed her a gilt cup and a crown. Eleanor died in 1393–4. He married (2nd) after 1

---

[17] The material below is based on the original research of John P. Ravilious and is gratefully included here: Eleanor (or Ellen), 1st wife of John Dinham, Knt., is identified in *Complete Peerage* only as "Ellen," with the note that she was alive on 22 Sept 1387 [see *C.P.* 4 (1916): 375 note g, 376 note a (sub Dinham)]. She is elsewhere named as "Ellen" and "Eleanor" in licenses granted by the Bishop of Exeter dating from Feb 1379/80 to 1382 [see Brantingham *Reg. Thomas de Brantyngham* 1 (Episc. Regs. of the Diocese of Exeter 6) (1901): 418, 472, 481]. Her connection to the Montagu family is suggested by a household account of the Dinham family dated c.1381–6 which records the "expenses of John de Dynham de Hertilond going to Warblington to fetch his wife" [see Cornwall Rec. Office: Arundell of Lanherne & Trerice, AR/37/56/1 (available at http://www.a2a.org.uk/search/index.asp); Hannes Kleineke, "Dinham Family in the Later Middle Ages" (Ph.D. Thesis, Royal Holloway and Bedford New College, 1998): 139]. The manor of Warblington, Hampshire was held during this period by John de Montagu, Knt., and his wife, Margaret de Monthermer, it later being Margaret's place of burial [see *VCH Hampshire* 3 (1908): 134–139; Kirby *Wykeham's Reg.* 2 (1899): 555]. There are also itineraries of various Dinham officials repeatedly visiting Warblington, Hampshire in the spring of 1381, the spring of 1383, the winter of 1383/84, between June 1384 and June 1385, and August 1394 [see Cornwall Rec. Office: Arundell of Lanherne & Trerice, AR/37/39; AR/37/44; AR/37/45; "8 Ric II", date assigned to AR/37/46 (available at http://www.a2a.org.uk/search/index.asp); Kleineke "Dinham Family in the Later Middle Ages" (1998): 155–156, 160]. These visits to Warblington only occurred during the period of John Dinham's marriage to his 1st wife, Eleanor (or Ellen), and ceased following her death in 1393/4. It is known that Sir John and Margaret de Montagu had a daughter named Eleanor. She is named in the will of her father dated 20 March 1387/88, in which he devised "to Alianore, my daughter, the crown which my wife had in her custody" [see Nicolas *Testamenta Vetusta* 1 (1826): 124]. A crown or coronet was subsequently represented on Ellen/Eleanor Dinham's effigy at Kingskerswell, Devon, which is described by one historian as "The [female] figure in the easternmost window wearing a coronet…" [see Stabb *Some Old Devon Churches* 2 (1911): 140]. Moreover, there is heraldic evidence of the marriage of Sir John de Dinham and a daughter of John de Montagu. In 1644 Richard Symonds recorded various arms dating from the 14th & 15th Centuries then displayed in the windows of Exeter Cathedral. Two arms which he matched in one window were "Argent, three fusils conjoined in fess gules, a bordure sable" and "Gules, three fusils conjoined in fess ermine" [DINHAM]" [see Symond *Diary of the Marches* (1997): 85]. The first set of arms "Argent, three fusils conjoined in fess gules, a bordure sable" can be identified as those employed by Sir John de Montagu (died 1378), husband of Margaret de Monthermer [see Willement *Roll of Arms of the Reign of Richard II* (1834): 11].

August 1396 (date of charter) and before 26 Nov. 1396 (date of bishop's license) **MAUD MAUTRAVERS**, widow of Peter de la Mare, Knt. (died 1396), of Lavington (in Market Lavington), Wiltshire, Offley, Hertfordshire, etc., and elder daughter and co-heiress of John Mautravers, Knt., of Hooke, Dorset, Crowell, Oxfordshire, etc., by Elizabeth, daughter of William Daumarle, Knt. [see MAUTRAVERS 12 for her ancestry]. She was born about 1368 (aged 18 in 1386). They had no issue. In 1396 his wife, Maud, received a license to choose a confessor. In 1397 he was accused by the Abbot of Hartland of breaking into the latter's houses, assaulting him and chasing him to his chamber, and ill-treating his servants. He was bound over in 1,000 marks to keep the peace 27 Feb. 1397/8, but was guilty of other assaults on the king's subjects 5 Jan. 1401/2 and 1 Dec. 1404; he was subsequently pardoned for these offences 28 April 1407. In 1402 he and others were accused by the Abbot of Torre of digging up a road at Kingskerwell, Devon and assaulting the Abbot's men. His wife, Maud, died about 1 Nov. 1402. He married (3rd) before 1406 **PHILIPPE LOVEL**, daughter of John Lovel, K.G., 5th Lord Lovel, Lord Holand, by Maud, daughter and heiress of Robert de Holand, of Nether Kellet, Lancashire [see LOVEL 13 for her ancestry]. They had one son, John, Knt., and two daughters, Maud (wife of Thomas Brooke, Esq.) and Philippe (wife of Thomas Beaumont, Knt.). His feoffees presented to the church of Corton Dinham, Somerset in 1418, 1422, and 1425. In 1422 they received a papal indult for plenary remission. SIR JOHN DINHAM died 25 Dec. 1428. His widow, Philippe, was granted a license 4 Jan. 1428/9 by the Bishop of Exeter for divine service in her presence in any suitable place in the diocese. She married (2nd) before 24 March 1428/9 **NICHOLAS BROUGHTON**, Esq. He and his wife, Philippe, presented to the church of Hemyock, Devon in Feb. 1444/5. NICHOLAS BROUGHTON, Esq., was living 3 Nov. 1459. His wife, Philippe, died 15 May 1465.

Nicolas *Testamenta Vetusta* 1 (1826): 124–125 (will of John Montacute, Knt.); 2 (1826): 395 (Beaumont ped.). *Coll. Top. et Gen.* 6 (1840): 334–361. Hutchins *Hist. & Antiqs. of Dorset* 3 (1868): 314–321. Weaver *Somerset Incumbents* (1889): 74, 136, 345. Rogers *Strife of the Roses & Days of the Tudors in the West* (1890): 137–154. *Wiltshire Notes & Queries* 1 (1893–5): 557–559; 2 (1896–8): 255–261; 3 (1899–1901): 193–202. Vivian *Vis. of Devon* (1895): 65–66 (Beaumont ped.). Bates *Two Cartularies of the Benedictine Abbeys of Muchelney & Athelney* (Somerset Rec. Soc. 14) (1899): 161–162. *Procs. Bath Natural Hist. & Antiq. Field Club* 9 (1901): 188–201. *Rpt. & Trans. of the Devonshire Assoc.* 2nd Ser. 4 (1902): 721–723. *Papal Regs.: Letters* 7 (1906): 321. Green *Feet of Fines for Somerset* 4 (Somerset Rec. Soc. 22) (1906): 165. *C.P.R.* 1436–1441 (1907): 316. Weaver *Feodary of Glastonbury Abbey* (Somerset Rec. Soc. 26) (1910): 36, footnote 1. VCH *Hampshire* 4 (1911): 531. VCH *Hertford* 3 (1912): 39–44. Bubwith *Reg. of Nicholas Bubwith Bishop of Bath & Wells* 2 (Somerset Rec. Soc. 30) (1914): 342. *C.P.* 4 (1916): 374–377 (sub Dinham). *C.F.R.* 9 (1926): 136. Schofield *Mulchelney Memoranda* (Somerset Rec. Soc. 42) (1927): 79–80, 98–99. *Genealogist's Mag.* 6 (1932–34): 606–626. *Procs. Cambridge Antiq. Soc.* 33 (1933): 61–82. *Somerset & Dorset Notes & Queries* 25 (1950): 32. Paget *Baronage of England* (1957) 187: 1–9 (sub Dinan); 372: 1–15 (sub Montacute). Lacy *Reg. of Edmund Lacy* 1 (Devon & Cornwall Rec. Soc. n.s. 7) (1963): 215; 4 (Devon & Cornwall Rec. Soc. n.s. 16) (1971): 277–278. *Cal. IPM* 16 (1974): 98–100; 23 (2004): 133–136. VCH *Somerset* 3 (1974): 111–120. VCH *Wiltshire* 10 (1975): 78. VCH *Oxford* 11 (1983): 295. Lewis *Essays in Later Medieval French Hist.* (1985): 227–228 (identifies Philippe Lovel, wife of John Dinham, as daughter of John Lovel, 5th Lord Lovel [died 1408]). Kleineke "The Dinham Fam. in the Later Middle Ages" (1998). Roskell *Parl. & Politics in Late Medieval England* 2 (1981): 3 (re. Peter de la Mare). Cornwall Rec. Office: Arundell of Lanherne & Trerice, AR/1/911; AR/1/912 (available at www.a2a.org.uk/search/index.asp). National Archives, SC 8/107/5313 (available at www.catalogue.nationalarchives.gov.uk/search.asp).

Child of John Dinham, Knt., by Eleanor (or Ellen) Montagu:

i. **MURIEL DINHAM**, married **EDWARD HASTINGS**, Knt., of Elsing, Norfolk [see ELSING 14].

Child of John Dinham, Knt., by Philippe Lovel:

i. **JOHN DINHAM**, Knt. [see next].

8. **JOHN DINHAM**, Knt., of Hartland, Dunterton, Kingskerwell, Nutwell, Sidmouth, Southbrook (in Broad Clyst), Venn Ottery, etc., Devon, Buckland Dinham, Corton Dinham, Cricket Malherbie, Maperton, etc., Somerset, Over Worton, Oxfordshire, etc., son and heir by his father's 3rd marriage, born about 1406 (aged 22 in 1428). He presented to the churches of Cricket Malherbie, Somerset,

1429, 1445; Corton Dinham, Somerset, 1434, 1436; Dunterton, Devon, 1434, and Maperton, Somerset, 1451, and to the chantry at Hemyock, Devon, 1442. In 1430 and 1431 he was in France with the King. He married before 12 July 1434 **JOAN ARCHES**, daughter of Richard Arches, Knt., of Oving, Eythrope, Cranwell, and Little Kimble, Buckinghamshire, Knight of the Shire for Buckinghamshire, by Joan, granddaughter and coheiress of Sir Giles Ardern, of Drayton, Oxfordshire. She was born about 1410 (aged 11 in 1421). She was sister and heiress of John Arches. They had four sons, John, K.G. [Lord Dinham], Roger, Esq., Charles, Esq., and Oliver [Archdeacon of Norfolk and Surrey; Canon of St. George's Chapel, Windsor], and four daughters, Margaret (or Margery), Elizabeth, Joan (wife of John Zouche, 7th Lord Zouche of Harringworth), and Katherine. In 1444 the Abbot of Hartland charged him with breaking into the Abbot's close and houses at Stoke St. Nectan, and taking his horses, sheep and cattle. In 1452 his wife, Joan, was co-heiress to her Shareshull cousin, Joan Lee, by which she inherited the manors of Dornford (in Wootton), Rousham, and Steeple Barton, Oxfordshire. SIR JOHN DINHAM died 25 Jan. 1457/8, and was buried in the Church of the Black Friars, Exeter, Devon. In 1460 his widow, Joan, sued John Langston in Chancery for possession the manors of Glynton, Ludwell, and Dunstrew, Oxfordshire. She left a will dated 26 Jan. 1496/7, proved 3 Nov. 1497 (P.C.C. 10 Horne), requesting burial by her husband at Black Friars, Exeter.

Fuller *Hist. of the Worthies of England* (1840): 427–428. Westcote *View of Devonshire in MDCXXX* (1845): 199–200. Monro *Letters of Queen Margaret of Anjou & Bishop Beckington* (Camden Soc. 86) (1863): 144. Weaver *Somerset Incumbents* (1889): 74, 136, 345. *Rpt. & Trans. of the Devonshire Assoc.* 2nd Ser. 4 (1902): 721–723. VCH *Hampshire* 4 (1911): 531. C.P. 4 (1916): 377–382 (sub Dinham); 12(2) (1959): 946–947 (sub Zouche). *Papal Regs.: Letters* 11 (1921): 570, 632. VCH *Berkshire* 4 (1924): 298. Brookes *Hist. of Steeple Aston & Middle Aston* (1929): 67–73. *Genealogist's Mag.* 6 (1932–34): 606–626. *Procs. Cambridge Antiq. Soc.* 33 (1933): 61–82. Paget *Baronage of England* (1957) 187: 1–9 (sub Dinan). Lacy *Reg. of Edmund Lacy* 1 (Devon & Cornwall Rec. Soc. n.s. 7) (1963): 272; 2 (Devon & Cornwall Rec. Soc. n.s. 10) (1966): 265. VCH *Oxford* 10 (1972): 42–49; 11 (1983): 59–75, 259–285, 295. *Nottingham Medieval Studies* 34 (1990): 113–140. Roskell *House of Commons 1386–1421* 2 (1992): 48–49 (biog. of Sir Richard Arches). *Cal. IPM* 23 (2004): 133–136. Cornwall Rec. Office: Arundell of Lanherne & Trerice, AR/1/911 (available at www.a2a.org.uk/search/index.asp).

Children of John Dinham, Knt., by Joan Arches:

i. **JOHN DINHAM**, K.G., of Hartland, Devon, Buckland Dinham, Somerset, Cardinham, Cornwall, Dornford (in Wootton), Rousham, Souldern, Steeple Aston, and Steeple Barton, Oxfordshire, etc., Sheriff of Devonshire, 1460–1, Keeper of Dartmoor Forest, Steward of Bradninch, Devon, Warden of the Stanneries in Devon, Lord High Treasurer, 1486–1501, son and heir, born at Nutwell, Devon about 1434 (aged 24 in 1458). He presented to the churches of Cricket Malherbie Cricket Malherbie, Somerset, 1458, 1489; Maperton, Somerset, 1465, 1482, 1487; and Corton Dinham, Somerset, 1472, 1473, and 1489. After the skirmish at Ludford 12 October 1459, he assisted Edward, Earl of March, and the Earls of Warwick and Salisbury to escape from Devonshire to Guernsey and thence to Calais. In Jan. 1460 he headed an expedition which captured Sandwich, and took back Lord Rivers and his son prisoners. He married (1st) in 1467 **ELIZABETH FITZ WALTER**, widow of John Radcliffe, Esq., of Attleborough, Norfolk (died 28 March 1461) [see BURNELL 15], and daughter and heiress of Walter Fitz Walter, Knt., 5th Lord Fitz Walter, by Elizabeth, daughter of John Chidiock, Knt. [see FITZ WALTER 13 for her ancestry]. She was born at Henham, Essex 28 July 1430, and baptized there (aged 1-½ in 1432). They had two sons, Roger and George, and one daughter, Philippe. He was summoned to Parliament from 28 Feb. 1466/7 to 16 Jan. 1496/7, by writs directed *Johanni Dynham de Care Dynham*, whereby he is held to have become Lord Dinham. He was made a commander of an armed force at sea 15 April 1475. His wife, Elizabeth, was living June 1483, but died before August 1485. He was admitted a member of Lincoln's Inn in 1486. He married (2nd) **ELIZABETH WILLOUGHBY**, daughter of Robert Willoughby, K.G., 1st Lord Willoughby of Brook, by Blanche, daughter and co-heiress of John Champernoun, Esq. [see BROOK 14 for her ancestry]. They had no issue. By an unknown mistress, he had one illegitimate son, Thomas, Knt. He also had a son, George, living 1470, of undetermined mother. SIR JOHN DINHAM, Lord Dinham, died 28 Jan. 1500/1, and was buried 30 Jan. 1500/1, in the church of the Grey Friars, London. He left a will dated 7 Jan. 1500[/1], proved 4 May 1509 (P.C.C. 14 Bennett). His wife, Elizabeth, was living 28 Jan. 1502. She is said to have married (2nd) (as his 1st wife) **WILLIAM ARUNDEL**, K.G., K.B., 18th Earl of Arundel [see ARUNDEL 13.i]. Clutterbuck *Hist. & Antiqs. of Hertford* 3 (1827): 512–514 (Willoughby ped.). Dugdale *Monasticon Anglicanum* 6(1) (1830): 148. Westcote *View of Devonshire in MDCXXX* (1845): 199–200. Whitaker *Hist. of Original Parish of Whalley* 2(2) (1876): chart foll. 292.

Weaver *Somerset Incumbents* (1889): 74, 136, 345. Baildon *Recs. of Lincoln's Inn: Admissions* 1 (1896): 24. *List of Sheriffs for England & Wales* (PRO Lists and Indexes 9) (1898): 36. *Rpt. & Trans. of the Devonshire Assoc.* 2nd Ser. 4 (1902): 721–723. Green *Feet of Fines for Somerset* 4 (Somerset Rec. Soc. 22) (1906): 207–208. *Misc. Gen. et Heraldica* 4th Ser. 2 (1908): 17–20. VCH *Hampshire* 4 (1911): 531. Kingsford *Grey Friars of London* (1915): 134–139. *C.P.* 4 (1916): 378–382 (sub Dinham); 5 (1926): 484–486 (sub Fitz Walter). Stephenson *List of Mon. Brasses in Surrey* (1921): 317–318. *Genealogist's Mag.* 6 (1932–34): 606–626. *Procs. Cambridge Antiq. Soc.* 33 (1933): 61–82. Stillington & Fox *Regs. of Robert Stillington & Richard Fox* (Somerset Rec. Soc. 52) (1937): 43, 53. Paget *Baronage of England* (1957) 187: 1–9 (sub Dinan). Reaney & Fitch *Feet of Fines for Essex* 4 (1964): 97. VCH *Oxford* 10 (1972): 42–49; 11 (1983): 21–44, 59–75, 159–168, 259–285, 295. *Ancient Deeds — Ser. A* 2 (List & Index Soc. 152) (1978): 105. Kirby *Abs. of Feet of Fines Rel. Wiltshire 1377–1509* (Wiltshire Rec. Soc. 41) (1986): 147–148. Roskell *House of Commons 1386–1421* 4 (1992): 155–159 (biog. of Sir John Radcliffe). *Cal. IPM* 23 (2004): 373–381.

ii. **OLIVER DINHAM**, clerk, Chaplain to the king, younger son, born about 1440 (aged 19 in 1459). He was charged for rent of room in Exeter College, Oxford, 1461; still in 1463. He supplicated for B.A. degree, 1458; allowed to wear *pellura* on his academic habit, 1458. While studying at Oxford, being in his 19th year, he was granted a papal dispensation to hold two benefices 14 June 1459. He was appointed Rector of Poole, Dorset, vacated by 1461; Rector of Cheshunt, Hertfordshire, 1461; Rector of Mildenhall, Suffolk, 1461; Canon of Lincoln and Prebendary of Keton, 1464; Vicar of Langford, Bedfordshire, 1464; Canon of Lichfield and prebendary of Wolvey, 1467, vacated 1500; Rector of Matlock, Derbyshire, 1467, vacated by 1483; Rector of Heneock, Devon, 1473; Canon of Salisbury and Prebendary of Shipton, 1477, vacated by 1479; Prebendary of St. Laurence Major in Romsey Abbey, Hampshire, 1478; Archdeacon of Norfolk, 1479; Canon of St. George's Chapel, Windsor, Berkshire, 1480; Archdeacon of Surrey, 1482; Canon of Wells and Prebendary of Litton, 1489; Master of St. Giles' Hospital, Norwich, 1489, vacated by 1495; Rector of Coltishall, Norfolk, 1490; Rector of Amersham, Buckinghamshire, 1493; Prebendary of Colwich, 1500; Rector of Tawstock, Devon; Canon and Prebendary of Crediton, Devon. OLIVER DINHAM died 3 April 1500. He left a will dated 2 April 1500, proved 30 May 1500 (P.C.C. 9 Moone), requesting burial in the church of Farnham, Surrey. Emden *Biog. Reg. of the Univ. of Oxford* 1 (1957): 618 (biog. of Oliver Dynham).

iii. **MARGARET** (or **MARGERY**) **DINHAM**, married **NICHOLAS CAREW**, Esq., Baron Carew [see CAREW 17].

iv. **ELIZABETH DINHAM**, married (1st) **FULK BOURCHIER**, Knt., 10th Lord Fitz Warin [see FITZ WARIN 17]; (2nd) **JOHN SAPCOTE**, Knt., of Elton, Huntingdonshire [see FITZ WARIN 17]; (3rd) **THOMAS BRANDON**, K.G., of Southwark, Surrey [see BERKELEY 10.i; FITZ WARIN 17; WILLOUGHBY 12.ii].

v. **KATHERINE DINHAM**, married **THOMAS ARUNDELL**, K.B., of Lanherne, Cornwall [see CHIDIOCK 15].

✥ DODDINGTON ✥

ROBERT DE VERE, Knt., Earl of Oxford, married **ISABEL DE BOLEBEC**.
ELEANOR DE VERE, married **RALPH GERNON**, Knt., of East Thorpe, Essex.
WILLIAM GERNON, Knt., of East Thorpe, Essex, married **ISABEL** _____.
JOHN GERNON, Knt., of East Thorpe, Essex, married **ALICE DE COLEVILLE**.
JOHN GERNON, Knt., of East Thorpe, Essex, married **ALICE** _____.
MARGARET GERNON, married **JOHN PEYTON**, Knt., of Peyton Hall (in Boxford), Essex.
JOHN PEYTON, of Peyton Hall (in Boxford), Essex, married **JOAN SUTTON**.
JOHN PEYTON, Esq., of East Thorpe, Essex, married **GRACE BURGOYNE**.
THOMAS PEYTON, Knt., of Isleham, Cambridgeshire, married **MARGARET BERNARD**.
THOMAS PEYTON, married **JOAN CALTHORPE**.
ROBERT PEYTON, Knt., of Isleham, Cambridgeshire, married **ELIZABETH CLERE** [see PEYTON 11].

12. JOHN PEYTON, Esq., of Knowlton, Northcote, and Thornton (in Eastry), Kent, Burgess (M.P.) for Hastings, Burgess (M.P.) of Winchelsea, 2nd son, born about 1503. By virtue of a fine levied in 1515 by John Langley, Esq. (husband of his aunt, Jane Peyton), he inherited the manors of Knowlton and Northcourt, Kent. He was a legatee in the 1518 will of his father, who bequeathed him the manor of Calthorpe Hall (in Barnham St. Martin), Suffolk. He was admitted a student at Gray's Inn in 1521. He married about 1537 **DOROTHY TYNDALL**, eldest daughter of John

Tyndall, K.B., of Hockwold, Norfolk, by Amphyllis, daughter of Humphrey Coningsby, Knt. [see TYNDALL 13 for her ancestry]. They had three sons, Thomas, Knt., John, Knt., and Edward, and two daughters, Elizabeth (wife of Thomas Monins, Esq.) and Frances (wife of Thomas Engeham, Esq.). He was the residuary legatee of the 1551 will of his aunt, Jane Peyton, widow successively of John Langley, Esq., of Knowlton, Kent, and Edward Ringeley, Knt. JOHN PEYTON, Esq., died intestate 22 October 1558. His widow, Dorothy, was living 18 October 1559.

    Waters *Chester of Chicheley* 1 (1878): 204–205, 288, 245–248, 276. Foster *Reg. of Admissions to Gray's Inn 1521–1889* (1889): 31. Philipot *Vis. of Kent 1619–1621* (H.S.P. 42) (1898): 66–67 (Peyton ped.: "Joh'es Peyton miles fil. 2^{dus} cui pater eius dedit Manor de Calthorpe in Burneham St Martins et Knolton in co' Cantij. = Dorothea filia Joh'is Tindall Militis Balnei ad Coronationem Annæ Bolenæ Reginæ Angliæ."). Copinger *Manors of Suffolk* 1 (1905): 22–28. Bindoff *House of Commons 1509–1558* 3 (1982): 100–101.

13. JOHN PEYTON, Knt., of Doddington, Cambridgeshire, 2nd son, born about 1541, and inherited his father's leasehold estates in Cambridgeshire. He served with distinction in the Irish Wars until the end of 1576, when he returned to England. He married at Outwell, Norfolk 8 June 1578 **DOROTHY BEAUPRÉ**, widow of Robert Bell, Knt., Chief Baron of the Exchequer (died 25 July 1571), and daughter and heiress of Edmund Beaupré, Esq., of Beaupré Hall in Outwell, Norfolk, by his 2nd wife, Katherine Bedingfield. His wife, Dorothy, died in February 1602/3. He served in the English army expedition in the Netherlands under the command of the Earl of Leicester in 1586. From this time he was in constant favor with Queen Elizabeth I. He was made Lieutenant of the Tower, and a member of the Queen's Privy Council. After Queen Elizabeth's death, he was made Governor of Jersey by King James I. His wife, Dorothy, died in February 1602/3. SIR JOHN PEYTON died intestate 4 Nov. 1630, and was buried at Doddington, Cambridgeshire.

    Waters *Chester of Chicheley* 1 (1878): 288–300. Philipot *Vis. of Kent 1619–1621* (H.S.P. 42) (1898): 66–67 (Peyton ped.: "Joh'es Peyton Miles nuper p'fectus Turris Londinensis. = Alicia filia et cohær. Edw: Beaupre de Well in com' Norff. militis vidua Rob'ti Bell milit. vnivs B'ronu' Sc'crio.").

14. JOHN PEYTON, Knt., of Doddington, Cambridgeshire, Lieutenant-Governor of Jersey, 1628–33, son and heir, born about 1579 (aged 51 in 1630). He was admitted in 1594 a Fellow Commoner of Queen's College, Cambridge. He married at Isleham, Cambridgeshire 25 Nov. 1602 **ALICE PEYTON**, 2nd daughter of John Peyton, Knt., Bart., of Isleham, Cambridgeshire, by Alice, eldest daughter of Edward Osborne, Knt., Lord Mayor of London [see PEYTON 14 for her ancestry]. They had three sons, Robert, Algernon, and Henry, and six daughters, Elizabeth (wife of Anthony Chester, Knt., Bart.), Alice (wife of Edward Lowe, Gent.), Dorothy (wife of Laurence Oxburgh, Esq.), Frances (wife of Francis Fortescue, Esq.), Susanna (wife of John Richers, Esq.), and Anne. On the death of Queen Elizabeth I in 1603, he was dispatched by his father to Edinburgh to assure King James I of his father's loyalty and that the Tower was being held at the king's disposal. The king received him with much distinction, and, recognizing his father's services, selected him as the first person on whom he bestowed knighthood. In 1603 the king granted him the manor of Lyngen and five other manors in Herefordshire, escheated to the crown by the attainder of Edward Lyngen. SIR JOHN PEYTON left a will dated 24 Feb. 1634/5, proved 22 April 1635 (P.C.C. 33 Sadler). His widow, Alice, was living in 1638.

    Betham *Baronetage of England* 1 (1801): 42–49 (sub Peyton). Lennard & Vincent *Vis. of Warwick 1619* (H.S.P. 12) (1877): 378–381 (Peiton ped.: "Joh'es Peiton miles fil. et hæres was the first Knight yt K. James made after he was K. of Engl. for bringing him the first newes of the death of Queene Elizab. = Alicia filia Joh'is Peiton de Isleham miles et Baronettus."). Waters *Chester of Chicheley* 1 (1878): 222, 288 (chart), 310–318. Philipot *Vis. of Kent 1619–1621* (H.S.P. 42) (1898): 66–67 (Peyton ped.: "Joh'es Peyton p'mus milit. Angliæ ab adventu. = Alicia filia Joh'is Peyton militis ac Baronetti."). Copinger *Manors of Suffolk* 1 (1905): 22–28.

Child of John Peyton, Knt., by Alice Peyton:

    i. **ANNE PEYTON**, married **GEORGE BRENT**, of Defford, Worcestershire [see BRENT 18].

ᎦDONZYᎦ

WILLIAM THE CONQUEROR, King of England, married **MAUD OF FLANDERS**.
ADÈLE OF ENGLAND, married **ÉTIENNE HENRI**, Count of Blois, Chartres, etc.
THIBAUT IV, Count of Blois, Champagne, and Troyes, married **MATHILDE OF CARINTHIA** [see BLOIS 3].

4. ISABELLE (or **ÉLIZABETH**) **OF BLOIS**, born about 1130. She married (1st) after August 1140 (date of marriage proposal) and before 1143 **ROGER DE HAUTEVILLE**, Duke of Apulia, son of Roger II, King of Sicily, Duke of Apulia, by his 1st wife, Elvira, daughter of Alfonso VI, King of Castile and León. He was probably born ar Christmas 1130. They had no issue. ROGER DE HAUTEVILLE, Duke of Apulia, died 2 May 1149. His widow, Isabelle, married (2nd) about 1150–55 **GUILLAUME GOUET** (or **GOËT, GOËTH**), seigneur of Montmirail, Alluyes, Authon, la Bazoche-Gouet, Brou, and le Saulee, son and heir of Guillaume Gouet, seigneur of Montmirail and Alluyes, by Mabel, illegitimate daughter of Henry I, King of England [see ENGLAND 2.v for his ancestry]. They had two daughters, Mathilde and Agnès (wife of Rotrou de Montfort). In 1157 he confirmed all that which Tiron Abbey possessed in his fiefs of Montmirail, Alluyes, Authon, la Bazoche-Gouet, Brou, and le Saulee, and the exemption of all customs. In 1168, at the moment of leaving on Crusade, he issued a confirmation charter to Gué-de-Launay Abbey, which charter was granted with the consent of his wife, Isabelle, and his daughters, Mathilde and Agnes. GUILLAUME GOËT died on Crusade in Palestine in 1169. In 1173 she witnessed a charter of her brother-in-law and sister, Rotrou III, Count of Perche, and his wife, Mathilde, to Bonneval Abbey. She became a nun at Fontevrault in 1180. About 1198 she gave her consent to a gift of Renaud de Orreville to the canons of Unverre. Isabelle, Duchess of Apulia, died at Fontevrault 13 August, year uncertain.

Duchesne *Histoire de la Maison de Chastillon sur Marne* (1621): 69–72. Le Pelletier *Histoire des Comtes de Champagne et de Brie* 1 (1753): 223–224. Doyen *Histoire de la Ville de Chartres* 1 (1786): 303–304. *Études sur le Maine, Noblesse du Maine aux Croisades* (1859): 49–50. Delisle *Chronique de Robert de Torigni* 2 (1873): 15–16 (sub A.D. 1169: "Cum Guillermus Goeth obiisset in itinere Jerusalem, et comes Theobaldus vellet habere in manu sua Montem Mirabilem et alias firmitates, quae fuerant Guillermi Goeth, de quibus saisitus erat Herveus de Juen [Gien], qui habebat in conjugio primogenitam filiam Guillermi Goeth, natam ex una sororum comitis Teobaldi."). Lalore *Collection des Principaux Obituaires et Confraternités du Diocèse de Troyes* (Coll. de Documents Inédits relatif a la Ville de Troyes et a la Champagne Méridionale 2) (1882): 284 (Obituaire de Saint-Étienne: 13 August — "Ce jour, mémoire d'Elisabeth, duchesse de Pouille [épouse du duc Roger], soeur du comte Henri [Ier, le Libéral]"). Merlet *Cartulaire de l'Abbaye de la Sainte-Trinite de Tiron* 1 (1883): 24–27; 2 (1883): 79–80 (confirmation charter of Guillaume Goët dated 1168). Boulais *Recueil des Antiquitéz du Perche* (1890): 86, 115–116, 125–126. Merlet *Inventaire-sommaire des Archives départementales antérieures à 1790: Eure-et-Loir, Archives Ecclésiastiques, Série H* 8 (1897): 162. Souancé & Métais *Saint-Denis de Nogent-le-Rotrou 1031–1789: Histoire et Cartulaire* (1899): 164–166. *Bulls. de la Société Dunoise Archéologie, Histoire, Sciences & Arts* 10 (1904): 171–188. Merlet *Cartulaire de l'Abbaye de Saint-Jean-en-Vallee de Chartres* (Coll. de Cartulaires Chartrains 1) (1906): 66 (charter of Renaud de Orreville). *Société des Lettres, Sciences et Arts du Saumurois* 5 (1914): 9–11. *Obituaires de la Province de Sens* 4 (1923): 192 (Prieuré de Fontaines: "13 Aug. — Domina Elisabeth, venerabilis monacha, ducissa, soror domine Marie ducisse."), 545 ("13 August — Mémoire d'Élisabeth, duchesse de Pouille, soeur du comte Henri."). Pertz *Monumenta Germaniæ Historica: Scriptorum* ser. 23 (1925): 841 (Chronicle of Alberic de Trois-Fontaines: "… Habuit etiam predictus Campanie comes Theobaldus filias sex ... tertia quedam ducissa in partibus remotis. Hanc postea duxit Guilelmus Goez in dyocesi Carnotensi, et genuit duas filias, matrem Gaufridi de Dunzei et Agnetam domnam de Monteforti in Cenomania."). *C.P.* 11 (1949): Appendix D, 115, footnote j. Schwennicke *Europäische Stammtafeln* 2 (1984): 47 (sub Champagne, Blois, Navarre). Winter *Descs. of Charlemagne (800–1400)* (1987): XIII.67 & XIII.1014. Takayama *Administration of the Norman Kingdom of Sicily* (1993): 74. Houben *Roger II von Sizilien* (1997): 92–93, 155A. Keats-Rohan *Family Tree & the Roots of Politics* (1997): 302, 306–307, 308 footnote 43. Grierson & Travaini *Medieval European Coinage* 14 (1998): 101–104. Houben *Roger II of Sicily* (2002): 87–88, 153. Thompson *Power & Border Lordship in Medieval France: County of the Perche 1000–1226* (2002): 94. Napran *Chronicle Of Hainaut* (2005): 26, footnote 102.

5. MATHILDE GOUET, married **HERVÉ III DE DONZY**, seigneur of Donzy, Châtel-Censoy, Cosne, and Gien, and, in right of his wife, of Montmirail, Alluyes, Brou, Authon, and la Bazoche-Gouet, son and heir of Geoffroi IV de Donzy, seigneur of Gien, Saint-Aignan, Cosne, and

Châtel-Censoir. They had six sons, Guillaume Gouet, Philippe, Hervé (IV) [Count of Nevers and Auxerre], Geoffroi (monk), Renaud de Montmirail [seigneur of Alluyes], and Bernard, and one daughter, Marguerite (wife of Gervais du Chastel, seigneur of Châteauneuf-en-Timeraie). He sold the castles of Montmirail and Saint-Aignan to King Henry II of England. In 1187 he gave the monks of La Charité one meadow at Rochefort, and the monks agreed in turn to pray for his soul. HERVÉ III DE DONZY went on the 3rd Crusade in 1189.

> Duchesne *Histoire de la Maison de Chastillon sur Marne* (1621): 69–72. Doyen *Histoire de la Ville de Chartres* 1 (1786): 303–304. *L'Art de vérifier les Dates* 3 (1818): 97–99 (sub Barons de Donzi); 11 (1818): 284–285. Hervey *Paper read before the Archaeological Institute of Suffolk ... 1856* (1858): App. I, 117–121 (Donzi ped.). *Études sur le Maine, Noblesse du Maine aux Croisades* (1859): 49–50. *Mémoires de la Société d'Agriculture, Sciences, Belles-lettres et Arts d'Orléans* 4 (1859): 267–268. *Bull. de la Société Nivernaise des Sciences, Lettres et Arts* 2nd Ser. 1 (1863): 495–497. Lespinasse *Cartulaire du Prieuré de La Charité-sur-Loire* (1887): 171–172 (charter of Hervé de Donzy dated 1187; charter witnessed by his sons, Guillaume Goët and Philippe). Souancé & Métais *Saint-Denis de Nogent-le-Rotrou 1031–1789: Histoire et Cartulaire* (1899): 164–166. *Bulls. de la Société Dunoise Archéologie, Histoire, Sciences & Arts* 10 (1904): 171–188. Merlet *Cartulaire de l'Abbaye de Saint-Jean-en-Vallée de Chartres* (Coll. de Cartulaires Chartrains 1) (1906): 65–66 (charter of Hervé, seigneur of Alluyes dated c.1197; charter witnessed by his brother, Philippe de Donzy). *C.P.* 11 (1949): Appendix D, 115, footnote j. Schwennicke *Europaische Stanmtafeln* 3 (1985): 435 (sub Donzy). Bouchard *Sword, Miter, & Cloister* (1987): 176, 327–329. Keats-Rohan *Family Tree & the Roots of Politics* (1997): 299–314.

6. HERVÉ IV DE DONZY, seigneur of Donzy, Gien, Cosne, Montmirail, and Saint-Aignan, and, in right of his wife, Count of Nevers, Auxerre, and Tonnerre, 3rd son. He was heir in 1194 to his older brother, Philippe de Donzy. In 1197 he gave a charter to Saint-Romain in which he acknowledged that the men of the priory were exempt from all contribution. He married in October 1199 (by dispensation dated 20 Dec. 1213, they being related in the 4th degree of kindred) **MAHAUT** (or **MATHILDE**) **DE COURTENAY**, daughter of Pierre de Courtenay, Count of Nevers, Auxonne, and Tonnerre, Marquis of Namur, seigneur of Courtenay and Montargis, etc., by his 1st wife, Agnès, daughter of Guy I, Count of Nevers, Auxonne, and Tonnerre [see NEVERS 7 for her ancestry]. They had one son, Guillaume, and one daughter, Agnès. In 1210 Count Hervé exchanged the castle of Grignon with Eudes III, Duke of Burgundy, for Rougemont [sur-Armançon] and Asnières [en-Montagne]. He left for the Holy Land in 1217, where he assisted at the Siege of Damietta in 1218–9. HERVÉ IV DE DONZY, Count of Nevers, Auxerre, and Tonnerre, died by poisoning at Château Saint-Aignan (Loir-et-Cher) 22 (or 23) Jan. 1222, and was buried in the church of the Abbey of Pontigny near Auxerre. Mahaut married (2nd) in July 1226 (as his 3rd wife) **GUY** (or **GUIGUES**) **IV D'ALBON**, Count of Nevers and Forez, seigneur of Maumont en Auvergne. He died at Castellaneta (prov. of Lecce) 29 October 1241, and was buried in the collegiale church of Notre Dame of Montbrison (Loire). His widow, Mahaut, Countess of Nevers and Forez, died testate at Coulanges-sur-Yonne 29 July 1257, and was buried in the Abbey of Réconfort near Monceaux-le-Comte (Nièvre).

> Duchesne *Histoire de la Maison de Chastillon sur Marne* (1621): 69–72. Du Bouchet *Histoire généalogique de la Maison royale de Courtenay* (1661). Martene & Durand *Veterum Scriptorum et Monumentorum* 1 (1724): 1162 (Mahaut [de Courtenay], Countess of Nevers, styled "niece" [neptis] by Robert de Courtenay). La Thaumassière *Histoire de Berry* 1 (1689): 310 (Gullaume de Donjon, Archbishop of Bourges, styled "uncle" in charter of Mahaut de Courtenay, Countess of Nevers dated 1223), 311 (Donjon-Courtenay ped.). La Chesnaye Des Bois *Dictionnaire de la Noblesse* 5 (1772): 244–256 (sub Courtenay). La Mure *Hist. des Ducs de Bourbon et des Comtes de Forez* 1 (1809): 203–243. *L'Art de vérifier les Dates* 3 (1818): 97–99 (sub Barons de Donzi); 11 (1818): 205–231 (sub Comtes de Auxerre & Nevers), 285–286. Hervey *Paper read before the Archaeological Institute of Suffolk ... 1856* (1858): App. I, 117–121 (Donzi ped.). *Études sur le Maine, Noblesse du Maine aux Croisades* (1859): 49–50. *Mémoires de la Société d'Agriculture, Sciences, Belles-lettres et Arts d'Orléans* 4 (1859): 267–268. *Bull. de la Société Nivernaise des Sciences, Lettres et Arts* 2nd Ser. 1 (1863): 495–497. Lépinois & Merlet *Cartulaire de Notre-Dame de Chartres* 2 (1863): 43–44 (charter of Hervé, Count of Nevers, dated 1209 names his wife, Countess Mahaut, and his brother, Renaud de Montmirail). Lebeuf *Mémoires concernant l'Histoire civile & ecclésiastique d'Auxerre* 3 (1855): 155–183 (pg. 157: Nécrologe de Cathédrale d'Auxerre — "[22 January] Obitus Hervei de Giemo comitis."). Teulet *Layettes du Trésor des Chartes* 2 (1866): 205–208, 289-290, 312–313, 398-399, 449–450. Gillois *Chroniques du Nivernois: Les Comtes et les Ducs de Nevers* (1867). Lespinasse *Hervé de Donzy, Comte de Nevers* (1868). *Bull. de la Société Nivernaise des*

Sciences, Lettres et Arts 2nd Ser. 5 (1872): 65–106. *Recueil des Historiens des Gaules et de la France* 17 (1878): 658. *Recueil des Historiens des Gaules et de la France* 18 (1879): 736, 783–785. *Recueil des Historiens des Gaules et de la France* 19 (1880): 477 (letter dated: 3 June 1205: "… Significavit nobis dilectus filius nobilis vir O(do) [Eudes] Dux Burgundiæ quod in ecclesia Gallicana grave scandalum est subortum, ex eo quod dilectus filius, nobilis vir Nivernensis Comes, cum consanguinea sua, quam in quarto gradu contingit, de facto solummodo, quia de jure non potuit, contraxit copulam conjugalem."), 586, 551-552, 576, 661, 704, 713, 754. Petit *Hist. des Ducs de Bourgogne de la Race Capétienne* 3 (1889): 378, 430–431, 433–434, 447, 455–456, 465–466, 474. Molinier *Obituaires de la Province de Sens* 1(1) (Recueil des Historiens de la France, Obituaires 1) (1902): 10 (Cathédrale de Sens: "IIII kal. Julius [29 July] Ob. Matildis, comitissa Nivernensis [1257]."); 2 (1906): 35 (Obituaire of Cathedral Church of Chartres: "[23 Jan.] X kal. Anniversarium Hervei, comitis Nivernensis [1223]."), 120 (Obituaire of Cathedral Church of Chartres: "[23 Jan.] X kal. Anniv. Hervei, comitis Nivernensis [1223]"). *Bull. de la Société Nivernaise des Lettres, Sciences & Arts* 3rd Ser. 12 (1908): 30 (Obituaire de l'Abbaye de Notre-Dame de Nevers: "IIII Kalendas Augusti [29 July] O[bit] Matildis, comitissa Nivernensis."), 609 (charter of Hervé, Count of Nevers, dated 1218.), 610–611 (charter of Mahaut, Countess of Nevers, dated October 1222 names her late husband, Hervé, Count of Nevers), 614–615 (charter of Count Guy and his wife, Mahaut, Countess of Nevers and Forez, dated 1230), 615 (charter of Mahaut, Countess of Nevers and Forez, dated 1230). Vidier & Merot *Obituaires de la Province de Sens* 3 (Recueil des Historiens de la France — Obituaires 3) (1909): 464 (Extraits de Baluze: "[23 Jan.] X kal. feb. Eodem die, Herveus, comes Nivernensis [1223]."), 465 (Extraits de Baluze: "[29 July] IIII kal. Eodem die, nobilis mulier Matildis, quondam comitissa Nivernensis [1257]."). Rübel-Blass (1939) 244. Schwennicke *Europaische Stamtafeln* 2 (1984): 17 (sub Courtenay); 3 (1985): 435 (sub Donzy). Bouchard *Sword, Miter, & Cloister* (1987): 327–329, 342, 350–351. Winter *Descs. of Charlemagne (800–1400)* (1987): XV.176 & XV.366. Keats-Rohan *Family Tree & the Roots of Politics* (1997): 299–314. Van Kerrebrouck *Les Capétians 987–1328* (2000): 458.

7. AGNÈS DE DONZY, daughter and heiress. She married before 15 Nov. 1223 **GUY I DE CHÂTILLON**, Chev., Count of Saint-Pol, seigneur of Montjay, Thorigny, Broigny, Pont-Sainte-Maixence, etc., and, in right of his wife, seigneur of Donzy, Cosne, and Saint-Aignan, son of Gautier (or Gaucher) III de Châtillon, Chev., Count of Saint-Pol, seigneur of Châtillon-sur-Marne, by Elizabeth, daughter and co-heiress of Hugues IV Candavène, Count of Saint-Pol. They had one son, Gaucher [seigneur of Montjay], and one daughter, Yolande. His wife, Agnès, died in 1225. **GUY I DE CHÂTILLON**, Count of Saint-Pol, was slain at the Siege of Avignon in mid-August 1226.

Duchesne *Histoire de la Maison de Chastillon sur Marne* (1621): 69–72. *L'Art de vérifier les Dates* 3 (1818): 97–99 (sub Barons de Donzi); 11 (1818): 205–231 (sub Comtes de Auxerre & Nevers), 286. Courcelles *Histoire Généalogique et Héraldique des Pairs de France* 11 (1831): 51–56 (biog. of Gui de Chastillon, comte de Saint-Pol). Hervey *Paper read before the Archaeological Institute of Suffolk … 1856* (1858): App. I, 117–121 (Donzi ped.). *Études sur le Maine, Noblesse du Maine aux Croisades* (1859): 49–50. *Recueil des Historiens des Gaules et de la France* 18 (1879): 783-785; 19 (1880): 738 (letter dated: 15 Nov 1223: "… quod nobilis vir Guido de Castellione cum nobili muliere filia quondam Comitis Nivernensis matrimonium de facto contraxit, quamquam sit ita proxima consanguinitatis linea sibi junctus"), 768 (A[gnes], wife of G[ui] de Castellione, styled "niece" [neptem] by R[obert] de Courtenay). Petit *Hist. des Ducs de Bourgogne de la Race Capétienne* 3 (1889): 455–456. Delaville le Roulx *Cartulaire Général de l'Ordre des Hospitaliers de S. Jean de Jérusalem* 2 (1897): 285. Schwennicke *Europaische Stamtafeln* 3 (1985): 435 (sub Donzy); 7 (1979): 17 (ancestry of Guy de Châtillon) (second marriage of wife). Bouchard *Sword, Miter, & Cloister* (1987): 327–329, 342, 350–351.

8. YOLANDE DE CHÂTILLON, married by settlement dated 30 May 1228 **ARCHAMBAUD DE DAMPIERRE**, seigneur of Bourbon-l'Archambaud, son and heir of Archambaud de Dampierre, seigneur of Bourbon-l'Archambaud and Saint-Dizier, by Beatrix, daughter of Archambaud de Saint-Gérand-le-Puy. They had two daughters, Mahaut and Agnès (wife of Jean of Burgundy and Robert II, Count of Artois). **ARCHAMBAUD DE DAMPIERRE** died at Cyprus 15 Jan. 1249. His widow, Yolande, was heiress in 1251 to her brother, Gaucher de Châtillon, seigneur of Montjay, by which she inherited the baronies of Donzy and Perche-Gouet. She left a will dated April 1254, codicil dated August 1254.

L'Art de vérifier les Dates 3 (1818): 97–99 (sub Barons de Donzi); 11 (1818): 205–231 (sub Comtes de Auxerre & Nevers), 287. Hervey *Paper read before the Archaeological Institute of Suffolk … 1856* (1858): App. I, 117–121 (Donzi ped.). olinier *Obituaires de la Province de Sens* 1(2) (Recueil des Historiens de la France — Obituaires) (1902): 655 (Abbaye de Maubuisson: "kal. mart. [1 March]. Ob. Domina Yolendis, comitissa Nivernensis [1280]."), 657 (Abbaye de Maubuisson: "[2 March] Madame Yolande, comtesse de Nevers [1280], qui nous a donné en aumosne cent livres tournois.")· Rübel-Blass (1939) 244. Schwennicke *Europaische Stanmtafeln* 3(1) (1984): 51 (sub Dampierre). Winter *Descs. of Charlemagne (800–1400)* (1987): XVI.1345 & XV.2018.

Child of Yolande de Châtillon, by Archambaud de Dampierre:

i. **MATHILDE** (or **MAHAUT**) **DE BOURBON**, married **EUDES OF BURGUNDY**, Count of Nevers, Auxerre, and Tonnerre [see BURGUNDY 8].

DRAKE

ALICE OF NORMANDY (sister of King William the Conqueror), married **LAMBERT**, Count of Lens.
JUDITH OF LENS, married **WALTHEOF**, Earl of Northumberland.
ALICE OF NORTHUMBERLAND, married **RALPH DE TONY**, of Flamstead, Hertfordshire.
ROGER DE TONY, of Flamstead, Hertfordshire, married **IDA OF HAINAULT**.
RALPH DE TONY, of Flamstead, Hertfordshire, married **MARGARET OF LEICESTER**.
IDA DE TONY, married **ROGER LE BIGOD**, Knt., Earl of Norfolk.
MARY LE BIGOD, married **RANULPH FITZ ROBERT**, of Middleham, Yorkshire.
RALPH FITZ RANULPH, Knt., of Middleham, Yorkshire, married **ANASTASIA DE PERCY**.
MARY FITZ RANULPH, married **ROBERT DE NEVILLE**, of Middleham, Yorkshire.
RANULPH DE NEVILLE, Knt., 1st Lord Neville of Raby, married **EUPHAME DE CLAVERING**.
RALPH DE NEVILLE, Knt., 2nd Lord Neville of Raby, married **ALICE DE AUDLEY** (desc. King William the Conqueror).
JOHN DE NEVILLE, K.G., 3rd Lord Neville of Raby, married **MAUD DE PERCY** (desc. King William the Conqueror).
RALPH NEVILLE, K.G., 1st Earl of Westmorland, married **JOAN BEAUFORT** (desc. King William the Conqueror).
RICHARD NEVILLE, K.G., 5th Earl of Salisbury, married **ALICE MONTAGU** (desc. King William the Conqueror).
RICHARD NEVILLE, K.G., Earl of Warwick and Salisbury, by an unknown mistress, _____ [see MONTAGU 12].

13. ALICE NEVILLE, illegitimate daughter. She married before 1 July 1506 (date of demise) **CHRISTOPHER CONYERS**, Esq., of Pinchingthorpe (in Guisborough), Yorkshire, son and heir of Brian Conyers (will proved 1478), of the City of York and Pinchingthorpe (in Guisborough), Yorkshire, merchant, by Elizabeth, daughter of Thomas Nelson, of York, merchant. They had two sons, John, Esq., and George, Esq., and three daughters, Elizabeth (wife of Richard Carlisle/Carlell), Agnes, and Dorothy (wife of _____ Salter). In 1506 he and his wife, Alice, conveyed all their lands and tenements in Brompton on Swale, Yorkshire to William, Abbot of St. Agatha by Richmond. In 1517 he complained that the Prior of Guisborough refused to allow him to occupy 300 acres of waste, and receive suit of his tenants in spite of the award of the Judge of Assize.
CHRISTOPHER CONYERS, Esq., died 6 April 1543. Administration on his estate was granted 26 April 1543.

Whitaker *Hist. of Richmondshire* 2 (2) (1823): unpaginated Conyers ped. Raine *Wills & Invs. from the Reg. of the Archdeaconry of Richmond* (Surtees Soc. 26) (1853): 110–112 (transcript of will of Alice Fulthorpe, widow of John Conyers, Esq.). *Testamenta Eboracensia* 3 (Surtees Soc. 45) (1865): 291n. Benolte *Vis. of Somerset 1531, 1573 & 1591* (1885): 14 (Carlille ped.: "Christ. Conyers of Pinchingthorpe, Yorks. = Alice, base dau. to Rich. Nevell, E. of Warwick."). *Old Yorkshire* n.s. 2 (1890): 62. *Index of Wills in the York Registry A.D. 1514 to 1553* (Yorkshire Arch. & Top. Assoc. Recs. 11) (1891): 215. *List of Procs. in the Star Chamber* 1 (PRO Lists and Indexes 13) (1901): 39. *Yorkshire Deeds* 1 (Yorkshire Arch. Soc. Recs. 39) (1909): 138n.,194, 208–209 (will of George Conyers, Esq.); 10 (Yorkshire Arch. Soc. Recs. 120) (1955): 126–129. Harvey et al. *Vis. of the North* 1 (Surtees Soc. 122) (1912): 51 (Conyers ped.). Edwards *Early Hist. of North Riding* (1924): 186. VCH *Yorkshire N.R.* 2 (1973): 360.

14. AGNES CONYERS, married before 1529 **GEOFFREY LEE**, Esq., of Cawood, Yorkshire and Southwell, Nottinghamshire, Burgesss (M.P.) for Portsmouth, 1529, Treasurer to Archbishop of York by 1532, joint (with his son) Steward and Receiver of Hexham, Northumberland, 1543–5, Justice of the Peace of Ripon, 1538, Justice of the Peace for Yorkshire, East Riding, 1538–45 or later, Justice of the Peace for Yorkshire, Northern circuit, 1540, younger son of Richard Lee, Esq., of Delee-Magna, Kent. He was born before 1488, and was a younger brother of Edward Lee, Archbishop of York. They had three sons, Richard, Esq. [Dr.] Roger, M.D., and Reynold (or Reginald), Esq. He was educated at Magdalen College, Oxford University, where he held various offices and lectureships. He obtained an M.A. degree in 1511. He and his wife, Agnes, received an annuity of £5 from her cousin, Margaret Plantagenet, Countess of Salisbury. In 1523 he witnessed the admission of Reginald Pole [afterwards Cardinal Pole] to an honorary fellowship at Corpus Christi. In 1529 he was employed in the delivery of the exhibition of £100 granted by the king to Reginald Pole. In 1536 he lost a flock of sheep and 75 oxen during the northern rebellion of that year. In 1537 his brother, Archbishop Edward, granted him a close called Plumtree field besides Scrooby Park and a lodge thereon, together with the warren and game of conies in the parishes of Scrooby and Harworth, Nottinghamshire for a term of 41 years. In 1544, following his brother, the Archbishop's death, he was instructed to take charge of the Scottish hostages who had been in his brother's care and to levy the archiepiscopal rents to the king's use. GEOFFREY LEE, Esq. was living in 1545, but died testate before 1551. In the period, 1544–51, Reynold Lee, Gent., of Southwell, Nottinghamshire, sued Edward Locksmythe alias Brereley and John Colton in Chancery regarding the presentation to the church of Clayworth, Nottinghamshire granted to Geoffrey Lee, Esq., of Southwell, to whom all parties claim to be executors.

    Berry *County Gens.: Kent Fams.* (1830): 172 (Lee ped.) (Lee arms: Azure on a fesse, between two fillets, or, three leopards' heads, gules). Dugdale *Vis. of York 1665–6* (Surtees Soc. 36) (1859): 96 (Lee ped.: "Gervase Lee. = ….. daughter of ….. Conyers."). *Gentleman's Mag.* n.s. 15 (1863): 337 (Lee ped.). Bloxam *Reg. of the Presidents, Fellows, Demies* 1 (1873): 36 (Lee pedigree). Benolte *Vis. of Somerset 1531, 1573 & 1591* (1885): 14 (Carlille ped.: "Agnes [Conyers]. = Geffery Lee of Maydston, Kent."). Brown *Pilgrim Fathers* (1895): 45. Philipot *Vis. of Kent 1619–1621* (H.S.P. 42) (1898): 55–56 (Lee ped.: "Galfridus Lee de Delee Magna Ar. frater & hæres. = Agnes filia et cohæres Leonardi Coniorom [Conyers] de Pinchethorpe co' Ebor.") (Lee arms: Azure on a fesse cotised or three leopards' faces gules). *Yorkshire Deeds* 1 (Yorkshire Arch. Soc. Recs. 39) (1909): 208–209 (will of George Conyers, Esq.), 210; 10 (Yorkshire Arch. Soc. Recs. 120) (1955): 126–129. VCH *Yorkshire N.R.* 2 (1973): 360. Emden *Biog. Reg. of the Univ. of Oxford 1502–1540* (1974): 347. Bindoff *House of Commons 1509–1558* 2 (1982): 506–507 (biog. of Geoffrey Lee). National Archives, C 1/1241/27-31 (available at www.catalogue.nationalarchives.gov.uk/search.asp).

15. RICHARD LEE, Esq., of Maidstone, Kent, joint (with his father) Steward and Receiver of Hexham, Northumberland, 1543–5. He married **ELIZABETH CRISPE**, daughter of John Crispe, of Anne in Thanet, by Anne, daughter of Robert Tuke. They had three sons, Richard, Henry, and Thomas, and three daughters, Mary, Elizabeth (wife of _____ Brewer), and Anne (wife of Thomas Francis). In the period, 1556–8, Francis Noone, Esq., of Gray's Inn, sued him in Chancery regarding the destruction of a subpoena. RICHARD LEE, Esq., was buried at Maidstone, Kent 26 Dec. 1573.

    Berry *County Gens.: Kent Fams.* (1830): 172 (Lee ped.). *Gentleman's Mag.* n.s. 15 (1863): 337 (Lee ped.). Gilbert *Mems. of the Church of All Saints, Maidstone* (1866): 226. Bloxam *Reg. of the Presidents, Fellows, Demies* 1 (1873): 36 (Lee ped.). *Surrey Arch. Colls.* 7 (1880): 211–212 (Drake ped.) (Lea arms: Argent a fess gules between 3 leopards' heads, azure). Philipot *Vis. of Kent 1619–1621* (H.S.P. 42) (1898): 55–56 (Lee ped.: "Rich' Lee de Delee fil. et hæres Galfridi. = Eliza filia Joh'is Crispe de Clime [Cliue = Cleve] in Thaneti."), 73–75 (Crispe ped.: "Eliza vx' Richardi Lee de Maydston.") (Crispe arms: Ermine, a fess chequy [argent and sable]). *TG* 1 (1980): 115. C 1/1457/30 (available at www.catalogue.nationalarchives.gov.uk/search.asp).

16. MARY LEE, married before 1583 **HENRY DRAKE**, of Wambrook, Dorset, St. Clement Danes, Middlesex, and Frenches (in Wiggey, parish of Reigate), Surrey, Cursitor of Chancery, son of John Drake, of Wambrook, Dorset. They had six sons, Richard, Edward, Gent., Robert, Henry, Gent., John, and Robert, and two daughters, Elizabeth (wife of James Morley, Esq.) and Mary (wife of Thomas Digges, Esq.). In 1588 he and his brother, George Drake, purchased the manor of Wambrook, Dorset from Francis Willoughby, Knt. for £2,400. The same year he and George sold two tenements called Haselcombe and Linnington with 160 acres of land to Thomas Estmond of

Lodge, Chardstock, Dorset. In 1593 he purchased the advowson of the church of Wambrook, Dorset from Alexander Brett, Esq. HENRY DRAKE died 31 Dec. 1609, and was buried in Reigate, Surrey. His widow, Mary, was buried in Reigate, Surrey 28 June 1637.

> Berry *County Gens.: Kent Fams.* (1830): 172 (Lee ped.). *Surrey Arch. Colls.* 7 (1880): 211–212 (Drake ped.) (Drake arms: Argent a wyvern gules). Phillips *Geological, Hist. & Top. Desc. of the Borough of Reigate* (1885): 34. Cooke & St. George *Vis. of Hertfordshire 1572, 1634 & 1546* (H.S.P. 22) (1886): 154–155 (Morley ped.). Philipot *Vis. of Kent 1619–1621* (H.S.P. 42) (1898): 55–56 (Lee ped.: "Maria [Lee] nupta Brake de Surr. [Henry Drake of Reigate]."). Benolte et al. *Vis. of Surrey 1530, 1572 & 1623* (H.S.P. 43) (1899): 102 (Drake ped.: "Henery Drake of the house of Drakes of Devonshire. = Mary 2 d. of Ric. Lee of Maydstone in com. Kent Esqr."). Matthews & Matthews *Abs. of Probate Acts in the P.C.C.* (Year Books of Probates) (1906): 102. Edwards *Ames, Mears & Allied Lines* (1967): 77. Wagner *Drake in England* (1970): 25. *TG* 1 (1980): 115; 24 (2010): 100–109. Neal *Cal. of Patent Rolls 26 Elizabeth I (1583–1584)* (List & Index Soc. 287) (2001): 76.

17. ROBERT DRAKE, of Merstham, Surrey, baptized at St. Clement Danes, Middlesex, 14 May 1598. He married at Merstham, Surrey 6 June 1622 **JOAN GAWTON**, daughter of Thomas Gawton, Gent., of Merstham, Surrey, by Patience, daughter of Nicholas Best. She was baptized at Merstham, Surrey 10 Nov. 1607. They had one son, Robert, and three daughters, Mary (wife of [Capt.] Richard Hill), Elizabeth, and Elizabeth (wife of John Parramore). He and his family immigrated to Virginia, where they settled in Accomack County, Virginia. He patented 200 acres of land at Maggettey Bay in Accomack County, Virginia in 1636. ROBERT DRAKE died intestate in Accomack County, Virginia before 29 March 1641. His widow, Joan, married (2nd) before 29 March 1641 [**LIEUT.**] **THOMAS HUNT**, of Accomack County, Virginia. They had one son, Thomas. By an uncertain marriage, he also had one daughter, Frances (wife of Edmund Bibby and Nathaniel Wilkins). He received a patent for 50 acres of land in Accomack County, Virginia in 1636. His wife, Mary, died about 1650. [LIEUT.] THOMAS HUNT died in 1656.

> *Surrey Arch. Colls.* 7 (1880): 211–212 (Drake ped.) (Drake arms: Argent a wyvern gules). *VMHB* 5 (1897–1898): 345. Benolte et al. *Vis. of Surrey 1530, 1572 & 1623* (H.S.P. 43) (1899): 102 (Drake ped.: "Robert Drake of Merstham. = Joane d. of Thom. Gawton of Merstham in com. Surrey."). Woodhouse et al. *Regs. of Merstham* (1902): 31, 43, 48, 49, 50, 51, 59, 77, 61. Nugent *Cavaliers & Pioneers* 1 (1929): 46. Sheppard *Ayres-Dawson & Allied Fams.* 1 (1961): 149–185. Edwards *Ames, Mears & Allied Lines* (1967): 77. Whitelaw *Virginia's Eastern Shore: a Hist. of Northampton & Accomack Counties* (1968): 71, 119–120. Ames *County Court Recs. of Accomack-Northampton, Virginia* 2 (Virginia Hist. Soc. Docs. 10) (1973): 72. *TG* 1 (1980): 115; 24 (2010): 100–109. Dorman *Adventurers of Purse & Person* 2 (2005): 776.

❧ DREUX

HUGUES CAPET, King of France, married **ALIX OF POITOU**.
ROBERT II *le Pieux*, King of France, married **CONSTANCE OF PROVENCE**.
HENRI I, King of France, married **ANNE OF KIEV**.
PHILIPPE I, King of France, married **BERTHA OF HOLLAND**.
LOUIS VI, King of France, married **ALIX OF SAVOY** [see FRANCE 5].

6. ROBERT I *le Grand*, Count of Dreux and Braine, seigneur of Brie-Comte-Robert, Chilly, Longjumeau, Savigny, and Torcy, and, in right of his 1st wife, Count of Perche, seigneur of Bellême, 5th son, born about 1123. He married (1st) in 1144 or 1145 **HAWISE OF SALISBURY**, widow of Rotrou II, Count of Perche, seigneur of Bellême [see ENGLAND 2.i], and daughter of Walter of Salisbury (also known as Walter Fitz Edward), of Chitterne, Wiltshire, Great Gaddesden, Hertfordshire, North Aston, Oxfordshire, etc., hereditary Sheriff of Wiltshire, Constable of Salisbury Castle, by Sibyl, daughter of Patrick de Chaources (or Sourches) [see LONGESPÉE 2 for her ancestry]. They had one daughter, Alix (or Alaidis, Alaydis) (wife successively of Waleran III, seigneur of Breteuil; Guy II de Châtillon, seigneur of Châtillon-sur-Marne, Jean I de Thourotte, seigneur of Thourotte, and Raoul I de Nesle, Count of Soissons). In 1149 he was involved in an aborted conspiracy to seize the throne. His wife, Hawise, died before 1152. He married (2nd) in late

1152 **AGNÈS DE BAUDEMENT**, lady of Fère-en-Tardenois, Nesle, Pontarcis, Longueville, Quincy, and Baudement, widow of Milon II, Count of Bar-sur-Seine (died 1 October 1151), and daughter and heiress of Guy (or Gui) de Baudement, seigneur of Braine, Seneschal of Champagne, by his wife, Alix. She was born about 1130. They had six sons, Robert [II] [Count of Dreux and Braine-sur-Vesle], Henri [Bishop of Orléans], Philippe [Bishop of Beauvais, Vidame of Gerberoy], Guillaume (seigneur of Brie-Comte-Robert, Torcy, and Chilly), Pierre, and Jean, and four daughters, Alix (wife of Raoul I, seigneur of Coucy), Isabelle (wife of Hugues III, seigneur of Broyes-Commercy and Châteauvillain), Massilie (or Béatrix, Basilie) [nun at Charmes Priory, afterwards at Wareville Priory], and Marguerite [nun at Charmes Priory]. In 1158 the Bishop of Soissons absolved him from an excommunication pronounced because of exactions against the priory of Councy. About 1177 another Bishop of Soissons lifted an interdict which the bishop had laid on Robert's land because of a dispute with the prelate. In 1170's he was involved in a dispute over property which he had unjustly taken from the abbey of Igny. In 1183 Pope Lucius III authorized the cathedral chapter at Chartres to excommunicate named barons, including Robert, for exactions in that diocese. ROBERT I, Count of Dreux and Braine, died 11 October 1188. His widow, Agnès, founded Saint-Yved Abbey in Braine. She died 24 July 1204. Robert and his wife, Agnès, were buried in the church of the Abbey of Saint-Yved, Braine. In 1204 Hugues de Garlande, Bishop of Orléans, gave 20 sous of rent on the grange of Cravant to Sainte-Croix of Orléans to celebrate the anniversary of his kinswoman, Agnès, Countess of Braine.

Duchesne *Histoire Généalogique de la Maison Royale de Dreux* (1631): 13–42. Anselme *Hist. de la Maison Royale de France* 1 (1726): 74–75 (sub Capetians), 423–425 (sub Comtes de Dreux). Moreri *Le grand Dictionnaire historique* 4 (1759): 247–250 (sub Dreux). *L'Art de Vérifier les Dates* 2 (1784): 670–674. *Histoire Littéraire de la France* 14 (1817): 236–237 (biog. of Pierre de Celle, Bishop of Chartres: "Mais une chose à laquelle jusqu'à-présent personne n'a fait attention, c'est que cette cousine n'était autre qu'Agnès de Braine, qui epousa en premières noces Milon, comte de Bar-sur-Seine, et en secondes noces Robert de France, comte de Dreux, frère du roi Louis-le-Jeune, comme nous l'apprenons d'une lettre de Jean de Sarisbèry, parmi celles de saint Thomas de Cantorbery, ou il est dit expressément que la comtesse de Dreux était cousine, cognata, de l'abbé de Saint-Rémi [Pierre de Celle]. Ainsi on peut assurer que la famille de notre auteur etait non-seulement noble, mais une des plus illustres de Champagne. C'était celle d'André de Baudement, de Baldimento, sénéchal de Champagne, ayeul de la comtesse Agnès."). Arbois de Jubainville *Histoire des Ducs et des Comtes de Champagne* 2 (1860): xxix–xxx (Agnes, Countess of Braine styled "kinswoman" [consanguinea] of Blanche of Navarre, Countess of Champagne). Edouard *Fontevrault et ses Monuments* 1 (1873): 234. *Recueil des Historiens des Gaules et de la France* 18 (1879): 350 (Ex Chronico Fiscannensis Coenobii (sub 1204): "obiit Agnes Comitissa Branæ"). Romanet de Beaune *Géographie du Perche, formant le Cartulaire de cette Province* (1890–1902): 44 (ped. chart), 48–51. Delaville le Roulx *Cartulaire Général de l'Ordre des Hospitaliers de S. Jean de Jérusalem* 1 (1894): 482–483 (Count Robert [of Dreux] styled "uncle" [patruo] by King Philippe *Auguste* of France in 1185). Barret *Cartulaire de Marmoutier pour le Perche* (1894): 44–45. Thillier and Jarry *Cartulaire de Sainte-Croix d'Orléans (814–1300)* (1906): 224 (Agnès, late Countess of Braine styled "kinswoman" [consanguinea] by Hugues [de Garlande], Bishop of Orléans in 1204), 210 (Manassès and Hugues styled nephews or kinsmen [nepotibus] of Hugues [de Garlande], Bishop of Orléans, in 1201). Molinier *Obituaires de la Province de Sens* 2 (1906): 106 (Obituaire of Cathedral Church of Chartres: "[23 Oct.] X kal. Ob[iit] Agnes, illustris comitissa de Breina."), 123 (Obituaire of Cathedral Church of Chartres: "[23 Oct.] X kal. Anniv. Agnetis, comitisse de Brena."). *C.P.* 11 (1949): Appendix D, 105–121. Schwennicke *Europaische Stanmtafeln* 2 (1984): 11 (ancestry of Robert de Dreux); 3 (1984): 63. *Traditio* 41 (1985): 145–179 ("Fifteen of his charters call him simply 'count'; six, 'count of Dreux'; three, 'count of Braine'; and four, 'count of Dreux and Braine.' … Comment on Agnes [his 2nd wife] is required, because scholars are often misidentified her. She was the daughter and heiress of Guy, lord of Braine, who died in or before 1145, and granddaughter of Andrew de Baudemont, seneschal of Theobald II of Champagn (Theobald IV of Blois) and his wife Agnes of Braine. The combined evidence of the charter to Prémontré and the obituary notices from Saint-Yved (in Duchesne) and [charter] no. 2 below establishes the genealogy.") ("Renaud" or "Renaud Pauper" served as a witness to charters dated 1152 and 1155 as "cognatus" [kinsman] of Robert, Count of Dreux; author suggests Renaud may be the same person as Reynold de Courtenay, supposed son of Count Robert's uncle, Fleury of France). Schwennicke *Europäische Stammtafeln* 2 (1984): 11 (sub France); 3(1) (1984): 63 (sub Dreux). Winter *Descs. of Charlemagne (800–1400)* (1987): XIII.147, XIV.241-XIV.252. Bautier & Dufour *Recueil des Actes de Louis VI, Roi de France (1108–1137)* 2 (1992): 364–365 (Robert, Count of Dreux and Braine, styled "brother" [frater] of Louis VI, King of France). Guyotjeannin *Chartrier de l'Abbaye prémontrée de Saint-Yved de Braine* (Mémoires et Docs. de l'École des Chartes 49) (2000): 376 (24 October — Pie memorie Agnetis, illustris comitisse Drocarum et Brane, que … dedit 10 libras fortium"). Van Kerrebrouck *Les Capétiens 987–1328* (2000): 307–310. Tanner *Fams., Friends, & Allies* (2004): 311

(France ped.). Evergates *Aristocracy in the County of Champagne, 1100–1300* (2009): 216 (biog. of Agnes Baudement), 229–230 (biog. of Elizabeth/Isabelle Dreux, wife of Hugh III of Broyes). Online source: http://www.mittelalter-genealogie.de/kapetinger_dreux_grafen_von/familie_graf_roberts_1/robert_1_der_grosse_graf_von_dreux_+_1188.html.

7. **ROBERT II**, Count of Dreux and Braine, seigneur of Brie-Comte-Robert, Chilly, Fère-en-Tardenois, Longjumeau, Longueville, Nesle, Pont-Arcy, Quincy, Torcy, Ville, etc., eldest surviving son and heir by his father's 3rd marriage, born about 1154. He married (1st) between 1177 and 1180 **MATHILDE** (or **MAHAUT**) **OF BURGUNDY**, Countess of Grignon, dame of Montpensier, widow successively of Eudes III, seigneur of Issoudun, Guy (or Gui) I, Count of Nevers, Auxerre, and Tonnerre (died 18 October 1175) [see NEVERS], and Pierre of Flanders, Count of Nevers (died August 1176), and daughter and heiress of Raymond of Burgundy, Count of Grignon, by Agnès, daughter of Gui de Thiers, seigneur of Montpensier [see BURGUNDY for her ancestry]. She was born about 1150. They had no issue. They were divorced on grounds of consanguinity in 1181; Mahaud died as a nun at Fontévrault in 1192. He married (2nd) in 1184 **YOLANDE DE COUCY**, daughter of Raoul I, seigneur of Coucy, Marle, Fère-en-Tardenois, Crécy, etc., by his 1st wife, Agnès, daughter of Baudouin IV, Count of Hainault [see COUCY for her ancestry]. They had five sons, Robert [III], Chev. [Count of Dreux and Braine], Pierre [Duke of Brittany], Henri [Archbishop of Reims], Geoffroi (seigneur of Rochecorbon), and Jean [Count of Mâcon], and seven daughters, Aliénor (wife of Hugues IV, seigneur of Châteauneuf-en-Thymerais, and Robert de Chaumont, Chev., seigneur of Saint-Clair), Isabelle (wife of Jean II, Count of Roucy, Vicomte of Mareuil), Alix (wife of Gaucher IV, seigneur of Salins, and Renaud de Choiseul), Philippe (or Philippine), Agnès (wife of Étienne III, Count of Auxonne), Yolande (wife of Raoul II de Lusignan, Count of Eu), and Jeanne [Abbess of Fontevrault]. ROBERT II, Count of Dreux and Braine, died 28 Dec. 1218. In 1219 his widow, Yolande, granted fifteen shillings of rent in Ambrosden, Buckinghamshire to the Abbey of Breuil. Yolande, Countess of Dreux and Braine, died 22 March 1222. They were buried at the Abbey of Saint-Yved, Braine.

Duchesne *Histoire Généalogique de la Maison Royale de Dreux* (1631): 43–69. Anselme *Hist. de la Maison Royale de France* 1 (1726): 425–426 (sub Comtes de Dreux). Moreri *Grand Dictionnaire historique* 4 (1759): 247–250 (sub Dreux). *L'Art de Vérifier les Dates* 2 (1784): 670–674. Kennett *Parochial Antiqs. of Ambrosden, Burcester* 1 (1818): 266–267 (charter of Yolande, Countess of Braine). Delisle *Cartulaire Normand* (1882): 16–17 (Robert. Count of Dreux styled "cousin" [consanguineo] by King Philippe-Auguste of France). *Cartulaire de l'Abbaye de Notre-Dame de la Trappe* (1889): 2–3 (charter of Count Robert, seigneur of Dreux and Braine, to Trappe Abbey dated July 1212, given with assent of his wife, Yolande, confirming the prior gift to the same abbey of Count Robert his father, brother of Louis, King of France, which was granted with the consent of Agnes his mother). Birch *Cat. Seals in the British Museum* 5 (1898): 538 (seal of Robert II, Count of Dreux dated 1202 — Obverse. To the right. In armour, with hauberk of mail, flat-topped helmet, sword, scabbard, and shield of arms: chequy, a bordure, DREUX. Horse springing. Legend: SIGILL' COMITIS . ROBERTI . DROCENSIS. Reverse. A smaller round counterseal. A shield of arms, as described in the obverse. Legend: * CONFIRMA HOC DEVS.). Michel *Histoire de la Ville de Brie-Comte-Robert* (1902): 105–171. Schwennicke *Europäische Stammtafeln* 3(1) (1984): 63 (sub Dreux); 7 (1979): 80 (ancestry of Yolande de Coucy). Winter *Descs. of Charlemagne (800–1400)* (1987): XIII.1081, XIV.244, XIV.652, XIV.1474-XIV.1483. *Traditio* 41 (1985): 145–179 ("In many of his acts, Robert II styled himself 'count, lord of Dreux,' or 'count, lord of Dreux and Braine.'"). Guyotjeannin *Chartrier de l'Abbaye Prémontrée de Saint-Yved de Braine (1134–1250)* (Mémoires et Docs. de l'École des Chartes 49) (2000): 16 (ped.), 192–195 (charter of Count Robert, lord of Dreux and Braine, and Countess Yolande his wife dated 1208), 195–196 (charters of Countess Yolande, lady of Dreux and Braine, dated 1208), 373 (19 March — Yolendis comitisse Brane, que dedit nobis 30 solidos parisiensium et 20 …"). Morganstern *Gothic Tombs of Kinship* (2000): 164–166. Van Kerrebrouck *Les Capétiens 987–1328* (2000): 310–313.

Children of Robert II de Dreux, by Yolande de Coucy:

i. **ROBERT [III]**, Count of Dreux and Braine [see next].

ii. **PIERRE DE BRAINE**, Duke of Brittany, Earl of Richmond, married **ALIX DE THOUARS**, Duchess of Brittany [see BRITTANY 7].

iii. **PHILIPPE** (or **PHILIPPINE**) **DE DREUX**, married **HENRI II**, Count of Bar-le-Duc [see BAR 6].

8. ROBERT III, Chev., Count of Dreux and Braine, seigneur of Bû, Brie-Comte-Robert, and Nesle, and, in right of his wife, seigneur of Saint-Valéry, Gamaches, Ault-sur-la-Mer, Bouint, Dommart, Bernardville, and Saint-Aubin, and, in England, Prince's Harwell (in Harwell), Berkshire, Thornton, Buckinghamshire, Covington, Huntingdonshire, Isleworth, Middlesex, Ambrosden, Beckley, Caswell (in Curbridge), Stoke Talmage, Worton (in Cassington), and Yarnton, Oxfordshire, Old Shorehan, Sussex, etc., born about 1190. He married about 1210 **ANNOR** (or **AÉNOR**) **DE SAINT-VALÉRY**, daughter and heiress of Thomas de Saint-Valéry, seigneur of Saint-Valéry, Gamaches, Ault-sur-la-Mer, Bouint, Dommart, Bernardville, and Saint-Aubin, and Prince's Harwell (in Harwell), Berkshire, Thornton, Buckinghamshire, Covington, Huntingdonshire, Isleworth, Middlesex, Ambrosden, Beckley, Mixbury, Stoke Talmage, and Yarnton, Oxfordshire, Old Shoreham, Sussex, etc., by Adèle, daughter of Jean I, Count of Ponthieu. She was born about 1192. They had three sons, Jean (I) (Count of Dreux and Braine, seigneur of Saint-Valéry), Robert [seigneur of Bû and Nesle-en-Tardenois, Vicomte of Châteaudun], and Pierre (priest), and one daughter, Yolande. He was a crusader against the Albigensians. He consistently supported King Philippe *Auguste* against King John, but made his peace with Henry III in 1217. In Feb. 1219 he was awarded the lands which his wife's father, Thomas of Saint-Valéry, had held in England. In 1225 he presented to the church of North Leigh, Oxfordshire. The same year he was granted the seigneuries of Bonneuil and Hautefontaine by King Louis VIII of France. In 1226 he gave the advowson of the church of Beckley, Oxfordshire to Studley Priory, Oxfordshire. By the end of 1226, he had again chosen to side with France. King Henry III of England subsequently seized all his England lands, but agreed to pay the count 200 marks yearly until they should be restored. In 1227, however, the honour of Saint-Valéry in England was granted to the king's brother, Richard, Earl of Cornwall. In compensation of the loss of his English lands, King Louis IX of France granted him the seigneuries of Canville and Anglefeuille (la Bralon) in Normandy in 1227. At an unknown date, Robert confirmed the gift of his wife's father, Thomas de Saint-Valéry, to Oseney Abbey of the manor of Mixbury, Oxfordshire. ROBERT III, Count of Dreux and Braine, died 3 March 1233/4, and was buried at the Abbey of Saint-Yved, Braine. His widow, Annor, married (2nd) before Jan. 1238 (date of charter) (as his 2nd wife) **HENRI DE SULLY** (or **DE SULLI**), seigneur of Sully, la Chapelle, and Aix-dans-Gilon, son and heir of Archambaud IV, seigneur of Sully, by his wife, Alix. They had no issue. In 1241 Annor gave some rents at St. Albins near Deep to the Abbey of Lieu-Dieu in Normandy. HENRI DE SULLY died 11 August, after 1248. Annor, Countess of Dreux and Braine, died 15 November 1251.

Duchesne *Histoire Généalogique de la Maison Royale de Dreux* (1631): 69–82. Martene & Durand *Veterum Scriptorum et Monumentorum* 1 (1724): 1200 (Robert III, Count of Dreux, styled "kinsman" [consanguineo] by King Louis VIII of France). Anselme *Hist. de la Maison Royale de France* 1 (1726): 426–427 (sub Comtes de Dreux). Moreri *Grand Dictionnaire historique* 4 (1759): 247–250 (sub Dreux). *L'Art de Vérifier les Dates* 2 (1784): 670–674. Kennett *Parochial Antiqs. of Ambrosden, Burcester* 1 (1818): 184, 237, 251–252, 264, 266–267, 268 (charter of Robert, Count of Dreux to Oseney Priory), 276, 282, 284, 290, 297, 307, 321. Delisle *Cartulaire Normand* 16 (1852): 55. Delisle *Catalogue des Actes de Philippe-Auguste* (1856): 397 (Henri de Sulli styled "cousin" by Guillaume de Chauvigni [Chauvigny], seigneur of Châteauroux in 1218), 458. Teulet *Layettes du Trésor des Chartes* 2 (1866): 193-194 ([J]Éléonore], lady of Costello [Châteauneuf], styled "sister" of Robert, Count of Dreux; [unnamed] son of Hugues de Castello [Châteauneuf] styled "nephew" [nepos]), 286, 396–397, 428–430. *Procs. Soc. of Antiquaries of London* 2nd Ser. 4 (1869): 392–393. Gorgue-Rosny *Recherches Généalogiques sur les Comtés de Ponthieu, de Boulogne, de Guines et Pays Circonvoisins* 4 (1877): 16, 35 (charters of Robert, Count of Dreux, dated 1220). Delisle *Manuscrits Latins et Français ajoutés aux Fonds des Nouvelles Acquisitions pendant les Années 1875–1894* Pt. 2 (1894): 474 (charter of Robert de Braine, son of Count Robert, dated 1212). Birch *Cat. Seals in the British Museum* 5 (1898): 538 (seal of Robert III, Count of Dreux dated 1225 — Obverse. To the right. In armour, with hauberk of mail, long-skirted tunic or surcoat, flat-topped helmet, sword, and shield of arms slung to the shoulders with a strap. Horse springing, armorially caparisoned. The armorial bearings of the shield are: chequy, a bordure, DREUX; those of the caparisons: a lion rampant, debruised by a bâton, ST. VALERY. Legend: S' . ROB'TI . COMIS . DROCE . DNI . SCI .WALERICI. Reverse. A smaller round counterseal. A shield of arms: chequy, DREUX). VCH *Oxford* 2 (1907): 77–79; 5 (1957): 56–76, 177–189; 6 (1959): 251–262, 262–267; 8 (1964): 198–210; 11 (1983): 159–168; 12 (1990): 40–44, 231–235, 475–478; 14 (2004): 202–206; 15 (2006): 218–227. VCH *Middlesex* 2

(1911): 324–327; 3 (1962): 103–111. VCH *Berkshire* 3 (1923): 484–492. VCH *Buckingham* 4 (1927): 243–249. VCH *Huntingdon* 3 (1936): 38–41. Leys *Sandford Cartulary* 1 (Oxfordshire Rec. Soc. 19) (1938): 76–78 (confirmation charter of Robert, Count of Dreux, lord of Saint Valery dated 1225). VCH *Sussex* 6(1) (1980): 149–154. VCH *Wiltshire* 12 (1983): 160–184. Schwennicke *Europäische Stammtafeln* 3(1) (1984): 63 (sub Dreux). *Winter* Descs. of Charlemagne (800–1400) (1987): XIV.1474; (1991): XV.2048-XV.2051, XVI.1291. Van Kerrebrouck *Les Capétiens 987–1328* (2000): 313–314. Power *Norman Frontier in the 12th & Early 13th Cents.* (2004): 454–455.

Children of Robert III de Dreux, Chev., by Annor de Saint-Valéry:

i. **ROBERT DE DREUX**, Vicomte of Châteaudun [see next].

ii. **YOLANDE DE DREUX**, Countess of Auxonne, married **HUGUES IV**, Duke of Burgundy [see BURGUNDY 7].

9. ROBERT DE DREUX, seigneur of Bû, Fère-en-Tardenois, Nesle-en-Tardenois, Longueville, and Quincy, and, in right of his 1st wife, Vicomte of Châteaudun, seigneur of Mondoubleau and Saint-Calais, born about 1217. He was on Crusade in 1248. He married (1st) in 1253 **CLÉMENCE DE CHÂTEAUDUN**, daughter and co-heiress of Geoffroi VI de Châteaudun, Vicomte of Châteaudun, seigneur of Château-du-Loir, Mayet, La Suze, Louplande, Mondoubleau, and Saint-Calais, by Clémence, daughter and co-heiress of Guillaume des Roches, Chev., Seneschal of Anjou [see MAYENNE 7 for her ancestry]. They had two daughters, Alix and Clémence (wife of Gautier de Nemours, seigneur of Aschères, and Jean de Barres, Chev., seigneur of Champrond). His wife, Clémence, died before 1 Feb. 1259, and was buried in the church of the Abbey of Saint-Yved, Braine. He married (2nd) about 1262 **ISABELLE DE VILLEBÉON**, daughter and heiress of Adam II de Villebéon, seigneur of Mesnil-Aubry, la Chapelle-Gauthier, Tournenfuye, etc., by Alix, possible daughter of Robert de Garlande. They had one son, Robert [seigneur of Bû, La Chapelle-Gautier, Bagneaux, etc.], and one daughter, Isabelle. ROBERT DE DREUX, Vicomte of Châteaudun, died in 1265 or 1266, and was buried at the Abbey of Saint-Yved, Braine. His widow, Isabeau, was heiress in 1265 to her aunt, Isabelle de Villebéon, widow of Mathieu de Montmirail, seigneur of La Ferté-Gaucher, Montmirail, Oisy, etc. She died before 1281.

Duchesne *Histoire Généalogique de la Maison Royale de Dreux* (1631): 129–145. Bernier *Histoire de Blois* (1682): 223–228. Anselme *Hist. de la Maison Royale de France* 1 (1726): 426–427 (sub Comtes de Dreux), 431–432 (sub Seigneurs de Beu). Moreri *Le grand Dictionnaire historique* 4 (1759): 247–250 (sub Dreux). *L'Art de Vérifier les Dates* 2 (1784): 670–674. Cartier *Recherches sur les Monnaies au type Chartrain* (1846): 112–117. Vallée *Cartulaire de Château-du-Loir* (Société des Archives Hist. du Maine 6) (1905): x–xiii, 139–140. Richemond *Recherches généalogiques sur la Famille des Seigneurs de Nemours* 2 (1908): 127–129. Schwennicke *Europäische Stammtafeln* 3(1) (1984): 64 (sub Dreux); 3(4) (1989): 690 (Châteaudun). Van Kerrebrouck *Les Capétiens 987–1328* (2000): 327–328.

Child of Robert de Dreux, by Clémence de Châteaudun:

i. **ALIX DE DREUX**, married **RAOUL DE CLERMONT**, seigneur of Nesle, Constable of France [see CLERMONT 6].

Child of Robert de Dreux, by Isabelle de Villebéon:

i. **ISABELLE DE DREUX** [see next].

10. ISABELLE DE DREUX, lady of Nesle-en-Tardenois, born in 1264. She married 1276/81 (as his 1st wife) **GAUTIER** (or **GAUCHER**) **V DE CHÂTILLON**, Chev., Count of Porcien, seigneur of Châtillon-sur-Marne, Crécy, Fère-en-Tardenois, Troissy, Marigny, and Pont-Arcy, Constable of France, son and heir of Gautier IV de Châtillon, seigneur of Châtillon-sur-Marne, Crécy, Crévecoeur, Troissy, and Marigny, by Isabeau, daughter of Guillaume de Villehardouin, seigneur of Lezinnes [see WYDEVILLE 6.ii for his ancestry]. He was probably born in 1249. They had three sons, Gaucher [VI], Jean [seigneur de Châtillon], and Hugues [seigneur de Rozoy and Pont-Arsy], and three daughters, Jeanne, Marie (wife of Guichard, seigneur de Beaujeu), and Isabelle [Abbess of Soissons]. His wife, Isabeau, died 29 April 1300. He married (2nd) in 1301 **HELISENDE DE VERGY**, widow of Henri I, Count of Vaudémont, and daughter of Jean I de

Vergy, seigneur of Fouvent, by his wife, Marguerite de Noyers. They had one son, Guy [seigneur of Fère-en-Tardenois]. She died in 1312. He married (3rd) in March 1313 **ISABELLE DE RUMIGNY**, lady of Rumigny, Florennes, and Boves, widow of Thibaut II, Duke of Lorraine, and daughter of Hugues II de Rumigny, seigneur of Florennes, by his wife, Ade de Boves. She was born in June 1263. They had no issue. She died in 1322. GAUTIER V DE CHÂTILLON, Chev., Count of Porcien, died in 1329.

Duchesne *Histoire Généalogique de la Maison Royale de Dreux* (1631): 129–145. Anselme *Hist. de la Maison Royale de France* 1 (1726): 431–432 (sub Seigneurs de Beu). *Bibliothèque de l'École des Chartes* 33 (1872): 180, 182. Schwennicke *Europäische Stammtafeln* 3(1) (1984): 64 (sub Dreux); 7 (1979): 19. Van Kerrebrouck *Les Capétians 987–1328* (2000): 328.

Child of Isabeau de Dreux, by Gautier V de Châtillon, Chev.:

i. **JEANNE DE CHÂTILLON**, married **GAUTHIER V DE BRIENNE**, Duke of Athens, Count of Brienne and Lecce [see JERUSALEM 9].

❧ DRURY ❦

ALICE OF NORMANDY (sister of King William the Conqueror), married **EUDES III**, Count of Champagne.
STEPHEN (or **ÉTIENNE**), Count of Aumale, married **HAWISE DE MORTIMER**.
AGNES OF AUMALE, married **ADAM DE BRUS**, of Skelton, Yorkshire.
ADAM DE BRUS, of Skelton, Yorkshire, married **IVETTE DE ARCHES**.
PETER DE BRUS, Knt., of Skelton, Yorkshire, married **JOAN OF CHESTER**.
PETER DE BRUS, of Skelton, Yorkshire, married **HAWISE DE LANCASTER**.
LADRANA DE BRUS, married **JOHN DE BELLEW**, Knt., of Carlton-in-Balne (in Snaith), Yorkshire.
SIBYL (or **ISABEL**) **DE BELLEW**, married **MILES DE STAPLETON**, Knt., of Stapleton, Yorkshire.
GILBERT DE STAPLETON, Knt., of Walkingham, Yorkshire, married **AGNES FITZ ALAN**.
MILES DE STAPLETON, K.G., of Bedale, Yorkshire, married **JOAN DE INGHAM**.
MILES STAPLETON, Knt., of Ingham, Norfolk, married **ELA UFFORD**.
BRIAN STAPLETON, Knt., of Ingham, Norfolk, married **CECILY BARDOLF** (desc. King William the Conqueror).
MILES STAPLETON, Knt., of Ingham, Norfolk, married **KATHERINE DE LA POLE**.
ELIZABETH STAPLETON, married **WILLIAM CALTHORPE**, Knt., of Burnham Thorpe, Norfolk [see STAPLETON 14].

15. ANNE CALTHORPE, married before 1494 (as his 1st wife) **ROBERT DRURY**, Knt., of Hawstead, Suffolk, Knight of the Body to Kings Henry VII and Henry VIII, Knight of the Shire for Suffolk, Speaker of the House of Commons, Privy Councillor, son and heir of Roger Drury, Esq., of Hawstead, Suffolk, by his 2nd wife, Felice, daughter and heiress of William Denston. He was born before 1456. They had two sons, William, Knt., and Robert, Knt., and four daughters, Anne, Elizabeth (wife of Philip Boteler, Knt.), Bridget (wife of John Jernegan, Knt.), and Ursula (wife of Giles Allington, Knt.). He was admitted a member of Lincoln's Inn in 1473. His wife, Anne, was named in the 1494 will of her father. He was legatee of the "Ellesmere Chaucer" (which bears the signature of Robert Drury on the fly-leaf) from John de Vere, Earl of Oxford. He attended the king at the Field of the Cloth of Gold in 1520. He married (2nd) before 1531 **ANNE JERNEGAN** (or **JERNINGHAM**), widow successively of [Lord] Edward Grey (died before 17 March 1517), _____ Berkeley, and Henry Barlee, Esq., of Albury, Hertfordshire (died 12 Nov. 1529), and daughter of Edward Jernegan, of Somerleyton, Suffolk, by his 1st wife, Margaret Bedingfield. They had no issue. SIR ROBERT DRURY died 2 March 1535/6, and was buried with his 1st wife at St. Mary's, Bury St. Edmunds, Suffolk. He left a will proved 8 Feb. 1535/6 [sic] (P.C.C. 32 Hogen). His widow, Anne, married (4th) before 1543 (as his 2nd wife) **EDMUND WALSINGHAM**, Knt. (died 10 Feb. 1550), of Scadbury (in Chislehurst), Kent, Lord Lieutenant of the Tower of London. She left a will dated 1 March 1558, proved 8 May 1558 (P.C.C. 17 Chaynay).

Betham *Baronetage of England* 1 (1801): 226n. (sub Jerningham). Cullum *Hist. & Antiqs. of Hawsted, & Hardwick* (1813). Gage *Hist. & Antiqs. of Suffolk: Thingoe Hundred* (1838): 428–444. Cooper & Cooper *Athenæ Cantabrigienses* 1 (1858): 56–57 (biog. of Robert Drury). *East Anglian* 1 (1864): 226–227 (Barlee ped.). *Notes & Queries* 4th Ser. 5 (1870): 146, 216. Flower *Vis. of Yorkshire 1563–4* (H.S.P. 16) (1881): 293–295 (Stapleton ped.: "Anne Calthorpe wyff to Sir Robert Drury"). Waters *Chester of Chicheley* 1 (1878): 140 (ped. chart). *Norfolk Arch.* 9 (1884): 1. Harvey et al. *Vis. of Norfolk 1563 & 1613* (H.S.P. 32) (1891): 63–64 (1563 Vis.) (Calthrop ped.: "Anne [Calthorpe] ux. Sir Robert Drury, knight"). Baildon *Recs. of Lincoln's Inn: Admissions* 1 (1896): 18. Muskett *Suffolk Manorial Fams.* 1 (1900): 354 (Drury ped.). Campling *Hist. of the Fam. of Drury* (1937): 43–47, 100–101 (ped.). Erwin *Anc. of William Clopton* (1939): 57–58. *Notes & Queries* 208 (1963): 5–9. Bindoff *House of Commons 1509–1558* 1 (1982): 380–381 (biog. of Henry Barley), 2 (1982): 57–58 (biog. of Sir Robert Drury: "… prominent as a lawyer, courtier and servant of the crown"), 539–540 (biog. of Sir Edmund Walsingham). Harvey *Vis. of Suffolk 1561* 2 (H.S.P. n.s. 3) (1984): 330–337 (Jernegan ped.). *TG* 9 (1988): 192. *Scottish Gen.* 49 (2002): 37–41.

Children of Anne Calthorpe, by Robert Drury, Knt.:

i. **WILLIAM DRURY**, Knt. [see next].

ii. **ANNE DRURY**, married (1st) **GEORGE WALDEGRAVE**, Esq., of Smallbridge (in Bures St. Mary), Suffolk [see WALDEGRAVE 15]; (2nd) **THOMAS JERMYN**, Knt., of Rushbrook, Suffolk [see WALDEGRAVE 15].

16. WILLIAM DRURY, Knt., of Hawstead, Suffolk, Esquire Extraordinary of the Body, Sheriff of Norfolk and Suffolk, 1536–7, 1544–5, Knight of the Shire for Suffolk, Privy Councillor to Queen Mary, son and heir, born about 1500 (aged 36 in 1536). He married (1st) before 7 Feb. 1516 **JANE SAINT MAUR**, daughter and heiress of William Saint Maur, Knt., of Beckington, Somerset, by Margaret, daughter of Richard Edgecombe, Knt. She was a legatee in the 1504 will of her paternal grandmother, Elizabeth (Choke) (Saint Maur) Biconyll. His wife, Jane, died in childbirth in 1517. They had no surviving issue. He was admitted a member of Lincoln's Inn 12 Feb. 1517. He married (2nd) before Feb. 1521 **ELIZABETH SOTHILL**, daughter and co-heiress of Henry Sothill, Esq., of Stoke Faston, Leicestershire, King's Attorney General, by Joan, daughter of Richard Empson, Knt. [see PLUMPTON 16 for her ancestry]. She was born about 1505 (aged 1 in 1506). They had four sons, Robert, Esq., William, Henry, and Roger, and thirteen daughters, Anne (wife of Christopher Heydon, Knt.), Mary, Elizabeth, Frances (wife of James Hobart), Bridget, Winifred, Ursula, Audrey, Dorothy, Margaret, Katherine, Dorothy (2nd of name) (wife of Robert Rookwood), and Elizabeth (2nd of name) (wife of Robert Drury, Knt.). SIR WILLIAM DRURY died at Hawstead, Suffolk 11 Jan. 1557/8. He left a will proved 29 April 1558 (P.C.C. 16 Noodes). His widow, Elizabeth, died 19 May 1575. She left a will proved 7 Nov. 1575 (P.C.C. 42 Pyckering). He and his two wives were buried at Hawstead, Suffolk.

Cullum *Hist. & Antiqs. of Hawsted, & Hardwick* (1813). Gage *Hist. & Antiqs. of Suffolk: Thingoe Hundred* (1838): 428–444. Plumpton *Plumpton Corr.* (1839): 208. *Testamenta Eboracensia* 4 (Surtees Soc. 53) (1869): 168n. Glover & St. George *Vis. of Yorkshire 1584–5, 1612* (1875): 275 (Sothill ped.: "Elizabeth [Sothill], mar. to Sir Wm. Drury, of Suffolk"). Harvey *Vis. of Norfolk 1563* 1 (1878): 267 (1563 Vis. Norfolk); 2 (1895): 188–189, 219. Hervey et al. *Vis. of Suffolk* (1882): 91 (Drury ped.: "Sir William Drury of Halsted (Hawsted), Kt. = Elizabeth, da. and heir of Henry Sothell of Stokeforton (?Stockerston), co. Leic."), 101 (Rokewode ped.). Baildon *Recs. of Lincoln's Inn: Admissions* 1 (1896): 38. *List of Sheriffs for England & Wales* (PRO Lists and Indexes 9) (1898): 88. Muskett *Suffolk Manorial Fams.* 1 (1900): 354 (Drury ped.). Weaver *Somerset Medieval Wills* 2 (Somerset Rec. Soc. 19) (1903): 72–74 (will of Elizabeth Biconyll). *East Anglian* n.s. 10 (1903–4): 145–146. Farnham *Leicestershire Medieval Peds.* (1925): 102 (Boyvill ped.). Campling *Hist. of the Fam. of Drury* (1937): 47–50, 100–101 (ped.). Walker *Yorkshire Peds.* 2 (H.S.P. 95) (1943): 341–345 (Soothill ped.). *Cal. IPM Henry VII* 3 (1955): 68, 98. Bindoff *House of Commons 1509–1558* 2 (1982): 60–61 (biog. of Sir William Drury). *TG* 9 (1988): 192. Menuge *Medieval Women & the Law* (2003): 75.

Children of William Drury, Knt., by Elizabeth Sothill:

i. **ROBERT DRURY**, Esq., of Hawstead, Suffolk, son and heir by his father's 1st marriage. He married **AUDREY RICH**, daughter of Richard Rich, 1st Lord Rich, Lord Chancellor of England. They had four sons, William, Knt., Henry, Thomas, and Robert, and eight daughters, Anne (wife of John Thornton), Mary (wife of Robert Russell), Elizabeth (wife of Thomas Gray and Nicholas Mynne), Susan (wife of Robert Baspole), Winifred (wife of Edmund Markhant), Bridget (wife of Richard Zouche), Dorothy (wife of Edward Barnes, of Soham,

Cambridgeshire[18]), and Audrey (wife of George Parker). ROBERT DRURY, Esq., died 10 Jan. 1557/8. Cullum *Hist. and Antiqs. of Hawsted, & Hardwick* (1813): 129–131 (Drury ped.). Gage *Hist. & Antiqs. of Suffolk: Thingoe Hundred* (1838): 428–444. Hervey et al. *Vis. of Suffolk* (1882): 91 (Drury ped.: "Robert Drury of Halsted, Esq."). Muskett *Suffolk Manorial Fams.* 1 (1900): 354 (Drury ped.). Campling *Hist. of the Fam. of Drury* (1937): 100–101 (ped.).

- ii. **MARY DRURY** [see next].
- iii. **BRIDGET DRURY**, married **HENRY YELVERTON**, Esq., of Rougham, Norfolk [see YELVERTON 17].

17. MARY DRURY, 2nd daughter, born 30 June 1526. She married (1st) **RICHARD CORBETT**, Knt., of Assington, Suffolk, son of Richard Corbett, Knt., of Assington, Suffolk, by his wife, Jane. He was born in May 1524. SIR RICHARD CORBETT died before 24 June 1565. She married (2nd) at Hawstead, Suffolk 24 June 1565 **JOHN TYRRELL**, Esq., of Gipping, Suffolk. She was buried at Cotton, Suffolk 16 June 1594. She left a will proved 29 June 1594.

Gage *Hist. & Antiqs. of Suffolk: Thingoe Hundred* (1838): 429 (Drury ped.). Hervey et al. *Vis. of Suffolk* (1882): 91 (Drury ped.: "Mary [Drury], wife to John Tyrrell."). Harvey *Vis. of Norfolk 1563* 2 (1895): 219. Muskett *Suffolk Manorial Fams.* 1 (1900): 354 (Drury ped.). Campling *Hist. of the Fam. of Drury* (1937): 49, 100–101 (ped.). *TG* 9 (1988): 192.

Child of Mary Drury, by Richard Corbett, Knt.:

- i. **ELIZABETH CORBETT**, married **PHILIP WENTWORTH**, Gent., of St. Margaret's, Ipswich, Suffolk [see NETTLESTEAD 20].

✤ DUDLEY ✤

WILLIAM THE CONQUEROR, King of England, married **MAUD OF FLANDERS**.
HENRY I, King of England, by an unknown mistress, _____.
ROBERT FITZ ROY, Earl of Gloucester, married **MABEL FITZ ROBERT**.
MAUD OF GLOUCESTER, married **RANULPH DE GERNONS**, Earl of Chester.
HUGH, Earl of Chester, by an unknown mistress, _____.
AMICE OF CHESTER, married **RALPH DE MAINWARING**, Seneschal of Chester.
BERTRADE DE MAINWARING, married **HENRY DE AUDLEY**, of Heleigh (in Audley), Staffordshire.
JAMES DE AUDLEY, Knt., of Heleigh (in Audley), Staffordshire, married **ELA LONGESPÉE** (desc. King William the Conqueror).
NICHOLAS DE AUDLEY, Knt., of Heleigh (in Audley), Staffordshire, married **KATHERINE GIFFARD**.
NICHOLAS DE AUDLEY, Knt., 1st Lord Audley, married **JOAN MARTIN** (desc. King William the Conqueror).
ALICE DE AUDLEY, married **HUGH DE MEYNELL**, Knt., of Langley Meynell (in Kirk Langley), Derbyshire.
ISABEL DE MEYNELL, married **THOMAS DE SHIRLEY**, Knt., of Lower Ettington, Warwickshire.
HUGH SHIRLEY, Knt., of Lower Ettington, Warwickshire, married **BEATRICE BREWES** (desc. King William the Conqueror).
RALPH SHIRLEY, Knt., of Lower Ettington, Warwickshire, married **JOAN BASSET**.
BEATRICE SHIRLEY, married **JOHN BROME**, Esq., of Baddesley Clinton, Warwickshire [see HAWES 15].

16. ISABEL BROME, married (1st) **PHILIP PUREFOY** (or **PUREFEY**, **PURFREY**), Esq., of Shalstone, Buckinghamshire, son and heir of William Purefoy, Esq., of Sherford (in Burton Hastings), Warwickshire and Shalstone, Buckinghamshire, by Margery, daughter of Robert Moton, Knt. They had four children, John, Nicholas, William, and Alice. PHILIP PUREFOY, Esq., died 16 Sept. 1466 [sic], and was buried in the chancel of the church of Baddesley Clinton, Warwickshire. PHILIP PUREFOY, Esq., left a will dated 26 March 1468, proved 18 June 1470 (P.C.C. 31 Godyn).

---

[18] Edward and Dorothy (Drury) Barnes of Soham, Cambridgeshire are the paternal grandparents of the immigrant, **Charles Barnes**, of East Hampton, Long Island, New York (living 1669) (see Campling *Hist. of the Drury Fam.* (1937): 47–51, 100–101; *NEHGR* 123 (1969): 86–88; *NEGHR* 158 (2004): 319–329; Roberts *Royal Descents of 600 Immigrants* (2004): 203–204).

His widow, Isabel, married (2nd) before 1472 **JOHN DENTON**, Esq., of Fyfield and Appleton, Berkshire, and Foscott, Buckinghamshire, son of Thomas Denton, of Fyfield, Berkshire, by Alice, daughter and co-heiress of William Dauntsey. They had one son, Thomas, and two daughters, Anne and Alice. In 1472 John Purefoy (brother of Philip) released the manor of Sherford (in Burton Hastings), Warwickshire and other lands to John Denton and his wife, Isabel. In 1475 John and his wife, Isabel, presented to the church of Shalstone, Buckinghamshire. In the period, 1475–80, or 1483–5, as "John Denton, of Shirford, gentleman," he sued Nicholas Waldyve, mercer, of London regarding the manor and advowson of Foxcote, Buckinghamshire, late of William Purfey [Purefoy], afterwards of Thomas Waldyve. In 1479 he presented to the churches of Foscott and Shalstone, Buckinghamshire. JOHN DENTON, Esq., left a will dated 6 Sept. 1493, proved 17 Nov. 1497 (P.C.C. 17 Horne). In 1498 his widow, Isabel, and his son, Thomas Denton, granted John Wright, of Oxford a shop in the parish of St. Martin's, Oxford. His widow, Isabel, presented to the churches of Foscott, Buckinghamshire, 1503, 1510, and 1526, and Shalstone, Buckinghamshire, 1503 and 1523. She left a will dated c.1540, by which she left four marks yearly for a priest to teach children in the town of Buckingham, Buckinghamshire.

> Dugdale *Antiqs. of Warwickshire* (1730): 54 (Purefey ped.). Willis *Hist. & Antiqs. of the Town, Hundred, & Deanery of Buckingham* (1755): 81, 186–187, 266. Nichols *Hist. & Antiqs. of Leicester* 4(2) (1811): 599. Nicolas *Testamenta Vetusta* 2 (1826): 415 (will of John Denton). Lipscomb *Hist. & Antiqs. of Buckingham* 3 (1847): 13–14, 71 (Purefoy ped.), 72. Harvey et al. *Vis. of Oxford 1566, 1574, 1634 & 1574* (H.S.P. 5) (1871): 228–229 (Denton ped.: "John Denton of Wightam in com. Barke. = Isabell daur. to John Brome of Baddesley in Com. Warr."). Lennard & Vincent *Vis. of Warwick 1619* (H.S.P. 12) (1877): 96–98 (Brome ped.: "Isabell [Brome] 1 mar. to Phillip Purfoye, 2 to John Denton."). Norris *Baddesley Clinton, its Manor, Church & Hall* (1897): 17–28, 49. C.P.R. 1467–1477 (1900): 626. C.P.R. 1476–1485 (1901): 489, 544. *List of Early Chancery Procs.* 1 (PRO Lists and Indexes 12) (1901): 91, 349; 2 (PRO Lists and Indexes 16) (1903): 236. Benolte et al. *Four Vis. of Berkshire 1532, 1566, 1623 & 1665–6* 2 (H.S.P. 57) (1908): 115–116 (Denton ped.: "John Denton of Wightham in Com. Berks: Esqr son & h: = Issabell wid: to Phillip Purifoy of Shalsone in Com. Buck: Esqr da to John Browne of Badesley in Com. Warw: Esqr."). Philipot et al. *Vis. of Buckingham 1634 & 1566* (H.S.P. 58) (1909): 37–38 (Denton ped.: "John Denton of Ambersden [co:] Oxf. = Margery da. of Sir John Brome of Halton [co.] Oxf."). Hawes *Edmond Hawes of Yarmouth* (1914): 73–91. *Cal. IPM Henry VII* 2 (1915): 40–41. VCH *Berkshire* 4 (1924): 338 (Denton arms: Argent, two bars gules with three cinqfoils sable in chief). VCH *Buckingham* 4 (1927): 171, 223–226. VCH *Warwick* 6 (1951): 58. C.C.R. 1468–1476 (1953): 256. Salter *Survey of Oxford* 2 (Oxford Hist. Soc. n.s. 20) (1969): 105. *NEHGR* 142 (1988): 227–244. National Archives, C 1/56/241; C 140/28/29 (available at www.catalogue.nationalarchives.gov.uk/search.asp).

Children of Isabel Brome, by John Denton, Esq.:

i. **ALICE DENTON** [see next].

ii. **ANNE DENTON**, married **EDWARD GREVILLE**, Knt., of Milcote-on-Avon, Warwickshire [see GREVILLE 11].

17. **ALICE DENTON**, married before 1494 (as his 1st wife) **NICHOLAS PUREFOY**, Esq., of Daventry, Northamptonshire, son and heir of John Purefoy, Esq., of Daventry, Northamptonshire. He was a minor in 1491. He was heir to his uncle, Philip Purefoy, Esq., by which he inherited the manors of Sherford (in Burton Hastings), Warwickshire and Shalstone, Buckinghamshire. They had one son, Edward, Esq., and two daughters, Isabel and Alice. In 1507–8 he and his wife, Alice, sold the manor of Sherford (in Burton Hastings), Warwickshire to Thomas Birde. He married (2nd) **CLEMENCE LYDIARD**, widow of _____ Byrde. They had one son, Simon, and one daughter, Susan (wife of Edmund Jenney, Gent.). He married (3rd) **KATHERINE BRAYFIELD**, daughter of Richard Brayfield, yeoman, of Buckinghamshire. They had three sons, Martin, Luke, and Francis, and one daughter, Isabel (wife of Thomas Godwin). He presented to the church of Shalstone, Buckinghamshire in 1536. NICHOLAS PUREFOY, Esq., died testate at Shalstone, Buckinghamshire 18 Feb. 1547. His widow, Katherine, died 6 May 1556.

> Dugdale *Antiqs. of Warwickshire* (1730): 54 (Purefey ped.). Willis *Hist. & Antiqs. of the Town, Hundred, & Deanery of Buckingham* (1755): 186–187, 260–267. Nichols *Hist. & Antiqs. of Leicester* 4(2) (1811): 599–600 (Purefoy ancestry).

Lipscomb *Hist. & Antiqs. of Buckingham* 3 (1847): 71 (Purefoy ped.), 72. Harvey et al. *Vis. of Oxford 1566, 1574, 1634 & 1574* (H.S.P. 5) (1871): 228–229 (Denton ped.: "Alice [Denton] maryed to Nicholas Purefoy of Shaldeston in com. Buck."). Leadam *Domesday of Inclosures* 1 (1897): 203. Philipot et al. *Vis. of Buckingham 1634 & 1566* (H.S.P. 58) (1909): 199–200 (Purefoy ped.: "Nicholas Purefoy of Shirford [*in co.*] War. Esquire [*eldest son & heir*]. = Alice da. of Tho. Denton of Basyles Lye [*in co.*] Berks Esquire."). *C.P.R. 1485–1494* (1914): 346. Benolte & Cooke *Vis. of Kent 1530–1, 1574 & 1592* 2 (H.S.P. 75) (1924): 107–108 (Purefoye ped.: "Nicholas Purefoye of Shalston aforesaide Esquire Sonne and heire to John [Purefoye] maried to his firste wife Alys Daughter to John Denton of Caverffelde in the Countie of Buck: Esquire") (Purefoy arms: Three pairs of hands in armour, couped at the wrist, conjoined). VCH *Buckingham* 4 (1927): 224. VCH *Warwick* 6 (1951): 58, 227. *NEHGR* 142 (1988): 227–244.

18. EDWARD PUREFOY, Gent., of Shalstone, Buckinghamshire, son and heir by his father's 1st marriage, born at Etfield 13 June 1494. He married **ANNE FETTIPLACE**, daughter of Richard Fettiplace, Esq., of East Shefford, Berkshire, by Elizabeth, daughter and heiress of William Bessiles (or Bessels), Esq., of Bessels Leigh, Berkshire [see BESSILES 16 for her ancestry]. She was born at Shelford Parva, Cambridgeshire 16 July 1496. They had eleven sons, John, Esq., Thomas, Edward, William, Nicholas, Francis, Henry, Henry (again), Thomas (again), Richard, and Charles, and one daughter, Mary. He presented to the church of Shalstone, Buckinghamshire in 1557. EDWARD PUREFOY, Gent., died 1 June 1558, and was buried at Shalstone, Buckinghamshire. His widow, Anne, died 16 August 1568.

Willis *Hist. & Antiqs. of the Town, Hundred, & Deanery of Buckingham* (1755): 260–267. Nichols *Hist. & Antiqs. of Leicester* 4(2) (1811): 600. Lipscomb *Hist. & Antiqs. of Buckingham* 3 (1847): 71 (Purefoy ped.), 72. Benolte et al. *Four Vis. of Berkshire 1532, 1566, 1623 & 1665–6* 1 (H.S.P. 56) (1907): 28 (Feteplace ped.: "Anne [Fetiplace] maried to Edwarde Purefoy of Shalston in the Countie of Buck Esquire."). Philipot et al. *Vis. of Buckingham 1634 & 1566* (H.S.P. 58) (1909): 199–200 (Purefoy ped.: "Edward Purefoy of Sherford Esquire [*eldest son & heir*]. = Anne da. of Thomas Fettiplace of Basilles Lee [*in co.*] Berks Esquire."). Benolte & Cooke *Vis. of Kent 1530–1, 1574 & 1592* 2 (H.S.P. 75) (1924): 107–108 (Purefoye ped.: "Edwarde Purefoye of Shalston aforesaide Esquire Sonne and heire to Nicholas, maried Anne one of the Daughters of Richarde ffeteplace of Este Shifforde in the Countie of Berk Esquire"). *TAG* 62 (1987): 43–46. *NEHGR* 142 (1988): 227–244.

19. MARY PUREFOY, married at Shalstone, Buckinghamshire 28 October 1540 **THOMAS THORNE** (or **DORNE**), Gent., of Yardley Hastings and Syresham, Northamptonshire, son and heir of William Thorne, Gent., of Yardley Hastings and Syresham, Northamptonshire, by Alice, sister of Thomas Stutysbury, Gent., of Sulgave, Northamptonshire. They had three sons, Anthony, Edward, and Robert, and three daughters, Katherine (wife of Francis Worsley), Susan, and Jane (wife of John Hender, Esq.). He was a legatee in the 1529 will of his father. THOMAS THORNE, Gent., was buried at Yardley Hastings, Northamptonshire 9 Nov. 1588. He left a will dated 29 October 1588, proved 9 May 1589. His wife, Mary, survived him.

Willis *Hist. & Antiqs. of the Town, Hundred, & Deanery of Buckingham* (1755): 260–267. Nichols *Hist. & Antiqs. of Leicester* 4(2) (1811): 600. Polsue *Complete Parochial Hist. of Cornwall* 3 (1870): 360 (re. Hender) (citation courtesy of John Brandon). Waters *Gen. Gleanings in England* 2 (1901): 1087–1088. *NEHGR* 66 (1912): 340–343 (Thorne arns: Sable, three fusills in fess argent); 142 (1988): 227–244. Benolte & Cooke *Vis. of Kent 1530–1, 1574 & 1592* 2 (H.S.P. 75) (1924): 107–108 (Purefoye ped.: "Marye [Purefoye] maried to Thomas Thorne of Yardley Hastinges in the Countie of North. gent."). *TG* 19 (2005): 112–128. Registered will of Thomas Dorne, Gent., proved 9 May 1589 (Archdeaconry Court of Northampton, Registered wills, Book 5, pp. 328–330).

20. SUSAN (or **SUSANNA**) **THORNE**, baptized at Yardley Hastings, Northamptonshire 5 March 1559/60. She married at Lidlington, Bedfordshire 8 June 1575 [**CAPT.**] **ROGER DUDLEY**. They had one son, [Gov.] Thomas, and one daughter, Mary. [CAPT.] ROGER DUDLEY was slain in battle before 1588, possibly at the Siege of Zutphen in 1586. His widow, Susan, and her unnamed children were legatees in the 1588 will of her father, Thomas Thorne, Gent.

Adlard *Sutton-Dudley* (1862): xiv–xvi, 21–38, 97. *Herald & Genealogist* 3 (1866): 308–315. *NEHGR* 47 (1893): 120–121 (will of Edmund Yorke); 56 (1902): 206; 65 (1911): 189; 66 (1912): 340–343 ("Cotton Mather wrote that Thomas Dudley's father was 'Capt. Roger Dudley, who was slain in the wars, when this, his son, and one only daughter were very young' ... an examination of the original Purefoy pedigree in the British Museum (Harleian MS 1189, fols. 18, 19) shows that Susanna Thorne married Roger ____, a very different statement from that of the printed pedigree, which gives her a husband surnamed Rogers and omits his Christian name. The will of Thomas Dorne, or Thorne, supplies the surname that is missing in the Harleian MS, and proves that the husband of Susanna Thorne was Roger Dudley."); 86 (1932): 263 (Dudley arms: Gold, a lion vert a crescent for difference); 139 (1985): 60 (marriage record); 142 (1988): 227–244. Benolte & Cooke *Vis. of Kent 1530–1, 1574 & 1592* 2 (H.S.P. 75) (1924): 108 (1592 Vis.). *TAG* 9 (1932–33): 212–222.

21. [GOV.] **THOMAS DUDLEY**, baptized at Yardley Hastings, Northamptonshire 12 October 1576. He was a legatee in the 1579 will of his great-uncle, John Purefoy, Esq. As a youth, he served as a page in the home of William Compton, 2nd Lord Compton (afterwards 1st Earl of Northampton). In 1597 he raised a company of soldiers to join the forces sent by Queen Elizabeth to aid King Henry IV of France at the Siege of Amiens. He subsequently returned to England, where he served as a clerk for Augustine Nichols, Judge of the Common Pleas, from 1598 to 1616. He married (1st) at Hardingstone, Northamptonshire 25 April 1603 **DOROTHY YORKE**, daughter of Edmund Yorke, of Cotton End, Northamptonshire. They had two sons, Thomas and [Rev.] Samuel, and four daughters, Anne (wife of Simon Bradstreet), Patience (wife of Daniel Denison), Sarah (wife of Benjamin Keayne and Thomas Pacy), and Mercy (wife of [Rev.] John Woodbridge). He was appointed one of the overseers in the 1614 will of his father-in-law, Edmund Yorke. He served as steward for Theophilus Fiennes, Earl of Lincoln from 1616 to 1628. He and his family immigrated to New England in 1630, where they lived successively at Cambridge, Ipswich, and finally Roxbury, Massachusetts. He served as Governor of Massachusetts Bay, 1634, 1640, 1645, 1650, Deputy Governor of Massachusetts Bay, 1630–3, 1637–9, 1646–9, 1651–2, Assistant of Massachusetts Bay, 1635–6, 1641–4, Commissioner of the United Colonies for Massachusetts Bay, 1643, 1647, and Sergeant Major General, 1644. His wife, Dorothy died at Roxbury, Massachusetts 27 Dec. 1643. He married (2nd) at Roxbury, Massachusetts 4 April 1644 **KATHERINE DEIGHTON**, widow of Samuel Hackburne (or Hagburne), of Roxbury, Mass. (buried 27 Dec. 1642) [see DEIGHTON 16.iii], and daughter of John Deighton, Gent., of St. Nicholas, Gloucester, Gloucestershire, by Jane, daughter of Edward Basset, Gent. [see DEIGHTON 16 for her ancestry]. She was baptized at St. Nicholas, Gloucester, Gloucestershire 16 Jan. 1614/5. They had two sons, Joseph and Paul, and one daughter Deborah (wife of Jonathan Wade). [GOV.] THOMAS DUDLEY died at Roxbury, Massachusetts 31 July 1653. His widow, Katherine, married (3rd) at Dedham, Massachusetts 8 Nov. 1653 (as his 2nd wife) [REV.] **JOHN ALLIN**, of Dedham, Massachusetts. They had three sons, Benjamin, Daniel, and Eliezer. She died 20 August 1671.

Herald & Genealogist 3 (1866): 308–315. *Annual Meeting of the Gov. Thomas Dudley Fam. Assoc.* (1893): 45–49 (Rpt. of Historian). *NEHGR* 47 (1893): 120; 56 (1902): 206; 66 (1912): 340–343; 142 (1988): 227–244. Jones *Life & Work of Thomas Dudley* (1900). Pope *Pioneers of Massachusetts* (1900): 145–146 (biog. of [Mr.] Thomas Dudley). Waters *Gen. Gleanings in England* 2 (1901): 1087–1088 (will of John Purefay, Esq.). *TAG* 9 (1932–33): 212–222. Raimo *Biog. Dict. of American Col. & Revolutionary Govs.* (1980): 123–124 (biog. of Thomas Dudley). Anderson *Great Migration Begins* 1 (1995): 581–588 (biog. of Thomas Dudley).

∞ DUNBAR ∞

MALCOLM III (CEANNMORE), King of Scots, married [SAINT] **MARGARET**.
DAVID I, King of Scots, married **MAUD OF NORTHUMBERLAND**.
HENRY OF SCOTLAND, Earl of Northumberland, married **ADA DE WARENNE**.
WILLIAM the Lion, King of Scots, by an unknown mistress, ____ [see SCOTLAND 4].

5. **ADA OF SCOTLAND**, married in 1184 (as his 1st wife) **PATRICK**, 5th Earl of Dunbar, Justiciary of Lothian, Keeper of Berwick, son and heir of Waldeve, 4th Earl of Dunbar, by his wife, Aline. They had three sons, Patrick, Knt. [6th Earl of Dunbar], William, Knt., and Robert, Knt., and

one daughter, Ada (wife of William de Courtenay, Theobald de Lascelles, and possibly William Fitz Patrick). In 1200 he attended King William *the Lion* to Lincoln, when William did homage to King John for his lands in England. His wife, Ada, founded a Cistertian nunnery at St. Bothans (now Abbey St. Bathans). She died in 1200. He married (2nd) before 1208 **CHRISTIAN FITZ WALTER**, widow of William de Brus (living 1202–3), of Annandale in Scotland, Hartlepool, Durham, etc., and daughter of Walter Fitz Alan, Steward of Scotland. His son, William, was mentioned as a hostage in England in 1213. In 1218 he founded a monastery of Red Friars in Dunbar. In 1221 he accompanied King Alexander II to York, and was present at the king's marriage there to Joan, sister of King Henry III. Patrick, 5th Earl of Dunbar, died 31 Dec. 1232, and was buried in the convent church of Eccles.

> Stevenson *Chronica de Mailros* (1835): 92 (sub A.D. 1184: "Willelmus rex Scottorum dedit filiam suam Ada Patricio comiti."). Stevenson *Chronicon de Lanercost* (1839): 41 (sub A.D. 1231: "Eodem anno obiit comes Patricius de Dunbar, cui successit filius ejus, consimili nomine Patricius."). Stevenson *Church Historians of England* 4(1) (1856): 139–140 (Chronicle of Melrose sub A.D. 1184: "William, king of Scotland, gave his daughter Ada in marriage to earl Patrick.."), 177 (Chronicle of Melrose sub A.D. 1232: "Patrick, the venerable earl of Dunbar, invited his sons and daughters, his kinsmen and his neighbours, to spend the festival of our Lord's Nativity happily together. When four days had been thus occupied, he was seized with a severe illness, whereupon he summoned A[dam de Harkarres] abbot of Melrose, his friend and kinsman, and received extreme unction and the dress of monk at his hands; and thus, bidding a last farewell to all, he died upon the day of St. Sylvester [31st Jan.] (after having held the earldom for fifty years), and was buried in the church of St. Mary at Hecclis. He was succeeded by his son Patrick, a sturdy knight, the king's nephew."). Miller *Hist. of Dunbar* (1859): 17–20. Hodgson *Hist. of Northumberland* 7 (1904): 14–106. *Scots Peerage* 1 (1904): 4 (sub Kings of Scotland); 3 (1906): 252–255 (sub Dunbar, Earl of Dunbar) ("This Earl had two seals. The first, round, 2-5/8 inches in diameter, showing a mounted Knight in chain mail, riding to sinister, holding a sword with an ornamented blade raised in his right hand. He wears a flat-topped helmet, and carries suspended round his neck a heater-shaped shield charged with a lion rampant. The saddle-cloth has a fringe of six tags at the bottom. Legend — 'SIGILL. COMI[TIS] PATRIC ... VMBAR. The second seal is round, showing an equestrian figure similar to the above, the saddle-cloth having eight pointed tags on the fringe. Legend — 'SIGILL. COMITIS PATRICII DE DVMBAR.'"). Dunbar *Scottish Kings* (1906): 58-70, 282 (chart). *Pubs Bedfordshire Hist. Soc.* 13 (1930): Ped. 8 (Engaine ped.). Easson *Charters of the Abbey of Coupar Angus* 1 (Scottish Hist. Soc. 3rd Ser. 40) (1947): 60–62. Hedley *Northumberland Fams.* 1 (1968): 238–241. Fryde *Handbook of British Chron.* (1986): 58. *TG* 9 (1988): 229–241; 17 (2003): 223–233. Owen *William the Lion, 1143–1214: Kingship & Culture* (1997).

6. PATRICK, Knt., 6th Earl of Dunbar, son and heir. He married **EUPHAME DE BRUS**, daughter of William de Brus, of Annandale in Scotland, Hartlepool, Durham, etc., by Christian, daughter of Walter Fitz Alan, Steward of Scotland. Her maritagium included the estate of Birkenside in Lauderdale. They had two sons, Patrick [7th Earl of Dunbar] and Waldeve [Rector of Dunbar], and one daughter, Isabel. In 1235 he took an active part in suppressing the rebellion in Galloway. In 1245 he took part in an attempt to settle a dispute as to marches between the Canons of Carham and Bernard de Hawden. In 1247 he decided to join a crusade to the Holy Land projected by King Louis IX of France. PATRICK, Earl of Dunbar, was living 14 April 1248, when he witnessed a grant at Berwick, but before 28 June he had left the country. He died soon afterwards at Marseilles en route to Palestine. In 1261 his widow, Euphame, sued her daughter and son-in-law, Isabel and Simon Baard, regarding five of her charters which she claimed they wrongfully withheld. Euphame, Countess of Dunbar, died in 1267.

> Stevenson *Chronicon de Lanercost* (1839): 54 (sub A.D. 1248: "In hoc itinere apud Marsiliam largus comes Patricius de Dunbar ex hac luce migravit."), 82 (sub A.D. 1267: "Domina mater domini comitis Patricii de Dunbar, Eufemia dicta, magistri Patricii relicta qui apud Marsilium obiit, multas, ut vidimus, a filio irrogatas sustinuit injurias, nec unquam in unum convenerunt amorem nisi cum, me praesente, matre ad mortem properante, filius ab ea petivit remissionem."). *Extracta e Variis Cronicis Scocie* (1842): 94 (Patrick de Dunbar, Earl of March, styled "nephew" [nepos] of King Alexander II of Scotland). Innes *Liber S. Marie de Dryburgh* (1847): 85 (charter of Countess Euphame widow of Patrick Earl of Dunbar). Miller *Hist. of Dunbar* (1859): 20–21. *Fourth Rpt.* (Hist. MSS Comm. 3) (1874): 460 (charter dated 1270–80 in which Robert Fitz Roger names his grandmother, "E[upheme], Countess of Dunbar"). Hodgson *Hist. of Northumberland* 7 (1904): 14–106. Dunbar *Scottish Kings* (1906): 282 (chart). *Scots Peerage* 3 (1906): 255–257 (sub Dunbar, Earl of Dunbar) ("This Earl had two great seals, and two privy seals. The first great seal, used during his

father's lifetime, round, shows an equestrian figure riding to sinister, with a sword raised in his right hand. He wears a square-topped helmet and carries a heater-shaped shield without any device. Legend, 'SIGILL. PATRICII FILII COMITIS PATRICII.' His seal as Earl is also round, showing an equestrian figure riding to dexter, wearing a flat-topped helmet, having a sword right hand, and carrying on left arm a heater-shaped shield charged with a lion rampant. Legend, 'SIGILLVM PATRICII COMITIS DE DVNBAR.' One of his privy seals shows a lion rampant, with legend, 'SECRETVM P. COMIT.'"). Hedley *Northumberland Fams.* 1 (1968): 238–241. *TG* 9 (1988): 229–241; 22 (2008): 28–29.

Child of Patrick of Dunbar, Knt., by Euphame de Brus:

i. **ISABEL OF DUNBAR**, married (1st) **ROGER FITZ JOHN** (or **DE BALLIOL**), of Warkworth, Northumberland [see CLAVERING 5]; (2nd) **SIMON BAARD** (or **BAYARD**), of Northumberland [see CLAVERING 5].

✥ EAST HARLING ✥

ALICE OF NORMANDY (sister of King William the Conqueror), married **LAMBERT**, Count of Lens.
JUDITH OF LENS, married **WALTHEOF**, Earl of Northumberland.
ALICE OF NORTHUMBERLAND, married **RALPH DE TONY**, of Flamstead, Hertfordshire.
ROGER DE TONY, of Flamstead, Hertfordshire, married **IDA OF HAINAULT**.
RALPH DE TONY, of Flamstead, Hertfordshire, married **MARGARET OF LEICESTER**.
IDA DE TONY, married **ROGER LE BIGOD**, Knt., Earl of Norfolk.
MARGARET LE BIGOD, married **WILLIAM DE HASTINGS**.
HENRY DE HASTINGS, Knt., married **ADA OF HUNTINGDON**.
HENRY DE HASTINGS, Knt., of Cavendish, Suffolk, married **JOAN DE CANTELOWE**.
JOHN DE HASTINGS, Knt., 1st Lord Hastings, married **ISABEL LE DESPENSER**.
HUGH DE HASTINGS, Knt., of Sutton Scotney, Hampshire, Gressenhall, Norfolk, etc., married **MARGERY FOLIOT** (desc. King William the Conqueror).
HUGH DE HASTINGS, Knt., of Elsing, Norfolk, married **MARGARET DE EVERINGHAM**.
MARGARET HASTINGS, married **JOHN WINGFIELD**, Knt., of Letheringham, Suffolk.
ROBERT WINGFIELD, Knt., of Letheringham, Suffolk, married **ELIZABETH RUSSELL**.
ROBERT WINGFIELD, Knt., of Letheringham, Suffolk, married **ELIZABETH GOUSHILL** (desc. King William the Conqueror).
ELIZABETH WINGFIELD, married **WILLIAM BRANDON**, Knt., of Henham, Suffolk [see BRANDON 16].

17. MARGARET BRANDON, married **GREGORY LOVELL**, Knt., of Barton Bendish, Norfolk, son and heir of Thomas Lovell, of Barton Bendish, Norfolk, by Anne Toppys (or Toppes). They had four sons, Thomas, Knt., Francis, Knt., Gregory, and John, and four daughters, Margaret (wife of _____ Willoughby), Katherine (wife of John Fitz Lewis), Bridget (wife of John Lynnolds), and Dorothy (nun). He was knighted in 1491. He was cured of "great bone ake" by St. Walstan in the 1490s. SIR GREGORY LOVELL left a will proved 5 June 1507 (P.C.C. 24 Adeane).

Wright *Hist. & Antiqs. of Rutland* (1684): 126 (Brandon ped.). Blomefield *Essay towards a Top. Hist. of Norfolk* 1 (1739): 217–218 (Lovell ped.). Blore *Hist. & Antiqs. of Rutland* 1(2) (1811): 47 (Lovell ped.). Nicolas *Testamenta Vetusta* 2 (1826): 432–433 (will of Elizabeth Brandon). Gurney *Rec. of the House of Gournay* (1848): 442 (Lovell ped.). Burke *Gen. Hist. of the Dormant, Abeyant, Forfeited & Extinct Peerages* (1866): 71 (sub Brandon, Dukes of Suffolk). *Misc. Gen. et Heraldica* 1st Ser. 2 (1876): 161–167. Harvey et al. *Vis. of Norfolk 1563 & 1613* (H.S.P. 32) (1891): 190–192 (1563 Vis.) (Lovell ped.: "Sir Gregory Lovell of Barton Bendish, Knight. = Margaret da. of Sir Wm Brandon, Knt."). *Trans. Essex Arch. Soc.* n.s. 6 (1898): 51–52. Benolte et al. *Vis. of Surrey 1530, 1572 & 1623* (H.S.P. 43) (1899): 69 (Lovell ped.: "Sr Gregory Louell of Barton Bendish in com. Norff. Knt. = Margerett d. of Sr Wi'm Brandon Knight.") (Lovell arms: Argent, a chevron azure between three squirrels sejant gules). *Norfolk Arch.* 18 (1894): 46–77. Harvey et al. *Vis. of the North* 3 (Surtees Soc. 144) (1930): 120–123 (Wingfeld ped.: "Margareta [Brandon] nupta domino Gregorio Louuell militi"). *Norfolk Arch.* 36 (1977): 305–326. Gunn *Charles Brandon, Duke of Suffolk c.1484–1545* (1988): 46–47 (Brandon ped.). Harper-Bill *Religious Belief & Eccl. Careers in Late Medieval England* (Studies in the Hist. of Medieval Religion 3) (1991): 129.

18. FRANCIS LOVELL, Knt., of East Harling, Norfolk, Esquire of the Body, Sheriff of Norfolk and Suffolk, 1526–7, 1538–9, 1543–4, Justice of the Peace for Norfolk, son and heir. He married

ANNE ASHBY, daughter of George Ashby, of Hertfordshire. They had three sons, Thomas, Knt., Francis, and Gregory, Esq., and seven daughters, Dorothy (wife of _____ Vernon and _____ Blunt), Eleanor (wife of Francis Sturgis), Bridget (wife of Robert Hodson), Katherine (wife of Leonard Spencer), Elizabeth (wife of Henry Repps), Mary (wife of _____ Markham), and Amphillis (wife of Thomas Derham, Esq.). He obtained the manor of Ryhall, Rutland on the death of his uncle, Thomas Lovell, K.G., in 1525. In 1530 he was among those appointed to hold an inquisition on the property of Cardinal Wolsey in Norfolk. He presented to the church of East Harling, Norfolk in 1530. He was one of the knights appointed to attend the queen at the Coronation of Queen Anne Boleyn in 1533. His wife, Elizabeth, died 12 Jan. 1551/2. SIR FRANCIS LOVELL died 20 Jan. 1551/2, and was buried at East Harling, Norfolk. He left a will dated 29 August 1551, proved 17 May 1552 (P.C.C. 15 Powell).

Blomefield *Essay towards a Top. Hist. of Norfolk* 1 (1739): 217–218 (Lovell ped.), 220. Blore *Hist. & Antiqs. of Rutland* 1(2) (1811): 47 (Lovell ped.). Gurney *Rec. of the House of Gournay* (1848): 442 (Lovell ped.). Harvey et al. *Vis. of Norfolk 1563 & 1613* (H.S.P. 32) (1891): 190–192 (1563 Vis.) (Lovell ped.: "Sir Francis Lovell of Barton. = Ann da. of George Ashbye of Hertfordshire.") (Ashby arms: Azure, a chevron between three eagles displayed or). *Norfolk Arch.* 18 (1894): 46–77. *List of Sheriffs for England & Wales* (PRO Lists and Indexes 9) (1898): 88. Benolte et al. *Vis. of Surrey 1530, 1572 & 1623* (H.S.P. 43) (1899): 69 (Lovell ped.: "S[r] Frances Louell."). Copinger *Manors of Suffolk: Hundreds of Babergh & Blackbourn* (1905): 280. VCH *Rutland* 2 (1935): 268–275.

19. THOMAS LOVELL, Knt., of East Harling, Norfolk, Ryhall, Rutland, etc., son and heir. He married before 10 Jan. 1557 (date of her father's will) **ELIZABETH PARIS**, daughter of Philip Paris, Knt., of Linton, Cambridgeshire, by Margaret, daughter of John Bowes, Citizen and mercer of London. They had seven sons, Thomas, Knt., Philip, Robert, Francis, Henry, Edmund, and Thomas, and four daughters, Anne (wife of Robert Grey, Esq.), Audrey (wife of _____ Cooke and William Fincham), Eleanor (wife of John Shelley, Esq.), and Katherine (wife of Francis Baxter). His wife, Elizabeth, was a legatee in the 1557 will of her father, Philip Paris, Knt. He presented to the church of East Harling, Norfolk in 1558. SIR THOMAS LOVELL died 23 April 1567, and was buried at East Harling, Norfolk. He left a will dated 5 October 1566, proved 27 March 1567 (P.C.C. 8 Stonard). In 1585 the queen ordered his widow, Elizabeth, and her son, Robert Lovell, be released from prison "for cause of conscience." His widow, Elizabeth, died 31 March 1591, and was buried at East Harling, Norfolk. She left a will dated 28 Dec. 1590, proved 14 July 1595 (P.C.C. 51 Scott).

Blomefield *Essay towards a Top. Hist. of Norfolk* 1 (1739): 217–218 (Lovell ped.), 220. Blore *Hist. & Antiqs. of Rutland* 1(2) (1811): 47 (Lovell ped.). Blyth *Hist. Notices & Recs. of Fincham* (1863): 120. Farrer *Church Heraldry of Norfolk* 1 (1887): 41–44. Harvey et al. *Vis. of Norfolk 1563 & 1613* (H.S.P. 32) (1891): 190–192 (1563 Vis.) (Lovell ped.: "Sir Thomas Lovell of Harling in Norfolk, Kn[t] . = Elizabeth da. of Sir Philip Paris of Lynton in co. Cambr., Kn[t].."). *Norfolk Arch.* 18 (1894): 46–77. Cooke & St. George *Vis. of Cambridge 1575 & 1619* (H.S.P. 41) (1897): 37 (Paris ped.) (Paris arms: Gules, three unicorns' heads couped or). Copinger *Manors of Suffolk: Hundreds of Babergh & Blackbourn* (1905): 280. *Misc. Gen. et Heraldica* 5th Ser. 2 (1916–17): 123–126 (Paris ped.). Bysshe *Vis. of Norfolk A.D. 1664* (Norfolk Rec. Soc. 5) (1934): 263–264 (Lovell ped.: "Sir Thomas Lovell of East Harling co. Norf. Knt. Died 23 Mch. 1567. Will (P.C.C. Stonarde, 8) pr. 27 Mch. 1567 = Eliz. da. of Sir Philip Paris of Lynton co. Cambs. Knt. Will pr. 4 July 1595."). VCH *Rutland* 2 (1935): 268–275.

20. THOMAS LOVELL, Knt., of East Harling, Norfolk, son and heir, born about 1540. He married **ALICE HUDDLESTON**, daughter of John Huddleston, Knt., of Sawston and Bartlow, Cambridgeshire, Hartford, Huntingdonshire, Rainham, Norfolk, etc., by Bridget, daughter of Robert Cotton, Knt. [see INGALDESTHORPE 16 for her ancestry]. She was born about 1538. They had five sons, Francis, Knt., Charles, Esq., William, Esq., Edmund, and Alborne, and three daughters, including Katherine (wife successively of Thomas Knyvet, Knt., Edward Spring, Esq., and Edward Downes, Esq.) and Eleanor (wife of Edward Waldegrave, Knt., 1st Baronet of Hever Castle). In 1578 the Privy Council ordered that the Bishop of Norwich see that Thomas be released from imprisonment "upon his promise and subscription of his new conformity." He presented to the church of East Harling, Norfolk in 1579 and 1595. In 1584 he and his mother, Elizabeth, sold the manor of Ryhall, Rutland to William Burghley, Lord Cecil. In 1590 Henry Knvyett, Gent., of Buckenham Castle, Norfolk sued him in Chancery regarding the execution of the will of Sir Thomas Knyvett and the failure to invest £2000 in lands for the use of the plaintiff and his heirs. His widow, Alice, died 1 Sept. 1602, and was buried at East Harling, Norfolk 2 Sept. 1602. SIR THOMAS LOVELL died 12 Dec. 1604, and was buried at East Harling, Norfolk 19 Dec. 1604.

Blomefield *Essay towards a Top. Hist. of Norfolk* 1 (1739): 217–218 (Lovell ped.), 220, 222–223. Blore *Hist. & Antiqs. of Rutland* 1(2) (1811): 47 (Lovell ped.). Burke *Hist. of the Commoners* 2 (1835): 582–585 (sub Huddleston). St. George *Vis. of Cumberland 1615* (H.S.P. 7) (1872): 22–24 (Hudleston ped.: "Allice [Hudleston] ux. Thom. Lovell of Harling in Com' Norff. Knt."). Farrer *Church Heraldry of Norfolk* 1 (1887): 41–44, 46. Harvey et al. *Vis. of Norfolk 1563 & 1613* (H.S.P. 32) (1891): 190–192 (1563 Vis.) (Lovell ped.: "Thomas Lovell of Harling. = Alice da. of Sir John Hudleston of Sawston in co. Cambridge."). *Norfolk Arch.* 18 (1894): 46–77. Cooke & St. George *Vis. of Cambridge 1575 & 1619* (H.S.P. 41) (1897): 26–28 (Hudleston ped.: "Alice [Hudleston] ux. Sr Thom. Lovell of Harling in Norff. Knight."). Copinger *Manors of Suffolk: Hundreds of Babergh & Blackbourn* (1905): 280. VCH *Rutland* 2 (1935): 268–275. Hoyle *Cal. of Chancery Decree Rolls, C 78/86–130* (List. & Index Soc. 254) (1994): 82. Lake & Questier *Conformity & Orthodoxy in the English Church, c.1560–1660* (Studies in Modern British Religious Hist.) (2000): 247–248.

21. CHARLES LOVELL, Esq., of Spridlington, Lincolnshire, born about 1571, younger son. He allegedly married four times. He married (1st) _____. They had one daughter, Frances (wife of Edward Gawdy). He married (2nd) before 22 October 1626 **ELIZABETH LE GROS**, daughter of Thomas le Gros, Knt., of Crostwick, Norfolk, by Elizabeth, daughter of Charles Cornwallis, Knt. [see WYNDHAM 18 for her ancestry]. She was born after 1595 (date of her parents' marriage). They had two daughters, Elizabeth (wife of Charles Yaxley, Esq.), and Alice. He was heir in 1624 to his older brother, Francis Lovell, Knt., by which he inherited the manor of East Harling, Norfolk. He was also appointed one of the executors of the 1624 will of his brother, Francis Lovell. His wife, Elizabeth, was a legatee in the 1626 will of her brother, Thomas Le Gros, Esq., of Crostwight, Norfolk. He married (3rd?) **ANNE** _____, who was buried at St. [?Waul's] church in [?Lincoln] 1 Sept. 1638. In 1638 he and his former brother-in-law, Charles Le Gros, mortgaged a park in Hockering and lands in North Tuddenham, Mattishall, and Mattishall Burgh, Norfolk. He married (4th) **MARY HEWKE**, daughter of John Hewke, of South Walsham, Norfolk, by his wife, Elizabeth Howlett. She was baptized at South Walsham, Norfolk 6 May 1599. They had no issue. CHARLES LOVELL, Esq., died 6 Jan. 1640/1, aged 69, and was buried at Spridlington, Lincolnshire Jan. 1640/1. He left a will dated 2 Jan. 1640/1, proved 29 May 1641 (P.C.C. 55 Evelyn). His widow, Mary, married (2nd) at Spridlington, Lincolnshire in August 1641 **GEORGE NEVILL**, Esq., of Stapleford, Lincolnshire. They had no issue. Mary was buried at Spridlington, Lincolnshire in August 1642. She left a will dated 6 August 1642, proved 21 Jan. 1642/3 (Cons. Court of Lincoln). GEORGE NEVILL, Esq., died in 1652, and was buried in Aubourn, Lincolnshire.

Blomefield *Essay towards a Top. Hist. of Norfolk* 1 (1739): 217–218 (Lovell ped.: "Sir Charles Lovell of Herling Ld. In 1623, had 4 wives, but having no Male Issue, the Estate went by Entail to Jn. Lovell, Grandson to Philip, who was uncle to Sir Charles."). Blore *Hist. & Antiqs. of Rutland* 1(2) (1811): 47 (Lovell ped.). *Coll. Top. et Gen.* 3 (1836): 157. Farrer *Church Heraldry of Norfolk* 1 (1887): 231. Harvey et al. *Vis. of Norfolk 1563 & 1613* (H.S.P. 32) (1891): 185–186 (Le Gros ped.: "Elizabeth [Le Gros]."). *Norfolk Arch.* 18 (1894): 46–77. Maddison *Lincolnshire Peds.* 2 (H.S.P. 51) (1903): 711–713 (Nevile ped.). *Notes & Queries* 153 (1927): 387–388. Bysshe *Vis. of Norfolk A.D. 1664* (Norfolk Rec. Soc. 4) (1934): 119–120 (Le Gros ped.: "*Elizabeth* [Le Gros] mar. *Chas. Lovell*"). Norfolk Rec. Office: Petre Fam. of Westwick, MC 124/21 600 x 2 — deed of trust dated 1638 Charles Lovell of East Harling, and Sir Charles Gros of Crostwight to Henry, Lord Maltravers, Sir Edward Waldegrave and John Dix. Park at Hockering and lands in N. Tuddenham, Mattishall and Mattishall Burgh, with schedule of obligations (available at www.a2a.org.uk/search/index.asp). Parish Regs. of Spridlington, Lincolnshire [FHL Microfilm 1450404]. Registered will of Thomas Le Groos, Esq., of Crostwight, Norfolk dated 22 Oct. 1626, proved 24 Jan. 1626/7, Cons. Court of Norfolk, 325 Mittings [FHL Microfilm 94939].

Child of Charles Lovell, Esq., by Elizabeth Le Gros:

  i. **ALICE LOVELL**, married (1st) **GEORGE CRYMES**, Knt., 1st Baronet, of Peckham (in Camberwell), Surrey [see CRYMES 17]; (2nd) **ANDREW KNIVETON**, Knt. [see CRYMES 17].

ECHINGHAM

 ROGER D'AUBENEY, married **AMICE** _____.
 WILLIAM D'AUBENEY, of Buckenham, Norfolk, married **MAUD LE BIGOD**.
 WILLIAM D'AUBENEY, of Buckenham, Norfolk, married **ALICE OF LOUVAIN**, Queen of England.
 WILLIAM D'AUBENEY, 2nd Earl of Arundel, married **MAUD DE SAINT HILARY**.
 WILLIAM D'AUBENEY, Earl of Arundel, married **MABEL OF CHESTER** (desc. King William the Conqueror).
 ISABEL D'AUBENEY, married **JOHN FITZ ALAN**, of Clun, Shropshire.
 JOHN FITZ ALAN, Knt., of Oswestry, Shropshire, married **MAUD DE VERDUN**.
 JOHN FITZ ALAN, of Arundel, Sussex, married **ISABEL DE MORTIMER** (desc. King William the Conqueror).
 RICHARD FITZ ALAN, Knt., Earl of Arundel, married **ALICE DI SALUZZO** (desc. King William the Conqueror).
 EDMUND DE ARUNDEL, Knt., Earl of Arundel, married **ALICE DE WARENNE**.
 RICHARD DE ARUNDEL, Earl of Arundel and Surrey, married **ELEANOR OF LANCASTER** (desc. King William the Conqueror).
 JOHN DE ARUNDEL, Knt., 1st Lord Arundel, married **ELEANOR MAUTRAVERS** (desc. King William the Conqueror) [see ARUNDEL 9].

10. JOAN ARUNDEL. She married (1st) **WILLIAM DE BRYAN** (or **BRIAN**), Knt., of Kemsing and Seale, Kent, Batheaston, Downhead, Kingsdon, and Shockerwick (in Bathford), Somerset, and Woodmansterne, Surrey, Captain of Merk Castle in the Marches of Calais, 2nd son of Guy de Bryan, K.G., Lord Bryan, of Laugharne, Carmarthenshire, Walwyn's Castle, Pembrokeshire, Clifton Dartmouth and Hardness and Slapton, Devon, Woodsford, Dorset, etc., by his 2nd wife, Elizabeth, daughter of William de Montagu, Knt., 1st Earl of Salisbury, 3rd Lord Montagu, Marshal of England [see CAREW 10.ii for his ancestry]. They had no issue. In the period, 1390–5, he complained to the king and the lords in Parliament that Sir John Devereux had "estranged him from his inheritance" while he was in the king's service. SIR WILLIAM DE BRYAN died 23 Sept. 1395, and was buried at Seale, Kent. His widow, Joan, was assigned dower 1 Dec. 1397. She married (2nd) before 22 Feb. 1401 (grant of land) (as his 2nd wife) **WILLIAM ECHINGHAM** (or **ECHYNGHAM**), Knt., of Etchingham and Udimore, Sussex,[19] son of William de Echingham, Knt., of Etchingham, Sussex, by his wife, Elizabeth. They had one son, Thomas, Knt. In 1401 he and his wife, Joan, were granted 102 acres of arable land, 22 acres of wood, and rents in Benenden, Kent by the king. She was a legatee in the 1401 will of Agnes Arundel, widow of her brother, William Arundel, K.G. His wife, Joan, died 1 Sept. 1404. SIR WILLIAM ECHINGHAM died 20 March 1412/13 (or 30 Dec. 1413). Administration on his estate was granted in 1414. He and his 1st wife, Joan Arundel, were buried at Etchingham, Sussex.

 Banks *Dormant & Extinct Baronage of England* 2 (1808): 63–65 (sub Bryan). Nicolas *Controversy between Scrope & Grosvenor* 2 (1832): 245–255. Banks *Baronies in Fee* 1 (1844): 198–199 (sub Robert Echingham). *Arch. Jour.* 7 (1850): 265–273. Hall *Echyngham of Echyngham* (1850): 13. *Top. & Gen.* 2 (1853): 312–339 (cites Vincent's Colls. in College of Arms); 3 (1858): 254–255. *Sussex Arch. Colls.* 8 (1856): 96–131; 9 (1857): 343–360; 30 (1880): 142–143; 77 (1936): 166–172 (Echingham arms: Azure fretty argent). *Arch. Aeliana* n.s. 4 (1860): 194–195 ("Sir William de Bryan, knt., brother of Guy the younger, and eventual heir-male. [He bore] the same coat [Gold, three blue piles from the chief, conjoined at base], a canton paly of four, silver and blue, charged with a red bend, thereon three golden eagles displayed. This

---

[19] William Echingham married (1st) Alice Batisford, daughter and co-heiress of William Batisford, of Buckholt (in Bexhill), Sussex, by Margery, daughter and heiress of Simon de Peplesham. His wife, Alice, was named in a Sussex fine dated 1397–8 [see Salzman *Feet of Fines Rel. Sussex* 3 (Sussex Rec. Soc. 23) (1916): 208–210]. They had two daughters, Joan (wife of John Rykhill) and Elizabeth (wife of Thomas Hoo, Knt., and Thomas Lewknor, Knt. [see CLAVERING 7, LEWKNOR 9, MORLEY 8]).

difference is from his maternal grandmother Grandison. (Willement's Roll). The piles only, for himself; and the same impaling Fitzalan and Maltravers quarterly, for his wife. Brass, 1395, Seal ch., Kent."). Hutchins *Hist. & Antiqs. of Dorset* 1 (1861): 448 (Bryan ped.); 3 (1868): 322–323 (Arundel ped.). *Misc. Gen. et Heraldica* 1st Ser. 2 (1876): 332 (identification of 2nd wife). *C.P.R.* 1399–1401 (1903): 434. *Genealogist* n.s. 21 (1905): 243–245. Benolte et al. *Vis. of Sussex 1530 & 1633–4* (H.S.P. 53) (1905): 124–126 (Echingham ped.: "Sr Willm. Echingham of Echingham in com. Sussex Lord of the mannor of Echingham. = Joane d. of John FitzAllen Lord Matrevers."). *Notes & Queries for Somerset & Dorset* 9 (1905): 297–302. *C.P.* 2 (1912): 361–362 (sub Bryan); 6 (1926): 565–567 (sub Hoo). VCH *Surrey* 4 (1912): 249. Woodruff & Churchill *Sede Vacante Wills* (Kent Arch. Soc. Recs. 3) (1914): 18. *C.C.R.* 1385–1389 (1921): 372, 425, 475–476. *C.C.R.* 1396–1399 (1927): 185, 376–377, 524–525. Wedgwood *Hist. of Parl.* 1 (1936): 466 (biog. of Thomas Hoo). *Cal. Inqs. Misc.* 7 (1968): 280. VCH *Somerset* 3 (1974): 111–120, 129–153. *TG* 5 (1984): 131–157. Saul *Scenes from Provincial Life* (1986). *Cal. IPM* 20 (1995): 7. National Archives, SC 8/94/4685 (petition dated c.1390–5 from William de Brien, Knt., to the king and the lords in this present parliament, who requests an audience so that he is able to show the king the truth of the matter concerning the lands of Guy de Briene in England and Wales which he held for his life with remainder to the petitioner. While Brien was in the king's service Sir John Devereux, Knt. estranged him from his inheritance, and Brien requests remedy so he can recover his right) (available at www.catalogue.nationalarchives.gov.uk/search.asp).

11. THOMAS ECHINGHAM, Knt., of Etchingham and Udimore, Sussex, son and heir by his father's 2nd marriage, born about 1400–1 (aged 13 in 1413, 13 in 1414). He married (1st) **AGNES SHOYSWELL**, daughter of John Shoyswell, of Shoyswell, Sussex. He married (2nd) before Michaelmas 1426 **MARGARET KNYVET** (or **KNYVETT**), widow successively of Robert Teye, Knt., of Barsham, Suffolk (died 8 October 1415), and Thomas Marney, Knt., of Layer Marney, Essex, Kingsey, Buckinghamshire, etc. (living 5 Nov. 1420, will proved 7 Nov. 1421, P.C.C. Marche), and daughter of John Knyvet, Knt., of Southwick, Northamptonshire, Mendlesham, Suffolk, etc., by Joan, daughter of John Botetourt, Knt. [see GURDON 13 for her ancestry]. They had two sons, Thomas, Knt., and Richard, Esq., and two daughters, Elizabeth and Anne. In 1411 Margaret and her 1st husband, Robert Teye, Knt., were granted the manor of Deenthorpe, with lands in Deenthorpe, Kyrkeby Deen, Bolwyk, and Great Weldon, Northamptonshire, and Thurning, Huntingdonshire. Thomas presented to the churches of Barsham, Suffolk, 1424, and Udimore, Sussex, 1439. In 1428 he sued William Cheyne, and two others, claiming they used force and arms in 1422 to break his close and houses at Etchingham, Sussex, where they abducted his servant. In 1433 John Knyvet, Knt., and three others owed a debt of £15 to Knyvet's brothers-in-law, John Radcliffe, Knt., and Thomas Echingham. SIR THOMAS ECHINGHAM died 14 (or 15) October 1444, and was buried at Etchingham, Sussex. He left a will proved 28 October 1444. In the period, 1452–4, his widow, Margaret, "late the wife of Thomas de Marny, Knt." sued John de Marny, brother of the said Thomas, regarding the manor of Colquite, Cornwall. Sometime in the period, 1461–86, Elizabeth, late the wife of Richard Echingham, Esq., daughter of John Gernegan, Esq. sued Margaret Echingham, mother of the said Richard regarding the petitioner's jointure in the manors of Kessingland and Blanchard (in Heveningham), Suffolk. Margaret was living in 1467.

Blomefield *Essay towards a Top. Hist. of Norfolk* 8 (1808): 286–287. Banks *Baronies in Fee* 1 (1844): 198–199 (sub Robert Echingham). Suckling *Hist. & Antiqs. of Suffolk* 1 (1846): 44. *Arch. Jour.* 7 (1850): 268. Hall *Echyngham of Echyngham* (1850): 13–14. *Sussex Arch. Colls.* 9 (1857): 343–360; 77 (1936): 166–172. *Desc. Cat. Ancient Deeds* 1 (1890): 396. Searle *Christ Church, Canterbury* (Cambridge Antiq. Soc., Octavo Pubs. 34) (1902): 35 (Chronicle of John Stone: "Item hoc anno [1444] obiit dominus Thomas dominus de Ecchyngham de comitatu Suthsexie, videlicet in die sancti Kalixti [14 Oct.]."). *Ancestor* 10 (1904): 87–97, esp. 95 (Friar Brackley's Book of Arms dated 1440–60: "68. Silver a bend and six crosslets fitchy sable for Sire Robert Tye or Ichingham. 'Tye weddid lady Ichingham now in Newsell.'"). Deedes *Extracts from the Episcopal Regs. of Richard Paty, S.T.P., Lord Bishop of Chichester* (Sussex Rec. Soc. 4) (1905): 116–117. *Genealogist* n.s. 21 (1905): 243–250. Benolte et al. *Vis. of Sussex 1530 & 1633–4* (H.S.P. 53) (1905): 124–126 (Echingham ped.: "Sr Thomas Echingham of Echingham knt. = ... d. of... Knevett of... in com. Norff."). *Notes & Queries for Somerset & Dorset* 9 (1905): 297–302. *Norfolk Antiq. Misc.* 2nd Ser. Pt. 1 (1906): 81–87 (Knyvet ped. dated 1651: "Johannes Knivet Miles filius et heres pdci Johannes Knivet militis duxit Johanam filiam et heredem solam dni Boutetort de Mendlesham ... Iste Johannes Knyvett miles habuit exitum Johem Margareta et Elizabetham."). *C.P.* 1 (1910): 341–342 (sub Audley). VCH *Buckingham* 4 (1927): 64. *Norfolk Arch.* 41 (1990): 1–12 ("In 1410 he [John Knyvett] settled his lands at Thirning and Deenthorpe in Northamptonshire upon his daughter, Margaret, and her husband, Robert Ty, in tail with remainders to himself and his wife for life and then to his other daughters, Katherine and Elizabeth ... Robert and Margaret Ty and Katherine had no children and in 1457 Edmund Radcliffe, Elizabeth's son, surrendered the reversion of Deenthorpe after the death of Margaret to a group of feoffees, possibly to the use of Thomas Echingham, Margaret's second husband - B.L. Additional Charter 713."). *Cal. IPM* 20 (1995): 7. Barnes *British Roots of Maryland Fams.* 2 (2002): 156–160. National Archives, C 1/22/16; C 1/29/35; C 241/225/30; C 241/228/85; C 241/228/126; C 241/228/129 (available at www.catalogue.nationalarchives.gov.uk/search.asp). Court of Common Pleas, CP 40/659, rot. 425; CP 40/667, rot. 578; CP 40/669, rot. 114 (available at www.british-history.ac.uk/source.aspx?pubid=1272).

Children of Thomas Echingham, Knt., by Margaret Knyvet:

i. **THOMAS ECHINGHAM**, Knt. [see next].

ii. **ANNE ECHINGHAM**, married (1st) **JOHN ROGERS**, Esq., of Bryanston, Dorset [see TUCHET 16]; (2nd) **JOHN TUCHET**, Knt., 6th Lord Audley [see TUCHET 16].

12. THOMAS ECHINGHAM, Knt., of Etchingham and Udimore, Sussex, Sheriff of Surrey and Sussex, 1463–4, 1474–5, son and heir by his father's 2nd marriage, born about 1425 (aged 20 in 1445). He married **MARGARET WEST**, daughter of Reynold West, Knt., 6th Lord la Warre, 3rd Lord West, by his 1st wife, Margaret, daughter of Robert Thorley, Esq. [see WEST 10 for her ancestry]. They had one son, Thomas, and three daughters, Elizabeth (died young 1452), Margaret, and Elizabeth (2nd of name). In 1463 Thomas Wenslowe, Citizen and draper of London, sued him regarding his failure to pay £90 still due on a bond made in 1457. In the period, 1460–65, Thomas son of Sir Thomas Echingham sued William Parker, clerk, feoffee, regarding the manors of Barsham, Blanchards (in Heveningham), and Kessingland, Suffolk, and the advowson of the church of Barsham, Suffolk. In 1464 he acquired the reversion of the manors of Dixter and Gatecourt, Sussex from Elizabeth Wakehurst. In the period, 1467–72, Henry Danvers, mercer, and John Dryland, draper, Citizens of London, sued him in Chancery regarding a debt owed by defendant to Thomas Hoo, Esquire, assigned by the latter to complainants. In 1479 he settled the manor of Dixter, Sussex on his daughter and son-in-law, Margaret and John Elrington. SIR THOMAS ECHINGHAM died 20 Jan. 1485/6, and was buried at Etchingham, Sussex.

Blore *Hist. & Antiqs. of Rutland* 1(2) (1811): 100–102 (La Warre/West ped.). *Coll. Top. et Gen.* 2 (1835): 8. Banks *Baronies in Fee* 1 (1844): 198–199 (sub Robert Echingham). Suckling *Hist. & Antiqs. of Suffolk* 1 (1846): 44. *Arch. Jour.* 7 (1850): 268 ("although a person of some consideration, outlived both the political influence and the greatness of his family"). Hall *Echyngham of Echyngham* (1850): 14–15. *Sussex Arch. Colls.* 9 (1857): 343–360; 77 (1936): 166–172. *List of Sheriffs for England & Wales* (PRO Lists and Indexes 9) (1898): 136–137. Copinger *County of Suffolk* 1 (1904): 119. Benolte et al. *Vis. of Sussex 1530 & 1633–4* (H.S.P. 53) (1905): 124–126 (Echingham ped.: "Sr Thomas Echingham of Echingham knt. = Margerett d. of Reignold West Lord Delaware"). *Notes & Queries for Somerset & Dorset* 9 (1905): 297–302. Comber *Sussex Gens.* 3 (1933): 304–308 (sub Lords West). *C.P.* 9 (1936): 336–337 (sub Mountjoy). Mate *Daughters, Wives, & Widows after the Black Death: Women in Sussex, 1350–1535* (1998): 32–33. Biancalana *Fee Tail & the Common Recovery in Medieval England* (2001): 346. Emery *Greater Medieval Houses of England & Wales 1300–1500* 3 (2006): 341. National Archives, C 1/29/41; C 1/45/303 (available at www.catalogue.nationalarchives.gov.uk/search.asp). Court of Common Pleas, CP 40/810, rot. 158 (available at www.british-history.ac.uk/source.aspx?pubid=1272).

Children of Thomas Echingham, Knt., by Margaret West:

i. **MARGARET ECHINGHAM**, daughter and co-heiress. She married (1st) **WILLIAM BLOUNT**, Esq., of Derbyshire, Knight of the Shire for Derby, Sheriff of Nottinghamshire and Derbyshire, 1469–70, son and heir apparent of Walter Blount, K.G., K.B., 1st Lord Mountjoy, Lord High Treasurer, by his 1st wife, Ellen, daughter of John Byron, Knt. Her maritagium included the manor of Midley, Kent. They had two sons, John and Edward [2nd Lord Mountjoy] and two daughters, Elizabeth and Anne (wife of Thomas Oxenbridge and David Owen, Knt.). WILLIAM BLOUNT, Esq., died of wounds fighting for King Edward IV at the Battle of Barnet 14 April 1471. His widow, Margaret, married (2nd) 1472–4 **JOHN ELRINGTON** (or **ELRYNGTON**), Knt., of Hoxton, Middlesex, and Dixter and Udimore, Sussex, Chief Clerk of the royal Kitchen, 1464, Cofferer, 1471–4, Clerk of the Hanaper, 1473, Treasurer of the Household of King Edward IV, 1474–83, Sheriff of Surrey and Sussex, 1479–80, Constable of Windsor Castle, 1483, Knight of the Body, Knight of the Shire for Middlesex. They had one son, Edward, and one daughter, Anne (wife of Edward Combe). His considerable household and financial duties included being treasurer of war for the French expedition, raising revenue, and auditing accounts of George, Duke of Clarence. He was knighted in 1478. In 1479 he had license to fortify his manors of Dixter and Udimore, Sussex, and impark lands there. In 1482 he was treasurer of war for the Scots campaign, and was made banneret by Richard, Duke of Gloucester in Scotland. He was present at the Coronation of King Richard III in 1483. SIR JOHN ELRINGTON died shortly before 12 Dec. 1483. He left a will dated 1482. In 1486 Robert Oxenbridge, Esq., and others, feoffees, granted Margaret widow of John Elrington, Knt., and Elizabeth widow of Roger Fiennes, Esq., daughters of Sir Thomas Echingham, Knt. 70 acres of land and marsh called Highfeldys in Bexhill, Sussex. In 1488 Richard Culpeper, Esq. sued his widow, Margaret, for the manors of Dixter and Gatecourt, Sussex. In Michaelmas term 1488 John Echingham sued Margaret, widow of John Elrington, Knt., and her sister, Elizabeth, widow of Roger Fiennes, Esq. for the manors of Etchingham, Munfield, Beddingham, and Pekeden, Sussex. Margaret married (3rd) before Hilary term 1490 (as his 2nd wife) **THOMAS COMBE**, Esq., of Pulborough, Sussex, M.P., Clerk of the Parcels in the Exchequer. In the period, 1488–1492, Thomas and his wife, Margaret, previously the wife of John Elrington, Knt., sued John Elrington, of Hackney, deputy to the said Sir John in Chancery regarding fees in defendant's hands due to the said Sir John. Margaret was living 17 July 1488 (date of bond), but was dead before November 1492. She and her 2nd husband were buried at St. Leonard, Shoreditch, Middlesex. In 1493 Simon Elryngton, Gent., of Hackney was summoned to answer Thomas Combe, Esq. in a plea that he render unto him £300 which he owed him and unjustly withheld, etc. Thomas Combe, Esq., left a will dated 15 October 1494, proved 3 Nov. 1494, requesting burial in the church of Pulburough, Sussex. Weever *Ancient Funerall Monuments* (1631): 427. Hasted *Hist. & Top. Survey of Kent* 8 (1799): 410–414. *Desc. Cat. of the Original Charters, Royal Grants, ... Monastic Chartulary ... constituting Muniments of Battle Abbey* (1835): 126. Banks *Baronies in Fee* 1 (1844): 126–127 (Blount), 198–199 (sub Echingham). Hall *Echyngham of Echyngham* (1850): 14–15. Burke *Gen. Hist. of the Dormant, Abeyant, Forfeited & Extinct Peerages* (1866): 690 (sub Windsor). Hawley et al. *Vis. of Essex 1552, 1558, 1570, 1612 & 1634* 1 (H.S.P. 13) (1878): 49 (1558 Vis.) (Elrington ped.: "Sir John Erlington of Shordiche Kt. = Margerett da. & coheire to Sir Thomas Echingham Knt. renupta Wm. Blunt L. Mountjoye"). Cooke & Mundy *Vis. of Worcester 1569* (H.S.P. 27) (1888): 20–21 (Blount ped.: "Will'm Blount. = Martha da. & heire of Thom. lord Etchingham. [she] = [2] Sr John Elrington of Hackney in com. Midlesex Knt, 2 husband."). (Blount arms: Barry nebulée of six or and sable, in chief three torteauxes). *List of Sheriffs for England & Wales* (PRO Lists and Indexes 9) (1898): 103, 137. *Trans. of the St. Paul's Ecclesiological Soc.* 4 (1900): 136 (will of Thomas Combe). Benolte et al. *Vis. of Sussex 1530 & 1633-4* (H.S.P. 53) (1905): 124–126 (Echingham ped.: "Margerett [Echingham] d. & coheire, [1] = Willm. Blount sonn & heire of the 1 Lord Montioy, [2] = Sr John Elrington knt."). *List of Early Chancery Procs.* 3 (PRO Lists and Indexes 20) (1906): 148, 151, 385. *Genealogist* n.s. 23 (1907): 18–19, 150–151, 153. Kingsford *Stonor Letters & Papers 1290–1483* 1 (Camden 3rd Ser. 29) (1919): 123–128 (letters of Thomas Mulle dated 1472 re. proposed marriage of Margaret Etchingham, widow of William Blount). Brewer *Letters & Papers, Foreign & Domestic, Henry VIII* 1 (1920): 217–234. *C.P.* 9 (1936): 336–337 (sub Mountjoy); 12(2) (1959): 792–794 (sub Windsor). Wedgwood *Hist. of Parl.* 1 (1936): 86–87 (biog. of William Blount), 297–299 (biog. of Sir John Elrington), 654–655 (biog. of Sir David Owen). *C.F.R.* 22 (1963): 183. VCH *Middlesex* 5 (1976): 324–330; 7 (1982): 208–216; 8 (1985): 57–69. Sutton *Coronation of Richard III* (1983): 338 (biog. of Sir John Elryngton). Ward *Women of the English Nobility & Gentry 1066–1500* (1995): 40–41. Baker *Rpts. of Cases by John Caryll* 1 (Selden Soc. 115) (1999): 145–151. Biancalana *Fee Tail & the Common Recovery in Medieval England* (2001): 407–408. Emery *Greater Medieval Houses of England & Wales 1300–1500* 3 (2006): 341. National Archives, C 1/126/57; C 1/217/19; C 1/268/24 (available at www.catalogue.nationalarchives.gov.uk/search.asp).

Children of Margaret Echingham, by William Blount, Esq.:

- a. **ELIZABETH BLOUNT**, married **ANDREW WINDSOR**, K.B., 1st Lord Windsor [see LUDLOW 13].
- b. **ANNE BLOUNT**, married (1st) **THOMAS OXENBRIDGE**, Gent., of Ford Place (in Brede), Sussex [see LANCASTER 12.i]; (2nd) **DAVID** (or **DAVY**) **OWEN**, Knt., of Cowdray (in Midhurst), Sussex [see LANCASTER 12.i].

ii. **ELIZABETH ECHINGHAM** [see next].

13. ELIZABETH ECHINGHAM, daughter and co-heiress. She married (1st) **ROGER FIENNES**, Esq. ROGER FIENNES, Esq., died before 5 August 1486. In 1486 Robert Oxenbridge, Esq., and others, feoffees, granted Margaret widow of John Elrington, Knt., and Elizabeth widow of Roger Fiennes, Esq., daughters of Sir Thomas Echingham, Knt. 70 acres of land and marsh called Highfeldys in Bexhill, Sussex. In Michaelmas term 1488 John Echingham sued his widow, Elizabeth, and her sister, Margaret, widow of John Elrington, Knt., for the manors of Etchingham, Munfield, Beddingham, and Pekeden, Sussex. Elizabeth married (2nd) before Hilary term 1490 (as his 1st wife) **GODDARD OXENBRIDGE**, Knt., of Forde Place (in Brede), Sussex, and, in right of his 1st wife, of Etchingham, Munfield, and Salehurst, Sussex, Sheriff of Surrey and Sussex, 1505–6, 1519–20, younger son of Robert Oxenbridge, of Forde Place (in Brede), Sussex, by his wife, Anne Lyvelode. They had one son, Thomas. He married (2nd) **ANNE FIENNES**, widow of John Windsor, and daughter of Thomas Fiennes, Knt., of Claverham (in Arlington), Sussex, by Anne, daughter of Thomas Urswick, Knt. [see FIENNES 16 for her ancestry]. They had two sons, Robert, Knt., and William, and three daughters, Margaret (wife of John Thatcher), Mary (wife of James Barnham), and Elizabeth. SIR GODDARD OXENBRIDGE died 10 Feb. 1531, and was buried at Brede, Sussex. He left a will proved 27 October 1531 (P.C.C. 8 Thower). His widow, Anne, died 24 May 1531.

> *Desc. Cat. of the Original Charters, Royal Grants, ... Monastic Chartulary ... constituting Muniments of Battle Abbey* (1835): 126. Banks *Baronies in Fee* 1 (1844): 198–199 (sub Robert Echingham). *Sussex Arch. Colls.* 8 (1856): 213–233; 9 (1857): 343–360; 58 (1916): chart facing 64. *List of Sheriffs for England & Wales* (PRO Lists and Indexes 9) (1898): 137. Benolte et al. *Vis. of Sussex 1530 & 1633–4* (H.S.P. 53) (1905): 14–16 (Oxenbridge ped.: "Sr Godard Oxenbrudge of Breade knight [1] = Anne d. & co-heire of Sr Tho. Eckingham knight, [2] Ann d. of Sr Tho. Fynes of Claverham knight 2 wiffe, [3] = marid to his 3 wiffe Faythe d. of Sr Ric. Devenishe."). Benolte et al. *Vis. of Sussex 1530 & 1633–4* (H.S.P. 53) (1905): 124–126 (Echingham ped.: "Anne [or] Elizabeth [Echingham] ux. Sr Goddard Oxenbridge."). *Genealogist* n.s. 23 (1907): 18–19. Biancalana *Fee Tail & the Common Recovery in Medieval England* (2001): 407–408.

14. THOMAS OXENBRIDGE, of Forde Place (in Brede), Etchingham, Munfield, and Salehurst, Sussex, son and heir by his father's 1st marriage, born about 1501 (aged 30 in 1531). He married (1st) **ELIZABETH PUTTENHAM**, daughter of George Puttenham, Knt. They had one daughter, Elizabeth. His wife, Elizabeth, died about 1529. He married (2nd) **FAITH DEVENISH**, daughter of Richard Devenish, Knt. They had one son, Andrew, LL.D., and one daughter, Ursula (wife of John Pickering). THOMAS OXENBRIDGE died 28 March 1540 and was buried at Brede, Sussex. His widow, Faith, married (2nd) _____ **BULSTRODE**. She was living at Hughenden, Buckinghamshire in July 1540.

> *Sussex Arch. Colls.* 8 (1856): 213–233. Benolte et al. *Vis. of Sussex 1530 & 1633–4* (H.S.P. 53) (1905): 14–16 (Oxenbridge ped.: "Thomas Oxenbridge sonn & heire was of Breade in com. Sussex. = Elizebeth d. of Sr George Putnam knight.").

Child of Thomas Oxenbridge, by Elizabeth Puttenham:

i. **ELIZABETH OXENBRIDGE**, married **ROBERT TYRWHIT**, Knt., of Kettleby, Lincolnshire [see TYRWHIT 20].

ELFORD

WILLIAM THE CONQUEROR, King of England, married **MAUD OF FLANDERS**.
HENRY I, King of England, by an unknown mistress, _____.
ROBERT FITZ ROY, Earl of Gloucester, married **MABEL FITZ ROBERT**.
MAUD OF GLOUCESTER, married **RANULPH DE GERNONS**, Earl of Chester.
HUGH, Earl of Chester, married **BERTRADE DE MONTFORT**.
AGNES OF CHESTER, married **WILLIAM DE FERRERS**, Knt., Earl of Derby.
WILLIAM DE FERRERS, Knt., Earl of Derby, married **MARGARET DE QUINCY**.
ROBERT DE FERRERS, Knt., Earl of Derby, married **ELEANOR DE BOHUN** (desc. King William the Conqueror).
JOHN DE FERRERS, Knt., 1st Lord Ferrers of Chartley, married **HAWISE DE MUSCEGROS**.
ELEANOR DE FERRERS, married **THOMAS DE LATHOM**, Knt., of Lathom, Lancashire.
THOMAS DE LATHOM, Knt., of Lathom, Lancashire, married **JOAN VENABLES**.
ISABEL LATHOM, married **JOHN STANLEY**, K.G., of Lathom, Lancashire [see STANLEY 12].

13. THOMAS STANLEY, Esq., in right of his wife, of Elford, Staffordshire, and Aldford, Alderley, and Etchells, Cheshire, King's esquire, Sheriff of Warwickshire and Leicestershire, 1427–8,

Sheriff of Staffordshire, 1433–4, 1438–9, Knight of the Shire for Staffordshire, 3rd son. He married (1st) before 1 May 1413 **MAUD ARDERNE**, daughter and heiress of John Arderne, Knt., of Elford, Staffordshire, and Aldford, Alderley, and Etchells, Cheshire, by Margaret, daughter of Roger Pilkington, Knt. [see ARDERNE 14 for her ancestry]. She was born 2 July 1396. They had one son, John, K.B., and one daughter, Anne. In 1414 he and his wife obtained an indult for a portable altar. In 1416 he was in the service of Richard Beauchamp, Earl of Warwick in Calais. He took part in the reduction of Normandy in 1420. In 1425 he and his wife, Maud, sued Isabel de Berkeley for waste and destruction in Okley, Staffordshire, which the said Isabel held for her life of the inheritance of Maud. His wife, Maud, died in 1430–2. He married (2nd) before 1434 **ELIZABETH LANGTON**, evidently daughter of Ralph Langton, Knt., of Walton le Dale, Lancashire, Baron of Newton. They had one son, George, Esq. In 1442 the inhabitants of Lichfield, Staffordshire rose against him in riot. In 1446 Thomas Warton of Lichfield and his wife, Felicia, conveyed to Thomas Stanley, Esq., of Elford; John Stanley, Esq., of Clifton-Campville, and five others all lands and tenements which Thomas had in the fee of Pipe and Chorley which were of Thomas Stanley, Esq., lord of Elford. THOMAS STANLEY, Esq. died 13 May 1463, and was buried with his 2nd wife, Elizabeth, at Elford, Staffordshire.

Topographer 2 (1790): 1–8. Shaw *Hist. & Antiqs. of Staffordshire* 1 (1798): 353, 380, 383–385. Brydges *Collins' Peerage of England* 3 (1812): 50–103 (sub Stanley, Earl of Derby). Nightingale et al. *Beauties of England & Wales* 13(2) (1813): 1106–1114. Ormerod *Hist. of Chester* 3 (1819): 301–302 (Stanley ped.). Erdeswicke *Survey of Staffordshire* (1820): 334–337, 341–343. Baines *Hist. of Lancaster* 4 (1836): chart facing 10 (Stanley ped.). *Coll. Top. et Gen.* 7 (1841): 1–21. Banks *Baronies in Fee* 1 (1844): 413–414 (sub Stafford of Clifton). *Antiq. & Architectural Year Book for 1844* (1845): 240–241. *Annual Rpt. of the Deputy Keeper* 37 (1876): 676, 678–679. Earwaker *East Cheshire* 1 (1877): 322–328; 2 (1880): 602–605 (Stanley ped.). Lennard & Vincent *Vis. of Warwick 1619* (H.S.P. 12) (1877): 22–23 (Carles ped.: "Tho. Stanley 2 sone of John Stanley of Lathom. = Mabell Da. & hey. of Sr John Ardren Kt."). Glover et al. *Vis. of Cheshire 1580, 1566, 1533 & 1591* (H.S.P. 18) (1882): 16–17 (Ardern ped.: "Maud [Arderne] uxr Sr Tho. Stanley who overlived him."), 212–213 (Stanley ped.: "Thos Stanley of Elford in Staff. = Maud d. & heire to Sr John Arderne."). Glover *Vis. of Staffordshire 1583* (Colls. Hist. Staffs. 3(2)) (1883): 51–53 (Bowes ped.: "Maulde [Arderne], da. and heire, ætat. 12 an'or' ano 10 H. 4. = Thomas Stanley, Knight, obijt 4 H. 6, 1425."), 57–58 (Brooke ped.: "Matildis, filia et hæres Joh'is Arderne de Elford in Com. Stafford, militis = Thomas Stanley, s'd's filius Joh'is Stanley, militis, Locitenentis Reg. H. 4 in Hibernia."). Wrottesley *Staffordshire Suits: Plea Rolls* (Colls. Hist. Staffs. 17) (1896): 107; (Colls. Hist. Staffs. n.s. 3) (1900): 124–125, 134, 140, 146, 157, 160, 213, 221; (Colls. Hist. Staffs. n.s. 4) (1901): 95. *List of Sheriffs for England & Wales* (PRO Lists and Indexes 9) (1898): 127, 145. Madan *Gresleys of Drakelowe* (Colls. Hist. Staffs. n.s. 1) (1898): 281. *Genealogical Mag.* 2 (1899): 61–67. Rushen *Hist. & Antiqs. of Chipping Campden* (1899): 18–23. *C.P.R.* 1476–1485 (1901): 2. *C.P.R.* 1429–1436 (1907): 523. *C.P.R.* 1436–1441 (1907): 250. *Feudal Aids* 5 (1908): 23. Wedgwood *Revs. of Rec. Office Pubs.* (Colls. Hist. Staffs. 3rd Ser. 1910) (1910): 315–316 (Stanley ped.); (Colls. Hist. Staffs. 3rd Ser. 1911) (1911): 470. Wedgwood *Staffordshire Parl. Hist.* 1 (Colls. Hist. Staffs. 3rd Ser. 1917) (1919): 203–204 (Stanley arms: Argent, on a bend azure three bucks' heads or). *C.F.R.* 13 (1933): 113; 20 (1949): 94. *C.C.R.* 1435–1441 (1937): 423. *Coat of Arms* n.s. 5 (Winter 1983/4): 204–210. *TG* 5 (1984): 131–157. VCH *Stafford* 14 (1990): 206. Gillespie *Age of Richard II* (1997): 195. Canterbury Cathedral Archives: Dean & Chapter Archive, CCA-DCc-ChAnt/L/213;CCA-DCc-ChAnt/L/214; CCA-DCc-ChAnt/L/215;CCA-DCc-ChAnt/L/217; CCA-DCc-ChAnt/L/218; CCA-DCc-ChAnt/L/219 (available at www.a2a.org.uk/search/index.asp).

Children of Thomas Stanley, Esq., by Maud Arderne:

i. **JOHN STANLEY**, K.B. [see next].

ii. **ANNE STANLEY**, married **JOHN GRESLEY**, Knt., of Drakelow, Staffordshire [see GRESLEY 13].

Child of Thomas Stanley, Esq., by Elizabeth Langton:

i. **GEORGE STANLEY**, Esq., of Hammerwich (in St. Michael's, Lichfield), Staffordshire, married **ELEANOR SUTTON** [see WOLSELEY 14].

14. JOHN STANLEY, K.B., of Elford, Tamworth, and Wigginton, Staffordshire, and Aldford, Etchells, and Alderley, Cheshire, King's esquire, Knight of the Shire for Staffordshire, 1447, 1450–1, 1467–8, 1472–5, Sheriff of Staffordshire, 1450–1, 1459–60, 1464–5, 1468–9, 1474–5, Ranger of the Forest of Cannock, 1468, son and heir, born c.1413–23 (aged 40 and more in 1463, adult by 1446).

He was heir sometime in the period, 1428–46, to his cousin, Richard, son of Thomas Stafford, of Babbington, by which he inherited the manors of Clifton-Campville, Haunton, Pipe, and Stotfold, Staffordshire, Aston-sub-Edge and Chipping Campden, Gloucestershire, and Sibbertoft, Northamptonshire. He married (1st) by dispensation dated 1428 **CECILY ARDERNE**. They had one son, John, Esq. He married (2nd) before 1446 **ELIZABETH VERNON**, widow of John Vampage, Esq. (will proved 1446), of Pershore, Worcestershire, Attorney-General, deputy Sheriff of Worcestershire, 1428, 1433, and daughter of Richard Vernon, Knt., of Haddon, Derbyshire, Harlaston, Staffordshire, etc., Speaker of the House of Commons, by Bennet, daughter of John Ludlow, Knt. [see VERNON 15 for her ancestry]. They had two sons, Thomas and Humphrey, Knt., and four daughters, Maud (wife of John Ferrers, Knt., and John Agard, Esq.), Alice (wife of John Melton, Knt.), Katherine, and Isabel (wife of Hugh Peshale, Knt.). In 1450 "as John Stanley, Esq.," he granted his father, Thomas Stanley, of Elford, and two others all the lands and tenements which he had togther with the said Thomas Stanley, etc., of the gift of Thomas Wharton and his wife, Felicia, in the fee of Pipe, Childerhay, and Chorley. He fought on the Lancastrian side at the Battle of Blore Heath in 1459. In 1466 he and his wife obtained a papal indult for plenary remission. His wife, Elizabeth, was living 4 August 1471. He fought on the Yorkist side at the Battle of Tewkesbury in 1471, where he was made banneret. He married (3rd) **ANNE HORNE**, widow of William Harcourt, Knt. (living 25 July 1471), of Maxstoke, Warwickshire, and Braunstone, Leicestershire, Steward to George, Duke of Clarence, and daughter of Robert Horne, Alderman of London, by Joan, daughter of Edward Fabian. They had no issue. SIR JOHN STANLEY died testate 29 June 1476, and was buried at Elford, Staffordshire. His widow, Anne, married (2nd) before 31 Jan. 1477/8 (date of award) (as his 3rd wife) **WILLIAM NORREYS** (or **NORRYS**, **NORYS**, **NOREYS**), Knt. [see NORREYS 13], of Yattendon, Adresham (in South Moreton), Elington (in Cookham), Bullocks (in Cookham), Hall Court (in Thatcham), and Marlston (in Bucklebury), Berkshire, Braunstone, Leicestershire, and London, Knight of the Body to Kings Edward IV and Henry VII, Lieutenant of Windsor, 1488–1506, Sheriff of Oxfordshire and Berkshire, 1468–9, 1481–2, 1486–7, Knight of the Shire for Berkshire, 1459, and, in right of his 2nd wife, of Rainham and Wimbotsham, Norfolk, son and heir of John Norreys, Esq., of Ockwells (in Bray) and Yattendon, Berkshire, Master of the Royal Wardrobe, Treasurer of the Queen's Chamber, by his 1st wife, Alice, daughter and heiress of Richard Merbrook, Esq. [see NORREYS 12 for his ancestry]. He was born about 1441 (aged 25 in 1466). They had two sons, Richard and Lionel, and four daughters, Katherine (wife of John Langford, Knt.), Anne (wife of William Wroughton and John Baldwin, Knt.), Elizabeth (wife of William Fermor, Esq.), and Jane (wife of John Cheney). In the period, 1468–9, James Staverton sued Sir William Norys, Sheriff of Berkshire in Chancery regarding the detention on suspicion of felony, complainant having bought from John Coldon beasts alleged to be stolen. In the period, 1476–80, or 1483–5, as "William Norrys, Knt., late the husband of Isabel, marchioness of Montagu," he sued Christopher Sharp in Chancery regarding the forging of his seal to a deed and suing thereon in Essex, where the jury would favor him. In 1479 he and his wife, Anne, sued John Stanley, Esq., for a third part of the manors of Clifton-Campville, Haunton, and Pipe, Staffordshire, which they claimed as the dower of Anne of the dotation of John Stanley, Knt., her former husband. He was attainted in 1484. He was granted the manor of Redenhall, Norfolk by the king in 1486. In 1499 he had a renewal of his father's grant to enclose Yattendon, Berkshire. His wife, Anne, died 12 July 1505. SIR WILLIAM NORREYS died shortly before 10 Jan. 1507.

Colls. towards a Parochial History of Berkshire (1783): 58 (rec. dated c.1525 identifies Sir William Norreys' wife, Anne, as Ann Horne, half-sister of William Fettiplace, of East Shefford, Berkshire). *Topographer* 2 (1790): 1–8. Shaw *Hist. & Antiqs. of Staffordshire* 1 (1798): 353–354, 380, 383–385; 2(1) (1801): Appendix of Adds. & Corrs., 10 (identifies 3rd wife as Anne Handesacre). Brydges *Collins' Peerage of England* 4 (1812): 428–453 (sub Harcourt Earl Harcourt). Nightingale et al. *Beauties of England & Wales* 13(2) (1813): 1106–1114. Ormerod *Hist. of Chester* 1 (1819): 416 (identifies 3rd wife as

Dorothy, daughter of Edmund Legh, of Baggiley); 3 (1819): 301 (Stanley ped.). Erdeswicke *Survey of Staffordshire* (1820): 334–337, 341–343. Burke *Gen'l & Heraldic Dict. of the Peerage & Baronetage* 1 (1832): 10–11 (sub Abingdon, Earl of). Banks *Baronies in Fee* 1 (1844): 413–414 (sub Stafford of Clifton). *Antiq. & Arch. Year Book for 1844* (1845): 240–241. *Annual Rpt. of the Deputy Keeper* 9 (1848): 92, 93, 101; 37 (1876): 678–679. *Gentleman's Mag.* n.s. 38 (1852): 66–69. Davenport *Lords Lieutenant & High Sheriffs of Oxfordshire* (1868): 29. *Wiltshire Arch. & Nat. Hist. Mag.* 11 (1869): 56. Flower *Vis. of Lancaster 1567* (Chetham Soc. 81) (1870): 85–86 (Norris ped.: "Sir Will. Norris. = Jane, dau. of John Vere, Erle of Oxford."). Palmer *Hist. & Antiqs. of the Collegiate Church of Tamworth* (1871): 89 (author states Maud Stanley, widow of Sir John Ferrers, of Tamworth "married again to John Agard, Esq., of Tutbury and was still alive with him in 1506 ..."). Campbell *Materials for a Hist. of Henry VII* 1 (1873): 482. Cox *Notes on the Churches of Derbyshire* 3 (1877): 263–264. Earwaker *East Cheshire* 1 (1877): 322–325, 328 ("[John Stanley] appears to have been married three times, but there are many discrepancies in the pedigrees usually accepted"). Lennard & Vincent *Vis. of Warwick 1619* (H.S.P. 12) (1877): 6–7 (Ferrers Ped.: "Sʳ John Ferrers of Tamworth Knight. = Maude da. of Sʳ John Stanley."), 22–23 (Carles ped.: "Sʳ John Stanley of Elford Kt. = Maude widowe of Sʳ John ... the King's Attorney."). Glover et al. *Vis. of Cheshire 1580, 1566, 1533 & 1591* (H.S.P. 18) (1882): 16–17 (Ardern ped.: "Sʳ John Stanley of Elford. = Mauld 1 wife."), 212–213 (Stanley ped.: "John Stanley of Elford = 1. Maud, mar. to his 2ᵈ wife Isabel d. to Sʳ Ric. Vernon, = 3. Dowce d. to... Ligh of Baguley."). Glover *Vis. of Staffordshire 1583* (Colls. Hist. Staffs. 3(2)) (1883): 51–53 (Bowes ped.: "Maulde. = Sʳ John Stanley, founder of the Chauntry at Elforde anno 1474 = Anne. = Elizabeth."), 57–58 (Brooke ped.: "Joh'es Stanley de Elford in Com. Staff., miles, ter nuptus = Matildis, uxor p'ma"). *Trans. Bristol & Gloucs. Arch. Soc.* 9 (1884): 167–168, 195. Cooke & Mundy *Vis. of Worcester 1569* (H.S.P. 27) (1888): 68–70 (Handford ped.: "Elizabeth da. of Thom. Walter. = John Vampage esq. = Isabell dau. to Sʳ Richard Vernon K. = Sʳ John Stanley of Pipe K., 2 husband."). *C.P.R. 1461–1467* (1897): 418. *List of Sheriffs for England & Wales* (PRO Lists and Indexes 9) (1898): 108, 127–128. Rushen *Hist. & Antiqs. of Chipping Campden* (1899): 18–23. *C.P.R. 1467–1477* (1900): 82. Wrottesley *Staffordshire Suits: Plea Rolls* (Colls. Hist. Staffs. n.s. 3) (1900): 175–176, 222; (Colls. Hist. Staffs. n.s. 4) (1901): 95, 99, 116, 136–137, 146, 156, 159, 169, 171; (Colls. Hist. Staffs. n.s. 6(1)) (1903): 113, 121, 150. *C.P.R. 1476–1485* (1901): 2, 371, 471. Colls. Hist. Staffs. n.s. 6(1) (1903): 121. Clay *Yorkshire Church Notes* (Yorkshire Arch. Soc. Rec. Ser. 34) (1904): 155–156. Benolte et al. *Four Vis. of Berkshire 1532, 1566, 1623 & 1665–6* 2 (H.S.P. 57) (1908): 184–186 (Norris ped.: "Sʳ Wm Norreys of Yattenden = 1 .... da. & coh. to John Nevill Marques Mountacute, = 2. Jane da: to Jnᵒ Vere E. of Oxford, [=] marr: to his 3: wife Anne da: to John Horne Alderman of London & Widow to Sʳ Jnᵒ Harcourt."). *C.P.R. 1446–1452* (1909): 127–128. Wedgwood *Revs. of Rec. Office Pubs.* (Colls. Hist. Staffs. 3rd Ser. 1910) (1910): 315–316 (Stanley ped.). Wedgwood *Staffordshire Parl. Hist.* 1 (Colls. Hist. Staffs. 3rd Ser. 1917) (1919): 228–229 (biog. of Sir John Stanley). VCH *Berkshire* 3 (1923): 124–133, 291–296, 311–329, 498–504; 4 (1924): 70–73, 125–130, 174–178. Cooke *Early Hist. of Mapledurham* (Oxfordshire Rec. Soc. 7) (1925): 77–81. *Papal Regs.: Letters* 12 (1933): 817. Wedgwood *Hist. of Parl.* 1 (1936): 640 (biog. of Sir William Norris), 799 (biog. of Sir John Stanley). *C.C.R. 1441–1447* (1937): 377. Lamborn *Lovel Tomb* (Oxfordshire Arch. Soc. Rpts. 83 (1937)) (1938): 16–17. Mander *Desc. Cat. Top. Sketches & Prints* (Colls. Hist. Staffs. 3rd Ser. 1942–3) (1946): 79. *Notes & Queries* 196 (1951): 463–468. *Cal. IPM Henry VII* 3 (1955): 97. VCH *Leicester* 4 (1958): 428–433. *Bull. John Rylands Lib.* 50 (1967–68): 451. Myers *Crown, Household & Parl.* (1985): 288. Kirby *Abs. of Feet of Fines Rel. Wiltshire* (Wiltshire Rec. Soc. 41) (1986): 141–142. Moreton *Townshends & their World* (1992): 123. Roskell *House of Commons 1386–1421* 4 (1992): 712–717 (biog. of Sir Richard Vernon). Shawcross *Arms of the Family: The Significance of John Milton's Relatives & Associates* (2004): 53 & 248 (In 1515 John Agard, of Foston and Sudbury, endowed a chantry for souls at the church of Scropton. Masses were to be said for the souls of the founder, his wife Joan, and several other individuals, including John Stanley, Lady Elizabeth his wife and their children, and Sir John Ferrers and his wife Matilda.). *Trans. Monumental Brass Soc.* 17 (2005): 251–255. Birmingham City Archives: Elford Hall Coll., MS 3878/45 — grant dated 4 Aug. 1471 from John de Stretey of Norhamton, son of William Stretey formerly of Elford and Margaret his wife to John Stanley, Knt., lord of Elford and Elizabeth, his wife, of lands with appurtenances in Elford and Haselhoor Haselour both in co. Stafford (available at www.a2a.org.uk/search/index.asp). Canterbury Cathedral Archives: Dean & Chapter Archive, CCA-DCc-ChAnt/L/218; CCA-DCc-ChAnt/L/219; CCA-DCc-ChAnt/L/223 (available at www.a2a.org.uk/search/index.asp). Leicestershire, Leicester & Rutland Rec. Office: Cat. of the Deeds & Papers of Winstanley of Braunstone, DE728/6; DE728/88 (available at www.a2a.org.uk/search/index.asp). Staffordshire & Stoke-on-Trent Archive Service, Staffordshire Rec. Office: Maple Hayes Estate, D150/1/322 (available at www.a2a.org.uk/search/index.asp). Worcestershire Rec. Office: Phillipps of Middle Hill, Broadway, 705:962/8965/5/xxiii (available at www.a2a.org.uk/search/index.asp). National Archives, C 1/46/199; C 1/66/73 (available at www.catalogue.nationalarchives.gov.uk/search.asp).

15. JOHN STANLEY, Esq., of Elford, Clifton-Campville, and Pipe, Staffordshire, Aldford, Etchells, and Alderley, Cheshire, Aston-sub-Edge and Chipping Campden, Gloucestershire, etc., son and heir by his father's 1ˢᵗ marriage, born about 1446 (aged 30 in 1476). He married before 1470 **ELIZABETH** _____. They had one son, John, and three daughters, Anne, Margery (wife of

William Staunton, Esq.), and Elizabeth (wife of William Ferrers). In 1475 he went to France in place of his father, a man-at-arms with six archers. In 1482 he sued Richard Wrottesley, Esq., and Robert Leigh, Esq., in a plea alleging that the said Richard and Robert had fabricated a false deed of feoffment relating to the plaintiff's manors of Etchells, Aldford, and Nether Alderley, Cheshire. About 1491 he agreed to convey the manors of Pipe and Clifton-Campville, Staffordshire to his younger half-brother, Humphrey Stanley, Knt. In 1500–1 he was sued by Thomas Leigh and Richard Wrottesley for the manors of Etchells and Aldford, Cheshire. JOHN STANLEY, Esq., died 22 Nov. 1508, and was buried at Northenden, Cheshire.

The Topographer 2 (1790): 1–8. Shaw *Hist. & Antiqs. of Staffordshire* 1 (1798): 353–354, 380, 383–385. Nightingale et al. *Beauties of England & Wales* 13(2) (1813): 1106–1114. Ormerod *Hist. of Chester* 3 (1819): 301 (Stanley ped.: wife not identified). Erdeswicke *Survey of Staffordshire* (1820): 334–336. Banks *Baronies in Fee* 1 (1844): 413–414 (sub Stafford of Clifton). Earwaker *East Cheshire* 1 (1877): 277–278 (discusses tomb of Sir John Stanley, died 1508, which displays various Stanley family quarterings, including Arderne impaling Stafford, Pype, and Camville, but not Vernon), 322–325, 328. Glover et al. *Vis. of Cheshire 1580, 1566, 1533 & 1591* (H.S.P. 18) (1882): 16–17 (Ardern ped.: "John Stanley of Eccles ob. sans issue male 1 H. 8."), 212–213 (Stanley ped.: "Sʳ John Stanley of Elford obijt 1509."). Glover *Vis. of Staffordshire 1583* (Colls. Hist. Staffs. 3(2)) (1883): 51–53 (Bowes ped.) (omits this generation), 57–58 (Brooke ped.: "Joh'es Stanley de Elford, Ar., filius et hæres Joh'is = [left blank]"). *Trans. Bristol & Gloucs. Arch. Soc.* 9 (1884): 167–168, 195. Raines *Rectors of Manchester* 1 (Chetham Soc. n.s. 5) (1885): 43–44. Rushen *Hist. & Antiqs. of Chipping Campden* (1899): 18–23. Wrottesley *Staffordshire Suits: Plea Rolls* (Colls. Hist. Staffs. n.s. 6(1)) (1903): 140. Wrottesley *Fam. of Wrottesley* (Colls. Hist. Staffs. n.s. 6(2)) (1903): 246–248. Wrottesley *Peds. from the Plea Rolls* (1905): 469. Wedgwood *Revs. of Rec. Office Pubs.* (Colls. Hist. Staffs. 3ʳᵈ Ser. 1910) (1910): 315–316 (Stanley ped.) (wife identified as Elizabeth Vernon). Wedgwood *Hist. of Parl.* 1 (1936): 799 (biog. of Sir John Stanley). National Archives, SP 46/183/fo.222: dated late 15ᵗʰ or early 16ᵗʰ centuries: Draft of legal instruments concerning conveyance of rights of alternate presentation to the church at Handsworth, Staffordshire, by John Stanley, cousin and heir general of Sir Richard Stafford, and Elizabeth his wife, to Thomas Earl of Ormond (available at www.catalogue.nationalarchives.gov.uk/search.asp).

Child of John Stanley, Esq., by Elizabeth _____:

i. **ANNE STANLEY**, married **CHRISTOPHER SAVAGE**, Knt., of Aston-sub-Edge, Gloucestershire [see SAVAGE 17].

❧ ELKINGTON ☙

WILLIAM MALET, of Curry-Mallet, Somerset, married _____.
MABEL MALET, married **HUGH DE VIVONNE**, Knt., of Chewton, Somerset.
HAWISE DE VIVONNE, married **WALTER DE WAHULL**, Knt., of Odell, Bedfordshire.
JOHN DE WAHULL, Knt., of Odell, Bedfordshire, married **AGNES DE PINKNEY**.
THOMAS DE WAHULL, Knt., of Odell, Bedfordshire, married **HAWISE DE PRAYERS**.
JOHN DE WAHULL, of Odell, Bedfordshire, married **ISABEL** _____.
THOMAS DE WODHULL, of Little Durnford, Wiltshire, married _____.
NICHOLAS DE WODHULL, of Odell, Bedfordshire, married **MARGARET FOXCOTE**.
THOMAS WODHULL, Knt., of Odell, Bedfordshire, married **ELIZABETH CHETWODE**.
THOMAS WODHULL, Esq., of Odell, Bedfordshire, married **ISABEL TRUSSELL**.
JOHN WODHULL, Esq., of Warkworth, Northamptonshire, married **JOAN ETWELL**.
FULK WODHULL, Esq., of Warkworth, Northamptonshire, married **ANNE NEWENHAM** [see CHETWODE 12].

13. **LAWRENCE WODHULL**, Esq., of Thenford, Northamptonshire and Mollington, Oxfordshire, younger son. He married (1ˢᵗ) **ELIZABETH HALL**, daughter and co-heiress of Edmund Hall, of Swerford, Oxfordshire, by his wife, Elizabeth. They had one son, Fulk, Gent., and one daughter, Alice. By an undetermined wife, he had three sons, Edmund, Nicholas, and John, and four daughters, Joan, Jane, Agnes, and Mary. He married (2ⁿᵈ) **MARGARET LUSHER**. They had two sons, Crescent and Francis. He was a legatee in the 1531 will of his brother, Nicholas

Wodhull, and in the 1542 will of his nephew, Anthony Wodhull. LAWRENCE WODHULL, Esq., left a will dated 20 March 1549/50, proved 10 Sept. 1551.

    Baker *Hist. & Antiqs. of Northampton* 1 (1822–30): 711–712. *Misc. Gen. et Heraldica* 2nd Ser. 1 (1886): 45–51, 69–80. *TAG* 22 (1945–46): 1–17. *TG* 7-8 (1986–87): 4–127.

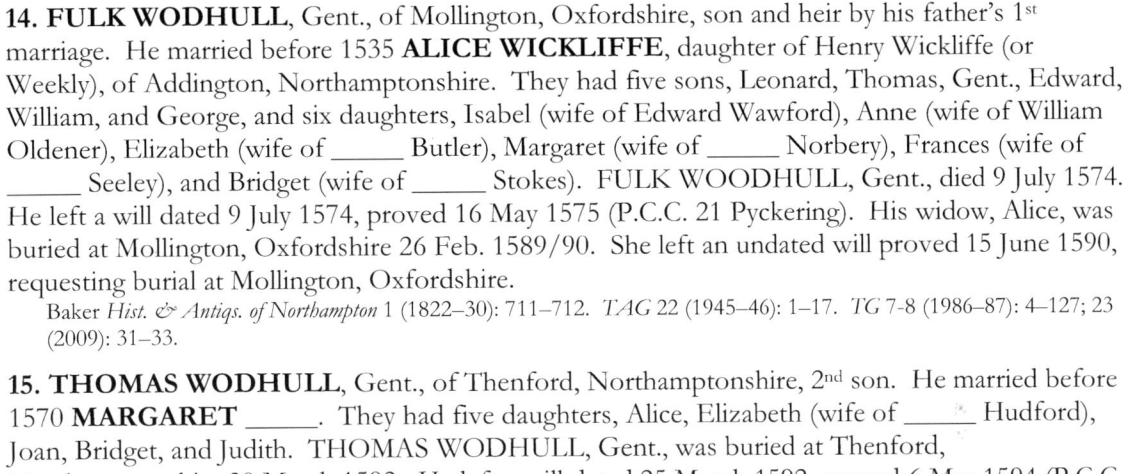

14. FULK WODHULL, Gent., of Mollington, Oxfordshire, son and heir by his father's 1st marriage. He married before 1535 **ALICE WICKLIFFE**, daughter of Henry Wickliffe (or Weekly), of Addington, Northamptonshire. They had five sons, Leonard, Thomas, Gent., Edward, William, and George, and six daughters, Isabel (wife of Edward Wawford), Anne (wife of William Oldener), Elizabeth (wife of _____ Butler), Margaret (wife of _____ Norbery), Frances (wife of _____ Seeley), and Bridget (wife of _____ Stokes). FULK WOODHULL, Gent., died 9 July 1574. He left a will dated 9 July 1574, proved 16 May 1575 (P.C.C. 21 Pyckering). His widow, Alice, was buried at Mollington, Oxfordshire 26 Feb. 1589/90. She left an undated will proved 15 June 1590, requesting burial at Mollington, Oxfordshire.

    Baker *Hist. & Antiqs. of Northampton* 1 (1822–30): 711–712. *TAG* 22 (1945–46): 1–17. *TG* 7-8 (1986–87): 4–127; 23 (2009): 31–33.

15. THOMAS WODHULL, Gent., of Thenford, Northamptonshire, 2nd son. He married before 1570 **MARGARET** _____. They had five daughters, Alice, Elizabeth (wife of _____ Hudford), Joan, Bridget, and Judith. THOMAS WODHULL, Gent., was buried at Thenford, Northamptonshire 30 March 1592. He left a will dated 25 March 1592, proved 6 May 1594 (P.C.C. 37 Dixy). His widow, Margaret, was buried at Mollington, Oxfordshire 9 October 1606.

    TAG 22 (1945–46): 1–17. *TG* 7-8 (1986–87): 4–127; 23 (2009): 31–33.

16. ALICE WODHULL, baptized at Mollington, Oxfordshire 8 May 1570. She married at Mollington, Oxfordshire 16 May 1588 (as his 2nd wife) **WILLIAM ELKINGTON** (or **ELKINTON**), of Mollington, Oxfordshire, blacksmith, son of Richard Elkington, of Cropredy, Oxfordshire, by his wife, Alice. He was baptized at Cropredy, Oxfordshire 25 July 1547. They had eight sons, Anthony, Richard, William, George, Edward, Francis, Zacharias, and Joseph, and two daughters, Elizabeth and Mary. He married (1st) at Mollington, Oxfordshire 18 Sept. 1575 **ALICE GREEN** (buried at Mollington, Oxfordshire 21 Sept. 1587), by whom he had three sons, Thomas, Edward, and William. WILLIAM ELKINGTON was buried at Mollington, Oxfordshire 15 July 1609. He left a will dated 14 July 1609, proved 25 Sept. 1609. His widow, Alice, was buried at Mollington, Oxfordshire 6 Nov. 1639.

    Adams *Elkinton Fam.* (1945): 2–3. *TAG* 22 (1945–46): 1–17. *TG* 7-8 (1986–87): 4–127; 23 (2009): 31–33.

17. JOSEPH ELKINGTON, of Mollington, Oxfordshire, younger son by his father's 2nd marriage, baptized at Mollington, Oxfordshire 12 June 1608. He married **ANN** _____. They had four sons, William, Joseph, George, and Richard, and three daughters, Elizabeth, Ann, and Mary. He and his children were legatees in the 1666 will of his brother, William Elkington. His wife, Ann, was buried at Mollington, Oxfordshire 23 March 1674/5. JOSEPH ELKINGTON was buried at Mollington, Oxfordshire 4 Feb. 1688/9.

    Adams *Elkinton Fam.* (1945). *TAG* 22 (1945–46): 1–17. *TG* 7-8 (1986–87): 4–127; 23 (2009): 31–33.

18. GEORGE ELKINGTON, blacksmith, baptized at Mollington, Oxfordshire 7 Dec. 1650. He immigrated to New Jersey in the Kent in 1677, where he settled at Northampton Township in Burlington County. He joined the Society of Friends (Quakers). He married at Burlington Monthly Meeting, New Jersey (intentions dated 6 June 1688) **MARY HUMPHRIES**, widow of Enoch Core, and daughter of Walter Humphries. She was born at Painswick, Gloucestershire 6 August 1660. They had six children. GEORGE ELKINTON died at Burlington County, New Jersey 19 October 1713. He left a will dated 15 October 1713, proved 19 Dec. 1713. His widow, Mary, died at Burlington County, New Jersey 24 March 1713/4.

Adams *Elkinton Fam.* (1945). *TAG* 22 (1945–46): 1–17. *TG* 7-8 (1986–87): 4–127; 23 (2009): 31–33.

✤ ELLIS ✤

WILLIAM DE MOWBRAY, Knt., of Thirsk, Yorkshire, married **AVICE** _____.
ROGER DE MOWBRAY, Knt., of Thirsk, Yorkshire, married **MAUD DE BEAUCHAMP** (desc. King William the Conqueror).
ROGER DE MOWBRAY, Knt., 1st Lord Mowbray, married **ROSE DE CLARE** (desc. King William the Conqueror).
JOHN DE MOWBRAY, Knt., 2nd Lord Mowbray, married **ALINE DE BREWES** (desc. King William the Conqueror).
JOHN DE MOWBRAY, Knt., 3rd Lord Mowbray, married **JOAN OF LANCASTER** (desc. King William the Conqueror).
JOHN DE MOWBRAY, Knt., 4th Lord Mowbray, married **ELIZABETH DE SEGRAVE** (desc. King William the Conqueror).
JOAN MOWBRAY, married **THOMAS GRAY**, Knt., of Heaton (in Norham), Northumberland.
JOHN GRAY, K.G., 1st Count of Tancarville, married **JOAN CHERLETON** (desc. King William the Conqueror).
HENRY GRAY, Knt., 2nd Count of Tancarville, married **ANTIGONE OF GLOUCESTER** (desc. King William the Conqueror).
ELIZABETH GRAY, married **ROGER KYNASTON**, Knt., of Middle, Shropshire [see LLOYD 10].

11. MARY KYNASTON, married **HYWEL AP JENKIN**. They had one son, Humphrey, and four daughters, Catrin (wife of Lewis Kyffin), Catrin (wife of John Wyn ap Gruffudd), Jane (wife of Llywelyn ap Morus), and Elsbeth (wife of William ap John). HYWEL AP JENKIN died of the plague in 1494.

Colls. Hist. & Arch. Rel. Montgomeryshire 15 (1882): 1–26 (Kynaston ped.). *Arch. Cambrensis* 5th Ser. 5 (1888): 343. Tresswell & Vincent *Vis. of Shropshire 1623, 1569 & 1584* 2 (H.S.P. 29) (1889): 291–299 (Kynaston ped.: "Maria [Kynaston] vxor Howelli ap Jenkin ap Jerworth ap Eignion.") (his arms: Ermine, a saltire gules). Harrison *Royal Anc. of George Leib Harrison* 2 (1914): 21–23. *Dict. Welsh Biog.* (1959): 1101. Bartrum *Welsh Gens. 1400–1500* 1 (1983): 131 [Bleddyn ap Cynfyn 38 (A3): "Mary [Kynaston] = Hywel ap Jenkin"); 9 (1983): 1428 [Osbwrn 2 (G2): "Hywel ap Jenkin d. 1494 = Mary f. Roger Kynaston"].

12. HUMPHREY AP HYWEL AP JENKIN, of Yns-y-maen-gwyn. He married **ANNE** (or **ANNES**) **HERBERT**, daughter of Richard Herbert, Knt., of Montgomery, by his 1st wife, Marged, daughter of Gwilym ap Rhys. They had one son, John, and two daughters, Elsabeth (wife of Morgan ap Thomas) and Jane. HUMPHREY AP HYWEL AP JENKIN died in 1545.

Glenn *Merion in the Welsh Tract* (1896): 215, 218, 307. *Dict. Welsh Biog.* (1959): 1101. Bartrum *Welsh Gens. 1400–1500* 5 (1983): 786 [Godwin 8 (B2): "Ann [Herbert] = Humphrey ap Hywel"), 9 (1983): 1428 [Osbwrn 2 (G2): "Humphrey [ap Hywel] d. 1545 = Ann f. Richard Herbert of Montgomery"].

13. JANE FERCH HUMPHREY AP HYWEL, married (as his 2nd wife) **GRUFFUDD AP HYWEL**, of Nannau, son of Hywel ap Dafydd ap Meurig Fychan, of Nannau, by his 1st wife, Elen, daughter of Robert Salesbury, of Llanrwst. They had two sons, Hugh and John, and three daughters, Margaret (wife of William ap Tudor), Elizabeth, and Anne. He married (1st) **ELEN FERCH TUDUR FYCHAN**. He was living 1541–2.

Glenn *Merion in the Welsh Tract* (1896): 215–234 (Hugh Nannau, the eldest son, signed the pedigree as head of the family, 24 July 1588). Bartrum *Welsh Gens. 1400–1500* 1 (1983): 148 [Bleddyn ap Cynfyn 51(A): "Gruffudd Nannau (1) = Elen f. Tudur Fychan, (2) = Jane f. Humphrey"); 9 (1983): 1428 [Osbwrn 2 (G2): "Jane [ferch Humphrey] = Gruffudd Nannau ap Hywel"].

14. JOHN NANNAU alias **JOHN AP GRUFFUDD**, of Dyffrydan (in Dôlgelly), Merionethshire. He married **ELSBETH FERCH DAFYDD LLWYD**, of Trawvynydd. They had one son, Lewis, and two daughters, Ellen and Jane. He held land in the township of Dyffrydan in Dôlgelly, Merionethshire.

Glenn *Merion in the Welsh Tract* (1896): 215–234.

15. LEWIS AP JOHN AP GRUFFUDD, Gent., of Dyffrydan (in Dôlgelly), Merionethshire. He married **ELLIN FERCH HYWEL AP GRUFFUDD**. They had two sons, Rees and Owen. LEWIS AP JOHN AP GRUFFUDD was living 28 August 1654.

Glenn *Merion in the Welsh Tract* (1896): 215–234.

Children of Lewis ap John ap Gruffudd, by Ellin ferch Hywel ap Gruffudd:

i. **REES AP LEWIS** [see next].

ii. **OWEN AP LEWIS**, married **MARY FERCH TUDOR VAUGHN**, of Caer y Nwch, Merionethshire.

Child of Owen ap Lewis, by Mary ferch Tudor Vaughn:

a. **ROBERT AB OWAIN**, of Dyffrydan township, Merionethshire, Wales. He married **MARGARET FERCH SION AP LEWIS**. Parents of **MARGARET ROBERTS**, 2nd wife of **ROWLAND ELLIS** [see ELLIS 18 below].

16. REES AP LEWIS AP JOHN GRUFFUDD, Gent. He married **CATHERINE FERCH ELISSA AP DAFYDD**, daughter of Elissa ap Dafydd ap Owen ap Thomas ap Howell ap Maredudd ap Gruffudd Derwas, by Mary ferch Sion ap David ap Gruffudd. In 1617 he built a stone house at Bryn Mawr near Dôlgelly, Dyffrydan township, Merionethshire. They had four sons, Lewis, Ellis, Griffith, and Rowland. REES AP LEWIS was living in 1649.

Glenn *Merion in the Welsh Tract* (1896): 215–234.

17. ELLIS AP REES (alias **ELLIS PRICE**), Gent., of Bryn Mawr, near Dôlgelly, Dyffrydan township, Merionethshire, 2nd son. He married by marriage settlement dated 1 Jan. 1649 **ANNE HUMPHREY**, daughter of Humphrey ap Hugh ap David ap Howell ap Gronw, Gent., Llwyn-du at Llwyn Gwrill (in Llangelynin), Merionethshire, by Elizabeth, daughter of John Powell (alias John ap Howell), of Llanwyddyn, Monmouthshire [see OWEN 21 for her ancestry]. They had one son, Rowland, Gent. ELLIS AP REES, Gent., was living 11 March 1678/9, and died before 1696.

Glenn *Merion in the Welsh Tract* (1896): 205–234. Browning *Welsh Settlement in Pennsylvania* (1912): 150–151, 296–297. *NEHGR* 108 (1954): 33 (Ellis arms: Or, a lion azure).

18. ROWLAND ELLIS, Gent., Quaker minister, born at Bryn Mawr, near Dôlgelly, Dyffrydan, Merionethshire, Wales in 1650. He married (1st) about 1672 **MARGARET ELLIS**, daughter and heiress of Ellis Morris, of Dolgun. They had two daughters, Ann (wife of [Rev.] Richard Johnson) and Jane. He married (2nd) about 1678 **MARGARET ROBERTS**, daughter of Robert ap Owen ap Lewis, of Dyffrydan township, Merionethshire, Wales [see ELLIS 15.ii.a above]. They had two sons, Rowland and Robert, and three daughters, Elizabeth, Eleanor/Ellin (wife of John Evans) and Catherine. He became a Friend (Quaker) in 1672, and was imprisoned in 1676. He visited Pennsylvania with his son, Rowland, in 1687, with a view of locating there; he returned to Wales about nine months later. He immigrated permanently to Pennsylvania with his wife and the remainder of his family in 1697, and settled at Bryn Mawr, in Merion, Pennsylvania. He represented Merion in the Assembly in 1700. His wife, Margaret, died about 1730. ROWLAND ELLIS, Gent., died at Plymouth, Philadelphia County, Pennsylvania Sept. 1731, and was buried there in the burying ground of the Gwynedd Monthly Meeting.

Piety Promoted 2 (1854): 317–322. *Friend* 29 (1856): 316–317 (biog. of Rowland Ellis), 331–332 (biog. of Margaret Ellis). Glenn *Merion in the Welsh Tract* (1896): 205–234 (includes MS ped. of ancestors prepared by Rowland Ellis shortly before 1697). Jenkins *Hist. Colls. Rel. to Gwynedd* (1897): 167–168 (Evans fam. gen.). Roberts *Plymouth Meeting* (1900). Glenn *Welsh Founders of Pennsylvania* (1911-13) (1970): 146–149. Browning *Welsh Settlement in Pennsylvania* (1912): 150–151, 233–240, 296–297.

❧ ELSING ❦

ALICE OF NORMANDY (sister of King William the Conqueror), married **LAMBERT**, Count of Lens.
JUDITH OF LENS, married **WALTHEOF**, Earl of Northumberland.
ALICE OF NORTHUMBERLAND, married **RALPH DE TONY**, of Flamstead, Hertfordshire.
ROGER DE TONY, of Flamstead, Hertfordshire, married **IDA OF HAINAULT**.
RALPH DE TONY, of Flamstead, Hertfordshire, married **MARGARET OF LEICESTER**.
IDA DE TONY, married **ROGER LE BIGOD**, Knt., Earl of Norfolk.
MARGARET (or **MARGERY**) **LE BIGOD**, married **WILLIAM DE HASTINGS**, Knt., of Lidgate, Suffolk.
HENRY DE HASTINGS, Knt., of Blunham, Bedfordshire, married **ADA OF HUNTINGDON**.
HENRY DE HASTINGS, Knt., of Cavendish, Suffolk, married **JOAN DE CANTELOWE**.
JOHN DE HASTINGS, Knt., 1st Lord Hastings, married **ISABEL LE DESPENSER** [see HASTINGS 10].

11. HUGH DE HASTINGS, Knt., of Sutton Scotney, Hampshire, Steward to Queen Philippe of Hainault (wife of King Edward III of England), 1344, Captain and Lieutenant of the king in Flanders, 1346, and, in right of his wife, of Gressenhall, Brisley, Elsing, and Weasenham, Norfolk, and Fenwick and Norton, Yorkshire, younger son by his father's 2nd marriage, born about 1310 (aged 24 in 1334). He was heir in 1333 to his full brother, Thomas de Hastings. He married before 18 May 1330 **MARGERY FOLIOT**, elder daughter of Richard Foliot, Knt., of Gressenhall, East Lexham, Elsing, Grimston, and Weasenham, Norfolk, Norton, Yorkshire, etc., by Joan, daughter and co-heiress of William de Brewes (or Breuse), Knt. [see MIDHURST 6 for her ancestry]. She was born about 1312–3 (aged 12 or 13 in 1325, aged 17 in 1330). They had two sons, John and Hugh, Knt., and three daughters, Isabel (wife of Saier de Rochford), Margery (wife of Nicholas Castell and John de Boyland), and Maud. In 1325 she was co-heiress to her brother, Richard Foliot, by which she inherited the manors of Fenwick and Norton, Yorkshire. In 1330 he and his wife, Margery, had livery of her purparty of the lands of her grandmother, Margery, widow of Jordan Foliot. In 1335 the king took his homage, and he had livery of a moiety of the manor of Sutton Scotney, Hampshire, which his mother had held in chief. He presented to the church of Brisley, Norfolk in 1339, and to the chapel of Norton, Yorkshire in 1343 and 1347. He fought at the Battle of Sluys 24 June 1340, in the retinue of the Earl of Derby. In Jan. 1341/2 he was pardoned for acquiring for life from Laurence de Hastings, Earl of Pembroke, the manor of Oswardebeck, Nottinghamshire. He was summoned to a council 25 Feb. 1341/2, by writ directed *Hugoni de Hastinges*. In 1343 he had license to grant away his manor of Sutton Scotney, Hampshire. In 1344 John de Camoys, Knt. and Margaret his wife (Margery's sister) settled the reversion of the manor and advowson of Cowesby, Yorkshire on Hugh and his wife, Margery. Hugh accompanied the Earl of Derby to Gascony in 1345, being in the retinue of the Earl of Pembroke. In 1346 he was commissioned to raise troops in Flanders for the war with France. Early in August 1346, he brought a large body of Flemings (60,000 it is said) to France to join the king. He fought at the Battle of Crécy 26 August 1346. In 1347 he took part in the expedition to Brittany in the retinue of John of Gaunt, Duke of Lancaster. SIR HUGH DE HASTINGS died 30 July 1347, and was buried at Elsing, Norfolk. He left a will dated 22 [sic] July 1347, proved 5 August 1347. In 1348 his widow, Margery, complained that John de Wentworth, William and Roger his sons, and others broke into the parks of the manors of Fenwick and Norton, Yorkshire and took away six oxen and four cows worth £10, felled her trees, fished in her stews, carried away deer, and assaulted her men and servants. She presented to the churches of Brisley, Norfolk, 1348, 1349, and Elsing, Norfolk, 1349. She died 8 August 1349, and was buried at Friars Minor, Doncaster.

Rymer *Fœdera* 5 (1708): 514–515 (Hugh de Hastings styled "kinsman" [consanguineo] by King Edward III in 1346). Bridges *Hist. & Antiqs. of Northamptonshire* 1 (1791): 394–399. Blomefield *Essay towards a Top. Hist. of Norfolk* 8 (1808): 201–203; 9 (1808): 468–471, 510–515. Brydges *Collins' Peerage of England* 6 (1812): 643–645 (sub Lord Hastings). *Testamenta Eboracensia* 1 (Surtees Soc. 4) (1836): 38–39 (will of Hugh de Hastings, Knt.). *Gentleman's Mag.* 2 (1865): 622–627. Carthew *Hundred of Launditch & Deanery of Brisley* 2 (1878): 645–646. Flower *Vis. of Yorkshire 1563-4* (H.S.P.

16) (1881): 154–156 (Hastings ped.: "Hugh Hastynges Knight 2 son. = Margery daughter & on of theyres of Sir Rychard Folyot."). Chandos Herald *Life & Feats of Arms of Edward the Black Prince* (1883): 354–355 (Hugh de Hastings styled "king's kinsman" by King Edward III of England). *Yorkshire Arch. & Topog. Jour.* 11 (1891): 444–446. *Genealogist* n.s. 19 (1903): 102; n.s. 20 (1904): 36. *Feudal Aids* 3 (1904): 522, 538, 540–541. *C.P.R. 1321–1324* (1904): 203. *C.P.R. 1348–1350* (1905): 66. Wrottesley *Peds. from the Plea Rolls* (1905): 416, 446. *Archæologia* 60 (1906): 25–42 (re. brass of Hugh de Hastings). *Cal. IPM* 7 (1909): 203–204, 447–448. *Feet of Fines for York[shire]* 1327–1347 (Yorkshire Arch. Soc. Recs. 42) (1910): 172. *C.P.* 6 (1926): 352–354 (sub Hastings) (pg. 353, footnote b: "French Roll, 20 Edw. III, *p.* 1, *m.* 1. The King addresses him in these writs 'dilecto et fideli consanguineo suo' : as Hugh was not a son of Isabel (de Valence), the form of address must be viewed as complementary.") [Note: Complete Peerage's comments withstanding, King Edward III of England was in fact related in the 5th and 6th degrees of kindred to Sir Hugh de Hastings by their common descent from the Dammartin family]. Watkin *Inventory of Church Goods temp. Edward III* (Norfolk Rec. Soc. 19(2)) (1948): 181, 182 (brass of Sir Hugh de Hastings). Paget *Baronage of England* (1957) 235: 4, 277: 1–5 (sub Hastings). Coss & Keen *Heraldry, Pageantry & Social Display in Medieval England* (2002): 169–194 ("Some of the grander brasses clearly benefited from a great deal of attention by the patron or his agent. The brass of Sir Hugh Hastings at Elsing (Norfolk), 1347, is a case in point. The task of choosing the comrades in arms to be represented as mourners for the deceased in the side shafts of the canopy could only have been undertaken by someone with intimate knowledge of Sir Hugh's career (very likely Henry, earl of Lancaster), while the devising of the elaborate iconography in the canopy itself would have required the services of a specialist in religious art ... The mourners in the dexter side were King Edward III, the Earl of Warwick, Hugh, Lord Despenser, and Sir John Grey of Ruthin, and, on the sinister. Henry, Earl of Lancaster, Laurence Hastings, Earl of Pembroke, Ralph, Lord Stafford, and Aymer, Lord St. Amand." [Note: John P. Ravilious has elsewhere noted that the "mourners" in the side shafts of the Hastings canopy, with the exception of the king, were evidently Sir Hugh de Hastings' near kinsmen, not comrades in arms]). *Trans. Monumental Brass Soc.* 18 (2011): 193–211 (London, College of Arms, MS Processus in Curia Marescalli, I, p. 527: "A[nn]o iii k[al]endas] Augusti: Obitus domini Hugonis de Hastynges ... qui obit anno D[omi]ni Millesimo CCC^{mo} xlvii^o"). Rye *Some Early English Inscriptions in Norfolk* (n.d.): 30–31 (drawing of window in Elsing, Norfolk now lost commemorating Hugh de Hastings and his wife, Margery, which shows arms of Hastings quartering Valence, and Hastings impaling Foliot). Norfolk Rec. Office: Hastings Fam. of Gressenhall, MR 316 242 x 5, indenture dated 30 Dec. 1336 between Sir Hugh de Hastynges and Sir Saere de Rocheford re. settlement on marriage of Sir Saere to Isabell daughter of Sir Hugh de Hastynges (available at www.a2a.org.uk/search/index.asp).

Children of Hugh de Hastings, Knt., by Margery Foliot:

i. **HUGH DE HASTINGS**, Knt. [see next].

ii. **MAUD DE HASTINGS**, married **ROBERT DE LA MARE**, Knt., of Steeple Lavington, Wiltshire [see BAYNTON 12].

12. HUGH DE HASTINGS, Knt., of Elsing, Brisley, and Grimston, Norfolk, younger son, born about 1335 (aged 25 in 1360). He married before 1355 **MARGARET** (or **MARGERY**) **DE EVERINGHAM**, daughter of Adam de Everingham, Knt., of Laxton, Nottinghamshire, by Joan, daughter of John D'Eiville, Knt. [see EVERINGHAM 9 for her ancestry]. They had two sons, Hugh, Knt., and John, Knt., and four daughters, Margaret, Joan, Alice, and Elizabeth. He presented to the church of Brisley, Norfolk in 1349, 1352, and 1361. He accompanied John of Gaunt, Duke of Lancaster, in his expedition to Normandy and Brittany in 1356. He was with the King in his invasion of France in 1359. He was heir before 1360 to his older brother, John de Hastings. His wife, Margaret, presented to the church of Elsing, Norfolk in 1361. He went to Gascony in the retinue of the Duke of Lancaster in 1366. He was taken prisoner by the Spaniards in a skirmish at Vitoria 20 March 1366/7, and was ransomed or exchanged the following autumn. He again served the Duke of Lancaster in 1369 in his raid into Picardy and Caus. SIR HUGH DE HASTINGS died at Kalkwell Hill near Calais, France Sept. 1369. His widow, Margaret, left a will dated 15 Nov. 1375. He and his wife were buried at Friars Preachers, Doncaster, Yorkshire.

Bridges *Hist. & Antiqs. of Northamptonshire* 1 (1791): 394–399. Blomefield *Essay towards a Top. Hist. of Norfolk* 8 (1808): 201–203; 9 (1808): 468–471, 510–515. Charles *Vis. of Huntingdon 1613* (Camden Soc. 43) (1849): 125 ("Margrett, daughter of Sr Hugh Hastings, of Elsing in Norff. k. by Margret, d. of Sr Adam Everingham, k. and lyeth buried at Letheringham, as appeareth by his monument"). *Norfolk Arch.* 6 (1864): 76–102. *Gentleman's Mag.* 2 (1865): 622–627. Glover & St. George *Vis. of Yorkshire 1584–5, 1612* (1875): 372–373 (Hastings ped.: "Sir Hugh Hastings. = Margaret, dau. of Adam de Everingham."). Carthew *Hundred of Launditch & Deanery of Brisley* 2 (1878): 645–646. Flower *Vis. of*

Yorkshire 1563–4 (H.S.P. 16) (1881): 154–156 (Hastings ped.: "Hugh Hastynges son & heyr. = Margaret daughter to Adam Everyngham Lord of Laxston."). *Yorkshire Arch. & Topog. Jour.* 11 (1891): 444–446. *Genealogist* n.s. 19 (1903): 102; n.s. 20 (1904): 36. Wrottesley *Peds. from the Plea Rolls* (1905): 416, 446. *Cal. IPM* 10 (1921): 502. *C.P.* 6 (1926): 355 (sub Hastings). Watkin *Inv. of Church Goods temp. Edward III* (Norfolk Rec. Soc. 19(2)) (1948): 181. Paget *Baronage of England* (1957) 277: 1–5 (sub Hastings). *Bull. Inst. Hist. Research* 38 (1965): 1–19. Roskell *House of Commons 1386–1421* 3 (1992): 13–17 (biog. of Sir William Elmham). *Trans. Monumental Brass Soc.* 18 (2011): 193–211 (London, College of Arms, MS Processus in Curia Marescalli, I, p. 360–361: "Et primerement vne sepulture dune chiualer appelle Mons[i]r[e] Hugh de Hastynges le seconde, ouec sa femme que fuest fille a Mons[i]r[e] Adam de Everyngham ... en la Chauncelle dudite Esglise al boute del grande Aucter vers le North"). Registered Will of Elizabeth Elmham (née Hastings) dated 1 Dec. 1419, proved 18 Feb. 1419/20, 56–57 Hyrning, Cons. Court of Norwich [FHL Microfilm 94857].

Children of Hugh de Hastings, Knt., by Margaret de Everingham:

i. **HUGH DE HASTINGS**, Knt. [see next].

ii. **MARGARET HASTINGS**, married (1st) **JOHN WINGFIELD**, Knt., of Letheringham, Suffolk [see WINGFIELD 13]; (2nd) **JOHN RUSSELL**, Knt., of Strensham, Worcestershire [see WINGFIELD 13].

iii. **JOAN HASTINGS**, married **THOMAS MORLEY**, K.G., 4th Lord Morley, Marshal of Ireland [see MORLEY 11].

iv. **ALICE HASTINGS**, married **JOHN ROCHFORD**, Knt., of Boston, Lincolnshire [see ROCHFORD 13].

v. **ELIZABETH HASTINGS**, married (1st) **THOMAS CATERTON** (or **CATESTON**). They had no issue. She married (2nd) before Feb. 1382 (as his 2nd wife) **WILLIAM ELMHAM**, Knt., of Westhorpe, Suffolk and Fring, Norfolk, Captain of Bayonne, 1374, Governor of Bayonne and Seneschal of Les Landes, 1375–7, Admiral of the Northern Fleet, 1380–2, Justice of the Peace for Norfolk, 1382–8, Knight of the Shire for Suffolk, 1393–4, 1397, King's bachelor, King's knight, son of Henry de Elmham, of Westhorpe, Suffolk, by Elizabeth, daughter and coheiress of William Hackford, Knt. He was born about 1336. They had no issue. In 1367 he served in Spain under the command of Edward *the Black Prince*. Following the Battle of Nájera 3 April 1367, he and Sir Hugh Calveley were sent by the prince to King Pedro IV of Aragón to open talks for an alliance between them. In 1371 he served at sea under the command of Guy de Bryan, K.G., Lord Bryan. In 1372 he was granted free warren on his lands at Westhorpe, Suffolk, and Fring, Norfolk, as well as the right to hold markets and fairs at both places. In 1375 he and Sir Thomas Felton were empowered to treat for a truce with the King of Navarre. Sometime before 1376 Edward *the Black Prince* granted him an annuity of £100 charged on the revenues of North Wales. In 1379 he was sent to Bury St. Edmunds to restore order following disturbances caused by opposition to the papal nomination to the abbacy. In May 1383 he enlisted as a captain in the army set to invade Flanders under the command of Bishop Henry le Despenser of Norwich, which campaign was an utter failure. The same year he was among the group of prominent knights who seized John le Latimer, the Carmelite friar, as he was being led into custody after accusing John of Gaunt of treason. In March 1384 the Sheriff of Norfolk and Suffolk was ordered to levy 3,400 francs from his lands, in repayment of sums he accepted from the French in the previous Flanders campaign. In 1385 he served at sea in the retinue of Thomas de Percy. In 1387 he was given instructions to visit João I of Portugal to request the dispatch of a squadron of Portuguese galleys to English waters in accordance with the treaty João had concluded with King Richard II. Later that year Elmham enlisted in the naval force commanded by Richard, Earl of Arundel. In Jan. 1388 he was arrested with other royalist partisans, when Arundel and his fellow Appellants assumed executive control of the government. In May 1388 he was released on bail after promising to appear for trial before the next Parliament. However, no further reprisals were evidently implemented against him. In 1390 Henry, Earl of Derby, sent him on a mission to Paris to secure from the French king a safe-conduct for the expedition he proposed to lead on crusade in Prussia. Later that year, he returned to Aquitaine to treat with the French for correction of violations of the truce, and also to negotiate with the Count of Armagnac. He remained in Gascony until 1392, when he received a special reward of £100 for having expedited business on behalf of the Crown. In 1393 he was sent to the Dukes of Lancaster and Gloucester, who were negotiating with the French at Calais. He was again sent to Calais in May 1394. He served in the royal retinue in Ireland from Sept. 1394 until the spring of 1395. In 1396 he and Sir Henry Percy were engaged in negotiations both in England and France for the moderation of ransom payments claimed by both sides. In 1398 he was appointed as an envoy to discuss with King Robert III of Scotland arrangements for a meeting of ambassadors from both sides. In October 1398 he was appointed one of the general attorneys of Thomas Mowbray, Duke of Norfolk, for the administration of the duke's estate while he was in exile. In 1399, after Bolingbroke's landing in England, he was taken captive at Berkeley Castle, where he and his men were stripped of their arms. On 28 October 1399 the new king, Henry IV, ordered that the horses and harness taken from him at Berkeley or elsewhere should be restored to him. In 1401 he was summoned to attend a great council. SIR WILLIAM ELMHAM died 16 April 1403, and was buried in Bury St. Edmunds Abbey. He left a will dated 2 April 1403. His widow, Elizabeth, presented to the church of Westhorpe, Suffolk in 1408. In 1409 she was sued by the Prince of Wales, the Duke of York, and the Countess of Hereford regarding the wardship of her grand-nephew, Robert Wingfield. Elizabeth left a will dated 1 Dec. 1419, proved 18 Feb. 1419/20 (56–57 Hyrning, Cons. Court of Norwich), containing bequests in money amounting to over £550 and many items in jewelry and fur. She named various relatives, including her niece, Lady Margaret Kerdeston [see GANT 8.i.a]. Thomas Beaufort, Duke of Exeter, was bequeathed her lavish furnishings at Westhorpe and the contents of the manor-house and stables there, as well as her property in Norwich, on condition he paid 100 marks or else provided a priest to pray for her soul for ten years. *Gentleman's Mag.* 2 (1865): 622–627. Flower *Vis. of Yorkshire 1563–4* (H.S.P. 16) (1881): 154–156 (Hastings ped.: "Elsabeth [Hastings] wyff to Sir Thomas Elmhud Knight."). *C.P.R. 1399–1401* (1903): 39. Copinger *Manors of Suffolk* 3 (1909): 326–327. *C.Ch.R.* 5 (1916): 227. Ellis *Cat. Seals in the P.R.O.* 2 (1981): 37 (seal of William de Elmham, Knt. dated 1401 — In a cusped circle, hung from a twin bush, a shield of arms: a fesse between three splayed eagles). Roskell *House of Commons 1386–1421* 3 (1992): 13–17 (biog. of Sir William Elmham: "… an experienced soldier and diplomat … Walsingham called him a renowed knight … Tout's opinion was that he was 'one of the worst of Bishop Despenser's mutinous follows.' Nevertheless, he deserves respect for his evident capabilities in the spheres of war and diplomacy, and for his loyalty to Richard II.").

13. HUGH DE HASTINGS, Knt., of Gressenhall, Elsing, Brisley, East Lexham, and Weasenham, Norfolk, Monewden, Suffolk, Fenwick and Norton, Yorkshire, etc., son and heir. He married before 1 Nov. 1376 **ANNE LE DESPENSER**, 3rd daughter of Edward le Despenser, K.G., 4th Lord le Despenser, by Elizabeth, daughter of Bartholomew de Burghersh, K.G., 4th Lord Burghersh [see DESPENSER 13 for her ancestry]. They had two sons, Hugh, Esq., and Edward, Knt. He took part in two expeditions to Brittany, the first in 1378 with William de Montagu, 2nd Earl of Salisbury, the other in 1379 with John de Arundel, Marshal of England. He presented to the chapel of Norton, Yorkshire in 1382. In 1386 he gave evidence in the Scrope and Grosvenor controversy. SIR HUGH HASTINGS died on an expedition to Spain 6 Nov. 1386. His widow, Anne, presented to the church of Elsing, Norfolk in 1388. She married (2nd) before 21 October 1390 (by papal dispensation, they being related in the 4th degree of affinity) (as his 2nd wife) **THOMAS MORLEY**, K.G., 4th Lord Morley, of Morley, Norfolk, Marshal of Ireland (died 24 Sept. 1416) [see MORLEY 11]. She was a legatee in the 1409 will of her mother, who bequeathed her her best chalice. Anne died 30 (or 31) October 1426. She left a will dated 24 October 1426, proved May 1427, requesting burial next to her 2nd husband in the Church of the Austin Friars at Norwich, Norfolk.

Blomefield *Essay towards a Top. Hist. of Norfolk* 8 (1808): 201–203; 9 (1808): 510–515. Blore *Hist. & Antiqs. of Rutland* 1(2) (1811): 19 (Despenser ped.). Brydges *Collins' Peerage of England* 6 (1812): 496–511 (sub Despenser). Dugdale *Monasticon Anglicanum* 2 (1819): 59–65 (Tewkesbury Cartulary: "Edwardus [le Despenser] vero secundus, filius istius Edwardi, successit Hugoni tertio, et copulavit sibi in matrimonium dominam Elizabetham, filiam domini Bartholomei de Borowashe, de qua genuit… dominam Annam quæ fuit desponsata Hugoni Hastings, et post Thomæ Morley."). Nicolas *Testamenta Vetusta* 1 (1826): 174–175 (will of Elizabeth de Burghersh, Lady Despenser). Nicolas *Controversy between Scrope & Grosvenor* 2 (1832): 168–169 (biog. of Sir Hugh Hastings). *Cat. MSS. Lib. of the Univ. of Cambridge* 1 (1856): 131. *Norfolk Arch.* 6 (1864): 76–102. *Gentleman's Mag.* 2 (1865): 622–627. Glover & St. George *Vis. of Yorkshire 1584–5, 1612* (1875): 372–373 (Hastings ped.: "Sir Hugh Hastings, 3rd son and heir. = Ann, dau. of Edward, 2nd Lord Spencer."). Carthew *Hundred of Launditch & Deanery of Brisley* 2 (1878): 645–646. Flower *Vis. of Yorkshire 1563–4* (H.S.P. 16) (1881): 154–156 (Hastynges ped.: "Hugh Hastynges son & heyr to Hugh. = Agnes doughter to Edward Lord Spencer & afterwards wyff to the Lord Morley."). Burke *Dormant, Abeyant, Forfeited & Extinct Peerages* (1883): 165–167 (sub Despenser). *Yorkshire Arch. & Topog. Jour.* 11 (1891): 444–446. *Papal Regs.: Letters* 4 (1902): 375. *Genealogist* n.s. 19 (1903): 102; n.s. 20 (1904): 36. Wrottesley *Peds. from the Plea Rolls* (1905): 416, 446. *C.P.* 6 (1926): 355–357 (sub Hastings). Watkin *Inv. of Church Goods temp. Edward III* (Norfolk Rec. Soc. 19(2)) (1948): 181. Train *Abs. of IPMs Rel. Nottinghamshire* 2 (Thoroton Soc. Recs. 12) (1952): 184–185. Paget *Baronage of England* (1957) 182: 1–2 (sub Despenser); 277: 1–5 (sub Hastings). Smith *Itinerary of John Leland* 4 (1964): 150–163. *Bull. Inst. Hist. Research* 38 (1965): 1–19. Rosenthal *Nobles & the Noble Life* (1976): 173–174. *English Hist. Rev.* 95 (1980): 115, footnote 9 (Sir Hugh de Hastings styled "cousin" by John of Gaunt, Duke of Lancaster). Hector *Westminster Chron. 1381–1394* (1982): 190–191. *TAG* 69 (1994): 129–139.

14. EDWARD HASTINGS, Knt., *de jure* Lord Hastings, of Gressenhall, Elsing, and Weasenham, Norfolk, Wellow, Nottinghamshire, Fenwick and Norton, Yorkshire, etc., King's knight, 2nd son, born at Fenwick, Yorkshire 21 May 1382 (aged 44 in 1427). He was heir in 1396 to his older brother, Hugh Hastings, Esq. In 1399 he was granted £40 a year by the king during his minority that he might maintain his estate. He married (1st) by marriage agreement dated 20 Feb. 1405/6 **MURIEL DINHAM** (or **DYNHAM**), daughter of John de Dinham, Knt., of Hartland, Devon, by his 1st wife, Eleanor (or Ellen), daughter of John de Montagu, Knt., Lord Montagu [see DINHAM 7 for her ancestry]. They had one son, John, Esq., and one daughter, Margaret (wife of Gilbert Debenham, Knt.). Edward was committed to the Tower 11 July 1403. In 1404 he released to the king all his right to Sutton Scotney, Hampshire. In 1405 he was going overseas on the king's service with Thomas of Lancaster, Admiral of England. The right to bear the undifferenced arms of Hastings was decided against him in the Court of Chivalry 9 May 1410, and in favor of his opponent, Reynold Grey, Lord Grey of Ruthin, heir to the sister of the whole blood, in preference to his own claim as heir to the brother of the half-blood, of John, Lord Hastings, ancestor of the Earls of Pembroke. On refusing to pay the costs of his suit of appeal (lest he should thereby acknowledge its justice), he was imprisoned about 1417 in the Marshalsea, where he was incarcerated (according to Dugdale) for the next sixteen years. He married (2nd) before 1 July 1427 (date of letter of attorney) **MARGERY CLIFTON**, daughter of Robert Clifton, Knt., of Buckenham, Norfolk, by his wife, Alice. He presented to the church of Brisley, Norfolk in 1435. On 20 October 1436 he entered into a recognizance in the amount of £1000 to Reynold Grey, Lord Grey of Ruthin, evidently for the purposes of satisfying his debt to Lord Grey, after which he was presumably released from prison. SIR EDWARD HASTINGS, self styled Lord Hastings and Stuteville, died 6 Jan. 1437/8. He left a will dated 4 July 1437. His widow, Margery, married (2nd) before 12 July 1440 (date of presentment) (as his 1st wife) **JOHN WYMONDHAM** (or **WYNDHAM**), Esq. They had one son, John, Knt. He presented to Brisley, Norfolk in 1441, in right of his wife. He and his wife, Margery, presented to the church of Gressenhall, Norfolk in 1441, 1443, and 1446. In 1442 he and his wife, Margery, leased the agistment of park and closes, pasture of Hulverswode, mansion called Norfolkes, with lands and meadows, a close of 10 acres, Ceryeswong and Marlyswong and right of warren, all in Elsing, Norfolk to Thomas King, Robert King, and John Bocher for a term of ten years. In 1451 he obtained the reversion of all of the Norfolk lands of the late Simon Felbrigg, Knt., including the manors of Felbrigg, Aylmerton, Banningham, Colby, Crackfordhall, Runton, and Tuttington, Norfolk. In 1454 Katherine, widow of Simon Felbrigg, Knt. leased these properties to John Wymondham for a term of 20 years. His wife, Margery, Lady Hastings, died in 1456, and was buried in the Church of the Austin Friars, Norwich, Norfolk. JOHN WYMONDHAM, Esq., died 4 June 1475.

Blomefield *Essay towards a Top. Hist. of Norfolk* 6 (1807): 350; 9 (1808): 510–515, 519. Young *Account of the Controversy between Reginald, Lord Grey of Ruthyn & Sir Edward Hastings* (1841). *Norfolk Arch.* 6 (1864): 76–102. *Gentleman's Mag.* 2 (1865): 622–627. Glover & St. George *Vis. of Yorkshire 1584–5, 1612* (1875): 372–373 (Hastings ped.: "Sir Edward Hastings, *of Rouseby, knt.* (temp. Ed. IV.). *Edwardus Hastings, qui contendebat cum Reginaldo, Dno. Grey de Ruthen, in curia constabularii pro stilo, titulo, honore, et armis de Hastings.* = Muriel, dau. to John Dynham."). Carthew *Hundred of Launditch & Deanery of Brisley* 2 (1878): 645–646. Flower *Vis. of Yorkshire 1563–4* (H.S.P. 16) (1881): 154–156 (Hastyngs ped.: "Edward Hastynges. = Meryell daughter of John Denham."). Rye *Cal. Feet of Fines for Suffolk* (1900): 294. *Papal Regs.: Letters* 6 (1902): 344, 348. *Genealogist* n.s. 19 (1903): 102; n.s. 20 (1904): 36. Usk *Chronicon Adæ de Usk 1377–1421* (1904): 91–92. Wrottesley *Peds. from the Plea Rolls* (1905): 416, 446. *D.N.B.* 9 (1908): 112–113 (biog. of Edward Hastings). *Yorkshire Inqs.* 5 (Yorkshire Arch. Soc. Recs. 59) (1918): 30–31. *C.P.* 6 (1926): 358–360 (sub Hastings). *Arch. Aeliana* 4th Ser. 19 (1941): 82 (seal of Edward Hastings dated 1406— Round, armorial, quarterly I and IV (gold) a maunch (gules) [HASTINGS], II and III (gules) a bend (silver) [FOLIOT]. Shield, in a quatrefoiled panel, surmounted by a mantled helm with crest of a bull's head, supported by two cocks. Legend: SIGILLUM · EDWARDI · DOMINI · HASTYNGES ET · DE · STOTEVYL.). Renshaw *IPMs Rel. Nottinghamshire 1437–1485* (Thoroton Soc. Recs. 17) (1956): 5–6 (abs. of IPM of Edward Hastings, Knt.). Paget *Baronage of England* (1957) 187: 1–9 (sub Dinan); 277: 1–5 (sub Hastings). *Bull. Inst. Hist. Research* 38 (1965): 1–19. McFarlane *Nobility of Later Medieval*

England (1973): 74–76. Rees *Cal. Ancient Petitions Rel. Wales* (Board of Celtic Studies, Hist. & Law 28) (1975): 332. *TAG* 69 (1994): 129–139. National Archives, AR/37/34 — marriage settlement of Edward Hastings and Muriel Dinham (citation courtesy of John P. Ravilious). Norfolk Rec. Office: Hastings Fam. of Gressenhall, MR 298 242 x 4 — letter of atty. dated 1 July 1427 Edward lord Hastyngges and Stotevile, Knt. and Margery his wife appoint Robert Goldeman and Thomas Feltewell to receive from John Spaldyng rector of the church of Gressenhale, Robert Edymon rector of the church of Brysle and others seisin of manors of Monnweden and Sulyard in Cretyngham, Suffolk and advowson of Monwedon, Suffolk (available at www.a2a.org.uk/search/index.asp). Norfolk Rec. Office: Ketton-Cremer fam. of Felbrigg Hall, Norfolk, WKC 1/336, 392 x 7; WKC 1/337, 392 x 7; WKC 1/338, 392 x 7; WKC 1/339, 392 x 7; WKC/80, 400 x 2 — lease dated 1442 by John Wymondham and Margery, Lady Hastings, his wife (available at www.a2a.org.uk/search/index.asp).

15. JOHN HASTINGS, Esq., of Gressenhall, Elsing, and Weasenham, Norfolk, Fenwick and Norton, Yorkshire, etc., *de jure* Lord Hastings, Captain of Saint-Lô in the Côtentin, Constable of Norwich Castle and gaol, Sheriff of Norwich, 1474–5, son and heir by his father's 1st marriage, born about 1412 (aged 26 in 1438). He married by papal dispensation dated 21 April 1434 (they being related in the 3rd and 4th degrees of kindred) **ANNE MORLEY**, daughter of Thomas Morley, Knt., 5th Lord Morley, *de jure* Lord Marshal, by Isabel, daughter of Michael de la Pole, Knt., 2nd Earl of Suffolk [see MORLEY 13 for her ancestry]. They had three sons, Hugh, Knt., Edmund, Knt., and Robert, and two daughters, Isabel (wife of Thomas Bosvile, Knt.) and Elizabeth. He and his wife, Anne, were mentioned in the 1463 will of her mother. His wife, Anne, died in 1471. JOHN HASTINGS, Esq., died at Elsing, Norfolk 9 April 1477. He left a will dated 8 April 1477. He and his wife were buried in the church of Gressenhall, Norfolk.

Blomefield *Essay towards a Top. Hist. of Norfolk* 9 (1808): 510–515. Chambers *Gen'l Hist. of Norfolk* 1 (1829): 337–338 (will of Isabel lady Morley). *Norfolk Arch.* 6 (1864): 76–102. *Gentleman's Mag.* 2 (1865): 622–627. Glover & St. George *Vis. of Yorkshire 1584–5, 1612* (1875): 372–373 (Hastings ped.: "John Hastings, of Fenwick juxta Ardsley. = Anne, dau. of William, Lord Morley"). Flower *Vis. of Yorkshire 1563–4* (H.S.P. 16) (1881): 154–156 (Hastynges ped.: "John Hastynges of Fenwyke nigh Ardesley. = Anne doughter to William Lord Morley."). *Genealogist* n.s. 19 (1903): 102; n.s. 20 (1904): 36. Wrottesley *Peds. from the Plea Rolls* (1905): 416, 446. *Papal Regs.: Letters* 8 (1909): 502. C.P. 6 (1926): 360–361 (sub Hastings). Macdonald *Fortunes of a Fam.* (1928): 228–229 (re. Bosvile fam.). Harvey et al. *Vis. of the North* 4 (Surtees Soc. 146) (1932): 45 (Hastings ped.: "John Hastings Esquier ('of Fennwyck') = Anne d. to..... (William) Lord Morley"). Paget *Baronage of England* (1957) 277: 1–5 (sub Hastings). *TAG* 69 (1994): 129–139. Davis *Paston Letters & Papers of the 15th Cent.* 2 (2004): 434 (John Hastings styled "my nowncle Hastynges" in letter from Lady Elizabeth (Debenham) Brews to her cousin, John Paston III dated 1476–7). Norfolk Rec. Office: Hastings Fam. of Gressenhall, MR 90 241 x 3 (deed of release dated 1434–5 by John son of Edward Lord of Hastyngg' and de Stotvyle, Knt. to Sir Robert Clifton, Knt. and Robert Edymon, clerk); MR 268 242 x 3 (granted dated 1476 by John Hastyngges of Elsyng, Esq., son and heir of Lord Edward Hastyngges, Knt. & Mirielle his wife daughter of Sir John Denham, Knt. to John Heydon, Henry Suthyll, and others), MR 320 242 x 5 (will of John Hastynges of Elsyng, Esq. dated 8 April 1477) (available at www.a2a.org.uk/search/index.asp).

Children of John Hastings, Esq., by Anne Morley:

    i. **HUGH HASTINGS**, Knt. [see next].

    ii. **ELIZABETH HASTINGS**, married **ROBERT HILDYARD**, Knt., of Winestead, Yorkshire [see SKEPPER 16].

16. HUGH HASTINGS, Knt., of Fenwick, Yorkshire, Elsing, Brisley, and Gressenhall, Norfolk, etc., *de jure* Lord Hastings, Knight of the Shire for Yorkshire, Sheriff of Yorkshire, 1479–80, Steward of Tickhill, son and heir, born about 1447 (aged 30 and more in 1477). He married before 12 April 1455 **ANNE GASCOIGNE**, daughter of William Gascoigne, Knt., of Gawthorpe, Yorkshire, by Margaret, daughter of Thomas Clarell, Esq. [see CLARELL 11.iii for her ancestry]. They had five sons, John, Knt., George, Knt., Brian, Knt., Charles, and Robert, and six daughters, Muriel, Isabel (wife of John Hotham, Knt.), Katherine (wife of John Melton, Knt.), Elizabeth (wife of Ralph Salvain, Knt.), Margaret (wife of John Grisacre), and Anne (wife of _____ Wastlyn). He was made a banneret by the Duke of Gloucester in Scotland in 1482. In 1484 the king granted him the manors of Wells, Warham, Sheringham, and Wiveton, Norfolk, in reward for his services against the rebels in Buckingham's insurrection. He presented to the churches of Gressenhall, Norfolk, 1485, and Brisley, Norfolk, 1486. SIR HUGH HASTINGS died 7 June 1488, and was survived by his wife, Anne. He left a will dated 20 June 1482.

> Blomefield *Essay towards a Top. Hist. of Norfolk* 9 (1808): 510–515, 519. *Norfolk Arch.* 6 (1864): 76–102. *Gentleman's Mag.* 2 (1865): 622–627. Glover & St. George *Vis. of Yorkshire 1584–5, 1612* (1875): 372–373 (Hastings ped.: "Sir Hugh Hastings. = Anne, daughter of Sir William Gascoigne, of Gawthorpe."). Carthew *Hundred of Launditch & Deanery of Brisley* 2 (1878): 645–646. Flower *Vis. of Yorkshire 1563–4* (H.S.P. 16) (1881): 154–156 (Hastynges ped.: "Hugh Hastynges son & heyr. = Ales doughter to Sir William Gaskon of Gawthorpe."). *List of Sheriffs for England & Wales* (PRO Lists and Indexes 9) (1898): 162. *Genealogist* n.s. 20 (1904): 36. Wrottesley *Peds. from the Plea Rolls* (1905): 416, 446. *C.P.* 6 (1926): 361 (sub Hastings). Harvey et al. *Vis. of the North* 4 (Surtees Soc. 146) (1932): 45 (Hastings ped.: "Sir Hugh Hastings = Anne d. to Sir Wm. Gascoyn of Galthorp"). Wedgwood *Hist. of Parl.* 1 (1936): 432–433 (biog. of Sir Hugh Hastings). Paget *Baronage of England* (1957) 277: 1–5 (sub Hastings).

Child of Hugh Hastings, Knt., by Anne Gascoigne:

i. **MURIEL HASTINGS**, married **RALPH EURE**, Knt., of Ayton (in Pickering Lythe), Yorkshire [see EURE 12].

ELTONHEAD

ALICE OF NORMANDY (sister of King William the Conqueror), married **LAMBERT**, Count of Lens.
JUDITH OF LENS, married **WALTHEOF**, Earl of Northumberland.
MAUD OF NORTHUMBERLAND, married **SIMON DE SENLIS**, Earl of Huntingdon and Northampton.
MAUD DE SENLIS, married **SAHER DE QUINCY**, of Long Buckby, Northamptonshire.
ROBERT DE QUINCY, of Tranent, Fawside, and Longniddry, East Lothian, Scotland, married **ORABEL FITZ NESS**.
SAHER DE QUINCY, Knt., Earl of Winchester, married **MARGARET OF LEICESTER**.
ROGER DE QUINCY, Knt., 2nd Earl of Winchester, married **ELLEN OF GALLOWAY**.
ELLEN DE QUINCY, married **ALAN LA ZOUCHE**, Knt., of Ashby de la Zouch, Leicestershire.
ROGER LA ZOUCHE, Knt., of Ashby de la Zouch, Leicestershire, married **ELA LONGESPÉE** (desc. King William the Conqueror).
ALAN LA ZOUCHE, Knt., Lord Zouche, married **ELEANOR DE SEGRAVE**.
MAUD LA ZOUCHE, married **ROBERT DE HOLAND**, Knt., 1st Lord Holand.
MAUD DE HOLAND, married **THOMAS DE SWINNERTON**, Knt., 3rd Lord Swinnerton.
ROBERT DE SWINNERTON, Knt., 4th Lord Swinnerton, married **ELIZABETH DE BEEK** (desc. King William the Conqueror).
MAUD SWINNERTON, married **JOHN SAVAGE**, Knt., of Clifton, Cheshire [see SAVAGE 14].

15. MARY SAVAGE, married (as his 1st wife) **WILLIAM STANLEY**, Esq., of Hooton (in Wirral) and Storeton, Cheshire, and Stanley, Staffordshire, son and heir of William Stanley, Knt., of Hooton (in Wirral) and Storeton, Cheshire, and Stanley, Staffordshire, by his 2nd wife, Blanche, daughter of John Arderne, Knt. He was born about 1405 (aged 23 in 1428). They had four sons, William, Esq., John, Richard, and Thomas. In 1424 his widowed mother, Blanche, released her rights to the manor of Stanley, Staffordshire and lands in Chorlton and Le Moels (both in Wirral), Cheshire to him. He was heir in 1428 to his grandfather, William Stanley, Knt. In 1432 he granted lands in Pulton Launcelyn, Bromburgh and le Spitall to Edward de Hoghton and others. In 1434 Richard Coly of Chester granted him lands in Pennesby and Thingwall. In 1437 king ordered the constable of Windsor Castle to take William Stanley, his brother-in-law, John Savage, Knt., Randolph Brereton, and Urian Brereton into custody for an unspecified offence. In 1439 Richard Bolde was appointed the marriage of Richard Donne, the king's ward, by mainprise of William Stanley, of Hooton, Cheshire, Esq., and another. He was granted a pardon by the king in 1446. WILLIAM STANLEY, Esq., was living 6 Feb. 1456.

> Ormerod *Hist. of Chester* 2 (1819): 228–232. Seacome *Hist. of the House of Stanley* (1821). Baines *Hist. of Lancaster* 4 (1836): chart facing 10 (Stanley ped.). Earwaker *East Cheshire* 1 (1877): 474 (assigns Blanche, wife of William Stanley, Knt., as daughter of Peter de Arderne of Alvanley). *Annual Rpt. of the Deputy Keeper* 37 (1876): 672, 674. Glover et al.

Vis. of Cheshire 1580, 1566, 1533 & 1591 (H.S.P. 18) (1882): 202–204 (Savage ped.: "Margrett [Savage] vxr Sr William Stanley of Hooton"), 214–215 (Stanley ped.: "Wm Stanley of Hooton Esqr vixit 10 H. 6. = Mary d. to Sr Jno Savage."). *C.P.R. 1436–1441* (1907): 239. *Trans. Hist. Soc. Lanc. & Cheshire* 105 (1954): 45–68. Bartrum *Welsh Gens. 1400–1500* 10 (1983): 1618 (Stanley 1: "Sir William Stanley of Hooton, Cheshire, l. 1431 = Mary d. Sir John Savage") (Stanley arms: Argent, on a bend Azure three bucks' heads cabossed Or). *Welsh Hist. Rev.* 14 (1988–89): 1–22. Clayton *Administration of Chester 1442–85* (Chetham Soc. 3rd Ser. 35) (1991). VCH *Stafford* 7 (1996): 230–231 (confuses William Stanley, living 1456, with his son, William the younger, died 1466). Stanley *House of Stanley* (1998): 65. Stanley fam. muniments found in Ryland Charters (available at www.a2a.org.uk/search/index.asp).

16. WILLIAM STANLEY, Esq., of Hooton (in Wirral) and Storeton, Cheshire, Stanley, Staffordshire, etc., Sheriff of Cheshire, 1463, son and heir. He married **ALICE HOGHTON** (or **HOUGHTON**), daughter of Richard Hoghton, Knt., of Hoghton (in Leyland), Lancashire, by his wife, Margaret. They had one son, William, Knt., and one daughter, Isabel (wife of John Marchumley). In 1450 he fought for the king against the traitor, Jack Cade, of Kent. In 1454 John Hertcombe granted authority to John Savage the younger, William Stanley, esqs., and Thomas Kendale to cause a deed to be made in his name regarding the castle, lordship and manor of Mold, Flintshire. In 1460 he was pardoned £166 in arrears as late receiver of Richard, Duke of York, of the lordship of Denbigh in Wales. In 1462 he and others were appointed to take muster of Roland Fitz Eustace, Knt., and 300 archers at some convenient place near Chester. WILLIAM STANLEY, Esq., died 17 Feb. 1465/6. His wife, Alice, was living 11 March 1465/6.

> Ormerod *Hist. of Chester* 2 (1819): 228–232. Seacome *Hist. of the House of Stanley* (1821). Baines *Hist. of Lancaster* 4 (1836): chart facing 10 (Stanley ped.). *Annual Rpt. of the Deputy Keeper* 37 (1876): 678, 680. Glover et al. *Vis. of Cheshire 1580, 1566, 1533 & 1591* (H.S.P. 18) (1882): 214–215 (Stanley ped.: "Wm Stanley of Hooton Esqr vixit 14 H. 6. = Alice d. to Sr Rich. Hoghton sister and heire to Henry.") (Hoghton arms: Sable, three bars Argent). *C.P.R. 1461–1467* (1897): 201, 333. *List of Sheriffs for England & Wales* (PRO Lists and Indexes 9) (1898): 17. *C.P.R. 1429–1436* (1907): 379. VCH *Lancaster* 6 (1911): 39 (Henry Hoghton, brother of Alice, was aged 40 & more in 1468). *C.C.R. 1447–1454* (1947): 494–495. Bartrum *Welsh Gens. 1400–1500* 10 (1983): 1618 (Stanley ped.: "William Stanley of Hooton, l. 1443 = Alice d. of Sir Richard Houghton"). Clayton *Administration of Chester 1442–85* (Chetham Soc. 3rd Ser. 35) (1991). VCH *Stafford* 7 (1996): 230–231 (confuses William Stanley, living 1456, with his son, William, died 1466). Stanley *House of Stanley* (1998): 65. Stanley fam. muniments found in Ryland Charters (available at www.a2a.org.uk/search/index.asp).

17. WILLIAM STANLEY, Knt., of Hooton (in Wirral), Roveacre, and Storeton, Cheshire, and Stanley, Staffordshire, son and heir, born about 1445. He married (1st) **MARGARET BROMLEY**, daughter and co-heiress of John Bromley, Knt., of Badington (in Acton), Cheshire, by Joan, daughter and co-heiress of William Hexstall, Knt. They had one daughter, Margery. His wife, Margaret, died in 1469. He married (2nd) by license dated 26 July 1470 **AGNES GROSVENOR**, daughter and co-heiress of Robert Grosvenor, Esq., of Holme, Cheshire, by Joan, daughter of Lawrence Fitton, Knt. They had a son, William, Knt. In 1487 he was granted a license to construct a stone tower at his manor of Hooton (in Wirral), Cheshire. He was an executor c.1492 of the will of [Master] Henry Medwall, Master of St. Giles. SIR WILLIAM STANLEY died in 1512. His widow, Agnes, died in 1520–1.

> Ormerod *Hist. of Chester* 2 (1819): 228–232; 3 (1819): 82–89, 194–195. Seacome *Hist. of the House of Stanley* (1821). Baines *Hist. of Lancaster* 4 (1836): chart facing 10 (Stanley ped.). *Annual Rpt. of the Deputy Keeper* 37 (1876): 681–684. Glover et al. *Vis. of Cheshire 1580, 1566, 1533 & 1591* (H.S.P. 18) (1882): 49–50 (Bromley ped.: "Margery Bromley vxr Sr Wm Stanley of Hooton."), 214–215 (Stanley ped.: "Sr Wm Stanley of Hooton vixit 5 E. 4. 1464. = 1. Margery [Margret] d. & coheire to Sr John Bromley of Bromley, = 2. Agnes 3d d. & coheire to Sr Rob't Grosvenor of Holme.") (Grosvenor arms: Azure, a garb Or). Willmore *Hist. of Walsall & its Neighbourhood* (1887): 143–145 (ped. of Hexstall and Bromley families; identifies husband of Margaret Bromley as Sir John Harpur of Rushall). Tresswell & Vincent *Vis. of Shropshire 1623, 1569 & 1584* 1 (H.S.P. 28) (1889): 71–78 (Bromley ped.: "Margareta [Bromley] nupta Willi'mi Stanley de Hooton militis."); 2 (H.S.P. 29) (1889): 371–372 (Needham ped.: "Margery [Bromley] vx. Sr Wm Stanley of Hooton."). Chetwynd *Hist. of Pirehill Hundred* 1 (Colls. Hist. Staffs. n.s. 12) (1909): 257. *Trans. Shropshire Arch. & Nat. Hist. Soc.* 51 (1941–43): 111–116. Jones *Church in Chester 1300–1500* (Chetham Soc. 3rd Ser. 7) (1957): 161. Clayton *Administration of Chester 1442–85* (Chetham Soc. 3rd Ser. 35) (1991). Bartrum *Welsh Gens. 1400–1500* 10 (1983): 1618 (Stanley 1: "Sir William Stanley (2) = Agnes d. Sir Robert Grosvenor of Holme"). VCH *Stafford* 7 (1996): 230–231.

Welsh Hist. Rev. 14 (1988–89): 1–22. Stanley fam. muniments found in Ryland Charters (available at www.a2a.org.uk/search/index.asp).

Child of William Stanley, Knt., by Margaret Bromley:

i. **MARGERY STANLEY**, married **PETER GERARD**, Esq., of Bryn (in Ashton-in-Makerfield), Lancashire [see GERARD 14].

Child of William Stanley, Knt., by Agnes Grosvenor:

i. **WILLIAM STANLEY**, Knt. [see next].

18. WILLIAM STANLEY, Knt., of Hooton (in Wirral) and Storeton, Cheshire, and Stanley, Staffordshire, Sheriff of Cheshire, 1526, and, in right of his wife, of Westleigh, Lancashire, born about 1474–5 (aged 38 in 1512, 46 in 1520/1). He married (1st) _____. They had no issue. He married (2nd) before 18 August 1505 (date of fine) **ANNE HARINGTON**, daughter and co-heiress of James Harington, Knt., of Brixworth and Hulcote, Northamptonshire, Drumbeth, Cumberland, Westleigh, Blackrod, Bretherton (in Croston), and Elston (in Preston), Lancashire, etc., by Isabel, daughter of Alexander Radcliffe, Esq. [see BRIXWORTH 18 for her ancestry]. She was born about 1479 (aged 41 in 1520). They had three sons, William, Knt., Peter, Esq., and John, and two daughters, Agnes (wife of Andrew Barton) and Katherine. In the period, 1504–15, William Stanley and Anne, his wife, daughter of James Harington, Knight, sued John, son and heir of Gilbert Ormeston, last surviving feoffee to uses in Chancery regarding "half the manor of Elston, Lancashire willed to the said Anne." He was knighted in 1513. His wife, Anne, was living 16 August 1528. SIR WILLIAM STANLEY was living in 1528–9.

Ormerod *Hist. of Chester* 2 (1819): 228–232. Seacome *Hist. of the House of Stanley* (1821). Baines *Hist. of Lancaster* 4 (1836): chart facing 10 (Stanley ped.). Raines *Hist. of the Chantries* (Chetham Soc. 59) (1862): 125–129. Towneley *Abs. of IPM* 2 (Chetham Soc. 99) (1876): 167–188. Flower *Vis. of Yorkshire 1563–4* (H.S.P. 16) (1881): 360–361 (Harrington ped.: "Anne [Harrington] = Sir William Stanley."). Glover et al. *Vis. of Cheshire 1580, 1566, 1533 & 1591* (H.S.P. 18) (1882): 214–215 (Stanley ped.: "Sr Wm Stanley of Hooton. = Anne eldest d. & coheire to Sr James Harrington.") (Harington arms: Sable, fretty Argent, a file of three points Or). Benolte *Vis. of Lancashire 1533* 2 (Chetham Soc. 110) (1882): 230–231 ("Sir William Stanley of Sturton had no yssue by his first wief, he maried to hys secound wief Anne daughter and one of the heyres to Sir James Harington… Memorandum that the said Sir William Stanley was sonne and heire to Agnes daughter and one of the heyres to Sir Robert Gravenor [Grosvenor] of the house of Holme in Cheshire."). *List of Sheriffs for England & Wales* (PRO Lists and Indexes 9) (1898): 17. Farrer *Final Concords of Lancaster* 3 (Lanc. & Cheshire Rec. Soc. 50) (1905): 157–158; 4 (Lanc. & Cheshire Rec. Soc. 60) (1910): 12. VCH *Lancaster* 3 (1907): 425, 429–430; 5 (1911): 300–301. *List of Early Chancery Procs.* 4 (PRO Lists and Indexes 29) (1908): 385. VCH *Northampton* 4 (1937): 150. Bartrum *Welsh Gens. 1400–1500* 10 (1983): 1618 (Stanley 1: "Sir William Stanley = Anne d. Sir James Harrington"). VCH *Stafford* 7 (1996): 230–231. Stanley fam. muniments found in Ryland Charters (available at www.a2a.org.uk/search/index.asp).

19. PETER STANLEY, Esq., of Moor Hall (in Aughton), Lancashire, and, in right of his 1st wife, of Bickerstaffe (in Ormskirk), Lancashire, younger son by his father's 2nd marriage. He was granted lands by his father in 1528 in Little and Great Storton, Cheshire. He married (1st) before 1543 **ELIZABETH SCARISBRICK**, daughter and heiress of James Scarisbrick, Esq., of Bickerstaffe (in Ormskirk), Lancashire, by his 1st wife, Margaret, daughter of Thomas Atherton. She was born in 1516. They had one daughter, Margaret (wife of Henry Stanley, Esq.). In 1553–4 he acquired the reversion of Moor Hall (in Aughton), Lancashire from William Bradshagh. His wife, Elizabeth, was living 22 August 1558. He married (2nd) 21 August 1559 at Aughton, Lancashire **CECILY TARLETON**, daughter of Richard Tarleton, of Walton. They had two sons, Edward, Knt. [1st Baronet], and William, Gent., and two daughters, Anne and Alice. His wife, Cecily, was buried at Ormskirk, Lancashire 28 Nov. 1568. In 1584, being a recusant or suspected person, he was required to furnish a light horseman accoutred (or £24) for the queen's service in Ireland. He married (3rd) before 1589 **JANE LEIGH**, widow of Richard Starkey, of Stretton in the Netherhall, Cheshire, and daughter of Philip Leigh, of Bouthes. They had no issue. PETER STANLEY, Esq., was buried in his chapel at Ormskirk, Lancashire 24 July 1592. He left a will 20 October 1589, proved 7 August 1598.

> Ormerod *Hist. of Chester* 2 (1819): 228–232. Seacome *Hist. of the House of Stanley* (1821). Baines *Hist. of Lancaster* 4 (1836): chart facing 10 (Stanley ped.). Draper *House of Stanley* (1864). King *Lancashire Funeral Certificates* (Chetham Soc. 75) (1869): 29–35. Dugdale *Vis. of Lancaster 1664-5* 3 (Chetham Soc. 88) (1873): 284 (Stanley ped.: "Peter Stanley, second son of Sir William Stanley of Stanley, Hooton, and Stourton, by Ann his wife, dau. of Sir James Harington. [1] = Elizabeth, dau. and heir of James Scarisbrick of Bickerstaffe, [2] = Cicely, dau. of Rich. Tarleton, of Walton."). Glover et al. *Vis. of Cheshire 1580, 1566, 1533 & 1591* (H.S.P. 18) (1882): 147–148 (Leigh ped.: "Jane [Leigh] vxor Ric. Starky of Stretton and after to... Stanley of Bickerstaff."), 214–215 (Stanley ped.: "Piers Stanley of Bickerstaff in Lancashire 2d sonne. = Elizab. d. & heire to James Scarsbridge of Bickerstaff & Margrett his wife d. & heire to Thos Atherton of Bickerstaff."), 217–218 (Starkey ped.: "Richard Starky of Stretton of the Netherhall 1566. = Jane d. to Philip Leigh of Bouthes after married to... Stanley of Bickerstaffe."). Benolte *Vis. of Lancashire 1533* 2 (Chetham Soc. 110) (1882): 109–113, 171–172 ("Elizabethe [Scarbryge], maryed Peter Stanley, sonne to Sir Wylliam Stanley of Hooton."). Metcalfe *Vis. of Northamptonshire 1564 & 1618-9* (1887): 180–181 (Harrington ped.: "Elizabeth [Harrington], ux.... Stanley of Houghton, co. Chester."). Arrowsmith & Williams *Regs. of Ormskirk* 1 (Lanc. Parish Reg. Soc. 13) (1902): 147, 184. VCH *Lancaster* 3 (1907): 276–278, 300–301 (Stanley arms: Argent, on a bend azure cotised gules, three bucks' heads cabossed or). Farrer *Final Concords of Lancaster* 4 (Lanc. & Cheshire Rec. Soc. 60) (1910): 58, 71, 115, 160. Harvey et al. *Vis. of the North* 1 (Surtees Soc. 122) (1912): 197. Stanley *House of Stanley* (1998). Stanley fam. muniments found in Ryland Charters (available at www.a2a.org.uk/search/index.asp).

20. ANNE STANLEY, daughter by her father's 2nd marriage, baptized at Ormskirk, Lancashire 31 Dec. 1561. She was mentioned in a fine executed by her father in 1566. She married at Ormskirk, Lancashire 14 May 1576 **EDWARD SUTTON**, Gent., of Knowsley (in Huyton), Lancashire and Hall House (in Rushton Spencer), Staffordshire, Deputy Steward of the manor of Prescot, Lancashire for Henry Stanley, Earl of Derby, 1578–96. They had four daughters, Alice (wife of John Eardley, Gent.), Jane, Margaret, and Anne. Edward and his wife, Anne, were present at the 1598 funeral of her brother-in-law, Henry Stanley, Esq. In 1607 as "Edward Sutton, of Coal Pitt Ford, Staffordshire, Gent.," he mortaged to Thomas Jollye, of Leck, Staffordshire, mercer one messuage called "Hall House" and a water corn mill commonly called Rushton both in Rushton Spencer, Staffordshire, also those on "Brookyate" also in Rushton Spencer. In 1607 Anne, wife of Edward Sutton, and her daughter, Alice Eardley, were returned as Popish recusants. In 1607–8 Edward Sutton, Gent., and Anne his wife, and John Eardley, Gent. and Alice his wife conveyed a messuage, garden, and lands in Rushton Spencer, Ravenscloughe and Cloudwood (in Leek), Staffordshire to John Davenport, Esq. Sometime in the period, 1607–25, Richard Eltonhead sued Sir William Bowyer, Thomas Ridiard [Rudyard], and John Eardley in Chancery regarding "messuages and lands in Rushton Spencer, Staffordshire "late of Edward Sutton." Anne Sutton was returned as a Popish recusant at Rushton Spencer in 1635.

> King *Lancashire Funeral Certificates* (Chetham Soc. 75) (1869): 29–35. Boyd & Wrottesley *Final Concords* (Colls. Hist. Staffs. n.s. 3) (1900): 9. Arrowsmith & Williams *Regs. of Ormskirk* 1 (Lanc. Parish Reg. Soc. 13) (1902): 6, 263. VCH *Lancaster* 3 (1907): 300–301. *Index of Chancery Procs. (Ser. I)* 1 (PRO Lists and Indexes 47) (1922): 303. Bailey *Selection from the Prescot Court Leet & Other Recs. 1447–1600* (Lanc. & Cheshire Rec. Soc. 89) (1937): 296, 298. VCH *Stafford* 7 (1996): 228. Parish Recs. of Huyton, Lancashire. Derbyshire Rec. Office: Wilmot-Horton of Osmaston & Catton, D3155/6348 (available at www.a2a.org.uk/search/index.asp).

21. ANNE SUTTON, baptized at Huyton, Lancashire 17 Nov. 1590. She married about 1607 **RICHARD ELTONHEAD**, Gent., of Eltonhead (in Prescot), Lancashire, son and heir of William Eltonhead, of Eltonhead (in Prescot), Lancashire, by Anne, daughter of James Bowers, of Brierly, Yorkshire. He was baptized at Prescot, Lancashire 6 Jan. 1580/1. They had six sons, Edward, Richard, John, Richard (again), James, and Henry, and nine daughters, Anne (wife of Edmund Wall), Katherine (wife of Thomas Meare), Barbara, Elizabeth (wife of Henry Parham), Jane, Agatha, Eleanor, Martha, and Alice. Sometime in the period, 1603–25, he and John Eltonhead sued Ralph Stanlake and _____ Nicholson in Chancery regarding a bond. He was a legatee and overseer in the 1609 will of his uncle, Thomas Eltonhead, Gent. Presumably he is the Richard Eltonhead, Gent., of

Charlton, Kent who was presented for not attending church in 1641. In 1642 his estates were ordered to be sold, he being a royalist supporter. In 1649 he petitioned regarding his "capital messuage and lands called Eltonhead Hall in Sutton," claiming a deduction of £120, it being a debt due on a bond to Thomas Barnes, who sued him "to the outlawry" in 1646. He also stood indebted to other persons in the aggregate sum of £190. His wife, Anne, was buried at Prescot, Lancashire 13 July 1654. RICHARD ELTONHEAD, Gent., was buried there in 1664.

> St. George *Vis. of Lancaster 1613* (Chetham Soc. 82) (1871): 115 (Eltonhead ped.: "Richard Eltonhed of Eltonhed, gent., living 1613. = Ann, dau. to Edward Sutton of Rushton Spenser, in co. Staff."). Dugdale *Vis. of Lancaster 1664–5* 1 (Chetham Soc. 84) (1872): 103 (Eltonhead ped.: "Richard Eltonhed of Eltonhead, æt. 82 an. 23 Sept. 1664. = Anne, dau. of Edward Sutton of Rushton Spencer, co. Stafford.") (Eltonhead arms: Quarterly: Per fess indented, sable and argent; in the first quarter in chief three plates). Hawley et al. *Vis. of Essex 1552, 1558, 1570, 1612 & 1634* 2 (H.S.P. 14) (1879): 393 (1634 Vis.) (Eltonhead ped.: "Richard Eltonhead of Eltonhead eldest sonn & heire. = Anne d. of Edw. Sutton of Rushton Spencer in com. Stafford."). Jeaffreson *Middlesex County Recs.* o.s. 3 (1888): 76. Hayden *Virginia Gens.* (1891): 221–290. Stanning *Royalist Composition Papers Rel. Lancaster* 2 (Lanc. & Cheshire Rec. Soc. 26) (1892): 279. VCH *Lancaster* 3 (1907): 359–360. *Index of Chancery Procs. (Ser. I)* 1 (PRO Lists and Indexes 47) (1922): 293, 303. Driffield *Parish Reg. of Prescot* 1 (Lanc. Parish Reg. Soc. 76) (1938); 2 (Lanc. Parish Reg. Soc. 114) (1975); 3 (Lanc. Parish Reg. Soc. 137) (1995). Ligon *Ligon Fam.* 1 (1947): 40–41. Barnes *British Roots of Maryland Fams.* 1 (1999): 178–179.

Children of Anne Sutton, by Richard Eltonhead, Gent.:

i. **JANE ELTONHEAD**, baptized at Prescot, Lancashire 23 March 1621/2. She married (1st) [CAPT.] **ROBERT MORRISON**, of York County, Virginia (died shortly before 25 October 1647); married (2nd) (as his 2nd wife) by jointure dated 1 August 1649 **CUTHBERT FENWICK**, Gent., of St. Mary's and Calvert Counties, Maryland, overseer and steward of Thomas Cornweleys, younger son of John Fenwick, Gent., of Brenkley, Northumberland. He was baptized at Ponteland, Northumberland 29 Dec. 1614. They had three sons, Robert, Richard, and John. He served as a member of the Maryland Assembly, 1637/8, 1638/9, 1640, 1641, 1642, 1647/8, 1649, 1650–1650/51, proprietary agent to New England, 1643, justice of St. Mary's County, 1644. CUTHBERT FENWICK, Gent., left a will dated 6 March 1654/5. His widow, Jane, left a will proved 28 Feb. 1659/60. Dugdale *Vis. of Lancaster 1664–5* 1 (Chetham Soc. 84) (1872): 103 (Eltonhead ped.: "Jane [Eltonhead], wife of Robert Fennick."). Hayden *Virginia Gens.* (1891): 221–290. Skordas *Early Settlers of Maryland* (1968): 159. Papenfuse *Biog. Dict. of the Maryland Legislature 1635–1789* 1 (1979): 304 (biog. of William Eltonhead), 319 (biog. of Cuthbert Fenwick). Fleet *Virginia Col. Abs.* 3 (1988): 76, 87. Sparacio & Sparacio *Virginia County Court Recs.: Deed & Will Abs. of Lancaster County, Virginia 1652–1657* (1991): 25. Barnes *British Roots of Maryland Fams.* 1 (1999): 191–192. Special thanks go to Todd Whitesides for his assistance with this account.

ii. **AGATHA ELTONHEAD**, baptized at Prescot, Lancashire 10 Feb. 1622/3; living 5 March 1682/3. She married (1st) **LUKE STUBBINS**, of Accomack and York Counties., Virginia (living 5 Jan. 1638/9). She married (2nd) before 18 Sept. 1647 **RALPH WORMELEY**, Esq., of Rosegill, Middlesex County, Virginia, member Virginia Council (died before 30 May 1652). They had two sons, William and Ralph. She married (3rd) before 7 May 1653 **HENRY CHICHLEY**, Knt., of Rappahannock, Lancaster County, and Rosegill, Middlesex County, Virginia, Burgess, Councillor, Deputy Governor of Virginia (died 5 Feb. 1682/3). They had no issue. Dugdale *Vis. of Lancaster 1664–5* 1 (Chetham Soc. 84) (1872): 103 (Eltonhead ped.: "Agatha [Eltonhead], wife of Raphe Wormley, son of Raphe Wormley, of… co. Ebor."). Hayden *Virginia Gens.* (1891): 221–290. Raimo *Biog. Dict. of American Col. & Revolutionary Govs.* (1980): 478 (biog. of Sir Henry Chicheley). Sparacio & Sparacio *Virginia County Court Recs.: Order Book Abs. of Middlesex County, Virginia 1677–1680* (1989): 3–4, 44–45; 1680–1686 (1994): 43. Sparacio & Sparacio *Virginia County Court Recs.: Deed & Will Abs. of Lancaster County, Virginia 1652–1657* (1991): 25, 48–49. Fleet *Virginia Col. Abs.* 1 (1988): 20, 76; 3 (1988): 73, 75.

iii. **ELEANOR ELTONHEAD**, married (1st) before 7 June 1648 (as his 2nd wife) [CAPT.] **WILLIAM BROCAS**, Esq. (died shortly before 24 May 1655), of Lancaster County, Virginia, member of the Virginia Council. She married (2nd) before 6 Feb. 1655/6 (as his 2nd wife) [COL.] **JOHN CARTER**, Esq., of Corotoman, Lancaster County, Virginia, member of the Virginia Council. They had no issue. [COL.] JOHN CARTER died 15 Sept. 1669. He left a will dated 1669. Dugdale *Vis. of Lancaster 1664–5* 1 (Chetham Soc. 84) (1872): 103 (Eltonhead ped.: "Elianor [Eltonhead], wife of Edward Brocas."). Hayden *Virginia Gens.* (1891): 221–290. Garber *Armistead Fam.* (1910): 34–35. Lee *Abs. of Lancaster County, Virginia Wills 1653–1800* (1959): 26. Sparacio & Sparacio *Virginia County Court Recs.: Deed Abs. of Middlesex County, Virginia 1679–1688* (1989): 68. Sparacio & Sparacio *Virginia County Court Recs.: Deed & Will Abs. of Lancaster County, Virginia 1652–1657* (1991): 104. Sparacio & Sparacio *Virginia County Court Recs.: Will Abs. of Lancaster County, Virginia 1690–1709* (1992): 3–4.

iv. **MARTHA ELTONHEAD**, born after 1613, living 28 Jan. 1653/4. She married **EDWIN CONWAY**, Gent. He was born in Worcestershire, England. They had one son, Edwin, and one daughter, Eltonhead (wife of Henry Thacker). He immigrated to Virginia, where he settled in Northampton County, Virginia. He was third clerk of Northampton County in 1642. He was granted land in 1644 and 1652/3 on Hungars Creek in Northampton County, Virginia. He was granted 1,250 acres of land on Corotoman River in Lancaster County, Virginia in 1652, to which county he removed. In 1657 he was granted 2,500 acres adjacent to John Meredith, of which 1,200 acres were due for an ealier patent and 1,200 acres for the transport of 25 persons. In 1660 he sold 200 acres of this land to William Gordon. EDWIN CONWAY, Gent., died in Lancaster County, Virginia shortly before 14 March 1660/1. Dugdale *Vis. of Lancaster 1664–5* 1 (Chetham Soc. 84) (1872): 103 (Eltonhead ped.: "Martha [Eltonhead], wife of Edwin Conway of… co. Wigorn."). Hayden *Virginia Gens.* (1891): 221–290. Nugent *Cavaliers & Pioneers* 1 (1963); 2 (1977): 182. Ames *County Court Recs. of Accomack-Northampton, Virginia* 2 (Virginia Hist. Soc. Docs. 10) (1973). McBride *Gordon Kinship* (1973): 233–243. Sparacio & Sparacio *Virginia County Court Recs.: Deed & Will Abs. of Lancaster County, Virginia* 1 (1991): 5, 6, 7, 9, 19–20, 22, 25–27, 39, 43–44, 46, 53–55, 62, 65, 69, 74, 106–107, 116, 139, 140; 2 (1991): 1, 2, 7, 78, 79, 80, 86, 100, 101, 119; 3 (1991): 1, 25, 69, 81. Sparacio & Sparacio *Virginia County Court Recs.: Order Book Abs. of Lancaster County, Virginia* 1 (1993): 1, 11, 18, 27, 39, 62, 79, 86, 98; 2 (1993): 4, 6, 7, 14, 57; 3 (1993): 1. Mackey, et al. *Northampton County, Virginia Rec. Book* 3 (1999): 1, 4, 10–12, 22, 25–27, 31, 34, 41, 46–47, 54–57, 59–61, 63, 65–66, 70, 75, 80, 82–84, 92–93, 96–97, 104, 111, 126, 137, 139–140, 141, 151, 154, 172, 186–188, 190, 210, 215–216, 224, 228, 233, 235, 238, 240–241, 245–246, 272, 287–288, 307, 7 (1999): 310–311.

v. **ALICE ELTONHEAD**, married (1st) **ROWLAND BURNHAM** (will proved 14 Jan. 1656/7), of York and Lancaster Counties, Virginia. They had three sons, Thomas, John, and Francis, and one daughter, Eleanor. ROWLAND BURNHAM left a will dated 12 Feb. 1655, proved 1 March 1656. She married (2nd) before 5 April 1658 **HENRY CORBIN** (died testate 8 Jan. 1675), of Middlesex County, Virginia [see CORBIN 21 for issue of this marriage]. She married (3rd) before 22 April 1677 [**CAPT.**] **HENRY CREYKE** (or **CRAYKE**, **CREEKE**) (died testate 8 June 1684), of Middlesex County, Virginia. They had no issue. His widow, Alice, left a will dated 23 March 1684/5, proved in Middlesex County, Virginia. Dugdale *Vis. of Lancaster 1664–5* 1 (Chetham Soc. 84) (1872): 103 (Eltonhead ped.: "Alice [Eltonhead], wife of… Durnham."). Hayden *Virginia Gens.* (1891): 221–290. *VMHB* 29 (1921): 374–382. Lee *Abs. of Lancaster County, Virginia Wills 1653–1800* (1959): 30. Hopkins *Middlesex County, Virginia Wills & Invs.* 1673–1812 (1989): 282. Sparacio & Sparacio *Virginia County Court Recs.: Deed & Will Abs. of Lancaster County, Virginia 1654–1661* (1991): 22–24, 78. Sparacio & Sparacio *Virginia County Court Recs.: Order Book Abs. of Middlesex County, Virginia 1680–1686* (1994): 76–77.

ENGAINE

EUSTACHE I, Count of Boulogne, married **MATHILDE** (or **MAHAUT**) **OF LOUVAIN**.
EUSTACHE II, Count of Boulogne, by an unknown mistress, _____.
GEOFFREY OF BOULOGNE, of Carshalton, Surrey, married **BEATRICE DE MANDEVILLE**.
WILLIAM OF BOULOGNE, of Carshalton, Surrey, married _____.
ROHESE OF BOULOGNE, married **RICHARD DE LUCY**, Knt., of Chipping Ongar, Essex, Justiciar of England.
AVELINE DE LUCY, married **GILBERT DE MONTFITCHET**, of Stanstead Mountfitchet, Essex.
RICHARD DE MONTFITCHET, of Stanstead Mountfitchet, Essex, married **MILLICENT** _____.
MARGARET DE MONTFITCHET, married **PETER DE FAUCONBERGE**, of Rise, Yorkshire.
WALTER DE FAUCONBERGE, Knt., 1st Lord Fauconberge, married **AGNES DE BRUS**.
WALTER DE FAUCONBERGE, 2nd Lord Fauconberge, married **ISABEL DE ROOS** [see FAUCONBERGE 8].

9. **ANICE** (or **AGNES**) **DE FAUCONBERGE**, married **NICHOLAS D'ENGAINE**, Knt., of Colne Engaine and Prested (in Feering), Essex, and Coton, Cambridgeshire, Sheriff of Essex and Hertfordshire, 1321–2, 2nd son of John d'Engaine, Knt., of Colne Engaine and White Notley, Essex, Blatherwycke, Bulwick, Laxton, and Pytchley, Northamptonshire, Great Gidding and Dillington, Huntingdonshire, Hallaton, Leicestershire, etc., by Joan, daughter and heiress of Gilbert de Greinville, Knt. They had two sons, John, Knt. [2nd Lord Engaine], and Henry. He was heir in 1322 to his older brother, John Engaine, Knt., 1st Lord Engaine [see CLAVERING 6.viii]. SIR NICHOLAS D'ENGAINE died testate 4 (or 10) Dec. 1322. His widow, Anice, was living in 1323.

Clutterbuck *Hist. & Antiq. of Hertford* 3 (1827): 178 (Engaine ped.). Dugdale *Monasticon Anglicanum* 6(1) (1830): 450–451 (Engaine ped. in Hist. Fundatorum of Castel Hymel Priory: "…Post hunc dominum Johannem Engaine juniorem, devolvitur hæreditas ad dominum Nicolaum fratrem ejus, qui habuit in uxorem dominam Amiciam, filiam domini Walteri Fawcomberg, de qua genuit ipse Johannem Engaine, and Henricum Engaine."). Banks *Baronies in Fees* 1 (1844): 199–200 (sub Engaine), 293. Fauconberge *Fauconberge Memorial* (1849): 9, 62–63 (Fauconberge ped.). *List of Sheriffs for England & Wales* (PRO Lists and Indexes 9) (1898): 44. *Notes & Queries for Somerset & Dorset* 10 (1907): 241–242 (Engaine arms: Gules, a fess indented between seven cross-crosslets, four in chief and three in base or). *C.F.R.* 3 (1912): 73, 192, 203, 210–211. *Eng. Hist. Rev.* 34 (1919): 165. *Trans. Leicestershire Arch. & Hist. Soc.* 13 (1923–24): 146 (Engaine chart). *C.P.* 5 (1926): 71–77 (sub Engaine). Mellows *Henry of Pytchley's Book of Fees* (Pubs. Northamptonshire Rec. Soc. 2) (1927): 130–132. *Pubs Bedfordshire Hist. Soc.* 13 (1930): Ped. 8 (Engaine ped.). VCH *Northampton* 4 (1937): 208–213.

10. JOHN D'ENGAINE, Knt., 2nd Lord Engaine, of Dillington, Great Gidding, and Graffham, Huntingdonshire, Blatherwycke, Laxton, and Pytchley, Northamptonshire, Colne Engaine and White Notley, Essex, justice in cos. Cambridge, Hunts, Northants, and Rutland, 1340, son and heir, born 30 May 1302. He married about 12 Nov. 1318 (date of fine) **JOAN PEVEREL**, daughter of Robert Peverel, Knt., of Castle Ashby, Northamptonshire, by his wife, Alice. They had two sons, John and Thomas, Knt. [3rd Lord Engaine], and three daughters, Joyce (wife of John de Goldington), Elizabeth, and Mary. He accompanied the Earl of Lancaster in his chivauche to Bedford 11 Jan. 1328/9. His lands were taken into the king's hand 16 Jan. 1328/9; they were restored to him 11 Feb. following. He was summoned for military service against the Scots in 1333. In 1343 he acquired the manor of Eaton Socon, Bedfordshire and in 1347 the reversion of the manor of Sandy, Bedfordshire from Roger de Beauchamp. He was present with the king in France in 1345. He presented to the church of Blatherwycke, Northamptonshire in 1345 and 1349. In 1346 he received writs to collect men-at-arms to join the king at Calais. He was summoned to Parliament from 20 Sept. 1355 to 15 Dec. 1357, by writs directed *Johanni Dengayne*, whereby he is held to have become Lord Engaine. SIR JOHN D'ENGAINE, 2nd Lord Engaine, died 16 Feb. 1357/8. His widow, Joan, was living 30 June 1359.

Weever *Antient Funeral Monuments* (1767): 405. Bridges *Hist. & Antiqs. of Northamptonshire* 2 (1791): 279. Chauncy *Hist. Antiqs. of Hertfordshire* 1 (1826): 557. Clutterbuck *Hist. & Antiq. of Hertford* 3 (1827): 178 (Engaine ped.). Dugdale *Monasticon Anglicanum* 6(1) (1830): 450–451 (Engaine ped. in Hist. Fundatorum of Castel Hymel Priory: "… Post prædictum dominum Nicolaum dominus Johannes Engaine filius ejus successit; qui duxit in uxorem suam dominam Joannam, filiam domini Roberti Peverell."). Banks *Baronies in Fees* 1 (1844): 199–200 (sub Engaine). *Antiquary* 4 (1881): 115–116. *C.C.R. 1339–1341* (1901): 183. *Notes & Queries for Somerset & Dorset* 10 (1907): 241–242. *C.F.R.* 3 (1912): 213. VCH *Bedford* 3 (1912): 189–202. *Trans. Leicestershire Arch. & Hist. Soc.* 13 (1923–24): 146 (Engaine chart). *C.P.* 5 (1926): 75–81 (sub Engaine). Mellows *Henry of Pytchley's Book of Fees* (Pubs. Northamptonshire Rec. Soc. 2) (1927): 130–132. *Pubs Bedfordshire Hist. Soc.* 13 (1930): Ped. 8 (Engaine ped.). VCH *Northampton* 4 (1937): 208–213. Sanders *English Baronies* (1960): 23. *Yorkshire Arch. Journal* 40 (1962): 265–297 (Engaine arms: Gules, a fess dancetty between six cross-crosslets or). VCH *Leicester* 5 (1964): 124. *Cal. IPM* 16 (1974): 393–394. Northamptonshire Rec. Office: Fitzwilliam (Milton) Charters, F(M) Charter/2033 (grant dated 30 June 1359 by William Bernak, Knt. to Lady Joan, formerly wife of John Engayne, Knt., and others) (available at www.a2a.org.uk/search/index.asp).

Children of John d'Engaine, Knt., by Joan Peverel:

i. **THOMAS D'ENGAINE**, Knt., 3rd Lord Engaine, 2nd but 1st surviving son and heir, born about 1336 (aged 22 in 1358). He married before 18 October 1353 **KATHERINE COURTENAY**, daughter of Hugh de Courtenay, Knt., 10th Earl of Devon, 2nd Lord Courtenay, by Margaret, daughter of Humphrey de Bohun, Knt., Earl of Hereford and Essex [see COURTENAY 7 for her ancestry]. They had no issue. He was summoned to a Council 20 June 1358, by writ directed *Thomas Dengayne*. His wife, Katherine, was a legatee in the 1361 will of her uncle, Humphrey de Bohun, Earl of Hereford and Essex. He was about to go beyond seas in 1362 and in 1364. SIR THOMAS D'ENGAINE, 3rd Lord Engaine, died in parts beyond seas 29 June 1367. His widow, Katherine, presented to the church of Blatherwycke, Northamptonshire in 1371. In 1382 William Burcester, Knt., and his wife, Margaret, complained that Katherine Engaine, Edward Dallingridge, Knt., and others disseised them of 80 marks rent in the parish of St. Martin in the Vintry, London. His widow, Katherine, was a legatee in the 1391 will of her mother. She was also a legatee in the 1396 will of her brother, William Courtenay, Archbishop of Canterbury, who bequeathed her certain books, stuffs, and plate, among the last were two silver bowls with the arms of Courtenay. Katherine, Lady Engaine, died 31 Dec. 1399. Newcourt *Repertorium Ecclesiasticum Parochiale*

Londinense 2 (1710): 187. Weever *Antient Funeral Monuments* (1767): 405. Bridges *Hist. & Antiqs. of Northamptonshire* 2 (1791): 279. Brydges *Collins' Peerage of England* 6 (1812): 214–271 (sub Courtenay, Viscount Courtenay). Chauncy *Hist. Antiqs. of Hertfordshire* 1 (1826): 557. Nicolas *Testamenta Vetusta* 1 (1826): 66–68 (will of Humphrey de Bohun, Earl of Hereford and Essex). Clutterbuck *Hist. & Antiqs. of Hertford* 3 (1827): 178 (Engaine ped.). Westcote *View of Devonshire in MDCXXX* (1845): 570–573 (sub Courtenay). Lipscomb *Hist. & Antiqs. of Buckingham* 1 (1847): 471–472 (Courtenay ped.). Birch *Cat. Seals in the British Museum* 2 (1892): 763 (seal of Katherine widow of Thomas Engaine Knt. dated 1397 — A shield of arms: per pale, dex., a fess dancettée between four crosslets in chief, and in base three, two, and one [ENGAINE], sin., three roundels, two and one, over all in chief a label of as many points [COURTENAY]. Above this, a smaller shield of arms: ENGLAND, and on the dex. and sin. sides other shields of similar size, BOHUN. Within a carved gothic quadrilobe, ornamented with ball-flowers along the inner edge). C.P.R. 1377–1381 (1895): 437 (Katherine, lady Denginæ, styled "king's kinswoman" by King Richard II of England). Vivian *Vis. of Devon 1531, 1564 & 1620* (1895): 243–250 (sub Courtenay). *Arch. Cantiana* 23 (1898): 55–67 (will of William Courtenay, Archbishop of Canterbury). C.P.R. 1391–1396 (1905): 556 (Katherine Dengayne styled "king's kinswoman" by King Richard II of England). *Trans. Leicestershire Arch. Soc.* 13 (1923-24): 146 (Engaine ped.). *C.P.* 5 (1926): 77–81 (sub Engaine). *Pubs Bedfordshire Hist. Soc.* 13 (1930): Ped. 8 (Engaine ped.). *VCH Leicester* 5 (1964): 124. Chew *London Possessory Assizes* (1965): 46–72 (no. 164). Schwennicke *Europaische Stanmtafeln* 3(4) (1989): 630 (sub Courtenay).

ii. **ELIZABETH D'ENGAINE** [see next].

iii. **MARY D'ENGAINE**, married (1st) **WILLIAM DE BERNAKE**, Knt. [see CANTELOWE 9.ii]; (2nd) **THOMAS LA ZOUCHE**, Knt., of Westoning, Bedfordshire [see CANTELOWE 9.ii].

11. ELIZABETH D'ENGAINE, born about 1341 (aged 26 in 1367). She married before 1372 (as his 1st wife) **LAURENCE PABENHAM**, Knt., of Pavenham, Bedfordshire, Fen Drayton, Cambridgeshire, Pavenham (in Offord Darcy), Huntingdonshire, Irchester, Northamptonshire, etc., Knight of the Shire for Bedfordshire, 1378, 1383, and, in right of his wife, of Eaton (in Eaton Socon), Bedfordshire, son and heir of Thomas de Pabenham, of Farndish, Hinwick, and Pavenham, Bedfordshire, and Irchester and Thenford, Northamptonshire, Sheriff of Northamptonshire, by Alice, sister of [Master] John and Andrew de Offard. He was born about 1334 (aged 11 in 1345). They had one son, Laurence, and one daughter, Katherine. In 1363 he claimed the advowson of Great Staughton, Huntingdonshire as nephew and heir of John de Offord (died 1349), late Chancellor of England, Archbishop-elect of Canterbury. His wife, Elizabeth, was co-heiress in 1367 to her brother, Thomas Engaine, Knt., 3rd Lord Engaine. His wife, Elizabeth, died 23 Sept. 1377. He married (2nd) before 1390 **JOAN DAUBENEY**, daughter of Giles Daubeney, Knt., of South Ingleby, Lincolnshire, by Eleanor, daughter of Henry de Wilington, Knt. [see MARKHAM 8 for her ancestry]. They had one son, John, and one daughter, Eleanor (wife of John Tyringham). By an unknown mistress, he had one illegitimate son, John Offard (alias John Pabenham). SIR LAURENCE PABENHAM died 10 June 1399. He and his 1st wife, Elizabeth, were buried in the church of Offard Darcy, Huntingdonshire. His widow, Joan, married (2nd) **JOHN WALEYS**. She died in 1414.

Newcourt *Repertorium Ecclesiasticum Parochiale Londinense* 2 (1710): 187. Weever *Antient Funeral Monuments* (1767): 405. Chauncy *Hist. Antiqs. of Hertfordshire* 1 (1826): 557. Clutterbuck *Hist. & Antiq. of Hertford* 3 (1827): 178 (Engaine ped.). Dugdale *Monasticon Anglicanum* 6(1) (1830): 450–451 (Engaine ped. in Hist. Fundatorum of Castel Hymel Priory: "…Quæ vero Elizabetha, secunda filia, cepit in virum Laurentium Pabenham militem, et habuerunt exitum inter eos quandam filiam, nomine Katerinam, quæ vero Katerina cepit in virum Willielmum Cheney militem, et habuerunt exitum inter eos Laurentium et Armam ... Elizabetha uxor Laurencii Pabenham militis, de cujus progenie venit Johannes Cheney miles."). Banks *Baronies in Fees* 1 (1844): 199–200 (sub Engaine). Waters *Chester of Chicheley* 1 (1878): 330–331 (re. Offard fam.). *Antiquary* 4 (1881): 115–116. *Notes & Queries* 9th Ser. 7 (1901): 73–74. C.C.R. 1346–1349 (1905): 299–300. *Notes & Queries for Somerset & Dorset* 10 (1907): 241–242 (Pabenham arms: Barry of six, argent and azure, on a bend gules three mullets or.). C.P.R. 1416–1422 (1911): 309. *VCH Bedford* 3 (1912): 76–80, 189–202. *Trans. Leicestershire Arch. & Hist. Soc.* 13 (1923–24): 146 (Engaine chart). *C.P.* 5 (1926): 77–81 (sub Engaine). Maxwell Lyte *Historical Notes on the Use of the Great Seal of England* (1926): 33. Mellows *Henry of Pytchley's Book of Fees* (Pubs. Northamptonshire Rec. Soc. 2) (1927): 130–132. *Pubs Bedfordshire Hist. Soc.* 13 (1930): Ped. 8 (Engaine ped.). *VCH Huntingdon* 2 (1932): 368. Fowler *Recs. of Harrold Priory* (Pubs. Bedfordshire Hist. Rec. Soc. 17) (1935): 131 (charter of Laurence Pabenham, Knt. dated 1383), 147–149. *VCH Northampton* 4 (1937): 21–22 (Pabenham arms: Barry azure and argent a bend gules with three molets argent thereon), 208–213. Otway-Ruthven *King's Secretary & the Signet Office in the XVth Century* (1939): 127. . Bassett *Knights of Bedfordshire* (Bedfordshire Hist. Rec. Soc. 29) (1949): 74 (biog. of Laurnece Pabenham). *Cal. IPM* 16 (1974): 268–269, 393–394; 20 (1995): 105–106. VCH *Cambridge* 9 (1989): 292–295. National Archives, C 143/380/4 (available at www.catalogue.nationalarchives.gov.uk/search.asp).

12. KATHERINE PABENHAM, daughter by her father's 1st marriage, born about 1372 (aged 27 in 1399). She married (1st) before 20 June 1383 (date of grant) **WILLIAM CHEYNE**, Knt., of Long Stanton and Fen Ditton, Cambridgeshire, Dadlington, Leicestershire, etc., son and heir of Henry Cheyne, of Fen Ditton, Cambridgeshire. They had two sons, John and Laurence, Esq., and one daughter, Anne. His wife, Katherine, was heiress sometime in the period, 1390–97, to her full brother, Laurence Pabenham, by which she inherited the manors of Blatherwycke and Engaines (in Pytchley), Northamptonshire, Eaton (in Eaton Socon), Bedfordshire, and Engaine (in Great Gidding), Huntingdonshire. SIR WILLIAM CHEYNE died about 1397. His widow, Katherine, married (2nd) before Dec. 1399 (as his 2nd wife) **THOMAS AYLESBURY**, Knt. [see BASSET 14], of Milton Keynes and Drayton Beauchamp, Buckinghamshire, Aldbury, Tiscot, and Wilstone (in Tring), Hertfordshire, Pytchley, Northamptonshire, Abinger, Surrey, etc., Knight of the Shire for Buckinghamshire, Sheriff of Bedfordshire and Buckinghamshire, 1412–3, son and heir of John Aylesbury, Knt., of Milton Keynes, Buckinghamshire, Sheriff of Bedfordshire and Buckinghamshire, 1373–4, 1377–8, 1381–3, 1386–7, Knight of the Shire for Buckinghamshire, by his 1st wife, Isabel [see BASSET 13 for his ancestry]. He was born about 1369 (aged 40 in 1409). They had one son, John, and two daughters, Eleanor and Isabel (or Elizabeth). He presented to the churches of Blatherwycke, Northamptonshire in 1403, 1407, 1409, 1413, and 1417, and Ashley, Northamptonshire, 1407. His wife, Katherine, was co-heiress in 1407 to her half-brother, John Pabenham, by which she inherited Pabenham (in Offord Darcy), Huntingdonshire, and a moiety share of Pavenham, Bedfordshire, and Irchester, Northamptonshire. SIR THOMAS AYLESBURY died 9 Sept. 1418. In 1422 her son, Laurence Cheyne, Esq., and his wife, Elizabeth, released the manor of Eaton (in Eaton Socon), Bedfordshire to Katherine, widow of Thomas Aylesbury, Thomas Brake, and others. Katherine was granted letters of fraternity by the Prior and Convent of Durham in 1423. In 1424 she presented to the perpetual chantry of St. Nicholas of Eaton, Bedfordshire. She died 17 June 1436.

Bridges *Hist. & Antiqs. of Northamptonshire* 2 (1791): 274, 279. Ebchester & Burnby *Obit. Roll* (Surtees Soc. 31) (1856): 109. Mundy et al. *Vis. of Nottingham 1569 & 1614* (H.S.P. 4) (1871): 123–128 (1569 Vis.) (Chaworth ped.: "Catherin d. of Sr Lawrance Pabenham ob. 17 July 14 H. 6. [1] = Thomas Aylisbery 1 husband, [2] = Sr William Cheney Knt. 2 husband."). Cooke & St. George *Vis. of Cambridge 1575 & 1619* (H.S.P. 41) (1897): 118–119 (Cheney ped.: "Sr Willm. Cheney of Fenn Ditton = Catherin d. & heire of Lawrance Pabenham. = Sr Thomas Aylesbury Knt.") (Cheney arms: Argent, a bend lozengy gules). *Notes & Queries* 9th Ser. 7 (1901): 73–74. *Notes & Queries for Somerset & Dorset* 10 (1907): 241–242. VCH *Bedford* 3 (1912): 76–80, 189–202. *C.P.* 5 (1926): 77–81 (sub Engaine). VCH *Northampton* 4 (1937): 21–22 (Pabenham arms: Barry azure and argent a bend gules with three molets argent thereon), 209–210. VCH *Cambridge* 9 (1989): 223, 292–295; 10 (2002): 123–124. Roskell *House of Commons 1386–1421* 2 (1992): 87–89 (biog. of Sir Thomas Aylesbury). *Cal. IPM* 21 (2002): 24–26.

Child of Katherine Pabenham, by William Cheyne, Knt.

i. **LAURENCE CHEYNE**, Esq., of Fen Ditton, Cambridgeshire, married **ELIZABETH COKAYNE** [see CHEYNE 12].

Children of Katherine Pabenham, by Thomas Aylesbury, Knt.:

i. **ELEANOR AYLESBURY**, married **HUMPHREY STAFFORD**, Knt., of Grafton, Worcestershire [see HASTANG 14].

ii. **ISABEL** (or **ELIZABETH**) **AYLESBURY**, married **THOMAS CHAWORTH**, Knt., of Wiverton, Nottinghamshire [see LEEKE 15].

❧ ESSEX ❦

1. PETER DE LUDGERSHALL, of Cherhill and Linley (in Tisbury), Wiltshire, and Gussage Saint Andrew (in Sixpenny Handley), Dorset. He married **MAUD** _____. They had two sons, Robert and Geoffrey, Knt. [Earl of Essex], and one daughter, Juliane. PETER DE LUDGERSHALL died as a lay monk at Winchester, Hampshire sometime before 1165. His widow, Maud, married (2nd) **HUGH DE BUCKLAND** (or **BOCLANDE**), of Buckland, Berkshire, Datchworth, Hertfordshire, etc., Sheriff of Berkshire, 1170–76, itinerant justice, 1173–4, son and heir of William de Buckland, living c.1145, of Cippenham (in Burnham), Buckinghamshire. They had three sons, William, Knt., Hugh, and Geoffrey [Archdeacon of Norwich], and one daughter, Hawise. He was pardoned two marks by the king in 1158–9. In 1166 he certfied that he held 2-½ knights' fees in Berkshire. Sometime in the period, c.1166–90, he witnessed a charter of Elias de Studley to his step-son, Geoffrey Fitz Peter, regarding lands in Heytesbury and Cherhill, Wiltshire. HUGH DE BUCKLAND died about 1176. Sometime before c.1185 his widow, Maud, and her son and heir, Robert Fitz Peter, granted the chapel of Wellsworth (in Chalton), Hampshire "so far as it belongs to them," together with a messuage with its croft, as well as five acres of land which the chapel used to have, to Southwick Priory, Hampshire; this gift made for the salvation of their souls and those of Peter de Ludgershall, Hugh de Buckland, Pernel wife of the said Robert,. etc. Sometime before c.1185, Maud and her son and heir, Robert Fitz Peter, gave one messuage and one hide of land in Costow (in Wroughton), Wiltshire to the canons of Bradenstoke at the instance of Roger Fitz Geoffrey. In 1198 Geoffrey Fitz Peter removed the body of his father to Winchester.

Dugdale *Monasticon Anglicanum* 6(1) (1830): 339–340. Luard *Annales Monastici* 2 (Rolls Ser. 36) (1865): 67 (Annals of Winchester sub A.D. 1198: "Gaufridus filius Petri, vir ingenus et specialis amator Wintoniensis ecclesiæ, fecit transferri patrem suum, qui fuerat ejusdem loci monachus conversus, ad succurrendum, de cœmiterio monachorum in ecclesiam, et ibi honorifice recondi in præsentia abbatis de Theokesbiria, et abbatis de Hida, et aliorum plurimorum virorum nobilium viij. idus Maii."). Foss *Biog. Dict. of the Judges of England* (1870): 103 (biog. of Hugh de Bocland). *Great Roll of the Pipe, A.D. 1158–1159* (Pipe Roll Soc. 1) (1884): 37. Maitland *Bracton's Note Book* 3 (1887): 452–453. *List of Sheriffs for England & Wales* (PRO Lists and Indexes 9) (1898): 6. *C.P.R. 1343–1345* (1902): 391. VCH *Hertford* 3 (1912): 78–81. *Genealogist* n.s. 34 (1918): 181–189. Fowler & Hughes *Cal. of the Pipe Rolls of the Reign of Richard I for Buckinghamshire & Bedfordshire, 1189–1199* (Pubs. Bedfordshire Hist. Rec. Soc. 7) (1923): 218–219. VCH *Buckingham* 3 (1925): 164–184. London *Cartulary of Bradenstoke Priory* (Wiltshire Rec. Soc. 35) (1979): 85, 165–168. Mason *Beauchamp Cartulary Charters* (Pipe Roll Soc. n.s. 43) (1980): 190 (charter of Elias de Studley to Geoffrey Fitz Peter dated c.1166–90). Hanna *Cartularies of Southwick Priory* 1 (Hampshire Rec. Ser. 9) (1988): 68 (charter of Maud de Bochland' and her son and heir, Robert Fitz Peter; charter witnessed by William de Bocland and Hugh his brother). VCH *Hampshire* 3 (1908): 107. Brown *Anglo-Norman Studies VIII* (1986): 218, 220. VCH *Wiltshire* 13 (1987): 195–248. Turner *Men Raised from the Dust* (1988): 37, App. Chart A (Fitz Peter ped.). Stacy *Charters & Custumals of Shaftesbury Abbey, 1089–1216* (2006): 66, 69, 86.

Children of Peter de Ludgershall, by Maud _____:

    i.   **ROBERT FITZ PETER**, of Cherhill and Linley (in Tisbury), Wiltshire, Gussage St. Andrew (in Handley), Dorset, etc., son and heir, adult before 1161. He married **PERNEL** _____. They had no issue. Sometime before 1161 he and his wife, Pernel, granted Savigny Abbey a bushel of wheat and the tenement of Gilbert de Londa at Criselon [?Christon]. In 1180 his heir owed upon accompt for the old ferm of Gorron. ROBERT FITZ PETER died c.1185. His widow, Pernel, married (2nd) in 1190 (date of payment for license to remarry) (as his 2nd wife) **EUSTACE DE BALLIOL**, of Bywell, Northumberland. In 1198 Eustace and his wife, Pernel, quitclaimed their right to lands in Salthrop (in Wroughton), Wiltshire to Geoffrey Fitz Peter, in return for 30 marks silver. His wife, Pernel, was living 17 October 1198. In 1199 he paid 200 marks fine for neglecting the king's precept to go to the wars in France. EUSTACE DE BALLIOL died in 1200. Clutterbuck *Hist. & Antiqs. of Hertford* 3 (1827): 17 (Balliol ped.). Dugdale *Monasticon Anglicanum* 6(1) (1830): 339–340. Wiffen *Hist. Memoirs of the House of Russell* 1 (1833): 43. Stapleton *Magni Rotuli Scaccarii Normanniæ* 1 (1840): clix. Fordyce *Hist. & Antiqs. of Durham* 2 (1857): 5. Maitland *Bracton's Note Book* 3 (1887): 452–453. *Feet of Fines of King Richard I A.D. 1198 to A.D. 1199* (Pubs. Pipe Roll Soc. 24) (1900): 15. VCH *Dorset* 2 (1908): 75. Sanders *English Baronies* (1960): 25. London *Cartulary of Bradenstoke Priory* (Wiltshire Rec. Soc. 35) (1979): 85, 165–168. Mason *Beauchamp Cartulary Charters* (Pipe Roll Soc.

n.s. 43) (1980): 190 ("An estate worth 22*l*. blanch was held in Cherhill [Wiltshire], in *terris datis* by John Marshall between 1556 and Michaelmas 1164 (*Red Book of the Exchequer* (Rolls ser., 3 vols., 1896), II, 664; P.R.S. VII, 14), Robert Fitz Peter held it between Michaelmas 1165 and Michaelmas 1185 (P.R.S. VIII, 56; P.R.S. XXXV, 189). At Michaelmas 1187 it was held in *terris datis* by Geoffrey Fitz Peter (P.R.S. XXX VII, 173)"). Stringer *Essays on the Nobility of Scotland* (1985): 153 (Balliol ped.). Brown *Anglo-Norman Studies VIII* (1986): 218, 220. Hanna *Cartularies of Southwick Priory* 1 (Hampshire Rec. Ser. 9) (1988): 68 (charter of Maud de Bochland' and her son and heir, Robert Fitz Peter). Turner *Men Raised from the Dust* (1988): 37, 166, App. Chart A (Fitz Peter ped.). White *Restoration & Reform, 1153–1165* (2004): 115–116. Stacy *Charters & Custumals of Shaftesbury Abbey, 1089–1216* (2006): 71.

ii. **GEOFFREY FITZ PETER**, Knt., Earl of Essex [see next].

iii. **JULIANE FITZ PETER**, married **STEPHEN DE BENDEGES**, of Winchfield, Hampshire. Her maritagium included one-third of the vill of Hartley Wintney, Hampshire. They had one son, Maurice. In 1198 he sold one hide of land in Wike, Surrey to Simon de Berkes. Maitland *Bracton's Note Book* 2 (1887): 193–194. *Feet of Fines of King Richard I A.D. 1197 to A.D. 1198* (Pubs. Pipe Roll Soc. 23) (1898): 78–80. *Genealogist* 6 (1889): 5; n.s. 34 (1918): 181-189. VCH *Hampshire* 4 (1911): 79–81.

Child of Maud _____, by Hugh de Buckland:

i. **WILLIAM DE BUCKLAND**, of Buckland, Berkshire, Westoning, Bedfordshire, Aldbury and Pendley (in Tring), Hertfordshire, etc., son and heir. He married **MAUD DE SAY**, daughter and co-heiress of William de Say, of Kimbolton, Huntingdonshire, and Saham, Norfolk [see SAY 4.i for her ancestry]. They had three daughters, Maud, Hawise, and Joan. In the period, 1186–89, he and his brother, Hugh, and their half-brother, Geoffrey Fitz Peter, witnessed a charter of William, Earl of Ferrers, to Ralph Fitz Stephen. In the period, 1186–90, he and his brother, Hugh de Buckland, witnessed a charter of their half-brother, Geoffrey Fitz Peter. In 1188 he and his brother, Hugh de Buckland, witnessed a charter of their mother, Maud, to Southwick Priory. In 1189 he paid £100 for seisin of the vill of Westoning, Bedfordshire, and was still in possession in 1210. Sometime in the period, 1199–1213, he granted the church of Aldbury, Hertfordshire to Missenden Abbey. In the same period, he granted 1-½ virgates of land in Aldbury, Hertfordshire to Missenden Abbey In 1206 William de Buckland was summoned to warrant the charter of his brother, Hugh, who gave Robert de Marsh two hides of land in Windrush, Gloucestershire. At an unknown date, he granted the advowson of the church of Aldbury, Hertfordshire to the Priory of Missenden, together with a virgate and a half of land. At an unknown date, he granted Richard son of Alexander de Stanwei nine acres of land in his ville of Elsenham, Hertfordshire. WILLIAM DE BUCKLAND died 15 April 1216. In 1218 his widow, Maud, sued her nephew, William de Mandeville, Earl of Essex, for a moiety share of various manors of the Mandeville inheritance, including Pleshey, Essex, Streatley, Berkshire, Amersham and Quarrendon, Buckinghamshire, Enfield, Middlesex, Compton, Warwickshire, etc. In 1219 she sued Richard Mauduit and his wife, Isabel, for her right of dower in the manor of Barcote (in Buckland), Berkshire. At an unknown date, she granted Thomas de Helsenham eleven acres of land in her woods of Elsenham, Hertfordshire. Maud died 28 March 1222. Baker *History & Antiquities of the County of Northampton* 1 (1822–1830): 544–545 (Mandeville-Fitz Peter-Bohun ped.). Clutterbuck *Hist. & Antiqs. of Hertford* 3 (1827): 190–194 (Mandeville-Say ped.). Palgrave *Rotuli Curiæ Regis* 1 (1835): 261, 305, 435–436. Lee *Hist., Desc. & Antiqs. of ...Thame* (1883): 332 (Mandeville ped.). Round *Ancient Charters Royal and Private Prior to A.D. 1200* (Pipe Roll Soc. 10) (1888): 108–110 (confirmation dated 1198 by King Richard I of the division of their inheritance made by Beatrice and Maud, daughters and co-heirs of William de Say, in the time of his father, King Henry II). Moore *Cartularium Monasterii Sancti Johannis Baptiste de Colecestria* 2 (1897): 373–374 (undated charter of Maud de Say), 375, 377 (undated charter of William de Boclande), 377 (charter of Maud de Say), 377–378. Salter *Eynsham Cartulary* 2 (Oxford Hist. Soc. 51) (1908): 224–225. VCH *Hertford* 2 (1908): 143–148, 281–294. VCH *Bedford* 3 (1912): 451–455. *Genealogist* n.s. 34 (1918): 181–189. Fowler & Hughes *Cal. of the Pipe Rolls of the Reign of Richard I for Buckinghamshire & Bedfordshire, 1189–1199* (Pubs. Bedfordshire Hist. Rec. Soc. 7) (1923): 218–219. VCH *Berkshire* 3 (1923): 511–516; 4 (1924): 453–460. VCH *Buckingham* 3 (1925): 141–155, 164–184. *C.P.* 5 (1926): chart foll. 116. *C.R.R.* 4 (1929): 226; 8 (1938): 56–57, 351. Jenkins *Cartulary of Missenden* 3 (Bucks Rec. Soc. 12) (1962): 174 (charter of William de Buckland dated 1199–1213; charter witnessed by Geoffrey Fitz Peter, Earl of Essex, and Geoffrey de Buckland), 174–175 (notification of William de Buckland to Hugh, Bishop of Lincoln), 175 (charter of William de Buckland dated 1199–1213; charter granted for the souls of himself, his wife, his children, his mother, Maud de Buckland, and Geoffrey Fitz Peter, Earl of Essex, and Geoffrey de Buckland; charter witnessed by Geoffrey Fitz Peter, Earl of Essex, and Geoffrey de Buckland), 219–220. VCH *Wiltshire* 8 (1965): 250–263. Mason *Beauchamp Cartulary Charters* (Pipe Roll Soc. n.s. 43) (1980): 195–196 (charter of William, Earl of Ferrers dated 1186–89), 196–197 (charter of Geoffrey Fitz Peter dated 1186–90). Stevenson *Edington Cartulary* (Wiltshire Rec. Soc. 42) (1987): 134–136, 139, 141–142. Hanna *Cartularies of Southwick Priory* 1 (Hampshire Rec. Ser. 9) (1988): 68. Mason *Westminster Abbey Charters, 1066–c.1214* (London Rec. Soc. 25) (1988): 160–175. Haskins

Soc. Jour. 1 (1989): 147–172. Ward *Women of the English Nobility & Gentry 1066–1500* (1995): 100–101. Greenway *Book of the Foundation of Walden Monastery* (1999): xxviii–xxx.

Children of William de Buckland, by Maud de Say:

- a. **MAUD DE BUCKLAND**, daughter and co-heiress. She married before 1219 **WILLIAM D'AVRANCHES**, of Folkestone, Kent. They had one son, William, and one daughter, Maud (wife of Hamo de Crevequer). WILLIAM D'AVRANCHES died in 1230. Hasted *Hist. & Top. Survey of Kent* 5 (1798): 311–322; 8 (1789): 152–188. VCH *Berkshire* 4 (1924): 453–460. VCH *Buckingham* 3 (1925): 165–184. *C.P.* 5 (1926): chart foll. 116. VCH *Kent* 2 (1926): 172–175. *C.R.R.* 8 (1938): 56–57. Sanders *English Baronies* (1960): 31, 45.

- b. **HAWISE DE BUCKLAND**. She married before 1219 **JOHN DE BOVILLE**. VCH *Berkshire* 4 (1924): 453–460. VCH *Buckingham* 3 (1925): 165–184. *C.P.* 5 (1926): chart foll. 116. *C.R.R.* 8 (1938): 56–57.

- c. **JOAN DE BUCKLAND**, daughter and co-heiress. She married (1st) before 1212 **WILLIAM MUSARD**, of Iping, Sussex and of Bulkington (in Keevil), Wiltshire, son and heir of Richard Musard, of Iping, Sussex. He was living in 1212. In 1217 his lands in Wiltshire were restored to him which he had forfeited for joining the rebels against King John. His widow, Joan, married (2nd) before 1219 **ROBERT DE FERRERS**, of Cippenham (in Burnham), Buckinghamshire, younger son of William de Ferrers, 3rd Earl of Derby, by Sibyl, daughter of William de Briouze (or Brewes). They had no issue. He confirmed a gift of his father, William de Ferrers, Earl of Ferrers to the Hospital of St. John of Jerusalem, Clerkenwell. In 1225, as Joan de Buckland, she gave the king half a mark for having a writ to attaint the twelve jurors of an assize of novel disseisin between Adam de Cheverell and William Musard, formerly her husband, concerning a tenement in Bulkington (in Keevil), Wiltshire. ROBERT DE FERRERS died testate shortly before 18 Jan. 1225/6. His widow, Joan, married (3rd) **SIMON D'AVRANCHES**. They had one son, John. As "Joan de Ferrers," she presented to the chapel of Cippenham (in Burnham), Buckinghamshire in 1249. In 1250 Joan came to an arrangement with the Abbot of Westminster regarding the manor of Cippenham (in Burnham), Buckinghamshire, by which she acquired the right to hold a view of frankpledge. In 1252 she transferred her rights in Cippenham (in Burnham), Buckinghamshire to Richard, Earl of Cornwall for £200; he was to hold the manor for life at a rent of £6 0s. 8d., and after her death he was to render to her heirs a pair of gilt spurs at Easter. Joan died in 1252. Dugdale *Monasticon Anglicanum* 6(2) (1830): 807 (charter of Robert de Ferrers, son of William, Earl of Ferrers; charter witnessed by William de Ferrers, son of William, Earl of Ferrers). Shaw *Hist. & Antiqs. of Staffordshire* 1 (1798): 39 (Ferrers ped.). Roberts *Excerpta e Rotulis Finium* 1 (1835): 133–134. *C.P.R.* 1338–1340 (1898): 310. *Desc. Cat. Ancient Deeds* 5 (1906): 104, 151. Grosseteste *Rotuli Roberti Grosseteste Episcopi Lincolniensis* (Lincoln Rec. Soc. 11) (1914): 378–379. VCH *Berkshire* 4 (1924): 453–460. VCH *Buckingham* 3 (1925): 164–184. *C.P.* 5 (1926): chart foll. 116. *C.R.R.* 8 (1938): 56–57. VCH *Sussex* 4 (1953): 63–65. VCH *Wiltshire* 8 (1965): 250–263. Dryburgh *Cal. of the Fine Rolls of the Reign of Henry III* 2 (2008): 35, 44, 54, 69, 82, 163.

ii. **HUGH DE BUCKLAND**, of Datchworth, Hertfordshire. In the period, 1186–89, he and his brother, William, and their half-brother, Geoffrey Fitz Peter, witnessed a charter of William, Earl of Ferrers, to Ralph Fitz Stephen. In the period, 1186–90, he and his brother, William de Buckland, witnessed a charter of their half-brother, Geoffrey Fitz Peter. In 1188 he and his brother, William de Buckland, witnessed a charter of their mother, Maud, to Southwick Priory. In 1192 Abbot William and the convent of Westminster quitclaimed the advowson of Datchworth, Hertfordshire to him; which quitclaim was made with the consent of his brother, William de Buckland. In 1206 William de Buckland was summoned to warrant the charter of his brother, Hugh, who gave Robert de Marsh two hides of land in Windrush, Gloucestershire. *C.R.R.* 4 (1929): 226. Mason *Beauchamp Cartulary Charters* (Pipe Roll Soc. n.s. 43) (1980): 195–196 (charter of William, Earl of Ferrers dated 1186–89), 196–197 (charter of Geoffrey Fitz Peter dated 1186–90). Hanna *Cartularies of Southwick Priory* 1 (Hampshire Rec. Ser. 9) (1988): 68. Mason *Westminster Abbey Charters, 1066–c.1214* (London Rec. Soc. 25) (1988): 160–175.

iii. **GEOFFREY DE BUCKLAND**, Archdeacon of Norfolk, 1198, Dean of St Martin le Grand, London; Justice in Eyre. He held the prebendary of Grantham before 1219. In the period, 1190–1213, he witnessed a charter of his half-brother, Geoffrey Fitz Peter, Earl of Essex, to Geoffrey's son, William de Mandeville. In the period, 1203–13, he witnessed a charter of Maud de Cauz, widow of Ralph Fitz Stephen, to his half-brother, Geoffrey Fitz Peter, Earl of Essex. GEOFFREY DE BUCKLAND shortly before 14 Sept. 1225. Palgrave *Rotuli Curiæ Regis* 1 (1835): 156. Foss *Biog. Dict. of the Judges of England* (1870): 103 (biog. of Geoffrey de Bocland). *Select Civil Pleas* 1 (Selden Soc. 3) (1890): 16. *Desc. Cat. Ancient Deeds* 2 (1894): 93. Moore *Cartularium Monasterii Sancti Johannis Baptiste de Colecestria* (1897): 201–202. *Feet of Fines of King Richard I A.D. 1197 to A.D. 1198* (Pubs. Pipe Roll Soc. 23) (1898): 78–80. *C.P.R. 1216–1225* (1901): 208, 271, 550. Salter *Eynsham Cartulary* 1 (Oxford Hist. Soc. 49) (1907): 59–60; 2 (Oxford Hist. Soc. 51) (1908): 224–225. Phillimore *Rotuli Hugonis de Welles Episcopi Lincolniensis 1209–1235* 3 (Lincoln Rec. Soc. 9) (1914): 149. *Speculum* 28 (1953): 808–813 ("[Geoffrey de Buckland's] brother,

William [de Buckland], was the brother-in-law of the justiciar, Geoffrey Fitz Peter, and his sister, was the wife of William II de Lanvalay. He was in addition to a brief tenure as archdeacon of Norwich, dean of St. Martin's in London, canon of Salisbury, and rector of at least five churches, three by the king's gift and one each from his brother, William de Buckland, and his brother-in-law, William de Lanvalay. He served King John as a justice and as a baron of the exchequer. In the early years of John's reign, when Geoffrey fitz Peter was ruling England during the king's absence in Normandy, Geoffrey de Buckland was the justiciar's representative in the exchequer. He seems to have retired from the royal service about 1203 and in 1216 was in rebellion. He died in 1225."). Mason *Beauchamp Cartulary Charters* (Pipe Roll Soc. n.s. 43) (1980): 191, 196–7. Mason *Westminster Abbey Charters, 1066–c.1214* (1988): 308–309. Greenway *Fasti Ecclesiae Anglicanae 1066–1300* 4 (1991): 68–70. Hobbs *Cartulary of Forde Abbey* (Somerset Rec. Soc. 85) (1998): 20.

    iv. **HAWISE DE BUCKLAND**, married **WILLIAM DE LANVALLAY**, of Walkern, Hertfordshire [see LANVALLAY 2].

2. GEOFFREY FITZ PETER, Knt., of Wellsworth (in Chalton), Hampshire, Cherhill and Costow, Wiltshire, Chief Forester, Sheriff of Northamptonshire, 1184–89, 1191–94, Sheriff of Essex and Hertfordshire, 1190–93, Constable of Hertford Castle, Justicier of England, 1198–1213, Sheriff of Staffordshire, 1198, Sheriff of Yorkshire, 1198–1200, 1202–4, Sheriff of Bedfordshire and Buckinghamshire, 1199–1204, Sheriff of Westmorland, 1199–1200, Sheriff of Hampshire, 1201–4, Sheriff of Shropshire, 1201–4, and, in right of his 1st wife, of Streatley, Berkshire, Amersham and Quarrendon, Buckinghamshire, Pleshey, Essex, Digswell, Hertfordshire, Kimbolton, Huntingdonshire, etc., younger son, born before 1145. Sometime in the period, 1157–66, he witnessed an exchange of land between Roger de Tichborne and the Bishop of Winchester. He held a fee in Cherhill, Wiltshire of new enfeoffment in 1166. Sometime in the period, c.1166–90, Elias de Studley conveyed to him his land held of the fee of William Malbanc in Heytesbury and Cherhill, Wiltshire at an annual rent of 20*s*. In 1184 he accounted for the farm of Kinver before the itinerant justices in Oxfordshire. He married (1st) before 25 Jan. 1184/5 **BEATRICE DE SAY**, daughter and co-heiress of William de Say, of Kimbolton, Huntingdonshire, and Saham, Norfolk [see SAY 4.i for her ancestry]. They had three sons, Geoffrey de Mandeville [5th Earl of Essex], William de Mandeville, Knt. [6th Earl of Essex], and Henry [Dean of Wolverhampton], and two daughters, Maud and Alice. In 1186–7 King Henry II granted him the manor of Cherhill, Wiltshire, to hold in fee and inheritance by the service of one knight, as his father Peter or his brother Robert held it. In the period, 1186–89, he and his two half-brothers, William and Hugh de Buckland, witnessed a charter of William, Earl of Ferrers, to Ralph Fitz Stephen. In the period, c.1189–99, he founded Shouldham Abbey, Norfolk, to which he gave the manor and the advowson of the church of Shouldham, Norfolk, together with the churches of Shouldham Thorpe, Stoke Ferry, and Wereham, Norfolk. In 1190 he obtained the lands to which his wife's grandmother, Beatrice, had become heir on the death of her nephew, William de Mandeville, Earl of Essex. From Easter 1190 he received the third penny of the county of Essex. Sometime in the period, 1190–1213, Sibyl de Fiennes, daughter of Pharamus of Boulogne, conveyed to him 300 acres on Hyngeshill [?in Quarrendon, Buckinghamshire] at an annual rent of an unmewed sparrowhawk, or 12*d*. Sometime in the period, 1190–1213, he granted the manor of Cherhill, Wiltshire to his younger son, William de Mandeville. He was one of those excommunicated for his part in removing Longchamp in 1191. About 1195 he and his half-brothers, William and Geoffrey de Buckland, witnessed a charter of Geoffrey Fitz Nigel de Gardino to William de Ultra la Haia. In 1195 he owed £4 4*s*. in the vill of Lydford, Devon for making the market of the king there. His wife, Beatrice, died in childbed before 19 April 1197. Her body was initially buried in Chicksands Priory, Bedfordshire, but later transferred to Shouldham Priory, Norfolk. In 1198 Eustace de Balliol and his wife, Pernel (widow of Geoffrey's brother Robert), quitclaimed all their right to lands in Salthrop (in Wroughton), Wiltshire to Geoffrey, in return for 30 marks silver. He was present at the Coronation of King John 27 May 1199, where he was girded with the sword of earl. In the period, 1199–1216, Geoffrey gave

Shouldham Priory, Norfolk twelve shops, with the rooms over them, in the parish of St. Mary's Colechurch, London, for the purpose of sustaining the lights of the church and of providing the sacramental wine. Sometime in or before 1199, he made a grant to William de Wrotham, Archdeacon of Taunton, of all his land of Sutton at Hone, Kent to make a hospital for the maintenance of thirteen poor men and three chaplains in honour of the Holy Trinity, St. Mary, and All Saints. He was granted a weekly market and yearly fair at Amersham, Buckinghamshire and Kimbolton, Huntingdonshire in 1200. In the period, 1200–13, he made notification that Abbot Ralph and the convent of Westminster had at his petition confirmed to the nuns of Shouldham all tithes pertaining to them in Clakelose Hundred, Norfolk, in return for £1 10s. due annually to the almoner of Westminster. In the same period, Abbot Ralph and the convent of Westminster granted him the vill of Claygate, Surrey to hold of them for his lifetime. In 1204 King John granted him the manor of Winterslow, Wiltshire, and, in 1205, the honour of Berkhampstead, Hertfordshire with the castle at a fee farm of £100 per annum. Geoffrey married (2nd) before 29 May 1205 (date of grant) **AVELINE DE CLARE**, widow of William de Munchensy, of Swanscombe, Kent, Winfarthing and Gooderstone, Norfolk, etc. (died shortly before 7 May 1204) [see CLARE 4.ii], and daughter of Roger de Clare, Earl of Clare or Hertford, by Maud, daughter and heiress of James de Saint Hilary [see CLARE 4 for her ancestry]. They had one son, John, Knt., and four daughters, Hawise, Cecily, _____, and Maud. He campaigned against the Welsh in 1206 and 1210. He was granted a significant part of the lands forfeited by Normans, including the manors of Depden and Hatfield Peverel, Essex, and other lands in Norfolk and Suffolk, all worth over £100 per annum. In 1207 the king confirmed his possession of the manor of Notgrove, Gloucestershire, which Geoffrey had by the gift of John Eskelling. The same year he was granted a weekly market and yearly fair at Moretonhampstead, Devon. Sometime before 1212, he was granted the manor of Gussage Dynaunt (or Gussage St. Michael), Dorset, which manor was forfeited by Roland de Dinan. At some unspecified date, when already earl, he granted all his right in St. Peter's chapel in Drayton to the canons of St. Peter's Cathedral, York. He was the founder of the first church of Wintney Priory, Hampshire. SIR GEOFFREY FITZ PETER, Earl of Essex, died 14 October 1213, and was buried in Shouldham Priory, Norfolk. In 1213–4 the king commanded Geoffrey de Buckland to let the king have, at the price any others would give for them, the corn, pigs, and other chattels at Berkhampstead, Hertfordshire which belonged his brother, Geoffrey Fitz Peter, lately deceased. About 1214 his widow, Aveline, granted the canons of Holy Trinity, London, in frank almoin, a half mark quit rent out of her manor of Towcester, Northamptonshire, part of whose body is buried there. In 1221 the Prior of the Hospital of Jerusalem in England sued her regarding two virgates and five acres of land in Towcester, Northamptonshire. Aveline, Countess of Essex, died before 4 June 1225.

Blomefield *Essay towards a Top. Hist. of Norfolk* 7 (1807): 414–427. Clutterbuck *Hist. & Antiq. of the County of Hertford* 1 (1815): 293 (Fitz Peter ped.). Montmorency-Morres *Genealogical Memoir of the Fam. of Montmorency* (1817): xxxii–xxxvi. Baker *Hist. & Antiqs. of Northampton* 1 (1822–1830): 544–545 (Mandeville-Fitz Peter-Bohun ped.). Dugdale *Monasticon Anglicanum* 5 (1825): 721–722; 6(1) (1830): 339–340; 6(3) (1830): 1191 (charter of Geoffrey Fitz Peter). Clutterbuck *Hist. & Antiqs. of Hertford* 3 (1827): 190–194 (Mandeville-Say ped.). Luard *Annales Monastici* 2 (Rolls Ser. 36) (1865): 273 (Annals of Waverley sub A.D. 1213: "Obiit Gaufridus filius Petri comes de Essexe, et justitiarius totius Angliæ, tunc temporis cunctis in Anglia præstantior."). *Notes & Queries* 4th Ser. 3 (1869): 484–485 (Fitz Peter ped.). Clark *Earls, Earldom, & Castle of Pembroke* (1880): 76–114. Lee *Hist., Desc. & Antiqs. of ...Thame* (1883): 332 (Mandeville ped.). Maitland *Bracton's Note Book* 2 (1887): 193–194; 3 (1887): 452–453. Round *Ancient Charters Royal & Private Prior to A.D. 1200* (Pipe Roll Soc. 10) (1888): 97–99 (confirmation by King Richard I dated 1191 to Geoffrey Fitz Peter and Beatrice his wife, as rightful and next heirs, of all the land of Earl William de Mandeville, which was hers by hereditary right), 108–110 (confirmation by King Richard I dated 1198 of the division of their inheritance made by Beatrice and Maud, daughters and co-heirs of William de Say, in the time of his father, King Henry II). *Desc. Cat. Ancient Deeds* 2 (1894): 91, 93. Moore *Cartularium Monasterii Sancti Johannis Baptiste de Colecestria* 2 (1897): 349–350, 354, 371–372. *Feet of Fines of King Richard I A.D. 1197 to A.D. 1198* (Pubs. Pipe Roll Soc. 23) (1898): 36–37, 58–59, 85, 130–131. *List of Sheriffs for England & Wales* (PRO Lists and Indexes 9) (1898): 1, 43, 54, 92, 117, 127, 150, 161. *Feet of Fines of King*

Richard I A.D. 1198 to A.D. 1199 (Pubs. Pipe Roll Soc. 24) (1900): 15. VCH *Norfolk* 2 (1906): 412–414. VCH *Essex* 2 (1907): 110–115; 4 (1956): 158–162. Salter *Eynsham Cartulary* 2 (Oxford Hist. Soc. 51) (1908): 224–225. VCH *Hertford* 3 (1912): 81–85, 501–511. *Genealogist* n.s. 34 (1918): 181–189 (two charters of Geoffrey Fitz Peter, Earl of Essex, and two charters of his widow, Aveline, Countess of Essex). *Book of Fees* 1 (1920): 91–92. Fowler & Hughes *Cal. of the Pipe Rolls of the Reign of Richard I for Buckinghamshire & Bedfordshire, 1189–1199* (Pubs. Bedfordshire Hist. Rec. Soc. 7) (1923): 215, 218–219. VCH *Berkshire* 3 (1923): 511–516. VCH *Buckingham* 3 (1925): 141–155; 4 (1927): 100–102. *C.P.* 5 (1926): 122–125 (sub Essex), 437 (chart) (sub Fitz John); 9 (1936):420 (sub Munchensy). VCH *Kent* 2 (1926): 175–176. Foster *Registrum Antiquissimum of the Cathedral Church of Lincoln* 3 (Lincoln Rec. Soc. 29) (1935): 216–218. Gibbs *Early Charters of the Cathedral Church of St. Paul* (Camden Soc. 3rd Ser. 58) (1939): 34–37, 41, 92–93, 255–256. *C.R.R.* 10 (1949): 24, 103, 228. Hassall *Cartulary of St. Mary Clerkenwell* (Camden 3rd ser. 71) (1949): 100–101. *Paget* (1957) 130:5 (see *Genealogist* n.s. 14:181). West *Justiciarship in England, 1066–1232* (1966). Elvey *Luffield Priory Charters* 1 (Buckingham Rec. Soc. 22) (1968): 174–176. Chew & Weimbaum *London Eyre of 1244* (London Rec. Soc. 6) (1970): 118. VCH *Hampshire* 2 (1973) 149–151; 3 (1908): 107; 4 (1911): 79–81. Burton *Cartulary of the Treasurer of York Minster* (Borthwick Texts & Cals.: Recs. of the Northern Province 5) (1978): 52–53 (charter of Geoffrey Fitz Peter, Earl of Essex dated 1199–1212). London *Cartulary of Bradenstoke Priory* (Wiltshire Rec. Soc. 35) (1979): 85, 165–168. Mason *Beauchamp Cartulary Charters* (Pipe Roll Soc. n.s. 43) (1980): 186–187, 189–190, 191 (charter dated 1190–1213 of Geoffrey Fitz Peter, Earl of Essex, to his son, William de Mandeville), 194–197. Holt *Acta of Henry II and Richard I* (List & Index Soc. Special Ser. 21) (1986): 193, 202–203. Mason *Westminster Abbey Charters, 1066–c.1214* (London Rec. Soc. 25) (1988): 308–309 (charter of Geoffrey Fitz Peter, Earl of Essex; charter witnessed by Geoffrey de Bocland. Seal on tag — obverse: earl of horseback, brandishing a sword. Legend: SI[GILLUM GAUFRIDI COMITI]S EXIE +; Counterseal: six-petalled flower (worn); Legend: …IL…ETRI…), 309, 314–315 (charter of Geoffrey Fitz Peter, Earl of Essex). Brand *Earliest English Law Reports* 1 (Selden Soc., vol. 111) (1996): 16–17, 84–91. Turner *Men Raised from the Dust* (1988): 35–70 (biog. of Geoffrey Fitz Peter), App. Chart A (Fitz Peter ped.). *Haskins Soc. Jour.* 1 (1989): 147–172. Franklin *English Episcopal Acta* 8 (1993): 78–79. Ward *Women of the English Nobility & Gentry 1066–1500* (1995): 100–101. Thorley *Docs. in Medieval Latin* (1998): 53–55. Breay *Cartulary of Chatteris Abbey* (1999): 151. Greenway *Book of the Foundation of Walden Monastery* (1999): xxviii–xxx. Norfolk Rec. Office: Hare Family, Baronets of Stow Bardolph, Hare 2706 198 x 4 (available at www.a2a.org.uk/search/index.asp).

Children of Geoffrey Fitz Peter, Knt., by Beatrice de Say:

i. **GEOFFREY DE MANDEVILLE**, Knt., 5th Earl of Essex, Constable of the Tower of London, 1213, Lord of the Honour of Glamorgan, 1214, Joint Marshal of the Army of the Barons, 1215, Governor of Essex for the Barons, 1215, and, in right of his 2nd wife, Earl of Gloucester, son and heir by his father's 1st marriage. He married (1st) **MAUD FITZ ROBERT**, 1st daughter of Robert Fitz Walter, of Little Dunmow, Burnham, and Woodham Walter, Essex, Constable of Hertford Castle, Magna Carta Baron, by his 1st wife, Gunnor, daughter and heiress of Robert de Valoines [see FITZ WALTER 6 for her ancestry]. They had no issue. His wife, Maud, was buried in Dunmow Priory, Essex. He married (2nd) 16/26 Jan. 1213/4 **ISABEL OF GLOUCESTER**, Countess of Gloucester, lady of Glamorgan, divorced wife of King John of England [see ENGLAND 5], and youngest daughter and co-heiress of William Fitz Robert, Earl of Gloucester, by Hawise, daughter of Robert of Meulan, Knt., 1st Earl of Leicester [see GLOUCESTER 4 for her ancestry]. They had no issue. SIR GEOFFREY DE MANDEVILLE, 5th Earl of Essex, was killed in a tournament in London 23 Feb. 1215/6. In 1217 his widow, Isabel, granted to the canons of Holy, Trinity, London for the souls of herself and Geoffrey de Mandeville, Earl of Essex, her late husband, a mark quit rent in the land and dwelling house that Godard de Antiochia held in the parish of St. Lawrence Jewry, London. Isabel married (3rd) c.17 Sept. 1217 (as his 2nd wife) **HUBERT DE BURGH**, Knt., Chamberlain to John, Count of Mortain [future King John], 1198–9, King's Chamberlain, 1199–1205, Earl of Kent [see BARDOLF 8; SCOTLAND 4.iii], son of Walter de Burgh, of Burgh near Aylsham, Norfolk, by his wife, Alice. Isabel, Countess of Gloucester and Essex, died 14 October 1217, and was buried in Canterbury Cathedral Church. HUBERT DE BURGH, Earl of Kent died testate shortly before 5 May 1243. Montmorency-Morres *Genealogical Memoir of the Fam. of Montmorency* (1817): xxxii–xxxvi. Baker *Hist. & Antiqs. of Northampton* 1 (1822–30): 544–545 (Mandeville-Fitz Peter ped.). Dugdale *Monasticon Anglicanum* 5 (1825): 325 (charter of Hubert de Burgh, Earl of Kent; charter witnessed by Walter de Burgh); 6(1) (1830): 74 (gifts by Sir Hubert de Burgh of the churches of Oulton, Norfolk and Badingham, Suffolk to Walsingham Priory); 6(2) (1830): 942 (two charters of Hubert de Burgh). Roberts *Excerpta è rotulis finium in Turri Londinensi asservatis, Henrico Tertio rege* 1 (1835): 405–406, 465. Gilbert *Parochial Hist. of Cornwall* 3 (1838): 350 (charter of Hubert de Burgh, King's Chamberlain). Thorpe *Florentii Wigorniensis Monachi Chronicon Ex Chronicis* 2 (1849): 179 (sub 1243: "Hubertus de Burgo, comes Cantiæ, obiit III. id. Maii [13 Maii]"). Luard *Annales Monastici* 2 (Rolls Ser. 36) (1865): 282 (Annals of Waverley sub A.D. 1215: "Obiit Gaufridus de Mandevilla comes de Essexia."), 289 (Annales de Waverleia sub A.D. 1217: "Obiit Isabel comitissa Gloucestriæ"); 3 (1866): 45 (Dunstable Annals sub A.D. 1214: "… ex quibus miles unus Galfridum de Mandevilla ludendo percussit, et mortuus est. Qui paulo ante guerram Johannam, comitissam Gloucestriæ, repudiatam a Johanne, rege Angliæ (archiepiscopo Burdegalensi divortium celebrante), duxit in uxorem, licet invitus ... Cui sine filiis mortuo, successit Willelmus frater ejus, et relictam ipsius duxit Hubertus de Burgo, justiciarius Angliæ; quæ post paucos dies decessit, et apud Cantuariam sepelitur."), 128 (Dunstable Annals sub A.D. 1232: "Hubertus de Burgo, justiciarius Angliæ, conventus super peregrinatione sanctæ Crucis per literas Papæ, per absolutionem Pandulfi legati tunc Angliæ, se rationabiliter expedivit. Super divortio vero tertiæ uxoris suæ, scilicet filiæ regis Scotiæ, conventus, super eo quod erat consanguinea secundæ uxoris suæ, scilicet comitissæ Gloverniæ ...."). Matthew of Paris *Matthæi Parisiensis* 2 (Rolls Ser. 44) (1866): 477 (sub A.D. 1243: "Et eodem anno, iii°. idus Maii [12 May], post multas, quas in mundo toleraverat patienter, persecutiones, comes Canciæ Hubertus de Burgo, de quo multa præscribuntur, laudabiliter diem clausit extremum apud Banstude, manerium suum. Et delatum est corpus suum tumulandum Londoniis, in domo fratrum Prædicatorum, quibus vivens multa bona contulerat, et corpus veneranter intumulandum delegaverat."). *Notes & Queries* 4th Ser. 3 (1869): 484–485 (Fitz Peter ped.). Lee *Hist., Desc. & Antiqs. of ...Thame* (1883): 331–332 (Mandeville ped.). Doyle *Official Baronage of England* 1 (1886): 685 (sub Essex); 2 (1886): 12–13 (sub Gloucester). *Desc. Cat. Ancient Deeds* 2 (1894): 72, 93. Wordsworth *Ceremonies & Processions of the Cathedral Church of Salisbury* (1901): 24-30, 235 (Obit Kalendar: "9 May — Obijt Hubertus de Burgo, justiciarius Anglie [A.D. 1242]."). *English Hist. Rev.* 19 (1904): 707–711; 50 (1935): 418–432. Parker *Cal. of Lancashire Assize Rolls* 1 (Rec. Soc. of Lancashire & Cheshire 47) (1904): 124–125. VCH *Essex* 2 (1907): 110–115. VCH *Hampshire* 3 (1908): 102–110. VCH *Lancaster* 8 (1914): 77, 85, 189, 192, 207, 231. *C.P.* 5 (1926): 126–130 (sub Essex), 689–692 (sub Gloucester); 7 (1929): 133–142 (sub Kent). Clay *Early Yorkshire Charters* 8 (1949): chart opp. 1, 26–35. Ellis *Hubert de Burgh: A Study in Constancy* (1952). *Viator* 5 (1974): 235–252. Schwennicke *Europaïsche Stammtafeln* 3(2) (1983): 354. Patterson ed. *Haskins Soc. Jour. Studies in Medieval Hist.* 1 (1989): 170 (Fitz Peter ped.). Holt *Magna Carta* (1992): 206–210. Meyer *Culture of Christendom* (1993): 142 (Canterbury Obituary Lists: "14 October [2 Id. Oct.] Obierunt Ysabel comitissa Gouernie, soror et benefactrix nostra"). Turner *Judges, Administrators & the Common Law in Angevin England* (1994): 306 (Fitz Peter ped.). University of Toronto Deed Research Project, #00810076, 00810114, 00810140, 00810141, 00810142, 00810143, 00810144, 00810145, 00810146, 00810147, 00810150, 01400342 (charters of Isabel, Countess of Gloucester and Essex, dated variously 1214–1217) (available at http://res.deeds.utoronto.ca:49838/research).

ii. **WILLIAM DE MANDEVILLE**, Knt., 6th Earl of Essex, of Aylesbury, Buckinghamshire, Moreton Hampstead, Devon, Gussage St. Michael, Dorset, Wellsworth, Hampshire, Berkhampstead, Hertfordshire, Cherhill, Wiltshire, etc., 2nd son by his father's 1st marriage. He married before 18 Nov. 1220 **CHRISTIAN** (or **CHRISTINE**) **FITZ ROBERT**, 2nd daughter of Robert Fitz Walter, of Little Dunmow, Burnham, and Woodham Walter, Essex, Constable of Hertford Castle, Magna Carta Baron, by his 1st wife, Gunnor, daughter and heiress of Robert de Valoines [see FITZ WALTER 6 for her ancestry]. They had no issue. Sometime in the period, 1190–1213, his father granted him the manor of Cherhill, Wiltshire. His wife, Christian, held four fees of the honour of Valoines of the gift of her father, including Lockleys (in Welwyn) and Radwell, Hertfordshire. She granted all her men in the vill of Ashwell, Hertfordshire to Walden Priory in Essex. At an unknown date, she gave part of the lordship of Wolferton, Norfolk to Shouldham Priory. He was heir in 1216 to his older brother, Geoffrey de Mandeville, Knt., 5th Earl of Essex. In 1218 his aunt, Maud de Say, sued him for a moiety share of various manors of the Mandeville inheritance, including Pleshey, Essex, Streatley, Berkshire, Amersham and Quarrendon, Buckinghamshire, Enfield, Middlesex, Compton, Warwickshire, etc. In 1220 he and his wife, Christian, granted the advowson of the church of Westlee, Norfolk to Binham Priory. In 1222 he rebuilt his house at Streatley, Berkshire. In 1223 he was in Wales with the Earl of Salisbury and the Earl Marshal in their campaign against Llywelyn. He was appointed Joint Ambassador to France in 1225. SIR WILLIAM DE MANDEVILLE, 6th Earl of Essex, died testate 8 Jan. 1226/7, and was buried in Shouldham Priory, Norfolk, his heart being buried in Walden Abbey, Essex. In 1227 his widow, Christian, granted all her lands in the vill of Westley (in Westley Waterless), Cambridgeshire, together with the advowson of the church, to Geoffrey de Lanvallay and his mother, Hawise de Buckland [half-sister of Geoffrey Fitz Peter, Earl of Essex]. Christian married (2nd) before 15 May 1227 **RAYMOND DE BURGH**, Knt., of Dartford, Kent, Constable of Hertford Castle, kinsman of Hubert de Burgh, Knt., Earl of Kent. They had no issue. He accompanied the king on the expedition to Brittany in April 1230. SIR RAYMOND DE BURGH was drowned in the Loire at Nantes on or shortly before 1 July 1230, and was buried at the Hospital of St. Mary at Dover. Christian, Countess of Essex, died shortly before 17 June 1232, and was buried with her 1st husband in Shouldham Priory, Norfolk. Blomefield *Essay towards a Top. Hist. of Norfolk* 7 (1807): 419 (charter of Christian de Mandeville, Countess of Essex); 9 (1808): 195–196. Montmorency-Morres *Genealogical Memoir of the Fam. of Montmorency* (1817): xxxii–xxxvi. Baker *Hist. & Antiq. of Northampton* 1 (1822–30): 544–545 (Mandeville-Fitz Peter ped.). Luard *Annales Monastici* 2 (Rolls Ser. 36) (1865): 303 (Annals of Waverley sub A.D. 1227: "Obiit Willelmus de Mandewilla comes Essexiæ."). *Notes & Queries* 4th Ser. 3 (1869): 484–485 (Fitz Peter ped.). *Genealogist* 6 (1882): 1–7. Lee *Hist., Desc. & Antiqs. of ...Thame* (1883): 331–332 (Mandeville ped.). Doyle *Official Baronage of England* 1 (1886): 685 (sub Essex). *Desc. Cat. Ancient Deeds* 2 (1894): 72, 93. Moore *Cartularium Monasterii Sancti Johannis Baptiste de Colecestria* (1897): 201–202, 205–206 (charter dated 1227 of Christian de Mandeville, Countess of Essex, widow, to Geoffrey de Lanvaley son of William and Hawise sister [sororis] of Geoffrey Fitz Peter formerly Justiciar of England), 206–207 (charter dated 1227–30 of Raymond de Burgh confirming grant of his wife, Christian de Mandeville, Countess of Essex to Geoffrey de Lanvalei son of William and his wife Hawise). *Ancestor* 11 (1904): 129–135. *English Hist. Rev.* 19 (1904): 707–711. VCH *Essex* 2 (1907): 110–115, 150–154. VCH *Hampshire* 3 (1908): 107. VCH *Hertford* 3 (1912): 33–37, 73–77, 102–110, 165–171, 199–209, 244–247, 501–511. VCH *Berkshire* 3 (1923): 511–516. *C.P.* 5 (1926): 130–133 (sub Essex). Jenkins *Cal. of the Rolls of the Justices on Eyre 1227* (Buckinghamshire Arch. Soc. 6) (1945): 46, 55. VCH *Hertford* 4 (1971): 426–428. VCH *Cambridge* 5 (1973): 4–16; 6 (1978): 177–182. Mason *Beauchamp Cartulary Charters* (Pipe Roll Soc. n.s. 43) (1980): 191 (charter dated 1190–1213 of Geoffrey Fitz Peter, Earl of Essex, to his son, William de Mandeville). Patterson ed. *Haskins Soc. Jour. Studies in Medieval Hist.* 1 (1989): 170 (Fitz Peter ped.). Turner *Judges, Administrators & the Common Law in Angevin England* (1994): 306 (Fitz Peter ped.). Online resource: www.finerollshenry3.org.uk/content/calendar/roll_025.html.

    iii. **HENRY FITZ GEOFFREY**, King's clerk, 3rd son. He was appointed Dean of Wolverhampton, Staffordshire by the king in 1205. The king granted him a prebend in the diocese of Lincoln in 1207. Sometime in the period, 1213–18, he resigned all his right in the church of Preston to Abbot and convent of Cirencester, Gloucestershire. He died sometime before 1224, when Giles de Erdington occurs as his successor as Dean of Wolverhampton. Baker *Hist. & Antiqs. of Northampton* 1 (1822–1830): 544–545 (Mandeville-Fitz Peter-Bohun ped.). Dugdale *Monasticon Anglicanum* 6(3) (1846): 1443. *Notes & Queries* 4th Ser. 3 (1869): 484–485 (Fitz Peter ped.). Lee *Hist., Description & Antiqs. of ...Thame* (1883): 332 (Mandeville ped.). Ross *Cartulary of Cirencester Abbey, Gloucestershire* 2 (1964): 340 (notification by Henry clerk, son of Geoffrey Fitz Peter formerly Earl of Essex dated 1213–18). VCH *Stafford* 3 (1970): 321–331. Greenway *Fasti Ecclesiae Anglicanae 1066–1300* 3 (1977): 118–150.

    iv. **MAUD DE MANDEVILLE**, Countess of Essex, married (1st) **HENRY DE BOHUN**, Earl of Hereford [see BOHUN 5]; (2nd) **ROGER DE DAUNTSEY**, Knt., of Dauntsey and Wilsford, Wiltshire [see BOHUN 5].

    v. **ALICE FITZ GEOFFREY**, died without issue sometime before 1227. Brand *Earliest English Law Reports* 1 (Selden Society 111) (1996): 84–91.

Children of Geoffrey Fitz Peter, Knt., by Aveline de Clare:

    i. **JOHN FITZ GEOFFREY**, Knt., of Shere, Surrey, Fambridge, Essex, etc., married **ISABEL LE BIGOD** [see VERDUN 8].

    ii. **HAWISE FITZ GEOFFREY**, married **REYNOLD DE MOHUN**, Knt., of Dunster, Somerset [see MOHUN 8].

    iii. **CECILY FITZ GEOFFREY**, married **SAVARY DE BOHUN**, of Midhurst, Sussex [see MIDHURST 3].

    iv. _____ **FITZ GEOFFREY**, married **WILLIAM DE LA ROCHELLE**, of South Ockendon, Essex, Market Lavington, Wiltshire, etc. [see HARLESTON 3].

    v. **MAUD FITZ GEOFFREY**, married (1st) **HENRY D'OILLY**, of Hook Norton, Oxfordshire, King's Constable [see CANTELOWE 4]; (2nd) **WILLIAM DE CANTELOWE**, Knt., of Eaton Bray, Bedfordshire, Steward of the Royal Household [see CANTELOWE 4].

ESTURMY

ALICE OF NORMANDY (sister of King William the Conqueror), married **LAMBERT**, Count of Lens.
JUDITH OF LENS, married **WALTHEOF**, Earl of Northumberland.
MAUD OF NORTHUMBERLAND, married **SIMON DE SENLIS**, Earl of Huntingdon and Northampton.
SIMON DE SENLIS, Earl of Huntingdon and Northampton, married **ISABEL** (or **ELIZABETH**) **OF LEICESTER**.
ISABEL DE SAINT LIZ, married **WILLIAM MAUDUIT**, of Hanslope, Buckinghamshire.
ROBERT MAUDUIT, of Hanslope, Buckinghamshire, married **ISABEL BASSET**.
WILLIAM MAUDUIT, of Hanslope, Buckinghamshire, married **ALICE DE NEWBURGH**.
ISABEL MAUDUIT, married **WILLIAM DE BEAUCHAMP**, Knt., of Elmley, Worcestershire [see BEAUCHAMP 8].

9. MARGARET (or **MARGERY**) **DE BEAUCHAMP**, married by contract dated 1249 **HUBERT HUSSEY** (or **HUSE, HUSEE, HOESE**), Knt., of Figheldean and Stapleford,

Wiltshire, son and heir of Henry Hussey, Knt., of Figheldean and Stapleford, Wiltshire, Tatwick (in Stainswick), Somerset, etc., by his wife, Maud. Her maritagium included the manor of Tidcombe, Wiltshire. He was a minor in 1249. They had three daughters, Margaret, Maud (wife of John le Dun), and Isabel (wife of John de Thorney). SIR HUBERT HUSSEY died shortly before 7 March 1275. In 1278–9 the king appointed commissioners to enquire as to certain unknown evildoers who made an attack upon Margaret and her men at Figheldean, Wiltshire, while they and their possessions were in the king's special protection. In 1278–9 the king likewise appointed commissioners to enquire as to an assault alleged to have been made by Margaret Husee and others at Figheldean, Wiltshire upon Peter Fitz Warin, James de la More, and others. His widow, Margaret, was living in 1284.

Wiltshire Arch. & Nat. Hist. Soc. 2 (1855): 387–389. Roberts *Calendarium Genealogicum* 1 (1865): 352. *Annual Rpt. of the Deputy Keeper* 48 (1887): 74, 163. C.P.R. 1272–1281 (1901): 107. C.F.R. 1 (1911): 227. Clanchy *Civil Pleas of the Wiltshire Eyre 1249* (Wiltshire Rec. Soc. 26) (1971): 82, 109–110, 154. VCH *Wiltshire* 15 (1995): 105–119, 252–263; 16 (1999): 215–222. Wiltshire & Swindon Archives: The Marquis of Ailesbury, 1300/11 (available at www.a2a.org.uk/search/index.asp).

10. MARGARET HUSSEY, daughter and co-heiress, born about 1266 (aged 18 in 1284). She married in 1277 **HENRY ESTURMY**, of Wolfhall (in Savernake) and Burbage, Wiltshire, hereditary Warden of Savernake Forest, Wiltshire, and, in right of his wife, of Figheldean, Stapleford, and Tidcombe, Wiltshire, son and heir of Henry Esturmy, of Wolfhall (in Savernake) and Burbage, Wiltshire, hereditary Warden of Savernake Forest, Wiltshire, by his wife, Aline. They had two sons, Henry and John. HENRY ESTURMY died shortly before 9 Jan. 1310 (date of inventory of goods). In 1316 his widow, Margaret, requested Brother John, minister of Easton priory, to deliver to Henry Esturmy her son a chest closed by a lock and all the muniments therein, and a key, wrapped in a red cloth and sealed with her seal. She died about 1320. He and his wife, Margaret, were buried at Easton Priory, Wiltshire.

Wiltshire Arch. & Nat. Hist. Soc. 2 (1855): 387–389. Roberts *Calendarium Genealogicum* 1 (1865): 352. C.F.R. 1 (1911): 227. Cardigan *Wardens of Savernake Forest* (1949): 21 (chart), 47–48. VCH *Wiltshire* 15 (1995):109, 252–263; 16 (1999): 69–82, 215–222. Wiltshire & Swindon Archives: Savernake Estate, 9/6/754 (available at www.a2a.org.uk/search/index.asp). Wiltshire & Swindon Archives: The Marquis of Ailesbury, 1300/11, 1300/29, 1300/30 (available at www.a2a.org.uk/search/index.asp).

11. HENRY ESTURMY, of Figheldean, Burbage, Cowesfield (in Whiteparish), and Stapleford, Wiltshire, Rushock, Worcestershire, etc., hereditary Warden of Savernake Forest, 1305–38, son and heir. He married **MAUD** _____. They had three sons, Henry, Knt., Richard, and Geoffrey. In 1315 he and other men broke into the Bishop of Salisbury's park at Ramsbury, Wiltshire and slew twelve deer. In 1316 Roger le Hunte, of Durley, Wiltshire, granted Henry and his wife, Maud, one tenement and land in the town of Burbage Sturmy at Durley (in Burbage), Wiltshire. In 1321 his right to the manor of Figheldean, Wiltshire was challenged by his brother, John Esturmy, but the manor was returned to him in 1330. In 1337 he and his son, Henry, and Henry the younger's wife, Margaret, was granted the reversion of a moiety of the manor of Figheldean, Wiltshire by John Torny [Thorney] and Isabel his wife. At an unknown date, he gave the prior and convent of Mottisfont, Hampshire an acre of meadow in the town of Burbage, Wiltshire called le Hachyete in exchange for the annual rent of 2s. due from Henry to the Prior and Convent for the soil on which a small part of Henry's grange of Burbage is situated, and for 9 acres of land which Henry holds of the Prior and Convent in the field called Bovethone in the town of Burbage. HENRY ESTURMY died shortly before 1 Feb. 1338. He and his wife, Maud, were buried at Easton Priory, Wiltshire.

C.F.R. 5 (1915): 64. Pugh *Abs. of Feet of Fines Rel. Wiltshire* (Wiltshire Arch. & Nat. Hist. Soc. Recs. Branch 1) (1939): 109, 119. Cardigan *Wardens of Savernake Forest* (1949): 21 (chart), 81. Elrington *Abs. of Feet of Fines Rel. Wiltshire* (Wiltshire Rec. Soc. 29) (1974): 49–50. Crowley *Wiltshire Tax List of 1332* (Wiltshire Rec. Soc. 45) (1989): 33, 82, 124. VCH *Wiltshire* 15 (1995):109; 252–263, 16 (1999): 69–82, 215–222. Wiltshire & Swindon Archives: Savernake Estate,

9/6/72, 9/6/422 (available at www.a2a.org.uk/search/index.asp). Wiltshire & Swindon Archives: The Marquis of Ailesbury, 1300/11, 1300/30, 1300/59/A (available at www.a2a.org.uk/search/index.asp).

12. GEOFFREY ESTURMY, of Figheldean, Wiltshire, 3rd son. He married an unknown wife, _____. They had one son, William, Knt., and one daughter, _____ (wife of _____ Erleigh).

Cardigan *Wardens of Savernake Forest* (1949): 21 (chart). Roskell *House of Commons 1386–1421* 4 (1992): 520–524 (biog. of Sir William Sturmy/Esturmy).

13. WILLIAM ESTURMY (or **STURMY**), Knt., of Wolfhall (in Great Bedwyn), Burbage, Cowesfield (in Whiteparish), Crofton Braboef (in Great Bedwyn), Huish, Stapleford, and Tidcombe, Wiltshire, and Elvetham, Liss, and Southwick, Hampshire, hereditary Warden of Savernake Forest, Wiltshire, 1381–1417, 1420–7, Knight of the Shire for Hampshire, 1384, 1390, Knight of the Shire for Wiltshire, 1390, 1393, 1400, 1401, 1413, 1414, 1417, 1422, Knight of the Shire for Devon, 1391, 1404, Knight of the Household, 1392, Ambassador to Avignon and Rome, 1397, member of the King's Council, 1401–2, Steward of the Household of Princess Blanche, 1401–2, Amabassador to the Emperor, 1401–2, Speaker of the House of Commons, 1404, Ambassador to Flanders, 1404, Ambassador to Prussia and Hanseatic towns, 1405–7, Chief Steward of the estates of Queen Joan, 1409–1427, Forester of Pewsham, Melksham, and Chippenham, 1416–17, Ambassador to Holland, 1418, Sheriff of Wiltshire, 1418–19, son and heir, born about 1356. He was heir in 1381 to his uncle, Henry Esturmy, Knt. He married in 1382 (date of settlement) **JOAN STOCKHEYE** (or **STOKEY**), widow of John de Beaumont, Knt., of Saunton (in Braunton) and Shirwell, Devon, and daughter and co-heiress of Robert de Stockheye, Esq. They had two daughters, Maud and Agnes (wife of William Ringbourne and John Holcombe). By an unknown mistress, he had one illegitimate son, John. He was retained as a Knight of Household for life in 1392. He accompanied King Richard I on his first expedition to Ireland in 1394–5. In 1397 he was granted a papal indult that he might have chapels and fonts in any castles or manors where he might live. In 1404 he leased the liberty of Kindwardeston and Bedwyn from Queen Joan. In 1420 he was granted lands in Caux in Normandy. SIR WILLIAM ESTURMY died 21 March 1427. He left a will dated 19 March 1427, proved 24 May 1427 (P.C.C. 7 Luffenham). His widow, Joan, died 20 Feb. 1429.

Pole *Colls. towards a Desc. of Devon* (1791): 326, 395, 407–408. Risdon *Chorographical Desc. or Survey of Devon* (1811): 339. Vautier *Extrait du Registre des Dons, Confiscations, Maintenues, et autres Actes* (1828): 102. Maclean *Hist. of Trigg Minor* 2 (1876): 237–238 (chart). VCH *Hampshire* 3 (1908): 161–165; 4 (1911): 84–86. Cardigan *Wardens of Savernake Forest* (1949): 21 (chart), 83, 91, 93–102.. Keene *Survey of Medieval Winchester* 2 (Pts. II & III) (Winchester Studies 2) (1985): 868. Roskell *House of Commons 1386–1421* 4 (1992): 520–524 (biog. of Sir William Sturmy/Esturmy: "He was clearly a man of strong and independent spirit."). VCH *Wiltshire* 4 (1959): 391–433; 15 (1995):109, 252–263; 16 (1999): 8–49, 50–69, 69–82, 149–181, 215–222. Timmins *Reg. of John Chandler Dean of Salisbury 1404–17* (Wiltshire Rec. Soc. 39) (1984): 32–33. Kirby *Abs. of Feet of Fines Rel. Wiltshire* (Wiltshire Rec. Soc. 41) (1986): 71–72. Kirby *Hungerford Cartulary* (Wiltshire Rec. Soc. 49) (1994): 33, 55 (two charters William Esturmy, Knt., of Burbage dated 1393), 55 (deed of William Esturmy, Knt.), 56, 152–153. Wiltshire & Swindon Archives: The Marquis of Ailesbury, 1300/32 (Grant dated 1382 William Esturmy to Sir Henry Esturmy, William Belhamyslond, rector of Hinton [Heantone], John Fouke and William de Haukeford, of manors of Wolfhall and Tidcombe Huse with advowson of church of Tidcombe and 20 a. land there, after seisin, they shall re-enfeoff William Esturmy and Joan widow of John de Beaumont jointly for life, after celebration of their marriage.), 1300/33 (Robert Erleghe styled "kinsman" by Sir William Esturmy in quitclaim dated 1404), 1300/34/A + B (Robert Erle styled "nephew" by Sir William Esturmy in demise dated 1401), 1300/42, 1300/43 (available at www.a2a.org.uk/search/index.asp).

Child of William Esturmy, Knt., by Joan Stockheye:

i. **MAUD ESTURMY**, married **ROGER SEYMOUR**, Esq., of Hatch Beauchamp, Somerset [see SEYMOUR 15].

EU

WILLIAM THE CONQUEROR, King of England, married **MAUD OF FLANDERS**.
ADELE OF ENGLAND, married **ÉTIENNE HENRI**, Count of Blois [see BLOIS 2].

3. GUILLAUME OF BLOIS, Count of Chartres, and, in right of his wife, seigneur of Sully-sur-Loire, eldest son, born about 1087. He married in or before 1104 **AGNÈS DE SULLY**, daughter and heiress of Gilles (or Gilon) de Sully, seigneur of Sully-sur-Loire, by Eldeberge, daughter of Geoffroi IV, Vicomte of Bourges. They had three sons, Archambaud [seigneur of Sully], Henri [Abbot of Fécamp] and Raoul [Prior of Charité, Abbot of Cluny], and two daughters, Marguerite and Elisabeth [Abbess of La Trinité of Caen]. He witnessed a charter of his mother for Conques Abbey in 1101. In 1103 he rashly intruded between his mother and Yves de Chartres in a negotiation concerning a nomination to the cathedral chapter of Chartres. He held the comital title until 1105. In 1107 his brother, Thibaut, took the comital title. GUILLAUME OF BLOIS, seigneur of Sully-sur-Loire, died in 1150.

> Anselme *Hist. de la Maison Royale de France* 2 (1726): 853 (sub Sully), 881. Guizot *Hist. des Ducs de Normandie par Guillaume de Jumiège* (1826): 296–297 (Guillaume de Jumiège, Histoire des Normands, Liv. VIII, Chap. XXXIV: "La quatrième, nommée Adèle, épousa Etienne, comte de Blois, et lui donna quatre fils, savoir, Guillaume, Thibaurt, Henri et Etienne, et une fille. Or Guillaume, leur premier né, fut appelé par son père à l'honneur de gouverneur le pays de Surrey. Sa fille fut mariée a Henri, comte d'Eu, fils du comte Guillaume, quoiqu'ils fussent très-proches parens, et ils eurent de ce mariage trois fils et une fille."). Arbois de Jubainville *Hist. des Ducs & des Comtes de Champagne* 2 (1860): 168–172. Marchegay *Cartulaire du Prieuré bénédictin de Saint-Gondon sur Loire* (1879): 28–29 (After the death of Gilon de Sully, Étienne, Count of Blois confirmed to Saint-Florent, Saint-Gondon a field situated in Sully; after Count Étienne left for Jerusalem, the gifts were confirmed by Adèle wife of the count, then by their son, Guillaume, and by his wife, Agnes de Sully, heiress of Gilon [Willelmus filius comitis Stephani et Agnes filia Gilonis]). Schwennicke *Europäische Stammtafeln* 2 (1984): 46 (sub Blois and Troyes), 3(1) (1984): 110 (sub Sully). Gazeau *Princes Normands et Abbés Bénédictins, Xe–XIIe Siècle* (Normannia Monastica) (2007): 169. Winter *Descs. of Charlemagne (800–1400)* (1987): XII.30, XIII.59–XIII.63.

4. MARGUERITE DE SULLY, married (as his 3rd wife) **HENRI I**, Count of Eu, Count of Eu, lord of Hastings, Sussex, son and heir of Guillaume II, Count of Eu, lord of Hastings, Sussex, by his 1st wife, Beatrice, daughter of Roger de Builli, of Tickhill, Yorkshire. They had three sons, including Jean (or John) [I] [Count of Eu] and Étienne, and one daughter, Mathilde. HENRI I, Count of Eu died as a monk at Foucarmont Abbey 12 July 1140. His widow, Marguerite, died 15 Dec., about 1145, and was buried at Foucarmont Abbey.

> Anselme *Hist. de la Maison Royale de France* 2 (1726): 493–497 (sub Eu), 853 (sub Sully). *L'Art de Vérifier les Dates* 12 (1818): 449–465. Estancelin *Histoire des Comtes d'Eu* (1828). Dugdale *Monasticon Anglicanum* 6(2) (1830): 1016–1017 (undated charter of Henry, Count of Eu to Okeburn Priory; charter witnessed by Count Henry's brother [fratre], William). *Desc. Cat. of the Original Charters, Royal Grants, ... Monastic Chartulary ... constituting Muniments of Battle Abbey* (1835): 29 (charter of Henry, Count of Eu; charter names his deceased wife, Maud). Laffleur de Kermaingant *Cartulaire de l'Abbaye de Saint-Michel du Tréport* (1880): 63–64, 64–65 (charters of Henri II, Count of Eu). *Yorkshire Arch. Jour.* 9 (1886): 257–302. *Recueil des Historiens des Gaules et de la France* 23 (1894): 450 (Ex Obituario ecclesiæ Augensis: "12 July — Anniversarium solemne Henrici, comitis Augi."), 451 (Ex Obituario ecclesiæ Augensis: "15 Dec. — Obiit Margareta, Augensis comitissa, mater Johannis comitis."). *Cartulaire de l'Abbaye de Saint-Martin de Pontoise* (1896): 233 (Obituaire: "IIII Id. [12 July] Ob. Henricus comes Augensis."). Legris *Les Comtes d'Eu* (1908). C.P. 5 (1926): 155–156 (sub Eu). Chibnall *Select Docs. of the English Lands of the Abbey of Dec* (Camden 3rd Ser. 73) (1951): 23 (charter of Henry, Count of Eu, dated c.1106). Sanders *English Baronies* (1960): 119. Schwennicke *Europäische Stammtafeln* 3(1) (1984): 110 (sub Sully). Power *Norman Frontier in the 12th & Early 13th Cents.* (2004): 497 (Eu ped.).

5. JEAN (or **JOHN**) [I], 5th Count of Eu, lord of Hastings, Sussex, hereditary patron of Eu Abbey, son and heir by his father's 3rd marriage. He married **ALICE D'AUBENEY**, daughter of William d'Aubeney, 1st Earl of Arundel, by Alice (or Aleide), widow of King Henry I of England, and daughter of Gottfried (or Godefroy) I, Duke of Brabant [see CLIFTON 3 for her ancestry]. Her maritagium included the manors of Snargate, Bilsington, and Elham, Kent. They had four sons,

Henri (or Henry) [I] [Count of Eu], Henri (or Henry) [Dean of St. Mary's, Hastings), Jean (or John), and Robert, and three daughters, Mathilde (wife of Henry de Stuteville) and Marguerite (possibly wife of _____, seigneur of Saint-Rémy), and Ida (wife of William de Hastings). JEAN (or JOHN) I, Count of Eu, died a monk at Fourcarmont Abbey 26 June 1170, and was buried at Foucarmont Abbey. His widow, Alice, married (2nd) **ALVRED DE SAINT MARTIN**, King's dapifer, living 30 Nov. 1189. They had one son, Adam. He founded Robertsbridge Abbey in 1176. He managed the lands of the king at Neufchâtel in 1180 and 1184. He witnessed a charter of Queen Margaret in 1186. Alice, Countess of Eu, died 11 Sept., in or before 1188, and was buried in Foucarmont Abbey.

Anselme *Hist. de la Maison Royale de France* 2 (1726): 493–497 (sub Eu). *L'Art de Vérifier les Dates* 12 (1818): 449–465. Dugdale *Monasticon Anglicanum* 5 (1825): 667 (charter of Alice, Countess of Eu), 668 (Alice, Countess of Eu, styled "aunt" [amitæ] by William d'Aubeney, Earl of Sussex). Estancelin *Hist. des Comtes d'Eu* (1828). Strickland *Lives of the Queens of England* 1 (1840): 212–256 (biog. of Adelicia of Louvaine). *Recueil des Historiens des Gaules et de la France* 13 (1869): 314 (Ex Roberti de Monte [Robert de Torigni]: "Johannes Comes Aucensis moritur, ei successit ei filius ejus Henricus, quem genuerat ex filia Willermi de Albineio, quem vocant Comitem de Arundel. Hic duxit Aelizam Reginam, relictam Henrici senioris Regis Anglorum, ex qua genuit Guillermum primogenitum suum, et Godefridum, et istam comitissam uxorem Johannis Aucensis, de quo sermo est."). Laffleur de Kermaingant *Cartulaire de l'Abbaye de Saint-Michel du Tréport* (1880): 36–41, 43–45, 51–55, 60, 62–64 (charters of Jean I, Count of Eu). *Yorkshire Arch. Jour.* 9 (1886): 257–302. *Recueil des Historiens des Gaules et de la France* 23 (1894): 440 (Chronique des Comtes d'Eu: "Jehan, aisné fils et hoir du dit Henry, ... espousa une moult noble dame nommée Aaliz, fille au conte d'Arondel en Angleterre, et niepce au vicomte de Rohan."), 449 (Ex Obituario ecclesiæ Augensis: "15 May — Anniversarium solemne Aelidis, comitissæ Augi."), 450 (Ex Obituario ecclesiæ Augensis: "26 June — Anniversarium solemne Johannis comitis."), 452 (Ex Obituario monasterii ulteriores portus: "26 June — Obiit Johannes, comes Augi"). Hall *Red Book of the Exchequer* 1 (1896): 398 (sub A.D. 1166: "Et ipse Pincerna feffavit xij milites in Kent in dominio suo, quos Comes de Hou habet in maritagio cum filia Comitis Arundel …"). Legris *Comtes d'Eu* (1908). Delisle *Recueil des Actes de Henri II, Roi d'Angleterre et Duc de Normandie* (1909): 354–355 (biog. of Alvred de Saint Martin, dapifer). *Misc. Gen. et Heraldica* 4th Ser. 3 (1910): 18–20 (Eu ped.). *C.P.* 5 (1926): 156–158 (sub Eu). Sanders *English Baronies* (1960): 119. Schwennicke *Europaische Stanmtafeln* 3 (1989): 693. Power *Norman Frontier in the 12th & Early 13th Cents.* (2004): 497 (Eu ped.).

6. HENRI (or **HENRY**) **[II]**, 6th Count of Eu, lord of Hastings, Sussex, son and heir, born after 1149 (minor in 1170). He married **MAUD DE WARENNE**, daughter of Hamelin, 5th Earl of Surrey, by Isabel, daughter and heiress of William de Warenne, 3rd Earl of Surrey [see WARENNE 7 for her ancestry]. They had two sons, Raoul (or Ralph) [7th Count of Eu] and Guy, and one daughter, Alice [Countess of Eu]. He was one of the adherents of the younger Henry in the rebellion of 1173 against King Henry II of England. HENRI (or HENRY) [II], 6th Count of Eu, died 16 (or 17) March 1183, and was buried in the choir of Foucarmont Abbey in Normandy. She married (2nd) **HENRY DE STUTEVILLE**, of Barton (in Fabis) and Bradmore, Nottinghamshire, seigneur of Valmont and Rames in Normandy, son and heir of Robert de Stuteville, of Valmont, Rames, etc., by Leonia, daughter and heiress of Edward of Salisbury. They had two sons, John and Robert, and one daughter, Isabel (wife of Peter de Préaux). His wife, Maud, was living in 1212, but died 30 March, before 1228. In 1224–5 the king ordered the Sheriff of Nottingham to take into the king's hand all the lands of Henry de Stuteville in his bailiwick and deliver them to William, Earl Warenne. HENRY DE STUTEVILLE died 5 April, before 1236.

Dugdale *Baronage of England* 1 (1675): 136–138 (sub Ewe). Anselme *Hist. de la Maison Royale de France* 2 (1726): 493–497. *L'Art de Vérifier les Dates* 12 (1818): 449–465. Dugdale *Monasticon Anglicanum* 5 (1825): 668 (charter of Henri I, Count of Eu). Estancelin *Hist. des Comtes d'Eu* (1828): 47–53. Wainright *Hist. & Topog. Intro. ... of the Wapentake of Stafford & Tickhill* (1829): 195–196 (Warenne ped.). Vatout *Souvenirs Hist. des Résidences Royales de France* 3 (1839): 65–72. *Sussex Arch. Colls.* 10 (1858): 63–68 (erroneously identifies Maud, wife of Henry, Count of Eu, as "d. of William of Gloucester."). Aveling *Hist. of Roche Abbey* (1870): xxi–xxii. Laffleur de Kermaingant *Cartulaire de l'Abbaye de Saint-Michel du Tréport* (1880): 63–64, 64–65 (charters of Henri II, Count of Eu). Demay *Inv. des Sceaux de la Normandie* (1881): 6 (seal of Henri, Comte d'Eu). Doyle *Official Baronage of England* 1 (1886): 703 (sub Eu). *Yorkshire Arch. Jour.* 9 (1886): 257–302 (mistakenly identifies wife Maud as widow of Osbert de Preaux). *Recueil des Historiens des Gaules et de la France* 23 (1894): 449 (Ex Obituario ecclesiæ Augensis: "16 March — Anniversarium solemne Henrici, comitis Augi."), 452 (Ex Obituario monasterii ulteriores portus: "17 March — Obiit piæ memoriæ comes Augi Henricus."), 452 (Ex

Obituario monasterii ulterioris Portus — sub 30 March: "Obiit Maltidis, Augensis comitissa, Henrici comitis venerabilis sponsa."). Wrottesley *Peds. from the Plea Rolls* (1905): 518. Legris *Les Comtes d'Eu* (1908). *Misc. Gen. et Heraldica* 4th Ser. 3 (1910): 18–20 (Eu ped.). *Genealogist* n.s. 36 (1920): 1–8. Vernier *Répertoire Numérique des Archives Départementales Antérieures à 1790* 1 (1921): 101. *Rpt. on the MSS of Lord de L'Isle & Dudley* 1 (Hist. MSS Comm. 77) (1925): 36–37 (two charters of Henry, Count of Eu dated c.1180, one charter bearing a seal: fine equestrian figure, shield with an indented border; the other charter bearing the same seal broken), 40–41 (letter to Henry, Count of Eu). *C.P.* 5 (1926): 158–160 (sub Eu). VCH *Sussex* 9 (1937): 1–2. *Early Yorkshire Charters* 8 (1949): 1–26, chart facing 1; 9 (1952): 42, 54–55. Paget *Baronage of England* (1957) 12: 1–6 (sub Aubigny); 199: 1–5 (sub Eu). Sanders *English Baronies* (1960): 119–120. Schwennicke *Europäische Stammtafeln* 3(4) (1989): 693 (sub Eu). Vincent et al. *Acta of Henry II & Richard I* 2 (List & Index Soc. Special Ser. 27) (1996): 80. Power *Norman Frontier in the 12th & Early 13th Cents.* (2004): 497 (Eu ped.). Dryburgh *Cal. of Fine Rolls of the Reign of Henry III* 2 (2008): 1.

7. ALICE (or **ALIX, AALIZ**) **OF EU**, Countess of Eu, Lady of Hastings. She was heiress in 1186 to her brother, Raoul of Eu. She married before 1190 **RAOUL** (or **RALPH**) **D'EXOUDUN** (or **D'ISSOUDUN**), Chev., seigneur of Issoudun, Melle, Chizé, and la Mothe-Saint-Heray, in Poitou, founder of Fontblanche Priory in Exoudun in Poitou, and, in right of his wife, 7th Count of Eu, Baron of Hastings, Sussex, younger son of Hugh de Lusignan (died 1169), by his wife, Orengarde. They had two sons, Raoul (or Ralph) [8th Count of Eu, seigneur of Melle, Chizé, and Civray] and Guarin, and two daughters, Maud and Jeanne (wife of Pierre de Braine, Knt., Duke of Brittany, Earl of Richmond). He joined the crusade in 1189 and was present at Acre in 1190. Upon his return, King Richard I granted him Drincourt castle (now Neufchatel-en-Bray) in Normandy. In 1200 he swore fealty to King John, who gave him the castle of Civray in Poitou. In 1201 King John confiscated his English possessions and his possessions in Normandy and Poitou. Raoul and his brother, Hugh, Count of La Marche, appealed to the King of France, who in 1202 overran the pays of Bray and the comté of Eu, putting him back in possession of his lands in Normandy. In 1209 Alice was subsequently confirmed in the county of Eu by King Philippe Auguste of France, she relinquishing her rights to the castles of Neufchatel, Mortemer, and Arques. The same year Raoul gave his rights on the grange of Soudrain to Noirlac Abbey. He fought at the Battle of Bouvines in 1214 against the French king. In 1214 King John granted Raoul the castles of Tickhill, Yorkshire and Hastings, Sussex with their appurtenances. In 1216 he was appointed Joint Procurator to treat with France. RAOUL D'EXOUDUN, 7th Count of Eu, died at Melle 1 May 1219, and was buried in Fontblanche Priory. In 1220 his widow, Alice, was sued by Robert de Vipont and his wife, Idoine (Alice's distant Builly cousin), for the Castle and vill of Tickhill, Yorkshire, which suit was unsuccessful. In 1224–5 the king ordered the Sheriff of Nottingham to take into the king's hand all the lands of Alice, Countess of Eu, in his bailiwick and deliver them to William, Earl Warenne; the same order was given to the sheriffs of Sussex, Kent, and Yorkshire. In 1225 Alice's uncle, William de Warenne, Earl of Surrey, granted her the manor of Greetwell, Lincolnshire in her widowhood. The same year she disputed the patronage of the church of Buckworth, Huntingdonshire. In 1230 she sued Emma de Bella Fago for two carucates of land in Gunthorpe, Nottinghamshire. In 1238 she gave £18 sterling of annual revenue and various pieces of land to the monks of Foucarmont Abbey in Normandy, in replacement of the tithe that her grandfather, Jean, Count of Eu, gave them from his goods in England. In 1243 King Henry II ordered all his vassals who took the side of King Louis IX of France to forfeit their lands. Alice elected to retain her possessions in France, thereby losing the honour and castle of Tickhill. Alice, Countess of Eu, died at la Mothe-Saint-Heray in Poitou 13–15 May 1246, and was buried in Fontblanche Priory. She left a will dated 1245.

Dugdale *Baronage of England* 1 (1675): 136–138 (sub Ewe). Martene & Durand *Veterum Scriptorum et Monumentorum* 1 (1724): 1137–1138, 1142–1143 (charter of Alice, Countess of Eu). Anselme *Hist. de la Maison Royale de France* 2 (1726): 493–497 (sub Eu). *L'Art de Vérifier les Dates* 12 (1818): 449–465. Dugdale *Monasticon Anglicanum* 5 (1825): 505 (charter of Alice, Countess of Eu, witnessed by her "uncle" [avunculo], Earl William de Warenne), 668 (charter of Raoul d'Exoudun, Count of Eu); 6(2) (1830): 1086 (charter of Alice, Countess of Eu). Estancelin *Hist. des Comtes d'Eu* (1828): 53–59. *Desc. Cat. of the Original Charters, Royal Grants, ... Monastic Chartulary ... constituting Muniments of Battle Abbey* (1835): 42 (charter of Ralph de Isseldun, Count of Eu), 42–43 (charter of Alice, Countess of Eu), 43 (charter of Alice,

Countess of Eu; charter names her late husband, Ralph de Issold, late Count of Eu). Lebon *Mémoire sur la bataille de Bouvines en 1214* (1835): 164. Vatout *Souvenirs Hist. des Résidences Royales de France* 3 (1839): 72–88. *Bulletins de la Société des Antiquaires de l'Ouest* 5th Ser. Years: 1847–9 (1849): 393–394. *Sussex Arch. Colls.* 6 (1853): 107–128 ([Alice], Countess of Eu, styled "niece" [neptis] by William de Warenne, 6th Earl of Surrey, and "kinswoman" [cognate] of Hubert de Burgh, Earl of Kent, in a letter dated pre-1227); 10 (1858): 63–68. Shirley *Royal & Other Hist. Letters Ill. of King Henry III* 1 (Rolls Ser. 27) (1862): 42 ([Alice], Countess of Eu, styled "kinswoman" [cognatæ] by Earl William de Warenne). Teulet *Layettes du Trésor des Chartes* 2 (1866): 261, 570–571 ("… Defuncto vero rege Ricardo [King Richard I], castrum illud devenit ad manum Johannis regis [King John], et tenuit castrum quousque contulit illud Radulpho comiti Augy qui de eodem castro fecit homagium ligium Johanni regi. — Postea vero, de mandato regis Johannis, idem Radulphus comes Augy fecit homagium ligium de eodem castro H. (Hugoni) comiti Marchie fratri suo…"). Aveling *Hist. of Roche Abbey* (1870): xxi–xxii. Delisle *Cat. des Actes de Philippe Auguste* (Bibliothèque de l'École des Chartes 33) (1872): No.1182. *Fourth Rpt.* (Hist. MSS Comm. 3) (1874): 460. *Recueil des Historiens des Gaules et de la France* 18 (1879): (1879): 762 (Chron. of Alberic of Trois Fontaines: "… Iste Hugo fratrem habuit natu majorem Radulphum de Essolduno, quo fuit Comes Augi"). Laffleur de Kermaingant *Cartulaire de l'Abbaye de Saint-Michel du Tréport* (1880): 143 (charter of Alice, Countess of Eu dated 1218 or 1219), 151 (charter of Alice, Countess of Eu dated 1225), 168–169 (charter of Alice, Countess of Eu dated 1231), 196–197 (charter of Alice, Countess of Eu dated 1245). Demay *Inv. des Sceaux de la Normandie* (1881): 6 (seal of Raoul, Comte d'Eu). Delisle *Cartulaire Normand* (1882): 28, 41. Doyle *Official Baronage of England* 1 (1886): 704 (sub Eu). *Yorkshire Arch. Jour.* 9 (1886): 257–302. Prarond *Hist. d'Abbeville: Abbeville avant la Guerre de Cent Ans* (1891): 90. *Recueil des Historiens des Gaules et de la France* 23 (1894): 449 (Ex Obituario ecclesiæ Augensis — sub 1 May: "Anniversarium solemne Radulfi, comitis Augi"; sub 15 May: "Anniversarium solemne Aelidis, comitissæ Augi"), 452 (Ex Obituario monasterii ulterioris Portus — sub 1 May: "Obiit Radulphus, comes Augi."; sub 14 May. "Obiit lis, venerabilis comitissa Augi."). Salzman *Feet of Fines Rel. Sussex* 1 (Sussex Rec. Soc. 2) (1902): 94. Wrottesley *Peds. from the Plea Rolls* (1905): 518. Legris *Les Comtes d'Eu* (1908). *Misc. Gen. et Heraldica* 4th Ser. 3 (1910): 18–20 (Eu ped.), 254–256 (seal of Alice, Countess of Eu, displays Lusignan arms with label of eight points for difference). Davis *Rotuli Hugonis de Welles Episcopi Lincolniensis 1209–1235* 3 (Lincoln Rec. Soc. 9) (1914): 51–52. *C.P.* 5 (1926): 160–166 (sub Eu) (arms of Ralph d'Exoudun: Barry argent and azure, with a label gules for a difference); 10 (1945): 800–805 (sub Richmond). *Genealogist* n.s. 36 (1920): 1–8. Vernier *Répertoire Numérique des Archives Départementales Antérieures à 1790* 1 (1921): 101, 106. *Rpt. on the MSS of Lord de L'Isle & Dudley* 1 (Hist. MSS Comm. 77) (1925): 82–83 (charters of Alice/Aaliz, Countess of Eu dated 1225 with attached seal — a shield of arms: eleven bars with a label of eight pieces) & 97 (charter of Alice, Countess of Eu dated 1241 with attached seal: a female figure, with a lily in her right hand, and a hawk on her left, reverse, a shield of arms: ten bars, a label of 8 pieces, above and below the shield a rose). Gandilhon *Inv. des Sceaux du Berry Antérieurs à 1515* (1933): 37 (seal of Raoul, seigneur d'Issoudun dated 1209 — Type équestre à gauche. L'écu aux armes : un chef.). Landon *Itinerary of King Richard I* (Pipe Roll Soc. n.s. 13) (1935): 98, 111, 117–118, 123, 126, 132, 137, 144. *VCH Sussex* 9 (1937): 1–2. *Early Yorkshire Charters* 8 (1949): 1–26. Langton *Acta Stephani Langton* (Canterbury & York Soc. 50) (1950): 122–123. *Speculum* 30 (1955): 374–384; 32 (1957): 27–47. Churchill *Cal. Kent Feet of Fines* (Kent Arch. Soc. Recs. 15) (1956): 121. Paget *Baronage of England* (1957) 199: 1–5 (sub Eu). Sanders *English Baronies* (1960): 119–120, 147–148. Dibben *Cowdray Archives* 1 (1960): 6–7. Chaplais *Diplomatic Docs.* 1 (1964): 26–27 (Raoul, Count of Eu, styled "cousin" [consanguineo] by Aimery VII, Vicomte de Thouars, in letter dated 1214). *Revue Française d'Héraldique et de Sigillographie* 39 (1971): 11–16 (seal of Alix, countess of Eu). Timson *Cartulary of Blyth Priory* 1 (Thoroton Soc. Recs. 27) (1973): cxxx–cxxxii; 2 (Thoroton Soc. Recs. 28) (1973): 214. Schwennicke *Europäische Stammtafeln* 3(4) (1989): 693 (sub Eu), 815 (sub Lusignan). Van Kerrebrouck *Les Capétiens 987–1328* (2000): 575–576. Power *Norman Frontier in the 12th & Early 13th Cents.* (2004): 497 (Eu ped.). Dryburgh *Cal. of Fine Rolls of the Reign of Henry III* 2 (2008): 1, 35–36, 211, 232–233, 430, 503. National Archives, SC 8/270/13494 (Alice, Countess of Eu, styled "kinswoman" by H[ugues] de Thoart [Thouars] in petition to king and council dated c.1220–2) (available at www.catalogue.nationalarchives.gov.uk/search.asp).

Child of Alice of Eu, by Raoul d'Exoudun, Chev:

i. **MAUD OF EU**, married **HUMPHREY DE BOHUN**, Knt., 6th Earl of Hereford, hereditary Constable of England [see BOHUN 6].

❧ EURE ☙

RICHARD, married _____ **LE BIGOD**.
ROGER FITZ RICHARD, Knt., of Warkworth, Northumberland, married **ALICE DE VERE**.
ROBERT FITZ ROGER, of Warkworth, Northumberland, married **MARGARET DE CHESNEY**.
JOHN FITZ ROBERT, of Warkworth, Northumberland, married **ADA DE BALLIOL** [see CLAVERING 4].

5. HUGH DE EURE (or **EVRE**, **EVERE**), Knt., of Stokesley, Yorkshire, and Kettins, Perthshire, Scotland, younger son. He married **ELLEN** _____. They had one son, John, Knt. In mid-1250 his mother, Ada de Balliol, settled the manor of Stokesley, Yorkshire, with half of that barony, the advowson of fifteen churches, and half of the forest of Bedale, Yorkshire on Hugh and his brother, Robert de Eure. Some months later they granted the manor of Stokesley back to her; she being in possession of the manor at her death in 1251 as farmer of the said Hugh and Robert. In 1267 Hugh purchased the manor of Kirkley (in Ponteland), Northumberland. The same year he acknowledged he was bound to John de Balliol, Knt., to hold him acquitted of £108 sterling, which he [Balliol] bound himself to pay William de Valence, in the said Hugh's behalf. He and his brother, [Master] Stephen de Balliol (or de Eure), clerk, were appointed executors of the will of their uncle, John de Balliol, Knt., who died in 1268. Hugh is mentioned in a deed to Brinkburn Priory in 1269. He was heir in 1271 to his brother, Robert de Eure, Knt., by which he inherited Robert's share of Stokesley, Yorkshire. Hugh was involved in a lawsuit dated c.17 March 1271/2. In 1278–9 Eleanor, widow of Alexander de Balliol, Ralph de Cotum, and two others, executors of the will of Alexander de Balliol, were summoned to respond to Hugh de Eure and Henry Spryng, executors of the will of Hugh de Balliol, in a plea regarding cattle worth £160 which they unjustly detained. In 1278–9 Master Hugh de Wodehall sued him and others in Northumberland regarding a debt. Sometime before 1278–9, Roger Bertram and Guiscard de Charron alienated the manor and carucate of land in Newton, Northumberland to him. In 1278–9 he sued Guiscard de Charron in a plea regarding the warranty of a charter. In 1279 he acted as mainpernor for his first cousin, John de Balliol [afterwards King of Scots]. He was surety for his nephew, Robert Fitz Roger, of Warkworth, Northumberland in 1280. In 1286 he bound himself to Master Walter de Fodringey, Principal, and his Fellows, Scholars of the House called "De Balliolo," Oxford in a sum of £22 10s. 10d., part of £100 due to the executors of the testament of John de Balliol. Hugh was granted free warren in Kirkley, Northumberland in 1291. In the period, 1292–6, as "Hugh de Euer, lord of Ketenes [Kettins]," he granted the Abbey of Coupar Angus his spring in the land of his abthane of Kettins, now in Perthshire. He bought Throphill, Northumberland from Thomas son of Roger Bertram. SIR HUGH DE EURE died in or before 1296. His wife, Ellen, survived him.

Blomefield *Essay towards a Top. Hist. of Norfolk* 5 (1775): 1356–1357. Hodgson *Hist. of Northumberland* Pt. 2 Vol. 1 (1827): 372 (ped.). Ord *Hist. & Antiqs. of Cleveland* (1846): 392–397. *Fourth Rpt.* (Hist. MSS Comm. 3) (1874): 442 (deed of Hugh de Eure and Stephen his brother dated 1287), 443 (deed of Hugh de Euere dated 1267), 444 (deed of Hugh de Euer, Knt. dated 1286), 444. Glover & St. George *Vis. of Yorkshire 1584–5, 1612* (1875): 607–617 (Eure ped.) (identifies wife as ".... dau. of Roger Bertram, baron of Mitford") ("[He] added, as generally alleged, three escallops to the bend. In Baliol College, Oxford, however, exists his seal attached to a deed in which he is a party as executor of John de Balliol, who founded the colleges; and there the bend is without escallops."). Blackburne *Reg. Booke of Inglebye iuxta Grenhow* (1889): xli–xlv. Page *Three Early Assize Rolls for Northumberland* (Surtees Soc. 88) (1891): 262, 301–303, 305, 311, 337, 350, 355, 421–422. Hodgson *Hist. of Northumberland* 5 (1899): 18–32. *Desc. Cat. Ancient Deeds* 3 (1900): 103. St. George & Dugdale *Peds. Rec. at the Heralds' Vis. of Northumberland* (1903): 30–31 (Clavering ped.: "Hugo de Evre a quo Barones de Evre originem ducunt."). *Arch. Aeliana* 3rd Ser. 20 (1923): 69–178 (seal of Hugh de Eure dated 1267: "Dark, green, round, imperfect, 28 mm., armorial quarterly a baston"; seal of Hugh de Eure dated 1280: "Round, a lion rampant."). *C.P.R. 1266–1272* (1913): 603. VCH *Yorkshire N.R.* 2 (1923): 302–303 (Eure arms: Quarterly or and gules a bend sable with three scallops argent thereon). Clay *Extinct & Dormant Peerages* (1913): 53–60 (sub Eure). Dodds *Hist. of Northumberland* 12 (1926): 492–501 (ped.). Oliver *Northumberland & Durham Deeds* (Newcastle-upon-Tyne Recs. Comm. 7) (1929): 77–79. Easson *Charters of the Abbey of Coupar Angus* 1 (Scottish

Hist. Soc. 3rd Ser. 40) (1947): 136–138. Hedley *Northumberland Fams.* 1 (1968): 160–163 (Clavering ped.), 184–191 (Eure ped.). *Genealogists' Mag.* 17 (1972): 86–87.

6. JOHN DE EURE (or **EVER, EUERE**), Knt., of Stokesley, Battersby, Easby (in Stokesley), Ingleby, and Kirkby, Yorkshire, Lynemouth, Northumberland, etc., Sheriff of Yorkshire, 1310–11, Escheator North of Trent, 1313–15. He married before 1301 **AGNES** _____. They had two sons, John, Knt., and Thomas. In 1304 he granted the church of Kirkby, Yorkshire to Whitby Abbey. The same year he granted land at Ingleby Greenhow, Yorkshire to Joan de Percy, Prioress of Basedale. In 1307 he was granted free warren in all his demesne lands at Easby (in Stokesley), Yorkshire. In 1308 Nicholas de Meynill was summoned to answer John de Eure in a plea touching a sum of 6*l*. arrear of annuity payable from the manor of Seamer, Yorkshire. He was appointed to view the Forest of Galtres in 1310, and was assessor of the tallage in Northumberland and Yorkshire in 1312. He was commissioner of oyer and terminer, 1311–17. In 1311 he and his wife, Agnes, had license to alienate lands at Kirkby, Cleveland, Bromby, Stokesley, and Busby to the Priory of St. Andrew's, York. His park at Mitford, Northumberland was broken in 1312. He was in Scotland before 1312, in which year he was acquitted of £12, due from him for amercements, in compensation for his horses lost in the king's service there. In 1313 he was one of those commissioned to view the bridge at Bradley, Yorkshire. In 1317 he was accused of having attacked Louis de Beaumont and two cardinals traveling with him at Akeld, Northumberland. His arrest was ordered 30 Sept. 1317. He had a safe-conduct for his journey south to meet Aymer de Valence in 1318, and in the same year received pardon as an adherent of Lancaster. In 1320 two parts of the manor of Easby (in Stokesley), Yorkshire was settled on him and his wife, Agnes. He took part in the rebellion of Thomas, Earl of Lancaster in 1322, and his arrest was ordered 13 March 1321/2. SIR JOHN DE EURE fought at the Battle of Boroughbridge 16 March 1321/2, and was apparently killed after the battle. His wife, Agnes, married (2nd) **ROGER DE BURTON**, Knt. She was living 13 August 1322.

> Ord *Hist. & Antiqs. of Cleveland* (1846): 392–397 (Sir John [de Eure] ... . There is an elegant impression of his seal appendant to a deed in the Durham Cathedral, dated 15th April, 2 Ed. II. It is engraved in Surtees' *Durham*, pl. x, fig. x, and presents the circumscription, S. JOHIS DE EVRE DOMINI DE STOKESLEY; a shield of arms quarterly; over all a bend charged with three scallops shells, shewing that he and not his father introduced that notable heraldic distinction."). Glover & St. George *Vis. of Yorkshire 1584–5, 1612* (1875): 607–617 (Eure ped.) (identifies wife as "Agnes, dau. of Sir John de Insula [Lisle], knt."). Blackburne *Reg. Booke of Inglebye iuxta Grenhow* (1889): xli–xlv. *C.P.R. 1307–1313* (1894): 400. *Yorkshire Lay Subsidy* 2 (Yorkshire Arch. Soc. Recs. 21) (1897): 29, 36, 41, 55. *List of Sheriffs for England & Wales* (PRO Lists and Indexes 9) (1898): 161. Hodgson *Hist. of Northumberland* 5 (1899): 18–32. *Year Books of Edward II* 1 (Selden Soc. 17) (1903): 34–35; 13 (Selden Soc. 34) (1918): 191–192. Clay *Extinct & Dormant Peerages* (1913): 53–60 (sub Eure). VCH *Yorkshire N.R.* 2 (1923): 302–303. *Durham Monuments* (Newcastle-upon-Tyne Recs. Comm. 5) (1925): 11–12. Dodds *Hist. of Northumberland* 12 (1926): 492–501 (ped.). Hedley *Northumberland Fams.* 1 (1968): 184–191 (Eure ped.). *Genealogists' Mag.* 17 (1972): 86–87. Roper *Feet of Fines for the County of York 1314–1326* (Yorkshire Arch. Soc. Recs. 158) (2006): 56. National Archives, SC 8/6/276 (available at www.catalogue.nationalarchives.gov.uk/search.asp).

7. JOHN DE EURE, Knt., of Stokesley, Yorkshire, and Kirkley (in Ponteland), Northumberland, son and heir, born 18 October 1302 (aged 19 in 1322, aged 24 in 1326). He married before 1340 **MARGARET** _____. They had two sons, Robert and Ralph, Knt. He petitioned for livery of his lands in 1326. He did not receive livery of Kirkley (in Ponteland), Northumberland until 22 Feb. 1358. He obtained restitution of the remainder of his lands in 1360 by payment of a £400 fine. In 1364 he granted all his lands in Yorkshire to his son, Robert. In 1365 David de Strathbogie, Earl of Atholl, sued him regarding the services due from the manor of Kirkley (in Ponteland), Northumberland. SIR JOHN DE EURE died 19–25 March 1368. His widow, Margaret, left a will dated 4 April 1378, proved 27 May 1378, requesting burial in the choir of the church of Preaching Brothers, Newcastle-upon-Tyne, Northumberland.

Glover & St. George *Vis. of Yorkshire 1584–5, 1612* (1875): 607–617 (Eure ped.). Blackburne *Reg. Booke of Inglebye iuxta Grenhow* (1889): xli–xlv. *Arch. Aeliana* 3rd Ser. 6 (1910): 58. Clay *Extinct & Dormant Peerages* (1913): 53–60 (sub Eure). VCH *Yorkshire N.R.* 2 (1923): 302–303. Dodds *Hist. of Northumberland* 12 (1926): 492–501 (ped.) (adds an additional John de Eure to ped.). Oliver *Northumberland & Durham Deeds* (Newcastle-upon-Tyne Recs. Comm. 7) (1929): 173–174. Hedley *Northumberland Fams.* 1 (1968): 184–191 (Eure ped.) (adds an additional John de Eure to ped.). *Genealogists' Mag.* 17 (1972): 86–87.

8. RALPH EURE (or **EVER**, **EVERS**, **IVRE**), Knt., of Witton (in Weardale), Durham, Stokesley, Yorkshire, and Berwick Hill, Darreshall, and Kirkley, Northumberland, Knight of the Shire for Northumberland, 1380, 1381, Justice of Assize for co. Durham, c.1382, c.1401, 1406–7, 1411, 1419–21, Sheriff of Northumberland, 1389–90, 1397–9, Sheriff of Yorkshire, 1391–2, 1395–6, Knight of the Shire for Yorkshire, 1393, 1397, 1399, and, in right of his 1st wife, of Felton, Northumberland, and, in right of his 2nd wife, of Malton and Boughton Spittle, Yorkshire, 2nd son. He was born about 1350 (aged 36 or more in 1386), and was heir c.1369 to his older brother, Robert de Eure. He married (1st) before 6 May 1372 **ISABEL DE ATHOLL**, daughter and co-heiress of Aymer de Atholl, Knt., of Felton, Northumberland, by his wife, Mary [see ATHOLL 13.ii for her ancestry]. They had four sons, Ralph (living 1378), Robert, John, and Hugh, and three daughters, Joan (wife of Thomas Surtees, Knt., and William Hilton, Knt.), Elizabeth (wife of William Claxton, Knt., and John Conyers, Knt.) and Margaret. In 1377–8 Thomas de Hansard and Anastasia his wife granted him their lands at Northtofts in Evenwode. He was appointed ambassador to treat for truces and redress of grievances with the Scots in 1380, 1390, 1400, 1401, 1403, 1404, 1407, and 1415. He fought in Scotland in 1383 and 1385. Ralph married (2nd) before 1385 **KATHERINE ATON**, Knt., daughter and co-heiress of William de Aton, Knt., Lord Aton, by Isabel, daughter of Henry de Percy, Knt., 2nd Lord Percy [see BROMFLETE 12 for her ancestry]. They had two sons, William, Knt., and Robert, and two daughters, Isabel (wife of Peter Buckton) and Katherine. He married (3rd) by dispensation dated 1 Dec. 1400 (they being related in the 4th degree of kindred) **MAUD GREYSTOKE**. In 1405 he sued John de Wytheryngton, Knt. and Robert de Ogle, Knt., regarding a debt of 100 marks. In 1410 he had license from the Bishop of Durham to fortify his principal residence at Witton (in Weardale), Durham. SIR RALPH EURE died 10 March 1421/2. His will was proved 9 Sept. 1422.

Surtees *Hist. & Antiqs. of Durham* 1 (1816): lvii, footnote q. Thoresby *Ducatus Leodiensis* (1816): 19–20 (Eure ped.). Nicolas *Controversy between Scrope & Grosvenor* 2 (1832): 315–317, 347–350. *Testamenta Eboracensia* 3 (Surtees Soc. 45) (1865): 222n. Burke *Gen. Hist. of the Dormant, Abeyant, Forfeited & Extinct Peerages* (1866): 15 (sub Aton). Tate *Hist. of Alnwick* 1 (1866): 406–410 (Aton ped.). Glover & St. George *Vis. of Yorkshire 1584–5, 1612* (1875): 120–121 (Vaughan ped.: "Katherin [de Aton], daughter and co-heir, wife of Ralph Evers."), 607–617 (Eure ped.). Flower *Vis. of Yorkshire 1563–4* (H.S.P. 16) (1881): 111–113 (Eure ped.: "Sir Raff Evers Knight = Kateren doughter and on of theyres of Sir William Atton"). Blackburne *Reg. Booke of Inglebye iuxta Grenhow* (1889): xli–xlv. *List of Sheriffs for England & Wales* (PRO Lists and Indexes 9) (1898): 98, 162. Hodgson *Hist. of Northumberland* 7 (1904): 234–258. *Papal Regs.: Letters* 5 (1904): 378. *List of Inqs. ad Quod Damnum* 2 (PRO Lists and Indexes 22) (1906): 589. *Arch. Aeliana* 3rd Ser. 6 (1910): 67; 3rd Ser. 20 (1923): 69–178 (seal of Sir Ralph Eure dated 1410/11: "Round, armorial, quarterly on a bend three escallops."); 4th Ser. 11 (1934): 65–67; 20 (1942): 55–56. *C.P.* 1 (1910): 325–326 (sub Aton). Clay *Extinct & Dormant Peerages* (1913): 53–60 (sub Eure). VCH *Yorkshire N.R.* 1 (1914): 532–533 (Aton arms: Barry or and azure a quarter gules with a cross paty argent thereon); 2 (1923): 256, 302–303 (Eure arms: Quarterly or and gules a bend sable with three scallops argent thereon). Littledale *Pudsay Deeds* (Yorkshire Arch. Soc. Recs. 56) (1916): 373–376; foldout Pudsay ped. chart. *Yorkshire Deeds* 4 (Yorkshire Arch. Soc. Recs. 65) (1924): 137. Dodds *Hist. of Northumberland* 12 (1926): 492–501 (ped.). Oliver *Northumberland & Durham Deeds* (Newcastle-upon-Tyne Recs. Comm. 7) (1929): 116, 131–132, 259. Harvey et al. *Vis. of the North* 3 (Surtees Soc. 144) (1930): 110–112 (Yvers ped.: "Dominus Radulphus Yvers alias Eure miles [1] = filia Domini Thome Gray, [2] = filia domini Willelmi de Aton") ("The spelling of the name here [Yvers] shows its early form and pronunciation; afterwards it became Evers, later Eurye, and so to the modern inharmonious Eure"). *Cal. IPM* 12 (1938): 112–113; 16 (1974): 2–5. Paget *Baronage of England* (1957) 10: 1 (sub Aton). Hedley *Northumberland Fams.* 1 (1968): 54–60 (Surtees ped.), 184–191 (Eure ped.). *Genealogists' Mag.* 17 (1972): 86–87. VCH *Yorkshire E.R.* 3 (1976): 48. Roskell *House of Commons 1386–1421* 3 (1992): 38–43 (biog. of Sir Ralph Euer).

Child of Ralph Eure, Knt., by Isabel de Atholl:

i. **MARGARET EURE**, married **JOHN PUDSEY**, Knt., of Bolton (in Boland), Yorkshire [see PUDSEY 9].

Children of Ralph Eure, Knt., by Katherine Aton:

i. **WILLIAM EURE**, Knt. [see next].

ii. **KATHERINE EURE**, married **ALEXANDER NEVILLE**, Knt., of Thornton Bridge (in Brafferton), Yorkshire [see THORNTON BRIDGE 14].

9. WILLIAM EURE, Knt., of Witton (in Weardale), Durham, Malton and Stokesley, Yorkshire, etc., Knight of the Shire for Yorkshire, 1422, 1431, 1442, 1449, Sheriff of Northumberland, 1436–7, Steward of Holderness, 1438, Sheriff of Yorkshire, 1444–5, son and heir, born about 1396 (aged 26 in 1422). He married by license dated 25 Jan. 1410/11 **MAUD FITZ HUGH**, daughter of Henry Fitz Hugh, K.G., 3rd Lord Fitz Hugh, Lord High Treasurer, by Elizabeth, daughter and heiress of Robert de Grey, Knt. [see FITZHUGH 7 for her ancestry]. They had six sons, Ralph, Knt., Henry, Esq., William [Archdeacon of Salisbury], John, Thomas, and Robert, and six daughters, Joan, Margery, Elizabeth (wife of John Hotham, Knt.), Isabel, Katherine (wife of Robert Ughtred, Knt.), and Joan (wife of Robert Ogle, Knt., and John Pennington). He was at the Battle of Agincourt in 1415 in the retinue of his father-in-law, Henry Fitz Hugh, Lord Fitz Hugh. His wife, Maud, was a legatee in the 1427 will of her mother. In 1431 he had license to crenellate the manor of Bradley, Durham. In 1431–2 he had license to settle the fortalice and manor of Bermetonhall (in Wotton) and lands in Escome on himself and his wife, Maud. In 1434 he was sent as a commissioner to treat with the Scots. In 1437 he was required to post surety of the peace in £2,000, he having threatened Thomas, Bishop of Durham with "death and maiming." In 1442 he was one of those ordered by the Privy Council to keep the seas. SIR WILLIAM EURE was living 12 August 1461, but died before 12 Feb. 1466/7 (date of his wife's will). His widow, Maud, left a will dated 12 Feb. 1466/7, proved 30 May 1467. They were buried in the chancel of Malton Abbey, Yorkshire.

Surtees *Hist. & Antiqs. of Durham* 1 (1816): lvii, footnote q. Thoresby *Ducatus Leodiensis* (1816): 19–20 (Eure ped.). *Wills & Invs.* 1 (Surtees Soc. 2) (1835): 74–75. *Testamenta Eboracensia* 2 (Surtees Soc. 30) (1855): 284–286 (will of Maud Eure); 3 (Surtees Soc. 45) (1865): 221n., 375 (abs. of license to marry). *Annual Rpt. of the Deputy Keeper* 33 (1872): 135. Glover & St. George *Vis. of Yorkshire 1584–5, 1612* (1875): 204–205 (Eure ped.: "Sir William Eure, Knt., superstites 17 Hen. VI = Maude, daughter and co-heir of Henry, Lord Fitzhugh"), 607–617 (Eure ped.). Flower *Vis. of Yorkshire 1563–4* (H.S.P. 16) (1881): 111–113 (Eure ped.: "Sir Edward [recte William] Evers, Knight, son & heyre to Sir Raff = Mawde, doughter to the Lord Fytzhugh"). Blackburne *Reg. Booke of Inglebye iuxta Grenhow* (1889): xli–xlv. *List of Sheriffs for England & Wales* (PRO Lists and Indexes 9) (1898): 98, 162. Clay *Extinct & Dormant Peerages* (1913): 53–60 (sub Eure), 72–75 (sub Fitz Henry). VCH *Yorkshire N.R.* 1 (1914): 532–533; 2 (1923): 303. Saltmarshe *Hist. & Chartulary of the Hothams of Scarborough* (1914): 76–81. *Arch. Aeliana* 3rd Ser. 20 (1923): 69–178 (seal of Sir William Eure dated 1423: "Round, armorial, quarterly on a bend three escallops."). Dodds *Hist. of Northumberland* 12 (1926): 492–501 (ped.). Oliver *Northumberland & Durham Deeds* (Newcastle-upon-Tyne Recs. Comm. 7) (1929): 177. Harvey et al. *Vis. of the North* 3 (Surtees Soc. 144) (1930): 110–112 (Yvers ped.: "Dominus Willelmus Yvers miles = Matildis filia domini Fitzhugh"), 132–133 (Fitzhugh ped.: "Matildis [Fitzhugh] nupta domino Willelmo Yvers"). Gooder *Parl. Representation of York* 1 (Yorkshire Arch. Soc. Recs. 91) (1935): 180–182 (biog. William Eure). Wedgwood *Hist. of Parl.* 1 (1936): 306 (biog. of Sir William Eure). *Arch. Aeliana* 4th Ser. 20 (1942): 64. Walker *Yorkshire Peds.* 3 (H.S.P. 96) (1944): 400–402 (Ughtred ped.). Langley *Reg. of Thomas Langley Bishop of Durham* 3 (Surtees Soc. 169) (1959): 62–64. Hedley *Northumberland Fams.* (1968): 184–191 (Eure ped.).

Children of William Eure, Knt., by Maud Fitz Hugh:

i. **RALPH EURE**, Knt. [see next].

ii. **THOMAS EURE**, of Shotton, co. Durham, married **MARGARET DANBY** [see GRIMSTON 10].

iii. **ROBERT EURE**, married **ANNE TEMPEST** [see STRANGEWAYS 10].

iv. **MARGERY EURE**, married **CHRISTOPHER CONYERS**, Knt., of Sockburn, Durham [see SURTEES 15].

iv. **ISABEL EURE**, married **JOHN LANGTON**, Esq. [see LANGTON 18].

10. RALPH EURE, Knt., of Malton and Stokesley, Yorkshire, son and heir. He married **ELEANOR GREYSTOKE**, daughter of John Greystoke, Knt., 4th Lord Greystoke, of Greystoke, Cumberland, by Elizabeth, daughter of Robert Ferrers, Knt., 2nd Lord Ferrers of Wem [see GREYSTOKE 13 for her ancestry]. They had six sons, William, Knt., John, Hugh, LL.D. (clerk), Ralph, Henry, and Robert, Knt., and six daughters, Elizabeth (wife of John Ellerker), Joan, Margaret (nun at Watton), Joan (again), Maud, and Anne (wife of Thomas Rokeby). SIR RALPH EURE was slain at Towton Field 9 March 1461/2.

> Thoresby *Ducatus Leodiensis* (1816): 19–20 (Eure ped.). *Coll. Top. et Gen.* 2 (1835): 160–161 (Greystock ped.: "Alienor [Greystock], mar. to Sir Ralph Yvers [or Ewers]"). Glover & St. George *Vis. of Yorkshire 1584–5, 1612* (1875): 204–205 (Eure ped.: "Sir Ralph Eure, Knt., 17 Hen. VI. = Ellinor, daughter to John, Baron of Greystock"), 607–617 (Eure ped.). Flower *Vis. of Yorkshire 1563–4* (H.S.P. 16) (1881): 111–113 (Eure ped.: "Sir Raff Evers, Knight, slene on Palme Sunday at Towton Fyld in A[nn]o primo Edw. IV. 1461. = Elenor daughter of John the Baron of Grestoke"), 151 (Grestoke ped.: "Alianora [Grestoke] nupta Domino Radulpho Ivers"). Rokeby *Œconomia Rokebiorum* (Northern Notes & Queries 1 Supp.) (1887): 31–32 (Rokeby ped.: "Thomas Rokeby Kᵗ Married Sʳ Ralph Uries Daughter"). Blackburne *Reg. Booke of Inglebye iuxta Grenhow* (1889): xli–xlv. Harvey et al. *Vis. of the North* 1 (Surtees Soc. 122) (1912): 124–127 (Eure ped.: "Sir Raufe Eure slayne on palmesondaye ffyelde [at Towton A. primo E. 4 (1461) weddyd [Elianor, doughter to the baron of Greystocke]"); 3 (Surtees Soc. 144) (1930): 23–32 (Neville ped.: "Aleonora [Greystoke] nupta domino Radulpho Ivers militi"), 110–112 (Yvers ped.: "Dominus Radulphus Yvers = Aleonora filia baronis domini de Graystock"), 139–141 (Greystoke ped.: "Aleonora [Greystoke] nupta domino Radulpho Yvers militi"). Clay *Extinct & Dormant Peerages* (1913): 53–60 (sub Eure), 95–98 (sub Greystoke). VCH *Yorkshire N.R.* 1 (1914): 532–533 (Eure arms: Quarterly or and gules a bend sable with three scallops argent thereon); 2 (1923): 303. Dodds *Hist. of Northumberland* 12 (1926): 492–501 (ped.). Harvey et al. *Vis. of the North* 3 (Surtees Soc. 144) (1930): 23–32 (Neville ped.: "Aleonora [Graystok] nupta domino Radulpho Ivers militi"), 110–112 (Yvers ped.: "Dominus Radulphus Yvers = Aleonora filia baronis *domini* de Graystock").

11. WILLIAM EURE, Knt., of Malton and Stokesley, Yorkshire, Sheriff of Yorkshire, 1482–3, son and heir. He married (1st) **MARGARET CONSTABLE**, daughter of Robert Constable, Knt., of Flamborough, Yorkshire, by Agnes, daughter of Roger Wentworth, Esq. [see CONSTABLE 16 for her ancestry]. They had three sons, Ralph, Knt., Robert, Knt., and William (clerk), and six daughters, Anne, Margaret (nun), Agnes, Anne (2nd of name), Elizabeth, and Mary. He was a legatee in the 1476 will of his uncle, Henry Eure, Esq., who bequeathed him a gray horse called "lierd Dale." He married (2nd) before 3 July 1497 by dispensation (they being twice related in the 3rd degree of kindred) **CONSTANCE** _____, widow of Henry Percy, Knt., of Bamburgh, Northumberland. They had three sons, Henry, John, and Eustace.

> Thoresby *Ducatus Leodiensis* (1816): 19–20 (Eure ped.). *Testamenta Eboracensia* 3 (Surtees Soc. 45) (1865): 222–225 (will of Henry Eure, Esq.). Glover & St. George *Vis. of Yorkshire 1584–5, 1612* (1875): 204–205 (Eure ped.: "Sir William Eure, Knt. = Margaret, daughter to Sir Robert Constable, of Flamborough"), 607–617 (Eure ped.). Flower *Vis. of Yorkshire 1563–4* (H.S.P. 16) (1881): 111–113 (Eure ped.: "Sir William Evers, Knight, son & heyr of Sir Raff, [1] = Margaret daughter of the old Sir Robert Counstable of Flamborough, [2] = Constance daughter of [left blank] late wyff to Sir Henry Percy of Bamborough base son"). Blackburne *Reg. Booke of Inglebye iuxta Grenhow* (1889): xli–xlv. *List of Sheriffs for England & Wales* (PRO Lists and Indexes 9) (1898): 162. Dugdale *Dugdale's Vis. of Yorkshire* 2 (1907): 287–294 (sub Constable). Harvey et al. *Vis. of the North* 1 (Surtees Soc. 122) (1912): 124–127 (Eure ped.: "Sir Wyllyam Eure, knight, weddyd Mergarett, doughtre to olde Sir Roberte Cunstable of Flaumborowghe"); 3 (Surtees Soc. 144) (1930): 110–112 (Yvers ped.: "Dominus Willelmus Yvers miles = Margeria filia domini Roberti Constable militis"). Clay *Extinct & Dormant Peerages* (1913): 53–60 (sub Eure). VCH *Yorkshire N.R.* 1 (1914): 532–533; 2 (1923): 303. Dodds *Hist. of Northumberland* 12 (1926): 492–501 (ped.).

12. RALPH EURE (or **EVERS**), Knt., of Ayton (in Pickering Lythe), Malton, and Stokesley, Yorkshire, Witton (in Weardale), Durham, and Abberwick (in Edlingham), Northumberland, Sheriff of Northumberland, 1502–3, Sheriff of Yorkshire, 1505–6, 1510–11, son and heir by his father's 1st marriage. He married (1st) at Fenwick, Yorkshire by license dated 18 Jan. 1481/2 **MURIEL HASTINGS**, daughter of Hugh Hastings, Knt., *de jure* Lord Hastings, of Fenwick, Yorkshire and Elsing, Norfolk, by Anne, daughter of William Gascoigne, Knt. [see ELSING 16 for her ancestry]. They had three sons, William, Knt. [1st Lord Eure], John, and Hugh. He married (2nd) by license dated 18 Jan. 1515/16 **AGNES CONSTABLE**, widow of Ralph Bigod, Knt., and daughter of Robert Constable, of Dromonby in Cleveland. They had three daughters, Frances (wife of George Conyers, Knt.), Jane (wife of Henry Pudsey, Knt., and Thomas Williamson), and Margery (wife of Francis Salvin, Knt.). SIR RALPH EURE died testate 22 October 1539 (will requesting burial at Hutton Bushell (in Pickering), Yorkshire).

> Thoresby *Ducatus Leodiensis* (1816): 19–20 (Eure ped.). *Gentleman's Mag.* 2 (1865): 622–627. *Testamenta Eboracensia* 3 (Surtees Soc. 45) (1865): 345–346 (abs. of license to marry); 6 (Surtees Soc. 106) (1902): 183 (his will). Glover & St. George *Vis. of Yorkshire 1584–5, 1612* (1875): 204–205 (Eure ped.: "Sir Ralph Eure, Knt. = Muriel, daughter to Sir Hugh Hastings, of Fenwick"), 372–373 (Hastings ped.: "Muriell [Hastings], mar. to Sir Ralph Evers, father to William, Lord Evers."), 607–617 (Eure ped.). Flower *Vis. of Yorkshire 1563–4* (H.S.P. 16) (1881): 111–113 (Eure ped.: "Sir Raff Evers, Knight, son & heyr to Sir William, [1] = Meryell doughter of Sir Hugh Hastyngs of Fenwyke besyde Hatfeld in Yorkshire, [2] = Agnes doughter to… Counstable of Dromondby besyde Stokesley in Cleveland in Yorkshire"), 154–156 (Hastynges ped.: "Meryell [Hastynges] wyff to Sir Raff Evers"). Blackburne *Reg. Booke of Inglebye iuxta Grenhow* (1889): xli–xlv. *List of Sheriffs for England & Wales* (PRO Lists and Indexes 9) (1898): 98, 163. Harvey et al. *Vis. of the North* 1 (Surtees Soc. 122) (1912): 124–127 (Eure ped.: "Sir Rauphe Eure wedydd fyrst Meryell, doughtre to Sir Hughe Hastinge of Fenwycke beside Hatfyld in Yorkeshire"); 3 (Surtees Soc. 144) (1930): 110–112 (Yvers ped.). Clay *Extinct & Dormant Peerages* (1913): 53–60 (sub Eure). VCH *Yorkshire N.R.* 1 (1914): 532–533; 2 (1923): 303. Dodds *Hist. of Northumberland* 12 (1926): 492–501 (ped.). Oliver *Northumberland & Durham Deeds* (Newcastle-upon-Tyne Recs. Comm. 7) (1929): 255. Rotherham *Reg. of Thomas Rotherham Archbishop of York* 1 (Canterbury & York Soc. 69) (1976): 13.

13. WILLIAM EURE, Knt., of Witton (in Weardale), Durham, Malton and Stokesley, Yorkshire, etc., Sheriff of Durham, 1519–23, Sheriff of Northumberland, 1526–7, Lieutenant of the Middle Marches, Marshal of the army for the rear against Scotland, Warden of the East Marches towards Scotland, Captain of Berwick Castle, son and heir by his father's 1st marriage, born about 1483. He married about 1503 **ELIZABETH WILLOUGHBY**, daughter of Christopher Willoughby, Knt., *de jure* 10th Lord Willoughby of Eresby, by Margaret, daughter of William Jenney, Knt. [see WILLOUGHBY 14 for her ancestry]. She was born about 1483. They had three sons, Ralph, Knt., John, and Henry, Esq., and three daughters, Margery (wife of William Buckton), Muriel, and Anne (wife of Anthony Thorpe). He was created Lord Eure by letters patent dated 24 Feb. 1543/4. He was summoned to Parliament 1 Dec. 1544, by writ directed *Willelmo domino Ewers chivaler*. His late wife, Elizabeth, was mentioned in the 1544 will of her brother, Thomas Willoughby, Knt. SIR WILLIAM EURE, 1st Lord Eure, died testate at Eresby, Lincolnshire 15 March 1547/8.

> Brydges *Collins' Peerage of England* 6 (1812): 591–619 (sub Bertie, Baroness Willoughby of Eresby). Thoresby *Ducatus Leodiensis* (1816): 19–20 (Eure ped.). Burke *Gen. Hist. of the Dormant, Abeyant, Forfeited & Extinct Peerages* (1866): 586–588 (sub Willoughby). Mundy et al. *Vis. of Nottingham 1569 & 1614* (H.S.P. 4) (1871): 184–185 (Willoughby ped.: "Elizebeth [Willoughby] ux. William the 1 Lord Evers"). Glover & St. George *Vis. of Yorkshire 1584–5, 1612* (1875): 204–205 (Eure ped.: "Sir William Eure, 1st Lord Eure = Elizabeth, daughter to Christopher, Lord Willoughby, of Eresby"), 607–617 (Eure ped.). Flower *Vis. of Yorkshire 1563–4* (H.S.P. 16) (1881): 110–114 (Evre ped.: "Sir William Evers, Fyrst Lord Evers = Elsabeth doughter to Crystofer Lord Wylloby and syster to William Lord Wylloby, Father to the Duchess of Suffolk"). Blackburne *Reg. Booke of Inglebye iuxta Grenhow* (1889): xli–xlv. *List of Sheriffs for England & Wales* (PRO Lists and Indexes 9) (1898): 42, 98. Hodgson *Hist. of Northumberland* 5 (1899): 243 (Eure ped.). *Testamenta Eboracensia* 6 (Surtees Soc. 106) (1902): 185. Harvey et al. *Vis. of the North* 1 (Surtees Soc. 122) (1912): 52 (Eure ped.: "Wylliam, fyrst Lord Eure, maryed the daughter to the Lord Wylloughby"), 124–127 (Eure ped.: "William the Lorde Eure, capteyne of the towne and castle of Berwyck and warden of thest marches, weddyd Elizabeth, sustre to William, Lord Wyllowghbye, father to the Dutchesse of Suffolke, doughtre to Sir Christopofer"). Clay *Extinct & Dormant Peerages* (1913): 53–60 (sub Eure). VCH *Yorkshire N.R.* 1 (1914): 532–533; 2 (1923): 303. Benolte & Cooke *Vis. of Kent 1530–1, 1574 & 1592* 2 (H.S.P. 75) (1924): 48 (1574 Vis.) (Willoughby ped.: "Elizabeth [Willoughby] maried to William the first Lord Euers"). *C.P.* 5 (1926): 180–181 (sub Eure). Dodds *Hist. of Northumberland* 12 (1926): 492–501 (ped.). Will of Thomas Willoughby, Knt., of Chiddingstone, Kent dated 20 July 1544, proved 5 Nov. 1545 (P.C.C. 40 Pynnyng).

Children of William Eure, Knt., by Elizabeth Willoughby:

i. **RALPH EURE**, Knt. [see next].

ii. **MURIEL EURE**, married (1st) **GEORGE BOWES**, Knt., of Streatlam, Durham [see BOWES 17]; (2nd) **WILLIAM WYCLIFFE**, Esq., of Wycliffe, Yorkshire [see BOWES 17].

14. RALPH EURE, Knt., of Foulbridge (in Brompton), Yorkshire, deputy Constable of Scarborough Castle, 1531–7, Justice of the Peace for Yorkshire (East Riding), 1536–45, Burgess (M.P.) for Scarborough, 1542, Keeper of Redesdale and Tynedale, ?1542–1545, deputy Warden of the Middle Marches by August 1543, Warden of the Middle Marches, 1544–5, son and heir apparent, born about 1510. He married before 1529 **MARGERY BOWES**, daughter of Ralph Bowes, Knt., of Streatlam and Dalden, Durham, by Elizabeth, daughter of Henry Clifford, K.B., 10th Lord Clifford [see BOWES 16 for her ancestry]. They had three sons, William, Knt. [2nd Lord Eure],[20] Ralph, and Thomas, and two daughters, Frances (wife of Robert Lambton) and Anne. SIR RALPH EURE was slain at the Battle of Ancrum Moor 6 March 1544/5, and was buried at Melrose Abbey. His widow, Margery, was a legatee in the 1566/7 will of Elizabeth Hutton, widow.

> Thoresby *Ducatus Leodiensis* (1816): 19–20 (Eure ped.). *Wills & Invs.* 1 (Surtees Soc. 2) (1835): 249. Surtees *Hist. & Antiqs. of Durham* 4 (1840): 107 (chart). Burke *Burke's Gen. & Heraldic Hist. of the Landed Gentry* 1 (1847): 128–129 (sub Bowes). Mundy et al. *Vis. of Nottingham 1569 & 1614* (H.S.P. 4) (1871): 184–185 (Willoughby ped.: "Elizabeth [Willoughby] ux. William the 1 Lord Evers"). Glover & St. George *Vis. of Yorkshire 1584–5, 1612* (1875): 607–617 (Eure ped.). Flower *Vis. of Yorkshire 1563–4* (H.S.P. 16) (1881): 31–32 (Bowes ped.: "Margaret [Bowes] = Sir Raff Ewry alias Evers"), 113–114 (Evre ped.: "Sir Raff Evers, Knight, slene in his father's lyef time in Scotland = Margery doughter to Sir Raff Bowes of the North"). Glover & St. George *Vis. of Yorkshire 1584–5, 1612* (1875): 204–205 (Eure ped.: "Sir Ralph Eure, Knt., slain in West Tivedale, by the Earl of Arrayne, in his father's lifetime = Margery, dau. to Sir Ralph Bowes, of Stretlam"). Blackburne *Reg. Booke of Inglebye iuxta Grenhow* (1889): xli–xlv. Hodgson *Hist. of Northumberland* 5 (1899): 243 (Eure ped.). Harvey et al. *Vis. of the North* 1 (Surtees Soc. 122) (1912): 52 (Eure ped.: "Sir Rafe Eure, son and heyre to William, Lord Eure, which dyed before hys father, maryed Margery, dowghter to Syr Raff Bowes"), 124–127 (Eure ped.: "Sir Rauphe Eure, knight, son and heyre to the Lorde William Eure, wedyd Margerye, doughtre to Sir Rauphe Bowes, knight, the yonger"), 130–131 (Bowes ped.: "Margerye [Bowes], wyefe to Sir Raufe Eure"). Clay *Extinct & Dormant Peerages* (1913): 53–60 (sub Eure). VCH *Yorkshire N.R.* 1 (1914): 532–533; 2 (1923): 303. Dodds *Hist. of Northumberland* 12 (1926): 492–501 (ped.). *C.P.* 5 (1926): 181 (sub Eure). Bindoff *House of Commons 1509–1558* 2 (1982): 109–110 (biog. of Sir Ralph Eure).

15. ANNE EURE married (as his 1st wife) **LANCELOT MANSFIELD** (or **MANFIELD**), Esq., of Skirpenbeck, Yorkshire. They had two sons, John, Gent., and Ralph, and three daughters, Julian (wife of Thomas Hassell), Margaret (wife of Richard Heslarton, Gent.) and Lucy (wife of George Wilkinson, Gent.). He married (2nd) **MARGARET** _____. They had no issue. LANCELOT MANSFIELD was living 20 Sept. 1563. His widow, Margaret, left a will dated 17 Jan. 1596/7, proved 13 April 1597.

> Thoresby *Ducatus Leodiensis* (1816): 19–20 (Eure ped.). Glover & St. George *Vis. of Yorkshire 1584–5, 1612* (1875): 204–205 (Eure ped.: "Anne [Eure], wife of Lancelot Mirfield [sic]"), 607–617 (Eure ped.). Flower *Vis. of Yorkshire 1563–4* (H.S.P. 16) (1881): 113–114 (Eure ped.: "Anne [Eure] = Launcelot Myrfeld"). Harvey et al. *Vis. of the North* 1 (Surtees Soc. 122) (1912): 52 (Eure ped.), 124–127 (Eure ped.: "Anne Eure, wyef to Launcelott Myrefyld [sic] of Yorkeshere"). Clay *Extinct & Dormant Peerages* (1913): 53–60 (sub Eure). Dodds *Hist. of Northumberland* 12 (1926): 492–501 (ped.). *NEHGR* 155 (2001): 3–35.

16. JOHN MANSFIELD, Esq., of London, Henley-on-Thames, Oxfordshire, and Hutton-on-Derwent, Yorkshire, Burgess (M.P.) for Beverley, Yorkshire, Queen's surveyor. He matriculated pensioner from St. John's College, Cambridge, at Michaelmas 1568, migrating to Peterhouse in 1572, where he received a B.A. degree in 1572–3, and was a scholar in 1573–5. He entered the Inner Temple by special admission 2 June 1583. He married (1st) **MARY HOBSON**, daughter of William Hobson, of St. Botolph Billingsgate, London, fishmonger. His wife, Mary, was living in

---

[20] Ancestor of **Frances Walker** (living 1735/6), wife of Thomas Bannister, of Boston, Massachusetts (shipwrecked 13 Sept. 1716). For further particulars of this line of descent, see *NEHGR* 165 (2011): 84–99, 206–222 (article by Nathaniel Lane Taylor et al.).

1587. He married (2nd) before 3 Feb. 1591/2 **ELIZABETH** _____. They had one son, John, and three daughters, Elizabeth, Anne, and Martha. JOHN MANSFIELD, Esq., left a will dated 13 July 1601, proved 31 July 1601. His widow, Elizabeth, was buried at St. Michael Cornhill, London 10 Feb. 1633/4. Administration on her estate was granted 12 Feb. 1633/4 to her daughter, Anne Keayne.

Cal. MSS in Various Colls. 8 (Hist. MSS Comm. 55) (1913): 2. Venn & Venn *Alumni Cantabrigiensis to 1751* 3 (1924): 133. Hasler *House of Commons 1558–1603* 3 (1981): 313 (biog. of John Mansfield). *NEHGR* 155 (2001): 3–35.

Children of John Mansfield, Esq., by Elizabeth _____:

i. **ELIZABETH MANSFIELD**, baptized at Henley-on-Thames, Oxfordshire 3 Dec. 1592. She married about 1617 [**Rev.**] **JOHN WILSON**, minister, son of [Rev.] William Wilson, D.D., Rector of Islip, Oxfordshire and Cliff [at-Hoo], Kent, Chaplain to the Archbishop of Canterbury, Canon of St. George's, Windsor, Prebendary of Rochester, Kent, Chancellor of St. Paul's, by his wife, Isabel Woodhall. He was born about 1591 (aged 14 in 1605). He was admitted at King's College, Cambridge 23 August 1605. He obtained a B.A. degree, 1609–10, and a M.A. degree, 1613. They had two sons, [Dr.] Edmund and [Rev.] John, and two daughters, Elizabeth (wife of [Rev.] Ezekiel Rogers) and Mary (wife of [Rev.] Samuel Danforth and Joseph Rock). He immigrated to New England in 1630, where he was appointed pastor of the First Church of Boston, Massachusetts. His wife, Elizabeth, joined him in New England in 1632. She died at Boston, Massachusetts about 1658. [**Rev.**] JOHN WILSON died testate at Boston, Massachusetts 7 August 1667, aged 78½ years. *Heraldic Jour.* 2 (1866): 182. Pope *Pioneers of Massachusetts* (1900): 504 (biog. of [Rev.] John Wilson). *NEHGR* 61 (1907): 36–41, 127–133; 155 (2001): 3–35. Anderson *Great Migration Begins* 3 (1995): 2012–2015.

ii. **ANNE MANSFIELD**, born about 1596 (aged 21 in 1617). She married by license dated 28 June 1617 [**Capt.**] **ROBERT KEAYNE**, of Windsor, Berkshire and St. Michael Cornhill, London, merchant taylor. They had four sons, Benjamin, John, Joseph, and John. They immigrated to New England in 1635, where they settled at Boston, Massachusetts. [**Capt.**] ROBERT KEAYNE died there in 1656. His widow, Anne, married (2nd) at Boston, Massachusetts 16 October 1660 (as his 3rd wife) **SAMUEL COLE**. She died at Boston, Massachusetts in 1667. Chester & Armytage *Allegations for the Marr. Licences issued by the Bishop of London 1611 to 1828* 2 (H.S.P. 26) (1887): 51. Pope *Pioneers of Massachusetts* (1900): 265 (biog. of Robert Keayne). *NEHGR* 155 (2001): 3–35.

iii. **JOHN MANSFIELD**, goldsmith and schoolmaster, born about 1601 (aged 34 in 1635). He immigrated to New England in 1635. He married about 1639 **MARY SHARD**, widow of John Gove, of Charlestown, Massachusetts. They had one son, John, and one daughter, Elizabeth. JOHN MANSFIELD died at Charlestown, Massachusetts 26 June 1674. His widow, Mary, died at Hampton, New Hampshire 4 March 1681/2. *NEHGR* 6 (1852): 156 (petition of John Mansfield mentions his "cousin," Mansfield Hassell); 19 (1865): 73; 29 (1875): 317; 155 (2001): 3–35. Pope *Pioneers of Massachusetts* (1900): 299 (biog. of John Mansfield). *New England Quarterly* 20 (1947): 260–263.

҈ EVERINGHAM ҈

WILLIAM DE PERCY, of Topcliffe, Yorkshire, married **EMMA DE PORT**.
ALAN DE PERCY, of Topcliffe, Yorkshire, married **EMMA DE GANT**.
WILLIAM DE PERCY, of Topcliffe, Yorkshire, married **ALICE DE TONBRIDGE**.
AGNES DE PERCY, married **JOSCELIN OF LOUVAIN**, of Petworth, Sussex [see PERCY 4].

5. MAUD DE PERCY, married **JOHN D'EIVILLE** (or **DE DAIVILLE, DEYVILLE, DE EYVILL**), of Egmanton, Nottinghamshire, Adlingfleet, Yorkshire, etc., son of Robert d'Eiville, of Egmanton, Nottinghamshire, by his 2nd wife, Juliane, daughter of Thurstan de Montfort, of Beaudesert, Warwickshire. Her maritagium included seven bovates of land in Catton (in Topcliffe), Yorkshire. She also had lands in Gargrave, Yorkshire as an inheritance or additional maritagium. They had four sons, Robert, Knt., Henry, Joscelin, and Adam [Rector of Adlingfleet, Yorkshire], and one daughter, Juliane (wife of William le Constable). In 1202 he and his mother, Juliane, entered into an agreement with Adam Fitz Eudes and others regarding ten bovates of land and appurtenances in Kilburn, Yorkshire. During the civil war in the reign of King John, his lands in Nottinghamshire, Yorkshire, and Leicestershire were declared forfeit and granted to Adam de Saint

Martin. He was granted a market at Adlingfleet, Yorkshire in 1220. In 1220 he claimed to be the heir of his uncle, Walter de Montfort. In 1226 he witnessed a charter of his brother-in-law, Richard de Percy. He was a benefactor of Drax Priory. JOHN D'EIVILLE was living in June 1228.

>Dugdale *Monasticon Anglicanum* 6(3) (1830): 1190. *Yorkshire Arch. Jour.* 10 (1889): 537–539. Martin *Percy Chartulary* (Surtees Soc. 117) (1911): 13. *C.R.R.* 9 (1952): 291. Clay *Early Yorkshire Charters* 11 (1963): 5–7. Church *Household Knights of King John* (1999): 91–92.

6. ROBERT D'EIVILLE, Knt., of Egmanton, Nottinghamshire, son and heir. He married before 1229 (date of lawsuit) **DENISE** (or **DIONIS**) **FITZ WILLIAM**, daughter of William Fitz William, of Sprotborough, Yorkshire, Plumtree, Nottinghamshire, etc., by Ela, daughter of Hamelin, 5th Earl of Surrey [see FITZWILLIAM 8 for her ancestry]. His wife, Denise, had lands in Skegby, Nottinghamshire in free marriage. They had two sons, John, Knt., and Adam, Knt. In 1229 John de Lungvilers brought an assize of novel disseisin against Robert and his wife, Denise, regarding a tenement in Skegby, Nottinghamshire. In 1242–3 Thomas Fitz William brought an assize of mort d'ancestor against Robert and his wife, Denise (sister of the said Thomas), regarding the manor of Greetwell, Lincolnshire; Thomas granted them the manor to hold to them and the heirs of Denise rendering 13 marks annually. SIR ROBERT D'EIVILLE was living in 1242–3. In or after 1252 John de Warenne, Earl of Surrey brought a writ of entry against his widow, Denise, concerning the manor of Greetwell, Lincolnshire, and agreement was made so that Thomas Fitz William rendered the manor to the earl. In 1260 Thomas Fitz William granted various lands in Barnburgh, Barnthorpe, Harlington, and elsewhere in Yorkshire to his sister, Denise, widow of Robert d'Eyville, in exchange for the manor of Greetwell, Lincolnshire. At an unknown date, she gave Alan Hille, called the miller, her native with all his family to Monk Bretton Priory, Yorkshire. Denise died sometime in or before 1283–4.

>*Testa de Nevill* (1807): 7. Dugdale *Monasticon Anglicanum* 5 (1825): 132–133. Atkinson *Cartularium Abbathiæ de Rievalle* (Surtees Soc. 83) (1889): 223–224 (charter dated pre-1284 of John de Eyville; charter granted with consent of his mother, Denise; charter witnessed by his brother, Sir Adam de Eyville). Giffard *Reg. of Walter Giffard Lord Archbishop of York 1266–1279* (1904): 52. *Lincolnshire Notes & Queries* 9 (1907): 188–189. *C.P.* 4 (1916): 130–131 (sub Deiville). Foster *Final Concords of Lincoln from the Feet of Fines A.D. 1244–1272* 2 (Lincoln Rec. Soc. 17) (1921): 288. *Book of Fees* 2 (1923): 1065.

7. JOHN D'EIVILLE, Knt., of Egmanton, Caunton, and West Markham, Nottinghamshire, Adlingfleet, Butterwick, Gargrave, High Catton, Kilburn, and Thornton-in-the-Hill, Yorkshire, Chief Justice and Keeper of the King's forest North of Trent, Sheriff of Yorkshire, Constable of York and Scarborough Castles, son and heir, adult by 1260 (minor at his father's death). In 1267–8 his cousin, William de Percy, sued him for the advowson of Catton, Yorkshire. He married (1st) before 5 Feb. 1275/6 (date of pardon for marrying without license) **MAUD** _____, widow of James de Audley (died 1273), of Audley, Staffordshire. They had two sons, John, Knt., and Thomas. Following the death of Simon de Montfort, he became one of the most active leaders of the disinherited barons. He occupied the Isle of Axholme in 1265 with Simon de Montfort the younger. He was the leader of those who took Lincoln and seized the Isle of Ely in 1266, after which they plundered Norwich and Cambridge. He was pardoned in 1267. In 1274–5 he arraigned a jury against the Prior of Newburgh touching common of pasture in Cokewald, Yorkshire. In the same period, he arraigned a jury against the Prior of Newburgh touching common of pasture in Selclif, Yorkshire. In the same period, Clemence de Lungvilers arraigned an assize of novel disseisin against him and others touching a tenement in Egmanton, Nottingthamshire and the same against him and others touching a tenement in Barlborough, Nottinghamshire. In the same period, Richard Bolax arraigned an assize of novel disseisin against him and others touching a tenement in Egmanton, Nottingthamshire. In the same period, he arraigned an assize of mort d'ancestor against John de Warenne, Earl of Surrey, touching the manor of Greetwell, Lincolnshire. In 1275–6 he arraigned a jury against the Prior of Newburgh touching common in pasture in Kilburn, Yorkshire.

In the same period, William le Noble and Clemence his wife arraigned an assize of novel disseisin against him and others touching a tenement in Egmanton, Nottinghamshire. In 1276–7 Clemence de Lungvilers arraigned an assize of novel disseisin against him and others touching a tenement in Barnbrough, Yorkshire. He was with the king in Wales in 1282. He served as a banneret in King Edward I's household. Sometime before 1284 he granted five bovates of land in Nawton to Rievaulx Priory. At an unknown date, his mother's sister, Ellen de Lungvilers, granted him lands and tenements in Skegby, Nottinghamshire. SIR JOHN D'EIVILLE died before October 1291.

Foss *Judges of England* 2 (1848): 307–308 (biog. of John de Daivill). *Annual Rpt. of the Deputy Keeper* 44 (1883): 70, 93, 118, 235; 45 (1885): 162, 217; 46 (1886): 92, 151, 153; 47 (1886): 213. Atkinson *Cartularium Abbathiæ de Rievalle* (Surtees Soc. 83) (1889): 223–224 (charter dated pre-1284 of John de Eyville; charter granted with consent of his mother, Denise; charter witnessed by his brother, Sir Adam de Eyville). Giffard *Reg. of Walter Giffard Lord Archbishop of York 1266–1279* (Surtees Soc. 109) (1904): 52. *C.Ch.R.* 2 (1906): 27, 252. *C.P.R.* 1258–1266 (1910): 323 (John de Eyvile styled "nephew" [i.e., kinsman] of John de Courtenay in 1264). *C.P.* 4 (1916): 130–132 (sub Deiville). *Feudal Aids* 6 (1920): 10, 47, 52, 58, 65–66, 68. Greenfield *Reg. of William Greenfield Lord Archbishop of York 1306–1315* (Surtees Soc. 152) (1938): 46, 126. *Nottingham Medieval Studies* 43 (1999): 90–109.

8. JOHN D'EIVILLE, Knt., of Adlingfleet, Cundall, Kilburn, Leckby (in Cundall), Thornton Bridge (in Brafferton), and Thornton-in-the-Hill, Yorkshire, and Egmanton, Nottinghamshire, son and heir, by father's 1st marriage, was a minor in 1295. He married (1st) **AGNES** _____. They had one son, Robert, Knt., and two daughters, Elizabeth (wife of Alexander de Leeds, Knt.) and Margaret (wife of _____). He married (2nd) **MARGARET** _____. They had one daughter, Joan. In 1298 he served at Falkirk as a banneret in King Edward I's victory over the Scots. In 1304 he was summoned to appear before the King at Lincoln for stealing venison from Sherwood. He sold the manors of Kilburn and Castle Hood, Yorkshire to the Earl of Lancaster in 1319 and the manor of Thornton-in-the-Hill in 1322 to John de Ellerker. In 1323–4 he conveyed to John de Ellerker his right to a fourth part of a knight's fee in Haldanby, Yorkshire. SIR JOHN D'EIVILLE died 1325–6. His widow, Margaret, married (2nd) before 29 Sept. 1326 (as his 2nd wife) **ADAM DE EVERINGHAM**, Knt., 1st Lord Everingham, of Laxton, North Leverton, Nottinghamshire, Everingham, Yorkshire, etc. She was living Feb. 1333/4, and was buried at Laxton, Nottinghamshire. SIR ADAM DE EVERINGHAM, 1st Lord Everingham, died shortly before 8 May 1341.

Genealogist 4 (1880): 50–58 (arms of John D'Eiville: Or, on a fess between four fleurs-de-lis gules two more of the field); n.s. 8 (1892): 37. *Index of Placita de Banco 1327–1328* 2 (PRO Lists and Indexes 22) (1906): 515–516, 521–522, 525, 754. *C.P.* 4 (1916): 132–133 (sub Deiville). Prestwich *Edward I* (1988): 286. *Nottingham Medieval Studies* 43 (1999): 90–109. Coss & Keen *Heraldry, Pageantry & Social Display in Medieval England* (2002): 143–167. Roper *Feet of Fines for the County of York 1314–1326* (Yorkshire Arch. Soc. Recs. 158) (2006): 89.

9. JOAN D'EIVILLE, daughter by her father's 2nd marriage, born before 9 July 1324. She married before 16 May 1332 **ADAM DE EVERINGHAM**, Knt., 2nd Lord Everingham, of Laxton and North Leverton, Nottinghamshire, Everingham, Yorkshire, and Westborough, Lincolnshire, and, in right of his wife, Egmanton, Nottinghamshire, son and heir of Adam de Everingham, Knt., 1st Lord Everingham, of Laxton, North Leverton, Nottinghamshire, Everingham, Yorkshire, etc., by his 1st wife, Clarice. He was born about 1307 (aged 79 in 1386). They had three sons, William, Knt., Reginald, Knt., and allegedly George, and two daughters, Margaret and allegedly Katherine. He was at the siege of Berwick, 1333, the Battle of Halidon Hill, 1333, the Battle of Sluys, 1340, and the Siege of Tournai, 1340. He was taken prisoner in France before 14 May 1342, and ransomed for 200 marks in gold. He was in the retinue of the Earl of Derby in France in 1342 and in Gascony in 1345–6. He was at the siege of Calais in 1347 in the retinue of the Earl of Lancaster, and, was about to go to France in the same retinue in 1348 and 1355. He was indicted of various trepasses and detained in Nottingham Castle in 1351. His wife, Joan, died about 1378. In Feb. 1387/8 he conveyed a moiety of the manor of Shelford, Nottinghamshire to Richard de Schulton, parson of

Everingham, Yorkshire, and John Rydver, vicar of Laxton, Nottinghamshire. SIR ADAM DE EVERINGHAM, 2nd Lord Everingham, died 8 Feb. 1387/8 at Laxton.

> Banks *Baronies in Fee* 1 (1844): 200–202 (sub Everingham). Ord *Hist. & Antiqs. of Cleveland* (1846): 274 (Everingham ped.). *Yorkshire Arch. Jour.* 13 (1895): 79 (charter of Adam de Everingham, Knt., lord of Laxton dated 1 Feb. 1387/8. "Seal of red wax. The shield couché bearing a lion rampant, surmounted by a helm, nearly front-faced, with a stag or brocket's head for crest. Legend: — ..... A. de Eu[er]ingham de Laxton."). *Genealogist* n.s. 13 (1896): 79 (grant by Adam de Everingham with wax seal displaying shield couche bearing a lion rampant). *C.P.* 4 (1916): 132–133 (sub Deiville), 5 (1926): 189–190 (sub Everingham). Train *Abs. of IPMs Rel. Nottinghamshire* 1 (Thoroton Soc. Recs. 12) (1949): 105. Paget *Baronage of England* (1957) 198: 3–5 (sub Everingham). Sanders *English Baronies* (1960): 76–77.

Children of Joan d'Eiville, by Adam de Everingham, Knt.:

i. **MARGARET DE EVERINGHAM**, married **HUGH DE HASTINGS**, Knt., of Elsing, Norfolk [see ELSING 12].

ii. **KATHERINE DE EVERINGHAM** (alleged daughter), married **JOHN BEAUMONT**, K.G., 4th Lord Beaumont [see BEAUMONT 10].

❧ EXETER ❧

ALICE OF NORMANDY (sister of King William the Conqueror), married **LAMBERT**, Count of Lens.
JUDITH OF LENS, married **WALTHEOF**, Earl of Northumberland.
MAUD OF NORTHUMBERLAND, married **SIMON DE SENLIS**, Earl of Huntingdon and Northampton.
MAUD DE SENLIS, married **SAHER DE QUINCY**, of Long Buckby, Northamptonshire.
ROBERT DE QUINCY, of Tranent, Fawside, and Longniddry, East Lothian, Scotland, married **ORABEL FITZ NESS**.
SAHER DE QUINCY, Knt., Earl of Winchester, married **MARGARET OF LEICESTER**.
ROGER DE QUINCY, Knt., Earl of Winchester, married **ELLEN OF GALLOWAY**.
ELLEN DE QUINCY, married **ALAN LA ZOUCHE**, Knt., of Ashby de la Zouch, Leicestershire.
ROGER LA ZOUCHE, Knt., of Ashby de la Zouch, Leicestershire, married **ELA LONGESPÉE** (desc. King William the Conqueror).
ALAN LA ZOUCHE, Knt., Lord Zouche, married **ELEANOR DE SEGRAVE**.
MAUD LA ZOUCHE, married **ROBERT DE HOLAND**, Knt., 1st Lord Holand.
THOMAS DE HOLAND, K.G., Earl of Kent, married **JOAN OF KENT** (desc. King William the Conqueror) [see KENT 9].

10. JOHN HOLAND, K.G., of Ardington, Berkshire, Stevington, Bedfordshire, Cockington, Fremington, South Molton, Torrington, etc., Devon, Northwich, Cheshire, Hope and Hopedale, Flintshire, etc., Chief Justice of Chester and Flint, 1381–5, Captain of the English Army in Spain, 1386–7, Admiral of the Fleet west of Thames towards Scotland, 1389, Captain of Brest, 1389–93, Privy Councillor, 1389, Great Chamberlain of England, 1390, Chief Justice of Chester, 1391–4, Admiral of the North and West, 1392, Warden of the West Marches 1397, Captain and Councillor of the Holy Roman Church, 1397, Captain of Calais, 1398, Constable of Arundel, Conway, Horston, Rockingham, and Tintagel Castles, younger son. He was half-brother of King Richard II of England. In 1384 he was pardoned for the murder of Ralph de Stafford. He married at or near Plymouth, Devon 24 June 1386 **ELIZABETH [OF] LANCASTER**, divorced wife of John de Hastings, Knt., 3rd Earl of Pembroke (marriage dissolved by mutual consent shortly after 24 Sept. 1383) [see HASTINGS 14], and 2nd daughter of John of Gaunt, K.G., Duke of Aquitaine and Lancaster, Earl of Derby, Lincoln, and Leicester (son of King Edward III of England), by his 1st wife, Blanche, daughter and coheiress of Henry, Duke of Lancaster [see LANCASTER 10 for her ancestry]. She was born before 21 Feb. 1363, and was full sister of King Henry IV. They had three sons, Richard, John, Knt. [Duke of Exeter], and Edward, Knt. [Count of Mortain], and two daughters, Constance and Alice (wife of Richard Vere, K.G., 11th Earl of Oxford [see VERE 7]). He was appointed Constable of the army which John, Duke of Lancaster, his father-in-law, raised in

John Cornwall, Lord Fanhope and his wife Elizabeth of Lancaster, daughter of John of Gaunt.

an attempt to obtain the Crown of Castile, and, by his advice, the Duke abandoned this unsuccessful enterprise. He was created Earl of Huntingdon 2 June 1388, and Duke of Exeter 29 Sept. 1397. He was granted the castle of Berkhampstead, Hertfordshire as a residence in 1388 during pleasure. In 1394 he obtained a papal indult for plenary remission, he going against the Turks and "other enemies of Christ." He was likewise granted letters of protection by the king, he then going on an embassy to the King of Hungary. He and his wife, Elizabeth, were members of the Trinity Guild of Coventry, Warwickshire. He was one of the eight persons who appealed of treason the Lords Appelant in 1397. In 1397 Pope Boniface IX appointed him galfalonier of the holy Roman church, vicar in temporals in all provinces, cities, castles and other places in Italy and elsewhere belonging to the Pope, and captain-general of all men-at-arms fighting in their service. He accompanied his brother, King Richard II, into Ireland in May 1399, and returned with him the following July. Following the overthrow of King Richard II, he joined in the plot to seize King Henry IV, but took no active part. SIR JOHN HOLAND was degraded from his Dukedom 3 Nov. 1399. He was beheaded at Pleshey Castle, Essex 9 (or 10) Jan. 1399/1400, for treason against his brother-in-law, King Henry IV. He was buried in Collegiate Church at Pleshey, Essex. In the Jan. 1400/1 Parliament he was attainted as Earl of Huntingdon. His widow, Elizabeth, married (3rd) before 12 Dec. 1400 (as his 2nd wife) **JOHN CORNWALL** (or **CORNEWAILLE**, **CORNEWAYLL**), K.G., of Charlton, Sompting, Steyning, Warminghurst, and Withyham, Sussex, King's knight, Constable of Sheppey (or Queenborough) Castle, Knight of the Shire for Shropshire, 1402, 1407, son and heir of John Cornwall, Knt., allegedy by a niece of the Duke of Brittany. They had one son, John, Knt., and one daughter, Constance. He previously married (1st) before 13 April 1398 **PHILIPPE ARUNDEL**, widow of Richard Sergeaux, Knt., of Colquite, Cornwall [see APPLETON 13], and daughter and co-heiress of Edmund de Arundel, Knt., of Bignor, Trayford, and Compton, Sussex, Chudleigh, Devon, etc., by Sibyl, daughter of William de Montagu, Knt., 1st Earl of Salisbury, 3rd Lord Montagu, Earl Marshal of England [see APPLETON 12 for her ancestry]. They had no issue. By an unknown mistress (or mistresses), he also had two illegitimate sons, John, Esq., and Thomas. In 1403 he and his wife, Elizabeth, and Hugh Veretot, monk and proctor in England of the Abbey of Fecamp in Normandy, were granted custody of all the lands, possessions, and liberties of the Fecamp abbey in England to hold during the war with France, save one manor; the said John and Elizabeth were also assigned the sum of 400 marks yearly from this farm for life during the war. In 1404 they were granted the castle and manor of Trematon and several other Duchy of Cornwall properties for the life of Elizabeth. In 1405 he was granted the manor of Weston, Hertfordshire for life, which property was re-granted the following year to the queen consort. In 1406 he and his wife, Elizabeth, were disputing the advowson of Stevington, Bedfordshire. In Trinity term 1406 Edmund Holand, Earl of Kent, sued them for the manor of Stevington, Bedfordshire under a grant of King Edward I to John Wake and his wife in tail. In 1410 he and his wife, Elizabeth, sold one messuage, two mills, and land in Lostwithiel, Cornwall to John Hogge for 100 marks of silver. He was present at the Battle of Agincourt in 1415. He took part in the siege of Rouen in 1418–19, which ended in its capture by the English 19 Jan. 1418/9. In 1420 he presented to the church of Calstock, Cornwall. His wife, Elizabeth, died 24 Nov. 1425, and was buried in Burford Church, Shropshire. In 1428 his trustees were fined 40 marks for acquiring the manors of Ampthill, Grange by Milbrook, and Milbrook, Bedfordshire without license from Eleanor widow of Amaury de Saint Amand, Knt. Sometime before 1428 he also acquired the manor of Dame Ellensbury (in Houghton Conquest), Bedfordshire. In 1431 he presented to the churches of Ampthill and Milbrook, Bedfordshire. He was created 17 July 1432 Baron of Fanhope, co. Hereford, although he appears to have been always summoned to Parliament by writs directed *Johanni Cornewall, Chivaler*. In 1432 he acquired a great tenement on Thames Street in London. In

1434 he conveyed the same property to William Londroppe (or ?Luddesop), John Fitz Geoffrey, and Walter Pijou, who in turn granted him a rent charge of 40 marks out of this property and another on Gracechurch Street and Lombard Street, which rent was subsequently applied for prayers for his soul under the terms of his first will. Tensions between him and Reynold, Lord Grey in Bedfordshire culminated in a riot in 1439, when Cornwall and his men gatecrashed the sessions of peace in Bedford town hall and eighteen people were killed. He was created 30 Jan. 1441/2 Baron of Milbroke [Millbrook], co. Bedford. SIR JOHN CORNWALL, Lord [of] Fanhope, Baron of Millbrook, died at Ampthill, Bedfordshire 10 (or 11) Dec. 1443, and was buried in a chapel in the cemetery of the Black Friars by Ludgate, London. He left wills dated 1 April 1437 and 10 Dec. 1443, the latter of which was proved 6 Jan. 1443/4. Following his death, the manors and advowsons of Ampthill and Milbrook, Bedfordshire were seised by his step-son, John Holand, Duke of Exeter, to the exclusion of Ralph Cromwell, Knt., Lord Cromwell, who had previously purchased these properties from Lord Fanhope. Cromwell was subsequently confirmed in his title to these lands 21 May 1444.

Sandford *Gen. Hist. of the Kings of England* (1677): 251–252. Rymer *Fœdera* 8 (1727): 404 (Elizabeth styled "sister" by King Henry IV of England). Blore *Hist. & Antiqs. of Rutland* 1(2) (1811): 98 (Lancaster ped.). Fisher *Colls. Hist. Gen. & Top. for Bedfordshire* (1812–36). Clutterbuck *Hist. & Antiqs. of Hertford* 1 (1815): 371 (Longespée-Zouch ped.); 3 (1827): 287–288 (Beaumont-Quincy ped.). Nicolas *Synopsis of the Peerage of England* 2 (1825): 426. Nicolas *Testamenta Vetusta* 1 (1826): 246 (will of John Cornwall, Knt., Lord Fanhope). Nicolas *Controversy between Scrope & Grosvenor* 2 (1832): 182–183 (biog. of Sir John Holand: "… one of the most distinguished persons of his time"). *Coll. Top. et Gen.* 1 (1834): 299. Thoms *Book of the Court* (1838): 122. Aungier *Hist. & Antiqs. of Syon Monastery* (1840): 40–41. Beaven *Rpts. of Cases in Chancery* 2 (1841): 588–604. Beltz *Mems. of the Order of the Garter* (1841): cliii, clvii. *Top. & Gen.* 1 (1846): 63–64. Hulton *Coucher Book, or Chartulary, of Whalley Abbey* 4 (Chetham Soc. 20) (1849): 977–979 (Holand ped.). Hawley *Royal Fam. of England* (1851): 23–27. *Notes & Queries* 10 (1854): 282–283 (re. monumental inscription and effigy of Elizabeth Lancaster at Burford). Napier *Swyncombe & Ewelme* (1858): chart facing 323. Theiner *Codex Diplomaticus Dominii Temporalis S. Sedis* 3 (1862): 91. *Reliquary* 8 (1867–8): 151–153. Dingley *Hist. from Marble* 2 (Camden Soc. 97) (1868): 116–117 (re. effigy of Elizabeth Lancaster at Burford, Shropshire: "Her effigies [sic] is adorned with a ducal coronet, a purple robe guarded with ermine, and other rich ornaments of a Princess: the arms of her father the Duke of Lancaster are also depicted on her monument. The shields of arms … are four in number: 1. France (semée de lis) and England quarterly. 2. Holand, Duke of Exeter (imaling the same). 3. Cornwall. 4. Cornwall impaling France and England."). *Vis. of Devon 1620* (H.S.P. 6) (1872): 345–347 (Holland ped.: "John Holland, 2, E. of Huntingdon & D. of Exeter = Eliz. d. of John of Gaunt, D. of Lancaster & sister to K. H. 4"). Wright *Feudal Manuals of English Hist.* (1872): 151. Harvey *Hist. & Antiqs. of the Hundred of Willey* (1872–8): opp. 146 (Quincy ped.). Hardy *Syllabus (in English) of the Docs. Rel. England & Other Kingdoms* 2 (1873): 525. *Annual Rpt. of the Deputy Keeper* 36 (1875): 13, 111, 164, 168, 209, 246, 247, 269, 315, 415, 449, 485. Rogers *Antient Sepulchral Effigies* (1877): 224–226. *Notes & Queries* 5th Ser. 9 (1878): 373–374. Burke *Dormant, Abeyant, Forfeited & Extinct Peerages* (1883): 280–281 (sub Holland). *Trans. Shropshire Arch. & Nat. Hist. Soc.* 6 (1883): 395, footnote 156. Wylie *Hist. of England under Henry IV* 1 (1884): 105. Doyle *Official Baronage of England* 1 (1886): 708–709 (sub Exeter); 2 (1886): 228–229 (sub Huntingdon). Gibbons *Early Lincoln Wills* (1888): 166–167 (will of John Cornewayll, Knt.), 215. *Englische Studien* (13) 1889: 1–24. Tresswell & Vincent *Vis. of Shropshire 1623, 1569 & 1584* 1 (H.S.P. 28) (1889): 145–148 (sub Cornwall: "Sr John Cornewall of Fanhope Kt."). Birch *Cat. Seals in the British Museum* 2 (1892): 689–690 (seal of John Cornwaille, Knt., Lord of Fanhope, dated 1440 — A shield of arms, couché: of ornamental shape, ermine, a lion rampant ducally crowned, within a bordure bezantée, CORNWALL. Crest on [a helmet] and elegantly designed mantling, a lion statant [ducally crowned]. Legend: "Sig …….. nnis * * cornewa……. tis*." Inner border cabled; outer border ornamented with small ball-flowers.); 3 (1894): 107 (seal of John de Holand dated 1380-1 — A shield of arms: three lions passant guardant in pale, within a bordure semée of fleurs-de-lis. Suspended by a strap from a tree. Within a traced gothic panel ornamented with ball-flowers along the inner edge), 108 (seal of John de Holand, 1st Earl of Huntingdon dated 1396 — A shield of arms: three lions passant in pale within a bordure of FRANCE. On a tree, the mount and lower part of the trunk alone remaining. Within an elaborately traced gothic panel. Legend: "………. Holand : comitis : Huntyngdon : co……"). *Desc. Cat. Ancient Deeds* 2 (1894): 254. *C.P.R. 1381–1385* (1897): 7, 20, 36 (instances of John Holand styled "king's brother"), 336 (Elizabeth, Countess of Pembroke, styled "king's kinswoman"). *Feudal Aids* 1 (1899): 36. *Genealogist* n.s. 16 (1899): 90–91. Rye *Cal. Feet of Fines for Suffolk* (1900): 277. *C.P.R. 1385–1389* (1900): 99, 114, 122. *Procs. Bath Natural Hist. & Antiq. Field Club* 9 (1901): 188–201. *Papal Regs.: Letters* 4 (1902): 294–295, 300, 396 (John de Holand, Earl of Huntingdon styled "brother" [germanus] of King Richard II of England in 1391), 489. *C.P.R. 1388–1392* (1902): 190 (Elizabeth, Countess of Huntingdon, styled "king's kinswoman" by King Richard II of England). *C.P.R. 1391–1396* (1905): 237. *C.P.R. 1401–1405* (1905): 94, 205, 476 (Elizabeth, Countess of Huntingdon, styled "king's sister"). Wrottesley *Peds. from the Plea Rolls* (1905): 283–284, 298. *Desc. Cat. Ancient Deeds* 5 (1906): 65, 82. *C.P.R. 1436–1441* (1907): 286. *C.P.R. 1441–1446* (1908): 267–268. VCH *Bedford* 2 (1908): 35–37, 324; 3 (1912): 100–104. VCH *Hertford* 2 (1908): 201–203; 3 (1912): 171–177. Lane *Royal Daughters of England* 1 (1910): 251–258. Flenley *Six Town Chrons. of England* (1911): 117 (Chron. of London: "…Item ye iii day afore cristemas deyed Sir John cornewall knight and lyeth buryed att blak ffreres."). *C.P.* 4 (1916): Appendix H, 727–728; 5 (1926): 195–200 (sub Exeter), 253–254 (sub Fanhope); 6 (1926): 653–654 (sub Huntingdon); 7 (1929): 415, footnote g; 10 (1945): 394–397 (sub Pembroke). Wall *Handbook of the Maude Roll* (1919) unpaginated (ped. dated c.1461–85: "Elizabetha comitissa Huntingdon"). VCH *Berkshire* 4 (1924): 269–270, 287–288. Jenkinson & Fowler *Some Bedfordshire Wills* (Bedfordshire Hist. Rec. Soc. 14) (1931): 108–112 (will of Sir John Cornwayll) (arms of John Cornwall: Ermine, a lion gules crowned or, with a star or on his shoulder, a bordure engrailed bezanty). *Year Books of Henry VI: 1 Henry VI 1422* (Selden Soc. 50) (1933): 30–34. Fowler *Recs. of Harrold Priory* (Bedfordshire Hist. Rec. Soc. 17) (1935): 42, 195. Harris *Reg. of the Guild of the Holy Trinity, St. Mary, St. John the Baptist & St. Katherine of Coventry* 1 (Dugdale Soc. 13) (1935): 34, 103 (list of the members of Trinity Guild: "John, Lord Holand, Duke of Exeter, and Lady Isabella [sic], Duchess"). Chichele *Reg. of Henry Chichele* 2 (Canterbury & York Soc. 42) (1937): 637–638 (biog. of John Arundel). Steel *Richard II* (1941). Legge *Anglo-Norman Letters & Petitions* (Anglo-Norman Text Soc. 3) (1941): 265, 328–329, 333 (letters of John Holand, Earl of Huntingdon/Duke of Exeter). *Cornwall Feet of Fines* 2 (1950): 102–103. Hatton *Book of Seals* (1950): 80. Paget *Baronage of England* (1957) 291: 1 (chart only). *Bedfordshire Hist. Rec. Soc.* 38 (1958): 12–48 (biog. of John Lord Wenlock). *Coat of Arms* 7 (1962): 164–169 (arms of John Holand: England and a bordure argent flory gold). Armitage-Smith *John of Gaunt* (1964): 459–460. *Bull. Inst. Hist. Research* 38 (1965): 12, footnote 3. *Cal. Inqs. Misc.* 7 (1968): 160. Dunning *Hylle Cartulary* (Somerset Rec. Soc. 68) (1968): 87–88. *Trans. Essex Arch. Soc.* 3rd Ser. 2(3) (1970): 267–279. Harriss & Harriss "John Benet's Chron. for the years 1400 to 1462" in *Camden Misc. Vol. XXIV* (Camden 4th Ser. 9) (1972): 190 ("Et ante festum sancti Nicholai [6 Dec. 1443] obiit dominus Johannes Cornewayle pro tunc dominus de la Wawnoppe et humatus apud Fratres Predicatores in Lundon."). Rees *Cal. Ancient Petitions Rel. Wales* (Board of Celtic Studies, Hist. & Law 28) (1975): 375–376 (petition of Margaret Marshal, Countess of Norfolk, John de Hastings, Earl of Pembroke, etc., to the King dated c.1384–5: "… at which time John [de Hastings], one of the petitioners, was married to Elizabeth, daughter of the Duke of Lancaster, which Duke, for the cause aforesaid, at that time was next friend to this John, and had great tenderness for the inheritance; and now it is that Elizabeth had disagreed to the marriage, and is married elsewhere; so that alliance is thereby terminated"). *Ancient Deeds — Ser. BB* (List & Index Soc. 137) (1977): 96, 108. Ellis *Cat. Seals in the P.R.O.* 1 (1978): 33 (seal of John Holand, Earl of Huntingdon dated 1390 — In a circle, between lunettes of tracery, a shield of arms: three lions passant gardant, within a bordure semé-de-lys [HOLAND]. Hung by a chain of pierced cinquefoils from a tree with a double bushy top, growing from a mount, with oak sprigs, below the shield), 33 (seal of Elizabeth Holand, wife of John Holand, Earl of Huntingdon dated 1390 — In a circle, with ivy leaves above and an ear of wheat on either side, a shield of arms: three lions passant gardant within a bordure semé-de-lys [HOLAND] impaling three lions passant gardant, and a label of three points [LANCASTER]). *Ancient Deeds — Ser. AS & WS* (List & Index Soc. 158) (1979): 5 (Deed A.S.19). Reeves *Lancastrian Englishmen* (1981): 139–202. Hector *Westminster Chron. 1381–1394* (1982): 192–193, 294–295. *Devon & Cornwall Notes & Queries* 35 (1984): 221. Kirby *Abs. of Feet of Fines Rel. Wiltshire* (Wiltshire Rec. Soc. 41) (1986): 51. Hicks *Profit, Piety & Professions in Later Medieval England* (1990): 103–118. Austin *Ancient Fams. in the British Isles* (1991): 66–84. Hicks *Who's Who in Late Medieval England* (1991): 187–188 (biog. of John Holland: "… a man of great strength and master of his weapon… famous for his knightly prowess"). Miller *Agrarian Hist. of England & Wales* 3 (1991): 567. *National Lib. of Wales Jour.* 27 (1991): 131–174. *Cal. IPM* 20 (1995): 187–189. Leese *Blood Royal* (1996): 128–134, 201–219. Watts *Henry VI & the Politics of Kingship* (1996). Carpenter *Wars of the Roses* (1997): 84–85, 112, 126–127. VCH *Sussex* 5(1) (1997): 204–214; 6(1) 1980: 53–64, 226–231, 231–237; 6(2) (1986): 52–54. Collins *Order of the Garter 1348-1461* (2000): 251. Dunn *War & Soc. in Medieval & Early Modern Britain* (2000): 129, 132–133. Emery *Greater Medieval Houses of England & Wales* 2 (2000): 205–206. Harriss *Shaping the Nation* (2005): 168. National Archives, C 146/3533 (grant dated 30 May 1434 by Isabella Ampthull to John Cornewayll, lord of Founhope and baron of Mylbrook, of a cottage in Dunstaplestret in Ampthill, Bedfordshire, adjoining a messuage of the lord of Ampthill); SC 8/129/6431; SC 8/177/8813 (available at www.catalogue.nationalarchives.gov.uk/search.asp). Court of Common Pleas, CP 40/567, rot. 493 (available at http:// www.british-history.ac.uk/source.aspx?pubid=1272).

Children of John Holand, K.G., by Elizabeth [of] Lancaster:

i. **JOHN HOLAND**, K.G. [see next].

ii. **CONSTANCE HOLAND**, married (1st) **THOMAS MOWBRAY**, Knt., Earl of Norfolk, Earl of Nottingham, Earl Marshal [see MOWBRAY 7.i]; (2nd) **JOHN GREY**, K.G., of Ruthin, Denbighshire [see GREY 12].

Children of Elizabeth [of] Lancaster, by John Cornwall, K.G.:

i. **JOHN CORNWALL**, Knt., born about 1404. He was killed by a cannon ball at the Siege of Meaux in December 1421. He died unmarried. Roberts *Mems. of the Rival Houses of York & Lancaster* 2 (1827): 22. *Chrons. of*

Enguerrand de Monstrelet 1 (1853): 475 ("During the siege [of Meaux], a young knight, son to sir John Cornwall, and cousin-german to king Henry, was killed by a cannon-shot, to the great sorrow of the king and the other princes."). Kingsford *Henry V. the Typical Mediæval Hero* (1901): 357. *C.P.* 5 (1926): 254, footnote f (sub Fanhope).

    ii. **CONSTANCE CORNWALL**, married **JOHN ARUNDEL**, K.G., K.B., 14th Earl of Arundel, 1st Duke of Touraine [see ARUNDEL 11.i].

Illegitimate children of John Cornwall, K.G., by unknown mistress (or mistresses), _____:

    i. **JOHN CORNWALL**, Esq. He was a legatee in the 1443 will of his father. In 1488 he conveyed all his right, title, and demand which he had or might have in the manor of Great Hampstead Someries (in Luton), Bedfordshire to Thomas Rotherham, Archbishop of York, and William Skelton, clerk. Nicolas *Testamenta Vetusta* 1 (1826): 246 (will of John Cornwall, Knt., Lord Fanhope). *Notes & Queries* 5th Ser. 9 (1878): 373–374. Jenkinson & Fowler *Some Bedfordshire Wills* (Bedfordshire Hist. Rec. Soc. 14) (1931): 108–112 (will of John Cornwall, Knt., Lord Fanhope). *Bedfordshire Hist. Rec. Soc.* 38 (1958): 15.

    ii. **THOMAS CORNWALL**. He was a legatee in the 1443 will of his father. Nicolas *Testamenta Vetusta* 1 (1826): 246 (will of John Cornwall, Knt., Lord Fanhope). Jenkinson & Fowler *Some Bedfordshire Wills* (Bedfordshire Hist. Rec. Soc. 14) (1931): 108–112 (will of John Cornwall, Knt., Lord Fanhope).

11. JOHN HOLAND, K.G., Earl of Huntingdon, of the castle, town and manor of Barnstaple, and manors of Dartington, Fremington, South Molton, Torrington, etc., Devon, Stevington, Bedfordshire, Ardington, Berkshire, Haslebury and Blagdon, Somerset, etc., Admiral of the South and West, 1415, Lieutenant of the King at Sea, 1416, 1417, Constable of the Tower of London, 1420, Privy Councillor, 1426, 1437, Earl Marshal of England, 1432–6, Warden of the Lower Marches of Normandy, 1433, joint Warden of the East & West Marches towards Scotland, 1435–6, Admiral of England, Ireland, and Aquitaine, 1435, Lieutenant of Aquitaine, 1439, Captain of Gournay, Gisors, Melun, Neufchatel, Pontoise, and Vinncennes, younger son, born and baptized at Dartington, Devon 29 March 1395 or 1396. He was heir in 1400 to his older brother, Richard Holand. He accompanied the King to France in 1415 and was present at the Siege of Harfleur and the Battle of Agincourt. He was a legatee in the 1421 will of his cousin, King Henry V of England. He was taken prisoner at the Battle of Beaugé in Anjou in 1421. He remained in captivity for five years, being ransomed at a cost of 20,000 marks. On his return to England, he was a significant owner of shipping, some of which traded into the Mediterranean. He married (1st) before 6 March 1426/7 **ANNE STAFFORD**, widow of Edmund Mortimer (died 19 Jan. 1424/5), K.B., 5th Earl of March, 8th Earl of Ulster, Lord Mortimer [see MORTIMER 14.i], and daughter of Edmund Stafford, K.G., K.B., 5th Earl of Stafford, 6th Lord Stafford, by Anne, Countess of Buckingham, Hertford and Northampton, daughter of Thomas of Woodstock, Duke of Gloucester (son of King Edward III of England) [see STAFFORD 9 for her ancestry]. They had one son, Henry (or Harry), Knt. [Duke of Exeter, Earl of Huntingdon and Ivry], and one daughter, Anne. By an unknown mistress (or mistresses), he also had five illegitimate sons, William, Knt., Thomas, Robert, Esq., John (clerk), and William (clerk). He received the county of Ivry in France from John, Duke of Bedford. His wife, Anne, died 20 (or 24) Sept. 1432 and was buried in a chapel at St. Katherine by the Tower, London. He married (2nd) by license dated 20 Jan. 1432/3 **BEATRICE** (or **BEATRIZ**) **OF PORTUGAL**, widow of Thomas Arundel, K.G., Earl of Arundel and Surrey, Lord High Treasurer (died 13 or 14 October 1415) [see FITZ ALAN 12.vii], and legitimated daughter of João I, King of Portugal and the Algarve [see LANCASTER 10.i], by his mistress, Inez Pires, daughter of Pedro Esteves. They had no issue. In 1439 Andrew Dautrey sued John and his wife, Beatrice, for the manors of Aldesworth, Sussex. His wife, Beatrice, died at Bordeaux, France 23 October 1439, and was buried at Arundel, Sussex by her 1st husband. He married (3rd) **ANNE MONTAGU**, widow successively of Richard Hankford, Knt. (died 8 Feb. 1430/1) [see HANKFORD 10; FITZ WARIN 15] and Lewis John, Knt. (died 27 October 1442) [see HANKFORD 10; VERE 6.ii], and daughter of John Montagu, K.G., 3rd Earl of Salisbury, by Maud, daughter of Adam Francis, Knt. [see MONTAGU 9 for her ancestry]. They had no issue. He was created Duke of Exeter 6 Jan. 1443/4. He presented to the church of Blagdon, Somerset in 1446. SIR JOHN HOLAND, Duke of Exeter, Earl of Huntingdon and Ivry,[21] died 5 August 1447. He left a will dated 16 July 1447, proved 16 Feb. 1447/8, requesting burial in a chapel at St. Katherine by the Tower, London, in a tomb ordained for his 1st and current wives, both named Anne, his sister, Constance, and for himself. His widow, Anne, was assigned dower 2 April 1454. His widow, Anne, Duchess of Exeter, died 28 Nov. 1457, and was buried with him. She left a will dated 20 April 1457, proved 15 May 1458 (P.C.C. 11 Stokton).

Weever *Ancient Funerall Monuments* (1631): 424–425. Rymer *Fœdera* 9 (1727): 223 (John styled "kinsman" by King Henry V of England); 11 (1727): 8–9, 10–12, 49, 96 (instances of John styled "kinsman" by King Henry VI of England). Nichols *Coll. of All the Wills* (1780): 282–290 (will of John Holand, Duke of Exeter). Clutterbuck *Hist. & Antiqs. of Hertford* 1 (1815): 371 (Longespée-Zouch ped.). Nicolas *Testamenta Vetusta* 1 (1826): 255–256 (will of John Holand, Duke of Exeter). Vautier *Extrait du Registre des Dons, Confiscations, Maintenues, et autres Actes* (1828): 16, 96. *Coll. Top. et Gen.* 1 (1834): 80–90, 299. Nicolas *Procs. & Ordinances of the Privy Council of England* 6 (1837): 355–357 (Anne, Duchess of Exeter, styled "king's kinswoman" [consanguinee d'ci d'ni Regis] by King Henry VI of England in 1454). Beltz *Mems. of the Order of the Garter* (1841): clvii. *Gentleman's Mag.* n.s. 32 (1849): 491–493. Napier *Swyncombe & Ewelme* (1858): chart facing 323. Hutchins *Hist. & Antiqs. of Dorset* 3 (1868): 291 (Montagu ped.). *Vis. of Devon 1620* (H.S.P. 6) (1872): 345–347 (Holland ped.: "John Holland D. of Exeter = d. of the E. of Stafford"). Wright *Feudal Manuals of English Hist.* (1872): 151–152. Harvey *Hist. & Antiqs. of the Hundred of Willey* (1872–8): opp. 146 (Quincy ped.). Hardy *Syllabus (in English) of the Docs. Rel. England & Other Kingdoms* 2 (1873): 641. Rogers *Antient Sepulchral Effigies* (1877): 224–226. Burke *Dormant, Abeyant, Forfeited & Extinct Peerages* (1883): 280–281 (sub Holland). Doyle *Official Baronage of England* 1 (1886): 711–712 (sub Exeter); 2 (1886): 229–230 (sub Huntingdon). Gibbons *Early Lincoln Wills* (1888): 167 (will of John [Holand], Duke of Exeter). Weaver *Somerset Incumbents* (1889): 28. Aveling *Heraldry, Ancient & Modern: including Boutell's Heraldry* (1890): 392 (engraving of seal of Beatrice of Portugal, Countess of Arundel & Surrey). Birch *Cat. Seals in the British Museum* 3 (1894): 108 (seal of John Holand, Earl of Huntingdon, Captain of Gournay and Gisors dated 1431 — Octagular: a shield of arms: ENGLAND within a bordure of FRANCE. Suspended from a tree. Cabled bordure), 108 (seal of John Holand, Duke of Exeter, Earl of Huntingdon & Ivory dated 1445 — A shield of arms, couché: three lions passant guardant in pale, ENGLAND, within a bordure of fleurs-de-lis, FRANCE. Crest on a helmet, ornamental mantling, and chapeau ermine, a lion statant guardant, collared, and crowned. Supporters, two heraldic antelopes, collared, chained, and ringed. In the background, on each side, his badge, a fire beacon in flames. Legend on a scroll: "Sigillum : ioh'is : ducis : exonie : * * comitis : huntyngdon : & : yveri : ac : d'ni de Sparre."). *Wiltshire Notes & Queries* 4 (1902–4): 481–493. *C.P.R. 1401–1405* (1905): 324 (John styled "king's kinsman"). Wrottesley *Peds. from the Plea Rolls* (1905): 364–365. *Rpt. on MSS in Various Colls.* 4 (Hist. MSS Comm. 55) (1907): 82, 84. Le Cacheux *Actes de la Chancellerie d'Henri VI concernant la Normandie sous la Domination Anglaise* 2 (1908): 296–298 ([John Holand], Earl of Huntingdon styled "tres chier et feal cousin" by King Henry VI of England in 1434). VCH *Hertford* 2 (1908): 201–203. *C.P.R. 1441–1446* (1908): 230 (John styled "king's kinsman"). *D.N.B.* 13 (1909): 1020–1022 (biog. of Edmund Mortimer). *C.P.R. 1416–1422* (1911): 11, 112 (instances of John, earl of Huntyngdon styled "king's kinsman"). VCH *Bedford* 3 (1912): 100–104. Wall *Handbook of the Maude Roll* (1919) unpaginated (ped. dated c.1461–85: "Anna Comitissa Huntingdon"). VCH *Berkshire* 4 (1924): 269–270. *C.P.* 5 (1926): 205–211 (sub Exeter); 6 (1926): 654 (sub Huntingdon). Harvey et al. *Vis. of the North* 3 (Surtees Soc. 144) (1930): 49–50 (Montagu ped.: "Anne [Montagu] ducesse of Excestre"). Beckington *Reg. of Thomas Bekynton Bishop of Bath & Wells* 1 (Somerset Rec. Soc. 49) (1934): 70, 111, 153. *Coat of Arms* 7 (1962): 164–169 (arms of John as Earl of Huntingdon: Quarterly 1 and 4, England and a label of France, 2 and 3, England and a bordure argent flory gold; his arms of Duke of Exeter: England and a bordure of France). Vale *English Gascony 1399–1453* (1970). McFarlane *Nobility of Later Medieval England* (1973): 32. *Ancient Deeds — Ser. BB* (List & Index Soc. 137) (1977): 100. Ellis *Cat. Seals in the P.R.O.* 1 (1978): 33 (seal of John Holand, Earl of Huntingdon dated 1440 — A shield of arms, couché: three lions passant gardant, within a bordure semé-de-lys [HOLAND]; helm above with mantling and crest: on a cap of estate a crowned and collared leopard standing; ears of wheat in the field). VCH *Wiltshire* 11 (1980): 165–181. *English Hist. Rev.* 96 (1981): 79–102 ([John Holand], Earl of Huntingdon, styled "kinsman" [consanguineo] by King Henry V of England). Williams *England in the 15th Cent.* (1987): 187–198. Hicks *Profit, Piety & Professions in Later Medieval England* (1990): 103–118. Austin *Ancient Fams. in the British Isles* (1991): 66–84. *Cal. IPM* 20 (1995): 187–189; 23 (2004): 227. Leese *Blood Royal* (1996): 170–181.

---

[21] For instances of Sir John Holand and his son, Sir Henry, using the style "Earl of Huntingdon and Ivry," see Rymer *Fœdera* 11 (1727): 8–9, 10–12, 34; Lacy *Reg. of Edmund Lacy* 1 (Episc. Regs. of the Diocese of Exeter 9) (1909): 129, 149, 251, 262–263, 381.

Catto "Chron. of John Somer," in *Camden Misc.* 34 (Camden Soc. 5th Ser. 10) (1997): 277 (birth date of John Holand). *TAG* 76 (2001): 46–49. Coss & Keen *Heraldry, Pageantry & Social Display in Medieval England* (2002): 143–167. Will of John Holand, Duke of Exeter, Lambeth Regs., Stafford, ff. 160–161 (FHL Microfilm 1473364) (names his "brother [Humphrey Stafford] Duke of Buckingham" and his "cousin [Richard] Duke of York").

Children of John Holand, K.G., by Anne Stafford:

i. **HENRY** (or **HARRY**) **HOLAND**, Knt., Duke of Exeter, Earl of Huntingdon and Ivry, joint Admiral of England, Ireland, and Aquitaine, 1446, joint Constable of the Tower of London, 1447, Admiral of England, Ireland, and Aquitaine, 1447, Constable of the Tower of London, 1447, Lord and Castellan of Lesparre and L'Esparrois, 1447, Constable of Fotheringhay Castle, 1459, son and heir, born in the Tower of London 27 June 1430. He resided at King's Hall, Cambridge in 1439–40 to 1441–2. He married before 30 July 1447 **ANNE PLANTAGENET** [see YORK 12.i], 1st daughter of Richard Plantagenet, K.G., 3rd Duke of York, 6th Earl of March, 9th Earl of Ulster, by Cecily, daughter of Ralph Neville, K.G., 1st Earl of Westmorland, 4th Lord Neville of Raby [see YORK 12 for her ancestry]. She was born at Fotheringhay Castle, Northamptonshire 10 August 1439. They had one daughter, Anne (wife of Thomas Grey, K.G., K.B., 1st Marquess of Dorset, Lord Ferrers of Groby) [see GROBY 17]. He was a legatee in the 1447 will of his father. He was granted 2/3 of an annuity of 500 marks 9 Sept. 1448, to hold as from his father's death, during his minority. He was a staunch Lancastrian, and a principal member of that party. In 1451 he was dispossessed of the Castle, town and lordship of Lesparre in Aquitaine by Pierre de Montferrand, Knt. He presented to the church of Thorpe Achurch, Northamptonshire in 1453 and 1454. He took part in Lord Egremont's rising in the North in 1454. He escaped and was ordered to appear before the Privy Council 25 June 1454. He was subsequently kept a prisoner at Pontefract and Wallingford Castles. He and his wife, Anne, were granted a papal indult for a portable altar in 1455. The king took his fealty 9 June 1458. In 1460 he was appointed to the command of the naval forces on the high seas for three years. He was present at the Battles of Blore Heath, 1459, Northampton, 1460, St. Albans (2nd), 1461, and Towton, 1461, after which defeat he took refuge in Scotland with King Henry VI and Queen Margaret. He assisted the latter in the Siege of Carlisle in May 1461. His wife, Anne, was admitted to the fraternity of St. Nicholas in London in 1461. He was attainted in Parliament 4 Nov. 1461, whereby all his honours were forfeited. The Duke escaped to Flanders, attending Queen Margaret of Anjou there in August 1463. He was living in exile with Queen Margaret at Saint-Mihiel in the Duchy of Bar c.1465. On the restoration of King Henry VI, he returned to England in Feb. 1470/1. At the Battle of Barnet 14 April 1471, he was severely wounded and left for dead, but afterwards taken to sanctuary at Westminster. He was in custody from 26 May 1471 until 20 May 1475, after which he was released. His wife, Anne, presented to the church of Blagdon, Somerset in August 1472. He and his wife, Anne, were divorced 12 Nov. 1472. In July 1475 he was ordered to join the King's expedition to France. SIR HENRY HOLAND was drowned between Calais and Dover in Sept. 1475. His former wife Anne married (2nd) about 1472/3 **THOMAS SAINT LEGER** (or **SEYNTLEGER**), Knt. [see YORK 12.i], of Guildford, Artington, Claygate (in Ash), Field Place and Down Place (both in Compton), Surrey, son of John Saint Leger, Esq., of Ulcombe, Kent, by Margery, daughter and heiress of James Donet [see RAYNSFORD 11.i.a for his ancestry]. She died 12 (or 14) Jan. 1475/6. He presented to the church of Blagdon, Somerset in 1479. He was present at the funeral of King Edward IV in 1483. SIR THOMAS SAINT LEGER was the chief instigator of the Buckingham rising in Surrey against King Richard III in 1483. He was taken at Torrington and beheaded at Exeter, Devon 12 Nov. 1483. He was attainted as from 18 October 1483, which attainder was reversed in 1485. He and his wife, Anne, were both buried in a chantry he founded in St. George's Chapel, Windsor, Berkshire. Sandford *Gen. Hist. of the Kings of England* (1677): 375–378. Rymer *Fœdera* 11 (1727): 365, 450–451 (Henry Holand styled "kinsman" by King Henry VI of England). Strachey *Rotuli Parl.* 5 (1777): 548–549 (Anne, "wife of Henry late Duke of Excestre," styled "entierly welbiloved suster" by King Edward IV in 1464). Bridges *Hist. & Antiqs. of Northamptonshire* 2 (1791): 364–365. Nichols *Hist. & Antiqs. of Leicester* 2(1) (1795): opp. 41 (representation of tomb of Sir Thomas Saint Leger and his wife, Anne, Duchess of Exeter). Clutterbuck *Hist. & Antiqs. of Hertford* 1 (1815): 371 (Longespée-Zouch ped.), 372. Nicolas *Procs. & Ordinances of the Privy Council* 6 (1837): 217–218 ([Henry Holand], Duke of Exeter, styled "welbeloved cousin" by King Henry VI of England in 1454), 355–357 (Anne, Duchess of Exeter, styled "king's kinswoman" [consanguinee regis] by King Henry VI of England in 1454). Fenn *Paston Letters* 1 (1840): 97 (letter dated 27 Jan. 1475/6: "Item, my Lady of Exeter is dead, and it was said, that both the old Duchess of Norfolk, and the Countess of Oxford, were dead, but it is not so yet."). *Gentleman's Mag.* n.s. 43 (1855): 253–254. Napier *Swyncombe & Ewelme* (1858): 323–329 (Henry Holand styled "kinsman" by King Henry VI of England), chart facing 323. *Vis. of Devon 1620* (H.S.P. 6) (1872): 345–347 (Holland ped.: "Henry Holland D. of Exeter, ob. s. p. = Ann sister to K. Ed. 4 [2] = St. Leger, 2nd husb."). Harvey *Hist. & Antiqs. of the Hundred of Willey* (1872–8): opp. 146 (Quincy ped.). Fortescue *De Laudibus Legum Angliæ* (1874): xxvi–xxix ([Henry Holand], Duke of Exeter stated to be "descended of the house of Lancaster" in letter by Sir John Fortescue dated c.1465). Cox *Notes on the Churches of Derbyshire* 3 (1877): 108, 110. Rogers *Antient Sepulchral Effigies* (1877): 224–226. *Archives Hist. du Département de la Gironde* 16 (1878): 352–353 (Henry Holand styled "kinsman" by King Henry VI of

England). *MSS of the Marquis of Ormonde* (Hist. MSS Comm. 10th Rpt., App., Pt. 5) (1885): 75. Doyle *Official Baronage of England* 1 (1886): 712–713 (sub Exeter); 2 (1886): 230 (sub Huntingdon). Gibbons *Early Lincoln Wills* (1888): 167 (will of John [Holand], Duke of Exeter). Weaver *Somerset Incumbents* (1889): 28. Birch *Cat. Seals in the British Museum* 3 (1894): 107 (seal of Henry Holand, Duke of Exeter dated 1455 — A shield of arms, couché: three lions passant guardant in pale, within a bordure semée of fleurs-de-lis. Crest on a helmet, ornamental mantling, and chapeau ermine, a lion statant [guardant?]. Supporters two heraldic antelopes, collared, chained, and ringed.). *Desc. Cat. Ancient Deeds* 3 (1900): 101. *Ancestor* 8 (1904): 167–201 (re. Saint Leger fam.). Gairdner *Paston Letters, A.D. 1422–1509* 1 (1904): 77, 134, 147–148, 150, 176, 182–183, 186, 192, 199. Kingsford *Chronicles of London* (1905): 164. Lane *Royal Daughters of England* 1 (1910): 291–299. VCH *Bedford* 3 (1912): 100–104. Clay *Extinct & Dormant Peerages* (1913): 169–171 (sub Plantagenet). Wall *Handbook of the Maude Roll* (1919) unpaginated (ped. dated c.1461–85: "Anna ducissa Oxon. [recte Exon.]"). VCH *Berkshire* 4 (1924): 269–270. *C.P.* 5 (1926): 212–216 (sub Exeter). Harvey et al. *Vis. of the North* 3 (Surtees Soc. 144) (1930): 2–5 ("Anna ducissa Exonie sepulta apud Wyndesor"), 161–164 (Espec [Roos] ped.: "Anna ducissa Exonie [1] = Henricus Holland dux Exonie, [2] = Thomas Sentleger miles secundus maritus"). Beckington *Reg. of Thomas Bekynton Bishop of Bath & Wells* 1 (Somerset Rec. Soc. 49) (1934): 111, 153, 333–334. Stillington & Fox *Regs. of Robert Stillington & Richard Fox* (Somerset Rec. Soc. 52) (1937): 79, 81. Somerville *Hist. of the Duchy of Lancaster* 1 (1953): 226–227. *Coat of Arms* 7 (1962): 164–169 (arms of Henry Holand: England and a bordure of France). Storey *End of the House of Lancaster* (1966): 65, 142–149, 160, 184–185. *Ancient Deeds — Ser. A* 2 (List & Index Soc. 152) (1978): 39. *Hist. Research* 63 (1990): 248–262. Griffiths *King & Country* (1991). *National Lib. of Wales Jour.* 27 (1991): 131–174. Zutshi *Medieval Cambridge: Essays on the Pre-Reformation Univ.* (1993): 56. James *Bede Roll of the Fraternity of St. Nicholas* 1 (London Rec. Soc. Pubs. 39) (2004): 56–58, 108. National Archives, SC 8/46/2278 (available at www.catalogue.nationalarchives.gov.uk/search.asp).

ii. **ANNE HOLAND**, married (1st) **JOHN NEVILLE**, Knt., of Kenton, Braunton, Chettiscombe, Lifton, and Shebbear, Devon, etc. [see NEVILLE 14.i.a]; (2nd) **JOHN NEVILLE**, Knt., Lord Neville [see NEVILLE 15]; (3rd) **JAMES DOUGLAS**, K.G., 9th Earl of Douglas, Earl of Avondale [see NEVILLE 15].

Illegitimate children of John Holand, K.G., by an unknown mistress or mistresses, _____:

i. **WILLIAM OF EXETER**, Knt., styled "Bastard of Exeter." He was a legatee in his father's 1447 will, who bequeathed him an annuity of £40. He served in Guyenne in 1453 in the expedition of William Fiennes, Lord Say. He was among those assembled by his half-brother, Henry Holand, Duke of Exeter in 1454 to take part in an insurrection in Yorkshire. In 1459–60 the mayor of Exeter ordered 12d. as payment to the trumpeter of William the Bastard of Exeter. On 6 March 1460/1, Edward IV, King of England, offered £100 reward for the execution of "the bastards of Exeter." In 1461 King Edward IV ordered William's arrest "for stirring up the people of Devon and Cornwall… to side with Henry VI." In 1463 he was formally attainted by Parliament. Cobbett *Parliamentary Hist. of England* 1 (1806): 418–421. *C.P.R. 1461–1467* (1897): 33. *C.P.R. 1452–1461* (1910): 125. Scofield *Life & Reign of Edward IV* 1 (1923): 156, 179, 220. *C.C.R. 1461–1468* (1949): 55–56. Vale *English Gascony 1399–1453* (1970): 233. Wasson *Recs. of Early English Drama: Devon* (1986): 376. Griffiths *King & Country* (1991): 347–348, 363. *TAG* 76 (2001): 46–49.

ii. **THOMAS HOLAND**, was a legatee in his father's 1447 will, who bequeathed him an annuity of £40. On 6 March 1460/1, Edward IV, King of England, offered £100 reward for the execution of "the bastards of Exeter." THOMAS HOLAND, Bastard of Exeter, was reportedly executed by Warwick at Coventry, Warwickshire in March 1460/1. He may also be one of the two bastard sons of the Duke of Exeter slain at the Battle of Towton 29 March 1461. Scofield *Life & Reign of Edward IV* 1 (1923): 121, 156–157. *C.C.R. 1461–1468* (1949): 55–56. Harriss & Harriss "John Benet's Chron. for the Years 1400 to 1462," in *Camden Misc.* 24 (Camden Soc. 4th Ser. 9) (1972): 233. *TAG* 76 (2001): 46–49.

iii. **ROBERT HOLAND**, Esq., styled "Bastard of Exeter." He married **MARGARET** _____. They had two daughters, Jane and Elizabeth (wife of John Reskymer). He was among those assembled by his half-brother, Henry Holand, Duke of Exeter in 1454 to take part in an insurrection in Yorkshire. Following the collapse of the insurrection, Robert and his brother, Duke Henry, traveled secretly to London and sought sanctuary at Westminster Abbey. They were led out of abbey and arrested by Richard, Duke of York 23 July 1454. In 1458 he was granted the manors of Manorbier and Penally, Pembrokeshire by his half-brother, Henry Holand, Duke of Exeter, both of which manors are named in their father's 1447 will, being then held by feoffees. Presumably he is one of the two bastard sons of the Duke of Exeter slain at the Battle of Towton 29 March 1461. In 1463 William Willoughby, Esq., of Boston, Lincolnshire was pardoned for failure to appear before the justices of the late King's [Henry VI] bench touching a debt of £20 formerly owed to "Robert the Bastard of Exeter." Sandford *Gen. Hist. of the Kings of England* (1677): 219. Collins *English Baronetage* 2 (1741): 91 (sub Trelawney). Polsue *Complete Parochial Hist. of the County of Cornwall* 4 (1872): chart foll. 352. *Vis. of Devon 1620* (H.S.P. 6) (1872): 161 (Kendall ped.)

(Holand arms quartered by Kendall fam.: Three lions passant guardant within bordure, over all a bar sinister). Boase & Courtney *Bibliotheca Cornubiensis* 2 (1878): 562 (re. John Reskymer). Vivian *Vis. of Cornwall* (1887): 258–259, 396, 475. *C.P.R. 1461–1467* (1897): 255. Law *Royal Gallery of Hampton Court* (1898): 315. *Notes & Queries* 9th Ser. 12 (1903): 276. Kingsford *Chronicles of London* (1905): 164. Rose-Troup *Western Rebellion of 1549* (1913): 100–101. Scofield *Life & Reign of Edward IV* (1923). Storey *End of the House of Lancaster* (1966): 142–149. *NEHGR* 121 (1967): 185. Griffiths *King & Country* (1991): 347–348, 352, 363. *TAG* 76 (2001): 46–49.

Child of Robert Holand, Esq., by Margaret _____:

- a. **JANE HOLAND**, married (1st) **JOHN KENDALL**, of Treworgy (in Duloe), Cornwall [see KENDALL 13]; (2nd) **JOHN TRELAWNEY**, Knt. [see KENDALL 13].

iv. **JOHN HOLAND**, clerk. He was already a rector when he resided as a commoner at at King's Hall, Cambridge in 1440–1 and 1441–2. Presumably he is the John Holand who occurs as Rector of Heanton Punchardon, Devon c.1450. Zutshi *Medieval Cambridge: Essays on the Pre-Reformation Univ.* (1993): 56. North Devon Rec. Office: Barnstaple Borough, B1/496 (available at www.a2a.org.uk/search/index.asp).

v. **WILLIAM HOLAND**, clerk. He was already a rector when he resided as a commoner at King's Hall, Cambridge in 1440–1 and 1441–2. Zutshi *Medieval Cambridge: Essays on the Pre-Reformation Univ.* (1993): 56.

❧ EXTON ❧

MALCOLM III (CEANNMORE), King of Scots, married [SAINT] **MARGARET**.
DAVID I, King of Scots, married **MAUD OF NORTHUMBERLAND**.
HENRY OF SCOTLAND, Earl of Northumberland, married **ADA DE WARENNE**.
DAVID OF SCOTLAND, Earl of Huntingdon, married **MAUD OF CHESTER** (desc. King William the Conqueror).
ISABEL OF HUNTINGDON, married **ROBERT DE BRUS**, Knt., of Annandale in Scotland.
BERNARD DE BRUS, of Conington, Huntingdonshire, married **ALICE DE BEAUCHAMP**.
BERNARD DE BRUS, Knt., of Conington, Huntingdonshire, married **AGATHA** _____.
BERNARD DE BRUS, Knt., of Conington, Huntingdonshire, married **AGNES** _____.
JOHN DE BRUS, of Conington, Huntingdonshire, married **MARGARET DE BEAUCHAMP** [see CONINGTON 9].

10. JOAN DE BRUS, married before 1361 (date of fine) **NICHOLAS GREENE**, Steward of Higham Ferrers and Glatton, Knight of the Shire for Rutland, 1371 and 1376, and, in right of his wife, of Exton, Rutland, son of Thomas Greene, of Boughton, Northamptonshire, by his 2nd wife, Christian, daughter and heiress of _____ Iwardby. They had two daughters, Elizabeth and Eleanor. He and his wife, Joan, made a settlement of their moiety of the manor of Exton, Rutland in 1361. In 1373 they settled the whole manor on their daughter Elizabeth, 1st wife of John Holand, Knt., of Thorpe Waterville, Northamptonshire. NICHOLAS GREENE died in or before 1379, and was buried in the church of Exton, Rutland. His widow, Joan, died 28 June 1421.

Herald & Genealogist 8 (1874): 325–348. *Misc. Gen. et Heraldica* n.s. 1 (1874): 337–340. *Greene Fam. in England & America* (1901): Greene Ped. I following 147). *Rutland Mag. & County Hist. Rec.* 3 (1908): 97–106, 130–137. VCH *Rutland* 2 (1935): 128. VCH *Huntingdon* 3 (1936): 144–151.

Children of Joan de Brus, by Nicholas Greene:

i. **ELIZABETH GREENE**, married **JOHN HOLAND**, Knt., of Thorpe Waterville, Northamptonshire [see HOLAND 12.ii].

ii. **ELEANOR GREENE** [see next].

11. ELEANOR GREENE, married before 1378 (date of fine) **THOMAS CULPEPER**, Knt., of Bayhall (in Pembury), Kent, Ansley and Hardreshull, Warwickshire, Saleby, Lincolnshire, etc., Sheriff of Kent, 1394–5, and, in right of his 2nd wife, of Cornerth Hall (in Bures), Suffolk, son and heir of John Culpeper, Knt., of Bayhall (in Pembury), Kent, Ashton, Northamptonshire, Ansley and Hardreshull, Warwickshire, etc., by Elizabeth, daughter and co-heiress of John Hardreshull, Knt.

They had one son, John, Knt., and one daughter, Eleanor. In 1396 he reached agreement with his cousin, John Garton, regarding the manors of North Kelsey and Saleby, Lincolnshire. He presented to the churches of Roade, Northamptonshire, 1392, and Ashton, Northamptonshire, 1399. In 1403 he settled a dispute with William Brinklow, parson of Manceter, regarding the tithes of his wood in Hartshill called the Hays. He married(2nd) before 1405 (date of release) **JOYCE CORNERDE**, widow of John Vyne, Esq., and daughter of Thomas Cornerde. They had four sons, Walter, Nicholas, Thomas, and Richard. In 1420 he purchased lands in Ashton, Roade, and Hartwell, Northamptonshire. SIR THOMAS CULPEPER died testate in 1428.

> Bartlett *Hist. & Antiqs. of Manceter* (1791): 60–66, 99–100. *Herald & Genealogist* 8 (1874): 325–348. *List of Sheriffs for England & Wales* (PRO Lists and Indexes 9) (1898): 68. *Greene Fam. in England & America* (1901): Greene Ped. I following 147). Copinger *Manors of Suffolk: Hundreds of Babergh & Blackbourn* (1905): 55. *Rutland Mag. & County Hist. Rec.* 3 (1908): 97–106, 130–137. Dudding *Hist. of the Manor & Parish of Saleby with Thoresthorpe* (1922): 26–43 (re. Hardreshull fam.), 44–53 (re. Culpeper fam.). *C.C.R. 1402–1405* (1929): 518. VCH *Rutland* 2 (1935): 128 (Culpeper arms: Argent a bend engrailed gules). VCH *Northampton* 5 (2002): 59–76.

Child of Eleanor Greene, by Thomas Culpeper, Knt.:

i. **ELEANOR CULPEPER**, married **REYNOLD COBHAM**, Knt., 3rd Lord Cobham of Sterborough [see COBHAM 10].

᭢ FAIRFAX ᭣

MALCOLM III (CEANNMORE), King of Scots, married [SAINT] **MARGARET**.
DAVID I, King of Scots, married **MAUD OF NORTHUMBERLAND**.
HENRY OF SCOTLAND, Earl of Northumberland, married **ADA DE WARENNE**.
WILLIAM THE LION, King of Scots, by a mistress, _____ **AVENEL**.
ISABEL OF SCOTLAND, married **ROBERT DE ROOS**, of Helmsley, Yorkshire.
WILLIAM DE ROOS, Knt., of Helmsley, Yorkshire, married **LUCY FITZ PETER**.
WILLIAM DE ROOS, Knt., of Ingmanthorpe (in Kirk Deighton), Yorkshire, married **EUSTACHE FITZ RALPH**.
LUCY DE ROOS, married **ROBERT DE PLUMPTON**, Knt., of Plumpton (in Spofforth), Yorkshire.
WILLIAM DE PLUMPTON, Knt., of Plumpton (in Spofforth), Yorkshire, married **CHRISTIAN DE MOWBRAY**.
ALICE PLUMPTON, married **RICHARD DE SHERBURNE**, Knt., of Aighton (in Mitton), Lancashire.
MARGARET DE SHERBURNE, married **RICHARD DE BAILEY**, of Stonyhurst, Lancashire.
RICHARD SHERBURNE, Esq., of Stonyhurst, Lancashire, married **AGNES HARINGTON**.
RICHARD SHERBURNE, married **ALICE HAMERTON**.
ROBERT SHERBURNE, married **JOAN RADCLIFFE** [see TOWNLEY 13.i].

15. ELIZABETH SHERBURNE, married by license dated 27 August 1460 **THOMAS FAIRFAX**, K.B., of Walton, Yorkshire, Master of the Horse to King Edward IV, son and heir of William Fairfax, of Walton, Yorkshire, by Katherine, daughter of Alexander Neville, of Thornton Bridge, Yorkshire. They had four sons, Thomas, Knt., William, Knt., Richard, and Robert, Gent., and three daughters, Jane (wife of Richard Aldborough, Knt.), Dorothy (wife of Christopher Nelson), and Isabel. He successfully claimed the manor of Gilling, Yorkshire in 1492. He was made a Knight of the Bath in 1495 at the creation of Arthur, Prince of Wales. SIR THOMAS FAIRFAX died in 1505.

> *Gentleman's Mag.* 94 (1824): 513–517, 588–591. Burke & Burke *Gen. & Heraldic Dict. of the Landed Gentry* (1847): 393–394 (sub Fairfax). *Testamenta Eboracensia* 3 (Surtees Soc. 45) (1865): 335 (license for marriage of Thomas Fairfax and Elizabeth Sherburn). *Herald & Genealogist* 6 (1871): 385–407, 611–630; 7 (1873): 145–163. Glover & St. George *Vis. of Yorkshire 1584–5, 1612* (1875): 39 (Fairfax ped.: "Sir Thomas Fairfax. = Elizabeth, dau. of Robert Sherburne, of Lanc."), 96–97 (Fairfax ped.: "Sir Thomas Fairfax. = Elizabeth, dau. to Robert Sherborne, of Lancashire."). Flower *Vis. of Yorkshire 1563–4* (H.S.P. 16) (1881): 117–119 (Fairfax ped.: "Sir Thomas Ferfax. = Elsabeth doughter of Robert Sherborne."). Sherborn *Hist. of the Fam. of Sherborn* (1901): 12–19. Harvey et al. *Vis. of the North* 1 (Surtees Soc. 122) (1912): 144–145 (Fairfax ped.: "Sir Thomas Fayrefax, knight, weddyd Elizabeth, doughtre to Roberte Sherborne of

Stonyeherste in Lancasshere"); 2 (Surtees Soc. 133) (1921): 148–149 (Fairfax ped.: "Sir Thomas Ferfax, son and heyre of William. = Elsabeth, doter of Robert Sherborou of Lancaster."); 4 (Surtees Soc. 146) (1932): 36–37 (Fairfax ped.: "Sr Thom. Fairfax = Elizabeth dau. to Sr Robert Sherborne [of Stanhurst] of Lancashier"). VCH *Yorkshire* N.R. 1 (1914): 481.

16. THOMAS FAIRFAX, Knt., of Walton and Gilling, Yorkshire, son and heir, born about 1476 (aged 29 in 1505). He married **ANNE** (or **AGNES**) **GASCOIGNE**, daughter of William Gascoigne, Knt., of Gawthorpe, Yorkshire, by Margaret, daughter of Henry Percy, Knt., 3rd Earl of Northumberland, 6th Lord Percy [see GASCOIGNE 17 for her ancestry]. They had six sons, Nicholas, Knt., William, Thomas, Miles, Guy, and Robert, and seven daughters, Anne (wife of William Harrington), Margaret (wife of William Sayer and Richard Mansell), Isabel, Elizabeth, Dorothy, Katherine, and _____ (wife of _____ Dawny (or Dawtry)). SIR THOMAS FAIRFAX left a will dated 26 Nov. 1520, proved 11 April 1521.

>Burke *Hist. of the Commoners* 2 (1836): 115. Burke & Burke *Gen. & Heraldic Dict. of the Landed Gentry* (1847): 393–394 (sub Fairfax). Tonge *Vis. of Northern Counties 1530* (Surtees Soc. 41) (1863): 57 (Fairfax ped.: "Syr Thomas Fairefax, son and heire of Thomas, maried Anne, doughter of Syr Willyam Gascoign of Galthorp"). Glover & St. George *Vis. of Yorkshire 1584-5, 1612* (1875): 39 (Fairfax ped.: "Sir Thomas Fairfax. = Ann, dau. of Sir William Gascoigne, of Gawthorpe."), 96–97 (Fairfax ped.), 384–385 (Gascoigne ped.: "Ann [Gascoigne], mar. to .... Fairfax."). *Herald & Genealogist* 6 (1871): 385–407, 611–630; 7 (1873): 145–163. Flower *Vis. of Yorkshire 1563-4* (H.S.P. 16) (1881): 117–119 (Fairfax ped.: "Thomas Ferfax son & heyre to Sir Thomas. = Anne doughter of Sir William Gaskon of Gawthorpe."), 133–136 (Gascoigne ped.: "Anne [Gascoigne] wyff to Sir Thomas Ferfax."). *Testamenta Eboracensia* 5 (Surtees Soc. 79) (1884): 121–124 (will of Thomas Fairfax, Knt.). Ruvigny and Raineval *Plantagenet Roll: Mortimer-Percy* 1 (1911): 33. Harvey et al. *Vis. of the North* 1 (Surtees Soc. 122) (1912): 144–145 (Fairfax ped.: "Sir Thomas Fayrefax, knight, weddyd Anne, doughtre to Sir Wylliam Gascoyne of Galtherope"); 2 (Surtees Soc. 133) (1921): 148–149 (Fairfax ped.: "Thomas [Fairfax], son and heyre, knight. = Anne, doter of Sir William Gaston of Gawthorp.") ; 4 (Surtees Soc. 146) (1932): 36–37 (Fairfax ped.: "Thomas Fairfax = Anne d. to Wm Gascoyn of Galthrop"). Clay *Extinct & Dormant Peerages* (1913): 65 (arms: Argent, three bars gemelles gules, over all a lion rampant sable). VCH *Yorkshire* N.R. 1 (1914): 481.

17. NICHOLAS FAIRFAX, Knt., of Walton and Gilling, Yorkshire, Sheriff of Yorkshire, 1531–2, 1544–5, 1561–2, Burgess (M.P.) for Scarborough, 1542, Knight of the Shire for Yorkshire, 1547, 1563, member of the Council in the North, 1548–53, 1555–71, Chief Steward of the lands late of St. Mary's Abbey, York, 1557, son and heir, born about 1499 (aged 22 in 1521). He married (1st) about 1516 **JANE PALMES**, daughter of Guy Palmes, Esq., of Lindley, Serjeant-at-law. They had eight sons, William, Knt., Nicholas, Thomas [Canon of Carlisle], George, Robert, Edward, Cuthbert, and Henry, and five daughters, Anne (wife of Christopher Anne, Esq.), Margaret (wife of William Bellasis, Knt.), Eleanor (wife of John Vavasour), Elizabeth (wife of Robert Roos), and Mary. In 1536 he shared command of a large force of rebels with his cousin, Sir Thomas Percy. At York he declared that as the Pilgrimage was a spiritual matter all churchmen should go forth on it. By Christmas he was on his way to court with a letter of recommendation from the Earl of Northumberland to Cromwell. He made his peace with the king, and later took part in the proceedings against Lords Darcy and Hussey. He served on the Scottish expedition of 1544 under the Earl of Hertford, as captain of 88 men of whom he had been required to furnish 60 himself. He married (2nd) **ALICE HARRINGTON**, widow of Richard Flower (died 1540), of Whitwell, Rutland, and Henry Sutton, Knt., of Averham, Nottinghamshire, and daughter of John Harrington, Knt., of Exton, Rutland. They had no issue. In 1564 he was called a 'favourer' of religion by the Archbishop of Canterbury and he was employed to enforce the Elizabethan settlement. SIR NICHOLAS FAIRFAX died 30 March 1571, and was buried at Gilling, Yorkshire. He left a will dated 6 July 1570.

>Burke *Hist. of the Commoners* 2 (1836): 115. Burke & Burke *Gen. & Heraldic Dict. of the Landed Gentry* (1847): 393–394 (sub Fairfax). Tonge *Vis. of Northern Counties 1530* (Surtees Soc. 41) (1863): 57 (Fairfax ped.: "Syr Nicholas Fayrefax, son of Thomas, maried Jane, doughter of Gye Pallmes, Sergeant at Lawe"). *Herald & Genealogist* 6 (1871): 385–407, 611–630; 7 (1873): 145–163. Glover & St. George *Vis. of Yorkshire 1584-5, 1612* (1875): 39 (Fairfax ped.: "Sir

Nicholas Fairfax. = Jane, dau. of Guy Palmes, serjeant-at-law."), 96–97 (Fairfax ped.). Flower *Vis. of Yorkshire 1563–4* (H.S.P. 16) (1881): 117–119 (Fairfax ped.: "Sir Nycolas Ferfax Knight of Gyllyng. = Jane doughter of Guy Palmes, serjent at lawe."). *List of Sheriffs for England & Wales* (PRO Lists and Indexes 9) (1898): 163. *Yorkshire Arch. Jour.* 19 (1907): 148–149. Clay *Extinct & Dormant Peerages* (1913): 65. Harvey et al. *Vis. of the North* 1 (Surtees Soc. 122) (1912): 144–145 (Fairfax ped.: "Sir Nycholus [Fairfax], nowe of Gyppinge, wedyd Jane, doughtre to Gwye Palmes, Sergeant of the lawe"); 2 (Surtees Soc. 133) (1921): 13 (Fairfax ped.: "Sir Nicholas Fairfax, sonne and heire of Sir Thomas maryed Jane, doughter of Gye Palmes, serjant at the lawe … and to his second wyfe he maryed Alice, doughter of Sir John Harington of Exon and widowe of Sir Henry Sutton of Averam, knight"), 148–149 (Fairfax ped.: "Sir Nycholas Ferfax of Gyppyng, son and heyr. = Jane, doter of Guy Palmes, sergent at lawe"); 4 (Surtees Soc. 146) (1932): 36–37 (Fairfax ped.: "Sr Nicolas Fairfax = Jane d. to Guy Palmes sergant at Law"). VCH *Yorkshire N.R.* 1 (1914): 481. *Ancient Deeds — Ser. B* 3 (List & Index Soc. 113) (1975): B.12079. Hasler *House of Commons 1558–1603* 2 (1981): 98–99 (biog. of Sir Nicholas Fairfax). Bindoff *House of Commons 1509–1558* 2 (1982): 114–115 (biog. of Sir Nicholas Fairfax).

18. **MARY FAIRFAX**, married at Gilling, Yorkshire in 1548 (as his 1st wife) **HENRY** (or **HARRY**) **CURWEN**, Knt., of Workington, Seaton, and Winscales, Cumberland, Knight of the Shire for Cumberland, 1553, 1555, 1563, Sheriff of Cumberland, 1562, 1570–1, 1580–1, 1589–90, son and heir of Thomas Curwen, Knt., of Workington, Cumberland, Sheriff of Cumberland, by Agnes, daughter of Walter Strickland, K.B. [see CARLETON 15.ii for his ancestry]. He was born in May 1528. They had one son, Nicholas, Knt., and three daughters, Jane (wife of Christopher Musgrave, Esq.), Agnes (wife of James Bellingham, Knt.), and Mabel. He married (2nd) **JANE CROSBY**, daughter of _____ Crosby, Rector of Camerton, Cumberland. They had two sons, George and Thomas, and five daughters. In 1558 he was granted the manor of Harington, Cumberland by the king and queen. In 1564 he purchased the advowsons of Harington and Workington, Cumberland from Richard Dalston. In 1568 he received Mary, Queen of Scots, at Workington, Cumberland on her flight from Scotland. In 1570 he was mustered at Carlisle to make a foray into Scotland. SIR HENRY CURWEN died 25 Dec. 1596. He left a will dated 7 October 1595, proved 31 Jan. 1597/8.

    Burke *Hist. of the Commoners* 1 (1836): 577–580 (sub Curwen); 2 (1838): 115. Jefferson *Hist. & Antiqs. of Allerdale Ward* (1842): 251–257. Tonge *Vis. of Northern Counties 1530* (Surtees Soc. 41) (1863): 100 (Curwyn ped.: "Henry [Curwen] son & heyre"). *Herald & Genealogist* 6 (1871): 385–407, 611–630; 7 (1873): 145–163. St. George *Vis. of Cumberland 1615* (H.S.P. 7) (1872): 30 (Curwen ped.: "Sr Henry Curwen."). Glover & St. George *Vis. of Yorkshire 1584–5, 1612* (1875): 39 (Fairfax ped.: "Mary [Fairfax], mar. Sir Hy. Curwen."). Flower *Vis. of Yorkshire 1563–4* (H.S.P. 16) (1881): 82 (Curwen ped.: "Henry Curwyn son and heyr"), 117–119 (Fairfax ped.: "Mary [Fairfax] wyff to … Curwen of Comberland."). Sandford *Cursory Relation of Cumberland* (Cumberland & Westmorland Antiq. & Arch. Soc. Tract Ser. 4) (1890): 64–65. Jackson *Papers & Peds. Mainly Rel. Cumberland & Westmorland* 1 (1892): 288–370. *List of Sheriffs for England & Wales* (PRO Lists and Indexes 9) (1898): 28. *Notes & Queries* 9th Ser. 7 (1901): 14. *Yorkshire Arch. Jour.* 19 (1907): 148–149. Harvey et al. *Vis. of the North* 1 (Surtees Soc. 122) (1912): 144–145 (Fairfax ped.: "Marye [Fairfax], wife to Curwen"); 2 (Surtees Soc. 133) (1921): 13 (Fairfax ped.: "Marye [Fairfax], maryed to Henrie Curwyn of Wirkington"), 148 (Fairfax ped.: "Mary [Fairfax] wyff to Curwen."); 4 (Surtees Soc. 146) (1932): 36–37 (Fairfax ped.: "Mary [Fairfax]"). Clay *Extinct & Dormant Peerages* (1913): 66. Bindoff *House of Commons 1509–1558* 1 (1982): 741–742 (biog. of Henry Curwen).

Child of Mary Fairfax, by Henry (or Harry) Curwen, Knt.:

  i. **MABEL CURWEN**, married **WILLIAM FAIRFAX**, Knt., of Steeton, Yorkshire [see BLADEN 14].

~ FARRER ~

ALICE OF NORMANDY (sister of King William the Conqueror), married **LAMBERT**, Count of Lens.
JUDITH OF LENS, married **WALTHEOF**, Earl of Northumberland.
MAUD OF NORTHUMBERLAND, married **SIMON DE SENLIS**, Earl of Huntingdon and Northampton.
SIMON DE SENLIS, Earl of Huntingdon and Northampton, married **ISABEL** (or **ELIZABETH**) **OF LEICESTER**.
ISABEL DE SAINT LIZ, married **WILLIAM MAUDUIT**, of Hanslope, Buckinghamshire.
ROBERT MAUDUIT, of Hanslope, Buckinghamshire, married **ISABEL BASSET**.
WILLIAM MAUDUIT, of Hanslope, Buckinghamshire, married **ALICE DE NEWBURGH**.
ISABEL MAUDUIT, married **WILLIAM DE BEAUCHAMP**, Knt., of Elmley, Worcestershire.
WILLIAM DE BEAUCHAMP, Knt., Earl of Warwick, married **MAUD FITZ JOHN**.
ISABEL DE BEAUCHAMP, married **HUGH LE DESPENSER**, Knt., Earl of Winchester.
PHILIP LE DESPENSER, Knt., of Goxhill, Lincolnshire, married **MARGARET DE GOUSHILL** (desc. King William the Conqueror).
PHILIP LE DESPENSER, Knt., of Goxhill, Lincolnshire, married **JOAN DE COBHAM** (desc. King William the Conqueror).
PHILIP LE DESPENSER, Knt., 1st Lord Despenser, married **ELIZABETH** _____.
PHILIP LE DESPENSER, Knt., 2nd Lord Despenser, married **ELIZABETH TIBETOT** (desc. King William the Conqueror).
MARGERY DESPENSER, married **ROGER WENTWORTH**, Esq., of Nettlestead, Suffolk.
PHILIP WENTWORTH, Knt., of Nettlestead, Suffolk, married **MARY CLIFFORD** (desc. King William the Conqueror).
ELIZABETH WENTWORTH, married **MARTIN DE LA SEE**, Knt., of Barmston, Yorkshire.
ELIZABETH DE LA SEE, married **ROGER KELKE**, of Barnetby le Wold, Lincolnshire.
CHRISTOPHER KELKE, of Barnetby le Wold, Lincolnshire, married **ISABEL GIRLINGTON** (desc. King William the Conqueror) [see KELKE 19].

20. WILLIAM KELKE, of Barnetby-le-Wold, Lincolnshire, and London, Mercer of London, younger son, born after 1519. He married **THOMASINE SKERNE**, daughter and co-heiress of Percival Skerne, of London, fishmonger, by his wife, Joan. They had two daughters, Elizabeth and Cecily. WILLIAM KELKE left a will dated 16 June 1552, proved 28 June 1552 (P.C.C. 18 Powell). His widow, Thomasine, died shortly before 31 August 1566, when Jeffrey Ducket was appointed administrator of her late husband's estate during the minority of their children, Elizabeth and Cecily Kelke.

Genealogist 4 (1880): 186 (1562–4 Vis. Lincolnshire.) (Kelke ped.: "William [Kelke]."). Maddison *Lincolnshire Peds.* 2 (H.S.P. 51) (1903): 555–557 (Kelke ped.). Holmes *Farrar's Island Fam.* (1972): 69–77. Dorman *Adventurers of Purse & Person* 1 (2004): 926–953.

21. CECILY KELKE, daughter and co-heiress, born before 1552. She married at St. Sepulchre's without Newgate, London by license dated 26 August 1574 **JOHN FARRER** (or **FARRAR**), Esq., of Croxton, Lincolnshire, and St. Mary, Aldermanbury, London, 2nd son of William Farrer, yeoman, of Ewood (in Midgley in Halifax), Yorkshire, by Margaret, daughter of Hugh Lacy, Esq., of Brearley Hall, Halifax, Yorkshire [see PENNINGTON 21 for his ancestry]. They had four sons, John, Esq., Henry, Esq., William and Humphrey (clerk). He was a legatee in the 1571 will of his father and in the 1610 will of his brother, Henry Farrer, Esq., of Ewood, Yorkshire. JOHN FARRER, Esq., left a will dated 14 Nov. 1627, codicil dated 24 April 1628, and proved 28 May 1628 (P.C.C. 50 Barrington).

Foster *Peds. of Fams. of Yorkshire* 1(1) (1874): Farrer ped. Cooke & St. George *Vis. of Hertfordshire 1572, 1634 & 1546* (H.S.P. 22) (1886): 53 (1634 Vis.) (Farrar ped.: "John Farrar of Croxton, co. Linc, 2 son = Sisseley, da. of William Kelk of Barnaby [Barnet by the Wold], co. Linc."). Foster *London Marr. Lics. 1521–1869* (1887): 472. Maddison *Lincolnshire Peds.* 2 (H.S.P. 51) (1903): 555–557 (Kelke ped.). *Misc. Gen. et Heraldica* 5th Ser. 9 (1935–7): 224–228. Farrer *Farrer Wills & Admins.* (1936): 53–55, 96–97, 126–128, 142, 156. Holmes *Farrar's Island Fam.* (1972): 25–32 (Farrar arms: Argent, on a bend engrailed gules three horse-shoes of the field). *NEHGR* 107 (1953): 190 (Farrar arms: Silver

22. WILLIAM FARRER, Gent., of London, 3rd son, baptized at Croxton, Lincolnshire 28 April 1583. He immigrated to Virginia 16 March 1617/8 in the Neptune with Lord De La Warr, arriving in Virginia August 1618, where he settled in Henrico County. He married before 2 May 1626 **CECILY** _____, widow successively of Thomas Bailey (died 1619), of Henrico County, Virginia, and Samuel Jordan (died 1623), of Charles City, Virginia. She was born about 1601 (aged 24 in 1625). They had two sons, William and John, and one daughter, Cecily. He was appointed to the Council 14 March 1625/6, where position he held for the remainder of his life. He was a legatee in his father's 1628 will. WILLIAM FARRER, Gent., died in Virginia shortly before 11 June 1637.

Foster *Peds. of Fams. of Yorkshire* 1(1) (1874): Farrer ped. Cooke & St. George *Vis. of Hertfordshire 1572, 1634 & 1546* (H.S.P. 22) (1886): 53 (Farrar ped.). Dorman *Adventurers of Purse & Person* 1 (2004): 120–197, 926–953.

❧ FAUCONBERGE ❧

RICHARD FITZ GILBERT, of Clare, Suffolk, married **ROHESE** (or **ROSE**) **GIFFARD**.
GILBERT FITZ RICHARD, of Clare, Suffolk, married **ALICE DE CLERMONT**.
MARGARET FITZ GILBERT, married **WILLIAM DE MONTFITCHET**, of Stanstead Mountfitchet, Essex.
GILBERT DE MONTFITCHET, of Stanstead Mountfitchet, Essex, married **AVELINE DE LUCY**.
RICHARD DE MONTFITCHET, of Stanstead Mountfitchet, Essex, married **MILLICENT** _____ [see PLAIZ 5].

6. MARGARET (or **MARGERY**) **DE MONTFITCHET**. She married (1st) **HUGH BOLBEC**, of Styford, Northumberland. Her maritagium included Bolbeck mill and other property in Barrington, Cambridgeshire. They had two sons, Hugh and Richard. HUGH BOLBEC was living in 1224. His widow, Margaret, married (2nd) after October 1214 **PETER DE FAUCONBERGE**, of Rise and Withernwick, Yorkshire. They had one son, Walter, Knt.[1st Lord Fauconberge], and one daughter, Aveline. PETER DE FAUCONBERGE was living April 1230.

Clutterbuck *Hist. & Antiq. of Hertfordshire* 2 (1821): 261 (Montfitchet ped.). VCH *Cambridge* 5 (1973): 147–160.

Children of Margaret de Montfitchet, by Peter de Fauconberge:

i. **WALTER DE FAUCONBERGE**, Knt., 1st Lord Fauconberge [see next].

ii. **AVELINE DE FAUCONBERGE**, married **GILES DE GOUSHILL** (or **GOUSEL**, **GOXHILL**), of Goxhill, Bassingham, Billinghay, East Halton, Graby, Gedney, Lobthorpe (in North Witham), Pointon, Roxholme (in Lensingham), Roxton (in Immingham), and Walcott (in Billinghay), Lincolnshire, Sheriff of Yorkshire, son and heir of Ralph de Goushill, by Emecina, daughter of Fulk d'Oyry, of Gedney, Lincolnshire.. They had one son, Peter, Knt. In 1242 he sued William de Beaumont and his wife, Alice, regarding eleven acres of land in Gedney, Lincolnshire, as his share of the inheritance of his uncle, Geoffrey d'Oyry. In 1258 he was granted a weekly market at Goxhill, Lincolnshire, and free warren in his demesne lands in Goxhill, Bassingham, Billinghay, East Halton, Graby, Gedney, Lobthorpe (in North Witham), Pointon, Roxholme (in Lensingham), Roxton (in Immingham), and Walcott (in Billinghay), Lincolnshire. Macdonald *Hist. Notices of the Parish of Holbeach* (1890): 37–38. *Lincolnshire Notes & Queries* 5 (1898): 122; 9 (1907): 57–58. *C.Ch. R. 1257–1300* 2 (1906): 12. Power *Norman Frontier in the 12th & Early 13th Cents.* (2004): 513 (Oyry ped.).

Child of Aveline de Fauconberge, by Giles de Goushill:

a. **PETER DE GOUSHILL**, Knt., of Gedney, Bassingham, East Halton, Goxhill, Immingham, Market Stainton, Pointon, and Roxholme (in Lensingham), Lincolnshire, Topsfield, Essex, etc., son and heir. He married **ELA DE CAMOYS**, daughter of Ralph de Camoys. They had one son, Ralph. In 1275–6 Simon le Constable arraigned an assize against Peter son of Giles de Gousle [Goushill] touching a fosse levied in Gedney, Lincolnshire. In 1275–6 Simon le Constable arraigned an assize against Peter son of Giles de Consyl [sic] touching a way stopped in Gedney, Lincolnshire. In 1275–6 Peter son of Giles de Gousl' arraigned an assize of novel disseisin against Master Hugh de Evesham, parson of the church of Goxhill, and others, touching a tenement in Goxhill, Lincolnshire. In 1278–9 Peter de Gousele arraigned an assize of mort d'ancestor against Radulph son of Radulph de Gousele touching possessions in Halton, Immingham, Killingholme, Roxton, and Stallingborough, Lincolnshire. In 1281 Peter de Gousele, with Simon le Constable and Walter le Burgyllon, claimed a fair in Holbeach and Whaplode, Lincolnshire; as Walter was under age and in the king's custody, Peter was not able to answer. The same year Peter de Gousle, with Robert de Vernur and Duncan de Cotes, held a weekly market and yearly fair in Market Stainton, Lincolnshire. His wife, Ela, left a will proved 12 August 1295. SIR PETER DE GOUSHILL left a will proved 13 June 1296. *Annual Rpt. of the Deputy Keeper* 45 (1885): 180, 183; 48 (1887): 160. Macdonald *Hist. Notices of the Parish of Holbeach* (1890): 33. *Lincolnshire Notes & Queries* 9 (1907): 57–58. *Rolls & Reg. of Bishop Oliver Sutton, 1280–1299* 5 (Lincoln Rec. Soc. 60) (1965): 102, 110–111, 157.

Children of Peter de Goushill, Knt., by Ela de Camoys:

1) **RALPH DE GOUSHILL**, of Goxhill, Lincolnshire, married **HAWISE FITZ WARIN** [see HOO 10].

7. WALTER DE FAUCONBERGE, Knt., of Rise and Withernwick, Yorkshire, son and heir. He married **AGNES DE BRUS**, daughter of Peter de Brus, of Skelton, Yorkshire, by Hawise de Lancaster, daughter of Gilbert Fitz Roger [Fitz Reinfrid], Knt. [see AUMALE 6 for her ancestry]. They had seven sons, Peter, Walter [2nd Lord Fauconberge], Frank, Peter (clerk), Alexander (clerk), John, and Patrick, and four daughters, Avice, Lorette, Hawise, and Agnes. He was on the king's service in Gascony with the Earl of Lancaster in April 1254. His wife, Agnes, was co-heiress in 1272 to her brother, Peter de Brus, by which she inherited the Castle, park, and forest of Skelton, and the manors of Marske and Eastburn, etc., Yorkshire, together with a moiety of the bailiwick of the wapentake of Langbaurgh, and a moiety of the advowson of Guisborough Priory. In 1272–3 the Prior of Gisbourne arraigned an assise of novel disseisin against Walter and his wife, Agnes, regarding common of pasture in Skelton, Yorkshire. In 1273 Walter, Archbishop of York, imposed various concessions upon Walter in compensation for injuries inflicted by him on the Prior and convent of Guisborough. In 1275 he and his wife, Agnes, made an arrangement with Marmaduke de Thweng and Lucy his wife (sister of Agnes) regarding the right to the advowson of Guisborough Priory. He was summoned to attend the muster at Worcester in 1277. He was summoned to the Parliament at Shrewsbury 30 Sept. 1283 for the trial of David, brother of Llywelyn. He was continually employed in the Scottish wars. His wife, Agnes, died 22 May 1286. He was summoned to Parliament from 24 June 1295 to 13 Sept. 1302, by writs directed *Waltero de Faucomberge*, whereby he is held to have become Lord Faucomberge. He was ordered to muster at London 7 July 1297 for service in parts beyond the sea; the king embarked for Flanders 22 August following. He joined in the Barons' Letter to the Pope in 1301. SIR WALTER DE FAUCONBERGE, 1st Lord Fauconberge, died at Rise, Yorkshire about midnight 1–2 Nov. 1304, and was buried at Nunkeeling Priory, Yorkshire.

Dugdale *Monasticon Anglicanum* 6(1) (1830): 267–268 (Hist. Hundatorum, Gisburne Priory) (Gen. of Fauconberge fam.: "Prima soror, domina Agnes de Bruse, quam duxerat in uxorem dominus Walterus Fauconberg, dominus de Ryse in Holdyrnes; habuitque in partem suam cum uxore sua, castrum de Skelton, Hersk, Uplythum, Westyby, et Estburne."). *Coll. Top. et Gen.* 4 (1837): 261–262 (Obits from calendar held by Gisburne Priory: "Obitus Walteri Fauconberge, calend. Novembris [1 November]."). Ord *Hist. & Antiqs. of Cleveland* (1846): 197–198, 245–252, 595–596. Fauconberge *Fauconberge Memorial* (1849): 6–7, 62 (Fauconberge ped.). *Annual Rpt. of the Deputy Keeper* 42 (1881): 654. Flower *Vis. of Yorkshire 1563-4* (H.S.P. 16) (1881): 40 (Brus ped.: "Agnes [de Brus] fyrst doter wyf to Water Lord Faconbredge."). Brown *Yorkshire Lay Subsidy* (Yorkshire Arch. Soc. Rec. Ser. 16) (1894): 131, 153. Brown *Cartularium Prioratus de Gyseburne* 2 (Surtees Soc. 89) (1894): 102. Brown *Yorkshire Lay Subsidy* (Yorkshire Arch. Soc. Rec. Ser. 21) (1897): 34, 37. Farrer *Chartulary of Cockersand Abbey* 1(1) (Chetham Soc. n.s. 38) (1898): 60–62 (charter of Walter de Fauconberge dated c.1271–82, names his wife, Agnes). *Genealogical Mag.* 5 (1902): 189–198. Howard de Walden *Some Feudal Lords & Their Seals* (1903): 165 (biog. of Walter de Fauconberge). Clay *Extinct & Dormant Peerages* (1913): 68–70 (sub Fauconberg). Farrer *Early Yorkshire Charters* 2 (1915): 15 (Brus ped.). *C.P.* 5 (1926): 267–269 (sub Fauconberg). Harvey et al. *Vis. of the North* 3 (Surtees Soc. 144) (1930): 152–156 (Brues ped.: "Agnes [de Brus] filia prima = Walterus Fauconberge de Ryse"). *Yorkshire Deeds* 8 (Yorkshire Arch. Soc. Recs. 102) (1940): 75 (indenture of Walter de Fauconberge, lord of Rise, dated 1264). *Paget* (1957) 202:3 (fought in Gascony 1254; joined the Barons against Henry III; fought in Wales 1282 and 1283; fought in Scotland 1291; joined the expedition to Gascony 1254; continually employed on service in the Scotch Wars of Edward I. Lancashire Rec. Office: Towneley of Towneley, DDTO K 21/6 (confirmation dated 1275 by Walter, Archbishop of York, of an undertaking dated 13 March 1274 by Walter de Fauconberge to carry out the terms of a decree dated 24 October 1273 by the Archbishop imposing various concessions upon Walter in compensation for injuries inflicted by him on the prior & convent of Guisborough) (available at www.a2a.org.uk/search/index.asp).

8. WALTER DE FAUCONBERGE, 2nd Lord Fauconberge, of Skelton, Arncliffe, Ingleby, Marske, and Rise, Yorkshire, son and heir, born c.1254/64 (aged 40 and more in 1304). He married (1st) **ISABEL DE ROOS**, daughter of Robert de Roos, Knt., of Helmsley, Yorkshire, by Isabel, daughter and heiress of William d'Aubeney, of Belvoir, Leicestershire [see ROOS 7 for her ancestry]. They had six sons, including Peter, Walter, Knt., John [3rd Lord Fauconberge], and William, and four daughters, Anice (or Agnes), Laurette, Ivette, and Joan. The king took his fealty and he had livery of his father's lands 5 Dec. 1304. He was summoned to Parliament from 12 Nov. 1304 to 25 August 1318, by writs directed *Waltero de Fauconberge*. He was summoned to attend the Coronation of King Edward II in 1308. He married (2nd) **ALICE DE KILLINGHOLM**, daughter of John de Killingholm, Knt., of Boythorpe, Yorkshire. In 1314 he petitioned for the restoration of the manor of Hert, granted on the forfeiture of Robert de Brus, Earl of Carrick, to the late Robert de Clifford. WALTER DE FAUCONBERGE, 2nd Lord Fauconberge, died 31 Dec. 1318. His widow, Alice, married (2nd) before 11 Feb. 1318/9 (probably as his 2nd wife) **RALPH DE BULMER**, Lord Bulmer, of Wilton in Cleveland, Yorkshire (died before 1356). She died 22 June 1356.

    Dugdale *Monasticon Anglicanum* 6(1) (1830): 267–268 (Hist. Hundatorum, Gisburne Priory) (Gen. of Fauconberge fam.: "Istis ergo domino Waltero, et dominae Agneti uxori ejus, successit dominus Walterus Faukonberg, secundus filius et haeres; qui dominam Isabellam filiam domini Roberti de Rose de Hamelak, duxerat in uxorem."). *Testamenta Eboracensia* 1 (Surtees Soc. 4) (1836): 40 (will of William de Fauconberge). *Coll. Top. et Gen.* 4 (1837): 261–262 (Obits from calendar held by Gisburne Priory: "Obitus Walteri Fauconberg S[e]c[un]di pridie calend. Januarii [31 December]."). Poulson *Hist. & Antiqs. of Holderness* 1 (1840): 403. Fauconberge *Fauconberge Memorial* (1849): 8, 62–63 (Fauconberge ped.). *Genealogical Mag.* 5 (1902): 189–198. Howard de Walden *Some Feudal Lords & Their Seals* (1903): 165 (biog. of Walter de Fauconberg). Clay *Extinct & Dormant Peerages* (1913): 68–70 (sub Fauconberge), 181–185 (sub Ros). *C.P.* 5 (1926): 270 (sub Fauconberge). Paget *Baronage of England* (1957) 202: 4–5. Hedley *Northumberland Fams.* (1968): 224–230. Brault *Rolls of Arms Edward I* 2 (1997): 159 ("Walter de Fauconberge [d. 1318] bore his mother's arms: Argent, a lion rampant azure.").

Children of Walter de Fauconberge, by Isabel de Roos:

  i. **JOHN DE FAUCONBERGE**, 3rd Lord Fauconberge [see next].

  ii. **ANICE** (or **AGNES**) **DE FAUCONBERGE**, married **NICHOLAS D'ENGAINE**, Knt., of Colne Engaine, Essex [see ENGAINE 9].

9. JOHN DE FAUCONBERGE, 3rd Lord Fauconberge, of Skelton, Yorkshire, Sheriff of Yorkshire, 1341-2, Constable of York Castle and Berwick-on-Tweed, 3rd but 1st surviving son by his father's 1st marriage, born on or just before 24 June 1290. He married **EVE** _____, probable daughter of Ralph de Bulmer, Knt., Lord Bulmer. They had one son, Walter, Knt. [4th Lord Fauconberge], and one daughter, Joan (wife of William de Colville, Knt.). The king took his homage and he had livery of his father's lands 10 Feb. 1318/9. He fought in Scotland in 1322 and 1333, and in Flanders in 1338. In 1323 the king ordered that he should be arrested and imprisoned in Pickering Castle for trespass of venison in Pickering Forest, but the order was superseded, and he was fined 100 marks. He was summoned to Parliament from 22 Jan. 1335/6 to 10 Mar. 1348/9, by writs directed *Johanni de Faucomberge*. In 1343 he obtained license to proceed to the Holy Land to fulfill a vow. He acquired a moiety of the wapentake of Langbaurgh from Adam de Everingham. JOHN DE FAUCONBERGE, 3rd Lord Fauconberge, died 17 (or 18) Sept. 1349. His wife, Eve, predeceased him.

    Coll. Top. et Gen. 4 (1837): 261–262 (Brus obits from calendar held by Gisburne Priory: "O[bitus] Joh'is Fauconberge . 15 . Calend. Octobris [17 September]."). Poulson *Hist. & Antiqs. of Holderness* 1 (1840): 403, 406. Fauconberge

Fauconberge Memorial (1849): 8–9, 62–63 (Fauconberge ped.). *Hist. of Northumberland* 1 (1893): 181 (Colville ped.). *List of Sheriffs for England & Wales* (PRO Lists and Indexes 9) (1898): 161. *Genealogical Mag.* 5 (1902): 189–198. *Yorkshire Arch. Jour.* 16 (1902): 154–226. Clay *Extinct & Dormant Peerages* (1913): 68–70 (sub Fauconberg) (author states he married (2nd) Ela, dau. of Simon Constable, by whom he had one son, John). Ramsay *Genesis of Lancaster* 1 (1913): 116. *C.P.* 5 (1926): 271–272 (sub Fauconberge). Paget *Baronage of England* (1957) 202: 6. Sanders *English Baronies* (1960): 77.

10. WALTER DE FAUCONBERGE, Knt., 4th Lord Fauconberge, of Skelton, Rise, and Withernwick, Yorkshire, son and heir, born about 1319 (aged 30 in 1349). He married (1st) about Dec. 1330 **MAUD DE PATESHULLE**, 2nd daughter of John de Pateshulle, Knt., of Patishall, Cold Higham, Grimscote (in Cold Higham), Milton and Collingtree (in Milton Malzor), and Rothersthorpe, Northamptonshire, Bletsoe, Bromham, Cardington, and Keysoe, Bedfordshire, etc., by Mabel, daughter of William de Grandison (or Graunson), Knt., 1st Lord Grandison [see PATESHULLE 11 for her ancestry]. They had four sons, including Thomas, Knt. [5th Lord Fauconberge], and Roger. The king took his homage and he had livery of the manor of Rise, Yorkshire and other property 23 Jan. 1349/50. He was about to go on pilgrimage to Santiago in 1350. He was summoned to Parliament from 25 Nov. 1350 to 14 August 1362, by writs directed *Waltero Faucomberg* or *de Faucomberge*. He went on a pilgrimage to the Holy Land in 1357. His wife, Maud, died before 28 Sept. 1359. He married (2nd) before 15 Jan. 1359/60 **ISABEL BIGOD**, widow of Roger de Burton, Knt. (died before 10 October 1359), and daughter of Roger le Bigod, Knt., of Settrington, Yorkshire, by his wife, Joan [see ASKE 10 for her ancestry]. They had no issue. She was a legatee in the 1388 will of her brother, John Bigod. SIR WALTER DE FAUCONBERGE, 4th Lord Fauconberge, died 29 Sept. 1362. His widow, Isabel, died 19 May 1401. She left a will dated 9 April 1401, proved 1 July 1401. He and his wife, Isabel, were buried in Guisborough Priory, Yorkshire.

Baker *Hist. & Antiqs. of Northampton* 2 (1836–41): 295–297 (Pateshull ped.). *Coll. Top. et Gen.* 4 (1837): 261–262 (Obits from calendar held by Gisburne Priory: "O[bitus] Walteri Fauconberge .3. Calend. Octobris [29 September]."). Poulson *Hist. & Antiqs. of Holderness* 1 (1840): 403. Banks *Baronies in Fee* 2 (1843): 136–137 (sub Steyngreve). Fauconberge *Fauconberge Memorial* (1849): 9, 62–63 (Fauconberge ped.). Nicolas & Courthope *Hist. Peerage of England* (1857): 218–219 (sub Grandison). *Arch. Cantiana* 2 (1859): 34–35. Harvey *Hist. & Antiqs. of the Hundred of Willey* (1872–8): opp. 4 (Beauchamp ped.). *Genealogist* n.s. 13 (1896): 173, 249; n.s. 16 (1899): 38. *Genealogical Mag.* 5 (1902): 189–198. Wrottesley *Peds. from the Plea Rolls* (1905): 125, 151, 168–169, 267–268. *List of Inqs. ad Quod Damnum* 2 (PRO Lists and Indexes 22) (1906): 464. *Trans. Royal Hist. Soc.* 3rd Ser. 3 (1909): 125–195. *C.C.R. 1364–1368* (1910): 434–435. Clay *Extinct & Dormant Peerages* (1913): 68–70 (sub Fauconberg). *Yorkshire Inqs.* 5 (Yorkshire Arch. Soc. Recs. 59) (1918): 15–16. VCH *Berkshire* 4 (1924): 251–266. *C.P.* 5 (1926): 272–276 (sub Fauconberge); 6 (1926): 66–68 (sub Grandison). Harvey et al. *Vis. of the North* 3 (Surtees Soc. 144) (1930): 99–101 (Brus ped.: "Walterus Fauconberge [1] = filia Iohannis Pateshull vxor prima, [2] = Isabella domina de Harlesay"). *C.F.R.* 13 (1933): 42–43. *Yorkshire Deeds* 8 (Yorkshire Arch. Soc. Recs. 102) (1940): 116–120. Paget *Baronage of England* (1957) 65: 1, 202: 6–7. Palmer *English Law in the Age of the Black Death 1348–1381* (1993): 352.

11. THOMAS FAUCONBERGE, Knt., 5th Lord Fauconberge, of Skelton, Marsk, and Redker, Yorkshire, son and heir, born at Upleatham, Yorkshire 20 July 1345. He married (1st) before 21 Sept. 1354 **CONSTANCE FELTON**, daughter of William de Felton, Knt., of Edlingham, Nafferton, and West Matfen, Northumberland, by his 2nd wife, Isabel (or Elizabeth), daughter and heiress of Duncan of Fife, Knt., 10th Earl of Fife [see CLARE 8.ii.a.1 for her ancestry]. They had three sons, John, Walter, and John, Knt. (again). He was co-heir in 1359 to his uncle, William de Pateshulle, Knt., by which he inherited the manors of Rothersthorpe and Pattishall, Northamptonshire. He was co-heir in 1375 to his cousin, Thomas de Grandison, Knt., 4th Lord Grandison, by which he inherited a share in the manor of Grandisons (in Lambourn), Berkshire. He was about to go beyond seas in 1366, and was staying there in 1368, 1369, and 1376. He joined the King of France as a traitor in 1376. The Constable of the Tower was ordered to receive him into custody 3 June 1378. He was subsequently imprisoned in Gloucester Castle. He was adjudged to be of unsound mind and his lands were granted to others. In 1390, on the petition of his wife, Constance, the king ordered that he be released from Gloucester Castle and delivered to the governance of John de Felton, Knt., and William de Hilton, baron of Hilton, if it not being against his will. His wife, Constance, left a will dated 1 May 1401, proved 8 June 1402. In 1403 his manors, etc., in Northamptonshire were restored to his feoffees. In 1403 Robert and John Conyers were appointed custodians of his lands in Yorkshire and Northumberland, because Thomas was not of sound mind. In 1405 all his lands were committed to Thomas Bromflete, Knt., and Robert Hilton, Knt., owing to his idiocy. In Dec. 1406 he appeared in person before the King and council, where he was examined and declared to be of sane mind. He married (2nd) **JOAN BROMFLETE**, daughter of Thomas Bromflete, Knt., of Londesborough, Yorkshire, Cupbearer and Chief Butler to King Richard II, Controller and Treasurer of the Household under King Henry IV, Keeper of King's Wardrobe, by Margaret, daughter and heiress of Edward Saint John, Knt. [see BROMFLETE 14 for her ancestry]. She was born about 1389–90. They had one daughter, Joan. SIR THOMAS FAUCONBERGE, 5th Lord Fauconberge, died 9 Sept. 1407. He left a nuncupative will dated 6 Sept. 1407, proved 19 May 1408. His widow, Joan, Lady Fauconberge, died 4 March 1408/9.

 Baker *Hist. & Antiqs. of Northampton* 2 (1836–41): 295–297(Pateshull ped.). *Coll. Top. et Gen.* 4 (1837): 261–262 (Obits from calendar held by Gisburne Priory: "O[bitus] Thomae Fauconberge .4. Non. Septembris [2 September]."). Poulson *Hist. & Antiqs. of Holderness* 1 (1840): 403, 406. Fauconberge *Fauconberge Memorial* (1849): 9–10, 62–63 (Fauconberge ped.). *Archæologia Cantiana* 2 (1859): 34–35. *Genealogist* n.s. 13 (1896): 173. C.P.R. 1388–1392 (1902): 228 (Constance, wife of Thomas Fauconberge, Knt., stated to be "of royal lineage"). *Genealogical Mag.* 5 (1902): 189–198. Wrottesley *Peds. from the Plea Rolls* (1905): 125, 151, 168–169, 216. Clay *Extinct & Dormant Peerages* (1913): 68–70 (sub Fauconberg). *Yorkshire Inqs.* 5 (Yorkshire Arch. Soc. Recs. 59) (1918): 68–76, 172–173. VCH *Berkshire* 4 (1924): 251–266. *C.P.* 5 (1926): 276–280 (sub Fauconberge); 6 (1926): 66–68 (sub Grandison). Harvey et al. *Vis. of the North* 3 (Surtees Soc. 144) (1930): 99–101 (Brus ped.: "Thomas Fauconberge [1] = Constancia filia *soror Willelmi* de Felton *vxor prima*, [2] = soror Thome Bromeflete vxor secunda"). *C.F.R.* 13 (1933): 42–43. Paget *Baronage of England* (1957) 202: 7–8. *Studies in Gen. & Fam. Hist. in Tribute to Charles Evans* (1989): 354–358.

12. JOAN FAUCONBERGE, daughter by her father's 2nd marriage, born at Skelton, Yorkshire 18 October 1406 (aged 1 in 1407, 2 in 1409, 16 in 1422). She was a fool and idiot from birth. She married (1st) before 28 April 1422 **WILLIAM NEVILLE**, K.G., Keeper of Roxburgh Castle, 1444, Steward of the Bishopric of Durham, 1444–53, joint Keeper of Roxburgh Castle, 1452, Privy Councillor, joint Keeper of Windsor Castle, 1455–8, Captain of Calais, 1460, Lord Steward of the Household, 1461–3, Admiral of England, Ireland & Aquitaine, 1462, and, in right of his wife, 6th Lord Fauconberge, 6th son of Ralph Neville, K.G., 1st Earl of Westmorland, 4th Lord Neville of Raby, by his 2nd wife, Joan Beaufort, legitimated daughter of John of Gaunt, K.G., Duke of Aquitaine and Lancaster, titular King of Castile and León (son of King Edward III) [see NEVILLE 13 for his ancestry]. They had three daughters, Joan (wife of Edward Bethom, Knt.), Elizabeth (wife of Richard Strangeways, Knt.), and Alice. By an unknown mistress (or mistresses), he also had at least two illegitimate sons, including Thomas (styled "Bastard of Fauconberge"). He was summoned to Parliament from 3 August 1429 to 13 June 1461, by writs directed *Willelmo de Nevill' chivaler*, later directed *Willelmo de Nevill' de Faucomberge militi* (or *chivaler*). He was appointed Joint Guardian of the truce with Scotland in 1433. In 1435 he was appointed joint commisioner and special envoy to treat with Scotland. In 1436 he accompanied the Duke of York to France. He was a legatee in the 1440 will of his father. He conducted the Siege of Harfleur with Talbot and the Earl of Dorset in 1440. He was appointed joint Ambassador to treat with France in 1449; he was taken prisoner at Pont-de-l'Arche, and remained in captivity for over three years. He was appointed joint Commissioner, Ambassador, and Deputy to treat with France in 1450. In 1454 he purchased the manor of Whiston, together with 12 messuages, one mill, and lands in Whiston and Woodford, Northamptonshire from John Clinton, 5th Lord Clinton, and his wife Joan for £300 sterling. He commanded the vanguard of the Yorkist army at the Battles of Northampton in 1460 and Towton in 1461. In 1460 he and his wife were granted a papal indult for a portable altar and to have mass celebrated before daybreak. He was created Earl of Kent 1 Nov. 1461. SIR WILLIAM NEVILLE, Earl of Kent, 6th Lord Fauconberge, died 9 Jan. 1462/3 probably at Alnwick, and was buried in Guisborough Priory, Yorkshire. His widow, Joan, married (2nd) before 14 March 1462/3 (date of pardon for marrying without royal license) **JOHN BERWYKE**. Joan, Countess of Kent, died 11 Dec 1490.

Rowland *Noble Fam. of Nevill* (1830). Burke *Dict. of the Peerages… Extinct, Dormant & in Abeyance* (1831): 390–391 (describes William as "a military person of great valour… took a leading part in the wars of France"). *Wills & Invs.* 1 (Surtees Soc. 2) (1835): 68–74. Baker *Hist. & Antiqs. of Northampton* 2 (1836–41): 295–297. Banks *Dormant & Extinct Baronage of England* 4 (1837): 338–348. Surtees *Hist. & Antiqs. of Durham* 4 (1840): 158–163 (Nevill peds.). Beltz *Mems. of the Order of the Garter* (1841): clx. Fauconberge *Fauconberge Memorial* (1849): 10–12, 62–63 (Fauconberge ped.). Stevenson *Letters & Papers Ill. of the Wars of the English in France* 1 (Rolls Ser. 22) (1861): 519–520 (William Neville styled "cousin" by King Henry VI of England). Tonge *Vis. of Northern Counties 1530* (Surtees Soc. 41) (1862): 28–29 (Neville ped.: "Willyam [Neville] Lord Fauconberge"). *Trans. Leicestershire Architectural & Arch. Soc.* 1 (1866): 316–340. Doyle *Official Baronage of England* 2 (1886): 279–280 (sub Kent). *Genealogist* n.s. 3 (1886): 31–35, 107–111 (Neville ped.: "Willelmum, Dominum de Fauconberge"). *C.P.R. 1461–1467* (1897): 183, 225 (instances of William [Neville], earl of Kent, styled king's uncle), 195 (William, earl of Kent, styled "king's kinsman"). *Genealogical Mag.* 5 (1902): 189–198. *Papal Regs.: Letters* 7 (1906): 307; 11 (1921): 568. *D.N.B.* 6 (1908): 1104 (biog. of Thomas Neville, Bastard of Fauconberg); 14 (1909): 304–306 (biog. of William Neville). *Cal. Milanese Papers* 1 (1912): 47–48 (Francesco I Sforza, Duke of Milan, styled "kinsman"). Clay *Extinct & Dormant Peerages* (1913): 68–70 (sub Fauconberg), 71 (sub Nevile). *C.P.* 4 (1916): Appendix H, 727; 5 (1926): 281–287 (sub Fauconberg), 754. *Yorkshire Inqs.* 5 (Yorkshire Arch. Soc. Recs. 59) (1918): 68, 180–182. Harvey et al. *Vis. of the North* 3 (Surtees Soc. 144) (1930): 23–32 (Neville ped.: "Willelmus [Neville] dominus de Fauconberge per vxorem suam"), 99–101 (Brus ped.: "Iohanna [Fauconberge] filia et heres = Willelmus Neuille"), 106–109 (Strangwais ped.); 4 (Surtees Soc. 146) (1932): 166 (arms of Lord Falconberg: quarterly I and IV gules on a saltire silver a molet gules [NEVILLE]; II and III silver a lion rampant azure [FAUCONBERGE, formerly BRUS]). *Yorkshire Deeds* 8 (Yorkshire Arch. Soc. Recs. 102) (1940): 116–120. Myers *Household of Edward IV* (1959): 286. VCH *Somerset* 3 (1974): 111–120. VCH *Somerset* 4 (1978): 4–38. *Ricardian* 10 (1995): 174–184. National Archives, CP 25/1/179/95, #137 [see abstract of fine at http://www.medievalgenealogy.org.uk/index.html].

Child of Joan Fauconberge, by William Neville, K.G.:

i. **ALICE NEVILLE**, married **JOHN CONYERS**, K.G., of Hornby, Yorkshire [see CONYERS 17].

✤ FELBRIGG ✤

REYNOLD DE COURTENAY, of Sutton, Berkshire, married _____.
REYNOLD DE COURTENAY, of Oakhampton, Devon, married **HAWISE DE COURCY**.
ROBERT DE COURTENAY, Knt., of Okehampton, Devon, married **MARY DE VERNON** (desc. King William the Conqueror).
JOHN DE COURTENAY, Knt., of Okehampton, Devon, married **ISABEL DE VERE**.
HUGH DE COURTENAY, Knt., of Okehampton, Devon, married **ELEANOR LE DESPENSER**.
EGELINE DE COURTENAY, married **ROBERT DE SCALES**, Knt., 2nd Lord Scales.
ROBERT DE SCALES, 3rd Lord Scales, married **KATHERINE DE UFFORD** [see SCALES 7].

8. ELIZABETH DE SCALES, married **ROGER DE FELBRIGG** (or **FELBRIGGE**, **FELBRYGGE**, **FYLBRYGGE**, etc.), Knt., of Felbrigg, Aylmerton, Banningham, Howe juxta Brooke, Runton, and Stirston next Stansted, Norfolk, Streatley (in Sharpenhoe), Bedfordshire, Braiseworth, Suffolk, etc., son and heir of Simon Bigod (or de Felbrigg), Knt., of Felbrigg, Aylmerton, and Runton, Norfolk, by Alice, daughter of George de Thorpe, Knt., of Braiseworth, Suffolk, and Sharpenhoe (in Streatley), Bedfordshire (younger brother of John de Thorpe, 1st Lord Thorpe).[22] They had two sons, Simon, K.G., and probably John (clerk), and allegedly one daughter,

---

[22] Blomefield *Hist. of Norfolk* 4 (1775): 305–307 states that the above named Sir Roger de Felbrigg (d. c.1380) was the great-grandson of a certain Simon le Bigod, Knt., by Maud de Felbrigg, only daughter and eventual heiress of Richard

_____ (wife of Constantine de Mortimer, of Attleborough). As "Roger son of Simon de Felbrug," in 1353 he was granted a weekly market and an annual fair to be held in the town of Felbrigg, Norfolk. In 1354–5 he was granted permission to have view of frankpledge of all inhabitants of Felbrigg and Aylmerton, Norfolk. SIR ROGER LE FELBRIGG fought in France and elsewhere beyond the seas, and died about 1380 in Prussia. He was styled "the late Sir Roger de Felbrigg" in a record dated 1386.

> Blomefield *Essay towards a Top. Hist. of Norfolk* 4 (1775): 305–307. Waters *Chester of Chicheley* 1 (1878): 253–255 (Scales ped.). Rye *Short Cal. Feet of Fines for Norfolk* 2 (1886): 341–342, 351. *Evidences of the Winthrops of Groton* (1894–6): 153 (Tyndal ped.). Muskett *Suffolk Manorial Fams.* 1 (1900): 153. Rye *Cal. Feet of Fines for Suffolk* (1900): 230. *List of Inqs. ad Quod Damnum* 2 (PRO Lists and Indexes 22) (1906): 480. *Norfolk Antiq. Misc.* 2nd Ser. 1 (1906): 135–141. *C.Ch.R.* 5 (1916): 130, 140. *Yorkshire Arch. Jour.* 32 (1936): 208–209. *C.P.* 11 (1949): 507 (sub Scales); 12(1) (1953): 720, footnote d (Thorpe arms: Checky or and gules, on a fess argent, three martlets sable). Paget *Baronage of England* (1957) 488: 1–8 (sub Scales). Ketton-Cremer *Felbrigg* (1962): 19–20 (brass showing "a soldier in complete armour, his feet resting on a lion... wife wearing a most elaborate head-dress") (provided by Robert Battle). *D.N.B.* 41: 230, 56: 13. Norfolk Rec. Office: Ketton-Cremer fam. of Felbrigg Hall, Norfolk, MS 15741, 37C2 (available at www.a2a.org.uk/search/index.asp).

9. SIMON FELBRIGG, K.G., of Felbrigg, Aylmerton, Banningham, Colby, and Runton, Norfolk, Braiseworth, Suffolk, and Streatley (in Sharpenhoe), Bedfordshire, and, in right of his 2nd wife, of Buckworth, Huntingdonshire, King's knight, Farmer of Barnstaple Priory, Devon, Knight of the Passion of Jesus Christ, son and heir, born before 1366 (of age in 1387). He married (1st) about 1386 **MARGARET OF TESCHEN**, daughter of Przemyslaw Noszak, Duke of Teschen and Glogau, by his 2nd wife, Elsbieta (or Elska), daughter of Boleslaw of Beuthen-Kosel. She was kinswoman and Lady of Honour to Queen Anne of Bohemia, wife of King Richard II. They had three daughters, Alana, Anne (nun at Brusyard), and Elizabeth. He served in the retinue of John of Gaunt, Duke of Lancaster, at the relief of Brest in 1386, and was with the Duke later that year in his expedition to Spain. In 1389 he had license to undertake a pilgrimage beyond sea in the company of William Arundel, Knt. His wife's connection with the Queen procured him the office of the King's Standard-bearer 7 April 1395, and he was soon afterwards elected a Knight of the Garter. In 1398, being then one of the knights of the king's chamber, he had a grant of the manor of Beeston Regis, Norfolk. In 1399 he was granted custody of the Cluniac manors of Letcombe Regis, Berkshire, Offord Cluny, Huntingdonshire, and Manton and Tixover, Rutland, to hold during the war with France, in return for an annual payment of 40 florins (about £6). In 1406 he and others, plaintiffs, sued Margery, widow of Thomas Spayne, and others, defendants, regarding the right of presentation to the church of Filby, Norfolk. In 1408 he deposed in the Grey and Hastings controversy. In 1413 George Felbrygge, Knt., quitclaimed to him all his right in certain lands lands in Codenham, Creeting All Saints, Creeting St. Mary, and Creeting St. Olive, Suffolk, which lately belonged to John

---

> de Felbrigg. The implication is that the family name was Bigod before the Felbrigg surname was assumed [see *Notes & Queries* 7th Ser. 2 (1886): 210–211]. Sir Roger de Felbrigg's own father certainly occurs as "Simon Bygod (or Bygot) of Felbrigge" in various Norfolk fines dated 1310–11, 1311–12, 1312–13, and 1332–3 [see Rye *Short Cal. Feet of Fines for Norfolk* 2 (1886): 228, 231, 235, 289]. As "Simon de Felebrigge," he likewise occurs in a Norfolk lawsuit dated Hilary term 1310, in which he is specifically named as the brother and heir of Mary, daughter of "Roger Bygod de Felibrigge" [see Maitland *Year Books of Edward II* 3 (Selden Soc. 20) (1905): 56–57]. The earlier ancestry of the family is uncertain. Blomefield alleges without documentation that Sir Roger de Felbrigg's great-grandfather, Simon le Bigod, was "3rd son (as is said) of Hugh le Bigod, earl of Norfolk, by Maud his wife." Modern Bigod family sources, however, such as *C.P.* 10 (1945): 590, Paget *Baronage of England* (1957) 65: 1, and Morris *Bigod Earls of Norfolk in the 13th Cent.* (2005) do not include a son, Simon, in the family of Earl Hugh le Bigod. As such, the alleged connection to Earl Hugh le Bigod seems quite doubtful. Anstis has suggested alternatively that the Felbrigg family of Norfolk was probably descended from a cadet branch of Ralph le Bigod, the Domesday tenant [see Anstis *Reg. of the Order of the Garter* 2 (1724): 169], which descent may well be more likely]. Whatever the case, this matter deserves further study].

Jaune, parson of Glemsford. On 29 April 1413 he was retained by indenture to serve in the wars in Aquitaine and France, with twelve men-at-arms and thirty-six archers. His wife, Margaret, died 27 June 1413, and was buried at Felbrigg, Norfolk, her brass displaying the Teschen arms of an eagle displayed. He married (2nd) before 1421 **KATHERINE CLIFTON**, widow of Ralph Greene, Esq. (died 1417), of Drayton (in Lowick), Northamptonshire, Knight of the Shire for Northamptonshire, 1404, 1410, Sheriff of Northamptonshire, Sheriff of Wiltshire, and daughter of John de Clifton, 1st Lord Clifton, by Elizabeth, daughter of Ralph de Cromwell, Knt., 1st Lord Cromwell [see CLIFTON 12 for her ancestry]. They had no issue. In 1422 he, Roger Prat, clerk, and two others conveyed one half of the church of Fressingfield, Suffolk to the Dean and chaplains of St. Mary's in the Fields in Norwich, Norfolk, subject to a payment of £10 annually to the Mayor and corporation of Norwich. He presented to the church of Lowick, Northamptonshire in 1422. In 1429–30 he was occupying a "hostel" in Norwich, Norfolk. In 1435 he and his wife, Katherine, quitclaimed all their right in the manor of Sudborough, Northamptonshire which they held for the life of Katherine to William Aldewyncle. In 1436 he and Roger Drury, Knt., demised to William Wallere, William Petystre, and another various lands in Codenham, Creeting All Saints, Creeting St. Mary, and Creeting St. Olive, Suffolk, which lately belonged to John Jaune, parson of Glemsford. In 1441 he granted to Bartholomew White, Esq., son and heir of Robert White, Esq., the manor of Shottesham, Norfolk, together with lands and tenements in Shotesham, Stoke Holy Cross, and the villages adjacent, and the advowson of the church of Filby, Norfolk. SIR SIMON FELBRIGG died 3 Dec. 1442. He left a will dated 21 Sept. 1442, proved 20 Feb. 1442/3 (P.C.C. 14 Rous). By the terms of his will, he left all of his Norfolk lands to his widow, Katherine, for life provided she remained unmarried, with remainder to his executors who were to sell the estate. In 1449 his widow, Katherine, was residing in a house in the parish of St. Etheldred, Norwich, Norfolk. In 1451 John Wymondham obtained the reversion of all of the Norfolk lands of the late Simon Felbrigg, Knt., including the manors of Felbrigg, Aylmerton, Banningham, Colby, Crackfordhall, Runton, and Tuttington, Norfolk. In 1454 Katherine, widow of Simon Felbrigg, Knt. leased these properties to John Wymondham for a term of 20 years. Katherine died 23 March 1459/60. She left a will proved in 1460 (Cons. Court of Norwich, 185, 186 Brosyard). Simon and his 2nd wife, Katherine, were buried in the choir of the Dominican Priory at Norwich, Norfolk.

Weever *Ancient Funerall Monuments* (1631): 856. Anstis *Reg. of the Order of the Garter* 2 (1724): 167–177 (biog. of Sir Simon de Felbrigg) ([The Felbrigg arms] are in the Repertory of *Jennings* blazoned d'Or, *a un Lion embelliff' rampant de Goules*, that is a Lion Saliant). Rymer *Fœdera* 7 (1727): 282 (Przemyslaw, Duke of Teschen, styled "kinsman" by Wenceslas, Holy Roman Emperor, King of Bohemia), 282, 294 (instances of Przemyslaw, Duke of Teschen, styled "kinsman" by Elizabeth, Holy Roman Empress, Queen of Bohemia), 295 (Przemyslaw, Duke of Teschen, styled "sororium" by Wenceslas, Holy Roman Emperor). Blomefield *Essay towards a Top. Hist. of Norfolk* 4 (1775): 305–307 (erroneous statements); 6 (1807): 350. Bridges *Hist. & Antiqs. of Northamptonshire* 2 (1791): 247–252 (erroneously identifies 2nd wife Katherine as daughter of Anketil Mallory). Nicolas *Testamenta Vetusta* 1 (1826): 245–246 (will of Simon Felbrigge, Knt.). Fuller *Hist. of the Worthies of England* (1840): 174–175. Beltz *Mems. of the Order of the Garter* (1841): clv, 369–374 ("This lady [Margaret, wife of Simon Felbrigg] is described in several heraldic collections as Margaret the daughter of Premislaus duke of Teschen, and as a relative of the queen her mistress (cites "Vinc. N° 20, fo. 50. H. 25, fo. 11, in Coll. Armor [Vincent "Baronagium Angliæ" (1613)] and sir Henry Spelman's *Icenia*, p. 412 — 'Margareta filia ducis *Thasæ*, regis Bohemiæ neptis' "). *Norfolk Arch.* 1 (1847): 356–357 (effigy of Sir Simon Felbrigge). Searle *Hist. of Queens' College 1446–1560* (1867): 367–371 (author discusses evidence of parentage of Margaret, 1st wife of Simon Felbrigg, K.G.). Turner *Cal. Charters & Rolls: Bodleian Lib.* (1878): 176, 178, 180, 217, 460, 461. Waters *Chester of Chicheley* 1 (1878): 252, 253–255 (Scales ped.), 287 (will of Sir Simon Felbrigge). *Archives de l'Orient Latin* 1 (1881): 362–364. Rye *Short Cal. Feet of Fines for Norfolk* 2 (1886): 380–381, 387, 392–393, 402–403, 407–409, 419. Rye *Pedes Finium or Fines Rel. Cambridge* (1891): 141. Birch *Cat. Seals in the British Museum* 2 (1892): 787 (seal of Simon de Felbrigg dated 1406 — A shield of arms, couché: a lion rampant [FELBRIGG]. Crest on a helmet and lambrequin, out of a ducal coronet, a plume of ostrich feathers. Supporters [two?] demi-lions. Within a carved gothic panel, ornamented wth ball-flowers along the inner edge). *Evidences of the Winthrops of Groton* (1894–6): 153 (Tyndal ped.). Harvey *Vis. of Norfolk 1563* 2 (1895): 293–294. Muskett *Suffolk Manorial Fams.* 1 (1900): 153 (asserts 1st wife Margaret was daughter of Semovitius, Duke of Silesia, by Elizabeth, sister of Charles IV, Emperor of Germany). Rye *Cal. Feet of*

Fines for Suffolk (1900): 271, 285–286. *C.P.R. 1399–1401* (1903): 64, 338, 525. *Feudal Aids* 3 (1904): 555, 559, 591, 615, 620, 655. *Norfolk Antiq. Misc.* 2nd Ser. 1 (1906): 135–141. VCH *Bedford* 2 (1908): 382. *Annales de l'Académie de Mâcon* 3rd Ser. 15 (1910): 369–370. Rye *Norfolk Fams.* (1911): 191–192. *C.P.* 3 (1913): 307–308 (sub Clifton). *Cal. MSS in Various Colls.* 7 (Hist. MSS Comm. 55) (1914): 236. VCH *Berkshire* 4 (1924): 222–228. Stephenson *List of Mon. Brasses* (1926): 333 (identifies 1st wife Margaret as "a native of Bohemia, [dau. of Primislaud, duke of Teschen and nephew of Winceslaus V, King of Bohemia], lady in waiting to Anne of Bohemia, Queen of Richard II"). *Rpt. on the MSS of Reginald Rawdon Hastings, Esq.* 1 (Hist. MSS Comm. 78) (1928): 207–208. *C.F.R.* 11 (1929): 209, 254, 261, 299. *Feet of Fines for Essex* 3 (1929–49): 255. *Historja Slaska* 3 (1936): plate 135, no. 179 (armorial seal of Przemyslaw I shows an eagle displayed, and the legend "S. Premisslai Ducis Thessinesis."). *Yorkshire Arch. Jour* 32 (1936): 208–209 (arms of Simon Felbrigg: Or a lion salient gules) (1st wife Margaret identified in accompanying ped. as "daughter of the Duke of Silesia."). VCH *Huntingdon* 3 (1936): 23–24. Legge *Anglo-Norman Letters & Petitions* (Anglo-Norman Text Soc. 3) (1941): 366 (2nd wife Katherine called "cousin" by an unidentified niece of Henry Despenser, Bishop of Norwich). Paget *Baronage of England* (1957) 134a: 1. Paget *Baronage of England* (1957) 488: 4. Ketton-Cremer *Felbrigg* (1962): 19–20. *Blackmansbury* 2 (1965): 3–7 ("… Margaret, after all, was probably daughter of Przemysl I of Nosak, Duke of Teschen and Glogau, as the early peds. supposed… Both Anne of Bohemia and Przemysl I of Teschen had a common descent from Bela IV, King of Hungary (1206–1270)") (identifies arms of 1st wife Margaret on her monumental brass as: "Argent (or sable), an eagle displayed gules, for Teschen"). *Norfolk Arch.* 35 (1970): 96–108. Ellis *Cat. Seals in the P.R.O.* 2 (1981): 40 (seal of Simon Felbrigg, knight dated 1411–12 — A shield of arms, couché: a lion rampant [FELBRIGG]; helm above, with mantling, supported by two demi-lions rampant, with crest: from a crown, a bush of feathers. Legend: "… SIMONIS:/DE:FELBRIGG':".). Roskell *House of Commons 1386–1421* 3 (1992): 228–230 (biog. of Ralph Green). *Roczniki Historyczne* 67 (2001): 107–130 (concludes wife Margaret is a daughter of Przemyslaw Noszak, duke of Cieszyn, by his wife, Elsbieta of Bytom and Kozielsk). Coss & Keen *Heraldry, Pageantry & Social Display in Medieval England* (2002): 169–194. *TAG* 79 (2004): 283–291. Norfolk Rec. Office: Ketton-Cremer fam. of Felbrigg Hall, Norfolk, MS 15678, 37C1; MS 15741, 37C2; WKC 1/41, 390 x 9: WKC 1/217, 392 x 1: WKC 1/274, 392 x 4; WKC 1/286, 392 x 5; WKC 1/332, 392 x 7; WKC 1/333, 392 x 7; WKC 1/334, 392 x 7; WKC 1/335, 392 x 7; WKC 1/336, 392 x 7; WKC 1/337, 392 x 7; WKC 1/338, 392 x 7: WKC 1/339, 392 x 7; WKC 2/84, 394 x 6; WKC 4/1, 399 x 7; WKC 7/160, 404 x 8 (available at www.a2a.org.uk/search/index.asp). National Archives, CP 25/1/179/94, #77 [see abstract of fine at http:// www.medievalgenealogy.org.uk/index.html].

Children of Simon Felbrigg, K.G., by Margaret of Teschen:

i. **ALANA FELBRIGG**, married **WILLIAM TYNDALL**, Knt., of Deene, Northamptonshire [see TYNDALL 10].

ii. **ELIZABETH FELBRIGG**, married **MILES STAPLETON**, Knt., of Ingham, Norfolk [see STAPLETON 13].

～ FELTON ～

JOHN DE SOMERY, married **HAWISE PAYNELL**.
RALPH DE SOMERY, of Dudley (in Sedgley), Staffordshire, married **MARGARET LE GRAS**.
ROGER DE SOMERY, Knt., of Dudley (in Sedgley), Staffordshire, married **NICHOLE D'AUBENEY** (desc. King William the Conqueror).
JOAN DE SOMERY, married **JOHN LE STRANGE**, of Knockin, Shropshire [see STRANGE 4].

5. HAWISE LE STRANGE, married **ROBERT DE FELTON**, Knt., of Litcham, Norfolk. They had one son, John, Knt. In 1298 he had a grant in reward for his services in Flanders. He was in the army in Scotland in 1298 and 1300. He served as Constable of Lochmaben Castle in 1300. He was again serving in Scotland in 1303 and 1310. His wife, Hawise, was living 16 May 1303. He was Constable of Scarborough Castle in 1312. The same year the king granted him the manor of Shotwick, Cheshire for life. He was summoned to Parliament from 8 January 1312/3 to 26 November 1313, by writs directed *Roberto de Felton'*, whereby he is held to have become Lord Felton. SIR ROBERT DE FELTON, Lord Felton, was slain at the Battle of Bannockburn 24 June 1314.

Hist. & Antiqs. of the County of Norfolk 8 (1781): 100–101. Blomefield *Essay towards a Top. Hist. of Norfolk* 5 (1806): 1031. *Desc. Cat. of the Original Charters, Royal Grants, … Monastic Chartulary … constituting Muniments of Battle Abbey* (1835): 62. *C.P.* 5 (1926): 289–290 (sub Felton). National Archives, SC 8/237/11821; SC 8/341/16052 (available at www.catalogue.nationalarchives.gov.uk/search.asp).

6. JOHN DE FELTON, Knt., of Litcham, Norfolk, son and heir. He married **SIBYL** _____. They had three sons, John, Hamon, Knt. [see KERDESTON 8], and Thomas, K.G. He was in the army of Scotland in 1310. He was appointed Keeper of the Castle and manor of Alnwick in 1314 and again in 1315. He was captured by the Scots in 1317. In 1318 he was ordered to deliver the Castle and manor of Alnwick to Henry de Percy. The same year he was about to go overseas with William de Montagu, Seneschal of Gascony. He served as Keeper of Ellesmere Castle, Shropshire in 1320–21. He was appointed Keeper of Red Castle, Shropshire, and of the manor of Hodnet, Shropshire in 1322, both during pleasure. He was ordered to deliver up the manor of Hodnet, Shropshire 20 December 1322. In May 1324 he was summoned to attend the Great Council. In June 1324 he was about to go to Gascony on the king's service. He was one of the three Admirals of England in 1325. In 1326 he was granted for life the Castle of Lyonshall, Herefordshire, late of William Tuchet, a rebel. On 14 October 1326, the king ordered him to remain in the March of Wales for its defence against the rebels. Soon afterwards he was appointed Constable of Caerphilly Castle, where he sustained a siege by the Queen's party. On 30 December 1326, and again, 15 February 1326/7, letters were sent him from Kenilworth ordering him, on pain of forfeiture, to surrender the Castle and the king's goods therein; these orders proved ineffectual, although pardons were issued to him and his garrison at short intervals, 4 January, 10, 15 and 20 February 1326/7. He held out against William la Zouche, until Hugh, son of Hugh le Despenser the younger, who was in the castle, and had been specially excepted from pardon, was included, 20 March 1326/7. SIR JOHN DE FELTON was living in 1334. His widow, Sibyl, was living in 1346.

Hist. & Antiqs. of the County of Norfolk 8 (1781): 100–101. Blomefield *Essay towards a Top. Hist. of Norfolk* 5 (1806): 1031. C.P. 5 (1926): 290–294 (sub Felton). National Archives, SC 8/148/7399; SC 8/164/8165; SC 8/201/10043; SC 8/259/12950 (available at www.catalogue.nationalarchives.gov.uk/search.asp).

7. THOMAS DE FELTON, K. G., of Litcham, Banham, and Wilby, Norfolk, Fordham, Cambridgeshire, Aslackby, Lincolnshire, Barrow, Suffolk, etc., Steward of the Household, Seneschal of Aquitaine, Seneschal of Gascony, Chamberlain of Cheshire, and, in right of his wife, of Dersingham, Ingaldesthorp, Great Ryburgh, and Little Ryburgh, Norfolk, etc., 3rd son. He married before 1356 **JOAN DE WALKEFARE**, daughter and co-heiress of Richard de Walkefare, Knt., of Dersingham, Great Ryburgh, Little Ryburgh, and Ingaldesthorp, Norfolk, etc. They had one son, Thomas, and three daughters, Mary (wife of Edmund de Hemgrave, Knt., and John Curson, Knt.), Sibyl (wife of Thomas Morley, Knt.; afterwards Abbess of Barking), and Eleanor. In 1355 he went with Edward *the Black Prince* to Bordeaux, and was honorably mentioned by him in a letter written towards the end of the year addressed to the Bishop of Winchester. In 1356 he fought at the Battle of Poitiers, and was rewarded by the prince with an annuity of £40 for his services. In 1360 he was one of the English commissioners who signed the important Treaty of Bretigny. In 1367 he was taken prisoner in the Spanish expedition in support of Don Pedro of Castile; he was subsequently exchanged for the French Marshall d'Audreham. He subsequently took part in combats and sieges at Monsac, Duravel, and Domme, and was then recalled to Angoulême by the prince, and sent into Poitou with the Earl of Pembroke. He secured La Linde on the Dordogne when it was about to be betrayed to the French. He joined John of Gaunt, Duke of Lancaster in an attack on the town of Mont-Paon, and made an unsuccessful attempt to relieve the garrison of Thouars. In 1372, when the Black Prince surrendered the principality of Aquitaine into the king's hands, it was granted by royal commission to Felton and Sir Robert Wykford. In 1377 he was taken prisoner by the French near Bordeaux. His ransom was fixed at 30,000 frances, and he was permitted to go to England in order to raise it within three years. He was heir male in 1379 to his elder brother, Hamon de Felton, Knt., of Litcham, Norfolk. In 1380 he was granted letters of protection to enable him to return to France to negotiate payment of his ransom. He presented to the churches of Ingaldesthorp, Norfolk, 1379, and Great Ryburgh, Norfolk, 1380. SIR THOMAS DE FELTON died testate 2

April 1381, and was buried at Walsingham Priory, Norfolk. In 1388 Adam Palmer and Thomas Palmer, of Dersingham, Norfolk owed his widow, Joan, and Thomas Weyland, Citizen and draper of London a debt of £160. She presented to the church of Great Ryburgh, Norfolk in 1390. In 1390 she settled the manor of Asklackby, Lincolnshire on herself for life, with remainder to various trustees for her daughter, Sibyl de Morley, nun at Barking, for life, then to Thomas de Morley, Knt., Marshal of Ireland. In 1398 she had license to grant land in London, and Barking and Dagenham, Essex to Barking Abbey, in order to found a chantry of one chaplain to celebrate divine service there at the tomb of St. Ethelburga for the good estate of her daughter, Sybil de Felton, then abbess, and others. Joan was living 31 March 1408, and died before 1434. *Hist. & Antiqs. of the County of Norfolk* 8 (1781): 100–101. Blomefield *Essay towards a Top. Hist. of Norfolk* 1 (1805): 362; 5 (1775): 1283–1284, 1286; 5 (1806): 1031; 7 (1807): 162–167; 10 (1809): 335–336. Nicolas *Controversy between Scrope & Grosvenor* 2 (1832): 183–187 (biog. of Thomas Morieux). Gage *Hist. & Antiqs. of Suffolk: Thingoe Hundred* (1838): 10–12. Beltz *Mems. of the Order of the Garter* (1841): 274–279 (biog. of Sir Thomas Felton) (Felton arms: Gules, two lions passant in pale Ermine, ducally crowned Or). *Procs. Suffolk Institute of Arch. & Natural Hist.* 4 (1864): 27–28. *Rpt. on the M.SS. of the Fam. of Gawdy* (Hist. MSS Comm.) (1885): 117–120. *D.N.B.* 18 (1889): 309–310 (biog. of Sir Thomas Felton). *MSS of Rye & Hereford Corporations* (Hist. MSS Comm. 13th Rep., App., Part IV) (1892): 422–427 (docs. re. Felton and Walkfare fams.). *C.P.R. 1388–1392* (1902): 337. *List of Inqs. ad Quod Damnum* 2 (PRO Lists and Indexes 22) (1906): 651. *VCH Essex* 2 (1907): 115–122. Muskett *Suffolk Manorial Fams.* 2 (1908): 173–174 (L'Estrange ped.). *C.C.R. 1381–1385* (1920): 9, 245, 422–423. *C.P.* 5 (1926): 292–294 (sub Felton). *C.C.R. 1405–1419* (1931): 385. *VCH Cambridge* 10 (2002): 395–402. Ormrod *Fourteenth Century England* 3 (2004): 88, 91–93, 97. National Archives, C 143/410/14; C 241/193/41; SC 8/21/1018; SC 8/85/4215; SC 8/104/5168; SC 8/111/5505; SC 8/111/5509; SC 8/111/5513; SC 8/111/5514; SC 8/111/5517; SC 8/169/8424; SC 8/210/10497; SC 8/210/10498 (available at www.catalogue.nationalarchives.gov.uk/search.asp). National Archives, CP 25/1/144/152, #31; CP 25/1/288/50, #760 [see abstract of fines at http://www.medievalgenealogy.org.uk/index.html].

Child of Thomas de Felton, K.G., by Joan de Walkefare:

i. **ELEANOR FELTON**, married (1st) **ROBERT DE UFFORD**, Knt., of Burgh St. Margaret, Norfolk [see CLAVERING 10]; (2nd) **THOMAS HOO**, Knt., of Luton Hoo (in Luton), Bedfordshire, Wartling, Sussex, etc. [see HOO 13].

❧ FENWICK ❧

WILLIAM DE MOWBRAY, Knt., of Thirsk, Yorkshire, married **AVICE** _____.
ROGER DE MOWBRAY, Knt., of Thirsk, Yorkshire, married **MAUD DE BEAUCHAMP** (desc. King William the Conqueror).
ROGER DE MOWBRAY, Knt., 1st Lord Mowbray, married **ROSE DE CLARE** (desc. King William the Conqueror).
JOHN DE MOWBRAY, Knt., 2nd Lord Mowbray, married **ALINE DE BREWES** (desc. King William the Conqueror).
JOHN DE MOWBRAY, Knt., 3rd Lord Mowbray, married **JOAN OF LANCASTER** (desc. King William the Conqueror).
JOHN DE MOWBRAY, Knt., 4th Lord Mowbray, married **ELIZABETH DE SEGRAVE** (desc. King William the Conqueror).
JOAN MOWBRAY, married **THOMAS GRAY**, Knt., of Heaton (in Norham), Northumberland.
MAUD GRAY, married **ROBERT OGLE**, Knt., of Ogle, Northumberland.
MARGARET OGLE, married **ROBERT HARBOTTLE**, Knt., of Preston, Northumberland.
BERTRAM HARBOTTLE, Esq., of Beamish, Durham, married **JOAN LUMLEY** (desc. King William the Conqueror) [see HARBOTTLE 10].

11. AGNES HARBOTTLE, married **ROGER FENWICK**, Knt., Esquire of the Body to King Henry VIII, Constable of Newcastle, Sheriff of Northumberland, 1492–3, son of John Fenwick, Esq., of Newburn, by Elizabeth, daughter of Roger Widdrington, Esq., Sheriff of Northumberland. SIR ROGER FENWICK died 1513–4.

Surtees *Hist. & Antiqs. of Durham* 2 (1820): 225 (chart). Hodgson *Hist. of Northumberland* 2(2) (1832): 75, 113–114, 234–235, 260–262. Marshall *Vis. of Northumberland in 1615* (1878): 45 (Fenwick ped.: "Sir Roger Fenwicke, Kt. 4 sonne = Anne da. of… Harbotle."). Flower *Vis. of Yorkshire 1563-4* (H.S.P. 16) (1881): 121 (Fenwick ped.: "Roger Fenwyke of Mydelton in com. Northumberland = … doughter of Wedryngton of Wedryngton."). *List of Sheriffs for England & Wales* (PRO Lists and Indexes 9) (1898): 98. St. George & Dugdale *Peds. Rec. at the Heralds' Vis. of Northumberland* (1903): 51–52 (Fenwick peds.). Harvey et al. *Vis. of the North* 1 (Surtees Soc. 122) (1912): 20–21; 4 (Surtees Soc. 146) (1932): 76–78 (Fenwike ped.: "Roger Fenwike *miles* (of Stanton) = Agnes Harbotle (sister to Ralf)"). Craster *Hist. of Northumberland* 9 (1909): 266–267 (Harbottle chart). Dodds *Hist. of Northumberland* 12 (1926): chart betw. 352–353.

12. RALPH FENWICK, Esq., in right of his wife, of Stanton, Northumberland, son and heir. He married **MARGERY MITFORD**. They had three sons, John, Anthony, and Wygard, and three daughters, Wylgeford (wife of Thomas Musgrave), Barbara (wife of Matthew Whitfeld), and _____ (wife of Robert Collingwood). RALPH FENWICK, Esq., died before 10 August 1535, when his widow entailed Stanton on their son, John, and Langfhaws on their son, Anthony. She died testate.

Hodgson *Hist. of Northumberland* 2(2) (1832): 75, 112–114 (Margery was a descendant (in an unknown way) of Gerard Mitford, husband, by marriage contract dated 20 July 1426, of Margery, daughter of Robert Corbet, descendant of Patrick fifth Earl of Dunbar). Marshall *Vis. of Northumberland in 1615* (1878): 45 (Fenwick ped.: "Sᵣ Raphe Fenwicke of Stanton, Kt. = Mary d. & sole heire of… Mitford of Stanton."). Flower *Vis. of Yorkshire 1563-4* (H.S.P. 16) (1881): 121 (Fenwick ped.: "Sir Raff Fenwyke son & heyre to Roger. = Margery doughter & sole heyre to Water Corbet of Stanton Knight."). St. George & Dugdale *Peds. Rec. at the Heralds' Vis. of Northumberland* (1903): 51–52 (Fenwick peds.). Harvey et al. *Vis. of the North* 1 (Surtees Soc. 122) (1912): 20–21; 4 (Surtees Soc. 146) (1932): 76–78 (Fenwike ped.: "Sir Raffe Fenwik of Stanton Knight"). Dodds *Hist. of Northumberland* 12 (1926): chart betw. 352–353.

13. JOHN FENWICK, Esq., of Stanton, Northumberland, son and heir. He married **MARY GRAY**, daughter and co-heiress of Ralph Gray, Knt., of Chillingham, Northumberland, by his wife, Elizabeth [see GRAY 12 for her ancestry]. She was born about 1505 (aged 12 in 1517). They had four sons, Ralph, Esq., Roger, Andrew, and George, and two daughters, Maud and Mary. She was co-heiress in 1517 to her brother, Thomas Gray. His widow, Mary, married (2ⁿᵈ) _____ **MADDISON**. She died 22 Nov. 1571.

Hodgson *Hist. of Northumberland* 2(2) (1832): 75, 113–114. Raine *Hist. & Antiqs. of North Durham* (1852): chart between 326–327. Marshall *Vis. of Northumberland in 1615* (1878): 45 (Fenwick ped.: "John Fenwicke of Stanton, esq. = Mary da. and coheire of Sʳ Raphe Grey of Chillingham Kt."). Flower *Vis. of Yorkshire 1563-4* (H.S.P. 16) (1881): 121 (Fenwick ped.: "John Fenwyke Esquyer son & heyre to Sir Raff. = Mary doughter & on of theyres of Sir Raff Grey of Chyllyngham."). St. George & Dugdale *Peds. Rec. at the Heralds' Vis. of Northumberland* (1903): 51–52 (Fenwick peds.). Harvey et al. *Vis. of the North* 1 (Surtees Soc. 122) (1912): 20–21; 4 (Surtees Soc. 146) (1932): 76–78 (Fenwike ped.: "John Fenwike Esquire (of Stanton) = Mary daughter to Sir Raff Grey of Chillingham"). Clay *Extinct & Dormant Peerages* (1913): 89 (sub Grey). Dodds *Hist. of Northumberland* 14 (1935): chart facing 328.

14. RALPH FENWICK, Esq., of Stanton, Northumberland, son and heir. He married **BARBARA OGLE**, daughter of John Ogle, Esq., of Ogle Castle, Northumberland. They had two sons, Richard, Esq., and Ralph, and one daughter, Mary. RALPH FENWICK, Esq., was living 10 May 1557.

Hodgson *Hist. of Northumberland* 2(2) (1832): 113–114. Marshall *Vis. of Northumberland in 1615* (1878): 45 (Fenwick ped.: "Raphe Fenwicke of Stanton esq. = Dorothie d. of John Ogle of Ogle Castle."). Flower *Vis. of Yorkshire 1563-4* (H.S.P. 16) (1881): 121 (Fenwick ped.: "Raff Fenwyke Esquyer son & heyre to John. = Barbara doughter to Sir John Ogle of Ogle Castell."). Ogle *Ogle & Bothal* (1902): 178–179, 181. St. George & Dugdale *Peds. Rec. at the Heralds' Vis. of Northumberland* (1903): 51–52 (Fenwick peds.). Harvey et al. *Vis. of the North* 1 (Surtees Soc. 122) (1912): 20–21; 4 (Surtees Soc. 146) (1932): 76–78 (Fenwike ped.: "Raffe Fenwike of Stanton Esquire = Dorothe daughter of John Ogle of Ogle Castle"). Note: Barbara Ogle, wife of Ralph Fenwick, Esq., is a lineal descendant of William Ogle, Knt., of Choppington, Northumberland (died 1474) [see HERON 8.i].

15. RICHARD FENWICK, Esq., son and heir, born at Heaton. He married (1ˢᵗ) before 1568 **DOROTHY THORNTON**, daughter and coheiress of Roger Thornton, of Witton. They had one son, Roger, and two daughters, Catherine (wife of Lancelot Lisle) and Jane (wife of Thomas Hall). He married (2ⁿᵈ) after 1575 **MARGARET MILLS**, daughter of William Mills, of Gray's Inn,

London, and Croydon, Surrey. They had two sons, William, Esq., and Thomas, and one daughter, Margaret (wife of Abraham Eden).

> Hodgson *Hist. of Northumberland* 2(2) (1832): 113–114. Marshall *Vis. of Northumberland in 1615* (1878): 45 (Fenwick ped.: "Richard Fenwicke of Stanton esq. living 1615, [1] = Dorothie da. and coheire of Roger Thornton. 1 wife, [2] = Margaret da. of Will'm Mills. 2 wife."). Flower *Vis. of Yorkshire 1563–4* (H.S.P. 16) (1881): 121 (Fenwick ped.: "Rychard Fenwyke son and heyr."). St. George & Dugdale *Peds. Rec. at the Heralds' Vis. of Northumberland* (1903): 51–52 (Fenwick peds.). Harvey et al. *Vis. of the North* 4 (Surtees Soc. 146) (1932): 76–78 (Fenwike ped.: "Richard Fenwike of Stanton now living 1575 = Dorothy daughter and coheir to Roger Thornton of Whitton (Witton)").

16. WILLIAM FENWICK, Esq., of Stanton, Northumberland, eldest son by his father's 2nd marriage, born 22 Sept. 1581. He was admitted to Gray's Inn 22 March 1597/8. He married 27 July 1605 **ELIZABETH GARGRAVE**, daughter of Cotton Gargrave, Knt., of Nostell Priory and Kinsley, Yorkshire, Burgess (M.P.) for Boroughbridge, by Anne, daughter of Thomas Waterton, Esq. [see GARGRAVE 18 for her ancestry]. She was baptized at Wragby, Yorkshire 19 Feb. 1577/8. They had two sons, Edward, Esq., and John, Esq., and three daughters, Margaret, Cecily, and Priscilla (wife of Roland Nevet). WILLIAM FENWICK, Esq., died 12 June 1647.

> Hodgson *Hist. of Northumberland* 2(2) (1832): 113–114. Glover & St. George *Vis. of Yorkshire 1584–5, 1612* (1875): 68–69 (Gargrave ped.: "Elizabeth [Gargrave], *mar. to Wm. Fenwick, of Stanton.*"). Marshall *Vis. of Northumberland in 1615* (1878): 45 (Fenwick ped.: "Will'm Fenwicke sonne and heire. = Elizabeth da. of S' Cotton Gargraue of Nostell Kt."). St. George & Dugdale *Peds. Rec. at the Heralds' Vis. of Northumberland* (1903): 52 (Fenwick ped.). *PMHB* 49 (1925): 151–162; 50 (1926): 267–272. *Parish Reg. of Wragby* 1 1538–1704 (Yorkshire Parish Reg. Soc. 105) (1938): 24, 65. *Misc. Gen. et Heraldica* 1st Ser. 1 (1868): 226–227. Hasler *House of Commons 1558–1603* 2 (1981): 166 (biog. of Cotton Gargrave).

Children of William Fenwick, Esq., by Elizabeth Gargrave:

i. **EDWARD FENWICK**, Esq., of Stanton, Northumberland, son and heir, born 29 October 1606. He married **SARAH NEVILLE**. They had eleven children, including Robert Fenwick.[23] EDWARD FENWICK, Esq., died 14 August 1689. St. George *Vis. of Northumberland 1615* (1878): 45 (Fenwick ped.: "Edward [Fenwick] sonne and heire ætat. 9 annor. 1615."). Foster *Peds. Rec. at the Heralds' Vis. of Northumberland* (1903?): 52 (Fenwick ped.).

ii. **JOHN FENWICK**, Esq., of Brockham, Surrey and Binfield, Berkshire, younger son. He was admitted to Gray's Inn 15 March 1638/9. He married (1st) before 10 May 1644 (date of lawsuit) **ELIZABETH COVERT**, daughter of Walter Covert, Knt., of Maidstone, Kent, by Anne, daughter and heiress of John Covert [see COVERT 13 for her ancestry]. She was baptized at Boxley, Kent in 1610, and was a legatee in the 1632 will of her mother. They had three daughters, Elizabeth (wife of John Adams), Anne (wife of Samuel Hedge), and Priscilla (wife of Edward Champney). He was a cavalry major under Cromwell. His wife, Elizabeth, was buried at Thakeham, Sussex 30 August 1654. He married (2nd) St. Bride's Fleet Street, London 5 May 1655 **MARY MARTEN**, widow of Richard Rogers, Knt., and sister of Henry Marten, Knt. They had no issue. In 1663 Richard Worsley and another sued him and his wife, Dame Mary, regarding the manor of Eaton Hastings, Berkshire. He joined the Society of Friends, and became a supporter of establishment of Quaker colony in America. He immigrated to New Jersey on the ship *Griffin* in 1673. He founded Fenwick's Colony at Salem, New Jersey. JOHN FENWICK, Esq. left a will dated 7 August 1683, proved 16 April 1684. Kerry *Hist. & Antiqs. of the Hundred of Bray* (1861): 69–70. Shourds *Hist. & Gen. of Fenwick's Colony* (1876). *Docs. Rel. the Col. Hist. of New Jersey* (Archives of New Jersey 1st Ser. 23 (1901): 162. *Sussex Arch. Colls.* 46 (1903): 170–180; 47 (1904): 116–147; 48 (1905): 1–15. *NEHGR* 82 (1928): 154 (arms of John Fenwick: Silver a chief gules six martlets three two and one counterchanged). *D.A.B.* 6 (1931): 330–331 (John Fenwick). Comber *Sussex Gens.* 2 (1932): 179–186 (sub Covert). *Chancery Procs., Bridges'Div. 1613–1714* 4 (List & Indexes 45) (1936): 343.

---

[23] Robert Fenwick, younger son of Edward Fenwick, Esq., and Sarah Neville above, was born 8 June 1646. He married Ann Culcheth. They were the parents of **John Fenwick** (died 1747), planter and merchant, of John's Island, Charleston County, South Carolina [see Bulloch *Hist. & Gen. of the Habersham Fam.* (1901): 63–64; *South Carolina Hist. & Gen. Mag.* 14 (1913): 6–16].

ཡ FERRERS ཡ

WILLIAM THE CONQUEROR, King of England, married **MAUD OF FLANDERS**.
HENRY I, King of England, by an unknown mistress, _____.
ROBERT FITZ ROY, Earl of Gloucester, married **MABEL FITZ ROBERT**.
MAUD OF GLOUCESTER, married **RANULPH DE GERNONS**, Earl of Chester.
HUGH, Earl of Chester, married **BERTRADE DE MONTFORT** [see CHESTER 5].

6. AGNES OF CHESTER, married in 1192 **WILLIAM DE FERRERS**, Knt., 4th Earl of Derby, Sheriff of Nottinghamshire and Derbyshire, 1194, Sheriff of Lancashire, 1223–8, son and heir of William de Ferrers, 3rd Earl of Derby, by Sibyl, daughter of William de Briouze (or Brewes). They had five sons, William, Knt. [5th Earl of Derby], Thomas, Knt., Hugh, Knt., Robert, and Ranulph (parson of St. Michael's on the Wyre, Lancashire), and three daughters, Bertha, Agnes (wife of Richard de Montfitchet), and _____. He had livery of his lands in 1190–91. Before the return of King Richard I from captivity to England, he supported the Justiciar against John, Count of Mortain, and, with the Earl of Chester, he besieged Nottingham Castle. He took part in the second Coronation of King Richard I, which was solemnized in Winchester Cathedral 17 April 1194. He was present at the Coronation of King John 27 May 1199. On 7 June 1199 the king restored and confirmed to him the third penny of Derby, and with his own hand girded him with the sword as an Earl. In 1213 he witnessed the king's surrender of the kingdom to Pope Innocent III. He was a witness to the last will of King John in 1216, and appointed one of its managers and disposers. He was present at the Coronation of King Henry III 28 October 1216. On 30 October following, the king granted him the Castles of Peak and Bolsover, Derbyshire, and, on 16 Jan. 1216/17, he was granted the manor of Melbourne, Derbyshire to hold until the king was 14 years of age. He assisted the Regent to raise the Siege of Lincoln Castle 20 May 1217, and, with his brother-in-law, Ranulph, Earl of Chester, he commanded the royal forces which razed Montsorel Castle. In June 1218 he went on Crusade. In 1225 he witnessed the third great charter of King Henry III. He was heir c.1226/7 to his younger brother, Robert de Ferrers. He accompanied the king in the expedition to Brittany and Poitou in 1230. In 1230 the king pardoned him up to 100 marks of the £170 which were exacted from him for the debts of his uncle, Robert de Ferrers. He was present at the Council of London Feb. 1231/2. His wife, Agnes, was co-heiress in 1232 to her brother, Ranulph, Earl of Chester and Lincoln, by which she inherited the Castle and manor of Chartley, Staffordshire, the Castle and vill of West Derby, Lancashire, and the borough of Liverpool, Lancashire, together with all the lands which Earl Ranulph had held between Ribble and Mersey (including the fiefs of Manchester, Widnes, Warrington, Tottington and Croston, Makerfield and Sefton, Lancashire), and the vills of Bugbrooke, Northamptonshire and Navenby, Lincolnshire. In 1236 he and his wife, Agnes, quitclaimed the advowson of the church of Bolton, Lancashire to Herbert, Prior of Mattersey. He presented to the churches of Brington, Northamptonshire, 1237, and Higham Ferrers, Northamptonshire, 1238. In 1241 Stephen de Meverel sued William de Ferrers, Earl of Derby, and Agnes his wife regarding the advowson of Gatton, Staffordshire; William and Agnes appeared by attorney, and stated that the advowson formed part of the inheritance of Agnes, which fell to her by the death of Ranulph, Earl of Chester, and that they could not answer without their co-parceners. In 1244 he was summoned for military service against the Scots. At an unknown date, he granted 24 acres in his Forest of Needwood to Robert son of Thomas of the Cross. At an unknown date, he granted 19 acres in the manor of Horecross (in Yoxall), Staffordshire to Bartholomew Andwinckle. At an unknown date, he granted all the town of Horecross (in Yoxall), Staffordshire to Hugh Melbourn. SIR WILLIAM DE FERRERS, Earl of Derby, died testate 22 Sept. 1247. His widow, Agnes, died testate 2 Nov. 1247.

Shaw *Hist. & Antiqs. of Staffordshire* 1 (1798): 39 (Ferrers ped.), 93 (charter of William de Ferrers, Earl of Derby; charter names his wife, Agnes), 103 (three charters of William de Ferrers, Earl of Derby, one of which is witnessed by his brother, Robert). Dugdale *Monasticon Anglicanum* 6(2) (1830): 807 (charter of Robert de Ferrers, son of William, Earl of Ferrers; charter witnessed by William de Ferrers, son of William, Earl of Ferrers). *Coll. Top. et Gen.* 2 (1835): 247–249. Baines *Hist. of the Commerce & Town of Liverpool* 1 (1852): 97–133. *Jour. British Arch. Assoc.* 7 (1852): 220–232. Giles *Matthew Paris's English Hist.* 2 (1853): 251 (sub 1247: "In this year certain nobles died in England, amongst whom was William Earl Ferrers, a peaceable and good man, who died at a great age, about St. Catherine's day [25 November], after having suffered for a long time from gout. His marriage with his wife the Countess was solemnized by St. Thomas, archbishop of Canterbury. In the same month also died his wife M, countess of Ferrers, of the same age and of equal fame and goodness. The said earl therefore was succeeded in the earldom by his eldest son and heir William, a good and discrete man, but who was miserably afflicted with the same disease as his father."). Luard *Annales Monastici* 1 (Rolls Ser. 36) (1864): 285 (Annals of Burton sub 1247: "Isto anno obiit Wilelmus de Ferrariis, nobilis comes Derbeiae, x. kal. Octobris. Agnes comitissa, uxor ejus, completa quarentena sua, decessit quarto non. Novembris."). Shirley *Royal & Other Historical Letters illus. of the Reign of King Henry III* 2 (Rolls Ser. 27) (1866): 14 (letter of William de Ferrers, Earl of Derby). *Year Books of Edward I: Years XXXIII–XXV* 5 (Rolls Ser. 31a) (1879): 100–107. Ormerod *Hist. of the County Palatine & City of Chester* 1 (1882): 26–33. Wrottesley *Staffordshire Suits: Plea Rolls* (Colls. Hist. Staffs. 4) (1883): 90–102. Maitland *Bracton's Note Book* 3 (1887): 280–283. Birch *Catalogue of Seals in the British Museum* 2 (1892): 280 (seal of William de Ferrers, Earl of Ferrers dated 1191–1199 — To the right. In armour: hauberk, surcoat, sword, long convex shield. Horse galloping; Another undated seal. Obverse. To the right. In armour: hauberk, surcoat, flat-topped helmet, sword, shield of arms: vairé, FERRERS; Reverse. Small oval counterseal. With mark of the handle. Impression of an antique oval intaglio gem. A lion devouring a stag). Delaville le Roulx *Cartulaire Général de l'Ordre des Hospitaliers de S. Jean de Jérusalem* 1 (1894): 304. Norris *Baddesley Clinton, its Manor, Church & Hall* (1897): 101–110. *List of Sheriffs for England & Wales* (PRO Lists and Indexes 9) (1898): 72, 102. Farrer *Final Concords of Lancaster* 1 (Lancs. & Cheshire Rec. Soc. 39) (1899): 74–93, 93–118, 216–219. Farrer *Lancashire Inquests, Extents & Feudal Aids* 1 (Lanc. & Cheshire Rec. Soc. 48) (1903): 120, 146. Parker *Cal. of Lancashire Assize Rolls* 1 (Lancs. & Cheshire Rec. Soc. 47) (1904): 18, 40, 55, 66. Wrottesley *Peds. from the Plea Rolls* (1905): 531–532. *Year Books of Edward II* 3 (Selden Soc. 20) (1905): 4–9. *C.P.* 3 (1913): 169, footnote a (sub Chester); 4 (1916): 194–196 (sub Derby(); 5 (1926): 320 (chart). Grosseteste *Rotuli Roberti Grosseteste Episcopi Lincolniensis* (Lincoln Rec. Soc. 11) (1914): 169, 178, 184–185, 190, 402. Farrer *Early Yorkshire Charters* 2 (1915): 195 (chart). Farnham *Leicestershire Medieval Peds.* (1925): 11 (ped. of Earls of Chester). *Rpt. on the MSS of Reginald Rawdon Hastings, Esq.* 1 (Hist. MSS Comm. 78) (1928): 83. Gibbs *Early Charters of the Cathedral Church of St. Paul* (Camden Soc. 3rd Ser. 58) (1939): 37–39. Sanders *English Baronies* (1960): 32–33, 148–149. Hockey *Beaulieu Cartulary* (Southampton Recs. Ser. 17) (1974): 11–12, 44–45. *C.R.R.* 16 (1979): 69. Ellis *Cat. Seals in the P.R.O.* 2 (1981): 41 (seal of William de Ferrers, Earl of Derby — On horseback, riding to right. He wears a long coat of mail and a flat-topped helmet with nasal, and holds a drawn sword and a shield. Legend: …DEF…R…). *Nottingham Medieval Studies* 44 (2000): 69–81. Online resource: http://www.finerollshenry3.org.uk/content/calendar/roll_029.html. Lancashire Rec. Office: Clifton of Lytham, DDCL 250 (charter of William de Ferrers, Earl of Derby) (available at http://www.a2a.org.uk/search/index.asp). Lancashire Rec. Office: Molyneux, Earls of Sefton, DDM 19/1 (charter of William de Ferrers, Earl of Derby), DDM 19/2 (charter of William de Ferrers, Earl of Derby); DDM 19/3 (charter of Agnes de Ferrers, Countess of Derby), DDM 19/4 (charter of William de Ferrers, Earl of Derby) (available at http://www.a2a.org.uk/search/index.asp).

Children of Agnes of Chester, by William de Ferrers, Knt.:

i. **WILLIAM DE FERRERS**, Knt., 5th Earl of Derby [see next].

ii. **BERTHA DE FERRERS**, married (1st) **THOMAS DE FURNIVAL**, of Worksop, Nottinghamshire, and Sheffield, Yorkshire [see FURNIVAL 8], (2nd) **RALPH LE BIGOD**, Knt., of Settrington, Yorkshire [see ASKE 8].

iii. _____ **DE FERRERS**, married **JOHN DE VIPONT**, of Appleby, Westmorland [see CLIFFORD 7].

7. WILLIAM DE FERRERS, Knt., 5th Earl of Derby, Constable of Bolsover Castle, 1235–6, son and heir, born about 1193. He married (1st) before 14 May 1219 **SIBYL MARSHAL**, died before 1238, 3rd daughter of William Marshal, Knt., 4th Earl of Pembroke (or Strigoil), hereditary Master Marshal, by Isabel, daughter of Richard Fitz Gilbert (nicknamed "*Strongbow*"), 2nd Earl of Pembroke (or Strigoil) [see MARSHAL 3 for her ancestry]. They had seven daughters, Agnes, Isabel, Maud, Sibyl, Joan, Agatha (wife of Hugh de Mortimer), and Eleanor. He was afflicted from youth with gout, and habitually travelled in a chariot or litter. He accompanied the king to France in 1230. He married (2nd) in or before 1238 **MARGARET** (or **MARGERY**) **DE QUINCY**, daughter and co-heiress of Roger de Quincy, 2nd Earl of Winchester, by his 1st wife, Ellen, daughter and co-heiress of Alan Fitz Roland, lord of Galloway, hereditary Constable of Scotland [see QUINCY 7 for her ancestry]. They had two sons, Robert, Knt. [6th Earl of Derby], and William, Knt., and three daughters, Elizabeth, Joan, and Agnes. He had livery of Chartley Castle and the rest of his mother's lands 10 Nov. 1247. He was invested with the Earldom of Derby 2 Feb. 1247/8. In 1245 he was granted respite of forest offences because he "laboured under infirmity." He presented to the church of Brington, Northamptonshire in 1250. While passing over a bridge at St. Neots, Huntingdonshire, he was accidentally thrown from his chariot sustaining broken limb bones from which he never recovered. SIR WILLIAM DE FERRERS, 5th Earl of Derby, died at Evington, Leicestershire 24 (or 28) March 1254, and was buried at Merevale Abbey, Warwickshire. His widow, Margaret, presented to the churches of Keyston, Huntingdonshire, 1255, Irchester, Northamptonshire, 1267, and Higham Ferrers, Northamptonshire, 1268, 1275. She was co-heiress in 1264 to her father, Roger de Quincy, Knt., Earl of Winchester, by which she inherited the hereditary office of Constable of Scotland, together with the manors of Groby (in Ratby) and Thurnby, Leicestershire, Ware, Hertfordshire, Keyston and Southoe, Huntingdonshire, Chinnor, Oxfordshire, etc. In 1268–9 the Prior and convent of Lenton released the church of Irchester, Northamptonshire to Margaret de Ferrers, Countess of Derby, who in turn levied a fine of it to the use of herself and her heirs. In 1270 she resigned the office of Constable of Scotland to her brother-in-law, Alexander Comyn, Knt., Earl of Buchan. In 1270 Margaret and her sisters, Ellen and Elizabeth, gave license for the election of William de Shaldeston as Prior of the Hospital of St. James and St. John at Brackley, Northamptonshire. In 1272–3 Margaret arraigned an assize of novel disseisin against John le Fauconer, of Thurcaston, and others, touching a tenement in Groby, Leicestershire. In 1273 Philip de Fififfe sued her for the next presentation to the church of Fyfield, Berkshire. In 1274–5 Ellen de Quincy and Alexander Comyn and his wife, Elizabeth, sued their sister, Margaret de Ferrers, Countess of Derby, regarding possessions in Eynesbury, Huntingdonshire. On the assignment of Quincy dower lands in 1275, Margaret was assigned a third part of the manor of Southoe Ferrers, Huntingdonshire, together with a third part of the chief messuage. In 1275–6 William de Karuill' arraigned an assize of mort d'ancestor against her touching a messuage and land in Brampton, Northamptonshire. Sometime in the period, 1275–9, she acquired the one-third share of the same manor assigned to her sister, Elizabeth Comyn, thus increasing Margaret's share to two-thirds. In 1276 Margaret had letters of protection, she then going to Scotland. In 1277–8 Alice widow of John de Kent arraigned an assize of novel disseisin against her and others touching a tenement in Chartley, Staffordshire. About 1281 Margaret de Ferrers, Countess of Derby, Ellen la Zouche, and Alexander Comyn, Earl of Buchan, and his wife, Elizabeth, sued Ranulph son of Robert de Neville and his wife, Euphame, regarding 11-½ virgates in Syston, Leicestershire. Margaret, Countess of Derby, died shortly before 12 March 1280/1, on which date custody of all lands late of the said Countess Margaret were granted by the king to Richard Fukeram to hold during pleasure, so that he cultivate and sow them and answer for the issues at the Exchequer. In 1282 custody of the manor of Southoe, Huntingdonshire late of Margaret, Countess of Derby, deceased was granted by the king to John de Aese, Vicomte of Tartas, to hold during the minority of the heirs. The same month custody of the manor of Keyston, Huntingdonshire late of Margaret, Countess of Derby, deceased was likewise granted by the king to John de Byuelard to hold during the minority of the heirs. In 1281 the king ratified the demise of John de Aysse, Vicomte of Tartas, to Baldwin Wake and Hawise his wife of custody of the manor of Southoe, Huntingdonshire which he had of the gift of the king by the extent of £40 2s. 8d. yearly to hold during the minority of the heirs of Margery, Countess of Derby.

Bridges *Hist. & Antiqs. of Northamptonshire* 2 (1791): 174, 180. Shaw *Hist. & Antiqs. of Staffordshire* 1 (1798): 39 (Ferrers ped.). Baker *Hist. & Antiqs. of Northampton* 1 (1822–30): 123–124 (Ferrers ped.), 563 (Beaumont-Quincy ped.). Clutterbuck *Hist. & Antiqs. of Hertford* 3 (1827): 287–288 (Beaumont-Quincy ped.). Burke *Dict. of the Peerages* …

Extinct, Dormant & in Abeyance (1831): 442–443 (sub Quincy). Hunter *Eccl. Docs.* (Camden Soc. 8) (1840): 68. Lipscomb *Hist. & Antiqs. of Buckingham* 1 (1847): 200–201 (Clare ped.). Baines *Hist. of the Commerce & Town of Liverpool* 1 (1852): 97–133. Giles *Matthew Paris's English Hist.* 2 (1853): 251 (sub 1247: "In this year certain nobles died in England, amongst whom was William Earl Ferrers, a peaceable and good man, who died at a great age, about St. Catherine's day [25 November], after having suffered for a long time from gout … The said earl therefore was succeeded in the earldom by his eldest son and heir William, a good and discrete man, but who was miserably afflicted with the same disease as his father."). Luard *Annales Monastici* 1 (Rolls Ser. 36) (1864): 317 (Annals of Burton sub 1254: "Willelmus de Ferrariis comes Derbeiæ obiit v. kal. Aprilis, apud Eventonam juxta Leycestriam, et sepultus est in capitulo de Mirevalle ii kal. Aprilis."). Skene *Liber Pluscardensis* 1 (Historians of Scotland 7) (1877): 136–137; 2 (Historians of Scotland 10) (1880): 102–103. *Year Books of Edward I: Years XXXIII–XXV* 5 (Rolls Ser. 31a) (1879): 100–107. Clark *Earls, Earldom, & Castle of Pembroke* (1880): 69–75. *Annual Rpt. of the Deputy Keeper* 42 (1881): 568; 44 (1883): 100; 45 (1885): 107, 152; 47 (1886): 186; 50 (1889): 45, 92, 442, 460. Wrottesley *Feet of Fines: Henry III* (Colls. Hist. Staffs. 4) (1883): 238–259. Godfrey *Hist. of the Parish & Priory of Lenton* (1884): 82. Doyle *Official Baronage of England* 1 (1886): 548 (sub Derby). *Military Service Performed by Staffordshire Tenants* (Colls. Hist. Staffs. 8(1)) (1887): 1–122. Birch *Cat. Seals in the British Museum* 2 (1892): 281 (seal of William de Ferrers, Earl of Derby dated 1254 — Obverse. To the right. In armour: hauberk, surcoat, shield, sword. Horse galloping. Fine style of workmanship. Reverse. Small round counterseal. A shield of arms: vairé, on a bordure eight horse-shoes [FERRERS]. Legend: * S WILL'I : COMITIS : DERB'.). Norris *Baddesley Clinton, its Manor, Church & Hall* (1897): 63–64 ("The windows at Baddesley are a treasure in themselves … Therein may be read, as in open volumes, the descent and the alliances of the house of Ferrers … Most of the shields were set up in the early part of the seventeenth century, though a few bear date in the sixteenth … In two large windows of the hall opening on the courtyard are twelve shields of arms surmounted by earls' and barons' coronets, and having inscriptions beneath indicating the alliances commemorated [including] … 6. Ferrers impaling Quinci. Gules, seven mascles, conjoined, or, 3, 3 and 1; [inscription:] "William Ferrers, earle of Derby, married Margaret, Lady of Groby, daughter of Roger Quincy, earle of Winchester."), 101–110. *C.C.R. 1272–1279* (1900): 225–226. *C.P.R. 1272–1281* (1901): 93, 140, 427, 442, 459–460. Wrottesley *Peds. from the Plea Rolls* (1905): 104, 276, 501, 531–532, 548. *Scots Peerage* 3 (1906): 142. *Cal. IPM* 2 (1906): 237, 323. *C.P.* 4 (1916): 196–198 (arms of William de Ferrers: Sable (or Azure), an escutcheon vairy or and gules, and an orle of 8 horse-shoes argent), 199 (chart) (sub Derby); 5 (1926): foll. 320 (chart), 340; 12(2) (1959): 276–278 (sub Vescy). VCH *Hertford* 3 (1912): 380–397. Turner *Cal. Feet of Fines Rel. Huntingdon* (Cambridge Antiq. Soc. 8° Ser. 37) (1913): 35. Grosseteste *Rotuli Roberti Grosseteste Episcopi Lincolniensis* (Lincoln Rec. Soc. 11) (1914): 246, 248, 511. *Year Books of Edward II* 13 (Selden Soc. 34) (1918): 59–67; 14(2) (Selden Soc. 43) (1927): 75–77. Foster *Final Concords of Lincoln from the Feet of Fines A.D. 1244–1272* 2 (Lincoln Rec. Soc. 17) (1920): 142 (fine dated 1256 between Ralph, Abbot of Croyland, and Margery countess of Ferrars). Davis *Rotuli Ricardi Gravesend Episcopi Lincolniensis* (Lincoln Rec. Soc. 20) (1925): 99, 109, 118, 129, 168. *Rpt. on the MSS of Reginald Rawdon Hastings, Esq.* 1 (Hist. MSS Comm. 78) (1928): 323–342 (partition of estates of Roger de Quincy, Earl of Winchester). Cam *Hundred & Hundred Rolls* (1930): 276. VCH *Huntingdon* 2 (1932): 346–354. Paget *Baronage of England* (1957) 205: 4–6; 464: 1–8 (sub Quincy) (Margaret de Quincy and her step-mother, Eleanor, were each the step-mother and step-daughter of the other, the Earls of Derby, their husbands, having each married the other's daughter). Reid *Wigtownshire Charters* (Scottish Hist. Soc. 51) (1960): xxxix–xlv. Sanders *English Baronies* (1960): 61, 63, 149. Painter *Feudalism & Liberty* (1961): 230–239. Beardwood *Trial of Walter Langton, Bishop of Lichfield 1307–1312* (Trans. American Philosophical Soc. n.s. 54 (3)) (1964): 14–17. VCH *Leicester* 5 (1964): 321–330. Saltman *Cartulary of Dale Abbey* (Derbyshire Arch. Soc. Recs. 2) (1967): 341 (charter of William de Ferrers). VCH *Cambridge* 5 (1973): 200–201. DeWindt *Royal Justice & Medieval English Countryside* 2 (1981): 590. Ellis *Cat. Seals in the P.R.O.* 2 (1981): 41 (seal of William de Ferrers, Earl of Derby dated 1249 — On horseback, galloping to right. He wears mail, long surcoat and flat-topped helmet, and holds a drawn sword and a shield of arms: vair, and a bordure [FERRERS]. Legend: +SIGILLVM:W/ILLELMI:DE/FERRARIIS). VCH *Wiltshire* 12 (1983): 125–138. Simpson & Galbraith *Cal. Docs. Rel. Scotland* 5 (1986): 142. Schwennicke *Europäische Stammtafeln* n.s. 3(4) (1989): 708 (sub Quency). *Nottingham Medieval Studies* 44 (2000): 69–81. Mitchell *Portraits of Medieval Women* (2003): 11–28. Derbyshire Rec. Office: Gell Fam. of Hopton, D258/7/1/1 (charter of William de Ferrers, Earl of Derby); D258/7/1/8i (charter of William de Ferrers, Earl of Derby) (available at (available at http://www.a2a.org.uk/search/index.asp). Derbyshire Rec. Office: Okeover of Okeover, D231M/T375 (charter of William de Ferrers, Earl of Derby) (available at (available at http://www.a2a.org.uk/search/index.asp). Shakespeare Centre Library & Archive: Gregory of Stivichall, DR10/723 (quitclaim of Margaret de Ferrers, Countess of Derby, to her son, Sir William de Ferrers).

Children of William de Ferrers, Knt., by Sibyl Marshal:

i. **AGNES DE FERRERS**, married **WILLIAM DE VESCY**, Knt., of Alnwick, Northumberland [see LONGESPEE 5.vii].

ii. **ISABEL DE FERRERS**, married (1st) **GILBERT BASSET**, of Wycombe, Buckinghamshire [see MOHUN 8]; (2nd) **REYNOLD DE MOHUN**, Knt., of Dunster, Somerset [see MOHUN 8].

iii. **MAUD DE FERRERS**, married (1st) **SIMON DE KYME**, of Sotby and Croft, Lincolnshire [see MALET 3]; (2nd) **WILLIAM DE FORZ** (or **DE VIVONNE**), Knt., of Chewton, Somerset [see MALET 3]; (3rd) **AMAURY DE ROCHECHOUART**, Knt., Vicomte of Rochechouart [see MALET 3].

iv. **SIBYL DE FERRERS**, married **FRANK DE BOHUN**, Knt., of Midhurst, Sussex [see MIDHURST 4].

v. **JOAN DE FERRERS**, married (1st) **JOHN DE MOHUN**, of Dunster, Somerset [see MOHUN 9], (2nd) **ROBERT D'AGUILLON**, Knt., of Addington, Surrey [see MOHUN 9].

vi. **ELEANOR DE FERRERS**, married (1st) **WILLIAM DE VAUX**, of Tharston and Houghton, Norfolk [see QUINCY 7]; (2nd) **ROGER DE QUINCY**, Knt., 2nd Earl of Winchester, Constable of Scotland [see QUINCY 7]; (3rd) **ROGER DE LEYBOURNE**, of Elham, Kent [see QUINCY 7].

Children of William de Ferrers, Knt., by Margaret de Quincy:

i. **ROBERT DE FERRERS**, Knt., 6th Earl of Derby [see next].

ii. **WILLIAM DE FERRERS**, Knt., of Groby (in Ratby), Leicestershire, married (1st) **ANNE DURWARD** [see GROBY 8]; (2nd) **ELEANOR DE LOVAINE** [see GROBY 8].

iii. **ELIZABETH DE FERRERS**, married (1st) (as his 2nd wife) **WILLIAM LE MARSHAL** [see HINGHAM 5], of Greens Norton and Whittlebury, Northamptonshire, King's Charlton, Gloucestershire, Cowley, Oxfordshire, Colton, Staffordshire, Hazlebury (in Box), Wiltshire, etc., deputy Marshal of Ireland, of Hingham and Foulsham, Norfolk, Chirton, Wiltshire, etc., younger son of John Marshal, Marshal of Ireland, by Aline, daughter and co-heiress of Hubert de Rye [see HINGHAM 4 for his ancestry]. They had no issue. He was heir in 1242 to his elder brother, John Marshal. In 1247, as William Marshal, of Norton, he reached agreement with William de Brackley, Prior of Luffield, whereby he quitclaimed the service of a pair of gilt spurs and suit of court every three week in respect of an estate at Monksbarn (in Whittlebury), Northamptonshire, so that the prior should thereafter hold of him in free alms, quit of all secular service. The same year he also reached agreement with the Templars regarding rent owed for land in Cowley, Oxfordshire. He was granted weekly markets to be held at the manors of Haselbury Plucknett, Somerset and Messingham, Lincolnshire in 1265. WILLIAM LE MARSHAL died Sept. 1265. His widow, Elizabeth, married (2nd) before 1274–5 (date of lawsuit) **DAVID AP GRUFFUDD**, Knt., Prince of North Wales, and, in right of his wife, of Foulsham, Norfolk, Colton, Staffordshire, etc., younger son of Gruffudd ap Llywelyn, by Senena ferch Cadadog. They had two sons, Llywelyn and Owain, and seven daughters, including Gwladus. By his mistress, Tangwystl, daughter of Owain Fflam, of Deheubarth, he also had an illegitimate son, Dafydd Goch. In 1242 his mother, Senena, agreed to give him and his brother, Roderick, as hostages to King Henry III of England. In 1252, as lord of Cwmwd Maen, he entered into a composition with the Abbot and convent of Bardsey. He presented to the church of Plumpton, Northamptonshire 24 Dec. 1273. In 1274–5 Hubert de Rully and Isabel his wife arraigned an assize of mort d'ancestor against David Fitz-Griffin touching a mill in Foulsham, Norfolk. In 1275–6 Hubert de Ruyly and Isabel his wife, and Nicholas de Pulham and Aveline his wife arraigned an assize of mort d'ancestor against David ab Gruffud and Elizabeth his wife touching a mill in Foulsham, Norfolk. In 1278–9 William son of Alexander de Blacolnesl' [Blakesley] arraigned an assize of novel disseisin against David ab Gruffud and others touching a tenement in Great Blakesley, Northamptonshire. In the same year Albric de Wytlebiry arraigned a similar assize against David ab Gruffud and others touching a tenement in Great Blakesley, Northamptonshire. In 1279 David and his wife, Elizabeth, sued her step-son, John le Marshal, for a third of the manor of Colton, Staffordshire as the dower of Elizabeth; John stated he only held a rent of 12s. of which he offered a third. In 1280 the king seised the third part of the manor of Haselbury, Somerset, which David and his wife, Elizabeth, held as the dower of the said Elizabeth of the lands which were of William Marshal her late husband; later the same year the king wishing to grant indulgence to the said David and Elizabeth ordered that the third part of the manor be restored to them. In 1282 David suddenly surprised the Castle of Hawarden, killed many of the knights and squires who formed the garrison, and carried off Roger de Clifford, the Justiciary, as a prisoner into the hills. DAVID AP GRUFFUDD, Prince of North Wales, was executed for treason 3 October 1283. His widow, as "Lady Elizabeth de Ferrers," presented to the church of Plumpton, Northamptonshire in 1285. She presented to the church of Greens Norton, Northamptonshire 20 Dec. 1296, which presentation was disputed by King Edward I, as guardian of William, heir of John Marshal. In 1297 she had a prolonged lawsuit in the royal courts with Sir Hugh de Cave regarding the right of patronage to the church of Plumpton, Northamptonshire. Blomefield *Essay towards a Top. Hist. of Norfolk* 1 (1739): 672–679. Bridges *Hist. & Antiqs. of Northamptonshire* 1 (1791): 241, 255. Ellis *Original Letters Ill. of English Hist.* 3rd Ser. 1 (1846): 27–29 (letter of King Edward I to the Prior and Prioress of Alvingham, Lincolnshire dated 1283 that they admit one or more of the children of Llewelyn ap Gruffudd, late Prince of Wales, or of David his brother into their House.). *Arch. Cambrensis* 4 (1849): 134–138. Riley *Willelmi Rishanger: quondam Monachi S. Albani, Chronica et Annales* (Rolls Ser. 28) (1865): 91 ("David, fuga dilapsus, multis annis cum Rege Angliæ stetit; a quo, contra morem gentis suæ, miles factus, in ista guerra, ob probitatem et fidelitatem suam, plurimum erat Regi acceptus: unde et eidem castrum de Dimby [Denbigh] contulit in Wallia, cum terris ad valorem mille librarum annui redditus; insuper et uxorem dedit, filiam Comitis Derbeyæ, quæ nuper alio viro fuerat viduata.") [also see Hog *F. Nicholai Triveti, de ordine frat. praedicatorum, Annales* (English Hist. Soc.) (1865): 298]. Luard *Annales Monastici* 3 (Rolls Ser. 36) (1866): 298 (Annals of Dunstable sub A.D. 1283: "Eodem anno David, germanus Leulini, principis Walliæ, captus est per gentem domini regis ...et filius suus legitimus captus est cum eo .... Uxor etiam ipsius David, quæ fuit filia comitis de Ferares, alias capta est et inprisonata."). *Annual Rpt. of the Deputy Keeper* 44 (1883): 109; 45 (1885): 176, 291; 46 (1886): 174–175; 48 (1887): 22. Rye *Short Cal. of the Feet of Fines for Norfolk* 1 (1885): 84. Wrottesley *Staffordshire Suits: Plea Rolls* (Colls. Hist. Staffs. 6(1)) (1885): 100. *Colls. Hist. Staffs.* 8 (1887): 10. *Trans. Honourable Soc. of Cymmrodorion* Session 1899–1900 (1901): 6–105; Session 1968, 1: 43–62. *C.Ch.R.* 1 (1903): 262–263; 2 (1906): 53. Ramsay *Dawn of the Constitution* (1908): 338 ("[King] Edward [I] knighted him [Dafydd ap Gruffudd], given him charge of Hope and Denbigh Castles, with lands valued at £1,000 a year, and married him to a kinswoman of his own, Elizabeth Ferrers, daughter of the ex-Earl of Derby, a Lusigan on the mother's side, and widow of John [sic] Marshal of Norton."). *C.P.R. 1258–1266* (1910): 602. Lloyd *Hist. of Wales* 2 (1911): 259. *Somersetshire Pleas* 4(1) (Somerset Rec. Soc. 44) (1929): 225–226, 351–352. *C.P.* 8 (1932): 527–528 (sub Marshal); 10 (1945): 182 footnote h (sub Orty); 14 (1998): 468 (sub Marshal). Leys *Sandford Cartulary* 1 (Oxfordshire Rec. Soc. 19) (1938): 37–38 (final concord between Master Robert de Saunford and William Marshal dated 1247), 38–40 (final concord between Geoffrey Fitz John and William Marshal dated 1247). Sutton *Rolls & Reg. of Bishop Oliver Sutton, 1280–1299* 2 (Lincoln Rec. Soc. 43) (1950): 48, 141–142. VCH *Oxford* 5 (1957): 76–96. Sanders *English Baronies* (1960): 53. Elvey *Luffield Priory Charters* 1 (Buckingham Rec. Soc. 22) (1968): 163, 178–179 (charter dated 1274–5 of Christian de Wayford to Luffield Priory, granted for the souls of Lady Elizabeth wife of Sir David Griffin, Sir William Marshal, and others); 2 (Buckingham Rec. Soc. 26) (1968): 367. Bartrum *Welsh Gens. 300–1400* (1980): 447 [Gruffudd ap Cynan 5: "Dafydd d. 1283 Ld. of Denbigh & Hope = Elizabeth d. Robt. Ferrers, E. of Derby"]. *T.G.* 1 (1980): 80–95. Cannon *Dict. of British Hist.* (2001) (biog. of Dafydd ap Gruffydd). Fritze & Robison *Hist. Dict. of Late Medieval England, 1272–1485* (2002): 144–145 (biog. of Dafydd ap Gruffydd). National Archives, SC 1/16/103 (available at www.catalogue.nationalarchives.gov.uk/search.asp).

iv. **JOAN DE FERRERS**, married **THOMAS DE BERKELEY**, Knt., 1st Lord Berkeley [see BERKELEY 5].

v. **AGNES DE FERRERS**, married **ROBERT DE MUSCEGROS**, Knt., of Charlton Musgrove, Somerset [see MUSCEGROS 4].

8. ROBERT DE FERRERS, Knt., 6th Earl of Derby, of Tutbury, Staffordshire, son and heir by his father's 2nd marriage, born about 1239 (aged 9 in 1249, came of age in 1260). He married (1st) at Westminster by contract dated 26 July 1249 **MARY** (or **MARIE**) **DE LUSIGNAN** (or **MARY DE LA MARCHE**), daughter of Hugues XI le Brun (or de Lusignan), Knt., Count of La Marche and Angoulême, seigneur of Lusignan in Poitou (uterine half-brother of Henry III, King of England), by Yolande, daughter of Pierre de Braine (nicknamed *Mauclerc*), Knt., Duke of Brittany, Earl of Richmond [see LUSIGNAN 6 for her ancestry]. She was born about 1242 (aged 7 in 1249). About 1260 he gave his younger brother, William de Ferrers, the manor of Bolton (in Great Bolton), Lancashire, together with all his lands in the wapentake of Leyland, Lancashire, including the manors of Bispham, Bolton, Bretherton, Charnock (in Charnock Richard), Chorley, Duxbury, Heath Charnock, Mawdesley, Shevington, and Welch Whittle, Lancashire. In the period, c.1254–60, he granted the manor of Easton, Leicestershire to his sister, Joan. In 1262 he made a gift in free alms to the Prior and convent of St. Thomas by Stafford of the manor of Sueneshurst and the township of Pendleton (in Eccles), Lancashire, together with the advowson of Stowe by Chartley, Staffordshire. On the outbreak of the Barons' War in 1263, he joined the Barons and seized three of Prince Edward's castles. He captured Worcester 29 Feb. 1263/4, and destroyed the town and Jewry. He absented himself from the Battle of Lewes, but, with 20,000 foot and many horsemen, put to flight the royal forces near Chester in November following. On 24 Dec. 1264 he was summoned to Parliament by writ directed *Comiti Derb'*. In that Parliament he was accused of divers trespasses and was sent to the Tower by Earl Simon de Montfort, but was pardoned 5 Dec. 1265. A few months later he again rebelled, and joining forces with John Deiville, Baldwin Wake, and others, he devastated the Midlands. He was subsequently captured by royal forces at the Battle of Chesterfield 15 May 1266, and remained a prisoner for nearly three years. All his castles, lands, and tenements were granted to the king's younger son, Edmund of Lancaster, 28 June 1266. His wife, Mary, was living 11 July 1266. In 1269 he regained his liberty by agreeing to redeem his lands by paying £50,000, a promise he later said was extorted from him under fear of corporal punishment while he was a prisoner, but was unable to raise the money. Robert married (2nd) 26 June 1269 **ELEANOR DE BOHUN**, daughter of Humphrey de Bohun, Knt., of Kimbolton, Huntingdonshire, by Eleanor, daughter and co-heiress of William de Brewes, Knt. [see BOHUN 7 for her ancestry]. They had two sons, John, Knt. [1st Lord Ferrers of Chartley], and Thomas, and one daughter, Eleanor. Sometime in the period, 1269–79, he made a gift in free alms to the Prior and convent of St. Thomas by Stafford for the souls of himself and his two wives, Mary and Eleanor, with his own body to be buried at St. Thomas, of two messuages in the town of Chartley, together with the advowson of Stowe by Chartley, Staffordshire. In 1274 he unsuccessfully sued Edmund son of King Henry III in a plea that he might redeem his lands according to the Dictum of Kenilworth; Edmund replied that Robert could not claim the benefit of the dictum of Kenilworth, because after it was passed and published he had come to him of his own free will and agreed to redeem his lands and himself from prison for a sum of £50,000 to be paid to the said Edmund on the Quindene of St. John the Baptist, 53 Henry III. In 1275–6 he arraigned an assize of mort d'ancestor against Devorguille de Balliol touching a messuage in Repton, Derbyshire. In the same period, he arraigned an assize of mort d'ancestor against the master of the hospital of St. Lazarus of Burton touching a messuage and land in Burrow-Ash, Derbyshire. In the same period, he arraigned an assize of novel disseisin against Sampson de Dun' and another touching a tenement in Breadsall, Derbyshire. In 1276–7 Geoffrey de Skeftington arraigned an assize of novel disseisin against him and others touching a tenement in Breadsall, Derbyshire. In the same period, Geoffrey de Skeftington arraigned an assize of novel disseisin against him and others touching a tenement in Morley, Derbyshire. SIR ROBERT DE FERRERS, sometime Earl of Derby, died shortly before 27 April 1279, and was buried at St. Thomas Priory at Stafford, Staffordshire. In Michaelmas term 1279 his widow, Eleanor, sued Edmund the king's brother for dower in a third of Tutbury, Scropton, Rolleston, Marchington, Calyngewode, Uttoxeter, Adgeresley, and Newborough, Staffordshire, and Duffield, Spondon, Chatesdene, and nine other vills named in Derbyshire; Edmund appeared in court and stated he held nothing in Spondon or Chatesdene, and as regards to the rest Eleanor had no claim to dower in them, because neither at the time Robert had married her nor any time afterwards had he been seised of them. About 1280 Eleanor petitioned the king for the restoration of the manor of Chartley, Staffordshire, stating it was part of the inheritance of her son, John de Ferrers, who is under age and in the king's keeping. In 1284 she sued Thomas de Bray in a plea regarding custody of the land and heir of William le Botiller. In 1286 a commission was appointed by the king to investigate the persons who hunted and carried away deer and felled and carried away trees in the park of Eleanor, late the wife of Robert de Ferrers, at Chartley, Staffordshire. In 1290 she and her brother, Humphrey de Bohun, Earl of Hereford, acknowledged they owed a debt of £200 to Robert de Tibetot and Matthew de Columbers, the king's butler. In 1295 she presented to the church of Keyston, Huntingdonshire. She and her son, John de Ferrers, presented to the church of Eynesbury, Huntingdonshire in 1296. Eleanor, Countess of Derby, died 20 Feb. 1313/4, and was buried at Walden Abbey, Essex.

Anselme *Hist. de la Maison Royale de France* 3 (1728): 75–81 (sub Lezignem). Shaw *Hist. & Antiqs. of Staffordshire* 1 (1798): 39 (Ferrers ped.), 85 (charter and seal of Robert de Ferrers, Earl of Derby dated c.1262). Baker *Hist. & Antiqs. of Northampton* 1 (1822–30): 123–124 (Ferrers ped.). Dugdale *Monasticon Anglicanum* 4 (1823): 140–141 (Walden Abbey: "Anno Domini MCCCXIIJ. x. kal. Martii obiit Elianora comitissa Derbi, cujus corpus juxta magnum altare in parte borcali jacet humatum"); 6(1) (1830): 472. Palgrave *Docs. & Recs. Ill. the Hist. of Scotland* 1 (1837): 219 ("Alianora de

Ferers Comitissa" included on list of people owing military service in 1300). Hunter *Eccl. Docs.* (Camden Soc. 8) (1840): 71. Baines *Hist. of the Commerce & Town of Liverpool* 1 (1852): 97–133. *Bibliothèque de l'École des Chartes* 4th Ser. 2 (1856): 537–545. Luard *Annales Monastici* 1 (Rolls Ser. 36) (1864): 285 (Annals of Burton sub 1249: "Isto anno Robertus de Ferrariis, puer ix. annorum, filius Willelmi de Ferrariis comitis Derbeiæ, desponsavit apud Westmonasterium, Mariam vii. annorum puellulam, neptem regis Henrici filiam fratris sui comitis Engolismi et Marchiæ."). Delisle "Chronologie Hist. des Comtes de la Marche" (Bull. Société Archéologique et Hist. de la Charente 4th Ser. 4) (1867): 3–16. *Annual Rpt. of the Deputy Keeper* 35 (1874): 35; 45 (1885): 108, 161, 287, 338; 46 (1886): 110, 234; 47 (1886): 169, 171. *Year Books of Edward I: Years XXXIII–XXV* 5 (Rolls Ser. 31a) (1879): 100–107. Francisque-Michel *Rôles Gascons* 1 (1885): 487–488. Wrottesley *Staffordshire Suits: Plea Rolls* (Colls. Hist. Staffs. 6) (1885): 60, 63–64, 76, 97–98, 137, 250. Doyle *Official Baronage of England* 1 (1886): 549 (sub Derby). La Porta *Les Gens de Qualité en Basse-Marche* 1(2) (1886): 1–60 (Généalogie de Lusignan). Birch *Cat. Seals in the British Museum* 2 (1892): 279 (seal of Robert de Ferrers, Earl of Derby dated c.1265 — Obverse. To the right. In armour: hauberk, surcoat, flat-topped helmet with vizor down, sword, shield slung by a strap over the shoulder. Horse galloping, caparisoned. Arms: vairé [FERRERS]. Legend: * ROBS · FIL' · ET · HERES · DNI : WILL'I : DE · FERRAR' QŌDA · COMITIS · DERBEYE. Reverse. A large shield of arms: vairé (in fourteen rows) [FERRERS], suspended by a strap from an elegantly designed conventional tree, and between two finely drawn wavy branches of foliage and flowers. Legend: * SIGILLVM · ROBERTI · DE · [FERRAR]IIS · COMITIS : DERBEYE. Beaded borders). Jeayes *Desc. Cat. of the Charters & Muniments in the Possession of the Rt. Hon. Lord Fitzhardinge* (1892): 118 (charter of Robert de Ferrers dated c.1254–60; charter witnessed by his brother, William de Ferrers, and his uncle, Sir Thomas de Ferrers). *C.P.R. 1281–1292* (1893): 208. *English Hist. Rev.* 10 (1895): 19–40. Norris *Baddesley Clinton, its Manor, Church & Hall* (1897): 101–110. *C.Ch.R.* 1 (1903): 345 (Mary, wife of Robert de Ferrers, styled "king's niece"); see *Cal. Liberate Rolls* 3 (1937): 279; *C.P.R. 1258–1266* (1910): 615. *C.C.R. 1288–1296* (1904): 119. Parker *Cal. of Lancashire Assize Rolls* 1 (Lancs. & Cheshire Rec. Soc. 47) (1904): 122–123. *Genealogist* n.s. 21 (1905): 78–82. Wrottesley *Peds. from the Plea Rolls* (1905): 531–532. Jeayes *Desc. Cat. Derbyshire Charters* (1906): 116. Swinfield *Reg. of Richard de Swinfield Bishop of Hereford* (Canterbury & York Soc. 6) (1909): 389. VCH *Lancashire* 5 (1911): 243–251. Wedgwood *Staffordshire Coats of Arms* (Colls. Hist. Staffs. 3rd Ser. 1913) (1913): 300 (seal of Robert [de Ferrers], Earl Ferrers dated c.1265 — To the right. In armour hauberk, surcoat, flat-topped helmet with vizor down, sword, shield slung over the shoulder. Horse galloping caparisoned. Arms: vaire [FERRERS]). *C.P.* 4 (1916): 198–202 (sub Derby); 5 (1926): chart foll. 320 (sub Ferrers), 472–474 (sub FitzWalter); 14 (1998): 468 (sub Marshal). *Year Books of Edward II* 13 (Selden Soc. 34) (1918): 59–67; 14(2) (Selden Soc. 43) (1927): 75–77. Wedgwood *Staffordshire Parl. Hist.* 1 (Colls. Hist. Staffs. 1917) (1919): 28. Lamborn *Armorial Glass of the Oxford Diocese* (1949): 97–101 (Ferrers arms: Vairy gold and gules). Paget *Baronage of England* (1957) 73: 1–13 (sub Bohun); 205: 6. Sanders *English Baronies* (1960): 32–33, 148–149. Saltman *Cartulary of Tutbury Priory* (Colls. Hist. Staffs. 4th Ser. 4) (1962): 14, 82–84, 88–92, 245–246. Beardwood *Trial of Walter Langton, Bishop of Lichfield 1307–1312* (Trans. American Philosophical Soc. n.s. 54 (3)) (1964): 14–17. VCH *Oxford* 8 (1964): 58. Saltman *Cartulary of Dale Abbey* (Derbyshire Arch. Soc. Recs. 2) (1967): 30, 361 (charter of Robert de Ferrers), 378–379 (charter of Robert de Ferrers). Mason *Beauchamp Cartulary Charters* (Pipe Roll Soc. n.s. 43) (1980): 197–200 (various charters of Robert de Ferrers, son and heir of William de Ferrers, formerly Earl of Derby dated 1261, 1262, 1260–66, 1260–66, and 1264), 200 (letters patent of Robert de Ferrers, Earl of Derby dated 1264). Ellis *Cat. Seals in the P.R.O.* 2 (1981): 41 (seal of Robert de Ferrers, Earl of Derby dated 1261 — Obverse. On horseback, galloping to right. He wears mail, surcoat and flat-topped close helmet, and holds a drawn sword and a shield of arms: vairy [FERRERS]. The horse's trapper is patterned vairy. Reverse. Hung upon a decorative tree, a shield of arms: vairy; scrolls of foliage on either side. Legend: +ROBS FIL' ET HERES DN/I WIL'I DE FERRAR...). Sutton *Rolls & Reg. of Bishop Oliver Sutton, 1280–1299* 8 (Lincoln Rec. Soc. 76) (1986): 86–88. Schwennicke *Europäische Stammtafeln* n.s. 3(4) (1989): 816 (sub Lusignan). Derbyshire Rec. Office: Gell Fam. of Hopton, D258/7/1/10 (available at www.a2a.org.uk/search/index.asp). National Archives, SC 8/85/4216 (petition dated c.1280 from Eleanor de Ferrers to the king who states that Earl William de Ferrers the elder married Anneys [Agnes], daughter of Randolph, Earl of Chester, and that they had two sons, William and Thomas. Anneys gave her manor of Chartley, Staffordshire to her son, Thomas, who was seised of it until his brother William died. Robert, the next Earl, impleaded him for it, but it the end an agreement was reached whereby Thomas would keep Chartley and have the homages and lordships of Sandon, Staffordshire as well. Thomas died seised of these, and Eleanor, the petitioner, was endowed with the whole manor of Chartley. She was seised until the death of William le Botiler, one of the parceners, then Lord Edmund [Earl of Lancaster] disseised her of it by force. As it is part of the inheritance of John de Ferrers, who is under age and in his keeping, so she asks the King that he might not be disinherited. Endorsement: Because Lord Edmund answers that he is seized of the fees, therefore she is to take action for herself by writ) (available at www.catalogue.nationalarchives.gov.uk/search.asp). Staffordshire and Stoke-on-Trent Archive Service, Staffordshire Rec. Office: Sneyd-Kynnersley of Loxley, D(W)1733/A/2/64 (charter of Robert de Ferrers) (available at http://www.a2a.org.uk/search/index.asp). Staffordshire and Stoke-on-Trent Archive Service, Staffordshire Rec. Office: St. Thomas' Priory, Stafford, D938/13 (charter of Robert de Ferrers); D938/493 (charter of Robert de Ferrers, late Earl of Derby, naming his wives, Mary and Eleanor); D938/597 (charter of Robert de Ferrers, Earl of Derby) (available at http://www.a2a.org.uk/search/

index.asp). Wolley Charter vi.48 (grant dated 27 Jan. 1262 by Robert de Ferr[ers] son and heir of Sir William de Ferr[ers,] earl of Derby, to Henry Shelford, of 100 acres of land, namely 40 acres in the ward of Hulland, and 60 acres lying next to the said 40 acres; with husebote and haybote in the same ward by view of the foresters, and pannage in his forest of Duffield; rent, a sparrow hawk or 6*d*. at the option of the said Henry, and suit to the 2 great courts of Belper.) (available www.bl.uk/catalogues/wolleycharters/Home.aspx).

Children of Robert de Ferrers, Knt., by Eleanor de Bohun:

i. **JOHN DE FERRERS**, Knt., 1st Lord Ferrers of Chartley [see next].

ii. **ELEANOR DE FERRERS**, married **ROBERT FITZ WALTER**, Knt., 1st Lord Fitz Walter [see FITZ WALTER 8].

9. JOHN DE FERRERS, Knt., of Chartley, Staffordshire, Keyston and Southoe, Huntingdonshire, etc., and, in right of his wife, of Boddington, Gloucestershire, Constable of Gloucester Castle, Constable of the Army of Scotland, Seneschal of Gascony, son and heir, born at Cardiff, Wales 20 June 1271. He married between 2 Feb. 1297/8 and 13 Sept. 1300 (date of dispensation to remain married, he and her 1st husband, William de Mortimer, being related in the 3rd degree of kindred) **HAWISE DE MUSCEGROS** (or **MUSGROVE**), widow of William de Mortimer (died shortly before 30 June 1297), of Bridgwater, Milverton, and Odcombe, Somerset, and daughter and heiress of Robert de Muscegros, Knt., of Hampstead and Aldworth, Berkshire, Brewham, Charlton Musgrove, Norton, and Stowell, Somerset, Boddington, English Bicknor, and Kemerton, Gloucestershire, by an unidentified 1st wife [see MUSCEGROS 4 for her ancestry].[24] She was born 21 Dec. 1276. They had two sons, John and Robert, Knt., and two daughters, Pernel (wife of Richard de Monmouth) and Eleanor. In 1294 he was going beyond the seas by the King's command in attendance of Eleanor, the King's daughter, lately married to Henri, Count of Bar. The same year he was heir to his cousin, Cecily de Ferrers, wife of Godfrey de Beaumont, by which he inherited the manor of Bugbrooke, Northamptonshire. In 1294 he had license to demise the manor of Chartley, Staffordshire held in chief to Robert de Bures for life at an annual rent of 30*l*., in exchange for Bures, Suffolk, granted to him in fee simple by the said Robert. In 1297 he was going to Brabant by the king's command in attendance on Margaret, the King's daughter, wife of Jean, Duke of Lorraine and Brabant. He was the principal supporter of the Earls of Hereford and Norfolk in their quarrel with the king in 1297. The same year he brought suit against his first cousin, William de Ferrers, in the Common Pleas, claiming the manor of Newbottle, Northamptonshire. He was summoned to Parliament from 6 Feb. 1298/9 to 19 Dec. 1311, by writs directed *Johanni de Ferariis, Ferrariis,* or *Ferers,* whereby he is held to have become Lord Ferrers. He was summoned to serve against the Scots in 1299–1301 and 1308–10. In 1300 they received a papal dispensation to remain in marriage, he and his wife's 1st husband being related in the 3rd degree of kindred. In 1301 he petitioned the Pope to allow him to borrow from prelates and ecclesiastics the money needed to redeem his father's estates, but was barred from the king from pursuing a cause concerning a lay fief in an ecclesiastical court. In 1304 he went overseas in the retinue of his cousin,

---

[24] Hawise de Muscegros is identified in most sources as the daughter of her father, Robert de Muscegros' surviving wife, Agnes de Ferrers, which relationship is untenable. Had Hawise been Agnes' daughter, she would have been a first cousin to her 2nd husband, John de Ferrers, which kinship would surely have barred marriage between the parties due to church laws governing consanguinity. Hawise and John did obtain a papal dispensation for their marriage, but only because John de Ferrers was related in the 3rd degree (i.e., 2nd cousin) to Hawise's 1st husband, William de Mortimer. No mention was made of any kinship between Hawise and John in the dispensation, presumably because none existed. As further evidence that Hawise was not Agnes' daughter, it may be noted that late in life, Agnes de Ferrers alienated her maritagium at Chinnor, Oxfordshire to an unrelated party, which action is typical of a childless widow in this period (see Hatton *Book of Seals* (1950): 64). If Agnes had issue, under normal circumstances, she would have retained Chinnor and passed it on her death to her descendants.

Humphrey de Bohun, Earl of Hereford and Essex. He was summoned to attend the Coronation of King Edward II in 1308. While Seneschal of Gascony, he had serious differences with Amanieu, sire of Albret, and other magnates. On 5 August 1312 he and Amanieu were ordered to appear before a commission to settle the dispute. SIR JOHN DE FERRERS, 1st Lord Ferrers of Chartley, died in Gascony about 27 August 1312. In 1313 his widow, Hawise, was disputing with Alice, widow of Walter de Beauchamp, regarding the advowson of Kemerton, Gloucestershire. Sometime in the period, c.1314-15, the king took the lands of Hawise, late the wife of John de Ferrers, into his hands because she reportedly married without the king's license; she stated, however, that she had not married. The king ordered that she give security to appear before the king at the next Parliament to answer for the trespass and give account of the whole affair to the king. Hawise married (3rd) before 1315 **JOHN DE BURES**, Knt., in right of his wife, of Boddington, English Bicknor, and Longford, Gloucestershire, Aldworth, Berkshire, Alvescote, Oxfordshire, and Asholt, Brewham, Charlton Musgrove, Norton Ferris, and Stowell, Somerset. They had one daughter, Katherine. In 1318 John and his wife, Hawise, sold all their goods and moveable chattels in Kemerton and Aston super Carentam, Gloucestershire to John de Annesleye and his wife, Lucy. He and his wife, Hawise, presented to the church of Charlton Musgrove, Somerset in 1322; he presented alone in 1328, 1339, and 1350. In 1327–8 John and Hawise sued Joan, widow of Thomas de Ferrers for dower in Essex. In 1329 they settled the manor of Stowell, Somerset on her daughter, Pernel de Ferrers. In 1336 Robert de Stoke and Margaret his wife sued John and his wife, Hawise, for land in West Compton, Berkshire. In 1339 John and his wife, Hawise, were sued by Henry de Pusey regarding the manor of Alvescote, Oxfordshire. His wife, Hawise, was living 23 June 1340. SIR JOHN DE BURES died at Boddington, Gloucestershire 21 (or 22) Dec. 1350. His wife predeceased him, and is allegedly buried in the church of English Bicknor, Gloucestershire.

Shaw *Hist. & Antiqs. of Staffordshire* 1 (1798): 39 (Ferrers ped.). Baker *Hist. & Antiqs. of Northampton* 1 (1822–30): 123–124 (Ferrers ped.). *Gentleman's Mag.* 201 (1856): 326. *Fourth Rpt.* (Hist. MSS Comm. 3) (1874): 389. *Trans. Bristol & Gloucs. Arch. Soc.* 1 (1876): 69–77, 82–84, chart betw. 88–89; 4 (1879–80): 313–319; 25 (1902): 168–169 (alleges Hawise de Muscegros died in 1350); 60 (1938): 287 (letters patent dated 1318 notifying sale by John and Hawise de Bures). Kellawe *Reg. of Richard de Kellawe, Lord Palatine & Bishop of Durham 1314–1316* 4 (1878): lxxxviii. *Year Books of Edward I: Years XXXIII–XXV* 5 (Rolls Ser. 31a) (1879): 100–107, 358–365, 576–687. *Annual Rpt. of the Deputy Keeper* 50 (1889): 159. Dickinson *Kirby's Quest for Somerset* (Somerset Rec. Soc. 3) (1889): 59, 60, 67, 75, 77, 97, 99. Weaver *Somerset Incumbents* (1889): 51. *Papal Regs.: Letters* 1 (1893): 588. *C.P.R. 1292–1301* (1895): 86. Green *Feet of Fines for Somerset* 2 (Somerset Rec. Soc. 12) (1898): 144, 238–239. *C.C.R. 1330–1333* (1898): 143. *C.P.R. 1313–1317* (1898): 491. *C.C.R. 1339–1341* (1901): 337. *Index of Placita de Banco 1327–1328* 1 (PRO Lists and Indexes 17) (1904): 136, 156. Wrottesley *Peds. from the Plea Rolls* (1905): 32–33. *Year Books of Edward II* 3 (Selden Soc. 20) (1905): 4–9. *C.P.* 4 (1916): 203 (sub Derby); 5 (1926): 305–310, chart foll. 320 (sub Ferrers). *Cal. IPM* 9 (1916): 401–402. *Year Books of Edward II* 13 (Selden Soc. 34) (1918): 59–67; 14(2) (Selden Soc. 43) (1927): 75–77. Wedgwood *Staffordshire Parl. Hist.* 1 (Colls. Hist. Staffs. 1917) (1919): 28. VCH *Berkshire* 4 (1924): 3–8. Reynolds *Reg. of Walter Reynolds Bishop of Worcester* (Dugdale Soc. 9) (1928): 72. Maxwell-Lyte *Hist. Notes of Some Somerset Manors* (Somerset Rec. Soc. Extra Ser. 1) (1931): 379–387. Lamborn *Armorial Glass of the Oxford Diocese* (1949): 97–101 (Muscegros arms: Gules a lion gold a label azure). Hatton *Book of Seals* (1950): 64. Paget *Baronage of England* (1957) 205: 6, 206: 1–2, 393: 4 (sub Muscegros). *English Hist. Rev.* 74 (1959): 70–89. Sanders *English Baronies* (1960): 32–33, 61–62. Beardwood *Trial of Walter Langton, Bishop of Lichfield 1307–1312* (Trans. American Philosophical Soc. n.s. 54 (3)) (1964): 14–17. Haines *Cal. Reg. of Wolstan de Bransford Bishop of Worcester* (Worcestershire Hist. Soc. n.s. 4) (1966): 358. DeWindt *Royal Justice & Medieval English Countryside* 2 (1981): 590. Simpson & Galbraith *Cal. Docs. Rel. Scotland* 5 (1986): 191 (Sir John de Ferreires [Ferrers] styled "cousin" by Humphrey de Bohun, Earl of Hereford and Essex in 1306). Sutton *Rolls & Reg. of Bishop Oliver Sutton, 1280–1299* 8 (Lincoln Rec. Soc. 76) (1986): 87–88. Stevenson *Edington Cartulary* (Wiltshire Rec. Soc. 42) (1987): 146–147, 154. VCH *Gloucester* 4 (1988): 396–397; 5 (1996): 106–107; 8 (1968): 190–191, 211. Brault *Rolls of Arms Edward I* 2 (1997): 163 (arms of John de Ferrers: Vairy or and gules). VCH *Somerset* 7 (1999): 6–15, 156–160, 170–177. National Archives, SC 8/1/39 (available online at www.catalogue.nationalarchives.gov.uk/search.asp).

Children of John de Ferrers, Knt., by Hawise de Muscegros:

   i. **JOHN DE FERRERS**, *de jure* 2nd Lord Ferrers of Chartley, of Keyston and Southoe, Huntingdonshire, son and heir, minor in 1321. He died without issue shortly before 23 July 1324. *C.P.* 5 (1926): chart foll. 320 (sub Ferrers).

ii. **ROBERT DE FERRERS**, Knt. [see next].

iii. **ELEANOR DE FERRERS**, married **THOMAS DE LATHOM**, Knt., of Lathom and Knowsley (in Huyton), Lancashire [see STANLEY 10].

Child of Hawise de Muscegros, by John de Bures, Knt.:

i. **KATHERINE DE BURES**, married **GILES DE BEAUCHAMP**, Knt., of Alcester, Warwickshire [see POWICK 10].

10. ROBERT DE FERRERS, Knt., *de jure* 3rd Lord Ferrers of Chartley, of Chartley, Staffordshire, Keyston and Southoe, Huntingdonshire, etc., younger son, king's chamberlain, Vice-Admiral of the Fleet, born 25 March 1309. He was heir in 1324 to his older brother, John de Ferrers, *de jure* 2nd Lord Ferrers of Chartley. In 1325 he was going beyond the seas with the king. In 1327, though still underage, the king took his homage and gave him livery of his brother's lands, on account of his recent good services during the king's expedition to northern parts. He married (1st) before 20 October 1330 **MARGARET** _____. They had one son, John, Knt. His wife, Margaret, was living in August 1331. He was summoned for military service against the Scots in 1335. In 1338 the king granted him the hundred of Pirehill, Staffordshire for term of life. In 1338 and 1339 he was with the king in Flanders. In 1342 he accompanied the king in his expedition to Brittany, being in the king's retinue. In 1343 Robert de Ferrers sued Maud late wife of Robert de Holand regarding the manor of Yoxall, Staffordshire, and she vouched to warrant Henry de Lancaster, the brother and heir of Thomas de Lancaster, formerly Earl of Lancaster. He was with the Earl of Derby at the Battle of Auberoche in Périgord 21 (or 23) October 1345. He accompanied the king to La Hogue in July 1346, and was present at the Battle of Crécy in 1346 and the Siege of Calais in 1346–7. He married (2nd) before 1350 **JOAN DE LA MOTE**, probably widow of Edmund de la Mote, of Willisham, Suffolk. They had one son, Robert, Knt. [1st Lord Ferrers of Wem]. SIR ROBERT DE FERRERS died testate 28 August 1350. In 1352 his widow, Joan, received a papal indult for plenary remission. She acquired the manor of Pancras (in St. Pancras), Middlesex in 1360 from John de Bukyngham, Dean of Lichfield. She was attending the Countess of Ulster in 1361. Joan died at London 29 June 1375.

Baker *Hist. & Antiqs. of Northampton* 1 (1822–30): 123–124 (Ferrers ped.). Palmer *St. Pancras* (1870): 52. *Trans. Bristol & Gloucs. Arch. Soc.* 1 (1876): 69–77, 82–84, chart betw. 88–89. Birch *Cat. Seals in the British Museum* 2 (1892): 790–791 (seal of Joan de Ferrers dated 1367 — A shield of arms: per pale, dexter, vairé [FERRERS]; sinister, three [conies?] passant in pale. Within a carved gothic panel, charged on the tracery with four lozenge-shaped shields of arms in cross, vairé, a mullet for difference. Legend between the points: SIGILL'V * IOHANNE * ..... FERRES.). Wrottesley *Staffordshire Suits: Plea Rolls* (Colls. Hist. Staffs. 13) (1892): 47–48. *Papal Regs.: Letters* 3 (1897): 443. *Year Books of Edward III: Years XVII & XVIII* 10 (Rolls Ser. 31b) (1903): 294–318. Copinger *Manors of Suffolk* 2 (1908): 375–376. *C.P.* 5 (1926): 310–312, chart foll. 320 (sub Ferrers). Lovell *Parish of St. Pancras* (Survey of London 17) (1936–52): 21. Paget *Baronage of England* (1957) 206: 2–3. Sanders *English Baronies* (1960): 32–33, 61–62. *Ancient Deeds — Ser. B* 3 (List & Index Soc. 113) (1975): B.11600. Raftis & Hogan *Early Huntingdonshire Lay Subsidy Rolls* (1976): 231. *Ancient Deeds — Ser. BB* (List & Index Soc. 137) (1977): 51. Orleton *Cal. Reg. of Adam de Orleton* (Worcestershire Hist. Soc. n.s. 10) (1979): 94. Bodine *Anc. of Dorothea Poyntz* (1995): 91.

Child of Robert de Ferrers, Knt., by Margaret _____:

i. **JOHN DE FERRERS**, Knt. [see next].

Child of Robert de Ferrers, Knt., by Joan de la Mote:

i. **ROBERT DE FERRERS**, Knt., 1st Lord Ferrers of Wem, married **ELIZABETH LE BOTELER** [see WEM 12].

11. JOHN DE FERRERS, Knt., *de jure* 4th Lord Ferrers of Chartley, of Chartley, Staffordshire, Aldworth, Berkshire, English Bicknor, Gloucestershire, Charlton Musgrove, Somerset, etc., son and heir, born and baptized at Southoe, Huntingdonshire on or about 10 August 1331. He married by royal license dated 19 October 1349 **ELIZABETH DE STAFFORD**, widow of Fulk le Strange,

3rd Lord Strange of Blackmere (died 6 Sept. or 22 or 30 August 1349) [see BLACKMERE 11.i], and daughter of Ralph de Stafford, K.G., 1st Earl of Stafford, by his 2nd wife, Margaret, daughter of Hugh de Audley, Knt., Earl of Gloucester [see STAFFORD 7 for her ancestry]. They had one son, Robert, Knt. On 13 Dec. 1353 the king took his homage, and he had livery of the lands of his grandmother, Hawise, sometime the wife of John de Ferrers. He was with the king in France from October 1359 to 1360. He petitioned the Duke of Lancaster to restore various estates forfeited by his great-grandfather, Robert de Ferrers, Earl of Derby, and those which Margaret, formerly Countess of Derby, held in dower as of the castle and honour of Tutbury, Derbyshire and as of the earldom of Derby, as well as the manor of Higham, Northamptonshire which Margaret held in jointure, and the manor of Kingston Lacy, Dorset, which she had inherited from her father, Roger de Quincy, formerly Earl of Winchester. He took part in the invasion of Navarre in 1367. SIR JOHN DE FERRERS was slain at the Battle of Nájera 3 April 1367. In Easter term 1370 his widow, Elizabeth, sued John, Prior of the Hospital of St. John of Stafford and two others for a third part of two messuages in Stafford, which she claimed as dower. She married (3rd) (as his 1st wife) **REYNOLD COBHAM**, Knt., 2nd Lord Cobham of Sterborough (died testate 3 or 6 July 1403) [see COBHAM 9], son and heir of Reynold de Cobham, K.G., 1st Lord Cobham of Sterborough, by Joan, daughter of Thomas de Berkeley, Knt., 3rd Lord Berkeley [see COBHAM 8 for his ancestry]. Elizabeth died 7 August 1375.

Baker *Hist. & Antiqs. of Northampton* 1 (1822–30): 123–124 (Ferrers ped.). *Surrey Arch. Colls.* 2 (1864): 132–145. *Trans. Bristol & Gloucs. Arch. Soc.* 1 (1876): 69–77, 82–84, chart betw. 88–89. Weaver *Somerset Incumbents* (1889): 51. Wrottesley *Staffordshire Suits: Plea Rolls* (Colls. Hist. Staffs. 13) (1892): 47–48, 68, 77, 79, 80, 123. *C.P.* 3 (1913): 353–354 (sub Cobham); 5 (1926): 313–315, chart foll. 320 (sub Ferrers); 12(1) (1953): 343–344 (sub Strange). VCH *Berkshire* 4 (1924): 3–8. Maxwell-Lyte *Hist. Notes of Some Somerset Manors* (Somerset Rec. Soc. Extra Ser. 1) (1931): 379–387. Paget *Baronage of England* (1957) 206: 3. Sayles *Select Cases in the Court of King's Bench* 5 (Selden Soc. 76) (1958): cxxxix. VCH *Gloucester* 5 (1996): 106–107. VCH *Somerset* 7 (1999): 170–177.

12. ROBERT FERRERS, Knt., *de jure* 5th Lord Ferrers of Chartley, of Chartley, Staffordshire, Aldworth, Berkshire, English Bicknor, Gloucestershire, Keyston, Huntingdonshire, Bugbrooke, Northamptonshire, Chinnor, Oxfordshire, Charlton Musgrove and Norton Ferris (in Kilmington), Somerset, etc., son and heir, born in Staffordshire 31 October 1357 or 1359. He married (1st) after 16 Sept. 1376 **ELIZABETH** _____. They had no known issue. The king took his homage and fealty 23 July 1381, and he had livery of his father's lands and those which Elizabeth, his mother, had held for life in dower or otherwise of his inheritance. In 1382 the king pardoned Hanekyn Fauconer, of Cardington, Bedfordshire, for his felony in having with others on 13 Jan. 1378/9 entered by night the manor of Robert de Ferrers, Knt. at Southoe, Huntingdonshire, ill-treated and abducted Elizabeth his wife, and stole linens and woolen goods in which she was clothed, gold rings, necklaces, and other jewels. Her subsequent history is unknown. He married (2nd) before 14 July 1389 (date of agreement) **MARGARET LE DESPENSER**, daughter of Edward le Despenser, K.G., 4th Lord le Despenser, of Glamorgan and Morgannwg, Wales, by Elizabeth, daughter of Bartholomew de Burghersh, K.G., 4th Lord Burghersh [see DESPENSER 13 for her ancestry]. They had three sons, Edmund, Knt., Thomas, Esq., and Edward, and one daughter, Philippe. In 1389 he made a gift in free alms for the souls of himself and lady Margaret his wife to the Canons regular of St. Thomas by Stafford of his right of patronage of the church of Weston on Trent. His wife, Margaret, was a legatee in the 1409 will of her mother, who bequeathed her two chargers and twelve dishes of silver. SIR ROBERT FERRERS died 12 (or 13) March 1412/13. In 1413 his widow, Margaret, was granted the manor of Aldworth, Berkshire by her son, Edmund Ferrers. Margaret died 3 Nov. 1415. Robert and Margaret were buried at Merevale Abbey, Warwickshire.

Dugdale *Antiqs. of Warwickshire* (1656): 1068. Blore *Hist. & Antiqs. of Rutland* 1(2) (1811): 19 (Despenser ped.). Brydges *Collins' Peerage of England* 6 (1812): 496–511 (sub Despenser). Dugdale *Monasticon Anglicanum* 2 (1819): 59–65

(Tewkesbury Cartulary: "Edwardus [le Despenser] vero secundus, filius istius Edwardi, successit Hugoni tertio, et copulavit sibi in matrimonium dominam Elizabetham, filiam domini Bartholomei de Borowashe, de qua genuit … Margaretam quæ fuit nupta domino Roberto de Ferrers."). Baker *Hist. & Antiqs. of Northampton* 1 (1822–30): 123–124 (Ferrers ped.). Nicolas *Testamenta Vetusta* 1 (1826): 174–175 (will of Elizabeth de Burghersh, Lady Despenser). *Trans. Bristol & Gloucs. Arch. Soc.* 1 (1876): 69–77, 82–84, chart betw. 88–89. Burke *Dormant, Abeyant, Forfeited & Extinct Peerages* (1883): 165–167 (sub Despenser). *C.P.R. 1381–1385* (1897): 99, 139, 591. *Procs. Bath Natural Hist. & Antiq. Field Club* 9 (1901): 188–201. *List of Inqs. ad Quod Damnum* 2 (PRO Lists and Indexes 22) (1906): 662. VCH *Surrey* 4 (1912): 183. VCH *Berkshire* 4 (1924): 3–8. *C.P.* 5 (1926): 315–317, chart foll. 320 (sub Ferrers). Legge *Anglo-Norman Letters & Petitions* (Anglo-Norman Text Soc. 3) (1941): 92–93 ([Margaret], Lady Ferrers of Chartley, styled "niece" of Henry Despenser, Bishop of Norwich and "cousin" by Anne le Despenser, Lady Botiller). Paget *Baronage of England* (1957) 182: 1–2 (sub Despenser); 206: 3–4. Smith *Itinerary of John Leland* 4 (1964): 150–163. *Cal. IPM* 20 (1995): 10–12. VCH *Gloucester* 5 (1996): 106–107. VCH *Somerset* 7 (1999): 170–177. Staffordshire & Stoke-on-Trent Archive Service, Staffordshire Rec. Office: St. Thomas' Priory, Stafford, D938/614 — agreement dated 14 July 1389 between Robert de Ferraius, Knt., lord of Chartley and the Blessed Thomas the Martyr by Stafford and the Canons Regular there (available at www.a2a.org.uk/search/index.asp).

Children of Robert de Ferrers, Knt., by Margaret le Despenser:

i. **EDMUND FERRERS**, Knt. [see next].

ii. **PHILIPPE FERRERS**, married **THOMAS GREENE**, Knt., of Green's Norton, Northamptonshire [see GREENE 15].

13. EDMUND FERRERS, Knt., *de jure* 6th Lord Ferrers of Chartley, of Chartley, Staffordshire, English Bicknor, and Taynton, Gloucestershire, Charlton Musgrove, Somerset, etc., and, in right of his wife, of Bromwich and Nether Whitacre, Warwickshire, Kingston Bagpuize, Berkshire, Dorton, Buckinghamshire, Barre, Staffordshire, etc., son and heir, born about 1386–9 (aged variously 24, 26, or 27 in 1413). He married before 24 Nov. 1414 (date of fine) **ELLEN [DE LA] ROCHE**, daughter and co-heiress of Thomas de la Roche, of Bromwich and Nether Whitacre, Warwickshire, by Elizabeth, daughter and heiress of Thomas Birmingham, Knt. They had five sons, William, Knt., Edmund, Knt., [Master] Henry (clerk), Richard, and Edward, and two daughters, Margaret and Joan (wife of John Clinton, Knt., Lord Clinton and Say). He was never summoned to Parliament, but he was usually called Lord Ferrers. In 1413 he granted the manor of Aldworth, Berkshire to his mother, Margaret. About 1413, he and his brothers, Thomas and Edward, carried on a private war with the Erdeswikes of Sandon, near Chartley. On 24 Jan. 1414/5 Edmund was granted a pardon for all robberies, murders, rapes on women, etc., committed by him before 8 Dec. last. He accompanied the king to France in August 1415. He was at the Siege of Harfleur, in August-Sept. 1415 and at the Battle of Agincourt 25 October 1415. He presented to the church of Charlton Musgrove, Somerset in 1420. In 1424 Edmund with a large company of armed men forcibly ejected William Birmingham, Knt., the Lady Joan his wife, and his children together with their household from the manor of Birmingham, Warwickshire. In 1427 he and his wife, Ellen, did homage for the manor of Birmingham, Warwickshire; the same year Joan Peshale, widow of William Birmingham, Knt. sued Edmund and his wife, Ellen, and George Longvyle for dower in the said manor. In 1428 he presented to the church of Birmingham, Warwickshire. In 1432 John Massy, Esq. granted all his right in the manor of Frankley, Worcestershire to Edmund, Lord Ferrers, John Sutton, lord of Dudley, Thomas Burdet, and others. SIR EDMUND FERRERS died 17 Dec. 1435. In 1436 his widow, Ellen, presented to the church of Birmingham, Warwickshire. She married (2nd) before 3 May 1438 (date of charter) (as his 1st wife) **PHILIP CHETWYND**, Knt., of Ingestre, Staffordshire, Grendon, Warwickshire, and, in right of his wife, of Great Barre, Staffordshire, Sheriff of Staffordshire, 1428–9, 1436–7, Governor of Bayonne, 1442, Lieutenant of Calais, 1444, 2nd son of Richard Chetwynd, of Ingestre, Staffordshire, by Thomasine, daughter of William de Frodesham, Esq. They had no issue. He was heir in 1418 to his older brother, William Chetwynd. In 1431 he entered the service of Humphrey Stafford, Earl of Stafford. Soon after Ellen's remarriage, her kinsman, William Birmingham, seised the manor of Birmingham, Warwickshire, who in turn was disseised by Ellen and her husband, Philip. In a subsequent assize of novel disseisin, the jury found in favor of William Birmingham's claim to the manor. Ellen died 4 Nov. 1440. Philip married (2nd) before 28 June 1442 (date of settlement) **JOAN BURLEY**, daughter and co-heiress of William Burley, Esq., of Broncroft (in Diddlebury), Alcaston (in Acton Scott), Baucott (in Tugford), Brockton (in Shipton), and Munslow, Shropshire, and London, Knight of the Shire for Shropshire, Speaker of the House of Commons, Sheriff of Shropshire, 1426, by his 1st wife, Ellen, daughter and co-heiress of John de Grendon, of Gayton. In 1444 he bound himself by indenture with Humphrey Stafford, Earl of Buckingham and Stafford, to serve the latter as Lieutenant of Calais, and to maintain a force of 29 men at arms on foot, and 20 archers. Sir Philip Chetwynd died 10 May 1444, presumably at Calais. His widow, Joan, married (2nd) before Easter term 1447 (date of lawsuit) **THOMAS LITTLETON**, Knt., of Frankley, Worcestershire, and, in right of his wife, of Arley, Staffordshire, Escheator of Worcestershire, deputy Sheriff of Worcestershire, 1447, Recorder of Coventry, 1450, Serjeant-at-law, King's sergeant, Steward of the Marshalsea Court, Justice of the county palatine of Lancaster, Justice of the Common Pleas, Trier of Petitions from Gascony in Parliaments of 1467 and 1472. They had three sons, William, Knt., Richard, and Thomas, and two daughters, Ellen and Alice. He was a member of the Inner Temple. He was in practice as a pleader in 1445. In 1447 John Chetwynd sued Thomas and his wife, Joan, for two parts of 13 messuages and various lands and rent in Rowele, Rugge, and Breredon, Staffordshire, together with two parts of the manors of Mutton, Ingestre, and Gratwich, Staffordshire, excepting a mill in Ingestre. In 1451 he was granted the manor of Sheriff Hales, Shropshire by William Trussell, Knt., for good counsel given to him. In 1452 Thomas and his wife, Joan, and her fellow Grendon co-heirs sued Richard Vernon, Knt., late of London, and John Chapman, yeoman, regarding possession of a moiety of the manor of Sheriff Hales, Staffordshire. In 1454 he and his wife, Joan, successfully sued Richard Cokette for the next presentation to the free chapel of Ingestre, Staffordshire. In 1457 he and his wife, Joan, sued Richard Rous, husbandman, for breaking into their close at Breredon, Staffordshire, and depasturing cattle on their grass. The same year he recovered the manor of Spetchley, Worcestershire, 20 messuages, 12 tofts, 3 carucates and 300 acres of land, etc., as his right of inheritance against John de Spechesley, of Spetchley, Worcestershire, and Maud his wife. In 1459 he and his wife, Joan, sued her step-mother, Margaret Burley, widow, to give up to them two chests containing deeds, writings, and other muniments which she unjustly detained. In 1464 Margaret Burley was summoned at the suit of Thomas and Joan his wife and William Trussell, Esq., for waste and destruction in houses and woods at Cressegge, Shropshire and Arley, Staffordshire, for which they claimed £200 as damages. In 1474 he and his wife, Joan, sued John Gresley, Knt., late of Colton, Staffordshire, for taking forcible possession of a rent of 22s. in Colton belonging to the plaintiffs against the Statute of 5 Richard II. His fame as a legal author rests upon a short treatise on 'Tenures' written primarily for the instruction of his son, Richard, but which early attained the rank of a work of authority. SIR THOMAS LITTLETON died at Frankley, Worcestershire 23 August 1481, and was buried in the nave of Worcester Cathedral. He left a will dated 22 August 1481. Under the terms of his will, he bequeathed 100s. per annum to the Prior and Convent of the Cathedral Church of Worcester to sing at the altar for the souls of his parents, and for William Burley his father-in-law, and Sir Philip Chetwynd. His widow, Joan, died 22 March 1504/5.

Baker *Hist. & Antiqs. of Northampton* 1 (1822–30): 123–124 (Ferrers ped.). Hutton *Hist. of Birmingham* (1836): 324. *Notes & Queries* 4th Ser. 9 (1872): 464–465. *Trans. Bristol & Gloucs. Arch. Soc.* 1 (1876): 69–77, 82–84, chart betw. 88–89. Lennard & Vincent *Vis. of Warwick 1619* (H.S.P. 12) (1877): 278–280 (Devereux ped.: "Willm's D'ns Ferrers de Chartley. = Ellina fil. et Coh. Tho. De la Roch Militis."). *Trans. Shropshire Arch. & Nat. Hist. Soc.* 5 (1882): 349–354. St. George *Vis. of Staffordshire 1614, 1663–4* (Colls. Hist. Staffs. 5(2)) (1885): 76–85 (Chetwynd ped.: "Philippus Chetwynd, miles, Vice com. Staff. 7 et 15 H. 6, ob. 24 H. 6, [1] = Helena, filia et hær. Thomæ de la Roche, relicta Edm. Dom. Ferrers de Chartley, [2] = Johanna, filia et cohæres Will. Burley, mil., ux. secunda; postea nupta Tho. Littleton, mil., de Balneo."). Weaver *Somerset Incumbents* (1889): 51. Boyd & Wrottesley *Final Concords* (Colls. Hist. Staffs. 11) (1890): 225, 245. Wrottesley *Chetwynd Chartulary* (Colls. Hist. Staffs. 12(1)) (1891): 259–264, 266–267, 311–

321, 323–326. Jeayes *Desc. Cat. Charters & Muniments of the Lyttelton Fam.* (1893): 82. *Jour. of Ex Libris Library* 4 (1895): 62–64. Grazebrook *Shenstone Charters* (Colls. Hist. Staffs. 17) (1896): 294–298 (Bray-Grendon ped.). *List of Sheriffs for England & Wales* (PRO Lists and Indexes 9) (1898): 118, 127. Bridgeman *Hist. of Weston-under-Lizard* (Colls. Hist. Staffs. n.s. 2) (1899): 106. Wrottesley *Staffordshire Suits: Plea Rolls* (Colls. Hist. Staffs. n.s. 3) (1900): 124–125, 175–178, 204, 216–217; (Colls. Hist. Staffs. n.s. 4) (1901): 101, 112, 130–131, 202. *Genealogist* n.s. 19 (1903): 247. Wrottesley *Peds. from the Plea Rolls* (1905): 437. *C.P.R. 1436–1441* (1907): 502–503. *D.N.B.* 11 (1909): 1252–1255 (biog. of Sir Thomas Littleton). *C.P.* 2 (1912): 46–47 (sub Beauchamp), 152 (sub Bermingham); 5 (1926): 317–319, chart foll. 320 (sub Ferrers); 11 (1949): 44–45 (sub Roche) (erroneously identifies wife Ellen as sister, not daughter, of Thomas de la Roche). VCH *Berkshire* 4 (1924): 3–8. VCH *Buckingham* 4 (1927): 46. Chichele *Reg. of Henry Chichele* 1 (Canterbury & York Soc. 45) (1943): 256–257. VCH *Warwick* 4 (1947): 253; 7 (1964): 58–59. Lamborn *Armorial Glass of the Oxford Diocese* (1949): 97–101 (Roche arms: Gules three fishes [roaches] swimming silver). Paget *Baronage of England* (1957) 206: 4–5. Powell *Kingship, Law & Soc.* (1989): 208–216. Roskell *House of Commons 1386–1421* 2 (1992): 432–435 (biog. of William Burley). Carpenter *Locality & Polity* (1992). *Cal. IPM* 20 (1995): 10–12. VCH *Gloucester* 5 (1996): 106–107. Aston & Richmond *Lollardy & the Gentry* (1997): 175–176. Carpenter *Armburgh Papers* (1998): 17–19, 23, 25, 27–28, 41–42, 92–93 (letter dated 1428 from Joan Armburgh [wife of Robert Armburgh and daughter of Geoffrey Brockhole, Knt., of Mancetter, Warwickshire] to Ellen [de la Roche], Lady Ferrers of Chartley; Joan styles herself "youre meke and pouer kynneswoman"), 106, 114–116 (letter dated probably late 1429/early 1430 or late 1430 from Robert Armburgh to Ellen, Lady Ferrers of Chartley; Robert refers to his wife, Joan Brokhole, as Ellen's "pouer kynneswoman"). VCH *Shropshire* 10 (1998): 9–22, 151–167, 180–186, 368–380. VCH *Somerset* 7 (1999): 170–177. Castor *King, the Crown & the Duchy of Lancaster* (2000): 261–263. National Archives, SC 8/23/1132; SC 8/295/14702 — petition dated c.1431 from Joan Beauchamp, Lady Bergavenny, to Humphrey, Duke of Gloucester, Guardian of England, and Council, who alleged that Edmund, Lord Ferrers of Chartley, attacked her and her servants at Birmingham, Warwickshire 17 March 1431, with a large number of men of his affinity, arrayed for war and in the manner of an insurrection, against the king's peace, laws and statutes, severely wounded several of her servants with arrows, and killed John Brydde, one of her valets de chamber. She requested a writ summoning Edmund before the Guardian and council, to be examined on these things and to have justice done to him (available at www.catalogue.nationalarchives.gov.uk/search.asp). Devon Rec. Office: Fortescue of Castle Hill, 1262M/TG/7 (Thomas Lyttylton styled "cousin and counsel" by Dame Joyce Beauchamp [née Cokesey] in letter dated c.1456) (available at www.a2a.org.uk/search/index.asp).

Children of Edmund Ferrers, Knt., by Ellen [de la] Roche:

i. **WILLIAM FERRERS**, Knt. [see next].

ii. [**MASTER**] **HENRY FERRERS**, clerk, of Taynton, Gloucestershire, younger son, born about 1430 (aged 54 in 1484). In 1463 Thomas Banns, chaplain of the King's mother, Cecily, Duchess of York, was appointed Prior of Folkestone either by the monks or by the Archbishop of Canterbury. At the same time, John Clinton, Lord Clinton and Say, appointed Henry Ferrers his brother-in-law as Prior. This led to an appeal to the Roman Curia and tuition of the Court of Canterbury in June 1463, which was decided in favor of Banns. He was appointed rector of Charlton Musgrove, Somerset in 1464, which position he resigned in 1473. HENRY FERRERS died 12 April 1486. *Fifth Rpt.* (Hist. MSS Comm. 4) (1876): 590–592 (Henry Ferrers styled "brother" by John Clinton, Lord Clinton and Say in letters dated 1463). Weaver *Somerset Incumbents* (1889): 51. Kingsford *English Hist. Lit. in the 15th Cent.* (Burt Franklin Bibliog. & Ref. 37) (1913): 391. *C.P.* 5 (1926): between pages 320–231 (chart). Stillington & Fox *Regs. of Robert Stillington & Richard Fox* (Somerset Rec. Soc. 52) (1937): 51–52. Smith *Heads of Religious Houses* 3 (2008): 176.

iii. **MARGARET FERRERS**, married **JOHN BEAUCHAMP**, K.G., 1st Lord Beauchamp of Powick [see POWICK 13].

iv. **JOAN** (or **JANE**) **FERRERS**, married by contract dated 29 October 1431 (as his 1st wife) **JOHN CLINTON**, 5th Lord Clinton, of Folkestone, Kent, son and heir of William Clinton, Knt., 4th Lord Clinton, by his 2nd wife, Anne, daughter of William de Botreaux, Knt., 2nd Lord Botreaux. They had one son, John [Lord Clinton and Say]. In 1438 he conveyed the castle and manor of Maxstoke, Warwickshire to Humphrey, Earl of Stafford, in exchange for the manors of Whiston and Woodford, Northamptonshire. He was summoned to Parliament from 4 Sept. 1450 to 30 July 1460. In 1454 he and his wife, Joan, conveyed the manor of Whiston, together with 12 messuages, one mill, and lands in Whiston and Woodford, Northamptonshire to William Neville, Lord Fauconberge for £300 sterling. His wife, Joan, died in 1458, and was buried in the parish of St. Bartholomew the Less, London. He married (2nd) **MARGARET SAINT LEGER**, widow of Walter Hungerford, Esq., and daughter of John Saint Leger, Esq., of Ulcombe, Kent, by Margery, daughter and heiress of James Donet [see RAYNSFORD 11.i.a for her ancestry]. In 1459 he joined the Yorkist party, and was attainted in Parliament in 1460. He was restored in 1461 by the new king, in whose reign he fought in France and Scotland. JOHN CLINTON, 5th Lord Clinton, died 24 Sept. 1464. His widow, Margaret, married (3rd) (as his 3rd wife) **JOHN HEVENINGHAM**, Knt., of Heveningham, Suffolk [see HARLESTON 11]. Margaret, Lady Clinton, died 1 Feb. 1495/6. SIR JOHN HEVENINGHAM died 20 March 1498/9. He left a will dated 11 March 1498/9. Fisher *Cat. of Most of the Memorable Tombs of London* (1668): 24. *Sussex Arch. Colls.* 17 (1865): 70–103. *Fifth Rpt.* (Hist. MSS Comm. 4) (1876): 590–592 (letters of John Clinton, Lord Clinton and Say, lord of Folkestone dated 1463). *Ancestor* 8 (1904): 167–201. *C.P.* 3 (1913): 315–316 (sub Clinton); 5 (1926): between pages 320–231 (Ferrers ped.). Kingsford *English Hist. Lit. in the Fifteenth Cent.* (Burt Franklin Bibliog. & Ref. 37) (1913): 391. Richmond *John Hopton* (1981): 164, 238–241. Sotheby Parke Bernet *Cat. English Charters & Docs.* (1981): 38 (marriage contract of John Clinton & Joan Ferrers dated 1431). National Archives, CP 25/1/179/95, #137 [see abstract of fine at http://www.medievalgenealogy.org.uk/index.html].

14. WILLIAM FERRERS, Knt., *de jure* 7th Lord Ferrers of Chartley, of Chartley, Staffordshire, English Bicknor and Taynton, Gloucestershire, Bugbrooke, Northamptonshire, Chinnor, Oxfordshire, Charlton Musgrove and Norton, Somerset, Barre, Staffordshire, Bromwich, Glascote, Nether Whitacre, and Perry Croft, Warwickshire, etc., son and heir, born about 1412–3 (aged 23 in 1435/6). He married **ELIZABETH BELKNAP**, daughter of Hamon (or Hamond) Belknap, Esq., of Knelle (in Beckley), Sussex, Kingsnorth, Ringwold (in Walmer), and Sentlynge (in St. Mary Cray), Kent, etc., by Joan, daughter of Thomas le Boteler (or Butler), Knt., *de jure* 4th Lord Sudeley [see SUDELEY 15 for her ancestry]. They had one daughter, Anne. He was never summoned to Parliament, but was frequently called Lord Ferrers. In 1450 he and his wife, Elizabeth, sold the manor of Hampstead Ferrers (also known as Hampstead Cifrewast), Berkshire to John Norreys, Esq. SIR WILLIAM FERRERS died 9 June 1450. His widow, Elizabeth, presented to the church of Charlton Musgrove, Somerset in 1464. She died 28 May 1471.

Baker *Hist. & Antiqs. of Northampton* 1 (1822–30): 123–124 (Ferrers ped.). *Trans. Bristol & Gloucs. Arch. Soc.* 1 (1876): 69–77, 82–84, chart betw. 88–89. Lennard & Vincent *Vis. of Warwick 1619* (H.S.P. 12) (1877): 278–280 (Devereux ped.: "Will'ms D'ns Ferrers de Chartley. = Eliz. fil. Hamonis Belknap p' Joannam sororem et Coh. Radi Butler Baronis de Sudley."). Weaver *Somerset Incumbents* (1889): 51. Boyd & Wrottesley *Final Concords* (Colls. Hist. Staffs. 11) (1890): 246, 248–249. Barfield *Thatcham* 2 (1901): 225–226. Green *Feet of Fines for Somerset* 4 (Somerset Rec. Soc. 22) (1906): 201–202. *C.P.* 5 (1926): 320–321, chart foll. 320 (sub Ferrers). VCH *Berkshire* 4 (1924): 3–8. VCH *Buckingham* 4 (1927): 41. VCH *Warwick* 4 (1947): 248–249, 253. Garratt *Derbyshire Feet of Fines 1323–1546* (Derbyshire Rec. Soc. 11) (1985): xi, 89. VCH *Gloucester* 5 (1996): 106–107. VCH *Somerset* 7 (1999): 170–177. Castor *King, the Crown & the Duchy of Lancaster* (2000): 261–264. Biancalana *Fee Tail & the Common Recovery in Medieval England* (2001): 354.

15. ANNE FERRERS, daughter and heiress, born about Nov. 1438 (aged 11 years and 8 months in July 1450). She married before 26 Nov. 1446 (as his 1st wife) **WALTER DEVEREUX**, K.G., of Weobley, Bodenham, Lyonshall, and Morecote, Herefordshire, Branston, Cotesbach, and Newbold Verdon, Leicestershire, Market Rasen, Lincolnshire, etc., and, in right of his wife, of Chartley, Staffordshire, English Bicknor, Gloucestershire, Keyston and Southoe, Huntingdonshire, Chinnor, Oxfordshire, Nether Whitacre, Warwickshire, etc., Knight of the Shire for Herefordshire, son and heir of Walter Devereux, Knt., of Weobley and Bodenham, Herefordshire, by Elizabeth, daughter and heiress of John Merbury, Esq. [see VERDUN 16 for his ancestry]. He was born about 1432–3 (aged 26 or 27 in 1459). They had three sons, John, Knt. [Lord Ferrers of Chartley], Richard, Knt., and Thomas, Knt., and two daughters, Elizabeth and Sibyl (or Isabel) (wife of James Baskerville, Knt.). His wife, Anne, Lady Ferrers, died 9 Jan. 1468/9. Walter marched on London in 1461 with the future King Edward IV and was present at the council which gave Edward the crown. He was knighted after the Battle of Towton 29 March 1461. He was summoned to Parliament from 26 July 1461 to 9 Dec. 1483, by writs directed *Waltero Devereux de Ferrers, chevalier*. He served as Councillor to the Prince of Wales in 1471. He presented to the church of Charlton Musgrove, Somerset in 1473. In Easter term 1480 Cecily, Duchess of York, sued him for a debt of £20 per a bond. He was present at the Coronation of King Richard III 6 July 1483. He married (2nd) before Michaelmas term 1483 (date of settlement) **JANE** (or **JOAN**) _____, widow of Thomas Ilam, of London, mercer, Alderman of London, 1478–81, Sheriff of London, 1479–80, Master of the Mercers'

Company, 1481. SIR WALTER DEVEREUX, Lord Ferrers of Chartley, was slain at the Battle of Bosworth 22 August 1485, and was attainted of high treason in Parliament. His widow, Jane, married (3rd) (as his 2nd wife) **THOMAS VAUGHAN** (alias **THOMAS AP ROGER**), Knt., of Tretower, Breconshire, Steward of the lordship of Brecknock, son of Roger Vaughan, Knt., of Tretower, Breconshire. He and his two brothers, Walter Vaughan, Esq., and Roger Vaughan, Gent., were pardoned in 1486 by King Henry VII. In 1487 he, Walter Herbert, Knt., Thomas ap Morgan, Knt., and three others owed a debt of £500 to Thomas Tremaill, King's attorney and three others. SIR THOMAS VAUGHAN died in 1494. His widow, Jane, married (4th) **EDWARD BLOUNT**, Knt., of Sodington, Worcestershire, Knight of the Body to King Henry VII, son and heir of John Blount, of Sodington, Worcestershire, by Katherine, daughter and co-heiress of Thomas Corbet. They had no issue. In 1486 he and his brothers, Thomas and Humphrey Blount, owed a debt of 100 marks to Thomas Fisher, Citizen and mercer of London. In the period, 1493–1500, John Broune sued James Walshe and John Huntley in Chancery regarding fraud in order to obtain the sealing of a release relating to a bond made between Sir Thomas Vagham [Vaughan], Knt., and Joan, wife of Edward Blount, esquire of the King's body, previously the wife of Sir Walter Devereux, Knt., Lord Ferrers. SIR EDWARD BLOUNT died testate 6 July 1499. His widow, Jane, married (5th) before 11 June 1500 **THOMAS POYNTZ**, Esq., of Alderley, Gloucestershire, younger son of John Poyntz, Esq., of Iron Acton, Gloucestershire, by Alice, daughter and heiress of John Cookes [see OWSLEY 9 for his ancestry]. In the period, 1499–1500, he and his wife, Jane, previously the wife of Edward Blount, Knt., sued John Middelmor and Edward Knyght, feoffees to uses, in Chancery regarding the manor of Blount's Hall and land in Blount's Hall, Staffordshire, and two messuages and land in Wyndley and Hazlewood, Derbyshire. In the period, 1500–1, he and his wife, Jane, sued the same parties in Chancery regarding the manor of Blontishall and lands in Blontishall, Wyndley, and Hesilwode, late of Edward Blount, knight, and the said Jane, late his wife. In the same time period, he and his wife, Jane, sued Thomas Fyssher, of London, mercer in Chancery regarding an action on a recognisance of Sir Edward Blount, deceased, and execution in lands now of the said Dame Jane. He and his wife, Jane, were legatees in the 1520 will of his brother, Robert Poyntz, Knt. In 1521 Anthony Poyntz, Knt. leased Thomas Poyntz, Esq., of Alderley, the manor of Alderley, together with lands in Alderley, Tresham, Hillesleyt, and Kilcote, Gloucestershire for a term of four years at an annual rent of £20; the rent was not to be payable after the first year if Lady Ferrers, wife of the said Thomas, died within that time. Jane, Lady Ferrers, and her 5th husband were both living in 1522.

Baker *Hist. & Antiqs. of Northampton* 1 (1822–30): 123–124 (Ferrers ped.). *Poetical Works of Lewis Glyn Cothi* (1837): chart following xxxviii (Vaughan ped.), 44–50 (two contemporary odes commemorating Sir Thomas Vaughan son of Sir Roger Vaughan, of Tretower). Beltz *Mems. of the Order of the Garter* (1841): clxiv. Banks *Baronies in Fee* 1 (1844): 205–206 (sub Devereux, sive Ferrers). Campbell *Materials for a Hist. of Henry VII* 1 (1873): 408. Robinson *Hist. of the Mansions & Manors of Herefordshire* (1873): 102 (Baskerville ped.). *Trans. Bristol & Gloucs. Arch. Soc.* 1 (1876): 69–77, 82–84, chart betw. 88–89; 6 (1881–2): 148–149. Lennard & Vincent *Vis. of Warwick 1619* (H.S.P. 12) (1877): 278–280 (Devereux ped.: "Walterus Deuereux Eques Garterij et D'ns Ferrers de Chartley p' E. 4 occisus apud Bosworth cu' R. 3. = Anna fil. et hær. Will'mi Dn'i Ferrers de Chartley."). *Notes & Queries* 6th Ser., 3 (1881): 167. Cooke & Mundy *Vis. of Worcester 1569* (H.S.P. 27) (1888): 16–19 (Blount ped.: "Sr Edward Blount of Sodington Knt ob. s.p. = ... widdow of ..... lorde Ferrers."). Weaver *Somerset Incumbents* (1889): 51. Brown *Abs. of Somersetshire Wills* 6 (1890): 30–31 (will of Sir Robert Poyntz, Knt.). Birch *Cat. Seals in the British Museum* 3 (1894): 411 (seal of Thomas Poyntz, Esq., dated 1517 — A shield of arms: on a chevron between three martlets, a mullet for difference.). Gairdner *Hist. of the Life & Reign of Richard III* (1898): 171. Habington *Survey of Worcestershire* 2 (1899): 203–206. Duncumb et al. *Colls. towards the Hist. & Antiqs. of Hereford* 5 (1902): 49 (Devereux ped.). Watkins *Colls. towards the Hist. & Antiqs. of Hereford* 5 (Hundred of Radlow) (1902): 49 (Devereux ped.). *List of Early Chancery Procs.* 3 (PRO Lists and Indexes 20) (1906): 459. Burke *Gen. & Heraldic Hist. of the Peerage & Baronetage* (1914): 1000–1002 (sub Hereford) (identifies Jane, 2nd wife of Walter Devereux above, as "Joan Verdon."). *C.P.* 4 (1916): 19, footnote f, 730–731 (Appendix H); 5 (1926): chart foll. 320, 321–325 (sub Ferrers), 754. *Letters & Papers... Henry VIII* 1(1) (1920): 265. Farnham *Leicestershire Medieval Peds.* (1925): 31 (Crophill ped.). Stillington & Fox *Regs. of Robert Stillington & Richard Fox* (Somerset Rec. Soc. 52) (1937): 51–52. *VCH Warwick* 4 (1947): 253. Thrupp *Merchant Class of Medieval London* (1948): 350. Bartrum *Welsh Gens. 1400–1500* 3

(1983): 462 (Drymbenog 2(C₂) ped.: "Sir Thomas ap Sir Roger Vaughan of Tretŵr (1) = Cecily f. Morgan, (2) = Jane, widow of Walter Devereux"). Sutton *Coronation of Richard III* (1983): 333–334. *National Lib. of Wales Jour.* 25 (1988): 387–398. Hoyle *Military Survey of Gloucestershire* (1993): 17, 54. Siddons *Vis. by the Heralds in Wales* (H.S.P. n.s. 14) (1996): 9 (arms of [Walter Devereux] Lord Ferrers). VCH *Gloucester* 5 (1996): 106–107. Court of Common Pleas, CP 40/872, rot. 457 (available at http:// www.british-history.ac.uk/source.aspx?pubid=1272). Biancalana *Fee Tail & the Common Recovery in Medieval England* (2001): 428–429. Gloucestershire Archives: Hale Family of Alderley, D1086/T2/25; D1086/T24 (available at www.a2a.org.uk/search/index.asp). National Archives, C 1/185/21; C 1/219/3; C 1/244/91; C 1/244/92; C 131/249/2; C 241/273/45; C 1/488/44; C 1/516/6; C 4/61/16; C 4/62/66; C 4/137/109 (available at www.catalogue.nationalarchives.gov.uk/search.asp).

Child of Anne Ferrers, by Walter Devereux, K.G.:

i. **ELIZABETH DEVEREUX**, married (1ˢᵗ) **RICHARD CORBET**, Knt., of Moreton Corbet, Shropshire [see CORBET 10]; (2ⁿᵈ) **THOMAS LEIGHTON**, Knt., of Wattlesborough, Shropshire [see CORBET 10].

❧ FIENNES ☙

EUSTACHE I, Count of Boulogne, married **MATHILDE** (or **MAHAUT**) **OF LOUVAIN**.
EUSTACHE II, Count of Boulogne, by an unknown mistress, _____.
GEOFFREY OF BOULOGNE, of Carshalton, Surrey, married **BEATRICE DE MANDEVILLE**.
WILLIAM OF BOULOGNE, of Carshalton, Surrey, married _____.
FARAMUS OF BOULOGNE, married **MAUD** _____.
SIBYL OF BOULOGNE, married **ENGUERRAND DE FIENNES**, Knt., seigneur of Fiennes.
WILLIAM (or **GUILLAUME**) **DE FIENNES**, seigneur of Fiennes, married **AGNÈS DE DAMMARTIN**.
ENGUERRAND DE FIENNES, Knt., seigneur of Fiennes, married [?**ISABEAU**] **DE CONDÉ**[see BOULOGNE 8].

9. **GILES DE FIENNES** (or **FENYS**, **FIENLES**, **FYENLES**), Knt., in right of his wife, of Old Court (in Wartling) and Marsham (in Fairlight), Sussex, younger son. He married before 19 Feb. 1269/70 (date of quitclaim) **SIBYL FILLIOL**, daughter and heiress of William Filliol, of Old Court (in Wartling), Sussex, by Cecily, daughter of Aimery de Chaunceux. They had one son, John, and one daughter, Eleanor (wife of Richard de Vernon). In 1270 Hagin of Lincoln quitclaimed to Giles and his wife, Sibyl, all right he had or might have by reason of the said Giles' and Sibyl's tenure of the lands and rents late of William Filliol. In 1270–2 he and his older brother, Guillaume (or William) de Fiennes, went on crusade in the Holy Land under the leadership of Lord Edward [future King Edward I]. In 1278 he was granted custody of the lands and heir of John le Blund, deceased, during the minority of the heir, with his marriage. In 1278–9 he and his wife, Sibyl, brought suit against Richard de Pageham to recover 40 pounds as compensation for her violent abduction by Pageham and others at Wartling, Sussex, and for keeping her prisoner at Rungeton (in North Mundham), Sussex for three years. In 1281 the king granted him three does in the forest of Essex. In 1283 the king gave a commission of oyer and terminer touching the persons who carried away swans of Giles de Fiennes at Wartling, Sussex during his absence on the king's service and under the king's protection in Wales. The same year the king granted him three bucks in the forest of Essex. In 1290 he was granted free warren in all his demesne lands in Old Court (in Wartling) and Marsham (in Fairlight), Sussex. The same year he was granted custody of the lands and heirs of Robert le Blund, tenant in chief. He was summoned to serve against the Scots in 1297 and 1301. In 1314 he and his wife, Sibyl, granted the reversion of the manor of Old Court (in Wartling), Sussex to William de Echingham. In 1320–1 his widow, Sibyl, held the manor of Old Court (in Wartling), Sussex for the term of her life.

Brydges *Collins' Peerage of England* 6 (1812): 555–590 (sub Brand, Baroness Dacre). Clutterbuck *Hist. & Antiq. of Hertford* 2 (1821): 9–11 (Fiennes ped.). Lipscomb *Hist. & Antiq. of the County of Buckingham* 2 (1847): 469–472 (omits this generation). Madden *Index to the additional MSS.* 1 (1849): 176. *Sussex Arch. Colls.* 4 (1851): 128–166. *Annual Rpt. of the Deputy Keeper* 47 (1886): 221. *C.P.R. 1281–1292* (1893): 73, 391, 470. *C.Ch.R.* 2 (1898): 234, 256, 267, 345. *C.C.R.*

1279–1288 (1902): 81, 215. Rigg *Cal. of the Plea Rolls of the Exchequer of the Jews* 1 (1905): 273. Salzmann *Abstract of Feet of Fines for the County of Sussex* 3 (1916): 14–52. VCH *Buckingham* 4 (1927): 90. VCH *Sussex* 9 (1937): 139, 177. Brault *Rolls of Arms Edward I (1272–1307)* 2 (1997): 164 (arms of Giles de Fiennes: Azure, three lions rampant or, a label gules). Aurell *Medieviste et la Monographie familiale* (2004): 249.

10. JOHN DE FIENNES, in right of his wife, of White Waltham, Berkshire, Ascot (in Great Milton), Oxfordshire, etc., son and heir. He married before 2 June 1294 **JOAN LE FORESTER**, daughter and heiress of Jordan le Forester, of Cookham, Hurley, and White Waltham, Berkshire, Ascot (in Great Milton) and Lyneham, Oxfordshire, etc., hereditary Forester of Windsor, by his wife, Amice. She was born before 25 May 1280. They had three sons, John, Knt., Edmund, and Jordan. JOHN DE FIENNES was returned as holding the fee in Ascot of the bishop in about 1305. He was one of the lords of Ascot in 1316, and contributed to the tax levied in 1327. His widow, Joan, was assessed for her property in Shottesbrook, Berkshire for subsidies in 1327 and 1332. She married (2nd) after Michaelmas term 1334 and before 25 July 1337 (as his 2nd wife) **ADAM DE SHARESHULL**, Knt., in right of his 1st wife, of Bickford, Whiston, and Saredon (in Shareshill), Staffordshire, in right of his 2nd wife, of Ascot (in Great Milton), Oxfordshire, and, in right of his 3rd wife, of Penleigh (in Westbury), Wiltshire, Knight of the Shire for Oxfordshire, 1355, Knight of the Shire for Gloucestershire, 1360. In 1337 he and two others were appointed to arrest certain suspected persons and imprison them in Oxford Castle. His wife, Joan, died testate in 1338. He married before 1340 (date of settlement) (3rd) **ALICE FITZ WARIN**, daughter and co-heiress of Peter Fitz Warin, Knt., of Ablington, Alton, and Penleigh (in Westbury), Wiltshire. Sometime before 1341 he released Reginald atte Hale, of Hurley, from all suits arising out of the execution of the will of his late wife, Joan de Fenes. In 1346 he served in France in the retinue of Richard, Earl of Arundel. In 1351 he complained that John de Acton, Knt., John Poyntz, Knt., and others broke his closes and houses at Bitton and Mangotsfield, Gloucestershire. SIR ADAM DE SHARESHULL died in 1370.

Brydges *Collins' Peerage of England* 6 (1812): 555–590 (sub Brand, Baroness Dacre). Clutterbuck *Hist. & Antiq. of Hertford* 2 (1821): 9–11 (Fiennes ped.). Lipscomb *Hist. & Antiq. of the County of Buckingham* 2 (1847): 469–472 (Fiennes ped.). *Sussex Arch. Colls.* 4 (1851): 128–166. *Colls. Hist. Staffs.* 11 (1890): 54. *Desc. Cat. Ancient Deeds* 1 (1890): 505–516. Wethered *St. Mary's, Hurley, in the Middle Ages* (1898): 163. Williams *Parliamentary Hist. of the County of Oxford* (1899): 22 (biog. of Adam de Shareshull). C.P.R. 1272–1281 (1901): 371. C.C.R. 1279–1288 (1902): 119, 315. C.C.R. 1288–1296 (1904): 348. *Cal. IPM* 1 (1904): 195. C.P.R. 1350–1354 (1907): 206. VCH *Berkshire* 3 (1923): 124–133, 172–173. Putnam *Place in Legal Hist. of Sir William Shareshill* (1950): 9–10. VCH *Oxford* 7 (1962): 126–127. VCH *Wiltshire* 8 (1965): 148–163. Parsons *Court & Household of Eleanor of Castile in 1290* (1977): 53. Parsons *Eleanor of Castile: Queen & Society in Thirteenth Century England* (1998): 159. Berkeley Castle Muniments, BCM/A/1/35/5 (available at www.a2a.org.uk/search/index.asp). Centre for Kentish Studies: Barrett-Lennard MSS., U1384/E3 (receipt dated ?1342 [sic] from Thomas de Ferrers, Knt., to Joan de Fyenles and her son John for £50, in full payment of a sum of £100 in which they were bound to him by a surety of £500 in "common baunk"); U1384/T4 (conveyance dated 1321 from Alan de Astone to Joan widow of John de Fienles regarding lands in Bridewelle within the manor of Cippenham, Buckinghamshire) (available at www.a2a.org.uk/search/index.asp).

11. JOHN DE FIENNES, Knt., of White Waltham, Berkshire, Forester of Windsor, Knight of the Shire for Sussex, and, in right of his wife, of Herstmonceux, Sussex, and Compton Monceux (in King's Somborne), Hampshire, etc., son and heir. He married before 1332 (date of fine) **MAUD DE MONCEUX**, daughter of John de Monceux, Knt. They had three sons, John, William, and Robert, and one daughter, Joan. His wife, Maud, was heiress to her brother, John de Monceux. In 1331 he and his wife, Maud, granted the manor of Compton Monceux (in King's Somborne), Hampshire to Maud de Ferrers for life. In 1337 he owed a debt of £100 to Augustine le Waleys, of Uxbridge, Middlesex. The same year he owed a debt of £100 to Roger Chauntecler, Citzen of London. In 1343 he witnessed a grant by Guy de Brian to Sir Andrew de Saukeville and Joan his wife of the reversion of a messuage and lands in Pevensey and Westham, Sussex. SIR JOHN DE FIENNES died 5 April 1351.

Brydges *Collins' Peerage of England* 6 (1812): 555–590 (sub Brand, Baroness Dacre). Clutterbuck *Hist. & Antiq. of Hertford* 2 (1821): 9–11 (Fiennes ped.). Lipscomb *Hist. & Antiq. of the County of Buckingham* 2 (1847): 469–472 (Fiennes ped.). *Sussex Arch. Colls.* 4 (1851): 128–166. *Desc. Cat. of Ancient Deeds* 5 (1906): 16, 427-429. VCH *Hampshire* 4 (1911): 475 (Monceux arms: Argent a bend sable). VCH *Berkshire* 3 (1923): 172–173. *Feet of Fines for Essex* 3 (1929–1949): 27, 45. VCH *Oxford* 7 (1962): 126–127. Centre for Kentish Studies: Barrett-Lennard MSS, U1384/T3/8 (conveyance dated 1335 from John de Fienles to Edmund his brother regarding lands in Bray; Berkshire), U1384/T3/9 (conveyance dated 1336 from Jordan de Fienles to John his brother regarding lands in Bray, Berkshire, they being the gift of Edmund de Fienles); U1384/T3/10 (bond dated 1341 in £10 13s. 4d. from Sir John de Fienles to Merota widow of Reginald atte Hale of Hurley, Berkshire); U1384/T14/1 (quitclaim dated 1344 from Margaret la Spencere to Sir John de Fienles, Knt.) (available at www.a2a.org.uk/search/index.asp). National Archives, C 241/110/213; C 241/111/13; C 241/129/203 (available at www.catalogue.nationalarchives.gov.uk/search.asp).

12. WILLIAM DE FIENNES, Knt., of Herstmonceux, Sussex, White Waltham, Berkshire, Compton Monceux (in King's Somborne), Hampshire, etc., Forester of Windsor, 2nd but eldest surviving son and heir, born about 1330 (aged 21 in 1351). He married before 1356 **JOAN DE SAY**, daughter of Geoffrey de Say, Knt., 2nd Lord Say, by Maud, daughter of Guy de Beauchamp, Knt., 10th Earl of Warwick [see SAY 10 for her ancestry]. They had two sons, John and William, Knt. SIR WILLIAM DE FIENNES died overseas 2 Dec. 1359. His widow, Joan, married (2nd) before 1370 (as his 2nd wife) **STEPHEN DE VALOINES** (or Valence, Vaylaunce), Knt., of Gore Court (in Otham) and Repton, Kent, Steward of the Archbishop of Canterbury, Lieutenant of Dover Castle and Cinque Ports, Knight of the Shire for Kent, 1373. By a previous marriage, he had one daughter, Joan (wife of William Costede and Thomas Fogge, Knt.). He was charged with defense of the coast in 1355 and 1377. In 1357–8 he acquired lands in Ashford, Great Chart, Hothfield, Kennington, Mersham, Westwell, Willesborough, and Wye, Kent from William de Suddynton, burgess of Berkeley. The same year he quitclaimed to Juliane, Countess of Huntingdon, lands in Ashford, Eaststour (in Ashford), Great Chart, Hothfield, Mersham, and Willesborough, Kent. He witnessed a grant in 1358 from Alexander Hauekyn, clerk, to Prior and Convent of Christ Church, Kent. His wife, Joan, died 29 June 1378.

Hasted *Hist. & Top. Survey of Kent* 11 (1800): 386–387. Hughson *London* 6 (1809): 395. Brydges *Collins' Peerage of England* 6 (1812): 555–590 (sub Brand, Baroness Dacre); 7 (1812): 16–39 (sub Twisleton, Lord Say and Sele). Clutterbuck *Hist. & Antiqs. of Hertford* 2 (1821): 9–11 (Fiennes ped.); 3 (1827): 190–194 (Mandeville-Say ped.). Devon *Issue Roll of Thomas de Brantingham, Bishop of Exeter* (1835): 154, 185, 268. *Coll. Top. et Gen.* 7 (1841): 57–66. Lipscomb *Hist. & Antiq. of the County of Buckingham* 2 (1847): 469–472 (Fiennes ped.). Holloway *Hist. of Romney Marsh* (1849): 108, 117, 119. *Sussex Arch. Colls.* 8 (1856): 96–131; 58 (1916): chart facing 64. Pearman *Hist. of Ashford* (1868): 24, 52. *Antiq.* 3 (1873): 312–313 (re. Valoigns fam.). *Reliquary* 16 (1875–76): 97–102. Scott *Mems. of the Fam. of Scott* (1876): 175. *Arch. Cantiana* 15 (1883): 5. Birch *Cat. Seals in the British Museum* 3 (1894): 613 (seal of Stephen de Valoyns, Knt. dated 1349 — A shield of arms: paly of six, undée [VALOINES]. Legend broken away). *Genealogist* n.s. 17 (1901): 249; n.s. 32 (1916): 216. Wrottesley *Peds. from the Plea Rolls* (1905): 354–355. *D.N.B.* 17 (1909): 875–876 (biog. of Geoffrey de Say). VCH *Hampshire* 4 (1911): 475 (Fiennes arms: Azure three lions or). VCH *Berkshire* 3 (1923): 172–173. VCH *Buckingham* 4 (1927): 181. *Feet of Fines for Essex* 3 (1929–49): 45. *Misc. Gen. et Heraldica* 5th Ser. 9 (1935–37): 232–245. Hussey *Kent Chantries* (Kent Arch. Soc. Recs. Branch 12) (1936): 31. VCH *Sussex* 7 (1940): 114; 9 (1937): 133. Rough *Reg. of Daniel Rough Common Clerk of Romney* (Kent Arch. Soc. Recs. 16) (1945): 102–103. *C.P.* 11 (1949): 478, footnote g (sub Say), 479 (sub Saye and Sele). Langham *Reg. Simonis Langham Cantuariensis Archiepiscopi* (Canterbury & York Soc. 53) (1956): 116, 172. Paget *Baronage of England* (1957) 210: 2, 485: 1–10 (sub Say). VCH *Oxford* 7 (1962): 126–127. Ellis *Cat. Seals in the P.R.O.* 1 (1978): 68 (seal of Stephen de Valognes (Valoyns), knight dated 1357 — A shield of arms: paly wavy of six). *Ancient Deeds — Ser. AS & WS* (List & Index Soc. 158) (1979): 14 (Deed A.S.73), 16 (Deed A.S.86), 22 (Deed A.S.121). Roskell *House of Commons 1386–1421* 3 (1992): 95–97 (biog. of Sir Thomas Fogg). Kirby *Hungerford Cartulary* (Wiltshire Rec. Soc. 49) (1994): 48. National Archives, SC 8/222/11064 (available at www.catalogue.nationalarchives.gov.uk/search.asp).

13. WILLIAM FIENNES, Knt., of Herstmonceux and Old Court (in Wartling), Sussex, White Waltham, Berkshire, Compton Monceux (in King's Somborne), Hampshire, Ascot (in Great Milton), Oxfordshire, etc., Sheriff of Surrey and Sussex, 1396–7, 1398–9, younger son, born at Herstmonceux, Sussex 1 August 1357. He was heir in 1375 to his older brother, John de Fiennes. He married before 23 April 1385 (date of enfeoffment) **ELIZABETH BATISFORD**, daughter and co-heiress of William Batisford, of Buckholt (in Bexhill), Sussex, by Margery, daughter and heiress of Simon de Peplesham. They had two sons, Roger, Knt., and James, Knt. [1st Lord Saye and Sele]. In 1388 he leased the manor of Compton Monceux, Hampshire for 7 years to John Trenchesvile. Elizabeth was named as a sister of Joan [Batisford], wife of William Brenchley, in a Sussex fine dated 1397–8. In 1398 he and his wife, Elizabeth, were granted a papal indult for plenary remission. In 1401–2 he assisted in drawing up the ordinances for Pevensey Marsh. SIR WILLIAM FIENNES died 18 Jan. 1401/2, and was buried at Herstmonceux, Sussex. His widow, Elizabeth, died before 1407.

>Brydges *Collins' Peerage of England* 6 (1812): 555–590 (sub Brand, Baroness Dacre); 7 (1812): 16–39 (sub Twisleton, Lord Say and Sele) (wife Elizabeth identified as "daughter and heir of William Batisford."). Clutterbuck *Hist. & Antiqs. of Hertford* 2 (1821): 9–11 (Fiennes ped.); 3 (1827): 194 (Say ped.). *Coll. Top. et Gen.* 7 (1841): 57–66. *Sussex Arch. Colls.* 8 (1856): 96–131; 58 (1916): 35, chart facing 64; 78 (1937): 87–89. Lipscomb *Hist. & Antiq. of the County of Buckingham* 2 (1847): 469–472 (Fiennes ped.). *Misc. Gen. et Heraldica* 1st Ser. 2 (1876): 332; 5th Ser. 9 (1935–37): 232–245. *List of Sheriffs for England & Wales* (PRO Lists and Indexes 9) (1898): 136. *Genealogist* n.s. 17 (1901): 249. *C.P.R.* 1399–1401 (1903): 209. *Papal Regs.: Letters* 5 (1904): 131. Benolte et al. *Vis. of Sussex 1530 & 1633–4* (H.S.P. 53) (1905): 11–12 (Fynes ped.: "Sr William Fynes knt. = Elizabeth d. of William Battesfford."). Wrottesley *Peds. from the Plea Rolls* (1905): 354–355. Jeayes *Desc. Cat. Derbyshire Charters* (1906): 97. VCH *Hampshire* 4 (1911): 475. Salzman *Feet of Fines Rel. Sussex* 3 (Sussex Rec. Soc. 23) (1916): 208–210. VCH *Berkshire* 3 (1923): 172–173. VCH *Sussex* 9 (1937): 118, 133. *C.P.* 11 (1949): 479 (sub Saye and Sele). Paget *Baronage of England* (1957) 210: 2–3, 485: 1–10 (sub Say). VCH *Oxford* 7 (1962): 126–127. Centre for Kentish Studies: Barrett-Lennard MSS, U1384/T5/6 (lease dated 1388 — Sir William Fienles to John Trenchesvile of manor of Compton Monceaus, Hampshire for 7 years at a rent of 22 marks) (available at online at ww.a2a.org.uk/search/index.asp). National Archives, SC 8/222/11064 (petition dated c.1378 from William de Fienles (Fiennes) to the king, requesting that he may be granted full seisin of all the lands which properly belonged to his late brother and father, as there have been mistakes in earlier inquisitions by the escheators into the nature of these lands. His father died during the reign of the king's grandfather, having leased certain property to his wife, Joan, late the wife of Stephen de Valoignes. His brother also died under-age, and he has since come into possession on his mother's death and his own majority) (available at www.catalogue.nationalarchives.gov.uk/search.asp). East Sussex Rec. Office: Add'l MSS, Catalogue H, AMS5629/1/1 (available at www.a2a.org.uk/search/index.asp).

Children of William Fiennes, Knt., by Elizabeth Batisford:

i. **ROGER FIENNES**, Knt. [see next].

ii. **JAMES FIENNES**, Knt., 1st Lord Saye and Sele, married (1st) **JOAN** _____ [see CROMER 14]; (2nd) **EMELINE CROMER** (or **CROWMER**) [see CROMER 14].

14. ROGER FIENNES, Knt., of Herstmonceux, Oldcourt (in Wartling), and Batsford (in Warbleton), Sussex, Compton Monceux (in King's Somborne), Hampshire, Lyneham, Oxfordshire, etc., Knight of the Shire for Sussex, Sheriff of Surrey and Sussex, 1423, 1434–5, Constable of Porchester, Treasurer of the Household to King Henry VI, Keeper of the King's Wardrobe, Chief Steward of the Duchy of Lancaster (Southern parts and Wales), son and heir, born at Herstmonceux, Sussex and baptized there 14 Sept. 1384 (aged 21 in 1406). In 1399 he was co-heir to his cousin, Elizabeth Say, wife of William Heron, Knt., *suo jure* Lady Say and Leybourne, by which he inherited half of the barony of Say, including the manors of Leckhampstead, Buckinghamshire, Cudham and Knole (in Sevenoke), Kent, and Streat, Sussex. He married before 1422 **ELIZABETH HOLAND**, daughter of John Holand, Knt., of Thorpe Waterville (in Thorpe Achurch), Northamptonshire, by his 2nd wife, Margaret [see HOLAND 12.ii for her ancestry]. They had two sons, Richard, Knt., and Robert, Knt., and one daughter, Margaret. He accompanied King Henry V to France with 8 men-at-arms and 24 foot-archers, and fought at Agincourt in 1415. In 1417 his feoffees presented to the church of Herstmonceux, Sussex. In 1424 he and his wife, Elzabeth, conveyed the manor of Lyneham, Oxfordshire to John Feriby, Esq., and others. In 1436 he sued William Hall and Elizabeth his wife for lands and rents in West Dean, Sussex. He presented to the church of Streat, Sussex in 1441. In 1441 he received license to "enclose crenellate and furnish with towers and battlements" his manor house at Herstmonceux, Sussex. His wife,

Elizabeth, was living in April 1441. SIR ROGER FIENNES left a will dated at Buxted, Sussex 29 October 1449, proved 18 Nov. 1449, requesting burial at Herstmonceux, Sussex.

> Hasted *Hist. & Top. Survey of Kent* 3 (1797): 62–65. Brydges *Collins' Peerage of England* 6 (1812): 555–590 (sub Brand, Baroness Dacre); 7 (1812): 16–39 (sub Twisleton, Lord Say and Sele) (wife Elizabeth identified as "daughter of John Holland."). Clutterbuck *Hist. & Antiqs. of Hertford* 2 (1821): 9–11 (Fiennes ped.); 3 (1827): 194 (Say ped.). *Coll. Top. et Gen.* 3 (1836): 259–260 (Roger Fiennes called "cousin" by Richard Poynings, Knt.); 7 (1841): 57–66; 8 (1843): 167–168. Lipscomb *Hist. & Antiq. of the County of Buckingham* 2 (1847): 469–472 (Fiennes ped.). *Sussex Arch. Colls.* 4 (1851): 148–152 ["Elizabeth Holland, of Northamptonshire, whose arms (azure semée of fleur-de-lis) existed in painted glass in the east window of the Chapel of the Castle"]; 8 (1856): 97–103; 58 (1916): 56–58, chart facing 64. *Rpt. of the Deputy Keeper* 48 (1887): 237, 268. *Desc. Cat. Ancient Deeds* 1 (1890): 452, 464. *List of Sheriffs for England & Wales* (PRO Lists and Indexes 9) (1898): 136. *Feudal Aids* 1 (1899): 294; 2 (1900): 373; 4 (1906): 48–51; 6 (1920): 453. *Genealogist* n.s. 17 (1901): 249. Benolte et al. *Vis. of Sussex 1530, 1633–4* (H.S.P. 53) (1905): 11–12 (Fynes ped.: "Sʳ Roger Fynes knt. = Elizabeth d. of... Holland of com. Northampton."). Deedes *Extracts from the Episcopal Regs. of Richard Paty, S.T.P., Lord Bishop of Chichester* (Sussex Rec. Soc. 4) (1905): 122–123, 136–137. Wrottesley *Peds. from the Plea Rolls* (1905): 354–355. *Papal Regs.: Letters* 7 (1906): 320, 323; 9 (1912): 240. VCH *Hampshire* 4 (1911): 475. *C.P.* 4 (1916): 8–9 (sub Dacre); 11 (1949): 478, footnote g (sub Say), 479, footnote b (sub Saye and Sele). VCH *Berkshire* 3 (1923): 172–173. *Rpt. on the MSS of Lord de L'Isle & Dudley* 1 (Hist. MSS Comm. 77) (1925): 164–165, 170. VCH *Buckingham* 4 (1927): 181. *C.C.R.* 1429–1435 (1933): 45–46, 63–64, 69, 226. *Misc. Gen. et Heraldica* 5ᵗʰ Ser. 9 (1935–37): 232–245. Wedgwood *Hist. of Parl.* 1 (1936): 324–325 (biog. of Sir Roger Fiennes) (wife Elizabeth identified as "sister of Sir John Holland, of N'hants"). VCH *Sussex* 7 (1940): 114; 9 (1937): 133. Chichele *Reg. of Henry Chichele* 3 (Canterbury & York Soc. 46) (1945): 460. Somerville *Hist. of the Duchy of Lancaster* 1 (1953): 428. Paget *Baronage of England* (1957) 210: 3 (died 1449) (married Elizabeth, daughter and heiress of Sir Thomas Echingham), 485: 1–10 (sub Say). VCH *Oxford* 7 (1962): 126–127. Centre for Kentish Studies: Barrett-Lennard MSS, U1384/E5 (indenture dated 1431 for Dame Elizabeth Fiennes, formerly Elizabeth Holand, the indenture mentions hangings embroidered with the arms of Fiennes and Holand, which hangings were presumably being moved from a house in London to the Fiennes house at Hurstmonceux) (available at www.a2a.org.uk/search/index.asp). Suffolk Rec. Office, Bury St. Edmunds Branch: Hengrave, 449/2/649 (will of Sir Richard Ponynges [Poynings], Knt., dated 13 July 1428, mentions his cousin, Sir Roger Fenys) (available at www.a2a.org.uk/search/index.asp). National Archives, CP 25/1/191/27, #16 [see abstract of fine at http://www.medievalgenealogy.org.uk/index.html].

Children of Roger Fiennes, Knt., by Elizabeth Holand:

i. **RICHARD FIENNES**, Knt. [see next].

ii. **MARGARET FIENNES**, married **NICHOLAS CAREW**, Knt., of Beddington, Surrey [see BEVILLE 15].

15. RICHARD FIENNES, Knt., of Herstmonceux, Sussex, Compton Monceux (in King's Somborne), Hampshire, etc., Sheriff of Surrey and Sussex, 1452–3, Chamberlain to Queen Elizabeth Wydeville, wife of King Edward IV of England, Privy Councillor, and, in right of his wife, of Dacre, Blackhall, Brackenthwaite, Kirkoswald, and Lazonby, Cumberland, Horsford, Burgh St. Margaret's, and Great Hautbois, Norfolk, Benacre, Suffolk, Hurstpierpont, Sussex, Barton, Westmorland, etc., son and heir. He married in or shortly after June 1446 **JOAN DACRE**, suo jure Lady Dacre, daughter and co-heiress of Thomas Dacre, Knt., of Horsford, Burgh St. Margaret's, and Great Hautbois, Norfolk, Benacre, South Cove, and Wrentham, Suffolk, Hurstpierpoint, Sussex, etc., by Elizabeth, daughter and co-heiress of William Bowet, Knt. [see DACRE 14.i for her ancestry]. She was born about 1433 (aged 26 in 1459). They had five sons, John, Knt., Thomas, Knt., Richard, William, and Roger, and one daughter, Elizabeth (wife of John Clinton, 6th Lord Clinton). In 1455–6 he, Richard Dallingridge, Esq., and Richard Sander sued John Chamber and John Holman, junior, in a plea of taking and unjustly detaining a horse called 'Gyllyng' of the value of 7s. His wife, Joan, was heiress sometime before 1458 to her sister, Philippe Dacre, wife of Robert Fiennes, Knt. He was summoned to Parliament from 9 October 1459 to 15 Nov. 1482, by writs directed *Ricardo Fenys domino Dacre chivaler*. In the period, 1460–5, he and his wife, Joan, sued Thomas Cryne, feoffee regarding a conspiracy to disinherit petitioners of the manors of Horsford, Great Hautbois, and Burgh St. Margaret, Norfolk. In the same period, he and his wife, Joan, sued John Heydon, William Calthorp, Esq., John Fyncham, and other feoffees regarding the manors of Horsford, Great

Hautbois, and Burgh St Margaret; Norfolk. He and the Convent presented to the church of Blythburgh, Suffolk in 1461 and 1482. He presented to the church of Benacre, Suffolk in 1473, 1478, 1480, 1481, and 1482. In 1473 he was granted the reversion of the office of the Constable of the Tower of London, but did no survive the then holder, John Sutton, Lord Dudley. The same year the attainder of Joan's uncle, Randolf Dacre, Knt. [2nd Lord Dacre of the North], was reversed, whereby she was awarded the manors of Fishwick and Eccleston, Lancashire, and Holbeach, Lincolnshire as his heir general. SIR RICHARD FIENNES, 7th Lord Dacre [of the South], died testate 25 Nov. 1483. His widow, Joan, Lady Dacre, died 8 March 1485/6. She left a will dated 13 October 1485, proved 14 June 1486 (P.C.C. 24 Logge). They were buried at Herstmonceux, Sussex.

> Blomefield *Essay towards a Top. Hist. of Norfolk* 5 (1775): 1356–1357; 11 (1810): 153. Brydges *Collins' Peerage of England* 6 (1812): 555–590 (sub Brand, Baroness Dacre). Nicolas *Testamenta Vetusta* 2 (1826): 390 (will of Joan Fynes, Lady Dacre). Burke *Dict. of the Peerages… Extinct, Dormant & in Abeyance* (1831): 153–155. *Coll. Top. et Gen.* 1 (1834): 302–303; 5 (1838): 317–328; 7 (1841): 197–202; 8 (1843): 167–168. Lipscomb *Hist. & Antiq. of the County of Buckingham* 2 (1847): 469–472 (Fiennes ped.). Suckling *Hist. & Antiqs. of Suffolk* 2 (1847): 130, 162. *Sussex Arch. Colls.* 4 (1851): 152–153. *Cal. State Papers, Domestic Ser., Edward VI, Mary, Elizabeth & James I* 7 (1871): 258–259. Howard *Selections from Household Books of the Lord William Howard* (Surtees Soc. 68) (1878): 365–395, 514–516. Flower *Vis. of Yorkshire 1563–4* (H.S.P. 16) (1881): 83–85 (Dacre ped.: "Jane [Dacre] his doughter & heyr = Sir Rychard Fynes Lord Dacres of the South"). Glover et al. *Vis. of Cheshire 1580, 1566, 1533 & 1591* (H.S.P. 18) (1882): 90–91 (Clavering ped.: "Jone [Dacre] vxr Sr Rich. ffynes."). *List of Sheriffs for England & Wales* (PRO Lists and Indexes 9) (1898): 136. *Norfolk Arch.* 15 (1904): 267–292. Benolte et al. *Vis. of Sussex 1530, 1633–4* (H.S.P. 53) (1905): 11–12 (Fynes ped.: "Richard Fynes Lord Dacres of the South in right of his wiffe. = Joane d. & heire of Tho. Dacres sonn of the Lord Dacres of the North."). Copinger *Manors of Suffolk* 2 (1908): 5–7, 42–43. VCH *Hampshire* 4 (1911): 475. VCH *Lancaster* 6 (1911): 162; 8 (1914): 120–121, 142. Attree *Sussex IPM* (Sussex Rec. Soc. 14) (1912): 95. Clay *Extinct & Dormant Peerages* (1913): 36–39 (sub Dacre). *C.P.* 3 (1913): 316 (sub Clinton); 4 (1916): 8–9, 18–19 (sub Dacre), 730–731 (Appendix H); 5 (1926): 754, 764–767. Salzman *Feet of Fines Rel. Sussex* 3 (Sussex Rec. Soc. 23) (1916): 262. *Sussex Arch. Colls.* 58 (1916): chart facing 64. *Genealogist* n.s. 34 (1918): 166–167. VCH *Berkshire* 3 (1923): 172–173. Harvey et al. *Vis. of the North* 3 (Surtees Soc. 144) (1930): 23–32 (Neville ped.: "Iohanna [Dacre] nupta domino Ricardo Fenys militi modo dominus Dacre et Camerarius regine"). Courthope & Formoy *Lathe Court Rolls & Views of Frankpledge in the Rape of Hastings 1387–1474* (Sussex Rec. Soc. 37) (1931): 102–104. VCH *Sussex* 9 (1937): 118, 133. Paget *Baronage of England* (1957) 164: 1–2 (sub Dacre); 210: 3. VCH *Oxford* 7 (1962): 126–127. National Archives, C 1/19/280; C 1/27/501; C 1/29/349; C 1/29/354; C 1/31/383; C 1/56/40; C 4/2/100 (available at www.catalogue.nationalarchives.gov.uk/search.asp).

16. THOMAS FIENNES, Knt., of Claverham (in Arlington), Sussex, Esquire of the Body to King Edward IV, 2nd son. He married before 22 Feb. 1482 **ANNE URSWICK**, widow of John Doreward, of Bocking, Essex (died before 1481), and daughter of Thomas Urswick, Knt., of Uphavering, Essex, Burgess (M.P.) for Midhurst and London, Chief Baron of the Exchequer, by his 2nd wife, Anne, daughter of Richard Rich, merchant of London. She was born about 1460 (aged 19 in 1479). They had three sons, Thomas (clerk), Giles, and Henry, and four daughters, Anne, Margaret, Elizabeth (wife of William Poyntz), and Joan (or Jane) (wife of Thomas Fiennes). SIR THOMAS FIENNES died 8 Feb. 1525/6. He left a will proved 19 May 1526 (P.C.C. 7 Porch).

> Foss *Judges of England* 4 (1857): 458–460. *C.P.R. 1476–1485* (1901): 261 (1901). Benolte et al. *Vis. of Sussex 1530 & 1633–4* (H.S.P. 53) (1905): 11–12 (Fynes ped.: "Sr Thomas Fynes of Claveringham in Sussex = Ann d. of… Ursewick."), 77–78 (Fynes ped.: "Thomas Fines of Claveringham in Sussex = Ann d. of Sr Tho. Urdswick Baron of the Exchequer."). Attree *Sussex IPM* (Sussex Rec. Soc. 14) (1912): 95. *Sussex Arch. Colls.* 58 (1916): chart facing 64. *Genealogist* n.s. 34 (1918): 166–167. Wedgwood *Hist. of Parl.* 1 (1936): 277–278 (biog. of Sir John Doreward), 897–898 (biog. of Sir Thomas Urswick). VCH *Essex* 5 (1966): 276.

Children of Thomas Fiennes, Knt., by Anne Urswick:

i. **ANNE FIENNES**, married (1st) **JOHN WINDSOR** [see ECHINGHAM 13]; (2nd) **GODDARD OXENBRIDGE**, Knt., of Forde Place (in Brede), Sussex [see ECHINGHAM 13].

ii. **MARGARET FIENNES**, married **WILLIAM LUNSFORD**, Esq., of Lunsford (in Etchingham), Sussex [see LUNSFORD 17].

❧ FILMER ❧

ALICE OF NORMANDY (sister of King William the Conqueror), married **LAMBERT**, Count of Lens.
JUDITH OF LENS, married **WALTHEOF**, Earl of Northumberland.
MAUD OF NORTHUMBERLAND, married **SIMON DE SENLIS**, Earl of Huntingdon and Northampton.
MAUD DE SENLIS, married **SAHER DE QUINCY**, of Long Buckby, Northamptonshire.
ALICE DE SENLIS, married **ROGER DE HUNTINGFIELD**, of Huntingfield, Suffolk.
WILLIAM DE HUNTINGFIELD, Knt., of Huntingfield, Suffolk, married **ISABEL FITZ WILLIAM**.
SARAH DE HUNTINGFIELD, married **RICHARD DE KEYNES**, of Horsted Keynes, Sussex.
RICHARD DE KEYNES, of Horsted Keynes, Sussex, married **ALICE DE MANKESEY**.
JOAN DE KEYNES, married **ROGER DE LEWKNOR**, Knt., of South Mimms, Middlesex.
THOMAS DE LEWKNOR, Knt., of South Mimms, Middlesex, married **SIBYL** _____.
ROGER DE LEWKNOR, Knt., of Broadhurst (in Horsted Keynes), Sussex, married **KATHERINE BARDOLF**.
THOMAS DE LEWKNOR, Knt., of Broadhurst (in Horsted Keynes), Sussex, married **JOAN D'OYLEY**.
ROGER LEWKNOR, Esq., of Horstead Keynes, Sussex, married **ELIZABETH CAREW**.
THOMAS LEWKNOR, Knt., of Horsted Keynes, Sussex, married **PHILIPPE DALLINGRIDGE**.
ROGER LEWKNOR, Knt., of Broadhurst (in Horsted Keynes), Sussex, married **ELEANOR CAMOYS** (desc. King William the Conqueror).
THOMAS LEWKNOR, Knt., of Trotton, Sussex, married **KATHERINE PELHAM**.
SIBYL LEWKNOR, married **WILLIAM SCOTT**, K.B.., of Scott's Hall (in Smeeth), Kent.
JOHN SCOTT, Knt., of Scott's Hall (in Smeeth), Kent, married **ANNE PYMPE** (desc. King William the Conqueror).
REYNOLD SCOTT, Knt., of Scott's Hall (in Smeeth), Kent, married **MARY TUKE** [see SCOTT 19].

20. MARY SCOTT, married (1st) (as his 2nd wife) **RICHARD ARGALL**, Esq., of East Sutton, Kent, son of Thomas Argall, Esq., of London, by Margaret, daughter of John Tallakarne. They had five sons, Thomas, Richard, Reginald, Knt., John, Esq., and Samuel, Knt., and six daughters, Elizabeth, Jane (wife of Paul Fleetwood, Esq.), Mary (wife of Reynold Kemp), Margaret (wife of Edmund Randolph, Esq.), Katherine (wife of Reynold Bathurst, Esq.), and Sarah (wife of _____ Jenkinson). RICHARD ARGALL, Esq., died at East Sutton, Kent, in 1588. His widow, Mary, married (2nd) (as his 2nd wife) **LAWRENCE WASHINGTON**, Esq., of Jordans Hall (in Maidstone), Kent and Much Hadham, Hertfordshire, Registrar of the Court of Chancery, 1593–1619, Burgess (M.P.) for Maidstone, 1603, younger son of Lawrence Washington, of Sulgrave, Northamptonshire, by his 2nd wife, Anne (or Amy), daughter of Robert Pargiter, Gent. They had no issue. He was called to the bar in 1582, and was styled "of Gray's Inn, co. Middlesex" in 1583. His wife, Mary, died in 1605. LAWRENCE WASHINGTON, Esq., died at his house on Chancery Lane 21 Dec. 1619. He left a will dated 10 August 1619, proved 10 Jan. 1619/20 (P.C.C. 3 Soame).

> Hasted *Hist. & Top. Survey of Kent* 2 (1797): 418. Berry *County Gens.: Kent Fams.* (1830): 169–171 (Scott ped.). Scott *Mems. of the Fam. of Scott* (1876): 185 (notes c & d), 254–255. Hawley et al. *Vis. of Essex 1552, 1558, 1570, 1612 & 1634* 1 (H.S.P. 13) (1878): 137 (1612 Vis.). Hunter *Familiæ Minorum Gentium* 4 (H.S.P. 40) (1896): 1301–1303 (Scott ped.: "Mary [Scott], mar. Ric. Argal, Esq."). Brown *Genesis of the United States* 2 (1897): 996–997. Ford *Writings of George Washington* 14 (1893): 333–334, 342–345. Philipot *Vis. of Kent 1619–1621* (H.S.P. 42) (1898): 127–129 (1619 Vis.) (Scott ped.: "Maria [Scott] nupta Ric'do Argall."). *VMHB* 28 (1920): 342–343; 34 (1926): 340–342. Benolte & Cooke *Vis. of Kent 1530-1, 1574 & 1592* 2 (H.S.P. 75) (1924): 30–31 (1574 Vis.) (Scott ped.: Mary [Scott] mar. to Rich: Argyll"), 101 (1592 Vis.). Filmer *Filmer Fam. Notes* 1 (1992): 63–77.

Children of Mary Scott, by Richard Argall, Esq.:

i. **SAMUEL ARGALL**, Knt., adventurer, deputy Governor of Virginia, born about 1580. He married _____. They had one daughter, Ann (wife of Samuel Percival). In 1611 he was selected to expel the French from soil claimed by England. He set out in 1613 for Mt. Desert; captured the missionaries who had established themselves there and at St. Croix and Port Royal, and carried off the priests to Virginia. The previous year he likewise captured Pocahontas, and carried her off to Jamestown, where she was detained. She was converted to Christianity, married John Rolder, and accompanied Gov. Dale and Argall to England in 1616. In 1617 he was appointed deputy governor of Virginia. He was subsequently recalled to England to justify his conduct. In 1620 he was in command of the *Golden* Phoenix, which ship was attached to the English fleet in the Mediterranean. In

1625 he was an admiral in a naval force which sailed from Plymouth and succeeded in capturing £100,000 worth of prizes. He became a member of the New England Royal Council and was knighted for his services. SIR SAMUEL ARGALL died testate on shipboard in March 1626. *D.A.B.* 1 (1928): 345–346 (biog. of Sir Samuel Argall). *VMHB* 59 (1951): 162–175. Raimo *Biog. Dict. of American Col. & Revolutionary Govs.* (1980): 466–467 (biog. of Sir Samuel Argall). Filmer *Filmer Fam. Notes* 1 (1992): 63–77.

    ii. **ELIZABETH ARGALL** [see next].

21. ELIZABETH ARGALL, married **EDWARD FILMER**, Knt., of East Sutton, Kent, son of Robert Filmer, Esq., of East Sutton, Kent, by Frances, daughter of Robert Chester, Knt., of Royston, Hertfordshire. They had nine sons, Robert, Knt., Edward, John, Thomas, Reginald (or Reynald), Thomas (again), Richard, Henry, Gent., and Augustine, and nine daughters, Mary (wife of John Knatchbull), Margaret, Elizabeth (wife of William Faulkner), Judith, Katherine, Anne, Jane, Susanna, and Sarah (wife of John Richard, Knt.). His wife, Elizabeth, was a legatee in the 1626 will of her brother, Samuel Argall, Knt. SIR EDWARD FILMER died testate 2 Nov. 1629. His widow, Elizabeth, died 9 August 1638. She left a will dated 23 March 1635, proved 16 August 1638 (P.C.C. 95 Lee). Edward and Elizabeth were buried at East Sutton, Kent.

Betham *Baronetage of England* 2 (1802): 440. Waller *Mon. Brasses from the 13th to the 16th Cent.* (1864): 61. Clutterbuck *Hist. & Antiqs. of Hertford* 1 (1815): 172. *VMHB* 24 (1916): 158–162; 59 (1951): 162–175. Benolte & Cooke *Vis. of Kent 1530–1, 1574 & 1592* 2 (H.S.P. 75) (1924): 101 (1592 Vis.) (Fylmer ped.: "Edward ffylmer of East Sutton aforsaide gent. Sonne and heire to Robert maried Elizabethe Daughter to Richarde Argall of Easte Sutton aforsaide Esquire"). Withington *Virginia Gleanings in England* (1980): 346–347 (will of Dame Elizabeth Filmer). Filmer *Filmer Fam. Notes* 1 (1992): 63–77.

Children of Elizabeth Argall, by Edward Filmer, Knt:

    i. **HENRY FILMER**, Gent. He attended Queen's College, Cambridge University, where he obtained a B.A. degree, 1624, and M.A. degree, 1631. He married **ELIZABETH** _____. They had one son and one daughter, Martha (wife of Thomas Green). He immigrated to Virginia in 1640, where he settled in James City and Warwick Counties, Virginia. He served as a member of the House of Burgesses for James City County, 1642–3, and for Warwick County, 1666–7. In 1653 he purchased 1,000 acres on the Chickahomany River. He was a justice for Warwick County in 1667. HENRY FILMER, Gent., left a will dated 21 Feb. 1671. *VMHB* 24 (1916): 158–162; 34 (1926): 340–342; 68 (1960): 408–428. Walter *Virginia Land Patents of the Counties of Norfolk, Princess Anne & Warwick* (1972): 29. Filmer *Filmer Fam. Notes* 3 (1992): 25–31. Allen *Major Henry Filmer* (2005).

    ii. **KATHERINE FILMER**, married at East Sutton, Kent 1 August 1620 **ROBERT BARHAM**, Gent., son and heir of Robert Barham, of Broughton Monchelsey, by Susannah, daughter of Thomas Norton. He was born about 1599 (aged 20 in 1619). They had six sons, Thomas, Edward, [Capt.] Charles, Richard, John, and Robert, and three daughters, Elizabeth, Susan (wife of William Cockerman), and Anne (wife of Richard Bennett). She was a legatee in the 1629 will of her uncle, Robert Filmer, Gent. *VMHB* 24 (1916): 158–162; 48 (1940): 276–280, 358–360. *Gens. of Virginia Fams. from VMHB* 4 (1981): 528–532. Filmer *Filmer Fam. Notes* 1 (1992): 63–77, 98.

Child of Katherine Filmer, by Robert Barham, Gent.:

    a. [CAPT.] **CHARLES BARHAM**, Gent., immigrated to Virginia in 1661, where he settled in Lawnes Creek Parish, Surry County, Virginia. He married before 2 Feb. 1666/7 **ELIZABETH** _____ (possibly **RIDLEY**). They had two sons, Charles and Robert, and two daughters, Elizabeth and Perilee. He served as Justice and Sheriff of Surry County, Virginia. He moved to Merchants Hundred in James City County, Virginia before 1684. [CAPT.] CHARLES BARHAM, Gent., died shortly before 1 Jan. 1683/4. His wife, Elizabeth, died 3 July 1694. *VMHB* 24 (1916): 158–162; 48 (1940): 276–280, 358–360. *Gens. of Virginia Fams. from VMHB* 4 (1981): 528–532. Filmer *Filmer Fam. Notes* 1 (1992): 98, 114–115.

❧ FILOLL ☙

RICHARD FITZ GILBERT, of Clare, Suffolk, married **ROHESE** (or **ROSE**) **GIFFARD**.
GILBERT FITZ RICHARD, of Clare, Suffolk, married **ALICE DE CLERMONT**.
RICHARD FITZ GILBERT, of Clare, Suffolk, married **ALICE OF CHESTER**.
ROGER DE CLARE, Earl of Hertford, married **MAUD DE SAINT HILARY**.
RICHARD DE CLARE, Knt., Earl of Hertford, married **AMICE OF GLOUCESTER** (desc. King William the Conqueror).
MAUD DE CLARE, married **WILLIAM DE BREWES**, of Bramber, Sussex.
JOHN DE BREWES, of Bramber, Sussex, married **MARGARET OF WALES**.
WILLIAM DE BREWES, Knt., 1st Lord Brewes, married **AGNES DE MOELS**.
GILES DE BREWES, Knt. of Buckingham, Buckinghamshire, married **MAUD DE WHITNEY**.
JOHN DE BREWES, of Knowlton, Dorset, married **SARAH** _____.
ELIZABETH DE BREWES, married **WILLIAM FROME**, of Winterborne Houndington, Dorset.
JOHN FROME, of Buckingham, Buckinghamshire, married _____ **DE TREGOZ** [see FROME 12].

13. JOAN FROME, daughter and co-heiress, born about 1386. She married (1st) in or before 1397 **WILLIAM FILOLL** (or **FYLOLL**, **FYLLOLL**), of Langton Walsh (in Purbeck), Dorset, and, in right of his wife, of Woodlands (in Horton) and Knowlton, Dorset, Justice of the Peace for Dorset, 1412–14, Knight of the Shire for Dorset, 1414, son and heir of John Filoll, by Margaret (or Margery), daughter and heiress of Roger le Walshe. He was born about 1380. They had one son, John, Esq., and three daughters, Avice, Eleanor, and Isabel. WILLIAM FILOLL left a will proved March 1416 (P.C.C. 34 Marche), requesting burial at St. Wulfhilda in Horton, Dorset. His widow, Joan, was assigned dower 14 May 1416. She held court at Langton Walsh (in Purbeck), Dorset 16 Sept. 1416. She married (2nd) before May 1417 (as his 2nd wife) **RICHARD ARCHES**, Knt., of Oving, Buckinghamshire, Knight of the Shire for Buckinghamshire, 1402, Justice of the Peace for Oxfordshire, 1410–1412, son and heir of Richard Arches, of Eythrope, Buckinghamshire, by Lucy, daughter of Richard Adderbury, Knt. They had no issue. SIR RICHARD ARCHES died in France 5 Sept. 1417. His widow, Joan, married (3rd) before March 1420 **WILLIAM CHEYNE**, Knt., in right of his wife, of Southcombe (in Coombe Keynes), Dorset, Justice of Common Pleas, Chief Justice of the King's Bench. She died 1 July 1434, leaving a will dated 31 March 1420. SIR WILLIAM CHEYNE died testate about 1439.

Foss *Judges of England* 4 (1851): 301–302 (biog. Sir William Cheyne). Hutchins *Hist. & Antiqs. of Dorset* 3 (1868): 152 (Filiol ped.). *D.N.B.* 4 (1885–6): 222 (biog. of Sir William Cheyne). *Misc. Gen. et Heraldica* 2nd Ser. 2 (1888): 190–191 (Filoll arms: Vair, a canton gules). *Feudal Aids* 2 (1900): 64, 108, 118. *List of Early Chancery Procs.* 1 (PRO Lists and Indexes 12) (1901): 97. Wrottesley *Peds. from the Plea Rolls* (1905): 184, 197. *C.P.R. 1408–1413* (1909): 481. *C.P.R. 1413–1416* (1910): 418. Fry & Fry *Abs. of Feet of Fines Rel. Dorset* 2 (Dorset Rec. Soc. 10) (1910): 218, 231, 286. *C.C.R. 1413–1419* (1929): 185, 305–306. VCH *Somerset* 4 (1978): 224. VCH *Sussex* 6(3) (1987): 161. Roskell *House of Commons 1386–1421* 3 (1992): 73–74 (biog. of William Filoll). Sainty *Judges of England* (Selden Soc. Supp. Ser. 10) (1993): 8, 26 (re. William Cheyne). Dorset Hist. Centre, Bankes: Manorial and Hundredal, BKL/CC/1/4; /BKL/CC/1/5; /BKL/CC/1/6 (available at www.a2a.org.uk/search/index.asp).

14. JOHN FILOLL, Esq., of Woodlands (in Horton), Langton Herring, Little Herringstone (in Charminster), and Winterborne Herringstone, Dorset, son and heir, born about 1409 (aged 7 in 1416). He was heir in 1420 to his great aunt, Mary Filoll, widow, successively, of William Percy, Knt., and Richard Bannebury (alias Chamberlain), by which he inherited the manors of Woodmancote, Morley, and Southwick, a moiety of the manor of Truleigh, rents in Goring, all in Sussex, and the manor of Wambrook, Somerset. He married **MARGARET CARENT** (or **CARAUNT**), daughter and co-heiress of John Carent, of Silton, Dorset. They had four sons, William, Knt., Reynold, Henry (clerk), and possibly Jasper, and one daughter, Katherine. In 1439–40 as "John Filoll, son of Joan, late the wife of Sir William Cheyne, chief justice," he sued Nicholas Arney, Simon Talbot, Margaret Cheyne, and others, executors to the said Sir William Cheyne, regarding the manor of Winterborne Belet and lands, etc. in Winterborne Hundyngton, Stafford, Kingston Mawreward, and Winterborne Kingston, Dorset, which lands were enfeoffed by the said Joan. JOHN FILOLL, Esq., left a will dated 1467, proved July 1467 (P.C.C. 21 Godyn), requesting burial in the Temple Church, London. His widow, Margaret, married (2nd) (as his 2nd wife) **JOHN WROUGHTON**, Esq., of Broad Hinton and Woodhill (in Clyffe Pypard), Wiltshire, Knight of the Shire of Wiltshire, 1455–6, Sheriff of Wiltshire, 1486–7. They had one son, Thomas. In 1486 Katherine Filoll, daughter of John Filoll, Esq., sued her step-father, John Wroughton, in Chancery regarding land in [....]geswell and elsewhere in Somerset and Dorset. In 1493 he and his wife, Margaret, conveyed the manor of Knightstreet and one messuage, one mill, and various lands in Knightstreet and Todber, Dorset to her younger son, Reynold Filoll for 300 marks of silver. JOHN WROUGHTON, Esq. died 16 August 1496. In 1501–2 Reynold, son of John Filoll sued his mother, Margaret Wroughton, executrix and late the wife of John Filoll, regarding lands and tenements in Dorset, Hampshire, and Essex. Margaret died in 1520/1.

Hutchins *Hist. & Antiqs. of Dorset* 3 (1868): 152 (Filiol ped.). Hawley et al. *Vis. of Essex 1552, 1558, 1570, 1612 & 1634* 1 (H.S.P. 13) (1878): 195–196 (1612 Vis.) (Filleall arms: Vair, a canton gules). *Misc. Gen. et Heraldica* 2nd Ser. 2 (1888): 190–191. *List of Sheriffs for England & Wales* (PRO Lists and Indexes 9) (1898): 153. *Feudal Aids* 2 (1900): 105, 114, 116. *List of Early Chancery Procs.* 3 (PRO Lists and Indexes 20) (1906): 22, 329, 463, 509, 513; 4 (PRO Lists and Indexes 29) (1908): 36, 41. VCH *Sussex* 7 (1940): 147; 6(3) (1987): 161. Boulton *Sherwood Forest Book* (Thoroton Soc. Rec. Ser.) (1965): 31. VCH *Wiltshire* 9 (1970): 32; 12 (1983): 109, 122. VCH *Somerset* 4 (1978): 224. National Archives, C 1/11/347; C 1/80/30; C 1/248/57 (available at www.catalogue.nationalarchives.gov.uk/search.asp). National Archives, CP 25/1/51/63, #4 (fine dated 3 Feb. 1493; Reynold Filoll, querent, and John Wroughton the elder, Esq., and Margaret, his wife, and John Filoll, clerk, deforciants) [see abstract of fine at http://www.medievalgenealogy.org.uk/index.html].

15. WILLIAM FILOLL, Knt., of Woodlands (in Horton) and Southcombe (in Coombe Keynes), Dorset, Wambrook, Somerset, and Woodmancote, Sussex, and, in right of his 2nd wife, of Stonehouse (in Standon), Hertfordshire, Justice of the Peace for Dorset, son and heir, born about 1451 (aged 16 in 1467). In the period, 1467–72, William Huse, King's attorney sued him regarding entry into the manors of Southcombe (in Coombe Keynes) and Woodlands (in Horton), Dorset without livery from the king. He married (1st) by marriage covenants dated 24 Nov. 1473 **ELIZABETH AUDLEY** (or **TUCHET**), 2nd daughter of John Audley (or Tuchet), 6th Lord Audley, Lord High Treasurer, by Anne, daughter of Thomas Echingham, Knt. [see TUCHET 16 for her ancestry]. They had no issue. He married (2nd) **DOROTHY IFIELD**, daughter and co-heiress of John Ifield, Esq., of Stonehouse (in Standon), Hertfordshire, by Agnes, daughter and heiress of Stephen Foster, of London. They had one son, William, and two daughters, Anne and Katherine. In 1520 Henry Assheleygh, Esq., late of Wimborne St. Giles, Dorset was attached to answer William Filoll, Knt. concerning a plea why with force and arms he assaulted Walter Rooper, servant of the said William, at Gussage St. Michael, Dorset, and beat, wounded and ill-treated him so that his life was despaired of, wherby he lost the service of his servant for a long time, and also took one dog called a 'bloodhound' (price ten marks) belonging to the said William, and inflicted other outrages on him. SIR WILLIAM FILOLL died 9 July 1527. He left a will dated 14 May 1527, proved 15 October 1527 (P.C.C. 23 Porch), requesting burial in the choir of the Grey Friars, Salisbury, Wiltshire. In Jan. 1528 his widow, Dorothy, and other co-feoffees leased property in Winterborne Muston, Dorset to Strangwich. In an Act of Parliament, 22 Henry VIII (1530–1) "concerning the assurance of certain lands to the heirs of Sir William Filoll", he was described as "an aged man and havyng many sondrie and inconstant fantasies in his latter daies." In 1528 she was granted license by the king to alienate the manors of Sellyng juxta Horton Monks and Harynge, Kent. His widow, Dorothy, married (2nd) after 8 August 1528 (date of license) and before 1531 (date of partition) (as his 2nd wife) **JOHN ROGERS**, Knt., of Bryanston, Dorset, Sheriff of

Somerset and Dorset, 1522. He presented to the church of Bryanston, Dorset in 1511. She died testate 1 October 1537.

> Brydges *Collins' Peerage of England* 6 (1812): 546–557 (sub Thicknesse Touchet, Lord Audley). Hutchins *Hist. & Antiqs. of Dorset* 3 (1868): 151–153, esp. 152 (Filiol ped.); 4: 315. Mundy et al. *Vis. of Nottingham 1569 & 1614* (H.S.P. 4) (1871): 145–149 (Filoll arms: Vair, a canton ermine (or gules)). Hawley et al. *Vis. of Essex 1552, 1558, 1570, 1612 & 1634* 1 (H.S.P. 13) (1878): 195–196 (1612 Vis.). *Misc. Gen. et Heraldica* 2nd Ser. 2 (1888): 190–191. *List of Sheriffs for England & Wales* (PRO Lists and Indexes 9) (1898): 124. *C.P.R. 1467–1477* (1900): 39. *List of Early Chancery Procs.* 2 (PRO Lists and Indexes 16) (1903): 33. *Notes & Queries for Somerset & Dorset* 8 (1903): 293–294. *Colls. Hist. Staffs.* 1912 (1912): 362. VCH *Hertford* 3 (1912): 362. *Genealogist* n.s. 36 (1920): 9–21. *Letters & Papers… Henry VIII* 1(1) (1920): 223; 1(2) (1920): 1173, 1536. *Notes & Queries for Somerset & Dorset* 16 (1920): 98. *C.P.* 12(1) (1953): 59–65 (sub Somerset). Boulton *Sherwood Forest Book* (Thoroton Soc. Rec. Ser. 23) (1965): 1, 5–7, 13, 15–16, 31–33, 48, 64. *Ancient Deeds — Ser. B* 3 (List & Index Soc. 113) (1975): B.12253. VCH *Somerset* 4 (1978): 224. VCH *Sussex* 6(3) (1987): 161. Roskell *House of Commons 1386–1421* 3 (1992): 73–74 (biog. of William Filoll). *Year Books of Henry VIII 1520–1523* (Selden Soc. 119) (2002): 14–20. Nottingham University Library, Dept. of MSS & Special Colls.: Fam. & Estate Papers of the Willoughby Fam., Lords Middleton, Mi 5/167/107/1-2; Mi 5/167/108; Mi 5/167/110 (Robert Morton styled "brother" by Dorothy Fyloll in 1528); Mi 5/167/111; Mi 6/174/53; Mi 6/174/54; Mi 6/174/56; Mi D 4794 (available at www.a2a.org.uk/search/index.asp). National Archives, C 1/40/249; C 1/673/26; C 1/708/6; C 1/766/22 (available at www.catalogue.nationalarchives.gov.uk/search.asp).

Children of William Filoll, Knt., by Dorothy Ifield:

 i. **ANNE FILOLL**, married **EDWARD WILLOUGHBY**, Knt., of Wollaton, Nottinghamshire [see FREVILLE 15].
 ii. **KATHERINE FILOLL**, married **EDWARD SEYMOUR**, K.G., Viscount Beauchamp, Earl of Hertford, Lord Seymour, 1st Duke of Somerset [see SEYMOUR 19.i].

❧ FINCH ❧

ALICE OF NORMANDY (sister of King William the Conqueror), married **LAMBERT**, Count of Lens.
JUDITH OF LENS, married **WALTHEOF**, Earl of Northumberland.
MAUD OF NORTHUMBERLAND, married **SIMON DE SENLIS**, Earl of Huntingdon and Northampton.
SIMON DE SENLIS, Earl of Huntingdon and Northampton, married **ISABEL** (or **ELIZABETH**) **OF LEICESTER**.
ISABEL DE SAINT LIZ, married **WILLIAM MAUDUIT**, of Hanslope, Buckinghamshire.
ROBERT MAUDUIT, of Hanslope, Buckinghamshire, married **ISABEL BASSET**.
WILLIAM MAUDUIT, of Hanslope, Buckinghamshire, married **ALICE DE NEWBURGH**.
ISABEL MAUDUIT, married **WILLIAM DE BEAUCHAMP**, Knt., of Elmley, Worcestershire.
JOAN DE BEAUCHAMP, married **BARTHOLOMEW DE SUDELEY**, Knt., of Dassett (in Burton Dassett), Warwickshire.
JOHN DE SUDELEY, 1st Lord Sudeley, married _____ **DE SAY**.
BARTHOLOMEW DE SUDELEY, married **MAUD DE MONTFORT** (desc. King William the Conqueror).
JOHN DE SUDELEY, 2nd Lord Sudeley, married **ELEANOR DE SCALES** (desc. King William the Conqueror).
JOAN DE SUDELEY, married **WILLIAM LE BOTELER**, Knt., of Wem, Shropshire.
THOMAS LE BOTELER, Knt., of Sudeley, Gloucestershire, married **ALICE BEAUCHAMP** (desc. King William the Conqueror).
JOAN BOTELER, married **HAMON** (or **HAMOND**) **BELKNAP**, Esq., of Knelle (in Beckley), Sussex [see SUDELEY 15].

16. **PHILIP BELKNAP**, Esq., of the Moat by Canterbury, Kent, Sheriff of Kent, 1455–6, Mayor of Canterbury, Kent, 1457, younger son. He married **ELIZABETH WOODHOUSE**, daughter of John Woodhouse. They had one daughter, Alice. PHILIP BELKNAP, Esq., died in 1457.

> Hasted *Hist. & Top. Survey of Kent* 11 (1800): 161–162; 12 (1801): 605. Brydges *Collins' Peerage of England* 3 (1812): 371–406 (sub Finch, Earl of Winchelsea & Nottingham). *Arch. Cantiana* 4 (1861): 196. *Misc. Gen. et Heraldica* 1st Ser. 2 (1876): 327–337. *List of Sheriffs for England & Wales* (PRO Lists and Indexes 9) (1898): 68. Philipot *Vis. of Kent 1619–1621* (H.S.P. 42) (1898): 67–68 (1619 Vis.) (Finche ped.).

17. ALICE BELKNAP, daughter and heiress. She married **HENRY FINCH** (or **FYNCHE**), Esq., of Icklesham and Netherfield, Sussex, son and heir of William Finch, of Netherfield, Sussex, by Agnes, daughter of William (or Walter) Row, Esq. They had three sons, William, Knt., Henry, and Philip. HENRY FINCH, Esq., left a will dated 18 Jan. 1493/4, proved 23 May 1494 (P.C.C. Vox), requesting burial in the Chapel of St. Nicholas in Icklesham, Sussex.

> Hasted *Hist. & Top. Survey of Kent* 7 (1798): 398–412. Brydges *Collins' Peerage of England* 3 (1812): 371–406 (sub Finch, Earl of Winchelsea & Nottingham). Nicolas *Testamenta Vetusta* 2 (1826): 416–417 (will of Henry Finch). *Arch. Cantiana* 4 (1861): 196. *Misc. Gen. et Heraldica* 2 (1876): 327–337. Philipot *Vis. of Kent 1619–1621* (H.S.P. 42) (1898): 67–68 (1619 Vis.) (Finche ped.: "Henricus ffinche. = Alicia filia et hæres Philippi Belknap de Mote prope Cant. Avunculi Edwardi Belknap militis.").

18. WILLIAM FINCH, Knt., of the Moat by Canterbury and Burmarsh, Kent, Sheriff of Kent, 1532–3, son and heir. He married (1st) **ELIZABETH CROMER** (or **CROWMER**), widow of Richard Lovelace, Knt., of Bethersden, Kent, and daughter of James Cromer, Knt., of Tunstall, Kent, by Katherine, daughter of William Cantelowe, Knt. [see CROMER 16 for her ancestry]. They had three sons, Laurence, Thomas, Knt., and Richard, and one daughter, Anne. He and his wife attended the king and queen at the Field of the Cloth of Gold in 1520. He married (2nd) **KATHERINE GAINESFORD**, daughter of John Gainesford, Knt., of Crowhurst, Surrey. They had two sons, Erasmus and Vincent, and four daughters, Elizabeth (wife of Thomas Thwaites, Esq.), Alice, Eleanor (wife of Robert Morton, Esq., and Thomas Wotton), and Mary (wife of _____ Whitney). SIR WILLIAM FINCH left a will proved 3 May 1553 (P.C.C. 9 Tashe).

> Hasted *Hist. & Top. Survey of Kent* 7 (1798): 398–412; 8 (1799): 258–264. Brydges *Collins' Peerage of England* 3 (1812): 371–406 (sub Finch, Earl of Winchelsea & Nottingham). *Arch. Cantiana* 4 (1861): 196. *Misc. Gen. et Heraldica* 2 (1876): 327–337. *List of Sheriffs for England & Wales* (PRO Lists and Indexes 9) (1898): 69. Philipot *Vis. of Kent 1619–1621* (H.S.P. 42) (1898): 67–68 (1619 Vis.) (Finche ped.: "Willi'mus ffinche de Le Mote p'dict Miles. [1] = Eliza: filia Jacobi Crowner militis vidua Ricardi Louelace militis, [2] = Catharina filia Joh'is Gaynsford de Crowhurst in co' Surrey militis."), 125 (1619 Vis.) (Lovelace ped.: "Rich: Louelace Miles ob't s.p. 17 H. 7. = Eliza filia Jacobi Crowmer Milit. renupt. .... ffinche."). Benolte & Cooke *Vis. of Kent 1530–1, 1574 & 1592* 1 (H.S.P. 74) (1923): 10 (1530–1 Vis.) (Fynche ped.: "Syr Willym Fynche, knyghte [1] = 1st Elysabeth d. vnto Sr James Cromer, knyght, [2] = 2nd wyffe Kateryne d. to Sr John Gaynsforde, knight"), 43–44 (1574 Vis.) (Crowmer ped.: "Elizabeth [Crowmer] mar. first to Sr Richard Louelace, Kt. 2 to Sr Willm Finch, Knight.").

19. THOMAS FINCH, Knt., of the Moat by Canterbury and Burmarsh, Kent, Icklesham and Netherfield, Sussex, etc., Burgess (M.P.) for Canterbury, Kent, 1559, Keeper of the site of St. Augustine's Priory, Canterbury, 1559, and, in right of his wife, of Eastwell and Beamstone, Kent, 2nd but 1st surviving son and heir by his father's 1st marriage. He married at Eastwell, Kent in 1547 **KATHERINE MOYLE**, daughter and heiress of Thomas Moyle, Knt., of Eastwell, Kent, Speaker of the House of Commons, Chancellor of the Court of Augmentations, by Katherine, daughter and co-heiress of Edward Jordan, Goldsmith of London [see MOYLE 18 for her ancestry]. They had four sons, Anthony, Moyle, Knt., Henry, Knt., and Thomas, and one daughter, Jane. In 1554 he helped restore order in Kent after the rebellion of Sir Thomas Wyatt. He and his wife, Katherine, were legatees in the 1560 will of her father. Early in 1563 he was promoted to Knight Marshal of the army at Le Havre, and set sail for France on 19 Mar. on the ship *Greyhound*. The ship went aground at Rye, Sussex and all were drowned except seven men. The body of SIR THOMAS FINCH was brought back to the Eastwell, Kent church for burial. Administration on his estate was granted to his widow, Katherine, 31 March 1563. Katherine married (2nd) **NICHOLAS SAINT LEGER**, Esq., 3rd son of Anthony Saint Leger, K.G., of Ulcombe, Kent, by Agnes, daughter and heiress of Hugh Warham, Esq. [see SAINT LEGER 18 for his ancestry]. They had no issue. He presented to the church of Eastling, Kent in 1574 and to Eastwell, Kent in 1580. His wife, Katherine, died in Feb. 1587. Administration on the estate NICHOLAS SAINT LEGER, Esq., was granted 5 June 1589 to Anthony Saint Leger.

Hasted *Hist. & Top. Survey of Kent* 7 (1798): 398–412; 8 (1799): 258–264. Brydges *Collins' Peerage of England* 3 (1812): 371–406 (sub Finch, Earl of Winchelsea & Nottingham). *Arch. Cantiana* 4 (1861): 196. *Misc. Gen. et Heraldica* 2 (1876): 327–337; 5th Ser. 4 (1920–22): 229–245 (Moyle ped.). Philipot *Vis. of Kent 1619–1621* (H.S.P. 42) (1898): 67–68 (1619 Vis.) (Finche ped.: "Tho: ffinche de Estwell Miles = Catharina filia et cohæres Tho: Moyle de Estwell myles."). *Misc. Gen. et Heraldica* 5th Ser. 4 (1920–22): 229–245 (Moyle ped.). Benolte & Cooke *Vis. of Kent 1530–1, 1574 & 1592* 1 (H.S.P. 74) (1923): 10 (1530–1 Vis.) (Fynche ped.: "Thomas [Fynche]."). Benolte & Cooke *Vis. of Kent 1530–1, 1574 & 1592* 2 (H.S.P. 75) (1924): 12–13 (1574 Vis.) (Moyle ped.: "Katherin [Moyle] married vnto Sʳ Thomas Finche, Knight"). Hasler *House of Commons 1558–1603* 2 (1981): 119–120 (biog. of Sir Thomas Finch). Mayer & Walters *Corr. of Reginald Pole* 4 (2008): 363–364 (biog. of Thomas Moyle).

Child of Thomas Finch, Knt., by Katherine Moyle:

i. **JANE FINCH**, married **GEORGE WYATT**, Esq., of Allington and Boxley Abbey, Kent [see WYATT 22].

⁕ FISHER ⁕

JOHN DE SOMERY, married **HAWISE PAYNELL**.
RALPH DE SOMERY, of Dudley (in Sedgley), Staffordshire, married **MARGARET LE GRAS**.
JOAN DE SOMERY, married **THOMAS DE BERKELEY**.
MAURICE DE BERKELEY, Knt., of Berkeley, Gloucestershire, married **ISABEL DE DOVER** (desc. King William the Conqueror).
THOMAS DE BERKELEY, Knt., 1st Lord Berkeley, married **JOAN DE FERRERS** (desc. King William the Conqueror).
MAURICE DE BERKELEY, Knt., 2nd Lord Berkeley, married **EVE LA ZOUCHE**.
THOMAS DE BERKELEY, Knt., 3rd Lord Berkeley, married **KATHERINE DE CLIVEDON** [see BERKELEY 7].

8. **JOHN BERKELEY**, Knt., of Beverstone, Compton Greenfield, Over (in Almondsbury), Syde, Tockington, and Woodmancote (in Dursley), Gloucestershire, Lower Ham and Tickenham, Somerset, Clevelode, Worcestershire, Knight of the Shire for Gloucestershire, 1388, 1397, Knight of the Shire for Somerset, 1390, 1394, Sheriff of Somerset and Dorset, 1390–1, 1394–5, Sheriff of Gloucestershire, 1392–3, 1397–8, 1414–15, Knight of the Shire for Wiltshire, 1402, 1406, Sheriff of Hampshire, 1402–3, 1406–7, Sheriff of Wiltshire, 1410–11, and, in right of his 2nd wife, of Bisterne (in Ringwood), Exbury, and Minstead, Hampshire, Gillingham, Dorset, Chaddenwick (in Mere) and West Grimstead, Wiltshire, etc., 4th and youngest but only surviving son by his father's 2nd marriage, born and baptized at Wotton-under-Edge, Gloucestershire 23 Jan. 1351/2 (aged 32 in 1386). He married (1st) before 16 March 1367 **ELEANOR ASHTON** (or **ASSHETON**), daughter of Robert de Ashton, Knt., of Ashton, Charlton, East Lydford, Knole (in Long Sutton), and Pitney Lorty, Somerset, Lord High Treasurer, 1375–7, Chancellor and Justiciar of Ireland, Admiral of the West, Governor of Dover Castle and Warden of the Cinque Ports, by his 1st wife, Elizabeth, daughter of Ralph Gorges, Knt., 1st Lord Gorges. They had no issue. His wife, Eleanor, died before 27 August 1369. He married (2nd) before 13 October 1374 (date of settlement) **ELIZABETH BETTESHORNE** (or **BISTORNE**), daughter and heiress of John de Betteshorne, Knt., of Bisterne (in Ringwood), Exbury, and Minstead, Hampshire, Gillingham, Dorset, Chaddenwick (in Mere) and West Grimstead, Wiltshire, etc., Knight of the Shire for Wiltshire and Hampshire, Sheriff of Hampshire, 1378–9, by Gouda (or Goda), kinswoman of William de Edington, Bishop of Winchester, and daughter and co-heiress of John de Cormailles, of East Hemsworth, Dorset. She was born about 1359/69 (aged 30 and more in 1399). They allegedly had fourteen sons, including Maurice, Knt., and three daughters, Joan, Eleanor, and Elizabeth. In 1387 he was pardoned for hunting in the Forest of Dean without license. In 1399 he and his wife, Elizabeth, obtained a license to augment a chapel at St. Mary, Mere, Wiltshire. He presented to the free chapel of Tockington, Gloucestershire in 1406, 1414, 1415, and 1427. In 1406 he and his wife, Elizabeth,

acquired the manor of Plaitford, Hampshire from Ralph Perot. In 1410 he and his wife, Elizabeth, obtained a license to found a chantry of one chaplain to celebrate divine service in the chapel of St. Mary in the manor of Bisterne (in Ringwood), Hampshire, and to endow it with a messuage, land, and rent there, and rent in Poulner, Hampshire. His wife, Elizabeth, was living 1410–11 (date of fine). He married (3rd) after 14 October 1412 and before 8 June 1427 **MARGARET CHEYNE**, widow successively of Thomas Brewes, Knt. [see TETBURY 9.i.b], of Bramley, Surrey, Tetbury, Gloucestershire, etc. (died 2 Sept. 1395), William Burcester, Knt. (died 1407) [see BURGHERSH 13], of Lesnes (in Erith), Kent, and Southwark, Surrey, Sheriff of Kent, 1389–90, Knight of the Shire for Kent, 1393, and William Breton, Esq. (living 1409–10), and daughter of Ralph de Cheyne, Knt. They had no issue. SIR JOHN BERKELEY died 5 March 1427/8. He left a will dated 21 Feb. 1427/8 (P.C.C. 9 Luffenam), requesting burial in St. Mary's chapel at Mere, Wiltshire. His widow, Margaret, died 12 (or 20) August 1444.

> Nash *Colls. for the Hist. of Worcestershire* 2 (1782): 119. Brydges *Collins' Peerage of England* 3 (1812): 591–627 (sub Earl of Berkeley). Cartwright *Parochial Topog. of the Rape of Bramber* 2(2) (1830): 369. Butterworth *Hist. Account of the Towns of Ashton-under-Lyne, Stalybridge, etc.* (1842): 14–15. *Sussex Arch. Colls.* 8 (1856): 96–131. Blunt Dursley & Its Neighbourhood (1877): 97–135. Smyth *Berkeley MSS* 1 (1883): 348–350. *Trans. Bristol & Gloucs. Arch. Soc.* 9 (1884–5): 268; 13 (1888–9): 247–251. Fisher *Cat. of the Tombs in the Churches of the City of London* (1885): 21. Jeayes Desc. Cat. of the Charters & Muniments in the Possession of the Rt. Hon. Lord Fitzhardinge (1892): xxii–xxiii (chart). Genealogist n.s. 13 (1896): 251; n.s. 36 (1920): 62–70 (biog. of Sir Robert Assheton). *List of Sheriffs for England & Wales* (PRO Lists and Indexes 9) (1898): 50, 54, 55, 123, 153. C.P.R. 1399–1401 (1903): 126. *List of Early Chancery Procs.* 2 (PRO Lists and Indexes 16) (1903): 505. Green *Feet of Fines for Somerset* 4 (Somerset Rec. Soc. 22) (1906): 38, 170. *List of Inqs. ad Quod Damnum* 2 (PRO Lists and Indexes 22) (1906): 557, 730. *Notes & Queries for Somerset & Dorset* 10 (1907): 137–139. VCH Hampshire 3 (1908): 290–291 (Bettesthorne arms: Argent a saltire gules with five stars or thereon); 4 (1911): 387–391, 542–543. C.P.R. 1408–1413 (1909): 168. Stawell *Quantock Fam.* (1910): 38–44. C.P. 2 (1912): 309–310 (sub Brewes); 6 (1926): 13, footnote 13 (sub Gorges); 10 (1945): 664–665 (sub Poynings). Benolte et al. *Peds. from the Vis. of Hampshire 1530, 1575, 1622 & 1634* (H.S.P. 64) (1913): 56–57 (Berkley ped.: "John Barkley = Elizebeth d. & heire of Sir John Bishorne knt."). Salzman *Abs. of Feet of Fines Rel. Sussex* 3 (Sussex Rec. Soc. 23) (1916): 223–227. VCH Worcester 4 (1924): 187. C.C.R. 1422–1429 (1933): 70–71. Stokes et al. *Warwickshire Feet of Fines* 3 (Dugdale Soc. 18) (1943): 130–131. VCH Wiltshire 7 (1953): 73. Davis *Anc. of Nicholas Davis* (1956): 168. Paget *Baronage of England* (1957) 56: 1 (sub Berkeley of Beverstone). Stow *Survey of London* (1971): 141. Cal. IPM 16 (1974): 81–83; 23 (2004): 52–59. VCH Somerset 3 (1974): 120–129. Saul *Knights & Esquires* (1981). VCH Gloucester 7 (1981): 228–229. Kirby *Abs. of Feet of Fines Rel. Wiltshire* (Wiltshire Rec. Soc. 41) (1986): 51. Keene & Harding Hist. Gaz. of London before the Great Fire (1987): 448–455. Roskell *House of Commons 1386–1421* 2 (1992): 197–199 (biog. of Sir John Berkeley), 219–220 (biog. of John Betteshorne), 353–354 (biog. of Sir Thomas Brewes), 410–412 (biog. of Sir William Burcester). VCH *Somerset* 8 (2004): 70-91. Berkeley Castle Muniments, BCM/A/5/9/4 (available at www.a2a.org.uk/search/index.asp). National Archives, C 1/69/154; C 143/441/5 (available at www.catalogue.nationalarchives.gov.uk/search.asp). Special thanks go to Doug Thompson for his identification of the maiden name and parentage of Margaret Cheyne, wife successively of Thomas de Brewes, Knt., William Burcester, Knt., William Brereton, Esq., and John Berkeley, Knt.

Children of John Berkeley, Knt., by Elizabeth Betteshorne:

i. **MAURICE BERKELEY**, Knt. [see next].

ii. **JOAN BERKELEY**, married before 1392–3 (date of fine) **THOMAS STAWELL**, Knt., of Cothelstone, Coschaevyssh, Stawell, and Stonystratton, Somerset, and Merton and Sutcombe, Devon, Knight of the Shire for Somerset, 1422, Sheriff of Devonshire, 1434–5, son and heir of Matthew Stawell, Knt., of Cothelstone, Somerset, by Eleanor, 1st daughter ad co-heiress of Richard Merton, Knt. They had no known issue. He married (2nd) before April 1396 **JOAN FRAMPTON**, daughter of Walter Frampton, of Buckland Ripers, Dorset. They had one son, Walter, Esq. [see ASHE 11.iii], and two daughters, Mary (wife of John Hill) and possibly Jane (wife of William Moore). He married (3rd) **MARGARET BURTON**, daughter of Henry Burton. In 1417 he served abroad in the retinue of John Arundel, Lord Mautravers. In 1423 he was named one of the executors of the will of Robert Hylle, of Spaxton. In 1437 he sued Elizabeth, late the wife of John Tuchet, Knt., her son, James Tuchet, Knt., her brother, John Stafford, Bishop of Bath and Wells, and William Lee for the manors of Nether Stowey, Honibere, etc., Somerset. A verdict was delivered in favor of the defendants. SIR THOMAS STAWELL died 14 Feb. 1439, and was buried in the south transept of the church of Glastonbury Abbey. His wife, Margaret, survived him. Pole *Colls. towards a Desc. of Devon* (1791): 380–381. St. George & Lennard *Vis. of Somerset 1623*

(H.S.P. 11) (1876): 106–107 (Stawell ped.: "Sir Thomas Stowell Knt. = Joan d. of Walter Frampton."). *List of Sheriffs for England & Wales* (PRO Lists and Indexes 9) (1898): 35. *Genealogist* n.s. 16 (1899): 240. Wrottesley *Peds. from the Plea Rolls* (1905): 312, 358. *Feudal Aids* 4 (1906): 366, 382, 394, 420. Green *Feet of Fines for Somerset* 4 (Somerset Rec. Soc. 22) (1906): 3, 22–23, 92, 93, 186–187. Stawell *Quantock Fam.* (1910): 38–44, 275–276, 323–327. Stokes et al. *Warwickshire Feet of Fines* 3 (Dugdale Soc. 18) (1943): 130–131. Dunning *Hylle Cartulary* (Somerset Rec. Soc. 68) (1968): 24, 34, 54. Roskell *House of Commons 1386–1421* 4 (1992): 470–471 (biog. of Sir Thomas Stawell).

iii. **ELEANOR BERKELEY**, married (1st) **JOHN ARUNDEL**, K.B., Lord Arundel and Mautravers [see ARUNDEL 11]; (2nd) **RICHARD POYNINGS**, Knt., of Poynings, Sussex [see POYNINGS 17]; (3rd) **WALTER HUNGERFORD**, K.G., K.B., 1st Lord Hungerford [see HUNGERFORD 11].

iv. **ELIZABETH BERKELEY**, married (1st) **EDWARD CHERLETON**, K.G., 5th Lord Cherleton[see CHERLETON 13]; (2nd) **JOHN SUTTON** (or **DUDLEY**), K.G., 1st Lord Dudley [see SUTTON 7].

9. MAURICE BERKELEY, Knt., of Beverstone, Gloucestershire, Bisterne (in Ringwood), Hampshire, Chaddenwick (in Mere), Wiltshire, Lower Ham, Somerset, Clevelode, Worcestershire, etc., Sheriff of Gloucestershire, 1435–6, son and heir, born about 1386 (aged 13 in 1400, aged 30 and more in 1428). He was originally intended for the church. In 1400, as "Morice, son of John de Berkeley, knight," he was granted a papal dispensation to hold a benefice without cure once he had became a clerk and to resign the benefice or exchange it as often as he pleased. He married after 10 Dec. 1427 (date of her mother's will) **LORA FITZ HUGH**, daughter of Henry Fitz Hugh, K.G., 3rd Lord Fitz Hugh, Lord High Treasurer, by Elizabeth, daughter and heiress of Robert de Grey, Knt. [see FITZ HUGH 7 for her ancestry]. They had three sons, Maurice, Knt., Thomas, and Edward, Knt. In 1427 he received papal indults for plenary indulgence, to have a portable altar, for the celebration of mass before daybreak, and to choose a confessor. Lora was a legatee in the 1427 will of her mother. He presented to the free chapel of Tockington, Gloucestershire in 1432 and 1457. He and his wife, Lora, were legatees in the 1455 will of his sister, Eleanor Berkeley, Countess of Arundel. In 1455 he was appointed one of the commissioners for Hampshire for raising money for the defense of Calais. At an unknown date, he and his wife, Lora, visited Rome where they stayed at the English Hospice there. SIR MAURICE BERKELEY died 5 May 1460. His widow, Lora, was living 12 March 1460/1.

Nash *Colls. for the Hist. of Worcestershire* 2 (1782): 119. Nicolas *Testamenta Vetusta* 1 (1826): 277–279 (will of Eleanor, Countess of Arundel). *Wills & Invs.* 1 (Surtees Soc. 2) (1835): 74–76 (will of Elizabeth Lady Fitzhugh). Nicolas *Procs. & Ordinances of the Privy Council* 6 (1837): 234–240, 339–341. Fuller *Hist. of the Worthies of England* (1840): 567–568. Blunt *Dursley & Its Neighbourhood* (1877): 97–135. Smyth *Berkeley MSS* 1 (1883): 351–352. *Trans. Bristol & Gloucs. Arch. Soc.* 13 (1888–9): 247–251. Birch *Cat. Seals in the British Museum* 2 (1892): 497 (seal of Maurice Berkeley dated 1428 — A shield of arms, couché: quarterly, 1, 4, a chevron between ten crosses crosslet, six in chief four in base, BERKELEY; 2, 3, on a saltire five mullets of six points, or roses, BEVERSTONE. Crest, on a helmet and mantling, a mitre, diapered with foliage. Supporters, two mermaids. Within a carved gothic panel, the inner edge ornamented with ball-flowers. Legend: S' mauricij de berkeley milit……[Bevers]ton et Bettesthorne.). *List of Sheriffs for England & Wales* (PRO Lists and Indexes 9) (1898): 50. *Papal Regs.: Letters* 5 (1904): 299–310; 7 (1906): 554–556. Benolte et al. *Peds. from the Vis. of Hampshire 1530, 1575, 1622 & 1634* (H.S.P. 64) (1913): 56–57 (Berkley ped.: "Morris Barkley of Beuerstone = Lora d. of…"). Clay *Extinct & Dormant Peerages* (1913): 72–75 (sub Fitz Henry). VCH *Worcester* 4 (1924): 187. *C.P.* 5 (1926): chart foll. 432 (sub FitzHugh); 12(1) (1953): 303 (sub Stourton). Harvey et al. *Vis. of the North* 3 (Surtees Soc. 144) (1930): 132–133 (Fitzhugh ped.: "Lora [Fitzhugh] nupta domino Mauricio de Barkeley"). Wedgwood *Hist. of Parl.* 1 (1936): 67–68 (biogs. of Sir Edward Berkeley; Sir Maurice Berkeley). *Trans. Bristol & Gloucestershire Arch. Soc.* 70 (1951): 94. Paget *Baronage of England* (1957) 56: 1 (sub Berkeley of Beverstone). *Bull. John Rylands Lib.* 40 (1957–8): 79–113, 391–431. Langley *Reg. of Thomas Langley Bishop of Durham* 3 (Surtees Soc. 169) (1959): 62–64. Allen *English Hospice in Rome* (1962): 76. VCH *Gloucester* 7 (1981): 228–229. *Cal. IPM* 23 (2004): 52–59. VCH *Somerset* 8 (2004): 70-91.

Children of Maurice Berkeley, Knt., by Lora Fitz Hugh:

i. **MAURICE BERKELEY**, Knt., of Beverstone, Gloucestershire, Bisterne (in Ringwood) and Minstead, Hampshire, etc., Sheriff of Gloucestershire, 1463–4, King's knight, King's councilor, son and heir. He married before 1455 **ANNE WEST**, daughter of Reynold West, Knt., 6th Lord la Warre, 3rd Lord West, by his 1st wife,

Margaret, daughter of Robert Thorley, Esq. [see WEST 10 for her ancestry]. They had one son, William, Knt., and one daughter, Katherine. He and his wife, Anne, were legatees in the 1455 will of his aunt, Eleanor Berkeley, Countess of Arundel. He presented to the church of Exton, Somerset in 1460 and 1465. SIR MAURICE BERKELEY died testate 5 May 1474. He and his wife, Anne, were buried in the Lady Chapel of Christ Church, Hampshire. Nicolas *Testamenta Vetusta* 1 (1826): 277–279 (will of Eleanor, Countess of Arundel). *Coll. Top. et Gen.* 2 (1835): 8. Blunt *Dursley & Its Neighbourhood* (1877): 97–135. *Trans. Bristol & Gloucs. Arch. Soc.* 13 (1888–9): 247–251. Weaver *Somerset Incumbents* (1889): 368. *Desc. Cat. Ancient Deeds* 2 (1894): 265–276. *List of Sheriffs for England & Wales* (PRO Lists and Indexes 9) (1898): 50. *C.P.R.* 1476–1485 (1901): 337. *Rpt. on MSS in Various Colls.* 4 (Hist. MSS Com. 55) (1907): 208–209. VCH *Hampshire* 4 (1911): 635–638. Benolte et al. *Peds. from the Vis. of Hampshire 1530, 1575, 1622 & 1634* (H.S.P. 64) (1913): 56–57 (Berkley ped.: "Sr Morris Barkley of Beuerstone in Com. ... knight = Anne d. of Reignald West lord Delaware."). Paget *Baronage of England* (1957) 56: 1 (sub Berkeley of Beverstone).

Children of Maurice Berkeley, Knt., by Anne West:

a. **WILLIAM BERKELEY**, Knt., of Beverstone, Gloucestershire, Bisterne (in Ringwood), Exbury, and Minstead, Hampshire, Exton, Somerset, etc., King's esquire, Sheriff of Hampshire, 1476–7, 1483, son and heir. He married **KATHERINE STOURTON**, daughter of William Stourton, 2nd Lord Stourton, by Margaret, 1st daughter and co-heiress of John Chidiock, Knt. [see CHIDIOCK 13]. They had no issue. He presented to the church of Exton, Somerset in 1475. In 1481 he released unspecified lands to Cecily, widow of John Forte, of Thornbury, Gloucestershire which his grandfather, Maurice Berkeley, Knt., and John Selwyn, clerk, previously had by the enfeoffment of the said John Forte. He took part in the plot of Henry Stafford, 2nd Duke of Buckingham against King Richard III in 1483. He was attainted, and his lands forfeited. SIR WILLIAM BERKELEY died in 1485. His widow, Katherine, married (2nd) before 1489 (as his 3rd wife) **HENRY** (or **HARRY**) **GREY**, Knt., 7th Lord Grey of Codnor [see CODNOR 14.i.a], son and heir of Henry Grey, Knt., 6th Lord Grey of Codnor, by Margaret, daughter and co-heiress of Henry Percy of Atholl, Knt. [see CODNOR 14.i for ancestry]. He was born about 1436 (aged 28 in 1464). They had no issue. By an unknown mistress (or mistresses), he had three illegitimate sons, Richard, Harry, and Harry Grey. SIR HENRY GREY, 7th Lord Grey of Codnor, died 8 April 1496. He left a will dated 10 Sept. 1492, proved 28 October 1496. His widow, Katherine, married (3rd) married before 26 April 1497 (date of presentment) **WILLIAM [DE LA] POLE**, Knt. [see DE LA POLE 10.i.e], of Wingfield, Suffolk, younger son of John [de la] Pole, Duke of Suffolk, by Elizabeth, daughter of Richard Plantagenet, K.G., 3rd Duke of York, 6th Earl of March, 9th Earl of Ulster, lord of Mortimer, Herefordshire and Clare, Suffolk [see DE LA POLE 10.i for his ancestry]. They had no issue. Sometime in or after 1496 Werburgh Brereton, daughter of Katherine, sister of William Berkeley, Knt., sued William Pole, Knt., son of John, Duke of Suffolk, and Katherine, lady Grey, his wife in Chancery regarding the detention of deeds relating to the castles and manors of Beverstone, Hatherley, Leckhampton, and Syde, Gloucestershire, etc. He presented to the church of Exton, Somerset in 1497. In 1503 William Stourton presented to the church of Great Kington, Dorset by grant of Katherine Grey, lady of the manor. William [de la] Pole was attainted in Parliament with his two brothers in Jan. 1503/4. He was still a prisoner in the Tower of London after the execution of his older brother, Edmund, Earl of Suffolk, in 1513. A bill was introduced in the House of Lords 10 Dec. 1515 for Katherine, wife of "William de la Poole." His wife, Katherine, Lady Grey died in London 25 Nov. 1521. William was listed first among the prisoners in the Tower in 1535 and again in 1538. SIR WILLIAM [DE LA] POLE was apparently living in October 1539, it is said in the Tower, but died before 20 Nov. 1539, when his name no longer appears in the list of the prisoners there. Nichols *Hist. & Antiqs. of Leicester* 3(2) (1804): 863 (Grey ped.). Glover *Hist. of Derby* 2 (1829): 308–312 (Grey ped.). Banks *Baronies in Fee* 1 (1844): 227–230 (sub Grey of Codnor). Burke *Gen. Hist. of the Dormant, Abeyant, Forfeited & Extinct Peerages* (1866): 247–249 (sub Grey). Wild *Hist. of Castle Bytham* (1871): 46–68. Blunt *Dursley & Its Neighbourhood* (1877): 97–135. *Trans. Bristol & Gloucs. Arch. Soc.* 13 (1888–9): 247–251. Weaver *Somerset Incumbents* (1889): 368. *Desc. Cat. Ancient Deeds* 1 (1890): 59–70, 105. *List of Sheriffs for England & Wales* (PRO Lists and Indexes 9) (1898): 55, 124. *C.P.R.* 1476–1485 (1901): 337, 530–531. VCH *Hampshire* 3 (1908): 290–291; 4 (1911): 635–638. Paget *Baronage of England* (1957) 56: 1 (sub Berkeley of Beverstone). Nottinghamshire Archives: Charlton of Chilwell, DD/CH/32/20 (will of Henry Grey, Lord Grey) (available at www.a2a.org.uk/search/index.asp). National Archives, C 1/84/73 (available at www.catalogue.nationalarchives.gov.uk/search.asp). Cornwall Rec. Office: Arundell of Lanherne & Trerice, AR/39/2 (ped. of Fitz Warin-Chidiock fams.) (available at www.a2a.org.uk/search/index.asp).

b. **KATHERINE BERKELEY**, married (1st) before 20 Feb. 1473/4 **JOHN STOURTON**, K.B., 3rd Lord Stourton, son and heir of William Stourton, 2nd Lord Stourton, by Margaret, daughter and co-heiress of John Chidiock, Knt. [see CHIDIOCK 13]. He was born about 1454. They had one son, Francis [4th Lord Stourton]. He was summoned to Parliament from 15 Nov. 1482 to 15 Sept. 1485. JOHN STOURTON, 3rd

Lord Stourton, died 6 October 1485. He left a will dated 18 August 1484, proved 1 July 1493, requesting burial at Mere, Wiltshire. His widow, Katherine, married (2nd) before 21 July 1486 **JOHN BRERETON**, Esq., of Plaitford, Hampshire, King's esquire, younger son of William Brereton, Knt., by Philippe, daughter of Hugh Hulse, Knt. They had two sons, John and John (again), and four daughters, Werburgh (or Warborough) (wife of Francis Cheyney, Knt. and William Compton, Knt.), Joan, Dorothy, and Dorothy (again). His wife, Katherine, was heiress in 1485 to her brother, William Berkeley, Knt., by which she inherited the manors of Bisterne (in Ringwood) and Minstead, Hampshire. In the period, 1486–93, he and his wife, Katherine, sister and heir to William Berkeley, of Bisterne, sued William Berkeley, Knt., of Weoley (in Northfield), Worcestershire in Chancery regarding the detention of deeds relating to the manor of Bisterne and other lands late of the said William Berkeley, of Bisterne. Katherine, Lady Stourton, died 25 June 1494. Burke *Gen. Hist. of the Dormant, Abeyant, Forfeited & Extinct Peerages* (1866): 74–75 (sub Brereton). Blunt *Dursley & Its Neighbourhood* (1877): 97–135. *Cal. IPM Henry VII* 1 (1898): 477–482. VCH *Hampshire* 3 (1908): 290–291; 4 (1911): 635–638. Benolte et al. *Peds. from the Vis. of Hampshire 1530, 1575, 1622 & 1634* (H.S.P. 64) (1913): 56–57 (Berkley ped.: "Catherin [Barkley] vx. John lord Stourton & ob. sp. = Sr John Brereton kn^t. 2. husband."). *C.P.* 12(1) (1953): 303 (sub Stourton). Paget *Baronage of England* (1957) 56: 1 (sub Berkeley of Beverstone). National Archives, C 1/85/48; C 241/267/16 (available at www.catalogue.nationalarchives.gov.uk/search.asp). Cornwall Rec. Office: Arundell of Lanherne & Trerice, AR/39/2 (ped. of Fitz Warin-Chidiock fams.) (available at www.a2a.org.uk/search/index.asp).

 ii. **THOMAS BERKELEY**. He was a legatee in the 1455 will of his aunt, Eleanor Berkeley, Countess of Arundel, who bequeathed him £10. Nicolas *Testamenta Vetusta* 1 (1826): 277–279 (will of Eleanor, Countess of Arundel). *Notes & Queries* 4th Ser. 7 (1871): 536–538.

 iii. **EDWARD BERKELEY**, Knt. [see next].

10. EDWARD BERKELEY, Knt., of Avon (in Sopley), Coldrey, Hussey's (in Froyle), Ibsley, and West Court (in Binsted), Hampshire, Beverstone, Over (in Almondsbury), Tockington, and Woodmancote (in Dursley), Gloucestershire, etc., Knight of the Shire for Sussex, 1463–5, Knight of the Shire for Hampshire, 1467–8, Sheriff of Hampshire, 1471–2, 1475–6, 1480–1, 1485, Sheriff of Gloucestershire, 1494–5, Bailiff of Burley (in New Forest), Hampshire, Lieutenant of Clarendon, Wiltshire, 3rd son. He was a legatee in the 1455 will of his aunt, Eleanor Berkeley, Countess of Arundel, who bequeathed him £10. He married (1st) before 1462 **CHRISTIAN HOLT**, daughter and co-heiress of Richard Holt, Esq., of Coldrey (in Froyle), Belney, and Brome, Hampshire, by Joan, daughter and heiress of _____ Barton of Derbyshire. They had one daughter, Lora. He married (2nd) before 1475 **ALICE COOKES** (or **COCKES**), widow of John Poyntz, Esq. (died 1465), of Iron Acton, Gloucestershire [see OWSLEY 9 for issue of this marriage], and daughter and heiress of John Cookes, of Bristol. They had three sons, Thomas, Esq., Maurice, and William, Knt. He was one of those licensed to found a chantry at Romsey, Hampshire in 1476. He was heir male in 1485 to his nephew, William Berkeley, Knt., of Beverstone, by which the Castle and manor of Beverstone, Gloucestershire and other properties passed to him by virtue of entail. He was named one of the executors of the 1489 will of his son-in-law, Thomas Montgomery, K.G. He presented to the free chapel of Tockington, Gloucestershire in 1492 and 1499. SIR EDWARD BERKELEY died 6 Feb. 1505/6. He left a will dated 4 Feb. 1505/6, proved 5 March 1505/6 (P.C.C. 4 Adeane), requesting burial at Christchurch Twynham, Hampshire. His widow, Alice, died in 1509.

Nicolas *Testamenta Vetusta* 1 (1826): 277–279 (will of Eleanor, Countess of Arundel); 2 (1826): 396. Blunt *Dursley & Its Neighbourhood* (1877): 97–135. Hawley et al. *Vis. of Essex 1552, 1558, 1570, 1612 & 1634* 1 (H.S.P. 13) (1878): 267–271 (1612 Vis.) (Poyntz ped.: "John Poyntz, Esquier, sonne and heire, obiit 5 Edw. 4th A[nn]o 1465. = Alice dau. to Cock"). Smyth *Berkeley MSS* 1 (1883): 353–354. Chitting & Phillipot *Vis. of Gloucester 1623, 1569 & 1582-3* (H.S.P. 21) (1885): 128–129 (Poyntz ped.: "John Poyntz esq^r ob. 12 E. 4. = Alice d. of .... Cox of Bristow = Sr Edward Barkley of Bev^rston Castell 2 husband."), 130–135 (Poyntz ped.: "Johannes Poyntz Ar. ob. 5 E. 4. = Alicia filia .... Cocks of Bristow.") (Cox arms: Argent, a bend sable, in sinister chief a [?trefoil] azure). *Trans. Bristol & Gloucs. Arch. Soc.* 13 (1888–9): 247–251. *Cal. IPM Henry VII* 1 (1898): 563. *List of Sheriffs for England & Wales* (PRO Lists and Indexes 9) (1898): 50, 55. VCH *Hampshire* 2 (1903): 286, 503, 516; 4 (1911): 28, 580; 5 (1912): 129. *List of Early Chancery Procs.* 5 (PRO Lists and Indexes 38) (1912): 385. Benolte et al. *Peds. from the Vis. of Hampshire 1530, 1575, 1622 & 1634* (H.S.P. 64) (1913): 56–57 (Berkley ped.: "Sir Edward Barkley knt. 2. sonn. = Christian d. & Coheire of Sir Ric. Holte knt."), 138 (White ped.: "Constance [Holte] vx. Sir Edward Barkley of Beverston"). *Letters & Papers... Henry*

VIII 1(1) (1920): 318; 3(2) (1867): 1046. *C.P.* 9 (1936): 337–338 (sub Mountjoy); 10 (1945): 131–133 (sub Ormond). Wedgwood *Hist. of Parl.* 1 (1936): 67 (biog. of Sir Edward Berkeley). Beachcroft *Two Compotus Rolls of Saint Augustine's Abbey, Bristol* (Bristol Rec. Soc. 9) (1938): 178 (Alice, wife of Edward Berkeley, Esq., styled "daughter and heir of John Cockes"), 179. *Cal. IPM Henry VII* 3 (1955): 25, 67–68. Paget *Baronage of England* (1957) 56: 1 (sub Berkeley of Beverstone). Sabin *Some Manorial Accounts of Saint Augustine's Abbey* (Bristol Rec. Soc. 22) (1960): 110–112. VCH *Gloucester* 7 (1981): 228–229. Leech *Top. of Medieval & Early Modern Bristol* 1 (Bristol Rec. Soc. 48) (1997): 108. Baker *Rpts. of Cases by John Caryll* 2 (Selden Soc. 116) (2000): 655–657.

Child of Edward Berkeley, Knt., by Christian Holt:

i. **LORA BERKELEY**, married (1st) **JOHN BLOUNT**, Knt., 3rd Lord Mountjoy; (2nd) **THOMAS MONTGOMERY**, K.G., of Faulkbourne, Essex [see NORBURY 15.ii]; (3rd) **THOMAS BUTLER** (otherwise **ORMOND**), K.B., 7th Earl of Ormond [see BUTLER 11].

Child of Edward Berkeley, Knt., by Alice Cookes:

i. **THOMAS BERKELEY**, Esq. [see next].

11. THOMAS BERKELEY, Esq., of Avon (in Sopley), Hampshire, son and heir apparent by his father's 2nd marriage. He married before 1 July 1491 **ELIZABETH NEVILLE**, daughter of George Neville, Knt., Lord Bergavenny, by his 1st wife, Margaret, daughter and heiress of Hugh at[te] Fenne, Esq. [see BERGAVENNY 15 for her ancestry]. They had one son, John, and four daughters, Lora (wife of John Ashburnham and John Daniel), Anne, Elizabeth (wife of George Herbert, Knt.), and Alice (wife of George Whetenhall, Gent.). His wife, Elizabeth, was a legatee in the 1491 will of her father. THOMAS BERKELEY, Esq., died in 1500. His widow, Elizabeth, married (2nd) (as his 2nd wife) **RICHARD COVERT**, Esq., of Slaugham, Ashington, Broadbridge (in Sullington), Sussex, and Hascombe, Surrey, Sheriff of Surrey and Sussex, 1522–3, son and heir of Thomas Covert. He was heir male in 1503 to his 1st cousin, John Covert, by which he inherited the manors of Hascombe and Wisley, Surrey and Twineham Benfield (in Twineham) and Trubweek (in Cockfield), Sussex. He presented to the church of Hascombe, Surrey in 1509. RICHARD COVERT, Esq., died 7 June 1547, and was buried in the chancel of the church of Slaugham, Sussex. He left a will dated 1546, proved 2 Nov. 1547 (P.C.C. 48 Alen), naming his 4th wife, Blanche, who survived him.

Blore *Hist. & Antiqs. of Rutland* 1(2) (1811): 19 (Despenser ped.). Rowland *Noble Fam. of Nevill* (1830). Burke *Gen. & Heraldic Hist. of the Extinct & Dormant Baronetcies* (1844): 139 (sub Covert). Blunt *Dursley & Its Neighbourhood* (1877): 97–135. Foster *Royal Lineage of Our Noble & Gentle Fams.* (1883): 3–10. Smyth *Berkeley MSS* 1 (1883): 354. *Trans. Bristol & Gloucs. Arch. Soc.* 13 (1888–9): 247–251. Hare *Sussex* (1894): 144. *List of Sheriffs for England & Wales* (PRO Lists and Indexes 9) (1898): 137. *Sussex Arch. Colls.* 47 (1904): 116–147. *Maryland Hist. Mag.* 1 (1906): 182–183. Williams *Llyfr Baglan* (1910): 180–181 (Herbert ped.). VCH *Surrey* 3 (1911): 102–104, 378–381. Benolte et al. *Peds. from the Vis. of Hampshire 1530, 1575, 1622 & 1634* (H.S.P. 64) (1913): 56–57 (Berkley ped.: "Thomas Barkley of [the] Vine in Com. Southampton = Elizebeth d. of George Neuell lord Aburgaueny"). *Letters & Papers... Henry VIII* 1(1) (1920): 318; 3(2) (1867): 1046. Benolte & Cooke *Vis. of Kent 1530–1, 1574 & 1592* 1 (H.S.P. 74) (1923): 3 (1530–1 Vis.) (Brent ped.), 33 (1574 Vis.) (Brent ped.); 2 (H.S.P. 75) (1924): 115–116 (1592 Vis.) (Whetenhall ped.). Paget *Baronage of England* (1957) 56: 1 (sub Berkeley of Beverstone). VCH *Gloucester* 7 (1981): 228–229. VCH *Sussex* 6(2) (1986): 20–24, 65–67; 7 (1940): 147–163, 181–186, 186–191. *National Lib. of Wales Jour.* 25 (1988): 387–398. Baker *Rpts. of Cases by John Caryll* 2 (Selden Soc. 116) (2000): 655–657.

12. ANNE BERKELEY, 2nd daughter and co-heiress, was a legatee in the 1506 will of her grandfather, Edward Berkeley, Knt. She was co-heiress before 1522 to her niece, Anne Berkeley, by which she inherited a one-fourth interest in the manor of Syde, Gloucestershire. She married **JOHN BRENT**, of Charing, Kent, son of John Brent, senior, of Charing, Kent. They had two sons, William and Thomas, and two daughters, Amy (wife of William Crispe) and Margaret. The estate of John Brent was administered by his son, Thomas Brent, 4 August 1565. His widow, Anne, died in 1571/2.

Wotton *English Baronetage* 2 (1741): 17. Foster *Royal Lineage of Our Noble & Gentle Fams.* (1883): 3–10. Smyth *Berkeley MSS* 1 (1883): 354. Philipot *Vis. of Kent 1619–21* (H.S.P. 42) (1898): 211–212 (Add'l. Peds.) (Brent ped.: "John Brent

= Ann 2 da. & coheire of Tho. Berkley 22 H. 8 vidua 37 H. 8 dyed 14 Q. Eliz."). *List of Early Chancery Procs.* 5 (PRO Lists and Indexes 38) (1912): 385. Benolte et al. *Peds. from the Vis. of Hampshire 1530, 1575, 1622 & 1634* (H.S.P. 64) (1913): 56–57 (Berkley ped.: "Anne [Barkley] vx. John Brent of Charing in Kent"). Benolte & Cooke *Vis. of Kent 1530–1, 1574 & 1592* 1 (H.S.P. 74) (1923): 3 (1530–1 Vis.) (Brent ped.): "John Brent of Charing = Anne dowghter and one of the heyres of Thomas Barkeley of Avyne in Hampsher"), 33 (1574 Vis.) (Brent ped.: "John Brent of Charing in Com. Canc. = Anne daughter and Coheire of Berkley of Hamshire") (Brent arms: Gules, a wyvern sejant, the tail nowed argent). Wedgwood *Hist. of Parl.* 1 (1936): 67, footnote 3. Brent *Descs. of Giles Brent* (1946): 31, 34. VCH *Gloucester* 7 (1981): 228–229. *Virginia Gen.* 38 (1994): 284–289. Baker *Rpts. of Cases by John Caryll* 2 (Selden Soc. 116) (2000): 655–657.

13. MARGARET BRENT, sister and heiress to Thomas Brent, Esq. She married (1st) before 1525 **JOHN DERING**, Esq., of Surrenden Dering, Kent, Burgess (M.P.) for New Romney, justice of the peace for Kent, son and heir of Nicholas Dering, Esq., of Surrenden, Knt., by Alice, daughter and co-heiress of William Bettenham, of Bettenham Wood, Cranbrook, Kent. He was born before 1504. They had five sons, Richard, Esq., Anthony, Esq., John, Esq., Edward, and Christopher, Gent., and four daughters, Anne (wife of William Swann and Ralph Haymond), Bennett (wife of Francis Bourne, Esq.), Martha (wife of _____ Hutchins and _____ Guildford), and Margaret (wife of _____ Harison). JOHN DERING, Esq., died testate in 1550, and was buried at Pluckley, Kent. His widow, Margaret, married (2nd) **JOHN MOORE**, Esq., of Benenden. They had issue. She was buried at Pluckley, Kent 1 Dec. 1560.

Wotton *English Baronetage* 2 (1741): 15. Betham *Baronetage of England* 1 (1801): 289. *Arch. Cantiana* 10 (1876): 327 (1619 Vis. Kent). Foster *Royal Lineage of Our Noble & Gentle Fams.* (1883): 3–10. Smyth *Berkeley MSS* 1 (1883): 354 (of Puckley in Kent). Philipot *Vis. of Kent 1619–21* (H.S.P. 42) (1898): 139–141 (1619 Vis.) (Dering ped.: "Johannes Dering Ar. = Margareta filia Joh'is Brent soror et vnica hær. Tho: Brent et consang et hær. Rob'ti Brent de Wilsborough"), 206–209 (Add'l. Peds.) (Dering ped.: Dering arms: Or, a saltire sable), 211–212 (Add'l Peds.) (Brent ped.: "Margareta Brent = John Dering of Surrenden Dering esq., renupta… Moore"). *Genealogist* n.s. 33 (1917): 269. Benolte & Cooke *Vis. of Kent 1530–1, 1574 & 1592* 1 (H.S.P. 74) (1923): 3 (1530–1 Vis.) (Brent ped.: "M'get [Brent] = John Derynge sonne & heire to Nicholas Derynge of…"), 33 (1574 Vis.) (Brent ped.: "Margarett [Brent] maried vnto John Deering"); 2 (H.S.P. 75) (1924): 95–96 (1592 Vis.) (Deringe ped.: "[John Deri]nge of Pluckly aforsaide Esquire Sonne and heire of [Nic]holas maried Margaret Daughter of John Brent of Charinge in the saide Countie Esquire"). Brent *Descs. of Giles Brent* (1946): 31. Bindoff *House of Commons 1509–1558* 2 (1982): 39 (biog. of John Dering). *Virginia Gen.* 38 (1994): 284–289. Deeds #318 & 330, English Deeds Coll., Harvard Law School Lib. — available at http://hollis.harvard.edu//?itemid=%7clibrary%2fm%2faleph%7c003307090 and http://hollis.harvard.edu//?itemid=%7clibrary%2fm%2faleph%7c003311595.

14. RICHARD DERING, Esq., of Surrenden, Kent, son and heir, born about 1530. He married about 1557 **MARGARET TWYSDEN**, of Chelmington (in Great Chart), Kent, daughter of William Twysden, Esq., of Peckham, Kent, by Elizabeth, daughter of Thomas Roydon, Esq. [see CROMER 19 for her ancestry]. They had four sons, Anthony, Knt., George, Edward, and Thomas, and three daughters, Bennett, Jane (wife of Henry Haule, Esq.), and Elizabeth (wife of William Skeffington, Knt., 1st Baronet). In 1566 he and his wife, Margaret, had the reversion of the manor of Eastbridge, Kent settled on them by her mother. His wife, Margaret, was buried at Pluckley, Kent 2 August 1608. RICHARD DERING was buried at Pluckley, Kent 6 March 1611.

Wotton *English Baronetage* 2 (1741): 17. Lodge *Peerage of Ireland* 2 (1789): 373–374 (sub Skeffington, Earl of Massereene). Betham *Baronetage of England* 1 (1801): 290. Larking *Procs. Principally in Kent* (Camden Soc. 80) (1862): 3 (Dering ped.). Burke *Gen. Hist. of the Dormant, Abeyant, Forfeited & Extinct Peerages* (1866): 496–497 (sub Skeffington, Earl of Massereene). *Arch. Cantiana* 10 (1876): 327. Smyth *Berkeley MSS* 1 (1883): 354. Philipot *Vis. of Kent 1619–21* (H.S.P. 42) (1898): 139–141 (1619 Vis.) (Dering ped.: "Richardus Dering de Surrenden = Margareta filia Will'i Twisden Ar."), 206–209 (Add'l Peds.) (Dering ped.: "Ric'dus Dering de Surrenden ar. = Margareta filia Wm. Twisden de Peckham ar."). *Genealogist* n.s. 33 (1917): 269. Benolte & Cooke *Vis. of Kent 1530–1, 1574 & 1592* 1 (H.S.P. 74) (1923): 33 (1574 Vis.) (Brent ped.: "Richard [Deering]"); 2 (H.S.P. 75) (1924): 41 (1574 Vis.) (Twysden ped.: "Margarett Twysden = Richard Deringe of Pluckeley"). Ward *Fam. of Twysden & Twisden* (1939). *Virginia Gen.* 38 (1994): 284–289.

15. BENNETT DERING, baptized at Pluckley, Kent 12 April 1568. She married by license dated 26 Jan. 1594 **JOHN FISHER**, Gent., son of Alexander Fisher, of Debtling, Kent, by Katherine, daughter of Peter Maplesden. He was baptized at Debtling, Kent 15 March 1563. They had four sons, Alexander, George, John, and Henry, and one daughter, Elizabeth.

> *Arch. Cantiana* 10 (1876): 327. Philipot *Vis. of Kent 1619–21* (H.S.P. 42) (1898): 139–141 (1619 Vis.) (Dering ped.: "Benetta [Dering] vx' Joh's Fisher"), 159 (Fisher ped.: "Joh'es ffisher de Maidstone = Benetta filia Ric'di Deering") (Fisher arms: Argent, on a chief gules a dolphin embowed of the field). Benolte & Cooke *Vis. of Kent 1530–1, 1574 & 1592* 2 (H.S.P. 75) (1924): 96 (1592 Vis.). *Virginia Gen.* 38 (1994): 284–289. Dorman *Adventurers of Purse & Person* 1 (2004): 954–969.

16. JOHN FISHER, 3rd son, baptized at Pluckley, Kent 7 March 1601, resided at Eastern Shore, Virginia in Feb. 1623/4. He married **ELIZABETH** _____. She was born about 1610 (aged 36 in 1646). They had three sons, John, Stephen, and Philip. He was agent for his 1st cousin, [Capt.] William Epes. JOHN FISHER left a will dated 4 Dec. 1639, proved 23 March 1639/40, in Northampton County, Virginia. His widow, Elizabeth, married (2nd) **HENRY WEED** (will proved 26 Dec. 1649), and (3rd) **RICHARD BAYLY** (will proved 29 October 1661). She was living 12 June 1661 (date of her last husband's will).

> Ames *County Court Recs. of Accomack-Northampton, Virginia* 1 (American Legal Recs. 7) (1954): 161–162. Dorman *Adventurers of Purse & Person* 1 (2004): 954–969.

ᛋ FITZ ALAN ᛋ

> **ROGER D'AUBENEY**, married **AMICE** _____.
> **WILLIAM D'AUBENEY**, of Buckenham, Norfolk, married **MAUD LE BIGOD**.
> **WILLIAM D'AUBENEY**, of Buckenham, Norfolk, married **ALICE OF LOUVAIN**, Queen of England.
> **WILLIAM D'AUBENEY**, 2nd Earl of Arundel, married **MAUD DE SAINT HILARY**.
> **WILLIAM D'AUBENEY**, Earl of Arundel, married **MABEL OF CHESTER** (desc. King William the Conqueror) [see CLIFTON 5].

6. ISABEL D'AUBENEY, married before 1223 (as his 1st wife) **JOHN FITZ ALAN**, of Clun, Acton Round, Cound, Montford, Oswestry, and Shrawardine, Shropshire, Trafford, Cheshire, Caverswall, Forsbrook (in Dilhorne), and Weston Coyney (in Caverswall), Staffordshire, Keevil, Wiltshire, etc., 2nd son of William Fitz Alan, of Clun and Oswestry, Shropshire, by _____, daughter of Hugh de Lacy. They had one son, John, Knt. He was heir in 1215 to his older brother, William Fitz Alan. He married (2nd) **HAWISE DE BLANCMINSTER**. JOHN FITZ ALAN died testate shortly before 15 March 1240. His widow, Hawise, died shortly before 19 September 1242.

> Blomefield *Essay towards a Top. Hist. of Norfolk* 9 (1808): 42–59. *Dignity of a Peer of the Realm* (1826): 389–448. Eyton *Antiqs. of Shropshire* 7 (1858): 211–262; 10 (1860): 326. Burke *Gen. Hist. of the Dormant, Abeyant, Forfeited & Extinct Peerages* (1866): 2–3 (sub Albini, Earls of Arundel). *Colls. Hist. Staffs.* 1 (1880): 218. Eyton *Domesday Studies* (1881): 99–100. Flower *Vis. of Yorkshire 1563–4* (H.S.P. 16) (1881): 176–177 (Knevet ped.: "Izabella [Dawbeny] nupta. = Johanni Fytz Allen Militi."). Wrottesley *Peds. from the Plea Rolls* (1905): 244–245, 531–532, 550. *C.P.* 1 (1910): 237; 4: 670 chart i. Farrer *Honors & Knights' Fees* 2 (1924): 10–11. Farnham *Leicestershire Medieval Peds.* (1925): 11 (ped. of Earls of Chester). Harvey et al. *Vis. of the North* 3 (Surtees Soc. 144) (1930): 152–156 (Daubeny ped.: "Isabella [Daubeney] nupta Iohanni Fitz-Aleyn (militi)"). VCH *Sussex* 4 (1953): 121–126. Sanders *English Baronies* (1960): 2, 71.

7. JOHN FITZ ALAN, Knt., of Oswestry, Acton Round, Clun, and Shrawardine, Shropshire, Trafford, Cheshire, Boarhunt, Hampshire, Keevil, Wiltshire, etc., Chief Butler of England, son and heir by his father's 1st marriage, born about 1223 (certified to be of age in May 1244). He married before 1240 **MAUD DE VERDUN**, daughter of Thebaud le Boteler, 2nd Lord Boteler, by his 2nd wife, Rohese (or Rose), daughter and heiress of Nicholas de Verdun. Her maritagium included property at Flecknoe (in Wolfhamcote), Warwickshire. They had one son, John, and allegedly one daughter, Joan. He was co-heir in 1243 to his uncle, Hugh d'Aubeney, Earl of Arundel, by which he inherited the Castle and Honour of Arundel, Sussex. In 1244 he made fine with the king by £1000 for having seisin of all castles and lands formerly held by his father. In 1253 he accompanied King Henry III to Gascony. In 1254 he was granted free warren in a number of manors, including Acton Round, Cound, Harnage, Rodington, Shrawardine, Upton Magna, and Wroxeter, Shropshire, Trafford, Cheshire, Norton, Oxfordshire, Stokes, Sussex, and Lavington, Wiltshire. In 1258, as "Sir John Fitz Alan, lord of Arundel," he settled a dispute with Boniface, Archbishop of Canterbury, regarding the right of hunting and taking venison within the forests of the honor of Arundel. He served as Captain-General of all the forces for guarding the Marches, 1258–60. In 1259 the king by Laurence del Brok appeared against him in a plea that after the death of Roger Corbet that the said John intruded himself into Roger's manors of Hedlegh, Haiton, and Tasley, the custody of which belonged to the king. In 1262–3, as "John Fitz Alan," he was summoned to attend at Hereford for the defense of the marches of Wales. In 1263 he sued the Master of the Knights Templar for disseizing him of his free tenement in La Hethe, Shropshire. In December 1263 he was one of those who signed the instrument which bound the barons to abide by the award of King Louis IX of France. He was one of the barons who held Rochester Castle for the king against Simon de Montfort in 1264. He was taken prisoner at the Battle of Lewes 12 May 1264. In 1265 he was required to give either his son and heir or the castle of Arundel as a security for peace. SIR JOHN FITZ ALAN died shortly before 10 Nov. 1267. He left a will dated 6 October 1267, requesting burial at Haughmond Abbey, Shropshire. His widow, Maud, married (2nd) **RICHARD DE AMUNDEVILLE**. In 1278 it was reported that Richard and his wife, Maud, were making great waste in the woods in Acton Round, Shropshire which belonged to Maud's dower. His wife, Maud, died 27 Nov. 1283.

Dignity of a Peer of the Realm (1826): 389–448 ("It is particularly remarkable, that in many of the documents relating to John Fitzalan the father, and John Fitzalan the son, after the partition of the inheritance of the Earl[dom] of Arundel, they are described by the addition 'de Arundell'."). Eyton *Antiqs. of Shropshire* 4 (1857): 14–19, 121–124; 7 (1858): 211–262. Wrottesley *Feet of Fines: Henry III* (Colls. Hist. Staffs. 4) (1883): 238–259. Wrottesley *Staffordshire Suits: Plea Rolls* (Colls. Hist. Staffs. 4) (1883): 134–147. Doyle *Official Baronage of England* 1 (1886): 68 (sub Arundel). Wrottesley *Peds. from the Plea Rolls* (1905): 244–245, 531–532. VCH *Hampshire* 3 (1908): 144-147. *C.P.* 1 (1910): 239-240, 253; 4:670 chart i. *Cal. IPM* 4 (1913): 53. Sanders *English Baronies* (1960): 71, 124.

Children of John Fitz Alan, Knt., by Maud de Verdun:

i. **JOHN FITZ ALAN**, Knt. [see next].

ii. **JOAN FITZ ALAN** (alleged daughter), married **RICHARD OF CORNWALL**, Knt., of Asthall, Oxfordshire [see CORNWALL 7].

8. **JOHN FITZ ALAN**, of Arundel, Sussex, Chipping Norton, Oxfordshire, Clun, Oswestry, and Shrawardine, Shropshire, etc., Chief Butler of England, son and heir, born 14 Sept. 1246. He married before 14 May 1260 (date of fine) **ISABEL DE MORTIMER**, daughter of Roger de Mortimer, Knt., of Wigmore, Herefordshire, by Maud, daughter and co-heiress of William de Brewes, Knt. [see MORTIMER 8 for her ancestry]. Her maritagium included 40 librates of land in Doddington [Earl's Ditton] (in Cleobury Mortimer), Shropshire. They had two sons, Richard, Knt. [8th Earl of Arundel] and John, and one daughter, Maud. As "John son and heir of John Fitz Alan," he did homage to the king for his lands 10 Dec. 1267. In March 1268, as "John Fitz Alan," he was pardoned half of the relief for his lands which he owed the king. In 1269 the king ordered him to deliver the manor of Ledbury North, Herefordshire to Reynold de Akele, guardian of the void bishopric of Hereford. In 1269 he was involved in a controversy with the abbey of St. Peter's, Shrewsbury regarding the advowson of the church of Oswestry, Shropshire; Anian, Bishop of St. Asaph, instituted his presentee to the church in defiance of the abbey. In 1270 he leased the manor of Chipping Norton, Oxfordshire to the Abbess and nuns of Fontevrault for a term of ten years. In 1271 he granted Bishop Anian certain lands at Martinchurch near Chirk within the lordship of Oswestry. In Jan. 1271 the king pardoned him all debts, penalties, and usuries which he owed to

Hagin son of Master Mosseus, Jew of London. JOHN FITZ ALAN died testate 18 March 1271/2, and was buried at Haughmond Abbey, Shropshire. His widow, Isabel, married (2nd) before 14 Feb. 1276 **RALPH D'ARDERNE**, of Souldern, Oxfordshire, probably younger son of Ralph d'Arderne, Knt., of Horndon and Ovesham (in Matching), Essex, Souldern, Oxfordshire, Yeovil, Somerset, etc., by Erneburg, probable daughter of Ralph de Assartis. In 1277 Anian, Bishop of St. Asaph, contested her right of presentation to the church of Llanymynech, Montgomeryshire which advowson had been assigned to her as part of her dower. In 1281 she instituted fresh proceedings in the king's court, which resulted in a royal writ of distraint on the bishop's goods. Archbishop Peckham wrote both her and her father in Nov. 1281, requesting that she desist from the suit against the bishop, threatening to excommunicate her if his words were not attended. The living remained unfilled, and in 1284 Archbishop Peckham committed it to Bishop Anian. In 1279 she was involved in a dispute with Llywelyn, Prince of Wales, regarding a transgression in the woods of Oswestry, Shropshire. In 1279 she committed herself to paying a rent of £200 yearly to the abbey of Vale Royal, in return for the custody of Oswestry Castle. In 1280 she obtained custody of the Castle and Honour of Arundel to hold during her son's minority. SIR RALPH D'ARDERNE was living 4 April 1283. In Nov. 1283 a commission was appointed to investigate the persons who entered the free chace of Isabel at Arundel and hunted and carried away deer. She held the patronage of Cold Norton Priory, Oxfordshire in 1284–5. Isabel married (3rd) at Poling, Sussex 2 Sept. 1285 (as his 2nd wife) **ROBERT [DE] HASTANG**, of Chebsey, Staffordshire, and Budbrook, Leamington Hastings, Newbold Pacey, and Whitnash, Warwickshire, son and heir of Robert Hastang, of Chebsey, Staffordshire, and Budbrook and Leamington Hastings, Warwickshire, by Joan, daughter of William de Curli. In 1272 John le Moyne appeared against him in a plea that he and others, during the disturbances in the kingdom, had burnt his houses at Shallowford (in Chebsey), Staffordshire, and carried away goods and chattels to the value of £300. In 1274–5 Thebaud de Neville arraigned an assize of novel disseisin against him and others regarding a tenement in Hill, Warwickshire. The same year Master John Giffard arraigned an assize of novel disseisin against him and others regarding a tenement in Walton, Staffordshire. In 1277–8 Alice the widow of Gervase de Levedale sued Robert de Hastang, of Chebsey, and Gilbert de Wandingfeld for a third of a messuage and a virgate of land in Shallowford (in Chebsey), Staffordshire as her dower. In 1277–8 Radulph Fitz Roger arraigned an assize of novel disseisin against him regarding a messuage and land in Whitnash, Warwickshire. In 1280–1 Robert arraigned an assize of novel disseissin against Hugh de Wyverston regarding common of pasture in Hilcot, Staffordshire. In 1282, he was granted letters of protection for one year, he then going to Ireland on the king's service. He held the patronage of Cold Norton Priory in 1288–9. Isabel de Mortimer, lady of Arundel, died before 1 April 1292, on which date her heirs and executors were discharged from the payment of arrears of £115 which she owed on the farm of West Dean and Charlton (in Singleton), Sussex; Robert de Hastang "sometime" her husband was ordered to pay £20 per year towards the arrears. She was was buried besides her 1st husband at Haughmond Abbey, Shropshire. ROBERT DE HASTANG was living 7 Sept. 1299.

Blomefield *Essay towards a Top. Hist. of Norfolk* 10 (1809): 16–20. Baker *Hist. & Antiqs. of Northampton* 1 (1822–30): 547. Owen *Hist. of Shrewsbury* 1 (1825): 370; 2 (1825): 79 (Fitz Alan pedigree). *Dignity of a Peer of the Realm* (1826): 389–434 ("It is particularly remarkable, that in many of the documents relating to John Fitzalan the father, and John Fitzalan the son, after the partition of the inheritance of the Earl[dom] of Arundel, they are described by the addition 'de Arundell'."). Dallaway *Hist. of the Western Div. of Sussex* 2(1) (1832): 120–121. Tierney *Hist. & Antiqs. of the Castle & Town of Arundel* 1 (1834): chart foll. 192 (states in error that Isabel de Mortimer, widow of John Fitz Alan, was living in 1300); 200. *Coll. Top. et Gen.* 2 (1835): 275. Eyton *Antiqs. of Shropshire* 4 (1857): 355–356; 7 (1858): 228–229 (Fitz Alan chart), 256–260. *Collectanea Archaeologia* 1 (1862): 48. Haddan *Councils & Eccl. Docs. Rel. Great Britain & Ireland* 1 (1869): 532–533. *Recs. of Buckinghamshire* 5 (1878): 183–189. *Colls. Hist. & Arch. rel. to Montgomeryshire* 12 (1879): 118–121. Flower *Vis. of Yorkshire 1563–4* (H.S.P. 16) (1881): 336–338 (Warren ped.: "John Fytzallen Erl of Arundel. = Izabell daughter of Edmund Mortymer, Earl of March."). Martin *Registrum Epistolarum Fratris Johannis Peckham, Archiepiscopi*

Cantuariensis 1 (Rolls Ser. 77) (1882): 250–252. Ormerod *Hist. of the County Palatine & City of Chester* 2 (1882): 36–37. *Annual Rpt. of the Deputy Keeper* 44 (1883): 7, 11, 136, 250, 280; 45 (1885): 254, 369; 47 (1886): 193, 389; 49 (1888): 66–67; 50 (1889): 116. *Arch. Cambrensis* 5th Ser. 1 (1884): 219–221 (Fitzalan ped.). Doyle *Official Baronage of England* 1 (1886): 69 (sub Arundel). Wrottesley *Staffordshire Suits: Plea Rolls* (Colls. Hist. Staffs. 7(1)) (1886): 50–65. Lloyd *Hist. of the Princes, the Lords Marcher, & the Ancient Nobility of Powys Fadog* 6 (1887): 320–323. Moore *Hist. of the Foreshore & the Law Relating Thereto* (1888): 97–98. *Desc. Cat. Ancient Deeds* 1 (1890): 47–59. Birch *Cat. Seals in the British Museum* 2 (1892): 427 (seal of Ralph d'Arderne Knt. dated late 13th Cent.). Blomfield *Hist. of Souldern* (1893): 10. C.P.R. 1281–1292 (1893): 9, 90. Mackenzie *Castles of England: Their Hist. & Structure* 2 (1897): 151–152. *Procs. Somerset Arch. & Nat. Hist. Soc.* 44 (1898): 209–210. C.C.R. 1272–1279 (1900): 350. Morris *Welsh Wars of Edward I* (1901): Pedigree V foll. 314 (Fitzalan-Warenne ped.). C.C.R. 1279–1288 (1902): 204, 213, 227, 260, 373, 451. *Scots Peerage* 1 (1904): 8. *Trans. Shropshire Arch. & Natural Hist. Soc.* 3rd Ser. 4 (1904): 322–323; 3rd Ser. 8(2) (1908): Miscellanea foll. pg. 150, i–iv; 3rd Ser. 9(2) (1909): 163–179. Cantilupe *Reg. Thome de Cantilupo Episcopi Herefordensis* (Canterbury & York Soc. 2) (1907): 243. Martin *Hist. of the Manor of Westhope* (1909): 15–33. C.P. 1 (1910): 240 (sub Arundel); 4 (1916): Appendix H, 670 (chart); 14 (1992): 38 (sub Arundel). C.F.R. 1 (1911): 74, 77, 127, 309. C.P.R. 1266–1272 (1913): 376, 428, 488–489, 502–503. *Jour. Flintshire Hist. Soc.* 5 (1915): 14–15, 22–23. Salter *Feet of Fines for Oxfordshire 1195–1291* (Oxfordshire Rec. Soc. 12) (1930): 241–242. Stokes et al. *Warwickshire Feet of Fines* 1 (Dugdale Soc. 11) (1932): 185–186. Edwards *Cal. Ancient Corr. Concerning Wales* (Board of Celtic Studies, Hist. & Law 2) (1935): 144. Richardson & Sayles *Rotuli Parl. Anglie Hactenus Inediti 1274–1373* (Camden Soc. 3rd Ser. 51) (1935): 7. *Trans. Shropshire Arch. & Nat. Hist. Soc.* 51 (1941–43): 135–136. VCH *Warwick* 5 (1949): 122–124. *VCH Oxford* 6 (1959): 301–312. Sanders *English Baronies* (1960): 70–71. VCH *Essex* 8 (1983): 196–206. Waugh *Lordship of England* (1988): 131–132. Brault *Rolls of Arms Edward I* 2 (1997): 17, 166 (arms of John Fitz Alan: Gules, a lion rampant or). Smith & London *Heads of Religious Houses, England & Wales* 2 (2001): 370. Weiler et al. *Thirteenth Century England* 11 (2007): 178–179. Lieberman *Medieval March of Wales* (2010): 133. Shropshire Archives: Lloyd of Leaton Knolls, 103/1/3/65 (grant dated c. 1272 by Isabel de Mortimer, Lady Arundel to Hugh son of Hugh, Forester of Shrawardine) (available at www.a2a.org.uk/search/index.asp).

Children of John Fitz Alan, by Isabel de Mortimer:

i. **RICHARD FITZ ALAN**, Knt. [see next].

ii. **JOHN FITZ ALAN**. In 1292, as "John Fitz Alan de Arundel," he was called to warranty regarding a messuage and lands in La Hethe, Shropshire. He was living in 1295. Eyton *Antiqs. of Shropshire* 4 (1857): 14–19. *Index to Ancient Correspondence of the Chancery and the Exchequer, Vol. 1: A–K* (Lists and Indexes, Supplementary Series, No. XV) (1902): 14 (John Fitz Alan styled "brother" of Richard Fitz Alan in letter dated 1295). Edwards *Cal. Ancient Corr. Concerning Wales* (Board of Celtic Studies, Hist. & Law 2) (1935): 144.

iii. **MAUD FITZ ALAN**, married (1st) **PHILIP BURNELL**, Knt., of Holgate, Shropshire [see BURNELL 9]; (2nd) **ROBERT DE BRUS**, Knt., Earl of Carrick, Lord Brus [see BRUS 7]; (3rd) **SIMON DE CRIKETOT** [see BURNELL 9].

9. RICHARD FITZ ALAN (or DE ARUNDEL),[25] Knt., 8th Earl of Arundel, of Arundel, Sussex, Acton Round, Clun, Oswestry, Shrawardine, and Wroxeter, Shropshire, Chipping Norton,

---

[25] Earl Richard Fitz Alan above, his father and grandfather all employed the surname *Fitz Alan*. In the 1270's, Earl Richard's father was styled John "Fitz Alan de Arundel" in several records [see *C.P.R. 1272–1281* (1901): 11, 96, 161, 331]. In 1291 Earl Richard received a grant addressed to him as "Richard de Arundel, Earl of Arundel" [see C.P. 1 (1910): 241]. In the same period, 1291–1302, Earl Richard's brother, John, was likewise styled John de Arundel [see Rees *Cartulary of Haughmond Abbey* (1985): 227]. Following Earl Richard's death in 1302, the family dropped the surname *Fitz Alan* in favor of *de Arundel* (or simply *Arundel*). The last known use of the name *Fitz Alan* by any member of this family dates c.1312–3, when Earl Richard's son, Edmund, brought a writ as "Edmund Fitz Alan" [see *Year Books of Edward III* 12 (Rolls Ser. 31b) (1905): 518–521]. Thereafter, all further references to this family employ the surname *Arundel* to the complete exclusion of the surname *Fitz Alan*. Specifically, Earl Richard's son Edmund (died 1326), both of his brothers, two of his sons and all four of his grandsons all employed the Arundel surname. Edmund's sister Alice is likewise styled "de Arundel" in an ancient Segrave family ped. VCH *Surrey* 1 (1902): 348, footnote 1 observes that Richard's son and heir, Edmund, is "commonly called Fitz Alan but the real designation of the family was then de Arundel." Nicolas, a well known antiquarian, states: "This family presents a singular instance of adopting the name of their title as the surname of the family, for after the marriage of John Fitz-Alan, Lord of Clun, with Isabel, the sister and co-heir of Hugh D'Albini, Earl of Arundel, all the descendants called themselves Arundel instead of Fitz-Alan" [see Nicolas *Testamenta Vetusta* 1 (1826): 105]. "J.G.N." in *Gentleman's Magazine* 103

Oxfordshire, etc., Chief Butler of England, son and heir, born 3 Feb. 1266/7. He married about Nov. 1281/2 (date of correspondence regarding this marriage) **ALICE** (or **ALASIA**) **DI SALUZZO**, daughter of Tommaso I, Marquis of Saluzzo, by Aluisia (or Aluyisia, Aloisia), daughter of Giorgio I, Marquis of Ceva [see SALUZZO 8 for her ancestry]. She was near kinswoman to Eleanor of Provence, wife of Henry III, King of England, who helped arrange this marriage. She was the sister of [Master] Boniface di Saluzzo [Papal chaplain, King's clerk, Archdeacon of Buckingham, Warden of Tickhill Chapel, Yorkshire, Doctor of Canon Law] and [Master] George di Saluzzo [Archdeacon of Buckingham, Precentor of Salisbury].[26] Richard and Alice had three sons, Edmund, Knt. [9th Earl of Arundel], Richard, Knt., and [Master] John [Warden of Tickhill Chapel, Yorkshire, Papal chaplain], and three daughters, Eleanor, Alice, and Margaret. In 1285, as "Richard le Fiz Aleyn," he was granted a weekly market to be held at his manor of Arundel, Sussex. In 1287 he was directed to raise foot soldiers to march against Rhys ap Meridith. He was created Earl of Arundel in 1289. In 1291–2, as "Richard Fitz Alan, Earl of Arundel," he was summoned by two different writs to answer to the king respecting the hundred of Pesseburn and other property in Shropshire. In 1292 he was excommunicated by Gilbert, Bishop of Chichester, for having hunted with horn and hound in the Bishop's Chase of Hoghton; the bishop absolved him Christmas Eve

---

(1833): 500 observes that unless Fitz Alan is "placed parenthetically, or as an addition to the other [i.e., Arundel]", it is certainly incorrect." For an instance of Earl Edmund (died 1326) being styled *Edmundus de Arundel*, see Luard *Annales Monastici* 4 (Rolls Ser. 36) (1869): 558–559. For an example of his seal bearing his name, "Edmūdi de Arundel," see Dallaway *Hist. of the Western Div. of Sussex* 2(1) (1832): 123. For an example of Edmund's brother, John, using the Arundel surname, see *Cal. Inqs. Misc.* 2 (1916): 334. For instances of Edmund's son, Edmund, using the Arundel surname, see *Papal Regs.: Petitions* 1 (1896): 8, 128, 186, 194. Other citations of the use of the Arundel surname are provided further below. The surname Fitz Alan is thought to have been revived in the early 1500's by William, 18th Earl of Arundel (died 1544) [see ARUNDEL 13.i] and by his son, Henry, 19th Earl of Arundel (died 1580) [see *Gentleman's Magazine* 103 (1833): 500; Beltz *Mems. of the Order of the Garter* (1841): clxxv; Banks *Baronies in Fee* 1 (1844): 304–306 (sub Fitz-Alan, sive Arundel, Baron Maltravers); *C.P.* 1 (1910): 250–252 (sub Arundel)]. William, 18th Earl of Arundel, occurs in one isolated record before he was earl as "William Alyn [i.e., Fitz Alan], knt., Lord Mautravers" [see abstract of *IPM* of Richard Coffyn, Esq. taken 1522 on file at Devon Rec. Office, Exeter, Devon available on FHL Microfilm 9175256]. As earl, however, William occurs regularly in contemporary records simply as William, Earl of Arundel, with no mention of any surname. William's son, Henry, was summoned several times to Parliament in his father's lifetime in the reign of King Henry VIII as "Henrico Fitz-Alan de Maltravers, Chl'r" [see Dugdale *Perfect Copy of all Summons of the Nobility to the Great Councils & Parliaments of this Realm* (1685): 498, 499, 502, 504, 505]. His marriage license, however, records his name only as "Lord Henry Ma[u]t[r]avers," without reference to any surname [see Chester *Allegations for Marr. Lics.: Canterbury* (H.S.P. 24) (1886): 5)].

[26] For information regarding the history of Alice di Saluzzo's two brothers, [Master] Boniface and [Master] George di Saluzzo, and her nephew, James son of Giovanni di Saluzzo, all of whom were English clergymen, see Jones *Fasti Ecclesiæ Sarisberiensis* (1879): 224; *C.P.R. 1327–1330* (1891): 487–488; *C.P.R. 1281–1292* (1893): 470 (Boniface de Saluzzo styled "king's kinsman and clerk" by King Edward I; *C.P.R. 1330–1334* (1893): 407 (Master George de Saluzzo styled "king's kinsman"); *Papal Regs.: Letters* 1 (1893): 568; *C.P.R. 1321–1324* (1904): 137, 203, 214 (instances of George de Saluzzo styled "kinsman" by King Edward II); Romeyn *Reg. of John le Romeyn Lord Archbishop of York* 1 (Surtees Soc. 123) (1913): 91, 147, 155, 282–283, 323, 331–334; 2 (Surtees Soc. 128) (1917): xvii, xxxiii, 24–25, 27, 239–240; *Trans. Thoroton Soc. of Nottinghamshire* 27 (1924): 77–79; Corbridge *Reg. of Thomas of Corbridge* 1 (Surtees Soc. 138) (1925): 27, 206; Corbridge *Reg. of Thomas of Corbridge* 2 (Surtees Soc. 141) (1928): 10, 31; Greenfield *Reg. of William Greenfield Lord Archbishop of York* 1 (Surtees Soc. 145) (1931): 43–50, 69–81, 90–91; 2 (Surtees Soc. 149) (1934): xxvii–xxx, 129–133, 139–146, 149–150, 197–198, 203–204, 211; 4 (Surtees Soc. 152) (1938): 98, 132–133, 150–151, 173–174 (Boniface de Saluzzo styled "our clerk and kinsman" [clericus et consanguineus noster] by King Edward II), 176–179; Greenfield *Reg. of William Greenfield Lord Archbishop of York 1306–1315* 5 (Surtees Soc. 153) (1940): xvi–xvii, 168, 274–275; Emden *Biog. Reg. of the Univ. of Oxford* 3 (1959): 1634 (biog. of Boniface of Saluzzo); Martival *Regs. of Roger Martival, Bishop of Salisbury* 1 (Canterbury & York Soc. 55) (1959): 133–135, 263–264 (George de Saluzzo styled "kinsman" [consanguineum] by King Edward II), 294–295; Clay *York Minster Fasti* 2 (Yorkshire Arch. Soc. Recs. 124) (1959): 53–54; Martival *Regs. of Roger Martival, Bishop of Salisbury* 3 (Canterbury & York Soc. 59) (1965): 95 (George de Saluzzo styled "king's cousin" in 1322), 139–140, 177, 183; 2 (bis) (Canterbury & York Soc. 58) (1972): 175–176, 550–552.

1292, enjoining on him the penance of a three days fast and a pilgrimage to St. Richard. His wife, Alice, died 25 Sept. 1292. In 1294 he was commander of the forces sent to relieve Bere Castle. He was summoned to Parliament 24 June 1295 by writ directed *Ricardo filio Alani Comiti Arundell'*. He fought in Gascony in 1295–7, and in the Scottish wars, 1299 and 1300–1. He fought at the Battle of Falkirk 22 July 1298. He was present at the Siege of Caerlaverock in 1300. He signed Barons' letter to Pope Boniface VIII in 1301 as *Com' Arundell*. At some unknown date, he confirmed his father's grant to Anian, Bishop of St. Asaph, of lands in Martinchurch near Chirk, with the addition of 44 acres and a manor house. SIR RICHARD FITZ ALAN, 8th Earl of Arundel, died testate 9 March 1301/2. He and his wife, Alice, were buried at Haughmond Abbey, Shropshire.

Dentis *Compendio Istorico dell' Origine de Marchese in Italia e di Saluzzo* (1704): 93–96 ("Alice maritata in Tomaso Conte d'Arondello d'Inghilterre"). Blomefield *Essay towards a Top. Hist. of Norfolk* 10 (1809): 16–20. Rymer *Fœdera* 1 (1816): 899 ("Richard fiz Aleyn conte de Arundell' "). Baker *Hist. & Antiqs. of Northampton* 1 (1822–30): 547. Owen *Hist. of Shrewsbury* 2 (1825): 79 (Fitz Alan ped.). *Dignity of a Peer of the Realm* (1826): 389–434. Nicolas *Siege of Carlaverock* (1828): 283–285 (biog. of Richard Fitz Alan) ("The Poem informs us that the Earl of Arundel [was] 'a handsome and well beloved knight.'"). Muletti *Memorie Storico-Diplomatiche di Saluzzo* 2 (1829): 508 ["Alasia, che fu moglie di Riccardo (e non Tommaso, come ha Lodovico Della Chiesa (2)) Fitz-Alan conte di Arundello, di antichissima famigilia d'Inghilterra, la quale apparisce dal testamento del marchese Tommaso dell'anno 1294 che al tempo del medesimo gia fosse morta, scorgendosi in esso instituiti eredi particolari i figliuoili della fu Alasia contessa di Arundello."]. Dallaway *Hist. of the Western Div. of Sussex* 2(1) (1832): 121–123 ("a handsome and well beloved knight"). Tierney *Hist. & Antiqs. of the Castle & Town of Arundel* 1 (1834): chart foll. 192; 201–212. Eyton *Antiqs. of Shropshire* 4 (1857): 14–19; 7 (1858): 211–262. *Recs. of Buckinghamshire* 5 (1878): 183–189. Flower *Vis. of Yorkshire 1563–4* (H.S.P. 16) (1881): 336–338 (Warren ped.: "Rychard Fytzallen Erl of Arundell. = Ales doughter of the Marquis of Saluces."). Ormerod *Hist. of Chester* 2 (1882): 36–37. *Arch. Cambrensis* 5th Ser. 1 (1884): 219–221 (Fitzalan ped.). Doyle *Official Baronage of England* 1 (1886): 69–70 (sub Arundel). di Crollalanza *Dizionario Storico-Blasnonico delle Famiglie Nobili e Notabili Italiane* 2 (1886–90): 472–473 (arms of Saluzzo: Argent, a chief azure). *Codex Astensis* (Atti della Reale Accademia dei Lincei Anno CCLXXIII 2nd Ser. 4) (1887): 286–287 (Saluzzo ped.). Lloyd *Hist. of the Princes, the Lords Marcher, & the Ancient Nobility of Powys Fadog* 6 (1887): 320–323. Birch *Cat. Seals in the British Museum* 2 (1892): 282 (seal of Richard Fitz Alan, Earl of Arundel dated 1301 — To the right. In armour: hauberk of mail, surcoat, helmet with fan plume, sword, shield of arms. Horse galloping, caparisoned and plumed. Arms: a lion rampant [ARUNDEL]. Legend: SIGILLVM : RICARDI : COMITIS : DE : ARONDEL). *Genealogist* n.s. 12 (1895): 115, 118–119. Mackenzie *Castles of England: Their Hist. & Structure* 2 (1897): 151–152. *Placita Coram Domino Rege 1297* (Index Lib. 19) (1898): 148 ("Ricardum filium Alani, Comitem Arundell' "). Morris *Welsh Wars of Edward I* (1901): Pedigree V foll. 314 (Fitzalan-Warenne ped.). *List of Ancient Corr. of the Chancery & Exchequer* (PRO Lists and Indexes 15) (1902): 485. Howard de Walden *Some Feudal Lords & Their Seals* (1903): 21 (biog. of Richard, Earl of Arundel). *C.Ch.R.* 2 (1906): 320. *D.N.B.* 7 (1908): 95–96 (biog. of Richard Fitzalan I). VCH *Hampshire* 3 (1908): 144-147. *Trans. Shropshire Arch. & Natural Hist. Soc.* 3rd Ser. 9(2) (1909): 163–179. Martin *Hist. of the Manor of Westhope* (1909): 15–33. *C.P.* 1 (1910): 240–241, 253 (sub Arundel); 2 (1912): 232 (sub Boteler); 4 (1916): Appendix H, 670 (chart); 7 (1929): 680–681 (sub Lincoln). *Jour. Flintshire Hist. Soc.* 5 (1915): 14–15. Tallone *Tomaso I Marchese di Saluzzo 1244–1296* (1916). Cam *Hundred & the Hundred Rolls* (1930): 280–282. Peckham *Chartulary of the High Church of Chichester* (Sussex Rec. Soc. 46) (1942/3): 282. Williams *Collectanea* (Wiltshire Arch. & Natural Hist. Soc. Recs. Branch 12) (1956): 89. Sanders *English Baronies* (1960): 70–71. Prestwich *Docs. Ill. the Crisis of 1297–98 in England* (Camden Soc. 4th Ser. 24) (1980): 141–142 (letter of Richard, Earl of Arundel). Ellis *Cat. Seals in the P.R.O.* 2 (1981): 42 (seal of Richard Fitz Alan, Earl of Arundel dated 1297 — In a circle filled with scrollwork, five lions rampant. Legend: "SIGILLVM: RICARDI…DEL".). Rees *Cartulary of Haughmond Abbey* (1985): 227 (agreement dated 23 Sept. 1341 between the abbot and convent of Haughmond and John, son of Wal. of Ireland,whereby the abbot and convent are to provide 12 candles each year to burn in the church of Haughmond around Earl Richard's tomb and that of his wife Alesia. They are to be renewed each year so that after the renovation each candle, including the old wax and the new, must weigh 6 lbs. They shall burn at high mass on the feasts of Christmas, St. John the Evangelist, Epiphany, the Purification and the Annunciation of the Virgin, Easter, Whitsunday, the Nativity of St. John the Baptist, the Assumption and the Nativity of the Virgin, the Exaltation of the Holy Cross, All Saints, All Souls, St. Nicholas, and the anniversaries of Earl Richard and Countess Alesia [Alice]."). Hanna *Cartularies of Southwick Priory* 1 (Hampshire Recs. 9) (1988): 211. Brault *Rolls of Arms Edward I* 2 (1997): 17, 166 (his arms: Gules, a lion rampant or). Weiler et al. *Thirteenth Century England* 11 (2007): 178–179 ("Alice [de Saluzzo] died on 25 September 1292 ... and is said on no good authority to have been buried at a place called Todingham Priory. The identity of this religious house is unclear, as no reference to a monastery by that name survives today (nor was it known to Dugdale), and it is probably an error. Suffice it to say that the bodies of both Alice and her husband [Richard] had been interred at Haughmond Abbey by 23 September 1341, at the latest, when arrangements were made for candles to burn around their tombs on specific days of the calendar year.").

Children of Richard Fitz Alan, Knt., by Alice di Saluzzo:

i. **EDMUND DE ARUNDEL**, Knt. [see next].

ii. **RICHARD DE ARUNDEL**, Knt., King's bachelor. In 1311 John Vanne acknowledged for himself and his fellows of the society of Bellardi of Lucca that he owed Richard a debt of 400 marks. In 1314 Richard was granted the manors of Brill, Buckinghamshire, Silverstone, Northamptonshire, Claverley, Shropshire, and Tettenhall, Staffordshire for his substance to the value of £80 a year, he then being on the king's service. He was captured at the Battle of Bannockburn 24 June 1314, whereupon King Edward II, declaring himself desirous "to hasten his delivery from the hands of the Scots," appointed keepers of Richard's lands and ordered them to keep his goods safe for his eventual return. SIR RICHARD DE ARUNDEL died shortly before 24 November 1314. In 1315 John Pecche, lord of Hampton, acknowledged that he owed a debt of 200 marks to Eleanor, widow of Henry de Percy, sister and executrix of Richard de Arundel. In 1316 Eleanor was granted pontage for three years by the king of all wares for sale carried across the bridge of Wetherby, Yorkshire, the repair of which Eleanor undertook for the good of the soul of the said Richard. Strachey *Rotuli Parl.* 1 (1777): 340. *C.C.R.* 1307–1313 (1892): 356–357. *C.C.R.* 1313–1318 (1893): 223. *C.P.R.* 1307–1313 (1894): 493 (Richard de Arundell styled "king's yeoman and kinsman."). *C.P.R.* 1313–1317 (1898): 53, 95, 146, 167, 521. Speight *Lower Wharfedale* (1902): 430. *C.F.R.* 2 (1912): 219. *Cal. Inqs. Misc.* 2 (1916): 35. Given-Wilson *Parliament Rolls of Medieval England* (2005): 179.

iii. [MASTER] **JOHN DE ARUNDEL**, Warden of Tickhill Chapel, Yorkshire, Rector of Bury, Lancashire, West Bourne, Sussex, and Arncliffe, Yorkshire, papal chaplain, born about 1291 (aged 15 in 1306). In 1303, as "John son of the late Richard, Earl of Arundel," he had papal provision of a canonry of Lichfield. In 1306 he was granted a papal indult to hold two benefices, together with the prebend of Lichfield, reserved to him by papal authority. In 1310 he accompanied his uncles, [Master] Boniface and George di Saluzzo, to the court at Rome. He was presented to the church of Arncliffe, Yorkshire by his sister, Eleanor de Percy, in 1317. In 1320 he was granted a canonry of Lincoln, with reservation of a prebend, at the request of his kinsmen, Philippe V and Edward II, kings of France and England, and of their wives, Jeanne and Isabel, notwithstanding that he already had canonries and prebends of Lichfield and Chichester. [MASTER] JOHN DE ARUNDEL died shortly before 17 May 1331. Whitaker *Hist. & Antiqs. of the Deanery of Craven* (1878): 579. *C.P.R.* 1307–1313 (1894): 278. *Papal Regs.: Letters* 2 (1895): 8, 201, 294, 310, 327–328. *Cal. Inqs. Misc.* 2 (1916): 333–334. *Cal. of Chancery Warrants 1244–1326* (1927): 320, 560. Emden *Biog. Reg. of the Univ. of Oxford* 1 (1957): 48 (biog. of John de Arundel). *Fasti Ecclesiae Anglicanae 1300–1541* 6 (1963): 68–70; 7 (1964): 23–24; 10 (1964): 53–54. *Fasti Parochiales* 4 (Pubs. Yorkshire Arch. Soc. 133) (1971): 7–8.

iv. **ELEANOR DE ARUNDEL**, married **HENRY DE PERCY**, Knt., 1st Lord Percy [see PERCY 8].

v. **ALICE DE ARUNDEL**. She was granted the wardship of a minor, John de Upton, of Upton, Shropshire, about 1301, by the gift of her father. She married before 27 Jan. 1314 (date of grant) **STEPHEN DE SEGRAVE**, Knt., 3rd Lord Segrave, of West Hatch, Wiltshire, Bretby (in Repton) and Ashbourne, Derbyshire, Chaucombe, Northamptonshire, Stiveschale and Thurlaston (in Dunchurch), Warwickshire, and North Piddle, Worcestershire, Constable of the Tower of London, son and heir of John de Segrave, Knt., 2nd Lord Segrave, Justice of the Forest beyond Trent, King's Lieutenant (or Keeper) of Scotland, by Christian, daughter of Hugh de Plessets (or Plescy, Plessis). He was born 22 July, about 1285 (aged 40 in 1325). They had three sons, Edmund, John, Knt. [4th Lord Segrave], and Stephen. He had letters of protection in 1305, 1307, and 1322, going to Scotland. In 1314 the Constable of the Tower of London was ordered to deliver to him a certain Scot, whom he was to take to Scotland with other Scottish prisoners, to exchange for his father, John de Segrave, who was captured at the Battle of Bannockburn. He was granted Stottesden Hundred in Shropshire in 1318 for life. He was pardoned as an adherent of Thomas, Earl of Lancaster, in 1318. In 1323 he was held responsible for having allowed Roger de Mortimer to escape from the Tower of London. In 1324 his father became bound to the king for the payment of 10,000 marks for pardon for misdemeanors. The same year he was going to Gascony and Aquitaine on the king's service. SIR STEPHEN DE SEGRAVE, 3rd Lord Segrave, died in Aquitaine shortly before 12 Dec. 1325, and was buried at Chaucombe Priory, Northamptonshire. Following his death, his widowed mother, Christian de Segrave, claimed a third of the manor of North Piddle, Worcestershire as her dower, but his widow, Alice, declared that her husband held the entire manor of his father's gift; the court decided that Alice should hold the estate, but that the value of one-third of it should be paid to Christian out of that part of the heir's property which was in the king's wardship. Alice subsequently presented to the church of North Piddle, Worcestershire in 1331, 1334, and 1338. In 1334 she was fined for entering an enclosure in Sherwood Forest with greyhounds and poaching the deer. Alice, Lady Segrave, died 7 Feb. 1340. Nash *Colls. for the Hist. of Worcestershire* 2 (1782): 188. Nichols *Hist. & Antiqs. of Leicestershire* 3(1) (1800): 240 (Segrave ped. from *Chronicis apud Chaucombe*: "… & predictus Johannes de Segrave nupsit Christiane de Plessy; de quibus dominus Stephanus de Segrave,

Eleanora-Kiriell, Margareta, Alicia, & Christiana de Moune [Mohun]. Et predictus Stephanus [de Segrave] nupsit Alicie de Arundell; de quibus Edmundus, qui obiit in cunis; & Johannes de Segrave, & Stephanus"), 413 (Segrave ped.). Baker *Hist. & Antiqs. of Northampton* 1 (1822–30): 588–590. *Cat. of the Arundel MSS in the Library of the College of Arms* (1829): 91 (Extracts from Regs. of the Priory of Chacombe: "De Nativitate d'ni Stephani de Segrave filij predicti d'ni Johannis. xj⁰ kl. Augusti [22 July] xlvj⁰. De obitu ejusdem apud Thame kl. Decembr. [1 December] ii⁰."). Glover *Hist. of Derby* 2(1) (1829): 194 (Segrave ped.). Burke *Gen. Hist. of the Dormant, Abeyant, Forfeited & Extinct Peerages* (1866): 484–485 (sub Segrave, Barons Segrave). Burke *Dormant, Abeyant, Forfeited & Extinct Peerages* (1883): 484–486 (sub Segrave). *Genealogist* n.s. 14 (1897): 96. *Index of Placita de Banco 1327–1328* 1 (PRO Lists and Indexes 17) (1904): 88, 276; 2 (PRO Lists and Indexes 22) (1906): 693, 726. Wrottesley *Peds. from the Plea Rolls* (1905): 186, 325–326. Jeayes *Desc. Cat. Derbyshire Charters* (1906): 257. *Cal. IPM* 4 (1913): 53; 6 (1910): 427–434. *Cal. Inqs. Misc.* 2 (1916): 342. VCH *Worcester* 4 (1924): 177–180. VCH *Buckingham* 3 (1925): 235–240. VCH *Huntingdon* 2 (1932): 280–285 (Segrave arms: Sable a lion argent crowned or). *Misc. Gen. et Heraldica* 5th Ser. 9 (1935–7): 162–168. Pugh *Abs. of Feet of Fines Rel. Wiltshire* (Wiltshire Arch. & Nat. Hist. Soc. Recs. 1) (1939): 99. *C.P.* 11 (1949): 608–609 (sub Segrave). Paget *Baronage of England* (1957) 493: 5. Segrave *Segrave Fam. 1066 to 1935* (1963): 14 (British Lib., MS Add. 5758 f. 21: "Syr Steven de Segraue which marryd the dought'r of Arrundell which last hadd issu Edmonde de Segraue."), 41–43. Orleton *Cal. Reg. of Adam de Orleton* (Worcestershire Hist. Soc. n.s. 10) (1979): 179. Montacute *Cal. Reg. of Simon de Montacute Bishop of Worcester 1334–1337* (Worcestershire Hist. Soc. n.s. 15) (1996): 4–5. Brault *Rolls of Arms Edward I* 2 (1997): 388 (his arms: Sable, a lion rampant argent crowned or charged on the shoulder with a fleur-de-lis gules). Burghersh *Regs. of Bishop Henry Burghersh* 1 (Lincoln Rec. Soc. 87) (1999): 118, 126. Coss *Lady in Medieval England 1000–1500* (2000): 67. Berkeley Castle Muniments, BCM/D/5/1/8; BCM/D/5/1/9; BCM/D/5/1/10; BCM/D/5/1/11; BCM/D/5/1/12; BCM/D/5/1/13 (available at www.a2a.org.uk/search/index.asp).

Child of Alice de Arundel, by Stephen de Segrave, Knt.:

a. **JOHN DE SEGRAVE**, Knt., 4th Lord Segrave, married **MARGARET MARSHAL**, Duchess and Countess of Norfolk, Countess Marshal [see NORFOLK 9].

vi. **MARGARET DE ARUNDEL**, married **WILLIAM LE BOTELER**, Knt., 2nd Lord Boteler of Wem [see WEM 10; SUDELEY 13].

10. EDMUND DE ARUNDEL (or **FITZ ALAN**), Knt., 9th Earl of Arundel, of the Castle and honor of Arundel, Sussex, of Clun and Oswestry, Shropshire, Chief Butler of England, Captain General north of the Trent, 1316, Privy Councillor, 1318, Chief Justice of North and South Wales, 1322, Warden of the Welsh Marches, 1325, son and heir, born at Marlborough Castle 1 May 1285. He married after 30 Dec. 1304 **ALICE DE WARENNE**, daughter of William de Warenne, Knt., of Medmenham, Buckinghamshire, by Joan, daughter of Robert de Vere, Earl of Oxford [see WARENNE 10 for her ancestry]. They had four sons, Richard, Knt. [Earl of Arundel and Surrey], John, Edmund [Treasurer of Chichester, Warden of the Hospital of St. Nicholas, Portsmouth], and Michael (clerk), and six daughters, Eleanor, Alice, Katherine, Aline, Elizabeth, and Mary. Her maritagium included the manors of High Roding, Margaretting, Ovesham Hall (in Matching), Prittlewell, and Woolston (in Chigwell), Essex. Sometime in the period, 1307–11, Gilbert de Clare, Earl of Gloucester and Hertford, Henry de Lacy, Earl of Lincoln, and other earls and barons, including "Edmund Fitz Aleyn, Earl of Arundell," while assembled in the Parliament in London, wrote to the Pope praying for the canonization of Thomas de Cantelowe, late Bishop of Hereford. He was knighted with Edward, the King's son, and many others in 1306, prior to an expedition to Scotland. He was summoned to Parliament 9 Nov. 1306, by writ directed *Edmundo comiti Arundell*. In 1308 he officiated as Chief Butler at the Coronation of King Edward II. For a long time, he was in opposition to the King and was violent against Peter de Gavaston, Earl of Cornwall, who had beaten him in a tournament. In 1309, as "Edmund, Earl of Arundel," he made a complaint against his cousin, Robert de Mohaut, regarding a ¼ knight's fee in Alspath, Warwickshire. In Hilary term 1310, as "Edmund FizAleyn, Earl of Arundell," he sued John de Chauvent and Eve his wife for the manor of Wepham, Sussex, which he claimed his great-grandfather, John Fitz Alan, was seised in his demesne as of fee on the day of his death. In 1312, as "Edmund, Earl of Arundel," he gave his waste in Ticknall, Derbyshire called Schadhawe to the Canons of Repton, Derbyshire. In 1313 the king cancelled all the debts which he owed the Crown. He presented to the churches of Hopesay, Shropshire, 1313, 1325, Stokesay, Shropshire, 1316, Beeston Regis, Norfolk, 1317, Stretton (by Wenlock), Shropshire, 1321, Mileham, Norfolk, 1323, and Alcaston, Shropshire, 1326. In 1314 he was granted the manors of Wing, Buckinghamshire, and Blackwell, Roding, Ovesham (in Matching), Prittlewell, and Margaretting, Essex by his brother-in-law, John de Warenne, Earl of Surrey. In 1321 he changed sides, being thereafter one of the few nobles who adhered to the king. SIR EDMUND DE ARUNDEL, 9th Earl of Arundel, was captured in Shropshire by Queen Isabel's party and beheaded without a trial at Hereford 17 Nov. 1326. He was subsequently attainted and his honours became forfeited. He was buried initially at the Franciscan church at Hereford, and, after repeated appeals to Queen Isabel and her son, Edward, by the abbot and convent of Haughmond, his remains were secured for reburial at Haughmond Abbey, Shropshire. In 1327 his widow, Alice, was granted the manor of Maplederwell, Hampshire by the king. Soon afterwards, however, the king made other provisions for Alice and her children. Alice was living in 1330, but died before 23 May 1338. She was buried in the church of the Black Friars, London, next to her two grandchildren, William and Jane Husee. In 1343 provision was made for a chantry in Haughmond Abbey for the repose of Earl Edmund's soul and the souls of his ancestors and his heirs.

Caraccioli *Antiqs. of Arundel* (1766): 76–82. Watson *Mems. of the Earls of Warren & Surrey & Their Descs.* (1782). Blomefield *Essay towards a Top. Hist. of Norfolk* 8 (1808): 90; 10 (1809): 16–20, 25. Baker *Hist. & Antiqs. of Northampton* 1 (1822–30): 547. Dugdale *Monasticon Anglicanum* 4 (1823): 141 (Walden Abbey: "Alicia Arundell [wife of John de Bohun, Earl of Hereford and Essex] sepelitur apud Walden, in medio capellæ beatæ Mariæ"); 6(1) (1830): 135. Hunter *South Yorkshire* 1 (1828): 105 (Warenne ped.). Wainright *Hist. & Top. Intro. ... of the Wapentake of Stafford & Tickhill* (1829): 195–196 (Warenne ped.). Dallaway *Hist. of the Western Div. of Sussex* 2(1) (1832): 123–125, 128 (Warenne ped.). Tierney *Hist. & Antiqs. of the Castle & Town of Arundel* 1 (1834): chart foll. 192, 212–224. Bigsby *Hist. & Top. Desc. of Repton* (1854): 69 (charter of Edmund, Earl of Arundel dated 1312; seal — a lion rampant, with a circumscription not legible). *Herald & Genealogist* 2 (1865): 56 (seal of Edmund of Arundel). Luard *Annales Monastici* 4 (Rolls Ser. 36) (1869): 558–559 (Annals of Worcester sub A.D. 1306 — "Item die Pentecostes accepit dominus Edwardus filius regis Angliæ cingulum militiæ a patre suo apud Westmonasterium; ubi et facti fuerunt milites Rogerus de Mortuomari filius Edmundi de Mortuomari, et Edmundus de Arundel, una cum aliis bachilariis numero circiter ccc., quorum pars maxima profecti sunt in Scotiam cum domino E[dwardo] filio regis prædicti."). Stow *Survey of London* (1876): 127(re. burial of Alice de Warenne). Kellawe *Reg. of Richard de Kellawe, Lord Palatine & Bishop of Durham 1314–1316* 4 (1878): xxxi. *Colls. Hist. & Arch. rel. to Montgomeryshire* 12 (1879): 118–121. Flower *Vis. of Yorkshire 1563–4* (H.S.P. 16) (1881): 336–338 (Warren ped.: "Edmund Fytzallen, Erl of Arundell. = Ales Warren daughter to William Erl Waren & syster & heyre to John."). *Arch. Cambrensis* 5th Ser. 1 (1884): 219–221 (Fitzalan ped.). Doyle *Official Baronage of England* 1 (1886): 70–71 (sub Arundel). *Trans. Hist. Soc. of Lanc. & Cheshire* n.s 5 (1889): 23–24 (seal of Edmund of Arundel). Aveling *Heraldry* (1890): 300 ("The seal of Edmund of Arundel, who was Earl from 1301 to 1326, has two crested helms placed at the sides of the shield."), 302 (seal of Edmund de Arundel). *Genealogist* n.s. 12 (1895): 115, 118–119. *Papal Regs.: Letters* 2 (1895): 242, 415, 438, 452, 456. *Papal Regs.: Petitions* 1 (1896): 8, 102, 128. *Regs. of John de Sandale & Rigaud de Asserio, Bishops of Winchester* (Hampshire Rec. Soc. 12) (1897): 488. C.P.R. 1301–1307 (1898): 308. C.P.R. 1343–1345 (1902): 16, 56. Warren *Hist. & Gen. of the Warren Fam.* (1902). C.P.R. 1324–1327 (1904): 281 (Edmund, Earl of Arundel, styled "king's kinsman" by King Edward II of England). *List of Inqs. ad Quod Damnum* 1 (PRO Lists and Indexes 17) (1904): 174, 176, 233. C.P.R. 1348–1350 (1905): 89. *Arch. Cambrensis* 6th Ser. 7(1) (1907): 1–34. *Year Books of Edward II* 4 (Selden Soc. 22) (1907): 204–205; 25 (Selden Soc. 81) (1964): 37–38, 130–132. Orleton *Cal. Reg. of Adam de Orleton 1317–1327* (1907): 265, 333, 346, 387, 389. D.N.B. 7 (1908): 87–88 (biog. of Edmund Fitzalan). Capes *Reg. Ricardi de Swinfield, Episcopi Herefordensis 1283–1317* (Canterbury & York Soc. 6) (1909): 542–543. Martin *Hist. of the Manor of Westhope* (1909): 15–33. C.P. 1 (1910): 241–242 (sub Arundel); 4 (1916): Appendix H, 670 (chart); 6 (1926): 470–471 (sub Hereford); 7 (1929): 4 (sub Husee). VCH *Hampshire* 4 (1911): 150–151. Clay *Extinct & Dormant Peerages* (1913): 236–238 (sub Warenne). *Feet of Fines for Essex* 2 (1913–28): 204. VCH *Buckingham* 3 (1925): 450–451. *Cal. Chancery Warrants* (1927): 505 ("Sir Edmund, earl of Arundel" styled "king's cousin" by King Edward II of England), 520, 565 (instances of Edmund styled "king's cousin"). Salzman *Chartulary of the Priory of St. Pancras of Lewes* 2 (Sussex Rec. Soc. 40) (1934): 19–21. VCH *Essex* 4 (1956): 31; 8 (1983): 199–200. Paget *Baronage of England* (1957) 569: 6. *English Hist. Rev.* 74 (1959): 70–89. Sanders *English Baronies* (1960): 70–71. VCH *Wiltshire* 8 (1965): 252. Aston *Thomas Arundel* (1967): chart foll. 431. VCH *Shropshire* 2 (1973): 64. Ellis *Cat. Seals in the P.R.O.* 1 (1978): 25 (seal of Edmund, Earl of Arundel — In a cusped circle, a shield of arms: a lion rampant [ARUNDEL]). Rees *Cartulary of Haughmond Abbey* (1985): 101, 227. Hanna *Cartularies of Southwick Priory* 2 (Hampshire Recs. 10) (1989): 18 (charter of

Edmund, Earl of Arundel). Barbour *The Bruce* (1997): 596–597. *Coat of Arms* 3rd Ser. 2(2) (2006): 83–95. National Archives, SC 8/174/8700; SC 8/174/8702A (available at www.catalogue.nationalarchives.gov.uk/search.asp).

Children of Edmund de Arundel, Knt., by Alice de Warenne:

i. **RICHARD DE ARUNDEL**, Knt., Earl of Arundel and Surrey [see next].

ii. **JOHN DE ARUNDEL**, occurs 1373. Eyton *Antiqs. of Shropshire* 7 (1858): 229 (Fitz Alan chart).

iii. **EDMUND DE ARUNDEL**, clerk, Treasurer of Chichester, Warden of the Hospital of St. Nicholas, Portsmouth. He died shortly before 24 March 1348. Caraccioli *Antiqs. of Arundel* (1766): 80. *Papal Regs.: Petitions* 1 (1896): 8 (Edmund d'Arundell styled "brother of the earl of Arundel and kinsman of the king" in 1342), 128, 186, 194. *Papal Regs.: Letters* 3 (1897): 81, 108, 317, 357. VCH *Hampshire* 2 (1903): 206–208. Emden *Biog. Reg. of the Univ. of Oxford* 1 (1957): 48 (biog. of Edmund de Arundel). Barrell *Papacy, Scotland & Northern England 1342–1378* (Cambridge Studies in Medieval Thought & Life) (1995): 58. *Index to Ancient Correspondence of the Chancery and the Exchequer, Vol. 1: A-K* (Lists and Indexes, Supplementary Series, No. XV): 44 (Edmund de Arundel, clerk, styled "brother" of R. Fitz Alan [sic] in letter dated 1340).

iv. **ELEANOR DE ARUNDEL**, married (1st) **WILLIAM DE SAINT JOHN** [see KINGSTON LISLE 9]; (2nd) **GERARD DE LISLE**, Knt., 1st Lord Lisle [see KINGSTON LISLE 9].

v. **ALICE DE ARUNDEL**, married **JOHN DE BOHUN**, Knt., Earl of Hereford and Essex, Constable of England [see BOHUN 9.iii].

vi. **KATHERINE DE ARUNDEL**, married (1st) before 16 October 1347 (as his 2nd wife) **HENRY HUSEE** (or **HUSE**), Knt., 2nd Lord Husee, of Harting, Sussex, Moreton, Berkshire, Rissington and Sapperton, Gloucestrershire, Freefolk, Hampshire, Hascombe, Surrey, Keeper of the Isle of Wight, 1347, son and heir of Henry Husee, Knt., 1st Lord Husee, of Danshurst, Hascombe, and Godalming, Surrey, Sheriff of Surrey and Sussex, 1320–1, by his wife, Isabel. He was born about 1302 (aged 30 in 1332). They had two children, William and Jane, both of whom died young. The king took his homage and he had livery of his inheritance 16 March 1331/2. In 1335 he was going with the king to Scotland. He was summoned to Parliament from 18 August 1337 to 10 March 1348/9, by writs directed *Henrico Husee* or *Huse*. He was a commissioner of array in 1338. SIR HENRY HUSEE, 2nd Lord Husee, died 1 July 1349. His widow, Katherine, married (2nd) after 6 August 1350 **ANDREW PEVEREL**, Knt., of Ifield, Ewhurst (in Shermanbury), etc., Sussex, Barton Peverel (in South Stoneham), Hampshire, etc., and, in right of his wife, of Freefolk, Hampshire, Knight of the Shire for Sussex, 1351, 1353, 1356, 1361, 1366, 1373, son and heir of Andrew Peverel, Knt., of Blatchington, Ewhurst (in Shermanbury) and Saperton (in Heathfield), Sussex, Barton Peverel (in South Stoneham), Hampshire, etc., Sheriff of Surrey and Sussex, by Katherine, daughter and co-heiress of John de Ifield, Knt. They had no issue. About 1345 he petitioned the king and council stating that he had brought an assize of novel disseisin against Eleanor, Countess of Ormond, and others, concerning a quarter of the manor of Gomshall [Towerhill] (in Shere), Surrey, but she claimed that she held half the manor, containing this quarter, for the term of her life of the king's lease, with reversion to the king, and that she cannot therefore answer without the king. In 1353 he released all his right in the manor of Gomshall [Towerhill] (in Shere), Surrey to the king. In 1355 he and his wife, Katherine, obtained papal indults for a portable altar and plenary remission at the hour of death. In 1366 he and his wife, Katherine, and her step-grandson, Henry Husee, Knt., conveyed the reversion of the manor of Freefolk, Hampshire after Katherine's death to Thomas Ludlow, Knt. In 1368 Andrew presented to the church of Hascombe, Surrey. In 1369 he and his wife, Katherine, presented to the church of Freefolk, Hampshire. SIR ANDREW PEVEREL died 13 Feb. 1376. His widow, Katherine, died shortly before 23 May 1376. She left a will dated 21 October 1375, naming her brother, the lord earl of Arundel, and his son, Sir Richard Arundel, and her late husbands, Sir Andrew Peverel and Sir Henry Husee. She requested burial in Lewes Priory, Sussex. Nicolas *Testamenta Vetusta* 1 (1826): 97 (will of Katherine Lady Peverell). Warter *Appendicia et Pertinentiæ; or, Parochial Fragments Rel. West Tarring* (1853): 345. *Sussex Arch. Colls* 12 (1860): 39; 32 (1882): 78. Elwes *Hist. of the Castles, Mansions & Manors of Western Sussex* (1876): 160 (Peverel ped.). Stow *Survey of London* (1876): 127 (re. burial of William and Jane Husee). *Misc. Gen. et Heraldica* 2nd Ser. 3 (1890): 11. Kirby *Wykeham's Reg.* 1 (1896): 22, 24. *Papal Regs.: Letters* 3 (1897): 554, 561. *List of Sheriffs for England & Wales* (PRO Lists and Indexes 9) (1898): 135. *Desc. Cat. Ancient Deeds* 3 (1900): 16 (A.3974). *C.C.R.* 1343–1346 (1904): 585, 623. VCH *Hampshire* 3 (1908): 481–489; 4 (1911): 282–285. VCH *Surrey* 3 (1911): 111–121. Salzman *Feet of Fines Rel. Sussex* 3 (Sussex Rec. Soc. 23) (1916): 174–182. *C.P.* 7 (1929): 4 (sub Husee). Nairn & Pevsner *Buildings of England: Sussex* (1965): 292. Elrington *Abs. of Feet of Fines Rel. Wiltshire* (Wiltshire Rec. Soc. 29) (1974): 147. VCH *Gloucester* 11 (1976): 90–93. Ellis *Cat. Seals in the P.R.O.* 1 (1978): 35 (seal of Henry Hussey (Husee) dated 1337 — In a cusped and traceried circle, between sprigs of oak, a shield of arms: ermine, three bars. Legend: *SIGILLV: HENR[ICI:H]VSEE DNI DE HERTYNGGES.). VCH *Sussex* 6(3) (1987): 192–195. Ward *Women of the English Nobility & Gentry 1066–1500* (1995): 224–226 (abstract of the will of Katherine Lady Peverel dated 1375). National Archives, SC 8/262/13054 (available at www.catalogue.nationalarchives.gov.uk/search.asp).

vii. **ALINE DE ARUNDEL**, married **ROGER LE STRANGE**, Knt., 5th Lord le Strange of Knockin [see STRANGE 8].

viii. **ELIZABETH DE ARUNDEL**, married **WILLIAM LE LATIMER**, K.G., 4th Lord Latimer [see THWENG 11].

ix. **MARY DE ARUNDEL**, married **JOHN LE STRANGE**, Knt., 4th Lord le Strange of Blackmere [see BLACKMERE 12].

11. RICHARD DE ARUNDEL,[27] Knt., 10th Earl of Arundel, of the Castle and honor of Arundel, Sussex, and Oswestry, Shropshire, Chief Butler of England, Constable of Chirk Castle, 1333, Chief Justiciar of North Wales, 1334, Privy Councillor, 1334, Constable of Portchester Castle, 1336, Governor of Caernarvon Castle, 1339, Sheriff of Caenarvonshire, 1339, Admiral of the West, 1340–1, 1345–7, Joint Warden of the Marches towards Scotland, 1342, Joint Lieutenant of Aquitaine, 1344, Sheriff of Shropshire, 1345–8, Chief Warden for cos. Surrey and Sussex, 1352, Joint Guardian and Lieutenant of England, 1355, son and heir, born about 1314 (aged 7 in 1321). He married (1st) in the King's Chapel at Havering-atte-Bower, Essex 9 Feb. 1320/1 **ISABEL LE DESPENSER**, daughter of Hugh le Despenser ("the younger"), Knt., 2nd Lord le Despenser, by Eleanor, daughter of Gilbert de Clare, Knt., Earl of Gloucester and Hertford [see DESPENSER 11 for her ancestry]. She was born about 1313 (aged 8 in 1321). Immediately following their marriage, his father settled the manors of Keevil, Wiltshire and Wing and Blakewell, Buckinghamshire on them and their issue. They had one son, Edmund, Knt. In 1330 he conspired to end Mortimer's rule through a rising of men in Shropshire and Staffordshire. However, he was found out and an order was issued to arrest him and his associates 4 June 1330. He was able to escape arrest and journey to the Continent, but returned to England before 8 Dec. 1330, when as "Richard de Arundell, lord of Oswaldestre [Oswestry]," the king ordered that he furnish men for an enquiry into the presentations of the churches of La Pole [Welshpool], Meynoc, and Guilsfield, co. Montgomery, which were claimed by John de Cherleton and his wife, Hawise. In 1330, as "Richart, filz Esmon Counte d'Arundell," he petitioned Parliament that the irregular proceedings against his father be reversed. In 1330–1 the king, of his favor, granted him all the lands of which his father died seised, including the Castle and honour of Arundel, and was made Earl of Arundel. In 1337 he claimed the Stewardship of Scotland by grant from Edward de Balliol. In 1342 he and William de Clinton, Earl of Huntingdon, secured a one year truce with Scotland. In March 1344 he and Henry de Lancaster, Earl of Derby, were appointed plenipotentiaries to treat with Alfonso XI, King of Castile, and as lieutenants to Aquitaine. He and his wife, Isabel, were granted papal indults 18 July 1344 to choose confessors who shall give them plenary remission at the hour of death and to have a portable altar. His marriage to Isabel le Despenser was annulled 4 Dec. 1344 (date of Papal mandate), and their issue bastardized; she was living in 1356.[28] He married (2nd) at Ditton (in Stoke Poges), Buckinghamshire

---

[27] Note: For instances of Richard, Earl of Arundel, using or being styled by the surname, de Arundel, see Strachey *Rotuli Parl.* 2 (1777): 55–56, 226–227; *C.P.R.* 1327–1330 (1891): 562; *C.F.R.* 4 (1913): 181, 218; *C.C.R.* 1330–1333 (1898): 81, 381; *C.C.R.* 1333–1337 (1898): 154; National Archives, SC 8/156/7787.

[28] Following the annulment of her marriage to Earl Richard, Isabel le Despenser is recorded in 1345 as holding the following manors for life [by grant] of her former husband: High Roding, Ovesham (in Matching), Prittlewell, Margaretting, Woolston (in Chigwell), and Little Canfield, Essex [see *C.P.R.* 1343–1345 (1902): 487–488; *C.P.R.* 1345–1348 (1903): 18; VCH *Essex* 4 (1956): 24–32; VCH *Essex* 8 (1983): 196–206]. In 1351–2 she sent a gift of fish to her aunt, Elizabeth de Burgh, lady of Clare [see Underhill *For Her Good Estate* (1999: 90]. As "Isabel daughter of Hugh le Despenser," she repeatedly brought action from 1349 to 1356 against Prior of St. John of Jerusalem in England concerning a tenurial and prescriptive duty to repair walls in a marsh in Great Wakering, Essex against the ebb and

5 Feb. 1344/5 in the presence of King Edward III (by papal dispensations dated 4 March 1344/5 and 6 July 1345, they being related in the 4th degree of kindred; also Eleanor and his former wife, Isabel, being related in the 2nd degree of kindred as well as the 3rd and 4th degrees of kindred) **ELEANOR OF LANCASTER**, widow of John de Beaumont, Knt., 2nd Lord Beaumont (died 14 April 1342) [see BEAUMONT 8], and daughter of Henry of Lancaster, Knt., Earl of Lancaster and Leicester, by Maud, daughter and heiress of Patrick de Chaworth, Knt. [see LANCASTER 8 for her ancestry]. They had three sons, Richard, K.G. [Earl of Arundel and Surrey], John, Knt. [1st Lord Arundel], and Thomas [Bishop of Ely, Lord Chancellor of England, Archbishop of York] and two daughters, Joan and Alice. By an unknown mistress (or mistresses), he had an illegitimate daughter, Eleanor, and probably one illegitimate son, Ralph [see below]. He took a distinguished part in the wars with France, and commanded the 2nd division at the Battle of Crécy, and was at the fall of Calais in 1347. He was heir in 1347 to his uncle, John de Warenne, Knt., 8th Earl of Surrey, by which he inherited vast estates in Sussex, Surrey, Norfolk, and other counties. He was appointed Joint Ambassador to treat at Avignon in 1348, 1350, and 1354. In 1351 he agreed with Edward *the Black Prince* to exchange the justiciarship of North Wales, and annual fee of 500 marks, for £200 a year from the City of Chester and Dee mills for life. He was appointed Joint Commissioner to treat with Scotland in 1351 and 1357. He did homage for the barony of Bromfield and Yale in 1353. In 1354–5 an act was passed in Parliament annulling the proceedings in 1327–8 touching his father, Edmund, Earl of Arundel, thus restoring Earl Richard, as if the earlier proceedings had not taken place. In 1355 he and Eleanor received a papal indult to celebrate mass before daybreak. He was appointed Chief Plenipotentiary to treat with the Duke of Luxemburg in 1358. In 1359 he made a loan of £2,000 to Edward *the Black Prince*, receiving as security the gold crown and star of the French king. He was appointed Joint Commissioner to treat with France in 1360. In 1361, on the death of Joan of Bar, widow of his uncle, John de Warenne, he assumed the title of Earl of Surrey. In 1364 and again in 1366 his wife, Eleanor, received a papal indult to enter once a year monasteries of Minoresses with four honest matrons aged forty. In 1365 he was granted a rent of £400 by his kinsman, Edward *the Black Prince*, out of the prince's lands in the county of Chester, with power of distraint. He presented to the church of Tackley, Oxfordshire in 1370. Eleanor, Countess of Arundel and Surrey, died at Arundel 11 Jan. 1371/2. SIR RICHARD DE ARUNDEL, Earl of Arundel and Surrey, died at Arundel 24 Jan. 1375/6. He left a will dated 5 Dec. 1375, proved 22 October 1376. He and his wife, Eleanor, were buried at Lewes Priory, Sussex.

Sandford *Gen. Hist. of the Kings of England* (1677): 111. Rymer *Fœdera* 5 (1708): 442–443 (re. dispensation for marriage of Richard and Eleanor). Caraccioli *Antiqs. of Arundel* (1766): 82–89. Langley *Hist. & Antiqs. of the Hundred of Desborough* (1797): 346. Blomefield *Essay towards a Top. Hist. of Norfolk* 10 (1809): 16–20, 25. Blore *Hist. & Antiqs. of Rutland* 1(2) (1811): 19 (Despenser ped.), 98 (Lancaster ped.). Brydges *Collins' Peerage of England* 6 (1812): 496–511 (sub Despenser). Baker *Hist. & Antiqs. of Northampton* 1 (1822–30): 547. Dugdale *Monasticon Anglicanum* 4 (1823): 141 (Anno Domini MCCClxxij. iij. idus Januarii, obiit Elianora Lancastriæ, comitissa Arundeliæ"; "Anno Domini MCCClxxv. ix. kal. Febr. obiit Ricardus comes Arundell."); 6(3) (1830): 1377–1379. *Dignity of a Peer of the Realm* (1826): 389–434 (pg. 424: "… but though heir to John de Warren, Earl of Surrey … Richard, Earl of Arundel, or his descendants, never bore the title of Earl of Warren, or that of Earl of Surrey, until the son of John Howard, Duke of Norfolk, was created Earl of Surrey."). Nicolas *Testamenta Vetusta* 1 (1826): 94–96 (will of Richard, Earl of Arundel & Surrey). Dallaway *Hist. of the Western Div. of Sussex* 2(1) (1832): 125–127 ("[he] bore a very conspicuous and honourable part in the warlike and political transactions of his day"). Tierney *Hist. & Antiqs. of the Castle & Town of Arundel* 1 (1834): chart foll. 192, 225–240. *Archæologia* 26 (1836): 338. *Coll. Top. et Gen.* 6 (1840): 1–20. *Gentleman's Mag.* n.s. 24 (1845): 584. Hawley *Royal Fam. of England* (1851): 20–21. Eyton *Antiqs. of Shropshire* 11 (1860): 235 (Sir John de

---

flow and flooding of seawater; the defendant refused to repair the walls that threatened ruin whereby the said Isabel, by flooding, lost her profit [see Palmer *English Law in the Age of the Black Death 1348–1381* (1993): 397]. At her death, Isabel le Despenser was buried in the Chapter House of Austin Friars, London [see *Gentleman's Mag.* n.s. 8 (1860): 372–376; Holt *Well in the Desert* (1872): 379–380].

Leybourne and Sir Robert Corbet styled "well-beloved cousins" by Richard, Earl of Arundel in 1333). *Herald & Genealogist* 2 (1865): 54 (seal of Richard, Earl of Arundel). Hutchins *Hist. & Antiqs. of Dorset* 3 (1868): 322–323 (Arundel ped.). Lennard & Vincent *Vis. of Leicester 1619* (H.S.P. 2) (1870): 169–170 (Beaumont ped.: "Alianora filia Henrici Comitis Lancast' ob. 47. E. 3., [1] = Johannes de Bellomonte obijt 16. E. 3., [2] = Ric'us Comes Arundell 2 maritius"). Flower *Vis. of Yorkshire 1563–4* (H.S.P. 16) (1881): 19 (Beaumont ped.: "Elenor daughter to Henry Earl of Lancaster, [1] = John Lord Beamont, [2] = The Earl of Arundell 2 husband to Elenor"), 336–338 (Warren ped.: "Rychard Fytzallen Erl of Arundell & Waren. =Elenor syster to Henry the fyrst Duk of Lancaster."). Burke *Dormant, Abeyant, Forfeited & Extinct Peerages* (1883): 165–167 (sub Despenser). *Arch. Cambrensis* 5th Ser. 1 (1884): 219–221 (Fitzalan ped.). Doyle *Official Baronage of England* 1 (1886): 71–72 (sub Arundel); 3 (1886): 473–474 (sub Surrey). Rye *Short Cal. Feet of Fines for Norfolk* 2 (1886): 342. *Trans. Hist. Soc. of Lanc. & Cheshire* n.s 5 (1889): 27 (seal of Richard, Earl of Arundel). Aveling *Heraldry* (1890): (seal of Richard, Earl of Arundel). Birch *Cat. Seals in the British Museum* 2 (1892): 796 (seal of Richard, Earl of Arundel: A shield of arms: a lion rampant [ARUNDEL]. Within a carved gothic device of a circle inscribed in a triangle, which is again inscribed in a circle. The inner edge of the small circle ornamented with ball-flowers. Each of the sides of the triangle is ornamented with a small circular panel carrying a circular shield of arms: chequy or fretty. Legend between the points: * S' RICARDI · COMITIS · DE · ARVNDEL. Beaded borders.), 796–797 (seal of Richard, Earl of Arundel dated 1359 — A shield of arms: quarterly, 1, 4, a lion rampant [ARUNDEL]; 2, 3, chequy [WARENNE]. Between two slipped roses, and within a finely-carved gothic trefoil ornamented along the inner edge with small ball-flowers. Legend: * Sigillum : Ricardi : Comitis : de : Arundel : *), 797 (seal of Richard, Earl of Arundel and Surrey dated 1375 — A shield of arms, couché: quarterly, 1, 4, a lion rampant [ARUNDEL]; 2, 3, chequy [WARENNE]. Crest on a helmet, a lambrequin out of a ducal coronet; a griffen's head and wings erect. Supporters, two griffins sejant. Within a carved quatrefoil, ornamented with ball-flowers along the inner edge. Legend: Sig…ricardi …..itis : arund..le : et : surreye.). Lewis *Pedes Finium; or, Fines Rel. Surrey* (Surrey Arch. Soc. Extra Vol. 1) (1894): 119, 131, 136, 143, 221. *Genealogist* n.s. 12 (1895): 115, 118–119. Kirby *Wykeham's Reg.* 1 (1896): 30. *Papal Regs.: Petitions* 1 (1896): 75, 81, 99, 128, 280–281 (John, Humphrey, Lewis, William, and Griffin de Cherleton, clerks, sons of John de Cherleton, 1st Lord Cherleton, all styled "kinsmen" by Richard, Earl of Arundel). *Papal Regs.: Letters* 3 (1897): 145, 157, 164, 176, 188, 254, 522, 560, 576; 4 (1902): 38, 56. Grandisson *Reg. of John de Grandisson, Bishop of Exeter* 2 (1897): 988–989. *List of Sheriffs for England & Wales* (PRO Lists and Indexes 9) (1898): 117–118. *Sussex Arch. Colls.* 41 (1898): 79–94. *Year Books of Edward III: Year XVI* 8 (Rolls Ser. 31b) (1900): 312–324. Legg *English Coronation Recs.* (1901): lxxxv. Green *Feet of Fines for Somerset* 3 (Somerset Rec. Soc. 17) (1902): 36. *C.P.R. 1317–1321* (1903): 562. Wrottesley *Peds. from the Plea Rolls* (1905): 46, 292. *List of Inqs. ad Quod Damnum* 2 (PRO Lists and Indexes 22) (1906): 478. *C.P.R. 1350–1354* (1907): 467 (Richard, Earl of Arundel styled "king's kinsman"). *Arch. Cambrensis* 6th Ser. 7(1) (1907): 1–34. *D.N.B.* 7 (1908): 96–98 (biog. of Richard Fitzalan II). Martin *Hist. of the Manor of Westhope* (1909): 15–33. *C.P.* 1 (1910): 242–244 (sub Arundel); 2 (1912): 60–61 (sub Beaumont); 4 (1916): Appendix H, 670 (chart); 7 (1929): 154–156 (sub Kent); 14 (1998): 38. Lane *Royal Daughters of England* 1 (1910): 141–149. *John of Gaunt's Reg.* 2 (Camden Soc. 3rd Ser. 21) (1911): 154 (Richard, Earl of Arundel styled "cousin" [cosyn] by John of Gaunt in 1373), 155, 296–297 & 303 (instances of Richard, Earl of Arundel styled "cousin" [cousyn] by John of Gaunt in 1375). *C.P.R. 1364–1367* (1912): 155 (Richard styled "kinsman" of Edward *the Black Prince*), 237–238, 239 (Richard styled "king's kinsman"). *C.Ch.R.* 5 (1916): 14 (wife Eleanor styled "king's kinswoman"). Salzman *Feet of Fines Rel. Sussex* 3 (Sussex Rec. Soc. 23) (1916): 123–124, 137, 144. *Genealogist* n.s. 36 (1920): 198–203 (his agreement with attached seal bearing a shield quarterly, 1 and 4, a lion rampant [Arundel], 2 and 3, chequy [Warenne]). Plaisted *Manor & Parish Recs. of Medmenham* (1925): 40–44. VCH *Buckingham* 3 (1925): 450–451. Sudbury *Reg. Simonis de Sudbiria Diocesis Londoniensis 1362–1375* 2 (Canterbury & York Soc. 38) (1938): 106. Salzman *Chartulary of the Priory of St. Pancras of Lewes* 2 (Sussex Rec. Soc. 40) (1934): 19–21. Pugh *Abs. of Feet of Fines Rel. Wiltshire* (Wiltshire Arch. & Nat. Hist. Soc. Recs. 1) (1939): 130. *TAG* 19 (1942–43): 10–16. Kiralfy *Action on the Case* (1951): 77, 215. VCH *Essex* 4 (1956): 31; 8 (1983): 199–200. Paget *Baronage of England* (1957) 182: 1–2 (sub Despenser). Sanders *English Baronies* (1960): 70–71. *Yorkshire Arch. Jour.* 40 (1962): 265–297 (his arms: Arundel quartering Warenne, 1 and 4, Gules, a lion rampant or, 2 and 3, Chequy or and azure). VCH *Sussex* 2 (1973): 108–109. VCH *Wiltshire* 8 (1965): 252. Aston *Thomas Arundel* (1967). McFarlane *Nobility of Later Medieval England* (1973): 88–91. *Ancient Deeds — Ser. B* 2 (List & Index Soc. 101) (1974): B6498, B.8858. Rosenthal *Nobles & the Noble Life* (1976): 177–178. Ellis *Cat. Seals in the P.R.O.* 1 (1978): 25 (seal of Richard, Earl of Arundel dated 1371 — In a richly traceried circle, a shield of arms: quarterly, 1 and 4 a lion rampant [ARUNDEL], 2 and 3 checky [WARENNE]. On either side a slipped rose.); 2 (1981): 42 (seal of Richard, Earl of Arundel dated 1347 — In a circle filled with flowing tracery, between two oak sprigs, a shield of arms: a lion rampant [ARUNDEL]. Legend: "… UM*…".). Vale *Edward III & Chivalry: Chivalric Soc. & its Context 1270–1350* (1982): 88–91. VCH *Oxford* 11 (1983): 194–208. Taylor *English Hist. Lit. in the 14th Cent.* (1987): 297 (*Wigmore Chron.* sub 1372: "Eodem anno iii idus Januarie [11 Jan.] obiit domina Elianea nobilis comitissa de Arundell."). Hanna *Cartularies of Southwick Priory* 1 (Hampshire Recs. 9) (1988): 228–229. *English Hist. Rev.* 106 (1991): 1–26. Booth *Account of Master John de Burnham the Younger* (Lanc. & Cheshire Rec. Soc. 125) (1991): 119 (biog. of Richard Fitz Alan). Palmer *English Law in the Age of the Black Death 1348–1381* (1993): 397, 409. *Nottingham Medieval Studies* 39 (1995): 106–107 (At his death, Earl Richard had in cash or bullion alone, the immense sum of over £60,000). Ward *Women of the*

English Nobility & Gentry 1066–1500 (1995): 224–226 (abstract of the will of Katherine Lady Peverel dated 1375). Given-Wilson *Ill. Hist. of Late Medieval England* (1996): chart opp. 61 (temp. King Edward IV). Leese *Blood Royal* (1996): 80–92. Sandler *Omne Bonum* (1996): 191. Mooney *Kalendarium of John Somer* (1998): 116. Underhill *For Her Good Estate* (1999). Gee *Women, Art & Patronage from Henry III to Edward III: 1216–1377* (2002): 71. Eales *Fam. & Dynasty in Late Medieval England* (Harlaxton Medieval Studies n.s. 9) (2003): 138. Higginbotham *Traitor's Wife* (2005): 471–472. *Coat of Arms* 3rd Ser. 2(2) (2006): 83–95; 3rd Ser. 3(2) (2007): 93–101. Psalter. K.26, St. John's College, Cambridge ("Jan. 10. Ob. domine Eleanore comitisse arundell matris doe alesie comitisse kancie. a. d. 1372."; "Jan. 25. Ob. doi Rici com. arudell. a. d. 1375.") (transcript of doc. available at www.joh.cam.ac.uk/library/special_collections/manuscripts/medieval_manuscripts/mmk26/).

Child of Richard de Arundel, Knt., by Isabel le Despenser:

i. **EDMUND DE ARUNDEL**, Knt., of Chedzoy, Somerset, married **SIBYL DE MONTAGU** [see APPLETON 12].

Children of Richard de Arundel, Knt., by Eleanor of Lancaster:

i. **RICHARD DE ARUNDEL**, K.G., Earl of Arundel and Surrey [see next].

ii. **JOHN DE ARUNDEL**, Knt., 1st Lord Arundel, married **ELEANOR MAUTRAVERS** [see ARUNDEL 9].

iii. **THOMAS ARUNDEL**, 3rd son, born in 1352–3 (aged 18 in 1371, aged 21 in 1373). He was King's clerk by 1370. He was appointed Canon of Chichester, Hereford and Canon of York, 1372, Archdeacon of Taunton, 1370, Bishop of Ely, 1373, Archbishop of York, 1388, and Archbishop of Canterbury, 1396. He served as Lord Chancellor of England, 1386–9, 1391–6, 1407–10, 1412–13. He was a leader of the opposition to King Richard II from 1386. He was a legatee in the 1393 will of his brother, Richard, Earl of Arundel and Surrey. He was impeached in Parliament 20 Sept. 1397, for having acted in derogation of the king's authority during the ascendancy of the Lords Appellant, 1386–8. He joined Henry, Earl of Derby, in exile at Paris, and crossed with him to Ravenspur 4 July 1399. After the abdication of King Richard, he crowned Henry as King Henry IV in Westminster Abbey 13 October 1399. On his resumption of the archbishopric, he was concerned largely with ecclesiastical affairs. He propounded measures for the extirpation of Lollardry by invoking secular legislation. He presided at the trials for heresy for John Purvey and William Sawtry, 1401, John Badby, 1410, and Sir John Oldcastle, Lord Cobham, 1413. He crowned King Henry V in Westminster Abbey in 1413. He was a member of Trinity Guild of Coventry, Warwickshire. THOMAS ARUNDEL, Archbishop of Canterbury died testate 19 Feb. 1413/4, and was buried in the chantry chapel in the new nave of Canterbury Cathedral, the building of which he contributed 1,000 marks in 1400–1. Weever *Ancient Funerall Monuments* (1631): 225–227. Rymer *Fædera* 7 (1728): 480, 553 (instances of Thomas Arundel styled "kinsman" by King Richard II of England); 8 (1727): 399, 542, 584, 592 (instances of Thomas Arundel styled "kinsman" by King Henry IV of England); 9 (1729): 9–11 (Thomas Arundel styled "cousin" by King Henry V of England). *Cobbett's Complete Collection of State Trials* 1 (1809): 123–124 (Impeachment of Thomas Arundel, Archbishop of Canterbury dated 1397). Nicolas *Testamenta Vetusta* 1 (1826): 129–134 (will of Richard, Earl of Arundel & Surrey). Dallaway *Hist. of the Western Div. of Sussex* 2(1) (1832): 137–138 ("… he possessed superior talents, and, as a politician, took a very active share in the turbulent times in which he lived… [he displayed] singular magnificence in the public structures belonging to the Bishoprics over which he presided. His contributions to his churches were frequent and splendid. His love of architecture appears to have constantly engaged him in some sumptuous edifice"). Foss *Judges of England* 4 (1851): 144–150 (biog. of Thomas de Arundel: "… a man of great vigour and capacity for business; and he left a high reputation as well as for learning and intelligence as for personal courage) (styled "well-beloved uncle" by Henry of Lancaster, Earl of Derby [afterwards King Henry IV]). Hutchins *Hist. & Antiqs. of Dorset* 3 (1868): 322–323 (Arundel ped.). *Procs. Soc. Antiqs.* 2nd Ser. 5 (1870): 304. *Collectanea* 1st Ser. (1885): 55, 65. Aveling *Heraldry* (1890): 246. Jeayes *Desc. Cat. of the Charters & Muniments in the Possession of the Rt. Hon. Lord Fitzhardinge* (1892): 256 (Thomas [Arundel], Archbishop of York, styled "kinsman" by Thomas Mowbray, Earl Marshal and of Nottingham in 1389). *Papal Regs.: Letters* 4 (1902): 161, 187. *C.P.R. 1399–1401* (1903): 37, 80 (instances of Thomas Arundel styled "king's kinsman"). *D.N.B.* 1 (1908): 609–613 (biog. of Thomas Arundel: "… Arundel's conduct throughout his life was governed by a standard of duty which … was in accordance with the general feeling and principles of his own day … He was a man of princely tastes, built fine edifices for himself at Ely and Canterbury, and was a munificent benefactor of the churches in which he had any interest."). Harris *Reg. of the Guild of the Holy Trinity, St. Mary, St. John the Baptist & St. Katherine of Coventry* 1 (Dugdale Soc. 13) (1935): 74, 108. Hussey *Kent Chantries* (Kent Arch. Soc. Recs. 12) (1936): 32–34. Legge *Anglo-Norman Letters & Petitions* (Anglo-Norman Text Soc. 3) (1941): 79–80 (Thomas Arundel styled "uncle" by Edmund of Langley, Duke of York), 81, 423 (instances of Thomas Arundel styled "uncle" by Joan Beauchamp, Lady Bergavenny), 86–87 (Thomas Arundel styled "uncle" by Edmund Holand in letter dated 1400), 87–88 (Thomas Arundel styled "uncle" by John Cherleton in letter dated 1396), 324

(Thomas Arundel styled "cousin" by Roger Mortimer, Earl of March in letter dated 1394–5), 340–346, 350–351, 409, 426–427, 433–437, 442–443, 465–466 (instances of Thomas Arundel styled "cousin" by King Henry IV of England), 347–348 (Thomas Arundel styled "cousin" by Philippe of Lancaster, Queen of Portugal in letter dated 1399), 348–349 (Thomas Arundel styled "cousin" by Ralph [Neville], Earl of Westmorland in letter dated c.1403), 354–355 (Thomas Arundel styled "cousin" by Edward, Duke of York in letter dated ?1403), 355–360 (instances of Thomas Arundel styled "uncle" by Henry, Prince of Wales [later King Henry V]), 408 (Thomas Arundel styled "cousin" by Henry, Earl of Derby [later King Henry IV]). Emden *Biog. Reg. of the Univ. of Oxford* 1 (1957): 51–53 (biog. of Thomas Arundel). Aston *Thomas Arundel* (1967). *Jour. Eccl. Hist.* 24 (1973): 9–21. *Ancient Deeds — Ser. B* 2 (List & Index Soc. 101) (1974): B.8043. Ellis *Cat. Seals in the P.R.O.* 1 (1978): 2 (seal of Thomas Arundel, Archbishop of Canterbury dated 1403 — A shield of arms, couché: within a bordure engrailed, quarterly, 1 and 4 a lion rampant [ARUNDEL], 2 and 3 checky [WARENNE]; helm above with crest: out of a ducal coronet, a griffin's head with wings erect. Supporters, two lions sejant gardant, each seated on grass from which a trefoil springs). McNiven *Heresy & Politics in the Reign of Henry IV* (1987). Hicks *Who's Who in Late Medieval England* (1991): 203–205 (biog. of Thomas Arundel: "… independent and courageous, thoughtful and sagacious, principled but never impratical… was a munificent benefactor, a loyal friend and ally, a lover of music, and deeply pious… he banned herectic preaching and heretical books, purged Oxford of heresy."). *Cal. IPM* 20 (1995): 90–91. Leese *Blood Royal* (1996): 80–92. Psalter. K.26, St. John's College, Cambridge ("Feb. 19. Ob. Thome Arnedelle [recte Arundell] quondam archiepiscopi Cante.") (transcript of doc. available at www.joh.cam.ac.uk/library/special_collections/manuscripts/medieval_manuscripts/mmk26/).

iv. **JOAN ARUNDEL**, married **HUMPHREY DE BOHUN**, K.G., Earl of Hereford, Essex, and Northampton [see BOHUN 11].

v. **ALICE ARUNDEL**, married **THOMAS DE HOLAND**, K.G., 2nd Earl of Kent [see KENT 10].

Illegitimate child of Richard de Arundel, Knt., by an unknown mistress, _____:

i. **ELEANOR DE ARUNDEL**, married in or before 1348 (as his 1st wife) **JOHN DE BEREFORD**, of Clapcot, Berkshire, Bickford (in Welford-on-Avon), Stonythorpe (in Long Itchington), and Wishaw, Warwickshire, illegitimate son of Edmund de Bereford, Knt., of Clapcot, Berkshire, Brightwell Baldwin, Oxfordshire, Steane, Northamptonshire, etc. They had no issue. He died in Gascony in 1356. His 2nd wife, Eve, survived him and was living 1357. Blomefield *Essay towards a Top. Hist. of Norfolk* 10 (1809): 16–20. Baker *Hist. & Antiqs. of Northampton* 1 (1822–30): 682. *Top. & Gen.* 2 (1853): 271–277 (Ufford ped.). *C.C.R. 1354–1360* (1908): 346. VCH *Berkshire* 3 (1923): 547. *Year Books of Richard II* 5 (Ames Found. 8) (1937): 152–158. Stokes et al. *Warwickshire Feet of Fines* 3 (Dugdale Soc. 18) (1943): 15. VCH *Warwick* 4 (1947): 259; 5 (1949): 190; 6 (1951): 127. Lamborn *Armorial Glass of the Oxford Diocese* (1949): 96 (Bereford arms: Silver crusilly fitchy and three fleurs-de-lis sable). Garratt *Derbyshire Feet of Fines 1323–1546* (Derbyshire Rec. Soc. 11) (1985): 35–36.

Probable illegitimate child of Richard de Arundel, Knt., by an unknown mistress, _____:

i. **RALPH DE ARUNDEL**. He married **JULIANE** _____ [see HOWELL 12].

12. RICHARD DE ARUNDEL,[29] K.G., 11th Earl of Arundel, 10th Earl of Surrey, Chief Butler of England, Member of the Council of Regency, 1377, Admiral of the West, 1377–8, Joint Governor to King Richard II, 1381, Admiral of the West and North, 1386, Admiral and Lieutenant of the king on the Seas, 1387, Admiral of England, 1387–9, Governor of Brest, 1388, Lieutenant in Brittany, 1388, Lieutenant and Captain-General of the Fleet at Sea, 1388, Privy Councillor, 1389, son and heir by 2nd marriage, born in 1346. He married (1st) by license dated 17 October 1359 (papal dispensation dated 9 Sept. 1359, they being related in the 4th degree of kindred) **ELIZABETH DE BOHUN**, daughter of William de Bohun, K.G., 1st Earl of Northampton, by Elizabeth, daughter of Bartholomew de Badlesmere, Knt., 1st Lord Badlesmere [see BOHUN 10 for her ancestry]. They

---

[29] For instances of Richard, Earl of Arundel, using the surname Arundel or being styled Richard [de] Arundel, see Lewis *Pedes Finium; or, Fines Rel. Surrey* (Surrey Arch. Soc. Extra Volume 1) (1894): 222; *Genealogist* n.s. 16 (1899): 162; Wrottesley *Peds. from the Plea Rolls* (1905): 421; *Arch. Cambrensis* 6th Ser. 7(1) (1907): 1–34; *Arch. Aeliana* 3rd Ser. 6 (1910): 60; *C.P.R. 1374–1377* (1916): 25, 28, 51, 107, 243; Salzman *Feet of Fines Rel. Sussex* 3 (Sussex Rec. Soc. 23) (1916): 164, 174–182; *C.F.R.* 8 (1924): 286, 339; Ward *Women of the English Nobility & Gentry 1066–1500* (1995): 224–226 (abstract of the will of Katherine Lady Peverel dated 1375).

had three sons, Richard, William (clerk), and Thomas, K.G., K.B. [Earl of Arundel and Surrey], and five daughters, Eleanor, Elizabeth, Alice, Joan, and Margaret. In 1359 his father obtained a license to grant to him and his wife, Elizabeth, the manor of Medmenham, Buckinghamshire worth £50 yearly, and £216 13s. 4d. of rent out of the Castle and lordship of Chirk in the march of Wales. His wife, Elizabeth, was a legatee in the 1361 will of her uncle, Humphrey de Bohun, Earl of Hereford and Essex. In 1370 he presented to the church of High Roding, Essex, as "Sir Richard son of the earl of Arundel and Surrey." In 1373 William Heron, Knt., Roger Heron, Knt. and others sued Joan widow of John de Coupland, Richard de Arundel son of Earl of Arundel and Surrey, Edward de Saint John, and others in a plea. In 1373–4 the Castle and town of Ryegate, Sussex, the Castle and vill of Lewes, Sussex, the Castles of Dynasbran and Castrum Leonis in Wales, together with many other manors were settled on him and his wife, Elizabeth. He was appointed one of the executors of the 1375 will of his aunt, Katherine (de Arundel) Peverel. He attended the Coronation of King Richard II in 1377, where he bore the crown. His wife, Elizabeth, died 3 April 1385, and was buried at Lewes Priory, Sussex. He distinguished himself in the French wars, and won a brilliant naval victory over the French, Spanish and Flemish fleets off Margate in 1387. Later, with the Duke of Gloucester, he took an active part in the opposition to King Richard II, becoming one of the five Lords Appellant in the Parliament of 1388. He married (2nd) 15 August 1390 without the king's license **PHILIPPE MORTIMER**, widow of John de Hastings, Knt., 3rd Earl of Pembroke (died 30 or 31 Dec. 1389) [see HASTINGS 14], and daughter of Edmund de Mortimer, Knt., Earl of March and Ulster, by Philippe, daughter and heiress of Lionel of Antwerp, K.G., Duke of Clarence, 5th Earl of Ulster (son of King Edward III) [see MORTIMER 13 for her ancestry]. She was born at Ludlow, Shropshire 21 Nov. 1375. She was a legatee in the 1380 will of her father. They had no issue. He presented to the church of Beeston Regis, Norfolk in 1377. In August 1391 the Pope declared the dispensation under which Richard and Philippe married valid, knowing that they were related in the 3rd degree of affinity and 4th degree of kindred. He obtained a pardon in 1394. He presented to the church of Compton, Surrey in 1395. SIR RICHARD DE ARUNDEL, Earl of Arundel and Surrey, was treacherously seized, tried at Westminster, and beheaded at Cheapside 21 Sept. 1397. He was buried in the church of the Austin Friars, London. He left a will dated 4 March 1392/3. He was subsequently attainted, all his honours being forfeited. His widow, Philippe, married (3rd) before 6 Dec. 1398 (date of letter) (as his 2nd wife) **THOMAS POYNINGS**, Knt., 5th Lord Saint John of Basing [see PAULET 11]. Philippe died at Halnaker, Sussex 24 Sept. 1401, and was buried at Boxgrove Priory, Sussex. SIR THOMAS POYNINGS *alias* SAINT JOHN, 5th Lord Saint John of Basing, died 7 March 1428/9.

Rymer *Fædera* 7 (1728): 187–188, 554, 556, 578–579, 680 (instances of Richard, Earl of Arundel, styled "cousin" by King Richard II of England). Nichols *Coll. of All the Wills* (1780): 104–117 (will of Edmund de Mortimer, Earl of March and Ulster), 120–144 (will of Richard, Earl of Arundel and Surrey). Blomefield *Essay towards a Top. Hist. of Norfolk* 8 (1808): 90; 10 (1809): 16–20, 25. *Cobbett's Complete Coll. of State Trials* 1 (1809): 125–136 (Impeachment of Richard, Earl of Arundel of high treason dated 1397). Brydges *Collins' Peerage of England* 6 (1812): 643–645 (sub Lord Hastings). Baker *Hist. & Antiq. of Northampton* 1 (1822–30): 544–545 (Mandeville-Fitz Peter-Bohun ped.), 547. Nicolas *Testamenta Vetusta* 1 (1826): 66–68 (will of Humphrey de Bohun, Earl of Hereford and Essex), 129–134 (will of Richard, Earl of Arundel & Surrey). Dugdale *Monasticon Anglicanum* 6(1) (1830): 134–136 (Bohun ped. in Llanthony Abbey records: "... Elizabetha filia Willielmi comitis Northamtoniæ desponsata fuit Richardo filio et hæredi ipsius comitis Arundeliæ"). Dallaway *Hist. of the Western Div. of Sussex* 2(1) (1832): 130–137 ("[Richard de Arundel] ... eminently distinguished for his integrity and magnificence"). Tierney *Hist. & Antiqs. of the Castle & Town of Arundel* 1 (1834): chart foll. 192, 240–276. *Coll. Top. et Gen.* 6 (1840): 1–20. Beltz *Mems. of the Order of the Garter* (1841): cliv–clv, 303–307. *Gentleman's Mag.* n.s. 24 (1845): 584. Hawley *Royal Fam. of England* (1851): 23–27. Hutchins *Hist. & Antiqs. of Dorset* 3 (1868): 322–323 (Arundel ped.). *Jour. British Arch. Assoc.* 27 (1871): 179–191. *Vis. of Devon* 1620 (H.S.P. 6) (1872): 169 (Lenthall ped.: "Ricus Comes Arundell = Eliz. fil. Bohun Comitis Hereff. et Northamp."). *Annual Rpt. of the Deputy Keeper* 35 (1874): 7. Flower *Vis. of Yorkshire 1563–4* (H.S.P. 16) (1881): 336–338 (Warren ped.: "Rychard Erl of Arendell Warren & Surrey, Knight of the Garter, son & heyr. = Elsabeth doughter to William Bohun Erl of Hertford & Northampton."). *Arch. Cambrensis* 5th Ser. 1 (1884): 219–221 (Fitzalan ped.). Doyle *Official Baronage of*

England 1 (1886): 73–74 (sub Arundel); 3 (1886): 474 (sub Surrey). Rye *Short Cal. Feet of Fines for Norfolk* 2 (1886): 382. *Sussex Arch. Colls.* 35 (1887): 11 (chart); 41 (1898): 79–94. *MSS of Rye & Hereford Corporations* (Hist. MSS Comm. 13th Rep., App., Part IV) (1892): 425 (indenture of Richard, Earl of Arundel and Surrey, dated 1392; mentions his late wife, Elizabeth, and his present wife, Phelipp). *Misc. Gen. et Heraldica* 2nd Ser. 5 (1894): 76–78; 5th Ser. 6 (1926–28): 168–172 (Roberts ped.). *Genealogist* n.s. 13 (1896): 34; n.s. 16 (1899): 162, 234; n.s. 18 (1902): 99; n.s. 19 (1903): 107. Kirby *Wykeham's Reg.* 1 (1896): 194. *C.P.R. 1381–1385* (1897): 35, 222 (instances of Richard styled "king's kinsman"). *Desc. Cat. Ancient Deeds* 4 (1902): 395 (Counterpart indenture being the defeasance of a bond dated 21 March 1377 by Adam de Houghton, bishop of St. Davids, and others to Richard, earl of Arundel and Surrey, and John de Arundell his brother). *Papal Regs.: Letters* 4 (1902): 391–392, 394. Usk *Chronicon Adæ de Usk 1377–1421* (1904): 87. Wrottesley *Peds. from the Plea Rolls* (1905): 292. *D.N.B.* 7 (1908): 98–100 (biog. of Richard Fitzalan III). Martin *Hist. of the Manor of Westhope* (1909): 15–33. VCH *London* 1 (1909): 510–513. *Arch. Aeliana* 3rd Ser. 6 (1910): 60. *C.P.* 1 (1910): 24–26 (sub Abergavenny), 244–245 (sub Arundel) ("a gallant, hot tempered, popular man, the persistent political opponent and bitter personal enemy of Richard II. He was one of the best sea-captains of the time"); 3 (1913): 161 (sub Cherleton); 4 (1916): Appendix H, 670 (chart); 6 (1926): 133, footnote a (sub Grey). 9 (1936): 601–604 (sub Norfolk); 10 (1945): 394–397 (sub Pembroke); 12(2) (1959): 153 (sub Ufford); 14 (1998): 38. Lane *Royal Daughters of England* 1 (1910): 278. VCH *Hertford* 3 (1912): 366–373. *C.P.R. 1370–1374* (1914): 83, 364, 371 (instances of Richard styled "king's kinsman"), 150–151 (re: daughter Eleanor). *C.Ch.R.* 5 (1916): 291 (Richard, earl of Arundel & Surrey styled "king's cousin"). Salzman *Feet of Fines Rel. Sussex* 3 (Sussex Rec. Soc. 23) (1916): 163–164; 174–182. *Genealogist* n.s. 36 (1920): 198–203. Plaisted *Manor & Parish Recs. of Medmenham* (1925): 40–44. VCH *Buckingham* 3 (1925): 450–451; 4 (1927): 41. Sudbury *Reg. Simonis de Sudbiria Diocesis Londoniensis 1362–1375* 1 (Canterbury & York Soc. 34) (1927): 274. Salzman *Chartulary of the Priory of St. Pancras of Lewes* 2 (Sussex Rec. Soc. 40) (1934): 19–21 ("Richard [de Arundel] the second beforenamed took to wife Elizabeth daughter to Sir William Boun Earl of Northampton and by her begot three sons Richard William and Thomas and four daughters Alice Elizabeth Joan and Margaret. Richard and William the elder sons died soon after their father who ceased to live 21 September, which was Friday and the day of St. Mathew the Apostle, 1397, and so the inheritance remained to the youngest son Thomas who took to wife Lady Beatrice daughter of the most puissant Lord Sir John King of Portugal and Algarbe. Alice was married to Sir John Charleton Lord de Powys. Elizabeth and Joan were born at one time. Elizabeth was married to Sir Thomas Segrave Earl of Nottingham and Marshal of England who afterwards became Duke of Norfolk. And Joan was married to Sir William Beuchampe Lord de Burgeuieny and brother to Sir Thomas Beuchampe Earl of Warwyke. Margaret was married to a right valiant knight Sir Roland Leythale."). VCH *Rutland* 2 (1935): 182–188. *Cal. Inqs. Misc.* 3 (1937): 389. *John of Gaunt's Reg.* 2 (Camden Soc. 3rd Ser. 57) (1937): 263–264, 294 (instances of Richard, Earl of Arundel, styled "cousin" by John of Gaunt). Legge *Anglo-Norman Letters & Petitions* (Anglo-Norman Text Soc. 3) (1941): 76–78, 87–88 ([Richard], Earl of Arundel and Surrey, styled "father" [i.e., father-in-law] by John Cherleton), 327. VCH *Warwick* 4 (1947): 69–75; 6 (1951): 215–219. Train *Abs. of IPMs Rel. Nottinghamshire* 2 (Thoroton Soc. Recs. 12) (1952): 133. VCH *Essex* 4 (1956): 31; 8 (1983): 199–200. Paget *Baronage of England* (1957) 73: 1–13 (sub Bohun). McKisack *The 14th Cent.* (1959). VCH *Wiltshire* 8 (1965): 252. Goodman *Loyal Conspiracy* (1971). Tuck *Richard II & the English Nobility* (1973). *Chancery Miscellanea* 8 (List & Index Soc. 105) (1974): 224. *Ancient Deeds — Ser. B* 3 (List & Index Soc. 113) (1975): B.9304, B.12444. *Year Books of Richard II* 1 (Ames Found. 1) (1975): 1–7 (Richard, Earl of Arundel, styled "king's kinsman" [consanguinei]). VCH *Middlesex* 5 (1976): 324–330. Edington *Reg. of William Edington Bishop of Winchester 1346–1366* 2 (Hampshire Recs. 8) (1987): 49–50. Hicks *Who's Who in Late Medieval England* (1991): 182–184 (biog. of Richard Earl of Arundel & Surrey: "…hot-tempered and tactless, honest to a fault and lacking in finesse… his criticism of government in 1384, of Gaunt in 1394, and his actions in 1398 all aimed at more effective use of royal resources for prosecution of the war…"). *TAG* 67 (1992): 97–107. Ward *Women of the English Nobility & Gentry 1066–1500* (1995): 224–226 (abstract of the will of Katherine Lady Peverel dated 1375). Leese *Blood Royal* (1996): 80–92, 143–149. Psalter. K.26, St. John's College, Cambridge ("Sept. 21. Ob. Ric. com. arundell a. d. 1397.") (transcript of doc. available at www.joh.cam.ac.uk/library/special_collections/manuscripts/medieval_manuscripts/mmk26/). *Foundations* 1 (2004): 246–268.

Children of Richard de Arundel, K.G., by Elizabeth de Bohun:

i. **ELEANOR DE ARUNDEL**, married on or about 28 October 1371 **ROBERT DE UFFORD**, 1st son and heir apparent of William de Ufford, K.G., 2nd Earl of Suffolk, Lord Ufford, by his 1st wife, Joan, daughter of Edward de Montagu, Knt., Lord Montagu [see NORFOLK 8.iii.e for his ancestry]. They had no issue. ROBERT DE UFFORD died about 1 August 1375. His wife, Eleanor, died about the same time. Banks *Baronies in Fees* 1 (1844): 437–440 (sub Ufford). *Top. & Gen.* 2 (1853): 271–277 (Ufford ped.). Hutchins *Hist. & Antiqs. of Dorset* 3 (1868): 322–323 (Arundel ped.). Waters *Chester of Chicheley* 1 (1878): 331–336. *C.P.R. 1370–1374* (1914): 150–151. *C.P.R. 1374–1377* (1916): 299. *C.P.* 12(1) (1953): 434 (sub Suffolk); 12(2) (1959): 153 (sub Ufford). *Foundations* 1 (2004): 246–268.

ii. **RICHARD ARUNDEL**, eldest son and heir apparent, living 4 March 1392/3 (date of his father's will). He predeceased his father. Nicolas *Testamenta Vetusta* 1 (1826): 129–134 (will of Richard, Earl of Arundel & Surrey). Hutchins *Hist. & Antiqs. of Dorset* 3 (1868): 322–323 (Arundel ped.). Wrottesley *Peds. from the Plea Rolls* (1905): 292. *Foundations* 1 (2004): 246–268.

iii. **ELIZABETH ARUNDEL** [see next].

iv. **JOAN ARUNDEL**, married **WILLIAM BEAUCHAMP**, K.G., 1st Lord Bergavenny [see BERGAVENNY 12].

v. **ALICE ARUNDEL**. Prior to her marriage, she was reputedly mistress to [**MASTER**] **HENRY** (or **HARRY**) **BEAUFORT**, Bishop of Lincoln, Lord Chancellor of England, 1403–5, 1413–17, and 1424–6, Cardinal Bishop of Winchester, Cardinal-Priest of the titular church of St. Eusebius (commonly called Cardinal of England), by whom it is said she had an illegitimate daughter, Joan (or Jane) (wife of Edward Stradling, Knt., of St. Donat's Castle, Glamorgan) [see STRADLING 11 for further details]. Henry Beaufort was the legitimated son of John of Gaunt, Duke of Aquitaine and Lancaster (younger son of King Edward III of England), by his mistress (later 3rd wife), Katherine, daughter and co-heiress of Paon (or Paonet) de Roet (or Ruet), Knt. Alice married before 4 March 1392/3 (date of her father's will) **JOHN CHERLETON**, 4th Lord Cherleton, feudal lord of Powis, Justice of North Wales, son and heir of John de Cherleton, Knt., 3rd Lord Cherleton, by Joan, daughter of Ralph de Stafford, K.G., 1st Earl of Stafford [see CHERLETON 12 for his ancestry]. He was born 25 April 1362. They had no issue. He was summoned to Parliament from 9 August 1382 to 3 October 1400, by writs directed *Johanni de Cherleton*, or *Cherleton de Powys*. His wife, Alice, was a legatee in the 1393 will of her father. He was killed in battle at Pool 19 October 1401. He left a will dated 1395. Alice died without legitimate issue sometime before 13 October 1415. Nichols *Coll. of All the Wills* (1780): 120–144 (will of Richard, Earl of Arundel & Surrey). Nicolas *Testamenta Vetusta* 1 (1826): 129–134 (will of Richard, Earl of Arundel & Surrey). Dallaway *Hist. of the Western Div. of Sussex* 2(1) (1832): 134, 142. Tierney *Hist. & Antiqs. of the Castle & Town of Arundel* 1 (1834): chart foll. 192. Nicolas *Procs. & Ordinances of the Privy Council* 5 (1835): 176. *Coll. Top. et Gen.* 6 (1840): 20, footnote f ["Vincent says she (Alice) was married to Cardinal (Henry) Beaufort, before he was in orders, and had a daughter, Jane, married to Sir Edward Stradling (Vinc[ent] upon Brooke: 27), and, quotes as his authority, Dr. Powell's treatise of the Conquest of Glamorganshire.... In the pedigrees of Stradling (Vinc[ent] "Chaos": 118, and Le Neve's Baronets i: 5.), Sir Edward Stradling is said to marry Jane, daughter of Henry Beaufort, where Alice Fitzalan is given to the Cardinal as a wife. Sandford and Le Neve style her *base* daughter"]. Hutchins *Hist. & Antiqs. of Dorset* 3 (1868): 322–323 (Arundel ped.). *Arch. Cambrensis* 5th Ser. 1 (1884): 219–221 (Fitzalan ped.). *Sussex Arch. Colls.* 35 (1887): 11 (chart); 41 (1898): 79–94. Bradney *Hist. of Monmouthshire* 2(1) (1911): 25–28 (Somerset ped.). *C.P.* 3 (1913): 161 (sub Cherleton); 14 (1998): 39. Harrison *Royal Ancestry of George Leib Harrison* 2 (1914): 28–42. Salzman *Chartulary of the Priory of St. Pancras of Lewes* 2 (Sussex Rec. Soc. 40) (1934): 19–21. Legge *Anglo-Norman Letters & Petitions* (Anglo-Norman Text Soc. 3) (1941): 87–88 (Richard, Earl of Arundel and Surrey, styled "father" and Thomas Arundel, Archbishop of Canterbury, styled "uncle" by John Cherleton in letter dated 1396), 292–293 (letter of John Cherleton dated 1401). Jones *Fasti Ecclesiae Anglicanae 1300–1541* 4 (1963): 45–47. *Foundations* 1 (2004): 246–268.

vi. **WILLIAM ARUNDEL**, born about 1380 (aged 11 in 1391). In 1391, he then being aged 11 and a student in arts, he was dispensed to hold any benefices without cure, and, upon attaining his 14th year, to be promoted to all holy orders and hold a benefice with cure, even if it be an elective cure. He presumably died before 4 March 1392/3 (date of his father's will). Nicolas *Testamenta Vetusta* 1 (1826): 129–134 (will of Richard, Earl of Arundel & Surrey). Hutchins *Hist. & Antiqs. of Dorset* 3 (1868): 322–323 (Arundel ped.). *Papal Regs.: Letters* 4 (1902): 394.

vii. **THOMAS ARUNDEL**, K.G., K.B., Chief Butler of England, Deputy Constable of England, Captain of Oswestry and Warden of Marches of North Wales, 1404–5, Warden of Shrewsbury and Marches in Shropshire, 1405, Privy Councillor, 1410, Lord High Treasurer, 1413–15, Constable of Dover Castle and Warden of Cinque Ports, 1413, Lieutenant for North and South Wales, 2nd and only surviving son and heir, born 13 October 1381. He was a legatee in the 1393 will of his father. Following his father's execution, he joined his uncle, Archbishop Arundel, at Utrecht, and was with Henry IV when he landed at Ravenspur about 4 July 1399. He was restored as Earl of Arundel and Surrey in October 1400. He fought with moderate success against the Welsh in 1401–5, and was victorious against the rebels under Archbishop Scrope in 1405. He married at Lambeth, Surrey 26 Nov. 1405 **BEATRICE** (or **BEATRIZ**) **OF PORTUGAL**, legitimated daughter of João I, King of Portugal and the Algarve [see LANCASTER 10.i], by his mistress, Inez Pires, daughter of Pedro Esteves. They had no issue. By an unknown mistress, he had an illegitimate son, John. He commanded the English forces against the Armagnacs in 1411. He was appointed chief ambassador to treat with Burgundy in 1411. He served in the French campaign of 1415, with 100 men-at-arms and 300 archers, and was present at the taking of Harfleur. THOMAS ARUNDEL, Earl of Arundel and Surrey, died testate 13 (or 14) October 1415, and was buried at the collegiate church at Arundel, Sussex. He left wills dated 10 August 1415 and 10 October 1415, proved 11 Dec. 1415. In

Drawn by E. Blore.
Engraved by H. Le Keux.

Monument of Thomas Earl of Arundel and his Countess Beatrice, in Arundel Church.

1426 his widow, Beatrice, had letters of protection granted her, she being about to go abroad. She married (2nd) by license dated 20 Jan. 1432/3 (as his 2nd wife) **JOHN HOLAND**, K.G., Earl of Huntingdon and Ivry, afterwards Duke of Exeter, Admiral of England, Ireland and Aquitaine, Lieutenant of Aquitaine (died 5 August 1447) [see EXETER 11]. In 1439 Andrew Dautrey sued John and his wife, Beatrice, for the manors of Aldesworth, Sussex. Beatrice died at Bordeaux 23 October 1439 and was buried with her 1st husband at Arundel, Sussex. SIR JOHN HOLAND, Duke of Exeter, Earl of Huntingdon and Ivry,[30] died 5 August 1447. He left a will dated 16 July 1447, proved 16 Feb. 1447/8. Rymer *Fœdera* 8 (1727): 284–285, 611 (Thomas, Earl of Arundel styled "kinsman" [consanguinei/consanguineo] by King Henry IV of England). Blomefield *Essay towards a Top. Hist. of Norfolk* 8 (1808): 90; 10 (1809): 16–20. Blore *Mon. Remains of Noble & Eminent Persons* (1826). Nicolas *Testamenta Vetusta* 1 (1826): 129–134 (will of Richard, Earl of Arundel & Surrey), 186 (will of Thomas, Earl of Arundel dated 10 October 1415). Dallaway *Hist. of the Western Div. of Sussex* 2(1) (1832): 198. *Coll. Top. et Gen.* 1 (1834): 80–90. Tierney *Hist. & Antiqs. of the Castle & Town of Arundel* 1 (1834): chart foll. 192, 277–287. Ellis *Original Letters Ill. of English Hist.* 3rd Ser. 1 (1846): 52–53 (letter of Thomas, Earl of Arundel and Surrey, dated 1403). Wood *Letters of Royal & Ill. Ladies* 1 (1846): 78–81 ([Thomas Arundel] Earl of Arundel styled "cousin" by Philippe [of Lancaster], Queen of Portugal in letter dated 1405). Hutchins *Hist. & Antiqs. of Dorset* 3 (1868): 322–323 (Arundel ped.). *Misc. Gen. et Heraldica* 1st Ser. 2 (1876): 161–167. Demay *Inventaire des Sceaux de la Collection Clairambault* 1 (1885): 35 (seal of Thomas, Comte d'Arundel, dated 1411 — Sceau rond, de 58 mill. Écu écartelé: au 1 et 4, un lion; au 2 et 3, un échiqueté; penché, timbré d'un heaume cimé d'une tête de griffon dans un vol, supporté par deux griffons, dans un quadrilobe. [Légende:] Sigill thome comit . . .). Doyle *Official Baronage of England* 1 (1886): 74 (sub Arundel); 3 (1886): 475 (sub Surrey). Aveling *Heraldry* (1890): 392 (engraving of seal of Beatrice of Portugal, Countess of Arundel & Surrey). Birch *Cat. Seals in the British Museum* 2 (1892): 797 (seal of Thomas, Earl of Arundel and Surrey dated 1412 — A shield of arms, couché: quarterly, 1, 4, a lion rampant enraged [ARUNDEL]; 2, 3, chequy [WARENNE]. Crest on a helmet, lambrequin, out of a ducal coronet, a griffin's head and wings erect. Legend wanting. Cabled border). *C.P.R. 1401–1405* (1905): 138, 242 (instances of Thomas styled "king's kinsman"). Wrottesley *Peds. from the Plea Rolls* (1905): 292, 364–365, 421. *Arch. Cambrensis* 6th Ser. 7(1) (1907): 1–34. *D.N.B.* 7 (1908): 100–103 (biog. of Thomas Fitzalan). Martin *Hist. of the Manor of Westhope* (1909): 15–33 (will of Thomas, Earl of Arundel & Surrey dated 10 August 1415). *C.P.R. 1413–1416* (1910): 105, 155, 278 (instances of Thomas, earl of Arundel [and Surrey] styled "king's kinsman"). *C.P.* 1 (1910): 245–246 (sub Arundel); 4 (1916): Appendix H, 670 (chart); 5 (1926): 205–211(sub Exeter); 6 (1926): 654 (sub Huntingdon); 12(1) (1953): 512 (sub Surrey). *C.F.R.* 14 (1934): 41, 46–47, 64–65, 72, 75, 80, 107, 119. Salzman *Chartulary of the Priory of St. Pancras of Lewes* 2 (Sussex Rec. Soc. 40) (1934): 19–21. Chichele *Reg. of Henry Chichele* 2 (Canterbury & York Soc. 42) (1937): 71–78, 652 (biog. of Thomas Fitzalan). Legge *Anglo-Norman Letters & Petitions* (Anglo-Norman Text Soc. 3) (1941): 286–287 ([Thomas], Earl of Arundel, styled "cousin" by King Henry IV of England). VCH *Wiltshire* 8 (1965): 252. *Cal. IPM* 20 (1995): 207–211. *Foundations* 1 (2004): 246–268. National Archives, SC 8/24/1156; SC 8/304/15195 (available at www.catalogue.nationalarchives.gov.uk/search.asp).

viii. **MARGARET ARUNDEL**, born about 1383–5 (aged 30/32 in 1415). She presented to the church of South Stoke, Sussex in 1403. She was a legatee in the 1393 will of her father. She married before 1408 (as his 1st wife) **ROLAND** (or **ROWLAND**) **LENTHALL** (or **LEYNTHALE**, **LEYNTALE**), Knt., of Lenthall and Hampton Court, Herefordshire, Chamberlain of the Household to Queen Katherine of France, Sheriff of Herefordshire, 1423–4, Constable of Haverfordwest, Pembrokeshire, and, in right of his 1st wife, and, in right of his 1st wife, of South Stoke, Clemsfold (in Slinfold), Coltstaple (in Horsham), Hadfold (in Billingshurst), Offham (in South Stoke), Peppering (in Burpham), Pinkhurst (in Shipley), Warningcamp, and Wepham (in Burpham), Sussex, son of Roger Lenthall. They had two sons, Edmund, Esq. (died 18 April 1447), and Henry, Esq. He presented to the church of South Stoke, Sussex in 1408. His wife, Margaret, was co-heiress in 1415 to her brother, Thomas Arundel, K.G., K.B., Earl of Arundel and Surrey, Chief Butler of England, Lord High Treasurer. Roland fought at the Battle of Agincourt in 1415. He was granted protection 28 April 1417, he being in the retinue of the king. In 1419 he and Thomas Felde were granted power to treat for a truce with Yolanda, Queen of Sicily, and her son, Charles. In 1422 he and his wife, Margaret, arraigned an assize of novel disseisin against her sisters, Elizabeth, Duchess of Norfolk, and Joan Beauchamp, lady of Bergavenny, regarding their free tenement in the Hay of Wellington, Shropshire. His wife, Margaret, died shortly before 5 May 1423. He married (2nd) before 1426 **LUCY GREY**, daughter of Richard Grey, K.G., 4th Lord Grey of Codnor, Admiral of the Fleet north of the Thames, King's Chamberlain, deputy Constable and Marshal of England, Justice of South Wales, joint Warden of

---

[30] For instances of Sir John Holand and his son, Sir Henry, using the style "Earl of Huntingdon and Ivry," see Rymer *Fœdera* 11 (1727): 8–9, 10–12, 34; Lacy *Reg. of Edmund Lacy* 1 (Episc. Regs. of the Diocese of Exeter 9) (1909): 129, 149, 251, 262–263, 381.

the East and West Marches, by Elizabeth, daughter and co-heiress of Ralph Basset, Lord Basset of Sapcote [see CODNOR 14 for her ancestry]. They had two sons, Roland, Esq., and John, and two daughters, Katherine (wife of William la Zouche, 6th Lord Zouche of Harringworth) and Elizabeth (wife of Thomas Cornwall, Knt.). In 1437 he presented William Saunders, clerk, as prior of Wootton Wawen, Warwickshire. SIR ROLAND LENTHALL died 22 Nov. 1450. *Feudal Aids* 6 (1920): 521. Nicolas *Testamenta Vetusta* 1 (1826): 129–134 (will of Richard, Earl of Arundel & Surrey). Dallaway *Hist. of the Western Div. of Sussex* 2(1) (1832): 223. Burke *Hist. of the Commoners* 1 (1836): 178–180. *Coll. Top. et Gen.* 5 (1838): 288. Banks *Baronies in Fee* 1 (1844): 227–230 (sub Grey of Codnor). *Archaeologia* 38 (1860): 37–45. *Notes & Queries* 3rd Ser. 2 (1862): 41. Townesend *Town & Borough of Leominster* (1863): 168. Burke *Gen. Hist. of the Dormant, Abeyant, Forfeited & Extinct Peerages* (1866): 27–28 (sub Basset), 247–249 (sub Grey). *Annual Rpt. of the Deputy Keeper* 29 (1868): 85. Hutchins *Hist. & Antiqs. of Dorset* 3 (1868): 322–323 (Arundel ped.). Burke *Gen. & Heraldic Hist. of the Landed Gentry* 2 (1871): 781–782 (sub Lenthall). Harvey et al. *Vis. of Oxford 1566, 1574, 1634 & 1574* (H.S.P. 5) (1871): 199 (Lenthall ped.: "Sr Rowland Lenthall, Knt. 2. sonne."). Wild *Hist. of Castle Bytham* (1871): 46–68. *Vis. of Devon 1620* (H.S.P. 6) (1872): 169 (Lenthall ped.: "Rolandus de Lenthall, miles primog. [1] = Margareta fil. & coh. [Ricus Comes Arundell] 1 ux., [2] = filia Baronis Gray, ux. 2"). Hardy *Syllabus (in English) of the Docs. Rel. England & Other Kingdoms* 2 (1873): 613. *Annual Rpt. of the Deputy Keeper* 44 (1883): 593. *Arch. Cambrensis* 5th Ser. 1 (1884): 219–221 (Fitzalan ped.). Tresswell & Vincent *Vis. of Shropshire 1623, 1569 & 1584* 1 (H.S.P. 28) (1889): 145–148 (Cornwall ped.). Birch *Cat. Seals in the British Museum* 3 (1894): 188 (seal of Rowland Leynthale dated 1416 — A shield of arms, couché: quarterly, 1, 4, on a bend cotised three pierced mullets [LENTHALL]; 2, 3, a bend fusilly. Crest on a helmet and ornamental mantling a (peacock's ?) head between two wings erect.), 188–189 (seal of Roland Lenthall dated 1449–1450 — A large shield of arms: per pale, dex., quarterly, 1, 4, a lion rampant [ARUNDEL]; 2, 3, chequy [WARENNE]; dex., quarterly, 1, 4, a bend fusilly, 2, 3, on a bend between two cotises three pierced mullets [LENTHALL]. Suspended by a strap from a forked tree. Within a cusped panel, the background replenished with flowering branches). *Misc. Gen. et Heraldica* 2nd Ser. 5 (1894): 76–78. *List of Sheriffs for England & Wales* (PRO Lists and Indexes 9) (1898): 60. Wylie *Hist. of England under Henry IV* 4 (1898): 123–124, 244. Bridgeman *Hist. of Weston-under-Lizard* (Colls. Hist. Staffs. n.s. 2) (1899): 159–167. Wrottesley *Peds. from the Plea Rolls* (1905): 292. *Arch. Cambrensis* 6th Ser. 7(1) (1907): 1–34. Reade *House of Cornewall* (1908): 199–201. VCH *Warwick* 2 (1908): 133–136. *Sussex Arch. Colls.* 54 (1911): 9–10. *Feudal Aids* 6 (1920): 521. *C.P.* 6 (1926): 132–133 (sub Grey); 12(2) (1959): 946 (sub Zouche). *C.C.R. 1422–1429* (1933): 105. *Year Books of Henry VI: 1 Henry VI 1422* (Selden Soc. 50) (1933): 48–50. Salzman *Chartulary of the Priory of St. Pancras of Lewes* 2 (Sussex Rec. Soc. 40) (1934): 19–21. Barker *Talbot Deeds* (Lanc. & Cheshire Rec. Soc. 103) (1953): 44 (conveyance dated 21 Dec. 1416 by Rolande Lenthale, kt., and Margaret de Arundel his wife), 52. VCH *Essex* 4 (1956): 31; 8 (1983): 199–200. *Chancery Miscellanea Vol. III* (List & Index Soc. 26) (1967): 289. *National Lib. of Wales Jour.* 17 (1972): 277–286. *Cal. IPM* 20 (1995): 207–211; 23 (2004): 103. *Foundations* 1 (2004): 246–268. National Archives, C 1/6/162; C 1/14/17; C 1/69/128 (available at www.catalogue.nationalarchives.gov.uk/search.asp).

13. ELIZABETH ARUNDEL, born about 1371 (aged 44 in 1415). She married (1st) before Dec. 1378 **WILLIAM DE MONTAGU**, Knt., of Kenninghall, Norfolk, son and heir apparent of William de Montagu, 2nd Earl of Salisbury, by his 2nd wife, Elizabeth, daughter and co-heiress of John Mohun, K.G., 2nd Lord Mohun [see MONTAGU 7.i for his ancestry]. They had no issue. SIR WILLIAM DE MONTAGU died 6 August 1382, being killed by his own father in a tilting-match at Windsor, Berkshire. Elizabeth married (2nd) in July 1384 (as his 2nd wife) **THOMAS MOWBRAY**, K.G., 1st Duke of Norfolk, Earl of Nottingham, Earl Marshal, 6th Lord Mowbray, Lord Segrave [see MOWBRAY 7], Warden of the East Marches towards Scotland, 1389–91, Keeper of Berwick and Roxburgh, 1389–91, Privy Councillor, 1389, Lieutenant of Calais, Picardy, Flanders, and Artois, 1392, Captain of Calais, 1392–8, Chief Justice of North Wales, 1394, Chief Justice of Chester and Flint, 1394, Keeper of the Castle, Town, and Lordship of Lewes, 1397. They had five children [see MOWBRAY 7 for issue of this marriage]. In 1389 he was sent with 500 spears to repel an incursion of the Scots into Northumberland. His wife, Elizabeth, was a legatee in the 1393 will of her father. He was appointed joint Ambassador to France in 1395. He died of pestilence at Venice, Italy 22 Sept. 1399, on his return from pilgrimage to the Holy Land. He was buried in Venice. He left a will dated 23 May 1389. The creation of the Dukedom was annulled by Parliament 6 October 1399. In Hilary term 1401 his widow, Elizabeth, sued John and Idonea Sutton, stating that in 1400 they broke into her house in London, took goods worth 10 marks, and assaulted her servant, Agnes Dersyngham. Elizabeth married (3rd) without the king's license before 19 August 1401 (when her dower lands were ordered back into the king's hands) **ROBERT GOUSHILL** (or **GOUSEHILL**, **GOUSHALL**), Knt., of Hoveringham, Nottinghamshire, and Barlborough and Killamarsh, Derbyshire, son and heir of Nicholas de Goushill, Knt., of Hoveringham, Nottinghamshire. They had three daughters, Joan, Elizabeth, and Joyce. Elizabeth was pardoned 28 Sept. 1401 and her lands were restored. SIR ROBERT GOUSHILL was slain at the Battle of Shrewsbury 21 July 1403. His widow, Elizabeth, presented to the church of Ellingham, Norfolk in 1403. In Michaelmas term 1407 John Carleton sued Elizabeth, Duchess of Norfolk, widow and executrix of Robert Goushill, Knt., for a debt of 100 marks per a bond made between the late Robert Goushill on the one part and the said John Carleton with the late Lewis Clifford, Knt., on the other part. She married (4th) before 1408 (date of presentation) **GERARD USFLETE**, Knt., of Swanland (in North Ferriby), North Ferriby, and Ousefleet (in Whitgift), Yorkshire, Steward of the Duchy of Lancaster in Lincolnshire, son and heir of Gerard de Usflete, Knt., of Swanland (in North Ferriby), North Ferriby, and Ousefleet (in Whitgift), Yorkshire, Sheriff of Yorkshire, Knight of the Shire for Yorkshire, allegedly by his wife, Mary [see USFLETE 12 for her ancestry]. They had no issue. Gerard and his wife, Elizabeth, presented to the churches of Forncett, Norfolk, 1408, and Thorpe-next-Haddiscoe, Norfolk, 1409. In 1411 he sued John de Aylesford, Knt., for the next presentation to the church of Beckingham, Lincolnshire. In 1414 Richard Husewyf, of Rothley, Leicestershire, was pardoned for not appearing before the justices of the bench to answer Gerard and his wife, Elizabeth, Duchess of Norfolk, touching a debt of £40. His wife, Elizabeth, was co-heiress in 1415 to her brother, Thomas Arundel, K.G., K.B., Earl of Arundel and Surrey, Chief Butler of England, Lord High Treasurer. Gerard presented to the church of Aldborough, Norfolk in 1416, in right of his wife, Elizabeth, Duchess of Norfolk. He was granted protection in 1417, he then being in the retinue of the king. In 1419 he was appointed by the king to conduct the Duke of Brittany to the king. SIR GERARD USFLETE left a will dated 13 Sept. 1420, proved 12 Feb. 1420/1. In 1424 his widow, Elizabeth, Duchess of Norfolk, presented to the church of Suffield, Norfolk. Elizabeth, Duchess of Norfolk, died 8 July 1425, and was buried with her 3rd husband at Hoveringham, Nottinghamshire.

Sandford *Gen. Hist. of the Kings of England* (1677): 210–212. Nichols *Coll. of All the Wills* (1780): 120–144 (will of Richard, Earl of Arundel & Surrey). Throsby *Thoroton's Hist. of Nottinghamshire* 3 (1790): 61–64 (sub Hoveringham: "… By the stone is a fair tomb for sir Robert Gousell, and the dutchess of Norfolk his lady, upon which are their statues, as by the coronet on the head of hers is supposed. Under his head lyeth the figure of a blackamores head crowned, and part of the body, with a wreath about his neck. About the tomb were the arms of Leek, Langford, Babington, Chaworth impaling Caltofts, Rempstons, and divers others which were worn out in Mr. St. Lo Knivetons v. time…"). Blomefield *Essay towards a Top. Hist. of Norfolk* 5 (1806): 261; 8 (1808): 6, 58, 166. Blore *Hist. & Antiqs. of Rutland* 1(2) (1811): 114 (Mowbray ped.). Baker *Hist. & Antiqs. of Northampton* 1 (1822–30): 547, 588–590. Nicolas *Testamenta Vetusta* 1 (1826): 129–134 (will of Richard, Earl of Arundel & Surrey). Grimaldi *Origines Genealogicæ* (1828): 84. Chambers *Gen'l Hist. of Norfolk* 2 (1829): 711. Glover *Hist. of Derby* 2(1) (1829): 194 (Segrave ped.). Dallaway *Hist. of the Western Div. of Sussex* 2(1) (1832): 142. Tierney *Hist. & Antiqs. of the Castle & Town of Arundel* 1 (1834): chart foll. 192. *Coll. Top. et Gen.* 1 (1834): 316–317 (Arundel ped.: "Elizabeth Duchess of Norfolk; after wedded Sir Ro. Gousill."). Phelps *Hist. & Antiqs. of Somersetshire* 1 (1836): 213–218. *Testamenta Eboracensia* 1 (Surtees Soc. 4) (1836): 340–341 (will of Gerard de Usflete, Knt.), 397–398 (will of Gerard Usflete, Knt.). Boutell *Heraldry, Hist. & Popular* (1864): 257–258. Brown *L'Archivio di Venezia* (1865): 176–178. *Annual Rpt. of the Deputy Keeper* 29 (1868): 78; 44 (1883): 599. Hutchins *Hist. & Antiqs. of Dorset* 3 (1868): 291 (Montagu ped.), 322–323 (Arundel ped.). Hardy *Syllabus (in English) of the Docs. Rel. England & Other Kingdoms* 2 (1873): 609. *Misc. Gen. et Heraldica* 1st Ser. 2 (1876): 161–167 (Goushill arms: Barry of six or and gules, a canton ermine); 5th Ser. 6 (1926–28): 168–172 (Roberts ped.). Marsh *Annals of Chepstow Castle* (1883): 158–176. *Arch. Cambrensis* 5th Ser. 1 (1884): 219–221 (Fitzalan ped.). *Archives de l'Orient Latin* 2 (1884): 237–238, 243. Doyle *Official Baronage of England* 2 (1886): 580–582 (sub Norfolk), 685–686 (sub Nottingham). *Sussex Arch. Colls.* 35 (1887): 11 (chart); 41 (1898): 79–94; 74 (1933): 197 (Goushill arms: Barry or and azure a canton ermine). Jeayes *Desc. Cat. of the Charters & Muniments in the Possession of the Rt. Hon. Lord Fitzhardinge* (1892): 256 (Thomas [Arundel], Archbishop of York, styled "kinsman" by Thomas Mowbray, Earl Marshal and of Nottingham in 1389). Tilley *Old Halls, Manors & Fams. of Derbyshire* 1 (1892): 171; 3 (1899): 59–61. Birch *Cat. Seals in the British Museum* 3 (1894): 286 (seal of Elizabeth Mowbray, Duchess of Norfolk dated 1397 — A shield of arms: per pale, dex., three lions passant guardant in pale, a label of three points [MOWBRAY]; sin., quarterly, 1, 4, chequy

[WARENNE]; 2, 3, a lion rampant [ARUNDEL]. Suspended by a strap from a nebulée line of cloud intermingled with six estoiles. Supporters, on mounts, two cranes rising with expanded wings. Within a carved gothic trilobe, ornamented with small ball-flowers or quatrefoils along the inner edge. Legend: + Sigillum : dne : Elizabeth : ducisse : norfolchie : comitisse : [maresch' : dne : de :] bretby : et : de : knapp.), 288–289 (seal of Thomas Mowbray, Earl of Nottingham dated 1396 — A shield of arms, couché: three lions passant guardant in pale, a label of three points [MOWBRAY]. Crest on a helmet, lambrequin, and chapeau, a lion statant guardant crowned. Supporters, two trees, upon rocky mounts replenished with herbage and flowers. Within a carved border ornamented with small ball-flowers along the inner edge. Legend: Sig : Thome : co'itis : notyngham : et : marescalli : anglie : dni : de : .... et : de Segraue.), 331 (seal of Gerard Usflete dated 1416 — A shield of arms, couché: quarterly, 1, 4, a bend between six martlets [FURNIVAL]; 2, 3, on a fess three fleurs-de-lis [USFLETE]. Crest on a helmet, mantling, and lambrequin, an old man's head, bearded, wearing a pointed cap, hair plaited in a queue. In the background on the left hand side a sprig of foliage. Legend wanting. Carved border.). *C.P.R. 1377–1381* (1895): 296. *Genealogist* n.s. 15 (1898): 154–155; n.s. 16 (1899): 162; n.s. 19 (1903): 107. *C.P.R. 1399–1401* (1903): 207, 280 (instances of Elizabeth, late the wife of Thomas, duke of Norfolk styled "king's kinswoman"). Wrottesley *Peds. from the Plea Rolls* (1905): 250, 269–270, 292, 421. *Arch. Cambrensis* 6th Ser. 7(1) (1907): 1–34. Newett *Canon Pietro Casola's Pilgrimage to Jerusalem* (Pubs. Univ. Manchester Hist. Ser. 5) (1907): 35–36. Clark *Cartæ et Alia Munimenta de Glamorgancia* 4 (1910): 1453. *C.P.* 1 (1910): 253 (chart); 4 (1916): Appendix H, 670 (chart); 9 (1936): 601–604 (sub Norfolk); 11 (1949): 390–391 (sub Salisbury); 14 (1998): 503. *C.P.R. 1413–1416* (1910): 209. *Yorkshire Inqs.* 5 (Yorkshire Arch. Soc. Recs. 59) (1918): 5–6, 33. *C.C.R. 1381–1385* (1920): 163. VCH *Buckingham* 3 (1925): 86–87, 235–240, 450–451. Harvey et al. *Vis. of the North* 3 (Surtees Soc. 144) (1930): 86–88 (Moubray ped.: "Thomas Comes Mariscallus et postea Comes Nottingham dux Norffolcie exulatus 1383 = Elizabeth vna heredum Ricardi Comitis Arundell et Warren"). *Year Books of Henry VI: 1 Henry VI 1422* (Selden Soc. 50) (1933): 48–50. Salzman *Chartulary of the Priory of St. Pancras of Lewes* 2 (Sussex Rec. Soc. 40) (1934): 19–21. Chichele *Reg. of Henry Chichele* 1 (Canterbury & York Soc. 45) (1943): 143. Walker *Yorkshire Peds.* 3 (H.S.P. 96) (1944): 403–404 (Usflete ped.). Train *Abs. of IPMs Rel. Nottinghamshire* 2 (Thoroton Soc. Recs. 12) (1952): 136–138, 143. Barker *Talbot Deeds* (Lanc. & Cheshire Rec. Soc. 103) (1953): 44. VCH *Essex* 4 (1956): 31; 8 (1983): 199–200. *Ancient Deeds — Ser. B* 3 (List & Index Soc. 113) (1975): B.9376, B.11886. *Ancient Deeds — Ser. BB* (List & Index Soc. 137) (1977): 106. Craven *Derbyshire Armory* (Derbyshire Rec. Soc. 17) (1991): 72 (Goushill arms: Barry of six or and gules a canton ermine). *TAG* 67 (1992): 97–107. Roskell *House of Commons 1386–1421* 3 (1992): 217 (biog. of Sir Nicholas Goushill); 4 (1992): 698–699 (biog. of Sir Gerard Usfleet). Foulds *Thurgarton Cartulary* (1994): cxxxiv–cxlv. *Cal. IPM* 20 (1995): 207–211. Leese *Blood Royal* (1996): 123–128. *Foundations* 1 (2004): 246–268. Marcombe *Leper Knights* (2004): 39–40 (states Thomas Mowbray was buried in St. Mark's Cathedral, Venice). Court of Common Pleas, CP 40/560, rot. 116; CP 40/587, rot. 205 (Elizabeth, Duchess of Norfolk, executrix of the will of Robert Goushill, Knt., defendant) (available at http:// www.british-history.ac.uk/source.aspx?pubid=1272).

Children of Elizabeth Arundel, by Thomas Mowbray, K.G.:

i. **THOMAS MOWBRAY**, Knt., Earl of Norfolk, Earl of Nottingham, Earl Marshal, Lord Mowbray, Segrave, and Gower, married **CONSTANCE HOLAND** [see MOWBRAY 7.i].

ii. **JOHN MOWBRAY**, K.G., Earl of Norfolk, Earl of Nottingham, Earl Marshal, Lord Mowbray and Segrave, married **KATHERINE NEVILLE** [see MOWBRAY 8].

iii. **ELIZABETH MOWBRAY**, married **MICHAEL [DE LA] POLE**, Knt., 3rd Earl of Suffolk [see DE LA POLE 9.i].

iv. **ISABEL MOWBRAY**, married (1st) **HENRY FERRERS**, Knt., of Buttsbury and Marks (in Dunmow), Essex [see GROBY 14]; (2nd) **JAMES BERKELEY**, Knt., 6th Lord Berkeley [see BERKELEY 10].

v. **MARGARET MOWBRAY**, married (1st) **ROBERT HOWARD**, Knt., of Stoke Nayland, Suffolk [see HOWARD 12]; (2nd) **JOHN GREY**, K.G., of Ruthin, Denbighshire [see GREY 12].

Children of Elizabeth Arundel, by Robert Goushill, Knt.:

i. **JOAN GOUSHILL**, married **THOMAS STANLEY**, K.G., Lord Stanley [see STANLEY 14].

ii. **ELIZABETH GOUSHILL**, married **ROBERT WINGFIELD**, Knt., of Letheringham, Suffolk [see WINGFIELD 15].

iii. **JOYCE GOUSHILL**. In 1408 she and her sisters, Joan and Elizabeth Goushill, sued their uncle, Nicholas Goushill, for the manors of Barlborough and Killamarsh, Derbyshire. *Genealogist* n.s. 15 (1898): 154–155. Wrottesley *Peds. from the Plea Rolls* (1905): 250. Foulds *Thurgarton Cartulary* (1994): cxxxiv–cxlv.

FITZ HERBERT

1. HERBERT OF WINCHESTER (also styled **HERBERT THE CHAMBERLAIN**), of Londesborough, Towthorpe, Weaverthorpe, and Weighton, Yorkshire, Brockhampton (in Havant), LaRode (in Selborne), Micheldever, and Soberton, Hampshire, Lissington, Lincolnshire, etc., Chamberlain and Treasurer under Kings William II and Henry I. He married **EMMA** _____, allegedly an illegitimate daughter of Étienne Henri, Count of Blois, and half-sister to Stephen, King of England. They had two sons, Herbert and [Saint] William [Archbishop of York], and two daughters, _____ (wife of Robert de Venuiz) and _____ (wife of William Croc). At the time of the Domesday Inquest of 1086, he held two manors in Hampshire *in capite* worth a total of £3 a year, plus part of a manor of the New Minister, Winchester worth £5, and two manors of Hugh de Port worth each £1. The Abingdon chronicler refers to him as the "king's chamberlain and treasurer" in passages describing his activities between 1097 and 1100 and again sometime before 1100 and 1130. He was granted property next to the church of St. John del Pyke, Yorkshire by Archbishop Thomas c.1109. He attests four surviving charters of King Henry I and is addressed in several more, all of them dealing with financial matters and all dating from the earlier part of the king's reign. SIR HERBERT OF WINCHESTER was living in 1111, when he was a member of the Michaelmas treasury court at Winchester. He probably died in 1118/20. In 1130 his widow owed money on estates which had belonged to her husband in Yorkshire.

Dugdale *Baronage of England* 1 (1675): 624–625. Dugdale *Monasticon Anglicanum* 6(3) (1830): 1196–1197. *Arch. Cambrensis* 3rd Ser. 4 (1858): 16–30. Eyton *Antiqs. of Shropshire* 7 (1868): 146-156. Robinson *Gilbert Crispin, Abbot of Winceshester* (1911): 146. Farrer *Early Yorkshire Charters* 2 (1915): 27, 127. Tout *Chapters in the Administrative Hist. of Medieval England* 1 (1920): 76-77. *Archaeologia* 72 (1922): 51–70. Poole "The Appointment and Deprivation of St. William, Archbishop of York," in *English Hist. Rev.* 45 (1930): 273–281. White "The Parentage of Herbert the Chamberlain," in *Notes & Queries* 162 (1932): 439–441, 453–455. Clay *York Minster Fasti* (Yorkshire Arch. Soc. Rec. Ser. 123) (1957): 22. *NGSQ* 59 (1971): 256–267; 60 (1972): 33–35. Hollister "The Origins of the English Treasury" in *English Hist. Rev.* 93 (1978): 262–275 ("At the height of [King] Henry [I]'s military difficulties in 1118, a frightening though unsuccessful attempt was made on his life by certain unidentified members of his own household, led by a mysterious, unnamed chamberlain. We have two independent accounts of this assassination plot. Suger of Saint-Denis reports that the leader was a chamberlain whose name began with the letter H., who had been closely associated with the king and had been enriched and made famous by him. Henry I afterwards treated the would-be assassin with great mercy, Suger says, blinding and castrating him rather than hanging him as he deserved. William of Malmesbury tells us simply that he was a certain chamberlain of low birth who rose to fame as custodian of the royal treasury. If he was as well known as Malmesbury and Suger assert, his name should appear somewhere in the records of the peiod, and yet he has never been identified. I suggest that the culprit was Herbert the Chamberlain, who was the only man known to have been styled treasurer at the time and the only known chamberlain in the entire reign to have a name beginning with H. Herbert is such an obvious candidate that he would doubtless have been identified long before were it not for the deepset tradition that he remained in office until 1129 or 1130. In reality we have seen that he had in all likelihood been succeeded by Geoffrey de Clinton in or before 1120. There is no charter or chronicle evidence of his being alive at any time after 1118; indeed, the charter evidence suggests that his lands had passed to his eldest son, Herbert fitz Herbert, by 1121."). Newman *Anglo-Norman Nobility in the Reign of Henry I: The Second Generation* (1988): 129. Norton *St. William of York* (2006). Scammell *Hugh Du Puiset* (2011): 9.

Children of Herbert of Winchester, by Emma (allegedly of Blois):

i. **HERBERT FITZ HERBERT** [see next].

ii. **WILLIAM FITZ HERBERT**. Poole "Appointment and Deprivation of St. William, Archbishop of York," in *English Hist. Rev.* 45 (1930): 273–281 ("The ancestry of Archbishop William has not been fully established. We have two statements by John of Hexham, an honest and well-informed chronicler, who wrote some twenty years after the archbishop's death… John's information was that William was the son of Herbert of Winchester, treasurer to King Henry II. In another place he tells us that when the archbishop was deprived of his see he resorted to the court of his kinsman Roger, king of Sicily, where he dwelt for a long time. The York statement, if we admit a simple emendation, furnishes the link required to connect Herbert with the king of Sicily. The statement is that William was 'filius viri secundum caducos huius mundi honores potentissimi, strenuissimi comitis

Herberti, ex Emma sorore praedicti regis [Stephani].' These words appear in three York texts. Now, as it is known that William was a son of Herbert the Chamberlain, it is plain that the statement as it stands in incorrect. The error, I can hardly doubt, has arisen from the scribe accidentally confusing in one the two clauses which mentioned 'cam' Herberti' and 'com' Herberti.' and omitting one of them. I therefore read the words as follows: 'filius Herberti camerarii, filii viri, &c., comitis Herberti'. Chronology alone requires the insertion of a generation, and its insertion alone explains John of Hexham's allusion to King Roger of Sicily. Herbert the 'strenuissimus comes' can only be Herbert II, count of Maine. He had succeeded to this dignity on the death of his father Hugh II in 1051, but never obtained more than transient possession of the land. [Count] Herbert [II] I presume to have left an illegitimate son whose very existence is ignored in our authorities. He was given his father's name, which was repeated among his descendants for a number of generations. He was probably an infant when he was left an orphan, and was, as I conjecture, taken in charge by Duke William who obtained possession of Maine. He was brought to England and provided with a modest estate there. He was also on the fringe of relationship with the house of Blois; for, according to Thomas Stubbs, he married Emma, an illegitimate daughter of Count Stephen and a half-sister of the future King Stephen. Herbert the chamberlain's second son William … was brought up, says John of Hexham, like a nobleman, in a life of pleasure and wealth, *in deliciis et divitiis*, and he was early established in the treasureship of York, the richest office in the cathedral."). Norton *St. William of York* (2006). Scammell *Hugh Du Puiset* (2011): 9.

2. HERBERT FITZ HERBERT, of Londesborough and Weaverthorpe, Yorkshire, etc., King's Chamberlain, son and heir. He married **SIBYL CORBET**, daughter and co-heiress of Robert Fitz Corbet, of Alcester, Warwickshire and Pontesbury and Woodcote, Shropshire. She was a former mistress of Henry I, King of England [see ENGLAND 2], by whom she was the mother of Reynold Fitz Roy, Earl of Cornwall [see ENGLAND 2.i]. Herbert and Sibyl had three sons, Robert [Chamberlain to King Henry II], Herbert, and probably Henry. He appears to have succeeded to his father's lands by 1121. He confirmed the gift of his brother, William, of the church of Weaverthorpe, Yorkshire to Nostell Priory sometime before 1127, and probably in or before 1122, when his own charter was confirmed by King Henry I. He is recorded in the Pipe Rolls of 1130, as paying 353 marks to have his father's lands. Sometime c.1130–33, he had a suit with Herbert, Abbot of Westminster, regarding lands at Parham, Sussex and Mapelefort, Middlesex; Abbot Herbert was subsequently able to prove his title to these lands in the presence of the barons of the Exchequer. He was styled chamberlain in the Winchester Survey of 1148 and in a royal charter to his son, Robert, in 1155. **HERBERT FITZ HERBERT** was dead sometime before 1155. His widow, Sibyl, was living in 1157.

Dugdale *Monasticon Anglicanum* 6(3) (1830): 1196–1197. Lipscomb *Hist. & Antiqs. of Buckingham* 1 (1847): 297 (Herbert ped.). *Arch. Cambrensis* 3rd Ser. 4 (1858): 16–30. Eyton *Antiq. of Shropshire* 7 (1868): 146-156. VCH *Hampshire* 3 (1908): 257–268. Poole "Appointment and Deprivation of St. William, Archbishop of York," in *English Hist. Rev.* 45 (1930): 273–281. White "Parentage of Herbert the Chamberlain," in *Notes & Queries* 162 (1932): 439–441, 453–455. Hollister "Origins of the English Treasury" in *English Hist. Rev.* 93 (1978): 262–275 ("Herbert fitz Herbert married Henry I's mistress, Sibyl Corbet, but on [his father] Herbert the Chamberlain's disgrace his chamberlainship and treasureship passed not to his son but to Geoffrey de Cliton. Herbert fitz Herbert survived but in a state of almost total obscureity…. He never attests for Henry I, Stephen or the Empress and is clearly not functioning at a royal chamberlain in those years."). Mason *Westminster Abbey Charters, 1066–c.1214* (London Rec. Soc. 25) (1988): 62–68, 225. Norton *St. William of York* (2006). Scammell *Hugh Du Puiset* (2011): 9.

3. HERBERT FITZ HERBERT, 2nd son, Sheriff of Gloucestershire, 1194–98, was an adult by 1161–2. He married **LUCY OF HEREFORD**, daughter of Miles of Gloucester (also known as Miles Fitz Walter), 1st Earl of Hereford, Constable of Gloucester, by Sibyl, daughter of Bernard de Neufmarché. They had two sons, Peter and Matthew. He was heir in 1165 to his older brother, Robert Fitz Herbert, Chamberlain to King Henry II. Sometime before 1166 his wife, Lucy, was co-heiress to her brother, Mahel of Hereford, Knt., lord of Abergavenny and Brecknock, Constable of England, by which she inherited Blaen Llyfni (in Cathedine) and Bwlch y Dinas, Breconshire and a moiety of the manors of Haresfield and Southam (in Bishop's Cleeve), Gloucestershire, and one-third share of Chirton, Wiltshire. Sometime before 1168 he attested a charter of Walter de Dunstanville to Lewes Priory as "Herbert Brother of Earl Reginald." He also witnessed two charters for his half-brother, Reynold Fitz Roy, Earl of Cornwall, in the period, c. 1170–75. In 1175–6 he was fined 20 marks for failing to appear before the king's justices and 500 marks under forest pleas in Hampshire. In 1177 King Henry II offered the kingdom of Limerick to Herbert Fitz Herbert, his brother, William [de Marsh], and their nephew, Joel de Pomeroy; all three declined the king's offer, since control of Limerick was merely nominal. He witnessed several charters in favor of Southwick Priory, Hampshire in the 1180s or 1190s. His estates were confiscated by the king for an unknown offense in 1184. Sometime after 1193, his wife, Lucy, granted Llanthony Secunda her land in Quedgeley, together with her body for burial. Sometime before 1194, he and his sons, Peter and Matthew, witnessed a charter of John de Gisors. He proffered relief in 1196 for the possession of one-third share of the barony of Miles of Gloucester, his wife's father. HERBERT FITZ HERBERT died shortly before June 1204. His widow, Lucy, was living 1219 or 1220. At her death, she was buried at the Chapter House of Lanthony Priory outside Gloucester.

Placitorum in Domo Capitulari Westmonasteriensi Asservatorum Abbrevatio (1811): 44. *Coll. Top. et Gen.* 1 (1834): 168–169. Banks *Baronies in Fee* 2 (1843): 80–81 (sub John Fitz-Reginald). Lipscomb *Hist. & Antiqs. of Buckingham* 1 (1847): 297 (Herbert ped.). Stubbs *Gesta Regis Henrici Secundi Benedicti Abbatis* (or *Chron. of the Reigns of Henry II. & Richard I. A.D. 1169–1192*) 1 (Rolls Ser. 49) (1867): 163 ("Deditque ibidem Hereberto filio Hereberti, et Willelmo fratri comitis Reginaldi, et Joelllano de la Pumerai, nepoti eorum, regnum be Limeric pro servitio sexaginta militum"), 172 ("Nam Herbertus, et Willelmus, fratres Reginaldi comitis Cornubiae, et Joellanus de Pumeria nepos eorum, regnum illud havere noluerunt; sed illud reddiderunt domino regi et Johanni filio suo liberum et quietum ab omni calumnia eorum"). Eyton *Antiq. of Shropshire* 2 (1855): 278, footnote 48; 7 (1868): 146-156. *Arch. Cambrensis* 3rd ser. 4 (1858): 16–30. Brewer *Registrum Malmesburiense* (or *The Register of Malmesbury Abbey*) 2 (Rolls Ser. 72) (1880): 11–12, 57–58, 65–67. Brown *Cartularium Prioratus de Gyseburne* 2 (Surtees Soc. 89) (1894): 303. Hall *Red Book of the Exchequer* 1 (Rolls Ser.) (1896): 31–32, 45, 73–74, 91, 99–100, 108, 115, 120, 129–130, 144, 148, 151–152, 158, 198–199, 205, 207, 246, 290–291, 412–413. *List of Sheriffs for England & Wales* (PRO Lists and Indexes 9) (1898): 49. Wrottesley *Peds. from the Plea Rolls* (1905): 490. VCH *Hampshire* 4 (1911): 145–147, 532. VCH *Berkshire* 3 (1923): 311–329. *C.P.* 6 (1926): 457, footnote c (sub Hereford) ("Giraldus Cambrensis … states that Miles had 5 sons, famous knights, Roger, Walter, Henry, William and Mahel, who all, *except William*, succeeded to the paternal inheritance and all *d.s.p.* (*Itinerarim Kambriae*, vol. vi, pp. 29, 30). At Mahel's death, the properties were divided up among his three sisters and their husbands: (1) Margaret, wife of Sir Humphrey de Bohun, (2) Berthe, wife of William de Briouze or Brewes; and (3) Lucy, wife of Herbert Fitz Herbert … Lucy had the forest of Dean [which last had been expressly exluded in the charter of Henry II to Earl Roger] (*Monasticon*, vol. vi, p. 134)."). David Walker ed. "Charters of the Earldom of Hereford, 1095–1201," in *Camden Miscellany* 22 (Camden Soc. 4th Ser. 1) (1964): 74–75. Sanders *English Baronies* (1960): 8–9. VCH *Gloucester* 8 (1968): 2–25; 10 (1972): 190–194. VCH *Wiltshire* 10 (1975): 62–63. Hanna *Cartularies of Southwick Priory* 2 (Hampshire Rec. Ser. 10) (1989): 60. Norton *St. William of York* (2006).

4. PETER FITZ HERBERT, of Blaen Llyfni (in Cathedine), Breconshire, Wales, Crookham (in Thatcham) and Leckhampstead, Berkshire, Haresfield and Southam (in Bishop's Cleeve), Gloucestershire, North Oakley (in Kingsclere) and Wolverton, Hampshire, Chirton, Wiltshire, etc., Keeper of Pickering Castle, Sheriff of Yorkshire, 1214–15, and, in right of his 2nd wife, of Oakham and Belton, Rutland, son and eventual heir, was an adult by 1204. He married (1st) by settlement dated 28 Nov. 1203 **ALICE FITZ ROBERT**, daughter of Robert Fitz Roger, of Warkworth and Whalton, Northumberland, by Margaret, daughter and co-heiress of William de Chesney [see CLAVERING 3 for her ancestry]. Her maritagium included the manor of More Hall (in Salle) Norfolk. They had two sons, Herbert, Knt., and Reynold, Knt., and one daughter, Lucy. In 1211 he proffered 500 marks for half of the manor of Market Weighton, Yorkshire, which offer was accepted. He witnessed the instrument by which King John surrendered England to Pope Innocent III in 1213. In 1214 he notified the barons of the Exchequer and justices of the Bench that he had received £100 from the Abbot and convent of Westminster, according to a concord made between them regarding the manor of Parham, Sussex. In 1215 he was granted the manor of Wolverton, Hampshire by King John, which grant was rendered void in 1217; he subsequently regained possession of the manor before 1228. About 1215 Peter and his brother, Matthew, witnessed a charter of Roger de Merlay to Southwick Priory, Hampshire. During the unrest at the end of the reign of King John, Giles de Brewes seized Blaen Llyfni which in turn passed in 1215 to his brother, Reynold de Brewes. In 1217 Reynold was ordered to restore the lands to Peter. Peter presented to the church of St. John's, Oxford in 1223. His wife, Alice, died before 1225. He married (2nd) in or before 1225 **ISABEL DE FERRERS**, widow of Roger de Mortimer (died 24 June 1214), and daughter of Walkelin de Ferrers, of Oakham, Rutland, seigneur of Ferrières-Saint-Hilaire. They had no known issue. In 1227 Sarah, Prioress of Cookhill, sued Peter Fitz Herbert and William Botreaux regarding the advowson of the church of Alcester, Warwickshire. The same year the king granted the manor of Oakham, Rutland to Peter's wife, Isabel, for life. In 1228 Peter was granted free warren in his lands at Crookham and Leckhampstead, Berkshire, and in all his lands in Hampshire and Wiltshire. In 1231 he was admonished not to disturb the nuns of Amesbury in their possessions in Wallop, Hampshire for which he had sued them. At some unknown date, he granted license to the nuns of Godstow to enclose, plough and sow their essart which lay next to his park of Wolverton, Hampshire. PETER FITZ HERBERT died shortly before 6 June 1235, and was buried at Reading, Berkshire. His widow, Isabel, died shortly before 29 April 1252.

Placitorum in Domo Capitulari Westmonasteriensi Asservatorum Abbreviatio (1811): 44. Banks *Baronies in Fee* 2 (1843): 80–81 (sub John Fitz-Reginald). Lipscomb *Hist. & Antiqs. of Buckingham* 1 (1847): 297 (Herbert ped.). *Arch. Cambrensis* 3rd Ser. 4 (1858): 16–30; 4th Ser. 14 (1883): 159–160 (charter of Peter Fitz Herbert). Maitland *Bracton's Note Book* 3 (1887): 336. Hall *Red Book of the Exchequer* 1 (Rolls Ser.) (1896): 93–94, 157. *List of Sheriffs for England & Wales* (PRO Lists and Indexes 9) (1898): 161. Barfield *Thatcham, Berks, & its Manor* 2 (1901). Wrottesley *Peds. from the Plea Rolls* (1905): 53–54, 490. VCH *Hampshire* 4 (1911): 249–267, 270–271, 525–530. Phillimore *Rotuli Hugonis de Welles Episcopi Lincolniensis 1209–1235* 2 (Lincoln Rec. Soc. 6) (1913): 16. VCH *Berkshire* 3 (1923): 311–329. VCH *Rutland* 2 (1935): 5–27, 27–32. Paget (1957) 132:2 (lord of Blaenlyfni). Eyton *Antiqs. of Shropshire* 7:148, 150–154. C.P. V 465 note d, 442 note c; NGSQ cit.; *Notebook of Tristram Risdon*: 75-77; The Gen. n.s. 10: 29; Devonshire Association, 50: 433–434. Sanders *English Baronies* (1960): 8. Turner *King & his Courts* (1968): 256. VCH *Gloucester* 8 (1968): 2–25; 10 (1972): 190–194. VCH *Worcester* 2 (1971): 156–158. VCH *Wiltshire* 10 (1975): 62–63. Kemp *Reading Abbey Cartularies* 1 (Camden 4th Ser. 31) (1986): 247, 390–391. Mason *Westminster Abbey Charters, 1066–c.1214* (London Rec. Soc. 25) (1988): 317–318 (charter of Peter Fitz Herbert). Hanna *Cartularies of Southwick Priory* 2 (Hampshire Rec. Ser. 10) (1989): 60, 69. Holt *Northerners* (1992): 236. Ormrod *Lord Lieutenants & High Sheriffs of Yorkshire, 1066–2000* (2000): 53–54. Greenway *Fasti Ecclesiæ Anglicanæ 1066–1300* 6 (1999): 105–107. Norton *St. William of York* (2006).

Children of Peter Fitz Herbert, by Alice Fitz Robert:

i. **REYNOLD FITZ PETER**, Knt. [see next].

ii. **LUCY FITZ PETER**, married **WILLIAM DE ROOS**, Knt., of Helmsley, Yorkshire [see ROOS 6].

5. REYNOLD FITZ PETER, Knt., of Blaen Llyfni (in Cathedine), Bwlch y Dinas (in Talgarth), and Talgarth, Breconshire, Wales, Crookham (in Thatcham) and Stanford (in Stanford Dingley), Berkshire, Haresfield and Southam (in Bishop's Cleeve), Gloucestershire, Bedhampton, Cliddesden, Herriard, Kempshott (in Winslade), North Oakley (in Kingsclere), Tadley, and Wolverton, Hampshire, Pontesbury, Shropshire, Calstone, Chirton, and Stanton Fitzwarren, Wiltshire, Calstone, Londesborough, Weaverthorpe, and Weighton, Yorkshire, etc., Joint Guardian of the Welsh Marches, Sheriff of Hampshire, 1261–4, Constable of Winchester Castle, and, in right of his 2nd wife, of Chewton, Somerset and Carbury, co. Kildare, Ireland, 2nd son by his father's 1st marriage. He married (1st) before September 1249 **ALICE** _____. They had two sons, John Fitz Reynold, Knt. [Lord Fitz Reynold], and Walter [Portioner of Pontesbury, Shropshire, Rector of Stanton Fitzwarren, Wiltshire], and five daughters, Eleanor, Alice, Katherine, Alice (wife of John de Manners) and allegedly Beatrice (wife of William de Mohun, Knt.). He witnessed a charter of his brother, Herbert Fitz Peter, to Brecon Priory dated c.1245. He was heir in 1248 to his brother, Herbert Fitz Peter, Knt. In 1252 he was granted a weekly market to be held at his manor of Market Weighton, Yorkshire, together with free warren in his demesne lands there. In 1257 he was granted free warren in his demesne lands in Leckhampstead, Berkshire, provided they are are within the king's forest. He supported King Henry III against the barons, and was sent to subdue the rebeles who still held out in Kenilworth. He fought in Wales in 1258 and 1260, 1263, 1277, 1280. He was Joint Guardian of the Welsh Marches 10 May 1257, Sheriff of Hampshire and Constable of Winchester Castle, 1261. In the period, c.1260–70, he granted one messuage and one virgate of land in Herriard, Hampshire called Hinewode to Henry de Bohun, rector of Farleigh. In 1263 he leased from the Crown a property known as The King's Mews in the city of Southampton, Hampshire, which property he still held in 1285. In 1263 he brought a plea against Walter de Beauchamp, Knt., in the king's court for a moiety of Alcester, Warwickshire. His wife, Alice, was living 24 October 1265. In 1269 he granted the advowson of the church of Weaverthorpe, Yorkshire to the Dean and chapter of York. In 1271 he quitclaimed to the church of York, Archbishop Giffard, and the dean all his right in the patronage of the church of Weighton, Yorkshire. In 1272–3 Oliver de Punchardon arraigned an assize of novel disseisin against him touching a tenement in Stanford, Berkshire. In 1273 he released all his claim to the manor of Nether Wallop, Hampshire to the Prioress of Amesbury in return for 200 marks. In 1274–5 he appointed attorneys in his absence, he then going to parts beyond seas. In 1274–5 Robert de Junnere [Immere] arraigned an assize of novel disseisin against him and others touching a tenement in Ashe, Hampshire. In 1275 he presented to the church of Londesborough, Yorkshire. In 1275–6 Oliver de Punchardon arraigned an assize of novel disseisin against him and others touching a tenement in Stanford, Berkshire. In 1276 the king granted him the manor of Freemantle (in Kingsclere), Berkshire for life. In 1276 an assize came to recognize whether Reynold Fitz Peter, John del Maner, and Richard de Cardeville unjustly disseized Robert de Immere of his free tenement in Ashe, Hampshire. In 1276–7 he was granted letters of protection, he then going in the king's suite to the parts of Wales. In 1276–7 Oliver de Punchardon arraigned an assize of novel disseisin against him and others touching a tenement in Bradfield, Berkshire. In the same period, William de Brewouse [Brewes] arraigned an assize of novel disseisin against him and others touching a tenement in Chirton, Wiltshire. About 1277–86 Maud, widow of William de Peautun, petitioned the king and council alleging that Reynold Fitz Peter had abducted her son, John, disseised him of the manor of Peautun, and threw her and her people out. In 1277–8 Oliver de Punchardun arraigned an assize of novel disseisin against him and others regarding a tenement in Stanford, Bradfield, and Bucklebury, Berkshire. In 1278 he broke the locks and doors of the Prebendaries' barns at Pontesbury, Shropshire, carried off their goods and fruits, and done other injuries to Master Thomas de Wynton and his Comporcioners, to the prejudice of the liberty of the Church; the same year Thomas de Cantelowe, Bishop of Hereford, requested the Bishop of Worcester publish in his diocese the sentence of excommunication pronounced against Reynold Fitz Peter who had persisted in his contumacy. In 1278–9 the prior of Llanthony without Gloucester arraigned a jury against him touching the church of Tockenham, Wiltshire. He married (2nd) before 3 Jan. 1279 **JOAN DE VIVONNE**, widow successively of Ingram de Percy, Knt., of Dalton, co. Durham and Kirkby Overblow, Yorkshire, King's yeoman (died shortly before 10 October 1262), and Amaury (or Emery) de Rochechouart (living 9 August 1269), and daughter and co-heiress of William de Forz (otherwise William de Vivonne), Knt., of Chewton, Somerset, by his wife, Maud, daughter of William de Ferrers, 5th Earl of Derby [see MALET 3 for her ancestry]. She was born about 1251 (aged 8 in 1259). They had four sons, Peter, Knt., Reynold, Matthew, and William (clerk), and two daughters, Isabel and Beatrice. By an unknown mistress, he also had an illegitimate son, David de Pontesbury (alias David Fitz Reynold) [Rector of Londesborough, Yorkshire, Portioner of Pontesbury]. In 1280 Reynold made good his right to free warren in all his demesne lands in North Oakley (in Kingsclere), Hampshire, basing his claim on a charter of King Henry III to his father, Peter Fitz Herbert. He took the Abbess and convent of Godstow under his special protection, receiving common of pasture for himself and his men in the wood called 'The Frith' in exchange for his charter. In 1279–80 Margaret daughter of John Neuman and Alice and Juliane her sisters arraigned an assize of mort d'ancestor against him touching a messuage and land in Hinton Martell, Dorset. In 1282 he abjured his concubine, with an oath to go to the Holy Land, if he relapsed. In 1284 Archbishop Peckham wrote to him requesting that he cease molesting the priory of Brecon. SIR REYNOLD FITZ PETER died testate 4 (or 5) May 1286. In 1289 his widow, Joan, made claim against William de Brewes (or Breouse) to one third of the manor of Manningford, Wiltshire, and to one third of six messuages and four virgates of arable land with appurtenances in Manningford Bruce and Chirton, Wiltshire as being her dower, etc. In March 1292 she was granted protection for three years, she then going beyond seas. In 1294 the manor of Bedhampton, Hampshire, which Joan held in dower, was taken into the king's hands by reason of default made by Joan against the Master of the Hospital of St. John and St. Nicholas at Portsmouth; sometime before her death, however, she appears to have recovered the manor. In 1310 she was summoned to answer John le Botiler, of Llantwit, and Beatrice his wife of a plea why she made waste, sale, and destruction of the houses and woods which she had of the inheritance of Beatrice in Haresfield, Gloucestershire. Joan died 1 June 1314.

Collinson *Hist. & Antiqs. of the County of Somerset* 2 (1791): 116–117. Dugdale *Monasticon Anglicanum* 6(3) (1830): 1196–1197. *Coll. Top. et Gen.* 7 (1841): 136–138. Banks *Baronies in Fee* 2 (1843): 80–81 (sub John Fitz-Reginald). Lipscomb *Hist. & Antiqs. of Buckingham* 1 (1847): 297 (Herbert ped.). *Arch. Cambrensis* 3rd Ser. 4 (1858): 16–30; 4th Ser. 13 (1882): 300–301 (charter of Herbert Fitz Peter dated c.1245). Eyton *Antiqs. of Shropshire* 7 (1858): 141–142, 146–156. *Memoirs chiefly illus. of the Hist. & Antiqs. of Northumberland* 2 (1858): 90. Shirley *Royal & Other Hist. Letters Ill. of King Henry III* 2 (Rolls Ser. 27) (1866): 219–221, 230–231, 237–238, 251–252, 367–369. Hart *Historia et Cartularium Monasterii Sancti Petri Gloucestriae* 3 (Rolls Ser.) (1867): 268. Kirkby *Survey of York* (Surtees Soc. 49) (1867): 79, 261. Gray *Reg., or Rolls, of Walter Gray, Lord Archbishop of York* (Surtees Soc. 56) (1872): 50 (charter of Reynold Fitz Peter, Knt., dated 1272). *Picards or Pichards of Stradewy* (1878): 25–26, 32–36, chart foll. 172. *Annual Rpt. of the Deputy Keeper* 42 (1881): 659; 44 (1883): 12, 104; 45 (1885): 197, 315; 46 (1886): 108, 128, 260, 286; 47 (1886): 351; 48 (1887): 190; 49 (1888): 87. Peckham *Reg. Epistolarum Fratris Johannis Peckham* 2 (Rolls Ser. 77(2)) (1884): 581; 3 (Rolls Ser. 77) (1885): 810 (letter to noble man ["nobili viro"] Sir Reginald Fitz Peter from John Peckham, Archbishop of Canterbury dated 1284), 831–832, 1021. Money *Hist. of the Ancient Town & Borough of Newbury* (1887): 121–123. Thoyts *Hist. of Esse or Ashe, Hampshire* (1888): 16–17, 20–21. *C.P.R. 1281–1292* (1893): 409, 481. *Two Cartularies of the Augustinian Priory of Bruton & Cluniac Priory of Montacute* (Somerset Rec. Soc. 8) (1894): 78–79. *C.P.R. 1292–1301* (1895): 602. *List of Sheriffs for England & Wales* (PRO Lists and Indexes 9) (1898): 54. *C.C.R. 1272–1279* (1900): 551–552. Barfield *Thatcham* 2 (1901). *C.C.R. 1279–1288* (1902): 395–396, 399, 425, 430. *C.Ch.R.* 1 (1903): 374, 474. *Ancestor* 11 (1904): 61–70. *C.C.R. 1288–1296* (1904): 29, 393, 439. Giffard *Reg. of Walter Giffard Archbishop of York* (Surtees Soc. 109) (1904): 17, 53–54, 288. Wrottesley *Peds. from the Plea Rolls* (1905): 35, 53–54. *Year Books of Edward II* 3 (Selden Soc. 20) (1905): 139–140. *Yorkshire Inqs.* 4 (Yorkshire Arch. Soc. Recs. 37) (1906): 105, 131–132. *Cal. IPM* 2 (1906): 364–365; 5 (1908): 275. *Bull. de la Soc. les Amis des Sciences et Arts de Rochechouart* 16 (1907): 26–35. Cantilupe *Reg. of Thome de Cantilupo Episcopi Herefordensis* (Canterbury & York Soc. 2) (1907): 142–143, 153–155, 159–160, 163, 188–189, 191, 193–194, 286. *Rpt. on MSS in Various Colls.* 4 (Hist. MSS Comm. 55) (1907): 142–143 (charter of Reynold Fitz Peter dated c.1250), 147, 148 (charter of Reynold Fitz Peter dated c.1260–70), 150. *C.C.R. 1302–1307* (1908): 391, 403. VCH *Bedford* 2 (1908): 351–352. VCH *Hampshire* 3 (1908): 142–144, 366–369; 4 (1911): 145–147, 179–181, 198–199, 249–267, 270–271, 525–530. *C.P.R. 1258–1266* (1910): 36, 38, 55, 113, 120, 146, 205, 206, 219, 220, 247, 265, 499–500. *C.P.R. 1266–1272* (1913): 735. Romeyn *Reg. of John le Romeyn Lord Archbishop of York* 1 (Surtees Soc. 123) (1913): 209–210. Pontisarra *Reg. Johannes de Pontissara Episcopi Wyntoniensis* 2 (Surrey Rec. Soc. 1(2)) (1915): 147, 174–185, 181. *Desc. Cat. Ancient Deeds* 6 (1915): 255–256. *C.P.* 4 (1916): 199; 5 (1926): 465–467 (sub FitzReynold); 11 (1949): 323–325 (sub Saint John). VCH *Berkshire* 3 (1923): 311–329; 4 (1924): 110–114. *Misc. Gen. et Heraldica* 5th Ser. 6 (1926–28): 81–87. VCH *Durham* 3 (1928): 254–263. *Somersetshire Pleas* 2 (1923) (Somerset Rec. Soc. 36): 96–99; 4(1) (Somerset Rec. Soc. 44) (1929): 8–9, 229. Moor *Knights of Edward I* 2 (H.S.P. 81) (1929): 52–53, 80. Gandavo *Reg. Simonis de Gandavo Diocesis Saresbiriensis* 2 (Canterbury & York Soc. 41) (1934): 563. *C.C.R. 1268–1272* (1938): 101–102. VCH *Sussex* 4 (1953): 158–159. Williams *Collectanea* (Wiltshire Arch. & Natural Hist. Soc. Recs. Branch 12) (1956): 114–115. Paget *Baronage of England* (1957) 218: 4–8. Clay *York Minster Fasti* 2 (Yorkshire Arch. Soc. Recs. 124) (1959): 80–82, 133–135 (charter of Reynold Fitz Peter dated 1269). Sanders *English Baronies* (1960): 9, 39. Beardwood *Trial of Walter Langton, Bishop of Lichfield 1307–1312* (Trans. American Philosophical Soc. n.s. 54 (3)) (1964): 34. Bean *Decline of English Feudalism* (1968): 108. VCH *Gloucester* 8 (1968): 2–25; 10 (1972): 181–185, 190–194. *NGSQ* 59 (1971): 254–262. VCH *Wiltshire* 10 (1975): 62–63. Ross *Cartulary of Cirencester Abbey* 3 (1977): 777–778, 784. Keene & Rumble *Survey of Medieval Winchester* (1985): 937. Keene *Survey of Medieval Winchester* 2 (1986): 937. Kemp *Reading Abbey Cartularies* 1 (Camden Soc. 4th Ser. 31) (1986): 247, 390–391. Hanna *Cartularies of Southwick Priory* 1 (Hampshire Recs. 9) (1988): 214–215. *C.R.R.* 19 (1991): 244. English *Yorkshire Hundred & Quo Warranto Rolls* (Yorkshire Arch. Soc. Recs. 151)

(1996): 146, 216–218. Brault *Rolls of Arms Edward I* 2 (1997): 171–172 (arms of Reynold Fitz Peter: Gules, three lions rampant or). *Roccafortis, Bull. de la Société de Géographie de Rochefort* 3rd Ser. 4 (2000): 149–153. Rickard *Castle Community* (2002): 98. Brand *Earliest English Law Rpts.* 4 (Selden Soc. 123) (2007): 409–411. Hampshire Rec. Office: Jervoise fam. of Herriard, 44M69/C/287 (www.a2a.org.uk/search/index.asp). National Archives, SC 8/65/3239 (available at www.catalogue.nationalarchives.gov.uk/search.asp). Online resource: http:// www.briantimms.net/rolls_of_arms/rolls/gloversB1.htm (Glover's Roll dated c.1252 — arms of Reynold Fitz Peter: Gules three lions rampant or).

Children of Reynold Fitz Peter, Knt., by Alice _____:

i. **JOHN FITZ REYNOLD**, Knt., Lord Fitz Reynold [see next].

ii. **ALICE FITZ REYNOLD**, married **JOHN DE SAINT JOHN**, Knt., of Basing, Hampshire [see PAULET 7].

iii. **ELEANOR FITZ REYNOLD**, married (1st) **JOHN DE MOHUN**, of Dunster, Somerset [see MOHUN 10]; (2nd) **WILLIAM MARTIN**, Knt., 1st Lord Martin [see MARTIN 10].

iv. **KATHERINE FITZ REYNOLD**, married **JOHN PICHARD**, of Stradewy [present day Llanfihangel-Ystrad], Cardiganshire, Wales [see BLUET 6].

Children of Reynold Fitz Peter, Knt., by Joan de Vivonne:

i. **PETER FITZ REYNOLD**, Knt., of Chewton, Somerset, married (1st) **ELA MARTEL**; (2nd) **MAUD** _____ [see BONVILLE 6].

ii. **REYNOLD FITZ REYNOLD**, of Hinton Martell, Dorset, married (1st) **JOAN MARTEL** [see FITZ REYNOLD 6]; (2nd) **MARGARET** _____ [see FITZ REYNOLD 6]; (3rd) **ALICE CRUBBE** (or **CRIBBE**) [see FITZ REYNOLD 6].

6. JOHN FITZ REYNOLD, Knt., of Blaen Llyfni (in Cathedine), Talgarth, and Bulke-Dinas, in the Marches, Crookham (in Thatcham), Berkshire, Haresfield and Southam (in Bishop's Cleeve), Gloucestershire, Wolverton, Hampshire, Stanton Fitzwarren, Wiltshire, Londesborough, Weaverthorpe, Weighton, Yorkshire, etc., son and heir by his father's 1st marriage, born about 1256 (aged 30 in 1286). He married **AGNES** _____. They had one son, Herbert, Knt. He fought in Wales in 1287, and in Gascony in 1294, and in Scotland in 1297, 1299 and 1300. He presented to the prebendal portion of Pontesbury, Shropshire in 1300. He signed the Baron's letter to the Pope in February 1301 as *Johannis filius Reginaldi Dominus de Blenleveney*. He was summoned to Parliament by writs directed *Johanni filio Reginaldi* from 29 Dec. 1299. He presented to the chapel of Crookham, Berkshire in 1299 and 1306. Sometime in the period, 1304–10, Margery, widow of William de Haiworth, clerk, petitioned the king, alleging that her husband was murdered, wrongfully and against reason, by John Fitz Reynold; the said John came before the sheriff and imputed to William the crime of robbery. In 1300 he presented to the prebendal portion of the church of Pontesbury, Shropshire. In 1305 he enfeoffed Hugh le Despenser with the manor of Bedhampton, Hampshire. On 15 Jan. 1310 SIR JOHN FITZ REYNOLD surrendered the lordships of Blaen Llyfni, Talgarth and Bulke-Dinas to the king for re-grant, but he died immediately afterwards before 10 Feb. 1310. By April 1310 his widow, Agnes, was seeking her dower. The same year the king granted the lordship of Blaen Llyfni to Roger de Mortimer, despite the claim of John's son and heir, Herbert. His widow, Agnes, was living 7 Nov. 1312.

Banks *Baronies in Fee* 2 (1843): 80–81 (sub John Fitz-Reginald). Lipscomb *Hist. & Antiqs. of Buckingham* 1 (1847): 297 (Herbert ped.). *Archaeologia Cambrensis* 3rd Ser. 4 (1858): 16–30; 4th Ser. 13 (1882): 295–299 (various charters of John Fitz Reginald). Eyton *Antiqs. of Shropshire* 7 (1858): 140, 146–156. Barfield *Thatcham, Berks, & its Manor* 2 (1901): 196–197 (charter of John Fitz Reginald dated c.1300). Wrottesley *Peds. from the Plea Rolls* (1905): 53–54. Brown *Yorkshire Inqs.* 4 (Yorkshire Arch. Soc. Rec. Ser. 37) (1906): 131–132. VCH *Hampshire* 3 (1908): 142–144; 4 (1911): 270–271. Capes *Reg. Ricardi de Swinfield, Episcopi Herefordensis 1283–1317* (Canterbury & York Soc. 6) (1909): 532. VCH *Berkshire* 3 (1923): 311–329; 4 (1924): 110–114. Paget (1957) 218:8. *List of Inq. ad Quod Damnum* 1 (PRO, Lists and Indexes, No. 17) (repr. 1963): 150. VCH *Gloucester* 8 (1968): 2–25; 10 (1972): 190–194. *Ancient Deeds — Ser. B* 2 (List & Index Soc. 101) (1974): B.8812. Rees *Cal. Ancient Petitions Rel. Wales* (Board of Celtic Studies, Hist. & Law 28) (1975): 70–71, 365–366. Kemp *Reading Abbey Cartularies* 2 (Camden 4th Ser. 33) (1987): 270–271. English *Yorkshire Hundred and Quo Warranto Rolls* (Yorkshire Archaeological Soc. Rec. Ser. 151) (1996): 216-218. Rickard *Castle Community* (2002): 98–99.

Brand *Kings, Barons & Justices* (2003): 248. National Archives, SC 8/111/5537; SC 8/327/E821 (available at www.catalogue.nationalarchives.gov.uk/search.asp). .Ancient Deed A.4610.

7. HERBERT FITZ JOHN, Knt., of Herriard and Wolverton, Hampshire, Haresfield and Southam (in Bishop's Cleeve), Gloucestershire, Chirton, Wiltshire, Weighton, Yorkshire, etc., son and heir, born about 1274 (aged 40 in 1314). He married 29 April 1291 **ELEANOR LE ROUS**, daughter of Roger le Rous, Knt., of Harescombe, Gloucestershire. They had two sons, Matthew, Knt., and Reynold. He fought in Scotland in 1306. He presented to the churches of Wolverton, Hampshire, 1317, and Stanton Fitzwarren, Wiltshire, 1320. In 1320 he seised the manor of Crookham (in Thatcham), Berkshire and a considerable quantity of goods; a settlement was made whereby he obtained the wardship of lands to the value of £20 a year. SIR HERBERT FITZ JOHN died 25 June 1321. In 1327 his widow, Eleanor, claimed dower in Blaen Llyfni (in Cathedine) and Talgarth, Breconshire, Crookham (in Thatcham), Berkshire, and Barnsley and Harescombe, Gloucestershire. She was living 23 April 1338.

Banks *Baronies in Fee* 2 (1843): 80–81 (sub John Fitz-Reginald). *Arch. Cambrensis* 3rd ser. 4 (1858): 16–30. Kirkby *Survey of York* (Surtees Soc. 49) (1867): 261. Hawley et al. *Vis. of Essex 1552, 1558, 1570, 1612 & 1634* 2 (H.S.P. 14) (1879): 548–549 (Misc. Peds.) (Barrett ped.: "Herbert Fitz John. = [left blank]."). *Regs. of John de Sandale & Rigaud de Asserio, Bishops of Winchester* (Hampshire Rec. Soc. 12) (1897): 137. Barfield *Thatcham, Berks, & its Manor* 2 (1901): 200–201, 212–214. *List of Inq. ad Quod Damnum* 1 (PRO Lists and Indexes 17) (1904): 150. Wrottesley *Peds. from the Plea Rolls* (1905): 53–54. VCH *Hampshire* 4 (1911): 270–271. VCH *Berkshire* 3 (1923): 311–329; 4 (1924): 110–114. *Norfolk Arch.* 30 (1952): 263–286. *Paget* (1957) 218:8-9. Martival *Regs. of Roger Martival, Bishop of Salisbury, 1315–1330* 1 (Canterbury & York Soc. 55) (1959): 148. VCH *Gloucester* 8 (1968): 2–25; 10 (1972): 190–194. VCH *Wiltshire* 10 (1975): 62–63. Hampshire Rec. Office: Jervoise fam. of Herriard, 44M69/C/39 (confirmation charter dated 8 July 1316 by Herbert son of John that Sir Thomas de Coudray holds of him the manor of Herriard, Hampshire for a knight's fee) (abs. available at www.a2a.org.uk/search/index.asp). National Archives, SC 8/111/5535; SC 8/111/5537; SC 8/168/8386; SC 8/172/8578 (available at www.catalogue.nationalarchives.gov.uk/search.asp).

Children of Herbert Fitz John, Knt., by Eleanor le Rus:

i. **MATTHEW FITZ HERBERT**, Knt., of Clanville (in Weyhill), Cliddesden, Herriard, Kempshott (in Winslade), Wallop, and Wolverton, Hampshire, Haresfield, Gloucestershire, Brockhampton, Herefordshire, More Hall (in Salle), Norfolk, Chirton and Staunton, Wiltshire, Londesborough, Weaverthorpe, and Weighton, Yorkshire, etc., son and heir, born about 1294-96. He married before 20 June 1325 **MARGARET COBHAM**, daughter of Henry de Cobham. They had no issue. About 1328 he petitioned the king and council regarding the manor of Leckhampstead, Berkshire, two thirds of which he claimed against Robert de Sapy and one third of which he claimed against Eleanor, widow of Herbert Fitz John. In 1330 he petitioned the king regarding the manor of Barnsley, Gloucestershire, stating that his grandfather, John Fitz Reynold, was attached by Hugh le Despenser at Leckhampstead, Berkshire for killing a stag in Windsor Forest, for which the said John was never indicted but remained imprisoned until forced to make a charter of his manor of Barnsley to the said Despenser. In 1340 he conveyed the reversion of the manors of Haresfield, Gloucestershire, Wolverton, Hampshire, Chirton, Wiltshire, etc., to his kinsman, Edward de Saint John, Knt. In 1341 he also conveyed the reversion of the manors of Londesborough, Weaverthorpe, and Weighton, Yorkshire to his cousin, Edward de Saint John, Knt., and his wife, Eve. Before 1342 he granted a tenement and lands in the suburb of Winchester, Hampshire to John de Oxenford, tailor. Before 1342 he granted the property called The King's Mews in the city of Southampton, Hampshire to John de Oxenford, tailor. He presented to the church of Wolverton, Hampshire in 1346, 1352, and 1354. In 1346 his cousin, Henry Fitz Roger, sued him for the manors of Londesborough and Weaverthorpe, and a moiety of the manor of Weighton, Yorkshire. In 1353 he released all his right to the manor of Talgarth, Breconshire to Philip ap Rees, Knt. SIR MATTHEW FITZ HERBERT died 16 Dec. 1356. His widow, Margaret, died 21 July 1357. Blomefield *Essay towards a Top. Hist. of Norfolk* 8 (1808): 269–276. *Archaeologia Cambrensis* 3rd ser. 4 (1858): 16–30. Barfield *Thatcham, Berks, & its Manor* 2 (1901). Wrottesley *Peds. from the Plea Rolls* (1905): 53–54, 359. VCH *Hampshire* 3 (1908): 366–369, 4 (1911): 145–147, 179–181, 270–271, 394–399. *Feet of Fines for York[shire]* 1327–1347 (Yorkshire Arch. Soc. Recs. 42) (1910): 144. VCH *Berkshire* 4 (1924): 110–114. VCH *Gloucester* 8 (1968): 2–25; 10 (1972): 190–194. VCH *Wiltshire* 10 (1975): 62–63. Keene & Rumble *Survey of Medieval Winchester* 1 (1985): 937. Edington *Reg. of William Edington* 1 (Hampshire Recs. 7) (1986): 22, 140, 151. Keene *Survey of Medieval Winchester* 2 (1986): 937. National Archives, SC 8/259/12925; SC 8/279/13926 (available at www.catalogue.nationalarchives.gov.uk/search.asp).

ii. **REYNOLD FITZ HERBERT** [see next].

8. REYNOLD FITZ HERBERT, of Stanford (in Stanford Dingley), Berkshire, Southam (in Bishop's Cleeve), Gloucestershire, etc., younger son. He married **JULIANE** _____. They had two daughters, Margaret (wife of Nicholas de Putton) and Elizabeth. REYNOLD FITZ HERBERT died in 1348. His widow, Juliane, married (2nd) **JOHN DE TIDMARSH**.

Arch. Cambrensis 3rd ser. 4 (1858): 16–30. Hawley et al. *Vis. of Essex 1552, 1558, 1570, 1612 & 1634* 2 (H.S.P. 14) (1879): 548–549 (Misc. Peds.) (Barrett ped.: "Reginald Fitzherbert. = [left blank]."). Barfield *Thatcham, Berks, & its Manor* 2 (1901): 214. Wrottesley *Peds. from the Plea Rolls* (1905): 359. VCH *Berkshire* 4 (1924): 110–114. *Paget* (1957) 218:9. VCH *Gloucester* 8 (1968): 2–25.

9. ELIZABETH FITZ REYNOLD, daughter and co-heiress, born about 1349 (aged 7 in 1356). She was co-heiress in 1356 to her uncle, Matthew Fitz Herbert, Knt. She married **JOHN CHENDUIT**, son of William Chenduit. In 1360–1 he and his wife, Elizabeth, together with her sister, Margaret, and her husband, Nicholas de Putton, conveyed the manor of More Hall (in Salle) Norfolk to William Clere. They had one daughter, Maud.

Blomefield *Essay towards a Top. Hist. of Norfolk* 8 (1808): 269–276. *Arch. Cambrensis* 3rd Ser. 4 (1858): 16–30. Hawley et al. *Vis. of Essex 1552, 1558, 1570, 1612 & 1634* 2 (H.S.P. 14) (1879): 548–549 (Misc. Peds.) (Barrett ped.: "John Chenduit. = Elizabeth d. & coheir [of] Reginald Fitzherbert") (Chenduit arms: Azure, a chevron or, in chief a label of three points gules). Barfield *Thatcham, Berks, & its Manor* 2 (1901): 214. Wrottesley *Peds. from the Plea Rolls* (1905): 359. VCH *Hampshire* 4 (1911): 270–271. VCH *Berkshire* 4 (1924): 110–114. VCH *Gloucester* 8 (1968): 2–25.

10. MAUD CHENDUIT, daughter and heiress. She married **ROBERT FOXCOTE** (or **FOXCOTT**). They had one son, Thomas.

Hawley et al. *Vis. of Essex 1552, 1558, 1570, 1612 & 1634* 2 (H.S.P. 14) (1879): 548–549 (Misc. Peds.) (Barrett ped.: "Robert Foscott. = Maude d. & heir [of John Chenduit]") (Chenduit arms: Azure, a chevron or, in chief a label of three points gules). Wrottesley *Peds. from the Plea Rolls* (1905): 359.

11. THOMAS FOXCOTE (or **FOXCOTT**), of Foxcott and Hatherden (in Andover), Hampshire, Stanford (in Stanford Dingley), Berkshire, etc., son and heir. He married **PHILIPPE STOKES**, daughter and heiress of William Stokes. They had one daughter, Margaret. He married (2nd) before 1407 (date of fine) **CHRISTIAN** _____. In 1405 he conveyed the manors of Foxcott, Hampshire and Stanford (in Stanford Dingley), Berkshire to three feoffees, William Stokes, Robert Taillour, and John Erle; in 1407 his feoffees reconveyed the manor of Stanford (in Stanford Dingley), Berkshire to Thomas and Christian his wife, with remainder to John son of William Stokes.

Hawley et al. *Vis. of Essex 1552, 1558, 1570, 1612 & 1634* 2 (H.S.P. 14) (1879): 548–549 (Misc. Peds.) (Barrett ped.: "Thomas Foscott. = Phillip d. & heir of Wm. Stokes."). Wrottesley *Peds. from the Plea Rolls* (1905): 359. VCH *Hampshire* 4 (1911): 345–358. VCH *Berkshire* 4 (1924): 110–114. *Hist. of Steeple Aston & Middle Aston, Oxfordshire* (1929): 191–195. VCH *Gloucester* 8 (1968): 2–25. National Archives, CP 25/1/290/60, #88; CP 25/1/207/30, #36; CP 25/1/290/61, #116 [see abstract of fines at http:// www.medievalgenealogy.org.uk/index.html].

12. MARGARET FOXCOTE (or **FOXCOTT**), daughter and heiress. She married before 1437 **WILLIAM DYNELEY** (or **DINGLEY**), Esq., of Malshanger (in Church Oakley) and Wolverton, Hampshire, Wokefield (in Stratfield Mortimer), Berkshire, etc., King's esquire, son and heir of Robert Dyneley, of Wolverton, Hampshire, Wokefield (in Stratfield Mortimer), Berkshire, etc., by Joan, daughter of Bernard Brocas, Knt. They had one son, Robert. In 1437 he and his wife, Elizabeth, sued Maud, widow of John Carpenter, to carry out the terms of a fine levied in 19 Edward II by Matthew Fitz Herbert and Margaret his wife respecting the manor of Wolverton, Hampshire, a moiety of the manor of More Hall (in Salle), Norfolk, and a fourth part of the manor of Chirton, Wiltshire. He was legatee and executor of his father's will dated 1456. At her death, his wife, Margaret, was buried in the church of Stanford, Berkshire. He married (2nd) before 1469 **ANNE MOMPESSON**. In 1469 the manor of Wolverton, Hampshire was settled in tail-male upon William and his wife Anne, and they dealt with it by fine four years later. His widow, Anne, was living in 1504.

Hawley et al. *Vis. of Essex 1552, 1558, 1570, 1612 & 1634* 2 (H.S.P. 14) (1879): 548–549 (Misc. Peds.) (Barrett ped.: "Thomas Foscott. = Phillip d. & heir of Wm. Stokes."). Wrottesley *Peds. from the Plea Rolls* (1905): 359. VCH *Hampshire* 4 (1911): 224–228, 270–271, 345–358. VCH *Berkshire* 3 (1923): 422–428; 4 (1924): 110–114. National Archives, CP 25/1/207/34, #20 [see abstract of fine at http:// www.medievalgenealogy.org.uk/index.html].

13. ROBERT DYNELEY, of Stanford (in Stanford Dingley), Berkshire, son and heir. He married _____ **LUDLOW**, daughter of William Ludlow, of Wiltshire. They had one son, Edward. In 1458 he owed a debt of 1,000 marks to Edward Langford, Esq. In 1458–9 he conveyed the manor of Stanford (in Stanford Dingley), Berkshire, to Edward Hampden and others, apparently trustees.

Hawley et al. *Vis. of Essex 1552, 1558, 1570, 1612 & 1634* 2 (H.S.P. 14) (1879): 548–549 (Misc. Peds.) (Barrett ped.: "Robert Dynley. = ... d. of Wm. Ludlow of Wilts."). VCH *Berkshire* 4 (1924): 110–114 (Dingley arms: Argent a fesse sable and in the chief a molet between two roundels sable). National Archives, C 241/254/10 (available at www.catalogue.nationalarchives.gov.uk/search.asp).

14. EDWARD DYNELEY, of Stanford (in Stanford Dingley), Berkshire, Wolverton, Hampshire, Middle Aston, Oxfordshire, etc., son and heir. He married **SANCHE LANGFORD**, daughter of William Langford. They had one son, Thomas, Esq. His widow, Sanche, married (2nd) **PETER CARVANELL**. She died in 1494. PETER CARVANELL died in 1500.

Hawley et al. *Vis. of Essex 1552, 1558, 1570, 1612 & 1634* 2 (H.S.P. 14) (1879): 548–549 (Misc. Peds.) (Barrett ped.: "Edward Dynley. = Elizabeth d. of Wm. Langford."). VCH *Hampshire* 4 (1911): 224–228, 270–271, 345–358. VCH *Berkshire* 3 (1923): 422–428; 4 (1924): 110–114. *Hist. of Steeple Aston & Middle Aston, Oxfordshire* (1929): 191, 196–197.

15. THOMAS DYNELEY, Esq., of Stanford (in Stanford Dingley) and Wokefield (in Stratfield Mortimer), Berkshire, Southam (in Bishop's Cleeve), Gloucestershire, Foxcott (in Andover) and Wolverton, Hampshire, etc., son and heir, born about 1479 (aged 15 in 1493–4). He married before 1509 (date of deeds) **PHILIPPE HARPESFIELD** (or **HARPESFELD**, daughter of Nicholas Harpesfield, Esq., of Harpesfield (in St. Peters, St. Albans), Hertfordshire, by Agnes, daughter of John Norton, Esq., of Nutley and East Tisted, Hampshire. They had one son, Elizabeth. Thomas Dyneley, Esq., died testate 29 May 1502. His widow, Philippe, married (2nd) (as his 2nd wife) **JOHN BARRETT**, Esq., of Belhouse (in Aveley), Essex, and London [see CULPEPER 10], son and heir of Robert Barrett, Esq., of Belhouse (in Aveley), Essex, by his 2nd wife, Margery, daughter of Robert Knolles, Esq. [see CULPEPER 9 for his ancestry]. They had six daughters, Cecily (wife of William Culpeper), Muriel (wife of John Champneys, Mayor of London), Anne (wife of Martin Bowes, Esq.), Joyce (wife of James Wilford, Knt.), Margaret (wife of Walter Crompton, Esq.), and Bridget. She was a legatee in the 1500 will of her aunt, Jane Norton, Viscountess Lisle, widow successively of Robert Drope, and Edward Grey, Viscount Lisle. His wife, Philippe, died before 1517. He married (3rd) **MARGARET NORRIS**, daughter of Edward Norris, of Ricot, Berkshire. They had no issue. He married (4th) before July 1526 **MARY BROOKE**, widow of Robert Blagge (died 13 Sept. 1522), of Broke Montacute, Somerset, Baron of the Exchequer, and daughter of John Brooke, Knt., 7th Lord Cobham, by Margaret, daughter of Edward Neville, Knt., Lord Bergavenny [see WYATT 18 for her ancestry]. They had no issue. JOHN BARRETT, Esq., died in 1526. His widow, Mary, married (3rd) (as his 2nd wife) **RICHARD WALDEN**, Knt., of Erith, Kent. In the period, 1529–32, Edward Cobham, Knt., younger son of John Brooke, Lord Cobham sued Richard and his wife, Mary, his wife, regarding an annuity charged by the will of complainant's father on Lufton manor, Somerset. SIR RICHARD WALDEN died 25 March 1536, and was buried in Erith, Kent. In the period, 1533–8, Ralph Folvyle sued Mary, late the wife of Richard Walden, Knt., George Blagge, her son, and others in Chancery regarding the occupation of messuages and lands in Dartford and Wilmington, Kent in contempt of divers judgments. Mary died in 1543–4.

Herald & Genealogist 5 (1870): 127–130 (re. Harpesfeld fam.). Hawley et al. *Vis. of Essex 1552, 1558, 1570, 1612 & 1634* 2 (H.S.P. 14) (1879): 548–549 (Misc. Peds.) (Barrett ped.: "Tho. Dynley 1 husb. = Phllip d. of John Harysfield."). VCH *Hampshire* 4 (1911): 224–228, 270–271, 4 (1911): 345–358. Woodruff & Churchill *Sede Vacante Wills* (Kent Arch. Soc. Recs. 3) (1914): 127–145 (will of Jane Viscountess Lisle). VCH *Berkshire* 3 (1923): 422–428. Brookes *Hist. of Steeple Aston & Middle Aston, Oxfordshire* (1929): 191, 197–198. VCH *Gloucester* 8 (1968): 2–25.

16. ELIZABETH DYNELEY, daughter and heiress. In 1504 her guardians sold the manor of Malshanger (in Church Oakley), Hampshire to William Warham, Archbishop of Canterbury. She married (1st) before 1517 **GEORGE BARRETT**, Gent., of London, and, in right of his wife, of Southam (in Bishop's Cleeve), Gloucestershire. They had three sons, Edward, Arthur, and Robert, and one daughter, Elizabeth. In the period, 1515–18, he and his wife, Elizabeth, sued Edward Brokas, Edward Langford, and John Davy, feoffees to uses in Chancery regarding their refusal to convey the manors of Stanford (in Stanford Dingley), Berkshire and Wolverton, Hampshire as devised by the will of the said Thomas. GEORGE BARRETT, Gent., died before 1518. In the period, 1515–18, his widow, Elizabeth, sued Francis Dyneley in Chancery regarding the detention of deeds relating to the manors of Foxcott, Malshanger (in Church Oakley), and Wolverton, Hampshire, Stanford (in Stanford Dingley), Berkshire, and Southam (in Bishop's Cleeve), Gloucestershire, and the advowsons of the churches of Wolverton and Stanford, and the chapel of Foxcote, etc. His widow, Elizabeth, married (2nd) before 1530 (as his 2nd wife) **JOHN BAKER**, Knt., of London and Sissinghurst Castle (in Cranbrook), Kent, Under Sheriff of London, 1520–26, Recorder of London, 1526–35, Burgess (M.P.) for London, 1529, 1536, Guilford, 1542, and Bramber, 1553, Attorney-General for the Duchy of Lancaster, 1535–6, Attorney-General, 1536–40, Knight of the Shire for Lancaster, 1545, Knight of the Shire for Huntingdonshire, 1547, Knight of the Shire for Kent, 1554–5, 1558, Chancellor of First Fruits and Tenths, 1540–54, Chancellor of the Exchequer, 1540–58, Privy Councillor, Under Treasurer, 1543–58, Speaker of the House of Commons, 1545, 1547, son and heir of Richard Baker, of Cranbrook, Kent. They had two sons, John and Richard, and three daughters, including Elizabeth and Cecily (wife of Thomas Sackville). In the period, 1558–79, Edward Barrett sued him [or his son] in Chancery regarding the manors of Foxcott and Wolverton, Hampshire, and Stanford (in Stanford Dingley), Berkshire. SIR JOHN BAKER died in London 23 Dec. 1558, and was buried at Cranbrook, Kent. He left a will dated 16 October 1555, codicils dated 27 Sept. 1558 and 5 Dec. 1558, proved 30 Jan. 1558/9 (P.C.C.). His wife, Elizabeth, predeceased him.

Hawley et al. *Vis. of Essex 1552, 1558, 1570, 1612 & 1634* 2 (H.S.P. 14) (1879): 548–549 (Misc. Peds.) (Barrett ped.: "Sr John Baker Kt. 2 husb. = Elizabeth d. & sole heir. = George Barrett 1 husband."). VCH *Hampshire* 4 (1911): 224–228, 270–271, 4 (1911): 345–358. VCH *Berkshire* 3 (1923): 422–428. Brookes *Hist. of Steeple Aston & Middle Aston, Oxfordshire* (1929): 191, 197–199. VCH *Gloucester* 8 (1968): 2–25. Bindoff *House of Commons 1509–1558* 1 (1982): 366–369 (biog. of John Baker). National Archives, C 1/386/17; C 1/391/47 (available at www.catalogue.nationalarchives.gov.uk/search.asp).

Child of Elizabeth Dyneley, by John Baker, Knt.:

i. **ELIZABETH BAKER**, married **THOMAS SCOTT**, Knt., of Scott's Hall (in Smeeth), Kent [see SCOTT 19.i].

✺ FITZ HUGH ✺

EUSTACHE I, Count of Boulogne, married **MATHILDE** (or **MAHAUT**) **OF LOUVAIN**.
EUSTACHE II, Count of Boulogne, by an unknown mistress, _____.
GEOFFREY OF BOULOGNE, of Carshalton, Surrey, married **BEATRICE DE MANDEVILLE**.
WILLIAM OF BOULOGNE, of Carshalton, Surrey, married _____.
ROHESE OF BOULOGNE, married **RICHARD DE LUCY**, Knt., of Chipping Ongar, Essex, Justiciar of England.
ALICE DE LUCY, married **ODINEL DE UMFREVILLE**, Knt., of Prudhoe, Northumberland.
RICHARD DE UMFREVILLE, of Prudhoe, Northumberland, married _____.
SIBYL DE UMFREVILLE, married **HUGH DE MORWICK**, Knt., of Chevington, Northumberland.
HUGH DE MORWICK, Knt., of Chevington, Northumbaerland, married **JULIANE** _____ [see LUMLEY 9].

10. TIPHAINE DE MORWICK, daughter and co-heiress, born about 6 Jan. 1254 (aged 15 at Epiphany 1269). She married before 26 April 1269 **JOHN DE BULMER**, Knt., of Wilton in

Cleveland and Bulmer, Yorkshire, son of John de Bulmer, by his wife, Katherine. They had one son, Ralph, Knt. [Lord Bulmer]. SIR JOHN DE BULMER died 17 Feb. 1298/9, and was buried in Guisborough Priory. His widow, Tiphaine, died shortly before 28 August 1315.

    Hodgson *Hist. of Northumberland* 5 (1899): 343–355. *C.P.* 2 (1912): 414 (sub Bulmer) (Bulmer arms: Gules, billetty, a lion rampant Gules). Farrer *Early Yorkshire Charters* 2 (1915): 128 (Bulmer ped.). Hedley *Northumberland Fams.* (1968): 29–31.

11. EVE DE BULMER, married (as his 1st wife) **HENRY FITZ HUGH**, Knt., of Ravensworth, Farnham, and Staveley, Yorkshire, Constable of Barnard Castle, 1315–19, son and heir of Hugh Fitz Henry, Knt., of Ravensworth, Airton in Craven, Barwick-on-Tees, Dent, Fremington, Lartington, Little Leeming, Mickleton, Sadbergh, and Staveley, Yorkshire, by Aubrey, daughter of William de Steyngrave, Knt., of Stonegrave, Yorkshire. They had two sons, Hugh and Henry, Knt. He was summoned for military service from Jan. 1299/1300 to 27 March 1335. In 1313 he was pardoned for any part he had taken against Peter de Gavaston, Earl of Cornwall. In 1315 he was granted 400 marks, in recompense for expenses he had incurred while on the king's service in Scotland. In 1321 he was pardoned for all felonies committed in pursuit of the Despensers. He was summoned to Parliament from 15 May 1321 to 15 Nov. 1351, by writs directed *Henrico filio Hugonis* or *fitz Hugh'*, whereby he is held to have become Lord Fitz Hugh. In 1322 John, Earl of Richmond accused him and others of having besieged and taken the earl's castle of Bowes. In 1323 he was ordered to arrest Andrew de Harcla, Earl of Carlisle. He married (2nd) before 25 Nov. 1337 **EMMA DE CLESEBY**, widow of Robert de Hastang, Knt., of Bagnall, Staffordshire (died before 15 April 1336), and daughter and heiress of Robert de Cleseby, Knt., of Cleasby, Clowbeck, and East Tanfield, Yorkshire, by his wife, Amabel. They had no issue. In 1340 he was appointed a justice in Northumberland, Cumberland, and Westmorland. His wife, Emma, died before 13 October 1348. SIR HENRY FITZ HUGH, 1st Lord Fitz Hugh, died in Ravensworth, Yorkshire in 1356.

    Clay *Extinct & Dormant Peerages* (1913): 72–75 (sub Fitz Henry). *C.P.* 5 (1926): 417–419 (sub Fitzhugh).

12. HENRY FITZ HUGH, Knt., of Ravensworth, Yorkshire, 2nd but 1st surviving son and heir apparent by his father's 1st wife. He married **JOAN DE FOURNEUX**, daughter of Richard de Fourneux, Knt., of Carlton in Lindrick, Kingston, and Bothamsall, Nottinghamshire, and Beighton Derbyshire. They had one son, Henry [2nd Lord Fitz Hugh], and one daughter, Joan. His wife, Joan, was heiress in 1349 to her brother, William de Fourneux. His wife, Joan, died 15 (or 21) Sept. 1349. SIR HENRY FITZ HUGH died 24 Sept. 1352, and was buried in Jervaulx Abbey.

    Clay *Extinct & Dormant Peerages* (1913): 72–75 (sub Fitz Henry). *C.P.* 5 (1926): 419–420 (sub Fitzhugh).

    Children of Henry Fitz Hugh, Knt., by Joan de Fourneux:

i.   **HENRY FITZ HUGH** [2nd Lord Fitz Hugh] [see next].

i.   **JOAN FITZ HUGH**, married **WILLIAM GREYSTOKE**, 2nd Lord Greystoke, Lord Fitz William [see GREYSTOKE 11]; (2nd) **ANTHONY DE LUCY**, Knt., 3rd Lord Lucy [see MELTON 8.i.a]; (3rd) **MATTHEW REDMAN**, Knt., of Levens, Westmorland [see GREYSTOKE 11].

13. HENRY FITZ HUGH, 2nd Lord Fitz Hugh, of Ravensworth, Yorkshire, and Kingston and Carlton (in Lindrick), Nottinghamshire, 2nd but 1st surviving son and heir, born about 1338 (aged 15 in 1353). He married about September 1350 **JOAN LE SCROPE**, daughter of Henry le Scrope, Knt., 1st Lord Scrope of Masham, by his wife, Joan [see SCROPE 9 for her ancestry]. They had two sons, Henry, K.G. [3rd Lord Fitz Hugh] and John. He accompanied the king in his expedition to France in October 1359, being in the retinue of the Earl of Richmond. In 1367 he had license to go to Rome. He was with John, Duke of Lancaster in his raid into Picardy and Caux in July 1369. He presented to the church of Burnsal, Yorkshire in 1369. He was summoned to Parliament from 4 August 1377 to 8 August 1386, by writs directed *Henrico fitz Hugh'*. HENRY FITZ HUGH, 2nd

Lord Fitz Hugh, died 29 August 1386, and was buried in Jervaulx Abbey, Yorkshire. His widow, Joan, died in 1392.

> Blore *Hist. & Antiqs. of Rutland* 1(2) (1811): 8 (Scrope ped.). Nicolas *Controversy between Scrope & Grosvenor* 2 (1832): 129, 134–137. Fisher *Hist. & Antiqs. of Masham & Mashamshire* (1865): 221–243. Burke *Gen. Hist. of the Dormant, Abeyant, Forfeited & Extinct Peerages* (1866): 482–483 (sub Scrope of Masham). Whitaker *Hist. & Antiqs. of the Deanery of Craven* (1878): 507. Clay *Extinct & Dormant Peerages* (1913): 72–75 (sub Fitz Henry). C.P. 5 (1926): 420–421, chart foll. 432 (sub FitzHugh). Paget *Baronage of England* (1957) 219: 2.

14. HENRY FITZ HUGH, K.G., 3rd Lord Fitz Hugh, of Ravensworth, Airton in Craven, Cleasby, Clowbeck, Cotherstone, Mickleton, and Scorton, Yorkshire, etc., and, in right of his wife, of Quinton, Gloucestershire, Lutton, Northampton, Berwick, Sussex, Stanton St. Quintin, Wiltshire, and Brandesburton, East Tanfield (in Kirklington), Manfield, Wath, and West Tanfield, Yorkshire, Chamberlain to King Henry V, Lord High Treasurer, 1417–21, Captain of Falaise, 1422, son and heir, born about 1358 (aged 28 in 1386). He married **ELIZABETH GREY**, daughter and heiress of Robert de Grey, Knt., of Wilcote, Oxfordshire, and, in right of his wife, of Brandesburton, Yorkshire, Great Bradley (in Cookham), Berkshire, Ibberton, Dorset, Stanton St. Quintin, Wiltshire, etc., by Lora, daughter and co-heiress of Herbert de Saint Quintin, Knt. [see ODDINGSELES 10.ii for her ancestry]. She was born about 1363–66 (age 21 or 24 in 1387). They had eight sons, Henry, John, William, Knt. [4th Lord Fitz Hugh], Geoffrey, Knt., Robert [Bishop of London], Ralph, Herbert, and Richard, and six daughters, Elizabeth (died young), Joan (wife of Robert Willoughby, K.G., 6th Lord Willoughby of Eresby), Eleanor, Maud, Elizabeth (again), and Lora. In 1386 the king took his fealty and he obtained possession of his inheritance. His wife, Elizabeth, was heiress in 1387 to her uncle, John Marmion, Knt., of West Tanfield, Yorkshire. He was summoned to Parliament from 17 Dec. 1387 to 1 Sept. 1423, by writs directed *Henrico fitz Hugh'*. In 1388 Queen Anne of Bohemia leased to him her castles of Richmond and Bowes, and all her manors and lands in Richmondshire, for a term of 12 years; in 1394, following the queen's death, he surrendered his interests in the premises to Ralph, Lord Neville. He presented to the church of Burnsal, Yorkshire in 1392, 1411, and 1425. He was one of the lords who gave their assent in Parliament in 1399 to the secret imprisonment of King Richard II. King Henry IV retained his services for life in 1399, granting him an annuity of 100 marks a year. He was a legatee in the 1401 will of his cousin, Richard le Scrope, Lord Scrope of Bolton. In 1404, 1405, and 1410 he was appointed a commissioner to treat of peace with Scotland. He performed the office of Constable of England at the Coronation of Henry V in 1413. In 1414 he was granted an annuity of £100 for life. He was appointed an envoy to the Council of Constance in 1414. In 1415 he was granted Masham and 12 other manors in the franchise of Richmond, forfeited by Henry le Scrope, of Masham. He accompanied King Henry V to France in August 1415. He was present at the Siege of Harfleur in August-Sept. 1415, and at the Battle of Agincourt 25 October 1415. He was a legatee in the 1415 will of his cousin, Henry le Scrope, K.G., 3rd Lord Scrope of Masham. He accompanied the king to France in July 1417, and was present at the Sieges of Rouen, 1418–19, Melun, 1420, and Meaux, 1421–2. He was an executor of the will of King Henry V, who appointed him a guardian of his infant son. SIR HENRY FITZ HUGH, 3rd Lord Fitz Hugh, died at Ravensworth, Yorkshire 11 Jan. 1424/5. He left a will dated 26 Dec. 1424. His widow, Elizabeth, died testate 12, 13, or 14 Dec. 1427. She left wills dated 24 Sept. 1427 and 10 Dec. 1427, proved 29 Dec. 1427. They were buried in Jervaulx Abbey, Yorkshire.

> Bridges *Hist. & Antiqs. of Northamptonshire* 2 (1791): 462–464. Nichols *Hist. & Antiqs. of Leicester* 3(1) (1800): 350 (Marmion ped.). Blore *Hist. & Antiqs. of Rutland* 1(2) (1811): 167 (Grey ped.). Baker *Hist. & Antiqs. of Northampton* 1 (1822–30): 140. Nicolas *Testamenta Vetusta* 1 (1826): 156–157 (will of Richard Scrope). Vautier *Extrait du Registre des Dons, Confiscations, Maintenues, et autres Actes* (1828): 23. Nicolas *Controversy between Scrope & Grosvenor* 2 (1832): 134–137, 142–147. *Wills & Invs.* 1 (Surtees Soc. 2) (1835): 74–76 (will of Elizabeth Lady Fitzhugh). Beltz *Mems. of the Order of the Garter* (1841): clvii. Banks *Baronies in Fee* 1 (1844): 307–308 (sub Marmyun of Witringham), 406–407 (sub St. Quintin) (St. Quintin ped.). Glover & St. George *Vis. of Yorkshire 1584-5, 1612* (1875): 611 (arms: Azure, three chevronels

embraced in base or, a chief of the last). Whitaker *Hist. & Antiqs. of the Deanery of Craven* (1878): 507. *Eighth Rpt.* (Hist. MSS Comm. 7) (1881): 263–263a (Marmion-Grey-Fitzhugh ped. dated 1429: "Elizabeth [Grey] = Henry, Lord Fitzhugh."). Lee *Hist., Desc. & Antiqs. of … Thame* (1883): 296–297 (Grey ped.). *Genealogist* n.s. 15 (1898): 25. Wrottesley *Peds. from the Plea Rolls* (1905): 221, 339–340. *List of Inqs. ad Quod Damnum* 2 (PRO Lists and Indexes 22) (1906): 735. VCH *Northampton* 2 (1906): 584–585. *Yorkshire Arch. Jour.* 20 (1909): 98–100. Clay *Extinct & Dormant Peerages* (1913): 72–75 (sub Fitz Henry), 131–132 (sub Marmion). VCH *Yorkshire N.R.* 1 (1914): 384–389. *C.P.* 4 (1916): 65–66 (sub Darcy); 5 (1926): 421–425, chart foll. 432 (sub FitzHugh); 6 (1926): 147, footnote a; 8 (1932): 522 (sub Marmion); 12(2) (1959): 663–666 (sub Willoughby). *Arch. Aeliana* 3rd Ser. 20 (1923): 69–178 (seal of Henry Fitz Hugh dated 1403: "Round, armorial, three chevrons braced and a chief."). VCH *Berkshire* 3 (1923): 124–133. Harvey et al. *Vis. of the North* 3 (Surtees Soc. 144) (1930): 132–133 (Fitzhugh ped.: "Henricus dominus Fitzhugh = Elizabeth filia et heres domini Iohannis de Marmeon") (Fitzhugh arms: Azure fretty and a chief gules). *Yorkshire Deeds* 6 (Yorkshire Arch. Soc. Recs. 65) (1930): 35. Train *Abs. of IPMs Rel. Nottinghamshire* 1 (Thoroton Soc. Recs. 12) (1949): 101; 2 (1952): 179–180. *NEHGR* 111 (1957): 195–200. Emden *Biog. Reg. of the Univ. of Oxford* 2 (1958): 689–690 (biog. of Robert FitzHugh). Langley *Reg. of Thomas Langley Bishop of Durham* 3 (Surtees Soc. 169) (1959): 62–64. Reeves *Lancastrian Englishmen* (1981): 65–138. VCH *Wiltshire* 14 (1991): 215–216. Coss & Keen *Heraldry, Pageantry & Social Display in Medieval England* (2002): 143–167. *Cal. IPM* 23 (2004): 37–43, 153–154. National Archives, SC 8/111/5526 (available at www.catalogue.nationalarchives.gov.uk/search.asp).

Children of Henry Fitz Hugh, K.G., by Elizabeth Grey:

i. **WILLIAM FITZ HUGH**, Knt., 4th Lord Fitz Hugh [see next].

ii. **ELEANOR FITZ HUGH**, married (1st) **PHILIP DARCY**, Knt., 6th Lord Darcy of Knaith [see DARCY 15]; (2nd) **THOMAS TUNSTALL**, Knt. [see TUNSTALL 15]; (3rd) **HENRY** (or **HARRY**) **BROMFLETE**, Knt., Lord Vescy [see BROMFLETE 15].

iii. **MAUD FITZ HUGH**, married **WILLIAM EURE**, Knt., of Witton (in Weardale), Durham [see EURE 9].

iv. **ELIZABETH FITZ HUGH**, married (1st) **RALPH GRAY**, Knt., of Chillingham, Northumberland [see GRAY 9]; (2nd) **EDMUND MONTFORT**, Knt., of Coleshill, Warwickshire [see GRAY 9].

v. **LORA FITZ HUGH**, married **MAURICE BERKELEY**, Knt., of Beverstone, Gloucestershire [see FISHER 9].

15. WILLIAM FITZ HUGH, Knt., 4th Lord Fitz Hugh, of Ravensworth, Yorkshire, Stanton St. Quintin, Wiltshire, West Tanfield, Yorkshire, etc., 3rd but 1st surviving son and heir, born about 1396–9 (aged 26 in 1425, aged 30 or 31 in 1427). He married at Ravensworth, Yorkshire before 18 Nov. 1406 **MARGERY WILLOUGHBY**, daughter of William Willoughby, K.G., 5th Lord Willoughby of Eresby, by Lucy, daughter of Roger le Strange, Knt., 5th Lord Strange of Knockin [see WILLOUGHBY 11 for her ancestry]. They had one son, Henry, Knt. [5th Lord Fitz Hugh], and seven daughters, Elizabeth (or Isabel), Eleanor (wife of Ranulph Dacre, Knt., 1st Lord Dacre of Gilsland), Maud, Lora, Lucy (nun), Margery (wife of John Melton), and Joan (wife of John le Scrope, K.G., 5th Lord Scrope of Bolton). He and his wife, Margery, received a papal indult for a portable altar in 1423 and again in 1431. He presented to the church of Burnsal, Yorkshire in 1426 and 1438. He was a legatee and one of the executors of the 1427 will of his mother. He was summoned to Parliament from 12 July 1429 to 5 Sept. 1450, by writs directed *Willelmo fitz Hugh' chivaler*. He was a legatee in the 1434 will of his brother, Robert Fitz Hugh, Bishop of London. In 1447 he had license to succeed to L'Aigle and other lands in Normandy which his father had held. SIR WILLIAM FITZ HUGH, 4th Lord Fitz Hugh, died 22 October 1452. His wife predeceased him.

Bridges *Hist. & Antiqs. of Northamptonshire* 2 (1791): 462–464. Brydges *Collins' Peerage of England* 6 (1812): 591–619 (sub Bertie, Baroness Willoughby of Eresby). Nicolas *Testamenta Vetusta* 1 (1826): 275, footnote 2. *Wills & Invs.* 1 (Surtees Soc. 2) (1835): 74–76 (will of Elizabeth Lady Fitzhugh). Whitaker *Hist. & Antiqs. of the Deanery of Craven* (1878): 507. *Eighth Rpt.* (Hist. MSS Comm. 7) (1881): 263–263a (Marmion-Grey-Fitzhugh ped. dated 1429: "William, Lord Fitzhugh."). Wrottesley *Peds. from the Plea Rolls* (1905): 340. *Papal Regs.: Letters* 7 (1906): 319; 8 (1909): 477. *North Country Wills* 1 (Surtees Soc. 116) (1908): 42–43. Clay *Extinct & Dormant Peerages* (1913): 72–75 (sub Fitz Henry). VCH *Yorkshire N.R.* 1 (1914): 384–389. *C.P.* 4 (1916): 18 (sub Dacre); 5 (1926): 426–427, chart foll. 432 (sub FitzHugh); 6 (1926): 197–199 (sub Greystoke); 11 (1949): 544–556 (sub Scrope). *Arch. Aeliana* 3rd Ser. 20 (1923): 69–

178 (seal of William Fitz Hugh dated 1433/34: "Oval, armorial, a sitting lion, in front of him a shield of arms, I and IV Fitz Hugh, II and III, vair a fess (Marmion). The lion's head is in the mantled and coroneted helm which surmounts the couched shield, the crest of a dragon's head issues out of the coronet. The dexter front paw of the lion holds a banner three chevrons and a chief vair (St. Quintin). His sinister paw holds a banner barry an eagle displayed; barry silver and azure an eagle displayed gules (Fitz Gernegan)."). Harvey et al. *Vis. of the North* 3 (Surtees Soc. 144) (1930): 132–133 (Fitzhugh ped.: "Willelmus dominus Fitzhugh = Margareta filia domini Wiloughby"). *Yorkshire Deeds* 9 (Yorkshire Arch. Soc. Recs. 111) (1948): 106–107 (two indentures of William, Lord Fitzhugh dated 1451). *NEHGR* 111 (1957): 195–200. Paget *Baronage of England* (1957) 219: 3; 576: 1–3 (sub Willoughby). *Bull. John Rylands Lib.* 40 (1957–8): 79–113, 391–431. Langley *Reg. of Thomas Langley Bishop of Durham* 3 (Surtees Soc. 169) (1959): 62–64. VCH *Wiltshire* 14 (1991): 215–216.

Children of William Fitz Hugh, Knt., by Margery Willoughby:

i. **HENRY FITZ HUGH**, Knt., 5th Lord Fitz Hugh [see next].

ii. **ELIZABETH FITZ HUGH**, married **RALPH GREYSTOKE**, Knt., 5th Lord Greystoke [see GREYSTOKE 14].

iii. **MAUD FITZ HUGH**, married **WILLIAM BOWES**, Knt., of Streatlam, Durham [see BOWES 14].

iv. **LORA FITZ HUGH**, married **JOHN CONSTABLE**, Knt., of Halsham, Yorkshire [see MALLORY 14].

16. **HENRY FITZ HUGH**, Knt., 5th Lord Fitz Hugh, of Ravensworth, Yorkshire, Stanton St. Quintin, Wiltshire, West Tanfield, Yorkshire, etc., Master-Forester and Keeper of the New Forest, Arkengarthdale, and Hope, Yorkshire, Steward of the Lordship of Richmond, Trier of Petitions in Parliament, son and heir, born about 1429 (aged 23 in 1452). He married **ALICE NEVILLE**, daughter of Richard Neville, K.G., 5th Earl of Salisbury, by Alice, daughter and heiress of Thomas de Montagu, K.G., 4th Earl of Salisbury [see MONTAGU 11 for her ancestry]. They had five sons, Richard [6th Lord Fitz Hugh], George [Dean of Lincoln], Edward, Thomas, and John, and six daughters, Alice (wife of John Fiennes, Knt.), Anne (wife of Francis Lovel, Knt., Viscount Lovel), Elizabeth, Margery, Joan (nun at Dartford), and Eleanor. He presented to the church of Burnsal, Yorkshire in 1454, 1469, and 1471. He and his wife, Alice, were granted a papal indult for a portable altar in 1458. Alice was a legatee in the 1459 will of her father. He was summoned to Parliament from 26 May 1455 to 15 October 1470, by writs directed *Henrico fitz Hugh' militi*. He appears to have been but a lukewarm member of the Lancastrian party, and was suspected of disaffection in 1461. He accompanied King Edward IV in his expedition to the North in 1462. He had license in 1468 to go to the Holy Sepulchre at Jerusalem with 12 other persons. In July 1470 he was the leader of a small insurrection in Yorkshire. The king hurrying northward, forced him to take refuge in Scotland. The king subsequently granted him a pardon 7 Sept. 1470. SIR HENRY FITZ HUGH, 5th Lord Fitz Hugh, died 8 June 1472. His widow, Alice, was living 22 Nov. 1503.

Coll. Top. et Gen. 1 (1834): 300–301 (Neville ped.), 406. Surtees *Hist. & Antiqs. of Durham* 4 (1840): 158–163 (Nevill peds.). *Testamenta Eboracensia* 2 (Surtees Soc. 30) (1855): 239–246 (will of Richard Neville, Earl of Salisbury). Cooper & Cooper *Athenæ Cantabrigienses* 1 (1858): 10 (biog. of George Fitzhugh). Whitaker *Hist. & Antiqs. of the Deanery of Craven* (1878): 507. *Genealogist* n.s. 3 (1886): 107–111 (Neville ped.). Gurney *Ref. Handbook for Readers, Students & Teachers of English Hist.* (1890): 42–44. Copinger *Manors of Suffolk* 2 (1908): 175 (chart). Clay *Extinct & Dormant Peerages* (1913): 72–75 (sub Fitz Henry). VCH *Yorkshire* N.R. 1 (1914): 384–389. *Papal Regs.: Letters* 11 (1921): 369–370. *C.P.* 5 (1926): 428–432, chart foll. 432 (sub FitzHugh); 11 (1949): 397, footnote l. Harvey et al. *Vis. of the North* 3 (Surtees Soc. 144) (1930): 23–32 (Neville ped.: "Alicia [Neville] nupta Henrico domini Fitzhugh"), 132–133 (Fitzhugh ped.: "Henricus dominus Fitzhugh = Alicia filia Ricardi Comitis Sarum"). *Papal Regs.: Letters* 13(2) (1955): 498, 633 (instances of son, George Fitzhugh, clerk, styled "kinsman" of King Edward IV of England). Davis *Paston Letters & Papers of the 15th Cent.* 2 (1976): 455–456. Langton *Reg. of Thomas Langton Bishop of Salisbury* (Canterbury & York Soc. 74) (1985): 15. VCH *Wiltshire* 14 (1991): 215–216.

Child of Henry Fitz Hugh, Knt., by Alice Neville:

i. **ELIZABETH FITZ HUGH**, married **WILLIAM PARR**, K.G., of Kirkby-Kendal, Westmorland [see PARR 14]; (2nd) **NICHOLAS VAUX**, 1st Lord Vaux of Harrowden [see OXENBRIDGE 17].

ii. **MARGERY FITZ HUGH**, married **MARMADUKE CONSTABLE**, Knt., of Flamborough, Yorkshire [see CONSTABLE 17].

FITZ IVES

WILLIAM THE CONQUEROR, King of England, married **MAUD OF FLANDERS**.
HENRY I, King of England, married **MAUD OF SCOTLAND**.
MAUD OF ENGLAND, married **GEOFFREY PLANTAGENET**, Count of Anjou, Duke of Normandy.
HENRY II, King of England, married **ELEANOR OF AQUITAINE**.
JOHN, King of England, by an unknown mistress, _____ [see ENGLAND 5].

6. ISABEL FITZ ROY, alleged illegitimate daughter. She married **RICHARD FITZ IVES**, Knt., of Degembris (in Newlyn East) and Trenoweth-with-Trewithgy (in Probus), Cornwall. They had two sons, William Fitz Richard, Knt., and Richard Fitz Richard (clerk), and one daughter, Isabel (wife of Bartholomew de Chaumont and Belyn Hellegan, Knt.). He gave tithes in Gruguth (in St. Keverne), Cornwall. Sometime before 1195, he granted one acre of land in Gun to the Priory of St. Michael's Mount, Cornwall. In 1202 he rendered account of 100s. for a fine he made with William Briwerre involving one half knight's fee in Cornwall. He occurs in subsequent Pipe Rolls for Cornwall during the reign of King John for the years, 1203–5, being assessed for a half-knight's fee. He may possibly be the Richard Fitz Ives who made a false claim in Northamptonshire in 1208. SIR RICHARD FITZ IVES died before Michaelmas 1211, when his heirs were charged 2 marks by the king for scutage for Wales. His heirs were subsequently charged scutage for Poitou on one knight's fee in Cornwall in 1214 (part of which was paid in 1222), and scutage for the Siege of Bytham in 1224.

Polsue *Complete Parochial Hist. of Cornwall* 4 (1872): 76. *Herald & Genealogist* 7 (1873): 229–231 (list of Fitz Ives family obits: "Obitus d'ni Ric'i fits yva militis A⁰ 1207," "Obitus d'ne Isabelle uxoris sue filie Regis Joh'is."). Maclean *Hist. of Trigg Minor* 1 (1876): 317, 321 (Fitz Ive arms: Gu. a bend between six fusils or). Vivian *Vis. of Cornwall* (1887): 30. Hall Red Book of the Exchequer 1 (Rolls Ser. 99) (1896): 162–163. Stawell *Quantock Fam.* (1910): 44–45, 278–280 (Fitzive arms: Gules, a bend between 6 lozenges [or fusils] or). Rowe & Tapley-Soper *Cornwall Feet of Fines* 1 (Devon & Cornwall Rec. Soc. 1914a) (1914): 17, 49, 54–55, 58–59, 91–92, 171, 438–440. *Reg. of Edward the Black Prince* 2 (1931): 113, 120. *Great Roll of the Pipe* Michaelmas 1202 (Pipe Roll Soc. n.s. 15) (1937): 170. *Great Roll of the Pipe* Michaelmas 1203 (Pipe Roll Soc. n.s. 16) (1938): 83. *Great Roll of the Pipe* Michaelmas 1204 (Pipe Roll Soc. n.s. 18) (1940): 41. *Great Roll of the Pipe* Michaelmas 1205 (Pipe Roll Soc. n.s. 19) (1941): 4. *Great Roll of the Pipe* Michaelmas 1208 (Pipe Roll Soc. n.s. 23) (1947): 179. *Great Roll of the Pipe* Michaelmas 1211 (Pipe Roll Soc. n.s. 28) (1953): 161. *Great Roll of the Pipe* Michaelmas 1214 (Pipe Roll Soc. n.s. 35) (1962): 63. Hull *Cartulary of St. Michael's Mount* (Devon & Cornwall Rec. Soc. n.s. 5) (1962): 31–32 (charter of Richard Fitz Ives). *NEHGR* 119 (1965): 94–102. *Great Roll of the Pipe* Michaelmas 1222 (Pipe Roll Soc. n.s. 51) (1999): 129. *Great Roll of the Pipe* Michaelmas 1224 (Pipe Roll Soc. n.s. 54) (2005): 244. Harleian MSS 4031: ff.76b, 81.

7. WILLIAM FITZ RICHARD, Knt., of Lanisley [in Gulival], Trenoweth-with-Trewithgy (in Probus), Trenoweth-Chammon and Rosneython (in St. Keverne), Degembris and Penhallow (both in Newlyn East), and Pelynt, Cornwall, son and heir, born say 1205 (evidently still a minor in 1224). He married **ROSE BEVYLE**, daughter of Ralph Bevyle, Knt., of Tredaule (in Altarnum), Cornwall. They had one daughter, Isabel. He granted the manor of Trenoweth-Chammon (in St. Keverne) in free marriage to his sister, Isabel, wife of Bartholomew de Chaumont. SIR WILLIAM FITZ RICHARD died 26 May 1265. His widow, Rose, died 4 April 1291.

Herald & Genealogist 7 (1873): 229–231 (list of Fitz Ives family obits: "Obitus d'ni Will'mi fitz yva militis de Lanuestby et Penhalyn in die S'ti Augustini xxvj⁰ die mensis Maij A⁰ d'ni 1265," "Obitus Rosee uxoris sui filie d'ni Rad'i Beauville militis quarto die mensis Aprilis A⁰ d'ni 1291."). *Book of Fees* 1 (1920): 394, 437. *Curia Regis Rolls* 11 (1955): 473; 12 (1957): 189; 18 (1999): 362–363. Hull *Caption of Seisin of Duchy of Cornwall* (Devon & Cornwall Rec. Soc. n.s. 17) (1971): xvii–xviii, 6.

8. ISABEL FITZ WILLIAM, daughter and heiress. She married **STEPHEN DE BEAUPRÉ**, Knt., of Kelynack (in St. Just), and, in right of his wife, of Trenoweth-with-Trewithgy (in Probus), Cornwall, presumably son of John de Beaupré, Steward and Sheriff of Cornwall. They had one son, Ralph, Knt., and one daughter, Joan (wife of John de Trevegnon, Knt.). He witnessed a charter for Edmund of Almain, Earl of Cornwall, in 1291. In 1295 he quitclaimed all his land in Lambessow, Cornwall, together with the homage and service of Randulf le Simple, to Geoffrey de Seroion, Prior of St. Michael's Mount, Cornwall. He witnessed an agreement between Herbert de Pyn, lord of Milton, and Richard, Prior of Launceston, in 1302. In 1309 he presented Richard de Beaupré to the church of St. Just in Penwith, Cornwall. SIR STEPHEN DE BEAUPRÉ died 17 March 1309. His widow, Isabel, died 7 Nov. 1325.

Herald & Genealogist 7 (1873): 229–231 (list of Fitz Ives family obits: "Obitus d'ni Stephani de bello prato milit' xvij⁰ die mensis Ma^rtij in vigillia S'ti Edwardi Regis et martiris A⁰ d'ni 1307," "Obitus Isabelle uxoris sue filie et heredis d'ci d'ni Will'mi fitz yva militis in crastino S'ti Leonardi confessoris et Abb'is vij⁰ die mensis Novembris A⁰ 1325."). St. George & Lennard *Vis. of Somerset 1623* (H.S.P. 11) (1876): 106–107 (Stawell ped.) (Beaupré arms: Vert, a lion rampant or, debruised by a bend gules). *C.F.R.* 2 (1912): 39. *Devon & Cornwall Notes & Queries* 8 (1915): 160. Hull *Cartulary of St. Michael's Mount* (Devon & Cornwall Rec. Soc. n.s. 5) (1962): 48 (letter of Stephen de Beaupré dated 1295), 58–59 (charters of Stephen de Beaupré dated 1295). Hull *Cartulary of Launceston Priory* (Devon & Cornwall Rec. Soc. n.s. 30) (1987): 12–13, 98, 145.

9. RALPH DE BEAUPRÉ, Knt., of Trenoweth-with-Trewithgy (in Probus), Carveth (in Mabe), Degembris (in Newlyn East), Kelynack (in St. Just), Lanisley [in Gulival], Penhallam (in Jacobstow), and Tremough, Cornwall, and Northcote, Devon, son and heir. He married **MARGARET DE FURNEAUX**, daughter of Matthew de Furneaux, Knt., of Ashington, Kilve, and Shurton, Somerset, Sheriff of Somerset and Dorset, by Maud, daughter of Warin de Raleigh, Knt. They had one son, John, Knt., and one daughter, Isabel. In 1329 he released to his mother-in-law, Maud de Furneaux, his claim to land which he had of her gift in Shurton, Steyning (in Stogursey), and Stogursey, Somerset. SIR RALPH DE BEAUPRÉ died 29 June 1329. On 25 June 1330 the Queen granted custody of two parts of his lands held in chief of the queen as of Launceston Castle during the minority of the heir to Otes de Botryngham, together with the marriage of John, minor son and heir of the said Ralph. In 1331 his widow, Margaret, released her right to dower to land in Shurton, Steyning (in Stogursey), and Stogursey, Somerset to her mother. Margaret married (2nd) before Trinity 1331 (date of settlement) (as his 2nd wife) **HUGH DE LONGLAND** (or **LANGELOND, LANGELONDE**), Knt., of South Brent, Axbridge, Burnham, Cheddar, Edington, etc., Somerset, Knight of the Shire of Somerset, 1327, Sheriff of Somerset and Dorset, 1330–1, son and heir of Nicholas de Longland, Knt., of South Brent, Somerset, Sheriff of Somerset and Dorset, 1306. He was born in 1287. They had one son, Hugh, and one daughter, Margaret (wife of John Saint Barbe, Knt., and Richard de Acton, Knt.). In 1327 he sued several parties, namely Gilbert Edward and others regarding trespass; John de Mareys, of Burnham, Somerset, regarding waste in Burnham, Somerset; and William Russel, of Brutton, regarding a debt. In 1328 he sued Joan wife of William de Brutton regarding waste. The same year John son of John le Denys sued him regarding unspecified land in Somserset. The same year Robert de Newburgh sued him regarding unspecified land in Somerset. In 1328 Anselm de Gournay sued him regarding a debt. In 1331 Hugh and his wife, Margaret, made a settlement of his lands in South Brent, Axbridge, Burnham, Cheddar, etc., Somerset. In 1333 Hugh complained that William son of Robert de Leye, John de Kyligrew, and others broke his park at Penhallam (in Jacobstow), Cornwall, hunted there, carried away deer, and assaulted his servant. SIR HUGH DE LONGLAND died testate shortly before 11 June 1334. In 1335 his widow, Margaret, complained that Thomas Chaunterel, John de Say, and others assaulted and imprisoned her at South Brent, Somerset, mowed her crops, and carried them away with other goods. In 1340 she complained that John de Langelond, John Barbe, parson of the church of Cossington, broke her coffers at Compton by Axbridge, Somerset, and carried away her goods with charters, writings, and other muniments. In 1343 she complained that Robert de Brente, John Barbe, parson of the church of Cossington, and others broke her houses at South Brent, Somerset, assaulted her, and carried away her goods. Margaret died 8 August 1349.

Coll. Top. et Gen. 1 (1834): 243–248 ["Also the 4th daughter of Mathew de Furneaux, Margarete, was maried to John [recte Ralph] Beaupre, kt., which had issue John Beaupre, kt. and the said John [recte Ralph] the father died, after whose decease the said Margarete was maried to Heugh Longland, kt. which had Hugh Longland, kt. and Margaret; which Hugh died without isseu, and Margaret suster to the said Hugh, and Margarete wife of Hugh Longland the father, had for their parte 50*li*. of lands, Astynton [Ashington], Warmester [Warminster], and divers other lands in Somersetshire."). *Herald & Genealogist* 7 (1873): 229–231 (list of Fitz Ives family obits: "Obitus d'ni Ran'di de bello prato militis filii et hered' d'ci d'ni Steph'i et Isabelle uxoris in festo S'coru' Petri et Pauli Aº d'ni 1329," "Obitus Margarete uxoris sue filie d'ni Simonis Sergeauxe [recte Furneaux] milit' viijº die mensis Augusti Aº d'ni 1349."). St. George & Lennard *Vis. of Somerset 1623* (H.S.P. 11) (1876): 106–107 (Stawell ped.) (Longland arms: Argent, a wyvern sable). Benolte *Vis. of Somerset 1531, 1573 & 1591* (1885): 108 (Furneaux ped.: "Margerett [Furneux] 4 d. [1] = Sr. John Bewpre Knt. 1 husband, [2] = Sr. Hugh Longland, Knt."). Benolte *Vis. of Somerset 1531, 1573 & 1591* (1885): 108 (Furneaux ped.: Margerett [ffurneux], 4 d. [1] = Sir John Bewpre, Knt. 1 husband, [2] = Sir Hug. Longland, Knt.") (Furneaux arms: Gules a bend between six crosses crosslet Or.). *C.P.R. 1327–1330* (1891): 539. *C.P.R. 1330–1334* (1893): 450–451. *C.P.R. 1334–1338* (1895): 215. Shrewsbury *Reg. of Ralph of Shrewsbury Bp. of Bath & Wells 1329–1363* (Somerset Rec. Soc. 9) (1896): 211–212, 229. *C.C.R. 1330–1333* (1898): 364. *C.P.R. 1338–1340* (1898): 481. Green *Feet of Fines for Somerset* 2 (Somerset Rec. Soc. 12) (1898): 154–155. *List of Sheriffs for England & Wales* (PRO Lists and Indexes 9) (1898): 123. Gerard *Particular Desc. of Somerset* (Somerset Rec. Soc. 15) (1900): 180 (Longland arms: Arg[ent] a wiverne volant sab[le]; Furneaux arms: Gules betw[een] 6 crosslets or). *Misc. Gen. et Heraldica* 3rd Ser. 3 (1900): 272–276 (Furneaux ped. dated 1421: "Aceciam predicta Margareta quarta filia predicti Mathei marritata fuit Johanni Beaupre militem, et habuerunt exitum Johannem Beaupre militem et Isabellam. Et predictus Johannes Beaupre pater obit, post cuius mortem predicta Margareta uxor predicti Johannis marritata fuit Hugoni Langelond militi, et habuerunt exitum Hugonem, et Margaretam, qui dictus Hugo obiit sine herede et predicta Margarata soror predicti Hugonis marritata fuit Johanni Barbe, et habuerunt exitum Ricardum Barbe, post cuius mortem predicta Margareta uxor predicti Johannis Barbe fuit marritata Ricardo de Acton militi, et nullum habuerunt exitum."). *C.P.R. 1343–1345* (1902): 83–84. *Index of Placita de Banco 1327–1328* 2 (PRO Lists and Indexes 22) (1906): 565, 568, 571, 574. Weaver *Feodary of Glastonbury Abbey* (Somerset Rec. Soc. 26) (1910): 105–106. *C.F.R.* 4 (1913): 142, 159–160, 178, 245, 283. *Somerset & Dorset Notes & Queries* 16 (1920): 281–285 (Furneaux ped.). Maxwell-Lyte *Hist. Notes of Some Somerset Manors* (Somerset Rec. Soc. Extra Ser. 1) (1931): 298–300, 310–312, 347. *Procs. of Somersetshire Arch. & Nat. Hist. Soc.* 79 (1933): Appendix, 28–29 (biog. of Hugh de Langlond). VCH *Wiltshire* 8 (1965): 96–103. Hull *Caption of Seisin of Duchy of Cornwall* (Devon & Cornwall Rec. Soc. n.s. 17) (1971): xvii–xviii, xxxi, 6, 12, 95. VCH *Somerset* 8 (1992): 145–146.

Children of Ralph de Beaupré, Knt., by Margaret de Furneaux:

i. **JOHN DE BEAUPRÉ**, Knt., of Lanisley (in Gulival), Penhallam (in Jacobstow), and Trenoweth-with-Trewithgy (in Probus), Cornwall, bachelor of Edward *the Black Prince*, son and heir, born 4 October 1327 (aged 2 in 1329, minor in 1337). He married **MARGARET DE CARMINOW**, daughter of John de Carminow, Knt., by Joan, daughter of John Glyn, Knt. They had no issue. In 1334 Sir Richard de Champernoun presented to the church of St. Just in Penwith, Cornwall by reason of the minority of John, son and heir of Ralph de Beaupre, Knt. In 1337 the tenants of [John] heir of Ralph de Beaupré were required "to make distraint" … "and to grind at the mill." In 1349 John presented to the church of St. Just in Penwirth, Cornwall. In 1355 he and his wife, Margaret, conveyed the advowson of St. Just in Penwith, Cornwall to the Provost and Chapter of St. Thomas at Glasneyth, Cornwall. SIR JOHN DE BEAUPRÉ died 23 August 1356, and was buried in the Friars Minor in Castelros in Berry, France. His widow, Margaret, died in 1359. *Coll. Top. et Gen.* 1 (1834): 243–248 (Furneaux ped.). Maclean *Hist. of Trigg Minor* 1 (1876): 189; 3 (1879): 158–159 (Carminow ped.). *Herald & Genealogist* 7 (1873): 229–231 (list of Fitz Ives family obits: "Obitus domini Joh'is Beaupre milit' filii et heredis d'ci d'ni Ran'di de bello pratro militis in vigillia S'ci Bartho'i apostoli apud Chatelros in com Berry," "Obitus Margarete vxoris sue filie d'ni Joh'is Carmenowe militis Aº d'ni 1359). Benolte *Vis. of Somerset 1531, 1573 & 1591* (1885): 108 (Furneaux ped.: "Sr. John Bewpre, Knt., ob. s.p."). *C.F.R.* 4 (1913): 159–160, 178. *Somerset & Dorset Notes & Queries* 16 (1920): 281–285 (Furneaux ped. dated 1421: "Johannes Beaupre, filius predicti Johannis Beaupre, obiit sine herede de corpore suo exeunte."). Hull *Caption of Seisin of Duchy of Cornwall* (Devon & Cornwall Rec. Soc. n.s. 17) (1971): xvii–xviii, xxxi, 6, 12, 95. Online resource: http://west-penwith.org.uk/justvic.htm.

ii. **ISABEL DE BEAUPRÉ** [see next].

10. ISABEL DE BEAUPRÉ, married before Trinity 1343 (date of settlement) **JOHN DE LONGLAND** (or **LANGELONDE**), Esq., of Grove (in South Brent), Axbridge, Burnham,

Cheddar, Compton by Axbridge, Edington, etc., Somerset, and, in right of his wife, Trenoweth-with-Trewithgy (in Probus), Carveth (in Mabe), Degembris (in Newlyn East), Kelynack (in St. Just), Lanisley [in Gulival], Penhallam (in Jacobstow), and Tremough, Cornwall, and Northcote, Devon, Knight of the Shire for Somerset, 1363, Sheriff of Somerset and Dorset, 1365–8, son and heir of Hugh de Longland, Knt., of South Brent, Axbridge, Burnham, Cheddar, Edington, etc., Somerset, Knight of the Shire of Somerset, 1327, Sheriff of Somerset and Dorset, 1330–1 [see Gen. 9 above], by his unknown 1st wife. They had three daughters, Margaret, Joan, and Agnes. In 1343 he and his wife, Isabel, made a settlement of his lands in Compton by Axbridge, Burnham, Edington, South Brent, etc., in Somerset. In 1351 he witnessed various charters of Ralph of Shrewsbury, Bishop of Bath and Wells. In 1353 he and his wife, Isabel, made a settlement of his lands in South Brent, East Brent, Burnham, Axbridge, Cheddar, Edington, etc., Somerset. His wife, Isabel, was heiress in 1356 to her brother, John de Beaupré, Knt. In 1359 he and his wife, Isabel, sold her manor of Northcote, Devon to Henry Percehay for 100 marks of silver. His wife, Isabel, was living 13 October 1359. JOHN DE LONGLAND, Esq., died shortly before 19 June 1380. His wife, Isabel, predeceased him.

Coll. Top. et Gen. 1 (1834): 243–248 (Furneaux ped.: "The forseid Isabell, suster of John Beaupre, maryed John Longland sone and heire of Hugh Longland, knt. borne and begotten of his first wife, which John and Ysabell had 3 doughters, Margarete, Jane, and Annes. The furst doughter Margaret maried Leonard Hakeluet, kt. of whom commyth Stepulton of Shroppeshier, and had for his parte lands besides Warmester, and in divers places. The 2nd Jane maried Robt. Yevelton, kt. and Robt. died without isseu, and Jone maryed with Richard Rynyon, grandfather to Wm. Ryvyon (*sic*), now alyve, and had for his parte lands besides Yevell or Yevelchester, and in other places, as well as in Somersetshier. The 3rd Anne maryed John Farwaye, and had bytwixte them 2 doughters, the one maryed with Stowell, the other with Berkley Lord of Tekenam and Stowell. And Berkeley as one heyre had for hir parte the lands at Warmester, and afterwards Stowell and Berkley made exchaunge, that Barkley shuld have Warmester hole for his parte to hym and his heyres; and Stowell to have as mych land therfor in Cornewaile, that was Barkles before that exchange made."). *Herald & Genealogist* 7 (1873): 229–231 (list of Fitz Ives family obits: "Obitus Joh'is Langlond ar' filii et heredis d'ni Hugonis Langlond militis A° 1300 [recte 1380]," "Obitus Isabelle uxoris sue filii d'ni Rad'i de bello prato et heres (*sic*), eo q'd p'd'cus d'nus Joh'es Beaupre frater ejus obiit sine herede."). Benolte *Vis. of Somerset 1531, 1573 & 1591* (1885): 108 (Furneaux ped.: "Issabell, sister and heire of Sr. John Bewpre. = Sr. John Longland."). Margerett [Furneux] 4 d. [1] = Sr. John Bewpre Knt. 1 husband, [2] = Sr. Hugh Longland, Knt."). Ralph of Shrewsbury Reg. of Ralph of Shrewsbury Bishop of Bath & Wells *2* (Somerset Rec. Soc. 10) (1896): 665–666, 679–681. Dallas & Porter *Note-book of Tristram Risdon* (1897): 265 (arms of Johannes Longland: Argent, a wyvern sable). Green *Feet of Fines for Somerset* 2 (Somerset Rec. Soc. 12) (1898): 217–218; 3 (Somerset Rec. Soc. 17) (1902): 24. *List of Sheriffs for England & Wales* (PRO Lists and Indexes 9) (1898): 123. *Somerset & Dorset Notes & Queries* 11 (1909): 193–195 (Longland arms: Gules a saltier ermine between four fleurs-de-lis or); 16 (1920): 281–285 (Furneaux ped. dated 1421). Weaver *Cartulary of Buckland Priory* (Somerset Rec. Soc. 25) (1909): 116. *C.F.R.* 9 (1926): 206, 214–215, 258. *Procs. of Somersetshire Arch. & Nat. Hist. Soc.* 80 (1934): Appendix, 53 (biog. of John de Langlond). Reichel *Devon Feet of Fines* 2 (Devon & Cornwall Rec. Soc. 1939) (1939): 406. VCH *Wiltshire* 8 (1965): 96–103. Cornwall Rec. Office: Arundell of Lanherne & Trerice, AR/1/415 — declaration dated c.1357 x 1380 mentions John Langelond as lord of Laneskele [Lanisley], Cornwall by right of Isabel his wife (available at www.a2a.org.uk/search/index.asp).

Children of Isabel de Beaupré, by John de Longland:

i. **MARGARET LONGLAND** [see next].

ii. **JOAN LONGLAND**, born about 1353 (age 17 in 1380). She married (1st) before 1380 **JOHN ROYNON** (or **RUYNON, REYNON**), of Bickfold, Somerset. They had one son, John, and one daughter, Joan. John Roynon died testate. His widow, Joan, married (2nd) before 11 June 1396 (date of fine) **ROBERT YEVELTON**, Knt., of Wiltshire, and, Rugges (in North Langley), Somerset, and in right of his wife, of Axbridge, Somerset, and Kelynack (in St. Just) and Trenoweth (in Probus), Cornwall. They had no issue. In the period, 1386–1411, he sued Ralph Trenewith regarding rights of common, estover, etc. in the manor of Trenewith and Trewishannes, Cornwall; assaults, etc. In 1394 he witnessed an agreement between the Dean and Chapter of Wells and the Abbot and Convent of Athelney. In 1396 he and his wife, Joan, sold to William Hankeford, Knt. the manor of Kelynack (in St. Just), Cornwall, together with 25*s*. of rent from the manor of Lanisley (in Gulval), Cornwall, and three chantries in Penryn, Cornwall for £100 sterling. He was cited in 1398 for not appearing in court to answer John Bonyngton touching a debt of 108*s*. 6*d*. in Bristol. The same year he was pardoned by the king for his outlawry in the Husting court of London for not appearing before the justices to render 12*l*. 1*s*. to Richard Pecock and another, executors of Peter Pecock, citizen and barber of London. In 1404 John Leythorn was cited for not appearing when sued before the justices of the Bench to answer Robert Yevelton, Knt. and Joan his wife touching a trespass in Cornwall. In 1412 the king took into his hand Robert's lands in Rugges (in North Langley), Somerset, on account of the outlawry promulgated against him in the city of London at the suit of Robert Polhill in a plea of debt. His wife, Joan, was a legatee in the 1414 will of her sister, Margaret Hakluyt, who bequeathed her a silver cup with a cover. Joan died before 1421. In 1423 Thomas Duke and John Wodecok, administrators of Nicholas Loude, of Somerset, sued Robert Yevelton, Knt. SIR ROBERT YEVELTON died 20 July 1428. *Coll. Top. et Gen.* 1 (1834): 243–248 (Furneaux ped.: "The 2nd [daughter] Jane [Longland] married Robt. Yevelton, kt. and Robt. died without isseu, and Jone maryed with Richard Rynyon, grandfather to Wm. Ryvyon (*sic*), now alive, and had for his parte lands besides Yevell or Yevelchester [Ilchester], and in other places, as well as in Somersetshier."). Scrope *Hist. of Castle Combe* (1852): 248–129 ("Mem^dum, that … Roger Young, junior, dwelt in Castel Combe [Wiltshire] as a clothier in the time of King Edward III. and a certain knight, Sir Robert Yevelton, in the time of Richard II. came by force of arms to beat Roger Young, then dwelling in Castel Combe; and the said knight fled into the church of that lace for safety of his body."). Benolte *Vis. of Somerset 1531, 1573 & 1591* (1885): 108 (Furneaux ped.: "Joane [Longland], 1 ux. Robert Penelton, 2 to John Ronyon [Roynon]."). Bates *Two Cartularies of the Benedictine Abbeys of Muchelney & Athelney* (Somerset Rec. Soc. 14) (1899): 168–169. *C.P.R. 1422–1429* (1901): 30. *Procs. Bath Natural Hist. & Antiq. Field Club* 9 (1901): 188–201. Weaver *Somerset Medieval Wills* 1 (Somerset Rec. Soc. 16) (1901): 66–67. *C.P.R. 1401–1405* (1905): 339. *C.P.R. 1396–1399* (1909): 302, 591. *Somerset & Dorset Notes & Queries* 16 (1920): 281–285 (Furneaux ped. dated 1421: "Et predicta Johanna [Longland] secunda filia predicti Johannis [de Longland] et Isabelle marritata fuit Johanni Roynon, et habuerunt exitum Johannem Roynon."). *C.F.R.* 9 (1926): 214–215; 11 (1929): 305; 13 (1933): 239. *Cornwall Feet of Fines* 2 (1950): 56. *Cal. IPM* 23 (2004): 87–88. National Archives, C 1/3/116 (Chancery Proc. dated 1386–1411— Robert Yevelton, Knt. v. Ralph Trenewith re. rights of common, estover, &c., in the manor of Trenewith and Trewishannes; assaults, &c.: Cornwall) (available at www.catalogue.nationalarchives.gov.uk/search.asp). Berkeley Castle Muniments, BCM/H/3/7/1 — petition dated 1399–c.1412 from Robert Yevelton, Knt., lord of the manor of Trenewith and Trewishawnes, to the king and privy council complaining that Ralph Trenewyth, who has common of pasture in the manor, has trespassed on Robert's lands with a number of followers, and has caused damage; he asks for redress (available at www.a2a.org.uk/search/index.asp).

Children of Joan Longland, by John Roynon:

- a. **JOHN ROYNON**. He married _____. They had one son, William. In 1414 John was co-heir to his Furneaux cousin, Alice Blount, wife successively of Richard Stafford, Knt. and Richard Stury, Knt., by which he inherited the manor of Steyning (in Stogursey), Somerset at the division of her estates in 1421. VCH *Somerset* 8 (1992): 145–146.

- b. **JOAN ROYNON**, married **HUGH MALET**, Esq., of Enmore, Somerset, son and heir of Baldwin Malet, Knt., of Enmore and Currypool (in Charlinch), Somerset, by his 2nd wife, Amice, daughter and co-heiress of Richard Lyffe (or Lyf), of Currypool (in Charlinch), Somerset. They had one son, Thomas, Esq. HUGH MALET, Esq., died in 1465. His widow, Joan, was living in 1467. Benolte *Vis. of Somerset 1531, 1573 & 1591* (1885): 44–46 (Malet ped.: "Hugh [Malet]. = Joan, d. John Roynon."). Malet *Notices of an English Branch of the Malet Fam.* (1885): ped. chart facing vii, 124–125. VCH *Somerset* 6 (1992): 92–94.

iii. **AGNES LONGLAND**, married **JOHN FARWAY**, of Penhallam (in Jacobstow), Cornwall [see ASHE 11].

11. MARGARET LONGLAND, daughter and co-heiress, born about 1362 (aged 18 in 1380). She married (1st) **JOHN DEVIOCK** (or **DEVYOK**, **DEVIOKE**). They had one daughter, Margaret. JOHN DEVIOCK died before 16 August 1380. She married (2nd) before 1394 **LEONARD HAKLUYT** (or **HAKELUYT**), Knt., of Stoke Edith, Herefordshire, and, in right of his wife, of Grove (in South Brent), Somerset, and Degembris (in Newlyn East), Tremough, and Carveth (in Mabe), Cornwall, Knight of the Shire for Herefordshire, 1385, 1388, 1394, Escheator of Herefordshire, 1401–2, Sheriff of Herefordshire, 1402, 1408–9, Knight of the Shire for Somerset, 1404, 1406, son of Edmund Hakluyt, Knt., of Longland, Herefordshire, by his wife, Emma. He was born about 1352. They had no issue. In 1390 he claimed the manor of Shepton Mallet, Somerset, by virtue of a prior settlement dated 1368. In 1394 and again in 1411, he and his wife, Margaret, made a settlement of her lands. In 1404 he was granted the keeping of Mawardyn and Much Marcle, Herefordshire as long as the manors remain in the king's hand. The same year he presented to the church of Shepton Mallet, Somerset. He was a legatee in the 1410 will of Thomas Clanvowe,

Knt. His wife, Margaret, claimed the right to dig turves in the manor of Edington, Somerset by a grant dated c.1269–89 made by John Fitz Geoffrey, lord of Edington, to her ancestor, Hugh de Langlonde and Eleanor his wife. SIR LEONARD HAKLUYT left a will dated 3 August 1413, proved 17 August 1413. His widow, Margaret, took a vow of perpetual chastity 2 October 1413. In Jan. 1413/4 she was dispensed from a vow she voluntarily made for life to fast every Saturday, which she was unable to do owing to the infirmity of her body. In 1414 Margaret was co-heiress to her Furneaux cousin, Alice Blount, wife successively of Richard Stafford, Knt. and Richard Stury, Knt.). Margaret left a will dated 29 July 1414, proved 11 August 1414, requesting burial in the church of the Friars Minor at Bridgwater, Somerset by her late husband, Sir Leonard Hakluyt.

Coll. Top. et Gen. 1 (1834): 243–248 (Furneaux ped.: "The furst doughter Margaret [Longland] maried Leonard Hakeluet, kt. of whom commyth Stepulton of Shroppeshier, and had for his parte lands besides Warmester, and in divers places."). Benolte *Vis. of Somerset 1531, 1573 & 1591* (1885): 108 (Furneaux ped.: "Margerett [Longland], ux. Leonard hackluit."). *Antiq.* 14 (1886): 115 (Deviock arms: Party per saltier argent and sable). Weaver *Somerset Incumbents* (1889): 180. *List of Sheriffs for England & Wales* (PRO Lists and Indexes 9) (1898): 60. Giffard & Bowett *Regs. of Walter Giffard & Henry Bowett Bishops of Bath & Wells* (Somerset Rec. Soc. 13) (1899): 57. *Procs. Bath Natural Hist. & Antiq. Field Club* 9 (1901): 188–201. Weaver *Somerset Medieval Wills* 1 (Somerset Rec. Soc. 16) (1901): 61–62 (will of Leonard Hakeluyt, Knt.), 66–67 (will of Margaret Hakeluyt). Bubwith *Reg. of Nicholas Bubwith Bishop of Bath & Wells* 1 (Somerset Rec. Soc. 29) (1914): 148, 167. *Somerset & Dorset Notes & Queries* 16 (1920): 281–285 (Furneaux ped. dated 1421: "Et predicta Margareta [de Longland] prima filia predictorum Johannis [de Longland] et Isabelle marritata fuit Johanni Devyok et habuerunt exitum Margaretam [Devyok] que fuit marritata Johanni Stepulton et habuerunt exitum Leonardum Stepulton."). *C.F.R.* 9 (1926): 214–215; 12 (1931): 279–280. *Year Books of Richard II* 7 (Ames Found. 10) (1929): 159–166. Rowe & Tapley-Soper *Cornwall Feet of Fines* 2 (Devon & Cornwall Rec. Soc. 1950) (1950): 75, 109. VCH *Wiltshire* 8 (1965): 96–103. *Chancery Misc.* 3 (List & Index Soc. 26) (1967): 255. Dunning *Hylle Cartulary* (Somerset Rec. Soc. 68) (1968): 62. Roskell *House of Commons 1386–1421* 3 (1992): 265–267 (biog. of Leonard Hakluyt).

12. MARGARET DEVIOCK, daughter and heiress, evidently born before 1380. She married before 1400 (as his 1st wife) **JOHN STAPLETON** (or **STEPULTON**), Esq., of Stapleton, Shropshire, Dormington, Herefordshire, etc., Knight of the Shire for Shropshire, 1421, 2nd son of John Stapleton, of Stapleton and Oaks (in Pontesbury), Shropshire, by Katherine, 2nd daughter and co-heiress of Edward Burnell, of Langley, Shropshire. They had one son, Leonard, Esq., and two daughters, Margaret and Elizabeth. His wife, Margaret, died before 1421. He married (2nd) **MARGERY** _____. They had three daughters, Joyce (wife of Thomas Horde), Joan (wife of Thomas Walwyn and Richard Bondes), and Mary (wife of Thomas Acton). In 1421 his 1st wife Margaret's son, Leonard Stapleton, was her representative as one of the co-heirs named in the division that year of the estates of her Furneaux cousin, Alice (Blount) (Stafford) Stury. In 1438 there was a fire at his moated manor house at Stapleton, Shropshire. In 1443 he made a settlement of his manor, advowson, and various lands in Stapleton, Shropshire, and as well as of one message and lands, also in Stapleton. JOHN STAPLETON, Esq., was living in 1446, but died before 1450.

Coll. Top. et Gen. 1 (1834): 243–248. Benolte *Vis. of Somerset 1531, 1573 & 1591* (1885): 108 (Furneaux ped.: "Margerett, ux. John Stepulton."). *Bye-gones* (1903): 195. *Colls. Hist. Staffs.* 1914 (1914): 221. *Somerset & Dorset Notes & Queries* 16 (1920): 281–285 (Furneaux ped. dated 1421: "Et predicta Margareta [de Beaupre] prima filia predictorum Johannis et Isabelle marritata fuit Johanni Devyok et habuerunt exitum Margaretam [Devyok] que fuit marritata Johanni Stepulton et habuerunt exitum Leonardum Stepulton."). Wedgwood *Hist. of Parl.* 1 (1936): 534–535 (biog. of John Leighton), 469 (biog. of Thomas Horde). VCH *Wiltshire* 8 (1965): 96–103. VCH *Shropshire* 8 (1968): 164, 266. Roskell *House of Commons 1386–1421* 3 (1992): 265–267 (biog. of Leonard Hakluyt); 4 (1992): 461–462 (biog. of John Stapleton). National Archives, CP 25/1/195/22, #26 (fine dated 13 Oct. 1443 — Parties: William Adam, of Longdon, and Richard Adam, of Cardynton, querents, and John Stepulton, of Stapleton, deforciant re. the manor of Stapleton and the advowson of the church of the same manor and lands in Stapleton, Shropshire); CP 25/1/195/22, #27 (fine dated 13 Oct. 1443 — Parties: Mary de Stepulton the younger and Joyce de Stepulton, querents, and William Adam, of Longdon, and Richard Adam, of Cardynton, deforciants re. one messuage, lands, and rent in Stapleton, Shropshire) [see abstract of fines at http:// www.medievalgenealogy.org.uk/index.html].

Children of Margaret Deviock by John Stapleton, Esq.:

i. **LEONARD STAPLETON**, Esq., of Grove (in South Brent), Somerset, and, in right of his 2nd wife, of Sezincote, Gloucestershire and Milcote, Warwickshire, son and heir by his father's 1st marriage, born in or before 1400 (minor in 1418, of age in 1421). He was a legatee in the 1413 will of his step-grandfather, Leonard Hakluyt, Knt. He was a legatee in the 1414 will of his grandmother, Margaret Hakluyt. In the period, 1426–32, he sued Hugh Stapleton, Gent., and Hugh his son in Chancery for killing his horses and cattle at Stapleton, Shropshire, and lying in wait to kill him. He served as one of the feoffees for Edward Benstede, Knt. in 1429. In 1435 he, John Greville, and others were pardoned for acquiring the manor of Braunton Gorges, Devon without license from Theobald Gorges alias Russell. He married (1st) before Trinity 1441 **MARY** _____. In 1441 he and his wife, Mary, sold the manor of Walton in Gordano, Somerset to Thomas Hethe for 200 marks of silver. In 1442 he and his wife, Mary, settled his manor of Grove (in South Brent), Somerset on themselves and their issue, with reversion to the right heirs of Leonard. He was appointed one of the executors of the 1444 will of Edward Leighton, of Stretton in the Dale, Shropshire. He married (2nd) before 1448 **JOYCE COKESEY** (or **COOKSEY**), widow of John Greville, Esq. (died 1444), of Sezincote and Lasborough (in Westonbirt), Gloucestershire, and daughter of Walter Cokesey, Esq., of Great Cooksey (in Upton Warren) Caldwell (in Kidderminster), and Great Witley, Worcestershire, by Maud, daughter of Thomas Harcourt, Knt. Joyce was co-heiress in 1446 to her brother, Hugh Cokesey, Knt., by which she inherited the manors of Tetbury, Gloucestershire, Bramley and Little Cookham, Surrey, Bidlington (in Bramber), Sussex, Hunningham, Warwickshire, and Great Cooksey (in Upton Warren), Worcestershire. He was granted an exemption for life from being put on assizes, juries, recognitions, etc. in 1448. LEONARD STAPLETON, Esq., died before 1450. His widow, Joyce, married (3rd) before c.1456 **WALTER BEAUCHAMP**, Knt. As "sister and heiress of Hugh Cokesey, knight," in 1465 she demised the site of a watermill at Horsley, Cheshire, together with a watercourse called Horseleywell, for a term of 40 years to William Underwoode, of Peckforton, Cheshire, and his son John. In 1469 she founded the chantry of St. Catherine in Kidderminster, Worcestershire. Joyce died in 1473, and was buried in Kidderminster, Worcestershire. Dugdale *Antiqs. of Warwickshire* (1730): 73 (Herdeburgh ped.). Collins *Peerage of England* 3 (1756): 661–663 (sub Grevile, Earl Brooke). Lysons & Lysons *Magna Britannia* 5 (1817): 129–142. Ormerod *Hist. of Chester* 2 (1819): 333 (Cokesay ped.), 336–337. *Coll. Top. et Gen.* 6 (1840): 74–75. *Sussex Arch. Colls.* 8 (1856): 100–101. Napier *Swyncombe & Ewelme* (1858): 30–34, 46. *Annual Rpt. of the Deputy Keeper* 36 (1875): 156–157. *Colls. Hist. Staffs.* 6 (1883): 320–321 (will of Edward Leighton). Benolte *Vis. of Somerset 1531, 1573 & 1591* (1885): 108 (Furneaux ped.: "Leonard Stepleton."). Tresswell & Vincent *Vis. of Shropshire 1623, 1569 & 1584* 2 (H.S.P. 29) (1889): 424–427 (St. Peter ped.: "Jocosa [Cocksey] soror et hæres nupta Joh's Greuill de Camden"). *Desc. Cat. Ancient Deeds* 1 (1890): 505–516; 3 (1900): 282. *C.P.R. 1422–1429* (1901): 539. Weaver *Somerset Medieval Wills* 1 (Somerset Rec. Soc. 16) (1901): 61–62 (will of Leonard Hakeluyt, Knt.), 66–67 (will of Margaret Hakeluyt). Green *Feet of Fines for Somerset* 4 (Somerset Rec. Soc. 22) (1906): 100, 103. *C.P.R. 1429–1436* (1907): 456. *C.P.R. 1446–1452* (1909): 154. VCH *Surrey* 3 (1911): 80–86, 335–338. VCH *Worcester* 3 (1913): 158–173, 173–179, 231–234; 4 (1924): 328–331 (Cooksey arms: Argent a bend azure with three cinqfoils or thereon), 372–375. Maxwell-Lyte *Docs. & Extracts illus. History of the Honour of Dunster* (1921): 162–163, 165. VCH *Warwick* 6 (1951): 117–120. VCH *Sussex* 6(1) (1960): 200–214. VCH *Gloucester* 6 (1965): 100; 11 (1976): 264–269, 285–288. VCH *Wiltshire* 8 (1965): 96–103. VCH *Shropshire* 8 (1968): 164. Brooks & Pevsner *Buildings of England: Worcestershire* (2007): 298. Chancery Procs., C 1/7/159 (Date: 1426–32: Leonard Stepilton, Esq. v. Hugh Stepilton, Gent. and Hugh his son); C 1/17/64 (Date: 1407–56: Joice, widow of Sir Walter Beauchamp, Knt., and late the wife of Leonard ? (Lethonarde) Stepulton, esq. v. William Bastard, William Arthoure, and John Hawkesby, feoffees of the said Leonard re. manor of Grove (in South Brent), Somerset and lands &c. in Warminster, Wiltshire) (available at www.catalogue.nationalarchives.gov.uk/search.asp). Devon Rec. Office: Fortescue of Castle Hill, 1262M/TG/7 (Thomas Lyttylton styled "cousin and counsel" by Dame Joyce Beauchamp in letter dated c.1456) (available at www.a2a.org.uk/search/index.asp).

ii. **MARGARET STAPLETON**. She was a legatee in the 1414 will of her grandmother, Margaret Hakeluyt, who bequeathed her 10 marks. She married after 1414 _____ (possibly **JOHN STAPLETON**). They had two daughters, Mary and Christian (or Christine). Margaret died before 1455. Weaver *Somerset Medieval Wills* 1 (Somerset Rec. Soc. 16) (1901): 66–67 (will of Margaret Hakeluyt). *Colls. Hist. Staffs.* 1914 (1914): 221. VCH *Wiltshire* 8 (1965): 96–103.

Children of Margaret Stapleton, by unknown husband, _____ (possibly John Stapleton):

a. **MARY STAPLETON**, married **ROBERT MONTFORT**, Esq., of Church Bickenhall, Warwickshire [see BOOTH 13].

b. **CHRISTIAN** (or **CHRISTINE**) **STAPLETON**, daughter and co-heiress. She married (1st) before 1455 **ROBERT CRESSETT**, Esq., of Upton Cressett, Shropshire, Sheriff of Shropshire, 1468–9, 1484–5, son and heir of Hugh Cressett, Esq., Sheriff of Shropshire, 1435. They had one son, Thomas, Esq., and one daughter, Joyce (wife of Ralph Lane and Edward Burton, Gent.). In 1455 Robert and his wife, Mary, and her fellow Stapleton co-heirs presented to the Free Chapel of St. John the Baptist at Stapleton, Shropshire. In 1470 he and his wife, Christine, and other Stapleton co-heirs were summoned at the suit of Thomas Horde and Joyce his wife in a plea that a partition be made of the manors of Stapleton, Armegrove, and Folhampton, Shropshire formerly belonging to John Stapleton, Esq. [grandfather of the said Christine]. In 1483 her cousin, William Roynon, quitclaimed all his land he had in Warminster, Wiltshire which he had by feoffment of Leonard Stapleton to George Booth and his wife, Katherine, John Leighton, and Robert Cressett and his wife, Christian. ROBERT CRESSETT, Esq., left a will proved 27 April 1490. His widow, Christian (or Christine), married (2nd) _____ **EYTON**, and (3rd) **ROBERT BURTON**, Knt. She died before 1495. Owen *Hist. of Shrewsbury* 2 (1825): 230–231. Burke *Hist. of the Commoners* 4 (1838): 261–267 (sub Burton). Eyton *Antiqs. of Shropshire* 6 (1858): 118. Tresswell & Vincent *Vis. of Shropshire 1623, 1569 & 1584* 1 (H.S.P. 28) (1889): 157–158 (Cressett ped.: "Robertus Cressett de Uton Cresset in com. Salop [Sheriff 1469].= Xpiana fil. et hær. Joh'es Stepleton de Stepleton mil. 2 nupta .... Eyton et 3 [*postea*] .... Byrton *Burton.*") (Cressett arms: Azure, a cross and bordure both engrailed or). *Trans. Shropshire Arch. & Nat. Hist. Soc.* 2nd Ser. 6 (1894): 180–181. *List of Sheriffs for England & Wales* (PRO Lists and Indexes 9) (1898): 118–119. *Bye-gones* (1903): 195. Wrottesley *Lane of King's Bromley* (Colls. Hist. Staffs. 3rd Ser. 1910) (1910): 155–163. *Colls. Hist. Staffs.* 1914 (1914): 221. VCH *Wiltshire* 8 (1965): 96–103. Faraday *Cal. of Hereford Probates 1407–1550* (2009): 130.

Child of Christian Stapleton, by Robert Cressett, Esq.:

1) **THOMAS CRESSETT**, Esq., of Upton Cressett, Shropshire married **JOAN** (or **JANE**) **CORBET** [see MORE 10].

iii. **ELIZABETH STAPLETON**, married (as his 1st wife) **EDWARD LEIGHTON**, of Stretton en le Dale, Shropshire,. They had one son, John, Esq. His wife, Elizabeth, died before 1444. He married (2nd) before 1444 **SIBYL** _____. EDWARD LEIGHTON left a will dated 1444, proved 4 March 1454, requesting burial in the chapel of St. Mary in the church of Stretton in le Dale, Shropshire. *Colls. Hist. Staffs.* 6 (1883): 320–321 (will of Edward Leighton). *Bye-gones* (1903): 195. *Colls. Hist. Staffs.* 1914 (1914): 221. Wedgwood *Hist. of Parl.* 1 (1936): 534–535 (biog. of John Leighton). VCH *Shropshire* 8 (1968): 164.

Child of Elizabeth Stapleton, by Edward Leighton:

a. **JOHN LEIGHTON**, Esq., of Stretton en le Dale, Shropshire, Knight of the Shire for Shropshire, 1460–1, (?1463–5), 1467–8, 1472–5, 1478, Steward of Bishop's Castle, 1463, Sheriff of Shropshire, 1467–8, 1473–4, 1481–2, Escheator of Shropshire, 1488–9, Steward of Pontesbury, Shropshire, 1474, Constable of Oswestry Castle, 1476, 2nd son, born in 1430. He was a legatee in the 1444 will of his father. He married before 1453 **ANKARET BURGH**, daughter of John Burgh, Knt., of Wattlesborough, Shropshire, Sheriff of Shropshire, by his 1st wife, Jane, daughter and coheiress of William Clopton. They had one son, Thomas, Knt. In 1455 he his fellow Stapleton co-heirs presented to the Free Chapel of St. John the Baptist at Stapleton, Shropshire. In 1470 he and other Stapleton co-heirs were summoned at the suit of Thomas Horde and Joyce his wife in a plea that a partition be made of the manors of Stapleton, Armegrove, and Folhampton, Shropshire formerly belonging to John Stapleton, Esq. [grandfather of John Leighton]. His wife, Ankaret, died in or before 1471. In 1481 the Bishop of Hereford allowed him as a "discrete man" to have a chapel at Stretton, Shropshire. In 1480–3 he was sued by the Abbot of Buildwas who accused him and his son, William, of breaking into a chapel and tearing up the hedges on the abbey pastures. In 1483 his cousin, William Roynon, quitclaimed all his land he had in Warminster, Wiltshire which he had by feoffment of Leonard Stapleton to George Booth and his wife, Katherine, John Leighton, and Robert Cressett and his wife, Christian. In 1495 he and his fellow Stapleton co-heirs presented to the Free Chapel of St. John the Baptist at Stapleton, Shropshire. JOHN LEIGHTON, Esq., died shortly before 4 Feb. 1496. Eyton *Antiqs. of Shropshire* 6 (1858): 118. *Collectanea Arch.* 1 (1862): 79–89, 182–231. *Colls. Hist. Staffs.* 6 (1883): 320–321 (will of Edward Leighton). *List of Sheriffs for England & Wales* (PRO Lists and Indexes 9) (1898): 118. *Colls. Hist. Staffs.* 1914 (1914): 221. Griffith *Peds. of Anglesey & Carnarvonshire Fams.* (1914): 26 (Powys ped.). Wedgwood *Hist. of Parl.* 1 (1936): 534–535 (biog. of John Leighton). VCH *Shropshire* 8 (1968): 164.

❧ FITZ REYNOLD ☙

HERBERT OF WINCHESTER, of Londesborough, Yorkshire, married **EMMA** _____.
HERBERT FITZ HERBERT, of Londesborough, Yorkshire, married **SIBYL CORBET**.
HERBERT FITZ HERBERT, married **LUCY OF HEREFORD**.
PETER FITZ HERBERT, of Blaen Llyfni (in Cathedine), Breconshire, married **ALICE FITZ ROBERT**.
REYNOLD FITZ PETER, Knt., of Blaen Llyfni (in Cathedine), Breconshire, married **JOAN DE VIVONNE** (desc. King William the Conqueror) [see FITZ HERBERT 5].

6. REYNOLD FITZ REYNOLD, of Hinton Martell and Wolfeton, Dorset, Midsomer Norton and Shepton Mallet, Somerset, Luton, Bedfordshire, and Carbury, co. Kildare, Ireland, younger son by his father's 2nd marriage. He married (1st) **JOAN MARTEL**, younger daughter and co-heiress of Roger Martel, Knt., of Broadmayne and Hinton Martell, Dorset, Carlton Curlieu and Glen Magna, Leicestershire, and Merston, Sussex, by his wife, Joan. She was born about 1276 (aged 4 in 1280). They had two sons, John and Herbert. His wife, Joan, died before 1 May 1306. He presented to the church of Shepton Mallet, Somerset in 1317. He was summoned for military service in Scotland in 1318, and was beyond seas in service in 1325. In 1318 he was granted a weekly market on Fridays and a yearly fair to be held at his manor of Shepton Mallet, Somerset. He married (2nd) before 6 Jan. 1319 **MARGARET** _____. He presented to the church of Mappowder, Dorset in 1323. He married (3rd) shortly before 23 March 1325 **ALICE CRUBBE** (or **CRIBBE**), daughter of John Crubbe. In 1327 Nicholas de Excestre, of Wynton, sued him regarding a debt. REYNOLD FITZ REYNOLD died shortly before 29 August 1328. His widow, Alice, married (2nd) without license shortly before 4 July 1329 **JOHN DE STAFORD** (or **STANORDE**). In 1337 John and his wife, Alice, were sued by Reynold Fitz Herbert for a moiety of the manor of Wolfeton, Dorset. Alice married (3rd) **JOHN CAUNTEREL**. She died 23 October 1358.

>Hutchins *Hist. & Antiqs. of Dorset* 3 (1868): 140. Weaver *Somerset Incumbents* (1889): 180. *Genealogist* n.s. 9 (1892): 85; n.s. 14 (1897): 22. *C.P.R. 1292–1301* (1895): 602. Wrottesley *Peds. from the Plea Rolls* (1905): 35, 178. *List of Inqs. ad Quod Damnum* 2 (PRO Lists and Indexes 22) (1906): 566. *C.Ch.R.* 3 (1908): 374. Weaver *Feodary of Glastonbury Abbey* (Somerset Rec. Soc. 26) (1910): 59–63. *Misc. Gen. et Heraldica* 5th Ser. 6 (1926–28): 81–87. VCH *Sussex* 4 (1953): 158–159. Paget *Baronage of England* (1957) 218: 6–7 (shared his mother's inheritance with his brother Peter, having a fourth part of the Manors of Shepton-Malet and Midsomer-Norton, Somers. Martival *Regs. of Roger Martival, Bishop of Salisbury 1315–1330* 1 (Canterbury & York Soc. 55) (1959): 290. VCH *Leicester* 5 (1964): 77. Mitchell *Portraits of Medieval Women* (2003): 11–28. Hanna *Christchurch Priory Cartulary* (Hampshire Rec. Ser. 18) (2007): 182–183.

7. HERBERT FITZ REYNOLD, of Hinton Martell and Broadmayne, Dorset, Glen Magna, Leicestershire, Merston, Sussex, 2nd but eldest surviving son and heir apparent. He married about 1311 **LUCY PEVEREL**, daughter of Andrew Peverel, Knt., of Blatchington, Ewhurst (in Shermanbury) and Saperton (in Heathfield), Sussex, Barton Peverel (in South Stoneham), Hampshire, etc., by Katherine, daughter and co-heiress of John de Ifield, Knt. They had one son, Reynold, Knt. HERBERT FITZ REYNOLD was living 24 April. 1316, when he was attorney for his father, but died shortly before 29 Sept. 1318.

>*Misc. Gen. et Heraldica* 2nd Ser. 3 (1890): 11. *Somerset & Dorset Notes & Queries* 1 (1890): 103–104. *Genealogist* n.s. 9 (1892): 85; 13 (1896): 38–39; n.s. 14 (1897): 22. Wrottesley *Peds. from the Plea Rolls* (1905): 35, 139–140, 178. VCH *Hampshire* 3 (1908): 481–489. VCH *Sussex* 9 (1937): 202; 6(3) (1987): 193–194. *Year Books of Edward II* 23 (Selden Soc. 65) (1950): 132–134. Paget *Baronage of England* (1957) 218: 6, 446: 3. *Chancery Miscellanea* 8 (List & Index Soc. 105) (1974): 228.

8. REYNOLD FITZ HERBERT, Knt., of Midsomer Norton, Somerset, Luton, Bedfordshire, Hinton Martell and Broadmayne, Dorset, etc., son and heir, born about 1312 (aged 16 in 1328). He married **JOAN HAKELUYT** (or **HAKELUTE**), daughter of Edmund Hakeluyt, Knt., of Longford, Herefordshire. They had one son, Edmund, Knt., and two daughters, Alice and Lucy (nun at Shaftesbury). In 1335 Reynold Fitz Herbert, Edmund son of Edmund Hakeluyt, Knt., and two others owed Arnold le Savage, Knt., of Kent a debt of £200. In 1337 he sued John de Stanorde and his wife, Alice, for a moiety of the manor of Wolfeton, Dorset. He was going beyond the seas on the king's service in 1337. In 1344 he was going to Ireland on the king's service with Ralph de Ufford. SIR REYNOLD FITZ HERBERT died 12 (or 13) Sept. 1346. His widow, Joan, married (2nd) shortly before 8 Feb. 1348 (date of pardon for marrying without license) (as his 1st wife) **THOMAS LE BLOUNT**, Knt., of Compton Valence, Dorset, and Kingston Blount, Oxfordshire, Knight of the Shire for Dorsetshire and for Oxfordshire. He was born about 1321. They had three sons, Thomas, Knt. [see BOTETOURT 10.iv], Hugh, Esq., and John, and one daughter, Thomasine (nun at Romsey). He was present at the Battle of Crécy in 1346 and the Siege of Calais in 1347. His wife, Joan, was living in 1363. In 1376 he and his son, Thomas le Blount the younger, were party to recognizances for £200 made with Edmund of Langley, Earl of Cambridge. SIR THOMAS LE BLOUNT died about 1407.

Nicolas *Testamenta Vetusta* 1 (1826): 121 (will of Sir Edmond Fitz-Herbert). *Misc. Gen. et Heraldica* 2nd Ser. 3 (1890): 11; 5th Ser. 7 (1929–31): 73–83, 120–123. *Genealogist* n.s. 9 (1892): 85; n.s. 13 (1896): 38–39; n.s. 14 (1897): 22. *C.P.R. 1334–1338* (1895): 532. *C.P.R. 1343–1345* (1902): 244, 260. *C.P.R. 1348–1350* (1905): 6. Wrottesley *Peds. from the Plea Rolls* (1905): 35, 139–140, 178. VCH *Bedford* 2 (1908): 351. *C.P.R. 1354–1358* (1909): 437. Weaver *Feodary of Glastonbury Abbey* (Somerset Rec. Soc. 26) (1910): 59–63. *Desc. Cat. Ancient Deeds* 6 (1915): 119–132. *Year Books of Edward II* 23 (Selden Soc. 65) (1950): 132–134. Paget *Baronage of England* (1957) 218: 7, 446: 3. *Chancery Miscellanea* 8 (List & Index Soc. 105) (1974): 228. Ellis *Cat. Seals in the P.R.O.* 2 (1981): 12 (seal of Joan wife of Thomas Blount, Knt. dated 1363 — A bird, facing to R, with spread wing (or a phoenix with flames). Roskell *House of Commons 1386–1421* 2 (1992): 261–262 (biog. of Sir Thomas Blount); 3 (1992): 78–79 (biog. of Sir Edmund Fitzherbert). Gorski *Fourteenth-Century Sheriff* (2003): 129. National Archives, C 241/108/7; SC 8/52/2560 (petition dated c.1331 by Reginald son of Herbert, who is in the king's wardship, to king and council, who states that Joan de Vyvon [Vivonne] gave half of the manor of Wolfeton in Dorset to Reginald le fitz Reynald and John le fitz Reynald, and to the heirs of John's body. John died without heirs of his body, and the half-manor passed to Reginald, who has now died, and whose heir is Reginald le fitz Herbert. But Reginald le fitz Reynald has alienated the lands, contrary to the form of the gift, and to the disinheritance of Reginald le fitz Herbert. He requests a remedy) (available at www.catalogue. nationalarchives.gov.uk/search.asp).

Children of Reynold Fitz Herbert, Knt., by Joan Hakeluyt:

i. **EDMUND FITZ HERBERT**, Knt., Midsomer Norton, Somerset, Luton, Bedforshire, Hinton Martell and Broadmayne, Dorset, Barton (in South Stoneham), Hampshire, Shepton Mallet, Somerset, Ewhurst (in Shermanbury), Offington (in Broadwater) and Saperton (in Heathfield), Sussex, etc., Sheriff of Surrey and Sussex, 1378–9, son and heir. He married **JOAN** _____. They had no issue. In 1368 he and his wife, Joan, made a settlement of the manor of Shepton Mallet, Somerset on themselves and their heirs male. He was heir in 1376 to his great-uncle, Andrew Peverel, Knt., by which he inherited the manors of Barton Peverel (in South Stoneham), Hampshire, Ewhurst (in Shermanbury), Sussex, etc. In 1377 he sold his estate at Luton, Bedfordshire worth £8 per annum to William de Wenlock. SIR EDMUND FITZ HERBERT died in 1387. He left a will dated 23 Feb. 1386, requesting burial in the Monastery of Christchurch, Twinham, Hampshire. His widow, Joan, was living in Michael term 1390. Nicolas *Testamenta Vetusta* 1 (1826): 121 (will of Sir Edmond Fitz-Herbert). Warter *Appendicia et Pertinentiæ Rel. West Tarring* (1853): 345. *Misc. Gen. et Heraldica* 2nd Ser. 3 (1890): 11. Birch *Cat. Seals in the British Museum* 2 (1892): 798 (seal of Edmund Fitz Herbert, Knt. dated 1381 — A shield of arms: quarterly, 1, 4, three lioncels, two and one, within an engrailed bordure [FITZ HERBERT]; 2, 3, gyronny of twelve within a bordure bezantée [PEVEREL]. Suspended by a strap from a forked tree, and within a carved gothic panel with small ballflowers along the inner edge). *Genealogist* n.s. 13 (1896): 38–39. *List of Sheriffs for England & Wales* (PRO Lists and Indexes 9) (1898): 136. Wrottesley *Peds. from the Plea Rolls* (1905): 139–140, 178. *Procs. Somersetshire Arch. & Nat. Hist. Soc.* 53 (1907). VCH *Bedford* 2 (1908): 351. VCH *Hampshire* 3 (1908): 481–489. *Year Books of Richard II* 7 (Ames Found. 10) (1929): 159–166. VCH *Sussex* 6(3) (1987): 192–195. Gorski *Fourteenth-Century Sheriff* (2003): 129.

ii. **ALICE FITZ HERBERT**, married **THOMAS WEST**, Knt., of Roughcombe, Wiltshire [see WEST 8].

✢ FITZ WALTER ✢

ALICE OF NORMANDY (sister of King William the Conqueror), married **LAMBERT**, Count of Lens.
JUDITH OF LENS, married **WALTHEOF**, Earl of Northumberland.
MAUD OF NORTHUMBERLAND, married **SIMON DE SENLIS**, Earl of Huntingdon and Northampton [see BEAUCHAMP 3].

4. MAUD DE SENLIS, married in 1112 **ROBERT FITZ RICHARD**, of Little Dunmow, Essex, Baynard's Castle, London, Cratfield, Suffolk, etc., Steward of Kings Henry I and Stephen, 5th son of Richard Fitz Gilbert, of Bienfaite and Orbec, Normandy, Clare, Suffolk, Tonbridge, Kent, by Rohese, daughter of Walter Giffard, of Long Crendon, Buckinghamshire [see CLARE 1 for his ancestry]. They had one son, Walter, and one daughter, Maud. He witnessed a number of charters of King Henry I. Sometime before 1136 he gave all his part of the water of Stour Mere, for the souls of himself and his ancestors, and for the love of his kinsman, Gerard Giffard the prior, to Stoke by Clare Priory, Suffolk. He accompanied King Stephen to York and Exeter in 1136. ROBERT FITZ RICHARD died in 1137, after 28 November, and was buried at St. Neot's Priory, Cambridgeshire. His widow, Maud, married (2nd) between 1137 and 1140 (as his 1st wife) **SAHER DE QUINCY** (or **QUENCY**), of Long Buckby, Northamptonshire and Wimpole, Cambridgeshire, and, in right of his 1st wife, of East Bradenham, Norfolk and Daventry, Northamptonshire; and, in right of his 2nd wife, of Great Childerley (in Childerley), Cambridgeshire. They had two sons, Robert and Saher, and one daughter, Alice. Sometime before 1176 Maud granted the church of East Bradenham, Norfolk to Norwich Cathedral with the consent of her son, Walter Fitz Robert. At an unknown date, with consent of Walter her son, she granted to Maurice Fitz Geoffrey all her dower lands in Essex and London, which William Fitz Walcher formerly held. He witnessed a charter of Simon son of Simon Earl of Northampton in 1153–7. His wife, Maud, was living in 1158. In 1158 he was pardoned 25s. danegeld in Northamptonshire. Sometime after 1163 he granted Sibton Abbey 20 acres of land from his demesne and 30 acres of broken heath in the village of Tuddenham, Suffolk. At an unknown date, Saher granted the canons of Dunmow, Essex a yearly rent of 10s. issuing out of the lordship of East Bradenham, Norfolk. Saher married (2nd) after 1165 **ASCELINE PEVEREL**, widow of Geoffrey de Waterville (occurs c.1138–61, dead in 1162), of Ailsworth and Upton (in Castor), Northamptonshire, and daughter of Robert Peverel, by his wife, Adelicia. They had no issue. She was co-heiress in 1148 to her brother, William Peverel, of Dover, by which she inherited a one-quarter share of the barony of Bourn, Cambridgeshire. Sometime between 1161 and 1172, she and her son, Ralph de Waterville, conceded to Shrewsbury Abbey a third of Crugelton and Slepe, Shropshire, as given previously by her uncle, Hamon Peverel. Sometime in the 1170s Saher confirmed William [de Belvoir] and his son, Reynold [de Oakley], in their possession of the manor of Great Childerley (in Childerley), Cambridgeshire. SAHER DE QUINCY died in 1190 (or about 1193).

Weever *Antient Funeral Monuments* (1767): 388–391. Baker *Hist. & Antiqs. of Northampton* 1 (1822–30): 563 (Beaumont-Quincy ped.). Dugdale *Monasticon Anglicanum* 5 (1825): 181 (charter of Maud de Senlis to Daventry Priory, naming her deceased husband, [Robert] Fitz Richard, and her mother, Queen Maud [of Scotland]); 6(1) (1830): 147 ("[Year:] 1112. Robertus filius Ricardi deponsavit Matildam de Sancto Licio quae fuit domina de Brade[n]ham"). Clutterbuck *Hist. & Antiqs. of Hertford* 3 (1827): 225–226 (Clare ped.). Hodgson *Hist. of Northumberland* Pt. 2 Vol. 3 (1840): 6–8 (ped.). *Trans. British Arch. Assoc., 2nd Annual Congress* (1846): 294–306. Lipscomb *Hist. & Antiqs. of Buckingham* 1 (1847): 200–201 (Clare ped.). Eyton *Antiqs. of Shropshire* 9 (1859): 62–78. *Notes & Queries* 4th Ser. 11 (1873): 269–271, 305–308. *Remarks & Colls. of Thomas Hearne* 3 (Oxford Hist. Soc.) (1889): 104 (ped. chart). Birch *Catalogue of Seals in the British Museum* 2 (1892): 397 (seal of Maud de Senlis dated temp. Henry II. — Pointed oval. To the left. In tightly-fitting dress with long maunches, in the right hand a fleur-de-lis. Standing. Legend wanting,). Round *Feudal England* (1895): 468–479, 575 (ped.). *Arch. Jour.* 2nd Ser. 6 (1899): 221–231. Warner & Ellis *Facsimiles of Royal & Other Charters in the British Museum* 1 (1903): #37 (charter of William, Count of Boulogne and [Earl] of Warenne dated 1154; charter witnessed by Saher de Quincy). Copinger *Manors of Suffolk* 1 (1905): 45–46; 2 (1908): 45–53. VCH *Northampton* 2

(1906): 483. Lindsay et al. *Charters, Bulls and other Docs. rel. to the Abbey of Inchaffray* (Scottish Hist. Soc. 56) (1908): lxxxvi–lxxxix. *C.P.* 5 (1926): 472, footnote f; 6 (1926): 641, footnote b. Leys *Sandford Cartulary* 2 (Oxfordshire Rec. Soc. 22) (1941): 280–281 (charter of Simon son of Simon Earl of Northampton dated 1153–7; charter witnessed by Saher de Quincy). Hatton *Book of Seals* (1950): 102–103 (charter of Maud de Senlis dated early Henry II; charter witnessed by Walter Fitz Robert and Saher [de Quincy] her sons; attached seal displays a lady standing in mantle and gown, no legend), 194–195 (charter of Saher de Quincy dated after 1163; charter witnessed his son, Saher de Quincy, and [son-in-law], Roger de Huntingfield). *Paget* (1957) 14:2 (daughter Maud, who retained her mother's surname, has been confused with the latter), 230:1 (he died after Easter 1136 when he was one of the witnesses to Stephen's Charter to Winchester). Sanders *English Baronies* (1960): 129–130. VCH *Cambridge* 5 (1973): 4–16, 16–25, 111–120, 241–251; 6 (1978): 220–230; 8 (1982): 97–110, 127–135, 248–267; 9 (1989): 41–44, 118–120. Dodwell *Charters of the Norwich Cathedral Priory* 1 (Pubs. Pipe Roll Soc. n.s. 40) (1974): 180-183 (charter dated 1176 mentions gift of the church of Bradenham, Norfolk "quam Matilda de Silvenecti concessione filii sui Gwalteri ecclesie tue dedit et carta sua confirmauit"). Harper-Bill *Stoke by Clare Cartulary* 1 (Suffolk Charters 4) (1982): 115 (Gerard Giffard, Prior of Stoke by Clare, styled "kinsman" by Robert Fitz Richard before 1136). Kealey *Harvesting the Air* (1987): 107–131. Caenegem *English Lawsuits from William I to Richard I* 1 (Selden Soc. 106) (1990): 249–250. Franklin *English Episcopal Acta 14: Coventry and Lichfield 1072–1159* (1997): 85–87. Raban *White Book of Peterborough* (2001): 250. Tanner *Fams., Friends, & Allies* (2004): 291 (chart), 313 (Scotland ped.), 316 (Clare ped.).

Children of Maud de Senlis, by Robert Fitz Richard:

i. **WALTER FITZ ROBERT** [see next].

ii. **MAUD DE SENLIS**, married (1st) **WILLIAM D'AUBENEY**, of Belvoir, Leicestershire [see DAUBENEY 5]; (2nd) **RICHARD DE LUVETOT**, of Sheffield, Yorkshire [see DAUBENEY 5].

Children of Maud de Senlis, by Saher de Quincy:

i. **ROBERT DE QUINCY**, of Tranent, Fawside, and Longniddry, East Lothian, Scotland, Grantchester, Cambridgeshire, Long Buckby, Northamptonshire, etc., married **ORABEL FITZ NESS** [see QUINCY 5].

ii. **ALICE DE SENLIS**, married **ROGER DE HUNTINGFIELD**, of Linstead and Mendham, Suffolk, Frampton, Lincolnshire, East Bradenham, Norfolk, etc. [see HUNTINGFIELD 5].

5. WALTER FITZ ROBERT, Knt., of Little Dunmow, Burnham, Henham, and Woodham Walter, Essex, Hempnall, Norfolk, Daventry, Northamptonshire, Poslingworth, Suffolk, seigneur of Meri in Normandy, etc., son and heir, born before 1134. He married (1st) **MAUD DE LUCY**, daughter of Richard de Lucy, Knt., of Chipping Ongar, Essex, Diss, Norfolk, etc., Chief Justicier of England,[31] by Rohese, daughter of William of Boulogne [see LUCY 5 for her ancestry]. Her maritagium included the manors of Chigwell, Essex and Diss, Norfolk. They had three sons, Richard, Robert, and Walter [Precentor of St. Paul's, Vicar of Burnham, Essex], and two daughters, Maud and Alice. He gave the advowsons of Woodham Walter (c. 1167) and Burnham (c. 1170), both in Essex, to the Hospitallers. In 1155 he gave the church of Burnham on Crouch, Essex to Dunmow Priory. In the period, 1167-1170, he gave the advowsons of Burnham and Woodham Walter, Essex to the Hospitallers. Sometime about 1170 he granted his warhorse and arms to the Hospitallers on his decease. His first wife, Maud, was presumably living about 1170. About 1175 he gave three mills and various tracts of land in Daventry and Drayton, Northamptonshire to St. Mary of La Charité and the monks of St. Augustine in Daventry. He also gave the oblations of his household to the monks of Daventry to maintain the lights in the priory church. He married (2nd) before c.1181 **MAUD DE BOHUN**, widow

---

[31] Maud de Lucy's father was Richard de Lucy, Knt. (died 1179), Chief Justicier of England, one of King Henry II's great ministers [see *D.N.B.* 12 (1909): 246–248 (biog. of Richard de Lucy)]. For evidence that Rohese, wife of Sir Richard de Lucy, was the sister of Pharamus (or Faramus) of Boulogne, see Cheney and John *English Epis. Acta III: Canterbury 1193–1205* (1986): 201–202 (charter of Sir Richard de Lucy's son, Godfrey de Lucy, Bishop of Winchester, dated 1198–1204 which names Pharamus of Boulogne as Godfrey's "uncle" [avunculo]). Pharamus of Boulogne was near "kinsman" [nepos] of Queen Maud of Boulogne, wife of King Stephen of England [see Arnold *Symeonis Monachi Opera Omnia* 2 (Rolls Ser.) (1885): 310]. For Pharamus of Boulogne's descent from the Counts of Boulogne, see Tanner *Families, Friends, & Allies: Boulogne & Politics in Northern France & England* (2004): 291 (chart).

of Henry d'Oilly (died c. 1163), of Hook Norton, Oxfordshire, Bradenham, Buckinghamshire, etc., and daughter of Humphrey de Bohun, of Trowbridge, Newton Tony, Wilsford, etc., Wiltshire, Steward to Kings Henry I, Stephen, and Henry II of England, by Margaret (or Margery), daughter of Miles of Gloucester, 1st Earl of Hereford, Constable of Gloucester [see BOHUN 3 for her ancestry]. They had one son, Simon. Sometime prior to 1180 he gave the advowsons of Wimbish, Essex and St. Andrew (Holborn), London to St. Neots Priory, Cambridgeshire. About 1181 he made notification of his sale to Gilbert Foliot, Bishop of London, of Walter Cheriesson, *natiuus*, with all his children and descendants. Sometime in the period, c.1181–98, he gave the monks of Stoke by Clare, Suffolk a dwelling-house and seven acres in Merdesford in free alms in his own *cultura* for the soul of Maud de Lucy his wife. Sometime in the period, c.1181–98, he granted the church of Keddington, Lincolnshire to Daventry Priory. Sometime prior to 1193, he gave the church of Heveningham, Suffolk to the monks of Bec dwelling at St. Neots. SIR WALTER FITZ ROBERT died in 1198, and was buried in the choir at Dunmow Priory, Essex. His widow, Maud, was living in Easter Term 1201.

Blomefield *Essay towards a Top. Hist. of Norfolk* 1 (1739): 2–8 (Walter Fitz Robert: "He was a Justice Intinerant in Norfolk and Suffolk"). Weever *Antient Funeral Monuments* (1767): 388–391. Hasted *Hist. & Top. Survey of Kent* 2 (1797): 227–263. *Placitorum in Domo Capitulari Westmonasteriensi Asservatorum Abbreviatio* (1811): 62. Dugdale *Monasticon Anglicanum* 3 (1821): 475 (charter of Walter Fitz Robert to Priory of St. Neot; charter names his father, Robert Fitz Richard; his wife, Maud, and his sister, Maud); 5 (1825): 181–182 (charter of Walter Fitz Robert to Daventry Priory, which names his parents, Robert Fitz Richard and Maud de Senlis, and his wife, Maud de Lucy); 6(2) (1830): 807 (charter of Walter Fitz Robert). Howlett *Chronicles of the Reigns of Stephen, Henry II, and Richard I* 3 (Rolls Ser. 82) (1886): 288–291. Maitland *Bracton's Note Book* 3 (1887): 76–77, 591–594. Round *Feudal England* (1895): 468–479, 575 (ped.). Moore *Cartularium Monasterii Sancti Johannis Baptiste de Colecestria* 1 (1897): 145–146 (undated charter of Walter Fitz Robert), 165–166 (undated charter of Walter Fitz Robert; charter names his father, Robert Fitz Richard, his mother, Maud, and his aunt [amite], Rohaise; charter witnessed by Matthew de Cruil [Criel] his "kinsman" [nepote]), 166–167 (undated charter of Walter Fitz Robert; charter names his wife, Maud), 244 (undated charter of Walter Fitz Robert, of Woodham, names his "aunt" [amita] Roasia and his "father" [patris], Robert.). *Genealogist* n.s. 15 (1898): 129–133. Kirk *Feet of Fines for Essex* 1 (1899): 19–20. Porée *Hist. de l'Abbaye du Bec* 1 (1901): 456. Copinger *Manors of Suffolk* 2 (1908): 45–53. Stenton *Docs. illus. of the Social & Economic Hist. of the Danelaw* (1920): 306–307 (charter of Walter Fitz Robert to Daventry Priory dated Henry II; charter names his late wife, Maud de Lucy, and current wife, Maud de Bohun). *VCH Buckingham* 3 (1925): 35. *C.P.* 5 (1926): 472, footnote f. *C.R.R.* 8 (1938): 25–26. Gibbs *Early Charters of the Cathedral Church of St. Paul, London* (Camden Soc. 3rd ser. 58) (1939): 210–211 (charter of Walter Fitz Robert dated c.1181). *English Hist. Rev.* 39 (1924): 568–571. Flower *Introduction to the Curia Regis Rolls, 1199–1230 A.D.* (Selden Soc. 62) (1944): 29–30. Loyd & Stenton *Sir Christopher Hatton's Book of Seals* (1950): 102. VCH *Essex* 4 (1956): 24–25 Paget *Baronage of England* (1957) 73:2; 230:1. Sanders *English Baronies* (1960): 129–130. Brooke *Letters and Charters of Gilbert Foliot* (1967): 414, 428, 480. Gervers *Cartulary of the Knights of St. John of Jerusalem in England, Secunda Camera, Essex* 1 (Recs. of Soc. & Econ. Hist. n.s. 6) (1982): 202 (charter of Walter Fitz Robert dated c. 1170). Harper-Bill ed. *Stoke by Clare Cartulary* 2 (Suffolk Charters 5) (1983): 152 (charter of Walter Fitz Robert dated pre-1198), 186–187. Cheney *English Episcopal Acta II: Canterbury 1162-1190* (1986): 116–117. Cheney *English Episcopal Acta III: Canterbury 1193–1205* (1986): 254–255. Kealey *Harvesting the Air* (1987): 107–131. Franklin *Cartulary of Daventry Priory* (1988): 4-7, 58. *Albion* 22 (1990): 383–401. Gervers *Cartulary of the Knights of St. John of Jerusalem in England, Prima Camera, Essex* (Recs. of Soc. & Econ. Hist. n.s. 23) (1996): 27–28 (charter of Walter Fitz Robert, witnessed by his wife, Maud de Lucy), 51–53 (charters of Walter Fitz Robert), 53-55, 217-218. Tanner *Fams., Friends, & Allies* (2004): 313 (Scotland ped.), 316 (Clare ped.), 317 (Lucy ped.).

Children of Walter Fitz Robert, Knt., by Maud de Lucy:

i. **ROBERT FITZ WALTER** [see next].

ii. **MAUD FITZ WALTER**, married (1st) **WILLIAM DE LUVETOT**, of Sheffield, Yorkshire [see FURNIVAL 6], (2nd) **ERNULF DE MANDEVILLE**, of South Mimms, Middlesex [see FURNIVAL 6].

iii. **ALICE FITZ WALTER**, married **GILBERT PECCHE**, of Great Bealings, Suffolk [see PECCHE 6].

6. ROBERT FITZ WALTER, of Little Dunmow, Burnham, and Woodham Walter, Essex, and, in right of his 1st wife, of Almshoe (in Ippollitts), Ashwell, Benington, Hertingfordbury, King's Walden, Radwell, and Sacombe, Hertfordshire, Bourn, Gamlingay, Teversham, and Westley (in

Westley Waterless), Cambridgeshire, etc., Constable of Hertford Castle, 2nd but 1st surviving son and heir by his father's 1st marriage. He married (1st) before 13 October 1199 **GUNNOR DE VALOINES**, widow of Durand d'Outillé (or de Ostelli), Butler and Chamberlain to King Henry II (living 1189/90, died c.1194), and daughter and heiress of Robert de Valoines, of Ashwell, Benington, Hertingfordbury, King's Walden, Radwell, and Sacombe, Hertfordshire, Gamlingay, Cambridgeshire, Higham, Essex, Great Fakenham and Bacton, Suffolk, etc., by his wife, Hawise. They had one son, _____ (living 1217), and two daughters, Maud and Christian. About 1200 he confirmed the gift of his father, Walter Fitz Robert, of the advowson of the church of Woodham Walter, Essex to the Hospitallers. In 1200 he and his wife, Gunnor, brought an assize of novel disseisin against John, Abbot of Saint Albans, for the wood of Northawe, Hertfordshire; in 1201 Robert made an agreement in the king's court, by which he released his claim of the wood to the abbey, in return for ten librates of land in Biscott, Bedfordshire. Sometime in the period, 1200–30, he confirmed to William son of William Fitz Rocelin nine acres of land in Cantelof (in Hethersett), Norfolk, which Peter le Blund gave him. In 1201 his wife, Gunnor, gave land in Leyton, Essex to Haliwell Priory, Middlesex. In 1202 he procured his appointment as warden of Hertford Castle. In 1203 he and Saher de Quincy were appointed joint-governors of Vaudreuil Castle in France, which they surrendered to the French army at the first summons. King Philippe *Auguste* confined them at Compiègne, where they remained until a ransom of 5,000 marks was paid. In 1204 he was co-heir to lands at Lesnes, Kent formerly held by his uncle, Godfrey de Lucy, Bishop of Winchester. In 1206 he witnessed a truce between King John and King Philip of France at Thouars. In 1207–8 he and his wife, Gunnor, gave 100 marks for an assize of mort d'ancestor against Philip de Valoines respecting Farleton, Cantsfield, and Staining, Lancashire, Partney, Lincolnshire, Newham, Northumberland, and Burton-in-Lonsdale, Yorkshire. By writ dated 27 Dec. 1207 his wife, Gunnor, had livery of Burton-in-Lonsdale, Yorkshire, whichg descended to her on the death of Emma de Humet, widow of her uncle, Geoffrey de Valoines. In 1208 Hugh de Morewick essoined himself *de malo veniendi* against Robert and his wife, Gunnor, in a plea of land. The same year Robert Fitz Walter and Philip de Valoines brought a suit against Robert de Stuteville and others regarding land formerly belonging to Geoffrey de Valoines in Yorkshire and Lancashire. In 1208 his wife, Gunnor, claimed Staple Terne, Lancashire against the Abbot of Furness. At an unknown date, his wife, Gunnor, gave the advowson of the church of Welwyn, Hertfordshire to Haliwell Priory, Middlesex. He married (2nd) **ROHESE** (or **ROSE**) _____. They had one son, Walter, Knt. He fought with the king in Ireland in the summer of 1210. In the period, 1210–18, he witnessed a charter of Saher de Quincy, Earl of Winchester. In the period, 1210–12, the removal of a certain Thomas as prior of Binham, Norfolk by the Abbot of St. Albans provoked considerable dispute. Robert asserted his claim to be patron of the cell, and alleged that he possessed a deed from the parent abbey by which it was stipulated that no prior could be removed without the patron's assent. He therefore impleaded the abbot in the king's court, charging him with coming to the priory of Binham to lodge there with more men and horses than he ought to have, and also with increasing the number of monks there resident, and extorting much money from the men of the priory, from which he ought only to receive one mark yearly. The defence was apparently a denial of Fitz Walter's claim to the patronage, and seems to have been successful. Having therefore obtained no satisfaction from the law, he assembled his retainers, and so closely beset the priory that the monks then in residence could not get anything to drink save rain water, or anything to eat save bread made of bran. When King John heard of this outrage, he sent an armed force to relieve Binham. In 1212 Robert likewise entered into intrigues with Eustace de Vescy and Llywelyn ap Iorwerth against the king, for which the king condemned him to perpetual exile. Robert fled with his wife and children to France, whereupon the king demolished his properties at Castle Baynard and Benington Castle. He was temporarily reconciled to the king 19 July 1213, but, breaking out again into rebellion, all his

Reversed Seal Matrix of Robert Fitz Walter (died 1235), Magna Carta Baron, in Department of Medieval and Later Antiquities, British Library, London
To the right. In armour: hauberk and chaussées of mail, with continuous coif, surcoat, flat-topped helmet with vizor closed, sword, shield of arms. Horse caparisoned, with diapered head-cloth. Arms: a fess between two chevrons [FITZ WALTER]. In the field, in front of the horse, a shield of arms: seven mascles, three, three, and one [QUINCY]. Below the horse, in the foreground, a wyvern regaurdant, tail flory. Fine workmanship. Beaded borders. Source: Birch *Catalogue of Seals in the British Museum* 2 (1892): 292.

lands in Cornwall were seized. He joined the confederacy of the barons against the king at Stamford in Easter week, 1215. The barons elected him their general, with the title "Marshall of the Army of God and Holy Church." He was one of the twenty-five barons elected to guarantee the observance of Magna Carta, which King John signed 15 June 1215. In consequence he was among the barons excommunicated by Pope Innocent III 16 Dec. 1215. He was sent over to France with Saher de Quincy to offer the English crown to Prince Louis of France. They returned 9 Jan. 1216 with forty-two ships full of French knights and their followers. On his return to England, in company with his cousin, William de Huntingfield, he subdued Essex and Suffolk. After King John's death 19 October 1216, the tide of fortune turned. Gradually the English went over to the side of King Henry III. In April 1217 he was sent from London at the head of a strong French force to raise the Siege of Mountsorrel in Leicestershire. On his way, he and his companions were thoroughly defeated at the Battle of Lincoln 20 May 1217. He was taken prisoner along with his son and most of the other leaders of his party. He made his peace with the king, and was released from prison 8 October 1217. The king granted him his scutage 24 Jan. 1217/8. He presented to the church of Sacombe, Hertfordshire after 1216 and again in 1223. In 1219 he sailed for the Holy Land with Saher de Quincy, Earl of Winchester, and William, Earl of Arundel. He spent the rest of his life peaceably in England. On 11 Feb. 1225 he was one of the witnesses of Henry III's third confirmation of Magna Carta. The same year Richard Fitz Roy and his wife, Rose, sued him for 140 acres of land in Lesnes, Kent. In 1230 he was one of those assigned to hold the assize of arms in Essex and Hertfordshire. At an unknown date, he gave all the enclosed marsh in his demesne of Burnham, Essex to Haliwell Priory, Middlesex. At an unknown date, he confirmed the grants made by his predecessors to Little Dunmow Priory, Essex, and granted so far as he could as patron of the hospital of St. Mary Magdalen, Hertford. ROBERT FITZ WALTER died 9 Dec. 1235. His wife, Rohese, survived him and allegedly died in 1256. They were buried before the high altar at Dunmow Priory, Essex.

> Weever *Ancient Funerall Monuments* (1631): 632 ("About the yeare 1213 saith the booke of Dunmow, there arose a great discord betwixt king Iohn and his Barons, because of Matilda surnamed the faire, daughter of Robert Fitz-water, whom the King vnlawfully loued, but could not obtaine her, nor her fathers consent thereunto. Whereupon, for other like causes, ensued warre through the whole Realme."). Blomefield *Essay towards a Top. Hist. of Norfolk* 1 (1739): 2–8 ("Hollinshed, that faithful Historian, gives him this Character, that he was, 'Both Excellent in Counsel, and Valiant in War.' He went with Ralph Earl of Chester's Army to the aid the Christians against the Infidels, who had besieged the City of Damieta in Egypt, where he performed noble Atchievements: 'After which, this strenuous Knight, this Mars of Men, this Marshal of God's Army and Holy Church, (for so he was stiled by the Common Multitude lived in all Affluence of Riches and Honour, 'till 1234, when he died, and was buried by his Daughter in the said Church: Hollinshed says, Anno 1235, in Advent died the noble Baron the Lord Fitz-Walter."). *Archæologia* 5 (1777): 211–215. *Placitorum in Domo Capitulari Westmonasteriensi Asservatorum Abbreviatio* (1811): 29–30, 59, 62. Clutterbuck *Hist. & Antiqs. of Hertford* 2 (1821): 276–278 (Valoines-Fitz Walter ped.). Dugdale *Monasticon Anglicanum* 2 (1819): 189; 3 (1821): 342, 349–350; 6(1) (1830): 147. Baker *Hist. & Antiqs. of Northampton* 1 (1822–30): 306 (Fitz Walter ped.). Michel *Histoire des Ducs de Normandie* (1840): 116–121 ("Robert le fils Gautier ... Il avoit .ij. filles et .i. fill; li ainsnée des fille ... fu mariée à Joffroi de Mandevlle, et l'autre fu encore petitie puciele; mais puis fuelle mariée à Guillaume de Mandeville, qui freres fu Joffroi."). Hardy *Syllabus (in English) of the Docs. Rel. England & Other Kingdoms* 1 (1869): 21. Fraser *Registrum Monasterii S. Marie de Cambuskenneth, A.D. 1147–1535* (1872): 93–94. Matthew of Paris *Chronica Majora* 2 (Rolls Ser. 57) (1874): 604–605, 642–644. Stubbs *Historical Works of Gervase of Canterbury* 2 (Rolls Ser. 73) (1880): 110–111. *Genealogist* 6 (1882): 1–7; n.s. 15 (1898): 129–133 (Godfrey [de Lucy], Bishop of Winchester, styled "uncle" [avunculus] of Robert Fitz Walter, cites Hardy *Rotuli Litterarum Clausarum* 1 (1833): 14). *Notes & Queries* 6th Ser. 5 (1882): 61–62, 142–143, 290–291. Maitland *Bracton's Note Book* 3 (1887): 76–77, 591–594. Baildon *Select Civil Pleas* 1 (Selden Soc. 3) (1890): 20–21. Birch *Cat. Seals in the British Museum* 2 (1892): 292 (seal of Robert Fitz Walter cast from the original matrix in the Dept. of Antiqs. — To the right. In armour: hauberk and chaussées of mail, with continuous coif, surcoat, flat-topped helmet with vizor closed, sword, shield of arms. Horse caparisoned, with diapered head-cloth. Arms: a fess between two chevrons [FITZ WALTER]. In the field, in front of the horse, a shield of arms: seven mascles, three, three, and one [QUINCY]. Below the horse, in the foreground, a wyvern reguardant, tail flory. Fine workmanship. Legend: * SIGILLVM : ROBERTI : FILII : WALTERI :. Beaded borders), 805 (seal of Robert Fitz Walter temp. Henry III — Obverse. Equestrian. Reverse: A small round counterseal. A shield of arms: a fess between two chevrons [FITZ

WALTER]), 805 (seal of Robert Fitz Walter temp. Henry III — A fede, or two hands clasped in pale, the arms issuing, vested. Between two shields of arms: a fess between two chevrons [FITZ WALTER]. Legend: FOI · E · L[EA]VTE · WS · TENGNE. Beaded borders). Round *Feudal England* (1895): 575 (ped.). Farrer *Final Concords of Lancaster* 1 (Lanc. & Cheshire Rec. Soc. 39) (1899): 31–32. *Feet of Fines for Essex* 1 (1899): 19–20, 22, 36, 45, 93–94, 97, 104–105. *List of Foreign Accounts* (Lists & Indexes XI) (1900): 201. *Trans. Essex Arch. Soc.* n.s. 7 (1900): 329–330. *C.Ch.R.* 1 (1903): 201. *Ancestor* 11 (1904): 129–135. *English Hist. Rev.* 19 (1904): 707–711; 80 (1965): 314–322. *Notes & Queries for Somerset & Dorset* 9 (1905): 308–310. Wrottesley *Peds. from the Plea Rolls* (1905): 521. VCH *Norfolk* 2 (1906): 343–346. Birch *Seals* (1907): 176 ("One of the finest equestrian seals is that of Robert Fitz-Walter, a matrix preserved in the British Museum, about two and three-quarter inches in diameter. This is of the early part of the twelfth century, and shows the rider clad in his hauberk and chausses of mail, continuous coif, surcoat, and helmet with flat-top visor closed, and armed with sword and shield of the arms of Fitz-Walter. In the field before the horse is another shield, bearing the seven mascles of the De Quincy family, below the horse is the wyvern reguardant, with a flowing tail."). VCH *Essex* 2 (1907): 150–154. *D.N.B.* 7 (1908): 219–223 (biog. of Robert Fitzwalter) ("He is described by Matthew Paris (iii.334) as a 'noble baron, illustrious by his birth, and renowned for his martial deeds'."). Lindsay et al. *Charters, Bulls & other Docs. Rel. the Abbey of Inchaffray* (Scottish Hist. Soc. 56) (1908): 157–158. VCH *Hertford* 2 (1908): 357–360; 3 (1912): 25–28, 33–37, 73–77, 165–171, 199–209, 244–247, 463, 501–511; 4 (1971): 372–416; 452–453. Phillimore *Rotuli Hugonis de Welles Episcopi Lincolniensis 1209–1235* 1 (Lincoln Rec. Soc. 3) (1912): 66; 3 (Lincoln Rec. Soc. 9) (1914): 47. VCH *Lancaster* 8 (1914): 244–247. *C.P.* 5 (1926): 126–133 (sub Essex), 472, footnote f (sub Fitzwalter). Foster *Registrum Antiquissimum of the Cathedral Church of Lincoln* 1 (1931) (Lincoln Rec. Soc. 27) (1931): 129–131; 3 (Lincoln Rec. Soc. 29) (1935): 216–218. *Curia Regis Rolls* 8 (1938): 25–26. Gibbs *Early Charters of the Cathedral Church of St. Paul* (Camden Soc. 3rd Ser. 58) (1939): 37–39. Hassall *Cartulary of St. Mary Clekenwell* (Camden 3rd Ser. 71) (1949): 28–29. Hatton *Book of Seals* (1950): 203–204 (charter of Robert Fitz Walter dated 1200–30 — seal on tag: equestrian, head obscured by tag, surcoat, shield and trappings with arms as on counterseal, below the horse a wyvern reguardant with tail flory, Legend: [+ SI]GILLVM : ROBERTI : FILII WALTERI. Counterseal: Shield of arms, a fess between two chevrons. Legend: + SECRETVM : ROBERTI : FILII : WALTERI. Paget *Baronage of England* (1957) 230: 2–3 (sub Fitz Walter). Sanders *English Baronies* (1960): 129–130. VCH *Middlesex* 1 (1969): 170–182. Scarfe *Suffolk in the Middle Ages* (1986): 64. Tremlett *Rolls of Arms Henry III* (H.S.P. 113-4) (1967): 65 (arms of Robert Fitz Walter: Or, a fess between two chevrons gules). Cheney *Letters of Pope Innocent III 1198–1216* (1967): 172. VCH *Cambridge* 5 (1973): 4–16, 70–71; 6 (1978): 177–182; 10 (2002): 173–178. *Art Hist.* 1 (1978): 26–42. *Comptes rendus de l'Académie des Inscriptions et Belles-lettres* (1982): 371–383. Kealey *Harvesting the Air* (1987): 107–131. Franklin *Cartulary of Daventry Priory* (1988): 7–8 (charter of Robert Fitz Walter). *Albion* 22 (1990): 383–401. Burton *Monastic & Religious Orders in Britain 1000–1300* (1994): 213. Gervers *Cartulary of the Knights of St. John of Jerusalem in England* 2 (Recs. of Soc. & Econ. Hist. n.s. 23) (1996): 55–56 (confirmation charter of Robert Fitz Walter dated c.1200). Shirley *Secular Jurisdiction of Monasteries in Anglo-Norman & Angevin England* (Studies in Hist. of Medieval Religion 21) (2004): 127–129. *Coat of Arms* 3rd Ser. 3(2) (2007): 159 ("The seal of Robert Fitzwalter is one of the finest medieval silver equestrian seal matrices to survive. Found in Stamford, Lincolnshire, in the reign of Chartles II, it came to the British Museum in 1841.").

Children of Robert Fitz Walter, Knt., by Gunnor de Valoines:

i. _____ **FITZ WALTER** (son). He and his father were captured at the Battle of Lincoln 20 May 1217. He died without issue sometime before 25 Jan. 1226/7, when his sister, Christian, had livery of the lands in cos. Norfolk and Cambridge which belonged to her by hereditary right. Michel *Histoire des Ducs de Normandie* (1840): 116–121. Stubbs *Historical Works of Gervase of Canterbury* 2 (Rolls Ser. 73) (1880): 110–111. *C.P.* 5 (1926): 130–133 (sub Essex).

ii. **MAUD FITZ ROBERT**, married **GEOFFREY DE MANDEVILLE**, Knt., 5th Earl of Essex [see ESSEX 2.i].

iii. **CHRISTIAN** (or **CHRISTINE**) **FITZ ROBERT**, married (1st) **WILLIAM DE MANDEVILLE**, Knt., 6th Earl of Essex [see ESSEX 2.ii]; (2nd) **RAYMOND DE BURGH**, Knt., of Dartford, Kent [see ESSEX 2.ii].

Child of Robert Fitz Walter, by Rohese (or Rose) _____:

i. **WALTER FITZ ROBERT**, Knt. [see next].

7. WALTER FITZ ROBERT, Knt., of Woodham Walter, Burnham, Roydon, Dunmow, Henham, Tey, Ulting, and Wimbish, Essex, son and heir by his father's 2nd marriage, born about 1219 (minor in 1235 and came of age in 1240). He married **IDA LONGESPÉE**, daughter of William Longespée, Earl of Salisbury (illegitimate son of King Henry II of England), by Ela, daughter and heiress of William Fitz Patrick, Earl of Salisbury [see LONGESPÉE 5 for her ancestry]. They had one son, Robert, Knt. [1st Lord Fitz Walter], and three daughters, Ela, Katherine (nun), and Lora (nun). In 1253 he was granted a weekly market and a yearly fair at his manor of Burnham, Essex. About 1255 he gave 3 acres of meadow in Westmead (in Roydon), Essex to the Hospitallers. SIR WALTER FITZ ROBERT died shortly before 10 April 1258. In 1259 his widow, "Ida Lungesp[ee]," paid £40 to have the farm of the manor of Henham, Essex. In the period, 1261–3, as "Ida Longespée," widow of Walter Fitz Robert, she petitioned Walter de Merton, the king's chancellor, to bail two of her men appealed of homicide. Ida was living 11 May 1262.

> Sandford *Gen. Hist. of the Kings of England* (1677): 117 (identifies wife Ida as daughter of William Longespée [I], Earl of Salisbury). Blomefield *Essay towards a Top. Hist. of Norfolk* 1 (1739): 2–8. Dugdale *Monasticon Anglicanum* 6(1) (1830): 148, 501 (Longespée ped. in Lacock Priory records: "Idam de Camyle, quam duxit in uxorem Walterus fil. Roberti, de qua genuit Catherinam et Loricam, quæ velatæ erant apud Lacok; Elam, quam duxit primo Guillelmus de Dodingeseles, de qua genuit Robertum"). Bowles & Nichols *Annals & Antiqs. of Lacock Abbey* (1835): 162–164 (biog. of Ida Longespée), App. I, i–v (Book of Lacock). Roberts *Excerpta è rotulis finium in Turri Londinensi asservatis, Henrico Tertio rege, AD 1216–1272* 2 (1836): 359. Banks *Dormant & Extinct Baronage of England* 4 (1837): 311–312. Hutchins *Hist. & Antiqs. of Dorset* 3 (1868): 287 (Salisbury-Longespée ped.). *Notes & Queries* 6th Ser. 12 (1885): 478. Birch *Cat. Seals in the British Museum* 2 (1892): 290 (seal of Walter Fitz Robert dated 1250? — To the right. In armour: hauberk of mail, sword, shield. Horse caparisoned; the caparisons are charged with chevrons, or chevronelly in allusion to the arms of FITZ WALTER, two chevrons. Legend wanting). *Feet of Fines for Essex* 1 (1899): 153, 184, 214, 221–222, 227. *List of Ancient Corr. of the Chancery & Exchequer* (PRO Lists and Indexes 15) (1902): 107–108. *C.Ch.R.* 1 (1903): 474. VCH *Lancaster* 1 (1906): 312. Copinger *Manors of Suffolk* 2 (1908): 45-53. *C.P.R. 1247–1258* (1908): 246. *C.P.R. 1258–1266* (1910): 209. VCH *Hertford* 3 (1912): 199–209, 244–247. *C.P.* 5 (1926): 472 (sub FitzWalter) [identifies wife Ida as "da. of William (Longespee), Earl of Salisbury)"]; 11 (1949): 381–382 footnote k (sub Salisbury) (confuses wife Ida with her sister of the same name who married William de Beauchamp; also misidentifies Walter Fitz Robert's parentage). Paget *Baronage of England* (1957) 230: 3 (sub Fitz Walter) (identifies wife Ida as daughter of William Longespée the younger). Sanders *English Baronies* (1960): 129–130. *Cal. Liberate Rolls* 5 (1961): 93 (Date: 11 May 1162 — "Liberate to Geoffrey de Lezinan, the king's brother, 40l. in recompense of a like sum received there of the issues of the manor of Henham [Essex] by the hands of Ida Lungespee"). *Curia Regis Rolls* 15 (1972): 369–370. London *Cartulary of Bradenstoke Priory* (Wiltshire Rec. Soc. 35) (1979): 8–9. Schwennicke *Europäische Stammtafeln* 3(2) (1983): 356a (sub Longespée). Gervers *Cartulary of the Knights of St. John of Jerusalem in England* 2 (Recs. of Soc. & Econ. Hist. n.s. 23) (1996): 30–31, 54–55. Leese *Blood Royal* (1996): 54–56. Online resource: http://www.briantimms.net/rolls_of_arms/rolls/gloversB2.htm (Glover's Roll dated c.1252 — arms of Walter Fitz Robert: Or a fess between two chevrons gules). Cassidy *1259 Pipe Roll*: 273 (available at http://www.cmjk.com/1259/1259_pipe_roll.html).

Children of Walter Fitz Robert, Knt., by Ida Longespée:

i. **ROBERT FITZ WALTER**, Knt., 1st Lord Fitz Walter [see next].

ii. **ELA FITZ WALTER**, married (1st) **WILLIAM DE ODDINGSELES**, Knt., of Solihull, Warwickshire [see ODDINGSELES 8].

8. ROBERT FITZ WALTER, Knt., of Woodham Walter, Little Dunmow, Burnham, Henham, Roydon, Sheering, Shopland, Tey, Theydon, and Wimbish, Essex, Westley (in Westley Waterless), Cambridgeshire, Diss and Hempnall, Norfolk, Shimpling, Suffolk, etc., Constable of Bere and Hadleigh Castles, Justice of Essex, and, in right of his 1st wife, of Great Bromley, Great Hallingbury, and Lexden, Essex, Datchworth and Walkern, Hertfordshire, Hamerton, Huntingdonshire, Finedon, Northamptonshire, etc., son and heir, born at Henham, Essex in 1247 (came of age in 1268). In 1258 his wardship was granted to his uncle, Stephen Longespée, Knt. He married (1st) in 1259 **DEVORGUILLE DE BURGH**, elder daughter and co-heiress of John de Burgh, Knt., of Walkern, Hertfordshire, Hamerton, Huntingdonshire, Wakerley, Northamptonshire, Portslade, Sussex, etc., by Cecily, daughter of John de Balliol, Knt., of Barnard Castle, Durham, and Bywell, Northumberland [see LA WARRE 10 for her ancestry]. She was born about 1255–6 (aged 24 or 25 in 1280). They had one son, Walter, and two daughters, Christian and Blanche (nun at Barking Abbey). In 1275 he had license to sell the site of Baynard's Castle in London to the Archbishop of Canterbury, reserving to himself and his heirs those privileges which constituted the possessor, banner bearer of the city. In 1276–7 he was granted letters of protection, he then going in the king's suite to the parts of Wales. He fought in Wales in 1277 and 1282. In 1277–8 he was pardoned an amercement of 200 marks for the capture of a stag in the Forest of Essex. In 1283 he and his wife, Devorguille, subinfeuded her ½ share of the manor of Finedon, Northamptonshire to Ralph de Kirketon and Ralph Seymour. His wife, Devorguille, died in 1284, and was buried in Dunmow Priory, Essex. He accompanied the King to France in 1286. He married (2nd) in the King's Chapel at Westminster before 11 March 1290 **ELEANOR DE FERRERS**, daughter of Robert de Ferrers, Knt., 6th Earl of Derby, by his 2nd wife, Eleanor, daughter of Humphrey de Bohun, Knt. [see FERRERS 8 for her ancestry]. They had one son, Robert, Knt., and three daughters, Ida, Denise, and Mary. In 1290 he acquired the manor of Sheering Hall (in Sheering), Essex from Christian de Valoines, widow of Peter de Maule. He presented to the church of Datchworth, Hertfordshire in 1292 and 1295. He was a benefactor of the Greyfriars of Colchester in 1293 and 1309. In 1294 he was ordered to relieve Bere Castle. He was in Gascony 1294, 1295, and 1297. He was summoned to Parliament from 24 June 1295 to 10 October 1325, by writs directed *Roberto filio Walteri*, whereby he is held to have become Lord Fitz Walter. In 1298 he was granted a weekly market and a yearly fair at his manor of Roydon, Essex. He fought at the Battle of Falkirk 22 July 1298, and was present at the Siege of Caerlaverock Castle in 1300. He signed Barons' letter to Pope Boniface in 1301. In 1302, as "Robert Fitz Walter, lord of Wodeham," he quitclaimed for 20 marks to Robert Fitz William, lord of Legh, all his right in the land of Manely (in St. Veep), Cornwall, which he had of Maud, widow of Henry Peverell. He was on the king's service in Scotland in 1303 and 1306. In 1303 he had a right of gallows and free warren in Shimpling, Suffolk. In 1303, on account of his good service, and in consideration of his great charges and expenses incurred by him on the king's service, the king granted that in case of his death, his heir being a minor, the executors of his testament shall hold the custody of his manors of Hempnall and Diss, Norfolk, and Shimpling, Suffolk, from the date of his death to the end of a term of four years next ensuing for the discharge of his debts. His wife, Eleanor, was living Sept. 1303. At her death, she was buried in Dunmow Priory, Essex. In 1306 he obtained a license to grant 40 acres of his park called "Gentesherne" at Shimpling, Suffolk to Adam de Waldingfield. He married (3rd) after 10 May 1308 (grant of her marriage) and before Hilary 1310 (date of fine) **ALICE DE MONTFORT**, widow of Warin de Lisle, Knt. [see LISLE 4], of Campton, Bedfordshire, Great Wilbraham, Cambridgeshire, Nedging, Suffolk, etc. (died shortly before 7 Dec. 1296), and daughter of Peter de Montfort, Knt., of Beaudesert, Warwickshire, by Maud, daughter and heiress of Henry de la Mare, Knt. [see MONTFORT 6 for her ancestry]. In July 1310 he and his wife, Alice, then going to Jerusalem, had letters appointing William de Hanyngfeld and another their attorneys for three years. In October 1313 his daughter, Christian de Burgh, had license to grant him a moiety of the manors of Great Hallingbury and Bromley, Essex, and Walkern, Hertfordshire, held in chief. The same month she likewise had license to grant a moiety of the manor of Lexden, Essex, held in chief, to him and to his wife, Alice, and the heirs of their bodies, with remainder to the heirs of the said Robert. In Jan. 1315 his grandson, John le Marshal, had license to grant the reversion of the manor of Lexden, Essex to Robert and his wife, Alice, and the heirs of their bodies. In Feb. 1315 his wife, Alice, was going on pilgrimage to Santiago. In April 1315 Robert had license to settle the manor of Hallingbury, Essex on himself for life, with reversion to John le Marshal. The same month John le Marshal had license to grant Robert for his life £46 13s. 4d. of rent in his manors of Hingham, Hockering, and Buxton, Norfolk, held in chief. In October 1315 Robert had license to settle the manor of Wimbish, Essex on himself and his wife, Alice, and the heirs of their body, with remainder to the right heirs of Robert. In Nov. 1317 he was granted custody of the town of Colchester, Essex. In Nov. 1317 he complained that John de Wauton and his brother Robert took and carried away a gentle falcon of the price of £20, and other goods of his, at Barking, Essex, and assaulted Ralph de Benesle his servant. In March 1318 he was granted simple protection, he then going beyond the seas. The same month he was granted license to demise at farm to whomsoever he will for a term of five years his manors of Burnham, Henham, Roydon, Tey, and Woodham Walter, Essex, held in chief; if however he die during that period, his heir being a minor, then the lessee shall answer to the king for the farm during the said term. His wife, Alice, was living in Trinity term 1319. SIR ROBERT FITZ WALTER, 1st Lord Fitz Walter, died 18 Jan. 1325/6.

Brooke *Discoverie of Certaine Errours* (1724): 36–37. Blomefield *Essay towards a Top. Hist. of Norfolk* 1 (1739): 2–9, 11. Morant *Hist. & Antiqs. of Essex* 1 (1768): 440–441; 2 (1768): 511–512. Bridges *Hist. & Antiqs. of Northamptonshire* 2 (1791): 257, 341–344. Clutterbuck *Hist. & Antiqs. of Hertford* 2 (1821): 461–467 (Lanvallei ped.). Chauncy *Hist. Antiqs. of Hertfordshire* 2 (1826): 85–88. Nicolas *Siege of Carlaverock* (1828): 99–101 (biog. of Robert Fitz Walter). Dugdale *Monasticon Anglicanum* 6(1) (1830): 148. Bowles & Nichols *Annals & Antiqs. of Lacock Abbey* (1835): 162–163. Palgrave *Antient Kalendars & Inventories of the Treasury of His Majesty's Exchequer* 1 (1836): 49. Surtees *Hist. & Antiqs. of Durham* 4 (1840): 60 (Baliol ped.). Watson *Tendring Hundred in the Olden Time* (1877): 161–164. Turner *Cal. Charters & Rolls: Bodleian Lib.* (1878): 59. *Annual Rpt. of the Deputy Keeper* 44 (1883): 104–105; 46 (1886): 260; 47 (1886): 224. Birch *Cat. Seals in the British Museum* 2 (1892): 805–806 (seal of Robert Fitz Walter dated 1313 — A shield of arms: a fess between two chevrons [FITZ WALTER]. Suspended by a strap from a forked tree. Between two wyverns sans wings. In place of a legend is a wavy scroll of foliage and flowers). *C.P.R. 1307–1313* (1894): 233. *C.P.R. 1292–1301* (1895): 84–85. *Genealogist* n.s. 13 (1896): 246. Moore *Cartularium Monasterii Sancti Johannis Baptiste de Colecestria* 2 (1897): 678 (letter dated 1289 from Robert Fitz Walter to the Bishop of Lincoln). *C.Ch. R.* 2 (1898): 428. *C.P.R. 1301–1307* (1898): 466, 527 (instances of Robert Fitz Walter styled "king's kinsman" by Edward I, King of England). *C.P.R. 1313–1317* (1898): 18, 20, 211, 221, 275, 356. Gerard *Particular Desc. of Somerset* (Somerset Rec. Soc. 15) (1900): 90–91. *C.P.R. 1317–1321* (1903): 46, 92, 109, 111, 142. Phillimore et al. *Abs. of IPM for Gloucestershire* 4 (1903): 125–127. Howard de Walden *Some Feudal Lords & Their Seals* (1903): 49–50 (biog. of Robert Fitz Walter). *C.P.R. 1321–1324* (1904): 2. *List of Inqs. ad Quod Damnum* 1 (PRO Lists and Indexes 17) (1904): 150–151, 167. Copinger *Manors of Suffolk* 1 (1905): 191–195; 2 (1908): 45–53; 3 (1909): 197. Wrottesley *Peds. from the Plea Rolls* (1905): 165–166. *C.P.R. 1258–1266* (1910): 13, 49, 209. VCH *Hertford* 3 (1912): 79, 152, 154, 244–247. *Feet of Fines for Essex* 2 (1913–28): 17, 77, 95, 127, 146, 189. Kingsford *Grey Friars of London* (1915): 178–201. *Cal. Inqs. Misc.* 2 (1916): 252. *C.P.* 5 (1926): 472–475 (sub FitzWalter) (arms of Robert Fitz Walter: Or, a fesse between two chevrons gules); 8 (1932): 71 (sub Lisle), 528–529 (sub Marshal); 9 (1936): 127 (sub Montfort); 14 (1992): 326 (sub Fitzwalter), 443 (sub Lisle). VCH *Northampton* 3 (1930): 196–203. VCH *Huntingdon* 3 (1936): 66–67. Taylor *Recs. of the Barony & Honour of the Rape of Lewis* (Sussex Rec. Soc. 44) (1939): 74–75. *Norfolk Arch.* 30 (1952): 263–286. VCH *Essex* 4 (1956): 265; 8 (1983): 240–249; 9 (1994): 394. Paget *Baronage of England* (1957) 230: 3–5 (sub Fitz Walter), 314: 3. Sanders *English Baronies* (1960): 92–93, 129–130. *Coat of Arms* 7 (1962): 157–161. Ellis *Cat. Seals in the P.R.O.* 1 (1978): 25 (seal of Robert Fitz Walter, Knt. dated 1317 — A shield of arms: a fesse between two chevrons. Hung from a sprig, between two small wyverns. Scroll-work in place of a legend). VCH *Cambridge* 6 (1978): 177–182. *Ancient Deeds — Ser. AS & WS* (List & Index Soc. 158) (1979): 48 (Deed A.S.271). Sutton *Rolls & Reg. of Bishop Oliver Sutton, 1280–1299* 8 (Lincoln Rec. Soc. 76) (1986): 79, 84. Brault *Rolls of Arms Edward I* 2 (1997): 174–175 (arms of Robert Fitz Walter: Or, a fess between two chevrons gules). Morrison *Women Pilgrims* (2000): 157. VCH *Cambridge* 10 (2002): 309. Cornwall Rec. Office: Croft Andrew, CA/B47/3 (quitclaim of Robert Fitz Walter, lord of Woodham, to Robert Fitz William, lord of Legh, dated 1302) (available at www.a2a.org.uk/search/index.asp). Online resource: http:// www.briantimms.net/era/lord_marshals/ Lord_Marshal02/Lord%20Marshal2.htm (Lord Marshal's Roll — arms of Robert Fitz Walter: Or a fess between two chevrons gules). National Archives, Chancery Miscellanea (C47) 9/52/3 (descent of Robert de Lisle, Knt.: "Sire Robert de Lyle fiz Sire Waryn de Lyle le quel Waryn avoit esposee Dame Alice fylle Sire Piers de Mountf[ort] iadys signour de Beaudesert") (see *Chancery Miscellanea, Bundles 1–14* (List & Index Soc. 7) (1966): 97).

Children of Robert Fitz Walter, Knt., by Devorguille de Burgh:

i. **WALTER FITZ ROBERT**, son and heir apparent by his father's 1st marriage, born at Henham, Essex in 1275. He married at Woodham, Essex in 1286 **JOAN D'ENGAINE**, daughter of John d'Engaine, Knt., of Colne Engaine, Essex and Laxton, Northamptonshire, by Joan, daughter and heiress of Gilbert de Greinville, Knt. They had one son, Robert (died young). WALTER FITZ WALTER died in Dunmow Priory in 1293. His widow, Joan, married in or before 1296 **ADAM DE WELLES** (or **WELLE**), Knt., of Well, Aby, Strubby, and Cumberworth, Lincolnshire, Faxton, Northamptonshire, etc., Constable of Rockingham Castle, 1299–1307. They had three sons, Robert [2nd Lord Welles], Adam, Knt. [3rd Lord Welles], and John, Knt., and three daughters, Margaret (nun), Cecily (nun), and _____ (wife of _____ Mablethorpe). He presented to the churches of Cumberworth, Lincolnshire, 1290 and 1297, and Dexthorpe, Lincolnshire, 1298. He accompanied Hugh le Despenser on his mission to the King of the Romans in 1294. In 1298 he disputed with Lady Joan de Willoughby regarding the patronage of the church of Anderby, Lincolnshire, but failed to appear in spite of repeated citations.

He fought in the king's division at the Battle of Falkirk 22 July 1298. He was summoned to serve against the Scots, 1299–1310. He was summoned to Parliament from 6 Feb. 1298/9 to 16 June 1311, by writs directed *Ade de Welles*, whereby he is held to have become Lord Welles or Welle. He was present at the Siege of Caerlaverock in 1300. He signed the Barons' letter to Pope Boniface VIII in 1301. In 1307–8 Juliane de Gant granted him land in Well and Manthorpe, Lincolnshire. SIR ADAM DE WELLES, 1st Lord Welles, died 1 Sept. 1311, and was buried in Greenfield Priory, Lincolnshire. His widow, Joan, died 1 June 1315, and was buried in Greenfield Priory, Lincolnshire. Dugdale *Monasticon Anglicanum* 6(1) (1830): 148. *C.P.* 5 (1926): 475 (sub FitzWalter); 12(2) (1959): 439–440 (sub Welles). Hill *Rolls & Reg. of Bishop Oliver Sutton* 1 (Lincoln Rec. Soc. 39) (1948): 140, 199–200, 220, 226, 241–244. Major *Registrum Antiquissimum of the Cathedral Church of Lincoln* 6 (Lincoln Rec. Soc. 41) (1950): 180, footnote 13. National Archives, C 143/67/7 (grant of Juliana de Gaunt to Adam de Welle) (available at www.catalogue.nationalarchives.gov.uk/search.asp).

ii. **CHRISTIAN DE BURGH**, married **WILLIAM LE MARSHAL**, Knt., 1st Lord Marshal, hereditary Marshal of Ireland [see HINGHAM 7].

Child of Robert Fitz Walter, Knt., by Eleanor de Ferrers:

i. **ROBERT FITZ WALTER**, Knt. [see next].

ii. **IDA FITZ WALTER**, married (1st) (as his 3rd wife) in 1305 **ROBERT DE LA WARDE**, Knt., Lord Warde, of Burton Overy and Upton, Leicestershire, Newhall, Derbyshire, Kingsley, Staffordshire, etc., Steward of the Household, 1303–7, son of William de la Warde, Knt. They had no issue. In 1284 he was granted lands in Melton Mowbray, Leicestershire by Roger de Mowbray. He was granted free warren in his demesne lands in cos. Derby and Leicester 9 May 1285. In 1290 he complained to Parliament of being unjustly imprisoned by Ralph de Hengham. In 1296 he was staying in Gascony on the king's service with Robert Fitz Walter. He was summoned for service in Scotland, 1297–1303, and in Flanders, 1297. He fought in the 4th division at the Battle of Falkirk 22 July 1298. He was summoned to Parliament from 29 Nov. 1299 to 3 Nov. 1306, by writs directed *Roberto le Warde*, or *la Warde*, whereby he is held to have become Lord Warde. He was at the Siege of Caerlaverock Castle in July 1300. He was sent as an envoy to the French king in 1301. He signed the Barons' letter to Pope Boniface VIII in 1301, as *Robertus la Warde, Dominus de Alba Aula*. He was at the Siege of Stirling Castle in 1304. In 1306 he was appointed Chief Justiciar for the "trial" of Scottish prisoners of war at Newcastle. SIR ROBERT DE LA WARDE, Lord Warde, died shortly before 25 Jan. 1306/7. His widow, Ida, married (2nd) before 4 July 1310 (as his 2nd wife) **HUGH DE NEVILLE**, Knt., 1st Lord Neville (of Essex), son and heir of John de Neville, of Hallingbury, Great Totham, and Wethersfield, Essex, by his wife, Margaret. He was born at Little Hallingbury, Essex 23 August 1276. He served in Scotland in 1300 and 1319, and was on service there in 1311. In 1313 he was going on the king's service beyond seas. In 1322 he was summoned with his forces against Thomas, Earl of Lancaster. He was summoned for service in Gascony in 1324, from which he was excused. He was summoned to Parliament from 19 Dec. 1311 to 1 April 1335, by writs directed *Hugoni de Neville*, whereby he is held to have become Lord Neville. SIR HUGH DE NEVILLE, Lord Neville, died shortly before 27 May 1335. In 1350 his widow, Ida, had permission to go on a pilgrimage to Santiago. She died 7 (or 12) Nov. 1361. Nicolas *Siege of Carlaverock* (1828): 280–281 (biog. of Robert de la Ward). Glover *Hist. of Derby* 2(1) (1829): 158–159 (Meynell ped.). Dugdale *Monasticon Anglicanum* 6(1) (1830): 148. *Annual Rpt. of the Deputy Keeper* 35 (1874): 25. Birch *Cat. Seals in the British Museum* 3 (1894): 638 (seal of Robert de la Warde dated 1301 — A shield of arms: vairé [WARDE]. Crest on a helmet, a fan-plume. On each side a wavy sprig of foliage and flowers. Legend: S' ROBERTI DE LA WARDE. Beaded borders.). Howard de Walden *Some Feudal Lords & Their Seals* (1903): 82 (biog. of Robert de la Warde). *Genealogist* n.s. 23 (1907): 143–145. *C.P.* 9 (1936): 484–485 (sub Neville); 12(2) (1959): 350–352 (sub Warde). National Archives, DL 10/264; DL 25/1290; DL 25/1644; DL 25/1739 (Date: 1357–8: Appointment by Ida de la Warde, Lady de Nevill, of attys. to deliver seisin to William de Bohoun, Earl of Northampton, of her dower lands after the death of Sir Hugh de Nevill, her late lord, in Great and Little Wakering, 9Essex); DL 25/1740; DL 25/1741 (Date: 1357–8: Appointment by William de Bohun, Earl of Northampton, of an atty. to receive seisin from Ida de la Warde, Lady de Nevill, his cousin, of the land she holds as dower by the death of Sir Hugh de Nevill, her late lord, in Great and Little Wakering, Essex) (available at www.catalogue.nationalarchives.gov.uk/search.asp).

9. ROBERT FITZ WALTER, Knt., of Woodham Walter, Burnham, Henham, Little Dunmow, Roydon, Ulting, Wimbish, and Tey, Essex, Westley (in Westley Waterless), Cambridgeshire, Diss and Hempnall, Norfolk, Ashwell and Radwell, Hertfordshire, Poslingworth and Shimpling, Suffolk, etc., 2nd but 1st surviving son and heir, born in 1300 (aged 25 in 1326). He was never summoned to Parliament. He was contracted to marry 18 March 1304/5 **JOAN BOTETOURT**, daughter of John Botetourt, Knt., 1st Lord Botetourt, Admiral of the North Fleet, by Maud, daughter of Thomas

Fitz Otes, Knt. [see BOTETOURT 8 for her ancestry]. They had no issue. He married (2nd) **JOAN DE MULTON**, daughter of Thomas de Multon, Knt., 1st Lord Multon, of Egremont, Cumberland, by Eleanor, daughter of Richard de Burgh, Knt., 3rd Earl of Ulster, lord of Connacht [see HARINGTON 9 for her ancestry]. She was born about 1304 (aged 30 and more in 1334). They had one son, John, Knt. [2nd Lord Fitz Walter]. SIR ROBERT FITZ WALTER died 6 May 1328. On 12 Dec. 1328, his widow, Joan, had license to marry John de Weyland, if she gave her consent. Joan was co-heiress in 1334 to her brother, John de Multon, Knt., 2nd Lord Multon, by which she inherited the Castle and manor of Egremont, Cumberland, and 1/3 of the manors of Fleet and Beausolze (in Algarkirk), Lincolnshire. In 1361 Lady Joan Fitz Walter presented to the church of Wimbish, Essex. She died 16 June 1363, and was buried in Dunmow Priory, Essex.

>Blomefield *Essay towards a Top. Hist. of Norfolk* 1 (1739): 2–8. Nicolson & Burn *Hist. & Antiqs. of the Counties of Westmorland & Cumberland* 2 (1777): 69–77. Hutchinson *Hist. of the County of Cumberland* 2 (1794): 27–28 (Lucy-Multon ped.). Banks *Dormant & Extinct Baronage of England* 2 (1808): 379–381 (sub Multon). Blore *Hist. & Antiqs. of Rutland* 1(2) (1811): 90, 209 (Botetourt Peds.). Baker *Hist. & Antiqs. of Northampton* 1 (1822–30): 672–673 (Multon ped.). Dugdale *Monasticon Anglicanum* 6(1) (1830): 148. Burke *Gen'l & Heraldic Dict. of the Peerages of England, Ireland & Scotland* (1831): 379–380 (sub Multon). *Arch. Aeliana* 2 (1832): 384–386 (Tailboys-Meschens ped.). *Coll. Top. et Gen.* 6 (1840): 152. *Genealogist* n.s. 13 (1896): 246; n.s. 18 (1902): 94. *C.P.R. 1301–1307* (1898): 320. Sharpe *Cal. Letter-Books of London: E 1314–1337* (1903): 229. Copinger *Manors of Suffolk* 1 (1905): 191–195; 2 (1908): 45–53. Wrottesley *Peds. from the Plea Rolls* (1905): 165–166, 368. *Cal. IPM* 7 (1909): 126–129. VCH *Hertford* 3 (1912): 199–209, 244–247. Clay *Extinct & Dormant Peerages* (1913): 142 (sub Multon). Mills *Cal. Gormanston Reg.* (1916): 2–3, 15, 111–115. *C.P.* 5 (1926): 475–476 (sub FitzWalter); 9 (1936): 404–405 (sub Multon). Fowler *Reg. Simonis de Sudbiria* 1 (Canterbury & York Soc. 34) (1927): 230. Paget *Baronage of England* (1957) 230: 5 (sub Fitz Walter), 394: 4. Sanders *English Baronies* (1960): 129–130. VCH *Cambridge* 6 (1978): 177–182. Biancalana *Fee Tail & the Common Recovery in Medieval England* (2001): 157.

10. JOHN FITZ WALTER, Knt., 2nd Lord Fitz Walter, of Little Dunmow, Essex, Westley (in Westley Waterless), Cambridgeshire, etc., son and heir by his father's 2nd marriage, born about 1315 (aged 13 in 1328). He married **ELEANOR DE PERCY**, daughter of Henry de Percy, Knt., 2nd Lord Percy, of Alnwick, Northumberland, Topcliffe, Yorkshire, etc., by Idoine, daughter of Robert de Clifford, Knt., 1st Lord Clifford [see PERCY 9 for her ancestry]. They had one son, Walter, Knt. [3rd Lord Fitz Walter], and one daughter, Alice.[32] In 1337 he was going beyond seas on the King's service with the Earl of Northampton. He was summoned to Parliament from 3 March 1340/1 to 20 Nov. 1360, by writs directed *Johanni fitz Wauter*. He served in France, in the retinue of the Prince of Wales, from the King's arrival at La Hogue on 12 July 1346, until his return to England. He was a legatee in the 1349 will of his father-in-law, Henry de Percy, Knt. He was sent to the Tower of London 1 Feb. 1351/2, for failure to answer for certain felonies and trespasses for which he had been indicted, but, on 24 June following, his lands were restored to him. SIR JOHN FITZ WALTER, 2nd Lord Fitz Walter, died 18 October 1361. His wife, Eleanor, predeceased him. Both were buried in Dunmow Priory, Essex.

>Dugdale *Baronage of England* 1 (1675): 221–222. Blomefield *Essay towards a Top. Hist. of Norfolk* 1 (1739): 2–8, 11. Brydges *Collins' Peerage of England* 2 (1812): 217–366 (sub Duke of Northumberland). Dugdale *Monasticon Anglicanum* 6(1) (1830): 148. *Testamenta Eboracensia* 1 (Surtees Soc. 4) (1836): 57–61 (will of Sir Henry de Percy). Flower *Vis. of Yorkshire 1563-4* (H.S.P. 16) (1881): 241–244 (Percy ped.: "Elenor [Percy] wyf to Lord Rychard Fitzwater."). *Genealogist* n.s. 13 (1896): 246; n.s. 18 (1902): 94. Rye *Cal. Feet of Fines for Suffolk* (1900): 209. Sharpe *Cal. Letter-Books of London: E 1314–1337* (1903): 229. Copinger *Manors of Suffolk* 1 (1905): 191–195. Wrottesley *Peds. from the Plea Rolls* (1905): 165–166, 368. *Cal. IPM* 7 (1909): 126–129. VCH *Hertford* 3 (1912): 244–247. *C.P.* 5 (1926): 476–477 (sub

---

[32] For indications that John Fitz Walter may had a 2nd daughter, [Alice?], who married John Fitzsymond, Knt., of North Shoebury and Barling, Essex, see Morant *Hist. & Antiqs. of Essex* 1 (1768): 302–303; Hawley et al. *Vis. of Essex 1552, 1558, 1570, 1612 & 1634* 1 (H.S.P. 13) (1878): 100–101 (Sharpe ped.); Flower *Vis. of Yorkshire 1563-4* (H.S.P. 16) (1881): 328–329 (Fitz Symon ped.); Roskell *House of Commons 1386–1421* 3 (1992): 83–84 (biog. of Sir John Fitzsymond).

FitzWalter). *Cal. Inqs. Misc.* 3 (1937): 70–73. Paget *Baronage of England* (1957) 230: 5 (sub Fitz Walter). Sanders *English Baronies* (1960): 129–130. Ellis *Cat. Seals in the P.R.O.* 1 (1978): 25 (seal of John Fitz Walter dated 1359 — In a richly cusped circle, a shield of arms: a fesse between two chevrons [FITZ WALTER]). VCH *Cambridge* 6 (1978): 177–182.

Children of John Fitz Walter, Knt., by Eleanor de Percy:

  i.   **WALTER FITZ WALTER**, Knt. [see next].

 ii.   **ALICE FITZ WALTER**, married **AUBREY VERE**, Knt., 10th Earl of Oxford [see VERE 6].

11. WALTER FITZ WALTER, Knt., 3rd Lord Fitz Walter, Admiral of the Fleet (Northern parts), Trier of Petitions in Parliament concerning Gascony and overseas, 1378–85, joint Warden of the West March of Scotland, 1383, son and heir, born and baptized at Henham, Essex 31 May 1345. He married (1st) at Vachery (in Cranley), Surrey by license dated 23 June 1362 **ELEANOR DE DAGWORTH**, daughter and heiress of Thomas de Dagworth, Knt., Lord Dagworth, by Eleanor (granddaughter of King Edward I), daughter of Humphrey de Bohun, Knt., Earl of Hereford and Essex [see BUTLER 7 for her ancestry]. They had two sons, Robert and Walter, Knt. [4th Lord Fitz Walter]. In 1366 he granted to William Moundry, of Diss, Norfolk one messuage and lands in Diss, Norfolk for a term of 200 years at a rent of 2s. 8d. a year and suit of court at Diss. In 1368 he had license to go beyond seas. He was summoned to Parliament from 6 April 1369 to 3 Sept. 1385, by writs directed *Waltero fitz Wauter*. In Autumn 1369 he served in the army in France. He accompanied Sir Robert Knolles in his raid into the North of France in 1370, in which expedition, or soon afterwards, he was captured by the French and sent to Paris. In order to pay for his ransom, he mortgaged his castle of Egremont and all his lands in Copeland, Cumberland for £1,000 to Alice Perrers, the king's mistress. In 1373 he was again in France under John of Gaunt. His wife, Eleanor, was living 29 Nov. 1375. At her death, she was buried in Dunmow Priory, Essex. In 1377 he was one of the commanders of the unsuccessful expedition of Thomas, Earl of Buckingham to attack the Spanish fleet at Sluys. In 1379 he was granted license to travel abroad with six men and horses. He was Marshal of the army of the Earl of Buckingham in his raid into Brittany in 1380–1, and was at the Siege of Nantes. In 1381 he took an active part in suppressing the insurrection of Jack Straw and Wat Tyler. He married (2nd) shortly before 6 March 1382 (recorded date of gift for their marriage) **PHILIPPE MOHUN**, 2nd daughter and co-heiress of John de Mohun, K.G., 2nd Lord Mohun, of Dunster, Somerset, by Joan, daughter of Bartholomew de Burghersh, Knt., 3rd Lord Burghersh [see MOHUN 13 for her ancestry]. They had no issue. He joined the unsuccessful expedition of John of Gaunt, Duke of Lancaster, to Spain in June 1386, and was captured and held for ransom. SIR WALTER FITZ WALTER, 3rd Lord Fitz Walter died at or near Oronse in Galicia 26 Sept. 1386. His widow, Philippe, married (2nd) 25 Nov. 1389 **JOHN GOLAFRE**, Knt., of Langley, Oxfordshire, and, in right of his wife, of Brinkley, Cambridgeshire, Knight of the King's Chamber, Constable of Wallingford Castle, Steward of the lordship and honour of Wallingford, and of the honor of St. Valery, Sheriff of Flintshire & Constable of Flint Castle, 1390–6, illegitimate son of John Golafre, Knt., by his mistress, Johenet Pulham. They had no issue. He took a leading part in the French negotiations of King Richard II. He was sent to France in 1387 with letters arranging a meeting with King Charles VI of France, and was charged with transmarine treason by the Appelants. His imprisonment was ordered by the Appelants 4 Jan. 1388. On 28 Feb. 1389, however, he was granted permission to bring some bales of cloth from Venice to England customs-free. He thereafter resumed his usual round of duties and favors as a chamber knight. On 13 Nov. 1389, on the occasion of their marriage, the king granted him and his wife, Philippe, an annuity of 100 marks for the term of their lives and to the longer liver. In 1392 his 1st cousin, John Golafre the younger, quitclaimed the manors of Sarsden, Oxfordshire and Bury Blunsdon, Wiltshire to him and his wife, Philippe. SIR JOHN GOLAFRE died at Wallingford, Berkshire 18 Nov. 1396, and was buried at Westminster Abbey. He left a will dated 19 Jan. 1393/4.

His widow, Philippe, married (3rd) before 7 October 1398 (date of papal indult) **EDWARD OF YORK**, K.G., 2nd Duke of York, 2nd Earl of Cambridge[see YORK 10.i], Admiral of the Northern and Western Fleets, 1391–8, Constable of Dover Castle and Warden of Cinque Ports, 1396–8, Keeper of the Channel Islands, Warden and Chief Justice of the New Forest, Justice of the Forest south of Trent, 1397–1415, Constable of the Tower of London, 1392, 1397–9, Lord of the Isle of Wight and Carisbrooke Castle, Constable of England, 1398, Warden of East and West Marches, Privy Councillor to King Henry IV, Governor of North Wales, Lieutenant of Aquitaine, Lieutenant of South Wales, Master of the Hart Hounds, Knight of the Passion of Jesus Christ, son and heir of Edmund of Langley, K.G., 1st Duke of York, 1st Earl of Cambridge (5th son of King Edward III of England), by his 1st wife, Isabel, daughter and co-heiress of Pedro I *el Cruel* ("the Cruel"), King of Castile and León [see YORK 10 for his ancestry]. He was born about 1374 (aged 28 in 1402). They had no issue. He was knighted at the Coronation of King Richard II in 1377. Edward was created Earl of Rutland 25 Feb. 1389/90 (granted for his father's lifetime), Earl of Cork prior to 11 July 1396, and Duke of Aumale 29 Sept. 1397 (from this title he was degraded by Parliament 6 October 1399), succeeded his father as Duke of York and Earl of Cambridge. He was appointed Joint Commissioner to treat with France in 1392. He served as Captain in the royal army in Ireland in 1394–5. He served as Joint Ambassador, afterwards Chief Ambassasador to France in 1395–6. He served as Joint Ambassador to Scotland in 1399. In 1411 he was joint founder of Fotheringhay College. In 1412 he attempted to enlist the support of Fernando de Antequera, King of Aragón, in support of his claim to the throne of Castile. His wife, Philippe, was co-heiress in 1415 to her sister, Elizabeth Mohun, Countess of Salisbury. He was constable and marshal of the king's army in France, Sept.–October 1415. EDWARD OF YORK, 2nd Duke of York, 2nd Earl of Cambridge, was slain while commanding the right wing at Agincourt 25 October 1415, and was buried at Fotheringhay, Northamptonshire. He left a will dated 17 August 1415. His widow, Philippe, Duchess of York, died 17 July 1431, and was buried in the chapel of St. Nicholas in Westminster Abbey. She left a will dated 12 March 1430, proved 13 Nov. 1431.

Dugdale *Baronage of England* 1 (1675): 222. Blomefield *Essay towards a Top. Hist. of Norfolk* 1 (1739): 2–8. Rymer *Fœdera* 4 (1740): 145 (will of Edward, Duke of York). Hearne *Itinerary of John Leland the Antiq.* 4 (1744): 5. Morant *Hist. & Antiqs. of Essex* 1 (1768): 268. Strachey *Rotuli Parl.* 3 (1777): 34, 99, 123, 133, 145, 151, 185, 204. Nichols *Coll. of All the Wills* (1780): 217–223 (will of Edward, Duke of York), 224–229 (will of Philippe, Duchess of York). Nicolas *Testamenta Vetusta* 1 (1826): 135 (will of Sir John Golafre, Knt.), 186–189 (will of Edward, Duke of York), 218–219 (will of Philippa, Duchess of York). Dugdale *Monasticon Anglicanum* 6(1) (1830): 148. Nicolas *Procs. & Ordinances of the Privy Council* 1 (1834): xiv, 13–14. Banks *Baronies in Fee* 1 (1844): 175–176 (sub Dagworth). Hawley *Royal Fam. of England* (1851): 23–27. *Vis. of Devon 1620* (H.S.P. 6) (1872): 185–187 (Mohun ped.: "Phillip [Mohun] [1] = Walter Fitzwalter, 1 husb., [2] mar. to Sir John Goleston, 2 husb., [3] = Edw. Duke of York slayne at Agincourt, 3d husb."). Vivian *Vis. of Cornwall* (H.S.P. 9) (1874): 143–146 (Mohun ped.: "Philippa [Mohun] uxor Edwardi Ducis Eboru' et postea uxor Walteri fitz Walter"). *Annual Rpt. of the Deputy Keeper* 36 (1875): Appendix II, 201. *Archives de l'Orient Latin* 1 (1881): 362–364. Hedges *Hist. of Wallingford* 2 (1881): 26. Burrows *Fam. of Brocas of Beaurepaire & Roche Court* (1886): 118. Doyle *Official Baronage of England* 1 (1886): 28 (sub Albemarle), 294 (sub Cambridge); 3 (1886): 188–189 (sub Rutland), 742–744 (sub York). Vivian *Vis. of Cornwall* (1887): 323–326 (Mohun ped.). Clark *Survey of the Antiqs. of Oxford* 2 (Oxford Hist. Soc.) (1890): 385, 411–412. Birch *Cat. Seals in the British Museum* 2 (1892): 806 (seal of Walter Fitz Walter dated 1368 — A shield of arms: diapré, a fess between two chevrons [FITZ WALTER]. Suspended from a forked tree. Between two wavy sprigs of elegant design, enclosed roses. Carved border ornamented with small ballflowers), 806–807 (seal of Walter Fitz Walter dated 1383 — A shield of arms, couché: a fess between two chevrons [FITZ WALTER]. Crest on a helmet and lambrequin, on a chapeau turned up ermine, an estoile of six points, between a pair of wings erect. Supporters, two griffins segreant, tails coward. In the field on each side, over the griffins' heads the letters xtx, with a sprig over them. Carved borders); 3 (1894): 382 (seal of Edward, 2nd Duke of York dated 1403 — A shield of arms, couché: quarterly, 1, 4, FRANCE (modern); 2, 3, ENGLAND. Over all a label of three points [each charged with as many castles (?)]. Crest, on a helmet and short mantling or lambrequin, on a chapeau, turned up ermine, a lion statant [guardant, crowned], the tail extended. Supporters, two ostrich feathers, the quills chained, labeled. Background diapered lozengy with a rose of five leaves in each interstice. All within a carved gothic quatrefoil panel, ornamented along the inner edge with small pellets and trefoils, alternated, each set on a cusp or finial. [S' edwardi * ducis * eboraci * comitis * canteb]rig[ie] * ruttl[andie * et * corcacie * et * domini * de *] tindale.). Little *Grey Friars in Oxford* 1 (1892): 25. *Genealogist* n.s. 13 (1896): 246; n.s. 18 (1902): 94; n.s. 23 (1907): 242. Kirby *Wykeham's Reg.* 1 (1896): 226. *C.P.R.* 1385–1389 (1900): 204–205, 287. *Desc. Cat. Ancient Deeds* 3 (1900): 451–465. *Papal Regs.: Letters* 5 (1904): 135. Copinger *Manors of Suffolk* 1 (1905): 191–195 ("Walter Fitz Walter was a valiant solider and served with distinction in the expedition into Gascony of Edw. III. in 1370 … Perhaps his most notable successes were in the expedition into Spain in 1385 with John Duke of Lancaster when he stormed the forts raised against the castle of Brest in Brittany and relieved by his valour that fortress then closely besieged."). Wrottesley *Peds. from the Plea Rolls* (1905): 165–166, 276, 368. VCH *Hertford* 3 (1912): 199–209, 244–247. *C.P.R.* 1374–1377 (1916): 191. *C.P.* 4 (1916): 29 (sub Dagworth) (asserts incorrectly that Thomas Dagworth, Lord Dagworth, left a son and heir, Sir Nicholas de Dagworth, of Blicking, Norfolk, noting, however, in footnote d: "There appears to be no evidence for this statement, which is made by Dugdale and repeated by other genealogists"); 5 (1926): 477–480 (sub FitzWalter); 14 (1998): 326 (sub Fitzwalter) (erroneously identifies wife Eleanor as "sister and (in her issue) heiress of Sir Nicholas de Dagworth [2nd Lord Dagworth]"). *Yorkshire Inqs.* 5 (Yorkshire Arch. Soc. Recs. 59) (1918): 120. Wall *Handbook of the Maude Roll* (1919) unpaginated (ped. dated c.1461–85: "Edwardus dux Eboraci"). *C.C.R.* 1389–1392 (1922): 29–30, 436–437. VCH *Berkshire* 3 (1923): 511–516. *C.C.R.* 1396–1399 (1927): 57. Fowler *Reg. Simonis de Sudbiria* 1 (Canterbury & York Soc. 34) (1927): 254, 256–257, 267, 278. Thomas *Cal. Plea & Memoranda Rolls of London 1381–1412* (1932): 279–282. Chichele *Reg. of Henry Chichele* 2 (Canterbury & York Soc. 42) (1937): 670–671 (biog. of Edward Plantagenet), 685 (biog. of Philippa, duchess of York). *John of Gaunt's Reg.* 1 (Camden Soc. 3rd Ser. 56) (1937): 229–231 (gift recorded 6 March 1382 by John of Gaunt, Duke of Lancaster, made to Philippe Mohun on "the day of her marriage"). *Year Books of Richard II* 5 (Ames Found. 8) (1937): 76–83. *English Hist. Rev.* 72 (1957): 597–8, 611. Paget *Baronage of England* (1957) 165: 1–4 (sub Dagworth); 230: 6 (sub Fitz Walter). *Coat of Arms* 7 (1962): 122–127 (arms of Edward as Earl of Rutland: Quarterly France ancient and England, a label of five points argent each charged with three roundels gules; arms as Duke of Aumale: Quarterly France ancient and England, a label of three points gules each charged with three castles gold). Holmes *Good Parl.* (1975): 97. Harvey *Westminster Abbey & its Estates in the Middle Ages* (1977): 381. VCH *Cambridge* 6 (1978): 136–141. Ellis *Cat. Seals in the P.R.O.* 2 (1981): 108 (seal of Philippe, Duchess of York dated 1420 — Hung from a twin bush, a shield of arms: quarterly, FRANCE modern and ENGLAND, with a label of three points, impaling a cross engrailed [MOHUN]). Hector *Westminster Chron. 1381–1394* (1982): 190–191, 406–407 (sub A.D. 1389: "… on the 25th of the same month [November] Sir John Golafre married Lord Mohun's daughter, who had formerly been the wife of Lord Fitz Walter."). Edington *Reg. of William Edington Bishop of Winchester* 2 (Hampshire Recs. 8) (1987): 53. Roskell *House of Commons 1386–1421* 2 (1992): 733–736 (biog. of Sir Nicholas Dagworth) (author states correctly that Eleanor de Dagworth, wife of Walter Fitz Walter, was 1st cousin, not sister, to Sir Nicholas Dagworth); 3 (1992): 199–202 (biog. of John Golafre). *Cal. IPM* 20 (1995): 70–76, 118–125, 153–156; 23 (2004): 365–373. Leese *Blood Royal* (1996): 149–168. Gillespie *Age of Richard II* (1997): 179–180. Harvard Law School Lib., Hist. in Deed: Medieval Soc. & the Law in England, 1100–1600 (#41 — grant by Walter Fitz Walter, lord of Wodeham, to William Moundry dated 3 Nov. 1366) (available at www.law.harvard.edu/library/special/exibits/exhibitions/history-in-deed.html#chap2).

12. **WALTER FITZ WALTER**, Knt., 4th Lord Fitz Walter, 2nd but 1st surviving son and heir by his father's 1st marriage, born at Henham, Essex 5 Sept. 1368 (aged 30 in 1399). He was summoned to Parliament from 12 Sept. 1390 to 25 August 1404, by writs directed *Waltero fitz Wauter*. He married before 1398 **JOAN DEVEREUX**, daughter of John Devereux, K.G., 1st Lord Devereux, of Lyonshall, Dorstone, and Whitchurch Maund (in Bodenham), Herefordshire, and Dinton, Buckinghamshire, Seneschal of Rochelle, Captain of Calais, Steward of the King's Household, Constable of Dover Castle, Warden of the Cinque Ports, by Margaret, daughter of John de Vere, Knt., 7th Earl of Oxford [see LOVAINE 6 for her ancestry]. She was born about 1380 (aged 17 in 1397). They had two sons, Humphrey and Walter, Knt. [5th Lord Fitz Walter], and one daughter, Joan. In 1395 he was on the King's service in Ireland with Thomas, Duke of Gloucester. His wife, Joan, was heiress in 1396 to her brother, John Devereux, Knt., 2nd Lord Devereux, by which she inherited the manor of Dinton, Buckinghamshire. In 1398 he was co-heir to his cousin, Maud de Lucy, wife successively of Gilbert de Umfreville, Knt., 4th Earl of Angus, and Henry Percy, K.G., 1st Earl of Northumberland. The same year he was in Ireland with the Earl of March, Lieutenant of Ireland. In 1399 he accused the Duke of Aumale in Parliament of being accessory to the murder of the Duke of Gloucester. In 1402 he and his wife, Joan, had a suit with his wife's half-sister, Margaret Lovaine, and her husband, Philip Saint Clair, Knt., regarding a tenement in Penshurst, Kent. In 1404 he and his wife, Joan, were sued by John son of Roger de Burley regarding the Castle and manor of Lyonshall, Herefordshire. In 1406, while passing by sea from Rome to Naples, he

was captured by Saracens and taken prisoner to Tunis. After being ransomed by some Genoese merchants, SIR WALTER FITZ WALTER, 4th Lord Fitz Walter, died at Venice 16 May 1406. He left a will dated 20 July 1408 [sic], which will was never proved. His widow, Joan, married (2nd) after 1 July 1407 (as his 3rd wife) **HUGH BURNELL**, K.G., 2nd Lord Burnell [see BURNELL 12], of Holgate and Acton Burnell, Shropshire, East and West Ham (in East Ham), Essex, Billingford and Thurning, Norfolk, Ham (in Kingston-upon-Thames) and Hatcham, Surrey, Bidford, Warwickshire, Great Cheverell, Wiltshire, Kidderminster Burnell and Upton Snodsbury, Worcestershire, etc., Governor of Bridgnorth, Cefnllys, Dolforwyn, and Montgomery Castles, Trier of Petitions in Parliament, 1407, 1411, and 1413, and, in right of his 2nd wife, of Weoley, Worcestershire, Woughton, Buckinghamshire, Cantley and Upton, Norfolk, Great Bradley, Suffolk, etc., son and heir of Nicholas Burnell, Knt., 1st Lord Burnell, by his wife, Mary [see BURNELL 11 for his ancestry]. He was born about 1347 (aged 36 in 1383). They had no issue. He was appointed to treat with French representatives in 1408. In 1408–9 he conveyed the manors of Trever (or River) (in Tillington), Nutbourn (in Pulborough), and West Chiltington, together with the advowson of the church of West Chiltington, Sussex, to trustees. His wife, Joan, died 10 (or 11) May 1409, and was buried in Dunmow Priory, Essex. He received a papal indult to choose a confessor in 1412. SIR HUGH BURNELL, 2nd Lord Burnell, died 27 Nov. 1420. He left a will dated 2 October 1417, requesting burial in the choir of Halesowen Abbey, Worcestershire near the body of Joyce his 2nd wife.

Dugdale *Baronage of England* 1 (1675): 222. Blomefield *Essay towards a Top. Hist. of Norfolk* 1 (1739): 2–8, 11. Bridges *Hist. & Antiqs. of Northamptonshire* 2 (1791): 37. Hasted *Hist. & Top. Survey of Kent* 2 (1797): 184–203. Nicolas *Testamenta Vetusta* 1 (1826): 134 (will of John Devereux, Knt.). Dugdale *Monasticon Anglicanum* 6(1) (1830): 148. Nicolas *Controversy between Scrope & Grosvenor* 2 (1832): 456–460 (biog. of Hugh Burnell). *Coll. Top. et Gen.* 6 (1840): 152. Beltz *Mems. of the Order of the Garter* (1841): cliv, clvi. Birch *Cat. Seals in the British Museum* 2 (1892): 807 (seal of Walter Fitz Walter dated 1398 — A shield of arms: couché, a fess between two chevrons [FITZ WALTER]. Crest on a helmet, on a chapeau turned up ermine, an estoile of six points wavy, between two wings erect. Supporters, dex., a lion rampant guardant, sin., wanting. Carved borders). Hardy & Page *Cal. to Feet of Fines for London & Middlesex* 1 (1892): 232. *Desc. Cat. Ancient Deeds* 2 (1894): 515–516 (C.2398); 3 (1900): 383–399 (Hugh Burnell, Knt., styled "cousin" by Richard Talbot, lord of Irchenefeld and Blakemere, in grant dated 1394). *Genealogist* n.s. 15 (1898): 97; n.s. 18 (1902): 194; n.s. 23 (1907): 242. Watkins *Colls. towards the Hist. & Antiqs. of Hereford* 5 (Hundred of Radlow) (1902): 49 (Devereux ped.). *Ancestor* 8 (1904): 167–185. Copinger *Manors of Suffolk* 1 (1905): 191–195. Wrottesley *Peds. from the Plea Rolls* (1905): 235, 368. Parker "Cal. of Feet of Fines for Cumberland" in *Trans. Cumberland & Westmorland Antiq. Soc.* n.s. 7 (1907): 244. VCH *Essex* 2 (1907): 150–154. VCH *Buckingham* 2 (1908): 273. Rede *Reg. of Robert Rede Bishop of Chichester* 2 (Sussex Rec. Soc. 11) (1910): 262, 290. VCH *Hertford* 3 (1912): 118–124, 244–247. *C.P.* 4 (1916): 301–302 (sub Devereux); 5 (1926): 480–482 (sub FitzWalter). *Rpt. on the MSS of Lord de L'Isle & Dudley* 1 (Hist. MSS Comm. 77) (1925): 233. Chichele *Reg. of Henry Chichele* 2 (Canterbury & York Soc. 42) (1937): 644 (biog. of Hugh Burnell, kt.); 3 (Canterbury & York Soc. 46) (1945): 452. St. George et al. *Wiltshire Vis. Peds. 1623, 1628* (H.S.P. 105-6) (1954): 89–90 (Hungerford ped.: "Hugh Burnell miles fil: et heres = [left blank]"). VCH *Essex* 4 (1956): 24-25. Holmes *Estates of the Higher Nobility in 14th Cent. England* (1957): 130–131. Paget *Baronage of England* (1957) 230: 6 (sub Fitz Walter). Clifford *Reg. of Richard Clifford Bp. of Worcester* (1976): 121. Ellis *Cat. Seals in the P.R.O.* 1 (1978): 13 (seal of Hugh Burnell, knight, lord Burnell dated 1416 — Hung from a twin bush, between lunettes of tracery, a shield of arms: quarterly, 1 and 4, a lion rampant [BURNELL], 2 and 3, a saltire engrailed [BOTETOURT]. Legend: SIGILLUM.HV[GONIS] BVRNELL.). *Cal. IPM* 17 (1988): 463–473; 20 (1995): 7, 163. Somerset *Recs. of Early English Drama: Shropshire* 2 (1994): 698. Leese *Blood Royal* (1996): 119–122.

13. WALTER FITZ WALTER, Knt., 5th Lord Fitz Walter, lord of La-Haye-du-Puits and La Roche-Tesson in Normandy, Master of the King's Dogs and Harthounds, 1420, Captain of Vire, 1421, 2nd son, born at Woodham Walter, Essex and baptized there 22 June 1400 (or 1401). He was heir in 1415 to his older brother, Humphrey Fitz Walter. He was actively employed in the French wars of King Henry V. He was present at the Siege of Melun in 1420. He was taken prisoner at the Battle of Beaugé in Anjou 22 March 1420/1. In June 1424, it was said he had been imprisoned for four years, and that his lands were much disturbed. In 1425 he took part in the conquest of Maine, and was serving with a retinue in 1426. In Jan. 1426 he was sent by Humphrey, Duke of

Gloucester, with 500 men to assist the Duke's wife, Jacque (or Jacoba) of Bavaria, but was defeated at Brouwershaven in Zeeland by Philippe, Duke of Burgundy. In 1428 he received a pardon for murder and rape, as well as for surrendering the castle of Saint-Laurent-des-Mortiers in Anjou. He was summoned to Parliament from 12 July 1429 to 27 Nov. 1430, by writs directed *Waltero fitz Wauter chivaler*. He married before 1430 **ELIZABETH CHIDIOCK**, widow of William Massey, King's esquire (living 16 May 1425), and daughter of John Chidiock, Knt., of Chidiock, Dorset, 5th Lord Fitz Payn, by Eleanor, daughter and heiress of Ives Fitz Warin, Knt. [see CHIDIOCK 12 for her ancestry]. They had one daughter, Elizabeth. By an unknown mistress (or mistresses), he had one illegitimate son, Gabriel, and one illegitimate daughter, Mary. In 1431 he led a retinue into France. SIR WALTER FITZ WALTER, 5th Lord Fitz Walter, died 25 Nov. 1431, being drowned in a storm at sea returning from France. He left a will dated 10 April 1431, proved 10 Nov. 1432, requesting burial at Dunmow Priory, Essex. His widow, Elizabeth, married (3rd) before 5 Nov. 1438 (as his 1st wife) **THOMAS COBHAM**, Knt., 5th Lord Cobham of Sterborough (died testate 26 April 1471). Elizabeth died 14 June 1464, and was buried with her 2nd husband at Dunmow Priory, Essex.

Dugdale *Baronage of England* 1 (1675): 222–223. Blomefield *Essay towards a Top. Hist. of Norfolk* 1 (1739): 2–8, 11. Nicolas *Testamenta Vetusta* 1 (1826): 221 (will of Walter Lord Fitz-Walter). Dugdale *Monasticon Anglicanum* 6(1) (1830): 148. *Genealogist* n.s. 18 (1902): 94; n.s. 23 (1907): 242. Copinger *Manors of Suffolk* 1 (1905): 191–195. Wrottesley *Peds. from the Plea Rolls* (1905): 368. *C.P.R. 1429–1436* (1907): 209. VCH *Essex* 2 (1907): 150–154. VCH *Hertford* 3 (1912): 25–28, 244–247. *C.P.* 5 (1926): 482–484 (sub FitzWalter). *C.C.R. 1422–1429* (1933): 260–261, 268. Chichele *Reg. of Henry Chichele* 2 (Canterbury & York Soc. 42) (1937): 469–470 (will of Walter Fitz Walter), 653 (biog. of Walter Fitzwalter). Paget *Baronage of England* (1957) 230: 7 (sub Fitz Walter). Allmand & Armstrong *English Suits before the Parlement of Paris* (Camden Soc. 4th Ser. 26) (1982): 293–294 (biog. of Walter, Lord FitzWalter). Pevsner *Essex* (Buildings of England) (1954): 32–33. *Cal. IPM* 23 (2004): 373–381. Court of Common Pleas, CP 40/740, rot. 259 (available at http://www.british-history.ac.uk/source.aspx?pubid=1272).

Child of Walter Fitz Walter, Knt., by Elizabeth Chidiock:

i. **ELIZABETH FITZ WALTER**, married (1st) **JOHN RADCLIFFE**, Esq., of Attleborough, Norfolk [see BURNELL 15]; (2nd) **JOHN DINHAM**, K.G., Lord Dinham [see DINHAM 8.i].

❧ FITZ WARIN ❧

ALICE OF NORMANDY (sister of King William the Conqueror), married **LAMBERT**, Count of Lens.
JUDITH OF LENS, married **WALTHEOF**, Earl of Northumberland.
ALICE OF NORTHUMBERLAND, married **RALPH DE TONY**, of Flamstead, Hertfordshire.
ROGER DE TONY, of Flamstead, Hertfordshire, married **IDA OF HAINAULT**.
RALPH DE TONY, of Flamstead, Hertfordshire, married **MARGARET OF LEICESTER**.
ROGER DE TONY, Knt., of Flamstead, Hertfordshire, married **CONSTANCE DE BEAUMONT** (desc. King William the Conqueror).
RALPH DE TONY, Knt., of Flamstead, Hertfordshire, married **PERNEL DE LACY** [see TONY 7].

8. **CONSTANCE DE TONY**, married **FULK FITZ WARIN**, Knt., of Whittington, Shropshire, Wantage, Berkshire, Alveston, Gloucestershire, and Stanton Fitzwarren, Wiltshire, son and heir of Fulk Fitz Warin, Knt., of Alveston, Gloucestershire, Norborough, Leicestershire, and Edlington, Yorkshire, by his 1st wife, Maud, daughter of Robert le Vavasour, Knt. Her maritagium included a moiety of the manor of Yarkhill, Herefordshire. They had one son, Fulk, Knt. [1st Lord Fitz Warin], and at least two daughters. In 1246 he was called to warrant land in Edlington, Yorkshire. In 1252 he was the defendant against John le Vavasour for the manor of Edlington, Yorkshire, less three carucates of land and the advowson. In 1252 he fined one mark to have a writ relevant to a Wiltshire lawsuit. In 1253 he had letters of protection, he then being in the king's service in Gascony. In 1257–8 he and his wife, Constance, conveyed a moiety of the manor of Yarkhill, Herefordshire to Richard Pryde and Margery his wife and their heirs, with remainder to Margery for

life. In 1260 he was summoned for military service in Wales. SIR FULK FITZ WARIN died 14 May 1264, being drowned in the Ouse, when endeavouring to escape, at the Battle of Lewes. In Michaelmas term 1266 his widow, Constance, sued the tenant of the manor of Stanton, Berkshire for dower. In 1267 she sued Fulk de Leyham for one-third of the manor of Alberbury, Shropshire. In 1276–7 she arraigned an assize of novel disseisin against Hugh Poyntz and William le Parker regarding common of pasture in Tockington, Gloucestershire. In 1277–8 William de Panes arraigned an assize of novel disseisin against her and others touching a tenement in Alveston and Erdcote, Gloucestershire. Constance married (2nd) at Stanton, Wiltshire 22 June 1278 **DAVID AP JOHN**, of Whittington, Shropshire. In 1286–7 Constance was summoned for holding view of frankpledge and waif in her manor of Alveston, Gloucestershire. She died before 11 August 1289, when her executors were owed a debt of £17 4s. by her son, Fulk Fitz Warin, Knt.

 Arch. Cambrensis n.s. 3 (1852): 282–291. Eyton *Antiqs. of Shropshire* 7 (1858): 79–83. *Year Books of Edward I: Years XXXIII–XXXV* 5 (Rolls Ser. 31a) (1879): 504–507. *Trans. Shropshire Arch. & Nat. Hist. Soc.* 5 (1881): 241–250. *Athenæum* (1885): 429–430. *Annual Report of the Deputy Keeper* 46 (1886): 303; 47 (1886): 143. Lloyd *Hist. of the Princes: Lords Marcher, Powys Fadog, Arwystli, Cedewen & Meirionwdd* 6 (1887): 180–187. Giffard *Episc. Reg. Diocese of Worcester, Reg. of Bishop Godfrey Giffard* 2 (Worcester Hist. Soc. 15) (1902): 486. *C.P.R. 1258–1266* (1910): 441, 453, 582. *C.P.* 5 (1926): 495, footnote d. *C.C.R. 1264–1265* (1937): 237, 376, 381. National Archives, C 241/3/12; C 241/9/237 (available at www.catalogue.nationalarchives.gov.uk/search.asp).

9. FULK FITZ WARIN, Knt., of Whittington, Shropshire, Wantage, Berkshire, Alveston, Gloucestershire,. Edlington, Yorkshire, etc., son and heir, born at Whittington, Shropshire 14 Sept. 1251. He married before 25 Feb. 1276/7 **MARGARET DE LA POLE**, daughter of Gruffudd (or Griffin) ap Wenwynwyn (called also de la Pole), Knt., Prince of Upper Powys, lord of Cyfeilioc, by Hawise, daughter of John le Strange, Knt., of Knockin, Shropshire. They had three sons, Fulk, Knt. [2nd Lord Fitz Warin], William, K.G., and John, and two daughters, Hawise and Mabel. In 1279 he granted Alderton (in Middle), Shropshire to his kinsman, John de Lee, of Lee Hall. He was with the king in the army of Wales in 1282. In 1283 he was granted free warren in his lordship of Whittington, Shropshire. In 1288 he owed a debt of 50 marks to Galuanus de Ferrad' and Peter Coruo his son. In 1289 he owed a debt of £17 4s. to Master Richard de Habyndon, Robert de Bytelescombe, and Sir William Serle, executors of his mother, Constance de Tony, deceased. In 1292 he sued his uncle, Fulk Fitz Warin, of Alberbury, regarding the manor of Alberbury, Shropshire. In 1292 he owed a debt of £30 to John de Ludlow, of Shrewsbury, merchant. In 1293 he complained to the king that Richard Fitz Alan, Earl of Arundel, had entered his lands at Whittington, Shropshire with horses and arms and banners displayed, spoiled the inhabitants of their goods, killed some of Fulk's men, and committed other enormities; oxen, kine, and foals worth £300 were carried off by the earl; the earl denied the force, entry, homicide, etc., and declared that he was in Sussex at the time alleged. The court ordered that the Sheriff of Shropshire should empanel 24 knights and others to appear before the king in three weeks of Trinity Sunday, and make recognition in the matter. In 1294 Fulk was going to Gascony on the king's service. He was summoned to Parliament by writs directed *Fulconi filio Warini* from 24 June 1295. In 1299 he owed a debt of £24 to Isabel Borrey, widow of John de Ludlow, of Shrewsbury. The same year he presented to the church of Stanton Fitzwarren, Wiltshire. In 1301, as *Fulco filius Warini, dominus de Whitington*, he joined the famous Barons' Letter to Pope Boniface VIII. In 1301 he owed a debt of £180 to Sir William de Hambleton, Dean of St. Peter's, York. On 10 August 1301 the king ordered Fulk and Richard Fitz Alan to abstain from attacking each other. In 1303 he owed a debt of £29 7d. to Henry Fitz Hugh, Knt. In 1305 he owed a debt of £31 10s. to Peter de Huntingfield, Knt. In 1307 he owed a debt of £200 to Hugh le Despenser, Knt. In 1309–10 he obtained license to grant the manor of Alveston, Gloucestershire to Walter de Gloucester for life. On 16 October 1313 he was pardoned, as an adherent of Thomas, Earl of Lancaster, for any part he had taken against Peter de Gaveston, Earl of Cornwall. SIR FULK FITZ WARIN, 1st Lord Fitz Warin, died 24 Nov. 1315. His widow, Margaret, died 11 May 1336.

Arch. Cambrensis n.s. 3 (1852): 282–291. Eyton *Antiqs. of Shropshire* 7 (1858): 83, 85, 98. *Year Books of Edward I: Years XXXII–XXXIII* 4 (Rolls Ser. 31a) (1864): 360–366. *Colls. Hist. & Arch. rel. to Montgomeryshire* 1 (1868): 22–50; 28 (1894): 34 (chart). *Trans. Shropshire Arch. & Nat. Hist. Soc.* 5 (1881): 241–250. Burke *Dormant, Abeyant, Forfeited & Extinct Peerages* (1883): 113–116 (sub Cherlton — Barons Cherlton of Powys). Wrottesley *Ronton Cartulary* (Colls. Hist. Staffs. 4) (1883): 289 (charter of Griffinus filius Wemonewyn, dominus de Keveylok). *Athenæum* (1885): 429–430. Lloyd *Hist. of the Princes: Lords Marcher, Powys Fadog, Arwystli, Cedewen & Meirionwdd* 6 (1887): 180–187. Brown *Yorkshire Lay Subsidy* 1 (Yorkshire Arch. Soc. Rec. Ser. 16) (1894): 77. Brown *Yorkshire Inqs.* 2 (Yorkshire Arch. Soc. Rec. Ser. 23) (1898): 165–169. Gandavo *Reg. Simonis de Gandavo Diocesis Saresbiriensis* 2 (Canterbury & York Soc. 41) (1934): 596. Chichele *Reg. of Henry Chichele* 2 (Canterbury & York Soc. 42) (1937): 18–21 (will of Sir Ives Fitz Warin, who requests a daily mass be said in the parish church of Wantage, Berkshire for various family members, including "Margaret, mother of [his father] Sir William Fitz Waryn, knight."); see also Gibbons & Davey *Wantage Past & Present* (1901): 44–46. *NEHGR* 140 (1986): 219–229. National Archives, C 241/3/12; C 241/9/12; C 241/9/237; C 241/19/25; C 241/27/130; C 241/29/39; C 241/34/168; C 241/43/217; C 241/45/54; C 241/49/299; C 241/55/73; C 241/84/43; SC 8/177/8848 (available at www.catalogue.nationalarchives.gov.uk/search.asp).

Children of Fulk Fitz Warin, Knt., by Margaret de la Pole:

i. **FULK FITZ WARIN**, Knt., 2nd Lord Fitz Warin [see next].

ii. **WILLIAM FITZ WARIN**, K.G., of Whittington, Shropshire, married **AMICE DE HADDON** [see CHIDIOCK 10]].

iii. **HAWISE FITZ WARIN**, married (1st) **RALPH DE GOUSHILL**, of Goxhill, Lincolnshire [see HOO 10]; (2nd) **ROBERT DE HOO**, Knt., of Hoo (in Luton), Bedfordshire [see HOO 10].

10. FULK FITZ WARIN, Knt., 2nd Lord Fitz Warin, of Whittington, Shropshire, Alveston and Earthcote (in Alveston), Gloucestershire, etc., son and heir. His marriage was granted to his father 1 July 1285. He married before 28 Feb. 1310 (date of license for settlement) **ELEANOR DE BEAUCHAMP**, daughter of John de Beauchamp, Knt., of Hatch Beauchamp, Somerset, by Cecily, daughter and co-heiress of William de Forz (or de Vivonne), Knt. [see SEYMOUR 10 for her ancestry]. They had two sons, Fulk, Knt. [3rd Lord Fitz Warin] and Ioun (or Ives/John) and two daughters, Margaret and Cecily. In 1299 he was about to set out for Scotland on the king's service. He was with the king in Scotland in 1300, and again in 1303. He was knighted by Edward, Prince of Wales in 1306. In 1309 he granted the manor of Alveston, Gloucestershire to Walter de Gloucester in fee; he was then about to set out with John de Hastings for Gascony. In 1311 he was about to go overseas on the king's business. He was summoned to Parliament from 20 Nov. 1317 to 22 Jan. 1335/6, by writs directed *Fulconi filio Warini* or *FitzWaryn*. He was beyond seas in May 1313, was about to go to Ireland on the king's service in Feb. 1316/7, and to parts beyond seas in April 1320. He was in Gascony on the king's service in 1324 and 1325. He was pardoned, as an adherent of Thomas, Earl of Lancaster, 22 October 1318. He was robbed at Burford, Oxfordshire by two men, but the thieves were caught, and a portion of the stolen goods, namely eight silver dishes, a silk girdle, a gold brooch, and a chest containing documents were ordered to be restored to him 20 Jan. 1321/2. In March 1321/2 he was Constable of the royal army against the rebels, and, holding this office, he was one of the judges who condemned Roger Damory at Tutbury 13 March 1321/2. Early in 1330, being accused of being an adherent of Edmund of Woodstock, Earl of Kent, he fled the country. He had a safe-conduct to return from beyond seas 25 Nov. 1330. He was found guiltless, and his lands were restored to him 8 Dec. 1330. SIR FULK FITZ WARIN, 2nd Lord Fitz Warin, died shortly before 6 June 1336. His widow, Eleanor, Lady Fitz Warin, was living 18 Nov. 1341. She left a will dated c.1346.

Notes & Queries 4th Ser. 3 (1869): 230 (will of Eleanor Fitz Warin); 10th Ser. 8 (1907): 472–473. *Procs. Somerset Arch. & Nat. Hist. Soc.* 36(2) (1891): 20–59. *C.P.R. 1307–1313* (1894): 213. *Colls. Hist. & Arch. rel. to Montgomeryshire* 28 (1894): 34 (chart). *C.P.* 5 (1926): 497–499 (sub FitzWarin). Paget *Baronage of England* (1957) 46: 1–7 (sub Beauchamp of Hatch); 232: 2.

11. FULK FITZ WARIN, Knt., 3rd Lord Fitz Warin, of Whittington, Shropshire, Wantage, Berkshire, etc. He married **MARGARET** _____, said to be a daughter of Henry de Beaumont, Knt., 1st Lord Beaumont, Earl of Buchan and Moray [in Scotland], Constable of England, Constable of the Army, hereditary Constable of Scotland, Justiciar of Scotland, by Alice, daughter and co-heiress of Alexander Comyn, Knt., of Buchan [see BEAUMONT 7 for her ancestry]. They had two sons, Fulk, Knt. [4th Lord Fitz Warin] and Philip. In 1324 he was about to go to Gascony with his father on the king's service. In 1330 he was found guitless of having been an adherent of Edmund, Earl of Kent, and his lands in Gloucestershire were restored to him. He and his wife, Margaret, were legatees in the c.1346 will of his mother. He accompanied the king to La Hogue in 1346, being in the retinue of William de Bohun, Earl of Northampton. He was present at the Battle of Crécy in 1346 and the Siege of Calais in 1346–7. SIR FULK FITZ WARIN, 3rd Lord Fitz Warin, died 25 July 1349, during the pestilence.

Notes & Queries 4th Ser. 3 (1869): 230 (will of Eleanor Fitz Warin). Wrottesley *Crécy & Calais* (1898): 6, 33, 82, 89, 145, 154, 197, 206. *C.P.* 5 (1926): 499–500 (sub Fitzwarin).

12. FULK FITZ WARIN, Knt., 4th Lord Fitz Warin, of Whittington, Shropshire, Wantage, Berkshire, Bentham (in Badgeworth), Gloucestershire, Edlington, Yorkshire, etc., son and heir, born at Whittington, Shropshire 2 March 1340/1, and baptized in the church there. He was a legatee in the c.1346 will of his grandmother, Eleanor Fitz Warin. He married **BLANCHE DE AUDLEY**, daughter of James de Audley, 2nd Lord Audley, by his 2nd wife, Isabel [see AUDLEY 11 for her ancestry]. They had one son, Fulk, Knt. [5th Lord Fitz Warin]. In 1362 the king took his fealty, and he had livery of his father's lands. In 1369 he granted Roger le Strange, lord of Knockin, all his lands and tenements in the town of New Marton, which formerly belonged to Ivo Fitz Warin his kinsman. He accompanied John of Gaunt, Duke of Lancaster in his expedition to France in 1373, being in the retinue of the Earl of Warwick. SIR FULK FITZ WARIN, 4th Lord Fitz Warin died 12 Feb. 1373/4. His widow, Blanche, was living in 1374–5 (date of settlement). She died before 1 April 1386.

Banks *Dormant & Extinct Baronage of England* 2 (1808): 214–220 (sub Fitz-Warine). *Notes & Queries* 4th Ser. 3 (1869): 230 (will of Eleanor Fitz Warin); 4th Ser. 4 (1869): 44. *Annual Rpt. of the Deputy Keeper* 36 (1875): 16, 234. *Genealogist* 4 (1880): 68–75; 6 (1882): 16–19. Duncumb et al. *Colls. towards the Hist. & Antiqs. of Hereford* 3 (1882): 10 (Audley ped.). Wrottesley *Staffordshire Suits: Plea Rolls* (Colls. Hist. Staffs. 15) (1894): 6–7 (lawsuit dated 1388 names Blanche de Audley, mother of Sir Fulk Fitz Warin, as "the daughter of James and Isabella [de Audley]"), 51–52 (lawsuit dated 1392 Margaret [sic] sister of Thomas de Audley named as mother of Sir Fulk Fitz Warin). *Wrottesley Peds. from the Plea Rolls* (1905): 188–189, 305–306. Chetwynd *Hist. of Pirehill Hundred* 1 (Colls. Hist. Staffs. n.s. 12) (1909): 228–229 (Audley ped.). VCH *Berkshire* 4 (1924): 321–322. *C.P.* 5 (1926): 499–501 (sub Fitzwarin). *C.F.R.* 6 (1931): 108–112 ("Margaret [de Audley], the third daughter of James [de Audley], by Isabel his second wife," named as mother of Fulk Fitz Waryn in 1401). Paget *Baronage of England* (1957) 16: 1–9 (sub Audley). National Archives, C 143/384/18 (Blanche daughter of James de Audeley of Heighley, knight, named in settlement dated 1374–5) (available at www.catalogue.nationalarchives.gov.uk/search.asp). Lancashire Rec. Office: Stanley, Earls of Derby (of Knowsley), DDK/1/5 (available at www.a2a.org.uk/search/index.asp).

13. FULK FITZ WARIN, Knt., 5th Lord Fitz Warin, of Whittington, Shropshire, Kingston and Tawstock, Devon, etc., son and heir, born and baptized at Combe Martin, Devon 2 March 1361/2. In 1383 the king took his homage and fealty, and he had livery of his father's lands. He was a legatee in the 1385 will of his grandfather, James de Audley, Knt. He was heir before 1386 to his uncle, Thomas de Audley, Knt., by which he inherited the manors of Kingston, North Holne, and Nymet Tracey (in Bow), Devon. In 1388 he was sued by Hugh Courtenay and his wife, Elizabeth, for dower in the manor of Kingston, Devon; Fulk pleaded he entered the manor as "kinsman and nearest heir of James and Isabella [de Audley], viz., as son of Blanch, the daughter of James and Isabella." He married before 30 Nov. 1388 **ELIZABETH COGAN**, daughter of William Cogan, Knt., of Bampton, Devon, Huntspill and Wigborough, Somerset, etc., by his 2nd wife, Isabel, daughter and co-heiress of Nigel (or Neel) Loring, Knt., of Chalgrave, Bedfordshire. She was born about 1374 (aged 8 in 1382). She was heiress in 1382 to her brother, John Cogan. They had one son, Fulk. Sometime before 1391 he granted the manor of Wantage, Berkshire to his uncle, Philip Fitz Warin, for life. SIR FULK FITZ WARIN, 5th Lord Fitz Warin died 8 August 1391. He left a will dated 8 August 1391, proved 5 Nov. 1391, requesting burial in the chancel of the church of Whittington, Shropshire. His widow, Elizabeth, married (2nd) after 1 July 1392 and before 11 Feb. 1392/3 (date of pardon for marrying without a license) (as his 2nd wife) **HUGH COURTENAY**, Knt. [see COURTENAY 9], of Goodrington (in Paignton), South Allington, and Stancombe (in Sherford), Devon, Corton, Dorset, and Hinton and Mudford Terry, Somerset, Knight of the Shire for Devonshire, 1395, 1397, 1421, Sheriff of Devonshire, 1418–19, younger son of Edward de Courtenay, Knt., of Goodrington (in Paignton), South Allington, and Stancombe (in Sherford), Devon, Mudford Terry and Hinton, Somerset, Prince's Bachelor to Edward *the Black Prince*, by Emeline, daughter and heiress of John Dauney, Knt. [see COURTENAY 8 for his ancestry]. They had no surviving issue. His wife, Elizabeth, died 29 October 1397. SIR HUGH COURTENAY died 5 (or 6) March 1425, and was buried at Haccombe, Devon.

<small>Pole *Colls. towards a Desc. of Devon* (1791): 22–23. *Coll. Top. et Gen.* 6 (1840): 79–80 (re. Cogan). *Annual Rpt. of the Deputy Keeper* 36 (1875): 16, 234. *Genealogist* 4 (1880): 68–75; 6 (1882): 16–19. Colby *Vis. of Devon 1564* (1881): 24 (Bourchier ped.: "Fulco Fitzwarren. = Eliz., d. of Will. Cogan of Baunton, Knt., sister & coh. of John Cogan, Knt."), 58 (Cogan ped.). Wrottesley *Staffordshire Suits: Plea Rolls* (Colls. Hist. Staffs. 15) (1894): 6–7, 51–52. Vivian *Vis. of Devon 1531, 1564 & 1620* (1895): 243–250 (sub Courtenay). *Wrottesley Peds. from the Plea Rolls* (1905): 188–189, 305–306. VCH *Berkshire* 4 (1924): 321–322. C.P. 5 (1926): 502–503 (sub Fitzwarin). *C.F.R.* 6 (1931): 108–112. *Cal. IPM* 16 (1974): 27. Roskell *House of Commons 1386–1421* 2 (1992): 668–670 (biog. of Sir Hugh Courtenay).</small>

14. FULK FITZ WARIN, 6th Lord Fitz Warin, of Whittington, Edgmond, and Red Castle (in Hodnet), Shropshire, Wantage, Berkshire, etc., son and heir, born 1 April or 3 May 1389. He married **ANNE BOTREAUX**, daughter of William de Botreaux, Knt., 2nd Lord Botreaux, by Elizabeth, daughter of John de Saint Loe (or Seintlo), Knt. [see MOELS 13 for her ancestry]. They had one son, Fulk [7th Lord Fitz Warin] and one daughter, Elizabeth. FULK FITZ WARIN died 31 October 1407. He left a will dated 30 October 1407, proved 6 June 1408. His widow, Anne, married (2nd) by license dated 13 August 1409 (as his 2nd wife) **WILLIAM CLINTON**, Knt., 4th Lord Clinton, of Maxstoke, Warwickshire, son and heir of William de Clinton, Knt. They had one son, John [5th Lord Clinton]. He was summoned to Parliament from 19 August 1399 to 27 Nov. 1430. His wife, Anne, died 17 October 1420. SIR WILLIAM CLINTON, 4th Lord Clinton, died 30 July (or 20 August) 1431.

<small>Pole *Colls. towards a Desc. of Devon* (1791): 22–23. Hasted *Hist. & Top. Survey of Kent* 3 (1797): 169. C.P. 3 (1913): 315 (sub Clinton); 5 (1926): 503–504 (sub Fitzwarin).</small>

15. ELIZABETH FITZ WARIN, born about 1403 (aged 17 in 1420). She married before 22 Nov. 1420 (as his 1st wife) **RICHARD HANKFORD** (or **HANKEFORD**), Knt., of Tawstock, Bampton, Combeinteignhead, Cookbury (in Milton Damerel), Harford, Huish, Instow, North Holne, Nymet Tracey (in Bow), Rolastone, Totnes, Uffculme, West Down, and Yarnscombe, Devon, Norton and Nonnington, Somerset, Netheravon, Wiltshire, etc., and, in right of his 1st wife, of Wantage, Berkshire, Dilwyn, Herefordshire, Edgmond, Red Castle (in Hodnet), and Whittington, Shropshire, Crofton (in Great Bedwyn) and Staunton, Wiltshire, Edlington, Yorkshire, etc., son and heir of Richard Hankford, by Thomasine, daughter and heiress of Richard de Stapeldon, Knt. He was born about 21 July 1397. They had two daughters, Thomasine and Elizabeth. His wife, Elizabeth, was heiress in 1420 to her brother, Fulk Fitz Warin, 7th Lord Fitz Warin. In 1422 he and his wife, Elizabeth, petitioned the king and Parliament complaining that on the Friday after the last feast of St Martin, during the present parliament, William Fitzwaryn and Richard Laken, with a great number of Welshmen, attacked their castle of Whittington, Shropshire by night, seized it, and are still holding it; they asked that the said William and Richard be required to appear in Chancery within fifteen days following proclamations for them to answer to the king for the forcible entry and other crimes. In 1426 he and his wife, Elizabeth, granted the manor of Edlington, Yorkshire to James Gascoigne for life. His wife, Elizabeth, died between 10 Feb. 1425/6 and 16 Jan. 1427/8. He served in France in the retinue of the Earl of Salisbury. He was knighted at St. Albans in 1429. He married (2nd) in or before 1430 **ANNE MONTAGU** [see HANKFORD 10], daughter of John Montagu, K.G., Earl of Salisbury, Lord Montagu, Lord Monthermer, by Maud, daughter of Adam Fraunceys, Knt., Lord Mayor of London [see MONTAGU 9 for her ancestry]. They had one daughter, Anne. He presented to the church of Pylle, Somerset in 1430. SIR RICHARD HANKFORD died 8 Feb. 1430/1. His widow, Anne, married (2nd) about 1433 (as his 2nd wife) **LEWIS JOHN** (or **JOHAN**), Knt. [see HANKFORD 10; VERE 6.ii], of West Horndon, Dunton, Ingrave, and Bishop's Ockendon (in Cranham), Essex, Citizen and vintner of London, Knight of the Shire for Essex, Sheriff of Essex and Hertfordshire, 1420–2, Steward of the Duchy of Cornwall within Devon, Warden of the Stannaries in Devon, Steward of Havering-atte-Bower, Essex. He was of Welsh origin. They had three daughters, Elizabeth, Alice, and Margaret. Lewis married (1st) shortly before 1 Jan. 1414 (date of pardon for marrying without a royal license) **ALICE VERE** (died about 1431), widow of Francis [de] Court, Knt. (died 11 Sept. 1413), of Byfleet, Surrey, and East Tytherley, Hampshire [see VERE 6.ii], and daughter of Aubrey de Vere, Knt., 10th Earl of Oxford, by Alice, daughter of John Fitz Walter, Knt., 2nd Lord Fitzwalter [see VERE 6 for her ancestry]. Lewis and Alice had five sons (surnamed both John *and* Fitz Lewis), namely Lewis, Henry, John, Philip, and Edmund, and one daughter, Margaret (1st of name). SIR LEWIS JOHN died (perhaps overseas) 27 October 1442. He left a will dated 2 June 1440, proved 31 Dec. 1442 (P.C.C. 14 Rous), requesting burial in the Abbey of St. Mary Graces, London. His widow, Anne, married (3rd) (as his 3rd wife) **JOHN HOLAND**, K.G., Duke of Exeter, Earl of Huntingdon and Ivry (died 5 August 1447) [see EXETER 11]. They had no issue. Anne, Duchess of Exeter, died 28 Nov. 1457, and was buried with her 3rd husband at St. Katherine by the Tower, London. She left a will dated 20 April 1457, proved 15 May 1458 (P.C.C. 11 Stokton).

Pole *Colls. towards a Desc. of Devon* (1791): 22–23. Banks *Dormant & Extinct Baronage of England* 2 (1808): 214–220 (sub Fitz-Warine). Clutterbuck *Hist. & Antiqs. of Hertford* 1 (1815): 481–482 (Montacute ped.). *Coll. Top. et Gen.* 6 (1840): 396–397. Fuller *Hist. of the Worthies of England* (1840): 524–526. Charles *Vis. of Huntingdon 1613* (Camden Soc. 43) (1849): 125–128 (Wingfield ped.). *Gentleman's Mag.* n.s. 32 (1849): 491–493. Monro *Letters of Queen Margaret of Anjou & Bishop Beckington* (Camden Soc. 86) (1863): 34–37. Hutchins *Hist. & Antiqs. of Dorset* 3 (1868): 291 (Montagu ped.). *Vis. of Devon 1620* (H.S.P. 6) (1872): 34–35 (Bourchier ped.: "Ric'us Hanford, mil. = Elizab. f. & h. Falconis D'ni Fitzwarren"). Rogers *Antient Sepulchral Effigies* (1877): 142–143. Colby *Vis. of Devon 1564* (1881): 24 (Bourchier ped.: "Elizabeth [Fitzwarren], d. & h. = Richard Hanckford, lord of the honour of Baunton, jure uxoris."), 58 (Cogan ped.). *Genealogist* 6 (1882): 16–19; n.s. 15 (1898): 215. Loftie *Kensington Picturesque & Hist.* (1888): 56–59 (Vere ped.). Weaver *Somerset Incumbents* (1889): 173. *List of Sheriffs for England & Wales* (PRO Lists and Indexes 9) (1898): 44. *Trans. Essex Arch. Soc.* n.s. 6 (1898): 28–59. *Wiltshire Notes & Queries* 4 (1902–4): 481–493. Wrottesley *Peds. from the Plea Rolls* (1905): 305–306, 322, 338, 426–427. *Genealogist* n.s. 22 (1906): 179–180. *Papal Regs.: Letters* 7 (1906): 315. VCH *Hampshire* 4 (1911): 500–502, 515–518. VCH *Surrey* 3 (1911): 399–403. *Yorkshire Inqs.* 5 (Yorkshire Arch. Soc. Recs. 59) (1918): 162. Benolte & Cooke *Vis. of Kent 1530–1, 1574 & 1592* 2 (H.S.P. 75) (1924): 31–32 (Sibill ped.: "Anne [Montague] maried to Hanckford"). VCH *Berkshire* 4 (1924): 321–322. *C.P.* 5 (1926): 205–211 (sub Exeter), 504–507 (sub FitzWarin); 10 (1945): 234 footnote g (Alice m., "1stly, Guy d'Albon; 2ndly, Sir John FitzLewis"). Harvey et al. *Vis. of the North* 3 (Surtees Soc. 144) (1930): 49–50 (Montagu ped.: "Anne [Montagu] ducesse de Excestre"). Chichele *Reg. of Henry Chichele* 2 (Canterbury & York Soc. 42) (1937): 656 (biog. of Sir William Hankeford). Paget *Baronage of England* (1957) 372: 12. *Ancient Deeds — Ser. B* 2 (List & Index Soc. 101) (1974): B.8247; 3 (List & Index Soc. 113) (1975): B.11807. VCH *Essex* 7 (1978): 103–109. VCH *Wiltshire* 11 (1980): 165–181. Buck *Politics, Finance & Church in the Reign of Edward II* (1983): 10–37 (re: Stapledon fam.). Harvey *Vis. of Suffolk 1561* 2 (H.S.P. n.s. 3) (1984): 211–222 (Wingfield ped.). Williams *England in the 15th Cent.* (1987): 187–198. Roskell *House of Commons 1386–1421* 3 (1992): 494–498 (biog. of Lewis John: "... a Welshman of dubious origin who became a financier, a landowner of substance and the son-in-law of two earls... close association with Thomas Chaucer of Ewelme, Henry IV's chief butler and cousin of the King's half-brothers, the Beauforts... the two men supplied wine to the households of Henry IV and Henry V"). Sainty *Judges of England* (Selden Soc. Supp. Ser. 10) (1993): 8 (re. William Hankford). *Cal. IPM* 20 (1995): 13; 23 (2004): 296–307. VCH *Somerset* 8 (2004): 91–112. National Archives, C 1/9/370 (Chancery Proc. dated 1432–43 — Lewis John, Esq. v. Thomas Hayne, some time servant to Sir John de Veer, Knt. brother of petitioner's late wife, and Nicholas Pope, and Robert Kent, notaries re. false declaration made by compulsion of the earl of Oxford concerning the enfeoffment of the manor of Dullingham, Cambridgeshire, and the manor of Langdon and Amees (or Amyes), Essex); SC 8/24/1181 (available at www.catalogue.nationalarchives.gov.uk/search.asp).

Child of Elizabeth Fitz Warin, by Richard Hankford, Knt.:

i. **THOMASINE HANKFORD** [see next].

Child of Richard Hankford, Knt., by Anne Montagu:

i. **ANNE HANKFORD**, married **THOMAS BUTLER**, K.B., 7th Earl of Ormond [see BUTLER 11].

16. THOMASINE HANKFORD (or **HANKEFORD**), daughter and co-heiress by her father's 1st marriage, born at Tawstock, Devon 23 Feb. 1422/3, and baptized in the church there. She married before 3 August 1437 (as his 1st wife) **WILLIAM BOURGCHIER**, Knt., 9th Lord Fitz Warin, Justice of the Peace for Shropshire, 1443–5, 1448–9, 1453–4, 1457–8, 1460–2, 1466, 1468, Justice of the Peace for Devon, 1444, 1447–8, 1451, 1453, 1455–66, 1468–9, Justice of the Peace for Surrey, 1448, 1452, Trier of Petitions in Parliament, Master Forester for Exmoor, Devon and Neroche, Somerset for life, 1461, 2nd son of William Bourgchier, Knt., Count of Eu, by Anne, Countess of Buckingham, Hereford, and Northampton, daughter and co-heiress of Thomas of Woodstock, Duke of Gloucester (son of King Edward III) [see BOURCHIER 11 for his ancestry]. He was born before 1420. They had four sons, Fulk, Knt. [10th Lord Fitz Warin], William, John, and Roger, and four daughters, Anne, Blanche (wife of Philip Beaumont and Bartholomew Saint Leger), Thomasine, and Isabel. She was heiress in 1433 to her sister, Elizabeth Hankford. He and his wife, Thomasine, were granted livery of her father's lands 15 August 1437. He presented to the churches of Pill, Somerset, 1440, 1446, 1457, 1460, and 1462, Huntspill, Somerset, 1453, and Trent, Somerset, 1464. He was summoned to Parliament from 2 Jan. 1448/9 to 7 Sept. 1469, by writs directed *Willelmo Bourgchier domino de fitz Waryn'*, or the like, *militi*, or *chivaler*. His wife, Thomasine, died 3 July 1453, and was buried in the church of Bampton, Devon. He was one of the Lords who swore allegiance to the king in Parliament 24 July 1455. He married (2nd) before 9 Jan. 1458/9 **KATHERINE AFFETON**, widow of Hugh Stukeley (or Stuckley, Esq. (died shortly before 13 Dec. 1457), of Affeton (in West Wolrington), Devon, Trent, Somerset, etc. [see STUKELEY 11], and daughter and heiress of John Affeton, Esq., of Affeton (in West Wolrington), Devon, by his wife, Joan Bratton. His wife, Katherine, died 26 March 1467. She left a will dated 13 Feb. 1466/7, proved 1 Sept. 1467 (P.C.C. 32 Godyn), requesting burial in the parish church of West Wolrington, Devon. SIR WILLIAM BOURGCHIER, 9th Lord Fitz Warin, died shortly before 12 Dec. 1469, and was buried in the church of the Austin Friars, London.

Pole *Colls. towards a Desc. of Devon* (1791): 22–23. Banks *Dormant & Extinct Baronage of England* 2 (1808): 214–220 (sub Fitz-Warine). Burke *Gen'l & Heraldic Dict. of the Peerages of England, Ireland & Scotland* (1831): 73–74 (sub Bourchier), 210–211 (sub Fitz-Warine). *Coll. Top. et Gen.* 6 (1840): 396–397. Westcote *View of Devonshire* (1845): 460–461. *Gentleman's Mag.* n.s. 32 (1849): 491–493. Rogers *Ancient Sepulchral Effigies & Monumental & Memorial Sculpture of Devon* (1877): 84–90. *Notes & Queries* 5th Ser. 11 (1879): 477. *Genealogist* 6 (1882): 16–19. Weaver *Somerset Incumbents* (1889): 108, 173, 201. Vivian *Vis. of Devon 1531, 1564 & 1620* (1895): 106–107 (sub Bourchier). Leadam *Select Cases in the Court of Requests A.D. 1497–1569* (Selden Soc. 12) (1898): 54–59. *MSS of the Duke of Somerset, the Marquis of Ailesbury & the Rev. Sir T.H.G. Puleston* (Hist. MSS Comm. 43) (1898): 143. Wrottesley *Peds. from the Plea Rolls* (1905): 377, 426–427. *Genealogist* n.s. 22 (1906): 179–180. *C.P.R. 1452–1461* (1910): 153 (William, lord Fitz Waryn styled "king's kinsman"). *C.P.* 5 (1926): 507–508 (sub FitzWarin); 5 (1926): App. A, 754. Beckington *Reg. of Thomas Bekynton Bishop of Bath & Wells* 1 (Somerset Rec. Soc. 49) (1934): 70, 229. Ross *Edward IV* (1974): 79.

17. FULK BOURCHIER, Knt., 10th Lord Fitz Warin], of Clifford (in Dunsford), Combeinteignhead, Little Yarnscombe (in Yarnscombe), Sutton, and West Down, Devon, Norton and Nonnington, Somerset, Netheravon, Wiltshire, etc., son and heir, born 25 October 1445. He married before 1466 (date of settlement) **ELIZABETH DINHAM**, daughter of John Dinham, Knt., of Hartland, Kingskerwell, and Nutwell, Devon, by Joan, daughter of Richard Arches, Knt.

[see DINHAM 8 for her ancestry]. She was born about 1451 (aged 50 and more in 1501). They had one son, John, K.B. [1st Earl of Bath, 11th Lord Fitz Warin], and two daughters, Joan (wife of James Tuchet, K.B., 7th Lord Audley) and Elizabeth. In 1466 he settled the manor of Netheravon, Wiltshire on his wife, Elizabeth, for life. In 1469 he had special livery of his father's lands. He was summoned to Parliament 19 August 1472, by writ directed *Fulconi Bourghchier de fitz Waryn' chivaler*. In 1474 he was granted an exemption for life from attending in person on the king by reason of any writ under the great or privy seal or otherwise for any council or Parliament. He presented to the churches of Norton Fitzwarren, Somerset, 1475, 1476, and Pill, Somerset, 1475, 1476. SIR FULK BOURCHIER, 10th Lord Fitz Warin, died 18 Sept. 1479, and was buried in the church of Bampton, Devon. He left a will dated 1 April 1475, proved 10 Nov. 1480. His widow, Elizabeth, married (2nd) before 7 Dec. 1480 **JOHN SAPCOTE**, Knt., of Elton, Huntingdonshire, Esquire of the Body, 1472–85, Knight of the Shire for Huntingdonshire, 1472–5, Sheriff of Rutland, 1475–6, Sheriff of Devon, 1477–8, Receiver of Cornwall, 1483, Knight of the Body, 1488–1501, Keeper of the Forests of Weybridge and Sapley, Hampshire, 1488, and, in right of his wife, of Bampton and Tawstock, Devon, son and heir of John Sapcotes, of Elton, Huntingdonshire. He was born about 1438 (aged 50 in 1488). They had one son, Richard, and one daughter, Jane. He served on the king's expedition to France in 1475. He presented to the churches of Cricket Thomas, Somerset, 1482, Norton Fitzwarren, Somerset, 1482, 1485, 1487, 1493, and Huntspill, Somerset, 1495. In 1487 John and his wife, Elizabeth, presented to the chapel of Haxton (in Fittleton), Wiltshire. He was heir in 1488 to his cousin, Richard Sapcote. SIR JOHN SAPCOTE died 5 Jan. 1500/1. He left a will dated 6 [sic] Jan. 1500/1, proved 28 May 1501 (P.C.C. 21 Moone), requesting burial in the Lady aisle of the Abbey church of Hartland Abbey, Devon. His widow, Elizabeth, was co-heiress in 1501 to her brother, John Dinham, K.G., Lord Dinham, by which she inherited a ¼ share of the manors of Dornford (in Wootton), Rousham, Souldern, Steeple Aston, and Steeple Barton, Oxfordshire. She presented to the church of Norton Fitzwarren, Somerset 18 June 1502. Elizabeth married (3rd) before 19 Nov. 1505 (date of presentment) (as his 2nd wife) **THOMAS BRANDON**, K.G., of Southwark, Surrey, Duddington, Northamptonshire, etc., Marshal of the King's Bench, Master of the Horse, younger son of William Brandon, Knt., of Henham, Framlingham, Trimley (in Colwey), and Wangford, Suffolk, Soham-Count, Cambridgeshire, and St. George's, Southwark, Surrey, Marshall of the King's Bench, by Elizabeth, daughter of Robert Wingfield, Knt. [see BRANDON 16 for his ancestry]. In 1505 Thomas and his wife, Elizabeth, and her fellow Dinham co-heirs presented to the church of Maperton, Somerset. In 1507 Thomas and his wife, Elizabeth, settled the reversion of a ¼ th share of the manors of Butterbury (in Hartland), Hartland, and Harton (in Hartland), Devon on his nephew, Charles Brandon, for life. In 1509 Elizabeth settled her lands in Souldern, Oxfordshire on Thomas and herself for life, with reversion to her son, Richard Sapcotes. SIR THOMAS BRANDON died 27 Jan. 1509/10, and was buried in the church of the Black Friars by Ludgate. He left a will dated 11 Jan. 1509/10, proved 11 May 1510 (P.C.C. 29 Bennett). His widow, Elizabeth, Lady Fitz Warin, died 19 October 1516, and was buried in the church of the Grey Friars, London. In the period, 1529–32, Mary Redyng, executrix and late the wife of John Redyng sued William Paston, Knt., John Carelton, and Francis Lovell, Esq., surviving executors of Thomas Lovell, Knt., executor of Thomas Brandon, Knt., regarding a debt due from the said Sir Thomas Brandon to her said late husband for boarding Lady Berkeley, then wife of the said Sir Thomas (sic) and sixteen of her servants and family for 32 weeks at 40s.

Pole *Colls. towards a Desc. of Devon* (1791): 22–23. Nicolas *Testamenta Vetusta* 2 (1826): 496–497 (will of Sir Thomas Brandon, Knt.). Westcote *View of Devonshire in MDCXXX* (1845): 199–200. *Gentleman's Mag.* n.s. 32 (1849): 491–493. *Annual Rpt. of the Deputy Keeper* 26 (1865): 22. Rogers *Ancient Sepulchral Effigies & Monumental & Memorial Sculpture of Devon* (1877): 84–90. Weaver *Somerset Incumbents* (1889): 108, 136, 173, 347, 409. Boase *Reg. of Exeter College, Oxford* (1894): liii, 268. Vivian *Vis. of Devon 1531, 1564 & 1620* (1895): 106–107 (sub Bourchier). *List of Sheriffs for England & Wales* (PRO Lists and Indexes 9) (1898): 36, 113. Wrottesley *Peds. from the Plea Rolls* (1905): 426–427. *Genealogist* n.s. 22

(1906): 179–180. *C.P.* 5 (1926): 508–510 (sub FitzWarin). Wedgwood *Hist. of Parl.* 1 (1936): 740–741 (biog. of Sir John Sapcotes). VCH *Huntingdon* 3 (1936): 154–156. VCH *Oxford* 6 (1959): 301–312; 10 (1972): 42–49; 11 (1983): 21–44, 59–75, 159–168, 259–285, 295. Ross *Edward IV* (1974): 79. VCH *Wiltshire* 11 (1980): 142–151, 165–181. Rosenthal *Patriarchy & Fams. of Privilege in Fifteenth-Cent. England* (1991): 184. National Archives, C 1/283/49; C 1/333/30 (available at www.catalogue.nationalarchives.gov.uk/search.asp). National Archives, CP 25/1/294/74, #35; CP 25/1/46/92, #43 [see abstract of fines at http://www.medievalgenealogy.org.uk/index.html].

Children of Fulk Fitz Warin, Knt., by Elizabeth Dinham:

i. **JOHN BOURCHIER**, K.B., 1st Earl of Bath, 11th Lord Fitz Warin, married **ELIZABETH WENTWORTH** [see WYNDHAM 15].

ii. **JOAN BOURCHIER**, married **JAMES TUCHET**, K.B., 7th Lord Audley [see TUCHET 16.i].

iii. **ELIZABETH BOURCHIER** [see next].

18. ELIZABETH BOURCHIER, born c.1475. She married (1st) before 1501 (as his 2nd wife) **HUGH BEAUMONT**, of Gittisham, Sherwell, and Youlston, Devon, Calstone Wellington, Wiltshire, etc., younger son of Thomas Beaumont, Knt., of Youlston, Devon. He was born about 1458 (aged 30 in 1488). They had no issue. He was heir in 1488 to his older brother, Thomas Beaumont, Esq. Between 1500 and 1501 Hugh and his wife, Elizabeth, and others released their right in the manor of Stalpits (in Shrivenham), Berkshire. She was a legatee as "Elizabeth Beaumont" in the 1501 will of her step-father, John Sapcotes, Knt. HUGH BEAUMONT died 25 March 1507. His widow, Elizabeth, married (2nd) (as his 2nd wife) **EDWARD STANHOPE**, Knt., of Rampton, Nottinghamshire, Sheriff of Nottinghamshire and Derbyshire, 1507–9, son and heir of Thomas Stanhope, Esq., of Rampton, Nottinghamshire, by Mary, daughter of John Jerningham. They had one daughter, Anne. In the period, 1500–1, Edward Stanhope sued Henry Stanhope in Chancery regarding the detention of deeds relating to the manors of Rainton, Tuxford, Skygby, Magnam, and Cotton, Nottinghamshire. SIR EDWARD STANHOPE died 6 June 1511. In the period, 1504–15, Elizabeth Stanhope sued John Coplestone and others in Chancery regarding the detention of deeds relating to the next presentation to the church of Aveton Gifford, Devon. Elizabeth married (3rd) **RICHARD PAGE**, Knt., of Molesey, Surrey, Beechwood (in Flamstead), Hertfordshire, etc., Knight of the Body, Vice-Chamberlain of Henry Fitzroy, Duke of Richmond, Chamberlain for Edward, Prince of Wales [future King Edward VI], Lieutenant of Gentleman Pensioners, Receiver, Bailiff, and Steward of Beverley, 1526–44, Sheriff of Surrey and Sussex, 1536–7, Privy Councillor, son and heir of Henry (or Harry) Page, by Margaret, daughter and heiress of John Danyell. They had one daughter, Elizabeth. He was the residuary heir in the 1483 will of his grandfather, Richard Page, of Horton, Kent. In 1530 the dissolved priory of Thoby, Essex was granted to him for life. In 1539 he was granted the manor of Beechwood (in Flamstead), Hertfordshire by the king, in exchange for his manor of Molesey, Surrey. The same year he was also granted the manors of St. Giles (in Edlesborough), Buckinghamshire and Woodhall (in Hemel Hempstead), Hertfordshire, together with land in Hockliffe, Bedfordshire. In 1539–40 he and his wife, Elizabeth, were granted the rectory of Tilsworth, Bedfordshire. In 1542 he was granted the manor of Northall (in Edllesborough), Buckinghamshire. In 1544 he was granted the manor of Flamstead, Hertfordshire for life, in exchange for the offices of Chief Steward of the lordship of Beverley and Recorder of Hull. SIR RICHARD PAGE died 3 Feb. 1548/9. He left a will dated 22 Sept. 1547, proved 14 April 1551, requesting burial in the church of St. Mary on the Hill besides Bishopgate, London, or in the church of Flamstead, Hertfordshire. In 1552 his widow, Elizabeth, had permission to visit her daughter, the Duchess of Somerset, who was then a prisoner in the Tower. Elizabeth died 8 August 1557, and was buried at Clerkenwell, Middlesex.

Dugdale *Antiqs. of Warwickshire* (1730): 84–85 (Skipwith ped.). Thoroton *Hist. of Nottinghamshire* 3 (1796): 242–248. Brydges *Collins' Peerage of England* 3 (1812): 407–434 (sub Stanhope, Earl of Chesterfield). Nichols *Literary Remains of King Edward the Sixth* 1 (1857): xxx–xxxi. Mundy et al. *Vis. of Nottingham 1569 & 1614* (H.S.P. 4) (1871): 5–8

(Stanhope ped.: "Edward Stanhop of Shelford miles [1] = Avelina [Audelina, Harl. 1400] filia Gervasii Clifton militis, [2] =Elizabetha filia ffulconi Bourchier d'ni fitz warren 1 nupta Hen. Beamont postea 2 maritus —— Verney, [she married 4th] = Richardus Pages miles Camerarius E. 4"). *Notes & Gleanings* 2 (1889): 70–73. Vivian *Vis. of Devon 1531, 1564 & 1620* (1895): 106–107 (sub Bourchier). *Cal. IPM Henry VII* 1 (1898): 119–120; 3 (1955): 167, 180. *List of Sheriffs for England & Wales* (PRO Lists and Indexes 9) (1898): 104. *Rpt. & Trans. of the Devonshire Assoc. for the Advancement of Science, Lit. & Art* 2nd Ser. 8 (1906): 154–160. *List of Early Chancery Procs.* 4 (PRO Lists and Indexes 29) (1908): 398. VCH *Hertford* 2 (1908): 193–201, 215–230. VCH *Surrey* 3 (1911): 451–456. VCH *Bedford* 3 (1912): 383–386, 432–435. VCH *Berkshire* 4 (1924): 531–543. VCH *Buckingham* 3 (1925): 350–361. Wedgwood *Hist. of Parl.* 1 (1936): 740–741 (biog. of Sir John Sapcotes). VCH *Somerset* 5 (1985): 19–25. VCH *Yorkshire* E.R. 6 (1989): 63–65. Carpenter *Kingsford's Stonor Letters & Papers 1290–1483* (1996): xxxiii–xxxiv. Alford *Kingship & Politics in the Reign of Edward VI* (2002): 89–90. VCH *Wiltshire* 17 (2002): 123–135. National Archives, C 1/106/34; C 1/224/62; C 1/245/68; C 1/360/63; C 1/360/64; C 1/360/65 (available at www.catalogue.nationalarchives.gov.uk/search.asp).

Child of Elizabeth Bourchier, by Edward Stanhope, Knt.:

i. **ANNE STANHOPE**, married (1st) **EDWARD SEYMOUR**, K.G., Duke of Somerset, Earl of Hertford [see SEYMOUR 19.i]; (2nd) **FRANCIS NEWDIGATE**, Esq., of Chelsea and Hanworth, Middlesex [see SEYMOUR 19.i].

Child of Elizabeth Bourchier, by Richard Page, Knt.:

i. **ELIZABETH PAGE** [see next].

19. ELIZABETH PAGE, daughter and heiress, born c.1527 (aged 30 & more in 1557). She married about 1538 (as his 1st wife) **WILLIAM SKIPWITH**, Knt., of South Ormsby, Ketsby, and Laceby, Lincolnshire, and Skipwith, Yorkshire, Sheriff of Lincolnshire, 1552–3, 1563–4, and, in right of his 1st wife, of St. Giles (in Edlesborough), Buckinghamshire, Beechwood (in Flamstead), Hertfordshire, Woodhall (in Hemel Hempstead), Hertfordshire, etc., son and heir of William Skipwith, Knt., of South Ormsby, Calthorpe (in Covenham), Covenham, Ketsby, and Laceby, Lincolnshire, by his 1st wife, Elizabeth, daughter of William Tyrwhit, Knt. [see SKIPWITH 15 for his ancestry]. They had one son, Richard, Knt., and six daughters, Elizabeth (wife of Thomas Portington, Esq.), Frances (wife of Francis Constable, Esq., and Ralph Ellerker, Knt.), Anne (wife of Francis Carsey or Kersey, Esq.), Mabel (wife of Thomas Skipwith, Esq.), Mary (wife of George Metham, Esq.), and Margaret (wife of John Try, Esq.). He was born about 1510. In 1561 he granted an annuity of 4 shillings to his brother, John Skipwith, Gent., chargeable on his lands in Ormsby, Lincolnshire. In 1566 he and his wife, Elizabeth, conveyed the manor of St. Giles (in Edlesborough), Buckinghamshire to Ralph Heydon. In 1570 he and his wife, Elizabeth, sold the advowson and rectory of Tilsworth, Bedfordshire to Gabriel Fowler. His wife, Elizabeth, died at South Ormsby, Lincolnshire April 1573. He married (2nd) **ANNE TOWTHBY**, daughter of John Towthby, Esq., of Towthby, Lincolnshire. They had one son, Edward. SIR WILLIAM SKIPWITH was buried at South Ormsby, Lincolnshire 18 October 1586.

Dugdale *Antiqs. of Warwickshire* (1730): 84–85 (Skipwith ped.). Burke & Burke *Extinct & Dormant Baronetcies of England* (1841): 486–488 (sub Skipwith). Mundy et al. *Vis. of Nottingham 1569 & 1614* (H.S.P. 4) (1871): 5–8 (Stanhope ped.: "Elizabetha [Page] ux. Will'mi Skipwith de fflambsted in Com. Hertford militis"). Gibbons *Notes on the Vis. oif Lincolnshire 1634* (1898): 49–60 (Skipwith ped.: "Sr Wm Skipwith of S. Ormsby in com. Linc. Knight. [1] = Eliza d. & h. of Sr Rd Page of Beverwood in co. Hertford, [2] = Anne dau. of John Tothby of Tothby in com. Linc. Esq."), 178–186. *List of Sheriffs for England & Wales* (PRO Lists and Indexes 9) (1898): 80. Maddison *Lincolnshire Peds.* 3 (H.S.P. 52) (1904): 894–896 (Skipwith ped.), 1008–1111 (Towthby ped.). VCH *Hertford* 2 (1908): 193–201, 215–230. VCH *Bedford* 3 (1912): 432–435. VCH *Buckingham* 3 (1925): 350–361. Hertfordshire Archives & Local Studies: Estate papers of the Sebright Fam. of Beachwood Park, Flamstead, DE/FL/17278; DE/FL/17309 (available at www.a2a.org.uk/search/index.asp). Massingberd Mundy, 1MM/1/10/5 (available at www.a2a.org.uk/search/index.asp).

20. RICHARD SKIPWITH, Knt., of South Ormsby and Ketsby, Lincolnshire, Beechwood (in Flamstead) and Woodhall (in Hemel Hempstead), Hertfordshire, Skipwith, Yorkshire, etc., son and heir by his father's 1st marriage, born about 1546 (aged 40 in 1586). He married by settlement dated 12 Nov. 1564 **MARY CHAMBERLAIN**, daughter of Ralph Chamberlain, Knt., of Gedding,

Suffolk, by Elizabeth, daughter of Robert Fiennes, Knt. They had three sons, William, Esq., Edward, Esq., and [Capt.] Henry, Knt., and two daughters, Catherine (wife of Charles Ayscough, Esq.) and Susan (wife of William Skipwith, Esq.). In 1573 he sold the manor of Beechwood (in Flamstead), Hertfordshire to Paul Pope. In 1574 he and his wife, Mary, and his father, William, conveyed the manor of Woodhall (in Hemel Hempstead), Hertfordshire to William Marston. In 1590 he and his son, William, leased a messuage in South Ormsby, Lincolnshire (where he dwelled), together with lands in South Ormsby and Ketsby, Lincolnshire to John Totty for a term of 21 years. SIR RICHARD SKIPWITH was buried at Winteringham, Lincolnshire 2 October 1608. Administration on his estate was granted in 1610 to his son, Henry Skipwith, Knt.

Dugdale *Antiqs. of Warwickshire* (1730): 84–85 (Skipwith ped.). Burke & Burke *Extinct & Dormant Baronetcies of England* (1841): 486–488 (sub Skipwith). Cooke & St. George *Vis. of Cambridge 1575 & 1619* (H.S.P. 41) (1897): 41 (Chamberlayne ped.). Gibbons *Notes on the Vis. oif Lincolnshire 1634* (1898): 49–60 (Skipwith ped.: "Sr R^d Skipwith sonne & heire K^t. = Mary da. of Sr Ralph Chamberlain of Suffolke."), 178–186. Maddison *Lincolnshire Peds.* 3 (H.S.P. 52) (1904): 894–896 (Skipwith ped.). VCH *Hertford* 2 (1908): 193–201, 215–230. Harkrider *Women, Reform & Community in Early Modern England* (2008): 125, footnote 64. Lincolnshire Archives: Hertfordshire Archives & Local Studies: Estate papers of the Sebright Fam. of Beachwood Park, Flamstead, DE/FL/17280 (available at www.a2a.org.uk/search/index.asp). Massingberd Mundy, 1MM/1/10/13; 1MM/1/10/14; 1MM/1/10/15; 1MM/1/10/16; 1MM/2/11/3 (settlement dated 12 Nov. 1564 for marriage of Richard Skipwith and Mary, daughter of Sir Ralph Chamberlain); 1MM/2/11/8; 1MM/2/11/12 (available at www.a2a.org.uk/search/index.asp).

21. WILLIAM SKIPWITH, Esq., of South Ormsby and Ketsby, Lincolnshire, and Skipwith, Yorkshire, son and heir, born c.1566. He married (1st) before 20 June 1605 (date of indenture) **ANNE HUSSEY**, widow of John Ryther and Robert Constable, Knt., and daughter and heiress of John Hussey, Esq. They had no issue. In 1605 his father conveyed to William and his wife, Lady Anne, a capital messuage at South Ormsby, Lincolnshire (where they live) and the manor of Skipwith, Yorkshire. His wife, Anne, was buried at South Ormsby, Lincolnshire 4 Feb. 1608/9. He married (2nd) his first cousin **ANNE PORTINGTON**, daughter of Thomas Portington, Esq., of Sawcliffe, Lincolnshire, by Elizabeth, daughter of William Skipwith, Knt. They had four sons, Willoughby, Esq., Edward, Henry, and William, and five daughters, Elizabeth (wife of John Newcomen, Esq.), Troth, Susan, Anne, and Mary. WILLIAM SKIPWITH, Esq., was buried at South Ormsby, Lincolnshire 1 October 1622. His widow, Anne, married (2nd) at South Ormsby, Lincolnshire 9 October 1623 (as his 2nd wife) **FRANCIS GUEVARA**, Esq., of Stenigot, Lincolnshire, son of John Guevara, Knt., of Stenigot, Lincolnshire, by Anne, daughter of Robert Saunderson. She was living 21 October 1650.

Dugdale *Antiqs. of Warwickshire* (1730): 84–85 (Skipwith ped.). Burke & Burke *Extinct & Dormant Baronetcies of England* (1841): 486–488 (sub Skipwith). Clay *Yorkshire Royalist Composition Papers* 2 (Yorkshire Arch. Soc. Rec. Ser. 18) (1895): 13. Gibbons *Notes on the Vis. oif Lincolnshire 1634* (1898): 49–60 (Skipwith ped.: "Wm Skipwith s. and heir m^d to An Portington 2 wife"), 178–186. Maddison *Lincolnshire Peds.* 2 (H.S.P. 51) (1903): 433–434 (Guevara ped.); 3 (H.S.P. 52) (1904): 793–795 (Portington ped.), 894–896 (Skipwith ped.). Lincolnshire Archives: Massingberd Mundy, 1MM/2/11/12 (available at www.a2a.org.uk/search/index.asp).

22. WILLOUGHBY SKIPWITH, Esq., of South Ormsby and Ketsby, Lincolnshire, Menthorpe and Skipwith, Yorkshire, son and heir by his father's 2nd marriage, baptized at South Ormesby, Lincolnshire 3 January 1612/13. He married at Barnet, Hertfordshire 20 July 1634 **HONORA SANDERS** (or **SAUNDERS**), daughter of Patrick Sanders, M.D., of St. Helen's, Bishopsgate, London, by Sarah, daughter of Henry Smith, Esq., of Withcote, Leicestershire. They had two sons, Patrick and John, Gent., and three daughters, Honora, Elizabeth, and Anne. He was admitted a member of Lincoln's Inn 13 October 1634, as "Willoughby Skipwith, son and heir of William Skipwith, late of South Ormsby, co. Linc., arm., dec'd." In 1636 he sold the manor of Ketsby, Lincolnshire to his uncle, Edward Skipwith, Esq. In 1637 he and his wife, Honora, leased the manor house and its outhouses at South Ormsby, Lincolnshire to Edward Dandy, Esq., for a term of 15 years. In 1638 he sold the manor of Ormsby, Lincolnshire to Drayner Massingberd.

Administration on the estate of WILLOUGHBY SKIPWITH, Esq., of Skipwith, Yorkshire was granted in 1658 to his widow, Honora. In 1670–1 a distress was levied at Skipwith, Yorkshire from Honora Skipwith. In 1675 Honora Skipwith, widow, was imprisoned after processes against her were conducted in the Ecclesiastical Courts for absenting herself from the parish church. Honora died as a Quaker martyr in prison at York Castle 15 April 1679. Administration to her estate was granted to her son, John Skipwith, 18 September 1680.

Annual Report Deputy Keeper 41 (1880): 304. St. George *Vis. of London 1633–5* 2 (H.S.P. 17) (1883): 227 (Sanders ped.: "Honora [Sanders]."). Collins *Cat. of the Yorkshire Wills at Somerset House 1649–1660* (Yorkshire Arch. & Top. Assoc. Rec. Ser. 1) (1885): 221. Clay *Yorkshire Royalist Composition Papers* 2 (Yorkshire Arch. Soc. Rec. Ser. 18) (1895): 13. Baildon *Recs. of Lincoln's Inn: Admissions* 1 (1896): 225. Gibbons *Notes on the Vis. oif Lincolnshire 1634* (1898): 49–60 (Skipwith ped.: "Willoughby [Skipwith] son and heir m^d Honor da. of Doctor Saunders of London."), 178–186. *NYGBR* 29 (1898): 171–172 (marriage of Patrick Sanders and Sarah Smith dated 1613). Maddison *Lincolnshire Peds.* 3 (H.S.P. 52) (1904): 894–896 (Skipwith ped.). *Lincolnshire Notes & Queries* 8 (1905): 188–189. Garrett *Marian Exiles* (1938): 290 (re. Henry Smith). Thistlethwaite *Yorkshire Quarterly Meeting (of the Society of Friends), 1665–1966* (1979): 56. National Archives, E 134/6&7Anne/Hil7 (available at www.catalogue.nationalarchives.gov.uk/search.asp). Lincolnshire Archives: Massingberd Mundy, 1MM/1/11/1; 1MM/1/11/2&3; 1MM/1/11/4; 1MM/1/11/5 (Letter of atty. dated 2 Dec. 1634 Patrick Saunders, M.D. appoints his cousin Samuel Pomphrett, of South Ormsby, Lincolnshire to receive all rents and money payable by Willoughby Skipwith his son-in-law); 1MM/1/11/6; 1MM/1/11/7; 1MM/1/11/8; 1MM/1/11/9; 1MM/1/11/10; 1MM/1/11/11; 1MM/1/11/12; 1MM/1/11/13; 1MM/1/11/14; 1MM/1/11/16; 1MM/1/11/17; 1MM/1/11/22; 1MM/1/11/23; 1MM/1/11/25; 1MM/1/11/29-45 (available at www.a2a.org.uk/search/index.asp).

23. ANNE SKIPWITH, born about 1642. She married (1st) at Hull, Yorkshire 11 Sept. 1662 in a Quaker ceremony **WILLIAM GOFORTH**, son of Miles Goforth, yeoman, of Knedlington-upon-Hull, Yorkshire, England. He was born about 1631. They had six sons, George, William, John, Miles, Zachariah, and Thomas, and one daughter, Susannah (wife of William Robinson). In 1677 William and his wife and family sailed in a company of Quakers from Hull, Yorkshire in the ship *Martha* in 1677. WILLIAM GOFORTH died before 1686. His widow, Anne, married (2nd) before 12 October 1686 **WILLIAM OXLEY**. They had two sons, John and Joseph, and one daughter, Honora (wife of George Harmer). WILLIAM OXLEY died at Philadelphia, Pennsylvania 15 April 1717. His widow, Anne, died at Philadelphia, Pennsylvania 3 April 1723.

Hinshaw *Encyclopedia of American Quaker Genealogy*, II:401. *Lincolnshire Notes & Queries* 8 (1905): 188–189. Sheppard *Passengers & Ships Prior to 1684* (1970): 142–143. Goforth *Goforth Gen.* (1981): 1–4. Davis *West Jersey New Jersey Deed Recs. 1676-1721* (2005): 240, 244. Special thanks go to Martin Hollick who developed the above royal line for the immigrant, Anne (Skipwith) (Goforth) Oxley, and generously gave permission for its inclusion in this publication.

⁌ FITZWILLIAM ⁍

HUGUES CAPET, King of France, married **ALIX OF POITOU**.
ROBERT II *le Pieux*, King of France, married **CONSTANCE OF PROVENCE**.
HENRI I, King of France, married **ANNE OF KIEV**.
HUGUES LE GRAND, Count of Crépy, married **ADÈLE DE VERMANDOIS**.
ISABEL DE VERMANDOIS, married **WILLIAM DE WARENNE**, 2nd Earl of Surrey.
WILLIAM DE WARENNE, 3rd Earl of Surrey, married **ELA** (or **ALA**) **OF PONTHIEU**.
ISABEL DE WARENNE, married **HAMELIN**, 5th Earl of Surrey [see WARENNE 7].

8. ELA DE WARENNE. She married (1st) **ROBERT DE NEWBURGH** (or **NEUBOURG**), son and heir apparent of Henry de Newburgh, of Ashhampstead and Basildon, Berkshire, and Radepont in Eure, Normandy, by his wife, Margaret. They had no issue. About 1180 Henry son of Robert of Newburgh together with his son, Robert, gave to Richard de Vernon and his heirs, in exchange for Henry's land at Radepont in Eure, a moiety of Ashampstead and a moiety of Basildon, Berkshire, with the 'messuage of Ashampstede' and the land of William de Puteo there. ROBERT DE NEWBURGH was living in 1191, but was dead before 1193. She married (2nd) (as his 2nd wife)

WILLIAM FITZ WILLIAM, of Sprotborough, Yorkshire, and Plumtree, Nottinghamshire, benefactor of Blythe Priory, son and heir of William Fitz Godric, by Aubrey, daughter and heiress of Robert de Lisours (or Lisures). They had two sons, Thomas, Knt., and Roger, and two daughters, Denise and Ellen (wife of John de Lungvilers). He previously married (1st) **MAUD** _____. In the period, 1191/c.1200, he confirmed a gift of his grandfather, Godric, to Byland Abbey, Yorkshire. In 1194 his nephew, Roger de Lacy, Constable of Chester, released to him and his mother, Aubrey, the lands which had belonged to her father, Robert de Lisours. His wife, Ela, gave five virgates of land in Rottingdean, Sussex, together with three villains and their sequels to Roche Abbey, Yorkshire c.1200. In 1202 Mary, wife of William Longum, released to William Fitz William and his mother, Aubrey, all her right to dower to lands in Cadeby, Kirk Bramwith, and Barnby-upon-Don, Yorkshire. Sometime before 1212, he witnessed a charter of his nephew, Roger de Lacy, Constable of Chester, to Fountains Abbey. At an unknown date, he confirmed the grant of his mother, Aubrey, of the advowson of the church of Aldwick to Hanepole Abbey. In 1219 he bound himself to Alexander de Neville, in return for 1/3 part of a carucate in Hopton, Yorkshire. **WILLIAM FITZ WILLIAM** was living 1219, but died before 23 Feb 1223/4. In the period, 1220–8, his wife, Ela, sued for dower in several English manors, including Basildon, Berkshire, in right of her first marriage to Robert de Newburgh. She died before 1240.

> Lodge *Peerage of Ireland* 2 (1789): 158–181 (sub Fitz-William). Brydges *Collins' Peerage of England* 4 (1812): 374–400 (sub Fitz-William). Dugdale *Monasticon Anglicanum* 5 (1825): 307 (charter of Roger de Lacy), 487 (charter of William Fitzwilliam). Hunter *South Yorkshire* 1 (1828): 331–341; 2 (1831): 92–94 (identifies wife as Maud). Wainright *Hist. & Top. Intro. ... of the Wapentake of Stafford & Tickhill* (1829): 195–196 (Warenne ped.). Burke *Gen. Hist. of the Dormant, Abeyant, Forfeited & Extinct Peerages* (1866): 52 (sub Bertram). Foster *Peds. of Fams. of Yorkshire* (1874) (Fitzwilliam ped.). Hawley et al. *Vis. of Essex 1552, 1558, 1570, 1612 & 1634* 1 (H.S.P. 13) (1878): 197–199 (1612 Vis.) (Fitzwilliam ped.: "Sr William Fitz William Knight, Lord of Ellmyn sonne and heire. = Ella daugh. and coheire to William Erle Warren."). Harvey et al. *Vis. of Bedfordshire 1566, 1582, 1634 & 1669* (H.S.P. 19) (1884): 27–29 (1566 Vis.) (Fitzwilliam ped.: "Sr Will'm ffitzwill'm of Emley K. sonne and heire. = [Ella — Harl. Ms. 5867] daughter of [William — Harl. Ms. 5867] Erle Warren."). *Pedes Finium Ebor. Regmante Johanne* (Surtees Soc. 94) (1897):15. *Ancestor* 12 (1905): 111–117. Baildon *Baildon & the Baildons* 1 (1912): 350–352. Clay *Extinct & Dormant Peerages* (1913): 76–78 (sub Fitz-william) (no mention of wife Ela). *Early Yorkshire Charters* 3 (1916): 134–135, 336, 8 (1949): 18–21. Salzman *Chartulary of the Priory of St. Peter at Sele* (1923): xix, 34–35. VCH *Berkshire* 3 (1923): 457–463. *C.P.* 5 (1926): 518–520 (sub FitzWilliam); 12(1) (1953): 500, footnote g (sub Surrey). Harvey et al. *Vis. of the North* 3 (Surtees Soc. 144) (1930): 74–76 (Fitzwilliam ped.: "Fitzwilliam = filia Comitis Waren"). Hatton *Book of Seals* (1950): 322–323. *C.R.R.* 9 (1952): 300; 348; 13 (1959): no. 705. Timson *Cartulary of Blyth Priory* 1 (Thoroton Soc. Recs. 27) (1973): xxxv, 132–133, 183–184. Power *Norman Frontier in the 12th & Early 13th Cents.* (2004): 511–512 (Neubourg ped.). Sheffield Archives: Wentworth Woodhouse Muniments, WWM/D/2 (available at www.a2a.org.uk/search/index.asp).

Children of Ela de Warenne, by William Fitz William:

i. **THOMAS FITZ WILLIAM**, Knt. [see next].

ii. **DENISE FITZ WILLIAM**, married **ROBERT D'EIVILLE**, Knt., of Egmanton, Nottinghamshire [see EVERINGHAM 6].

iii. **ELLEN FITZ WILLIAM**, married **JOHN DE LUNGVILERS**, Knt., of Hornby, Lancashire [see HORNBY 9].

9. THOMAS FITZ WILLIAM, Knt., of Sprotborough, Emley, Woodhall (in Darfield), and Barbrough, Yorkshire, and Plumtree, Nottinghamshire, born about 1195–1200 (of age in 1226). He married **AGNES BERTRAM**, daughter of Roger Bertram, Knt., of Mitford, Acton, Felton, Framlington, Glantlees, Overglass, and Swarland, Northumberland, Stainton, co. Durham, etc., by his wife, Agnes [see BERTRAM 8 for her ancestry]. Her maritagium included the manor of Stainton, co. Durham. They had two sons, William, Knt., and Roger, and five daughters, Rametta, Margaret, Agnes, Bertha, and Audrey (wife of Richard Walens). He witnessed a deed about 1250 for his cousin, William son of John Lisours. He was granted free warren in Barnburgh, Emley, and Woodhall, Yorkshire and Plumtree, Nottinghamshire and a weekly and yearly fair at Emley in 1253.

In 1253 he granted to the Abbey and Convent of Roche all his lands and tenements in the town, and the lands of Mar, which he held by grant of Jordan, son of Philip of Mar. In 1260 he granted various lands in Barnburgh, Barnthorpe, Harlington, and elsewhere in Yorkshire to his sister, Denise, widow of Robert d'Eyville, in exchange for the manor of Greetwell, Lincolnshire. At an unknown date, he granted Monk Bretton Priory, Yorkshire 9s. per annum, and one half of a certain measure (windell) of white pease out of lands in Adwick-le-Street, Yorkshire. SIR THOMAS FITZ WILLIAM died before 17 October 1264. In or about 1267 his widow, Agnes, granted the manor of Stainton, co. Durham to her dughter, Agnes.

> Lodge *Peerage of Ireland* 2 (1789): 158–181 (sub Fitz-William). Brydges *Collins' Peerage of England* 4 (1812): 374–400 (sub Fitz-William). Dugdale *Monasticon Anglicanum* 5 (1825): 131. Hunter *South Yorkshire* 1 (1828): 331–341; 2 (1831): 92–94. Hodgson *Hist. of Northumberland* Pt. 2 Vol. II (1832): 122–128 (Bertram ped.). Foster *Peds. of Fams. of Yorkshire* (1874) (Fitzwilliam ped.). Hawley et al. *Vis. of Essex 1552, 1558, 1570, 1612 & 1634* 1 (H.S.P. 13) (1878): 197–199 (1612 Vis.) (Fitzwilliam ped.: "Sr Thomas Fitz Williams Knight, Lo. of Ellmynne and Sprotsburgh, sonne and heire. = Agnis daugh. and heire to Roger Bartram, Lord of Mitfort."). Hodgson *Hist. of Northumberland* 7 (1904): 385–386. *Ancestor* 12 (1905): 111–117. Baildon *Baildon & the Baildons* 1 (1912): 352–353. *C.P.* 2 (1912): 159–162 (sub Bertram); 4 (1916): 130–131 (sub Deiville), 5 (1926): 518–520 (sub FitzWilliam). Clay *Extinct & Dormant Peerages* (1913): 15 (sub Bertram), 76–78 (sub Fitz-william). Foster *Final Concords of Lincoln from the Feet of Fines A.D. 1244–1272* 2 (Lincoln Rec. Soc. 17) (1921): 288. *Arch. Aeliana* 3rd Ser. 20 (1923): 69–178. VCH *Durham* 3 (1928): 344–348. *Yorkshire Arch. Jour.* 35 (1943): 199. Hatton *Book of Seals* (1950): 168–170 (corrects Bertram ped. in Hist. Northumberland, 7: 385–386). Paget *Baronage of England* (1957) 61: 1–4 (sub Bertram). Timson *Cartulary of Blyth Priory* 1 (Thoroton Soc. Recs. 27) (1973): xxxv–xxxvi, 184–185. Sheffield Archives: Wentworth Woodhouse Muniments, WWM/D/4; WWM/D/7 (available at www.a2a.org.uk/search/index.asp).

10. WILLIAM FITZ THOMAS, Knt., of Sprotborough and Emley, Yorkshire, son and heir. He married **AGNES DE GREY**, evidently daughter of Richard de Grey, Knt., of Codnor, Derbyshire, Thurrock, Essex, Aylesford and Hoo, Kent, Governor of the Channel Isles, Seneschal of Gascony and Poitou, Constable of Devises, Dover, and Kenilworth Castles, Warden of the Cinque Ports, by Lucy, daughter and heiress of John du Hommet (or de Humez), of Humberstone, Leicestershire, Sherringham, Norfolk, and Newbottle Northamptonshire. They had two sons, William, Knt., and Edmund. SIR WILLIAM FITZ THOMAS died testate in or before 1294.

> Lodge *Peerage of Ireland* 2 (1789): 158–181 (sub Fitz-William). Brydges *Collins' Peerage of England* 4 (1812): 374–400 (sub Fitz-William) (identifies wife as "Agnes, daughter of Richard Lord Grey, of Codnor"). Baker *Hist. & Antiqs. of Northampton* 1 (1822–30): 658 (Grey ped.). Hunter *South Yorkshire* 1 (1828): 331–341; 2 (1831): 92–94 (identifies wife as "Agnes, dau. of Sir John Metham"). Foster *Peds. of Fams. of Yorkshire* (1874) (Fitzwilliam ped.). Hawley et al. *Vis. of Essex 1552, 1558, 1570, 1612 & 1634* 1 (H.S.P. 13) (1878): 197–199 (1612 Vis.) (Fitzwilliam ped.: "Sr William Fitz Williams Knight, Lo. of Ellmynne and Sprotsburghe, sonne and heire. = Agnis daugh. to Richard Lord Graye of Codnor."). Harvey et al. *Vis. of Bedfordshire 1566, 1582, 1634 & 1669* (H.S.P. 19) (1884): 27–29 (1566 Vis.) (Fitzwilliam ped.: "[Sr Wm] ffitzwill'm of Emley sonne and heire [Lord of Sprotburgh etc. — Harl. Ms. 5867]. = [Agnes] daughter of the lord Grey of Wilton [Codnor — Harl. Ms. 5867]."). Dodsworth *Yorkshire Church Notes* (Yorkshire Arch. Soc. Recs. 34) (1904): 135–137 (North window of Sprotborough church displays arms of Fitzwilliam and Grey). Baildon *Baildon & the Baildons* 1 (1912): 353 (identifies wife as "Agnes, d. of Sir John Metham"). *C.P.* 2 (1912): 159–162 (sub Bertram); 5 (1926): 518–520 (sub FitzWilliam). Clay *Extinct & Dormant Peerages* (1913): 76–78 (sub Fitz-william). Harvey et al. *Vis. of the North* 3 (Surtees Soc. 144) (1930): 74–76 (Fitzwilliam ped.: "Fitzwilliam = filia domini Gray").

11. WILLIAM FITZWILLIAM, Knt., of Sprotborough, Emley, Dalton (in Kirkheaton), and Darrington, Yorkshire, and Plumtree and Hucknall, Nottinghamshire, son and heir, adult before 1294. He married **ISABEL DEINCOURT**, daughter of Edmund Deincourt, Knt., 1st Lord Deincourt, of Blankney, Lincolnshire. They had three sons, William, John, Knt., and Thomas, and five daughters, Margaret, Joan (wife of Brian de Thornhill), Agnes, Isabel, and Maud (nun). He was executor of his father's will in 1294. He served in the retinue of Edmund Deincourt in 1295. In 1296 Ellen widow of Adam Fitz Nicholas, clerk, released to him her right of dower to a tenement and land in Emley held by her late husband. He fought at the Battle of Falkirk 22 July 1298. In 1308 Maud widow of Roger de la Wodehall complained against William Fitzwilliam, his brother, Edmund, and others for trespass at la Woodhall near Wombwell. He was co-heir in 1311 to his cousin, Agnes, daughter and heiress of Roger Bertram, Knt. He presented to the church of Emley, Yorkshire in 1313, 1323, and again in 1338. In 1317 his father-in-law, Edmund Deincourt, enfeoffed him with property in Elmeton, Derbyshire in trust for Edmund for life, with remainders in succession to his grandson, Edmund's widow, Joan Clinton, and then to Edmund's great-grandddaughter, Isabel Deincourt. He was an adherent of Thomas, Earl of Lancaster. In 1321 he was pardoned for actions against Hugh le Despenser, senior and junior, on testimony of his cousin, Richard de Grey, Knt., 2nd Lord Grey of Codnor. In 1325 the manors of Emley and Darrington, Yorkshire, and Sprotborough, Yorkshire were settled on him and his wife, Isabel. He was summoned for military service against the Scots in 1327 by writ directed *Willelmo filio Willelmi*. The same year, he, his son, John, and Brian de Thornhill fled for the death of Richard de Plaiz, Knt., killed at Helaw. SIR WILLIAM FITZWILLIAM was living 4 March 1338/9, but dead before 1342. In 1342–3 John de Wombwell and others came to the manor of Emley belonging to Isabel Fitzwilliam, seized and kept her servants, razed the bridges, and killed the plough-oxen with arrows. His widow, Isabel, died testate shortly before 29 May 1348. Both were buried at Sprotborough, Yorkshire.

Lodge *Peerage of Ireland* 2 (1789): 158–181 (sub Fitz-William). Blore *Hist. & Antiqs. of Rutland* 1(2) (1811): 150–151 (De La Hay/Deincourt ped.). Brydges *Collins' Peerage of England* 4 (1812): 374–400 (sub Fitz-William) (identifies wife as "Maud, daughter of Edward Lord Deyncourt"). Hunter *South Yorkshire* 1 (1828): 331–341; 2 (1831): 92–94 (identifies wife as "Maud, or Isabel Deincourt"). Foster *Peds. of Fams. of Yorkshire* (1874) (Fitzwilliam ped.). Hawley et al. *Vis. of Essex 1552, 1558, 1570, 1612 & 1634* 1 (H.S.P. 13) (1878): 197–199 (1612 Vis.) (Fitzwilliam ped.: "Sr William Fitz Williams Knight, Lord of Ellmynne and Sprotsburghe, sonne and heire. = Mawde daugh. to William, Lord Agincourt."). Harvey et al. *Vis. of Bedfordshire 1566, 1582, 1634 & 1669* (H.S.P. 19) (1884): 27–29 (1566 Vis.) (Fitzwilliam ped.: "Sr William ffitzwill'm of Emley Knight sonne and heire. = [Maude] daughter of [William — Harl. Ms. 5867] Deyncourte."). *Yorkshire Arch. Jour.* 12 (1893): 482. Dodsworth *Yorkshire Church Notes* (Yorkshire Arch. Soc. Recs. 34) (1904): 135–137 (East and north windows of Sprotbrough church both display arms of Fitzwilliam and Deincourt). *List of Inqs. ad Quod Damnum* 1 (PRO Lists and Indexes 17) (1904): 245. *Ancestor* 12 (1905): 111–117. Wrottesley *Peds. from the Plea Rolls* (1905): 415, 428. Baildon *Baildon & the Baildons* 1 (1912): 353–355. *C.P.* 2 (1912): 159–162 (sub Bertram); 4 (1916): 118–120 (sub Deincourt), 5 (1926): 518–520 (sub FitzWilliam). Clay *Extinct & Dormant Peerages* (1913): 76–78 (sub Fitz-william). *Yorkshire Inqs.* 5 (Yorkshire Arch. Soc. Recs. 59) (1918): 144–145 (late inquisition alleges William had no issue by his wife, Isabel Deincourt). *Arch. Aeliana* 3rd Ser. 20 (1923): 69–178 (seal of William Fitz William dated 1324: "Red, round, 26 mm., armorial, lozengy. The shield hangs from a cross and is placed in a traceried panel."). *Yorkshire Arch. Jour.* 27 (1924): 17; 29 (1929): 47, 53. Harvey et al. *Vis. of the North* 3 (Surtees Soc. 144) (1930): 74–76 (Fitzwilliam ped.: "Dominus Willelmus Fitzwilliam = filia domini Deyncourt"). Greenfield *Reg. of William Greenfield Lord Archbishop of York 1306–1315* 2 (Surtees Soc. 149) (1934): 151, 171. Edwards *Cal. Ancient Corr. Concerning Wales* (Board of Celtic Studies, Hist. and Law 2) (1935): 154. Dalton *MSS of St. George's Chapel, Windsor Castle* (1957): 405. *English Hist. Rev.* 74 (1959): 70–89. Foulds *Thurgarton Cartulary* (1994): xcii–xcvii (re: Deincourt family). Roper *Feet of Fines for the County of York 1314–1326* (Yorkshire Arch. Soc. Recs. 158) (2006): 103–104, 106.

Children of William Fitzwilliam, Knt., by Isabel Deincourt:

i. **JOHN FITZWILLIAM**, Knt. [see next].

ii. **AGNES FITZWILLIAM**, married **ADAM DE NEWMARCH**, Knt., of Womersley, Yorkshire [see NEWMARCH 5].

12. JOHN FITZWILLIAM, Knt., of Sprotborough, Dalton (in Kirkheaton), Darrington, and Emley, Yorkshire, 2nd but eldest surviving son. He married **JOAN RERESBY**, daughter of Adam Reresby, Knt., of Thribergh, Yorkshire. They had two sons, John, Knt., and William, and one daughter, Elizabeth (wife of Reynold Mohun). In 1343 John de Verdun, of Brixworth, Northamptonshire, acknowledged receipt from John Fitz William, Knt., of Emley, Yorkshire, of £10 silver, in part payment of £60 which he lent Sir John by statute merchant. He was one of the executors of his mother's will in 1348. The same year he confirmed the grant of his mother, Isabel, of one messuage and land in Dalton, Yorkshire to Robert Loveday, of Dalton. SIR JOHN FITZWILLIAM died of the plague 10 August 1349.

Lodge *Peerage of Ireland* 2 (1789): 158–181 (sub Fitz-William) (identifies wife as "Joanna, daughter of Sir Adam Kelby, of Thrybeg, in the county of York"). Brydges *Collins' Peerage of England* 4 (1812): 374–400 (sub Fitz-William) (identifies wife as "Joan, daughter of Sir Adam Reresby"). Hunter *South Yorkshire* 1 (1828): 331–341; 2 (1831): 92–94. Foster *Peds. of Fams. of Yorkshire* (1874) (Fitzwilliam ped.). Harvey et al. *Vis. of Bedfordshire 1566, 1582, 1634 & 1669* (H.S.P. 19) (1884): 27–29 (1566 Vis.) (Fitzwilliam ped.: omits this generation). Wrottesley *Peds. from the Plea Rolls* (1905): 415, 428. Baildon *Baildon & the Baildons* 1 (1912): 356. Clay *Extinct & Dormant Peerages* (1913): 76–78 (sub Fitz-william). C.P. 5 (1926): 518–520 (sub FitzWilliam). Sheffield Archives: Wentworth Woodhouse Muniments, WWM/D/31 (available at www.a2a.org.uk/search/index.asp).

13. JOHN FITZWILLIAM, Knt., of Sprotborough, Emley, and Wadworth, Yorkshire, son and heir, born about Feb. 1328 (aged 22 years and 6 months on 4 August 1350). He married **ELIZABETH DE CLINTON**,[33] daughter of William de Clinton, Knt., Earl of Huntingdon [see CLINTON 9.ii for her ancestry]. They had five sons, William, Knt., Edmund, Esq., John, Richard, Thomas, and three daughters, Mary (wife of Henry Hastings), _____ (wife of Edmund Pierpont, Knt.), and Elizabeth (wife of Brian Thornhill, Knt.). He obtained the manor of East Haddlesey, Yorkshire in 1374 on the death of Sir Thomas de Stapleton, on condition he found two chantries in the chapel of Haddlesey. In 1378–9 John and his wife, Elizabeth, and their sons, William and Edmund, were taxed as residents of Sprotborough, Yorkshire. In 1382 Peter de Mauley, Knt., complained that John Fitzwilliam, Knt., Richard Lewer and others broke into his closes, houses and parks at Rosington, Egeton, and elsewhere. SIR JOHN FITZWILLIAM was murdered at Howden, Yorkshire shortly before 19 Feb. 1384/5. His widow, Elizabeth, was living in 1400.

Lodge *Peerage of Ireland* 2 (1789): 158–181 (sub Fitz-William) (identifies wife as "Elizabeth daughter of William Lord Clinton, Earl of Huntingdon."). Brydges *Collins' Peerage of England* 4 (1812): 374–400 (sub Fitz-William) (identifies wife as "Elizabeth, daughter of William Lord Clinton"). Hunter *South Yorkshire* 1 (1828): 331–341; 2 (1831): 92–94 (identifies wife as "Elizabetth, d. of a Clinton"). Foster *Peds. of Fams. of Yorkshire* (1874) (Fitzwilliam ped.). Glover & St. George *Vis. of Yorkshire 1584–5, 1612* (1875): 411 (Fitzwilliam ped.: "Johannes Fitzwilliam, miles, duxit Elizabetham filiam Domini de Clynton et Baronis."). Hawley et al. *Vis. of Essex 1552, 1558, 1570, 1612 & 1634* 1 (H.S.P. 13) (1878): 197–199 (1612 Vis.) (Fitzwilliam ped.: "S[r] John Fitz Williams Knight, Lord of Ellmynne and Sprotsburgh, sonne and heire. = Elizabeth daugh. to William, Lord Clynton and Erle of Huntingdon."). Flower *Vis. of Yorkshire 1563–4* (H.S.P. 16) (1881): 122–124 (Fitz William ped.: "Sir William [sic] Fytz William of Sprotboro Lord of Emley. = Lady Elsabeth doughter to William Clynton, Erl of Huntyngdon & Lord Admyrall."). Glover *Vis. of Staffordshire 1583* (Colls. Hist. Staffs. 3(2)) (1883): 76–77 (Fitzwilliam ped.: "John [Fitzwilliam] = Elizabeth, da. of Will'm Clinton, Earle of Huntingdon"). Harvey et al. *Vis. of Bedfordshire 1566, 1582, 1634 & 1669* (H.S.P. 19) (1884): 27–29 (1566 Vis.) (Fitzwilliam ped.: "S[r] John ffitzwill'm of Sprotborough in com. Ebor. K. sonne and heire. = Elizabeth daughter of the lord Clinton Erle of Huntingdon."). *Yorkshire Arch. Jour.* 13 (1895): 51–52. *C.P.R. 1381–1385* (1897): 200. Dodsworth *Yorkshire Church Notes* (Yorkshire Arch. Soc. Recs. 34) (1904): 135–137 (North window of Sprotborough church displays arms of Clinton and Fitzwilliam). Wrottesley *Peds. from the Plea Rolls* (1905): 415, 428.

---

[33] Elizabeth de Clinton's placement as a daughter of William de Clinton, Earl of Huntingdon, is based chiefly on visitation records cited below, five of which identify Elizabeth as the Earl's daughter, including the reliable *Vis. of the North* dated c.1490. It may also be noted that the Clinton arms are found in north window of the church of Sprotborough, Yorkshire (the chief seat of the Fitzwilliam family), which is a good indication of a Fitzwilliams-Clinton marital match. Surviving records clearly indicate that William de Clinton, Earl of Huntingdon, died without legitimate male issue in 1354. As such, Elizabeth might have been Earl William's legitimate child, provided the Earl had settled all of his property on his nephew and heir male, John de Clinton, prior to his death; if so, then Elizabeth could be the issue of an unknown 1st wife of Earl William. The possibility also exists that Elizabeth was Earl William's illegitimate child. As for other supporting evidence for this marriage, it is known that Edmund Deincourt (died c.1317) (1st cousin of Elizabeth de Clinton's father-in-law, John Fitzwilliam) married Joan de Clinton, sister of Earl William de Clinton (see *C.P.* 4 (1916): 119, footnote f). John Fitzwilliam served as a trustee for the settlement of property on Joan (de Clinton) Deincourt in 1317. So, the Fitzwilliam and Clinton families clearly knew each other well. Moreover, sometime prior to 1398, John de Clinton, Knt., served as a trustee for Elizabeth de Clinton's son, William Fitzwilliam, Knt., in the settlement of Fitzwilliam property. Sir John de Clinton was clearly an important person, as on the list of trustees, his name precedes that of William Fitzwilliam's father-in-law, Ralph de Cromwell, Knt. Presumably this John de Clinton was Elizabeth de Clinton's 1st cousin, John de Clinton, Knt., 3rd Lord Clinton, of Maxstoke, Warwickshire (died 1398), who was the heir male to Elizabeth's father, the Earl, in 1354.

List of Inqs. ad Quod Damnum 2 (PRO Lists and Indexes 22) (1906): 618. Baildon *Baildon & the Baildons* 1 (1912): 356–361. Clay *Extinct & Dormant Peerages* (1913): 76–78 (sub Fitz-william). *C.P.* 5 (1926): 518–520 (sub FitzWilliam) (Elizabeth, wife of John Fitzwilliam "said to have been a daughter of William Clinton, Earl of Huntingdon, but this is probably an error"). Harvey et al. *Vis. of the North* 3 (Surtees Soc. 144) (1930): 74–76 (Fitzwilliam ped.: "Dominus Iohannes Fitzwilliam miles = Elizabeth filia domini Clynton comitis Huntingdon"). Fenwick *Poll Taxes of 1377, 1379 & 1381* 3 (Recs. of Social & Economic Hist. n.s. 37) (2005): 326.

Children of John Fitzwilliam, Knt., by Elizabeth de Clinton:

i. **WILLIAM FITZWILLIAM**, Knt. [see next].

ii. **EDMUND FITZWILLIAM**, Esq., of Wadworth, Yorkshire, married **MAUD HOTHAM** [see HOTHAM 12].

14. WILLIAM FITZWILLIAM, Knt., of Sprotborough, Elmley, Baildon, and East Haddlesay, Yorkshire, and Plumtree, Nottinghamshire, son and heir. He married before 1377 **MAUD CROMWELL**, daughter of Ralph de Cromwell, Knt., 1st Lord Cromwell, of Cromwell, Nottinghamshire, by Maud, daughter of John de Bernake, Knt. [see CROMWELL 8 for her ancestry]. They had two sons, John, Knt., and Ralph, clerk, and two daughters, Joan (wife of Henry Sothill, Knt.) and Elizabeth (wife of Robert Rockley, Knt.). SIR WILLIAM FITZWILLIAM died 8 April 1398. In 1413 the Master of Saint Leonard's Hospital, York sued his widow, Maud, for not paying the thrave of corn due to the Hospital. She was living in 1415.

Lodge *Peerage of Ireland* 2 (1789): 158–181 (sub Fitz-William). *Topographer* 1 (1789): 327–336. Throsby *Thoroton's Hist. of Nottinghamshire* 3 (1790): 169–171. Blomefield *Essay towards a Top. Hist. of Norfolk* 5 (1806): 23–33. Banks *Dormant & Extinct Baronage of England* 2 (1808): 120–124 (sub Cromwell). Brydges *Collins' Peerage of England* 4 (1812): 374–400 (sub Fitz-William). Hunter *South Yorkshire* 1 (1828): 331–341; 2 (1831): 92–94. *Coll. Top. et Gen.* 7 (1841): 142–144 (sub Tateshale). Foster *Peds. of Fams. of Yorkshire* (1874) (Fitzwilliam ped.). Hawley et al. *Vis. of Essex 1552, 1558, 1570, 1612 & 1634* 1 (H.S.P. 13) (1878): 197–199 (1612 Vis.) (Fitzwilliam ped.: "Sr Will'm Fitz Williams Knight, Lord of Ellmyn and Sprotsburghe, sonne and heire. = Mawde dau. and coheire to Raulfe Cromwell, Lo. of Tattersall."). Flower *Vis. of Yorkshire 1563–4* (H.S.P. 16) (1881): 122–124 (Fitz William ped.: "William Fytz William of Sprotboro Knight Lord of Emley son & heyr to Sir John. = Mawde doughter & on of theyres of Sir Raff Cromwell Lord of Tatesall."), 176–177 (Knevet ped.: "Mawde [Cromwell] = Sir William Fitzwilliam of Sprotboroo."). Harvey et al. *Vis. of Bedfordshire 1566, 1582, 1634 & 1669* (H.S.P. 19) (1884): 27–29 (1566 Vis.) (Fitzwilliam ped.: "Sr Will'm ffitzwill'm of Sprotborough K. sonne and heire. = Mawde daughter of Rauf Cromwell lorde of Tattersall."). Phillimore *Abs. of IPMs Rel. Nottinghamshire* 1 (Thoroton Soc. Rec. Ser. 3) (1905): vii, 18–20. Baildon *Baildon & the Baildons* 1 (1912): 361–363. Clay *Extinct & Dormant Peerages* (1913): 76–78 (sub Fitz-william). Wrottesley *Peds. from the Plea Rolls* (1905): 415, 428. *C.P.* 5 (1926): 518–520 (sub FitzWilliam). Harvey et al. *Vis. of the North* 3 (Surtees Soc. 144) (1930): 74–76 (Fitzwilliam ped.: "Dominus Willelmus Fitzwilliam = Domina Matildis filia domini Radulphi Cromwell domini de Tatersall"), 152–156 [Daubeny ped.: "Matildis [Cromwell] nupta domino Willelmo Fitzwilliam de Sprotborough"]. Walker *Yorkshire Peds.* 2 (H.S.P. 95) (1943): 341–345 (Soothill ped.). Train *Abs. of IPMs Rel. Nottinghamshire* 2 (Thoroton Soc. Recs. 12) (1952): 134. *Cal. IPM* 17 (1988): 375–376. Roskell *House of Commons 1386–1421* 4 (1992): 223 (biog. of Robert Rockley). Fenwick *Poll Taxes of 1377, 1379 & 1381* 3 (Recs. of Social & Economic Hist. n.s. 37) (2005): 326.

15. JOHN FITZWILLIAM, Knt., of Sprotborough, Baildon, Emley, and West Haddlesey (in Birkin), Yorkshire, and Plumtree, Nottinghamshire, son and heir, born 25 July 1377. He married before 1397 **ELEANOR GREENE**, daughter of Henry Greene, Knt., of Drayton (in Lowick), Northamptonshire, Warminster, Wiltshire, etc., Knight of the Shire variously for Huntingdonshire, Northamptonshire and Wiltshire, by Maud, daughter and heiress of Thomas Mauduit. They had six sons, John, Knt., Nicholas, Ralph, Robert, William, and John, Esq. (2nd of name), and two daughters, Maud (wife of John Bosville) and Joan. He also had an illegitimate son, Thomas, clerk. He presented to the chapel of Chapel Haddlesey, Yorkshire in 1399. SIR JOHN FITZWILLIAM died 5 July 1417. His widow, Eleanor, was living 1 May 1421, but died before 21 Dec. 1422.

Lodge *Peerage of Ireland* 2 (1789): 158–181 (sub Fitz-William). Throsby *Thoroton's Hist. of Nottinghamshire* 3 (1790): 169–171. Bridges *Hist. & Antiqs. of Northamptonshire* 2 (1791): 249, 251 (Greene ped.: "Eleanor Greene [married] to John Fitz-Williams of Sprotsburgh"), 516–519. Brydges *Collins' Peerage of England* 4 (1812): 374–400 (sub Fitz-William). Hunter *South Yorkshire* 1 (1828): 331–341; 2 (1831): 92–94. Lipscomb *Hist. & Antiqs. of Buckingham* 1 (1847): 29 (Greene ped.). Foster *Peds. of Fams. of Yorkshire* (1874) (Fitzwilliam ped.). Hawley et al. *Vis. of Essex 1552, 1558, 1570, 1612 & 1634* 1 (H.S.P. 13) (1878): 197–199 (1612 Vis.) (Fitzwilliam ped.: "Sr John Fitz Williams Knight, Lord of

Ellmyn and Sprotsburgh, sonne and heire. = Ellenor daugh. to Sr Henry Greene of Drayton, K^t a^o 1412."). Flower *Vis. of Yorkshire 1563–4* (H.S.P. 16) (1881): 122–124 (Fitz William ped.: "Sir John Fytz William of Sprotborowe *lived 6 Hen. V.* maryed = Elenor daughter to Sir Henry Grene of Dreton in Northamptonshire."). Harvey et al. *Vis. of Bedfordshire 1566, 1582, 1634 & 1669* (H.S.P. 19) (1884): 27–29 (1566 Vis.) (Fitzwilliam ped.: "Sr John ffitzwill'm of Sprotborough Knight sonne and heire. = Eleanor daughter of Sir Henry Grene Knight."). *Greene Fam. in England & America* (1901): Greene ped. I following 147. Phillimore *Abs. of IPMs Rel. Nottinghamshire* 1 (Thoroton Soc. Rec. Ser. 3) (1905): vii, 18–20. Wrottesley *Peds. from the Plea Rolls* (1905): 415, 428. Baildon *Baildon & the Baildons* 1 (1912): 364–366. Clay *Extinct & Dormant Peerages* (1913): 76–78 (sub Fitz-william). *Yorkshire Inqs.* 5 (Yorkshire Arch. Soc. Recs. 59) (1918): 144–145. *C.P.* 5 (1926): 518–520 (sub FitzWilliam). Harvey et al. *Vis. of the North* 3 (Surtees Soc. 144) (1930): 76–78 (Fitzwilliam ped.: "Dominus Iohannes Fitzwilliam miles = Aleonora filia domini Henrici Greene militis"). Train *Abs. of IPMs Rel. Nottinghamshire* 2 (Thoroton Soc. Recs. 12) (1952): 176. VCH *Wiltshire* 8 (1965): 96–103. Swanson *Cal. Reg. of Richard Scrope Archbishop of York 1398–1405* 1 (Borthwick Texts & Cals. 8) (1981): 19. *Cal. IPM* 17 (1988): 375–376.

Children of John Fitzwilliam, Knt., by Eleanor Greene:

i. **JOHN FITZWILLIAM**, Knt., of Sprotborough, Yorkshire, married **MARGARET CLARELL** [see SALTONSTALL 16; CLARELL 11.iii].

ii. **JOHN FITZWILLIAM**, Esq. (2nd of name) [see next].

16. JOHN FITZWILLIAM, Esq., 6th son, of Green's Norton, Northamptonshire. He married **HELEN** (or **ELLEN**) **VILLIERS**, daughter of William Villiers, Esq., of Brooksby, Leicestershire, by Joan, daughter of John Bellers, of Eye Kettleby and Sysonby, Leicestershire [see BERTRAM 16 for her ancestry]. They had five sons, John [Citizen and draper of London], William, Knt., Bartholomew [Citizen of London], Richard [Citizen and merchant taylor of London], and Thomas, and two daughters, Mary (wife of Thomas Waddington and Richard Ogle) and Katherine (wife of Thomas Rolleston and Richard Francis).

Lodge *Peerage of Ireland* 2 (1789): 158–181 (sub Fitz-William). Bridges *Hist. & Antiqs. of Northamptonshire* 2 (1791): 516–519. Nichols *Hist. & Antiqs. of Leicestershire* 3(1) (1800): 197–198 (Villiers ped.: "Helen [Villiers], married to John Fitzwilliam, of Greens Norton, esq."). Brydges *Collins' Peerage of England* 3 (1812): 762–796 (sub Villiers, Earl of Jersey); 4 (1812): 374–400 (sub Fitz-William). Hunter *South Yorkshire* 2 (1831): 92–94. Foster *Peds. of Fams. of Yorkshire* (1874) (Fitzwilliam ped.). Hawley et al. *Vis. of Essex 1552, 1558, 1570, 1612 & 1634* 1 (H.S.P. 13) (1878): 197–199 (1612 Vis.) (Fitzwilliam ped.: "John Fitz Williams of Greenes norton 6th sonne. = Hellen dau. to William Villers of Brokesby in Lestershyr."). Flower *Vis. of Yorkshire 1563–4* (H.S.P. 16) (1881): 124–127 (Fitz William ped.: "John Fytz William, of Grensnorton, 4 son to Sir John *sixth son*. = Ellyn doughter of William Vyllers, of Brokysby."). *Genealogist* 6 (1882): 150 (1592 Vis. Lincolnshire) (Fitzwilliam ped.: "John Fitz Williams of Grenes Norton in Northton, 6 son of Sir John by Elenor his wife, da. to Scene [recte Grene] of Drayton = Helen, da. to William Villers of Brookesbie"). Harvey et al. *Vis. of Bedfordshire 1566, 1582, 1634 & 1669* (H.S.P. 19) (1884): 27–29 (1566 Vis.) (Fitzwilliam ped.: "John ffitzwill'm of Gaynspark hall in com. Essex and of Melton in com. Northampt. ar. = Helene daughter of Will'm Villers of Brokisby ar."). Metcalfe *Vis. of Northamptonshire 1564 & 1618–9* (1887): 88–89 (1618–19 Vis.) (Fitzwilliam ped.: "John Fitzwilliam of Gainsparkhall in Essex, and of Milton, co. North'ton = Ellen, da. of William Villers of Brokesby, co. Leicester."). Baildon *Baildon & the Baildons* 1 (1912): 365–366. *C.P.* 5 (1926): 518–520 (sub FitzWilliam) ("…I have never found any reference to him in any document…. This, of course, does not prove his non-existence."). *Vis. of the North* 3 (Surtees Soc. 144) (1930): 76–78 (Fitzwilliam ped.: "Iohannes Fitzwilliam iunior"). Chambers *Sir Henry Lee; An Elizabethan Portrait* (1936): 256.

Children of John Fitzwilliam, by Helen Villiers:

i. **WILLIAM FITZWILLIAM**, Knt. [see next].

ii. **MARY FITZWILLIAM**, married (1st) **THOMAS WADDINGTON**. They had issue. She married (2nd) **RICHARD OGLE**, of Pinchbeck, Lincolnshire. They had one son, Richard, Esq., and one daughter, Elizabeth (wife of _____ Serjeant). RICHARD OGLE was living in 1504. *Coll. Top. et Gen.* 6 (1840): 194–196 (Ogle ped.). *Genealogist* 4 (1880): 261 (Vis. Lincolnshire) (Ogle ped.: "Richard Ogle, descended of a younger house of the Baron Ogle. = Marie, sister to Sir William Fitz Williams of Moulton, Kt."). Maddison *Lincolnshire Peds.* 2 (H.S.P. 51) (1903): 730–735 (Ogle ped.: "Richard Ogle of Pinchbeck, living 1504. = Mary, dau. of John Fitzwiilliam of Milton, co. Northampton, widow of Thomas Waddington.").

17. WILLIAM FITZWILLIAM, Knt., of Gaynes Park (in Theydon Garnon), Essex, and Milton (in Castor) and Marholm, Northamptonshire, Warden and Master of the Merchant Taylors' Company, London, Mayor of the Staple of Calais in London, Alderman of London, Sheriff of London, treasurer to Cardinal Wolsey. He married (1st) **ANNE HAWES**, daughter of John Hawes, Knt., Alderman of London. They had two sons, William, Knt., and Richard, Esq., and two daughters, Anne and Elizabeth (wife of Thomas Brudenell, Knt.). He was a legatee in the 1485 will of his brother, John Fitzwilliam, Citizen and draper of London, who bequeathed him 20 marks. He married (2nd) **MILDRED SACKVILLE**, daughter of Richard Sackville, Esq., of Withyham, Sussex, by Isabel, daughter of John Digges, Esq. They had three sons, Christopher, Francis, and Thomas, Esq., and two daughters, Eleanor (wife of Nicholas Strange, Knt.) and Mary (wife of John Shelley, Esq.). He attended the king at the Field of the Cloth of Gold in 1520. He was a legatee in the 1529 will of his cousin, Maud Greene, widow of Thomas Parr, Knt., they being related through Sir William's grandmother, Eleanor (Greene) Fitzwilliam. He married (3rd) about 1529 **JANE** (or **JOAN**) **ORMOND**, widow successively of Thomas Dinham, Knt. (will proved 13 Feb. 1519/20), of Ashridge, Hertfordshire and Eythorpe (in Waddesdon), Buckinghamshire, and Edward Greville, Knt. (died 22 June 1528) [see GREVILLE 11], of Milcote-on-Avon, Warwickshire, and daughter and co-heiress of John Ormond, Esq., of Alfreton, Derbyshire, by Joan, daughter of William Chaworth, Knt. They had no issue. He rebuilt the greater part of the church of St. Andrew Undershaft in London and the chancel of Marholm church in Northamptonshire. By deed dated 1533, he settled 1,200 marks on the Merchants' Taylor Company for religious uses. In 1534 he acquired the reversion of the manor of Kempston, Bedfordshire from Elizabeth, widow of Reginald Grey. SIR WILLIAM FITZWILLIAM died at St. Thomas the Apostle, London 9 August 1534, and was buried at Marholm, Northamptonshire. He left a will dated 28 May 1534, proved 5 Sept. 1534 (P.C.C. 17 and 33 Hogen). His widow, Jane, left a will dated 18 Jan. 1540, codicil dated 26 Jan. 1539/40, proved 23 October 1542 (P.C.C. 10 Spert), requesting burial in the church of St. Thomas the Apostle, London.

Morant *Hist. & Antiqs. of Essex* 1 (1768): 160. Lodge *Peerage of Ireland* 2 (1789): 158–181 (sub Fitz-William). Bridges *Hist. & Antiqs. of Northamptonshire* 2 (1791): 516–519. Brydges *Collins' Peerage of England* 4 (1812): 374–400 (sub Fitz-William). Lysons & Lysons *Magna Britannia* 5 (1817): 217–228. Nicolas *Testamenta Vetusta* 2 (1826): 665–669 (will of William Fitz William, Knt.). Hunter *South Yorkshire* 2 (1831): 92–94. Nichols *Wills from Doctors' Commons* (Camden Soc. 83) (1863): 9–20 (will of Dame Maud Parr [née Greene], widow, dated 20 May 1529, proved 14 Dec. 1531: "….and if it that chaunce happen that all my said childerne dye, then my cousin Sir William FitzWilliam knight to have oon hundrith poundes…"). Foster *Peds. of Fams. of Yorkshire* (1874) (Fitzwilliam ped.). Hawley et al. *Vis. of Essex 1552, 1558, 1570, 1612 & 1634* 1 (H.S.P. 13) (1878): 197–199 (1612 Vis.) (Fitzwilliam ped.: "Sr William Fitz Williams of Gaines parke in com. Essex, Knight, sonne and heire, [1] = Ann daugh. to John Hawes first wyfe, [2] = Mildred daugh. to Richard Sackvile of Buckhurste 2d wyfe."). Flower *Vis. of Yorkshire 1563–4* (H.S.P. 16) (1881): 124–127 (Fitz William ped.: "Sir William Fytz William of Geyns park Hall, in Essex, and of Mylton in the countye of Northampton, [1] = Ann doughter to John Hawes of London, Knight, first wyff to Sir William, = 2nd Myldred doughter to Rychard Sackevyle of Buckhurst 2 wyff to Sir William, maryed 3rd Jane doughter of John Ormond, and on of theyrs of Chaworth."). *Genealogist* 6 (1882): 150 (1592 Vis. Lincolnshire) (Fitzwilliam ped.). Harvey et al. *Vis. of Bedfordshire 1566, 1582, 1634 & 1669* (H.S.P. 19) (1884): 27–29 (1566 Vis.) (Fitzwilliam ped.: "Sr Will'm ffitzwill'm of Gaynspark hall and Melton in com. Northampt. Knight sonne and heire. [1] = Anne daughter of John Hawes of London ar. first wyfe, [2] = Mildred daughter of Richard Sackville of Witham in com. Sussex esquire second wife."). Metcalfe *Vis. of Northamptonshire 1564 & 1618–9* (1887): 88–89 (1618–19 Vis.) (Fitzwilliam ped.: "Sir William Fitzwilliam of Gainsparkhall and of Milton, [1] = Anne, da. of Sir James Hawes, Kt., 1 ux., [2] = Mildred, da. of Richard Sackville of Buckhurst, 2 ux."). *Herts Gen. & Antiq.* 3 (1899): 258–259. *Trans. Thoroton Soc.* 5 (1901): Chaworth ped. at end. *North Country Wills* 1 (Surtees Soc. 116) (1908): 135–138. VCH *Hertford* 2 (1908): 314–317. *C.P.* 5 (1926): 518–520 (sub FitzWilliam). VCH *Buckingham* 4 (1927): 110–111. Phillips *Hist. of the Sackville Fam.* 1 (1930): 108–115. VCH *Northampton* 4 (1937): 33, 42. Finch *Five Northamptonshire Fams.* (Northamptonshire Rec. Soc. 19) (1956): 100–102, 188–189 [The author expresses doubts as to the accuracy of the commonly accepted Fitzwilliam pedigree, citing long generations between John Fitzwilliam (died 1417) and his alleged grandson, Sir William Fitzwilliam (died 1534). However, Finch was evidently unaware of the existence of evidence which proves kinship between Sir William Fitzwilliam and his cousin, Maud (Greene) Parr, they being related through Sir William's grandmother, Eleanor

Greene, wife of John Fitzwilliam (died 1417). In support of the Fitzwilliam descent, Finch does note that c.1565 members of Sir William's family aided their kinsman, Hugh Fitzwilliam, in his attempt to recover Fitzwilliam family lands. Hugh Fitzwilliam was then heir male of John Fitzwilliam (died 1417), he being descended from John's 3rd son, Ralph, whereas Sir William and his line descended from John, 6th son of the same John (died 1417)], chart foll. 246. Registered will of John Fitzwilliam, Citizen and draper of London, proved 9 Nov. 1485, Comm. Court of London, Vol. 7, pg. 33 [FHL Microfilm 1068473]. Registered will of Thomas Dynham, Knt., proved 13 Feb. 1519/20, P.C.C. 25 Ayloffe [FHL Microfilm 91909]. Registered will of Edward Greville, Knt., proved 24 Jan. 1528/9, P.C.C. 1 Jankyn [FHL Microfilm 91913]. National Archives, C 1/601/32 (Chancery Proc. dated 1529–32 — Margaret, executrix and late the wife of William Arches v. William FitzWilliam, Knt., Johanne, his wife, and John Denham of Ethorpe, esq.: Detention of deeds whereby Edward Grevyll, Knt., and Thomas Redmayne secured the price of land at Cranwell [in Waddesdon] and Quainton, Buckinghamshire, bought of the testator); C 1/795/39–40 (Chancery Proc. dated 1532-8 — Jane, late the wife of William Fytzwilliam, Knt., formerly of Edward Grevyll, Knt., and before that of Thomas Dynham, Knt.: Petitions to examine Anthony Babyngton, Knt., and others as to title to the manor of Ethorpe in Waddesdon, Buckinghamshire) (available at www.catalogue.nationalarchives.gov.uk/search.asp).

Children of William Fitzwilliam, Knt., by Anne Hawes:

i. **RICHARD FITZWILLIAM**, Esq. [see next].

ii. **ANNE FITZWILLIAM**, married **ANTHONY COOKE**, K.B., of Gidea Hall (in Havering), Essex [see SUDELEY 19].

18. RICHARD FITZWILLIAM, Esq., of Kilburn, Middlesex, Champneys (in Wigginton), Hertfordshire, Ringstead, Northamptonshire, etc., 2nd son by his father's 1st marriage. He married about 16 Nov. 1528 (date of marriage settlement) **ELIZABETH KNYVET**, daughter of Charles Knyvet, Esq., of Hamerton, Huntingdonshire, Leigh, Kent, etc., by his 1st unidentified wife [see GURDON 16.ii for her ancestry]. They had one son, John, and two daughters, Margaret and Rachel. She was a legatee in the 1528 will of her uncle, Edward Knyvet, Knt., who bequeathed her 100 marks towards her marriage. He was a legatee in the 1534 will of his father, who bequeathed him the remainder of his lease and the reversion in fee of the manor of Champneys (in Wigginton), Hertfordshire, together with his manor of Cotes, Ringstead, and Raunds, Northamptonshire. In the period, 1534–8, he sued Robert Halley in Chancery regarding the manor of Champnes and other lands in Tring, Hertfordshire. In 1536 he conveyed the manor of Champneys (in Wigginton), Hertfordshire to Thomas, Earl of Norfolk, evidently for the purposes of a settlement. In the period, 1538–44, he sued Robert Halley in Chancery regarding the detention of deeds relating to the manors of Champneys (in Wigginton) and Forsters, formerly of John Cowper of Wigginton, deceased. In the period, 1538–44, Robert, son and heir of Robert Halley (or Hawley) sued him in Chancery regarding the manor of Champneys and land in Tring, Hertfordshire, late of John Cowper, deceased, great-uncle of the said Robert the elder, which Robert recovered them in this court against Thomas Cheyney, son-in-law of the said Cowper. In 1543 he and his wife, Elizabeth, conveyed the reversionary right to lands in Wigginton and Tring, Hertfordshire to Robert Dormer, Knt. In 1544 he and his wife, Elizabeth, conveyed a messuage and lands in Theydon Bois and Lambourne, Essex to Robert Archer and John Pyckeman. In the period, 1544–51, Robert, nephew and heir of Robert Halley sued him in Chancery regarding the manor of Champneys (in Wigginton) and advowson of the chapel of Wigginton, Hertfordshire. In the period, 1544–51, he sued John Felde, yeoman, in Chancery regarding conditions of lease of the manors of Champneys and Fosters in Wigginton in the parish of Tring (sic), Hertfordshire, of the demise of Robert Dormer, knight. In 1545 he and his wife, Elizabeth, conveyed lands in Lambourne, Essex to Robert Barefote, Esq. The same year he and his wife, Elizabeth, conveyed various lands in Lambourne, Stapleford, and Navestock, Essex to Anthony Brown, Gent. In 1546 he and his wife, Elizabeth, conveyed the manor of Champneys (in Wigginton), Hertfordshire, together with three messuages, land, and rent in Tring, Wigginton, and Northchurch, Hertfordshire to Thomas Palmer, of Sarratt. The same year he and his wife, Elizabeth, conveyed lands in Stapleford Abbots, Essex to Richard Gybbes.

RICHARD FITZWILLIAM, Esq., died sometime before 1559. His widow, Elizabeth, was living 7 March 1559, when her son, John Fitzwilliam, agreed to pay her an annuity of £10 for her interest in the manors of Ringstead, Cotes, Myll Cotes, etc., Northamptonshire.

Lodge & Archdall *Peerage of Ireland* 2 (1789): 158–181 (sub Fitz-William) ("Richard [Fitz-William], of Ringsted in the county of Northampton, who married Elizabeth, daughter of Charles Knevit, Esq., by whom he had a daughter Rachael, married to Richard, son of Robert Hudleston, of Pinchleet, Esq; and a son John, who died in 1568, leaving by Margaret, daughter of Richard Hudleston, Robert his heir, John, William, Thomas, Margaret, and Grace."). Brydges *Collins' Peerage of England* 4 (1812): 374–400 (sub Fitz-William) ("Richard [Fitz-William], who was seated at Ringstede, in the county of Northampton, and by his wife, _____ daughter of _____, had a son, John Fitz-William, who died without issue, A.D. 1568."). Nicolas *Testamenta Vetusta* 2 (1826): 635–640 (will of Edward Knyvet, Knt.). Foster *Peds. of Fams. of Yorkshire* (1874) (Fitzwilliam pedigree). Glover & St. George *Vis. of Yorkshire 1584–5, 1612* (1875): 516 (Estouteville pedigree). Hawley et al. *Vis. of Essex 1552, 1558, 1570, 1612 & 1634* 1 (H.S.P. 13) (1878): 197–199 (1612 Vis.) (Fitzwilliam pedigree: "Richard Fitz Will'm of Ringsted 2d sonne, mar. Elizabeth, dau. to Charles Knyvett."). Flower *Vis. of Yorkshire 1563–4* (H.S.P. 16) (1881): 124–127 (Fitz William pedigree: "Rychard Fitzwilliam 2 son by his first wyf."). Harvey et al. *Vis. of Bedfordshire 1566, 1582, 1634 & 1669* (H.S.P. 19) (1884): 27–29 (1566 Vis.) (Fitzwilliam pedigree: "Richard [Fitzwilliam] second sonne."). Metcalfe *Vis. of Northamptonshire 1564 & 1618–9* (1887): 88–89 (1618–19 Vis.) (Fitzwilliam pedigree: "Richard [Fitzwilliam]."). *Herts Gen. & Antiq.* 1 (1895): 155, 161. VCH *Hertford* 2 (1908): 314–317. *List of Early Chancery Procs.* 7 (PRO Lists and Indexes 50) (1926): 361; 8 (PRO Lists and Indexes 51) (1929): 91, 124; 9 (PRO Lists and Indexes 54) (1933): 47, 59. VCH *Northampton* 4 (1937): 33, 42. Finch *Five Northamptonshire Fams.* (Northamptonshire Rec. Soc. 19) (1956): 100–102, chart foll. 246. Reaney & Fitch *Feet of Fines for Essex* 4 (1964): 267, 283, 285, 296. *Blackmansbury* 9 (1972): 4–7. Hertfordshire Archives & Local Studies: Artificial coll. of title deeds & estate papers including court rolls of several Hertfordshire manors, together with title deeds of the Hertfordshire estate of Lord Winterton of Shillinglee Park, West Sussex, DE/Z120/44841 (Covenants for the bargain and sale dated 12 April 1546 by Richard Fitzwilliam of Kilburn, Middlesex, Gnt., and Elizabeth his wife, to Thomas Palmer of Sarratt, Gnt., of the manors of Champneys and Fosters and all their lands in Herts and Bucks which Sir William Fitzwilliam, Knt., bought of Sir Robert Dormer, Knt.; covenant that Thomas Palmer shall save harmless the said Richard and Elizabeth for an obligation whereby they are bound to Sir Robert Dormer in connexion with an indenture between Richard Fitzwilliam and Thomas Garlyk and others of 12th Feb 1541) (available at www.a2a.org.uk/search/index.asp).

Children of Richard Fitzwilliam, Esq., by Elizabeth Knyvet:

i. **JOHN FITZWILLIAM**, of Ringstead, Northamptonshire, son and heir, born say 1530. He married **MARGARET HUDDLESTON**, daughter of Richard Huddleston. They had four sons, Robert, John, William, and Thomas, and two daughters, Margaret and Grace. In 1559 he and his wife, Bridget (a second wife?), conveyed to John Pickering the manors of Ringstead, Cotes alias Cotton Chamberlyn, Myll Cotes, West Cotes, Mallard Cotes, and Cotes Bydon, Northamptonshire. He may possibly be the John Fitzwilliam of London who was a legatee in the 1561 will of Beatrix Cooke, widow of Richard Ogle, Esq., of Pinchbeck, Lincolnshire. In 1564 as "John Fitzwilliam son and heyre to Richard Fytzwilliam, of Ringsted," he signed a Fitzwilliam family pedigree created by his kinsman, Hugh Fitzwilliam, of Sprotborough, Northamptonshire. JOHN FITZWILLIAM died in 1568. Lodge *Peerage of Ireland* 2 (1789): 158–181 (sub Fitz-William) ("Richard Fitz-William, of Ringsted in the county of Northampton, who married Elizabeth, daughter of Charles Knevit, Esq., by whom he had a daughter Rachael, married to Richard, son of Robert Hudleston, of Pinchleet, Esq; and a son John, who died in 1568, leaving by Margaret, daughter of Richard Hudleston, Robert his heir, John, William, Thomas, Margaret, and Grace."). Brydges *Collins' Peerage of England* 4 (1812): 374–400 (sub Fitz-William) ("Richard [Fitz-William], who was seated at Ringstede, in the county of Northampton, and by his wife, _____ daughter of _____, had a son, John Fitz-William, who died without issue, A.D. 1568."). VCH *Northampton* 4 (1937): 33, 42. Registered will of Beatrix Ogle, widow, of Pinchbeck, Lincolnshire proved 18 August 1561, Cons. Court of Lincoln, Year: 1561, pp. 21–22 [FHL Microfilm 198822].

Child of John Fitzwilliam, by Margaret Huddleston:

a. **ROBERT FITZWILLIAM**, of Humberstone, Leicestershire and Pinchbeck, Lincolnshire, son and heir, born say 1550. He married at Humberstone, Leicestershire 7 August 1576 **JOAN PRESGRAVE**. They had three sons, William, Richard, and John, and two daughters, _____ and Mary. He witnessed the 1585 will of his aunt, Rachel Fitzwilliam's husband, Richard Huddleston, Esq., of Pinchbeck, Lincolnshire. Registered will of Richard Huddleston, Esq., of Pinchbeck, Lincolnshire proved 24 August 1585, Cons. Court of Lincoln, Year: 1585, vol. 2, pp. 45–46 [FHL Microfilm 198842]. Parish Regs. of Humberstone, Leicestershire [FHL Microfilm 596711].

ii. **MARGARET FITZWILLIAM** [see next].

iii. **RACHEL FITZWILLIAM**, married (1st) **RICHARD HUDDLESTON**, Esq., of Pinchbeck, Lincolnshire, son of Robert Huddleston, Gent., of Pinchbeck, Lincolnshire, by Alice, daughter of _____ Winter, of Swineshead, Lincolnshire. He was born about 1546 (aged 18 in 1564). They had one daughter, Jane. He was a legatee in the 1564 will of his father. RICHARD HUDDLESTON, Esq., was buried at Pinchbeck, Lincolnshire 10 August 1585. He left a will dated 11 August 1585, proved 24 August 1585. His widow, Rachel, married (2nd) _____ **HALL**, of Pinchbeck, Lincolnshire. She was a legatee in the 1597 will of her nephew, John Robertson, Gent., of London, who referred to her as "Aunte Hall." His widow, Rachel, married (3rd) at Pinchbeck, Lincolnshire 1 April 1602 **JOHN REPPES**, Gent., of Tyling, Norfolk, and afterwards of Pinchbeck, Lincolnshire. She was granted administration on the estate of her late son-in-law, William Gannock, 4 June 1603. Administration on the estate of John Reppes, Gent., was granted to his widow, Rachel, 27 April 1605. She married (4th) at Pinchbeck, Lincolnshire 12 April 1608 **RICHARD CURE**, of St. Helen's without Temple Bar, London, upholsterer. Presumably he is the Richard Cure of St. Gregory by St. Paul, London who occurs on the 1582 Subsidy Roll of London. Rachel Cure, widow, was buried at Pinchbeck, Lincolnshire 26 June 1617. Lodge *Peerage of Ireland* 2 (1789): 158–181 (sub Fitz-William). *Genealogist* 4 (1880): 181 (Vis. Lincolnshire) (Huddleston pedigree: "Richard Huddleston. = Rachel da. to Richard Fitz Williams."). Maddison *Lincolnshire Peds.* 2 (H.S.P. 51) (1903): 383 (Gannock pedigree), 519–520 (Huddleston pedigree). Lang *Two Tudor Subsidy Assessment Rolls for the City of London: 1541 & 1582* (London Rec. Soc. 29) (1993): 185. Registered will of Robert Huddleston, Gent., of Pinchbeck, Lincolnshire proved 23 Nov. 1564, Cons. Court of Lincoln, Year: 1564, pp. 65–66 [FHL Microfilm 198825]. Registered will of Richard Huddleston, Esq., of Pinchbeck, Lincolnshire proved 24 August 1585, Cons. Court of Lincoln, Year: 1585, vol. 2, pp. 45–46 [FHL Microfilm 198842]. Registered will of John Robertson, Gent., of London proved 29 April 1597, P.C.C. 26 Cobham [FHL Microfilm 91998]. Bishop's Transcripts of Boston, Lincolnshire [FHL Microfilm 504734].

Child of Rachel Fitzwilliam, by Richard Huddleston, Esq.:

a. **JANE HUDDLESTON**, daughter and heiress, baptized at Pinchbeck, Lincolnshire 23 Dec. 1571. She was a legatee in the 1585 will of her father. She married at Boston, Lincolnshire 21 October 1585 **WILLIAM GANNOCK**, Gent., of Boston, Lincolnshire, Mayor of Boston, Lincolnshire, 1594, son of William Gannock [Sr.], of Boston, Lincolnshire, Merchant of the Staple of Calais, Mayor of Boston, Lincolnshire, 1578, by his wife, Ursula. They had five sons, William, Robert, John, Reginald, and Posthumous, and one daughter, Rachel (wife of William Greene). His wife, Jane, was a legatee in the 1597 will of her cousin, John Robertson, Gent., of London. WILLIAM GANNOCK, Gent., was buried at Boston, Lincolnshire 11 August 1602. Administration on the estate of William Gannock was granted to his widow, Jane, 11 August 1602. Jane married (2nd) **REGINALD HALL**, of Boston, Lincolnshire. She was buried at Boston, Lincolnshire 22 March 1602/3. Following her death, administration on the estate of her 1st husband, William Gannock, was re-granted 29 March 1603 to Reginald Hall, and 4 June 1603 to her mother, Rachel Cure. Thompson *Hist. & Antiqs. of Boston* (1856): 454. *Genealogist* 4 (1880): 181 (Vis. Lincolnshire) (Huddleston pedigree: "Jane [Huddleston], wife to ... Gannoke of Boston."). Maddison *Lincolnshire Peds.* 2 (H.S.P. 51) (1903): 383 (Gannock pedigree), 519–520 (Huddleston pedigree). Registered will of Richard Huddleston, Esq., of Pinchbeck, Lincolnshire proved 24 Aug. 1585, Cons. Court of Lincoln, Year: 1585, vol. 2, pp. 45–46 [FHL Microfilm 198842]. Registered will of John Robertson, Gent., of London proved 29 April 1597, P.C.C. 26 Cobham [FHL Microfilm 91998]. Bishop's Transcripts of Boston, Lincolnshire [FHL Microfilm 504734].

19. MARGARET FITZWILLIAM, married at Boston, Lincolnshire 20 Jan. 1562/3 (as his 1st wife) **BRIAN ROBERTSON** (or **ROBINSON**), Gent., of Sutterton and Kirton, Lincolnshire, younger son of Nicholas Robertson, Esq., of Boston, Lincolnshire, Merchant of the Staple of Calais, Mayor of Boston, Lincolnshire, 1545, by Florence, daughter of John Style, Knt., of London. He was a legatee in the 1552 will of his father, he being then of minor age. They had two sons, John, Gent., and Thomas, and one daughter, Anne. Following their marriage, he and his wife, Margaret, resided at Sutterton, Lincolnshire during the period, 1565–71, where their three children were baptized. Following his wife, Margaret's death, he married (2nd) **GRACE** _____. By an uncertain wife, he had a son, Robert, who was buried at Kirton, Lincolnshire 21 Jan. 1587/8. BRIAN ROBERTSON, Gent., was buried at Kirton, Lincolnshire 6 Nov. 1592. He left a will dated 16 October 1592, proved 29 Nov. 1592, requesting burial in the church of Kirton, Lincolnshire "so neere to my sonne Roberte Robertsone as conveniently may bee." His widow, Grace, was living in 1597, in Quadring, Lincolnshire.

> Pishey Thompson *Hist. & Antiqs. of Boston* (1856): 454. Glover & St. George *Vis. of Yorkshire 1584–5, 1612* (1875): 516 (Estouteville pedigree: "Bryan Robertson. = Margaret, dau. of Richd. Fitzwilliam, of Sprotborough."). *Yorkshire Genealogist* 1 (1888): 92–94. Maddison *Lincolnshire Peds.* 3 (H.S.P. 52) (1904): 825–826 (Robinson/Robertson pedigree) (Robertson arms: Vert, on a chevron between three bucks passant or as many estoiles gules). Besant *Parish Regs. of Boston* 1 (Lincoln Rec. Soc. Parish Reg. Sec. 1) (1914): 2. Registered will of Nicholas Robertson, Esq., dated 27 March 1552, proved 5 July 1552, P.C.C. 19 Powell [FHL Microfilm 91926]. Registered will of Brian Robertson, Gent., of Kirton, Lincolnshire proved 29 Nov. 1592, Cons. Court of Lincoln [FHL Microfilm 198850]. Parish Regs. of Sutterton, Lincolnshire [FHL Microfilm 989865].

Children of Margaret Fitzwilliam, by Brian Robertson, Gent.:

i. **JOHN ROBERTSON**, Gent., of London, son and heir, baptized at Sutterton, Lincolnshire 12 Jan. 1564/5. He was a legatee in the 1592 will of his father. In 1596 he purchased the manor of Deepdale Grange in Deepdale (parish of Cayton), Yorkshire from his cousin, Edward Gate, Esq., of Seamer, Yorkshire, son of his mother's aunt, Lady Lucy (Knyvet) Gate. He left a will dated 13 April 1597, proved 29 April 1597 (P.C.C. 26 Cobham). He died unmarried.

ii. **ANNE ROBERTSON** [see next].

iii. **THOMAS ROBERTSON**, baptized at Sutterton, Lincolnshire 9 Jan. 1570/1. He was a legatee in the 1592 will of his father. His subsequent history is unknown. He was presumably living in 1612, or died before 1612 with issue, as his sister, Anne (Robertson) Touteville, was not styled an heiress by her husband in the 1612 Vis. of Yorkshire.

20. ANNE ROBERTSON, baptized at Sutterton, Lincolnshire 18 Feb. 1567/8. She was a legatee in the 1592 will of her father. She married before 1592 (baptism of their first child) **CHARLES TOUTEVILLE** (or **TOUTEVILE, ESTOUTEVILE**), Gent., of Stainton Dale and Fordon (in Hunmanby), Yorkshire, son of Robert Touteville (or Estouteville), by Katherine, daughter of William Whittington, of Newborough, Staffordshire. They had two sons, Henry, Gent., and Charles, and four daughters, Anna Maria (wife of Thomas Acklam), Elizabeth (wife of John Acklam), Margaret, and Mary (wife of Richard Hill). In 1585 he witnessed a lease for 23 years for tithes relating to Hunmanby, Yorkshire between Sir Henry Gate of Kilburn, Middlesex (late husband of his wife's aunt, Lucy Knyvet) and Sir Henry's daughter, Mistress Mary Gate, of Hunmanby. In 1587 William Kethe conveyed to Charles Touteville a half share of a messuage with lands in Hutton Bushel and Preston, Yorkshire. In 1589 Thomas Allanson and Francis Allanson conveyed to him and his wife's cousin, Mistress Mary Gate, and the heirs of Charles, two messuages with lands in Stainton Dale, Yorkshire; he and Mary Gate subsequently paid 40s. to the Queen's farmers under patent for this alienation. In June 1590, being then of Stainton Dale, Yorkshire, he acquired two messuages and eight oxgangs of property [place not specified] from Charles Rant, of Westminster, Middlesex, and others. In August 1590, being then of Hunmanby, Yorkshire, he purchased from John Harrison one messuage and various lands in Fordon [in Hunmanby], Yorkshire for £90. In 1591 Christopher Constable and his wife, Everild, and John Harrison and his wife, Elice, conveyed to him a messuage and two cottages with lands in Fordon [in Hunmanby] for £40. In 1592 Thomas Mawe, of Fordon, yeoman, gave him two pieces of arable land called Hall Croft and a headland stretching from north to south down Audungat [parish not specified]. In 1595 John Welles and Charles Best, Citizens and scriveners of London, conveyed to him one messuage and lands in Fordon [in Hunmanby]; this conveyance was witnessed by his wife's brother, John Robertson. He and his wife, Anne, were legatees in the 1597 will of her brother, John Robertson, Gent., of London. In 1601 Reginald Farley, Esq., and his wife Barbara conveyed to him and William Jordaine one messuage with lands in Hunmanby. In 1609 Robert Rancke, of Fordon, husbandman quitclaimed to him various lands in Chapple Flat in Fordon [in Hunmanby], all sometime property of the chapel there. In 1610 John Eldred and William Whitmore assigned him a parcel called Calfehills and two smiths' shops in Hunmanby. In 1618–9 he and Dakins Constable of Sherburn, Gent. conveyed to John Legard of Ganton, Yorkshire, Esq. four and a half oxgangs in Foulthropp Field in or near Hunmanby, sometime property of Sir Francis Bigod attainted. In 1620 he and his wife, Anne, conveyed a windmill and lands in Muston, Yorkshire to William Leppington, Gent. In 1620 Sir Charles Egerton sued him regarding a title close called Perdicote Hill in Hunmanby. His wife, Anne, was buried at Hunmanby, Yorkshire 11 August 1620. CHARLES TOUTEVILLE, Gent., was buried at Hunmanby, Yorkshire 21 April 1621. He left a will dated 12 Feb. 1620/1, proved 19 Sept. 1622.

> Dugdale *Vis. of York 1665–6* (Surtees Soc. 36) (1859): 87 (Stoutville ped.: "Charles Stouteville of Humanby in com. Ebor. died in a⁰ 1622, or thereabouts. = Anne, daughter of Bryan Robinson of Boston in com. Linc.") (Stoutville arms: Barry of twelve argent and gules, a lion rampant sable.). Glover & St. George *Vis. of Yorkshire 1584–5, 1612* (1875): 516 (Estouteville pedigree: "Charles Estouteville, of Hunmanby, co. York, living 1612. = Ann, dau. of Bryan Robertson."). *Yorkshire Genealogist* 1 (1888): 92–94. *Feet of Fines of the Tudor Period* 3 (Yorkshire Arch. Soc. Rec. Ser. 7) (1889): 74, 118, 157; 4 (Yorkshire Arch. Soc. Rec. Ser. 8) (1890): 176. Brigg *Yorkshire Fines for the Stuart Period* 2 (Yorkshire Arch. Soc. 58) (1917): 122, 200. Clay *Dugdale's Vis. of Yorkshire* 3 (1917): 142–143 (Stoutville pedigree). *NEHGR* 100 (1946): 73. Neal *Cal. Patent Rolls 33 Elizabeth I (1590–1591)* (List and Index Soc. 308) (2005): 13. Registered will of Brian Robertson, Gent., of Kirton, Lincolnshire proved 29 Nov. 1592, Cons. Court of Lincoln [FHL Microfilm 198850]. Registered will of John Robertson, Gent., of London proved 29 April 1597, P.C.C. 26 Cobham [FHL Microfilm 91998]. Registered will of Charles Toutwell [sic], Gent., of Hunmanby, Yorkshire proved 19 Sept. 1622 (York Registry, vol. 37, pg. 54) [FHL Microfilm 99506]. Parish Regs. of Sutterton, Lincolnshire [FHL Microfilm 989865]. East Riding of Yorkshire Archives & Recs. Service: Grimston Fam. of Grimston Garth & Kilnwick, DDGR/9/4, DDGR/9/5, DDGR/9/6, DDGR/9/7, DDGR/9/8, DDGR/9/9, DDGR/9/10, DDGR/13/4, DDGR/34/3; East Riding of Yorkshire Archives & Recs. Service: Osbaldeston & Mitford Fams. of Hunmanby, DDHU/9/39, DHU/9/17, DDHU/9/118 (available at www.a2a.org.uk/search/index.asp).

21. MARGARET TOUTEVILLE, 3rd daughter, baptized at Hunmanby, Yorkshire 3 August 1606. She was a legatee and named co-executrix in the 1621 will of her father. Her guardianship was granted by her father's will to Sir Richard Darley, of Buttercrambe, Yorkshire, whose wife, Elizabeth Gate, was the granddaughter of Lucy (Knyvet) Gate, aunt of her maternal grandmother, Margaret (Fitzwilliam) Robertson. Margaret married at Buttercrambe (in Bossal), Yorkshire 23 July 1632 [**REV.**] **THOMAS SHEPARD**, younger son of William Shepard, of Towcester, Northamptonshire, grocer. He was born at Towcester, Northamptonshire 5 Nov. 1605. They had two sons, Thomas (died young) and [Rev.] Thomas, Gent. He matriculated at Emmanuel College, Cambridge, England in 1619, and received the degrees of B.A. (1623) and M.A. (1627). He was ordained deacon in Peterborough diocese 12 July 1627; priest 13 July 1627. He preached at Earls Colne, Essex, where he was reprimanded by Laud for his Puritan activities and prohibited from exercising as a minister in the diocese of London. He subsequently became a chaplain to Sir Richard Darley, of Buttercrambe, Yorkshire. He preached surreptitiously in that area until forced by persecution to flee to Heddon, near Newcastle-upon-Tyne, Northumberland. He attempted to immigrate to New England in 1634, but his ship was driven back by bad weather. In 1635 he and his wife, Margaret, and their infant son, Thomas, sailed on the ship *Defence* to New England. The ship arrived safely at Boston 3 October 1635, and he proceeded to Cambridge, Massachusetts. His wife, Margaret, died at Cambridge, Massachusetts Feb. 1635/6. He was made a freeman of Massachusetts Bay, 3 March 1635/6. He became the minister of Cambridge, Massachusetts in 1636. He took a leading part in establishing Harvard College. He married (2nd) about 1637 **JOANNA HOOKER**, daughter of [Rev.] Thomas Hooker, by his wife, Susanna Garbrand. They had four sons, one unnamed (died in infancy), Samuel, John, and John (again). He was a legatee in the 1643 will of his brother, John Shepard, of Towcester, Northamptonshire. He married (3rd) 8 Sept. 1647 **MARGARET BORODELL**, by whom he had one son, Jeremiah. [Rev.] Thomas Shepard died at Cambridge, Massachusetts 25 August 1649. He left a will dated 25 August 1649, proved 29 Nov. 1649. His widow, Margaret, married (2nd) [**REV.**] **JONATHAN MITCHELL**, of Cambridge, Massachusetts.

On 9 October 1651 the executors of Thomas Shepard's estate conveyed to Mitchell the house where Shepard lived; Mitchell gave them a receipt of the same date mentioning "my wife, mother of Jeremiah Shepard, son of Rev. Thomas."

>Dugdale *Vis. of York 1665–6* (Surtees Soc. 36) (1859): 87 (Stoutville ped.: "3. Margaret [Stouteville], wife of ..... Shepheard."). Savage *Gen. Dict. of New England* 4 (1862): 76. *Yorkshire Genealogist* 1 (1888): 92–94. Clay *Paver's Marr. Licences* (Yorkshire Arch. Soc. 40) (1909): 13 (marriage license of Thomas Shepard, clerk, and Margaret Tuteville dated 1630 — to be married at Buttercrambe). Clay *Dugdale's Vis. of Yorkshire* 3 (1917): 142–143 (Stouteville pedigree). *Notes & Queries* 12th Ser. 5 (1919): 179. Venn & Venn *Alumni Cantabrigiensis to 1751* 4 (1927): 60 (biog. of Thomas Shepard: "He was held in high esteem by his contemporaries."). Ernest Flagg *Founding of New England* (1927): 318–324. Paige & Gozzaldi *Hist. of Cambridge Supp.* (1930). *NEHGR* 100 (1946): 73. Gerald Faulkner Shepard *Shepard Fams. of New England* 3 (1973): 293–295 ("[Thomas Shepard] "was most highly regarded and Cotton Mather gives some account of him in *Magnalia Christ Americana* ... According to Thomas Shepard's statement in his 'Mem. of His Own Life,' included in Young's *Chrons. of the First Planters of Massachusetts Bay*, his first wife [Margaret Touteville] was related to Sir Richard Darley of Buttercrambe, Yorkshire."). Roger Thompson *Mobility & Migration 1629–1640* (1994): 165. *TG* 16 (2002): 163–165. Bishop's Transcripts of Buttercrambe, Yorkshire [FHL Microfilm 918414].

INDEX - People

ab Owain, Robert & Margaret ferch Sion ap Lewis, 493
ab Rhys, Lywelyn, 322
Abergavenny, 200
Aberly, 362
Abernathy, 225
Abingdon, 32, 33
Abrahall, 432
Acklam, 682
Acre, 19, 196, 443
Acres, 198
Acton, 216, 578, 635, 639
Acworth, 165, 266
Adam, 639
Adams, 559
Adcock, 362
Adderbury, 585
Admiral of England, 232, 420, 498, 540, 551, 610, 615
Adverton, 136
Aese, 562
Affeton, 666
Affeton, Katherine & William Bourgchier, 666
Agard, 488, 489
Aguillon, 189, 564
Aguillon, Robert d' & Margaret of Savoy, 189
Airmyn, 456
Akele, 597
Akerman, 266
Albany, 202, 375, 428
Albeney, 392
Albon, 28, 237
Albon, Béatrix d' & Hugues III, Duke of Burgundy, 28
Albret, 419, 569
Aldborough, 543
Aldewyncle, 123, 554
Aldham, 266

Aldus, 378
Alençon, 121
Algarve, 115, 118, 119, 120, 121, 538, 613
Algesiras, 121
Allanson, 682
Allemania, 304
Allen, 10
Allen, Jane & Peter Bulkeley, 10
Alleslee, 262
Allin, John & Katherine Deighton, 412, 477
Allington, 161, 472
Almain, 195, 299, 302, 303, 304, 305
Almain, Edmund of, 635
Almain, Edmund of & Margaret de Clare, 303
Almain, Henry of & Constance of Béarn, 301
Alston, 159
Alwent, 130
Alyn, 600
Amboise, 137
Amiens, 235, 236
Ampthull, 537
Amundeville, Richard de & Maud de Verdun, 597
Anabyll, 210
Andrew, 341
Andrewe, 165
Andrews, 341
Andwinckle, 560
Anesty, 179
Angoulême, 30, 185, 195
Angus, 6, 375, 658
Anian, 598
Anjou, 121, 186, 280, 298, 299
Anjou, Margaret of [Queen of England], 53, 99, 123, 247, 334, 540
Anne, 544
Annesleye, 569

Anstis, 553
Antequera, 657
Antevill, 4
Antiochia, 514
Antwerp, Lionel of, 71, 611
Antwerp, Lionel of & Elizabeth de Burgh, 23
Antwerp, Lionel of & Violante Visconti, 23
ap Adam, 197, 407
ap Adam, John, 197
ap Dafydd ap Meurig Fychan, 492
ap Dafydd ap Owen ap Thomas ap Howell ap Maredudd ap Gruffudd Derwas, 493
ap Griffith, Llwelyn, 184
ap Griffith, Rhys, 183
ap Gruffudd ap Wenwynwyn, Owain, 141
ap Gruffudd, John ap, 492
ap Gryffydd, Dafydd & Elizabeth de Ferrers, 564
ap Gwilym, William Fychan, 345
ap Harry, 312
ap Howell, John, 493
ap Hugh ab Owen, Owen, 346
ap Hugh ap David ap Howell ap Gronw, 493
ap Hywel ap Jenkin, Humphrey & Anne Herbert, 492
ap Hywel, Gruffudd & Jane ferch Humphrey ap Hywel, 492
ap Iorwerth, Llywelyn, 186, 647
ap Jenkin, Hywel & Mary Kynaston, 492
ap John ap Gruffudd, Lewis & Ellin ferch Hywel ap Gruffudd, 493
ap John, David & Constance de Tony, 661
ap John, William, 492
ap Lewis ap John Gruffudd, Rees & Catherine ferch ap Elissa ap Dafydd, 493
ap Lewis, Owen & Mary ferch Tudor Vaughn, 493

ap Lloyd, 446
ap Maredudd, Rhys & Ada de Hastings, 183
ap Maredudd, Robert, 346
ap Meridith, Rhys, 601
ap Morus, Llywelyn, 492
ap Rees, Ellis & Anne Humphrey, 493
ap Rees, Philip, 626
ap Rhys Gryg, Maredudd & _____, 183
ap Rhys, Gwilym, 492
ap Thomas, 100
ap Thomas, Morgan, 492
ap Tudor, William, 492
Appleyard, 162
Aprice, 312
Apulia, 462
Aquitaine, 122, 390, 433, 455, 533, 551, 613
Aquitaine, Eleanor of [Queen of England], 315
Aragón, 59, 95, 114, 118, 119, 120, 121, 194, 195, 237, 301, 496, 657
Aragón, Katherine of [Queen of England], 427
Aragón, Violante of & Alfonso X, King of Castile and León, 118
Arc, Joan of, 420
Arcedeaken, 333
Arcedekne, 99
Arcedekne, l', 98, 333
Arcedekne, Philippe l' & Hugh Courtenay, 333
Archdeacon, 1
Archer, 409, 679
Arches, 100, 168, 459, 585, 666, 679
Arches, Joan & John Dinham, 459
Arches, Richard & Joan Frome, 585
Ardern, 39, 418, 449, 459
Arderne, 487, 500, 598
Arderne, Cecily & John Stanley, 488
Arderne, Maud & Thomas Stanley, 487

Arderne, Ralph d' & Isabel de Mortimer, 598
Argall, 583
Argall, Elizabeth & Edward Filmer, 584
Argall, Richard & Mary Scott, 583
Argall, Samuel & _____, 583
Argentan, 137
Argentine, 164, 281, 450
Argentine, Maud & Ives Fitz Warin, 164
Argyll, 206
Arlon, 237
Armagnac, 419, 496
Armburgh, 574
Armiger, 378
Arnaldi, 138
Arney, 585
Arnold, 411, 435
Arrendell, 170
Arthoure, 640
Artois, 464
Arundel, 3, 31, 32, 33, 35, 36, 43, 50, 51, 52, 59, 67, 83, 89, 94, 97, 142, 154, 169, 176, 177, 244, 249, 250, 252, 253, 254, 255, 261, 269, 271, 333, 375, 397, 417, 425, 447, 451, 453, 459, 482, 496, 497, 519, 535, 538, 539, 553, 578, 591, 592, 593, 596, 597, 600, 601, 602, 603, 604, 605, 606, 607, 608, 609, 610, 611, 612, 613, 615, 616, 617, 649, 661
Arundel, Alice & Henry Beaufort, 613
Arundel, Alice & John Cherleton, 613
Arundel, Alice de & Stephen de Segrave, 602
Arundel, Edmund de & Alice de Warenne, 603
Arundel, Eleanor de & John de Bereford, 610
Arundel, Eleanor de & Robert de Ufford, 612
Arundel, Elizabeth & Gerard Usflete, 617
Arundel, Elizabeth & John de Meriet, 97
Arundel, Elizabeth & Leonard de Carew, 97
Arundel, Elizabeth & Robert Goushill, 617
Arundel, Elizabeth & Thomas Mowbray, 616
Arundel, Elizabeth & William de Montagu, 616
Arundel, Joan & William de Bryan, 482
Arundel, Joan & William Echingham, 482
Arundel, Katherine de & Andrew Peverel, 605
Arundel, Katherine de & Henry Husee, 605
Arundel, Margaret & John de la Pole, 425
Arundel, Margaret & Roland Lenthall, 615
Arundel, Philippe & John Cornwall, 535
Arundel, Richard de & Eleanor of Lancaster, 607
Arundel, Richard de & Elizabeth de Bohun, 610
Arundel, Richard de & Isabel le Despenser, 606
Arundel, Richard de & Philippe Mortimer, 611
Arundel, Thomas & Beatrice of Portugal, 613
Arundel, Thomas, Archbishop of Canterbury, 609
Arundel, William & Elizabeth Willoughby, 459
Arundell, 43, 64, 99, 166, 167, 168, 170, 334, 337, 343, 398, 399, 428, 430, 460, 603, 605, 612
Arundell, Anne & Cecil Calvert, 64
Arundell, Elizabeth & Edmund Stradling, 398

Arundell, Elizabeth & William Lygon, 398
Arundell, John & Elizabeth Grey, 168
Arundell, John & Elizabeth Morley, 166
Arundell, John & Katherine Chidiock, 166
Arundell, John & Katherine Grenville, 169
Arundell, Margaret & William Capell, 167
Arundell, Mary & Henry Fitz Alan, 43
Arundell, Mary & Robert Radcliffe, 43
Arundell, Matthew & Margaret Willoughby, 170
Arundell, Thomas & Anne Philipson, 170
Arundell, Thomas & Katherine Dinham, 168
Arundell, Thomas & Margaret Howard, 169
Arundell, Thomas & Mary Wriothesley, 170
Ascue, 288
Aselakesby, 238
Ashburnham, 56, 343, 594
Ashburnham, Ellen & Walter Hendley, 343
Ashburnham, Thomas & Elizabeth Dudley, 343
Ashby, 480
Ashby, Anne & Francis Lovell, 480
Ashe, 411
Ashford, 403
Ashford, Elizabeth & Philip Courtenay, 403
Ashton, 589
Ashton, Eleanor & John Berkeley, 589
Aske, 248
Assartis, 598
Asshe, 411
Assheleygh, 586
Assheton, 589
Asthall, 306, 307

Astley, 168, 248, 401, 438
Astley, Thomas & Mary Denny, 438
Aston, 159, 212, 314, 409
Aston, Susan & William Batte, 314
Athens, 472
Atherton, 502
Atholl, 6, 197, 200, 202, 210, 524, 525
Atholl, Isabel de & Ralph Eure, 525
Aton, 6, 18, 386, 525
Aton, Isabel de & Roger Darcy, 386
Aton, Katherine & Ralph Eure, 525
Attewode, 140, 440
Aubeney, 83, 133, 154, 176, 253, 255, 392, 394, 519, 520, 549, 596, 645
Aubeney, d', 253, 254
Aubeney, Eustache d' & Gerard de Fancourt, 396
Aubeney, Hugh d' & Isabel de Warenne, 253
Aubeney, Isabel d' & John Fitz Alan, 596
Aubeney, Maud d' & Gilbert, Earl of Strathearn, 392
Aubeney, Maud d' & Robert de Tateshale, 254
Aubeney, Odinel d' & Hawise _____, 394
Aubeney, Robert d' & Eustache _____, 395
Aubeney, Sarah d' & Richard de Bernake, 395
Aubeney, William d' & & Maud de Senlis, 392
Aubeney, William d' & _____, 395
Aubeney, William d' & _____, 395
Aubeney, William d' & Agatha Trussebut, 393
Aubeney, William d' & Alice of Louvain, 250
Aubeney, William d' & Aubrey Biset, 396
Aubeney, William d' & Isabel _____, 396

Aubeney, William d' & Mabel of Chester, 252
Aubeney, William d' & Margaret de Umfreville, 393
Aubeney, William d' & Maud de Saint Hilary, 176, 252
Aubeny, 149, 392, 395
Aucher, 369, 376
Audeley, 229
Audeleye, 334
Audley, 141, 205, 227, 228, 269, 273, 333, 403, 451, 484, 531, 571, 586, 663, 667, 668
Audley, Blanche de & Fulk Fitz Warin, 663
Audley, Elizabeth & William Filoll, 586
Audley, James de & Eve de Clavering, 227
Audley, Thomas de & Eve de Clavering, 227
Audreham, 556
Aulton, 192
Aumale, 117, 188, 189, 190, 191, 192, 323, 382, 385, 657, 658
Aumbroys, 84
Austria, 30, 427, 428, 429
Auvergne, 28
Auxerre, 30, 31, 463, 465
Auxonne, 30, 463, 469
Avaugor, Henry de, 126
Avenel, Gervase & Joan de Clare, 200
Avesnes, 187, 300
Avondale, 541
Avranches, 150, 233, 315, 317, 319
Avranches, William d' & Maud de Buckland, 511
Aylard, 27
Aylesbury, 161, 409, 508
Aylesbury, Thomas & Katherine Pabenham, 508
Aylesford, 617
Ayremynne, 242
Ayscough, 670

Aysse, 562
Baard, 221, 222, 478
Baard, Simon & Isabel of Dunbar, 222
Babthorp, 286
Babyngton, 679
Bacon, 59, 62, 255
Bacon, Edmund & Elizabeth la Warre, 59
Bacon, Edmund & Joan de Beaumont, 59
Bacon, Edmund & Margery de Poynings, 59
Bacun, 150
Badajoz, 115
Badby, 609
Badby, Mary & Thomas Waldegrave, 11
Badew, 33
Badlesmere, 1, 25, 91, 327, 446, 610
Bagot, 107
Bailey, 547
Baker, 8, 629
Baker, John & Elizabeth Dyneley, 629
Bakewell, 33
Balderston, 211
Balderston, Joan & John Pilkington, 211
Balderston, Joan & Thomas Wortley, 211
Baldwin, 55, 94, 488
Baldwin, Frances & Richard Townshend, 94
Balliol, 5, 178, 184, 200, 202, 219, 220, 221, 224, 479, 512, 523, 566, 606, 651
Balliol, Ada de & John Fitz Robert, 219
Balliol, Edward de, 201
Baltimore, 63, 64, 65, 170
Banaster, 278
Banbury, 109
Bankes, Mary & Charles Calvert, 65
Bannebury, 585
Bannister, Thomas & Frances Walker, 529

Banns, 574
Bar, 29, 263, 469, 568, 607
Bar, Clémence of & Renaud II, Count of Clermont, 234
Bar, Clémence of & Thibaud III, seigneur of Nanteuil, 234
Barantyne, 421, 431
Barat, 73, 74, 76
Barbe, 635, 636
Barber, 441
Barcelona, 115, 118, 120
Barcelos, 120
Barclay, 7
Bardolf, 20, 22, 59, 270, 275, 358
Bardolf, Anne & Reynold Cobham, 270
Bardulf, 188
Barefote, 679
Barentyne, 421
Baret, 61
Barham, 584
Barham, Charles & Elizabeth _____, 584
Barham, Robert & Katherine Filmer, 584
Bar-le-Duc, 234, 382
Barlee, 162, 472
Barnard, 412
Barnardiston, 11
Barnerdeston, 11
Barnes, 473, 504
Barnes, Charles, 474
Barney, 266
Barnham, 486
Barre, 310
Barre, Elizabeth & Edmund Cornwall, 310
Barres, 384, 471
Barrett, 368, 628, 629
Barrett, Cecily & William Culpeper, 369
Barrett, George & Elizabeth Dyneley, 629
Barrett, Jane & Henry Chauncy, 132

Barrett, John & Elizabeth Braytoft, 368
Barrett, John & Margaret Norris, 369, 628
Barrett, John & Mary Brooke, 369, 628
Barrett, John & Philippe Harpesfield, 368, 628
Barrett, Robert & Margaret Chicheley, 368
Barrett, Robert & Margery Knolles, 368
Barrett, Thomas & Maud Poyntz, 368
Barry, 52, 351
Barry, Ellice & Maurice Mor FitzGibbon, 52
Barry, Ellice & Thomas Fitz James, Earl of Desmond, 52
Barrymore, 52
Bartelott, 344
Barton, 130, 348, 502, 593
Barwike, 376
Basing, 93
Basings, 93
Baskerville, 312, 575
Baspole, 473
Basset, 76, 255, 259, 274, 316, 319, 321, 341, 381, 411, 441, 477, 564, 616
Basset, Edward & Isabel Ligon, 411
Basset, Elizabeth & Richard Grey, 274
Basset, Eustache & Richard de Camville, 316
Basset, Eustache & Thomas de Verdun, 316
Basset, Gilbert & Egeline de Courtenay, 316
Basset, Joan & Aubrey, Count of Dammartin, 381
Basset, Ralph, 445
Bassett, Jane & John Deighton, 411
Bassingbourne, John & Anne Pashley, 375
Bastard, 640
Basyng, 93
Basynges, 93, 94, 139

Basynges, Alice & Thomas Mackworth, 94
Basynges, John & Elizabeth la Zouche, 93
Bath, 667, 668
Bathurst, 583
Batisford, 108, 230, 231, 482, 580
Batisford, Alice & William Echingham, 482
Batisford, Elizabeth & William Fiennes, 579
Batte, 313
Batte, Henry & Mary Lound, 314
Batte, John & Martha Mallory, 314
Batte, Robert & Elizabeth Parry, 313
Batte, Thomas & Mary _____, 314
Batte, William & Elizabeth Horton, 314
Batte, William & Susan Aston, 314
Baudement, Agnès de & Robert I, Count of Dreux, 468
Baudrip, 68
Bavaria, 95, 660
Bavaria, Jacob (or Jacque) of, 421
Bavent, 397
Bavent, Joan de & John Dauntsey, 397
Bavent, Roger de & Hawise de Montagu, 397
Baxter, 480
Bayard, 222, 479
Bayeux, 151
Bayly, Richard & Elizabeth _____, 596
Baynham, 434
Beacham, 366
Beachamp, 366
Beare, 405
Béarn, 301, 302, 303
Béarn, Constance & Aimon II, Count of Geneva, 302
Béarn, Constance of & Henry of Almain, 301
Beauchamp, 34, 37, 50, 51, 52, 53, 68, 70, 96, 97, 102, 125, 140, 141, 154, 164, 182, 196, 197, 199, 228, 244, 260, 264, 281, 310, 380, 391, 408, 424, 451, 455, 487, 506, 569, 570, 574, 579, 587, 609, 613, 615, 640, 662
Beauchamp, Alice de & Bernard de Brus, 281
Beauchamp, Eleanor de & Fulk Fitz Warin, 662
Beauchamp, Isabel de & Hugh le Despenser, 140, 441
Beauchamp, Isabel de & Patrick de Chaworth, 140, 440
Beauchamp, Joan & James le Boteler (or Butler), 50
Beauchamp, John de & Nesta de Cockfield, 13
Beauchamp, Margaret de & Hubert Hussey, 516
Beauchamp, Maud de & Roger de Clifford, 244
Beauchamp, Walter & Joyce Cokesey, 640
Beaufort, 51, 103, 277, 390, 424, 425, 451, 455, 497, 551
Beaufort, Eleanor & James Butler, 51
Beaufort, Eleanor & James Butler, 102
Beaufort, Eleanor & James Ormond, 51
Beaufort, Eleanor & Robert Spencer, 51, 103
Beaufort, Henry & Alice Arundel, 613
Beaufort, Margaret & John de la Pole, 424
Beaujeu, 471
Beaumont, 7, 59, 129, 233, 333, 451, 458, 518, 524, 533, 547, 568, 607, 663, 666, 668
Beaumont, Hugh & Elizabeth Bourchier, 668
Beaumont, Joan de & Edmund Bacon, 59
Beaumont, Joan de & Giles de Brewes, 59
Beaumont, Margaret de & Fulk Fitz Warin, 663

Beaumont, Maud & Hugh Courtenay, 333
Beaumont, William & Isabel Wilington, 129
Beaunoy, Isabel de & Roger Camoys, 72
Beaupre, 636
Beaupré, 461, 635, 636, 637
Beaupré, Dorothy & John Peyton, 461
Beaupré, Isabel de & John de Longland, 636
Beaupré, John de & Margaret de Carminow, 636
Beaupré, Ralph de & Margaret de Furneaux, 635
Beaupré, Stephen de & Isabel Fitz William, 635
Beausault, 236
Beavis, 405
Beche, de la, 202
Beche, Nicholas de la & Margery de Poynings, 59
Beckering, 162
Becket, 176
Beckwith, 361
Bedford, 409, 422, 431
Bedford, John, Duke of, 51, 232, 246, 408, 538
Bedingfield, 364, 461, 472
Beere, 147
Beheathland, 378
Bek, 197, 208
Beler, 273
Belers, 90, 355
Belers, Amice (or Avice) & Ralph de Cromwell, 355
Belhone, 208
Belhous, 12
Belhouse, 368
Belknap, 575
Belknap, Alice & Henry Finch, 588
Belknap, Elizabeth & William Ferrers, 575

Belknap, Philip & Elizabeth Woodhouse, 587
Bell, 439, 461
Bella Fago, 521
Bellasis, 544
Bellers, 677
Bellingham, 111, 157, 545
Bénauges, 419
Benesle, 653
Benhale, 228, 229
Benhale, Robert de & Eve de Clavering, 228
Bennett, 371, 584
Benstead, 358
Benstead, Edward & Elizabeth de Cromwell, 257
Benstede, 257, 640
Bere, 35
Bereford, 164, 610
Bereford, John de & Eleanor de Arundel, 610
Berenger, 429
Berewe, atte, 140, 440
Bergavenny, 50, 52, 102, 352, 369, 408, 574, 594, 609, 613, 615, 628
Berkeley, 28, 36, 53, 86, 142, 199, 243, 264, 265, 274, 276, 286, 294, 370, 371, 407, 408, 409, 410, 411, 427, 434, 435, 447, 457, 472, 487, 565, 571, 590, 591, 592, 593, 594, 618, 632, 667
Berkeley, Anne & John Brent, 594
Berkeley, Anne & William Dennis, 434
Berkeley, Edward & Alice Cookes, 593
Berkeley, Edward & Christian Holt, 593
Berkeley, Elizabeth & Edward Cherleton, 142
Berkeley, Elizabeth & Henry Ligon, 411
Berkeley, Elizabeth & John Sutton, 143
Berkeley, Isabel de & Robert de Clifford, 243

Berkeley, Isabel de & Thomas de Musgrave, 243
Berkeley, Joan & Thomas Stawell, 590
Berkeley, Joan de & Reynold de Cobham, 268
Berkeley, Joan de & Thomas Burnell, 268
Berkeley, John & Eleanor Ashton, 589
Berkeley, John & Elizabeth Betteshorne, 589
Berkeley, John & Isabel Dennis, 410
Berkeley, John & Margaret Cheyne, 27, 590
Berkeley, Katherine & John Brereton, 593
Berkeley, Katherine & John Stourton, 592
Berkeley, Lora & Thomas Butler, 53
Berkeley, Lora & Thomas Ormond, 53
Berkeley, Maurice & Anne West, 591
Berkeley, Maurice & Ellen Montfort, 408
Berkeley, Maurice & Joan Dinham, 408
Berkeley, Maurice & Lora Fitz Hugh, 591
Berkeley, Maurice de & Margery de Vere, 406
Berkeley, Richard & Elizabeth Coningsby, 410
Berkeley, Thomas & Elizabeth Neville, 594
Berkeley, Thomas de & Katherine Botetourt, 407
Berkeley, William & Anne Stafford, 409
Berkeley, William & Frances Culpeper, 371
Berkeley, William & Katherine Stourton, 276, 592
Berkes, 510
Bermingham, 16, 259, 264
Bernak, 93, 506
Bernake, 93, 257, 355, 395, 507, 676

Bernake, Maud de & Ralph de Cromwell, 355
Bernake, Richard de & Sarah d'Aubeney, 395
Bernard, 126, 378
Bernard, Beheathland & Andrew Gilson, 378
Bernard, Beheathland & Francis Dade, 378
Bernere, 40, 418
Bertone, 325
Bertram, 239, 523, 672, 674
Bertram, Agnes & Thomas Fitz William, 672
Bertulmeu, 262
Berwyke, John & Joan Fauconberge, 552
Bessels, 476
Bessiles, 476
Best, 467, 682
Bethom, 551
Beton, 203
Bettenham, 595
Betteshorne, 143, 589
Betteshorne, Elizabeth & John Berkeley, 589
Beuthen-Kosel, 553
Beverley, 130, 398
Beverley, Elizabeth & John Dauntsey, 398
Bevyle, 169, 634
Bevyle, Rose & William Fitz Richard, 634
Béziers, 236
Bibby, 467
Biconyll, 473
Bifield, 291
Bifield, William de & Maud de Somery, 291
Bigenet, 35
Bigod, 15, 46, 130, 179, 180, 218, 239, 249, 253, 284, 289, 392, 441, 516, 528, 550, 552, 553, 561, 683

Bigod, Isabel & Walter de Fauconberge, 550
Bigod, Joan & William Chauncy, 129
Bigorre, 301, 302, 303
Billinge, 283
Bird, 412
Birde, 475
Birkell, William & Jane Gibbon, 113
Birmingham, 572
Birmingham, Roger de & Hawise _____, 394
Biset, 83, 396
Biset, Aubrey & William d'Aubeney, 396
Biset, Thomas & Isabel of Fife, 202
Bishop, 128
Bishopsdon, 261
Bisset, 202
Bistorne, 143, 589
Biterle, Richard de & Cecily _____, 310
Black Prince, Edward the, 122, 496
Blagge, 369, 628
Blakiston, 64
Blanchminster, 126
Blanchminster, Eve de & Giles de Clifford, 126
Blanchminster, Eve de & Henry Fitz Roy, 126
Blanchminster, Eve de & William de Champernoun, 126
Blancminster, Hawise de & John Fitz Alan, 596
Blancmuster, 26
Blean, 192
Blechenden, 351
Blennerhasset, 377
Blois, 47, 619
Blois, Isabelle of & Guillaume Gouet, 462
Blois, Isabelle of & Roger de Hauteville, 462
Blois, Marie of & Eudes II, Duke of Burgundy, 28

Blome, 440
Blount, 53, 109, 165, 261, 311, 336, 370, 399, 484, 576, 594, 638, 639, 643
Blount, Edward & Jane _____, 576
Blount, Gertrude & Henry Courtenay, 336
Blount, Thomas le & Joan Hakeluyt, 643
Blount, William & Margaret Echingham, 484
Bluet, 197, 198
Blumville, 228
Blund, 577, 647
Blundel, 65
Blundeville, Robert de & _____ de Burgh, 13
Blunt, 480
Blunville, 13
Bocher, 498
Boclande, 509
Bodrugan, Sibyl de & Richard de Cornwall, 309
Bodulgate, 275
Bohemia, 428
Bohemia, Anne of [Queen of England], 331, 553, 631
Bohoun, 654
Bohun, 1, 19, 26, 47, 48, 68, 179, 326, 380, 506, 507, 516, 522, 564, 566, 569, 605, 610, 611, 623, 646, 652, 654, 656, 663
Bohun, Eleanor de & James le Boteler (or Butler), 47
Bohun, Eleanor de & Robert de Ferrers, 566
Bohun, Eleanor de & Thomas de Dagworth, 47
Bohun, Elizabeth de & Richard de Arundel, 610
Bohun, Humphrey de, 326
Bohun, Margaret de & Hugh de Courtenay, 326
Bohun, Maud de & Walter Fitz Robert, 645

Bohun, William de, 329
Bois, 84, 86, 87, 436
Bois, Alice & Hugh Champernoun, 436
Bois, du, 92
Boisleux, 28
Bokenham, 440
Bolax, 531
Bolde, 500
Boleyn, 55, 56, 57, 104, 105, 107, 349, 432
Boleyn, Anne [Queen of England], 104, 106, 169, 480
Boleyn, George & Jane Parker, 57
Boleyn, Margaret & John Sackville, 56
Boleyn, Mary, 104, 106
Boleyn, Mary & William Carey, 104
Boleyn, Mary & William Stafford, 105
Boleyn, Thomas & Elizabeth Howard, 56
Boleyn, William & Margaret Butler, 55
Bollegh, 306
Bolney, 126
Bon, le, 84
Bondes, 639
Bonham, 266
Boniface VIII, Pope, 197, 223, 225, 242, 272, 354, 601, 654
Bonville, 98, 101, 168, 248, 333, 334, 402, 435
Bonville, Elizabeth & Thomas Carew, 98
Bonville, Isabel & Richard Champernoun, 435
Bonville, Margaret & William Courtenay, 402
Bonyngton, 637
Boorn, 449
Booth, 267, 289, 641
Booth, Anne & William Clopton, 267
Booton, 14
Borodell, Margaret & Jonathan Mitchell, 683
Borodell, Margaret & Thomas Shepard, 683

Borough, 112
Borrey, 661
Boscawen, 337
Boscawen, John & Margaret Tretherff, 337
Boseham, 27
Bosom, 39, 418, 449
Bosse, 324, 325
Bosum, 100
Bosun, 39, 418
Bosvile, 499
Bosville, 676
Boteler, 15, 19, 45, 46, 50, 102, 109, 160, 161, 188, 247, 260, 276, 306, 345, 376, 387, 450, 455, 472, 570, 575, 596, 603
Boteler, Edmund le & Joan Fitz John, 46
Boteler, Edward le & Anne le Despenser, 450
Boteler, James le & Anne Welles, 49
Boteler, James le & Eleanor de Bohun, 47
Boteler, James le & Elizabeth Darcy, 49
Boteler, James le & Elizabeth Fitzgerald, 50
Boteler, James le & Joan Beauchamp, 50
Boteler, Philip le & Elizabeth Cokayne, 161
Boteler, Thebaud le & Joan Fitz John, 45
Boteler, Thebaud le & Margery de Burgh, 45
Boteler, William & Joan Troutbeck, 345
Botetourt, 37, 69, 407, 408, 483, 654
Botetourt, Joan & Robert Fitz Walter, 654
Botetourt, Joyce & Hugh Burnell, 37
Botetourt, Katherine & John de Thorpe, 407
Botetourt, Katherine & Thomas de Berkeley, 407

Botiler, 50, 567, 624
Botiller, 45, 48, 49, 50, 52, 53, 451, 566, 572
Botoner, 215
Botreaux, 125, 456, 574, 622, 664
Botreaux, Anne & Fulk Fitz Warin, 664
Botreaux, Anne & William Clinton, 664
Botreaux, John & Anne Talbot, 332
Botreaux, Margaret de & John de Dinham, 456
Botringham, 309
Botryngham, 635
Boulogne, 117, 178, 234, 382, 383, 384, 385, 644, 645
Boulogne, Ida of & Renaud de Dammartin, 384
Boulogne, Maud of [Queen of England, 645
Bourbon, 28, 30, 121, 122
Bourbon, Blanche of & Pedro I, King of Castile and León, 121
Bourbon, Mathilde (or Mahaut) de & Eudes of Burgundy, 30
Bourchier, 53, 280, 460
Bourchier, Elizabeth & Edward Stanhope, 668
Bourchier, Elizabeth & Hugh Beaumont, 668
Bourchier, Elizabeth & Richard Page, 668
Bourchier, Fulk & Elizabeth Dinham, 666
Boure, 309
Bourgchier, 55, 278, 350, 358, 666
Bourgchier, William & Katherine Affeton, 666
Bourgchier, William & Thomasine Hankford, 666
Bourges, 519
Bourgilion, 224
Bourgogne, 328
Bourn, 25

Bourne, 130, 595
Boves, 472
Boville, John de & Hawise de Buckland, 511
Bowden, 156
Bowers, 503
Bowes, 249, 266, 344, 368, 480, 529, 628, 633
Bowes, Cecily & Richard Covert, 344
Bowes, Charity & John Covert, 344
Bowes, Margery & Ralph Eure, 529
Bowet, 230, 232, 233, 373, 581
Bowet, Elizabeth & Thomas Dacre, 373
Bowet, William & Amy Wythe, 232
Bowet, William & Joan Ufford, 232
Bowyer, 503
Box, 192
Boyland, 494
Boyle, 145
Boynton, 113
Boynton, Henry & Elizabeth _____, 203
Boynton, Thomas & Alice Tempest, 113
Boyse, 131
Boyse, Alice & John Chauncy, 131
Boyton, 196
Bozoun, 39, 418
Bozun, 266
Bozun, Margaret & Richard Clopton, 266
Brabant, 30, 328, 519, 568
Bracebridge, 259
Braci, 75
Brackley, 564
Bracks, 114
Bracy, 75, 76
Bracy, Masceline de & William de Cantelowe, 75
Bradshagh, 248, 277, 502
Bradstreet, 347, 477
Braine, 30, 195, 468, 469, 470, 521, 565
Brake, 161, 508

Bramshott, 340
Bramshott, Elizabeth & John Dudley, 340
Brandon, 346, 460, 479, 667
Brandon, John, 132, 133, 217, 438, 476
Brandon, Margaret & Gregory Lovell, 479
Brandon, Thomas & Elizabeth Dinham, 667
Brattle, 347
Bratton, 666
Braunsford, 261
Braunspath, 357
Bray, 159, 364, 566
Braybrooke, 156
Brayfield, 475
Brayfield, Katherine & Nicholas Purefoy, 475
Braytoft, 368
Braytoft, Elizabeth & John Barrett, 368
Breauté, 254, 413, 414
Brechin, 3
Breirton, 334
Brenchley, 580
Brénieu, 429
Brent, 10, 64, 461, 594, 595
Brent, John & Anne Berkeley, 594
Brent, Margaret & John Dering, 595
Brent, Margaret & John Moore, 595
Brente, 636
Breouse, 624
Brereley, 466
Brereton, 28, 276, 346, 409, 427, 449, 500, 590, 592, 593
Brereton, John & Katherine Berkeley, 593
Bret, 303
Breteuil, 171, 467
Breton, 33, 590
Breton, William & Margaret Cheyne, 27
Brett, 467
Breuse, 14, 58, 69, 82, 494

Brewer, 138, 466
Brewes, 14, 27, 28, 58, 60, 66, 67, 69, 82, 138, 183, 205, 494, 511, 560, 566, 590, 597, 622, 623, 624
Brewes, Eve de & William de Cantelowe, 82
Brewes, Giles de & Joan de Beaumont, 59
Brewes, Giles de & Katherine de Huntingfield, 59
Brewes, John de & Agnes ____, 60
Brewes, John de & Eve de Ufford, 60
Brewes, John de & Joan de Shardelow, 60
Brewes, Margaret & John Shelton, 61
Brewes, Margaret de & Ralph de Camoys, 67
Brewes, Margaret de & Thomas de Monthermer, 205
Brewes, Richard de & Alice le Rus, 58
Brewes, Robert & Ela Stapleton, 61
Brewouse, 623
Brews, 499
Brewse, 58
Brian, 446, 482, 578
Brie, 30
Brien, 483
Briene, 483
Brienne, 116, 472
Bringhurst, 395
Brinklow, 543
Brionne, 171
Briouze, 511, 560
Brisele, 228
Brittany, 95, 119, 152, 192, 195, 451, 452, 469, 521, 535, 565, 617
Brittany, Constance of & Guy de Thouars, 152
Brittany, Constance of & Ranulph, Earl of Chester, 152
Briwerre, 75, 82, 137, 138, 634
Brocas, 108, 627
Brocas, William & Eleanor Eltonhead, 504

Brock, 279
Brock, John & Anne Vere, 279
Brock, John & Mary Pascall, 279
Brock, John & Sarah Symmes, 10
Brockhole, 574
Brograve, 362
Brok, 597
Brokas, 629
Brokesbourne, 350
Brokhole, 574
Brome, 61
Brome, Isabel & John Denton, 475
Brome, Isabel & Philip Purefoy, 474
Brome, Mary & Ralph Shelton, 61
Bromflete, 247, 551, 632
Bromflete, Henry & Eleanor Fitz Hugh, 391
Bromflete, Joan & Thomas Fauconberge, 551
Bromflete, Margaret & John Clifford, 247
Bromflete, Margaret & Lancelot Threlkeld, 247
Bromley, 432, 501
Bromley, Margaret & William Stanley, 501
Brompton, 308
Brompton, Elizabeth de & Edmund de Cornwall, 308
Brook, 459
Brooke, 64, 369, 458, 628
Brooke, Mary & John Barrett, 369, 628
Brooke, Mary & Richard Walden, 369, 628
Broughton, 110, 403
Broughton, Nicholas & Philippe Lovel, 458
Broun, 457
Broune, 576
Brown, 679
Browne, 44, 155, 170, 214, 278, 366
Browne, Jane & John Stoughton, 366
Brudenell, 678
Brûlon, 133

Brumfeld, 222
Brun, 565
Brune, 194
Brus, 16, 17, 32, 33, 46, 86, 191, 197, 220, 221, 242, 281, 282, 283, 478, 548, 549, 599
Brus, Agnes de & Hugh de Wesenham, 283
Brus, Agnes de & Robert Lovetot, 283
Brus, Agnes de & Walter de Fauconberge, 548
Brus, Bernard de & Agatha _____, 282
Brus, Bernard de & Agnes de Hardreshull, 282
Brus, Bernard de & Alice de Beauchamp, 281
Brus, Bernard de & Constance de Merston, 281
Brus, Bernard de & Isabel Falkney, 282
Brus, Edward de, 17
Brus, Euphame de & Patrick, Earl of Dunbar, 478
Brus, Joan de & Nicholas Greene, 542
Brus, Robert de, 5, 200
Brus, Robert de & Maud Fitz Alan, 32
Brus, Robert de, King of Scots, 5
Brutton, 635
Bryan, 1, 2, 140, 273, 278, 328, 333, 440, 446, 482, 496
Bryan, Elizabeth de & Robert Fitz Payn, 273
Bryan, Guy de & Elizabeth de Montagu, 1, 446
Bryan, Guy de & Joan de Carew, 1
Bryan, Margaret de & Hugh de Courtenay, 328
Bryan, William de & Joan Arundel, 482
Brydde, 574
Bryers, 362
Brynklowe, 103
Buch, 419
Buchan, 3, 4, 5, 6, 7, 197, 221, 562, 663

Buckingham, 43, 176, 389, 403, 431, 538, 573, 592, 656, 666
Buckland, 178, 509, 510, 511, 512, 513, 515
Buckland, Hawise de & John de Boville, 511
Buckland, Hugh de & Maud _____, 509
Buckland, Maud de & William d'Avranches, 511
Buckland, William de & Maud de Say, 510
Buckler, 435
Buckton, 525, 528
Bucton, 376
Buelot, Baldwin & Rohese Fitz Baldwin, 238
Builli, 238, 519
Builli, Idoine de & Robert de Vipont, 238
Builli, John de & Cecily de Bussey, 238
Builly, 238
Bukyngham, 570
Bulkeley, 8, 133, 160, 216, 345
Bulkeley, Dorcas & Anthony Ingoldsby, 9
Bulkeley, Edward & Olive Irby, 9
Bulkeley, Elizabeth & Atherton Hough, 10
Bulkeley, Elizabeth & Richard Whittingham, 9
Bulkeley, Martha & Abraham Mellowes, 9
Bulkeley, Peter & Grace Chetwode, 10
Bulkeley, Peter & Jane Allen, 10
Bulkeley, Thomas & Elizabeth Grosvenor, 8
Buller, 337
Buller, Francis & Thomasine Williams, 338
Buller, Katherine & James Parker, 339
Buller, Richard & Alice Hayward, 338

Buller, Richard & Margaret Tretherff, 337
Bulleyn, 57
Bully, 149
Bulmer, 113, 289, 549, 630
Bulmer, Eve de & Henry Fitz Hugh, 630
Bulmer, John de & Tiphaine de Morwick, 629
Bulmer, Ralph de & Alice de Killingholm, 549
Bulstrode, _____ & Faith Devenish, 486
Burcester, 28, 506, 590
Burcester, William & Margaret Cheyne, 27
Burcester, William & Margaret Gisors, 26
Burcestre, 27
Burcy, 20
Burdet, 572
Burell, 338
Bures, 568
Bures, John de & Hawise de Muscegros, 569
Burgh, 12, 14, 15, 16, 17, 19, 20, 21, 22, 23, 49, 69, 75, 112, 192, 204, 205, 228, 386, 514, 522, 606, 641, 650, 651, 652, 655
Burgh, _____ de & Robert de Blundeville, 13
Burgh, Ankaret & John Leighton, 641
Burgh, Devorguille de & Robert Fitz Walter, 651
Burgh, Elizabeth de, 448
Burgh, Elizabeth de & Lionel of Antwerp, 23
Burgh, Giles de & James Stewart, 15
Burgh, Henry & Katherine Neville, 112
Burgh, Hubert de, 185
Burgh, Hubert de & Isabel of Gloucester, 514
Burgh, Hubert de, Earl of Kent, 515

Burgh, Joan de & Alexander de Clavering, 224
Burgh, Joan de & John Darcy, 18, 386
Burgh, Joan de & Thomas Fitz John, 18
Burgh, John de & Elizabeth de Clare, 19
Burgh, Margaret de & Richard de Clare, 192
Burgh, Margery de & Thebaud le Boteler (or Butler), 45
Burgh, Maud de & Gilbert de Clare, 204
Burgh, Raymond de & Christian Fitz Robert, 515
Burgh, Richard de & Gille de Lacy, 14
Burgh, Richard de & Margaret _____, 16
Burgh, Thomas de & Nesta de Cockfield, 12
Burgh, Walter de & Alice _____, 12
Burgh, Walter de & Aveline Fitz John, 15
Burgh, William de & _____, 14
Burgh, William de & Maud of Lancaster, 22
Burghersh, 18, 24, 25, 26, 27, 94, 166, 421, 451, 452, 497, 571, 572, 656
Burghersh, Bartholomew de & Cecily de Weyland, 26
Burghersh, Bartholomew de & Elizabeth de Verdun, 24
Burghersh, Bartholomew de & Margaret Gisors, 26
Burghersh, Elizabeth & Edward le Despenser, 451
Burghersh, Elizabeth de & Maurice Fitz Thomas, 18
Burghley, 146, 481
Burgundy, 28, 29, 30, 31, 95, 115, 237, 428, 463, 464, 465, 471
Burgundy, 660
Burgundy, Eudes II, Duke of & Marie of Blois, 28
Burgundy, Eudes III, Duke of & Alix de Vergy, 29
Burgundy, Eudes III, Duke of & Mahaut (or Mafalda) of Portugal, 29
Burgundy, Eudes of & Mathilde (or Mahaut) de Bourbon, 30
Burgundy, Hugh, Duke of & Béatrice of Navarre, 30
Burgundy, Hugh, Duke of & Yolande de Dreux, 30
Burgundy, Hugues III, Duke of & Alix of Lorraine, 28
Burgundy, Hugues III, Duke of & Béatrix d'Albon, 28
Burgundy, Mahaud of & Robert II, Count of Dreux, 469
Burgyllon, 548
Burk, 52
Burleigh, 395
Burley, 573, 658
Burley, Joan & Philip Chetwynd, 573
Burley, Joan & Thomas Littleton, 573
Burnaby, 158
Burnel, 31, 32, 33, 34, 35, 41, 291
Burnele, 34
Burnell, 31, 32, 34, 35, 36, 37, 38, 40, 268, 408, 417, 418, 441, 443, 599, 639, 659
Burnell, Edward & Aline le Despenser, 34
Burnell, Edward & Aline le Strange, 39
Burnell, Edward & Elizabeth [de la] Pole, 417
Burnell, Edward & Elizabeth de la Pole, 39
Burnell, Hugh & Elizabeth _____, 37
Burnell, Hugh & Joan Devereux, 38, 659
Burnell, Hugh & Joyce Botetourt, 37
Burnell, Katherine & John Ferrers, 41
Burnell, Katherine & John Radcliffe, 40
Burnell, Katherine & John Talbot, 40
Burnell, Maud & John de Haudlo, 35

Burnell, Maud & John Lovel, 34
Burnell, Nicholas & Mary _____, 37
Burnell, Philip & Maud Fitz Alan, 31
Burnell, Thomas & Joan de Berkeley, 268
Burnham, 297
Burnham, Rowland & Alice Eltonhead, 505
Burns, 119
Burrell, 44
Burrell, Elizabeth & Thomas Burrough, 44
Burrough, 44, 45
Burrough, George & Frances Sparrow, 45
Burrough, Nathaniel & Rebecca Stiles, 45
Burrough, Thomas & Bridget Higham, 44
Burrough, Thomas & Elizabeth Burrell, 44
Bursalle, 26
Burton, 130, 277, 296, 347, 550, 590, 640
Burton, Margaret & Thomas Stawell, 590
Burton, Robert & Christian Stapleton, 641
Burton, Roger de & Agnes _____, 524
Bury, 146
Busche, 165
Bush, 165
Bush, Ralph & Eleanor Fitz Warin, 165
Busket, 325
Busse, 324
Bussei, 238
Bussey, 238
Bussey, Cecily de & John de Builli, 238
Bussey, William de & Rohese Fitz Baldwin, 238
Bussh, 165
Butiller, 53

Butler, 19, 45, 46, 47, 49, 51, 53, 54, 57, 147, 161, 247, 276, 279, 345, 361, 376, 387, 491, 575, 594, 666
Butler, Anne & Ambrose Cresacre, 54
Butler, Anne & James Saint Leger, 54
Butler, Anne & Thomas Fitz James, Earl of Desmond, 52
Butler, Edmund & Joan Fitz John, 46
Butler, James & Anne Welles, 49
Butler, James & Avice Stafford, 51
Butler, James & Eleanor Beaufort, 51, 102
Butler, James & Eleanor de Bohun, 47
Butler, James & Elizabeth Darcy, 49
Butler, James & Joan Beauchamp, 50
Butler, Margaret & William Boleyn, 55
Butler, Nicholas & Elizabeth Wroth, 63
Butler, Philip & Elizabeth Cokayne, 161
Butler, Thebaud & Joan Fitz John, 45
Butler, Thebaud & Margery de Burgh, 45
Butler, Thomas & Anne Hankford, 52
Butler, Thomas & Lora Berkeley, 53
Buxhall, 398
Bygod, 553
Bygot, 553
Bylton, 224
Byngham, 104
Byrchore, 310
Byrd, 371
Byrde, 475
Byron, 110, 207, 484
Byron, James de & Alice de Roos, 207
Byseth, 202
Bytelescombe, 661
Byuelard, 562
Byzantium, 117
Cabrera, 115
Cade, 348, 501
Caerleon, 180
Cahaines, 381
Cailly, 256

Cailly, Adam de & Emma de Tateshale, 256
Cailly, Margaret de & Roger de Clifton, 256
Callaly, 222
Calmady, 339
Calthorp, 266, 581
Calthorpe, 55, 62, 229, 232
Calthorpe, Anne & Robert Drury, 472
Calthorpe, Christopher & Anne _____, 62
Calthorpe, Christopher & Maud Thurton, 62
Calthorpe, Prudence & Ralph Shelton, 62
Calveley, 496
Calverley, George & Agnes Wodhull, 158
Calvert, 63, 170
Calvert, Cecil & Anne Arundell, 64
Calvert, Charles & Jane Lowe, 65
Calvert, Charles & Margaret Charleton, 65
Calvert, Charles & Mary Bankes, 65
Calvert, Charles & Mary Darnall, 64
Calvert, George & Anne Mynne, 63
Calvert, George & Joan _____, 63
Calvert, Leonard & _____, 64
Calvin, John, 106
Cambridge, 96, 142, 245, 247, 417, 643, 657
Camden, 170
Camois, 69
Camoys, 65, 66, 67, 68, 69, 70, 71, 72, 331, 363, 415, 443, 494, 547
Camoys, Ela de & Peter de Goushill, 547
Camoys, John de & Elizabeth le Latimer, 69
Camoys, John de & Margaret de Gatesden, 65
Camoys, John de & Margaret Foliot, 69

Camoys, Margaret & Ralph Radmylde, 363
Camoys, Maud & Edward Courtenay, 331
Camoys, Ralph de & Elizabeth le Despenser, 68
Camoys, Ralph de & Margaret de Brewes, 67
Camoys, Richard & Joan Poynings, 72
Camoys, Roger & Isabel _____, 71
Camoys, Roger & Isabel de Beaunoy, 72
Camoys, Thomas & Elizabeth Louches, 70
Camoys, Thomas & Elizabeth Mortimer, 71
Campo Ernulfi, 125
Camville, 316
Camville, Richard de & Eustache Basset, 316
Candale, 419
Candishe, 278
Candishe, John & Margaret Zouche, 278
Candyshe, 278
Caneville, Maud de & John de Courtenay, 320
Canon, 165, 361
Cantelowe, 73, 74, 76, 77, 79, 81, 83, 92, 138, 180, 183, 185, 192, 204, 304, 351, 516, 588, 603, 623
Cantelowe, 76
Cantelowe, Eustace de & Katherine de Lisle, 74
Cantelowe, George de & Margaret de Lacy, 82
Cantelowe, Isabel de & Ralph de Pembridge, 75
Cantelowe, Isabel de & Stephen Devereux, 74
Cantelowe, Katherine & James Cromer, 351
Cantelowe, Milicent de & Eudes la Zouche, 83

Cantelowe, Milicent de & John de Mohaut, 83
Cantelowe, Sibyl de & Geoffrey Pauncefote, 74
Cantelowe, William de & Eve de Brewes, 82
Cantelowe, William de & Masceline de Bracy, 75
Cantelowe, William de & Maud Fitz Geoffrey, 78
Cantelowe, William de & Milicent de Gournay, 78
Cantelowe, Nichole & _____ de Wanneville, 74
Canterburi, 25
Cantilupe, 74, 76
Capel, 167, 168
Capell, William & Margaret Arundell, 167
Carant, 432
Caraunt, 585
Carbonel, 151
Carcasonne, 236
Carden, 341
Cardeville, 623
Carelton, 667
Carent, 585
Carent, Margaret & John Filoll, 585
Carent, Margaret & John Wroughton, 586
Carew, 1, 2, 3, 55, 97, 98, 99, 100, 101, 231, 273, 328, 334, 360, 400, 403, 436, 460, 581
Carew, Cecily & Thomas Kirkham, 101
Carew, Edmund & Katherine Huddesfield, 100
Carew, Joan de & Guy de Bryan, 1
Carew, John de & Elizabeth Corbet, 2
Carew, John de & Joan Talbot, 1
Carew, Katherine & Philip Champernoun, 436
Carew, Leonard de & Elizabeth Arundel, 97

Carew, Nicholas & Joan Courtenay, 98
Carew, Nicholas & Margaret Dinham, 100
Carew, Thomas & Elizabeth Bonville, 98
Carew, Thomas & Joan Carminow, 99
Carew, William & Joan Courtenay, 101
Carey, 57, 103, 104, 105, 107, 108
Carey, Henry & Anne Morgan, 107
Carey, Katherine & Francis Knolles, 109
Carey, Thomas & Margaret Spencer, 103
Carey, William & Mary Boleyn, 104
Carlell, 465
Carleton, 113, 617
Carleton, Edward & Ellen Newton, 113
Carleton, John & Ellen Strickland, 113
Carleton, Walter & Jane Gibbon, 113
Carlisle, 243, 465, 630
Carlton, 113
Carminow, 99, 128, 334
Carminow, Joan & Halnath Mauleverer, 99
Carminow, Joan & Thomas Carew, 99
Carminow, Margaret & Hugh Courtenay, 334
Carminow, Margaret de & John de Beaupré, 636
Carminow, Maud & John de Wilington, 128
Carne, 435
Carnell, William & Elizabeth _____, 96
Carpenter, 627
Carr, 214, 246
Carreu, 1, 97
Carrew, 97
Carrick, 17, 32, 33, 46, 549, 599
Carrillo, 116
Carroll, Dr. Charles, 49
Carru, 1
Carsey, 669

Carter, John & Eleanor Eltonhead, 504
Carvanell, Peter & Sanche Langford, 628
Cary, 100, 103
Castell, 494
Castellione, 464
Castile, 114, 115, 116, 117, 118, 119, 120, 121, 122, 151, 164, 194, 196, 252, 385, 453, 462, 551, 657
Castile & León, Pedro, King of, 122
Castile, Alfonso VIII, King of & Eleanor of England, 114
Castile, Alfonso XI, King of, 606
Castile, Beatriz of & Guglielmo VII, Marquis of Monferrato, 194
Castile, Berenguela I, Queen of & Alfonso IX, King of León, 115
Castile, Berenguela I, Queen of & Konrad II, Duke of Swabia, 115
Castile, Eleanor of [Queen of England], 17, 119, 194, 263, 302, 303
Castile, Juan of & Margarita of Monferrato, 195
Castile, Juan of & María Díaz de Haro, 195
Castile-León, Alfonso of & Mafalda González de Lara, 116
Castile-León, Alfonso of & Mayor Alfonso de Meneses, 116
Castile-León, Alfonso of & Teresa González de Lara, 116
Castile-León, Alfonso X, King of & Mayor Guillén de Guzmán, 118
Castile-León, Alfonso X, King of & Violante of Aragón, 118
Castile-León, Alfonso XI, King & Constanza Manuel, 121
Castile-Leon, Alfonso XI, King of & María of Portugal, 121
Castile-León, Fernando III, King of & Beatriz of Swabia, 117
Castile-León, Fernando III, King of & Jeanne (or Juana) de Dammartin, 117

Castile-León, Fernando IV, King of & Constanza of Portugal, 120
Castile-León, Pedro I, King of & Blanche of Bourbon, 121
Castile-León, Pedro I, King of & Juana de Castro, 121
Castile-León, Pedro I, King of & María Díaz de Padilla, 121
Castile-León, Sancho IV, King of & María Alfonso de Molina, 119
Castro, 114, 120, 121
Castro, Juana de & Pedro I, King of Castile and León, 121
Caterton, Thomas & Elizabeth Hastings, 496
Catesby, 96
Cateston, 496
Catfield, 228
Catlin, 352
Caul, 125
Caundish, 278
Cauntelo, 181
Caunterel, John & Alice Crubbe, 642
Caunton, 259
Causton, 70
Cauz, 255, 511
Cave, 145, 214, 296, 366, 564
Cavendish, 65, 278
Cavendyssh, 264
Cavendysshe, 278
Cay, 420, 421, 422, 430
Cecil, 107, 481
Cerda, de la, 118
Ceva, 600
Chabanais, 303
Chaceporc, 138, 154
Chadworth, 354
Chaix, 429
Challons, 99
Chalon, 30
Châlon, 30, 238
Chaloner, 344
Chalon-sur-Saône, 30
Chamber, 113, 581

Chamberlain, 96, 123, 144, 157, 585, 669
Chamberlain, Anne & Edward Raleigh, 144
Chamberlain, Anne & Ralph Foulshurst, 145
Chamberlain, Herbert the & Emma _____, 619
Chamberlain, Mary & Richard Skipwith, 669
Chamberlain, Richard & Elizabeth _____, 122
Chamberlain, Richard & Margaret Knyvet, 122
Chamberlain, Richard & Sibyl Fowler, 123
Chamberleng, 255
Chamberleyn, 123, 420
Chambernon, 435
Chambernoun, 124
Chamburn, 436
Champagne, 30, 184
Champaigne, 184
Champaigne, Robert & Ada de Hastings, 184
Champaine, 184, 455
Champaine, Robert de & Maud _____, 184
Champayne, 184
Champernoun, 102, 124, 125, 126, 306, 400, 401, 404, 435, 436, 459, 636
Champernoun, Hugh & Alice Bois, 436
Champernoun, Joan & Anthony Denny, 437
Champernoun, Joan & John Courtenay, 401
Champernoun, Joan de & Ralph de Wilington, 127
Champernoun, John & Margaret Courtenay, 436
Champernoun, Jordan de & Emma de Soligny, 125
Champernoun, Jordan de & Mabel Fitz Robert, 124

Champernoun, Philip & Katherine Carew, 436
Champernoun, Richard & Isabel Bonville, 435
Champernoun, Richard de & Joan de Cornwall, 306
Champernoun, William & Elizabeth Chuderlegh, 436
Champernoun, William de & Eve de Blanchminster, 126
Champney, 559
Champneys, 368, 628
Chanceaux, 180
Chandos, 1
Chaources, 137, 467
Chaources, Pain de & _____, 135
Chaources, Patrick & Maud de Hesdin, 133
Chaources, Patrick & Wiburge _____, 134
Chaources, Patrick de & Agnès _____, 136
Chapman, 573
Charleton, 65, 141, 142, 143, 292, 295
Charleton, Margaret & Charles Calvert, 65
Charleton, Margaret & Lawrence Eliot, 65
Charlton, 292
Charlton, Anne & Randall Grosvenor, 8
Charron, 523
Chartres, 121, 519
Chastel, 463
Châteaudun, 237, 470, 471
Châteaudun, Clémence de & Robert de Dreux, 471
Châteauneuf, 469, 470
Châtellerault, 385
Châtillon, 30, 39, 328, 384, 419, 464, 467, 471
Châtillon, Gautier de & Helisende de Vergy, 471

Châtillon, Gautier de & Isabelle de Dreux, 471
Châtillon, Gautier de & Isabelle de Rumigny, 472
Châtillon, Marie de & Renaud de Dammartin, 384
Châtillon, Yolande de & Archambaud de Dampierre, 464
Châtillon-sur-Marne, 471
Chaucer, 421, 424, 425, 665
Chaucer, Alice & William de la Pole, 421
Chaucers, 425
Chaumont, 469, 634
Chaumpayne, 184
Chaumpyon, 190
Chaunceux, 577
Chauncey, 133
Chauncy, 129, 130, 132
Chauncy, Charles & Catherine Eyre, 133
Chauncy, George & Agnes Welsh, 132
Chauncy, George & Jane Cornwell, 132
Chauncy, Henry & Jane Barrett, 132
Chauncy, Henry & Lucy _____, 132
Chauncy, Henry & Rose _____, 132
Chauncy, John & Alice Boyse, 131
Chauncy, John & Anne Leventhorpe, 131
Chauncy, John & Elizabeth Proffit, 131
Chauncy, John & Katherine _____, 131
Chauncy, John & Margaret Giffard, 130
Chauncy, William & Joan Bigod, 129
Chauntecler, 578
Chaunterel, 635
Chauvent, 603
Chauvigni, 470
Chauvigny, 470
Chaworth, 22, 79, 139, 140, 210, 225, 440, 441, 508, 607, 678

Chaworth, Pain de & Gundred de la Ferté, 137
Chaworth, Patrick de & Hawise de London, 138
Chaworth, Patrick de & Isabel de Beauchamp, 140, 440
Cheddre, 331
Chediok, 165
Chenduit, 627
Chenduit, John & Elizabeth Fitz Reynold, 627
Chenduit, Maud & Robert Foxcote, 627
Cheney, 161, 488
Cheriesson, 646
Cherleton, 141, 142, 143, 293, 591, 606, 608, 612, 613
Cherleton, Edward & Eleanor Holand, 142
Cherleton, Edward & Elizabeth Berkeley, 142
Cherleton, John, 609
Cherleton, John & Alice Arundel, 613
Cherleton, John de & Avice _____, 141
Cherleton, John de & Joan de Stafford, 141
Cherleton, John de & Maud de Mortimer, 141
Cherlton, 143
Cheseldine, Kenelm & Bridget Faulkner, 148
Cheseldine, Kenelm & Grace Dryden, 147
Cheseldine, Kenelm & Mary Gerard, 148
Cheseldyne, 147, 148
Chesney, 219, 413, 621
Chesney, Margaret de & Robert Fitz Roger, 219
Chester, 75, 76, 78, 148, 149, 150, 151, 152, 153, 174, 218, 233, 234, 239, 252, 253, 254, 461, 560, 567, 584
Chester, Agnes of & William de Ferrers, 560

Chester, Alice of & Richard Fitz Gilbert [de Clare], 174
Chester, Hugh, Earl of & Bertrade de Montfort, 151
Chester, Mabel of & William d'Aubeney, 252
Chester, Ranulph, Earl of & Clemence de Fougères, 152
Chester, Ranulph, Earl of & Constance of Brittany, 152
Chester, Ranulph, Earl of & Maud of Gloucester, 148
Chettell, 360
Chetwode, 10, 156, 158, 159
Chetwode, Elizabeth & Thomas Wodhull, 156
Chetwode, Elizabeth & William Loudesop, 156
Chetwode, Grace & Peter Bulkeley, 10
Chetwode, Richard & Agnes Wodhull, 158
Chetwode, Richard & Dorothy Needham, 159
Chetwode, Richard & Jane Drury, 159
Chetwood, 158
Chetwynd, 572, 573
Chetwynd, Philip & Ellen de la Roche, 572
Chetwynd, Philip & Joan Burley, 573
Cheverell, 511
Cheverston, 331
Cheverston, John de & Joan de Courtenay, 331
Cheyne, 27, 28, 90, 161, 166, 231, 343, 483, 508, 585, 590
Cheyne, John & Elizabeth Rempston, 162
Cheyne, Laurence & Elizabeth Cokayne, 161
Cheyne, Margaret & John Berkeley, 27, 590
Cheyne, Margaret & William Breton, 27

Cheyne, Margaret & William Burcester, 27
Cheyne, Robert & Elizabeth Webb, 157
Cheyne, William & Joan Frome, 585
Cheyne, William & Katherine Pabenham, 508
Cheyney, 593, 679
Chicheley, Margaret & Robert Barrett, 368
Chichester, 250, 251, 405
Chichley, Henry & Agatha Eltonhead, 504
Chickering, 412
Chidiock, 41, 165, 167, 276, 427, 430, 459, 592, 660
Chidiock, Elizabeth & Thomas Cobham, 660
Chidiock, Elizabeth & Walter Fitz Walter, 660
Chidiock, John & Eleanor Fitz Warin, 165
Chidiock, John & Katherine Lumley, 165
Chidiock, Katherine & John Arundell, 166
Chidiock, Katherine & Roger Lewknor, 166
Chidiock, Katherine & William Stafford, 166
Chiggewell, 223
Chike, 318
Chilmerford, 138
Chirche, 95
Chiverston, 331
Chiverton, 338
Choiseul, 469
Choke, 473
Cholmeley, 111, 289
Cholmeley, Richard & Elizabeth Pennington, 111
Cholmondeley, 292, 346
Chuderlegh, 436

Chuderlegh, Elizabeth & William Champernoun, 436
Chudleigh, 401, 405
Chute, 362
Chytwood, 158
Cigogné, 316
Citroun, 446
Clackere, 83
Clanvowe, 638
Clara, 81
Clare, 16, 17, 19, 20, 32, 59, 78, 175, 176, 177, 180, 181, 182, 183, 191, 193, 194, 196, 197, 198, 199, 200, 204, 228, 233, 234, 242, 252, 253, 298, 303, 304, 305, 388, 443, 444, 448, 513, 603, 606
Clare, Amice de & Baldwin de Rivers, 188
Clare, Aveline de & Geoffrey Fitz Peter, 178, 513
Clare, Aveline de & William de Munchensy, 177
Clare, Eleanor de & Hugh le Despenser, 443
Clare, Eleanor de & William la Zouche Mortimer, 444
Clare, Elizabeth de & John de Burgh, 19
Clare, Elizabeth de & Roger Damory, 19
Clare, Elizabeth de & Thebaud de Verdun, 19
Clare, Gilbert de & Alice de Lusignan, 195
Clare, Gilbert de & Isabel Marshal, 185
Clare, Gilbert de & Joan of England, 196
Clare, Gilbert de & Maud de Burgh, 204
Clare, Isabel de & Guglielmo VII, Marquis of Monferrato, 194
Clare, Joan de & Duncan of Fife, 200
Clare, Joan de & Gervase Avenel, 200
Clare, Joan de & Rhys Gryg, 183
Clare, Margaret de & Edmund of Almain, 303
Clare, Margaret de & Edmund, Earl of Cornwall, 303
Clare, Maud de & Robert de Clifford, 242
Clare, Maud de & Robert de Welle, 242
Clare, Richard de & Alice of Chester, 174
Clare, Richard de & Amice of Gloucester, 180
Clare, Richard de & Margaret de Burgh, 192
Clare, Richard de & Maud de Lacy, 192
Clare, Roger de & Alice de Dammartin, 182
Clarell, 208, 209, 210, 211, 499, 677
Clarell, Margaret & John Fitzwilliam, 209
Clarell, Margaret & Robert Waterton, 209
Clarell, Margaret & William Gascoigne, 209
Clarell, Thomas & Elizabeth Scrope, 210
Clarell, Thomas & Isabel Comyn, 208
Clarell, Thomas & Maud Montgomery, 209
Clarell, William & Elizabeth de Reygate, 208
Clarence, 2, 23, 71, 357, 399, 402, 403, 488, 611
Clarence, George, Duke of, 52, 211, 429, 485
Clarence, Lionel, Duke of, 244, 448
Clarence, Philippe of, 24
Clarke, 11, 147, 213, 214
Clarke, Jeremy & Frances Latham, 214
Clarkson, 217
Clarkson, David & Elizabeth Kenrick, 217

Clarkson, Matthew & Catharine Van Schaick, 218
Claston, 83
Clavering, 222, 224, 225, 226, 227, 228, 230
Clavering, Alan de & Isabel Ryddell, 224
Clavering, Alexander de & Joan de Burgh, 224
Clavering, Ellen de & John d'Engaine, 225
Clavering, Eve de & James de Audley, 227
Clavering, Eve de & Robert de Benhale, 228
Clavering, Eve de & Thomas de Audley, 227
Clavering, Eve de & Thomas de Ufford, 227
Clavering, Roger de & Beatrice _____, 224
Claxton, 525
Clayfield, 411
Clemens, 348
Clement V, Pope, 442
Clere, 56, 58, 61, 105, 255, 627
Clere, Margaret & Ralph Shelton, 61
Clerk, 212
Clerke, 213
Clerke, George & Elizabeth Wilsford, 213
Clerke, James & Elizabeth Ferrers, 213
Clerke, James & Mary Saxby, 214
Clerke, William & Mary Weston, 214
Clermont, 28, 29, 121, 172, 233, 234, 235, 236, 237, 382, 384, 471
Clermont, Mahaut of & Aubrey, Count of Dammartin, 382
Clermont, Raoul de & Alix de Dreux, 237
Clermont, Raoul de & Gertrude de Nesle, 236
Clermont, Raoul de & Isabelle of Hainault, 237
Clermont, Renaud II, Count of & Adèle de Vermandois, 234
Clermont, Renaud II, Count of & Clémence of Bar, 234
Clermont, Simon de & Alix de Montfort, 236
Clermunt, 177
Clervaux, 295
Clervaux, Alice & John Faunt, 296
Clervaux, Thomas & Isabel Conyers, 295
Cleseby, 630
Cleseby, Emma de & Henry Fitz Hugh, 630
Cleves, 108
Cleves, Anne of, 43, 105, 437
Cliderowe, 348
Clif, 68
Clifford, 126, 127, 205, 241, 242, 243, 244, 245, 246, 247, 248, 249, 270, 272, 277, 374, 388, 529, 549, 564, 617, 655
Clifford, Giles de & Eve de Blanchminster, 126
Clifford, Henry & Anne Saint John, 248
Clifford, Henry & Florence Pudsey, 248
Clifford, John & Elizabeth Percy, 246
Clifford, John & Margaret Bromflete, 247
Clifford, Robert de & Isabel de Berkeley, 243
Clifford, Robert de & Maud de Clare, 242
Clifford, Roger de & Isabel de Vipont, 241
Clifford, Roger de & Maud de Beauchamp, 244
Clifford, Thomas & Joan Dacre, 246
Clifford, Thomas de & Elizabeth de Roos, 245
Clifton, 122, 249, 257, 258, 284, 348, 358, 451, 498, 499, 554

Clifton, Adam de & Eleanor de Mortimer, 256
Clifton, Constantine de & Margaret Howard, 258
Clifton, John de & Elizabeth de Cromwell, 257
Clifton, Katherine & Simon Felbrigg, 554
Clifton, Margery & Edward Hastings, 498
Clifton, Margery & John Wymondham, 498
Clifton, Roger de & Margaret de Cailly, 256
Clinton, 106, 259, 260, 261, 262, 263, 264, 265, 291, 348, 411, 551, 572, 574, 575, 581, 606, 664, 674, 675
Clinton, Elizabeth de & Eble de Mounts, 263
Clinton, Elizabeth de & John Fitzwilliam, 675
Clinton, John & Joan Ferrers, 574
Clinton, John & Margaret Saint Leger, 574
Clinton, John de & Elizabeth de la Plaunche, 264
Clinton, John de & Ida de Oddingseles, 259
Clinton, John de & Idoine de Say, 264
Clinton, John de & Joan _____, 264
Clinton, John de & Margery Corbet, 263
Clinton, William & Anne Botreaux, 664
Clinton, William de & Juliane de Leybourne, 261
Clopton, 265, 266, 267, 641
Clopton, Richard & Margaret Bozun, 266
Clopton, Richard & Margery Playters, 266
Clopton, Walter & Margaret Maidstone, 267
Clopton, William & Anne Booth, 267

Clopton, William & Elizabeth Sutcliffe, 267
Clopton, William & Margery Waldegrave, 266
Clopton, William & Thomasine Knyvet, 265
Clyfford, 248
Clynton, 259
Clyve, 294
Clyvedon, 330
Clyvedon, Margaret & Peter Courtenay, 330
Cobham, 268, 269, 270, 274, 330, 369, 543, 571, 609, 626, 628, 660
Cobham, Joan de & Henry de Grey, 274
Cobham, Margaret & Matthew Fitz Herbert, 626
Cobham, Reynold & Anne Bardolf, 270
Cobham, Reynold & Eleanor Culpeper, 270
Cobham, Reynold & Eleanor Mautravers, 269
Cobham, Reynold & Elizabeth de Stafford, 269, 571
Cobham, Reynold de & Joan de Berkeley, 268
Cobham, Thomas & Elizabeth Chidiock, 660
Cocat, 293
Cocke, 267
Cockerman, 584
Cockes, 132, 593, 594
Cockfield, 12
Cockfield, Nesta de & John de Beauchamp, 13
Cockfield, Nesta de & Matthew de Leyham, 13
Cockfield, Nesta de & Thomas de Burgh, 12
Coddington, 214
Codnor, 674
Coe, 132

Coetmor, 346
Coetmore, 346
Coffyn, 600
Cogan, 333, 663, 664
Cogan, Elizabeth & Fulk Fitz Warin, 663
Cogan, Elizabeth & Hugh Courtenay, 333, 664
Cokayne, 160, 161, 508
Cokayne, Elizabeth & Laurence Cheyne, 161
Cokayne, Elizabeth & Philip le Boteler (or Butler), 161
Cokayne, John & Ida Grey, 160
Coke, 437
Cokedaek, 282
Cokefeld, 12
Cokerel, 379
Cokesey, 574, 640
Cokesey, Joyce & Leonard Stapleton, 640
Cokesey, Joyce & Walter Beauchamp, 640
Cokette, 573
Cokyngton, 127, 128
Colbroke', 403
Colchester, 339
Coldon, 488
Cole, 147
Cole, Samuel & Anne Mansfield, 530
Coleshill, 260
Coleshull, 398
Coleville, 59, 394
Collingwood, 558
Collins, 147, 438
Colmore, 410
Colomb, 429
Colton, 466
Columbers, 319, 566
Columbers, Philip de & Egeline de Courtenay, 319
Colville, 388, 549
Colvyle, 233, 373
Coly, 500

Combe, 217, 484, 485
Combe, Thomas & Margaret Echingham, 485
Compton, 201, 477, 593
Comyn, 3, 4, 5, 6, 7, 80, 142, 206, 207, 208, 220, 221, 222, 242, 562, 663
Comyn, Alexander & Joan le Latimer, 6
Comyn, Alexander, Earl of Buchan & Elizabeth de Quincy, 3
Comyn, Isabel & Thomas Clarell, 208
Comyn, John & Alice de Roos, 206
Comyn, John & Eve _____, 206
Comyn, John & Maud _____, 207
Comyn, John, Earl of Buchan & Isabel of Fife, 4
Comyn, Margaret & John of Ross, 7
Comyn, Marjory & Patrick of Dunbar, 221
Comyn, Robert & _____, 207
Comyn, Thomas & Margaret Danyel, 208
Condet, 126
Coningsby, 410, 461
Coningsby, Elizabeth & John Fitz James, 410
Coningsby, Elizabeth & Richard Berkeley, 410
Connacht, 15, 16, 22, 49, 204, 386, 655
Constable, 20, 112, 249, 284, 285, 287, 290, 527, 528, 530, 547, 548, 633, 634, 669, 670, 682, 683
Constable of England, 43, 293, 335, 425, 605, 613, 620, 631, 657, 663
Constable of France, 471
Constable of Gloucester, 620
Constable of Ireland, 19
Constable of Scotland, 3, 4, 221, 222, 562, 663
Constable of the Tower of London, 18, 25, 240, 293, 348, 386, 387, 422, 514, 538, 540, 582, 602, 657
Constable, Agnes & Ralph Eure, 528

Constable, Margaret & William Eure, 527
Constable, Marmaduke & Barbara Sothill, 286
Constable, Marmaduke & Jane Conyers, 287
Constable, Marmaduke & Joyce Stafford, 285
Constable, Marmaduke & Margery Fitz Hugh, 285
Constable, Robert & Agnes Wentworth, 284
Constable, Robert & Katherine Manners, 286
Constantinople, 116
Conway, 345
Conway, Edwin & Martha Eltonhead, 505
Conyers, 96, 130, 246, 248, 287, 288, 289, 290, 296, 375, 391, 465, 525, 526, 528, 552
Conyers, Agnes & Geoffrey Lee, 465
Conyers, Christopher & Alice Neville, 465
Conyers, Christopher & Anne Dacre, 290
Conyers, Isabel & Thomas Clervaux, 295
Conyers, Jane & Marmaduke Constable, 287
Conyers, John & Alice Neville, 288
Conyers, John & Margery Darcy, 288
Conyers, William & Anne Neville, 289
Conyers, William & Mary Scrope, 289
Conyngesby, 410
Coode, 65
Cook, 264
Cooke, 344, 480, 679
Cookes, 576, 593
Cookes, Alice & Edward Berkeley, 593
Cooksey, 640
Coope, 145
Cooper, 228, 353
Cope, 145, 157
Cope, Elizabeth & John Dryden, 145
Cope, John & Bridget Raleigh, 145
Cope, John & Margaret Tame, 145
Cope, John & Mary Mallory, 145
Copleston, 405
Coplestone, 668
Copley, 364
Copley, Margaret & Edward Lewknor, 364
Coppleston, 166
Corbet, 91, 263, 292, 576, 577, 597, 608, 641
Corbet, Elizabeth & John de Carew, 2
Corbet, Elizabeth & John de Gournay, 2
Corbet, Margery & John de Clinton, 263
Corbet, Richard & Elizabeth Devereux, 294
Corbet, Robert & Elizabeth Vernon, 295
Corbet, Robert & Margaret ____, 292
Corbet, Roger & Elizabeth Hopton, 292
Corbet, Roger & Margaret de Erdington, 292
Corbett, 295, 474
Corbett, Richard & Mary Drury, 474
Corbicun, 76
Corbin, 297
Corbin, George & Mary Faunt, 297
Corbin, Henry & Alice Eltonhead, 297, 505
Corbin, Thomas & Winifred Grosvenor, 297
Corbizun, 74
Cordall, 266
Córdoba, 116, 118, 119, 120, 121
Core, 491
Cork, 657
Cormailles, 589
Cornerde, 543
Cornerde, Joyce & Thomas Culpeper, 543

Cornewaille, 535
Cornewayll, 535, 537
Cornhill, 413, 530
Cornhill, Henry de & Alice de Courcy, 413
Cornhill, Joan de & Hugh de Neville, 413
Cornubia, 307
Cornwall, 59, 87, 90, 133, 182, 185, 186, 187, 191, 192, 194, 195, 205, 242, 294, 298, 299, 302, 303, 304, 305, 306, 307, 308, 309, 310, 311, 312, 414, 470, 511, 535, 536, 538, 597, 603, 616, 620, 621, 630, 635
Cornwall, Edmund & Alice _____, 310
Cornwall, Edmund & Elizabeth Barre, 310
Cornwall, Edmund de & Elizabeth de Brompton, 308
Cornwall, Edmund, Earl of, 309
Cornwall, Edmund, Earl of & Margaret de Clare, 303
Cornwall, Eleanor & Hugh Mortimer, 311
Cornwall, Eleanor & Richard Croft, 311
Cornwall, Geoffrey de & Cecily _____, 310
Cornwall, Geoffrey de & Margaret de Mortimer, 309
Cornwall, Joan de & Peter de Fissacre, 306
Cornwall, Joan de & Richard de Champernoun, 306
Cornwall, John & Elizabeth [of] Lancaster, 535
Cornwall, John & Philippe Arundel, 535
Cornwall, Richard & Alice _____, 310
Cornwall, Richard & Cecily Seymour, 310
Cornwall, Richard de & Joan _____, 306

Cornwall, Richard de & Sibyl de Bodrugan, 309
Cornwall, Richard of England, Earl of & Beatrice de Falkenburg, 299
Cornwall, Richard, Earl of, 182, 188, 195
Cornwall, Richard, Earl of & Beatrice de Falkenburg, 186
Cornwall, Richard, Earl of & Isabel Marshal, 185
Cornwall, Richard, Earl of & Sanche of Provence, 186
Cornwallis, 376, 481
Cornwallis, Anne & Thomas Dade, 377
Cornwallis, John & Mary Sulliard, 376
Cornwallis, Richard & Margaret Louthe, 377
Cornwallis, Thomas & Philippe Tyrrell, 376
Cornwallis, William & Elizabeth Stanford, 376
Cornwallys, 376
Cornweleys, 504
Cornwell, 132
Cornwell, Jane & George Chauncy, 132
Cortenay, 314
Corton, 273
Coruo, 661
Cossington, 327
Cossington, William de & Elizabeth de Vere, 327
Costede, 579
Cosyn, 124
Cotes, 103, 126, 548
Cotesford, 144
Cottesford, 144
Cottesmore, 430
Cotton, 170, 283, 296, 343, 480
Cotum, 523
Coucy, 17, 343, 385
Coucy, Yolande de & Robert II, Count of Dreux, 469
Countess Marshal, 603

Coupland, 26, 611
Courcy, 317, 412, 413
Courcy, Alice de & Henry de Cornhill, 413
Courcy, Alice de & Warin Fitz Gerold, 413
Courcy, Hawise de & Reynold de Courtenay, 317
Courcy, William de & Gundred de Warenne, 412
Court, 665
Courtenay, 2, 3, 31, 49, 70, 98, 99, 101, 129, 166, 247, 273, 315, 316, 317, 318, 319, 321, 322, 323, 324, 325, 326, 327, 328, 329, 330, 331, 332, 333, 334, 335, 336, 337, 338, 400, 401, 402, 404, 408, 415, 436, 456, 457, 463, 468, 478, 506, 507, 532, 663, 664
Courtenay, Aveline de & John Giffard, 322
Courtenay, Edward & Eleanor Mortimer, 332
Courtenay, Edward & Elizabeth Courtenay, 334
Courtenay, Edward & Maud Camoys, 331
Courtenay, Edward de & Emeline Dauney, 331
Courtenay, Egeline de & Gilbert Basset, 316
Courtenay, Egeline de & Philip de Columbers, 319
Courtenay, Eleanor de & John de Grey, 273
Courtenay, Elizabeth & Edward Courtenay, 334
Courtenay, Elizabeth & John Tretherff, 336
Courtenay, Elizabeth & William Strode, 404
Courtenay, Hawise de & John de Gatesden, 414
Courtenay, Hawise de & John de Neville, 414
Courtenay, Henry & Elizabeth Grey, 335
Courtenay, Henry & Gertrude Blount, 336
Courtenay, Hugh & Anne Talbot, 332
Courtenay, Hugh & Elizabeth Cogan, 333, 664
Courtenay, Hugh & Elizabeth Fitz Payn, 333
Courtenay, Hugh & Margaret Carminow, 334
Courtenay, Hugh & Maud Beaumont, 333
Courtenay, Hugh & Philippe l'Arcedekne, 333
Courtenay, Hugh de & Agnes de Saint John, 323
Courtenay, Hugh de & Eleanor le Despenser, 321
Courtenay, Hugh de & Elizabeth de Vere, 327
Courtenay, Hugh de & Margaret de Bohun, 326
Courtenay, Hugh de & Margaret de Bryan, 328
Courtenay, Hugh de & Maud de Holand, 328
Courtenay, Joan & Nicholas Carew, 98
Courtenay, Joan & Robert Vere, 99
Courtenay, Joan & William Carew, 101
Courtenay, Joan de & John de Cheverston, 331
Courtenay, John & Joan Champernoun, 401
Courtenay, John de & Emma _____, 320
Courtenay, John de & Isabel de Vere, 320
Courtenay, John de & Maud de Caneville, 320
Courtenay, Katherine & Thomas d'Engaine, 506
Courtenay, Margaret & _____ Fortescue, 436

Courtenay, Margaret & John Champernoun, 436
Courtenay, Margaret & John West, 436
Courtenay, Muriel de & John de Dinham, 456
Courtenay, Peter & Margaret Clyvedon, 330
Courtenay, Philip & Anne Wake, 400
Courtenay, Philip & Elizabeth _____, 403
Courtenay, Philip & Elizabeth Ashford, 403
Courtenay, Philip & Elizabeth Hungerford, 402
Courtenay, Philip & Humphrey Prideaux, 404
Courtenay, Philip & Jane Fowell, 404
Courtenay, Reynold de & _____, 314
Courtenay, Reynold de & Hawise de Courcy, 317
Courtenay, Reynold de & Maud Fitz Robert, 315
Courtenay, Robert de & Mary de Vernon, 318
Courtenay, Thomas de & Muriel de Moels, 325
Courtenay, William & Katherine Plantagenet, 335
Courtenay, William & Margaret Bonville, 402
Courtenay, William, Archbishop of Canterbury, 329
Courteney, 337, 403
Courteys, 269
Courtney, 321
Coverham, 130
Covert, 344, 559, 594
Covert, Anne & Walter Covert, 344
Covert, Elizabeth & John Fenwick, 559
Covert, John & Charity Bowes, 344
Covert, Richard & Anne Hendley, 344
Covert, Richard & Cecily Bowes, 344

Covert, Richard & Elizabeth Neville, 594
Covert, Richard & Mary Heron, 344
Covert, Walter & Anne Covert, 344
Cowper, 679
Coytemore, Alice & Hugh Wynne, 347
Coytemore, Elizabeth & William Tyng, 347
Coytemore, Rowland & Christian Haynes, 347
Coytemore, Rowland & Dorothy [?Lane], 347
Coytemore, Rowland & Katherine Myles, 347
Coytemore, Thomas & Martha Rainsborough, 347
Coytemore, William & Jane Williams, 346
Coytemore, William & Mary Lewis, 346
Crakes, Walter de de & Isabel Ryddell, 225
Crane, Robert & Margaret Maidstone, 267
Cranford, 35
Cranston, 214
Crawley, 438
Crawley, Thomas & Mary Denny, 438
Crawthorne, 286
Crayke, 505
Crécy, 31
Creeke, 297, 505
Crekhay, 337
Crépy, 234
Cresacre, 53, 54, 55
Cresacre, Ambrose & Anne Butler, 54
Cressett, 294, 640, 641
Cressett, Robert & Christian Stapleton, 640
Cressy, 219, 222, 226
Crevequer, 511
Crewse, 338
Creyke, Henry & Alice Eltonhead, 297, 505

Cribbe, 625, 642
Criketoft, 32
Criketot, 32, 33, 599
Criketot, Simon de & Maud Fitz Alan, 32
Crimes, 319, 362
Crispe, 466, 594
Crispe, Elizabeth & Richard Lee, 466
Cristoferys, 337
Croatia, 118
Croc, 619
Crocker, 399, 430
Croft, 110, 253, 311
Croft, Edward & Joyce Skulle, 312
Croft, Elizabeth & James Vaughan, 312
Croft, Richard & Eleanor Cornwall, 311
Crofton, 66
Crofts, 62
Croke, 108, 431
Croke, Elizabeth & William Stonor, 431
Cromer, 348, 349, 580, 588
Cromer, Anne & William Whetenhall, 351
Cromer, Elizabeth & William Finch, 588
Cromer, Emeline & James Fiennes, 348
Cromer, James & Katherine Cantelowe, 351
Cromer, William & Elizabeth Fiennes, 349
Crompton, 369, 628
Cromuel, 241
Cromwell, 87, 105, 128, 169, 239, 240, 241, 242, 243, 257, 270, 272, 355, 356, 357, 358, 360, 369, 404, 444, 536, 554, 675, 676
Cromwell, Elizabeth de & Edward Benstead, 257
Cromwell, Elizabeth de & John de Clifton, 257

Cromwell, Frances & Richard Strode, 404
Cromwell, John de & Idoine de Vipont, 240
Cromwell, Maud & Richard Stanhope, 358
Cromwell, Maud & William Fitzwilliam, 676
Cromwell, Ralph & Joan Gray, 357
Cromwell, Ralph & Margaret Deincourt, 357
Cromwell, Ralph de & Amice (or Avice) Belers, 355
Cromwell, Ralph de & Joan de la Mare, 354
Cromwell, Ralph de & Joan de Somerville, 354
Cromwell, Ralph de & Maud de Bernake, 355
Crophill, Joan & Thomas Swynford, 390
Crosby, 111, 545
Crosby, Jane & Henry Curwen, 545
Crosley, 313
Crosley, Mary & Roger Parry, 313
Cross, 560
Crosse, 95, 201, 276
Crossland, 63
Crowmer, 348, 349, 351, 580
Croxston, 266
Croy, 318
Crubbe, 625, 642
Crubbe, Alice & John Caunterel, 642
Crubbe, Alice & John de Staford, 642
Crubbe, Alice & Reynold Fitz Reynold, 642
Cruel, 646
Cruil, 646
Crumbewell, 353
Crump, 214
Crumwell, 353
Crunes, 319
Cruse, 438
Cruues, 319

Crymes, 361, 362, 482
Crymes, George & Alice Lovell, 361
Crymes, Thomas & Margaret More, 361
Crymes, William & _____, 362
Crymes, William & Christiana _____, 362
Cryne, 581
Cudworth, 367
Cudworth, James & Mary Parker, 367
Cudworth, Ralph & Mary Machell, 366
Culcheth, 559
Culpeper, 20, 57, 169, 213, 270, 343, 351, 357, 369, 371, 485, 542, 628
Culpeper, Eleanor & Reynold Cobham, 270
Culpeper, Frances & Philip Ludwell, 371
Culpeper, Frances & Samuel Stephens, 370
Culpeper, Frances & William Berkeley, 371
Culpeper, John & Ann _____, 370
Culpeper, John & Eleanor Norwood, 370
Culpeper, John & Elizabeth Sedley, 369
Culpeper, John & Judith _____, 371
Culpeper, John & Margaret _____, 371
Culpeper, John & Mary _____, 372
Culpeper, John & Sarah Mayo, 371
Culpeper, John & Ursula Woodcock, 370
Culpeper, Thomas & Eleanor Greene, 542
Culpeper, Thomas & Joyce Cornerde, 543
Culpeper, Thomas & Katherine Saint Leger, 370
Culpeper, William & Cecily Barrett, 369
Cumberford, 368
Cumberland, 248
Cupere, 303

Curcy, 319, 412
Cure, 681
Cure, Richard & Rachel Fitzwilliam, 681
Curli, 598
Curson, 556
Curtenay, 314, 324
Curteys, 228
Curwen, 111, 545
Curwen, Henry & Jane Crosby, 545
Curwen, Henry & Mary Fairfax, 545
Curwen, Thomas & Agnes Strickland, 111
Curwen, Thomas & Florence Wharton, 111
Curzon, 390
Cutts, 108
D'Aubeney, 396
d'Aubeney, Alice & Alvred de Saint Martin, 520
d'Aubeney, Alice & Jean, Count of Eu, 519
D'Eiville, Joan & Adam de Everingham, 532
D'Eiville, John & Agnes _____, 532
D'Eiville, John & Margaret _____, 532
D'Eiville, John & Maud _____, 531
D'Eiville, Robert & Denise Fitz William, 531
d'Issoudun, 521
d'Oilly, 303
Dacre, 108, 233, 246, 247, 287, 290, 372, 373, 374, 375, 581, 582, 632
Dacre, Anne & Christopher Conyers, 290
Dacre, Humphrey & Mabel Parr, 374
Dacre, Joan & Richard Fiennes, 581
Dacre, Joan & Thomas Clifford, 246
Dacre, Thomas & Elizabeth Bowet, 373
Dacre, Thomas & Elizabeth Greystoke, 374
Dacre, Thomas & Philippe Neville, 372

Dacres, 233
Dade, Francis & Beheathland Bernard, 378
Dade, Thomas & Anne Cornwallis, 377
Dade, Thomas & Anne Haselop, 377
Dade, William & Elizabeth Revett, 378
Dade, William & Mary Wingfield, 378
Dagworth, 47, 48, 379, 380, 656, 658
Dagworth, Eleanor de & Walter Fitz Walter, 656
Dagworth, John de & Alice Fitz Warin, 379
Dagworth, John de & Maud de l'Escheker, 379
Dagworth, Nicholas de & Margaret ____, 380
Dagworth, Osbert de & Hawise ____, 379
Dagworth, Richard de & Isabel de Huntingfield, 378
Dagworth, Thomas de & Eleanor de Bohun, 47
Daiville, 530
Dalden, 433
Dale, 583
Daleroun, 32, 33
Dallingridge, 26, 506, 581
Dalmatia, 118
Dalston, 545
Dalton, 59, 345
Dalton, John de & Margery de Poynings, 59
Damet, 95
Dammartin, 78, 117, 118, 182, 234, 235, 380, 381, 382, 384
Dammartin, Alice de & Roger de Clare, 182
Dammartin, Aubrey, Count of & Joan Basset, 381
Dammartin, Aubrey, Count of & Mahaut de Clermont, 382
Dammartin, Aubrey, Count of & Maud ____, 381
Dammartin, Jeanne (or Juana) de & Fernando III, King of Castile and León, 117
Dammartin, Jeanne de & Jean de Nesle, 117
Dammartin, Renaud de & Ida of Boulogne, 384
Dammartin, Renaud de & Marie de Châtillon, 384
Dammartin, Simon de & Marie of Ponthieu, 385
Dammary, 19
Dammory, 19
Damory, 19, 20, 205, 662
Damory, Roger & Elizabeth de Clare, 19
Dampierre, 30, 464
Dampierre, Archambaud de & Yolande de Châtillon, 464
Danby, 370, 526
Dandy, 670
Danet, 87, 91
Danforth, 530
Danhurst, 408
Daniel, 594
Daniell, 360
Danvers, 123, 399, 434, 436, 484
Danvers, Agnes & Walter Dennis, 434
Danvers, John & Anne Stradling, 399
Danyel, 208
Danyel, Margaret & Thomas Comyn, 208
Danyell, 668
Darcy, 18, 49, 50, 164, 248, 265, 386, 387, 388, 389, 390, 391, 438, 544, 632
Darcy, ____ & Katherine Neville, 112
Darcy, Elizabeth & James le Boteler (or Butler), 49
Darcy, Elizabeth & Robert Lukyn, 49
Darcy, John & Eleanor de Holand, 387
Darcy, John & Elizabeth de Meinill, 388

Darcy, John & Emmeline Heron, 18, 386
Darcy, John & Joan de Burgh, 18, 386
Darcy, John & Margaret Grey, 389
Darcy, Margery & John Conyers, 288
Darcy, Philip & Eleanor Fitz Hugh, 391
Darcy, Philip & Elizabeth Gray, 389
Darcy, Roger & Isabel de Aton, 386
Darell, 156
Darges, 236
Darley, 683
Darnall, 64
Darnall, Mary & Charles Calvert, 64
Darrell, 42, 103, 311, 352
Dartmouth, John de & Joan Talbot, 1
Daubeney, 128, 133, 166, 167, 168, 391, 395, 507
Daubeney, Joan & John Waleys, 507
Daubeney, Joan & Laurence Pabenham, 507
Daubney, 170
Daumarle, 98, 458
Dauney, 331, 664
Dauney, Emeline & Edward de Courtenay, 331
Dauntsey, 397, 398, 475, 516
Dauntsey, Joan & John Dewall, 398
Dauntsey, Joan & John Stradling, 398
Dauntsey, Joan & Maurice Russell, 398
Dauntsey, John & Elizabeth Beverley, 398
Dauntsey, John & Joan de Bavent, 397
Dautrey, 538, 615
Dautry, 66, 68, 126
Davenport, 503
Davie, 405, 406
Davie, Humphrey & Mary White, 406
Davie, Humphrey & Sarah Gibbons, 406
Davie, John & Isabel Hele, 405
Davie, John & Julian Strode, 405
Davies, 411

Davis, Rice & Isabel Ligon, 411
Davis, Rice & Mary Pitt, 411
Davy, 629
Dawkins, 297
Dawny, 544
Dawson, 209
Dawtrey, 364
Dawtry, 544
Dayre, 70
Debenham, 498, 499
Deighton, 411, 477
Deighton, Frances & Richard Williams, 412
Deighton, Jane & John Lugg, 412
Deighton, Jane & Jonathan Negus, 412
Deighton, John & Jane Basset, 411
Deighton, Katherine & John Allin, 412, 477
Deighton, Katherine & Samuel Hackburne, 412
Deighton, Katherine & Thomas Dudley, 412, 477
Deincourt, 90, 259, 357, 673, 674, 675
Deincourt, Isabel & William Fitzwilliam, 673
Deincourt, Margaret & Ralph Cromwell, 357
Deincourt, William & Milicent la Zouche, 90
Deiville, 566, 672
Delabar, 434
Delahay, 352
Delaval, 103
Delves, 26, 216, 278
Dene, 35, 266
Dengayne, 507
Denginæ, 507
Denham, 679
Denison, 477
Denmark, 401
Dennett, 267
Dennis, 410, 433
Dennis, Isabel & Arthur Porter, 410

Dennis, Isabel & John Berkeley, 410
Dennis, Maurice & Alice Poyntz, 433
Dennis, Maurice & Katherine Stradling, 433
Dennis, Walter & _____ Fiennes, 434
Dennis, Walter & Agnes Danvers, 434
Dennis, Walter & Agnes Mynne, 434
Dennis, Walter & Alice Walwyn, 434
Dennis, William & Anne Berkeley, 434
Dennis, William & Edith Twinihoe, 435
Denny, 437, 438
Denny, Anthony & Joan Champernoun, 437
Denny, Mary & Thomas Astley, 438
Denny, Mary & Thomas Crawley, 438
Densell, 402
Denston, 472
Denton, 372, 475
Denton, Alice & Nicholas Purefoy, 475
Denton, John & Isabel Brome, 475
Denys, 433, 434, 635
Derby, 3, 4, 43, 122, 154, 191, 239, 273, 278, 390, 455, 494, 496, 503, 511, 532, 533, 560, 561, 562, 563, 564, 565, 566, 567, 570, 571, 606, 609, 623, 652
Derby, Henry, Earl of, 91
Derehaugh, 440
Derehaugh, William & Mary Wright, 440
Derham, 480
Dering, 353, 595
Dering, Bennett & John Fisher, 596
Dering, John & Margaret Brent, 595
Dering, Richard & Margaret Twysden, 595
Dersyngham, 616
Desmond, 18, 49, 52, 53
Desmond, Thomas, Earl of & Anne Butler, 52
Desmond, Thomas, Earl of & Ellice Barry, 52

Despenser, 1, 20, 28, 33, 34, 35, 36, 51, 67, 68, 69, 94, 140, 193, 197, 200, 204, 240, 321, 397, 407, 441, 442, 443, 444, 445, 446, 447, 448, 449, 450, 451, 452, 453, 454, 455, 496, 497, 556, 571, 572, 606, 625, 626, 630, 653, 661, 674
Despenser, Aline le & Edward Burnell, 34
Despenser, Anne le & Edward le Boteler, 450
Despenser, Anne le & Hugh Hastings, 497
Despenser, Anne le & Thomas Morley, 497
Despenser, Anne le, Lady Botiller, 451
Despenser, Edward le & Anne de Ferrers, 448
Despenser, Edward le & Elizabeth Burghersh, 451
Despenser, Eleanor le & Hugh de Courtenay, 321
Despenser, Elizabeth le & Ralph de Camoys, 68
Despenser, Elizabeth le & William la Zouche, 94
Despenser, Henry le, Bishop of Norwich, 451
Despenser, Hugh le & Alice de Hotham, 449
Despenser, Hugh le & Eleanor de Clare, 443
Despenser, Hugh le & Elizabeth de Montagu, 446
Despenser, Hugh le & Isabel de Beauchamp, 140, 441
Despenser, Hugh le & Sibyl _____, 450
Despenser, Isabel le & Ralph de Monthermer, 197
Despenser, Isabel le & Richard de Arundel, 606
Despenser, Margaret le & Robert Ferrers, 571

Despenser, Richard le & Eleanor Neville, 455
Despenser, Thomas le & Constance of York, 453
Devenish, 55, 486
Devenish, Faith & _____ Bulstrode, 486
Devenish, Faith & Thomas Oxenbridge, 486
Devereux, 38, 74, 109, 294, 482, 483, 575, 576, 577, 658, 659
Devereux, Elizabeth & Richard Corbet, 294
Devereux, Elizabeth & Thomas Leighton, 294
Devereux, Joan & Hugh Burnell, 38, 659
Devereux, Joan & Walter Fitz Walter, 658
Devereux, Stephen & Isabel de Cantelowe, 74
Devereux, Walter & Anne Ferrers, 575
Devereux, Walter & Jane _____, 575
Devereux, William & Margaret de Mortimer, 309
Deviock, John & Margaret Longland, 638
Deviock, Margaret & John Stapleton, 639
Devon, 70, 124, 166, 175, 188, 189, 190, 191, 273, 318, 321, 322, 323, 325, 326, 327, 329, 331, 332, 334, 335, 336, 338, 341, 404, 414, 506
Dewale, 398
Dewall, John & Joan Dauntsey, 398
Dewe, Richard & Elizabeth Mitton, 216
Deye, 216
Deyncourt, 90
Deyville, 530
Dible, 101
Dier, 216
Digby, 352
Digges, 56, 466, 678

Dillon, 46, 57
Dinan, 152, 178, 513
Dingley, 627
Dinham, 41, 100, 168, 169, 303, 306, 320, 321, 325, 408, 455, 456, 457, 458, 459, 498, 499, 660, 666, 667, 678
Dinham, Elizabeth & Fulk Bourchier, 666
Dinham, Elizabeth & John Sapcote, 667
Dinham, Elizabeth & Thomas Brandon, 667
Dinham, Joan & Maurice Berkeley, 408
Dinham, John & Eleanor de Montagu, 457
Dinham, John & Elizabeth Fitz Walter, 41, 459
Dinham, John & Elizabeth Willoughby, 459
Dinham, John & Joan Arches, 459
Dinham, John & Maud Mautravers, 458
Dinham, John & Philippe Lovel, 458
Dinham, John de & Margaret de Botreaux, 456
Dinham, John de & Muriel de Courtenay, 456
Dinham, Josce de & Margaret de Hydon, 455
Dinham, Katherine & Thomas Arundell, 168
Dinham, Margaret & Nicholas Carew, 100
Dinham, Muriel & Edward Hastings, 498
Dinham, Oliver de & Isabel de Vere, 320
Dive, 437
Divelston, 219, 222
Dix, 481
Dixwell, 215
Docwra, 109
Dodson, 338

Doggett, 267
D'Oilly, 180, 516
Dol, 125
Donet, 54, 540, 574
Donjon, 463
Donne, 360, 361, 500
Donyngton, 448
Donzy, 462, 463
Donzy, Hervé de & Mathilde Gouet, 462
Doreward, 420, 582
Dormer, 431, 679, 680
Dormond, 50
Dorne, 476
Dorney, 411
Dorset, 170, 431, 540, 551
Douglas, 201, 245, 372, 375, 541
Downes, 480
Drake, 105, 106, 405, 466
Drake, Henry & Mary Lee, 466
Drake, Robert & Joan Gawton, 467
Dransfeld, 209
Drayton, 94
Dreux, 30, 237, 315, 419, 420, 423, 468, 469, 470, 471
Dreux, Alix de & Raoul de Clermont, 237
Dreux, Isabelle de & Gautier de Châtillon, 471
Dreux, Robert de & Clémence de Châteaudun, 471
Dreux, Robert de & Isabelle de Villebéon, 471
Dreux, Robert I, Count of & Agnès de Baudement, 468
Dreux, Robert I, Count of & Hawise of Salisbury, 467
Dreux, Robert II, Count of & Mahaud of Burgundy, 469
Dreux, Robert II, Count of & Yolande de Coucy, 469
Dreux, Robert III, Count of & Annor de Saint-Valéry, 470

Dreux, Yolande de & Hugh, Duke of Burgundy, 30
Driby, 256, 274
Drope, 167, 369, 628
Drummond, 202
Drury, 44, 105, 159, 266, 390, 472, 473, 554
Drury, Jane & Richard Chetwode, 159
Drury, Mary & John Tyrrell, 474
Drury, Mary & Richard Corbett, 474
Drury, Robert & Anne Calthorpe, 472
Drury, Robert & Anne Jernegan, 472
Drury, Robert & Audrey Rich, 473
Drury, William & Elizabeth Sothill, 473
Drury, William & Jane Saint Maur, 473
Dryden, Bridget & Francis Marbury, 146
Dryden, Bridget & Thomas Newton, 146
Dryden, Grace & Kenelm Cheseldine, 147
Dryden, John & Elizabeth Cope, 145
Dryden, Stephen & Ellen Neale, 147
Dryland, 484
Drylond, 426
Dublin., 19
Ducie, 278
Dudley, 109, 143, 169, 170, 247, 279, 280, 343, 360, 362, 365, 409, 410, 582, 591
Dudley, Edmund & Anne Windsor, 341
Dudley, Edmund & Elizabeth Grey, 341
Dudley, Elizabeth & Thomas Ashburnham, 343
Dudley, John & Elizabeth Bramshott, 340
Dudley, John & Jane Guildford, 342
Dudley, Roger & Susan Thorne, 476
Dudley, Thomas & Dorothy Yorke, 477
Dudley, Thomas & Katherine Deighton, 412, 477

Duke, 638
Duket, 151
Dun, 517, 566
Dunbar, 6, 220, 221, 222, 477, 478
Dunbar, Isabel of & Roger Fitz John, 221
Dunbar, Isabel of & Simon Baard, 222
Dunbar, John de & Isabel of Fife, 202
Dunbar, Patrick of & Cecily Fitz John, 220
Dunbar, Patrick of & Marjory Comyn, 221
Dunbar, Patrick, Earl of & Ada of Scotland, 477
Dunbar, Patrick, Earl of & Christian Fitz Walter, 478
Dunbar, Patrick, Earl of & Euphame de Brus, 478
Dungan, 214
Dunmowe, 256
Dunstanville, 316, 620
Durfort, 429, 430
Durfort, Gaillard de & Anne de la Pole, 429
Durward, 4, 200, 564
Dutton, 345
Duvall, Jeffrey A., 94
Dydelyngg, 68
Dymmok, 380
Dyneham, 456
Dyneley, 368, 627, 629
Dyneley, Edward & Sanche Langford, 628
Dyneley, Elizabeth & George Barrett, 629
Dyneley, Elizabeth & John Baker, 629
Dyneley, Robert & _____ Ludlow, 628
Dyneley, Thomas & Philippe Harpesfield, 628
Dyneley, William & Anne Mompesson, 627
Dyneley, William & Margaret Foxcote, 627
Dynggeleye, 91

Dynham, 41, 101, 168, 320, 324, 325, 408, 455, 456, 498, 679
Dyve, 112
Dyvelston, 223
Eardley, 503
Earl Marshal, 294, 609, 617
Earl Marshal of England, 342, 538
Echingham, 230, 363, 364, 482, 483, 484, 485, 577, 581, 586
Echingham, Edward & Anne Everard, 364
Echingham, Elizabeth & Goddard Oxenbridge, 486
Echingham, Elizabeth & Roger Fiennes, 485
Echingham, Elizabeth & Thomas Hoo, 230
Echingham, Margaret & John Elrington, 484
Echingham, Margaret & Thomas Combe, 485
Echingham, Margaret & William Blount, 484
Echingham, Thomas & Agnes Shoyswell, 483
Echingham, Thomas & Margaret Knyvet, 483
Echingham, Thomas & Margaret West, 484
Echingham, William & Alice Batisford, 482
Echingham, William & Joan Arundel, 482
Echyngham, 482
Eddowes, 347
Eden, 350, 559
Edgecombe, 169, 473
Edington, 589
Edolphe, 369
Edward, 635
Edwards, John & Margery Knolles, 368
Edymon, 499
Egerton, 683

Eiville, 530, 672
Eiville, d', 495
Eiville, John d' & Maud de Percy, 530
Eldred, 682
Eliot, Lawrence & Margaret Charleton, 65
Elkington, 491
Elkington, George & Mary Humphries, 491
Elkington, Joseph & Ann _____, 491
Elkington, William & Alice Green, 491
Elkington, William & Alice Wodhull, 491
Elkinton, 491
Ellerker, 286, 527, 532, 669
Ellesfield, 443
Ellis, 493
Ellis, Margaret & Rowland Ellis, 493
Ellis, Rowland & Margaret Ellis, 493
Ellis, Rowland & Margaret Roberts, 493
Elmes, 431
Elmham, 39, 418, 424, 496
Elmham, William & Elizabeth Hastings, 496
Elrington, 106, 484, 485
Elrington, John & Margaret Echingham, 484
Elryngton, 484, 485
Elsefeld, 443
Eltham, John of, 263
Eltonhead, 297, 503
Eltonhead, Agatha & Henry Chichley, 504
Eltonhead, Agatha & Luke Stubbins, 504
Eltonhead, Agatha & Ralph Wormeley, 504
Eltonhead, Alice & Henry Corbin, 297, 505
Eltonhead, Alice & Henry Creyke, 297, 505
Eltonhead, Alice & Rowland Burnham, 505

Eltonhead, Eleanor & John Carter, 504
Eltonhead, Eleanor & William Brocas, 504
Eltonhead, Jane & Cuthbert Fenwick, 504
Eltonhead, Jane & Robert Morrison, 504
Eltonhead, Martha & Edwin Conway, 505
Eltonhead, Richard & Anne Sutton, 503
Empson, 473
Encre, 234
Engaine, 26, 93, 225, 331, 505, 506, 507, 549, 653
Engaine, Elizabeth d' & Laurence Pabenham, 507
Engaine, Joan d' & Adam de Welles, 653
Engaine, Joan d' & Walter Fitz Robert, 653
Engaine, John d' & Ellen de Clavering, 225
Engaine, John d' & Joan Peverel, 506
Engaine, Mary d' & Thomas la Zouche, 93
Engaine, Nicholas d' & Amice de Faucomberge, 505
Engaine, Thomas d' & Katherine Courtenay, 506
Engayne, 93, 506
Engeham, 461
England, 57, 118, 119, 121, 152, 195, 200, 298, 462, 541
England, Charles I, King of, 63, 280, 361, 405, 419
England, Edward I, King of, 3, 5, 6, 16, 17, 46, 47, 117, 119, 194, 196, 207, 221, 237, 302, 303, 308, 326, 443, 577, 600, 653
England, Edward II, King of, 17, 46, 66, 197, 201, 241, 261, 291, 305, 407, 444, 549, 569, 600, 601, 662

England, Edward III, King of, 23, 48, 49, 92, 202, 329, 390, 407, 449, 451, 453, 494, 495, 533, 538, 551, 607, 613, 657, 666
England, Edward IV, King of, 51, 103, 334, 341, 403, 424, 425, 427, 429, 484, 540, 581, 633
England, Edward V, King of, 96, 168
England, Edward VI, King of, 376
England, Edwards VI, King of, 668
England, Eleanor of & Alfonso VIII, King of Castile, 114
England, Elizabeth I, Queen of, 106, 108, 366, 437, 461
England, Henry I, King of, 133, 150, 172, 250, 315, 519, 619, 620
England, Henry II, King of, 135, 150, 250, 252, 315, 463, 520, 620
England, Henry III, King of, 3, 22, 45, 116, 118, 119, 152, 186, 189, 196, 239, 281, 299, 302, 393, 470, 478, 560, 564, 565, 597, 600, 622, 649
England, Henry IV, King of, 95, 275, 330, 390, 400, 401, 450, 451, 453, 496, 609, 610, 613, 615, 631
England, Henry V, King of, 93, 96, 123, 246, 275, 332, 340, 401, 422, 538, 539, 580, 609, 610, 631, 659
England, Henry VI, King of, 50, 51, 52, 123, 349, 419, 422, 423, 425, 539, 540, 541, 580
England, Henry VII, King of, 168, 277, 284, 335, 364, 426, 431
England, Henry VIII, King of, 43, 57, 104, 105, 169, 277, 335, 336, 365, 428
England, James I, King of, 461
England, Joan of, 121
England, Joan of & Gilbert de Clare, 196
England, Joan of & Ralph de Monthermer, 197
England, John, King of, 73, 152, 178, 185, 219, 470, 478, 511, 514, 560, 621

England, Katherine of France, Queen of, 166
England, Mary I, Queen of, 43, 170, 312, 336, 365
England, Richard I, King of, 152, 177, 180, 252, 318, 413, 560
England, Richard II, King of, 50, 93, 94, 327, 328, 329, 330, 331, 333, 388, 389, 390, 400, 451, 496, 497, 507, 533, 536, 553, 609, 631, 656, 657
England, Richard III, King of, 168, 288, 341, 374, 403, 425, 426, 427, 429, 431, 485, 540, 575, 592
England, Richard of, Earl of Cornwall & Isabel Marshal, 298
England, Richard of, Earl of Cornwall & Sanche of Provence, 298
England, Stephen, King of, 149, 175, 250, 384, 619, 645
England, William Rufus, King of, 172
England, William the Conqueror, King of, 171
English, 306
Entwistle, 420
Epes, 596
Erdeswicke, 215
Erdeswike, 572
Erdington, 32, 39, 290, 291, 516
Erdington, Giles de & Elizabeth de Tolethorpe, 291
Erdington, Henry de & Joan de Wolvey, 291
Erdington, Henry de & Maud de Somery, 290
Erdington, Margaret de & Roger Corbet, 292
Erle, 518, 627
Erleigh, 518
Erskine, 202
Escheker, 379, 380
Escheker, del, 84
Escheker, Maud de l' & John de Dagworth, 379
Escores, 32

Eskelling, 178, 513
Espec, 238
Essex, 12, 47, 48, 78, 80, 109, 178, 179, 218, 219, 326, 384, 506, 507, 509, 510, 511, 512, 514, 515, 516, 569, 605, 610, 611, 650, 656
Esteves, 538, 613
Estgate, 255
Esthall, 307
Estmond, 466
Estoutevile, 682
Esturmy, 517, 518
Esturmy, Geoffrey & _____, 518
Esturmy, Henry & Margaret Hussey, 517
Esturmy, Henry & Maud _____, 517
Esturmy, William & Joan Stockheye, 518
Estwyk, 449
Eton, Robert de & Hawise de Prayers, 155
Etwell, 157
Etwell, Joan & John Wodhull, 157
Eu, 239, 252, 318, 469, 519, 520, 521, 522, 666
Eu, Alice, Countess of & Raoul d'Exoudun, 521
Eu, Henri I, Count of & Marguerite de Sully, 519
Eu, Henri II, Count of & Maud de Warenne, 520
Eu, Jean, Count of & Alice d'Aubeney, 519
Euer, 523
Eure, 130, 170, 219, 285, 500, 523, 524, 525, 526, 527, 528, 529, 632
Eure, Anne & Lancelot Mansfield, 529
Eure, Hugh de & Ellen _____, 523
Eure, John de & Agnes _____, 524
Eure, John de & Margaret _____, 524
Eure, Ralph & Agnes Constable, 528
Eure, Ralph & Eleanor Greystoke, 527
Eure, Ralph & Isabel de Atholl, 525
Eure, Ralph & Katherine Aton, 525
Eure, Ralph & Margery Bowes, 529
Eure, Ralph & Maud Greystoke, 525
Eure, Ralph & Muriel Hastings, 527
Eure, William & Constance _____, 527
Eure, William & Elizabeth Willoughby, 528
Eure, William & Margaret Constable, 527
Eure, William & Maud Fitz Hugh, 526
Evans, 313, 493
Ever, 525
Everard, 364
Everard, Anne & Edward Echingham, 364
Everard, Anne & Edward Lewknor, 364
Evergin, 371
Everingham, 273, 495, 532, 533, 549
Everingham, Adam de & Joan D'Eiville, 532
Everingham, Adam de & Margaret _____, 532
Everingham, Margaret de & Hugh de Hastings, 495
Evermere, 224
Evermue, 224
Evers, 525, 527
Evesham, 547
Evington, 271
Evreux, 78, 181, 185
Évreux, 78, 79, 151, 252
Ewyns, 313
Excestre, 642
Exchequer, del, 83
Exeter, 99, 335, 336, 390, 422, 497, 533, 535, 536, 538, 539, 540, 541, 615, 665
Exoudun, 521
Exoudun, Raoul d' & Alice, Countess of Eu, 521
Extremadura, 114
Eylesburi, 291
Eyre, 133, 313
Eyre, Catherine & Charles Chauncy, 133

Eyre, Marshal of the, 379, 380
Eyton, 111
Eyton, _____ & Christian Stapleton, 641
Eyvile, 321, 532
Eyville, 531, 532, 673
Fabian, 488
Fairclough, 10
Fairfax, 111, 280, 281, 543, 545
Fairfax, Mary & Henry Curwen, 545
Fairfax, Nicholas & Alice Harrington, 544
Fairfax, Nicholas & Jane Palmes, 544
Fairfax, Thomas & Anne Gascoigne, 544
Fairfax, Thomas & Elizabeth Sherburne, 543
Falkenburg, 186, 299, 301
Falkenburg, Beatrice de & England, Richard of, Earl of Cornwall, 299
Falkenburg, Beatrice de & Richard, Earl of Cornwall, 186
Falkner, 282
Falkney, 282
Falkney, Isabel & Bernard de Brus, 282
Falowefeld, 71
Falvy, 117
Fanacourt, 379
Fancourt, Gerard de & Eustache d'Aubeney, 396
Fane, 343, 352
Fanhope, 536, 538
Farington, 130
Farley, 682
Farrer, 361, 546
Farrer, John & Cecily Kelke, 546
Farrer, William & Cecily _____, 547
Farway, 638
Faryngton, 130
Fastolf, 284
Fathers, 339
Faucomberge, 548, 549

Faucomberge, Amice de & Nicholas d'Engaine, 505
Fauconberge, 130, 203, 289, 323, 547, 548, 549, 550, 551, 552, 574
Fauconberge, Aveline de & Giles de Goushill, 547
Fauconberge, Joan & John Berwyke, 552
Fauconberge, Joan & William Neville, 551
Fauconberge, John de & Eve _____, 549
Fauconberge, Thomas & Constance Felton, 550
Fauconberge, Thomas & Joan Bromflete, 551
Fauconberge, Walter de & Agnes de Brus, 548
Fauconberge, Walter de & Alice de Killingholm, 549
Fauconberge, Walter de & Isabel Bigod, 550
Fauconberge, Walter de & Isabel de Roos, 549
Fauconberge, Walter de & Maud de Pateshulle, 550
Fauconer, 562, 571
Faulkner, 148, 584
Faulkner, Bridget & Kenelm Cheseldine, 148
Faunt, 296
Faunt, John & Alice Clervaux, 296
Faunt, Mary & George Corbin, 297
Faunt, William & Anne Fielding, 296
Faunt, William & Isabel Sayer, 296
Faunt, William & Jane Vincent, 296
Faunte, 296
Fauquemont, 186, 299
Fay, 414
Faye, 58
Felbrig, 233
Felbrigg, 498, 552, 553, 554
Felbrigg, Roger de & Elizabeth de Scales, 552

Felbrigg, Simon & Katherine Clifton, 554
Felbrigg, Simon & Margaret of Teschen, 553
Felbrigge, 554
Felbrygg, 257
Felbrygge, 553
Felde, 615, 679
Feltewell, 499
Felton, 202, 203, 230, 496, 550, 551, 555, 556, 557
Felton, Eleanor & Robert de Ufford, 230
Felton, Eleanor de & Thomas Hoo, 230
Felton, John & _____, 203
Felton, John & Elizabeth _____, 203
Felton, John de & Sibyl _____, 556
Felton, Robert de & Hawise le Strange, 555
Felton, Thomas de & Joan de Walkefare, 556
Felton, William de & Isabel of Fife, 202
Fenes, 578
Fenne, 357, 431, 594
Fenwick, 344, 504, 557, 558, 559
Fenwick, Cuthbert & Jane Eltonhead, 504
Fenwick, Edward & Sarah Neville, 559
Fenwick, John & Elizabeth Covert, 559
Fenwick, John & Mary Gray, 558
Fenwick, John & Mary Marten, 559
Fenwick, Ralph & Barbara Ogle, 558
Fenwick, Ralph & Margery Mitford, 558
Fenwick, Richard & Dorothy Thornton, 558
Fenwick, Richard & Margaret Mills, 558
Fenwick, Roger & Agnes Harbottle, 557

Fenwick, William & Elizabeth Gargrave, 559
Fenys, 348, 577, 581
ferch Dafydd Llwyd, Elsbeth & John Nannau, 492
ferch Elissa ap Dafydd, Catherine & Rees ap Lewis ap John Gruffudd, 493
ferch Humphrey ap Hywel, Jane & Gruffudd ap Hywel, 492
ferch Hywel ap Gruffudd, Ellin & Lewis ap John ap Gruffudd, 493
ferch Sion ap David ap Gruffudd, 493
ferch Sion ap Lewis, Margaret & Robert ab Owain, 493
ferch Tudor Vaughn, Mary & Owain ap Lewis, 493
Fereby, 410
Feriby, 130, 580
Ferlington, 58
Fermor, 55, 488
Fermoy, 46
Ferrad', 661
Ferraius, 572
Ferreires, 569
Ferrers, 2, 3, 4, 22, 154, 168, 178, 201, 212, 213, 239, 245, 248, 269, 273, 294, 352, 409, 448, 450, 453, 488, 489, 490, 510, 511, 512, 527, 540, 560, 561, 562, 563, 565, 566, 567, 568, 569, 570, 571, 572, 574, 575, 576, 577, 578, 618, 622, 623, 652
Ferrers, _____ de & John de Vipont, 239
Ferrers, Anne & Walter Devereux, 575
Ferrers, Anne de & Edward le Despenser, 448
Ferrers, Edmund & Ellen de la Roche, 572
Ferrers, Eleanor de & Robert Fitz Walter, 652
Ferrers, Elizabeth & James Clerke, 213
Ferrers, Elizabeth de & Dafydd ap Gruffudd, 564

Ferrers, Elizabeth de & William le Marshal, 564
Ferrers, Henry & Margaret Hexstall, 213
Ferrers, Isabel de & Peter Fitz Herbert, 622
Ferrers, Joan & John Clinton, 574
Ferrers, John & Katherine Burnell, 41
Ferrers, John de & Elizabeth de Stafford, 570
Ferrers, John de & Hawise de Muscegros, 568
Ferrers, Margaret, Countess of Warwick, 451
Ferrers, Robert & Elizabeth _____, 571
Ferrers, Robert & Margaret le Despenser, 571
Ferrers, Robert de & Eleanor de Bohun, 566
Ferrers, Robert de & Joan de la Mote, 570
Ferrers, Robert de & Margaret _____, 570
Ferrers, Robert de & Mary de Lusignan, 565
Ferrers, Thomas & Elizabeth Freville, 212
Ferrers, William & Elizabeth Belknap, 575
Ferrers, William de & Agnes of Chester, 560
Ferrers, William de & Margaret de Quincy, 561
Ferrers, William de & Sibyl Marshal, 561
Ferté, de la, 137
Ferté, Gundred de la & Pain de Chaworth, 137
Fetplace, 35
Fettiplace, 109, 344, 399, 476
Fettiplace, Anne & Edward Purefoy, 476
Fezensaguet, 419

Fielding, 215, 296
Fielding, Anne & Humphrey Grey, 215
Fielding, Anne & William Faunt, 296
Fienes, 349
Fienles, 577, 579, 580
Fiennes, 178, 231, 301, 328, 373, 374, 385, 399, 434, 477, 485, 486, 512, 541, 577, 579, 580, 581, 582, 633, 670
Fiennes, _____ & Walter Dennis, 434
Fiennes, Anne & Goddard Oxenbridge, 486
Fiennes, Elizabeth & Alexander Iden, 350
Fiennes, Elizabeth & Laurence Raynsford, 350
Fiennes, Elizabeth & William Cromer, 349
Fiennes, Giles de & Sibyl Filliol, 577
Fiennes, James & Emeline Cromer, 348
Fiennes, James & Joan _____, 348
Fiennes, John de & Joan le Forester, 578
Fiennes, John de & Maud de Monceux, 578
Fiennes, Richard & Joan Dacre, 581
Fiennes, Roger & Elizabeth Echingham, 485
Fiennes, Roger & Elizabeth Holand, 580
Fiennes, Thomas & Anne Urswick, 582
Fiennes, William & Elizabeth Batisford, 579
Fiennes, William & Margaret Wykeham, 349
Fiennes, William de & Joan de Say, 579
Fiesco, 189
Fife, 4, 197, 200, 201, 202, 205, 392, 393, 550
Fife, Duncan of & Joan de Clare, 200

Fife, Duncan of & Mary de Monthermer, 200
Fife, Isabel of & John Comyn, Earl of Buchan, 4
Fife, Isabel of & John de Dunbar, 202
Fife, Isabel of & Thomas Biset, 202
Fife, Isabel of & Walter Stewart, 202
Fife, Isabel of & William de Felton, 202
Fifife, 562
Filby, 224
Filliol, 577
Filliol, Sibyl & Giles de Fiennes, 577
Fillol, 35, 68
Filmer, 371, 584
Filmer, Edward & Elizabeth Argall, 584
Filmer, Henry & Elizabeth _____, 584
Filmer, Katherine & Robert Barham, 584
Filoll, 585, 586
Filoll, John & Margaret Carent, 585
Filoll, William & Dorothy Ifield, 586
Filoll, William & Elizabeth Audley, 586
Filoll, William & Joan Frome, 585
Finamour, 191
Finch, 351, 588
Finch, Henry & Alice Belknap, 588
Finch, Thomas & Katherine Moyle, 588
Finch, William & Elizabeth Cromer, 588
Finch, William & Katherine Gainesford, 588
Fincham, 480
Fineux, 348
Firmage, 147
Fishacre, 306
Fisher, 214, 576, 596
Fisher, John & Bennett Dering, 596
Fisher, John & Elizabeth _____, 596
Fissacre, 306, 455

Fissacre, Peter de & Joan de Cornwall, 306
Fitton, 501
Fitz Ailwin, 189
Fitz Alan, 33, 36, 169, 197, 254, 306, 307, 478, 596, 598, 599, 600, 601, 603, 605, 661
Fitz Alan, Henry & Mary Arundell, 43
Fitz Alan, John & Hawise de Blancminster, 596
Fitz Alan, John & Isabel d'Aubeney, 596
Fitz Alan, John & Isabel de Mortimer, 597
Fitz Alan, John & Maud de Verdun, 596
Fitz Alan, Maud & Philip Burnell, 31
Fitz Alan, Maud & Robert de Brus, 32
Fitz Alan, Maud & Simon de Cricketot, 32
Fitz Alan, Richard & Alice di Saluzzo, 600
Fitz Aleyn, 603
Fitz Baldwin, 317
Fitz Baldwin, Rohese & Baldwin Buelot, 238
Fitz Baldwin, Rohese & William de Bussey, 238
Fitz Corbet, 620
Fitz Count, 126, 148
Fitz Durand, 184
Fitz Edward, 467
Fitz Eustace, 396, 501
Fitz Geoffrey, 15, 45, 79, 138, 140, 239, 509, 536, 639, 644
Fitz Geoffrey, Maud & William de Cantelowe, 78
Fitz Gerald, 46, 277, 432
Fitz Gerold, 148, 188, 413
Fitz Gerold, Warin & Alice de Courcy, 413
Fitz Gilbert, 16, 185, 298, 561, 644
Fitz Gilbert, Richard & Alice of Chester, 174

Fitz Gilbert, Rohese & Baderon de Monmouth, 173
Fitz Godric, 672
Fitz Hamo, 393
Fitz Henry, 14, 281, 630
Fitz Henry, Henry & Joan de Fourneux, 630
Fitz Herbert, 219, 315, 623, 642
Fitz Herbert, Edmund & Joan _____, 643
Fitz Herbert, Herbert & Lucy of Hereford, 620
Fitz Herbert, Matthew & Margaret Cobham, 626
Fitz Herbert, Peter & Alice Fitz Robert, 621
Fitz Herbert, Peter & Isabel de Ferrers, 622
Fitz Herbert, Reynold & Joan Hakeluyt, 642
Fitz Herbert, Reynold & Juliane _____, 627
Fitz Hervey, 378
Fitz Hubert, 172
Fitz Hugh, 80, 247, 285, 288, 374, 391, 526, 591, 630, 631, 632, 633, 661
Fitz Hugh, Eleanor & Henry Bromflete, 391
Fitz Hugh, Eleanor & Philip Darcy, 391
Fitz Hugh, Eleanor & Thomas Tunstall, 391
Fitz Hugh, Henry & Alice Neville, 633
Fitz Hugh, Henry & Elizabeth Grey, 631
Fitz Hugh, Henry & Emma de Cleseby, 630
Fitz Hugh, Henry & Eve de Bulmer, 630
Fitz Hugh, Henry & Joan le Scrope, 630
Fitz Hugh, Lora & Maurice Berkeley, 591

Fitz Hugh, Margery & Marmaduke Constable, 285
Fitz Hugh, Maud & William Eure, 526
Fitz Hugh, William & Margery Willoughby, 632
Fitz Ives, 634
Fitz Ives, Richard & Isabel Fitz Roy, 634
Fitz James, John & Elizabeth Coningsby, 410
Fitz James, Thomas & Anne Butler, 52
Fitz James, Thomas & Ellice Barry, 52
Fitz Joerg, 74
Fitz John, 16, 46, 124, 138, 177, 219, 222, 240, 242, 386, 479, 565
Fitz John, Aveline & Walter de Burgh, 15
Fitz John, Cecily & Patrick of Dunbar, 220
Fitz John, Herbert & Eleanor le Rous, 626
Fitz John, Isabel & Robert de Vipont, 239
Fitz John, Joan & Edmund le Boteler (or Butler), 46
Fitz John, Joan & Thebaud le Boteler (or Butler), 45
Fitz John, Roger & Isabel of Dunbar, 221
Fitz John, Thomas & Joan de Burgh, 18
Fitz Lewis, 61, 479, 665
Fitz Matthew, 140, 443
Fitz Maurice, 49, 50, 194, 242
Fitz Morgald, 154
Fitz Ness, 645
Fitz Nicholas, 673
Fitz Nigel, 35, 178, 512
Fitz Nigel, Joan & John de Haudlo, 35
Fitz Otes, 655
Fitz Pain, 72, 381
Fitz Patrick, 478, 650
Fitz Payn, 2, 272, 333, 660

Fitz Payn, Elizabeth & Hugh Courtenay, 333
Fitz Payn, Joan & Richard de Grey, 272
Fitz Payn, Robert & Elizabeth de Bryan, 273
Fitz Peter, 66, 78, 178, 179, 323, 384, 509, 510, 511, 513, 514, 515, 516, 622, 623, 624
Fitz Peter, Geoffrey & Aveline de Clare, 178, 513
Fitz Peter, Geoffrey & Beatrice de Say, 178, 512
Fitz Peter, Reynold & Alice _____, 622
Fitz Peter, Reynold & Joan de Vivonne, 623
Fitz Ralph, 23, 181, 381, 382, 422
Fitz Reinfrid, 548
Fitz Reynold, 622, 623, 625, 626
Fitz Reynold, Elizabeth & John Chenduit, 627
Fitz Reynold, Herbert & Lucy Peverel, 642
Fitz Reynold, John & Agnes _____, 625
Fitz Reynold, Reynold & Alice Crubbe, 642
Fitz Reynold, Reynold & Joan Martel, 642
Fitz Reynold, Reynold & Margaret _____, 642
Fitz Richard, 173, 177, 218, 252, 645, 646
Fitz Richard, Richard, 634
Fitz Richard, Robert & Maud de Senlis, 644
Fitz Richard, Roger & Alice de Vere, 218
Fitz Richard, Roger & Maud de Saint Hilary, 176
Fitz Richard, William & Rose Bevyle, 634
Fitz Robert, 13, 180, 644, 646, 647, 651
Fitz Robert, Alice & Peter Fitz Herbert, 621
Fitz Robert, Christian & Raymond de Burgh, 515
Fitz Robert, Christian & William de Mandeville, 515
Fitz Robert, John & Ada de Balliol, 219
Fitz Robert, John & Hawise de Tibetot, 225
Fitz Robert, Mabel & Guillaume de Solers, 124
Fitz Robert, Mabel & Jordan de Champernoun, 124
Fitz Robert, Maud & Geoffrey de Mandeville, 514
Fitz Robert, Maud & Reynold de Courtenay, 315
Fitz Robert, Robert & Hawise de Redvers, 124
Fitz Robert, Walter & Ida Longespée, 650
Fitz Robert, Walter & Joan d'Engaine, 653
Fitz Robert, Walter & Maud de Bohun, 645
Fitz Robert, Walter & Maud de Lucy, 645
Fitz Robert, William, 514
Fitz Rocelin, 647
Fitz Roger, 128, 219, 221, 223, 224, 413, 435, 523, 548, 598, 621, 626
Fitz Roger, Robert & Margaret de Chesney, 219
Fitz Roger, Robert & Margery la Zouche, 222
Fitz Roland, 562
Fitz Roland, Alan, 189
Fitz Roscelin, 378
Fitz Roy, 126, 315, 341, 621, 649
Fitz Roy, Henry & Eve de Blanchminster, 126
Fitz Roy, Isabel & Richard Fitz Ives, 634
Fitz Simon, 160
Fitz Stephen, 178, 510, 511, 512

Fitz Thomas, 16, 18, 26, 46, 673
Fitz Thomas, Maurice & Elizabeth de Burghersh, 18
Fitz Thomas, William & Agnes de Grey, 673
Fitz Walcher, 644
Fitz Walter, 16, 38, 41, 42, 43, 48, 165, 219, 459, 515, 568, 620, 647, 649, 651, 652, 653, 654, 655, 656, 658, 659, 660, 665
Fitz Walter, Christian & Patrick, Earl of Dunbar, 478
Fitz Walter, Elizabeth & John Dinham, 41, 459
Fitz Walter, Elizabeth & John Radcliffe, 41
Fitz Walter, Ida & Hugh de Neville, 654
Fitz Walter, Ida & Robert de la Warde, 654
Fitz Walter, John & Eleanor de Percy, 655
Fitz Walter, Robert, 126
Fitz Walter, Robert & Alice de Montfort, 652
Fitz Walter, Robert & Devorguille de Burgh, 651
Fitz Walter, Robert & Eleanor de Ferrers, 652
Fitz Walter, Robert & Gunnor de Valoines, 647
Fitz Walter, Robert & Joan Botetourt, 654
Fitz Walter, Robert & Joan de Multon, 655
Fitz Walter, Robert & Rohese ____, 647
Fitz Walter, Walter & Eleanor de Dagworth, 656
Fitz Walter, Walter & Elizabeth Chidiock, 660
Fitz Walter, Walter & Joan Devereux, 658

Fitz Walter, Walter & Philippe Mohun, 656
Fitz Waltheof, 206
Fitz Warin, 47, 53, 138, 164, 333, 379, 460, 517, 548, 578, 660, 661, 662, 663, 664, 666, 667, 668
Fitz Warin, Alice & Adam de Shareshull, 578
Fitz Warin, Alice & John de Dagworth, 379
Fitz Warin, Eleanor & John Chidiock, 165
Fitz Warin, Eleanor & Ralph Bush, 165
Fitz Warin, Elizabeth & Richard Hankford, 664
Fitz Warin, Fulk & Anne Botreaux, 664
Fitz Warin, Fulk & Blanche de Audley, 663
Fitz Warin, Fulk & Constance de Tony, 660
Fitz Warin, Fulk & Eleanor de Beauchamp, 662
Fitz Warin, Fulk & Elizabeth Cogan, 663
Fitz Warin, Fulk & Margaret de Beaumont, 663
Fitz Warin, Fulk & Margaret de la Pole, 661
Fitz Warin, Ives & Maud Argentine, 164
Fitz Warin, William & Amice de Haddon, 162
Fitz Waryn, 663, 666
Fitz William, 76, 83, 211, 531, 630, 652, 653, 673, 674, 678
Fitz William, Denise & Robert D'Eiville, 531
Fitz William, Isabel & Stephen de Beaupré, 635
Fitz William, Thomas & Agnes Bertram, 672

Fitz William, William & Ela de Warenne, 672
Fitz William, William & Maud _____, 672
FitzGerald, 52, 109
Fitzgerald, Elizabeth & James le Boteler, 50
FitzGibbon, Maurice Mor & Ellice Barry, 52
Fitzhugh, 633
Fitzlewis, Philip, 432
Fitzroy, 668
Fitzsymond, 655
Fitzwalter, 43, 169, 665
Fitz-Walter, 660
Fitzwaryn, 664
Fitzwilliam, 209, 210, 211, 248, 263, 288, 358, 673, 674, 675, 678, 680, 683
FitzWilliam, 679
Fitzwilliam, John & Eleanor Greene, 676
Fitzwilliam, John & Elizabeth de Clinton, 675
Fitzwilliam, John & Helen Villiers, 677
Fitzwilliam, John & Joan Reresby, 674
Fitzwilliam, John & Margaret Clarell, 209
Fitzwilliam, John & Margaret Huddleston, 680
Fitzwilliam, Margaret & Brian Robertson, 681
Fitzwilliam, Mary & Richard Ogle, 677
Fitzwilliam, Mary & Thomas Waddington, 677
Fitzwilliam, Rachel & _____ Hall, 681
Fitzwilliam, Rachel & John Reppes, 681
Fitzwilliam, Rachel & Richard Cure, 681
Fitzwilliam, Rachel & Richard Huddleston, 681
Fitzwilliam, Richard & Elizabeth Knyvet, 679
Fitzwilliam, Robert & Joan Presgrave, 680
Fitzwilliam, William & Anne Hawes, 678
Fitzwilliam, William & Isabel Deincourt, 673
Fitzwilliam, William & Jane Ormond, 678
Fitzwilliam, William & Maud Cromwell, 676
Fitzwilliam, William & Mildred Sackville, 678
Fiz Aleyn, 601
FizAleyn, 603
Flaitel, 171
Flamake, 338
Flambard, 375
Flanders, 18, 29, 31, 178, 189, 234, 238, 249, 384, 387, 496
Fleetwood, 439, 583
Fleitel, 171
Fleix, 419
Fleming, 207
Fletcher, 377
Flower, 544
Fobes, 148
Fodringey, 523
Fogge, 105, 579
Foix, 39, 419, 420, 428, 429
Foix, Jean de & Margaret Kerdeston, 419
Foliot, 69, 164, 406, 494, 646
Foliot, Margaret & John de Camoys, 69
Foliot, Margery & Hugh de Hastings, 494
Folky, 259
Folville, John & Joan Wesenham, 283
Folvyle, 369, 628
Fontaines, 219
Forcalquier, 186, 298

Forester, Joan le & Adam de Shareshull, 578
Forester, Joan le & John de Fiennes, 578
Forez, 463
Forster, 27, 111, 166, 430
Forte, 592
Fortescue, 52, 53, 170, 432, 461, 540
Fortescue, ____ & Margaret Courtenay, 436
Fortescue, Adrian & Anne Reade, 432
Fortescue, Adrian & Anne Stonor, 432
Forz, 189, 190, 192, 323, 324, 564, 662
Forz, William de & Christian of Galloway, 189
Forz, William de & Isabel de Rivers, 189
Foster, 586
Fougères, 152, 153, 172, 173
Fougères, Clemence de & Ranulph, Earl of Chester, 152
Fouleshurst, 110
Fouleshurst, Margaret & Thomas Strickland, 110
Foulman, 275
Foulshurst, Ralph & Anne Chamberlain, 145
Fourneux, 630
Fourneux, Joan de & Henry Fitz Henry, 630
Fowell, 138, 404
Fowell, Jane & Humphrey Prideaux, 404
Fowell, Jane & Philip Courtenay, 404
Fowlar, 368
Fowler, 123, 144, 669
Fowler, Sibyl & Richard Chamberlain, 123
Fox, 278, 377
Foxcote, 155
Foxcote, Margaret & Nicholas de Wodhull, 155
Foxcote, Margaret & William Dyneley, 627

Foxcote, Robert & Maud Chenduit, 627
Foxcote, Thomas & Christian ____, 627
Foxcote, Thomas & Philippe Stokes, 627
Frampton, 379, 590
Frampton, Joan & Thomas Stawell, 590
Franc Chevaler, 127
France, 18, 115, 117, 121, 387, 419
France, Charles IV, King of, 442
France, Charles VI, King of, 656
France, Charles VII, King of, 422, 429
France, François I, King of, 105, 428
France, Henri II, King of, 106
France, Isabel of, 263
France, Isabel of [Queen of England], 261, 444
France, Katherine of [Queen of England], 123, 340, 615
France, Louis IX, King of, 237, 470, 521, 597
France, Louis VI, King of, 315
France, Louis VII, King of, 385
France, Louis VIII, King of, 470
France, Louis XI, King of, 429
France, Louis XII, King of, 270, 428
France, Philippe II Auguste, King of, 30, 470, 521
France, Philippe III, King of, 299, 302
Francis, 410, 466, 539, 677
Frankeleyn, 303
Franklin, 406
Fraunceys, 290, 665
Freckleton, 145
Frelond, 233
Freman, 184
French, Thomas & Bridget Higham, 45
Freney, 79
Freville, 60, 128, 212, 264, 409
Freville, Elizabeth & Thomas Ferrers, 212

Freville, Margaret de & Henry de Wilington, 128
Friesland, 23, 121
Frodesham, 572
Froilaz, 115
Froílaz, 116
Frome, Joan & Richard Arches, 585
Frome, Joan & William Cheyne, 585
Frome, Joan & William Filoll, 585
Frowick, 111, 231
Frowick, Henry & Agnes Strickland, 111
Froxmere, 376
Fukeram, 562
Fulberti, 306, 308
Fulford, 103, 402
Fulthorpe, 465
Furneaux, 162, 635
Furneaux, Margaret de & Hugh de Longland, 635
Furneaux, Margaret de & Ralph de Beaupré, 635
Furnival, 561
Fychan, Rhys, 183
Fyenles, 577
Fyllol, 585
Fyloll, 585
Fyncham, 581
Fynes, 582
Fyneux, 293
Fyssher, 576
Fytzwauter, 42
Fytzwilliam, 679
Gael, 171
Gainesford, 588
Gainesford, Katherine & William Finch, 588
Gainsford, 144
Galicia, 115, 116, 118, 119, 120, 121
Gallloway, 184
Galloway, 189, 562
Galloway, Christian of & William de Forz, 189
Galwithia, 240

Gamage, 279, 310, 436, 437
Gannock, 681
Gannock, William & Jane Huddleston, 681
Gant, 176, 654
Gardiner, 105
Gargrave, 559
Gargrave, Elizabeth & William Fenwick, 559
Garland, 131
Garlande, 468, 471
Garlyk, 680
Garneys, 377
Gascoigne, 111, 209, 284, 285, 499, 527, 544, 665
Gascoigne, Anne & Hugh Hastings, 499
Gascoigne, Anne & Thomas Fairfax, 544
Gascoigne, William & Elizabeth Pennington, 111
Gascoigne, William & Margaret Clarell, 209
Gascony, 114
Gask, 393
Gask, Ysenda de & Gilbert, Earl of Strathearn, 393
Gate, 682, 683
Gatesden, 66, 320, 415
Gatesden, John de & Hawise de Courtenay, 414
Gatesden, Margaret de & John de Camoys, 65
Gatesden, Margaret de & William Paynel, 66
Gaunt, 390, 454, 658
Gaunt, John of, 70, 122, 142, 160, 164, 244, 274, 329, 388, 390, 408, 425, 452, 455, 494, 495, 496, 533, 551, 553, 556, 608, 612, 613, 656, 663
Gavaston, 59, 87, 90, 205, 242, 442, 603, 630
Gavaston, Peter de, 17, 204
Gavell, 62

Gaveston, 662
Gawdy, 481
Gawton, 467
Gawton, Joan & Robert Drake, 467
Gawton, Joan & Thomas Hunt, 467
Gayland, 306
Gedney, William & Margaret Knyvet, 123
Geneva, 302
Geneva, Aimon II, Count of & Constance of Béarn, 302
Gerald, 109
Gerard, 148, 345, 502
Gerard, Mary & Kenelm Cheseldine, 148
Gerardmoulin, 381
Gerberoy, 233
Gernegan, 483
Gernon, 397
Gernons, 150
Gibbes, 410
Gibbon, 113
Gibbon, Jane & Walter Carleton, 113
Gibbon, Jane & William Birkell, 113
Gibbons, 406
Gibbons, Sarah & Humphrey Davie, 406
Gibbons, Sarah & Jonathan Tyng, 406
Gibbs, 366
Giffard, 130, 131, 171, 176, 180, 227, 296, 322, 598, 623, 644, 645
Giffard, John & Aveline de Courtenay, 322
Giffard, Margaret & John Chauncy, 130
Gilbert, 169, 341
Gill, 92
Gilson, Andrew & Beheathland Bernard, 378
Gisors, 26, 621
Gisors, Margaret & Bartholomew de Burghersh, 26
Gisors, Margaret & William Burcester, 26

Gl.oucester, 17
Glamorgan, 180
Glanville, 378, 405
Glanville, Dewnes & William Strode, 405
Glascock, 438
Glasen, 336
Gledhill, 314
Glemham, 230
Glendower, 98, 143
Glogau, 553
Gloucester, 12, 19, 23, 32, 59, 78, 79, 124, 141, 149, 150, 174, 180, 181, 182, 185, 186, 187, 188, 191, 192, 193, 195, 196, 197, 198, 203, 204, 205, 228, 269, 270, 299, 301, 303, 304, 305, 416, 443, 453, 496, 514, 571, 603, 606, 611, 621, 646, 661, 662, 666
Gloucester, Amice of & Richard de Clare, 180
Gloucester, Humphrey, Duke of, 123, 348, 421, 574, 660
Gloucester, Isabel of & Geoffrey de Mandeville, 514
Gloucester, Isabel of & Hubert de Burgh, 514
Gloucester, Maud of & Ranulph de Gernons, Earl of Chester, 148
Gloucester, Miles of, 82
Gloucester, Richard, Duke of, 485
Gloucester, Thomas, Duke of, 245, 538, 658
Glyn, 636
Glyn Dwr, Owain, 95, 143
Gobard, 112
Godbold, 377
Goddard, 370
Goddard, John & Constance Sutton, 388
Godden, 213
Godwin, 475
Goët, 462
Goëth, 462
Goffe, 99

Goforth, 671
Goforth, William & Anne Skipwith, 671
Golafre, 656, 657, 658
Golafre, John & Philippe Mohun, 656
Goldeman, 499
Goldinge, 353
Goldinge, Thomas & Elizabeth Roydon, 353
Goldington, 506
Goldsborough, 354
Goldwell, 343
Good, 313
Goode, 231
Gordon, 505
Gorges, 589, 640
Goring, 363, 364
Gosebek, 222
Gosnell, 378
Gosse, 99
Got, 253
Gouet, 462, 463
Gouet, Guillaume & Isabelle of Blois, 462
Gouet, Mathilde & Hervé de Donzy, 462
Goulden, 213
Gournay, 78, 241, 385, 635
Gournay, John de & Elizabeth Corbet, 2
Gournay, Milicent de & William de Cantelowe, 78
Gousehill, 617
Gousel, 547
Gousele, 548
Goushall, 617
Goushill, 276, 293, 443, 547, 617, 618, 662
Goushill, Giles de & Aveline de Fauconberge, 547
Goushill, Peter de & Ela de Camoys, 547
Goushill, Robert & Elizabeth Arundel, 617

Gousle, 548
Gove, 530
Goxhill, 547
Gra, 357
Gracyan, 328
Grafton, 291
Graham, 393
Grandison, 1, 89, 324, 325, 446, 550
Grapenell, 90
Grapnel, 90
Graunson, 446, 550
Gravele, 37
Gravenel, 238, 239
Gravesende, John & Maud de Grey, 273
Gray, 11, 143, 347, 357, 389, 473, 558, 632
Gray, Elizabeth & Anthony Waldegrave, 11
Gray, Elizabeth & Philip Darcy, 389
Gray, Joan & Ralph Cromwell, 357
Gray, Mary & _____ Maddison, 558
Gray, Mary & John Fenwick, 558
Green, 584
Green, Alice & William Elkington, 491
Greene, 8, 94, 156, 209, 257, 270, 283, 388, 451, 542, 554, 572, 676, 678, 681
Greene, Agnes & William la Zouche, 94
Greene, Eleanor & John Fitzwilliam, 676
Greene, Eleanor & Thomas Culpeper, 542
Greene, Elizabeth & William Raleigh, 144
Greene, Nicholas & Joan de Brus, 542
Greenfield, 148
Gregor, 339
Greinville, 225, 505, 653
Grelle, 59
Grelley, 59
Grendon, 573
Grene, 95
Grenoble, 28, 237

Grenville, 35, 43, 169, 341
Grenville, Honor & Arthur Plantagenet, 341
Grenville, Katherine & John Arundell, 169
Gresley, 209, 487, 573
Greville, 145, 411, 432, 475, 640, 678
Grevyll, 679
Grey, 11, 37, 50, 72, 95, 97, 142, 168, 170, 248, 255, 258, 259, 264, 271, 272, 273, 274, 275, 276, 277, 326, 333, 336, 341, 345, 354, 357, 362, 369, 374, 389, 391, 402, 427, 431, 445, 472, 480, 498, 526, 536, 537, 540, 591, 592, 615, 618, 628, 631, 673, 674, 678
Grey, Agnes & Richard Mitton, 216
Grey, Agnes de & William Fitz Thomas, 673
Grey, Edward & Anne Middleton, 216
Grey, Edward & Joyce Horde, 216
Grey, Elizabeth & Arthur Plantagenet, 341
Grey, Elizabeth & Edmund Dudley, 341
Grey, Elizabeth & Henry Courtenay, 335
Grey, Elizabeth & Henry Fitz Hugh, 631
Grey, Elizabeth & John Arundell, 168
Grey, Elizabeth & John Zouche, 276
Grey, Elizabeth & William Griffith, 345
Grey, Henry & Katherine Stourton, 592
Grey, Henry & Katherine Strangeways, 276
Grey, Henry & Margaret Percy, 275
Grey, Henry & Margaret Stanley, 276
Grey, Henry de & Eleanor _____, 271
Grey, Henry de & Joan de Cobham, 274
Grey, Henry de & Joan de Somerville, 272, 354
Grey, Humphrey & Anne Fielding, 215

Grey, Ida & John Cokayne, 160
Grey, Jane [Queen of England], 342
Grey, John de & Alice de Lisle, 273
Grey, John de & Eleanor de Courtenay, 273
Grey, John de & Lucy de Mohun, 271
Grey, Lucy & Roland Lenthall, 615
Grey, Margaret & John Darcy, 389
Grey, Margaret & Thomas Swynford, 390
Grey, Maud de & John de Gravesende, 273
Grey, Maud de & Roger de Loudham, 273
Grey, Nichole de & Robert de Tateshale, 255
Grey, Richard & Elizabeth Basset, 274
Grey, Richard & Florence Pudsey, 248
Grey, Richard de & Joan Fitz Payn, 272
Grey, Robert & Eleanor Lowe, 215
Greystoke, 245, 290, 374, 391, 527, 630, 633
Greystoke, Eleanor & Ralph Eure, 527
Greystoke, Elizabeth & Thomas Dacre, 374
Greystoke, Maud & Ralph Eure, 525
Griffin, 297, 565
Griffin, Edward & Anne Smith, 158
Griffith, 159, 284, 345, 346
Griffith, Dorothy & Robert Wynne, 346
Griffith, Dorothy & William Williams, 346
Griffith, William & Elizabeth Grey, 345
Griffith, William & Jane Puleston, 346
Griffith, William & Jane Stradling, 345
Griffith, William & Joan Troutbeck, 345
Griffun, 255
Grimston, 362
Grisacre, 499
Gros, 481

Grosseteste, 77
Grosvenor, 8, 130, 297, 501
Grosvenor, Agnes & William Stanley, 501
Grosvenor, Eleanor & Jasper Lodge, 216
Grosvenor, Elizabeth & Thomas Bulkeley, 8
Grosvenor, Nicholas & Elizabeth Mitton, 216
Grosvenor, Randall & Anne Charlton, 8
Grosvenor, Winifred & _____ Hovell, 297
Grosvenor, Winifred & Henry Hurdman, 297
Grosvenor, Winifred & Thomas Corbin, 297
Grove, 369
Gruscet, 83
Gryg, Rhys & Joan de Clare, 183
Grymes, 361
Grymstede, 163
Gryslyng, 112
Guelders, 384, 385
Guevara, 670
Guevara, Francis & Anne Portington, 670
Guildford, 66, 342, 359, 595
Guildford, Jane & John Dudley, 342
Guildford, Mary & Owen West, 359
Guilford, 280
Guines, 17, 188
Gunville, 96
Gurdon, 11
Gurdon, Elizabeth & Thomas Waldegrave, 11
Gurson, 419
Guzmán, 115, 118, 121
Guzmán, Mayor Guillén de & Alfonso X, King of Castile and León, 118
Gwynne, 312
Gybbes, 679
Gyney, 232

Gyse, 410
Habyndon, 661
Hackburne, 477
Hackburne, Samuel & Katherine Deighton, 412
Hackford, 496
Haddon, 162, 662
Haddon, Amice de & William Fitz Warin, 162
Hadlow, 36
Hadlowe, 35
Hagborne, 412
Hagburne, 477
Hainault, 22, 23, 121, 189, 237, 390, 421, 444
Hainault, Isabelle of & Raoul de Clermont, 237
Hainault, Philippe of [Queen of England], 23, 163, 327, 448, 494
Haithorp, 26
Haiworth, 625
Hakelute, 642
Hakeluyt, 638, 642
Hakeluyt, Joan & Reynold Fitz Herbert, 642
Hakeluyt, Joan & Thomas le Blount, 643
Haket, 79
Hakluyt, 638, 639, 640
Hakluyt, Leonard & Margaret Longland, 638
Haldeyn, 232, 233
Hale, 63, 104, 578, 579
Hales, 296
Hall, 157, 340, 490, 558, 580, 681
Hall, _____ & Rachel Fitzwilliam, 681
Hall, Elizabeth & Lawrence Wodhull, 490
Hall, Reginald & Jane Huddleston, 681
Halleman, 228
Halley, 679
Halse, 377
Hambleton, 661

Hambly, 339
Hamby, 147
Hamelton, 32
Hamerton, 112, 113, 247
Hamerton, Margaret & Walter Strickland, 112
Hammond, 268
Hampden, 166, 422, 430, 431, 432, 628
Hampton, 430
Handlo, 69, 442
Hankeford, 52, 637, 664, 666
Hankford, 52, 102, 538, 664, 665, 666
Hankford, Anne & Thomas Butler, 52
Hankford, Anne & Thomas Ormond, 52
Hankford, Richard & Anne Montagu, 665
Hankford, Richard & Elizabeth Fitz Warin, 664
Hankford, Thomasine & William Bourgchier, 666
Hanlegh, 20
Hansard, 319
Hanyngfeld, 652
Harbottle, Agnes & Roger Fenwick, 557
Harburne, 216
Harburne, Eleanor & Richard Mitton, 216
Harcla, 243, 630
Harcourt, 37, 74, 83, 85, 86, 107, 167, 273, 393, 430, 431, 488, 640
Hardel, 379
Hardeshull, 282
Hardreshull, 542
Hardreshull, Agnes de & Bernard de Brus, 282
Harewell, 158, 216
Harington, 165, 168, 211, 247, 248, 333, 502
Harington, Anne & William Stanley, 502
Harison, 595
Harkarres, 478

Harley, 312
Harling, 96
Harling, Anne & John Scrope, 96
Harmer, 671
Haro, 115, 116, 118, 121, 195
Haro, María Díaz de & Juan of Castile, 195
Harper, 147
Harpesfeld, 368, 628
Harpesfield, 368, 628
Harpesfield, Philippe & John Barrett, 368, 628
Harpesfield, Philippe & Thomas Dyneley, 628
Harpur, 39, 40, 418
Harrington, 544
Harrington, Alice & Nicholas Fairfax, 544
Harris, 231, 347, 438
Harrison, 377, 682
Harry, 277
Harte, 344
Hartingdon, 70
Harwedon, 67
Harwood, 362
Haselop, 377
Haselop, Anne & Thomas Dade, 377
Hasilden, 162
Hassell, 529, 530
Hastang, 32, 598, 630
Hastang, Robert & Isabel de Mortimer, 598
Hastings, 39, 42, 43, 55, 69, 71, 72, 83, 87, 183, 197, 200, 203, 210, 230, 261, 262, 266, 342, 364, 386, 418, 443, 453, 458, 494, 495, 498, 499, 520, 521, 527, 533, 537, 611, 662, 675
Hastings, Ada de & Rhys ap Maredudd, 183
Hastings, Ada de & Robert de Champaine, 184
Hastings, Edward & Margery Clifton, 498

Hastings, Edward & Muriel Dinham, 498
Hastings, Elizabeth & Thomas Caterton, 496
Hastings, Elizabeth & William Elmham, 496
Hastings, Hugh & Anne Gascoigne, 499
Hastings, Hugh & Anne le Despenser, 497
Hastings, Hugh de & Margaret de Everingham, 495
Hastings, Hugh de & Margery Foliot, 494
Hastings, John & Anne Morley, 499
Hastings, Muriel & Ralph Eure, 527
Hastynges, 262
Hastyngges, 499
Haudlo, 32, 33, 34, 35, 36, 37, 67, 68, 69, 268, 442
Haudlo, John de & Joan Fitz Hugh, 35
Haudlo, John de & Maud Burnell, 35
Hauekyn, 579
Haugh, 10
Haule, 595
Hausex, 83
Haute, 351, 365
Haute-Pierre, 235
Hauterive, 66, 126
Hauterive, Eve de & Edward de Saint John, 66
Hauterive, Eve de & William Paynel, 66
Hauteryve, 126
Hauteville, Roger de & Isabelle of Blois, 462
Hauville, 32
Hawcliff, 285
Hawden, 478
Hawes, 678
Hawes, Anne & William Fitzwilliam, 678
Hawkesby, 640

Hawley, 329, 679
Hawtrey, 109
Hawy, 196
Hay, 58, 148, 392
Haye, de la, 80, 249, 316
Haymond, 595
Hayne, 665
Haynes, Christian & Rowland Coytemore, 347
Hayward, 338, 370, 410
Hayward, Alice & Richard Buller, 338
Head, 376
Hedge, 559
Heigham, 44, 439
Hele, 404, 405
Hele, Isabel & John Davie, 405
Hellebek, 240
Hellegan, 634
Helsenham, 510
Hemgrave, 556
Hender, 476
Hendley, 343
Hendley, Anne & Richard Covert, 344
Hendley, Walter & Ellen Ashburnham, 343
Hendley, Walter & Margery Pigott, 343
Henestrosa, 121
Hengham, 654
Henley, Patrick & Sarah Mayo, 371
Henry, 29
Henston, 403
Herbert, 311, 345, 410, 492, 576, 594
Herbert, Anne & Humphrey ap Hywel ap Jenkin, 492
Herdeburgh, 259
Herdeburgh, Isabel de & John de Hulles, 260
Herdeburgh, Roger de & Ida de Oddingseles, 259
Hereford, 47, 48, 49, 78, 80, 109, 124, 171, 173, 196, 204, 326, 387, 497, 506, 507, 516, 522, 566, 568, 569, 603, 605, 610, 611, 620, 646, 656, 666

Hereford, Lucy of & Herbert Fitz Herbert, 620
Herigaud, 139
Heringaud, 139
Herle, 5
Herling, 40
Herolff, 33
Heron, 344, 352, 357, 386, 580, 611
Heron, Emmeline & John Darcy, 18, 386
Heron, Mary & Richard Covert, 344
Herpesfeld, 88
Hertcombe, 501
Hertford, 17, 19, 23, 32, 78, 105, 174, 175, 176, 177, 180, 181, 182, 184, 185, 187, 191, 192, 193, 195, 197, 198, 203, 204, 252, 303, 305, 443, 513, 544, 587, 603, 606, 669
Herthull, 263
Hervey, John & Margaret Wykeham, 349
Hesdin, Maud de & Patrick de Chaources, 133
Heslarton, 529
Hethe, 398, 640
Heveningham, 61
Heveningham, John & Margaret Saint Leger, 575
Hever, 268
Hewke, 481
Hewke, Mary & Charles Lovell, 481
Hewke, Mary & George Nevill, 481
Hexstall, 213, 351, 501
Hexstall, Margaret & Henry Ferrers, 213
Heydon, 473, 499, 581, 669
Heyr, 306
Heythe, 380
Higgon, 216
Higham, 44
Higham, Bridget & Thomas Burrough, 44
Higham, Bridget & Thomas French, 45

Higham, Thomas & Phyllis Waldegrave, 44
Hildyard, 499
Hill, 8, 99, 102, 159, 334, 339, 467, 590, 682
Hillary, 264
Hille, 531
Hilton, 525, 551
Hilton, Robert de & Constance Sutton, 388
Hingham, 59
Hingston, 403
Hirst, 313
Hobart, 42, 266, 473
Hobson, 432, 529
Hobson, Mary & John Mansfield, 529
Hoby, 108
Hochem, 386
Hodde, 352
Hodenet, 81
Hodson, 480
Hoese, 516
Hogan, 112
Hogge, 535
Hoghles, 68
Hoghton, 500, 501
Hoghton, Alice & William Stanley, 501
Holand, 41, 95, 99, 142, 143, 246, 328, 332, 387, 454, 458, 535, 536, 537, 538, 539, 540, 541, 542, 570, 580, 581, 609, 610, 615, 618
Holand, Eleanor & Edward Cherleton, 142
Holand, Eleanor de & John Darcy, 387
Holand, Elizabeth & Roger Fiennes, 580
Holand, Henry & Anne Plantagenet, 540
Holand, John & Anne Montagu, 538, 665
Holand, John & Anne Stafford, 538
Holand, John & Beatrice of Portugal, 538, 615

Holand, John & Elizabeth [of] Lancaster, 533
Holand, Maud de & Hugh de Courtenay, 328
Holand, Maud de & Waleran de Luxembourg, 328
Holand, Robert & Margaret _____, 541
Holbeck, 224
Holcombe, 518
Holder, 147
Holdich, 206
Holgate, 278
Holland, 23, 121, 237, 581
Holles, 279
Hollick, Martin, 671
Holman, 581
Holme, 112
Holmstead, 12
Holmstead, Margaret & Thomas Waldegrave, 12
Holt, 53, 593
Holt, Christian & Edward Berkeley, 593
Holverston, 380
Hommet, 152, 271, 673
Honywood, 338
Hoo, 55, 230, 231, 364, 482, 484, 557, 662
Hoo, Thomas & Eleanor de Felton, 230
Hoo, Thomas & Elizabeth Echingham, 230
Hooe, 378
Hooker, Joanna & Thomas Shepard, 683
Hopton, 260, 261, 264, 292
Hopton, Elizabeth & John Tiptoft, 293
Hopton, Elizabeth & Roger Corbet, 292
Hopton, Elizabeth & William Stanley, 293
Horde, 216, 639, 641
Horde, Joyce & Edward Grey, 216
Hormansden, 371

Horne, 131, 343, 488
Horne, Anne & John Stanley, 488
Horne, Anne & William Norreys, 488
Horsey, 337
Horton, 314
Horton, Elizabeth & William Batte, 314
Hose, 413
Hoskins, Anthony, 104
Hotham, 448, 449, 450, 499, 526, 676
Hotham, Alice de & Hugh le Despenser, 449
Hotham, Alice de & John Trussell, 449
Hothom, 130, 388
Hoton, John & Isabel Trussell, 156
Hough, Atherton & Elizabeth Bulkeley, 10
Hough, Atherton & Susanna Hutchinson, 10
Hough, Samuel & Sarah Symmes, 10
Houghton, 501, 612
Hovell, _____ & Winifred Grosvenor, 297
Howard, 55, 56, 104, 107, 169, 258, 279, 308, 336, 607, 618
Howard, Douglas & Edward Stafford, 280
Howard, Douglas & John Sheffield, 279
Howard, Elizabeth & Thomas Boleyn, 56
Howard, Katherine [Queen of England], 57, 169
Howard, Margaret & Constantine de Clifton, 258
Howard, Margaret & Gilbert Talbot, 258
Howard, Margaret & Thomas Arundell, 169
Howell, 297
Howghton, 368
Howlett, 481
Hoxton, 347

Hubard, 66
Hubbard, Martha & John Whittingham, 10
Hubert, 42, 255
Huchon, 230
Huddesfeld, 101
Huddesfield, 100, 403, 436
Huddesfield, Katherine & Edmund Carew, 100
Huddleston, 248, 374, 480, 680
Huddleston, Alice & Thomas Lovell, 480
Huddleston, Jane & Reginald Hall, 681
Huddleston, Jane & William Gannock, 681
Huddleston, Margaret & John Fitzwilliam, 680
Huddleston, Richard & Rachel Fitzwilliam, 681
Hudford, 491
Hudleston, 680
Huggones, 106
Hulhampton, Thomas de & Margaret de Mortimer, 309
Hulles, 260
Hulles, Alice de & John de Langley, 261
Hulles, Alice de & John de Peyto, 261
Hulles, Denise de & John de Wateville, 260
Hulles, John de & Isabel de Herdeburgh, 260
Hulse, 593
Humberston, 132
Humet, 647
Humez, 271
Humphrey, Anne & Ellis ap Rees, 493
Humphries, 491
Humphries, Mary & George Elkington, 491
Hungary, 118, 426, 535
Hungary, Ladislaus VI, King of, 428

Hungerford, 26, 39, 96, 350, 399, 402, 452, 574, 591
Hungerford, Elizabeth & Philip Courtenay, 402
Hunsdon, 104, 107, 108
Hunt, Thomas & Joan Gawton, 467
Hunte, 517
Hunting, 412
Huntingdon, 71, 154, 189, 259, 261, 262, 264, 342, 453, 535, 536, 537, 538, 539, 540, 579, 606, 615, 665, 675
Huntingfield, 59, 379, 645, 649, 661
Huntingfield, Isabel de & Richard de Dagworth, 378
Huntingfield, Katherine de & Giles de Brewes, 59
Huntley, 197, 576
Huntyngdon, 262
Hurdman, Henry & Winifred Grosvenor, 297
Huse, 516, 586, 605
Husee, 66, 516, 517, 604, 605
Husee, Henry & Katherine de Arundel, 605
Husewyf, 617
Hussey, 250, 434, 517, 544, 605, 670
Hussey, Anne & William Skipwith, 670
Hussey, Hubert & Margaret de Beauchamp, 516
Hussey, Margaret & Henry Esturmy, 517
Hutchins, 595
Hutchinson, 147
Hutchinson, Susanna & Atherton Hough, 10
Hutchinson, William & Anne Marbury, 147
Hutton, 266, 529
Hyde, 342, 415
Hyde, de la, 66
Hyde, Walter de la & Joan de Neville, 415
Hydon, 321, 455

Hydon, Margaret de & Gilbert de Knoville, 455
Hydon, Margaret de & Josce de Dinham, 455
Hydon, Margaret de & Peter de Uvedale, 455
Hylle, 590
Hyndeston, 403
Iden, Alexander & Elizabeth Fiennes, 350
Ifeld, 68
Ifield, 586, 605, 642
Ifield, Dorothy & John Rogers, 586
Ifield, Dorothy & William Filoll, 586
Ilam, 351, 575
Ilam, Margaret & John Raynsford, 351
Ile, 99
Ilger, 449
Illingworth, 276
Immere, 623
Ingaldesthorpe, 293, 431
Inge, 90
Inge, Joan & Eudes la Zouche, 90
Inge, Joan & William Moton, 90
Ingham, 230
Ingleby, 286
Inglose, 232, 233, 373
Inglose, Henry & Amy Wythe, 232
Ingoldsby, Anthony & Dorcas Bulkeley, 9
Ingoldsby, Olive & Thomas James, 9
Innocent III, Pope, 114, 180, 185, 393, 396, 649
Innocent IV, Pope, 298
Irby, 9
Irby, Olive & Edward Bulkeley, 9
Ireland, 216
Ireland, Marshal of, 453
Ireys, 253
Irish, le, 242
Irwin, 280
Irwin, Mariana & Edmund Sheffield, 280
Issoudun, 521

Italy, 186, 298
Ivre, 525
Ivry, 538, 539, 540, 615, 665
Jackson, 361, 365
Jaén, 116, 118, 119, 120, 121
James, 9
James, Thomas & Elizabeth ____, 9
James, Thomas & Olive Ingoldsby, 9
Jaune, 554
Jay, 436
Jenkinson, 583
Jenney, 266, 267, 475, 528
Jennings, 297
Jenny, 61
Jermyn, 473
Jernegan, 472
Jernegan, Anne & Edmund Walsingham, 472
Jernegan, Anne & Robert Drury, 472
Jerningham, 472, 668
Jerusalem, 31, 116
Jobson, 341
Johan, 665
John, 46, 170, 538, 665
John XXII, Pope, 442
John, Lewis, 665
John, Lewis & Alice Vere, 665
John, Lewis & Anne Montagu, 665
Johnson, 209, 277, 493
Johnstone, 393
Jollye, 503
Jolye, 267
Jones, 94, 314, 367
Jordaine, 682
Jordan, 547, 588
Jowles, 148
Joynt, 226
Junnere, 623
Jurden, 359
Justiciar of England, 321, 393, 441
Justiciar of Ireland, 2, 18, 19, 22, 45, 46, 97, 141, 227, 242, 386, 387, 589
Kaignes, 441
Kaines, 443

Karuill, 562
Kaynes, 34, 441, 443
Keayne, 477, 530
Keayne, Robert & Anne Mansfield, 530
Kebbyll, 310
Kebell, 283
Kechin, 328
Kekewich, 337, 339
Kelke, 546
Kelke, Cecily & John Farrer, 546
Kelke, William & Thomasine Skerne, 546
Kemp, 583
Kendal, 39, 354, 419, 424
Kendale, 419, 430, 501
Kendall, 338, 542
Kenninghall, 253
Kenrick, 217
Kenrick, Elizabeth & David Clarkson, 217
Kenrick, Elizabeth & Walrave Lodwick, 217
Kenrick, John & Elizabeth Lodge, 217
Kenrick, Matthew & Rebecca Percival, 217
Kent, 12, 15, 59, 66, 68, 142, 192, 194, 206, 246, 288, 328, 332, 374, 377, 453, 454, 514, 522, 535, 552, 562, 610, 662, 663, 666
Kerdeston, 39, 40, 59, 60, 418, 420, 429, 449, 497
Kerdeston, Margaret & Jean de Foix, 419
Kerdeston, Thomas & Elizabeth de la Pole, 39, 418
Kerdeston, Thomas & Phillippe Trussell, 39, 418
Keresley, 95
Kersey, 669
Kethe, 682
Kett, 342, 437
Kighley, 266

Kildare, 18, 19, 26, 46, 50, 53, 277, 386, 432, 447
Killegrew, 371
Killingholm, 549
Killingholm, Alice de & Ralph de Bulmer, 549
Killingholm, Alice de & Walter de Fauconberge, 549
King, 266, 439, 498
King of the Romans, 117
Kingsfold, 142
Kingston, 410
Kirby, 430
Kiriell, 603
Kirkby, 66, 441
Kirkeby, 291
Kirketoft, 32
Kirketon, 652
Kirkham, 101, 102, 405
Kirkham, Thomas & Cecily Carew, 101
Kirkham, Thomasine & Thomas Southcott, 102
Knatchbull, 584
Knesworth, 155
Knight, 361
Kniveton, 362, 482
Kniveton, Andrew & Alice Lovell, 362
Knockin, 308, 309
Knolles, 109, 368, 628, 656
Knolles, Francis & Katherine Carey, 109
Knolles, Margery & John Knolles, 368
Knolles, Margery & Robert Barrett, 368
Knollys, 105, 109
Knouyll, 83
Knovill, 84
Knoville, 84
Knoville, Gilbert de & Margaret de Hydon, 455
Knowles, 109
Knvyett, 481
Knyght, 576

Knyvet, 112, 122, 258, 266, 432, 480, 483, 679, 680, 682, 683
Knyvet, Elizabeth & Richard Fitzwilliam, 679
Knyvet, Margaret & Richard Chamberlain, 122
Knyvet, Margaret & Thomas Echingham, 483
Knyvet, Margaret & William Gedney, 123
Knyvet, Thomasine & William Clopton, 265
Knyvet, William & Katherine Neville, 112
Knyvet, William and Alice _____, 112
Knyvett, 265, 481, 483
Krak, 186
Kyffin, 492
Kygheley, 84
Kyligrew, 635
Kyme, 220, 221, 564
Kynaston, 270, 292
Kynaston, Mary & Hywel ap Jenkin, 492
Kyngesford, 259
Kyngeston, 442
Kyriel, 261
Kyrkeby, 99
Kyrkeham, 101
l'Arcedeaken, 333
l'Arcedekne, Philippe & Hugh Courtenay, 333
La Chouche, 446
La Marche, 30, 195, 565
La Roche, 237
La Warr, 110
La Warre, 59, 484
La Warre, Elizabeth & Edmund Bacon, 59
Lacon, 294
Lacy, 14, 173, 192, 193, 204, 207, 283, 303, 305, 445, 446, 546, 596, 603, 672
Lacy, Gille de & Richard de Burgh, 14

Lacy, Gille de & Richard de Rochester, 15
Lacy, Margaret de & George de Cantelowe, 82
Lacy, Maud de & Richard de Clare, 192
Laken, 664
Lalande, 429
Lambton, 529
Lamphere, 313
Lamporte, 157
Lancaster, 22, 87, 122, 140, 160, 164, 191, 270, 274, 329, 389, 390, 408, 433, 443, 445, 452, 453, 454, 455, 495, 496, 524, 533, 536, 537, 548, 551, 556, 566, 570, 571, 602, 606, 607, 609, 613, 630, 658, 663
Lancaster, Edmund, Earl of, 567
Lancaster, Eleanor of & Richard de Arundel, 607
Lancaster, Elizabeth [of] & John Cornwall, 535
Lancaster, Elizabeth [of] & John Holand, 533
Lancaster, Henry, Earl of, 25, 70, 205, 229, 532
Lancaster, John of, Duke of Bedford, 422
Lancaster, John, Duke of, 656
Lancaster, Maud of & Ralph de Ufford, 22
Lancaster, Maud of & William de Burgh, 22
Lancaster, Philippe of [Queen of Portugal], 451, 610, 615
Lancaster, Thomas of, 357, 498
Lancaster, Thomas, Earl of, 25, 50, 204, 323, 442, 446, 654, 662, 674
Lane, 111, 132, 347, 640
Langdon, 371
Langelond, 635
Langelonde, 635, 636
Langford, 398, 399, 430, 431, 488, 628, 629

Langford, Alice & John Stradling, 399
Langford, Alice & Richard Pole, 399
Langford, Sanche & Edward Dyneley, 628
Langford, Sanche & Peter Carvanell, 628
Langforth, 430
Langhous, 328
Langley, 460, 461
Langley, Edmund of, 122, 142, 453, 609, 643
Langley, John de & Alice de Hulles, 261
Langlonde, 639
Langres, 29
Langston, 459
Langton, 223, 487, 526
Langton, Elizabeth & Thomas Stanley, 487
Langworth, 207
Lanvallay, 512, 515
Lara, 114, 115, 116, 195
Lara, Mafalda González de & Alfonso of Castile-León, 116
Lara, Teresa González de Alfonso & Alfonso of Castile-León, 116
Larchévêque, 237
Lascelles, 478
Latham, 214, 335
Latham, Frances & Jeremy Clarke, 214
Latham, Frances & William Vaughan, 214
Lathom, 570
Latimer, 6, 69, 70, 71, 111, 164, 245, 331, 496, 606
Latimer, Elizabeth le & John de Camoys, 69
Latimer, Elizabeth le & Ralph de Ufford, 70
Latimer, Joan le & Alexander Comyn, 6
Laud, 366, 683
Lawrence, 313
Layton, 146

Le Forester, 578
Le Gros, 361, 481
Le Gros, Elizabeth & Charles Lovell, 481
Lecce, 472
Leche, 337
Ledet, 6
Lee, 113, 295, 297, 459, 466, 661
Lee, Geoffrey & Agnes Conyers, 465
Lee, Mary & Henry Drake, 466
Lee, Richard & Elizabeth Crispe, 466
Leeds, 532
Leeds, Thomas de & Elizabeth de Reygate, 208
Leeke, 277
Leeton, 35
Legard, 683
Leicester, 22, 87, 109, 122, 140, 149, 180, 191, 195, 250, 280, 304, 342, 414, 443, 455, 514, 533, 607
Leigh, 73, 111, 490, 502
Leigh, Jane & Peter Stanley, 502
Leighton, 109, 577, 640, 641
Leighton, Edward & Elizabeth Stapleton, 641
Leighton, John & Ankaret Burgh, 641
Leighton, Thomas & Elizabeth Devereux, 294
Lenard, 422
Lendon, 1
Lenthall, 95, 276, 277, 615
Lenthall, Roland & Lucy Grey, 615
Lenthall, Roland & Margaret Arundel, 615
Lenton, 146
León, 114, 115, 116, 117, 118, 119, 120, 121, 122, 385, 453, 462, 551, 657
Léon, 47
León, Alfonso IX, King of & Berenguela I, Queen of Castile, 115
León, Alfonso IX, King of & Teresa of Portugal, 115
Leppington, 683
Lestalrig, 393

Levedale, 598
Leventhorpe, 131
Leventhorpe, Anne & John Chauncy, 131
Lever, 68
Leveson, John & Anne Smith, 158
Lewer, 675
Lewis, 216, 345, 346
Lewis, Mary & William Coytemore, 346
Lewkenour, 364
Lewknor, 55, 71, 72, 231, 363, 364, 365, 482
Lewknor, Edward & Anne Everard, 364
Lewknor, Edward & Dorothy Wroth, 365
Lewknor, Edward & Margaret _____, 364
Lewknor, Edward & Margaret Copley, 364
Lewknor, Edward & Sibyl _____, 364
Lewknor, Mary & Matthew Machell, 365
Lewknor, Nicholas & Elizabeth Radmylde, 363
Lewknor, Roger & Katherine Chidiock, 166
Lewyr, 68
Leybourne, 239, 240, 243, 261, 262, 564, 580, 608
Leybourne, Juliane de & William de Clinton, 261
Leybourne, Roger de & Idoine de Vipont, 240
Leyburn, 241
Leyburne, 240, 261
Leye, 635
Leyham, 661
Leyham, Matthew de & Nesta de Cockfield, 13
Leyntale, 615
Leynthale, 615
Leythorn, 638

Lieutenant of Aquitaine, 538, 615
Lieutenant of Calais, 40, 95, 96, 359, 572, 573
Lieutenant of Ireland, 16, 17, 47, 50, 386, 400, 424, 658
Lievens, 218
Lightfoot, 297
Ligny, 328
Ligon, 314, 370, 411, 435
Ligon, Henry & Elizabeth Berkeley, 411
Ligon, Isabel & Edward Basset, 411
Ligon, Isabel & Rice Davis, 411
Lilleburn, 74
Lilly, 217
Lima, 116
Limburg, 186, 299
Limbury, 264
Limerick, 14
Limesi, 290
Limoges, 30, 119
Lincoln, 76, 122, 152, 176, 192, 193, 204, 207, 250, 253, 254, 303, 424, 425, 426, 428, 455, 477, 533, 560, 603
Lindsay, 7
Lindsey, 196
Lindsey, Gilbert de & Alice de Lusignan, 196
Lisle, 51, 74, 273, 303, 323, 336, 341, 342, 369, 442, 448, 455, 558, 605, 628, 652
Lisle, Alice de & John de Grey, 273
Lisle, Katherine de & Eustace de Cantelowe, 74
Lisours, 396, 672
Littlebury, 224
Littlefield, 362
Littleton, Thomas & Joan Burley, 573
Lloyd, 346
Lobb, 339
Lobbe, 339
Locksmythe, 466
Lodge, 216
Lodge, Edward & Eleanor Grosvenor, 216

Lodge, Elizabeth & John Kenrick, 217
Lodwick, 217
Lodwick, Walrave & Elizabeth Kenrick, 217
Logan, 22
Loky, 291
Lomene, 128
Londa, 509
London, 79, 138, 440
London, Hawise de & Patrick de Chaworth, 138
Londroppe, 536
Longe, 32
Longespée, 58, 137, 317, 415, 650, 651
Longespée, Ida & Walter Fitz Robert, 650
Longland, 635, 637
Longland, Hugh de & Margaret Furneaux, 635
Longland, Joan & John Roynon, 637
Longland, Joan & Robert Yevelton, 637
Longland, John de & Isabel de Beaupré, 636
Longland, Margaret & John Deviock, 638
Longland, Margaret & Leonard Hakluyt, 638
Longueville, 419
Longum, 672
Longvyle, 572
Lopham, 27
Lord High Treasurer, 41, 43, 51, 96, 247, 293, 335, 348, 357, 391, 402, 425, 459, 484, 526, 538, 586, 589, 591, 613, 615, 617, 631
Lord Marshal, 429
Loring, 333, 663
Loriol, 429
Lorraine, 29, 30, 328, 428, 472, 568
Lorraine, Alix of & Hugues III, Duke of Burgundy, 28
Louches, 70

Louches, Elizabeth & Thomas Camoys, 70
Loude, 638
Loudesop, William & Elizabeth Chetwode, 156
Loudham, Roger de & Maud de Grey, 273
Lound, 314
Lound, Mary & Henry Batte, 314
Louth, 16
Louthe, 377
Louthe, Margaret & Richard Cornwallis, 377
Louvain, 177, 250
Louvain, Alice of & William d'Aubeney, 250
Lovaine, 122, 564, 658
Loveday, 196, 674
Lovel, 34, 36, 41, 51, 52, 84, 86, 95, 96, 325, 429, 458, 633
Lovel, Henry & Elizabeth de la Pole, 429
Lovel, John & Maud Burnell, 34
Lovel, Maud & William la Zouche, 86
Lovel, Philippe & John Dinham, 458
Lovel, Philippe & Nicholas Broughton, 458
Lovelace, 351, 588
Lovell, 42, 361, 431, 479, 480, 481, 667
Lovell, Alice & Andrew Kniveton, 362
Lovell, Alice & George Crymes, 361
Lovell, Charles & Anne ____, 481
Lovell, Charles & Elizabeth le Gros, 481
Lovell, Charles & Mary Hewke, 481
Lovell, Francis & Anne Ashby, 480
Lovell, Gregory & Margaret Brandon, 479
Lovell, Thomas & Alice Huddleston, 480
Lovell, Thomas & Elizabeth Paris, 480
Lovetoft, 283
Lovetot, 66
Lovetot, Robert & Agnes de Brus, 283

Lovett, 400
Lowe, 39, 65, 215, 418, 461
Lowe, Eleanor & Robert Grey, 215
Lowe, Jane & Charles Calvert, 65
Lower, 337, 339
Lower Lorraine, 177, 250
Lowther, 111, 248
Lucy, 127, 182, 243, 262, 277, 292, 393, 630, 645, 647, 649, 658
Lucy, Maud de & Walter Fitz Robert, 645
Luddesop, 536
Luddington, 365
Ludford, 217
Ludgershall, 178, 509
Ludgershall, Peter de & Maud _____, 509
Ludlow, 156, 488, 605, 628, 661
Ludlow, _____ & Robert Dyneley, 628
Ludwell, Philip & Frances Culpeper, 371
Lugg, John & Jane Deighton, 412
Lukyn, 49, 387
Lukyn, Robert & Elizabeth Darcy, 49
Lumley, 165, 166, 289
Lumley, Katherine & John Chidiock, 165
Lungvilers, 531, 532, 672
Lunsford, 56, 582
Lusher, Margaret & Lawrence Wodhull, 490
Lusignan, 30, 195, 385, 469, 521, 522, 565
Lusignan, Alice de & Gilbert de Clare, 195
Lusignan, Alice de & Gilbert de Lindsey, 196
Lusignan, Mary de & Robert de Ferrers, 565
Luttrell, 330, 332, 403
Luvetot, 392, 645, 646
Luvetot, Richard de & Maud de Senlis, 392
Luxembourg, 237, 328

Luxembourg, Waleran de & Maud de Holand, 328
Luxemburg, 607
Lydiard, Clemence & Nicholas Purefoy, 475
Lyf, 638
Lyffe, 638
Lygon, 411, 435
Lygon, William & Elizabeth Arundell, 398
Lyngen, 461
Lynnolds, 479
Lyttylton, 574, 640
Lyvelode, 486
Mablethorpe, 653
MacEwen, Andrew B.W., 7, 207, 221
Machell, 365, 366
Machell, Mary & John Stoughton, 366
Machell, Mary & Ralph Cudworth, 366
Machell, Matthew & Mary Lewknor, 365
Mackworth, 94
Mackworth, Thomas & Alice Basynges, 94
Mâcon, 469
Macy, 68
Maddison, _____ & Mary Gray, 558
Magges, 371
Maidstone, 267
Maidstone, Margaret & Robert Crane, 267
Maidstone, Margaret & Walter Clopton, 267
Maignard, 224
Mainwaring, 8, 154, 217, 295
Maisnières, 385
Major, 314
Majorca, 118
Malbanc, 178, 512
Malemains, 73
Malet, 150, 321, 403, 638
Malet, Hugh & Joan Roynon, 638
Mallory, 145, 313, 314
Mallory, Martha & John Batte, 314

Mallory, Mary & John Cope, 145
Mallory, William & Margaret _____, 292
Maloysel, 256
Maltravers, 481
Mandeville, 22, 78, 178, 179, 323, 510, 511, 512, 514, 515, 516, 646, 650
Mandeville, Geoffrey de & Isabel of Gloucester, 514
Mandeville, Geoffrey de & Maud Fitz Robert, 514
Mandeville, William de & Christian Fitz Robert, 515
Maner, 623
Manfeld, 47
Manfield, 131, 132, 529
Manners, 286
Manners, Katherine & Robert Constable, 286
Manning, 159
Mannington, 338
Mansell, 544
Mansfield, 529, 530
Mansfield, Anne & Robert Keayne, 530
Mansfield, Anne & Samuel Cole, 530
Mansfield, Elizabeth & John Wilson, 530
Mansfield, John & Elizabeth _____, 530
Mansfield, John & Mary Hobson, 529
Mansfield, John & Mary Shard, 530
Mansfield, Lancelot & Anne Eure, 529
Mansfield, Lancelot & Margaret _____, 529
Manuel, 121
Manuel, Constanza & Alfonso XI, King of Castile-León, 121
Maplesden, 596
Mar, 16, 673
Marbury, 146
Marbury, Anne & William Hutchinson, 147

Marbury, Francis & Bridget Dryden, 146
Marbury, Francis & Elizabeth Moore, 146
Marbury, Katherine & Richard Scott, 147
Marc, 396
March, 6, 24, 36, 71, 98, 142, 201, 220, 221, 225, 244, 246, 276, 311, 332, 424, 448, 459, 478, 538, 540, 592, 610, 611
March, Erard de la, Bishop of Liège, 428
Marcham, 228
Marche, 121, 521
Marche, de la, 196
Marchena, 117
Marchumley, 501
Marck, de la, 428
Mare, de la, 66, 67, 69, 88, 206, 415, 458, 495
Mare, Henry de la, 652
Mare, Henry de la & Joan de Neville, 415
Mare, Joan de la & Ralph de Cromwell, 354
Mare, Reynold de la, 310
Mareuil, 469
Mareys, 45, 635
Markenfield, 99, 249, 288
Markham, 480
Markhant, 473
Marmion, 79, 355, 631
Marney, 166, 483
Marny, 483
Marsan, 301, 302
Marsburgh, 210
Marsh, 45, 313, 510, 511, 621
Marshal, 1, 14, 82, 166, 179, 180, 183, 185, 192, 253, 298, 417, 446, 482, 499, 515, 535, 537, 561, 564, 565, 616, 618, 652, 654
Marshal of England, 183, 269, 274, 331, 497, 615
Marshal of France, 237
Marshal of Ireland, 496, 654

Marshal of the Eyre, 47
Marshal, Isabel & Gilbert de Clare, 185
Marshal, Isabel & Richard of England, Earl of Cornwall, 298
Marshal, Isabel & Richard, Earl of Cornwall, 185
Marshal, Sibyl & William de Ferrers, 561
Marshal, William le & Elizabeth de Ferrers, 564
Marsham, 64
Marston, 281, 670
Martel, 317, 625, 642
Martel, Joan & Reynold, Fitz Reynold, 642
Marten, 559
Marten, Mary & John Fenwick, 559
Martin, 625
Martyn, 404
Marwell, 127
Marwood, 403
Massereene, 595
Massey, 165, 378, 660
Massingberd, 364, 670
Massy, 572
Master of the Horse, 109, 209, 543, 667
Master of the Hounds, 209
Masterson, 158
Matha, 301, 302
Mathew, 312, 345, 434
Matravers, 159
Mauduit, 281, 442, 510, 676
Maule, 652
Mauleverer, 99
Mauleverer, Halnath & Joan Carminow, 99
Mauley, 243, 388, 675
Mauley, Peter de & Constance Sutton, 388
Mauley, Peter de & Elizabeth de Meinill, 388
Maunder, 338
Maundley, 338
Mauntell, 39, 418
Maurienne, 29
Mauteby, 256
Mautravers, 43, 164, 166, 269, 407, 408, 458, 590, 591, 600, 609
Mautravers, Eleanor & Reynold Cobham, 269
Mautravers, Maud & John Dinham, 458
Mawe, 682
Mayenne, 28, 135
Mayo, 371
Mayo, Sarah & John Culpeper, 371
Mayo, Sarah & Matthew Pritchard, 371
Mayo, Sarah & Patrick Henley, 371
McMurrough, 453
Meade, 434
Meare, 503
Mede, 434
Medlicote, 370
Medwall, 501
Meilles, 419
Meinell, 388, 389, 390
Meinill, 388
Meinill, Elizabeth de & John Darcy, 388
Meinill, Elizabeth de & Peter de Mauley, 388
Melbourn, 560
Meldrum, 3
Melford, 249
Mello, 233, 236
Mellowes, Abraham & Martha Bulkeley, 9
Melton, 245, 277, 488, 499, 632
Melton, John & Eleanor Saint John, 277
Meneses, 116, 120
Meneses Girón, 119
Meneses, Mayor Alfonso & Alfonso of Castile-León, 116
Menteith, 200, 202
Menzies, 16, 201

Merbrook, 488
Merbury, 146, 575
Mercœur, 29
Mere, 163
Meredith, 505
Meriet, 68
Meriet, John de & Elizabeth Arundel, 97
Merlay, 220, 272, 621
Merston, 281
Merston, Constance de & Bernard de Brus, 281
Merston, Constance de & Robert de Wotton, 281
Merton, 139, 164, 382, 590, 651
Meryet, 69
Meschin, 413
Metham, 279, 284, 669
Meulan, 173, 180, 318, 514
Meverel, 560
Meyners, 16
Meynill, 524
Michell, 361, 364
Michell, Constance & George More, 361
Middelmor, 576
Middleton, 110, 216
Middleton, Anne & Edward Grey, 216
Midwinter, 157
Milan, 552
Mill, 311
Milliton, 404
Mills, 267, 360, 558
Mills, Margaret & Richard Fenwick, 558
Mirfeld, 211
Mitchell, 684
Mitchell, Jonathan & Margaret Borodell, 683
Mitford, Margery & Ralph Fenwick, 558
Mitton, 216
Mitton, Elizabeth & Nicholas Grosvenor, 216
Mitton, Elizabeth & Richard Dewe, 216
Mitton, Richard & Agnes Grey, 216
Mitton, Richard & Eleanor Harburne, 216
Moels, 323, 325, 456
Moels, Muriel de & Thomas de Courtenay, 325
Mohaut, 35, 83, 84, 85, 86, 254, 255, 268, 603
Mohaut, John de & Milicent de Cantelowe, 83
Mohone, 337
Mohun, 2, 25, 26, 39, 97, 179, 334, 339, 354, 516, 564, 603, 616, 622, 625, 656, 657, 658, 674
Mohun, Lucy de & Arnold Murdac, 271
Mohun, Lucy de & John de Grey, 271
Mohun, Philippe & Edward of York, 657
Mohun, Philippe & Walter Fitz Walter, 656
Mohun, Philppe & John Golafre, 656
Mokhale, 311
Moleyns, 59
Molford, 102
Molina, 119, 120, 121
Molina, María Alfonso de & Sancho IV King of Castile and León, 119
Mompesson, Anne & William Dyneley, 627
Monboucher, 355
Monceux, 578
Monceux, Maud de & John de Fiennes, 578
Mondoubleau, 134
Monferrato, 23, 118, 194
Monferrato, Guglielmo VII, Marquis of & Beatriz of Castile, 194
Monferrato, Guglielmo VII, Marquis of & Isabel de Clare, 194
Monferrato, Margarita of & Juan of Castile, 195

Monferrato, William, marquis of, 195
Monins, 461
Monke, 341
Monmouth, 82, 107, 443, 568
Monmouth, Baderon de & Rohese Fitz Gilbert, 173
Montacute, 458
Montagu, 1, 53, 65, 206, 242, 342, 420, 421, 431, 446, 457, 482, 488, 497, 498, 535, 538, 556, 609, 612, 616, 633, 665
Montagu, Anne & John Holand, 538, 665
Montagu, Anne & Lewis John, 665
Montagu, Anne & Richard Hankford, 665
Montagu, Eleanor de & John Dinham, 457
Montagu, Elizabeth de & Guy de Bryan, 1, 446
Montagu, Elizabeth de & Hugh le Despenser, 446
Montagu, Hawise de & Roger de Bavent, 397
Montagu, William de & Elizabeth Arundel, 616
Montague, 44, 170
Montalt, 83, 84
Montcada, 301
Montchenu, 429
Montdidier, 233
Monte Hermeri, 201
Montesquieu, 429
Montferrand, 540
Montfitchet, 174, 189, 560
Montfort, 66, 75, 76, 77, 78, 151, 196, 201, 239, 252, 264, 265, 301, 302, 320, 408, 414, 416, 462, 530, 531, 565, 597, 632, 640, 652
Montfort, Alice de & Robert Fitz Walter, 652
Montfort, Alix de & Simon de Clermont, 236
Montfort, Bertrade de & Hugh, Earl of Chester, 151

Montfort, Ellen & Maurice Berkeley, 408
Montfort, Simon de, 195
Montfort], 188
Montgomery, 53, 117, 209, 292, 593, 594
Montgomery, Maud & Thomas Clarell, 209
Monthermer, 5, 197, 198, 199, 200, 201, 205, 206, 443, 457, 665
Monthermer, Mary de & Duncan of Fife, 200
Monthermer, Ralph de & Isabel le Despenser, 197
Monthermer, Ralph de & Joan of England, 197
Monthermer, Thomas de & Margaret de Brewes, 205
Montignac, 238
Montmirail, 463, 471
Montmorency, 172, 234, 385
Montmorency, Mathieu de & Marie of Ponthieu, 385
Montreuil, 117, 385
Mont-Saint-Jean, 30
Monynton, 448
Moore, 363, 370, 436, 590
Moore, Elizabeth & Francis Marbury, 146
Moore, John & Margaret Brent, 595
Moray, 7, 201, 206, 221, 393, 663
Moray, _____ of & Robert, Earl of Strathearn, 393
Mordaunt, 62
More, 360
More, de la, 517
More, George & Anne Poynings, 360
More, George & Constance Michell, 361
More, Margaret & Thomas Crymes, 361
Morewick, 647
Morgan, 107, 311
Morgan, Anne & Henry Carey, 107
Morham, 200

Morland, 243
Morley, 57, 166, 417, 425, 429, 451, 453, 466, 496, 497, 499, 556, 557
Morley, Anne & John Hastings, 499
Morley, Elizabeth & John Arundell, 166
Morley, Thomas & Anne le Despenser, 497
Morris, 493
Morrison, Robert & Jane Eltonhead, 504
Morsel, 303
Morstede, 71
Mortain, 73, 75, 382, 384, 514, 533, 560
Mortemer, 36
Morteyn, 281, 282
Mortimer, 24, 40, 46, 58, 71, 98, 142, 196, 244, 246, 256, 259, 276, 307, 309, 311, 332, 359, 407, 409, 424, 445, 446, 448, 454, 538, 553, 561, 568, 592, 597, 598, 602, 610, 611, 622, 625
Mortimer, Cecily & John Radcliffe, 40
Mortimer, Eleanor & Edward Courtenay, 332
Mortimer, Eleanor de & Adam de Clifton, 256
Mortimer, Elizabeth & Thomas Camoys, 71
Mortimer, Hugh & Eleanor Cornwall, 311
Mortimer, Isabel de & John Fitz Alan, 597
Mortimer, Isabel de & Ralph d'Arderne, 598
Mortimer, Isabel de & Robert Hastang, 598
Mortimer, Margaret de & Geoffrey de Cornwall, 309
Mortimer, Margaret de & Thomas de Hulhampton, 309
Mortimer, Margaret de & William Devereux, 309
Mortimer, Maud de & John de Cherleton, 141

Mortimer, Philippe & Richard de Arundel, 611
Mortimer, Philippe & Thomas Poynings, 611
Mortimer, Roger de, 444
Mortimer, William la Zouche & Eleanor de Clare, 444
Morton, 278, 293, 587, 588
Morville, 239
Morwick, Tiphaine de & John de Bulmer, 629
Moss, 267
Mostyn, 345
Mote, 570
Mote, Joan de la & Robert de Ferrers, 570
Moton, 474
Moton, William & Joan Inge, 90
Moulton, 296
Moundry, 656, 658
Mouner, 303
Mounteney, 54
Mounthermer, 206
Mountjoy, 53, 336, 484, 594
Mounts, Eble de & Elizabeth de Clinton, 263
Mowbray, 172, 195, 206, 225, 261, 320, 327, 417, 496, 537, 609, 616, 617, 618, 654
Mowbray, Elizabeth & Michael de la Pole, 417
Mowbray, John de & Elizabeth de Vere, 327
Mowbray, Thomas & Elizabeth Arundel, 616
Moyle, 166, 213, 588
Moyle, Katherine & Nicholas Saint Leger, 588
Moyle, Katherine & Thomas Finch, 588
Moyne, 598
Mulgrave, 279, 280, 281
Mull, 431
Multon, 17, 456, 655

Multon, Joan de & Robert Fitz Walter, 655
Munchensy, 177, 253, 513
Munchensy, William de & Aveline de Clare, 177
Munster, 15
Murcia, 118, 119, 120, 121
Murdac, Arnold & Lucy de Mohun, 271
Mure, 202
Murgatroyd, 314
Musard, 511
Muscegros, 565, 568, 569
Muscegros, Hawise de & John de Bures, 569
Muscegros, Hawise de & John de Ferrers, 568
Muschamp, 361
Musgrave, 112, 243, 246, 545, 558
Musgrave, Thomas de & Isabel de Berkeley, 243
Musket, 144
Myles, 347
Myles, Katherine & Rowland Coytemore, 347
Mylton, 152
Mymecan, 71, 72
Mynn, 63
Mynne, 63, 473
Mynne, Agnes & Walter Dennis, 434
Mynne, Anne & George Calvert, 63
Mynne, George & Elizabeth Wroth, 63
Mytton, 345
Namur, 250
Nannau, John & Elsbeth ferch Dafydd Llwyd, 492
Nanteuil, 234
Nanteuil, Thibaut III, seigneur of & Clémence of Bar, 234
Narbonne, 236
Nash, 8
Navarre, 30, 92, 114, 151, 252, 496
Navarre, Béatrice of Champagne & Hugh, Duke of Burgundy, 30

Navarre, Charles, King of, 122
Navarre, Joan of [Queen of England], 95
Neale, 147, 378
Neale, Ellen & Stephen Dryden, 147
Needham, 10, 159
Needham, Dorothy & Richard Chetwode, 159
Néele, 117
Néelle, 117
Negus, Jonathan & Jane Deighton, 412
Nelson, 465, 543
Nemours, 471
Nerford, 12
Nesle, 117, 237, 467
Nesle, Gertrude de & Raoul de Clermont, 236
Nesle, Jean de & Jeanne de Dammartin, 117
Neufmarché, 620
Neuman, 623
Neusom, 198
Nevers, 30, 31, 463, 465
Nevet, 559
Nevill, 361, 654
Nevill, George & Mary Hewke, 481
Neville, 3, 4, 84, 108, 111, 112, 130, 165, 166, 201, 210, 225, 226, 228, 243, 246, 276, 285, 288, 289, 309, 320, 321, 349, 350, 352, 358, 369, 373, 374, 399, 413, 415, 424, 431, 455, 526, 540, 541, 543, 551, 552, 562, 574, 594, 598, 610, 618, 628, 631, 633, 654, 672
Neville, Alice & Christopher Conyers, 465
Neville, Alice & Henry Fitz Hugh, 633
Neville, Alice & John Conyers, 288
Neville, Anne & Anthony Saltmarshe, 289
Neville, Anne & William Conyers, 289
Neville, Anne & William Stonor, 431
Neville, Eleanor & Henry Percy, 455
Neville, Eleanor & Richard le Despenser, 455

Neville, Elizabeth & Richard Covert, 594
Neville, Elizabeth & Thomas Berkeley, 594
Neville, Hugh de & Beatrice de Turnham, 414
Neville, Hugh de & Elizabeth de Quincy, 3
Neville, Hugh de & Ida Fitz Walter, 654
Neville, Hugh de & Joan de Cornhill, 413
Neville, Joan de & Henry de la Mare, 415
Neville, Joan de & Walter de la Hyde, 415
Neville, John de & Hawise de Courtenay, 414
Neville, Katherine & _____ Darcy, 112
Neville, Katherine & Henry Burgh, 112
Neville, Katherine & Walter Strickland, 112
Neville, Katherine & William Knyvet, 112
Neville, Philippe & Thomas Dacre, 372
Neville, Ralph & Elizabeth Percy, 246
Neville, Sarah & Edward Fenwick, 559
Neville, William & Joan Fauconberge, 551
Nevyll, 211
Newburgh, 366, 635, 671, 672
Newburgh, Prior of, 531
Newburgh, Robert de & Ela de Warenne, 671
Newby, 371
Newcomen, 670
Newdigate, 669
Newenham, 157
Newenham, Anne & Fulk Wodhull, 157
Neweport, 357
Newland, 9

Newman, Thomas & Bridget Dryden, 146
Newmarch, 674
Newport, 274, 277, 295
Newton, 113
Newton, Ellen & Edward Carleton, 113
Nicholls, 159, 339
Nichols, 477
Nicholson, 146, 503
Niño, 116
Noble, 532
Noone, 440, 466
Norbery, 491
Noreys, 488
Norfolk, 15, 46, 56, 104, 108, 193, 249, 260, 336, 417, 441, 496, 537, 540, 553, 568, 603, 607, 615, 616, 617, 618, 679
Normandy, 149, 315
Normanville, 291, 396
Norreys, 488, 575
Norreys, William & Anne Horne, 488
Norris, 369, 376, 432, 628
Norris, Margaret & John Barrett, 369, 628
Norrys, 488
North Wales, 151
Northampton, 18, 48, 329, 382, 387, 477, 610, 644, 645, 654, 655, 663, 666
Northumberland, 103, 108, 152, 169, 258, 280, 341, 342, 350, 431, 455, 544, 658
Norton, 217, 368, 369, 449, 450, 584, 628
Norton, ____ & Ellen Strickland, 113
Norway, Eric, King of, 221
Norwich, 35, 219, 226, 257
Norwood, 370
Norwood, Eleanor & John Culpeper, 370
Norys, 488
Noszak, 553
Nottingham, 107, 294, 417, 537, 609, 616, 617, 618
Noyelles-sur-Mer, 117
Noyers, 472

O'Brien, 18, 52
O'Carrol, 49
O'Carroll, 49
O'Connor, 16
O'Conor, 15
O'Brien, 52
Oddingseles, 13, 253, 259, 651
Oddingseles, Ida de & John de Clinton, 259
Oddingseles, Ida de & Roger de Herdeburgh, 259
Odingsells, 160, 368
Offard, 507
Offord, 227, 507
Ogard, 41
Ogle, 201, 525, 526, 558, 677
Ogle, Barbara & Ralph Fenwick, 558
Ogle, Richard & Mary Fitzwilliam, 677
Oilly, 78, 80, 180, 381, 516, 646
Okeover, 297
Oldcastle, 143, 609
Oldcotes, 386
Oldener, 491
Olton, 259
Onslow, 294
ontgomery, 271
Orchard, 339
Orgeoise, 429
Orget, 73, 74, 75, 76
Orléans, 270
Ormeston, 502
Ormond, 19, 46, 47, 48, 49, 50, 51, 52, 53, 54, 55, 56, 57, 102, 104, 108, 279, 387, 490, 594, 605, 666, 678
Ormond, James & Avice Stafford, 51
Ormond, James & Eleanor Beaufort, 51
Ormond, Jane & William Fitzwilliam, 678
Ormond, Thomas & Anne Hankford, 52
Ormond, Thomas & Lora Berkeley, 53
Ormonde, 50, 52, 55

Orreby, 255
Orreville, 462
Orsini, 194
Osbarn, 230
Osbern, 232, 233, 373
Osborne, 130, 461
Oseberne, 37
Osgoodby, 89
Ostelli, 647
Ostre, 65
Oteley, 216
Ouensby, 184
Outhorp, 355
Outillé, 647
Overton, 9
Owen, 312, 411, 484, 485
Oxburgh, 461
Oxenbridge, 280, 484, 485, 486
Oxenbridge, Goddard & Anne Fiennes, 486
Oxenbridge, Goddard & Elizabeth Echingham, 486
Oxenbridge, Thomas & Elizabeth Puttenham, 486
Oxenbridge, Thomas & Faith Devenish, 486
Oxenford, 626
Oxford, 23, 38, 226, 273, 275, 279, 320, 327, 472, 533, 540, 603, 656, 658, 665, 666
Oxley, 671
Oxley, William & Anne Skipwith, 671
Oyry, 547
Pabenham, 161, 507, 508
Pabenham, Katherine & Thomas Aylesbury, 508
Pabenham, Katherine & William Cheyne, 508
Pabenham, Laurence & Elizabeth d'Engaine, 507
Pabenham, Laurence & Joan Daubeney, 507
Pacy, 477
Padilla, 121, 122

Padilla, María Díaz de & Pedro I, King of Castile and León, 121
Page, 668
Page, Elizabeth & William Skipwith, 669
Page, Richard & Elizabeth Bourchier, 668
Pageham, 577
Pair de France, 30
Palæologus, 194
Palæologus, Othon II & Violante Visconti, 23
Palmer, 557, 679, 680
Palmes, 544
Palmes, Jane & Nicholas Fairfax, 544
Palton, 402
Panchard, 339
Panes, 661
Pantolf, 254
Pargiter, 583
Parham, 314, 503
Paris, 480
Paris, Elizabeth & Thomas Lovell, 480
Park, 40, 195
Parker, 57, 339, 425, 474, 484, 661
Parker, James & Katherine Buller, 339
Parker, Jane & George Boleyn, 57
Parker, Mary & James Cudworth, 367
Parker, Richard & Mary _____, 340
Parmenter, 412
Parr, 157, 374, 633, 678
Parr, Agnes & Thomas Strickland, 110
Parr, Elizabeth & Nicholas Wodhull, 157
Parr, Katherine [Queen of England], 169
Parr, Mabel & Humphrey Dacre, 374
Parram, 233
Parramore, 467
Parry, 312, 313
Parry, Elizabeth & Anthony Rawlinson, 313
Parry, Elizabeth & Robert Batte, 313
Parry, George & Isabel Vaughan, 312
Parry, Roger & Eleanor _____, 313

Parry, Roger & Mary Crosley, 313
Parry, Thomas & Anne Reade, 432
Pascall, Mary & John Brock, 279
Pashley, Anne & Edward Tyrrell, 375
Pashley, Anne & John Bassingbourne, 375
Paston, 41, 65, 103, 104, 499, 667
Pateshull, 320
Pateshulle, 400, 550
Pateshulle, Maud de & Walter de Fauconberge, 550
Patsyll, 131
Paulet, 108, 168
Pauncefote, 74
Pauncefote, Geoffrey & Sibyl de Cantelowe, 74
Paycocke, 362
Paynel, 66, 241, 392, 415
Paynel, William & Eve de Hauterive, 66
Paynel, William & Margaret de Gatesden, 66
Peasley, 63
Peautun, 623
Pecche, 260, 408, 602, 646
Peckham, 365, 598, 624
Pecock, 637, 638
Pecok, 263
Peirsey, 371
Pelham, 11, 12, 56, 231, 340
Pellatt, 365
Pembridge, Ralph de & Isabel de Cantelowe, 75
Pembroke, 14, 170, 173, 175, 180, 183, 185, 192, 193, 226, 238, 253, 274, 302, 386, 422, 494, 498, 533, 536, 537, 556, 561, 611
Penbrigg, 92
Penebrug, 75
Peniston, 109
Penn, 65
Penne, 310
Pennington, 110, 526

Pennington, Elizabeth & Richard Cholmeley, 111
Pennington, Elizabeth & Walter Strickland, 110
Pennington, Elizabeth & William Gascoigne, 111
Penres, 306
Penruddock, 438
Peplesham, 482, 580
Pepwall, 410
Percehay, 637
Perche, 152, 462, 467
Percival, 217, 583
Percival, Rebecca & Matthew Kenrick, 217
Percy, 71, 103, 174, 243, 246, 258, 275, 285, 350, 356, 455, 496, 524, 525, 527, 531, 544, 556, 585, 592, 602, 623, 655, 658
Percy, Anne & Hugh Vaughan, 350
Percy, Anne & Laurence Raynsford, 350
Percy, Eleanor de & John Fitz Walter, 655
Percy, Elizabeth & John Clifford, 246
Percy, Elizabeth & Ralph Neville, 246
Percy, Henry & Eleanor Neville, 455
Percy, Margaret & Henry Grey, 275
Percy, Margaret & Richard Vere, 275
Percy, Maud de & John d'Eiville, 530
Peres, 84
Periton, 242
Perkins, 340
Perle, 141
Perot, 590
Perrers, 656
Peshale, 292, 488, 572
Peteghem, 236
Petre, 102
Petystre, 554
Pevensey, 65
Peverel, 1, 47, 93, 380, 506, 605, 611, 642, 643, 644

Peverel, Andrew & Katherine de Arundel, 605
Peverel, Asceline & Saher de Quincy, 644
Peverel, Joan & John d'Engaine, 506
Peverel, Lucy & Herbert Fitz Reynold, 642
Peverell, 326, 402, 605, 652
Peyforer, 380
Peyto, 260, 261
Peyto, John de & Alice de Hulles, 261
Peyto, John de & Beatrice _____, 261
Peyton, 460, 461
Peyton, Alice & John Peyton, 461
Peyton, John & Alice Peyton, 461
Peyton, John & Dorothy Beaupré, 461
Peyton, John & Dorothy Tyndall, 460
Peyvre, 96
Phelip, 421
Phelipp, 423
Philip, 258, 421
Philipps, 345
Philipson, 64, 170
Philipson, Anne & Thomas Arundell, 170
Phillips, 147
Philpot, 170
Picard, 26
Pichard, 625
Pickerell, 62
Pickering, 486
Pierpoint, 229
Pierpont, 675
Pierrepoint, 229
Pierrepoint, Sibyl de & Edmund de Ufford, 229
Pierrepont, 232
Pigott, 343
Pigott, Margery & Thomas Roberts, 344
Pigott, Margery & Walter Hendley, 343
Pijou, 536
Pilkington, 211, 487

Pilkington, John & Elizabeth Scrope, 210
Pilkington, John & Joan Balderston, 211
Pilkyngton, 211
Pinkney, 154
Pinkney, Agnes de & John de Wahull, 154
Pinner, 214
Pipard, 46, 441
Pires, 538, 613
Pistoye, 92
Pitt, Mary & Rice Davis, 411
Place, 113, 288, 290
Plaiz, 414, 674
Plaiz, Hugh de & Beatrice de Turnham, 414
Planché, 198
Plantagenet, 276, 342, 399, 424, 466, 540, 592
Plantagenet, Anne & Henry Holand, 540
Plantagenet, Anne & Thomas Saint Leger, 540
Plantagenet, Arthur, 342
Plantagenet, Arthur & Elizabeth Grey, 341
Plantagenet, Arthur & Honor Grenville, 341
Plantagenet, Elizabeth & John de la Pole, 424
Plantagenet, Elizabeth [Queen of England], 43, 335, 425
Plantagenet, Katherine & William Courtenay, 335
Plantagenet, Margaret & Richard Pole, 399
Plaunche, 264
Plaunche, Elizabeth de la & John de Clinton, 264
Plaunche, Elizabeth de la & John Russell, 264
Players, 266

Playters, Margery & Richard Clopton, 266
Plescy, 602
Plessets, 602
Plessis, 602
Plessy, 602
Plugenet, 47
Plumbe, 296
Plumpton, 247, 285
Poer, 244
Poer, le, 17
Poitou, 149, 185, 187, 298, 299
Pole, 39, 101, 105, 276, 336, 399, 419, 426, 427, 429, 430, 592
Pole, Anne de la & Gaillard de Durfort, 429
Pole, Cardinal Reginald, 466
Pole, de la, 39, 40, 257, 416, 417, 418, 419
Pole, John de la & Elizabeth Plantagenet, 424
Pole, John de la & Margaret Arundel, 425
Pole, John de la & Margaret Beaufort, 424
Pole, Margaret, 342
Pole, Margaret de la & Fulk Fitz Warin, 661
Pole, Marguerite de la & Sibeud de Thivoley, 429
Pole, Michael de la & Elizabeth Mowbray, 417
Pole, Michael de la & Katherine Stafford, 416
Pole, Owain de la, 141
Pole, Reginald, 158
Pole, Richard & Alice Langford, 399
Pole, Richard & Margaret Plantagenet, 399
Pole, William [de la] & Katherine Stourton, 276, 427, 592
Pole, William de la, 348
Pole, William de la & Alice Chaucer, 421
Poley, 42

Polhill, 638
Pollard, 100, 403
Pomeroy, 403, 621
Pomphrett, 671
Pontesbury, 623
Ponthieu, 117, 118, 385, 470
Ponthieu, Marie of & Mathieu de Montmorency, 385
Ponthieu, Marie of & Simon de Dammartin, 385
Pontissara, 305, 306
Ponynges, 59, 581
Poole, 399
Poole, de la, 420
Pope, 666, 670
Popham, 430
Porcien, 471
Pordage, 370
Port, 619
Porter, 132, 410, 411, 435
Porter, Arthur & Isabel Dennis, 410
Portington, 669, 670
Portington, Anne & Francis Guevara, 670
Portington, Anne & William Skipwith, 670
Portugal, 29, 98, 115, 119, 120, 121, 384, 451, 496, 538, 539, 610, 613, 615
Portugal, Beatrice of & John Holand, 538, 615
Portugal, Beatrice of & Thomas Arundel, 613
Portugal, Constanza of & Fernando IV, King of Castile and León, 120
Portugal, João I, King of, 538
Portugal, Mahaut (or Mafalda) of & Eudes III, Duke of Burgundy, 29
Portugal, María of & Alfonso XI, King of Castile and León, 121
Portugal, Teresa of & Alfonso IX, King of León, 115
Pouchard, 12, 13
Povere, 35
Powell, 295, 493

Powis, 99, 141, 142, 143, 293, 334
Powys, 149
Poynings, 59, 72, 106, 273, 296, 359, 581, 591
Poynings, Adrian & Mary West, 359
Poynings, Anne & George More, 360
Poynings, Joan & Richard Camoys, 72
Poynings, Margery de & Edmund Bacon, 59
Poynings, Margery de & John de Dalton, 59
Poynings, Margery de & Nicholas de la Beche, 59
Poynings, Thomas & Philippe Mortimer, 611
Poyntz, 86, 163, 274, 411, 434, 576, 578, 582, 593, 661
Poyntz, Alice & Maurice Dennis, 433
Poyntz, Edward & _____, 368
Poyntz, Maud & Thomas Barrett, 368
Poyntz, Thomas & Jane _____, 576
Poythress, 314
Prat, 554
Pratt, 362
Prayers, 155
Prayers, Hawise de & Robert de Eton, 155
Prayers, Hawise de & Thomas de Wahull, 155
Preaux, 318
Préaux, 155, 318, 520
Préaux, Peter de & Mary de Vernon, 318
Prendergast, 14, 15
Prescott, 297
Presfen, 357, 389
Presgrave, Joan & Robert Fitzwilliam, 680
Pressen, 357, 389
Preston, 16
Prestwood, 404
Prichard, 371
Pride, 291
Prische, 382

Pritchard, 371
Pritchard, Matthew & Sarah Mayo, 371
Proffit, 131
Proffit, Elizabeth & John Chauncy, 131
Provence, 186, 298
Provence, Eleanor of [Queen of England], 186, 189, 298, 304, 600
Provence, Raymond Bérenger V, Count of, 186, 298
Provence, Sanche of & Richard of England, Earl of Cornwall, 298
Provence, Sanche of & Richard, Earl of Cornwall, 186
Prussia, 496
Pruz, 321
Pryde, 660
Prynce, 212
Pudsey, 248, 297, 528
Pudsey, Florence & Clifford, Henry, 248
Pudsey, Florence & Richard Grey, 248
Puleston, 346
Puleston, Jane & William Griffith, 346
Pulham, 444, 564, 656
Pulteney, 122
Punchardon, 124, 623
Punchardun, 623
Purefey, 474
Purefoy, 296, 474, 475, 477
Purefoy, Edward & Anne Fettiplace, 476
Purefoy, Mary & Thomas Thorne, 476
Purefoy, Nicholas & Alice Denton, 475
Purefoy, Nicholas & Clemence Lydiard, 475
Purefoy, Nicholas & Katherine Brayfield, 475
Purefoy, Philip & Isabel Brome, 474
Purfey, 475
Purfrey, 474
Purley, 448
Purvey, 609

Purvis, 362
Puse, 228
Pusey, 569
Puteo, 671
Putten, 627
Puttenham, 486
Puttenham, Elizabeth & Thomas Oxenbridge, 486
Pycheford, 74
Pyckeman, 679
Pyferer, 380
Pylson, 132
Pylston, 132
Pyn, 635
Quarrera, de la, 84
Quatermayns, 430
Quency, 644
Quincie, 84
Quincy, 4, 153, 154, 192, 221, 222, 320, 562, 563, 564, 571, 647, 649
Quincy, Elizabeth & Hugh de Neville, 3
Quincy, Elizabeth de & Alexander Comyn, Earl of Buchan, 3
Quincy, Margaret de & William de Ferrers, 561
Quincy, Saher de & Asceline Peverel, 644
Quincy, Saher de & Maud de Senlis, 644
Quintin, 631
Radcliff, 41
Radcliffe, 40, 42, 43, 169, 358, 459, 483, 502, 660
Radcliffe, John & Cecily Mortimer, 40
Radcliffe, John & Elizabeth Fitz Walter, 41
Radcliffe, John & Katherine Burnell, 40
Radcliffe, John & Margaret Whethill, 42
Radcliffe, Robert & Elizabeth Stafford, 43

Radcliffe, Robert & Margaret Stanley, 43
Radcliffe, Robert & Mary Arundell, 43
Radclyff, 42
Rademelde, 363
Radmyld, 363
Radmylde, 72, 348, 364
Radmylde, Elizabeth & Nicholas Lewknor, 363
Radmylde, Ralph & Agnes _____, 363
Radmylde, Ralph & Margaret Camoys, 363
Radmyll, 363
Raglan, 435
Rainsborough, 347
Rainsborough, Martha & Thomas Coytemore, 347
Ralegh, 126
Raleigh, 124, 126, 144, 157, 437, 635
Raleigh, Bridget & John Cope, 145
Raleigh, Edward & Anne Chamberlain, 144
Raleigh, Edward & Margaret Verney, 144
Raleigh, Mary & Nicholas Wodhull, 157
Raleigh, William & Elizabeth Greene, 144
Raleye, 126
Ramsay, 200
Rancke, 682
Randall, 44
Randolph, 201, 583
Ranqueroles, 117
Rant, 682
Ratcliffe, 248
Ravendale, 202
Ravilious, John P., 321, 495, 499
Rawlinson, Anthony & Elizabeth Parry, 313
Raymundi, 48
Raynesford, 266
Raynsford, 266, 350
Raynsford, John & Anne Starkey, 351

Raynsford, John & Margaret Ilam, 351
Raynsford, Laurence & Anne Percy, 350
Raynsford, Laurence & Elizabeth Fiennes, 350
Read, 159
Reade, 339, 432
Reade, Anne & Adrian Fortescue, 432
Reade, Anne & Thomas Parry, 432
Rede, 62
Rede, Edmund, 421, 431
Reding, 32
Redman, 111, 630
Redman, Agnes & Walter Strickland, 111
Redmayne, 679
Redvers, 124, 125
Redvers, Hawise de & Robert Fitz Robert, 124
Redyng, 667
Reed, 100
Rees, 60
Refham, 184, 224
Reigny, 144
Reims, 233
Reinsham, 159
Rempston, 162
Rempston, Elizabeth & John Cheyne, 162
Rendu, 386
Repington, 297
Reppes, John & Rachel Fitzwilliam, 681
Repps, 480
Reresby, 674
Reresby, Joan & John Fitzwilliam, 674
Reskymer, 541
Restwold, 430
Rethel, 328
Reus, 328
Reve, 347
Revett, 378
Revett, Elizabeth & William Dade, 378

Reviers, 413
Reygate, 208
Reygate, Elizabeth de & Thomas de Leeds, 208
Reygate, Elizabeth de & William Clarell, 208
Reynes, 161
Reynolds, 339
Reynon, 637
Reyny, 83
Rich, 108, 431, 473, 582
Rich, Audrey & Robert Drury, 473
Richard, 584
Richards, 406
Richardson, 147
Richers, 461
Richmond, 119, 152, 168, 195, 204, 274, 295, 341, 399, 469, 565, 630, 668
Richmond, Henry, Duke of, 43
Richmond, Margaret, Countess of, 277
Rickhill, 351
Ridiard, 503
Ridley, 405
Riley, 131
Ringbourne, 518
Ringeley, 461
Risby, 378
Rivere, de la, 34
Rivers, 43, 188, 189, 190, 191, 335, 349, 413, 425
Rivers, Baldwin de & Amice de Clare, 188
Rivers, Baldwin de & Margaret of Savoy, 189
Rivers, Isabel de & William de Forz, 189
Robert, 428
Roberts, 343, 371
Roberts, Margaret & Rowland Ellis, 493
Roberts, Thomas & Margery Pigott, 344
Robertson, 681, 682, 683

Robertson, Anne & Charles Touteville, 682
Robertson, Brian & Grace ____, 681
Robertson, Brian & Margaret Fitzwilliam, 681
Robinson, 671
Robsart, 39, 418
Robyn, 328
Robynson, 112
Roche, 46, 572, 574
Roche, Ellen de la & Edmund Ferrers, 572
Roche, Ellen de la & Philip Chetwynd, 572
Rochechouart, 564, 623
Rocheford, 57
Rochelle, de la, 180, 516
Roches, 471
Rochester Richard de & Gille de Lacy, 15
Rochford, 52, 53, 56, 57, 104, 494, 496
Rock, 530
Rockley, 676
Roclife, 285
Roding, 33
Rodney, 411
Roet, 390, 613
Roet, Katherine de, 425
Roet, Philippe de, 425
Rogate, 68
Rogers, 359, 360, 403, 484, 530, 559
Rogers, John & Dorothy Ifield, 586
Rogers, Richard & Mary West, 360
Rok, 16
Rokeby, 527
Rokele, 35
Rokelle, 319
Rokewood, 228
Rolder, 583
Rolfe, 439
Rolleston, 288, 677
Romans, Maximilian, King of the, 426
Romans, Richard, King of the, 186
Romero, 115

Romeyns, 186
Ronquereles, 118
Roodes, 276
Rookwood, 473
Rooper, 586
Roos, 34, 49, 67, 87, 91, 192, 207, 245, 286, 356, 388, 393, 394, 396, 397, 544, 549, 622
Roos, Alice de & John Comyn, 206
Roos, Alice de Roos & James de Byron, 207
Roos, Elizabeth de & Thomas de Clifford, 245
Roos, Elizabeth de & William la Zouche, 91
Roos, Isabel de & Walter de Fauconberge, 549
Roos, William & Agnes _____, 60
Ros, 49, 80, 206, 245, 395
Ross, 7
Ross, John of & Margaret Comyn, 7
Roterbiaus, 125
Rothenburg, 115
Rotherham, 538
Roucy, 233, 385, 469
Roumare, 73, 251
Rous, 269, 573, 626
Rous, Eleanor le & Herbert Fitz John, 626
Row, 588
Rowe, 436
Roydon, 352, 353, 376, 595
Roydon, Elizabeth & Cuthbert Vaughan, 353
Roydon, Elizabeth & Thomas Goldinge, 353
Roydon, Elizabeth & William Twysden, 352
Roydon, Thomas & Margaret Whetenhall, 352
Roye, 117
Roynon, Joan & Hugh Malet, 638
Roynon, John & _____, 638
Roynon, John & Joan Longland, 637

Ruddell, 224
Rudyard, 503
Ruet, 390, 613
Rufford, 111
Rullos, 173
Rully, 564
Rumigny, 472
Rumigny, Isabelle de & Gautier de Châtillon, 472
Rumilly, 412, 413
Rus, 58
Rus, Alice le & Richard de Brewes, 58
Russe, 92
Russel, 635
Russell, 11, 398, 433, 439, 473, 496, 640
Russell, John de & Elizabeth de la Plaunche, 264
Russell, Maurice & Joan Dauntsey, 398
Ruthven, 392
Rutland, 453, 657
Ruyly, 564
Ruynon, 637, 641
Ryddell, Isabel & Alan de Clavering, 224
Ryddell, Isabel & Walter de Crakes, 225
Rydver, 533
Rydyll, 283
Rye, 564
Ryhall, 381
Rykhill, 231, 482
Ryngeley, 343
Rynyon, 638
Rysley, 159
Ryther, 210, 285, 670
Sackville, 56, 218, 629, 678
Sackville, John & Anne Torrell, 56
Sackville, John & Margaret Boleyn, 56
Sackville, Mildred & William Fitzwilliam, 678
Saint Amand, 35, 36, 69, 443, 535
Saint Aubyn, 336
Saint Austell, 306

Saint Barbe, 216, 364, 398, 635
Saint Clair, 122, 381, 382, 658
Saint Helen, 318
Saint Hilaire, 177
Saint Hilary, 176, 252, 513
Saint Hilary, Maud de & Roger Fitz Richard, 176
Saint Hilary, Maud de & William d'Aubeney, 176, 252
Saint John, 10, 57, 59, 66, 68, 81, 96, 200, 241, 248, 273, 277, 289, 306, 322, 323, 324, 399, 551, 605, 611, 625, 626
Saint John, Agnes de & Hugh de Courtenay, 323
Saint John, Anne & Henry Clifford, 248
Saint John, Edward de & Eve de Hauterive, 66
Saint John, Eleanor & John Melton, 277
Saint John, Eleanor & John Zouche, 277
Saint John, Elizabeth & John Scrope, 96
Saint John, Elizabeth & William Zouche, 96
Saint Leger, 54, 83, 286, 370, 540, 574, 666
Saint Leger, James & Anne Butler, 54
Saint Leger, Katherine & Thomas Culpeper, 370
Saint Leger, Margaret & John Clinton, 574
Saint Leger, Margaret & John Heveningham, 575
Saint Leger, Nicholas & Katherine Moyle, 588
Saint Leger, Thomas & Anne Plantagenet, 540
Saint Lo, 330
Saint Loe, 165, 330, 664
Saint Martin, 252, 531
Saint Martin, Alvred de & Alice d'Aubeney, 520

Saint Mary, 73
Saint Maur, 96, 473
Saint Maur, Jane & William Drury, 473
Saint Omer, 230, 232, 382
Saint Quintin, 631
Saint Rémy, 520
Saint-Gelais, 429
Saint-Gérand-le-Puy, 464
Saint-Gilles, 28
Saint-Pol, 30, 234, 328, 384, 464
Saint-Valéry, 30, 470
Saint-Valéry, Annor de & Henri de Sully, 470
Saint-Valéry, Annor de & Robert III, Count of Dreux, 470
Sale, de la, 58
Salesbury, 492
Salins, 469
Salisbury, 1, 53, 72, 132, 134, 137, 157, 205, 285, 342, 373, 399, 415, 420, 421, 446, 453, 466, 467, 482, 497, 515, 520, 535, 538, 616, 633, 650, 657, 665
Salisbury, Hawise of & Robert I, Count of Dreux, 467
Salkeld, 110
Salter, 465
Saltmarsh, 34, 286
Saltmarshe, 289
Saltmarshe, Anthony & Anne Neville, 289
Saluces, 429
Salusbury, 346
Saluzzo, 82, 419, 428, 429, 600, 601
Saluzzo, Alice di & Richard Fitz Alan, 600
Salvain, 499
Salvin, 528
Sampson, 267
Sander, 581
Sanders, 670
Sanders, Honora & Willoughby Skipwith, 670
Sandford, 292
Sandwich, 77

Sandys, 170
Sandys, William, 431
Sanford, 147
Sapcote, 460, 667
Sapcote, John & Elizabeth Dinham, 667
Sapcotes, 667, 668
Sapy, 307, 626
Saukeville, 578
Saunders, 311, 616, 670, 671
Saunderson, 670
Savadge, 366
Savage, 147, 490, 500, 501, 642
Savage, Mary & William Stanley, 500
Savoy, 23, 29, 186, 189, 192, 194, 298, 305
Savoy, Margaret of & Baldwin de Rivers, 189
Savoy, Margaret of Robert d'Aguillon, 189
Sawbridgeworth, 33
Sawtry, 609
Saxby, 214
Saxby, Mary & James Clerke, 214
Saxilby, 214
Say, 162, 178, 183, 264, 336, 349, 399, 510, 512, 515, 541, 572, 574, 575, 579, 580, 635
Say, Beatrice de & Geoffrey Fitz Peter, 178, 512
Say, Idoine de & John de Clinton, 264
Say, Joan de & Stephen de Valoines, 579
Say, Joan de & William de Fiennes, 579
Say, Maud de & William de Buckland, 510
Saye, 348, 580
Saye and Sele, 348, 349
Sayer, 296, 544
Sayer, Isabel & William Faunt, 296
Scaccario, 379
Scales, 258, 275, 323
Scales, Elizabeth de & Roger de Felbrigg, 552

Scardeburgh, 233
Scargehill, 89
Scargill, 209, 284
Scarisbrick, 502
Scarisbrick, Elizabeth & Peter Stanley, 502
Schulton, 532
Scotenay, 192
Scotland, 12, 17, 152, 154, 189, 375, 478
Scotland, Ada of & Patrick, Earl of Dunbar, 477
Scotland, Alexander III, King of, 3, 4, 196
Scotland, David II, King of, 201
Scotland, James VI, King of, 108
Scotland, Robert III, King of, 496
Scotland, William the Lion, King of, 192
Scots, Alexander II, King of, 393, 478
Scots, Alexander III, King of, 220
Scots, David I, King of, 149
Scots, David II, King of, 202, 203
Scots, James IV, King of, 427
Scots, Malcolm IV, King of, 392
Scots, Mary, Queen of, 108, 109, 545
Scots, Robert I, King of, 201
Scots, William *the Lion*, King of, 219, 221, 315
Scott, 105, 362, 629
Scott, Mary & Lawrence Washington, 583
Scott, Mary & Richard Argall, 583
Scott, Richard & Katherine Marbury, 147
Scrope, 54, 96, 108, 130, 210, 212, 226, 289, 372, 374, 417, 426, 613, 630, 631, 632
Scrope, Elizabeth & John Pilkington, 210
Scrope, Elizabeth & Thomas Clarell, 210
Scrope, Joan le & Henry Fitz Hugh, 630
Scrope, John & Anne Harling, 96
Scrope, John & Elizabeth Saint John, 96

Scrope, Margaret & Edmund de la Pole, 426
Scrope, Mary & William Conyers, 289
Scryven, 312
Scudamore, 312
Secondat, 429
Sedley, 369
Sedley, Elizabeth & John Culpeper, 369
Seeley, 491
Sees, 151
Segrave, 2, 223, 240, 445, 448, 602, 603, 616, 618
Segrave, Stephen de & Alice de Arundel, 602
Segrey, 108
Seintlo, 165, 330, 664
Sele, 348, 399, 580
Selwyn, 592
Seman, 368
Semur, 28
Seneschal of Aquitaine, 40, 331
Seneschal of Gascony, 138, 331, 568, 569
Sengleton, 211
Senlis, 172, 234, 382
Senlis, Maud de & Richard de Luvetot, 392
Senlis, Maud de & Robert Fitz Richard, 644
Senlis, Maud de & Saher de Quincy, 644
Senlis, Maud de & William d'Aubeney, 392
Septvans, 348
Sergeant, 368
Sergeaux, 275, 535
Serle, 661
Seroion, 635
Seville, 116, 118, 119, 120, 121
Sewall, 65
Sexton, 11
Seymour, 96, 105, 157, 310, 404, 518, 587, 652, 669
Seymour, Alice & William Zouche, 96

Seymour, Cecily & Richard Cornwall, 310
Seynt John, 248
Seyntleger, 57, 540
Sforza, 552
Shaa, 351
Shaldeston, 3, 562
Shard, Mary & John Mansfield, 530
Shardelow, 60
Shardelow, Joan de & John de Brewes, 60
Shardelowe, 380
Shardlowe, 61
Shareshull, 459
Shareshull, Adam de & Alice Fitz Warin, 578
Shareshull, Adam de & Joan le Forester, 578
Sharp, 488
Shaw, Ellen, 412
Shawe, 278
Sheffelde, 278
Sheffield, 278, 279, 280, 281
Sheffield, Edmund & Anne Vere, 279
Sheffield, Edmund & Mariana Irwin, 280
Sheffield, Edmund & Ursula Tyrwhit, 280
Sheffield, John & Douglas Howard, 279
Sheffield, Robert & Joan Stanley, 278
Sheffield, Robert & Margaret Zouche, 278
Shelford, 568
Shelley, 480, 678
Shellom, 411
Shelton, 55, 61, 62, 410
Shelton, Grace & John Thurton, 62
Shelton, John & Margaret Brewes, 61
Shelton, Ralph & Cecily Steward, 62
Shelton, Ralph & Joan _____, 61
Shelton, Ralph & Margaret Clere, 61
Shelton, Ralph & Mary Brome, 61

Shelton, Ralph & Prudence Calthorpe, 62
Shelvestrode, 66
Sheney, 253
Shepard, 347, 683, 684
Shepard, Thomas & Joanna Hooker, 683
Shepard, Thomas & Margaret Borodell, 683
Shepard, Thomas & Margaret Touteville, 683
Sheppard, 344
Sherburne, Elizabeth & Thomas Fairfax, 543
Shoyswell, Agnes & Thomas Echingham, 483
Shrewsbury, 40, 50, 52, 90, 170, 289, 295, 374
Sicile, 419
Sicily, 31, 120, 428, 462, 615
Sicily, Charles I, King of, 302
Sidley, 369, 370
Sidney, 342
Similly, 185
Simnel, 426
Simond, 70
Singleton, 376
Siward, 206
Skargill, 211
Skeffington, 159, 184, 595
Skefinton, 184
Skeftington, 566
Skeftinton, 184
Skelton, 538
Skerne, 546
Skerne, Thomasine & William Kelke, 546
Skewys, 337
Skipwith, 669, 670, 671
Skipwith, Anne & William Goforth, 671
Skipwith, Anne & William Oxley, 671
Skipwith, Richard & Mary Chamberlain, 669
Skipwith, William & Anne Hussey, 670
Skipwith, William & Anne Portington, 670
Skipwith, William & Anne Towthby, 669
Skipwith, William & Elizabeth Page, 669
Skirlaw, 244
Skulle, 312, 409
Skulle, Joyce & Edward Croft, 312
Slaney, 280
Sleford, 279
Sloper, 411
Slorey, 296
Smith, 9, 158, 266, 339, 344, 378, 670
Smith, Anne & Anthony Wodhull, 158
Smith, Anne & Edward Griffin, 158
Smith, Anne & John Leveson, 158
Smyth, 256, 422
Smythe, 8, 338
Snell, 388
Snow, 148
Soanes, 378
Soissons, 385, 467
Solers, Guillaume de & Mabel Fitz Robert, 124
Soligney, Emma de & Jordan de Champernoun, 125
Soligny, 125
Soliis, 125
Somaster, 405
Someresham, 83
Somerset, 51, 65, 103, 106, 171, 336, 424, 451, 587, 668, 669
Somerville, 272, 354
Somerville, Joan de & Henry de Grey, 272, 354
Somerville, Joan de & Ralph de Cromwell, 354
Somery, 240, 253, 254, 272
Somery, Maud de & Henry de Erdington, 290

Somery, Maud de & William de Bifield, 291
Sothill, 286, 473, 676
Sothill, Barbara & Marmaduke Constable, 286
Sothill, Elizabeth & William Drury, 473
Souche, 92, 277
Soulis, 3
Sourches, 467
South Wales, 180
Southampton, 170, 248
Southcote, 101, 102, 405
Southcott, 101, 102, 405
Southcott, Mary & William Strode, 405
Southcott, Thomas & Thomasine Kirkham, 102
Spaldyng, 499
Sparrow, 45
Sparrow, Frances & George Burrough, 45
Spayne, 553
Speaker of the House of Commons, 278, 338, 340, 402, 421, 472, 488, 518, 573, 588, 629
Speccot, 405
Spechesley, 573
Speke, 168, 410
Speleman, 231
Spelman, 230
Spencer, 103, 145, 159, 480
Spencer, Margaret & Thomas Carey, 103
Spencer, Robert & Eleanor Beaufort, 51, 103
Spenser, 103
Sprencheheuse, 291
Spring, 439, 480
Spring, Frances & Edmund Wright, 439
Spring, John & Dorothy Waldegrave, 439
Springehoes, 84
Springehose, 32
Spryng, 523
Squery, 349
Squire, 403
St. Amand, 35
St. John, 352
St. Leger, 371
St. Low, 168
St. Paul, 329
St. Pol, 329
Stafford, 39, 43, 51, 52, 57, 105, 106, 107, 141, 142, 145, 165, 166, 245, 269, 280, 329, 403, 409, 431, 488, 490, 508, 533, 538, 571, 572, 573, 574, 590, 592, 613, 638, 639
Stafford, Anne & John Holand, 538
Stafford, Anne & William Berkeley, 409
Stafford, Avice & James Butler, 51
Stafford, Avice & James Ormond, 51
Stafford, Dorothy & William Stafford, 105
Stafford, Edward & Douglas Howard, 280
Stafford, Elizabeth & Reynold Cobham, 571
Stafford, Elizabeth & Robert Radcliffe, 43
Stafford, Elizabeth de & John de Ferrers, 570
Stafford, Elizabeth de & Reynold Cobham, 269
Stafford, Joan de & Gilbert Talbot, 142
Stafford, Joan de & John de Cherleton, 141
Stafford, Joyce & Marmaduke Constable, 285
Stafford, Katherine & Michael de la Pole, 416
Stafford, William & Dorothy Stafford, 105
Stafford, William & Katherine Chidiock, 166
Stafford, William & Mary Boleyn, 105
Staford, John de & Alice Crubbe, 642

Stamford, 376
Stane, de la, 66
Staneway, 191
Stanford, 376
Stanford, Elizabeth & William Cornwallis, 376
Stanhope, 668
Stanhope, Edward & Elizabeth Bourchier, 668
Stanhope, Richard & Maud Cromwell, 358
Stanlake, 503
Stanley, 43, 211, 276, 278, 293, 294, 345, 438, 487, 488, 489, 490, 500, 501, 502, 503, 618
Stanley, Anne & Edward Sutton, 503
Stanley, Joan & Robert Sheffield, 278
Stanley, John & Anne Horne, 488
Stanley, John & Cecily Arderne, 488
Stanley, John & Elizabeth _____, 489
Stanley, John & Elizabeth Vernon, 488
Stanley, Margaret & Henry Grey, 276
Stanley, Margaret & Robert Radcliffe, 43
Stanley, Peter & Cecily Tarleton, 502
Stanley, Peter & Elizabeth Scarisbrick, 502
Stanley, Peter & Jane Leigh, 502
Stanley, Thomas & Elizabeth Langton, 487
Stanley, Thomas & Maud Arderne, 487
Stanley, William & Agnes Grosvenor, 501
Stanley, William & Anne Harington, 502
Stanley, William & Elizabeth Hopton, 293
Stanley, William & Margaret Bromley, 501
Stanley, William & Mary Savage, 500
Stanorde, 642
Stanton, 214
Stanwei, 510

Stapeldon, 664
Stapleton, 61, 287, 388, 639, 640, 641, 675
Stapleton, Christian & _____ Eyton, 641
Stapleton, Christian & Robert Burton, 641
Stapleton, Christian & Robert Cressett, 640
Stapleton, Ela & Robert Brewes, 61
Stapleton, Elizabeth & Edward Leighton, 641
Stapleton, John & Margaret Deviock, 639
Stapleton, John & Margery _____, 639
Stapleton, Leonard & Joyce Cokesey, 640
Stapleton, Leonard & Mary _____, 640
Starkey, 351, 502
Starkey, Anne & John Raynsford, 351
Staundon, 34
Staunton, 291, 490
Staveley, 399
Staverton, 488
Stavyn, 207
Stawell, 590
Stawell, Thomas & Joan Berkeley, 590
Stawell, Thomas & Joan Frampton, 590
Stawell, Thomas & Margaret Burton, 590
Stede, 369
Steed, 344
Stephens, 371
Stephens, Samuel & Frances Culpeper, 370
Stepilton, 640
Stepulton, 639
Steward, 16, 62
Steward, Cecily & Ralph Shelton, 62
Stewart, 15, 16, 202, 206, 375
Stewart, James & Giles de Burgh, 15
Stewart, James & Muriel of Strathearn, 16
Stewart, Walter & Isabel of Fife, 202

Steyngrave, 630
Stiles, 45
Stiles, Rebecca & Nathaniel Burrough, 45
Still, 133
Stockheye, 129, 518
Stockheye, Joan & William Esturmy, 518
Stoke, 569
Stokes, 491, 627
Stokes, Philippe & Thomas Foxcote, 627
Stokey, 518
Stonar, 430
Stones, 95
Stonor, 166, 167, 421, 430, 431, 432
Stonor, Anne & Adrian Fortescue, 432
Stonor, Thomas & Joan de la Pole, 430
Stonor, William & Agnes Winnard, 431
Stonor, William & Anne Neville, 431
Stonor, William & Elizabeth Croke, 431
Stonour, 430
Storre, 10
Stotenay, 191
Stotevile, 499
Stoughton, 366
Stoughton, John & Jane Browne, 366
Stoughton, John & Mary Machell, 366
Stourton, 166, 276, 341, 424, 427, 592, 593
Stourton, John & Katherine Berkeley, 592
Stourton, Katherine & Henry Grey, 592
Stourton, Katherine & William [de la] Pole, 276, 427, 592
Stourton, Katherine & William Berkeley, 276, 592
Stowell, 25, 100
Stradling, 168, 345, 398, 399, 433, 613
Stradling, Anne & John Danvers, 399
Stradling, Edmund & Elizabeth Arundell, 398

Stradling, Jane & William Griffith, 345
Stradling, John & Alice Langford, 399
Stradling, John & Joan Dauntsey, 398
Stradling, Katherine & Maurice Dennis, 433
Strange, 39, 43, 69, 269, 270, 278, 292, 332, 449, 570, 571, 606, 632, 661, 663, 678
Strange, Aline le & Edward Burnell, 39
Strange, Hawise le & Robert de Felton, 555
Strange, le, 606
Strangeways, 166, 276, 374, 391, 551
Strangeways, Katherine & Henry Grey, 276
Strangways, 276
Strangwich, 586
Stratford, 26
Strathbogie, 6, 202, 210, 524
Strathearn, 3, 16, 392, 393
Strathearn, Gilbert, Earl of & Maud d'Aubeney, 392
Strathearn, Gilbert, Earl of & Ysenda de Gask, 393
Strathearn, Muriel of & James Stewart, 16
Strathearn, Robert, Earl of & _____ of Moray, 393
Stratton, 314, 440
Straw, Jack, 656
Stredlam, 219
Stretey, 489
Stretley, 84
Strickland, 110, 111, 112, 113, 545
Strickland, Agnes & Henry Frowick, 111
Strickland, Agnes & Thomas Curwen, 111
Strickland, Ellen & _____ Norton, 113
Strickland, Ellen & John Carleton, 113
Strickland, Thomas & Agnes Parr, 110

Strickland, Thomas & Margaret Fouleshurst, 110
Strickland, Walter & Agnes Redman, 111
Strickland, Walter & Alice Tempest, 113
Strickland, Walter & Elizabeth Pennington, 110
Strickland, Walter & Katherine Neville, 112
Strickland, Walter & Margaret Hamerton, 112
Strigoil, 561
Striguil, 253
Stringer, 361
Strode, 102, 404
Strode, Julian & John Davie, 405
Strode, Richard & Frances Cromwell, 404
Strode, William & Elizabeth Courtenay, 404
Stroud, 404
Strowde, 404
Strutt, 62
Stubbins, Luke & Agatha Eltonhead, 504
Stubbs, 132
Stuckley, 666
Studley, 178, 509, 512
Stukeley, 666
Sturgis, 480
Sturmy, 518
Sturry, 292
Stury, 165, 638, 639
Stuteville, 59, 222, 255, 498, 520, 647
Stuteville, Henry de & Maud de Warenne, 520
Stutysbury, 476
Style, 681
Suddynton, 262, 579
Sudeley, 575
Suffolk, 13, 22, 39, 40, 60, 227, 228, 230, 276, 335, 346, 348, 416, 417, 418, 419, 420, 421, 422, 423, 424, 425, 426, 427, 428, 429, 430, 451, 499, 592, 612, 618
Sulli, 470
Sulliard, 376
Sulliard, Mary & John Cornwallis, 376
Sully, 470, 519
Sully, Henri de & Annor de Saint-Valéry, 470
Sully, Marguerite de & Henri I, Count of Eu, 519
Sulyard, 376
Surrey, 35, 50, 97, 142, 252, 253, 333, 417, 445, 447, 520, 521, 522, 531, 538, 539, 603, 604, 605, 607, 608, 609, 610, 611, 612, 613, 615, 616, 617
Surtees, 525
Susche, 83
Sussex, 42, 43, 108, 169, 176, 177, 520
Sutcliffe, 267
Sutcliffe, Elizabeth & William Clopton, 267
Sutheby, 207
Suthyll, 499
Sutton, 207, 209, 247, 260, 278, 297, 388, 389, 456, 487, 503, 544, 572, 582, 591, 616
Sutton, Anne & Richard Eltonhead, 503
Sutton, Constance & John Goddard, 388
Sutton, Constance & Peter de Mauley, 388
Sutton, Constance & Robert de Hilton, 388
Sutton, Edward & Anne Stanley, 503
Sutton, John & Elizabeth Berkeley, 143
Swabia, 28, 115, 117
Swabia, Beatriz of & Fernando III, King of Castile and León, 117
Swabia, Konrad II, Duke of & Berenguela I, Queen of Castile, 115
Swann, 595
Swetenham, 39, 418

Swift, 280
Swynford, 390
Swynford, Thomas & Joan Crophill, 390
Swynford, Thomas & Margaret Grey, 390
Sydenham, 168
Symmes, 10, 367
Symmes, Sarah & John Brock, 10
Symmes, Sarah & Samuel Hough, 10
Symonds, 457
Symonete, 446
Tabourer, Richard & Maud _____, 184
Tackley, 35
Tailboys, 374
Taillebois, 148
Taillour, 627
Talbot, 38, 48, 50, 52, 63, 99, 142, 248, 258, 289, 295, 310, 332, 333, 334, 341, 360, 374, 390, 551, 585, 659
Talbot, Anne & Hugh Courtenay, 332
Talbot, Anne & John Botreaux, 332
Talbot, Gilbert & Joan de Stafford, 142
Talbot, Gilbert & Margaret Howard, 258
Talbot, Joan & John de Carew, 1
Talbot, Joan & John de Dartmouth, 1
Talbot, John & Katherine Burnell, 40
Talemasch, 32
Tallakarne, 583
Tame, 145, 435
Tame, Margaret & John Cope, 145
Tancarville, 143
Tanner, 339
Tarleton, 502
Tarleton, Cecily & Peter Stanley, 502
Tartas, 419, 562
Tateshale, 254, 255
Tateshale, Emma de & Adam de Cailly, 256
Tateshale, Robert de & Maud d'Aubeney, 254
Tateshale, Robert de & Nichole de Grey, 255

Taverner, 312
Taville, 40
Tayloe, 297
Taylor, 406
Tempest, 113, 246, 526
Tempest, Alice & Thomas Boynton, 113
Tempest, Alice & Walter Strickland, 113
Teringham, 44
Teschen, 553
Teschen, Margaret of & Simon Felbrigg, 553
Teye, 483
Thacker, 505
Thatcher, 364, 486
Thelwall, 280, 345
Thessalonica, 30
Thivoley, 419, 429
Thivoley, Sibeud de & Marguerite de la Pole, 429
Thoire, 29
Thomond, 52
Thompson, Doug, 27, 590
Thorley, 484, 592
Thorne, 278, 476
Thorne, Susan & Roger Dudley, 476
Thorne, Thomas & Mary Purefoy, 476
Thornes, 294
Thorney, 517
Thornhill, 673, 674, 675
Thornton, 473, 558
Thornton, Dorothy & Richard Fenwick, 558
Thorp, 89
Thorpe, 65, 408, 528, 552
Thorpe, John de & Katherine Botetourt, 407
Thouars, 153, 469, 522
Thouars, Guy de & Constance of Brittany, 152
Threlkeld, Lancelot & Margaret Bromflete, 247
Throckmorton, 216, 266, 353

Thurlton, 62
Thurston, 439, 440
Thurton, John & Grace Shelton, 62
Thurton, Maud & Christopher Calthorpe, 62
Thwaites, 588
Thweng, 548
Tibetot, 90, 138, 139, 183, 225, 566
Tibetot, Hawise de & John Fitz Robert, 225
Tichborne, 178, 512
Tidmarsh, John de & Juliane _____, 627
Tilney, 56, 162
Ting, 347
Tiptoft, 99, 143, 293, 334
Tiptoft, John & Elizabeth Hopton, 293
Tirel, 171
Tirrell, 159
Tivoley, 429
Toledo, 114, 116, 118, 119, 120, 121
Tolethorpe, 291
Tolethorpe, Elizabeth de & Giles de Erdington, 291
Tolymer, 263
Tonnerre, 30, 31, 463, 465
Tony, 14, 180, 261
Tony, Constance de & David ap John, 661
Tony, Constance de & Fulk Fitz Warin, 660
Toppes, 479
Toppys, 479
Torm, 320
Torny, 6
Torpel, 65
Torrell, 56
Torrell, Anne & John Sackville, 56
Tosny, 249
Tothby, 669
Totington, 93
Totty, 670
Touchet, 226
Toulouse, 28, 236

Touraine, 538
Tournelle, 234
Touteville, 682
Touteville, Charles & Anne Robertson, 682
Touteville, Margaret & Thomas Shepard, 683
Tower, Joan of the, 121
Townshend, Richard & Frances Baldwin, 94
Towthby, Anne & William Skipwith, 669
Tracey, 102
Tracy, 35, 138, 139
Trailly, 70
Trainel, 29
Trap, 261
Trastamara, 116, 121, 122
Tree, 240
Trefusis, 405
Tregasowe, 336
Tregluthenou, 303
Tregoz, 81
Treisgeu, 303
Trelawney, 334, 542
Trellok, 306
Tremaill, 576
Tremayle, 101
Tremayne, 98
Trenchesvile, 580
Trenewith, 637, 638
Trenewyth, 638
Trente, 380
Trentham, 295
Tresham, 95, 96, 157
Tretherf, 337
Tretherff, 336, 337
Tretherff, John & Elizabeth Courtenay, 336
Tretherff, Margaret & Edward Courtenay, 337
Tretherff, Margaret & John Boscawen, 337

Tretherff, Margaret & Richard Buller, 337
Tretherff, Thomas & Maud Trevisa, 337
Tretherffe, 337
Trevegnon, 635
Treverbyn, 331
Trevisa, 337
Trevisa, Maud & Thomas Tretherff, 337
Trevitho, 125
Trie, 382
Trier of Petitions in Parliament, 37, 51, 141, 244, 341, 342, 633, 659, 666
Trillow, 348
Tropenell, 157
Troutbeck, 276, 438
Troutbeck, Joan & William Boteler, 345
Troutbeck, Joan & William Griffith, 345
Troyes, 30
Trussebut, 80, 393, 394
Trussebut, Agatha & William d'Aubeney, 393
Trussel, 31
Trussell, 39, 156, 261, 279, 418, 449, 573
Trussell, Isabel & John Hoton, 156
Trussell, Isabel & Thomas Wodhull, 156
Trussell, John & Alice de Hotham, 449
Trussell, John & Margaret _____, 449
Trussell, Philippe & Thomas Kerdeston, 39, 418
Try, 669
Trye, 410
Tuchet, 484, 556, 586, 590, 667, 668
Tudor, 375, 376, 399, 427, 428
Tudor, Jasper, 409
Tudor, Mary, 105
Tuke, 466
Tumbur, 303
Tunstall, 374, 632

Tunstall, Thomas & Eleanor Fitz Hugh, 391
Turberville, 138
Turnham, 414
Turnham, Beatrice de & Hugh de Neville, 414
Turnham, Beatrice de & Hugh de Plaiz, 414
Turville, 81, 89, 259
Tuscany, 117
Tuwyng, 457
Twinihoe, Edith & William Dennis, 435
Twyford, 146
Twynyho, 294
Twysden, 352, 353, 595
Twysden, Margaret & Richard Dering, 595
Twysden, William & Elizabeth Royden, 352
Ty, 232
Tyeys, 205, 273, 442
Tyler, Wat, 656
Tyndale, 555
Tyndall, 461
Tyndall, Dorothy & John Peyton, 460
Tyng, Jonathan & Sarah Gibbons, 406
Tyng, William & Elizabeth Coytemore, 347
Tynten, 128
Tyrell, 420
Tyringham, 507
Tyrrell, 112, 158, 168, 375, 376, 428, 431
Tyrrell, Edward & Anne Pashley, 375
Tyrrell, John & Mary Drury, 474
Tyrrell, Philippe & Thomas Cornwallis, 376
Tyrwhit, 280, 285, 486, 669
Tyrwhit, Ursula & Edmund Sheffield, 280
Ufford, 22, 26, 60, 61, 227, 228, 229, 230, 373, 557, 612, 643
Ufford, Edmund de & Sibyl de Pierrepoint, 229

Ufford, Eve de & John de Brewes, 60
Ufford, Joan & William Bowet, 232
Ufford, Ralph de & Elizabeth le Latimer, 70
Ufford, Ralph de & Maud of Lancaster, 22
Ufford, Robert de & Eleanor de Arundel, 612
Ufford, Robert de & Eleanor Felton, 230
Ufford, Thomas de & Eve de Clavering, 227
Ughtred, 210, 285, 388, 526
Ulster, 14, 15, 16, 17, 19, 22, 23, 24, 49, 71, 142, 204, 276, 332, 386, 424, 538, 540, 570, 592, 611, 655
Ultra la Haia, 178, 512
Umfreville, 6, 225, 240, 393, 395, 658
Umfreville, Margaret de & William d'Aubeney, 393
Underwoode, 640
Unton, 434
Upgate, 228
Upper Lorraine, 28
Upton, 25, 26, 198, 602
Urban V, Pope, 448
Urgel, 118
Urry, 27
Urswick, 486, 582
Urswick, Anne & Thomas Fiennes, 582
Usflete, 617
Usflete, Gerard & Elizabeth Arundel, 617
Usumaris, 380
Uvedale, 61, 62, 455
Uvedale, Peter de & Margaret de Hydon, 455
Vache, de la, 241
Valence, 126, 196, 199, 223, 226, 238, 302, 386, 441, 495, 523, 524, 579
Valencia, 118
Valladares, 115
Valletorte, 306

Valoignes, 580
Valoines, 14, 22, 60, 262, 412, 514, 515, 647, 652
Valoines, Gunnor de & Robert Fitz Walter, 647
Valoines, Stephen de & Joan de Say, 579
Valois, 31, 121, 234, 237
Vampage, 488
Van Schaick, 218
Van Schaick, Catharine & Matthew Clarkson, 218
Vanne, 602
Vaudémont, 234, 471
Vaughan, 312, 314, 350, 404, 432, 576
Vaughan, Cuthbert & Elizabeth Roydon, 353
Vaughan, Hugh & Anne Percy, 350
Vaughan, Isabel & George Parry, 312
Vaughan, James & Elizabeth Croft, 312
Vaughan, Thomas & Jane _____, 576
Vaughan, William & Frances Latham, 214
Vaus, 274
Vautort, 299
Vaux, 295, 564, 633
Vavasour, 209, 544, 660
Vaylaunce, 579
Veel, 66, 415
Veer, 99, 275, 386, 665
Venables, 229
Venuiz, 619
Venuz, 68
Verdon, 576
Verdun, 18, 19, 205, 316, 596, 674
Verdun, Elizabeth de & Bartholomew de Burghersh, 24
Verdun, Maud de & John Fitz Alan, 596
Verdun, Maud de & Richard de Amundeville, 597
Verdun, Thebaud de & Elizabeth de Clare, 19

Verdun, Thomas de & Eustache Basset, 316
Vere, 19, 23, 38, 99, 218, 226, 273, 275, 279, 295, 320, 321, 327, 330, 334, 378, 406, 472, 533, 603, 656, 658, 665
Vere, Alice & Lewis John, 665
Vere, Alice de & Roger Fitz Richard, 218
Vere, Anne & Edmund Sheffield, 279
Vere, Anne & John Brock, 279
Vere, Elizabeth & William de Cossington, 327
Vere, Elizabeth de & Hugh de Courtenay, 327
Vere, Elizabeth de & John de Mowbray, 327
Vere, Isabel de & John de Courtenay, 320
Vere, Isabel de & Oliver de Dinham, 320
Vere, Margery de & Maurice de Berkeley, 406
Vere, Richard & Margaret Percy, 275
Vere, Robert & Joan Courtenay, 99
Veretot, 535
Vergy, 29, 472
Vergy, Alix de & Eudes III, Duke of Burgundy, 29
Vergy, Helisende de & Gautier de Châtillon, 471
Vermandois, 234
Vermandois, Adèle de & Renaud II, Count of Clermont, 234
Verney, 144, 280, 430
Verney, Margaret & Edward Raleigh, 144
Vernon, 160, 295, 318, 414, 480, 488, 490, 573, 577, 671
Vernon, Elizabeth & John Stanley, 488
Vernon, Elizabeth & Robert Corbet, 295
Vernon, Mary de & Peter de Préaux, 318

Vernon, Mary de & Robert de Courtenay, 318
Vernur, 548
Vescy, 247, 248, 391, 563, 632, 647
Viennois, 28, 237
Vieuxpont, 239
Villalobos, 116
Villamayor, 116
Villebéon, 471
Villebéon, Isabelle de & Robert de Dreux, 471
Villehardouin, 471
Villiers, 677
Villiers, Helen & John Fitzwilliam, 677
Vincent, 35, 127, 296
Vincent, Jane & William Faunt, 296
Vipont, 238, 239, 242, 243, 521, 561
Vipont, Idoine de & John de Cromwell, 240
Vipont, Idoine de & Roger de Leybourne, 240
Vipont, Isabel de & Roger de Clifford, 241
Vipont, John de & _____ de Ferrers, 239
Vipont, Robert de & Idoine de Builli, 238
Vipont, Robert de & Isabel Fitz John, 239
Viscaya, 121
Visconti, 23, 452
Visconti, Ludovico & Violante Visconti, 23
Visconti, Violante & Lionel of Antwerp, 23
Visconti, Violante & Ludovico Visconti, 23
Visconti, Violante & Othon II Palæologus, 23
Vitré, 152
Vivian, 337, 338
Vivonne, 154, 185, 196, 564, 662

Vivonne, Hawise de & Walter de Wahull, 154
Vivonne, Joan de & Reynold Fitz Peter, 623
Vosper, 405
Vychan, 345
Vyne, 344, 543
Vyvian, 337
Vyvyan, 337
Wace, 72
Waddesle, 388
Waddington, 677
Waddington, Thomas & Mary Fitzwilliam, 677
Wade, 412, 477
Wadham, 410
Wahull, 154
Wahull, John de & Agnes de Pinkney, 154
Wahull, John de & Isabel ____, 155
Wahull, Thomas de & Hawise de Prayers, 155
Wahull, Walter de & Hawise de Vivonne, 154
Wake, 238, 330, 400, 415, 535, 562, 566
Wake, Anne & Philip Courtenay, 400
Wakehurst, 27, 484
Waldegrave, 11, 266, 267, 351, 473, 480, 481
Waldegrave, Anthony & Elizabeth Gray, 11
Waldegrave, Dorothy & John Spring, 439
Waldegrave, Margery & William Clopton, 266
Waldegrave, Phyllis & Thomas Higham, 44
Waldegrave, Thomas & Elizabeth Gurdon, 11
Waldegrave, Thomas & Margaret Holmstead, 12
Waldegrave, Thomas & Mary Badby, 11
Walden, 42, 369, 628

Walden, Richard & Mary Brooke, 369, 628
Waldgrave, 44, 267
Waldingfield, 652
Waldyve, 475
Walens, 672
Walerand, 65, 66
Wales, 175, 497
Wales, Edward the Black, Prince of, 26, 328, 329, 330, 331, 607, 636, 664
Wales, Edward, Prince of, 329
Wales, Llywelyn, Prince of, 3, 598
Walewayn, 260
Waleys, 271, 578
Waleys, John & Joan Daubeney, 507
Walgrave, 11, 267
Walkefar, 70
Walkefare, 556
Walkefare, Joan & Thomas de Felton, 556
Walker, 267
Walker, Frances & Thomas Bannister, 529
Walkfare, 230
Walkington, 22
Wall, 503
Walleis, 208
Waller, 343
Wallere, 328, 554
Wallingford, 109
Walsh, 26, 280, 365, 409
Walshe, 410, 576, 585
Walsingham, Edmund & Anne Jernegan, 472
Walter, 45
Walter Hydon, 328
Walwyn, 311, 434, 639
Walwyn, Alice & Walter Dennis, 434
Wandak, 195
Wandard, 195
Wandingfeld, 598
Wanneville, ____ de & Nichole de Cantelowe, 74
Wanses, 343

Warbeck, Perkin, 42, 100, 293
Warburton, 293
Warcopp, 111
Ward, 112
Warde, 112, 654
Warde, de la, 654
Warde, Robert de la & Ida Fitz Walter, 654
Warenne, 12, 252, 253, 254, 445, 520, 521, 522, 531, 603, 604, 607, 644
Warenne, Alice de & Edmund de Arundel, 603
Warenne, Ela de & Robert de Newburgh, 671
Warenne, Ela de & William Fitz William, 672
Warenne, Gundred de & William de Courcy, 412
Warenne, Isabel de & Hugh d'Aubeney, 253
Warenne, Maud & Henri II, Count of Eu, 520
Warenne, Maud de & Henry de Stuteville, 520
Warham, 371, 432, 588, 629
Warre, 591
Warre, la, 59, 311, 342, 359, 365, 451, 484
Warren, 147, 377, 607
Warton, 487
Warwick, 34, 51, 70, 76, 106, 140, 197, 199, 244, 260, 264, 281, 310, 342, 343, 348, 349, 399, 402, 451, 455, 487, 579, 663
Washbourne, 426
Washington, Lawrence & Mary Scott, 583
Wastlyn, 499
Waterton, 246, 559
Waterton, Robert & Margaret Clarell, 209
Waterville, 394, 644
Wateville, John de & Denise de Hulles, 260
Watton, 278

Wauton, 6, 182, 652
Wawford, 491
Wayford, 565
Wayte, 341
Weaverham, 89
Webb, 157
Webb, Elizabeth & Fulk Wodhull, 157
Webb, Elizabeth & Robert Cheyne, 157
Weed, Henry & Elizabeth _____, 596
Weekly, 491
Welby, 9
Weld, 170
Welle, 49, 242, 654
Welle, Robert de & Maud de Clare, 242
Welles, 49, 275, 653, 654, 682
Welles, Adam de & Joan d'Engaine, 653
Welles, Anne & James le Boteler (or Butler), 49
Wellesbourne, 260
Welsh, 132
Welsh, Agnes & George Chauncy, 132
Wenard, 431
Wendovre, 20
Wenlock, 643
Wenlok, 227
Wenslowe, 349, 484
Wentworth, 159, 246, 366, 433, 474, 494, 527
Wentworth, Agnes & Robert Constable, 284
Wesenham, 283
Wesenham, Hugh de & Agnes de Brus, 283
Wesenham, Joan & John Folville, 283
Wesenham, Robert & Elfred _____, 283
West, 110, 311, 313, 342, 359, 360, 365, 484, 591, 643
West, Anne & Maurice Berkeley, 591
West, John & Margaret Courtenay, 436

West, Margaret & Thomas Echingham, 484
West, Mary & Adrian Poynings, 359
West, Mary & Richard Rogers, 360
West, Owen & Mary Guildford, 359
Westmoreland, 108
Westmorland, 130, 246, 248, 276, 289, 350, 424, 455, 540, 551, 610
Weston, 169, 214, 360
Weston, Mary & William Clerke, 214
Wexford, 238
Weyland, 26, 451, 557, 655
Weyland, Cecily de & Bartholomew de Burghersh, 26
Whalesborough, 128, 422
Whalesborough, Isabel de & Henry de Wilington, 128
Wharton, 43, 111, 347, 488
Wharton, Florence & Thomas Curwen, 111
Whelton, 84
Wherwell, 127
Whetehill, 42
Whetenhall, 213, 351, 352, 594
Whetenhall, Margaret & Thomas Roydon, 352
Whetenhall, William & Anne Cromer, 351
Whethill, 42, 359
Whethill, Margaret & John Radcliffe, 42
Whetnall, 213, 351
Whitchurch, 126
Whitcomb, 367
White, 105, 267, 406, 554
White, Mary & Humphrey Davie, 406
Whitewell, 207
Whitfeld, 558
Whitfield, 2, 446
Whitmore, 682
Whitney, 107, 346, 588
Whittingham, 9
Whittingham, John & Martha Hubbard, 10

Whittingham, Richard & Elizabeth Bulkeley, 9
Whittington, 164, 311, 682
Whyte, 404
Wichingham, 233
Wickliffe, 491
Wickliffe, Alice & Fulk Wodhull, 491
Widdrington, 557
Wideslade, 431
Widworthy, 456
Wiggonholt, 318
Wight, Isle of, 188
Wildgose, 369
Wilford, 368, 628
Wilington, 128, 129, 333, 507
Wilington, Henry de & Isabel de Whalesborough, 128
Wilington, Henry de & Margaret de Freville, 128
Wilington, Isabel & William Beaumont, 129
Wilington, John de & Maud Carminow, 128
Wilington, Ralph de & Joan de Champernoun, 127
Wilington, Ralph de & Juliane _____, 127
Wilkins, 467
Wilkinson, 529
William Stanley & Alice Hoghton, 501
William Strode & Dewnes Glanville, 405
William Strode & Mary Southcott, 405
Williams, 94, 132, 313, 338, 346, 412
Williams, Jane & William Coytemore, 346
Williams, Richard & Frances Deighton, 412
Williams, Thomasine & Francis Buller, 338
Williams, William & Dorothy Griffith, 346
Williamson, 528

Willoughby, 92, 94, 161, 170, 212, 278, 294, 341, 358, 405, 459, 466, 479, 528, 541, 587, 631, 632, 653
Willoughby Skipwith & Honora Sanders, 670
Willoughby, Elizabeth & John Dinham, 459
Willoughby, Elizabeth & William Arundel, 459
Willoughby, Elizabeth & William Eure, 528
Willoughby, Margaret & Matthew Arundell, 170
Willoughby, Margery & William Fitz Hugh, 632
Wilsford, 213, 352
Wilsford, Elizabeth & George Clerke, 213
Wilson, 113, 406, 530
Wilson, John & Elizabeth Mansfield, 530
Wiltesire, 3
Wiltshire, 50, 51, 55, 56, 102, 103, 104, 105
Winchcombe, 312
Winchester, 4, 34, 68, 108, 140, 168, 197, 221, 222, 320, 442, 562, 563, 564, 571, 647, 649
Winchester, Herbert of & Emma ____, 619
Wincole, 11
Wincoll, 12
Windsor, 341, 485, 486, 582
Windsor, Anne & Edmund Dudley, 341
Wingfield, 96, 364, 378, 416, 437, 439, 496, 497, 618, 667
Wingfield, Mary & William Dade, 378
Winnard, 431
Winnard, Agnes & William Stonor, 431
Winnington, 345
Winthrop, 267
Wintle, 339
Wiseman, 279

Wodecok, 638
Wodehall, 523, 673
Wodehyll, 155
Wodhull, 145, 154, 155, 156, 491
Wodhull, Agnes & George Calverley, 158
Wodhull, Agnes & Richard Chetwode, 158
Wodhull, Alice & William Elkington, 491
Wodhull, Anthony & Anne Smith, 158
Wodhull, Fulk & Alice Wickliffe, 491
Wodhull, Fulk & Anne Newenham, 157
Wodhull, Fulk & Elizabeth Webb, 157
Wodhull, John & Joan Etwell, 157
Wodhull, Lawrence & Elizabeth Hall, 490
Wodhull, Lawrence & Margaret Lusher, 490
Wodhull, Nicholas & Elizabeth Parr, 157
Wodhull, Nicholas & Mary Raleigh, 157
Wodhull, Nicholas de & Margaret Foxcote, 155
Wodhull, Thomas & Elizabeth Chetwode, 156
Wodhull, Thomas & Isabel Trussell, 156
Wodhull, Thomas & Margaret ____, 491
Wodhull, Thomas de & ____, 155
Wolder, 365
Wolsey, 111, 112, 169
Wolsey, Cardinal, 480
Wolvey, 291
Wolvey, Joan de & Henry de Erdington, 291
Wombwell, 240, 674
Woodbridge, 477
Woodcock, 370
Woodcock, Ursula & John Culpeper, 370

Woodhall, 530
Woodhouse, 587
Woodhouse, Elizabeth & Philip Belknap, 587
Woodstock, 666
Woodstock, Edmund of, 59, 206, 662
Woodstock, Thomas of, 416, 538, 656
Woodville - see Wydeville
Woodward, 412, 432
Worcester, 293, 336, 455
Wormeley, Ralph & Agatha Eltonhead, 504
Worsley, 476, 559
Wortley, Thomas & Joan Balderston, 211
Wotton, 184, 281, 282, 337, 588
Wotton, Robert de & Constance de Merston, 281
Woulder, 364
Wragg, 62
Wright, 132, 475
Wright, Edmund & Frances Spring, 439
Wright, Mary & William Derehaugh, 440
Wriothesley, 170
Wriothesley, Mary & Thomas Arundell, 170
Writtle, 33, 351
Wroth, 63, 365
Wroth, Dorothy & Edward Lewknor, 365
Wroth, Elizabeth & George Mynne, 63
Wroth, Elizabeth & Nicholas Butler, 63
Wrotham, 178, 513
Wrothe, 128
Wrottesley, 490
Wroughton, 488, 586
Wroughton, John & Margaret Carent, 586
Wyatt, 343, 360, 588, 589
Wycliffe, 529
Wydeville, 43, 335, 349, 425

Wydeville, Elizabeth [Queen of England], 293, 424, 581
Wye, 266
Wyger, 139, 194
Wykeham, 348, 349
Wykeham, Margaret & John Hervey, 349
Wykeham, Margaret & William Fiennes, 349
Wykford, 556
Wylemot, 326
Wyman, 209
Wymondham, 498, 499, 554
Wymondham, John & Margery Clifton, 498
Wynburn, 303
Wynde, 408
Wyndham, 498
Wyndod, 183
Wyngefeld, 258, 417
Wynne, 347
Wynne, Hugh & Alice Coytemore, 347
Wynne, Robert & Dorothy Griffith, 346
Wynton, 623
Wyston, 302
Wythe, 232, 447
Wythe, Amy & Henry Inglose, 232
Wythe, Amy & William Bowet, 232
Wytheryngton, 525
Wytlebiry, 564
Wytton, 281
Wyverston, 598
Yarde, 404
Yaxley, 481
Yelvelton, Robert & Joan Longland, 637
Yelverton, 61, 474
Yevelton, 638
Yonge, 102, 405
York, 122, 245, 247, 276, 277, 422, 424, 426, 429, 453, 497, 540, 541, 574, 575, 592, 609, 657

York, Constance of & Thomas le Despenser, 453
York, Edward of & Philippe Mohun, 657
York, Edward, Duke of, 454, 610
York, Elizabeth of [Queen of England], 335, 425
York, Richard, Duke of, 51, 422, 501
Yorke, 477
Yorke, Dorothy & Thomas Dudley, 477
Young, 638
Younge, 405
Zeeland, 23, 121, 237
Zouch, 90
Zouche, 3, 4, 38, 83, 84, 85, 86, 87, 88, 89, 90, 91, 92, 93, 94, 95, 96, 167, 204, 222, 243, 259, 276, 277, 278, 355, 387, 407, 409, 444, 445, 446, 448, 452, 453, 459, 473, 507, 556, 562, 616
Zouche, Elizabeth la & John Basynges, 93
Zouche, Eudes la & Joan Inge, 90
Zouche, Eudes la & Milicent de Cantelowe, 83
Zouche, Hugh la, 448
Zouche, John & Eleanor Saint John, 277
Zouche, John & Elizabeth Grey, 276
Zouche, Margaret & John Candishe, 278
Zouche, Margaret & Robert Sheffield, 278
Zouche, Margery la & Robert Fitz Roger, 222
Zouche, Milicent la & William Deincourt, 90
Zouche, Thomas la & Christine ____, 89
Zouche, Thomas la & Mary d'Engaine, 93
Zouche, William & Alice Seymour, 96
Zouche, William & Elizabeth Saint John, 96
Zouche, William & Maud Lovel, 86
Zouche, William la & Agnes Greene, 94
Zouche, William la & Elizabeth ____, 95
Zouche, William la & Elizabeth de Roos, 91
Zouche, William la & Elizabeth le Despenser, 94
Zousche, 88
Zuheros, 117
Zutphen, 384

❧ INDEX – Events ❦

(1106) Battle of Tinchebrai, 249
(1141) Battle of Lincoln, 149
(1156) Siege of Chinon, 176
(1177) Siege of Baieux, 124
(1192) Siege of Acre, 318
(1192) Siege of Jaffa, 413
(1214) Battle of Bouvines, 521
(1217) Battle of Lincoln, 75, 78, 185, 649, 650
(1217) Siege of Mountsorrel, 649
(1218–9) Siege of Damietta, 463
(1221) Siege of Bytham Castle, 219, 254, 634
(1263) Battle of Largs, 220
(1264) Battle of Lewes, 186, 195, 255, 299, 301, 565, 597
(1265) Battle of Evesham, 186, 196, 299, 396
(1266) Battle of Chesterfield, 566
(1270) Siege of Tunis, 302
(1296) Battle of Dunbar, 32
(1296) Siege of Berwick, 307
(1297) Battle of Stirling, 16, 223
(1298) Battle of Falkirk, 19, 197, 225, 532, 601, 652, 654, 673
(1300) Siege of Caerlaverock Castle, 197, 221, 223, 225, 242, 272, 323, 354, 441, 601, 652, 654
(1304) Siege of Stirling Castle, 59, 654
(1314) Battle of Bannockburn, 6, 19, 34, 197, 204, 225, 227, 242, 322, 442, 555, 602
(1321) Siege of Tickhill, 19
(1322) Battle of Boroughbridge, 25, 240, 243, 263, 323, 444, 524
(1323–5) War of Saint-Sardos, 59
(1327–60) battles in France and Flanders, 268
(1332) Battle of Dupplin Moor, 201

(1333) Battle of Halidon Hill, 201, 202, 532
(1333) Siege of Berwick, 532
(1340) Battle of Sluys (naval), 205, 446, 494, 532, 656
(1340) Siege of Tournai, 532
(1345) Battle of Auberoche, 570
(1346) Battle of Crécy, 18, 25, 26, 59, 69, 228, 274, 387, 388, 407, 446, 494, 570, 607, 643, 663
(1346) Battle of Neville's Cross, 90, 201
(1346–7) Siege of Calais, 20, 60, 69, 91, 228, 274, 388, 407, 446, 532, 570, 607, 643, 663
(1347) Battle of La Roche-Derien, 47
(1350) Battle of Winchelsea (naval), 244
(1356) Battle of Poitiers, 26, 227, 264, 268, 407, 452, 556
(1367) Battle of Nájera, 328, 330, 496, 571
(1380) Siege of Nantes, 164, 656
(1381) Peasants' Revolt, 451
(1383) Siege of Ypres, 451
(1401) battle at Pool, 613
(1403) Battle of Shrewsbury, 617
(1407–8) Siege of Aberystwyth, 98
(1415) Battle of Agincourt, 71, 230, 232, 332, 357, 417, 526, 535, 538, 572, 580, 615, 631, 657
(1415) Siege of Harfleur, 39, 165, 401, 417, 418, 420, 538, 572, 613, 631
(1418) Siege of Cherbourg, 420
(1418–19) Siege of Rouen, 230, 420, 535, 631
(1420) Siege of Melun, 420, 631, 659
(1421) Battle of Beaugé, 156, 232, 538, 659
(1421–22) Siege of Meaux, 246, 537, 631
(1424) Battle of Verneuil, 420
(1424) Siege of Ivry, 420

(1427) Siege of Montargis, 420
(1440) Siege of Harfleur, 551
(1453) Battle of Castillon, 429
(1455) Battle of St. Albans (1st), 51, 102, 247
(1459) Battle of Blore Heath, 488, 540
(1460) Battle of Northampton, 349, 540, 551
(1460) Battle of Wakefield, 247
(1461) Battle of Ferrybridge, 41, 247, 424
(1461) Battle of St. Albans (2nd), 424, 540
(1461) Battle of Towton, 41, 51, 103, 247, 374, 424, 527, 540, 541, 551, 575
(1461) Siege of Carlisle, 540
(1462) Siege of Alnwick Castle, 552
(1469) Battle of Edgecote, 289
(1471) Battle of Barnet, 349, 403, 484, 540
(1471) Battle of Tewkesbury, 53, 166, 294, 334, 351, 402, 488
(1485) Battle of Bosworth, 100, 168, 294, 409, 425, 426, 576
(1487) Battle of Stoke, 311, 426, 431
(1497) Battle of Blackheath, 56, 351, 426, 427
(1513) Battle of Flodden Field, 248, 285, 286, 289, 374
(1513) Battle of the Spurs, 345
(1513) Siege of Thérouanne, 43, 100, 169, 345, 428
(1513) Siege of Tournai, 43, 169, 346
(1520) Field of the Cloth of Gold, 43, 56, 105, 286, 336, 351, 432, 472, 588, 678
(1524) Siege of Marseilles, 428
(1525) Battle of Pavia, 428
(1536) Pilgrimage of Grace, 112, 336
(1544) Siege of Boulogne, 437
(1545) Battle of Ancrum Moor, 529
(1547) Battle of Pinkie, 342
(1557) Battle of St. Quintin, 360
(1597) Siege of Amiens, 477
(1642) Battle of Edgehill, 361
(1643) Battle of Adwalton Moor, 314

Made in the USA
Middletown, DE
10 February 2023